A Note from Peterson's® Editors

Peterson's Private Secondary Schools 2017–18 is the authoritative source of information for parents and students who are exploring the alternative of privately provided education. In this edition, you will find information for more than 1,000 schools worldwide. The data published in this guide are obtained directly from the schools themselves to help you make a fully informed decision.

If you've decided to look into private schooling for your son or daughter but aren't sure how to begin, relax. You won't have to go it alone. **What You Should Know About Private Education** can help you plan your search and demystify the admission process. In the articles that follow, you'll find valuable advice from admission experts about applying to private secondary schools and choosing the school that's right for your child.

In "Why Choose an Independent School?" Donna Orem, Interim President of the National Association of Independent Schools (NAIS), describes the reasons why an increasing number of families are considering private schooling.

If you want a private education for your child but are hesitant about sending him or her away to a boarding school, read our new article, "Independent Day Schools: The Best of Both Worlds," which discusses the benefits of day schools.

If you are considering attending a boarding school, you will want to read our insightful article, "Why Boarding School: Reasons I Chose This Path and Why You Might Too," by Justin Muchnick, a boarding school student at Phillips Academy Andover. Or check out the article, "Study Confirms Benefits of Boarding School," with valuable data from The Association of Boarding Schools (TABS).

Mark Meyer-Braun, Former Head of School at the Outdoor Academy, offers "Semester Schools: Great Opportunities," which explores various options for students to spend an exciting semester in a new "school-away-from-school."

Schools will be pleased to know that Peterson's helped you in your private secondary school selection.

If you are considering a special needs or therapeutic school for your child, you will want to read "Why a Therapeutic or Special Needs School?" by Diederik van Renesse, an educational consultant who specializes in this area.

To help you compare private schools and make the best choice for your child, check out "Finding the Perfect Match" by Helene Reynolds, a former educational planning and placement counselor.

"Plan a Successful School Search" gives you an overview of the admission process.

If the admission application forms have you baffled and confused, read "Admissions Applications for Private Secondary Schools," by Tom Sheppard, Dean of Admissions and Financial Aid.

For the lowdown on standardized testing, Heather Hoerle, Executive Director of the Secondary School Admission Test Board (SSATB), describes the two tests most often required by private schools and the role that tests play in admission decisions in "About Admission Tests and the SSAT." In addition, you can read about another private schools admissions test in the "About the Independent School Entrance Exam (ISEE)" article.

In "Paying for a Private Education," Mark Mitchell, Vice President, School and Student Services at NAIS, shares some thoughts on financing options.

Finally, "How to Use This Guide" gives you all the information you need on how to make *Peterson's Private Secondary Schools 2017–18* work for you!

Next up, the **Quick-Reference Chart,** "Private Secondary Schools At-a-Glance," lists schools by state, U.S. territory, or country and provides essential information about a school's students, range of grade levels, enrollment figures, faculty, and special offerings.

A Note from Peterson's® Editors

The **School Profiles** follow, and it's here you can learn more about particular schools. *Peterson's Private Secondary Schools 2017–18* contains three **School Profiles** sections—one for traditional college-preparatory and general academic schools, one for special needs schools that serve students with a variety of special learning and social needs, and one for junior boarding schools that serve students in middle school grades. Many schools have chosen to submit a display ad, which appears near their profile and offers specific information the school wants you to know.

Close-Ups follow each **School Profiles** section and feature expanded two-page school descriptions written exclusively for this guide. There is a reference at the end of a profile directing you to that school's **Close-Up.**

The **Specialized Directories** are generated from responses to Peterson's annual school survey. These directories group schools by the categories considered most important when choosing a private school, including type, entrance requirements, curricula, financial aid data, and special programs.

Finally, in the **Index** you'll find the "Alphabetical Listing of Schools" for the page references of schools that have already piqued your interest.

Peterson's publishes a full line of resources to help guide you and your family through the private secondary school admission process. Peterson's publications can be found at your local bookstore and library and your school guidance office, and you can access us online at www.petersons.com.

We welcome any comments or suggestions you may have about this publication. Please send us an e-mail at custsvc@petersons.com. Your feedback will help us make your educational dreams possible.

Schools will be pleased to know that Peterson's helped you in your private secondary school selection. Admission staff members are more than happy to answer questions, address specific problems, and help in any way they can. The editors at Peterson's wish you great success in your search!

Contents

Contents

What You Should Know About Private Education

Why Choose an Independent School?

Donna Orem
Interim President of the National Association of Independent Schools (NAIS)

What does the ideal school for your child look like? Is it small or large? Competitive, or more nurturing? Are there aptitudes or interests that you'd like to foster in your child? Or challenges that you'd like to address? Are you looking for a school in a particular area, or is living away from home at a boarding school appealing to your child?

Each independent school has a unique mission that guides its offerings. You can choose a school where the philosophy, values, and teaching approach are right for your child.

Independent schools nurture students' intellectual abilities, curiosity, social growth, and civic conscience. Opportunities extend well beyond the classroom to athletic competitions, artistic pursuits, and school leadership experiences.

Students are deeply engaged in learning at independent schools. More than twice as many students at the schools belonging to the National Association of Independent Schools (NAIS) reported that they received helpful feedback from teachers on assignments compared to students at all other types of schools, according to *The High School Survey of Student Engagement*. In addition, students who attended NAIS schools were more than twice as likely as students at other schools to say that the school contributed "very much" to their growth in critical thinking.

Graduates of NAIS schools felt more prepared for the academic demands of college than their public school counterparts, according to *The Freshman Survey Trends Report*, an annual study conducted by the Higher Education Research Institute. In addition, as college freshmen, NAIS graduates reported that they were more likely to ask questions in their college classes and explore topics on their own, even though it was not required for a class.

The diverse range of independent school types allows parents to find schools that best meet each child's needs. Once you identify schools of interest, look at each and ask:

- What is the school's mission, and does its philosophy appeal to me?
- What types of learning experiences are available—in class, on the playing field, in extracurricular activities, and in community service? Would these experiences fit my child's needs?
- Does the school offer before- or after-school care or transportation (if necessary)?
- What are the deadlines for admission and financial aid applications?

For tips on applying to independent schools, timelines, and more, visit http://parents.nais.org.

> *Independent schools nurture not just students' intellectual ability and curiosity but also their personal and social growth and civic conscience.*

Independent Day Schools: The Best of Both Worlds

It's a common dilemma. You want more for your student than public schools have to offer, but a boarding school isn't the right option either. That's when an independent day school can be the perfect solution—one that benefits both students and their families.

"An independent day school provides a college-prep environment, where kids can get an education similar to the best boarding schools but without having to leave home," says Susan Grodman, Director of Enrollment and Global Programs for Derryfield School in Manchester, New Hampshire. "They can still be home for dinner each night." She says the typical family that chooses an independent day school is one that emphasizes the importance of education and also wants to be involved with their child and their school and activities.

Jen Groen, Director of Admissions and Strategic Engagement for Jack M. Barrack Hebrew Academy in Bryn Mawr, Pennsylvania agrees. "An independent day school offers a self-selected group of families and students a safe, nurturing, college-prep setting. And because they're not bound to some of the things that public schools are required to do, such as testing, independent day schools have the freedom to offer unique, specialized instruction."

"Education is a team effort, and parents are a part of that team. The family is a big part of the development of the child," says Elizabeth Norton, Director of Enrollment and Financial Aid at York Preparatory School in New York City. "The personal connection you get at a day school is incredible. It's like being part of a small town, with much more of a human element."

> *Independent day schools have the freedom to offer unique, specialized instruction.*

What Makes an Independent Day School Special?

Because they are independent, each school has the freedom to establish a unique identity that is suited to the needs of the students and families it serves.

For instance, Barrack Hebrew Academy incorporates the Jewish calendar into the academic year, allowing for easy practice of faith without conflict. "This helps students feel more whole in their identity," says Groen.

Many independent day schools have smaller populations, which helps students develop a strong self-image, self-concept, and self-advocacy skills. The small size also fosters involvement in a range of extracurricular activities; students can explore and try many things.

"There's not a lot of labeling here—no one is a 'jock' or a 'theater geek' and there aren't a lot of cliques," says Grodman. "The kids make a lot of connections with one another as well."

Groen agrees that there is a high level of intimacy and strong relationships are formed at an independent day school, due in part to the fact that the students come from the same geographic area and may share the same faith or another common bond. "Friendships that are made here are those that truly last a lifetime."

Norton pointed out that because students have a wide range of learning styles, an independent day school may be able to serve those with unique needs better because of the smaller number of students.

Of course, there's another big benefit to an independent day school that's close to home. Parents and other family members are able to easily attend athletic events, concerts, plays, and other programs their students are involved with.

Academics and College Prep

Academics are still the heart of every independent day school, with college entrance being the primary focus.

"While placement is the primary goal, the way they get there varies. We seek an appropriate, challenging college acceptance path for each student," says Norton. She adds that schools address the subject of challenge differently. "Some are more aggressive at pushing children to the point where it's almost like college, but we think developmentally that's not where these young people are. We want to challenge them but also teach them to use the tools that they have available, such as how to have contact with their teachers. It's a progression."

"Homework doesn't necessarily equate rigor; we strive to develop a well-rounded child. Honing outside interests and talents is important for the long term, for life. This also helps distinguish each student during the college entrance process," Norton says.

The smaller student population of most independent day schools again is a factor. Grodman points out that independent day schools allow students to develop relationships with teachers that they might not be able to have in other settings. Sharon Levin, Head of School at Barack Academy reports their students perform as well, if not better, at college than those from larger schools.

"Kids find their passion here—it's so much easier to find what they love," says Derryfield's Grodman. "Students come back and report that they were well-prepared for college. They know how to manage their time, how to study effectively, how to advocate for themselves, and how to approach teachers."

Time management is an especially important skill for students at independent day schools. Some will commute an hour or more to get to and from their school. They get up early and often stay late for extracurricular activities, so self-discipline and effective use of time are key components to their success.

Independent day schools also pride themselves on the degree of college guidance their students receive. For instance, at York Preparatory Academy, Norton says that most students have everything in place—the schools they want to attend, applications filled out, essays complete—at the end of their junior year. When students return for senior year they simply review and polish up their materials before applying, so there's no last-minute pressure or rush.

Not Just for Students, But a Community for the Family

One of the hallmarks that sets independent day schools apart is the opportunity to involve the entire family in the school and its activities.

Levin asserts that this is one of the main reasons families choose Barack Hebrew Academy. "People are looking for community and relationships, and this goes beyond just the students. We offer family and community with a Jewish soul."

Families who choose independent day schools tend to be very committed in terms of time, participation, and finances. Most schools have organizations to help facilitate involvement on a variety of levels.

The focus of York's parent organization is also building community. "We want to help these families feel like they're part of our family," Norton states. They have social activities, get-togethers for parents of each grade level, an international dinner where families bring foods that represent their culture and heritage, baseball and volleyball games, picnics, and even a class for parents taught by one of the school's history teachers.

Grodman says that some of the strong sense of community at Derryfield is because students are at the school a long time each day. With required sports participation and many other extracurricular activities, the school day lasts well past the time when classes end. It builds strong relationships, which leads to a lot of parental involvement: they volunteer in the library, serve as parent ambassadors who help with admissions, and help however they can. "Even those who can't get to the school regularly still find ways to be involved," she says.

At Barack Hebrew Academy, parental involvement includes the school's board and numerous committees: technology, recruitment, finances and investments, athletics support, drama boosters, and more. Parents help with learning enrichment and learning support. The Home-School Association provides a large volunteer presence at the school, with some grandparents involved, too. "They know how much the school has given to their kids. This is their way of giving back," Levin states.

Diverse and Accessible

Even though some independent day schools may be affiliated with a particular faith or draw students from a fairly small geographic area, they also strive to make their school community diverse.

"We have a great deal of cultural diversity but also a range of diverse learning styles and diversity of talents as well. It makes for a very interesting community—

more the way the real world looks," says Norton. "That's why we celebrate diversity here at York."

Groen describes Barack Hebrew Academy as an incubator for future world leaders, and because of that they stress an attitude of tolerance and diversity within the school's population. They are intentionally pluralistic and promote respect for what everyone stands for and believes.

There is also economic diversity. While an independent day school is often more accessible financially, it can still be a challenge. "Derryfield families have made sacrifices in order to provide this kind of education for their child," explained Grodman. "They want their kids to have a broad, well-rounded education: world issues, travel, different perspectives, the arts, sciences, athletics, and more—not just an emphasis on one of those areas."

Friendships that are made here are those that truly last a lifetime.

Independent day schools work with families to make attendance affordable; often, a large percentage of students receive some type of scholarship.

Much to Offer

Students at independent day schools benefit from top-flight academics; personalized college guidance; small, diverse student populations with strong bonds; and opportunities to participate and thrive in extracurricular activities. But parents and families also benefit, by being able to be present, involved, and engaged with their student's school on a day-to-day, hands-on basis. These are just some of the reasons why independent day schools are a valuable option on the spectrum of education choice available for students today.

Why Boarding School: Reasons I Chose This Path and Why You Might, Too

Justin Muchnick

My seventh-grade literature class changed my life. To be more exact, Mr. Rogers, my seventh-grade literature teacher, changed my life. Only a temporary substitute teacher (the regular faculty member took the year off for maternity leave), Mr. Rogers entered the classroom on the first day of school and did something remarkable: he asked his students to have a conversation about a book we had read over the summer. My school's traditional "raise your hand and wait to be called on" style of learning had left me completely unprepared for a teacher who *wanted* me to talk. Nevertheless, I relished the opportunity to learn in this interesting and dynamic classroom environment, and I certainly jumped at a chance to voice my opinions without fear of being chastised for speaking out of turn.

Within a few weeks, active participation had fully cemented its reputation as the primary way of learning in Mr. Rogers' class. Instead of employing a standard row-and-column classroom seating pattern, Mr. Rogers positioned our seats in a large circle. This "Harkness" method encouraged free-flowing conversations in which Mr. Rogers would serve only as a mediator and participant. Rather than writing bland responses to even blander study questions, my class honed its public speaking skills by participating in spur-of-the-moment debates about these topics. Mr. Rogers' classroom, reminiscent of a scene out of *Dead Poets Society*, allowed the act of learning to intellectually stretch and stimulate me.

As Mr. Rogers became my friend and mentor as well as my teacher, I learned that he had previously worked as the Writer in Residence at Phillips Exeter Academy, a boarding school in New England. At that time, I thought that boarding school meant a place where disobedient children were sent to resolve their behavioral issues. Mr. Rogers, though, spoke glowingly of the East Coast boarding school system and told me that schools like Exeter utilize an active, discussion-based, Mr. Rogers-esque style of teaching. Soon, I started dreaming of a school full of teachers like Mr. Rogers, full of intellectually curious students, and full of eager learners. I did some research about Exeter and other New England schools, and in the spring of my seventh-grade year, I presented the boarding school idea to my mom and dad.

At first, my parents commended me on the excellent joke I had pulled on them; however, they quickly realized that I was serious. They began to think that I wanted to get away from them or that I disliked my family. But after extensive negotiations, I was able to convince them that this was not the case, and by midway through the summer after seventh grade, they fully backed my decision. Once my family agreed that I was in fact going to pursue the boarding school idea, we made it our mission to select the schools to which I would apply. I devised a list of qualities I was looking for in a boarding school. At this point in the application process, you, too, should create a list of criteria—you can save yourself the wasted time and effort of applying to the "wrong" schools by knowing what kinds of schools best suit you. Though your personal list may be very different, mine was as follows:

Size: I tried to find a relatively big school. At my primary school, the average grade size was about 50 students, and, as time wore on, my desire to expand beyond my small group of classmates grew stronger. By applying to larger schools, I felt that I could both broaden my social experience and avoid another "small school burnout."

Uniform Policy: My former school enforced a strict dress code. Since collared shirts and I never really hit if off, I had definitely worn a uniform for long enough. Thus, I did not want to spend my high school years wearing a blazer and slacks.

> *For me, the process of applying to and selecting boarding schools was fueled by my innate passion for learning: I simply wanted to find a place where it was "cool to be smart."*

Single-Sex or Coed: I didn't really want to spend my high school years at an all-boys school.

Location: For me, the East Coast seemed like the best place to find a boarding school. After all, that's what Mr. Rogers had recommended.

Academics: I have an unquenchable thirst for knowledge. I did not wish to "dehydrate" myself at a school with a less-than-excellent academic reputation.

Proximity to an Airport: My mom thought of this one. She suggested that I should apply to schools located near a major airport that offered nonstop flights from Los Angeles. Cross-country flights are tough enough; complicating matters with a connecting flight seemed unnecessary.

Here are some other things that you might want to consider:

Religious Affiliation: Do you want religion to play a large part in your high school experience, or would you rather go to a nondenominational school?

Specialty Schools: Do you want to apply to schools that focus on a specific aspect or method of learning? Are you particularly talented in a certain field? If so, look into arts, math and sciences, or military schools.

Athletics: If you play a sport, you might try to look for schools with strong teams and exceptional athletic facilities. One good way to do this is to contact a school's coach or athletic director. As both a soccer player and a wrestler, I talked to many coaches from a number of different boarding schools to get a sense of each school's athletic program.

Cost/Financial Aid Policy: Obviously, some schools are more expensive than others. In addition to looking at the tuition, you may want to find out which schools offer need-based financial aid or any merit-based scholarships.

By comparing various schools to my personal list of attributes, I was able to find four schools that really matched my requirements. I sent applications to Choate Rosemary Hall, The Lawrenceville School, Phillips Exeter Academy, and Phillips Academy Andover, and I was fortunate enough to have been accepted by all four schools. After taking the SSAT, writing applications, and interviewing with admission officers, little did I realize that I would still have one last, equally significant hurdle to jump. The choice that I was about to make would directly impact the next four years of my life, so my parents and I did everything in our power to ensure that my decision was the correct one. By obtaining contact information from admission offices as well as school counselors and friends of friends, we sought out current students who lived locally and attended each of the schools. We scheduled face-to-face meetings with as many of them as we could, during which we "grilled"

them on the pros and cons of their schools. We spent hours reading websites, blogs, and Facebook pages in hopes of getting students' unsolicited perspectives of their schools. Most importantly, however, we attended the revisit days for each of the schools. For those at this stage of the boarding school process, I would highly recommend going to the admitted students events if you have the financial means and your schedule permits. At any given revisit day, I was truly able to get a feel for the campus and environment and see if I could envision myself as a student at that school next year—sometimes my gut instinct would tell me "yes," and other times it would tell me "no." While on campus, I also had the opportunity to ask countless current students about their high school experiences. Don't be afraid to ask tough questions. By doing so, you can better understand the general campus vibe. After the revisit days, I was able to make my decision with confidence. I was going to Andover!

You might choose to apply to boarding schools for different reasons than I did. No two cases are exactly alike, but many applicants fall into these categories.

Ready to Leave Home: Whether it's a desire for independence, friction within the household, or any other reason, waiting until college to live on your own isn't the best option for you.

Family Tradition: As a baby, you wore a boarding school bib around your neck. Your favorite shirt is one emblazoned with a particular school's emblem. A few older family members have paved the way, or, perhaps, generations of relatives have attended. Boarding school is in your blood.

Diversity: You have grown up in a homogenous community, or you yearn for difference in both tradition and mindset. Today's boarding schools afford you interaction with peers of all racial, financial, geographical, and religious backgrounds—conducive to a multicultural educational experience.

Love of Learning: Is your nose perpetually stuck in a book? Do you stay after class to delve deeper into a conversation with your teacher? Is your idea of a fun weekend activity reading up on political affairs or the latest scientific breakthrough? Do you love learning for learning's sake? If so, boarding school is undoubtedly worth exploring.

For me, the process of applying to and selecting boarding schools was fueled by my innate passion for learning: I simply wanted to find a place where it was "cool to be smart." When I look back at this initial notion, I realize that it was certainly idealistic and a bit naïve, but Andover has come about as close as possible. Though busy work and uninteresting conversations bog me down from time to time, they are more than made up for by engaging writing prompts, stimulating discussions, and inspirational teachers that would make even Mr. Rogers proud.

To learn more about boarding schools, look for Peterson's *The Boarding School Survival Guide*, by Justin Muchnick, available in stores, online, and as an ebook.

Top 10 Tips To Know Before Your Teen Leaves for Boarding School

by Justin Muchnick

Reprinted with permission by Ten to Twenty Parenting (Tentotwentyparenting.com)

1. Only let your son or daughter go away to boarding school if he or she really wants it for the right reasons. Sending you teen off to boarding school as a punishment or because your child thinks it will be an extended camp experience are not good reasons.

2. Don't be worried that your teen isn't under constant parental supervision at school, but definitely try to stay connected through text, Skype, phone calls, or e-mail.

3. That said, cherish the time you spend over school breaks together. Breaks are good opportunities to "make up for lost time."

4. Pack a small "first-aid kit" that includes Neosporin®, Band-Aids®, Tylenol®, TUMS®, and some throat lozenges. A few of these essential medical items can spare your teen an unnecessary trip to the infirmary.

5. To complement the medical kit, make sure to send your teen to school with some nonperishable snacks for late-night study sessions. Some dorm favorites include fruit leathers, microwavable noodles and mac and cheese, and granola bars.

6. Even if you are used to cheering on your child at every Little League game or musical theater production, don't feel guilty about missing many sporting events or other extracurricular activities once your teen is in boarding school. Student bodies at boarding schools are incredibly supportive, and your teen will most likely have a few friends or even teachers on the sidelines or in the audience.

7. Teach your son or daughter the basics of laundry, personal finance, and efficient packing. These skills, however trivial they might seem, are important ones to master before leaving home.

8. Chances are, the boarding school your teen attends is one of the most, if not the very most, diverse communities he or she will be a part of. Be very excited about this and open to this unique aspect of boarding school.

9. Never underestimate the power of a care package! Sometimes, receiving a little pick-me-up in the mail can really brighten up your teen's day.

10. Finally be sure to pick up a copy of *The Boarding School Survival Guide* for additional insights, tips, and strategies about boarding school life, written by students for students (and parents, too!).

Justin Muchnick is a student at Phillips Academy Andover in Massachusetts. He is a four-year varsity wrestler and two-time captain, serves on the Athletic Advisory Bord, works as a senior proctor, participates in the chess club, and works as a campus tour guide. A passionate learner, Justin enjoys reading, writing, Latin, and modern American history. He co-authored Straight-A Study Skills *(Adams Media, January 2013) and is the author of* Teens' Guide to College and Career Planning *(Peterson's 2016). He is the youngest journalist for* The Bootleg® *(http://stanford.scout.com), Stanford University's sports news website, where he writes articles about college football. When he is not at boarding school, Justin resides in Newport Beach, California, with his parents and three younger siblings. To contact Justin, visit his website www.justinmuchnick.com. He can also be reached via Twitter: @BoardingSchl or Facebook: https://www.facebook.com/TheBoardingSchoolSurvivalGuide.*

Study Confirms Benefits of Boarding School

Many people have long sung the praises of the boarding school experience. The high-level academics, the friendships, and the life lessons learned are without rival at private day or public schools, they say.

A study released by The Association of Boarding Schools (TABS), a nonprofit organization of independent, college-preparatory schools, validates these claims. Not only do boarding school students spend more time studying (and less time watching TV), they are also better prepared for college and progress more quickly in their careers than their counterparts who attended private day or public schools.

The survey, which was conducted by the Baltimore-based research firm the Art & Science Group, involved interviews with 1,000 students and alumni from boarding schools, 1,100 from public schools, and 600 from private day schools (including independent day and parochial schools).

The results not only affirm the benefits enjoyed by boarding school graduates but those bestowed upon current boarding school students as well. "The study helps us better understand how the opportunities for interaction and learning beyond the classroom found at boarding schools impact a student's life at school and into adulthood," explained Steve Ruzicka, former TABS executive director. Ruzicka said the survey also provides boarding school alumni with empirical data to help when considering their children's educational options.

Rigorous Academics Prevail

Why do students apply to boarding schools? The TABS study found that the primary motivation for both applicants and their parents is the promise of a better education. And, happily, the vast majority of current and past students surveyed reported that their schools deliver on this promise. Current students indicated significantly higher levels of satisfaction with their academic experience at boarding schools than their peers at public and private day schools by more than ten per-

centage points (54 percent of boarding students versus 42 percent of private day students and 40 percent of public school students). Boarders reported in greater relative percentages that they find their schools academically challenging, that their peers are more motivated, and the quality of teaching is very high.

But the boarding environment is valued just as much for the opportunities for interaction and learning beyond the classroom. Interactions in the dining room, the dormitory, and on the playing field both complement and supplement academics, exposing students to a broad geographic and socioeconomic spectrum, challenging their boundaries, and broadening their vision of the world.

The Boarding School Boost

The 24/7 life at boarding schools also gives students a significant leg up when they attend college, the survey documents.

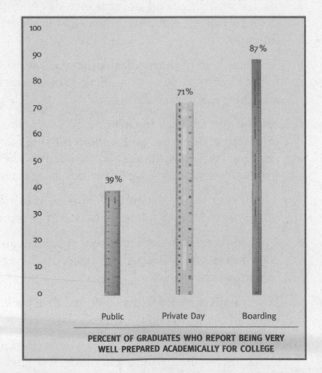

PERCENT OF GRADUATES WHO REPORT BEING VERY WELL PREPARED ACADEMICALLY FOR COLLEGE

Some 87 percent of boarding school graduates said they were very well prepared academically for college, with only 71 percent of private day and just 39 percent of public school alumni saying the same. And 78 percent of boarders reported that their schools also helped better prepare them to face the nonacademic aspects of college life, such as independence, social life, and time management. Only 36 percent of private day graduates and 23 percent of public school graduates said the same. The TABS survey also documented that a larger percentage of boarding school graduates go on to earn advanced degrees once they finish college: 50 percent, versus 36 percent of private day and 21 percent of public school alumni.

Beyond college, boarding school graduates also reap greater benefits from their on-campus experiences, advancing faster and further in their careers comparatively. The study scrutinized former boarders versus private day and public school graduates in terms of achieving positions in top management and found that by midcareer, 44 percent of boarding school graduates had reached positions in top management versus 33 percent of private day school graduates and 27 percent of public school graduates.

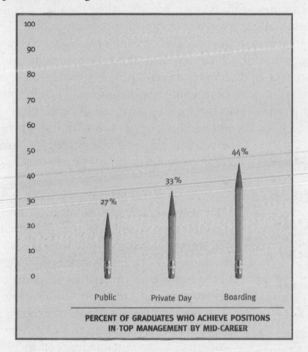

PERCENT OF GRADUATES WHO ACHIEVE POSITIONS
IN TOP MANAGEMENT BY MID-CAREER

By late in their careers, more than half of the surveyed boarding school sample, 52 percent, held positions in top management as opposed to 39 percent of private day and 27 percent of public school graduates.

But perhaps the most compelling statistic that the study produced is the extremely high percentage—some 90 percent—of boarding school alumni who say they would, if given the opportunity, repeat their boarding school experience. This alone is a strong argument that validates the enduring value of the boarding school model. It is hoped that the study will help dispel many of the myths and stereotypes that have dogged the image of boarding schools over the last century and spread the good news that boarding schools today are diverse, exciting places for bright, well-adjusted students who are looking for success in their academic lives—and beyond.

For more information on TABS visit the website at www.schools.com.

Used by permission of The Association of Boarding Schools.

Semester Schools: Great Opportunities

Mark Meyer-Braun
Former Head of School, The Outdoor Academy

Over the last twenty years, there has been tremendous growth in the range of educational opportunities available to young Americans. The advent of semester schools has played no small part in this trend. Similar in many ways to semester-abroad programs, semester schools provide secondary school students the opportunity to leave their home school for half an academic year to have a very different kind of experience—the experience of living and learning within a small community, among diverse students, and in a new and different place. The curricula of such schools tend to be thematic, interdisciplinary, rigorous, and experiential.

What Are the Benefits?

As a starting point for their programs, semester schools have embraced many of the qualities typical of independent schools. In fact, a number of semester schools were developed as extension programs by existing independent schools, providing unusual opportunities to their own students and those from other schools. Other semester schools have grown from independent educational organizations or foundations that bring their own educational interests and expertise to their semester programs. In both cases, semester schools provide the kind of challenging environment for which independent schools are known.

Across the board, semester school programs provide students with exceptional opportunities for contact with their teachers. Individual instruction and intimate classes are common, as is contact with teachers outside the classroom. At semester schools, students have a full-immersion experience in a tightly knit learning community. In such a setting, teachers are able

At semester schools, students have a full-immersion experience in a tightly knit learning community.

to challenge each student in his or her own area of need, mentoring students to both academic and personal fulfillment.

Semester schools have developed around specialized curricular interests, often involving unique offerings or nontraditional subjects. In almost every case, these specialized curricula are related to the school's location. Indeed, place-based learning is a common thread in semester school education. Whether in New York City or the Appalachian Mountains, semester schools enable students to cultivate a sense of place and develop greater sensitivity to their surroundings. This is often accomplished through a combination of experiential education and traditional instruction. Students develop academic knowledge and practical skills in tandem through active participation in intellectual discourse, creative projects, hands-on exercises, and service learning opportunities. Throughout, emphasis is placed on the importance of combining intellectual exploration with thoughtful self-reflection, often facilitated by journaling exercises or group processing activities.

At semester schools, students inevitably learn their most important lessons through their membership in the school community. Living closely with peers and teachers and working together for the benefit of the group enables students to develop extraordinary communication skills and high levels of interpersonal accountability. Through this experience, students gain invaluable leadership and cooperation skills.

Ultimately, semester schools seek to impart translatable skills to their students. The common goal is for students to return to their schools and families with greater motivation, empathy, self-knowledge, and self-determination. These skills help to prepare students for the college experience and beyond. In addition, semester school participants report that their experiences helped to distinguish them in the college application process. Semester school programs are certainly not for everybody, but they serve an important role for students who are seeking something beyond the ordinary—students who wish to know themselves and the world in a profound way. All of the following semester school programs manifest these same values in their own distinctive way.

CITYterm

CITYterm, founded in 1996, is an interdisciplinary, experience-based program that takes 30 juniors and seniors from across the country and engages them in a semester-long study of New York City. CITYterm students typically spend three days a week in the classroom, reading, writing, and thinking about New York City, and three days a week in the city working on projects, studying diverse neighborhoods, or meeting with politicians, urban historians, authors, artists, actors, and various city experts. Much of the excitement of CITYterm comes from experiencing firsthand in the city what has been studied in the classroom. Many of the projects are done in collaborative teams where the groups engage not only in formal academic research at the city's libraries but also use the resources of New York City's residents and institutions to gather the information necessary for presentations. Students come to see themselves as the active creators of their own learning both in the classroom and in the world. Learn more about CITYterm by visiting www.cityterm.org.

Conserve School

Conserve School is a semester school for high school juniors that is focused on the theme of environmental stewardship. Attending Conserve School gives high school students a one-semester opportunity to step out of their regular school and into a unique educational setting, while still continuing their required academic studies. Conserve School's challenging, college-prep curriculum immerses high school juniors in environmental history, nature literature, and the science of conservation. Because Conserve School is located on a 1,200-acre wilderness campus, a significant portion of the curriculum is delivered via outdoors, hands-on, active learning. Conserve School is located just west of Land O' Lakes, Wisconsin, near the border of Michigan's Upper Peninsula. Learn more about the Conserve School at www.conserveschool.org/.

The Island School

The Island School, founded in 1999 by The Lawrenceville School, is an independent academic program in the Bahamas for high school sophomores or juniors. The fourteen-week academic course of study includes honors classes in science, field research (a laboratory science), history, math, art, English literature, and physical/outdoor education and a weekly community service component. All courses are place-based and explicitly linked, taking advantage of the school's surroundings to both deepen understandings of complex academic and social issues and to make those understandings lasting by connecting course content with experience. Students apply their investigative, interpretive, and problem-solving skills during four- and eight-day kayaking expeditions, SCUBA diving opportunities, teaching environmental issues to local students, and in daily life at the school. In addition to traditional

classroom assessments, students conduct research on mangrove communities, coastal management, artificial reefs, permaculture, and marine protected areas. These projects support national research and are conducted under the auspices of the Bahamian government. At the conclusion of the semester, students present their work to a panel of visiting scientists and educators, including local and national government officials from the Bahamas. The opportunity to interact with the local community through research, outreach, and the rigorous physical and academic schedule creates a transformative experience for students. The admissions process is competitive, and selected students demonstrate solid academic performance, leadership potential, and a high degree of self-motivation. Contact The Island School for more information at www.islandschool.org.

Chewonki Semester School

The Chewonki Semester School (formerly Maine Coast Semester) offers a small group of eleventh-grade students the chance to live and work on a 400-acre saltwater peninsula with the goal of exploring the natural world through courses in natural science, environmental issues, literature and writing, art, history, mathematics, and foreign language. Since 1988, this semester school has welcomed students from more than 230 public and private schools across the country and in Canada. The Chewonki community is small—39 students and 20 faculty members—and the application process is competitive. In addition to their studies, students work for several hours each afternoon on an organic farm, in a wood lot, or on maintenance and construction projects. Students who attend are highly motivated, capable, and willing to take the risk of leaving friends and family for a portion of their high school career. They enjoy hard work, both intellectual and physical, and they demonstrate a tangible desire to contribute to the world. Chewonki students return to their schools with self-confidence, an appreciation for the struggles and rewards of community living, and an increased sense of ownership of their education. For information on the Chewonki Semester School, go to www.chewonki.org.

The High Mountain Institute Semester

The High Mountain Institute (HMI) Semester is a unique opportunity for juniors and some seniors in high school to spend a semester living, traveling, and studying in the mountains of central Colorado and the canyons of southeastern Utah. The school combines some of the best qualities of an academic program at a rigorous boarding school with the adventure of a summer backpacking expedition. The HMI Semester offers an honors and AP-level curriculum to prepare students to thrive during their senior year and in college. Courses are designed to match the content and rigor of the sending schools to ensure smooth transitions for HMI graduates. The High Mountain Institute is accredited by the Association of Colorado Independent Schools.

Interested students can learn more about The High Mountain Institute Semester at http://www.hminet.org/.

The Mountain School

The Mountain School of Milton Academy, founded in 1984, hosts 45 high school juniors from private and public schools throughout the United States who have chosen to spend four months on a working organic farm in Vermont. Courses provide a demanding and integrated learning experience, taking full advantage of the school's small size and mountain campus. Students and adults develop a social contract of mutual trust that expects individual and communal responsibility, models the values of simplicity and sustainability, and challenges teenagers to engage in meaningful work. Students live with teachers in small houses and help make important decisions concerning how to live together and manage the farm. Courses offered include English, environmental science, U.S. history, and all levels of math, physics, chemistry, Spanish, French, Latin, studio art, and humanities. To learn more, please visit the Web site at www. mountainschool.org.

The Outdoor Academy of the Southern Appalachians

The Outdoor Academy offers tenth-grade and select eleventh-grade students from across the country a semester away in the mountains of North Carolina. Arising from more than eighty years of experiential education at Eagle's Nest Foundation, this school-away-from-school provides a college-preparatory curriculum along with special offerings in environmental education, outdoor leadership, the arts, and community service. Each semester, up to 35 students embrace the Southern Appalachians as a unique ecological, historical, and cultural American region. In this setting, students and teachers live as a close-knit community, and lessons of cooperation and responsibility abound. Students develop a healthy work ethic as course work and projects are pursued both in and out of the classroom. Courses in English, mathematics, science, history, foreign language, visual and performing arts, and music emphasize hands-on and cooperative learning. Classes often meet outside on the 180-acre wooded campus or in nearby national wilderness areas, where the natural world enhances intellectual pursuits. On weekends and extended trips, the outdoor leadership program teaches hiking, backpacking, caving, canoeing, and rock-climbing skills. The Outdoor Academy is open to students from both public and private secondary schools and is accredited by the Southern Association of Colleges and Schools. Learn more about The Outdoor Academy at www.enf.org/outdoor_academy/.

The Oxbow School

The Oxbow School in Napa, California, is a one-semester visual arts program for high school juniors and seniors from public and private schools nationwide. Oxbow offers students a unique educational experience focused on in-depth study in sculpture, printmaking, drawing and painting, and photography and digital media, including animation. The interdisciplinary, project-based curriculum emphasizes experiential learning, critical thinking, and the development of research skills as a means of focused artistic inquiry. Each semester, 2 Visiting Artists are invited to work collaboratively with students and teachers. By engaging students in the creative process, Oxbow fosters a deep appreciation for creativity in all areas of life beyond the classroom. Since its founding in 1998, students who have spent a semester at The Oxbow School have matriculated to leading universities, colleges, and independent colleges of art and design around the country. Learn more at www.oxbowschool.org.

The Traveling School

Through The Traveling School (TTS), 15- to 18-year-old girls have the opportunity to go overseas for an academic semester that enables them experience the world and reconnect with their childhood curiosity of learning.

TTS Fall Semester programs run from the end of August through the beginning of December and alternate between South-East Africa and South-West Africa. The South-East Africa semester travels through Zambia, Mozambique, and South Africa. Starting on the

Zambian side of Victoria Falls, students and faculty journey through rural villages to the South Luangwa National Park. Students discover Mozambique's palm-fringed coasts, where they have the opportunity to earn their open water scuba certificates and experience small towns and colorful markets. In addition, students volunteer in schools, orphanages, and villages during the semester.

In the South-West Africa semester, students travel through South Africa, Namibia, and Botswana—exploring from the tip of Cape Horn to the Skeleton Coast in Namibia to the massive elephant herds in Botswana's Okavango Delta. Students stay with local families outside of Cape Town, hike Table Mountain, and meet with freedom fighters who helped to bring an end to Apartheid in South Africa. Students climb rocks, listen to African drums in ancient villages, help with service projects, and experience a river trip on the gentle Orange River between Namibia and South Africa.

TTS Spring semesters run from the start of February through mid-May in Central or South America. In Central America, students travel throughout Guatemala, Chiapas Mexico, and Nicaragua. Students visit ancient Mayan ruins, learn to scuba dive in the turquoise waters of the Corn Islands of Nicaragua, and try out surfing skills on the coast. Students have the opportunity to live in an indigenous community while doing service projects with a local woman's cooperative. In the alternating Spring Semester in South America, students travel through Ecuador, the Galapagos Islands, Peru, and Bolivia, with equally exciting adventures and learning opportunities.

Throughout the TTS semester, students take a full academic course load, including English, a foreign language, global studies, history, math, physical education, and science. The courses focus on the region where the students are traveling and are rigorous, relevant, and inspiring.

For more information on TTS, visit www.travelingschool.com.

The Woolman Semester School

The Woolman Semester School is a progressive academic school for young people who want to make a difference in the world. Students in their junior, senior, or gap year come for a "semester away" to take charge of

their education and study the issues that matter most to them. Woolman students earn transferable high school credits while taking an active role in their learning experience through community work, organic gardening and cooking, permaculture, art, wilderness exploration, service work, and by doing advocacy and activism work with real issues of peace, justice, and sustainability in the world.

The academic foundation of the semester school consists of three core academic classes: Peace Studies, Environmental Science, and Global Issues as well as two academic electives, math (Algebra II and Pre-Calculus), and Spanish II and III. All students take Art, Nonviolent Communication, and Farm to Table classes. In addition, students who do not need math or Spanish may choose from nonacdemic electives, which are offered each semester. In the past, these courses have included Art as Activism, Wilderness Training, Permaculture, the History of American Music and others.

Three times a semester, Woolman learning goes on the road. The backpacking trip along the wild and scenic Yuba River orients students to the natural world that is Woolman's backyard. During the Food Intensive, students and teachers travel to the San Francisco Bay area and California's Central Valley for a week-long exploration of food systems as part of the Environmental Science curriculum. The Peace Studies–Global Issues trip integrates peace with social and environmental justice by traveling to the Bay area to connect with and learn from activists living what they believe.

Students at Woolman live and learn with their classmates and teachers exploring the 230 acres and the nearby Yuba River. They connect with environmental and peace organizations in the local communities of Grass Valley and Nevada City. Through their experience at Woolman, students become engaged citizens with skills to begin addressing issues of peace, social justice, and sustainability on a local and global scale.

For more information on The Woolman Semester School, visit http://semester.woolman.org/.

The author wishes to acknowledge and thank all the semester school programs for contributing their school profiles and collaborating in order to spread the word about semester school education.

Why a Therapeutic or Special Needs School?

Diederik van Renesse

Families contact me when a son or daughter is experiencing increased difficulties in school or has shown a real change in attitude at home. Upon further discussion, parents often share the fact that they have spoken with their child's teachers and have held meetings to establish support systems in the school and at home. Evaluations, medications, therapists, and motivational counseling are but a few of the multiple approaches that parents and educators take—yet in some cases, the downward spiral continues. Anxiety builds in the student and family members; school avoidance and increased family turmoil reach a point where the situation is intolerable, and alternatives must be explored—be it a special needs school, a therapeutic school, or a combination of both.

But should that school be a day or residential school, and how do parents decide which will best meet their child's needs? Resources such as *Peterson's Private Secondary Schools*, the Internet, guidance/school counselors, and therapists are valuable; however, the subtle nuances involved in determining the environment that will best serve the child are difficult to ascertain. Some families seek the help of an independent education consultant to identify the most appropriate setting. Many independent education consultants specialize in working with children who have special needs such as learning differences, anxiety disorders, emotional issues, ADHD, opposition, defiance, school phobia, drug or alcohol abuse, Asperger Syndrome, autism, and more. Consultants have frequent contact with the schools, and they work closely with parents during the enrollment process.

Some families seek the help of an independent education consultant to identify the most appropriate setting.

Given the broad spectrum of needs presented by individual students, many parents question whether there is indeed a day school that can meet the needs of their child. The answer often depends on location, space availability, willingness to relocate, and appropriateness of the options. While there are many day school options throughout the United States, there are even more residential or boarding options. Clearly the decision to have your child attend a residential school is not made easily. As a family you may feel as though you do not have a choice—but you should undertake a thorough assessment of all the day options and how they might meet the majority of your child's needs.

When the primary concerns are learning differences, many local options (though often small and issue-specific) are available to families. Local counselors are often valuable resources as are local chapters of national LD organizations. If you come up with a variety of options, carefully compare them by visiting the schools and meeting with the specialists at each school—those individuals who will work directly with your child.

With the day options, it is important to keep the following factors in mind: program and staff credentials, transportation time to and from the school, availability of additional resources (support services) in or outside the school setting, sports and extracurricular offerings, facilities and accessibility, and your child's potential peer group. You will also need to assess many of these factors when considering residential schools, although most residential schools are more self-contained than day schools. Also significant is whether the school has been approved by and accepts funding from its state and/or school district.

For families who cannot avail themselves of local day options or whose child is best served in a residential setting, an even greater spectrum of options is available. These range from traditional boarding schools with built-in academic support services to therapeutic boarding schools, wilderness or outdoor therapeutic programs, emotional growth or behavior modification schools, transitional or independent living programs, and even residential treatment centers, hospitals, or other health facilities.

Given the breadth of the residential schools or programs, most families are best served by a team that includes not only the parents (and at times the student), but also the professionals who have taught, counseled, and worked closely with the child. Together, the team can identify the specific needs, deficits, or behavioral issues that must be addressed, and they can work together to match those with the appropriate schools. As with day schools, you should arrange to visit the facilities so that you are well-informed about each option and will be comfortable with your final decision. These visits are not only opportunities for you to meet the staff and students, but also for you and your child to begin a relationship that will continue when your child is enrolled.

There is no question that seeking alternative options, whether they are special needs or therapeutic, is a daunting task. However, with the help of expert resources and reliable professionals, the right school can make a significant and lasting impact on your child's health and well-being.

Diederik van Renesse is a Senior Partner at Steinbrecher & Partners Educational Consulting Services in Westport, Connecticut. A former teacher, admission director, and private school counselor, he now specializes in helping families throughout the United States and abroad with youngsters who require special needs or alternative schools or who need interventions and therapeutic settings.

Finding the Perfect Match

Helene Reynolds

One of the real benefits of independent education is that it allows you to deliberately seek out and choose a school community for your child. If you are like most parents, you want your child's school years to reflect an appropriate balance of academic challenge, social development, and exploration into athletics and the arts. You hope that through exposure to new ideas and sound mentoring your child will develop an awareness of individual social responsibility, as well as the study skills and work ethic to make a contribution to his or her world. It is every parent's fondest wish to have the school experience spark those areas of competence that can be pursued toward excellence and distinction.

An increasing number of parents realize that this ideal education is found outside their public school system, that shrinking budgets, divisive school boards, and overcrowded classrooms have resulted in schools where other agendas vie with education for attention and money. In this environment there is less time and energy for teachers to focus on individual needs.

The decision to choose a private school can be made for as many different reasons as there are families making the choice. Perhaps your child would benefit from smaller classes or accelerated instruction. Perhaps your child has needs or abilities that can be more appropriately addressed in a specialized environment. Perhaps you are concerned about the academic quality of your local public school and the impact it may have on your child's academic future. Or perhaps you feel that a private school education is a gift you can give your child to guide him or her toward a more successful future.

Every child is an individual, and this makes school choice a process unique to each family. The fact that your father attended a top-flight Eastern boarding school to prepare for the Ivy League does not necessarily make this educational course suitable for all of his grandchildren. In addition to determining the school's overall quality, you must explore the appropriateness of philosophy, curriculum, level of academic difficulty, and style before making your selection. The right school is the school where your child will thrive, and a famous name and a hallowed reputation are not necessarily the factors that define the right environment. The challenge is in discovering what the factors are that make the match between your child and his or her school the right one.

No matter how good its quality and reputation, a single school is unlikely to be able to meet the needs of all children. The question remains: How do families begin their search with confidence so they will find what they are looking for? How do they make the right connection?

As a parent, there are a number of steps you can follow to establish a reasoned and objective course of information gathering that will lead to a subjective discussion of this information and the way it applies to the student in question. This can only occur if the first step is done thoroughly and in an orderly manner. Ultimately, targeting a small group of schools, any of which could be an excellent choice, is only possible after information gathering and discussion have taken place. With work and a little luck, the result of this process is a school with an academically sound and challenging program based on an educational philosophy that is an extension of the family's views and which will provide an emotionally and socially supportive milieu for the child.

Step 1: Identify Student Needs

Often the decision to change schools seems to come out of the blue, but, in retrospect, it can be seen as a decision the family has been leading up to for some time. I would urge parents to decide on their own goals for the search first and to make sure, if possible, that they can work in concert toward meeting these goals before introducing the idea to their child. These goals are as different as the parents who hold them. For one parent, finding a school with a state-of-the-art computer program is a high priority. For another, finding a school with a full dance and music program is important. Others will be most concerned about finding a school that has the best record of college acceptances and highest SAT® or ACT® scores.

Once you have decided your own goals for the search, bring the child into the discussion. I often say to parents that the decision to explore is *not* the decision to change schools but only the decision to gather information and consider options. It is important to be aware that everyone has an individual style of decision making and that the decision to make a change is loaded with concerns, many of which will not be discovered until the process has begun.

If you have already made the decision to change your child's school, it is important to let your child know that this aspect of the decision is open to discussion but not to negotiation. It is equally important that you let your child know that he or she will have responsibility in choosing the specific school. Without that knowledge, your son or daughter may feel that he or she has no control over the course of his or her own life.

Some students are responsible enough to take the lead in the exploration; some are too young to do so. But in all cases, children need reassurance about their future and clarity about the reasons for considering other school settings. Sometimes the situation is fraught with disparate opinions that can turn school choice into a family battleground, one in which the child is the ultimate casualty. It is always important to keep in mind that the welfare of the child is the primary goal.

The knowledge that each individual has his or her own agenda and way of making decisions should be warning enough to pursue some preliminary discussion so that you, as parents, can avoid the pitfall of conflicting goals and maintain a united front and a reasonably directed course of action. The family discussion should be energetic, and differences of opinion should be encouraged as healthy and necessary and expressed in a climate of trust and respect.

There are many reasons why you may, at this point, decide to involve a professional educational consultant. Often this choice is made to provide a neutral ground where you and your child can both speak and be heard. Another reason is to make sure that you have established a sound course of exploration that takes both your own and your child's needs into consideration. Consultants who are up-to-date on school information, who have visited each campus, and who are familiar with

If you have already made the decision to change your child's school, it is important to let your child know that this aspect of the decision is open to discussion but not to negotiation.

the situations of their clients can add immeasurably to the process. They can provide a reality check, reinforcement of personal impressions, and experience-based information support for people who are doing a search of this type for the first time. All the research in the world cannot replace the experience and industry knowledge of a seasoned professional. In addition, if the specific circumstances of the placement are delicate, the educational consultant is in a position to advocate for your child during the placement process. There are also situations in which a family in crisis doesn't have the time or the ability to approach school choice in a deliberate and objective manner.

These are some of the many reasons to engage the services of a consultant, but it is the family guidance aspect that most families overlook at the start of the process and value most highly after they have completed it. A good consultant provides neutral ground and information backup that are invaluable.

Step 2: Evaluate Your Child's Academic Profile

If your child's academic profile raises questions about his or her ability, learning style, or emotional profile, get a professional evaluation to make sure that your expectations for your child are congruent with the child's actual abilities and needs.

Start gathering information about your child from the current school. Ask guidance counselors and teachers for their observations, and request a formal meeting to review the standardized testing that virtually every school administers. Question their views of your child's behavior, attentiveness, and areas of strength and weakness. Make sure you fully understand the reasons behind their recommendations. Do not feel shy about calling back to ask questions at a later date, after you have had time to think and consider this important information. Your child's future may depend on the decisions you are making; don't hesitate to keep asking until you have the information you need.

If a picture of concern emerges, ask the guidance counselor, other parents, or your pediatrician for suggestions regarding learning specialists or psychologists in the community who work with children and can provide an evaluation of their academic ability, academic achievement, and learning style. The evaluation should be reviewed in-depth with the specialist, who should be asked about specific recommendations for changes in the youngster's schooling.

Remember, as the parent, it is ultimately your responsibility to weigh the ideas of others and to decide if the difficulty lies with your child or the environment, either of which could indicate a need for a change of school.

Step 3: Review the Goals of Placement

Discuss your differences of opinion about making a change. Identify a list of schools that creates a ballpark of educational possibilities. (An educational consultant can also be helpful at this stage.)

It is important that both you and your child take the time to consider what characteristics, large and small, you would like in the new school and which you would like to avoid. As you each make lists of priorities and discuss them, the process of school choice enters the subjective arena. The impersonal descriptions of school environments transform into very personal visualizations of the ways you and your child view the child in a new setting.

A chance to play ice hockey, a series of courses in Mandarin Chinese, the opportunity to take private flute lessons, or a desire to meet others from all over the world may sound like a bizarre mix of criteria, but the desire to explore and find all of these options in a single environment expresses the expansiveness of the student's mind and the areas he or she wants to perfect, try out, or explore. Don't expect perfectly logical thinking from your child as he or she considers options; don't take everything he or she says literally or too seriously. Open and respectful discussion will allow a child to embrace a new possibility one day and reject it the next—this is part of the process of decision making and affirmation and part of the fun of exploration.

Step 4: Set an Itinerary

Set an itinerary for visits and interviews so that you and your child can compare campuses and test your preconceived ideas of the schools you have researched against the reality of the campus community; forward standardized testing scores and transcripts to the schools prior to visits so that the admission office has pertinent information in advance of your meeting.

In order to allow your child the freedom to form opinions about the schools you visit, you may want to keep these pointers in mind:

- Parents should allow their child to be front and center during the visits and interviews—allow your child to answer questions, even if they leave out details you think are important.

- Parents should stay in the background and have confidence that the admission officers know how to engage kids in conversation.

- This may be the first time your child has been treated by a school as an individual and responsible person—enjoy watching him or her adjust to this as an observer, not as a protector or participant.

- Don't let your own anxiety ruin your child's experience.

- Discuss dress in advance so it doesn't become the issue and focus of the trip.

Keep your ideas and impressions to yourself and allow your child first shot at verbalizing opinions. Remember that immediate reactions are not final decisions; often the first response is only an attempt to process the experience.

Step 5: Use the Application Process for Personal Guidance

Make sure your child uses the application process not only to satisfy the school's need for information but also to continue the personal guidance process of working through and truly understanding his or her goals and expectations.

Application questions demand your child's personal insight and exploration. Addressing questions about significant experiences, people who have influenced his or her life, or selecting four words that best describe him or her are ways of coming to grips with who your child is and what he or she wants to accomplish both at the new school and in life. Although parents want their children to complete seamless and perfect applications, it is important to remember that the application must be the work of the child and that the parent has an excellent opportunity to discuss the questions and answers to help guide the student in a positive and objective self-review.

It is more important that the application essays accurately reflect the personality and values of the student than that they be technically flawless. Since the school is basing part of its acceptance decision on the contents of the application, the school needs to meet the real student in the application. The child's own determination of what it is important for the school to know about them is crucial to this process. That being said, parents can play an important role in helping the child understand the difference between unnecessarily brutal honesty and putting his or her best foot forward.

Step 6: Trust Your Observations

Although the process of school exploration depends on objectivity, it is rare that a family will embrace a school solely because of its computer labs, endowment, library, SAT or ACT scores, or football team. These objective criteria frame the search, but it tends to be the intangibles that determine the decision. It is the subjective—instinctive responses to events on campus, people met, quality of interview, unfathomable vibes—that makes the match.

It is important to review what aspects of the school environment made you feel at home. These questions apply equally to parent and child. Did you like the people you met on campus? Was the tour informational but informal, with students stopping to greet you or the tour guide? Was the tone of the campus (austere or homey, modern or traditional) consistent with the kind of educational atmosphere you are looking for? Are the sports facilities beyond your wildest expectation? Does the college-sending record give you confidence that your child will find an intellectually comfortable peer group? How long do the teachers tend to stay with the school, and do they send their own children there? If it is a boarding school, do teachers live on campus? How homey is the dorm setup?

The most fundamental questions are: Do people in the school community like where they are, trust each other, have respect for each other, and feel comfortable there? Is it a family you would care to join? These subjective responses will help you recognize which schools will make your child feel he or she is part of the community, where he or she will fit in and be respected for who he or she is and wants to become.

————————

Helene Reynolds is a former educational consultant from Princeton, New Jersey.

Tips for a Successful School Search

You'd like to have your child attend a private school—but making that decision is just the first step on the process. From researching and touring, to applying and acceptance, there's a lot to consider along the way. Here are some things to keep in mind as you and your student head toward that exciting first day at a new school!

First of all, don't wait until the last minute. Searching and finding the right school for your student can be a lengthy process. Ideally, you should start searching at least a year before your student will be attending.

Research: Which Schools Do You Want to Consider and Why?

When it comes to private schools, there are hundreds to choose from and many options to consider. Day school or boarding school? A school that offers general college prep or one with a specific focus or specialty, whether it's the arts or athletics? Close to home or across the country? Co-ed or single-sex? What is your child's learning style? Answering some of these questions first will help narrow your search.

You may already have some schools in mind: those that you're familiar with because they're in your area or those that you've heard about from other families. Whether you're conducting a broad search or have a short list of possibilities, books like this one are a great place to start familiarizing yourself with what schools are available and what they have to offer.

Once you have identified some potential schools, start looking more closely at each one. A school's website is a great place to start; it can offer a wealth of information and pictures. You can also request a catalog and application packet from each school, too.

Tips from the Experts:

Be realistic about your child. Don't search in terms of bragging rights instead of your child's needs and abilities. Children are better served if their parents think about what their real needs are. How much pressure can they handle? What kind of structure does your child need?

~Elizabeth Norton, Director of Enrollment and Financial Aid, York Preparatory School

It is important to understand the strengths and weaknesses of your child in order to be able to do the appropriate research and make the most suitable decision on the right school for your family.

~Dr. Douglas Laurie, Vice President, American Heritage School

Students must first determine if the school's academic curriculum is in line with their personal goals. Next, students should consider the school's culture and its values, from daily activities to annual celebrations.

~Emily McKee, Associate Director of Admissions, TASIS The American School in Switzerland

Don't just look at test scores or lists of colleges that the school's students go on to. That doesn't really tell you about the school.

~Susan Grodman, Director of Enrollment and Global Programs, Derryfield School

A year, or even a semester, abroad can be a life-enhancing experience, broadening a student's world perspective as well as helping their college application stand out. You may want to look for an international school with an academic program that complements your child's current curriculum to ease the transition in both directions.

~Karen House, Director of Admissions, TASIS The American School in England

The biggest mistake families can make is creating their list of schools based only on perceived prestige. This process is not about brand names; it is about fit. Being a big fish in a small pond might provide the right student with a needed burst of confidence during these developmentally critical years, and it might be a better choice than ending up at a school where the child might struggle for four years.

~Beth Whitney, Director of Admission,
Fay School, Southborough, MA

Visiting: See for Yourself

A website or brochure can only convey so much—if at all possible, you and your child need to visit each school you're considering in person. Most schools have special visit days for prospective families several times throughout the year. If you're not able to make it to a specific event, schedule an appointment to check out the school in person.

Be prepared for the visit. Review the school's website and materials. Write down any questions you may have. Are there specific things you and your student want to see, such as a particular sports facility, dormitory rooms, or the concert hall?

Will your student be interviewed during the visit? If so, help them prepare by practicing answering questions that they might be asked, such as why they want to attend the school or what their educational goals are for the future. Encourage them to relax and be themselves.

Take part in as much as possible during your visit: tours, presentations from administrators and teachers, question and answer sessions, other activities, meals, etc. Take notes about your observations.

Tips from the Experts:

Visit! The best way to know if you have found your home is to experience the place firsthand. It is difficult to differentiate schools on paper or on screen, and visits give students the opportunity to experience classes, extracurricular activities, and, perhaps most importantly, the school's culture and vibe.

~Emily McKee, Associate Director of
Admissions, TASIS–The American School in
Switzerland

Be open-minded when looking at schools. Don't dismiss a school because you think it might be too rigid, or not athletic enough, or too large, and so on. It could prove to be just right once you actually visit and see it firsthand.

~Sharon Levin, Head of School, Jack M.
Barack Hebrew Academy

We host Open Houses two times each year for prospective families, and we also encourage people to schedule a personal tour. We believe that by visiting our campus and seeing firsthand the diversity of our curriculum and the energy of our student body, a family will better understand our school's philosophy and vision so as to make an informed decision whether our school is the right fit for their child.

~Dr. Douglas Laurie, Vice President,
American Heritage School

Most schools have January or February deadlines, so it pays to begin filling out forms in November.

If possible, don't just come for the official tour and the interview. Come to other events, like concerts or ball games, and talk to other parents. Observe the students, too.

~Susan Grodman, Director of
Enrollment and Global
Programs, Derryfield School

On a campus visit, focus on your feelings and impressions. This is a time for you to "smell" the school's culture and not concern yourself with facts and figures. Before you arrive, read the school's mission and ask your hosts to describe how the school fulfills that mission.

~Tom Sheppard, Dean of Admission and
Financial Aid, Lawrenceville School

What would it actually be like to go to this school, to be a member of this learning community? Only by walking around the campus, talking with students and teachers, and observing school life firsthand can this question begin to be answered in an authentic way.

~Beth Whitney, Director of
Admission, Fay School

It's Time to Apply

After the research, tours, visits, interviews, and conversations with administrators and teachers at the various schools, you have a lot of information to consider. Your field of possibilities may have been narrowed to just one or two, or you may still have several choices.

Weigh all the options involved: academics, extracurricular activities, size, financial viability, transportation expenses, distance, and so on. Don't forget that important, but vague quality known as "fit." You may just have a gut feeling that a certain school is right—or wrong—for your student.

Then you and your child need to carefully fill out and submit all the required forms and materials for the school or schools that top your list. In addition to the application, schools may request the student's academic records, references from teachers, a student statement, a writing sample or essay, an application fee, and medical history. Some or all of this may be completed and submitted online.

Most schools have deadlines in January or February for the academic year that starts the following fall, so gathering materials and references and filling out the forms should be underway in November.

Tips from the Experts:

One of the biggest mistakes people make when applying is not meeting deadlines or thinking they don't matter. Deadlines are there for a reason; they help both the school and student plan and be prepared. For instance, if a student needs a little help in a certain subject area they can work on that over the summer.

~Jen Groen, Director of Admissions and Strategic Engagement, Jack M. Barack Hebrew Academy

Deadlines are important for many reasons, but perhaps the biggest reason is basic respect. When a student meets all deadlines in the application process, it's a sign that the decision to apply has been well thought-out and that the applicant's family is serious about wanting to join the school community. When the deadlines aren't met, the admission officer is left asking him or herself "Will this child be able to turn in his homework on time at our school next year?" On the other hand, if you learn of a school after the deadline has passed, call the school to find out if applying late is an option. Many schools will welcome a late application if there is still space available in that grade.

~Beth Whitney, Director of Admission, Fay School

Narrowing choices to a manageable and realistic number is most important, along with utilizing common applications, which teachers who are writing recommendations will appreciate. Admissions offices are a helpful resource to ensure students are presenting their best selves. Also, deadlines are critical, and they vary from school to school. Organization is key to ensuring applications are received on time, especially at schools where space is limited.

~Emily McKee, Associate Director of Admissions, TASIS–The American School in Switzerland

While children should have input on the decision, it's okay for parents to make the final call.

~Sharon Levin, Head of School, Jack M. Barack Hebrew Academy

The application process can feel arduous, but seize it as an opportunity for the student to reflect on him or herself as a learner and as a person. Find moments for the whole family to bask in the child's stories of those challenges overcome and accomplishments celebrated that go into the application. And in the end, remember that all of your efforts will end up significantly enhancing the life of the student by matching him/her to an amazing school.

~Beth Whitney, Director of Admission, Fay School

The Decision

Much as you may want your student to attend a particular school, once you've applied, the decision is not yours to make. Sometimes a school will say yes and everyone will be happy, but other times, the answer is no.

Realistically, private schools can't admit every student who applies. It's important to remind your child that being turned down by a school is not a statement about his or her worth. You need to be gracious and look at other possibilities; perhaps reconsidering another school on your list or looking at other choices.

If you apply and your student is accepted at more than one school, then you need to make a final decision and notify the schools that the student chooses not to attend, so their spot could be given to another student.

Tips from the Experts:

A good fit is a two-way street. The school has to be right for the student, and the student has to be right for the school.

~Jen Groen, Director of Admissions and Strategic Engagement, Jack M. Barack Hebrew Academy

We work hard to be honest when families might not be a good fit for the school and even suggest ways to help a student possibly gain admission down the road.

~Susan Grodman, Director of Enrollment and Global Programs, Derryfield School

With any luck, you have been accepted to more than one school . . . and they're all great choices because you pre-screened them before even applying. So at this point, follow your gut. And the corollary is also true: don't ignore your gut.

~Beth Whitney, Director of Admission, Fay School

A Final Thought

The search for the right private school requires time and effort, but the end result—finding the school that fits your child and his or her needs—is worth it. And there's another benefit. You'll be practiced and prepared when it's time to go through this same process and search for colleges in just a few years!

Admissions Applications for Private Secondary Schools

Tom Sheppard

Dean of Admissions and Financial Aid
Lawrenceville School
Lawrenceville, New Jersey

Enrollment at an independent secondary school is one of the most important educational decisions a family can make. The process of finding the school (or schools) that will be the most appropriate educational fit for any child takes on many dimensions including an application process that can be time consuming and lengthy. However, with careful planning and an understanding of a few important considerations, this process can also serve as important means for parents and children to reflect upon the educational needs of the child.

The most significant development in the application process for secondary schools in recent years has been the integration of technology into what had been a paper-driven process. Advances in technology have enabled the application process for independent schools to evolve rapidly, and, in numerous ways, some of these advances have proven to be helpful to the applicant and their families. At the same time, some developments have resulted in additional challenges and options that the applicant must navigate throughout the application process.

With each passing year, the admission process at secondary schools continues its transition from a paper-based process to a digital process. As this transition continues, more and more schools have adopted at least one form of a digital application to replace or parallel any paper applications that were previously accepted. To complicate matters, there are several applications that are common to many schools, but no application is universally accepted by all independent schools. Some commonly utilized application processes include the following:

- Standard Application Online by SSAT (SAO)— Accepted by over 500 boarding and day schools (http://www.ssat.org/admission/the-sao)
- Gateway to Prep Schools—Accepted by 60 boarding schools (https://www.gatewaytoprepschools.com)
- TABS Admission Application--PDF Application forms accepted by many boarding schools (http://www.boardingschools.com/

Besides the above noted options, families may discover that clusters of schools offer regionally accepted applications or common recommendation forms that are used in an effort to reduce duplication of efforts among teachers who write numerous letters of recommendation.

The variety of application options and the lack of a single application that is common to all independent schools have resulted in an application process that may require extra time and research on the part of families applying to independent schools. In addition, due dates for applications and other required materials can vary widely. The cumulative effect of the various possible application pathways and due dates is that families will be well served and best able to manage the application process with forethought and attention to detail. Whether or not time and advances in technology bring greater clarity and uniformity to this process remains to be seen.

While any one application may have its own unique requirements, applications often include:

- A request for biographical information
- One or more student essays or short answer questions
- One or more recommendations to be completed by teachers or others who know the applicant
- A transcript request form
- that the applicant submits to his or her current school
- An interview with any school to which a student is applying
- Submission of standardized testing required by the schools

The exact type of testing required can vary widely depending upon region and grade level. Many secondary schools utilize the Secondary School Admission Test (SSAT) and/or the Independent School Entrance Exam (ISEE). These same schools may also accept the PSAT/

NMSQT® or the SAT® for older students. Ultimately, the exact nature of the testing that is part of any application process should be clearly explained on a school's website. Unfortunately, since there is no universal test that covers all grades and all areas of the country, there may be instances in which the list of schools to which a family decides to apply is limited by time available to take one or more required tests.

If the above variables seem like they would make the application process a daunting one, be assured it does not need to be. In an attempt to demystify this process, it may be helpful to hear directly from educational consultants and placement directors who have helped thousands families to successfully navigate the secondary school application process for many years.

What advice would you give to students and parents who are beginning the application process to secondary schools for the first time?

Jennifer Evans and Brady Weinstock, Educational Consultants, Virginia Bush and Associates (www.virginiabush.com):

Take the time to do the process right. It is a process to determine the right school fit for you and your child. Investigate schools on their websites to help define your choices. Make appointments to tour and interview on the campuses. Learn from the tour guides, and meet with the admissions officers to best discover what is right for you and your child. When visiting schools, observe the teacher/student interaction on campuses. Reflect on the campus cultures and offerings. Notice the sense of structure and community. Then try to relate that to your own values and set of expectations and goals for your child's future.

There are many extraordinary school options with extremely passionate teachers who are fully dedicated to enriching children's lives every day. Finding the school that is going to best maximize your child's learning process—socially, emotionally and academically—is the key to his or her future success.

The families with whom we work look back on this journey and are amazed at their child's growth and development throughout the process. Students begin to take ownership and gain a sense of inde-

pendence and autonomy while writing their applications, talking to friends, and visiting and interviewing at the schools. It is a time in life when students are given this amazing opportunity to learn, explore, grow, and self-reflect. If the process is done correctly, it can be a transformational experience. Furthermore it gives students the advantage of gaining so much maturity and perspective about themselves and the world around them. This journey of self-discovery is a wonderful asset to have when entering a new school.

Fran Ryan, Assistant Headmaster and Director of Secondary School Placement, Rumsey Hall School:

Whether a family has professional guidance throughout the process or not, the parents must make the decision about the list of schools to which a child may apply. If the parents are relatively satisfied with any of the schools on the list, then the child can, hopefully, choose from among those schools. By framing the process in this way, the parents are secure in any of the school choices, and the child completely owns the decision in the end.

How can families manage the application process since there isn't one application that can work for all schools?

Cammie Bertram, Educational Consultant, The Bertram Group (http://thebertramgroup.com):

As a result of the confusion associated with secondary school applications, many of our candidates approach the process with fear rather than enthusiasm. Our families struggle to determine which application will be the "right" one to file in order for their sons or daughters to present themselves in the most positive light.

SSATB's most recent parental survey featured in *The Ride to Independent Schools* (http://admission.org/whytheyapply) reports that parents of students attending boarding schools tend to experience the highest level of anxiety about the application process. Our goal is for our candidates to take pride in creating their individual profiles and in developing their unique personal stories and essays. Our team strives to simplify the process to allow our students to maintain their busy lifestyles in and out of the

Using a common application makes the process of applying to multiple schools a much more manageable endeavor.

classroom yet still devote quality time to the application process one step at a time—a delicate balance.

At The Bertram Group we believe that streamlining the method by which our candidates apply to schools has significantly reduced the amount of anxiety associated with filing applications. Because most schools now accept the SAO and/or Gateway forms, there is no longer an emphasis on completing individual schools' applications. However, there still are some institutions that continue to require candidates to submit their own application forms.

We encourage our families to navigate the application process in a manner that best suits their child's learning style. It is often helpful to print out the forms and supplements and create a roadmap so the candidate knows how to target the questions and then discuss what to emphasize in his or her answers. Clustering similar essay topics and then choosing a different opening or closing paragraph often serves as a way to modify an essay so it can be used more than once. Candidates should be well acquainted with the schools to which they are applying and be able to echo themes of importance in their essays. Their interests and accomplishments should dovetail with the philosophy of the schools to which they are applying. We encourage our students to demonstrate how they can be contributors on every level throughout the application process. At the end of the day we want this chapter in our children's lives to be a healthy and rewarding experience.

Jennifer Evans and Brady Weinstock, Educational Consultants, Virginia Bush and Associates:

Take a deep breath! Be organized. This part of the process is difficult to navigate. Everything in this part of the process varies—from application deadlines, to the essays, to the parent statements, to the supplements, and to the teacher recommendations.

Make a chart of which schools take which applications: Most schools list which applications they accept in the How to Apply section of their website, but some do not show all of the options. Calling the schools is the most accurate way to determine which applications they take, if the website does not make it explicitly clear. Parents can also look

directly on the SSAT website for schools that accept the SAO application and on the Gateway to Prep Schools site for member schools. Some schools do not use a common application but will often accept common recommendation forms. Contact the schools directly for information on which forms to use. You may also be able to use the TABS application for TABS member schools.

Once you have chosen which applications to use, you will need to sort out the requirements and recommendations. Again, refer to the How to Apply pages on the schools' websites for instructions, as well as the pages on Gateway and SAO for each school where applicable. Creating a chart of required and optional items to submit will help keep things clear and organized—and we highly recommend doing this!

In the end, the application process may require an investment of time and effort on the part of families interested in independent schools. At the same time this investment will be more likely to ensure that children enroll at an independent school well suited for their educational needs. As a result of such a careful and detailed process, these same schools are well positioned to effectively serve families and provide an important option in today's educational landscape that includes more options than ever before.

About Admission Tests and the SSAT

Heather Hoerle
Executive Director
Secondary School Admission Test Board (SSATB)

Mention the word "testing" to even the most capable student, and he or she is likely to become anxious. It's no wonder, then, that testing in the independent school admission process causes nail-biting among students and parents alike.

It is important to remember, though, that results of admission testing, while integral to an application, are just one of many factors considered by admission officers when determining if your child and their schools make a great match. The degree of emphasis placed on scores depends on the school and on other information, such as the transcript and teacher recommendations. For the vast majority of schools, students with a wide range of SSAT scores are admitted.

The most important thing to remember about admission tests is that they are different from other kinds of tests. Admission tests, while "standardized," are different from aptitude and achievement tests. A classroom math test, for example, is an achievement test: The teacher specifically designed it to evaluate how much you know about what has been covered in class. The SSAT, on the other hand, is designed to measure the verbal, quantitative, and reading skills you have acquired over time, instead of focusing on your mastery of particular course materials. The SSAT provides independent school admission professionals with meaningful information about the possible academic success of potential students like you at their institutions, regardless of students' background or experience.

It's important to remember that results of admission testing, while integral to an application, are just one of many factors considered by admission officers.

Admission tests are also different from classroom and achievement tests, because they are "norm-referenced." This means that your child's score is interpreted relative to the group of students taking the test (the *norm group*). For example, if you are a student in the sixth grade, and your percentile rank on the SSAT verbal section is 70 percent, it means that 70 percent of all the other sixth-grade students' (who have taken the test for the first time on one of the students' Standard SSAT administrations in the USA and Canada in the last three years) verbal scaled scores fall below your scaled score. Therefore, the same scaled score on the SSAT may have a different percentile rank from year to year. In contrast, your percent correct from a classroom math test is 90 percent because you answered 90 percent of the questions correctly. Your score is not referenced to the performance of anyone else in your class.

Finally, admission tests are constructed so that only about half of the examinees will get the average test question correct. This is so that the test will effectively differentiate among test-takers, who vary in their level of skills. Therefore, "average" on the SSAT (50 percent) is different than "average" on your child's math test. Many parents express concern that their child's SSAT percentile is lower than they typically score on other tests such as standardized achievement tests and school exams. It is important to remember that SSAT test takers are members of a small and highly competitive group of students who plan to attend some of the world's best private/independent schools. Being in the middle of this group is still impressive!

Taking the SSAT

There are three levels of the SSAT administered. The Upper Level is administered to students in grades 8–12. The Middle Level is administered to grades 5–7, and the Elementary Level is administered to grades 3 and 4. The Middle and Upper Level exams are both approximately 3 hours in length, while the Elementary Level test is just short of 2 hours. Each test has verbal, reading, and quantitative sections that are constructed in a multiple-choice format, as well as an unscored writing sample.

The two mathematics sections of the Middle and Upper Level SSAT measure a student's knowledge of algebra, geometry, and other quantitative concepts and consists of two 25-question sections. The Elementary Level SSAT test measures knowledge of elementary arithmetic, algebra, and geometry in one 30-minute, 30-question section.

The reading comprehension section of the test measures a student's ability to understand what they have read. After reading a passage, the student will be asked questions about its content or about the author's style, intent, or point of view. The goals are to discern the main idea of the piece, to identify the important details that move the narrative along or create a mood or tone, or to identify the details that support the writer's opinion. The Upper and Middle level tests contain 40 questions, while the Elementary Level test consists of 28 reading comprehension questions.

The verbal section asks students to identify synonyms and interpret analogies. The synonym questions test the strength of the student's vocabulary, while the analogy questions measure a student's ability to relate ideas to each other logically. The Upper and Middle Level SSATs consist of 60 verbal questions, while the Elementary Level test has just 30 verbal section questions.

In addition, the exams contain a writing sample that is not scored but is provided to schools to offer a sense of the student's writing skills. The writing sample section varies based on the level of test. The Upper and Middle Level SSATs offer a choice of two writing prompts. In the Upper Level SSAT, one prompt is a creative prompt and the other an essay prompt. On the Middle Level exam, both are creative prompt choices. The Elementary Level exam offers a picture, and the student must write a story about what is happening in the picture.

There are two types of SSAT test administrations: Standard and Flex. The Standard administrations are given eight Saturdays during the academic year (October, November, December, January, February, March, April, and June) at various test locations around the world. Students also have the option of "on demand" Flex testing through member schools and educational consultants. Students can take up to all eight of the Standard tests, but they may only take the Flex test once.

Test takers can arrange to have SSAT scores sent to different schools and have the option to select school score recipients either during test registration or after receiving their scores. Students can learn more about the test, research schools, find a test center, and register for the SSAT online at ssat.org or by calling 609-683-4440. In addition, students can order the *Official Guide to the SSAT* for the Middle and Upper Level tests. *The Official Guide to the SSAT* is the only study guide written by the SSAT test development team. *The Official Guide to*

the Elementary Level SSAT* is available for free download on ssat.org.

SSAT.org also offers a wealth of resources for the independent school applicant, including free webinars, advice on the process, and an online application that can make applying to schools much easier.

How is the SSAT Scored?

The SSAT uses a method of scoring known in the testing industry as "formula scoring." Students earn one point for every correct answer, receive no points for omitted questions, and lose ¼ point for each incorrect answer (each question has five choices). This is different from "right scoring," which computes the total score by counting the number of correct answers, with no penalty for incorrect answers. Formula scoring is used to remove the test taker's expected gain from random guessing.

Test takers are instructed to omit questions for which they cannot make an educated guess. Since most students have not encountered this kind of test before, it is an important concept for students to understand and have some experience with prior to taking the SSAT. SSAT score reports provide detailed information by section on the number of questions right, wrong, and not answered to aid families and schools in understanding the student's test-taking strategy and scores.

> *The SSAT is designed to measure the verbal, quantitative, and reading skills you have acquired over time.*

How Important Are the Tests?

The SSAT norm group is a highly competitive group. Your child is being compared to all the other students (same grade and same grade/gender) who are taking this test for admission into independent schools—some of which can be the most selective schools in the world. I can assure you, though, that in 100 percent of independent schools, the test is just one part of the selection process. This is vital for students and families to remember, as it relieves the "test-taking pressure" we've read so much about in the media and heard from families, teachers, and the educational community. Admission officers are tasked with finding the right students that not only fit the academic pace of their school, but also the culture and community that is unique to each independent school environment. The SSAT is not designed to measure other characteristics such as motivation, persistence, or creativity that a student may contribute to a particular school's community environment.

That said, parents should be partners in the test-preparation process, both as tutors and reassuring voices for the student. This same relationship should extend to partnering with your student to submit an application that highlights a student's schoolwork portfolios and other academic achievements, recommendations, and elements that are just as critical to the selection process. Remember, admission officers must find applicants that are the right academic AND social/cultural fit for their school. The SSAT can only assist in determining one element of this process.

Heather Hoerle's career began in independent schools as an administrator, student advisor, and teacher at George School (Newtown, PA) and Westtown School (Westchester, PA). She then embarked on a successful 23-year tenure in leadership roles with two of the world's largest nonprofit independent school associations: first as associate director of The Association of Boarding Schools (TABS), then as director of admission and marketing services for The National Association of Independent Schools (NAIS), leading to a vice presidency at NAIS overseeing membership, corporate affiliations, customer service, and the annual NAIS Conference.

Heather holds a B.A. in art history from Mount Holyoke College and a M.Ed. in educational administration from Harvard University. She has been a board member for Westtown School (her alma mater) and is presently a trustee for the National Business Officers Association, Princeton Academy of the Sacred Heart, and New Jersey Association of Independent Schools. Heather currently resides in Hopewell, New Jersey with her husband; she has one daughter, a student at Skidmore College.

10 Tips for Doing Your Best on the SSAT

1. Practice, practice, practice—early!

For the SSAT, just like other standardized tests, if you practice, you will feel more confident that you'll do well. Purchase the *Official Guide to the SSAT* a couple of months before you plan to take the test, if possible.

2. Read—a lot!

The best way to build your vocabulary and to get a better sense for the meanings of unfamiliar words is to see them in the context of other words.

3. If you know you're weak in a particular subject, get help before you take the test.

If you know that math is your weakest subject, make sure you address it as soon as you can. Begin early and practice every day if possible until your skills improve. Look to teachers, tutors, or your parents for advice and assistance.

4. Be prepared.

The night before the test, gather everything you need: your admission ticket, pencils, a snack, and so on. This will allow you time in the morning to eat a healthy breakfast and review, if necessary.

5. Get a good night's rest.

We can't stress enough the importance of trying to relax and get plenty of sleep the night before your exam.

6. Arrive at the test center early on test day and come prepared.

Arrive 30 minutes early. Be sure to have your admission ticket, three #2 pencils, a snack in a clear plastic bag, and water. Leave your cell phone and backpack at home, if possible!

7. Relax!

Your attitude and outlook will be reflected in the outcome of the test. Stay confident and calm throughout your exam. If you start to feel nervous or anxious, take a few deep breaths to collect yourself.

8. Set a pace.

Don't spend too much time on one question, and don't speed through carelessly. If you get stuck on a question, skip it, and return to it later if you have time—be sure to leave the bubble unmarked on your answer sheet for this question! Read each question carefully, and answer accurately.

9. Remember your test-taking strategy!

You receive one point for every correct answer and lose ¼ of a point for each wrong answer on a question. You don't lose points by skipping a question. If you can't eliminate at least one or two of the choices in a question and take an "educated guess," it's better to leave the question unanswered. This strategy can help you receive the highest possible score.

10. Remember: The SSAT is one piece of the admission picture!

The SSAT is just one piece of your admission application. Schools will look at your grades, recommendations, test scores, your interview, and more to decide if you are a fit for their school.

Good luck!

About the Independent School Entrance Exam (ISEE)

Elizabeth Mangas
Vice President, Admission Testing
Educational Records Bureau (ERB)

If you have chosen to take the ISEE or a school to which you are applying requires it, we want you to know as much as possible about our admission test. We understand that there is often much anxiety involved in testing, but knowledge about the makeup of the test may help to ease your concerns. In the following paragraphs, we will try to summarize information about the ISEE. However, a very detailed description of the test may be found on our website, www.iseetest.org, under "Preparing for the ISEE." There you will see preparation guides called *What to Expect on the ISEE* that are available to you at no cost online. By looking at these guides, you will have a clear idea of the types of items in each section, a full practice test, sample essays, a copy of an actual answer sheet, and other important components of the test.

Modalities and Availability

You may take the ISEE either as a paper-and-pencil test or online. In 42 cities in the United States, groups of schools have joined together to offer the ISEE on a variety of testing dates. They also offer it on some dates before and after the busy part of the admission season. To see which schools offer the test online, check the website mentioned in the previous paragraph.

You may also take an online ISEE at a Prometric Test Center. Prometric is a subsidiary of ETS and has testing centers in over 400 cities in both the United States and abroad. For more information, visit our website.

Levels and Content

There are four levels on the ISEE: Primary, Lower, Middle, and Upper. The Lower Level is for entrance to grades 5 and 6, Middle Level for entrance to grades 7 and 8, and Upper Level for entrance to grades 9–12. Each of these levels contains four multiple choice sections and an essay, which is unscored.

Two of the multiple choice sections, Verbal Reasoning and Quantitative Reasoning, measure your capability for learning a subject. The Reading Comprehension and Mathematics Achievement multiple choice sections provide a school with specific information about your strengths and weaknesses in these areas. The essay is not scored and is meant to show schools how well you write in response to an essay prompt appropriate for your age.

Even more specifically, the **Verbal Reasoning** section consists of two types of items: vocabulary (synonyms) and sentence completion. The **Quantitative Reasoning** consists of word problems, and for the Middle and Upper levels, quantitative comparisons. The **Reading Comprehension** section consists of reading passages and questions specific to those passages. For example, you may be asked to find the main idea of the passage or inferences that may be made from the author's choice of words. The **Mathematics Achievement** section consists of items that require one or more steps in calculating the answer. These items may cover topics such as algebraic concepts, decimals, and measurement.

Again, it is best to go to the *What to Expect on the ISEE* guide books on our website to see specific examples of ISEE test items and essay questions. You will feel much more comfortable when you sit down to take the ISEE if you do this.

Timing

The Lower Level test is 2 hours 20 minutes in length, and the Middle and Upper level tests are 2 hours 40 minutes in length. The essay section for all three levels is 30 minutes. Once "time" is called, you may not return to a completed section. There is a 5-minute warning before the end of each of the multiple-choice sections, and there is both a 15-minute and a 5-minute warning in the essay section. There are two 5-minute breaks, one after the second section of the test and one after the fourth section.

Non-Standard Administrations

We make every effort to arrange ISEE administrations to accommodate you if you are unable to take the ISEE under standard conditions because of a documented learning difference or physical challenge and you are given accommodations in your current school. Detailed instructions and requirements for seeking approval for accommodations may be found at www.iseetest.org under "ISEE," then "Accommodations."

Parent/Student Portal

You and your family will be able use a portal that is accessed with a password to find test site locations, register for the test, make changes to your registration, and order special services such as expedited score reports.

Scoring

The schools you have selected when you register for the test will generally receive your ISEE score reports electronically within 48 hours of the scoring process. Your family will not receive a copy of your essay because of the security of our essay prompts. The schools will receive a copy of your essay along with your ISEE score report.

You will receive credit only for correct answers. There are no points taken off for incorrect answers.

Your score on each section of the ISEE is based on a pool of students in your same grade who have taken the ISEE over the past three years—the ISEE norming population. Therefore, remember that you are not being compared to the children who took the test at your test site or other students who tested the same day. You should keep in mind that students taking the ISEE are also applying to independent schools and that they tend to be a select and possibly higher achieving group than those who take tests with a wider norming population. Therefore, your scores may be as much as 20 to 40 percentile points lower than you are used to receiving on nationally normed tests. The schools to which you are applying are aware of this difference.

You may ask to have score reports sent to extra schools after you have tested. Your registration includes the sending of score reports to six schools plus your family.

You may wonder what a "good" or "bad" score is. These terms are relative and may only be determined by the specific school looking at your score report.

Fee waivers

Fee waivers are available to cover the cost of an ISEE at a school or a Prometric site. These waivers are granted by a school's admission office, not by Educational Records Bureau (ERB).

Testing Policy

Identification for a tester is required at check-in on the day of testing. If a student's identity is in question before, during, or after the exam, ERB will not release test scores and reserves the right to investigate the matter at the expense of the family. ERB may, at is discretion, disclose the results of any such investigation to the schools to which the test results were to be sent and to all appropriate government regulators.

How Schools Use Your Information

It is important to remember that each school to which you are applying will use other information about you, besides your ISEE scores, as they evaluate your application. This information may include your transcript, teacher recommendations, scores from other standardized tests, and lists of extracurricular activities and interests. Most important, they will be considering *you*, the person they met at an open house, at a day visit, and/or at an interview. You are the most important part of the admission process.

Keep your perspective and remember that the schools will be looking at many items in your application folder— not just your ISEE scores.

Other Important Information

When using the ISEE as your admission test of choice, please remember the following:

- Test sites and Prometric sites fill up rapidly *and are on a first-come, first-served basis*.
- The test-preparation guides called *What to Expect on the ISEE* are your best preparation for the test. They are online, free of charge, and contain answers to just about everything you ever wanted to know about the test. (You may purchase a copy for $20 if you wish.)
- Check the Verification Letter you will receive after you register for the test. It will be your admission ticket on the day of the test along with some personal identification, such as a library card, passport, or green card. The Verification Letter will give you details about the address of the school, the arrival time for the test, and the start time. You don't want to arrive late for the test.

- *If you are taking a paper-based test*, make sure to bring two #2 pencils for the multiple choice sections and a blue or black pen for the essay. (You may use an erasable pen.) You may also bring a light snack for the two 5-minute breaks.
- Get a good night's sleep the night before, and eat a regular, healthy breakfast that morning.
- Keep your perspective and remember that the schools will be looking at many items in your application folder—not just your ISEE scores.

We wish you the best of luck in the admission process. If you have any questions about registering, please call 800-446-0320 (toll-free). If you have any questions about your score reports, please feel free to call 800-989-3721, Ext. 2620.

ERB (Educational Records Bureau) is a global not-for-profit organization providing admission and achievement assessment as well as instructional services for PreK–Grade 12. For over 85 years, and with over 2,000 member schools and districts around the world, ERB continues to be a trusted source to inform admission decisions and/or to support curriculum and instruction. Collaborating with both independent and public schools around the world to build communities, guide instruction, and put assessment insights into action, ERB is dedicated to supporting student learning.

Paying for a Private School Education

Mark J. Mitchell

Vice President, School and Student Services
National Association of Independent
Schools (NAIS)

Imagine being able to buy a $23,000 car for $12,000 because that is all you can afford. When you buy a car, you know that you will be paying more than it cost to design, build, ship, and sell the car. The sales staff will not offer you a price based on your income. At best, you may receive discounts, rebates, or other incentives that allow you to pay the lowest price the dealer is willing to accept. No matter how you look at it, you pay more than the car cost to make.

Tuition at many private schools can approach the cost of a new car, but paying for a private school education is not the same as buying a car. One difference is the availability of financial aid at thousands of schools in the United States and abroad. Financial aid helps offset the cost of tuition. Learning about the financing options and procedures available can make private school a reality for many families.

Need-Based Financial Aid

Many private schools offer assistance to families who demonstrate financial need. In fact, for a recent academic year, schools that belonged to the National Association of Independent Schools (NAIS) provided more than $2 trillion in need-based financial aid to more than 24 percent of their students. For 2015–16, the median grant for boarding school students was $31,363 and the median grant for day school students was $12,753. These need-based grants do not need to be repaid and are used to offset the school's tuition. Schools make this substantial commitment as one way of ensuring a socio-economically diverse student body and to help ensure that every student qualified for admission has the best chance to enroll, regardless of his or her financial circumstances.

How Financial Need Is Determined

Many schools use a process of determining financial need that requires the completion of applications and the submission of tax forms and other documentation to help them decide how much help each family needs. Currently, more than 2,100 schools nationwide ask families to complete The School and Student Services (SSS by NAIS) Parents' Financial Statement (PFS) online at http://SSSbyNAIS.org to determine eligibility for aid. The Parents' Financial Statement gathers information about family size, income and expenses, parents' assets and indebtedness, and the child's assets. From this and other information, schools are provided with an estimate of the amount of discretionary income (after several allowances are made for basic necessities) available for education costs. Schools review each case individually and use this estimate, along with such supporting documentation as most recent income tax forms, to make a final decision on a family's need for a financial aid grant. For more information, please visit http://sssbynais.org.

The amount of a need-based financial aid award varies from person to person and school to school. Just as individuals have different financial resources and obligations that dictate their need for assistance, schools have different resources and policies that dictate their ability to meet your financial need. Tuition costs, endowment incomes, and the school's philosophy about financial aid are a few of the things that can affect how much aid a school can offer. If your decision to send your child to a private school depends heavily on getting financial help, you would benefit from applying for aid at more than one school.

Merit-Based Awards

While the majority of aid offered is based on a family's financial situation, not everyone who receives financial assistance must demonstrate financial need. Private schools offer millions of dollars in merit-based scholarships to thousands of students. In the 2015–16 academic year, 525 NAIS-member schools granted a median annual merit award worth $4,232 to students, totaling more than $84.1 million. Even with this level of commitment, such awards are rare (just 8.3 percent of students enrolled at schools that offer this type of aid received a merit-based grant) and, therefore, highly competitive. They may serve to reward demonstrated talents or achievements in areas ranging from academics to athletics to the arts.

Some additional resources may be available from organizations and agencies in your community. Civic and religious groups, foundations, and even your employer may sponsor scholarships for students at private schools. Unfortunately, these options tend to be few and far between, and limited in number and size of award. Be sure to ask a financial aid officer at the school(s) in which you are interested if he or she is aware of such organizations and opportunities. Whether it is offered by the school or a local organization, understanding the requirements or conditions on which a merit-based scholarship is based is critical. Ask if the award is renewable and, if so, under what conditions. Often, certain criteria must be met (such as minimum GPA, community service, or participation in activities) to ensure renewal of the award in subsequent years, and some merit awards are available for just one year.

Tuition Financing Options

Whether or not you qualify for grants or scholarships, another way to get financial help involves finding ways to make tuition payments easier on your family's monthly budget. One common option is the tuition payment plan. These plans allow you to spread tuition payments (less any forms of financial aid you receive) over a period of eight to ten months. In most cases, payments start before the school year begins, but this method can be more feasible than coming up with one or two lump sum payments before the beginning of the school year. Payment plans may be administered by the schools themselves or by a private company approved by the school. They do not normally require credit checks or charge interest; however, they typically charge an application or service fee, which may include tuition insurance. Additional information about tuition payment plans is available on the NAIS website at http://sssbynais.org.

Since a high-quality education is one of the best investments they can make in their child's future, many parents finance the cost just as they would any other important expense. A number of schools, banks, and other agencies offer tuition loan programs specifically for elementary and secondary school expenses. While such loans are subject to credit checks and must be repaid with interest, they tend to offer rates and terms that are more favorable than those of other consumer loans. It pays to compare the details of more than one type of loan program to find the best one for your needs. Although they should always be regarded as an option of last resort, tuition loan programs can be helpful. Of course, every family must consider both the short- and long-term costs of borrowing and make its decision part of a larger plan for education financing.

A Final Word

Although the primary responsibility to pay for school costs rests with the family, there are options available if you need help. As you can see, financing a private school education can result in a partnership between the family, the school, and sometimes outside agencies or companies, with each making an effort to provide ways to meet the costs. The financial aid officer at the school is the best source of information about your options and is willing to help you in every way he or she can. Always go to the financial aid officer at a school in which you are interested whenever you have any questions or concerns about programs or the application process. Understanding your responsibilities, meeting deadlines, and learning about the full range of options are your best strategies for obtaining assistance. Although there are no guarantees, with proper planning and by asking the right questions, your family just might get the high-quality private education for less.

> *The financial aid officer at the school is the best source of information about your options.*

How to Use This Guide

Quick-Reference Chart

"Private Secondary Schools At-a-Glance" presents data listed in alphabetical order by state and U.S. territories; schools in Canada and other countries follow state listings. If your search is limited to a specific state, turn to the appropriate section and scan the chart for quick information about each school in that state: Are students boarding, day, or both? Is it coeducational? What grade levels are offered? How many students are enrolled? What is the student/faculty ratio? How many sports are offered? Does the school offer Advanced Placement test preparation?

School Profiles and Displays

The **School Profiles** and **Displays** contain basic information about the schools and are listed alphabetically in each section. An outline of a **School Profile** follows. The items of information found under each section heading are defined and displayed. Any item discussed below that is omitted from a **School Profile** either does not apply to that particular school or is one for which no information was supplied.

Heading Name and address of school, along with the name of the Head of School.

General Information Type (boys', girls', coeducational, boarding/day, distance learning) and academic emphasis, religious affiliation, grades, founding date, campus setting, nearest major city, housing, campus size, total number of buildings, accreditation and memberships, languages of instruction, endowment, enrollment, upper school average class size, upper school faculty-student ratio, number of required school days per year (Upper School), number of days per week Upper School students typically attend, and length of the average school day.

Upper School Student Profile Breakdown by grade, gender, boarding/day, geography, and religion.

Faculty Total number; breakdown by gender, number with advanced degrees, and number who reside on campus.

Subjects Offered Academic and general subjects.

Graduation Requirements Subjects and other requirements, including community service.

Special Academic Programs Honors and Advanced Placement courses, accelerated programs, study at local college for college credit, study abroad, independent study, ESL programs, programs for gifted/remedial students and students with learning disabilities.

College Admission Counseling Number of recent graduates, representative list of colleges attended. May include mean or median SAT®/ACT® scores and percentage of students scoring over 600 on each section of the SAT, over 1800 on the combined SAT (scores for the redesigned SAT® were not available at the time of this printing), or over 26 on the composite ACT®.

Student Life Dress code, student council, discipline, and religious service attendance requirements.

Summer Programs Programs offered and focus; location; open to boys, girls, or both and availability to students from other schools; usual enrollment; program dates and application deadlines.

Tuition and Aid Costs, available financial aid.

Admissions New-student figures, admissions requirements, application deadlines, fees.

Athletics Sports, levels, and gender; number of PE instructors, coaches, and athletic trainers.

Computers List of classes that use computers, campus technology, and availability of student e-mail accounts, online student grades, and a published electronic and media policy.

Contact Person to whom inquiries should be addressed.

Displays, provided by school administrators, present information designed to complement the data already appearing in the **School Profile.**

Close-Ups

Close-Ups, written expressly for Peterson's by school administrators, provide in-depth information about the schools that have chosen to submit them. These descriptions are all in the same format to provide maximum comparability. **Close-Ups** follow each **School Profile** section; there is a page reference at the end of a **School Profile** directing you to that school's **Close-Up,** if one was provided. Schools are listed alphabetically in each section.

Special Needs Schools

One of the great strengths of private schools is their variety. This section is dedicated to the belief that there is an appropriate school setting for every child, one in which he or she will thrive academically, socially, and emotionally. The task for parents, counselors, and educators is to know the child's needs and the schools' resources well enough to make the right match.

Schools in this section serve those students who may have special challenges, including learning differences, dyslexia, language delay, attention deficit disorders, social maladjustment to family and surroundings, or emotional disturbances; these students may need individual attention or are underachieving for some other reason. Parents of children who lag significantly behind their grade level in basic academic skills or who have little or no motivation for schoolwork will also want to consult this section. (For easy reference, schools that offer extra help for students are identified in two directories: "Schools Reporting Programs for Students with Special Needs" and "Schools Reporting That They Accommodate Underachievers.") The schools included here chose to be in this section because they consider special needs education to be their primary focus. It is the mission of these schools, whose curricula and methodologies vary widely, to uncover a student's strengths and, with appropriate academic, social, and psychological counseling, enable him or her to succeed.

Junior Boarding Schools

As parents know, the early adolescent years are ones of tremendous physical and emotional change. Junior boarding schools specialize in this crucial period by taking advantage of children's natural curiosity, zest for learning, and growing self-awareness. While junior boarding schools enroll students with a wide range of academic abilities and levels of emotional self-assurance, their goal is to meet each youngster's individual needs within a supportive community. They accomplish this through low student-teacher ratios and enrollment numbers deliberately kept low.

The boarding schools featured in this section serve students in the middle school grades (6–9); some offer primary programs as well. For more information about junior boarding schools, visit the Junior Boarding Schools Association Web site at www.jbsa.org.

Specialized Directories

These directories are compiled from the information gathered in *Peterson's Annual Survey of Private Secondary Schools*. The schools that did not return a survey or provided incomplete data are not fully represented in these directories. For ease of reference, the directories are grouped by category: type, curricula, financial data, special programs, and special needs.

Index

The "Alphabetical Listing of Schools" shows page numbers for School Profiles in regular type, page numbers for Displays in italics, and page numbers for Close-Ups in boldface type.

Data Collection Procedures

The data contained in *Peterson's Private Secondary Schools 2016–17* **School Profiles, Quick-Reference Chart, Specialized Directories, and Index** were collected through *Peterson's Annual Survey of Private Secondary Schools* during summer and fall 2015. Also included were schools that submitted information for the 2014–15 data collection effort but did not submit updates in the summer/fall of 2015. Questionnaires were posted online. With minor exceptions, data for those schools that responded to the questionnaire were submitted by officials at the schools themselves. All usable information received in time for publication has been included. The omission of a particular item from a **School Profile** means that it is either not applicable to that school or not available or usable. Because of Peterson's extensive system of checking data, we believe that the information presented in this guide is accurate. However, errors and omissions are possible in a data collection and processing endeavor of this scope. Therefore, students and parents should check with a specific school at the time of application to verify all pertinent information.

Criteria for Inclusion in This Book

Most schools in this book have curricula that are primarily college preparatory. If a school is accredited or is a candidate for accreditation by a regional accrediting group, including the European Council of Schools, and/or is approved by a state Department of Education, and/or is a member of the National Association of Independent Schools or the European Council of Schools, then such accreditation, approval, or membership is stated. Schools appearing in the **Special Needs Schools** section may not have such accreditation or approval.

Quick-Reference Chart

Private Secondary Schools At-a-Glance

| | STUDENTS ACCEPTED | | | | GRADES | | | STUDENT/FACULTY | | | SCHOOL OFFERINGS | |
| | BOARDING | | DAY | | | | | | | | | |
	Boys	Girls	Boys	Girls	Lower	Middle	Upper	Total	Upper	Student/Faculty Ratio	Advanced Placement Preparation	Sports
UNITED STATES												
Alabama												
Alabama Christian Academy, Montgomery			X	X	K4–5	–	6–12	1,014	535	20:1	X	16
American Christian Academy, Tuscaloosa			X	X	K–5	6–8	9–12	958	401	12:1	X	40
Briarwood Christian High School, Birmingham			X	X	K–6	7–8	9–12	1,912	564	16:1	X	19
Edgewood Academy, Elmore			X	X	PK–5	6–8	9–12	320	82	11:1	X	14
Indian Springs School, Indian Springs	X	X	X	X	–	–	8–12	299	309	8:1	X	18
Madison Academy, Madison			X	X	PS–6	–	7–12	850	448	13:1		13
Marion Academy, Marion			X	X	K–3	4–6	7–12	53	35	8:1		8
Springwood School, Lanett					–	–	–					11
The Westminster School at Oak Mountain, Birmingham			X	X	K–6		7–12	508	178	16:1		10
Alaska												
Grace Christian School, Anchorage			X	X	K–6	7–8	9–12	532	180	15:1	X	8
Arizona												
Arizona Lutheran Academy, Phoenix			X	X	–	–	9–12	188	184	13:1		13
Blueprint Education, Glendale					–	7–12	–					
Brophy College Preparatory, Phoenix			X		–	6–8	9–12	1,391	1,326	15:1	X	44
Faith Christian School, Mesa			X	X	K–6	7–8	9–12			15:1		4
Green Fields Country Day School, Tucson			X	X	K–5	6–8	9–12	105	44	5:1	X	18
The Orme School, Mayer	X	X	X	X	–	–	8–PG	75	120	6:1	X	63
Phoenix Christian Preparatory School, Phoenix			X	X	PS–5	6–8	9–12	385	214	11:1	X	14
Phoenix Country Day School, Paradise Valley			X	X	PK–4	5–8	9–12	750	280	8:1	X	30
Saint Mary's High School, Phoenix			X	X	–	–	9–12	541	573	13:1	X	17
Salpointe Catholic High School, Tucson			X	X	–	–	9–12	1,093	1,125	15:1	X	17
Sedona Sky Academy, Rimrock		X			–	–	9–12	90	90	7:1		20
Seton Catholic High School, Chandler			X	X	–	–	9–12	563	563	13:1	X	25
Southwestern Academy, Rimrock	X	X	X	X	–	6–8	9–PG	1,161	148	9:1	X	52
Tri-City Christian Academy, Chandler			X	X	K–6	7–8	9–12	276	108	7:1		5
Arkansas												
Episcopal Collegiate School, Little Rock			X	X	PK–5	6–8	9–12	784	197	10:1	X	16
Harding Academy, Searcy	X		X	X	K–6	–	7–12	598	327	11:1	X	11
Subiaco Academy, Subiaco	X		X		–	7–8	9–12	199	174	9:1	X	23
West Memphis Christian High School, West Memphis			X	X	K–3	4–6	7–12	208	107	12:1		14
California												
Academy of Our Lady of Peace, San Diego				X	–	–	9–12	748	725	13:1	X	16
Alma Heights Christian High School, Pacifica			X	X	K–5	6–8	9–12	303	147	15:1	X	8
Alverno Heights Academy, Sierra Madre				X	–	–	9–12	170	175	12:1	X	12
Archbishop Mitty High School, San Jose			X	X	–	–	9–12	1,723	1,748	17:1	X	27
Arete Preparatory Academy, Los Angeles			X	X	–	–	9–12	58	53	2:1		1
Army and Navy Academy, Carlsbad	X		X		7–9	–	10–12	267		15:1	X	30
Arroyo Pacific Academy, Arcadia			X	X	–	–	–		137	10:1	X	20
Bakersfield Christian High School, Bakersfield			X	X	–	–	9–12	488	475	17:1	X	17
Balboa City School, San Diego			X	X	1–6	7–8	9–12	75	55	10:1		3
The Bay School of San Francisco, San Francisco			X	X	–	–	9–12	355	355	8:1		20
Bentley School, Lafayette			X	X	K–5	6–8	9–12	684	325	9:1	X	17
Berean Christian High School, Walnut Creek			X	X	–	–	9–12	411	422	20:1	X	11
Bishop O'Dowd High School, Oakland			X	X	–	–	9–12	1,151	1,151	15:1	X	37
The Bishop's School, La Jolla			X	X	–	6–8	9–12	811	540	9:1		18
Brethren Christian Junior and Senior High Schools, Huntington Beach			X	X	–	6–8	9–12	313	244	13:1	X	12
Bridges Academy, Studio City			X	X	4–6	7–8	9–12	170	87	8:1		3
The Buckley School, Sherman Oaks			X	X	K–5	6–8	9–12	830	331	8:1	X	12
California Crosspoint High School, Alameda	X	X	X	X	–	6–8	9–12	200	190	8:1	X	15
California Lutheran High School, Wildomar	X	X			–	–	9–12	85	86	8:1	X	7
Calvin Christian High School, Escondido			X	X	PK–5	6–8	9–12	470	150	17:1	X	11
Campbell Hall (Episcopal), North Hollywood			X	X	K–6	7–8	9–12	1,125	552	8:1	X	20
Capistrano Valley Christian Schools, San Juan Capistrano			X	X	JK–6	7–8	9–12	435	200	13:1	X	17
Carnegie Schools Riverside, Riverside			X	X	K–5	6–8	9–12	253	231	22:1	X	16
Carondelet High School, Concord				X	–	–	9–12	800	800	16:1	X	24
Castilleja School, Palo Alto				X	–	6–8	9–12	438	247	6:1	X	14
Cate School, Carpinteria	X	X	X	X	–	–	9–12	270	280	5:1	X	54

Private Secondary Schools At-a-Glance

| | STUDENTS ACCEPTED | | | | GRADES | | | STUDENT/FACULTY | | | SCHOOL OFFERINGS | |
| | BOARDING | | DAY | | | | | | | | | |
	Boys	Girls	Boys	Girls	Lower	Middle	Upper	Total	Upper	Student/Faculty Ratio	Advanced Placement Preparation	Sports
Chadwick School, Palos Verdes Peninsula			X	X	K–6	7–8	9–12	835	362	6:1	X	21
Chaminade College Preparatory, West Hills			X	X	–	6–8	9–12	2,030	1,322	16:1	X	25
Children's Creative and Performing Arts Academy of San Diego, San Diego	X	X	X	X	K–5	6–8	9–12	262	82	18:1	X	31
Contra Costa Christian High School, Walnut Creek			X	X	K–5	6–8	9–12	230	90	15:1	X	5
Damien High School, La Verne			X		–	–	9–12	936	919	17:1	X	24
De La Salle High School, Concord			X		–	–	9–12	1,038	1,047	28:1	X	23
Eldorado Emerson Private School, Orange			X	X	–	–	–	166	109	18:1	X	7
Escondido Adventist Academy, Escondido			X	X	K–5	6–8	9–12	215	101	10:1	X	6
Faith Christian High School, Yuba City			X	X	–	–	9–12	77	77	9:1	X	12
Flintridge Preparatory School, La Canada Flintridge			X	X	–	7–8	9–12	500	400	8:1	X	16
Flintridge Sacred Heart Academy, La Canada Flintridge		X		X	–	–	9–12	406	391	8:1	X	21
Fresno Christian Schools, Fresno			X	X	K–6	7–8	9–12	464	174	10:1	X	18
The Grauer School, Encinitas			X	X	–	7–8	9–12	164	104	7:1		28
Halstrom Academy, Beverly Hills			X	X	–	6–8	9–12	9	7	1:1	X	
Halstrom Academy, Calsbad			X	X	–	6–8	9–12	51	41	1:1	X	
Halstrom Academy, Cupertino			X	X	–	6–8	9–12	19	16	1:1	X	
Halstrom Academy, Huntington Beach			X	X	–	6–8	9–12	32	21	1:1	X	
Halstrom Academy, Irvine			X	X	–	6–8	9–12	31	26	1:1	X	
Halstrom Academy, Los Angeles			X	X	–	6–8	9–12	13	20	1:1	X	
Halstrom Academy, Manhattan Beach			X	X	–	6–8	9–12	20	29	1:1	X	
Halstrom Academy, Mission Viejo			X	X	–	6–8	9–12	72	60	1:1	X	
Halstrom Academy, Orange			X	X	–	6–8	9–12	27	22	1:1	X	
Halstrom Academy, Pasadena			X	X	–	6–8	9–12	27	21	1:1	X	
Halstrom Academy, San Diego			X	X	–	6–8	9–12	40	36	1:1	X	
Halstrom Academy, San Mateo			X	X	–	6–8	9–12	11	14	1:1	X	
Halstrom Academy, Walnut Creek			X	X	–	6–8	9–12	12	18	1:1	X	
Halstrom Academy, Westlake Village			X	X	–	6–8	9–12	35	30	1:1	X	
Halstrom Academy, Woodland Hills			X	X	–	6–8	9–12	40	44	1:1	X	
The Harker School, San Jose			X	X	K–5	6–8	9–12	1,911	767	10:1	X	21
Harvard-Westlake School, Studio City			X	X	–	7–8	9–12	1,592	1,160	8:1	X	20
Hebrew Academy, Huntington Beach		X	X	X	N–5	6–8	9–12	257	26	4:1	X	14
Hillcrest Christian School, Thousand Oaks			X	X	K–6	7–8	9–12	263	68	8:1	X	7
International High School, San Francisco			X	X	PK–5	6–8	9–12	1,077	376	10:1		15
Jewish Community High School of the Bay, San Francisco					–	–	–				X	10
Junipero Serra High School, San Mateo			X		–	–	9–12	881	860	15:1		29
La Salle High School, Pasadena			X	X	–	–	9–12	650	652	11:1	X	24
La Sierra Academy, Riverside					–	7–8	9–12	573	230	14:1		10
Laurel Springs School, Ojai					K–5	6–8	9–12	1,529	876	1:1	X	
Le Lycee Francais de Los Angeles, Los Angeles			X	X	PS–5	6–8	9–12	819	198	3.6:1	X	24
Liberty Christian High School, Redding			X	X	PK–5	6–8	9–12	145	49	5:1		6
Liberty Christian School, Huntington Beach			X	X	K–6	7–8	9–12	112	26	6:1		4
Linfield Christian School, Temecula			X	X	JK–5	6–8	9–12	757	395	13:1	X	14
Louisville High School, Woodland Hills				X	–	–	9–12	337	337	25:1	X	17
Lutheran High School of San Diego, Chula Vista			X	X	–	–	9–12	101	96	12:1	X	6
Lycée Français La Perouse, San Francisco			X	X	–	6–8	9–12	1,004	182	20:1		
Maranatha High School, Pasadena			X	X	–	–	9–12	680	600	13:1	X	21
Marin Academy, San Rafael			X	X	–	–	9–12	406	406	9:1	X	35
Marlborough School, Los Angeles				X	–	7–9	10–12	530	280	8:1	X	14
Marymount High School, Los Angeles				X	–	–	9–12	396	410	7:1	X	21
Menlo School, Atherton			X	X	–	6–8	9–12	795	575	10:1	X	17
Mesa Grande Seventh-Day Academy, Calimesa			X	X	K–6	7–8	9–12	252	85	10:1		10
Midland School, Los Olivos	X	X			–	–	9–12	81	81	4:1	X	17
Montcrey Bay Academy, La Selva Beach	X	X	X	X	–	–	9–12	181	200	13:1	X	5
Moreau Catholic High School, Hayward			X	X	–	–	9–12	945	951	18:1	X	20
Mountain View Academy, Mountain View			X	X	–	–	9–12	150	133	12:1	X	5
New Roads School, Santa Monica			X	X	K–5	6–8	9–12	615	375	11:1		11
Notre Dame High School, Riverside			X	X	–		9–12	629	505	19:1	X	15
Notre Dame High School, San Jose				X	–	–	9–12	631	631	11:1	X	12
Oak Grove School, Ojai	X	X	X	X	PK–6	7–8	9–12	227	50	7:1	X	15
Ojai Valley School, Ojai	X	X	X	X	PK–5	6–8	9–12	288	109	6:1	X	31
Orangewood Adventist Academy, Garden Grove			X	X	PK–6	7–8	9–12	261	104	10:1	X	12
Orinda Academy, Orinda			X	X	–	8–8	9–12	78	68	8:1	X	7
Pacific Lutheran High School, Gardena			X	X	–	7–8	9–12	107	89	10:1	X	15
Palma School, Salinas			X		–	7–8	9–12	428	363	15:1	X	27
Paradise Adventist Academy, Paradise			X	X	K–4	5–8	9–12	143	53	8:1		3
Polytechnic School, Pasadena			X	X	K–5	6–8	9–12	858	384		X	25
Providence High School, Burbank			X	X	–	–	9–12	435	434	9:1	X	11
Ramona Convent Secondary School, Alhambra				X	–	–	9–12	250	250	9:1	X	8

Private Secondary Schools At-a-Glance

| | STUDENTS ACCEPTED | | | | GRADES | | | STUDENT/FACULTY | | | SCHOOL OFFERINGS | |
| | BOARDING | | DAY | | | | | | | | | |
Private Secondary Schools At-a-Glance	Boys	Girls	Boys	Girls	Lower	Middle	Upper	Total	Upper	Student/Faculty Ratio	Advanced Placement Preparation	Sports
Redwood Christian Schools, Castro Valley			X	X	K–5	6–8	9–12	650	290	16:1	X	8
Rolling Hills Preparatory School, San Pedro			X	X	–	6–8	9–12	256	181	9:1	X	22
Sacramento Country Day School, Sacramento			X	X	PK–5	6–8	9–12	503	128	9:1	X	14
Sacramento Waldorf School, Fair Oaks			X	X	PK–8	–	9–12	441	155	6:1		17
Sacred Heart High School, Los Angeles				X	–	–	9–12	250	260	25:1	X	6
Sage Hill School, Newport Coast			X	X	–	–	9–12	521	518	10:1	X	17
St. Bernard's Catholic School, Eureka	X	X	X	X	PK	7–8	9–12	231	190	12:1	X	11
St. Catherine's Academy, Anaheim	X		X		K–6	7–8	–	145		14:1		24
Saint Francis High School, La Canada Flintridge			X		–	–	9–12	663	663	12:1	X	14
Saint John Bosco High School, Bellflower			X		–	–	9–12	821	835	25:1	X	19
Saint Joseph Academy, San Marcos			X	X	K–5	6–8	9–12	302	60	15:1	X	6
St. Joseph High School, Santa Maria			X	X	–	–	9–12	561	396	19:1		16
Saint Lucy's Priory High School, Glendora				X	–	–	9–12	647	647	17:1	X	21
St. Michael's Preparatory School of the Norbertine Fathers, Silverado	X				–	–	9–12	64	64	3:1	X	21
San Francisco University High School, San Francisco			X	X	–	–	9–12	403	410	7:1	X	24
Santa Catalina School, Monterey		X		X	–	–	9–12	244	233	8:1	X	33
Santa Margarita Catholic High School, Rancho Santa Margarita			X	X	–	–	9–12	1,755	1,755	14:1	X	40
Sierra Canyon School, Chatsworth					K–6	7–8	9–12	1,000	410	10:1	X	21
Sonoma Academy, Santa Rosa			X	X	–	–	9–12	284	302	10:1	X	28
Squaw Valley Academy, Olympic Valley	X	X	X	X	–	–	9–12	100	100	8:1	X	66
STAR Prep Academy, Los Angeles			X	X	–	6–8	9–12	47	30	7:1		
Stevenson School, Pebble Beach	X	X	X	X	PK–4	5–8	9–12	747	498	10:1	X	38
The Thacher School, Ojai	X	X	X	X	–	–	9–12	252	260	5:1	X	46
Valley Christian High School, San Jose			X	X	K–5	6–8	9–12	2,668	1,600	15:1	X	23
Victor Valley Christian School, Victorville			X	X	K–6	7–8	9–12	275	76	16:1	X	12
Westmark School, Encino			X	X	2–5	6–8	9–12	234	101	12:1		14
Westridge School, Pasadena				X	4–6	7–8	9–12	482	296	7:1	X	19
Windward School, Los Angeles			X	X	–	7–8	9–12	541	373	7:1	X	5
Colorado												
Bishop Machebeuf High School, Denver			X	X	–	–	9–12	380	380			13
Denver Academy, Denver			X	X	1–6	7–8	9–12	378	211	8:1		27
Denver Christian High School, Lakewood			X	X	PK–5	6–8	9–12	417	135	19:1		11
Eagle Rock School, Estes Park	X	X	X	X	–	–	–		72	4:1		40
Fountain Valley School of Colorado, Colorado Springs	X	X	X	X	–	–	9–12	236	230	5:1	X	42
Front Range Christian High School, Littleton			X	X	PK–6	7–8	9–12	437	172	12:1	X	24
Kent Denver School, Englewood			X	X	–	6–8	9–12	698	475	13:1	X	27
Lutheran High School, Denver			X	X	–	–	9–12	182	470	20:1	X	10
Regis Jesuit High School, Boys Division, Aurora			X		–	–	9–12	944	930	12:1	X	34
Regis Jesuit High School, Girls Division, Aurora				X	–	–	9–12	738	720	12:1	X	25
St. Mary's High School, Colorado Springs			X	X	–	–	9–12	389	252	11:1	X	13
Steamboat Mountain School, Steamboat Springs	X	X	X	X	–	–	9–12	55	55	8:1	X	58
Connecticut												
Academy of the Holy Family, Baltic		X		X	–	–	9–12	29	34	6:1	X	5
Canterbury School, New Milford	X	X	X	X			9–PG	350	350	6:1	X	28
Chase Collegiate School, Waterbury			X	X	PK–5	6–8	9–12	402	145	8:1	X	32
Choate Rosemary Hall, Wallingford	X	X	X	X			9–PG	867	862	6:1	X	46
Convent of the Sacred Heart, Greenwich			X	X	PS–4	5–8	9–12	750	313	7:1	X	22
Eagle Hill School, Greenwich	X	X	X	X	1–6	–	6–9	250	136	4:1		33
Franklin Academy, East Haddam	X	X	X	X	–	–	8–PG	85	80	2:1		32
The Gunnery, Washington	X	X	X	X	–	–	9–PG	287	288	6:1	X	24
Holy Cross High School, Waterbury			X	X	–	–	9–12	489	489	11:1	X	24
The Hotchkiss School, Lakeville	X	X	X	X	–	–	9–PG	598	629	5:1	X	46
Hyde School, Woodstock	X	X	X	X	–	–	9–12	151	151	6:1	X	21
Kent School, Kent	X	X	X	X	–	–	9–PG	570	572	7:1	X	44
King School, Stamford			X	X	PK–5	6–8	9–12	674	357	8:1	X	22
Kingswood-Oxford School, West Hartford			X	X	–	6–8	9–12	507	342	8:1	X	18
Kolbe-Cathedral High School, Bridgeport			X	X	–	–	9–12	308	308	18:1		6
Lauralton Hall, Milford				X	–	–	9–12	467	456	9:1		18
Marianapolis Preparatory School, Thompson	X	X	X	X	–	–	9–PG	400	400	7:1	X	43
The Marvelwood School, Kent	X	X	X	X	–	–	9–12	172	150	4:1	X	45
Mercy High School, Middletown				X	–	–	9–12	573	533	13:1	X	18
Miss Porter's School, Farmington		X		X	–	–	9–12	323	325	6:1	X	45
Northwest Catholic High School, West Hartford			X	X	–	–	9–12	587	570	12:1	X	34
The Norwich Free Academy, Norwich			X	X	–	–	9–12	2,280	2,339	13:1	X	36
The Rectory School, Pomfret	X	X	X	X	K–4	5–9	–	243	173	4:1		41
Rumsey Hall School, Washington Depot	X	X	X	X	K–5	6–9		420		5:1		54
St. Joseph High School, Trumbull			X	X	–	–	9–12		800	12:1	X	21
St. Luke's School, New Canaan			X	X	–	5–8	9–12	553	314	8:1	X	20

Private Secondary Schools At-a-Glance

	STUDENTS ACCEPTED				GRADES			STUDENT/FACULTY			SCHOOL OFFERINGS	
	BOARDING		DAY									
	Boys	Girls	Boys	Girls	Lower	Middle	Upper	Total	Upper	Student/Faculty Ratio	Advanced Placement Preparation	Sports
The Stanwich School, Greenwich			X	X	PK–5	–	6–12	345	165	5:1	X	22
The Taft School, Watertown	X	X	X	X	–	–	9–PG	594	594	5:1	X	47
Trinity Catholic High School, Stamford			X	X	–	–	9–12	429	416	13:1	X	14
Watkinson School, Hartford			X	X	–	6–8	9–PG	240	180	6:1		29
Westminster School, Simsbury	X	X	X	X	–	–	9–PG	394	395	5:1	X	39
Westover School, Middlebury		X		X	–	–	9–12	210	202	8:1	X	50
The Woodhall School, Bethlehem	X		X		–	–	9–12	42	42	3:1	X	29
Woodstock Academy, Woodstock	X	X	X	X	–	–	9–12	1,025	1,050	14:1	X	28
Delaware												
Tower Hill School, Wilmington			X	X	PS–4	5–8	9–12	703	282	6:1	X	26
Wilmington Christian School, Hockessin			X	X	PK–5	6–8	9–12	500	210	15:1	X	13
Wilmington Friends School, Wilmington			X	X	PS–5	6–8	9–12	736	285	14:1	X	15
District of Columbia												
Edmund Burke School, Washington			X	X	–	6–8	9–12	297	215	6:1	X	17
Gonzaga College High School, Washington			X		–	–	9–12	962	960	13:1	X	27
The Lab School of Washington, Washington			X	X	1–4	5–8	9–12	375	135	8:1		8
St. Albans School, Washington	X		X		4–8	–	9–12	593	324	7:1	X	37
Washington International School, Washington			X	X	PS–5	6–8	9–12	920		7:1		9
Florida												
Academy at the Lakes, Land O'Lakes			X	X	PK–4	5–8	9–12	466	157	5:1	X	17
Allison Academy, North Miami Beach			X	X	–	6–8	9–12	105	74	10:1	X	20
Belen Jesuit Preparatory School, Miami			X		–	6–8	9–12	1,479	846	12:1	X	19
Berkeley Preparatory School, Tampa			X	X	PK–5	6–8	9–12	1,300	575	15:1	X	33
Bishop John J. Snyder High School, Jacksonville			X	X	–	–	9–12	440	440	15:1	X	18
Bishop Kenny High School, Jacksonville			X	X	–	–	9–12	1,210	1,210	14:1	X	17
Bishop Verot High School, Fort Myers			X	X	–	–	9–12	673	668	14:1	X	16
The Bolles School, Jacksonville	X	X	X	X	PK–5	6–8	9–12	1,637	779	12:1	X	18
Bradenton Christian School, Bradenton			X	X	PK–5	6–8	9–12	542	254	11:1	X	20
Canterbury School, Fort Myers			X	X	PK–4	5–8	9–12	620	270	12:1	X	13
The Canterbury School of Florida, St. Petersburg			X	X	PK–4	5–8	9–12	480	161	15:1	X	30
Cardinal Newman High School, West Palm Beach			X	X	–	–	9–12	544	543	25:1	X	19
Chaminade-Madonna College Preparatory, Hollywood			X	X	–	–	9–12	545	545	19:1	X	14
Christopher Columbus High School, Miami			X		–	–	9–12	1,579	1,600	15:1	X	18
The Community School of Naples, Naples			X	X	PK–5	6–8	9–12	807	310	9:1	X	16
Episcopal High School of Jacksonville, Jacksonville			X	X	–	6–8	9–12	857	566	10:1	X	22
Father Lopez High School, Daytona Beach			X	X	–	–	9–12	474	489	14:1	X	17
The First Academy, Orlando			X	X	K4–6	7–8	9–12	990	410	13:1	X	28
Forest Lake Academy, Apopka	X	X	X	X	–	–	9–12	397	412	15:1		13
Foundation Academy, Winter Garden			X	X	K–6	7–8	9–12	677	247	9:1	X	12
Glades Day School, Belle Glade			X	X	PK–6	7–8	9–12	289	117	7:1	X	10
Gulliver Preparatory School, Miami			X	X	1–4	5–8	9–12	2,014	986	8:1	X	39
Immaculata-La Salle High School, Miami			X	X	–	–	9–12	832	854	18:1	X	18
Jesuit High School of Tampa, Tampa			X		–	–	9–12	775	786	12:1	X	17
Lake Mary Preparatory School, Lake Mary	X	X	X	X	PK–5	6–8	9–12	550	237	15:1	X	25
Monsignor Edward Pace High School, Miami Gardens	X	X	X	X	–	–	9–12	817	850	19:1	X	18
Mount Dora Christian Academy, Mount Dora			X	X	PK–5	6–8	9–12	557	192	12:1	X	14
The North Broward Preparatory Upper School, Coconut Creek	X	X	X	X	PK–5	6–8	9–12	1,550	956	18:1	X	32
Northside Christian School, St. Petersburg			X	X	PS–6	7–8	9–12	877	286	11:1	X	21
PACE/Brantley Hall High School, Longwood			X	X	2–5	6–8	9–12	171	85	12:1	X	14
Pensacola Catholic High School, Pensacola			X	X	–	–	9–12	599	630	18:1	X	17
Providence School, Jacksonville			X	X	K–5	6–8	9–12	1,170	439	15:1	X	15
Ransom Everglades School, Miami			X	X	–	6–8	9–12	1,085	612	9:1	X	22
Saddlebrook Preparatory School, Wesley Chapel	X	X	X	X	3–5	6–8	9–12	80	63	8:1		19
Saint Andrew's School, Boca Raton	X	X	X	X	JK–5	6–8	9–12	1,285	585	9:1	X	23
St. John Neumann High School, Naples			X	X	–	–	9–12	213	244	15:1	X	13
St. Joseph Academy, St. Augustine			X	X	–	–	9–12	318	320	11:1	X	17
Saint Stephen's Episcopal School, Bradenton			X	X	PK–6	7–8	9–12	654	294	11:1	X	34
St. Thomas Aquinas High School, Fort Lauderdale			X	X	–	–	9–12	2,171	2,133	18:1	X	31
Seacrest Country Day School, Naples			X	X	PS–5	6–8	9–12	399	157	9:1		19
Shorecrest Preparatory School, Saint Petersburg			X	X	PK–4	5–8	9–12	940	330	10:1	X	19
Trinity Preparatory School, Winter Park			X	X	–	6–8	9–12	861	530	12:1	X	23
The Vanguard School, Lake Wales	X	X	X	X	–	6–8	9–12	95	69	6:1		22
Westminster Christian School, Palmetto Bay			X	X	PK–5	6–8	9–12	1,244	514	15:1	X	19
Georgia												
Advanced Academy of Georgia, Carrollton	X	X			–	–	10–12	83	80	14:1		16
Athens Academy, Athens			X	X	N–4	5–8	9–12	963	327	8:1	X	13

Private Secondary Schools At-a-Glance

| | STUDENTS ACCEPTED | | | | GRADES | | | STUDENT/FACULTY | | | SCHOOL OFFERINGS | |
| | BOARDING | | DAY | | | | | | | | | |
	Boys	Girls	Boys	Girls	Lower	Middle	Upper	Total	Upper	Student/Faculty Ratio	Advanced Placement Preparation	Sports
Atlanta Girls' School, Atlanta				X	–	6–8	9–12	260	150	7.5:1		12
Atlanta International School, Atlanta			X	X	PK–5	6–8	9–12	1,160	355	15:1		11
Augusta Christian School, Martinez			X	X	PK–5	6–8	9–12	561	227	11:1	X	13
Blessed Trinity High School, Roswell			X	X	–	–	9–12	1,001	1,001	12:1	X	16
Brandon Hall School, Atlanta	X	X	X	X	–	6–8	9–12	155	110	8:1	X	15
Darlington School, Rome	X	X	X	X	PK–5	6–8	9–PG	789	463	15:1	X	42
Eaton Academy, Roswell			X	X	K–5	6–8	9–12	80	40	5:1		33
Excel Christian Academy, Cartersville			X	X	K–5	6–8	9–12	297	60	12:1	X	10
First Presbyterian Day School, Macon	X	X	X	X	PK–5	6–8	9–12	962	383	8:1	X	21
The Galloway School, Atlanta			X	X	P3–4	5–8	9–12	750	269	12:1	X	11
Greater Atlanta Christian Schools, Norcross			X	X	P4–5	6–8	9–12	1,815	776	13:1	X	29
Holy Innocents' Episcopal School, Atlanta			X	X	PS–5	6–8	9–12	1,360	510	7:1	X	20
The Howard School, Atlanta			X	X	K–5	6–8	9–12	264	86	8:1		10
La Grange Academy, La Grange			X	X	PK–5	6–8	9–12	215	52	16:1	X	8
Lakeview Academy, Gainesville			X	X	PK–5	6–8	9–12	598	237	8:1	X	20
Landmark Christian School, Fairburn			X	X	K4–5	6–8	9–12	807	224	12:1	X	17
The Lovett School, Atlanta			X	X	K–5	6–8	9–12	1,673	672	8:1	X	43
Marist School, Atlanta			X	X	–	7–8	9–12	1,088	792	11:1	X	17
Mill Springs Academy, Alpharetta			X	X	1–5	6–8	9–12	355	173	6:1		23
Mount Vernon Presbyterian School, Atlanta			X	X	K–4	5–8	9–12	932	320	12:1	X	28
Pace Academy, Atlanta			X	X	K–5	6 8	9–12	1,015	459	7:1	X	25
The Paideia School, Atlanta			X	X	PK–6	7–8	9–12	991	434	9:1	X	18
Pinecrest Academy, Cumming			X	X	PK–5	6–8	9–12	807	306	8:1	X	13
St. Andrew's School, Savannah			X	X	PK–4	5–8	9–12	457	136	6:1		20
St. Francis School, Milton			X	X	K–5	6–8	9–12	778	317	14:1	X	19
St. Pius X Catholic High School, Atlanta			X	X	–	–	9–12	1,100	1,100	12:1	X	23
Stratford Academy, Macon			X	X	1–5	6–8	9–12	896	311	13:1	X	24
Valwood School, Hahira			X	X	PK–5	6–8	9–12	509	174	12:1	X	12
The Weber School, Sandy Springs			X	X	–	–	9–12	226	226	6:1		19
Woodward Academy, College Park			X	X	PK–6	7–8	9–12	2,738	1,105		X	22
Guam												
Father Duenas Memorial School, Hagatna			X		–	–	9–12	435	440	25:1	X	19
Saint John's School, Tumon			X	X	PK–5	6–8	9–12	533	194	12:1	X	17
Hawaii												
Hawaii Baptist Academy, Honolulu			X	X	K–6	7–8	9–12	1,060	456	10:1	X	22
Hawai`i Preparatory Academy, Kamuela	X	X	X	X	K–5	6–8	9–12	628	403	12:1	X	35
Ho'Ala School, Wahiawa			X	X	K–6	7–8	9–12	93	20	5:1	X	8
Kauai Christian Academy, Kilauea			X	X	PS–3	4–6	7–12	79	15	8:1		3
La Pietra–Hawaii School for Girls, Honolulu				X	–	6–8	9–12	247	109	7:1	X	24
Mid-Pacific Institute, Honolulu			X	X	K–5	6–8	9–12	1,556	840	20:1	X	31
Punahou School, Honolulu			X	X	K–5	6–8	9–12	3,768	1,720	9:1	X	21
Seabury Hall, Makawao			X	X	–	6–8	9–12	455	320	11:1	X	25
Idaho												
Bishop Kelly High School, Boise			X	X	–	–	9–12	794	803	19:1	X	22
Gem State Academy, Caldwell	X	X	X	X	–	–	9–12	55	70	6:1	X	7
Nampa Christian Schools, Nampa			X	X	PK–5	6–8	9–12	586	192	13:1		13
Illinois												
Aurora Central Catholic High School, Aurora			X	X	–	–	9–12	525	600	14:1	X	29
Brehm Preparatory School, Carbondale	X	X	X	X	–	6–8	9–PG	85	75	4:1		19
Elgin Academy, Elgin			X	X	PS–4	5–8	9–12	323	113	7:1	X	12
The Governor French Academy, Belleville	X	X	X	X	K–8	–	9–12	155	41	6:1	X	6
Holy Trinity High School, Chicago			X	X	–	–	9–12	331	331	11:1	X	14
Illiana Christian High School, Lansing			X	X	–	–	9–12	520	520	18:1	X	13
Josephinum Academy, Chicago				X	–	–	9–12	200	200	10:1	X	11
Lake Forest Academy, Lake Forest	X	X	X	X	–	–	9–12	391	391	7:1	X	27
Marian Central Catholic High School, Woodstock			X	X	–	–	9–12	687	693	19:1	X	17
Marist High School, Chicago			X	X	–	–	9–12	1,703	1,675	18:1	X	33
Mater Dei High School, Breese					–	–	9–12	414	414	18:1	X	12
Mooseheart High School, Mooseheart	X	X	X	X	K–5	6–8	9–12	199	109	6:1	X	17
Mother McAuley High School, Chicago				X	–	–	9–12	1,027	975	13:1	X	21
Nazareth Academy, LaGrange Park				X	–	–	9–12	763	784	17:1	X	15
North Shore Country Day School, Winnetka			X	X	PK–5	6–8	9–12	525	225	7.2:1	X	16
Queen of Peace High School, Burbank				X	–	–	–			14:1		
Routt Catholic High School, Jacksonville			X	X	–	–	9–12	118	132	8:1	X	10
Sacred Heart/Griffin High School, Springfield			X	X	–	–	9–12	725	643	15:1	X	16
Saint Anthony High School, Effingham			X	X	–	–	9–12	190	190	10:1	X	12
Saint Ignatius College Prep, Chicago			X	X	–	–	9–12	1,364	1,364	14:1		33
Saint Patrick High School, Chicago			X		–	–	9–12	648	648	15:1	X	17

Private Secondary Schools At-a-Glance

	STUDENTS ACCEPTED				GRADES			STUDENT/FACULTY			SCHOOL OFFERINGS	
	BOARDING		DAY									
	Boys	Girls	Boys	Girls	Lower	Middle	Upper	Total	Upper	Student/Faculty Ratio	Advanced Placement Preparation	Sports
Timothy Christian High School, Elmhurst			X	X	–	–	9–12	990	343	10.4:1	X	12
University of Chicago Laboratory Schools, Chicago			X	X	N–5	6–8	9–12	2,007	531	10:1	X	19
The Willows Academy, Des Plaines				X	–	6–8	9–12	230	150	10:1	X	8
Indiana												
Canterbury School, Fort Wayne			X	X	K–4	5–8	9–12	754	371	9:1	X	16
Cardinal Ritter High School, Indianapolis			X	X	–	7–8	9–12	389	315	16:1		17
Concordia Lutheran High School, Fort Wayne			X	X	–	–	9–12	772	781	14:1	X	24
The Culver Academies, Culver	X	X	X	X	–	–	–		828	8:1	X	96
Lakeland Christian Academy, Winona Lake			X	X	–	7–8	9–12	149	102	14:1		8
La Lumiere School, La Porte	X	X	X	X	–	–	9–PG	230	230	7:1	X	13
Lutheran High School of Indianapolis, Indianapolis			X	X	–	–	9–12	216	250	15:1	X	18
Oldenburg Academy, Oldenburg			X	X	–	–	9–12	198	208	12:1	X	16
Shawe Memorial Junior/Senior High School, Madison			X	X	K–6	7–8	9–12	342	109	8:1	X	11
Iowa												
Alpha Omega Academy, Rock Rapids			X	X	K–5	6–8	9–12	2,350	1,600			
Dowling Catholic High School, West Des Moines			X	X	–	–	9–12	1,438	1,407	14:1	X	23
Regina Junior-Senior High School, Iowa City			X	X	PK–6	–	7–12	902	383	15:1	X	13
Rivermont Collegiate, Bettendorf			X	X	PS–5	6–8	9–12	192	39	2:1	X	6
Saint Albert Junior-Senior High School, Council Bluffs	X	X	X	X	PK–5	6–8	9–12	720	200	11:1	X	16
Scattergood Friends School, West Branch	X	X	X	X	–	–	9–12	35	35	3:1		25
Kansas												
Hyman Brand Hebrew Academy of Greater Kansas City, Overland Park			X	X	K–5	6–8	9–12	232	41	5:1	X	4
Immaculata High School, Leavenworth			X	X	–	–	7–12	74	123	9:1		14
Independent School, Wichita			X	X	PK–5	6–8	9–12	538	181	7:1	X	17
Maur Hill-Mount Academy, Atchison	X	X	X	X	–	–	9–12	195	209	9:1	X	37
Saint Thomas Aquinas High School, Overland Park			X	X	–	–	9–12	900	950	14:1	X	20
Trinity Academy, Wichita			X	X	K–5	6–8	9–12	279	335	12:1		19
Kentucky												
Beth Haven Christian School, Louisville			X	X	K–5	6–8	9–12	178	59	7:1		7
Bishop Brossart High School, Alexandria			X	X	–	–	9–12	382	254	16:1		10
Covington Catholic High School, Park Hills			X		–	–	9–12	502	595	18:1	X	26
Lexington Christian Academy, Lexington			X	X	PS–6	7–8	9–12	1,445	448	16:1	X	18
Louisville Collegiate School, Louisville			X	X	JK–5	6–8	9–12	676		7:1	X	15
Oneida Baptist Institute, Oneida	X	X	X	X	K–5	6–8	9–12	320	211	11:1	X	11
St. Francis High School, Louisville			X	X	PS–4	5–8	9–12	154	155	7:1	X	19
Saint Xavier High School, Louisville			X		–	–	9–12	1,334	1,334	11:1	X	46
Sayre School, Lexington			X	X	PK–5	6–8	9–12	549	245	8:1	X	12
Trinity High School, Louisville			X		–	–	9–12	1,230	1,230	12:1	X	48
Villa Madonna Academy, Covington			X	X	K–6	7–8	9–12	421	131	8:1	X	12
Whitefield Academy, Louisville			X	X	PS–5	6–8	9–12	711	192	11:1	X	17
Louisiana												
Academy of the Sacred Heart, New Orleans				X	1–4	5–8	9–12	742	209	16:1	X	27
Archbishop Shaw High School, Marrero			X		–	–	8–12	472	472	21:1	X	17
Brother Martin High School, New Orleans			X		–	8–8	9–12	1,190	915	23:1	X	19
Central Catholic High School, Morgan City			X	X	–	7–8	9–12	206	154	15:1		21
Holy Cross School, New Orleans			X		PK–4	5–7	8–12	1,140	750	12:1	X	29
Holy Savior Menard Catholic High School, Alexandria			X	X	–	7–8	9–12	510	349	14:1	X	16
Loyola College Prep, Shreveport			X	X	–	–	9–12	375	463	12:1	X	19
Mount Carmel Academy, New Orleans				X	–	–	8–12	1,081	1,245			20
Saint Thomas More Catholic High School, Lafayette			X	X	–	–	9–12	1,050	1,063	12:1	X	28
Teurlings Catholic High School, Lafayette			X	X	–	–	9–12	779	779	17:1		23
Westminster Christian Academy, Opelousas			X	X	PK–6	7–8	9–12	1,059	213	13:1	X	17
Maine												
Bangor Christian School, Bangor			X	X	K4–5	6–8	9–12	310	95	10:1		15
Cheverus High School, Portland			X	X	–	–	9–12	470	427	10:1	X	27
Erskine Academy, South China			X	X	–	–	9–12	589	582	9:1	X	15
George Stevens Academy, Blue Hill	X	X	X	X	–	–	9–12	325	325	9:1	X	54
Hebron Academy, Hebron	X	X	X	X	–	6–8	9–PG	268	234	7:1	X	32
Hyde School, Bath	X	X	X	X	–	–	9–12	150	150	6:1	X	42
Lincoln Academy, Newcastle	X	X	X	X	–	–	9–12	588	569	11:1	X	37
North Yarmouth Academy, Yarmouth			X	X	PK–4	5–8	9–12	345	136	6:1	X	20
Pine Tree Academy, Freeport	X	X	X	X	K–4	5–8	9–12	121	61	6:1		2
Thornton Academy, Saco	X	X	X	X	–	6–8	9–12	1,503	1,433	15:1	X	31
Waynflete School, Portland			X	X	PK–5	6–8	9–12	583	259	11:1		23

Private Secondary Schools At-a-Glance

| | STUDENTS ACCEPTED | | | | GRADES | | | STUDENT/FACULTY | | | SCHOOL OFFERINGS | |
| | BOARDING | | DAY | | | | | | | | | |
	Boys	Girls	Boys	Girls	Lower	Middle	Upper	Total	Upper	Student/Faculty Ratio	Advanced Placement Preparation	Sports
Maryland												
Academy of the Holy Cross, Kensington				X	–	–	9–12		479	11:1	X	18
Archbishop Curley High School, Baltimore			X		–	–	9–12	535	560	14:1	X	21
The Bryn Mawr School for Girls, Baltimore			X	X	K–5	6–8	9–12	681	322	7:1	X	45
Calvert Hall College High School, Baltimore			X		–	–	9–12	1,160	1,179	11:1	X	36
Charles E. Smith Jewish Day School, Rockville	X	X	X	X	JK–5	–	6–12	975	342	5.7:1	X	13
Chelsea School, Hyattsville			X	X	–	5–8	9–12	65	43	8:1		5
DeMatha Catholic High School, Hyattsville			X		–	–	9–12	815	837	12:1	X	24
Gilman School, Baltimore			X		K–5	6–8	9–12	1,017	466	7:1	X	27
Glenelg Country School, Ellicott City			X	X	PK–5	6–8	9–12	751	324	6:1	X	28
Griggs International Academy, Silver Spring			X	X	PK–6	7–8	9–12	1,559	788	21:1		
The Gunston School, Centreville			X	X	–	–	9–12	182	189	6:1	X	11
The Key School, Annapolis			X	X	PK–4	5–8	9–12	630	210	7:1	X	29
Landon School, Bethesda			X		3–5	6–8	9–12	681	340	6:1	X	26
Loyola-Blakefield, Baltimore			X		–	6–8	9–12	956	720	10:1	X	23
Maryvale Preparatory School, Brooklandville				X	–	6–8	9–12	362	310	8:1	X	14
McDonogh School, Owings Mills	X	X	X	X	PK–4	5–8	9–12	1,350	629	9:1	X	28
The McLean School of Maryland, Inc., Potomac			X	X	K–4	5–8	9–12	355	150	9:1	X	9
The Nora School, Silver Spring			X	X	–	–	9–12	66	65	5:1		28
The Park School of Baltimore, Baltimore			X	X	PK–5	6–8	9–12	788	344	7:1	X	17
Roland Park Country School, Baltimore			X	X	PS–5	6–8	9–12	644	317	7:1	X	26
St. Andrew's Episcopal School, Potomac			X	X	PS–5	6–8	9–12	553	317	7:1	X	20
St. John's Catholic Prep, Buckeystown			X	X	–	–	9–12	260	294	9:1	X	13
The Siena School, Silver Spring			X	X	4–5	6–8	9–12	126	46	10:1		10
Takoma Academy, Takoma Park			X	X	–	–	9–12	226	226	14:1	X	6
Washington Waldorf School, Bethesda			X	X	1–4	5–8	9–12	242	53	7:1	X	10
West Nottingham Academy, Colora	X	X	X	X	–	–	9–PG	117	130	7:1	X	20
Worcester Preparatory School, Berlin			X	X	PK–5	6–8	9–12	542	213	9:1	X	15
Massachusetts												
Academy of Notre Dame, Tyngsboro			X	X	K–5	6–8	9–12	610	177	12:1	X	20
Austin Preparatory School, Reading			X	X	–	6–8	9–12	738	528	11:1	X	21
The Bement School, Deerfield	X	X	X	X	K–5	–	6–9	204	113	6:1		22
Berkshire School, Sheffield	X	X	X	X	–	–	9–PG	405	405	4:1	X	43
Bishop Connolly High School, Fall River			X	X	–	–	9–12	280	280	16:1	X	17
Bishop Stang High School, North Dartmouth			X	X	–	–	9–12	620	590	12:1	X	30
Boston Trinity Academy, Boston			X	X	–	6–8	9–12	233	163	6:1	X	9
Boston University Academy, Boston			X	X	–	–	9–12	170	175	9:1		12
Brimmer and May School, Chestnut Hill			X	X	PK–5	6–8	9–12	387	139	6:1	X	21
British International School of Boston, Boston			X	X	PK–5	6–8	9–12	421		4:1		20
Brooks School, North Andover	X	X	X	X	–	–	9–12	373	380	6:1	X	22
Buckingham Browne & Nichols School, Cambridge			X	X	PK–6	7–8	9–12	968	522	7:1	X	21
Buxton School, Williamstown	X	X	X	X	–	–	9–12	90	90	4:1		26
Cape Cod Academy, Osterville			X	X	PK–5	6–8	9–12	247	105	5:1	X	19
Central Catholic High School, Lawrence			X	X	–	–	9–12	1,330	1,295	24:1	X	31
Commonwealth School, Boston			X	X	–	–	9–12	145	145	5:1		15
Concord Academy, Concord	X	X	X	X	–	–	9–12	378	381	6:1		35
Cushing Academy, Ashburnham	X	X	X	X	–	–	9–PG	400	400	8:1	X	35
Dana Hall School, Wellesley		X		X	–	5–8	9–12	464	356	6:1	X	41
Deerfield Academy, Deerfield	X	X	X	X	–	–	9–PG	638	651	5:1	X	50
Eaglebrook School, Deerfield	X		X		–	6–9	–	250	230	4:1		66
Falmouth Academy, Falmouth			X	X	–	7–8	9–12	200	135	4:1	X	3
Fay School, Southborough	X	X	X	X	PK–2	3–6	7–9	475	235	6:1		21
The Fessenden School, West Newton	X		X		K–4	5–6	7–9	475	203	7:1		24
Fontbonne Academy, Milton				X	–	–	9–12	335	313	8:1	X	31
Gann Academy (The New Jewish High School of Greater Boston), Waltham			X	X	–	–	9–12	277	277	5:1	X	17
The Governor's Academy, Byfield	X	X	X	X	–	–	9–12	405	405	5:1	X	23
Hillside School, Marlborough	X		X		–	5–9	–	150	128	7:1		50
The John Dewey Academy, Great Barrington	X	X			–	–	10–PG	20	20	3:1		
The Judge Rotenberg Educational Center, Canton	X	X			–	–	–		130			3
Landmark School, Prides Crossing	X	X	X	X	2–5	6–8	9–12	471	315	3:1		20
Lexington Christian Academy, Lexington	X	X	X	X	–	6–8	9–12	317	210	11:1	X	22
Lycee Internationale de Boston/International School of Boston, Cambridge			X	X	PK–5	6–8	9–12	567	135	6:1		16
Malden Catholic High School, Malden			X		–	–	9–12	562	562	13:1	X	36
Marian High School, Framingham			X	X	–	–	9–12	260	260	17:1	X	18
Matignon High School, Cambridge			X	X	–	–	9–12	462	410	18:1	X	25
Middlesex School, Concord	X	X	X	X	–	–	9–12	384	394	4:1	X	22
Milton Academy, Milton	X	X	X	X	K–5	6–8	9–12	1,000	700	5:1	X	28

Private Secondary Schools At-a-Glance

| | STUDENTS ACCEPTED | | | | GRADES | | | STUDENT/FACULTY | | | SCHOOL OFFERINGS | |
| | BOARDING | | DAY | | | | | | | | | |
	Boys	Girls	Boys	Girls	Lower	Middle	Upper	Total	Upper	Student/Faculty Ratio	Advanced Placement Preparation	Sports
Montrose School, Medfield				X	–	6–8	9–12	217	129	5:1	X	15
Newton Country Day School of the Sacred Heart, Newton				X	–	5–8	9–12	409	238	7:1	X	30
Noble and Greenough School, Dedham	X	X	X	X	–	7–8	9–12	615	496	7:1	X	20
Northfield Mount Hermon School, Mount Hermon	X	X	X	X	–	–	9–PG	650	650	6:1	X	54
Perkins School for the Blind, Watertown	X	X	X	X	–	6–8	9–12	182	86			
The Pingree School, South Hamilton			X	X	–	–	9–12	364	375	6:1	X	33
Pioneer Valley Christian Academy, Springfield			X	X	PS–5	6–8	9–12	293	96	10:1	X	9
Pope Francis High School, Chicopee			X	X	–	–	9–12	245	367	10:1	X	17
Redemption Christian Academy, Northfield	X	X	X	X	–	–	–			7:1	X	9
The Rivers School, Weston			X	X	–	6–8	9–12	490	367	6:1	X	21
The Roxbury Latin School, West Roxbury			X		–	–	7–12	303	301	7:1	X	10
St. John's Preparatory School, Danvers			X		–	6–8	9–12	1,450	1,150	11:1	X	54
The Sudbury Valley School, Framingham			X	X	–	–	–	160		16:1		
Ursuline Academy, Dedham			X		–	7–8	9–12	397	310	9:1	X	23
Walnut Hill School for the Arts, Natick	X	X	X	X	–	–	9–12	285	285	6:1	X	16
Willow Hill School, Sudbury			X	X	–	6–8	9–12	61	48	3:1	X	46
The Winchendon School, Winchendon	X	X	X	X	–	–	9–PG	255	232	8:1	X	46
The Woodward School, Quincy				X	–	6–8	9–12	120	77	8:1		3
Michigan												
Academy of the Sacred Heart, Bloomfield Hills			X	X	N–4	5–8	9–12	478	145	7:1	X	11
Bishop Foley Catholic High School, Madison Heights			X	X	–	–	9–12	353	353	15:1		
Catholic Central High School, Novi			X		–	–	9–12	1,070	1,039	16:1	X	18
Detroit Country Day School, Beverly Hills			X	X	PK–5	6–8	9–12	1,523	694	8:1	X	50
Gabriel Richard Catholic High School, Riverview			X	X	–	–	9–12	323	323	17:1	X	16
Greenhills School, Ann Arbor			X	X	–	6–8	9–12	574	340	8:1	X	18
Jean and Samuel Frankel Jewish Academy of Metropolitan Detroit, West Bloomfield			X	X	–	–	9–12	225	225		X	
Kalamazoo Christian High School, Kalamazoo			X	X	–	–	9–12	234	234	12:1	X	17
Lutheran High School Northwest, Rochester Hills			X	X	–	–	9–12	177	279	15:1	X	21
Mercy High School, Farmington Hills			X		–	–	9–12	730	730	15:1	X	18
Powers Catholic High School, Flint			X	X	–	–	9–12	605	673	18:1	X	27
The Roeper School, Bloomfield Hills			X	X	PK–5	6–8	9–12	579	148	8:1	X	11
Rudolf Steiner School of Ann Arbor, Ann Arbor			X	X	1–5	6–8	9–12	345	120	10:1		22
St. Mary's Preparatory School, Orchard Lake	X		X		–	–	9–12	540	540	10:1	X	44
Southfield Christian High School, Southfield			X	X	PK–5	6–8	9–12	588	184	10:1	X	12
The Valley School, Swartz Creek			X	X	PK–4	5–8	9–12	64	16	8:1		8
Minnesota												
Academy of Holy Angels, Richfield			X	X	–	–	9–12	613	625	13:1	X	20
The Blake School, Hopkins			X	X	PK–5	6–8	9–12	1,363	527	8:1	X	15
Concordia Academy, St. Paul			X	X	–	–	9–12	241	246	15:1		15
DeLaSalle High School, Minneapolis			X	X	–	–	9–12	760	780	14:1	X	23
Marshall School, Duluth	X	X	X	X	–	4–8	9–12	446	283	9.4:1	X	27
Mayer Lutheran High School, Mayer			X	X	–	–	9–12	252	185	14:1	X	16
St. Croix Schools, West St. Paul	X	X	X	X	–	6–8	9–12	500	440	13:1	X	40
Saint Thomas Academy, Mendota Heights			X		–	7–8	9–12	671	494	10:1	X	31
Shattuck-St. Mary's School, Faribault	X	X	X	X	–	6–9	9–PG	443	338	8:1	X	23
Mississippi												
Jackson Preparatory School, Jackson			X	X	–	6–9	10–12	836	408	13:1	X	22
Magnolia Heights School, Senatobia			X	X	PK–5	6–8	9–12	685	227	12:1		9
Northpoint Christian School, Southaven			X	X	PK–6	–	7–12	1,084	460	13:1	X	17
St. Stanislaus College, Bay St. Louis	X		X		–	7–8	9–12	352	250	12:1	X	35
Vicksburg Catholic School, Vicksburg			X	X	PK–6	–	7–12	536	256	10:1	X	13
Missouri												
Chaminade College Preparatory School, St. Louis	X		X		–	6–8	9–12	775	560	9:1	X	23
Duchesne High School, Saint Charles			X	X	–	–	–	300	300			31
Greenwood Laboratory School, Springfield			X	X	K–5	6–8	9–12	339	123	22:1		9
John Burroughs School, St. Louis			X	X	–	7–8	9–12	600	400	7:1	X	27
Lutheran High School, Kansas City			X	X	–	–	9–12	128	137	11:1		23
Mary Institute and St. Louis Country Day School (MICDS), St. Louis			X	X	JK–4	5–8	9–12	1,250	642	8:1	X	29
Nerinx Hall, Webster Groves				X	–	–	9–12	597	595	9:1	X	13
New Covenant Academy, Springfield			X	X	JK–6	7–8	9–12	478	140	10:1		9
The Pembroke Hill School, Kansas City			X	X	PS–5	6–8	9–12	1,188	436	11:1	X	18
Rockhurst High School, Kansas City			X		–	–	9–12		1,031	12:1	X	23
Saint Paul Lutheran High School, Concordia	X	X	X	X	–	–	9–12	189	21,525	9:1		20
Saint Teresa's Academy, Kansas City				X	–	–	9–12	596	589	12:1	X	26
Thomas Jefferson School, St. Louis	X	X	X	X	–	7–8	9–PG	91	68	7:1	X	13

Private Secondary Schools At-a-Glance

| | STUDENTS ACCEPTED | | | | GRADES | | | STUDENT/FACULTY | | | SCHOOL OFFERINGS | |
| | BOARDING | | DAY | | | | | | | | | |
	Boys	Girls	Boys	Girls	Lower	Middle	Upper	Total	Upper	Student/Faculty Ratio	Advanced Placement Preparation	Sports
Villa Duchesne and Oak Hill School, St. Louis			X	X	JK–6	7–8	9–12	585	293	8:1	X	12
Whitfield School, St. Louis			X	X	–	6–8	9–12	409	289	7:1	X	21
Montana												
Lustre Christian High School, Lustre	X	X	X	X	–	–	9–12	40	40	4:1		4
Manhattan Christian High School, Manhattan			X	X	PK–5	6–8	9–12	304	93	11:1	X	10
Valley Christian School, Missoula			X	X	K–5	6–8	9–12	211	94	8:1	X	7
Nebraska												
Nebraska Christian Schools, Central City	X	X	X	X	K–6	7–8	9–12	201	130	10:1		7
Scotus Central Catholic High School, Columbus			X	X	–	7–8	9–12	364	247	13:1		13
Nevada												
The Dr. Miriam and Sheldon G. Adelson Educational Campus, The Adelson Upper School, Las Vegas			X	X	PS–5	6–8	9–12	419	140	14:1	X	15
Faith Lutheran High School, Las Vegas			X	X	–	6–8	9–12	1,572	957	17:1	X	22
The Meadows School, Las Vegas			X	X	PK–5	6–8	9–12	871	247	11:1	X	12
Mountain View Christian High School, Las Vegas			X	X	K–6	7–8	9–12	631	65	8:1		12
New Hampshire												
Crotched Mountain School, Greenfield	X	X	X	X	–	–	–		97			2
Dublin Christian Academy, Dublin	X	X	X	X	K–6	7–8	9–12	98	33	9:1	X	5
Dublin School, Dublin	X	X	X	X	–	–	9–12	152	160	5:1	X	70
Hampshire Country School, Rindge	X				3–6	–	7–12	20	14	2:1		21
Kimball Union Academy, Meriden	X	X	X	X	–	–	9–PG	345	341	6:1	X	40
Portsmouth Christian Academy, Dover			X	X	PK–5	6–8	9–12	551	200	9:1	X	22
Proctor Academy, Andover	X	X	X	X	–	–	9–12	360	370	5:1	X	44
St. Paul's School, Concord	X	X			–	–	9–12	541	531	5:1	X	33
St. Thomas Aquinas High School, Dover			X	X	–	–	9–12	526	500	13:1	X	17
Tilton School, Tilton	X	X	X	X	–	–	9–PG	233	257	7:1	X	28
New Jersey												
Academy of Saint Elizabeth, Convent Station				X	–	–	9–12	245	142	6:1	X	17
The American Boychoir School, Princeton	X		X		4–5	6–8	–	51	17	3:1		14
Barnstable Academy, Oakland			X	X	–	5–8	9–12	100	80	7:1	X	28
Christian Brothers Academy, Lincroft			X		–	–	9–12	999	968	12:1	X	24
Community High School, Teaneck			X	X	–	–	–	181	178	5:1		7
Delbarton School, Morristown			X		–	7–8	9–12	573	518	13:1	X	28
Doane Academy, Burlington			X	X	PK–5	6–8	9–12	226	110	12:1	X	17
Donovan Catholic, Toms River			X	X	–	–	9–12	689	680	15:1	X	24
The Frisch School, Paramus			X	X	–	–	9–12	500	698	7:1	X	24
Hawthorne Christian Academy, Hawthorne			X	X	PS–5	6–8	9–12	482	138	7:1	X	10
The Hun School of Princeton, Princeton	X	X	X	X	–	6–8	9–PG	630	544	8:1	X	35
Immaculata High School, Somerville			X	X	–	–	9–12	690	500	13:1	X	13
Immaculate Conception High School, Lodi				X	–	–	9–12	205	205	11:1		18
Immaculate Heart Academy, Washington Township				X	–	–	9–12	830	790	11:1		15
The King's Christian High School, Cherry Hill			X	X	P3–6	7–8	9–12	311	131	6:1	X	10
The Lawrenceville School, Lawrenceville	X	X	X	X	–	–	9–PG	815	823	8:1		52
Ma'ayanot Yeshiva High School for Girls of Bergen County, Teaneck				X	–	–	9–12	221	289	6:1	X	17
Mary Help of Christians Academy, North Haledon				X	–	–	9–12	342	164	8:1	X	10
Mater Dei Prep, New Monmouth			X	X	–	–	9–12	322	322			16
Montclair Kimberley Academy, Montclair			X	X	PK–3	4–8	9–12	990	439	6:1	X	21
Moorestown Friends School, Moorestown			X	X	PS–4	5–8	9–12	730	320	7:1	X	18
Morris Catholic High School, Denville			X	X	–	–	–			11:1		14
Notre Dame High School, Lawrenceville			X	X	–	–	9–12	1,292	1,236	15:1	X	32
Peddie School, Hightstown	X	X	X	X	–	–	9–PG	542	564	6:1	X	26
The Pennington School, Pennington	X	X	X	X	–	6–8	9–12	500	398	6:1	X	30
The Pingry School, Basking Ridge			X	X	K–5	6–8	9–12	1,116	557	7:1	X	25
Pope John XXIII Regional High School, Sparta			X	X	–	–	8–12	953	889	12:1	X	19
Saint Augustine Preparatory School, Richland			X		–	–	9–12	695	682	12:1	X	27
Saint Dominic Academy, Jersey City				X	–	7–8	9–12	451	220	12:1	X	12
Saint Joseph High School, Metuchen			X		–	–	9–12	683	631	12:1	X	24
Saint Joseph Regional High School, Montvale			X		–	–	9–12	516	516	12:1	X	28
Saint Mary of the Assumption High School, Elizabeth					–	–	–		209	13:1		7
SciCore Academy, Hightstown			X	X	K–4	5–8	9–12	95	30	7:1	X	9
Villa Victoria Academy, Ewing				X	K–6	7–8	9–12	162	65	8:1	X	10
Villa Walsh Academy, Morristown				X	–	7–8	9–12	238	208	8:1	X	11
New Mexico												
Albuquerque Academy, Albuquerque			X	X	–	6–7	8–12	1,121	802	9:1	X	28
Desert Academy, Santa Fe			X	X	–	6–8	9–12	190	120	8:1		11
Santa Fe Preparatory School, Santa Fe			X	X	–	7–8	9–12	317	215	14:1	X	21

Private Secondary Schools At-a-Glance

| | STUDENTS ACCEPTED | | | | GRADES | | | STUDENT/FACULTY | | | SCHOOL OFFERINGS | |
| | BOARDING | | DAY | | | | | | | | | |
	Boys	Girls	Boys	Girls	Lower	Middle	Upper	Total	Upper	Student/Faculty Ratio	Advanced Placement Preparation	Sports
New York												
Adelphi Academy, Bay Ridge, Brooklyn			X	X	PK–4	5–8	9–12	110	60	8:1		26
Bay Ridge Preparatory School, Brooklyn			X	X	K–5	6–8	9–12	396	210	7:1	X	16
The Beekman School, New York			X	X	–	–	9–12	80	80	8:1	X	
Berkeley Carroll School, Brooklyn			X	X	PK–4	5–8	9–12	942	285	8:1		10
The Birch Wathen Lenox School, New York			X	X	K–5	6–8	9–12	570	180	15:1	X	25
Bishop Kearney High School, Brooklyn				X	–	–	9–12	1,052		15:1		23
The Browning School, New York			X		K–4	5–8	9–12	399	116	4:1	X	8
Buffalo Seminary, Buffalo		X		X	–	–	9–12	219	219	7:1	X	30
The Calhoun School, New York			X	X	N–5	6–8	9–12	724	240	7:1		17
Cathedral High School, New York				X	–	–	9–12	660	650	14:1	X	12
Catholic Central High School, Troy			X	X	–	7–8	9–12	379	277	14:1	X	17
Christian Brothers Academy, Syracuse			X	X	–	–	7–12	750	780		X	19
Christian Central Academy, Williamsville			X	X	K–5	6–8	9–12	335	115	5:1	X	9
Darrow School, New Lebanon	X	X	X	X	–	–	9–PG	110	110	4:1	X	30
Dominican Academy, New York				X	–	–	9–12	216	222	8:1	X	15
The Dwight School, New York			X	X	PS–5	6–8	9–12			6:1	X	19
Fontbonne Hall Academy, Brooklyn				X	–	–	9–12	486	486	13:1	X	17
Fordham Preparatory School, Bronx			X		–	–	9–12	985	1,015	12:1	X	28
French-American School of New York, Mamaroneck			X	X	N–5	6–8	9–12	842	236	5:1	X	9
Friends Academy, Locust Valley			X	X	N–5	6–8	9–12	781	381	7:1	X	19
The Gow School, South Wales	X	X	X	X	–	6–9	10–12	145	116	4:1		46
Green Meadow Waldorf School, Chestnut Ridge			X	X	N–8	–	9–12	375	74	9:1		20
The Harley School, Rochester			X	X	N–4	5–8	9–12	537	186	8:1	X	15
The Harvey School, Katonah	X	X	X	X	–	6–8	9–12	365	280	6:1	X	23
The Hewitt School, New York				X	K–4	5–8	9–12	517	139	7:1	X	15
Holy Trinity Diocesan High School, Hicksville			X	X	–	–	9–12	1,003	897	17:1	X	25
Hoosac School, Hoosick	X	X	X	X	–	–	8 PG	125	125	5:1	X	35
Houghton Academy, Houghton	X	X	X	X	–	7–8	9–12	124	108	7:1	X	15
Keio Academy of New York, Purchase	X	X	X	X	–	–	9–12	316	316		X	20
Kildonan School, Amenia	X	X	X	X	2–8	–	9–PG	91	49	2:1		38
La Salle Institute, Troy			X		–	6–8	9–12	440	300	10:1	X	25
Lawrence Woodmere Academy, Woodmere			X	X	PK–4	5–8	9–12	356	130	6:1	X	9
Long Island Lutheran Middle and High School, Brookville	X	X	X	X	–	6–8	9–12	590	458	9:1		23
Maplebrook School, Amenia	X	X	X	X	–	–	–	75	62	8:1		41
Martin Luther High School, Maspeth			X	X	–	6–8	9–12	225	198	12:1	X	18
The Mary Louis Academy, Jamaica Estates				X	–	–	9–12	782	730	13:1	X	31
Marymount School of New York, New York			X	X	N–2	3–8	9–12	744	247	5:1	X	23
Millbrook School, Millbrook	X	X	X	X	–	–	9–12	294	213	5:1	X	35
Mount Mercy Academy, Buffalo				X	–	–	9–12	229	237	20:1		13
New York Military Academy, Cornwall-on-Hudson	X	X	X	X	–	8–9	9–12	141	124	8:1	X	27
Niagara Catholic Jr./Sr. High School, Niagara Falls			X	X	–	–	–					10
Norman Howard School, Rochester			X	X	–	5–8	9–12	121	82	7:1		5
North Country School, Lake Placid	X	X	X	X	–	4–8	9	80	20	3:1		49
Notre Dame High School, Elmira			X	X	–	7–8	9–12	373	261	15:1	X	12
The Packer Collegiate Institute, Brooklyn			X	X	PK–4	5–8	9–12	941	306	7:1		4
The Park School of Buffalo, Snyder	X	X	X	X	PK–4	5–8	9–12	298	126	8:1	X	32
Portledge School, Locust Valley			X	X	N–5	6–8	9–12	475	210	8:1		16
Poughkeepsie Day School, Poughkeepsie			X	X	PK–5	6–8	9–12	264	106	7:1	X	23
Preston High School, Bronx				X	–	–	9–12	511	496	10:1	X	7
Professional Children's School, New York			X	X	–	6–8	9–12	198	168	8:1		
Riverdale Country School, Bronx			X	X	PK–5	6–8	9–12	1,150	505	8:1		22
Rockland Country Day School, Congers	X	X	X	X	PK–4	5–8	9–12	117	59	7:1	X	12
Sacred Heart Academy, Hempstead				X	–	–	–			15:1		
Sacred Heart High School, Yonkers			X		–	–	9–12	401	306	15:1	X	9
Seton Catholic Central High School, Binghamton			X	X	–	7–8	9–12	445	339	23:1	X	21
Smith School, New York			X	X	–	7–8	9–12	57	42	4:1		14
The Spence School, New York				X	K–4	5–8	9–12	738	253	6.7:1	X	14
The Stony Brook School, Stony Brook	X	X	X	X	–	7–8	9–12	360	305	7:1	X	21
The Storm King School, Cornwall-on-Hudson	X	X	X	X	–	8–8	9–PG	167	165	5:1	X	63
Trevor Day School, New York			X	X	N–5	6–8	9–12	795	68	6:1	X	14
Trinity-Pawling School, Pawling	X		X		–	8–8	9–PG	285	270	8:1	X	38
United Nations International School, New York			X	X	PK–4	5–8	9–12	1,570	490	6:1		49
The Waldorf School of Saratoga Springs, Saratoga Springs			X	X	PK–8	–	9–12	248	44	13:1		23
The Windsor School, Flushing			X	X	–	6–8	9–13	110	100	14:1	X	12
Winston Preparatory School, New York			X	X	–	4–8	9–12	227	151	3:1		19
Xavier High School, New York			X		–	–	–	1,077	1,077	14:1	X	20

Private Secondary Schools At-a-Glance

| | STUDENTS ACCEPTED | | | | GRADES | | | STUDENT/FACULTY | | | SCHOOL OFFERINGS | |
| | BOARDING | | DAY | | | | | | | | | |
	Boys	Girls	Boys	Girls	Lower	Middle	Upper	Total	Upper	Student/Faculty Ratio	Advanced Placement Preparation	Sports
North Carolina												
Asheville School, Asheville	X	X	X	X	–	–	9–12	260	260	7:1	X	44
Cardinal Gibbons High School, Raleigh			X	X	–	–	9–12	1,428	1,428	14:1	X	34
Charlotte Country Day School, Charlotte			X	X	PK–4	5–8	9–12	1,660	519	7:1		21
Charlotte Latin School, Charlotte			X	X	K–5	6–8	9–12	1,413	504	9:1	X	21
Durham Academy, Durham			X	X	PK–4	5–8	9–12	1,183	438	8:1	X	25
Fayetteville Academy, Fayetteville			X	X	PK–5	6–8	9–12	370	131	14:1	X	11
Forsyth Country Day School, Lewisville			X	X	PK–4	5–8	9–12	702	243	12:1	X	16
Gaston Day School, Gastonia			X	X	PS–4	5–8	9–12	481	152	13:1	X	13
Greenfield School, Wilson			X	X	PS–4	5–8	9–12	250	72	3:1	X	8
Harrells Christian Academy, Harrells			X	X	K–5	6–8	9–12	363	129	8:1	X	9
The Hill Center, Durham Academy, Durham			X	X	K–5	6–8	9–12	175	56	4:1		
Laurinburg Institute, Laurinburg	X	X	X	X	–	–	9–12	10	10	10:1		4
Noble Academy, Greensboro			X	X	K–6	7–9	10–12	160	64	9:1		12
Oak Ridge Military Academy, Oak Ridge	X	X	X	X	–	7–8	9–12	65	50	11:1		25
The O'Neal School, Southern Pines			X	X	PK–5	6–8	9–12	411	152	8:1	X	10
Providence Day School, Charlotte			X	X	PK–5	6–8	9–12	1,580	585	9:1	X	24
Ravenscroft School, Raleigh			X	X	PK–5	6–8	9–12	1,169	468	8:1	X	24
Rocky Mount Academy, Rocky Mount			X	X	PK–5	6–8	9–12	447	144	6:1	X	18
Salem Academy, Winston-Salem		X		X	–	–	9–12	160	160	7:1	X	22
North Dakota												
Oak Grove Lutheran School, Fargo			X	X	K–5	6–8	9–12	430	165	10:1	X	17
Shanley High School, Fargo			X	X	–	–	9–12	327	327	14:1	X	19
Ohio												
Andrews Osborne Academy, Willoughby	X	X	X	X	PK–5	6–8	9–12	347	151	6:1	X	17
Archbishop Alter High School, Kettering			X	X	–	–	9–12	673	612	12:1	X	20
Archbishop Hoban High School, Akron			X	X	–	–	9–12	856	852	13:1	X	27
Archbishop McNicholas High School, Cincinnati			X	X	–	–	9–12	677	633	18:1	X	19
Archbishop Moeller High School, Cincinnati			X		–	–	9–12	949	885	14:1	X	35
Benedictine High School, Cleveland			X		–	–	9–12	380	368	10:1	X	22
Bishop Fenwick High School, Franklin			X	X	–	–	9–12	533	533	14:1	X	24
The Columbus Academy, Gahanna			X	X	PK–5	6–8	9–12	1,080	392	8:1	X	15
Columbus School for Girls, Columbus				X	PK–5	6–8	9–12	562	197	8:1	X	16
Gilmour Academy, Gates Mills	X	X	X	X	PK–6	7–8	9–12	656	424	9:1	X	37
Hawken School, Gates Mills			X	X	PS–5	6–8	9–12	1,011	433	9:1	X	17
Lake Ridge Academy, North Ridgeville			X	X	K–5	6–8	9–12	339	170	8:1	X	20
Lawrence School, Sagamore Hills			X	X	K–6	7–8	9–12	344	164	11:1		21
Lutheran High School West, Rocky River			X	X	–	–	9–12	460	435	14:1	X	18
Maumee Valley Country Day School, Toledo	X	X	X	X	P3–6	7–8	9–12	532	215	9:1	X	13
The Miami Valley School, Dayton			X	X	PK–5	6–8	9–12	474	186	8:1	X	15
Mount Notre Dame High School, Cincinnati				X	–	–	9–12	649	649	15:1	X	
Notre Dame-Cathedral Latin School, Chardon			X	X	–	–	9–12	678	691	14:1	X	31
Padua Franciscan High School, Parma			X	X	–	–	9–12	773	755	12:1	X	39
St. John's Jesuit High School, Toledo			X		–	6–8	9–12	950	640	14:1	X	17
Saint Ursula Academy, Cincinnati				X	–	–	9–12			15:1	X	
Saint Ursula Academy, Toledo				X	–	6–8	9–12	552	435	10:1	X	35
Saint Vincent-Saint Mary High School, Akron			X	X	–	–	9–12	686	653	12:1	X	20
The Seven Hills School, Cincinnati			X	X	PK–5	6–8	9–12	1,017	344	15:1	X	14
Trinity High School, Garfield Heights			X	X	–	–	9–12	327	320	10:1	X	15
The Wellington School, Columbus			X	X	PK–4	5–8	9–12	668	240	8:1	X	15
Oklahoma												
Bishop McGuinness Catholic High School, Oklahoma City			X	X	–	–	9–12	714	369	13:1	X	19
Casady School, Oklahoma City			X	X	PK–4	5–8	9–12	905	319	15:1	X	29
Cascia Hall Preparatory School, Tulsa			X	X	–	6–8	9–12	527	345	9:1	X	23
Heritage Hall, Oklahoma City			X	X	PS–4	5–8	9–12	924	339	16:1	X	21
Holland Hall, Tulsa			X	X	PK–3	4–8	9–12	995	333	9:1	X	22
Rejoice Christian Schools, Owasso			X	X	P3–5	6–8	9–12	873	194	14:1		13
Oregon												
Blanchet School, Salem			X	X	–	6–8	9–12	367	231	17:1	X	17
Cascades Academy of Central Oregon, Bend			X	X	PK–5	6–8	9–12	186	35	6:1		24
Christa McAuliffe Academy School of Arts and Sciences, Lake Oswego			X	X	K–5	6–8	9–12	263	229	20:1	X	
City Christian Schools, Portland			X	X	–	6–8	9–12	508	144	12:1		6
C.S. Lewis Academy, Newberg			X	X	PK–5	6–8	9–12	150	30	6:1		5
De La Salle North Catholic High School, Portland			X	X	–	–	9–12	311	327	12:1	X	5
The Delphian School, Sheridan	X	X	X	X	K–4	5–8	9–12	272		10:1	X	32
Horizon Christian School, Hood River			X	X	–	7–8	9–12	199	71			4
Livingstone Adventist Academy, Salem			X	X	K–5	6–8	9–12	142	61	12:1		4

Private Secondary Schools At-a-Glance

| | STUDENTS ACCEPTED | | | | GRADES | | | STUDENT/FACULTY | | | SCHOOL OFFERINGS | |
| | BOARDING | | DAY | | | | | | | | | |
	Boys	Girls	Boys	Girls	Lower	Middle	Upper	Total	Upper	Student/Faculty Ratio	Advanced Placement Preparation	Sports
Northwest Academy, Portland			X	X	–	6–8	9–12	211	100	5:1		12
Oregon Episcopal School, Portland	X	X	X	X	PK–5	6–8	9–12	870	314	6.5:1	X	35
Regis High School, Stayton			X	X	–	–	9–12	189	130	12:1	X	13
Salem Academy, Salem			X	X	K–5	6–8	9–12	646	215	14:1	X	14
Westside Christian High School, Tigard			X	X	–	–	9–12	300	240	12:1		
Pennsylvania												
Academy of Notre Dame de Namur, Villanova				X	–	6–8	9–12	519	393	9:1		25
Academy of the New Church Boys' School, Bryn Athyn	X		X		–	–	9–12	121	121	8:1	X	6
Academy of the New Church Girls' School, Bryn Athyn		X		X	–	–	9–12	96	95	8:1	X	10
The Agnes Irwin School, Rosemont				X	PK–4	5–8	9–12	666	283	6:1	X	22
Allentown Central Catholic High School, Allentown			X	X	–	–	9–12	810	810	14:1	X	24
Camphill Special School, Glenmoore	X	X	X	X	K–5	6–8	9–13	120	67	7:1		
Central Catholic High School, Pittsburgh			X		–	–	9–12	857	867	16:1	X	27
The Church Farm School, Exton	X		X		–	–	9–12	193	185	6:1	X	18
The Concept School, Westtown			X	X	–	6–8	9–12	24	21	5:1		14
Delaware County Christian School, Newtown Square			X	X	PK–5	6–8	9–12	810	298	12:1	X	15
Delaware Valley Friends School, Paoli			X	X	–	5–8	9–12	149	119	5:1		18
Devon Preparatory School, Devon			X		–	6–8	9–12	272	195	10:1	X	11
Dock Mennonite Academy, Lansdale	X	X	X	X	–	–	9–12	375	363	12:1	X	12
The Ellis School, Pittsburgh				X	PK–4	5–8	9–12	393	130		X	29
The Episcopal Academy, Newtown Square			X	X	PK–5	6–8	9–12	1,250	545	7:1	X	39
Friends Select School, Philadelphia			X	X	PK–4	5–8	9–12	558	167	15:1	X	9
Girard College, Philadelphia	X	X			1–5	6–8	9–12	270	97	16:1	X	21
Grier School, Tyrone		X		X	–	–	7–PG	309	316	6:1	X	47
The Haverford School, Haverford			X		PK–5	6–8	9–12	977	436	8:1		25
Holy Ghost Preparatory School, Bensalem			X		–	–	9–12	467	485	11:1	X	20
Jack M. Barrack Hebrew Academy, Bryn Mawr			X	X	–	6–8	9–12	274	207	15:1	X	13
Kimberton Waldorf School, Kimberton			X	X	PK–8	–	9–12	306	64	7:1		11
The Kiski School, Saltsburg	X		X		–	–	9–PG	200	206	7:1	X	40
Lancaster Catholic High School, Lancaster			X	X	–	–	9–12	630	630		X	25
Lancaster Mennonite High School, Lancaster	X	X	X	X	PK–5	6–8	9–12	1,393	591	15:1	X	14
Lansdale Catholic High School, Lansdale			X	X	–	–	9–12	703	724	21:1	X	22
Lehigh Valley Christian High School, Allentown			X	X	–	–	9–12	53	40	5:1	X	6
Malvern Preparatory School, Malvern			X		–	6–8	9–12	654	511	9:1	X	25
Mercersburg Academy, Mercersburg	X	X	X	X	–	–	9–PG	430	430	5:1	X	58
Mercyhurst Preparatory School, Erie			X	X	–	–	9–12	545	545	14:1		20
Merion Mercy Academy, Merion Station				X	–	–	9–12	484	460	9:1	X	15
Milton Hershey School, Hershey	X	X			PK–4	5–8	9–12	2,012	943	15:1	X	13
MMI Preparatory School, Freeland			X	X	–	6–8	9–12	252	158	13:1	X	11
Monsignor Bonner and Archbishop Prendergast Catholic High School, Drexel Hill			X	X	–	–	9–12	901	810	22:1	X	29
Moravian Academy, Bethlehem			X	X	PS–5	6–8	9–12	734	310	7:1	X	15
Notre Dame Junior/Senior High School, East Stroudsburg			X	X	–	–	7–12	317	288	15:1	X	9
The Pathway School, Jeffersonville			X	X	–	–	–	135	83	4:1		5
Perkiomen School, Pennsburg	X	X	X	X		6–8	9–PG	350	300	7:1	X	20
The Phelps School, Malvern	X		X		–	–	6–PG	97	98	4:1	X	28
Philadelphia-Montgomery Christian Academy, Erdenheim			X	X	K–5	6–8	9–12	252	107	10:1	X	8
Plumstead Christian School, Plumsteadville			X	X	–	–	–	337	118			7
Quigley Catholic High School, Baden			X	X	–	–	9–12	203	111	12:1	X	15
Saint Basil Academy, Jenkintown				X	–	–	9–12	324	324	10:1	X	12
St. Joseph's Preparatory School, Philadelphia			X		–	–	9–12	890	902	16:1	X	35
Shady Side Academy, Pittsburgh	X	X	X	X	PK–5	6–8	9–12	945	485	8:1	X	23
Springside Chestnut Hill Academy, Philadelphia			X	X	PK–5	6–8	9–12	1,059	464	9.7:1	X	22
Villa Joseph Marie High School, Holland				X	–	–	9–12	363	392	9:1	X	17
Westtown School, West Chester	X	X	X	X	PK–5	6–8	9–12	636	363	8:1	X	35
Winchester Thurston School, Pittsburgh			X	X	PK–5	6–8	9–12	670	242	8:1	X	25
Woodlynde School, Strafford			X	X	K–5	6–8	9–12	270	132	5:1	X	16
Wyoming Seminary, Kingston	X	X	X	X	–	3–8	9–PG	790	458	8:1	X	26
York Country Day School, York			X	X	PS–5	6–8	9–12	246	81	6:1	X	12
Puerto Rico												
Colegio San Jose, San Juan			X		–	7–8	9–12	489	339	12:1	X	14
Fowlers Academy, Guaynabo			X	X	–	7–8	9–12	71	46	15:1		7
Guamani Private School, Guayama			X	X	1–6	7–8	9–12	606	164	13:1	X	6
Wesleyan Academy, Guaynabo			X	X	PK–6	7–8	9–12	903	246	25:1	X	10

Private Secondary Schools At-a-Glance

| | STUDENTS ACCEPTED | | | | GRADES | | | STUDENT/FACULTY | | | SCHOOL OFFERINGS | |
| | BOARDING | | DAY | | | | | | | | | |
	Boys	Girls	Boys	Girls	Lower	Middle	Upper	Total	Upper	Student/Faculty Ratio	Advanced Placement Preparation	Sports
Rhode Island												
La Salle Academy, Providence			X	X	–	6–8	9–12	1,462	1,372	11:1	X	25
Lincoln School, Providence			X	X	N–5	6–8	9–12	350	169	4:1	X	9
Mount Saint Charles Academy, Woonsocket			X	X	–	6–8	9–12	627	483	14:1	X	27
Providence Country Day School, East Providence			X	X	–	6–8	9–12	208	175	8:1	X	21
St. George's School, Middletown	X	X	X	X	–	–	9–12	370	370	6:1	X	22
The Wheeler School, Providence			X	X	N–5	6–8	9–12	819	374	7:1	X	15
South Carolina												
Ashley Hall, Charleston			X	X	PS–4	5–6	7–12	682	293	8:1	X	36
Beaufort Academy, Beaufort			X	X	PK–4	5–8	9–12	260	80	10:1	X	19
Ben Lippen Schools, Columbia	X	X	X	X	K–5	6–8	9–12	776	345	15:1	X	17
Christ Church Episcopal School, Greenville			X	X	K–4	5–8	9–12	1,128	309	10:1		32
Hammond School, Columbia			X	X	PK–4	5–8	9–12	898	301	9:1	X	45
Pinewood Preparatory School, Summerville			X	X	PS–5	6–8	9–12	675	240	12:1	X	22
St. Joseph's Catholic School, Greenville			X	X	–	6–8	9–12	677	437	10:1	X	15
Wilson Hall, Sumter			X	X	PS–5	6–8	9–12	781	245	13:1	X	34
Tennessee												
Battle Ground Academy, Franklin			X	X	K–4	5–8	9–12	754	364	8:1	X	23
Baylor School, Chattanooga	X	X	X	X	–	6–8	9–12	1,070	721	8:1	X	47
Briarcrest Christian High School, Eads			X	X	PK–5	6–8	9–12	1,657	573	12:1	X	19
Clarksville Academy, Clarksville			X	X	PK–5	6–8	9–12	650	242	12:1	X	13
Collegedale Academy, Collegedale			X	X	–	–	9–12	310	298	16:1	X	11
Columbia Academy, Columbia			X	X	K–6	–	7–12	748	396	12:1	X	13
Currey Ingram Academy, Brentwood			X	X	K–4	5–8	9–12	307	95			8
Davidson Academy, Nashville			X	X	PK–6	7–8	9–12	750		15:1	X	17
Donelson Christian Academy, Nashville			X	X	PS–5	6–8	9–12	818	209	14:1	X	19
Ezell-Harding Christian School, Antioch			X	X	PK–4	5–8	9–12	431	153	9:1	X	13
Grace Baptist Academy, Chattanooga			X	X	K4–5	6–8	9–12	469	135	12:1	X	17
The Harpeth Hall School, Nashville				X	–	5–8	9–12	690	402	8:1	X	39
The McCallie School, Chattanooga	X		X		–	6–8	9–12	913	656	8:1	X	62
Memphis Catholic High School and Middle School, Memphis			X	X	–	7–8	9–12	275	185	15:1		11
Memphis University School, Memphis			X		–	7–8	9–12	633	437	8:1	X	16
Montgomery Bell Academy, Nashville			X		–	7–8	9–12	752	515	7:1	X	37
Notre Dame High School, Chattanooga			X	X	–	–	9–12	423	423	10:1	X	42
Saint Agnes Academy–St. Dominic School, Memphis			X	X	PK–6	7–8	9–12	847	359	8:1	X	13
St. Andrew's–Sewanee School, Sewanee	X	X	X	X	–	6–8	9–12	230	176	6:1	X	50
St. Benedict at Auburndale, Cordova			X	X	–	–	9–12	945	750	16:1	X	24
St. George's Independent School, Collierville			X	X	PK–5	6–8	9–12	1,188	418	9:1	X	18
St. Mary's Episcopal School, Memphis				X	PK–4	5–8	9–12	837	253	9:1	X	12
University School of Jackson, Jackson			X	X	PK–5	6–8	9–12	1,124	312	13:1	X	17
Webb School of Knoxville, Knoxville			X	X	PK–5	6–8	9–12	989	449	11:1	X	24
Texas												
Allen Academy, Bryan	X	X	X	X	PK–5	6–8	9–12	323	90	8:1	X	17
Austin Waldorf School, Austin			X	X	K–5	6–8	9–12	390	84	20:1		12
The Canterbury Episcopal School, DeSoto			X	X	PK–6	7–8	9–12	251	55	16:1	X	11
Dallas Academy, Dallas			X	X	1–6	7–8	9–12	165	8	6:1		12
Episcopal High School, Bellaire			X	X	–	–	9–12	680	696	14.5:1	X	24
Father Yermo High School, El Paso			X	X	–	2–8	9–12	315	139			4
Fort Worth Christian School, North Richland Hills			X	X	PK–5	6–8	9–12	835	333	14:1	X	17
Fort Worth Country Day School, Fort Worth			X	X	K–4	5–8	9–12	1,110	400	10:1	X	31
Greenhill School, Addison			X	X	PK–4	5–8	9–12	1,280	462	7:1	X	27
The Hockaday School, Dallas		X		X	PK–4	5–8	9–12	1,096	486	10:1	X	42
Huntington-Surrey School, Austin			X	X	–	–	9–12	36	29	2:1		1
Hyde Park Baptist School, Austin			X	X	PK–5	6–8	9–12	599	298	12:1	X	15
Incarnate Word Academy, Houston				X	–	–	9–12	272	336	11:1	X	13
Jesuit College Preparatory School, Dallas			X		–	–	9–12	1,107	1,108	11:1	X	28
Lakehill Preparatory School, Dallas			X	X	K–4	5–8	9–12	405	120	10:1	X	19
Lutheran High North, Houston			X	X	–	–	9–12	295	148	22:1	X	18
Lydia Patterson Institute, El Paso			X	X	–	7–8	9–12	399	341	20:1	X	9
Marine Military Academy, Harlingen	X				–	–	8–PG	262	252	13:1	X	40
The Monarch School, Houston			X	X	K–8	–	6–12	135	67	2:1	X	
North Central Texas Academy, Granbury	X	X	X	X	K–5	6–8	9–12	175	58	7:1		17
The Oakridge School, Arlington			X	X	PS–4	5–8	9–12	869	322	11:1	X	27
Presbyterian Pan American School, Kingsville	X	X	X	X	–	–	9–12	168	140	10:1	X	19
Prestonwood Christian Academy, Plano			X	X	PK–4	5–8	9–12	1,551	507	12:1	X	13

Private Secondary Schools At-a-Glance

	STUDENTS ACCEPTED				GRADES			STUDENT/FACULTY			SCHOOL OFFERINGS	
	BOARDING		DAY									
	Boys	Girls	Boys	Girls	Lower	Middle	Upper	Total	Upper	Student/Faculty Ratio	Advanced Placement Preparation	Sports
River Oaks Baptist School, Houston			X	X	K–4	5–8	–	732	160	16:1		
St. Agnes Academy, Houston				X	–	–	9–12	899	921	12:1	X	21
Saint Andrew's Episcopal School, Austin			X	X	K–5	6–8	9–12	939	401	10:1		
St. Joseph High School, Victoria			X	X	–	–	9–12	407	310	14:1	X	19
Saint Mary's Hall, San Antonio			X	X	PK–5	6–8	9–PG	996	387	6:1	X	21
St. Pius X High School, Houston			X	X	–	–	9–12	682	664	12:1	X	20
St. Stephen's Episcopal School, Austin	X	X	X	X	–	6–8	9–12	688	486	8:1	X	41
San Marcos Baptist Academy, San Marcos	X	X	X	X	–	6–8	9–12	270	187	8:1	X	25
Second Baptist School, Houston			X	X	PK–4	5–8	9–12				X	9
Shelton School and Evaluation Center, Dallas			X	X	PS–5	6–8	9–12	895	300	10:1		15
The Tenney School, Houston			X	X	–	6–8	9–12	57	37	2:1	X	
TMI - The Episcopal School of Texas, San Antonio	X	X	X	X	–	6–8	9–12	472	341	9:1	X	24
The Ursuline Academy of Dallas, Dallas				X	–	–	9–12	843	844	10:1	X	13
Westbury Christian School, Houston			X	X	PK–4	5–8	9–12	464	223	10:1	X	14
The Winston School, Dallas			X	X	–	–	–		51	5:1		21
The Winston School San Antonio, San Antonio			X	X	K–6	7–8	9–12	201	90	8:1		15
The Woodlands Christian Academy, The Woodlands			X	X	PK–4	5–8	9–12	579	187		X	13
Utah												
Alpine Academy, Erda		X			–	7–8	9–12	61	54	4:1		36
Realms of Inquiry, Murray			X	X	–	6–8	9–12	32	21	8:1		50
Rowland Hall, Salt Lake City			X	X	PK–5	6–8	9–12	918	300	7:1	X	30
Sunrise Academy, Hurricane		X			–	–	7–12	32	60	4:1		52
Wasatch Academy, Mt. Pleasant	X	X	X	X	–	7–8	9–PG	319	249	10:1	X	64
The Waterford School, Sandy			X	X	PK–5	6–8	9–12	880	290	4:1	X	29
Vermont												
Burr and Burton Academy, Manchester	X	X	X	X	–	–	9–12	668	699	12:1	X	26
The Greenwood School, Putney	X		X		–	6–8	9–12	50	32	2:1		76
Long Trail School, Dorset			X	X	–	6–8	9–12	155	93	8:1		79
Lyndon Institute, Lyndon Center	X	X	X	X	–	–	9–12		626	10:1	X	35
Rice Memorial High School, South Burlington			X	X	–	–	9–12	461	435	11:1	X	22
Rock Point School, Burlington	X	X	X	X	–	–	9–12	26	26	5:1		40
Stratton Mountain School, Stratton Mountain	X	X	X	X	–	7–8	9–PG	134	104	7:1		16
Virgin Islands												
Good Hope Country Day School, Kingshill			X	X	N–6	7–8	9–12	360	127	12:1	X	12
Virginia												
Bishop Denis J. O'Connell High School, Arlington			X	X	–	–	–	1,100	1,100	12:1	X	24
Bishop Ireton High School, Alexandria			X	X	–	–	9–12	813	786	12:1	X	26
Blessed Sacrament Huguenot Catholic School, Powhatan			X	X	PS–5	6–8	9–12	316	106	6:1	X	13
The Blue Ridge School, St. George	X				–	–	9–12	195	182	8:1		49
Cape Henry Collegiate School, Virginia Beach			X	X	PK–5	6–8	9–12	893	337	10:1	X	40
Chatham Hall, Chatham		X		X	–	–	9–12	140	143	5:1	X	18
Christchurch School, Christchurch	X	X	X	X	1–4	5–8	9–12	196	206	6:1	X	31
The Collegiate School, Richmond			X	X	JK–4	5–8	9–12	1,644	538	15:1	X	31
Eastern Mennonite High School, Harrisonburg			X	X	K–5	6–8	9–12	379	161	12:1	X	14
Episcopal High School, Alexandria	X	X			–	–	9–12	435	440	5:1	X	44
Foxcroft School, Middleburg		X		X	–	–	9–PG	167	151	6:1	X	40
Fuqua School, Farmville			X	X	PK–5	6–8	9–12	379	151	7:1	X	13
Hampton Roads Academy, Newport News			X	X	JK–4	5–8	9–12	606	250	10:1	X	35
Loudoun School for the Gifted, Ashburn			X	X	–	6–8	9–12	35	31	3:1	X	
Massanutten Military Academy, Woodstock	X	X	X	X	–	6–8	9–PG	99	98	8:1	X	44
Oakland School, Troy	X	X	X	X	–	–	–			5:1		45
Peninsula Catholic High School, Newport News			X	X	–	–	8–12	305	265	11:1	X	13
The Potomac School, McLean			X	X	K–3	4–8	9–12	1,032	459	6:1	X	27
Randolph-Macon Academy, Front Royal	X	X	X	X	–	6–8	9–PG	293	254	8:1	X	27
St. Christopher's School, Richmond			X		JK–5	6–8	9–12	1,006	336	7.5:1	X	28
Saint Gertrude High School, Richmond				X	–	–	9–12	247	240	9:1	X	12
Stuart Hall, Staunton	X	X	X	X	PK–5	6–8	9–12	302	128	8:1	X	10
Tandem Friends School, Charlottesville			X	X	–	5–8	9–12		98	5:1	X	9
Trinity Episcopal School, Richmond			X	X	–	–	8–12	495	503	9:1	X	45
Virginia Episcopal School, Lynchburg	X	X	X	X	–	–	9–12	262	245	6:1	X	20
Woodberry Forest School, Woodberry Forest	X				–	–	9–12	393	399	6:1	X	59
Washington												
Bellevue Christian School, Clyde Hill			X	X	PK–6	7–8	9–12	1,160	349	21:1	X	21
Chrysalis School, Woodinville			X	X	K–6	7–8	9–12	185	126	3:1		
Explorations Academy, Bellingham			X	X	–	–	–	35	20	7:1	X	
The Northwest School, Seattle	X	X	X	X	–	6–8	9–12	506	350	9:1		16

Private Secondary Schools At-a-Glance

	Boarding Boys	Boarding Girls	Day Boys	Day Girls	Lower	Middle	Upper	Total	Upper	Student/Faculty Ratio	Advanced Placement Preparation	Sports
Seattle Academy of Arts and Sciences, Seattle			X	X	–	6–8	9–12	764	513	6:1		31
Shoreline Christian, Shoreline			X	X	PS–6	7–8	9–12	199	55	8:1		6
University Prep, Seattle			X	X	–	6–8	9–12	545	308	9:1		33
West Sound Academy, Poulsbo	X	X	X	X	–	6–8	9–12	113	73	6:1		18
Wisconsin												
Catholic Central High School, Burlington			X	X	–	–	9–12	185	131	11:1	X	26
Edgewood High School of the Sacred Heart, Madison			X	X	–	–	9–12	660	531	10:1	X	19
St. Lawrence Seminary High School, Mount Calvary	X				–	–	9–12	203	193	9:1		29
University Lake School, Hartland			X	X	PK–4	5–8	9–12	258	83	9:1	X	14
Wyoming												
The Journeys School of Teton Science School, Jackson			X	X	K–5	6–8	9–12	159	36	7:1		30
CANADA												
The Academy for Gifted Children (PACE), Richmond Hill, ON			X	X	1–3	4–5	6–12	307	194	20:1	X	43
Académie Ste Cécile International School, Windsor, ON	X	X	X	X	JK–8	–	9–12	296	137	15:1	X	24
Balmoral Hall School, Winnipeg, MB		X		X	N–5	6–8	9–12	504	199	18:1	X	63
Banbury Crossroads School, Calgary, AB			X	X	1–3	4–6	7–12	41	26	10:1		28
Bayview Glen School, Toronto, ON			X	X	PS–5	6–8	9–12	1,042		22:1	X	10
Bearspaw Christian School, Calgary, AB			X	X	K–6	7–9	10–12	729	119	9:1		16
Bishop's College School, Sherbrooke, QC	X	X	X	X	–	7–9	10–12	239	180	8:1	X	56
Branksome Hall, Toronto, ON		X		X	JK–6	7–8	9–12	895	456	9:1		50
Brentwood College School, Mill Bay, BC	X	X	X	X	–	–	9–12	510	510	11:1	X	44
Central Alberta Christian High School, Lacombe, AB			X	X	–	–	10–12	97	96	12:1		27
The Country Day School, King City, ON			X	X	JK–6	7–8	9–12	700	300	9:1	X	33
Covenant Canadian Reformed School, County of Barrhead, AB			X	X	K–6	7–9	10–12	244	41	14:1		17
Crawford Adventist Academy, Willowdale, ON			X	X	JK–6	7–8	9–12	361	127	14:1	X	19
Crescent School, Toronto, ON			X		3–6	7–8	9–12	715	365	10:1	X	24
Crestwood Preparatory College, Toronto, ON			X	X	–	7–8	9–12	525		16:1	X	15
De La Salle College, Toronto, ON			X	X	5–6	7–8	9–12	627	434	15:1	X	22
Edison School, Okotoks, AB			X	X	K–4	5–8	9–12	236	48	12:1	X	5
Edmonton Academy, Edmonton, AB			X	X	3–6	7–9	10–12	69	23	6:1		12
Elmwood School, Ottawa, ON				X	PK–5	6–8	9–12	340	110	8:1		29
Fraser Academy, Vancouver, BC			X	X	1–6	7–9	10–12	229	84	3:1		31
Grace Christian School, Charlottetown, PE			X	X	JK–6	7–9	10–12	124	43	12:1	X	12
Great Lakes Christian High School, Beamsville, ON	X	X	X	X	–	–	9–12	124	124	8:1		22
Highroad Academy, Chilliwack, BC			X	X	K–6	7–8	9–12	427	137	13:1		
Holy Trinity School, Richmond Hill, ON			X	X	JK–6	7–8	9–12	750	400	17:1	X	26
Hope Christian School, Champion, AB			X	X	1–6	7–9	10–12	24	1	12:1		
King's-Edgehill School, Windsor, NS	X	X	X	X	–	6–9	10–12	332	218	10:1		35
The Laureate Academy, Winnipeg, MB		X		X	1–5	6–8	9–12	80	27	5:1		36
The Linden School, Toronto, ON				X	1–6	7–8	9–12	121	42	5:1	X	37
Lower Canada College, Montreal, QC			X	X	K–6	7–8	9–12	775	280	22:1	X	58
Luther College High School, Regina, SK	X	X	X	X	–	–	9–12	440	440	17:1		21
Miss Edgar's and Miss Cramp's School, Montreal, QC				X	K–5	6–8	9–11	320	108	9:1	X	26
Moncton Wesleyan Academy, Moncton, NB			X	X	K–6	7–8	9–12	147	44			4
Newton's Grove School, Toronto, ON			X	X	JK–6	7–8	9–12	249	110	18:1	X	29
Niagara Christian Community of Schools, Fort Erie, ON	X	X	X	X	–	–	9–12	205	212	18:1		19
North Toronto Christian School, Toronto, ON			X	X	JK–6	7–8	9–12	407	151	15:1		26
Peoples Christian Academy, Markham, ON			X	X	JK–5	6–8	9–12	376	104	10:1	X	11
Pickering College, Newmarket, ON	X	X	X	X	JK–5	6–8	9–12	423	242	8:1	X	47
Queen Margaret's School, Duncan, BC		X	X	X	PS–3	4–7	8–12	339	145	8:1	X	57
Quinte Christian High School, Belleville, ON			X	X	–	–	9–12	148	135	15:1		10
Redeemer Christian High School, Ottawa, ON			X	X	–	–	9–12	149	145	10:1		13
Ridley College, St. Catharines, ON	X	X	X	X	JK–8	–	9–PG	649	479	8:1		81
Rockway Mennonite Collegiate, Kitchener, ON	X	X	X	X	–	7–8		265	223	10:1		24
Ron Pettigrew Christian School, Dawson Creek, BC			X	X	JK–6	7–8	9–12	88	25	5:1		
Rosseau Lake College, Rosseau, ON	X	X	X	X	–	7–8	9–12	84	78	6:1		80
Rothesay Netherwood School, Rothesay, NB	X	X	X	X	–	6–8	9–12	271	212	7:1		51
Royal Canadian College, Vancouver, BC			X	X	–	9–10	11–12	149	122	20:1		8
Rundle College, Calgary, AB			X	X	K–6	7–9	10–12	811	246	14:1		23
St. George's School, Vancouver, BC	X		X		1–7	–	8–12	1,150	771	8:1	X	47
St. John's International, Vancouver, BC			X	X	–	–	10–12	125	125	10:1		
St. John's-Ravenscourt School, Winnipeg, MB	X	X	X	X	K–5	6–8	9–12	822	374	10:1	X	15
St. Patrick's Regional Secondary, Vancouver, BC			X	X	–	–	8–12	500	500		X	8
St. Paul's High School, Winnipeg, MB			X		–	–	9–12	554	560	14:1	X	23
Scholar's Hall Preparatory School, Kitchener, ON			X	X	JK–3	4–8	9–12	105	65	10:1		26

Private Secondary Schools At-a-Glance

	STUDENTS ACCEPTED				GRADES			STUDENT/FACULTY			SCHOOL OFFERINGS	
	BOARDING		DAY									
	Boys	Girls	Boys	Girls	Lower	Middle	Upper	Total	Upper	Student/Faculty Ratio	Advanced Placement Preparation	Sports
Shawnigan Lake School, Shawnigan Lake, BC	X	X	X	X	–	–	8–12	493	494	8:1	X	52
Signet Christian School, North York, ON			X	X	JK–8	–	9–12	30	10	5:1		8
Southern Ontario Collegiate, Hamilton, ON			X	X	–	–	–			15:1		
Trafalgar Castle School, Whitby, ON		X		X	–	5–8	9–12	191	138	18:1	X	26
Trinity College School, Port Hope, ON	X	X	X	X	–	5–8	9–12	562	460	8:1	X	39
United Mennonite Educational Institute, Leamington, ON			X	X	–	–	9–12	48	74	9:1		14
Upper Canada College, Toronto, ON	X		X		K–7	–	8–12	1,166	650	8:1		58
Venta Preparatory School, Ottawa, ON	X	X	X	X	JK–7	–	8–10	66	11	6:1		21

INTERNATIONAL

Austria

The American International School, Vienna			X	X	PK–5	6–8	9–12	787	279	7:1		17

Belgium

International School of Brussels, Brussels			X	X	N–6	7–9	10–13	1,387	483	10:1	X	16

Bermuda

The Bermuda High School for Girls, Pembroke				X	1–6	7–9	10–13	746	190	12:1		32
Mount St. Agnes Academy, Hamilton			X	X	K–5	6–8	9–12	372	111	10:1	X	12

Brazil

Escola Americana de Campinas, Campinas-SP			X	X	PK–5	6–8	9–12	701	144	7:1	X	27

Colombia

Colegio Bolivar, Cali			X	X	PK–5	6–8	9–12	1,269	333	9:1	X	13

Czech Republic

The English College in Prague, Prague			X	X	8–9	10–11	12–13	360	150	11:1		

Ecuador

Alliance Academy, Quito	X	X	X	X	PK–6	7–8	9–12	604	180	7:1	X	27

Egypt

Cairo American College, Cairo			X	X	PK–5	6–8	9–12	1,417	300	9:1	X	10

France

The Lycee International, American Section, Saint-Germain-en-Laye Cedex			X	X	PK–5	6–9	10–12	705	200	18:1	X	17

Germany

Bavarian International School, Haimhausen			X	X	PK–5	6–9	10–12	1,008	244	7:1		41
Black Forest Academy, Kandern	X	X	X	X	–	5–8	9–12	361	240	8:1	X	9
International School Hamburg, Hamburg			X	X	PK–5	6–8	9–12	755	261	8:1		19
Schule Schloss Salem, Salem	X	X	X	X	5–7	8–10	11–12	675	315	5:1		52

Greece

Campion School, Athens, Athens			X	X	PK–6	7–9	10–13	485	177	18:1		15

India

The American Embassy School, New Delhi 110 021			X	X	PK–5	6–8	9–12	957	350	7:1	X	16
Woodstock School, Uttarakhand	X	X	X	X	–	6–8	9–12	522	330	15:1	X	29

Italy

CCI The Renaissance School, Lanciano	X	X	X	X	–	–	10–12	70	45	7:1		33
St. Stephen's School, Rome, Rome	X	X	X	X	–	–	9–PG	287	295	7:1	X	7

Japan

The American School in Japan, Tokyo			X	X	N–5	6–8	9–12	1,620	570	10:1	X	23
Canadian Academy, Kobe	X	X	X	X	PK–5	6–8	9–13	690	212	10:1	X	10
Columbia International School, Tokorozawa, Saitama	X	X	X	X	1–6	7–9	10–12	225	75	12:1	X	47
Saint Maur International School, Yokohama			X	X	PK–5	6–8	9–12	446	145	4:1	X	6
Seisen International School, Tokyo			X	X	K–6	7–8	9–12	646	173	4:1		12
Yokohama International School, Yokohama			X	X	N–5	6–8	9–12	644	258	8:1		12

Kenya

International School of Kenya, Ltd., Nairobi			X	X	PK–5	6–8	9–12	948	335		X	17

Kuwait

The English School, Kuwait, Safat			X	X	–	–	–	600				9

Lebanon

American Community School at Beirut, Beirut					–	–	–					

Private Secondary Schools At-a-Glance

| | STUDENTS ACCEPTED | | | | GRADES | | | STUDENT/FACULTY | | | SCHOOL OFFERINGS | |
| | BOARDING | | DAY | | | | | | | | | |
	Boys	Girls	Boys	Girls	Lower	Middle	Upper	Total	Upper	Student/Faculty Ratio	Advanced Placement Preparation	Sports
Malaysia												
Alice Smith School, Kuala Lumpur			X	X	7–9	10–11	12–13	632	182	9:1		17
Dalat School, Tanjung Bunga	X	X	X	X	–	5–8	9–12	599	195			16
Malta												
Verdala International School, Pembroke	X	X	X	X	PK–5	6–8	9–12	310	109	7:1		6
Mexico												
The American School Foundation, Mexico City, D.F.			X	X	1–5	6–8	9–12	2,530	721	11:1	X	17
The American School of Puerto Vallarta, Puerto Vallarta, Jalisco			X	X	K–6	7–9	10–12	343	74	7:1	X	15
Netherlands												
American International School Rotterdam, Rotterdam			X	X	PK–5	6–8	9–12	213	61	6:1		6
American School of The Hague, Wassenaar			X	X	PS–4	5–8	9–12	1,035	417	7:1	X	11
International School of Amsterdam, Amstelveen			X	X	PS–5	6–8	9–12	1,327	361	13:1		18
Rotterdam International Secondary School, Wolfert van Borselen, Rotterdam			X	X	6–8	9–10	11–12	278	102	10:1		8
Peru												
Colegio Franklin D. Roosevelt, Lima 12			X	X	3–5	6–8	9–12	1,500	399	12:1		17
Philippines												
International School Manila, 1634 Taguig City			X	X	PK–4	5–8	9–12	2,194	771	9:1	X	18
Spain												
The American School of Madrid, Madrid			X	X	PK–5	6–8	9–12	884	324	10:1		10
International College Spain, Madrid			X	X	PK–5	6–8	9–12	709	130	9:1		25
Switzerland												
Institut Monte Rosa, Montreux	X	X	X	X	–	–	–			4:1	X	38
Leysin American School in Switzerland, Leysin	X	X			–	7–10	11–PG	340	340	8:1		66
Neuchatel Junior College, Neuchâtel	X	X			–	–	12	62	62	10:1	X	38
TASIS, The American School in Switzerland, Montagnola-Lugano	X	X	X	X	PK–5	6–8	9–PG	722	390	6:1	X	38
Zurich International School, Wädenswil			X	X	PS–5	6–8	9–13	1,422	513	7:1	X	33
Taiwan												
Kaohsiung American School, Kaohsiung City			X	X	PK–5	6–8	9–12	290	307	8:1	X	18
Taipei American School, Taipei			X	X	PK–5	6–8	9–12	2,323	2,308	9:1	X	12
Thailand												
New International School of Thailand, Bangkok			X	X	N–5	–	6–12	1,319	645	8:1		15
St. Stephen's International School, Bangkok					–	–	–					
Trinidad and Tobago												
International School of Port-of-Spain, Westmoorings			X	X	PK–5	6–8	9–12	466	140	12:1	X	12
Tunisia												
American Cooperative School of Tunis, Tunis			X	X	–	–	–	353	90			12
Turkey												
Istanbul International Community School, Istanbul			X	X	1–6	–	7–12	619	292	9:1		12
United Kingdom												
Brockwood Park School, Alresford	X	X			–	–	–	65	58	7:1		
The International School of Aberdeen, Aberdeen			X	X	PK–5	6–8	9–12	439	81	5:1		54
The International School of London, London			X	X	K–5	6–10	11–12	340	80	8:1		12
Merchiston Castle School, Edinburgh	X		X		–	–	–		174	7:1		46
TASIS The American School in England, Thorpe, Surrey	X	X	X	X	N–4	5–8	9–13	750	405	7:1	X	39
Windermere School, Windermere	X	X	X	X	–	–	–	375	232	8:1		52
Venezuela												
Escuela Campo Alegre, Caracas			X	X	N–5	6–8	9–12	480	102	6:1		5

Traditional Day and Boarding Schools

THE ACADEMY AT CHARLEMONT

1359 Route 2
The Mohawk Trail
Charlemont, Massachusetts 01339

Head of School: Dr. Brian B. Bloomfield

General Information Coeducational day college-preparatory and arts school. Grades 7–PG. Founded: 1981. Setting: rural. Nearest major city is Northampton. 52-acre campus. 2 buildings on campus. Approved or accredited by Association of Independent Schools in New England, New England Association of Schools and Colleges, and Massachusetts Department of Education. Member of National Association of Independent Schools and Secondary School Admission Test Board. Endowment: $1.1 million. Total enrollment: 88. Upper school average class size: 14. Upper school faculty-student ratio: 1:4. There are 164 required school days per year for Upper School students. Upper School students typically attend 5 days per week. The average school day consists of 7 hours and 15 minutes.

Upper School Student Profile Grade 9: 15 students (8 boys, 7 girls); Grade 10: 13 students (7 boys, 6 girls); Grade 11: 11 students (7 boys, 4 girls); Grade 12: 17 students (7 boys, 10 girls).

Faculty School total: 25. In upper school: 9 men, 7 women; 13 have advanced degrees.

Subjects Offered 3-dimensional art, 3-dimensional design, algebra, American legal systems, American literature, architectural drawing, art, art history, biology, calculus, ceramics, chemistry, choral music, civics, computer programming, creative writing, dance, drama, drawing, earth science, ecology, English, English literature, environmental science, ethics, European history, expository writing, film, fine arts, French, geography, geometry, government/civics, grammar, Greek, health, history, jazz band, journalism, Latin, mathematics, music, music appreciation, philosophy, photography, physical education, physics, pre-algebra, pre-calculus, publications, publishing, religion, science, senior humanities, senior project, social studies, Spanish, speech, theater, trigonometry, world history, world literature, yearbook.

Graduation Requirements Algebra, American government, American literature, American studies, arts and fine arts (art, music, dance, drama), biology, calculus, chemistry, civics, computer literacy, English, foreign language, four units of summer reading, geography, geometry, Latin, mathematics, physics, pre-calculus, science, senior project, social studies (includes history), year-long independent senior project equal to one full course, requiring outside evaluation and a presentation.

Special Academic Programs Independent study; term-away projects; study abroad; special instructional classes for deaf students, blind students; ESL (4 students enrolled).

College Admission Counseling 12 students graduated in 2015; 10 went to college, including Brown University; Mount Holyoke College; Northeastern University; Sarah Lawrence College; University of Vermont; Vassar College. Other: 1 entered a postgraduate year, 1 had other specific plans. Mean SAT critical reading: 673, mean SAT math: 585, mean SAT writing: 621, mean combined SAT: 1879, mean composite ACT: 28.

Student Life Upper grades have specified standards of dress, student council, honor system. Discipline rests equally with students and faculty.

Tuition and Aid Day student tuition: $22,500. Tuition installment plan (monthly payment plans, individually arranged payment plans). Need-based scholarship grants available. In 2015–16, 62% of upper-school students received aid. Total amount of financial aid awarded in 2015–16: $419,375.

Admissions Traditional secondary-level entrance grade is 9. For fall 2015, 13 students applied for upper-level admission, 13 were accepted, 6 enrolled. Deadline for receipt of application materials: February 1. Application fee required: $50. On-campus interview required.

Athletics Interscholastic: alpine skiing (boys, girls), baseball (b,g), basketball (b,g), cross-country running (b,g), lacrosse (g), skiing (downhill) (b,g), soccer (b,g), ultimate Frisbee (b,g); intramural: independent competitive sports (b,g); coed interscholastic: baseball, cross-country running, soccer, ultimate Frisbee; coed intramural: alpine skiing, hiking/backpacking, outdoor activities, outdoor recreation, rafting, tennis, yoga. 7 coaches.

Computers Computers are regularly used in all classes. Computer network features include on-campus library services, Internet access, wireless campus network, Internet filtering or blocking technology, school Web site for schedules and other administrative information. Student e-mail accounts and computer access in designated common areas are available to students. Students grades are available online. The school has a published electronic and media policy.

Contact Martha Tirk, Director of Admissions and Advancement. 413-339-4912 Ext. 113. Fax: 413-339-4324. E-mail: mtirk@charlemont.org.
Website: www.charlemont.org

ACADEMY AT THE LAKES

2331 Collier Parkway
Land O'Lakes, Florida 34639

Head of School: Mr. Mark Heller

General Information Coeducational day college-preparatory school. Grades PK–12. Founded: 1992. Setting: suburban. Nearest major city is Tampa. 11-acre campus. 10 buildings on campus. Approved or accredited by Florida Council of Independent Schools, Southern Association of Schools and Colleges, and Florida Department of Education. Member of National Association of Independent Schools and Secondary School Admission Test Board. Total enrollment: 466. Upper school average class size: 14. Upper school faculty-student ratio: 1:5. There are 175 required school days per year for Upper School students. Upper School students typically attend 5 days per week. The average school day consists of 7 hours and 15 minutes.

Faculty School total: 69. In upper school: 10 men, 18 women; 19 have advanced degrees.

Graduation Requirements Standard curriculum, Personal Finance (.5 credit), senior speech, senior internship.

Special Academic Programs 17 Advanced Placement exams for which test preparation is offered; honors section; ESL.

College Admission Counseling 37 students graduated in 2016; 35 went to college. Other: 2 went to work.

Student Life Upper grades have specified standards of dress, student council, honor system. Discipline rests primarily with faculty.

Summer Programs Enrichment, sports, art/fine arts, computer instruction programs offered; held on campus; accepts boys and girls; open to students from other schools. 350 students usually enrolled. 2017 schedule: June to August.

Tuition and Aid Day student tuition: $10,490–$21,190. Tuition installment plan (monthly payment plans). Need-based scholarship grants available.

Admissions Traditional secondary-level entrance grade is 9. SSAT required. Deadline for receipt of application materials: February 17. Application fee required: $75. Interview recommended.

Athletics Interscholastic: baseball (boys), basketball (b,g), cheering (g), cross-country running (b,g), football (b), golf (b,g), physical fitness (b,g), physical training (b,g), soccer (b,g), softball (g), strength & conditioning (b,g), swimming and diving (b,g), tennis (b,g), track and field (b,g), volleyball (g), weight training (b,g), winter soccer (b,g); coed interscholastic: physical fitness, physical training, strength & conditioning. 3 PE instructors, 12 coaches, 1 athletic trainer.

Computers Computers are regularly used in all classes. Computer network features include on-campus library services, online commercial services, Internet access, wireless campus network, Internet filtering or blocking technology. Student e-mail accounts are available to students. Students grades are available online. The school has a published electronic and media policy.

Contact Mrs. Melissa Starkey, Associate Director of Admissions. 813-909-7919. Fax: 813-949-0563. E-mail: mstarkey@academyatthelakes.org.
Website: www.academyatthelakes.org/

THE ACADEMY FOR GIFTED CHILDREN (PACE)

12 Bond Crescent
Richmond Hill, Ontario L4E 3K2, Canada

Head of School: Barbara Rosenberg

General Information Coeducational day college-preparatory and differentiated curriculum for Intellectually gifted students school. Grades 1–12. Founded: 1993. Setting: suburban. Nearest major city is Toronto, Canada. 3-acre campus. 2 buildings on campus. Approved or accredited by Ontario Department of Education. Language of instruction: English. Total enrollment: 307. Upper school average class size: 20. Upper school faculty-student ratio: 1:20. There are 187 required school days per year for Upper School students. Upper School students typically attend 5 days per week. The average school day consists of 6 hours and 45 minutes.

Upper School Student Profile Grade 6: 40 students (26 boys, 14 girls); Grade 7: 40 students (23 boys, 17 girls); Grade 8: 34 students (19 boys, 15 girls); Grade 9: 20 students (14 boys, 6 girls); Grade 10: 20 students (13 boys, 7 girls); Grade 11: 20 students (8 boys, 12 girls); Grade 12: 20 students (15 boys, 5 girls).

Faculty School total: 28. In upper school: 7 men, 14 women; 10 have advanced degrees.

Subjects Offered 20th century world history, advanced biology, advanced chemistry, advanced math, Advanced Placement courses, algebra, analytic geometry, biology, calculus, calculus-AP, Canadian geography, Canadian history, Canadian law, career education, chemistry, chemistry-AP, civics, computer education, computer programming, computer science, computer science-AP, computer studies, critical thinking, current history, debate, decision making skills, drama performance, dramatic arts, English, English composition, equality and freedom, finite math, food and nutrition, French, French as a second language, geometry, global issues, government/civics, health and wellness, health education, honors algebra, honors English, honors geometry, human anatomy, language, law, life management skills, literature, marine biology, mathematics, microbiology, modern Western civilization, music, music appreciation, music composition, music history, music theory, organic chemistry, personal development, philosophy, physical education, physics, probability and statistics, research seminar, robotics, scene study, science, scuba diving, Shakespeare, skills for success, sociology, visual arts, world civilizations, writing.

Graduation Requirements Advanced chemistry, advanced math, algebra, analytic geometry, biology, calculus, Canadian geography, Canadian history, Canadian literature, career education, chemistry, civics, drama, English, English literature, French as a second language, government, health and wellness, healthful living, law, mathematics, music, philosophy, pre-algebra, pre-calculus, science, scuba diving, social sciences, theater arts, visual arts, minimum of 40 hours of community service, Ontario Secondary School Literacy Test.

Special Academic Programs 5 Advanced Placement exams for which test preparation is offered; honors section; academic accommodation for the gifted.

College Admission Counseling 21 students graduated in 2016; all went to college, including Harvard University; McMaster University; Queen's University at Kingston; The University of Western Ontario; University of Toronto; University of Waterloo. Median SAT critical reading: 780, median SAT math: 800, median SAT writing: 780, median combined SAT: 2360, median composite ACT: 33. 100% scored over 600 on SAT critical reading, 100% scored over 600 on SAT math, 100% scored over 600 on SAT writing, 100% scored over 1800 on combined SAT, 100% scored over 26 on composite ACT.

Student Life Upper grades have specified standards of dress, student council, honor system. Discipline rests primarily with faculty.

Tuition and Aid Day student tuition: CAN$12,500. Tuition installment plan (monthly payment plans).

Admissions Traditional secondary-level entrance grade is 7. For fall 2016, 15 students applied for upper-level admission, 12 were accepted, 12 enrolled. Individual IQ, psychoeducational evaluation, Wechsler Individual Achievement Test and WISC III or other aptitude measures; standardized achievement test required. Deadline for receipt of application materials: none. No application fee required. On-campus interview recommended.

Athletics Interscholastic: badminton (boys, girls), ball hockey (b), baseball (b,g), basketball (b,g), flag football (b), floor hockey (b), golf (b,g), independent competitive sports (b,g), indoor soccer (b,g), sailboarding (b,g), soccer (b,g), softball (b,g), tennis (b,g), track and field (b,g), volleyball (b,g), winter soccer (b,g); intramural: badminton (b,g), basketball (b,g), soccer (b,g), softball (b,g); coed interscholastic: badminton, baseball, bowling, cross-country running, flag football, Frisbee, indoor soccer, sailboarding, tennis, track and field, ultimate Frisbee; coed intramural: alpine skiing, badminton, ball hockey, baseball, basketball, blading, climbing, cooperative games, cross-country running, curling, dance, fitness, floor hockey, handball, indoor soccer, jogging, jump rope, life saving, outdoor activities, outdoor education, outdoor skills, physical fitness, rock climbing, ropes courses, scuba diving, skiing (cross-country), skiing (downhill), snowboarding, snowshoeing, track and field, ultimate Frisbee, volleyball, wall climbing. 2 PE instructors, 10 coaches.

Computers Computers are regularly used in career exploration, desktop publishing, digital applications, English, information technology, keyboarding, news writing, newspaper, programming, science, technology, theater, writing, yearbook classes. Computer network features include Internet access, wireless campus network, Internet filtering or blocking technology, Edmodo. Computer access in designated common areas is available to students. The school has a published electronic and media policy.

Contact Barbara Rosenberg, Director. 905-773-3997. Fax: 905-773-4722. Website: www.pace.on.ca

ACADEMY FOR INDIVIDUAL EXCELLENCE

3101 Bluebird Lane
Louisville, Kentucky 40299

Head of School: Mr. John Savage

General Information Coeducational day college-preparatory and general academic school. Grades K–12. Founded: 1984. Setting: suburban. 9-acre campus. 1 building on campus. Approved or accredited by Kentucky Department of Education. Total enrollment: 368. Upper school average class size: 16. Upper school faculty-student ratio: 1:9. There are 174 required school days per year for Upper School students. Upper School students typically attend 5 days per week. The average school day consists of 6 hours and 10 minutes.

Upper School Student Profile Grade 9: 47 students (25 boys, 22 girls); Grade 10: 51 students (30 boys, 21 girls); Grade 11: 45 students (31 boys, 14 girls); Grade 12: 39 students (31 boys, 8 girls).

Faculty School total: 46. In upper school: 10 men, 10 women; 12 have advanced degrees.

Subjects Offered Algebra, American government, American history, American literature, American sign language, art, art appreciation, biology, business mathematics, calculus, chemistry, composition, computer applications, creative writing, critical thinking, drama, English, English literature, foreign language, general math, general science, geography, geometry, government, health, music appreciation, personal finance, physical education, psychology, world history.

College Admission Counseling 45 students graduated in 2015; 24 went to college, including Harding University; Lipscomb University; Northern Kentucky University; University of Louisville; Western Kentucky University. Other: 14 went to work, 4 entered a postgraduate year, 3 had other specific plans.

Student Life Upper grades have specified standards of dress. Discipline rests primarily with faculty.

Tuition and Aid Day student tuition: $8395. Tuition installment plan (monthly payment plans). Need-based scholarship grants available. In 2015–16, 7% of upper-school students received aid.

Admissions Traditional secondary-level entrance grade is 9. For fall 2015, 42 students applied for upper-level admission, 37 were accepted, 37 enrolled. Deadline for receipt of application materials: none. No application fee required. On-campus interview required.

Athletics Interscholastic: baseball (boys), basketball (b,g), softball (g), volleyball (g); coed interscholastic: archery, soccer; coed intramural: bowling, horseback riding. 1 PE instructor.

Computers Computers are regularly used in computer applications classes. Computer network features include Internet filtering or blocking technology. Computer access in designated common areas is available to students. The school has a published electronic and media policy.

Contact 502-267-6187. Fax: 502-261-9687. Website: www.aiexcellence.com

ACADEMY OF HOLY ANGELS

6600 Nicollet Avenue South
Richfield, Minnesota 55423-2498

Head of School: Mr. Thomas C. Shipley

General Information Coeducational day college-preparatory school, affiliated with Roman Catholic Church. Grades 9–12. Founded: 1877. Setting: suburban. Nearest major city is Minneapolis. 26-acre campus. 2 buildings on campus. Approved or accredited by North Central Association of Colleges and Schools. Endowment: $1.8 million. Total enrollment: 613. Upper school average class size: 20. Upper school faculty-student ratio: 1:13. Upper School students typically attend 5 days per week. The average school day consists of 7 hours.

Upper School Student Profile 70% of students are Roman Catholic.

Faculty School total: 48. In upper school: 23 men, 23 women; 38 have advanced degrees.

Subjects Offered Algebra, American history, American literature, anatomy, art, art history, astronomy, Bible studies, biology, broadcasting, business, business skills, calculus, ceramics, chemistry, computer math, computer programming, computer science, dance, drafting, drama, economics, electronics, English, English literature, environmental science, ethics, European history, expository writing, fine arts, French, geography, geometry, German, government/civics, grammar, health, history, home economics, industrial arts, journalism, mathematics, mechanical drawing, music, photography, physical education, physics, physiology, psychology, religion, Russian, science, social sciences, social studies, sociology, Spanish, speech, theater, theology, trigonometry, typing, world history, world literature, writing.

Graduation Requirements Arts and fine arts (art, music, dance, drama), business skills (includes word processing), English, mathematics, physical education (includes health), religion (includes Bible studies and theology), science, social sciences, social studies (includes history).

Special Academic Programs Advanced Placement exam preparation; honors section; independent study; study at local college for college credit; academic accommodation for the gifted, the musically talented, and the artistically talented; ESL (30 students enrolled).

College Admission Counseling 161 students graduated in 2016; 158 went to college, including College of Saint Benedict; Marquette University; Saint John's University; University of Minnesota, Twin Cities Campus; University of St. Thomas; University of Wisconsin Madison. Other: 1 entered military service, 2 had other specific plans. Mean SAT critical reading: 596, mean SAT math: 732, mean SAT writing: 585, mean combined SAT: 1912, mean composite ACT: 27.

Student Life Upper grades have uniform requirement, student council, honor system. Discipline rests equally with students and faculty. Attendance at religious services is required.

Summer Programs Sports, art/fine arts programs offered; session focuses on activities geared toward 9th grade recruiting; held both on and off campus; accepts boys and girls; open to students from other schools. 450 students usually enrolled. 2017 schedule: June 12 to July 20. Application deadline: May 26.

Tuition and Aid Day student tuition: $14,500. Tuition installment plan (monthly payment plans, individually arranged payment plans, three payment plan; lump sum payment). Need-based scholarship grants, minority student scholarships, single-parent family scholarships available. In 2016–17, 37% of upper-school students received aid. Total amount of financial aid awarded in 2016–17: $1,300,000.

Admissions Traditional secondary-level entrance grade is 9. STS or STS, Diocese Test required. Deadline for receipt of application materials: January 21. No application fee required. On-campus interview required.

Athletics Interscholastic: baseball (boys), basketball (b,g), cheering (g), cross-country running (b,g), danceline (g), football (b), golf (b,g), ice hockey (b,g), lacrosse (b,g), soccer (b,g), softball (g), strength & conditioning (b,g), swimming and diving (b,g), tennis (b,g), track and field (b,g), volleyball (g); coed interscholastic: bowling, paddle tennis, table tennis, trap and skeet; coed intramural: football. 3 PE instructors, 27 coaches, 1 athletic trainer.

Computers Computers are regularly used in English, foreign language, mathematics, science, yearbook classes. Computer network features include on-campus library services, online commercial services, Internet access, wireless campus network. Student e-mail accounts and computer access in designated common areas are available to students. Students grades are available online. The school has a published electronic and media policy.

Contact Mrs. Meg Angevine, Director of Admissions. 612-798-0764. Fax: 612-798-2610. E-mail: mangevine@ahastars.org. Website: www.academyofholyangels.org

ACADEMY OF NOTRE DAME

180 Middlesex Road
Tyngsboro, Massachusetts 01879-1598

Head of School: Mr. Randall Adams

General Information Coeducational day college-preparatory school, affiliated with Reformed Church in America. Boys grades K–8, girls grades K–12. Founded: 1854. Setting: small town. Nearest major city is Boston. 195-acre campus. 2 buildings on campus. Approved or accredited by National Catholic Education Association, New England Association of Schools and Colleges, and Massachusetts Department of Education. Endowment: $1.6 million. Total enrollment: 610. Upper school average class size: 14. Upper school faculty-student ratio: 1:12. There are 172 required school days per year for Upper School students. Upper School students typically attend 5 days per week. The average school day consists of 6 hours and 35 minutes.

Upper School Student Profile Grade 9: 48 students (48 girls); Grade 10: 38 students (38 girls); Grade 11: 56 students (56 girls); Grade 12: 35 students (35 girls). 44% of students are Reformed Church in America.

Faculty School total: 20. In upper school: 5 men, 15 women; 15 have advanced degrees.

Subjects Offered French language-AP, French-AP, government/civics-AP, healthful living, yearbook.

Graduation Requirements Algebra, American history, American literature, ancient world history, art appreciation, biology, British literature, Christian and Hebrew scripture, Christian ethics, church history, geometry, history of the Catholic Church, literary genres, mathematics, modern world history, music appreciation, physical science, pre-calculus, science, technology, U.S. history, world history, world literature, world religions.

Special Academic Programs Advanced Placement exam preparation; honors section; independent study; academic accommodation for the gifted.

College Admission Counseling 38 students graduated in 2016; all went to college, including Boston University; Emmanuel College; Providence College; Suffolk University; University of Massachusetts Amherst; University of New Hampshire. Mean SAT critical reading: 579, mean SAT math: 547, mean SAT writing: 596, mean combined SAT: 1722, mean composite ACT: 26. 34% scored over 600 on SAT critical reading, 23% scored over 600 on SAT math, 39% scored over 600 on SAT writing, 35% scored over 1800 on combined SAT, 50% scored over 26 on composite ACT.

Student Life Upper grades have uniform requirement, student council, honor system. Discipline rests primarily with faculty. Attendance at religious services is required.

Tuition and Aid Day student tuition: $13,750. Tuition installment plan (FACTS Tuition Payment Plan, monthly payment plans). Merit scholarship grants available. In 2016–17, 72% of upper-school students received aid. Total amount of financial aid awarded in 2016–17: $11,300.

Admissions Traditional secondary-level entrance grade is 9. For fall 2016, 162 students applied for upper-level admission, 84 were accepted, 40 enrolled. Archdiocese of Boston High School entrance exam provided by STS required. Deadline for receipt of application materials: December 31. Application fee required: $50.

Athletics Interscholastic: basketball, cheering, cross-country running, diving, indoor track & field, soccer, softball, swimming and diving, tennis, track and field, volleyball, winter (indoor) track; intramural: bowling, dance, dance team, Frisbee, outdoor activities, physical fitness, rafting, walking. 1 PE instructor, 17 coaches.

Computers Computers are regularly used in all classes. Computer network features include on-campus library services, Internet access, wireless campus network, Internet filtering or blocking technology, virtual high school online courses. Student e-mail accounts and computer access in designated common areas are available to students. Students grades are available online. The school has a published electronic and media policy.

Contact Ms. Jocelyn Mendonsa, Vice President of Enrollment Management. 978-649-7611 Ext. 327. Fax: 978-649-2909. E-mail: jmendonsa@ndatyngsboro.org. Website: www.ndatyngsboro.org

ACADEMY OF NOTRE DAME DE NAMUR

560 Sproul Road
Villanova, Pennsylvania 19085-1220

Head of School: Dr. Judith A. Dwyer

General Information Girls' day college-preparatory school, affiliated with Roman Catholic Church. Grades 6–12. Founded: 1856. Setting: suburban. Nearest major city is Philadelphia. 39-acre campus. 9 buildings on campus. Approved or accredited by Middle States Association of Colleges and Schools, National Catholic Education Association, Pennsylvania Association of Independent Schools, and Pennsylvania Department of Education. Member of National Association of Independent Schools. Endowment: $7 million. Total enrollment: 519. Upper school average class size: 15. Upper school faculty-student ratio: 1:9. There are 170 required school days per year for Upper School students. Upper School students typically attend 5 days per week. The average school day consists of 6 hours and 45 minutes.

Upper School Student Profile Grade 9: 101 students (101 girls); Grade 10: 103 students (103 girls); Grade 11: 98 students (98 girls); Grade 12: 91 students (91 girls). 88% of students are Roman Catholic.

Faculty School total: 60. In upper school: 9 men, 49 women; 48 have advanced degrees.

Subjects Offered Advanced biology, Advanced Placement courses, American history-AP, Bible, biology, biology-AP, calculus, calculus-AP, ceramics, chemistry, chemistry-AP, choral music, Christian and Hebrew scripture, Christian ethics, comparative government and politics-AP, computer science-AP, computer skills, contemporary history, dance, economics, English, English literature, English literature and composition-AP, environmental science, French, French language-AP, geometry, government and politics-AP, health, health education, Hebrew scripture, instrumental music, journalism, Latin, Latin-AP, literature, literature and composition-AP, mathematics, multimedia design, music, music performance, music theory, music theory-AP, music-AP, physical education, physics-AP, pre-algebra, pre-calculus, psychology, SAT/ACT preparation, Spanish, Spanish language-AP, Spanish-AP, studio art-AP, U.S. government and politics-AP, U.S. history-AP, United States government-AP, visual and performing arts, world cultures.

Graduation Requirements Art, English, foreign language, guidance, mathematics, music, physical education (includes health), religion (includes Bible studies and theology), science, social studies (includes history), 40 hours of service.

Special Academic Programs Honors section; independent study; study at local college for college credit; study abroad; academic accommodation for the gifted, the musically talented, and the artistically talented.

College Admission Counseling 99 students graduated in 2016; all went to college, including Boston College; Georgetown University; Penn State University Park; Saint Joseph's University; University of Delaware; Villanova University.

Student Life Upper grades have uniform requirement, student council, honor system. Discipline rests primarily with faculty. Attendance at religious services is required.

Summer Programs Enrichment, advancement, sports, computer instruction programs offered; session focuses on academic enrichment; held on campus; accepts girls; not open to students from other schools. 2017 schedule: June 25 to July 16. Application deadline: June 1.

Tuition and Aid Day student tuition: $18,087–$22,013. Tuition installment plan (Insured Tuition Payment Plan, monthly payment plans, quarterly and semi-annual payment plans). Merit scholarship grants, need-based scholarship grants available. In 2016–17, 42% of upper-school students received aid; total upper-school merit-scholarship money awarded: $485,500. Total amount of financial aid awarded in 2016–17: $1,078,519.

Admissions Traditional secondary-level entrance grade is 9. High School Placement Test required. Deadline for receipt of application materials: December 17. Application fee required: $40. Interview required.

Athletics Interscholastic: basketball, crew, cross-country running, dance, diving, fencing, field hockey, golf, indoor track & field, lacrosse, paddle tennis, rowing, sailing, soccer, softball, swimming and diving, tennis, track and field, volleyball, winter (indoor) track; intramural: basketball, dance, flag football, floor hockey, kickball, modern dance, strength & conditioning. 2 PE instructors, 38 coaches, 1 athletic trainer.

Computers Computers are regularly used in all classes. Computer network features include on-campus library services, online commercial services, Internet access, wireless campus network, Internet filtering or blocking technology, SmartBoards in classrooms, One to one MacBook. Student e-mail accounts and computer access in designated common areas are available to students. Students grades are available online. The school has a published electronic and media policy.

Contact Mrs. Diane Sander, Director of Admissions. 610-971-0498. Fax: 610-687-1912. E-mail: dsander@ndapa.org. Website: www.ndapa.org

ACADEMY OF OUR LADY OF PEACE

4860 Oregon Street
San Diego, California 92116-1393

Head of School: Dr. Lauren Lek

General Information Girls' day college-preparatory and STEAM school, affiliated with Roman Catholic Church. Grades 9–12. Founded: 1882. Setting: urban. 20-acre campus. 7 buildings on campus. Approved or accredited by National Catholic Education Association, Western Association of Schools and Colleges, Western Catholic Education Association, and California Department of Education. Endowment: $250,000. Total enrollment: 748. Upper school average class size: 28. Upper school faculty-student ratio: 1:13. There are 180 required school days per year for Upper School students. Upper School students typically attend 5 days per week. The average school day consists of 6 hours and 45 minutes.

Upper School Student Profile Grade 9: 170 students (170 girls); Grade 10: 190 students (190 girls); Grade 11: 186 students (186 girls); Grade 12: 179 students (179 girls). 94% of students are Roman Catholic.

Faculty School total: 69. In upper school: 11 men, 58 women; 50 have advanced degrees.

Subjects Offered Algebra, American literature, art, Bible studies, biology, biology-AP, British literature, calculus, calculus-AP, campus ministry, ceramics, chemistry, chemistry-AP, computer science-AP, dance, drama, economics, engineering, English, English language and composition-AP, English literature and composition-AP, environmental science-AP, ethics, fitness, French, French language-AP, French-AP, genetics, geometry, government, graphic arts, health, honors algebra, marine science, music appreciation, music theory-AP, painting, physical education, physics, physics-

AP, pre-calculus, psychology, Spanish, Spanish language-AP, Spanish literature-AP, speech, studio art-AP, study skills, U.S. government and politics-AP, U.S. history, U.S. history-AP, video film production, Western civilization, yearbook, yoga.

Graduation Requirements Arts and fine arts (art, music, dance, drama), English, foreign language, mathematics, physical education (includes health), religion (includes Bible studies and theology), science, social sciences, social studies (includes history), speech, 75 hours of community service, 9-11 reflection paper required for seniors.

Special Academic Programs 16 Advanced Placement exams for which test preparation is offered; honors section.

College Admission Counseling 185 students graduated in 2016; 184 went to college, including Gonzaga University; Northern Arizona University; San Diego State University; San Francisco State University; University of California, Santa Barbara; University of San Francisco. Other: 1 had other specific plans.

Student Life Upper grades have uniform requirement, student council, honor system. Discipline rests equally with students and faculty. Attendance at religious services is required.

Summer Programs Remediation, enrichment, advancement, sports programs offered; session focuses on advancement and remediation/make-up; held on campus; accepts girls; open to students from other schools. 200 students usually enrolled. 2017 schedule: June 19 to July 28. Application deadline: May 1.

Tuition and Aid Day student tuition: $17,880. Tuition installment plan (FACTS Tuition Payment Plan). Merit scholarship grants, need-based scholarship grants available. In 2016–17, 40% of upper-school students received aid; total upper-school merit-scholarship money awarded: $50,000. Total amount of financial aid awarded in 2016–17: $2,600,000.

Admissions Traditional secondary-level entrance grade is 9. For fall 2016, 230 students applied for upper-level admission, 205 were accepted, 170 enrolled. High School Placement Test required. Deadline for receipt of application materials: January 15. Application fee required: $55. On-campus interview recommended.

Athletics Interscholastic: basketball, cheering, cross-country running, diving, golf, gymnastics, lacrosse, sand volleyball, soccer, softball, surfing, swimming and diving, tennis, track and field, volleyball, water polo. 4 PE instructors, 16 coaches, 1 athletic trainer.

Computers Computers are regularly used in all academic, computer applications, media production, music, music technology, photography, Web site design, word processing classes. Computer network features include on-campus library services, online commercial services, Internet access, wireless campus network, Internet filtering or blocking technology. Campus intranet, student e-mail accounts, and computer access in designated common areas are available to students. Students grades are available online. The school has a published electronic and media policy.

Contact Erica Huebner, Admissions Coordinator. 619-725-9175. Fax: 619-297-2473. E-mail: admissions@aolp.org. Website: www.aolp.org

ACADEMY OF SAINT ELIZABETH

Box 297
Convent Station, New Jersey 07961-0297

Head of School: Mrs. Lynn Durek

General Information Girls' day college-preparatory school, affiliated with Roman Catholic Church. Grades 9–12. Founded: 1860. Setting: suburban. Nearest major city is Morristown. 200-acre campus. 2 buildings on campus. Approved or accredited by Middle States Association of Colleges and Schools, National Catholic Education Association, and New Jersey Association of Independent Schools. Member of National Association of Independent Schools. Total enrollment: 245. Upper school average class size: 15. Upper school faculty-student ratio: 1:6. The average school day consists of 6 hours and 45 minutes.

Upper School Student Profile Grade 9: 47 students (47 girls); Grade 10: 33 students (33 girls); Grade 11: 30 students (30 girls); Grade 12: 32 students (32 girls). 90% of students are Roman Catholic.

Faculty School total: 30. In upper school: 4 men, 22 women; 20 have advanced degrees.

Subjects Offered 20th century American writers, algebra, American history, American literature, art, bioethics, biology, biology-AP, British literature-AP, calculus, calculus-AP, ceramics, chemistry, chemistry-AP, dance, drama, driver education, ecology, English, English literature, English-AP, environmental education, environmental science, equestrian sports, European history, expository writing, fine arts, French, French as a second language, French language-AP, freshman seminar, geometry, grammar, health, history, history-AP, Holocaust studies, honors English, honors geometry, journalism, Latin, library, literary magazine, mathematics, modern world history, music, musical productions, photography, physical education, physics, psychology, religion, research, SAT preparation, science, Shakespeare, social sciences, social studies, sociology, softball, Spanish, Spanish language-AP, Spanish-AP, sports, studio art, swimming, theater, theology, trigonometry, U.S. history-AP, voice ensemble, volleyball, world history, world literature, world religions, yearbook.

Graduation Requirements Arts and fine arts (art, music, dance, drama), computer education, English, foreign language, mathematics, physical education (includes health), religion (includes Bible studies and theology), science, social sciences, social studies (includes history), senior independent study.

Special Academic Programs Advanced Placement exam preparation; honors section; independent study; study at local college for college credit.

College Admission Counseling 31 students graduated in 2016; all went to college, including American University; Boston College; College of the Holy Cross; Seton Hall University; University of Notre Dame; Villanova University.

Student Life Upper grades have uniform requirement, student council, honor system. Discipline rests primarily with faculty. Attendance at religious services is required.

Summer Programs Enrichment, sports, art/fine arts programs offered; held on campus; accepts boys and girls; open to students from other schools. 2017 schedule: June 20.

Tuition and Aid Day student tuition: $11,000. Tuition installment plan (monthly payment plans, individually arranged payment plans). Merit scholarship grants, need-based scholarship grants available. In 2016–17, 35% of upper-school students received aid.

Admissions Traditional secondary-level entrance grade is 9. School's own exam required. Deadline for receipt of application materials: January 15. Application fee required: $100. On-campus interview recommended.

Athletics Interscholastic: aquatics, basketball, cross-country running, equestrian sports, field hockey, lacrosse, soccer, softball, swimming and diving, track and field, volleyball; intramural: aerobics, aerobics/dance, alpine skiing, dance, equestrian sports, horseback riding, independent competitive sports. 1 PE instructor, 9 coaches, 1 athletic trainer.

Computers Computers are regularly used in all academic, English, foreign language, history, mathematics, science, study skills classes. Computer network features include on-campus library services, online commercial services, Internet access. Student e-mail accounts are available to students. Students grades are available online. The school has a published electronic and media policy.

Contact Ms. Kathleen Thomas, Director of Admissions. 973-290-5225. Fax: 973-290-5232. E-mail: kthom@aose.info. Website: www.academyofsaintelizabeth.org

ACADEMY OF THE HOLY CROSS

4920 Strathmore Avenue
Kensington, Maryland 20895-1299

Head of School: Ms. Kathleen R. Prebble

General Information Girls' day college-preparatory and International Baccalaureate Diploma Programme school, affiliated with Roman Catholic Church. Grades 9–12. Founded: 1868. Setting: suburban. Nearest major city is Rockville. 28-acre campus. 2 buildings on campus. Approved or accredited by Association of Independent Schools of Greater Washington, Middle States Association of Colleges and Schools, National Catholic Education Association, The College Board, and Maryland Department of Education. Member of National Association of Independent Schools. Upper school average class size: 19. Upper school faculty-student ratio: 1:11. There are 174 required school days per year for Upper School students. Upper School students typically attend 5 days per week. The average school day consists of 7 hours.

Upper School Student Profile Grade 9: 115 students (115 girls); Grade 10: 130 students (130 girls); Grade 11: 115 students (115 girls); Grade 12: 119 students (119 girls). 81% of students are Roman Catholic.

Faculty School total: 48. In upper school: 11 men, 37 women.

Subjects Offered Acting, Advanced Placement courses, algebra, American history, American literature, art, art history-AP, Asian studies, biology, biology-AP, calculus, calculus-AP, ceramics, chemistry, chemistry-AP, Christian scripture, computer science, concert choir, creative writing, design, drama, drawing, earth science, economics, English, English language and composition-AP, English literature, English literature and composition-AP, environmental science, ethnic studies, expository writing, fine arts, forensics, French, geography, geometry, government/civics, grammar, health, Hebrew scripture, history, history of the Catholic Church, honors English, honors geometry, humanities, instrumental music, jazz dance, Latin, Latin American studies, madrigals, mathematics, moral theology, music, music appreciation, musical theater, musical theater dance, painting, peace studies, personal finance, photography, physical education, physical science, physics, physiology, pre-calculus, psychology, public speaking, religion, science, sculpture, Shakespeare, social sciences, social studies, Spanish, sports medicine, statistics, studio art, studio art-AP, tap dance, technology, theater, theater design and production, theology, trigonometry, U.S. government, U.S. government and politics-AP, U.S. history, U.S. history-AP, Web site design, world history, world studies.

Graduation Requirements Art, electives, English, foreign language, mathematics, performing arts, physical education (includes health), science, senior project, social sciences, social studies (includes history), technology, theology, Christian service commitment, senior project internship.

Special Academic Programs International Baccalaureate program; Advanced Placement exam preparation; honors section; independent study; academic accommodation for the gifted and the artistically talented; remedial math.

College Admission Counseling 120 students graduated in 2016; all went to college, including James Madison University; Salisbury University; Syracuse University; The Catholic University of America; University of Maryland, College Park; University of South Carolina. Mean SAT critical reading: 563, mean SAT math: 543, mean SAT writing: 572, mean combined SAT: 1678, mean composite ACT: 25. 44% scored over 600 on SAT critical reading, 37% scored over 600 on SAT math, 46%

scored over 600 on SAT writing, 43% scored over 1800 on combined SAT, 50% scored over 26 on composite ACT.

Student Life Upper grades have uniform requirement, student council, honor system. Discipline rests equally with students and faculty. Attendance at religious services is required.

Summer Programs Enrichment, advancement, sports, art/fine arts, computer instruction programs offered; session focuses on enrichment, performing arts and athletic skill-building; held on campus; accepts boys and girls; open to students from other schools. 200 students usually enrolled. 2017 schedule: June 19 to June 30. Application deadline: May 31.

Tuition and Aid Day student tuition: $22,425. Tuition installment plan (FACTS Tuition Payment Plan). Tuition reduction for siblings, merit scholarship grants, need-based scholarship grants available. In 2016–17, 31% of upper-school students received aid.

Admissions Traditional secondary-level entrance grade is 9. High School Placement Test required. Deadline for receipt of application materials: December 12. Application fee required: $60.

Athletics Interscholastic: basketball, cheering, crew, cross-country running, dance team, diving, equestrian sports, field hockey, ice hockey, lacrosse, soccer, softball, swimming and diving, tennis, track and field, volleyball; intramural: archery, basketball, soccer; coed interscholastic: golf. 2 PE instructors, 35 coaches, 1 athletic trainer.

Computers Computers are regularly used in art, foreign language, mathematics, science, social sciences classes. Computer network features include on-campus library services, online commercial services, Internet access, wireless campus network, Internet filtering or blocking technology, 1:1 iPad program. Campus intranet, student e-mail accounts, and computer access in designated common areas are available to students. Students grades are available online. The school has a published electronic and media policy.

Contact Mrs. Louise Hendon, Director of Admissions. 301-929-6442. Fax: 301-929-6440. E-mail: admissions@academyoftheholycross.org. Website: www.ahctartans.org

ACADEMY OF THE HOLY FAMILY

54 West Main Street
PO Box 691
Baltic, Connecticut 06330-0691

Head of School: Mother Mary David, SCMC

General Information Girls' boarding and day college-preparatory school, affiliated with Roman Catholic Church. Grades 9–12. Founded: 1874. Setting: small town. Nearest major city is New London. Students are housed in single-sex dormitories. 15-acre campus. 3 buildings on campus. Approved or accredited by Association of Independent Schools in New England, Connecticut Association of Independent Schools, National Catholic Education Association, New England Association of Schools and Colleges, and Connecticut Department of Education. Endowment: $300,000. Total enrollment: 29. Upper school average class size: 7. Upper school faculty-student ratio: 1:6. There are 180 required school days per year for Upper School students. Upper School students typically attend 5 days per week. The average school day consists of 6 hours.

Upper School Student Profile Grade 9: 6 students (6 girls); Grade 10: 6 students (6 girls); Grade 11: 13 students (13 girls); Grade 12: 8 students (8 girls). 70% of students are boarding students. 59% are state residents. 9 states are represented in upper school student body. 7% are international students. International students from China, Comoros, Mexico, Nigeria, United Kingdom, and United Republic of Tanzania. 70% of students are Roman Catholic.

Faculty School total: 13. In upper school: 2 men, 11 women; 8 have advanced degrees; 8 reside on campus.

Subjects Offered Algebra, American government, American history, American literature, art, biology, calculus, calculus-AP, Catholic belief and practice, chemistry, church history, civics, community service, computer applications, computer programming, creative writing, economics, English, English literature, English-AP, ESL, family studies, fine arts, foods, geometry, health, honors algebra, honors English, honors geometry, honors U.S. history, honors world history, life skills, mathematics, music, painting, parenting, personal finance, physical education, physical science, practical arts, pre-calculus, religion, SAT preparation, science, scripture, sculpture, senior project, Spanish, theater design and production, U.S. government, vocal jazz, Web site design, world history, world literature.

Graduation Requirements Arts and fine arts (art, music, dance, drama), computer science, English, foreign language, life skills, mathematics, physical education (includes health), religion (includes Bible studies and theology), science, social studies (includes history), vocational arts. Community service is required.

Special Academic Programs Honors section; independent study; study at local college for college credit; academic accommodation for the gifted and the musically talented; remedial reading and/or remedial writing; remedial math; ESL (3 students enrolled).

College Admission Counseling 4 students graduated in 2016; all went to college, including Eastern Connecticut State University; Rhode Island College; Seton Hall University; St. Bonaventure University; University of Connecticut. Other: 1 entered military service. Median SAT critical reading: 580, median SAT math: 610, median

SAT writing: 510, median combined SAT: 1550. 24% scored over 600 on SAT critical reading, 33% scored over 600 on SAT math, 22% scored over 600 on SAT writing, 20% scored over 1800 on combined SAT.

Student Life Upper grades have uniform requirement, student council, honor system. Discipline rests primarily with faculty. Attendance at religious services is required.

Summer Programs Remediation programs offered; session focuses on remediation/make-up courses; held on campus; accepts boys and girls; open to students from other schools. 20 students usually enrolled. 2017 schedule: July 5 to August 5. Application deadline: June 25.

Tuition and Aid Day student tuition: $9000; 5-day tuition and room/board: $28,000; 7-day tuition and room/board: $28,000. Guaranteed tuition plan. Tuition installment plan (FACTS Tuition Payment Plan, individually arranged payment plans, Tuition Management Services). Tuition reduction for siblings, need-based scholarship grants available. In 2016–17, 30% of upper-school students received aid. Total amount of financial aid awarded in 2016–17: $86,600.

Admissions Traditional secondary-level entrance grade is 9. For fall 2016, 19 students applied for upper-level admission, 17 were accepted, 10 enrolled. Admissions testing, STS or STS, Diocese Test required. Deadline for receipt of application materials: none. Application fee required: $50. Interview recommended.

Athletics Interscholastic: basketball, physical fitness, soccer, softball; intramural: fitness. 1 PE instructor, 3 coaches.

Computers Computers are regularly used in business applications, foreign language, French, graphic arts, independent study, journalism, media production, newspaper, programming, SAT preparation, yearbook classes. Computer network features include on-campus library services, Internet access, wireless campus network, Internet filtering or blocking technology, laptops. Student e-mail accounts and computer access in designated common areas are available to students. Students grades are available online. The school has a published electronic and media policy.

Contact Sr. Kateri Mary Ludick, SCMC, Admissions. 860-822-6279. Fax: 860-822-1318. E-mail: admissions@ahfbaltic.org. Website: www.ahfbaltic.org

ACADEMY OF THE NEW CHURCH BOYS' SCHOOL

2815 Benade Circle
Box 707
Bryn Athyn, Pennsylvania 19009

Head of School: Mr. Jeremy T. Irwin

General Information Boys' boarding and day college-preparatory school, affiliated with Church of the New Jerusalem. Grades 9–12. Founded: 1887. Setting: suburban. Nearest major city is Philadelphia. Students are housed in coed dormitories and single-sex dormitories. 200-acre campus. 8 buildings on campus. Approved or accredited by Middle States Association of Colleges and Schools, Pennsylvania Association of Independent Schools, and Pennsylvania Department of Education. Member of National Association of Independent Schools. Endowment: $200 million. Total enrollment: 121. Upper school average class size: 15. Upper school faculty-student ratio: 1:8. There are 180 required school days per year for Upper School students. Upper School students typically attend 5 days per week. The average school day consists of 7 hours and 15 minutes.

Upper School Student Profile Grade 9: 31 students (31 boys); Grade 10: 32 students (32 boys); Grade 11: 30 students (30 boys); Grade 12: 32 students (32 boys). 38% of students are boarding students. 75% are state residents. 17 states are represented in upper school student body. 7% are international students. International students from Cape Verde, China, and United States; 4 other countries represented in student body. 85% of students are Church of the New Jerusalem.

Faculty School total: 40. In upper school: 18 men, 18 women; 33 have advanced degrees; 10 reside on campus.

Subjects Offered Advanced chemistry, Advanced Placement courses, African-American literature, algebra, American history, American history-AP, American literature, American literature-AP, anatomy, anatomy and physiology, ancient world history, art, art history, Bible studies, biology, British literature, calculus, calculus-AP, ceramics, chemistry, civics, computer programming, computer science, creative writing, dance, drama, ecology, English, English literature, English literature-AP, environmental science, European history, expository writing, fine arts, French, geometry, German, government/civics, grammar, health, history, honors U.S. history, industrial arts, journalism, Latin, mathematics, music, music theater, musical theater, philosophy, photography, physical education, physical science, physics, physiology, portfolio art, pre-calculus, printmaking, probability and statistics, religion, religious education, religious studies, science, sculpture, senior project, social sciences, social studies, sociology, Spanish, speech, statistics, studio art, theater, theater arts, theater design and production, theater production, theology, trigonometry, U.S. history-AP, vocal ensemble, vocal music, women in literature, world history, world literature.

Graduation Requirements Arts and fine arts (art, music, dance, drama), English, foreign language, mathematics, physical education (includes health), religion (includes Bible studies and theology), science, social sciences, social studies (includes history).

Special Academic Programs Advanced Placement exam preparation; honors section; independent study; study at local college for college credit; academic accommodation for the gifted, the musically talented, and the artistically talented; remedial reading and/or remedial writing; remedial math; programs in English, mathematics, general development for dyslexic students; ESL (10 students enrolled).

College Admission Counseling 30 students graduated in 2016; all went to college, including Arcadia University; Bryn Athyn College of the New Church; Gettysburg College; Millersville University of Pennsylvania; Penn State University Park; West Chester University of Pennsylvania. Median SAT critical reading: 540, median SAT math: 560, median SAT writing: 530, median combined SAT: 1630. 28% scored over 600 on SAT critical reading, 33% scored over 600 on SAT math, 31% scored over 600 on SAT writing, 31% scored over 1800 on combined SAT.

Student Life Upper grades have specified standards of dress, student council. Discipline rests primarily with faculty. Attendance at religious services is required.

Tuition and Aid Day student tuition: $15,400; 7-day tuition and room/board: $22,850. Tuition installment plan (monthly payment plans, individually arranged payment plans, term payment plan). Need-based scholarship grants available. In 2016–17, 60% of upper-school students received aid. Total amount of financial aid awarded in 2016–17: $750,000.

Admissions Traditional secondary-level entrance grade is 9. For fall 2016, 55 students applied for upper-level admission, 38 were accepted, 32 enrolled. Iowa Subtests, PSAT or SAT required. Deadline for receipt of application materials: none. Application fee required: $50. Interview recommended.

Athletics Interscholastic: baseball, basketball, football, ice hockey, lacrosse, wrestling. 2 PE instructors, 6 coaches, 1 athletic trainer.

Computers Computers are regularly used in English, foreign language, history, mathematics, science classes. Computer network features include on-campus library services, online commercial services, Internet access, wireless campus network, Internet filtering or blocking technology. Campus intranet, student e-mail accounts, and computer access in designated common areas are available to students. Students grades are available online. The school has a published electronic and media policy.

Contact Denise DiFiglia, Director of Admissions. 267-502-4855. Website: www.ancss.org

ACADEMY OF THE NEW CHURCH GIRLS' SCHOOL

2815 Benade Circle
Box 707
Bryn Athyn, Pennsylvania 19009

Head of School: Kira R. Schadegg

General Information Girls' boarding and day college-preparatory and general academic school, affiliated with Church of the New Jerusalem. Grades 9–12. Founded: 1884. Setting: suburban. Nearest major city is Philadelphia. Students are housed in single-sex dormitories. 200-acre campus. 8 buildings on campus. Approved or accredited by Middle States Association of Colleges and Schools, Pennsylvania Association of Independent Schools, and Pennsylvania Department of Education. Member of National Association of Independent Schools. Endowment: $200 million. Total enrollment: 96. Upper school average class size: 15. Upper school faculty-student ratio: 1:8. There are 180 required school days per year for Upper School students. Upper School students typically attend 5 days per week. The average school day consists of 7 hours and 15 minutes.

Upper School Student Profile Grade 9: 21 students (21 girls); Grade 10: 18 students (18 girls); Grade 11: 32 students (32 girls); Grade 12: 24 students (24 girls). 27% of students are boarding students. 75% are state residents. 10 states are represented in upper school student body. 10% are international students. International students from Belize, China, and Republic of Korea. 80% of students are Church of the New Jerusalem.

Faculty School total: 39. In upper school: 18 men, 18 women; 34 have advanced degrees; 10 reside on campus.

Graduation Requirements Arts and fine arts (art, music, dance, drama), English, foreign language, mathematics, physical education (includes health), religion (includes Bible studies and theology), science, social sciences, social studies (includes history).

Special Academic Programs 5 Advanced Placement exams for which test preparation is offered; honors section; independent study; study at local college for college credit; academic accommodation for the gifted, the musically talented, and the artistically talented; remedial reading and/or remedial writing; remedial math; special instructional classes for students with Attention Deficit Disorder and learning-disabled children; ESL (12 students enrolled).

College Admission Counseling 26 students graduated in 2016; all went to college, including Bloomsburg University of Pennsylvania; Bryn Athyn College of the New Church; Connecticut College; Salisbury University. Median SAT critical reading: 537, median SAT math: 560, median SAT writing: 530, median combined SAT: 1630. 28% scored over 600 on SAT critical reading, 33% scored over 600 on SAT math, 31% scored over 600 on SAT writing, 31% scored over 1800 on combined SAT.

Student Life Upper grades have uniform requirement, student council. Discipline rests primarily with faculty. Attendance at religious services is required.

Summer Programs Sports programs offered; held on campus; accepts boys and girls; open to students from other schools. 130 students usually enrolled. 2017 schedule: July 11 to August 1. Application deadline: June 1.

Tuition and Aid Day student tuition: $15,400; 7-day tuition and room/board: $22,850. Tuition installment plan (monthly payment plans, individually arranged payment plans, term payment plan). Need-based scholarship grants available. In 2016–17, 60% of upper-school students received aid. Total amount of financial aid awarded in 2016–17: $1,200,000.

Admissions Traditional secondary-level entrance grade is 9. For fall 2016, 90 students applied for upper-level admission, 68 were accepted, 54 enrolled. Iowa Subtests, PSAT or SAT required. Deadline for receipt of application materials: none. Application fee required: $50. Interview required.

Athletics Interscholastic: baseball, basketball, dance team, field hockey, ice hockey, lacrosse, softball, tennis, volleyball; intramural: aerobics/dance. 1 PE instructor, 6 coaches, 1 athletic trainer.

Computers Computers are regularly used in English, foreign language, history, Latin, mathematics, science classes. Computer network features include on-campus library services, online commercial services, Internet access, wireless campus network, Internet filtering or blocking technology. Campus intranet and student e-mail accounts are available to students. Students grades are available online. The school has a published electronic and media policy.

Contact Denise DiFiglia, Director of Admissions. 267-502-4855. Fax: 267-502-2617. E-mail: denise.difiglia@ancss.org. Website: www.ancss.org

ACADEMY OF THE SACRED HEART

4521 St. Charles Avenue
New Orleans, Louisiana 70115-4831

Head of School: Sr. Melanie A. Guste, RSCJ

General Information Girls' day college-preparatory, arts, and religious studies school, affiliated with Roman Catholic Church. Grades PK–12. Founded: 1867. Setting: urban. 7-acre campus. 3 buildings on campus. Approved or accredited by Independent Schools Association of the Southwest, National Catholic Education Association, Network of Sacred Heart Schools, Office for Standards in Education (OFSTED), Southern Association of Colleges and Schools, and Louisiana Department of Education. Member of National Association of Independent Schools. Endowment: $8.8 million. Total enrollment: 742. Upper school average class size: 16. Upper school faculty-student ratio: 1:16. There are 178 required school days per year for Upper School students. Upper School students typically attend 5 days per week. The average school day consists of 6 hours and 30 minutes.

Upper School Student Profile Grade 9: 40 students (40 girls); Grade 10: 48 students (48 girls); Grade 11: 65 students (65 girls); Grade 12: 56 students (56 girls). 93% of students are Roman Catholic.

Faculty School total: 123. In upper school: 6 men, 27 women; 18 have advanced degrees.

Subjects Offered Advanced chemistry, algebra, American government, American history, American history-AP, American literature, American literature-AP, anatomy and physiology, art, astronomy, athletics, baseball, basketball, biology, biology-AP, British literature, British literature-AP, broadcasting, calculus, calculus AP, campus ministry, Catholic belief and practice, ceramics, cheerleading, chemistry, chemistry-AP, clayworking, college admission preparation, college awareness, college counseling, college planning, computer applications, computer education, computer processing, computer resources, computer science, computer skills, computer studies, creative writing, drama, drawing, electives, English, English literature, English literature-AP, English-AP, entrepreneurship, fine arts, foreign language, French, French-AP, geometry, government, government-AP, guidance, handbells, history of the Catholic Church, honors algebra, honors English, honors geometry, honors U.S. history, honors world history, painting, peer counseling, physics, physics-AP, physiology, pre-calculus, religion, robotics, social justice, Spanish, Spanish-AP, statistics, statistics-AP, television, U.S. government, U.S. government and politics, U.S. government and politics-AP, U.S. history, U.S. history-AP, U.S. literature, video communication, Web site design, world history, world history-AP, world religions.

Graduation Requirements 1 1/2 elective credits, Advanced Placement courses, algebra, American government, American history, American literature, arts, arts and fine arts (art, music, dance, drama), athletics, Basic programming, biology, British literature, calculus, campus ministry, career/college preparation, ceramics, chemistry, church history, civics, computer applications, computer literacy, computers, drawing, electives, English, foreign language, French, geometry, government/civics, guidance, health and wellness, history of the Catholic Church, moral theology, painting, peer counseling, physical education (includes health), physics, pre-calculus, religion (includes Bible studies and theology), science, scripture, senior project, social justice, social studies (includes history), Spanish, statistics, U.S. government, U.S. government and politics, U.S. history, United States government-AP, world geography, world history, world literature, world religions, senior project, 50 hours of required community service.

Special Academic Programs Advanced Placement exam preparation; honors section; study at local college for college credit; domestic exchange program (with Network of Sacred Heart Schools, Network of Sacred Heart Schools).

College Admission Counseling 47 students graduated in 2016; all went to college, including Louisiana State University and Agricultural & Mechanical College; The University of Alabama; Tulane University; University of Georgia; University of Mississippi; Wake Forest University.

Student Life Upper grades have uniform requirement, student council, honor system. Discipline rests equally with students and faculty. Attendance at religious services is required.

Summer Programs Enrichment, sports, art/fine arts programs offered; session focuses on arts, creative writing, robotics, strength and conditioning; held both on and off campus; accepts girls; not open to students from other schools. 18 students usually enrolled. 2017 schedule: June to August. Application deadline: May.

Tuition and Aid Day student tuition: $17,500. Tuition installment plan (The Tuition Plan, Insured Tuition Payment Plan, individually arranged payment plans, bank loan). Merit scholarship grants, need-based scholarship grants available. In 2016–17, 28% of upper-school students received aid; total upper-school merit-scholarship money awarded: $35,600. Total amount of financial aid awarded in 2016–17: $342,850.

Admissions Traditional secondary-level entrance grade is 9. For fall 2016, 21 students applied for upper-level admission, 16 were accepted, 4 enrolled. Achievement tests, admissions testing, ERB, OLSAT/Stanford or PSAT or SAT for applicants to grade 11 and 12 required. Deadline for receipt of application materials: none. Application fee required: $50. Interview required.

Athletics Interscholastic: aerobics, ballet, baseball, basketball, cheering, cross-country running, fitness, golf, indoor track & field, physical fitness, soccer, softball, strength & conditioning, swimming and diving, tennis, track and field, volleyball; intramural: aerobics, cooperative games, fitness, jogging, jump rope, kickball, modern dance, outdoor activities, outdoor recreation, physical fitness, running, volleyball, walking, yoga. 5 PE instructors, 14 coaches, 1 athletic trainer.

Computers Computers are regularly used in all classes. Computer network features include on-campus library services, online commercial services, Internet access, wireless campus network, Internet filtering or blocking technology. Campus intranet, student e-mail accounts, and computer access in designated common areas are available to students. Students grades are available online. The school has a published electronic and media policy.

Contact Ms. Christy Sevante, Director of Admission. 504-269-1214. Fax: 504-896-7880. E-mail: csevante@ashrosary.org. Website: www.ashrosary.org

ACADEMY OF THE SACRED HEART

1250 Kensington Road
Bloomfield Hills, Michigan 48304-3029

Head of School: Bridget Bearss, RSCJ

General Information Coeducational day college-preparatory, experiential learning, and community service school, affiliated with Roman Catholic Church. Boys grades N–8, girls grades N–12. Founded: 1851. Setting: suburban. Nearest major city is Detroit. 28-acre campus. 1 building on campus. Approved or accredited by Independent Schools Association of the Central States, Network of Sacred Heart Schools, and Michigan Department of Education. Endowment: $3.8 million. Total enrollment: 478. Upper school average class size: 12. Upper school faculty-student ratio: 1:7. There are 180 required school days per year for Upper School students. Upper School students typically attend 5 days per week. The average school day consists of 7 hours.

Upper School Student Profile Grade 9: 25 students (25 girls); Grade 10: 37 students (37 girls); Grade 11: 41 students (41 girls); Grade 12: 28 students (28 girls). 75% of students are Roman Catholic.

Faculty School total: 66. In upper school: 6 men, 16 women; 11 have advanced degrees.

Subjects Offered 20th century history, Advanced Placement courses, algebra, American literature, art, art history, biology, calculus, calculus-AP, chemistry, child development, choir, clayworking, communication arts, community service, computer applications, computer graphics, concert band, concert choir, crafts, creative writing, earth science, economics, English literature, English literature-AP, English-AP, environmental science, European history, European history-AP, forensics, French, genetics, geometry, global studies, government/civics, health, health and wellness, honors algebra, honors geometry, humanities, interior design, jewelry making, Latin, literature, mathematics, photography, physical education, physical science, physics, pre-calculus, psychology, publications, robotics, social justice, social studies, sociology, Spanish, theater, theology, U.S. history, U.S. history-AP, video, Web site design, women's studies, world history, world literature, writing.

Graduation Requirements Arts and fine arts (art, music, dance, drama), computer applications, foreign language, government, health and wellness, literature, mathematics, physical education (includes health), science, social studies (includes history), theology, U.S. government, U.S. history, world history, world literature, Project Term, First Year Experience (arts lab). Community service is required.

Special Academic Programs 5 Advanced Placement exams for which test preparation is offered; honors section; independent study; term-away projects; domestic exchange program (with Network of Sacred Heart Schools); academic accommodation for the gifted, the musically talented, and the artistically talented.

College Admission Counseling 34 students graduated in 2016; all went to college, including Columbia College Chicago; Grand Valley State University; Loyola University Chicago; Michigan State University; Oakland University; University of Michigan. Mean composite ACT: 25.

Student Life Upper grades have uniform requirement, student council, honor system. Discipline rests primarily with faculty. Attendance at religious services is required.

Tuition and Aid Day student tuition: $23,915. Tuition installment plan (FACTS Tuition Payment Plan). Tuition reduction for siblings, merit scholarship grants, need-based scholarship grants available. In 2016–17, 40% of upper-school students received

aid; total upper-school merit-scholarship money awarded: $7000. Total amount of financial aid awarded in 2016–17: $626,915.

Admissions Traditional secondary-level entrance grade is 9. For fall 2016, 29 students applied for upper-level admission, 22 were accepted, 14 enrolled. Scholastic Testing Service High School Placement Test or Stanford Achievement Test required. Deadline for receipt of application materials: none. Application fee required: $50. On-campus interview required.

Athletics Interscholastic: basketball, bowling, dance team, field hockey, figure skating, golf, gymnastics, lacrosse, skiing (downhill), tennis, volleyball. 1 PE instructor, 16 coaches, 1 athletic trainer.

Computers Computers are regularly used in all academic classes. Computer network features include on-campus library services, online commercial services, Internet access, wireless campus network, Internet filtering or blocking technology, tablet PC program with wireless network and print services, classroom multimedia services, computer in each classroom. Campus intranet, student e-mail accounts, and computer access in designated common areas are available to students. Students grades are available online. The school has a published electronic and media policy.

Contact Kris Sanders, Director of Admissions. 248-646-8900 Ext. 129. Fax: 248-646-4143. E-mail: ksanders@ashmi.org. Website: www.ashmi.org

ACADÉMIE STE CÉCILE INTERNATIONAL SCHOOL

925 Cousineau Road
Windsor, Ontario N9G 1V8, Canada

Head of School: Mr. Stephan Pelland

General Information Coeducational boarding and day college-preparatory school, affiliated with Roman Catholic Church. Boarding grades 6–12, day grades JK–12. Founded: 1993. Setting: suburban. Nearest major city is Toronto, Canada. Students are housed in single-sex dormitories. 30-acre campus. 5 buildings on campus. Approved or accredited by International Baccalaureate Organization, Ontario Ministry of Education, The Association of Boarding Schools, and Ontario Department of Education. Languages of instruction: English and French. Total enrollment: 296. Upper school average class size: 15. Upper school faculty-student ratio: 1:15. There are 180 required school days per year for Upper School students. Upper School students typically attend 5 days per week. The average school day consists of 6 hours and 15 minutes.

Upper School Student Profile Grade 9: 18 students (9 boys, 9 girls); Grade 10: 32 students (13 boys, 19 girls); Grade 11: 34 students (13 boys, 21 girls); Grade 12: 53 students (34 boys, 19 girls). 45% of students are boarding students. 2% are province residents. 2 provinces are represented in upper school student body. 45% are international students. International students from Canada, China, Hong Kong, Mexico, Taiwan, and United States; 2 other countries represented in student body. 40% of students are Roman Catholic.

Faculty School total: 50. In upper school: 13 men, 11 women; 10 have advanced degrees; 4 reside on campus.

Subjects Offered Accounting, advanced chemistry, advanced computer applications, advanced math, algebra, art, art education, art history, audio visual/media, ballet, basketball, biology, business technology, calculus, campus ministry, career education, careers, Catholic belief and practice, chemistry, choir, choral music, civics, classical music, computer information systems, computer programming, computer science, concert band, concert bell choir, concert choir, creative dance, creative drama, creative thinking, creative writing, critical thinking, critical writing, dance, dance performance, decision making skills, desktop publishing, desktop publishing, ESL, discrete mathematics, drama performance, drama workshop, dramatic arts, drawing, drawing and design, driver education, earth science, economics, English, English literature, environmental studies, ethics, expository writing, family living, French, French studies, geography, geometry, German, golf, handbells, health and wellness, health education, history, history of dance, history of music, history of religion, history of the Catholic Church, honors algebra, honors English, honors geometry, honors world history, instrumental music, International Baccalaureate courses, Internet, Internet research, intro to computers, Italian, jazz band, jazz dance, journalism, keyboarding, Latin, leadership, library skills, Life of Christ, literature, literature and composition-AP, mathematics, media studies, music, music appreciation, music composition, music history, music performance, music theory, organ, painting, philosophy, photography, physical education, physics, piano, poetry, prayer/spirituality, pre-algebra, pre-calculus, probability and statistics, public speaking, reading, reading/study skills, religion, research skills, SAT preparation, science, sculpture, Shakespeare, social studies, softball, Spanish, stage and body movement, stained glass, strings, student government, swimming, tennis, TOEFL preparation, track and field, values and decisions, visual arts, vocal ensemble, voice, volleyball, wind ensemble, wind instruments, world religions, writing, yearbook.

Graduation Requirements Ontario Ministry of Education requirements.

Special Academic Programs International Baccalaureate program; Advanced Placement exam preparation; honors section; accelerated programs; academic accommodation for the gifted, the musically talented, and the artistically talented; remedial reading and/or remedial writing; remedial math; ESL (30 students enrolled).

College Admission Counseling 52 students graduated in 2016; 51 went to college, including McGill University; Ryerson University; The University of Western Ontario; University of Toronto; University of Victoria; University of Windsor. Other: 1 went to work, 51 entered a postgraduate year. Mean SAT critical reading: 593, mean SAT math: 724, mean SAT writing: 615. 67% scored over 600 on SAT critical reading, 83% scored over 600 on SAT math, 67% scored over 600 on SAT writing.

Student Life Upper grades have uniform requirement, student council, honor system. Discipline rests primarily with faculty.

Summer Programs Remediation, enrichment, advancement, ESL, art/fine arts programs offered; session focuses on ESL; held on campus; accepts boys and girls; open to students from other schools. 25 students usually enrolled. 2017 schedule: July 10 to August 11. Application deadline: May 1.

Tuition and Aid Day student tuition: CAN$14,500; 7-day tuition and room/board: CAN$50,000. Tuition installment plan (Insured Tuition Payment Plan). Tuition reduction for siblings, merit scholarship grants available. Total upper-school merit-scholarship money awarded for 2016–17: CAN$4500.

Admissions Traditional secondary-level entrance grade is 9. For fall 2016, 38 students applied for upper-level admission, 38 were accepted, 34 enrolled. CAT, International English Language Test or TOEFL required. Deadline for receipt of application materials: none. Application fee required: CAN$300. Interview required.

Athletics Interscholastic: aquatics (boys, girls), badminton (b,g), basketball (b,g), cross-country running (b,g), equestrian sports (b,g), golf (b,g), horseback riding (b,g), independent competitive sports (b,g), modern dance (b,g), physical fitness (b,g), soccer (b,g), softball (b,g), swimming and diving (b,g), tennis (b,g), volleyball (b,g); intramural: aquatics (b,g), badminton (b,g), ballet (g), basketball (b,g), bowling (b,g), cross-country running (b,g), dance (b,g), dressage (b,g), equestrian sports (b,g), golf (b,g), horseback riding (b,g), paddle tennis (b,g), soccer (b,g), softball (b,g), swimming and diving (b,g), table tennis (b,g), tennis (b,g), volleyball (b,g); coed interscholastic: aquatics, badminton, basketball, cross-country running, dressage, equestrian sports, fitness, golf, horseback riding, indoor track & field, modern dance, physical fitness, soccer, softball, swimming and diving, tennis, volleyball; coed intramural: aquatics, badminton, basketball, bowling, cross-country running, dance, dressage, equestrian sports, floor hockey, golf, horseback riding, modern dance, soccer, softball, swimming and diving, tennis, volleyball. 2 PE instructors, 8 coaches.

Computers Computers are regularly used in accounting, business, desktop publishing, ESL, information technology, mathematics classes. Computer network features include Internet access, wireless campus network. Computer access in designated common areas is available to students. The school has a published electronic and media policy.

Contact Ms. Gwen A. Gatt, Admissions Clerk. 519-969-1291. Fax: 519-969-7953 Ext. 220. E-mail: admissions@stececile.ca. Website: www.stececile.ca

ADELPHI ACADEMY

8515 Ridge Boulevard
Bay Ridge, Brooklyn, New York 11209

Head of School: Ms. Iphigenia Romanos

General Information Coeducational day college-preparatory, arts, and writing school. Grades PK–12. Founded: 1863. Setting: urban. Nearest major city is Brooklyn. 1-acre campus. 3 buildings on campus. Approved or accredited by New York State Board of Regents and New York Department of Education. Candidate for accreditation by Middle States Association of Colleges and Schools. Member of National Association of Independent Schools. Endowment: $2.6 million. Total enrollment: 110. Upper school average class size: 14. Upper school faculty-student ratio: 1:8. There are 160 required school days per year for Upper School students. Upper School students typically attend 5 days per week. The average school day consists of 7 hours and 45 minutes.

Upper School Student Profile Grade 9: 15 students (7 boys, 8 girls); Grade 10: 15 students (6 boys, 9 girls); Grade 11: 15 students (5 boys, 10 girls); Grade 12: 15 students (7 boys, 8 girls).

Faculty School total: 9. In upper school: 5 men, 4 women; all have advanced degrees.

Subjects Offered Acting, algebra, American history, American literature, art, art history, athletics, biology, business, calculus, chemistry, choir, chorus, college counseling, college placement, communication arts, community service, computer applications, computer education, computer math, computer science, computer skills, computer studies, computers, creative writing, dance, digital photography, drama, drama performance, drawing, driver education, earth science, English, English composition, English literature, environmental science, European history, film, fine arts, fitness, foreign language, general science, geography, geometry, government, government/civics, grammar, guidance, health, health and wellness, health education, health science, history, history of the Americas, independent study, Internet, Internet research, intro to computers, keyboarding, lab science, language arts, languages, leadership, library, library research, library skills, literature, math analysis, math applications, math methods, mathematics, modern history, music, music appreciation, newspaper, nutrition, photography, physical education, physics, public speaking, publications, publishing, SAT preparation, science, senior seminar, Spanish, speech, strategies for success, student teaching, studio art, study skills, technology, The 20th Century, theater, theater arts, trigonometry, U.S. government, U.S. literature, visual arts, voice, volleyball, Web site design, weight fitness, Western literature, word processing, world civilizations, world cultures, world history, writing, writing.

Graduation Requirements 20th century American writers, advanced biology, advanced math, African-American literature, American literature, 50 hours of community/school service, extracurricular participation.

Special Academic Programs Honors section; independent study; study at local college for college credit; academic accommodation for the gifted, the musically talented, and the artistically talented; remedial reading and/or remedial writing; remedial math; special instructional classes for students with mild learning disabilities and/or Attention Deficit Disorder issues.

College Admission Counseling 13 students graduated in 2016; 14 went to college, including Adelphi University; Bucknell University; Harvard University; St. John's University; Syracuse University. 50% scored over 600 on SAT critical reading, 50% scored over 600 on SAT math.

Student Life Upper grades have uniform requirement, student council, honor system. Discipline rests primarily with faculty.

Summer Programs Remediation, enrichment, advancement, sports, art/fine arts, rigorous outdoor training, computer instruction programs offered; session focuses on enrichment; held on campus; accepts boys and girls; open to students from other schools. 100 students usually enrolled. 2017 schedule: July 10 to August 25. Application deadline: March 1.

Tuition and Aid Day student tuition: $17,500. Tuition installment plan (individually arranged payment plans). Tuition reduction for siblings, merit scholarship grants, need-based scholarship grants, paying campus jobs available. In 2016–17, 25% of upper-school students received aid; total upper-school merit-scholarship money awarded: $33,000. Total amount of financial aid awarded in 2016–17: $125,000.

Admissions Traditional secondary-level entrance grade is 9. For fall 2016, 125 students applied for upper-level admission, 65 were accepted, 50 enrolled. Stanford Diagnostic Test required. Deadline for receipt of application materials: none. Application fee required: $100. On-campus interview required.

Athletics Interscholastic: aerobics/dance (girls), baseball (b), basketball (b,g), cheering (g), dance (g), dance squad (g), dance team (g), danceline (g), jogging (b,g), soccer (b), softball (g), volleyball (b,g); coed interscholastic: bowling, cross-country running, fitness, golf, indoor hockey, martial arts, physical fitness, self defense, tennis, weight lifting, weight training; coed intramural: bowling, cross-country running, gymnastics, juggling. 3 PE instructors, 4 coaches, 4 athletic trainers.

Computers Computers are regularly used in all classes. Computer network features include on-campus library services, online commercial services, Internet access. The school has a published electronic and media policy.

Contact Ms. Iphigenia Romanos, Director of Academy Admissions. 718-238-3308 Ext. 301. Fax: 718-238-2894. E-mail: info@adelphi.org. Website: www.adelphinyc.org

ADMIRAL FARRAGUT ACADEMY

501 Park Street North
St. Petersburg, Florida 33710

Head of School: Capt. Robert J. Fine Jr.

General Information Coeducational boarding and day college-preparatory, Naval Junior ROTC, Aviation, Sailing, Marine Science, Engineering, Scuba, and military school. Boarding grades 8–12, day grades P3–12. Founded: 1933. Setting: suburban. Students are housed in single-sex by floor dormitories. 35-acre campus. 20 buildings on campus. Approved or accredited by Florida Council of Independent Schools, Southern Association of Colleges and Schools, The Association of Boarding Schools, and Florida Department of Education. Member of National Association of Independent Schools and Secondary School Admission Test Board. Endowment: $4 million. Total enrollment: 436. Upper school average class size: 17. Upper school faculty-student ratio: 1:8. There are 189 required school days per year for Upper School students. Upper School students typically attend 5 days per week. The average school day consists of 7 hours.

Upper School Student Profile 50% of students are boarding students. 73% are state residents. 17 states are represented in upper school student body. 30% are international students. International students from China, Czech Republic, Japan, Mexico, Republic of Korea, and Russian Federation; 20 other countries represented in student body.

Faculty School total: 63. In upper school: 20 men, 14 women; 20 have advanced degrees; 20 reside on campus.

Subjects Offered ACT preparation, advanced math, algebra, American history, American literature, analytic geometry, anatomy and physiology, art, art history, aviation, band, biology, boating, British literature, business communications, calculus, calculus-AP, chemistry, Chinese, chorus, community service, computer programming, computer science, computer science-AP, creative writing, drama, driver education, earth science, economics, English, English composition, English language-AP, English literature, environmental science, ESL, ethics and responsibility, fine arts, French, geography, geometry, government/civics, grammar, health, history, journalism, keyboarding, Latin, library assistant, marching band, marine biology, mathematics, meteorology, military science, music, music history, navigation, NJROTC, oceanography, physical education, physics, pre-algebra, science, sign language, social studies, sociology, Spanish, Spanish language-AP, speech, statistics, swimming test, trigonometry, world history, world literature, yearbook.

Graduation Requirements Arts and fine arts (art, music, dance, drama), economics, English, ethics, foreign language, government, health education, mathematics, NJROTC, physical education (includes health), science, social studies (includes history), U.S. history, world history, Qualified Boat Handler (QBH) test, 80 hours of community service.

Special Academic Programs Advanced Placement exam preparation; honors section; study at local college for college credit; academic accommodation for the gifted; remedial reading and/or remedial writing; remedial math; ESL (15 students enrolled).

College Admission Counseling 63 students graduated in 2015; they went to Florida State University; Georgia Institute of Technology; Syracuse University; United States Naval Academy; University of Florida; University of South Florida. Other: 1 entered military service. Mean SAT critical reading: 488, mean SAT math: 520, mean SAT writing: 478, mean composite ACT: 20. 10% scored over 600 on SAT critical reading, 20% scored over 600 on SAT math, 3% scored over 600 on SAT writing, 15% scored over 26 on composite ACT.

Student Life Upper grades have uniform requirement, student council. Discipline rests equally with students and faculty.

Tuition and Aid Day student tuition: $8610–$21,325; 5-day tuition and room/board: $37,000–$40,000; 7-day tuition and room/board: $43,850–$46,850. Tuition installment plan (monthly payment plans). Tuition reduction for siblings, need-based scholarship grants, tuition reduction for children of faculty available. In 2015–16, 22% of upper-school students received aid. Total amount of financial aid awarded in 2015–16: $500,000.

Admissions Any standardized test required. Deadline for receipt of application materials: none. Application fee required: $100. Interview required.

Athletics Interscholastic: aquatics (boys, girls); baseball (b); basketball (b,g), cheering (g), cross-country running (b,g), diving (b,g), drill team (b,g), football (b,g), golf (b,g), riflery (b,g), soccer (b,g), softball (g), swimming and diving (b,g), tennis (b,g), track and field (b,g), volleyball (g), wrestling (b,g); intramural: kayaking (b,g), riflery (b,g), running (b,g), weight training (b,g); coed interscholastic: aquatics, drill team, football, golf, JROTC drill, marksmanship, riflery, sailing; coed intramural: basketball, bicycling, billiards, canoeing/kayaking, fishing, fitness, martial arts, outdoor recreation, outdoors, pillo polo, scuba diving, strength & conditioning, table tennis, volleyball. 1 PE instructor, 3 coaches, 1 athletic trainer.

Computers Computers are regularly used in aerospace science, aviation, computer applications, English, foreign language, history, keyboarding, NJROTC, programming, science, writing, yearbook classes. Computer network features include on-campus library services, online commercial services, Internet access, wireless campus network, Internet filtering or blocking technology. Students grades are available online. The school has a published electronic and media policy.

Contact Cosmo Kunzelmann, Admissions Office Manager. 727-384-5500 Ext. 220. Fax: 727-347-5160. E-mail: admissions@farragut.org. Website: www.farragut.org

ADVANCED ACADEMY OF GEORGIA

Honors House
University of West Georgia
Carrollton, Georgia 30118

Head of School: Ms. Adriana Stanley

General Information Coeducational boarding college-preparatory and mathematics, science, and humanities school. Grades 10–12. Distance learning grades 10–12. Founded: 1995. Setting: small town. Nearest major city is Atlanta. 394-acre campus. 89 buildings on campus. Approved or accredited by Georgia Department of Education. Total enrollment: 83. Upper school average class size: 14. Upper school faculty-student ratio: 1:14.

Upper School Student Profile Grade 11: 38 students (18 boys, 20 girls); Grade 12: 42 students (22 boys, 20 girls).

Faculty School total: 270. In upper school: 149 men, 121 women; all have advanced degrees.

Subjects Offered Accounting, acting, advanced chemistry, advanced math, advanced studio art-AP, African American studies, algebra, American foreign policy, American government, American history, American literature, American sign language, analysis and differential calculus, analytic geometry, anatomy, ancient world history, ancient/medieval philosophy, anthropology, art and culture, art history, astronomy, athletics, band, biochemistry, biology, business applications, business communications, business education, business skills, business studies, calculus, chemistry, choir, civil rights, civil war history, classical civilization, communications, comparative politics, computer applications, computer art, computer graphics, computer processing, computer programming, computer science, consumer economics, critical writing, data analysis, debate, desktop publishing, drama, drawing, earth science, East European studies, ecology, economics, education, English, English composition, English literature, environmental science, ethics, European history, film studies, forensics, French, geography, geology, geometry, German, German literature, global studies, government/civics, graphic design, Holocaust studies, honors algebra, honors English, honors geometry, honors U.S. history, honors world history, Japanese, language arts, Latin, law studies, linear algebra, marine biology, marketing, media communications, microbiology, microeconomics, model United Nations, modern world history, money management, music, Native American history, North American literature, organic chemistry, performing arts, personal finance, philosophy, photography, physical education, physics, political science, post-calculus, pre-calculus, probability and statistics, psychology, public policy, public speaking, religion and culture, religious studies, science and technology, Shakespeare, social studies, sociology, Spanish, speech and debate, statistics, studio art, telecommunications, U.S. government, U.S. government and politics, U.S. history, U.S. literature, U.S. Presidents, visual and performing arts, Western civilization, women's studies, world history, writing.

Graduation Requirements Students must complete Georgia high school requirements which are satisfied through equivalent college courses offered by the university.

Special Academic Programs Honors section; accelerated programs; independent study; study at local college for college credit; study abroad; academic accommodation for the gifted, the musically talented, and the artistically talented.

College Admission Counseling 32 students graduated in 2016; all went to college, including Agnes Scott College; Brown University; Georgia Institute of Technology; Georgia State University; Savannah College of Art and Design; University of Georgia. Mean SAT critical reading: 626, mean SAT math: 615, mean combined SAT: 1240, mean composite ACT: 27. 79% scored over 600 on SAT critical reading, 75% scored over 600 on SAT math.

Student Life Upper grades have student council, honor system. Discipline rests equally with students and faculty.

Summer Programs Enrichment, advancement, art/fine arts programs offered; session focuses on arts and humanities, mathematics and science; held on campus; accepts boys and girls; open to students from other schools. 40 students usually enrolled. 2017 schedule: June 8 to July 24. Application deadline: May 15.

Tuition and Aid Merit scholarship grants, need-based scholarship grants, paying campus jobs available. In 2016–17, 90% of upper-school students received aid; total upper-school merit-scholarship money awarded: $56,000. Total amount of financial aid awarded in 2016–17: $109,000.

Admissions Traditional secondary-level entrance grade is 11. ACT or SAT required. Deadline for receipt of application materials: June 1. Application fee required: $40.

Athletics Coed Intramural: aerobics, backpacking, basketball, bicycling, climbing, flag football, Frisbee, outdoor activities, outdoor recreation, paint ball, running, soccer, softball, tennis, ultimate Frisbee, walking.

Computers Computers are regularly used in all classes. Computer network features include on-campus library services, online commercial services, Internet access, wireless campus network, Internet filtering or blocking technology. Student e-mail accounts and computer access in designated common areas are available to students. Students grades are available online. The school has a published electronic and media policy.

Contact Kate Theobald, Academic Advisor. 678-839-5529. Fax: 678-839-2685. E-mail: kate@westga.edu. Website: www.advancedacademy.org

THE AGNES IRWIN SCHOOL

Ithan Avenue and Conestoga Road
Rosemont, Pennsylvania 19010

Head of School: Dr. Wendy L. Hill

General Information Girls' day college-preparatory school. Grades PK–12. Founded: 1869. Setting: suburban. Nearest major city is Philadelphia. 18-acre campus. 5 buildings on campus. Approved or accredited by Middle States Association of Colleges and Schools, Pennsylvania Association of Independent Schools, and Pennsylvania Department of Education. Member of National Association of Independent Schools, Secondary School Admission Test Board, and National Coalition of Girls' Schools. Endowment: $21.2 million. Total enrollment: 666. Upper school average class size: 17. Upper school faculty-student ratio: 1:6. There are 162 required school days per year for Upper School students. Upper School students typically attend 5 days per week. The average school day consists of 6 hours and 45 minutes.

Upper School Student Profile Grade 6: 42 students (42 girls); Grade 7: 60 students (60 girls); Grade 8: 56 students (56 girls); Grade 9: 68 students (68 girls); Grade 10: 75 students (75 girls); Grade 11: 75 students (75 girls); Grade 12: 65 students (65 girls).

Faculty School total: 104. In upper school: 17 men, 44 women; 37 have advanced degrees.

Subjects Offered 20th century world history, advanced studio art-AP, African-American history, algebra, American history, American history-AP, Ancient Greek, art history, Asian studies, bioethics, bioethics, DNA and culture, biology, biology-AP, calculus, calculus-AP, chemistry, chemistry-AP, choreography, computer programming, dance, drama, English, English language and composition-AP, English language-AP, English literature, English literature and composition-AP, English-AP, environmental science-AP, European history, European history-AP, film history, French, French-AP, geometry, Greek, health, history, honors algebra, honors English, honors geometry, honors U.S. history, honors world history, independent study, international relations, Latin, mathematics-AP, media arts, Middle East, Middle Eastern history, music theory, photography, physical education, physics, physics-AP, pre-calculus, public speaking, robotics, Spanish, Spanish-AP, statistics, studio art, theater arts, trigonometry.

Graduation Requirements Arts and fine arts (art, music, dance, drama), English, foreign language, history, mathematics, media literacy, physical education (includes health), science, senior assembly given by each girl before graduation. Community service is required.

Special Academic Programs 12 Advanced Placement exams for which test preparation is offered; honors section; independent study; term-away projects; study abroad; academic accommodation for the gifted.

College Admission Counseling 69 students graduated in 2016; all went to college, including Brown University; Colgate University; The George Washington University; University of Pennsylvania; University of Richmond.

Student Life Upper grades have uniform requirement, student council, honor system. Discipline rests equally with students and faculty.

Summer Programs Remediation, enrichment, advancement, sports, art/fine arts, computer instruction programs offered; session focuses on arts, academics, and athletics; held on campus; accepts boys and girls; open to students from other schools. 340 students usually enrolled. 2017 schedule: June 15 to July 31. Application deadline: April 1.

Tuition and Aid Day student tuition: $36,550. Tuition installment plan (Insured Tuition Payment Plan, monthly payment plans, One-pay plan, Two-pay plan). Need-based scholarship grants available. In 2016–17, 27% of upper-school students received aid. Total amount of financial aid awarded in 2016–17: $1,771,400.

Admissions Traditional secondary-level entrance grade is 9. For fall 2016, 89 students applied for upper-level admission, 64 were accepted, 28 enrolled. ISEE, SSAT or WISC-R or WISC-III required. Deadline for receipt of application materials: December 12. Application fee required: $50. On-campus interview recommended.

Athletics Interscholastic: basketball, crew, cross-country running, diving, field hockey, golf, independent competitive sports, lacrosse, soccer, softball, squash, swimming and diving, tennis, track and field, volleyball; intramural: crew, dance, fitness, modern dance, physical fitness, physical training, strength & conditioning, weight training. 4 PE instructors, 21 coaches, 1 athletic trainer.

Computers Computers are regularly used in art, drawing and design, English, foreign language, history, mathematics, media arts, photography, science, yearbook classes. Computer network features include on-campus library services, online commercial services, Internet access, wireless campus network, online databases. Campus intranet, student e-mail accounts, and computer access in designated common areas are available to students. The school has a published electronic and media policy.

Contact Mrs. Claire Lewis, Admission Office Manager. 610-526-1667. Fax: 610-581-0495. E-mail: clewis@agnesirwin.org. Website: www.agnesirwin.org

ALABAMA CHRISTIAN ACADEMY

4700 Wares Ferry Road
Montgomery, Alabama 36109

Head of School: Dr. Misty Overman

General Information Coeducational day college-preparatory, general academic, arts, religious studies, and technology school, affiliated with Church of Christ. Grades K4–12. Founded: 1942. Setting: urban. 23-acre campus. 3 buildings on campus. Approved or accredited by Southern Association of Colleges and Schools and Alabama Department of Education. Total enrollment: 1,014. Upper school average class size: 20. Upper school faculty-student ratio: 1:20. There are 180 required school days per year for Upper School students. Upper School students typically attend 5 days per week. The average school day consists of 8 hours.

Upper School Student Profile 46% of students are members of Church of Christ.

Faculty School total: 64. In upper school: 17 men, 22 women; 10 have advanced degrees.

Graduation Requirements American government, Bible, computer applications, economics, English, geography, mathematics, physical education (includes health), science, U.S. history, world history, Bible.

Special Academic Programs Advanced Placement exam preparation; honors section; study at local college for college credit; programs in English, mathematics, general development for dyslexic students.

College Admission Counseling 89 students graduated in 2016; 86 went to college, including Auburn University; Harding University; The University of Alabama; The University of Alabama at Birmingham; Troy University; University of South Alabama. Other: 1 went to work, 2 had other specific plans.

Student Life Upper grades have uniform requirement, student council, honor system. Discipline rests primarily with faculty.

Summer Programs Sports, art/fine arts, computer instruction programs offered; session focuses on weight training; held on campus; accepts boys and girls; not open to students from other schools. 80 students usually enrolled. 2017 schedule: June 2 to August 1.

Tuition and Aid Day student tuition: $5300. Guaranteed tuition plan. Tuition installment plan (monthly payment plans). Tuition reduction for siblings, contact school for financial aid available. In 2016–17, 7% of upper-school students received aid.

Admissions Traditional secondary-level entrance grade is 9. Any standardized test required. Deadline for receipt of application materials: none. Application fee required: $210. On-campus interview recommended.

Athletics Interscholastic: baseball (boys), basketball (b,g), cheering (g), cross-country running (b,g), fishing (b,g), football (b), golf (b,g), physical training (b,g), running (b,g), soccer (b,g), softball (g), strength & conditioning (b,g), track and field (b,g), volleyball (g), weight training (b,g); coed interscholastic: jump rope, track and field. 1 athletic trainer.

Computers Computers are regularly used in all academic classes. Computer network features include on-campus library services, Internet access, wireless campus network, Internet filtering or blocking technology. Student e-mail accounts are available to students. Students grades are available online. The school has a published electronic and media policy.

Contact Mrs. Harriett Parker, Admissions. 334-277-1985 Ext. 227. Fax: 334-279-0604. E-mail: hparker@alabamachristian.org. Website: www.alabamachristian.com

ALBUQUERQUE ACADEMY

6400 Wyoming Boulevard NE
Albuquerque, New Mexico 87109

Head of School: Andrew Watson

General Information Coeducational day college-preparatory, experiential education, and global languages school. Grades 6–12. Founded: 1955. Setting: suburban. 312-acre campus. 9 buildings on campus. Approved or accredited by New Mexico Department of Education. Member of National Association of Independent Schools and Secondary School Admission Test Board. Endowment: $87 million. Total enrollment: 1,121. Upper school average class size: 15. Upper school faculty-student ratio: 1:9. There are 171 required school days per year for Upper School students. Upper School students typically attend 5 days per week. The average school day consists of 7 hours and 30 minutes.

Upper School Student Profile Grade 8: 145 students (73 boys, 72 girls); Grade 9: 162 students (81 boys, 81 girls); Grade 10: 169 students (81 boys, 88 girls); Grade 11: 160 students (75 boys, 85 girls); Grade 12: 166 students (78 boys, 88 girls).

Faculty School total: 180. In upper school: 66 men, 61 women; 100 have advanced degrees.

Graduation Requirements Experiential education (environmental and outdoor activities).

Special Academic Programs 18 Advanced Placement exams for which test preparation is offered; independent study; term-away projects; domestic exchange program; study abroad.

College Admission Counseling 166 students graduated in 2016; all went to college, including Arizona State University at the Tempe campus; Colorado State University; The University of Texas at Austin; University of New Mexico; Washington University in St. Louis. Mean SAT critical reading: 663, mean SAT math: 660, mean SAT writing: 650, mean combined SAT: 1973, mean composite ACT: 29.

Student Life Upper grades have specified standards of dress, student council, honor system. Discipline rests primarily with faculty.

Summer Programs Remediation, enrichment, advancement, sports, art/fine arts, computer instruction programs offered; session focuses on enrichment; held on campus; accepts boys and girls; open to students from other schools. 1,900 students usually enrolled. 2017 schedule: June 2 to July 14. Application deadline: none.

Tuition and Aid Day student tuition: $22,870. Tuition installment plan (FACTS Tuition Payment Plan). Need-based scholarship grants available. In 2016–17, 22% of upper-school students received aid. Total amount of financial aid awarded in 2016–17: $2,385,154.

Admissions Traditional secondary-level entrance grade is 9. For fall 2016, 117 students applied for upper-level admission, 68 were accepted, 35 enrolled. ISEE, school's own exam or SSAT required. Deadline for receipt of application materials: February 3. Application fee required: $65. On-campus interview recommended.

Athletics Interscholastic: baseball (boys), basketball (b,g), cross-country running (b,g), dance (b,g), diving (b,g), football (b), golf (b,g), hiking/backpacking (b,g), life saving (b,g), modern dance (b,g), outdoor education (b,g), outdoor skills (b,g), physical training (b,g), rafting (b,g), rappelling (b,g), rock climbing (b,g), soccer (b,g), softball (g), swimming and diving (b,g), tennis (b,g), track and field (b,g), volleyball (g), wrestling (b,g); intramural: bowling (b,g); coed intramural: ballet, basketball, canoeing/kayaking, wilderness, wilderness survival. 9 PE instructors, 84 coaches, 3 athletic trainers.

Computers Computers are regularly used in all classes. Computer network features include on-campus library services, online commercial services, Internet access, wireless campus network, Internet filtering or blocking technology. Campus intranet and student e-mail accounts are available to students. The school has a published electronic and media policy.

Contact Amy Eglinton Keller, Director of Admission and Enrollment Management. 505-828-3208. Fax: 505-828-3128. E-mail: keller@aa.edu. Website: www.aa.edu

ALEXANDER DAWSON SCHOOL

10455 Dawson Drive
Lafayette, Colorado 80026

Head of School: Mr. George Moore

General Information Coeducational day college-preparatory, arts, technology, and engineering, global studies, robotics school. Grades K–12. Founded: 1970. Setting: rural. Nearest major city is Boulder. 108-acre campus. 11 buildings on campus. Approved or accredited by Association of Colorado Independent Schools and Colorado Department of Education. Member of National Association of Independent Schools and Secondary School Admission Test Board. Total enrollment: 517. Upper school average class size: 15. Upper school faculty-student ratio: 1:8. There are 168 required school days per year for Upper School students. Upper School students typically attend 5 days per week. The average school day consists of 9 hours and 30 minutes.

Upper School Student Profile Grade 9: 67 students (33 boys, 34 girls); Grade 10: 57 students (31 boys, 26 girls); Grade 11: 61 students (28 boys, 33 girls); Grade 12: 61 students (33 boys, 28 girls).

Faculty School total: 55. In upper school: 17 men, 10 women; 25 have advanced degrees.

Subjects Offered Algebra, American history, American literature, art, art history, biology, calculus, ceramics, chemistry, Chinese, computer math, computer multimedia, computer programming, computer science, creative writing, dance, drafting, drama, earth science, economics, English, English literature, European history, expository writing, fine arts, French, geography, geometry, government-AP, government/civics, grammar, health, history, industrial arts, journalism, Latin, mathematics, mechanical drawing, music, photography, physical education, physics, science, social sciences, social studies, Spanish, speech, theater, trigonometry, world history, world literature, writing.

Graduation Requirements Arts and fine arts (art, music, dance, drama), computer science, English, foreign language, history, mathematics, science, sports.

Special Academic Programs 15 Advanced Placement exams for which test preparation is offered; honors section; independent study; term-away projects; study at local college for college credit; study abroad; academic accommodation for the gifted, the musically talented, and the artistically talented; remedial reading and/or remedial writing; remedial math; special instructional classes for deaf students.

College Admission Counseling 57 students graduated in 2015; all went to college, including Middlebury College; Pomona College; University of Denver; Wellesley College. Mean SAT critical reading: 625, mean SAT math: 630, mean SAT writing: 630, mean composite ACT: 27.

Student Life Upper grades have specified standards of dress, student council, honor system. Discipline rests equally with students and faculty.

Tuition and Aid Day student tuition: $23,950. Tuition installment plan (Insured Tuition Payment Plan, monthly payment plans, individually arranged payment plans). Need-based scholarship grants, need-based loans available. In 2015–16, 21% of upper-school students received aid. Total amount of financial aid awarded in 2015–16: $1,450,000.

Admissions Traditional secondary-level entrance grade is 9. For fall 2015, 108 students applied for upper-level admission, 70 were accepted, 56 enrolled. Deadline for receipt of application materials: none. Application fee required: $75. Interview required.

Athletics Interscholastic: baseball (boys), basketball (b,g), lacrosse (b), soccer (b,g), swimming and diving (b,g), synchronized swimming (g), tennis (b,g), track and field (b,g), volleyball (g); intramural: lacrosse (b); coed interscholastic: bicycling, canoeing/kayaking, cross-country running, equestrian sports, golf, kayaking, martial arts, paddling, skiing (downhill), Special Olympics; coed intramural: aerobics, aerobics/dance, backpacking, Circus, climbing, dance, equestrian sports, fitness, flag football, football, Frisbee, golf, hiking/backpacking, indoor soccer, martial arts, modern dance, outdoor activities, outdoor education, outdoor recreation, outdoor skills, physical fitness, rafting, rock climbing, ropes courses, running, strength & conditioning, weight lifting. 3 PE instructors, 22 coaches, 1 athletic trainer.

Computers Computers are regularly used in art, engineering, mathematics, science classes. Computer network features include on-campus library services, online commercial services, Internet access, wireless campus network, Internet filtering or blocking technology. Campus intranet, student e-mail accounts, and computer access in designated common areas are available to students. Students grades are available online. The school has a published electronic and media policy.

Contact Ms. Denise LaRusch, Assistant to the Director of Admissions. 303-665-6679. Fax: 303-381-0415. E-mail: dlarusch@dawsonschool.org.
Website: www.dawsonschool.org

ALICE SMITH SCHOOL

3 Jalan Equine
Taman Equine
Seri Kembangan
Kuala Lumpur 43300, Malaysia

Head of School: Mr. Roger Schultz

General Information Coeducational day college-preparatory, arts, business, technology, and sciences school. Grades 7–13. Founded: 1946. Setting: rural. 25-acre campus. 7 buildings on campus. Member of European Council of International Schools. Language of instruction: English. Total enrollment: 632. Upper school average class size: 20. Upper school faculty-student ratio: 1:9. Upper School students typically attend 5 days per week.

Faculty In upper school: 30 men, 25 women; 12 have advanced degrees.

Subjects Offered Art, biology, business studies, chemistry, drama, economics, English, French, geography, German, history, information technology, Malay, Mandarin, mathematics, modern languages, music, physical education, physics, science.

Student Life Upper grades have uniform requirement, student council. Discipline rests primarily with faculty.

Tuition and Aid Day student tuition: 25,000 Malaysian ringgits. Tuition reduction for siblings available.

Admissions Deadline for receipt of application materials: none. Application fee required: 300 Malaysian ringgits. On-campus interview recommended.

Athletics Intramural: basketball (boys, girls), gymnastics (b,g), life saving (b,g); coed interscholastic: aquatics, backpacking, badminton; coed intramural: aerobics, aerobics/dance, aquatics, backpacking, badminton, ball hockey, canoeing/kayaking,

cross-country running, dance, fencing, field hockey, fitness, hiking/backpacking, kayaking, life saving. 4 PE instructors, 6 coaches.

Computers Computers are regularly used in all classes. Computer network features include on-campus library services, Internet access, wireless campus network, Internet filtering or blocking technology. Campus intranet, student e-mail accounts, and computer access in designated common areas are available to students. The school has a published electronic and media policy.

Contact Ms. Agnes Chang, Admissions Manager. 603-95433688. Fax: 603-95433788. E-mail: admissions.ep@alice-smith.edu.my. Website: www.alice-smith.edu.my

ALLEN ACADEMY

3201 Boonville Road
Bryan, Texas 77802

Head of School: Dr. Matthew J. Rush

General Information Coeducational boarding and day college-preparatory and ESL school. Boarding grades 9–12, day grades PK–12. Founded: 1886. Setting: small town. Nearest major city is Houston. Students are housed in 5 Villas (off campus) segregated by gender. 40-acre campus. 4 buildings on campus. Approved or accredited by Independent Schools Association of the Southwest, Southern Association of Colleges and Schools, and Texas Education Agency. Member of National Association of Independent Schools. Endowment: $8,000. Total enrollment: 323. Upper school average class size: 18. Upper school faculty-student ratio: 1:8. There are 175 required school days per year for Upper School students. Upper School students typically attend 5 days per week. The average school day consists of 7 hours and 30 minutes.

Upper School Student Profile Grade 9: 14 students (6 boys, 8 girls); Grade 10: 25 students (13 boys, 12 girls); Grade 11: 21 students (12 boys, 9 girls); Grade 12: 21 students (10 boys, 11 girls). 17% of students are boarding students. 90% are state residents. 1 state is represented in upper school student body. 10% are international students. International students from China, Mexico, and Republic of Korea; 3 other countries represented in student body.

Faculty School total: 55. In upper school: 8 men, 12 women; 10 have advanced degrees.

Subjects Offered Algebra, American history, American history-AP, American literature, art, band, biology, biology-AP, business, calculus, calculus-AP, chemistry, choir, drama, drawing, English language-AP, English literature, English literature and composition-AP, English literature-AP, ESL, European history, European history-AP, French, French-AP, geometry, honors English, keyboarding, multimedia, painting, physical education, physics-AP, pre-calculus, Spanish, Spanish-AP, theater, video film production, world history, yearbook.

Graduation Requirements Algebra, American history, American literature, arts and fine arts (art, music, dance, drama), biology, chemistry, economics, electives, English, English composition, English literature, European history, geometry, mathematics, physics, pre-calculus, Spanish, world history, 48 hours of community service (12 per year).

Special Academic Programs Advanced Placement exam preparation; honors section; study at local college for college credit; ESL.

College Admission Counseling 23 students graduated in 2016; 22 went to college, including Penn State University Park; Texas A&M University; Texas Tech University; The University of Texas at Austin; University of California, Los Angeles; University of Notre Dame. Other: 1 went to work, 1 entered a postgraduate year. Median SAT critical reading: 555, median SAT math: 660, median SAT writing: 600, median combined SAT: 1865, median composite ACT: 25. 33% scored over 600 on SAT critical reading, 60% scored over 600 on SAT math, 50% scored over 600 on SAT writing, 59% scored over 1800 on combined SAT, 73% scored over 26 on composite ACT.

Student Life Upper grades have uniform requirement, student council, honor system. Discipline rests equally with students and faculty.

Summer Programs Sports programs offered; held on campus; accepts boys and girls; open to students from other schools. 16 students usually enrolled. 2017 schedule: June 13 to July 29. Application deadline: June 1.

Tuition and Aid Day student tuition: $8066–$12,051; 7-day tuition and room/board: $36,240. Tuition installment plan (FACTS Tuition Payment Plan, monthly and quarterly payment plans). Need-based scholarship grants available. In 2016–17, 32% of upper-school students received aid. Total amount of financial aid awarded in 2016–17: $230,000.

Admissions Traditional secondary-level entrance grade is 9. For fall 2016, 14 students applied for upper-level admission, 10 were accepted, 10 enrolled. Any standardized test, Archdiocese of Washington Entrance Exam, ERB CTP IV, ISEE, PSAT, PSAT, SAT, or ACT for applicants to grade 11 and 12 or writing sample required. Deadline for receipt of application materials: none. Application fee required: $250. Interview required.

Athletics Interscholastic: baseball (boys), basketball (b,g), cheering (g), cross-country running (b,g), football (b), golf (b,g), softball (g), swimming and diving (g), tennis (b,g), track and field (b,g), volleyball (g); coed interscholastic: fitness, soccer, strength & conditioning, weight training, winter soccer; coed intramural: basketball, combined training, weight training. 2 PE instructors, 4 coaches, 2 athletic trainers.

Computers Computers are regularly used in keyboarding, multimedia classes. Computer network features include online commercial services, Internet access, wireless campus network, Internet filtering or blocking technology. Campus intranet, student e-mail accounts, and computer access in designated common areas are available to students. Students grades are available online. The school has a published electronic and media policy.

Contact Mrs. Anne Prescott, Director of Admission. 979-776-0731. Fax: 979-774-7769. E-mail: aprescott@allenacademy.org. Website: www.allenacademy.org

ALLENTOWN CENTRAL CATHOLIC HIGH SCHOOL

301 North Fourth Street
Allentown, Pennsylvania 18102-3098

Head of School: Mr. Blair A. Tiger

General Information Coeducational day college-preparatory school, affiliated with Roman Catholic Church. Grades 9–12. Founded: 1927. Setting: urban. 3-acre campus. 3 buildings on campus. Approved or accredited by Middle States Association of Colleges and Schools, National Catholic Education Association, and Pennsylvania Department of Education. Endowment: $100,000. Total enrollment: 810. Upper school average class size: 25. Upper school faculty-student ratio: 1:14. There are 190 required school days per year for Upper School students. Upper School students typically attend 5 days per week. The average school day consists of 6 hours and 50 minutes.

Upper School Student Profile Grade 9: 172 students (90 boys, 82 girls); Grade 10: 224 students (119 boys, 105 girls); Grade 11: 222 students (129 boys, 93 girls); Grade 12: 191 students (100 boys, 91 girls). 87% of students are Roman Catholic.

Faculty School total: 55. In upper school: 27 men, 28 women; 22 have advanced degrees.

Subjects Offered Advanced biology, advanced chemistry, advanced math, Advanced Placement courses, algebra, American culture, American government, American history, American history-AP, American legal systems, American literature, American literature-AP, analysis, analysis and differential calculus, analysis of data, anatomy, anatomy and physiology, art, athletics, band, Basic programming, biology, biology-AP, British literature, British literature (honors), broadcast journalism, business, business applications, business technology, calculus, calculus-AP, campus ministry, Catholic belief and practice, chemistry, chemistry-AP, choir, choral music, church history, comparative government and politics-AP, composition-AP, computer graphics, computer programming, concert band, criminal justice, desktop publishing, ecology, environmental systems, economics, economics-AP, English language and composition-AP, English language-AP, English literature, English literature and composition-AP, English literature-AP, environmental science, environmental science-AP, foreign language, French, geography, geometry, German, government, government and politics-AP, government-AP, graphic design, health education, history of the Catholic Church, history-AP, honors algebra, honors English, honors geometry, honors U.S. history, honors world history, human anatomy, internship, jazz band, journalism, Latin, library assistant, literature and composition-AP, macro/microeconomics-AP, marching band, math analysis, modern history, moral theology, music appreciation, New Testament, physical education, physics, physics-AP, physiology, pre-calculus, psychology, psychology-AP, sign language, Spanish, Spanish language-AP, speech and debate, statistics-AP, studio art, theology, U.S. government, U.S. government and politics, U.S. government and politics-AP, U.S. history, U.S history-AP, United States government-AP.

Graduation Requirements Algebra, American government, American studies, biology, chemistry, English, foreign language, geometry, theology, world studies, community services for each grade level, attend two retreats per year.

Special Academic Programs 15 Advanced Placement exams for which test preparation is offered; honors section; independent study; study at local college for college credit; academic accommodation for the gifted; programs in English, mathematics for dyslexic students; special instructional classes for deaf students, blind students.

College Admission Counseling 190 students graduated in 2016; 188 went to college, including Moravian College; Penn State University Park; Temple University; University of Pittsburgh; West Chester University of Pennsylvania. Other: 1 entered military service, 2 had other specific plans. Median SAT critical reading: 580, median SAT math: 540, median SAT writing: 520, median combined SAT: 1640, median composite ACT: 25.

Student Life Upper grades have uniform requirement, student council, honor system. Discipline rests primarily with faculty. Attendance at religious services is required.

Tuition and Aid Day student tuition: $8750. Tuition installment plan (The Tuition Plan, FACTS Tuition Payment Plan). Tuition reduction for siblings, paying campus jobs available. In 2016–17, 46% of upper-school students received aid. Total amount of financial aid awarded in 2016–17: $923,830.

Admissions Traditional secondary-level entrance grade is 9. For fall 2016, 215 students applied for upper-level admission, 210 were accepted, 190 enrolled. Placement test required. Deadline for receipt of application materials: none. Application fee required: $200. Interview recommended.

Athletics Interscholastic: aerobics/dance (girls), aerobics/Nautilus (b), baseball (b), basketball (b,g), cross-country running (b,g), dance team (g), field hockey (g), football (b), lacrosse (b,g), power lifting (b), soccer (b,g), swimming and diving (b,g), tennis (b,g), track and field (b,g), volleyball (g), weight lifting (b); coed interscholastic: cheering, diving, drill team, golf; coed intramural: alpine skiing, skiing (downhill), snowboarding, yoga. 2 PE instructors, 17 coaches, 2 athletic trainers.

Computers Computers are regularly used in all classes. Computer network features include on-campus library services, Internet access, wireless campus network, Internet filtering or blocking technology. Campus intranet, student e-mail accounts, and computer access in designated common areas are available to students. Students grades are available online. The school has a published electronic and media policy.

Contact Ms. Ashley Pittman, Director of Admissions. 610-437-4601 Ext. 148. Fax: 610-437-6760. E-mail: apittman@acchs.info. Website: www.acchs.info

ALL HALLOWS HIGH SCHOOL

111 All Hallows Way
Bronx, New York 10452-9402

Head of School: Mr. Ron Schutte

General Information Boys' day college-preparatory, general academic, business, religious studies, and technology school, affiliated with Roman Catholic Church. Grades 9–12. Founded: 1909. Setting: urban. 1 building on campus. Approved or accredited by Christian Brothers Association, Middle States Association of Colleges and Schools, and New York Department of Education. Total enrollment: 600. Upper school average class size: 25. Upper school faculty-student ratio: 1:25. There are 180 required school days per year for Upper School students. Upper School students typically attend 5 days per week. The average school day consists of 6 hours and 8 minutes.

Upper School Student Profile Grade 9: 151 students (151 boys); Grade 10: 157 students (157 boys); Grade 11: 159 students (159 boys); Grade 12: 133 students (133 boys). 85% of students are Roman Catholic.

Faculty School total: 42. In upper school: 37 men, 5 women; 33 have advanced degrees.

Subjects Offered Algebra, American history, art, Bible studies, biology, calculus, chemistry, computer science, economics, English, English literature, environmental science, geometry, government/civics, grammar, history, humanities, Latin, mathematics, media studies, physical education, physics, political science, religion, science, social studies, Spanish, speech, trigonometry.

Graduation Requirements Arts and fine arts (art, music, dance, drama), business skills (includes word processing), computer science, English, foreign language, mathematics, physical education (includes health), religion (includes Bible studies and theology), science, social sciences, social studies (includes history), 100 Christian Service hours accumulated over the 4 years of study. Community service is required.

Special Academic Programs Study at local college for college credit; remedial reading and/or remedial writing; remedial math.

College Admission Counseling 154 students graduated in 2015; all went to college.

Student Life Upper grades have specified standards of dress, student council, honor system. Discipline rests primarily with faculty. Attendance at religious services is required.

Tuition and Aid Day student tuition: $6200. Tuition installment plan (SMART Tuition Payment Plan). Tuition reduction for siblings, merit scholarship grants available.

Admissions Traditional secondary-level entrance grade is 9. For fall 2015, 475 students applied for upper-level admission, 289 were accepted, 151 enrolled. School's own exam required. Deadline for receipt of application materials: none. No application fee required. On-campus interview required.

Athletics Interscholastic: baseball, basketball, bowling, cross-country running, fencing, golf, indoor track & field, soccer, track and field, winter (indoor) track; intramural: basketball, field hockey, flag football, floor hockey, indoor soccer, lacrosse. 1 PE instructor, 4 coaches.

Computers Computers are regularly used in English, history, mathematics, media studies, science classes. Computer resources include Internet access, wireless campus network, Internet filtering or blocking technology.

Contact Mr. Sean Sullivan, Principal. 718-293-4545. Fax: 718-293-8634. E-mail: ssullivan@allhallows.org. Website: www.allhallows.org

ALLIANCE ACADEMY

Casilla 17-11-06186
Quito, Ecuador

Head of School: Dr. David Wells

General Information Coeducational boarding and day and distance learning college-preparatory school, affiliated with Christian faith. Boarding grades 7–12, day grades PK–12. Founded: 1929. Setting: urban. Students are housed in single-sex dormitories and mission agency dormitories. 8-acre campus. 6 buildings on campus. Approved or accredited by Association of American Schools in South America, Association of Christian Schools International, and Southern Association of Colleges and Schools. Language of instruction: English. Total enrollment: 604. Upper school average class size: 15. Upper school faculty-student ratio: 1:7. There are 200 required school days per year for Upper School students. Upper School students typically attend 5 days per week. The average school day consists of 6 hours and 30 minutes.

Upper School Student Profile 40% of students are Christian.

Faculty School total: 91. In upper school: 21 men, 24 women; 14 have advanced degrees; 3 reside on campus.

Subjects Offered Algebra, American history, American literature, art, auto mechanics, band, Bible, Bible as literature, Bible studies, biology, biology-AP, business, calculus, calculus-AP, chemistry, choir, Christian doctrine, Christian ethics, Christian studies, church history, computer applications, computer art, computer programming, computer science, concert band, creative writing, debate, desktop publishing, drama, earth science, economics, English, English as a foreign language, English language-AP, English literature, English literature-AP, ESL, family and consumer science, fine arts, French, French as a second language, geography, geometry, government/civics, grammar, health, health education, history, home economics, industrial arts, journalism, keyboarding, Life of Christ, marching band, mathematics, music, novels, photography, physical education, physics, pre-algebra, pre-calculus, public speaking, religion, religion and culture, science, senior seminar, small engine repair, social sciences, social studies, Spanish, Spanish literature, Spanish literature-AP, speech, speech and debate, theater, trigonometry, video communication, vocal ensemble, woodworking, world geography, world history, world religions, writing, yearbook.

Graduation Requirements 1 1/2 elective credits, algebra, arts and fine arts (art, music, dance, drama), comparative government and politics, computer applications, English, foreign language, health education, mathematics, physical education (includes health), religion (includes Bible studies and theology), science, social sciences, social studies (includes history), U.S. government and politics, U.S. history.

Special Academic Programs 12 Advanced Placement exams for which test preparation is offered; independent study; study at local college for college credit; academic accommodation for the gifted; remedial reading and/or remedial writing; remedial math; programs in English, mathematics, general development for dyslexic students; special instructional classes for students with developmental and/or learning disabilities; ESL (52 students enrolled).

College Admission Counseling Colleges students went to include Azusa Pacific University; Calvin College; Houghton College; New York University; Simpson University. Median SAT critical reading: 495, median SAT math: 517, median SAT writing: 496, median combined SAT: 1508, median composite ACT: 22. 36% scored over 600 on SAT critical reading, 29% scored over 600 on SAT math, 30% scored over 600 on SAT writing, 32% scored over 1800 on combined SAT, 26% scored over 26 on composite ACT.

Student Life Upper grades have specified standards of dress, student council, honor system. Discipline rests primarily with faculty. Attendance at religious services is required.

Summer Programs Remediation, ESL, sports, art/fine arts programs offered; session focuses on ESL, Sports and activities; held on campus; accepts boys and girls; open to students from other schools. 180 students usually enrolled. 2017 schedule: July 3 to July 21. Application deadline: June 12.

Tuition and Aid Day student tuition: $8750; 7-day tuition and room/board: $18,700. Tuition installment plan (monthly payment plans, individually arranged payment plans). Tuition reduction for siblings, need-based scholarship grants, paying campus jobs, tuition reduction for children of missionaries, two full scholarships for children of Ecuadorian military personnel available.

Admissions Traditional secondary-level entrance grade is 9. For fall 2016, 46 students applied for upper-level admission, 28 were accepted, 26 enrolled. English entrance exam, English proficiency, WRAT and writing sample required. Deadline for receipt of application materials: none. No application fee required. Interview recommended.

Athletics Interscholastic: basketball (boys, girls), soccer (b,g), volleyball (b,g); intramural: badminton (b,g), ball hockey (b), horseshoes (b), in-line hockey (b), modern dance (g), table tennis (b,g); coed intramural: backpacking, basketball, bocce, climbing, croquet, field hockey, flag football, floor hockey, football, hiking/backpacking, indoor soccer, kickball, martial arts, outdoor adventure, paddle tennis, running, soccer, softball, strength & conditioning, table tennis, volleyball, wall climbing. 4 PE instructors, 1 coach.

Computers Computers are regularly used in basic skills, business education, career exploration, college planning, computer applications, design, desktop publishing, desktop publishing, ESL, digital applications, graphic design, independent study, information technology, introduction to technology, keyboarding, lab/keyboard, language development, media arts, media production, media services, photography, photojournalism, programming, publications, technology, video film production, word processing, writing, yearbook classes. Computer network features include on-campus library services, online commercial services, Internet access, wireless campus network, Internet filtering or blocking technology. Campus intranet, student e-mail accounts, and computer access in designated common areas are available to students. Students grades are available online. The school has a published electronic and media policy.

Contact Maria Luisa Davalos, Admissions Coordinator. 593-2-226-6985. Fax: 593-2-226-4350. E-mail: mdavalos@alliance.k12.ec. Website: www.alliance.k12.ec

ALLISON ACADEMY

1881 Northeast 164th Street
North Miami Beach, Florida 33162

Head of School: Dr. Sarah F. Allison

General Information Coeducational day college-preparatory, general academic, and English for Speakers of Other Languages school; primarily serves students with learning disabilities, individuals with Attention Deficit Disorder, dyslexic students, and Asperger's Syndrome. Grades 6–12. Founded: 1983. Setting: urban. Nearest major city is Miami. 1-acre campus. 2 buildings on campus. Approved or accredited by Middle States Association of Colleges and Schools, National Council for Private School Accreditation, Southern Association of Colleges and Schools, and Florida Department of Education. Total enrollment: 105. Upper school average class size: 15. Upper school faculty-student ratio: 1:10. There are 175 required school days per year for Upper School students. Upper School students typically attend 5 days per week. The average school day consists of 5 hours and 40 minutes.

Upper School Student Profile Grade 6: 4 students (3 boys, 1 girl); Grade 7: 5 students (5 boys); Grade 8: 8 students (7 boys, 1 girl); Grade 9: 13 students (9 boys, 4 girls); Grade 10: 18 students (8 boys, 10 girls); Grade 11: 22 students (14 boys, 8 girls); Grade 12: 19 students (14 boys, 5 girls).

Faculty School total: 11. In upper school: 5 men, 6 women; 4 have advanced degrees.

Subjects Offered ACT preparation, Advanced Placement courses, algebra, American government, American history, applied music, arts, band, basic language skills, basketball, biology, British literature, chemistry, computer science, consumer mathematics, creative drama, current events, digital photography, drafting, drama, drama workshop, drawing, earth and space science, ecology, environmental systems, economics, economics and history, English, English language and composition-AP, English literature, environmental science, ESL, fine arts, forensics, French, general math, geography, geometry, health education, history, humanities, journalism, law studies, life management skills, life skills, literature and composition-AP, mathematics, painting, participation in sports, peer counseling, personal and social education, personal finance, physical education, physical science, physics, pre-algebra, pre-calculus, psychology, reading, reading/study skills, SAT preparation, SAT/ACT preparation, science, social sciences, social studies, Spanish, sports, trigonometry, U.S. government, volleyball, world cultures, writing, yearbook.

Graduation Requirements Algebra, American government, American history, applied arts, arts and fine arts (art, music, dance, drama), biology, business skills (includes word processing), chemistry, computer applications, creative writing, current events, drama, earth and space science, economics, English, English literature, environmental education, foreign language, geometry, health education, life management skills, mathematics, physical education (includes health), psychology, SAT preparation, SAT/ACT preparation, science, social sciences, social studies (includes history), Spanish, U.S. history, world history, 75 hours minimum of community service.

Special Academic Programs 1 Advanced Placement exam for which test preparation is offered; honors section; accelerated programs; study at local college for college credit; academic accommodation for the gifted, the musically talented, and the artistically talented; remedial reading and/or remedial writing; remedial math; programs in English, mathematics, general development for dyslexic students; special instructional classes for students with mild learning disabilities, dyslexia, and Attention Deficit Disorder; ESL (1 student enrolled).

College Admission Counseling 17 students graduated in 2016; all went to college, including Barry University; Broward College; Florida International University; Lynn University; Miami Dade College; University of Miami. Median SAT critical reading: 500, median SAT math: 510, median composite ACT: 20. 16% scored over 600 on SAT critical reading, 15% scored over 600 on SAT math, 5% scored over 26 on composite ACT.

Student Life Upper grades have uniform requirement, student council. Discipline rests primarily with faculty.

Summer Programs Remediation, enrichment, advancement, ESL programs offered; session focuses on academics for credit courses, remedial reading, and ESL; held on campus; accepts boys and girls; open to students from other schools. 30 students usually enrolled. 2017 schedule: June 19 to July 27. Application deadline: June 16.

Tuition and Aid Day student tuition: $17,000. Tuition installment plan (monthly payment plans, individually arranged payment plans). Tuition reduction for siblings, merit scholarship grants, need-based scholarship grants available. In 2016–17, 30% of upper-school students received aid; total upper-school merit-scholarship money awarded: $70,000. Total amount of financial aid awarded in 2016–17: $215,000.

Admissions Traditional secondary-level entrance grade is 9. For fall 2016, 27 students applied for upper-level admission, 23 were accepted, 23 enrolled. Admissions testing, CTBS (or similar from their school), school placement exam, standardized test scores or Woodcock-Johnson Revised Achievement Test required. Deadline for receipt of application materials: none. Application fee required: $450. Interview recommended.

Athletics Interscholastic: basketball (boys), cross-country running (b), flag football (b), indoor track & field (b), kickball (b), physical fitness (b,g), swimming and diving (b), volleyball (b,g), walking (g), weight training (b); intramural: basketball (b,g), cross-country running (b), flag football (b), indoor track (b,g), kickball (b), soccer (b,g), softball (b,g), swimming and diving (b,g), table tennis (b,g), volleyball (b,g), walking (g); coed interscholastic: bowling, indoor track & field, kickball, physical fitness, track and field, volleyball; coed intramural: badminton, indoor soccer, indoor track, paddle tennis, physical fitness, soccer, softball, swimming and diving, table tennis, track and field, volleyball, yoga. 2 PE instructors, 3 coaches.

Computers Computers are regularly used in art, business applications, computer applications, current events, drawing and design, English, foreign language, geography, health, history, journalism, keyboarding, life skills, mathematics, news writing, newspaper, psychology, reading, SAT preparation, science, Spanish, word processing, yearbook classes. Computer network features include on-campus library services, online commercial services, Internet access, wireless campus network, Internet filtering or blocking technology, each student has their own tablets and notebooks to access textbooks, etc. Student e-mail accounts and computer access in designated common areas are available to students. Students grades are available online. The school has a published electronic and media policy.

Contact Margaret Sheriff, Registrar. 305-940-3922. Fax: 305-940-1820. E-mail: msheriff@allisonacademy.com. Website: www.allisonacademy.com

ALL SAINTS' ACADEMY

5001 State Road 540 West
Winter Haven, Florida 33880

Head of School: Mrs. Carolyn Baldwin

General Information Coeducational day college-preparatory, arts, technology, and project-based learning school, affiliated with Episcopal Church. Grades PS–12. Setting: suburban. Nearest major city is Orlando. 60-acre campus. 7 buildings on campus. Approved or accredited by Florida Council of Independent Schools, National Association of Episcopal Schools, and Florida Department of Education. Member of National Association of Independent Schools and Secondary School Admission Test Board. Total enrollment: 600. Upper school average class size: 13. Upper School students typically attend 5 days per week.

Special Academic Programs 17 Advanced Placement exams for which test preparation is offered; honors section.

College Admission Counseling 43 students graduated in 2015; all went to college.

Student Life Upper grades have uniform requirement, student council, honor system. Discipline rests primarily with faculty. Attendance at religious services is required.

Tuition and Aid Tuition installment plan (FACTS Tuition Payment Plan). Tuition reduction for siblings, need-based scholarship grants available.

Admissions Deadline for receipt of application materials: none. Application fee required: $30.

Athletics Interscholastic: baseball (boys), basketball (b,g), cheering (g), cross-country running (b,g), dance (g), diving (b,g), football (b), golf (b,g), lacrosse (b,g), soccer (b,g), softball (g), swimming and diving (b,g), tennis (b,g), track and field (b,g), volleyball (g); coed interscholastic: dance; coed intramural: strength & conditioning, weight training.

Computers Computers are regularly used in all classes. Computer network features include on-campus library services, Internet access, wireless campus network, Internet filtering or blocking technology. Campus intranet, student e-mail accounts, and computer access in designated common areas are available to students. Students grades are available online. The school has a published electronic and media policy.

Contact Ms. Evelyn Schwalb, Director of Admission. 863-293-5980 Ext. 2239. Fax: 863-595-1163. E-mail: eschwalb@allsaintsacademy.com. Website: www.allsaintsacademy.com

ALMA HEIGHTS CHRISTIAN HIGH SCHOOL

1030 Linda Mar Boulevard
Pacifica, California 94044

Head of School: Dr. David Gross

General Information Coeducational day college-preparatory and general academic school. Grades K–12. Founded: 1955. Setting: suburban. Nearest major city is San Francisco. 37-acre campus. 5 buildings on campus. Approved or accredited by Association of Christian Schools International, Western Association of Schools and Colleges, and California Department of Education. Total enrollment: 303. Upper school average class size: 22. Upper school faculty-student ratio: 1:15. There are 176 required school days per year for Upper School students. Upper School students typically attend 5 days per week. The average school day consists of 7 hours and 25 minutes.

Upper School Student Profile Grade 6: 18 students (13 boys, 5 girls); Grade 7: 21 students (5 boys, 16 girls); Grade 8: 14 students (9 boys, 5 girls); Grade 9: 25 students (11 boys, 14 girls); Grade 10: 29 students (14 boys, 15 girls); Grade 11: 45 students (21 boys, 24 girls); Grade 12: 44 students (28 boys, 16 girls).

Faculty School total: 50. In upper school: 10 men, 9 women; 7 have advanced degrees.

Subjects Offered 20th century history, 20th century world history, advanced biology, advanced math, algebra, American history, American history-AP, arts, ASB Leadership, athletic training, athletics, baseball, basketball, Bible, Bible studies, biology, biology-AP, calculus, campus ministry, career and personal planning, cheerleading, choir, college counseling, English, English language and composition-AP, entrepreneurship, environmental science-AP, geometry, honors algebra, honors English, pre-calculus, robotics, senior seminar, Spanish, speech and debate, volleyball, weight fitness.

Special Academic Programs International Baccalaureate program; 6 Advanced Placement exams for which test preparation is offered; honors section; study at local college for college credit; special instructional classes for students with ADD and dyslexia; ESL (19 students enrolled).

College Admission Counseling 45 students graduated in 2016; 40 went to college, including Academy of Art University; Biola University; University of California, Berkeley; University of California, Davis; University of California, Irvine. Other: 5 went to work. Mean SAT critical reading: 494, mean SAT math: 529, mean SAT writing: 503.

Student Life Upper grades have uniform requirement, student council, honor system. Discipline rests primarily with faculty.

Tuition and Aid Day student tuition: $12,800. Tuition installment plan (SMART Tuition Payment Plan). Need-based scholarship grants available. In 2016–17, 15% of upper-school students received aid.

Admissions Traditional secondary-level entrance grade is 9. ISEE required. Deadline for receipt of application materials: February 15. Application fee required: $50. On-campus interview recommended.

Athletics Interscholastic: baseball (boys), basketball (b,g), cheering (g), soccer (b), softball (g), strength & conditioning (b), volleyball (b,g); coed interscholastic: cross-country running, soccer. 3 PE instructors, 6 coaches.

Computers Computers are regularly used in English classes. Computer network features include on-campus library services, online commercial services, Internet access, wireless campus network, Internet filtering or blocking technology. Campus intranet, student e-mail accounts, and computer access in designated common areas are available to students. Students grades are available online. The school has a published electronic and media policy.

Contact Mrs. Anna Valladares, Director of Admissions. 650-355-1935 Ext. 104. Fax: 650-355-3488. E-mail: avalladares@almaheights.ort. Website: www.almaheights.org

ALPHA OMEGA ACADEMY

804 North Second Avenue East
Rock Rapids, Iowa 51246

Head of School: Mr. Joseph A. Bakker

General Information Coeducational day and distance learning college-preparatory, general academic, and distance learning school, affiliated with Christian faith. Grades K–12. Distance learning grades K–12. Founded: 1992. Setting: small town. 4-acre campus. Approved or accredited by CITA (Commission on International and Trans-Regional Accreditation) and North Central Association of Colleges and Schools. Total enrollment: 2,350. Upper School students typically attend 5 days per week.

Upper School Student Profile 99% of students are Christian.

Faculty School total: 47. In upper school: 13 men, 29 women; 7 have advanced degrees.

Subjects Offered 20th century history, accounting, algebra, American Civil War, American government, American history, American literature, art, Bible, biology, British literature, calculus, career planning, chemistry, civics, computer information systems, computer multimedia, computer skills, computer technologies, computer tools, computers, consumer mathematics, digital art, earth science, English, English composition, English literature, French, general math, general science, geography, geometry, health, history, home economics, language arts, mathematics, music appreciation, music theory, physical education, physical fitness, programming, science, Spanish, state history, Vietnam War, world geography, world history.

Graduation Requirements 1 1/2 elective credits, algebra, biology, chemistry, language arts, mathematics, physical education (includes health), science, social studies (includes history), one credit of Bible.

Special Academic Programs Accelerated programs; independent study; remedial math.

College Admission Counseling 359 students graduated in 2016; they went to Dallas Baptist University; Liberty University.

Student Life Upper grades have honor system. Discipline rests primarily with faculty.

Summer Programs Remediation, enrichment, advancement, art/fine arts, computer instruction programs offered; held off campus; accepts boys and girls; open to students from other schools.

Tuition and Aid Day student tuition: $600–$3000. Tuition installment plan (six month payment plan, two payment plan). Tuition reduction for siblings, need-based scholarship grants available.

Admissions Math and English placement tests or placement test required. Deadline for receipt of application materials: none. Application fee required: $285. Interview required.

Athletics 2 PE instructors.

Computers Computers are regularly used in accounting, Bible studies, business skills, career technology, college planning, English, foreign language, French, geography, health, history, mathematics, music, science, social sciences, social studies, Spanish classes. Students grades are available online. The school has a published electronic and media policy.

Contact Mrs. Robin Inlow, Continuous Improvement Coordinator. 800-682-7396 Ext. 6253. Fax: 712-472-6830. E-mail: rinlow@aoacademy.com. Website: www.aoacademy.com

ALPINE ACADEMY

Erda, Utah
See Special Needs Schools section.

ALVERNO HEIGHTS ACADEMY

200 North Michillinda Avenue
Sierra Madre, California 91024

Head of School: Ms. Julia V. Fanara

General Information Girls' day college-preparatory, arts, and STEM school, affiliated with Roman Catholic Church; primarily serves individuals with Attention Deficit Disorder. Grades 9–12. Founded: 1960. Setting: suburban. Nearest major city is Los Angeles. 13-acre campus. 8 buildings on campus. Approved or accredited by California Association of Independent Schools, National Catholic Education Association, Western Association of Schools and Colleges, and California Department of Education. Member of National Association of Independent Schools. Total enrollment: 170. Upper school average class size: 15. Upper school faculty-student ratio: 1:12. There are 181 required school days per year for Upper School students. Upper School students typically attend 5 days per week. The average school day consists of 7 hours and 45 minutes.

Upper School Student Profile Grade 9: 33 students (33 girls); Grade 10: 43 students (43 girls); Grade 11: 43 students (43 girls); Grade 12: 55 students (55 girls). 70% of students are Roman Catholic.

Faculty School total: 20. In upper school: 4 men, 16 women; 19 have advanced degrees.

Subjects Offered ACT preparation, acting, advanced biology, advanced chemistry, advanced math, Advanced Placement courses, advanced studio art-AP, aerospace education, algebra, American government, American history, American history-AP, American literature, band, biology, biology-AP, British literature, British literature (honors), calculus, calculus-AP, Catholic belief and practice, ceramics, chemistry, choir, choral music, Christian testament, Christianity, church history, college admission preparation, college awareness, college counseling, college planning, conceptual physics, contemporary issues, creative writing, dance, drama, dramatic arts, driver education, earth science, engineering, English, English language and composition-AP, English language-AP, English literature and composition-AP, English literature-AP, environmental science-AP, European history-AP, finite math, fitness, freshman seminar, geometry, government and politics-AP, graphic design, health, health education, healthful living, history of the Catholic Church, history-AP, honors algebra, honors English, honors geometry, honors U.S. history, honors world history, human geography - AP, improvisation, lab science, language-AP, languages, leadership and service, literature and composition-AP, literature-AP, Mandarin, mathematics-AP, modern European history-AP, multicultural studies, musical theater, photography, pre-calculus, religion, SAT preparation, SAT/ACT preparation, science, science research, senior project, Shakespeare, sign language, social justice, social studies, softball, Spanish language-AP, Spanish-AP, sports conditioning, stagecraft, state government, student government, studio art, studio art-AP, technology/design, theater arts, theater design and production, track and field, trigonometry, U.S. history-AP, United States government-AP, video film production, visual and performing arts, world literature, world religions, writing, yearbook, zoology.

Graduation Requirements ACT preparation, algebra, American government, American history, American literature, ancient world history, art, Bible, biology, British literature, campus ministry, chemistry, civics, electives, English, English literature, ethics, European history, foreign language, geography, geometry, government, health, history, history of the Catholic Church, SAT preparation, Spanish, theology, U.S. government, U.S. history, world history, world religions, completion of 140 service hours.

Special Academic Programs 10 Advanced Placement exams for which test preparation is offered; honors section; accelerated programs; independent study; study at local college for college credit; academic accommodation for the gifted; remedial reading and/or remedial writing; remedial math; programs in English, mathematics, general development for dyslexic students; special instructional classes for blind students; ESL (14 students enrolled).

College Admission Counseling 42 students graduated in 2016; all went to college, including California State University, Fullerton; Chapman University; Mount Saint Mary's University; University of California, Los Angeles.

Student Life Upper grades have uniform requirement, student council, honor system. Discipline rests primarily with faculty. Attendance at religious services is required.

Summer Programs Remediation, enrichment, advancement, sports, art/fine arts, rigorous outdoor training, computer instruction programs offered; session focuses on to empower each young woman to be exactly the person she wants to be; held both on and off campus; accepts girls; open to students from other schools. 100 students usually enrolled. 2017 schedule: June 16 to July 16. Application deadline: June 1.

Tuition and Aid Day student tuition: $17,520. Tuition installment plan (FACTS Tuition Payment Plan, monthly payment plans). Tuition reduction for siblings, merit scholarship grants, need-based scholarship grants, tuition remission for faculty and staff available. In 2016–17, 52% of upper-school students received aid; total upper-school merit-scholarship money awarded: $247,620. Total amount of financial aid awarded in 2016–17: $63,920.

Admissions Traditional secondary-level entrance grade is 9. For fall 2016, 70 students applied for upper-level admission, 60 were accepted, 40 enrolled. High School Placement Test (closed version) from Scholastic Testing Service or ISEE required. Deadline for receipt of application materials: February 3. Application fee required: $100. On-campus interview recommended.

Athletics Interscholastic: aquatics, basketball, cross-country running, soccer, softball, track and field, volleyball; intramural: aerobics/dance, dance, modern dance, self defense, yoga. 1 PE instructor, 9 coaches.

Computers Computers are regularly used in all academic classes. Computer resources include on-campus library services, Internet access, wireless campus network, Internet filtering or blocking technology. Campus intranet and computer access in designated common areas are available to students. Students grades are available online. The school has a published electronic and media policy.

Contact Ms. Sara McCarthy, Director of Admissions and Enrollment Management. 626-355-3463 Ext. 235. Fax: 626-355-3153. E-mail: smccarthy@alvernoheights.org. Website: www.alverno-hs.org/

THE AMERICAN BOYCHOIR SCHOOL

Princeton, New Jersey
See Junior Boarding Schools section.

AMERICAN CHRISTIAN ACADEMY

2300 Veterans Memorial Parkway
Tuscaloosa, Alabama 35404

Head of School: Dr. Dan Carden

General Information Coeducational day college-preparatory and arts school, affiliated with Baptist Church; primarily serves individuals with Attention Deficit Disorder. Grades K–12. Founded: 1979. Setting: small town. 20-acre campus. 6 buildings on campus. Approved or accredited by Association of Christian Schools International and Southern Association of Colleges and Schools. Endowment: $200,000. Total enrollment: 958. Upper school average class size: 20. Upper school faculty-student ratio: 1:12. There are 170 required school days per year for Upper School students. Upper School students typically attend 5 days per week. The average school day consists of 7 hours and 40 minutes.

Upper School Student Profile Grade 6: 83 students (43 boys, 40 girls); Grade 7: 80 students (41 boys, 39 girls); Grade 8: 78 students (36 boys, 42 girls); Grade 9: 77 students (38 boys, 39 girls); Grade 10: 82 students (40 boys, 42 girls); Grade 11: 77 students (41 boys, 36 girls); Grade 12: 77 students (33 boys, 44 girls). 75% of students are Baptist.

Faculty School total: 81. In upper school: 32 men, 48 women; 26 have advanced degrees.

Subjects Offered 3-dimensional art, ACT preparation, advanced chemistry, advanced math, Advanced Placement courses, Alabama history and geography, algebra, American history-AP, anatomy, art, art history-AP, band, baseball, basketball, Bible, Bible studies, biology, bowling, calculus, calculus-AP, cheerleading, chemistry, choir, Christian ethics, college planning, computer science, computers, concert band, driver education, earth science, economics, economics-AP, English, English language-AP, English literature and composition-AP, English-AP, environmental science, family living, fine arts, French, geography, geology, golf, government, gymnastics, health, health education, history, history-AP, human anatomy, integrated physics, life science, marine biology, mathematics, organic chemistry, physical education, physics, reading, religion, research skills, science, self-defense, Southern literature, Spanish, sports, statistics, track and field, travel, typing, U.S. government, U.S. government and politics-AP, U.S. history-AP, volleyball, world history, yearbook.

Graduation Requirements Arts and fine arts (art, music, dance, drama), business skills (includes word processing), computer science, English, foreign language, mathematics, physical education (includes health), religion (includes Bible studies and theology), science, social sciences, social studies (includes history), accelerated reading is required in all grades, religion classes required in all grades. Community service is required.

Special Academic Programs Advanced Placement exam preparation; honors section; accelerated programs; independent study; study at local college for college credit; study abroad; special instructional classes for deaf students.

College Admission Counseling 61 students graduated in 2016; 59 went to college, including Auburn University; Birmingham-Southern College; Samford University; Shelton State Community College; The University of Alabama; University of South Alabama. Other: 1 went to work, 1 entered military service. Median composite ACT: 25. 30% scored over 26 on composite ACT.

Student Life Upper grades have specified standards of dress, student council, honor system. Discipline rests primarily with faculty. Attendance at religious services is required.

Tuition and Aid Day student tuition: $5900. Tuition installment plan (monthly payment plans, individually arranged payment plans). Tuition reduction for siblings, need-based scholarship grants, paying campus jobs available. In 2016–17, 15% of upper-school students received aid. Total amount of financial aid awarded in 2016–17: $95,000.

Admissions Traditional secondary-level entrance grade is 9. For fall 2016, 172 students applied for upper-level admission, 141 were accepted, 130 enrolled. Scholastic Achievement Test or TerraNova required. Deadline for receipt of application materials: none. Application fee required: $200. Interview recommended.

Athletics Interscholastic: baseball (boys), basketball (b,g), bowling (b,g), cheering (g), cross-country running (b,g), dance squad (g), dance team (g), danceline (g), diving (b,g), fishing (b,g), fly fishing (b), football (b), golf (b,g), indoor track (b,g), indoor track & field (b,g), power lifting (b), soccer (b,g), softball (g), strength & conditioning (b,g), swimming and diving (b,g), tennis (b,g), track and field (b,g), volleyball (g), weight lifting (b,g), weight training (b,g), winter (indoor) track (b,g), wrestling (b); intramural: aerobics (g), aerobics/dance (g), basketball (b,g), cheering (g), dance squad (g), dance team (g), danceline (g), fishing (b,g), flag football (b,g), gymnastics (g), in-line skating (b,g), kickball (b,g), outdoor activities (b,g), paint ball (b), physical training (b,g), roller blading (b,g), softball (g), strength & conditioning (b,g), swimming and diving (b,g), touch football (b,g); coed intramural: outdoor activities, physical fitness, running. 3 PE instructors, 40 coaches, 1 athletic trainer.

Computers Computers are regularly used in computer applications, foreign language, mathematics, typing, video film production classes. Computer network features include on-campus library services, Internet access, wireless campus network, Internet filtering or blocking technology. Campus intranet, student e-mail accounts, and computer access in designated common areas are available to students. Students grades are available online. The school has a published electronic and media policy.

Contact Nancy Hastings, Director of Admissions. 205-553-5963 Ext. 12. Fax: 205-553-5942. E-mail: nhastings@acacademy.com. Website: www.acacademy.com

AMERICAN COMMUNITY SCHOOL AT BEIRUT

PO Box 8129
67 Nigeria St. Jel-elBahr
Ras Beirut
Beirut 2035-8003, Lebanon

Head of School: Mr. Greg MacGilpin

General Information Coeducational day college-preparatory school. Founded: 1905. Setting: urban. 4 buildings on campus. Approved or accredited by Middle States Association of Colleges and Schools. Affiliate member of National Association of Independent Schools. Languages of instruction: Arabic, English, and French. Upper school average class size: 20.

Graduation Requirements American history, art, arts and fine arts (art, music, dance, drama), chemistry, computer skills, creative writing, drama, electives, English, foreign language, French, geography, health and wellness, mathematics, music, physical education (includes health), senior thesis, sports, world history, National Official Exams, International Bacc. Community service is required.

Student Life Upper grades have specified standards of dress, student council. Discipline rests equally with students and faculty.

Tuition and Aid Tuition installment plan (The Tuition Plan, monthly payment plans, individually arranged payment plans). Need-based scholarship grants available.

Admissions Admissions testing, English proficiency, ISEE and writing sample required. Application fee required: $100. On-campus interview recommended.

Computers Computer network features include on-campus library services, Internet access, wireless campus network, Internet filtering or blocking technology. Campus intranet and student e-mail accounts are available to students. Students grades are available online. The school has a published electronic and media policy.

Contact Mrs. Najwa Musallam Zabad, Director of Admission. 961-1374370 Ext. 3603. Fax: 961-1366050. Website: www.acs.edu.lb

AMERICAN COOPERATIVE SCHOOL OF TUNIS

c/o US Embassy, Avenue de la Liberte 144
Tunis 1002, Tunisia

General Information Coeducational day general academic, arts, business, and technology school; primarily serves individuals with emotional and behavioral problems and Students who need English Support (EAL or Academic support). Grades PK–12. Distance learning grades 11–12. Setting: urban. Students are housed in NA. 22-hectare campus. 1 building on campus. Approved or accredited by International Baccalaureate Organization and Middle States Association of Colleges and Schools. Member of European Council of International Schools. Language of instruction: English. Upper school average class size: 160. There are 177 required school days per year for Upper School students. Upper School students typically attend 5 days per week. The average school day consists of 8 hours.

Upper School Student Profile Grade 6: 23 students (16 boys, 7 girls); Grade 7: 21 students (11 boys, 10 girls); Grade 8: 33 students (25 boys, 8 girls); Grade 9: 32 students (22 boys, 10 girls); Grade 10: 20 students (10 boys, 10 girls); Grade 11: 27 students (15 boys, 12 girls); Grade 12: 11 students (6 boys, 5 girls).

Faculty School total: 31. In upper school: 11 men, 20 women; 35 have advanced degrees.

Subjects Offered 1 1/2 elective credits, advanced chemistry, advanced computer applications, advanced math, advertising design, algebra, all academic, American history, American literature-AP, American studies, Arabic, art, arts, athletics, band,

biology, chemistry, computers, English, English literature, French, general science, German, mathematics, media arts, model United Nations, music, philosophy, physics, science, visual arts, yearbook.

Special Academic Programs Independent study; study at local college for college credit; remedial math; ESL (17 students enrolled).

College Admission Counseling 13 students graduated in 2016; 12 went to college, including Ottawa University; University of California, Berkeley; York University. Other: 11 entered a postgraduate year. Median SAT critical reading: 532, median SAT math: 479, median SAT writing: 515, median composite ACT: 34. 25% scored over 600 on SAT critical reading, 13% scored over 600 on SAT math, 25% scored over 600 on SAT writing, 100% scored over 26 on composite ACT.

Student Life Upper grades have honor system. Discipline rests primarily with faculty.

Tuition and Aid Day student tuition: $24,470. Tuition installment plan (The Tuition Plan). Tuition discount for 3 years available.

Admissions Traditional secondary-level entrance grade is 9. For fall 2016, 24 students applied for upper-level admission, 22 were accepted, 145 enrolled. Admissions testing, English proficiency, Math Placement Exam or writing sample required. Application fee required: $200.

Athletics Interscholastic: basketball (boys, girls), cooperative games (b,g), football (b,g), gymnastics (b,g), soccer (b,g), swimming and diving (b,g), track and field (b,g); coed interscholastic: table tennis, yoga; coed intramural: dance, horseback riding, paint ball. 3 PE instructors, 6 coaches.

Computers Computers are regularly used in all academic classes. Computer network features include on-campus library services, online commercial services, Internet access, wireless campus network. Campus intranet, student e-mail accounts, and computer access in designated common areas are available to students. Students grades are available online. The school has a published electronic and media policy.

THE AMERICAN EMBASSY SCHOOL

Chandragupta Marg
Chanakyapuri
New Delhi 110 021, India

Head of School: Mr. James Laney

General Information Coeducational day college-preparatory school. Grades PK–PG. Founded: 1952. Setting: urban. Nearest major city is New Delhi, India. 13-acre campus. 8 buildings on campus. Approved or accredited by Middle States Association of Colleges and Schools. Member of Secondary School Admission Test Board. Language of instruction: English. Endowment: $2 million. Total enrollment: 957. Upper school average class size: 15. Upper school faculty-student ratio: 1:7. There are 187 required school days per year for Upper School students. Upper School students typically attend 5 days per week. The average school day consists of 7 hours.

Upper School Student Profile Grade 9: 95 students (47 boys, 48 girls); Grade 10: 100 students (50 boys, 50 girls); Grade 11: 79 students (40 boys, 39 girls); Grade 12: 87 students (44 boys, 43 girls).

Faculty School total: 135. In upper school: 25 men, 27 women; 41 have advanced degrees.

Subjects Offered Algebra, American history, American history-AP, art-AP, arts, biology, biology-AP, calculus, chemistry, choir, computer science, computer science-AP, drawing, earth science, economics-AP, English, English-AP, ESL, fine arts, French, French-AP, geometry, health, history, Indian studies, instrumental music, International Baccalaureate courses, mathematics, mathematics-AP, photography, physical education, physics, physics-AP, publications, science, social sciences, social studies, Spanish, Spanish-AP, statistics, theater arts, theory of knowledge, trigonometry, world affairs, world history.

Graduation Requirements Humanities, social sciences.

Special Academic Programs International Baccalaureate program; Advanced Placement exam preparation; independent study; remedial reading and/or remedial writing; remedial math; programs in general development for dyslexic students; ESL (240 students enrolled).

College Admission Counseling 77 students graduated in 2016; 75 went to college, including Boston University; Duke University; Princeton University; The George Washington University; University of Virginia; Yale University. Other: 2 went to work. Median SAT critical reading: 660, median SAT math: 700, median SAT writing: 670, median combined SAT: 2030, median composite ACT: 28. 65% scored over 1800 on combined SAT, 52% scored over 26 on composite ACT.

Student Life Upper grades have specified standards of dress, student council, honor system. Discipline rests primarily with faculty.

Admissions Traditional secondary-level entrance grade is 9. For fall 2016, 97 students applied for upper-level admission, 50 were accepted, 47 enrolled. Any standardized test required. Deadline for receipt of application materials: none. Application fee required: $500. On-campus interview required.

Athletics Interscholastic: badminton (boys, girls), basketball (b,g), cross-country running (b,g), golf (b,g), outdoor adventure (b,g), soccer (b,g), swimming and diving (b,g), table tennis (b,g), tennis (b,g), track and field (b,g), volleyball (b,g), wrestling (b); intramural: badminton (b,g), basketball (b,g), climbing (b,g), cross-country running (b,g), golf (b,g), physical fitness (b,g), soccer (b,g), swimming and diving (b,g), table tennis (b,g), tennis (b,g), track and field (b,g), volleyball (b,g), wrestling (b); coed interscholastic: outdoor adventure, softball, swimming and diving, table tennis, tennis; coed intramural: soccer, swimming and diving, table tennis, tennis, volleyball, weight lifting. 6 PE instructors.

Computers Computers are regularly used in all classes. Computer network features include on-campus library services, online commercial services, Internet access, wireless campus network, Internet filtering or blocking technology. Campus intranet, student e-mail accounts, and computer access in designated common areas are available to students. Students grades are available online. The school has a published electronic and media policy.

Contact Ms. Patricia Dhar, Director of Admissions. 91-011-2688-8854 Ext. 3156. E-mail: admissions@aes.ac.in. Website: www.aes.ac.in//splash.php

THE AMERICAN INTERNATIONAL SCHOOL

Salmannsdorfer Strasse 47
Vienna A-1190, Austria

Head of School: Dr. Steve Razidlo

General Information Coeducational day college-preparatory, International Baccalaureate, and U.S. high school diploma program school. Ungraded, ages 4–18. Founded: 1959. Setting: suburban. 15-acre campus. 1 building on campus. Approved or accredited by Council of International Schools, European Council of International Schools, International Baccalaureate Organization, and Middle States Association of Colleges and Schools. Affiliate member of National Association of Independent Schools; member of Secondary School Admission Test Board and European Council of International Schools. Language of instruction: English. Total enrollment: 787. Upper school average class size: 18. Upper school faculty-student ratio: 1:7. There are 175 required school days per year for Upper School students. Upper School students typically attend 5 days per week. The average school day consists of 7 hours.

Upper School Student Profile Grade 9: 61 students (35 boys, 26 girls); Grade 10: 72 students (35 boys, 37 girls); Grade 11: 77 students (37 boys, 40 girls); Grade 12: 69 students (37 boys, 32 girls).

Faculty School total: 100. In upper school: 19 men, 18 women; 22 have advanced degrees.

Subjects Offered Basic programming.

Graduation Requirements Art, music.

Special Academic Programs International Baccalaureate program; independent study; remedial reading and/or remedial writing; remedial math; programs in English, mathematics for dyslexic students; special instructional classes for The Learning Support program provides support to students with mild learning difficulties; ESL (106 students enrolled).

College Admission Counseling 61 students graduated in 2016; 58 went to college, including Boston University; Boston University; New York University; Queen's University at Kingston; The University of British Columbia; University of Pennsylvania. Other: 2 entered military service, 1 had other specific plans. Mean SAT critical reading: 539, mean SAT math: 579, mean SAT writing: 547, mean combined SAT: 1665, mean composite ACT: 26.

Student Life Upper grades have specified standards of dress, student council, honor system. Discipline rests primarily with faculty.

Tuition and Aid Day student tuition: €17,048–€19,967. Tuition installment plan (individually arranged payment plans).

Admissions Traditional secondary-level entrance grade is 9. For fall 2016, 64 students applied for upper-level admission, 43 were accepted, 40 enrolled. Admissions testing, math and English placement tests, non-standardized placement tests or writing sample required. Deadline for receipt of application materials: none. Application fee required: €177. On-campus interview required.

Athletics Interscholastic: baseball (boys), basketball (b,g), cross-country running (b,g), soccer (b,g), softball (g), swimming and diving (b,g), tennis (b,g), track and field (b,g), volleyball (b,g); intramural: ballet (g); coed interscholastic: aquatics; coed intramural: aerobics/dance, badminton, basketball, dance, golf, gymnastics, martial arts, soccer, softball. 2 PE instructors, 19 coaches.

Computers Computers are regularly used in all academic classes. Computer network features include on-campus library services, Internet access, wireless campus network, Internet filtering or blocking technology. Campus intranet, student e-mail accounts, and computer access in designated common areas are available to students. Students grades are available online. The school has a published electronic and media policy.

Contact Deidree R. Dio, Director of Admissions / Registrar. 43-1-40132 Ext. 2181. Fax: 43-1-40132-5. E-mail: Admissions@ais.at. Website: www.ais.at

AMERICAN INTERNATIONAL SCHOOL, LUSAKA

PO Box 320176
Lusaka, Zambia

Head of School: Mr. Thomas J. Pado

General Information Coeducational day college-preparatory school. Grades 6–12. Founded: 1986. Setting: suburban. 12-acre campus. 11 buildings on campus. Approved or accredited by Council of International Schools, International Baccalaureate Organization, and Middle States Association of Colleges and Schools. Member of European Council of International Schools. Language of instruction: English. Total

enrollment: 280. Upper school average class size: 20. Upper school faculty-student ratio: 1:7. There are 180 required school days per year for Upper School students. Upper School students typically attend 5 days per week. The average school day consists of 7 hours and 5 minutes.

Upper School Student Profile Grade 6: 43 students (25 boys, 18 girls); Grade 7: 42 students (24 boys, 18 girls); Grade 8: 44 students (20 boys, 24 girls); Grade 9: 43 students (27 boys, 16 girls); Grade 10: 35 students (18 boys, 17 girls); Grade 11: 44 students (27 boys, 17 girls); Grade 12: 29 students (16 boys, 13 girls).

Faculty School total: 40. In upper school: 20 men, 20 women; 13 have advanced degrees.

Subjects Offered International Baccalaureate courses.

Graduation Requirements International Baccalaureate courses.

Special Academic Programs International Baccalaureate program; ESL (16 students enrolled).

College Admission Counseling 37 students graduated in 2015; 35 went to college. Other: 2 had other specific plans. Median SAT critical reading: 530, median SAT math: 520, median SAT writing: 540, median combined SAT: 1610, median composite ACT: 23. 26.7% scored over 600 on SAT critical reading, 26.7% scored over 600 on SAT math, 40% scored over 600 on SAT writing, 33.3% scored over 1800 on combined SAT, 27.8% scored over 26 on composite ACT.

Student Life Upper grades have student council, honor system. Discipline rests primarily with faculty.

Tuition and Aid Day student tuition: $18,150. Need-based scholarship grants available. In 2015–16, 1% of upper-school students received aid.

Admissions Traditional secondary-level entrance grade is 11. Admissions testing or English Composition Test for ESL students required. Deadline for receipt of application materials: none. No application fee required.

Athletics Intramural: badminton (boys, girls), basketball (b,g), cross-country running (b,g), dance (b,g), field hockey (b,g), fitness (b,g), floor hockey (b,g), Frisbee (b,g), indoor soccer (b,g), physical fitness (b,g), rugby (b), soccer (b,g), swimming and diving (b,g), tennis (b,g), triathlon (b,g), ultimate Frisbee (b,g), volleyball (b,g), water polo (b,g), weight training (b,g); coed intramural: badminton, basketball, cross-country running, dance, field hockey, fitness, floor hockey, Frisbee, indoor soccer, physical fitness, soccer, swimming and diving, tennis, triathlon, ultimate Frisbee, volleyball, water polo, weight training. 3 PE instructors, 14 coaches.

Computers Computers are regularly used in all classes. Computer network features include on-campus library services, online commercial services, Internet access, wireless campus network, Internet filtering or blocking technology. Campus intranet and student e-mail accounts are available to students. Students grades are available online. The school has a published electronic and media policy.

AMERICAN INTERNATIONAL SCHOOL ROTTERDAM

Verhulstlann 21
Rotterdam 3055 WJ, Netherlands

Head of School: Mr. Neal Dilk

General Information Coeducational day college-preparatory and IB school. Grades PK–12. Founded: 1959. Setting: suburban. 5-acre campus. 1 building on campus. Approved or accredited by Council of International Schools and New England Association of Schools and Colleges. Member of European Council of International Schools. Language of instruction: English. Total enrollment: 213. Upper school average class size: 18. Upper school faculty-student ratio: 1:6.

Upper School Student Profile Grade 6: 8 students (5 boys, 3 girls); Grade 7: 12 students (5 boys, 7 girls); Grade 8: 12 students (7 boys, 5 girls); Grade 9: 16 students (9 boys, 7 girls); Grade 10: 16 students (8 boys, 8 girls); Grade 11: 16 students (6 boys, 10 girls); Grade 12: 13 students (5 boys, 8 girls).

Faculty School total: 40. In upper school: 10 men, 21 women; 17 have advanced degrees.

Subjects Offered Algebra, American history, American literature, art, biology, British literature, chemistry, computer applications, concert band, current history, digital photography, drama, Dutch, earth science, ecology, environmental systems, English literature, ESL, European history, fine arts, French, geography, geometry, global issues, health, history, instrumental music, integrated physics, International Baccalaureate courses, journalism, library assistant, math applications, photography, physical education, physical science, physics, Spanish, sports, trigonometry, yearbook.

Special Academic Programs International Baccalaureate program; independent study; remedial reading and/or remedial writing; remedial math; programs in English, mathematics, general development for dyslexic students; ESL (32 students enrolled).

College Admission Counseling 10 students graduated in 2016; all went to college, including The University of Montana Western; The University of Texas at Austin; University of Florida; University of North Carolina at Asheville.

Student Life Upper grades have specified standards of dress, student council, honor system. Discipline rests primarily with faculty.

Tuition and Aid Day student tuition: €13,350–€17,250. Tuition installment plan (individually arranged payment plans, On a case by case basis).

Admissions Admissions testing, English entrance exam and mathematics proficiency exam required. Deadline for receipt of application materials: none. Application fee required. On-campus interview required.

Athletics Interscholastic: basketball (boys, girls), soccer (b,g), track and field (b,g), volleyball (b,g); coed interscholastic: softball, swimming and diving, track and field, volleyball. 2 PE instructors, 4 coaches.

Computers Computers are regularly used in all classes. Computer network features include on-campus library services, online commercial services, Internet access, wireless campus network. Campus intranet and student e-mail accounts are available to students. Students grades are available online. The school has a published electronic and media policy.

Contact Mrs. Aurora Anne George-Kelso, Admissions Officer. 31-(10) 422-5351. Fax: 31-(10)422-4075. E-mail: aurora.george-kelso@aisr.nl. Website: www.aisr.nl

THE AMERICAN SCHOOL FOUNDATION

Bondojito 215
Colonia Las Americas
Mexico City, D.F. 01120, Mexico

Head of School: Mr. Paul Williams

General Information Coeducational day college-preparatory, Mexican Program Curriculum, and U.S. program curriculum school. Grades PK–12. Founded: 1888. Setting: urban. Nearest major city is Mexico City, Mexico. 17-acre campus. 4 buildings on campus. Approved or accredited by Southern Association of Colleges and Schools and Southern Association of Independent Schools. Affiliate member of National Association of Independent Schools; member of Secondary School Admission Test Board. Languages of instruction: English and Spanish. Endowment: 191.1 million Mexican pesos. Total enrollment: 2,530. Upper school average class size: 18. Upper school faculty-student ratio: 1:11. There are 180 required school days per year for Upper School students. Upper School students typically attend 5 days per week. The average school day consists of 6 hours and 45 minutes.

Upper School Student Profile Grade 9: 177 students (80 boys, 97 girls); Grade 10: 197 students (94 boys, 103 girls); Grade 11: 180 students (80 boys, 100 girls); Grade 12: 167 students (83 boys, 84 girls).

Faculty School total: 76. In upper school: 40 men, 36 women; 48 have advanced degrees.

Subjects Offered Advanced Placement courses, algebra, American history, American literature, American studies, anatomy, art, art history, biology, calculus, ceramics, chemistry, computer programming, computer science, drafting, drama, earth science, ecology, economics, English, English literature, European history, expository writing, film, fine arts, French, geography, geometry, government/civics, grammar, health, history, humanities, journalism, mathematics, Mexican history, music, philosophy, photography, physical education, physics, physiology, psychology, science, social sciences, social studies, Spanish, speech, statistics, trigonometry, world history, world literature, writing.

Graduation Requirements Art, English, foreign language, health, humanities, mathematics, physical education (includes health), science, social studies (includes history), technology, International Baccalaureate Personal Project (grade 10), Week Without Walls (grade 9).

Special Academic Programs International Baccalaureate program, 13 Advanced Placement exams for which test preparation is offered; independent study; study abroad; remedial reading and/or remedial writing; programs in English, mathematics, general development for dyslexic students, special instructional classes for deaf students, blind students, learning disabilities (LD), Attention Deficit Hyperactivity Disorder (ADHD), and speech and language disorders.

College Admission Counseling 193 students graduated in 2016; 163 went to college, including Brown University; Emory University; New York University; Northeastern University; Parsons School of Design; University of Southern California. Other: 30 had other specific plans. Mean SAT critical reading: 576, mean SAT math: 588, mean SAT writing: 572, mean combined SAT: 1736, mean composite ACT: 28. 38% scored over 600 on SAT critical reading, 46% scored over 600 on SAT math, 37% scored over 600 on SAT writing, 72.4% scored over 1800 on combined SAT, 54.7% scored over 26 on composite ACT.

Student Life Upper grades have specified standards of dress, student council. Discipline rests primarily with faculty.

Tuition and Aid Day student tuition: 195,200 Mexican pesos. Tuition installment plan (monthly payment plans, tuition insurance). Need-based scholarship grants available. In 2016–17, 17% of upper-school students received aid. Total amount of financial aid awarded in 2016–17: 14,667,170 Mexican pesos.

Admissions Traditional secondary-level entrance grade is 10. For fall 2016, 236 students applied for upper-level admission, 109 were accepted, 104 enrolled. Essay required. Deadline for receipt of application materials: January 9. No application fee required. On-campus interview recommended.

Athletics Interscholastic: aquatics (boys, girls), artistic gym (b,g), basketball (b,g), flag football (b), football (b), gymnastics (b,g), soccer (b,g), swimming and diving (b,g), tennis (b,g), track and field (b,g), volleyball (g); intramural: aquatics (b,g), artistic gym (b,g), flag football (b), football (g), gymnastics (b,g), strength & conditioning (b,g); coed interscholastic: cross-country running, running, tennis, track and field; coed intramural: basketball, cross-country running, dance, fitness, life saving, running, strength & conditioning. 2 PE instructors, 42 coaches, 1 athletic trainer.

Computers Computers are regularly used in all classes. Computer network features include on-campus library services, online commercial services, Internet access, wireless campus network, Internet filtering or blocking technology. Campus intranet, student e-mail accounts, and computer access in designated common areas are available to students. Students grades are available online. The school has a published electronic and media policy.

Contact Patricia Hubp, Director of Admission. 52-555-227-4900. Fax: 52-55273-4357. E-mail: martindehubp@asf.edu.mx. Website: www.asf.edu.mx

THE AMERICAN SCHOOL IN JAPAN

1-1, Nomizu 1-chome
Chofu-shi
Tokyo 182-0031, Japan

Head of School: Areta Williams

General Information Coeducational day college preparatory school. Grades N–12. Founded: 1902. Setting: suburban. 14-acre campus. 5 buildings on campus. Approved or accredited by US Department of State and Western Association of Schools and Colleges. Affiliate member of National Association of Independent Schools. Language of instruction: English. Endowment: $29 million. Total enrollment: 1,620. Upper school average class size: 18. Upper school faculty-student ratio: 1:10. There are 176 required school days per year for Upper School students. Upper School students typically attend 5 days per week. The average school day consists of 6 hours and 30 minutes.

Upper School Student Profile Grade 6: 120 students (61 boys, 59 girls); Grade 7: 131 students (65 boys, 66 girls); Grade 8: 140 students (72 boys, 68 girls); Grade 9: 133 students (57 boys, 76 girls); Grade 10: 155 students (74 boys, 81 girls); Grade 11: 134 students (63 boys, 71 girls); Grade 12: 146 students (72 boys, 74 girls).

Faculty School total: 192. In upper school: 60 men, 51 women; 75 have advanced degrees.

Subjects Offered Algebra, American history, American literature, applied music, art, art-AP, arts and crafts, biology, biology-AP, calculus-AP, ceramics, chemistry, chemistry-AP, choir, computer graphics, computer programming, computer science-AP, conceptual physics, concert band, creative writing, digital photography, drama, economics, economics-AP, English, English literature, environmental science-AP, European history-AP, expository writing, geometry, health, honors English, independent living, Japanese, Japanese as Second Language, Japanese history, Japanese literature, Japanese studies, jazz band, jewelry making, journalism, Mandarin, marine biology, mathematics, metalworking, music composition, mythology, news writing, orchestra, personal fitness, photography, physical education, physics, physics-AP, poetry, pre-calculus, probability and statistics, psychology, Spanish, Spanish language-AP, speech, stagecraft, stained glass, statistics-AP, strings, symphonic band, theater arts, trigonometry, U.S. history-AP, video film production, vocal jazz, weightlifting, world history, world literature, writing.

Graduation Requirements American history, arts and fine arts (art, music, dance, drama), computer applications, English, foreign language, health, Japanese studies, mathematics, physical education (includes health), science, social studies (includes history), one semester of Japanese studies.

Special Academic Programs 15 Advanced Placement exams for which test preparation is offered; honors section; independent study.

College Admission Counseling 150 students graduated in 2016; 146 went to college, including Northeastern University; The University of British Columbia; University of Colorado Boulder; University of Michigan; University of Washington. Other: 1 went to work, 1 entered military service, 2 had other specific plans. Mean SAT critical reading: 596, mean SAT math: 639, mean SAT writing: 592, mean composite ACT: 26. 51% scored over 600 on SAT critical reading, 69% scored over 600 on SAT math, 51% scored over 600 on SAT writing.

Student Life Upper grades have specified standards of dress, student council. Discipline rests primarily with faculty.

Summer Programs Enrichment, art/fine arts, computer instruction programs offered; session focuses on enrichment; held on campus; accepts boys and girls; open to students from other schools. 75 students usually enrolled. 2017 schedule: June 12 to June 30. Application deadline: April 1.

Tuition and Aid Day student tuition: ¥2,451,000. Tuition installment plan (individually arranged payment plans). Need-based scholarship grants available. In 2016–17, 3% of upper-school students received aid.

Admissions Traditional secondary-level entrance grade is 9. Any standardized test required. Deadline for receipt of application materials: none. Application fee required: ¥20,000. Interview required.

Athletics Interscholastic: baseball (boys), basketball (b,g), cross-country running (b,g), field hockey (g), football (b), soccer (b,g), softball (g), swimming and diving (b,g), tennis (b,g), track and field (b,g), volleyball (g), wrestling (b); coed interscholastic: cheering; coed intramural: aerobics/dance, badminton, dance, golf, judo, martial arts, modern dance, strength & conditioning, weight lifting, weight training. 6 PE instructors, 2 coaches, 1 athletic trainer.

Computers Computers are regularly used in all academic classes. Computer network features include on-campus library services, online commercial services, Internet access, wireless campus network, Blackboard, Destiny. Campus intranet and student e-mail accounts are available to students. Students grades are available online. The school has a published electronic and media policy.

Contact Mary Margaret Mallat, Director of Admissions. 81-422-34-5300 Ext. 720. Fax: 81-422-34-5339. E-mail: enroll@asij.ac.jp. Website: http://www.asij.ac.jp/

THE AMERICAN SCHOOL OF MADRID

Apartado 80
Madrid 28080, Spain

Head of School: Mr. Benjamin Weinberg

General Information Coeducational day college-preparatory, arts, and business school. Grades PK–12. Founded: 1961. Setting: suburban. 4-hectare campus. 4 buildings on campus. Approved or accredited by International Baccalaureate Organization and Middle States Association of Colleges and Schools. Affiliate member of National Association of Independent Schools; member of European Council of International Schools. Language of instruction: English. Total enrollment: 884. Upper school average class size: 25. Upper school faculty-student ratio: 1:10. There are 175 required school days per year for Upper School students. Upper School students typically attend 5 days per week. The average school day consists of 6 hours and 45 minutes.

Faculty School total: 110. In upper school: 12 men, 19 women; 22 have advanced degrees.

Subjects Offered Economics, Mandarin, music performance, participation in sports, performing arts, statistics-AP, theater, theater production, trigonometry, United Nations and international issues, video and animation, voice, weight fitness, writing, yoga.

Graduation Requirements Art, information technology, technology, International Baccalaureate Diploma requirements.

Special Academic Programs International Baccalaureate program; independent study; remedial reading and/or remedial writing; remedial math; ESL.

College Admission Counseling 74 students graduated in 2016; 73 went to college, including Georgetown University; Northeastern University; Suffolk University; The University of British Columbia; University of Florida. Other: 1 had other specific plans. Mean SAT critical reading: 551, mean SAT math: 566, mean SAT writing: 558.

Student Life Upper grades have student council, honor system. Discipline rests equally with students and faculty.

Summer Programs ESL, sports, art/fine arts, computer instruction programs offered; session focuses on ESL, Soccer; held on campus; accepts boys and girls; open to students from other schools. 250 students usually enrolled. 2017 schedule: July 1 to July 31. Application deadline: June 1.

Tuition and Aid Day student tuition: €15,618–€23,618. Tuition installment plan (monthly payment plans, individually arranged payment plans, semester payment plan). Tuition reduction for siblings, need-based scholarship grants, scholarships for children of employees available. In 2016–17, 5% of upper-school students received aid.

Admissions Traditional secondary-level entrance grade is 9. For fall 2016, 83 students applied for upper-level admission, 50 were accepted, 50 enrolled. Achievement/Aptitude/Writing, Comprehensive Test of Basic Skills, ERB, independent norms, Iowa Tests of Basic Skills, PSAT or TAP required. Deadline for receipt of application materials: none. Application fee required: €150. On-campus interview recommended.

Athletics Interscholastic: basketball (boys, girls), soccer (b,g), volleyball (b,g); intramural: baseball (b); coed interscholastic: golf, gymnastics, martial arts, tennis, yoga; coed intramural: weight lifting. 2 PE instructors, 10 coaches.

Computers Computers are regularly used in all academic classes. Computer network features include on-campus library services, online commercial services, Internet access, wireless campus network, Internet filtering or blocking technology. Campus intranet, student e-mail accounts, and computer access in designated common areas are available to students. Students grades are available online. The school has a published electronic and media policy.

Contact Ms. Veronica Tudsbery, Admissions Assistant. 34-91 740 1904. Fax: 34-91 357 2678. E-mail: admissions@asmadrid.org. Website: www.asmadrid.org

THE AMERICAN SCHOOL OF PUERTO VALLARTA

Albatros # 129
Marina Vallarta
Puerto Vallarta, Jalisco 48335, Mexico

Head of School: Mrs. Lisa Langley

General Information Coeducational day college-preparatory school. Grades N–12. Founded: 1986. Setting: small town. 7-acre campus. 4 buildings on campus. Approved or accredited by Council of Accreditation and School Improvement, Southern Association of Colleges and Schools, Southern Association of Independent Schools, The College Board, US Department of State, and state department of education. Affiliate member of National Association of Independent Schools. Languages of instruction: English and Spanish. Endowment: 2 million Mexican pesos. Total enrollment: 343. Upper school average class size: 25. Upper school faculty-student ratio: 1:7. There are 150 required school days per year for Upper School students. Upper School students typically attend 5 days per week. The average school day consists of 6 hours and 40 minutes.

Upper School Student Profile Grade 7: 26 students (16 boys, 10 girls); Grade 8: 27 students (10 boys, 17 girls); Grade 9: 23 students (10 boys, 13 girls); Grade 10: 24 students (13 boys, 11 girls); Grade 11: 23 students (12 boys, 11 girls); Grade 12: 27 students (11 boys, 16 girls).

Faculty School total: 38. In upper school: 9 men, 9 women; 7 have advanced degrees.

Subjects Offered Advanced Placement courses, advanced studio art-AP, algebra, American literature, anatomy, art, biology, British literature, business mathematics, calculus, chemistry, chorus, civics, comparative government and politics-AP, computer science, computers, conceptual physics, earth science, economics-AP, English, English literature, English literature and composition-AP, etymology, geography, journalism, law, life science, literature, literature and composition-AP, mathematics, Mexican history, Mexican literature, philosophy, physical science, physics, pre-algebra, pre-calculus, robotics, Spanish, Spanish language-AP, Spanish literature, Spanish literature-AP, statistics-AP, studio art-AP, trigonometry, U.S. history, U.S. history-AP, world history.

Graduation Requirements American literature, art, art education, biology, British literature, calculus, chemistry, computer education, conceptual physics, economics, English literature, mathematics, Mexican history, Mexican literature, physical education (includes health), pre-calculus, Spanish, Spanish literature, U.S. history.

Special Academic Programs Advanced Placement exam preparation; honors section; independent study; remedial reading and/or remedial writing; remedial math.

College Admission Counseling 20 students graduated in 2016; all went to college, including Antelope Valley College; Boise State University; Simon Fraser University; The University of British Columbia; University of California, Santa Cruz; University of Victoria.

Student Life Upper grades have uniform requirement, student council, honor system. Discipline rests primarily with faculty.

Summer Programs Remediation programs offered; session focuses on remediation and make-up; held on campus; accepts boys and girls; open to students from other schools. 5 students usually enrolled. 2017 schedule: July 10 to August 11. Application deadline: June 19.

Tuition and Aid Day student tuition: $5850–$6470. Tuition installment plan (monthly payment plans, individually arranged payment plans). Tuition reduction for siblings available. In 2016–17, 10% of upper-school students received aid.

Admissions Traditional secondary-level entrance grade is 10. For fall 2016, 30 students applied for upper-level admission, 18 were accepted, 12 enrolled. Achievement tests, admissions testing, English language, math and English placement tests, Math Placement Exam and math, reading, and mental ability tests required. Deadline for receipt of application materials: none. No application fee required. On-campus interview recommended.

Athletics Interscholastic: archery (boys, girls), ballet (g), basketball (b,g), cheering (g), dance (g), flagball (b), golf (b,g), sailing (g), soccer (b,g), tennis (b,g), track and field (b,g), volleyball (b,g); intramural: baseball (b), basketball (b,g), cheering (g), dance (g), jump rope (g), soccer (b,g), swimming and diving (b,g), tennis (b,g), track and field (b,g). 3 PE instructors, 4 coaches, 3 athletic trainers.

Computers Computers are regularly used in computer applications, history, keyboarding, lab/keyboard, music, science, social studies, Spanish, technology, yearbook classes. Computer network features include on-campus library services, Internet access, wireless campus network, Internet filtering or blocking technology. Campus intranet, student e-mail accounts, and computer access in designated common areas are available to students. Students grades are available online. The school has a published electronic and media policy.

Contact Mrs. Amanda Gonzalez, Director of Admissions and Communications. 322-226 7672. Fax: 322-221 2555. E-mail: agonzalez@aspv.edu.mx. Website: www.aspv.edu.mx

AMERICAN SCHOOL OF THE HAGUE

Rijksstraatweg 200
Wassenaar 2241 BX, Netherlands

Head of School: Richard Spradling

General Information Coeducational day college-preparatory and applied and performing arts school. Grades PS–12. Founded: 1953. Setting: suburban. Nearest major city is The Hague, Netherlands. 11-acre campus. 1 building on campus. Approved or accredited by Council of International Schools, International Baccalaureate Organization, Middle States Association of Colleges and Schools, The College Board, and US Department of State. Member of European Council of International Schools. Language of instruction: English. Total enrollment: 1,035. Upper school average class size: 18. Upper school faculty-student ratio: 1:7. There are 183 required school days per year for Upper School students. Upper School students typically attend 5 days per week. The average school day consists of 6 hours.

Upper School Student Profile Grade 9: 77 students (35 boys, 42 girls); Grade 10: 86 students (48 boys, 38 girls); Grade 11: 104 students (51 boys, 53 girls); Grade 12: 96 students (58 boys, 38 girls).

Faculty School total: 157. In upper school: 24 men, 29 women; 42 have advanced degrees.

Subjects Offered Advanced chemistry, advertising design, algebra, American literature, art history, art-AP, band, biology, biology-AP, calculus, calculus-AP, chemistry, chemistry-AP, choir, comparative government and politics, computer applications, computer multimedia, computer music, computer science, computer-aided design, creative writing, current events, dance, debate, dramatic arts, Dutch, economics, economics-AP, English, English literature, English-AP, environmental systems, ESL, European history, French, French-AP, geometry, German, German-AP, global studies, guidance, health and wellness, honors algebra, honors geometry, human geography - AP, information technology, instrumental music, international affairs, International Baccalaureate courses, jazz band, math analysis, math methods, mathematics-AP, multimedia, music composition, music technology, music theory-AP, music-AP, orchestra, peer counseling, photography, physical education, physics, physics-AP, pre-calculus, programming, psychology, public speaking, senior composition, sociology, Spanish, Spanish-AP, speech and debate, stagecraft, student publications, studio art, theater arts, theater design and production, theory of knowledge, trigonometry, U.S. history, U.S. history-AP, video film production, Web site design, Western civilization, world history, writing, yearbook.

Graduation Requirements Arts, computer information systems, electives, English, health and wellness, human issues, lab science, mathematics, modern languages, physical education (includes health), science, service learning/internship, social studies (includes history), technology.

Special Academic Programs International Baccalaureate program; Advanced Placement exam preparation; honors section; independent study; academic accommodation for the gifted, the musically talented, and the artistically talented; remedial reading and/or remedial writing; remedial math; programs in English, mathematics, general development for dyslexic students; ESL (100 students enrolled).

College Admission Counseling 89 students graduated in 2016; 87 went to college, including Massachusetts Institute of Technology; Parsons School of Design; Queen's University at Kingston; United States Air Force Academy; Vassar College; Virginia Polytechnic Institute and State University. Other: 1 entered military service, 1 had other specific plans. Mean SAT critical reading: 570, mean SAT math: 597, mean SAT writing: 560, mean combined SAT: 1727.

Student Life Upper grades have specified standards of dress, student council, honor system. Discipline rests primarily with faculty.

Tuition and Aid Day student tuition: €13,470–€21,050. Tuition installment plan (individually arranged payment plans).

Admissions For fall 2016, 84 students applied for upper-level admission, 78 were accepted, 65 enrolled. Any standardized test required. Deadline for receipt of application materials: none. No application fee required.

Athletics Interscholastic: baseball (boys), basketball (b,g), cross-country running (b,g), soccer (b,g), softball (g), swimming and diving (b,g), tennis (b,g), track and field (b,g), volleyball (b,g); intramural: baseball (b), basketball (b,g), cheering (g), cross-country running (b,g), dance team (g), soccer (b,g), softball (g), volleyball (b,g); coed intramural: cheering. 2 PE instructors, 9 coaches.

Computers Computers are regularly used in all academic classes. Computer network features include on-campus library services, online commercial services, Internet access, wireless campus network, Internet filtering or blocking technology. Campus intranet, student e-mail accounts, and computer access in designated common areas are available to students. Students grades are available online. The school has a published electronic and media policy.

Contact Admissions Office. 31-70-512-1080. Fax: 31-70-512-1076. E-mail: admissions@ash.nl. Website: www.ash.nl

ANDREWS OSBORNE ACADEMY

38588 Mentor Avenue
Willoughby, Ohio 44094

Head of School: Dr. Larry Goodman

General Information Coeducational boarding and day college-preparatory and arts school. Boarding grades 7–12, day grades PK–12. Founded: 1910. Setting: suburban. Nearest major city is Cleveland. Students are housed in coed dormitories. 300-acre campus. 12 buildings on campus. Approved or accredited by Midwest Association of Boarding Schools, Ohio Association of Independent Schools, The Association of Boarding Schools, and Ohio Department of Education. Member of National Association of Independent Schools and Secondary School Admission Test Board. Endowment: $12 million. Total enrollment: 347. Upper school average class size: 10. Upper school faculty-student ratio: 1:6. The average school day consists of 8 hours.

Upper School Student Profile Grade 9: 19 students (19 girls); Grade 10: 15 students (15 girls); Grade 11: 31 students (31 girls); Grade 12: 24 students (24 girls). 17 states are represented in upper school student body.

Faculty School total: 25. In upper school: 7 men, 18 women; 18 have advanced degrees; 10 reside on campus.

Subjects Offered Algebra, American government, American literature, art, astronomy, biology, biology-AP, calculus, calculus-AP, ceramics, chemistry, chemistry-AP, choir, choral music, community service, CPR, drama, economics, English, English composition, English language-AP, English literature, English literature and composition-AP, environmental science, equine science, ESL, ethics, film history, fine arts, first aid, French, French language-AP, geometry with art applications, government, grammar, health science, history, honors algebra, honors English, honors geometry, independent study, instrumental music, Mandarin, mathematics, music, painting, physical education, physics, portfolio art, pre-calculus, probability and statistics, science, social studies, Spanish, Spanish language-AP, speech, studio art, textiles,

theater, TOEFL preparation, U.S. history, U.S. history-AP, women in literature, world history.

Graduation Requirements Algebra, arts and fine arts (art, music, dance, drama), biology, computer literacy, CPR, English, foreign language, geometry, mathematics, physical education (includes health), science, social studies (includes history), speech, acceptance into at least one U.S. college or university. Community service is required.

Special Academic Programs Advanced Placement exam preparation; honors section; independent study; study at local college for college credit; domestic exchange program; academic accommodation for the gifted, the musically talented, and the artistically talented; ESL (35 students enrolled).

College Admission Counseling 50 students graduated in 2016; all went to college, including Baldwin Wallace University; Cleveland State University; Kent State University; Miami University; Penn State University Park; University of Illinois at Urbana–Champaign. Mean SAT critical reading: 541, mean SAT math: 627, mean SAT writing: 563, mean combined SAT: 1732, mean composite ACT: 24.

Student Life Upper grades have uniform requirement, student council, honor system. Discipline rests primarily with faculty.

Summer Programs ESL, sports programs offered; session focuses on sports/science/ESL; held on campus; accepts boys and girls; open to students from other schools. 30 students usually enrolled. 2017 schedule: June 15.

Tuition and Aid Day student tuition: $16,050; 5-day tuition and room/board: $23,100; 7-day tuition and room/board: $28,350. Tuition installment plan (monthly payment plans, individually arranged payment plans). Merit scholarship grants, need-based scholarship grants available. In 2016–17, 50% of upper-school students received aid; total upper-school merit-scholarship money awarded: $87,190. Total amount of financial aid awarded in 2016–17: $401,000.

Admissions Traditional secondary-level entrance grade is 9. ISEE, SSAT, TOEFL or SLEP or writing sample required. Deadline for receipt of application materials: none. Application fee required: $50. Interview required.

Athletics Interscholastic: baseball (boys), basketball (b), flag football, lacrosse (b), soccer (b), softball, tennis (b), volleyball; intramural: flag football, table tennis; coed interscholastic: alpine skiing, aquatics, ballet, cross-country running, equestrian sports, horseback riding; coed intramural: alpine skiing, equestrian sports, horseback riding, skiing (downhill), snowboarding. 2 PE instructors, 20 coaches, 1 athletic trainer.

Computers Computers are regularly used in art, English, foreign language, history, mathematics, music, science classes. Computer network features include on-campus library services, online commercial services, Internet access, wireless campus network, Internet filtering or blocking technology. Student e-mail accounts and computer access in designated common areas are available to students. Students grades are available online. The school has a published electronic and media policy.

Contact Mrs. Rachelle Sundberg, Director of Admissions. 440-942-3600 Ext. 114. Fax: 440-942-3660. E-mail: rsundberg@andrewsosborne.org. Website: http://www.AndrewsOsborne.org

AQUINAS HIGH SCHOOL

1920 Highland Avenue
Augusta, Georgia 30904-5303

Head of School: Mrs. Maureen G. Lewis

General Information Coeducational day college-preparatory school, affiliated with Roman Catholic Church. Grades 9–12. Founded: 1957. Setting: urban. Nearest major city is Atlanta. 25-acre campus. 4 buildings on campus. Approved or accredited by Southern Association of Colleges and Schools. Total enrollment: 244. Upper school average class size: 20. Upper school faculty-student ratio: 1:10. There are 180 required school days per year for Upper School students. Upper School students typically attend 5 days per week. The average school day consists of 6 hours and 40 minutes.

Upper School Student Profile Grade 9: 66 students (33 boys, 33 girls); Grade 10: 64 students (38 boys, 26 girls); Grade 11: 58 students (27 boys, 31 girls); Grade 12: 56 students (22 boys, 34 girls). 77% of students are Roman Catholic.

Faculty School total: 25. In upper school: 14 men, 11 women; 9 have advanced degrees.

Subjects Offered 3-dimensional art, advanced biology, advanced chemistry, Advanced Placement courses, advanced studio art-AP, algebra, American history, American literature, anatomy and physiology, art, Bible studies, biology, biology-AP, British literature, British literature (honors), broadcasting, calculus, calculus-AP, campus ministry, Catholic belief and practice, chemistry, chemistry-AP, choir, computer applications, computer programming, computer science, computer technologies, creative writing, digital art, digital photography, drama, economics, economics and history, economics-AP, English, English language and composition-AP, English literature, English literature and composition-AP, environmental science, ethics, European history, expository writing, foreign language, French, French language-AP, geography, geometry, government, government and politics-AP, government/civics, health, health education, history, honors algebra, honors English, honors geometry, honors U.S. history, honors world history, horticulture, human anatomy, human geography - AP, instruments, language, language and composition, Latin, literature and composition-AP, macroeconomics-AP, mathematics, moral theology, music, music theory, performing arts, philosophy, photography, physical education, physics, physics-AP, play production, prayer/spirituality, religion, religion and culture, religious education, science, social studies, software design, Spanish, Spanish language-AP, speech, statistics-AP, theater, theology, trigonometry, U.S. government and politics, U.S. government and politics-AP, weightlifting, wilderness education, wilderness experience, world geography, world history, world history-AP, world literature, writing, yearbook, yoga, zoology.

Graduation Requirements 20th century American writers, arts and fine arts (art, music, dance, drama), computer science, English, foreign language, mathematics, physical education (includes health), religion (includes Bible studies and theology), science, social studies (includes history). Community service is required.

Special Academic Programs 12 Advanced Placement exams for which test preparation is offered; honors section; independent study; study abroad; special instructional classes for students with learning disabilities, Attention Deficit Disorder, and dyslexia.

College Admission Counseling 60 students graduated in 2015; 57 went to college, including Augusta State University; Georgia Southern University; Kennesaw State University; University of Georgia; University of South Carolina; Valdosta State University. Other: 2 went to work, 1 entered military service.

Student Life Upper grades have uniform requirement, student council. Discipline rests equally with students and faculty. Attendance at religious services is required.

Tuition and Aid Day student tuition: $11,220. Tuition installment plan (FACTS Tuition Payment Plan). Tuition reduction for siblings, merit scholarship grants, need-based scholarship grants, paying campus jobs available. In 2015–16, 28% of upper-school students received aid. Total amount of financial aid awarded in 2015–16: $257,379.

Admissions Traditional secondary-level entrance grade is 9. For fall 2015, 69 students applied for upper-level admission, 66 were accepted, 66 enrolled. High School Placement Test (closed version) from Scholastic Testing Service required. Deadline for receipt of application materials: none. No application fee required. On-campus interview recommended.

Athletics Interscholastic: baseball (boys), basketball (b,g), cheering (g), football (b), golf (b,g), soccer (b,g), softball (g), tennis (b,g), track and field (b,g), volleyball (g), weight training (b,g); coed interscholastic: cross-country running, diving, outdoor education, riflery, swimming and diving, yoga. 2 PE instructors, 20 coaches, 1 athletic trainer.

Computers Computers are regularly used in all academic classes. Computer resources include on-campus library services, Internet access, wireless campus network, Internet filtering or blocking technology. Student e-mail accounts are available to students. Students grades are available online. The school has a published electronic and media policy.

Contact Mrs. Shannon Williams, Assistant Principal. 706-736-5516. Fax: 706-736-2678. E-mail: swilliams@aquinashigh.org. Website: www.aquinashigh.org

ARCHBISHOP ALTER HIGH SCHOOL

940 East David Road
Kettering, Ohio 45429-5512

Head of School: Mrs. Lourdes Lambert

General Information Coeducational day college-preparatory, general academic, arts, and religious studies school, affiliated with Roman Catholic Church; primarily serves students with learning disabilities, individuals with Attention Deficit Disorder, and dyslexic students. Grades 9–12. Founded: 1962. Setting: suburban. Nearest major city is Dayton. 3 buildings on campus. Approved or accredited by National Catholic Education Association, Ohio Catholic Schools Accreditation Association (OCSAA), and Ohio Department of Education. Total enrollment: 673. Upper school average class size: 22. Upper school faculty-student ratio: 1:12. There are 185 required school days per year for Upper School students. The average school day consists of 7 hours and 5 minutes.

Upper School Student Profile Grade 9: 164 students (81 boys, 83 girls); Grade 10: 153 students (75 boys, 78 girls); Grade 11: 132 students (63 boys, 69 girls); Grade 12: 163 students (71 boys, 92 girls). 87% of students are Roman Catholic.

Faculty School total: 57. In upper school: 22 men, 33 women; 37 have advanced degrees.

Subjects Offered Accounting, advanced chemistry, advanced math, Advanced Placement courses, algebra, American Civil War, American government, American history, American history-AP, American literature, American literature-AP, analysis and differential calculus, analytic geometry, anatomy and physiology, band, Basic programming, biology-AP, British literature, business, business law, calculus, calculus-AP, Catholic belief and practice, chemistry, chemistry-AP, choir, choral music, Christian and Hebrew scripture, church history, Civil War, civil war history, costumes and make-up, ecology, environmental systems, economics, English, English literature, French, health, history, history of the Catholic Church, honors algebra, honors English, honors geometry, honors U.S. history, integrated mathematics, introduction to theater, keyboarding, Latin, marching band, mechanical drawing, music appreciation, personal finance, physical fitness, physics, physics-AP, pre-calculus, public speaking, reading/study skills, Spanish, speech, theater arts, U.S. government and politics-AP, U.S. history, U.S. history-AP.

Graduation Requirements Arts and fine arts (art, music, dance, drama), English, health, keyboarding, mathematics, physical education (includes health), science, social studies (includes history), speech, theology, word processing, additional requirements for students enrolled in the Alter Scholars Program or Conservatory for the Arts.

Special Academic Programs Advanced Placement exam preparation; honors section; study at local college for college credit.

College Admission Counseling 163 students graduated in 2016; 162 went to college, including Miami University; Ohio University; The Ohio State University; University of Cincinnati; University of Dayton; Wright State University. Other: 1 entered military service. Mean SAT critical reading: 596, mean SAT math: 599, mean SAT writing: 585, mean combined SAT: 1782, mean composite ACT: 26.

Student Life Upper grades have uniform requirement, student council, honor system. Discipline rests equally with students and faculty. Attendance at religious services is required.

Tuition and Aid Day student tuition: $9500–$10,200. Tuition installment plan (FACTS Tuition Payment Plan). Tuition reduction for siblings, merit scholarship grants, need-based scholarship grants available. Total upper-school merit-scholarship money awarded for 2016–17: $32,000. Total amount of financial aid awarded in 2016–17: $200,000.

Admissions Traditional secondary-level entrance grade is 9. For fall 2016, 181 students applied for upper-level admission, 180 were accepted, 164 enrolled. Scholastic Testing Service High School Placement Test (open version), STS or STS, Diocese Test required. Deadline for receipt of application materials: December 1. Application fee required: $100.

Athletics Interscholastic: baseball (boys), basketball (b,g), bowling (b,g), cheering (g), cross-country running (b,g), dance team (g), diving (b,g), football (b), golf (b,g), gymnastics (g), ice hockey (b,g), lacrosse (b), soccer (b,g), softball (g), strength & conditioning (b,g), swimming and diving (b,g), tennis (b,g), track and field (b,g), volleyball (b,g), wrestling (b). 1 PE instructor, 3 coaches, 1 athletic trainer.

Computers Computers are regularly used in all classes. Computer network features include on-campus library services, online commercial services, Internet access, wireless campus network, Internet filtering or blocking technology, 1:1 laptop program. Campus intranet, student e-mail accounts, and computer access in designated common areas are available to students. Students grades are available online. The school has a published electronic and media policy.

Contact Mrs. Mary Ruth Shearer, Director of Enrollment Management. 937-428-5394. Fax: 937-434-0507. E-mail: maryruth.shearer@alterhs.org. Website: www.alterhighschool.org

ARCHBISHOP CURLEY HIGH SCHOOL

3701 Sinclair Lane
Baltimore, Maryland 21213

Head of School: Fr. Donald Grzymski

General Information Boys' day college-preparatory school, affiliated with Roman Catholic Church. Grades 9–12. Founded: 1961. Setting: urban. 33-acre campus. 3 buildings on campus. Approved or accredited by Southern Association of Independent Schools and Maryland Department of Education. Endowment: $4.2 million. Total enrollment: 535. Upper school average class size: 22. Upper school faculty-student ratio: 1:14. There are 180 required school days per year for Upper School students. Upper School students typically attend 5 days per week. The average school day consists of 6 hours and 30 minutes.

Upper School Student Profile Grade 9: 161 students (161 boys); Grade 10: 131 students (131 boys); Grade 11: 139 students (139 boys); Grade 12: 129 students (129 boys). 65% of students are Roman Catholic.

Faculty School total: 46. In upper school: 34 men, 12 women; 26 have advanced degrees.

Subjects Offered 20th century world history, 3-dimensional design, accounting, advanced biology, advanced chemistry, advanced computer applications, advanced math, Advanced Placement courses, algebra, American government, American history, American history-AP, American literature, analytic geometry, art, art appreciation, arts appreciation, astronomy, band, Basic programming, biology, biology-AP, British literature, British literature (honors), British literature-AP, business, business communications, business law, business mathematics, business technology, calculus, calculus-AP, campus ministry, Catholic belief and practice, chemistry, chemistry-AP, choir, choral music, chorus, Christian and Hebrew scripture, Christian doctrine, Christian ethics, college admission preparation, college awareness, college counseling, college planning, computer applications, computer studies, computer technologies, concert band, consumer law, consumer mathematics, creative writing, earth science, engineering, English, English literature and composition-AP, environmental science, ethical decision making, European history, fine arts, French, freshman seminar, geography, geometry, government, government-AP, health, history of the Catholic Church, HTML design, instrumental music, jazz band, journalism, keyboarding, Latin, Life of Christ, music theory, photography, physical science, physics, physics-AP, pre-algebra, pre-calculus, probability and statistics, psychology, psychology-AP, reading/study skills, SAT/ACT preparation, Spanish, Spanish language-AP, U.S. government and politics-AP.

Graduation Requirements Algebra, American government, American history, art, art appreciation, biology, British literature, chemistry, church history, computer applications, computer skills, English, foreign language, four units of summer reading, geometry, health, Life of Christ, mathematics, physical fitness, physics, religion (includes Bible studies and theology), theology, world history, world religions, 84 hours of community service with a written paper. Community service is required.

Special Academic Programs Advanced Placement exam preparation; honors section; independent study; study at local college for college credit; remedial reading and/or remedial writing; remedial math; programs in English, mathematics for dyslexic students.

College Admission Counseling 120 students graduated in 2016; they went to Loyola University Maryland; Mount St. Mary's University; Stevenson University; Towson University; University of Maryland, Baltimore County; University of Maryland, College Park.

Student Life Upper grades have specified standards of dress, student council, honor system. Discipline rests primarily with faculty. Attendance at religious services is required.

Summer Programs Remediation, enrichment, advancement, sports, art/fine arts, computer instruction programs offered; held on campus; accepts boys and girls; open to students from other schools. 2017 schedule: June 15 to August 9. Application deadline: June 15.

Tuition and Aid Day student tuition: $13,200. Tuition installment plan (FACTS Tuition Payment Plan, individually arranged payment plans). Tuition reduction for siblings, merit scholarship grants, need-based scholarship grants, paying campus jobs available.

Admissions Traditional secondary-level entrance grade is 9. For fall 2016, 300 students applied for upper-level admission, 161 enrolled. High School Placement Test (closed version) from Scholastic Testing Service required. Deadline for receipt of application materials: December 16. Application fee required: $25. On-campus interview recommended.

Athletics Interscholastic: baseball, basketball, cross-country running, football, golf, ice hockey, indoor track & field, lacrosse, soccer, swimming and diving, tennis, track and field, volleyball, wrestling; intramural: flag football, Frisbee, handball, martial arts, touch football, weight lifting, weight training. 3 PE instructors, 32 coaches, 1 athletic trainer.

Computers Computers are regularly used in all classes. Computer network features include on-campus library services, Internet access, wireless campus network, Internet filtering or blocking technology, 1:1 iPad program. Campus intranet, student e-mail accounts, and computer access in designated common areas are available to students. Students grades are available online. The school has a published electronic and media policy.

Contact Mr. Nick Brownlee, Admissions Director. 410-485-5000 Ext. 289. Fax: 410-485-6493. E-mail: nbrownlee@archbishopcurley.org.
Website: www.archbishopcurley.org

ARCHBISHOP HOBAN HIGH SCHOOL

1 Holy Cross Boulevard
Akron, Ohio 44306

Head of School: Dr. Todd R. Sweda, EdD

General Information Coeducational day college-preparatory, religious studies, English, and mathematics school, affiliated with Roman Catholic Church. Grades 9–12. Founded: 1953. Setting: urban. 75-acre campus. 4 buildings on campus. Approved or accredited by National Catholic Education Association, North Central Association of Colleges and Schools, Ohio Catholic Schools Accreditation Association (OCSAA), and Ohio Department of Education. Endowment $10.5 million. Total enrollment: 856. Upper school average class size: 23. Upper school faculty-student ratio: 1:13. There are 178 required school days per year for Upper School students. Upper School students typically attend 5 days per week. The average school day consists of 6 hours and 55 minutes.

Upper School Student Profile Grade 9: 203 students (103 boys, 100 girls); Grade 10: 220 students (111 boys, 109 girls); Grade 11: 202 students (104 boys, 98 girls); Grade 12: 227 students (117 boys, 110 girls). 78% of students are Roman Catholic.

Faculty School total: 52. In upper school: 27 men, 25 women; 43 have advanced degrees.

Subjects Offered ACT preparation, advanced math, Advanced Placement courses, advanced studio art-AP, algebra, American literature, anatomy and physiology, archaeology, art, art history-AP, art-AP, biology, biology-AP, British literature, calculus-AP, Catholic belief and practice, ceramics, chemistry, chemistry-AP, Chinese, Christian and Hebrew scripture, church history, computer applications, computer graphics, computer science, conceptual physics, concert choir, digital imaging, digital music, drawing, economics, electronic music, electronic publishing, engineering, English, English language and composition-AP, English literature and composition-AP, English literature-AP, ensembles, environmental science, environmental studies, European history-AP, fine arts, French, French language-AP, geometry, government, health, health education, honors algebra, honors English, honors geometry, human anatomy, Italian, Latin, leadership, leadership and service, learning strategies, Mandarin, moral and social development, newspaper, orchestra, organic chemistry, painting, physical education, physics, physics-AP, pre-calculus, printmaking, psychology, psychology-AP, social justice, Spanish, statistics-AP, studio art, television, trigonometry, U.S. government, U.S. history, U.S. history-AP, values and decisions, Web site design, world cultures, world literature, yearbook.

Graduation Requirements Algebra, arts and fine arts (art, music, dance, drama), biology, economics, electives, English, health education, mathematics, physical

education (includes health), religious studies, science, social studies (includes history), U.S. government, Christian service totaling 75 hours over four years.

Special Academic Programs 15 Advanced Placement exams for which test preparation is offered; honors section; independent study; study at local college for college credit; academic accommodation for the gifted and the artistically talented; remedial reading and/or remedial writing; remedial math; programs in general development for dyslexic students.

College Admission Counseling 196 students graduated in 2016; 192 went to college, including Kent State University; Ohio University; The Ohio State University; The University of Akron; The University of Toledo; University of Dayton. Other: 2 went to work, 2 had other specific plans. Median SAT critical reading: 600, median SAT math: 620, median SAT writing: 600, median composite ACT: 25. 50% scored over 600 on SAT critical reading, 60% scored over 600 on SAT math, 50% scored over 600 on SAT writing, 44% scored over 26 on composite ACT.

Student Life Upper grades have specified standards of dress, student council, honor system. Discipline rests primarily with faculty. Attendance at religious services is required.

Summer Programs Advancement programs offered; session focuses on physical education; held on campus; accepts boys and girls; not open to students from other schools. 100 students usually enrolled. 2017 schedule: June 10 to June 30. Application deadline: March.

Tuition and Aid Day student tuition: $10,475. Tuition installment plan (FACTS Tuition Payment Plan). Tuition reduction for siblings, merit scholarship grants, need-based scholarship grants, paying campus jobs available. In 2016–17, 66% of upper-school students received aid; total upper-school merit-scholarship money awarded: $640,000. Total amount of financial aid awarded in 2016–17: $1,550,000.

Admissions Traditional secondary-level entrance grade is 9. For fall 2016, 281 students applied for upper-level admission, 237 were accepted, 203 enrolled. High School Placement Test required. Deadline for receipt of application materials: none. No application fee required. Interview recommended.

Athletics Interscholastic: baseball (boys), basketball (b,g), bowling (b,g), cross-country running (b,g), football (b), golf (b,g), gymnastics (g), indoor track & field (b,g), lacrosse (b,g), physical fitness (b,g), physical training (b,g), soccer (b,g), softball (g), swimming and diving (b,g), tennis (b,g), track and field (b,g), volleyball (b,g), winter (indoor) track (b,g), wrestling (b); intramural: flag football (g); coed interscholastic: cheering, dance team, physical fitness, physical training; coed intramural: basketball, skiing (downhill), snowboarding, strength & conditioning, ultimate Frisbee, weight training. 1 PE instructor, 1 athletic trainer.

Computers Computers are regularly used in graphic arts, literary magazine, newspaper, photography, science, video film production, Web site design, yearbook classes. Computer network features include Internet access, wireless campus network, Internet filtering or blocking technology. Campus intranet, student e-mail accounts, and computer access in designated common areas are available to students. Students grades are available online. The school has a published electronic and media policy.

Contact Mrs. Karen Carabin, Admissions Counselor. 330-773-6658 Ext. 215. Fax: 330-773-9100. E-mail: CarabinK@hoban.org. Website: www.hoban.org

ARCHBISHOP McNICHOLAS HIGH SCHOOL

6536 Beechmont Avenue
Cincinnati, Ohio 45230-2098

Head of School: Ms. Patricia Beckert

General Information Coeducational day college-preparatory and general academic school, affiliated with Roman Catholic Church. Grades 9–12. Founded: 1951. Setting: suburban. 48-acre campus. 3 buildings on campus. Approved or accredited by Ohio Catholic Schools Accreditation Association (OCSAA) and Ohio Department of Education. Total enrollment: 677. Upper school average class size: 18. Upper school faculty-student ratio: 1:18. There are 180 required school days per year for Upper School students. Upper School students typically attend 5 days per week. The average school day consists of 7 hours.

Upper School Student Profile 92% of students are Roman Catholic.

Faculty School total: 51. In upper school: 20 men, 31 women; 24 have advanced degrees.

Subjects Offered Accounting, advanced computer applications, advanced math, Advanced Placement courses, advanced studio art-AP, algebra, American history, American history-AP, American legal systems, American literature, anatomy and physiology, architectural drawing, band, Basic programming, biology, biology-AP, British literature, business applications, calculus-AP, Catholic belief and practice, ceramics, chemistry, choir, church history, civics, communication skills, computer art, computer processing, computer programming, computer programming-AP, computer technologies, computer-aided design, concert band, concert choir, creative writing, design, developmental math, digital photography, directing, drama, drawing and design, English, English literature and composition-AP, European history-AP, French, government and politics-AP, guitar, health, honors algebra, honors English, honors geometry, integrated science, intro to computers, journalism, Latin, Latin-AP, Life of Christ, marching band, moral theology, music appreciation, music theory-AP, Native American studies, photography, physical education, physical science, physics, physics-AP, portfolio art, pottery, pre-algebra, pre-calculus, reading, reading/study skills, skills for success, Spanish, Spanish language-AP, Spanish literature-AP, speech and debate, street law, studio art, studio art-AP, theater, U.S. government and politics-AP, video film production, Web site design, world history, world religions, writing.

Graduation Requirements Algebra, American government, American history, American literature, arts and fine arts (art, music, dance, drama), biology, British literature, Catholic belief and practice, civics, communication skills, computer applications, English, foreign language, geometry, mathematics, religion (includes Bible studies and theology), science, social justice, world history, senior year retreat, a minimum of 40 hours of community service.

Special Academic Programs Advanced Placement exam preparation; honors section; remedial reading and/or remedial writing; remedial math; programs in English, mathematics, general development for dyslexic students.

College Admission Counseling 160 students graduated in 2016; 158 went to college, including Miami University; Northern Kentucky University; Ohio University; University of Cincinnati; University of Dayton; Xavier University. Other: 1 entered military service, 1 had other specific plans.

Student Life Upper grades have uniform requirement, student council. Discipline rests primarily with faculty. Attendance at religious services is required.

Tuition and Aid Day student tuition: $10,700. Tuition installment plan (FACTS Tuition Payment Plan). Tuition reduction for siblings, merit scholarship grants, need-based scholarship grants available.

Admissions Traditional secondary-level entrance grade is 9. High School Placement Test (closed version) from Scholastic Testing Service required. Deadline for receipt of application materials: December 10. No application fee required.

Athletics Interscholastic: baseball (boys), basketball (b,g), bowling (b,g), cheering (g), dance team (g), football (b), golf (b,g), lacrosse (b,g), soccer (b,g), softball (g), track and field (b,g), volleyball (b,g), wrestling (b); coed interscholastic: cross-country running, swimming and diving, track and field; coed intramural: bicycling, flag football, skiing (downhill), snowboarding. 44 coaches, 3 athletic trainers.

Computers Computers are regularly used in computer applications, data processing, English, foreign language, French, graphic design, history, journalism, mathematics, multimedia, photography, programming, publications, reading, religion, science, Spanish, video film production, Web site design, writing classes. Computer network features include on-campus library services, Internet access, Internet filtering or blocking technology, student files, Edline. Campus intranet and student e-mail accounts are available to students. Students grades are available online. The school has a published electronic and media policy.

Contact Mrs. Christina Mullis, Director of Admissions and Enrollment. 513-231-3500 Ext. 5809. Fax: 513-231-1351. E-mail: cmullis@mcnhs.org. Website: www.mcnhs.org

ARCHBISHOP MITTY HIGH SCHOOL

5000 Mitty Avenue
San Jose, California 95129

Head of School: Mr. Tim Brosnan

General Information Coeducational day college-preparatory and college preparatory school, affiliated with Roman Catholic Church. Grades 9–12. Founded: 1964. Setting: suburban. 24-acre campus. 12 buildings on campus. Approved or accredited by National Catholic Education Association, Western Association of Schools and Colleges, and California Department of Education. Endowment: $18 million. Total enrollment: 1,723. Upper school average class size: 27. Upper school faculty-student ratio: 1:17. There are 180 required school days per year for Upper School students. Upper School students typically attend 5 days per week. The average school day consists of 6 hours and 45 minutes.

Upper School Student Profile Grade 9: 461 students (226 boys, 235 girls); Grade 10: 428 students (203 boys, 225 girls); Grade 11: 436 students (210 boys, 226 girls); Grade 12: 423 students (211 boys, 212 girls). 75% of students are Roman Catholic.

Faculty School total: 110. In upper school: 55 men, 55 women; 84 have advanced degrees.

Subjects Offered 3-dimensional art, acting, African-American literature, algebra, American government, American history-AP, American literature, American literature-AP, ancient world history, art, biology, biology-AP, British literature, calculus, calculus-AP, Catholic belief and practice, chemistry, chemistry-AP, choral music, chorus, church history, college placement, college writing, community service, computer graphics, computer multimedia, concert band, concert choir, drawing, economics and history, English, English language and composition-AP, English literature, English literature-AP, French, French language-AP, French literature-AP, French studies, French-AP, geometry, history-AP, honors algebra, honors English, honors geometry, honors U.S. history, honors world history, music, music appreciation, music theory-AP, philosophy, physics, physics-AP, political science, religion, social sciences, Spanish, Spanish language-AP, Spanish literature, Spanish literature-AP, student government, theater arts, U.S. government and politics, U.S. government and politics-AP, U.S. history, U.S. history-AP, U.S. literature, visual and performing arts, visual arts, world history.

Graduation Requirements Art, English, foreign language, mathematics, philosophy, physical education (includes health), religious studies, science, social sciences, 80 hours of Christian service.

Special Academic Programs 18 Advanced Placement exams for which test preparation is offered; honors section; study at local college for college credit; academic accommodation for the gifted, the musically talented, and the artistically talented.

College Admission Counseling 418 students graduated in 2016; all went to college, including California Polytechnic State University, San Luis Obispo; Santa Clara University; Stanford University; University of California, Berkeley; University of California, Davis; University of California, Los Angeles. Mean SAT critical reading: 600, mean SAT math: 597, mean SAT writing: 608, mean combined SAT: 1805, mean composite ACT: 27.

Student Life Upper grades have specified standards of dress, student council, honor system. Discipline rests primarily with faculty. Attendance at religious services is required.

Summer Programs Remediation, enrichment, advancement, sports, art/fine arts, computer instruction programs offered; session focuses on academics and athletics; held on campus; accepts boys and girls; open to students from other schools. 500 students usually enrolled. 2017 schedule: June 12 to July 21. Application deadline: May 1.

Tuition and Aid Day student tuition: $19,250. Tuition installment plan (SMART Tuition Payment Plan). Need-based scholarship grants, paying campus jobs available. In 2016–17, 38% of upper-school students received aid. Total amount of financial aid awarded in 2016–17: $3,800,000.

Admissions Traditional secondary-level entrance grade is 9. For fall 2016, 1,600 students applied for upper-level admission, 461 were accepted, 461 enrolled. High School Placement Test required. Deadline for receipt of application materials: December 9. Application fee required: $75.

Athletics Interscholastic: aquatics (boys, girls), badminton (b,g), baseball (b), basketball (b,g), cross-country running (b,g), dance team (g), diving (b,g), field hockey (g), football (b), golf (b,g), lacrosse (b,g), soccer (b,g), softball (g), swimming and diving (b,g), tennis (b,g), track and field (b,g), volleyball (b,g), water polo (b,g), weight training (b,g), winter soccer (b,g); intramural: roller hockey (b,g); coed interscholastic: physical fitness, strength & conditioning, wrestling; coed intramural: basketball, ice hockey, in-line hockey, table tennis. 4 PE instructors, 110 coaches, 2 athletic trainers.

Computers Computers are regularly used in all classes. Computer network features include on-campus library services, online commercial services, Internet access, wireless campus network, Internet filtering or blocking technology. Campus intranet, student e-mail accounts, and computer access in designated common areas are available to students. Students grades are available online. The school has a published electronic and media policy.

Contact Mrs. Katrina Montano, Assistant for Admissions. 408-342-4300. Fax: 408-342-4308. E-mail: admissions@mitty.com. Website: www.mitty.com/

ARCHBISHOP MOELLER HIGH SCHOOL

9001 Montgomery Road
Cincinnati, Ohio 45242-7711

Head of School: Mr. Blane Collison

General Information Boys' day college-preparatory, arts, business, religious studies, and technology school, affiliated with Roman Catholic Church. Grades 9–12. Founded: 1960. Setting: suburban. 5-acre campus. 3 buildings on campus. Approved or accredited by North Central Association of Colleges and Schools, Ohio Catholic Schools Accreditation Association (OCSAA), and Ohio Department of Education. Endowment: $4 million. Total enrollment: 949. Upper school average class size: 21. Upper school faculty-student ratio: 1:14. There are 181 required school days per year for Upper School students. Upper School students typically attend 5 days per week. The average school day consists of 7 hours.

Upper School Student Profile Grade 9: 242 students (242 boys); Grade 10: 202 students (202 boys); Grade 11: 221 students (221 boys); Grade 12: 218 students (218 boys). 76% of students are Roman Catholic.

Faculty School total: 85. In upper school: 80 men, 5 women; 35 have advanced degrees.

Subjects Offered 20th century history, 20th century physics, 20th century world history, 3-dimensional art, 3-dimensional design, accounting, advanced biology, advanced chemistry, advanced computer applications, advanced math, Advanced Placement courses, advanced studio art-AP, algebra, all academic.

Graduation Requirements American government, American history, art, business skills (includes word processing), career and personal planning, career/college preparation, college admission preparation, college counseling, computer literacy, ecology, environmental systems, foreign language, health education, mathematics, New Testament, physical education (includes health), reading, religion (includes Bible studies and theology), science, social studies (includes history), values and decisions, world history, writing. Community service is required.

Special Academic Programs Honors section; accelerated programs; remedial reading and/or remedial writing; remedial math; programs in English, mathematics, general development for dyslexic students; special instructional classes for deaf students, blind students.

College Admission Counseling 216 students graduated in 2016; 212 went to college, including Miami University; Ohio University; The Ohio State University; University of Cincinnati; University of Dayton. Other: 4 entered military service. Median composite ACT: 26.

Student Life Upper grades have specified standards of dress, student council. Discipline rests primarily with faculty. Attendance at religious services is required.

Summer Programs Enrichment, advancement, sports, art/fine arts programs offered; session focuses on Recruitment Grades 2-8; held both on and off campus; accepts boys and girls; open to students from other schools. 1,000 students usually enrolled. 2017 schedule: June 12 to August 4. Application deadline: May 31.

Tuition and Aid Day student tuition: $12,950. Tuition installment plan (SMART Tuition Payment Plan). Tuition reduction for siblings, merit scholarship grants, need-based scholarship grants, off-campus work study available. In 2016–17, 40% of upper-school students received aid; total upper-school merit-scholarship money awarded: $42,000. Total amount of financial aid awarded in 2016–17: $1,400,000.

Admissions Traditional secondary-level entrance grade is 9. For fall 2016, 485 students applied for upper-level admission, 475 were accepted, 242 enrolled. High School Placement Test required. Deadline for receipt of application materials: June 30. No application fee required. On-campus interview required.

Athletics Interscholastic: alpine skiing, baseball, basketball, bowling, cross-country running, diving, football, golf, hockey, ice hockey, indoor track, indoor track & field, lacrosse, soccer, swimming and diving, tennis, track and field, volleyball, winter (indoor) track, wrestling; intramural: alpine skiing, backpacking, bicycling, boxing, cheering, cooperative games, fencing, freestyle skiing, Frisbee, hiking/backpacking, in-line hockey, outdoor education, physical fitness, skiing (downhill), snowboarding, ultimate Frisbee. 2 PE instructors, 30 coaches, 1 athletic trainer.

Computers Computers are regularly used in all classes. Computer network features include Internet access, wireless campus network, Internet filtering or blocking technology, home computer port limiters, Kurzweil. Campus intranet and student e-mail accounts are available to students. Students grades are available online. The school has a published electronic and media policy.

Contact Charles Lytle, Director of Admissions. 513-791-1680 Ext. 1240. Fax: 513-792-1400. E-mail: clytle@moeller.org. Website: www.moeller.org

ARCHBISHOP SHAW HIGH SCHOOL

1000 Barataria Boulevard
Marrero, Louisiana 70072-3052

Head of School: Rev. Louis J. Molinelli, SDB

General Information Boys' day college-preparatory, religious studies, technology, engineering, entrepreneurship, and theatre/film studies school, affiliated with Roman Catholic Church. Grades 8–12. Founded: 1962. Setting: suburban. Nearest major city is New Orleans. 71-acre campus. 5 buildings on campus. Approved or accredited by National Catholic Education Association, Southern Association of Colleges and Schools, and Louisiana Department of Education. Total enrollment: 472. Upper school average class size: 23. Upper school faculty-student ratio: 1:21. There are 178 required school days per year for Upper School students. Upper School students typically attend 5 days per week. The average school day consists of 7 hours.

Upper School Student Profile Grade 8: 96 students (96 boys); Grade 9: 97 students (97 boys); Grade 10: 98 students (98 boys); Grade 11: 98 students (98 boys); Grade 12: 83 students (83 boys). 85% of students are Roman Catholic.

Faculty School total: 45. In upper school: 26 men, 9 women; 30 have advanced degrees.

Subjects Offered Accounting, advanced math, Advanced Placement courses, algebra, American government, American history, American history-AP, American literature, American literature-AP, art, art history, athletics, band, baseball, Bible studies, biology, British literature, British literature (honors), broadcasting, business law, calculus, calculus AP, Catholic belief and practice, chemistry, Christian and Hebrew scripture, Christian doctrine, Christian ethics, Christian testament, Christianity, civics, civics/free enterprise, college counseling, college writing, community service, composition, computer applications, computer literacy, computer science-AP, concert band, driver education, earth science, economics, engineering, English, English composition, English language and composition-AP, English language-AP, English literature, ethical decision making, family and consumer science, film and literature, film and new technologies, fitness, French, geometry, guidance, health, history, history of the Catholic Church, history-AP, honors algebra, honors English, honors geometry, honors world history, human sexuality, instrumental music, Internet, jazz band, keyboarding, lab science, marching band, moral theology, music, physical education, physics, pre-algebra, pre-calculus, psychology, religious studies, SAT/ACT preparation, Spanish, symphonic band, U.S. history, U.S. history-AP, wind instruments, world geography, world history.

Graduation Requirements Algebra, biology, civics/free enterprise, earth science, electives, English, English composition, English literature, foreign language, geometry, health, mathematics, physical education (includes health), physical fitness, physical science, religion (includes Bible studies and theology), religious studies, science, social studies (includes history), world geography, service hours per school year/grade level.

Special Academic Programs Advanced Placement exam preparation; honors section; study at local college for college credit.

College Admission Counseling 93 students graduated in 2016; 87 went to college, including Louisiana State University and Agricultural & Mechanical College; Louisiana Tech University; University of Louisiana at Lafayette; University of New Orleans. Other: 10 went to work, 3 entered military service, 3 had other specific plans. Median composite ACT: 21. 15% scored over 26 on composite ACT.

Student Life Upper grades have uniform requirement, student council, honor system. Discipline rests primarily with faculty. Attendance at religious services is required.

Summer Programs Remediation programs offered; session focuses on Remediation; held on campus; accepts boys; not open to students from other schools. 35 students usually enrolled. 2017 schedule: June 5 to July 14. Application deadline: June 2.

Tuition and Aid Day student tuition: $8800. Tuition installment plan (monthly payment plans, individually arranged payment plans, local bank). Merit scholarship grants, need-based scholarship grants, paying campus jobs, educational bank loan financing available. In 2016–17, 10% of upper-school students received aid. Total amount of financial aid awarded in 2016–17: $100,000.

Admissions Traditional secondary-level entrance grade is 9. For fall 2016, 222 students applied for upper-level admission, 217 were accepted, 197 enrolled. High School Placement Test (closed version) from Scholastic Testing Service required. Deadline for receipt of application materials: none. Application fee required: $20. Interview recommended.

Athletics Interscholastic: baseball, basketball, bowling, cheering, cross-country running, fishing, football, golf, running, soccer, strength & conditioning, track and field, wrestling; intramural: basketball, flag football, football, Frisbee, rugby, volleyball. 3 PE instructors, 9 coaches, 1 athletic trainer.

Computers Computers are regularly used in all academic classes. Computer network features include on-campus library services, online commercial services, Internet access, wireless campus network, Internet filtering or blocking technology, 1:1 Chromebook program, ebooks. Campus intranet and student e-mail accounts are available to students. Students grades are available online. The school has a published electronic and media policy.

Contact Mr. Matthew Ducote, Admissions Director. 504-340-6727 Ext. 52. Fax: 504-347-9883. E-mail: shawadm@archdiocese-no.org. Website: www.archbishopshaw.org

ARCHMERE ACADEMY

3600 Philadelphia Pike
Claymont, Delaware 19703

Head of School: Dr. Michael Marinelli

General Information Coeducational day college-preparatory, arts, religious studies, and technology school, affiliated with Roman Catholic Church. Grades 9–12. Founded: 1932. Setting: suburban. Nearest major city is Wilmington. 38-acre campus. 6 buildings on campus. Approved or accredited by Middle States Association of Colleges and Schools, National Catholic Education Association, and Delaware Department of Education. Member of National Association of Independent Schools. Endowment: $12 million. Total enrollment: 505. Upper school average class size: 16. Upper school faculty-student ratio: 1:10. The average school day consists of 6 hours and 30 minutes.

Upper School Student Profile 75% of students are Roman Catholic.

Faculty School total: 62. In upper school: 31 men, 25 women; 51 have advanced degrees.

Subjects Offered Algebra, American history, American literature, architecture, art, art history, Bible studies, biology, calculus, chemistry, Chinese, computer programming, computer science, creative writing, drama, driver education, ecology, economics, English, English literature, environmental science, ethics, European history, expository writing, French, geometry, German, government/civics, grammar, health, history, mathematics, music, philosophy, physical education, physics, psychology, reading, religion, science, social studies, Spanish, speech, statistics, theater, theology, trigonometry, world history, writing.

Graduation Requirements Computer science, English, foreign language, mathematics, physical education (includes health), religion (includes Bible studies and theology), science, social studies (includes history), speech.

Special Academic Programs Advanced Placement exam preparation; honors section; independent study; study abroad; academic accommodation for the gifted, the musically talented, and the artistically talented; programs in English, mathematics for dyslexic students.

College Admission Counseling 124 students graduated in 2015; all went to college, including Boston University; Hofstra University; Penn State University Park; Saint Joseph's University; University of Delaware; University of Maryland, College Park. Median SAT critical reading: 595, median SAT math: 600, median SAT writing: 615. 48% scored over 600 on SAT critical reading, 48% scored over 600 on SAT math, 52% scored over 600 on SAT writing.

Student Life Upper grades have uniform requirement, student council, honor system. Discipline rests primarily with faculty. Attendance at religious services is required.

Tuition and Aid Day student tuition: $23,380. Tuition installment plan (10-month Automatic Debit Plan). Merit scholarship grants, need-based scholarship grants, grants for children of faculty and staff, minority scholarships/grants available. In 2015–16, 65% of upper-school students received aid; total upper-school merit-scholarship money awarded: $2,000,000. Total amount of financial aid awarded in 2015–16: $2,000,000.

Admissions Traditional secondary-level entrance grade is 9. For fall 2015, 300 students applied for upper-level admission, 250 were accepted, 135 enrolled. Deadline for receipt of application materials: March 1. Application fee required: $50. On-campus interview required.

Athletics Interscholastic: baseball (boys), basketball (b,g), cheering (g), cross-country running (b,g), field hockey (g), football (b), golf (b,g), ice hockey (b,g), indoor track (b,g), lacrosse (b,g), soccer (b,g), softball (g), swimming and diving (b,g), tennis (b,g), track and field (b,g), volleyball (g), wrestling (b); coed interscholastic: winter (indoor) track; coed intramural: basketball, bowling, fencing. 1 PE instructor, 16 coaches, 2 athletic trainers.

Computers Computers are regularly used in art, English, foreign language, history, mathematics, multimedia, science classes. Computer network features include on-campus library services, online commercial services, Internet access, wireless campus network. Student e-mail accounts are available to students. The school has a published electronic and media policy.

Contact Mrs. Kristin B. Mumford, Director of Admissions. 302-798-6632 Ext. 781. E-mail: kmumford@archmereacademy.com. Website: www.archmereacademy.com

ARENDELL PARROTT ACADEMY

PO Box 1297
Kinston, North Carolina 28503-1297

Head of School: Dr. Bert S. Bright Jr.

General Information Coeducational day college-preparatory and arts school. Grades PK–12. Founded: 1964. Setting: small town. Nearest major city is Greenville. 80-acre campus. 6 buildings on campus. Approved or accredited by North Carolina Association of Independent Schools, Southern Association of Colleges and Schools, and North Carolina Department of Education. Member of National Association of Independent Schools. Total enrollment: 721. Upper school average class size: 18. Upper school faculty-student ratio: 1:17. There are 178 required school days per year for Upper School students. Upper School students typically attend 5 days per week. The average school day consists of 6 hours and 20 minutes.

Upper School Student Profile Grade 9: 62 students (30 boys, 32 girls); Grade 10: 70 students (34 boys, 36 girls); Grade 11: 54 students (28 boys, 26 girls); Grade 12: 59 students (30 boys, 29 girls).

Faculty School total: 60. In upper school: 10 men, 21 women; 20 have advanced degrees.

Special Academic Programs Advanced Placement exam preparation; honors section; study at local college for college credit.

College Admission Counseling 59 students graduated in 2015; 58 went to college, including Duke University; East Carolina University; North Carolina State University; The University of North Carolina at Chapel Hill; University of Mississippi; University of South Carolina. Other: 1 entered military service. Mean SAT critical reading: 555, mean SAT math: 568, mean SAT writing: 546, mean combined SAT: 1669, mean composite ACT: 25.

Student Life Upper grades have specified standards of dress, student council, honor system. Discipline rests primarily with faculty.

Tuition and Aid Day student tuition: $10,150. Tuition installment plan (monthly payment plans, individually arranged payment plans). Need-based scholarship grants available. In 2015–16, 17% of upper-school students received aid. Total amount of financial aid awarded in 2015–16: $260,000.

Admissions Traditional secondary-level entrance grade is 9. For fall 2015, 26 students applied for upper-level admission, 13 were accepted, 13 enrolled. Deadline for receipt of application materials: February 15. Application fee required: $550. Interview required.

Athletics Interscholastic: baseball (boys), basketball (b,g), cheering (g), cross-country running (b,g), dance squad (g), field hockey (g), football (b), lacrosse (b), soccer (b,g), softball (g), swimming and diving (b,g), tennis (b,g), volleyball (g); coed interscholastic: dance, fitness, golf, physical fitness, physical training, strength & conditioning; coed intramural: archery. 5 PE instructors, 4 coaches, 1 athletic trainer.

Computers Computer network features include on-campus library services, Internet access, wireless campus network, Internet filtering or blocking technology. Computer access in designated common areas is available to students. Students grades are available online. The school has a published electronic and media policy.

Contact Nancy Gilmore, Director of Admissions. 252-522-0410 Ext. 202. Fax: 919-522-0672. E-mail: ngilmore@parrottacademy.org. Website: www.parrottacademy.org

ARETE PREPARATORY ACADEMY

11500 West Olympic Boulevard
Suite 318
Los Angeles, California 90064

Head of School: Jim Hahn

General Information Coeducational day college-preparatory, general academic, and philosophy school. Grades 9–12. Founded: 2008. Setting: urban. Approved or accredited by Western Association of Schools and Colleges and California Department of Education. Total enrollment: 58. Upper school average class size: 5. Upper school faculty-student ratio: 1:2. There are 168 required school days per year for Upper School students. Upper School students typically attend 5 days per week. The average school day consists of 7 hours and 45 minutes.

Upper School Student Profile Grade 9: 7 students (2 boys, 5 girls); Grade 10: 18 students (9 boys, 9 girls); Grade 11: 8 students (3 boys, 5 girls); Grade 12: 20 students (9 boys, 11 girls).

Faculty School total: 28. In upper school: 11 men, 17 women; 15 have advanced degrees.

Subjects Offered 20th century world history, advanced chemistry, algebra, American history, American literature, art, band, biology, calculus, chemistry, college counseling, comparative government and politics, composition, creative writing, critical thinking, critical writing, discrete mathematics, drama, electives, electronics, English, English composition, English literature, environmental science, ethics, ethics and responsibility, film history, foreign language, French, geometry, global issues, great issues, honors English, honors U.S. history, honors world history, humanities, independent study, introduction to literature, Japanese, Japanese studies, language and composition, linguistics, literary magazine, literature, logic, modern civilization, moral reasoning, multicultural literature, neuroscience, participation in sports, philosophy, physical education, physics, poetry, politics, pre-calculus, science, senior composition, senior project, social sciences, social studies, Southern literature, Spanish, sports, strategies for success, theater, theory of knowledge, trigonometry, U.S. constitutional history, U.S. history, U.S. literature, world civilizations, world history.

Special Academic Programs Honors section; accelerated programs; independent study; study at local college for college credit; academic accommodation for the gifted; remedial reading and/or remedial writing; remedial math; programs in English, mathematics, general development for dyslexic students.

College Admission Counseling 17 students graduated in 2016; 15 went to college. Other: 2 had other specific plans.

Student Life Upper grades have student council, honor system. Discipline rests primarily with faculty.

Summer Programs Remediation, enrichment, advancement programs offered; held on campus; accepts boys and girls; open to students from other schools. 2017 schedule: June 5 to August 15.

Tuition and Aid Day student tuition: $49,500. Need-based scholarship grants available. In 2016–17, 40% of upper-school students received aid.

Admissions Traditional secondary-level entrance grade is 9. For fall 2016, 25 students applied for upper-level admission, 20 were accepted, 17 enrolled. Deadline for receipt of application materials: none. Application fee required: $100. On-campus interview required.

Athletics Interscholastic: cross-country running (boys, girls); coed interscholastic: cross-country running. 2 PE instructors, 2 coaches.

Computers Computers are regularly used in all classes. Computer network features include Internet access, wireless campus network, Internet filtering or blocking technology. Campus intranet, student e-mail accounts, and computer access in designated common areas are available to students. Students grades are available online. The school has a published electronic and media policy.

Contact Clark Brandon, Dean of Students. 310-478-9900.
E-mail: clark@areteprep.org. Website: www.areteprep.org

ARIZONA LUTHERAN ACADEMY

6036 South 27th Avenue
Phoenix, Arizona 85041

Head of School: Mr. Kurt E. Rosenbaum

General Information Coeducational day and distance learning college-preparatory and College Prep school, affiliated with Wesleyan Church. Grades 9–12. Distance learning grades 11–12. Founded: 1978. Setting: urban. 20-acre campus. 8 buildings on campus. Approved or accredited by North Central Association of Colleges and Schools. Total enrollment: 188. Upper school average class size: 18. Upper school faculty-student ratio: 1:13. There are 180 required school days per year for Upper School students. Upper School students typically attend 5 days per week. The average school day consists of 8 hours.

Upper School Student Profile 10% of students are boarding students. 90% are state residents. 2 states are represented in upper school student body. 10% are international students. International students from China, Germany, and Viet Nam; 6 other countries represented in student body. 70% of students are members of Wesleyan Church.

Faculty School total: 16. In upper school: 10 men, 6 women; 8 have advanced degrees.

Subjects Offered Advanced Placement courses, all academic, Christian education.

Graduation Requirements Arts and fine arts (art, music, dance, drama), computer skills, electives, English, mathematics, physical education (includes health), religion (includes Bible studies and theology), science, social studies (includes history), community service is required for graduation. Religion courses are required, not optional. Community service is required.

Special Academic Programs Honors section; study at local college for college credit; academic accommodation for the gifted and the musically talented; remedial reading and/or remedial writing; remedial math; ESL (10 students enrolled).

College Admission Counseling 47 students graduated in 2016; all went to college, including Arizona State University at the Tempe campus; Grand Canyon University; Northern Arizona University.

Student Life Upper grades have specified standards of dress, student council, honor system. Discipline rests primarily with faculty. Attendance at religious services is required.

Tuition and Aid Tuition installment plan (FACTS Tuition Payment Plan, monthly payment plans, individually arranged payment plans). Tuition reduction for siblings, need-based scholarship grants, Arizona Tuition Tax Credit program through various STOs (School Tuition Organizations) available.

Admissions Traditional secondary-level entrance grade is 9. For fall 2016, 48 students applied for upper-level admission, 46 were accepted, 45 enrolled. Achievement tests required. Deadline for receipt of application materials: July 30. Application fee required. On-campus interview recommended.

Athletics Interscholastic: baseball (boys), basketball (b,g), cheering (g), cross-country running (b,g), football (b), physical training (b,g), softball (g), track and field (b,g), volleyball (g), wrestling (b,g); coed interscholastic: cheering, golf, soccer; coed intramural: weight training.

Computers Computers are regularly used in all classes. Computer network features include on-campus library services, Internet access, wireless campus network, Internet filtering or blocking technology, classroom use of tablets, computer lab time. Student e-mail accounts and computer access in designated common areas are available to students. Students grades are available online. The school has a published electronic and media policy.

Contact 602-268-8686. Website: www.alacoyotes.org

ARMBRAE ACADEMY

1400 Oxford Street
Halifax, Nova Scotia B3H 3Y8, Canada

Head of School: Gary O'Meara

General Information Coeducational day college-preparatory school. Grades K–12. Founded: 1887. Setting: urban. 2-acre campus. 3 buildings on campus. Approved or accredited by Canadian Association of Independent Schools, Canadian Educational Standards Institute, and Nova Scotia Department of Education. Language of instruction: English. Endowment: CAN$1 million. Total enrollment: 250. Upper school average class size: 22. Upper school faculty-student ratio: 1:9. There are 185 required school days per year for Upper School students. Upper School students typically attend 5 days per week. The average school day consists of 5 hours and 30 minutes.

Faculty School total: 35. In upper school: 5 men, 8 women; 5 have advanced degrees.

Subjects Offered Algebra, American history, art, biology, calculus, chemistry, computer science, earth science, economics, English, English literature, European history, French, geography, geology, geometry, government/civics, grammar, health, history, keyboarding, Mandarin, mathematics, music, physical education, physics, science, social studies, study skills, trigonometry, world literature, writing.

Graduation Requirements Computer science, English, foreign language, mathematics, physical education (includes health), science, social studies (includes history), 6 courses each in grades 11 and 12.

Special Academic Programs Advanced Placement exam preparation; accelerated programs; study at local college for college credit; academic accommodation for the artistically talented.

College Admission Counseling 20 students graduated in 2015; they went to Acadia University; Carleton University; Dalhousie University; McGill University; Queen's University at Kingston; St. Francis Xavier University.

Student Life Upper grades have uniform requirement, student council. Discipline rests equally with students and faculty.

Tuition and Aid Day student tuition: CAN$13,870. Tuition installment plan (monthly payment plans, term payment plan). Tuition reduction for siblings, bursaries, merit scholarship grants available. In 2015–16, 4% of upper-school students received aid; total upper-school merit-scholarship money awarded: CAN$2000. Total amount of financial aid awarded in 2015–16: CAN$60,000.

Admissions Traditional secondary-level entrance grade is 10. For fall 2015, 25 students applied for upper-level admission, 22 were accepted, 15 enrolled. CTBS (or similar from their school) required. Deadline for receipt of application materials: none. Application fee required: CAN$150. On-campus interview required.

Athletics Interscholastic: badminton (boys, girls), basketball (b,g), cross-country running (b,g), field hockey (g), ice hockey (b), soccer (b,g), swimming and diving (b,g), tennis (b,g), track and field (b,g), volleyball (b,g), yoga (b,g); intramural: badminton (b,g), cross-country running (b,g); coed interscholastic: curling, ice hockey; coed intramural: ice hockey. 2 PE instructors, 4 coaches.

Computers Computers are regularly used in all classes. Computer network features include on-campus library services, online commercial services, Internet access, wireless campus network. Campus intranet, student e-mail accounts, and computer access in designated common areas are available to students. Students grades are available online. The school has a published electronic and media policy.

Contact Gary D. O'Meara, Headmaster. 902-423-7920. Fax: 902-423-9731. E-mail: head@armbrae.ns.ca. Website: www.armbrae.ns.ca

ARMY AND NAVY ACADEMY

2605 Carlsbad Boulevard
PO Box 3000
Carlsbad, California 92018-3000

Head of School: Maj. Gen. Arthur M. Bartell, Retd.

General Information Boys' boarding and day college-preparatory, Junior ROTC, and military school. Grades 7–12. Distance learning grades 7–12. Founded: 1910. Setting: small town. Nearest major city is San Diego. Students are housed in coed dormitories. 16-acre campus. 34 buildings on campus. Approved or accredited by California Association of Independent Schools, The Association of Boarding Schools, and Western Association of Schools and Colleges. Member of National Association of Independent Schools and Secondary School Admission Test Board. Endowment: $637,605. Total enrollment: 267. Upper school average class size: 15. Upper school faculty-student ratio: 1:15. There are 180 required school days per year for Upper School students. Upper School students typically attend 5 days per week. The average school day consists of 7 hours.

Upper School Student Profile 67% of students are boarding students. 44% are state residents. 14 states are represented in upper school student body. 20% are international students. International students from China, Germany, Mexico, Mongolia, Republic of Korea, and Russian Federation; 16 other countries represented in student body.

Faculty School total: 33. In upper school: 14 men, 19 women; 16 have advanced degrees.

Subjects Offered Algebra, art, astronomy, biology, biology-AP, calculus-AP, chemistry, chemistry-AP, composition-AP, drama, economics, economics-AP, English, English literature-AP, English-AP, ESL, European history-AP, French, geography, geometry, German, guitar, independent study, JROTC, Mandarin, marching band, music technology, photography, physical education, physics, physics-AP, pre-calculus, psychology-AP, Spanish, Spanish-AP, sports psychology, studio art-AP, study skills, U.S. government, U.S. history, U.S. history-AP, video film production, weight training, world history, yearbook.

Graduation Requirements Arts and fine arts (art, music, dance, drama), electives, English, foreign language, lab science, leadership education training, mathematics, physical education (includes health), social studies (includes history).

Special Academic Programs 7 Advanced Placement exams for which test preparation is offered; honors section; independent study; ESL (37 students enrolled).

College Admission Counseling 67 students graduated in 2016; 64 went to college, including Arizona State University at the Tempe campus; California State University, Chico; California State University, San Marcos; Penn State University Park; University of California, Irvine; University of Colorado Boulder. Other: 3 entered military service. Median SAT critical reading: 488, median SAT math: 543, median SAT writing: 483.

Student Life Upper grades have uniform requirement, student council, honor system. Discipline rests primarily with faculty.

Summer Programs Enrichment, ESL, sports, computer instruction programs offered; session focuses on academic, JROTC leadership, and recreation; held on campus; accepts boys and girls; open to students from other schools. 300 students usually enrolled. 2017 schedule: July 5 to August 1. Application deadline: none.

Tuition and Aid Day student tuition: $21,000–$22,000; 7-day tuition and room/board: $36,500–$37,500. Tuition reduction for siblings, need-based scholarship grants, military discount available. In 2016–17, 15% of upper-school students received aid. Total amount of financial aid awarded in 2016–17: $382,500.

Admissions Traditional secondary-level entrance grade is 10. For fall 2016, 541 students applied for upper-level admission, 153 were accepted, 121 enrolled. ISEE, Otis-Lennon School Ability Test, SSAT, Star-9 or TOEFL required. Deadline for receipt of application materials: none. No application fee required. On-campus interview recommended.

Athletics Interscholastic: aquatics, baseball, basketball, cross-country running, drill team, flag football, football, golf, lacrosse, marksmanship, soccer, swimming and diving, tennis, track and field, water polo, wrestling; intramural: badminton, combined training, fitness, hockey, independent competitive sports, JROTC drill, outdoor activities, outdoor recreation, physical fitness, physical training, riflery, strength & conditioning, surfing, weight lifting. 15 coaches, 1 athletic trainer.

Computers Computers are regularly used in music technology, video film production, yearbook classes. Computer network features include on-campus library services, Internet access, wireless campus network, Internet filtering or blocking technology. Computer access in designated common areas is available to students. Students grades are available online. The school has a published electronic and media policy.

Contact Candice Heidenrich, Director of Admissions. 888-762-2338. Fax: 760-434-5948. E-mail: admissions@armyandnavyacademy.org. Website: www.armyandnavyacademy.org

ARROYO PACIFIC ACADEMY

41 West Santa Clara Street
Arcadia, California 91007-0661

Head of School: Philip Clarke

General Information Coeducational day college-preparatory, arts, and technology school. Grades 9–12. Founded: 1998. Setting: suburban. 2 buildings on campus. Approved or accredited by Western Association of Schools and Colleges and California Department of Education. Upper school average class size: 12. Upper school faculty-student ratio: 1:10. There are 160 required school days per year for Upper School students. Upper School students typically attend 5 days per week. The average school day consists of 6 hours.

Upper School Student Profile Grade 9: 17 students (11 boys, 6 girls); Grade 10: 32 students (23 boys, 9 girls); Grade 11: 41 students (29 boys, 12 girls); Grade 12: 47 students (30 boys, 17 girls).

Faculty School total: 21. In upper school: 12 men, 9 women.

Subjects Offered Acting, advanced biology, advanced chemistry, advanced math, Advanced Placement courses, algebra, American government, American history, American history-AP, American literature, American literature-AP, American sign language, applied arts, applied music, art, ASB Leadership, athletics, basketball, biology-AP, British literature, broadcast journalism, broadcasting, business, business mathematics, calculus-AP, career and personal planning, career/college preparation, chemistry, chemistry-AP, China/Japan history, Chinese, Chinese history, Chinese literature, Chinese studies, choir, chorus, cinematography, classical music, college admission preparation, college counseling, college planning, college writing, computer art, computer education, computer graphics, computer music, computer skills, computer technologies, conceptual physics, creative arts, creative dance, creative drama, creative thinking, creative writing, culinary arts, dance, dance performance, digital art, digital music, drama, drama performance, dramatic arts, drawing, earth science, economics-AP, English, English language and composition-AP, English language-AP, English literature and composition-AP, English literature-AP, English-AP, environmental science, environmental science-AP, film, filmmaking, fine arts, fitness, food and nutrition, foreign language, forensics, geometry, government-AP, graphic design, health education, history, history of music, history-AP, instrumental music, instruments, intro to computers, introduction to digital multitrack recording techniques, introduction to technology, introduction to theater, jazz, jazz band, jazz ensemble, lab science, lab/keyboard, literature and composition-AP, macro/microeconomics-AP, Mandarin, mathematics-AP, media, media arts, media communications, media production, microeconomics-AP, modern Chinese history, music, music appreciation, music composition, music history, music performance, music technology, music theater, musical productions, musical theater, musical theater dance, nutrition, orchestra, outdoor education, participation in sports, personal finance, personal fitness, personal money management, photo shop, photography, photojournalism, physical education, physical fitness, physics, physics-AP, play production, play/screen writing, playwriting, playwriting and directing, poetry, pre-algebra, pre-calculus, psychology, SAT preparation, scene study, science, science and technology, sign language, Spanish, Spanish language-AP, Spanish-AP, stage and body movement, stage design, statistics, statistics-AP, student government, theater, theater arts, theater design and production, theater production, trigonometry, U.S. government, U.S. government and politics, U.S. government and politics-AP, U.S. history, U.S. history-AP, United States government-AP, video film production, visual and performing arts, visual arts, vocal ensemble, vocal music, voice, volleyball, world history, world history-AP.

Graduation Requirements American government, American history, arts and fine arts (art, music, dance, drama), chemistry, college admission preparation, economics, English, foreign language, government, mathematics, physical education (includes health), SAT preparation, science, technology.

Special Academic Programs 11 Advanced Placement exams for which test preparation is offered; honors section; independent study; academic accommodation for the gifted, the musically talented, and the artistically talented; remedial reading and/or remedial writing; remedial math.

College Admission Counseling 50 students graduated in 2016; all went to college, including Kent State University; University of California, Irvine; University of Southern California.

Student Life Upper grades have specified standards of dress, student council, honor system. Discipline rests primarily with faculty.

Summer Programs Remediation, enrichment, advancement, art/fine arts programs offered; held on campus; accepts boys and girls; open to students from other schools. 80 students usually enrolled. 2017 schedule: June 14 to July 20. Application deadline: May 26.

Tuition and Aid Day student tuition: $14,500. Tuition installment plan (FACTS Tuition Payment Plan).

Admissions Traditional secondary-level entrance grade is 10. Admissions testing or TOEFL required. Deadline for receipt of application materials: none. Application fee required: $150. On-campus interview required.

Athletics Interscholastic: basketball (boys), flag football (b), rugby (b); intramural: cheering (g); coed interscholastic: soccer, tennis, track and field; coed intramural: aerobics, aerobics/dance, backpacking, badminton, bicycling, dance, dance squad, dance team, fitness, hiking/backpacking, outdoor skills, outdoors, physical fitness.

Computers Computers are regularly used in all classes. Computer resources include on-campus library services, Internet access, advanced photo/video design software. Campus intranet, student e-mail accounts, and computer access in designated common areas are available to students. Students grades are available online. The school has a published electronic and media policy.

Contact Robert Nguyen, Admissions Director. 626-566-2280 Ext. 103. Fax: 626-294-0677. E-mail: rnguyen@arroyopacific.org. Website: www.arroyopacific.org/

ARTHUR MORGAN SCHOOL

Burnsville, North Carolina

See Junior Boarding Schools section.

ASHEVILLE SCHOOL

360 Asheville School Road
Asheville, North Carolina 28806

Head of School: Archibald R. Montgomery, IV

General Information Coeducational boarding and day college-preparatory school. Grades 9–12. Founded: 1900. Setting: suburban. Students are housed in single-sex dormitories. 300-acre campus. 19 buildings on campus. Approved or accredited by North Carolina Association of Independent Schools, Southern Association of Colleges and Schools, Southern Association of Independent Schools, The Association of Boarding Schools, and North Carolina Department of Education. Member of National Association of Independent Schools and Secondary School Admission Test Board. Endowment: $48 million. Total enrollment: 260. Upper school average class size: 13. Upper school faculty-student ratio: 1:7. The average school day consists of 6 hours.

Upper School Student Profile Grade 9: 61 students (28 boys, 33 girls); Grade 10: 81 students (39 boys, 42 girls); Grade 11: 72 students (36 boys, 36 girls); Grade 12: 67 students (37 boys, 30 girls).

Faculty School total: 36. In upper school: 21 men, 15 women; 25 have advanced degrees; 28 reside on campus.

Subjects Offered Algebra, American history, American literature, ancient history, art, biology, calculus, chemistry, Chinese, creative writing, English, English literature, European history, finite math, French, geometry, grammar, humanities, Latin, literature, mathematics, medieval/Renaissance history, music, physics, pre-calculus, science, social studies, Spanish, studio art, Western civilization, world history, world literature, writing.

Graduation Requirements Arts and fine arts (art, music, dance, drama), English, foreign language, history, mathematics, music, science, senior demonstration (series of research papers and oral defense of work), three-day camping trip, senior chapel talk (public speaking).

Special Academic Programs 17 Advanced Placement exams for which test preparation is offered; honors section; academic accommodation for the gifted.

College Admission Counseling 73 students graduated in 2016; 72 went to college, including Cornell University; Harvard University; New York University; Sewanee: The University of the South; The University of North Carolina at Chapel Hill. Other: 1 had other specific plans.

Student Life Upper grades have specified standards of dress, student council, honor system. Discipline rests equally with students and faculty.

Tuition and Aid Day student tuition: $22,420; 7-day tuition and room/board: $38,720. Tuition installment plan (monthly payment plans, individually arranged payment plans). Need-based scholarship grants, tuition remission for children of faculty available. In 2016–17, 25% of upper-school students received aid. Total amount of financial aid awarded in 2016–17: $1,803,000.

Admissions Traditional secondary-level entrance grade is 9. For fall 2016, 355 students applied for upper-level admission, 149 were accepted, 94 enrolled. ISEE, PSAT or SAT for applicants to grade 11 and 12, SSAT or TOEFL required. Deadline for receipt of application materials: February 1. Application fee required: $50. On-campus interview required.

Athletics Interscholastic: baseball (boys), basketball (b,g), cross-country running (b,g), field hockey (g), football (b), running (b,g), soccer (b,g), swimming and diving (b,g), tennis (b,g), track and field (b,g), volleyball (g), wrestling (b); intramural: alpine skiing (b,g), dance (g), lacrosse (b); coed interscholastic: equestrian sports, horseback riding; coed intramural: backpacking, bicycling, canoeing/kayaking, climbing, dance, equestrian sports, fitness, fly fishing, Frisbee, hiking/backpacking, horseback riding, kayaking, life saving, modern dance, mountain biking, mountaineering, Nautilus, outdoor activities, physical fitness, rock climbing, ropes courses, skateboarding, skiing (downhill), snowboarding, strength & conditioning, table tennis, wall climbing, weight lifting, wilderness, yoga. 3 coaches, 1 athletic trainer.

Computers Computers are regularly used in French, history, humanities, Latin, mathematics, science, Spanish classes. Computer network features include on-campus library services, online commercial services, Internet access, wireless campus network, Internet filtering or blocking technology. Campus intranet, student e-mail accounts, and computer access in designated common areas are available to students. Students grades are available online. The school has a published electronic and media policy.

Contact John T. Smith III, Director of Admission. 828-254-6345 Ext. 4083. Fax: 828-210-6109. E-mail: admission@ashevilleschool.org. Website: www.ashevilleschool.org

ASHLEY HALL

172 Rutledge Avenue
Charleston, South Carolina 29403-5877

Head of School: Jill Swisher Muti

General Information Coeducational day (boys' only in lower grades) college-preparatory, arts, and science, mathematics school. Boys grades PS–K, girls grades PS–12. Founded: 1909. Setting: urban. Students are housed in single-sex dormitories. 5-acre campus. 8 buildings on campus. Approved or accredited by South Carolina Independent School Association, Southern Association of Colleges and Schools, and Southern Association of Independent Schools. Member of National Association of Independent Schools. Endowment: $12 million. Total enrollment: 682. Upper school average class size: 16. Upper school faculty-student ratio: 1:8. Upper School students typically attend 5 days per week. The average school day consists of 7 hours.

Upper School Student Profile Grade 6: 48 students (48 girls); Grade 7: 47 students (47 girls); Grade 8: 45 students (45 girls); Grade 9: 39 students (39 girls); Grade 10: 53 students (53 girls); Grade 11: 55 students (55 girls); Grade 12: 54 students (54 girls). 5% of students are boarding students. 95% are state residents. 1 state is represented in upper school student body. 5% are international students. International students from China.

Faculty School total: 95. In upper school: 8 men, 20 women; 18 have advanced degrees; 3 reside on campus.

Subjects Offered 3-dimensional design, algebra, American history, American history-AP, American literature, art, art history, art history-AP, bioethics, biology, biology-AP, calculus, calculus-AP, ceramics, chemistry, chemistry-AP, choir, computer science, creative writing, desktop publishing, drama, economics, economics and history, English, English literature, English-AP, European history, European history-AP, forensics, foundations of civilization, French, French-AP, geography, geometry, government/civics, history, Internet, keyboarding, Latin, Latin-AP, marine biology, mathematics, microeconomics-AP, music, photo shop, photography, physical education, physical science, physics, physics-AP, pre-calculus, programming, psychology, social studies, Spanish, Spanish-AP, speech, statistics, statistics-AP, studio art, studio art-AP, technology, trigonometry, U.S. government and politics-AP, Web site design, world history.

Graduation Requirements Advanced Placement courses, arts and fine arts (art, music, dance, drama), English, foreign language, history, mathematics, physical education (includes health), science.

Special Academic Programs Advanced Placement exam preparation; honors section; independent study; term-away projects; study at local college for college credit; study abroad; academic accommodation for the gifted, the musically talented, and the artistically talented; ESL (15 students enrolled).

College Admission Counseling 53 students graduated in 2016; 52 went to college, including Clemson University; College of Charleston; Sewanee: The University of the South; The University of North Carolina at Chapel Hill; University of South Carolina; Wofford College. Other: 1 entered a postgraduate year.

Student Life Upper grades have uniform requirement, student council, honor system. Discipline rests equally with students and faculty.

Summer Programs Enrichment, sports, art/fine arts, computer instruction programs offered; session focuses on enrichment, athletics, adventure, and day camps; held on campus; accepts girls; open to students from other schools. 900 students usually enrolled. 2017 schedule: June 1 to July 28. Application deadline: none.

Tuition and Aid Day student tuition: $14,460–$22,985; 7-day tuition and room/board: $47,500. Tuition installment plan (FACTS Tuition Payment Plan). Need-based scholarship grants, paying campus jobs available. In 2016–17, 23% of upper-school students received aid. Total amount of financial aid awarded in 2016–17: $1,215,000.

Admissions Traditional secondary-level entrance grade is 9. For fall 2016, 64 students applied for upper-level admission, 58 were accepted, 26 enrolled. ISEE, Kaufman Test of Educational Achievement or SSAT required. Deadline for receipt of application materials: February 7. Application fee required: $75. Interview required.

Athletics Interscholastic: basketball, cross-country running, running, sailing, soccer, strength & conditioning, swimming and diving, tennis, track and field, volleyball, weight training; intramural: aerobics/dance, aquatics, archery, backpacking, basketball, canoeing/kayaking, climbing, cross-country running, dance, dance squad, dance team, equestrian sports, fitness, golf, hiking/backpacking, horseback riding, jogging, judo, jump rope, kayaking, kickball, life saving, outdoor adventure, outdoor education, outdoor skills, physical fitness, physical training, running, soccer, strength & conditioning, swimming and diving, tennis, track and field, volleyball. 3 PE instructors, 4 coaches, 1 athletic trainer.

Computers Computers are regularly used in animation, art, career exploration, college planning, desktop publishing, graphic design, independent study, introduction to technology, library skills, newspaper, photography, research skills, SAT preparation, video film production, Web site design, yearbook classes. Computer network features include on-campus library services, online commercial services, Internet access, wireless campus network, Internet filtering or blocking technology. The school has a published electronic and media policy.

Contact Jill Lyon, Assistant Director of Admission. 843-965-8501. Fax: 843-720-2868. E-mail: lyonl@ashleyhall.org. Website: www.ashleyhall.org

ASSETS SCHOOL

Honolulu, Hawaii

See Special Needs Schools section.

ATHENS ACADEMY

1281 Spartan Lane
PO Box 6548
Athens, Georgia 30604

Head of School: Mr. John Thorsen

General Information Coeducational day college-preparatory school. Grades N–12. Founded: 1967. Setting: suburban. Nearest major city is Atlanta. 154-acre campus. 11 buildings on campus. Approved or accredited by Georgia Independent School Association, Southern Association of Colleges and Schools, Southern Association of Independent Schools, and Georgia Department of Education. Member of National Association of Independent Schools and Secondary School Admission Test Board. Endowment: $6.5 million. Total enrollment: 963. Upper school average class size: 18. Upper school faculty-student ratio: 1:8. There are 182 required school days per year for Upper School students. Upper School students typically attend 5 days per week. The average school day consists of 7 hours.

Upper School Student Profile Grade 9: 82 students (42 boys, 40 girls); Grade 10: 79 students (38 boys, 41 girls); Grade 11: 93 students (42 boys, 51 girls); Grade 12: 72 students (46 boys, 26 girls).

Faculty School total: 102. In upper school: 22 men, 20 women, 31 have advanced degrees.

Subjects Offered Advanced math, advanced studio art-AP, algebra, American history, American history-AP, American literature, anatomy, art, art history, band, bioethics, biology, biology-AP, calculus, calculus-AP, ceramics, chemistry, chemistry-AP, choral music, creative writing, drama, ecology, economics, engineering, English, English literature, English-AP, European history, expository writing, fine arts, French, geography, geometry, government/civics, grammar, health, history, Latin, Latin-AP, mathematics, music, photography, physical education, physics, physics-AP, physiology, robotics, science, social studies, Spanish, statistics, theater, trigonometry, world history, world literature.

Graduation Requirements Arts and fine arts (art, music, dance, drama), English, foreign language, mathematics, physical education (includes health), science, social studies (includes history).

Special Academic Programs 13 Advanced Placement exams for which test preparation is offered; honors section; independent study.

College Admission Counseling 82 students graduated in 2016; all went to college, including Georgia Institute of Technology; University of Georgia. Median SAT critical reading: 616, median SAT math: 628, median SAT writing: 604, median combined SAT: 1848, median composite ACT: 27.

Student Life Upper grades have specified standards of dress, student council, honor system. Discipline rests primarily with faculty.

Summer Programs Remediation, enrichment, sports, art/fine arts, computer instruction programs offered; session focuses on enrichment and review; held on campus; accepts boys and girls; open to students from other schools. 250 students usually enrolled. 2017 schedule: June 15 to August 13. Application deadline: none.

Tuition and Aid Day student tuition: $8500–$17,500. Tuition installment plan (Insured Tuition Payment Plan, monthly payment plans, individually arranged payment plans). Tuition reduction for siblings, need-based scholarship grants available. In 2016–17, 20% of upper-school students received aid. Total amount of financial aid awarded in 2016–17: $12,000,000.

Admissions Traditional secondary-level entrance grade is 9. For fall 2016, 39 students applied for upper-level admission, 27 were accepted, 23 enrolled. CTP III and Otis-Lennon School Ability Test, ERB CPT III required. Deadline for receipt of application materials: February 12. Application fee required: $85. On-campus interview recommended.

Athletics Interscholastic: baseball (boys), basketball (b,g), cheering (g), cross-country running (b,g), diving (b,g), football (b), soccer (b,g), swimming and diving (b,g), tennis (b,g), track and field (b,g), volleyball (g), wrestling (b); coed interscholastic: cross-country running, diving, golf, swimming and diving, tennis, track and field. 6 PE instructors, 5 coaches.

Computers Computers are regularly used in English, foreign language, French, history, Latin, mathematics, science, Spanish classes. Computer network features include on-campus library services, online commercial services, Internet access, wireless campus network. Student e-mail accounts are available to students. The school has a published electronic and media policy.

Contact Mr. Geoffrey R. Walton, Director of Admission. 706-549-9225. Fax: 706-354-3775. E-mail: gwalton@athensacademy.org. Website: www.athensacademy.org/

ATHENS BIBLE SCHOOL

507 South Hoffman Street
Athens, Alabama 35611

Head of School: Mr. Randall L. Adams

General Information Coeducational day college-preparatory school. Grades K–12. Founded: 1943. Setting: small town. Nearest major city is Huntsville. 2 buildings on campus. Approved or accredited by Southern Association of Colleges and Schools and Alabama Department of Education. Total enrollment: 270. Upper school average class size: 30. There are 180 required school days per year for Upper School students. The average school day consists of 6 hours and 11 minutes.

Upper School Student Profile Grade 7: 9 students (9 boys).
Subjects Offered 1968.
Student Life Upper grades have specified standards of dress, student council. Discipline rests primarily with faculty.
Admissions No application fee required. Interview required.
Contact Mrs. Jill Duke, Secretary/Receptionist. 256-232-3525. Fax: 256-232-5417 Ext. 221. E-mail: jill.duke@athensbibleschool.org.
Website: www.athensbibleschool.org

ATLANTA GIRLS' SCHOOL

3254 Northside Parkway NW
Atlanta, Georgia 30327
Head of School: Ms. Ayanna Hill-Gill

General Information Girls' day college-preparatory, arts, and leadership and service school. Grades 6–12. Distance learning grades 10–12. Founded: 2000. Setting: suburban. 7-acre campus. 1 building on campus. Approved or accredited by Georgia Independent School Association, Headmasters' Conference, National Independent Private Schools Association, Southern Association of Colleges and Schools, Southern Association of Independent Schools, The College Board, and Georgia Department of Education. Member of National Association of Independent Schools and Secondary School Admission Test Board. Upper school average class size: 13. Upper school faculty-student ratio: 1:8. There are 180 required school days per year for Upper School students. Upper School students typically attend 5 days per week.
Upper School Student Profile Grade 9: 52 students (52 girls); Grade 10: 36 students (36 girls); Grade 11: 27 students (27 girls); Grade 12: 34 students (34 girls).
Faculty School total: 27. In upper school: 3 men, 16 women; 11 have advanced degrees.
Subjects Offered All academic.
Graduation Requirements 2, 70 hr minimum internships, 1 global travel experience.
Special Academic Programs Honors section; independent study; study at local college for college credit; study abroad.
College Admission Counseling 23 students graduated in 2016; all went to college, including Emory University; Georgia Institute of Technology; Georgia State University; Spelman College; Tennessee State University; Vanderbilt University.
Student Life Upper grades have uniform requirement, student council, honor system. Discipline rests primarily with faculty.
Summer Programs Enrichment, advancement, art/fine arts, computer instruction programs offered; session focuses on science, math, technology, and arts; held on campus; accepts girls; open to students from other schools. 200 students usually enrolled. 2017 schedule: June 5 to June 23. Application deadline: May 26.
Tuition and Aid Day student tuition: $23,330. Tuition installment plan (SMART Tuition Payment Plan, FACTS Tuition Payment Plan). Need-based scholarship grants available. In 2016–17, 30% of upper-school students received aid.
Admissions Traditional secondary-level entrance grade is 9. PSAT or SAT for applicants to grade 11 and 12 or SSAT required. Deadline for receipt of application materials: January 27. Application fee required: $75. On-campus interview recommended.
Athletics Interscholastic: archery, basketball, cross-country running, dance team, golf, soccer, softball, swimming and diving, tennis, track and field, volleyball; intramural: outdoor activities. 2 PE instructors, 5 coaches, 1 athletic trainer.
Computers Computers are regularly used in all classes. Computer network features include on-campus library services, online commercial services, Internet access, wireless campus network, Internet filtering or blocking technology. Campus intranet, student e-mail accounts, and computer access in designated common areas are available to students. Students grades are available online. The school has a published electronic and media policy.
Contact Cassandra Streich, Director of Admission. 404-845-0900 Ext. 227. Fax: 404-869-9718. E-mail: cstreich@atlantagirlsschool.org.
Website: www.atlantagirlsschool.org/

ATLANTA INTERNATIONAL SCHOOL

2890 North Fulton Drive
Atlanta, Georgia 30305
Head of School: Mr. Kevin Glass

General Information Coeducational day college-preparatory, International Baccalaureate Diploma Programme (Grades 11-12), and International Baccalaureate Middle Years (Grades 9-10) school. Grades PK–12. Founded: 1984. Setting: urban. 14-acre campus. 4 buildings on campus. Approved or accredited by European Council of International Schools, French Ministry of Education, Georgia Independent School Association, International Baccalaureate Organization, Southern Association of Colleges and Schools, Southern Association of Independent Schools, and Georgia Department of Education. Member of National Association of Independent Schools and European Council of International Schools. Languages of instruction: English, German, and Spanish. Total enrollment: 1,160. Upper school average class size: 15. Upper school faculty-student ratio: 1:15. There are 182 required school days per year for

Upper School students. Upper School students typically attend 5 days per week. The average school day consists of 7 hours and 30 minutes.
Upper School Student Profile Grade 6: 97 students (52 boys, 45 girls); Grade 7: 100 students (51 boys, 49 girls); Grade 8: 97 students (48 boys, 49 girls); Grade 9: 99 students (43 boys, 56 girls); Grade 10: 81 students (37 boys, 44 girls); Grade 11: 98 students (49 boys, 49 girls); Grade 12: 77 students (29 boys, 48 girls).
Faculty School total: 164.
Subjects Offered American history, art, biology, chemistry, Chinese, choir, chorus, computer science, contemporary issues, design, economics, English, English literature, ESL, fine arts, French, French as a second language, geography, German, health, integrated mathematics, International Baccalaureate courses, jazz band, lab/keyboard, Latin, math methods, mathematics, model United Nations, physical education, physics, robotics, SAT preparation, science, science and technology, social studies, Spanish, theater, theater arts, theory of knowledge, world history, yearbook.
Graduation Requirements IBDP Extended essay/research project, IBDP Creativity, Activity, Service (CAS) hours, IBDP Exams.
Special Academic Programs International Baccalaureate program; independent study; term-away projects; study abroad; ESL.
College Admission Counseling 84 students graduated in 2016; all went to college, including Emory University; Georgia Institute of Technology; Georgia State University; McGill University; New York University; University of Georgia. Mean SAT critical reading: 606, mean SAT math: 608.
Student Life Upper grades have specified standards of dress, student council, honor system. Discipline rests primarily with faculty.
Summer Programs Enrichment, advancement, ESL, sports, art/fine arts, computer instruction programs offered; session focuses on Language acquisition (French, Spanish, German, Chinese, ESL), day camps, sport camps, theater, robotics, chess; held on campus; accepts boys and girls; open to students from other schools. 150 students usually enrolled. 2017 schedule: June 12 to July 27. Application deadline: April 30.
Tuition and Aid Day student tuition: $21,266–$24,277. Tuition installment plan (Insured Tuition Payment Plan). Need-based scholarship grants available. In 2016–17, 11% of upper-school students received aid.
Admissions Traditional secondary-level entrance grade is 9. SSAT required. Deadline for receipt of application materials: none. Application fee required: $100. Interview recommended.
Athletics Interscholastic: basketball (boys, girls), cross-country running (b,g), soccer (b,g), swimming and diving (b,g), tennis (b,g), track and field (b,g), ultimate Frisbee (b,g), volleyball (g); intramural: strength & conditioning (b,g); coed interscholastic: golf, sailing; coed intramural: basketball, soccer, volleyball. 9 PE instructors, 3 athletic trainers.
Computers Computers are regularly used in all academic classes. Computer network features include on-campus library services, Internet access, wireless campus network, Internet filtering or blocking technology, server space for file storage, online classroom, multi-user learning software. Student e-mail accounts and computer access in designated common areas are available to students. Students grades are available online. The school has a published electronic and media policy.
Contact Ms. Nici Robinson, Associate Director of Admission and Financial Aid. 404-841-3891. Fax: 404-841-3873. E-mail: nrobinson@aischool.org.
Website: www.aischool.org

ATLANTIS ACADEMY

Miami, Florida
See Special Needs Schools section.

AUGUSTA CHRISTIAN SCHOOL

313 Baston Road
Martinez, Georgia 30907
Head of School: Mr. Les Walden

General Information Coeducational day college-preparatory, Health Sciences Academy, and talent development for students with learning disabilities school, affiliated with Christian faith. Grades K–12. Founded: 1958. Setting: suburban. Nearest major city is Augusta. 26-acre campus. 10 buildings on campus. Approved or accredited by Association of Christian Schools International, South Carolina Independent School Association, Southern Association of Colleges and Schools, and Georgia Department of Education. Total enrollment: 561. Upper school average class size: 11. Upper school faculty-student ratio: 1:11. There are 180 required school days per year for Upper School students. Upper School students typically attend 5 days per week. The average school day consists of 7 hours and 5 minutes.
Upper School Student Profile Grade 9: 51 students (27 boys, 24 girls); Grade 10: 50 students (38 boys, 12 girls); Grade 11: 56 students (35 boys, 21 girls); Grade 12: 70 students (37 boys, 33 girls).
Faculty School total: 60. In upper school: 11 men, 16 women; 11 have advanced degrees.
Subjects Offered Advanced chemistry, advanced computer applications, advanced math, Advanced Placement courses, algebra, American government, American history, American history-AP, American literature, anatomy and physiology, art, athletic training, athletics, band, baseball, basketball, Bible, Bible studies, biology, biology-AP,

British literature, British literature-AP, calculus-AP, ceramics, cheerleading, chemistry, choir, choral music, chorus, Christian education, Christian studies, college counseling, comparative religion, computer education, computer skills, drama, drama performance, earth science, ecology, economics and history, electives, English, English composition, English literature, English literature-AP, English-AP, European history, French, general science, geography, geometry, government, grammar, health, health science, history, instrumental music, keyboarding, life skills, mathematics, mathematics-AP, music appreciation, musical productions, New Testament, physics, piano, pre-algebra, pre-calculus, public speaking, reading, remedial/makeup course work, SAT preparation, science, social studies, Spanish, speech, sports, state history, student government, swimming, U.S. government, U.S. history, U.S. history-AP, U.S. literature, volleyball, weight training, weightlifting, world history, wrestling, yearbook.

Graduation Requirements Bible, computers, electives, English, foreign language, mathematics, physical education (includes health), science, social studies (includes history), speech.

Special Academic Programs Advanced Placement exam preparation; honors section; study at local college for college credit; programs in English, mathematics for dyslexic students; ESL (8 students enrolled).

College Admission Counseling 65 students graduated in 2016; all went to college, including Augusta State University; Georgia Institute of Technology; Georgia Southern University; University of Georgia.

Student Life Upper grades have specified standards of dress, student council. Discipline rests primarily with faculty. Attendance at religious services is required.

Tuition and Aid Day student tuition: $1896–$13,368. Tuition installment plan (Insured Tuition Payment Plan, monthly payment plans, individually arranged payment plans). Tuition reduction for siblings, need-based scholarship grants available.

Admissions Traditional secondary-level entrance grade is 9. Stanford Achievement Test required. Deadline for receipt of application materials: none. Application fee required: $100. Interview recommended.

Athletics Interscholastic: baseball (boys), basketball (b,g), cross-country running (b,g), football (b), soccer (b,g), softball (g), swimming and diving (b,g), tennis (b,g), track and field (b,g), volleyball (g), wrestling (b); coed interscholastic: cheering, golf. 3 PE instructors.

Computers Computers are regularly used in all academic, computer applications, keyboarding, yearbook classes. Computer network features include on-campus library services, Internet access, wireless campus network, Internet filtering or blocking technology, all middle and high school students get a Mac laptop. Campus intranet and student e-mail accounts are available to students. Students grades are available online. The school has a published electronic and media policy.

Contact Mrs. Lauren Banks, Director of Admissions. 706-863-2905 Ext. 206. Fax: 706-860-6618. E-mail: laurenbanks@augustachristian.org. Website: www.augustachristian.org

AURORA CENTRAL CATHOLIC HIGH SCHOOL

1255 North Edgelawn Drive
Aurora, Illinois 60506-1673

Head of School: Rev. F. William Etheredge

General Information Coeducational day college-preparatory school, affiliated with Roman Catholic Church. Grades 9–12. Founded: 1968. Setting: suburban. 35-acre campus. 1 building on campus. Approved or accredited by National Catholic Education Association, North Central Association of Colleges and Schools, and Illinois Department of Education. Total enrollment: 525. Upper school average class size: 20. Upper school faculty-student ratio: 1:14. There are 180 required school days per year for Upper School students. Upper School students typically attend 5 days per week. The average school day consists of 6 hours and 50 minutes.

Faculty School total: 44. In upper school: 16 men, 28 women.

Subjects Offered Acting, algebra, American history, American literature-AP, anatomy and physiology, Ancient Greek, architectural drawing, art, athletics, band, Bible, biology, biology-AP, business law, calculus-AP, campus ministry, chemistry, chemistry-AP, chorus, civil war history, comparative religion, composition-AP, computer skills, constitutional history of U.S., consumer economics, contemporary history, CPR, creative drama, creative writing, drafting, earth science, ecology, environmental systems, electives, engineering, English, English composition, English literature, English literature-AP, English/composition-AP, environmental science, environmental science-AP, ethics, fine arts, foreign language, French, French-AP, geography, geometry, health, health education, history, home economics, honors algebra, honors English, honors geometry, honors U.S. history, honors world history, instrumental music, Internet, jazz band, journalism, keyboarding, Latin, literature and composition-AP, math applications, mathematics, medieval history, moral theology, music, newspaper, oral communications, photography, physical education, political science, pre-algebra, pre-calculus, psychology, psychology-AP, reading/study skills, science, Shakespeare, social justice, sociology, Spanish, Spanish-AP, theology, trigonometry, U.S. government and politics, U.S. government and politics-AP, U.S. history, U.S. history-AP, Western civilization, world history, World War II, writing, yearbook.

Graduation Requirements Algebra, American history, arts and fine arts (art, music, dance, drama), biology, Catholic belief and practice, Christian and Hebrew scripture, constitutional history of U.S., consumer economics, economics, English, English

literature, foreign language, geometry, health and wellness, history, keyboarding, language and composition, mathematics, moral theology, physical education (includes health), religion (includes Bible studies and theology), science, scripture, U.S. government, U.S. history, retreat programs. Community service is required.

Special Academic Programs 6 Advanced Placement exams for which test preparation is offered; honors section; independent study; study at local college for college credit; academic accommodation for the gifted; remedial reading and/or remedial writing; remedial math.

College Admission Counseling Colleges students went to include Benedictine University; Illinois State University; Loyola University Chicago; Marquette University; Northern Illinois University; University of Illinois at Urbana–Champaign. Mean composite ACT: 24.

Student Life Upper grades have uniform requirement, student council, honor system. Discipline rests primarily with faculty. Attendance at religious services is required.

Tuition and Aid Tuition installment plan (monthly payment plans). Tuition reduction for siblings, merit scholarship grants, need-based scholarship grants, need-based loans available.

Admissions Traditional secondary-level entrance grade is 9. High School Placement Test required. Deadline for receipt of application materials: none. Application fee required: $50.

Athletics Interscholastic: aerobics/dance (girls), baseball (b,g), basketball (b,g), cheering (g), cross-country running (b,g), dance (g), dance squad (g), dance team (g), football (b), golf (b,g), indoor track (b,g), indoor track & field (b,g), pom squad (g), soccer (b,g), softball (g), tennis (b,g), volleyball (g), wrestling (b); intramural: aerobics/dance (g), baseball (b,g), basketball (b,g), flag football (b), floor hockey (g), football (b), indoor track (b,g), indoor track & field (b,g), jogging (b,g), physical fitness (b,g), physical training (b,g), power lifting (b,g), soccer (b,g), softball (b,g), volleyball (b,g), weight lifting (b,g), weight training (b,g), winter (indoor) track (b,g), wrestling (b); coed interscholastic: dance team; coed intramural: modern dance, physical fitness, physical training, power lifting, soccer, swimming and diving, volleyball, weight lifting, weight training, winter (indoor) track. 2 PE instructors, 1 athletic trainer.

Computers Computers are regularly used in drafting, engineering, English, French, history, photography, Spanish, technology classes. Computer network features include on-campus library services, online commercial services, Internet access, Internet filtering or blocking technology. Student e-mail accounts are available to students. Students grades are available online. The school has a published electronic and media policy.

Contact Mrs. Mackenzie Livingston, Recruitment Director and Assistant Development Director. 630-907-0095. Fax: 630-907-1076. E-mail: mlivingston@auroracentral.com. Website: www.auroracentral.com

AUSTIN PREPARATORY SCHOOL

101 Willow Street
Reading, Massachusetts 01867

Head of School: Dr. James Hickey

General Information Coeducational day college-preparatory, arts, religious studies, and technology school, affiliated with Roman Catholic Church. Grades 6–12. Founded: 1961. Setting: suburban. Nearest major city is Boston. 50-acre campus. 3 buildings on campus. Approved or accredited by New England Association of Schools and Colleges and Massachusetts Department of Education. Member of National Association of Independent Schools. Upper school average class size: 14. Upper school faculty-student ratio: 1:11. There are 168 required school days per year for Upper School students. Upper School students typically attend 5 days per week. The average school day consists of 6 hours and 30 minutes.

Upper School Student Profile Grade 9: 128 students (59 boys, 69 girls); Grade 10: 117 students (56 boys, 61 girls); Grade 11: 125 students (64 boys, 61 girls); Grade 12: 144 students (60 boys, 84 girls). 85% of students are Roman Catholic.

Faculty School total: 70. In upper school: 25 men, 15 women.

Subjects Offered ACT preparation, algebra, American history, American literature, anatomy, arts, Bible studies, biology, botany, business, calculus, chemistry, computer math, computer programming, computer science, creative writing, earth science, economics, English, English literature, environmental science, French, geography, geology, geometry, government/civics, grammar, history, Latin, marine biology, mathematics, oceanography, physics, physiology, religion, Russian, SAT preparation, SAT/ACT preparation, science, social studies, sociology, Spanish, sports team management, statistics, technology, trigonometry, world studies, World War II, world wide web design, World-Wide-Web publishing, writing, yearbook.

Graduation Requirements Art, English, foreign language, humanities, mathematics, religion (includes Bible studies and theology), science, social studies (includes history), technology. Community service is required.

Special Academic Programs 18 Advanced Placement exams for which test preparation is offered; honors section; independent study; study at local college for college credit.

College Admission Counseling 140 students graduated in 2016; 139 went to college, including Bentley University; Endicott College; Merrimack College; Quinnipiac University; Villanova University; Worcester Polytechnic Institute. Other: 1 entered a postgraduate year. 30% scored over 600 on SAT critical reading, 30% scored over 600 on SAT math.

Student Life Upper grades have uniform requirement, student council. Discipline rests primarily with faculty. Attendance at religious services is required.

Summer Programs Enrichment, sports, art/fine arts programs offered; held on campus; accepts boys and girls; open to students from other schools.

Tuition and Aid Day student tuition: $18,650. Tuition installment plan (Academic Management Services Plan, SMART Tuition Payment Plan, monthly payment plans, see school web site for full description). Tuition reduction for siblings, merit scholarship grants, need-based scholarship grants available. In 2016–17, 30% of upper-school students received aid.

Admissions Traditional secondary-level entrance grade is 9. Archdiocese of Boston or STS, High School Placement Test, ISEE or SSAT required. Deadline for receipt of application materials: December 21. Application fee required: $50. On-campus interview required.

Athletics Interscholastic: baseball (boys), basketball (b,g), cheering (g), cross-country running (b,g), dance team (g), football (b), golf (b,g), ice hockey (b,g), lacrosse (b,g), skiing (downhill) (b,g), soccer (b,g), softball (g), swimming and diving (b,g), tennis (b,g), track and field (b,g), volleyball (g), winter (indoor) track (b,g); intramural: basketball (b,g), skiing (downhill) (b,g), softball (b,g); coed interscholastic: golf, indoor track & field, skiing (downhill), swimming and diving; coed intramural: basketball, dance, equestrian sports, skiing (downhill), softball, yoga. 52 coaches, 1 athletic trainer.

Computers Computers are regularly used in all academic, art, creative writing, English, foreign language, French, geography, history, humanities, Latin, library, mathematics, media, music technology, psychology, religion, science, Spanish, writing, yearbook classes. Computer network features include on-campus library services, online commercial services, Internet access, wireless campus network, Internet filtering or blocking technology. Student e-mail accounts and computer access in designated common areas are available to students. Students grades are available online. The school has a published electronic and media policy.

Contact Mrs. Elizabeth Flynn, Director of Enrollment. 781-944-4900 Ext. 834. Fax: 781-942-0918. E-mail: eflynn@austinprep.org. Website: www.austinprep.org

AUSTIN WALDORF SCHOOL

8700 South View Road
Austin, Texas 78737

Head of School: Ms. Kathy McElveen

General Information Coeducational day college-preparatory, arts, and music school. Grades K–12. Founded: 1980. Setting: rural. 19-acre campus. 14 buildings on campus. Approved or accredited by Association of Waldorf Schools of North America, Independent Schools Association of the Southwest, and Texas Department of Education. Total enrollment: 390. Upper school average class size: 30. Upper school faculty-student ratio: 1:20. There are 185 required school days per year for Upper School students. Upper School students typically attend 5 days per week. The average school day consists of 6 hours.

Upper School Student Profile Grade 6: 27 students (11 boys, 16 girls); Grade 7: 28 students (20 boys, 8 girls); Grade 8: 33 students (21 boys, 12 girls); Grade 9: 32 students (5 boys, 27 girls); Grade 10: 20 students (7 boys, 13 girls); Grade 11: 16 students (6 boys, 10 girls); Grade 12: 17 students (8 boys, 9 girls).

Faculty School total: 50. In upper school: 10 have advanced degrees.

Subjects Offered 20th century American writers, 20th century history, 20th century physics, 20th century world history, 3-dimensional art, 3-dimensional design, acting, advanced biology, advanced chemistry, advanced computer applications, advanced math, African American history, African American studies, African-American literature, agriculture, algebra, all academic, American biography, American Civil War, American culture, American democracy, American foreign policy, American government, American history, American literature, American studies, analysis, analysis and differential calculus, analytic geometry, anatomy, anatomy and physiology, Ancient Greek, ancient history, ancient world history, ancient/medieval philosophy, anthropology, applied arts, applied music, art, art and culture, art appreciation, art education, art history, Asian history, Asian literature, Asian studies, astronomy, athletics, atomic theory, band, basic language skills, Basic programming, basketball, Bible as literature, biochemistry, biology, bookbinding, botany, British literature, business mathematics, calculus, career education internship, career/college preparation, cell biology, Central and Eastern European history, ceramics, chemistry, child development, choral music, chorus, circus acts, Civil War, classical language, classical studies, clayworking, college admission preparation, college counseling, college planning, communication skills, community garden, community service, comparative civilizations, comparative government and politics, comparative religion, composition, computer animation, computer applications, computer art, computer education, computer graphics, computer information systems, computer literacy, computer math, computer multimedia, computer processing, computer programming, computer resources, computer science, computer skills, computer studies, computer technologies, computer-aided design, constitutional history of U.S., consumer economics, critical thinking, critical writing, cultural geography, current events, current history, data analysis, debate, decision making skills, democracy in America, desktop publishing, digital applications, diversity studies, drama, drawing, East European studies, ecology, environmental systems, economics and history, electives, English, English composition, English literature, environmental education, environmental science, environmental studies, ethics, etymology, European civilization, European history, European literature,

eurythmy, expository writing, fiber arts, fiction, film and literature, finance, fine arts, finite math, food and nutrition, foreign language, foundations of civilization, four units of summer reading, gardening, general business, general science, genetics, geography, geology, geometry, German, global studies, golf, government, grammar, Greek culture, health and wellness, history, human anatomy, human biology, human development, humanities, illustration, instrumental music, interactive media, interdisciplinary studies, Internet research, internship, interpersonal skills, intro to computers, jazz band, language and composition, language arts, Latin American history, library research, linear algebra, literature, logarithms, logic, mathematics, mechanics of writing, medieval history, medieval/Renaissance history, metalworking, modern politics, multicultural studies, music, Native American history, nature study, newspaper, novels, oil painting, oral communications, orchestra, organic chemistry, painting, participation in sports, performing arts, physical education, physics, physiology, poetry, political science, pottery, practical arts, pre-algebra, pre-calculus, projective geometry, public speaking, qualitative analysis, religion and culture, remedial study skills, research, Roman civilization, SAT preparation, sculpture, senior composition, senior internship, senior project, Shakespeare, social studies, Spanish, sports, stage design, stained glass, state government, stone carving, strings, student government, student publications, studio art, swimming, Texas history, textiles, the Web, theater arts, theater design and production, theater production, trigonometry, twentieth century ethnic conflicts, U.S. constitutional history, U.S. government and politics, visual arts, water color painting, weaving, Web site design, Western civilization, Western literature, Western philosophy, woodworking, work experience, world civilizations, writing, yearbook, zoology.

Special Academic Programs Study abroad; remedial reading and/or remedial writing; remedial math; programs in English for dyslexic students.

College Admission Counseling 15 students graduated in 2016; all went to college, including Southwestern University; Texas State University; The University of Texas at Austin; The University of Texas at San Antonio; University of California, Berkeley.

Student Life Upper grades have specified standards of dress, student council. Discipline rests primarily with faculty.

Tuition and Aid Day student tuition: $15,000. Tuition installment plan (FACTS Tuition Payment Plan). Need-based scholarship grants available. In 2016–17, 30% of upper-school students received aid.

Admissions Traditional secondary-level entrance grade is 9. For fall 2016, 13 students applied for upper-level admission, 8 were accepted, 8 enrolled. Achievement tests required. Deadline for receipt of application materials: none. Application fee required: $100. Interview required.

Athletics Interscholastic: basketball (boys, girls), cross-country running (b,g), flag football (b), golf (b), independent competitive sports (b,g), running (b,g), swimming and diving (b,g), tennis (b), touch football (b), track and field (b,g), volleyball (g); coed interscholastic: soccer. 2 PE instructors, 4 coaches.

Computers Computer resources include Internet access. Computer access in designated common areas is available to students. Students grades are available online.

Contact Ms. Kim DeVittorio, Enrollment Director. 512-288-5942 Ext. 103. Fax: 512-301-8997. E-mail: enroll@austinwaldorf.org. Website: www.austinwaldorf.org/

BAKERSFIELD CHRISTIAN HIGH SCHOOL

12775 Stockdale Highway
Bakersfield, California 93314

Head of School: Mr. John Buetow

General Information Coeducational day college-preparatory and agriculture science school, affiliated with Christian faith. Grades 9–12. Founded: 1979. Setting: suburban. 47-acre campus. 11 buildings on campus. Approved or accredited by Association of Christian Schools International, Western Association of Schools and Colleges, and California Department of Education. Endowment: $500,000. Total enrollment: 488. Upper school average class size: 22. Upper school faculty-student ratio: 1:17. There are 180 required school days per year for Upper School students. Upper School students typically attend 5 days per week. The average school day consists of 5 hours and 45 minutes.

Upper School Student Profile Postgraduate: 100 students (51 boys, 49 girls). 85% of students are Christian faith.

Faculty School total: 35. In upper school: 17 men, 18 women; 8 have advanced degrees.

Subjects Offered ACT preparation, algebra, American sign language.

Graduation Requirements 40 hours community service, religious courses.

Special Academic Programs Advanced Placement exam preparation; honors section; study at local college for college credit.

College Admission Counseling 110 students graduated in 2016; 102 went to college, including Azusa Pacific University; California Polytechnic State University, San Luis Obispo; Penn State University Park; The University of Alabama in Huntsville; United States Naval Academy; University of California, Davis.

Student Life Upper grades have specified standards of dress, student council, honor system. Discipline rests primarily with faculty. Attendance at religious services is required.

Summer Programs Remediation, enrichment, advancement, sports, art/fine arts programs offered; held on campus; accepts boys and girls; open to students from other schools. 300 students usually enrolled. 2017 schedule: June 5 to July 15. Application deadline: May 31.

Tuition and Aid Day student tuition: $13,277. Tuition installment plan (SMART Tuition Payment Plan, monthly payment plans, individually arranged payment plans). Tuition reduction for siblings, need-based scholarship grants, need-based financial aid available. In 2016–17, 30% of upper-school students received aid. Total amount of financial aid awarded in 2016–17: $160,000.

Admissions Traditional secondary-level entrance grade is 9. For fall 2016, 115 students applied for upper-level admission, 112 were accepted, 100 enrolled. Admissions testing required. Deadline for receipt of application materials: none. Application fee required: $100. On-campus interview recommended.

Athletics Interscholastic: aquatics (boys, girls), baseball (b), basketball (b,g), cheering (g), football (b), golf (b,g), soccer (b,g), softball (g), tennis (b,g), volleyball (g), water polo (b,g), weight training (b,g), wrestling (b); coed interscholastic: cross-country running, diving, swimming and diving, track and field. 2 PE instructors, 10 coaches, 1 athletic trainer.

Computers Computers are regularly used in all classes. Computer network features include on-campus library services, Internet access, Internet filtering or blocking technology. Student e-mail accounts and computer access in designated common areas are available to students. Students grades are available online. The school has a published electronic and media policy.

Contact Mrs. Alice E. Abril, Director of Admissions. 661-410-7000 Ext. 5527. Fax: 661-410-7410. E-mail: aabril@bakersfieldchristian.com.

Website: www.bakersfieldchristian.com

BALBOA CITY SCHOOL

San Diego, California
See Special Needs Schools section.

BALMORAL HALL SCHOOL

630 Westminster Avenue
Winnipeg, Manitoba R3C 3S1, Canada
Head of School: Mrs. Joanne Kamins

General Information Girls' boarding and day college-preparatory and athletics/prep hockey school. Boarding grades 6–12, day grades N–12. Founded: 1901. Setting: urban. Students are housed in apartment-style residence. 12-acre campus. 2 buildings on campus. Approved or accredited by Canadian Association of Independent Schools, Canadian Educational Standards Institute, International Baccalaureate Organization, The Association of Boarding Schools, and Manitoba Department of Education. Affiliate member of National Association of Independent Schools; member of Secondary School Admission Test Board. Language of instruction: English. Endowment: CAN$1.5 million. Total enrollment: 504. Upper school average class size: 18. Upper school faculty-student ratio: 1:18. There are 182 required school days per year for Upper School students. Upper School students typically attend 5 days per week. The average school day consists of 5 hours.

Upper School Student Profile Grade 9: 42 students (42 girls); Grade 10: 60 students (60 girls); Grade 11: 48 students (48 girls); Grade 12: 49 students (49 girls). 24% of students are boarding students. 80% are province residents. 3 provinces are represented in upper school student body. 18% are international students. International students from China, Japan, and Mexico.

Faculty School total: 55. In upper school: 8 men, 21 women; 7 have advanced degrees.

Subjects Offered Acting, advanced math, Advanced Placement courses, advanced studio art-AP, advanced TOEFL/grammar, art, biology, biology-AP, calculus, calculus-AP, career and personal planning, career/college preparation, chemistry, chemistry-AP, choir, college planning, communications, community service, computer science, consumer mathematics, dance performance, debate, desktop publishing, digital art, digital photography, drama, English, English language and composition-AP, English literature, English literature and composition-AP, English literature-AP, English/composition-AP, ESL, ethics, French, French language-AP, French literature-AP, general science, geography, health, history, history-AP, mathematics, mathematics-AP, media arts, modern Western civilization, multimedia, music, musical theater, performing arts, personal development, physical education, physics, physics-AP, pre-calculus, psychology-AP, SAT/ACT preparation, science, social studies, Spanish, Spanish-AP, studio art-AP, technology, vocal ensemble, world affairs, world history.

Graduation Requirements English, English composition, mathematics, science, minimum of 10 hours per year of Service Learning participation in grades 9 through 12.

Special Academic Programs Advanced Placement exam preparation; honors section; study at local college for college credit; academic accommodation for the gifted; ESL (60 students enrolled).

College Admission Counseling 36 students graduated in 2016; 34 went to college, including McGill University; The University of British Columbia; The University of Western Ontario; The University of Winnipeg; University of Manitoba; University of Toronto. Other: 2 had other specific plans.

Student Life Upper grades have uniform requirement, student council, honor system. Discipline rests primarily with faculty.

Tuition and Aid Day student tuition: CAN$16,350; 5-day tuition and room/board: CAN$32,000; 7-day tuition and room/board: CAN$34,500. Tuition installment plan (The Tuition Plan). Tuition reduction for siblings, bursaries, merit scholarship grants

available. In 2016–17, 8% of upper-school students received aid. Total amount of financial aid awarded in 2016–17: CAN$291,000.

Admissions Traditional secondary-level entrance grade is 9. CAT or school's own exam required. Deadline for receipt of application materials: none. Application fee required: CAN$175. Interview recommended.

Athletics Interscholastic: badminton, basketball, cross-country running, curling, Frisbee, golf, ice hockey, indoor track & field, outdoor skills, running, soccer, speedskating, track and field, ultimate Frisbee, volleyball; intramural: aerobics, aerobics/dance, aerobics/Nautilus, aquatics, archery, badminton, ballet, baseball, basketball, bicycling, bowling, broomball, cooperative games, cross-country running, curling, dance, dance team, diving, fencing, field hockey, figure skating, fitness, fitness walking, floor hockey, Frisbee, golf, gymnastics, handball, hockey, ice hockey, in-line skating, indoor hockey, indoor track & field, jogging, jump rope, modern dance, outdoor activities, outdoor education, outdoor skills, physical fitness, physical training, roller blading, rowing, rugby, running, skiing (cross-country), skiing (downhill), snowboarding, snowshoeing, soccer, softball, speedskating, strength & conditioning, swimming and diving, table tennis, tennis, track and field, ultimate Frisbee, volleyball, walking, wall climbing, weight training, yoga. 2 PE instructors, 4 coaches.

Computers Computers are regularly used in all classes. Computer network features include on-campus library services, Internet access, wireless campus network, Internet filtering or blocking technology. Campus intranet, student e-mail accounts, and computer access in designated common areas are available to students. Students grades are available online. The school has a published electronic and media policy.

Contact Ms. Regan Boulton, Admissions Officer. 204-784-1600 Ext. 608. Fax: 204-774-5534. E-mail: rboulton@balmoralhall.net. Website: www.balmoralhall.com

THE BALTIMORE ACTORS' THEATRE CONSERVATORY

The Dumbarton House
300 Dumbarton Road
Baltimore, Maryland 21212-1532
Head of School: Walter E. Anderson

General Information Coeducational day and distance learning college-preparatory and arts school. Grades K–12. Distance learning grades 9–12. Founded: 1979. Setting: suburban. 35-acre campus. 3 buildings on campus. Approved or accredited by Middle States Association of Colleges and Schools and Maryland Department of Education. Endowment: $200,000. Total enrollment: 22. Upper school average class size: 6. Upper school faculty-student ratio: 1:3. There are 175 required school days per year for Upper School students. Upper School students typically attend 5 days per week. The average school day consists of 7 hours and 30 minutes.

Upper School Student Profile Grade 10: 3 students (1 boy, 2 girls); Grade 11: 4 students (4 girls); Grade 12: 2 students (1 boy, 1 girl); Postgraduate: 3 students (1 boy, 2 girls).

Faculty School total: 12. In upper school: 2 men, 8 women; 9 have advanced degrees.

Subjects Offered Acting, algebra, American history-AP, ballet, biology-AP, British literature, chemistry, English language-AP, environmental science-AP, French, geometry, health science, music history, music theory-AP, novels, physics, pre-calculus, psychology, sociology, theater history, trigonometry, world history, world history-AP.

Graduation Requirements Algebra, American history, ballet, chemistry, English, French, geometry, jazz dance, modern dance, music history, physical science, psychology, sociology, theater history, world history, students are required to complete graduation requirements in the three performing arts areas of music, drama, and dance.

Special Academic Programs Advanced Placement exam preparation; honors section; accelerated programs; independent study; study at local college for college credit; academic accommodation for the gifted, the musically talented, and the artistically talented; programs in English for dyslexic students.

College Admission Counseling 4 students graduated in 2015; all went to college, including University of Maryland, Baltimore County. Median SAT critical reading: 600, median SAT math: 570, median composite ACT: 26.

Student Life Upper grades have uniform requirement, student council, honor system. Discipline rests primarily with faculty.

Tuition and Aid Day student tuition: $12,000. Tuition installment plan (individually arranged payment plans). Need-based scholarship grants available. In 2015–16, 10% of upper-school students received aid. Total amount of financial aid awarded in 2015–16: $18,000.

Admissions Traditional secondary-level entrance grade is 9. For fall 2015, 50 students applied for upper-level admission, 15 were accepted, 7 enrolled. Any standardized test, English, French, and math proficiency and writing sample required. Deadline for receipt of application materials: April 3. Application fee required: $100. On-campus interview required.

Computers Computers are regularly used in college planning, creative writing, dance, desktop publishing, English, historical foundations for arts, history, independent study, introduction to technology, keyboarding, music, music technology, psychology, senior seminar, theater, theater arts, word processing, writing classes. Computer network features include Internet access, wireless campus network, Internet filtering or blocking technology. Student e-mail accounts are available to students. The school has a published electronic and media policy.

Contact Mr. Walter E. Anderson, Headmaster. 410-337-8519. Fax: 410-337-8582. E-mail: batpro@baltimoreactorstheatre.org. Website: www.baltimoreactorstheatre.org

BANBURY CROSSROADS SCHOOL

2451 Dieppe Avenue SW, #201
Calgary, Alberta T3E 7K1, Canada

Head of School: Diane Swiatek

General Information Coeducational day college-preparatory and general academic school. Grades 1–12. Founded: 1979. Setting: urban. 1 building on campus. Approved or accredited by Alberta Department of Education. Language of instruction: English. Total enrollment: 41. Upper school average class size: 10. Upper school faculty-student ratio: 1:10. The average school day consists of 6 hours and 30 minutes.

Upper School Student Profile Grade 6: 5 students (2 boys, 3 girls); Grade 8: 5 students (1 boy, 4 girls); Grade 9: 6 students (3 boys, 3 girls); Grade 10: 3 students (3 boys); Grade 11: 2 students (2 boys); Grade 12: 8 students (3 boys, 5 girls).

Faculty School total: 8. In upper school: 1 man, 3 women.

Subjects Offered Arts, Brazilian history, Brazilian social studies, Brazilian studies, conceptual physics, drawing, early childhood, Egyptian history, ESL, Far Eastern history, foreign language, French, German, health education, history of England, Italian history, music, nutrition, painting, personal growth, physics, psychology, self-defense, social skills, sociology, swimming, wellness, wind instruments, world civilizations, world geography, world religions, World War I, writing.

Graduation Requirements Ballet technique.

Special Academic Programs Accelerated programs; independent study; academic accommodation for the gifted; ESL (6 students enrolled).

College Admission Counseling 1 student graduated in 2016 and went to The University of Western Ontario. Other: 1 entered a postgraduate year.

Student Life Upper grades have honor system. Discipline rests equally with students and faculty.

Tuition and Aid Day student tuition: CAN$9000–CAN$13,000. Tuition installment plan (monthly payment plans, individually arranged payment plans). Bursaries available. In 2016–17, 3% of upper-school students received aid. Total amount of financial aid awarded in 2016–17: CAN$10,500.

Admissions Traditional secondary-level entrance grade is 7. Deadline for receipt of application materials: none. Application fee required: CAN$350. On-campus interview required.

Athletics Coed Intramural: aerobics/dance, archery, backpacking, badminton, basketball, bowling, cooperative games, dance, field hockey, fitness walking, floor hockey, Frisbee, golf, gymnastics, horseback riding, ice skating, outdoor recreation, outdoor skills, roller blading, skiing (downhill), soccer, street hockey, swimming and diving, tennis, volleyball, wall climbing, winter walking, yoga. 1 PE instructor.

Computers Computers are regularly used in all academic classes. Computer network features include Internet access.

Contact Anne Bransby-Williams, Office Administrator. 403-270-7787. Fax: 403-270-7486. E-mail: general@banburycrossroads.com. Website: www.banburycrossroads.com

BANGOR CHRISTIAN SCHOOL

1476 Broadway
Bangor, Maine 04401

Head of School: Dr. Jeffrey Benjamin

General Information Coeducational day college-preparatory school, affiliated with Baptist Church. Grades K4–12. Founded: 1970. Setting: suburban. 35-acre campus. 3 buildings on campus. Approved or accredited by Association of Christian Schools International, New England Association of Schools and Colleges, and Maine Department of Education. Total enrollment: 310. Upper school average class size: 20. Upper school faculty-student ratio: 1:10. There are 175 required school days per year for Upper School students. Upper School students typically attend 5 days per week. The average school day consists of 6 hours and 45 minutes.

Upper School Student Profile Grade 6: 16 students (7 boys, 9 girls); Grade 7: 24 students (9 boys, 15 girls); Grade 8: 32 students (17 boys, 15 girls); Grade 9: 20 students (9 boys, 11 girls); Grade 10: 28 students (13 boys, 15 girls); Grade 11: 28 students (12 boys, 16 girls); Grade 12: 19 students (9 boys, 10 girls). 55% of students are Baptist.

Faculty School total: 23. In upper school: 5 men, 8 women; 5 have advanced degrees.

Special Academic Programs Study at local college for college credit; ESL.

College Admission Counseling 22 students graduated in 2016; 19 went to college, including Husson University; Liberty University; Penn State University Park; University of Maine. Other: 3 went to work.

Student Life Upper grades have specified standards of dress, student council, honor system. Discipline rests primarily with faculty. Attendance at religious services is required.

Tuition and Aid Day student tuition: $4800. Guaranteed tuition plan. Tuition installment plan (FACTS Tuition Payment Plan, monthly payment plans). Tuition reduction for siblings, need-based scholarship grants available.

Admissions Traditional secondary-level entrance grade is 9. Deadline for receipt of application materials: none. Application fee required: $100. On-campus interview required.

Athletics Interscholastic: baseball (boys), basketball (b,g), cheering (g), cross-country running (b,g), diving (b,g), hockey (b,g), indoor track & field (b,g), skiing (cross-country) (b,g), skiing (downhill) (b,g), soccer (b,g), softball (g), swimming and diving (b,g), tennis (b,g), track and field (b,g), winter (indoor) track (b,g). 2 PE instructors, 12 coaches.

Computers Computers are regularly used in introduction to technology, keyboarding, lab/keyboard, research skills, typing, word processing, yearbook classes. Computer network features include on-campus library services, Internet access, wireless campus network, Internet filtering or blocking technology. Student e-mail accounts are available to students. Students grades are available online. The school has a published electronic and media policy.

Contact Mrs. Nicky Benjamin, Main Office Secretary. 207-947-7356 Ext. 331. Fax: 207-262-9528. E-mail: nbenjamin@bangorchristian.org. Website: www.bangorchristian.com

BAPTIST REGIONAL SCHOOL

300 Station Avenue
Haddon Heights, New Jersey 08035

Head of School: Mrs. Lynn L. Conahan

General Information Coeducational day college-preparatory, general academic, arts, business, religious studies, and technology school, affiliated with General Association of Regular Baptist Churches. Grades K–12. Founded: 1972. Setting: small town. Nearest major city is Philadelphia, PA. 1 building on campus. Approved or accredited by Association of Christian Schools International, Middle States Association of Colleges and Schools, and New Jersey Department of Education. Total enrollment: 253. Upper school average class size: 25. Upper school faculty-student ratio: 1:10. There are 188 required school days per year for Upper School students. The average school day consists of 6 hours and 35 minutes.

Upper School Student Profile Grade 9: 24 students (13 boys, 11 girls); Grade 10: 36 students (16 boys, 20 girls); Grade 11: 31 students (13 boys, 18 girls); Grade 12: 42 students (20 boys, 22 girls). 60% of students are General Association of Regular Baptist Churches.

Faculty School total: 21. In upper school: 8 men, 13 women; 6 have advanced degrees.

Subjects Offered Accounting, advanced chemistry, advanced computer applications, advanced math, algebra, American government, American history-AP, American literature-AP, analytic geometry, anatomy and physiology, applied music, art, art and culture, art appreciation, arts, Basic programming, Bible studies, biology, business mathematics, calculus, calculus-AP, chemistry, choir, church history, civics, communication skills, computer applications, computer programming, creative writing, desktop publishing, dramatic arts, economics, English composition, English literature, English literature and composition-AP, ethics, foreign language, French, general math, general science, geometry, grammar, health, history, jazz band, keyboarding, physics, pre-algebra, pre-calculus, SAT preparation, Spanish, speech, Western civilization, women's health, world history, world history-AP, yearbook.

Graduation Requirements 20th century history, 20th century world history, algebra, American government, American literature, arts appreciation, Bible, biology, British literature, chemistry, computer science, economics, electives, English composition, English literature, ethics, geometry, health, Holocaust studies, lab/keyboard, physical science.

Special Academic Programs Advanced Placement exam preparation; honors section; study at local college for college credit; remedial reading and/or remedial writing; remedial math; ESL (13 students enrolled).

College Admission Counseling 34 students graduated in 2015; 32 went to college, including Cedarville University; Drexel University; Liberty University; Penn State University Park; Rowan University; Rutgers, The State University of New Jersey, Rutgers College. Other: 2 went to work. Mean SAT critical reading: 540, mean SAT math: 550, mean SAT writing: 570. 32% scored over 600 on SAT critical reading, 32% scored over 600 on SAT math, 19% scored over 600 on SAT writing.

Student Life Upper grades have specified standards of dress, student council, honor system. Discipline rests primarily with faculty. Attendance at religious services is required.

Tuition and Aid Day student tuition: $8300. Tuition installment plan (SMART Tuition Payment Plan). Tuition reduction for siblings, need-based scholarship grants available. In 2015–16, 8% of upper-school students received aid. Total amount of financial aid awarded in 2015–16: $100,000.

Admissions Traditional secondary-level entrance grade is 9. Comprehensive educational evaluation required. Deadline for receipt of application materials: none. Application fee required: $100. Interview required.

Athletics Interscholastic: baseball (boys), basketball (b,g), cheering (g), soccer (b,g), softball (g); intramural: floor hockey (b), indoor hockey (b,g), indoor soccer (b); coed interscholastic: cross-country running, golf, track and field; coed intramural: volleyball. 2 PE instructors, 11 coaches.

Computers Computers are regularly used in accounting, art, business applications, mathematics classes. Computer network features include on-campus library services,

Internet access, Internet filtering or blocking technology. The school has a published electronic and media policy.

Contact Mrs. Betty Ryder, School Secretary. 856-547-2996 Ext. 0. Fax: 856-547-6584. E-mail: brsschoolsecretary@gmail.com. Website: www.baptistregional.org

BARNSTABLE ACADEMY

8 Wright Way

Oakland, New Jersey 07436

Head of School: Mrs. Luanne McGann

General Information Coeducational day college-preparatory and general academic school; primarily serves students with learning disabilities, individuals with Attention Deficit Disorder, dyslexic students, and Executive Function Challenges. Grades 5–12. Founded: 1978. Setting: suburban. Nearest major city is New York, NY. 4-acre campus. 1 building on campus. Approved or accredited by Middle States Association of Colleges and Schools, National Independent Private Schools Association, New Jersey Department of Education, and New Jersey Department of Education. Total enrollment: 100. Upper school average class size: 8. Upper school faculty-student ratio: 1:7. There are 174 required school days per year for Upper School students. Upper School students typically attend 5 days per week. The average school day consists of 6 hours and 20 minutes.

Upper School Student Profile Grade 6: 4 students (3 boys, 1 girl); Grade 7: 4 students (3 boys, 1 girl); Grade 8: 11 students (7 boys, 4 girls); Grade 9: 14 students (12 boys, 2 girls); Grade 10: 18 students (13 boys, 5 girls); Grade 11: 22 students (15 boys, 7 girls); Grade 12: 21 students (12 boys, 9 girls).

Faculty School total: 20. In upper school: 9 men, 7 women; 12 have advanced degrees.

Subjects Offered Acting, advanced computer applications, Advanced Placement courses, American literature-AP, athletics, college counseling, community service, computer skills, contemporary history, creative drama, economics and history, environmental science, film, foreign language, government/civics, health education, honors English, law and the legal system, music theater, performing arts, pre-calculus, street law, U.S. government and politics, world cultures.

Special Academic Programs Advanced Placement exam preparation; honors section; accelerated programs; independent study; study at local college for college credit; academic accommodation for the gifted, the musically talented, and the artistically talented; remedial reading and/or remedial writing; remedial math; programs in English, general development for dyslexic students; special instructional classes for students with learning disabilities and Attention Deficit Disorder; ESL (6 students enrolled).

College Admission Counseling 20 students graduated in 2016; 19 went to college, including Drew University; Fairleigh Dickinson University, College at Florham; Marist College; Stevens Institute of Technology; The College of New Jersey. Other: 1 went to work. Median SAT critical reading: 520, median SAT math: 530, median SAT writing: 560, median composite ACT: 26. 25% scored over 600 on SAT critical reading, 25% scored over 600 on SAT math, 25% scored over 600 on SAT writing, 25% scored over 1800 on combined SAT, 20% scored over 26 on composite ACT.

Student Life Upper grades have specified standards of dress, student council. Discipline rests primarily with faculty.

Summer Programs Remediation, enrichment, advancement programs offered; held on campus; accepts boys and girls; open to students from other schools. 25 students usually enrolled. 2017 schedule: June 29 to July 31. Application deadline: June 28.

Tuition and Aid Day student tuition: $24,000–$31,000. Tuition installment plan (SMART Tuition Payment Plan, monthly payment plans). Merit scholarship grants, need-based scholarship grants available. In 2016–17, 30% of upper-school students received aid; total upper-school merit-scholarship money awarded: $150,000. Total amount of financial aid awarded in 2016–17: $200,000.

Admissions Traditional secondary-level entrance grade is 11. For fall 2016, 300 students applied for upper-level admission, 100 were accepted, 35 enrolled. Deadline for receipt of application materials: none. No application fee required. On-campus interview recommended.

Athletics Interscholastic: baseball (boys), cheering (g), softball (g); coed interscholastic: basketball, dance team, horseback riding, Nautilus, soccer; coed intramural: aerobics, aerobics/dance, aerobics/Nautilus, alpine skiing, billiards, bowling, dance, fitness, fitness walking, flag football, golf, hiking/backpacking, physical fitness, snowboarding, swimming and diving, tennis, track and field, volleyball, weight training, yoga. 2 PE instructors, 3 coaches.

Computers Computers are regularly used in computer applications, reading classes. Computer network features include on-campus library services, Internet access, wireless campus network, Internet filtering or blocking technology. Campus intranet and student e-mail accounts are available to students. Students grades are available online. The school has a published electronic and media policy.

Contact Ms. Lizanne M. Coyne, Director of Student Achievement. 201-651-0200 Ext. 103. Fax: 201-337-9797. E-mail: lcoyne@barnstableacademy.com.
Website: www.barnstableacademy.com

BATTLE GROUND ACADEMY

336 Ernest Rice Lane

Franklin, Tennessee 37069

Head of School: Mr. Will Kesler

General Information Coeducational day college-preparatory and entrepenurial leadership school. Grades K–12. Founded: 1889. Setting: suburban. Nearest major city is Nashville. 67-acre campus. 13 buildings on campus. Approved or accredited by Southern Association of Colleges and Schools, Southern Association of Independent Schools, and Tennessee Department of Education. Member of National Association of Independent Schools. Endowment: $12 million. Total enrollment: 754. Upper school average class size: 15. Upper school faculty-student ratio: 1:8. There are 180 required school days per year for Upper School students. Upper School students typically attend 5 days per week. The average school day consists of 7 hours and 15 minutes.

Upper School Student Profile Grade 9: 89 students (52 boys, 37 girls); Grade 10: 96 students (52 boys, 44 girls); Grade 11: 94 students (47 boys, 47 girls); Grade 12: 85 students (41 boys, 44 girls).

Faculty School total: 86. In upper school: 19 men, 20 women; 32 have advanced degrees.

Subjects Offered Accounting, algebra, American history, American literature, art, art history, biology, calculus, chemistry, chorus, computer applications, computer programming, computer science, drama, early childhood, economics, English, English literature, English literature and composition-AP, entrepreneurship, European history, fine arts, French, French-AP, geography, geometry, government/civics, grammar, health, history, Latin, mathematics, modern European history-AP, music, music history, physical education, physics, science, social studies, Spanish, speech, technical theater, theater, trigonometry, U.S. history, U.S. history-AP, world history, world history-AP, world literature, writing.

Graduation Requirements Arts and fine arts (art, music, dance, drama), computer science, English, foreign language, mathematics, physical education (includes health), science, social studies (includes history), speech. Community service is required.

Special Academic Programs Advanced Placement exam preparation; honors section.

College Admission Counseling 77 students graduated in 2016; all went to college, including Auburn University; Belmont University; The University of Alabama; The University of Tennessee; University of Mississippi. Mean SAT critical reading: 616, mean SAT math: 607, mean SAT writing: 539, mean combined SAT: 1816, mean composite ACT: 27.

Student Life Upper grades have uniform requirement, student council, honor system. Discipline rests equally with students and faculty.

Summer Programs Remediation, enrichment, sports, art/fine arts, computer instruction programs offered; session focuses on remediation, enrichment, and sports; held both on and off campus; accepts boys and girls; open to students from other schools. 550 students usually enrolled. 2017 schedule: June 1 to July 31. Application deadline: none.

Tuition and Aid Day student tuition: $22,506. Tuition installment plan (FACTS Tuition Payment Plan, individually arranged payment plans). Merit scholarship grants, need-based scholarship grants available. In 2016–17, 21% of upper-school students received aid; total upper-school merit-scholarship money awarded: $124,214. Total amount of financial aid awarded in 2016–17: $963,689.

Admissions Traditional secondary-level entrance grade is 9. For fall 2016, 58 students applied for upper-level admission, 53 were accepted, 31 enrolled. ISEE required. Deadline for receipt of application materials: none. Application fee required: $50. On-campus interview required.

Athletics Interscholastic: aquatics (boys, girls), baseball (b), basketball (b,g), cheering (g), cross-country running (b,g), dance team (g), fitness (b,g), football (b), golf (b,g), soccer (b,g), softball (g), strength & conditioning (b,g), swimming and diving (b,g), tennis (b,g), track and field (b,g), volleyball (g), weight training (b,g), wrestling (b); intramural: baseball (b,g), basketball (b,g), fitness (b,g), football (b), softball (g); coed interscholastic: fitness, trap and skeet; coed intramural: fitness, flag football, physical training, rock climbing, ropes courses, soccer. 1 PE instructor, 4 coaches, 1 athletic trainer.

Computers Computers are regularly used in all academic, art, college planning, desktop publishing, English, foreign language, geography, history, library, literary magazine, mathematics, newspaper, photography, SAT preparation, science, social studies, Spanish, study skills, technology, theater, writing classes. Computer network features include on-campus library services, online commercial services, Internet access, wireless campus network, Internet filtering or blocking technology. Campus intranet, student e-mail accounts, and computer access in designated common areas are available to students. Students grades are available online. The school has a published electronic and media policy.

Contact Ms. Robin Goertz, Director of Admissions. 615-567-9014.
E-mail: robin.goertz@mybga.org. Website: www.battlegroundacademy.org

BAVARIAN INTERNATIONAL SCHOOL

Schloss Haimhausen
Hauptstrasse 1
Haimhausen D-85778, Germany

Head of School: Dr. Chrissie Sorenson

General Information Coeducational day college-preparatory, general academic, arts, business, technology, and physical education school. Grades PK–12. Founded: 1991. Setting: small town. Nearest major city is Munich, Germany. 10-acre campus. 5 buildings on campus. Approved or accredited by International Baccalaureate Organization and New England Association of Schools and Colleges. Member of European Council of International Schools. Language of instruction: English. Total enrollment: 1,008. Upper school average class size: 19. Upper school faculty-student ratio: 1:7. There are 190 required school days per year for Upper School students. Upper School students typically attend 5 days per week. The average school day consists of 7 hours.

Upper School Student Profile Grade 6: 85 students (43 boys, 42 girls); Grade 7: 81 students (33 boys, 48 girls); Grade 8: 82 students (50 boys, 32 girls); Grade 9: 82 students (41 boys, 41 girls); Grade 10: 93 students (35 boys, 58 girls); Grade 11: 87 students (37 boys, 50 girls); Grade 12: 64 students (34 boys, 30 girls).

Faculty School total: 270. In upper school: 9 men, 26 women; 24 have advanced degrees.

Subjects Offered Art, biology, business studies, chemistry, Chinese, community service, computer science, computer skills, drama, English, English as a foreign language, English literature, environmental studies, fine arts, French, geography, German, German literature, history, Japanese, mathematics, model United Nations, music, personal and social education, physical education, physics, science, social studies, Spanish, theater, work experience.

Graduation Requirements Youth culture.

Special Academic Programs International Baccalaureate program; independent study; remedial reading and/or remedial writing; remedial math; programs in English, mathematics, general development for dyslexic students; special instructional classes for students with learning disabilities and dyslexia; ESL (66 students enrolled).

College Admission Counseling 72 students graduated in 2016.

Student Life Upper grades have specified standards of dress, student council, honor system. Discipline rests primarily with faculty.

Summer Programs Enrichment, ESL, sports, art/fine arts, computer instruction programs offered; session focuses on English as an additional language; held on campus; accepts boys and girls; open to students from other schools. 2017 schedule: July 1 to July 31. Application deadline: none.

Tuition and Aid Day student tuition: €14,650–€16,150. Tuition installment plan (yearly payment plan, 2-payment plan). Tuition reduction for siblings available.

Admissions English proficiency or mathematics proficiency exam required. Deadline for receipt of application materials: none. No application fee required. On-campus interview required.

Athletics Interscholastic: cheering (girls); coed interscholastic: aerobics, aerobics/dance, alpine skiing, badminton, ball hockey, ballet, baseball, basketball, climbing, combined training, cooperative games, cricket, cross-country running, dance, field hockey, football, golf, gymnastics, handball, indoor hockey, indoor soccer, indoor track & field, jogging, judo, netball, outdoor activities, outdoors, physical training, rock climbing, rugby, running, skiing (downhill), snowboarding, soccer, softball, swimming and diving, tennis, track and field, volleyball, winter soccer. 7 PE instructors, 6 coaches.

Computers Computers are regularly used in all classes. Computer network features include on-campus library services, online commercial services, Internet access, wireless campus network, Internet filtering or blocking technology. Campus intranet, student e-mail accounts, and computer access in designated common areas are available to students. Students grades are available online. The school has a published electronic and media policy.

Contact Erika Swedberg, Admissions Coordinator. 49-8133-917 Ext. 126. Fax: 49-8133-917 Ext. 182. E-mail: e.swedberg@bis-school.com.
Website: www.bis-school.com

BAYLOR SCHOOL

171 Baylor School Road
Chattanooga, Tennessee 37405

Head of School: Mr. Scott Wilson

General Information Coeducational boarding and day college-preparatory school. Boarding grades 9–12, day grades 6–12. Founded: 1893. Setting: suburban. Nearest major city is Atlanta, GA. Students are housed in single-sex dormitories. 690-acre campus. 30 buildings on campus. Approved or accredited by Southern Association of Colleges and Schools, Southern Association of Independent Schools, and Tennessee Department of Education. Member of National Association of Independent Schools and Secondary School Admission Test Board. Endowment: $90 million. Total enrollment: 1,070. Upper school average class size: 14. Upper school faculty-student ratio: 1:8. There are 180 required school days per year for Upper School students. Upper School students typically attend 5 days per week. The average school day consists of 7 hours and 30 minutes.

Upper School Student Profile Grade 9: 172 students (83 boys, 89 girls); Grade 10: 195 students (96 boys, 99 girls); Grade 11: 180 students (93 boys, 87 girls); Grade 12: 174 students (85 boys, 89 girls). 28% of students are boarding students. 72% are state residents. 23 states are represented in upper school student body. 8% are international students. International students from Bahamas, Brazil, Cayman Islands, China, and Finland; 8 other countries represented in student body.

Faculty School total: 115. In upper school: 54 men, 49 women; 77 have advanced degrees; 40 reside on campus.

Subjects Offered 3-dimensional art, acting, American government, Chinese, Eastern religion and philosophy, law, model United Nations, pre-calculus, science research, Spanish language-AP, Spanish literature-AP, Western religions, wilderness education.

Graduation Requirements Arts and fine arts (art, music, dance, drama), English, foreign language, mathematics, physical education (includes health), science, social studies (includes history).

Special Academic Programs 22 Advanced Placement exams for which test preparation is offered; honors section; study abroad; academic accommodation for the gifted; remedial reading and/or remedial writing.

College Admission Counseling 179 students graduated in 2016; all went to college, including Georgia Institute of Technology; Sewanee: The University of the South; The University of Alabama; The University of Tennessee; University of Georgia; University of Illinois at Urbana–Champaign.

Student Life Upper grades have uniform requirement, student council, honor system. Discipline rests primarily with faculty.

Summer Programs Enrichment, sports, art/fine arts, rigorous outdoor training, computer instruction programs offered; session focuses on sports, arts, wilderness activities; held both on and off campus; accepts boys and girls; open to students from other schools. 700 students usually enrolled. 2017 schedule: June 5 to July 28. Application deadline: none.

Tuition and Aid Day student tuition: $23,282; 7-day tuition and room/board: $47,419. Tuition installment plan (Insured Tuition Payment Plan, FACTS Tuition Payment Plan). Merit scholarship grants, need-based scholarship grants available. In 2016–17, 33% of upper-school students received aid; total upper-school merit-scholarship money awarded: $425,000. Total amount of financial aid awarded in 2016–17: $5,900,000.

Admissions Traditional secondary-level entrance grade is 9. For fall 2016, 337 students applied for upper-level admission, 198 were accepted, 116 enrolled. Deadline for receipt of application materials: none. Application fee required: $75. On-campus interview recommended.

Athletics Interscholastic: baseball (boys), basketball (b,g), bowling (b,g), cheering (g), crew (b,g), cross-country running (b,g), dance (g), dance team (g), diving (b,g), fencing (b,g), football (b), golf (b,g), lacrosse (b,g), soccer (b,g), softball (g), swimming and diving (b,g), tennis (b,g), track and field (b,g), volleyball (g), wrestling (b); intramural: ballet (g), dance (g), fitness (b,g), modern dance (g), strength & conditioning (b,g), weight lifting (b,g), weight training (b,g); coed interscholastic: aerobics/dance, strength & conditioning; coed intramural: backpacking, bicycling, canoeing/kayaking, climbing, fly fishing, Frisbee, hiking/backpacking, kayaking, mountain biking, outdoor activities, outdoor adventure, outdoor education, outdoor recreation, outdoor skills, physical fitness, rafting, rock climbing, ultimate Frisbee, wall climbing, wilderness survival. 4 PE instructors, 10 coaches, 2 athletic trainers.

Computers Computers are regularly used in all classes. Computer network features include on-campus library services, online commercial services, Internet access, wireless campus network, Internet filtering or blocking technology. Campus intranet, student e-mail accounts, and computer access in designated common areas are available to students. Students grades are available online. The school has a published electronic and media policy.

Contact Ms. Carissa Sebes Margio, Administrative Assistant for Boarding. 423-757-2877. Fax: 423-757-2525. E-mail: csmargio@bayorschool.org.
Website: www.baylorschool.org

BAY RIDGE PREPARATORY SCHOOL

7420 Fourth Avenue
Brooklyn, New York 11209

Head of School: Dr. Michael T. Dealy

General Information Coeducational day college-preparatory and general academic school. Grades K–12. Founded: 1998. Setting: urban. 1 building on campus. Approved or accredited by New York State Association of Independent Schools, New York State Board of Regents, and New York Department of Education. Member of National Association of Independent Schools. Total enrollment: 396. Upper school average class size: 17. Upper school faculty-student ratio: 1:7. There are 165 required school days per year for Upper School students. Upper School students typically attend 5 days per week. The average school day consists of 6 hours and 15 minutes.

Upper School Student Profile Grade 9: 34 students (18 boys, 16 girls); Grade 10: 44 students (32 boys, 12 girls); Grade 11: 66 students (34 boys, 32 girls); Grade 12: 66 students (37 boys, 29 girls).

Faculty School total: 48. In upper school: 46 have advanced degrees.

Subjects Offered Acting, advanced biology, Advanced Placement courses, advanced studio art-AP, algebra, American government, American history, American history-AP, American literature, American literature-AP, American sign language, ancient world history, art, art history, biology, calculus, chemistry, college admission preparation, college counseling, college writing, computer science, creative writing, dance, earth science, economics, English, English as a foreign language, English composition, English literature, European history, European literature, finance, geometry, health education, journalism, microbiology, modern history, music composition, physics, SAT preparation, Shakespeare, Spanish, statistics, U.S. government and politics.

Special Academic Programs Advanced Placement exam preparation; honors section; independent study; study at local college for college credit; academic accommodation for the gifted, the musically talented, and the artistically talented; remedial reading and/or remedial writing; remedial math; programs in English, mathematics, general development for dyslexic students; ESL.

College Admission Counseling 67 students graduated in 2016; 66 went to college. Other: 1 entered a postgraduate year.

Student Life Upper grades have specified standards of dress, honor system. Discipline rests primarily with faculty.

Tuition and Aid Tuition installment plan (FACTS Tuition Payment Plan, monthly payment plans). Tuition reduction for siblings, merit scholarship grants available.

Admissions Traditional secondary-level entrance grade is 9. For fall 2016, 125 students applied for upper-level admission, 32 were accepted, 25 enrolled. Deadline for receipt of application materials: none. Application fee required: $60. On-campus interview required.

Athletics Interscholastic: baseball (boys), basketball (b,g), cross-country running (b,g), fencing (b,g), soccer (b,g), tennis (b,g), volleyball (g); intramural: baseball (b), basketball (g), cheering (g), cross-country running (b,g), fencing (b,g), hockey (b), soccer (b,g), softball (g), tennis (b,g), volleyball (g); coed interscholastic: cross-country running, squash, track and field; coed intramural: cross-country running, dance, dance squad, martial arts, squash, track and field, yoga. 4 PE instructors, 7 coaches.

Computers Computer network features include Internet access, wireless campus network. Student e-mail accounts and computer access in designated common areas are available to students. Students grades are available online.

Contact Ms. Alissa Roeder, Admissions Director. 718-833-9090 Ext. 8305. Fax: 718-833-6680. E-mail: admissions@bayridgeprep.org. Website: www.bayridgeprep.org

THE BAY SCHOOL OF SAN FRANCISCO

35 Keyes Avenue, The Presidio of San Francisco
San Francisco, California 94129

Head of School: Mr. Luke Felker

General Information Coeducational day college-preparatory school. Grades 9–12. Founded: 2004. Setting: urban. 2 buildings on campus. Approved or accredited by California Association of Independent Schools, Western Association of Schools and Colleges, and California Department of Education. Member of National Association of Independent Schools and Secondary School Admission Test Board. Total enrollment: 355. Upper school average class size: 14. Upper school faculty-student ratio: 1:8. The average school day consists of 6 hours and 40 minutes.

Faculty School total: 43. In upper school: 17 men, 25 women; 29 have advanced degrees.

Graduation Requirements Senior signature project.

Special Academic Programs Honors section.

College Admission Counseling 75 students graduated in 2016; all went to college.

Student Life Upper grades have student council. Discipline rests equally with students and faculty.

Tuition and Aid Day student tuition: $40,740. Tuition installment plan (Insured Tuition Payment Plan, monthly payment plans). Need-based scholarship grants available. In 2016–17, 30% of upper-school students received aid.

Admissions Traditional secondary-level entrance grade is 9. ISEE, PSAT or SAT for applicants to grade 11 and 12 or SSAT required. Deadline for receipt of application materials: January 17. Application fee required: $90. Interview required.

Athletics Interscholastic: baseball (boys), basketball (b,g), climbing (b,g), golf (b,g), lacrosse (b,g), soccer (b,g), softball (g), tennis (b,g); coed interscholastic: cross-country running, sailing, track and field, volleyball; coed intramural: aerobics, aerobics/dance, backpacking, dance, dance squad, hiking/backpacking, rock climbing, yoga.

Computers Computers are regularly used in all classes. Computer network features include on-campus library services, Internet access, wireless campus network, Internet filtering or blocking technology. Student e-mail accounts are available to students.

Contact Mr. Hewett Yip, Admission Associate. 415-684-8949 Ext. 155. Fax: 415-561-5808. E-mail: admission@bayschoolsf.org. Website: www.bayschoolsf.org/

BAYVIEW GLEN SCHOOL

275 Duncan Mill Road
Toronto, Ontario M3B 3H9, Canada

Head of School: Mrs. Eileen Daunt

General Information Coeducational day college-preparatory, general academic, and athletics school. Grades PK–12. Founded: 1962. Setting: urban. 40-acre campus. 1 building on campus. Approved or accredited by Canadian Association of Independent Schools, Conference of Independent Schools of Ontario, and Ontario Department of Education. Affiliate member of National Association of Independent Schools. Language of instruction: English. Total enrollment: 1,042. Upper school average class size: 22. Upper school faculty-student ratio: 1:22. There are 175 required school days per year for Upper School students. Upper School students typically attend 5 days per week. The average school day consists of 7 hours.

Faculty School total: 100. In upper school: 17 men, 16 women.

Subjects Offered Advanced Placement courses, all academic.

Graduation Requirements Outdoor leadership trips for grade 9 to 11, grade 10 physical education.

Special Academic Programs Advanced Placement exam preparation.

College Admission Counseling 92 students graduated in 2016; they went to Carleton University; McGill University; McMaster University; Queen's University at Kingston; The University of Western Ontario; University of Toronto. Other: 100 entered a postgraduate year.

Student Life Upper grades have uniform requirement, student council, honor system. Discipline rests primarily with faculty.

Tuition and Aid Day student tuition: CAN$15,800–CAN$22,600. Tuition installment plan (monthly payment plans, individually arranged payment plans). Bursaries, need-based scholarship grants available.

Admissions Traditional secondary-level entrance grade is 9. Admissions testing required. Deadline for receipt of application materials: December. Application fee required: CAN$100. Interview required.

Athletics Interscholastic: badminton (boys, girls), basketball (b,g), cross-country running (b,g), field hockey (g), soccer (b,g), softball (b,g), tennis (b,g), track and field (b,g), ultimate Frisbee (b,g), volleyball (b,g). 5 PE instructors, 30 coaches.

Computers Computers are regularly used in all academic classes. Computer network features include on-campus library services, Internet access, wireless campus network, Internet filtering or blocking technology. Campus intranet, student e-mail accounts, and computer access in designated common areas are available to students. Students grades are available online. The school has a published electronic and media policy.

Contact Mrs. Judy Maxwell, Director of Admissions. 416-443-1030 Ext. 605. Fax: 416-443-1032. E-mail: jmaxwell@bayviewglen.ca. Website: www.bayviewglen.ca/

BEARSPAW CHRISTIAN SCHOOL

15001 69 Street NW
Calgary, Alberta T3R 1C5, Canada

Head of School: Mr. David Anger

General Information Coeducational day and distance learning college-preparatory and general academic school, affiliated with Christian faith. Grades K–12. Distance learning grades 1–12. Founded: 1991. Setting: rural. 40-acre campus. 3 buildings on campus. Approved or accredited by Association of Christian Schools International, Canadian Association of Independent Schools, and Alberta Department of Education. Language of instruction: English. Total enrollment: 729. Upper school average class size: 25. Upper school faculty-student ratio: 1:9. There are 177 required school days per year for Upper School students. Upper School students typically attend 5 days per week. The average school day consists of 6 hours and 45 minutes.

Upper School Student Profile Grade 10: 44 students (21 boys, 23 girls); Grade 11: 30 students (15 boys, 15 girls); Grade 12: 45 students (14 boys, 31 girls). 95% of students are Christian faith.

Faculty School total: 24. In upper school: 5 men, 8 women; 3 have advanced degrees.

Subjects Offered Advanced chemistry, advanced computer applications, audio visual/media, Bible, business studies, career planning, English literature, fitness, foods, French, kinesiology, lab/keyboard, Latin, law, law studies, leadership and service, sports conditioning, sports medicine, sports nutrition.

Graduation Requirements Bible, career and personal planning, physical education (includes health).

Special Academic Programs Honors section; independent study; remedial math; special instructional classes for students with learning disabilities, Attention Deficit Disorder, emotional problems, and dyslexia.

College Admission Counseling 36 students graduated in 2016; they went to Trinity Western University; University of Alberta; University of Calgary; University of Victoria.

Student Life Upper grades have uniform requirement, student council, honor system. Discipline rests primarily with faculty. Attendance at religious services is required.

Summer Programs Sports programs offered; session focuses on basketball, volleyball, strength training; held on campus; accepts boys and girls; open to students from other schools. 60 students usually enrolled. 2017 schedule: July 15 to August 15. Application deadline: July 15.

Tuition and Aid Day student tuition: CAN$6200. Tuition installment plan (monthly payment plans, individually arranged payment plans). Tuition reduction for siblings, need-based scholarship grants available. In 2016–17, 5% of upper-school students received aid. Total amount of financial aid awarded in 2016–17: CAN$111,354.

Admissions Traditional secondary-level entrance grade is 10. Achievement tests, admissions testing, CTB/McGraw-Hill/Macmillan Co-op Test, WAIS, WICS, Woodcock-Johnson and writing sample required. Deadline for receipt of application materials: September 30. Application fee required: CAN$150. On-campus interview recommended.

Athletics Interscholastic: badminton (boys, girls), basketball (b,g), cross-country running (b,g), floor hockey (b,g), golf (b,g), indoor soccer (b,g), track and field (b,g), volleyball (b,g), wrestling (b); intramural: aerobics/dance (b,g), badminton (b,g), basketball (b,g), cross-country running (b,g), flag football (b,g), floor hockey (b,g), physical training (b), track and field (b,g), volleyball (b,g), wrestling (b,g); coed interscholastic: badminton, indoor soccer, soccer; coed intramural: aerobics/dance, badminton, ball hockey, basketball, flag football, floor hockey, handball, indoor soccer, strength & conditioning, volleyball. 2 PE instructors, 1 athletic trainer.

Computers Computers are regularly used in all academic classes. Computer network features include Internet access, wireless campus network, Internet filtering or blocking technology. Student e-mail accounts and computer access in designated common areas are available to students. Students grades are available online. The school has a published electronic and media policy.

Contact Mrs. Sherri Patzer, Registrar. 403-295-2566. Fax: 403-275-8170. E-mail: spatzer@bearspawschool.com. Website: www.bearspawschool.com

BEAUFORT ACADEMY

240 Sams Point Road
Beaufort, South Carolina 29907

Head of School: Mr. Stephen Schools

General Information Coeducational day college-preparatory and technology school. Grades PK–12. Founded: 1965. Setting: small town. Nearest major city is Savannah, GA. 35-acre campus. 3 buildings on campus. Approved or accredited by South Carolina Independent School Association and Southern Association of Colleges and Schools. Member of National Association of Independent Schools. Endowment: $650,000. Total enrollment: 260. Upper school average class size: 12. Upper school faculty-student ratio: 1:10. There are 174 required school days per year for Upper School students. Upper School students typically attend 5 days per week. The average school day consists of 7 hours.

Upper School Student Profile Grade 9: 27 students (6 boys, 21 girls); Grade 10: 31 students (15 boys, 16 girls); Grade 11: 23 students (8 boys, 15 girls); Grade 12: 18 students (12 boys, 6 girls).

Faculty School total: 48. In upper school: 4 men, 13 women; 16 have advanced degrees.

Subjects Offered Advanced biology, Advanced Placement courses, American history-AP, world history-AP, writing.

Graduation Requirements Arts and fine arts (art, music, dance, drama), computer science, English, ethics and responsibility, foreign language, mathematics, physical education (includes health), science, social studies (includes history), senior seminar (ethics and philosophy).

Special Academic Programs Advanced Placement exam preparation; honors section; independent study; study at local college for college credit; study abroad; academic accommodation for the gifted; programs in general development for dyslexic students.

College Admission Counseling 22 students graduated in 2016; all went to college, including Clemson University; College of Charleston; University of South Carolina; Wofford College. Median SAT critical reading: 579, median SAT math: 586. 33% scored over 600 on SAT critical reading, 25% scored over 600 on SAT math.

Student Life Upper grades have specified standards of dress, honor system. Discipline rests primarily with faculty.

Summer Programs Enrichment, sports programs offered; session focuses on sports/soccer; held on campus; accepts boys and girls; open to students from other schools. 30 students usually enrolled. 2017 schedule: June 4 to June 15.

Tuition and Aid Day student tuition: $5400–$11,725. Tuition installment plan (Insured Tuition Payment Plan, monthly payment plans, individually arranged payment plans). Tuition reduction for siblings, need-based scholarship grants, tuition remission for children of faculty available. In 2016–17, 25% of upper-school students received aid. Total amount of financial aid awarded in 2016–17: $72,600.

Admissions Traditional secondary-level entrance grade is 9. For fall 2016, 31 students applied for upper-level admission, 19 were accepted, 16 enrolled. CTP III, ERB CTP III, OLSAT, Stanford Achievement Test or school's own exam or coop required. Deadline for receipt of application materials: none. Application fee required: $80. Interview recommended.

Athletics Interscholastic: baseball (boys), basketball (b,g), cheering (g), football (b), lacrosse (b), soccer (b,g), softball (g), swimming and diving (b,g), tennis (b,g), volleyball (g); coed interscholastic: crew, golf, physical fitness, soccer, swimming and diving, track and field; coed intramural: archery, crew, fitness, floor hockey, rowing, softball, touch football. 2 PE instructors, 8 coaches, 1 athletic trainer.

Computers Computers are regularly used in English, history, journalism, library skills, media, newspaper, publishing, science, yearbook classes. Computer network features include on-campus library services, online commercial services, Internet access, wireless campus network, Internet filtering or blocking technology. The school has a published electronic and media policy.

Contact MJ Simmons, Director of Admissions. 843-524-3393. Fax: 843-524-1171. E-mail: mjsimmons@beaufortacademy.org. Website: www.beaufortacademy.org

THE BEEKMAN SCHOOL

220 East 50th Street
New York, New York 10022

Head of School: George Higgins

General Information Coeducational day and distance learning college-preparatory and general academic school. Grades 9–12. Distance learning grades 9–12. Founded: 1925. Setting: urban. 1 building on campus. Approved or accredited by Middle States Association of Colleges and Schools, New York State Board of Regents, and New York Department of Education. Total enrollment: 80. Upper school average class size: 8. Upper school faculty-student ratio: 1:8. There are 165 required school days per year for Upper School students. Upper School students typically attend 5 days per week. The average school day consists of 6 hours and 15 minutes.

Upper School Student Profile Grade 9: 15 students (8 boys, 7 girls); Grade 10: 19 students (11 boys, 8 girls); Grade 11: 21 students (12 boys, 9 girls); Grade 12: 25 students (13 boys, 12 girls); Postgraduate: 2 students (1 boy, 1 girl).

Faculty School total: 12. In upper school: 4 men, 8 women; 10 have advanced degrees.

Subjects Offered Advanced Placement courses, algebra, American history, anatomy and physiology, ancient world history, art, astronomy, bioethics, biology, business mathematics, calculus, calculus-AP, chemistry, computer animation, computer art, computer science, conceptual physics, creative writing, drama, drawing, Eastern religion and philosophy, ecology, economics, English, environmental science, ESL, European history, film, French, geometry, government, health, modern politics, modern world history, photography, physical education, physical science, physics, poetry, pre-calculus, psychology, SAT preparation, sculpture, Spanish, TOEFL preparation, trigonometry, U.S. history, video film production, Web site design, Western philosophy.

Graduation Requirements Art, computer technologies, electives, English, foreign language, health education, mathematics, physical education (includes health), science, social studies (includes history).

Special Academic Programs 30 Advanced Placement exams for which test preparation is offered; honors section; accelerated programs; independent study; academic accommodation for the gifted, the musically talented, and the artistically talented; remedial reading and/or remedial writing; remedial math; programs in English, mathematics, general development for dyslexic students; ESL (4 students enrolled).

College Admission Counseling 28 students graduated in 2016; 27 went to college, including Arizona State University at the Tempe campus; Boston University; Fordham University; New York University; Sarah Lawrence College; University of Vermont. Other: 1 had other specific plans. Mean SAT critical reading: 558, mean SAT math: 519, mean SAT writing: 540. 33% scored over 600 on SAT critical reading, 27% scored over 600 on SAT math, 30% scored over 600 on SAT writing.

Student Life Upper grades have student council, honor system. Discipline rests primarily with faculty.

Summer Programs Remediation, enrichment, advancement, ESL programs offered; session focuses on academics; held on campus; accepts boys and girls; open to students from other schools. 35 students usually enrolled. 2017 schedule: July 5 to August 15. Application deadline: June 30.

Tuition and Aid Day student tuition: $38,250. Tuition installment plan (monthly payment plans, individually arranged payment plans). Merit scholarship grants available. Total upper-school merit-scholarship money awarded for 2016–17: $75,000.

Admissions Traditional secondary-level entrance grade is 9. For fall 2016, 39 students applied for upper-level admission, 38 were accepted, 33 enrolled. Deadline for receipt of application materials: none. No application fee required. On-campus interview required.

Athletics 1 PE instructor.

Computers Computers are regularly used in all academic classes. Computer network features include Internet access, wireless campus network, Internet filtering or blocking technology. Campus intranet and computer access in designated common areas are available to students. The school has a published electronic and media policy.

Contact George Higgins, Headmaster. 212-755-6666. Fax: 212-888-6085. E-mail: georgeh@beekmanschool.org. Website: http://www.BeekmanSchool.org

BELEN JESUIT PREPARATORY SCHOOL

500 Southwest 127th Avenue
Miami, Florida 33184

Head of School: Fr. Guillermo M. Garcia-Tuon, SJ

General Information Boys' day college-preparatory school, affiliated with Roman Catholic Church, Roman Catholic Church (Jesuit order). Grades 6–12. Founded: 1854. Setting: urban. 32-acre campus. 3 buildings on campus. Approved or accredited by Jesuit Secondary Education Association, Southern Association of Colleges and Schools, and Florida Department of Education. Endowment: $8 million. Total enrollment: 1,479. Upper school average class size: 25. Upper school faculty-student ratio: 1:12. There are 175 required school days per year for Upper School students. Upper School students typically attend 5 days per week. The average school day consists of 8 hours.

Upper School Student Profile Grade 9: 219 students (219 boys); Grade 10: 216 students (216 boys); Grade 11: 232 students (232 boys); Grade 12: 179 students (179 boys). 98% of students are Roman Catholic, Roman Catholic Church (Jesuit order).

Faculty School total: 132. In upper school: 39 men, 30 women; 49 have advanced degrees.

Subjects Offered Advanced Placement courses, art, art history, biology, chemistry, Chinese, composition, computers, engineering, English, English literature, French, history, mathematics, music, philosophy, physical education, physics, religion, science, social studies, Spanish.

Graduation Requirements Arts and fine arts (art, music, dance, drama), electives, English, foreign language, mathematics, philosophy, physical education (includes health), religion (includes Bible studies and theology), science, social sciences, social studies (includes history). Community service is required.

Special Academic Programs Advanced Placement exam preparation; honors section; study at local college for college credit.

College Admission Counseling 227 students graduated in 2016; 226 went to college, including Florida International University; Florida State University; Miami Dade College; The University of Alabama; University of Florida; University of Miami. Other: 1 entered military service, 1 had other specific plans. Mean SAT critical reading: 580, mean SAT math: 592, mean SAT writing: 566, mean combined SAT: 1737, mean composite ACT: 26. 39% scored over 1800 on combined SAT, 48% scored over 26 on composite ACT.

Student Life Upper grades have uniform requirement, student council. Discipline rests primarily with faculty.

Summer Programs Remediation, enrichment programs offered, session focuses on make-up courses; held on campus; accepts boys; not open to students from other schools. 120 students usually enrolled. 2017 schedule: June 26 to July 21. Application deadline: June 21.

Tuition and Aid Day student tuition: $15,000. Tuition installment plan (SMART Tuition Payment Plan). Need-based scholarship grants available. In 2016–17, 12% of upper-school students received aid. Total amount of financial aid awarded in 2016–17: $514,810.

Admissions Traditional secondary-level entrance grade is 9. For fall 2016, 74 students applied for upper-level admission, 52 were accepted, 2 enrolled. School's own exam required. Deadline for receipt of application materials: December 7. Application fee required: $100.

Athletics Interscholastic: baseball, basketball, bowling, crew, cross-country running, football, golf, lacrosse, soccer, swimming and diving, tennis, track and field, volleyball, water polo, wrestling; intramural: fencing, fishing, in-line hockey, weight training. 3 PE instructors, 36 coaches, 2 athletic trainers.

Computers Computers are regularly used in art, engineering, English, foreign language, history, mathematics, music, science classes. Computer network features include on-campus library services, online commercial services, Internet access, wireless campus network, Internet filtering or blocking technology. Campus intranet, student e-mail accounts, and computer access in designated common areas are available to students. Students grades are available online. The school has a published electronic and media policy.

Contact Mrs. Ana Mora, Assistant to the Director of Admissions. 786-621-4032. Fax: 786-621-4033. E-mail: admissions@belenjesuit.org. Website: www.belenjesuit.org

BELLEVUE CHRISTIAN SCHOOL

1601 98th Avenue NE
Clyde Hill, Washington 98004-3400

Head of School: Kevin Dunning

General Information Coeducational day college-preparatory and general academic school. Grades PK–12. Founded: 1950. Setting: suburban. Nearest major city is Bellevue. 10-acre campus. 5 buildings on campus. Approved or accredited by Christian Schools International, Northwest Accreditation Commission, and Washington Department of Education. Endowment: $1 million. Total enrollment: 1,160. Upper school average class size: 20. Upper school faculty-student ratio: 1:21. There are 180 required school days per year for Upper School students. Upper School students typically attend 5 days per week. The average school day consists of 6 hours and 30 minutes.

Upper School Student Profile Grade 7: 81 students (45 boys, 36 girls); Grade 8: 77 students (43 boys, 34 girls); Grade 9: 90 students (51 boys, 39 girls); Grade 10: 86 students (49 boys, 37 girls); Grade 11: 89 students (45 boys, 44 girls); Grade 12: 84 students (45 boys, 39 girls).

Faculty School total: 39. In upper school: 18 men, 21 women; 23 have advanced degrees.

Subjects Offered 20th century world history, advanced biology, advanced chemistry, advanced computer applications, Advanced Placement courses, advanced studio art-AP, algebra, American history-AP, American literature-AP, architectural drawing, art, arts, athletics, band, Basic programming, Bible, biology, biology-AP, calculus, calculus-AP, choral music, church history, community service, computer applications, computer multimedia, computer programming, concert choir, creative writing, culinary arts, digital photography, drama, English, English language and composition-AP, English-AP, environmental science, ESL, ethics, fine arts, foods, foreign language, French, geometry, German, government, health, history-AP, human relations, instrumental music, integrated mathematics, interior design, jazz band, jazz ensemble, library assistant, math analysis, mathematics, media communications, music performance, photography, physical education, physical science, physics, physics-AP, religion, social

sciences, social studies, Spanish, Spanish language-AP, Spanish-AP, studio art, technical drawing, trigonometry, U.S. history-AP, vocal ensemble, vocal music, Washington State and Northwest History, wind ensemble, woodworking, work experience, world history, world history-AP, yearbook.

Graduation Requirements Algebra, art, arts and fine arts (art, music, dance, drama), band, baseball, basketball, Bible, calculus-AP, computer technologies, concert choir, English, English-AP, ethics, geometry, German, golf, health, international foods, jazz band, marine biology, mathematics, photography, physical education (includes health), physical fitness, physics-AP, religion (includes Bible studies and theology), science, social sciences, social studies (includes history), softball, Spanish-AP, speech, technology, theater arts, track and field, U.S. history-AP, video film production, visual and performing arts, vocal ensemble, volleyball, woodworking, wrestling. Community service is required.

Special Academic Programs 7 Advanced Placement exams for which test preparation is offered; honors section; study at local college for college credit; academic accommodation for the gifted, the musically talented, and the artistically talented; remedial math; programs in English, mathematics, general development for dyslexic students; special instructional classes for student academic support; ESL (18 students enrolled).

College Admission Counseling 70 students graduated in 2016; 66 went to college, including Azusa Pacific University; Bellevue College; Gonzaga University; Seattle Pacific University; University of Washington; Washington State University. Other: 2 went to work, 2 had other specific plans. Median SAT critical reading: 546, median SAT math: 590, median SAT writing: 534, median combined SAT: 1670, median composite ACT: 24. 19% scored over 600 on SAT critical reading, 37% scored over 600 on SAT math, 19% scored over 600 on SAT writing, 31% scored over 1800 on combined SAT, 27% scored over 26 on composite ACT.

Student Life Upper grades have specified standards of dress, student council, honor system. Discipline rests primarily with faculty.

Summer Programs Enrichment, advancement, sports, art/fine arts, computer instruction programs offered; session focuses on providing additional course offerings that might not fit in the schedule during the academic year; held on campus; accepts boys and girls; not open to students from other schools. 100 students usually enrolled. 2017 schedule: June 25 to August 5. Application deadline: June 1.

Tuition and Aid Day student tuition: $14,240. Tuition installment plan (monthly payment plans). Tuition reduction for siblings, need-based scholarship grants, financial aid awarded on basis of report and ability to pay available. In 2016–17, 15% of upper-school students received aid. Total amount of financial aid awarded in 2016–17: $900,000.

Admissions Deadline for receipt of application materials: none. Application fee required: $75. On-campus interview required.

Athletics Interscholastic: baseball (boys), basketball (b,g), cheering (g), combined training (b,g), cooperative games (b,g), cross-country running (b,g), fitness (b,g), golf (b,g), outdoor activities (b,g), outdoor education (b,g), physical fitness (b,g), physical training (b,g), running (b,g), soccer (b,g), softball (g), strength & conditioning (b,g), track and field (b,g), volleyball (g), weight lifting (b,g), weight training (b,g), wrestling (b,g).

Computers Computers are regularly used in art, Bible studies, computer applications, creative writing, desktop publishing, drawing and design, English, ESL, foreign language, health, keyboarding, library, mathematics, media production, music, newspaper, photography, religious studies, science, social studies, Spanish, technical drawing, technology, video film production, Web site design, writing, yearbook classes. Computer network features include on-campus library services, Internet access, wireless campus network, Internet filtering or blocking technology. Student e-mail accounts and computer access in designated common areas are available to students. Students grades are available online. The school has a published electronic and media policy.

Contact Ann Kats, Admissions Coordinator. 425-454-4402 Ext. 215. Fax: 425-454-4418. E-mail: admissions@bellevuechristian.org. Website: www.bellevuechristian.org

THE BEMENT SCHOOL

Deerfield, Massachusetts
See Junior Boarding Schools section.

BENEDICTINE HIGH SCHOOL

2900 Martin Luther King, Jr. Drive
Cleveland, Ohio 44104

Head of School: Mrs. Sue Zulandt

General Information Boys' day college-preparatory school, affiliated with Roman Catholic Church. Grades 9–12. Founded: 1927. Setting: urban. 13-acre campus. 3 buildings on campus. Approved or accredited by National Catholic Education Association, North Central Association of Colleges and Schools, and Ohio Department of Education. Total enrollment: 380. Upper school average class size: 20. Upper school faculty-student ratio: 1:10. There are 180 required school days per year for Upper School students. Upper School students typically attend 5 days per week. The average school day consists of 6 hours and 50 minutes.

Upper School Student Profile Grade 9: 82 students (82 boys); Grade 10: 100 students (100 boys); Grade 11: 82 students (82 boys); Grade 12: 104 students (104 boys). 70% of students are Roman Catholic.

Faculty School total: 37. In upper school: 30 men, 7 women; 31 have advanced degrees.

Subjects Offered 3-dimensional design, advanced chemistry, advanced math, Advanced Placement courses, aesthetics, algebra, American literature, American literature-AP, analysis and differential calculus, analytic geometry, Ancient Greek, ancient history, art, athletic training, band, Basic programming, Bible studies, biology, biology-AP, British literature-AP, business education, business law, calculus, calculus-AP, Catholic belief and practice, ceramics, chemistry, choir, chorus, church history, Civil War, civil war history, classical Greek literature, classical language, computer graphics, computer information systems, computer literacy, computer skills, computer-aided design, concert band, concert choir, current events, drawing, drawing and design, economics, electives, English, English literature and composition-AP, European history-AP, film studies, foreign language, French, geometry, German, government, government-AP, government/civics, government/civics-AP, graphic design, health, honors algebra, honors English, honors geometry, honors U.S. history, honors world history, human geography - AP, jazz band, journalism, keyboarding, lab science, Latin, Latin-AP, Life of Christ, marching band, marketing, moral theology, music, music appreciation, New Testament, painting, physical education, pre-calculus, probability and statistics, psychology, Russian, Shakespeare.

Graduation Requirements 1 1/2 elective credits, 20th century American writers, 20th century history, 20th century world history, algebra, American government, American history, American literature, ancient history, ancient world history, art, biology, British literature, chemistry, church history, computer applications, English, foreign language, geometry, physical education (includes health), physics, senior project, theology, U.S. history, world history, community service hours.

Special Academic Programs 9 Advanced Placement exams for which test preparation is offered; honors section; independent study; study at local college for college credit; study abroad.

College Admission Counseling 91 students graduated in 2016; 84 went to college, including Bowling Green State University; Case Western Reserve University; Cleveland State University; Kent State University; The University of Akron; University of Dayton. Other: 7 went to work, 1 entered military service. Mean SAT critical reading: 566, mean SAT math: 527, mean composite ACT: 22.

Student Life Upper grades have specified standards of dress, student council, honor system. Discipline rests primarily with faculty. Attendance at religious services is required.

Summer Programs Enrichment, sports, computer instruction programs offered; session focuses on enrichment; held on campus; accepts boys and girls; open to students from other schools. 150 students usually enrolled. 2017 schedule: June 8 to July 24. Application deadline: June 1.

Tuition and Aid Day student tuition: $10,500. Tuition installment plan (SMART Tuition Payment Plan, monthly payment plans, individually arranged payment plans). Tuition reduction for siblings, merit scholarship grants, need-based scholarship grants, paying campus jobs available. In 2016–17, 79% of upper-school students received aid.

Admissions Traditional secondary-level entrance grade is 9. For fall 2016, 250 students applied for upper-level admission, 175 were accepted, 112 enrolled. High School Placement Test and writing sample required. Deadline for receipt of application materials: none. No application fee required. On-campus interview required.

Athletics Interscholastic: baseball, basketball, bowling, cross-country running, football, golf, ice hockey, lacrosse, soccer, swimming and diving, track and field, wrestling; intramural: baseball, basketball, flag football, football, physical fitness, physical training, skiing (downhill), snowboarding, strength & conditioning, touch football, volleyball, weight lifting, weight training. 3 PE instructors, 15 coaches, 1 athletic trainer.

Computers Computers are regularly used in all academic, computer applications, creative writing, current events, data processing, design, English, graphic design, history, independent study, information technology, library, mathematics, newspaper, technical drawing, yearbook classes. Computer network features include on-campus library services, online commercial services, Internet access, wireless campus network, Internet filtering or blocking technology, every student has a laptop. Campus intranet and student e-mail accounts are available to students. Students grades are available online. The school has a published electronic and media policy.

Contact Mr. John Ellis, Admissions Director. 216-421-2080 Ext. 356. Fax: 216-421-1100. E-mail: ellis@cbhs.edu. Website: www.cbhs.net

BEN FRANKLIN ACADEMY

1585 Clifton Road
Atlanta, Georgia 30329

Head of School: Dr. Martha B. Burdette

General Information Coeducational day college-preparatory school. Grades 9–12. Founded: 1987. Setting: urban. 3-acre campus. 2 buildings on campus. Approved or accredited by Georgia Independent School Association, Southern Association of Colleges and Schools, Southern Association of Independent Schools, and Georgia Department of Education. Total enrollment: 125. Upper school average class size: 3. Upper school faculty-student ratio: 1:3. There are 180 required school days per year for

Upper School students. Upper School students typically attend 5 days per week. The average school day consists of 6 hours.

Faculty School total: 29. In upper school: 12 men, 17 women; 15 have advanced degrees.

Subjects Offered 1 1/2 elective credits.

Graduation Requirements A work-study component in addition to the academic requirements.

Special Academic Programs Advanced Placement exam preparation; honors section; accelerated programs; academic accommodation for the gifted.

College Admission Counseling 40 students graduated in 2015; all went to college.

Student Life Upper grades have specified standards of dress. Discipline rests primarily with faculty.

Tuition and Aid Day student tuition: $25,500–$34,500. Tuition installment plan (individually arranged payment plans). Tuition reduction for siblings, need-based scholarship grants available. In 2015–16, 10% of upper-school students received aid.

Admissions Traditional secondary-level entrance grade is 9. Deadline for receipt of application materials: none. No application fee required. On-campus interview required.

Athletics Interscholastic: cross-country running (boys, girls), golf (b,g); coed interscholastic: basketball, cross-country running, Frisbee, golf, tennis, ultimate Frisbee.

Computers Computer resources include on-campus library services, Internet access, Internet filtering or blocking technology. Campus intranet and student e-mail accounts are available to students. The school has a published electronic and media policy.

Contact Mrs. Amy H. Barnes, Registrar. 404-633-7404. Fax: 404-321-0610. E-mail: abarnes@benfranklinacademy.org. Website: www.benfranklinacademy.org

THE BENJAMIN SCHOOL

11000 Ellison Wilson Road
North Palm Beach, Florida 33408

Head of School: Mr. Robert S. Goldberg

General Information Coeducational day college-preparatory, arts, and technology school. Grades PK–12. Founded: 1960. Setting: suburban. Nearest major city is West Palm Beach. 50-acre campus. 6 buildings on campus. Approved or accredited by Florida Council of Independent Schools, Southern Association of Colleges and Schools, and Florida Department of Education. Member of National Association of Independent Schools and Secondary School Admission Test Board. Endowment: $5.6 million. Total enrollment: 1,081. Upper school average class size: 16. Upper school faculty-student ratio: 1:8. There are 175 required school days per year for Upper School students. Upper School students typically attend 5 days per week. The average school day consists of 5 hours and 30 minutes.

Upper School Student Profile Grade 9: 102 students (47 boys, 55 girls); Grade 10: 105 students (55 boys, 50 girls); Grade 11: 113 students (64 boys, 49 girls); Grade 12: 100 students (52 boys, 48 girls).

Faculty School total: 141. In upper school: 20 men, 23 women; 35 have advanced degrees.

Subjects Offered 3-dimensional art, acting, advanced studio art-AP, algebra, American history, art, art history, art history-AP, Asian studies, band, biology, biology-AP, biotechnology, calculus, calculus-AP, Caribbean history, ceramics, chemistry, chemistry-AP, choral music, chorus, comparative government and politics-AP, computer programming, computer science, computer science-AP, critical studies in film, current events, dance, drama, economics, engineering, English, English language and composition-AP, English literature, English literature and composition-AP, environmental science, environmental studies, European history-AP, expository writing, film appreciation, film studies, French, French language-AP, French-AP, geometry, government/civics, honors English, honors geometry, human biology, human geography - AP, intro to computers, law, law studies, macro/microeconomics-AP, Mandarin, marine biology, modern dance, modern European history-AP, music theory-AP, painting, physical education, physics, physics-AP, piano, pre-calculus, SAT preparation, sculpture, Spanish, Spanish language-AP, Spanish literature-AP, speech, speech communications, statistics-AP, studio art-AP, theater, U.S. government, U.S. government and politics-AP, U.S. history-AP, video film production, world history.

Graduation Requirements Arts and fine arts (art, music, dance, drama), computer science, English, foreign language, mathematics, physical education (includes health), science, social sciences, social studies (includes history), work program for seniors.

Special Academic Programs 22 Advanced Placement exams for which test preparation is offered; honors section.

College Admission Counseling 113 students graduated in 2015; 112 went to college, including Florida State University; Harvard University; The University of Alabama; University of Florida; University of Miami; Wake Forest University. Mean SAT critical reading: 574, mean SAT math: 579, mean SAT writing: 598, mean composite ACT: 26.

Student Life Upper grades have uniform requirement, student council, honor system. Discipline rests primarily with faculty.

Tuition and Aid Day student tuition: $24,500. Tuition installment plan (monthly payment plans, The Tuition Solution). Merit scholarship grants, need-based scholarship grants, need-based loans available. In 2015–16, 24% of upper-school students received aid; total upper-school merit-scholarship money awarded: $24,500. Total amount of financial aid awarded in 2015–16: $1,388,838.

Admissions Traditional secondary-level entrance grade is 9. For fall 2015, 83 students applied for upper-level admission, 76 were accepted, 42 enrolled. ERB or SSAT required. Deadline for receipt of application materials: February 1. Application fee required: $100. On-campus interview required.

Athletics Interscholastic: ballet (girls), baseball (b), basketball (b,g), bowling (b,g), cross-country running (b,g), dance (g), dance team (g), diving (b,g), football (b), golf (b,g), lacrosse (b,g), modern dance (g), soccer (b,g), softball (g), tennis (b,g), track and field (b,g), volleyball (g), winter soccer (b,g), wrestling (b); coed interscholastic: aerobics/dance, cheering, strength & conditioning, swimming and diving, weight training. 1 PE instructor, 40 coaches, 1 athletic trainer.

Computers Computers are regularly used in art, computer applications, English, foreign language, history, mathematics, science classes. Computer network features include on-campus library services, online commercial services, Internet access, wireless campus network, Internet filtering or blocking technology, tablet laptop program for grades 9 to 12. Student e-mail accounts are available to students. Students grades are available online. The school has a published electronic and media policy.

Contact Mrs. Mary Lou Primm, Director of Admission. 561-472-3451. Fax: 561-472-3410. E-mail: marylou.primm@thebenjaminschool.org.
Website: www.thebenjaminschool.org

BEN LIPPEN SCHOOLS

7401 Monticello Road
Columbia, South Carolina 29203

Head of School: Mr. Chip Jones

General Information Coeducational boarding and day college-preparatory and religious studies school, affiliated with Baptist Church, Presbyterian Church. Boarding grades 7–12, day grades K–12. Founded: 1941. Setting: suburban. Students are housed in single-sex modern houses. 100-acre campus. 9 buildings on campus. Approved or accredited by Association of Christian Schools International, South Carolina Independent School Association, Southern Association of Colleges and Schools, The Association of Boarding Schools, and South Carolina Department of Education. Endowment: $150,000. Total enrollment: 776. Upper school average class size: 25. Upper school faculty-student ratio: 1:15. There are 178 required school days per year for Upper School students. Upper School students typically attend 5 days per week. The average school day consists of 6 hours and 30 minutes.

Upper School Student Profile Grade 6: 56 students (24 boys, 32 girls); Grade 7: 65 students (37 boys, 28 girls); Grade 8: 57 students (29 boys, 28 girls); Grade 9: 73 students (43 boys, 30 girls); Grade 10: 103 students (62 boys, 41 girls); Grade 11: 89 students (45 boys, 44 girls); Grade 12: 80 students (44 boys, 36 girls). 25% of students are boarding students. 75% are state residents. 1 state is represented in upper school student body. 25% are international students. International students from China, Hong Kong, Japan, Republic of Korea, and Taiwan. 85% of students are Baptist, Presbyterian.

Faculty School total: 47. In upper school: 22 men, 24 women; 23 have advanced degrees; 1 resides on campus.

Subjects Offered 20th century history, advanced biology, advanced chemistry, advanced computer applications, advanced math, algebra, American culture, American government, American history, American history-AP, American literature, American literature-AP, American studies, anatomy, anatomy and physiology, ancient world history, art, art-AP, baseball, basic language skills, Basic programming, basketball, Bible, Bible studies, biology, biology-AP, British literature, British literature (honors), business, calculus, calculus-AP, cheerleading, chemistry, chemistry-AP, choir, choral music, Christian doctrine, Christian studies, Christianity, comparative government and politics, composition, composition-AP, computer literacy, computer programming, consumer economics, current history, developmental language skills, discrete mathematics, drama, drama performance, drawing, drawing and design, economics, electives, engineering, English, English as a foreign language, English language and composition-AP, English literature, English literature and composition-AP, English-AP, environmental science, ESL, ethics, European history-AP, film history, fine arts, foreign language, French, French as a second language, general science, geography, geometry, government, government and politics-AP, government/civics, grammar, guitar, health, health and wellness, history, history-AP, honors algebra, honors English, honors geometry, honors U.S. history, honors world history, HTML design, human anatomy, lab science, leadership, Life of Christ, literature and composition-AP, Mandarin, marine biology, mathematics, mathematics-AP, music, mythology, New Testament, participation in sports, philosophy, photography, photojournalism, physical education, physical science, physics, physics-AP, pre-calculus, probability and statistics, programming, psychology, religion, religious studies, robotics, science, sculpture, social studies, sociology, softball, Spanish, Spanish language-AP, Spanish-AP, sports conditioning, statistics, statistics-AP, student government, theology, trigonometry, U.S. government, U.S. government and politics-AP, U.S. history, U.S. history-AP, United States government-AP, video, visual arts, volleyball, weightlifting, world geography, world history, world literature, writing, writing, yearbook.

Graduation Requirements Bible, computer applications, electives, English, foreign language, mathematics, physical education (includes health), religion (includes Bible studies and theology), science, social studies (includes history), senior research paper, 30 hours of community service (seniors).

Special Academic Programs 13 Advanced Placement exams for which test preparation is offered; honors section; independent study; study at local college for college credit; ESL (40 students enrolled).

College Admission Counseling 78 students graduated in 2016; 76 went to college, including Anderson University; Clemson University; College of Charleston; Midlands Technical College; The Citadel, The Military College of South Carolina; University of South Carolina. Other: 2 went to work. Median SAT critical reading: 550, median SAT math: 600, median SAT writing: 550, median combined SAT: 1160, median composite ACT: 25. 34% scored over 600 on SAT critical reading, 49% scored over 600 on SAT math, 24% scored over 600 on SAT writing, 34% scored over 1800 on combined SAT, 39% scored over 26 on composite ACT.

Student Life Upper grades have specified standards of dress, student council, honor system. Discipline rests primarily with faculty. Attendance at religious services is required.

Tuition and Aid Day student tuition: $9340–$12,630; 7-day tuition and room/board: $35,580–$45,580. Tuition installment plan (FACTS Tuition Payment Plan, monthly payment plans, individually arranged payment plans, annual, 10-month, and semester payment plans). Merit scholarship grants, need-based scholarship grants, need-based financial aid, ministerial discounts available. In 2016–17, 25% of upper-school students received aid; total upper-school merit-scholarship money awarded: $140,000. Total amount of financial aid awarded in 2016–17: $570,000.

Admissions Traditional secondary-level entrance grade is 9. For fall 2016, 92 students applied for upper-level admission, 82 were accepted, 56 enrolled. Math and English placement tests, SSAT, Stanford Achievement Test, TOEFL or TOEFL Junior required. Deadline for receipt of application materials: none. Application fee required: $75. Interview recommended.

Athletics Interscholastic: aquatics (boys, girls), baseball (b), basketball (b,g), cheering (g), cross-country running (b,g), football (b), golf (b,g), soccer (b,g), softball (g), strength & conditioning (b,g), swimming and diving (b,g), tennis (b,g), track and field (b,g), volleyball (g), weight lifting (b,g), weight training (b,g), wrestling (b). 2 PE instructors, 1 athletic trainer.

Computers Computers are regularly used in all classes. Computer network features include on-campus library services, Internet access, wireless campus network, Internet filtering or blocking technology. Student e-mail accounts are available to students. Students grades are available online. The school has a published electronic and media policy.

Contact Mrs. Kelly M. Adams, Director of Admissions. 803-807-4110. Fax: 803-744-1387. E-mail: kelly.adams@benlippen.com. Website: www.benlippen.com

BENTLEY SCHOOL

1000 Upper Happy Valley Road
Bentley School
Lafayette, California 94549

Head of School: Arlene F. Hogan

General Information Coeducational day college-preparatory and college-preparatory, liberal arts school. Grades K–12. Founded: 1920. Setting: suburban. 12-acre campus. 4 buildings on campus. Approved or accredited by California Association of Independent Schools, Western Association of Schools and Colleges, and California Department of Education. Member of National Association of Independent Schools. Total enrollment: 684. Upper school average class size: 14. Upper school faculty-student ratio: 1:9. There are 170 required school days per year for Upper School students. Upper School students typically attend 5 days per week.

Upper School Student Profile Grade 6: 41 students (20 boys, 21 girls); Grade 7: 52 students (23 boys, 29 girls); Grade 8: 36 students (19 boys, 17 girls); Grade 9: 93 students (52 boys, 41 girls); Grade 10: 87 students (44 boys, 43 girls); Grade 11: 72 students (47 boys, 25 girls); Grade 12: 73 students (39 boys, 34 girls).

Faculty School total: 76. In upper school: 21 men, 25 women; 20 have advanced degrees.

Graduation Requirements American history, art, athletics, chemistry, English, foreign language, health and wellness, mathematics, science, senior internship, world history, mini-term courses. Community service is required.

Special Academic Programs Advanced Placement exam preparation; honors section; independent study; study at local college for college credit.

College Admission Counseling 73 students graduated in 2016; all went to college, including Brown University; New York University; Oberlin College; University of California, Berkeley; University of Michigan; University of Southern California. Mean SAT critical reading: 636, mean SAT math: 615, mean SAT writing: 624, mean composite ACT: 27.

Student Life Upper grades have specified standards of dress, student council, honor system. Discipline rests equally with students and faculty.

Tuition and Aid Day student tuition: $37,400. Tuition installment plan (monthly payment plans). Need-based scholarship grants available. In 2016–17, 28% of upper-school students received aid.

Admissions Traditional secondary-level entrance grade is 9. For fall 2016, 220 students applied for upper-level admission, 145 were accepted, 69 enrolled. Deadline for receipt of application materials: January 12. Application fee required: $100. Interview recommended.

Athletics Interscholastic: baseball (boys), basketball (b,g), cross-country running (b,g), soccer (b,g), swimming and diving (b,g), tennis (b,g), volleyball (b,g); coed interscholastic: golf, track and field; coed intramural: equestrian sports, fencing, fitness, Frisbee, physical fitness, ultimate Frisbee, weight training, yoga. 19 coaches.

Computers Computers are regularly used in all classes. Computer network features include on-campus library services, online commercial services, Internet access, wireless campus network. Campus intranet, student e-mail accounts, and computer access in designated common areas are available to students. Students grades are available online.

Contact 510-843-2512. Fax: 510-843-5162. Website: www.bentleyschool.net

BEREAN CHRISTIAN HIGH SCHOOL

245 El Divisadero Avenue
Walnut Creek, California 94598

Head of School: Dr. Nelson M. Noriega

General Information Coeducational day college-preparatory school, affiliated with Baptist Church. Grades 9–12. Founded: 1969. Setting: suburban. Nearest major city is Oakland. 5-acre campus. 5 buildings on campus. Approved or accredited by Association of Christian Schools International, Western Association of Schools and Colleges, and California Department of Education. Total enrollment: 411. Upper school average class size: 20. Upper school faculty-student ratio: 1:20. There are 180 required school days per year for Upper School students. Upper School students typically attend 5 days per week. The average school day consists of 6 hours and 30 minutes.

Upper School Student Profile Grade 9: 97 students (51 boys, 46 girls); Grade 10: 105 students (59 boys, 46 girls); Grade 11: 105 students (51 boys, 54 girls); Grade 12: 104 students (49 boys, 55 girls). 50% of students are Baptist.

Faculty School total: 34. In upper school: 12 men, 22 women; 12 have advanced degrees.

Subjects Offered Algebra, American literature, anatomy, art, arts, Bible studies, biology, chemistry, choir, computer literacy, computer science, drama, economics, English, ethics, fine arts, geometry, government, health, mathematics, physical education, physics, physiology, pre-calculus, religion, science, social studies, Spanish, trigonometry, U.S. history, world history, world religions.

Graduation Requirements U.S. history, U.S. history-AP, world history.

Special Academic Programs Advanced Placement exam preparation; study at local college for college credit.

College Admission Counseling 114 students graduated in 2016; 110 went to college, including Azusa Pacific University; California Polytechnic State University, San Luis Obispo; California State University, Sacramento; Grand Canyon University; University of California, Berkeley; University of California, Santa Barbara. Other: 1 went to work.

Student Life Upper grades have specified standards of dress, student council, honor system. Discipline rests primarily with faculty. Attendance at religious services is required.

Summer Programs Session focuses on biology; held on campus; accepts boys and girls; not open to students from other schools. 25 students usually enrolled. 2017 schedule: May 31 to June 30.

Tuition and Aid Day student tuition: $9500. Tuition installment plan (SMART Tuition Payment Plan). Tuition reduction for siblings, merit scholarship grants, need-based scholarship grants available. In 2016–17, 17% of upper-school students received aid. Total amount of financial aid awarded in 2016–17: $286,000.

Admissions Traditional secondary-level entrance grade is 9. Traditional secondary-level entrance age is 14. For fall 2016, 451 students applied for upper-level admission, 422 were accepted, 422 enrolled. Math Placement Exam required. Deadline for receipt of application materials: none. Application fee required: $95. On-campus interview required.

Athletics Interscholastic: baseball (boys), basketball (b,g), cheering (g), cross-country running (b,g), football (b), soccer (b,g), softball (g), swimming and diving (b,g), tennis (g), volleyball (b,g); coed interscholastic: golf. 2 PE instructors, 42 coaches.

Computers Computers are regularly used in all academic classes. Computer network features include Internet access, wireless campus network, Internet filtering or blocking technology. Campus intranet and student e-mail accounts are available to students. Students grades are available online.

Contact Shelley M. Elson, Acct/HR Assistant. 925-945-6464 Ext. 22. Fax: 925-945-7473. E-mail: selson@berean-eagles.org. Website: www.berean-eagles.org

BERKELEY CARROLL SCHOOL

181 Lincoln Place
Brooklyn, New York 11217

Head of School: Mr. Robert D. Vitalo

General Information Coeducational day college-preparatory and Global Education, STEAM school. Grades PK–12. Founded: 1886. Setting: urban. Nearest major city is New York. 3 buildings on campus. Approved or accredited by New York State Association of Independent Schools and New York Department of Education. Member of National Association of Independent Schools. Endowment: $8 million. Total enrollment: 942. Upper school average class size: 15. Upper school faculty-student ratio: 1:8. There are 174 required school days per year for Upper School students. Upper School students typically attend 5 days per week. The average school day consists of 6 hours and 30 minutes.

Upper School Student Profile Grade 9: 81 students (43 boys, 38 girls); Grade 10: 79 students (43 boys, 36 girls); Grade 11: 65 students (37 boys, 28 girls); Grade 12: 80 students (44 boys, 36 girls).

Faculty School total: 144. In upper school: 21 men, 19 women; 38 have advanced degrees.

Graduation Requirements Arts and fine arts (art, music, dance, drama), computer science, English, foreign language, mathematics, physical education (includes health), science, social sciences, 2-week Spring Intensives, senior speaker program, Community Service. Community service is required.

Special Academic Programs Honors section; independent study; term-away projects; study at local college for college credit; study abroad.

College Admission Counseling 56 students graduated in 2016; all went to college, including Carleton College; Drexel University; New York University; Northeastern University; Pitzer College; Smith College. Median combined SAT: 2180, median composite ACT: 29. 64% scored over 600 on SAT critical reading, 56% scored over 600 on SAT math, 87% scored over 600 on SAT writing, 68% scored over 26 on composite ACT.

Student Life Upper grades have student council, honor system. Discipline rests equally with students and faculty.

Summer Programs Enrichment, sports, art/fine arts, computer instruction programs offered; session focuses on creative arts, athletics, field trips, academics; held on campus; accepts boys and girls; open to students from other schools. 250 students usually enrolled. 2017 schedule: June 26 to August 11. Application deadline: none.

Tuition and Aid Day student tuition: $40,980. Tuition installment plan (Insured Tuition Payment Plan, Academic Management Services Plan, SMART Tuition Payment Plan, monthly payment plans, individually arranged payment plans). Need-based scholarship grants available. In 2016–17, 35% of upper-school students received aid. Total amount of financial aid awarded in 2016–17: $3,300,000.

Admissions Traditional secondary-level entrance grade is 9. For fall 2016, 387 students applied for upper-level admission, 135 were accepted, 67 enrolled. ISEE, PSAT and SAT for applicants to grade 11 and 12, SSAT, SSAT, ERB, PSAT, SAT, PLAN or ACT, TOEFL or SLEP or writing sample required. Deadline for receipt of application materials: December 1. Application fee required: $100. On-campus interview recommended.

Athletics Interscholastic: baseball (boys), basketball (b,g), cross-country running (b,g), soccer (b,g), softball (g), swimming and diving (b,g), tennis (b,g), track and field (b,g), volleyball (b,g); intramural: ultimate Frisbee (b,g); coed intramural: swimming and diving. 8 PE instructors, 30 coaches, 1 athletic trainer.

Computers Computers are regularly used in all classes. Computer network features include on-campus library services, online commercial services, Internet access, wireless campus network, Internet filtering or blocking technology, free iPad for every student, staffed Knowledge Bar for help with iPads and apps. Campus intranet, student e-mail accounts, and computer access in designated common areas are available to students. Students grades are available online. The school has a published electronic and media policy.

Contact Ms. Jennifer Brown, Administrative Assistant for Upper School Admissions. 718-789-6060 Ext. 6527. Fax: 718-398-3640. E-mail: jbrown@berkeleycarroll.org. Website: www.berkeleycarroll.org

BERKELEY PREPARATORY SCHOOL

4811 Kelly Road
Tampa, Florida 33615

Head of School: Joseph W. Seivold

General Information Coeducational day college-preparatory, arts, business, religious studies, bilingual studies, technology, and global studies school, affiliated with Episcopal Church. Grades PK–12. Founded: 1960. Setting: suburban. 86-acre campus. 10 buildings on campus. Approved or accredited by Florida Council of Independent Schools, National Association of Episcopal Schools, Southern Association of Colleges and Schools, Southern Association of Independent Schools, The College Board, and Florida Department of Education. Member of National Association of Independent Schools and Secondary School Admission Test Board. Endowment: $17 million. Total enrollment: 1,300. Upper school average class size: 15. Upper school faculty-student ratio: 1:15. There are 171 required school days per year for Upper School students. Upper School students typically attend 5 days per week. The average school day consists of 7 hours and 20 minutes.

Faculty School total: 125. In upper school: 86 have advanced degrees.

Subjects Offered Advanced Placement courses, advanced studio art-AP, African history, algebra, American government, American history, American history-AP, American literature, American literature-AP, art, art history, biology, biology-AP, calculus, calculus-AP, ceramics, chemistry, chemistry-AP, China/Japan history, community service, computer math, computer programming, computer science, creative writing, dance, drama, drama performance, drama workshop, early childhood, economics, English, English literature, English-AP, environmental science-AP, etymology, European history, expository writing, fine arts, French, French-AP, freshman seminar, geography, geometry, government/civics, grammar, guitar, health, history, history of China and Japan, honors algebra, honors English, honors geometry, instruments, Latin, Latin American history, Latin-AP, logic, Mandarin, math analysis, mathematics, media arts, microbiology, modern European history, modern European history-AP, music, performing arts, philosophy, physical education, physics, physics-AP, pre-calculus, psychology, religious studies, SAT preparation, science, social studies, Spanish, Spanish-AP, speech, stage design, statistics, statistics-AP, technical theater, television, theater, theater production, U.S. history, U.S. history-AP, video, video film production, Western civilization, world history, world literature, writing, yearbook.

Graduation Requirements Arts and fine arts (art, music, dance, drama), computer science, English, foreign language, mathematics, physical education (includes health), religious studies, science, social studies (includes history). Community service is required.

Special Academic Programs Advanced Placement exam preparation; honors section; independent study; domestic exchange program; study abroad.

College Admission Counseling 155 students graduated in 2016; all went to college, including Clemson University; Florida State University; University of Florida; University of Miami; University of Southern California; Vanderbilt University. Mean SAT critical reading: 625, mean SAT math: 621, mean SAT writing: 630, mean combined SAT: 1876, mean composite ACT: 28. 68% scored over 600 on SAT critical reading, 59% scored over 600 on SAT math, 53% scored over 600 on SAT writing, 29% scored over 1800 on combined SAT, 69% scored over 26 on composite ACT.

Student Life Upper grades have uniform requirement, student council, honor system. Discipline rests equally with students and faculty. Attendance at religious services is required.

Summer Programs Remediation, enrichment, advancement, sports, art/fine arts, computer instruction programs offered; session focuses on setting a fun pace for excellence; held on campus; accepts boys and girls; open to students from other schools. 3,000 students usually enrolled. 2017 schedule: June 5 to July 28.

Tuition and Aid Day student tuition: $17,560–$23,660. Tuition installment plan (SMART Tuition Payment Plan, 8-installment plan). Merit scholarship grants, need-based scholarship grants available. Total upper-school merit-scholarship money awarded for 2016–17: $9,000,000.

Admissions Traditional secondary-level entrance grade is 9. Achievement/Aptitude/Writing, Otis-Lennon Mental Ability Test and SSAT required. Deadline for receipt of application materials: January 30. Application fee required: $75. On-campus interview required.

Athletics Interscholastic: baseball (boys), basketball (b,g), cheering (g), crew (b,g), cross-country running (b,g), dance squad (g), dance team (g), diving (b,g), field hockey (g), football (b), golf (b,g), ice hockey (b), lacrosse (b,g), rowing (b,g), soccer (b,g), softball (g), swimming and diving (b,g), tennis (b,g), track and field (b,g), volleyball (b,g); coed interscholastic: weight lifting, wrestling; coed intramural: mountain biking,

outdoor activities, outdoor adventure, physical fitness, physical training, power lifting, project adventure, ropes courses, strength & conditioning, wall climbing, weight training. 14 PE instructors, 74 coaches, 2 athletic trainers.

Computers Computers are regularly used in all academic, art, English, foreign language, history, mathematics, music, science classes. Computer network features include on-campus library services, online commercial services, Internet access, wireless campus network, Internet filtering or blocking technology. Student e-mail accounts are available to students. Students grades are available online. The school has a published electronic and media policy.

Contact Janie McIlvaine, Director of Admissions. 813-885-1673. Fax: 813-886-6933. E-mail: mcilvjan@berkeleyprep.org. Website: www.berkeleyprep.org

See Display below and Close-Up on page 590.

BERKSHIRE SCHOOL

245 North Undermountain Road
Sheffield, Massachusetts 01257

Head of School: Mr. Pieter M. Mulder

General Information Coeducational boarding and day college-preparatory, advanced math/science research, and advanced humanities research school. Grades 9–PG. Founded: 1907. Setting: rural. Nearest major city is Hartford, CT. Students are housed in coed dormitories. 400-acre campus. 43 buildings on campus. Approved or accredited by Association of Independent Schools in New England, New England Association of Schools and Colleges, and The Association of Boarding Schools. Member of National Association of Independent Schools and Secondary School Admission Test Board. Endowment: $126 million. Total enrollment: 405. Upper school average class size: 12. Upper school faculty-student ratio: 1:4. There are 182 required school days per year for Upper School students. Upper School students typically attend 6 days per week. The average school day consists of 6 hours and 40 minutes.

Upper School Student Profile Grade 9: 60 students (30 boys, 30 girls); Grade 10: 114 students (62 boys, 52 girls); Grade 11: 102 students (61 boys, 41 girls); Grade 12: 114 students (68 boys, 46 girls); Postgraduate: 7 students (7 boys). 91% of students are boarding students. 9% are state residents. 31 states are represented in upper school student body. 19% are international students. International students from Bermuda, China, Germany, United Kingdom, United States, and Viet Nam; 27 other countries represented in student body.

Faculty School total: 64. In upper school: 34 men, 30 women; 53 have advanced degrees; 74 reside on campus.

Subjects Offered 3-dimensional design, acting, Advanced Placement courses, algebra, American government, American history, American literature, art, art history,

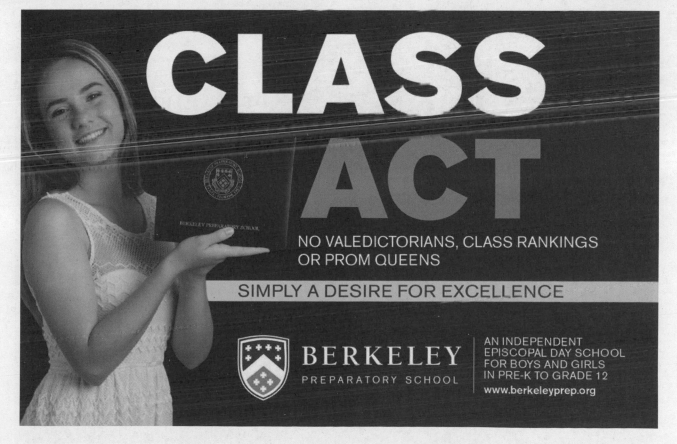

astronomy, aviation, biology, British literature, calculus, calculus-AP, ceramics, chamber groups, chemistry, chemistry-AP, Chinese, choral music, chorus, college counseling, college writing, comparative religion, computer programming, constitutional law, creative writing, dance, digital art, digital music, digital photography, drama, drawing and design, economics, engineering, English, English language and composition-AP, English literature, environmental science, environmental studies, ESL, ethics, ethnic studies, European history, expository writing, French, French-AP, geometry, Harlem Renaissance, health, history, improvisation, independent study, instrumental music, jazz ensemble, journalism, Latin, literature and composition-AP, mathematics, modern European history-AP, modern world history, music, music technology, music theory, painting, performing arts, philosophy, photography, physics, pre-calculus, psychology, science, sculpture, Spanish, Spanish-AP, statistics, studio art, theater, trigonometry, U.S. history-AP, visual arts, world history, writing.

Graduation Requirements Arts and fine arts (art, music, dance, drama), English, foreign language, history, mathematics, science. Community service is required.

Special Academic Programs 17 Advanced Placement exams for which test preparation is offered; honors section; independent study; term-away projects; study abroad; ESL.

College Admission Counseling 119 students graduated in 2016; all went to college, including Dartmouth College; Georgetown University; Middlebury College; Sewanee: The University of the South; St. Lawrence University; Trinity College.

Student Life Upper grades have specified standards of dress, student council, honor system. Discipline rests equally with students and faculty.

Tuition and Aid Day student tuition: $46,500; 7-day tuition and room/board: $58,500. Tuition installment plan (Key Tuition Payment Plan, SMART Tuition Payment Plan, monthly payment plans). Need-based scholarship grants available. In 2016–17, 31% of upper-school students received aid. Total amount of financial aid awarded in 2016–17: $5,100,000.

Admissions Traditional secondary-level entrance grade is 9. For fall 2016, 1,204 students applied for upper-level admission, 289 were accepted, 132 enrolled. ACT, PSAT, SAT, SSAT or TOEFL required. Deadline for receipt of application materials: January 15. Application fee required: $100. Interview required.

Athletics Interscholastic: baseball (boys), basketball (b,g), crew (b,g), cross-country running (b,g), field hockey (g), football (b), ice hockey (b,g), lacrosse (b,g), rowing (b,g), skiing (downhill) (b,g), soccer (b,g), softball (g), squash (b,g), tennis (b,g), track and field (b,g), volleyball (g); coed interscholastic: alpine skiing, golf, mountain biking; coed intramural: alpine skiing, bicycling, canoeing/kayaking, climbing, combined training, dance, fly fishing, hiking/backpacking, kayaking, modern dance, mountain biking, mountaineering, nordic skiing, outdoor adventure, outdoor education, outdoor skills, rappelling, rock climbing, ropes courses, skiing (cross-country), snowboarding, snowshoeing, wall climbing, weight training, wilderness, wilderness survival. 2 athletic trainers.

Computers Computers are regularly used in all classes. Computer network features include on-campus library services, online commercial services, Internet access, wireless campus network, Internet filtering or blocking technology, network printing, interactive Polyvision white boards (Smart boards). Campus intranet, student e-mail accounts, and computer access in designated common areas are available to students. Students grades are available online. The school has a published electronic and media policy.

Contact Ms. Danielle Francoline, Assistant to Director of Admission. 413-229-1253. Fax: 413-229-1016. E-mail: admission@berkshireschool.org. Website: www.berkshireschool.org

See Display below and Close-Up on page 592.

THE BERMUDA HIGH SCHOOL FOR GIRLS

19 Richmond Road
Pembroke HM 08, Bermuda

Head of School: Mrs. Linda (Noble) Parker

General Information Girls' day college-preparatory and general academic school. Grades 1–13. Founded: 1894. Setting: small town. Nearest major city is Hamilton, Bermuda. 8-acre campus. 4 buildings on campus. Approved or accredited by Council of International Schools, New England Association of Schools and Colleges, and state department of education. Language of instruction: English. Endowment: 5 million Bermuda dollars. Total enrollment: 746. Upper school average class size: 17. Upper school faculty-student ratio: 1:12. There are 210 required school days per year for Upper School students. The average school day consists of 7 hours.

Upper School Student Profile Grade 10: 48 students (48 girls); Grade 11: 49 students (49 girls); Grade 12: 41 students (6 boys, 35 girls); Grade 13: 52 students (11 boys, 41 girls).

Faculty School total: 85. In upper school: 13 men, 40 women; 25 have advanced degrees.

Subjects Offered Accounting, algebra, art, arts, biology, business, business skills, business studies, calculus, chemistry, college admission preparation, college counseling, community service, computer science, drama, economics, English, English literature, European history, expository writing, fine arts, French, geography, geometry, grammar, health, history, keyboarding, Latin, mathematics, music, physical education, physics, science, social studies, Spanish, theater, trigonometry, world history.

Graduation Requirements Arts and fine arts (art, music, dance, drama), business skills (includes word processing), computer science, electives, English, foreign language, geography, mathematics, science.

Special Academic Programs International Baccalaureate program; remedial reading and/or remedial writing.

College Admission Counseling 30 students graduated in 2016; 28 went to college, including Cornell University; Dalhousie University; Florida State University; McGill University; University of Toronto; Wake Forest University. Other: 2 had other specific plans.

Student Life Upper grades have uniform requirement, student council, honor system. Discipline rests primarily with faculty.

Tuition and Aid Day student tuition: 18,000 Bermuda dollars–21,300 Bermuda dollars. Tuition installment plan (monthly payment plans, individually arranged payment plans). Bursaries, merit scholarship grants, need-based scholarship grants available. In 2016–17, 39% of upper-school students received aid. Total amount of financial aid awarded in 2016–17: 332,100 Bermuda dollars.

Admissions Traditional secondary-level entrance grade is 7. For fall 2016, 28 students applied for upper-level admission, 14 were accepted, 12 enrolled. School's own test required. Deadline for receipt of application materials: none. Application fee required: 75 Bermuda dollars. On-campus interview recommended.

Athletics Interscholastic: aquatics (girls), basketball (g), cross-country running (g), field hockey (g), gymnastics (g), netball (g), soccer (g), swimming and diving (g), tennis (g), track and field (g), volleyball (g); intramural: aerobics (g), aerobics/dance (g), aerobics/Nautilus (g), backpacking (g), badminton (g), ball hockey (g), basketball (g), cooperative games (g), cross-country running (g), dance (g), dressage (g), field hockey (g), fitness (g), fitness walking (g), floor hockey (g), football (g), gymnastics (g), jogging (g), Nautilus (g), netball (g), outdoor education (g), outdoor skills (g), physical fitness (g), soccer (g), softball (g), squash (g), track and field (g), volleyball (g), wall climbing (g). 3 PE instructors, 10 coaches.

Computers Computers are regularly used in business skills, business studies, English, foreign language, French, geography, history, introduction to technology, mathematics, research skills, Spanish, word processing, yearbook classes. Computer network features include on-campus library services, Internet access, Internet filtering or blocking technology. Campus intranet, student e-mail accounts, and computer access in designated common areas are available to students. Students grades are available online. The school has a published electronic and media policy.

Contact Mrs. Elizabeth Richens, Registrar/Secondary Admissions. 441-278-3011. Fax: 441-278-3017. E-mail: lrichens@bhs.bm. Website: www.bhs.bm

BESANT HILL SCHOOL

8585 Ojai Santa Paula Road
PO Box 850
Ojai, California 93024

Head of School: Mr. Randy Bertin

General Information Coeducational boarding and day college-preparatory and arts school; primarily serves students with learning disabilities, individuals with Attention Deficit Disorder, and dyslexic students. Grades 9–PG. Founded: 1946. Setting: small town. Nearest major city is Los Angeles. Students are housed in single-sex dormitories. 500-acre campus. 14 buildings on campus. Approved or accredited by Western Association of Schools and Colleges and California Department of Education. Member of National Association of Independent Schools and Secondary School Admission Test Board. Endowment: $1 million. Total enrollment: 100. Upper school average class size: 10. Upper school faculty-student ratio: 1:4. Upper School students typically attend 5 days per week. The average school day consists of 8 hours.

Upper School Student Profile Grade 9: 17 students (9 boys, 8 girls); Grade 10: 26 students (14 boys, 12 girls); Grade 11: 29 students (16 boys, 13 girls); Grade 12: 28 students (14 boys, 14 girls). 84% of students are boarding students. 40% are state residents. 12 states are represented in upper school student body. 40% are international students. International students from China, Germany, Japan, Mexico, Russian Federation, and Taiwan; 12 other countries represented in student body.

Faculty School total: 25. In upper school: 13 men, 12 women; 12 have advanced degrees; 24 reside on campus.

Subjects Offered Acting, addiction, adolescent issues, algebra, American history, art, art history, astronomy, biology, calculus, calculus-AP, ceramics, chemistry, computer science, digital art, drama, English, English as a foreign language, English language and composition-AP, English literature, English-AP, environmental science, ESL, ethics, expository writing, film, fine arts, geography, geometry, government/civics, history, mathematics, music, music history, music theory, music theory-AP, philosophy, photography, physical education, physics, psychology, scene study, science, social sciences, social studies, Spanish, theater, world history.

Graduation Requirements Arts and fine arts (art, music, dance, drama), English, foreign language, mathematics, physical education (includes health), science, social sciences, social studies (includes history).

Special Academic Programs 4 Advanced Placement exams for which test preparation is offered; honors section; independent study; study at local college for college credit; academic accommodation for the musically talented and the artistically talented; programs in English, mathematics, general development for dyslexic students; ESL (22 students enrolled).

College Admission Counseling 27 students graduated in 2015; 26 went to college, including San Diego State University; Sarah Lawrence College; University of California, Santa Barbara; University of California, Santa Cruz; University of Colorado

Boulder. Other: 1 had other specific plans. Median SAT critical reading: 580, median SAT math: 550, median SAT writing: 500. 18% scored over 600 on SAT critical reading, 10% scored over 600 on SAT math, 15% scored over 600 on SAT writing.

Student Life Upper grades have student council, honor system. Discipline rests equally with students and faculty.

Tuition and Aid Day student tuition: $22,000; 7-day tuition and room/board: $47,950. Tuition installment plan (Academic Management Services Plan, Key Tuition Payment Plan). Tuition reduction for siblings, need-based scholarship grants available. In 2015–16, 25% of upper-school students received aid. Total amount of financial aid awarded in 2015–16: $450,000.

Admissions Traditional secondary-level entrance grade is 9. For fall 2015, 245 students applied for upper-level admission, 86 were accepted, 37 enrolled. Deadline for receipt of application materials: February 1. Application fee required: $75. Interview required.

Athletics Interscholastic: basketball (boys), soccer (b,g), volleyball (g); intramural: baseball (b), basketball (b), soccer (b,g), softball (b), wrestling (b); coed interscholastic: aerobics/dance, backpacking, cross-country running, dance, fitness, fitness walking, Frisbee, golf, hiking/backpacking, modern dance, mountain biking, outdoor activities, outdoor adventure, outdoor education, outdoor skills, paddle tennis, physical training, ropes courses, skeet shooting; coed intramural: bicycling, billiards, climbing, jogging, kayaking, running, skateboarding, skiing (downhill), surfing, swimming and diving, table tennis, tennis, track and field, ultimate Frisbee, walking, wall climbing, weight lifting, wilderness, yoga. 2 coaches, 1 athletic trainer.

Computers Computers are regularly used in desktop publishing, graphic arts, graphic design, mathematics, media arts, publications, video film production classes. Computer network features include on-campus library services, online commercial services, Internet access, wireless campus network, Internet filtering or blocking technology. Campus intranet, student e-mail accounts, and computer access in designated common areas are available to students. Students grades are available online.

Contact Terra Furguiel, Associate Director of Admissions. 805-646-4343 Ext. 111. Fax: 805-646-4371. E-mail: tfurguiel@besanthill.org. Website: www.besanthill.org

BETH HAVEN CHRISTIAN SCHOOL

5515 Johnsontown Road
Louisville, Kentucky 40272

Head of School: Mrs. John O. Baker III

General Information Coeducational day college-preparatory and college preparatory school, affiliated with Baptist Church. Grades K–12. Founded: 1971. Setting: suburban. 2-acre campus. 2 buildings on campus. Approved or accredited by Association of Christian Schools International and Kentucky Department of Education. Total enrollment: 178. Upper school average class size: 15. Upper school faculty-student ratio: 1:7. There are 174 required school days per year for Upper School students. Upper School students typically attend 5 days per week. The average school day consists of 7 hours.

Upper School Student Profile Grade 9: 13 students (7 boys, 6 girls); Grade 10: 11 students (4 boys, 7 girls); Grade 11: 18 students (11 boys, 7 girls); Grade 12: 17 students (7 boys, 10 girls). 55% of students are Baptist.

Faculty School total: 17. In upper school: 6 men, 3 women; 4 have advanced degrees.

Graduation Requirements ACT preparation, algebra, American literature, analytic geometry, arts appreciation, Bible, biology, British literature, creative arts, earth science, geography, health, language, mathematics, religion (includes Bible studies and theology), science, world geography.

Special Academic Programs Study at local college for college credit.

College Admission Counseling 12 students graduated in 2016; all went to college, including Bellarmine University; Jefferson Community and Technical College; University of Kentucky; University of Louisville. Median composite ACT: 19. 7% scored over 26 on composite ACT.

Student Life Upper grades have uniform requirement, student council, honor system. Discipline rests primarily with faculty. Attendance at religious services is required.

Tuition and Aid Day student tuition: $5325. Tuition installment plan (FACTS Tuition Payment Plan). Tuition reduction for siblings, need-based scholarship grants, two full-tuition memorial scholarships are awarded each year based on a combination of merit and need available. In 2016–17, 5% of upper-school students received aid. Total amount of financial aid awarded in 2016–17: $10,650.

Admissions Traditional secondary-level entrance grade is 9. California Achievement Test required. Deadline for receipt of application materials: none. Application fee required: $350. On-campus interview recommended.

Athletics Interscholastic: archery (boys, girls), baseball (b), basketball (b,g), cheering (g), softball (g), volleyball (g); coed interscholastic: golf. 1 PE instructor, 6 coaches.

Computers Computers are regularly used in Spanish classes. Computer network features include Internet access, Internet filtering or blocking technology. Computer access in designated common areas is available to students. Students grades are available online. The school has a published electronic and media policy.

Contact Ms. Jessica Piercey, Registrar/Secretary. 502-937-3516. Fax: 502-937-3364. E-mail: jpiercey@bethhaven.com. Website: www.bethhaven.com/

THE BIRCH WATHEN LENOX SCHOOL

210 East 77th Street
New York, New York 10075

Head of School: Mr. Frank J. Carnabuci III

General Information Coeducational day college-preparatory and well-rounded college preparatory traditional education school. Grades K–12. Founded: 1916. Setting: urban. 1 building on campus. Approved or accredited by New York State Association of Independent Schools and New York Department of Education. Member of National Association of Independent Schools. Endowment: $7.2 million. Total enrollment: 570. Upper school average class size: 17. Upper school faculty-student ratio: 1:15. Upper School students typically attend 5 days per week. The average school day consists of 7 hours.

Upper School Student Profile Grade 9: 46 students (24 boys, 22 girls); Grade 10: 45 students (25 boys, 20 girls); Grade 11: 46 students (23 boys, 23 girls); Grade 12: 48 students (22 boys, 26 girls).

Faculty School total: 120. In upper school: 30 men, 85 women; 115 have advanced degrees.

Subjects Offered Algebra, American history, American history-AP, American literature, American literature-AP, art, art history, biology, calculus, ceramics, chemistry, community service, computer math, computer science, creative writing, dance, drama, driver education, economics, English, English literature, environmental science, European history, expository writing, fine arts, French, geography, geology, geometry, government/civics, grammar, industrial arts, Japanese, journalism, mathematics, music, philosophy, photography, physical education, physics, science, Shakespeare, social studies, Spanish, speech, swimming, theater, trigonometry, typing, world history, writing.

Graduation Requirements 20th century world history, arts and fine arts (art, music, dance, drama), computer science, English, foreign language, mathematics, physical education (includes health), science, social studies (includes history). Community service is required.

Special Academic Programs Advanced Placement exam preparation; honors section; independent study; study abroad; academic accommodation for the gifted.

College Admission Counseling 48 students graduated in 2016; all went to college, including Bowdoin College; Cornell University; Princeton University; University of Pennsylvania; Vanderbilt University; Wesleyan University. Mean SAT critical reading: 680, mean SAT math: 700, mean SAT writing: 700.

Student Life Upper grades have uniform requirement, student council, honor system. Discipline rests equally with students and faculty.

Summer Programs Enrichment, advancement programs offered; session focuses on math and science; held on campus; accepts boys and girls; not open to students from other schools.

Tuition and Aid Day student tuition: $44,791–$46,004. Tuition installment plan (Key Tuition Payment Plan, monthly payment plans, individually arranged payment plans). Merit scholarship grants, need-based scholarship grants available. In 2016–17, 18% of upper-school students received aid. Total amount of financial aid awarded in 2016–17: $1,500,000.

Admissions Traditional secondary-level entrance grade is 9. For fall 2016, 200 students applied for upper-level admission, 85 were accepted, 62 enrolled. ERB, ISEE, Math Placement Exam, PSAT or SAT, SSAT or writing sample required. Deadline for receipt of application materials: none. Application fee required: $50. On-campus interview recommended.

Athletics Interscholastic: baseball (boys), basketball (b,g), cross-country running (b,g), field hockey (g), hockey (b), ice hockey (b), lacrosse (b), soccer (b,g), softball (g), squash (b,g), swimming and diving (b,g), tennis (b,g), track and field (b,g), volleyball (g); intramural: aerobics (b,g), badminton (g), baseball (b), basketball (b,g), dance (b), ice hockey (b), indoor soccer (b), running (b,g), skiing (downhill) (b,g), soccer (b,g), softball (g), swimming and diving (b,g), tennis (b,g), track and field (b,g), volleyball (b,g); coed interscholastic: cross-country running, golf, ice hockey, indoor track & field, lacrosse, squash; coed intramural: bicycling, dance, golf, gymnastics, indoor track & field, skiing (cross-country), skiing (downhill). 5 PE instructors, 8 coaches.

Computers Computers are regularly used in all academic classes. Computer network features include on-campus library services, Internet access, wireless campus network, Internet filtering or blocking technology, MOBY, Smartboard, Chromebooks, iPads. Student e-mail accounts and computer access in designated common areas are available to students.

Contact Billie Williams, Admissions Coordinator. 212-861-0404 Ext. 135. Fax: 212-879-3388. E-mail: admissions@bwl.org. Website: www.bwl.org

BISHOP BRADY HIGH SCHOOL

25 Columbus Avenue
Concord, New Hampshire 03301

Head of School: Ms. Andrea Elliot

General Information Coeducational day college-preparatory school, affiliated with Roman Catholic Church. Grades 9–12. Founded: 1963. Setting: suburban. 8-acre campus. 1 building on campus. Approved or accredited by National Catholic Education Association, New England Association of Schools and Colleges, and New Hampshire Department of Education. Endowment: $100,000. Total enrollment: 349. Upper school

average class size: 17. Upper school faculty-student ratio: 1:16. There are 179 required school days per year for Upper School students. Upper School students typically attend 5 days per week. The average school day consists of 6 hours and 30 minutes.

Upper School Student Profile Grade 9: 73 students (30 boys, 43 girls); Grade 10: 87 students (40 boys, 47 girls); Grade 11: 101 students (63 boys, 38 girls); Grade 12: 88 students (48 boys, 40 girls). 55% of students are Roman Catholic.

Faculty School total: 32. In upper school: 13 men, 19 women; 25 have advanced degrees.

Subjects Offered Advanced chemistry, advanced math, Advanced Placement courses, algebra, anatomy and physiology, art appreciation, arts, biology, biology-AP, calculus-AP, career/college preparation, chemistry, chemistry-AP, Christian scripture, civics, college awareness, college counseling, computer education, computer programming, conceptual physics, drama, engineering, English, English literature-AP, English-AP, ethics, film studies, forensics, French-AP, freshman seminar, geometry, guidance, health education, history, history-AP, honors English, Latin, moral theology, music appreciation, musical theater, physical education, physics-AP, pre-calculus, probability and statistics, psychology, religious studies, research and reference, SAT preparation, social justice, Spanish-AP, theology, trigonometry, U.S. history-AP, world religions, writing.

Graduation Requirements Algebra, American literature, arts and fine arts (art, music, dance, drama), biology, chemistry, civics, computer education, economics, English, geometry, languages, literature, mathematics, physical education (includes health), science, theology, U.S. history, wellness, world history, 100 hours of community service.

Special Academic Programs 10 Advanced Placement exams for which test preparation is offered; honors section; independent study; study at local college for college credit; academic accommodation for the gifted; special instructional classes for deaf students; ESL (34 students enrolled).

College Admission Counseling 78 students graduated in 2015; 75 went to college, including Merrimack College; Plymouth State University; Purdue University; Saint Anselm College; University of New Hampshire; University of Vermont. Other: 2 went to work, 1 entered a postgraduate year. Mean SAT critical reading: 542, mean SAT math: 564, mean SAT writing: 542, mean composite ACT: 24. 30% scored over 600 on SAT critical reading, 30% scored over 600 on SAT math.

Student Life Upper grades have specified standards of dress, student council, honor system. Discipline rests primarily with faculty. Attendance at religious services is required.

Tuition and Aid Day student tuition: $11,565. Tuition installment plan (Insured Tuition Payment Plan, FACTS Tuition Payment Plan, monthly payment plans, individually arranged payment plans). Tuition reduction for siblings, merit scholarship grants, need-based scholarship grants available. In 2015–16, 34% of upper-school students received aid; total upper-school merit-scholarship money awarded: $4000. Total amount of financial aid awarded in 2015–16: $550,000.

Admissions Traditional secondary-level entrance grade is 9. For fall 2015, 179 students applied for upper-level admission, 167 were accepted, 101 enrolled. SSAT, STS Examination or TOEFL or SLEP required. Deadline for receipt of application materials: none. Application fee required: $45. Interview required.

Athletics Interscholastic: alpine skiing (boys, girls), baseball (b), basketball (b,g), cross-country running (b,g), field hockey (g), fishing (b), football (b), golf (b,g), ice hockey (b,g), indoor track & field (b,g), lacrosse (b,g), nordic skiing (b,g), skiing (cross-country) (b,g), skiing (downhill) (b,g), soccer (b,g), softball (g), swimming and diving (b,g), tennis (b,g), track and field (b,g); coed interscholastic: equestrian sports, juggling, physical fitness; coed intramural: crew, rock climbing, snowboarding, strength & conditioning, table tennis, volleyball, weight lifting, weight training. 1 PE instructor.

Computers Computers are regularly used in business applications, college planning, computer applications, journalism, literary magazine, newspaper classes. Computer network features include on-campus library services, online commercial services, Internet access, wireless campus network, Internet filtering or blocking technology. Student e-mail accounts and computer access in designated common areas are available to students. Students grades are available online. The school has a published electronic and media policy.

Contact Mrs. Lonna J. Abbott, Director of Admissions and Enrollment. 603-224-7419. Fax: 603-228-6664. E-mail: labbott@bishopbrady.edu. Website: www.bishopbrady.edu

BISHOP BROSSART HIGH SCHOOL

4 Grove Street
Alexandria, Kentucky 41001

Head of School: Mr. Dan Ridder

General Information Coeducational day college-preparatory school, affiliated with Roman Catholic Church. Grades 9–12. Founded: 1950. Setting: small town. Nearest major city is Cincinnati, OH. 1 building on campus. Approved or accredited by National Catholic Education Association, Southern Association of Colleges and Schools, and Kentucky Department of Education. Total enrollment: 382. Upper school average class size: 25. Upper school faculty-student ratio: 1:16. There are 177 required school days per year for Upper School students. Upper School students typically attend 5 days per week. The average school day consists of 6 hours and 10 minutes.

Upper School Student Profile Grade 9: 64 students (31 boys, 33 girls); Grade 10: 68 students (42 boys, 26 girls); Grade 11: 57 students (26 boys, 31 girls); Grade 12: 65 students (26 boys, 39 girls). 98% of students are Roman Catholic.

Faculty School total: 26. In upper school: 10 men, 16 women; 25 have advanced degrees.

Subjects Offered Advanced Placement courses, anatomy, art, arts appreciation, biology, business, calculus-AP, chemistry, chorus, communication arts, computer programming, computer technologies, discrete mathematics, earth science, economics, English, English language-AP, English literature-AP, English-AP, European history-AP, film, finance, foreign language, French, French language-AP, French-AP, geometry, global issues, government, health, history-AP, instrumental music, introduction to technology, physics, religion, science, social studies, Spanish, Spanish-AP, theater, U.S. history, U.S. history-AP.

Special Academic Programs Honors section.

College Admission Counseling 86 students graduated in 2016; 81 went to college, including Northern Kentucky University; University of Cincinnati; University of Kentucky; University of Louisville. Other: 1 went to work, 2 entered military service, 1 entered a postgraduate year, 1 had other specific plans.

Student Life Upper grades have uniform requirement, student council, honor system. Discipline rests primarily with faculty. Attendance at religious services is required.

Tuition and Aid Day student tuition: $6540. Tuition installment plan (FACTS Tuition Payment Plan, monthly payment plans, individually arranged payment plans). Tuition reduction for siblings, merit scholarship grants, need-based scholarship grants available.

Admissions Traditional secondary-level entrance grade is 9. High School Placement Test required. Application fee required: $100.

Athletics Interscholastic: baseball (boys), basketball (b,g), bowling (b,g), cheering (g), dance team (g), golf (b,g), indoor track & field (b,g), soccer (b,g), track and field (b,g), volleyball (g). 1 PE instructor, 5 coaches.

Computers Computers are regularly used in all academic classes. Computer network features include Internet access, wireless campus network. Student e-mail accounts are available to students. Students grades are available online. The school has a published electronic and media policy.

Contact Mr. Chris Holtz, Admissions. 859-635-2108 Ext. 1018. Fax: 859-635-2135. E-mail: choltz@bishopbrossart.org. Website: http://bishopbrossart.org

BISHOP CONNOLLY HIGH SCHOOL

373 Elsbree Street
Fall River, Massachusetts 02720

Head of School: Mr. Christopher Myron

General Information Coeducational day college-preparatory school, affiliated with Roman Catholic Church. Grades 9–12. Founded: 1966. Setting: suburban. 72-acre campus. 1 building on campus. Approved or accredited by New England Association of Schools and Colleges and Massachusetts Department of Education. Total enrollment: 280. Upper school average class size: 16. Upper school faculty-student ratio: 1:16. There are 185 required school days per year for Upper School students. Upper School students typically attend 5 days per week. The average school day consists of 6 hours and 30 minutes.

Upper School Student Profile 95% of students are Roman Catholic.

Faculty School total: 26. In upper school: 13 men, 13 women; 22 have advanced degrees.

Subjects Offered Advanced Placement courses, algebra, American literature, American studies, anatomy and physiology, art, art history, Bible studies, biology, biology-AP, British literature, British literature (honors), calculus, calculus-AP, campus ministry, chemistry, chemistry-AP, choir, chorus, community service, computer programming, creative writing, desktop publishing, drama, English, English literature, English-AP, environmental science, European history-AP, French, French-AP, geometry, health, history, honors algebra, honors English, honors geometry, honors U.S. history, honors world history, human biology, instrumental music, keyboarding, math analysis, mathematics, music, music history, music theory, physical education, physics, Portuguese, psychology, religion, science, social studies, Spanish, theology, trigonometry, U.S. history-AP, world history, world literature.

Graduation Requirements English, foreign language, mathematics, religion (includes Bible studies and theology), science, social studies (includes history). Community service is required.

Special Academic Programs Advanced Placement exam preparation; honors section; independent study; study at local college for college credit.

College Admission Counseling 72 students graduated in 2016; 70 went to college, including Bridgewater State University; Northeastern University; Providence College; Quinnipiac University; University of Massachusetts Dartmouth; University of Rhode Island. Other: 2 entered military service. Mean SAT critical reading: 511, mean SAT math: 508, mean SAT writing: 522.

Student Life Upper grades have uniform requirement, student council, honor system. Discipline rests primarily with faculty. Attendance at religious services is required.

Tuition and Aid Day student tuition: $8900. Tuition installment plan (FACTS Tuition Payment Plan, monthly payment plans). Merit scholarship grants, need-based scholarship grants available.

Admissions Traditional secondary-level entrance grade is 9. High School Placement Test required. Deadline for receipt of application materials: none. No application fee required. Interview recommended.

Athletics Interscholastic: baseball (boys), basketball (b,g), cheering (g), cross-country running (b,g), field hockey (g), football (b), ice hockey (b), lacrosse (b), soccer (b,g), softball (g), tennis (b,g), track and field (b,g), volleyball (g), winter (indoor) track (b,g); intramural: field hockey (g); coed interscholastic: golf, indoor soccer, indoor track & field. 1 PE instructor, 18 coaches, 1 athletic trainer.

Computers Computers are regularly used in all classes. Computer network features include online commercial services, Internet access, wireless campus network, Internet filtering or blocking technology. Computer access in designated common areas is available to students. The school has a published electronic and media policy.

Contact Mr. Anthony C. Ciampanelli, Director of Admissions/Alumni. 508-676-1071 Ext. 333. Fax: 508-676-8594. E-mail: aciampanelli@bchs.dfrcs.org. Website: www.bishopconnolly.com

BISHOP DENIS J. O'CONNELL HIGH SCHOOL

6600 Little Falls Road
Arlington, Virginia 22213

Head of School: Dr. Joseph Vorbach III

General Information Coeducational day college-preparatory school, affiliated with Roman Catholic Church. Grades 9–12. Founded: 1957. Setting: suburban. Nearest major city is Washington, DC. 28-acre campus. 1 building on campus. Approved or accredited by National Catholic Education Association, Southern Association of Colleges and Schools, Southern Association of Independent Schools, and Virginia Department of Education. Member of Secondary School Admission Test Board. Total enrollment: 1,100. Upper school average class size: 17. Upper school faculty-student ratio: 1:12. There are 180 required school days per year for Upper School students. Upper School students typically attend 5 days per week. The average school day consists of 7 hours and 15 minutes.

Upper School Student Profile 80% of students are Roman Catholic.

Faculty School total: 110. In upper school: 71 have advanced degrees.

Subjects Offered Accounting, African American history, African-American history, algebra, American history, American history-AP, American literature, analysis, art, art history, athletic training, Basic programming, Bible studies, biology, biology-AP, business, business technology, calculus, calculus-AP, chemistry, chemistry-AP, choir, choral music, chorus, church history, comparative government and politics-AP, comparative political systems-AP, computer graphics, computer multimedia, computer music, computer programming, computer science, computer science-AP, computer skills, creative writing, digital art, dramatic arts, driver education, earth science, East Asian history, ecology, economics, economics-AP, English, English language-AP, English literature, English literature-AP, environmental science-AP, European history, European history-AP, fine arts, forensics, French, French language-AP, French-AP, geography, geometry, German, German-AP, government and politics-AP, government-AP, government/civics, guitar, health, history, history of the Catholic Church, honors English, honors geometry, honors U.S. history, honors world history, introduction to theater, Italian, jazz band, journalism, Latin, Latin-AP, literature-AP, macro/microeconomics-AP, macroeconomics-AP, marketing, mathematics, media arts, microeconomics-AP, modern European history-AP, music, music theory-AP, music-AP, New Testament, newspaper, orchestra, painting, personal finance, personal fitness, photo shop, photography, photojournalism, physical education, physical fitness, physics, physics-AP, piano, play production, pre-calculus, probability, psychology, psychology-AP, public speaking, religion, remedial study skills, science, science research, social sciences, social studies, sociology, Spanish, Spanish language-AP, Spanish literature-AP, Spanish-AP, speech, speech and debate, sports conditioning, sports psychology, statistics, statistics-AP, student government, studio art-AP, theater arts, theater design and production, theology, trigonometry, U.S. and Virginia government-AP, U.S. and Virginia history, U.S. government, U.S. government and politics-AP, U.S. history, U.S. history-AP, United States government-AP, video film production, voice ensemble, Web site design, weight training, weightlifting, world history, world literature.

Graduation Requirements Arts and fine arts (art, music, dance, drama), computer science, English, foreign language, mathematics, physical education (includes health), religion (includes Bible studies and theology), science, social sciences, social studies (includes history), community service program incorporated into graduation requirements.

Special Academic Programs 26 Advanced Placement exams for which test preparation is offered; honors section; independent study; study at local college for college credit; academic accommodation for the gifted; remedial math; programs in general development for dyslexic students; ESL (20 students enrolled).

College Admission Counseling 310 students graduated in 2016; 306 went to college, including George Mason University; James Madison University; The College of William and Mary; University of Virginia; Virginia Commonwealth University; Virginia Polytechnic Institute and State University. Other: 4 entered military service. Median SAT critical reading: 574, median SAT math: 559, median SAT writing: 564, median combined SAT: 1697, median composite ACT: 29.

Student Life Upper grades have uniform requirement, student council, honor system. Discipline rests equally with students and faculty. Attendance at religious services is required.

Summer Programs Remediation, enrichment, advancement, sports, art/fine arts, computer instruction programs offered; held on campus; accepts boys and girls; open to students from other schools. 200 students usually enrolled. 2017 schedule: June 15 to August 15. Application deadline: none.

Tuition and Aid Day student tuition: $14,625–$16,625. Tuition installment plan (FACTS Tuition Payment Plan). Tuition reduction for siblings, merit scholarship grants, need-based scholarship grants, scholarship competition only for eighth graders currently enrolled in a Diocese of Arlington Catholic school available. In 2016–17, 30% of upper-school students received aid; total upper-school merit-scholarship money awarded: $50,000. Total amount of financial aid awarded in 2016–17: $2,100,000.

Admissions High School Placement Test required. Deadline for receipt of application materials: January 13. Application fee required: $50.

Athletics Interscholastic: baseball (boys), basketball (b,g), crew (b,g), cross-country running (b,g), dance team (g), diving (b,g), field hockey (g), football (b), ice hockey (b), lacrosse (b,g), soccer (b,g), softball (g), swimming and diving (b,g), tennis (b,g), track and field (b,g), volleyball (g), weight lifting (b,g), weight training (b,g), winter (indoor) track (b,g), wrestling (b); intramural: basketball (b,g), weight lifting (b,g); coed interscholastic: golf, ice hockey, sailing; coed intramural: crew, flag football, softball, ultimate Frisbee, volleyball. 7 PE instructors, 7 coaches, 1 athletic trainer.

Computers Computers are regularly used in accounting, all academic, art, business, computer applications, English, foreign language, health, history, mathematics, science, social sciences classes. Computer network features include on-campus library services, online commercial services, Internet access, wireless campus network, Internet filtering or blocking technology. Campus intranet, student e-mail accounts, and computer access in designated common areas are available to students. Students grades are available online. The school has a published electronic and media policy.

Contact Mr. Michael Cresson, Director of Admissions. 703-237-1433. Fax: 703-241-4297. E-mail: mcresson@bishopoconnell.org. Website: www.bishopoconnell.org

BISHOP EUSTACE PREPARATORY SCHOOL

5552 Route 70
Pennsauken, New Jersey 08109-4798

Head of School: Br. James Beamesderfer, SAC

General Information Coeducational day college-preparatory, arts, religious studies, and technology school, affiliated with Roman Catholic Church. Grades 9–12. Founded: 1954. Setting: suburban. Nearest major city is Philadelphia, PA. 32-acre campus. 7 buildings on campus. Approved or accredited by Middle States Association of Colleges and Schools and New Jersey Department of Education. Member of National Association of Independent Schools. Endowment: $4.8 million. Total enrollment: 675. Upper school average class size: 19. Upper school faculty-student ratio: 1:12. There are 165 required school days per year for Upper School students. Upper School students typically attend 5 days per week. The average school day consists of 6 hours and 20 minutes.

Upper School Student Profile 88% of students are Roman Catholic.

Faculty School total: 54. In upper school: 25 men, 29 women; 43 have advanced degrees.

Subjects Offered Advanced chemistry, advanced computer applications, Advanced Placement courses, algebra, American history, American history-AP, American literature, anatomy, anatomy and physiology, applied music, art and culture, art history, band, Bible studies, biology, biology-AP, British literature, British literature (honors), calculus, calculus-AP, campus ministry, career education, career exploration, career/college preparation, chemistry, chemistry-AP, choir, Christian doctrine, Christian education, Christian ethics, Christian scripture, clinical chemistry, college counseling, college placement, college planning, comparative religion, computer education, computer science, creative writing, driver education, economics and history, electives, English, English literature, English literature and composition-AP, environmental science, environmental science-AP, ethics, European history-AP, film, film and literature, fine arts, French, French as a second language, gender issues, genetics, geometry, German, government and politics-AP, government/civics, grammar, health, history, honors algebra, honors English, honors geometry, honors U.S. history, honors world history, instrumental music, journalism, Latin, law, law studies, macroeconomics-AP, mathematics, mathematics-AP, music, music composition, music history, music theory, music theory-AP, physical education, physical science, physics, physics-AP, physiology, pre-calculus, psychology, psychology-AP, science, sex education, social studies, sociology, Spanish, Spanish-AP, statistics-AP, theology, trigonometry, U.S. government and politics-AP, U.S. history, U.S. history-AP, vocal music, women's studies, world affairs, world history, world religions.

Graduation Requirements Art history, arts and fine arts (art, music, dance, drama), career exploration, computer science, English, foreign language, mathematics, physical education (includes health), religion (includes Bible studies and theology), science, social studies (includes history). Community service is required.

Special Academic Programs 17 Advanced Placement exams for which test preparation is offered; honors section; independent study; study at local college for college credit; academic accommodation for the gifted and the musically talented.

College Admission Counseling 160 students graduated in 2015; 156 went to college, including Drexel University; Penn State University Park; Rutgers University–New Brunswick; Saint Joseph's University; University of Delaware; Villanova University. Other: 1 entered a postgraduate year, 3 had other specific plans. Mean SAT critical reading: 564, mean SAT math: 574, mean SAT writing: 566. 33.5% scored over 600 on SAT critical reading, 37.5% scored over 600 on SAT math, 35.5% scored over 600 on SAT writing.

Student Life Upper grades have uniform requirement, student council, honor system. Discipline rests primarily with faculty. Attendance at religious services is required.

Tuition and Aid Day student tuition: $16,400. Tuition installment plan (FACTS Tuition Payment Plan). Merit scholarship grants, need-based scholarship grants available. In 2015–16, 35% of upper-school students received aid; total upper-school merit-scholarship money awarded: $295,200. Total amount of financial aid awarded in 2015–16: $800,000.

Admissions Traditional secondary-level entrance grade is 9. For fall 2015, 400 students applied for upper-level admission, 335 were accepted, 170 enrolled. High School Placement Test, math and English placement tests or placement test required. Deadline for receipt of application materials: none. Application fee required: $60.

Athletics Interscholastic: baseball (boys), basketball (b,g), bowling (b,g), cheering (g), crew (b,g), cross-country running (b,g), field hockey (g), football (b), golf (b,g), ice hockey (b), indoor track (b,g), indoor track & field (b,g), lacrosse (b,g), running (b,g), soccer (b,g), softball (g), swimming and diving (b,g), tennis (b,g), track and field (b,g); coed interscholastic: aquatics, diving, golf; coed intramural: ultimate Frisbee. 3 PE instructors, 59 coaches, 1 athletic trainer.

Computers Computers are regularly used in all academic classes. Computer network features include on-campus library services, online commercial services, Internet access, wireless campus network, Internet filtering or blocking technology. Campus intranet and computer access in designated common areas are available to students. Students grades are available online. The school has a published electronic and media policy.

Contact Mr. Nicholas Italiano, Dean of Admissions. 856-662-2160 Ext. 240. Fax: 856-662-0025. E-mail: admissions@eustace.org. Website: www.eustace.org

BISHOP FENWICK HIGH SCHOOL

4855 State Route 122
Franklin, Ohio 45005

Head of School: Mr. Andrew J. Barczak

General Information Coeducational day college-preparatory, religious studies, technology, and engineering school, affiliated with Roman Catholic Church. Grades 9–12. Founded: 1952. Setting: suburban. Nearest major city is Cincinnati. 66-acre campus. 1 building on campus. Approved or accredited by North Central Association of Colleges and Schools, Ohio Catholic Schools Accreditation Association (OCSAA), and Ohio Department of Education. Upper school average class size: 19. Upper school faculty-student ratio: 1:14. There are 184 required school days per year for Upper School students. Upper School students typically attend 5 days per week. The average school day consists of 6 hours and 35 minutes.

Upper School Student Profile Grade 9: 128 students (51 boys, 77 girls); Grade 10: 144 students (84 boys, 60 girls); Grade 11: 130 students (76 boys, 54 girls); Grade 12: 134 students (69 boys, 65 girls). 85% of students are Roman Catholic.

Faculty School total: 38. In upper school: 20 men, 18 women; 23 have advanced degrees.

Subjects Offered Accounting, ACT preparation, algebra, American democracy, art, art-AP, athletic training, biology, botany, calculus-AP, career planning, cell biology, chemistry, choir, chorus, church history, college admission preparation, computer graphics, computer programming, concert band, creative writing, economics, engineering, English, English-AP, ensembles, film and literature, fine arts, French, functions, general business, geometry, government, government/civics-AP, health, honors algebra, honors English, honors geometry, integrated mathematics, jazz band, Latin, Latin-AP, leadership, marching band, mathematics, multimedia, music appreciation, mythology, physical education, physical science, physics, physiology, portfolio art, pre-algebra, psychology, publications, religion, science, social studies, Spanish, statistics, study skills, technology, theater, theater arts, trigonometry, U.S. history, U.S. history-AP, Web site design, world geography, world history, writing, yearbook, zoology.

Graduation Requirements Arts and fine arts (art, music, dance, drama), English, foreign language, mathematics, physical education (includes health), religion (includes Bible studies and theology), science, social studies (includes history), technology, community service, retreats, must pass the Ohio Graduation Test.

Special Academic Programs Advanced Placement exam preparation; honors section; study at local college for college credit; academic accommodation for the gifted.

College Admission Counseling 145 students graduated in 2016; 142 went to college, including Miami University; Ohio University; The Ohio State University; University of Cincinnati; University of Dayton; Xavier University. Other: 2 went to work, 1 entered military service. Median SAT critical reading: 579, median SAT math: 595, median SAT writing: 552, median combined SAT: 1726, median composite ACT: 24.

Student Life Upper grades have uniform requirement, student council, honor system. Discipline rests primarily with faculty. Attendance at religious services is required.

Tuition and Aid Day student tuition: $9800. Tuition installment plan (FACTS Tuition Payment Plan). Tuition reduction for siblings, merit scholarship grants, need-based scholarship grants, paying campus jobs available. In 2016–17, 24% of upper-school students received aid.

Admissions Traditional secondary-level entrance grade is 9. High School Placement Test required. Deadline for receipt of application materials: November 21. No application fee required.

Athletics Interscholastic: baseball (boys), basketball (b,g), bowling (b,g), cheering (g), cross-country running (b,g), dance team (g), football (b), golf (b,g), lacrosse (b,g), soccer (b,g), softball (g), tennis (b,g), volleyball (b,g), weight training (b,g), wrestling (b); intramural: basketball (b), weight training (b,g); coed interscholastic: in-line hockey, roller hockey, swimming and diving, track and field; coed intramural: freestyle skiing, paint ball, skiing (downhill), snowboarding, strength & conditioning. 1 PE instructor, 62 coaches, 2 athletic trainers.

Computers Computers are regularly used in career exploration, career technology, college planning, engineering, graphic arts, graphic design, introduction to technology, multimedia, photography, publications, technology, video film production, Web site design, yearbook classes. Computer network features include on-campus library services, Internet access, wireless campus network, Internet filtering or blocking technology, 1:1 Microsoft Surface Pros; laptop carts, iPad cart, Kindles. Campus intranet, student e-mail accounts, and computer access in designated common areas are available to students. Students grades are available online. The school has a published electronic and media policy.

Contact Mrs. Betty Turvy, Director of Admissions. 513-428-0525. Fax: 513-727-1501. E-mail: bturvy@fenwickfalcons.org. Website: www.fenwickfalcons.org

BISHOP FOLEY CATHOLIC HIGH SCHOOL

32000 Campbell Road
Madison Heights, Michigan 48071-1098

Head of School: Mrs. Elizabeth Hubbell

General Information Coeducational day college-preparatory school, affiliated with Roman Catholic Church. Grades 9–12. Setting: suburban. Nearest major city is Detroit. 20.5-acre campus. 2 buildings on campus. Approved or accredited by North Central Association of Colleges and Schools and Michigan Department of Education. Upper school average class size: 18. Upper school faculty-student ratio: 1:15. Upper School students typically attend 5 days per week. The average school day consists of 7 hours.

Upper School Student Profile 84% of students are Roman Catholic.

Faculty School total: 24. In upper school: 11 men, 13 women.

Subjects Offered All academic.

Special Academic Programs Honors section; study at local college for college credit.

College Admission Counseling 78 students graduated in 2016; they went to Grand Valley State University; Oakland Community College; Oakland University; University of Detroit Mercy; University of Michigan; Wayne State University. Mean composite ACT: 24.

Student Life Upper grades have uniform requirement, student council, honor system. Discipline rests primarily with faculty. Attendance at religious services is required.

Tuition and Aid Day student tuition: $9050. Tuition installment plan (FACTS Tuition Payment Plan, monthly payment plans, individually arranged payment plans). Tuition reduction for siblings, merit scholarship grants, need-based scholarship grants available.

Admissions High School Placement Test required. Deadline for receipt of application materials: July 31. No application fee required. On-campus interview recommended.

Computers Computers are regularly used in all classes. Computer network features include on-campus library services, online commercial services, Internet access, wireless campus network, Internet filtering or blocking technology. Student e-mail accounts and computer access in designated common areas are available to students. Students grades are available online. The school has a published electronic and media policy.

Contact 248-585-1210. Fax: 248-585-3667. Website: www.bishopfoley.org

BISHOP GUERTIN HIGH SCHOOL

194 Lund Road
Nashua, New Hampshire 03060-4398

Head of School: Mrs. Linda Brodeur

General Information Coeducational day college-preparatory, arts, business, religious studies, and technology school, affiliated with Roman Catholic Church. Grades 9–12. Founded: 1963. Setting: suburban. Nearest major city is Boston, MA. 1 building on campus. Approved or accredited by National Catholic Education Association, New England Association of Schools and Colleges, and New Hampshire Department of Education. Total enrollment: 800. Upper school average class size: 19. Upper school faculty-student ratio: 1:14. There are 180 required school days per year for Upper School students. Upper School students typically attend 5 days per week. The average school day consists of 6 hours and 30 minutes.

Upper School Student Profile 70% of students are Roman Catholic.

Faculty School total: 72.

Subjects Offered 20th century history, 20th century world history, acting, advanced biology, advanced chemistry, advanced computer applications, advanced math, Advanced Placement courses, algebra, American history-AP, American literature, American literature-AP, analysis and differential calculus, anatomy and physiology, ancient world history, art appreciation, art history, band, Bible studies, biology, biology-AP, British history, British literature, British literature (honors), business applications, business law, calculus, calculus-AP, campus ministry, career/college preparation, chemistry, chemistry-AP, chorus, Christian and Hebrew scripture, Christian doctrine, Christian education, Christian ethics, Christianity, church history, civics, college admission preparation, college counseling, college writing, community service, comparative government and politics, comparative government and politics-AP, comparative religion, computer applications, computer art, computer education, computer literacy, computer multimedia, computer processing, computer programming, computer programming-AP, computer science, computer science-AP, computer technologies, computer-aided design, concert band, concert choir, constitutional history of U.S., consumer economics, contemporary history, CPR, creative writing, death and loss, debate, desktop publishing, digital photography, discrete mathematics, dramatic arts, drawing, driver education, economics, emergency medicine, English, English composition, English literature, English literature and composition-AP, English literature-AP, English-AP, environmental science, environmental science-AP, ethics, European history, film studies, fine arts, foreign language, French, French-AP, geography, geometry, government and politics-AP, government/civics, grammar, Greek, health, health and wellness, health education, health enhancement, healthful living, history, Holocaust and other genocides, honors geometry, honors U.S. history, honors world history, human anatomy, human biology, human sexuality, instrumental music, introduction to literature, jazz band, journalism, Latin, Latin-AP, law, literary magazine, marching band, mechanics of writing, moral reasoning, moral theology, music, music appreciation, philosophy, photography, physical education, physics, physics-AP, pre-calculus, psychology, religion, religious studies, science, senior seminar, Shakespeare, social justice, social studies, Spanish, Spanish-AP, statistics, studio art, studio art-AP, The 20th Century, theater, trigonometry, U.S. government and politics, U.S. government and politics-AP, U.S. history, U.S. history-AP, U.S. literature, world history, world literature, yearbook.

Graduation Requirements Arts and fine arts (art, music, dance, drama), computer science, English, foreign language, mathematics, physical education (includes health), religion (includes Bible studies and theology), science, social studies (includes history).

Special Academic Programs 16 Advanced Placement exams for which test preparation is offered; honors section; study at local college for college credit; academic accommodation for the gifted.

College Admission Counseling 209 students graduated in 2015; 208 went to college, including Boston College; College of the Holy Cross; Dartmouth College; Saint Anselm College; University of Massachusetts Amherst; University of New Hampshire. Other: 1 entered military service. Median combined SAT: 1720, median composite ACT: 26.

Student Life Upper grades have uniform requirement, student council, honor system. Discipline rests primarily with faculty. Attendance at religious services is required.

Tuition and Aid Day student tuition: $13,495. Tuition installment plan (FACTS Tuition Payment Plan, individually arranged payment plans). Merit scholarship grants, need-based scholarship grants available. In 2015–16, 21% of upper-school students received aid. Total amount of financial aid awarded in 2015–16: $600,000.

Admissions Traditional secondary-level entrance grade is 9. High School Placement Test required. Deadline for receipt of application materials: January 15. Application fee required: $30.

Athletics Interscholastic: baseball (boys), basketball (b,g), cheering (b,g), cross-country running (b,g), field hockey (g), football (b), gymnastics (g), hockey (b,g), ice hockey (b,g), lacrosse (b,g), skiing (downhill) (b,g), soccer (b,g), softball (g), swimming and diving (b,g), tennis (b,g), track and field (b,g), volleyball (b,g), wrestling (b); intramural: crew (b,g); coed interscholastic: alpine skiing, aquatics, bowling, cheering, fishing, golf, ice hockey, indoor track, nordic skiing, skiing (downhill); coed intramural: aerobics/dance, basketball, bowling, crew, dance, fishing, fly fishing, freestyle skiing, golf, mountain biking, outdoor education, physical fitness, skiing (downhill), strength & conditioning, swimming and diving, table tennis, tennis, ultimate Frisbee, volleyball, weight lifting, weight training. 4 PE instructors, 55 coaches, 2 athletic trainers.

Computers Computers are regularly used in career education, career exploration, career technology, college planning, data processing, desktop publishing, independent study, information technology, introduction to technology, library, library science, library skills, literary magazine, multimedia, music, news writing, newspaper, programming, publications, publishing, research skills, stock market, technology, Web site design, word processing, yearbook classes. Computer network features include on-campus library services, online commercial services, Internet access, wireless campus network, Internet filtering or blocking technology. Student e-mail accounts and computer access in designated common areas are available to students. Students grades are available online. The school has a published electronic and media policy.

Contact Mrs. Joni McCabe, Admissions Coordinator. 603-889-4107 Ext. 4304. Fax: 603-889-0701. E-mail: admit@bghs.org. Website: www.bghs.org

BISHOP IRETON HIGH SCHOOL

201 Cambridge Road
Alexandria, Virginia 22314-4899

Head of School: Dr. Thomas J. Curry

General Information Coeducational day college-preparatory school, affiliated with Roman Catholic Church. Grades 9–12. Founded: 1964. Setting: suburban. 12-acre campus. 1 building on campus. Approved or accredited by National Catholic Education Association and Southern Association of Colleges and Schools. Total enrollment: 813. Upper school average class size: 24. Upper school faculty-student ratio: 1:12. There are 180 required school days per year for Upper School students. Upper School students typically attend 5 days per week. The average school day consists of 7 hours.

Upper School Student Profile Grade 9: 197 students (93 boys, 104 girls); Grade 10: 197 students (94 boys, 103 girls); Grade 11: 203 students (95 boys, 108 girls); Grade 12: 189 students (78 boys, 111 girls). 86% of students are Roman Catholic.

Faculty School total: 67. In upper school: 27 men, 40 women; 50 have advanced degrees.

Subjects Offered Advanced Placement courses, Catholic belief and practice, computer science, driver education, English, film, fine arts, foreign language, health, law, mathematics, physical education, psychology, religion, science, social studies, World War II.

Graduation Requirements Arts and fine arts (art, music, dance, drama), computer science, English, foreign language, mathematics, physical education (includes health), religion (includes Bible studies and theology), science, social studies (includes history), 60 hours of community service. Community service is required.

Special Academic Programs 16 Advanced Placement exams for which test preparation is offered; honors section; remedial reading and/or remedial writing; remedial math; special instructional classes for students with Attention Deficit Disorder.

College Admission Counseling 202 students graduated in 2016; 196 went to college, including Christopher Newport University; George Mason University; James Madison University; The College of William and Mary; University of Virginia; Virginia Polytechnic Institute and State University. Other: 2 went to work, 1 entered military service, 3 had other specific plans. Mean SAT critical reading: 587, mean SAT math: 555, mean SAT writing: 581, mean combined SAT: 1723, mean composite ACT: 25. 44% scored over 26 on composite ACT.

Student Life Upper grades have uniform requirement, student council, honor system. Discipline rests primarily with faculty. Attendance at religious services is required.

Tuition and Aid Day student tuition: $14,650–$19,150. Tuition installment plan (FACTS Tuition Payment Plan, monthly payment plans). Tuition reduction for siblings, merit scholarship grants, need-based scholarship grants available. In 2016–17, 15% of upper-school students received aid; total upper-school merit-scholarship money awarded: $143,000. Total amount of financial aid awarded in 2016–17: $772,000.

Admissions Traditional secondary-level entrance grade is 9. For fall 2016, 441 students applied for upper-level admission, 414 were accepted, 213 enrolled. High School Placement Test (closed version) from Scholastic Testing Service required. Deadline for receipt of application materials: January 13. Application fee required: $50.

Athletics Interscholastic: baseball (boys), basketball (b,g), field hockey (g), football (b), lacrosse (b,g), soccer (b,g), softball (g), swimming and diving (b,g), tennis (b,g), track and field (b,g), volleyball (g), water polo (b), winter (indoor) track (b,g), wrestling (b); intramural: weight training (b,g); coed interscholastic: cheering, crew, cross-country running, diving, golf, ice hockey, indoor track, ultimate Frisbee, water polo, weight training; coed intramural: Frisbee, skiing (downhill), table tennis. 4 PE instructors, 2 athletic trainers.

Computers Computers are regularly used in all academic classes. Computer network features include on-campus library services, online commercial services, Internet access, wireless campus network, Internet filtering or blocking technology. Student e-mail accounts and computer access in designated common areas are available to students. Students grades are available online. The school has a published electronic and media policy.

Contact Mr. Peter J. Hamer, Director of Admissions and Financial Aid. 703-212-5190. Fax: 703-212-8173. E-mail: hamerp@bishopireton.org. Website: www.bishopireton.org

BISHOP JOHN J. SNYDER HIGH SCHOOL

5001 Samaritan Way
Jacksonville, Florida 32210

Head of School: Deacon David Yazdiya, M.Ed.

General Information Coeducational day college-preparatory and diagnosed learning disabilities academic support school, affiliated with Roman Catholic Church. Grades 9–12. Founded: 2002. Setting: suburban. 50-acre campus. 15 buildings on campus. Approved or accredited by Council of Accreditation and School Improvement, National Catholic Education Association, Southern Association of Colleges and Schools, and Florida Department of Education. Endowment: $20,000. Upper school average class size: 16. Upper school faculty-student ratio: 1:15. There are 180 required school days per year for Upper School students. Upper School students typically attend 5 days per week. The average school day consists of 6 hours and 47 minutes.

Upper School Student Profile Grade 9: 123 students (60 boys, 63 girls); Grade 10: 122 students (62 boys, 60 girls); Grade 11: 96 students (52 boys, 44 girls); Grade 12: 99 students (45 boys, 54 girls). 77% of students are Roman Catholic.

Faculty School total: 31. In upper school: 18 men, 13 women; 15 have advanced degrees.

Subjects Offered Advanced biology, advanced chemistry, Advanced Placement courses, algebra, American government, American history, American history-AP, American literature, American literature-AP, anatomy and physiology, applied skills, art, athletics, Basic programming, Bible, biology, biology-AP, British literature, British literature (honors), calculus-AP, campus ministry, chemistry-AP, Chinese, choir, choral music, Christian doctrine, church history, college admission preparation, college awareness, college counseling, college planning, composition-AP, computer skills, creative writing, debate, economics, economics-AP, English, English composition, English language and composition-AP, English literature and composition-AP, French, geography, geometry, government, government-AP, guidance, healthful living, history of the Catholic Church, honors algebra, honors English, honors geometry, honors U.S. history, honors world history, Latin, marine science, physics, religious education, Spanish, speech and debate, statistics, studio art, the Web, U.S. history, U.S. history-AP, world history, world history-AP.

Graduation Requirements 20th century world history, algebra, all academic, American government, American history, chemistry, economics, English, English composition, English literature, foreign language, geometry, government, world history, all students must complete 25 hours of off-campus Christian service to the community.

Special Academic Programs 9 Advanced Placement exams for which test preparation is offered.

College Admission Counseling 101 students graduated in 2016; 98 went to college, including Florida Gulf Coast University; Florida State University; University of Central Florida; University of Florida; University of North Florida; University of South Florida. Other: 2 went to work, 1 entered military service.

Student Life Upper grades have uniform requirement, student council, honor system. Discipline rests primarily with faculty. Attendance at religious services is required.

Summer Programs Remediation programs offered; held on campus; accepts boys and girls; not open to students from other schools. 15 students usually enrolled. 2017 schedule: June to July.

Tuition and Aid Day student tuition: $7790. Tuition installment plan (FACTS Tuition Payment Plan). Tuition reduction for siblings, need-based scholarship grants, Step Up for Students, McKay Scholarship, PLSA-Gardiner Scholarship available. In 2016–17, 38% of upper-school students received aid. Total amount of financial aid awarded in 2016–17: $325,000.

Admissions Traditional secondary-level entrance grade is 9. For fall 2016, 450 students applied for upper-level admission, 445 were accepted, 440 enrolled. High School Placement Test required. Deadline for receipt of application materials: none. Application fee required: $375. Interview recommended.

Athletics Interscholastic: baseball (boys), basketball (b,g), cheering (b,g), cross-country running (b,g), dance team (g), diving (b,g), drill team (b,g), football (b), golf (b,g), lacrosse (b), soccer (b,g), softball (g), swimming and diving (b,g), tennis (b,g), track and field (b,g), volleyball (g), weight lifting (b,g), wrestling (b). 3 PE instructors, 23 coaches, 1 athletic trainer.

Computers Computers are regularly used in all academic classes. Computer network features include on-campus library services, Internet access, wireless campus network, Internet filtering or blocking technology, Bring Your Own Device policy. Campus intranet, student e-mail accounts, and computer access in designated common areas are available to students. Students grades are available online. The school has a published electronic and media policy.

Contact Mrs. Mary Anne Briggs, Office of Admissions. 904-771-1029. Fax: 904-908-8988. E-mail: maryannebriggs@bishopsnyder.org. Website: www.bishopsnyder.org

BISHOP KEARNEY HIGH SCHOOL

2202 60th Street
Brooklyn, New York 11204-2599

Head of School: Dr. Elizabeth Hill

General Information Girls' day college-preparatory and medical program, computer science school, affiliated with Roman Catholic Church. Grades 9–12. Founded: 1961. Setting: urban. 1-acre campus. 1 building on campus. Approved or accredited by Middle States Association of Colleges and Schools, National Catholic Education Association, The College Board, and New York Department of Education. Total enrollment: 1,052. Upper school average class size: 25. Upper school faculty-student ratio: 1:15.

Upper School Student Profile 60% of students are Roman Catholic.

Faculty In upper school: 80 have advanced degrees.

Subjects Offered Advanced chemistry, advanced computer applications, advanced math, advertising design, algebra, American studies, anatomy, art, art appreciation, art history, art-AP, biology-AP, calculus-AP, Catholic belief and practice, chemistry, chemistry-AP, child development, chorus, Christian ethics, Christian studies, college counseling, communication skills, computer education, computer skills, concert band, concert choir, CPR, creative writing, drawing, earth science, economics, English, English literature, English literature-AP, English-AP, European history, European history-AP, family living, first aid, foreign language,

French, geometry, global studies, health, honors English, honors U.S. history, honors world history, humanities, instrumental music, intro to computers, Italian, keyboarding, Latin, Latin-AP, law, learning lab, marching band, music appreciation, music performance, music theory, musical productions, newspaper, physical education, physics-AP, piano, pottery, pre-calculus, reading/study skills, SAT preparation, science research, scripture, Shakespeare, Spanish, student government, studio art, studio art-AP, trigonometry, U.S. history-AP, water color painting, women's literature, world civilizations, yearbook.

Graduation Requirements Art, English, language, mathematics, music, physical education (includes health), religion (includes Bible studies and theology), science, social studies (includes history).

Special Academic Programs Honors section; study at local college for college credit; academic accommodation for the gifted, the musically talented, and the artistically talented; remedial reading and/or remedial writing; remedial math; special instructional classes for deaf students, blind students, students with physical, emotional, or academic challenges; ESL.

College Admission Counseling Colleges students went to include City College of the City University of New York; Fordham University; Pace University; St. Francis College; St. John's University; St. Joseph's College, New York.

Student Life Upper grades have uniform requirement, student council. Discipline rests primarily with faculty. Attendance at religious services is required.

Summer Programs Remediation programs offered; held on campus; accepts girls; open to students from other schools.

Tuition and Aid Day student tuition: $9450. Tuition installment plan (FACTS Tuition Payment Plan, monthly payment plans, individually arranged payment plans). Tuition reduction for siblings, merit scholarship grants, need-based scholarship grants, paying campus jobs available.

Admissions Traditional secondary-level entrance grade is 9. Deadline for receipt of application materials: November 5. Application fee required: $63. On-campus interview required.

Athletics Interscholastic: basketball, cheering, cross-country running, golf, independent competitive sports, indoor track, indoor track & field, soccer, softball, swimming and diving, tennis, track and field, volleyball, winter (indoor) track; intramural: badminton, dance, dance team, fitness, gymnastics, physical fitness, physical training, strength & conditioning, weight training.

Computers Computers are regularly used in all classes. Computer network features include on-campus library services, Internet access, wireless campus network. Student e-mail accounts and computer access in designated common areas are available to students. Students grades are available online.

Contact Ms. Rachel Kasold, Director of Admissions. 718-236-6363 Ext. 265. Fax: 718-236-7784. E-mail: admissions@kearneyhs.org. Website: www.bishopkearneyhs.org

BISHOP KELLY HIGH SCHOOL

7009 Franklin Road
Boise, Idaho 83709-0922

Head of School: Mr. Mike Caldwell

General Information Coeducational day college-preparatory and religious studies school, affiliated with Roman Catholic Church. Grades 9–12. Distance learning grades 9–12. Founded: 1964. Setting: urban. 68-acre campus. 2 buildings on campus. Approved or accredited by National Catholic Education Association, Western Catholic Education Association, and Idaho Department of Education. Endowment: $9 million. Total enrollment: 794. Upper school average class size: 21. Upper school faculty-student ratio: 1:19. There are 173 required school days per year for Upper School students. Upper School students typically attend 5 days per week. The average school day consists of 7 hours.

Upper School Student Profile Grade 9: 202 students (88 boys, 114 girls); Grade 10: 236 students (123 boys, 113 girls); Grade 11: 171 students (84 boys, 87 girls); Grade 12: 194 students (106 boys, 88 girls). 76% of students are Roman Catholic.

Faculty School total: 54. In upper school: 26 men, 28 women; 47 have advanced degrees.

Subjects Offered Advanced Placement courses, algebra, American government, American history-AP, art, art-AP, ASB Leadership, band, biology, biology-AP, calculus-AP, campus ministry, Catholic belief and practice, ceramics, chemistry, chemistry-AP, choir, Christianity, comparative religion, computer applications, computer programming, computer science-AP, conceptual physics, creative writing, drawing, economics, engineering, English, English language and composition-AP, English-AP, fitness, French, geometry, guitar, health, history of the Catholic Church, horticulture, human anatomy, instrumental music, Latin, leadership, literature, moral reasoning, painting, physical education, physics, physics-AP, physiology, pre-calculus, psychology, reading/study skills, religious education, religious studies, senior seminar, service learning/internship, social justice, Spanish, Spanish-AP, speech, speech and debate, sports medicine, statistics-AP, theater, theater arts, theology, U.S. history, weight training, world history, yearbook.

Graduation Requirements Computer science, English, foreign language, mathematics, physical education (includes health), religion (includes Bible studies and theology), science, social studies (includes history), 30 hours of community service.

Special Academic Programs Advanced Placement exam preparation; honors section; independent study; study at local college for college credit.

College Admission Counseling 185 students graduated in 2016; 180 went to college, including Boise State University; Gonzaga University; The College of Idaho; The University of Montana Western; University of Idaho; University of Utah. Other: 1 entered military service, 4 had other specific plans. Mean SAT critical reading: 574, mean SAT math: 598, mean SAT writing: 570, mean combined SAT: 1742, mean composite ACT: 25.

Student Life Upper grades have specified standards of dress, student council, honor system. Discipline rests primarily with faculty. Attendance at religious services is required.

Tuition and Aid Day student tuition: $7900. Tuition installment plan (The Tuition Plan, monthly payment plans, individually arranged payment plans). Need-based scholarship grants available. In 2016–17, 71% of upper-school students received aid. Total amount of financial aid awarded in 2016–17: $1,398,238.

Admissions Traditional secondary-level entrance grade is 9. For fall 2016, 803 students applied for upper-level admission, 803 were accepted, 803 enrolled. Math Placement Exam required. Deadline for receipt of application materials: none. Application fee required: $205.

Athletics Interscholastic: baseball (boys), basketball (b,g), cheering (g), cross-country running (b,g), fitness (b,g), football (b), golf (b,g), lacrosse (b,g), physical fitness (b,g), skiing (downhill) (b,g), snowboarding (b,g), soccer (b,g), softball (g), swimming and diving (b,g), tennis (b,g), track and field (b,g), volleyball (g), weight lifting (b,g), weight training (b,g), wrestling (b); coed interscholastic: ice hockey, water polo. 3 PE instructors, 12 coaches, 2 athletic trainers.

Computers Computers are regularly used in computer applications, economics, English, foreign language, history, journalism, mathematics, science classes. Computer network features include on-campus library services, Internet access, wireless campus network, Internet filtering or blocking technology, Blackboard, 1:1 Technology-Bring Your Own Device. Student e-mail accounts and computer access in designated common areas are available to students. Students grades are available online. The school has a published electronic and media policy.

Contact Mrs. Kelly Shockey, Director of Admissions. 208-375-6010. Fax: 208-375-3626. E-mail: kshockey@bk.org. Website: www.bk.org

BISHOP KENNY HIGH SCHOOL

1055 Kingman Avenue
Jacksonville, Florida 32207

Head of School: Mr. Todd M. Orlando

General Information Coeducational day college-preparatory and college prep, honors, AP school, affiliated with Roman Catholic Church. Grades 9–12. Founded: 1952. Setting: urban. 55-acre campus. 10 buildings on campus. Approved or accredited by National Catholic Education Association and Southern Association of Colleges and Schools. Upper school average class size: 25. Upper school faculty-student ratio: 1:14. There are 180 required school days per year for Upper School students. Upper School students typically attend 5 days per week. The average school day consists of 6 hours and 30 minutes.

Upper School Student Profile 83% of students are Roman Catholic.

Faculty School total: 82. In upper school: 33 men, 49 women; 39 have advanced degrees.

Graduation Requirements Performing arts, personal fitness, physical education (includes health), service hour requirements.

Special Academic Programs 12 Advanced Placement exams for which test preparation is offered; honors section.

College Admission Counseling 288 students graduated in 2016; all went to college, including Florida State University; University of Central Florida; University of Florida; University of Florida; University of North Florida; University of South Florida. Median SAT critical reading: 530, median SAT math: 530, median SAT writing: 530, median combined SAT: 1610, median composite ACT: 25. 25% scored over 600 on SAT critical reading, 27% scored over 600 on SAT math, 23% scored over 600 on SAT writing, 24% scored over 1800 on combined SAT, 41% scored over 26 on composite ACT.

Student Life Upper grades have uniform requirement, student council, honor system. Discipline rests primarily with faculty. Attendance at religious services is required.

Summer Programs Remediation, enrichment, sports programs offered; session focuses on enrichment/remediation; held on campus; accepts boys and girls; not open to students from other schools. 300 students usually enrolled. 2017 schedule: June 8 to July 7.

Tuition and Aid Day student tuition: $8228–$11,252. Tuition installment plan (FACTS Tuition Payment Plan, individually arranged payment plans). Tuition reduction for siblings, need-based scholarship grants available. In 2016–17, 25% of upper-school students received aid.

Admissions Traditional secondary-level entrance grade is 9. High School Placement Test required. Deadline for receipt of application materials: none. No application fee required. Interview required.

Athletics Interscholastic: baseball (boys), basketball (b,g), cheering (g), cross-country running (b,g), diving (b,g), football (b), golf (b,g), JROTC drill (b,g), riflery (b,g), soccer (b,g), softball (g), swimming and diving (b,g), tennis (b,g), track and field (b,g), volleyball (g), weight lifting (b), wrestling (b). 4 PE instructors, 55 coaches, 3 athletic trainers.

Computers Computers are regularly used in journalism, newspaper, writing, yearbook classes. Computer network features include on-campus library services, Internet access, wireless campus network, Internet filtering or blocking technology, design software for Journalism and MultiMedia, CS4 Suite, 5 computer labs. Campus intranet, student e-mail accounts, and computer access in designated common areas are available to students. Students grades are available online. The school has a published electronic and media policy.

Contact Mrs. Brooke Johnson, Director of Admissions. 904-398-7545. Fax: 904-398-5728. E-mail: admissions@bishopkenny.org. Website: www.bishopkenny.org

BISHOP MACHEBEUF HIGH SCHOOL

1958 Elm Street
Denver, Colorado 80220

Head of School: Deacon Marc Nestorick

General Information Coeducational day college-preparatory and religious studies school, affiliated with Roman Catholic Church. Grades 9–12. Setting: urban. Nearest major city is Lowry. 11-acre campus. 1 building on campus. Approved or accredited by North Central Association of Colleges and Schools and Colorado Department of Education. Upper school average class size: 20.

Upper School Student Profile 86% of students are Roman Catholic.

Faculty School total: 34. In upper school: 24 have advanced degrees.

Special Academic Programs Honors section; independent study; study at local college for college credit.

College Admission Counseling 67 students graduated in 2016; they went to Benedictine College; Colorado State University; Metropolitan State University of Denver; Regis University; University of Colorado Boulder. Other: 1 entered military service. Mean SAT critical reading: 602, mean SAT math: 554, mean combined SAT: 1178, mean composite ACT: 24.

Student Life Upper grades have uniform requirement, student council. Discipline rests primarily with faculty. Attendance at religious services is required.

Tuition and Aid Day student tuition: $11,200. Tuition installment plan (FACTS Tuition Payment Plan). Tuition reduction for siblings, merit scholarship grants, need-based scholarship grants available.

Admissions Traditional secondary-level entrance grade is 9. High School Placement Test (closed version) from Scholastic Testing Service required. Deadline for receipt of application materials: December 9. No application fee required. On-campus interview recommended.

Athletics Interscholastic: baseball (boys), basketball (b,g), cross-country running (b,g), football (b), golf (b,g), lacrosse (b), soccer (b,g), swimming and diving (g), tennis (g), track and field (b,g), volleyball (g); intramural: flag football (g), weight training (b,g). 1 PE instructor, 18 coaches, 1 athletic trainer.

Computers Computer resources include on-campus library services, online commercial services, Internet access, wireless campus network, Internet filtering or blocking technology, Technology Center, Professional Conferencing System for college classes. Campus intranet, student e-mail accounts, and computer access in designated common areas are available to students. Students grades are available online.

Contact Kristen Dieterich, Director of Admissions. 303-344-0082. Fax: 303-344-1582. E-mail: kdieterich@machebeuf.org. Website: www.machebeuf.org/

BISHOP MCCORT HIGH SCHOOL

25 Osborne Street
Johnstown, Pennsylvania 15905

Head of School: Mr. Thomas P. Fleming Jr.

General Information Coeducational day college-preparatory school, affiliated with Roman Catholic Church. Founded: 1922. Setting: small town. Nearest major city is Pittsburgh. 1 building on campus. Approved or accredited by North Central Association of Colleges and Schools and Pennsylvania Department of Education. Upper school average class size: 20.

Upper School Student Profile 80% of students are Roman Catholic.

Student Life Upper grades have uniform requirement, student council, honor system. Discipline rests primarily with faculty. Attendance at religious services is required.

Admissions No application fee required.

Contact Sarah Golden, Administrative Assistant. 814-536-8991. Fax: 724-535-4118. E-mail: sgolden@mccort.org. Website: www.mccort.org

BISHOP MCGUINNESS CATHOLIC HIGH SCHOOL

801 Northwest 50th Street
Oklahoma City, Oklahoma 73118-6001

Head of School: Mr. David L. Morton

General Information Coeducational day college-preparatory school, affiliated with Roman Catholic Church. Ungraded, ages 14–19. Founded: 1950. Setting: urban. 20-acre campus. 5 buildings on campus. Approved or accredited by North Central

Association of Colleges and Schools, Oklahoma Private Schools Accreditation Commission, and Oklahoma Department of Education. Endowment: $250,000. Total enrollment: 714. Upper school average class size: 13. Upper school faculty-student ratio: 1:13. There are 178 required school days per year for Upper School students. Upper School students typically attend 5 days per week. The average school day consists of 6 hours and 45 minutes.

Upper School Student Profile Grade 9: 191 students (99 boys, 92 girls); Grade 10: 161 students (91 boys, 70 girls); Grade 11: 178 students (92 boys, 86 girls); Grade 12: 190 students (90 boys, 100 girls). 75% of students are Roman Catholic.

Faculty School total: 56. In upper school: 24 men, 32 women; 20 have advanced degrees.

Subjects Offered Algebra, American history-AP, American literature, anatomy, art, band, Bible, biology, biology-AP, broadcasting, business, calculus-AP, Catholic belief and practice, ceramics, chemistry, chemistry-AP, Chinese studies, chorus, church history, computer technologies, creative writing, culinary arts, current events, dance, debate, digital photography, drama, drawing, drawing and design, electives, English, English language and composition-AP, English literature, English literature and composition-AP, French, geometry, German, government, health and wellness, history of the Catholic Church, honors algebra, honors English, honors geometry, human geography - AP, introduction to theater, Latin, Latin-AP, leadership, learning lab, Life of Christ, macroeconomics-AP, media production, music appreciation, newspaper, painting, personal finance, photography, physical education, physical science, physics, physics-AP, physiology, practical arts, prayer/spirituality, pre-calculus, psychology, psychology-AP, scripture, social justice, sociology, Spanish, Spanish-AP, speech, stagecraft, state history, statistics-AP, strategies for success, theater, trigonometry, U.S. government and politics-AP, U.S. history, U.S. history-AP, weight training, world history, world history-AP, world religions, writing workshop, yearbook.

Graduation Requirements Arts and fine arts (art, music, dance, drama), electives, English, foreign language, mathematics, physical education (includes health), practical arts, science, social studies (includes history), theology, 90 hours of Christian service.

Special Academic Programs 16 Advanced Placement exams for which test preparation is offered; honors section; academic accommodation for the gifted and the artistically talented; remedial reading and/or remedial writing; remedial math; programs in English, mathematics for dyslexic students; special instructional classes for students with learning differences.

College Admission Counseling 154 students graduated in 2016; 150 went to college, including Colorado School of Mines; Oklahoma State University; Texas Christian University; University of Arkansas; University of Oklahoma. Other: 3 entered military service, 4 had other specific plans. Median SAT critical reading: 616, median SAT math: 578, median SAT writing: 570, median combined SAT: 1764, median composite ACT: 25. 54% scored over 600 on SAT critical reading, 46% scored over 600 on SAT math, 54% scored over 600 on SAT writing, 31% scored over 1800 on combined SAT, 42% scored over 26 on composite ACT.

Student Life Upper grades have uniform requirement, student council, honor system. Discipline rests primarily with faculty. Attendance at religious services is required.

Summer Programs Remediation, enrichment, sports programs offered; session focuses on science enrichment, PE enrichment, math enrichment and remediation; held on campus; accepts boys and girls; not open to students from other schools. 20 students usually enrolled. 2017 schedule: June 8 to August 1. Application deadline: May 1.

Tuition and Aid Day student tuition: $8600. Tuition installment plan (FACTS Tuition Payment Plan). Need-based scholarship grants, paying campus jobs available. In 2016–17, 19% of upper-school students received aid. Total amount of financial aid awarded in 2016–17: $237,350.

Admissions For fall 2016, 9 students applied for upper-level admission, 9 were accepted, 9 enrolled. STS, STS, Diocese Test or writing sample required. Deadline for receipt of application materials: May 1. Application fee required: $400. On-campus interview required.

Athletics Interscholastic: baseball (boys), basketball (b,g), bowling (b,g), cheering (g), crew (b,g), cross-country running (b,g), football (b), golf (b,g), soccer (b,g), softball (g), swimming and diving (b,g), tennis (b,g), track and field (b,g), volleyball (g), weight training (b,g), winter (indoor) track (b,g), wrestling (b); coed interscholastic: dance team, physical fitness. 43 coaches, 1 athletic trainer.

Computers Computers are regularly used in all academic classes. Computer network features include on-campus library services, online commercial services, Internet access, wireless campus network, Internet filtering or blocking technology, laptop classroom carts, wireless printing, eBooks, and My Road, Digital Citizenship classes, each student has an iPad. Student e-mail accounts and computer access in designated common areas are available to students. Students grades are available online. The school has a published electronic and media policy.

Contact Mrs. Laura O'Hara, 9th Grade Counselor. 405-842-6638 Ext. 225. Fax: 405-858-9550. E-mail: Lohara@bmchs.org. Website: www.bmchs.org

BISHOP MCNAMARA HIGH SCHOOL

6800 Marlboro Pike
Forestville, Maryland 20747

Head of School: Dr. Robert Van der Waag

General Information Coeducational day college-preparatory and arts school, affiliated with Roman Catholic Church; primarily serves individuals with Attention

Deficit Disorder. Grades 9–12. Founded: 1964. Setting: suburban. Nearest major city is Washington, DC. 16-acre campus. 3 buildings on campus. Approved or accredited by Middle States Association of Colleges and Schools, National Catholic Education Association, and Maryland Department of Education. Endowment: $2.6 million. Total enrollment: 880. Upper school average class size: 21. Upper school faculty-student ratio: 1:10. There are 180 required school days per year for Upper School students. Upper School students typically attend 5 days per week. The average school day consists of 6 hours.

Upper School Student Profile Grade 9: 224 students (105 boys, 119 girls); Grade 10: 223 students (105 boys, 118 girls); Grade 11: 227 students (94 boys, 133 girls); Grade 12: 211 students (90 boys, 121 girls). 50% of students are Roman Catholic.

Faculty School total: 88. In upper school: 39 men, 49 women; 50 have advanced degrees.

Subjects Offered 3-dimensional design.

Special Academic Programs Advanced Placement exam preparation; honors section; study at local college for college credit; academic accommodation for the gifted.

College Admission Counseling 197 students graduated in 2015; 190 went to college. Other: 6 entered military service.

Student Life Upper grades have uniform requirement, student council, honor system. Discipline rests primarily with faculty. Attendance at religious services is required.

Tuition and Aid Day student tuition: $13,250. Tuition installment plan (FACTS Tuition Payment Plan). Tuition reduction for siblings, merit scholarship grants, need-based scholarship grants available.

Admissions Traditional secondary-level entrance grade is 9. For fall 2015, 800 students applied for upper-level admission, 275 were accepted, 225 enrolled. High School Placement Test required. Deadline for receipt of application materials: December 15. Application fee required: $50. Interview recommended.

Athletics Interscholastic: baseball (boys), cheering (g), football (b), pom squad (g), softball (g), volleyball (g), wrestling (b); coed interscholastic: basketball, cross-country running, horseback riding, indoor track & field, soccer, swimming and diving, tennis, track and field, winter (indoor) track; coed intramural: bowling. 3 PE instructors, 2 athletic trainers.

Computers Computers are regularly used in aerospace science, all academic classes. Computer network features include on-campus library services, online commercial services, Internet access, wireless campus network. Student e-mail accounts and computer access in designated common areas are available to students. Students grades are available online.

Contact Mr. Jeffrey Southworth, Associate Director of Admissions. 301-735-8401 Ext. 102. Fax: 301-735-0934. E-mail: jeffrey.southworth@bmhs.org. Website: www.bmhs.org

BISHOP MIEGE HIGH SCHOOL

5041 Reinhardt Drive
Shawnee Mission, Kansas 66205-1599

Head of School: Dr. Joseph Passantino

General Information Coeducational day college-preparatory, religious studies, and technology school, affiliated with Roman Catholic Church. Grades 9–12. Founded: 1958. Setting: suburban. Nearest major city is Roeland Park. 25-acre campus. 1 building on campus. Approved or accredited by National Catholic Education Association and Kansas Department of Education. Total enrollment: 721. Upper school average class size: 16. Upper school faculty-student ratio: 1:16. There are 170 required school days per year for Upper School students. Upper School students typically attend 5 days per week. The average school day consists of 8 hours.

Upper School Student Profile Grade 9: 182 students (100 boys, 82 girls); Grade 10: 173 students (93 boys, 80 girls); Grade 11: 205 students (110 boys, 95 girls); Grade 12: 161 students (82 boys, 79 girls). 81% of students are Roman Catholic.

Faculty School total: 43. In upper school: 19 men, 24 women; 38 have advanced degrees.

Special Academic Programs Advanced Placement exam preparation; honors section; independent study; study at local college for college credit.

College Admission Counseling 160 students graduated in 2015; 157 went to college, including Kansas State University; The University of Kansas.

Student Life Upper grades have uniform requirement, student council. Discipline rests primarily with faculty. Attendance at religious services is required.

Tuition and Aid Day student tuition: $9850. Tuition installment plan (SMART Tuition Payment Plan). Tuition reduction for siblings, merit scholarship grants, need-based scholarship grants, paying campus jobs available. In 2015–16, 35% of upper-school students received aid. Total amount of financial aid awarded in 2015–16: $1,000,000.

Admissions Traditional secondary-level entrance grade is 9. Scholastic Testing Service High School Placement Test or STS required. Deadline for receipt of application materials: February 20. Application fee required: $630. Interview required.

Athletics Interscholastic: baseball (boys), basketball (b,g), cheering (g), cross-country running (b,g), dance team (g), diving (b,g), fitness (b,g), football (b), golf (b,g), soccer (b,g), softball (g), strength & conditioning (b,g), swimming and diving (b,g), tennis (b,g), track and field (b,g), volleyball (g), wrestling (b). 3 PE instructors, 23 coaches, 1 athletic trainer.

Computers Computer network features include on-campus library services, online commercial services, Internet access.

Contact Mrs. Patti Marnett, Director of Admissions. 913-262-2701 Ext. 226. Fax: 913-262-2752. E-mail: pmarnett@bishopmiege.com. Website: www.bishopmiege.com

BISHOP MONTGOMERY HIGH SCHOOL

5430 Torrance Boulevard
Torrance, California 90503

Head of School: Ms. Rosemary Distaso-Libbon

General Information Coeducational day college-preparatory, arts, religious studies, and technology school, affiliated with Roman Catholic Church. Grades 9–12. Founded: 1957. Setting: suburban. Nearest major city is Los Angeles. 27-acre campus. 9 buildings on campus. Approved or accredited by National Catholic Education Association, Western Association of Schools and Colleges, Western Catholic Education Association, and California Department of Education. Total enrollment: 946. Upper school average class size: 22. Upper school faculty-student ratio: 1:22. There are 180 required school days per year for Upper School students. Upper School students typically attend 5 days per week. The average school day consists of 6 hours and 10 minutes.

Upper School Student Profile Grade 9: 240 students (103 boys, 137 girls); Grade 10: 257 students (133 boys, 124 girls); Grade 11: 247 students (112 boys, 135 girls); Grade 12: 202 students (107 boys, 95 girls). 75% of students are Roman Catholic.

Faculty School total: 60. In upper school: 26 men, 34 women; 22 have advanced degrees.

Subjects Offered Advanced Placement courses, algebra, American history, American history-AP, American literature, anatomy, art, Bible studies, biology, calculus, chemistry, chorus, composition, computer science, drama, economics, English, English literature, English literature-AP, fine arts, French, geometry, government/civics, health, history, languages, literature, mathematics, physical education, physics, physics-AP, physiology, religion, science, social studies, Spanish, statistics, theater, weight training, world history, yearbook.

Graduation Requirements Arts and fine arts (art, music, dance, drama), business skills (includes word processing), computer science, English, mathematics, physical education (includes health), religion (includes Bible studies and theology), science, social studies (includes history).

Special Academic Programs Advanced Placement exam preparation; honors section; ESL (27 students enrolled).

College Admission Counseling 240 students graduated in 2015; 237 went to college, including California State University, Long Beach; Loyola Marymount University; University of California, Irvine, University of California, Los Angeles; University of California, Riverside. Other: 3 had other specific plans. Mean combined SAT: 1900, mean composite ACT: 25.

Student Life Upper grades have uniform requirement, student council, honor system. Discipline rests primarily with faculty. Attendance at religious services is required.

Tuition and Aid Day student tuition: $9400. Tuition installment plan (SMART Tuition Payment Plan). Tuition reduction for siblings, merit scholarship grants, need-based scholarship grants, financial need available. In 2015–16, 4% of upper-school students received aid; total upper-school merit-scholarship money awarded: $38,000. Total amount of financial aid awarded in 2015–16: $68,000.

Admissions Traditional secondary-level entrance grade is 9. For fall 2015, 455 students applied for upper-level admission, 380 were accepted, 248 enrolled. High School Placement Test, Iowa Tests of Basic Skills, Stanford 9 and Star-9 required. Deadline for receipt of application materials: January 14. Application fee required: $80.

Athletics Interscholastic: baseball (boys), basketball (b,g), cheering (g), cross-country running (b,g), dance (g), dance team (g), football (b), golf (b,g), soccer (b,g), softball (g), strength & conditioning (b,g), tennis (b,g), volleyball (b,g); coed interscholastic: aerobics, surfing, swimming and diving, track and field. 3 PE instructors, 32 coaches, 2 athletic trainers.

Computers Computers are regularly used in library, newspaper, programming, publications, technology, Web site design classes. Computer network features include on-campus library services, Internet access, wireless campus network, Internet filtering or blocking technology. Student e-mail accounts are available to students. Students grades are available online. The school has a published electronic and media policy.

Contact Mrs. Casey Dunn, Director of Admissions. 310-540-2021 Ext. 227. Fax: 310-543-5102. E-mail: cdunn@bmhs-la.org. Website: www.bmhs-la.org

BISHOP MORA SALESIAN HIGH SCHOOL

960 South Soto Street
Los Angeles, California 90023

Head of School: Mr. Alex Chacon

General Information Boys' day college-preparatory, general academic, and religious studies school, affiliated with Roman Catholic Church. Grades 9–12. Founded: 1958. Setting: urban. 2 buildings on campus. Approved or accredited by Accrediting Commission for Schools, Western Association of Schools and Colleges, Western Catholic Education Association, and California Department of Education. Upper school average class size: 28. Upper school faculty-student ratio: 1:16. There are 188 required school days per year for Upper School students. The average school day consists of 6 hours and 50 minutes.

Upper School Student Profile Grade 9: 125 students (125 boys); Grade 10: 90 students (90 boys); Grade 11: 141 students (141 boys); Grade 12: 122 students (122 boys). 98% of students are Roman Catholic.

Faculty School total: 32. In upper school: 24 men, 8 women; 28 have advanced degrees.

Subjects Offered Advanced biology, advanced chemistry, advanced math, Advanced Placement courses, algebra, American history, American history-AP, American literature, anatomy and physiology, applied music, art, arts appreciation, athletic training, athletics, baseball, basketball, Bible studies, biology, biology-AP, British history, British literature, British literature (honors), business, calculus, calculus-AP, Catholic belief and practice, chemistry, chemistry-AP, Christianity, church history, cinematography, college admission preparation, college awareness, college counseling, college placement, college planning, computer applications, computer science, creative writing, drama, drawing, economics, economics-AP, English, English literature, English-AP, environmental science, ethics, European history, expository writing, fine arts, geometry, government/civics, grammar, health, health education, Hispanic literature, history, mathematics, music, physical education, physical science, physics, physics-AP, pre-algebra, pre-calculus, psychology, psychology-AP, religion, science, social studies, Spanish, Spanish-AP, speech and debate, theater, trigonometry, U.S. government and politics-AP, volleyball, weight training, world history, world literature, writing.

Graduation Requirements Arts and fine arts (art, music, dance, drama), computer science, English, foreign language, mathematics, physical education (includes health), religion (includes Bible studies and theology), religious studies, science, social studies (includes history), Christian service program.

Special Academic Programs Study at local college for college credit; academic accommodation for the musically talented and the artistically talented; remedial reading and/or remedial writing.

College Admission Counseling 87 students graduated in 2015; 86 went to college, including California State University, Los Angeles; Loyola Marymount University; San Francisco State University; University of California, Los Angeles; University of California, Riverside; Whittier College. Other: 1 entered military service.

Student Life Upper grades have uniform requirement, student council, honor system. Discipline rests equally with students and faculty. Attendance at religious services is required.

Tuition and Aid Day student tuition: $8500. Tuition installment plan (FACTS Tuition Payment Plan, monthly payment plans, individually arranged payment plans). Tuition reduction for siblings, merit scholarship grants, need-based scholarship grants available. In 2015–16, 85% of upper-school students received aid; total upper-school merit-scholarship money awarded: $2500. Total amount of financial aid awarded in 2015–16: $1,548,500.

Admissions Traditional secondary-level entrance grade is 9. ETS high school placement exam required. Deadline for receipt of application materials: none. Application fee required: $60. On-campus interview required.

Athletics Interscholastic: baseball, basketball, bicycling, cross-country running, football, golf, physical fitness, physical training, power lifting, running, soccer, track and field, volleyball, weight training, wrestling; intramural: aerobics/Nautilus, basketball, billiards, cheering, dance squad, dance team, soccer, yoga. 12 coaches, 1 athletic trainer.

Computers Computers are regularly used in design, desktop publishing, English, mathematics, word processing, writing, writing, yearbook classes. Computer network features include Internet access. Campus intranet and student e-mail accounts are available to students. The school has a published electronic and media policy.

Contact Ms. Adriana Bronzina, Vice Principal/Director of Curriculum. 323-261-7124 Ext. 236. Fax: 323-261-7600. E-mail: bronzina@mustangsla.org. Website: www.mustangsla.org

BISHOP O'DOWD HIGH SCHOOL

9500 Stearns Avenue
Oakland, California 94605-4799

Head of School: Dr. Stephen Phelps

General Information Coeducational day college-preparatory and environmental science school, affiliated with Roman Catholic Church. Grades 9–12. Founded: 1951. Setting: urban. 20-acre campus. 13 buildings on campus. Approved or accredited by Western Association of Schools and Colleges, Western Catholic Education Association, and California Department of Education. Member of National Association of Independent Schools. Endowment: $1 million. Total enrollment: 1,151. Upper school average class size: 25. Upper school faculty-student ratio: 1:15. Upper School students typically attend 5 days per week. The average school day consists of 6 hours and 30 minutes.

Upper School Student Profile Grade 9: 308 students (155 boys, 153 girls); Grade 10: 290 students (139 boys, 151 girls); Grade 11: 309 students (152 boys, 157 girls); Grade 12: 245 students (122 boys, 123 girls). 55% of students are Roman Catholic.

Faculty School total: 86. In upper school: 41 men, 38 women; 55 have advanced degrees.

Subjects Offered Art, computer science, English, fine arts, foreign language, mathematics, physical education, religion, science, social studies.

Graduation Requirements Arts and fine arts (art, music, dance, drama), English, foreign language, mathematics, physical education (includes health), religion (includes Bible studies and theology), religious studies, science, social studies (includes history), 100 hour service learning project to be completed over all four years.

Special Academic Programs Advanced Placement exam preparation; honors section; independent study; academic accommodation for the gifted, the musically talented, and the artistically talented; remedial reading and/or remedial writing; remedial math.

College Admission Counseling 296 students graduated in 2016; 294 went to college, including California Polytechnic State University, San Luis Obispo; San Francisco State University; University of California, Berkeley; University of California, Davis; University of California, Santa Cruz; University of Oregon. Other: 2 had other specific plans. Mean SAT critical reading: 566, mean SAT math: 565, mean SAT writing: 575.

Student Life Upper grades have specified standards of dress, student council. Discipline rests equally with students and faculty.

Summer Programs Remediation, enrichment, advancement, sports, art/fine arts, computer instruction programs offered; held on campus; accepts boys and girls; open to students from other schools. 120 students usually enrolled. 2017 schedule: June 13 to July 20. Application deadline: June 1.

Tuition and Aid Day student tuition: $17,800. Tuition installment plan (SMART Tuition Payment Plan, monthly payment plans, individually arranged payment plans). Tuition reduction for siblings, merit scholarship grants, need-based scholarship grants available. In 2016–17, 30% of upper-school students received aid; total upper-school merit-scholarship money awarded: $150,000. Total amount of financial aid awarded in 2016–17: $2,300,000.

Admissions Traditional secondary-level entrance grade is 9. For fall 2016, 760 students applied for upper-level admission, 475 were accepted, 310 enrolled. High School Placement Test and High School Placement Test (closed version) from Scholastic Testing Service required. Deadline for receipt of application materials: none. Application fee required: $90.

Athletics Interscholastic: aquatics (boys, girls); baseball (b); basketball (b,g); cross-country running (b,g); diving (b,g); football (b); golf (b,g); lacrosse (b,g); rugby (b,g); soccer (b,g); softball (g); strength & conditioning (b,g); swimming and diving (b,g); tennis (b,g); track and field (b,g); volleyball (g); water polo (b,g); winter soccer (b,g); intramural: basketball (b,g); dance squad (g); physical training (b,g); soccer (b,g); weight training (b,g); yoga (g); coed interscholastic: cheering, cross-country running, strength & conditioning; coed intramural: aerobics, aerobics/dance, alpine skiing, backpacking, bicycling, bowling, combined training, fitness, flag football, Frisbee, hiking/backpacking, mountain biking, skiing (downhill), snowboarding, weight training, yoga. 5 PE instructors, 36 coaches, 1 athletic trainer.

Computers Computers are regularly used in all academic, animation, art, career education, career exploration, Christian doctrine, college planning, computer applications, creative writing, current events, design, drawing and design, economics, engineering, English, foreign language, French, geography, graphic arts, health, history, human geography - AP, independent study, library, library skills, mathematics, media arts, media production, music, music technology, newspaper, philosophy, programming, psychology, research skills, science, social sciences, social studies, Spanish, theater arts, video film production, writing, yearbook classes. Computer network features include on-campus library services, online commercial services, Internet access, wireless campus network, Internet filtering or blocking technology, one-to-one laptop program—every student has a laptop on campus. Student e-mail accounts are available to students. Students grades are available online. The school has a published electronic and media policy.

Contact Kerryn Pincus, Director of Admissions. 510-577-9100. Fax: 510-638-3259. E-mail: kpincus@bishopodowd.org. Website: www.bishopodowd.org

BISHOP'S COLLEGE SCHOOL

80 Moulton Hill Road
Sherbrooke, Quebec J1M 1Z8, Canada

Head of School: Mr. Tyler Lewis

General Information Coeducational boarding and day college-preparatory and bilingual studies school. Grades 7–12. Founded: 1836. Setting: small town. Nearest major city is Montreal, Canada. Students are housed in single-sex dormitories. 240-acre campus. 30 buildings on campus. Approved or accredited by Canadian Association of Independent Schools and Quebec Department of Education. Affiliate member of National Association of Independent Schools; member of Secondary School Admission Test Board. Languages of instruction: English and French. Endowment: CAN$15.6 million. Total enrollment: 239. Upper school average class size: 14. Upper school faculty-student ratio: 1:8. There are 180 required school days per year for Upper School students. Upper School students typically attend 5 days per week. The average school day consists of 7 hours.

Upper School Student Profile Grade 10: 66 students (40 boys, 26 girls); Grade 11: 57 students (35 boys, 22 girls); Grade 12: 57 students (37 boys, 20 girls). 80% of students are boarding students. 44% are province residents. 15 provinces are represented in upper school student body. 45% are international students. International students from China, Germany, Hong Kong, Mexico, Turkey, and United States; 35 other countries represented in student body.

Faculty School total: 30. In upper school: 17 men, 13 women; 15 reside on campus.

Subjects Offered 3-dimensional art, acting, Advanced Placement courses, algebra, art, band, biology, calculus, chemistry, college counseling, college placement, computer science, creative writing, drama, economics, English, environmental science, ESL, ethics, finite math, French, French as a second language, geography, geometry, history, mathematics, music, philosophy, physical education, physical science, physics, political science, religion, robotics, science, sociology, study skills, technology, theater, trigonometry, world history.

Graduation Requirements English, follow Ministry of Quebec guidelines, follow Ministry of New Brunswick guidelines, follow International Bacclaureate (IB) guidelines.

Special Academic Programs 6 Advanced Placement exams for which test preparation is offered; independent study; term-away projects; study at local college for college credit; study abroad; academic accommodation for the gifted; remedial reading and/or remedial writing; remedial math; programs in English, mathematics, general development for dyslexic students; ESL (35 students enrolled).

College Admission Counseling 53 students graduated in 2016; 51 went to college, including Bishop's University; Boston University; Carleton University; McGill University; University of Toronto; University of Waterloo. Other: 1 entered a postgraduate year, 1 had other specific plans.

Student Life Upper grades have uniform requirement, student council, honor system. Discipline rests primarily with faculty.

Summer Programs ESL programs offered; session focuses on English or French as a Second Language; held on campus; accepts boys and girls; open to students from other schools. 150 students usually enrolled. 2017 schedule: July 4 to July 30. Application deadline: none.

Tuition and Aid Day student tuition: CAN$22,800; 7-day tuition and room/board: CAN$57,800. Tuition installment plan (monthly payment plans, individually arranged payment plans, single payment plan). Tuition reduction for siblings, bursaries, merit scholarship grants, need-based scholarship grants, need-based loans available. In 2016–17, 40% of upper-school students received aid; total upper-school merit-scholarship money awarded: CAN$700,000. Total amount of financial aid awarded in 2016–17: CAN$900,000.

Admissions Traditional secondary-level entrance grade is 10. For fall 2016, 230 students applied for upper-level admission, 150 were accepted, 107 enrolled. Admissions testing, English for Non-native Speakers and math and English placement tests required. Deadline for receipt of application materials: none. Application fee required: CAN$100. Interview recommended.

Athletics Interscholastic: baseball (boys), football (b), gymnastics (g), hockey (b,g), ice hockey (b), softball (g); intramural: football (g); coed interscholastic: alpine skiing, aquatics, basketball, bicycling, climbing, combined training, cross-country running, equestrian sports, golf, horseback riding, independent competitive sports, nordic skiing, outdoor adventure, rugby, skiing (cross-country), skiing (downhill), soccer, swimming and diving, tennis; coed intramural: aerobics, alpine skiing, backpacking, badminton, basketball, canoeing/kayaking, climbing, Cosom hockey, curling, dance, figure skating, fitness, fitness walking, floor hockey, freestyle skiing, hiking/backpacking, hockey, horseback riding, ice hockey, indoor hockey, jogging, mountain biking, outdoor activities, outdoor education, outdoor skills, physical fitness, racquetball, rock climbing, snowboarding, snowshoeing, soccer, squash, strength & conditioning, table tennis, tennis, wall climbing, weight training, wilderness survival, yoga. 1 PE instructor, 10 coaches, 1 athletic trainer.

Computers Computers are regularly used in all classes. Computer network features include on-campus library services, Internet access, wireless campus network, Internet filtering or blocking technology, school-wide laptop initiative (annual fee), fiber optic network. Campus intranet, student e-mail accounts, and computer access in designated common areas are available to students. Students grades are available online. The school has a published electronic and media policy.

Contact Mr. Greg McConnell, Director of Admissions. 819-566-0227 Ext. 296. Fax: 819-566-8917. E-mail: gmcconnell@bishopscollegeschool.com. Website: www.bishopscollegeschool.com

THE BISHOP'S SCHOOL

7607 La Jolla Boulevard
La Jolla, California 92037

Head of School: Aimeclaire Roche

General Information Coeducational day college-preparatory school, affiliated with Episcopal Church. Grades 6–12. Founded: 1909. Setting: suburban. Nearest major city is San Diego. 11-acre campus. 9 buildings on campus. Approved or accredited by California Association of Independent Schools, National Association of Episcopal Schools, Western Association of Schools and Colleges, and California Department of Education. Member of National Association of Independent Schools. Endowment: $38.2 million. Total enrollment: 811. Upper school average class size: 14. Upper school faculty-student ratio: 1:9. There are 170 required school days per year for Upper School students. Upper School students typically attend 5 days per week. The average school day consists of 7 hours.

Faculty School total: 95. In upper school: 34 men, 39 women; 65 have advanced degrees.

Subjects Offered Acting, Advanced Placement courses, advanced studio art-AP, algebra, American history, American literature, art history, art history-AP, arts, ASB Leadership, biology, biology-AP, calculus, calculus-AP, ceramics, chemistry, chemistry-AP, Chinese, Chinese studies, chorus, community service, comparative government and politics-AP, comparative religion, computer programming, computer science, creative writing, dance, discrete mathematics, drama, drawing, earth science, ecology, economics, economics and history, economics-AP, English, English literature, English-AP, environmental science, ethics, European history, European history-AP, forensics, French, French language-AP, French literature-AP, genetics, geography, geometry, government/civics, health, history, human anatomy, humanities, integrated mathematics, Internet, jazz band, journalism, Latin, Latin American studies, Latin-AP, literature and composition-AP, literature-AP, macro/microeconomics-AP, marine biology, mathematics, music, painting, philosophy, photography, physical education, physical science, physics, physics-AP, physiology, pre-algebra, pre-calculus, probability, programming, religious studies, Shakespeare, social studies, Spanish, Spanish language-AP, Spanish literature-AP, speech, speech and debate, stained glass, statistics, statistics-AP, studio art-AP, tap dance, theater, theater design and production, typing, U.S. government and politics-AP, U.S. history, U.S. history-AP, visual reality, world history, yearbook.

Graduation Requirements Arts and fine arts (art, music, dance, drama), computer science, English, foreign language, mathematics, physical education (includes health), religion (includes Bible studies and theology), science, social sciences, social studies (includes history), swimming test, computer proficiency. Community service is required.

Special Academic Programs Advanced Placement exam preparation; honors section; independent study; study abroad.

College Admission Counseling 137 students graduated in 2016; all went to college, including Southern Methodist University; Stanford University; University of California, Berkeley; University of California, Los Angeles; University of San Diego; University of Southern California. Median SAT critical reading: 670, median SAT math: 680, median SAT writing: 690, median combined SAT: 2050, median composite ACT: 31. 77.1% scored over 600 on SAT critical reading, 79% scored over 600 on SAT math, 78.1% scored over 600 on SAT writing, 80% scored over 1800 on combined SAT, 82.9% scored over 26 on composite ACT.

Student Life Upper grades have uniform requirement, student council, honor system. Discipline rests equally with students and faculty. Attendance at religious services is required.

Summer Programs Remediation, enrichment, advancement, sports, art/fine arts, computer instruction programs offered; held on campus; accepts boys and girls; open to students from other schools. 325 students usually enrolled. 2017 schedule: June 10 to July 24. Application deadline: June 6.

Tuition and Aid Day student tuition: $33,800. Tuition installment plan (FACTS Tuition Payment Plan, semester payment plans, Key Resources Achiever Loan). Need-based scholarship grants available. In 2016–17, 20% of upper-school students received aid.

Admissions Traditional secondary-level entrance grade is 9. ISEE required. Deadline for receipt of application materials: February 3. Application fee required: $100. On-campus interview required.

Athletics Interscholastic: baseball (boys), basketball (b,g), cross-country running (b,g), equestrian sports (b,g), field hockey (g), football (b), golf (b,g), gymnastics (g), lacrosse (b,g), soccer (b,g), softball (g), swimming and diving (b,g), tennis (b,g), track and field (b,g), volleyball (b,g), water polo (b,g); intramural: weight training (b,g); coed interscholastic: sailing. 5 PE instructors, 92 coaches, 2 athletic trainers.

Computers Computers are regularly used in English, foreign language, history, journalism, library, music, science, yearbook classes. Computer network features include on-campus library services, online commercial services, Internet access, wireless campus network. Student e-mail accounts and computer access in designated common areas are available to students. Students grades are available online.

Contact Kim Cooper, Director of Admissions and Financial Aid. 858-875-0809. Fax: 858-459-2990. E-mail: kim.cooper@bishops.com. Website: www.bishops.com

BISHOP STANG HIGH SCHOOL

500 Slocum Road
North Dartmouth, Massachusetts 02747-2999

Head of School: Mr. Peter V. Shaughnessy

General Information Coeducational day college-preparatory, arts, religious studies, and science school, affiliated with Roman Catholic Church. Grades 9–12. Founded: 1959. Setting: suburban. Nearest major city is New Bedford. 8-acre campus. 1 building on campus. Approved or accredited by New England Association of Schools and Colleges and Massachusetts Department of Education. Endowment: $2 million. Total enrollment: 620. Upper school average class size: 19. Upper school faculty-student ratio: 1:12. There are 180 required school days per year for Upper School students. Upper School students typically attend 5 days per week. The average school day consists of 6 hours and 30 minutes.

Upper School Student Profile Grade 9: 142 students (62 boys, 80 girls); Grade 10: 143 students (74 boys, 69 girls); Grade 11: 166 students (71 boys, 95 girls); Grade 12: 139 students (55 boys, 84 girls). 75% of students are Roman Catholic.

Faculty School total: 50. In upper school: 20 men, 30 women; 31 have advanced degrees.

Subjects Offered 20th century American writers, 20th century world history, 3-dimensional art, 3-dimensional design, ACT preparation, advanced biology, advanced chemistry, advanced math, Advanced Placement courses, algebra, alternative physical education, American history, American history-AP, American literature, American literature-AP, anatomy and physiology, art, athletics, biochemistry, bioethics, biology, biology-AP, business law, calculus, calculus-AP, campus ministry, career and personal planning, career/college preparation, Catholic belief and practice, chemistry, chemistry-AP, chorus, church history, clayworking, collage and assemblage, college admission preparation, college awareness, college counseling, college placement, college planning, college writing, communications, community service, comparative religion, computer education, computer literacy, computer science, computer technologies, concert band, criminal justice, criminology, death and loss, drama, drama performance, dramatic arts, drawing, drawing and design, driver education, ecology, English, English language and composition-AP, English literature, English literature-AP, English-AP, environmental science, fine arts, French, geometry, government/civics, health, health science, history, history of the Catholic Church, honors algebra, honors English, honors geometry, honors U.S. history, honors world history, human biology, human development, instrumental music, introduction to theater, jazz band, lab science, Latin, leadership and service, Life of Christ, marine biology, marketing, mathematics, mechanical drawing, media production, modern European history, modern European history-AP, moral theology, music, oceanography, painting, photography, physical education, physics, physics-AP, physiology, Portuguese, prayer/spirituality, psychology, psychology-AP, public service, public speaking, religion, religious studies, SAT/ACT preparation, science, social sciences, social studies, sociology, Spanish, statistics-AP, study skills, technical drawing, theater arts, trigonometry, U.S. history-AP, Web authoring, Web site design, world history, world literature, writing, yearbook.

Graduation Requirements Arts and fine arts (art, music, dance, drama), English, foreign language, mathematics, physical education (includes health), religion (includes Bible studies and theology), science, social sciences, social studies (includes history), U.S. history, world history, service project. Community service is required.

Special Academic Programs 11 Advanced Placement exams for which test preparation is offered; honors section; academic accommodation for the gifted; remedial reading and/or remedial writing; remedial math; programs in English, mathematics, general development for dyslexic students.

College Admission Counseling 156 students graduated in 2016; 154 went to college, including Assumption College; Quinnipiac University; Stonehill College; University of Massachusetts Dartmouth; University of Rhode Island; Worcester Polytechnic Institute. Other: 2 entered a postgraduate year. Mean SAT critical reading: 578, mean SAT math: 555, mean SAT writing: 544, mean combined SAT: 1687. 39.1% scored over 600 on SAT critical reading, 32.1% scored over 600 on SAT math, 35.9% scored over 600 on SAT writing, 31.4% scored over 1800 on combined SAT, 52.6% scored over 26 on composite ACT.

Student Life Upper grades have uniform requirement, student council, honor system. Discipline rests primarily with faculty. Attendance at religious services is required.

Summer Programs Enrichment, advancement, sports, art/fine arts, computer instruction programs offered; session focuses on sport and activity camps; held on campus; accepts boys and girls; open to students from other schools. 200 students usually enrolled. 2017 schedule: July 1 to August 19. Application deadline: June 1.

Tuition and Aid Day student tuition: $9650. Tuition installment plan (FACTS Tuition Payment Plan, monthly payment plans). Merit scholarship grants, need-based scholarship grants available. In 2016–17, 26% of upper-school students received aid; total upper-school merit-scholarship money awarded: $10,000. Total amount of financial aid awarded in 2016–17: $600,000.

Admissions Traditional secondary-level entrance grade is 9. For fall 2016, 228 students applied for upper-level admission, 220 were accepted, 142 enrolled. Scholastic Testing Service High School Placement Test or SSAT required. Deadline for receipt of application materials: none. No application fee required.

Athletics Interscholastic: aquatics (boys, girls), baseball (b), basketball (b,g), cheering (g), cross-country running (b,g), diving (b,g), field hockey (g), fitness (b,g), football (b), ice hockey (b,g), indoor track (b,g), lacrosse (b,g), soccer (b,g), softball (g), swimming and diving (b,g), tennis (b,g), track and field (b,g), volleyball (g), winter (indoor) track (b,g); intramural: volleyball (b); coed interscholastic: golf, sailing, strength & conditioning; coed intramural: climbing, crew, Frisbee, physical training, rowing, sailing, strength & conditioning, ultimate Frisbee, weight lifting, weight training. 1 PE instructor, 13 coaches, 1 athletic trainer.

Computers Computers are regularly used in all classes. Computer network features include on-campus library services, online commercial services, Internet access, wireless campus network, Internet filtering or blocking technology, computer device/tablet used by all students in grades 9-11. Campus intranet, student e-mail accounts, and computer access in designated common areas are available to students. Students grades are available online. The school has a published electronic and media policy.

Contact Mrs. Christine Payette, Admissions Director. 508-996-5602 Ext. 424. Fax: 508-994-6756. E-mail: admissions@bishopstang.org. Website: www.bishopstang.org

BISHOP VEROT HIGH SCHOOL

5598 Sunrise Drive
Fort Myers, Florida 33919-1799

Head of School: Dr. Denny Denison

General Information Coeducational day college-preparatory, religious studies, technology, honors, and Advanced Placement school, affiliated with Roman Catholic Church. Grades 9–12. Founded: 1962. Setting: suburban. Nearest major city is Tampa. 20-acre campus. 8 buildings on campus. Approved or accredited by Southern Association of Colleges and Schools and Florida Department of Education. Endowment: $800,000. Total enrollment: 673. Upper school average class size: 25. Upper school faculty-student ratio: 1:14. There are 182 required school days per year for Upper School students. Upper School students typically attend 5 days per week. The average school day consists of 7 hours.

Upper School Student Profile Grade 9: 181 students (92 boys, 89 girls); Grade 10: 162 students (100 boys, 62 girls); Grade 11: 159 students (81 boys, 78 girls); Grade 12: 166 students (84 boys, 82 girls). 60% of students are Roman Catholic.

Faculty School total: 50. In upper school: 19 men, 31 women; 33 have advanced degrees.

Subjects Offered Acting, Advanced Placement courses, algebra, American government, American history, American history-AP, American literature, American sign language, art, athletic training, band, Bible studies, biology, biology-AP, British literature, British literature (honors), broadcast journalism, business, calculus-AP, career planning, career/college preparation, ceramics, chemistry, chemistry-AP, choir, church history, college admission preparation, college counseling, comparative government and politics-AP, computer studies, creative writing, drafting, drama, drawing, driver education, economics, electives, English, English literature and composition-AP, English literature-AP, environmental science, European history-AP, fine arts, foreign language, French, geometry, government, government-AP, health education, history, history of the Catholic Church, history-AP, honors algebra, honors English, honors geometry, honors U.S. history, honors world history, industrial arts, law studies, marine biology, mathematics, painting, personal fitness, photography, physical education, physics, physics-AP, pottery, practical arts, pre-algebra, pre-calculus, probability and statistics, psychology, SAT preparation, Spanish, Spanish language-AP, speech, studio art, television, theater, U.S. government and politics-AP, U.S. history, U.S. history-AP, weightlifting, world history, world history-AP, writing, yearbook.

Graduation Requirements Algebra, American government, arts and fine arts (art, music, dance, drama), biology, British literature, chemistry, economics, electives, English, English composition, foreign language, geometry, health education, mathematics, moral theology, personal fitness, physics, practical arts, psychology, religion (includes Bible studies and theology), science, U.S. history, world history, world literature.

Special Academic Programs Advanced Placement exam preparation; honors section; independent study; study at local college for college credit; special instructional classes for Learning Strategies for mild learning needs.

College Admission Counseling 145 students graduated in 2016; 144 went to college, including Florida Atlantic University; Florida Gulf Coast University; Florida State University; University of Central Florida; University of Florida. Other: 1 had other specific plans. Mean SAT critical reading: 541, mean SAT math: 540, mean SAT writing: 527, mean combined SAT: 1608, mean composite ACT: 24.

Student Life Upper grades have specified standards of dress, student council, honor system. Discipline rests primarily with faculty. Attendance at religious services is required.

Summer Programs Enrichment, sports programs offered; session focuses on enrichment; held on campus; accepts boys and girls; not open to students from other schools.

Tuition and Aid Day student tuition: $11,900. Tuition installment plan (FACTS Tuition Payment Plan, monthly payment plans, individually arranged payment plans, quarterly payment plan). Merit scholarship grants, need-based scholarship grants, tuition reduction for contributing Catholic families available. In 2016–17, 40% of upper-school students received aid.

Admissions Traditional secondary-level entrance grade is 9. High School Placement Test required. Deadline for receipt of application materials: none. Application fee required: $75.

Athletics Interscholastic: baseball (boys), basketball (b,g), cheering (g), cross-country running (b,g), diving (b,g), football (b), golf (b,g), lacrosse (b,g), sand volleyball (g), soccer (b,g), softball (g), swimming and diving (b,g), tennis (b,g), track and field (b,g), volleyball (g); coed interscholastic: strength & conditioning. 2 PE instructors, 20 coaches, 1 athletic trainer.

Computers Computers are regularly used in career exploration, college planning, drafting, information technology, media production, media services, photography, publications, SAT preparation, technology, vocational-technical courses, Web site design, yearbook classes. Computer network features include Internet access, wireless campus network, Internet filtering or blocking technology, Naviance Family Connection—college and career planning, 1-to-1 iPad program. Student e-mail accounts are available to students. Students grades are available online. The school has a published electronic and media policy.

Contact Mrs. Jill Rhone, Director of Admission. 239-274-6760. Fax: 239-274-6795. E-mail: jill.rhone@bvhs.org. Website: www.bvhs.org/

BISHOP WALSH MIDDLE HIGH SCHOOL

Bishop Walsh School
700 Bishop Walsh Road
Cumberland, Maryland 21502

Head of School: Mrs. Ann Workmeister

General Information Coeducational day college-preparatory school, affiliated with Roman Catholic Church. Grades PK–12. Founded: 1966. Setting: small town. 10-acre campus. 1 building on campus. Approved or accredited by National Catholic Education Association and Maryland Department of Education. Total enrollment: 320. Upper school average class size: 20. Upper school faculty-student ratio: 1:15. There are 190 required school days per year for Upper School students. Upper School students typically attend 5 days per week. The average school day consists of 6 hours and 5 minutes.

Upper School Student Profile 70% of students are Roman Catholic.

Faculty School total: 40. In upper school: 8 men, 12 women; 15 have advanced degrees.

Subjects Offered 3-dimensional design, advanced biology, advanced chemistry, algebra, American government, American history, American history-AP, American literature, art, art history-AP, biology, biology-AP, British literature, British literature-AP, calculus, calculus-AP, campus ministry, Catholic belief and practice, chemistry, chemistry-AP, Christian and Hebrew scripture, Christian ethics, computer applications, computer science, English language and composition-AP, English language-AP, English literature, English literature and composition-AP, English literature-AP, environmental science, environmental science-AP, ESL, ESL, geography, geometry, government and politics-AP, government-AP, Hausa, health, Hebrew scripture, history-AP, honors algebra, honors English, honors geometry, honors U.S. history, honors world history, Internet, lab science, literature and composition-AP, model United Nations, music, music appreciation, New Testament, physical education, physics, psychology, scripture, social justice, Spanish, statistics, statistics-AP, U.S. government, U.S. government and politics, U.S. government and politics-AP, U.S. history, U.S. history-AP, United States government-AP, Web site design, weight training, weightlifting, Western civilization, world civilizations, yearbook.

Graduation Requirements All academic.

Special Academic Programs 10 Advanced Placement exams for which test preparation is offered; honors section; remedial reading and/or remedial writing; programs in English, general development for dyslexic students; ESL (10 students enrolled).

College Admission Counseling 30 students graduated in 2015; 29 went to college, including Frostburg State University; West Virginia University. Other: 1 entered military service. Median SAT critical reading: 505, median SAT math: 504, median SAT writing: 500, median combined SAT: 1509, median composite ACT: 25.

Student Life Upper grades have uniform requirement, student council. Discipline rests primarily with faculty. Attendance at religious services is required.

Tuition and Aid Day student tuition: $5500. Tuition installment plan (FACTS Tuition Payment Plan, monthly payment plans). Need-based scholarship grants available. In 2015–16, 50% of upper-school students received aid. Total amount of financial aid awarded in 2015–16: $30,000.

Admissions Traditional secondary-level entrance grade is 9. High School Placement Test (closed version) from Scholastic Testing Service required. Deadline for receipt of application materials: none. Application fee required: $60. Interview required.

Athletics Interscholastic: baseball (boys), basketball (b,g), bowling (b,g), cheering (g), golf (b), horseback riding (b,g), soccer (b,g), softball (g), tennis (b,g), volleyball (g), weight training (b,g); coed interscholastic: cross-country running, track and field; coed intramural: table tennis. 1 PE instructor, 8 coaches, 1 athletic trainer.

Computers Computer network features include Internet access, wireless campus network. Student e-mail accounts are available to students. Students grades are available online. The school has a published electronic and media policy.

Contact Mrs. Erin Dale, Administrative Assistant. 301-724-5360 Ext. 104. Fax: 301-722-0555. E-mail: edale@bishopwalsh.org. Website: www.bishopwalsh.org

BLACK FOREST ACADEMY

Hammersteiner Strasse 50
Postfach 1109
Kandern 79396, Germany

Head of School: Mr. Scott Jones

General Information Coeducational boarding and day college-preparatory and general academic school, affiliated with Christian faith. Boarding grades 9–12, day grades 5–12. Founded: 1956. Setting: small town. Nearest major city is Basel, Switzerland. Students are housed in single-sex dormitories. 2-acre campus. 3 buildings on campus. Approved or accredited by Association of Christian Schools International, Council of International Schools, and Middle States Association of Colleges and Schools. Language of instruction: English. Total enrollment: 361. Upper school average class size: 20. Upper school faculty-student ratio: 1:8. There are 174 required school days per year for Upper School students.

Upper School Student Profile Grade 9: 40 students (19 boys, 21 girls); Grade 10: 53 students (29 boys, 24 girls); Grade 11: 75 students (36 boys, 39 girls); Grade 12: 74 students (33 boys, 41 girls). 60% of students are boarding students. 76% are international students. International students from Canada, France, Italy, Republic of Korea, Russian Federation, and Turkey; 52 other countries represented in student body. 90% of students are Christian.

Faculty School total: 62. In upper school: 31 men, 31 women; 33 have advanced degrees.

Subjects Offered Advanced math, Advanced Placement courses, algebra, American history, art, band, Bible, biology, calculus, calculus-AP, Canadian history, chemistry, choir, Christian education, church history, community service, computer programming, computer science, drama, English, English literature, English-AP, environmental science, ESL, European history, European history-AP, fine arts, French, general math, geography, geometry, German, German-AP, graphic arts, graphic design, health, home economics, industrial technology, journalism, keyboarding, mathematics, music, music appreciation, music theory, physical education, physics, science, social studies, Spanish, statistics, U.S. history-AP, world history.

Graduation Requirements Algebra, American history, arts and fine arts (art, music, dance, drama), Bible, biology, chemistry, computer applications, English, foreign language, physical education (includes health), trigonometry, 30 hours of community service per year.

Special Academic Programs Advanced Placement exam preparation; honors section, remedial math; programs in English, mathematics, general development for dyslexic students; special instructional classes for students with learning disabilities; ESL (10 students enrolled).

College Admission Counseling 74 students graduated in 2016; 65 went to college, including Calvin College; Gordon College; John Brown University; Taylor University; Trinity Western University. Other: 2 went to work, 4 entered military service, 3 had other specific plans. Mean SAT critical reading: 590, mean SAT math: 570. 47% scored over 600 on SAT critical reading, 58% scored over 600 on SAT math, 27% scored over 26 on composite ACT.

Student Life Upper grades have specified standards of dress, student council, honor system. Discipline rests primarily with faculty. Attendance at religious services is required.

Tuition and Aid Tuition installment plan (monthly payment plans, individually arranged payment plans, quarterly payment plan). Tuition reduction for siblings available.

Admissions Traditional secondary-level entrance grade is 10. Any standardized test or math and English placement tests required. Deadline for receipt of application materials: none. Application fee required: €100. Interview recommended.

Athletics Interscholastic: basketball (boys, girls), soccer (b,g), track and field (b,g), volleyball (b,g); intramural: basketball (b,g), cross-country running (b,g), soccer (b,g); coed interscholastic: cross-country running, jogging, jump rope; coed intramural: floor hockey, outdoor education. 3 PE instructors, 1 coach.

Computers Computers are regularly used in Bible studies, career exploration, data processing, graphic arts, journalism, media production, music, yearbook classes. Computer network features include on-campus library services, Internet access, wireless campus network, Internet filtering or blocking technology, off-campus email. Student e-mail accounts are available to students. Students grades are available online. The school has a published electronic and media policy.

Contact Mrs. Judy Thompson, Admissions Secretary. 49-7626-91610. Fax: 49-7626-8821. E-mail: admissions@bfacademy.de. Website: www.bfacademy.com

BLAIR ACADEMY

2 Park Street
Blairstown, New Jersey 07825

Head of School: Christopher Fortunato, JD

General Information Coeducational boarding and day college-preparatory, arts, and technology school. Boarding grades 9–PG, day grades 9–12. Founded: 1848. Setting: rural. Nearest major city is New York, NY. Students are housed in single-sex dormitories. 425-acre campus. 42 buildings on campus. Approved or accredited by Middle States Association of Colleges and Schools, The Association of Boarding Schools, and New Jersey Department of Education. Member of National Association of Independent Schools and Secondary School Admission Test Board. Endowment: $90 million. Total enrollment: 460. Upper school average class size: 11. Upper school faculty-student ratio: 1:6. Upper School students typically attend 6 days per week. The average school day consists of 6 hours and 45 minutes.

Upper School Student Profile 80% of students are boarding students. 30% are state residents. 26 states are represented in upper school student body. 17% are international students. International students from China, Hong Kong, Republic of Korea, Spain, Thailand, and United Kingdom; 20 other countries represented in student body.

Faculty School total: 90. In upper school: 50 men, 40 women; 57 have advanced degrees; 83 reside on campus.

Subjects Offered 3-dimensional art, 3-dimensional design, advanced math, Advanced Placement courses, advanced studio art-AP, African history, algebra, American government, American history, American history-AP, American literature, anatomy, architectural drawing, architecture, art, art history-AP, art-AP, Asian studies, biochemistry, biology, biology-AP, biotechnology, calculus, calculus-AP, ceramics, chemistry, chemistry-AP, Chinese, comparative government and politics-AP, computer programming, computer science, computer science-AP, creative writing, dance, drafting, drama, drawing, drawing and design, driver education, economics, economics and history, economics-AP, English, English language-AP, English literature, English literature-AP, environmental science, environmental science-AP, ethics, European history, European history-AP, filmmaking, fine arts, French, French language-AP, geometry, government/civics, health, history, Japanese history, jazz band, Latin, marine biology, marine science, mathematics, mechanical drawing, music, music theory-AP, painting, philosophy, photography, physics, pre-calculus, psychology, religion, robotics, science, social studies, Spanish, Spanish language-AP, statistics-AP, theater, theology, world history, world history-AP, world literature, writing.

Graduation Requirements Arts and fine arts (art, music, dance, drama), biology, English, foreign language, mathematics, performing arts, religion (includes Bible studies and theology), science, social studies (includes history), U.S. history, athletic requirement.

Special Academic Programs 23 Advanced Placement exams for which test preparation is offered; honors section; independent study; study abroad.

College Admission Counseling 135 students graduated in 2015; all went to college, including Boston College; Cornell University; Lehigh University; New York University; Syracuse University; University of Pennsylvania.

Student Life Upper grades have specified standards of dress, student council, honor system. Discipline rests equally with students and faculty. Attendance at religious services is required.

Tuition and Aid Day student tuition: $35,600; 7-day tuition and room/board: $49,500. Tuition installment plan (Key Tuition Payment Plan, monthly payment plans). Need-based scholarship grants, need-based loans available. In 2015–16, 32% of upper-school students received aid. Total amount of financial aid awarded in 2015–16: $5,100,000.

Admissions Traditional secondary-level entrance grade is 9. For fall 2015, 991 students applied for upper-level admission, 241 were accepted, 154 enrolled. SSAT or TOEFL required. Deadline for receipt of application materials: January 15. Application fee required: $50. On-campus interview required.

Athletics Interscholastic: alpine skiing (boys, girls), baseball (b), basketball (b,g), crew (b,g), cross-country running (b,g), field hockey (g), football (b), golf (b,g), indoor track (b,g), lacrosse (b,g), rowing (b,g), running (b,g), skiing (downhill) (b,g), soccer (b,g), softball (g), squash (b,g), swimming and diving (b,g), tennis (b,g), track and field (b,g), volleyball (g), winter (indoor) track (b,g), wrestling (b); intramural: basketball (b,g), crew (b,g), ice hockey (b,g), rowing (b,g), volleyball (g); coed intramural: alpine skiing, bicycling, canoeing/kayaking, dance, equestrian sports, fitness, flag football, golf, horseback riding, kayaking, life saving, modern dance, mountaineering, outdoor activities, outdoor adventure, outdoor education, outdoor skills, physical fitness, skiing (downhill), snowboarding, squash, swimming and diving, tennis, weight lifting, weight training, wrestling, yoga. 3 athletic trainers.

Computers Computers are regularly used in architecture, drawing and design, English, foreign language, graphic arts, graphic design, history, information technology, mathematics, media production, science, video film production, writing classes. Computer network features include on-campus library services, online commercial services, Internet access, Internet filtering or blocking technology. Campus intranet, student e-mail accounts, and computer access in designated common areas are available to students. The school has a published electronic and media policy.

Contact Nancy Klein, Administrative Assistant. 800-462-5247. Fax: 908-362-7975. E-mail: admissions@blair.edu. Website: www.blair.edu

THE BLAKE SCHOOL

110 Blake Road South
Hopkins, Minnesota 55343

Head of School: Dr. Anne E. Stavney

General Information Coeducational day college-preparatory school. Grades PK–12. Founded: 1900. Setting: urban. Nearest major city is Minneapolis. 5-acre campus. 1 building on campus. Approved or accredited by Independent Schools Association of the Central States. Member of National Association of Independent Schools. Endowment: $59.8 million. Total enrollment: 1,363. Upper school average class size: 16. Upper school faculty-student ratio: 1:8. There are 176 required school days per year for Upper School students. Upper School students typically attend 5 days per week. The average school day consists of 7 hours and 30 minutes.

Upper School Student Profile Grade 9: 135 students (72 boys, 63 girls); Grade 10: 133 students (52 boys, 81 girls); Grade 11: 136 students (71 boys, 65 girls); Grade 12: 129 students (63 boys, 66 girls).

Faculty School total: 135. In upper school: 31 men, 34 women; 37 have advanced degrees.

Subjects Offered Advanced chemistry, African-American literature, algebra, American history, American literature, art, Asian studies, astronomy, band, biology, biology-AP, calculus, calculus-AP, ceramics, chemistry, chemistry-AP, Chinese, choir, chorus, communication arts, communications, computer math, creative writing, debate, design, drama, drawing, economics, English, English literature, English-AP, ethics, European history, European history-AP, fine arts, French, French language-AP, French literature-AP, geology, geometry, German-AP, government/civics, history, instrumental music, jazz ensemble, journalism, Latin, mathematics, multicultural studies, music, painting, performing arts, photography, physical education, physics, physics-AP, policy and value, political science, printmaking, psychology, religion, science, sculpture,

senior project, social psychology, social studies, Spanish, Spanish language-AP, speech, statistics, statistics-AP, studio art, studio art-AP, theater, theater arts, trigonometry, visual and performing arts, vocal ensemble, women's studies, world cultures, world history, world literature, writing.

Graduation Requirements Arts and fine arts (art, music, dance, drama), communications, English, foreign language, mathematics, physical education (includes health), science, social studies (includes history), senior speech.

Special Academic Programs 14 Advanced Placement exams for which test preparation is offered; honors section; term-away projects; study at local college for college credit; study abroad.

College Admission Counseling 134 students graduated in 2016; 129 went to college, including Abilene Christian University; Carleton University; Northwestern University; St. Olaf College; University of Minnesota, Twin Cities Campus; University of Wisconsin–Madison. Other: 4 had other specific plans. Median SAT critical reading: 665, median SAT math: 660, median SAT writing: 680, median combined SAT: 2005, median composite ACT: 29. 68% scored over 600 on SAT critical reading, 64% scored over 600 on SAT math, 69% scored over 600 on SAT writing, 75% scored over 26 on composite ACT.

Student Life Upper grades have specified standards of dress, student council, honor system. Discipline rests primarily with faculty.

Summer Programs Remediation, enrichment, advancement, sports, art/fine arts programs offered; session focuses on broad-based program including academics, arts, and sports; held both on and off campus; accepts boys and girls; open to students from other schools. 250 students usually enrolled. 2017 schedule: June 24 to August 9.

Tuition and Aid Day student tuition: $25,525. Tuition installment plan (Insured Tuition Payment Plan, monthly payment plans, local bank-arranged plan). Need-based scholarship grants, need-based loans, tuition remission for children of faculty available. In 2016–17, 22% of upper-school students received aid. Total amount of financial aid awarded in 2016–17: $2,321,797.

Admissions Traditional secondary-level entrance grade is 9. For fall 2016, 90 students applied for upper-level admission, 59 were accepted, 34 enrolled. ERB required. Deadline for receipt of application materials: January 31. Application fee required: $100. On-campus interview required.

Athletics Interscholastic: alpine skiing (boys, girls), baseball (b), basketball (b,g), cross-country running (b,g), diving (b,g), football (b), golf (b,g), ice hockey (b,g), lacrosse (b,g), skiing (cross-country) (b,g), skiing (downhill) (b,g), soccer (b,g), softball (g), swimming and diving (b,g); coed interscholastic: fencing. 1 PE instructor, 45 coaches, 1 athletic trainer.

Computers Computers are regularly used in all classes. Computer network features include on-campus library services, online commercial services, Internet access, wireless campus network, Internet filtering or blocking technology, laptops. Campus intranet, student e-mail accounts, and computer access in designated common areas are available to students. Students grades are available online. The school has a published electronic and media policy.

Contact Joseph Silvestri, Director of Admissions. 952-988-3422. Fax: 952-988-3455. E-mail: jsilvestri@blakeschool.org. Website: www.blakeschool.org

BLANCHET SCHOOL

4373 Market Street NE
Salem, Oregon 97305

Head of School: Mr. Anthony Guevara

General Information Coeducational day college-preparatory school, affiliated with Roman Catholic Church. Grades 6–12. Founded: 1995. Setting: suburban. 22-acre campus. 2 buildings on campus. Approved or accredited by National Catholic Education Association, Northwest Accreditation Commission, Northwest Association of Schools and Colleges, and Oregon Department of Education. Endowment: $285,000. Total enrollment: 367. Upper school average class size: 18. Upper school faculty-student ratio: 1:17. There are 175 required school days per year for Upper School students. Upper School students typically attend 5 days per week. The average school day consists of 7 hours.

Upper School Student Profile Grade 9: 61 students (28 boys, 33 girls); Grade 10: 63 students (37 boys, 26 girls); Grade 11: 56 students (30 boys, 26 girls); Grade 12: 51 students (30 boys, 21 girls). 70% of students are Roman Catholic.

Faculty School total: 30. In upper school: 13 men, 15 women; 23 have advanced degrees.

Subjects Offered Advanced Placement courses, algebra, American government, American history-AP, American literature, anatomy, anatomy and physiology, art, art education, band, Bible studies, biology, calculus, campus ministry, career and personal planning, Catholic belief and practice, chemistry, chemistry-AP, choir, civics, college counseling, college placement, comparative religion, composition, critical thinking, critical writing, debate, digital photography, drama, economics, economics and history, English literature, English literature and composition-AP, first aid, fitness, French, geometry, global studies, government, great books, health, health and safety, health and wellness, health education, history of the Catholic Church, history-AP, lab science, leadership, literature and composition-AP, mathematics, media production, music, personal finance, physical education, physical fitness, physical science, physics, pre-algebra, pre-calculus, psychology, publications, religion, religion and culture,

SAT/ACT preparation, sociology, Spanish, speech and debate, U.S. government, U.S. history, U.S. history-AP, weight training, world history, world religions, World War II.

Graduation Requirements Applied arts, arts and fine arts (art, music, dance, drama), electives, English, foreign language, mathematics, physical education (includes health), religion (includes Bible studies and theology), science, social studies (includes history), 20 hours of community service for each year in attendance.

Special Academic Programs 2 Advanced Placement exams for which test preparation is offered; honors section; study at local college for college credit; special instructional classes for deaf students; ESL (8 students enrolled).

College Admission Counseling 65 students graduated in 2016; all went to college, including Chemeketa Community College; Gonzaga University; Linfield College; Oregon State University; University of Portland; Willamette University. Mean SAT critical reading: 553, mean SAT math: 535, mean SAT writing: 534, mean composite ACT: 25.

Student Life Upper grades have specified standards of dress, student council. Discipline rests primarily with faculty. Attendance at religious services is required.

Summer Programs Enrichment, sports programs offered; session focuses on preparation for the next academic year, athletic training; held on campus; accepts boys and girls; open to students from other schools. 75 students usually enrolled. 2017 schedule: June 13 to August 31.

Tuition and Aid Day student tuition: $8590. Tuition installment plan (FACTS Tuition Payment Plan). Tuition reduction for siblings, need-based scholarship grants available. In 2016–17, 41% of upper-school students received aid. Total amount of financial aid awarded in 2016–17: $360,000.

Admissions Traditional secondary-level entrance grade is 9. For fall 2016, 100 students applied for upper-level admission, 97 were accepted, 95 enrolled. Math Placement Exam required. Deadline for receipt of application materials: none. Application fee required: $125. On-campus interview required.

Athletics Interscholastic: baseball (boys), basketball (b,g), cheering (g), cross-country running (b,g), fencing (b,g), football (b), golf (b,g), physical fitness (b,g), soccer (b,g), softball (g), swimming and diving (b,g), tennis (b,g), track and field (b,g), volleyball (g), weight training (b,g); intramural: weight training (b,g); coed intramural: badminton, basketball, outdoor recreation. 3 PE instructors, 60 coaches, 1 athletic trainer.

Computers Computers are regularly used in business, media production, photography, science, social studies classes. Computer network features include online commercial services, Internet access, wireless campus network, Internet filtering or blocking technology. Computer access in designated common areas is available to students. Students grades are available online. The school has a published electronic and media policy.

Contact Mrs. Megan Johnston, Admissions Office. 503-485-4491. Fax: 503-399-1259. E-mail: admissions@blanchetcatholicschool.com. Website: www.blanchetcatholicschool.com

BLESSED SACRAMENT HUGUENOT CATHOLIC SCHOOL

2501 Academy Road
Powhatan, Virginia 23139

Head of School: Mrs. Paula Ledbetter

General Information Coeducational day college-preparatory, arts, and religious studies school, affiliated with Roman Catholic Church. Grades PS–12. Founded: 1954. Setting: rural. Nearest major city is Richmond. 46-acre campus. 5 buildings on campus. Approved or accredited by Southern Association of Colleges and Schools and Virginia Department of Education. Total enrollment: 316. Upper school average class size: 12. Upper school faculty-student ratio: 1:6. There are 180 required school days per year for Upper School students. Upper School students typically attend 5 days per week. The average school day consists of 7 hours.

Upper School Student Profile Grade 9: 23 students (16 boys, 7 girls); Grade 10: 26 students (17 boys, 9 girls); Grade 11: 33 students (17 boys, 16 girls); Grade 12: 24 students (16 boys, 8 girls). 33% of students are Roman Catholic.

Faculty School total: 36. In upper school: 6 men, 11 women; 6 have advanced degrees.

Subjects Offered Advanced math, Advanced Placement courses, algebra, American government, American history, American history-AP, American literature-AP, art, athletics, baseball, basketball, biology, calculus, calculus-AP, Central and Eastern European history, cheerleading, chemistry, Christian education, college admission preparation, college awareness, college counseling, college planning, college writing, community service, conceptual physics, drama, drama performance, English, English-AP, European history, foreign language, geography, geometry, government-AP, history of the Catholic Church, history-AP, honors algebra, honors English, honors geometry, honors U.S. history, honors world history, Latin, modern European history, physical education, religious education, SAT preparation, Spanish, student government, swimming, tennis, theology, trigonometry, U.S. and Virginia government, U.S. and Virginia government-AP, U.S. history-AP, world history.

Graduation Requirements American government, arts and fine arts (art, music, dance, drama), economics, English, foreign language, mathematics, physical education (includes health), religion and culture, science, social studies (includes history), admission to a 4-year institution, community service hours, state diploma standards. Community service is required.

Special Academic Programs Advanced Placement exam preparation; honors section.

College Admission Counseling 36 students graduated in 2016; all went to college, including James Madison University; Longwood University; Radford University; Randolph-Macon College; University of Virginia; Virginia Polytechnic Institute and State University. Mean SAT critical reading: 550, mean SAT math: 515, mean composite ACT: 23.

Student Life Upper grades have uniform requirement, student council, honor system. Discipline rests equally with students and faculty. Attendance at religious services is required.

Summer Programs Enrichment, sports, art/fine arts, computer instruction programs offered; session focuses on extracurricular activities, art enrichment, and sports enrichment; held on campus; accepts boys and girls; open to students from other schools. 50 students usually enrolled. 2017 schedule: June 12 to August 17. Application deadline: none.

Tuition and Aid Day student tuition: $13,000. Tuition installment plan (FACTS Tuition Payment Plan). Tuition reduction for siblings, need-based scholarship grants available. In 2016–17, 30% of upper school students received aid. Total amount of financial aid awarded in 2016–17: $150,000.

Admissions Traditional secondary-level entrance grade is 9. For fall 2016, 30 students applied for upper-level admission, 25 were accepted, 25 enrolled. Deadline for receipt of application materials: none. Application fee required: $50. Interview recommended.

Athletics Interscholastic: baseball (boys), basketball (b,g), football (b), softball (g), volleyball (g); intramural: basketball (b,g), football (b), softball (g), Special Olympics (b,g), volleyball (g); coed interscholastic: cheering, cross-country running, field hockey, golf, soccer, swimming and diving, tennis; coed intramural: cross-country running, soccer, swimming and diving, tennis. 2 PE instructors, 20 coaches, 1 athletic trainer.

Computers Computer network features include on-campus library services, online commercial services, Internet access, wireless campus network, Internet filtering or blocking technology. Campus intranet and student e-mail accounts are available to students. Students grades are available online. The school has a published electronic and media policy.

Contact Mrs. Christina Dowdy, Director of Admissions. 804-598-4211. Fax: 804-598-1053. E-mail: cdowdy@bshknights.org. Website: www.bshknights.org

BLESSED TRINITY HIGH SCHOOL

11320 Woodstock Road
Roswell, Georgia 30075

Head of School: Mr. Brian Marks

General Information Coeducational day college-preparatory school, affiliated with Roman Catholic Church. Grades 9–12. Founded: 2000. Setting: suburban. Nearest major city is Atlanta. 68-acre campus. 2 buildings on campus. Approved or accredited by National Catholic Education Association, Southern Association of Colleges and Schools, and Georgia Department of Education. Member of National Association of Independent Schools and Secondary School Admission Test Board. Upper school average class size: 20. Upper school faculty-student ratio: 1:12. There are 180 required school days per year for Upper School students. Upper School students typically attend 5 days per week. The average school day consists of 7 hours.

Upper School Student Profile Grade 9: 259 students (121 boys, 138 girls); Grade 10: 260 students (130 boys, 130 girls); Grade 11: 245 students (114 boys, 131 girls); Grade 12: 237 students (117 boys, 120 girls). 85% of students are Roman Catholic.

Faculty School total: 87. In upper school: 42 men, 45 women; 58 have advanced degrees.

Graduation Requirements Advanced math, algebra, American government, American history, American literature, ancient world history, arts and fine arts (art, music, dance, drama), biology, British literature, chemistry, economics, foreign language, geometry, health, mathematics, personal finance, physics, theology, world history.

Special Academic Programs 23 Advanced Placement exams for which test preparation is offered; honors section.

College Admission Counseling 226 students graduated in 2016; all went to college, including Auburn University; Georgia Institute of Technology; Georgia Southern University; Kennesaw State University; University of Georgia; University of South Carolina.

Student Life Upper grades have uniform requirement, student council, honor system. Discipline rests primarily with faculty. Attendance at religious services is required.

Tuition and Aid Day student tuition: $12,050. Tuition installment plan (FACTS Tuition Payment Plan). Need-based scholarship grants available. In 2016–17, 20% of upper-school students received aid.

Admissions Traditional secondary-level entrance grade is 9. SSAT required. Deadline for receipt of application materials: February 1. Application fee required: $100.

Athletics Interscholastic: baseball (boys), basketball (b,g), cheering (g), cross-country running (b,g), dance (b,g), dance team (g), football (b), golf (b,g), lacrosse (b,g), soccer (b,g), softball (g), swimming and diving (b,g), tennis (b,g), track and field (b,g), volleyball (g), wrestling (b). 5 PE instructors, 2 athletic trainers.

Computers Computers are regularly used in all classes. Computer network features include on-campus library services, Internet access, wireless campus network. Campus intranet and student e-mail accounts are available to students. Students grades are available online. The school has a published electronic and media policy.

Contact Mr. Paul Stevens, Director of Admissions. 678-277-9083 Ext. 531. Fax: 678-277-9756. E-mail: pstevens@btcatholic.org. Website: www.btcatholic.org

BLUEPRINT EDUCATION

5651 West Talavi Boulevard
Suite 170
Glendale, Arizona 85306

Head of School: Mr. Mark French

General Information Distance learning only college-preparatory, general academic, and distance learning school. Distance learning grades 7–12. Founded: 1969. Approved or accredited by CITA (Commission on International and Trans-Regional Accreditation), North Central Association of Colleges and Schools, and Arizona Department of Education. Upper school average class size: 200.

Faculty School total: 4. In upper school: 3 men, 1 woman; all have advanced degrees.

Subjects Offered 3-dimensional art, algebra, American government, American history, animation, art, art appreciation, art history, audio visual/media, auto mechanics, biology, business studies, calculus, career experience, career exploration, career planning, careers, chemistry, Chinese, computer applications, computer education, digital art, earth science, economics, English, entrepreneurship, foreign language, French, general business, geometry, German, government, health and wellness, health education, health science, information technology, interpersonal skills, literacy, mathematics, personal development, personal finance, physical education, physical fitness, physics, pre-algebra, psychology, reading, remedial/makeup course work, sociology, Spanish, speech communications, statistics, travel, trigonometry, U.S. government, U.S. history, work experience, world geography, world history.

Graduation Requirements Arts and fine arts (art, music, dance, drama), computers, economics, English, foreign language, geography, health, mathematics, science, social studies (includes history), speech.

Special Academic Programs Honors section; accelerated programs; independent study; academic accommodation for the musically talented and the artistically talented; remedial reading and/or remedial writing; remedial math.

College Admission Counseling Colleges students went to include Arizona State University at the Tempe campus; Northern Arizona University; Pima Community College; The University of Arizona.

Student Life Upper grades have honor system.

Summer Programs Remediation, advancement programs offered; session focuses on remediation and advancement; held off campus; held at various locations for independent study; accepts boys and girls; open to students from other schools.

Admissions Deadline for receipt of application materials: none. No application fee required.

Computers Computers are regularly used in all academic classes. Computer resources include Internet access. Students grades are available online. The school has a published electronic and media policy.

Contact Mrs. Erin Horn, Principal. 800-426-4952. Fax: 602-943-9700. E-mail: erinh@blueprinteducation.org. Website: www.blueprinteducation.org

THE BLUE RIDGE SCHOOL

273 Mayo Drive
St. George, Virginia 22935

Head of School: Mr. Trip Darrin

General Information Boys' boarding college-preparatory and general academic school, affiliated with Episcopal Church; primarily serves underachievers. Grades 9–12. Founded: 1909. Setting: rural. Nearest major city is Charlottesville. Students are housed in single-sex dormitories. 750-acre campus. 11 buildings on campus. Approved or accredited by Southern Association of Colleges and Schools, Virginia Association of Independent Schools, and Virginia Department of Education. Member of National Association of Independent Schools and Secondary School Admission Test Board. Endowment: $17 million. Total enrollment: 195. Upper school average class size: 9. Upper school faculty-student ratio: 1:8. There are 180 required school days per year for Upper School students. Upper School students typically attend 6 days per week. The average school day consists of 6 hours.

Upper School Student Profile Grade 9: 30 students (30 boys); Grade 10: 45 students (45 boys); Grade 11: 60 students (60 boys); Grade 12: 47 students (47 boys). 100% of students are boarding students. 25% are state residents. 18 states are represented in upper school student body. 30% are international students. International students from China, Mexico, Nigeria, Saudi Arabia, South Africa, and Spain; 25 other countries represented in student body. 25% of students are members of Episcopal Church.

Faculty School total: 35. In upper school: 25 men, 7 women; 18 have advanced degrees; all reside on campus.

Subjects Offered Algebra, American history, American literature, anatomy, anatomy and physiology, art, astronomy, biology, calculus, chemistry, choir, decision making skills, discrete mathematics, drama, economics, English, environmental science, ESL, European history, French, geometry, guitar, health, honors English, honors geometry,

honors U.S. history, integrated science, keyboarding, leadership, marketing, mathematics, music, music history, outdoor education, physics, pre-algebra, pre-calculus, Spanish, trigonometry, U.S. history, world history, world literature, writing, yearbook.

Graduation Requirements Algebra, American history, American literature, biology, decision making skills, English, foreign language, geometry, leadership, mathematics, physical education (includes health), science, social studies (includes history), three years of a single foreign language.

Special Academic Programs Honors section; independent study; study at local college for college credit; remedial reading and/or remedial writing; remedial math; programs in English, general development for dyslexic students; ESL (30 students enrolled).

College Admission Counseling 40 students graduated in 2016; all went to college, including Clemson University; Hampden-Sydney College; James Madison University; Kenyon College; Queens University of Charlotte; University of Virginia.

Student Life Upper grades have specified standards of dress, student council, honor system. Discipline rests primarily with faculty. Attendance at religious services is required.

Tuition and Aid 7-day tuition and room/board: $44,750. Tuition installment plan (monthly payment plans). Merit scholarship grants, need-based scholarship grants, paying campus jobs available. In 2016–17, 40% of upper-school students received aid; total upper-school merit-scholarship money awarded: $100,000. Total amount of financial aid awarded in 2016–17: $200,000.

Admissions Traditional secondary-level entrance grade is 9. For fall 2016, 271 students applied for upper-level admission, 112 were accepted, 70 enrolled. Deadline for receipt of application materials: none. Application fee required: $50. Interview recommended.

Athletics Interscholastic: baseball, basketball, cross-country running, football, golf, indoor soccer, lacrosse, mountain biking, soccer, table tennis, tennis, track and field, volleyball, wrestling; intramural: alpine skiing, aquatics, backpacking, basketball, bicycling, canoeing/kayaking, climbing, cooperative games, fishing, fitness, Frisbee, hiking/backpacking, kayaking, mountain biking, mountaineering, outdoor activities, outdoor adventure, outdoor education, outdoor recreation, outdoor skills, outdoors, paint ball, physical fitness, physical training, rafting, rappelling, rock climbing, ropes courses, skiing (downhill), snowboarding, soccer, strength & conditioning, tennis, ultimate Frisbee, wall climbing, weight lifting, weight training, wilderness, wilderness survival. 2 coaches, 2 athletic trainers.

Computers Computers are regularly used in business studies, English, ESL, foreign language, mathematics, science, study skills, word processing, writing, yearbook classes. Computer network features include on-campus library services, online commercial services, Internet access, wireless campus network, Internet filtering or blocking technology. Campus intranet, student e-mail accounts, and computer access in designated common areas are available to students. The school has a published electronic and media policy.

Contact Mr. James H. Miller III, Senior Director of Admissions. 434-985-2811 Ext. 106. Fax: 434-985-7215. E-mail: jmiller@blueridgeschool.com. Website: www.blueridgeschool.com

BOCA PREP INTERNATIONAL SCHOOL

10333 Diego Drive South
Boca Raton, Florida 33428

Head of School: Mr. Stan L. Daniel

General Information Coeducational day college-preparatory school. Grades PK–12. Founded: 1998. Setting: suburban. Students are housed in Their own homes. 1.5-acre campus. 2 buildings on campus. Approved or accredited by Florida Council of Independent Schools, Southern Association of Colleges and Schools, and Florida Department of Education. Total enrollment: 243. Upper school average class size: 22. Upper school faculty-student ratio: 1:24. There are 186 required school days per year for Upper School students. Upper School students typically attend 5 days per week. The average school day consists of 7 hours and 10 minutes.

Upper School Student Profile Grade 6: 20 students (9 boys, 11 girls); Grade 7: 23 students (15 boys, 8 girls); Grade 8: 17 students (7 boys, 10 girls); Grade 9: 28 students (19 boys, 9 girls); Grade 10: 23 students (12 boys, 11 girls); Grade 11: 20 students (7 boys, 13 girls); Grade 12: 31 students (19 boys, 12 girls).

Faculty School total: 28. In upper school: 9 men, 19 women; 19 have advanced degrees.

Special Academic Programs International Baccalaureate program.

Student Life Upper grades have uniform requirement, student council, honor system. Discipline rests primarily with faculty.

Tuition and Aid Tuition installment plan (monthly payment plans). Tuition reduction for siblings, bursaries, merit scholarship grants, need-based scholarship grants available.

Admissions Traditional secondary-level entrance grade is 9. Deadline for receipt of application materials: none. Application fee required: $250. Interview required.

Athletics Coed Interscholastic: physical fitness, soccer, swimming and diving. 1 PE instructor, 3 coaches.

Computers Computer network features include on-campus library services, Internet access, Internet filtering or blocking technology. Campus intranet and student e-mail accounts are available to students. Students grades are available online. The school has a published electronic and media policy.

Contact Mrs. Lesley F. Fisher, Director of Admissions and Marketing. 561-852-1410 Ext. 222. Fax: 561-470-6124. E-mail: lesley.fisher@icsmail.com. Website: www.bocaprep.net

BODWELL HIGH SCHOOL

955 Harbourside Drive

North Vancouver, British Columbia V7P 3S4, Canada

Head of School: Ms. Cathy Lee

General Information Coeducational boarding and day college-preparatory, arts, business, and technology school. Grades 8–12. Founded: 1991. Setting: suburban. Students are housed in single-sex by floor dormitories. 2-acre campus. 1 building on campus. Approved or accredited by British Columbia Department of Education. Language of instruction: English. Total enrollment: 538. Upper school average class size: 17. Upper school faculty-student ratio: 1:15. There are 290 required school days per year for Upper School students. Upper School students typically attend 6 days per week. The average school day consists of 5 hours and 50 minutes.

Upper School Student Profile 80% of students are boarding students. 25% are province residents. 8 provinces are represented in upper school student body. 75% are international students. International students from Brazil, China, Japan, Mexico, Nigeria, and Russian Federation; 40 other countries represented in student body.

Faculty School total: 40. In upper school: 17 men, 23 women; 15 have advanced degrees; 2 reside on campus.

Subjects Offered 3-dimensional art, Advanced Placement courses, art, band, biology, calculus, chemistry, choral music, communications, composition, computer applications, drama, economics, English, entrepreneurship, ESL, French as a second language, geography, global studies, health and wellness, history, information technology, Japanese, leadership, Mandarin, mathematics, music, physical education, physics, psychology, science, social studies, Spanish, sports, studio art

Graduation Requirements British Columbia Ministry of Education Requirements.

Special Academic Programs Advanced Placement exam preparation; accelerated programs; academic accommodation for the gifted; ESL (150 students enrolled).

College Admission Counseling 161 students graduated in 2015; 120 went to college, including Simon Fraser University; The University of British Columbia; University of Toronto; University of Victoria. Other: 41 had other specific plans.

Student Life Upper grades have uniform requirement, student council, honor system. Discipline rests primarily with faculty.

Tuition and Aid Day student tuition: CAN$16,650; 7-day tuition and room/board: CAN$33,650. Merit scholarship grants available. In 2015–16, 2% of upper-school students received aid; total upper-school merit-scholarship money awarded: CAN$50,000.

Admissions Traditional secondary-level entrance grade is 10. For fall 2015, 299 students applied for upper level admission, 249 were accepted, 219 enrolled. English proficiency required. Deadline for receipt of application materials: none. Application fee required: CAN$300. Interview required.

Athletics Interscholastic: aquatics (boys, girls), baseball (b), basketball (b,g), soccer (b), swimming and diving (b,g), volleyball (b,g); intramural: aquatics (b,g), badminton (b,g), baseball (b,g), basketball (b,g), cheering (g), fitness (b,g), floor hockey (b,g), hiking/backpacking (b,g), ice skating (b,g), indoor soccer (b), martial arts (b), mountain biking (b,g), outdoor activities (b,g), outdoor education (b,g), outdoor recreation (b,g), running (b,g), skiing (downhill) (b,g), snowboarding (b,g), snowshoeing (b,g), soccer (b), swimming and diving (b,g), table tennis (b,g), tennis (b,g), track and field (b,g), triathlon (b), ultimate Frisbee (b), volleyball (b,g), wrestling (b); coed interscholastic: aerobics/dance, aquatics, backpacking, badminton, ball hockey, bicycling, cross-country running, fitness, floor hockey, swimming and diving; coed intramural: aquatics, badminton, bicycling, bowling, canoeing/kayaking, climbing, cross-country running, dance, fishing, fitness, floor hockey, golf, hiking/backpacking, ice skating, indoor hockey, indoor soccer, kayaking, martial arts, mountain biking, outdoor activities, outdoor education, outdoor recreation, physical fitness, rock climbing, running, skiing (downhill), snowboarding, snowshoeing, soccer, strength & conditioning, swimming and diving, table tennis, tennis, track and field, ultimate Frisbee, volleyball, wall climbing, weight training, wilderness, wilderness survival, wrestling, yoga. 3 PE instructors, 5 coaches.

Computers Computers are regularly used in all academic classes. Computer network features include on-campus library services, Internet access, wireless campus network, Internet filtering or blocking technology. Campus intranet and student e-mail accounts are available to students. Students grades are available online. The school has a published electronic and media policy.

Contact Ms. Rachel Wong, Registration Manager. 604-998-1000. Fax: 604-998-1150. E-mail: office@bodwell.edu. Website: www.bodwell.edu

THE BOLLES SCHOOL

7400 San Jose Boulevard
Jacksonville, Florida 32217-3499

Head of School: David J. Farace

General Information Coeducational boarding and day college-preparatory school. Boarding grades 7–PG, day grades PK–PG. Founded: 1933. Setting: suburban. Students are housed in single-sex by floor dormitories. 52-acre campus. 12 buildings on campus. Approved or accredited by Florida Council of Independent Schools, National Independent Private Schools Association, Southern Association of Colleges and Schools, Southern Association of Independent Schools, The Association of Boarding Schools, and Florida Department of Education. Member of National Association of Independent Schools and Secondary School Admission Test Board. Endowment: $15.1 million. Total enrollment: 1,637. Upper school average class size: 17. Upper school faculty-student ratio: 1:12. There are 175 required school days per year for Upper School students. Upper School students typically attend 5 days per week. The average school day consists of 6 hours.

Upper School Student Profile Grade 9: 185 students (103 boys, 82 girls); Grade 10: 190 students (104 boys, 86 girls); Grade 11: 197 students (96 boys, 101 girls); Grade 12: 189 students (93 boys, 96 girls). 10% of students are boarding students. 88% are state residents. 4 states are represented in upper school student body. 22% are international students. International students from Brazil, China, Japan, Mexico, United Kingdom, and United States; 22 other countries represented in student body.

Faculty School total: 158. In upper school: 55 men, 103 women; 84 have advanced degrees; 9 reside on campus.

Subjects Offered 3-dimensional art, 3-dimensional design, acting, advanced chemistry, algebra, American government, American history, American history-AP, American literature, anatomy, art, art history, art history-AP, art-AP, band, biology, biology-AP, calculus, calculus-AP, ceramics, chemistry, chemistry-AP, Chinese, Chinese studies, chorus, comparative government and politics-AP, composition, composition-AP, computer science, contemporary history, dance, data analysis, design, directing, drama, drawing, driver education, ecology, economics, English, environmental science, ESL, European history, fine arts, fitness, French, French language-AP, French-AP, geography, geometry, government/civics, health, history, history-AP, humanities, Japanese, journalism, Latin, Latin-AP, life management skills, life skills, literature, marine science, mathematics, Middle Eastern history, modern European history-AP, multimedia, music, mythology, neurobiology, painting, performing arts, photography, physical education, physics, physics-AP, portfolio art, pre-algebra, pre-calculus, programming, psychology, public speaking, publications, science, sculpture, social sciences, social studies, Spanish, Spanish language-AP, Spanish-AP, speech and debate, statistics, statistics-AP, studio art, theater, U.S. government and politics-AP, U.S. history, U.S. history-AP, visual arts, Web site design, weight training, world cultures, world history, world religions.

Graduation Requirements Arts and fine arts (art, music, dance, drama), English, foreign language, mathematics, physical education (includes health), science, social studies (includes history).

Special Academic Programs International Baccalaureate program; Advanced Placement exam preparation; honors section; independent study; term-away projects; study at local college for college credit; ESL (45 students enrolled).

College Admission Counseling 187 students graduated in 2016; 184 went to college, including Auburn University; Florida Atlantic University; Florida State University; The University of Alabama; University of Florida; University of South Carolina. Other: 2 entered military service, 1 entered a postgraduate year, 1 had other specific plans. 50% scored over 600 on SAT critical reading, 50% scored over 600 on SAT math, 49% scored over 600 on SAT writing, 47% scored over 1800 on combined SAT, 50% scored over 26 on composite ACT.

Student Life Upper grades have specified standards of dress, student council, honor system. Discipline rests equally with students and faculty.

Summer Programs Enrichment, ESL, art/fine arts, computer instruction programs offered; session focuses on Enrichment; held on campus; accepts boys and girls; open to students from other schools. 150 students usually enrolled. 2017 schedule: June 6 to July 22.

Tuition and Aid Day student tuition: $23,870; 7-day tuition and room/board: $48,750. Tuition installment plan (FACTS Tuition Payment Plan). Need-based scholarship grants, faculty tuition remission available. In 2016–17, 21% of upper-school students received aid. Total amount of financial aid awarded in 2016–17: $3,878,650.

Admissions Traditional secondary-level entrance grade is 9. For fall 2016, 485 students applied for upper-level admission, 351 were accepted, 243 enrolled. ISEE required. Deadline for receipt of application materials: none. Application fee required: $45. Interview required.

Athletics Interscholastic: baseball (boys), basketball (b,g), cheering (g), crew (b,g), cross-country running (b,g), dance (b,g), diving (b,g), football (b), golf (b,g), lacrosse (b,g), soccer (b,g), softball (g), swimming and diving (b,g), tennis (b,g), track and field (b,g), volleyball (g), weight lifting (b), wrestling (b). 2 PE instructors, 5 coaches, 1 athletic trainer.

Computers Computers are regularly used in all academic classes. Computer network features include on-campus library services, online commercial services, Internet access, wireless campus network, Internet filtering or blocking technology. Campus intranet, student e-mail accounts, and computer access in designated common areas are

available to students. Students grades are available online. The school has a published electronic and media policy.

Contact Mark I. Frampton, Director of Upper School and Boarding Admission. 904-256-5032. Fax: 904-739-9929. E-mail: framptonm@bolles.org. Website: www.bolles.org

BOSTON TRINITY ACADEMY

17 Hale Street
Boston, Massachusetts 02136

Head of School: Mr. Frank Guerra

General Information Coeducational day college-preparatory school, affiliated with Christian faith. Grades 6–12. Founded: 2002. Setting: urban. 5-acre campus. 1 building on campus. Approved or accredited by Association of Independent Schools in New England, New England Association of Schools and Colleges, and Massachusetts Department of Education. Member of National Association of Independent Schools and Secondary School Admission Test Board. Total enrollment: 233. Upper school average class size: 14. Upper school faculty-student ratio: 1:6. There are 169 required school days per year for Upper School students. Upper School students typically attend 5 days per week. The average school day consists of 6 hours and 30 minutes.

Upper School Student Profile 80% of students are Christian faith.

Faculty School total: 32. In upper school: 10 men, 18 women; 16 have advanced degrees.

Special Academic Programs 12 Advanced Placement exams for which test preparation is offered; ESL.

College Admission Counseling 39 students graduated in 2016; all went to college.

Student Life Upper grades have uniform requirement, student council, honor system. Discipline rests primarily with faculty. Attendance at religious services is required.

Summer Programs Remediation, ESL programs offered; held on campus; accepts boys and girls; open to students from other schools. Application deadline: none.

Tuition and Aid Day student tuition: $17,800. Tuition installment plan (SMART Tuition Payment Plan). Need-based scholarship grants available.

Admissions Traditional secondary-level entrance grade is 9. ISEE or SSAT required. Deadline for receipt of application materials: January 31. Application fee required: $50. Interview recommended.

Athletics Interscholastic: baseball (boys), basketball (b,g), cross-country running (b,g), lacrosse (b,g), soccer (b,g), softball (g), tennis (b,g); intramural: physical fitness (b,g), table tennis (b,g).

Computers Computer network features include on-campus library services, Internet access, wireless campus network, Internet filtering or blocking technology. Campus intranet and computer access in designated common areas are available to students. Students grades are available online. The school has a published electronic and media policy.

Contact Ms. Bisi Oloko, Associate Director of Admission. 617-364-3700. Fax: 617-364-3800. E-mail: boloko@bostontrinity.org. Website: www.bostontrinity.org

BOSTON UNIVERSITY ACADEMY

One University Road
Boston, Massachusetts 02215

Head of School: Dr. Ari M. Betof

General Information Coeducational day college-preparatory school. Grades 9–12. Founded: 1993. Setting: urban. 132-acre campus. 1 building on campus. Approved or accredited by Association of Independent Schools in New England, New England Association of Schools and Colleges, and Massachusetts Department of Education. Member of National Association of Independent Schools and Secondary School Admission Test Board. Total enrollment: 170. Upper school average class size: 12. Upper school faculty-student ratio: 1:9. There are 164 required school days per year for Upper School students. Upper School students typically attend 5 days per week. The average school day consists of 7 hours.

Upper School Student Profile Grade 9: 46 students (22 boys, 24 girls); Grade 10: 43 students (17 boys, 26 girls); Grade 11: 53 students (18 boys, 35 girls); Grade 12: 33 students (16 boys, 17 girls).

Faculty School total: 20. In upper school: 12 men, 8 women; 18 have advanced degrees.

Subjects Offered Advanced math, African American studies, algebra, American history, American literature, Ancient Greek, ancient history, anthropology, Arabic, archaeology, art, art history, astronomy, biochemistry, biology, calculus, chemistry, Chinese, classical studies, college counseling, community service, computer programming, drama, English, English literature, European history, French, geometry, German, Hebrew, history, Italian, Japanese, Latin, music, physical education, physics, robotics, Russian, sculpture, senior project, Spanish, statistics, theater, trigonometry, women's studies, writing.

Graduation Requirements Ancient Greek, arts and fine arts (art, music, dance, drama), chemistry, English, history, Latin, mathematics, physical education (includes health), physics, two-semester senior thesis project, coursework at Boston University. Community service is required.

Special Academic Programs Honors section; accelerated programs; independent study; study at local college for college credit; academic accommodation for the gifted.

College Admission Counseling 43 students graduated in 2016; all went to college, including Boston University; Brown University; Harvard University; Rensselaer Polytechnic Institute; University of California, Berkeley; University of Rochester. Median SAT critical reading: 735, median SAT math: 720, median SAT writing: 730, median combined SAT: 2205. 97.5% scored over 600 on SAT critical reading, 97.5% scored over 600 on SAT math, 97.5% scored over 600 on SAT writing, 97.5% scored over 1800 on combined SAT.

Student Life Upper grades have student council, honor system. Discipline rests equally with students and faculty.

Tuition and Aid Day student tuition: $41,368. Tuition installment plan (Insured Tuition Payment Plan, monthly payment plans, individually arranged payment plans, Tuition Management Systems). Need-based scholarship grants available. In 2016–17, 35% of upper-school students received aid. Total amount of financial aid awarded in 2016–17: $1,514,582.

Admissions Traditional secondary-level entrance grade is 9. For fall 2016, 198 students applied for upper-level admission, 101 were accepted, 53 enrolled. SSAT required. Deadline for receipt of application materials: January 31. Application fee required: $50. On-campus interview recommended.

Athletics Interscholastic: basketball (boys, girls), crew (b,g); intramural: volleyball (g); coed interscholastic: cross-country running, fencing, soccer, tennis, ultimate Frisbee; coed intramural: climbing, dance, sailing, softball. 10 PE instructors, 7 coaches.

Computers Computers are regularly used in art, English, foreign language, history, mathematics, science classes. Computer network features include on-campus library services, online commercial services, Internet access, wireless campus network, Internet filtering or blocking technology, internal electronic bulletin board system. Campus intranet and student e-mail accounts are available to students. Students grades are available online. The school has a published electronic and media policy.

Contact Ms. Tessa Evoy, Admission Associate. 617-358-2493. Fax: 617-353-8999. E-mail: tmsevoy@bu.edu. Website: www.buacademy.org

BOYD-BUCHANAN SCHOOL

4650 Buccaneer Trail
Chattanooga, Tennessee 37411

Head of School: Mrs. Jill Hartness

General Information Coeducational day college-preparatory and religious studies school, affiliated with Church of Christ. Grades PK–12. Founded: 1952. Setting: urban. 50-acre campus. 7 buildings on campus. Approved or accredited by National Christian School Association, Southern Association of Colleges and Schools, Tennessee Association of Independent Schools, and Tennessee Department of Education. Endowment: $3 million. Total enrollment: 868. Upper school average class size: 18. Upper school faculty-student ratio: 1:12. There are 177 required school days per year for Upper School students. Upper School students typically attend 5 days per week. The average school day consists of 6 hours.

Upper School Student Profile 30% of students are members of Church of Christ.

Faculty School total: 74. In upper school: 13 men, 17 women; 18 have advanced degrees.

Subjects Offered ACT preparation, Advanced Placement courses, algebra, American government, American history, American studies, art, band, Bible, biology, biology-AP, calculus, calculus-AP, chemistry, chemistry-AP, choir, choral music, chorus, computer applications, computer programming, concert choir, contemporary issues, contemporary problems, data processing, desktop publishing, ecology, economics, English, English composition, English language-AP, English literature, English literature and composition-AP, fitness, French, French-AP, geometry, government, health and wellness, honors algebra, honors English, honors geometry, integrated arts, jazz band, journalism, library assistant, music appreciation, music theory, physical science, physics, pre-algebra, pre-calculus, probability and statistics, psychology, SAT/ACT preparation, sociology, Spanish, Spanish-AP, theater arts, trigonometry, U.S. history, U.S. history-AP, Web site design, wellness, world geography, world history, yearbook.

Graduation Requirements Arts and fine arts (art, music, dance, drama), Bible, electives, English, foreign language, health and wellness, mathematics, physical education (includes health), physics, science, social sciences.

Special Academic Programs 11 Advanced Placement exams for which test preparation is offered; honors section.

College Admission Counseling 95 students graduated in 2015; all went to college, including Chattanooga State Community College; Lipscomb University; Middle Tennessee State University; Tennessee Technological University; The University of Tennessee; The University of Tennessee at Chattanooga.

Student Life Upper grades have uniform requirement, student council, honor system. Discipline rests primarily with faculty. Attendance at religious services is required.

Tuition and Aid Day student tuition: $7480–$10,090. Tuition installment plan (FACTS Tuition Payment Plan, Tuition Bank). Tuition reduction for siblings, need-based scholarship grants, paying campus jobs available. In 2015–16, 4% of upper-school students received aid. Total amount of financial aid awarded in 2015–16: $80,000.

Admissions Traditional secondary-level entrance grade is 9. ISEE required. Deadline for receipt of application materials: none. Application fee required: $50. Interview required.

Athletics Interscholastic: baseball (boys), basketball (b,g), cheering (g), cross-country running (b,g), football (b), golf (b,g), soccer (b,g), softball (g), swimming and diving (b,g), tennis (b,g), volleyball (g), wrestling (b); coed interscholastic: archery. 3 PE instructors, 18 coaches, 1 athletic trainer.

Computers Computers are regularly used in creative writing, data processing, desktop publishing, journalism, keyboarding, newspaper, programming, study skills, technology, Web site design, word processing, writing, yearbook classes. Computer network features include on-campus library services, online commercial services, Internet access, wireless campus network, Internet filtering or blocking technology. Campus intranet, student e-mail accounts, and computer access in designated common areas are available to students. Students grades are available online. The school has a published electronic and media policy.

Contact Mrs. Heather Wamack, Secondary Admissions Director. 423-629-7610 Ext. 249. Fax: 423-508-2218. E-mail: hwamack@bbschool.org.
Website: www.bbschool.org

BRADENTON CHRISTIAN SCHOOL

3304 43rd Street West
Bradenton, Florida 34209
Head of School: Mr. Dan Vande Pol

General Information Coeducational day college-preparatory and religious studies school, affiliated with Christian faith. Grades PK–12. Distance learning grades 9–12. Founded: 1960. Setting: suburban. Nearest major city is Tampa. 24-acre campus. 6 buildings on campus. Approved or accredited by Christian Schools International, Christian Schools of Florida, Middle States Association of Colleges and Schools, and Florida Department of Education. Member of National Association of Independent Schools. Endowment: $600,000. Total enrollment: 542. Upper school average class size: 18. Upper school faculty-student ratio: 1:11. There are 180 required school days per year for Upper School students. Upper School students typically attend 5 days per week. The average school day consists of 7 hours.

Upper School Student Profile 100% of students are Christian.

Faculty School total: 22. In upper school: 11 men, 11 women; 16 have advanced degrees.

Subjects Offered 3-dimensional art, ACT preparation, advanced biology, advanced math, Advanced Placement courses, algebra, American government, American history, American history-AP, American literature, anatomy, anatomy and physiology, art, band, Bible, biology, biology-AP, British literature, British literature (honors), calculus, calculus AP, career/college preparation, ceramics, choir, Christian ethics, civics, college admission preparation, computer applications, economics, English literature-AP, European history, geography, geometry, government-AP, health and wellness, journalism, marine science, orchestra, painting, physical fitness, physics, political science, pre-calculus, psychology-AP, religious studies, SAT/ACT preparation, Spanish, Spanish-AP, speech, statistics, U.S. government, weight training, world history-AP, yearbook.

Graduation Requirements American history, arts and fine arts (art, music, dance, drama), computer skills, English, foreign language, health and wellness, mathematics, New Testament, physical education (includes health), religion (includes Bible studies and theology), science, world history, 3 1/2 credits of Bible, 2 years of consecutive foreign language, 1 year of fine arts, 1 year of PE/health.

Special Academic Programs Advanced Placement exam preparation; honors section; study at local college for college credit.

College Admission Counseling 43 students graduated in 2016; all went to college, including Florida State University; University of Florida; University of South Florida. Mean combined SAT: 1530, mean composite ACT: 23. 20% scored over 600 on SAT critical reading, 20% scored over 600 on SAT math, 20% scored over 600 on SAT writing, 20% scored over 1800 on combined SAT, 15% scored over 26 on composite ACT.

Student Life Upper grades have uniform requirement, student council, honor system. Discipline rests primarily with faculty. Attendance at religious services is required.

Tuition and Aid Day student tuition: $11,200. Tuition installment plan (FACTS Tuition Payment Plan, monthly payment plans, individually arranged payment plans). Tuition reduction for siblings, need-based scholarship grants available. In 2016–17, 25% of upper-school students received aid.

Admissions Traditional secondary-level entrance grade is 9. For fall 2016, 70 students applied for upper-level admission, 41 were accepted, 41 enrolled. Academic Profile Tests or Woodcock-Johnson required. Deadline for receipt of application materials: none. Application fee required: $200. On-campus interview recommended.

Athletics Interscholastic: aquatics (boys, girls), baseball (b), basketball (b,g), cheering (g), cross-country running (b,g), football (b), golf (b,g), sand volleyball (g), soccer (b,g), softball (g), swimming and diving (g), tennis (b,g), track and field (b,g), volleyball (g), wrestling (b); intramural: dance (g), flag football (b), touch football (b); coed interscholastic: physical fitness; coed intramural: kickball. 4 PE instructors, 25 coaches.

Computers Computers are regularly used in art, Bible studies, business, business applications, business skills, career exploration, Christian doctrine, creative writing, design, desktop publishing, ESL, drawing and design, economics, English, ethics, foreign language classes. Computer network features include on-campus library services, Internet access, wireless campus network, Internet filtering or blocking technology, one to one chrome books in middle school, laptop carts. Student e-mail accounts and computer access in designated common areas are available to students. Students grades are available online. The school has a published electronic and media policy.

Contact Darcy Leahy, Director of Admissions. 941-792-5454 Ext. 150. Fax: 941-795-7190. E-mail: dleahy@bcspanthers.org. Website: www.bcspanthers.org

BRANDON HALL SCHOOL

Atlanta, Georgia
See Special Needs Schools section.

BRANKSOME HALL

10 Elm Avenue
Toronto, Ontario M4W 1N4, Canada
Head of School: Ms. Karen L. Jurjevich

General Information Girls' boarding and day college-preparatory and International Baccalaureate school. Boarding grades 7–12, day grades JK–12. Founded: 1903. Setting: urban. Students are housed in single-sex dormitories. 13-acre campus. 6 buildings on campus. Approved or accredited by Canadian Association of Independent Schools, Canadian Educational Standards Institute, International Baccalaureate Organization, Ontario Ministry of Education, The Association of Boarding Schools, and Ontario Department of Education. Affiliate member of National Association of Independent Schools; member of Secondary School Admission Test Board. Language of instruction: English. Endowment: CAN$20 million. Total enrollment: 895. Upper school average class size: 20. Upper school faculty-student ratio: 1:9. There are 180 required school days per year for Upper School students. Upper School students typically attend 5 days per week. The average school day consists of 8 hours.

Upper School Student Profile Grade 9: 113 students (113 girls); Grade 10: 117 students (117 girls); Grade 11: 116 students (116 girls); Grade 12: 111 students (111 girls). 12% of students are boarding students. 87% are province residents. 8 provinces are represented in upper school student body. 13% are international students. International students from China, Germany, United Kingdom, and United States; 13 other countries represented in student body.

Faculty School total: 130. In upper school: 14 men, 81 women; 25 have advanced degrees; 6 reside on campus.

Subjects Offered Cantonese.

Graduation Requirements Arts and fine arts (art, music, dance, drama), business skills (includes word processing), English, International Baccalaureate courses, language, mathematics, physical education (includes health), science, social sciences, social studies (includes history), International Baccalaureate diploma or certificate requirements.

Special Academic Programs International Baccalaureate program; honors section; academic accommodation for the gifted, the musically talented, and the artistically talented; ESL (38 students enrolled).

College Admission Counseling 111 students graduated in 2016; all went to college, including McGill University; McMaster University; Queen's University at Kingston; The University of Western Ontario; University of Toronto; University of Waterloo. Mean SAT critical reading: 616, mean SAT math: 662, mean SAT writing: 638, mean combined SAT: 1916, mean composite ACT: 29.

Student Life Upper grades have uniform requirement, student council, honor system. Discipline rests primarily with faculty.

Tuition and Aid Day student tuition: CAN$33,125; 7-day tuition and room/board: CAN$59,630. Tuition installment plan (Insured Tuition Payment Plan, monthly payment plans, tri-annual payment, early payment option ($500 savings)). Bursaries, merit scholarship grants available. In 2016–17, 8% of upper-school students received aid; total upper-school merit-scholarship money awarded: CAN$192,500. Total amount of financial aid awarded in 2016–17: CAN$600,000.

Admissions Traditional secondary-level entrance grade is 9. For fall 2016, 251 students applied for upper-level admission, 74 were accepted, 56 enrolled. English entrance exam, Math Placement Exam or SSAT required. Deadline for receipt of application materials: December 4. Application fee required: CAN$210. Interview recommended.

Athletics Interscholastic: alpine skiing, aquatics, badminton, baseball, basketball, crew, cross-country running, dance, dance team, field hockey, golf, hockey, ice hockey, indoor track, indoor track & field, nordic skiing, rowing, skiing (downhill), soccer, softball, swimming and diving, synchronized swimming, tennis, track and field, volleyball; intramural: aerobics, aerobics/dance, aquatics, badminton, ball hockey, ballet, basketball, climbing, cooperative games, cross-country running, dance, dance squad, fitness, fitness walking, floor hockey, Frisbee, gymnastics, jogging, modern dance, nordic skiing, outdoor activities, paddle tennis, physical fitness, physical training, rock climbing, rugby, soccer, softball, squash, strength & conditioning, swimming and diving, table tennis, tennis, track and field, triathlon, volleyball, yoga. 6 PE instructors, 2 coaches, 1 athletic trainer.

Computers Computers are regularly used in all academic classes. Computer network features include on-campus library services, Internet access, wireless campus network, Internet filtering or blocking technology. Campus intranet, student e-mail accounts, and computer access in designated common areas are available to students. The school has a published electronic and media policy.

Contact Kimberly Carter, Director of Enrolment Management. 416-920-6265 Ext. 268. Fax: 416-920-5390. E-mail: admissions@branksome.on.ca. Website: www.branksome.on.ca

BRECK SCHOOL

123 Ottawa Avenue North
Golden Valley, Minnesota 55422

Head of School: Edward Kim

General Information Coeducational day college-preparatory, arts, religious studies, and service school, affiliated with Episcopal Church. Grades PK–12. Founded: 1886. Setting: suburban. Nearest major city is Minneapolis. 53-acre campus. 1 building on campus. Approved or accredited by Independent Schools Association of the Central States. Member of National Association of Independent Schools and Secondary School Admission Test Board. Total enrollment: 1,185. Upper school average class size: 16. Upper school faculty-student ratio: 1:16. The average school day consists of 6 hours and 15 minutes.

Upper School Student Profile 10% of students are members of Episcopal Church.

Faculty School total: 145. In upper school: 12 men, 17 women; 22 have advanced degrees.

Subjects Offered Algebra, American history, American literature, art, astronomy, biology, calculus, ceramics, chemistry, Chinese, chorus, community service, computer math, computer programming, creative writing, dance, drama, ecology, economics, English, English literature, environmental science, ethics, European history, expository writing, fine arts, French, geometry, health, history, mathematics, music, orchestra, physical education, physics, religion, science, social studies, Spanish, statistics, theater, theology, trigonometry, world history, world literature, writing.

Graduation Requirements Arts and fine arts (art, music, dance, drama), English, foreign language, mathematics, physical education (includes health), religion (includes Bible studies and theology), science, social studies (includes history), senior speech, May Program, service. Community service is required.

Special Academic Programs Advanced Placement exam preparation; honors section; independent study; term-away projects; academic accommodation for the gifted, the musically talented, and the artistically talented.

College Admission Counseling 106 students graduated in 2015; 105 went to college, including Bowdoin College; Carleton College; Colgate University; Pepperdine University; Washington University in St. Louis; Williams College. Median SAT critical reading: 640, median SAT math: 640, median SAT writing: 650, median combined SAT: 1910, median composite ACT: 29. 64% scored over 600 on SAT critical reading, 67% scored over 600 on SAT math, 67% scored over 600 on SAT writing, 67% scored over 1800 on combined SAT, 70% scored over 26 on composite ACT.

Student Life Upper grades have specified standards of dress, student council, honor system. Discipline rests equally with students and faculty. Attendance at religious services is required.

Tuition and Aid Day student tuition: $27,995. Tuition installment plan (Key Tuition Payment Plan). Need-based scholarship grants available. In 2015–16, 23% of upper-school students received aid.

Admissions Traditional secondary-level entrance grade is 9. CTP III required. Deadline for receipt of application materials: February 1. Application fee required: $75. On-campus interview required.

Athletics Interscholastic: alpine skiing (boys, girls), baseball (b), basketball (b,g), cross-country running (b,g), diving (b,g), football (b), golf (b,g), gymnastics (g), ice hockey (b,g), lacrosse (b,g), nordic skiing (b,g), skiing (cross-country) (b,g), skiing (downhill) (b,g), soccer (b,g), softball (g), swimming and diving (b,g), tennis (b,g), track and field (b,g), volleyball (g). 6 PE instructors, 82 coaches, 1 athletic trainer.

Computers Computers are regularly used in all classes. Computer network features include on-campus library services, online commercial services, Internet access, wireless campus network, Internet filtering or blocking technology, multimedia imaging, video presentation, student laptop program. Campus intranet and student e-mail accounts are available to students. Students grades are available online. The school has a published electronic and media policy.

Contact Scott D. Wade, Director of Admissions. 763-381-8200. Fax: 763-381-8288. E-mail: scott.wade@breckschool.org. Website: www.breckschool.org

BREHM PREPARATORY SCHOOL

Carbondale, Illinois
See Special Needs Schools section.

BRENTWOOD COLLEGE SCHOOL

2735 Mount Baker Road
Mill Bay, British Columbia V0R 2P1, Canada

Head of School: Mr. Bud Patel

General Information Coeducational boarding and day college-preparatory, arts, and athletics, leadership, and citizenship school school. Grades 9–12. Founded: 1923. Setting: small town. Nearest major city is Victoria, Canada. Students are housed in single-sex dormitories. 77-acre campus. 16 buildings on campus. Approved or accredited by California Association of Independent Schools, Western Boarding Schools Association, and British Columbia Department of Education. Affiliate member of National Association of Independent Schools. Language of instruction: English. Endowment: CAN$10 million. Total enrollment: 510. Upper school average class size: 16. Upper school faculty-student ratio: 1:11. Upper School students typically attend 6 days per week. The average school day consists of 6 hours.

Upper School Student Profile Grade 9: 73 students (37 boys, 36 girls); Grade 10: 142 students (77 boys, 65 girls); Grade 11: 148 students (60 boys, 88 girls); Grade 12: 147 students (79 boys, 68 girls). 81% of students are boarding students. 58% are province residents. 20 provinces are represented in upper school student body. 27% are international students. International students from Ghana, Hungary, Micronesia, Republic of Moldova, Senegal, and United States Minor Outlying Islands; 21 other countries represented in student body.

Faculty School total: 50. In upper school: 28 men, 22 women; 39 have advanced degrees; 30 reside on campus.

Subjects Offered Advanced Placement courses, algebra, art history-AP, athletics, audio visual/media, band, basketball, biology, biology-AP, business, calculus, calculus-AP, Canadian geography, Canadian history, Canadian law, career and personal planning, ceramics, chemistry, chemistry-AP, choir, choreography, computer graphics, computer science, dance, dance performance, debate, design, drafting, drama, dramatic arts, drawing, economics, economics-AP, English, English literature, English literature-AP, French, French language-AP, geography, geometry, golf, government and politics-AP, health and wellness, history, human geography - AP, information technology, instrumental music, international studies, jazz band, jazz ensemble, marketing, mathematics, musical productions, musical theater, orchestra, outdoor education, painting, photography, physics, physics-AP, pottery, psychology, psychology-AP, public speaking, science, sculpture, sex education, social studies, Spanish, Spanish-AP, stagecraft, technical theater, tennis, theater design and production, video film production, visual and performing arts, vocal jazz, volleyball, yearbook.

Graduation Requirements Arts and fine arts (art, music, dance, drama), career and personal planning, English, foreign language, mathematics, physical education (includes health), science, social studies (includes history).

Special Academic Programs Advanced Placement exam preparation.

College Admission Counseling 112 students graduated in 2016; all went to college, including Duke University; McGill University; Queen's University at Kingston; The University of British Columbia; University of California, Berkeley; University of California, Los Angeles.

Student Life Upper grades have uniform requirement, student council, honor system. Discipline rests primarily with faculty.

Summer Programs Sports programs offered; session focuses on athletics and arts; held on campus; accepts boys and girls; open to students from other schools. 30 students usually enrolled. 2017 schedule: July to July. Application deadline: July.

Tuition and Aid Day student tuition: CAN$24,500; 5-day tuition and room/board: CAN$46,900; 7-day tuition and room/board: CAN$45,900–CAN$62,900. Tuition installment plan (The Tuition Plan). Tuition reduction for siblings available. In 2016–17, 20% of upper-school students received aid.

Admissions Traditional secondary-level entrance grade is 9. Traditional secondary-level entrance age is 13. Henmon-Nelson or SSAT required. Deadline for receipt of application materials: none. Application fee required: CAN$2500. Interview required.

Athletics Interscholastic: basketball (boys, girls), crew (b,g), cross-country running (b,g), field hockey (g), hockey (g), rowing (b,g), rugby (b,g), running (b,g), soccer (b,g), squash (b,g), tennis (b,g), volleyball (g), yoga (g); intramural: crew (b,g), cross-country running (b,g), field hockey (g), indoor hockey (g), soccer (b,g), squash (b,g), tennis (b,g), track and field (b,g), volleyball (g), weight training (g); coed interscholastic: badminton, ballet, canoeing/kayaking, fitness, golf, ice hockey, judo, kayaking, modern dance, ocean paddling, outdoor activities, rock climbing, sailing; coed intramural: aerobics, aerobics/dance, badminton, canoeing/kayaking, cooperative games, dance, fitness, floor hockey, hiking/backpacking, indoor soccer, kayaking, outdoor activities, physical fitness, physical training, rowing, rugby, running, skiing (downhill), snowboarding, strength & conditioning, table tennis, touch football, weight lifting, weight training. 6 PE instructors, 36 coaches.

Computers Computers are regularly used in photojournalism, video film production classes. Computer network features include on-campus library services, Internet access, wireless campus network, Internet filtering or blocking technology. Campus intranet and student e-mail accounts are available to students. The school has a published electronic and media policy.

Contact Mr. Clayton Johnston, Director of Admissions. 250-743-5521. Fax: 250-743-2911. E-mail: admissions@brentwood.bc.ca. Website: www.brentwood.bc.ca

BRENTWOOD SCHOOL

100 South Barrington Place
Los Angeles, California 90049

Head of School: Dr. Michael Riera

General Information Coeducational day college-preparatory school. Grades K–12. Founded: 1972. Setting: suburban. 30-acre campus. 12 buildings on campus. Approved or accredited by California Association of Independent Schools, Northwest Association of Independent Schools, Western Association of Schools and Colleges, and Western Catholic Education Association. Member of National Association of Independent Schools and Secondary School Admission Test Board. Endowment: $13 million. Total enrollment: 995. Upper school average class size: 17. Upper school faculty-student ratio: 1:8. There are 170 required school days per year for Upper School students. Upper School students typically attend 5 days per week. The average school day consists of 8 hours.

Upper School Student Profile Grade 9: 126 students (65 boys, 61 girls); Grade 10: 122 students (63 boys, 59 girls); Grade 11: 115 students (63 boys, 52 girls); Grade 12: 103 students (52 boys, 51 girls).

Faculty School total: 130. In upper school: 45 men, 49 women; 60 have advanced degrees.

Subjects Offered Acting, Advanced Placement courses, advanced studio art-AP, algebra, American history, American literature, Ancient Greek, anthropology, art, art history, art history-AP, art-AP, astronomy, biology, biology-AP, calculus, calculus-AP, ceramics, chemistry, chemistry-AP, Chinese, choir, choral music, chorus, community service, comparative government and politics-AP, computer programming, computer programming-AP, computer science, computer science-AP, concert choir, creative writing, dance, digital photography, directing, drama, drawing, ecology, economics, economics-AP, English, English literature, environmental science-AP, European history, filmmaking, fine arts, French, French-AP, geometry, global studies, government and politics-AP, government-AP, history, honors algebra, honors English, honors geometry, human development, human geography - AP, Japanese, jazz band, jazz dance, journalism, language-AP, Latin, Latin-AP, literature-AP, math analysis, mathematics, music, music theater, music theory-AP, orchestra, organic chemistry, philosophy, photography, physical education, physics, physics-AP, probability and statistics, robotics, science, senior seminar, senior thesis, social sciences, social studies, Spanish, Spanish-AP, speech, speech and debate, stagecraft, stained glass, statistics AP, studio art-AP, theater, U.S. government and politics-AP, U.S. history-AP, video, word processing, world history, world literature.

Graduation Requirements Arts and fine arts (art, music, dance, drama), English, foreign language, mathematics, physical education (includes health), science, social sciences, social studies (includes history). Community service is required.

Special Academic Programs 26 Advanced Placement exams for which test preparation is offered; honors section; independent study; study at local college for college credit; academic accommodation for the gifted and the artistically talented.

College Admission Counseling 103 students graduated in 2015; all went to college, including New York University; Northwestern University; University of Michigan; University of Pennsylvania; University of Southern California; Yale University. Mean SAT critical reading: 660, mean SAT math: 660, mean SAT writing: 683, mean combined SAT: 2003, mean composite ACT: 31.

Student Life Upper grades have specified standards of dress, student council, honor system. Discipline rests primarily with faculty.

Tuition and Aid Day student tuition: $37,725. Tuition installment plan (Insured Tuition Payment Plan, monthly payment plans, individually arranged payment plans). Need-based scholarship grants available. In 2015–16, 15% of upper school students received aid. Total amount of financial aid awarded in 2015–16: $3,500,000.

Admissions Traditional secondary-level entrance grade is 9. For fall 2015, 200 students applied for upper-level admission, 12 were accepted, 8 enrolled. ISEE required. Deadline for receipt of application materials: January 11. Application fee required: $125. Interview required.

Athletics Interscholastic: baseball (boys), basketball (b,g), cheering (g), cross-country running (b,g), dance squad (g), dance team (g), football (b), independent competitive sports (b,g), lacrosse (b,g), soccer (b,g), softball (g), swimming and diving (b,g), tennis (b,g), track and field (b,g), volleyball (b,g), water polo (b), wrestling (b); intramural: modern dance (g), ultimate Frisbee (b); coed interscholastic: dance, drill team, equestrian sports, fencing, football, golf, swimming and diving, water polo; coed intramural: fitness, Frisbee, jogging, mountain biking, outdoor activities, physical fitness, physical training, running, sailing, surfing, table tennis, ultimate Frisbee, weight lifting, weight training, wilderness, yoga. 6 PE instructors, 40 coaches, 2 athletic trainers.

Computers Computers are regularly used in college planning, computer applications, desktop publishing, digital applications, foreign language, graphic design, introduction to technology, journalism, literary magazine, mathematics, media arts, media production, photojournalism, programming, publications, research skills, science, technical drawing, technology, video film production, Web site design classes. Computer network features include on-campus library services, online commercial services, Internet access, wireless campus network, Internet filtering or blocking technology, Schoology (learning management system). Campus intranet, student e-mail accounts, and computer access in designated common areas are available to students. Students grades are available online. The school has a published electronic and media policy.

Contact Ms. Melissa Gruenthal, Admissions Administrative Assistant. 310-889-2657. Fax: 310-476-4087. E-mail: mgruenthal@bwscampus.com. Website: www.bwscampus.com

BRETHREN CHRISTIAN JUNIOR AND SENIOR HIGH SCHOOLS

21141 Strathmoor Lane
Huntington Beach, California 92646

Head of School: Mr. Rick Niswonger

General Information Coeducational day college-preparatory and arts school, affiliated with Fellowship of Grace Brethren Churches, Evangelical/Fundamental faith. Grades 6–12. Founded: 1947. Setting: suburban. 15-acre campus. 1 building on campus. Approved or accredited by Association of Christian Schools International, Western Association of Schools and Colleges, and California Department of Education. Endowment: $250,000. Total enrollment: 313. Upper school average class size: 19. Upper school faculty-student ratio: 1:13. There are 175 required school days per year for Upper School students. Upper School students typically attend 5 days per week. The average school day consists of 6 hours and 35 minutes.

Upper School Student Profile Grade 9: 44 students (33 boys, 11 girls); Grade 10: 70 students (34 boys, 36 girls); Grade 11: 59 students (34 boys, 25 girls); Grade 12: 71 students (39 boys, 32 girls). 80% of students are Fellowship of Grace Brethren Churches, Evangelical/Fundamental faith.

Faculty School total: 25. In upper school: 8 men, 17 women; 8 have advanced degrees.

Subjects Offered Algebra, American government, American literature, anatomy and physiology, art, art-AP, ASB Leadership, athletics, band, baseball, basketball, Bible, biology, biology-AP, British literature, British literature (honors), calculus-AP, cheerleading, chemistry, Christian ethics, comedy, comparative government and politics-AP, computer science, computer science-AP, concert band, concert choir, creative writing, drama, drama performance, drama workshop, economics, English literature, English literature and composition-AP, fitness, golf, government, jazz band, keyboarding, math analysis, physical education, physics, pre-algebra, Spanish, studio art, theater, U.S. history, U.S. history-AP, volleyball, weightlifting, world history-AP.

Graduation Requirements Algebra, American government, American history, American literature, arts and fine arts (art, music, dance, drama), Bible, biology, chemistry, computer applications, computer literacy, economics, English, English composition, English literature, geography, geometry, government, health education, mathematics, physical education (includes health), physics, science, social studies (includes history), technology, U.S. government, U.S. history, world history, geography and current issues grade 9, Bible class each year.

Special Academic Programs 6 Advanced Placement exams for which test preparation is offered; honors section; academic accommodation for the gifted; remedial reading and/or remedial writing; remedial math; special instructional classes for deaf students, blind students.

College Admission Counseling 46 students graduated in 2016; 39 went to college, including Azusa Pacific University; Chapman University; Orange Coast College; San Francisco State University; University of California, Irvine; University of California, San Diego. Other: 5 went to work, 2 had other specific plans. Mean SAT critical reading: 546, mean SAT math: 557, mean SAT writing: 535. 34% scored over 600 on SAT critical reading, 38% scored over 600 on SAT math, 34% scored over 600 on SAT writing.

Student Life Upper grades have specified standards of dress, student council, honor system. Discipline rests primarily with faculty. Attendance at religious services is required.

Summer Programs Remediation, advancement, sports, computer instruction programs offered; session focuses on remediation and advancement; held on campus; accepts boys and girls; not open to students from other schools. 25 students usually enrolled. 2017 schedule: June 18 to August 5. Application deadline: June 1.

Tuition and Aid Tuition installment plan (monthly payment plans, individually arranged payment plans, pre-payment discount). Merit scholarship grants, need-based scholarship grants available. In 2016–17, 35% of upper-school students received aid; total upper-school merit-scholarship money awarded: $2000. Total amount of financial aid awarded in 2016–17: $7500.

Admissions Traditional secondary-level entrance grade is 9. For fall 2016, 68 students applied for upper-level admission, 63 were accepted, 62 enrolled. Achievement tests, English proficiency, Math Placement Exam or TOEFL Junior required. Deadline for receipt of application materials: none. Application fee required: $395. On-campus interview recommended.

Athletics Interscholastic: baseball (boys), basketball (b,g), cheering (g), football (b), golf (b), physical fitness (g), soccer (b,g), softball (g), volleyball (b,g); coed interscholastic: cross-country running, dance, track and field. 2 PE instructors, 12 coaches, 1 athletic trainer.

Computers Computers are regularly used in computer applications, geography, keyboarding, media production, social studies, yearbook classes. Computer network features include Internet access, wireless campus network, Internet filtering or blocking technology, computers available in Library and computer lab. Campus intranet, student e-mail accounts, and computer access in designated common areas are available to students. Students grades are available online. The school has a published electronic and media policy.

Contact Mrs. June Helton, Records Secretary. 714-962-6617 Ext. 14. Fax: 714-962-3171. E-mail: jhelton@bchs.net. Website: www.bchs.net

BRIARCREST CHRISTIAN HIGH SCHOOL

76 S. Houston Levee Road
Eads, Tennessee 38028

Head of School: Mr. Eric Sullivan

General Information Coeducational day college-preparatory, arts, religious studies, and technology school, affiliated with Christian faith. Grades 9–12. Founded: 1973. Setting: suburban. Nearest major city is Memphis. 100-acre campus. 1 building on campus. Approved or accredited by Southern Association of Colleges and Schools and Southern Association of Independent Schools. Member of National Association of Independent Schools. Total enrollment: 1,657. Upper school average class size: 18. Upper school faculty-student ratio: 1:12. There are 176 required school days per year for Upper School students. Upper School students typically attend 5 days per week. The average school day consists of 7 hours.

Upper School Student Profile Grade 9: 137 students (53 boys, 84 girls); Grade 10: 153 students (69 boys, 84 girls); Grade 11: 154 students (78 boys, 76 girls); Grade 12: 129 students (69 boys, 60 girls). 92% of students are Christian faith.

Faculty School total: 43. In upper school: 18 men, 25 women; 30 have advanced degrees.

Subjects Offered ACT preparation, acting, Advanced Placement courses, algebra, American government, American history, American literature, anatomy, anatomy and physiology, art, band, Bible studies, biology, biology-AP, business, calculus, calculus-AP, chemistry, chemistry-AP, choir, chorus, Christianity, communication arts, computer applications, computer math, computer programming, computer science, creative writing, drama, driver education, English, English literature, entrepreneurship, environmental science, European history, European history-AP, expository writing, French, geography, geometry, government/civics, grammar, health, history, human geography - AP, journalism, Latin, Latin-AP, marketing, mathematics, media studies, microeconomics, music, music appreciation, music theory-AP, personal finance, physical education, physics, physiology, pre-calculus, psychology, religion, science, social sciences, social studies, sociology, Spanish, speech, sports conditioning, statistics, statistics-AP, studio art, studio art-AP, symphonic band, theater, theater arts, theater production, trigonometry, typing, U.S. government, U.S. government and politics-AP, U.S. history, U.S. history-AP, weightlifting, wellness, wind ensemble, world civilizations, world geography, world history, writing.

Graduation Requirements Arts and fine arts (art, music, dance, drama), English, foreign language, mathematics, physical education (includes health), religion (includes Bible studies and theology), science, social sciences, social studies (includes history).

Special Academic Programs Advanced Placement exam preparation; honors section; study at local college for college credit; academic accommodation for the gifted, the musically talented, and the artistically talented; remedial reading and/or remedial writing; remedial math; programs in English, mathematics, general development for dyslexic students.

College Admission Counseling 134 students graduated in 2016; 132 went to college, including Mississippi State University; The University of Tennessee; Union University; University of Arkansas; University of Memphis; University of Mississippi. Other: 2 had other specific plans. Median composite ACT: 26. 53% scored over 26 on composite ACT.

Student Life Upper grades have uniform requirement, student council, honor system. Discipline rests primarily with faculty. Attendance at religious services is required.

Tuition and Aid Day student tuition: $14,695. Tuition installment plan (Insured Tuition Payment Plan, SMART Tuition Payment Plan, monthly payment plans, individually arranged payment plans, 2-payment plan). Tuition reduction for siblings, need-based tuition assistance available. In 2016–17, 16% of upper-school students received aid.

Admissions Traditional secondary-level entrance grade is 9. ISEE required. Deadline for receipt of application materials: none. Application fee required: $50. On-campus interview required.

Athletics Interscholastic: baseball (boys), basketball (b,g), cheering (g), cross-country running (b,g), drill team (g), football (b), golf (b,g), lacrosse (b,g), soccer (b,g), softball (g), strength & conditioning (b), swimming and diving (b,g), tennis (b,g), track and field (b,g), trap and skeet (b,g), volleyball (g), weight lifting (b), wrestling (b); coed interscholastic: bowling, cross-country running, swimming and diving. 2 PE instructors.

Computers Computers are regularly used in all classes. Computer network features include on-campus library services, Internet access, wireless campus network, Internet filtering or blocking technology. Campus intranet, student e-mail accounts, and computer access in designated common areas are available to students. Students grades are available online. The school has a published electronic and media policy.

Contact Mrs. Claire Foster, Admissions Coordinator. 901-765-4605. Fax: 901-765-4667. E-mail: cofoster@briarcrest.com. Website: www.briarcrest.com

BRIARWOOD CHRISTIAN HIGH SCHOOL

6255 Cahaba Valley Road
Birmingham, Alabama 35242

Head of School: Dr. Barrett L. Mosbacker

General Information Coeducational day college-preparatory school, affiliated with Presbyterian Church in America. Grades K4–12. Distance learning grades 9–12. Founded: 1964. Setting: suburban. 85-acre campus. 6 buildings on campus. Approved or accredited by Association of Christian Schools International, Southern Association of Colleges and Schools, and Alabama Department of Education. Member of National Association of Independent Schools. Endowment: $500,000. Total enrollment: 1,912. Upper school average class size: 22. Upper school faculty-student ratio: 1:16. There are 177 required school days per year for Upper School students. Upper School students typically attend 5 days per week. The average school day consists of 6 hours and 10 minutes.

Upper School Student Profile Grade 6: 144 students (75 boys, 69 girls); Grade 7: 147 students (70 boys, 77 girls); Grade 8: 144 students (79 boys, 65 girls); Grade 9: 144 students (76 boys, 68 girls); Grade 10: 138 students (76 boys, 62 girls); Grade 11: 150 students (81 boys, 69 girls); Grade 12: 132 students (67 boys, 65 girls). 40% of students are Presbyterian Church in America.

Faculty School total: 125. In upper school: 32 men, 25 women; 35 have advanced degrees.

Subjects Offered Accounting, ACT preparation, advanced biology, advanced chemistry, Advanced Placement courses, algebra, American history, American literature, art, band, Bible as literature, Bible studies, biology, calculus, calculus-AP, chemistry, chemistry-AP, community service, computer science, concert band, creative writing, debate, drama, driver education, economics, electives, English, English literature, ethics, European history, film history, French, geometry, government, grammar, health, history, history-AP, Latin, Mandarin, mathematics, mentorship program, music, musical productions, philosophy, photo shop, physical education, physical fitness, physics, psychology, religion, robotics, SAT/ACT preparation, science, social sciences, social studies, Spanish, speech, trigonometry, video film production, weight training, world history, world literature.

Graduation Requirements 20th century history, business skills (includes word processing), computer science, English, foreign language, mathematics, physical education (includes health), religion (includes Bible studies and theology), science, social sciences, social studies (includes history). Community service is required.

Special Academic Programs Advanced Placement exam preparation; honors section; study at local college for college credit; academic accommodation for the gifted; special instructional classes for students with learning disabilities, students with Attention Deficit Disorder.

College Admission Counseling 135 students graduated in 2016; 134 went to college, including Auburn University; Mississippi State University; Samford University; The University of Alabama; Troy University; University of Mississippi. Other: 1 went to work, 3 entered military service. Mean combined SAT: 1187, mean composite ACT: 27.

Student Life Upper grades have specified standards of dress, student council. Discipline rests primarily with faculty. Attendance at religious services is required.

Summer Programs Remediation, advancement programs offered; session focuses on social studies and mathematics; held on campus; accepts boys and girls; not open to students from other schools. 50 students usually enrolled. 2017 schedule: June 12 to July 28. Application deadline: March 1.

Tuition and Aid Day student tuition: $8025. Tuition installment plan (monthly payment plans). Tuition reduction for siblings, need-based scholarship grants available. In 2016–17, 10% of upper-school students received aid. Total amount of financial aid awarded in 2016–17: $30,000.

Admissions Traditional secondary-level entrance grade is 9. For fall 2016, 72 students applied for upper-level admission, 43 were accepted, 40 enrolled. Admissions testing required. Deadline for receipt of application materials: none. Application fee required: $95. On-campus interview recommended.

Athletics Interscholastic: baseball (boys), basketball (b,g), cheering (g), cross-country running (b,g), dance team (g), fishing (b), football (b), golf (b,g), indoor track (b,g), indoor track & field (b,g), outdoor activities (b,g), physical fitness (b,g), soccer (b,g), softball (g), strength & conditioning (b), swimming and diving (b,g), tennis (b,g), track and field (b,g), volleyball (g). 5 PE instructors, 16 coaches, 1 athletic trainer.

Computers Computers are regularly used in all academic, computer applications classes. Computer network features include on-campus library services, online commercial services, Internet access, wireless campus network, Internet filtering or blocking technology, each student is issued an iPad for their use for the academic school year. Campus intranet, student e-mail accounts, and computer access in designated common areas are available to students. Students grades are available online. The school has a published electronic and media policy.

Contact Mrs. Kelly McCarthy Mooney, Director of Admissions. 205-776-5812. Fax: 205-776-5816. E-mail: kmooney@bcsk12.org. Website: www.bcsk12.org

BRIDGEPORT INTERNATIONAL ACADEMY

285 Lafayette Street
Bridgeport, Connecticut 06604

Head of School: Dr. Frank LaGrotteria

General Information Coeducational boarding and day college-preparatory and arts school. Grades 9–12. Founded: 1997. Setting: urban. Nearest major city is New York, NY. Students are housed in single-sex dormitories. 2 buildings on campus. Approved or accredited by New England Association of Schools and Colleges and Connecticut Department of Education. Total enrollment: 60. Upper school average class size: 15. Upper school faculty-student ratio: 1:6. There are 180 required school days per year for Upper School students. Upper School students typically attend 5 days per week. The average school day consists of 7 hours.

Upper School Student Profile Grade 9: 9 students (6 boys, 3 girls); Grade 10: 11 students (3 boys, 8 girls); Grade 11: 20 students (11 boys, 9 girls); Grade 12: 20 students (8 boys, 12 girls). 27% of students are boarding students. 60% are state residents. 1 state is represented in upper school student body. 40% are international students. International students from Australia, China, Congo, Japan, Republic of Korea, and Viet Nam; 2 other countries represented in student body.

Faculty School total: 10. In upper school: 5 men, 5 women; 3 have advanced degrees; 7 reside on campus.

Subjects Offered Algebra, American government, American history, American literature, analytic geometry, applied arts, arts, band, basketball, biology, British literature, business mathematics, career/college preparation, character education, chemistry, Chinese, college admission preparation, college counseling, college writing, communication arts, computer applications, computer science, computer-aided design, dance, digital art, earth science, electives, English, English as a foreign language, English composition, English literature, ESL, expository writing, filmmaking, fine arts, geometry, guidance, health, history, human biology, introduction to theater, Japanese, journalism, keyboarding, language arts, learning lab, literature, media communications, modern civilization, oil painting, painting, performing arts, personal fitness, physics, play production, pre-calculus, psychology, public speaking, SAT/ACT preparation, social studies, Spanish, sports, stagecraft, theater, U.S. government, U.S. history, world cultures, world religions.

Graduation Requirements American government, American history, character education, 25 hours of community service per year.

Special Academic Programs Accelerated programs; study at local college for college credit; ESL (8 students enrolled).

College Admission Counseling 19 students graduated in 2015; all went to college, including Babson College; Boston University; Fairfield University; Sacred Heart University; Southern Connecticut State University; University of Connecticut. Mean SAT critical reading: 544, mean SAT math: 540, mean SAT writing: 524, mean combined SAT: 1608, mean composite ACT: 25. 30% scored over 600 on SAT critical reading, 38% scored over 600 on SAT math, 24% scored over 600 on SAT writing, 23% scored over 1800 on combined SAT, 42% scored over 26 on composite ACT.

Student Life Upper grades have specified standards of dress, student council, honor system. Discipline rests primarily with faculty.

Tuition and Aid Day student tuition: $7000; 7-day tuition and room/board: $36,000. Tuition installment plan (SMART Tuition Payment Plan, monthly payment plans, individually arranged payment plans). Tuition reduction for siblings, merit scholarship grants available. In 2015–16, 25% of upper-school students received aid.

Admissions Traditional secondary-level entrance grade is 9. For fall 2015, 30 students applied for upper-level admission, 25 were accepted, 17 enrolled. Writing sample required. Deadline for receipt of application materials: June 30. Application fee required: $125. Interview recommended.

Athletics Intramural: basketball (boys, girls), dance (g), modern dance (g), soccer (b), softball (b,g), volleyball (b,g); coed intramural: table tennis, volleyball. 1 PE instructor, 1 coach.

Computers Computers are regularly used in all classes. Computer network features include Internet access, wireless campus network. Campus intranet, student e-mail accounts, and computer access in designated common areas are available to students. Students grades are available online. The school has a published electronic and media policy.

Contact Dr. Frederick Swarts, Academic Dean. 203-334-3434. Fax: 203-334-8651. E-mail: fswarts@bridgepotacademy.org. Website: http://www.bridgeportacademy.org/

BRIDGES ACADEMY

Studio City, California
See Special Needs Schools section.

BRIMMER AND MAY SCHOOL

69 Middlesex Road
Chestnut Hill, Massachusetts 02467

Head of School: Mrs. Judy Guild

General Information Coeducational day college-preparatory, Creative Arts diploma program, and Global Studies diploma program, STEAM diploma program school.

Grades PK–12. Founded: 1880. Setting: suburban. Nearest major city is Boston. 7-acre campus. 7 buildings on campus. Approved or accredited by New England Association of Schools and Colleges. Member of National Association of Independent Schools and Secondary School Admission Test Board. Endowment: $13 million. Total enrollment: 387. Upper school average class size: 12. Upper school faculty-student ratio: 1:6. There are 175 required school days per year for Upper School students. Upper School students typically attend 5 days per week. The average school day consists of 7 hours and 20 minutes.

Upper School Student Profile Grade 9: 39 students (18 boys, 21 girls); Grade 10: 36 students (20 boys, 16 girls); Grade 11: 29 students (15 boys, 14 girls); Grade 12: 35 students (18 boys, 17 girls).

Faculty School total: 67. In upper school: 16 men, 18 women; 28 have advanced degrees.

Subjects Offered Acting, adolescent issues, Advanced Placement courses, advanced studio art-AP, algebra, American history, American literature, art, biology, biology-AP, calculus, calculus-AP, ceramics, chamber groups, chemistry, chorus, college counseling, community service, computer education, creative arts, creative writing, desktop publishing, drama, economics, economics-AP, English, English literature, English literature-AP, ESL, European history, expository writing, fine arts, French, French language-AP, geometry, grammar, health, health education, history, humanities, literature and composition-AP, Mandarin, mathematics, microeconomics-AP, music, music theater, music theory, musical theater, newspaper, participation in sports, performing arts, photography, physical education, physical science, physics, physics-AP, psychology, social studies, Spanish, Spanish language-AP, statistics-AP, theater, trigonometry, typing, U.S. history, video film production, world history, world history-AP, world literature, writing, yearbook.

Graduation Requirements Creative arts, English, foreign language, history, mathematics, physical education (includes health), science, technology, senior independent project, senior thesis defense. Community service is required.

Special Academic Programs 16 Advanced Placement exams for which test preparation is offered; honors section; independent study; study at local college for college credit.

College Admission Counseling 37 students graduated in 2016; all went to college, including Bates College; Boston University; Brown University; Harvard University; Hobart and William Smith Colleges; Lehigh University

Student Life Upper grades have specified standards of dress, student council, honor system. Discipline rests equally with students and faculty.

Summer Programs Enrichment, sports, art/fine arts programs offered; session focuses on coed day camp for students ages 3-10 and select enrichment programs for middle and high school students; held both on and off campus; accepts boys and girls; open to students from other schools. 300 students usually enrolled. 2017 schedule: June 20 to August 19. Application deadline: none.

Tuition and Aid Day student tuition: $43,000. Tuition installment plan (SMART Tuition Payment Plan, monthly payment plans). Need-based scholarship grants available. In 2016–17, 40% of upper-school students received aid. Total amount of financial aid awarded in 2016–17: $1,606,150.

Admissions Traditional secondary-level entrance grade is 9. For fall 2016, 113 students applied for upper-level admission, 73 were accepted, 23 enrolled. ISEE, SSAT or TOEFL or SLEP required. Deadline for receipt of application materials: January 13. Application fee required: $50. Interview recommended.

Athletics Interscholastic: baseball (boys), basketball (b,g), field hockey (g), lacrosse (b,g), soccer (b,g), softball (g), tennis (b,g); coed interscholastic: cross-country running, curling, golf; coed intramural: alpine skiing, fitness, Frisbee, outdoor education, physical fitness, running, skiing (downhill), snowboarding, strength & conditioning, tennis, weight training, yoga. 3 PE instructors, 20 coaches, 1 athletic trainer.

Computers Computers are regularly used in architecture, desktop publishing, foreign language, graphic design, humanities, journalism, media production, technology, typing, video film production, Web site design, yearbook classes. Computer network features include on-campus library services, online commercial services, Internet access, wireless campus network, Internet filtering or blocking technology. Campus intranet, student e-mail accounts, and computer access in designated common areas are available to students. Students grades are available online. The school has a published electronic and media policy.

Contact Ms. Myra Korin, Admissions Coordinator. 617-738-8695. Fax: 617-734-5147. E-mail: admissions@brimmer.org. Website: www.brimmerandmay.org

BRITISH INTERNATIONAL SCHOOL OF BOSTON

416 Pond Street
Boston, Massachusetts 02130

Head of School: Mr. Darren Nicholas

General Information Coeducational day college-preparatory, International Baccalaureate Diploma Programme, and International Primary Curriculum/International Middle Years school. Grades PK–12. Founded: 2000. Setting: suburban. 40-acre campus. 2 buildings on campus. Approved or accredited by Council of International Schools, International Baccalaureate Organization, New England Association of Schools and Colleges, and Massachusetts Department of Education. Member of National Association of Independent Schools and Secondary School Admission Test Board. Total enrollment: 421. Upper school average class size: 10.

Upper school faculty-student ratio: 1:4. There are 180 required school days per year for Upper School students. Upper School students typically attend 5 days per week. The average school day consists of 7 hours.

Faculty School total: 60. In upper school: 14 men, 11 women.

Subjects Offered ACT preparation, arts, British National Curriculum, business, career and personal planning, career education internship, choir, college counseling, college placement, college planning, computer education, computer science, English, English as a foreign language, French, geography, history, International Baccalaureate courses, language, life management skills, mathematics, research skills, science, Spanish, sports, study skills.

Graduation Requirements International Baccalaureate courses.

Special Academic Programs International Baccalaureate program; academic accommodation for the gifted; ESL.

College Admission Counseling 15 students graduated in 2016; 13 went to college. Other: 2 went to work.

Student Life Upper grades have specified standards of dress, student council, honor system. Discipline rests equally with students and faculty.

Tuition and Aid Day student tuition: $30,800. Tuition installment plan (individually arranged payment plans). Tuition reduction for siblings, merit scholarship grants, discounts for students who enroll for full four years of high school available.

Admissions Traditional secondary-level entrance grade is 9. ISEE or SSAT required. Deadline for receipt of application materials: February 1. Application fee required: $150. Interview required.

Athletics Interscholastic: basketball (boys, girls), cross-country running (b,g), independent competitive sports (b), soccer (b,g), swimming and diving (b,g), tennis (b,g); intramural: basketball (b,g); coed interscholastic: curling, rugby, soccer; coed intramural: alpine skiing, backpacking, combined training, cross-country running, fitness, golf, hiking/backpacking, life saving, outdoor activities, outdoor education, outdoors, sailing, strength & conditioning. 2 PE instructors.

Computers Computers are regularly used in all classes. Computer network features include Internet access, wireless campus network. Student e-mail accounts and computer access in designated common areas are available to students. Students grades are available online. The school has a published electronic and media policy.

Contact Ms. Anique Seldon, Director of Admissions and Marketing. 617-522-2261 Ext. 141. Fax: 617-522-0385. E-mail: anique.seldon@bisboston.org.

Website: www.bisboston.org

BRITISH INTERNATIONAL SCHOOL OF WASHINGTON

2001 Wisconsin Avenue NW
Washington, District of Columbia 20007

Head of School: David Rowsell

General Information Coeducational day college-preparatory and arts school. Grades PS–12. Founded: 1998. Setting: urban. 1 building on campus. Approved or accredited by Council of International Schools, International Baccalaureate Organization, and District of Columbia Department of Education. Candidate for accreditation by Middle States Association of Colleges and Schools. Member of National Association of Independent Schools and European Council of International Schools. Total enrollment: 460. Upper school average class size: 15. Upper school faculty-student ratio: 1:12. There are 180 required school days per year for Upper School students. Upper School students typically attend 5 days per week. The average school day consists of 7 hours and 15 minutes.

Upper School Student Profile Grade 6: 45 students (20 boys, 25 girls); Grade 7: 30 students (15 boys, 15 girls); Grade 8: 45 students (25 boys, 20 girls); Grade 9: 35 students (15 boys, 20 girls); Grade 10: 35 students (20 boys, 15 girls); Grade 11: 25 students (10 boys, 15 girls); Grade 12: 20 students (10 boys, 10 girls).

Special Academic Programs International Baccalaureate program; independent study; ESL (20 students enrolled).

College Admission Counseling 23 students graduated in 2015; all went to college, including Savannah College of Art and Design; The George Washington University; University of California, San Diego.

Student Life Upper grades have uniform requirement, student council. Discipline rests equally with students and faculty.

Admissions Application fee required: $150.

Athletics Coed Interscholastic: basketball, cross-country running, flag football, Frisbee, kickball, soccer, squash, swimming and diving, track and field, triathlon, ultimate Frisbee, volleyball; coed intramural: aerobics/dance, backpacking, basketball, cross-country running, dance, field hockey, fitness, flag football, golf, gymnastics, handball, physical fitness, rounders, rugby, self defense, skiing (downhill), soccer, softball, table tennis, track and field, ultimate Frisbee, volleyball. 3 PE instructors.

Computers Computer resources include Internet access, wireless campus network, Internet filtering or blocking technology. Student e-mail accounts are available to students. Students grades are available online. The school has a published electronic and media policy.

Contact Admissions Office. 202-829-3700. Fax: 202-829-6522.
E-mail: admissions@BISWashington.org. Website: www.BISWashington.org

BROCKWOOD PARK SCHOOL

Brockwood Park
Bramdean
Hampshire
Alresford SO24 0LQ, United Kingdom

Head of School: Mr. Antonio Autor

General Information Coeducational boarding college-preparatory, general academic, and arts school. Ungraded, ages 14–19. Founded: 1969. Setting: rural. Nearest major city is Winchester, United Kingdom. Students are housed in individual rooms, single-sex compound. 40-acre campus. 13 buildings on campus. Approved or accredited by Independent Schools Council (UK). Language of instruction: English. Total enrollment: 65. Upper school average class size: 7. Upper school faculty-student ratio: 1:7. Upper School students typically attend 5 days per week. The average school day consists of 8 hours.

Upper School Student Profile 100% of students are boarding students. 75% are international students. International students from Austria, China, Germany, India, Netherlands, and Spain; 12 other countries represented in student body.

Faculty School total: 26. In upper school: 15 men, 11 women; 7 have advanced degrees; 30 reside on campus.

Subjects Offered Advanced biology, advanced chemistry, advanced math, area studies, art, band, biology, body human, bookbinding, business studies, career and personal planning, career education, carpentry, cartooning/animation, chamber groups, chemistry, choir, choral music, cinematography, classical music, communication skills, computers, design, desktop publishing, diversity studies, drama, drama performance, drama workshop, English, English literature, environmental education, ethics, ethics and responsibility, fabric arts, filmmaking, fine arts, folk dance, food and nutrition, French, gardening, gender issues, geography, graphic design, history, mathematics, music, physics, pottery, psychology, science, social studies, Spanish, statistics.

Graduation Requirements Graduation requirements determined on an individual basis.

Special Academic Programs Independent study; term-away projects; study abroad; academic accommodation for the gifted, the musically talented, and the artistically talented; remedial reading and/or remedial writing; remedial math; programs in English, mathematics, general development for dyslexic students; special instructional classes for deaf students, blind students; ESL (25 students enrolled).

College Admission Counseling 29 students graduated in 2016.

Student Life Upper grades have specified standards of dress, student council. Discipline rests equally with students and faculty.

Tuition and Aid 7-day tuition and room/board: £20,790. Tuition installment plan (individually arranged payment plans). Bursaries available. In 2016–17, 10% of upper-school students received aid.

Admissions Traditional secondary-level entrance age is 14. For fall 2016, 72 students applied for upper-level admission, 28 enrolled. 3-R Achievement Test, any standardized test or ESL required. Deadline for receipt of application materials: none. Application fee required: £20. On-campus interview recommended.

Athletics 1 coach, 2 athletic trainers.

Computers Computers are regularly used in design, drawing and design, graphic design classes. Computer resources include Internet access, Internet filtering or blocking technology. The school has a published electronic and media policy.

Contact Mrs. Victoria Lewin, Recruitment Officer. 44-1962 771744. Fax: 44-1962 771875. E-mail: enquiry@brockwood.org.uk. Website: www.brockwood.org.uk

THE BROOK HILL SCHOOL

1051 N. Houston
Bullard, Texas 75757

Head of School: Rod Fletcher

General Information Coeducational boarding and day college-preparatory and arts school, affiliated with Christian faith. Boarding grades 8–12, day grades PK–12. Founded: 1997. Setting: small town. Nearest major city is Dallas. Students are housed in single-sex dormitories. 280-acre campus. 9 buildings on campus. Approved or accredited by Association of Christian Schools International, Southern Association of Colleges and Schools, The Association of Boarding Schools, and The College Board. Member of National Association of Independent Schools. Endowment: $1 million. Total enrollment: 645. Upper school average class size: 11. Upper school faculty-student ratio: 1:9. There are 176 required school days per year for Upper School students. Upper School students typically attend 5 days per week. The average school day consists of 6 hours and 30 minutes.

Upper School Student Profile Grade 6: 37 students (24 boys, 13 girls); Grade 7: 48 students (26 boys, 22 girls); Grade 8: 37 students (20 boys, 17 girls); Grade 9: 62 students (26 boys, 36 girls); Grade 10: 68 students (32 boys, 36 girls); Grade 11: 66 students (34 boys, 32 girls); Grade 12: 55 students (28 boys, 27 girls). 30% of students are boarding students. 65% are state residents. 5 states are represented in upper school student body. 20% are international students. International students from China, Nigeria, Republic of Korea, Saudi Arabia, South Africa, and Viet Nam; 21 other countries represented in student body. 70% of students are Christian faith.

Faculty School total: 50. In upper school: 14 men, 17 women; 25 have advanced degrees; 6 reside on campus.

Subjects Offered Accounting, ACT preparation, advanced biology, advanced chemistry, advanced math, Advanced Placement courses, advanced studio art-AP, advanced TOEFL/grammar, algebra, American government, American history, American history-AP, American literature, American literature-AP, analysis and differential calculus, anatomy and physiology, ancient history, ancient world history, art, art-AP, athletics, baseball, basketball, Bible as literature, Bible studies, biology, British literature, British literature-AP, business, calculus, calculus-AP, career/college preparation, chemistry, chemistry-AP, choir, choral music, Christian ethics, Christian studies, Christianity, church history, civics/free enterprise, classics, college admission preparation, college awareness, college writing, communication skills, communications, community service, comparative religion, composition, composition-AP, computer applications, computer art, computer education, conceptual physics, concert choir, creation science, dance, dance performance, digital art, digital photography, drama, drama performance, dramatic arts, drawing, economics, economics-AP, English, English composition, English language and composition-AP, English language-AP, English literature, English literature and composition-AP, English literature-AP, English/composition-AP, ensembles, environmental science, epic literature, ESL, European history, European history-AP, European literature, finance, fine arts, foreign language, four units of summer reading, French, French as a second language, geometry, government, government and politics-AP, government-AP, great books, health, history-AP, honors algebra, honors English, honors geometry, human biology, lab science, Latin, leadership and service, literary genres, literature and composition-AP, literature-AP, logic, logic, rhetoric, and debate, macro/microeconomics-AP, macroeconomics-AP, mathematics-AP, microeconomics-AP, modern European history-AP, modern languages, orchestra, painting, physical education, physics, physics-AP, pre-calculus, public speaking, religion, rhetoric, SAT preparation, SAT/ACT preparation, senior project, Spanish, Spanish language-AP, Spanish literature-AP, Spanish-AP, speech communications, stagecraft, statistics-AP, strings, student government, student publications, studio art-AP, theater arts, TOEFL preparation, U.S. government and politics, U.S. government and politics-AP, U.S. history, U.S. history-AP, volleyball, yearbook.

Graduation Requirements Arts and fine arts (art, music, dance, drama), Bible, college admission preparation, economics, electives, English, foreign language, government, history, lab science, leadership, mathematics, physical education (includes health). Community service is required.

Special Academic Programs 12 Advanced Placement exams for which test preparation is offered; honors section; study at local college for college credit; academic accommodation for the gifted and the artistically talented; ESL (15 students enrolled).

College Admission Counseling 50 students graduated in 2015; all went to college, including Baylor University; Texas A&M University; Texas Tech University; The University of Texas at Austin; University of Mississippi; Wheaton College. Median SAT critical reading: 630, median SAT math: 632, median SAT writing: 611, median combined SAT: 1873, median composite ACT: 28. 67% scored over 600 on SAT critical reading, 67% scored over 600 on SAT math, 65% scored over 600 on SAT writing, 65% scored over 1800 on combined SAT, 67% scored over 26 on composite ACT.

Student Life Upper grades have uniform requirement, student council, honor system. Discipline rests primarily with faculty. Attendance at religious services is required.

Tuition and Aid Day student tuition: $10,350; 7-day tuition and room/board: $37,350. Tuition installment plan (FACTS Tuition Payment Plan, individually arranged payment plans). Tuition reduction for siblings, need-based scholarship grants available. In 2015–16, 40% of upper-school students received aid. Total amount of financial aid awarded in 2015–16: $850,000.

Admissions Traditional secondary-level entrance grade is 9. For fall 2015, 170 students applied for upper-level admission, 100 were accepted, 95 enrolled. International English Language Test, Iowa Test, CTBS, or TAP, Iowa Tests of Basic Skills, SSAT, Stanford Achievement Test, Otis-Lennon School Ability Test, TOEFL or TOEFL or SLEP required. Deadline for receipt of application materials: none. Application fee required: $75. Interview recommended.

Athletics Interscholastic: baseball (boys, girls), basketball (b,g), cheering (g), cross-country running (b,g), dance (g), dance squad (g), dance team (g), football (b), golf (b,g), independent competitive sports (b,g), physical fitness (b,g), physical training (b,g), soccer (b,g), softball (g), strength & conditioning (b,g), swimming and diving (b,g), tennis (b,g), track and field (b,g), volleyball (g), weight training (b,g); intramural: baseball (b,g), basketball (b,g), fishing (b,g), flag football (b,g), Frisbee (b,g), ultimate Frisbee (b,g); coed interscholastic: cheering, dance, dance squad, dance team, tennis; coed intramural: fishing, flag football, Frisbee. 1 PE instructor, 2 coaches, 1 athletic trainer.

Computers Computers are regularly used in all academic, art classes. Computer network features include on-campus library services, Internet access, wireless campus network, Internet filtering or blocking technology. Computer access in designated common areas is available to students. Students grades are available online. The school has a published electronic and media policy.

Contact Mr. Landry Humphries, Associate Director of Admissions, Boarding. 903-894-5000 Ext. 1042. Fax: 903-894-6332. E-mail: Landry.humphries@brookhill.org. Website: www.brookhill.org/

BROOKS SCHOOL

1160 Great Pond Road
North Andover, Massachusetts 01845-1298

Head of School: Mr. John R. Packard

General Information Coeducational boarding and day college-preparatory school, affiliated with Episcopal Church. Grades 9–12. Founded: 1926. Setting: suburban. Nearest major city is Boston. Students are housed in coed dormitories. 251-acre campus. 40 buildings on campus. Approved or accredited by Association of Independent Schools in New England, National Association of Episcopal Schools, New England Association of Schools and Colleges, The Association of Boarding Schools, and Massachusetts Department of Education. Member of National Association of Independent Schools and Secondary School Admission Test Board. Endowment: $70.8 million. Total enrollment: 373. Upper school average class size: 12. Upper school faculty-student ratio: 1:6. There are 180 required school days per year for Upper School students. Upper School students typically attend 6 days per week. The average school day consists of 7 hours.

Upper School Student Profile Grade 9: 72 students (30 boys, 42 girls); Grade 10: 94 students (48 boys, 46 girls); Grade 11: 111 students (69 boys, 42 girls); Grade 12: 103 students (60 boys, 43 girls). 67% of students are boarding students. 60% are state residents. 20 states are represented in upper school student body. 14% are international students. International students from Bermuda, China, Hong Kong, Republic of Korea, Thailand, and Viet Nam; 10 other countries represented in student body.

Faculty School total: 87. In upper school: 30 men, 32 women; 47 have advanced degrees; 47 reside on campus.

Subjects Offered Acting, advanced math, Advanced Placement courses, African literature, African-American literature, algebra, all academic, American history, American history-AP, American literature, American literature-AP, anatomy and physiology, art, art history, art history-AP, astronomy, Bible studies, biology, biology-AP, business, calculus, calculus-AP, ceramics, chemistry, chemistry-AP, Chinese, chorus, college admission preparation, college counseling, computer math, creative writing, drama, driver education, earth science, English, English literature, English-AP, environmental science-AP, ethics, European history, expository writing, film, fine arts, French, French language-AP, French literature-AP, French-AP, geometry, government and politics-AP, grammar, Greek, health, history, history-AP, honors algebra, honors geometry, honors world history, integrated arts, journalism, Latin, Latin-AP, life skills, Mandarin, mathematics, mathematics-AP, Middle East, model United Nations, music, music theory, music theory AP, painting, photography, physics, physics-AP, playwriting, poetry, psychology, public speaking, religion, rhetoric, robotics, senior project, senior seminar, Southern literature, Spanish, Spanish language-AP, Spanish literature, Spanish literature-AP, Spanish-AP, statistics, studio art, theater, theater design and production, theology, trigonometry, U.S. government and politics-AP, U.S. history-AP, visual arts, world history, world history-AP, world literature, writing.

Graduation Requirements Arts and fine arts (art, music, dance, drama), English, foreign language, health, history, mathematics, science.

Special Academic Programs 15 Advanced Placement exams for which test preparation is offered; honors section; independent study; term-away projects; study abroad.

College Admission Counseling 106 students graduated in 2016; 104 went to college, including Boston University; Northeastern University; Sacred Heart University; The George Washington University; Trinity College; University of Denver. Other: 2 had other specific plans. Mean SAT critical reading: 598, mean SAT math: 626, mean SAT writing: 603, mean combined SAT: 1827.

Student Life Upper grades have specified standards of dress, student council. Discipline rests primarily with faculty. Attendance at religious services is required.

Summer Programs Enrichment, advancement, computer instruction programs offered; session focuses on English, mathematics, SSAT and SAT preparation; held on campus; accepts boys and girls; open to students from other schools. 70 students usually enrolled. 2017 schedule: June 29 to August 21. Application deadline: none.

Tuition and Aid Day student tuition: $44,575; 7-day tuition and room/board: $57,785. Tuition installment plan (Academic Management Services Plan, FACTS Tuition Payment Plan, individually arranged payment plans). Need-based scholarship grants available. In 2016–17, 27% of upper-school students received aid. Total amount of financial aid awarded in 2016–17: $4,000,000.

Admissions Traditional secondary-level entrance grade is 9. For fall 2016, 939 students applied for upper-level admission, 248 were accepted, 102 enrolled. ISEE, SSAT, ERB, PSAT, SAT, PLAN or ACT or TOEFL required. Deadline for receipt of application materials: January 15. Application fee required: $60. Interview required.

Athletics Interscholastic: baseball (boys), basketball (b,g), crew (b,g), cross-country running (b,g), field hockey (g), football (b), ice hockey (b,g), lacrosse (b,g), soccer (b,g), softball (g), squash (b,g), tennis (b,g), wrestling (b); coed interscholastic: golf; coed intramural: dance, Frisbee, modern dance, physical fitness, sailing, skiing (downhill), weight training, yoga. 2 athletic trainers.

Computers Computers are regularly used in all academic classes. Computer network features include on-campus library services, online commercial services, Internet access, wireless campus network, Internet filtering or blocking technology, Multimedia lab, Maker Space. Campus intranet, student e-mail accounts, and computer access in designated common areas are available to students. Students grades are available online. The school has a published electronic and media policy.

Contact Mrs. Bini Egertson, Director of Admission. 978-725-6272. Fax: 978-725-6298. E-mail: admission@brooksschool.org. Website: www.brooksschool.org

BROPHY COLLEGE PREPARATORY

4701 North Central Avenue

Phoenix, Arizona 85012-1797

Head of School: Mr. Robert E. Ryan III

General Information Boys' day college-preparatory school, affiliated with Roman Catholic Church (Jesuit order). Grades 6–12. Founded: 1928. Setting: urban. 38-acre campus. 9 buildings on campus. Approved or accredited by Western Catholic Education Association. Endowment: $19 million. Total enrollment: 1,391. Upper school average class size: 24. Upper school faculty-student ratio: 1:15. There are 180 required school days per year for Upper School students. Upper School students typically attend 5 days per week. The average school day consists of 6 hours and 40 minutes.

Upper School Student Profile Grade 9: 347 students (347 boys); Grade 10: 338 students (338 boys); Grade 11: 315 students (315 boys); Grade 12: 326 students (326 boys). 66% of students are Roman Catholic Church (Jesuit order).

Faculty School total: 100. In upper school: 77 men, 23 women; 75 have advanced degrees.

Subjects Offered Advanced Placement courses, advanced studio art-AP, algebra, American history, American literature, anatomy, art, Bible studies, biology, business, calculus, chemistry, community service, computer math, computer programming, computer science, creative writing, drama, earth science, economics, engineering, English, English literature, ethics, European history, expository writing, fine arts, French, geography, geometry, government/civics, health, history, Latin, mathematics, mechanical drawing, music, physical education, physics, probability and statistics, psychology, religion, science, social sciences, social studies, sociology, Spanish, speech, theater, theology, trigonometry, video film production, world history, world literature.

Graduation Requirements Arts and fine arts (art, music, dance, drama), English, foreign language, mathematics, physical education (includes health), religion (includes Bible studies and theology), science, social studies (includes history). Community service is required.

Special Academic Programs Advanced Placement exam preparation; honors section; study at local college for college credit; study abroad.

College Admission Counseling 295 students graduated in 2016; 292 went to college, including Arizona State University at the Tempe campus; Creighton University; Northern Arizona University; Santa Clara University; Seattle University; The University of Arizona. Other: 2 entered military service, 1 had other specific plans. Median SAT critical reading: 601, median SAT math: 601, median SAT writing: 569, median combined SAT: 1771, median composite ACT: 27.

Student Life Upper grades have specified standards of dress, student council, honor system. Discipline rests primarily with faculty. Attendance at religious services is required.

Summer Programs Enrichment, advancement, sports, art/fine arts, computer instruction programs offered; session focuses on academic skills and sports; held both on and off campus; accepts boys and girls; open to students from other schools. 1,300 students usually enrolled. 2017 schedule: May 30 to June 30. Application deadline: May 26.

Tuition and Aid Day student tuition: $14,650. Tuition installment plan (FACTS Tuition Payment Plan). Need-based scholarship grants, paying campus jobs available. In 2016–17, 22% of upper-school students received aid. Total amount of financial aid awarded in 2016–17: $4,316,250.

Admissions Traditional secondary-level entrance grade is 9. For fall 2016, 580 students applied for upper-level admission, 383 were accepted, 347 enrolled. STS and STS, Diocese Test required. Deadline for receipt of application materials: January 27. Application fee required: $75. On-campus interview required.

Athletics Interscholastic: aquatics, baseball, basketball, cross-country running, diving, flagball, football, golf, ice hockey, lacrosse, soccer, swimming and diving, tennis, track and field, volleyball, wrestling; intramural: aquatics, badminton, baseball, basketball, bicycling, bowling, cheering, climbing, crew, cricket, fishing, fitness, flag football, Frisbee, golf, handball, hockey, ice hockey, lacrosse, mountain biking, outdoor activities, physical fitness, physical training, rock climbing, skiing (downhill), softball, strength & conditioning, table tennis, touch football, ultimate Frisbee, volleyball, wall climbing, water polo, weight lifting, weight training. 2 PE instructors, 15 coaches, 3 athletic trainers.

Computers Computers are regularly used in all academic classes. Computer network features include online commercial services, Internet access, wireless campus network, computer tablets, iPads. Student e-mail accounts are available to students. Students grades are available online. The school has a published electronic and media policy.

Contact Ms. Shelly Scheuring, Assistant to Director of Admissions. 602-264-5291 Ext. 6233. Fax: 602-234-1669. E-mail: sscheuring@brophyprep.org. Website: www.brophyprep.org/

BROTHER MARTIN HIGH SCHOOL

4401 Elysian Fields Avenue

New Orleans, Louisiana 70122-3898

Head of School: Mr. Gregory Rando

General Information Boys' day college-preparatory school, affiliated with Roman Catholic Church. Grades 8–12. Founded: 1869. Setting: urban. 15-acre campus. 3 buildings on campus. Approved or accredited by National Catholic Education Association, Southern Association of Colleges and Schools, and Louisiana Department of Education. Endowment: $2 million. Total enrollment: 1,190. Upper school average class size: 25. Upper school faculty-student ratio: 1:23. There are 180 required school days per year for Upper School students. Upper School students typically attend 5 days per week. The average school day consists of 7 hours and 6 minutes.

Upper School Student Profile Grade 8: 220 students (220 boys); Grade 9: 233 students (233 boys); Grade 10: 244 students (244 boys); Grade 11: 230 students (230 boys); Grade 12: 208 students (208 boys). 88% of students are Roman Catholic.

Faculty School total: 104. In upper school: 76 men, 28 women; 54 have advanced degrees.

Subjects Offered Accounting, ACT preparation, advanced biology, advanced chemistry, advanced math, Advanced Placement courses, algebra, American history, American history-AP, anatomy, art, band, biology, biology-AP, calculus, calculus-AP, chemistry, chemistry-AP, Chinese, chorus, civics/free enterprise, computer programming, computer science, computer science-AP, concert band, creative writing, driver education, earth science, economics, engineering, English, English language and composition-AP, English literature and composition-AP, English-AP, environmental science, European history-AP, fine arts, forensics, French, geography, geometry, German, health, jazz band, JROTC, Latin, law studies, marching band, mathematics, physical education, physical science, physics, physics-AP, religion, science, social sciences, social studies, Spanish, typing, U.S. government and politics-AP, Western civilization, world geography, world history.

Graduation Requirements Computer science, English, foreign language, mathematics, physical education (includes health), religion (includes Bible studies and theology), science, social sciences, social studies (includes history), honors students must have additional credits for graduation. Community service is required.

Special Academic Programs Advanced Placement exam preparation; honors section; study at local college for college credit; academic accommodation for the gifted, the musically talented, and the artistically talented.

College Admission Counseling 218 students graduated in 2016; 213 went to college, including Louisiana State University and Agricultural & Mechanical College; Loyola University New Orleans; Southeastern Louisiana University; Tulane University; University of Louisiana at Lafayette; University of New Orleans. Other: 2 went to work, 3 entered military service. Mean composite ACT: 25.

Student Life Upper grades have uniform requirement, student council. Discipline rests primarily with faculty. Attendance at religious services is required.

Summer Programs Remediation, enrichment, advancement programs offered; session focuses on remediation and new course offerings; held on campus; accepts boys; not open to students from other schools. 300 students usually enrolled. 2017 schedule: June to July. Application deadline: June 1.

Tuition and Aid Tuition installment plan (monthly payment plans). Merit scholarship grants, need-based scholarship grants, paying campus jobs available. In 2016–17, 12% of upper-school students received aid.

Admissions Traditional secondary-level entrance grade is 9. Deadline for receipt of application materials: November 30. No application fee required. On-campus interview recommended.

Athletics Interscholastic: baseball, basketball, bowling, cheering, cross-country running, football, golf, indoor track & field, lacrosse, rugby, sailing, sand volleyball, soccer, swimming and diving, tennis, track and field, wrestling; intramural: baseball, basketball, bowling, flag football, football, volleyball. 5 PE instructors, 21 coaches, 1 athletic trainer.

Computers Computers are regularly used in all classes. Computer network features include on-campus library services, online commercial services, Internet access, wireless campus network, Internet filtering or blocking technology. Campus intranet and student e-mail accounts are available to students. Students grades are available online. The school has a published electronic and media policy.

Contact Mr. Carlos Bogran, Director of Admissions. 504-283-1561. Fax: 504-286-8462. E-mail: cbogran@brothermartin.com. Website: www.brothermartin.com

BROTHER RICE HIGH SCHOOL

7101 Lahser Road

Bloomfield Hills, Michigan 48301

Head of School: Mr. John Birney

General Information Boys' day college-preparatory, arts, business, religious studies, and technology school, affiliated with Roman Catholic Church. Grades 9–12. Founded: 1960. Setting: suburban. Nearest major city is Detroit. 20-acre campus. 1 building on campus. Approved or accredited by North Central Association of Colleges and Schools and Michigan Department of Education. Endowment: $2 million. Total enrollment: 640. Upper school average class size: 22. Upper school faculty-student ratio: 1:13. Upper

School students typically attend 5 days per week. The average school day consists of 6 hours and 51 minutes.

Upper School Student Profile Grade 9: 165 students (165 boys); Grade 10: 162 students (162 boys); Grade 11: 159 students (159 boys); Grade 12: 148 students (148 boys). 75% of students are Roman Catholic.

Faculty School total: 60. In upper school: 32 men, 10 women; 36 have advanced degrees.

Subjects Offered 20th century world history, accounting, algebra, American government, anatomy, anthropology, architectural drawing, art, band, biology, biology-AP, business law, calculus, calculus-AP, chemistry, Chinese, choir, church history, computer science, computer science-AP, computers, concert band, creative writing, death and loss, debate, drama, earth science, economics, electronics, engineering, English, English composition, English language-AP, ensembles, European history, family living, forensics, French, French-AP, geometry, German, global science, health, jazz band, Latin, library science, literature, mathematics, mechanical drawing, music, music history, music theory, organic chemistry, photography, photojournalism, physical education, physics, physiology, pre-calculus, probability and statistics, psychology, social justice, Spanish, Spanish-AP, speech, studio art-AP, theology, trigonometry, U.S. government and politics-AP, U.S. history, U.S. history-AP, Western civilization, world geography, world religions.

Graduation Requirements Computer science, electives, English, foreign language, mathematics, physical education (includes health), science, social studies (includes history), speech, theology.

Special Academic Programs 13 Advanced Placement exams for which test preparation is offered; honors section; remedial reading and/or remedial writing; remedial math.

College Admission Counseling 168 students graduated in 2015; 162 went to college, including Central Michigan University; Michigan State University; Oakland University; University of Michigan; Wayne State University. Other: 6 had other specific plans. Median combined SAT: 1838, median composite ACT: 25.

Student Life Upper grades have specified standards of dress, student council, honor system. Discipline rests primarily with faculty. Attendance at religious services is required.

Tuition and Aid Day student tuition: $11,750. Tuition installment plan (SMART Tuition Payment Plan, monthly payment plans, individually arranged payment plans). Tuition reduction for siblings, merit scholarship grants, need-based scholarship grants available. In 2015–16, 40% of upper-school students received aid; total upper-school merit-scholarship money awarded: $600,000. Total amount of financial aid awarded in 2015–16: $900,000.

Admissions Traditional secondary-level entrance grade is 9. For fall 2015, 476 students applied for upper-level admission, 300 were accepted, 165 enrolled. High School Placement Test (closed version) from Scholastic Testing Service or SAS, STS-HSPT required. Deadline for receipt of application materials: none. No application fee required. Interview required.

Athletics Interscholastic: alpine skiing, baseball, basketball, bowling, cross-country running, diving, football, golf, hockey, ice hockey, lacrosse, skiing (downhill), soccer, swimming and diving, tennis, track and field, wrestling; intramural: basketball, bowling, fishing, fitness, flag football, football, mountain biking, paint ball, skiing (downhill), snowboarding, strength & conditioning, touch football, ultimate Frisbee, winter (indoor) track. 50 coaches, 1 athletic trainer.

Computers Computers are regularly used in computer applications, drafting, drawing and design, engineering, keyboarding, lab/keyboard, newspaper, publications, video film production, yearbook classes. Computer resources include online commercial services, Internet access, wireless campus network, Internet filtering or blocking technology. Campus intranet and student e-mail accounts are available to students. Students grades are available online. The school has a published electronic and media policy.

Contact Mr. Brendan F. Robinson, Director of Admissions. 248-833-2022. Fax: 248-833-2011. E-mail: robinson@brrice.edu. Website: www.brrice.edu

THE BROWNING SCHOOL

52 East 62nd Street
New York, New York 10065

Head of School: Dr. John M. Botti

General Information Boys' day college-preparatory school. Grades K–12. Founded: 1888. Setting: urban. 1 building on campus. Approved or accredited by New York State Association of Independent Schools. Member of National Association of Independent Schools and Secondary School Admission Test Board. Endowment: $50 million. Total enrollment: 399. Upper school average class size: 15. Upper school faculty-student ratio: 1:4. There are 164 required school days per year for Upper School students. Upper School students typically attend 5 days per week. The average school day consists of 6 hours and 54 minutes.

Upper School Student Profile Grade 9: 35 students (35 boys); Grade 10: 27 students (27 boys); Grade 11: 29 students (29 boys); Grade 12: 25 students (25 boys).

Faculty School total: 70. In upper school: 23 men, 12 women; 35 have advanced degrees.

Subjects Offered Adolescent issues, advanced biology, advanced chemistry, advanced math, Advanced Placement courses, advanced studio art-AP, African drumming, algebra, American history, American history-AP, American literature, American literature-AP, anatomy and physiology, Ancient Greek, ancient world history, applied arts, applied music, art, art history, athletics, baseball, basketball, bell choir, biology, biology-AP, calculus, calculus-AP, ceramics, chemistry, chemistry-AP, chorus, college admission preparation, computer math, computer music, computer programming, computer science, drama, dramatic arts, English, English literature, English-AP, environmental science, environmental studies, ethics, European history, European history-AP, expository writing, fencing, filmmaking, fine arts, French, French language-AP, general science, geography, geometry, golf, government/civics, grammar, Greek, handbells, health, history, instruments, jazz ensemble, language arts, Latin, Latin-AP, mathematics, medieval/Renaissance history, mentorship program, model United Nations, music, peer counseling, philosophy, physical education, physics, physics-AP, political science, public speaking, science, senior project, social sciences, social studies, Spanish, Spanish language-AP, squash, statistics, technology, tennis, theater, track and field, trigonometry, U.S. history-AP, video film production, visual arts, wrestling, yearbook.

Graduation Requirements Arts and fine arts (art, music, dance, drama), computer science, English, foreign language, mathematics, physical education (includes health), public speaking, science, social sciences, social studies (includes history), senior community service project.

Special Academic Programs Advanced Placement exam preparation; honors section; independent study; academic accommodation for the gifted and the musically talented.

College Admission Counseling 26 students graduated in 2016; all went to college, including Boston College; Georgetown University; Johns Hopkins University; New York University. Median SAT critical reading: 636, median SAT math: 654, median SAT writing: 664, median combined SAT: 1954, median composite ACT: 27. 71% scored over 600 on SAT critical reading, 71% scored over 600 on SAT math, 83% scored over 600 on SAT writing, 75% scored over 1800 on combined SAT, 57% scored over 26 on composite ACT.

Student Life Upper grades have specified standards of dress, student council, honor system. Discipline rests primarily with faculty.

Tuition and Aid Day student tuition: $44,500. Need-based scholarship grants available. In 2016–17, 32% of upper-school students received aid. Total amount of financial aid awarded in 2016–17: $953,900.

Admissions Traditional secondary-level entrance grade is 9. For fall 2016, 75 students applied for upper-level admission, 16 were accepted, 8 enrolled. ISEE and SSAT required. Deadline for receipt of application materials: January 15. Application fee required: $75. On-campus interview required.

Athletics Interscholastic: baseball, basketball, soccer, tennis; intramural: basketball, cross-country running, ice hockey, soccer, softball; coed intramural: fencing. 4 PE instructors, 6 coaches.

Computers Computers are regularly used in all academic, English, foreign language, history, mathematics, music technology, science, video film production classes. Computer network features include on-campus library services, online commercial services, Internet access, wireless campus network. Student e-mail accounts are available to students. The school has a published electronic and media policy.

Contact Janetta Lien, Director of Middle and Upper School Admission. 212-838-6280 Ext. 103. Fax: 212-355-5602. E-mail: jlien@browning.edu. Website: www.browning.edu

BRUNSWICK SCHOOL

100 Maher Avenue
Greenwich, Connecticut 06830

Head of School: Thomas W. Philip

General Information Boys' day college-preparatory school. Grades PK–12. Founded: 1902. Setting: suburban. Nearest major city is New York, NY. 10-acre campus. 1 building on campus. Approved or accredited by New England Association of Schools and Colleges and Connecticut Department of Education. Member of National Association of Independent Schools. Endowment: $118.3 million. Total enrollment: 962. Upper school average class size: 15. Upper school faculty-student ratio: 1:5. There are 167 required school days per year for Upper School students. Upper School students typically attend 5 days per week. The average school day consists of 6 hours and 30 minutes.

Upper School Student Profile Grade 9: 93 students (93 boys); Grade 10: 95 students (95 boys); Grade 11: 95 students (95 boys); Grade 12: 97 students (97 boys).

Faculty School total: 171. In upper school: 42 men, 14 women; 47 have advanced degrees.

Subjects Offered 20th century history, 3-dimensional design, acting, advanced chemistry, African-American literature, algebra, American history, American history-AP, American literature, anthropology, Arabic, architecture, art, art history, art history-AP, astronomy, biology, biology-AP, calculus, calculus-AP, ceramics, chemistry, chemistry-AP, Chinese, choir, community service, computer graphics, computer programming, computer programming-AP, creative writing, digital art, digital music, drama, earth science, economics, economics-AP, English, environmental science-AP, ethics, European history, European history-AP, film and literature, fine arts, French, French language-AP, French literature-AP, geometry, government-AP, Greek, Greek culture, health, history, honors algebra, honors geometry, human geography - AP,

Italian, Japanese history, jazz, jazz band, jazz ensemble, Latin, Latin American literature, Latin-AP, mathematics, media studies, microeconomics, military history, music, oceanography, philosophy, photography, physical education, physics, physics-AP, poetry, pre-calculus, psychology, psychology-AP, science, senior seminar, Shakespeare, short story, social studies, Spanish, Spanish language-AP, Spanish literature-AP, speech and debate, statistics-AP, studio art, studio art-AP, theater, trigonometry, U.S. government and politics-AP, U.S. history-AP, world cultures, world history-AP, writing.

Graduation Requirements Arts and fine arts (art, music, dance, drama), English, foreign language, mathematics, physical education (includes health), science, social studies (includes history). Community service is required.

Special Academic Programs Advanced Placement exam preparation; honors section; independent study; term-away projects; study abroad.

College Admission Counseling 96 students graduated in 2015; all went to college, including Cornell University; Dartmouth College; Duke University; Georgetown University; University of Virginia; Yale University. Mean SAT critical reading: 660, mean SAT math: 665, mean SAT writing: 670, mean combined SAT: 1985. 75% scored over 600 on SAT critical reading, 87% scored over 600 on SAT math, 88% scored over 600 on SAT writing, 85% scored over 1800 on combined SAT.

Student Life Upper grades have specified standards of dress, student council, honor system. Discipline rests equally with students and faculty.

Tuition and Aid Day student tuition: $39,250. Tuition installment plan (Key Tuition Payment Plan, monthly payment plans). Need-based scholarship grants available. In 2015–16, 11% of upper-school students received aid. Total amount of financial aid awarded in 2015–16: $1,250,000.

Admissions Traditional secondary-level entrance grade is 9. For fall 2015, 162 students applied for upper-level admission, 38 were accepted, 33 enrolled. ISEE, PSAT or SSAT required. Deadline for receipt of application materials: December 15. Application fee required: $75. On-campus interview required.

Athletics Interscholastic: baseball, basketball, crew, cross-country running, fencing, fitness, football, golf, ice hockey, lacrosse, sailing, soccer, squash, tennis, track and field, water polo, wrestling; intramural: basketball, softball, squash, touch football, ultimate Frisbee. 4 PE instructors, 2 coaches, 4 athletic trainers.

Computers Computers are regularly used in career technology classes. Computer network features include on-campus library services, online commercial services, Internet access, wireless campus network, Internet filtering or blocking technology. Campus intranet and student e-mail accounts are available to students. Students grades are available online. The school has a published electronic and media policy.

Contact Tucker Hastings, Director, Upper School Admission. 203-625-5842. Fax: 203-625-5863. E-mail: thastings@brunswickschool.org. Website: www.brunswickschool.org

THE BRYN MAWR SCHOOL FOR GIRLS

109 West Melrose Avenue
Baltimore, Maryland 21210

Head of School: Mrs. Maureen E. Walsh

General Information Coeducational day (boys' only in lower grades) college-preparatory, arts, and technology school. Boys grade PK, girls grades PK–12. Founded: 1885. Setting: suburban. 26-acre campus. 9 buildings on campus. Approved or accredited by Association of Independent Maryland Schools, The College Board, and Maryland Department of Education. Member of National Association of Independent Schools and Secondary School Admission Test Board. Endowment: $30.4 million. Total enrollment: 681. Upper school average class size: 14. Upper school faculty-student ratio: 1:7. There are 180 required school days per year for Upper School students. Upper School students typically attend 5 days per week. The average school day consists of 7 hours and 20 minutes.

Upper School Student Profile Grade 9: 82 students (82 girls); Grade 10: 83 students (83 girls); Grade 11: 81 students (81 girls); Grade 12: 76 students (76 girls).

Faculty School total: 136. In upper school: 15 men, 34 women; 25 have advanced degrees.

Subjects Offered 20th century American writers, accounting, acting, African-American history, African-American literature, algebra, American history, American literature, anatomy, anatomy and physiology, Arabic, architectural drawing, art, art history, art history-AP, astronomy, biology, biology-AP, British literature, calculus, calculus-AP, ceramics, chemistry, chemistry-AP, Chesapeake Bay studies, China/Japan history, Chinese, comparative government and politics-AP, comparative religion, computer programming, computer science, computer science-AP, creative writing, dance, design, digital art, digital photography, drama, drawing, ecology, economics, economics-AP, emerging technology, English, English literature, English-AP, environmental science-AP, ethics, European history, European history-AP, fine arts, forensics, French, French language-AP, genetics, geography, geology, geometry, grammar, Greek, health, Holocaust, Holocaust studies, honors algebra, honors geometry, human geography - AP, Irish literature, Latin, Latin American history, Latin-AP, mathematics, mechanical drawing, moral theology, music, music theory, mythology, Native American studies, orchestra, painting, personal finance, photography, physical education, physics, physics-AP, poetry, pre-calculus, psychology-AP, public speaking, rite of passage, Russian, science, Shakespearean histories, short story, social studies, Spanish, Spanish language-AP, statistics, statistics-

AP, strings, technology, theater, trigonometry, U.S. government and politics-AP, U.S. history, urban studies, Vietnam War, world history, world history-AP, world literature, World War I, World War II, writing.

Graduation Requirements Arts and fine arts (art, music, dance, drama), emerging technology, English, foreign language, history, mathematics, physical education (includes health), public speaking, science, 50 hours of community service, convocation speech.

Special Academic Programs 27 Advanced Placement exams for which test preparation is offered; honors section; independent study; term-away projects; study abroad; academic accommodation for the gifted, the musically talented, and the artistically talented.

College Admission Counseling 73 students graduated in 2016; all went to college, including Boston University; Clemson University; Colgate University; Georgetown University; Macalester College; University of Maryland, College Park. Other: 73 entered a postgraduate year. Median SAT critical reading: 660, median SAT math: 650, median SAT writing: 670, median combined SAT: 1970, median composite ACT: 29. 76.8% scored over 600 on SAT critical reading, 66.7% scored over 600 on SAT math, 78.3% scored over 600 on SAT writing, 76.8% scored over 1800 on combined SAT, 69.4% scored over 26 on composite ACT.

Student Life Upper school grades have uniform requirement, student council, honor system. Discipline rests equally with students and faculty.

Summer Programs Enrichment, sports, art/fine arts programs offered; session focuses on arts, crafts, language, culture, and sports; held on campus; accepts boys and girls; open to students from other schools. 360 students usually enrolled. 2017 schedule: June 19 to August 4. Application deadline: none.

Tuition and Aid Day student tuition: $29,530. Tuition installment plan (FACTS Tuition Payment Plan, individual payment 65% due August 1st and remaining 35% December 1st, semi-monthly payroll deduction (for employees only)). Merit scholarship grants, need-based scholarship grants available. In 2016–17, 32% of upper-school students received aid; total upper-school merit-scholarship money awarded: $77,000. Total amount of financial aid awarded in 2016–17: $1,664,085.

Admissions Traditional secondary-level entrance grade is 9. For fall 2016, 116 students applied for upper-level admission, 65 were accepted, 33 enrolled. ISEE, Otis-Lennon Ability or Stanford Achievement Test, school's own exam, SSAT, TOEFL or writing sample required. Deadline for receipt of application materials: December 15. Application fee required: $60. Interview recommended.

Athletics Interscholastic: badminton, ballet, basketball, cross-country running, dance, field hockey, golf, hockey, indoor track & field, lacrosse, running, soccer, softball, squash, tennis, track and field, volleyball, winter (indoor) track, winter soccer; intramural: aerobics, aerobics/dance, aerobics/Nautilus, archery, badminton, ball hockey, basketball, cooperative games, croquet, cross-country running, dance, fencing, fitness, flag football, floor hockey, ice hockey, jogging, kickball, outdoor activities, physical training, pillo polo, ropes courses, running, strength & conditioning, team handball, tennis, touch football, ultimate Frisbee, walking, weight training, whiffle ball, yoga. 5 PE instructors, 34 coaches, 1 athletic trainer.

Computers Computers are regularly used in animation, art, computer applications, graphic design, programming, Web site design classes. Computer network features include on-campus library services, online commercial services, Internet access, wireless campus network, Internet filtering or blocking technology, off-campus email. Campus intranet, student e-mail accounts, and computer access in designated common areas are available to students. Students grades are available online. The school has a published electronic and media policy.

Contact Rebekah Jackson, Director of Enrollment Management. 410-323-8800 Ext. 1237. Fax: 410-435-4678. E-mail: jacksonr@brynmawrschool.org. Website: www.brynmawrschool.org

BUCKINGHAM BROWNE & NICHOLS SCHOOL

80 Gerry's Landing Road
Cambridge, Massachusetts 02138-5512

Head of School: Rebecca T. Upham

General Information Coeducational day college-preparatory school. Grades PK–12. Founded: 1883. Setting: urban. Nearest major city is Boston. 5-acre campus. 6 buildings on campus. Approved or accredited by Association of Independent Schools in New England, New England Association of Schools and Colleges, and Massachusetts Department of Education. Member of National Association of Independent Schools and Secondary School Admission Test Board. Endowment: $42 million. Total enrollment: 968. Upper school average class size: 12. Upper school faculty-student ratio: 1:7. Upper School students typically attend 5 days per week.

Upper School Student Profile Grade 9: 142 students (73 boys, 69 girls); Grade 10: 129 students (58 boys, 71 girls); Grade 11: 132 students (69 boys, 63 girls); Grade 12: 130 students (70 boys, 60 girls).

Faculty In upper school: 26 men, 48 women; 83 have advanced degrees.

Subjects Offered Advanced Placement courses, African-American studies, algebra, American history, American literature, ancient history, art, art history, art history-AP, biology, bivouac, calculus, ceramics, chemistry, Chinese, Chinese history, community service, computer science, dance, design, drama, economics, English, English literature, European history, film, fine arts, French, geometry, government/civics, history, Latin, mathematics, medieval history, music, photography, physical education, physics, physiology, psychology, Russian, science, social studies, Spanish, statistics, theater, trigonometry, video, woodworking.

Graduation Requirements Arts and fine arts (art, music, dance, drama), bivouac, English, foreign language, history, mathematics, science, social studies (includes history), Senior spring project. Community service is required.

Special Academic Programs Advanced Placement exam preparation; honors section; independent study; term-away projects; study at local college for college credit; study abroad.

College Admission Counseling 139 students graduated in 2016; all went to college, including Brown University; Colby College; Harvard University; New York University; University of Chicago; Washington University in St. Louis. Mean SAT critical reading: 674, mean SAT math: 682, mean SAT writing: 679, mean combined SAT: 2035, mean composite ACT: 29.

Student Life Upper grades have specified standards of dress, student council. Discipline rests equally with students and faculty.

Tuition and Aid Day student tuition: $43,970. Tuition installment plan (monthly payment plans). Need-based scholarship grants available. In 2016–17, 30% of upper-school students received aid. Total amount of financial aid awarded in 2016–17: $5,370,000.

Admissions Traditional secondary-level entrance grade is 9. For fall 2016, 407 students applied for upper-level admission, 147 were accepted, 68 enrolled. ISEE or SSAT required. Deadline for receipt of application materials: January 16. Application fee required: $50. Interview recommended.

Athletics Interscholastic: baseball (boys), basketball (b,g), crew (b,g), cross-country running (b,g), fencing (b,g), field hockey (g), football (b), hockey (b,g), ice hockey (b,g), lacrosse (b,g), soccer (b,g), softball (g), squash (b,g), tennis (b,g), volleyball (g), wrestling (b); coed interscholastic: golf, sailing; coed intramural: fitness, physical fitness, strength & conditioning, tennis. 2 PE instructors, 20 coaches, 2 athletic trainers.

Computers Computers are regularly used in mathematics, programming, science, video film production classes. Computer network features include on-campus library services, online commercial services, Internet access, wireless campus network. Student e-mail accounts and computer access in designated common areas are available to students. Students grades are available online. The school has a published electronic and media policy.

Contact Amy Pratt, Admission Coordinator, Upper School. 617-800-2136. Fax: 617-547-7696. E-mail: apratt@bbns.org. Website: www.bbns.org

THE BUCKLEY SCHOOL

3900 Stansbury Avenue
Sherman Oaks, California 91423

Head of School: Mr. James Busby

General Information Coeducational day college-preparatory and full college preparatory program school. Grades K–12. Founded: 1933. Setting: suburban. Nearest major city is Los Angeles. 20-acre campus. 10 buildings on campus. Approved or accredited by California Association of Independent Schools, Western Association of Schools and Colleges, and California Department of Education. Member of National Association of Independent Schools. Total enrollment: 830. Upper school average class size: 14. Upper school faculty-student ratio: 1:8. There are 180 required school days per year for Upper School students. Upper School students typically attend 5 days per week. The average school day consists of 6 hours.

Upper School Student Profile Grade 9: 78 students (49 boys, 29 girls); Grade 10: 81 students (41 boys, 40 girls); Grade 11: 79 students (41 boys, 38 girls); Grade 12: 93 students (47 boys, 46 girls).

Faculty School total: 110. In upper school: 28 men, 27 women; 31 have advanced degrees.

Subjects Offered Algebra, American history, American literature, art history, biology, calculus, ceramics, chemistry, chorus, computer graphics, computer science, creative writing, dance, drama, ecology, English, English literature, fine arts, French, geology, geometry, government/civics, humanities, journalism, Latin, mathematics, music, music theory, orchestra, photography, physical education, physics, science, social sciences, Spanish, theater, trigonometry, world history, world literature, yoga.

Graduation Requirements Arts and fine arts (art, music, dance, drama), computer science, English, foreign language, humanities, mathematics, performing arts, physical education (includes health), science, social sciences. Community service is required.

Special Academic Programs Advanced Placement exam preparation; honors section; independent study; study abroad.

College Admission Counseling 85 students graduated in 2016; all went to college, including New York University; Stanford University; University of California, Berkeley; University of California, Los Angeles; University of Southern California.

Student Life Upper grades have uniform requirement, student council, honor system. Discipline rests primarily with faculty.

Summer Programs Enrichment, advancement, art/fine arts, computer instruction programs offered; session focuses on college preparatory courses and enrichment; held on campus; accepts boys and girls; open to students from other schools. 100 students usually enrolled. 2017 schedule: June 20 to July 22. Application deadline: May 1.

Tuition and Aid Day student tuition: $39,320. Tuition installment plan (monthly payment plans, individually arranged payment plans, reduced payments for families receiving financial aid). Need-based scholarship grants available. In 2016–17, 14% of

upper-school students received aid. Total amount of financial aid awarded in 2016–17: $530,000.

Admissions Traditional secondary-level entrance grade is 9. For fall 2016, 188 students applied for upper-level admission, 64 were accepted, 28 enrolled. ISEE or SSAT required. Deadline for receipt of application materials: January 20. Application fee required: $125. On-campus interview recommended.

Athletics Interscholastic: baseball (boys), softball (g), volleyball (g); coed interscholastic: basketball, cross-country running, dance, dance team, equestrian sports, horseback riding, soccer, swimming and diving, tennis. 12 PE instructors, 11 coaches, 2 athletic trainers.

Computers Computers are regularly used in art, English, foreign language, graphic design, music, science, video film production, yearbook classes. Computer network features include on-campus library services, online commercial services, Internet access, wireless campus network, Internet filtering or blocking technology, Web page design, online syllabi. Campus intranet, student e-mail accounts, and computer access in designated common areas are available to students. Students grades are available online. The school has a published electronic and media policy.

Contact Mr. Stephen D. Milich, Director of Admission and Financial Aid. 818-461-6719. Fax: 818-461-6714. E-mail: admissions@buckley.org.
Website: www.buckley.org

BUFFALO SEMINARY

205 Bidwell Parkway
Buffalo, New York 14222

Head of School: Mrs. Helen Ladds Marlette

General Information Girls' boarding and day college-preparatory, arts, technology, and community service school. Grades 9–12. Founded: 1851. Setting: urban. Students are housed in single-sex dormitories. 3 acre campus. 6 buildings on campus. Approved or accredited by New York Department of Education, New York State Association of Independent Schools, The Association of Boarding Schools, and New York Department of Education. Member of National Association of Independent Schools and Secondary School Admission Test Board. Endowment: $7 million. Total enrollment: 219. Upper school average class size: 12. Upper school faculty-student ratio: 1:7. There are 168 required school days per year for Upper School students. Upper School students typically attend 5 days per week. The average school day consists of 7 hours and 35 minutes.

Upper School Student Profile Grade 9: 49 students (49 girls); Grade 10: 61 students (61 girls); Grade 11: 63 students (63 girls); Grade 12: 43 students (43 girls). 20% of students are boarding students. 83% are state residents. 4 states are represented in upper school student body. 17% are international students. International students from China, Germany, and Republic of Korea; 2 other countries represented in student body.

Faculty School total: 37. In upper school: 4 men, 33 women; 23 have advanced degrees; 7 reside on campus.

Subjects Offered 20th century American writers, 20th century history, 20th century physics, 20th century world history, 3-dimensional art, 3-dimensional design, acting, advanced biology, advanced chemistry, advanced computer applications, advanced math, Advanced Placement courses, algebra, American biography, American culture, American democracy, American history, American history-AP, American literature, anatomy, ancient history, ancient world history, applied arts, applied music, art, art and culture, art appreciation, arts appreciation, astronomy, athletics, biology, biology-AP, British literature (honors), calculus, calculus-AP, career education internship, chemistry, Chinese, choral music, chorus, cinematography, community service, computer applications, computer literacy, computer science, computer skills, conceptual physics, contemporary women writers, creative writing, dance, digital art, digital photography, drama, drama workshop, dramatic arts, drawing, driver education, ecology, engineering, English, English language-AP, English literature, English literature and composition-AP, environmental science, European history, European literature, expository writing, film and literature, fine arts, foreign language, French, French language-AP, French literature-AP, French-AP, geometry, government and politics-AP, grammar, health and wellness, honors English, honors U.S. history, honors world history, Latin, leadership and service, literary magazine, mathematics, mathematics-AP, modern European history, music, photography, physical education, physics, physics-AP, play production, public speaking, science, senior internship, Shakespeare, social studies, society and culture, South African history, Spanish, Spanish language-AP, statistics, student government, theater, trigonometry, U.S. government and politics-AP, U.S. history-AP, United States government-AP, visual and performing arts, visual arts, vocal ensemble, women's health, women's literature, women's studies, world history, world history-AP, world literature, writing.

Graduation Requirements Arts and fine arts (art, music, dance, drama), computer science, English, foreign language, health education, history, mathematics, physical education (includes health), science, senior internship. Community service is required.

Special Academic Programs Advanced Placement exam preparation; honors section; independent study; academic accommodation for the gifted.

College Admission Counseling 66 students graduated in 2016; all went to college, including Boston University; Canisius College; Hobart and William Smith Colleges; Loyola University Chicago; University of Pittsburgh; University of Toronto. Mean SAT critical reading: 545, mean SAT math: 575, mean SAT writing: 557, mean composite

ACT: 27. 71% scored over 600 on SAT critical reading, 65% scored over 600 on SAT math.

Student Life Upper grades have specified standards of dress, student council, honor system. Discipline rests equally with students and faculty.

Tuition and Aid Day student tuition: $19,840; 5-day tuition and room/board: $42,715; 7-day tuition and room/board: $46,715. Tuition installment plan (FACTS Tuition Payment Plan, monthly payment plans, individually arranged payment plans, 2-payment plan, prepayment discount plan). Tuition reduction for siblings, merit scholarship grants, need-based scholarship grants, faculty remission available. In 2016–17, 58% of upper-school students received aid; total upper-school merit-scholarship money awarded: $400,000. Total amount of financial aid awarded in 2016–17: $1,074,305.

Admissions Traditional secondary-level entrance grade is 9. For fall 2016, 140 students applied for upper-level admission, 120 were accepted, 58 enrolled. School placement exam, school's own exam, TOEFL and writing sample required. Deadline for receipt of application materials: none. Application fee required: $35. Interview required.

Athletics Interscholastic: basketball, bowling, crew, fencing, field hockey, golf, independent competitive sports, lacrosse, rowing, sailing, soccer, squash, swimming and diving, tennis; intramural: aerobics, dance, drill team, fitness, fitness walking, lacrosse, Nautilus, outdoors, paddle tennis, physical fitness, physical training, self defense, skiing (downhill), snowboarding, strength & conditioning, volleyball, yoga. 2 PE instructors, 20 coaches, 1 athletic trainer.

Computers Computers are regularly used in digital applications classes. Computer network features include on-campus library services, online commercial services, Internet access, wireless campus network, Internet filtering or blocking technology. Campus intranet, student e-mail accounts, and computer access in designated common areas are available to students. Students grades are available online. The school has a published electronic and media policy.

Contact Ms. Laura Munson, Director of Admission. 716-885-6780 Ext. 253. Fax: 716-885-6785. E-mail: lmunson@buffaloseminary.org. Website: www.buffaloseminary.org

BURR AND BURTON ACADEMY

57 Seminary Avenue
Manchester, Vermont 05254

Head of School: Mr. Mark Tashjian

General Information Coeducational boarding and day college-preparatory and general academic school. Grades 9–12. Founded: 1829. Setting: small town. Nearest major city is Albany, NY. Students are housed in coed dormitories and BBA Only Boards International Students - Some international students live off campus with host families. 49-acre campus. 7 buildings on campus. Approved or accredited by Independent Schools of Northern New England, New England Association of Schools and Colleges, and Vermont Department of Education. Member of National Association of Independent Schools. Total enrollment: 668. Upper school average class size: 17. Upper school faculty-student ratio: 1:12. There are 175 required school days per year for Upper School students. Upper School students typically attend 5 days per week. The average school day consists of 6 hours and 40 minutes.

Upper School Student Profile Grade 9: 158 students (82 boys, 76 girls); Grade 10: 197 students (85 boys, 112 girls); Grade 11: 159 students (77 boys, 82 girls); Grade 12: 188 students (88 boys, 100 girls). 9% of students are boarding students. 9% are international students. International students from Brazil, China, Germany, Japan, Spain, and Thailand; 7 other countries represented in student body.

Faculty School total: 60. In upper school: 35 men, 25 women; 30 have advanced degrees; 6 reside on campus.

Subjects Offered 3-dimensional design, acting, Advanced Placement courses, applied music, audio visual/media, Basic programming, French studies, graphic design, honors geometry, instrumental music, jazz ensemble, language-AP, mathematics-AP, microeconomics-AP, modern dance, senior internship, strategies for success, study skills, technology/design, theater production, United States government-AP, video film production, vocal music, voice ensemble, wind instruments, woodworking, work-study.

Graduation Requirements Arts, computer literacy, English, mathematics, physical education (includes health), science, social studies (includes history), U.S. history. Community service is required.

Special Academic Programs 14 Advanced Placement exams for which test preparation is offered; honors section; accelerated programs; independent study; term-away projects; study abroad; remedial reading and/or remedial writing; remedial math; programs in English, mathematics, general development for dyslexic students; special instructional classes for deaf students, blind students; ESL (21 students enrolled).

College Admission Counseling 164 students graduated in 2016; 142 went to college, including Boston University; Hobart and William Smith Colleges; Rensselaer Polytechnic Institute; Rochester Institute of Technology; State University of New York College at Cortland; University of Vermont. Other: 16 went to work, 1 entered military service, 5 had other specific plans. 21% scored over 600 on SAT critical reading, 24% scored over 600 on SAT math, 17% scored over 600 on SAT writing, 20% scored over 1800 on combined SAT, 21% scored over 26 on composite ACT.

Student Life Upper grades have specified standards of dress, student council, honor system. Discipline rests primarily with faculty.

Tuition and Aid Tuition installment plan (individually arranged payment plans). Financial aid available to upper-school students. In 2016–17, 10% of upper-school students received aid.

Admissions Traditional secondary-level entrance grade is 9. School's own test and TOEFL or SLEP required. Deadline for receipt of application materials: none. No application fee required. Interview required.

Athletics Interscholastic: alpine skiing (boys, girls), baseball (b), basketball (b,g), cross-country running (b,g), dance team (g), field hockey (g), football (b), golf (b,g), ice hockey (b,g), lacrosse (b,g), mountain biking (b,g), nordic skiing (b,g), skiing (cross-country) (b,g), skiing (downhill) (b,g), snowboarding (b,g), soccer (b,g), softball (g), tennis (b,g), track and field (b,g), wrestling (b,g); coed intramural: equestrian sports, floor hockey, outdoor adventure, outdoor education, volleyball, weight training. 4 PE instructors, 54 coaches, 1 athletic trainer.

Computers Computers are regularly used in all academic, French, humanities, media production, music technology, photography, programming, remedial study skills, SAT preparation, social studies, writing classes. Computer network features include on-campus library services, Internet access, wireless campus network, Internet filtering or blocking technology. Campus intranet, student e-mail accounts, and computer access in designated common areas are available to students. Students grades are available online. The school has a published electronic and media policy.

Contact Mr. Kirk R. Knutson, Director of Admissions and School Counseling. 802-362-1775 Ext. 125. Fax: 802-362-0574. E-mail: kknutson@burrburton.org. Website: www.burrburton.org

BUTTE CENTRAL CATHOLIC HIGH SCHOOL

9 South Idaho Street
Butte, Montana 59701

Head of School: Mr. Kevin St. John

General Information Boys' boarding and coeducational day college-preparatory, arts, business, vocational, religious studies, and technology school, affiliated with Roman Catholic Church. Boarding boys grades 9–12, day boys grades 9–12, day girls grades 9–12. Founded: 1892. Setting: small town. Nearest major city is Bozeman. 6-acre campus. 1 building on campus. Approved or accredited by National Catholic Education Association, Western Catholic Education Association, and Montana Department of Education. Endowment: $300,000. Total enrollment: 145. Upper school average class size: 20. Upper school faculty-student ratio: 1:10. There are 180 required school days per year for Upper School students. Upper School students typically attend 5 days per week. The average school day consists of 7 hours.

Upper School Student Profile Grade 9: 27 students (15 boys, 12 girls); Grade 10: 44 students (25 boys, 19 girls); Grade 11: 37 students (18 boys, 19 girls); Grade 12: 37 students (16 boys, 21 girls). 4% of students are boarding students. 93% are state residents. 1 state is represented in upper school student body. 5% are international students. International students from China and Taiwan; 5 other countries represented in student body. 75% of students are Roman Catholic.

Faculty School total: 17. In upper school: 6 men, 11 women; 3 have advanced degrees; 1 resides on campus.

Subjects Offered Accounting, advanced math, Advanced Placement courses, algebra, American literature-AP, animal behavior, art, athletic training, biology, calculus, calculus-AP, career education, chemistry, choir, college counseling, college placement, college planning, college writing, community service, computer science, computers, debate, desktop publishing, drama, English, English literature and composition-AP, foreign language, French, French as a second language, geometry, government/civics, health, history, honors algebra, honors English, honors geometry, human biology, integrated mathematics, keyboarding, mathematics, model United Nations, physical education, physics, pre-calculus, public speaking, reading, religion, science, social studies, Spanish, student government, trigonometry, Web site design, weightlifting, world history, writing, yearbook.

Graduation Requirements American government, American history, arts and fine arts (art, music, dance, drama), electives, English, foreign language, global studies, health education, keyboarding, mathematics, physical education (includes health), religion (includes Bible studies and theology), science, social studies (includes history), writing. Community service is required.

Special Academic Programs 2 Advanced Placement exams for which test preparation is offered; honors section; independent study; study at local college for college credit; remedial reading and/or remedial writing; remedial math.

College Admission Counseling 32 students graduated in 2015; 30 went to college, including Carroll University; Division of Technology of Montana Tech of The University of Montana; Gonzaga University; Montana State University; The University of Montana Western. Other: 1 went to work, 1 entered military service. Median composite ACT: 20. 7% scored over 26 on composite ACT.

Student Life Upper grades have specified standards of dress, student council, honor system. Discipline rests primarily with faculty. Attendance at religious services is required.

Tuition and Aid Day student tuition: $4000–$8000; 7-day tuition and room/board: $10,000–$15,000. Guaranteed tuition plan. Tuition installment plan (FACTS Tuition Payment Plan, monthly payment plans, individually arranged payment plans). Tuition reduction for siblings, need-based scholarship grants available. In 2015–16, 25% of upper-school students received aid. Total amount of financial aid awarded in 2015–16: $68,000.

Admissions Traditional secondary-level entrance grade is 9. For fall 2015, 145 students applied for upper-level admission, 145 were accepted, 145 enrolled. Admissions testing required. Deadline for receipt of application materials: none. Application fee required: $150. Interview required.

Athletics Interscholastic: basketball (boys, girls), cheering (g), cross-country running (b,g), football (b), golf (b,g), softball (g), strength & conditioning (b,g), tennis (b,g), track and field (b,g), volleyball (g), wrestling (b). 1 PE instructor, 30 coaches, 1 athletic trainer.

Computers Computer network features include on-campus library services, Internet access, Internet filtering or blocking technology. The school has a published electronic and media policy.

Contact Mr. Kevin St. John, Principal. 406-782-6761. Fax: 406-723-3873. E-mail: ksj@buttecentralschools.org. Website: www.buttecentralschools.org

BUXTON SCHOOL

291 South Street
Williamstown, Massachusetts 01267
Head of School: Mr. Peter Smith '74

General Information Coeducational boarding and day college-preparatory school. Grades 9–12. Founded: 1928. Setting: small town. Nearest major city is Boston. Students are housed in coed dormitories. 120-acre campus. 18 buildings on campus. Approved or accredited by Association of Independent Schools in New England, New England Association of Schools and Colleges, The Association of Boarding Schools, and Massachusetts Department of Education. Member of National Association of Independent Schools and Secondary School Admission Test Board. Endowment: $3 million. Total enrollment: 90. Upper school average class size: 9. Upper school faculty-student ratio: 1:4. There are 222 required school days per year for Upper School students. Upper School students typically attend 7 days per week. The average school day consists of 5 hours and 15 minutes.

Upper School Student Profile Grade 9: 17 students (8 boys, 9 girls); Grade 10: 23 students (11 boys, 12 girls); Grade 11: 25 students (12 boys, 13 girls); Grade 12: 25 students (12 boys, 13 girls). 91% of students are boarding students. 26% are state residents. 12 states are represented in upper school student body. 23% are international students. International students from Bangladesh, China, Japan, Mexico, South Africa, and Spain; 4 other countries represented in student body.

Faculty School total: 22. In upper school: 11 men, 11 women; 8 have advanced degrees; 16 reside on campus.

Subjects Offered Advanced math, African dance, African drumming, African studies, algebra, American history, American literature, anatomy and physiology, anthropology, architecture, astronomy, biology, British literature, calculus, cell biology, ceramics, chemistry, civil rights, costumes and make-up, creative writing, critical writing, dance performance, drama, drama performance, drawing, economics, education, English, English literature, ensembles, ESL, European history, expository writing, fiction, film history, French, geometry, grammar, history, improvisation, independent study, instruments, lab science, linear algebra, literary genres, literature, marine biology, medieval/Renaissance history, music, music composition, music performance, music theory, mythology, oceanography, painting, performing arts, philosophy, photography, physics, poetry, pre-calculus, printmaking, psychology, religion, set design, social sciences, Spanish, studio art, technical theater, TOEFL preparation, trigonometry, video film production, voice, Western civilization, writing workshop.

Graduation Requirements American history, English, foreign language, lab science, mathematics, social sciences.

Special Academic Programs Honors section; independent study; study at local college for college credit; academic accommodation for the gifted, the musically talented, and the artistically talented; ESL (7 students enrolled).

College Admission Counseling 27 students graduated in 2016; all went to college, including Bard College; Bard College; Bennington College; Mount Holyoke College; Oberlin College; Pitzer College.

Student Life Discipline rests primarily with faculty.

Tuition and Aid Day student tuition: $31,000; 7-day tuition and room/board: $52,500. Tuition installment plan (individually arranged payment plans, Tuition Management Systems). Need-based scholarship grants available. In 2016–17, 49% of upper-school students received aid. Total amount of financial aid awarded in 2016–17: $1,600,000.

Admissions Traditional secondary-level entrance grade is 9. SSAT or TOEFL or SLEP required. Deadline for receipt of application materials: February 1. Application fee required: $50. Interview recommended.

Athletics Interscholastic: soccer (boys, girls); intramural: cheering (g), soccer (b,g); coed interscholastic: basketball, Frisbee, ultimate Frisbee; coed intramural: basketball, bicycling, dance, fitness, freestyle skiing, hiking/backpacking, horseback riding, indoor soccer, jogging, martial arts, mountain biking, outdoor activities, running, skateboarding, skiing (cross-country), skiing (downhill), snowboarding, soccer, table tennis, ultimate Frisbee, volleyball, walking, weight lifting, yoga.

Computers Computers are regularly used in architecture, ESL, language development, mathematics, media production, multimedia, music, photography,

science, Spanish, video film production, writing, yearbook classes. Computer network features include Internet access, wireless campus network, Internet filtering or blocking technology. Campus intranet and computer access in designated common areas are available to students. The school has a published electronic and media policy.

Contact Admissions Office. 413-458-3919. Fax: 413-458-9428. E-mail: Admissions@BuxtonSchool.org. Website: http://www.BuxtonSchool.org

CAIRO AMERICAN COLLEGE

1 Midan Digla, Road 253, Maadi
Cairo 11431, Egypt
Head of School: Wayne Rutherford

General Information Coeducational day college-preparatory, general academic, and IB school. Grades PK–12. Founded: 1945. Setting: suburban. 11-acre campus. 12 buildings on campus. Approved or accredited by Council of International Schools and Middle States Association of Colleges and Schools. Affiliate member of National Association of Independent Schools; member of European Council of International Schools. Language of instruction: English. Total enrollment: 1,417. Upper school average class size: 16. Upper school faculty-student ratio: 1:9. There are 176 required school days per year for Upper School students. Upper School students typically attend 5 days per week. The average school day consists of 7 hours.

Faculty School total: 100. In upper school: 17 men, 20 women.

Subjects Offered International Baccalaureate courses.

Graduation Requirements Arts and fine arts (art, music, dance, drama), English, foreign language, mathematics, physical education (includes health), science, social studies (includes history).

Special Academic Programs International Baccalaureate program; Advanced Placement exam preparation; remedial reading and/or remedial writing; remedial math; programs in English, mathematics, general development for dyslexic students; ESL.

College Admission Counseling 66 students graduated in 2016; 65 went to college.

Student Life Upper grades have specified standards of dress, student council. Discipline rests primarily with faculty.

Tuition and Aid Limited need-based scholarship grants for continuing students only available.

Admissions Admissions testing required. Deadline for receipt of application materials: none. Application fee required: $350. Interview required.

Athletics Interscholastic: baseball (boys), basketball (b,g), soccer (b,g), softball (b,g); intramural: flag football (b,g), synchronized swimming (g), volleyball (b,g), weight lifting (b,g); coed interscholastic: badminton; coed intramural: diving.

Computers Computers are regularly used in all classes. Computer network features include on-campus library services, online commercial services, Internet access. Campus intranet and student e-mail accounts are available to students.

Contact Danya Amin, Director of Admissions. 20-2-2755-5555. Fax: 20-2-2519-6584. E-mail: registrar@cacegypt.org. Website: www.cacegypt.org

CALGARY ACADEMY

9400 17 Avenue SW
Calgary, Alberta T3H 4A6, Canada
Head of School: Ms. Dana Braunberger

General Information Coeducational day college-preparatory, arts, and technology school; primarily serves underachievers, students with learning disabilities, individuals with Attention Deficit Disorder, and dyslexic students. Grades 2–12. Founded: 1981. Setting: suburban. 17-acre campus. 3 buildings on campus. Approved or accredited by Association of Independent Schools and Colleges of Alberta and Alberta Department of Education. Language of instruction: English. Endowment: CAN$3 million. Total enrollment: 370. Upper school average class size: 16. Upper school faculty-student ratio: 1:8. There are 188 required school days per year for Upper School students. Upper School students typically attend 5 days per week. The average school day consists of 6 hours and 10 minutes.

Upper School Student Profile Grade 10: 41 students (21 boys, 20 girls); Grade 11: 49 students (29 boys, 20 girls); Grade 12: 50 students (32 boys, 18 girls).

Faculty School total: 25. In upper school: 10 men, 15 women; 10 have advanced degrees.

Subjects Offered Art history, athletics, band, biology, calculus, career and personal planning, character education, chemistry, computer animation, computer multimedia, creative drama, drama, English composition, English literature, general science, grammar, language arts, mathematics, outdoor education, physical education, physics, psychology, reading/study skills, remedial study skills, sociology, Spanish, study skills.

Graduation Requirements Biology, chemistry, English, mathematics, physics, science, social studies (includes history).

Special Academic Programs Remedial reading and/or remedial writing; remedial math; programs in English, mathematics for dyslexic students.

College Admission Counseling 64 students graduated in 2015; 55 went to college, including Mount Royal University; University of Alberta; University of Calgary; University of Lethbridge. Other: 5 went to work, 4 had other specific plans.

Student Life Upper grades have specified standards of dress, student council, honor system. Discipline rests primarily with faculty.

Tuition and Aid Day student tuition: CAN$18,000. Tuition installment plan (monthly payment plans, individually arranged payment plans). Bursaries available. In 2015–16, 5% of upper-school students received aid. Total amount of financial aid awarded in 2015–16: CAN$300,000.

Admissions Traditional secondary-level entrance grade is 10. For fall 2015, 100 students applied for upper-level admission, 30 were accepted, 25 enrolled. Achievement tests, Wechsler Individual Achievement Test and Wechsler Intelligence Scale for Children III required. Deadline for receipt of application materials: none. Application fee required: CAN$1500. On-campus interview required.

Athletics Interscholastic: badminton (boys, girls), ball hockey (b), basketball (b,g), cross-country running (b,g), floor hockey (b), golf (b,g), handball (b,g), track and field (b,g), volleyball (b,g), wrestling (b,g); intramural: fly fishing (b), ice hockey (b,g); coed interscholastic: badminton, curling, golf, soccer; coed intramural: alpine skiing, outdoor recreation, triathlon. 6 PE instructors.

Computers Computers are regularly used in all academic classes. Computer network features include on-campus library services, Internet access, wireless campus network, Internet filtering or blocking technology. Campus intranet and computer access in designated common areas are available to students. Students grades are available online. The school has a published electronic and media policy.

Contact Ms. Irina Dart, Director of Admissions. 403-686-6444 Ext. 236. Fax: 403-240-3427. E-mail: idart@calgaryacademy.com. Website: www.calgaryacademy.com

CALGARY ACADEMY COLLEGIATE

1677 93rd St Sw
Calgary, Alberta T3H 0R3, Canada

Head of School: Ms. Jessica Richmond

General Information Coeducational day college-preparatory, arts, and technology school; primarily serves students with learning disabilities, individuals with Attention Deficit Disorder, and dyslexic students. Grades 6–12. Founded: 1981. Setting: urban. 17-acre campus. 3 buildings on campus. Approved or accredited by Association of Independent Schools and Colleges of Alberta and Alberta Department of Education. Language of instruction: English. Endowment: CAN$15 million. Total enrollment: 176. Upper school average class size: 17. Upper school faculty-student ratio: 1:8. There are 188 required school days per year for Upper School students. Upper School students typically attend 5 days per week. The average school day consists of 6 hours and 10 minutes.

Upper School Student Profile Grade 10: 30 students (20 boys, 10 girls); Grade 11: 30 students (19 boys, 11 girls); Grade 12: 35 students (21 boys, 14 girls).

Faculty School total: 25. In upper school: 10 men, 15 women; 20 have advanced degrees.

Subjects Offered Art history, athletics, band, biology, calculus, career and personal planning, character education, chemistry, computer animation, computer multimedia, drama, English composition, English literature, grammar, language arts, mathematics, outdoor education, physical education, physics, psychology, social studies, sociology, Spanish, study skills.

Graduation Requirements Biology, chemistry, English, mathematics, physics, social studies (includes history).

Special Academic Programs International Baccalaureate program; 1 Advanced Placement exam for which test preparation is offered.

College Admission Counseling 39 students graduated in 2015; 38 went to college, including Mount Royal University; University of Alberta; University of Calgary; University of Lethbridge. Other: 1 went to work.

Student Life Upper grades have specified standards of dress, student council, honor system. Discipline rests primarily with faculty.

Tuition and Aid Day student tuition: CAN$18,000. Tuition installment plan (monthly payment plans, individually arranged payment plans). Bursaries, need-based scholarship grants available. In 2015–16, 5% of upper-school students received aid. Total amount of financial aid awarded in 2015–16: CAN$300,000.

Admissions Traditional secondary-level entrance grade is 10. For fall 2015, 50 students applied for upper-level admission, 30 were accepted, 20 enrolled. Achievement tests, Wechsler Individual Achievement Test or Wechsler Intelligence Scale for Children III required. Deadline for receipt of application materials: none. Application fee required: CAN$1600. On-campus interview required.

Athletics Interscholastic: badminton (boys, girls), ball hockey (b), basketball (b,g), cross-country running (b,g), golf (b,g), handball (b,g), rugby (b), track and field (b,g), volleyball (b,g), wrestling (b,g); intramural: ice hockey (b,g); coed interscholastic: badminton, cheering, curling, soccer; coed intramural: aerobics/Nautilus, bicycling, canoeing/kayaking, martial arts, mountain biking, outdoor activities, outdoor education, outdoor recreation, rock climbing, skiing (cross-country), skiing (downhill), triathlon, wall climbing. 6 PE instructors, 30 coaches.

Computers Computers are regularly used in all academic classes. Computer network features include on-campus library services, Internet access, wireless campus network, Internet filtering or blocking technology. Computer access in designated common areas is available to students. Students grades are available online. The school has a published electronic and media policy.

Contact Ms. Irina Dart, Director of Admissions. 403-686-6444 Ext. 236. Fax: 403-686-3427. E-mail: idart@calgaryacademy.com.
Website: http://www.calgaryacademy.com/

THE CALHOUN SCHOOL

433 West End Avenue
New York, New York 10024

Head of School: Steven Solnick

General Information Coeducational day college-preparatory, arts, and Experiential, progressive education school. Grades N–12. Founded: 1896. Setting: urban. 1 building on campus. Approved or accredited by New York State Association of Independent Schools. Member of National Association of Independent Schools. Endowment: $19 million. Total enrollment: 724. Upper school average class size: 13. Upper school faculty-student ratio: 1:7. There are 164 required school days per year for Upper School students. Upper School students typically attend 5 days per week. The average school day consists of 6 hours and 50 minutes.

Upper School Student Profile Grade 9: 60 students (31 boys, 29 girls); Grade 10: 61 students (28 boys, 33 girls); Grade 11: 63 students (32 boys, 31 girls); Grade 12: 57 students (27 boys, 30 girls).

Faculty School total: 140. In upper school: 20 men, 18 women; 30 have advanced degrees.

Subjects Offered Acting, advanced biology, advanced chemistry, advanced computer applications, African-American literature, algebra, American history, American literature, anthropology, arts, biology, calculus, chemistry, child development, chorus, community service, computer math, computer programming, computer science, constitutional law, creative writing, English literature, English-AP, ethnic literature, French, geometry, healthful living, human sexuality, independent study, instrumental music, music history, peer counseling, photography, physical education, physics, pre-calculus, psychology, Shakespeare, Spanish, speech, studio art, theater, theater design and production, Web site design, world history, world literature.

Graduation Requirements Arts and fine arts (art, music, dance, drama), English, foreign language, mathematics, physical education (includes health), science, social studies (includes history), 9th grade Life Skills with peer leaders, Junior Workshop independent research project, Senior Work internship. Community service is required.

Special Academic Programs Independent study; term-away projects; domestic exchange program (with The Network Program Schools); academic accommodation for the gifted, the musically talented, and the artistically talented.

College Admission Counseling 60 students graduated in 2016; 59 went to college, including Bard College; Emory University; Tulane University; University of Chicago; University of Michigan; Wesleyan University. Other: 1 entered a postgraduate year.

Student Life Upper grades have student council. Discipline rests equally with students and faculty.

Summer Programs Art/fine arts programs offered; session focuses on Shakespeare production; held on campus; accepts boys and girls; open to students from other schools. 16 students usually enrolled. 2017 schedule: June 19 to July 28. Application deadline: March 1.

Tuition and Aid Day student tuition: $47,350. Tuition installment plan (Key Tuition Payment Plan, monthly payment plans, individually arranged payment plans). Need-based scholarship grants available. In 2016–17, 30% of upper-school students received aid. Total amount of financial aid awarded in 2016–17: $2,000,000.

Admissions Traditional secondary-level entrance grade is 9. For fall 2016, 240 students applied for upper-level admission, 80 were accepted, 25 enrolled. Deadline for receipt of application materials: January 15. Application fee required: $75. On-campus interview recommended.

Athletics Interscholastic: baseball (boys, girls), basketball (b,g), cross-country running (b,g), softball (g), track and field (b,g), volleyball (b,g); coed interscholastic: golf, soccer; coed intramural: aerobics, aerobics/Nautilus, basketball, fitness, golf, project adventure, sailing, soccer, strength & conditioning, tennis, weight training, yoga. 5 PE instructors, 10 coaches.

Computers Computers are regularly used in basic skills, mathematics, programming, video film production, Web site design classes. Computer network features include on-campus library services, online commercial services, Internet access, wireless campus network, MS Office, PowerPoint, Basic, Dreamweaver, and Flash Software. Student e-mail accounts and computer access in designated common areas are available to students. Students grades are available online. The school has a published electronic and media policy.

Contact Andrew Hume, Director of Enrollment and External Relationships. 212-497-6511. Fax: 212-497-6531. E-mail: andrew.hume@calhoun.org.
Website: www.calhoun.org

CALIFORNIA CROSSPOINT HIGH SCHOOL

1501 Harbor Bay Parkway
Alameda, California 94502

Head of School: Mr. Robin S. Hom

General Information Coeducational boarding and day college-preparatory, religious studies, and ESL school, affiliated with Bible Fellowship Church,

Evangelical/Fundamental faith. Grades 9–12. Founded: 1979. Setting: suburban. Nearest major city is Oakland. Students are housed in Home Stay. 6-acre campus. 1 building on campus. Approved or accredited by Association of Christian Schools International, The College Board, US Department of State, Western Association of Schools and Colleges, and California Department of Education. Endowment: $100,000. Total enrollment: 200. Upper school average class size: 15. Upper school faculty-student ratio: 1:8. There are 173 required school days per year for Upper School students. Upper School students typically attend 5 days per week. The average school day consists of 7 hours and 5 minutes.

Upper School Student Profile Grade 9: 36 students (22 boys, 14 girls); Grade 10: 43 students (26 boys, 17 girls); Grade 11: 62 students (38 boys, 24 girls); Grade 12: 39 students (19 boys, 20 girls). 25% of students are boarding students. 2 states are represented in upper school student body. 35% are international students. International students from China, Hong Kong, Macao, Venezuela, and Viet Nam. 20% of students are Bible Fellowship Church, Evangelical/Fundamental faith.

Faculty School total: 40. In upper school: 15 men, 20 women; 22 have advanced degrees.

Subjects Offered Advanced computer applications, Advanced Placement courses, aerobics, algebra, American government, American history, American history-AP, American literature, American literature-AP, applied music, art, art-AP, audio visual/media, Basic programming, basketball, Bible, Bible studies, biology, biology-AP, British literature, calculus, calculus-AP, career/college preparation, chemistry, Chinese, Chinese studies, choir, choral music, Christian doctrine, Christian ethics, Christian studies, civics, civics/free enterprise, college counseling, college placement, college planning, communications, community service, comparative religion, computer applications, computer graphics, computer science, computer science-AP, CPR, debate, drama, driver education, economics, economics-AP, electives, English, English language-AP, English literature, English literature-AP, European history-AP, first aid, foreign language, general science, geometry, government, government and politics-AP, government-AP, graphic arts, honors English, intro to computers, language arts, leadership and service, learning strategies, library assistant, literature and composition-AP, literature-AP, macro/microeconomics-AP, Mandarin, marching band, marine science, martial arts, mathematics-AP, microeconomics, microeconomics-AP, music, newspaper, participation in sports, physical education, physics, physics-AP, pre-algebra, pre-calculus, probability and statistics, psychology-AP, public speaking, religious education, religious studies, ROTC (for boys), SAT preparation, SAT/ACT preparation, science, science research, Spanish, speech, speech and debate, speech communications, sports, state history, statistics, student government, theater, theater arts, trigonometry, U.S. government, U.S. government and politics-AP, U.S. history, U.S. history-AP, visual and performing arts, volleyball, Web authoring, world history, world wide web design, yearbook.

Graduation Requirements Algebra, American government, American history, Bible, Chinese, CPR, driver education, economics, English, first aid, foreign language, geometry, history, lab science, Life of Christ, mathematics, physical education (includes health), physics, pre-algebra, science, visual and performing arts, world history.

Special Academic Programs 15 Advanced Placement exams for which test preparation is offered; honors section; term-away projects; study at local college for college credit; study abroad; academic accommodation for the gifted, remedial reading and/or remedial writing; ESL (30 students enrolled).

College Admission Counseling 59 students graduated in 2016; all went to college, including San Jose State University; University of California, Berkeley; University of California, Irvine; University of California, Los Angeles; University of California, San Diego; University of the Pacific. Mean SAT critical reading: 529, mean SAT math: 641, mean SAT writing: 546, mean combined SAT: 1704. 45% scored over 600 on SAT critical reading, 85% scored over 600 on SAT math, 50% scored over 600 on SAT writing, 45% scored over 1800 on combined SAT.

Student Life Upper grades have uniform requirement, student council. Discipline rests primarily with faculty. Attendance at religious services is required.

Summer Programs Remediation, enrichment, advancement, ESL, sports programs offered; session focuses on academic enrichment or remediation; held on campus; accepts boys and girls; open to students from other schools. 40 students usually enrolled. 2017 schedule: June 14 to July 28. Application deadline: May 15.

Tuition and Aid Day student tuition: $10,300–$12,450. Tuition installment plan (monthly payment plans, individually arranged payment plans, eTuition automatic electronic deposit). Tuition reduction for siblings, merit scholarship grants, need-based scholarship grants, paying campus jobs, tuition reduction for staff children, tuition reduction for children of full-time Christian ministers of like faith available. In 2016–17, 15% of upper-school students received aid; total upper-school merit-scholarship money awarded: $75,000. Total amount of financial aid awarded in 2016–17: $520,000.

Admissions Traditional secondary-level entrance grade is 9. For fall 2016, 50 students applied for upper-level admission, 40 were accepted, 30 enrolled. Achievement/Aptitude/Writing, admissions testing, California Achievement Test, CTBS (or similar from their school), Math Placement Exam, Stanford Achievement Test or writing sample required. Deadline for receipt of application materials: none. No application fee required. Interview recommended.

Athletics Interscholastic: badminton (boys, girls), basketball (b,g), cross-country running (b,g), golf (b,g), soccer (b,g), tennis (b), track and field (b,g), volleyball (b,g); intramural: basketball (b,g), dance (b,g), outdoor education (b,g), outdoor recreation

(b,g), soccer (b,g), table tennis (b,g), tennis (g), volleyball (b,g); coed interscholastic: badminton, golf, swimming and diving; coed intramural: backpacking, outdoor education, outdoor recreation, softball, table tennis, volleyball. 2 PE instructors, 1 coach.

Computers Computers are regularly used in all academic, lab/keyboard, programming, science, Web site design classes. Computer network features include on-campus library services, online commercial services, Internet access, wireless campus network, Internet filtering or blocking technology, Naviance College Planning Software, PowerSchool Student Information Service, Schoology Learning Management System. Student e-mail accounts and computer access in designated common areas are available to students. Students grades are available online. The school has a published electronic and media policy.

Contact Mrs. Christine Hom, Admissions Director. 510-995-5333. Fax: 510-995-5333. E-mail: ChristineHom@cchsrams.org. Website: www.cchsrams.org

CALIFORNIA LUTHERAN HIGH SCHOOL

31970 Central Avenue
PO Box 1570
Wildomar, California 92595

Head of School: Mr. Steven Rosenbaum

General Information Coeducational boarding college-preparatory school, affiliated with Wisconsin Evangelical Lutheran Synod. Grades 9–12. Founded: 1977. Setting: small town. Nearest major city is Temecula. Students are housed in single-sex dormitories. 6-acre campus. 4 buildings on campus. Approved or accredited by Western Association of Schools and Colleges and California Department of Education. Total enrollment: 85. Upper school average class size: 15. Upper school faculty-student ratio: 1:8. There are 175 required school days per year for Upper School students. Upper School students typically attend 5 days per week. The average school day consists of 7 hours.

Upper School Student Profile Grade 9: 22 students (13 boys, 9 girls); Grade 10: 25 students (11 boys, 14 girls); Grade 11: 23 students (13 boys, 10 girls); Grade 12: 17 students (10 boys, 7 girls). 60% of students are boarding students. 76% are state residents. 1 state is represented in upper school student body. 24% are international students. International students from China; 2 other countries represented in student body. 59% of students are Wisconsin Evangelical Lutheran Synod.

Faculty School total: 11. In upper school: 7 men, 4 women; 2 have advanced degrees; 4 reside on campus.

Subjects Offered All academic.

Graduation Requirements Computer skills, English, foreign language, government, mathematics, religion (includes Bible studies and theology), SAT preparation, science, typing, world history.

Special Academic Programs International Baccalaureate program; Advanced Placement exam preparation; honors section; ESL (22 students enrolled).

College Admission Counseling 19 students graduated in 2016; 15 went to college, including Martin Luther College. Other: 3 went to work, 1 entered military service. 50% scored over 26 on composite ACT.

Student Life Upper grades have specified standards of dress, student council, honor system. Discipline rests primarily with faculty. Attendance at religious services is required.

Tuition and Aid Day student tuition: $6800–$28,000. Tuition installment plan (FACTS Tuition Payment Plan). Tuition reduction for siblings, need-based scholarship grants available. In 2016–17, 40% of upper-school students received aid. Total amount of financial aid awarded in 2016–17: $250,000.

Admissions Traditional secondary-level entrance grade is 9. For fall 2016, 29 students applied for upper-level admission, 29 were accepted, 29 enrolled. Math and English placement tests required. Deadline for receipt of application materials: none. Application fee required: $100. Interview required.

Athletics Interscholastic: baseball (boys), basketball (b,g), football (b), softball (g), track and field (b,g), volleyball (g); coed interscholastic: cross-country running.

Computers Computers are regularly used in computer applications, yearbook classes. Computer network features include Internet access, wireless campus network, Internet filtering or blocking technology. Student e-mail accounts and computer access in designated common areas are available to students. Students grades are available online.

Contact Sarah Garvin, Secretary. 951 678-7000. Fax: 951-678-0172. E-mail: sgarvin@clhsonline.net. Website: www.clhsonline.net

CALVARY DAY SCHOOL

4625 Waters Avenue
Savannah, Georgia 31404

Head of School: Dr. James Taylor

General Information Coeducational day college-preparatory, arts, religious studies, and technology school, affiliated with Baptist Church. Grades PK–12. Founded: 1961. Setting: suburban. 22-acre campus. 6 buildings on campus. Approved or accredited by Southern Association of Colleges and Schools and Georgia Department of Education.

Total enrollment: 767. Upper school average class size: 17. Upper school faculty-student ratio: 1:17. There are 180 required school days per year for Upper School students. Upper School students typically attend 5 days per week. The average school day consists of 6 hours and 45 minutes.

Upper School Student Profile 10% of students are Baptist.

Faculty School total: 72. In upper school: 22 men, 28 women; 32 have advanced degrees.

Subjects Offered 20th century history, 20th century world history, accounting, acting, advanced biology, advanced chemistry, advanced math, Advanced Placement courses, algebra, American government, American history, American history-AP, American literature, American literature-AP, analysis and differential calculus, anatomy and physiology, ancient world history, art, band, Bible, biochemistry, biology, biology-AP, calculus-AP, chemistry, chemistry-AP, Chinese, chorus, composition-AP, computer applications, data processing, economics, English, English language and composition-AP, European history-AP, French, geometry, government, government/civics-AP, mathematics-AP, physical education, physical science, physics, pre-calculus, religion, Spanish, U.S. history, weight training, world history.

Graduation Requirements Business skills (includes word processing), computer science, English, foreign language, history, mathematics, physical education (includes health), religion (includes Bible studies and theology), science, social sciences, social studies (includes history), technology.

Special Academic Programs 11 Advanced Placement exams for which test preparation is offered; honors section; accelerated programs; independent study; study at local college for college credit; domestic exchange program; academic accommodation for the gifted; remedial reading and/or remedial writing; remedial math.

College Admission Counseling 76 students graduated in 2015; 75 went to college, including Armstrong State University; Georgia Institute of Technology; Georgia Southern University; Liberty University; Mercer University; University of Georgia. Other: 1 went to work. 38% scored over 600 on SAT critical reading, 27% scored over 600 on SAT math.

Student Life Upper grades have uniform requirement, student council, honor system. Discipline rests primarily with faculty. Attendance at religious services is required.

Tuition and Aid Day student tuition: $8400. Tuition installment plan (Insured Tuition Payment Plan, monthly payment plans, individually arranged payment plans). Tuition reduction for siblings, merit scholarship grants, need-based scholarship grants available. In 2015–16, 10% of upper-school students received aid; total upper-school merit-scholarship money awarded: $5000. Total amount of financial aid awarded in 2015–16: $183,000.

Admissions Traditional secondary-level entrance grade is 9. For fall 2015, 112 students applied for upper-level admission, 74 were accepted, 73 enrolled. Otis-Lennon School Ability Test, Reading for Understanding, Stanford Achievement Test, Otis-Lennon School Ability Test or WRAT required. Deadline for receipt of application materials: none. Application fee required: $100. Interview required.

Athletics Interscholastic: aquatics (boys, girls), baseball (b), basketball (b,g), cross-country running (b,g), equestrian sports (b,g), football (b), golf (b,g), soccer (b,g), softball (g), tennis (b,g), track and field (b,g), volleyball (g), weight lifting (b,g); intramural: backpacking (b,g), physical fitness (b,g), physical training (b,g); coed intramural: physical fitness, physical training. 4 PE instructors, 4 coaches, 1 athletic trainer.

Computers Computers are regularly used in all academic classes. Computer network features include on-campus library services, online commercial services, Internet access, wireless campus network, Internet filtering or blocking technology. Campus intranet, student e-mail accounts, and computer access in designated common areas are available to students. Students grades are available online. The school has a published electronic and media policy.

Contact KIm Rice, Admissions Director. 912-351-2299 Ext. 112. Fax: 912-351-2280. E-mail: KRice@calvarydayschool.com. Website: http://www.calvarydayschool.com/

CALVERT HALL COLLEGE HIGH SCHOOL

8102 LaSalle Road
Baltimore, Maryland 21286

Head of School: Br. John Kane, FSC

General Information Boys' day college-preparatory school, affiliated with Roman Catholic Church. Grades 9–12. Founded: 1845. Setting: suburban. 32-acre campus. 6 buildings on campus. Approved or accredited by Christian Brothers Association, Middle States Association of Colleges and Schools, National Catholic Education Association, and Maryland Department of Education. Member of National Association of Independent Schools. Endowment: $8.5 million. Total enrollment: 1,160. Upper school average class size: 18. Upper school faculty-student ratio: 1:11. There are 174 required school days per year for Upper School students. Upper School students typically attend 5 days per week. The average school day consists of 6 hours and 20 minutes.

Upper School Student Profile Grade 9: 325 students (325 boys); Grade 10: 284 students (284 boys); Grade 11: 298 students (298 boys); Grade 12: 272 students (272 boys). 64% of students are Roman Catholic.

Faculty School total: 106. In upper school: 72 men, 32 women; 72 have advanced degrees.

Subjects Offered Accounting, algebra, American history, American history-AP, American literature, art, art history, band, Bible studies, biology, business, business skills, calculus, chemistry, chorus, computer programming, computer science, creative writing, drama, earth science, economics, economics-AP, engineering, English, English language-AP, English literature, ethics, European history, fine arts, French, French-AP, geography, geometry, German, German-AP, government/civics, graphic arts, history, history-AP, journalism, Latin, leadership, marketing, mathematics, music, painting, philosophy, physical education, physics, physics-AP, political science, pre-calculus, probability and statistics, psychology, psychology-AP, religion, religious education, science, sculpture, social sciences, social studies, Spanish, Spanish language-AP, speech, statistics, statistics-AP, theater, theology, typing, U.S. government and politics-AP, U.S. history, U.S. history-AP, world history, world literature, writing.

Graduation Requirements Arts and fine arts (art, music, dance, drama), English, foreign language, mathematics, physical education (includes health), religion (includes Bible studies and theology), science, social sciences, social studies (includes history).

Special Academic Programs 22 Advanced Placement exams for which test preparation is offered; honors section; academic accommodation for the gifted, the musically talented, and the artistically talented; programs in English, mathematics, general development for dyslexic students.

College Admission Counseling 284 students graduated in 2016; 281 went to college, including La Salle University; Loyola University Maryland; Penn State University Park; Salisbury University; Towson University; University of Maryland, College Park. Other: 3 had other specific plans. Median SAT critical reading: 565, median SAT math: 575, median SAT writing: 545, median combined SAT: 1685, median composite ACT: 24. 31% scored over 600 on SAT critical reading, 42% scored over 600 on SAT math, 31% scored over 600 on SAT writing, 36% scored over 1800 on combined SAT, 35% scored over 26 on composite ACT.

Student Life Upper grades have specified standards of dress, student council, honor system. Discipline rests primarily with faculty. Attendance at religious services is required.

Summer Programs Remediation, enrichment, sports, art/fine arts, computer instruction programs offered; session focuses on remediation and make-up courses; held on campus; accepts boys and girls; open to students from other schools. 250 students usually enrolled. 2017 schedule: June 24 to July 26. Application deadline: June 15.

Tuition and Aid Day student tuition: $14,950. Tuition installment plan (monthly payment plans, individually arranged payment plans). Merit scholarship grants, need-based scholarship grants available. In 2016–17, 55% of upper-school students received aid; total upper-school merit-scholarship money awarded: $830,850. Total amount of financial aid awarded in 2016–17: $2,668,735.

Admissions Traditional secondary-level entrance grade is 9. Traditional secondary-level entrance age is 13. High School Placement Test (closed version) from Scholastic Testing Service required. Deadline for receipt of application materials: none. Application fee required: $25. On-campus interview recommended.

Athletics Interscholastic: aquatics, baseball, basketball, cross-country running, football, golf, hockey, ice hockey, indoor track & field, lacrosse, rugby, soccer, squash, swimming and diving, tennis, track and field, volleyball, water polo, winter (indoor) track, wrestling; intramural: basketball, bicycling, billiards, bocce, bowling, fitness, flag football, freestyle skiing, Frisbee, martial arts, outdoor adventure, rock climbing, rugby, sailing, skiing (downhill), table tennis, ultimate Frisbee, weight lifting. 2 PE instructors, 11 coaches, 1 athletic trainer.

Computers Computers are regularly used in accounting, business, college planning, computer applications, digital applications, economics, English, foreign language, graphic design, history, independent study, journalism, keyboarding, library, literary magazine, mathematics, music, programming, religion, SAT preparation, science, social sciences, stock market, video film production, writing, yearbook classes. Computer network features include on-campus library services, Internet access, wireless campus network, Internet filtering or blocking technology. Campus intranet, student e-mail accounts, and computer access in designated common areas are available to students. Students grades are available online. The school has a published electronic and media policy.

Contact Chris Bengel, Director of Admissions. 410-825-4266 Ext. 126. Fax: 410-825-6826. E-mail: bengelc@calverthall.com. Website: www.calverthall.com

CALVIN CHRISTIAN HIGH SCHOOL

2000 North Broadway
Escondido, California 92026

Head of School: Mr. Terry D. Kok

General Information Coeducational day college-preparatory school, affiliated with Reformed Church. Grades PK–12. Founded: 1980. Setting: suburban. Nearest major city is San Diego. 24-acre campus. 2 buildings on campus. Approved or accredited by Christian Schools International, Western Association of Schools and Colleges, and California Department of Education. Endowment: $1 million. Total enrollment: 470. Upper school average class size: 18. Upper school faculty-student ratio: 1:17. There are 175 required school days per year for Upper School students. Upper School students typically attend 5 days per week. The average school day consists of 6 hours and 25 minutes.

Upper School Student Profile Grade 9: 34 students (15 boys, 19 girls); Grade 10: 32 students (16 boys, 16 girls); Grade 11: 42 students (24 boys, 18 girls); Grade 12: 42 students (27 boys, 15 girls). 30% of students are Reformed.

Faculty School total: 15. In upper school: 8 men, 7 women; 8 have advanced degrees.

Subjects Offered Advanced Placement courses, algebra, American government, art, band, Bible, biology, biology-AP, business mathematics, calculus-AP, chemistry, choir, Christian doctrine, Christian ethics, Christian studies, church history, computer applications, computer programming, computers, dramatic arts, economics, electives, English, English literature-AP, geometry, health, instrumental music, intro to computers, media, modern history, photography, physical education, physical science, physics, pre-calculus, psychology, robotics, Spanish, Spanish-AP, speech, U.S. history, U.S. history-AP, world history, World War II, yearbook.

Graduation Requirements Advanced Placement courses, arts and fine arts (art, music, dance, drama), English, foreign language, mathematics, media, physical education (includes health), religion (includes Bible studies and theology), science, social studies (includes history), technology, service-learning requirements.

Special Academic Programs 6 Advanced Placement exams for which test preparation is offered; remedial reading and/or remedial writing; remedial math.

College Admission Counseling 43 students graduated in 2016; 41 went to college, including California State University, San Marcos; Calvin College; Dordt College; Point Loma Nazarene University; Trinity Christian College; University of California, San Diego. Other: 1 went to work, 1 entered military service. Mean SAT critical reading: 568, mean SAT math: 570, mean SAT writing: 549, mean composite ACT: 24. 43% scored over 600 on SAT critical reading, 36% scored over 600 on SAT math, 29% scored over 600 on SAT writing.

Student Life Upper grades have specified standards of dress, student council, honor system. Discipline rests primarily with faculty. Attendance at religious services is required.

Tuition and Aid Day student tuition: $10,345. Tuition installment plan (monthly payment plans, individually arranged payment plans). Need-based scholarship grants, need-based loans available. In 2016–17, 30% of upper-school students received aid. Total amount of financial aid awarded in 2016–17: $275,000.

Admissions For fall 2016, 20 students applied for upper-level admission, 18 were accepted, 18 enrolled. Deadline for receipt of application materials: none. Application fee required: $300. Interview required.

Athletics Interscholastic: baseball (boys), basketball (b,g), cross-country running (b,g), football (b), soccer (b,g), softball (g), track and field (b,g), volleyball (g); coed interscholastic: golf; coed intramural: swimming and diving, weight training. 2 PE instructors, 16 coaches.

Computers Computers are regularly used in computer applications, keyboarding, photography, programming, science, yearbook classes. Computer network features include on-campus library services, Internet access, wireless campus network, Internet filtering or blocking technology. Student e-mail accounts are available to students. Students grades are available online. The school has a published electronic and media policy.

Contact Mr. Frank Steidl, Principal. 760-489-6430. Fax: 760-489-7055. E-mail: franksteidl@calvinchristianescondido.org. Website: www.calvinchristianescondido.org

CAMDEN MILITARY ACADEMY

520 Highway 1 North
Camden, South Carolina 29020

Head of School: Col. Eric Boland

General Information Boys' boarding college-preparatory and military school; primarily serves students with learning disabilities, individuals with Attention Deficit Disorder, individuals with emotional and behavioral problems, and dyslexic students. Grades 7–PG. Founded: 1892. Setting: small town. Nearest major city is Columbia. Students are housed in single-sex dormitories. 40-acre campus. 15 buildings on campus. Approved or accredited by South Carolina Independent School Association, Southern Association of Colleges and Schools, and Southern Association of Independent Schools. Member of National Association of Independent Schools. Total enrollment: 295. Upper school average class size: 15. Upper school faculty-student ratio: 1:12. Upper School students typically attend 5 days per week. The average school day consists of 6 hours.

Upper School Student Profile Grade 9: 55 students (55 boys); Grade 10: 55 students (55 boys); Grade 11: 60 students (60 boys); Grade 12: 60 students (60 boys). 100% of students are boarding students. 39% are state residents. 23 states are represented in upper school student body. International students from Bermuda, Cayman Islands, Ghana, Mexico, and Trinidad and Tobago.

Faculty School total: 49. In upper school: 35 men, 3 women; 23 have advanced degrees; 9 reside on campus.

Subjects Offered Algebra, American government, anatomy and physiology, band, biology, calculus, chemistry, computer applications, computer literacy, driver education, economics, English, French, geometry, humanities, physical science, physics, pre-calculus, psychology, sociology, Spanish, U.S. history, world geography, world history.

Graduation Requirements Computer literacy, English, foreign language, history, JROTC, mathematics, science.

Special Academic Programs Advanced Placement exam preparation; honors section; study at local college for college credit; remedial reading and/or remedial writing.

College Admission Counseling 58 students graduated in 2015; 56 went to college, including University of South Carolina. Other: 2 entered military service.

Student Life Upper grades have uniform requirement, student council, honor system. Discipline rests primarily with faculty.

Tuition and Aid 7-day tuition and room/board: $17,595. Tuition installment plan (monthly payment plans, individually arranged payment plans). Tuition reduction for siblings, need-based scholarship grants available. In 2015–16, 20% of upper-school students received aid.

Admissions Traditional secondary-level entrance grade is 10. Deadline for receipt of application materials: none. Application fee required: $100. Interview required.

Athletics Interscholastic: baseball, basketball, cross-country running, football, golf; intramural: aerobics, aquatics. 2 PE instructors, 15 coaches, 1 athletic trainer.

Computers Computers are regularly used in all academic classes. Computer resources include on-campus library services, Internet access. Student e-mail accounts are available to students.

Contact Mr. Casey Robinson, Director of Admissions. 803-432-6001. Fax: 803-425-1020. E-mail: admissions@camdenmilitary.com Website: www.camdenmilitary.com

CAMPBELL HALL (EPISCOPAL)

4533 Laurel Canyon Boulevard
North Hollywood, California 91607

Head of School: Rev. Canon Julian P. Bull

General Information Coeducational day college-preparatory school, affiliated with Episcopal Church. Grades K–12. Founded: 1944. Setting: urban. Nearest major city is Los Angeles. 15-acre campus. 12 buildings on campus. Approved or accredited by National Association of Episcopal Schools, Western Association of Schools and Colleges, and California Department of Education. Member of National Association of Independent Schools. Endowment: $10 million. Total enrollment: 1,125. Upper school average class size: 15. Upper school faculty-student ratio: 1:8. There are 140 required school days per year for Upper School students. Upper School students typically attend 5 days per week. The average school day consists of 6 hours and 50 minutes.

Upper School Student Profile 7% of students are members of Episcopal Church.

Faculty School total: 142. In upper school: 41 men, 96 women; 30 have advanced degrees.

Subjects Offered Algebra, American history, American literature, American studies, ancient history, art, art history, astronomy, band, biology, calculus, ceramics, chemistry, Chinese, community service, computer programming, computer science, creative writing, dance, drama, drawing, earth science, ecology, economics, English, English literature, environmental science, ethics, European history, filmmaking, fine arts, French, geography, geometry, government/civics, history, human development, humanities, instrumental music, Japanese, law, mathematics, music, orchestra, painting, philosophy, photography, physical education, physics, physiology, pre-calculus, printmaking, psychology, science, sculpture, senior seminar, social studies, sociology, Spanish, speech, statistics, theater, theater arts, trigonometry, voice, yearbook.

Graduation Requirements Arts and fine arts (art, music, dance, drama), English, foreign language, mathematics, music history, physical education (includes health), science, social studies (includes history). Community service is required.

Special Academic Programs Advanced Placement exam preparation; honors section; independent study; study at local college for college credit.

College Admission Counseling 142 students graduated in 2016; all went to college, including Boston University; Indiana University Bloomington; New York University; University of California, Los Angeles; University of Michigan; University of Southern California.

Student Life Upper grades have uniform requirement, student council, honor system. Discipline rests equally with students and faculty. Attendance at religious services is required.

Summer Programs Enrichment, advancement, sports, art/fine arts, computer instruction programs offered; session focuses on creative arts and sports; held on campus; accepts boys and girls; open to students from other schools. 200 students usually enrolled. 2017 schedule: June 12 to August 4. Application deadline: May 1.

Tuition and Aid Day student tuition: $36,760. Tuition installment plan (Insured Tuition Payment Plan, monthly payment plans, individually arranged payment plans). Need-based scholarship grants, Episcopal Credit Union tuition loans available. In 2016–17, 25% of upper-school students received aid. Total amount of financial aid awarded in 2016–17: $5,400,000.

Admissions Traditional secondary-level entrance grade is 9. ISEE required. Deadline for receipt of application materials: December 15. Application fee required: $135. Interview required.

Athletics Interscholastic: aerobics/dance (boys, girls), ballet (b,g), baseball (b), basketball (b,g), cheering (b,g), cross-country running (b,g), dance (b,g), dance squad (b,g), equestrian sports (b,g), flag football (b,g), football (b), golf (b,g), horseback riding (b,g), modern dance (b,g), soccer (b,g), softball (g), tennis (b,g), track and field (b,g), volleyball (b,g); intramural: weight lifting (b,g); coed interscholastic: aerobics/dance, ballet, cheering, cross-country running, dance, dance squad, golf, horseback riding, modern dance, track and field. 5 PE instructors, 13 coaches, 2 athletic trainers.

Computers Computers are regularly used in all classes. Computer network features include on-campus library services, online commercial services, Internet access, wireless campus network, Internet filtering or blocking technology. Campus intranet, student e-mail accounts, and computer access in designated common areas are available to students. The school has a published electronic and media policy.

Contact Mr. George White, Director of Admissions & Enrollment Management. 818-980-7280. Fax: 818-762-3269. E-mail: whiteg@campbellhall.org. Website: www.campbellhall.org

CAMPBELL RIVER CHRISTIAN SCHOOL

250 South Dogwood Street
Campbell River, British Columbia V9W 6Y7, Canada

Head of School: Mr. Christian Klaue

General Information Coeducational day college-preparatory, arts, religious studies, and technology school, affiliated with Baptist Church. Grades K–12. Founded: 1981. Setting: small town. Nearest major city is Nanaimo, Canada. 3-acre campus. 1 building on campus. Approved or accredited by Association of Christian Schools International and British Columbia Department of Education. Language of instruction: English. Upper school average class size: 15. Upper school faculty-student ratio: 1:15. There are 178 required school days per year for Upper School students. Upper School students typically attend 5 days per week. The average school day consists of 6 hours and 15 minutes.

Upper School Student Profile Grade 8: 16 students (7 boys, 9 girls); Grade 9: 10 students (6 boys, 4 girls); Grade 10: 12 students (10 boys, 2 girls); Grade 11: 11 students (5 boys, 6 girls); Grade 12: 13 students (8 boys, 5 girls). 50% of students are Baptist.

Faculty School total: 177. In upper school: 6 men, 3 women; 1 has an advanced degree.

Subjects Offered All academic.

Graduation Requirements Bible, Canadian history, career and personal planning, English.

College Admission Counseling Colleges students went to include Trinity Western University.

Student Life Upper grades have specified standards of dress. Discipline rests primarily with faculty. Attendance at religious services is required.

Admissions For fall 2015, 62 students applied for upper-level admission, 62 were accepted, 62 enrolled. Deadline for receipt of application materials: none. Application fee required: CAN$100. Interview required.

Athletics Interscholastic: basketball (boys, girls), cross-country running (b,g), track and field (b,g), volleyball (b,g), wrestling (b); coed intramural: outdoor education. 1 PE instructor, 1 coach.

Computers Computers are regularly used in all academic classes. Computer network features include on-campus library services, Internet access, wireless campus network, Internet filtering or blocking technology. Campus intranet and student e-mail accounts are available to students. The school has a published electronic and media policy.

Contact Mr. Christian Klaue, Principal. 250-287-4266. Fax: 250-287-4266. E-mail: principal@crcs.bc.ca. Website: http://www.crcs.bc.ca/

CAMPHILL SPECIAL SCHOOL

Glenmoore, Pennsylvania
See Special Needs Schools section.

CAMPION SCHOOL, ATHENS

PO Box 67484
Pallini
Athens 15302, Greece

Head of School: Mr. Stephen W. Atherton

General Information Coeducational day college-preparatory, general academic, and arts school. Grades PK–13. Founded: 1970. Setting: suburban. 2-hectare campus. 2 buildings on campus. Member of European Council of International Schools. Language of instruction: English. Total enrollment: 485. Upper school average class size: 20. Upper school faculty-student ratio: 1:18. Upper School students typically attend 5 days per week. The average school day consists of 6 hours and 30 minutes.

Upper School Student Profile Grade 6: 52 students (26 boys, 26 girls); Grade 7: 31 students (19 boys, 12 girls); Grade 8: 45 students (23 boys, 22 girls); Grade 9: 38 students (21 boys, 17 girls); Grade 10: 53 students (28 boys, 25 girls); Grade 11: 39 students (17 boys, 22 girls); Grade 12: 44 students (18 boys, 26 girls); Grade 13: 41 students (16 boys, 25 girls).

Faculty School total: 65. In upper school: 12 men, 32 women; 16 have advanced degrees.

Subjects Offered Algebra, Arabic, art, biology, calculus, chemistry, design, drama, economics, English, English literature, European history, French, geography, geometry, German, Greek, history, information technology, International Baccalaureate courses, mathematics, music, philosophy, physical education, physics, psychology, SAT preparation, science, Spanish, theater, trigonometry, world history, world literature.

Graduation Requirements Creative arts, English, foreign language, humanities, mathematics, physical education (includes health), science.

Special Academic Programs International Baccalaureate program; academic accommodation for the musically talented and the artistically talented; ESL (18 students enrolled).

College Admission Counseling 29 students graduated in 2016; 28 went to college, including Northeastern University; Vassar College; Yale University. Other: 1 had other specific plans. Median SAT critical reading: 641, median SAT math: 730, median SAT writing: 675, median combined SAT: 2170. 80% scored over 600 on SAT critical reading, 100% scored over 600 on SAT math, 100% scored over 600 on SAT writing, 100% scored over 1800 on combined SAT.

Student Life Upper grades have specified standards of dress, student council. Discipline rests primarily with faculty.

Tuition and Aid Day student tuition: €11,560–€12,920. Tuition installment plan (individually arranged payment plans). Tuition reduction for siblings, merit scholarship grants available. In 2016–17, 20% of upper-school students received aid; total upper-school merit-scholarship money awarded: €52,000.

Admissions Traditional secondary-level entrance grade is 8. For fall 2016, 225 students applied for upper-level admission, 120 were accepted, 115 enrolled. Admissions testing and English entrance exam required. Deadline for receipt of application materials: none. Application fee required: 80 Greek drachmas. On-campus interview recommended.

Athletics Interscholastic: basketball (boys, girls), cross-country running (b,g), dance (b,g), soccer (b,g), swimming and diving (b,g), tennis (b,g), track and field (b,g), volleyball (b,g); intramural: basketball (b,g), cross-country running (b,g), dance (b,g), gymnastics (b,g), rafting (b,g), rugby (b,g), skiing (downhill) (b,g), snowboarding (b,g), soccer (b,g), swimming and diving (b,g), table tennis (b,g), tennis (b,g), track and field (b,g), volleyball (b,g), water skiing (b,g). 3 PE instructors.

Computers Computers are regularly used in computer applications, design, English, geography, information technology, mathematics, science, yearbook classes. Computer resources include on-campus library services, Internet access, wireless campus network, Internet filtering or blocking technology. Student e-mail accounts and computer access in designated common areas are available to students.

Contact Ms. Diane Baker, Director of Communications/Senior Admissions. 30-2106071730. Fax: 30-2106071770. E-mail: dbaker@campion.edu.gr. Website: www.campion.edu.gr

CANADIAN ACADEMY

4-1 Koyo-cho Naka
Higashinada-ku
Kobe 658-0032, Japan

Head of School: Mr. Jon Schatzky

General Information Coeducational boarding and day college-preparatory school. Boarding grades 8–13, day grades PK–13. Founded: 1913. Setting: urban. Nearest major city is Osaka, Japan. Students are housed in coed dormitories. 3-hectare campus. 2 buildings on campus. Approved or accredited by Council of International Schools and Western Association of Schools and Colleges. Language of instruction: English. Total enrollment: 690. Upper school average class size: 15. Upper school faculty-student ratio: 1:10. There are 180 required school days per year for Upper School students. Upper School students typically attend 5 days per week. The average school day consists of 6 hours and 55 minutes.

Upper School Student Profile Grade 9: 57 students (23 boys, 34 girls); Grade 10: 50 students (25 boys, 25 girls); Grade 11: 57 students (29 boys, 28 girls); Grade 12: 48 students (22 boys, 26 girls).

Faculty School total: 74. In upper school: 16 men, 12 women; 20 have advanced degrees; 8 reside on campus.

Subjects Offered Algebra, art, biology, calculus, chemistry, choir, college writing, concert band, drama, economics, English, ESL, French, geometry, health, integrated mathematics, introduction to literature, Japanese, Japanese history, jazz band, music, orchestra, peer counseling, physical education, physics, publications, social studies, Spanish, theater arts, theory of knowledge, U.S. history, world literature.

Graduation Requirements Art, electives, English, health, mathematics, modern languages, performing arts, physical education (includes health), science, social studies (includes history), personal project and mission portfolio.

Special Academic Programs International Baccalaureate program; Advanced Placement exam preparation; independent study; ESL (14 students enrolled).

College Admission Counseling 57 students graduated in 2016; 50 went to college, including Biola University; New York University; The University of British Columbia; University of California, Berkeley. Other: 7 had other specific plans. Median SAT critical reading: 530, median SAT math: 570, median SAT writing: 530. 36% scored over 600 on SAT critical reading, 52% scored over 600 on SAT math, 33% scored over 600 on SAT writing.

Student Life Upper grades have specified standards of dress, student council, honor system. Discipline rests primarily with faculty.

Summer Programs Enrichment, sports, computer instruction programs offered; session focuses on SAT preparation; held on campus; accepts boys and girls; open to students from other schools. 2017 schedule: June 19 to July 14. Application deadline: May 31.

Tuition and Aid Day student tuition: ¥2,341,100; 7-day tuition and room/board: ¥3,509,944. Tuition installment plan (semester payment plan). Need-based scholarship grants available. In 2016–17, 5% of upper-school students received aid; total upper-school merit-scholarship money awarded: ¥1,350,000. Total amount of financial aid awarded in 2016–17: ¥3,350,000.

Admissions Traditional secondary-level entrance grade is 9. For fall 2016, 32 students applied for upper-level admission, 22 were accepted, 20 enrolled. English for Non-native Speakers, essay or math and English placement tests required. Deadline for receipt of application materials: none. Application fee required: ¥65,000. On-campus interview recommended.

Athletics Interscholastic: badminton (boys, girls), baseball (b), basketball (b,g), soccer (b,g), softball (g), tennis (b,g), volleyball (b,g); intramural: badminton (b,g), baseball (b), basketball (b,g), soccer (b,g), softball (g), table tennis (b,g), volleyball (b,g), weight training (b,g); coed interscholastic: dance, tennis. 4 PE instructors.

Computers Computers are regularly used in all classes. Computer network features include on-campus library services, online commercial services, Internet access, wireless campus network, Internet filtering or blocking technology. Campus intranet and student e-mail accounts are available to students. Students grades are available online. The school has a published electronic and media policy.

Contact Mr. Rob Smailes, Director of Admissions and Community Relations. 81-78-857-0100. Fax: 81-78-857-3250. E-mail: admissions@canacad.ac.jp.

Website: www.canacad.ac.jp

THE CANTERBURY EPISCOPAL SCHOOL

1708 North Westmoreland Road
DeSoto, Texas 75115

Head of School: Mrs. Alison Reese

General Information Coeducational day college-preparatory school, affiliated with Episcopal Church. Grades PK–12. Founded: 1992. Setting: suburban. Nearest major city is Dallas. 32-acre campus. 2 buildings on campus. Approved or accredited by Southwest Association of Episcopal Schools and Texas Department of Education. Member of National Association of Independent Schools. Total enrollment: 251. Upper school average class size: 16. Upper school faculty-student ratio: 1:16. There are 173 required school days per year for Upper School students. Upper School students typically attend 5 days per week. The average school day consists of 6 hours and 50 minutes.

Upper School Student Profile Grade 7: 23 students (8 boys, 15 girls); Grade 8: 19 students (10 boys, 9 girls); Grade 9: 15 students (8 boys, 7 girls); Grade 10: 15 students (8 boys, 7 girls); Grade 11: 13 students (3 boys, 10 girls); Grade 12: 11 students (4 boys, 7 girls). 2% of students are members of Episcopal Church.

Faculty School total: 27. In upper school: 8 men, 11 women; 9 have advanced degrees.

Subjects Offered 1 1/2 elective credits, advanced chemistry, Advanced Placement courses, algebra, American government, American literature, anatomy and physiology, art history-AP, athletics, basketball, biology, biology-AP, calculus, calculus-AP, cheerleading, chemistry, chemistry-AP, college counseling, comparative religion, computer applications, debate, economics, English composition, English language and composition-AP, English literature, English literature and composition-AP, environmental science AP, European history-AP, fine arts, foreign language, geometry, government, health, math applications, music, personal money management, physics AP, psychology-AP, Spanish, speech, studio art, theology, U.S. history, U.S. history-AP, visual and performing arts, world geography, world history, yearbook.

Graduation Requirements 1 1/2 elective credits, algebra, anatomy and physiology, arts and fine arts (art, music, dance, drama), biology, calculus, chemistry, computer applications, economics, English, English composition, English language and composition-AP, English literature, European history, foreign language, geometry, government, health, math applications, physical education (includes health), physics, pre-calculus, religion (includes Bible studies and theology), speech, trigonometry, U.S. history, world geography, senior thesis in English IV.

Special Academic Programs 9 Advanced Placement exams for which test preparation is offered; honors section; independent study; study at local college for college credit; domestic exchange program.

College Admission Counseling 17 students graduated in 2016; all went to college, including Baylor University; Fordham University; Rice University; Texas A&M University. Median SAT critical reading: 574, median SAT math: 553, median SAT writing: 574, median combined SAT: 1686, median composite ACT: 25. 35% scored over 600 on SAT critical reading, 18% scored over 600 on SAT math, 41% scored over 600 on SAT writing, 29% scored over 1800 on combined SAT, 33% scored over 26 on composite ACT.

Student Life Upper grades have uniform requirement, student council, honor system. Discipline rests primarily with faculty. Attendance at religious services is required.

Tuition and Aid Day student tuition: $17,750. Tuition installment plan (FACTS Tuition Payment Plan, individually arranged payment plans). Tuition reduction for siblings, need-based scholarship grants available. In 2016–17, 40% of upper-school students received aid.

Admissions Traditional secondary-level entrance grade is 9. For fall 2016, 15 students applied for upper-level admission, 12 were accepted, 9 enrolled. ISEE or OLSAT,

Stanford Achievement Test required. Deadline for receipt of application materials: none. Application fee required: $150. Interview required.

Athletics Interscholastic: baseball (boys), basketball (b,g), cheering (g), golf (b), softball (g), volleyball (g); intramural: flag football (b); coed interscholastic: soccer, swimming and diving, tennis, track and field. 1 PE instructor, 8 coaches, 1 athletic trainer.

Computers Computers are regularly used in computer applications, yearbook classes. Computer network features include Internet access, Internet filtering or blocking technology. Computer access in designated common areas is available to students. Students grades are available online.

Contact Mack Bridges, Business Manager. 972-572-7200 Ext. 107. Fax: 972-572-2470. E-mail: bridgesm@TheCanterburySchool.org.

Website: www.thecanterburyschool.org/

CANTERBURY SCHOOL

101 Aspetuck Avenue
New Milford, Connecticut 06776

Head of School: Rachel E. Stone

General Information Coeducational boarding and day college-preparatory school. Grades 9–PG. Founded: 1915. Setting: small town. Nearest major city is Hartford. Students are housed in single-sex dormitories. 150-acre campus. 20 buildings on campus. Approved or accredited by New England Association of Schools and Colleges, The Association of Boarding Schools, and Connecticut Department of Education. Member of National Association of Independent Schools and Secondary School Admission Test Board. Endowment: $25 million. Total enrollment: 350. Upper school average class size: 11. Upper school faculty-student ratio: 1:6. Upper School students typically attend 6 days per week.

Upper School Student Profile Grade 9: 50 students (30 boys, 20 girls); Grade 10: 82 students (39 boys, 43 girls); Grade 11: 108 students (63 boys, 45 girls); Grade 12: 107 students (62 boys, 45 girls); Postgraduate: 21 students (19 boys, 2 girls). 70% of students are boarding students. 50% are state residents. 18 states are represented in upper school student body. 17% are international students. International students from Austria, Christmas Island, Ghana, Republic of Moldova, Sri Lanka, and Tajikistan; 12 other countries represented in student body.

Faculty School total: 76. In upper school: 40 men, 36 women; 45 have advanced degrees; 56 reside on campus.

Subjects Offered 1 1/2 elective credits, adolescent issues, algebra, American history, American literature, anthropology, art, art history, astronomy, biochemistry, biology, calculus, ceramics, chemistry, civil rights, computer programming, computer science, creative writing, dance, drama, driver education, earth science, economics, English, English literature, environmental science, ethics, European history, expository writing, fine arts, French, geography, geology, geometry, grammar, history, Irish studies, Latin, marine biology, mathematics, microbiology, music, oceanography, philosophy, photography, physics, physiology, religion, science, social studies, Spanish, Spanish literature, speech, statistics, theater, theology, trigonometry, women's studies, world history, world literature, writing.

Graduation Requirements Arts and fine arts (art, music, dance, drama), computer science, English, foreign language, mathematics, New Testament, religion (includes Bible studies and theology), science, social studies (includes history).

Special Academic Programs Advanced Placement exam preparation; honors section; independent study; ESL (15 students enrolled).

College Admission Counseling 108 students graduated in 2016; all went to college, including Boston University; Hobart and William Smith Colleges; Sacred Heart University; University of Connecticut. 25% scored over 600 on SAT critical reading, 35% scored over 600 on SAT math.

Student Life Upper grades have specified standards of dress, student council, honor system. Discipline rests primarily with faculty. Attendance at religious services is required.

Summer Programs Sports programs offered; session focuses on basketball and football camps; held on campus; accepts boys and girls; open to students from other schools. 70 students usually enrolled.

Tuition and Aid Day student tuition: $33,000; 7-day tuition and room/board: $42,500. Tuition installment plan (Academic Management Services Plan, Key Tuition Payment Plan). Need-based scholarship grants, need-based loans, middle-income loans available. In 2016–17, 36% of upper-school students received aid. Total amount of financial aid awarded in 2016–17: $3,500,000.

Admissions Traditional secondary-level entrance grade is 9. For fall 2016, 700 students applied for upper-level admission, 250 were accepted, 125 enrolled. SLEP, SSAT, TOEFL and writing sample required. Deadline for receipt of application materials: January 31. Application fee required: $50. Interview required.

Athletics Interscholastic: baseball (boys), basketball (b,g), cross-country running (b,g), diving (b,g), field hockey (g), football (b), ice hockey (b,g), lacrosse (b,g), soccer (b,g), softball (g), squash (b,g), swimming and diving (b,g), tennis (b,g), track and field (b,g), volleyball (g); intramural: dance (g), equestrian sports (g), hockey (b,g), horseback riding (b,g); coed interscholastic: crew, golf, water polo, wrestling; coed intramural: fitness, softball, Special Olympics, strength & conditioning, weight lifting, weight training. 40 coaches, 2 athletic trainers.

Computers Computers are regularly used in accounting, English, mathematics, multimedia, science classes. Computer network features include on-campus library services, Internet access, wireless campus network, Internet filtering or blocking technology. Student e-mail accounts and computer access in designated common areas are available to students. Students grades are available online. The school has a published electronic and media policy.

Contact Mr. Matt Mulhern, Director of Admission. 860-210-3836. Fax: 860-350-1120. E-mail: mmulhern@cbury.org. Website: www.cbury.org

CANTERBURY SCHOOL

8141 College Parkway
Fort Myers, Florida 33919

Head of School: Mr. Rick Kirschner

General Information Coeducational day college-preparatory and liberal arts school. Grades PK–12. Founded: 1964. Setting: suburban. 33-acre campus. 7 buildings on campus. Approved or accredited by Council of Accreditation and School Improvement, Florida Council of Independent Schools, Southern Association of Colleges and Schools, Southern Association of Independent Schools, The College Board, and Florida Department of Education. Member of National Association of Independent Schools and Secondary School Admission Test Board. Endowment: $6.6 million. Total enrollment: 620. Upper school average class size: 18. Upper school faculty-student ratio: 1:12. There are 181 required school days per year for Upper School students. Upper School students typically attend 5 days per week. The average school day consists of 6 hours and 30 minutes.

Upper School Student Profile Grade 9: 75 students (41 boys, 34 girls); Grade 10: 64 students (36 boys, 28 girls); Grade 11: 77 students (41 boys, 36 girls); Grade 12: 54 students (35 boys, 19 girls).

Faculty School total: 87. In upper school: 16 men, 10 women; 15 have advanced degrees.

Subjects Offered Advanced Placement courses, algebra, American history, American history-AP, American literature, anatomy, art, art history, biology, biology-AP, British literature, calculus, calculus-AP, ceramics, chemistry, chemistry-AP, comparative government and politics-AP, computer programming, constitutional law, creative writing, critical writing, drama, earth science, ecology, economics, English, English literature, English literature-AP, environmental science-AP, European history, fine arts, French, French language-AP, geography, geometry, government-AP, government/civics, grammar, health, history, Latin, leadership, macroeconomics-AP, marine biology, mathematics, music, nationalism and ethnic conflict, photography, physical education, physics, physics-AP, physiology, SAT preparation, science, social studies, sociology, Spanish, Spanish language-AP, speech, statistics, theater, U.S. government and politics-AP, U.S. history, United Nations and international issues, world history, world literature, writing, yearbook.

Graduation Requirements Arts and fine arts (art, music, dance, drama), English, foreign language, mathematics, physical education (includes health), science, social studies (includes history), speech, required community service hours.

Special Academic Programs 16 Advanced Placement exams for which test preparation is offered; independent study; study at local college for college credit; ESL (19 students enrolled).

College Admission Counseling 62 students graduated in 2016; all went to college, including Boston College; Columbia University; Duke University; University of Central Florida; University of Florida; University of Miami. Mean SAT critical reading: 590, mean SAT math: 597, mean SAT writing: 577, mean combined SAT: 1764, mean composite ACT: 27. 47% scored over 600 on SAT critical reading, 49% scored over 600 on SAT math, 46% scored over 600 on SAT writing, 47% scored over 1800 on combined SAT, 65% scored over 26 on composite ACT.

Student Life Upper grades have specified standards of dress, student council, honor system. Discipline rests primarily with faculty.

Summer Programs Remediation, enrichment, advancement, ESL, sports, art/fine arts programs offered; session focuses on academic enrichment; held on campus; accepts boys and girls; open to students from other schools. 200 students usually enrolled. 2017 schedule: June 6 to July 30. Application deadline: none.

Tuition and Aid Day student tuition: $23,270. Tuition installment plan (Insured Tuition Payment Plan, FACTS Tuition Payment Plan, monthly payment plans, individually arranged payment plans, quarterly payment plan). Need-based scholarship grants, tuition remission available. In 2016–17, 42% of upper-school students received aid; total upper-school merit-scholarship money awarded: $514,390. Total amount of financial aid awarded in 2016–17: $1,747,197.

Admissions Traditional secondary-level entrance grade is 9. For fall 2016, 86 students applied for upper-level admission, 58 were accepted, 42 enrolled. ERB CTP IV or SSAT required. Deadline for receipt of application materials: none. Application fee required: $100. On-campus interview recommended.

Athletics Interscholastic: baseball (boys), basketball (b,g), cheering (g), football (b), lacrosse (b,g), soccer (b,g), swimming and diving (b,g), tennis (b,g), track and field (b,g), volleyball (g), winter soccer (b,g); intramural: baseball (b), basketball (b,g), football (b), soccer (b,g), volleyball (g); coed interscholastic: cross-country running, golf; coed intramural: golf. 6 PE instructors, 26 coaches, 1 athletic trainer.

Computers Computers are regularly used in all classes. Computer network features include on-campus library services, Internet access, wireless campus network, Internet filtering or blocking technology. Campus intranet, student e-mail accounts, and computer access in designated common areas are available to students. Students grades are available online. The school has a published electronic and media policy.

Contact Ms. Julie A. Peters, Director of Admission. 239-415-8945 Ext. 118. Fax: 239-481-8339. E-mail: jpeters@canterburyfortmyers.org. Website: www.canterburyfortmyers.org

CANTERBURY SCHOOL

3210 Smith Road
Fort Wayne, Indiana 46804

Head of School: Mr. Bill Ennist

General Information Coeducational day college-preparatory, technology, global studies, and advanced science school. Grades K–12. Founded: 1977. Setting: suburban. 60-acre campus. 3 buildings on campus. Approved or accredited by Southern Association of Colleges and Schools. Member of National Association of Independent Schools. Endowment: $12.1 million. Total enrollment: 754. Upper school average class size: 17. Upper school faculty-student ratio: 1:9. There are 178 required school days per year for Upper School students. Upper School students typically attend 5 days per week. The average school day consists of 7 hours and 15 minutes.

Upper School Student Profile Grade 9: 87 students (52 boys, 35 girls); Grade 10: 96 students (49 boys, 47 girls); Grade 11: 96 students (48 boys, 48 girls); Grade 12: 93 students (48 boys, 45 girls).

Faculty School total: 115. In upper school: 22 men, 25 women; 39 have advanced degrees.

Subjects Offered ACT preparation, advanced biology, advanced chemistry, American history-AP, anatomy, anatomy and physiology, astronomy, British literature, chemistry-AP, choir, civics, college counseling, computer technology certification, driver education, economics-AP, engineering, government, health, horticulture, intro to computers, macro/microeconomics-AP, macroeconomics-AP, microeconomics-AP, music technology, newspaper, orchestra, statistics-AP, student publications, U.S. history-AP, yearbook.

Graduation Requirements Chemistry, college counseling, college planning, electives, health, performing arts, senior seminar, world history, Freshman Block, Sophomore Block.

Special Academic Programs Advanced Placement exam preparation; independent study; study at local college for college credit; study abroad.

College Admission Counseling 90 students graduated in 2016; all went to college, including Harvard University; Indiana University Bloomington; Miami University; Purdue University; Stanford University; Taylor University. Mean composite ACT: 28.

Student Life Upper grades have specified standards of dress, student council, honor system. Discipline rests primarily with faculty.

Summer Programs Art/fine arts, computer instruction programs offered; session focuses on grade 9 and grade 10 academic block, select courses for upperclassmen; held on campus; accepts boys and girls; not open to students from other schools. 100 students usually enrolled. 2017 schedule: June 12 to June 30. Application deadline: March 1.

Tuition and Aid Day student tuition: $13,500–$16,340. Tuition installment plan (FACTS Tuition Payment Plan, pre-approved tuition loans through local bank). Merit scholarship grants, need-based scholarship grants available.

Admissions Traditional secondary-level entrance grade is 9. ERB required. Deadline for receipt of application materials: none. Application fee required: $35. On-campus interview required.

Athletics Interscholastic: baseball (boys), basketball (b,g), cheering (g), cross-country running (b,g), diving (b,g), golf (b,g), soccer (b,g), softball (g), swimming and diving (b,g), tennis (b,g), track and field (b,g), volleyball (g); intramural: equestrian sports (g); coed intramural: bowling, fencing, rowing. 2 PE instructors, 17 coaches, 1 athletic trainer.

Computers Computers are regularly used in all academic classes. Computer network features include on-campus library services, online commercial services, Internet access, wireless campus network, Internet filtering or blocking technology, Homework available online. Campus intranet and student e-mail accounts are available to students. Students grades are available online. The school has a published electronic and media policy.

Contact Mrs. Susan Johnson, Director of High School Admissions. 260-407-3553 Ext. 2011. Fax: 260-407-3551. E-mail: sjohnson@canterburyschool.org. Website: www.canterburyschool.org

THE CANTERBURY SCHOOL OF FLORIDA

990 62nd Avenue NE
St. Petersburg, Florida 33702

Head of School: Mr. Mac H. Hall

General Information Coeducational day college-preparatory and marine studies, educational technolog school. Grades PK–12. Founded: 1968. Setting: suburban. 20-acre campus. 5 buildings on campus. Approved or accredited by Florida Council of Independent Schools, The College Board, and Florida Department of Education. Member of National Association of Independent Schools. Total enrollment: 480. Upper school average class size: 15. Upper school faculty-student ratio: 1:15. There are 174 required school days per year for Upper School students. Upper School students typically attend 5 days per week. The average school day consists of 7 hours and 23 minutes.

Upper School Student Profile Grade 9: 39 students (21 boys, 18 girls); Grade 10: 47 students (26 boys, 21 girls); Grade 11: 32 students (15 boys, 17 girls); Grade 12: 42 students (17 boys, 25 girls).

Faculty School total: 98. In upper school: 9 men, 17 women; 9 have advanced degrees.

Subjects Offered 20th century history, 20th century physics, 20th century world history, 3-dimensional art, 3-dimensional design, acting, adolescent issues, advanced biology, advanced chemistry, advanced computer applications, advanced math, Advanced Placement courses, advanced studio art-AP, algebra, American government, American history, American history-AP, American literature, American literature-AP, anatomy, anatomy and physiology, Ancient Greek, ancient history, ancient world history, applied arts, applied music, art, art history, art history-AP, art-AP, arts, astronomy, athletics, band, baseball, Basic programming, basketball, biology, biology-AP, British literature, British literature (honors), calculus, calculus-AP, career/college preparation, ceramics, character education, cheerleading, chemistry, chemistry-AP, Chinese, choir, choral music, chorus, classical language, classical studies, college counseling, college placement, communication skills, community service, comparative government and politics-AP, competitive science projects, computer graphics, computer multimedia, computer science, computer science-AP, computer skills, contemporary issues, creative writing, critical thinking, dance, dance performance, design, desktop publishing, digital imaging, digital photography, drama, drawing, earth science, economics, economics-AP, English, English composition, English language and composition-AP, English language-AP, English literature, English literature and composition-AP, English literature-AP, environmental education, environmental science, environmental science-AP, environmental studies, ethics, European history, expository writing, fine arts, finite math, foreign language, French, French-AP, freshman seminar, geography, geometry, golf, government and politics-AP, government-AP, government/civics, government/civics-AP, grammar, Greek culture, guitar, health, health and wellness, history, history of music, history-AP, honors algebra, honors English, honors geometry, honors U.S. history, honors world history, human geography - AP, independent living, interdisciplinary studies, keyboarding, Latin, Latin-AP, leadership, leadership and service, library, library research, library skills, life management skills, life science, life skills, macro/microeconomics-AP, macroeconomics-AP, Mandarin, marine biology, marine ecology, marine science, marine studies, mathematics, mathematics-AP, mechanical drawing, mentorship program, modern world history, music, music theater, music theory-AP, musical productions, musical theater, oceanography, outdoor education, personal and social education, personal fitness, photography, photojournalism, physical education, physical science, physics, physics-AP, play production, portfolio art, pre-algebra, pre-calculus, pre-college orientation, psychology, psychology-AP, reading/study skills, robotics, SAT preparation, SAT/ACT preparation, science, senior composition, senior seminar, senior thesis, social sciences, social studies, Spanish, Spanish language-AP, Spanish literature-AP, Spanish-AP, speech, speech and debate, sports conditioning, stagecraft, statistics-AP, student government, student publications, student teaching, studio art-AP, swimming, technical theater, tennis, theater arts, theater design and production, theater history, theater production, track and field, typing, U.S. history, U.S. history-AP, values and decisions, visual and performing arts, volleyball, weight fitness, weight training, Western philosophy, world history, world literature, world religions, yearbook, yoga.

Graduation Requirements Arts and fine arts (art, music, dance, drama), career/college preparation, electives, English, ethics, foreign language, history, mathematics, physical education (includes health), research, science, senior seminar, writing, community service hours, character education, senior thesis. Community service is required.

Special Academic Programs 25 Advanced Placement exams for which test preparation is offered; honors section; independent study; ESL (2 students enrolled).

College Admission Counseling 38 students graduated in 2016; all went to college, including Auburn University; Emory University; Florida State University; University of Colorado Boulder; University of Florida. Mean SAT critical reading: 596, mean SAT math: 611, mean SAT writing: 593, mean combined SAT: 1801, mean composite ACT: 27. 37% scored over 600 on SAT critical reading, 44% scored over 600 on SAT math, 48% scored over 600 on SAT writing, 48% scored over 1800 on combined SAT, 61% scored over 26 on composite ACT.

Student Life Upper grades have specified standards of dress, student council, honor system. Discipline rests primarily with faculty.

Summer Programs Remediation, enrichment, advancement, sports, art/fine arts, computer instruction programs offered; session focuses on fun, enrichment, multi-discipline skills and abilities; held both on and off campus; accepts boys and girls; open to students from other schools. 550 students usually enrolled. 2017 schedule: June 5 to July 31. Application deadline: March 15.

Tuition and Aid Day student tuition: $8075-$18,975. Tuition installment plan (Insured Tuition Payment Plan, monthly payment plans, individually arranged payment plans). Tuition reduction for siblings, need-based scholarship grants, Step Up Program (FL) available. In 2016–17, 22% of upper-school students received aid. Total amount of financial aid awarded in 2016–17: $1,014,852.

Admissions Traditional secondary-level entrance grade is 9. For fall 2016, 61 students applied for upper-level admission, 30 were accepted, 16 enrolled. 3-R Achievement Test, any standardized test, ERB, SSAT or TOEFL required. Deadline for receipt of application materials: none. Application fee required: $75. Interview recommended.

Athletics Interscholastic: baseball (boys), basketball (b,g), cheering (g), cross-country running (b,g), dance (g), dance team (g), diving (b,g), football (b), golf (b,g), soccer (b,g), softball (g), swimming and diving (b,g), tennis (b,g), track and field (b,g), volleyball (g); intramural: yoga (g); coed interscholastic: soccer; coed intramural: canoeing/kayaking, fitness, hiking/backpacking, kayaking, modern dance, outdoor activities, outdoor adventure, outdoor education, physical fitness, running, scuba diving, strength & conditioning, ultimate Frisbee, weight training. 3 PE instructors, 20 coaches.

Computers Computers are regularly used in all academic classes. Computer network features include on-campus library services, online commercial services, Internet access, wireless campus network, Internet filtering or blocking technology, 1:1 iPad program for grades 3-7 (each child receives an iPad), 1:1 Chromebooks for grade 8, 2 makerspaces. Computer access in designated common areas is available to students. Students grades are available online. The school has a published electronic and media policy.

Contact Mrs. Michelle Robinson, Director of Advancement and Admission. 727-521-5903. Fax: 727-525-2545. E-mail: mrobinson@canterburyflorida.org. Website: www.canterburyflorida.org

CAPE COD ACADEMY

50 Osterville-West Barnstable Road
Osterville, Massachusetts 02655

Head of School: Mr. Tom Trigg

General Information Coeducational day college-preparatory school. Grades PK–12. Founded: 1976. Setting: small town. Nearest major city is Boston. 47-acre campus. 5 buildings on campus. Approved or accredited by Association of Independent Schools in New England and New England Association of Schools and Colleges. Member of National Association of Independent Schools and Secondary School Admission Test Board. Endowment: $2.2 million. Total enrollment: 247. Upper school average class size: 13. Upper school faculty-student ratio: 1:5. There are 172 required school days per year for Upper School students. Upper School students typically attend 5 days per week. The average school day consists of 6 hours and 30 minutes.

Upper School Student Profile Grade 9: 25 students (12 boys, 13 girls); Grade 10: 30 students (14 boys, 16 girls); Grade 11: 56 students (30 boys, 26 girls); Grade 12: 44 students (25 boys, 19 girls).

Faculty School total: 50. In upper school: 16 men, 19 women; 28 have advanced degrees.

Subjects Offered Advanced biology, advanced chemistry, advanced math, Advanced Placement courses, advanced studio art-AP, algebra, American history, American literature, art, art history, art history-AP, art-AP, biology, calculus, calculus-AP, ceramics, chemistry, chemistry-AP, community service, computer math, computer programming, computer science, digital photography, drama, earth science, English, English literature, English-AP, environmental science, ethics, European history, expository writing, fine arts, French, French-AP, geography, geometry, health, history, history-AP, honors algebra, honors geometry, Latin, mathematics, music, music composition, music history, music theory, philosophy, photography, physical education, physics, SAT preparation, science, senior internship, social sciences, social studies, Spanish, Spanish-AP, statistics-AP, studio art-AP, theater, trigonometry, world history, world literature.

Graduation Requirements Arts and fine arts (art, music, dance, drama), computer science, English, foreign language, history, independent study, mathematics, physical education (includes health), science. Community service is required.

Special Academic Programs 10 Advanced Placement exams for which test preparation is offered; honors section; independent study; term-away projects; study abroad; ESL (6 students enrolled).

College Admission Counseling 27 students graduated in 2016; all went to college, including Boston College; Boston University; Roger Williams University; University of Massachusetts Amherst; University of Pennsylvania; Wheaton College. Mean SAT critical reading: 600, mean SAT math: 620.

Student Life Upper grades have specified standards of dress, student council, honor system. Discipline rests primarily with faculty.

Tuition and Aid Day student tuition: $21,150–$25,290. Tuition installment plan (Academic Management Services Plan, SMART Tuition Payment Plan, FACTS Tuition Payment Plan, monthly payment plans, individually arranged payment plans). Merit scholarship grants, need-based scholarship grants available. In 2016–17, 43% of upper-school students received aid. Total amount of financial aid awarded in 2016–17: $1,600,000.

Admissions Traditional secondary-level entrance grade is 9. For fall 2016, 105 students applied for upper-level admission, 66 were accepted, 40 enrolled. ISEE, SSAT, TOEFL or TOEFL Junior required. Deadline for receipt of application materials: February 1. Application fee required: $50. On-campus interview recommended.

Athletics Interscholastic: baseball (boys), basketball (b,g), lacrosse (b,g), soccer (b,g), swimming and diving (b,g), tennis (b,g); coed interscholastic: cross-country running, golf, ice hockey, sailing; coed intramural: aerobics, aerobics/Nautilus, archery, basketball, combined training, fitness, floor hockey, physical training, sailing, soccer, strength & conditioning, swimming and diving, weight training. 1 PE instructor, 11 coaches, 1 athletic trainer.

Computers Computers are regularly used in all academic classes. Computer network features include on-campus library services, online commercial services, Internet access, wireless campus network, Internet filtering or blocking technology. Campus intranet, student e-mail accounts, and computer access in designated common areas are available to students. Students grades are available online. The school has a published electronic and media policy.

Contact Barbara Hansen, Admissions Administrator. 508-428-5400 Ext. 226. Fax: 508-428-0701. E-mail: atolischus@capecodacademy.org. Website: www.capecodacademy.org

CAPE FEAR ACADEMY

3900 South College Road
Wilmington, North Carolina 28412

Head of School: Mr. Donald Berger

General Information Coeducational day college-preparatory and arts school. Grades PK–12. Founded: 1967. Setting: suburban. 27-acre campus. 4 buildings on campus. Approved or accredited by Southern Association of Colleges and Schools, Southern Association of Independent Schools, and North Carolina Department of Education. Member of National Association of Independent Schools. Endowment: $881,340. Total enrollment: 599. Upper school average class size: 17. Upper school faculty-student ratio: 1:7. There are 177 required school days per year for Upper School students. Upper School students typically attend 5 days per week. The average school day consists of 7 hours and 20 minutes.

Upper School Student Profile Grade 9: 64 students (29 boys, 35 girls); Grade 10: 45 students (24 boys, 21 girls); Grade 11: 61 students (34 boys, 27 girls); Grade 12: 59 students (24 boys, 35 girls).

Faculty School total: 70. In upper school: 12 men, 19 women; 13 have advanced degrees.

Subjects Offered 3-dimensional art, Advanced Placement courses, algebra, American history, American history-AP, American literature, analysis, art, art history, band, biology, biology-AP, British literature, calculus-AP, chemistry, choral music, comparative government and politics-AP, computer science, conceptual physics, critical studies in film, discrete mathematics, drama, earth and space science, English, English language-AP, English literature, English literature-AP, environmental science, environmental science-AP, European history, European history-AP, film studies, finance, fine arts, fitness, geometry, global studies, government and politics-AP, government-AP, history, honors geometry, human anatomy, independent study, journalism, language, literature, marine science, mathematics, music, music theory-AP, musical theater, newspaper, organizational studies, photography, physical education, physics, pre-calculus, psychology, publications, religion, SAT preparation, science, sculpture, social studies, Spanish, student publications, theater, video film production, vocal ensemble, weight training, world history.

Graduation Requirements Arts and fine arts (art, music, dance, drama), biology, English, foreign language, mathematics, physical education (includes health), science, social studies (includes history), U.S. government, U.S. history, 72 hours of community service over 4 years. Community service is required.

Special Academic Programs 12 Advanced Placement exams for which test preparation is offered; honors section; independent study; study at local college for college credit; study abroad; ESL (4 students enrolled).

College Admission Counseling 66 students graduated in 2015; all went to college, including East Carolina University; North Carolina State University; The University of North Carolina at Chapel Hill; The University of North Carolina Wilmington. Mean combined SAT: 1686, mean composite ACT: 25.

Student Life Upper grades have specified standards of dress, student council, honor system. Discipline rests primarily with faculty.

Tuition and Aid Day student tuition: $15,975. Tuition installment plan (Insured Tuition Payment Plan, FACTS Tuition Payment Plan, monthly payment plans). Merit scholarship grants, need-based scholarship grants available. In 2015–16, 14% of upper-school students received aid; total upper-school merit-scholarship money awarded: $70,507. Total amount of financial aid awarded in 2015–16: $331,999.

Admissions Traditional secondary-level entrance grade is 9. For fall 2015, 57 students applied for upper-level admission, 45 were accepted, 26 enrolled. ERB, ISEE, PSAT or SAT or SSAT required. Deadline for receipt of application materials: none. Application fee required: $80. On-campus interview recommended.

Athletics Interscholastic: basketball (boys, girls), cheering (g), field hockey (g), lacrosse (b,g), soccer (b,g), tennis (b,g), volleyball (g); coed interscholastic: cross-country running, golf, outdoor education, outdoor recreation, surfing, swimming and diving. 2 PE instructors, 11 coaches, 1 athletic trainer.

Computers Computers are regularly used in all academic classes. Computer network features include on-campus library services, online commercial services, Internet access, wireless campus network, Internet filtering or blocking technology. Campus intranet, student e-mail accounts, and computer access in designated common areas are available to students. Students grades are available online. The school has a published electronic and media policy.

Contact Mrs. Nelda Nutter, Director of Admission. 910-791-0287 Ext. 1015. Fax: 910-791-0290. E-mail: nelda.nutter@capefearacademy.org. Website: www.capefearacademy.org

CAPE HENRY COLLEGIATE SCHOOL

1320 Mill Dam Road
Virginia Beach, Virginia 23454-2306

Head of School: Dr. Christopher Garran

General Information Coeducational day college-preparatory and global education school. Grades PK–12. Founded: 1924. Setting: suburban. 30-acre campus. 9 buildings on campus. Approved or accredited by Southern Association of Colleges and Schools, Southern Association of Independent Schools, Virginia Association of Independent Schools, and Virginia Department of Education. Member of National Association of Independent Schools. Endowment: $16 million. Total enrollment: 895. Upper school average class size: 14. Upper school faculty-student ratio: 1:10. There are 176 required school days per year for Upper School students. Upper School students typically attend 5 days per week. The average school day consists of 7 hours and 20 minutes.

Upper School Student Profile Grade 9: 77 students (48 boys, 29 girls); Grade 10: 97 students (47 boys, 50 girls); Grade 11: 90 students (59 boys, 31 girls); Grade 12: 73 students (41 boys, 32 girls).

Faculty School total: 117. In upper school: 20 men, 23 women; 32 have advanced degrees.

Subjects Offered Algebra, American history, American literature, art, art history, biology, botany, business skills, calculus, ceramics, chemistry, community service, computer programming, computer science, creative writing, drama, driver education, earth science, ecology, economics, English, English literature, environmental science, European history, expository writing, fine arts, French, geography, geology, geometry, government/civics, health, history, journalism, Latin, law, marine biology, mathematics, music, oceanography, photography, physical education, physics, science, social sciences, social studies, sociology, Spanish, speech, statistics, theater, trigonometry, world history, world literature, writing.

Graduation Requirements Arts and fine arts (art, music, dance, drama), computer science, English, foreign language, mathematics, physical education (includes health), science, social sciences, social studies (includes history). Community service is required.

Special Academic Programs Advanced Placement exam preparation; honors section; independent study; academic accommodation for the gifted, the musically talented, and the artistically talented; ESL (10 students enrolled).

College Admission Counseling 102 students graduated in 2016; 101 went to college, including James Madison University; Randolph-Macon College; University of Mary Washington; University of South Carolina; University of Virginia; Virginia Polytechnic Institute and State University. Other: 1 entered military service.

Student Life Upper grades have specified standards of dress, student council, honor system. Discipline rests equally with students and faculty.

Summer Programs Enrichment, advancement, ESL, sports, art/fine arts, computer instruction programs offered; session focuses on academics and enrichment; held on campus; accepts boys and girls; open to students from other schools. 1,200 students usually enrolled. 2017 schedule: June 5 to August 11. Application deadline: none.

Tuition and Aid Day student tuition: $19,650. Tuition installment plan (The Tuition Plan, Insured Tuition Payment Plan, monthly payment plans, individually arranged payment plans, 3-payment plan). Merit scholarship grants, need-based scholarship grants available. In 2016–17, 25% of upper-school students received aid.

Admissions Traditional secondary-level entrance grade is 9. For fall 2016, 96 students applied for upper-level admission, 63 were accepted, 41 enrolled. ERB CTP, ISEE, Scholastic Achievement Test, SSAT, ERB, PSAT, SAT, PLAN or ACT, TOEFL or writing sample required. Deadline for receipt of application materials: none. Application fee required: $50. Interview required.

Athletics Interscholastic: baseball (boys), basketball (b,g), crew (b,g), cross-country running (b,g), field hockey (g), golf (b,g), lacrosse (b,g), physical fitness (b,g), soccer (b,g), softball (g), tennis (b,g), volleyball (b,g), wrestling (b); intramural: field hockey (g), fitness (b,g), floor hockey (b,g), wrestling (b); coed interscholastic: cheering, dance, dance team, swimming and diving, track and field; coed intramural: badminton, ballet, dance, fishing, fitness, fitness walking, flag football, golf, hiking/backpacking, jogging, kayaking, lacrosse, modern dance, ocean paddling, outdoor activities, outdoor adventure, physical fitness, physical training, soccer, strength & conditioning, surfing, swimming and diving, table tennis, tennis, volleyball, weight lifting, weight training, wilderness, yoga. 3 PE instructors, 25 coaches, 1 athletic trainer.

Computers Computers are regularly used in computer applications, desktop publishing, graphic arts, information technology, literary magazine, newspaper, publications, technology, video film production, Web site design, word processing, yearbook classes. Computer network features include on-campus library services, online commercial services, Internet access, wireless campus network, Internet filtering or blocking technology. Campus intranet, student e-mail accounts, and computer access in designated common areas are available to students. Students grades are available online. The school has a published electronic and media policy.

Contact Mrs. Angie Finley, Admissions Associate. 757-963-8234. Fax: 757-481-9194. E-mail: angiefinley@capehenry.org. Website: www.capehenrycollegiate.org

CAPISTRANO VALLEY CHRISTIAN SCHOOLS

32032 Del Obispo Street
San Juan Capistrano, California 92675
Head of School: Mr. Christopher Rutz

General Information Coeducational day college-preparatory, arts, religious studies, and technology school, affiliated with Evangelical Christian Church. Grades JK–12. Founded: 1972. Setting: suburban. 8-acre campus. 3 buildings on campus. Approved or accredited by Association of Christian Schools International, The College Board, Western Association of Schools and Colleges, and California Department of Education. Total enrollment: 435. Upper school average class size: 18. Upper school faculty-student ratio: 1:13. There are 180 required school days per year for Upper School students. Upper School students typically attend 5 days per week. The average school day consists of 6 hours.

Upper School Student Profile Grade 6: 30 students (16 boys, 14 girls); Grade 7: 39 students (17 boys, 22 girls); Grade 8: 51 students (22 boys, 29 girls); Grade 9: 47 students (28 boys, 19 girls); Grade 10: 49 students (31 boys, 18 girls); Grade 11: 53 students (34 boys, 19 girls); Grade 12: 51 students (32 boys, 19 girls). 80% of students are members of Evangelical Christian Church.

Faculty School total: 55. In upper school: 16 men, 18 women; 11 have advanced degrees.

Subjects Offered Advanced biology, advanced chemistry, advanced computer applications, advanced math, Advanced Placement courses, advanced TOEFL/grammar, algebra, American government, American history, American history-AP, American literature, American literature-AP, anatomy, art, ASB Leadership, athletic training, athletics, Bible, Bible studies, biology, biology-AP, business, business applications, business communications, business education, business law, business skills, business studies, calculus, calculus-AP, career planning, chemistry, choir, chorus, Christian doctrine, Christian ethics, Christian scripture, Christian studies, Christian testament, Christianity, church history, college admission preparation, college counseling, college placement, college planning, comparative government and politics-AP, competitive science projects, composition, composition-AP, computer applications, computer education, computer information systems, computer literacy, computer multimedia, computer skills, computer technologies, dance, desktop publishing, drama performance, economics, English, English literature-AP, English-AP, European history, geometry, government, health, history, honors algebra, honors English, independent study, Internet, intro to computers, journalism, keyboarding, kinesiology, lab science, leadership, photography, physical education, physical science, physics, public speaking, research skills, Spanish, sports medicine, sports nutrition, statistics, statistics-AP, student government, TOEFL preparation, U.S. government and politics-AP, U.S. history-AP, Web site design, world cultures, writing, yearbook.

Graduation Requirements Algebra, American government, American history, American literature, arts and fine arts (art, music, dance, drama), Bible, biology, composition, computer skills, economics, electives, English, European history, foreign language, freshman foundations, geometry, physical education (includes health), research skills, speech, graduation requirements meet UC and CSU entrance requirements.

Special Academic Programs 11 Advanced Placement exams for which test preparation is offered; honors section; independent study; study at local college for college credit; remedial reading and/or remedial writing; remedial math; programs in general development for dyslexic students; special instructional classes for Opportunity School Program; ESL (31 students enrolled).

College Admission Counseling 53 students graduated in 2016; all went to college, including Biola University; Boise State University; Concordia University Irvine; Grand Canyon University; University of California, Irvine. Other: 1 entered military service. Mean SAT critical reading: 517, mean SAT math: 582, mean SAT writing: 510, mean combined SAT: 1609, mean composite ACT: 26. 22% scored over 600 on SAT critical reading, 35% scored over 600 on SAT math, 13% scored over 600 on SAT writing, 30% scored over 1800 on combined SAT, 35% scored over 26 on composite ACT.

Student Life Upper grades have uniform requirement, student council, honor system. Discipline rests primarily with faculty. Attendance at religious services is required.

Summer Programs Remediation, enrichment, advancement, sports, art/fine arts programs offered; session focuses on advancement; held on campus; accepts boys and girls; open to students from other schools. 25 students usually enrolled. 2017 schedule: July 12 to August 6. Application deadline: May 1.

Tuition and Aid Day student tuition: $14,300. Tuition installment plan (FACTS Tuition Payment Plan, individually arranged payment plans, payroll deductions). Tuition reduction for siblings, merit scholarship grants, need-based scholarship grants available. In 2016–17, 25% of upper school students received aid. Total amount of financial aid awarded in 2016–17: $200,000.

Admissions Traditional secondary-level entrance grade is 9. For fall 2016, 54 students applied for upper-level admission, 49 were accepted, 46 enrolled. Admissions testing, ESOL English Proficiency Test, High School Placement Test, Stanford Test of Academic Skills or TOEFL required. Deadline for receipt of application materials: none. Application fee required: $100. Interview recommended.

Athletics Interscholastic: baseball (boys), basketball (b,g), cheering (g), combined training (b,g), cross-country running (b,g), dance (g), football (b), soccer (b,g), softball (g), tennis (g), volleyball (b,g); coed interscholastic: equestrian sports, golf, physical training, strength & conditioning, track and field, weight training. 3 PE instructors, 14 coaches, 4 athletic trainers.

Computers Computers are regularly used in all academic, data processing, design, journalism, writing, yearbook classes. Computer network features include on-campus library services, Internet access, wireless campus network, Internet filtering or blocking technology, 1:1 tablet PC program, Google Classroom. Campus intranet, student e-mail accounts, and computer access in designated common areas are available to students. Students grades are available online. The school has a published electronic and media policy.

Contact Mrs. Jo Beveridge, Director of Admissions. 949-493-5683 Ext. 109. Fax: 949-493-6057. E-mail: jbeveridge@cvcs.org. Website: www.cvcs.org

CARDIGAN MOUNTAIN SCHOOL

Canaan, New Hampshire
See Junior Boarding Schools section.

CARDINAL GIBBONS HIGH SCHOOL

1401 Edwards Mill Road
Raleigh, North Carolina 27607
Head of School: Mr. Jason Curtis

General Information Coeducational day college-preparatory, arts, business, religious studies, and technology school, affiliated with Roman Catholic Church. Grades 9–12. Founded: 1909. Setting: suburban. 36-acre campus. 1 building on campus. Approved or accredited by Southern Association of Colleges and Schools. Total enrollment: 1,428. Upper school faculty-student ratio: 1:14. Upper School students typically attend 5 days per week. The average school day consists of 7 hours.

Upper School Student Profile Grade 9: 415 students (219 boys, 196 girls); Grade 10: 367 students (196 boys, 171 girls); Grade 11: 334 students (163 boys, 171 girls); Grade 12: 302 students (138 boys, 164 girls). 86% of students are Roman Catholic.

Faculty School total: 100. In upper school: 51 men, 49 women.

Subjects Offered All academic.

Graduation Requirements Arts and fine arts (art, music, dance, drama), English, foreign language, health education, mathematics, physical education (includes health), science, social studies (includes history), technology, theology.

Special Academic Programs Advanced Placement exam preparation; honors section; accelerated programs; independent study; special instructional classes for extra time for testing with supporting documentation.

College Admission Counseling 323 students graduated in 2016; all went to college, including North Carolina State University; The University of North Carolina at Chapel Hill.

Student Life Upper grades have uniform requirement, student council. Discipline rests primarily with faculty. Attendance at religious services is required.

Summer Programs Enrichment, advancement, sports, art/fine arts programs offered; session focuses on sports, music, theatre, academic enrichment; held on campus; accepts boys and girls; open to students from other schools. 2017 schedule: June to August.

Tuition and Aid Day student tuition: $10,340–$14,340. Tuition installment plan (FACTS Tuition Payment Plan). Need-based scholarship grants available. Total amount of financial aid awarded in 2016–17: $1,400,000.

Admissions Traditional secondary-level entrance grade is 9. High School Placement Test (closed version) from Scholastic Testing Service required. Deadline for receipt of application materials: January 5. Application fee required: $100.

Athletics Interscholastic: aerobics/dance (boys, girls), ballet (g), baseball (b,g), basketball (b,g), cheering (g), cross-country running (b,g), dance (g), dance squad (g), dance team (g), diving (b,g), field hockey (g), football (b), golf (b,g), kickball (b,g), lacrosse (b,g), modern dance (g), mountain biking (b,g), outdoor education (b,g), physical fitness (b,g), physical training (b,g), roller hockey (b), running (b,g), soccer (b,g), softball (g), strength & conditioning (b), surfing (b,g), swimming and diving (b,g), tennis (b,g), track and field (b,g), ultimate Frisbee (b,g), volleyball (g), weight lifting (b,g), weight training (g), wrestling (b). 85 coaches.

Computers Computers are regularly used in accounting, all academic classes. Computer network features include Internet access, wireless campus network, Internet filtering or blocking technology. Campus intranet, student e-mail accounts, and computer access in designated common areas are available to students. Students grades are available online.

Contact Mrs. Marianne McCarty, Admissions Director. 919-834-1625 Ext. 209. Fax: 919-834-9771. E-mail: mmccarty@cghsnc.org. Website: www.cghsnc.org

CARDINAL MOONEY CATHOLIC HIGH SCHOOL

4171 Fruitville Road
Sarasota, Florida 34232
Head of School: Mr. Stephen J. Christie

General Information Coeducational day college-preparatory, arts, religious studies, and technology school, affiliated with Roman Catholic Church. Grades 9–12. Founded: 1959. Setting: suburban. Nearest major city is Tampa. 36-acre campus. 5 buildings on campus. Approved or accredited by Southern Association of Colleges and Schools.

Endowment: $1.8 million. Total enrollment: 474. Upper school average class size: 18. Upper school faculty-student ratio: 1:13. There are 180 required school days per year for Upper School students. Upper School students typically attend 5 days per week. The average school day consists of 6 hours and 35 minutes.

Upper School Student Profile Grade 9: 126 students (76 boys, 50 girls); Grade 10: 145 students (75 boys, 70 girls); Grade 11: 132 students (69 boys, 63 girls); Grade 12: 110 students (60 boys, 50 girls). 75% of students are Roman Catholic.

Faculty School total: 50. In upper school: 12 men, 26 women; 25 have advanced degrees.

Subjects Offered Algebra, American government, American history, anatomy, art, biology, business, calculus, ceramics, chemistry, chorus, Christian and Hebrew scripture, community service, computer applications, computer graphics, contemporary history, creative writing, drama, earth science, economics, economics and history, English, English literature, environmental science, fine arts, French, geometry, guitar, health, history, instrumental music, integrated mathematics, journalism, keyboarding, learning strategies, marine biology, mathematics, music, physical education, physics, psychology, science, social justice, social studies, sociology, Spanish, speech, theology, trigonometry, U.S. government and politics-AP, world history, world literature, world religions.

Graduation Requirements Arts and fine arts (art, music, dance, drama), electives, English, foreign language, mathematics, physical education (includes health), religion (includes Bible studies and theology), science, social studies (includes history), 100 hours of community service.

Special Academic Programs 8 Advanced Placement exams for which test preparation is offered; honors section; remedial reading and/or remedial writing; remedial math; programs in English, mathematics for dyslexic students.

College Admission Counseling 123 students graduated in 2015; all went to college, including Auburn University; Florida Gulf Coast University; Florida State University; University of Central Florida; University of Florida. Median SAT critical reading: 512, median SAT math: 507, median SAT writing: 506, median composite ACT: 23. 31% scored over 600 on SAT critical reading, 41% scored over 600 on SAT math, 35% scored over 600 on SAT writing, 38% scored over 26 on composite ACT.

Student Life Upper grades have specified standards of dress, student council. Discipline rests primarily with faculty. Attendance at religious services is required.

Tuition and Aid Tuition installment plan (monthly payment plans, semester payment plan). Tuition reduction for siblings, merit scholarship grants, need-based scholarship grants available. In 2015–16, 25% of upper-school students received aid. Total amount of financial aid awarded in 2015–16: $200,000.

Admissions Traditional secondary-level entrance grade is 9. For fall 2015, 180 students applied for upper-level admission, 180 were accepted, 128 enrolled. Placement test required. Deadline for receipt of application materials: none. No application fee required. On-campus interview required.

Athletics Interscholastic: baseball (boys), basketball (b,g), cheering (g), cross-country running (b,g), dance team (g), diving (b,g), football (b), golf (b,g), lacrosse (b,g), modern dance (g), physical fitness (b,g), soccer (b,g), softball (g), strength & conditioning (b,g), swimming and diving (b,g), track and field (b,g), volleyball (g), weight lifting (b,g), weight training (b,g); intramural: basketball (b,g), volleyball (b,g); coed interscholastic: aquatics; coed intramural: volleyball. 4 PE instructors, 66 coaches, 4 athletic trainers.

Computers Computers are regularly used in art, basic skills, Christian doctrine, computer applications, creative writing, English, foreign language, French, history, mathematics, religious studies, remedial study skills, science, social sciences, social studies, Spanish, technology, theater arts, video film production, writing, yearbook classes. Computer network features include on-campus library services, Internet access, wireless campus network. Student e-mail accounts are available to students. Students grades are available online. The school has a published electronic and media policy.

Contact Mrs. Joanne Mades, Registrar. 941-371-4917. Fax: 941-371-6924 Ext. 135. E-mail: jmades@cmhs-sarasota.org. Website: www.cmhs-sarasota.org

CARDINAL NEWMAN HIGH SCHOOL

512 Spencer Drive
West Palm Beach, Florida 33409-3699

Head of School: Fr. David W. Carr

General Information Coeducational day college-preparatory and International Baccalaureate school, affiliated with Roman Catholic Church. Grades 9–12. Founded: 1961. Setting: suburban. Nearest major city is Miami. 50-acre campus. 5 buildings on campus. Approved or accredited by National Catholic Education Association, Southern Association of Colleges and Schools, and Florida Department of Education. Total enrollment: 544. Upper school average class size: 25. Upper school faculty-student ratio: 1:25. There are 180 required school days per year for Upper School students. Upper School students typically attend 5 days per week. The average school day consists of 6 hours and 40 minutes.

Upper School Student Profile Grade 9: 131 students (65 boys, 66 girls); Grade 10: 140 students (80 boys, 60 girls); Grade 11: 134 students (72 boys, 62 girls); Grade 12: 138 students (67 boys, 71 girls). 80% of students are Roman Catholic.

Faculty School total: 46. In upper school: 15 men, 34 women; 36 have advanced degrees.

Subjects Offered Algebra, American government, American history, American literature, anatomy and physiology, art, band, Bible studies, biology, biology-AP, calculus, calculus-AP, chemistry, chorus, church history, computer applications, computer science, desktop publishing, drama, economics, English, English literature, English-AP, ethics, European history, fine arts, French, French-AP, geometry, government/civics, health, history, honors algebra, honors English, honors geometry, integrated science, International Baccalaureate courses, journalism, leadership, marine biology, mathematics, physical education, physics, political science, pre-calculus, probability and statistics, religion, social justice, social studies, Spanish, speech, world history, world literature, writing, yearbook.

Graduation Requirements Arts and fine arts (art, music, dance, drama), English, foreign language, mathematics, physical education (includes health), religion (includes Bible studies and theology), science, social studies (includes history), 100 hour community service requirement.

Special Academic Programs International Baccalaureate program; Advanced Placement exam preparation; honors section; study at local college for college credit; academic accommodation for the gifted; remedial reading and/or remedial writing; remedial math.

College Admission Counseling 123 students graduated in 2016; all went to college, including Florida Atlantic University; Florida Gulf Coast University; Florida State University; Palm Beach State College; University of Central Florida; University of Florida.

Student Life Upper grades have uniform requirement, student council, honor system. Discipline rests primarily with faculty. Attendance at religious services is required.

Summer Programs Remediation, enrichment, sports programs offered; session focuses on freshman preparation; held on campus; accepts boys and girls; not open to students from other schools. 75 students usually enrolled. 2017 schedule: June 17 to June 30.

Tuition and Aid Day student tuition: $11,800–$12,800. Tuition installment plan (FACTS Tuition Payment Plan). Need-based scholarship grants available. In 2016–17, 18% of upper-school students received aid.

Admissions Traditional secondary-level entrance grade is 9. STS or STS, Diocese Test required. Deadline for receipt of application materials: none. Application fee required: $100. On-campus interview required.

Athletics Interscholastic: baseball (boys), basketball (b,g), bowling (b,g), cheering (g), cross-country running (b,g), dance team (b,g), diving (b,g), football (b), golf (b,g), lacrosse (b,g), physical fitness (b,g), soccer (b,g), softball (g), swimming and diving (b,g), tennis (b,g), track and field (b,g), volleyball (g), weight lifting (b), wrestling (b). 2 PE instructors, 1 athletic trainer.

Computers Computers are regularly used in all academic, Bible studies, social studies, yearbook classes. Computer network features include on-campus library services, online commercial services, Internet access, wireless campus network, Internet filtering or blocking technology. Student e-mail accounts are available to students. Students grades are available online. The school has a published electronic and media policy.

Contact Mrs. Christina Amodie, Admissions Director. 561-683-6266 Ext. 1050. Fax: 561-683-7307. E-mail: christina.amodie@cardinalnewman.com. Website: www.cardinalnewman.com

CARDINAL RITTER HIGH SCHOOL

3360 West 30 Street
Indianapolis, Indiana 46222-2181

Head of School: Mrs. E. Jo Hoy

General Information Coeducational day college-preparatory and religious studies school, affiliated with Roman Catholic Church. Grades 7–12. Founded: 1964. Setting: urban. 1 building on campus. Approved or accredited by Indiana Department of Education. Total enrollment: 389. Upper school average class size: 16. Upper school faculty-student ratio: 1:16. Upper School students typically attend 5 days per week. The average school day consists of 7 hours and 45 minutes.

Upper School Student Profile Grade 9: 79 students (46 boys, 33 girls); Grade 10: 80 students (48 boys, 32 girls); Grade 11: 87 students (38 boys, 49 girls); Grade 12: 69 students (36 boys, 33 girls). 70% of students are Roman Catholic.

Faculty School total: 42. In upper school: 18 men, 24 women.

Graduation Requirements American history, art, business, classical language, composition, English, foreign language, government, health and wellness, health education, mathematics, physical education (includes health), science, social studies (includes history). Community service is required.

Special Academic Programs Honors section; independent study; study at local college for college credit; academic accommodation for the gifted, the musically talented, and the artistically talented; remedial reading and/or remedial writing; remedial math; ESL (32 students enrolled).

College Admission Counseling 122 students graduated in 2016; 117 went to college, including Ball State University; Indiana University Bloomington; Purdue University; University of Indianapolis. Other: 3 went to work, 2 entered military service. Mean SAT critical reading: 502, mean SAT math: 501, mean SAT writing: 495, mean combined SAT: 1498, mean composite ACT: 22.

Student Life Upper grades have uniform requirement, student council. Discipline rests equally with students and faculty. Attendance at religious services is required.

Summary Programs Remediation, enrichment programs offered; session focuses on Academics; held on campus; accepts boys and girls; open to students from other schools. 60 students usually enrolled. 2017 schedule: June 1 to August 1. Application deadline: April 1.

Tuition and Aid Tuition installment plan (The Tuition Plan, monthly payment plans). Merit scholarship grants, need-based scholarship grants, paying campus jobs available.

Admissions Traditional secondary-level entrance grade is 9. For fall 2016, 160 students applied for upper-level admission, 140 were accepted, 546 enrolled. Admissions testing required. Deadline for receipt of application materials: January 31. No application fee required. On-campus interview required.

Athletics Interscholastic: baseball (boys), basketball (b,g), bowling (b,g), cheering (b,g), cross-country running (b,g), diving (b,g), drill team (g), football (b), golf (b,g), indoor track & field (b,g), soccer (b,g), softball (g), tennis (b,g), track and field (b,g), volleyball (b,g), winter (indoor) track (b,g), wrestling (b). 3 PE instructors, 47 coaches, 1 athletic trainer.

Computers Computers are regularly used in all classes. Computer network features include on-campus library services, online commercial services, Internet access, wireless campus network, Internet filtering or blocking technology. Campus intranet, student e-mail accounts, and computer access in designated common areas are available to students. Students grades are available online. The school has a published electronic and media policy.

Contact Mr. Kyle Powers, Recruitment Director. 317-924-4333 Ext. 32. Fax: 317-927-7822. E-mail: kpowers@cardinalritter.org.

CARLISLE SCHOOL

300 Carlisle Road
Axton, Virginia 24054

Head of School: Mr. Thomas P. Hudgins Jr.

General Information Coeducational boarding and day college-preparatory school. Boarding grades 9–12, day grades PK–12. Founded: 1968. Setting: rural. Nearest major city is Danville. Students are housed in single-sex dormitories and hosted by local families. 32-acre campus. 5 buildings on campus. Approved or accredited by Southern Association of Colleges and Schools, Southern Association of Independent Schools, Virginia Association of Independent Schools, and Virginia Department of Education. Member of National Association of Independent Schools. Endowment: $1.9 million. Total enrollment: 390. Upper school average class size: 15. Upper school faculty-student ratio: 1:8. There are 177 required school days per year for Upper School students. Upper School students typically attend 5 days per week. The average school day consists of 6 hours and 45 minutes.

Upper School Student Profile Grade 9: 25 students (13 boys, 12 girls); Grade 10: 35 students (19 boys, 16 girls); Grade 11: 33 students (16 boys, 17 girls); Grade 12: 39 students (21 boys, 18 girls). 9% of students are boarding students. 75% are state residents. 2 states are represented in upper school student body. 25% are international students. International students from Canada, China, Colombia, Japan, Republic of Korea, and Yemen.

Faculty School total: 42. In upper school: 4 men, 14 women; 8 have advanced degrees; 4 reside on campus.

Subjects Offered Advanced computer applications, advanced math, Advanced Placement courses, algebra, American government, American history, American history-AP, American literature, art, arts, band, biology, biology-AP, calculus, calculus-AP, chemistry, chemistry-AP, choir, composition-AP, computer information systems, computer programming, computer science, computer science-AP, concert band, creative dance, creative drama, creative writing, dance, drama, earth science, economics, economics-AP, English, English language and composition-AP, English literature, English literature and composition-AP, English literature-AP, ESL, film studies, fine arts, geometry, government, government/civics, health, health and wellness, history, history of the Americas, honors algebra, honors English, honors geometry, HTML design, independent study, International Baccalaureate courses, intro to computers, jazz band, jazz ensemble, journalism, lab science, madrigals, mathematics, mathematics-AP, music, physical education, physics, play production, pre-algebra, pre-calculus, psychology, psychology-AP, publications, robotics, science, senior project, social studies, Spanish, statistics, statistics-AP, studio art, theater, theory of knowledge, U.S. government and politics-AP, U.S. history-AP, wind ensemble, world civilizations, world history, world history-AP, world wide web design, yearbook.

Graduation Requirements Advanced math, algebra, arts and fine arts (art, music, dance, drama), computer science, electives, English, foreign language, mathematics, physical education (includes health), science, social studies (includes history), U.S. and Virginia history, U.S. government, community service, senior project.

Special Academic Programs Advanced Placement exam preparation; honors section; independent study; term-away projects; study at local college for college credit; ESL (17 students enrolled).

College Admission Counseling 41 students graduated in 2015; all went to college, including George Mason University; Old Dominion University; University of Virginia; Virginia Commonwealth University; Virginia Polytechnic Institute and State University. Median SAT critical reading: 510, median SAT math: 520, median SAT writing: 500, median combined SAT: 1560, median composite ACT: 23. 18% scored over 600 on SAT critical reading, 24% scored over 600 on SAT math, 29% scored over 600 on SAT writing, 24% scored over 1800 on combined SAT, 13% scored over 26 on composite ACT.

Student Life Upper grades have specified standards of dress, student council, honor system. Discipline rests equally with students and faculty.

Tuition and Aid Day student tuition: $11,490; 5-day tuition and room/board: $28,000; 7-day tuition and room/board: $36,810. Tuition installment plan (Insured Tuition Payment Plan, FACTS Tuition Payment Plan). Need-based scholarship grants available. In 2015–16, 39% of upper-school students received aid. Total amount of financial aid awarded in 2015–16: $372,479.

Admissions Traditional secondary-level entrance grade is 9. Nelson-Denny Reading Test, TOEFL or SLEP, Woodcock-Johnson or writing sample required. Deadline for receipt of application materials: none. Application fee required: $65. Interview required.

Athletics Interscholastic: basketball (boys, girls), cheering (g), field hockey (g), soccer (b,g), softball (g), tennis (b,g), volleyball (b,g); intramural: basketball (b,g), cheering (g), softball (g); coed interscholastic: baseball, cross-country running, dance, fencing, golf; coed intramural: aerobics/Nautilus, archery, basketball, Frisbee, swimming and diving, table tennis, weight lifting. 2 PE instructors, 29 coaches, 1 athletic trainer.

Computers Computers are regularly used in all academic classes. Computer network features include on-campus library services, online commercial services, Internet access, wireless campus network, Internet filtering or blocking technology. Campus intranet, student e-mail accounts, and computer access in designated common areas are available to students. Students grades are available online. The school has a published electronic and media policy.

Contact Ms. Cindy Pike, International Student Affairs Coordinator, Admissions Assistant. 276-632-7288 Ext. 221. Fax: 276-632-9545. E-mail: cpike@carlisleschool.org. Website: www.carlisleschool.org

CARLUCCI AMERICAN INTERNATIONAL SCHOOL OF LISBON

Rua António dos Reis, 95
Linhó, Sintra 2710-301, Portugal

Head of School: Ms. Blannie M. Curtis

General Information Coeducational day college-preparatory school. Grades PK–12. Founded: 1956. Setting: suburban. Nearest major city is Lisbon, Portugal. 4-hectare campus. 4 buildings on campus. Approved or accredited by Council of International Schools, International Baccalaureate Organization, New England Association of Schools and Colleges, US Department of State, and state department of education. Member of European Council of International Schools. Language of instruction: English. Total enrollment: 640. Upper school average class size: 15. Upper school faculty-student ratio: 1:8. There are 179 required school days per year for Upper School students. Upper School students typically attend 5 days per week. The average school day consists of 5 hours and 30 minutes.

Upper School Student Profile Grade 9: 59 students (34 boys, 25 girls); Grade 10: 52 students (28 boys, 24 girls); Grade 11: 51 students (22 boys, 29 girls); Grade 12: 54 students (26 boys, 28 girls).

Faculty School total: 78. In upper school: 12 men, 15 women; 25 have advanced degrees.

Subjects Offered Algebra, art, biology, business studies, chemistry, choir, computer applications, computer art, economics, English, European history, French, geography, geometry, International Baccalaureate courses, journalism, model United Nations, modern civilization, music, physical education, physics, Portuguese, Portuguese literature, Spanish, theory of knowledge, U.S. history, U.S. literature, writing workshop, yearbook.

Graduation Requirements Arts and fine arts (art, music, dance, drama), computer science, electives, English, foreign language, mathematics, physical education (includes health), science, social studies (includes history), International Baccalaureate diploma candidates have to complete 150 Community Action Service hours, plus Theory of Knowledge and Extended Essay.

Special Academic Programs International Baccalaureate program; honors section; independent study; programs in general development for dyslexic students; ESL (68 students enrolled).

College Admission Counseling 39 students graduated in 2015; 35 went to college, including Amherst College; Boston University; California State University, Fullerton; Rensselaer Polytechnic Institute; Rollins College; Suffolk University. Other: 4 had other specific plans.

Student Life Upper grades have specified standards of dress, student council, honor system. Discipline rests primarily with faculty.

Tuition and Aid Day student tuition: €7596–€17,716. Tuition installment plan (monthly payment plans, individually arranged payment plans, early payment discount, quarterly payment plan). Tuition reduction for siblings, merit scholarship grants, Merit-based scholarships are available to student residents in Sintra, Portugal only available.

Admissions English for Non-native Speakers or Math Placement Exam required. Deadline for receipt of application materials: none. No application fee required.

Athletics Interscholastic: basketball (boys, girls), cross-country running (b,g), soccer (b,g), track and field (b,g), volleyball (b,g); intramural: basketball (b,g), soccer (b,g);

coed interscholastic: baseball; coed intramural: ballet, fitness, gymnastics, modern dance, mountain biking, volleyball. 4 PE instructors, 6 coaches.

Computers Computers are regularly used in computer applications, digital applications, graphic design classes. Computer network features include on-campus library services, Internet access, wireless campus network, Internet filtering or blocking technology. Campus intranet, student e-mail accounts, and computer access in designated common areas are available to students. Students grades are available online. The school has a published electronic and media policy.

Contact Ms. Maria Barral, DMC Manager. 351-21-923-9800. Fax: 351-21-923-9809. E-mail: admissions@caislisbon.org. Website: www.caislisbon.org

CARNEGIE SCHOOLS RIVERSIDE

8775 Magnolia Ave
Riverside, California 92503

Head of School: Dr. Tiffany Edwards

General Information Coeducational day college-preparatory school. Grades K–12. Founded: 1958. Setting: urban. Students are housed in home stay. 5-acre campus. 6 buildings on campus. Approved or accredited by Association of Christian Schools International and Western Association of Schools and Colleges. Total enrollment: 253. Upper school average class size: 25. Upper school faculty-student ratio: 1:22. There are 5 required school days per year for Upper School students. Upper School students typically attend 5 days per week. The average school day consists of 6 hours and 45 minutes.

Upper School Student Profile 13% of students are boarding students. 87% are state residents. 12 states are represented in upper school student body. 13% are international students. International students from Argentina, Canada, China, France, Mexico, and Turkey; 22 other countries represented in student body.

Faculty School total: 22. In upper school: 10 men, 12 women; 15 have advanced degrees.

Subjects Offered Advanced biology, advanced chemistry, advanced math, Advanced Placement courses, all academic, American government, American history, American history-AP, American literature, American literature-AP, anatomy and physiology, ancient history, area studies, biology, biology-AP, biotechnology, British literature, British literature (honors), British literature-AP, calculus, calculus-AP, chemistry, chemistry-AP, choir, Christian and Hebrew scripture, Christian doctrine, Christian education, Christian scripture, Christian studies, Christian testament, drama, drama performance, economics, English, English language and composition-AP, English language-AP, English literature, English literature and composition-AP, English literature-AP, English-AP, fine arts, general science, government, government-AP, history-AP, honors algebra, honors English, honors geometry, honors U.S. history, honors world history, language and composition, life science, modern world history, New Testament, physical fitness, physical science, physics, physics-AP, pre-algebra, pre-calculus, science, U.S. government, U.S. history, U.S. history-AP, U.S. literature, video film production, visual arts, world cultures, world geography, world history, world studies, yearbook.

Graduation Requirements All academic, American government, American history, arts and fine arts (art, music, dance, drama), chemistry, creative arts, English, foreign language, health, mathematics, physical education (includes health), science, theology, world history, 4 years of Bible. Community service is required.

Special Academic Programs 8 Advanced Placement exams for which test preparation is offered; honors section; accelerated programs; independent study; study at local college for college credit; remedial reading and/or remedial writing; remedial math; special instructional classes for Learning Lab; ESL (40 students enrolled).

College Admission Counseling 36 students graduated in 2016; 35 went to college, including California Lutheran University; California State University, Northridge; California State University, San Bernardino; Fullerton College; Grand Canyon University; University of California, Riverside. Other: 1 went to work.

Student Life Upper grades have uniform requirement, student council, honor system. Discipline rests primarily with faculty.

Summer Programs Remediation, enrichment, advancement, ESL programs offered; held on campus; accepts boys and girls; open to students from other schools. 25 students usually enrolled. 2017 schedule: June 5 to July 14. Application deadline: May 31.

Tuition and Aid Tuition installment plan (SMART Tuition Payment Plan, FACTS Tuition Payment Plan, monthly payment plans, international students paid in full at beginning of school year). Tuition reduction for siblings, need-based scholarship grants available.

Admissions Traditional secondary-level entrance grade is 9. TOEFL or SLEP required. Deadline for receipt of application materials: none. Application fee required: $50. Interview required.

Athletics Interscholastic: baseball (boys), basketball (b,g), cheering (g), cross-country running (b,g), dance squad (g), flag football (b), football (b), lacrosse (b), rugby (b), soccer (b,g), softball (g), swimming and diving (b,g), tennis (b,g), track and field (b,g), volleyball (b,g), winter soccer (b,g); coed interscholastic: soccer, swimming and diving. 3 PE instructors, 1 athletic trainer.

Computers Computers are regularly used in all classes. Computer network features include Internet access, wireless campus network, Internet filtering or blocking technology, iPads, laptops. Campus intranet, student e-mail accounts, and computer

access in designated common areas are available to students. Students grades are available online. The school has a published electronic and media policy.

Contact Dr. Elizabeth Pashko, Director of Admissions and Marketing. 951-687-0077. Fax: 951-687-3340. E-mail: epashko@rivchristian.org. Website: www.rivchristian.org/

CARONDELET HIGH SCHOOL

1133 Winton Drive
Concord, California 94518

Head of School: Bonnie Cotter

General Information Girls' day college-preparatory school, affiliated with Roman Catholic Church. Grades 9–12. Founded: 1965. Setting: suburban. Nearest major city is Oakland. 9-acre campus. 5 buildings on campus. Approved or accredited by National Catholic Education Association, Western Association of Schools and Colleges, and Western Catholic Education Association. Member of National Association of Independent Schools. Endowment: $9 million. Total enrollment: 800. Upper school average class size: 23. Upper school faculty-student ratio: 1:16. There are 176 required school days per year for Upper School students. Upper School students typically attend 5 days per week. The average school day consists of 7 hours.

Upper School Student Profile Grade 9: 200 students (200 girls); Grade 10: 200 students (200 girls); Grade 11: 200 students (200 girls); Grade 12: 200 students (200 girls). 87% of students are Roman Catholic.

Faculty School total: 51. In upper school: 9 men, 42 women; 17 have advanced degrees.

Subjects Offered Advanced Placement courses, all academic.

Graduation Requirements Art, electives, foreign language, modern languages, religion and culture, religious studies, visual and performing arts.

Special Academic Programs 12 Advanced Placement exams for which test preparation is offered; honors section; independent study; study at local college for college credit; academic accommodation for the gifted; special instructional classes for educational support for students with learning differences and physical challenges across subjects, extended time on assessments, oral/visual explanations of concepts, indiv. instruction for curriculum access.

College Admission Counseling 199 students graduated in 2016; all went to college, including California Polytechnic State University, San Luis Obispo; Saint Mary's College of California; San Diego State University; Sonoma State University; University of California, Berkeley; University of Nevada, Reno. Mean SAT critical reading: 567, mean SAT math: 546, mean SAT writing: 570, mean composite ACT: 26.

Student Life Upper grades have uniform requirement, student council, honor system. Discipline rests primarily with faculty. Attendance at religious services is required.

Summer Programs Remediation, enrichment, advancement, sports programs offered; session focuses on academics (advancement, remediation & enrichment), sports, and fun & middle school; held on campus; accepts boys and girls; open to students from other schools. 100 students usually enrolled. 2017 schedule: June to July. Application deadline: May.

Tuition and Aid Day student tuition: $16,900. Tuition installment plan (SMART Tuition Payment Plan, monthly payment plans, prepayment plan, semester or quarterly payment plans). Need-based scholarship grants available. In 2016–17, 26% of upper-school students received aid. Total amount of financial aid awarded in 2016–17: $1,100,000.

Admissions Traditional secondary-level entrance grade is 9. For fall 2016, 311 students applied for upper-level admission, 260 were accepted, 214 enrolled. High School Placement Test (closed version) from Scholastic Testing Service required. Deadline for receipt of application materials: December 2. Application fee required: $100. On-campus interview required.

Athletics Interscholastic: aquatics, badminton, basketball, cheering, combined training, cross-country running, dance squad, dance team, diving, golf, lacrosse, soccer, softball, swimming and diving, tennis, track and field, volleyball, water polo; intramural: badminton, basketball, broomball, flag football, physical fitness, physical training, touch football, volleyball, yoga. 4 PE instructors, 57 coaches, 1 athletic trainer.

Computers Computers are regularly used in Web site design, yearbook classes. Computer network features include on-campus library services, Internet access, wireless campus network, Internet filtering or blocking technology. Campus intranet, student e-mail accounts, and computer access in designated common areas are available to students. Students grades are available online. The school has a published electronic and media policy.

Contact Ms. Jessica Mix, Assistant Principal/Director of Admissions. 925-686-5353 Ext. 367. Fax: 925-671-9429. E-mail: jmix@carondeleths.org. Website: www.carondelet.net

CARROLLTON SCHOOL OF THE SACRED HEART

3747 Main Highway
Miami, Florida 33133

Head of School: Mr. Olen Kalkus

General Information Girls' day college-preparatory, arts, religious studies, bilingual studies, and technology school, affiliated with Roman Catholic Church. Grades PK–12. Founded: 1961. Setting: urban. 17-acre campus. 5 buildings on campus. Approved or accredited by Florida Council of Independent Schools, Network of Sacred Heart Schools, and Southern Association of Colleges and Schools. Member of National Association of Independent Schools and Secondary School Admission Test Board. Endowment: $2 million. Total enrollment: 800. Upper school average class size: 16. Upper school faculty-student ratio: 1:9. There are 180 required school days per year for Upper School students. Upper School students typically attend 5 days per week. The average school day consists of 8 hours.

Upper School Student Profile 87% of students are Roman Catholic.

Faculty School total: 74. In upper school: 9 men, 24 women; 20 have advanced degrees.

Subjects Offered Algebra, American history, American literature, anatomy and physiology, art, art history, Bible studies, biology, British literature, calculus, chemistry, computer science, debate, drama, earth systems analysis, economics, English, English literature, environmental science, ethics, expository writing, fine arts, French, general science, geometry, government/civics, grammar, health, history, humanities, journalism, mathematics, music, photography, physical education, physical science, physics, pre-calculus, psychology, religion, science, scripture, social sciences, social studies, Spanish, speech, theater, trigonometry, vocal ensemble, world history, world literature.

Graduation Requirements Arts and fine arts (art, music, dance, drama), computer science, English, foreign language, mathematics, physical education (includes health), religion (includes Bible studies and theology), science, social studies (includes history) Community service is required.

Special Academic Programs International Baccalaureate program; Advanced Placement exam preparation; honors section; independent study; study at local college for college credit; domestic exchange program; study abroad.

College Admission Counseling 70 students graduated in 2015; all went to college, including Boston College; Massachusetts Institute of Technology; Northwestern University; University of Miami; Vanderbilt University. Median SAT math: 590, median composite ACT: 24. Mean SAT critical reading: 590. 51% scored over 600 on SAT critical reading, 47% scored over 600 on SAT math, 30% scored over 26 on composite ACT.

Student Life Upper grades have uniform requirement, student council, honor system. Discipline rests primarily with faculty. Attendance at religious services is required.

Tuition and Aid Day student tuition: $30,350. Tuition installment plan (Insured Tuition Payment Plan, monthly payment plans). Merit scholarship grants, need-based scholarship grants available. In 2015–16, 25% of upper school students received aid; total upper-school merit-scholarship money awarded: $45,000. Total amount of financial aid awarded in 2015–16: $920,000.

Admissions Traditional secondary-level entrance grade is 9. For fall 2015, 132 students applied for upper-level admission, 37 were accepted, 30 enrolled. Admissions testing or ISEE required. Deadline for receipt of application materials: February 1. Application fee required: $50. On-campus interview required.

Athletics Interscholastic: aquatics, basketball, crew, cross-country running, golf, sailing, soccer, softball, swimming and diving, tennis, track and field, volleyball, water polo, winter soccer. 6 PE instructors, 30 coaches, 3 athletic trainers.

Computers Computers are regularly used in all academic classes. Computer network features include on-campus library services, online commercial services, Internet access, wireless campus network, Internet filtering or blocking technology, laptop program. Student e-mail accounts are available to students. The school has a published electronic and media policy.

Contact Ms. Ana J. Roye, Director of Admission and Financial Aid. 305-446-5673 Ext. 1224. Fax: 305-446-4160. E-mail: aroye@carrollton.org. Website: www.carrollton.org

CASADY SCHOOL

9500 North Pennsylvania Avenue
Oklahoma City, Oklahoma 73120

Head of School: Mr. Nathan Sheldon

General Information Coeducational day college-preparatory school, affiliated with Episcopal Church. Grades PK–12. Founded: 1947. Setting: suburban. 80-acre campus. 30 buildings on campus. Approved or accredited by Independent Schools Association of the Southwest, National Independent Private Schools Association, Southwest Association of Episcopal Schools, and The College Board. Member of National Association of Independent Schools and Secondary School Admission Test Board. Endowment: $16 million. Total enrollment: 905. Upper school average class size: 15. Upper school faculty-student ratio: 1:15. Upper School students typically attend 5 days per week. The average school day consists of 6 hours.

Upper School Student Profile Grade 6: 70 students (33 boys, 37 girls); Grade 7: 66 students (34 boys, 32 girls); Grade 8: 69 students (33 boys, 36 girls); Grade 9: 81 students (46 boys, 35 girls); Grade 10: 80 students (39 boys, 41 girls); Grade 11: 81 students (41 boys, 40 girls); Grade 12: 78 students (48 boys, 30 girls). 30% of students are members of Episcopal Church.

Faculty School total: 148. In upper school: 32 men, 21 women; 35 have advanced degrees.

Subjects Offered African-American studies, algebra, American history, American literature, art, art history, Asian history, athletic training, band, Bible studies, biochemistry, biology, biology-AP, British literature, calculus, calculus-AP, ceramics, chemistry, chemistry-AP, Chinese, choir, choral music, college counseling, college placement, college planning, computer applications, computer programming, computer science, creative writing, data processing, digital imaging, drama, drama performance, drawing, driver education, earth science, economics, English, English language-AP, English literature, English literature-AP, environmental science, European history, expository writing, fine arts, French, French language-AP, French literature-AP, freshman seminar, functions, geology, geometry, German, government/civics, grammar, Greek, health, history, human anatomy, journalism, Latin, Latin-AP, mathematics, Middle Eastern history, modern languages, music, mythology, Native American history, painting, photography, physical education, physics, physiology, religion, Russian history, science, social studies, Spanish, Spanish language-AP, Spanish literature-AP, speech, statistics, theater, theology, trigonometry, U.S. history-AP, water color painting, weight training, word processing, world history, world literature, writing, yearbook.

Graduation Requirements Arts and fine arts (art, music, dance, drama), computer science, English, foreign language, mathematics, physical education (includes health), science, social studies (includes history), service learning.

Special Academic Programs Advanced Placement exam preparation; honors section; independent study; study abroad; academic accommodation for the gifted, the musically talented, and the artistically talented; programs in English, mathematics, general development for dyslexic students.

College Admission Counseling 77 students graduated in 2016; all went to college, including Oklahoma State University; Sewanee: The University of the South; Southern Methodist University; Texas Christian University; University of Oklahoma; Washington University in St. Louis. Other: 2 had other specific plans. Mean composite ACT: 28.

Student Life Upper grades have specified standards of dress, student council, honor system. Discipline rests equally with students and faculty. Attendance at religious services is required.

Summer Programs Remediation, enrichment, advancement, sports, art/fine arts, computer instruction programs offered; held on campus; accepts boys and girls; open to students from other schools. 300 students usually enrolled. 2017 schedule: June 11 to July 13. Application deadline: June 1.

Tuition and Aid Day student tuition: $6700–$19,990. Tuition installment plan (The Tuition Plan, Insured Tuition Payment Plan, SMART Tuition Payment Plan, FACTS Tuition Payment Plan, monthly payment plans, individually arranged payment plans, 2-installment plan). Merit scholarship grants, need-based scholarship grants available. In 2016–17, 25% of upper-school students received aid; total upper-school merit-scholarship money awarded: $378,671. Total amount of financial aid awarded in 2016–17: $2,050,129.

Admissions Traditional secondary-level entrance grade is 9. For fall 2016, 218 students applied for upper-level admission, 155 were accepted, 134 enrolled. CTP, ERB - verbal abilities, reading comprehension, quantitative abilities (level F, form 1) and school's own exam required. Deadline for receipt of application materials: none. Application fee required: $50. On-campus interview required.

Athletics Interscholastic: baseball (boys), basketball (b,g), cheering (g), cross-country running (b,g), field hockey (g), football (b), golf (b,g), soccer (b,g), softball (g), swimming and diving (b,g), tennis (b,g), track and field (b,g), volleyball (b,g), wrestling (b); intramural: aerobics/dance (g), dance (g), martial arts (b,g), modern dance (g), physical fitness (b,g), physical training (b,g); coed intramural: aerobics, bowling, climbing, fencing, fitness walking, racquetball, sailing, weight lifting, yoga. 9 PE instructors, 23 coaches, 2 athletic trainers.

Computers Computers are regularly used in all academic classes. Computer resources include on-campus library services, Internet access, wireless campus network, Internet filtering or blocking technology. Campus intranet, student e-mail accounts, and computer access in designated common areas are available to students. Students grades are available online.

Contact Mrs. Amanda Bishop, Advancement Office Coordinator. 405-749-3185. Fax: 405-749-3223. E-mail: bishopa@casady.org. Website: www.casady.org

CASCADES ACADEMY OF CENTRAL OREGON

19860 Tumalo Reservoir Road
Bend, Oregon 97703

Head of School: Julie Amberg

General Information Coeducational day college-preparatory and Experiential Education school. Grades PK–12. Founded: 2003. Setting: suburban. 21-acre campus. 2 buildings on campus. Approved or accredited by Northwest Association of Independent Schools and Oregon Department of Education. Member of National Association of Independent Schools. Endowment: $35,000. Total enrollment: 186. Upper school average class size: 12. Upper school faculty-student ratio: 1:6. There are 168 required school days per year for Upper School students. Upper School students typically attend 5 days per week. The average school day consists of 7 hours and 20 minutes.

Upper School Student Profile Grade 9: 12 students (4 boys, 8 girls); Grade 10: 7 students (2 boys, 5 girls); Grade 11: 10 students (5 boys, 5 girls); Grade 12: 6 students (5 boys, 1 girl).

Faculty School total: 30. In upper school: 3 men, 3 women; 4 have advanced degrees.

Graduation Requirements Internship.

Special Academic Programs Independent study.

College Admission Counseling 9 students graduated in 2016; 8 went to college, including Central Oregon Community College; Emerson College; Grinnell College;

University of Oregon; University of Portland; University of San Diego. Other: 1 went to work.

Student Life Upper grades have specified standards of dress, student council, honor system. Discipline rests primarily with faculty.

Tuition and Aid Day student tuition: $13,500. Tuition installment plan (monthly payment plans, individually arranged payment plans). Merit scholarship grants, need-based scholarship grants available. In 2016–17, 48% of upper-school students received aid; total upper-school merit-scholarship money awarded: $6000. Total amount of financial aid awarded in 2016–17: $152,000.

Admissions Traditional secondary-level entrance grade is 9. For fall 2016, 14 students applied for upper-level admission, 4 were accepted, 3 enrolled. Deadline for receipt of application materials: none. Application fee required: $75. Interview required.

Athletics Coed Intramural: backpacking, bicycling, canoeing/kayaking, fitness, Frisbee, jogging, kayaking, mountain biking, outdoor activities, outdoor adventure, outdoor education, outdoor recreation, outdoor skills, physical fitness, rafting, running, skiing (downhill), snowboarding, strength & conditioning, tennis, ultimate Frisbee, walking, wilderness survival, yoga.

Computers Computers are regularly used in all classes. Computer network features include Internet access, wireless campus network, Internet filtering or blocking technology. Student e-mail accounts and computer access in designated common areas are available to students. Students grades are available online. The school has a published electronic and media policy.

Contact Andrea Hendrickson, Director of Admission. 541-382-0699 Ext. 132. Fax: 541-382-0225. E-mail: hendrickson@cascadesacademy.org.
Website: www.cascadesacademy.org/

CASCADILLA SCHOOL

116 Summit Street
Ithaca, New York 14850

Head of School: Patricia T. Kendall

General Information Coeducational boarding and day college-preparatory, arts, bilingual studies, English/language arts (The Cascadilla Seminar/Cornell Univ.), and mathematics school. Grades 9–PG. Founded: 1876. Setting: urban. Nearest major city is Syracuse. Students are housed in single-sex dormitories. 2-acre campus. 3 buildings on campus. Approved or accredited by New York Department of Education, New York State Board of Regents, New York State University, The College Board, US Department of State, and New York Department of Education. Endowment: $1.5 million. Upper school average class size: 7. Upper school faculty-student ratio: 1:5. There are 185 required school days per year for Upper School students. Upper School students typically attend 5 days per week. The average school day consists of 8 hours.

Upper School Student Profile Grade 9: 9 students (5 boys, 4 girls); Grade 10: 3 students (1 boy, 2 girls); Grade 11: 13 students (9 boys, 4 girls); Grade 12: 11 students (4 boys, 7 girls). 30% of students are boarding students. 45% are state residents. 4 states are represented in upper school student body. 55% are international students. International students from Angola, China, Portugal, and Republic of Korea.

Faculty School total: 13. In upper school: 5 men, 8 women; 12 have advanced degrees; 4 reside on campus.

Subjects Offered Advanced biology, advanced chemistry, advanced math, Advanced Placement courses, advanced TOEFL/grammar, African literature, algebra, alternative physical education, American government, American history, American history-AP, American literature, analysis and differential calculus, analytic geometry, art, biochemistry, biology, biology-AP, calculus, calculus-AP, career/college preparation, ceramics, chemistry, chemistry-AP, civics, classical language, college admission preparation, college awareness, college counseling, college placement, college planning, college writing, computer programming, computer science, creative writing, decision making skills, desktop publishing, digital photography, DNA science lab, earth science, economics, electives, English, English composition, English literature, English literature and composition-AP, English literature-AP, environmental education, environmental science, ethics, expository writing, fabric arts, French, French as a second language, geometry, government/civics, graphic design, health, health and wellness, health education, history, honors algebra, honors English, honors geometry, honors U.S. history, honors world history, journalism, lab science, Latin, leadership, library research, library skills, literary magazine, mathematics, philosophy, photography, photojournalism, physical education, physics, pre-calculus, psychology, public speaking, reading, reading/study skills, SAT preparation, SAT/ACT preparation, science, senior composition, senior humanities, senior seminar, senior thesis, Shakespeare, social studies, Spanish, statistics, statistics-AP, TOEFL preparation, trigonometry, U.S. government, U.S. government and politics, U.S. history, U.S. history-AP, U.S. literature, video film production, world history, world history-AP, world literature, writing, yearbook, zoology.

Graduation Requirements Alternative physical education, arts, arts and fine arts (art, music, dance, drama), computer science, current events, debate, economics, economics and history, English, European history, foreign language, government, health education, international affairs, mathematics, physical education (includes health), political science, public speaking, research, research and reference, research seminar, science, senior seminar, social studies (includes history), study skills, U.S. government and politics, English V-The Cascadilla Seminar (preparation for college writing and research). Community service is required.

Special Academic Programs 16 Advanced Placement exams for which test preparation is offered; honors section; accelerated programs; independent study; term-away projects; study at local college for college credit; academic accommodation for the gifted, the musically talented, and the artistically talented; remedial reading and/or remedial writing; remedial math; programs in English, mathematics for dyslexic students; special instructional classes for students with learning disabilities and Attention Deficit Disorder.

College Admission Counseling 11 students graduated in 2015; all went to college, including Barry University; Ithaca College; Pace University; University of California, Riverside; University of Missouri; University of Pittsburgh. Median SAT critical reading: 630, median SAT math: 610, median SAT writing: 510, median combined SAT: 1800. 60% scored over 600 on SAT critical reading, 60% scored over 600 on SAT math, 20% scored over 600 on SAT writing, 20% scored over 1800 on combined SAT.

Student Life Upper grades have specified standards of dress, student council, honor system. Discipline rests equally with students and faculty.

Tuition and Aid Day student tuition: $14,550; 7-day tuition and room/board: $39,950. Tuition installment plan (monthly payment plans, individually arranged payment plans). Tuition reduction for siblings, merit scholarship grants, need-based scholarship grants available. In 2015–16, 40% of upper-school students received aid; total upper-school merit-scholarship money awarded: $50,000. Total amount of financial aid awarded in 2015–16: $60,000.

Admissions Traditional secondary-level entrance grade is 10. For fall 2015, 70 students applied for upper-level admission, 16 were accepted, 14 enrolled. English Composition Test for ESL students, English entrance exam, English for Non-native Speakers, English language, English proficiency, High School Placement Test, math and English placement tests, mathematics proficiency exam, non-standardized placement tests, Reading for Understanding, school's own exam or writing sample required. Deadline for receipt of application materials: none. Application fee required: $75. Interview recommended.

Athletics Interscholastic: crew (boys, girls), modern dance (g); intramural: crew (b,g), fencing (b), independent competitive sports (b,g), rowing (b,g), sailing (b,g), skiing (cross-country) (b,g), skiing (downhill) (b,g), soccer (b,g), tennis (b,g); coed interscholastic: aerobics, aerobics/Nautilus, alpine skiing, aquatics, backpacking, badminton, ballet, basketball, billiards, blading, bowling, climbing, combined training, fencing, fitness, fitness walking, Frisbee, hiking/backpacking, jogging, kayaking, nordic skiing, outdoor activities, outdoor adventure, outdoor education, physical fitness, physical training, swimming and diving, table tennis, weight lifting, yoga; coed intramural: aerobics, aerobics/dance, badminton, basketball, blading, bowling, equestrian sports, horseback riding, independent competitive sports, jogging, Nautilus, nordic skiing, outdoor activities, outdoor adventure, physical fitness, physical training, pillo polo, racquetball, rowing, sailboarding, skiing (cross-country), skiing (downhill), snowboarding, soccer, strength & conditioning, tennis, volleyball, walking, wall climbing, windsurfing. 3 PE instructors.

Computers Computers are regularly used in career exploration, college planning, creative writing, desktop publishing, economics, English, foreign language, graphic design, journalism, language development, library skills, literary magazine, mathematics, media arts, news writing, newspaper, photography, photojournalism, publications, publishing, research skills, SAT preparation, senior seminar, Spanish, stock market, theater, theater arts, video film production, Web site design, word processing, writing, yearbook classes. Computer network features include on-campus library services, online commercial services, Internet access, wireless campus network, Internet filtering or blocking technology, dormitories are fitted for high speed Internet. Student e-mail accounts and computer access in designated common areas are available to students. Students grades are available online.

Contact Mary B. Lorson, Assistant Director of Admissions. 607-272-3110. Fax: 607-272-0747. E-mail: admissions@cascadillaschool.org.
Website: www.cascadillaschool.org

CASCIA HALL PREPARATORY SCHOOL

2520 South Yorktown Avenue
Tulsa, Oklahoma 74114-2803

Head of School: Mr. Roger C. Carter

General Information Coeducational day college-preparatory and liberal arts school, affiliated with Roman Catholic Church. Grades 6–12. Founded: 1926. Setting: urban. 40-acre campus. 10 buildings on campus. Approved or accredited by North Central Association of Colleges and Schools, Southern Association of Colleges and Schools, and Oklahoma Department of Education. Endowment: $8 million. Total enrollment: 527. Upper school average class size: 16. Upper school faculty-student ratio: 1:9. There are 180 required school days per year for Upper School students. Upper School students typically attend 5 days per week. The average school day consists of 6 hours and 30 minutes.

Upper School Student Profile Grade 9: 70 students (38 boys, 32 girls); Grade 10: 108 students (49 boys, 59 girls); Grade 11: 75 students (41 boys, 34 girls); Grade 12: 76 students (51 boys, 25 girls). 45% of students are Roman Catholic.

Faculty School total: 48. In upper school: 19 men, 20 women; 32 have advanced degrees.

Subjects Offered 20th century physics, ACT preparation, Advanced Placement courses, advanced studio art-AP, algebra, American history-AP, American literature, anatomy and physiology, ancient world history, art, art-AP, Asian studies, astronomy, Basic programming, Bible studies, biology, business, calculus, calculus-AP, career experience, career exploration, Catholic belief and practice, Central and Eastern European history, chemistry, chemistry-AP, Chinese, Chinese studies, chorus, Christian ethics, church history, college admission preparation, composition, computer science, CPR, creative writing, digital photography, drama, drawing, driver education, English language and composition-AP, English literature and composition-AP, environmental studies, ethics, European history, European history-AP, French, geography, geometry, German, government-AP, grammar, health, history of the Catholic Church, Holocaust studies, independent study, Latin, literature, philosophy, photography, physical science, physics, physics-AP, pre-calculus, probability and statistics, psychology, Russian studies, SAT/ACT preparation, senior seminar, senior thesis, Shakespeare, Spanish, Spanish language-AP, speech, speech and debate, theater, theology, trigonometry, U.S. government and politics-AP, U.S. history, world history, writing.

Graduation Requirements Arts and fine arts (art, music, dance, drama), career exploration, college admission preparation, computer science, English, foreign language, mathematics, religion (includes Bible studies and theology), science, senior seminar, social sciences, social studies (includes history), community service.

Special Academic Programs 12 Advanced Placement exams for which test preparation is offered; honors section; independent study; study at local college for college credit; study abroad; academic accommodation for the gifted.

College Admission Counseling 85 students graduated in 2016; all went to college, including Oklahoma State University; Texas Christian University; The University of Kansas; The University of Tulsa; University of Arkansas; University of Oklahoma. Median SAT critical reading: 611, median SAT math: 602, median SAT writing: 600, median composite ACT: 26. 56% scored over 600 on SAT critical reading, 56% scored over 600 on SAT math, 53% scored over 600 on SAT writing, 45% scored over 26 on composite ACT.

Student Life Upper grades have uniform requirement, student council. Discipline rests primarily with faculty. Attendance at religious services is required.

Summer Programs Remediation, enrichment, advancement, sports, art/fine arts programs offered; session focuses on sports camp, driver's education, and performing arts, English Enrichment, College essay writing; held on campus; accepts boys and girls; open to students from other schools. 500 students usually enrolled. 2017 schedule: June to August. Application deadline: May 1.

Tuition and Aid Day student tuition: $13,500. Tuition installment plan (monthly payment plans). Tuition reduction for siblings, need-based scholarship grants available. In 2016–17, 20% of upper-school students received aid. Total amount of financial aid awarded in 2016–17: $75,000.

Admissions Traditional secondary-level entrance grade is 9. For fall 2016, 75 students applied for upper-level admission, 59 were accepted, 44 enrolled. STS - Educational Development Series required. Deadline for receipt of application materials: none. Application fee required: $25. On-campus interview recommended.

Athletics Interscholastic: baseball (boys), basketball (b,g), bowling (b), cheering (g), cross-country running (b,g), dance team (g), football (b), golf (b,g), power lifting (b,g), soccer (b,g), softball (g), strength & conditioning (b,g), tennis (b,g), track and field (b,g), volleyball (g), weight training (b,g), wrestling (b); coed intramural: bowling, crew, lacrosse, outdoor recreation, rowing, rugby, ultimate Frisbee. 1 PE instructor, 17 coaches, 1 athletic trainer.

Computers Computers are regularly used in all classes. Computer network features include on-campus library services, online commercial services, Internet access, wireless campus network, Internet filtering or blocking technology, InfoTrac Search Bank, Internet access to local and state university library catalogues. Campus intranet, student e-mail accounts, and computer access in designated common areas are available to students. Students grades are available online. The school has a published electronic and media policy.

Contact Mrs. Patricia A. Wilson, Coordinator of Admissions. 918-746-2604. Fax: 918-746-2640. E-mail: pwilson@casciahall.com. Website: www.casciahall.com

CASTILLEJA SCHOOL

1310 Bryant Street
Palo Alto, California 94301

Head of School: Nanci Z. Kauffman

General Information Girls' day college-preparatory school. Grades 6–12. Founded: 1907. Setting: suburban. Nearest major city is San Francisco/San Jose. 5-acre campus. 7 buildings on campus. Approved or accredited by California Association of Independent Schools and Western Association of Schools and Colleges. Member of National Association of Independent Schools and Secondary School Admission Test Board. Endowment: $42 million. Total enrollment: 438. Upper school average class size: 14. Upper school faculty-student ratio: 1:6. Upper School students typically attend 5 days per week. The average school day consists of 7 hours.

Upper School Student Profile Grade 6: 65 students (65 girls); Grade 7: 61 students (61 girls); Grade 8: 65 students (65 girls); Grade 9: 68 students (68 girls); Grade 10: 65 students (65 girls); Grade 11: 58 students (58 girls); Grade 12: 56 students (56 girls).

Faculty School total: 75. In upper school: 12 men, 34 women; 40 have advanced degrees.

Subjects Offered Advanced Placement courses, African studies, algebra, American history, American literature, art, art history, biology, calculus, ceramics, chemistry,

computer math, computer science, creative writing, drama, economics, English, English literature, environmental science, European history, expository writing, fine arts, French, geometry, global issues, government/civics, grammar, health, history, journalism, Latin, marine biology, mathematics, music, philosophy, physical education, physics, psychology, Russian history, science, social studies, Spanish, speech, statistics, theater, trigonometry, world history, writing.

Graduation Requirements Arts and fine arts (art, music, dance, drama), English, foreign language, health and wellness, mathematics, science, social studies (includes history).

Special Academic Programs 13 Advanced Placement exams for which test preparation is offered; honors section; independent study; academic accommodation for the gifted.

College Admission Counseling 67 students graduated in 2016; all went to college. Mean SAT critical reading: 712, mean SAT math: 703, mean SAT writing: 731, mean composite ACT: 32.

Student Life Upper grades have uniform requirement, student council, honor system. Discipline rests equally with students and faculty.

Tuition and Aid Day student tuition: $44,465. Tuition installment plan (monthly payment plans, individually arranged payment plans). Need-based scholarship grants available. In 2016–17, 20% of upper-school students received aid. Total amount of financial aid awarded in 2016–17: $2,600,000.

Admissions Traditional secondary-level entrance grade is 9. For fall 2016, 450 students applied for upper-level admission, 80 enrolled. ISEE, SSAT or TOEFL required. Deadline for receipt of application materials: January 17. Application fee required: $75. On-campus interview required.

Athletics Interscholastic: basketball, cross-country running, golf, lacrosse, soccer, softball, swimming and diving, tennis, track and field, volleyball, water polo; intramural: climbing, fitness, rock climbing. 6 PE instructors, 15 coaches, 1 athletic trainer.

Computers Computers are regularly used in art, English, foreign language, history, mathematics, science classes. Computer network features include on-campus library services, online commercial services, Internet access, wireless campus network, Internet filtering or blocking technology, one-to-one laptop program, iPads. Campus intranet and student e-mail accounts are available to students. Students grades are available online. The school has a published electronic and media policy.

Contact Jill V.W. Lee, Director of Admission. 650-470-7731. Fax: 650-326-8036. E-mail: jlee@castilleja.org. Website: www.castilleja.org

CATE SCHOOL

1960 Cate Mesa Road
Carpinteria, California 93013

Head of School: Benjamin D. Williams, IV

General Information Coeducational boarding and day college-preparatory school. Grades 9–12. Founded: 1910. Setting: small town. Nearest major city is Santa Barbara. Students are housed in single-sex dormitories. 150-acre campus. 19 buildings on campus. Approved or accredited by California Association of Independent Schools, The Association of Boarding Schools, and Western Association of Schools and Colleges. Member of National Association of Independent Schools and Secondary School Admission Test Board. Endowment: $60 million. Total enrollment: 270. Upper school average class size: 10. Upper school faculty-student ratio: 1:5. There are 184 required school days per year for Upper School students. Upper School students typically attend 6 days per week. The average school day consists of 6 hours and 45 minutes.

Upper School Student Profile Grade 9: 70 students (38 boys, 32 girls); Grade 10: 71 students (35 boys, 36 girls); Grade 11: 71 students (32 boys, 39 girls); Grade 12: 68 students (36 boys, 32 girls). 83% of students are boarding students. 42% are state residents. 28 states are represented in upper school student body. 16% are international students. International students from China, Hong Kong, Philippines, Republic of Korea, Saudi Arabia, and United Kingdom; 12 other countries represented in student body.

Faculty School total: 58. In upper school: 26 men, 32 women; 42 have advanced degrees; 49 reside on campus.

Subjects Offered Advanced studio art-AP, African American history, algebra, American history, American literature, anatomy and physiology, art, art history-AP, Asian history, astronomy, biology, biology-AP, calculus, California writers, ceramics, chemistry, chemistry-AP, Chinese, choir, computer programming, computer science, computer science-AP, creative writing, digital art, drama, drama performance, economics-AP, English, English literature, environmental science-AP, ethics, European history, finance, fine arts, French, French language-AP, French literature-AP, French-AP, freshman seminar, genetics, geometry, government-AP, human development, international relations, Japanese, marine biology, Middle Eastern history, multimedia, music, photography, photojournalism, physics, physics-AP, pre-calculus, psychology, research skills, Russian literature, Spanish, Spanish language-AP, Spanish literature-AP, Spanish-AP, statistics, statistics-AP, studio art-AP, the Sixties, theater, trigonometry, U.S. government and politics-AP, U.S. history-AP, world history, writing.

Graduation Requirements 1 1/2 elective credits, arts and fine arts (art, music, dance, drama), English, foreign language, history, human development, mathematics, science, social sciences.

Special Academic Programs 19 Advanced Placement exams for which test preparation is offered; honors section; independent study; term-away projects; study abroad; academic accommodation for the gifted, the musically talented, and the artistically talented; special instructional classes for deaf students.

College Admission Counseling 75 students graduated in 2016; all went to college, including Barnard College; New York University; Stanford University; The Colorado College; University of Pennsylvania; University of Southern California. Median SAT critical reading: 680, median SAT math: 700, median SAT writing: 700, median combined SAT: 2080. 81% scored over 600 on SAT critical reading, 81% scored over 600 on SAT math, 83% scored over 600 on SAT writing, 82% scored over 1800 on combined SAT.

Student Life Upper grades have student council, honor system. Discipline rests equally with students and faculty.

Tuition and Aid Day student tuition: $46,280; 7-day tuition and room/board: $58,050. Tuition installment plan (The Tuition Plan, Insured Tuition Payment Plan, Key Tuition Payment Plan, monthly payment plans). Need-based scholarship grants available. In 2016–17, 30% of upper-school students received aid. Total amount of financial aid awarded in 2016–17: $3,200,000.

Admissions Traditional secondary-level entrance grade is 9. For fall 2016, 700 students applied for upper-level admission, 105 were accepted, 70 enrolled. ISEE, PSAT and SAT for applicants to grade 11 and 12, SSAT, ERB, PSAT, SAT, PLAN or ACT or TOEFL required. Deadline for receipt of application materials: January 15. Application fee required: $85. On-campus interview required.

Athletics Interscholastic: aquatics (boys, girls), baseball (b), basketball (b,g), cross-country running (b,g), football (b), lacrosse (b,g), running (b,g), soccer (b,g), softball (g), squash (b,g), tennis (b,g), track and field (b,g), volleyball (b,g), water polo (b,g); intramural: independent competitive sports (b,g), sand volleyball (g); coed interscholastic: aquatics, baseball, cross-country running, golf, swimming and diving; coed intramural: aerobics, aerobics/dance, backpacking, ballet, bicycling, canoeing/kayaking, climbing, dance, dance team, fitness, Frisbee, hiking/backpacking, independent competitive sports, indoor soccer, judo, kayaking, martial arts, modern dance, mountain biking, ocean paddling, outdoor activities, outdoor adventure, outdoor education, outdoor recreation, outdoor skills, outdoors, physical fitness, physical training, rock climbing, ropes courses, scuba diving, strength & conditioning, surfing, ultimate Frisbee, wall climbing, wilderness, yoga. 7 coaches, 1 athletic trainer.

Computers Computers are regularly used in English, history, humanities, literary magazine, mathematics, media arts, media production, multimedia, music, newspaper, photography, science, yearbook classes. Computer network features include on-campus library services, online commercial services, Internet access, wireless campus network, Internet filtering or blocking technology. Campus intranet, student e-mail accounts, and computer access in designated common areas are available to students. Students grades are available online. The school has a published electronic and media policy.

Contact Lynn Dinning, Admission Office Manager. 805-684-4127 Ext. 217. Fax: 805-684-2279. E-mail: lynn_dinning@cate.org. Website: www.cate.org

CATHEDRAL HIGH SCHOOL

350 East 56th Street
New York, New York 10022-4199

Head of School: Ms. Maria Spagnuolo

General Information Girls' day college-preparatory, arts, business, religious studies, and technology school, affiliated with Roman Catholic Church. Grades 9–12. Founded: 1905. Setting: urban. 1 building on campus. Approved or accredited by Middle States Association of Colleges and Schools, National Catholic Education Association, New York Department of Education, New York State Board of Regents, The College Board, and New York Department of Education. Total enrollment: 660. Upper school average class size: 25. Upper school faculty-student ratio: 1:14. There are 180 required school days per year for Upper School students. Upper School students typically attend 5 days per week. The average school day consists of 7 hours.

Upper School Student Profile Grade 9: 130 students (130 girls); Grade 10: 170 students (170 girls); Grade 11: 185 students (185 girls); Grade 12: 165 students (165 girls). 75% of students are Roman Catholic.

Faculty School total: 49. In upper school: 19 men, 30 women.

Subjects Offered Advanced Placement courses, algebra, American history-AP, American sign language, anatomy and physiology, art, astronomy, band, biology, biology-AP, broadcasting, business law, business skills, business studies, calculus, calculus-AP, campus ministry, career education internship, career exploration, Catholic belief and practice, chemistry, choir, chorus, Christian doctrine, college admission preparation, college counseling, computer education, computer graphics, computers, constitutional history of U.S., crafts, drama, earth science, economics, electives, English composition, English literature, English-AP, English/composition-AP, fashion, fitness, foreign language, general math, geometry, government, guidance, health, health education, honors algebra, honors English, honors geometry, honors U.S. history, honors world history, HTML design, integrated mathematics, internship, journalism, lab science, Latin, law and the legal system, literature, Mandarin, mathematics-AP, photography, physics, physics-AP, physiology, portfolio art, pre-algebra, pre-calculus, psychology, psychology-AP, religion, robotics, science, science and technology, social education, sociology, Spanish literature, Spanish-AP, statistics-AP, studio art, technical drawing, technology/design, U.S. government, U.S. government and politics-AP, U.S.

history, U.S. history-AP, Web site design, women's studies, world history, world history-AP, world wide web design, writing workshop.

Graduation Requirements Art, electives, English, foreign language, health, mathematics, music, physical education (includes health), religion (includes Bible studies and theology), science, social studies (includes history), New York State Regents.

Special Academic Programs 10 Advanced Placement exams for which test preparation is offered; honors section; study at local college for college credit.

College Admission Counseling 160 students graduated in 2016; all went to college, including Barnard College; College of the Holy Cross; Columbia University; Cornell University; New York University; University of Pennsylvania.

Student Life Upper grades have uniform requirement, student council, honor system. Discipline rests primarily with faculty. Attendance at religious services is required.

Summer Programs Remediation, sports programs offered; held on campus; accepts boys and girls; open to students from other schools. 2017 schedule: July to August.

Tuition and Aid Day student tuition: $8295. Tuition installment plan (FACTS Tuition Payment Plan). Tuition reduction for siblings, merit scholarship grants, need-based scholarship grants available. In 2016–17, 40% of upper-school students received aid.

Admissions Traditional secondary-level entrance grade is 9. Admissions testing and Catholic High School Entrance Examination required. Deadline for receipt of application materials: none. No application fee required. On-campus interview recommended.

Athletics Interscholastic: basketball, cheering, cross-country running, indoor track, lacrosse, soccer, softball, track and field, volleyball; intramural: basketball, fencing, fitness, swimming and diving. 1 PE instructor, 7 coaches.

Computers Computers are regularly used in all academic classes. Computer network features include on-campus library services, Internet access, wireless campus network, Internet filtering or blocking technology. Campus intranet, student e-mail accounts, and computer access in designated common areas are available to students. Students grades are available online. The school has a published electronic and media policy.

Contact Mrs. Johanna Velez, Director of Admissions. 212-688-1545 Ext. 224. Fax: 212-754-2024. E-mail: jcastex@cathedralhs.org. Website: www.cathedralhs.org

CATHOLIC CENTRAL HIGH SCHOOL

27225 Wixom Road
Novi, Michigan 48374

Head of School: Fr. Dennis Noelke, CSB

General Information Boys' day college-preparatory school, affiliated with Roman Catholic Church. Grades 9–12. Founded: 1928. Setting: suburban. Nearest major city is Detroit. 113-acre campus. 1 building on campus. Approved or accredited by North Central Association of Colleges and Schools and Michigan Department of Education. Endowment: $3 million. Total enrollment: 1,070. Upper school average class size: 25. Upper school faculty-student ratio: 1:16. Upper School students typically attend 5 days per week. The average school day consists of 6 hours and 45 minutes.

Upper School Student Profile Grade 9: 270 students (270 boys); Grade 10: 269 students (269 boys); Grade 11: 257 students (257 boys); Grade 12: 243 students (243 boys). 81% of students are Roman Catholic.

Faculty School total: 68. In upper school: 35 men, 24 women; 59 have advanced degrees.

Subjects Offered Advanced biology, advanced chemistry, advanced computer applications, advanced math, Advanced Placement courses, algebra, American Civil War, American government, American history, American history-AP, anatomy and physiology, art, art history, biology, biology-AP, Catholic belief and practice, chemistry, chemistry-AP, Chinese, church history, Civil War, civil war history, computer science-AP, drawing, economics, English, environmental science, European history-AP, French, geometry, health, history, journalism, keyboarding, Latin, mathematics, painting, physics, pre-calculus, psychology, science, sculpture, social justice, sociology, Spanish, Spanish-AP, theology, trigonometry, U.S. government and politics-AP, U.S. history, Web site design, world history.

Special Academic Programs 14 Advanced Placement exams for which test preparation is offered; honors section.

College Admission Counseling 270 students graduated in 2016; all went to college, including Central Michigan University; Grand Valley State University; Michigan State University; University of Michigan; University of Michigan–Dearborn; University of Notre Dame. Other: 3 entered military service. Mean SAT critical reading: 595, mean SAT math: 610, mean SAT writing: 579, mean composite ACT: 26.

Student Life Upper grades have specified standards of dress, student council, honor system. Discipline rests equally with students and faculty. Attendance at religious services is required.

Tuition and Aid Day student tuition: $11,200. Tuition installment plan (monthly payment plans, individually arranged payment plans). Tuition reduction for siblings, merit scholarship grants, need-based scholarship grants available. In 2016–17, 30% of upper-school students received aid; total upper-school merit-scholarship money awarded: $50,000. Total amount of financial aid awarded in 2016–17: $1,100,000.

Admissions Traditional secondary-level entrance grade is 9. For fall 2016, 500 students applied for upper-level admission, 400 were accepted, 270 enrolled. STS or STS, Diocese Test required. Deadline for receipt of application materials: March 22. No application fee required. Interview recommended.

Athletics Interscholastic: alpine skiing, baseball, basketball, bowling, cross-country running, diving, ice hockey, lacrosse, physical fitness, physical training, skiing (downhill), soccer, swimming and diving, tennis, track and field, wrestling; intramural: basketball, cross-country running, flag football, ice hockey, touch football. 3 PE instructors, 54 coaches, 1 athletic trainer.

Computers Computer network features include on-campus library services, Internet access. The school has a published electronic and media policy.

Contact Mr. Jake Marmul, Director of Admissions. 248-596-3874. Fax: 248-596-3811. E-mail: jmarmul@catholiccentral.net. Website: www.catholiccentral.net

CATHOLIC CENTRAL HIGH SCHOOL

625 Seventh Avenue
Troy, New York 12182-2595

Head of School: Mr. Christopher Bott

General Information Coeducational day college-preparatory, business, and religious studies school, affiliated with Roman Catholic Church. Grades 7–12. Founded: 1924. Setting: suburban. 4-acre campus. 2 buildings on campus. Approved or accredited by National Catholic Education Association and New York State Board of Regents. Endowment: $50,000. Total enrollment: 379. Upper school average class size: 15. Upper school faculty-student ratio: 1:14. There are 168 required school days per year for Upper School students. Upper School students typically attend 5 days per week. The average school day consists of 6 hours and 40 minutes.

Upper School Student Profile Grade 7: 32 students (15 boys, 17 girls); Grade 8: 34 students (13 boys, 21 girls); Grade 9: 47 students (20 boys, 27 girls); Grade 10: 75 students (30 boys, 45 girls); Grade 11: 76 students (29 boys, 47 girls); Grade 12: 79 students (28 boys, 51 girls). 85% of students are Roman Catholic.

Faculty School total: 35. In upper school: 15 men, 21 women; 24 have advanced degrees.

Subjects Offered Accounting, algebra, anatomy and physiology, art, band, biology, business communications, business law, calculus, Catholic belief and practice, chemistry, chorus, computer art, computer programming, computer science, drama, drawing and design, driver education, earth science, economics, English, English language-AP, global studies, government, health, history, honors English, honors U.S. history, Internet, library skills, mathematics, physics, pre-calculus, religion, social studies, Spanish, technology, U.S. history.

Graduation Requirements Art, English, mathematics, physical education (includes health), science, social studies (includes history), theology.

Special Academic Programs Advanced Placement exam preparation; remedial reading and/or remedial writing; remedial math; ESL (11 students enrolled).

College Admission Counseling 77 students graduated in 2016; 75 went to college, including Binghamton University, State University of New York; Le Moyne College; Siena College; State University of New York at New Paltz; State University of New York College at Geneseo; University at Albany, State University of New York. Other: 1 went to work, 1 entered military service.

Student Life Upper grades have uniform requirement, student council. Discipline rests primarily with faculty. Attendance at religious services is required.

Tuition and Aid Day student tuition: $7200. Tuition installment plan (FACTS Tuition Payment Plan). Need-based scholarship grants, paying campus jobs available. In 2016–17, 26% of upper-school students received aid. Total amount of financial aid awarded in 2016–17: $240,000.

Admissions Traditional secondary-level entrance grade is 9. For fall 2016, 35 students applied for upper-level admission, 34 were accepted, 26 enrolled. Scholastic Testing Service High School Placement Test required. Deadline for receipt of application materials: none. Application fee required: $100. Interview recommended.

Athletics Interscholastic: baseball (boys), basketball (b,g), bowling (b,g), cross-country running (b,g), dance squad (g), football (b), golf (b), indoor track & field (b,g), lacrosse (g), soccer (b,g), softball (g), tennis (b,g), track and field (b,g), volleyball (g); intramural: figure skating (g); coed interscholastic: cheering; coed intramural: Frisbee. 2 PE instructors, 8 coaches, 1 athletic trainer.

Computers Computers are regularly used in accounting, art, business applications, English, graphic design, programming classes. Computer network features include on-campus library services, Internet access, Internet filtering or blocking technology. Computer access in designated common areas is available to students. Students grades are available online.

Contact Mrs. Teresa Mainello, Publicity Director. 518-235-7100 Ext. 224. Fax: 518-237-1796. E-mail: tmainello@cchstroy.org. Website: www.cchstroy.org

CATHOLIC CENTRAL HIGH SCHOOL

148 McHenry Street
Burlington, Wisconsin 53105

Head of School: Mr. David Wieters

General Information Coeducational day college-preparatory school, affiliated with Roman Catholic Church. Grades 9–12. Founded: 1924. Setting: small town. Nearest major city is Milwaukee. 25-acre campus. 2 buildings on campus. Approved or accredited by Academy of Orton-Gillingham Practitioners and Educators, National Catholic Education Association, North Central Association of Colleges and Schools, and Wisconsin Department of Education. Endowment: $1.5 million. Total enrollment: 185. Upper school average class size: 12. Upper school faculty-student ratio: 1:11. There are 180 required school days per year for Upper School students. Upper School students typically attend 5 days per week. The average school day consists of 6 hours and 45 minutes.

Upper School Student Profile Grade 9: 35 students (21 boys, 14 girls); Grade 10: 33 students (13 boys, 20 girls); Grade 11: 28 students (12 boys, 16 girls); Grade 12: 37 students (18 boys, 19 girls). 93% of students are Roman Catholic.

Faculty School total: 20. In upper school: 5 men, 15 women; 9 have advanced degrees.

Subjects Offered 20th century history, 3-dimensional art, 3-dimensional design, accounting, advanced biology, advanced chemistry, advanced computer applications, advanced math, Advanced Placement courses, African-American history, algebra, American government, American history, American literature, American literature-AP, analytic geometry, anatomy, anatomy and physiology, animation, Arabic, art, band, Bible, Bible studies, biology, biology-AP, biotechnology, botany, business, business education, business technology, calculus, calculus-AP, cartooning/animation, Catholic belief and practice, ceramics, chemistry, Chinese, choir, church history, college admission preparation, college planning, composition, composition-AP, computer animation, computer graphics, computer skills, consumer education, digital photography, diversity studies, drawing, earth science, economics, English, English literature-AP, environmental science, finance, forensics, French, geography, geometry, government, government and politics-AP, health, history of religion, history of the Catholic Church, human anatomy, human biology, integrated science, intro to computers, Italian, journalism, language-AP, marketing, mathematics-AP, music theory, New Testament, painting, personal finance, personal fitness, photography, physical fitness, physics, physics-AP, physiology, pre-calculus, probability and statistics, psychology, psychology-AP, religion, religious studies, skills for success, social justice, sociology, Spanish, speech, statistics, study skills, theology, trigonometry, U.S. history, video and animation, world religions, zoology.

Graduation Requirements 20th century history, American government, American history, arts and fine arts (art, music, dance, drama), English, health, health and wellness, mathematics, personal finance, physical education (includes health), religious education, science, speech, theology, world history, community service hours required.

Special Academic Programs 3 Advanced Placement exams for which test preparation is offered; honors section; independent study; study at local college for college credit; academic accommodation for the gifted and the artistically talented.

College Admission Counseling 52 students graduated in 2016; 51 went to college, including St. Norbert College; University of Wisconsin–Green Bay; University of Wisconsin–Madison; University of Wisconsin–Milwaukee; University of Wisconsin–Stevens Point; University of Wisconsin–Whitewater. Other: 1 entered military service. Median composite ACT: 24. 30% scored over 26 on composite ACT.

Student Life Upper grades have specified standards of dress, student council, honor system. Discipline rests primarily with faculty. Attendance at religious services is required.

Summer Programs Sports programs offered; session focuses on fitness and wellness; held on campus; accepts boys and girls; open to students from other schools. 150 students usually enrolled. 2017 schedule: June 7 to July 31. Application deadline: June 1.

Tuition and Aid Day student tuition: $7750–$12,000. Tuition installment plan (FACTS Tuition Payment Plan, individually arranged payment plans). Tuition reduction for siblings, merit scholarship grants, need-based scholarship grants available. In 2016–17, 40% of upper-school students received aid; total upper-school merit-scholarship money awarded: $20,000. Total amount of financial aid awarded in 2016–17: $140,000.

Admissions Traditional secondary-level entrance grade is 9. For fall 2016, 151 students applied for upper-level admission, 131 were accepted, 131 enrolled. ACT or ACT-Explore required. Deadline for receipt of application materials: none. Application fee required: $100. Interview required.

Athletics Interscholastic: baseball (boys), basketball (b,g), dance team (g), football (b), soccer (g), softball (g), tennis (g), volleyball (g), wrestling (b); coed interscholastic: cheering, cross-country running, fishing, golf, gymnastics, swimming and diving, track and field; coed intramural: bicycling, bowling, dance, dance squad, physical fitness, physical training, strength & conditioning, table tennis, ultimate Frisbee, weight training. 1 PE instructor, 29 coaches, 1 athletic trainer.

Computers Computers are regularly used in accounting, business, economics, graphic design, journalism, multimedia, newspaper, photography, typing, video film production, Web site design, writing classes. Computer network features include Internet access, wireless campus network, Internet filtering or blocking technology. Campus intranet, student e-mail accounts, and computer access in designated common areas are available to students. Students grades are available online. The school has a published electronic and media policy.

Contact Mrs. Karen Schwenn, Admissions Director. 262-763-1510 Ext. 225. Fax: 262-763-1509. E-mail: kschwenn@cchsnet.org. Website: www.cchsnet.org

THE CATLIN GABEL SCHOOL

8825 SW Barnes Road
Portland, Oregon 97225

Head of School: Mr. Tim Bazemore

General Information Coeducational day college-preparatory, arts, technology, and sciences school. Grades PK–12. Founded: 1957. Setting: suburban. 63-acre campus. 13 buildings on campus. Approved or accredited by Northwest Accreditation Commission and Northwest Association of Independent Schools. Member of National Association of Independent Schools and Secondary School Admission Test Board. Endowment: $30 million. Total enrollment: 759. Upper school average class size: 15. Upper school faculty-student ratio: 1:7. There are 170 required school days per year for Upper School students. Upper School students typically attend 5 days per week. The average school day consists of 7 hours and 15 minutes.

Upper School Student Profile Grade 9: 77 students (35 boys, 42 girls); Grade 10: 78 students (46 boys, 32 girls); Grade 11: 79 students (41 boys, 38 girls); Grade 12: 77 students (40 boys, 37 girls).

Faculty School total: 97. In upper school: 26 men, 27 women; 38 have advanced degrees.

Subjects Offered 20th century history, 20th century world history, 3-dimensional art, advanced biology, algebra, American democracy, American foreign policy, American government, American history, American literature, American studies, analysis and differential calculus, analytic geometry, anatomy and physiology, ancient world history, art, art and culture, art appreciation, art history, astronomy, athletics, audio visual/media, audition methods, basketball, bioethics, biology, calculus, career/college preparation, ceramics, chemistry, chorus, civil rights, Civil War, civil war history, classics, college writing, communication skills, community service, composition, computer programming, computer science, computer skills, contemporary history, creative arts, creative writing, critical thinking, critical writing, cultural geography, current events, debate, desktop publishing, digital photography, drama, drawing and design, ecology, economics, engineering, English, English composition, English literature, environmental science, equality and freedom, ethics and responsibility, European history, expository writing, fiction, film and literature, film history, film studies, fine arts, fitness, food and nutrition, foreign language, foreign policy, French, French as a second language, French studies, geometry, global studies, government, government/civics, graphic design, health, history, honors algebra, honors geometry, human biology, humanities, independent study, inorganic chemistry, instrumental music, interdisciplinary studies, international relations, jazz band, language and composition, leadership, life science, linear algebra, literary magazine, literature, literature seminar, logic, marketing, math applications, mathematics, mechanics, media studies, microbiology, minority studies, model United Nations, modern European history, modern Western civilization, music, musical theater, neurobiology, neuroscience, news writing, non-Western societies, organic chemistry, outdoor education, painting, performing arts, photography, photojournalism, physical education, physical science, physics, physiology, play/screen writing, poetry, political science, portfolio art, pre-calculus, probability and statistics, psychology, public policy, public speaking, publishing, research skills, science, science fiction, Shakespeare, social studies, socioeconomic problems, software design, Spanish, speech and debate, statistics, student government, student publications, swimming, theater arts, trigonometry, U.S. constitutional history, U.S. government, U.S. government and politics, U.S. history, U.S. literature, video and animation, video film production, visual and performing arts, visual arts, Western civilization, world affairs, world history, world literature, writing.

Graduation Requirements Arts, biology, chemistry, English, foreign language, health, history, mathematics, physical education (includes health), physics, senior project, U.S. history.

Special Academic Programs Honors section; independent study; study abroad; academic accommodation for the gifted.

College Admission Counseling 77 students graduated in 2015; 74 went to college, including Northeastern University; Occidental College; Stanford University; University of Oregon; Whitman College; Worcester Polytechnic Institute. Other: 3 had other specific plans. Median SAT critical reading: 680, median SAT math: 660, median SAT writing: 660, median combined SAT: 1985, median composite ACT: 30. 100% scored over 600 on SAT critical reading, 100% scored over 600 on SAT math, 100% scored over 600 on SAT writing, 100% scored over 1800 on combined SAT, 100% scored over 26 on composite ACT.

Student Life Upper grades have specified standards of dress, student council, honor system. Discipline rests equally with students and faculty.

Tuition and Aid Day student tuition: $21,050–$28,250. Tuition installment plan (Insured Tuition Payment Plan, monthly payment plans, individually arranged payment plans). Merit scholarship grants, need-based scholarship grants available. In 2015–16, 28% of upper-school students received aid. Total amount of financial aid awarded in 2015–16: $18,119.

Admissions Traditional secondary-level entrance grade is 9. SSAT required. Deadline for receipt of application materials: January 19. Application fee required: $75. Interview required.

Athletics Interscholastic: aquatics (boys, girls), baseball (b,g), basketball (b,g), cross-country running (b,g), golf (b,g), racquetball (b,g), skiing (downhill) (b,g), soccer (b,g), swimming and diving (b,g), tennis (b,g), track and field (b,g), volleyball (g); coed interscholastic: racquetball; coed intramural: aerobics/dance, alpine skiing, backpacking, bicycling, bowling, canoeing/kayaking, climbing, dance team, fishing, fitness, Frisbee, hiking/backpacking, jogging, kayaking, mountain biking, mountaineering, nordic skiing, ocean paddling, outdoor activities, outdoor adventure, outdoor education, outdoor recreation, outdoors, physical fitness, physical training, rafting, rock climbing, ropes courses, running, skiing (cross-country), skiing (downhill), snowshoeing, strength & conditioning, telemark skiing, ultimate Frisbee, walking, wall climbing, weight lifting, weight training, wilderness, wilderness survival, yoga. 6 PE instructors, 20 coaches.

Computers Computers are regularly used in all classes. Computer network features include on-campus library services, online commercial services, Internet access, wireless campus network, all students attending the Upper School have laptops, video conferencing capabilities are available on campus, SmartBoards or projectors are installed in most classrooms. Campus intranet, student e-mail accounts, and computer access in designated common areas are available to students. The school has a published electronic and media policy.

Contact Ms. Sara Nordhoff, Director of Admission and Financial Aid. 503-297-1894 Ext. 345. Fax: 503-297-0139. E-mail: nordhoffs@catlin.edu. Website: www.catlin.edu

CCI THE RENAISSANCE SCHOOL

Via Cavour 13
Lanciano 66034, Italy

Head of School: Marisa Di Carlo D'Alessandro

General Information Coeducational boarding and day college-preparatory, arts, and science school. Grades 10–12. Founded: 1995. Setting: small town. Nearest major city is Rome, Italy. Students are housed in single-sex residences. 2 buildings on campus. Approved or accredited by Ontario Ministry of Education and state department of education. Member of European Council of International Schools. Language of instruction: English. Total enrollment: 70. Upper school average class size: 12. Upper school faculty-student ratio: 1:7.

Upper School Student Profile 95% of students are boarding students. 5% are state residents. 6 states are represented in upper school student body. 95% are international students. International students from Canada, Italy, Mexico, Russian Federation, United Kingdom, and United States; 3 other countries represented in student body.

Faculty School total: 6. In upper school: 3 men, 3 women; 5 have advanced degrees; 4 reside on campus.

Subjects Offered Algebra, anthropology, art, biology, calculus, Canadian history, career exploration, chemistry, civics, classical civilization, community service, computers, creative writing, data analysis, drama, economics, English, English literature, environmental science, expository writing, finite math, geometry, government/civics, history, information technology, Italian, literature, mathematics, physics, politics, psychology, science, social studies, sociology, trigonometry, world history, world issues, world literature, writing.

Graduation Requirements English, foreign language, mathematics, physical education (includes health), science, social studies (includes history). Community service is required.

Special Academic Programs Study abroad.

College Admission Counseling Colleges students went to include Acadia University; Dalhousie University; McGill University; Queen's University at Kingston; The University of Western Ontario; University of Toronto.

Student Life Upper grades have uniform requirement, student council, honor system. Discipline rests equally with students and faculty.

Tuition and Aid 7-day tuition and room/board: €36,000. Tuition installment plan (monthly payment plans, individually arranged payment plans). Bursaries, need-based scholarship grants available. In 2016–17, 5% of upper-school students received aid. Total amount of financial aid awarded in 2016–17: €30,000.

Admissions Achievement/Aptitude/Writing required. Deadline for receipt of application materials: none. Application fee required: $100.

Athletics Intramural: dance (girls), modern dance (g); coed intramural: aerobics, aerobics/dance, alpine skiing, aquatics, ball hockey, basketball, bicycling, climbing, cross-country running, equestrian sports, fitness, fitness walking, flag football, hiking/backpacking, horseback riding, jogging, mountain biking, outdoor activities, outdoor recreation, physical fitness, running, skiing (downhill), snowboarding, soccer, softball, swimming and diving, tennis, touch football, walking, weight training, yoga.

Computers Computers are regularly used in yearbook classes. Computer resources include on-campus library services, online commercial services, Internet access. Computer access in designated common areas is available to students. Students grades are available online. The school has a published electronic and media policy.

Contact Jocelyn Manchee, Admissions Officer. 905-508-7108. Fax: 905-508-5480. E-mail: admissions@canadiancollegeitaly.com. Website: www.ccilanciano.com

CENTRAL ALBERTA CHRISTIAN HIGH SCHOOL

22 Eagle Road
Lacombe, Alberta T4L 1G7, Canada

Head of School: Mr. Mel Brandsma

General Information Coeducational day college-preparatory, general academic, religious studies, and bilingual studies school, affiliated with Christian Reformed

Church. Grades 10–12. Distance learning grades 10–12. Founded: 1989. Setting: rural. Nearest major city is Red Deer, Canada. 12-acre campus. 1 building on campus. Approved or accredited by Christian Schools International and Alberta Department of Education. Language of instruction: English. Total enrollment: 97. Upper school average class size: 96. Upper school faculty-student ratio: 1:12. There are 180 required school days per year for Upper School students. Upper School students typically attend 5 days per week. The average school day consists of 6 hours and 25 minutes.

Upper School Student Profile Grade 10: 33 students (12 boys, 21 girls); Grade 11: 32 students (18 boys, 14 girls); Grade 12: 31 students (20 boys, 11 girls). 75% of students are members of Christian Reformed Church.

Faculty School total: 8. In upper school: 4 men, 4 women; 2 have advanced degrees.

Subjects Offered Accounting, agriculture, all academic, art, career education, Christian ethics, computer education, drafting, foods, French as a second language, photography, physical education, work experience.

Graduation Requirements All academic, French, iIncluding English 30 level, Social Studies 30 level, Mathematics 20 level, Science 20 level, Physical Education 10 level, Career & Life Management.

College Admission Counseling 32 students graduated in 2016; 25 went to college, including University of Alberta. Other: 6 went to work, 1 entered military service.

Student Life Upper grades have student council, honor system. Discipline rests primarily with faculty. Attendance at religious services is required.

Tuition and Aid Day student tuition: CAN$5950. Tuition installment plan (monthly payment plans, individually arranged payment plans). Tuition reduction for siblings available. In 2016–17, 10% of upper-school students received aid.

Admissions Traditional secondary-level entrance grade is 10. Deadline for receipt of application materials: none. No application fee required. On-campus interview recommended.

Athletics Coed Interscholastic: badminton, basketball, bowling, climbing, cross-country running, fitness, golf, hiking/backpacking, jogging, outdoor activities, physical fitness, physical training, running, soccer, softball, swimming and diving, track and field, volleyball, wall climbing, weight training, whiffle ball, wilderness survival; coed intramural: broomball, cooperative games, hiking/backpacking, outdoor adventure, outdoor education, outdoor recreation. 1 PE instructor, 1 coach.

Computers Computers are regularly used in all classes. Computer network features include Internet access, wireless campus network, Internet filtering or blocking technology, Campus intranet, student e-mail accounts, and computer access in designated common areas are available to students.

Contact Office. 403-782-4535. Fax: 403-782-5425. E-mail: office@cachs.ca. Website: www.cachs.ca/

CENTRAL CATHOLIC HIGH SCHOOL

200 South Carpenter Road
Modesto, California 95351

Head of School: Jim Pecchenino

General Information Coeducational day college-preparatory, arts, religious studies, and bilingual studies school, affiliated with Roman Catholic Church. Grades 9–12. Founded: 1966. Setting: urban. Nearest major city is Sacramento. 21-acre campus. 13 buildings on campus. Approved or accredited by National Catholic Education Association, Western Association of Schools and Colleges, and Western Catholic Education Association. Endowment: $2.2 million. Total enrollment: 372. Upper school average class size: 22. Upper school faculty-student ratio: 1:16. There are 180 required school days per year for Upper School students. Upper School students typically attend 5 days per week. The average school day consists of 6 hours and 50 minutes.

Upper School Student Profile Grade 9: 98 students (53 boys, 45 girls); Grade 10: 95 students (43 boys, 52 girls); Grade 11: 92 students (50 boys, 42 girls); Grade 12: 87 students (58 boys, 29 girls). 82% of students are Roman Catholic.

Faculty School total: 28. In upper school: 5 men, 23 women; 15 have advanced degrees.

Subjects Offered Agriculture, algebra, American history, American literature, animal science, art, Bible studies, biology, broadcast journalism, calculus, chemistry, dance, drama, drawing and design, economics, English, English literature, environmental science, ethics, European history, geometry, government/civics, health, mathematics, music, physical education, physical science, physics, pre-calculus, Spanish, speech, theology, vocal ensemble, world history, world literature, yearbook.

Graduation Requirements Arts and fine arts (art, music, dance, drama), English, geography, mathematics, physical education (includes health), religion (includes Bible studies and theology), science, social studies (includes history), speech, 100 Christian service hours.

Special Academic Programs Advanced Placement exam preparation; honors section; study at local college for college credit; remedial reading and/or remedial writing; remedial math; programs in English, mathematics, general development for dyslexic students.

College Admission Counseling 87 students graduated in 2015; 85 went to college, including California Polytechnic State University, San Luis Obispo; California State University, Chico; California State University, Fresno; California State University, Stanislaus; University of California, Berkeley. Other: 2 entered military service. Median SAT critical reading: 510, median SAT math: 500, median SAT writing: 520, median combined SAT: 1530. 14% scored over 600 on SAT critical reading, 23% scored over

600 on SAT math, 19% scored over 600 on SAT writing, 17% scored over 1800 on combined SAT.

Student Life Upper grades have specified standards of dress, student council. Discipline rests primarily with faculty. Attendance at religious services is required.

Tuition and Aid Day student tuition: $9835–$10,290. Tuition installment plan (FACTS Tuition Payment Plan, monthly payment plans, individually arranged payment plans, quarterly and semiannual payment plans). Tuition reduction for siblings, merit scholarship grants, need-based scholarship grants, paying campus jobs available. In 2015–16, 40% of upper-school students received aid; total upper-school merit-scholarship money awarded: $14,250. Total amount of financial aid awarded in 2015–16: $541,705.

Admissions Traditional secondary-level entrance grade is 9. For fall 2015, 125 students applied for upper-level admission, 98 were accepted, 98 enrolled. ETS HSPT (closed), Otis-Lennon School Ability Test or Otis-Lennon School Ability Test, ERB CPT III required. Deadline for receipt of application materials: none. Application fee required: $45. On-campus interview required.

Athletics Interscholastic: baseball (boys), basketball (b,g), cross-country running (b,g), football (b), golf (b,g), soccer (b,g), softball (g), tennis (b,g), track and field (b,g), volleyball (g), water polo (b,g), wrestling (b,g); intramural: cheering (g); coed intramural: dance, yoga. 1 PE instructor, 90 coaches.

Computers Computers are regularly used in graphic arts, literacy, yearbook classes. Computer network features include on-campus library services, Internet access, wireless campus network, Internet filtering or blocking technology. Computer access in designated common areas is available to students. Students grades are available online. The school has a published electronic and media policy.

Contact Jodi Tybor, Admissions Coordinator/Registrar. 209-524-9611 Ext. 113. Fax: 209-524-4913. E-mail: tybor@cchsca.org. Website: www.cchsca.org

CENTRAL CATHOLIC HIGH SCHOOL

2100 Cedar Street, Unit I
Morgan City, Louisiana 70380

Head of School: Deacon Vic Bonnaffee III

General Information Coeducational day college-preparatory school, affiliated with Seventh-day Adventists. Ungraded, ages 12–18. Founded: 1893. Setting: rural. Nearest major city is Lafayette. 14-acre campus. 4 buildings on campus. Approved or accredited by National Catholic Education Association and Southern Association of Colleges and Schools. Endowment: $1.1 million. Total enrollment: 206. Upper school average class size: 15. Upper school faculty-student ratio: 1:15. There are 176 required school days per year for Upper School students. Upper School students typically attend 5 days per week.

Upper School Student Profile Grade 9: 50 students (26 boys, 24 girls); Grade 10: 33 students (20 boys, 13 girls); Grade 11: 34 students (18 boys, 16 girls); Grade 12: 37 students (27 boys, 10 girls). 80% of students are Seventh-day Adventists.

Faculty School total: 23. In upper school: 7 men, 16 women; 7 have advanced degrees.

Subjects Offered Advanced math, algebra, American government, American history, anatomy and physiology, biology, calculus, chemistry, civics, English, English composition, environmental science, European history-AP, fine arts, foreign language, geography, geometry, physical education, physical science, physics, pre-calculus, psychology-AP, publications, religion, speech, U.S. history, world history.

Graduation Requirements 20th century world history, algebra, arts and fine arts (art, music, dance, drama), biology, calculus, Catholic belief and practice, civics, computer applications, electives, English, foreign language, geometry, government/civics, history of the Catholic Church, literature, mathematics, physical education (includes health), physical fitness, physics, pre-algebra, religion (includes Bible studies and theology), science, scripture, social studies (includes history), trigonometry, U.S. history, Board of Regents curriculum (Louisiana), TOPS University Diploma.

Special Academic Programs Honors section; study at local college for college credit; remedial reading and/or remedial writing; remedial math; programs in English, mathematics, general development for dyslexic students.

College Admission Counseling 24 students graduated in 2016; 22 went to college, including Louisiana State University and Agricultural & Mechanical College; Nicholls State University; University of Louisiana at Lafayette. Other: 1 went to work. Median composite ACT: 21. 1% scored over 26 on composite ACT.

Student Life Upper grades have uniform requirement, student council, honor system. Discipline rests primarily with faculty. Attendance at religious services is required.

Summer Programs Sports, rigorous outdoor training programs offered; session focuses on conditioning and weightlifting; held both on and off campus; accepts boys and girls; not open to students from other schools. 165 students usually enrolled. 2017 schedule: May 30 to August 1. Application deadline: May 27.

Tuition and Aid Day student tuition: $5050–$6550. Tuition installment plan (FACTS Tuition Payment Plan, monthly payment plans, full-payment plan, state scholarship). Need-based scholarship grants, state voucher, ACE, ARETE available. In 2016–17, 38% of upper-school students received aid. Total amount of financial aid awarded in 2016–17: $167,512.

Admissions Traditional secondary-level entrance grade is 9. For fall 2016, 154 students applied for upper-level admission, 154 were accepted, 154 enrolled.

Achievement tests or ACT required. Deadline for receipt of application materials: none. Application fee required: $200. On-campus interview required.

Athletics Interscholastic: baseball (boys), basketball (b,g), bowling (b,g), cheering (b,g), cross-country running (b,g), dance squad (g), dance team (g), fishing (b), football (b), golf (b,g), indoor track (b,g), indoor track & field (b,g), physical fitness (b,g), softball (g), strength & conditioning (b,g), swimming and diving (b,g), tennis (b,g), track and field (b,g), volleyball (g), weight lifting (b,g), weight training (b,g); coed interscholastic: cheering, physical fitness, swimming and diving, weight lifting, weight training. 5 PE instructors, 8 coaches, 1 athletic trainer.

Computers Computers are regularly used in accounting, aerospace science, animation, architecture, art, aviation, basic skills, Bible studies, business, business applications, business education, business skills, business studies, cabinet making, career education, career exploration, career technology, Christian doctrine, classics, college planning, commercial art, computer applications, construction, creative writing, current events, dance, data processing, design, desktop publishing, desktop publishing, ESL, digital applications, drafting, drawing and design, economics, engineering, English, ESL, ethics, foreign language, French, French as a second language, freshman foundations, geography, graphic arts, graphic design, graphics, health, historical foundations for arts, history, human geography - AP, humanities, independent study, industrial technology, information technology, introduction to technology, journalism, JROTC, keyboarding, lab/keyboard, language development, Latin, learning cognition, library, library science, library skills, life skills, literacy, literary magazine, mathematics, media, media arts, media production, media services, mentorship program, multimedia, music, music technology, news writing, newspaper, NJROTC, occupational education, philosophy, photography, photojournalism, programming, psychology, publications, publishing, reading, religion, religious studies, remedial study skills, research skills, SAT preparation, science, senior seminar, social sciences, social studies, Spanish, speech, stock market, study skills, technical drawing, technology, theater, theater arts, theology, typing, video film production, vocational-technical courses, Web site design, wilderness education, woodworking, word processing, writing, writing, yearbook classes. Computer network features include on-campus library services, Internet access, wireless campus network, Internet filtering or blocking technology. Student e-mail accounts and computer access in designated common areas are available to students. Students grades are available online. The school has a published electronic and media policy.

Contact Mrs. Sandra N. Daigle, Director of Admissions. 985-385-5372 Ext. 303. Fax: 985-385-3444. E-mail: centcathi@htdiocese.org. Website: www.cchseagles.com

CENTRAL CATHOLIC HIGH SCHOOL

300 Hampshire Street
Lawrence, Massachusetts 01841

Head of School: Mrs. Doreen A. Keller

General Information Coeducational day and distance learning college-preparatory, arts, business, religious studies, and technology school, affiliated with Roman Catholic Church. Grades 9–12. Distance learning grades 11–12. Founded: 1935. Setting: urban. Nearest major city is Boston. 11-acre campus. 1 building on campus. Approved or accredited by Commission on Independent Schools, New England Association of Schools and Colleges, and Massachusetts Department of Education. Member of National Association of Independent Schools. Endowment: $17.3 million. Total enrollment: 1,330. Upper school average class size: 25. Upper school faculty-student ratio: 1:24. There are 168 required school days per year for Upper School students. Upper School students typically attend 5 days per week. The average school day consists of 6 hours and 15 minutes.

Upper School Student Profile Grade 9: 352 students (163 boys, 189 girls); Grade 10: 302 students (163 boys, 139 girls); Grade 11: 333 students (166 boys, 167 girls); Grade 12: 308 students (126 boys, 182 girls). 80% of students are Roman Catholic.

Faculty School total: 85. In upper school: 38 men, 47 women; 60 have advanced degrees.

Subjects Offered Art, arts, computer science, English, fine arts, French, health, mathematics, physical education, religion, science, social studies, Spanish.

Graduation Requirements Arts and fine arts (art, music, dance, drama), computer science, English, foreign language, mathematics, religion (includes Bible studies and theology), science, social studies (includes history).

Special Academic Programs International Baccalaureate program; Advanced Placement exam preparation; honors section; study at local college for college credit.

College Admission Counseling 341 students graduated in 2016; 335 went to college, including Merrimack College; Suffolk University; University of Massachusetts Amherst; University of Massachusetts Lowell; University of New Hampshire. Other: 1 went to work, 1 entered military service, 4 entered a postgraduate year. 23% scored over 600 on SAT critical reading, 28% scored over 600 on SAT math, 22% scored over 600 on SAT writing, 21% scored over 1800 on combined SAT, 47% scored over 26 on composite ACT.

Student Life Upper grades have uniform requirement, student council, honor system. Discipline rests primarily with faculty. Attendance at religious services is required.

Summer Programs Remediation, enrichment, advancement, art/fine arts, computer instruction programs offered; session focuses on remediation/advancement; held on campus; accepts boys and girls; open to students from other schools. 300 students usually enrolled. 2017 schedule: June 26 to August 1.

Tuition and Aid Day student tuition: $13,190. Tuition installment plan (monthly payment plans). Merit scholarship grants, need-based scholarship grants available. In 2016–17, 27% of upper-school students received aid; total upper-school merit-scholarship money awarded: $105,015. Total amount of financial aid awarded in 2016–17: $1,051,402.

Admissions Traditional secondary-level entrance grade is 9. For fall 2016, 688 students applied for upper-level admission, 657 were accepted, 353 enrolled. Archdiocese of Boston High School entrance exam provided by STS, High School Placement Test and High School Placement Test (closed version) from Scholastic Testing Service required. Deadline for receipt of application materials: none. No application fee required. Interview required.

Athletics Interscholastic: baseball (boys), basketball (b,g), bowling (b,g), cheering (g), cross-country running (b,g), dance squad (b,g), diving (b,g), field hockey (g), figure skating (g), fishing (b,g), football (b), golf (b), gymnastics (g), hockey (b), ice hockey (b), indoor hockey (g), indoor track (b,g), indoor track & field (b,g), lacrosse (b,g), martial arts (b,g), modern dance (b,g), soccer (b,g), softball (g), swimming and diving (b,g), tennis (b,g), track and field (b,g), volleyball (b,g), wall climbing (b,g), winter (indoor) track (b,g), wrestling (b); intramural: basketball (b,g); coed interscholastic: dance team. 3 PE instructors, 80 coaches, 1 athletic trainer.

Computers Computers are regularly used in all academic classes. Computer network features include on-campus library services, Internet access, wireless campus network, Internet filtering or blocking technology. Campus intranet, student e-mail accounts, and computer access in designated common areas are available to students. The school has a published electronic and media policy.

Contact Ms. Elizabeth Schroth, Assistant Director of Admissions. 978-682-0260 Ext. 626. Fax: 978-685-2707. E-mail: eschroth@centralcatholic.net. Website: www.centralcatholic.net

CENTRAL CATHOLIC HIGH SCHOOL

4720 Fifth Avenue
Pittsburgh, Pennsylvania 15213

Head of School: Br. Tony Baginski, FSC

General Information Boys' day college-preparatory, religious studies, liberal arts, and STEM school, affiliated with Roman Catholic Church. Grades 9–12. Founded: 1927. Setting: urban. 1.5-acre campus. 4 buildings on campus. Approved or accredited by Christian Brothers Association, Middle States Association of Colleges and Schools, National Catholic Education Association, and Pennsylvania Department of Education. Endowment: $13.6 million. Total enrollment: 857. Upper school average class size: 21. Upper school faculty-student ratio: 1:16. There are 180 required school days per year for Upper School students. Upper School students typically attend 5 days per week. The average school day consists of 6 hours and 45 minutes.

Upper School Student Profile Grade 9: 228 students (228 boys); Grade 10: 199 students (199 boys); Grade 11: 220 students (220 boys); Grade 12: 220 students (220 boys). 77% of students are Roman Catholic.

Faculty School total: 70. In upper school: 58 men, 12 women; 53 have advanced degrees.

Subjects Offered 20th century history, 20th century world history, 3-dimensional design, accounting, advanced chemistry, advanced computer applications, advanced math, Advanced Placement courses, algebra, American government, American history, American history-AP, American literature, analysis of data, art, art history-AP, athletic training, band, bioethics, DNA and culture, biology, biology-AP, biotechnology, British literature, British literature (honors), business, business mathematics, calculus, calculus-AP, cartooning/animation, Catholic belief and practice, chemistry, chemistry-AP, choir, chorus, civics, college admission preparation, college counseling, comparative government and politics, computer applications, computer programming, computer science, computer technology certification, computer-aided design, computers, concert band, concert choir, consumer education, creative writing, cultural geography, data analysis, debate, digital applications, economics-AP, electives, English, English language and composition-AP, English literature-AP, English-AP, entrepreneurship, environmental science, European history-AP, film and literature, film studies, fitness, foreign language, French, French-AP, geometry, government, government and politics-AP, government-AP, health, health education, history, honors algebra, honors English, honors geometry, honors U.S. history, honors world history, human geography - AP, instrumental music, introduction to technology, Italian, jazz band, jazz ensemble, journalism, Latin, Latin American literature, law, marching band, math analysis, mathematics, modern world history, music, music history, music theory, personal finance, personal fitness, physical education, physics, physics-AP, probability and statistics, programming, psychology, public speaking, religion, robotics, Russian history, SAT/ACT preparation, senior seminar, social studies, sociology, Spanish, Spanish language-AP, Spanish-AP, speech and debate, sports medicine, statistics-AP, strings, studio art, technology/design, The 20th Century, theater arts, trigonometry, U.S. government, U.S. history, U.S. history-AP, United States government-AP, vocal music, weight training, wellness, world history, world literature, writing.

Special Academic Programs 16 Advanced Placement exams for which test preparation is offered; honors section; study at local college for college credit; academic accommodation for the gifted.

College Admission Counseling 204 students graduated in 2016; 196 went to college, including Duquesne University; Kent State University; Ohio University; Penn

State University Park; University of Dayton; University of Pittsburgh. Other: 3 entered military service, 5 had other specific plans. Mean SAT critical reading: 566, mean SAT math: 557, mean SAT writing: 545, mean combined SAT: 1668, mean composite ACT: 26. 40% scored over 600 on SAT critical reading, 39% scored over 600 on SAT math, 33% scored over 600 on SAT writing, 36% scored over 1800 on combined SAT, 42% scored over 26 on composite ACT.

Student Life Upper grades have specified standards of dress, student council. Discipline rests primarily with faculty. Attendance at religious services is required.

Tuition and Aid Day student tuition: $11,500. Tuition installment plan (SMART Tuition Payment Plan). Merit scholarship grants, need-based scholarship grants available. In 2016–17, 34% of upper-school students received aid; total upper-school merit-scholarship money awarded: $112,000. Total amount of financial aid awarded in 2016–17: $1,600,000.

Admissions Traditional secondary-level entrance grade is 9. For fall 2016, 335 students applied for upper-level admission, 287 were accepted, 228 enrolled. Scholastic Testing Service High School Placement Test required. Deadline for receipt of application materials: none. No application fee required. Interview required.

Athletics Interscholastic: baseball, basketball, bowling, crew, cross-country running, fencing, football, golf, hockey, ice hockey, in-line hockey, indoor track, lacrosse, rowing, rugby, soccer, squash, swimming and diving, tennis, track and field, ultimate Frisbee, volleyball, winter (indoor) track, wrestling; intramural: basketball, flag football, football, Frisbee, touch football. 2 PE instructors, 17 coaches, 2 athletic trainers.

Computers Computers are regularly used in all academic classes. Computer network features include on-campus library services, online commercial services, Internet access, wireless campus network, Internet filtering or blocking technology. Campus intranet, student e-mail accounts, and computer access in designated common areas are available to students. Students grades are available online. The school has a published electronic and media policy.

Contact Mr. Brian Miller, Director of Admissions. 412-621-7505. Fax: 412-208-0555. E-mail: bmiller@centralcatholichs.com. Website: www.centralcatholichs.com

CHADWICK SCHOOL

26800 South Academy Drive
Palos Verdes Peninsula, California 90274

Head of School: Dr. John "Jack" E. Creeden

General Information Coeducational day college-preparatory, science, mathematics, English, history, global studies,, and global languages, performing/visual arts, STEM school. Grades K–12. Distance learning grades 9–12. Founded: 1935. Setting: suburban. Nearest major city is Los Angeles. 45-acre campus. 5 buildings on campus. Approved or accredited by Association for Experiential Education, California Association of Independent Schools, Western Association of Schools and Colleges, and California Department of Education. Member of National Association of Independent Schools and Secondary School Admission Test Board. Endowment: $28 million. Total enrollment: 835. Upper school average class size: 17. Upper school faculty-student ratio: 1:6. There are 170 required school days per year for Upper School students. Upper School students typically attend 5 days per week. The average school day consists of 7 hours and 45 minutes.

Upper School Student Profile Grade 9: 102 students (47 boys, 55 girls); Grade 10: 100 students (46 boys, 54 girls); Grade 11: 66 students (29 boys, 37 girls); Grade 12: 94 students (39 boys, 55 girls).

Faculty School total: 73. In upper school: 33 men, 40 women, 43 have advanced degrees.

Subjects Offered 3-dimensional art, Advanced Placement courses, African history, algebra, American history, American literature, American studies, art, art history-AP, art-AP, Asian history, biology, calculus, calculus-AP, ceramics, chemistry, chemistry-AP, choral music, comparative government and politics-AP, computer math, computer programming, computer science-AP, constitutional law, creative writing, dance, drama, economics, English, English literature, English literature-AP, environmental science-AP, European history, expository writing, fine arts, forensics, French, French-AP, geometry, grammar, health, history, honors algebra, honors geometry, instrumental music, integrated science, Latin, Latin American history, Latin American studies, life science, Mandarin, marine biology, mathematics, Middle East, Middle Eastern history, music, music theory-AP, outdoor education, photography, physical education, physics, pre-calculus, probability, robotics, science, social studies, South African history, Spanish, Spanish-AP, speech, statistics, statistics-AP, theater, trigonometry, U.S. history-AP, wilderness education, world history, world literature, writing, yearbook.

Graduation Requirements Arts and fine arts (art, music, dance, drama), English, foreign language, history, mathematics, outdoor education, performing arts, physical education (includes health), science.

Special Academic Programs Advanced Placement exam preparation; honors section; independent study; term-away projects; domestic exchange program; study abroad; academic accommodation for the gifted, the musically talented, and the artistically talented.

College Admission Counseling 86 students graduated in 2016; all went to college, including Boston University; Stanford University; University of California, Berkeley; University of Chicago; University of Southern California; Williams College. Mean SAT critical reading: 655, mean SAT math: 678, mean SAT writing: 690, mean combined SAT: 2023, mean composite ACT: 29.

Student Life Upper grades have specified standards of dress, student council, honor system. Discipline rests equally with students and faculty.

Summer Programs Sports, art/fine arts, computer instruction programs offered; session focuses on visual and performing arts, academics, athletics, academic enrichment; held on campus; accepts boys and girls; open to students from other schools. 500 students usually enrolled. 2017 schedule: June 26 to July 28. Application deadline: March 20.

Tuition and Aid Day student tuition: $34,270. Tuition installment plan (monthly payment plans, individually arranged payment plans). Need-based scholarship grants, Malone Scholarship (need/merit-based), MacFarlane Leadership Scholarship (need/merit-based) available. In 2016–17, 22% of upper-school students received aid. Total amount of financial aid awarded in 2016–17: $2,000,000.

Admissions Traditional secondary-level entrance grade is 9. ISEE or SSAT required. Deadline for receipt of application materials: January 17. Application fee required: $125. On-campus interview recommended.

Athletics Interscholastic: baseball (boys), basketball (b,g), cheering (g), cross-country running (b,g), diving (b,g), football (b), golf (b,g), lacrosse (b,g), soccer (b,g), softball (g), swimming and diving (b,g), tennis (b,g), track and field (b,g), volleyball (b,g), water polo (b,g); intramural: aerobics/dance (g), dance (g), horseback riding (g), yoga (b,g); coed interscholastic: cheering, equestrian sports; coed intramural: fencing. 5 PE instructors, 14 coaches, 2 athletic trainers.

Computers Computers are regularly used in art, college planning, computer applications, creative writing, drawing and design, economics, engineering, English, foreign language, geography, graphic arts, health, history, humanities, journalism, mathematics, music, newspaper, photography, photojournalism, programming, publications, research skills, science, social studies, theater arts, Web site design, wilderness education, writing, yearbook classes. Computer network features include on-campus library services, Internet access, wireless campus network, Internet filtering or blocking technology, online learning management system for faculty, students, parents. Campus intranet, student e-mail accounts, and computer access in designated common areas are available to students. Students grades are available online. The school has a published electronic and media policy.

Contact Ms. Vivian Ham, Admission Manager. 310-377-1543 Ext. 4025. Fax: 310-377-0380. E-mail: admissions@chadwickschool.org. Website: www.chadwickschool.org

CHAMINADE COLLEGE PREPARATORY

7500 Chaminade Avenue
West Hills, California 91304

Head of School: Tom Fahy

General Information Coeducational day college-preparatory school, affiliated with Roman Catholic Church. Grades 9–12. Founded: 1952. Setting: suburban. Nearest major city is Los Angeles. 21-acre campus. 15 buildings on campus. Approved or accredited by Western Association of Schools and Colleges, Western Catholic Education Association, and California Department of Education. Endowment: $6.8 million. Total enrollment: 2,030. Upper school average class size: 28. Upper school faculty-student ratio: 1:16. There are 180 required school days per year for Upper School students. Upper School students typically attend 5 days per week. The average school day consists of 6 hours and 25 minutes.

Upper School Student Profile Grade 9: 347 students (174 boys, 173 girls); Grade 10: 337 students (180 boys, 157 girls); Grade 11: 317 students (169 boys, 148 girls); Grade 12: 321 students (174 boys, 147 girls). 47% of students are Roman Catholic.

Faculty School total: 82. In upper school: 33 men, 49 women; 66 have advanced degrees.

Subjects Offered Algebra, American history, American literature, anatomy, art, art history, athletic training, band, baseball, basketball, biology, biology-AP, British literature, British literature (honors), calculus, calculus-AP, chemistry, chemistry-AP, Chinese, Christian and Hebrew scripture, community service, comparative government and politics-AP, composition, computer programming, computer programming-AP, computer science, creative writing, dance, dance performance, debate, drama, drawing, driver education, economics, economics and history, English, English language-AP, English literature and composition-AP, environmental science-AP, ethics, European history, expository writing, film studies, finance, fine arts, finite math, French, French language-AP, French literature-AP, geography, geometry, government-AP, government/civics, guitar, human geography - AP, jazz ensemble, journalism, Latin, Latin-AP, literature and composition-AP, macroeconomics-AP, marching band, mathematics, modern European history-AP, music, music appreciation, music performance, mythology, physical education, physical science, physics, physics-AP, physiology, play/screen writing, probability and statistics, psychology, psychology-AP, religion, science, science fiction, scripture, Shakespeare, social studies, Spanish, Spanish language-AP, Spanish literature-AP, speech, speech and debate, sports medicine, statistics-AP, studio art, theater, trigonometry, U.S. government, U.S. history, U.S. history-AP, United States government-AP, visual and performing arts, visual arts, Western philosophy, Western religions, women's studies, world history, world history-AP, world literature, writing.

Graduation Requirements Arts and fine arts (art, music, dance, drama), college writing, computer science, English, foreign language, mathematics, physical education (includes health), religious studies, science, social studies (includes history), speech. Community service is required.

Special Academic Programs 18 Advanced Placement exams for which test preparation is offered; honors section.

College Admission Counseling 332 students graduated in 2016; 325 went to college, including California Lutheran University; California State University, Northridge; Chapman University; The University of Arizona; University of California, Los Angeles; University of Oregon. Other: 1 entered military service, 6 had other specific plans. Mean SAT critical reading: 570, mean SAT math: 567, mean SAT writing: 577, mean combined SAT: 1714, mean composite ACT: 25. 39% scored over 600 on SAT critical reading, 40% scored over 600 on SAT math, 44% scored over 600 on SAT writing, 41% scored over 1800 on combined SAT, 39% scored over 26 on composite ACT.

Student Life Upper grades have uniform requirement, student council, honor system. Discipline rests primarily with faculty. Attendance at religious services is required.

Summer Programs Remediation, enrichment, advancement, sports, art/fine arts, computer instruction programs offered; session focuses on remediation; held on campus; accepts boys and girls; open to students from other schools. 400 students usually enrolled. 2017 schedule: June 6 to July 15. Application deadline: none.

Tuition and Aid Day student tuition: $15,500. Tuition installment plan (monthly payment plans, 2-payment plan, discounted one-payment plan). Merit scholarship grants, need-based scholarship grants available. In 2016–17, 25% of upper-school students received aid; total upper-school merit-scholarship money awarded: $20,000. Total amount of financial aid awarded in 2016–17: $2,529,026.

Admissions Traditional secondary-level entrance grade is 9. For fall 2016, 394 students applied for upper-level admission, 319 were accepted, 190 enrolled. Admissions testing required. Deadline for receipt of application materials: January 16. Application fee required: $100. On-campus interview required.

Athletics Interscholastic: aquatics (boys, girls), baseball (b), basketball (b,g), cross-country running (b,g), equestrian sports (b,g), fencing (b,g), field hockey (g), football (b), golf (b,g), lacrosse (b,g), soccer (b,g), softball (g), strength & conditioning (b,g), swimming and diving (b,g), tennis (b,g), track and field (b,g), volleyball (b,g), weight training (b,g), wrestling (b); coed interscholastic: cheering, dance, equestrian sports, physical fitness, strength & conditioning, weight training; coed intramural: dance team, hiking/backpacking, table tennis. 3 PE instructors, 85 coaches, 2 athletic trainers.

Computers Computers are regularly used in all classes. Computer network features include on-campus library services, online commercial services, Internet access, wireless campus network, Internet filtering or blocking technology, laptops are issued to students in grades 9-12, Blackboard online learning system, Dyno. Student e-mail accounts are available to students. Students grades are available online. The school has a published electronic and media policy.

Contact Mrs. Yolanda Uramoto, Assistant to Admissions and Registrar. 818-347-8300 Ext. 355. Fax: 818-348-8374. E-mail: yuramoto@chaminade.org. Website: www.chaminade.org

CHAMINADE COLLEGE PREPARATORY SCHOOL

425 South Lindbergh Boulevard
St. Louis, Missouri 63131-2799

Head of School: Rev. Ralph A. Siefert, SM

General Information Boys' boarding and day college-preparatory, arts, business, religious studies, bilingual studies, and technology school, affiliated with Roman Catholic Church. Grades 6–12. Founded: 1910. Setting: suburban. Students are housed in single-sex dormitories. 55-acre campus. 12 buildings on campus. Approved or accredited by Independent Schools Association of the Central States, Midwest Association of Boarding Schools, National Catholic Education Association, The Association of Boarding Schools, The College Board, and Missouri Department of Education. Member of National Association of Independent Schools and Secondary School Admission Test Board. Endowment: $18 million. Total enrollment: 775. Upper school average class size: 17. Upper school faculty-student ratio: 1:9. There are 174 required school days per year for Upper School students. Upper School students typically attend 5 days per week. The average school day consists of 7 hours.

Upper School Student Profile Grade 9: 149 students (149 boys); Grade 10: 145 students (145 boys); Grade 11: 135 students (135 boys); Grade 12: 130 students (130 boys). 8% of students are boarding students. 92% are state residents. 6 states are represented in upper school student body. 8% are international students. International students from Canada, China, Japan, Mexico, Mexico, and Peru; 15 other countries represented in student body. 80% of students are Roman Catholic.

Faculty School total: 89. In upper school: 68 men, 16 women; 80 have advanced degrees; 6 reside on campus.

Subjects Offered Accounting, algebra, American government, American history, American history-AP, American literature, anatomy and physiology, architecture, art, art history, band, Bible studies, biology, biology-AP, botany, broadcasting, business, business law, business skills, calculus, calculus-AP, campus ministry, Catholic belief and practice, chemistry, chemistry-AP, Chinese, church history, civics, communication skills, communications, community service, comparative government and politics-AP, comparative political systems-AP, computer literacy, computer processing, computer

programming, computer programming-AP, computer science, computer science-AP, concert band, creative writing, drama, dramatic arts, earth science, ecology, economics, economics-AP, engineering, English, English composition, English literature, English literature-AP, English/composition-AP, ESL, European history, European history-AP, expository writing, fine arts, French, French-AP, geography, geology, geometry, government/civics, grammar, health, history, industrial arts, keyboarding, Latin, Latin-AP, mathematics, music theory-AP, physical education, physics, physics-AP, psychology, psychology-AP, religion, science, social studies, sociology, Spanish, Spanish-AP, speech, statistics, statistics-AP, studio art-AP, theater, theology, trigonometry, weight training, world affairs, world history, world literature, writing.

Graduation Requirements Arts and fine arts (art, music, dance, drama), computer science, English, foreign language, mathematics, physical education (includes health), practical arts, religion (includes Bible studies and theology), science, social studies (includes history). Community service is required.

Special Academic Programs 23 Advanced Placement exams for which test preparation is offered; honors section; study at local college for college credit; academic accommodation for the gifted; programs in general development for dyslexic students; ESL (32 students enrolled).

College Admission Counseling 125 students graduated in 2016; all went to college, including Purdue University; Saint Louis University; University of Dayton; University of Illinois at Urbana–Champaign; University of Missouri; Vanderbilt University. Mean composite ACT: 27. 42% scored over 26 on composite ACT.

Student Life Upper grades have specified standards of dress, honor system. Discipline rests primarily with faculty. Attendance at religious services is required.

Summer Programs Remediation, enrichment, sports, art/fine arts programs offered; held on campus; accepts boys; open to students from other schools. 500 students usually enrolled. 2017 schedule: June to July.

Tuition and Aid Day student tuition: $15,765; 5-day tuition and room/board: $31,991; 7-day tuition and room/board: $33,091. Tuition installment plan (FACTS Tuition Payment Plan). Merit scholarship grants, need-based scholarship grants, paying campus jobs available. In 2016–17, 35% of upper-school students received aid; total upper-school merit-scholarship money awarded: $95,000. Total amount of financial aid awarded in 2016–17: $1,600,000.

Admissions Traditional secondary-level entrance grade is 9. For fall 2016, 78 students applied for upper-level admission, 66 were accepted, 53 enrolled. SSAT required. Deadline for receipt of application materials: none. Application fee required: $50. Interview required.

Athletics Interscholastic: baseball, basketball, bocce, bowling, cross-country running, football, golf, ice hockey, lacrosse, racquetball, rugby, soccer, swimming and diving, tennis, track and field, ultimate Frisbee, volleyball, water polo, wrestling; intramural: fishing, in-line hockey, rugby, table tennis, weight training. 5 PE instructors, 30 coaches, 1 athletic trainer.

Computers Computers are regularly used in all academic classes. Computer network features include on-campus library services, online commercial services, Internet access, wireless campus network, Internet filtering or blocking technology. Campus intranet and student e-mail accounts are available to students. Students grades are available online. The school has a published electronic and media policy.

Contact Mr. Erik Carretero, Director of Admissions. 314-692-6650. Fax: 314-993-4403. E-mail: ecarretero@chaminade-stl.org. Website: www.chaminade-stl.org

CHAMINADE-MADONNA COLLEGE PREPARATORY

500 Chaminade Drive
Hollywood, Florida 33021-5800

Head of School: Mrs. Raiza Echemendia

General Information Coeducational day college-preparatory school, affiliated with Roman Catholic Church. Grades 9–12. Founded: 1960. Setting: suburban. Nearest major city is Fort Lauderdale. 13-acre campus. 10 buildings on campus. Approved or accredited by Southern Association of Colleges and Schools and Florida Department of Education. Total enrollment: 545. Upper school average class size: 26. Upper school faculty-student ratio: 1:19. There are 180 required school days per year for Upper School students. Upper School students typically attend 5 days per week. The average school day consists of 6 hours and 45 minutes.

Upper School Student Profile Grade 9: 122 students (63 boys, 59 girls); Grade 10: 127 students (67 boys, 60 girls); Grade 11: 143 students (82 boys, 61 girls); Grade 12: 154 students (98 boys, 56 girls). 70% of students are Roman Catholic.

Faculty School total: 36. In upper school: 14 men, 22 women.

Subjects Offered Advanced chemistry, advanced computer applications, advanced math, Advanced Placement courses, advanced studio art-AP, algebra, American government, American history, American history-AP, American literature, American literature-AP, anatomy, art, art history, athletic training, athletics, band, baseball, basketball, biology, business skills, calculus, calculus-AP, campus ministry, Catholic belief and practice, ceramics, chemistry, chemistry-AP, choir, chorus, college placement, community service, computer applications, computer graphics, computer skills, creative writing, dance, dance performance, design, directing, drama, drama performance, dramatic arts, economics, English, English composition, English language and composition-AP, English literature and composition-AP, ethics, European history-AP, film studies, fine arts, foreign language, French, French-AP, geography, geometry, government/civics, health, health and wellness, history, history of the Catholic Church, history-AP, honors algebra, honors English, honors geometry, honors U.S. history, honors world history, international relations, journalism, keyboarding, leadership, macro/microeconomics-AP, marine biology, mathematics, model United Nations, music, music history, music theater, musical productions, New Testament, newspaper, peace and justice, philosophy, physical education, physics, physics-AP, physiology, play production, practical arts, pre-calculus, psychology, public speaking, reading, religion, SAT/ACT preparation, science, Shakespeare, social studies, sociology, Spanish, Spanish language-AP, Spanish literature-AP, speech, sports medicine, stagecraft, theater, trigonometry, U.S. history-AP, weight training, word processing, world history, writing, yearbook.

Graduation Requirements Arts and fine arts (art, music, dance, drama), business skills (includes word processing), English, foreign language, mathematics, physical education (includes health), practical arts, religion (includes Bible studies and theology), science, social studies (includes history), 100 community service hours.

Special Academic Programs 10 Advanced Placement exams for which test preparation is offered; honors section; study at local college for college credit; academic accommodation for the gifted, the musically talented, and the artistically talented; remedial reading and/or remedial writing; remedial math; programs in general development for dyslexic students; special instructional classes for students with learning disabilities, Attention Deficit Disorder, and dyslexia.

College Admission Counseling 115 students graduated in 2016; all went to college, including Florida Atlantic University; Florida Gulf Coast University; Florida International University; Florida State University; University of Central Florida; University of Florida.

Student Life Upper grades have uniform requirement, student council, honor system. Discipline rests primarily with faculty. Attendance at religious services is required.

Summer Programs Remediation, enrichment, sports, art/fine arts programs offered; session focuses on remediation/make-up; held on campus; accepts boys and girls; not open to students from other schools.

Tuition and Aid Day student tuition: $11,645. Tuition installment plan (FACTS Tuition Payment Plan). Merit scholarship grants, need-based scholarship grants, need-based loans available. In 2016–17, 33% of upper-school students received aid.

Admissions Traditional secondary-level entrance grade is 9. For fall 2016, 250 students applied for upper-level admission, 200 were accepted, 152 enrolled. High School Placement Test (closed version) from Scholastic Testing Service required. Deadline for receipt of application materials: none. Application fee required: $50. Interview required.

Athletics Interscholastic: baseball (boys), basketball (b,g), cheering (g), cross-country running (b,g), dance (g), dance team (g), football (b), golf (b,g), soccer (b,g), softball (g), swimming and diving (b,g), track and field (b,g), volleyball (b,g), wrestling (b). 2 PE instructors, 1 athletic trainer.

Computers Computers are regularly used in all classes. Computer network features include on-campus library services, online commercial services, Internet access, wireless campus network, Internet filtering or blocking technology. Student e-mail accounts are available to students. Students grades are available online. The school has a published electronic and media policy.

Contact Ms. Tainah Georges, Director of Admissions. 954-989-5150 Ext. 103. Fax: 954-983-4663. E-mail: tgeorges@cmlions.org. Website: www.cmlions.org

CHARLES E. SMITH JEWISH DAY SCHOOL

11710 Hunters Lane
Rockville, Maryland 20852

Head of School: Rabbi Mitchel Malkus

General Information Coeducational boarding and day college-preparatory and religious studies school, affiliated with Jewish faith. Grades K–12. Founded: 1965. Setting: suburban. Nearest major city is Washington, DC. 9-acre campus. 1 building on campus. Approved or accredited by Association of Independent Schools of Greater Washington and Maryland Department of Education. Languages of instruction: English and Hebrew. Total enrollment: 975. Upper school average class size: 16. Upper school faculty-student ratio: 1:6. Upper School students typically attend 5 days per week. The average school day consists of 7 hours and 45 minutes.

Upper School Student Profile 100% of students are Jewish.

Faculty School total: 175. In upper school: 30 men, 61 women.

Subjects Offered Advanced chemistry, advanced math, ancient world history, Arabic, arts, biotechnology, college counseling, comparative religion, critical studies in film, debate, electives, English composition, exercise science, forensics, Hebrew scripture, Holocaust and other genocides, honors algebra, honors English, honors geometry, honors U.S. history, Israeli studies, Judaic studies, law and the legal system, modern history, organic chemistry, pre-calculus, religion, religion and culture, religious education, senior composition, Talmud, U.S. history, world history.

Graduation Requirements English, foreign language, mathematics, physical education (includes health), Rabbinic literature, religion (includes Bible studies and theology), science, social studies (includes history).

Special Academic Programs Advanced Placement exam preparation; honors section; academic accommodation for the gifted; remedial reading and/or remedial writing; remedial math; programs in English for dyslexic students; ESL (12 students enrolled).

College Admission Counseling 79 students graduated in 2016; they went to Harvard University; Princeton University; University of Michigan; University of Pennsylvania; Washington University in St. Louis. Median SAT critical reading: 620, median SAT math: 630.

Student Life Upper grades have specified standards of dress, student council. Discipline rests equally with students and faculty. Attendance at religious services is required.

Tuition and Aid Day student tuition: $31,820. Tuition installment plan (FACTS Tuition Payment Plan, monthly payment plans). Need-based scholarship grants available. In 2016–17, 40% of upper-school students received aid. Total amount of financial aid awarded in 2016–17: $5,000,000.

Admissions Traditional secondary-level entrance grade is 7. Deadline for receipt of application materials: none. Application fee required: $100. On-campus interview required.

Athletics Interscholastic: baseball (boys), basketball (b,g), dance squad (g), golf (b,g), soccer (b,g), softball (g), tennis (b,g), volleyball (b,g), wrestling (b); coed interscholastic: cross-country running, indoor track & field, swimming and diving, track and field. 3 PE instructors, 18 coaches, 1 athletic trainer.

Computers Computers are regularly used in all classes. Computer resources include on-campus library services, online commercial services, Internet access, wireless campus network. Student e-mail accounts are available to students. Students grades are available online. The school has a published electronic and media policy.

Contact Maya Lavi, Admission Assistant. 301-881-1400 Ext. 4870.
E-mail: mlavi@cesjds.org. Website: www.cesjds.org

CHARLES FINNEY SCHOOL

2070 Five Mile Line Road
Penfield, New York 14526

Head of School: Mr. Michael VanLeeuwen

General Information Coeducational day college-preparatory, arts, religious studies, bilingual studies, and technology school, affiliated with Christian faith. Grades K–12. Founded: 1992. Setting: suburban. Nearest major city is Rochester. 8-acre campus. 1 building on campus. Approved or accredited by New York Department of Education. Total enrollment: 301. Upper school average class size: 25.

Faculty School total: 35.

Special Academic Programs Advanced Placement exam preparation; honors section; study at local college for college credit.

Student Life Upper grades have uniform requirement, student council, honor system. Discipline rests primarily with faculty. Attendance at religious services is required.

Tuition and Aid Tuition installment plan (monthly payment plans). Tuition reduction for siblings, need-based scholarship grants available.

Admissions Traditional secondary-level entrance grade is 9. Deadline for receipt of application materials: none. Application fee required: $40. Interview required.

Athletics Interscholastic: baseball (boys), basketball (b,g), football (b), soccer (b,g), softball (g), volleyball (g); coed interscholastic: track and field. 1 PE instructor.

Computers Computer network features include on-campus library services, Internet access, wireless campus network, Internet filtering or blocking technology. Students grades are available online. The school has a published electronic and media policy.

Contact Ms. Tara Butar, Director of Admissions and Recruitment. 585-387-3770. Fax: 585-387-3771. E-mail: info@finneyschool.org. Website: www.finneyschool.org

CHARLOTTE COUNTRY DAY SCHOOL

1440 Carmel Road
Charlotte, North Carolina 28226

Head of School: Mr. Mark Reed

General Information Coeducational day college-preparatory school. Grades JK–12. Founded: 1941. Setting: suburban. 60-acre campus. 10 buildings on campus. Approved or accredited by Southern Association of Colleges and Schools, Southern Association of Independent Schools, and North Carolina Department of Education. Member of National Association of Independent Schools and Secondary School Admission Test Board. Endowment: $48.4 million. Total enrollment: 1,660. Upper school average class size: 12. Upper school faculty-student ratio: 1:7. There are 170 required school days per year for Upper School students. Upper School students typically attend 5 days per week. The average school day consists of 7 hours and 15 minutes.

Upper School Student Profile Grade 9: 127 students (62 boys, 65 girls); Grade 10: 138 students (76 boys, 62 girls); Grade 11: 124 students (47 boys, 77 girls); Grade 12: 131 students (54 boys, 77 girls).

Faculty School total: 217. In upper school: 34 men, 39 women; 49 have advanced degrees.

Subjects Offered Algebra, American history, American history-AP, anatomy, art, art history-AP, astronomy, biology, biology-AP, biotechnology, calculus-AP, ceramics, chemistry, chemistry-AP, Chinese, computer graphics, computer science, computer science-AP, creative writing, dance, debate, discrete mathematics, drama, ecology, economics, English, English literature, English-AP, environmental science-AP, ESL, European history, European history-AP, French, French-AP, geography, geometry,

German, German-AP, Japanese, journalism, Latin, Latin-AP, library studies, music, novels, photography, physical education, physics, physics-AP, physiology, poetry, political science, pre-calculus, probability and statistics, psychology-AP, sculpture, Shakespeare, short story, Spanish, Spanish-AP, studio art-AP, theater, theory of knowledge, trigonometry, visual arts, yearbook.

Graduation Requirements Arts and fine arts (art, music, dance, drama), computer science, English, foreign language, mathematics, physical education (includes health), science, social sciences, social studies (includes history). Community service is required.

Special Academic Programs International Baccalaureate program; honors section; independent study; term-away projects; domestic exchange program; study abroad; academic accommodation for the gifted; ESL (9 students enrolled).

College Admission Counseling 119 students graduated in 2016; all went to college, including Clemson University; Elon University; Furman University; North Carolina State University; The University of North Carolina at Chapel Hill; Wake Forest University. Median SAT critical reading: 600, median SAT math: 615, median SAT writing: 615, median combined SAT: 1845, median composite ACT: 29. 50% scored over 600 on SAT critical reading, 59% scored over 600 on SAT math, 58% scored over 600 on SAT writing, 55% scored over 1800 on combined SAT, 81% scored over 26 on composite ACT.

Student Life Upper grades have specified standards of dress, student council, honor system. Discipline rests primarily with faculty.

Summer Programs Remediation, enrichment, advancement, sports, art/fine arts, computer instruction programs offered; session focuses on enrichment classes, academic courses, and sports camps; held on campus; accepts boys and girls; open to students from other schools. 200 students usually enrolled. 2017 schedule: June 12 to July 28. Application deadline: none.

Tuition and Aid Day student tuition: $22,570. Tuition installment plan (The Tuition Plan, Insured Tuition Payment Plan, monthly payment plans). Need-based scholarship grants available. In 2016–17, 17% of upper-school students received aid. Total amount of financial aid awarded in 2016–17: $1,470,003.

Admissions Traditional secondary-level entrance grade is 9. For fall 2016, 127 students applied for upper-level admission, 65 were accepted, 38 enrolled. CTP III, ERB or ISEE required. Deadline for receipt of application materials: January 15. Application fee required: $90. On-campus interview recommended.

Athletics Interscholastic: baseball (boys), basketball (b,g), cheering (g), crew (g), cross-country running (b,g), dance (g), dance team (g), field hockey (g), fitness (b,g), football (b), golf (b,g), lacrosse (b,g), soccer (b,g), softball (g), strength & conditioning (b,g), swimming and diving (b,g), tennis (b,g), track and field (b,g), volleyball (g), weight training (b,g), wrestling (b). 1 PE instructor, 38 coaches, 3 athletic trainers.

Computers Computers are regularly used in art, computer applications, English, foreign language, mathematics, photography, science, yearbook classes. Computer network features include on-campus library services, online commercial services, Internet access, wireless campus network, Internet filtering or blocking technology. Campus intranet and student e-mail accounts are available to students. Students grades are available online. The school has a published electronic and media policy.

Contact Nancy R. Ehringhaus, Director of Admissions. 704-943-4530 Ext. 4531. Fax: 704-943-4536. E-mail: nancy.ehringhaus@charlottecountryday.org. Website: www.charlottecountryday.org

CHARLOTTE LATIN SCHOOL

9502 Providence Road
Charlotte, North Carolina 28277-8695

Head of School: Mr. Arch N. McIntosh Jr.

General Information Coeducational day college-preparatory school. Grades K–12. Founded: 1970. Setting: suburban. 128-acre campus. 7 buildings on campus. Approved or accredited by Southern Association of Colleges and Schools, Southern Association of Independent Schools, and North Carolina Department of Education. Member of National Association of Independent Schools and Secondary School Admission Test Board. Endowment: $28.1 million. Total enrollment: 1,413. Upper school average class size: 14. Upper school faculty-student ratio: 1:9. There are 173 required school days per year for Upper School students. Upper School students typically attend 5 days per week. The average school day consists of 7 hours and 5 minutes.

Upper School Student Profile Grade 9: 133 students (66 boys, 67 girls); Grade 10: 131 students (58 boys, 73 girls); Grade 11: 124 students (59 boys, 65 girls); Grade 12: 116 students (60 boys, 56 girls).

Faculty School total: 170. In upper school: 31 men, 27 women; 47 have advanced degrees.

Subjects Offered 20th century American writers, 20th century history, 20th century physics, 20th century world history, 3-dimensional art, acting, advanced chemistry, Advanced Placement courses, algebra, American culture, American foreign policy, American government, American history, American history-AP, American literature, American studies, anatomy, anatomy and physiology, art, biology, biology-AP, British literature, calculus, calculus-AP, ceramics, chemistry, chemistry-AP, choir, college admission preparation, college counseling, composition-AP, computer applications, computer math, computer programming, computer science, computer science-AP, computer technology certification, conceptual physics, concert band, concert choir, creative writing, debate, discrete mathematics, drama, dramatic arts, earth science,

ecology, ecology, environmental systems, economics, economics and history, engineering, English, English literature, English literature and composition-AP, English-AP, environmental science, environmental science-AP, European history, European history-AP, expository writing, finite math, French, French-AP, geography, geology, geometry, global studies, government and politics-AP, government/civics, grammar, Greek, health, history, Holocaust and other genocides, honors algebra, honors English, honors geometry, human anatomy, human rights, hydrology, international relations, international studies, Irish literature, journalism, Latin, Latin-AP, leadership and service, mathematics, media literacy, music, music theory, music theory-AP, physical education, physical fitness, physics, physics-AP, pre-calculus, programming, psychology, psychology-AP, science, social studies, Southern literature, Spanish, Spanish language-AP, Spanish-AP, speech, sports medicine, statistics-AP, studio art, technical theater, theater, trigonometry, U.S. government and politics-AP, U.S. history-AP, United States government-AP, visual arts, Web site design, wind ensemble, world history, world literature, world religions, writing, yearbook.

Graduation Requirements Electives, English, foreign language, history, mathematics, physical education (includes health), science, Observe and Serve internship program for Seniors.

Special Academic Programs 19 Advanced Placement exams for which test preparation is offered; honors section; independent study; study abroad; academic accommodation for the gifted.

College Admission Counseling 114 students graduated in 2016; all went to college, including Clemson University; Furman University; Northeastern University; The University of North Carolina at Chapel Hill; University of Colorado Boulder; Wake Forest University. Median SAT critical reading: 640, median SAT math: 670, median SAT writing: 660, median combined SAT: 1980, median composite ACT: 31. 74% scored over 600 on SAT critical reading, 78.7% scored over 600 on SAT math, 78.7% scored over 600 on SAT writing, 81.5% scored over 1800 on combined SAT, 82.4% scored over 26 on composite ACT.

Student Life Upper grades have specified standards of dress, student council, honor system. Discipline rests primarily with faculty.

Summer Programs Enrichment, sports, art/fine arts, computer instruction programs offered; session focuses on STEAM, enrichment, sports; held both on and off campus; accepts boys and girls; open to students from other schools. 2,960 students usually enrolled. 2017 schedule: June 12 to July 28. Application deadline: none.

Tuition and Aid Day student tuition: $22,340. Tuition installment plan (Insured Tuition Payment Plan, FACTS Tuition Payment Plan, monthly payment plans, individually arranged payment plans). Merit scholarship grants, need-based scholarship grants available. In 2016–17, 20% of upper-school students received aid; total upper-school merit-scholarship money awarded: $192,880. Total amount of financial aid awarded in 2016–17: $1,185,535.

Admissions Traditional secondary-level entrance grade is 9. For fall 2016, 157 students applied for upper-level admission, 54 were accepted, 34 enrolled. ERB, ISEE, Wechsler Intelligence Scale for Children or Woodcock-Johnson required. Deadline for receipt of application materials: none. Application fee required: $90. On-campus interview required.

Athletics Interscholastic: aquatics (boys, girls), baseball (b), basketball (b,g), cross-country running (b,g), dance team (g), field hockey (g), football (b), golf (b,g), independent competitive sports (b,g), indoor track (b,g), lacrosse (b,g), soccer (b,g), softball (g), strength & conditioning (b,g), swimming and diving (b,g), tennis (b,g), track and field (b,g), volleyball (g), wrestling (b); intramural: basketball (b,g), outdoor activities (b,g); coed interscholastic: ultimate Frisbee; coed intramural: outdoor activities. 11 PE instructors, 62 coaches, 3 athletic trainers.

Computers Computers are regularly used in all academic classes. Computer network features include on-campus library services, online commercial services, Internet access, wireless campus network, Internet filtering or blocking technology. Campus intranet, student e-mail accounts, and computer access in designated common areas are available to students. Students grades are available online. The school has a published electronic and media policy.

Contact Mrs. Mary Yorke Oates, Director of Admissions. 704-846-7207. Fax: 704-849-0503. E-mail: moates@charlottelatin.org. Website: www.charlottelatin.org

CHASE COLLEGIATE SCHOOL

565 Chase Parkway
Waterbury, Connecticut 06708-3394

Head of School: Dr. Polly A. Peterson

General Information Coeducational day college-preparatory, arts, and Design Thinking & Innovation school. Grades PK–12. Distance learning grades 9–12. Founded: 1865. Setting: suburban. 47-acre campus. 8 buildings on campus. Approved or accredited by Connecticut Association of Independent Schools, New England Association of Schools and Colleges, and Connecticut Department of Education. Member of National Association of Independent Schools and Secondary School Admission Test Board. Endowment: $12 million. Total enrollment: 402. Upper school average class size: 12. Upper school faculty-student ratio: 1:8. There are 168 required school days per year for Upper School students. Upper School students typically attend 5 days per week. The average school day consists of 6 hours and 45 minutes.

Upper School Student Profile Grade 9: 29 students (15 boys, 14 girls); Grade 10: 54 students (29 boys, 25 girls); Grade 11: 32 students (18 boys, 14 girls); Grade 12: 30

students (14 boys, 16 girls). 13% of students are boarding students. 100% are international students. International students from China.

Faculty School total: 54. In upper school: 11 men, 15 women; 23 have advanced degrees.

Graduation Requirements Arts and fine arts (art, music, dance, drama), athletics, computer literacy, electives, English, ethics, foreign language, history, lab science, mathematics, music appreciation, psychology, public speaking, science, technology, theater arts, senior speech.

Special Academic Programs 18 Advanced Placement exams for which test preparation is offered; honors section; accelerated programs; independent study; study abroad; academic accommodation for the gifted; ESL (10 students enrolled).

College Admission Counseling 42 students graduated in 2016; all went to college, including American University; Boston University; Colgate University; Fairfield University; Quinnipiac University; University of Connecticut. Mean SAT critical reading: 582, mean SAT math: 568, mean SAT writing: 561, mean combined SAT: 1711.

Student Life Upper grades have specified standards of dress, student council, honor system. Discipline rests equally with students and faculty.

Summer Programs Enrichment, advancement, ESL, sports, art/fine arts, computer instruction programs offered; session focuses on enrichment and advancement; held on campus; accepts boys and girls; open to students from other schools. 300 students usually enrolled. 2017 schedule: June 26 to August 4. Application deadline: none.

Tuition and Aid Day student tuition: $38,500. Tuition installment plan (monthly payment plans). Merit scholarship grants, need-based scholarship grants, Founders' Scholarships (for students entering 9th grade) available. In 2016–17, 50% of upper-school students received aid; total upper-school merit-scholarship money awarded: $341,050. Total amount of financial aid awarded in 2016–17: $1,619,717.

Admissions Traditional secondary-level entrance grade is 9. For fall 2016, 83 students applied for upper-level admission, 55 were accepted, 32 enrolled. TOEFL or TOEFL Junior required. Deadline for receipt of application materials: none. Application fee required: $60. On-campus interview recommended.

Athletics Interscholastic: baseball (boys), basketball (b,g), cross-country running (b,g), independent competitive sports (b,g), lacrosse (b,g), soccer (b,g), softball (g), tennis (b,g), volleyball (g), wrestling (b,g); intramural: ice hockey (b,g), strength & conditioning (b,g); coed interscholastic: crew, Frisbee, golf, independent competitive sports, rowing, swimming and diving, ultimate Frisbee, wrestling; coed intramural: aerobics/dance, aerobics/Nautilus, curling, dance, equestrian sports, figure skating, fitness, ice skating, modern dance, outdoor education, physical fitness, skiing (downhill), snowboarding, weight training. 3 PE instructors, 20 coaches, 1 athletic trainer.

Computers Computers are regularly used in art, college planning, creative writing, English, foreign language, history, humanities, library, literary magazine, mathematics, music, newspaper, photography, research skills, SAT preparation, science, social sciences, study skills, technology, yearbook classes. Computer network features include on-campus library services, online commercial services, Internet access, wireless campus network, Internet filtering or blocking technology. Campus intranet, student e-mail accounts, and computer access in designated common areas are available to students. Students grades are available online. The school has a published electronic and media policy.

Contact Ruth Teague, Director of Admissions. 203-236-9560. Fax: 203-236-9509. E-mail: rteague@chasemail.org. Website: www.chasecollegiate.org

CHATHAM ACADEMY

Savannah, Georgia
See Special Needs Schools section.

CHATHAM HALL

800 Chatham Hall Circle
Chatham, Virginia 24531

Head of School: Mrs. Suzanne Walker Buck

General Information Girls' boarding and day college-preparatory school, affiliated with Episcopal Church. Grades 9–12. Founded: 1894. Setting: small town. Nearest major city is Greensboro, NC. Students are housed in single-sex dormitories. 362-acre campus. 9 buildings on campus. Approved or accredited by National Association of Episcopal Schools, The Association of Boarding Schools, Virginia Association of Independent Schools, and Virginia Department of Education. Member of Secondary School Admission Test Board. Endowment: $20 million. Total enrollment: 140. Upper school average class size: 9. Upper school faculty-student ratio: 1:5. Upper School students typically attend 5 days per week. The average school day consists of 8 hours and 30 minutes.

Upper School Student Profile 85% of students are boarding students. 34% are state residents. 20 states are represented in upper school student body. 14% are international students.

Faculty School total: 33. In upper school: 10 men, 23 women; 26 have advanced degrees; 29 reside on campus.

Subjects Offered Algebra, American history-AP, American literature, art, art history, biology, biology-AP, calculus, calculus-AP, ceramics, chemistry, chemistry-AP, choir, college counseling, computer art, creative writing, dance, DNA science lab, drama, drama performance, earth science, economics, English, English language-AP, English literature, English-AP, ESL, ethics, European history, European history-AP, fine arts, French, French-AP, general science, geography, geometry, history, instrumental music, journalism, Latin, mathematics, medieval/Renaissance history, model United Nations, modern European history, modern European history-AP, music, music composition, music theory, music theory-AP, photography, physical education, physics, pre-calculus, psychology, religion, robotics, SAT/ACT preparation, science, service learning/internship, social studies, Spanish, Spanish-AP, studio art-AP, swimming, theater design and production, trigonometry, U.S. government and politics, U.S. history, veterinary science, Western civilization, world history, writing workshop, yearbook.

Graduation Requirements Arts and fine arts (art, music, dance, drama), English, ethics, foreign language, mathematics, physical education (includes health), religion (includes Bible studies and theology), science, social studies (includes history).

Special Academic Programs 13 Advanced Placement exams for which test preparation is offered; honors section; independent study; study abroad; academic accommodation for the gifted, the musically talented, and the artistically talented; ESL.

College Admission Counseling 29 students graduated in 2016; all went to college, including Cornell University; Dartmouth College; Duke University; Georgetown University; University of Virginia; Vanderbilt University. Mean combined SAT: 1854, mean composite ACT: 27.

Student Life Upper grades have specified standards of dress, student council, honor system. Discipline rests equally with students and faculty. Attendance at religious services is required.

Summer Programs Sports programs offered; session focuses on horseback riding; held on campus; accepts girls; open to students from other schools. 30 students usually enrolled. 2017 schedule: July to August.

Tuition and Aid Day student tuition: $20,000; 5-day tuition and room/board: $41,500; 7-day tuition and room/board: $49,500. Tuition installment plan (Key Tuition Payment Plan, increments of 45%, 30%, and 20% due July 1, September 1, and December 1 respectively). Merit scholarship grants, need-based scholarship grants available.

Admissions Traditional secondary-level entrance grade is 9. ISEE, PSAT or SAT, SSAT or TOEFL required. Deadline for receipt of application materials: January 15. Application fee required: $50. Interview required.

Athletics Interscholastic: aquatics, basketball, cross-country running, diving, equestrian sports, field hockey, fitness, golf, horseback riding, soccer, swimming and diving, tennis, volleyball; intramural: aerobics, aquatics, basketball, dance, diving, equestrian sports, field hockey, fitness, horseback riding, lacrosse, modern dance, soccer, softball, swimming and diving, tennis, volleyball. 9 coaches, 1 athletic trainer.

Computers Computers are regularly used in art, English, foreign language, history, independent study, journalism, literary magazine, mathematics, music, newspaper, photography, science, yearbook classes. Computer network features include on-campus library services, online commercial services, Internet access, Internet filtering or blocking technology. Campus intranet, student e-mail accounts, and computer access in designated common areas are available to students. The school has a published electronic and media policy.

Contact Mrs. Carney O'Brien, Dean of Enrollment Management. 434-432-5604. Fax: 434-432-1002. E-mail: cobrien@chathamhall.org. Website: www.chathamhall.org

CHATTANOOGA CHRISTIAN SCHOOL

3354 Charger Drive
Chattanooga, Tennessee 37409

Head of School: Mr. Chad Dirkse

General Information Coeducational day college-preparatory, arts, religious studies, technology, college-level (AP) courses, and dual enrollment courses school, affiliated with Christian faith. Grades K–12. Founded: 1970. Setting: urban. Nearest major city is Atlanta, GA. 60-acre campus. 6 buildings on campus. Approved or accredited by Christian Schools International, Southern Association of Colleges and Schools, Southern Association of Independent Schools, and Tennessee Department of Education. Endowment: $8 million. Total enrollment: 1,143. Upper school average class size: 20. Upper school faculty-student ratio: 1:17. There are 175 required school days per year for Upper School students. Upper School students typically attend 5 days per week. The average school day consists of 7 hours.

Upper School Student Profile Grade 6: 119 students (58 boys, 61 girls); Grade 7: 112 students (62 boys, 50 girls); Grade 8: 106 students (48 boys, 58 girls); Grade 9: 124 students (65 boys, 59 girls); Grade 10: 105 students (44 boys, 61 girls); Grade 11: 103 students (43 boys, 60 girls); Grade 12: 108 students (52 boys, 56 girls). 100% of students are Christian faith.

Faculty School total: 104. In upper school: 33 men, 35 women; 19 have advanced degrees.

Subjects Offered Advanced biology, advanced chemistry, advanced studio art-AP, algebra, American government, American history, American literature, anatomy and physiology, ancient history, art, art and culture, art appreciation, art history, art-AP, astronomy, band, Bible, Bible studies, biology, biology-AP, calculus, calculus-AP, chemistry, choir, civil rights, community service, computer applications, computer programming, computer-aided design, concert band, concert choir, creative writing, current events, dance, drama, drama performance, earth science, Eastern world civilizations, economics, English, English literature, English-AP, environmental science, environmental studies, ethics, European history, European history-AP, fine arts, foreign language, French, geometry, German, government, health, honors geometry, industrial arts, introduction to theater, Latin, leadership education training, life science, mathematics, mathematics-AP, mechanical drawing, Microsoft, modern dance, modern European history-AP, music, music theory, New Testament, personal finance, physical education, physical science, physics, physics-AP, physiology, psychology, religion, science, shop, Spanish, statistics-AP, studio art-AP, theater, trigonometry, U.S. history-AP, Web site design, weight training, wellness, world literature, writing.

Graduation Requirements Arts and fine arts (art, music, dance, drama), computer science, English, foreign language, mathematics, physical education (includes health), religion (includes Bible studies and theology), science, social sciences, social studies (includes history). Community service is required.

Special Academic Programs Advanced Placement exam preparation; honors section; independent study; study at local college for college credit; academic accommodation for the gifted and the artistically talented; remedial reading and/or remedial writing; remedial math.

College Admission Counseling 104 students graduated in 2015; 98 went to college, including Chattanooga State Community College; Covenant College; Samford University; Tennessee Technological University; The University of Tennessee; The University of Tennessee at Chattanooga. Other: 4 went to work, 1 entered a postgraduate year, 1 had other specific plans. Mean SAT critical reading: 560, mean SAT math: 540, mean SAT writing: 530, mean combined SAT: 1650, mean composite ACT: 25. 35% scored over 600 on SAT critical reading, 22% scored over 600 on SAT math, 29% scored over 600 on SAT writing, 26% scored over 1800 on combined SAT, 35% scored over 26 on composite ACT.

Student Life Upper grades have specified standards of dress, student council, honor system. Discipline rests primarily with faculty. Attendance at religious services is required.

Tuition and Aid Day student tuition: $9990. Tuition installment plan (monthly payment plans, individually arranged payment plans). Tuition reduction for siblings, need-based scholarship grants, paying campus jobs available. In 2015–16, 20% of upper-school students received aid. Total amount of financial aid awarded in 2015–16: $500,000.

Admissions For fall 2015, 153 students applied for upper-level admission, 115 were accepted, 95 enrolled. Deadline for receipt of application materials: none. Application fee required: $100. Interview required.

Athletics Interscholastic: baseball (boys), basketball (b,g), bowling (b,g), cheering (g), cross-country running (b,g), football (b), golf (b,g), soccer (b,g), softball (g), strength & conditioning (b,g), swimming and diving (b,g), tennis (b,g), track and field (b,g), volleyball (g), weight lifting (b,g), weight training (b,g), wrestling (b); intramural: basketball (b,g), flag football (g); coed intramural: aerobics/dance, swimming and diving. 5 PE instructors, 15 coaches, 2 athletic trainers.

Computers Computers are regularly used in all academic, drawing and design, English, foreign language, history, lab/keyboard, library, mathematics, psychology, science, technology classes. Computer network features include on-campus library services, online commercial services, Internet access, wireless campus network, Internet filtering or blocking technology. Student e-mail accounts are available to students. Students grades are available online. The school has a published electronic and media policy.

Contact Mrs. Charlene Wolfe, Admission Director. 423-265-6411 Ext. 209. Fax: 423-756-4044. E-mail: cwolfe@ccsk12.com. Website: www.ccsk12.com

CHELSEA SCHOOL

Hyattsville, Maryland
See Special Needs Schools section.

CHEVERUS HIGH SCHOOL

267 Ocean Avenue
Portland, Maine 04103

Head of School: Dr. John J. Moran

General Information Coeducational day college-preparatory, honors, and AP courses school, affiliated with Roman Catholic Church (Jesuit order). Grades 9–12. Founded: 1917. Setting: suburban. 32-acre campus. 2 buildings on campus. Approved or accredited by Association of Independent Schools in New England, Independent Schools of Northern New England, Jesuit Secondary Education Association, New England Association of Schools and Colleges, The College Board, and Maine Department of Education. Endowment: $4 million. Total enrollment: 470. Upper school average class size: 22. Upper school faculty-student ratio: 1:10. There are 168 required school days per year for Upper School students. Upper School students typically attend 5 days per week. The average school day consists of 6 hours and 30 minutes.

Upper School Student Profile Grade 9: 96 students (62 boys, 34 girls); Grade 10: 114 students (63 boys, 51 girls); Grade 11: 108 students (57 boys, 51 girls); Grade 12: 109 students (58 boys, 51 girls). 65% of students are Roman Catholic Church (Jesuit order).

Faculty School total: 42. In upper school: 23 men, 19 women; 28 have advanced degrees.

Subjects Offered Advanced Placement courses, algebra, American history, art, biology, calculus, chemistry, college counseling, creative writing, economics, English, European history, fine arts, French, geography, geometry, government/civics, history, journalism, Latin, library skills, mathematics, music, physics, religion, science, social studies, Spanish, statistics, trigonometry, world history, yearbook.

Graduation Requirements Arts and fine arts (art, music, dance, drama), computer science, English, foreign language, health, mathematics, science, social studies (includes history), theology, all seniors are required to fill a community service requirement. Community service is required.

Special Academic Programs Advanced Placement exam preparation; honors section; study at local college for college credit; programs in general development for dyslexic students.

College Admission Counseling 118 students graduated in 2016; 111 went to college, including Maine Maritime Academy; Saint Joseph's College of Maine; Saint Louis University; The Catholic University of America; University of Maine; University of Southern Maine. Other: 7 went to work. Median SAT critical reading: 541, median SAT math: 552, median SAT writing: 535.

Student Life Upper grades have specified standards of dress, student council, honor system. Discipline rests primarily with faculty. Attendance at religious services is required.

Summer Programs Enrichment, sports programs offered; session focuses on enrichment; held on campus; accepts boys and girls; open to students from other schools. 75 students usually enrolled. 2017 schedule: June 21 to August 8. Application deadline: June 1.

Tuition and Aid Day student tuition: $18,070. Tuition installment plan (FACTS Tuition Payment Plan, monthly payment plans, individually arranged payment plans). Tuition reduction for siblings, merit scholarship grants, need-based scholarship grants, paying campus jobs available. In 2016–17, 67% of upper-school students received aid; total upper-school merit-scholarship money awarded: $10,000. Total amount of financial aid awarded in 2016–17: $2,172,770.

Admissions Traditional secondary-level entrance grade is 9. For fall 2016, 234 students applied for upper-level admission, 169 were accepted, 97 enrolled. English language and Math Placement Exam required. Deadline for receipt of application materials: none. Application fee required: $50. On-campus interview required.

Athletics Interscholastic: baseball (boys), basketball (b,g), cross-country running (b,g), diving (b,g), field hockey (g), football (b), golf (b,g), ice hockey (b,g), indoor track & field (b,g), lacrosse (b,g), sailing (b,g), skiing (downhill) (b,g), soccer (b,g), softball (g), swimming and diving (b,g), tennis (b,g), track and field (b,g), ultimate Frisbee (b), volleyball (g), winter (indoor) track (b,g), wrestling (b); intramural: basketball (b,g), flag football (b,g); coed interscholastic: alpine skiing, outdoor adventure; coed intramural: basketball, bicycling, flag football, hiking/backpacking, table tennis, volleyball. 84 coaches, 2 athletic trainers.

Computers Computers are regularly used in creative writing, economics, history, information technology, journalism, mathematics, SAT preparation, science, word processing, yearbook classes. Computer network features include on-campus library services, online commercial services, Internet access, wireless campus network. Student e-mail accounts and computer access in designated common areas are available to students. Students grades are available online. The school has a published electronic and media policy.

Contact Mrs. Ruth Summers, Director of Admissions. 207-774-6238 Ext. 190. Fax: 207-774-8461. E-mail: summers@cheverus.org. Website: www.cheverus.org

CHILDREN'S CREATIVE AND PERFORMING ARTS ACADEMY OF SAN DIEGO

3051 El Cajon Boulevard
San Diego, California 92104

Head of School: Mrs. Janet M. Cherif

General Information Coeducational boarding and day college-preparatory, arts, mathematics, and science school. Boarding grades 6–12, day grades K–12. Founded: 1981. Setting: urban. Students are housed in homestay families. 1-acre campus. 1 building on campus. Approved or accredited by Western Association of Schools and Colleges and California Department of Education. Total enrollment: 262. Upper school average class size: 18. Upper school faculty-student ratio: 1:18. There are 186 required school days per year for Upper School students. Upper School students typically attend 5 days per week. The average school day consists of 7 hours and 30 minutes.

Upper School Student Profile Grade 6: 9 students (4 boys, 5 girls); Grade 7: 11 students (2 boys, 9 girls); Grade 8: 8 students (4 boys, 4 girls); Grade 9: 15 students (5 boys, 10 girls); Grade 10: 14 students (9 boys, 5 girls); Grade 11: 30 students (13 boys, 17 girls); Grade 12: 23 students (12 boys, 11 girls). 30% of students are boarding students. 70% are state residents. 3 states are represented in upper school student body. 30% are international students. International students from China, Germany, Iran, Japan, Mexico, and Viet Nam; 2 other countries represented in student body.

Faculty School total: 33. In upper school: 4 men, 14 women; 10 have advanced degrees.

Subjects Offered 3-dimensional art, 3-dimensional design, algebra, American government, anatomy and physiology, art, art history, art history-AP, art-AP, audition methods, ballet, band, biology, business skills, calculus, calculus-AP, ceramics, chamber groups, cheerleading, chemistry, Chinese, choir, choreography, chorus, communications, comparative government and politics-AP, computer applications, computer literacy, computer programming-AP, concert band, concert choir, creative writing, dance performance, digital photography, drama, drama performance, earth science, English, English literature-AP, English-AP, English/composition-AP, ensembles, environmental science-AP, ESL, European history-AP, film, fitness, French, French language-AP, geometry, government and politics-AP, government/civics, government/civics-AP, graphic design, gymnastics, health, history of music, history-AP, honors algebra, honors English, honors geometry, honors U.S. history, honors world history, HTML design, human anatomy, instrumental music, Japanese, jazz band, jazz dance, jazz ensemble, journalism, Latin, mathematics, mathematics-AP, modern dance, music history, music performance, music theory-AP, orchestra, performing arts, physical education, physics, physics-AP, playwriting and directing, political science, portfolio art, pottery, pre-algebra, pre-calculus, reading/study skills, SAT preparation, SAT/ACT preparation, science, senior seminar, social sciences, social studies, Spanish, Spanish language-AP, Spanish literature-AP, speech, sports, stage design, statistics, studio art-AP, tap dance, theater design and production, TOEFL preparation, track and field, trigonometry, U.S. government and politics-AP, U.S. history, U.S. history-AP, vocal ensemble, vocal jazz, voice ensemble, volleyball, Web site design, Western civilization, world history, world history-AP, writing, writing workshop, yearbook.

Graduation Requirements Algebra, American government, American history, arts, arts and fine arts (art, music, dance, drama), biology, chemistry, choir, chorus, computer applications, computer skills, CPR, English, English composition, English literature, foreign language, government/civics, history, mathematics, modern world history, music, physical education (includes health), physics, science, social sciences, sports, TOEFL preparation, trigonometry, U.S. government, U.S. history, visual and performing arts, world history, senior recital or project, 30 hours of community service per year of attendance, CPR and First Aid. Community service is required.

Special Academic Programs 14 Advanced Placement exams for which test preparation is offered; honors section; accelerated programs; independent study; academic accommodation for the gifted, the musically talented, and the artistically talented; remedial reading and/or remedial writing; remedial math; ESL (20 students enrolled).

College Admission Counseling 23 students graduated in 2016; all went to college, including California State University, San Marcos; Pratt Institute; San Diego State University; The Boston Conservatory; University of California, Los Angeles; University of California, San Diego. Median SAT critical reading: 550, median SAT math: 650, median SAT writing: 490, median combined SAT: 1690. 36.4% scored over 600 on SAT critical reading, 77.3% scored over 600 on SAT math, 18.2% scored over 600 on SAT writing, 36.4% scored over 1800 on combined SAT.

Student Life Upper grades have uniform requirement, student council, honor system. Discipline rests primarily with faculty.

Summer Programs Remediation, enrichment, advancement, ESL, art/fine arts, computer instruction programs offered; session focuses on academic advancement; held on campus; accepts boys and girls; open to students from other schools. 40 students usually enrolled. 2017 schedule: June 19 to August 4. Application deadline: May 30.

Tuition and Aid Day student tuition: $12,000; 7-day tuition and room/board: $22,000. Tuition installment plan (individually arranged payment plans, pay by semester). Tuition reduction for siblings, merit scholarship grants, need-based scholarship grants, paying campus jobs, music scholarships, science and math scholarships, art scholarships available. In 2016–17, 20% of upper-school students received aid; total upper-school merit-scholarship money awarded: $10,000. Total amount of financial aid awarded in 2016–17: $25,000.

Admissions Traditional secondary-level entrance grade is 10. For fall 2016, 20 students applied for upper-level admission, 17 were accepted, 17 enrolled. Admissions testing, any standardized test, audition, math and English placement tests, Math Placement Exam, TOEFL or SLEP or writing sample required. Deadline for receipt of application materials: none. Application fee required: $350. Interview required.

Athletics Interscholastic: badminton (boys, girls), baseball (b,g), basketball (b,g), cross-country running (b,g), flag football (b), indoor soccer (b,g), soccer (b,g), softball (g), track and field (b,g), volleyball (b,g); intramural: aerobics/dance (b,g), badminton (b,g), ballet (b,g), baseball (b,g), basketball (b,g), bowling (b,g), cheering (g), dance (b,g), dance squad (b,g), dance team (b,g), field hockey (b,g), fitness (b,g), flag football (b,g), gymnastics (b,g), hiking/backpacking (b,g), horseback riding (b,g), indoor soccer (b,g), jump rope (b,g), modern dance (b,g), outdoor activities (b,g), outdoor education (b,g), physical fitness (b,g), soccer (b,g), softball (b,g), surfing (b,g), swimming (b,g), diving (b,g), table tennis (b,g), tennis (b,g), track and field (b,g), volleyball (b,g). interscholastic: indoor soccer; coed intramural: aerobics/dance, badminton, baseball, bowling, dance, dance squad, dance team, fitness, hiking/backpacking, indoor soccer, jump rope, modern dance, outdoor education, physical fitness, softball, surfing, swimming, tennis, track and field. 3 PE instructors, 3 coaches.

Computers Computers are regularly used in architecture, writing, desktop publishing, drawing and design, journalism, music, programming, SAT preparation, typing, video, word processing, yearbook classes. Computer network. college credit classes online.

Contact Mrs. Karen Peterson, Admissions [...] 2422. E-mail: capaadmissions@yahoo.com

CHOATE ROSEMARY HALL

333 Christian Street
Wallingford, Connecticut 06492-3800
Head of School: Alex D. Curtis, PhD

General Information Coeducational boarding and day college-preparatory and Signature Programs school. Grades 9–PG. Founded: 1890. Setting: small town. Nearest major city is New Haven. Students are housed in coed dormitories. 458-acre campus. 121 buildings on campus. Approved or accredited by Connecticut Association of Independent Schools, New England Association of Schools and Colleges, The Association of Boarding Schools, and Connecticut Department of Education. Member of National Association of Independent Schools and Secondary School Admission Test Board. Endowment: $346 million. Total enrollment: 867. Upper school average class size: 12. Upper school faculty-student ratio: 1:6. There are 159 required school days per year for Upper School students. Upper School students typically attend 5 days per week. The average school day consists of 6 hours.

Upper School Student Profile Grade 9: 163 students (85 boys, 78 girls); Grade 10: 213 students (107 boys, 106 girls); Grade 11: 227 students (112 boys, 115 girls); Grade 12: 241 students (125 boys, 116 girls); Postgraduate: 18 students (15 boys, 3 girls). 74% of students are boarding students. 47% are state residents. 42 states are represented in upper school student body. 18% are international students. International students from China, Hong Kong, Japan, Nigeria, Republic of Korea, and Thailand; 42 other countries represented in student body.

Faculty School total: 138. In upper school: 71 men, 67 women; 97 have advanced degrees; 110 reside on campus.

Subjects Offered Acting, advanced biology, advanced chemistry, advanced math, algebra, American history, American literature, anatomy, Arabic, architecture, art, astronomy, biology, British history, calculus, calculus-AP, ceramics, chemistry, chemistry-AP, child development, Chinese, computer programming, computer science, computer science-AP, creative writing, dance, design, drama, ecology, economics, English, English literature, environmental science, environmental science-AP, European history-AP, fine arts, French, French language-AP, French studies, geometry, government and politics-AP, history, history-AP, Holocaust, interdisciplinary studies, international studies, Italian, language, Latin, Latin-AP, linear algebra, macroeconomics-AP, marine biology, mathematics, microbiology, microeconomics-AP, music, music composition, music history, music performance, music technology, music theater, music theory-AP, music-AP, musical productions, musical theater, musical theater dance, musicianship, philosophy, photography, physics, physics-AP, psychology, psychology-AP, public speaking, religion, Spanish, Spanish language-AP, Spanish literature, Spanish literature-AP, Spanish-AP, statics, statistics-AP, studio art, theater, trigonometry, U.S. history, U.S. history-AP, visual arts, world history, world literature, world religions, world studies, wrestling, writing, writing, writing workshop.

Graduation Requirements Art, English, foreign language, global studies, history, mathematics, philosophy, physical education (includes), science, 30 hours of community service.

Special Academic Programs 25 Advanced Placement exams for which test preparation is offered; honors section; independent study; far-away projects; study abroad; academic accommodation for the gifted, the musically talented, and the artistically talented.

College Admission Counseling 232 students graduated in 2016; 227 went to college, including Boston College; Colgate University; Harvard University; New York University; University of Chicago. Median SAT math: 67, median SAT writing: 670, median combined SAT: 20 on combined SAT, 80% scored over 600 on composite ACT: 30, 77% scored over 600 on SAT critical reading, 75% scored over 600 on SAT math, 79% scored over 600 on SAT writing, 82% scored over 26 on composite ACT.

Student Life Upper grades have student council, honor system. Discipline rests primarily with faculty.

Summer Programs Remediation, enrichment, advancement, ESL, sports, art/fine arts programs offered for boys and girls; open to students from other schools; held both on and off campus; session focuses on academic growth and enrichment. 625 students usually enrolled. Day student tuition: $43,130; 7-day tuition and room/board: $[...]. Tuition installment plan (Higher One, Your Tuition Solution). Need-based financial aid available. In 2016–17, 35% of upper-school students received aid.

Admissions Traditional secondary-level entrance grade is 9. For fall 2016, 2,087 students applied for upper-level admission, 381 were accepted, 242 enrolled. ACT, SAT or TOEFL required for applicants to grade 11 and 12. Deadline for receipt of application materials: January 10. Application fee required: $75.

Athletics Interscholastic: baseball (boys), basketball (b,g), crew (b,g), cross-country running (b,g), field hockey (g), football (b), golf (b,g), ice hockey (b,g), soccer (b,g), softball (g), squash (b,g), swimming and diving (b,g), tennis (b,g), track and field (b,g), volleyball (b,g), water polo (b,g), wrestling; coed intramural: archery, sailing, ultimate Frisbee, crew (b,g), squash (b,g), coed interscholastic: aerobics, aerobics/dance, aerobics/Nautilus, ballet, basketball, canoeing/kayaking, climbing, dance, dance squad, fencing, fitness, martial arts, modern dance, Nautilus, outdoor activities, physical fitness, physical training, rock

climbing, rowing, running, soccer, softball, diving, tennis, ultimate Frisbee, volleyball, (indoor) track, yoga. 10 coaches, 3 athletic tr...

Computers Computers are regularly used... computer applications, desktop publishing... information technology, library skills, lit... newspaper, photography, programming, st... film production, word processing, yearbook... on-campus library services, online com... campus network, Internet filtering or ble... Campus intranet, student e-mail account... areas are available to students. Students... published electronic and media policy.

Contact Amin Abdul-Malik Gonzalew... 203-697-2629. E-mail: admission@choddle...

CHRISTA MCAULIFFE ARTS AND SCIENCES

5200 SW Meadows Road, S...
Lake Oswego, Oregon 9703...

Head of School: Christopher...

General Information Coeduca... general academic, and Advance... learning grades K–12. Founded... Portland. 1 building on campus... 25. Upper school faculty-stude... year for Upper School student... week. The average school day...

Upper School Student Pro... students (4 boys, 11 girls); On... students (18 boys, 44 girls); Sr... students (13 boys, 40 girls)... students (2 boys).

Faculty School total: 27. In...

Subjects Offered ACT... government, American histor... appreciation, art history, s... (honors), career educatio... literacy, economics, el... foreign language, foren... Japanese, keyboarding,... education, science, soci...

Graduation Require... applications, Englsh, fo... science, social studies...

Special Academic... section; accelerated p... gifted, the musically... remedial writing; reined SA... students.

College Admission... 5... mean SAT wri...

Student Life Up... equay with stude...

Summer Progra... progra... at stude... students u... home... none.

Tuition and... installment pl... reduction fo...

Admission... Achievem... none. A...

Comp... Internet... Con... 866...

...School Stud...nt Profile Grade 9: 32 students... ...ts (13 boys, ... girls); Grade 11: 30 students (16... ...(14 boys, 12 girls). 100% of students are Evangel... **Faculty** School total: ... In upper school: 7 men, 18 ... degrees.

Graduation Requirements Algebra, Bible, biology,... literature, geometry, global studies, physics, trigonometry, com... all four years, completion of standardized NYS Regents exams... diplomas have more rigorous requirements.

Special Academic Programs 8 Advanced Placement ex... preparation is offered; independent study; study at local college for... 2 students enrolled).

Christian Brothers A... ...istant. 804-758-2306 Ext. 122. ...ool.org.

...CADEMY

...ated with ...40-acre ca... Brothers ...York State ...ool average

...ce, drama), English, ...th), religion (includes ...dies (includes history),

...m preparation; honors

...d in 2016; 121 went to ...ollege; Loyola University ...University at Buffalo, the ...ate year.

...of dress, student council. ...on services is required.

...ART Tuition Payment ...grants, need-based scholarship ...dents received aid; total upper-

...grade is 7. Admissions testing ...ls: February 1. No application fee

...all (b,g), cheering (g), cross-country ...g), gymnastics (b), ice hockey (b), ...er (b,g), softball (g), swimming and ...volleyball (g), wrestling (b); coed ...thletic trainer. ...ade on-campus library services, Internet ...ering or blocking technology. Student e-...ents grades are available online. The school

...e Assistant. 315-446-5960 Ext. 1202. Fax: ...us.org. Website: www.cbasyracuse.org

...14221

...d Gaebelein

...oeducational day ...faith. Grades K–... ...uffalo. 5-acre campus ...ory school, affiliated with ...949. Setting: suburban. Approved or ...ols, New York State Assoc... ...Regents, and New York D...campus. ... Admission Test Board. Endow... States Association ...average class size: 15. Upper scho...nt Schools, New ...ool days per year for Upper Schoo...n. Member of ...ad 5 days per week. The average school d...

College Admission Counseling 30 students graduated in 2016; all went to college, including Erie Community College; Liberty University; Roberts Wesleyan College; University at Buffalo, the State University of New York. Median SAT critical reading: 500, median SAT math: 540, median SAT writing: 500, median combined SAT: 1540, median composite ACT: 24. 26% scored over 600 on SAT math, 30% scored over 600 on SAT writing, 22% scored over 1800 on over 600 on SAT math, 30% scored over 600 on SAT writing, 33% scored combined SAT, 29% scored over 26 on composite ACT.

Student Life Upper grades have specified standards of dress, student council, honor system. Discipline rests primarily with faculty. Attendance at religious services is required.

Tuition and Aid Day student tuition: $9400. Tuition installment plan (FACTS Tuition Payment Plan, monthly payment plans, individually arranged payment plans, prepayment discount plans, multiple-student discounts, pastors/full-time Christian service discounts). Tuition reduction for siblings, merit scholarship grants available. In 2016–17, 47% of upper-school students received aid; total upper-school merit-scholarship money awarded: $6000. Total amount of financial aid awarded in 2016–17: $177,758.

Admissions Traditional secondary-level entrance grade is 9. For fall 2016, 24 students applied for upper-level admission, 23 were accepted, 21 enrolled. Deadline for receipt of application materials: none. Application fee required: $50. On-campus interview recommended.

Athletics Interscholastic: baseball (boys), basketball (b,g), golf (b), soccer (b,g), softball (g), volleyball (g); intramural: soccer (b,g); coed intramural: track and field. 2 PE instructors, 3 cross-country running, soccer; coed intramural: bowling, coaches, 1 athletic trainer.

Computers Computers are regularly used in all classes. Computer network features include on-campus library services, Internet access, wireless campus network, Internet filtering or blocking technology, teacher-guided use of programs in various subject areas. Student e-mail accounts and computer access in designated common areas are available to students. Students grades are available online. The school has a published electronic and media policy.

Contact Ms. Jeanne Conklin, Director of Admissions. 716-634-4821 Ext. 151. Fax: 716-634-5851. E-mail: jconklin@christianca.com. Website: www.christianca.com

CHRISTIAN HERITAGE SCHOOL

575 White Plains Road
Trumbull, Connecticut 06611-4898

Head of School: Mr. Brian Modarelli, PhD

General Information Coeducational day college-preparatory, religious studies, and technology school. Grades K–12. Founded: 1977. Setting: suburban. Nearest major city is Bridgeport. 12-acre campus. 7 buildings on campus. Approved or accredited by Association of Christian Schools International, New England Association of Schools and Colleges, The College Board, and Connecticut Department of Education. Member of European Council of International Schools. Endowment: $15 million. Total enrollment: 450. 1:9. There are 170 required school days per year for Upper School students. Upper school average class size: 19. Upper school faculty-student ratio: 1:9. There are 170 required school days per year for Upper School students. Upper school students typically attend 5 days per week. The average school day consists of 7 hours and 15 minutes.

Upper School Student Profile Grade 6: 32 students (17 boys, 15 girls); Grade 7: 34 students (18 boys, 16 girls); Grade 8: 39 students (18 boys, 21 girls); Grade 9: 53 students (27 boys, 26 girls); Grade 10: 36 students (19 boys, 17 girls); Grade 11: 44 students (25 boys, 19 girls); Grade 12: 46 students (20 boys, 26 girls).

Faculty School total: 59. In upper school: 18 men, 13 women; 23 have advanced degrees.

Subjects Offered 20th century American writers, 20th century history, 20th century physics, 20th century world history, advanced chemistry, advanced math, advanced Placement courses, algebra, American democracy, American foreign policy, American government, American history, American history-AP, American literature, applied music, art, athletics, band, Basic programming, Bible, Bible studies, biology, biology-AP, British literature, business, calculus, calculus-AP, career and personal planning, career exploration, business, calculus, calculus-AP, career and personal planning, music, chorus, Christian and Hebrew scripture, chamber groups, chemistry, choir, choral church ethics, Christian scripture, Christian studies, Christian doctrine, Christian education, church history, classical Greek literature, classics, Christian testament, Christianity, college awareness, college counseling, college placement, college admission preparation, writing, communication skills, comparative government and politics, computer education, computer processing, computer programming, computer programming-AP, computer science, computer skills, computer technologies, computer mathematics, concert band, concert choir, contemporary history of U.S., consumer mathematics, contemporary history, contemporary issues, data processing, desktop publishing, drama performance, drawing, earth current history, English, English composition, English language-AP, English literature, English literature-AP, ensembles, ethics, ethics and responsibility, expository writing, functions, science, geography, geometry, government/civics, grammar, health and health education, history, history-AP, honors algebra, honors English, honors U.S. history, human anatomy, human biology, instrumental... intro to computers, journalism, keyboarding, languag... of Christ, life science, literature, math...

reasoning, music, music theory, musical productions, newspaper, novels, painting, philosophy, physical education, physical science, physics, poetry, prayer/spirituality, pre-algebra, pre-calculus, public speaking, publications, reading/study skills, religion, religious education, science, science project, Shakespeare, social studies, Spanish, Spanish-AP, speech, statistics, student government, student publications, U.S. government, U.S. history-AP, vocal ensemble, vocal music, volleyball, work experience, world affairs, world history, writing, yearbook.

Graduation Requirements Electives, English, foreign language, mathematics, physical education (includes health), religion (includes Bible studies and theology), science, social studies (includes history), community service hours.

Special Academic Programs Advanced Placement exam preparation; honors section; accelerated programs; independent study; term-away projects; academic accommodation for the gifted; ESL (9 students enrolled).

College Admission Counseling 44 students graduated in 2015; 42 went to college, including Southern Connecticut State University; University of Connecticut; Wheaton College. Other: 2 entered military service. Median SAT critical reading: 579, median SAT math: 597, median SAT writing: 588, median combined SAT: 1695, median composite ACT: 25. 9% scored over 600 on SAT critical reading, 9% scored over 600 on SAT math, 8% scored over 600 on SAT writing, 10% scored over 1800 on combined SAT.

Student Life Upper grades have specified standards of dress, student council, honor system. Discipline rests primarily with faculty. Attendance at religious services is required.

Tuition and Aid Day student tuition: $17,400. Tuition installment plan (FACTS Tuition Payment Plan, monthly payment plans, individually arranged payment plans, Tuition Management Systems). Need-based scholarship grants available. In 2015–16, 46% of upper-school students received aid. Total amount of financial aid awarded in 2015–16: $500,000.

Admissions Traditional secondary-level entrance grade is 9. For fall 2015, 56 students applied for upper-level admission, 43 were accepted, 38 enrolled. Admissions testing, ISEE, Otis-Lennon School Ability Test or Stanford Achievement Test required. Deadline for receipt of application materials: none. Application fee required: $50. Interview required.

Athletics Interscholastic: baseball (boys), basketball (b,g), cross-country running (b,g), soccer (b,g), tennis (b,g), volleyball (g); intramural: soccer (b,g), softball (g). 4 PE instructors, 31 coaches.

Computers Computers are regularly used in business education, college planning, data processing, desktop publishing, journalism, keyboarding, mathematics, newspaper, programming, word processing, yearbook classes. Computer network features include on-campus library services, online commercial services, Internet access, wireless campus network, Internet filtering or blocking technology, iPads for all high school students. Campus intranet and student e-mail accounts are available to students. Students grades are available online. The school has a published electronic and media policy.

Contact Mrs. Robin Parrish, Director of Admissions. 203-261-6230 Ext. 555. Fax: 203-268-1046. E-mail: admissions@kingsmen.org. Website: www.kingsmen.org

CHRISTOPHER COLUMBUS HIGH SCHOOL

3000 Southwest 87th Avenue
Miami, Florida 33165-3293

Head of School: Mr. David Pugh II

General Information Boys' day college-preparatory school, affiliated with Roman Catholic Church. Grades 9–12. Founded: 1958. Setting: suburban. 19-acre campus. 10 buildings on campus. Approved or accredited by National Catholic Education Association, Southern Association of Colleges and Schools, and Florida Department of Education. Total enrollment: 1,579. Upper school average class size: 25. Upper school faculty-student ratio: 1:15. There are 180 required school days per year for Upper School students. Upper School students typically attend 5 days per week. The average school day consists of 6 hours and 25 minutes.

Upper School Student Profile Grade 9: 427 students (427 boys); Grade 10: 412 students (412 boys); Grade 11: 389 students (389 boys); Grade 12: 372 students (372 boys). 95% of students are Roman Catholic.

Faculty School total: 82. In upper school: 56 men, 26 women; 35 have advanced degrees.

Subjects Offered 3-dimensional art, accounting, acting, advanced biology, advanced chemistry, advanced computer applications, advanced math, Advanced Placement courses, algebra, American government, American history, American history-AP, American literature, analysis, anatomy, ancient world history, architectural drawing, art, athletic training, athletics, band, Basic programming, Bible, biology, biology-AP, British literature (honors), business law, business skills, calculus, calculus-AP, campus ministry, Catholic belief and practice, chemistry, chemistry-AP, Christian and Hebrew scripture, Christian doctrine, Christian ethics, church history, college counseling, composition-AP, computer applications, computer information systems, computer programming, computer science, computer science-AP, computer-aided design, contemporary history, debate, drama, economics, economics-AP, English, English language and composition-AP, English literature, English literature-AP, English-AP, ethics, European history, European history-AP, French, French language-AP, French-AP, geometry, global studies, government, government and politics-AP, health, history

of the Catholic Church, Holocaust studies, keyboarding, library assistant, marine biology, physical education, physical fitness, physics, physics-AP, pre-algebra, pre-calculus, psychology, Spanish, Spanish language-AP, Spanish literature, Spanish literature-AP, speech, U.S. government, U.S. government and politics, U.S. government and politics-AP, U.S. history, U.S. history-AP, Vietnam War, word processing, world governments, yearbook.

Graduation Requirements Algebra, arts and fine arts (art, music, dance, drama), computer applications, English, lab science, language, mathematics, personal fitness, physical education (includes health), practical arts, religion (includes Bible studies and theology), science, social studies (includes history), students must earn a Florida scale GPA of 2.0, students must complete 100 hours of community service during their four years of high school.

Special Academic Programs Advanced Placement exam preparation; honors section; study at local college for college credit; academic accommodation for the gifted; remedial reading and/or remedial writing.

College Admission Counseling 365 students graduated in 2016; 363 went to college, including Florida International University; Florida State University; University of Central Florida; University of Florida; University of Miami; University of South Florida. Other: 2 entered military service. Mean SAT critical reading: 530, mean SAT math: 540, mean SAT writing: 520, mean combined SAT: 1590, mean composite ACT: 24. 25% scored over 600 on SAT critical reading, 25% scored over 600 on SAT math, 25% scored over 600 on SAT writing, 25% scored over 1800 on combined SAT, 30% scored over 26 on composite ACT.

Student Life Upper grades have uniform requirement, student council, honor system. Discipline rests primarily with faculty. Attendance at religious services is required.

Summer Programs Remediation, enrichment programs offered; session focuses on enrichment, remediation, and study skills; held on campus; accepts boys; not open to students from other schools. 154 students usually enrolled. 2017 schedule: June 11 to June 29. Application deadline: June 7.

Tuition and Aid Tuition installment plan (monthly payment plans, individually arranged payment plans). Bursaries available.

Admissions Traditional secondary-level entrance grade is 9. High School Placement Test required. Deadline for receipt of application materials: none. Application fee required: $50.

Athletics Interscholastic: baseball, basketball, bowling, cross-country running, football, golf, lacrosse, soccer, swimming and diving, tennis, track and field, volleyball, water polo, wrestling; intramural: basketball, flag football, power lifting, roller hockey, weight training. 2 PE instructors, 25 coaches, 2 athletic trainers.

Computers Computers are regularly used in all classes. Computer network features include on-campus library services, online commercial services, Internet access, wireless campus network, Internet filtering or blocking technology. Campus intranet, student e-mail accounts, and computer access in designated common areas are available to students. Students grades are available online. The school has a published electronic and media policy.

Contact Mrs. Rebecca Rafuls, Registrar. 305-223-5650 Ext. 2239. Fax: 305-559-4306. E-mail: rrafuls@columbushs.com. Website: www.columbushs.com

CHRYSALIS SCHOOL

14241 North East Woodinville-Duvall Road
PMB 243
Woodinville, Washington 98072

Head of School: Karen Fogle

General Information Coeducational day college-preparatory, general academic, and personalized curriculum for every student school. Grades 1–12. Founded: 1983. Setting: suburban. Nearest major city is Seattle. 1.5-acre campus. 1 building on campus. Approved or accredited by Washington Department of Education. Total enrollment: 185. Upper school average class size: 10. Upper school faculty-student ratio: 1:3. There are 180 required school days per year for Upper School students. Upper School students typically attend 4 days per week. The average school day consists of 5 hours.

Upper School Student Profile Grade 9: 19 students (12 boys, 7 girls); Grade 10: 25 students (17 boys, 8 girls); Grade 11: 33 students (24 boys, 9 girls); Grade 12: 49 students (28 boys, 21 girls).

Faculty School total: 61. In upper school: 18 men, 30 women; 18 have advanced degrees.

Subjects Offered Advanced biology, advanced chemistry, advanced computer applications, advanced math, art, audio visual/media, career planning, college counseling, computer technologies, drama, English, filmmaking, French, geography, German, graphics, history, Japanese, mathematics, physical education, SAT preparation, science, social sciences, Spanish.

Graduation Requirements American history, arts and fine arts (art, music, dance, drama), career and personal planning, computer literacy, English, foreign language, government, health education, history, mathematics, physical education (includes health), science, world history, portfolio.

Special Academic Programs Honors section; accelerated programs; study at local college for college credit; academic accommodation for the gifted; programs in English, mathematics, general development for dyslexic students.

College Admission Counseling 35 students graduated in 2016; 29 went to college, including Bellevue College; Central Washington University; Seattle University; University of Washington; Washington State University; Western Washington University. Other: 1 went to work, 5 had other specific plans.

Student Life Upper grades have specified standards of dress, honor system. Discipline rests primarily with faculty.

Summer Programs Remediation, enrichment, advancement, computer instruction programs offered; session focuses on enrichment; held on campus; accepts boys and girls; open to students from other schools. 10 students usually enrolled. 2017 schedule: July 12 to August 25. Application deadline: June 1.

Tuition and Aid Tuition installment plan (monthly payment plans).

Admissions Traditional secondary-level entrance grade is 9. For fall 2016, 96 students applied for upper-level admission, 92 were accepted, 90 enrolled. Deadline for receipt of application materials: none. Application fee required: $1000. On-campus interview recommended.

Computers Computers are regularly used in computer applications, English, foreign language, graphic arts, history, information technology, introduction to technology, keyboarding, mathematics, media, science, video film production, Web site design, word processing, yearbook classes. Computer network features include on-campus library services, online commercial services, Internet access, wireless campus network, Internet filtering or blocking technology. Campus intranet and computer access in designated common areas are available to students. The school has a published electronic and media policy.

Contact Kari Lewis, Schedule Designer. 425-481-2228. Fax: 425-486-8107. E-mail: karil@chrysalis-school.com. Website: www.chrysalis-school.com

THE CHURCH FARM SCHOOL

1001 East Lincoln Highway
Exton, Pennsylvania 19341

Head of School: Rev. Edmund K. Sherrill II

General Information Boys' boarding and day college-preparatory, arts, technology, and STEAM school, affiliated with Episcopal Church. Grades 9–12. Founded: 1918. Setting: suburban. Nearest major city is Philadelphia. Students are housed in single-sex dormitories. 150-acre campus. 19 buildings on campus. Approved or accredited by Middle States Association of Colleges and Schools, National Association of Episcopal Schools, The Association of Boarding Schools, and Pennsylvania Department of Education. Member of National Association of Independent Schools and Secondary School Admission Test Board. Endowment: $135 million. Total enrollment: 193. Upper school average class size: 12. Upper school faculty-student ratio: 1:6. There are 180 required school days per year for Upper School students. Upper School students typically attend 5 days per week. The average school day consists of 7 hours and 5 minutes.

Upper School Student Profile Grade 9: 53 students (53 boys); Grade 10: 45 students (45 boys); Grade 11: 42 students (42 boys); Grade 12: 45 students (45 boys). 90% of students are boarding students. 35% are state residents. 15 states are represented in upper school student body. 18% are international students. International students from China, Ethiopia, Ghana, Jamaica, Lithuania, and Republic of Korea; 6 other countries represented in student body. 10% of students are members of Episcopal Church.

Faculty School total: 33. In upper school: 22 men, 11 women; 17 have advanced degrees; 24 reside on campus.

Subjects Offered 20th century history, 3-dimensional design, African-American history, algebra, American government, American history, American history-AP, American literature, American studies, anatomy and physiology, art, art history, biology, biology-AP, British literature, calculus-AP, ceramics, chemistry, chemistry-AP, choir, choral music, clayworking, college writing, composition, computer science, construction, creative writing, design, drama, driver education, earth science, ecology, economics, English, English-AP, environmental science, ethics, European history, expository writing, film and literature, fine arts, French, geometry, government/civics, grammar, health, history, history of jazz, industrial arts, instrumental music, journalism, leadership, mathematics, medieval history, music, music history, music technology, musicianship, mythology, photography, physical education, physics, poetry, pre-calculus, psychology, public speaking, Russian history, science, Shakespeare, Shakespearean histories, social studies, sociology, Spanish, speech, statistics, technology, theater, trigonometry, Vietnam history, Vietnam War, weaving, Web site design, woodworking, world history, world literature, world religions, World War II, writing.

Graduation Requirements Arts and fine arts (art, music, dance, drama), English, foreign language, mathematics, physical education (includes health), religion (includes Bible studies and theology), science, social studies (includes history), technology, Challenge of Required Experience (combination of community service and outdoor educational experience).

Special Academic Programs 5 Advanced Placement exams for which test preparation is offered; honors section; accelerated programs; independent study; study at local college for college credit; study abroad; academic accommodation for the gifted, the musically talented, and the artistically talented.

College Admission Counseling 31 students graduated in 2016; all went to college, including Lehigh University; Swarthmore College; Temple University; University of California, San Diego; University of Pennsylvania; Williams College. Median SAT critical reading: 540, median SAT math: 570, median SAT writing: 520, median combined SAT: 1660. 29% scored over 600 on SAT critical reading, 43% scored over 600 on SAT math, 29% scored over 600 on SAT writing, 30% scored over 1800 on combined SAT.

Student Life Upper grades have specified standards of dress, student council, honor system. Discipline rests primarily with faculty. Attendance at religious services is required.

Tuition and Aid Day student tuition: $20,000; 7-day tuition and room/board: $38,000. Tuition installment plan (SMART Tuition Payment Plan, monthly payment plans, individually arranged payment plans). Tuition reduction for siblings, need-based scholarship grants, paying campus jobs available. In 2016–17, 90% of upper-school students received aid. Total amount of financial aid awarded in 2016–17: $3,881,717.

Admissions Traditional secondary-level entrance grade is 9. For fall 2016, 264 students applied for upper-level admission, 94 were accepted, 60 enrolled. 3-R Achievement Test, ISEE, SSAT or TOEFL required. Deadline for receipt of application materials: none. Application fee required: $50. Interview recommended.

Athletics Interscholastic: baseball, basketball, bowling, cross-country running, golf, indoor track, lacrosse, soccer, tennis, track and field, wrestling; intramural: fitness, floor hockey, indoor soccer, physical fitness, strength & conditioning, touch football, weight lifting. 2 coaches, 1 athletic trainer.

Computers Computers are regularly used in art, English, foreign language, history, mathematics, music, science, technology classes. Computer network features include on-campus library services, online commercial services, Internet access, wireless campus network, Internet filtering or blocking technology, 1:1 MacBook program. Campus intranet, student e-mail accounts, and computer access in designated common areas are available to students. Students grades are available online. The school has a published electronic and media policy.

Contact Mr. Michael S. Foster, Director of Admissions. 610-363-5346. Fax: 610-280-6746. E-mail: mfoster@gocfs.net. Website: www.gocfs.net

CITY CHRISTIAN SCHOOLS

9200 NE Fremont Street
Portland, Oregon 97220

Head of School: Mr. Lynden Evans

General Information Coeducational day college-preparatory, arts, business, vocational, religious studies, technology, and CNA Program school, affiliated with Christian faith. Grades PK–12. Founded: 1974. Setting: suburban. Students are housed in Host homes for international students. 8-acre campus. 3 buildings on campus. Approved or accredited by Oregon Department of Education. Upper school average class size: 25. Upper school faculty-student ratio: 1:12. There are 178 required school days per year for Upper School students. Upper School students typically attend 5 days per week. The average school day consists of 7 hours.

Upper School Student Profile Grade 6: 29 students (11 boys, 18 girls); Grade 7: 28 students (15 boys, 13 girls); Grade 8: 19 students (12 boys, 7 girls); Grade 9: 33 students (18 boys, 15 girls); Grade 10: 35 students (21 boys, 14 girls); Grade 11: 28 students (16 boys, 12 girls); Grade 12: 48 students (25 boys, 23 girls). 40% of students are boarding students. 68% are state residents. 2 states are represented in upper school student body. 40% are international students. International students from China, Democratic People's Republic of Korea, Japan, and Viet Nam.

Faculty School total: 33. In upper school: 3 men, 11 women.

Subjects Offered All academic.

Graduation Requirements Critical writing, electives, English, mathematics, physical education (includes health), reading, religion (includes Bible studies and theology), religion and culture, science, social studies (includes history), writing. Community service is required.

Special Academic Programs Independent study; study at local college for college credit; study abroad; academic accommodation for the gifted and the artistically talented; remedial reading and/or remedial writing; remedial math; programs in general development for dyslexic students; ESL (16 students enrolled).

College Admission Counseling 33 students graduated in 2016; 27 went to college, including Oregon State University; Portland State University; University of Nebraska–Lincoln; University of Oregon; University of Washington. Other: 6 went to work.

Student Life Upper grades have uniform requirement, student council, honor system. Discipline rests primarily with faculty. Attendance at religious services is required.

Summer Programs Remediation programs offered; held on campus; accepts boys and girls; not open to students from other schools. 3 students usually enrolled. 2017 schedule: July to August.

Tuition and Aid Day student tuition: $5665; 7-day tuition and room/board: $9515. Guaranteed tuition plan. Tuition installment plan (SMART Tuition Payment Plan). Tuition reduction for siblings, need-based scholarship grants, scholarships available.

Admissions Traditional secondary-level entrance grade is 9. Traditional secondary-level entrance age is 14. California Achievement Test or ESL required. Application fee required: $50. On-campus interview recommended.

Athletics Interscholastic: basketball (boys, girls), cheering (g), cross-country running (b,g), soccer (b), track and field (b,g), volleyball (g).

Computers Computers are regularly used in all academic classes. Computer network features include Internet access, wireless campus network, Internet filtering or blocking technology, online AP courses, online Technology courses, online CNA program. Campus intranet, student e-mail accounts, and computer access in designated common areas are available to students. Students grades are available online. The school has a published electronic and media policy.

Contact Becky Faria, Director of Development. 503-8895568. Fax: 503-257-2221. E-mail: bfaria@citychristianschools.com. Website: www.citychristianschool.com/

CLARKSVILLE ACADEMY

710 North Second Street
Clarksville, Tennessee 37040-2998

Head of School: Dr. Kay D. Drew

General Information Coeducational day college-preparatory, 1:1 Apple program, and FUSE school. Grades PK–12. Founded: 1970. Setting: urban. 31-acre campus. 7 buildings on campus. Approved or accredited by Southern Association of Colleges and Schools, Tennessee Association of Independent Schools, and Tennessee Department of Education. Member of National Association of Independent Schools. Endowment: $1 million. Total enrollment: 650. Upper school average class size: 15. Upper school faculty-student ratio: 1:12. There are 175 required school days per year for Upper School students. Upper School students typically attend 5 days per week. The average school day consists of 7 hours and 10 minutes.

Upper School Student Profile Grade 9: 69 students (39 boys, 30 girls); Grade 10: 64 students (33 boys, 31 girls); Grade 11: 60 students (27 boys, 33 girls); Grade 12: 50 students (20 boys, 30 girls).

Faculty School total: 60. In upper school: 13 men, 18 women; 18 have advanced degrees.

Subjects Offered Advanced math, Advanced Placement courses, algebra, American government, American history-AP, anatomy and physiology, animal science, arts appreciation, college counseling, community service, current history, drama performance, Shakespeare, zoology.

Graduation Requirements Economics, finance, government, health and wellness, personal finance, wellness, 24 credit, 4 years of high school math required.

Special Academic Programs 7 Advanced Placement exams for which test preparation is offered; honors section; independent study; study at local college for college credit.

College Admission Counseling 42 students graduated in 2016; all went to college, including Austin Peay State University; Belmont University; Jacksonville State University; Samford University; The University of Tennessee; The University of Tennessee at Martin. 25% scored over 26 on composite ACT.

Student Life Upper grades have specified standards of dress, student council, honor system. Discipline rests primarily with faculty.

Summer Programs Remediation, enrichment, sports, art/fine arts, computer instruction programs offered; session focuses on enrichment and remediation; held both on and off campus; accepts boys and girls; open to students from other schools. 300 students usually enrolled. 2017 schedule: June 5 to August 4. Application deadline: May 19.

Tuition and Aid Tuition installment plan (monthly payment plans). Tuition reduction for siblings, paying campus jobs available.

Admissions Traditional secondary-level entrance grade is 9. For fall 2016, 31 students applied for upper-level admission, 29 were accepted, 25 enrolled. Brigance Test of Basic Skills, Otis-Lennon School Ability Test and writing sample required. Deadline for receipt of application materials: none. Application fee required: $75. On-campus interview recommended.

Athletics Interscholastic: baseball (boys), basketball (b,g), cheering (g), dance team (g), football (b), soccer (b,g), softball (g), volleyball (g); coed interscholastic: archery, bowling, cross-country running, golf, tennis. 4 coaches.

Computers Computers are regularly used in all classes. Computer network features include on-campus library services, Internet access, wireless campus network, Internet filtering or blocking technology, 1:1 Apple MacBook program, 1:1 Apple iPad program, 1:1 Apple iPad mini program. Campus intranet, student e-mail accounts, and computer access in designated common areas are available to students. Students grades are available online. The school has a published electronic and media policy.

Contact Mrs. Angie Henson, Business Office and Enrollment. 931-647-6311. Fax: 931-906-0610. E-mail: ahenson@clarksvilleacademy.com. Website: www.clarksvilleacademy.com

COLEGIO BOLIVAR

Calle 5 # 122-21 Via a Pance
Cali, Colombia

Head of School: Dr. Joseph John Nagy

General Information Coeducational day college-preparatory school. Grades PK–12. Founded: 1947. Setting: suburban. 14-hectare campus. 7 buildings on campus. Approved or accredited by Association of American Schools in South America, Colombian Ministry of Education, and Southern Association of Colleges and Schools. Languages of instruction: English and Spanish. Total enrollment: 1,269. Upper school average class size: 18. Upper school faculty-student ratio: 1:9. There are 180 required

school days per year for Upper School students. The average school day consists of 7 hours.

Upper School Student Profile Grade 6: 81 students (46 boys, 35 girls); Grade 7: 72 students (34 boys, 38 girls); Grade 8: 91 students (49 boys, 42 girls); Grade 9: 83 students (43 boys, 40 girls); Grade 10: 83 students (55 boys, 28 girls); Grade 11: 88 students (47 boys, 41 girls); Grade 12: 91 students (49 boys, 42 girls).

Faculty School total: 166. In upper school: 21 men, 19 women; 32 have advanced degrees.

Subjects Offered Advanced chemistry, Advanced Placement courses, algebra, American history, American literature, art, art history, biology, business, calculus, chemistry, computer science, dance, drama, English, English literature, environmental science, ESL, ethics, French, geology, government/civics, graphic design, history, journalism, mathematics, music, philosophy, photography, physical education, physics, programming, psychology, religion, robotics, social studies, Spanish, theater, trigonometry, world literature.

Graduation Requirements Algebra, American history, American literature, art, biology, calculus, chemistry, computer education, economics, electives, geography, geometry, history of the Americas, music, physical education (includes health), physics, political science, pre-calculus, senior project, Spanish, Spanish literature, trigonometry, world history, world literature, writing, social service hours, senior project.

Special Academic Programs Advanced Placement exam preparation; independent study; remedial reading and/or remedial writing; remedial math; ESL.

College Admission Counseling 86 students graduated in 2016; 66 went to college, including Georgia Institute of Technology; Northwestern State University of Louisiana; University of Miami. Other: 20 had other specific plans.

Student Life Upper grades have specified standards of dress, student council, honor system. Discipline rests equally with students and faculty.

Summer Programs Remediation programs offered; session focuses on math camp; held on campus; accepts boys and girls; not open to students from other schools. 20 students usually enrolled. 2017 schedule: June 27 to July 11.

Tuition and Aid Day student tuition: 17,000,000 Colombian pesos–25,000,000 Colombian pesos. Tuition installment plan (monthly payment plans, annual payment plan). Need-based scholarship grants available.

Admissions Traditional secondary-level entrance grade is 9. Traditional secondary-level entrance age is 13. School's own exam required. Deadline for receipt of application materials: none. Application fee required: 80,000 Colombian pesos. On-campus interview required.

Athletics Interscholastic: aerobics/dance (girls), baseball (b), basketball (b,g), dance (g), equestrian sports (b,g), gymnastics (b,g), horseback riding (b,g), running (b,g), soccer (b,g), swimming and diving (b,g), track and field (b,g), volleyball (b,g); intramural: gymnastics (b,g), soccer (b,g), softball (h), swimming and diving (b,g), track and field (b,g), volleyball (b,g). 11 PE instructors, 25 coaches.

Computers Computers are regularly used in graphic design, photography, Web site design, yearbook classes. Computer network features include Internet access, Internet filtering or blocking technology. The school has a published electronic and media policy.

Contact Mrs. Patricia Nasser, Admissions Assistant. 57-2-485-5050 Ext. 274. Fax: 57-2-4850453. E-mail: pnasser@colegiobolivar.edu.co. Website: www.colegiobolivar.edu.co

COLEGIO FRANKLIN D. ROOSEVELT

Av. Las Palmeras 325, Urbanizacion Camacho La Molina
Lima 12, Peru

Head of School: Dr. Kerry Ray Jacobson

General Information Coeducational day college-preparatory, general academic, arts, and technology school; primarily serves students with learning disabilities. Grades K–12. Founded: 1946. Setting: suburban. Nearest major city is Lima, Peru. 23-acre campus. 6 buildings on campus. Approved or accredited by International Baccalaureate Organization and Southern Association of Colleges and Schools. Affiliate member of National Association of Independent Schools. Languages of instruction: English, French, and Spanish. Total enrollment: 1,500. Upper school average class size: 24. Upper school faculty-student ratio: 1:12. There are 185 required school days per year for Upper School students. Upper School students typically attend 5 days per week. The average school day consists of 7 hours and 30 minutes.

Upper School Student Profile Grade 9: 121 students (69 boys, 52 girls); Grade 10: 126 students (65 boys, 61 girls); Grade 11: 116 students (65 boys, 51 girls); Grade 12: 92 students (57 boys, 35 girls).

Faculty School total: 182. In upper school: 20 men, 25 women; 26 have advanced degrees.

Subjects Offered Algebra, American history, American literature, art, biology, calculus, chemistry, computer programming, computer science, debate, digital photography, drama, early childhood, earth science, economics, English, ESL, fine arts, French, geography, geometry, global issues, health, history, International Baccalaureate courses, mathematics, model United Nations, music, orchestra, photography, physical education, physical science, social studies, Spanish, theory of knowledge, trigonometry, U.S. history, world history, yearbook.

Graduation Requirements Arts and fine arts (art, music, dance, drama), electives, English, foreign language, mathematics, physical education (includes health), science, social studies (includes history).

Special Academic Programs International Baccalaureate program; honors section; special instructional classes for students with mild learning disabilities; ESL (16 students enrolled).

College Admission Counseling 110 students graduated in 2016; 108 went to college, including Bowdoin College; Florida International University; Northwestern University; Syracuse University; The University of British Columbia; University of Miami. Other: 2 had other specific plans. Median SAT critical reading: 561, median SAT math: 598, median SAT writing: 574, median composite ACT: 26.

Student Life Upper grades have uniform requirement, student council, honor system. Discipline rests primarily with faculty.

Tuition and Aid Day student tuition: $15,570. Tuition installment plan (monthly payment plans). Need-based scholarship grants available. Total amount of financial aid awarded in 2016–17: $6200.

Admissions Traditional secondary-level entrance grade is 9. For fall 2016, 33 students applied for upper-level admission, 24 were accepted, 24 enrolled. ESL and math and English placement tests required. Deadline for receipt of application materials: none. Application fee required: $500. On-campus interview required.

Athletics Interscholastic: aquatics (boys, girls), basketball (b,g), field hockey (b), soccer (b,g), softball (b,g), swimming and diving (b,g), track and field (b,g), volleyball (b,g); intramural: aerobics (g), aquatics (b,g), basketball (b,g), dance (g), fitness (b,g), Fives (b), floor hockey (b), soccer (b,g), softball (b,g), swimming and diving (b,g), volleyball (b,g), water polo (b); coed interscholastic: aerobics, aquatics, dance, field hockey, fitness, floor hockey, martial arts, soccer, swimming and diving, track and field, volleyball; coed intramural: aerobics, aquatics, fitness, floor hockey, outdoor adventure, soccer, softball, swimming and diving, volleyball, wall climbing. 4 PE instructors, 20 coaches.

Computers Computers are regularly used in art, career exploration, creative writing, digital applications, English, history, library, mathematics, media production, music, photography, science, technology classes. Computer network features include on-campus library services, online commercial services, Internet access, wireless campus network, Internet filtering or blocking technology. Campus intranet and student e-mail accounts are available to students. Students grades are available online. The school has a published electronic and media policy.

Contact Ms. Nora Marquez, Registrar. 51-1-435-0890 Ext. 1002. Fax: 1-6199301. E-mail: nmarquez@amersol.edu.pe. Website: www.amersol.edu.pe

COLEGIO SAN JOSE

PO Box 21300
San Juan, Puerto Rico 00928-1300

Head of School: Br. Francisco T. Gonzalez, MD

General Information Boys' day college-preparatory, science, anatomy, and environmental science, and psychology, humanities, health, economy, political science school, affiliated with Roman Catholic Church. Grades 7–12. Founded: 1938. Setting: urban. 6-acre campus. 2 buildings on campus. Approved or accredited by Middle States Association of Colleges and Schools, National Catholic Education Association, The College Board, and Puerto Rico Department of Education. Languages of instruction: English and Spanish. Endowment: $293,000. Total enrollment: 489. Upper school average class size: 25. Upper school faculty-student ratio: 1:12. There are 172 required school days per year for Upper School students. Upper School students typically attend 5 days per week. The average school day consists of 6 hours and 50 minutes.

Upper School Student Profile Grade 7: 70 students (70 boys); Grade 8: 92 students (92 boys); Grade 9: 92 students (92 boys); Grade 10: 85 students (85 boys); Grade 11: 83 students (83 boys); Grade 12: 79 students (79 boys). 90% of students are Roman Catholic.

Faculty School total: 43. In upper school: 24 men, 21 women; 25 have advanced degrees.

Subjects Offered Accounting, algebra, American history, American literature, anatomy, art, art history, biology, biology-AP, broadcasting, business skills, calculus, chemistry, choir, Christian ethics, computer education, computer science, ecology, English, English literature, ethics, European history, French, French as a second language, geography, geometry, government/civics, grammar, health, history, instrumental music, keyboarding, mathematics, music, physical education, physics, pre-calculus, psychology, religion, science, social studies, Spanish, world history.

Graduation Requirements Business skills (includes word processing), computer science, English, foreign language, history, mathematics, physical education (includes health), religion (includes Bible studies and theology), science, social studies (includes history), Spanish, 40 hours of Christian community service.

Special Academic Programs International Baccalaureate program; Advanced Placement exam preparation; honors section; domestic exchange program.

College Admission Counseling 62 students graduated in 2016; all went to college, including University of Dayton; University of Puerto Rico, Mayagüez Campus; University of Puerto Rico, Río Piedras Campus.

Student Life Upper grades have uniform requirement, student council, honor system. Discipline rests equally with students and faculty. Attendance at religious services is required.

Summer Programs Remediation programs offered; session focuses on remediation/make-up; held on campus; accepts boys and girls; open to students from other schools. 150 students usually enrolled. 2017 schedule: June 1 to June 30. Application deadline: May 30.

Tuition and Aid Day student tuition: $7400. Tuition installment plan (The Tuition Plan, individually arranged payment plans). Need-based scholarship grants available. In 2016–17, 13% of upper-school students received aid.

Admissions Traditional secondary-level entrance grade is 9. Catholic High School Entrance Examination required. Deadline for receipt of application materials: February 28. Application fee required: $10. On-campus interview required.

Athletics Interscholastic: baseball, basketball, bowling, cross-country running, fitness, golf, indoor soccer, physical fitness, soccer, swimming and diving, table tennis, tennis, track and field, volleyball; intramural: cross-country running, indoor soccer, soccer, swimming and diving, tennis, track and field, volleyball. 4 PE instructors, 6 coaches, 1 athletic trainer.

Computers Computers are regularly used in accounting, art, creative writing, current events, data processing, English, foreign language, French as a second language, health, keyboarding, mathematics, music, psychology, science, Spanish, speech, writing, yearbook classes. Computer network features include on-campus library services, online commercial services, Internet access, wireless campus network, Internet filtering or blocking technology, Edline, Rediker. Campus intranet and student e-mail accounts are available to students. Students grades are available online. The school has a published electronic and media policy.

Contact Mrs. María E. Guzmán, M.Ed., Guidance Counselor. 787-751-8177 Ext. 229. Fax: 866-955-7646. E-mail: mguzman@csj-rpi.org. Website: www.csj-rpi.org

COLLEGEDALE ACADEMY

PO Box 628
4855 College Drive East
Collegedale, Tennessee 37315

Head of School: Dr. Brent Baldwin

General Information Coeducational day college-preparatory and religious studies school, affiliated with Seventh-day Adventists. Grades 9–12. Founded: 1892. Setting: small town. Nearest major city is Chattanooga. 20-acre campus. 3 buildings on campus. Approved or accredited by Board of Regents, General Conference of Seventh-day Adventists, Middle States Association of Colleges and Schools, Southern Association of Colleges and Schools, and Tennessee Department of Education. Endowment: $2.5 million. Total enrollment: 310. Upper school average class size: 25. Upper school faculty-student ratio: 1:16. There are 180 required school days per year for Upper School students. Upper School students typically attend 5 days per week. The average school day consists of 8 hours and 15 minutes.

Upper School Student Profile Grade 9: 65 students (27 boys, 38 girls); Grade 10: 86 students (42 boys, 44 girls); Grade 11: 74 students (39 boys, 35 girls); Grade 12: 73 students (32 boys, 41 girls). 98% of students are Seventh-day Adventists.

Faculty School total: 39. In upper school: 18 men, 17 women; 30 have advanced degrees.

Graduation Requirements Arts and fine arts (art, music, dance, drama), computer science, English, foreign language, mathematics, physical education (includes health), religion (includes Bible studies and theology), science, social studies (includes history), 20 hours of community service per year in attendance.

Special Academic Programs 1 Advanced Placement exam for which test preparation is offered; honors section; accelerated programs; independent study; study at local college for college credit.

College Admission Counseling 62 students graduated in 2016; all went to college, including Chattanooga State Community College; Southern Adventist University; The University of Tennessee; The University of Tennessee at Chattanooga; University of Kentucky; Walla Walla University. Other: 3 entered a postgraduate year. Median composite ACT: 22. 29% scored over 26 on composite ACT.

Student Life Upper grades have uniform requirement, student council, honor system. Discipline rests primarily with faculty. Attendance at religious services is required.

Summer Programs Enrichment, advancement programs offered; session focuses on U.S. history; held on campus; accepts boys and girls; open to students from other schools. 20 students usually enrolled. 2017 schedule: June 1 to July 1. Application deadline: May 1.

Tuition and Aid Day student tuition: $8950. Tuition installment plan (monthly payment plans). Need-based scholarship grants available. In 2016–17, 30% of upper-school students received aid. Total amount of financial aid awarded in 2016–17: $210,000.

Admissions Traditional secondary-level entrance grade is 9. For fall 2016, 321 students applied for upper-level admission, 301 were accepted, 299 enrolled. Mathematics proficiency exam required. Deadline for receipt of application materials: August 1. Application fee required: $125. On-campus interview recommended.

Athletics Interscholastic: cross-country running (boys, girls), golf (b,g), tennis (b,g); intramural: basketball (b,g), soccer (b,g), track and field (b,g), volleyball (b,g); coed intramural: flag football, gymnastics, hiking/backpacking, paddle tennis, volleyball. 2 PE instructors, 2 coaches.

Computers Computers are regularly used in Bible studies, history, mathematics, publications, social studies, study skills, writing classes. Computer network features include on-campus library services, Internet access, wireless campus network, Internet filtering or blocking technology. Student e-mail accounts and computer access in designated common areas are available to students. Students grades are available online. The school has a published electronic and media policy.

Contact Miss Kerre Conerly, Registrar. 423-396-2124 Ext. 5421. Fax: 423-396-3363. E-mail: kconerly@collegedaleacademy.com. Website: www.collegedaleacademy.com

THE COLLEGIATE SCHOOL

103 North Mooreland Road
Richmond, Virginia 23229

Head of School: Stephen D. Hickman

General Information Coeducational day college-preparatory school. Grades JK–12. Founded: 1915. Setting: suburban. 211-acre campus. 13 buildings on campus. Approved or accredited by Southern Association of Colleges and Schools, Southern Association of Independent Schools, Virginia Association of Independent Schools, and Virginia Department of Education. Member of National Association of Independent Schools and Secondary School Admission Test Board. Endowment: $54 million. Total enrollment: 1,644. Upper school average class size: 15. Upper school faculty-student ratio: 1:15. There are 174 required school days per year for Upper School students. Upper School students typically attend 5 days per week. The average school day consists of 7 hours.

Upper School Student Profile Grade 9: 139 students (68 boys, 71 girls); Grade 10: 134 students (69 boys, 65 girls); Grade 11: 132 students (65 boys, 67 girls); Grade 12: 123 students (58 boys, 65 girls).

Faculty School total: 199. In upper school: 31 men, 35 women; 42 have advanced degrees.

Subjects Offered 20th century history, acting, advanced chemistry, African studies, algebra, American Civil War, American history, American history-AP, American literature, anatomy, art, Asian literature, Bible as literature, biology, biology-AP, calculus-AP, ceramics, chemistry, chemistry-AP, community service, computer applications, computer science-AP, creative writing, drama, driver education, earth science, economics, economics-AP, English, English literature, ethics, European history, film and literature, fine arts, French, French-AP, geometry, government and politics-AP, government/civics, health, journalism, Latin, music, photography, physics, physics-AP, religion, robotics, Russian literature, senior project, senior seminar, Spanish, Spanish language-AP, statistics, statistics-AP, technical theater, theater, theater design and production, trigonometry, world history, World War II.

Graduation Requirements Arts and fine arts (art, music, dance, drama), English, ethics, foreign language, government, history, mathematics, physical education (includes health), religion (includes Bible studies and theology), science, sports, senior speech, senior project. Community service is required.

Special Academic Programs 16 Advanced Placement exams for which test preparation is offered; honors section; independent study; study at local college for college credit; programs in general development for dyslexic students.

College Admission Counseling 126 students graduated in 2016; all went to college, including James Madison University; University of South Carolina; University of Virginia; Washington and Lee University. Mean SAT critical reading: 607, mean SAT math: 627, mean SAT writing: 601, mean combined SAT: 1836, mean composite ACT: 29. 53% scored over 600 on SAT critical reading, 61% scored over 600 on SAT math, 50% scored over 600 on SAT writing, 57% scored over 1800 on combined SAT, 76% scored over 26 on composite ACT.

Student Life Upper grades have specified standards of dress, student council, honor system. Discipline rests equally with students and faculty.

Summer Programs Remediation, enrichment, advancement, sports, art/fine arts, computer instruction programs offered; session focuses on advancement, remediation, sports; held both on and off campus; accepts boys and girls; open to students from other schools. 1,327 students usually enrolled. 2017 schedule: June 12 to August 11. Application deadline: none.

Tuition and Aid Day student tuition: $24,980. Tuition installment plan (Insured Tuition Payment Plan, monthly payment plans). Need-based scholarship grants available.

Admissions Traditional secondary-level entrance grade is 9. For fall 2016, 118 students applied for upper-level admission, 54 were accepted, 27 enrolled. PSAT and SAT for applicants to grade 11 and 12, SSAT or writing sample required. Deadline for receipt of application materials: none. Application fee required: $50. Interview required.

Athletics Interscholastic: baseball (boys), basketball (b,g), cross-country running (b,g), diving (b,g), field hockey (g), football (b), indoor track & field (b,g), lacrosse (b,g), soccer (b,g), softball (g), swimming and diving (b,g), tennis (b,g), track and field (b,g), volleyball (g), winter (indoor) track (b,g), wrestling (b); coed interscholastic: golf, indoor soccer; coed intramural: combined training, dance, dance squad, dance team, fitness, hiking/backpacking, modern dance, mountain biking, outdoor activities, outdoor adventure, strength & conditioning, weight lifting, yoga. 5 PE instructors, 50 coaches, 2 athletic trainers.

Computers Computers are regularly used in all academic classes. Computer network features include on-campus library services, Internet access, wireless campus network, Internet filtering or blocking technology. Campus intranet, student e-mail accounts, and computer access in designated common areas are available to students. Students grades are available online. The school has a published electronic and media policy.

Contact Brent I. Miller, Director of Middle/Upper School Admission. 804-726-3273. Fax: 804-741-9797. E-mail: brent_miller@collegiate-va.org. Website: www.collegiate-va.org/

THE COLORADO ROCKY MOUNTAIN SCHOOL

500 Holden Way
Carbondale, Colorado 81623

Head of School: Jeff Leahy

General Information Coeducational boarding and day college-preparatory and arts school. Grades 9–12. Founded: 1953. Setting: small town. Nearest major city is Denver. Students are housed in single-sex dormitories. 350-acre campus. 23 buildings on campus. Approved or accredited by Association for Experiential Education, Association of Colorado Independent Schools, The Association of Boarding Schools, and Colorado Department of Education. Member of National Association of Independent Schools and Secondary School Admission Test Board. Endowment: $20 million. Total enrollment: 176. Upper school average class size: 12. Upper school faculty-student ratio: 1:5. There are 175 required school days per year for Upper School students. Upper School students typically attend 5 days per week. The average school day consists of 8 hours.

Upper School Student Profile Grade 9: 43 students (23 boys, 20 girls); Grade 10: 46 students (26 boys, 20 girls); Grade 11: 38 students (21 boys, 17 girls); Grade 12: 49 students (30 boys, 19 girls). 57% of students are boarding students. 59% are state residents. 22 states are represented in upper school student body. 20% are international students. International students from China, Germany, Japan, Macedonia, Mexico, and Mongolia; 6 other countries represented in student body.

Faculty School total: 35. In upper school: 20 men, 15 women; 19 have advanced degrees; 33 reside on campus.

Subjects Offered Advanced Placement courses, algebra, American literature, art, art history, biology, calculus, ceramics, chemistry, computer programming, computer science, creative writing, drama, ecology, English, English literature, environmental science, ESL, ethics, European history, fine arts, gardening, geography, geology, geometry, geopolitics, government/civics, grammar, graphic design, guitar, history, history of ideas, journalism, mathematics, music, philosophy, photography, physical education, physics, physiology, religion, robotics, science, senior project, Shakespeare, social studies, Spanish, theater, trigonometry, video film production, Western civilization, world history, world literature, writing.

Graduation Requirements Arts and fine arts (art, music, dance, drama), biology, chemistry, English, foreign language, mathematics, science, senior project, social studies (includes history), wilderness experience, participation in wilderness orientation. Community service is required.

Special Academic Programs 5 Advanced Placement exams for which test preparation is offered; independent study; academic accommodation for the gifted, the musically talented, and the artistically talented; ESL (10 students enrolled).

College Admission Counseling 39 students graduated in 2015; 37 went to college, including Lewis & Clark College; Middlebury College; The Colorado College; University of Colorado Boulder; University of Pennsylvania. Other: 2 entered military service. Mean SAT critical reading: 520, mean SAT math: 525, mean SAT writing: 515, mean combined SAT: 1561, mean composite ACT: 24. 23% scored over 600 on SAT critical reading, 23% scored over 600 on SAT math, 8% scored over 600 on SAT writing, 13% scored over 1800 on combined SAT, 28% scored over 26 on composite ACT.

Student Life Upper grades have student council, honor system. Discipline rests equally with students and faculty.

Tuition and Aid Day student tuition: $32,500; 7-day tuition and room/board: $52,000. Tuition installment plan (monthly payment plans, individually arranged payment plans, 3rd party loan options). Merit scholarship grants, need-based scholarship grants available. In 2015–16, 30% of upper-school students received aid; total upper-school merit-scholarship money awarded: $45,500. Total amount of financial aid awarded in 2015–16: $2,072,750.

Admissions Traditional secondary-level entrance grade is 9. For fall 2015, 157 students applied for upper-level admission, 100 were accepted, 70 enrolled. PSAT or SAT, SSAT or TOEFL required. Deadline for receipt of application materials: February 15. Application fee required: $75. Interview required.

Athletics Intramural: aerobics/dance (girls), basketball (b,g), dance (b,g), fly fishing (b,g), freestyle skiing (b,g); coed interscholastic: alpine skiing, bicycling, canoeing/kayaking, climbing, cross-country running, independent competitive sports, kayaking, mountain biking, nordic skiing, rock climbing, running, skiing (downhill), snowboarding, telemark skiing, wall climbing; coed intramural: alpine skiing, backpacking, basketball, bicycling, canoeing/kayaking, climbing, cross-country running, dance, fishing, fitness, floor hockey, fly fishing, freestyle skiing, Frisbee, hiking/backpacking, horseback riding, horseshoes, jogging, kayaking, martial arts, mountain biking, mountaineering, nordic skiing, outdoor activities, outdoor adventure, outdoor education, outdoor recreation, outdoor skills, outdoors, physical fitness, physical training, rafting, rock climbing, running, skiing (cross-country), skiing (downhill), snowboarding, strength & conditioning, swimming and diving, telemark skiing, wall climbing, weight lifting, wilderness, wilderness survival, yoga. 4 coaches.

Computers Computers are regularly used in art, college planning, ESL, mathematics, science classes. Computer network features include on-campus library services, online commercial services, Internet access, wireless campus network, Internet filtering or blocking technology. Student e-mail accounts are available to students. Students grades are available online. The school has a published electronic and media policy.
Contact Molly Dorais, Director of Admission and Financial Aid. 970-963-2562. Fax: 970-963-9865. E-mail: mdorais@crms.org. Website: www.crms.org

THE COLORADO SPRINGS SCHOOL

21 Broadmoor Avenue
Colorado Springs, Colorado 80906

Head of School: Mr. Aaron Schubach

General Information Coeducational day college-preparatory, arts, experiential and project-based learning, and global perspectives school. Grades PK–12. Founded: 1962. Setting: suburban. 30-acre campus. 7 buildings on campus. Approved or accredited by Association of Colorado Independent Schools. Member of National Association of Independent Schools and National Association for College Admission Counseling. Endowment: $3.1 million. Total enrollment: 274. Upper school average class size: 16. Upper school faculty-student ratio: 1:7. There are 169 required school days per year for Upper School students. Upper School students typically attend 5 days per week. The average school day consists of 6 hours and 30 minutes.

Upper School Student Profile Grade 9: 21 students (11 boys, 10 girls); Grade 10: 22 students (11 boys, 11 girls); Grade 11: 32 students (14 boys, 18 girls); Grade 12: 23 students (12 boys, 11 girls).

Faculty School total: 46. In upper school: 11 men, 13 women; 18 have advanced degrees.

Subjects Offered 20th century history, 3-dimensional art, 3-dimensional design, ACT preparation, acting, adolescent issues, advanced chemistry, advanced math, Advanced Placement courses, advanced studio art-AP, African history, African studies, algebra, American government, American history, American history-AP, American literature, American literature-AP, American studies, analysis and differential calculus, anatomy and physiology, art history, art-AP, athletics, band, biology, biology-AP, botany, British literature, British literature-AP, calculus, calculus-AP, career education internship, career/college preparation, ceramics, chemistry, choir, choral music, clayworking, college admission preparation, college counseling, community service, comparative government and politics, comparative government and politics-AP, composition, computer applications, concert band, costumes and make-up, creative arts, digital art, digital photography, directing, discrete mathematics, drama, drawing, economics, economics-AP, English, English literature, English literature and composition-AP, English literature-AP, environmental science, environmental science-AP, environmental studies, equality and freedom, ethics, European history-AP, European literature, experiential education, filmmaking, fine arts, French, French language-AP, French literature-AP, French-AP, functions, gardening, geography, geology, geometry, glassblowing, global studies, government and politics-AP, grammar, health and wellness, history, history-AP, Latin American history, literature, macro/microeconomics-AP, microeconomics, music, music appreciation, musical productions, painting, philosophy, photography, photojournalism, physical education, physics, physics-AP, playwriting, post-calculus, pottery, pre-algebra, pre-calculus, printmaking, SAT/ACT preparation, science, sculpture, Spanish, Spanish literature, Spanish literature-AP, speech, statistics, statistics-AP, stone carving, studio art, studio art-AP, textiles, theater, theater arts, theater production, trigonometry, U.S. history, U.S. history-AP, welding, Western civilization, wilderness education, wilderness experience, world affairs, world civilizations, world cultures, world geography, world governments, world history, world history-AP, world issues, world literature, world religions, writing, writing workshop, yearbook.

Graduation Requirements Arts and fine arts (art, music, dance, drama), athletics, college admission preparation, English, experiential education, foreign language, mathematics, science, social studies (includes history), speech and oral interpretations, experience-centered seminar each year, college overview course, 24 hours of community service per each year of high school.

Special Academic Programs Advanced Placement exam preparation; honors section; independent study; term-away projects; academic accommodation for the gifted; programs in general development for dyslexic students; special instructional classes for deaf students.

College Admission Counseling 26 students graduated in 2015; 25 went to college, including University of Colorado Boulder. Other: 1 had other specific plans. Mean combined SAT: 1952, mean composite ACT: 27.

Student Life Upper grades have specified standards of dress, student council, honor system. Discipline rests equally with students and faculty.

Tuition and Aid Day student tuition: $20,850. Tuition installment plan (Insured Tuition Payment Plan, monthly payment plans, individually arranged payment plans). Merit scholarship grants, need-based scholarship grants available. In 2014–15, 46% of upper-school students received aid; total upper-school merit-scholarship money awarded: $165,750. Total amount of financial aid awarded in 2014–15: $347,902.

Admissions Traditional secondary-level entrance grade is 9. For fall 2015, 11 students applied for upper-level admission, 10 were accepted, 9 enrolled. Standardized test scores or TOEFL required. Deadline for receipt of application materials: none. Application fee required: $75. On-campus interview required.

Athletics Interscholastic: basketball (boys, girls), cross-country running (b,g), golf (b), lacrosse (b), soccer (b,g), tennis (b,g), volleyball (b,g); intramural: archery (b,g), climbing (b,g), Frisbee (b,g), physical fitness (b,g), physical training (b,g); coed interscholastic: mountain biking; coed intramural: fly fishing, golf, mountaineering, outdoor activities, outdoor adventure, outdoor education, paddle tennis, rock climbing, skiing (cross-country), skiing (downhill), wilderness, yoga. 2 PE instructors, 8 coaches.
Computers Computer network features include on-campus library services, online commercial services, Internet access, wireless campus network, Internet filtering or blocking technology. Campus intranet, student e-mail accounts, and computer access in designated common areas are available to students. Students grades are available online. The school has a published electronic and media policy.
Contact Ms. Lisa Kleintjes Kamemoto, Director of Admission and Marketing. 719-434-3500. Fax: 719-475-9864. E-mail: lisakk@css.org. Website: www.css.org

COLUMBIA ACADEMY

1101 West 7th Street
Columbia, Tennessee 38401

Head of School: Dr. James Thomas

General Information Coeducational day college-preparatory school, affiliated with Church of Christ. Grades K–12. Founded: 1978. Setting: small town. Nearest major city is Nashville. 67-acre campus. 6 buildings on campus. Approved or accredited by National Christian School Association, Southern Association of Colleges and Schools, and Tennessee Department of Education. Endowment: $2.8 million. Total enrollment: 748. Upper school average class size: 17. Upper school faculty-student ratio: 1:12. There are 175 required school days per year for Upper School students. Upper School students typically attend 5 days per week. The average school day consists of 7 hours.

Upper School Student Profile Grade 7: 71 students (27 boys, 44 girls); Grade 8: 55 students (31 boys, 24 girls); Grade 9: 74 students (44 boys, 30 girls); Grade 10: 77 students (50 boys, 27 girls); Grade 11: 72 students (40 boys, 32 girls); Grade 12: 48 students (21 boys, 27 girls). 60% of students are members of Church of Christ.

Faculty School total: 35. In upper school: 18 men, 17 women; 14 have advanced degrees.

Subjects Offered Accounting, ACT preparation, advanced math, algebra, American history, American literature, anatomy and physiology, art, band, Bible, biology, British literature, calculus-AP, chemistry, computer applications, economics, English, English literature and composition-AP, environmental science, fine arts, geometry, government/civics, grammar, health, math review, multimedia, music, personal finance, physical education, physics, pre-calculus, religion, Spanish, speech, theater, theater arts, U.S. history-AP, world geography, world history.

Graduation Requirements ACT preparation, arts and fine arts (art, music, dance, drama), computer applications, economics, electives, English, foreign language, mathematics, physical education (includes health), religion (includes Bible studies and theology), science, social sciences, social studies (includes history), speech, four hours of approved service required for each quarter enrolled.

Special Academic Programs Advanced Placement exam preparation; honors section; independent study; study at local college for college credit.

College Admission Counseling 41 students graduated in 2016; 40 went to college, including Columbia State Community College; Freed-Hardeman University; Harding University; Lipscomb University; Pepperdine University; Samford University. Other: 1 entered a postgraduate year. Median composite ACT: 23. 37% scored over 26 on composite ACT.

Student Life Upper grades have specified standards of dress, student council, honor system. Discipline rests primarily with faculty.

Summer Programs Remediation programs offered; session focuses on make-up or credit recovery for failing grades during the semesters; held on campus; accepts boys and girls; not open to students from other schools. 10 students usually enrolled. 2017 schedule: May 22 to June 20. Application deadline: May 11.

Tuition and Aid Day student tuition: $7900. Tuition installment plan (monthly payment plans, individually arranged payment plans). Tuition reduction for siblings, need-based scholarship grants, paying campus jobs available. In 2016–17, 5% of upper-school students received aid. Total amount of financial aid awarded in 2016–17: $36,100.

Admissions Traditional secondary-level entrance grade is 9. For fall 2016, 44 students applied for upper-level admission, 39 were accepted, 38 enrolled. Otis-Lennon School Ability Test required. Deadline for receipt of application materials: none. Application fee required: $75. On-campus interview recommended.

Athletics Interscholastic: baseball (boys), basketball (b,g), cheering (g), football (b), golf (b,g), soccer (b,g), softball (g), tennis (b,g), trap and skeet (b,g), volleyball (g); coed interscholastic: bowling, cross-country running, marksmanship. 1 PE instructor.

Computers Computers are regularly used in all academic, computer applications, keyboarding, library, yearbook classes. Computer network features include on-campus library services, Internet access, wireless campus network, Internet filtering or blocking technology, students in grades 7-12 are issued iPads. Campus intranet, student e-mail accounts, and computer access in designated common areas are available to students. Students grades are available online. The school has a published electronic and media policy.
Contact Mrs. Emily Lansdell, Director of Admissions. 931-398-5355. Fax: 931-398-5359. E-mail: emily.lansdell@cabulldogs.org. Website: www.columbia-academy.net

COLUMBIA INTERNATIONAL SCHOOL

153 Matsugo

Tokorozawa, Saitama 359-0027, Japan

Head of School: Mr. Barrie McCliggott

General Information Coeducational boarding and day and distance learning college-preparatory and language school. Boarding grades 7–12, day grades 1–12. Founded: 1988. Setting: small town. Nearest major city is Tokyo, Japan. Students are housed in single-sex by floor dormitories. 2-acre campus. 3 buildings on campus. Approved or accredited by Ontario Ministry of Education, Western Association of Schools and Colleges, and state department of education. Language of instruction: English. Endowment: ¥100 million. Total enrollment: 225. Upper school average class size: 15. Upper school faculty-student ratio: 1:12. There are 180 required school days per year for Upper School students. Upper School students typically attend 5 days per week. The average school day consists of 5 hours and 30 minutes.

Upper School Student Profile Grade 6: 15 students (6 boys, 9 girls); Grade 7: 20 students (10 boys, 10 girls); Grade 8: 16 students (10 boys, 6 girls); Grade 9: 14 students (6 boys, 8 girls); Grade 10: 19 students (11 boys, 8 girls); Grade 11: 30 students (14 boys, 16 girls); Grade 12: 26 students (18 boys, 8 girls). 20% of students are boarding students. 1 state is represented in upper school student body. 100% are international students. International students from Canada, China, Republic of Korea, Russian Federation, Thailand, and United States; 17 other countries represented in student body.

Faculty School total: 24. In upper school: 12 men, 3 women; 7 have advanced degrees; 2 reside on campus.

Subjects Offered 1 1/2 elective credits, 20th century world history, advanced TOEFL/grammar, algebra, ancient world history, art, Asian history, biology, business, calculus, Canadian geography, Canadian history, chemistry, communications, community service, computer science, computers, economics, English, ESL, foreign language, geography, geometry, global issues, history, Internet, keyboarding, literacy, mathematics, media studies, physical education, reading, TOEFL preparation, world issues, yearbook.

Graduation Requirements 20th century history, arts, Asian history, biology, chemistry, economics, English, geography, humanities, law, mathematics, physical education (includes health), science, social sciences, Ontario Literacy Test, 40 hours of community involvement activities.

Special Academic Programs Advanced Placement exam preparation; honors section; accelerated programs; independent study; study abroad; remedial reading and/or remedial writing; remedial math; ESL (20 students enrolled).

College Admission Counseling 14 students graduated in 2016; all went to college, including Queens University of Charlotte; Temple University; The University of British Columbia; University of Saskatchewan; University of Victoria; Western Michigan University.

Student Life Upper grades have uniform requirement, student council, honor system. Discipline rests primarily with faculty.

Summer Programs Remediation, enrichment, advancement, ESL, sports, art/fine arts, computer instruction programs offered; session focuses on ESL, computers, science, and art; held both on and off campus; accepts boys and girls; open to students from other schools. 250 students usually enrolled. 2017 schedule: July 5 to August 31. Application deadline: June 30.

Tuition and Aid Day student tuition: ¥1,575,000; 7-day tuition and room/board: ¥2,805,000. Tuition installment plan (individually arranged payment plans, term payment plans). Tuition reduction for siblings, merit scholarship grants available. In 2016–17, 5% of upper-school students received aid; total upper-school merit-scholarship money awarded: ¥2,735,000. Total amount of financial aid awarded in 2016–17: ¥3,360,000.

Admissions Traditional secondary-level entrance grade is 10. For fall 2016, 53 students applied for upper-level admission, 30 were accepted, 26 enrolled. Any standardized test required. Deadline for receipt of application materials: none. Application fee required: ¥25,000. Interview recommended.

Athletics Coed Interscholastic: basketball, dance, football, soccer; coed intramural: aerobics, alpine skiing, artistic gym, badminton, ball hockey, baseball, bicycling, bowling, climbing, cooperative games, dance team, field hockey, fitness, flag football, floor hockey, freestyle skiing, Frisbee, golf, hiking/backpacking, hockey, horseback riding, indoor hockey, indoor soccer, juggling, kickball, life saving, mountain biking, outdoor activities, physical fitness, power lifting, rock climbing, self defense, skiing (downhill), snowboarding, softball, table tennis, team handball, tennis, volleyball, wall climbing, weight lifting, weight training, yoga. 2 PE instructors.

Computers Computers are regularly used in all classes. Computer network features include Internet access, wireless campus network, Internet filtering or blocking technology, repair service. Campus intranet and student e-mail accounts are available to students. The school has a published electronic and media policy.

Contact Mr. Tetsuya Morimata, Administrator. 81-4-2946-1911. Fax: 81-4-2946-1955. E-mail: morimata@columbia-ca.co.jp. Website: www.columbia-ca.co.jp

THE COLUMBUS ACADEMY

4300 Cherry Bottom Road
Gahanna, Ohio 43230

Head of School: Melissa B. Soderberg

General Information Coeducational day college-preparatory school. Grades PK–12. Founded: 1911. Setting: suburban. Nearest major city is Columbus. 231-acre campus. 16 buildings on campus. Approved or accredited by Independent Schools Association of the Central States and Ohio Department of Education. Member of National Association of Independent Schools and Secondary School Admission Test Board. Endowment: $38 million. Total enrollment: 1,080. Upper school average class size: 14. Upper school faculty-student ratio: 1:8. There are 180 required school days per year for Upper School students. Upper School students typically attend 5 days per week. The average school day consists of 7 hours and 5 minutes.

Upper School Student Profile Grade 6: 84 students (43 boys, 41 girls); Grade 7: 94 students (43 boys, 51 girls); Grade 8: 83 students (39 boys, 44 girls); Grade 9: 101 students (53 boys, 48 girls); Grade 10: 99 students (50 boys, 49 girls); Grade 11: 97 students (49 boys, 48 girls); Grade 12: 95 students (51 boys, 44 girls).

Faculty School total: 148. In upper school: 25 men, 22 women; 36 have advanced degrees.

Subjects Offered Advanced chemistry, advanced computer applications, advanced math, Advanced Placement courses, advanced studio art-AP, algebra, American history, American history-AP, American literature, analysis and differential calculus, art history, biology, biology-AP, British literature, calculus, calculus-AP, career/college preparation, ceramics, chemistry, chemistry-AP, Chinese, choir, choral music, chorus, college counseling, comparative government and politics-AP, comparative political systems-AP, computer applications, computer education, computer science, computer science-AP, concert band, concert choir, creative writing, drawing and design, economics, economics-AP, English, European history, fine arts, French-AP, geology, geometry, government and politics-AP, government-AP, health education, history of China and Japan, instrumental music, Latin, Latin-AP, military history, photography, physical education, physics, physics-AP, pre-calculus, robotics, senior career experience, South African history, Spanish, Spanish language-AP, Spanish literature-AP, speech, statistics-AP, strings, theater, trigonometry, U.S. government and politics-AP, U.S. history-AP, United States government-AP, weight training, world history, world religions.

Graduation Requirements Arts and fine arts (art, music, dance, drama), English, foreign language, mathematics, science, social studies (includes history), formal speech delivered to the students and faculty of the upper school during junior year, community service requirement.

Special Academic Programs 21 Advanced Placement exams for which test preparation is offered; honors section; independent study; academic accommodation for the gifted.

College Admission Counseling 91 students graduated in 2016; 90 went to college, including Columbia University; Harvard University; Miami University; Purdue University; The Ohio State University; Washington University in St. Louis. Other: 1 entered military service. Mean SAT critical reading: 653, mean SAT math: 669, mean SAT writing: 647, mean combined SAT: 1969, mean composite ACT: 30.

Student Life Upper grades have specified standards of dress, student council. Discipline rests equally with students and faculty.

Summer Programs Remediation, enrichment, advancement, art/fine arts, computer instruction programs offered; session focuses on academic enrichment, fine arts, fun and games; held on campus; accepts boys and girls; open to students from other schools. 600 students usually enrolled. 2017 schedule: June 15 to August 22.

Tuition and Aid Day student tuition: $21,600–$25,000. Tuition installment plan (The Tuition Plan, Tuition Management Systems Plan). Merit scholarship grants, need-based scholarship grants available. In 2016–17, 22% of upper-school students received aid. Total amount of financial aid awarded in 2016–17: $1,230,000.

Admissions Traditional secondary-level entrance grade is 9. For fall 2016, 84 students applied for upper-level admission, 45 were accepted, 32 enrolled. SSAT, ERB, PSAT, SAT, PLAN or ACT required. Deadline for receipt of application materials: February 10. Application fee required: $50. On-campus interview recommended.

Athletics Interscholastic: baseball (boys), basketball (b,g), bowling (b,g), cross-country running (b,g), diving (b,g), field hockey (g), football (b), lacrosse (b,g), soccer (b,g), swimming and diving (b,g), tennis (b,g), track and field (b,g), volleyball (g), wrestling (b); coed intramural: bicycling. 3 PE instructors, 30 coaches, 2 athletic trainers.

Computers Computers are regularly used in college planning, current events, economics, English, foreign language, humanities, journalism, Latin, learning cognition, library skills, mathematics, media production, multimedia, music, photography, publications, reading, research skills, SAT preparation, science, technology, theater, writing, yearbook classes. Computer network features include on-campus library services, online commercial services, Internet access, wireless campus network. Campus intranet, student e-mail accounts, and computer access in designated common areas are available to students. Students grades are available online. The school has a published electronic and media policy.

Contact John Wuorinen, Director of Admissions and Financial Aid. 614-509-2220. Fax: 614-475-0396. E-mail: admissions@columbusacademy.org. Website: http://www.ColumbusAcademy.org

COLUMBUS SCHOOL FOR GIRLS

56 South Columbia Avenue
Columbus, Ohio 43209

Head of School: Mrs. Jennifer Ciccarelli

General Information Girls' day college-preparatory and STEM school. Grades PK–12. Founded: 1898. Setting: urban. 150-acre campus. 1 building on campus. Approved or accredited by Independent Schools Association of the Central States and Ohio Association of Independent Schools. Member of National Association of Independent Schools. Endowment: $17.2 million. Total enrollment: 562. Upper school average class size: 13. Upper school faculty-student ratio: 1:8. There are 170 required school days per year for Upper School students. Upper School students typically attend 5 days per week. The average school day consists of 7 hours and 30 minutes.

Upper School Student Profile Grade 6: 40 students (40 girls); Grade 7: 50 students (50 girls); Grade 8: 44 students (44 girls); Grade 9: 51 students (51 girls); Grade 10: 56 students (56 girls); Grade 11: 48 students (48 girls); Grade 12: 42 students (42 girls).

Faculty School total: 74. In upper school: 10 men, 16 women; 19 have advanced degrees.

Subjects Offered Acting, Advanced Placement courses, algebra, American literature, astronomy, band, biology, biology-AP, British literature, calculus, calculus-AP, ceramics, chemistry, chemistry-AP, civics, college admission preparation, comparative government and politics-AP, computer science, concert choir, digital photography, discrete mathematics, drawing, economics, English, English language and composition-AP, English literature and composition-AP, European history-AP, fine arts, geometry, German, health, lab science, Latin, Latin-AP, Mandarin, modern European history-AP, music theory-AP, newspaper, philosophy, photography, physical education, physics, physics-AP, pre-calculus, public speaking, robotics, senior seminar, Spanish, Spanish language-AP, statistics, strings, studio art-AP, theater, trigonometry, U.S. government and politics-AP, U.S. history, visual arts, vocal ensemble, world history, world literature, world religions, yearbook.

Graduation Requirements Algebra, arts and fine arts (art, music, dance, drama), biology, chemistry, civics, college planning, electives, English, foreign language, geometry, health, mathematics, physical education (includes health), physics, public speaking, science, self-defense, senior project, technology, U.S. history, world history, self-defense, service hours, water safety.

Special Academic Programs Advanced Placement exam preparation; honors section; independent study; study at local college for college credit.

College Admission Counseling 53 students graduated in 2016; all went to college, including Denison University; Furman University; Kenyon College; Miami University; The Ohio State University; University of Chicago. Median SAT critical reading: 680, median SAT math: 630, median SAT writing: 640, median combined SAT: 1930, median composite ACT: 29. 80% scored over 600 on SAT critical reading, 60% scored over 600 on SAT math, 56% scored over 600 on SAT writing, 72% scored over 1800 on combined SAT, 70% scored over 26 on composite ACT.

Student Life Upper grades have uniform requirement, student council, honor system. Discipline rests primarily with faculty.

Summer Programs Remediation, enrichment, advancement, sports, art/fine arts, rigorous outdoor training, computer instruction programs offered; session focuses on academic areas; held both on and off campus; accepts boys and girls; open to students from other schools. 446 students usually enrolled. 2017 schedule: June 12 to August 4. Application deadline: June 12.

Tuition and Aid Day student tuition: $20,595–$24,625. Merit scholarship grants, need-based scholarship grants available. In 2016–17, 24% of upper-school students received aid; total upper-school merit-scholarship money awarded: $74,120. Total amount of financial aid awarded in 2016–17: $697,799.

Admissions Traditional secondary-level entrance grade is 9. For fall 2016, 57 students applied for upper-level admission, 32 were accepted, 19 enrolled. ISEE or school's own test required. Deadline for receipt of application materials: February 6. Application fee required: $50. On-campus interview required.

Athletics Interscholastic: aquatics, basketball, cross-country running, diving, field hockey, golf, independent competitive sports, lacrosse, running, soccer, swimming and diving, tennis, track and field, volleyball; intramural: aquatics, basketball, cross-country running, diving, field hockey, golf, lacrosse, martial arts, running, self defense, soccer, swimming and diving, tennis, track and field, volleyball. 1 PE instructor, 31 coaches, 1 athletic trainer.

Computers Computers are regularly used in art, English, foreign language, freshman foundations, health, history, mathematics, music, publications, science, technology, theater, yearbook classes. Computer network features include on-campus library services, online commercial services, Internet access, wireless campus network, Internet filtering or blocking technology, 1:1 tablet program. Campus intranet, student e-mail accounts, and computer access in designated common areas are available to students. Students grades are available online. The school has a published electronic and media policy.

Contact Jenni Biehn, Director of Admission and Financial Aid. 614-252-0781 Ext. 104. Fax: 614-252-0571. E-mail: jbiehn@columbusschoolforgirls.org. Website: www.columbusschoolforgirls.org

COMMONWEALTH SCHOOL

151 Commonwealth Avenue

Boston, Massachusetts 02116

Head of School: Mr. William D. Wharton

General Information Coeducational day college-preparatory school. Grades 9–12. Founded: 1957. Setting: urban. 1 building on campus. Approved or accredited by Association of Independent Schools in New England, New England Association of Schools and Colleges, and Massachusetts Department of Education. Member of National Association of Independent Schools and Secondary School Admission Test Board. Endowment: $16 million. Total enrollment: 145. Upper school average class size: 12. Upper school faculty-student ratio: 1:5. Upper School students typically attend 5 days per week. The average school day consists of 6 hours and 30 minutes.

Upper School Student Profile Grade 9: 43 students (24 boys, 19 girls); Grade 10: 37 students (23 boys, 14 girls); Grade 11: 28 students (8 boys, 20 girls); Grade 12: 39 students (19 boys, 20 girls).

Faculty School total: 38. In upper school: 14 men, 24 women; 27 have advanced degrees.

Subjects Offered 20th century American writers, 20th century history, acting, advanced biology, advanced chemistry, advanced computer applications, advanced math, Advanced Placement courses, African-American literature, algebra, American history, American history-AP, American literature, ancient history, ancient world history, art, art history, biology, biology-AP, calculus, calculus-AP, ceramics, chamber groups, chemistry, chemistry-AP, choral music, chorus, classics, computer programming, computer science, creative writing, dance, drama, drawing, economics, economics-AP, English, English literature, English-AP, environmental science, environmental studies, ethics, European history, European history-AP, expository writing, film, film history, film studies, fine arts, foreign language, French, French language-AP, French literature-AP, French studies, French-AP, geometry, health and safety, Hispanic literature, history of the Americas, Japanese history, jazz, jazz band, jazz ensemble, jazz theory, Latin, Latin American history, Latin-AP, mathematics, mathematics-AP, medieval history, medieval/Renaissance history, modern European history-AP, music, music theory, music theory-AP, orchestra, organic chemistry, painting, performing arts, philosophy, photography, physical education, physics, physics-AP, pottery, pre-calculus, printmaking, probability and statistics, psychology, Russian literature, science, short story, society, politics and law, Spanish, Spanish language-AP, Spanish literature, Spanish literature-AP, Spanish-AP, studio art, theater, U.S. history-AP, visual and performing arts, visual arts, voice ensemble, writing.

Graduation Requirements Algebra, ancient history, art, biology, calculus, chemistry, English, ethics, foreign language, geometry, medieval history, physical education (includes health), physics, U.S. history, City of Boston course, completion of a one- to three-week project each year (with report), Health and Community. Community service is required.

Special Academic Programs Advanced Placement exam preparation; honors section; independent study; term-away projects; study abroad; academic accommodation for the gifted, the musically talented, and the artistically talented.

College Admission Counseling 35 students graduated in 2016; all went to college, including Cornell University; Harvard University; Princeton University; University of Chicago; University of Massachusetts Amherst; Yale University. Mean SAT critical reading: 748, mean SAT math: 730, mean SAT writing: 728.

Student Life Discipline rests primarily with faculty.

Tuition and Aid Day student tuition: $39,972. Tuition installment plan (Key Tuition Payment Plan). Need-based scholarship grants, need-based loans available. In 2016–17, 30% of upper-school students received aid. Total amount of financial aid awarded in 2016–17: $1,015,000.

Admissions Traditional secondary-level entrance grade is 9. For fall 2016, 214 students applied for upper-level admission, 90 were accepted, 45 enrolled. ISEE or SSAT required. Deadline for receipt of application materials: January 10. Application fee required: $50. On-campus interview recommended.

Athletics Interscholastic: basketball (boys, girls), independent competitive sports (b,g), soccer (b,g); coed interscholastic: baseball, cross-country running, fencing, squash, ultimate Frisbee; coed intramural: aerobics/Nautilus, ballet, cross-country running, dance, fencing, fitness, martial arts, sailing, squash, yoga. 12 coaches.

Computers Computers are regularly used in computer applications, photography, programming classes. Computer network features include on-campus library services, online commercial services, Internet access, wireless campus network, Internet filtering or blocking technology. Campus intranet, student e-mail accounts, and computer access in designated common areas are available to students. The school has a published electronic and media policy.

Contact Ms. Carrie Healy, Director of Admissions and Financial Aid. 617-266-7525. Fax: 617-266-5769. E-mail: admissions@commschool.org. Website: www.commschool.org

COMMUNITY CHRISTIAN ACADEMY

11875 Taylor Mill Road
Independence, Kentucky 41051

Head of School: Tara Montez Bates

General Information Coeducational day college-preparatory and religious studies school, affiliated with Pentecostal Church. Grades PS–12. Founded: 1983. Setting: rural. Nearest major city is Cincinnati, OH. 112-acre campus. 2 buildings on campus. Approved or accredited by International Christian Accrediting Association and Kentucky Department of Education. Total enrollment: 269. Upper school average class size: 15. Upper school faculty-student ratio: 1:15. There are 175 required school days per year for Upper School students. Upper School students typically attend 5 days per week. The average school day consists of 6 hours.

Upper School Student Profile Grade 9: 18 students (8 boys, 10 girls); Grade 10: 13 students (5 boys, 8 girls); Grade 11: 12 students (5 boys, 7 girls); Grade 12: 15 students (6 boys, 9 girls). 50% of students are Pentecostal.

Faculty School total: 14. In upper school: 3 men, 3 women; 2 have advanced degrees.

Subjects Offered Advanced biology, advanced math, algebra, American history, art appreciation, Bible, biology, business skills, calculus, chemistry, choral music, computer applications, cultural geography, English, geography, health, integrated science, life skills, literature, pre-algebra, pre-calculus, Spanish.

Graduation Requirements Bible, electives, English, foreign language, mathematics, physical education (includes health), science, social studies (includes history), statistics, visual and performing arts.

College Admission Counseling 12 students graduated in 2015; 10 went to college, including Cincinnati State Technical and Community College; Morehead State University; Northern Kentucky University; Oral Roberts University; University of Cincinnati. Other: 2 went to work. Mean composite ACT: 21. 20% scored over 26 on composite ACT.

Student Life Upper grades have uniform requirement, student council, honor system. Discipline rests primarily with faculty. Attendance at religious services is required.

Tuition and Aid Day student tuition: $3349. Guaranteed tuition plan. Tuition installment plan (The Tuition Plan, monthly payment plans). Financial aid available to upper-school students. In 2015–16, 5% of upper-school students received aid. Total amount of financial aid awarded in 2015–16: $9000.

Admissions Traditional secondary-level entrance grade is 9. For fall 2015, 16 students applied for upper-level admission, 11 were accepted, 11 enrolled. Admissions testing required. Deadline for receipt of application materials: none. Application fee required: $50. Interview required.

Athletics Interscholastic: baseball (boys), basketball (b,g), cheering (g), softball (g), volleyball (g); coed interscholastic: cross-country running. 2 PE instructors, 13 coaches.

Computers Computers are regularly used in foreign language classes. Computer network features include Internet access.

Contact Edie Carkeek, Secretary. 859-356-7990 Ext. 112. Fax: 859-356-7991. E-mail: edie.carkeek@ccaky.org. Website: www.ccaky.org

COMMUNITY HIGH SCHOOL

Teaneck, New Jersey
See Special Needs Schools section.

THE COMMUNITY SCHOOL

PO Box 2118
Sun Valley, Idaho 83353

Head of School: Ben Pettit

General Information Coeducational boarding and day college-preparatory, arts, and technology school. Boarding grades 9–12, day grades K–12. Founded: 1973. Setting: small town. Nearest major city is Boise. 45-acre campus. 4 buildings on campus. Approved or accredited by Northwest Association of Independent Schools and Idaho Department of Education. Member of National Association of Independent Schools, Secondary School Admission Test Board, and Council for the Advancement and Support of Education. Endowment: $3.4 million. Total enrollment: 400. Upper school average class size: 12. Upper school faculty-student ratio: 1:8. Upper School students typically attend 5 days per week. The average school day consists of 6 hours and 30 minutes.

Upper School Student Profile Grade 9: 33 students (12 boys, 21 girls); Grade 10: 38 students (19 boys, 19 girls); Grade 11: 46 students (21 boys, 25 girls); Grade 12: 47 students (28 boys, 19 girls). 13% of students are boarding students. 87% are state residents. 10 states are represented in upper school student body. 3% are international students. International students from Bermuda, Brazil, and China.

Faculty School total: 64. In upper school: 11 men, 6 women; 13 have advanced degrees.

Subjects Offered Algebra, American history, American literature, art, biology, calculus, ceramics, chemistry, computer graphics, computer math, computer programming, computer science, constitutional law, creative writing, drama, earth science, ecology, economics, English, English literature, environmental science, ethics, European history, expository writing, fine arts, forensics, French, geography, geology,

geometry, government/civics, history, human development, information technology, mathematics, music, musical productions, philosophy, photography, physical education, physics, science, social studies, Spanish, speech, statistics, theater, trigonometry, world history, world literature, writing.

Graduation Requirements Arts and fine arts (art, music, dance, drama), computer science, English, foreign language, mathematics, outdoor education, physical education (includes health), science, social studies (includes history), speech, senior project presentation, senior speech, outdoor program.

Special Academic Programs Advanced Placement exam preparation; honors section; independent study; term-away projects; domestic exchange program; academic accommodation for the gifted; programs in English, mathematics, general development for dyslexic students; ESL (8 students enrolled).

College Admission Counseling 34 students graduated in 2015; 33 went to college, including Dartmouth College; Harvard University; The Colorado College; Tufts University; University of Colorado Boulder; University of Virginia. Other: 1 entered military service. Mean SAT critical reading: 604, mean SAT math: 582, mean SAT writing: 591. 51% scored over 600 on SAT critical reading, 54% scored over 600 on SAT math, 54% scored over 600 on SAT writing.

Student Life Upper grades have specified standards of dress, student council, honor system. Discipline rests primarily with faculty.

Tuition and Aid Day student tuition: $26,500; 7-day tuition and room/board: $43,500. Tuition installment plan (individually arranged payment plans). Merit scholarship grants, need-based scholarship grants available. In 2015–16, 41% of upper-school students received aid; total upper-school merit-scholarship money awarded: $153,650. Total amount of financial aid awarded in 2015–16: $599,175.

Admissions Traditional secondary-level entrance grade is 9. PSAT and SAT for applicants to grade 11 and 12, SSAT and writing sample required. Deadline for receipt of application materials: February 25. Application fee required: $50. Interview required.

Athletics Interscholastic: alpine skiing (boys, girls), basketball (b,g), cross-country running (b,g), freestyle skiing (b,g), golf (b,g), ice hockey (b,g), ice skating (b,g), lacrosse (b), nordic skiing (b,g), physical fitness (b,g), rock climbing (b,g), skiing (cross-country) (b,g), skiing (downhill) (b,g), snowboarding (b,g), soccer (b,g), swimming and diving (g), tennis (b,g), track and field (b,g), volleyball (g); coed interscholastic: backpacking, bicycling, canoeing/kayaking, climbing, cooperative games, equestrian sports, figure skating, fitness, hiking/backpacking, independent competitive sports, kayaking, mountain biking, mountaineering, outdoor activities, outdoor adventure, outdoor education, outdoor skills, physical fitness, rafting, rock climbing, ropes courses, snowshoeing, strength & conditioning, telemark skiing, tennis, wilderness, wilderness survival. 2 PE instructors, 9 coaches, 1 athletic trainer.

Computers Computers are regularly used in English, foreign language, independent study, science, yearbook classes. Computer network features include on-campus library services, online commercial services, Internet access, wireless campus network, Internet filtering or blocking technology. Student e-mail accounts and computer access in designated common areas are available to students. Students grades are available online. The school has a published electronic and media policy.

Contact Katie Robins, Director of Admission. 208-622-3960 Ext. 117. Fax: 208-622-3962. E-mail: krobins@communityschool.org. Website: www.communityschool.org

THE COMMUNITY SCHOOL OF NAPLES

13275 Livingston Road
Naples, Florida 34109

Head of School: Dr. David Watson

General Information Coeducational day college-preparatory and Advanced Placement school. Grades PK–12. Founded: 1982. Setting: suburban. Nearest major city is Miami. 77-acre campus. 4 buildings on campus. Approved or accredited by Florida Council of Independent Schools. Member of National Association of Independent Schools and Secondary School Admission Test Board. Endowment: $9.6 million. Total enrollment: 807. Upper school average class size: 13. Upper school faculty-student ratio: 1:9. There are 172 required school days per year for Upper School students. Upper School students typically attend 5 days per week. The average school day consists of 5 hours and 15 minutes.

Upper School Student Profile Grade 9: 82 students (50 boys, 32 girls); Grade 10: 76 students (41 boys, 35 girls); Grade 11: 70 students (45 boys, 25 girls); Grade 12: 82 students (45 boys, 37 girls).

Faculty School total: 99. In upper school: 11 men, 27 women, 27 have advanced degrees.

Subjects Offered 3-dimensional art, 3-dimensional design, advanced computer applications, advanced math, Advanced Placement courses, advanced studio art-AP, algebra, American government, American history, American literature, American literature-AP, American sign language, anatomy and physiology, art, art history, art history-AP, art-AP, band, biology, biology-AP, biotechnology, calculus, calculus-AP, chemistry, chemistry-AP, chorus, clayworking, comparative government and politics-AP, composition, composition-AP, computer graphics, computer programming, computer programming-AP, computer science, computer science-AP, creative writing, digital photography, drama performance, dramatic arts, drawing, drawing and design, economics, economics-AP, electives, English, English composition, English language and composition-AP, English language-AP, English literature, English literature and composition-AP, English literature-AP, English-AP, English/composition-AP, environmental science, environmental science-AP, fine arts, French, French language-AP, French literature-AP, French-AP, geometry, government, government and politics-AP, government-AP, government/civics, government/civics-AP, graphic design, health, history, history-AP, honors algebra, honors English, honors geometry, honors U.S. history, honors world history, human geography - AP, jazz band, Latin, literature, literature and composition-AP, literature-AP, macro/microeconomics-AP, macroeconomics-AP, marine biology, marine science, mathematics, mathematics-AP, microeconomics, microeconomics-AP, modern European history-AP, music, music theory-AP, oceanography, painting, performing arts, personal fitness, photography, physical education, physical fitness, physics, physics-AP, portfolio art, pre-algebra, pre-calculus, psychology, psychology-AP, robotics, science, senior project, Spanish, Spanish language-AP, Spanish literature-AP, Spanish-AP, statistics-AP, strings, studio art-AP, theater, U.S. government and politics, U.S. government and politics-AP, U.S. history, U.S. history-AP, United States government-AP, visual and performing arts, visual arts, vocal music, Web site design, world history, world history-AP, world literature.

Graduation Requirements Arts and fine arts (art, music, dance, drama), computer science, electives, English, foreign language, history, mathematics, physical education (includes health), science, community service hours (25 per year).

Special Academic Programs 26 Advanced Placement exams for which test preparation is offered; honors section; independent study; study at local college for college credit; study abroad; academic accommodation for the gifted.

College Admission Counseling 79 students graduated in 2016; all went to college, including Boston University; Southern Methodist University; University of Central Florida; University of Colorado Boulder; University of Florida; University of Michigan. Median SAT critical reading: 597, median SAT math: 634, median SAT writing: 589, median composite ACT: 26. 13% scored over 600 on SAT critical reading, 32% scored over 600 on SAT math, 16% scored over 600 on SAT writing.

Student Life Upper grades have specified standards of dress, student council, honor system. Discipline rests equally with students and faculty.

Summer Programs Enrichment, advancement, sports programs offered; session focuses on mathematics, English, and SAT preparation; sports; held on campus; accepts boys and girls; open to students from other schools. 25 students usually enrolled. 2017 schedule: June 5 to August 4. Application deadline: June 1.

Tuition and Aid Day student tuition: $26,800. Tuition installment plan (Insured Tuition Payment Plan, monthly payment plans, individually arranged payment plans). Need-based scholarship grants available. In 2016–17, 20% of upper-school students received aid. Total amount of financial aid awarded in 2016–17: $1,212,598.

Admissions Traditional secondary-level entrance grade is 9. For fall 2016, 77 students applied for upper-level admission, 57 were accepted, 45 enrolled. Math, reading, and mental ability tests or SSAT required. Deadline for receipt of application materials: February 1. Application fee required: $100. Interview recommended.

Athletics Interscholastic: baseball (boys), basketball (b,g), cross-country running (b,g), diving (b,g), football (b), golf (b,g), lacrosse (b,g), soccer (b,g), softball (g), swimming and diving (b,g), tennis (b,g), track and field (b,g), volleyball (g), winter soccer (b,g); coed intramural: cheering, sailing. 1 PE instructor, 67 coaches, 1 athletic trainer.

Computers Computers are regularly used in art, computer applications, creative writing, design, desktop publishing, digital applications, English, foreign language, history, mathematics, music, science, Web site design, writing, writing, yearbook classes. Computer network features include on-campus library services, online commercial services, Internet access, wireless campus network, Internet filtering or blocking technology. Campus intranet, student e-mail accounts, and computer access in designated common areas are available to students. Students grades are available online. The school has a published electronic and media policy.

Contact Ms. Franchesca Gannon, Admissions Officer. 239-597-7575 Ext. 133. Fax: 239-598-2973. E-mail: FGannont@communityschoolnaples.org.
Website: www.communityschoolnaples.org

THE CONCEPT SCHOOL

1120 E. Street Rd
PO Box 54
Westtown, Pennsylvania 19395

Head of School: Mr. William M. Bennett

General Information Coeducational day college-preparatory and general academic school; primarily serves students with learning disabilities, individuals with Attention Deficit Disorder, dyslexic students, students on the Autism Spectrum, and students with Anxiety Disorders. Grades 6–12. Founded: 1972. Setting: suburban. Nearest major city is Philadelphia. 10-acre campus. 1 building on campus. Approved or accredited by Pennsylvania Department of Education. Endowment: $400,000. Total enrollment: 24. Upper school average class size: 5. Upper school faculty-student ratio: 1:5. There are 175 required school days per year for Upper School students. Upper School students typically attend 5 days per week. The average school day consists of 6 hours and 30 minutes.

Upper School Student Profile Grade 6: 1 student (1 boy); Grade 7: 2 students (2 boys); Grade 8: 5 students (5 boys); Grade 9: 5 students (3 boys, 2 girls); Grade 10: 3 students (2 boys, 1 girl); Grade 11: 7 students (4 boys, 3 girls); Grade 12: 6 students (5 boys, 1 girl).

Faculty School total: 12. In upper school: 4 men, 8 women; 5 have advanced degrees.

Subjects Offered 20th century world history, acting, algebra, American history, art, biology, career and personal planning, consumer mathematics, cultural arts, English, environmental science, foreign language, general science, geometry, government/civics, health, history, independent study, lab science, language arts, mathematics, physical education, pre-algebra, pre-calculus, science, Shakespeare, social sciences, social studies, U.S. government, visual arts.

Graduation Requirements Arts and fine arts (art, music, dance, drama), computer science, English, foreign language, mathematics, physical education (includes health), science, social sciences, social studies (includes history).

Special Academic Programs Accelerated programs; independent study; academic accommodation for the gifted; remedial reading and/or remedial writing; remedial math; programs in general development for dyslexic students.

College Admission Counseling 3 students graduated in 2016; they went to Barry University. Other: 1 went to work, 1 entered a postgraduate year, 1 had other specific plans.

Student Life Upper grades have specified standards of dress, honor system. Discipline rests primarily with faculty.

Tuition and Aid Day student tuition: $25,000. Tuition installment plan (monthly payment plans, individually arranged payment plans). Tuition reduction for siblings available.

Admissions Traditional secondary-level entrance grade is 7. For fall 2016, 19 students applied for upper-level admission, 8 were accepted, 6 enrolled. Stanford Binet, Wechsler Individual Achievement Test or WISC or WAIS required. Deadline for receipt of application materials: none. Application fee required: $75. On-campus interview recommended.

Athletics Coed Intramural: aerobics, basketball, bowling, cooperative games, fitness, fitness walking, flag football, kickball, outdoor activities, physical fitness, physical training, walking, whiffle ball, yoga. 1 PE instructor.

Computers Computers are regularly used in all academic classes. Computer network features include Internet access, wireless campus network, Internet filtering or blocking technology, all students are issued Chrome Books. Student e-mail accounts are available to students. The school has a published electronic and media policy.

Contact Mrs. Maureen Sullivan Funsten, School Secretary. 610-399-1135. Fax: 610-399-0767. E-mail: mfunsten@theconceptschool.org.
Website: www.theconceptschool.org

CONCORD ACADEMY

166 Main Street
Concord, Massachusetts 01742

Head of School: Mr. Rick Hardy

General Information Coeducational boarding and day college-preparatory school. Ungraded, ages 13–19. Founded: 1922. Setting: suburban. Nearest major city is Boston. Students are housed in single-sex dormitories. 39-acre campus. 29 buildings on campus. Approved or accredited by New England Association of Schools and Colleges, The Association of Boarding Schools, and Massachusetts Department of Education. Member of National Association of Independent Schools and Secondary School Admission Test Board. Endowment: $62.3 million. Total enrollment: 378. Upper school average class size: 12. Upper school faculty-student ratio: 1:6. Upper School students typically attend 5 days per week. The average school day consists of 6 hours and 30 minutes.

Upper School Student Profile Grade 9: 90 students (41 boys, 49 girls); Grade 10: 95 students (49 boys, 46 girls); Grade 11: 99 students (49 boys, 50 girls); Grade 12: 97 students (47 boys, 50 girls). 42% of students are boarding students. 71% are state residents. 15 states are represented in upper school student body. 11% are international students. International students from Australia, Canada, China, Hong Kong, Republic of Korea, and Russian Federation; 17 other countries represented in student body.

Faculty School total: 64. In upper school: 23 men, 37 women; 52 have advanced degrees; 26 reside on campus.

Subjects Offered 20th century American writers, 3-dimensional art, advanced chemistry, advanced math, African history, African-American literature, algebra, American history, American literature, ancient history, ancient world history, anthropology, applied music, architecture, art, art history, Asian history, astronomy, astrophysics, batik, Bible as literature, biochemistry, biology, bookmaking, British literature, calculus, ceramics, chamber groups, chemistry, Chinese history, choreography, chorus, classical civilization, classical Greek literature, classical language, computer multimedia, computer programming, computer science, computer studies, creative writing, critical studies in film, dance, dance performance, digital imaging, directing, drama, drama performance, drawing, earth science, economics, English, English literature, environmental science, environmental studies, European history, experimental science, expository writing, fiber arts, fiction, film, film history, filmmaking, forensics, French, freshman seminar, geology, geometry, German, German literature, guitar, health and wellness, history of China and Japan, history of music, Holocaust, HTML design, improvisation, instruments, introduction to digital multitrack recording techniques, Irish literature, Islamic history, jazz ensemble, journalism, Latin, Latin American history, Latin American literature, life management skills, literature seminar, math analysis, mathematics, medieval/Renaissance history, Middle East, Middle Eastern history, model United Nations, modern dance, modern European history, modern languages, music, music composition, music history, music technology, music theory, musical productions, neuroscience, newspaper, novels, oceanography, orchestra, painting, performing arts, philosophy, photography, physical education, physics, piano, play/screen writing, poetry, post-calculus, pre-calculus, printmaking, probability and statistics, Roman civilization, science, science fiction, sculpture, senior project, sex education, Shakespeare, Spanish, Spanish literature, statistics, student publications, studio art, technical theater, theater, theater design and production, theater history, trigonometry, U.S. history, urban studies, visual arts, voice, Web site design, wind ensemble, writing.

Graduation Requirements Computer science, creative arts, English, foreign language, health and wellness, history, mathematics, performing arts, physical education (includes health), science, visual arts.

Special Academic Programs Honors section; independent study; term-away projects; study abroad; academic accommodation for the gifted, the musically talented, and the artistically talented.

College Admission Counseling 95 students graduated in 2016; all went to college, including Columbia University; New York University; Northeastern University; Smith College; Tufts University; Washington University in St. Louis. Mean SAT critical reading: 686, mean SAT math: 699, mean SAT writing: 699, mean combined SAT: 2074.

Student Life Upper grades have student council, honor system. Discipline rests equally with students and faculty.

Tuition and Aid Day student tuition: $47,160; 7-day tuition and room/board: $58,558. Tuition installment plan (Key Tuition Payment Plan, monthly payment plans). Need-based scholarship grants, need-based loans available. In 2016–17, 25% of upper-school students received aid. Total amount of financial aid awarded in 2016–17: $4,200,000.

Admissions Traditional secondary-level entrance grade is 9. For fall 2016, 885 students applied for upper-level admission, 183 were accepted, 102 enrolled. ISEE, SSAT or TOEFL required. Deadline for receipt of application materials: January 15. Application fee required: $50. On-campus interview recommended.

Athletics Interscholastic: baseball (boys), basketball (b,g), cross-country running (b,g), field hockey (g), lacrosse (g), skiing (downhill) (b,g), soccer (b,g), squash (g), tennis (b,g), volleyball (g), wrestling (b); intramural: softball (g), squash (b); coed interscholastic: alpine skiing, golf, lacrosse, ultimate Frisbee; coed intramural: aerobics, aerobics/dance, ballet, canoeing/kayaking, combined training, cross-country running, dance, fencing, fitness, jogging, martial arts, modern dance, outdoor activities, physical fitness, physical training, sailing, self defense, skiing (downhill), strength & conditioning, track and field, ultimate Frisbee, weight training, yoga. 8 PE instructors, 35 coaches, 2 athletic trainers.

Computers Computers are regularly used in English, foreign language, history, library skills, mathematics, music, newspaper, science, social studies, technology, video film production, Web site design, yearbook classes. Computer network features include on-campus library services, online commercial services, Internet access, wireless campus network, Internet filtering or blocking technology. Campus intranet, student e-mail accounts, and computer access in designated common areas are available to students. Students grades are available online. The school has a published electronic and media policy.

Contact Admissions Office. 978-402-2250. Fax: 978-402-2345. E-mail: admissions@concordacademy.org. Website: www.concordacademy.org

CONCORDIA ACADEMY

2400 North Dale Street
St. Paul, Minnesota 55113

Head of School: Rev. Dr. Timothy Berner

General Information Coeducational day college-preparatory and arts school, affiliated with Lutheran Church–Missouri Synod. Grades 9–12. Founded: 1893. Setting: suburban. 14-acre campus. 1 building on campus. Approved or accredited by National Lutheran School Accreditation, North Central Association of Colleges and Schools, and Minnesota Department of Education. Endowment: $300,000. Total enrollment: 241. Upper school average class size: 18. Upper school faculty-student ratio: 1:15. There are 175 required school days per year for Upper School students. Upper School students typically attend 5 days per week. The average school day consists of 6 hours and 45 minutes.

Upper School Student Profile Grade 9: 55 students (32 boys, 23 girls); Grade 10: 67 students (41 boys, 26 girls); Grade 11: 62 students (32 boys, 30 girls); Grade 12: 57 students (28 boys, 29 girls). 45% of students are Lutheran Church–Missouri Synod.

Faculty School total: 27. In upper school: 15 men, 12 women; 16 have advanced degrees.

Subjects Offered Dance.

Graduation Requirements Christian scripture, religion (includes Bible studies and theology).

Special Academic Programs Honors section; study at local college for college credit; remedial reading and/or remedial writing; remedial math; programs in general development for dyslexic students; special instructional classes for deaf students.

College Admission Counseling 56 students graduated in 2016; 52 went to college. Other: 3 went to work, 1 entered military service. Median composite ACT: 24. 55% scored over 26 on composite ACT.

Student Life Upper grades have specified standards of dress, student council. Discipline rests primarily with faculty. Attendance at religious services is required.

Summer Programs Sports, art/fine arts, computer instruction programs offered; held on campus; accepts boys and girls; open to students from other schools. 150 students usually enrolled. 2017 schedule: June 5 to August 4.

Tuition and Aid Day student tuition: $9800–$17,000. Tuition installment plan (monthly payment plans, quarterly payment plan, semi-annual payment plan, 10 monthly payments (through TADS)). Merit scholarship grants, need-based scholarship grants available. In 2016–17, 40% of upper-school students received aid; total upper-school merit-scholarship money awarded: $98,500. Total amount of financial aid awarded in 2016–17: $334,804.

Admissions Traditional secondary-level entrance grade is 9. Math and English placement tests required. Deadline for receipt of application materials: none. Application fee required: $100. On-campus interview required.

Athletics Interscholastic: baseball (boys), basketball (b,g), cross-country running (b,g), dance team (g), football (b), golf (b), ice hockey (b), lacrosse (b), soccer (b,g), softball (g), strength & conditioning (b,g), track and field (b,g), volleyball (g), wrestling (b); intramural: basketball (b,g), weight training (b,g). 1 PE instructor, 30 coaches, 1 athletic trainer.

Computers Computers are regularly used in Christian doctrine, creative writing, English, foreign language, freshman foundations, graphic design, history, mathematics, music, photography, remedial study skills, science, speech, writing, yearbook classes. Computer resources include online commercial services, Internet access, wireless campus network, Internet filtering or blocking technology. Campus intranet, student e-mail accounts, and computer access in designated common areas are available to students. Students grades are available online. The school has a published electronic and media policy.

Contact Mrs. Sarah Adams, Director of Admissions & Outreach. 651-796-2679. Fax: 651-484-0594. E-mail: sofia.humphries@concordiaacademy.com. Website: www.concordiaacademy.com

CONCORDIA LUTHERAN HIGH SCHOOL

1601 Saint Joe River Drive
Fort Wayne, Indiana 46805

Head of School: Mr. Mychal Thom

General Information Coeducational day college-preparatory, religious studies, and video production school, affiliated with Lutheran Church Missouri Synod. Grades 9–12. Founded: 1935. Setting: urban. 70-acre campus. 1 building on campus. Approved or accredited by National Lutheran School Accreditation, North Central Association of Colleges and Schools, and Indiana Department of Education. Endowment: $15 million. Total enrollment: 772. Upper school average class size: 21. Upper school faculty-student ratio: 1:14. There are 180 required school days per year for Upper School students. Upper School students typically attend 5 days per week. The average school day consists of 7 hours and 5 minutes.

Upper School Student Profile Grade 9: 211 students (101 boys, 110 girls); Grade 10: 219 students (105 boys, 114 girls); Grade 11: 200 students (101 boys, 99 girls); Grade 12: 210 students (102 boys, 108 girls). 86% of students are Lutheran Church–Missouri Synod.

Faculty School total: 55. In upper school: 26 men, 28 women; 30 have advanced degrees.

Subjects Offered Accounting, advanced studio art-AP, chorus, cinematography, college admission preparation, comparative religion, computer animation, computer graphics, computer programming, concert band, CPR, digital photography, engineering, English composition, government, health and wellness, interpersonal skills, language and composition, literature and composition-AP, marketing, media production, New Testament, parent/child development, pre-calculus, psychology-AP, student publications, studio art-AP.

Graduation Requirements English, foreign language, health education, mathematics, physical education (includes health), religion (includes Bible studies and theology), science, social sciences, social studies (includes history). Community service is required.

Special Academic Programs Advanced Placement exam preparation; honors section; independent study; study at local college for college credit; remedial reading and/or remedial writing; remedial math; programs in English, mathematics, general development for dyslexic students; special instructional classes for deaf students, blind students, we provide needed up in our Study Center, and a student's schedule is built around that need.

College Admission Counseling 153 students graduated in 2016; 140 went to college, including Ball State University; Concordia University Chicago; Concordia University Wisconsin; Indiana University–Purdue University Fort Wayne; Indiana University Bloomington; Purdue University. Other: 3 went to work, 11 entered military service. Mean SAT critical reading: 528, mean SAT math: 542, mean SAT writing: 506, mean composite ACT: 24.

Student Life Upper grades have uniform requirement, student council, honor system. Discipline rests primarily with faculty. Attendance at religious services is required.

Summer Programs Remediation, advancement, sports, art/fine arts, computer instruction programs offered; session focuses on summer classes, drivers education, summer conditioning, and summer athletic, academic and music camps; held both on and off campus; accepts boys and girls; open to students from other schools. 700 students usually enrolled. 2017 schedule: June to August. Application deadline: June.

Tuition and Aid Day student tuition: $8545–$9995. Tuition installment plan (FACTS Tuition Payment Plan, monthly payment plans, individually arranged payment plans). Tuition reduction for siblings, merit scholarship grants, need-based scholarship grants, Indiana School Choice voucher available. In 2016–17, 97% of upper-school students received aid; total upper-school merit-scholarship money awarded: $567,250. Total amount of financial aid awarded in 2016–17: $3,928,184.

Admissions Traditional secondary-level entrance grade is 9. For fall 2016, 221 students applied for upper-level admission, 217 were accepted, 201 enrolled. Deadline for receipt of application materials: none. Application fee required: $35.

Athletics Interscholastic: baseball (boys), basketball (b,g), cheering (g), cross-country running (b,g), football (b), golf (b,g), gymnastics (g), lacrosse (b), soccer (b,g), softball (g), swimming and diving (b,g), tennis (b,g), track and field (b,g), volleyball (g), wrestling (b); coed interscholastic: bowling, crew, dance team, JROTC drill, marksmanship, outdoor adventure, rappelling, riflery, rowing; coed intramural: volleyball. 3 PE instructors, 70 coaches, 2 athletic trainers.

Computers Computers are regularly used in all academic classes. Computer network features include on-campus library services, online commercial services, Internet access, wireless campus network, Internet filtering or blocking technology, students are all required to have iPads as part of the instructional process. Campus intranet, student e-mail accounts, and computer access in designated common areas are available to students. Students grades are available online. The school has a published electronic and media policy.

Contact Mrs. Dawn Schuller, Director of Admissions and Retention. 260-483-1102 Ext. 298. Fax: 260-471-0180. E-mail: dschuller@clhscadets.com. Website: www.clhscadets.com

CONTRA COSTA CHRISTIAN HIGH SCHOOL

2721 Larkey Lane
Walnut Creek, California 94596

Head of School: Mr. Chris Winters

General Information Coeducational day and distance learning college-preparatory school. Grades PK–12. Distance learning grades K–12. Founded: 1978. Setting: suburban. 8-acre campus. 3 buildings on campus. Approved or accredited by Western Association of Schools and Colleges and California Department of Education. Total enrollment: 230. Upper school average class size: 15. Upper school faculty-student ratio: 1:15. There are 178 required school days per year for Upper School students. Upper School students typically attend 5 days per week. The average school day consists of 7 hours.

Upper School Student Profile Grade 9: 16 students (10 boys, 6 girls); Grade 10: 18 students (10 boys, 8 girls); Grade 11: 34 students (19 boys, 15 girls); Grade 12: 21 students (10 boys, 11 girls). 82% are state residents. 1 state is represented in upper school student body. 18% are international students.

Faculty School total: 13. In upper school: 4 men, 8 women; 2 have advanced degrees.

Subjects Offered 20th century history, 20th century world history, advanced math, Advanced Placement courses, algebra, American government, American history, American history-AP, American literature-AP, anatomy and physiology, art, arts, athletics, band, basketball, Bible, biology, calculus-AP, career and personal planning, career/college preparation, chemistry, choir, Christian education, Christian ethics, Christianity, college admission preparation, college counseling, community service, conceptual physics, creative writing, drama, economics, English, English composition, English literature, English literature-AP, ESL, European history, European history-AP, French, geometry, government, guitar, health, physics-AP, pre-calculus, psychology, Spanish, Spanish language-AP, Spanish literature-AP, Spanish-AP, U.S. government, U.S. history, U.S. history-AP.

Graduation Requirements All academic.

Special Academic Programs 4 Advanced Placement exams for which test preparation is offered; ESL (22 students enrolled).

College Admission Counseling 28 students graduated in 2016; all went to college, including Boston University; California Polytechnic State University, San Luis Obispo; University of California, Davis; University of California, Irvine; University of California, San Diego; University of Washington.

Student Life Upper grades have specified standards of dress, student council. Discipline rests primarily with faculty. Attendance at religious services is required.

Tuition and Aid Tuition installment plan (FACTS Tuition Payment Plan). Tuition reduction for siblings, need-based scholarship grants available.

Admissions Deadline for receipt of application materials: none. Application fee required: $450. Interview recommended.

Athletics Interscholastic: aquatics (boys, girls), basketball (b,g), cross-country running (b,g), soccer (b,g), volleyball (b,g). 3 PE instructors, 12 coaches.

Computers Computers are regularly used in accounting, aerospace science, all academic, animation, architecture, art, aviation, basic skills, Bible studies, business, business applications, business education, business skills, business studies, cabinet making, career education, career exploration, career technology, Christian doctrine, classics, college planning, commercial art, computer applications, construction, creative writing, current events, dance, data processing, design, desktop publishing, desktop publishing, ESL, digital applications, drafting, drawing and design, economics, engineering, English, ESL, ethics, foreign language, French, French as a second language, freshman foundations, geography, graphic arts, graphic design, graphics, health, historical foundations for arts, history, human geography - AP, humanities, independent study, industrial technology, information technology, introduction to technology, journalism, JROTC, keyboarding, lab/keyboard, language development, Latin, learning cognition, library, library science, library skills, life skills, literacy, literary magazine, mathematics, media, media arts, media production, media services, mentorship program, multimedia, music, music technology, news writing, newspaper, NJROTC, occupational education, philosophy, photography, photojournalism, programming, psychology, publications, publishing, reading, religion, religious studies, remedial study skills, research skills, SAT preparation, science, senior seminar, social sciences, social studies, Spanish, speech, stock market, study skills, technical drawing, technology, theater, theater arts, theology, typing, video film production, vocational-technical courses, Web site design, wilderness education, woodworking, word processing, writing, writing, yearbook classes. Computer network features include on-campus library services, online commercial services, Internet access, wireless campus network, Internet filtering or blocking technology. Student e-mail accounts and computer access in designated common areas are available to students. Students grades are available online. The school has a published electronic and media policy.

Contact Ms. Lisa Asher. 925-934-4964. E-mail: lasher@cccss.org. Website: www.cccss.org

CONVENT OF THE SACRED HEART

1177 King Street
Greenwich, Connecticut 06831

Head of School: Mrs. Pamela Juan Hayes

General Information Coeducational day (boys only in lower grades) and distance learning college-preparatory, STEAM (Science, Technology, Engineering, Arts, Math), and world languages school, affiliated with Roman Catholic Church. Boys grades PS–PK, girls grades PS–12. Distance learning grades 9–12. Founded: 1848. Setting: suburban. Nearest major city is New York, NY. 118-acre campus. 10 buildings on campus. Approved or accredited by Connecticut Association of Independent Schools, Network of Sacred Heart Schools, New England Association of Schools and Colleges, and Connecticut Department of Education. Member of National Association of Independent Schools and Secondary School Admission Test Board. Endowment: $34.3 million. Total enrollment: 750. Upper school average class size: 13. Upper school faculty-student ratio: 1:7. There are 163 required school days per year for Upper School students. Upper School students typically attend 5 days per week. The average school day consists of 7 hours and 15 minutes.

Upper School Student Profile Grade 6: 65 students (65 girls); Grade 7: 71 students (71 girls); Grade 8: 79 students (79 girls); Grade 9: 78 students (78 girls); Grade 10: 76 students (76 girls); Grade 11: 77 students (77 girls); Grade 12: 82 students (82 girls). 70% of students are Roman Catholic.

Faculty School total: 158. In upper school: 10 men, 40 women; 45 have advanced degrees.

Subjects Offered 20th century world history, advanced biology, advanced chemistry, advanced math, Advanced Placement courses, advanced studio art-AP, algebra, American literature, American literature-AP, Arabic, biology, biology-AP, broadcast journalism, calculus, calculus-AP, Catholic belief and practice, chemistry, chemistry-AP, Chinese, choir, choral music, Christian and Hebrew scripture, Christian education, Christian ethics, Christianity, college counseling, community service, comparative government and politics-AP, computer science, concert bell choir, design, drama, drawing, English language and composition-AP, English literature, English literature and composition-AP, environmental science-AP, ethics, European history, European history-AP, fine arts, French, French language-AP, geometry, health, honors algebra, honors geometry, honors U.S. history, HTML design, instrumental music, journalism, Latin, literary magazine, photography, physical education, physics, physics-AP, pre-calculus, SAT/ACT preparation, Spanish, Spanish language-AP, Spanish literature-AP, statistics-AP, theology, trigonometry, U.S. history, U.S. history-AP, world cultures, world literature.

Graduation Requirements Electives, English, foreign language, mathematics, physical education (includes health), science, theology, 100 hours of community service by graduation. Community service is required.

Special Academic Programs 19 Advanced Placement exams for which test preparation is offered; honors section; independent study; term-away projects; domestic exchange program (with Network of Sacred Heart Schools); study abroad; academic accommodation for the gifted and the artistically talented.

College Admission Counseling 60 students graduated in 2016; all went to college, including Boston University; Elon University; Fordham University; Georgetown University; University of Southern California; University of Virginia.

Student Life Upper grades have uniform requirement, student council, honor system. Discipline rests primarily with faculty. Attendance at religious services is required.

Summer Programs Enrichment programs offered; session focuses on enrichment; held on campus; accepts girls; not open to students from other schools. 2017 schedule: June to July.

Tuition and Aid Day student tuition: $40,200. Tuition installment plan (Sallie May Payment Plan). Merit scholarship grants, need-based scholarship grants available. In 2016–17, 20% of upper-school students received aid.

Admissions Traditional secondary-level entrance grade is 9. For fall 2016, 111 students applied for upper-level admission, 56 were accepted, 28 enrolled. ISEE or SSAT required. Deadline for receipt of application materials: February 1. Application fee required: $50. On-campus interview required.

Athletics Interscholastic: basketball, cooperative games, crew, cross-country running, dance, diving, field hockey, fitness, golf, jogging, lacrosse, physical fitness, running, soccer, softball, squash, swimming and diving, tennis, volleyball; intramural: fitness, independent competitive sports, physical training, strength & conditioning. 4 PE instructors, 34 coaches, 1 athletic trainer.

Computers Computers are regularly used in all academic classes. Computer network features include on-campus library services, online commercial services, Internet access, wireless campus network, Internet filtering or blocking technology, course selection online, grades online, CSH is a member of the Online School for Girls, laptops mandatory for students in grades 6 to 12. Campus intranet, student e-mail accounts, and computer access in designated common areas are available to students. Students grades are available online. The school has a published electronic and media policy.

Contact Mrs. Catherine Cullinane, Director of Admission. 203-532-3534. Fax: 203-532-3301. E-mail: admission@cshct.org. Website: www.cshgreenwich.org

THE COUNTRY DAY SCHOOL

13415 Dufferin Street
King City, Ontario L7B 1K5, Canada

Head of School: Mr. John Liggett

General Information Coeducational day college-preparatory, arts, business, and technology school. Grades JK–12. Founded: 1972. Setting: rural. Nearest major city is Toronto, Canada. 100-acre campus. 4 buildings on campus. Approved or accredited by Canadian Association of Independent Schools, Canadian Educational Standards Institute, Conference of Independent Schools of Ontario, and Ontario Department of Education. Affiliate member of National Association of Independent Schools. Language of instruction: English. Endowment: CAN$6 million. Total enrollment: 700. Upper school average class size: 17. Upper school faculty-student ratio: 1:9 Upper School students typically attend 5 days per week. The average school day consists of 6 hours and 25 minutes.

Upper School Student Profile Grade 9: 75 students (30 boys, 45 girls); Grade 10: 75 students (30 boys, 45 girls); Grade 11: 75 students (30 boys, 45 girls); Grade 12: 91 students (46 boys, 45 girls).

Faculty School total: 81. In upper school: 28 men, 20 women.

Subjects Offered Advanced chemistry, advanced computer applications, advanced math, algebra, American history, anatomy and physiology, ancient history, ancient/medieval philosophy, art and culture, art history, athletics, band, biology, business studies, Canadian geography, Canadian history, Canadian literature, career education, career/college preparation, choir, comparative politics, computer programming, creative writing, English, environmental geography, European history, French, government/civics, history, languages, mathematics, modern Western civilization, performing arts, philosophy, physical education, physics, politics, science, society, world history.

Graduation Requirements Ministry Grade 10 Literacy Test (Government of Ontario).

Special Academic Programs Advanced Placement exam preparation; study abroad.

College Admission Counseling 91 students graduated in 2016; all went to college, including McGill University; McMaster University; Queen's University at Kingston; The University of Western Ontario; University of Toronto; Wilfrid Laurier University.

Student Life Upper grades have uniform requirement, student council, honor system. Discipline rests primarily with faculty.

Summer Programs Advancement, sports, art/fine arts programs offered; session focuses on advancement; held both on and off campus; accepts boys and girls; open to students from other schools. 20 students usually enrolled. 2017 schedule: July 3 to July 28. Application deadline: March 1.

Tuition and Aid Day student tuition: CAN$27,100. Bursaries, need-based scholarship grants available.

Admissions Traditional secondary-level entrance grade is 9. For fall 2016, 97 students applied for upper-level admission, 58 were accepted, 37 enrolled. CAT 5 or SSAT required. Deadline for receipt of application materials: none. Application fee required: CAN$125. On-campus interview required.

Athletics Interscholastic: baseball (girls), basketball (b,g), cross-country running (b,g), golf (b,g), hockey (b,g), ice hockey (b,g), rugby (b,g), running (b,g), soccer (b,g), softball (b,g), tennis (b,g), track and field (b,g), volleyball (b,g); intramural: badminton (b,g), basketball (b,g), bowling (b,g), ice hockey (b), physical fitness (b,g), skiing (downhill) (b,g), snowboarding (b,g), soccer (b,g), softball (b,g), volleyball (b,g); coed interscholastic: alpine skiing, skiing (cross-country); coed intramural: bicycling, curling, Frisbee, mountain biking, nordic skiing, outdoor activities, outdoor education, physical fitness, physical training, strength & conditioning, swimming and diving, table tennis, weight training, yoga. 5 PE instructors.

Computers Computers are regularly used in accounting, business, career education, English, geography, history, mathematics, media, music, writing, yearbook classes.

Computer network features include on-campus library services, Internet access, wireless campus network, Internet filtering or blocking technology, access to online library resources from home, access to homework online via Blackboard Software. Campus intranet is available to students.

Contact Mr. David Huckvale, Director of Admission. 905-833-1220. Fax: 905-833-1350. E-mail: admissions@cds.on.ca. Website: www.cds.on.ca/

COVENANT CANADIAN REFORMED SCHOOL

3030 TWP Road 615A
County of Barrhead, Alberta T0G 1R2, Canada

Head of School: Mr. Mike Nederveen

General Information Coeducational day college-preparatory, general academic, and religious studies school, affiliated with Reformed Church. Grades K–12. Founded: 1977. Setting: rural. Nearest major city is Edmonton, Canada. 5-acre campus. 2 buildings on campus. Approved or accredited by Association of Independent Schools and Colleges of Alberta and Alberta Department of Education. Language of instruction: English. Total enrollment: 244. Upper school average class size: 14. Upper school faculty-student ratio: 1:14. There are 172 required school days per year for Upper School students. Upper School students typically attend 4 days per week. The average school day consists of 6 hours and 10 minutes.

Upper School Student Profile Grade 10: 16 students (8 boys, 8 girls); Grade 11: 13 students (7 boys, 6 girls); Grade 12: 12 students (6 boys, 6 girls). 100% of students are Reformed.

Faculty School total: 14. In upper school: 4 men, 5 women.

Subjects Offered Accounting, architectural drawing, Bible studies, biology, Canadian geography, career and personal planning, career technology, chemistry, child development, Christian education, computer information systems, computer skills, computer studies, consumer law, desktop publishing, digital photography, drama, drawing and design, early childhood, electronic publishing, English, French as a second language, geology, health education, history, HTML design, information processing, intro to computers, introduction to technology, keyboarding, mathematics, physical education, physics, prayer/spirituality, religious studies, science, sewing, social studies, theology and the arts, Web site design, Western religions, work experience, world geography, world religions, yearbook.

Graduation Requirements Must pass religious studies courses offered in grades 10, 11, and 12 for years attended.

Special Academic Programs Independent study; remedial reading and/or remedial writing; remedial math; programs in English, mathematics, general development for dyslexic students.

College Admission Counseling 9 students graduated in 2016; 2 went to college, including Abilene Christian University; The University of British Columbia; University of Lethbridge. Other: 7 went to work, 1 had other specific plans.

Student Life Upper grades have specified standards of dress, student council. Discipline rests primarily with faculty.

Tuition and Aid Day student tuition: CAN$6600. Tuition installment plan (monthly payment plans, individually arranged payment plans). Tuition rates per family available.

Admissions Traditional secondary-level entrance grade is 10. Achievement tests required. Deadline for receipt of application materials: none. No application fee required. Interview required.

Athletics Interscholastic: badminton (boys, girls), basketball (b,g), track and field (b,g), volleyball (b,g); coed intramural: badminton, ball hockey, baseball, basketball, flag football, floor hockey, football, Frisbee, hockey, ice hockey, indoor hockey, indoor soccer, lacrosse, soccer, softball, volleyball. 4 PE instructors, 6 coaches.

Computers Computers are regularly used in all classes. Computer network features include on-campus library services, Internet access, Internet filtering or blocking technology. Computer access in designated common areas is available to students. The school has a published electronic and media policy.

Contact Mr. Mike Nederveen, Principal. 780-674-4774. Fax: 780-401-3295. E-mail: principal@covenantschool.ca. Website: www.covenantschool.ca/

COVINGTON CATHOLIC HIGH SCHOOL

1600 Dixie Highway
Park Hills, Kentucky 41011

Head of School: Mr. Robert Rowe

General Information Boys' day college-preparatory, arts, business, religious studies, bilingual studies, and technology school, affiliated with Roman Catholic Church. Grades 9–12. Founded: 1925. Setting: suburban. Nearest major city is Cincinnati, OH. 30-acre campus. 4 buildings on campus. Approved or accredited by Southern Association of Colleges and Schools and Kentucky Department of Education. Total enrollment: 502. Upper school average class size: 140. Upper school faculty-student ratio: 1:18. There are 177 required school days per year for Upper School students. Upper School students typically attend 5 days per week. The average school day consists of 6 hours and 40 minutes.

Upper School Student Profile Grade 9: 139 students (139 boys); Grade 10: 167 students (167 boys); Grade 11: 147 students (147 boys); Grade 12: 142 students (142 boys). 90% of students are Roman Catholic.

Faculty School total: 46. In upper school: 33 men, 13 women; 35 have advanced degrees.

Subjects Offered Accounting, advanced chemistry, Advanced Placement courses, algebra, American government, American history, American history-AP, anatomy and physiology, art, biology, business law, calculus-AP, career exploration, chemistry, chemistry-AP, chorus, church history, computer applications, computer programming, computer science, computer science-AP, computer-aided design, creative writing, current events, drama, economics, engineering, English, film, geometry, German, graphic design, health, journalism, Latin, modern European history, music appreciation, orchestra, personal finance, physical education, physical science, physics, pre-algebra, pre-calculus, probability and statistics, psychology, psychology-AP, reading, scripture, social justice, sociology, Spanish, Spanish-AP, speech, theology, Web site design, wood processing, world civilizations, world geography, world history-AP, writing workshop.

Graduation Requirements Arts and fine arts (art, music, dance, drama), electives, English, health, mathematics, physical education (includes health), religion (includes Bible studies and theology), science, social studies (includes history), word processing, community service requirement, senior retreat.

Special Academic Programs 10 Advanced Placement exams for which test preparation is offered; honors section; study at local college for college credit.

College Admission Counseling 138 students graduated in 2016; 135 went to college, including The Ohio State University; University of Cincinnati; University of Dayton; University of Kentucky; University of Louisville; Xavier University. Other: 1 went to work, 2 entered military service. Mean composite ACT: 26.

Student Life Upper grades have specified standards of dress, student council. Discipline rests primarily with faculty. Attendance at religious services is required.

Tuition and Aid Day student tuition: $8130–$8855. Tuition installment plan (FACTS Tuition Payment Plan, monthly payment plans). Tuition reduction for siblings, merit scholarship grants, paying campus jobs available. In 2016–17, 17% of upper-school students received aid; total upper-school merit-scholarship money awarded: $30,000. Total amount of financial aid awarded in 2016–17: $400,000.

Admissions Traditional secondary-level entrance grade is 9. High School Placement Test required. Deadline for receipt of application materials: none. Application fee required: $200.

Athletics Interscholastic: archery, baseball, basketball, bowling, cross-country running, football, golf, soccer, swimming and diving, tennis, track and field, wrestling; intramural: alpine skiing, backpacking, basketball, bicycling, bowling, fishing, Frisbee, golf, hiking/backpacking, lacrosse, outdoor adventure, outdoor skills, skiing (downhill), snowboarding, Special Olympics, ultimate Frisbee, whiffle ball. 1 PE instructor.

Computers Computers are regularly used in all academic classes. Computer network features include Internet access, wireless campus network, Internet filtering or blocking technology. Student e-mail accounts are available to students. Students grades are available online. The school has a published electronic and media policy.

Contact Mr. Tony Barczak, Freshman/Sophomore Counselor; Admissions Director. 859-491-2247 Ext. 2257. Fax: 859-448-2242. E-mail: tbarczak@covcath.org. Website: www.covcath.org/

CRAWFORD ADVENTIST ACADEMY

531 Finch Avenue West
Willowdale, Ontario M2R 3X2, Canada

Head of School: Mr. Norman Brown

General Information Coeducational day college-preparatory, arts, business, religious studies, and technology school, affiliated with Seventh-day Adventist Church. Grades JK–12. Founded: 1954. Setting: urban. Nearest major city is Toronto, Canada. Students are housed in none. 5-acre campus. 1 building on campus. Approved or accredited by Ontario Ministry of Education and Ontario Department of Education. Language of instruction: English. Total enrollment: 361. Upper school average class size: 20. Upper school faculty-student ratio: 1:14. There are 196 required school days per year for Upper School students. Upper School students typically attend 5 days per week. The average school day consists of 7 hours and 15 minutes.

Upper School Student Profile Grade 9: 36 students (15 boys, 21 girls); Grade 10: 31 students (12 boys, 19 girls); Grade 11: 30 students (17 boys, 13 girls); Grade 12: 30 students (13 boys, 17 girls). 85% of students are Seventh-day Adventists.

Faculty School total: 17. In upper school: 12 men, 5 women; 13 have advanced degrees.

Subjects Offered Advanced computer applications, band, Bible, biology, business, business technology, calculus, Canadian geography, Canadian history, chemistry, choir, civics, community service, computer applications, computer information systems, drama, dramatic arts, earth and space science, English, English composition, French, French as a second language, geography, guidance, independent study, information technology, marketing, mathematics, physical education, physics, religion, science, writing, yearbook.

Graduation Requirements French as a second language, complete 40 community service hours, must pass the Ontario Secondary School Literacy Test.

Special Academic Programs 3 Advanced Placement exams for which test preparation is offered; remedial reading and/or remedial writing; programs in English for dyslexic students; ESL.

College Admission Counseling 30 students graduated in 2016; 4 went to college, including Andrews University; Oakwood University; Ryerson University; University of Toronto; University of Waterloo; York University. Other: 26 entered a postgraduate year. Median composite ACT: 20. 22% scored over 26 on composite ACT.

Student Life Upper grades have uniform requirement, student council, honor system. Discipline rests primarily with faculty. Attendance at religious services is required.

Tuition and Aid Day student tuition: CAN$12,000. Tuition installment plan (monthly payment plans, individually arranged payment plans). Tuition reduction for siblings, need-based scholarship grants, paying campus jobs available. In 2016–17, 25% of upper-school students received aid. Total amount of financial aid awarded in 2016–17: CAN$40,000.

Admissions Traditional secondary-level entrance grade is 9. For fall 2016, 12 students applied for upper-level admission, 10 were accepted. CAT, CAT 2, CCAT, CTBS (or similar from their school) or Learn Aid Aptitude Test required. Deadline for receipt of application materials: none. Application fee required: CAN$150. On-campus interview required.

Athletics Interscholastic: basketball (boys, girls), flag football (b), soccer (b,g), touch football (b), weight lifting (b,g); intramural: basketball (b,g), soccer (b,g), wall climbing (b); coed interscholastic: cooperative games, outdoor recreation, touch football, volleyball; coed intramural: basketball, flag football, floor hockey, indoor hockey, indoor soccer, outdoor education, outdoor recreation, physical fitness, physical training, running, skiing (downhill), snowboarding, table tennis, touch football, volleyball. 1 PE instructor, 2 coaches.

Computers Computers are regularly used in accounting, business, computer applications, yearbook classes. Computer network features include Internet access, wireless campus network, Internet filtering or blocking technology. Student e-mail accounts and computer access in designated common areas are available to students. Students grades are available online. The school has a published electronic and media policy.

Contact Mr. Derrick Hall, Vice President, Advancement. 416-633-0090 Ext. 234. Fax: 416-633-0467. E-mail: dhall@caasda.com. Website: www.tadsb.com/

THE CRENSHAW SCHOOL

2342 Hempel Ave.
Gotha, Florida 34734

Head of School: Mrs. Brenda Crenshaw

General Information Coeducational day college-preparatory school. Grades PK–12. Founded: 1999. Setting: suburban. Nearest major city is Orlando. 2 buildings on campus. Approved or accredited by Association of Independent Schools of Florida, National Council for Private School Accreditation, Southern Association of Colleges and Schools, and Florida Department of Education. Total enrollment: 102. Upper school average class size: 10. Upper school faculty-student ratio: 1:10. There are 180 required school days per year for Upper School students. Upper School students typically attend 5 days per week. The average school day consists of 6 hours.

Faculty School total: 18. In upper school: 2 men, 6 women; 3 have advanced degrees.

Subjects Offered 1968.

Special Academic Programs Honors section; accelerated programs; study at local college for college credit; academic accommodation for the gifted; ESL (10 students enrolled).

College Admission Counseling 16 students graduated in 2015; 1 went to college, including University of Central Florida; University of South Florida; Valencia College. Other: 1 had other specific plans.

Student Life Upper grades have uniform requirement, student council, honor system. Discipline rests equally with students and faculty.

Admissions For fall 2015, 25 students applied for upper-level admission, 20 were accepted, 20 enrolled. Deadline for receipt of application materials: none. Application fee required: $1250. Interview required.

Athletics 1 coach.

Computers Computer resources include wireless campus network. Students grades are available online. The school has a published electronic and media policy.

Contact Mrs. Brenda Crenshaw, Head of School. 407-877-7412. Fax: 407-877-0541. E-mail: bcrenshaw@crenshawschool.com. Website: www.crenshawschool.com/

CRESCENT SCHOOL

2365 Bayview Avenue
Toronto, Ontario M2L 1A2, Canada

Head of School: Mr. Michael Fellin

General Information Boys' day college-preparatory school. Grades 3–12. Founded: 1913. Setting: urban. 30-acre campus. 4 buildings on campus. Approved or accredited by Canadian Association of Independent Schools, Canadian Educational Standards Institute, Conference of Independent Schools of Ontario, Ontario Ministry of Education, and Ontario Department of Education. Affiliate member of National Association of Independent Schools; member of Secondary School Admission Test

Board. Language of instruction: English. Endowment: CAN$11 million. Total enrollment: 715. Upper school average class size: 18. Upper school faculty-student ratio: 1:10. Upper School students typically attend 5 days per week. The average school day consists of 6 hours and 50 minutes.

Upper School Student Profile Grade 9: 101 students (101 boys); Grade 10: 87 students (87 boys); Grade 11: 90 students (90 boys); Grade 12: 87 students (87 boys).

Faculty School total: 68. In upper school: 31 men, 11 women; 9 have advanced degrees.

Subjects Offered Accounting, algebra, American history, art, biology, business skills, calculus, chemistry, computer programming, computer science, creative writing, drama, economics, English, English literature, entrepreneurship, fine arts, finite math, French, geography, health, history, information technology, law, leadership, mathematics, media arts, music, philosophy, physical education, physics, political science, robotics, science, social studies, Spanish, technology/design, theater, world history.

Graduation Requirements Arts and fine arts (art, music, dance, drama), business skills (includes word processing), English, foreign language, mathematics, physical education (includes health), science, social studies (includes history).

Special Academic Programs Advanced Placement exam preparation; honors section; accelerated programs.

College Admission Counseling 86 students graduated in 2016; 82 went to college, including Dalhousie University; McGill University; Queen's University at Kingston; The University of Western Ontario; University of Waterloo; Wilfrid Laurier University. Other: 4 had other specific plans. 75% scored over 600 on SAT critical reading, 80% scored over 600 on SAT math.

Student Life Upper grades have uniform requirement, student council. Discipline rests primarily with faculty.

Summer Programs Advancement programs offered; session focuses on earning additional credits; held on campus; accepts boys and girls; open to students from other schools. 135 students usually enrolled. 2017 schedule: June 26 to July 28.

Tuition and Aid Day student tuition: CAN$30,750. Tuition installment plan (monthly payment plans, individually arranged payment plans). Bursaries, merit scholarship grants, need-based scholarship grants available. In 2016–17, 3% of upper-school students received aid; total upper-school merit-scholarship money awarded: CAN$30,000. Total amount of financial aid awarded in 2016–17: CAN$680,000.

Admissions Traditional secondary-level entrance grade is 9. For fall 2016, 81 students applied for upper-level admission, 50 were accepted, 31 enrolled. CAT, ERB CTP III, school's own exam or SSAT required. Deadline for receipt of application materials: December 4. Application fee required: CAN$200. On-campus interview required.

Athletics Interscholastic: alpine skiing, badminton, basketball, cross-country running, golf, ice hockey, judo, rugby, skiing (downhill), snowboarding, soccer, softball, squash, swimming and diving, table tennis, tennis, track and field, volleyball; intramural: ball hockey, basketball, curling, flag football, Frisbee, golf, ice hockey, mountain biking, soccer, softball, squash, table tennis, tennis, track and field, volleyball, weight lifting. 3 PE instructors.

Computers Computers are regularly used in accounting, art, business, computer applications, creative writing, economics, English, foreign language, French, geography, history, human geography - AP, information technology, mathematics, media arts, music, science, technology, yearbook classes. Computer network features include on-campus library services, online commercial services, Internet access, wireless campus network. Student e-mail accounts are available to students. Students grades are available online. The school has a published electronic and media policy.

Contact Ms. Angela Van Straubenzee, Receptionist and Enrolment Assistant. 416-449-2556 Ext. 227. Fax: 416-449-7950. E-mail: avanstraubenzee@crescentschool.org. Website: www.crescentschool.org

CRESTWOOD PREPARATORY COLLEGE

217 Brookbanks Drive
Toronto, Ontario M3A 2T7, Canada

Head of School: Mr. Vince Pagano

General Information Coeducational day college-preparatory school. Grades 7–12. Founded: 1980. Setting: urban. 5-acre campus. 1 building on campus. Approved or accredited by Ontario Department of Education. Language of instruction: English. Total enrollment: 525. Upper school average class size: 17. Upper school faculty-student ratio: 1:16. There are 190 required school days per year for Upper School students.

Faculty School total: 45. In upper school: 22 men, 23 women.

Subjects Offered 1 1/2 elective credits, addiction, ADL skills, aerobics, aesthetics, African American history, African American studies, African dance.

Special Academic Programs Advanced Placement exam preparation; academic accommodation for the gifted; remedial reading and/or remedial writing; ESL (35 students enrolled).

College Admission Counseling 72 students graduated in 2016; 71 went to college, including Sewanee: The University of the South. Other: 1 had other specific plans.

Student Life Upper grades have uniform requirement, student council. Discipline rests primarily with faculty.

Summer Programs Advancement, computer instruction programs offered; session focuses on Reach ahead credits; held on campus; accepts boys and girls; not open to students from other schools. 60 students usually enrolled. 2017 schedule: June 26 to July 21.

Tuition and Aid Day student tuition: CAN$25,900. Tuition installment plan (The Tuition Plan). Tuition reduction for siblings available.

Admissions Writing sample required. Deadline for receipt of application materials: February 14. Application fee required: CAN$125. Interview recommended.

Athletics Interscholastic: ball hockey (boys), baseball (b,g), basketball (b,g), golf (b), hockey (b,g), indoor track & field (b,g), running (b,g), softball (b,g), swimming and diving (b,g), volleyball (b,g); intramural: ball hockey (b), flag football (b), tai chi (b,g), ultimate Frisbee (b,g); coed intramural: Frisbee, scuba diving. 6 PE instructors, 3 coaches.

Computers Computer network features include on-campus library services, Internet access, wireless campus network, Internet filtering or blocking technology. Campus intranet, student e-mail accounts, and computer access in designated common areas are available to students. The school has a published electronic and media policy.

Contact Mr. Dave Hecock. 416-391-1441 Ext. 4323. Fax: 416-444-0949. E-mail: dave.hecock@crestwood.on.ca.

CROSSROADS SCHOOL FOR ARTS & SCIENCES

1714 21st Street
Santa Monica, California 90404-3917

Head of School: Bob Riddle

General Information Coeducational day college-preparatory, arts, and technology school. Grades K–12. Founded: 1971. Setting: urban. Nearest major city is Los Angeles. 3-acre campus. 20 buildings on campus. Approved or accredited by California Association of Independent Schools, Western Association of Schools and Colleges, and California Department of Education. Member of National Association of Independent Schools. Endowment: $17.9 million. Total enrollment: 1,174. Upper school average class size: 17. Upper school faculty-student ratio: 1:11. There are 164 required school days per year for Upper School students. Upper School students typically attend 5 days per week. The average school day consists of 7 hours.

Upper School Student Profile Grade 9: 133 students (59 boys, 74 girls); Grade 10: 130 students (64 boys, 66 girls); Grade 11: 127 students (67 boys, 60 girls); Grade 12: 131 students (64 boys, 67 girls).

Faculty School total: 165. In upper school: 42 men, 45 women; 73 have advanced degrees.

Subjects Offered Algebra, American history, American studies, art history, biology, calculus, ceramics, chemistry, community service, computer programming, computer science, creative writing, critical studies in film, cultural arts, dance, earth and space science, English, environmental education, film studies, French, gender issues, geometry, graphic design, great books, Greek, human development, Japanese, jazz ensemble, jazz theory, journalism, Latin, marine biology, marine ecology, music appreciation, music theory, orchestra, photography, physical education, physics, physiology, pre-calculus, sculpture, Spanish, statistics, studio art, theater, trigonometry, video film production, world civilizations, yoga.

Graduation Requirements Arts and fine arts (art, music, dance, drama), English, foreign language, human development, mathematics, physical education (includes health), science, social studies (includes history), community service hours, senior project. Community service is required.

Special Academic Programs Honors section; term-away projects; academic accommodation for the gifted, the musically talented, and the artistically talented.

College Admission Counseling 126 students graduated in 2015; all went to college, including New York University; The George Washington University; Tulane University; University of California, Los Angeles; University of Michigan; University of Southern California. Median SAT critical reading: 640, median SAT math: 630, median SAT writing: 670, median combined SAT: 1930, median composite ACT: 29. 69% scored over 600 on SAT critical reading, 60% scored over 600 on SAT math, 77% scored over 600 on SAT writing, 69% scored over 1800 on combined SAT, 82% scored over 26 on composite ACT.

Student Life Upper grades have student council. Discipline rests primarily with faculty.

Tuition and Aid Day student tuition: $36,000. Tuition installment plan (individually arranged payment plans, in-house only—2 payment plan for full pay students, and 10 payment plan exclusively for financial aid students only). Need-based scholarship grants, tuition reduction fund, need-based financial aid available. In 2015–16, 25% of upper-school students received aid. Total amount of financial aid awarded in 2015–16: $3,490,851.

Admissions Traditional secondary-level entrance grade is 9. For fall 2015, 140 students applied for upper-level admission, 28 were accepted, 20 enrolled. ISEE required. Deadline for receipt of application materials: December 2. Application fee required: $150. On-campus interview required.

Athletics Interscholastic: baseball (boys), basketball (b,g), cross-country running (b,g), soccer (b,g), softball (g), tennis (b,g), track and field (b,g), volleyball (b,g); coed interscholastic: flag football, golf, swimming and diving; coed intramural: canoeing/kayaking, climbing, hiking/backpacking, kayaking, outdoor activities, outdoor education, rock climbing, ropes courses, snowshoeing, table tennis. 7 PE instructors, 24 coaches, 3 athletic trainers.

Computers Computers are regularly used in college planning, creative writing, foreign language, graphic design, journalism, mathematics, music, newspaper, programming, science classes. Computer network features include on-campus library services, online commercial services, Internet access, wireless campus network. Student e-mail accounts and computer access in designated common areas are available to students. Students grades are available online. The school has a published electronic and media policy.

Contact Eric Barber, Director of Enrollment Management. 310-829-7391 Ext. 525. Fax: 310-828-5636. E-mail: Ebarber@xrds.org. Website: www.xrds.org

CROTCHED MOUNTAIN SCHOOL

Greenfield, New Hampshire
See Special Needs Schools section.

CRYSTAL SPRINGS UPLANDS SCHOOL

400 Uplands Drive
Hillsborough, California 94010

Head of School: Ms. Amy Richards

General Information Coeducational day college-preparatory school. Grades 6–12. Founded: 1952. Setting: suburban. Nearest major city is San Francisco. 10-acre campus. 4 buildings on campus. Approved or accredited by American Association of Christian Schools, Western Association of Schools and Colleges, and California Department of Education. Member of National Association of Independent Schools and Secondary School Admission Test Board. Endowment: $15 million. Total enrollment: 350. Upper school average class size: 14. Upper school faculty-student ratio: 1:9. Upper School students typically attend 5 days per week. The average school day consists of 7 hours.

Faculty School total: 44. In upper school: 18 men, 26 women; 24 have advanced degrees.

Subjects Offered Acting, advanced computer applications, algebra, American history, American literature, art, astronomy, biology, calculus, ceramics, chamber groups, chemistry, chorus, comparative cultures, computer math, computer programming, computer science, concert bell choir, creative writing, dance, dance performance, drama, English, English literature, ensembles, European history, fine arts, French, geometry, graphic design, health, history, mathematics, multicultural literature, music, photography, physical education, physics, poetry, post-calculus, pre-calculus, science, Shakespeare, Spanish, statistics, theater, video film production, wellness, world history, world literature, writing.

Graduation Requirements Arts and fine arts (art, music, dance, drama), English, foreign language, history, mathematics, physical education (includes health), science, senior project.

Special Academic Programs Honors section; independent study; term-away projects; domestic exchange program; study abroad.

College Admission Counseling 61 students graduated in 2015; all went to college, including Stanford University; University of California, Los Angeles; University of California, San Diego; University of Pennsylvania; University of Southern California. Mean SAT critical reading: 674, mean SAT math: 703, mean SAT writing: 688, mean combined SAT: 2067, mean composite ACT: 29.

Student Life Upper grades have specified standards of dress, student council, honor system. Discipline rests equally with students and faculty.

Tuition and Aid Day student tuition: $37,485. Tuition installment plan (Insured Tuition Payment Plan, monthly payment plans, Tuition Management Systems Plan). Need-based scholarship grants available. In 2015–16, 20% of upper-school students received aid. Total amount of financial aid awarded in 2015–16: $2,200,000.

Admissions Traditional secondary-level entrance grade is 9. For fall 2015, 477 students applied for upper-level admission, 137 were accepted, 77 enrolled. ISEE or SSAT required. Deadline for receipt of application materials: January 14. Application fee required: $85. On-campus interview required.

Athletics Interscholastic: baseball (boys), basketball (b,g), cross-country running (b,g), football (b), soccer (b,g), softball (g), swimming and diving (b,g), tennis (b,g), track and field (b,g), volleyball (g); coed interscholastic: badminton, dance, golf, running, strength & conditioning; coed intramural: dance, fitness, Frisbee, hiking/backpacking, outdoors, rock climbing, table tennis, ultimate Frisbee, weight lifting, weight training. 3 PE instructors, 14 coaches, 1 athletic trainer.

Computers Computers are regularly used in all academic classes. Computer network features include on-campus library services, online commercial services, Internet access, wireless campus network, Internet filtering or blocking technology. Campus intranet, student e-mail accounts, and computer access in designated common areas are available to students. Students grades are available online. The school has a published electronic and media policy.

Contact Admission Office. 650-342-4175. Fax: 650-342-7611. E-mail: admission@csus.org. Website: www.csus.org

C.S. LEWIS ACADEMY

PO Box 3250
Newberg, Oregon 97132

Head of School: Mr. Mike Wenger

General Information Coeducational day college-preparatory and general academic school, affiliated with Christian faith. Grades 9–12. Founded: 1985. Setting: small

town. Nearest major city is Portland. 8-acre campus. 3 buildings on campus. Approved or accredited by Northwest Association of Independent Schools and Oregon Department of Education. Total enrollment: 150. Upper school average class size: 10. Upper school faculty-student ratio: 1:6. There are 170 required school days per year for Upper School students. Upper School students typically attend 5 days per week. The average school day consists of 7 hours.

Upper School Student Profile Grade 9: 9 students (6 boys, 3 girls); Grade 10: 11 students (3 boys, 8 girls); Grade 11: 15 students (5 boys, 10 girls); Grade 12: 11 students (6 boys, 5 girls).

Faculty School total: 25. In upper school: 2 men, 7 women; 5 have advanced degrees.

Subjects Offered Algebra, American literature, ancient world history, art, band, Bible, Bible studies, biology, career/college preparation, chemistry, choir, consumer education, creative writing, drama, economics, English, English literature, European literature, food science, general science, geometry, government, health, history, home economics, journalism, language arts, New Testament, physical education, physics, pre-algebra, pre-calculus, religious studies, social studies, Spanish, speech, student government, U.S. history, vocational arts, Western civilization, woodworking, writing, yearbook.

College Admission Counseling 22 students graduated in 2016; 19 went to college, including Chemeketa Community College; George Fox University; Portland Community College; Western Oregon University. Other: 1 went to work, 2 entered military service. Mean combined SAT: 1721, mean composite ACT: 30. 43% scored over 600 on SAT critical reading, 29% scored over 600 on SAT math, 43% scored over 600 on SAT writing, 43% scored over 1800 on combined SAT, 50% scored over 26 on composite ACT.

Student Life Upper grades have specified standards of dress, student council. Discipline rests primarily with faculty. Attendance at religious services is required.

Tuition and Aid Day student tuition: $7450. Tuition installment plan (FACTS Tuition Payment Plan, individually arranged payment plans). Tuition reduction for siblings, need-based scholarship grants available. In 2016–17, 15% of upper-school students received aid. Total amount of financial aid awarded in 2016–17: $22,113.

Admissions Traditional secondary-level entrance grade is 9. Deadline for receipt of application materials: none. Application fee required: $75. Interview recommended.

Athletics Interscholastic: basketball (boys, girls), track and field (b,g), volleyball (g); coed interscholastic: golf, soccer; coed intramural: basketball, soccer, volleyball. 1 PE instructor, 10 coaches.

Computers Computers are regularly used in creative writing, mathematics, science, social sciences, writing, yearbook classes. Computer network features include Internet access, wireless campus network, Internet filtering or blocking technology. Students grades are available online. The school has a published electronic and media policy.

Contact Ms. Dianne Sargent, Administrative Assistant. 503-538-0114. Fax: 503-538-4113. E-mail: highschool@cslewisacademy.com. Website: www.cslewisacademy.com

THE CULVER ACADEMIES

1300 Academy Road
Culver, Indiana 46511

Head of School: Dr. Jim Power

General Information Coeducational boarding and day college-preparatory, arts, and horsemanship, entrepreneurial studies school. Grades 9–PG. Founded: 1894. Setting: small town. Nearest major city is South Bend. Students are housed in single-sex dormitories. 1,700-acre campus. 38 buildings on campus. Approved or accredited by Independent Schools Association of the Central States. Member of National Association of Independent Schools and Secondary School Admission Test Board. Endowment: $385 million. Upper school average class size: 12. Upper school faculty-student ratio: 1:8. There are 185 required school days per year for Upper School students. Upper School students typically attend 5 days per week. The average school day consists of 6 hours and 45 minutes.

Upper School Student Profile Grade 9: 163 students (95 boys, 68 girls); Grade 10: 231 students (136 boys, 95 girls); Grade 11: 221 students (123 boys, 98 girls); Grade 12: 211 students (114 boys, 97 girls); Postgraduate: 2 students (1 boy, 1 girl). 92% of students are boarding students. 40% are state residents. 38 states are represented in upper school student body. 20% are international students. International students from Canada, China, Mexico, Republic of Korea, Saudi Arabia, and United States; 17 other countries represented in student body.

Faculty School total: 106. In upper school: 56 men, 50 women; 82 have advanced degrees; 16 reside on campus.

Subjects Offered Concert band, concert choir.

Graduation Requirements Arts and fine arts (art, music, dance, drama), English, foreign language, health education, history, leadership, mathematics, science, senior community service project.

Special Academic Programs 25 Advanced Placement exams for which test preparation is offered; honors section; study abroad; academic accommodation for the gifted, the musically talented, and the artistically talented; ESL (24 students enrolled).

College Admission Counseling 204 students graduated in 2016; 192 went to college, including Ball State University; Indiana University Bloomington; Princeton University; Purdue University; United States Military Academy; United States Naval Academy. Other: 8 had other specific plans.

Student Life Upper grades have uniform requirement, student council, honor system. Discipline rests primarily with students.

Summer Programs Enrichment, advancement, ESL, sports, art/fine arts, rigorous outdoor training, computer instruction programs offered; session focuses on leadership training, citizenship, lifetime interests, and skills development; held on campus; accepts boys and girls; open to students from other schools. 1,385 students usually enrolled. 2017 schedule: June 18 to July 29. Application deadline: April 1.

Tuition and Aid Day student tuition: $34,500; 7-day tuition and room/board: $44,500. Tuition installment plan (Key Tuition Payment Plan). Merit scholarship grants, need-based scholarship grants available. In 2016–17, 48% of upper-school students received aid; total upper-school merit-scholarship money awarded: $7,850,000. Total amount of financial aid awarded in 2016–17: $8,900,000.

Admissions Traditional secondary-level entrance grade is 9. SSAT or TOEFL required. Deadline for receipt of application materials: June 1. Application fee required: $30. Interview required.

Athletics Interscholastic: baseball (boys), basketball (b,g), crew (b,g), cross-country running (b,g), diving (b,g), equestrian sports (b,g), fencing (b,g), football (b), golf (b,g), hockey (b,g), ice hockey (b,g), indoor track & field (b,g), lacrosse (b,g), polo (b,g), rowing (b,g), rugby (b,g), soccer (b,g), softball (g), swimming and diving (b,g), tennis (b,g), track and field (b,g), volleyball (g), winter (indoor) track (b,g), wrestling (b,g); intramural: basketball (b), dance team (b), drill team (b,g), flag football (b), ice hockey (b,g), indoor soccer (b,g), modern dance (b,g), paint ball (b,g), soccer (b); coed interscholastic: cheering, dressage, equestrian sports, sailing, trap and skeet; coed intramural: aerobics, aerobics/dance, aerobics/Nautilus, alpine skiing, aquatics, archery, backpacking, badminton, ballet, bicycling, bowling, broomball, canoeing/kayaking, climbing, combined training, cooperative games, cross-country running, dance, figure skating, fishing, fitness, fitness walking, Frisbee, handball, hiking/backpacking, horseback riding, independent competitive sports, indoor track & field, jogging, kickball, life saving, marksmanship, Nautilus, outdoor activities, outdoor adventure, outdoor education, outdoor recreation, outdoor skills, outdoors, paddling, physical fitness, physical training, power lifting, project adventure, racquetball, riflery, ropes courses, running, scuba diving, skeet shooting, skiing (cross-country), skiing (downhill), snowboarding, squash, strength & conditioning, swimming and diving, table tennis, ultimate Frisbee, volleyball, walking, wall climbing, weight lifting, weight training, wilderness, winter walking, yoga. 8 PE instructors, 4 athletic trainers.

Computers Computers are regularly used in all classes. Computer network features include on-campus library services, online commercial services, Internet access, wireless campus network, Internet filtering or blocking technology, each student is issued a laptop. Campus intranet, student e-mail accounts, and computer access in designated common areas are available to students. Students grades are available online. The school has a published electronic and media policy.

Contact Mr. Michael Turnbull, Director of Admissions. 574-842-7100. Fax: 574-842-8066. E-mail: Michael.Turnbull@culver.org. Website: www.culver.org

CURREY INGRAM ACADEMY

6544 Murray Lane
Brentwood, Tennessee 37027

Head of School: Dr. Jeffrey Mitchell

General Information Coeducational day college-preparatory, arts, technology, ethics and character education, and service learning school; primarily serves students with learning disabilities, individuals with Attention Deficit Disorder, and dyslexic students. Grades K–12. Founded: 1968. Setting: suburban. Nearest major city is Nashville. 83-acre campus. 3 buildings on campus. Approved or accredited by Council of Accreditation and School Improvement, Southern Association of Colleges and Schools, Southern Association of Independent Schools, and Tennessee Department of Education. Member of National Association of Independent Schools. Total enrollment: 307. Upper school average class size: 7. There are 175 required school days per year for Upper School students. Upper School students typically attend 5 days per week. The average school day consists of 7 hours and 30 minutes.

Subjects Offered Algebra, American government, art, basic language skills, biology, British literature, character education, chemistry, cinematography, college admission preparation, college awareness, college counseling, college planning, community service, digital music, digital photography, drama performance, earth science, economics, electives, English composition, English literature, environmental science, ethics and responsibility, government, health, history, integrated technology fundamentals, learning strategies, life skills, literature, modern world history, music, newspaper, physical education, physics, pragmatics, pre-calculus, reading/study skills, social studies, sports, studio art, technology, video film production, vocal music, writing, writing workshop, yearbook.

Graduation Requirements Arts and fine arts (art, music, dance, drama), electives, English, ethics, foreign language, mathematics, physical education (includes health), science, social studies (includes history), students who need remediation in reading/writing take reading/writing workshop instead of foreign language, seniors must complete Service Learning credit plus 30 hours of community service.

Special Academic Programs Honors section; independent study; academic accommodation for the gifted, the musically talented, and the artistically talented; remedial reading and/or remedial writing; remedial math; programs in English, mathematics, general development for dyslexic students.

College Admission Counseling 12 students graduated in 2016; 11 went to college, including Austin Peay State University; Chattanooga State Community College; High Point University; Lipscomb University; Lynn University; Reinhardt University. Other: 1 entered military service.

Student Life Upper grades have uniform requirement, student council, honor system. Discipline rests primarily with faculty.

Tuition and Aid Day student tuition: $37,380–$38,524. Tuition installment plan (Insured Tuition Payment Plan, monthly payment plans). Need-based scholarship grants available. In 2016–17, 35% of upper-school students received aid. Total amount of financial aid awarded in 2016–17: $1,750,000.

Admissions Traditional secondary-level entrance grade is 9. Psychoeducational evaluation required. Deadline for receipt of application materials: none. Application fee required: $250. Interview required.

Athletics Interscholastic: basketball (boys), cheering (g), volleyball (g); intramural: fitness (b,g); coed interscholastic: cross-country running, golf, soccer, tennis.

Computers Computers are regularly used in all academic classes. Computer network features include on-campus library services, Internet access, wireless campus network, Internet filtering or blocking technology, iPods for instructional use in classrooms, 1:1 laptop and/or iPad program, assistive technology. Campus intranet and student e-mail accounts are available to students. Students grades are available online. The school has a published electronic and media policy.

Contact Mrs. Kathy Boles, Director of Admission. 615-507-3173 Ext. 250. Fax: 615-507-3170. E-mail: kathy.boles@curreyingram.org. Website: www.curreyingram.org

CUSHING ACADEMY

39 School Street
Ashburnham, Massachusetts 01430-8000

Head of School: Ms. Cathrine Pollock

General Information Coeducational boarding and day college-preparatory, arts, and Academic Support, ESL school. Grades 9–PG. Founded: 1865. Setting: small town. Nearest major city is Boston. Students are housed in single-sex dormitories. 162-acre campus. 33 buildings on campus. Approved or accredited by Association of Independent Schools in New England, New England Association of Schools and Colleges, The Association of Boarding Schools, and Massachusetts Department of Education. Member of National Association of Independent Schools and Secondary School Admission Test Board. Endowment: $45 million. Total enrollment: 400. Upper school average class size: 12. Upper school faculty-student ratio: 1:8. There are 152 required school days per year for Upper School students. Upper School students typically attend 5 days per week. The average school day consists of 7 hours.

Upper School Student Profile Grade 9: 49 students (20 boys, 29 girls); Grade 10: 94 students (52 boys, 42 girls); Grade 11: 122 students (70 boys, 52 girls); Grade 12: 116 students (65 boys, 51 girls); Postgraduate: 19 students (18 boys, 1 girl).

Faculty School total: 64. In upper school: 27 men, 37 women; 37 have advanced degrees; 47 reside on campus.

Subjects Offered Advanced biology, advanced math, Advanced Placement courses, aerobics, algebra, American government, American history, American literature, American literature-AP, anatomy, anatomy and physiology, architectural drawing, art, art history, athletic training, bioethics, biology, biology-AP, calculus, calculus-AP, career education internship, chemistry, chemistry-AP, Chinese, chorus, Civil War, community service, computer programming, computer science, creative arts, creative drama, creative writing, dance, developmental language skills, digital photography, discrete mathematics, drafting, drama, drawing, driver education, earth and space science, ecology, ecology, environmental systems, economics, economics and history, economics-AP, English, English literature, environmental science, ESL, ethics, European history, expository writing, fine arts, French, geometry, government/civics, grammar, graphic arts, health, health and wellness, history, honors algebra, honors English, honors geometry, honors U.S. history, honors world history, Latin, Latin-AP, Mandarin, marine biology, mathematics, mechanical drawing, music, music history, music theory, musical theater, photography, physics, physiology, pre-calculus, probability and statistics, psychology, SAT preparation, science, social studies, sociology, Spanish, Spanish-AP, speech, stagecraft, statistics-AP, student government, technology, The 20th Century, theater, theater history, trigonometry, U.S. government and politics-AP, U.S. history, United Nations and international issues, Vietnam War, visual arts, vocal music, wind instruments, world history, world literature, World-Wide-Web publishing, writing.

Graduation Requirements Art, English, foreign language, mathematics, science, social studies (includes history).

Special Academic Programs 14 Advanced Placement exams for which test preparation is offered; honors section; independent study; term-away projects; academic accommodation for the gifted, the musically talented, and the artistically talented; remedial reading and/or remedial writing; remedial math; programs in English, mathematics, general development for dyslexic students; ESL (55 students enrolled).

College Admission Counseling 131 students graduated in 2016; 129 went to college, including Boston University; Hobart and William Smith Colleges; Ithaca College; Northeastern University; Skidmore College; Syracuse University. Other: 2 had other specific plans.

Student Life Upper grades have specified standards of dress, student council, honor system. Discipline rests equally with students and faculty.

Summer Programs Remediation, enrichment, advancement, ESL, sports, art/fine arts, computer instruction programs offered; session focuses on enrichment; held on campus; accepts boys and girls; open to students from other schools. 280 students usually enrolled. 2017 schedule: July 2 to August 4.

Tuition and Aid Day student tuition: $41,300; 7-day tuition and room/board: $57,800. Tuition installment plan (monthly payment plans). Merit scholarship grants, need-based scholarship grants, Watkins Scholars available. In 2016–17, 26% of upper-school students received aid; total upper-school merit-scholarship money awarded: $100,000. Total amount of financial aid awarded in 2016–17: $3,500,000.

Admissions Traditional secondary-level entrance grade is 9. For fall 2016, 804 students applied for upper-level admission, 505 were accepted, 153 enrolled. ACT, PSAT, SAT, SSAT, TOEFL or TOEFL Junior required. Deadline for receipt of application materials: February 1. Application fee required: $50. Interview recommended.

Athletics Interscholastic: baseball (boys), basketball (b,g), field hockey (g), football (b), hockey (b,g), ice hockey (b,g), lacrosse (b,g), running (b,g), skiing (downhill) (b,g), soccer (b,g), softball (g), tennis (b,g), track and field (b,g), volleyball (g); coed interscholastic: alpine skiing, cross-country running, golf, running; coed intramural: aerobics, aerobics/dance, alpine skiing, dance, equestrian sports, figure skating, fitness, horseback riding, ice hockey, ice skating, independent competitive sports, martial arts, modern dance, mountain biking, physical fitness, physical training, skiing (downhill), snowboarding, strength & conditioning, tennis, weight training, yoga. 3 coaches, 2 athletic trainers.

Computers Computers are regularly used in all academic classes. Computer network features include on-campus library services, online commercial services, Internet access, wireless campus network, Internet filtering or blocking technology, Live event webcasting. Campus intranet, student e-mail accounts, and computer access in designated common areas are available to students. Students grades are available online. The school has a published electronic and media policy.

Contact Mrs. Catherine Pollock, Co-Head of School. 978-827-7300. Fax: 978-827-6253. E-mail: admissions@cushing.org. Website: www.cushing.org

DALAT SCHOOL

Tanjung Bunga, Malaysia

General Information Coeducational boarding and day college-preparatory school, affiliated with Christian faith. Boarding grades 6–12, day grades P3–12. Setting: suburban. Nearest major city is Georgetown, Malaysia. Students are housed in Family Style Boarding. 4-acre campus. 3 buildings on campus. Approved or accredited by Association of Christian Schools International and Western Association of Schools and Colleges. Language of instruction: English. Upper school average class size: 20. There are 180 required school days per year for Upper School students. Upper School students typically attend 5 days per week. The average school day consists of 6 hours and 15 minutes.

Upper School Student Profile 10% of students are boarding students. 32% are state residents. 22 states are represented in upper school student body. 68% are international students. International students from Canada, India, Malaysia, Republic of Korea, Singapore, and United States; 18 other countries represented in student body. 0.5% of students are Christian faith.

Faculty School total: 85. In upper school: 8 men, 10 women; 7 reside on campus.

Graduation Requirements Community service hours.

Special Academic Programs Honors section; independent study; domestic exchange program; programs in English, general development for dyslexic students; special instructional classes for study hall support in Special Services department.

College Admission Counseling 59 students graduated in 2016; 57 went to college, including Azusa Pacific University; Liberty University; Nyack College; Taylor University; The University of British Columbia; University of California, Davis. Other: 1 went to work, 1 entered military service.

Student Life Upper grades have uniform requirement, student council, honor system. Discipline rests primarily with faculty. Attendance at religious services is required.

Tuition and Aid Day student tuition: 41,400 Malaysian ringgits.

Admissions Traditional secondary-level entrance grade is 9. Achievement tests required. Deadline for receipt of application materials: May 1. Application fee required: 500 Malaysian ringgits. Interview required.

Athletics Interscholastic: basketball (boys, girls), cross-country running (b,g), soccer (b,g), softball (b,g), swimming and diving (b,g), volleyball (b,g); intramural: basketball (b,g), cross-country running (b,g), soccer (b,g), softball (b,g), volleyball (b,g); coed interscholastic: Frisbee, running, tennis, track and field; coed intramural: Frisbee, gymnastics, indoor soccer, kickball, outdoor recreation, physical fitness, physical training, running, track and field. 4 PE instructors.

Computers Computers are regularly used in all classes. Computer network features include on-campus library services, online commercial services, Internet access, wireless campus network, Internet filtering or blocking technology. Campus intranet, student e-mail accounts, and computer access in designated common areas are available to students. Students grades are available online. The school has a published electronic and media policy.

Contact Mr. Karl Steinkamp. 60-4-899-2105. Fax: 60-4-890-2141. E-mail: ksteinkamp@dalat.org.

DALLAS ACADEMY

Dallas, Texas

See Special Needs Schools section.

DAMIEN HIGH SCHOOL

2280 Damien Avenue
La Verne, California 91750

Head of School: Dr. Merritt Hemenway

General Information Boys' day college-preparatory, Project Lead The Way: 4-year pre-engineering program, and interscholastic debate school, affiliated with Roman Catholic Church. Grades 9–12. Distance learning grades 9–12. Founded: 1959. Setting: suburban. Nearest major city is Los Angeles. 28-acre campus. 9 buildings on campus. Approved or accredited by Western Association of Schools and Colleges, Western Catholic Education Association, and California Department of Education. Endowment: $450,000. Total enrollment: 936. Upper school average class size: 26. Upper school faculty-student ratio: 1:17. There are 180 required school days per year for Upper School students. Upper School students typically attend 5 days per week. The average school day consists of 5 hours and 50 minutes.

Upper School Student Profile Grade 9: 228 students (228 boys); Grade 10: 209 students (209 boys); Grade 11: 258 students (258 boys); Grade 12: 224 students (224 boys). 68% of students are Roman Catholic.

Faculty School total: 54. In upper school: 40 men, 14 women; 27 have advanced degrees.

Subjects Offered Advanced biology, advanced chemistry, Advanced Placement courses, advanced studio art-AP, algebra, American history, American history-AP, American literature, American literature-AP, anatomy and physiology, ancient world history, art history, art history-AP, band, biology, biology-AP, calculus-AP, chemistry, chemistry-AP, Chinese, comparative government and politics-AP, comparative religion, computer applications, computer programming, computer science-AP, debate, earth science, economics, economics-AP, English composition, English language and composition-AP, English literature, English literature and composition-AP, environmental science-AP, European history-AP, fitness, French, French language-AP, German, German-AP, government, health, honors geometry, human geography - AP, macroeconomics-AP, mathematics, microeconomics-AP, music, physics, physics-AP, pre-calculus, social issues, Spanish, Spanish-AP, sports medicine, statistics-AP, theology, U.S. government and politics, U.S. history, visual arts, weight training, Western civilization, world history.

Graduation Requirements Algebra, American government, American history, ancient world history, art, biology, Catholic belief and practice, chemistry, Christian and Hebrew scripture, Christian doctrine, Christian ethics, Christian scripture, economics, English, English composition, foreign language, geometry, government, health and wellness, history of the Catholic Church, language and composition, modern world history, New Testament, U.S. history, world history, world literature, 100 hours of community service.

Special Academic Programs 25 Advanced Placement exams for which test preparation is offered; honors section; ESL (18 students enrolled).

College Admission Counseling 221 students graduated in 2016; 203 went to college, including California State Polytechnic University, Pomona; Northern Arizona University; The University of Arizona; University of California, Riverside; University of San Diego; University of Southern California. Other: 2 entered military service, 16 had other specific plans. Mean SAT critical reading: 539, mean SAT math: 563, mean SAT writing: 520, mean combined SAT: 1622, mean composite ACT: 25. 26.6% scored over 600 on SAT critical reading, 37.5% scored over 600 on SAT math, 20.8% scored over 600 on SAT writing, 25% scored over 1800 on combined SAT, 20% scored over 26 on composite ACT.

Student Life Upper grades have uniform requirement, student council. Discipline rests primarily with faculty. Attendance at religious services is required.

Summer Programs Remediation, enrichment, advancement, sports, art/fine arts, computer instruction programs offered; session focuses on academic advancement, remediation; held on campus; accepts boys and girls; open to students from other schools. 500 students usually enrolled. 2017 schedule: June 12 to July 14. Application deadline: June 5.

Tuition and Aid Day student tuition: $8100. Tuition installment plan (FACTS Tuition Payment Plan). Tuition reduction for siblings, merit scholarship grants, need-based scholarship grants available. In 2016–17, 23% of upper-school students received aid; total upper-school merit-scholarship money awarded: $212,000. Total amount of financial aid awarded in 2016–17: $495,000.

Admissions Traditional secondary-level entrance grade is 9. For fall 2016, 287 students applied for upper-level admission, 270 were accepted, 228 enrolled. High School Placement Test (closed version) from Scholastic Testing Service required. Deadline for receipt of application materials: none. Application fee required: $75.

Athletics Interscholastic: baseball, basketball, bicycling, cross-country running, football, golf, hockey, ice hockey, in-line skating, lacrosse, mountain biking, roller hockey, soccer, swimming and diving, tennis, track and field, volleyball, water polo, wrestling; intramural: bocce, bowling, fishing, hiking/backpacking, surfing. 2 PE instructors, 30 coaches, 2 athletic trainers.

Computers Computers are regularly used in all academic classes. Computer network features include online commercial services, Internet access, wireless campus network,

Internet filtering or blocking technology. Campus intranet, student e-mail accounts, and computer access in designated common areas are available to students. Students grades are available online. The school has a published electronic and media policy.

Contact Mrs. Christina Provenzano, Admissions Coordinator. 909-596-1946 Ext. 247. Fax: 909-596-6112. E-mail: christina@damien-hs.edu. Website: www.damien-hs.edu

DANA HALL SCHOOL

45 Dana Road
Wellesley, Massachusetts 02482

Head of School: Ms. Katherine L. Bradley

General Information Girls' boarding and day college-preparatory, athletics, health and wellness, and leadership and community service school. Boarding grades 9–12, day grades 5–12. Founded: 1881. Setting: suburban. Nearest major city is Boston. Students are housed in single-sex dormitories. 55-acre campus. 34 buildings on campus. Approved or accredited by Association of Independent Schools in New England, New England Association of Schools and Colleges, The Association of Boarding Schools, and Massachusetts Department of Education. Member of National Association of Independent Schools and Secondary School Admission Test Board. Endowment: $46.9 million. Total enrollment: 464. Upper school average class size: 12. Upper school faculty-student ratio: 1:6. There are 165 required school days per year for Upper School students. Upper School students typically attend 5 days per week. The average school day consists of 7 hours and 30 minutes.

Upper School Student Profile Grade 9: 92 students (92 girls); Grade 10: 94 students (94 girls); Grade 11: 81 students (81 girls); Grade 12: 89 students (89 girls). 40% of students are boarding students. 72% are state residents. 11 states are represented in upper school student body. 20% are international students. International students from China, Hong Kong, Mexico, Republic of Korea, Taiwan, and Thailand; 6 other countries represented in student body.

Faculty School total: 64. In upper school: 21 men, 43 women; 49 have advanced degrees; 46 reside on campus.

Subjects Offered 3-dimensional design, advanced computer applications, African American history, African-American literature, American culture, area studies, basketball, calculus-AP, chamber groups, chemistry-AP, choreography, classical civilization, college admission preparation, digital art, diversity studies, drawing and design, equestrian sports, fencing, literary magazine, softball, statistics, technical theater, U.S. history, volleyball, women in the classical world, yearbook.

Graduation Requirements Area studies, art, performing arts, visual arts, 20 hours of community service.

Special Academic Programs 17 Advanced Placement exams for which test preparation is offered; honors section; independent study; term-away projects; study abroad.

College Admission Counseling 93 students graduated in 2016; all went to college, including Babson College; Boston College; Boston University; Colby College; Colgate University; The George Washington University. Mean SAT critical reading: 612, mean SAT math: 629, mean SAT writing: 644, mean combined SAT: 1885, mean composite ACT: 30.

Student Life Upper grades have specified standards of dress, student council, honor system. Discipline rests equally with students and faculty.

Summer Programs Enrichment programs offered; session focuses on leadership training and confidence building for girls entering high school; held on campus; accepts girls; open to students from other schools. 40 students usually enrolled. 2017 schedule: June 24 to June 30. Application deadline: April 4.

Tuition and Aid Day student tuition: $44,800; 7-day tuition and room/board: $58,600. Tuition installment plan (monthly payment plans). Merit scholarship grants, need-based scholarship grants available. In 2016–17, 27% of upper-school students received aid; total upper-school merit-scholarship money awarded: $20,000. Total amount of financial aid awarded in 2016–17: $4,090,422.

Admissions Traditional secondary-level entrance grade is 9. For fall 2016, 389 students applied for upper-level admission, 142 were accepted, 71 enrolled. ISEE, SSAT or TOEFL required. Deadline for receipt of application materials: January 15. Application fee required: $50. On-campus interview recommended.

Athletics Interscholastic: basketball, cross-country running, diving, equestrian sports, fencing, field hockey, horseback riding, ice hockey, lacrosse, soccer, softball, squash, swimming and diving, tennis, volleyball; intramural: aquatics, ballet, climbing, crew, dance, equestrian sports, fitness, Frisbee, golf, hiking/backpacking, horseback riding, indoor track, life saving, martial arts, modern dance, Nautilus, outdoor activities, physical fitness, physical training, rock climbing, rowing, running, self defense, squash, strength & conditioning, swimming and diving, tennis, ultimate Frisbee, weight lifting, weight training, yoga. 3 PE instructors, 33 coaches, 2 athletic trainers.

Computers Computers are regularly used in all academic, art, English, French, history, Latin, mathematics, science, Spanish, Web site design, yearbook classes. Computer network features include on-campus library services, online commercial services, Internet access, wireless campus network, Internet filtering or blocking technology, Schoology learning management system, 1:1 iPad program. Campus intranet, student e-mail accounts, and computer access in designated common areas are available to students. Students grades are available online. The school has a published electronic and media policy.

Contact Mrs. Bethann Coppi, Admission Office Manager/Database Coordinator. 781-489-1331 Ext. 2531. Fax: 781-787-2693. E-mail: admission@danahall.org. Website: www.danahall.org

DARLINGTON SCHOOL

1014 Cave Spring Road, SW
Rome, Georgia 30161-4700

Head of School: Mr. Brent Bell

General Information Coeducational boarding and day college-preparatory, arts, and technology school. Boarding grades 9–PG, day grades PK–PG. Founded: 1905. Setting: small town. Nearest major city is Atlanta. Students are housed in coed dormitories. 500-acre campus. 15 buildings on campus. Approved or accredited by Georgia Independent School Association, Middle States Association of Colleges and Schools, Southern Association of Colleges and Schools, Southern Association of Independent Schools, The Association of Boarding Schools, The College Board, and Georgia Department of Education. Member of National Association of Independent Schools and Secondary School Admission Test Board. Endowment: $34.9 million. Total enrollment: 789. Upper school average class size: 15. Upper school faculty-student ratio: 1:15. There are 176 required school days per year for Upper School students. Upper School students typically attend 5 days per week. The average school day consists of 7 hours and 30 minutes.

Upper School Student Profile Grade 6: 53 students (25 boys, 28 girls); Grade 7: 43 students (24 boys, 19 girls); Grade 8: 37 students (21 boys, 16 girls); Grade 9: 100 students (52 boys, 48 girls); Grade 10: 118 students (62 boys, 56 girls); Grade 11: 117 students (64 boys, 53 girls); Grade 12: 125 students (78 boys, 47 girls). 40% of students are boarding students. 66% are state residents. 15 states are represented in upper school student body. 23% are international students. International students from Bahamas, Brazil, China, Germany, Nigeria, and Spain; 20 other countries represented in student body.

Faculty School total: 71. In upper school: 34 men, 37 women; 47 have advanced degrees; 57 reside on campus.

Subjects Offered Advanced biology, advanced chemistry, Advanced Placement courses, advanced studio art-AP, algebra, ancient world history, art, art history, art history-AP, band, biology, biology-AP, calculus, calculus-AP, chemistry, chemistry-AP, choir, chorus, college counseling, computer programming, computer science, concert choir, creative writing, drama, drawing, economics, economics-AP, English, English language and composition-AP, English language-AP, English literature, English literature-AP, English-AP, ensembles, environmental science, environmental science-AP, ESL, fine arts, French, geometry, government-AP, graphic arts, graphic design, health, honors algebra, honors English, honors geometry, honors world history, humanities, jazz ensemble, journalism, lab science, macro/microeconomics-AP, macroeconomics-AP, modern European history-AP, music, music theory-AP, musical theater, newspaper, personal fitness, physical education, physics, physics-AP, pre-calculus, probability and statistics, psychology-AP, robotics, Spanish, Spanish language-AP, Spanish literature-AP, Spanish-AP, statistics-AP, studio art-AP, trigonometry, U.S. history, U.S. history-AP, video, video film production, vocal ensemble, wind ensemble, world cultures, world history, world history-AP, yearbook.

Graduation Requirements Arts and fine arts (art, music, dance, drama), English, foreign language, information technology, mathematics, physical education (includes health), science, social studies (includes history), community service/servant leadership program, after school activity.

Special Academic Programs 21 Advanced Placement exams for which test preparation is offered; honors section; academic accommodation for the musically talented; ESL.

College Admission Counseling 114 students graduated in 2016; all went to college, including Auburn University; Emory University; Georgia Institute of Technology; Georgia Southern University; The University of North Carolina at Chapel Hill; University of Georgia.

Student Life Upper grades have uniform requirement, student council, honor system. Discipline rests equally with students and faculty.

Summer Programs Enrichment, sports, art/fine arts, computer instruction programs offered; session focuses on academic enrichment and specialized sports camps for all ages; held on campus; accepts boys and girls; open to students from other schools. 3,500 students usually enrolled. 2017 schedule: June 2 to August 5. Application deadline: none.

Tuition and Aid Day student tuition: $19,970; 7-day tuition and room/board: $44,900–$50,700. Tuition installment plan (FACTS Tuition Payment Plan, monthly payment plans, individually arranged payment plans). Merit scholarship grants, need-based scholarship grants available. In 2016–17, 48% of upper-school students received aid; total upper-school merit-scholarship money awarded: $749,800. Total amount of financial aid awarded in 2016–17: $2,566,200.

Admissions Traditional secondary-level entrance grade is 9. For fall 2016, 421 students applied for upper-level admission, 180 were accepted, 103 enrolled. PSAT, SAT, or ACT for applicants to grade 11 and 12 required. Deadline for receipt of application materials: February 15. Application fee required: $50. Interview recommended.

Athletics Interscholastic: baseball (boys), basketball (b,g), cheering (g), crew (b,g), cross-country running (b,g), diving (b,g), football (b), golf (b,g), lacrosse (b,g), rowing (b,g), soccer (b,g), softball (g), swimming and diving (b,g), tennis (b,g), track and field (b,g), volleyball (g), wrestling (b); intramural: aerobics/dance (g), aquatics (b,g), basketball (b,g), cheering (g), dance squad (g), fitness (b,g), flag football (b,g), flagball (b,g), running (b,g), tennis (b,g), volleyball (b,g); coed intramural: aerobics, fishing, fly fishing, Frisbee, independent competitive sports, jogging, outdoor activities, outdoor education, outdoor recreation, physical fitness, physical training, soccer, speleology, strength & conditioning, table tennis, ultimate Frisbee, water volleyball, weight lifting, weight training. 2 PE instructors, 11 coaches, 2 athletic trainers.

Computers Computers are regularly used in all academic classes. Computer network features include on-campus library services, Internet access, wireless campus network, Internet filtering or blocking technology. Campus intranet, student e-mail accounts, and computer access in designated common areas are available to students. Students grades are available online. The school has a published electronic and media policy.

Contact Ms. Audrey Ashworth, Assistant Director of Boarding Admission. 706-236-0407. Fax: 706-232-3600. E-mail: aashworth@darlingtonschool.org. Website: www.darlingtonschool.org

DARROW SCHOOL

110 Darrow Road
New Lebanon, New York 12125

Head of School: Mr. Simon Holzapfel

General Information Coeducational boarding and day college-preparatory, project-based learning, active curriculum, and sustainability school. Grades 9–12. Founded: 1932. Setting: rural. Nearest major city is Pittsfield, MA. Students are housed in coed dormitories and single-sex dormitories. 365.5-acre campus. 26 buildings on campus. Approved or accredited by Middle States Association of Colleges and Schools, New York State Association of Independent Schools, The Association of Boarding Schools, and New York Department of Education. Member of National Association of Independent Schools and Secondary School Admission Test Board. Endowment: $4.6 million. Upper school average class size: 9. Upper school faculty-student ratio: 1:4. There are 220 required school days per year for Upper School students. Upper School students typically attend 6 days per week. The average school day consists of 6 hours.

Upper School Student Profile Grade 9: 14 students (9 boys, 5 girls); Grade 10: 24 students (11 boys, 13 girls); Grade 11: 37 students (19 boys, 18 girls); Grade 12: 27 students (17 boys, 10 girls). 83% of students are boarding students. 55% are state residents. 12 states are represented in upper school student body. 20% are international students. International students from Bahamas, China, Italy, Japan, Taiwan, and Turkey; 8 other countries represented in student body.

Faculty School total: 30. In upper school: 15 men, 15 women; 24 have advanced degrees; 25 reside on campus.

Subjects Offered 3-dimensional art, advanced math, African drumming, African-American literature, African-American studies, algebra, American Civil War, American history, American literature, art, art history, athletics, biology, calculus, ceramics, chemistry, civil rights, clayworking, computer graphics, creative writing, critical writing, culinary arts, design, digital art, drama, drama performance, drama workshop, dramatic arts, drawing, drawing and design, ecology, ecology, environmental systems, economics, economics and history, English, English as a foreign language, English literature, ensembles, environmental education, environmental science, environmental studies, ESL, ESL, ethics, experiential education, fine arts, French, geometry, global studies, health and wellness, history, independent study, language, language arts, languages, Latin American literature, leadership, linguistics, literature, mathematics, microeconomics, multicultural studies, music appreciation, music theory, oil painting, photo shop, photography, physics, play production, poetry, portfolio art, pottery, pre-calculus, reading/study skills, robotics, Russian literature, science, social studies, Spanish, Spanish literature, sports, studio art, study skills, theater, U.S. history, Western civilization, women in literature, women's literature, woodworking, writing, yearbook, yoga.

Graduation Requirements Arts, arts and fine arts (art, music, dance, drama), electives, English, foreign language, health, history, mathematics, physical education (includes health), science.

Special Academic Programs Advanced Placement exam preparation; independent study; term-away projects; study abroad; academic accommodation for the gifted, the musically talented, and the artistically talented; ESL (14 students enrolled).

College Admission Counseling 30 students graduated in 2016; all went to college, including Brandeis University; Carleton College; Hobart and William Smith Colleges; St. Lawrence University; Suffolk University; Wheaton College. Mean combined SAT: 1181, mean composite ACT: 25.

Student Life Upper grades have specified standards of dress, student council, honor system. Discipline rests equally with students and faculty.

Tuition and Aid Day student tuition: $32,300; 7-day tuition and room/board: $56,100. Tuition installment plan (Academic Management Services Plan, SMART Tuition Payment Plan, individually arranged payment plans). Need-based scholarship grants available. In 2016–17, 40% of upper-school students received aid. Total amount of financial aid awarded in 2016–17: $1,400,000.

Admissions Traditional secondary-level entrance grade is 9. For fall 2016, 145 students applied for upper-level admission, 93 were accepted, 33 enrolled. SLEP for foreign students or TOEFL or SLEP required. Deadline for receipt of application materials: none. Application fee required: $75. On-campus interview recommended.

Athletics Interscholastic: basketball (boys, girls), cross-country running (b,g), lacrosse (b), soccer (b,g), softball (g), tennis (b,g); coed interscholastic: cross-country running, Frisbee, independent competitive sports, lacrosse, tennis, ultimate Frisbee; coed intramural: aerobics/dance, alpine skiing, backpacking, bicycling, climbing, dance, fitness, freestyle skiing, hiking/backpacking, independent competitive sports, martial arts, mountain biking, outdoor activities, outdoor education, physical fitness, rock climbing, self defense, skiing (downhill), snowboarding, telemark skiing, weight lifting, yoga. 1 coach.

Computers Computers are regularly used in all classes. Computer network features include on-campus library services, Internet access, wireless campus network, Internet filtering or blocking technology. Campus intranet, student e-mail accounts, and computer access in designated common areas are available to students. Students grades are available online. The school has a published electronic and media policy.

Contact Ms. Betsy Strickler, Director of Admission. 518-794-6008. Fax: 518-794-7065. E-mail: stricklerb@darrowschool.org. Website: www.darrowschool.org

DAVIDSON ACADEMY

1414 W. Old Hickory Boulevard
Nashville, Tennessee 37207-1098

Head of School: Dr. Bill Chaney

General Information Coeducational day college-preparatory and science, mathematics school. Grades PK–12. Founded: 1980. Setting: suburban. 67-acre campus. 1 building on campus. Approved or accredited by Association of Christian Schools International, Southern Association of Colleges and Schools, and Tennessee Department of Education. Endowment: $25,000. Total enrollment: 750. Upper school average class size: 15. Upper school faculty-student ratio: 1:15. There are 180 required school days per year for Upper School students. Upper School students typically attend 5 days per week. The average school day consists of 5 hours and 50 minutes.

Faculty School total: 34. In upper school: 16 men, 18 women.

Subjects Offered 3-dimensional art, ACT preparation, advanced math, Advanced Placement courses, algebra, American government, American history, American history-AP, art, art appreciation, audio visual/media, band, Bible, Bible studies, biology, calculus, calculus-AP, cheerleading, chemistry, choral music, chorus, church history, college admission preparation, college counseling, college placement, composition-AP, computer applications, computer skills, conceptual physics, concert band, concert choir, consumer economics, creative writing, drama, drama performance, dramatic arts, earth science, economics, English, English literature-AP, English-AP, English/composition-AP, European history-AP, film and new technologies, geography, geometry, government-AP, health and wellness, history, honors algebra, honors English, honors geometry, human anatomy, independent study, Latin, leadership and service, Life of Christ, literature, marching band, mathematics, mathematics-AP, music, musical productions, New Testament, newspaper, physical education, physical fitness, physical science, physics, physics-AP, poetry, pre-algebra, pre-calculus, pre-college orientation, probability and statistics, psychology, reading, religious studies, science, senior project, Spanish, speech, speech communications, trigonometry, U.S. history, U.S. history-AP, video film production, wellness, world geography, world history, writing, yearbook.

Graduation Requirements Algebra, art, biology, calculus, chemistry, computer technologies, drama, economics, electives, English, English composition, English literature, foreign language, geometry, government, literature, physical science, physics, senior project, trigonometry, U.S. history, wellness, world history, senior research project, Bible.

Special Academic Programs 3 Advanced Placement exams for which test preparation is offered; honors section; independent study; study at local college for college credit; programs in general development for dyslexic students; ESL (15 students enrolled).

College Admission Counseling 54 students graduated in 2016; all went to college, including Belmont University; Lipscomb University; Tennessee Technological University; The University of Tennessee; The University of Tennessee at Chattanooga; Western Kentucky University.

Student Life Upper grades have uniform requirement, student council, honor system. Discipline rests primarily with faculty.

Summer Programs Remediation, enrichment, advancement, sports, art/fine arts programs offered; session focuses on physical and mental growth through a caring, Christian, and learning-enriched environment; held on campus; accepts boys and girls; open to students from other schools. 250 students usually enrolled. 2017 schedule: May 30 to July 30. Application deadline: April 15.

Tuition and Aid Day student tuition: $9300. Tuition installment plan (monthly payment plans, individually arranged payment plans). Tuition reduction for siblings, need-based scholarship grants, need-based financial aid, tuition reduction for children of faculty and staff available. In 2016–17, 20% of upper-school students received aid.

Admissions Traditional secondary-level entrance grade is 9. Admissions testing, any standardized test and WRAT required. Deadline for receipt of application materials: none. Application fee required: $75.

Athletics Interscholastic: baseball (boys), basketball (b,g), cheering (g), cross-country running (b,g), dance team (g), football (b), golf (b,g), soccer (b,g), softball (g), tennis (b,g), track and field (b,g), volleyball (g), wrestling (b); intramural: ballet (g), dance (g), weight training (b); coed interscholastic: bowling. 2 PE instructors, 1 athletic trainer.

Computers Computers are regularly used in computer applications, English, graphic arts, history, mathematics, media production, yearbook classes. Computer network features include on-campus library services, Internet access, wireless campus network, Internet filtering or blocking technology, RenWeb, Accelerated Reader, CollegeView. Computer access in designated common areas is available to students. Students grades are available online. The school has a published electronic and media policy.

Contact Mr. Jason McGehee, Director of Admission. 615-860-5317. Fax: 615-860-7631. E-mail: jason.mcgehee@davidsonacademy.com. Website: www.davidsonacademy.com

DEERFIELD ACADEMY

7 Boyden Lane

Deerfield, Massachusetts 01342

Head of School: Dr. Margarita O'Byrne Curtis

General Information Coeducational boarding and day college-preparatory school. Grades 9–PG. Founded: 1797. Setting: rural. Nearest major city is Hartford, CT. Students are housed in single-sex dormitories. 330-acre campus. 81 buildings on campus. Approved or accredited by Association of Independent Schools in New England, New England Association of Schools and Colleges, and Massachusetts Department of Education. Member of National Association of Independent Schools and Secondary School Admission Test Board. Endowment: $5 million. Total enrollment: 638. Upper school average class size: 12. Upper school faculty-student ratio: 1:5. There are 150 required school days per year for Upper School students. Upper School students typically attend 5 days per week. The average school day consists of 5 hours and 25 minutes.

Upper School Student Profile Grade 9: 116 students (55 boys, 61 girls); Grade 10: 161 students (84 boys, 77 girls); Grade 11: 168 students (80 boys, 88 girls); Grade 12: 206 students (116 boys, 90 girls). 89% of students are boarding students. 22% are state residents. 38 states are represented in upper school student body. 17% are international students. International students from British Virgin Islands, China, Democratic People's Republic of Korea, Hong Kong, Japan, and Mexico; 34 other countries represented in student body.

Faculty School total: 133. In upper school: 69 men, 64 women; 92 have advanced degrees; 130 reside on campus.

Subjects Offered Advanced chemistry, advanced computer applications, advanced math, advanced studio art-AP, algebra, American government, American history-AP, American studies, analytic geometry, anatomy, applied arts, applied music, Arabic, architectural drawing, architecture, art, art history, art history-AP, Asian history, Asian literature, Asian studies, astronomy, Basic programming, biochemistry, biology, biology-AP, Black history, calculus, calculus-AP, chemistry, chemistry-AP, Chinese, computer applications, computer math, computer programming, computer science, computer science-AP, concert band, creative writing, dance, dance performance, discrete mathematics, drama, drama performance, drama workshop, drawing and design, earth science, Eastern religion and philosophy, economics, economics-AP, English, English literature, English literature-AP, English-AP, environmental science, ethics, European history, expository writing, fine arts, French, geology, geometry, Greek, health, health education, history, instrumental music, journalism, Latin, literature, mathematics, modern European history, music, philosophy, photography, physics, physics-AP, physiology, probability and statistics, religion, science, social studies, Spanish, Spanish literature, statistics, studio art, studio art-AP, theater, theater arts, trigonometry, U.S. history, U.S. literature, video, vocal music, Western civilization, world civilizations, world governments, world history, world literature, world religions, writing.

Graduation Requirements Arts and fine arts (art, music, dance, drama), English, foreign language, history, mathematics, philosophy, science.

Special Academic Programs Advanced Placement exam preparation; honors section; independent study; term-away projects; study abroad; academic accommodation for the gifted, the musically talented, and the artistically talented.

College Admission Counseling 186 students graduated in 2016; all went to college, including Bowdoin College; Dartmouth College; Georgetown University; Harvard University; University of Virginia; Yale University. Mean SAT critical reading: 663, mean SAT math: 679, mean SAT writing: 666, mean combined SAT: 2008, mean composite ACT: 30.

Student Life Upper grades have specified standards of dress, student council, honor system. Discipline rests equally with students and faculty.

Summer Programs Enrichment programs offered; session focuses on Interdisciplinary, project-based learning; held on campus; accepts boys and girls; open to students from other schools. 75 students usually enrolled. 2017 schedule: July 10 to August 6. Application deadline: May 1.

Tuition and Aid Day student tuition: $39,220; 7-day tuition and room/board: $54,720. Tuition installment plan (SMART Tuition Payment Plan, Educational Data Systems, Inc). Need-based scholarship grants available. In 2016–17, 33% of upper-school students received aid. Total amount of financial aid awarded in 2016–17: $8,985,000.

Admissions Traditional secondary-level entrance grade is 9. For fall 2016, 1,907 students applied for upper-level admission, 313 were accepted, 215 enrolled. ACT, ISEE, PSAT, SAT, SSAT or TOEFL required. Deadline for receipt of application materials: January 15. Application fee required: $60. Interview required.

Athletics Interscholastic: alpine skiing (boys, girls), baseball (b), basketball (b,g), crew (b,g), cross-country running (b,g), diving (b,g), field hockey (b,g), football (b), golf (b), hockey (b,g), ice hockey (b,g), lacrosse (b,g), rowing (b,g), skiing (downhill) (b,g), soccer (b,g), softball (g), squash (b,g), swimming and diving (b,g), tennis (b,g), track and field (b,g), volleyball (g), water polo (b,g), wrestling (b); intramural: dance (b,g), fitness (b,g), modern dance (b,g); coed interscholastic: bicycling, diving, golf, indoor track & field, swimming and diving; coed intramural: aerobics/dance, aerobics/Nautilus, alpine skiing, aquatics, archery, ballet, canoeing/kayaking, combined training, dance, dance team, fitness, hiking/backpacking, life saving, modern dance, nordic skiing, outdoor activities, outdoor adventure, outdoor recreation, outdoor skills, paddle tennis, sailing, skiing (cross-country), skiing (downhill), snowboarding, soccer, squash, strength & conditioning, swimming and diving, tennis, volleyball, weight lifting, weight training. 1 coach, 2 athletic trainers.

Computers Computers are regularly used in all classes. Computer network features include on-campus library services, online commercial services, Internet access, wireless campus network, Internet filtering or blocking technology. Campus intranet, student e-mail accounts, and computer access in designated common areas are available to students. Students grades are available online. The school has a published electronic and media policy.

Contact Charles Davis, Dean of Admission and Financial Aid. 413-774-1400. Fax: 413-772-1100. E-mail: admission@deerfield.edu. Website: www.deerfield.edu

DE LA SALLE COLLEGE

131 Farnham Avenue

Toronto, Ontario M4V 1H7, Canada

Head of School: Br. Domenic Viggiani, FSC

General Information Coeducational day college-preparatory and Advanced Placement courses school, affiliated with Roman Catholic Church. Grades 5–12. Founded: 1851. Setting: urban. 12-acre campus. 4 buildings on campus. Approved or accredited by Conference of Independent Schools of Ontario and Ontario Department of Education. Member of Secondary School Admission Test Board. Language of instruction: English. Total enrollment: 627. Upper school average class size: 22. Upper school faculty-student ratio: 1:15. The average school day consists of 5 hours and 40 minutes.

Upper School Student Profile 80% of students are Roman Catholic.

Faculty School total: 51. In upper school: 36 men, 15 women.

Subjects Offered Advanced Placement courses.

Graduation Requirements English, religion (includes Bible studies and theology), science.

Special Academic Programs Advanced Placement exam preparation; accelerated programs.

College Admission Counseling 100 students graduated in 2016; all went to college, including McGill University; McMaster University; Queen's University at Kingston; The University of Western Ontario; University of Toronto; York University.

Student Life Upper grades have uniform requirement, student council, honor system. Discipline rests primarily with faculty. Attendance at religious services is required.

Summer Programs Enrichment, advancement programs offered; session focuses on Reach ahead program; held both on and off campus; accepts boys and girls; open to students from other schools. 75 students usually enrolled. 2017 schedule: July 1 to August 25. Application deadline: June 15.

Tuition and Aid Day student tuition: CAN$13,750. Tuition installment plan (monthly payment plans). Bursaries, need-based scholarship grants available. In 2016–17, 15% of upper-school students received aid.

Admissions Traditional secondary-level entrance grade is 9. For fall 2016, 150 students applied for upper-level admission, 75 were accepted, 50 enrolled. School's own test or SSAT required. Deadline for receipt of application materials: December 9. Application fee required: CAN$100. On-campus interview recommended.

Athletics Interscholastic: baseball (boys), basketball (b,g), field hockey (g), hockey (b,g), ice hockey (b,g), rugby (g), soccer (b,g), softball (b,g), volleyball (g); coed interscholastic: alpine skiing, aquatics, badminton, cross-country running, golf, skiing (downhill), swimming and diving, track and field, ultimate Frisbee; coed intramural: ball hockey, physical fitness, physical training, strength & conditioning. 4 PE instructors.

Computers Computer network features include on-campus library services, Internet access, wireless campus network, Internet filtering or blocking technology. Student e-mail accounts are available to students. The school has a published electronic and media policy.

Contact Mr. Danny Viotto, Principal of the Senior School. 416-969-8771 Ext. 238. Fax: 416-969-9175. E-mail: dviotto@delasalle.ca. Website: www.delasalle.ca

DE LA SALLE HIGH SCHOOL

1130 Winton Drive
Concord, California 94518-3528

Head of School: Dr. Heather Alumbaug

General Information Boys' day college-preparatory and religious studies school, affiliated with Roman Catholic Church. Grades 9–12. Founded: 1965. Setting: suburban. Nearest major city is Oakland. 25-acre campus. 11 buildings on campus. Approved or accredited by Western Association of Schools and Colleges and Western Catholic Education Association. Endowment: $8.3 million. Total enrollment: 1,038. Upper school average class size: 30. Upper school faculty-student ratio: 1:28. There are 172 required school days per year for Upper School students. Upper School students typically attend 5 days per week. The average school day consists of 6 hours and 5 minutes.

Upper School Student Profile Grade 9: 270 students (270 boys); Grade 10: 267 students (267 boys); Grade 11: 253 students (253 boys); Grade 12: 257 students (257 boys). 77% of students are Roman Catholic.

Faculty School total: 73. In upper school: 51 men, 22 women; 41 have advanced degrees.

Subjects Offered 3-dimensional design, acting, Advanced Placement courses, advanced studio art-AP, African literature, algebra, American history, American history-AP, American literature-AP, anatomy, art, band, basketball, Bible studies, biology, biology-AP, biotechnology, calculus, calculus-AP, cartooning/animation, chemistry, chemistry-AP, choir, chorus, church history, composition-AP, computer multimedia, concert band, CPR, criminal justice, design, drafting, drawing, drawing and design, driver education, economics, economics and history, English, English language and composition-AP, English literature and composition-AP, English-AP, environmental science-AP, ethics, film and literature, fine arts, first aid, French, French language-AP, geometry, global studies, government and politics-AP, government/civics, health, history, Italian, jazz, jazz band, Latin, Latin-AP, law studies, leadership education training, literature, marine biology, mathematics, moral theology, music composition, music theory, painting, physical education, physical science, physics, physics-AP, physiology, pre-calculus, psychology, psychology-AP, religion, religious studies, science, sculpture, Shakespeare, sign language, social studies, Spanish, Spanish-AP, sports medicine, statistics, statistics-AP, the Sixties, theater, theater design and production, transition mathematics, trigonometry, U.S. government and politics-AP, weight training, world geography, world history, world religions, world religions, writing, writing, yearbook.

Graduation Requirements Arts and fine arts (art, music, dance, drama), English, foreign language, mathematics, physical education (includes health), religion (includes Bible studies and theology), science, social studies (includes history).

Special Academic Programs Advanced Placement exam preparation; honors section; independent study; remedial math; programs in English, mathematics, general development for dyslexic students.

College Admission Counseling 238 students graduated in 2016; 236 went to college, including California Polytechnic State University, San Luis Obispo; California State University, Chico; Gonzaga University; Saint Mary's College of California; San Francisco State University; University of California, Berkeley. Other: 2 entered military service, 2 had other specific plans. Mean SAT critical reading: 544, mean SAT math: 555, mean SAT writing: 526, mean combined SAT: 1644, mean composite ACT: 25. 30% scored over 600 on SAT critical reading, 38% scored over 600 on SAT math, 25% scored over 600 on SAT writing, 32% scored over 1800 on combined SAT, 36% scored over 26 on composite ACT.

Student Life Upper grades have specified standards of dress, student council, honor system. Discipline rests primarily with faculty. Attendance at religious services is required.

Summer Programs Remediation, sports programs offered; session focuses on make-up for current students, sports programs for local kids, conditionally accepted study skills program; held on campus; accepts boys and girls; not open to students from other schools. 75 students usually enrolled. 2017 schedule: June 12 to August 2. Application deadline: June 1.

Tuition and Aid Day student tuition: $17,500. Tuition installment plan (individually arranged payment plans, 10-month plan). Need-based scholarship grants, need-based grants available. In 2016–17, 32% of upper-school students received aid. Total amount of financial aid awarded in 2016–17: $2,330,000.

Admissions Traditional secondary-level entrance grade is 9. For fall 2016, 435 students applied for upper-level admission, 340 were accepted, 270 enrolled. High School Placement Test required. Deadline for receipt of application materials: December 2. Application fee required: $100. On-campus interview required.

Athletics Interscholastic: badminton, baseball, basketball, cross-country running, diving, football, golf, ice hockey, lacrosse, rugby, soccer, swimming and diving, tennis, track and field, trap and skeet, volleyball, water polo, wrestling; intramural: basketball, flag football, floor hockey, football, indoor soccer, street hockey, ultimate Frisbee. 5 PE instructors, 120 coaches, 3 athletic trainers.

Computers Computers are regularly used in all classes. Computer network features include on-campus library services, Internet access, wireless campus network, Internet filtering or blocking technology, Learning Management System/Schoology. Student e-mail accounts and computer access in designated common areas are available to students. Students grades are available online. The school has a published electronic and media policy.

Contact Mr. Joseph Grantham, Director of Admissions. 925-288-8102. Fax: 925-686-3474. E-mail: granthamj@dlshs.org. Website: www.dlshs.org

DELASALLE HIGH SCHOOL

One DeLaSalle Drive
Minneapolis, Minnesota 55401-1597

Head of School: Mr. Barry Lieske

General Information Coeducational day college-preparatory, arts, religious studies, and technology school, affiliated with Roman Catholic Church. Grades 9–12. Founded: 1900. Setting: urban. 10-acre campus. 4 buildings on campus. Approved or accredited by National Catholic Education Association, North Central Association of Colleges and Schools, and Minnesota Department of Education. Endowment: $4.3 million. Total enrollment: 760. Upper school average class size: 23. Upper school faculty-student ratio: 1:14. There are 175 required school days per year for Upper School students. Upper School students typically attend 5 days per week. The average school day consists of 6 hours and 30 minutes.

Upper School Student Profile Grade 9: 196 students (91 boys, 105 girls); Grade 10: 210 students (109 boys, 101 girls); Grade 11: 182 students (87 boys, 95 girls); Grade 12: 192 students (94 boys, 98 girls). 70% of students are Roman Catholic.

Faculty School total: 55. In upper school: 27 men, 28 women; 48 have advanced degrees.

Subjects Offered ACT preparation, advanced chemistry, advanced math, Advanced Placement courses, African American studies, American studies, business education, computer programming, CPR, engineering, environmental science, health, law and the legal system, media literacy, orchestra, painting, photography, scripture, Spanish-AP, theater, theology and the arts, U.S. government and politics, U.S. history, U.S. history-AP, United States government-AP, world history, world history-AP.

Graduation Requirements Arts and fine arts (art, music, dance, drama), English, foreign language, mathematics, physical education (includes health), religious studies, science, social studies (includes history), 60 hours of documented Christian service.

Special Academic Programs Advanced Placement exam preparation; honors section; independent study; study at local college for college credit; study abroad; programs in English, mathematics, general development for dyslexic students.

College Admission Counseling 156 students graduated in 2016; 153 went to college, including College of Saint Benedict; Loyola University Chicago; Saint John's University; University of Minnesota, Twin Cities Campus; University of St. Thomas; University of Wisconsin–Madison. Other: 2 went to work, 1 entered military service. Mean composite ACT: 25. 64% scored over 26 on composite ACT.

Student Life Upper grades have uniform requirement, student council, honor system. Discipline rests primarily with faculty. Attendance at religious services is required.

Summer Programs Enrichment, advancement programs offered; held on campus; accepts boys and girls; open to students from other schools. 350 students usually enrolled. 2017 schedule: June 6 to July 30. Application deadline: June 1.

Tuition and Aid Day student tuition: $12,775. Tuition installment plan (monthly payment plans). Merit scholarship grants, need-based scholarship grants, off-campus work programs for tuition benefit available. In 2016–17, 53% of upper-school students received aid; total upper-school merit-scholarship money awarded: $406,000. Total amount of financial aid awarded in 2016–17: $26,070,000.

Admissions Traditional secondary-level entrance grade is 9. For fall 2016, 413 students applied for upper-level admission, 285 were accepted, 196 enrolled. Academic Profile Tests or High School Placement Test required. Deadline for receipt of application materials: none. No application fee required. Interview required.

Athletics Interscholastic: alpine skiing (boys, girls), baseball (b), basketball (b,g), cross-country running (b,g), football (b), golf (b,g), hockey (b,g), lacrosse (b,g), soccer (b,g), softball (g), swimming and diving (b,g), tennis (b,g), track and field (b,g), volleyball (g), wrestling (b); coed interscholastic: cheering, dance team, weight training; coed intramural: aerobics, archery, bowling, dance, dance team, strength & conditioning. 2 PE instructors, 63 coaches, 1 athletic trainer.

Computers Computers are regularly used in all academic, art, business, English, French, graphic design, independent study, journalism, media, media production, music, science, social studies, Spanish, writing classes. Computer network features include on-campus library services, online commercial services, Internet access, wireless campus network, Internet filtering or blocking technology, one-to-one iPad/cloud technology for all students. Student e-mail accounts and computer access in designated common areas are available to students. Students grades are available online. The school has a published electronic and media policy.

Contact Mr. Patrick Felicetta, Director of Admission. 612-676-7605. Fax: 612-676-7699. E-mail: patrick.felicetta@delasalle.com. Website: www.delasalle.com

DE LA SALLE NORTH CATHOLIC HIGH SCHOOL

7528 N. Fenwick Avenue
Portland, Oregon 97217

Head of School: Mr. Tim Joy

General Information Coeducational day college-preparatory, religious studies, and Corporate Work Study Program school, affiliated with Roman Catholic Church. Grades 9–12. Founded: 2000. Setting: urban. 2-acre campus. 1 building on campus. Approved or accredited by Oregon Department of Education. Endowment: $289,297. Total enrollment: 311. Upper school average class size: 21. Upper school faculty-student ratio: 1:12. There are 181 required school days per year for Upper School students.

Upper School students typically attend 5 days per week. The average school day consists of 7 hours and 30 minutes.

Upper School Student Profile Grade 9: 102 students (56 boys, 46 girls); Grade 10: 91 students (51 boys, 40 girls); Grade 11: 82 students (36 boys, 46 girls); Grade 12: 52 students (18 boys, 34 girls). 38% of students are Roman Catholic.

Faculty School total: 26. In upper school: 12 men, 14 women; 15 have advanced degrees.

Subjects Offered All academic.

Graduation Requirements American government, American history, arts and fine arts (art, music, dance, drama), economics, foreign language, physical education (includes health), science, theology, World Language, Corporate Work Study.

Special Academic Programs 2 Advanced Placement exams for which test preparation is offered; honors section; independent study; remedial reading and/or remedial writing; remedial math.

College Admission Counseling 62 students graduated in 2016; 58 went to college, including George Fox University; Georgetown University; Oregon State University; Portland Community College; Portland State University; University of Oregon. Other: 1 entered military service, 2 had other specific plans.

Student Life Upper grades have uniform requirement, student council, honor system. Discipline rests primarily with faculty. Attendance at religious services is required.

Summer Programs Remediation, enrichment programs offered; session focuses on academic preparation and work study training program; held on campus; accepts boys and girls; not open to students from other schools. 120 students usually enrolled. 2017 schedule: June 27 to August 5. Application deadline: May 1.

Tuition and Aid Day student tuition: $2995. Tuition installment plan (monthly payment plans, individually arranged payment plans). Need-based scholarship grants available. In 2016–17, 85% of upper-school students received aid. Total amount of financial aid awarded in 2016–17: $294,820.

Admissions Traditional secondary-level entrance grade is 9. For fall 2016, 262 students applied for upper-level admission, 142 were accepted, 114 enrolled. Catholic High School Entrance Examination required. Deadline for receipt of application materials: none. No application fee required. On-campus interview required.

Athletics Interscholastic: basketball (boys, girls), soccer (b,g), track and field (b,g), volleyball (g); coed interscholastic: wrestling. 2 PE instructors, 7 coaches.

Computers Computers are regularly used in all academic classes. Computer network features include Internet access, wireless campus network, Internet filtering or blocking technology. Student e-mail accounts and computer access in designated common areas are available to students. Students grades are available online. The school has a published electronic and media policy.

Contact Ms. Alba Quinones, Admissions Assistant. 503-285-9385 Ext. 135. Fax: 503-285-9546. E-mail: admissions@dlsnc.org. Website: www.delasallenorth.org/

DELAWARE COUNTY CHRISTIAN SCHOOL

462 Malin Road
Newtown Square, Pennsylvania 19073-3499

Head of School: Dr. Timothy P. Wiens

General Information Coeducational day college-preparatory and School for Applied and Innovative Learning school, affiliated with Protestant-Evangelical faith. Grades PK–12. Founded: 1950. Setting: suburban. Nearest major city is Philadelphia. Students are housed in Host Families - International Students Only. 16-acre campus. 6 buildings on campus. Approved or accredited by Association of Christian Schools International, Middle States Association of Colleges and Schools, and Pennsylvania Department of Education. Member of National Association of Independent Schools. Endowment: $1.6 million. Total enrollment: 810. Upper school average class size: 18. Upper school faculty-student ratio: 1:12. There are 175 required school days per year for Upper School students. Upper School students typically attend 5 days per week. The average school day consists of 6 hours and 30 minutes.

Upper School Student Profile Grade 9: 64 students (29 boys, 35 girls); Grade 10: 82 students (48 boys, 34 girls); Grade 11: 76 students (37 boys, 39 girls); Grade 12: 72 students (28 boys, 44 girls). 100% of students are Protestant-Evangelical faith.

Faculty School total: 100. In upper school: 28 men, 32 women; 45 have advanced degrees.

Subjects Offered Algebra, American history, American literature, art, Bible studies, biology, calculus, chemistry, choir, choral music, concert band, concert bell choir, concert choir, creative writing, digital art, discrete mathematics, drama, earth science, economics, English, English literature, English literature and composition AP, European history-AP, fine arts, geography, geometry, German, German-AP, government/civics, grammar, graphics, handbells, journalism, literature, mathematics, music, music theory, physical education, physics, physics-AP, religion, science, social studies, Spanish, Spanish-AP, theater, trigonometry, U.S. history-AP, world history, writing workshop, yearbook.

Graduation Requirements Arts and fine arts (art, music, dance, drama), computer science, English, foreign language, mathematics, physical education (includes health), religion (includes Bible studies and theology), science, social studies (includes history).

Special Academic Programs Advanced Placement exam preparation; honors section; study abroad; academic accommodation for the gifted, the musically talented, and the artistically talented; ESL (10 students enrolled).

College Admission Counseling 88 students graduated in 2016; all went to college, including Gordon College; Grove City College; Penn State University Park; Temple University; University of Pittsburgh; Wheaton College. Mean SAT critical reading: 577, mean SAT math: 555, mean SAT writing: 566, mean combined SAT: 1698.

Student Life Upper grades have uniform requirement, student council, honor system. Discipline rests primarily with faculty. Attendance at religious services is required.

Summer Programs Sports, art/fine arts, computer instruction programs offered; held on campus; accepts boys and girls; open to students from other schools. 200 students usually enrolled. 2017 schedule: June 21 to August 13. Application deadline: May 1.

Tuition and Aid Day student tuition: $16,324. Tuition installment plan (monthly payment plans). Tuition reduction for siblings, merit scholarship grants, need-based scholarship grants available. In 2016–17, 33% of upper-school students received aid; total upper-school merit-scholarship money awarded: $18,000. Total amount of financial aid awarded in 2016–17: $800,000.

Admissions Traditional secondary-level entrance grade is 9. ERB required. Deadline for receipt of application materials: none. Application fee required: $50. Interview required.

Athletics Interscholastic: baseball (boys), basketball (b,g), cheering (g), cross-country running (b,g), field hockey (g), football (b), golf (b,g), indoor track & field (b,g), lacrosse (b,g), soccer (b,g), softball (g), tennis (g), track and field (b,g), wrestling (b); coed interscholastic: life saving. 3 PE instructors, 1 athletic trainer.

Computers Computers are regularly used in art, English, journalism, library, literary magazine, mathematics, newspaper, photography, photojournalism, publications, SAT preparation, science, technology, video film production, writing, writing, yearbook classes. Computer network features include on-campus library services, Internet access, wireless campus network, Internet filtering or blocking technology. Students grades are available online. The school has a published electronic and media policy.

Contact Mrs. Anne Goneau, Assistant Director of Admissions. 610-353-6522 Ext. 2285. Fax: 610-356-9684. E-mail: agoneau@dccs.org. Website: www.dccs.org

DELAWARE VALLEY FRIENDS SCHOOL

Paoli, Pennsylvania
See Special Needs Schools section.

DELBARTON SCHOOL

230 Mendham Road
Morristown, New Jersey 07960

Head of School: Br. Paul Diveny, OSB

General Information Boys' day college-preparatory, arts, and religious studies school, affiliated with Roman Catholic Church. Grades 7–12. Founded: 1939. Setting: suburban. Nearest major city is New York, NY. 200-acre campus. 7 buildings on campus. Approved or accredited by Middle States Association of Colleges and Schools, National Catholic Education Association, New Jersey Association of Independent Schools, and New Jersey Department of Education. Member of National Association of Independent Schools and Secondary School Admission Test Board. Endowment: $26 million. Total enrollment: 573. Upper school average class size: 15. Upper school faculty-student ratio: 1:13. There are 160 required school days per year for Upper School students. Upper School students typically attend 5 days per week. The average school day consists of 6 hours and 30 minutes.

Upper School Student Profile Grade 9: 129 students (129 boys); Grade 10: 132 students (132 boys); Grade 11: 131 students (131 boys); Grade 12: 126 students (126 boys). 79% of students are Roman Catholic.

Faculty School total: 86. In upper school: 60 men, 18 women; 59 have advanced degrees.

Subjects Offered Accounting, advanced chemistry, algebra, American history, American literature, art, art history, astronomy, biology, calculus, chemistry, computer math, computer programming, computer science, creative writing, driver education, economics, English, English literature, environmental science, ethics, European history, fine arts, French, geography, geometry, German, grammar, health, history, international relations, Latin, mathematics, music, philosophy, physical education, physics, religion, Russian, social studies, Spanish, speech, trigonometry, world history.

Graduation Requirements Arts and fine arts (art, music, dance, drama), computer science, English, foreign language, mathematics, physical education (includes health), religion (includes Bible studies and theology), science, social studies (includes history), speech.

Special Academic Programs Advanced Placement exam preparation; independent study.

College Admission Counseling 116 students graduated in 2016; all went to college, including Boston College; Columbia University; Georgetown University; Loyola University Maryland; Princeton University; Villanova University.

Student Life Upper grades have specified standards of dress, student council, honor system. Discipline rests primarily with faculty. Attendance at religious services is required.

Summer Programs Enrichment, advancement, sports, computer instruction programs offered; session focuses on summer school (coed) and summer sports (boys); held on campus; accepts boys and girls; open to students from other schools. 1,200

students usually enrolled. 2017 schedule: June 21 to July 28. Application deadline: June 1.

Tuition and Aid Day student tuition: $36,900. Tuition installment plan (monthly payment plans, individually arranged payment plans). Need-based scholarship grants available. In 2016–17, 15% of upper-school students received aid. Total amount of financial aid awarded in 2016–17: $2,605,000.

Admissions Traditional secondary-level entrance grade is 9. For fall 2016, 385 students applied for upper-level admission, 161 were accepted, 133 enrolled. Stanford Achievement Test, Otis-Lennon School Ability Test, school's own exam required. Deadline for receipt of application materials: November 20. Application fee required: $65. On-campus interview required.

Athletics Interscholastic: baseball, basketball, bowling, cross-country running, football, golf, ice hockey, indoor track, lacrosse, soccer, squash, swimming and diving, tennis, track and field, winter (indoor) track, wrestling; intramural: bicycling, combined training, fitness, flag football, Frisbee, independent competitive sports, mountain biking, skiing (downhill), strength & conditioning, ultimate Frisbee, weight lifting, weight training. 3 PE instructors, 2 athletic trainers.

Computers Computers are regularly used in computer applications, music, science, word processing classes. Computer network features include on-campus library services, online commercial services, Internet access, wireless campus network. Student e-mail accounts are available to students. Students grades are available online.

Contact Mrs. Connie Curnow, Administrative Assistant, Office of Admissions. 973-538-3231 Ext. 3019. Fax: 973-538-8836. E-mail: ccurnow@delbarton.org. Website: www.delbarton.org

See Display on this page and Close-Up on page 594.

THE DELPHIAN SCHOOL

20950 Southwest Rock Creek Road
Sheridan, Oregon 97378

Head of School: Trevor Ott

General Information Coeducational boarding and day college-preparatory, general academic, arts, business, technology, and sciences, career orientation, community outreach school. Boarding grades 4–12, day grades K–12. Founded: 1976. Setting: rural. Nearest major city is Salem. Students are housed in coed dormitories. 740-acre campus. 4 buildings on campus. Approved or accredited by Northwest Association of Independent Schools and Oregon Department of Education. Member of National Association of Independent Schools. Endowment: $2.5 million. Total enrollment: 272. Upper school average class size: 17. Upper school faculty-student ratio: 1:10. Upper School students typically attend 5 days per week. The average school day consists of 7 hours.

Upper School Student Profile 80% of students are boarding students. 10% are state residents. 18 states are represented in upper school student body. 40% are international students. International students from Canada, China, India, Russian Federation, Taiwan, and United States; 18 other countries represented in student body.

Faculty School total: 55. In upper school: 7 men, 9 women; 48 reside on campus.

Subjects Offered Advanced chemistry, advanced computer applications, algebra, American history, American literature, anatomy and physiology, art, arts and crafts, biology, biology-AP, business, business applications, business skills, calculus, calculus-AP, career and personal planning, career/college preparation, ceramics, cheerleading, chemistry, choir, communication skills, comparative religion, computer programming, computer science, computer skills, concert choir, creative writing, drama, drawing, economics, economics-AP, electronics, English, English composition, English language and composition-AP, English literature and composition-AP, ESL, ethical decision making, ethics, ethics and responsibility, fine arts, first aid, French, geography, geometry, government, grammar, health, language arts, leadership, logic, mathematics, music, music history, nutrition, personal money management, photography, physical education, physical fitness, physical science, physics, public speaking, research skills, SAT preparation, science, Shakespeare, social studies, Spanish, student government, study skills, trigonometry, U.S. constitutional history, U.S. government, volleyball, world history, yearbook, yoga.

Graduation Requirements American history, anatomy and physiology, business skills (includes word processing), career/college preparation, communication skills, composition, computer science, current events, economics, English, ethics, foreign language, leadership, literature, logic, mathematics, mathematics-AP, physical education (includes health), public speaking, science, social studies (includes history), student government, U.S. government, world history, specific graduation requirements which students are required to meet in order to complete each equivalent grade level. Community service is required.

Special Academic Programs Advanced Placement exam preparation; honors section; accelerated programs; independent study; academic accommodation for the gifted, the musically talented, and the artistically talented; remedial reading and/or remedial writing; programs in English, mathematics, general development for dyslexic students; ESL (38 students enrolled).

College Admission Counseling 39 students graduated in 2016; 35 went to college, including Berklee College of Music; Johns Hopkins University; New York University; Parsons School of Design; University of California, Davis; University of Oregon. Other: 4 had other specific plans.

Student Life Upper grades have specified standards of dress, student council, honor system. Discipline rests equally with students and faculty.

Summer Programs Enrichment, advancement, ESL, sports, art/fine arts, computer instruction programs offered; session focuses on academics; held on campus; accepts boys and girls; open to students from other schools. 260 students usually enrolled. 2017 schedule: June 26 to August 6. Application deadline: April 15.

Tuition and Aid Day student tuition: $13,050–$27,525; 7-day tuition and room/board: $43,530–$45,940. Tuition installment plan (SMART Tuition Payment Plan, FACTS Tuition Payment Plan, monthly payment plans, individually arranged payment plans, Your Tuition Solution). Tuition reduction for siblings, merit scholarship grants, need-based scholarship grants, need-based loans available. In 2016–17, 41% of upper-school students received aid; total upper-school merit-scholarship money awarded: $150,000. Total amount of financial aid awarded in 2016–17: $315,000.

Admissions Traditional secondary-level entrance grade is 9. Admissions testing and any standardized test required. Deadline for receipt of application materials: none. Application fee required: $100. On-campus interview required.

Athletics Interscholastic: baseball (boys), basketball (b,g), cheering (g), cross-country running (b,g), soccer (b), softball (g), tennis (b,g), track and field (b,g), volleyball (g); coed intramural: alpine skiing, archery, fitness, flag football, hiking/backpacking, horseback riding, jogging, jump rope, kickball, martial arts, outdoors, physical fitness, physical training, racquetball, rock climbing, running, skiing (downhill), snowboarding, strength & conditioning, tennis, walking, weight lifting, weight training, yoga. 4 PE instructors, 15 coaches.

Computers Computer network features include on-campus library services, Internet access, wireless campus network, Internet filtering or blocking technology. Campus intranet, student e-mail accounts, and computer access in designated common areas are available to students. The school has a published electronic and media policy.

Contact Sue MacKenzie, Admissions Assistant. 800-626-6610. Fax: 503-843-4158. E-mail: info@delphian.org. Website: www.delphian.org

DELPHOS SAINT JOHN'S HIGH SCHOOL

515 East Second Street

Delphos, Ohio 45833

Head of School: Mr. Adam J. Lee

General Information Coeducational day college-preparatory, general academic, arts, business, religious studies, bilingual studies, and technology school, affiliated with Roman Catholic Church; primarily serves underachievers. Grades 7–12. Founded: 1912. Setting: rural. Nearest major city is Toledo. 2 buildings on campus. Approved or accredited by National Catholic Education Association, Ohio Catholic Schools Accreditation Association (OCSAA), and Ohio Department of Education. Total enrollment: 310. Upper school average class size: 15. Upper school faculty-student ratio: 1:15. There are 180 required school days per year for Upper School students. Upper School students typically attend 5 days per week. The average school day consists of 6 hours and 30 minutes.

Upper School Student Profile 98% of students are Roman Catholic.

Faculty School total: 25. In upper school: 10 men, 15 women; 15 have advanced degrees.

College Admission Counseling 50 students graduated in 2015; 48 went to college, including Bowling Green State University; The Ohio State University; The University of Toledo; University of Cincinnati; University of Dayton. Other: 2 went to work.

Student Life Upper grades have uniform requirement, student council, honor system. Discipline rests primarily with faculty. Attendance at religious services is required.

Tuition and Aid Tuition installment plan (SMART Tuition Payment Plan, monthly payment plans, individually arranged payment plans). Tuition reduction for siblings, need-based scholarship grants available.

Admissions Deadline for receipt of application materials: none. No application fee required. Interview required.

Athletics Interscholastic: basketball (boys, girls), cheering (g), cross-country running (b,g); football (b), golf (b,g), indoor track (b,g), soccer (g), strength & conditioning (b), volleyball (g), weight lifting (b,g), weight training (b,g); intramural: baseball (b), basketball (b), strength & conditioning (b,g), volleyball (b,g). 12 coaches, 1 athletic trainer.

Computers Computers are regularly used in all academic classes. Computer network features include on-campus library services, online commercial services, Internet access, wireless campus network, Internet filtering or blocking technology. Campus intranet and student e-mail accounts are available to students. Students grades are available online. The school has a published electronic and media policy.

Contact Mr. Alan Unterbrink, Guidance Counselor. 419-692-5371 Ext. 1135. Fax: 419-879-6874. E-mail: unterbrink@delphosstjohns.org. Website: www.delphosstjohns.org/

DeMATHA CATHOLIC HIGH SCHOOL

4313 Madison Street

Hyattsville, Maryland 20781

Head of School: Daniel J. McMahon, PhD

General Information Boys' day college-preparatory, arts, religious studies, technology, and music (instrumental and choral) school, affiliated with Roman Catholic Church. Grades 9–12. Distance learning grade 0. Founded: 1946. Setting: suburban. Nearest major city is Washington, DC. 6-acre campus. 5 buildings on campus. Approved or accredited by National Catholic Education Association and Maryland Department of Education. Endowment: $4.8 million. Total enrollment: 815. Upper school average class size: 18. Upper school faculty-student ratio: 1:12. There are 172 required school days per year for Upper School students. Upper School students typically attend 5 days per week. The average school day consists of 5 hours and 45 minutes.

Upper School Student Profile Grade 9: 258 students (258 boys); Grade 10: 228 students (228 boys); Grade 11: 191 students (191 boys); Grade 12: 160 students (160 boys). 46% of students are Roman Catholic.

Faculty School total: 70. In upper school: 53 men, 17 women; 46 have advanced degrees.

Subjects Offered Accounting, Advanced Placement courses, algebra, American government, American history, American history-AP, anatomy and physiology, art, art history, art-AP, astronomy, band, biology, biology-AP, British literature, British literature-AP, business, business law, calculus, calculus-AP, campus ministry, chemistry, chemistry-AP, Chinese, choral music, chorus, Christian ethics, church history, college admission preparation, community service, computer applications, computer programming, computer science, computer science-AP, computer skills, computer studies, contemporary art, digital photography, English, English composition, English literature, environmental science, film studies, French, French language-AP, geology, geometry, German, German-AP, government, government-AP, Greek, health, health education, history, history of religion, history of rock and roll, honors algebra, honors English, honors geometry, honors U.S. history, honors world history, instrumental music, jazz, journalism, Latin, Latin American studies, Latin-AP, literature-AP, Mandarin, mathematics, modern languages, music, music performance, mythology, newspaper, photography, photojournalism, physical education, physical science, physics, physics-AP, pre-calculus, psychology, SAT preparation, science, science research, social studies, Spanish, Spanish-AP, speech, sports medicine, statistics, studio art, studio art-AP, study skills, symphonic band, theology, trigonometry, U.S. government, U.S. government and politics-AP, U.S. history, U.S. literature, vocal music, world history, writing, yearbook.

Graduation Requirements American government, art, arts, computer science, English, foreign language, health education, mathematics, physical education (includes health), science, social studies (includes history), theology, 55 hours of Christian service, service reflection paper.

Special Academic Programs 13 Advanced Placement exams for which test preparation is offered; honors section; independent study; academic accommodation for the gifted, the musically talented, and the artistically talented; remedial reading and/or remedial writing.

College Admission Counseling 181 students graduated in 2016; 177 went to college, including Frostburg State University; Hampton University; The University of Alabama; Towson University; University of Maryland, Baltimore County; University of Maryland, College Park. Other: 4 went to work. Median SAT critical reading: 500, median SAT math: 500, median SAT writing: 460, median composite ACT: 21. 16.6% scored over 600 on SAT critical reading, 21.2% scored over 600 on SAT math, 10.9% scored over 600 on SAT writing, 16% scored over 1800 on combined SAT, 28% scored over 26 on composite ACT.

Student Life Upper grades have uniform requirement, student council, honor system. Discipline rests primarily with faculty. Attendance at religious services is required.

Summer Programs Remediation, enrichment, sports, art/fine arts, computer instruction programs offered; session focuses on remediation/enrichment; held on campus; accepts boys and girls; open to students from other schools. 350 students usually enrolled. 2017 schedule: June 19 to July 21. Application deadline: June 19.

Tuition and Aid Day student tuition: $16,975. Tuition installment plan (FACTS Tuition Payment Plan). Tuition reduction for siblings, merit scholarship grants, need-based scholarship grants, paying campus jobs available. In 2016–17, 65% of upper-school students received aid; total upper-school merit-scholarship money awarded: $694,600. Total amount of financial aid awarded in 2016–17: $1,632,348.

Admissions Traditional secondary-level entrance grade is 9. For fall 2016, 516 students applied for upper-level admission, 485 were accepted, 258 enrolled. High School Placement Test required. Deadline for receipt of application materials: December 15. Application fee required: $50.

Athletics Interscholastic: baseball (boys), basketball (b), crew (b), cross-country running (b), diving (b), football (b), golf (b), hockey (b), ice hockey (b), indoor track (b), indoor track & field (b), lacrosse (b), rugby (b), soccer (b), swimming and diving (b), tennis (b), track and field (b), ultimate Frisbee (b), water polo (b), winter (indoor) track (b), wrestling (b); intramural: basketball (b), paddle tennis (b), strength & conditioning (b), table tennis (b). 2 PE instructors, 2 coaches, 2 athletic trainers.

Computers Computers are regularly used in business, computer applications, digital applications, English, foreign language, independent study, lab/keyboard, library, mathematics, newspaper, publishing, religious studies, science, technology, Web site design, word processing, yearbook classes. Computer network features include on-campus library services, Internet access, wireless campus network, Internet filtering or blocking technology, ProQuest, SIRS, World Book, Veracross. Student e-mail accounts and computer access in designated common areas are available to students. Students grades are available online. The school has a published electronic and media policy.

Contact Mrs. Christine Thomas, Assistant Director of Admissions. 240-764-2210. Fax: 240-764-2277. E-mail: cthomas@dematha.org. Website: www.dematha.org

DENVER ACADEMY

Denver, Colorado
See Special Needs Schools section.

DENVER CHRISTIAN HIGH SCHOOL

3898 S. Teller Street
Lakewood, Colorado 80235

Head of School: Mr. Steve Kortenhoeven

General Information Coeducational day college-preparatory, general academic, arts, religious studies, bilingual studies, and technology school, affiliated with Christian Reformed Church. Grades PK–12. Founded: 1950. Setting: suburban. 20-acre campus. 1 building on campus. Approved or accredited by Association of Christian Schools International, Christian Schools International, North Central Association of Colleges and Schools, and Colorado Department of Education. Endowment: $1.5 million. Total enrollment: 417. Upper school average class size: 20. Upper school faculty-student ratio: 1:19. There are 180 required school days per year for Upper School students. Upper School students typically attend 5 days per week. The average school day consists of 6 hours and 45 minutes.

Upper School Student Profile Grade 9: 29 students (10 boys, 19 girls); Grade 10: 39 students (18 boys, 21 girls); Grade 11: 32 students (16 boys, 16 girls); Grade 12: 35 students (20 boys, 15 girls). 20% of students are members of Christian Reformed Church.

Faculty School total: 17. In upper school: 8 men, 9 women; 16 have advanced degrees.

Subjects Offered Acting, advanced biology, advanced chemistry, advanced computer applications, advanced math, algebra, American government, American history, American literature, art, band, Bible, biology, British literature, calculus, chamber groups, chemistry, choir, Christian doctrine, Christian scripture, church history, composition, computer applications, concert band, concert choir, consumer economics, drama, driver education, earth science, European history, general math, government, grammar, health, introduction to literature, jazz band, keyboarding, personal fitness, physical education, physical fitness, physics, poetry, pre-algebra, pre-calculus, psychology, research, senior seminar, Shakespeare, Spanish, speech, studio art, symphonic band, the Web, trigonometry, U.S. government, U.S. history, Web site design, weight fitness, Western civilization, world geography, world history, yearbook.

Graduation Requirements Bible studies.

Special Academic Programs Honors section; independent study; special instructional classes for deaf students.

College Admission Counseling 42 students graduated in 2016; 39 went to college, including Baylor University; Calvin College; Colorado State University; Dordt College; University of Northern Colorado. Other: 2 went to work, 1 had other specific plans. Mean SAT critical reading: 560, mean SAT math: 545, mean composite ACT: 24.

Student Life Upper grades have specified standards of dress, student council. Discipline rests primarily with faculty. Attendance at religious services is required.

Tuition and Aid Day student tuition: $11,800. Tuition installment plan (FACTS Tuition Payment Plan, monthly payment plans). Tuition reduction for siblings, merit scholarship grants, need-based scholarship grants available. In 2016–17, 40% of upper-school students received aid; total upper-school merit-scholarship money awarded: $1500. Total amount of financial aid awarded in 2016–17: $30,000.

Admissions Traditional secondary-level entrance grade is 9. For fall 2016, 37 students applied for upper-level admission, 23 were accepted, 23 enrolled. WISC-III and Woodcock-Johnson, WISC/Woodcock-Johnson or Woodcock-Johnson Educational Evaluation, WISC III required. Deadline for receipt of application materials: none. Application fee required: $500. On-campus interview recommended.

Athletics Interscholastic: baseball (boys), basketball (b,g), cheering (b,g), cross-country running (b,g), golf (b), soccer (b,g), track and field (b,g), volleyball (g); coed interscholastic: physical training, strength & conditioning, weight training. 3 PE instructors, 24 coaches, 1 athletic trainer.

Computers Computer network features include on-campus library services, Internet access, wireless campus network, Internet filtering or blocking technology. Student e-mail accounts and computer access in designated common areas are available to students. Students grades are available online. The school has a published electronic and media policy.

Contact Mrs. Sandie Posthumus, Administrative Assistant. 303-763-7922. Fax: 303-733-7734. E-mail: sposthumus@denverchristian.org.
Website: www.denverchristian.org

THE DERRYFIELD SCHOOL

2108 River Road
Manchester, New Hampshire 03104-1302

General Information Coeducational day college-preparatory school. Grades 6–12. Founded: 1964. Setting: suburban. Nearest major city is Boston, MA. 84-acre campus. 4 buildings on campus. Approved or accredited by Association of Independent Schools in New England, Independent Schools of Northern New England, New England Association of Schools and Colleges, and New Hampshire Department of Education. Member of National Association of Independent Schools and Secondary School Admission Test Board. Endowment: $5 million. Total enrollment: 387. Upper school average class size: 13. Upper school faculty-student ratio: 1:8. There are 163 required school days per year for Upper School students. Upper School students typically attend 5 days per week. The average school day consists of 6 hours and 45 minutes.

See Display on next page and Close-Up on page 596.

DESERT ACADEMY

7300 Old Santa Fe Trail
Santa Fe, New Mexico 87505

Head of School: Mr. Terry Passalacqua

General Information Coeducational day college-preparatory, arts, and world citizenship school. Grades 6–12. Founded: 1994. Setting: small town. Students are housed in homestays. 26-acre campus. 4 buildings on campus. Approved or accredited by Independent Schools Association of the Southwest, International Baccalaureate Organization, North Central Association of Colleges and Schools, and New Mexico Department of Education. Member of National Association of Independent Schools. Endowment: $12,000. Total enrollment: 190. Upper school average class size: 12. Upper school faculty-student ratio: 1:8. There are 180 required school days per year for Upper School students. Upper School students typically attend 5 days per week. The average school day consists of 7 hours and 30 minutes.

Upper School Student Profile Grade 6: 8 students (4 boys, 4 girls); Grade 7: 28 students (19 boys, 9 girls); Grade 8: 24 students (13 boys, 11 girls); Grade 9: 19 students (11 boys, 8 girls); Grade 10: 25 students (13 boys, 12 girls); Grade 11: 31 students (11 boys, 20 girls); Grade 12: 40 students (16 boys, 24 girls). 15% of students are boarding students. 100% are international students. International students from China, Germany, and Spain.

Faculty School total: 31. In upper school: 17 men, 14 women; 10 have advanced degrees.

Subjects Offered Acting, advanced chemistry, algebra, American history, American literature, American sign language, anatomy, applied music, art, Basic programming, biology, business mathematics, calculus, chemistry, Chinese, chorus, civics, computer graphics, computer programming, culinary arts, current events, digital photography, drama, drama performance, earth science, electives, French, geometry, government, honors algebra, honors English, honors geometry, honors U.S. history, honors world history, independent study, keyboarding, language and composition, Latin, literature, modern world history, musical productions, newspaper, performing arts, photography, physical education, physical science, physics, poetry, pre-algebra, pre-calculus, reading/study skills, SAT/ACT preparation, social studies, Spanish, U.S. history, Web site design, world history, writing, yearbook.

Graduation Requirements Algebra, biology, electives, English, foreign language, geometry, mathematics, science, social studies (includes history). Community service is required.

Special Academic Programs International Baccalaureate program; honors section; independent study; remedial reading and/or remedial writing; remedial math; ESL (2 students enrolled).

College Admission Counseling 13 students graduated in 2016; all went to college, including Bates College; Savannah College of Art and Design; University of California, Santa Cruz; University of Denver; University of New Mexico; University of New Mexico. 90% scored over 26 on composite ACT.

Student Life Upper grades have specified standards of dress, student council, honor system. Discipline rests primarily with faculty.

Tuition and Aid Day student tuition: $19,100. Tuition installment plan (Insured Tuition Payment Plan, monthly payment plans, two annual payments). Tuition reduction for siblings, need-based scholarship grants available. In 2016–17, 41% of upper-school students received aid; total upper-school merit-scholarship money awarded: $83,000. Total amount of financial aid awarded in 2016–17: $180,000.

Admissions Traditional secondary-level entrance grade is 9. For fall 2016, 51 students applied for upper-level admission, 43 were accepted, 42 enrolled. Deadline for receipt of application materials: none. Application fee required: $65. Interview recommended.

Athletics Interscholastic: basketball (boys, girls), cross-country running (b,g), golf (b), soccer (b,g), swimming and diving (b,g), track and field (b,g), volleyball (g); coed interscholastic: baseball; coed intramural: alpine skiing, backpacking, weight training. 1 PE instructor, 8 coaches.

Computers Computers are regularly used in current events, English, geography, graphic design, history, journalism, literary magazine, newspaper, photography, science, social sciences, social studies, Web site design, writing, yearbook classes. Computer network features include Internet access, wireless campus network, Internet filtering or blocking technology, DSL Internet access. Students grades are available online. The school has a published electronic and media policy.

Contact Jennifer Warren, Director of Admissions. 505-992-8284 Ext. 22. Fax: 505-992-8270. E-mail: jwarren@desertacademy.org. Website: www.desertacademy.org

DETROIT COUNTRY DAY SCHOOL

22305 West Thirteen Mile Road
Beverly Hills, Michigan 48025-4435

Head of School: Mr. Glen P. Shilling

General Information Coeducational day college-preparatory, arts, and global communities school. Grades PK–12. Founded: 1914. Setting: suburban. Nearest major city is Detroit. 100-acre campus. 1 building on campus. Approved or accredited by Independent Schools Association of the Central States and Michigan Department of Education. Member of National Association of Independent Schools. Endowment: $36 million. Total enrollment: 1,523. Upper school average class size: 15. Upper school faculty-student ratio: 1:8. There are 162 required school days per year for Upper School students. Upper School students typically attend 5 days per week. The average school day consists of 7 hours and 30 minutes.

Upper School Student Profile Grade 6: 118 students (77 boys, 41 girls); Grade 7: 128 students (71 boys, 57 girls); Grade 8: 145 students (90 boys, 55 girls); Grade 9: 146 students (75 boys, 71 girls); Grade 10: 187 students (89 boys, 98 girls); Grade 11: 175 students (104 boys, 71 girls); Grade 12: 155 students (83 boys, 72 girls).

Faculty School total: 202. In upper school: 35 men, 37 women; 60 have advanced degrees.

Subjects Offered African-American studies, algebra, American history, American literature, American studies, analytic geometry, anatomy, anatomy and physiology, ancient history, art, art and culture, art appreciation, art-AP, astronomy, band, biology, botany, calculus, ceramics, chemistry, Chinese, chorus, college counseling, community service, composition, computer programming, computer science, current events, design, drama, drawing, ecology, economics, economics and history, English, English literature, environmental science, European history, fine arts, finite math, French, genetics, geometry, German, government/civics, grammar, graphic arts, health, history, humanities, Japanese, Latin, literature, mathematics, media, metalworking, microbiology, music, music history, music theory, natural history, orchestra, painting, photography, physical education, physical science, physics, physiology, poetry, pre-calculus, printmaking, science, sculpture, social studies, Spanish, speech, statistics, study skills, theater, theory of knowledge, Western civilization, world literature, zoology.

Graduation Requirements American government, American history, arts and fine arts (art, music, dance, drama), English, foreign language, mathematics, science, speech, athletic participation, skill-oriented activities, service-oriented activities.

Special Academic Programs International Baccalaureate program; Advanced Placement exam preparation; honors section; independent study; academic accommodation for the gifted, the musically talented, and the artistically talented; remedial reading and/or remedial writing; programs in English, mathematics, general development for dyslexic students.

College Admission Counseling 182 students graduated in 2016; all went to college, including Michigan State University; University of Michigan. Other: 2 entered a postgraduate year. Mean composite ACT: 30. 80% scored over 26 on composite ACT.

Student Life Upper grades have uniform requirement, student council, honor system. Discipline rests primarily with faculty.

Summer Programs Enrichment, advancement, sports, art/fine arts, computer instruction programs offered; session focuses on academic enrichment and sports camps; held on campus; accepts boys and girls; open to students from other schools. 300 students usually enrolled. 2017 schedule: June 19 to July 17. Application deadline: June 1.

Tuition and Aid Day student tuition: $28,000. Tuition installment plan (The Tuition Plan, Insured Tuition Payment Plan, Academic Management Services Plan, Key Tuition Payment Plan, SMART Tuition Payment Plan, FACTS Tuition Payment Plan, monthly payment plans, Dewar Tuition Refund Plan). Need-based scholarship grants available. In 2016–17, 20% of upper-school students received aid.

Admissions Traditional secondary-level entrance grade is 9. ISEE and Otis-Lennon School Ability Test required. Deadline for receipt of application materials: none. Application fee required: $50. On-campus interview recommended.

Athletics Interscholastic: aerobics/dance (girls), alpine skiing (b,g), ball hockey (g), baseball (b), basketball (b,g), bicycling (b,g), bowling (b,g), cross-country running (b,g), dance (b,g), dance squad (b,g), dance team (g), diving (b,g), field hockey (g), football (b), golf (b,g), hockey (b), ice hockey (b,g), lacrosse (b,g), sailing (b), skiing (downhill) (b,g), soccer (b,g), softball (g), swimming and diving (b,g), tennis (b,g), track and field (b,g), volleyball (g), wrestling (b); intramural: weight lifting (b,g), weight training (b,g); coed interscholastic: cheering, modern dance, mountain biking, outdoor adventure, running, sailing, snowboarding; coed intramural: basketball, climbing, crew, figure skating, Frisbee, hiking/backpacking, kickball, mountaineering, outdoor education, outdoor skills, project adventure, rock climbing, running, strength & conditioning, ultimate Frisbee, volleyball, wall climbing, weight training, yoga. 4 coaches, 3 athletic trainers.

Computers Computers are regularly used in all academic classes. Computer network features include on-campus library services, online commercial services, Internet access, wireless campus network, Internet filtering or blocking technology. Campus intranet and student e-mail accounts are available to students. Students grades are available online. The school has a published electronic and media policy.

Contact Mrs. Michele Reimer, Enrollment and Admissions Manager. 248-430-3587. Fax: 248-203-2184. E-mail: mreimer@dcds.edu. Website: www.dcds.edu

DEVON PREPARATORY SCHOOL

363 North Valley Forge Road
Devon, Pennsylvania 19333-1299

Head of School: Rev. Francisco J. Aisa, Sch.P.

General Information Boys' day college-preparatory, arts, religious studies, and technology school, affiliated with Roman Catholic Church. Grades 6–12. Founded: 1956. Setting: suburban. Nearest major city is Philadelphia. 20-acre campus. 7 buildings on campus. Approved or accredited by Middle States Association of Colleges and Schools, National Catholic Education Association, Pennsylvania Association of Independent Schools, and Pennsylvania Department of Education. Member of National Association of Independent Schools. Endowment: $600,000. Total enrollment: 272. Upper school average class size: 15. Upper school faculty-student ratio: 1:10. There are 180 required school days per year for Upper School students. Upper School students typically attend 5 days per week. The average school day consists of 6 hours and 30 minutes.

Upper School Student Profile Grade 6: 15 students (15 boys); Grade 7: 29 students (29 boys); Grade 8: 26 students (26 boys); Grade 9: 44 students (44 boys); Grade 10: 45 students (45 boys); Grade 11: 63 students (63 boys); Grade 12: 43 students (43 boys). 84% of students are Roman Catholic.

Faculty School total: 37. In upper school: 23 men, 14 women; 23 have advanced degrees.

Subjects Offered Marketing.

Graduation Requirements Computer science, English, foreign language, geography, Latin, mathematics, physical education (includes health), political science, religion (includes Bible studies and theology), science, social studies (includes history). Community service is required.

Special Academic Programs 21 Advanced Placement exams for which test preparation is offered.

College Admission Counseling 50 students graduated in 2016; all went to college, including Drexel University; Loyola University Maryland; Penn State University Park; Saint Joseph's University; Temple University; Villanova University. Median SAT critical reading: 643, median SAT math: 636, median SAT writing: 625, median combined SAT: 1904.

Student Life Upper grades have specified standards of dress, student council. Discipline rests primarily with faculty. Attendance at religious services is required.

Tuition and Aid Day student tuition: $22,900. Tuition installment plan (monthly payment plans). Tuition reduction for siblings, merit scholarship grants, need-based scholarship grants available. In 2016–17, 65% of upper-school students received aid; total upper-school merit-scholarship money awarded: $660,000. Total amount of financial aid awarded in 2016–17: $1,030,000.

Admissions Traditional secondary-level entrance grade is 9. For fall 2016, 220 students applied for upper-level admission, 85 were accepted, 30 enrolled. Deadline for receipt of application materials: none. Application fee required: $50. On-campus interview recommended.

Athletics Interscholastic: baseball, basketball, bowling, cross-country running, golf, indoor track & field, lacrosse, soccer, swimming and diving, tennis, track and field. 2 PE instructors, 11 coaches, 2 athletic trainers.

Computers Computers are regularly used in all classes. Computer network features include on-campus library services, Internet access, wireless campus network, Internet filtering or blocking technology. Student e-mail accounts and computer access in designated common areas are available to students. Students grades are available online. The school has a published electronic and media policy.

Contact Mr. Kevin Mulholland, Director of Admissions. 610-688-7337 Ext. 129. Fax: 610-688-2409. E-mail: kmulholland@devonprep.com. Website: www.devonprep.com

DOANE ACADEMY

350 Riverbank
Burlington, New Jersey 08016-2199

Head of School: Mr. George B. Sanderson

General Information Coeducational day college-preparatory, arts, College Counseling, English, Health, STEAM, History, Math, and Science, Social Studies,World and Classical Language school, affiliated with Episcopal Church. Grades PK–12. Distance learning grades 9–12. Founded: 1837. Setting: suburban. Nearest major city is Philadelphia, PA. Students are housed in Day School Only. 11-acre campus. 5 buildings on campus. Approved or accredited by Middle States Association of Colleges and Schools and National Association of Episcopal Schools. Member of National Association of Independent Schools. Endowment: $17 million. Total enrollment: 226. Upper school average class size: 12. Upper school faculty-student ratio: 1:12. There are 177 required school days per year for Upper School students. Upper School students typically attend 5 days per week. The average school day consists of 7 hours and 10 minutes.

Upper School Student Profile Grade 6: 13 students (5 boys, 8 girls); Grade 7: 18 students (9 boys, 9 girls); Grade 8: 17 students (9 boys, 8 girls); Grade 9: 28 students

(14 boys, 14 girls); Grade 10: 27 students (16 boys, 11 girls); Grade 11: 25 students (14 boys, 11 girls); Grade 12: 32 students (20 boys, 12 girls).

Faculty School total: 36. In upper school: 6 men, 11 women; 14 have advanced degrees.

Subjects Offered Acting.

Graduation Requirements Arts and fine arts (art, music, dance, drama), computer skills, English, ethics, foreign language, lab science, mathematics, physical education (includes health), science, social studies (includes history), world religions, one semester of ethics and world religions.

Special Academic Programs Advanced Placement exam preparation; honors section; independent study; study at local college for college credit; academic accommodation for the gifted, the musically talented, and the artistically talented; remedial reading and/or remedial writing; remedial math.

College Admission Counseling 29 students graduated in 2016; all went to college, including Haverford College; Lehigh University; The College of New Jersey; Wellesley College. 68% scored over 600 on SAT critical reading, 70% scored over 600 on SAT math, 80% scored over 600 on SAT writing, 65% scored over 1800 on combined SAT, 50% scored over 26 on composite ACT.

Student Life Upper grades have uniform requirement, student council, honor system. Discipline rests primarily with faculty. Attendance at religious services is required.

Tuition and Aid Day student tuition: $18,400–$19,999. Tuition installment plan (FACTS Tuition Payment Plan, monthly payment plans). Tuition reduction for siblings, merit scholarship grants, need-based scholarship grants, tuition remission for children of faculty and staff available. In 2016–17, 50% of upper-school students received aid; total upper-school merit-scholarship money awarded: $20,000. Total amount of financial aid awarded in 2016–17: $8000.

Admissions Traditional secondary-level entrance grade is 9. For fall 2016, 40 students applied for upper-level admission, 32 were accepted, 32 enrolled. ISEE or SSAT required. Deadline for receipt of application materials: none. Application fee required: $35. On-campus interview required.

Athletics Interscholastic: baseball (boys), basketball (b,g), bowling (g), crew (b,g), cross-country running (b,g), golf (b,g), rowing (b,g), soccer (b,g), softball (g), tennis (g); coed interscholastic: outdoor adventure, soccer, strength & conditioning; coed intramural: alpine skiing, basketball, kickball, outdoor activities, soccer, softball, table tennis, volleyball. 2 PE instructors, 11 coaches.

Computers Computers are regularly used in graphic design, lab/keyboard, mathematics, photography, research skills, SAT preparation, science, Web site design, yearbook classes. Computer network features include on-campus library services, Internet access, wireless campus network, Internet filtering or blocking technology, homework assignments available online. Campus intranet is available to students. Students grades are available online. The school has a published electronic and media policy.

Contact Ms. Lacy Hall, Dean of Admission. 609-386-3500 Ext. 115. Fax: 609-386-5878. E-mail: lhall@doaneacademy.org. Website: www.doaneacademy.org

DOCK MENNONITE ACADEMY

1000 Forty Foot Road
Lansdale, Pennsylvania 19446

Head of School: Dr. Conrad J. Swartzentruber

General Information Coeducational boarding and day college-preparatory and general academic school, affiliated with Mennonite Church. Ungraded, ages 14–19. Founded: 1954. Setting: suburban. Nearest major city is Philadelphia. Students are housed in homes. 75-acre campus. 6 buildings on campus. Approved or accredited by Mennonite Education Agency and Pennsylvania Department of Education. Endowment: $4.5 million. Total enrollment: 375. Upper school average class size: 16. Upper school faculty-student ratio: 1:12. There are 180 required school days per year for Upper School students. Upper School students typically attend 5 days per week. The average school day consists of 6 hours and 55 minutes.

Upper School Student Profile Grade 9: 90 students (40 boys, 50 girls); Grade 10: 91 students (54 boys, 37 girls); Grade 11: 105 students (54 boys, 51 girls); Grade 12: 77 students (35 boys, 42 girls). 42% of students are Mennonite.

Faculty School total: 32. In upper school: 15 men, 17 women; 21 have advanced degrees.

Subjects Offered Accounting, advanced biology, advanced chemistry, advanced math, Advanced Placement courses, algebra, American government, American history, American literature, anatomy, anatomy and physiology, art, art history, arts, arts appreciation, athletic training, athletics, Basic programming, Bible, Bible studies, biology, British literature, business, business mathematics, business skills, calculus, calculus-AP, career education internship, career technology, ceramics, chemistry, child development, choir, choral music, chorus, Christian and Hebrew scripture, Christian doctrine, Christian education, Christian ethics, Christian scripture, Christian studies, Christian testament, Christianity, church history, communication skills, communications, composition-AP, computer applications, computer graphics, computer information systems, computer literacy, computer programming, computer science, computer skills, computer technologies, computers, concert choir, consumer economics, creative writing, design, digital art, digital imaging, digital music, digital photography, drama, driver education, early childhood, earth science, ecology, environmental systems, economics, economics and history, economics-AP, English,

English language and composition-AP, English literature, environmental science, European history, family and consumer science, family living, family studies, fine arts, food science, foreign language, forensics, genetics, geography, geology, geometry, global studies, government-AP, government/civics, grammar, graphic design, guitar, health, health and wellness, health education, history, honors English, honors geometry, instrumental music, instruments, international foods, jazz band, journalism, keyboarding, language and composition, Life of Christ, life saving, life science, mathematics, mathematics-AP, music, New Testament, oral communications, parent/child development, peace and justice, peace education, peace studies, personal finance, photography, physical education, physics, religion, religion and culture, religious education, religious studies, research and reference, rhetoric, science, science research, scripture, sculpture, senior internship, service learning/internship, social sciences, social studies, Spanish, Spanish language-AP, Spanish literature-AP, Spanish-AP, speech, speech communications, sports team management, stage and body movement, statistics, student government, student publications, theater, trigonometry, U.S. government, U.S. history, U.S. literature, Vietnam, vocal ensemble, vocal music, vocational skills, vocational-technical courses, Web site design, word processing, work-study, world cultures, world history, world literature.

Graduation Requirements Arts and fine arts (art, music, dance, drama), business skills (includes word processing), computer science, English, family and consumer science, mathematics, physical education (includes health), religion (includes Bible studies and theology), science, social sciences, social studies (includes history), three-day urban experience, senior independent study/service experience (one week), senior presentation.

Special Academic Programs 16 Advanced Placement exams for which test preparation is offered; honors section; study at local college for college credit; remedial reading and/or remedial writing; remedial math.

College Admission Counseling 95 students graduated in 2016; 83 went to college, including Bucks County Community College; Eastern University; Liberty University; Messiah College; Penn State University Park. Other: 8 went to work, 4 had other specific plans. Mean SAT critical reading: 528, mean SAT math: 565, mean SAT writing: 533, mean combined SAT: 1626, mean composite ACT: 25.

Student Life Upper grades have specified standards of dress, student council, honor system. Discipline rests primarily with faculty. Attendance at religious services is required.

Tuition and Aid Day student tuition: $15,805; 7-day tuition and room/board: $32,605. Tuition installment plan (FACTS Tuition Payment Plan, monthly payment plans). Tuition reduction for siblings, need-based scholarship grants available. In 2016–17, 67% of upper-school students received aid. Total amount of financial aid awarded in 2016–17: $655,758.

Admissions Traditional secondary-level entrance grade is 9. For fall 2016, 140 students applied for upper-level admission, 120 were accepted, 110 enrolled. Deadline for receipt of application materials: none. Application fee required: $50. Interview recommended.

Athletics Interscholastic: baseball (boys), basketball (b,g), bowling (b,g), cheering (g), cross-country running (b,g), field hockey (g), golf (b), soccer (b,g), softball (g), tennis (b,g), track and field (b,g), volleyball (b,g). 3 PE instructors, 37 coaches, 1 athletic trainer.

Computers Computers are regularly used in accounting, art, computer applications, design, digital applications, graphic design, journalism, keyboarding, lab/keyboard, library, library skills, mathematics, music, music technology, programming, research skills, SAT preparation, science, technology, Web site design, word processing, yearbook classes. Computer network features include on-campus library services, wireless campus network, Internet filtering or blocking technology, PowerSchool, Schoology, WinSNAP, 1:1 iPad program. Campus intranet, student e-mail accounts, and computer access in designated common areas are available to students. Students grades are available online. The school has a published electronic and media policy.

Contact Doug Hackman, Director of Admissions. 215-362-2675 Ext. 106. Fax: 215-362-2943. E-mail: dhackman@dock.org. Website: www.dockhs.org

THE DR. MIRIAM AND SHELDON G. ADELSON EDUCATIONAL CAMPUS, THE ADELSON UPPER SCHOOL

9700 West Hillpointe Road
Las Vegas, Nevada 89134

Head of School: Dr. Joyce Raynor

General Information Coeducational day college-preparatory and technology school, affiliated with Jewish faith. Grades PS–12. Founded: 1979. Setting: suburban. Students are housed in Host families. 4-acre campus. 1 building on campus. Approved or accredited by Nevada Department of Education. Member of National Association of Independent Schools. Total enrollment: 419. Upper school average class size: 16. Upper school faculty-student ratio: 1:14. There are 180 required school days per year for Upper School students. Upper School students typically attend 5 days per week. The average school day consists of 7 hours and 10 minutes.

Upper School Student Profile Grade 9: 33 students (16 boys, 17 girls); Grade 10: 35 students (19 boys, 16 girls); Grade 11: 32 students (19 boys, 13 girls); Grade 12: 40 students (18 boys, 22 girls). 80% of students are Jewish.

Faculty School total: 70. In upper school: 11 men, 13 women; 22 have advanced degrees.

Subjects Offered All academic.

Graduation Requirements Jewish studies.

Special Academic Programs 13 Advanced Placement exams for which test preparation is offered; honors section; study at local college for college credit; study abroad; academic accommodation for the gifted; programs in English, mathematics for dyslexic students; special instructional classes for deaf students; ESL (5 students enrolled).

College Admission Counseling 30 students graduated in 2016; 29 went to college. Other: 1 had other specific plans.

Student Life Upper grades have uniform requirement, student council, honor system. Discipline rests primarily with faculty. Attendance at religious services is required.

Tuition and Aid Day student tuition: $20,850; 5-day tuition and room/board: $38,850. Tuition installment plan (monthly payment plans, individually arranged payment plans). Need-based scholarship grants available. In 2016–17, 35% of upper-school students received aid.

Admissions Traditional secondary-level entrance grade is 9. For fall 2016, 35 students applied for upper-level admission, 27 were accepted, 24 enrolled. Achievement tests, Achievement/Aptitude/Writing or admissions testing required. Deadline for receipt of application materials: none. No application fee required. Interview recommended.

Athletics Interscholastic: aerobics/dance (girls), baseball (b), basketball (b,g), cheering (g), cross-country running (b,g), dance (b,g), dance team (b,g), modern dance (b,g), soccer (b,g), swimming and diving (b,g), tennis (b,g), volleyball (b,g); intramural: fencing (b,g); coed interscholastic: aquatics, golf. 4 PE instructors, 10 coaches, 1 athletic trainer.

Computers Computers are regularly used in all academic, computer applications, technology classes. Computer network features include on-campus library services, Internet access, wireless campus network, Internet filtering or blocking technology, one-to-world devices, startup Incubator. Student e-mail accounts and computer access in designated common areas are available to students. Students grades are available online. The school has a published electronic and media policy.

Contact Mrs. Alli Abrahamson, Director of Admissions. 702-255-4500. Fax: 702-255-7232. E-mail: alli.abrahamson@adelsoncampus.org. Website: www.adelsoncampus.org

DOMINICAN ACADEMY

44 East 68th Street
New York, New York 10065

Head of School: Sr. Margaret Ormond, O.P.

General Information Girls' day college-preparatory and all honors school, affiliated with Roman Catholic Church. Grades 9–12. Founded: 1897. Setting: urban. 1 building on campus. Approved or accredited by Middle States Association of Colleges and Schools, National Catholic Education Association, New York State Board of Regents, and New York Department of Education. Member of National Association of Independent Schools and Secondary School Admission Test Board. Total enrollment: 216. Upper school average class size: 18. Upper school faculty-student ratio: 1:8. There are 180 required school days per year for Upper School students. Upper School students typically attend 5 days per week. The average school day consists of 6 hours and 30 minutes.

Upper School Student Profile Grade 9: 73 students (73 girls); Grade 10: 40 students (40 girls); Grade 11: 56 students (56 girls); Grade 12: 53 students (53 girls). 80% of students are Roman Catholic.

Faculty School total: 27. In upper school: 4 men, 23 women; 20 have advanced degrees.

Subjects Offered Algebra, American history, American history-AP, American literature, art history-AP, biology, biology-AP, calculus, calculus-AP, chemistry, chemistry-AP, Chinese, chorus, communications, computer science, creative writing, dance, debate, drama, economics, economics-AP, English, English literature, English-AP, European history-AP, forensics, French, French-AP, geometry, global studies, government and politics-AP, government/civics, health, history, Latin, Latin-AP, library studies, logic, mathematics, music, music theory, physical education, physics, physics-AP, pre-calculus, psychology, religion, science, social studies, Spanish, Spanish-AP, world history.

Graduation Requirements Alternative physical education, arts and fine arts (art, music, dance, drama), English, foreign language, Latin, mathematics, religion (includes Bible studies and theology), science, social studies (includes history), 5 years of language including 2 years minimum of both Latin and a modern language.

Special Academic Programs 12 Advanced Placement exams for which test preparation is offered; honors section; domestic exchange program; ESL (8 students enrolled).

College Admission Counseling 58 students graduated in 2016; all went to college, including Cornell University; Fordham University; Princeton University; Sarah Lawrence College; The College of William and Mary; Villanova University. Mean combined SAT: 1835.

Student Life Upper grades have uniform requirement, student council. Discipline rests primarily with faculty. Attendance at religious services is required.

Summer Programs Remediation, enrichment, advancement programs offered; session focuses on prospective student and math prep; held on campus; accepts girls;

open to students from other schools. 80 students usually enrolled. Application deadline: June 15.

Tuition and Aid Day student tuition: $16,200. Tuition installment plan (FACTS Tuition Payment Plan, individually arranged payment plans, full year payment, eight equal installments). Tuition reduction for siblings, merit scholarship grants, need-based scholarship grants, paying campus jobs available. In 2016–17, 33% of upper-school students received aid.

Admissions Traditional secondary-level entrance grade is 9. For fall 2016, 390 students applied for upper-level admission, 215 were accepted, 73 enrolled. Catholic High School Entrance Examination or Differential Aptitude Test required. Deadline for receipt of application materials: December 15. Application fee required: $150.

Athletics Interscholastic: basketball, cross-country running, indoor track, indoor track & field, running, soccer, softball, swimming and diving, tennis, track and field, volleyball; intramural: billiards, dance, modern dance, soccer, tennis, track and field, volleyball, yoga. 1 PE instructor.

Computers Computers are regularly used in economics, health, history, Latin, library science, library studies, mathematics, religious studies, science, technology classes. Computer network features include on-campus library services, online commercial services, Internet access, wireless campus network, Internet filtering or blocking technology, T1 fiber optic network. Campus intranet, student e-mail accounts, and computer access in designated common areas are available to students. The school has a published electronic and media policy.

Contact Ms. Madeleine Metzler, Director of Admissions. 212-744-0195 Ext. 31. Fax: 212-744-0375. E-mail: mmetzler@dominicanacademy.org. Website: www.dominicanacademy.org

DONELSON CHRISTIAN ACADEMY

300 Danyacrest Drive
Nashville, Tennessee 37214

Head of School: Mr. Keith M. Singer

General Information Coeducational day college-preparatory, arts, religious studies, and technology school. Grades PS–12. Founded: 1971. Setting: suburban. 50-acre campus. 1 building on campus. Approved or accredited by Association of Christian Schools International, Southern Association of Colleges and Schools, Tennessee Association of Independent Schools, and Tennessee Department of Education. Member of National Association of Independent Schools. Endowment: $78,000. Total enrollment: 818. Upper school average class size: 14. Upper school faculty-student ratio: 1:14. There are 175 required school days per year for Upper School students. Upper School students typically attend 5 days per week. The average school day consists of 7 hours and 20 minutes.

Upper School Student Profile Grade 9: 57 students (32 boys, 25 girls); Grade 10: 45 students (23 boys, 22 girls); Grade 11: 64 students (33 boys, 31 girls); Grade 12: 43 students (22 boys, 21 girls).

Faculty School total: 68. In upper school: 15 men, 21 women; 18 have advanced degrees.

Subjects Offered 3-dimensional art, ACT preparation, Advanced Placement courses, advanced studio art-AP, algebra, American history, American history-AP, American literature, American literature-AP, anatomy, art, athletic training, Bible studies, biology, biology-AP, business, calculus, calculus-AP, chemistry, chemistry-AP, Chinese, choir, community service, computer science, creative writing, drama, earth science, ecology, economics, English, English language and composition-AP, English literature, English literature and composition-AP, environmental science, ESL, European history-AP, fine arts, French, geography, geometry, government/civics, grammar, health, history, honors algebra, honors English, honors geometry, honors U.S. history, journalism, keyboarding, Latin, Latin-AP, mathematics, music, personal finance, physical education, physics, physiology, psychology, religion, science, social sciences, social studies, sociology, Spanish, speech, theater, U.S. history-AP, world history, world literature, yearbook.

Graduation Requirements Arts and fine arts (art, music, dance, drama), Bible, chemistry, consumer economics, electives, English, foreign language, mathematics, physical education (includes health), science, social sciences, social studies (includes history), wellness, senior service (community service for 12th grade students).

Special Academic Programs 6 Advanced Placement exams for which test preparation is offered; independent study; study at local college for college credit; ESL (8 students enrolled).

College Admission Counseling 40 students graduated in 2016; 38 went to college, including Middle Tennessee State University; Samford University; Tennessee Technological University; The University of Tennessee; The University of Tennessee at Chattanooga; Vanderbilt University. Other: 2 went to work. Median composite ACT: 25. 27% scored over 26 on composite ACT.

Student Life Upper grades have uniform requirement, student council, honor system. Discipline rests primarily with faculty.

Summer Programs Sports, art/fine arts programs offered; session focuses on to enhance in the areas of academics, the arts, and athletics; held on campus; accepts boys and girls; not open to students from other schools. 75 students usually enrolled. 2017 schedule: May 30 to July 31.

Tuition and Aid Day student tuition: $11,432. Tuition installment plan (FACTS Tuition Payment Plan). Need-based scholarship grants available. In 2016–17, 25% of

upper-school students received aid. Total amount of financial aid awarded in 2016–17: $217,000.

Admissions Traditional secondary-level entrance grade is 9. For fall 2016, 22 students applied for upper-level admission, 15 were accepted, 12 enrolled. Admissions testing required. Deadline for receipt of application materials: none. Application fee required: $40. On-campus interview required.

Athletics Interscholastic: baseball (boys), basketball (b,g), bowling (b,g), cheering (g), cross-country running (b,g), football (b), golf (b,g), soccer (b,g), softball (g), tennis (b,g), track and field (b,g), volleyball (g), wrestling (b); intramural: basketball (b,g), football (b); coed interscholastic: fitness, physical fitness, swimming and diving, weight training; coed intramural: fitness, kickball, rappelling. 1 PE instructor, 3 coaches, 1 athletic trainer.

Computers Computers are regularly used in all academic, career exploration, college planning, creative writing, English, French, history, journalism, library, mathematics, newspaper, science, social sciences, Spanish, technology, yearbook classes. Computer network features include on-campus library services, Internet access, wireless campus network, Internet filtering or blocking technology. Campus intranet and student e-mail accounts are available to students. Students grades are available online. The school has a published electronic and media policy.

Contact Mrs. Nicole Schierling, Assistant to Advancement. 615-577-1215. Fax: 615-883-2998. E-mail: nschierling@dcawildcats.org. Website: www.dcawildcats.org

DONNA KLEIN JEWISH ACADEMY

9701 Donna Klein Boulevard
Boca Raton, Florida 33428-1524

Head of School: Helena Levine

General Information Coeducational day college-preparatory, arts, religious studies, and bilingual studies school, affiliated with Jewish faith. Grades K–12. Founded: 1979. Setting: suburban. 23-acre campus. 1 building on campus. Approved or accredited by Florida Council of Independent Schools, Southern Association of Colleges and Schools, and Florida Department of Education. Member of National Association of Independent Schools and Secondary School Admission Test Board. Languages of instruction: English and Hebrew. Endowment: $1 million. Total enrollment: 580. Upper school average class size: 15. Upper school faculty-student ratio: 1:6. There are 172 required school days per year for Upper School students. Upper School students typically attend 5 days per week. The average school day consists of 7 hours and 30 minutes.

Upper School Student Profile Grade 6: 53 students (30 boys, 23 girls); Grade 7: 53 students (19 boys, 34 girls); Grade 8: 50 students (25 boys, 25 girls); Grade 9: 47 students (18 boys, 29 girls); Grade 10: 40 students (28 boys, 12 girls); Grade 11: 25 students (12 boys, 13 girls); Grade 12: 46 students (19 boys, 27 girls). 100% of students are Jewish.

Faculty School total: 24. In upper school: 11 men, 13 women; 11 have advanced degrees.

Subjects Offered Advanced biology, advanced chemistry, advanced math, Advanced Placement courses, advanced studio art-AP, anatomy and physiology, art, band, basketball, Bible studies, biology, calculus, calculus-AP, chemistry, college counseling, computer programming, computer skills, computer tools, dance, debate, drama, economics, English, English language and composition-AP, English literature and composition-AP, environmental science, environmental science-AP, French studies, geometry, government, government-AP, guidance, health, Hebrew, honors English, honors geometry, honors U.S. history, honors world history, Jewish history, journalism, Judaic studies, literature and composition-AP, model United Nations, physical education, pre-calculus, psychology-AP, SAT/ACT preparation, softball, Spanish, statistics, statistics-AP, student government, studio art-AP, theater production, U.S. government and politics, U.S. history-AP, visual arts, volleyball, world history, world history-AP, writing, yearbook.

Graduation Requirements Electives, English, foreign language, history, Judaic studies, mathematics, physical education (includes health), science, writing, completion of 225 hours of community service.

Special Academic Programs 15 Advanced Placement exams for which test preparation is offered; honors section; independent study; study at local college for college credit; study abroad.

College Admission Counseling 25 students graduated in 2015; 23 went to college, including Boston University; Florida Atlantic University; Florida State University; University of Central Florida; University of Florida; University of Miami. Other: 2 went to work. Median combined SAT: 1090, median composite ACT: 25.

Student Life Upper grades have specified standards of dress, student council, honor system. Discipline rests primarily with faculty. Attendance at religious services is required.

Tuition and Aid Day student tuition: $23,125. Tuition installment plan (FACTS Tuition Payment Plan, monthly payment plans, individually arranged payment plans). Merit scholarship grants, need-based scholarship grants available. In 2015–16, 50% of upper-school students received aid; total upper-school merit-scholarship money awarded: $33,000. Total amount of financial aid awarded in 2015–16: $840,465.

Admissions Traditional secondary-level entrance grade is 9. For fall 2015, 30 students applied for upper-level admission, 14 were accepted, 14 enrolled. SSAT and SSAT, ERB, PSAT, SAT, PLAN or ACT required. Deadline for receipt of application materials: none. Application fee required: $100. On-campus interview required.

Athletics Interscholastic: baseball (boys), basketball (b,g), dance team (g), golf (b), soccer (b,g), softball (g), volleyball (g); coed interscholastic: cross-country running, tennis; coed intramural: dance team, fitness, scuba diving, self defense, swimming and diving, tennis, weight lifting, weight training. 1 PE instructor, 6 coaches.

Computers Computers are regularly used in all classes. Computer network features include Internet access, wireless campus network, Internet filtering or blocking technology. Campus intranet and student e-mail accounts are available to students. Students grades are available online. The school has a published electronic and media policy.

Contact Mrs. Jodi Orshan. 561-852-3310. Fax: 561-852-3327. E-mail: orshanj@dkja.net. Website: www.dkja.org

THE DONOHO SCHOOL

2501 Henry Road
Anniston, Alabama 36207

Head of School: Dr. James Hutchins

General Information Coeducational day college-preparatory and arts school. Grades PK–12. Founded: 1963. Setting: suburban. Nearest major city is Birmingham. 73-acre campus. 4 buildings on campus. Approved or accredited by Southern Association of Colleges and Schools and Alabama Department of Education. Member of National Association of Independent Schools. Total enrollment: 357. Upper school average class size: 12. Upper school faculty-student ratio: 1:12. There are 180 required school days per year for Upper School students. Upper School students typically attend 5 days per week. The average school day consists of 5 hours and 25 minutes.

Upper School Student Profile Grade 9: 40 students (23 boys, 17 girls); Grade 10: 27 students (17 boys, 10 girls); Grade 11: 38 students (18 boys, 20 girls); Grade 12: 34 students (13 boys, 21 girls).

Faculty School total: 33. In upper school: 6 men, 12 women; 12 have advanced degrees.

Subjects Offered Algebra, American history, American literature, anatomy, art, arts, band, biology, calculus, chemistry, chorus, computer science, drama, economics, English, English literature, European history, fine arts, French, geography, geometry, government/civics, grammar, health, history, journalism, Latin, mathematics, music, physical education, physics, physiology, public speaking, robotics, science, social studies, Spanish, speech, theater, world history.

Graduation Requirements Arts and fine arts (art, music, dance, drama), English, foreign language, mathematics, physical education (includes health), public speaking, science, social sciences, social studies (includes history).

Special Academic Programs Advanced Placement exam preparation; honors section; term-away projects; study at local college for college credit; ESL (6 students enrolled).

College Admission Counseling 22 students graduated in 2015; all went to college, including Auburn University; Birmingham-Southern College; Samford University; University of Montevallo; Vanderbilt University. Mean SAT critical reading: 625, mean SAT math: 631, mean SAT writing: 633, mean combined SAT: 1889, mean composite ACT: 27.

Student Life Upper grades have specified standards of dress, student council, honor system. Discipline rests primarily with faculty.

Tuition and Aid Day student tuition: $4630–$9245. Tuition installment plan (FACTS Tuition Payment Plan, monthly payment plans). Need-based scholarship grants available. In 2015–16, 18% of upper-school students received aid.

Admissions Traditional secondary-level entrance grade is 10. For fall 2015, 14 students applied for upper-level admission, 11 were accepted, 11 enrolled. Admissions testing, Woodcock-Johnson and writing sample required. Deadline for receipt of application materials: none. Application fee required: $50. Interview required.

Athletics Interscholastic: baseball (boys), basketball (b,g), cheering (g), cross-country running (b,g), football (b), golf (b,g), soccer (b,g), tennis (b,g), track and field (b,g), volleyball (g). 2 coaches.

Computers Computers are regularly used in English, foreign language, mathematics, science classes. Computer network features include on-campus library services, online commercial services, Internet access, wireless campus network, Internet filtering or blocking technology, laptop and iPad use welcomed on campus. Student e-mail accounts and computer access in designated common areas are available to students. Students grades are available online. The school has a published electronic and media policy.

Contact Mrs. Jean Jaudon, Lower School Director. 256-236-4459 Ext. 108. Fax: 256-237-6474. E-mail: jean.jaudon@donohoschool.com.
Website: www.donohoschool.com/

DONOVAN CATHOLIC

711 Hooper Avenue
Toms River, New Jersey 08753

Head of School: Dr. Edward Gere

General Information Coeducational day college-preparatory school, affiliated with Roman Catholic Church. Grades 9–12. Founded: 1962. Setting: suburban. Nearest major city is New York City, NY. 5-acre campus. 1 building on campus. Approved or accredited by National Catholic Education Association and New Jersey Department of Education. Total enrollment: 689. Upper school average class size: 23. Upper school faculty-student ratio: 1:15. There are 180 required school days per year for Upper School students. Upper School students typically attend 5 days per week. The average school day consists of 6 hours.

Upper School Student Profile Grade 9: 163 students (72 boys, 91 girls); Grade 10: 171 students (78 boys, 93 girls); Grade 11: 173 students (86 boys, 87 girls); Grade 12: 174 students (88 boys, 86 girls). 85% of students are Roman Catholic.

Faculty School total: 45. In upper school: 18 men, 27 women; 21 have advanced degrees.

Subjects Offered 1968, all academic.

Special Academic Programs Advanced Placement exam preparation; honors section; independent study; study at local college for college credit; academic accommodation for the gifted, the musically talented, and the artistically talented; remedial reading and/or remedial writing; remedial math; programs in English, mathematics for dyslexic students.

College Admission Counseling 182 students graduated in 2016; 181 went to college. Other: 1 entered military service. Mean SAT critical reading: 597, mean SAT math: 638.

Student Life Upper grades have uniform requirement, student council, honor system. Discipline rests equally with students and faculty. Attendance at religious services is required.

Tuition and Aid Day student tuition: $12,760. Tuition installment plan (SMART Tuition Payment Plan, monthly payment plans). Merit scholarship grants, need-based scholarship grants, paying campus jobs available. In 2016–17, 20% of upper-school students received aid. Total amount of financial aid awarded in 2016–17: $400,000.

Admissions Traditional secondary-level entrance grade is 9. Scholastic Testing Service High School Placement Test required. Deadline for receipt of application materials: October 31. No application fee required. On-campus interview recommended.

Athletics Interscholastic: baseball (boys), basketball (b,g), bowling (b,g), cheering (g), cross-country running (b,g), equestrian sports (b,g), football (b), golf (b), ice hockey (b), lacrosse (g), softball (g), wrestling (b); coed interscholastic: dance, hiking/backpacking, sailing, skiing (cross-country), snowboarding, soccer, strength & conditioning, surfing, swimming and diving, tennis, weight lifting, weight training. 5 PE instructors, 22 coaches, 1 athletic trainer.

Computers Computers are regularly used in all academic classes. Computer network features include on-campus library services, Internet access, wireless campus network, Internet filtering or blocking technology, on-site computer technical support. Student e-mail accounts are available to students. Students grades are available online. The school has a published electronic and media policy.

Contact Mrs. Tara Mulligan, Registrar. 732-349-8801 Ext. 2426. Fax: 732-505-8014. E-mail: tmulligan@donovancatholic.org. Website: www.donovancatholic.org

DOWLING CATHOLIC HIGH SCHOOL

1400 Buffalo Road
West Des Moines, Iowa 50265

Head of School: Dr. Jerry M. Deegan

General Information Coeducational day college-preparatory, general academic, performing arts, and Advanced Placement school, affiliated with Roman Catholic Church. Grades 9–12. Founded: 1918. Setting: suburban. 60-acre campus. 1 building on campus. Approved or accredited by Iowa Department of Education. Endowment: $9 million. Total enrollment: 1,438. Upper school average class size: 25. Upper school faculty-student ratio: 1:14. The average school day consists of 6 hours and 30 minutes.

Upper School Student Profile 92% of students are Roman Catholic.

Faculty School total: 99. In upper school: 54 have advanced degrees.

Subjects Offered 20th century world history, accounting, ACT preparation, acting, advanced chemistry, advanced computer applications, advanced math, Advanced Placement courses, advertising design, algebra, American government, American history, American history-AP, American literature, American literature-AP, applied arts, aquatics, art, art history, athletics, band, baseball, Basic programming, biology, biology-AP, brass choir, British literature, business, business communications, business law, calculus, calculus-AP, career and personal planning, career planning, career/college preparation, ceramics, chamber groups, cheerleading, chemistry, chemistry-AP, choir, choral music, chorus, church history, college counseling, college planning, composition, composition-AP, computer applications, computer information systems, computer processing, computer programming, computers, concert band, concert choir, creative writing, digital photography, drama, economics, economics-AP, engineering, English, English composition, English language and composition-AP, English literature, environmental science, European history, European history-AP, finance, fine arts, foreign language, French, general business, general science, geography, geometry, German, government, government-AP, health, health education, history, history-AP, honors algebra, honors English, honors geometry, honors U.S. history, honors world history, humanities, information processing, integrated mathematics, jazz band, journalism, keyboarding, Latin, life saving, literature, literature-AP, marching band, metalworking, modern European history, newspaper, painting, personal finance, physical education, physics, physics-AP, play production, poetry, pottery, pre-algebra, pre-calculus, probability and statistics, programming, religion, SAT/ACT preparation, social justice, sociology, Spanish, Spanish language-AP, speech and debate, swimming, tennis, theater production, theology, U.S. government, U.S. government and politics-AP, U.S. history, U.S. history-AP, visual arts, vocal jazz, weight training, world religions, yearbook.

Graduation Requirements Arts, business, electives, English, mathematics, reading, science, social studies (includes history), theology, Summer Reading Program, 10 Christian service hours per semester/20 per year. Community service is required.

Special Academic Programs Advanced Placement exam preparation; study at local college for college credit; academic accommodation for the gifted, the musically talented, and the artistically talented; remedial reading and/or remedial writing; remedial math; special instructional classes for blind students.

College Admission Counseling 356 students graduated in 2016; 345 went to college, including Creighton University; Iowa State University of Science and Technology; Loras College; The University of Iowa; University of Northern Iowa. Median SAT critical reading: 988, median SAT math: 1073, median SAT writing: 946, median composite ACT: 25.

Student Life Upper grades have uniform requirement, student council, honor system. Discipline rests primarily with faculty. Attendance at religious services is required.

Summer Programs Enrichment, advancement, sports, art/fine arts, computer instruction programs offered; session focuses on advancement for the purpose of freeing up a slot in the schedule to take an elective; held on campus; accepts boys and girls; not open to students from other schools. 500 students usually enrolled. 2017 schedule: June 1 to June 30.

Tuition and Aid Day student tuition: $7502. Tuition installment plan (monthly payment plans, individually arranged payment plans). Need-based scholarship grants available. In 2016–17, 40% of upper-school students received aid. Total amount of financial aid awarded in 2016–17: $1,000,000.

Admissions Traditional secondary-level entrance grade is 9. High School Placement Test required. Deadline for receipt of application materials: none. Application fee required: $95.

Athletics Interscholastic: aerobics/dance (girls), aquatics (b,g), baseball (b), basketball (b,g), bowling (b,g), cheering (g), cross-country running (b,g), dance (g), dance team (g), diving (g), drill team (g), football (b), golf (b,g), soccer (b,g), softball (g), swimming and diving (b,g), tennis (b,g), track and field (b,g), volleyball (g), wrestling (b); coed interscholastic: cheering, running, yoga; coed intramural: ultimate Frisbee.

Computers Computer network features include on-campus library services, Internet access, wireless campus network, Internet filtering or blocking technology. Computer access in designated common areas is available to students. Students grades are available online. The school has a published electronic and media policy.

Contact Mrs. Tatia Eischeid, Admissions Director. 515-222-1025. Fax: 515-222-1056. E-mail: teischeid@dowlingcatholic.org. Website: www.dowlingcatholic.org

DUBLIN CHRISTIAN ACADEMY

106 Page Road
Dublin, New Hampshire 03444

Head of School: Mr. Eric J. Moody

General Information Coeducational boarding and day college-preparatory and religious studies school. Boarding grades 7–12, day grades K–12. Founded: 1964. Setting: rural. Nearest major city is Boston, MA. Students are housed in single-sex dormitories. 200-acre campus. 5 buildings on campus. Approved or accredited by American Association of Christian Schools and New Hampshire Department of Education. Total enrollment: 98. Upper school average class size: 12. Upper school faculty-student ratio: 1:9. There are 170 required school days per year for Upper School students. Upper School students typically attend 5 days per week. The average school day consists of 7 hours.

Upper School Student Profile Grade 7: 9 students (2 boys, 7 girls); Grade 8: 4 students (1 boy, 3 girls); Grade 9: 9 students (3 boys, 6 girls); Grade 10: 7 students (3 boys, 4 girls); Grade 11: 12 students (7 boys, 5 girls); Grade 12: 5 students (1 boy, 4 girls). 7% of students are boarding students. 95% are state residents. 2 states are represented in upper school student body. 3% are international students. International students from China.

Faculty School total: 17. In upper school: 6 men, 6 women; 6 have advanced degrees; 7 reside on campus.

Subjects Offered Advanced biology, advanced math, algebra, American government, American history, American literature, anatomy and physiology, art, athletics, Bible, Bible studies, biology, British literature, business, calculus, calculus-AP, chemistry, choir, chorus, computer literacy, consumer mathematics, cultural geography, economics, economics and history, English, geometry, history, home economics, instrumental music, law, life management skills, life science, mathematics, music, piano, religion, science, social studies, space and physical sciences, Spanish, speech, speech and debate, speech communications, studio art, study skills, U.S. history, voice, word processing, world history.

Graduation Requirements English, foreign language, mathematics, religion (includes Bible studies and theology), science, social studies (includes history), speech.

Special Academic Programs International Baccalaureate program; Advanced Placement exam preparation; independent study; academic accommodation for the

musically talented and the artistically talented; remedial reading and/or remedial writing; remedial math.

College Admission Counseling 11 students graduated in 2016; 6 went to college, including Bob Jones University; Cedarville University; Gordon College; Pensacola State College. Other: 3 went to work, 2 had other specific plans. Mean SAT critical reading: 570, mean SAT math: 520, mean SAT writing: 470, mean composite ACT: 20. 27% scored over 600 on SAT critical reading, 18% scored over 600 on SAT math, 18% scored over 600 on SAT writing, 27% scored over 1800 on combined SAT.

Student Life Upper grades have uniform requirement, student council, honor system. Discipline rests primarily with faculty.

Tuition and Aid Day student tuition: $7500; 7-day tuition and room/board: $13,800. Tuition installment plan (FACTS Tuition Payment Plan). Need-based scholarship grants available. In 2016–17, 20% of upper-school students received aid. Total amount of financial aid awarded in 2016–17: $125,000.

Admissions Traditional secondary-level entrance grade is 9. For fall 2016, 10 students applied for upper-level admission, 8 were accepted, 6 enrolled. SLEP for foreign students, Stanford Diagnostic Test, TOEFL Junior or TOEFL or SLEP required. Deadline for receipt of application materials: August 15. Application fee required: $35. On-campus interview recommended.

Athletics Interscholastic: basketball (boys, girls), soccer (b), volleyball (g); coed intramural: alpine skiing, snowboarding. 1 PE instructor, 2 coaches.

Computers Computers are regularly used in accounting, business, English, foreign language, history, mathematics, music, science classes. Computer network features include on-campus library services, Internet access, wireless campus network, Internet filtering or blocking technology. Student e-mail accounts are available to students. Students grades are available online.

Contact Miss Rachel Smitley, Administrative Assistant. 603-563-8505 Ext. 15. Fax: 603-563-8008. E-mail: rsmitley@dublinchristian.org.
Website: www.dublinchristian.org

DUBLIN SCHOOL

Box 522
18 Lehmann Way
Dublin, New Hampshire 03444-0522

Head of School: Mr. Bradford D. Bates

General Information Coeducational boarding and day college-preparatory school. Grades 9–12. Founded: 1935. Setting: rural. Nearest major city is Boston, MA. Students are housed in single-sex dormitories. 400-acre campus. 22 buildings on campus. Approved or accredited by Independent Schools of Northern New England, New England Association of Schools and Colleges, and The Association of Boarding Schools. Member of National Association of Independent Schools and Secondary School Admission Test Board. Endowment: $2.2 million. Total enrollment: 152. Upper school average class size: 10. Upper school faculty-student ratio: 1:5. Upper School students typically attend 5 days per week. The average school day consists of 5 hours.

Upper School Student Profile 75% of students are boarding students. 30% are state residents. 19 states are represented in upper school student body. 15% are international students. International students from Bahamas, Canada, China, Germany, Mexico, and Republic of Korea.

Faculty School total: 42. In upper school: 15 men, 20 women; 35 have advanced degrees; 33 reside on campus.

Subjects Offered Acting, advanced biology, advanced math, algebra, American foreign policy, American literature, anatomy and physiology, ancient world history, art, arts, biology, biology-AP, calculus, calculus-AP, carpentry, ceramics, chemistry, choir, chorus, college counseling, college placement, community service, computer education, computer literacy, computer programming, costumes and make-up, creative arts, creative dance, creative drama, cultural arts, dance performance, digital music, drama, drama performance, dramatic arts, drawing and design, electronic music, English, English composition, English literature, European civilization, European history, film history, fine arts, foreign policy, French, geology, geometry, guitar, honors U.S. history, instrumental music, Latin, library research, library skills, literature, marine biology, mathematics, modern dance, modern European history, music, music composition, music performance, music technology, music theory, musical productions, musical theater, musical theater dance, painting, personal and social education, personal development, philosophy, photography, physics, poetry, pre-calculus, psychology, research, science, senior project, Shakespeare, social studies, Spanish, stagecraft, statistics, student government, studio art, study skills, theater, theater arts, U.S. government and politics, U.S. history, U.S. history-AP, video film production, vocal ensemble, voice, voice ensemble, Web site design, weight training, white-water trips, wilderness experience, women's studies, woodworking, world literature, writing, writing workshop, yearbook.

Graduation Requirements Art, computer skills, English, general science, history, languages, mathematics, senior presentation, graduation requirements for honors diploma different.

Special Academic Programs 10 Advanced Placement exams for which test preparation is offered; honors section; independent study; term-away projects; study at local college for college credit; academic accommodation for the gifted; programs in general development for dyslexic students; ESL (10 students enrolled).

College Admission Counseling 35 students graduated in 2016; all went to college, including Berklee College of Music; Boston University; Hamilton College; Hobart and William Smith Colleges; Johns Hopkins University; St. Lawrence University. Median SAT critical reading: 480, median SAT math: 605, median SAT writing: 525, median combined SAT: 1610, median composite ACT: 24.

Student Life Upper grades have specified standards of dress, student council, honor system. Discipline rests equally with students and faculty.

Tuition and Aid Day student tuition: $33,092; 7-day tuition and room/board: $56,940. Tuition installment plan (monthly payment plans). Need-based scholarship grants, loans and payment plans are through a third party available. In 2016–17, 32% of upper-school students received aid. Total amount of financial aid awarded in 2016–17: $1,490,000.

Admissions Traditional secondary-level entrance grade is 9. For fall 2016, 143 students applied for upper-level admission, 97 were accepted, 48 enrolled. SSAT, SSAT, ERB, PSAT, SAT, PLAN or ACT or TOEFL or SLEP required. Deadline for receipt of application materials: January 31. Application fee required: $60. Interview recommended.

Athletics Interscholastic: basketball (boys, girls), crew (b,g), cross-country running (b,g), lacrosse (b,g), mountain biking (b), nordic skiing (b,g), rowing (b,g), running (b,g), sailing (b,g), skiing (cross-country) (b,g), skiing (downhill) (b,g), snowboarding (b,g), soccer (b,g), tennis (b,g); coed interscholastic: aerobics/dance, alpine skiing, ballet, crew, cross-country running, dance, dance team, equestrian sports, golf, modern dance, mountain biking, nordic skiing, rowing, running, sailing, skiing (cross-country), skiing (downhill), snowboarding; coed intramural: aerobics/dance, alpine skiing, archery, backpacking, badminton, basketball, biathlon, bicycling, billiards, bowling, canoeing/kayaking, climbing, cooperative games, equestrian sports, fencing, fishing, fitness, flag football, flagball, fly fishing, freestyle skiing, Frisbee, golf, hiking/backpacking, horseback riding, ice hockey, indoor soccer, kayaking, martial arts, outdoor activities, outdoor adventure, outdoor education, outdoor recreation, paddle tennis, physical fitness, physical training, rafting, rock climbing, ropes courses, rowing, sailing, skateboarding, skiing (cross-country), skiing (downhill), snowshoeing, softball, strength & conditioning, table tennis, telemark skiing, tennis, ultimate Frisbee, volleyball, wall climbing, weight lifting, weight training, whiffle ball, wrestling, yoga. 20 coaches, 1 athletic trainer.

Computers Computers are regularly used in all academic classes. Computer network features include on-campus library services, online commercial services, Internet access, wireless campus network, Internet filtering or blocking technology. Campus intranet, student e-mail accounts, and computer access in designated common areas are available to students. Students grades are available online. The school has a published electronic and media policy.

Contact Mrs. Jill Hutchins, Dean of Enrollment Management. 603-563-1233. Fax: 603-563-8671. E-mail: admission@dublinschool.org. Website: www.dublinschool.org/

DUCHESNE HIGH SCHOOL

2550 Elm Street
Saint Charles, Missouri 63301

Head of School: Mr. Charles L. Nolan Jr.

General Information Coeducational day college-preparatory, arts, business, and technology school, affiliated with Roman Catholic Church. Grades 9–12. Setting: suburban. Nearest major city is Saint Louis. 2 buildings on campus. Approved or accredited by North Central Association of Colleges and Schools and Missouri Department of Education. Upper school average class size: 18. Upper School students typically attend 5 days per week. The average school day consists of 7 hours.

Upper School Student Profile Grade 9: 71 students (31 boys, 40 girls); Grade 10: 57 students (32 boys, 25 girls); Grade 11: 80 students (45 boys, 35 girls); Grade 12: 90 students (46 boys, 44 girls). 98% of students are Roman Catholic.

Faculty School total: 27. In upper school: 14 men, 13 women; 75 have advanced degrees.

Graduation Requirements American government, American history, art, athletics, business, electives, English, fitness, foreign language, geography, government, health and wellness, health education, mathematics, moral and social development, moral reasoning, New Testament, physical education (includes health), practical arts, reading, religion (includes Bible studies and theology), social studies (includes history), world history, writing, 100 hours of required community service.

Special Academic Programs Academic accommodation for the gifted; programs in English, mathematics, general development for dyslexic students.

College Admission Counseling 100 students graduated in 2016; all went to college, including Missouri State University; Saint Louis University; Southeast Missouri State University; Truman State University; University of Central Missouri; University of Missouri. Median composite ACT: 24.

Student Life Upper grades have uniform requirement, student council, honor system. Discipline rests primarily with faculty. Attendance at religious services is required.

Tuition and Aid Day student tuition: $9500. Tuition installment plan (FACTS Tuition Payment Plan). Tuition reduction for siblings, merit scholarship grants, need-based scholarship grants, paying campus jobs available. In 2016–17, 41% of upper-school students received aid.

Admissions Traditional secondary-level entrance grade is 9. Any standardized test, Iowa Tests of Basic Skills or Iowa Tests of Basic Skills-Grades 7-8, Archdiocese

HSEPT-Grade 9 required. Deadline for receipt of application materials: August 1. No application fee required.

Athletics Intramural: baseball (boys), basketball (b,g), cheering (g), dance (g), dance team (g), danceline (g), diving (g), football (b), golf (b,g), hockey (b), ice hockey (b), soccer (b,g), softball (g), swimming and diving (g), tennis (b,g), volleyball (b,g); coed interscholastic: aerobics, fitness, jogging, physical fitness, physical training, running, strength & conditioning, table tennis, walking, weight lifting, weight training, whiffle ball, yoga; coed intramural: cross-country running, running, track and field. 2 PE instructors, 18 coaches.

Computers Computer network features include Internet access, wireless campus network, Internet filtering or blocking technology. Student e-mail accounts and computer access in designated common areas are available to students. Students grades are available online. The school has a published electronic and media policy.

Contact Mr. Fritz Long, Principal. 636-946-6767 Ext. 6905. Fax: 636-946-6267. E-mail: flong@duchesne-hs.org. Website: http://duchesne-hs.org

DURHAM ACADEMY

3601 Ridge Road
Durham, North Carolina 27705

Head of School: Mr. Michael Ulku-Steiner

General Information Coeducational day college-preparatory school. Grades PK–12. Distance learning grades 10–12. Founded: 1933. Setting: suburban. 75-acre campus. 10 buildings on campus. Approved or accredited by Southern Association of Colleges and Schools, Southern Association of Independent Schools, and North Carolina Department of Education. Member of National Association of Independent Schools and Secondary School Admission Test Board. Endowment: $12 million. Total enrollment: 1,183. Upper school average class size: 15. Upper school faculty-student ratio: 1:8. There are 179 required school days per year for Upper School students. Upper School students typically attend 5 days per week. The average school day consists of 6 hours and 50 minutes.

Upper School Student Profile Grade 9: 119 students (57 boys, 62 girls); Grade 10: 111 students (60 boys, 51 girls); Grade 11: 105 students (54 boys, 51 girls); Grade 12: 103 students (50 boys, 53 girls).

Faculty School total: 256. In upper school: 26 men, 34 women; 38 have advanced degrees.

Subjects Offered 3-dimensional art, accounting, acting, advanced biology, advanced chemistry, advanced computer applications, advanced math, Advanced Placement courses, advanced studio art-AP, algebra, American history, American literature, art, art history, art history-AP, astronomy, biology, calculus, ceramics, chemistry, chemistry-AP, Chinese, Chinese studies, chorus, community service, computer graphics, computer programming, computer science, computer science-AP, concert band, creative writing, dance, drama, ecology, economics, engineering, English, English language and composition-AP, English literature, English literature and composition-AP, environmental science, environmental science-AP, fine arts, finite math, forensics, French, French language-AP, French-AP, geometry, German, history, Latin, literature and composition-AP, mathematics, mathematics-AP, modern European history-AP, music, outdoor education, physical education, physics, psychology, robotics, science, social studies, Spanish, statistics, studio art-AP, theater, U.S. government and politics-AP, U.S. history-AP.

Graduation Requirements Arts and fine arts (art, music, dance, drama), computer science, English, foreign language, mathematics, outdoor education, physical education (includes health), science, senior project, social studies (includes history), community service hours required for graduation, senior project required for graduation.

Special Academic Programs Advanced Placement exam preparation; honors section; independent study; special instructional classes for students with learning disabilities and Attention Deficit Disorder.

College Admission Counseling 103 students graduated in 2016; 101 went to college, including Columbia University; Davidson College; Duke University; Northeastern University; The University of North Carolina at Chapel Hill; Washington University in St. Louis. Other: 2 had other specific plans. Mean SAT critical reading: 655, mean SAT math: 660, mean SAT writing: 656.

Student Life Upper grades have specified standards of dress, student council, honor system. Discipline rests equally with students and faculty.

Summer Programs Remediation, enrichment, sports, art/fine arts, computer instruction programs offered; session focuses on academic enrichment, non-academic activities; held on campus; accepts boys and girls; open to students from other schools. 1,000 students usually enrolled. 2017 schedule: June 12 to July 28. Application deadline: none.

Tuition and Aid Day student tuition: $24,040. Tuition installment plan (FACTS Tuition Payment Plan). Need-based scholarship grants available. In 2016–17, 14% of upper-school students received aid. Total amount of financial aid awarded in 2016–17: $2,000,000.

Admissions Traditional secondary-level entrance grade is 9. For fall 2016, 145 students applied for upper-level admission, 35 were accepted, 30 enrolled. ISEE or SSAT required. Deadline for receipt of application materials: January 6. Application fee required: $55. Interview recommended.

Athletics Interscholastic: aquatics (boys, girls), baseball (b), basketball (b,g), cross-country running (b,g), dance team (g), field hockey (g), golf (b,g), lacrosse (b,g), soccer (b,g), softball (g), swimming and diving (b,g), tennis (b,g), track and field (b,g), volleyball (g), weight training (b,g); coed interscholastic: outdoor adventure, outdoor education, ultimate Frisbee, weight training; coed intramural: indoor soccer, judo, martial arts, modern dance, physical fitness, physical training, winter soccer. 1 PE instructor, 3 coaches, 2 athletic trainers.

Computers Computers are regularly used in all academic, animation, computer applications, graphic arts, graphic design, introduction to technology, video film production, Web site design classes. Computer network features include on-campus library services, online commercial services, Internet access, wireless campus network, Internet filtering or blocking technology. Student e-mail accounts and computer access in designated common areas are available to students. Students grades are available online. The school has a published electronic and media policy.

Contact Ms. S. Victoria Muradi, Director of Admission and Financial Aid. 919-493-5787. Fax: 919-489-4893. E-mail: admissions@da.org. Website: www.da.org

THE DWIGHT SCHOOL

291 Central Park West
New York, New York 10024

Head of School: Ms. Dianne Drew

General Information Coeducational day college-preparatory school. Grades PK–12. Distance learning grades 9–12. Founded: 1880. Setting: urban. 3 buildings on campus. Approved or accredited by International Baccalaureate Organization, Middle States Association of Colleges and Schools, and New York Department of Education. Member of National Association of Independent Schools, Secondary School Admission Test Board, and European Council of International Schools. Upper school average class size: 15. Upper school faculty-student ratio: 1:6.

Faculty School total: 93. In upper school: 24 men, 26 women; 32 have advanced degrees.

Subjects Offered Algebra, American history, American literature, art, art history, biology, calculus, chemistry, community service, computer math, computer science, creative writing, dance, drama, economics, English, English literature, environmental science, ethics, European history, expository writing, film, fine arts, French, geometry, government/civics, grammar, health, history, Italian, Japanese, journalism, Latin, mathematics, music, philosophy, photography, physical education, physics, physiology, psychology, science, social studies, Spanish, technology/design, theater, theory of knowledge, trigonometry, typing, world history, world literature, writing.

Graduation Requirements Arts and fine arts (art, music, dance, drama), computer science, English, foreign language, mathematics, physical education (includes health), science, social studies (includes history). Community service is required.

Special Academic Programs International Baccalaureate program; Advanced Placement exam preparation; honors section; independent study; term-away projects; study abroad; academic accommodation for the gifted, the musically talented, and the artistically talented; remedial reading and/or remedial writing; remedial math; programs in English for dyslexic students; special instructional classes for students with learning disabilities; ESL (15 students enrolled).

College Admission Counseling 65 students graduated in 2016; 61 went to college, including Brown University; Dartmouth College; New York University; Northwestern University; The George Washington University; Trinity College. Other: 4 went to work.

Student Life Upper grades have specified standards of dress, student council, honor system. Discipline rests equally with students and faculty.

Summer Programs Remediation, enrichment, ESL programs offered; session focuses on Help students newly enrolled in our EAL and Quest programs to transition into each program and get a jumpstart; held on campus; accepts boys and girls; not open to students from other schools. 2017 schedule: August 20 to August 30.

Tuition and Aid Day student tuition: $43,675. Tuition installment plan (The Tuition Plan, Insured Tuition Payment Plan, monthly payment plans, individually arranged payment plans). Need-based scholarship grants, prepGATE loans available. In 2016–17, 20% of upper-school students received aid.

Admissions Traditional secondary-level entrance grade is 9. ERB or ISEE required. Deadline for receipt of application materials: none. Application fee required: $65. On-campus interview recommended.

Athletics Interscholastic: baseball (boys), basketball (b,g), cross-country running (b,g), dance (g), fencing (b,g); intramural: basketball (b,g), boxing (b,g), fencing (b,g); coed interscholastic: aquatics, fencing, golf, running, swimming and diving, tennis; coed intramural: aerobics/dance, boxing, dance squad, dance team, fencing, fitness, skateboarding, weight lifting, weight training, yoga.

Computers Computers are regularly used in foreign language, mathematics, music, science classes. Computer network features include on-campus library services, online commercial services, Internet access, wireless campus network, Internet filtering or blocking technology. Students grades are available online.

Contact Ellana Mandell, Admissions Associate. 212-724-6360 Ext. 201. Fax: 212-724-2539. E-mail: admissions@dwight.edu. Website: www.dwight.edu

EAGLEBROOK SCHOOL

Deerfield, Massachusetts
See Junior Boarding Schools section.

EAGLE HILL SCHOOL

Greenwich, Connecticut
See Special Needs Schools section.

EAGLE ROCK SCHOOL

Estes Park, Colorado
See Special Needs Schools section.

EASTERN MENNONITE HIGH SCHOOL

801 Parkwood Drive
Harrisonburg, Virginia 22802

Head of School: Dr. Paul G. Leaman

General Information Coeducational day college-preparatory and general academic school, affiliated with Mennonite Church. Grades K–12. Founded: 1917. Setting: small town. Nearest major city is Washington, DC. 24-acre campus. 1 building on campus. Approved or accredited by Mennonite Education Agency, Southern Association of Colleges and Schools, Virginia Association of Independent Schools, and Virginia Department of Education. Member of National Association of Independent Schools. Endowment: $3 million. Total enrollment: 379. Upper school average class size: 15. Upper school faculty-student ratio: 1:12. There are 180 required school days per year for Upper School students. Upper School students typically attend 5 days per week. The average school day consists of 7 hours.

Upper School Student Profile Grade 6: 25 students (16 boys, 9 girls); Grade 7: 32 students (14 boys, 18 girls); Grade 8: 41 students (24 boys, 17 girls); Grade 9: 36 students (14 boys, 22 girls); Grade 10: 44 students (19 boys, 25 girls); Grade 11: 37 students (25 boys, 12 girls); Grade 12: 44 students (24 boys, 20 girls). 10% of students are boarding students. 90% are state residents. 1 state is represented in upper school student body. 10% are international students. International students from China and Republic of Korea; 4 other countries represented in student body. 50% of students are Mennonite.

Faculty School total: 40. In upper school: 15 men, 19 women; 24 have advanced degrees.

Subjects Offered 3-dimensional art, 3-dimensional design, acting, advanced biology, advanced math, Advanced Placement courses, algebra, American government, American history, American history-AP, American literature, American literature-AP, analysis, anatomy and physiology, applied music, art, art history, band, bell choir, Bible studies, biology, biology-AP, biotechnology, British literature, British literature (honors), business, business skills, calculus-AP, career/college preparation, ceramics, chemistry, choir, choral music, chorus, Christian and Hebrew scripture, Christian doctrine, Christian ethics, Christian scripture, Christian studies, Christian testament, Christianity, church history, college admission preparation, college counseling, college writing, communications, community service, composition, computer education, computer science, concert choir, consumer mathematics, creative writing, desktop publishing, digital imaging, digital photography, drama, drawing, driver education, earth science, economics, engineering, English, English composition, English language and composition-AP, English literature, environmental science, family and consumer science, fiction, fine arts, food and nutrition, food science, French, general science, geography, geometry, government, grammar, guitar, handbells, health, health education, history, home economics, honors algebra, honors English, honors geometry, honors U.S. history, human development, human relations, independent study, industrial arts, industrial technology, instrumental music, instruments, interior design, jazz ensemble, keyboarding, Latin, life science, mathematics, mechanical drawing, media communications, music, music composition, music performance, music theory, music theory-AP, New Testament, novels, oil painting, oral communications, orchestra, outdoor education, painting, photography, physical education, physical science, physics, poetry, pottery, pre-algebra, religion, religious education, research skills, science, sculpture, sewing, Shakespeare, shop, social psychology, social sciences, social studies, sociology, Spanish, Spanish-AP, speech, speech communications, stained glass, statistics-AP, strings, studio art, study skills, theater, typing, U.S. government, U.S. history, U.S. literature, vocal music, voice, water color painting, woodworking, world cultures, world history, writing.

Graduation Requirements Arts and fine arts (art, music, dance, drama), electives, English, foreign language, history, home economics, keyboarding, mathematics, physical education (includes health), religion (includes Bible studies and theology), science, social studies (includes history), technical arts, experiential learning credit annually, community service participation.

Special Academic Programs 5 Advanced Placement exams for which test preparation is offered; honors section; independent study; term-away projects; study at local college for college credit; study abroad; academic accommodation for the gifted; remedial reading and/or remedial writing; remedial math; ESL (6 students enrolled).

College Admission Counseling 54 students graduated in 2016; 50 went to college, including Eastern Mennonite University; Goshen College; James Madison University; The College of William and Mary; University of Virginia; Virginia Polytechnic Institute and State University. Other: 1 went to work, 3 had other specific plans. Mean SAT critical reading: 525, mean SAT math: 559, mean SAT writing: 512, mean combined

SAT: 1596. 47% scored over 600 on SAT critical reading, 43% scored over 600 on SAT math, 46% scored over 600 on SAT writing, 60% scored over 1800 on combined SAT.

Student Life Upper grades have specified standards of dress, student council, honor system. Discipline rests primarily with faculty. Attendance at religious services is required.

Tuition and Aid Day student tuition: $5995–$14,195. Tuition installment plan (FACTS Tuition Payment Plan, monthly payment plans, individually arranged payment plans). Need-based scholarship grants, paying campus jobs, VDOE Education Improvement Scholarship available. In 2016–17, 70% of upper-school students received aid. Total amount of financial aid awarded in 2016–17: $200,000.

Admissions Traditional secondary-level entrance grade is 9. For fall 2016, 97 students applied for upper-level admission, 76 were accepted, 59 enrolled. Any standardized test required. Deadline for receipt of application materials: none. Application fee required: $50. On-campus interview required.

Athletics Interscholastic: baseball (boys), basketball (b,g), cheering (g), cross-country running (b,g), soccer (b,g), softball (g), tennis (b,g), track and field (b,g), volleyball (g); intramural: baseball (b), basketball (b,g), soccer (g), wrestling (b); coed interscholastic: baseball, cross-country running, golf; coed intramural: Frisbee, table tennis, ultimate Frisbee, volleyball. 3 PE instructors, 9 coaches, 2 athletic trainers.

Computers Computers are regularly used in Bible studies, business skills, Christian doctrine, college planning, computer applications, construction, creative writing, current events, design, desktop publishing, digital applications, economics, engineering, English, foreign language, geography, graphic arts, graphic design, history, independent study, industrial technology, information technology, introduction to technology, keyboarding, library, literary magazine, mathematics, media arts, music, photography, psychology, publications, publishing, religious studies, research skills, science, social sciences, social studies, Spanish, speech, study skills, technology, Web site design, word processing, writing, yearbook classes. Computer resources include on-campus library services, online commercial services, Internet access, wireless campus network, Internet filtering or blocking technology. Campus intranet, student e-mail accounts, and computer access in designated common areas are available to students. Students grades are available online. The school has a published electronic and media policy.

Contact Ms. Marsha Thomas, Admissions Counselor. 540-236-6021. Fax: 540-236-6028. E-mail: admissions@emhs.net. Website: www.emhs.net

EATON ACADEMY

1000 Old Roswell Lakes Parkway
Roswell, Georgia 30076

Head of School: Ms. Bridgit Eaton-Partalis

General Information Coeducational day and distance learning college-preparatory school. Grades K–12. Distance learning grades 5–12. Founded: 1995. Setting: suburban. Nearest major city is Atlanta. 12-acre campus. 1 building on campus. Approved or accredited by Southern Association of Colleges and Schools, Southern Association of Independent Schools, and Georgia Department of Education. Total enrollment: 80. Upper school average class size: 5. Upper school faculty-student ratio: 1:5. There are 180 required school days per year for Upper School students. Upper School students typically attend 5 days per week. The average school day consists of 6 hours and 45 minutes.

Upper School Student Profile Grade 9: 8 students (6 boys, 2 girls); Grade 10: 8 students (6 boys, 2 girls); Grade 11: 8 students (6 boys, 2 girls); Grade 12: 8 students (6 boys, 2 girls).

Faculty School total: 35. In upper school: 3 men, 6 women; 6 have advanced degrees.

Subjects Offered All academic.

Graduation Requirements All academic.

Special Academic Programs Honors section; accelerated programs; independent study; term-away projects; academic accommodation for the gifted, the musically talented, and the artistically talented; remedial reading and/or remedial writing; remedial math; programs in English, mathematics for dyslexic students; special instructional classes for deaf students; ESL.

College Admission Counseling 22 students graduated in 2016; all went to college, including Georgia College & State University; Georgia Institute of Technology; Georgia Perimeter College; Georgia Southern University; Kennesaw State University; University of Georgia. Mean SAT critical reading: 530, mean SAT math: 520, mean SAT writing: 480, mean combined SAT: 1530.

Student Life Upper grades have specified standards of dress. Discipline rests primarily with faculty.

Summer Programs Remediation, enrichment, advancement, ESL, sports, art/fine arts, computer instruction programs offered; session focuses on academic acceleration and remediation; held both on and off campus; accepts boys and girls; open to students from other schools. 35 students usually enrolled. 2017 schedule: June 12 to July 28. Application deadline: none.

Tuition and Aid Day student tuition: $20,500. Tuition installment plan (FACTS Tuition Payment Plan).

Admissions For fall 2016, 50 students applied for upper-level admission, 25 were accepted, 20 enrolled. Deadline for receipt of application materials: none. Application fee required: $250. Interview required.

Athletics Coed Intramural: aquatics, artistic gym, basketball, bowling, canoeing/kayaking, crew, cross-country running, equestrian sports, field hockey, fitness walking, flag football, floor hockey, Frisbee, golf, gymnastics, hockey, horseback riding, ice hockey, jogging, kayaking, martial arts, modern dance, outdoor activities, physical fitness, racquetball, rock climbing, ropes courses, running, scuba diving, strength & conditioning, tennis, volleyball, weight training. 3 PE instructors.

Computers Computers are regularly used in all academic classes. Computer network features include Internet access, wireless campus network, Internet filtering or blocking technology. Student e-mail accounts are available to students. Students grades are available online. The school has a published electronic and media policy.

Contact Ms. Margie Cohan, Admissions Director. 770-645-2673 Ext. 242. Fax: 770-645-2711. E-mail: mcohan@eatonacademy.org. Website: www.eatonacademy.org

EDGEWOOD ACADEMY

5475 Elmore Road
PO Box 160
Elmore, Alabama 36025

Head of School: Mr. Clint Welch

General Information Coeducational day college-preparatory, bilingual studies, and technology school. Grades PK–12. Founded: 1967. Setting: small town. Nearest major city is Montgomery. 30-acre campus. 4 buildings on campus. Approved or accredited by CITA (Commission on International and Trans-Regional Accreditation), National Council for Private School Accreditation, Southern Association of Colleges and Schools, and Alabama Department of Education. Total enrollment: 320. Upper school average class size: 18. Upper school faculty-student ratio: 1:11. There are 177 required school days per year for Upper School students. Upper School students typically attend 5 days per week. The average school day consists of 5 hours and 45 minutes.

Upper School Student Profile Grade 9: 22 students (14 boys, 8 girls); Grade 10: 24 students (11 boys, 13 girls); Grade 11: 21 students (8 boys, 13 girls); Grade 12: 15 students (6 boys, 9 girls).

Faculty School total: 24. In upper school: 5 men, 8 women; 9 have advanced degrees.

Graduation Requirements Advanced diploma requires 100 hours of community service, standard diplomas requires 50 hours of community service.

Special Academic Programs Advanced Placement exam preparation; study at local college for college credit.

College Admission Counseling Colleges students went to include Auburn University; Auburn University at Montgomery; The University of Alabama. Median composite ACT: 25.

Student Life Upper grades have specified standards of dress, student council.

Summer Programs Session focuses on driver education; held both on and off campus; accepts boys and girls; open to students from other schools. 15 students usually enrolled. 2017 schedule: June to July. Application deadline: May 1.

Tuition and Aid Day student tuition: $6800. Tuition installment plan (SMART Tuition Payment Plan, monthly payment plans). Tuition reduction for siblings available.

Admissions Admissions testing required. Deadline for receipt of application materials: none. No application fee required. Interview recommended.

Athletics Interscholastic: baseball (boys), basketball (b,g), cheering (g), football (b), physical fitness (b,g), physical training (b,g), softball (g), strength & conditioning (b,g), volleyball (g), weight lifting (b), weight training (b,g); coed interscholastic: fishing, golf, track and field. 2 PE instructors, 4 coaches.

Computers Computers are regularly used in lab/keyboard, yearbook classes. Computer network features include on-campus library services, Internet access, wireless campus network, Internet filtering or blocking technology, SmartBoard technology. Campus intranet and student e-mail accounts are available to students. Students grades are available online. The school has a published electronic and media policy.

Contact Carole Angus, Office Manager. 334-567-5102 Ext. 201. Fax: 334-567-8316. E-mail: cangus@edgewoodacademy.org. Website: www.edgewoodacademy.org/

EDGEWOOD HIGH SCHOOL OF THE SACRED HEART

2219 Monroe Street
Madison, Wisconsin 53711

Head of School: Mr. Michael Elliott

General Information Coeducational day college-preparatory school, affiliated with Roman Catholic Church. Grades 9–12. Founded: 1881. Setting: urban. 53-acre campus. 2 buildings on campus. Approved or accredited by Independent Schools Association of the Central States, National Catholic Education Association, and Wisconsin Department of Education. Endowment: $8.3 million. Total enrollment: 660. Upper school average class size: 23. Upper school faculty-student ratio: 1:10. There are 180 required school days per year for Upper School students. Upper School students typically attend 5 days per week. The average school day consists of 6 hours and 46 minutes.

Upper School Student Profile Grade 9: 133 students (61 boys, 72 girls); Grade 10: 116 students (54 boys, 62 girls); Grade 11: 118 students (59 boys, 59 girls); Grade 12: 164 students (87 boys, 77 girls). 67% of students are Roman Catholic.

Faculty School total: 56. In upper school: 19 men, 37 women; 42 have advanced degrees.

Subjects Offered All academic.

Graduation Requirements American history, chemistry, electives, English, health education, mathematics, physical education (includes health), religion (includes Bible studies and theology), science, social studies (includes history), world history, 100 volunteer service hours by graduation.

Special Academic Programs Advanced Placement exam preparation; honors section; independent study; study at local college for college credit; programs in English, mathematics, general development for dyslexic students; special instructional classes for deaf students, blind students.

College Admission Counseling 134 students graduated in 2016; 128 went to college, including Lawrence University; Loyola University Chicago; Marquette University; University of St. Thomas; University of Wisconsin–Madison; University of Wisconsin–Milwaukee. Other: 1 entered military service, 5 had other specific plans. Mean composite ACT: 26.

Student Life Upper grades have specified standards of dress, student council, honor system. Discipline rests primarily with faculty. Attendance at religious services is required.

Tuition and Aid Day student tuition: $11,123. Tuition installment plan (monthly payment plans, individually arranged payment plans, annual, semester, quarterly plans). Tuition reduction for siblings, merit scholarship grants, need-based scholarship grants available. In 2016–17, 42% of upper-school students received aid; total upper-school merit-scholarship money awarded: $22,792. Total amount of financial aid awarded in 2016–17: $641,388.

Admissions Traditional secondary-level entrance grade is 9. Standardized test scores or TOEFL required. Deadline for receipt of application materials: December 15. No application fee required. Interview required.

Athletics Interscholastic: aquatics (boys, girls), baseball (b), basketball (b,g), cross-country running (b,g), dance team (g), diving (b,g), football (b), golf (b,g), gymnastics (g), ice hockey (b), pom squad (g), skiing (downhill) (b,g), soccer (b,g), softball (g), swimming and diving (b,g), tennis (b,g), track and field (b,g), ultimate Frisbee (b), volleyball (g); coed intramural: skiing (downhill). 4 PE instructors, 20 coaches, 2 athletic trainers.

Computers Computers are regularly used in all classes. Computer network features include on-campus library services, Internet access, wireless campus network, Internet filtering or blocking technology. Student e-mail accounts and computer access in designated common areas are available to students. Students grades are available online. The school has a published electronic and media policy.

Contact Ms. Marcia Lovett, Director of Admissions. 608-257-1023 Ext. 131. Fax: 608-257-9133. E-mail: marcia.lovett@edgewoodhs.org. Website: www.edgewoodhs.org

EDISON SCHOOL

Box 2, Site 11, RR2
Okotoks, Alberta T1S 1A2, Canada

Head of School: Mrs. Beth Chernoff

General Information Coeducational day college-preparatory and general academic school. Grades K–12. Founded: 1993. Setting: small town. Nearest major city is Calgary, Canada. 10-acre campus. 3 buildings on campus. Approved or accredited by Association of Independent Schools and Colleges of Alberta and Alberta Department of Education. Language of instruction: English. Total enrollment: 236. Upper school average class size: 12. Upper school faculty-student ratio: 1:12. There are 185 required school days per year for Upper School students. Upper School students typically attend 5 days per week. The average school day consists of 6 hours and 15 minutes.

Upper School Student Profile Grade 9: 20 students (10 boys, 10 girls); Grade 10: 12 students (6 boys, 6 girls); Grade 11: 12 students (6 boys, 6 girls); Grade 12: 12 students (6 boys, 6 girls).

Faculty School total: 22. In upper school: 3 men, 3 women; 4 have advanced degrees.

Subjects Offered Advanced Placement courses, art, biology, chemistry, English, French, mathematics, physical education, physics, science, social studies, Spanish, standard curriculum.

Graduation Requirements Alberta Learning requirements.

Special Academic Programs 11 Advanced Placement exams for which test preparation is offered; accelerated programs; independent study; study at local college for college credit; academic accommodation for the gifted.

College Admission Counseling 10 students graduated in 2016; 9 went to college, including Queen's University at Kingston; The University of British Columbia; University of Alberta; University of Calgary; University of Waterloo. Other: 1 went to work. Median composite ACT: 26. 58% scored over 26 on composite ACT.

Student Life Upper grades have uniform requirement, student council, honor system. Discipline rests primarily with faculty.

Tuition and Aid Day student tuition: CAN$7000. Tuition installment plan (monthly payment plans). Tuition reduction for siblings available.

Admissions Traditional secondary-level entrance grade is 9. For fall 2016, 20 students applied for upper-level admission, 4 were accepted, 4 enrolled. Achievement tests or admissions testing required. Deadline for receipt of application materials: none. No application fee required. On-campus interview required.

Athletics Interscholastic: badminton (boys, girls), basketball (b,g), cross-country running (b,g); intramural: badminton (b,g), basketball (b,g), cross-country running

(b,g); coed interscholastic: badminton, flag football; coed intramural: badminton, flag football, outdoor education. 1 PE instructor, 1 coach.

Computers Computers are regularly used in all classes. Computer resources include Internet access, wireless campus network. Computer access in designated common areas is available to students. Students grades are available online.

Contact Mrs. Beth Chernoff, Headmistress. 403-938-7670. Fax: 403-938-7224 Ext. 200. E-mail: office@edisonschool.ca. Website: www.edisonschool.ca

EDMONTON ACADEMY

Edmonton, Alberta, Canada
See Special Needs Schools section.

EDMUND BURKE SCHOOL

4101 Connecticut Avenue NW
Washington, District of Columbia 20008

Head of School: Damian Jones

General Information Coeducational day college-preparatory and leadership and service school. Grades 6–12. Founded: 1968. Setting: urban. 2 buildings on campus. Approved or accredited by Association of Independent Maryland Schools, Association of Independent Schools of Greater Washington, Middle States Association of Colleges and Schools, and District of Columbia Department of Education. Member of National Association of Independent Schools and Secondary School Admission Test Board. Endowment: $829,556. Total enrollment: 297. Upper school average class size: 11. Upper school faculty-student ratio: 1:6. There are 178 required school days per year for Upper School students. Upper School students typically attend 5 days per week. The average school day consists of 5 hours.

Upper School Student Profile Grade 9: 58 students (28 boys, 30 girls); Grade 10: 61 students (29 boys, 32 girls); Grade 11: 56 students (33 boys, 23 girls); Grade 12: 57 students (27 boys, 30 girls).

Faculty School total: 50. In upper school: 19 men, 19 women; 25 have advanced degrees.

Subjects Offered African-American literature, algebra, American history, American literature, anatomy, Asian history, band, baseball, biology, calculus, ceramics, chemistry, chorus, computer science, creative writing, economics, English, English literature, European history, French, geography, geometry, health, history, journalism, Latin, music, performing arts, philosophy, photography, physical education, physics, senior seminar, Spanish, theater, trigonometry, values and decisions, visual arts, world history, writing.

Graduation Requirements English, foreign language, history, mathematics, physical education (includes health), science, social sciences, values and decisions, visual and performing arts, senior research seminar, senior project. Community service is required.

Special Academic Programs Advanced Placement exam preparation; independent study; term-away projects.

College Admission Counseling 59 students graduated in 2016; all went to college, including Dickinson College; Drexel University; Goucher College; Temple University; University of Vermont. Mean SAT critical reading: 631, mean SAT math: 584, mean SAT writing: 615, mean composite ACT: 29.

Student Life Upper grades have student council, honor system. Discipline rests primarily with faculty.

Summer Programs Remediation, enrichment, advancement, ESL, art/fine arts, computer instruction programs offered; session focuses on academic programs and visual arts; held on campus; accepts boys and girls; open to students from other schools. 50 students usually enrolled. 2017 schedule: June 20 to August 21. Application deadline: none.

Tuition and Aid Day student tuition: $38,535. Tuition installment plan (The Tuition Plan, Insured Tuition Payment Plan, Academic Management Services Plan, individually arranged payment plans). Need-based scholarship grants available. In 2016–17, 29% of upper-school students received aid. Total amount of financial aid awarded in 2016–17: $978,185.

Admissions Traditional secondary-level entrance grade is 9. For fall 2016, 130 students applied for upper-level admission, 86 were accepted, 45 enrolled. ISEE or SSAT required. Deadline for receipt of application materials: January 4. Application fee required: $70. Interview required.

Athletics Interscholastic: aquatics (boys, girls), baseball (b), basketball (b,g), cross-country running (b,g), golf (b,g), soccer (b,g), softball (g), swimming and diving (g), track and field (b,g), volleyball (b,g); intramural: dance team (b,g), Frisbee (b,g), martial arts (b,g), physical fitness (b,g), weight lifting (b,g); coed interscholastic: swimming and diving; coed intramural: indoor soccer, jogging. 1 PE instructor, 10 coaches.

Computers Computers are regularly used in creative writing, English, foreign language, French, graphic arts, history, journalism, mathematics, science classes. Computer network features include on-campus library services, online commercial services, Internet access, wireless campus network, Internet filtering or blocking technology, iPad program in grade 9. Student e-mail accounts are available to students. Students grades are available online. The school has a published electronic and media policy.

Contact Admissions Office. 202-362-8882 Ext. 670. Fax: 202-362-1914. E-mail: admissions@burkeschool.org. Website: www.burkeschool.org

ELDORADO EMERSON PRIVATE SCHOOL

4100 East Walnut Street
Orange, California 92869

Head of School: Mr. Sean Kelley

General Information Coeducational day college-preparatory and general academic school. Grades K–12. Founded: 1958. Setting: suburban. Nearest major city is Los Angeles. 5-acre campus. 8 buildings on campus. Approved or accredited by Western Association of Schools and Colleges and California Department of Education. Total enrollment: 166. Upper school average class size: 20. Upper school faculty-student ratio: 1:18. There are 90 required school days per year for Upper School students. Upper School students typically attend 5 days per week. The average school day consists of 6 hours.

Upper School Student Profile Grade 6: 6 students (3 boys, 3 girls); Grade 7: 8 students (4 boys, 4 girls); Grade 8: 10 students (6 boys, 4 girls); Grade 9: 10 students (8 boys, 2 girls); Grade 10: 22 students (18 boys, 4 girls); Grade 11: 25 students (15 boys, 10 girls); Grade 12: 34 students (25 boys, 9 girls).

Faculty School total: 25. In upper school: 7 men, 5 women; 10 have advanced degrees.

Subjects Offered Acting, advanced chemistry, advanced math, advanced TOEFL/grammar, algebra, American government, American history-AP, analysis and differential calculus, anatomy, ancient world history, applied arts, applied music, Arabic, art, art and culture, art appreciation, art education, art history, Basic programming, biology, biology-AP, calculus, calculus-AP, cell biology, ceramics, chemistry, chemistry-AP, Chinese, civil war history, classical civilization, classical Greek literature, classical music, classics, clayworking, computer processing, computer programming, computer skills, concert band, contemporary art, contemporary history, creative drama, creative writing, cultural geography, current events, current history, drama workshop, drawing, earth science, economics and history, Egyptian history, English, English literature, ESL, fine arts, gardening, general math, geography, geometry, grammar, jazz band, keyboarding, library skills, Mandarin, math analysis, physics, physics-AP, pre-algebra, pre-calculus, reading, SAT preparation, science, Shakespeare, Spanish, TOEFL preparation, U.S. government and politics-AP, U.S. history, world history.

Graduation Requirements Art, English, foreign language, mathematics, music, physical education (includes health), science, social studies (includes history). Community service is required.

Special Academic Programs Advanced Placement exam preparation; honors section; accelerated programs; independent study; study at local college for college credit; academic accommodation for the gifted, the musically talented, and the artistically talented; ESL (50 students enrolled).

College Admission Counseling 30 students graduated in 2016; all went to college, including California State University, Fullerton; Chapman University; Johns Hopkins University; Occidental College; Purdue University; University of California, Santa Cruz.

Student Life Upper grades have specified standards of dress, honor system. Discipline rests equally with students and faculty.

Summer Programs Enrichment, sports, art/fine arts programs offered; held on campus; accepts boys and girls; open to students from other schools. 160 students usually enrolled. 2017 schedule: June 21 to July 21. Application deadline: June 1.

Tuition and Aid Day student tuition: $12,150. Tuition installment plan (monthly payment plans, individually arranged payment plans). Tuition reduction for siblings, need-based scholarship grants available. In 2016–17, 10% of upper-school students received aid. Total amount of financial aid awarded in 2016–17: $50,000.

Admissions Traditional secondary-level entrance grade is 10. Achievement tests or any standardized test required. Deadline for receipt of application materials: none. Application fee required: $185. Interview required.

Athletics Interscholastic: basketball (boys), soccer (b), volleyball (g); coed interscholastic: fitness, outdoor education, physical fitness, physical training. 1 PE instructor, 3 coaches.

Computers Computers are regularly used in desktop publishing, graphic design, keyboarding, Web site design, word processing, yearbook classes. Computer resources include Internet access, Internet filtering or blocking technology.

Contact Ms. Jackie Fogle, Administration. 714-633-4774. Fax: 714-744-3304. E-mail: jfogle@eldoradoemerson.org. Website: http://www.eldoradoemerson.org

ELGIN ACADEMY

350 Park Street
Elgin, Illinois 60120

Head of School: Mr. Seth L. Hanford

General Information Coeducational day college-preparatory, arts, and technology school. Grades PS–12. Founded: 1839. Setting: suburban. Nearest major city is Chicago. 20-acre campus. 8 buildings on campus. Approved or accredited by Independent Schools Association of the Central States, National Independent Private Schools Association, and Illinois Department of Education. Member of National Association of Independent Schools. Endowment: $8 million. Total enrollment: 323. Upper school average class size: 12. Upper school faculty-student ratio: 1:7. There are 173 required school days per year for Upper School students. Upper School students typically attend 5 days per week. The average school day consists of 6 hours and 30 minutes.

Upper School Student Profile Grade 9: 25 students (15 boys, 10 girls); Grade 10: 20 students (10 boys, 10 girls); Grade 11: 30 students (18 boys, 12 girls); Grade 12: 38 students (19 boys, 19 girls).

Faculty School total: 54. In upper school: 13 men, 11 women; 21 have advanced degrees.

Subjects Offered 3-dimensional art, 3-dimensional design, ACT preparation, acting, advanced biology, advanced chemistry, advanced computer applications, advanced math, Advanced Placement courses, advanced studio art-AP, algebra, American government, American history, American history-AP, American literature, American literature-AP, American politics in film, analytic geometry, applied music, architectural drawing, art, art appreciation, art education, art history, art-AP, athletics, baseball, Basic programming, basketball, biology, biology-AP, calculus, calculus-AP, Central and Eastern European history, ceramics, chamber groups, character education, chemistry, chemistry-AP, child development, choir, chorus, classical language, clayworking, college admission preparation, college counseling, college placement, college planning, college writing, composition-AP, computer information systems, computer programming, computer science, concert choir, consumer economics, creative writing, critical thinking, critical writing, digital art, digital imaging, digital photography, drama, drama performance, dramatic arts, early childhood, ecology, environmental systems, economics, English, English as a foreign language, English language and composition-AP, English literature, English literature and composition-AP, English-AP, environmental education, environmental science, European history, European history-AP, expository writing, fine arts, finite math, French, French language-AP, geometry, golf, government/civics, grammar, history, history-AP, honors algebra, honors geometry, honors U.S. history, independent study, Latin, Latin-AP, library skills, mathematics, media production, model United Nations, music, music appreciation, music performance, music theory, musical productions, musical theater, oil painting, oral communications, painting, performing arts, photography, physical education, physics, physics-AP, poetry, pre-calculus, programming, psychology, psychology-AP, public service, public speaking, SAT/ACT preparation, science, social studies, software design, Spanish, Spanish-AP, sports, statistics, statistics-AP, student government, student publications, studio art, studio art-AP, tennis, theater, theater arts, track and field, travel, trigonometry, U.S. constitutional history, U.S. history-AP, video, video film production, visual and performing arts, wilderness education, world civilizations, world history, world history-AP, world literature, writing, writing workshop, yearbook.

Graduation Requirements Arts and fine arts (art, music, dance, drama), English, foreign language, mathematics, physical education (includes health), science, social studies (includes history).

Special Academic Programs 16 Advanced Placement exams for which test preparation is offered; honors section; independent study; ESL (7 students enrolled).

College Admission Counseling 32 students graduated in 2016; all went to college, including Iowa State University of Science and Technology; Knox College; Marquette University; Northwestern University; University of Illinois at Urbana–Champaign; University of Southern California. Mean SAT critical reading: 596, mean SAT math: 601, mean SAT writing: 578, mean combined SAT: 1197, mean composite ACT: 27.

Student Life Upper grades have specified standards of dress, student council, honor system. Discipline rests primarily with faculty.

Summer Programs Enrichment, sports, art/fine arts programs offered; session focuses on college prep work, academics, athletics, art, music; held both on and off campus; accepts boys and girls; open to students from other schools. 140 students usually enrolled. 2017 schedule: June 12 to August 15.

Tuition and Aid Day student tuition: $25,480. Tuition installment plan (FACTS Tuition Payment Plan, monthly payment plans). Tuition reduction for siblings, merit scholarship grants, need-based scholarship grants available. In 2016–17, 40% of upper-school students received aid; total upper-school merit-scholarship money awarded: $50,000. Total amount of financial aid awarded in 2016–17: $1,590,000.

Admissions Traditional secondary-level entrance grade is 9. For fall 2016, 27 students applied for upper-level admission, 25 were accepted, 16 enrolled. Admissions testing, International English Language Test, ISEE, TOEFL or TOEFL Junior required. Deadline for receipt of application materials: none. Application fee required: $50. Interview required.

Athletics Interscholastic: baseball (boys), basketball (b,g), cross-country running (b,g), field hockey (g), soccer (b,g), tennis (b,g), track and field (b,g), volleyball (g); coed interscholastic: cross-country running, golf, physical fitness, physical training, strength & conditioning. 2 PE instructors, 15 coaches.

Computers Computers are regularly used in art, English, foreign language, mathematics, science, social studies, video film production classes. Computer network features include on-campus library services, online commercial services, Internet access, wireless campus network, Internet filtering or blocking technology, iPads, Chromebooks. Campus intranet, student e-mail accounts, and computer access in designated common areas are available to students. Students grades are available online. The school has a published electronic and media policy.

Contact Dr. Diane R. Schael, Director of Admissions. 847-695-0303. Fax: 847-695-5017. E-mail: admissions@elginacademy.org. Website: www.elginacademy.org

ELIZABETH SETON HIGH SCHOOL

5715 Emerson Street
Bladensburg, Maryland 20710-1844

Head of School: Sr. Ellen Marie Hagar

General Information Girls' day college-preparatory, arts, religious studies, bilingual studies, technology, and engineering, law, pharmacy school, affiliated with Roman Catholic Church. Grades 9–12. Founded: 1959. Setting: suburban. Nearest major city is Washington, DC. 24-acre campus. 2 buildings on campus. Approved or accredited by Middle States Association of Colleges and Schools, National Catholic Education Association, and Maryland Department of Education. Total enrollment: 563. Upper school average class size: 16. Upper school faculty-student ratio: 1:11. There are 180 required school days per year for Upper School students. Upper School students typically attend 5 days per week. The average school day consists of 6 hours and 30 minutes.

Upper School Student Profile Grade 9: 144 students (144 girls); Grade 10: 115 students (115 girls); Grade 11: 158 students (158 girls); Grade 12: 146 students (146 girls). 50% of students are Roman Catholic.

Faculty School total: 58. In upper school: 3 men, 45 women; 35 have advanced degrees.

Subjects Offered 3-dimensional design, advanced biology, advanced chemistry, advanced math, advanced studio art-AP, algebra, American history, American history-AP, American legal systems, American literature, American sign language, analytic geometry, anatomy, art, art-AP, band, bioethics, biology, biology-AP, British literature-AP, calculus, calculus-AP, Catholic belief and practice, ceramics, chemistry, chemistry-AP, choir, choral music, chorus, Christian and Hebrew scripture, Christianity, church history, college counseling, college planning, college writing, computer multimedia, computer programming, computer science, computer skills, computer technologies, concert band, concert choir, constitutional history of U.S., dance, dance performance, desktop publishing, drama performance, drama workshop, dramatic arts, drawing, drawing and design, earth science, economics, engineering, English, English literature, English literature and composition-AP, English literature-AP, environmental science, environmental science-AP, ethics, European history, film and literature, fine arts, foreign language, French, French-AP, genetics, geography, geometry, government-AP, government/civics, government/civics-AP, grammar, health, health science, history, Holocaust studies, honors algebra, honors English, honors geometry, HTML design, introduction to theater, journalism, keyboarding, Latin, life management skills, mathematics, music, newspaper, orchestra, philosophy, photography, physical education, physics, physiology, pre-calculus, probability and statistics, psychology, psychology-AP, religion, religious education, robotics, science, social studies, sociology, Spanish, speech, statistics-AP, symphonic band, theater arts, theater production, theology, trigonometry, U.S. government and politics-AP, U.S. history-AP, Web site design, weightlifting, wind ensemble, women in literature, world history, world history-AP, world literature, writing.

Graduation Requirements 1 1/2 elective credits, arts and fine arts (art, music, dance, drama), English, foreign language, health education, mathematics, physical education (includes health), religion (includes Bible studies and theology), science, social studies (includes history), technology. Community service is required.

Special Academic Programs Advanced Placement exam preparation; honors section; independent study; academic accommodation for the gifted, the musically talented, and the artistically talented; programs in general development for dyslexic students; special instructional classes for students with mild learning disabilities, organizational deficiencies, Attention Deficit Disorder, and dyslexia.

College Admission Counseling 109 students graduated in 2015; all went to college, including George Mason University; Hampton University; Mount St. Mary's University; The Catholic University of America; Towson University; University of Maryland, Baltimore County. Mean SAT critical reading: 589, mean SAT math: 573, mean SAT writing: 585.

Student Life Upper grades have uniform requirement, student council, honor system. Discipline rests equally with students and faculty. Attendance at religious services is required.

Tuition and Aid Day student tuition: $12,750. Tuition installment plan (FACTS Tuition Payment Plan, monthly payment plans, one, two, or ten payments). Tuition reduction for siblings, merit scholarship grants, need-based scholarship grants, paying campus jobs available. In 2015–16, 35% of upper-school students received aid; total upper-school merit-scholarship money awarded: $104,000. Total amount of financial aid awarded in 2015–16: $500,000.

Admissions Traditional secondary-level entrance grade is 9. High School Placement Test required. Deadline for receipt of application materials: December 3. Application fee required: $50. On-campus interview required.

Athletics Interscholastic: aerobics/dance, archery, badminton, basketball, cheering, crew, cross-country running, dance, dance squad, dance team, equestrian sports, field hockey, flag football, golf, horseback riding, indoor track, indoor track & field, lacrosse, martial arts, rowing, running, self defense, soccer, softball, swimming and diving, tennis, touch football, volleyball, winter (indoor) track; intramural: dance, flag football, martial arts, outdoor recreation, physical fitness, strength & conditioning, weight lifting, weight training. 3 PE instructors, 56 coaches, 1 athletic trainer.

Computers Computers are regularly used in all academic, computer applications, desktop publishing, graphic design, independent study, lab/keyboard, literary magazine, multimedia, photojournalism, programming, research skills, writing, yearbook classes.

Computer network features include on-campus library services, online commercial services, Internet access, wireless campus network, Internet filtering or blocking technology. Campus intranet and student e-mail accounts are available to students. Students grades are available online. The school has a published electronic and media policy.

Contact Mrs. Melissa Davey Landini, Dean of Admissions. 301-864-4532 Ext. 7015. Fax: 301-864-8946. E-mail: mlandini@setonhs.org. Website: www.setonhs.org

THE ELLIS SCHOOL

6425 Fifth Avenue
Pittsburgh, Pennsylvania 15206

Head of School: Mrs. Robin Newham

General Information Girls' day and distance learning college-preparatory, arts, STEM, and integrated studies school. Grades PK–12. Distance learning grades 9–12. Founded: 1916. Setting: urban. 8-acre campus. 5 buildings on campus. Approved or accredited by Pennsylvania Association of Independent Schools and Pennsylvania Department of Education. Member of National Association of Independent Schools. Endowment: $24 million. Total enrollment: 393. Upper school average class size: 15. There are 167 required school days per year for Upper School students. Upper School students typically attend 5 days per week. The average school day consists of 6 hours and 20 minutes.

Upper School Student Profile Grade 9: 26 students (26 girls); Grade 10: 38 students (38 girls); Grade 11: 36 students (36 girls); Grade 12: 30 students (30 girls).

Faculty School total: 68.

Subjects Offered 3-dimensional art, acting, advanced biology, advanced chemistry, advanced math, Advanced Placement courses, advanced studio art-AP, algebra, American history, American history-AP, American literature, anatomy and physiology, anthropology, art, art history, art history-AP, art-AP, Basic programming, biology, biology-AP, calculus, calculus-AP, ceramics, chemistry, chemistry-AP, choir, chorus, college admission preparation, college counseling, computer graphics, computer science, computer science-AP, CPR, creative writing, dance, digital art, digital music, digital photography, discrete mathematics, drama, drama performance, English, English language and composition-AP, English literature, English literature and composition-AP, English-AP, environmental science, European history, expository writing, fine arts, first aid, fitness, French, French language-AP, French-AP, gender issues, geometry, global issues, government/civics, health, history, history-AP, human anatomy, interdisciplinary studies, jewelry making, journalism, Latin, Latin-AP, mathematics, music, musical productions, painting, photography, physical education, physics, public service, robotics, SAT/ACT preparation, senior project, sex education, social studies, socioeconomic problems, Spanish, Spanish language-AP, Spanish-AP, speech, statistics, studio art, studio art-AP, technical theater, theater, trigonometry, U.S. government and politics-AP, U.S. history, U.S. history-AP, video, voice, world history, world literature, writing, writing workshop, yearbook.

Graduation Requirements Arts and fine arts (art, music, dance, drama), English, first aid, foreign language, health education, interdisciplinary studies, mathematics, physical education (includes health), science, social studies (includes history), completion of three-week mini-course program (grades 9-11), senior projects.

Special Academic Programs 14 Advanced Placement exams for which test preparation is offered; honors section; independent study; term-away projects; study at local college for college credit; study abroad; academic accommodation for the gifted, the musically talented, and the artistically talented; remedial reading and/or remedial writing.

College Admission Counseling 29 students graduated in 2016; all went to college, including Cornell University; Ithaca College; University of Pennsylvania; University of Pittsburgh. Mean combined SAT: 1870, mean composite ACT: 28.

Student Life Upper grades have uniform requirement, student council, honor system. Discipline rests primarily with faculty.

Tuition and Aid Day student tuition: $9500–$28,000. Tuition installment plan (FACTS Tuition Payment Plan, 10-month payment plan, two-payment plan). Tuition reduction for siblings, merit scholarship grants, need-based scholarship grants, need-based financial aid, legacy tuition reduction available. In 2016–17, 49% of upper-school students received aid; total upper-school merit-scholarship money awarded: $40,000.

Admissions Traditional secondary-level entrance grade is 9. For fall 2016, 34 students applied for upper-level admission, 22 were accepted, 13 enrolled. ISEE required. Deadline for receipt of application materials: none. Application fee required: $50. Interview recommended.

Athletics Interscholastic: basketball, crew, cross-country running, field hockey, independent competitive sports, lacrosse, soccer, softball, swimming and diving, tennis, track and field; intramural: aerobics/dance, archery, badminton, ball hockey, ballet, basketball, cooperative games, crew, dance, field hockey, fitness, gymnastics, indoor soccer, kickball, lacrosse, outdoor activities, physical fitness, running, tennis, volleyball, wall climbing, weight training, yoga. 1 PE instructor, 17 coaches, 1 athletic trainer.

Computers Computers are regularly used in all academic classes. Computer network features include on-campus library services, online commercial services, Internet access, wireless campus network, Internet filtering or blocking technology, blended learning and flipped classrooms, Google Glass/Labcasts. Campus intranet and student e-mail accounts are available to students. The school has a published electronic and media policy.

Contact Ms. Bayh Sullivan, Director of Enrollment Management. 412-661-4880. Fax: 412-661-7634. E-mail: admissions@theellisschool.org. Website: www.theellisschool.org

ELMWOOD SCHOOL

261 Buena Vista Road
Ottawa, Ontario K1M 0V9, Canada

Head of School: Ms. Cheryl Boughton

General Information Girls' day college-preparatory and International Baccalaureate school. Grades PK–12. Founded: 1915. Setting: suburban. 2-acre campus. 1 building on campus. Approved or accredited by Canadian Association of Independent Schools, Canadian Educational Standards Institute, Conference of Independent Schools of Ontario, International Baccalaureate Organization, Ontario Ministry of Education, and Ontario Department of Education. Language of instruction: English. Total enrollment: 340. Upper school average class size: 10. Upper school faculty-student ratio: 1:8. There are 178 required school days per year for Upper School students. The average school day consists of 6 hours and 45 minutes.

Faculty School total: 50. In upper school: 10 men, 21 women; 14 have advanced degrees.

Subjects Offered Algebra, art, art history, biology, business, calculus, Canadian geography, Canadian history, chemistry, communications, computer math, computer science, creative writing, drama, economics, English, English literature, environmental science, ESL, European history, fine arts, French, geography, geometry, German, grammar, health, history, Latin, mathematics, music, philosophy, physical education, physics, science, social studies, Spanish, theater, theory of knowledge, trigonometry, typing, world history, world literature.

Graduation Requirements Arts and fine arts (art, music, dance, drama), business skills (includes word processing), Canadian geography, Canadian history, English, foreign language, mathematics, physical education (includes health), science, social studies (includes history).

Special Academic Programs International Baccalaureate program; academic accommodation for the gifted; ESL.

College Admission Counseling 30 students graduated in 2016; all went to college, including Carleton University; McGill University; Penn State University Park; Texas A&M University; University of Ottawa; University of Toronto.

Student Life Upper grades have uniform requirement, student council, honor system. Discipline rests primarily with faculty.

Summer Programs ESL, sports, art/fine arts programs offered; held on campus; accepts girls; open to students from other schools. 2017 schedule: June 20 to August 26.

Tuition and Aid Day student tuition: CAN$12,960–CAN$23,640. Tuition installment plan (monthly payment plans, individually arranged payment plans, 4 payment plan and 11 month payment plan). Bursaries, merit scholarship grants, need-based scholarship grants available. In 2016–17, 10% of upper-school students received aid; total upper-school merit-scholarship money awarded: CAN$80,000. Total amount of financial aid awarded in 2016–17: CAN$250,000.

Admissions CAT required. Deadline for receipt of application materials: none. Application fee required: CAN$150. Interview recommended.

Athletics Interscholastic: alpine skiing, aquatics, badminton, basketball, cross country running, field hockey, golf, nordic skiing, rowing, rugby, skiing (cross-country), skiing (downhill), snowboarding, soccer, swimming and diving, tennis, ultimate Frisbee, volleyball, water polo; intramural: aerobics/dance, aerobics/Nautilus, badminton, ball hockey, ballet, dance, hiking/backpacking, outdoor adventure, ropes courses, wilderness, yoga. 4 PE instructors, 1 coach.

Computers Computers are regularly used in all classes. Computer network features include on-campus library services, Internet access, wireless campus network, Internet filtering or blocking technology. Campus intranet, student e-mail accounts, and computer access in designated common areas are available to students. The school has a published electronic and media policy.

Contact Ms. Elise Aylen, Director of Admissions. 613-744-7783. Fax: 613-741-8210. E-mail: admissions@elmwood.ca. Website: www.elmwood.ca

ELYRIA CATHOLIC HIGH SCHOOL

725 Gulf Road
Elyria, Ohio 44035-3697

Head of School: Mrs. Amy Butler

General Information Coeducational day college-preparatory, arts, business, religious studies, bilingual studies, and technology school, affiliated with Roman Catholic Church; primarily serves students with learning disabilities, individuals with Attention Deficit Disorder, and dyslexic students. Grades 9–12. Founded: 1948. Setting: suburban. Nearest major city is Cleveland. 16-acre campus. 2 buildings on campus. Approved or accredited by North Central Association of Colleges and Schools and Ohio Department of Education. Endowment: $3 million. Total enrollment: 434. Upper school average class size: 24. Upper school faculty-student ratio: 1:14. There are 180 required school days per year for Upper School students. Upper School students typically attend 5 days per week. The average school day consists of 6 hours and 45 minutes.

Upper School Student Profile Grade 9: 103 students (54 boys, 49 girls); Grade 10: 105 students (52 boys, 53 girls); Grade 11: 117 students (56 boys, 61 girls); Grade 12: 109 students (48 boys, 61 girls). 90% of students are Roman Catholic.

Faculty School total: 37. In upper school: 18 men, 19 women; 22 have advanced degrees.

Subjects Offered Accounting, advanced math, algebra, American government, American history, American history-AP, analysis of data, anatomy and physiology, ancient world history, art, band, biology, business, calculus, calculus-AP, campus ministry, Catholic belief and practice, chemistry, choir, Christian and Hebrew scripture, Christian doctrine, Christian ethics, church history, computer applications, concert band, concert choir, current events, data analysis, drama, drama performance, earth science, English, fine arts, French, French language-AP, geometry, German, health, history, honors English, industrial arts, introduction to theater, journalism, leadership, life issues, marching band, music appreciation, parent/child development, peer ministry, physical fitness, physics, prayer/spirituality, pre-calculus, psychology, reading/study skills, social justice, Spanish, Spanish language-AP, theater, world religions, yearbook.

Graduation Requirements Arts and fine arts (art, music, dance, drama), computers, English, mathematics, physical education (includes health), religion (includes Bible studies and theology), science, social studies (includes history), school and community service hours, Ohio Proficiency Test.

Special Academic Programs Advanced Placement exam preparation; honors section; study at local college for college credit; remedial reading and/or remedial writing; remedial math; programs in English, mathematics, general development for dyslexic students; special instructional classes for students with learning disabilities and Attention Deficit Disorder; ESL (5 students enrolled).

College Admission Counseling 92 students graduated in 2015; 91 went to college, including Baldwin Wallace University; Bowling Green State University; John Carroll University; Kent State University; The Ohio State University; The University of Toledo. Other: 1 entered military service. Mean SAT critical reading: 570, mean SAT math: 557.

Student Life Upper grades have specified standards of dress, student council, honor system. Discipline rests primarily with faculty. Attendance at religious services is required.

Tuition and Aid Day student tuition: $7750. Tuition installment plan (FACTS Tuition Payment Plan). Tuition reduction for siblings, merit scholarship grants, need-based scholarship grants, paying campus jobs available. In 2015–16, 54% of upper-school students received aid; total upper-school merit-scholarship money awarded: $15,750. Total amount of financial aid awarded in 2015–16: $250,300.

Admissions Traditional secondary-level entrance grade is 9. High School Placement Test (closed version) from Scholastic Testing Service required. Deadline for receipt of application materials: January 14. No application fee required. Interview recommended.

Athletics Interscholastic: baseball (boys), basketball (b,g), cross-country running (b,g), diving (b,g), football (b), golf (b), rugby (b), soccer (b,g), softball (g), tennis (b,g), volleyball (g), wrestling (b); coed interscholastic: bowling, cheering, ice hockey, swimming and diving, track and field. 1 PE instructor, 47 coaches, 1 athletic trainer.

Computers Computers are regularly used in business studies, journalism, newspaper, typing, word processing, yearbook classes. Computer network features include on-campus library services, online commercial services, Internet access, wireless campus network, Internet filtering or blocking technology, 1:1 Google Chromebook Initiative. Campus intranet and student e-mail accounts are available to students. Students grades are available online. The school has a published electronic and media policy.

Contact Mrs. Annie Cunningham, Director of Admissions/Marketing. 440-365-1821 Ext. 116. Fax: 440-365-7536. E-mail: annie.cunningham@elyriacatholic.com. Website: www.elyriacatholic.com

THE ENGLISH COLLEGE IN PRAGUE

Sokolovska 320
Prague 190 00, Czech Republic

Head of School: Dr. Nigel Brown

General Information Coeducational day college-preparatory school. Grades 8–13. Founded: 1994. Setting: urban. 1-acre campus. 2 buildings on campus. Approved or accredited by Department of Education and Employment, United Kingdom, Headmasters' Conference, Independent Schools Council (UK), and International Baccalaureate Organization. Language of instruction: English. Total enrollment: 360. Upper school average class size: 13. Upper school faculty-student ratio: 1:11. The average school day consists of 8 hours and 45 minutes.

Faculty School total: 40. In upper school: 20 men, 20 women.

Subjects Offered Independent study, International Baccalaureate courses.

Graduation Requirements International Baccalaureate courses, Czech maturita for Czech students.

Special Academic Programs International Baccalaureate program; independent study; academic accommodation for the gifted, the musically talented, and the artistically talented; programs in English for dyslexic students; ESL (30 students enrolled).

College Admission Counseling 67 students graduated in 2016; 64 went to college. Other: 1 went to work, 2 had other specific plans.

Student Life Upper grades have student council, honor system. Discipline rests primarily with faculty.

Summer Programs ESL programs offered; session focuses on English preparation for new students; held on campus; accepts boys and girls; not open to students from other schools. 60 students usually enrolled. 2017 schedule: April 24 to June 30.

Tuition and Aid Tuition reduction for siblings, bursaries, merit scholarship grants, need-based scholarship grants available. In 2016–17, 30% of upper-school students received aid.

Admissions Traditional secondary-level entrance grade is 12. For fall 2016, 15 students applied for upper-level admission, 6 were accepted, 6 enrolled. English entrance exam and mathematics proficiency exam required. Deadline for receipt of application materials: May 1. Application fee required: 500 Czech korun. Interview required.

Athletics 2 PE instructors.

Computers Computers are regularly used in all academic classes. Computer network features include on-campus library services, online commercial services, Internet access, wireless campus network, Internet filtering or blocking technology. Campus intranet, student e-mail accounts, and computer access in designated common areas are available to students. Students grades are available online.

Contact Mrs. Iva Rozkosna, Admissions Registrar. 420-283893113. Fax: 420-283890118. E-mail: office@englishcollege.cz. Website: www.englishcollege.cz

THE ENGLISH SCHOOL, KUWAIT

PO Box 379
Safat 13004, Kuwait

Head of School: Mr. Kieron Peacock

General Information Coeducational day college-preparatory and general academic school. Founded: 1953. Setting: suburban. Nearest major city is Kuwait City, Kuwait. 12-acre campus. 1 building on campus. Approved or accredited by Department for Education and Skills (UK), Independent Schools Council (UK), and Kuwait Ministry of Education. Language of instruction: English. Total enrollment: 600. Upper school average class size: 21. Upper School students typically attend 5 days per week.

Faculty School total: 50.

Student Life Upper grades have uniform requirement, student council, honor system. Discipline rests primarily with faculty.

Tuition and Aid Day student tuition: 3340 Kuwaiti dinars. Tuition installment plan (individually arranged payment plans).

Admissions Traditional secondary-level entrance age is 11. Any standardized test, English language or English proficiency required. Deadline for receipt of application materials: none. No application fee required. On-campus interview recommended.

Athletics Interscholastic: cricket (boys), netball (g); coed interscholastic: aquatics, ball hockey, basketball, floor hockey, gymnastics, independent competitive sports, roller blading. 2 PE instructors, 2 coaches.

Computers Computers are regularly used in all classes. Computer network features include on-campus library services, Internet access, wireless campus network, Internet filtering or blocking technology. Student e-mail accounts are available to students. The school has a published electronic and media policy.

Contact Mrs. Claire Billett, Registrar. E-mail: registrar@tes.edu.kw. Website: www.tes.edu.kw

THE EPISCOPAL ACADEMY

1785 Bishop White Drive
Newtown Square, Pennsylvania 19073-1300

Head of School: Dr. Thomas John Locke

General Information Coeducational day college-preparatory, arts, and athletics school, affiliated with Episcopal Church. Grades PK–12. Founded: 1785. Setting: suburban. Nearest major city is Philadelphia. 123-acre campus. 12 buildings on campus. Approved or accredited by National Association of Episcopal Schools, Pennsylvania Association of Independent Schools, and Pennsylvania Department of Education. Member of National Association of Independent Schools. Total enrollment: 1,250. Upper school average class size: 15. Upper school faculty-student ratio: 1:7. There are 167 required school days per year for Upper School students. Upper School students typically attend 5 days per week. The average school day consists of 8 hours.

Upper School Student Profile Grade 9: 135 students (77 boys, 58 girls); Grade 10: 144 students (81 boys, 63 girls); Grade 11: 132 students (68 boys, 64 girls); Grade 12: 134 students (68 boys, 66 girls).

Faculty School total: 188. In upper school: 46 men, 41 women; 65 have advanced degrees.

Subjects Offered 3-dimensional design, advanced biology, advanced chemistry, advanced math, Advanced Placement courses, advanced studio art-AP, algebra, American history, American history-AP, American literature, American literature-AP, art, art history, biology, biology-AP, calculus, ceramics, chemistry, chemistry-AP, choral music, chorus, classical language, college counseling, computer art, computer graphics, computer information systems, computer programming, computer programming-AP, creative writing, drama, drawing, earth science, ecology, economics,

English, English-AP, environmental science, ethics, European history, fine arts, French, French language-AP, French literature-AP, French studies, French-AP, geometry, government and politics-AP, Greek, health and safety, history, Latin, Latin-AP, Mandarin, mathematics, mechanical drawing, modern world history, music, orchestra, painting, photography, physical education, physics, physics-AP, pre-calculus, psychology, religion, religion and culture, science, senior project, social studies, Spanish, Spanish language-AP, Spanish literature, Spanish literature-AP, Spanish-AP, statistics-AP, studio art, studio art-AP, theater history, theater production, theology, U.S. government and politics-AP, U.S. history, U.S. history-AP, Vietnam history, visual and performing arts, vocal ensemble, vocal music, water polo, weight training, woodworking, world cultures, world history, writing.

Graduation Requirements Arts and fine arts (art, music, dance, drama), athletics, English, foreign language, mathematics, physical education (includes health), religion (includes Bible studies and theology), science, senior project, social studies (includes history), participation in Outward Bound program.

Special Academic Programs Advanced Placement exam preparation; honors section; independent study; study abroad.

College Admission Counseling 132 students graduated in 2016; all went to college, including Boston College; Cornell University; New York University; Princeton University; University of Pennsylvania; Vanderbilt University. Mean SAT critical reading: 639, mean SAT math: 648, mean SAT writing: 665, mean combined SAT: 1952, mean composite ACT: 29.

Student Life Upper grades have uniform requirement, student council, honor system. Discipline rests primarily with faculty. Attendance at religious services is required.

Summer Programs Remediation, enrichment, advancement, sports, art/fine arts, computer instruction programs offered; session focuses on academics, athletics; held on campus; accepts boys and girls; open to students from other schools. 700 students usually enrolled.

Tuition and Aid Day student tuition: $33,100. Tuition installment plan (monthly payment plans, individually arranged payment plans, Tuition Management Systems. 60% due July 1, remainder by December 1). Need-based scholarship grants available. In 2016–17, 25% of upper-school students received aid.

Admissions Traditional secondary-level entrance grade is 9. For fall 2016, 212 students applied for upper-level admission, 102 were accepted, 58 enrolled. ISEE or SSAT required. Deadline for receipt of application materials: December 15. Application fee required: $50. On-campus interview required.

Athletics Interscholastic: aquatics (boys, girls), baseball (b), basketball (b,g), crew (b,g), cross-country running (b,g), diving (b,g), field hockey (g), football (b), golf (b,g), indoor track (b,g), lacrosse (b,g), rowing (b,g), soccer (b,g), softball (g), squash (b,g), swimming and diving (b,g), tennis (b,g), track and field (b,g), water polo (b,g), winter (indoor) track (b,g), wrestling (b); intramural: aerobics (g), floor hockey (b); coed interscholastic: ice hockey, paddle tennis; coed intramural: aerobics/dance, aerobics/Nautilus, basketball, dance, dance squad, dance team, fencing, fitness, fitness walking, Frisbee, paddle tennis, physical fitness, physical training, ultimate Frisbee, weight lifting, weight training. 1 PE instructor, 14 coaches, 2 athletic trainers.

Computers Computers are regularly used in art, English, foreign language, history, mathematics, science, technology classes. Computer network features include on-campus library services, online commercial services, Internet access, wireless campus network, Internet filtering or blocking technology, 1:1 laptop program. Campus intranet, student e-mail accounts, and computer access in designated common areas are available to students. Students grades are available online. The school has a published electronic and media policy.

Contact Mr. Peter C. Anderson, Director of Admission. 484-424-1400 Ext. 1445. Fax: 484-424-1604. E-mail: anderson@episcopalacademy.org. Website: www.episcopalacademy.org

EPISCOPAL COLLEGIATE SCHOOL

Jackson T. Stephens Campus
1701 Cantrell Road
Little Rock, Arkansas 72201

Head of School: Mr. Christopher Tompkins

General Information Coeducational day college-preparatory school, affiliated with Episcopal Church. Grades PK–12. Founded: 1998. Setting: suburban. 34-acre campus. 3 buildings on campus. Approved or accredited by Arkansas Nonpublic School Accrediting Association, National Association of Episcopal Schools, Southern Association of Colleges and Schools, Southern Association of Independent Schools, and Southwest Association of Episcopal Schools. Member of National Association of Independent Schools. Endowment: $64 million. Total enrollment: 784. Upper school average class size: 15. Upper school faculty-student ratio: 1:10. There are 179 required school days per year for Upper School students. Upper School students typically attend 5 days per week. The average school day consists of 7 hours and 30 minutes.

Upper School Student Profile Grade 9: 52 students (33 boys, 19 girls); Grade 10: 49 students (24 boys, 25 girls); Grade 11: 44 students (21 boys, 23 girls); Grade 12: 52 students (23 boys, 29 girls). 35% of students are members of Episcopal Church.

Faculty School total: 106. In upper school: 14 men, 22 women; 28 have advanced degrees.

Graduation Requirements Senior chapel talk.

Special Academic Programs 16 Advanced Placement exams for which test preparation is offered; honors section; independent study.

College Admission Counseling 55 students graduated in 2016; all went to college, including Hendrix College; Louisiana State University and Agricultural & Mechanical College; Ouachita Baptist University; University of Arkansas; University of Mississippi. Mean SAT critical reading: 637, mean SAT math: 610, mean SAT writing: 633, mean combined SAT: 1879, mean composite ACT: 27. 65% scored over 600 on SAT critical reading, 44% scored over 600 on SAT math, 60% scored over 600 on SAT writing, 61% scored over 1800 on combined SAT, 41% scored over 26 on composite ACT.

Student Life Upper grades have uniform requirement, student council, honor system. Discipline rests primarily with faculty. Attendance at religious services is required.

Summer Programs Enrichment, sports, art/fine arts, computer instruction programs offered; session focuses on enrichment; held on campus; accepts boys and girls; open to students from other schools. 150 students usually enrolled. 2017 schedule: June 1 to July 31. Application deadline: May 30.

Tuition and Aid Day student tuition: $12,570. Tuition installment plan (FACTS Tuition Payment Plan). Need-based scholarship grants available. In 2016–17, 17% of upper-school students received aid. Total amount of financial aid awarded in 2016–17: $482,000.

Admissions Traditional secondary-level entrance grade is 9. For fall 2016, 55 students applied for upper-level admission, 21 were accepted, 16 enrolled. Stanford 9 required. Deadline for receipt of application materials: none. Application fee required: $50. Interview required.

Athletics Interscholastic: baseball (boys), basketball (b,g), cross-country running (b,g), fishing (b,g), fitness (b,g), football (b), golf (b,g), physical fitness (b,g), physical training (b,g), soccer (b,g), tennis (b,g), track and field (b,g), volleyball (g), weight training (b,g), wrestling (b,g); coed interscholastic: cheering. 5 PE instructors, 10 coaches, 2 athletic trainers.

Computers Computers are regularly used in all academic classes. Computer network features include on-campus library services, online commercial services, Internet access, wireless campus network, Internet filtering or blocking technology. Campus intranet, student e-mail accounts, and computer access in designated common areas are available to students. Students grades are available online. The school has a published electronic and media policy.

Contact Mr. Matt Radtke, Director of Advancement. 501-372-1194 Ext. 2678. Fax: 501-372-2160. E-mail: mradtke1@episcopalcollegiate.org. Website: www.episcopalcollegiate.org

EPISCOPAL HIGH SCHOOL

4650 Bissonnet
Bellaire, Texas 77401

Head of School: Mr. C. Edward Smith

General Information Coeducational day college-preparatory, arts, and religious studies school, affiliated with Episcopal Church. Grades 9–12. Founded: 1984. Setting: urban. Nearest major city is Houston. 35-acre campus. 7 buildings on campus. Approved or accredited by Independent Schools Association of the Southwest and Texas Department of Education. Member of National Association of Independent Schools and Secondary School Admission Test Board. Endowment: $29.8 million. Total enrollment: 680. Upper school average class size: 15. Upper school faculty-student ratio: 1:15. There are 169 required school days per year for Upper School students. Upper School students typically attend 5 days per week. The average school day consists of 8 hours.

Upper School Student Profile Grade 9: 174 students (67 boys, 107 girls); Grade 10: 183 students (84 boys, 99 girls); Grade 11: 183 students (82 boys, 101 girls); Grade 12: 156 students (87 boys, 69 girls). 20% of students are members of Episcopal Church.

Faculty School total: 85. In upper school: 40 men, 45 women; 48 have advanced degrees.

Subjects Offered 3-dimensional art, acting, advanced biology, advanced chemistry, African-American literature, algebra, all academic, American history-AP, anatomy, art history, band, Bible studies, biology, biology-AP, calculus-AP, ceramics, chemistry, choir, dance, debate, design, drawing, English, English-AP, ethics, French, French-AP, geology, geometry, government, government-AP, graphic design, health, instrumental music, journalism, Latin, music theory, newspaper, oceanography, orchestra, painting, photography, physical education, physics, physics-AP, physiology, pre-calculus, sculpture, Spanish, Spanish-AP, speech, stagecraft, statistics, theater, theology, U.S. history, U.S. history-AP, video film production, world religions, World War II, writing, yearbook.

Graduation Requirements Arts and fine arts (art, music, dance, drama), English, foreign language, mathematics, physical education (includes health), religion (includes Bible studies and theology), religious studies, science, social studies (includes history).

Special Academic Programs 14 Advanced Placement exams for which test preparation is offered; honors section; independent study.

College Admission Counseling 170 students graduated in 2016; all went to college, including Baylor University; Southern Methodist University; Texas Christian University; The University of Texas at Austin. Mean SAT critical reading: 586, mean SAT math: 590, mean SAT writing: 566, mean combined SAT: 1742, mean composite ACT: 27.

Student Life Upper grades have uniform requirement, student council, honor system. Discipline rests equally with students and faculty. Attendance at religious services is required.

Summer Programs Remediation, enrichment, advancement, sports, art/fine arts programs offered; session focuses on Enrichment, advancement; held on campus; accepts boys and girls; open to students from other schools. 120 students usually enrolled. 2017 schedule: June 5 to July 14. Application deadline: May 15.

Tuition and Aid Day student tuition: $27,025. Tuition installment plan (Insured Tuition Payment Plan, monthly payment plans). Merit scholarship grants, need-based scholarship grants available. In 2016–17, 16% of upper-school students received aid. Total amount of financial aid awarded in 2016–17: $2,229,200.

Admissions Traditional secondary-level entrance grade is 9. ISEE and Otis-Lennon School Ability Test required. Deadline for receipt of application materials: December 16. Application fee required: $75. On-campus interview recommended.

Athletics Interscholastic: ballet (boys, girls), baseball (b), basketball (b,g), cheering (g), cross-country running (b,g), dance (b,g), diving (b,g), drill team (g), field hockey (g), fitness (b,g), football (b), golf (b,g), lacrosse (b,g), physical fitness (b,g), running (b,g), soccer (b,g), softball (g), strength & conditioning (b,g), swimming and diving (b,g), tennis (b,g), track and field (b,g), volleyball (b,g), weight training (b,g), wrestling (b). 7 PE instructors, 8 coaches, 3 athletic trainers.

Computers Computers are regularly used in art, English, foreign language, history, mathematics, music, religion, science classes. Computer network features include on-campus library services, online commercial services, Internet access, wireless campus network. Student e-mail accounts are available to students. Students grades are available online. The school has a published electronic and media policy.

Contact Ms. Carol Wasden, Director of Admission. 713-512-3444. Fax: 713-512-3603. E-mail: cwasden@ehshouston.org. Website: www.ehshouston.org/

EPISCOPAL HIGH SCHOOL

1200 North Quaker Lane
Alexandria, Virginia 22302

Head of School: Mr. Charles M. Stillwell

General Information Coeducational boarding college-preparatory school. Grades 9–12. Founded: 1839. Setting: urban. Nearest major city is Washington, DC. Students are housed in single-sex dormitories. 130-acre campus. 26 buildings on campus. Approved or accredited by Southern Association of Colleges and Schools, Virginia Association of Independent Schools, and Virginia Department of Education. Member of National Association of Independent Schools and Secondary School Admission Test Board. Endowment: $214 million. Total enrollment: 435. Upper school average class size: 11. Upper school faculty-student ratio: 1:5. Upper School students typically attend 5 days per week. The average school day consists of 7 hours.

Upper School Student Profile Grade 9: 85 students (44 boys, 41 girls); Grade 10: 123 students (60 boys, 63 girls); Grade 11: 125 students (64 boys, 61 girls); Grade 12: 108 students (54 boys, 54 girls). 100% of students are boarding students. 29% are state residents. 31 states are represented in upper school student body. 13% are international students. International students from Canada, China, Republic of Korea, and United States; 15 other countries represented in student body.

Faculty School total: 68. In upper school: 38 men, 30 women; 56 have advanced degrees; 61 reside on campus.

Subjects Offered 3-dimensional art, 3-dimensional design, acting, advanced biology, advanced chemistry, advanced computer applications, advanced math, aesthetics, algebra, all academic, American government, American history, American literature, anatomy and physiology, Ancient Greek, ancient history, ancient world history, art, art and culture, art history, arts, astronomy, ballet, Bible studies, biology, biotechnology, calculus, ceramics, chemistry, Chinese, Chinese history, Chinese literature, Chinese studies, choir, Christian education, comparative religion, computer programming, computer science, computer studies, conceptual physics, dance, digital photography, drama, drawing, drawing and design, ecology, ecology, environmental systems, economics, electives, engineering, English, English composition, English literature, equality and freedom, forensics, French, French studies, genetics, geology, geometry, German, German literature, global studies, government, government/civics, Greek, guitar, health and wellness, honors algebra, honors English, honors geometry, independent study, intro to computers, introduction to digital multitrack recording techniques, Latin, linear algebra, modern politics, music theory, orchestra, painting, photography, physics, portfolio art, pre-calculus, Shakespeare, Spanish, Spanish literature, statistics, studio art, technology, theater, theater arts, theater design and production, theater production, theology, U.S. history.

Graduation Requirements Arts and fine arts (art, music, dance, drama), computer studies, English, foreign language, mathematics, physical education (includes health), science, social studies (includes history), theology.

Special Academic Programs Advanced Placement exam preparation; honors section; independent study; term-away projects; study abroad.

College Admission Counseling 126 students graduated in 2016; all went to college, including Sewanee: The University of the South; Southern Methodist University; The University of North Carolina at Chapel Hill; University of Georgia; University of Virginia. Median SAT critical reading: 620, median SAT math: 610, median SAT writing: 640, median combined SAT: 1860, median composite ACT: 27. 64% scored over 600 on SAT critical reading, 56% scored over 600 on SAT math, 71%

scored over 600 on SAT writing, 63% scored over 1800 on combined SAT, 57% scored over 26 on composite ACT.

Student Life Upper grades have specified standards of dress, student council, honor system. Discipline rests primarily with faculty. Attendance at religious services is required.

Tuition and Aid 7-day tuition and room/board: $54,250. Tuition installment plan (Insured Tuition Payment Plan, monthly payment plans). Merit scholarship grants, need-based scholarship grants, paying campus jobs available. In 2016–17, 34% of upper-school students received aid; total upper-school merit-scholarship money awarded: $189,500. Total amount of financial aid awarded in 2016–17: $6,600,000.

Admissions Traditional secondary-level entrance grade is 9. For fall 2016, 705 students applied for upper-level admission, 247 were accepted, 143 enrolled. ISEE, PSAT or SAT or SSAT required. Deadline for receipt of application materials: January 15. Application fee required: $60. Interview recommended.

Athletics Interscholastic: baseball (boys), basketball (b,g), crew (g), cross-country running (b,g), field hockey (g), football (b), golf (b), indoor track (b,g), indoor track & field (b,g), lacrosse (b,g), rowing (g), soccer (b,g), softball (g), squash (b,g), tennis (b,g), track and field (b,g), volleyball (g), winter (indoor) track (b,g), wrestling (b); intramural: strength & conditioning (b,g); coed interscholastic: climbing, fitness, outdoor education, outdoor recreation, outdoors, physical fitness, physical training, rock climbing, strength & conditioning, weight lifting, weight training; coed intramural: aerobics, aerobics/dance, aerobics/Nautilus, backpacking, ballet, canoeing/kayaking, climbing, dance, fitness, hiking/backpacking, kayaking, modern dance, outdoor activities, outdoor adventure, physical fitness, physical training, power lifting, rock climbing, soccer, wall climbing, weight lifting, weight training. 4 coaches, 2 athletic trainers.

Computers Computers are regularly used in all academic classes. Computer network features include on-campus library services, online commercial services, Internet access, wireless campus network, Internet filtering or blocking technology. Campus intranet and student e-mail accounts are available to students. Students grades are available online. The school has a published electronic and media policy.

Contact Mr. Scott Conklin, Director of Admission. 703-933-4062. Fax: 703-933-3016. E-mail: admissions@episcopalhighschool.org. Website: www.episcopalhighschool.org

EPISCOPAL HIGH SCHOOL OF JACKSONVILLE

Episcopal School of Jacksonville
4455 Atlantic Boulevard
Jacksonville, Florida 32207

Head of School: Adam Greene

General Information Coeducational day college-preparatory school, affiliated with Episcopal Church. Grades 6–12. Founded: 1966. Setting: urban. 88-acre campus. 25 buildings on campus. Approved or accredited by Florida Council of Independent Schools, National Association of Episcopal Schools, Southern Association of Colleges and Schools, and Southern Association of Independent Schools. Member of National Association of Independent Schools. Endowment: $15.4 million. Total enrollment: 857. Upper school average class size: 17. Upper school faculty-student ratio: 1:10. There are 175 required school days per year for Upper School students. Upper School students typically attend 5 days per week. The average school day consists of 6 hours and 50 minutes.

Upper School Student Profile Grade 9: 140 students (76 boys, 64 girls); Grade 10: 142 students (73 boys, 69 girls); Grade 11: 140 students (73 boys, 67 girls); Grade 12: 144 students (77 boys, 67 girls). 33% of students are members of Episcopal Church.

Faculty School total: 100. In upper school: 35 men, 58 women; 53 have advanced degrees.

Subjects Offered Advanced studio art-AP, algebra, American history, American history-AP, American literature, ancient history, art, art history, art history-AP, band, Basic programming, biology, biology-AP, calculus, calculus-AP, ceramics, chemistry, chemistry-AP, Chinese, computer programming, computer science, computer science-AP, dance, drama, earth science, economics, electronic publishing, English, English language and composition-AP, English literature and composition-AP, English/composition-AP, environmental science-AP, European history-AP, fine arts, French, French language-AP, geography, geometry, German, German-AP, government and politics-AP, government/civics, health, history, journalism, Latin, Latin-AP, marine biology, mathematics, music, music history, music theory, music theory-AP, photography, physical education, physics, physics-AP, public speaking, religion, religious studies, science, social studies, Spanish, Spanish language-AP, statistics, statistics-AP, studio art-AP, technical theater, theater, theology, trigonometry, U.S. government and politics-AP, U.S. history-AP, world history, writing, yearbook.

Graduation Requirements Arts and fine arts (art, music, dance, drama), computer science, English, foreign language, leadership, library skills, mathematics, physical education (includes health), religion (includes Bible studies and theology), science, social studies (includes history), 100 community service hours. Community service is required.

Special Academic Programs Advanced Placement exam preparation; honors section; independent study; study abroad; academic accommodation for the gifted.

College Admission Counseling 156 students graduated in 2016; all went to college, including Florida State University; University of Florida; University of North

Florida. Median SAT critical reading: 579, median SAT math: 584, median SAT writing: 567, median combined SAT: 1729, median composite ACT: 26.

Student Life Upper grades have uniform requirement, student council, honor system. Discipline rests equally with students and faculty. Attendance at religious services is required.

Summer Programs Remediation, enrichment, advancement, sports, art/fine arts, rigorous outdoor training, computer instruction programs offered; session focuses on academics, athletics, fine arts, specialty programs; held both on and off campus; accepts boys and girls; open to students from other schools. 500 students usually enrolled. 2017 schedule: May 27 to August 5. Application deadline: none.

Tuition and Aid Day student tuition: $23,500. Tuition installment plan (Insured Tuition Payment Plan, monthly payment plans). Need-based scholarship grants available. In 2016–17, 33% of upper-school students received aid. Total amount of financial aid awarded in 2016–17: $2,000,000.

Admissions Traditional secondary-level entrance grade is 9. For fall 2016, 89 students applied for upper-level admission, 58 were accepted, 38 enrolled. ISEE required. Deadline for receipt of application materials: January 1. Application fee required: $50. On-campus interview required.

Athletics Interscholastic: baseball (boys), basketball (b,g), crew (b,g), cross-country running (b,g), football (b), golf (b,g), lacrosse (b,g), modern dance (b,g), soccer (b,g), softball (g), swimming and diving (b,g), tennis (b,g), track and field (b,g), volleyball (g), weight lifting (b), weight training (b), wrestling (b); intramural: dance (g); coed interscholastic: cheering, dance, dance squad, dance team, wrestling; coed intramural: fencing. 7 PE instructors, 100 coaches, 4 athletic trainers.

Computers Computers are regularly used in all classes. Computer network features include on-campus library services, online commercial services, Internet access, wireless campus network, Internet filtering or blocking technology, Senior Systems: My BackPack online grading and student accounts, online parent portals, RSS feeds. Campus intranet, student e-mail accounts, and computer access in designated common areas are available to students. Students grades are available online. The school has a published electronic and media policy.

Contact Sam Hyde, Director of Admissions. 904-396-7104. Fax: 904-396-0981. E-mail: hydes@esj.org. Website: https://www.esj.org/

ERSKINE ACADEMY

309 Windsor Road
South China, Maine 04358

Head of School: Michael McQuarrie

General Information Coeducational day college-preparatory and general academic school. Grades 9–12. Founded: 1893. Setting: rural. Nearest major city is Augusta. Students are housed in Home Stay program where students live with families or staff members. 29-acre campus. 3 buildings on campus. Approved or accredited by New England Association of Schools and Colleges and Maine Department of Education. Total enrollment: 589. Upper school average class size: 15. Upper school faculty-student ratio: 1:9. There are 175 required school days per year for Upper School students. Upper School students typically attend 5 days per week. The average school day consists of 6 hours and 30 minutes.

Upper School Student Profile Grade 9: 161 students (81 boys, 80 girls); Grade 10: 154 students (88 boys, 66 girls); Grade 11: 146 students (76 boys, 70 girls); Grade 12: 121 students (55 boys, 66 girls). 1% of students are boarding students. 99% are state residents. 2 states are represented in upper school student body. 1% are international students. International students from China and Germany.

Faculty School total: 47. In upper school: 20 men, 27 women; 23 have advanced degrees.

Subjects Offered Accounting, advanced biology, advanced chemistry, advanced math, Advanced Placement courses, algebra, all academic, art, calculus, calculus-AP, chemistry, college admission preparation, composition-AP, concert band, drama, English, English composition, English language and composition-AP, English language-AP, English literature, ESL, French, geometry, German, global studies, government, health, health education, history, Latin, Latin-AP, life science, physics, physics-AP, psychology, psychology-AP, Russian, Spanish, Spanish-AP, speech and debate, U.S. government, U.S. history-AP, vocal ensemble, vocal jazz, world history.

Special Academic Programs 30 Advanced Placement exams for which test preparation is offered; honors section; study at local college for college credit; ESL (5 students enrolled).

College Admission Counseling 140 students graduated in 2016; 100 went to college, including University of Maine; University of Maine at Farmington; University of Southern Maine. Other: 22 went to work, 6 entered military service, 12 had other specific plans. Median SAT critical reading: 470, median SAT math: 480, median SAT writing: 450. 9% scored over 600 on SAT critical reading, 17% scored over 600 on SAT math, 7% scored over 600 on SAT writing.

Student Life Upper grades have honor system. Discipline rests primarily with faculty.

Tuition and Aid Guaranteed tuition plan. Tuition installment plan (Insured Tuition Payment Plan, 2 payment plan).

Admissions Traditional secondary-level entrance grade is 9. For fall 2016, 582 students applied for upper-level admission, 582 were accepted, 582 enrolled. TOEFL or SLEP required. Deadline for receipt of application materials: none. Application fee required: $75. Interview recommended.

Athletics Interscholastic: baseball (boys), basketball (b,g), cheering (g), cross-country running (b,g), field hockey (g), indoor track (b,g), lacrosse (b,g), soccer (b,g), softball (g), swimming and diving (b,g), tennis (b,g), winter (indoor) track (b,g); coed interscholastic: golf, wrestling; coed intramural: skiing (downhill). 2 PE instructors, 1 athletic trainer.

Computers Computers are regularly used in all academic classes. Computer network features include on-campus library services, Internet access, wireless campus network, Internet filtering or blocking technology. Student e-mail accounts are available to students. Students grades are available online. The school has a published electronic and media policy.

Contact Jamie Soule, Associate Headmaster. 207-445-2962 Ext. 1109. Fax: 207-445-5520. E-mail: jsoule@erskine247.com. Website: www.erskineacademy.org/

ESCOLA AMERICANA DE CAMPINAS

Rua Cajamar, 35
Chácara da Barra
Campinas-SP 13090-860, Brazil

Head of School: Mr. Thomas Joseph Pado

General Information Coeducational day college-preparatory, arts, and technology school; primarily serves students with learning disabilities. Grades PK–12. Founded: 1956. Setting: urban. Nearest major city is São Paulo, Brazil. 4-acre campus. 4 buildings on campus. Approved or accredited by Association of American Schools in South America, New England Association of Schools and Colleges, and Southern Association of Colleges and Schools. Affiliate member of National Association of Independent Schools; member of European Council of International Schools. Languages of instruction: English and Portuguese. Endowment: $358,000. Total enrollment: 701. Upper school average class size: 20. Upper school faculty-student ratio: 1:7. There are 200 required school days per year for Upper School students. Upper School students typically attend 5 days per week. The average school day consists of 6 hours.

Upper School Student Profile Grade 6: 53 students (27 boys, 26 girls); Grade 7: 54 students (31 boys, 23 girls); Grade 8: 48 students (23 boys, 25 girls); Grade 9: 46 students (21 boys, 25 girls); Grade 10: 34 students (19 boys, 15 girls); Grade 11: 26 students (11 boys, 15 girls); Grade 12: 38 students (21 boys, 17 girls).

Faculty School total: 88. In upper school: 20 men, 25 women; 39 have advanced degrees.

Subjects Offered Algebra, American history, American literature, art, biology, calculus, chemistry, computer science, creative writing, drama, economics, English, English literature, fine arts, geography, geometry, government/civics, grammar, history, journalism, mathematics, music, physical education, physics, Portuguese, psychology, science, social studies, speech, trigonometry, world history, world literature, writing.

Graduation Requirements Arts and fine arts (art, music, dance, drama), computer science, English, foreign language, mathematics, physical education (includes health), science, social studies (includes history), theory of knowledge. Community service is required.

Special Academic Programs International Baccalaureate program; Advanced Placement exam preparation; honors section; term-away projects; study at local college for college credit, study abroad; special instructional classes for students with mild learning differences; ESL (5 students enrolled).

College Admission Counseling 14 students graduated in 2016; 12 went to college, including Bard College; Carnegie Mellon University; Stevens Institute of Technology; University of Notre Dame; University of Pennsylvania; Wesleyan University. Other: 1 entered a postgraduate year, 1 had other specific plans. Median SAT critical reading: 660, median SAT math: 680, median SAT writing: 625, median combined SAT: 1965, median composite ACT: 25. 83% scored over 600 on SAT critical reading, 67% scored over 600 on SAT math, 33% scored over 600 on SAT writing, 67% scored over 1800 on combined SAT, 25% scored over 26 on composite ACT.

Student Life Upper grades have specified standards of dress, student council, honor system. Discipline rests primarily with faculty.

Tuition and Aid Day student tuition: 27,475 Brazilian reals–86,711 Brazilian reals. Tuition installment plan (monthly payment plans). Need-based scholarship grants available. In 2016–17, 10% of upper-school students received aid. Total amount of financial aid awarded in 2016–17: $51,000.

Admissions Traditional secondary-level entrance grade is 9. For fall 2016, 57 students applied for upper-level admission, 33 were accepted, 28 enrolled. Admissions testing, English Composition Test for ESL students, ERB CTP IV, Iowa Test, CTBS, or TAP, SAT and writing sample required. Deadline for receipt of application materials: September 31. No application fee required. On-campus interview recommended.

Athletics Interscholastic: basketball (boys, girls), canoeing/kayaking (g), cheering (g), indoor soccer (b,g), soccer (b,g), volleyball (g); intramural: ballet (g), basketball (b,g), canoeing/kayaking (g), cheering (g), climbing (b,g), indoor soccer (b,g), soccer (b,g); coed intramural: aerobics, baseball, basketball, climbing, cooperative games, fitness, flag football, Frisbee, gymnastics, handball, indoor soccer, jogging, judo, kickball, martial arts, physical fitness, self defense, soccer, softball, strength & conditioning, table tennis, track and field, ultimate Frisbee, volleyball. 5 PE instructors, 12 coaches.

Computers Computers are regularly used in art, English, history, independent study, mathematics, science, yearbook classes. Computer network features include on-campus library services, online commercial services, Internet access. Campus intranet is available to students. Students grades are available online.

Contact Mr. Mauricio Fernando Gozzi, Upper School Principal. 19-2102-1006. Fax: 19-2102-1016. E-mail: mauricio.gozzi@eac.com.br. Website: www.eac.com.br

ESCONDIDO ADVENTIST ACADEMY

1301 Deodar Road
Escondido, California 92026

Head of School: Mr. Larry Rich

General Information Coeducational day college-preparatory school, affiliated with Seventh-day Adventist Church. Grades K–12. Founded: 1903. Setting: suburban. Nearest major city is San Diego. 14-acre campus. 1 building on campus. Approved or accredited by Association of Christian Schools International, Board of Regents, General Conference of Seventh-day Adventists, Western Association of Schools and Colleges, and California Department of Education. Total enrollment: 215. Upper school average class size: 25. Upper school faculty-student ratio: 1:10. There are 180 required school days per year for Upper School students. Upper School students typically attend 5 days per week. The average school day consists of 7 hours.

Upper School Student Profile Grade 9: 20 students (11 boys, 9 girls); Grade 10: 25 students (9 boys, 16 girls); Grade 11: 30 students (18 boys, 12 girls); Grade 12: 26 students (16 boys, 10 girls). 85% of students are Seventh-day Adventists.

Faculty School total: 18. In upper school: 4 men, 7 women; 2 have advanced degrees.

Subjects Offered Advanced TOEFL/grammar, ASB Leadership, basic skills, bell choir, Bible, campus ministry, career and personal planning, English literature and composition-AP, environmental science-AP, government, physics-AP.

Graduation Requirements Arts and fine arts (art, music, dance, drama), computer science, English, mathematics, physical education (includes health), religion (includes Bible studies and theology), science, social studies (includes history), Service Learning requirement.

Special Academic Programs Advanced Placement exam preparation; honors section; independent study; ESL (16 students enrolled).

College Admission Counseling 20 students graduated in 2016; all went to college, including La Sierra University; Pacific Union College; Southern Adventist University; Walla Walla University.

Student Life Upper grades have uniform requirement, student council, honor system. Discipline rests primarily with faculty. Attendance at religious services is required.

Tuition and Aid Day student tuition: $4830–$8500. Tuition installment plan (FACTS Tuition Payment Plan, monthly payment plans, individually arranged payment plans). Tuition reduction for siblings, need-based scholarship grants, church scholarships available. In 2016–17, 15% of upper-school students received aid. Total amount of financial aid awarded in 2016–17: $50,000.

Admissions Traditional secondary-level entrance grade is 9. For fall 2016, 120 students applied for upper-level admission, 115 were accepted, 101 enrolled. Deadline for receipt of application materials: none. Application fee required: $175. On-campus interview required.

Athletics Interscholastic: basketball (boys, girls), golf (b), soccer (b), softball (g), volleyball (b,g); intramural: basketball (b,g), flag football (b,g), softball (b). 2 PE instructors, 6 coaches.

Computers Computers are regularly used in computer applications classes. Computer network features include on-campus library services, Internet access, wireless campus network, Internet filtering or blocking technology. Computer access in designated common areas is available to students. Students grades are available online. The school has a published electronic and media policy.

Contact Gail Hall, Registrar. 760-746-1800. Fax: 760-743-3499. E-mail: registrar@eaaschool.org. Website: www.eaaschool.org

ESCUELA CAMPO ALEGRE

Final Calle La Cinta Las Mercedes
Caracas, Venezuela

Head of School: Mr. Terence Christian

General Information Coeducational day college-preparatory school. Grades N–12. Founded: 1937. Setting: urban. 7-acre campus. 2 buildings on campus. Approved or accredited by Council of International Schools and Middle States Association of Colleges and Schools. Language of instruction: English. Total enrollment: 480. Upper school average class size: 14. Upper school faculty-student ratio: 1:6. There are 183 required school days per year for Upper School students. Upper School students typically attend 5 days per week. The average school day consists of 1 hours and 30 minutes.

Upper School Student Profile Grade 9: 30 students (19 boys, 11 girls); Grade 10: 27 students (16 boys, 11 girls); Grade 11: 23 students (8 boys, 15 girls); Grade 12: 22 students (10 boys, 12 girls).

Faculty School total: 72. In upper school: 15 men, 14 women; 25 have advanced degrees.

Special Academic Programs International Baccalaureate program; ESL.

College Admission Counseling 39 students graduated in 2016; all went to college, including Boston University; Florida International University; Georgetown University; Georgia Institute of Technology; New York University; Northeastern University.

Student Life Upper grades have uniform requirement, student council, honor system. Discipline rests primarily with faculty.

Tuition and Aid Day student tuition: $29,500.

Admissions Traditional secondary-level entrance grade is 10. For fall 2016, 6 students applied for upper-level admission, 6 were accepted, 5 enrolled. Application fee required: 500 Venezuelan bolivars. Interview required.

Athletics Interscholastic: basketball (boys, girls), soccer (b,g), volleyball (b,g); intramural: basketball (b,g), soccer (b,g), volleyball (b,g); coed interscholastic: swimming and diving; coed intramural: cooperative games. 3 PE instructors.

Computers Computers are regularly used in all classes. Computer network features include on-campus library services, Internet access, Internet filtering or blocking technology. Campus intranet and student e-mail accounts are available to students. Students grades are available online.

Contact Mrs. MONICA RIVERO, DIRECTOR OF ADMISSIONS. 58-2129933922 Ext. 1011. E-mail: admissions@ecak12.com. Website: http://www.ecak12.com/

EXCEL CHRISTIAN ACADEMY

325 Old Mill Road
Cartersville, Georgia 30120

Head of School: Mrs. Tamara C. Griffith

General Information Coeducational day college-preparatory school. Grades K–12. Founded: 1993. Setting: suburban. 15-acre campus. 1 building on campus. Approved or accredited by Association of Christian Schools International, Southern Association of Colleges and Schools, and Georgia Department of Education. Total enrollment: 297. Upper school average class size: 15. Upper school faculty-student ratio: 1:12. There are 178 required school days per year for Upper School students. Upper School students typically attend 5 days per week. The average school day consists of 7 hours and 25 minutes.

Upper School Student Profile Grade 6: 17 students (6 boys, 11 girls); Grade 7: 11 students (4 boys, 7 girls); Grade 8: 12 students (5 boys, 7 girls); Grade 9: 13 students (6 boys, 7 girls); Grade 10: 14 students (8 boys, 6 girls); Grade 11: 14 students (4 boys, 10 girls); Grade 12: 18 students (7 boys, 11 girls).

Faculty School total: 25. In upper school: 5 men, 12 women; 10 have advanced degrees.

Subjects Offered Advanced biology, advanced math, Advanced Placement courses, algebra, American government, American history, American history-AP, American literature, anatomy, anatomy and physiology, art, band, Bible, Bible studies, biology, biology-AP, British literature, broadcast journalism, business education, calculus, calculus-AP, chemistry, choir, chorus, computer applications, concert band, dance, drama, earth science, economics, economics-AP, electives, English, English language-AP, English literature, English literature and composition-AP, foreign language, geometry, government, government-AP, health, health education, history, life science, literature, mathematics, music, personal finance, personal fitness, physical education, physical fitness, physical science, physics, pre-algebra, pre-calculus, psychology, reading, science, social studies, Spanish, trigonometry, U.S. government, U.S. history, U.S. history-AP, Web site design, work-study, world geography, world history, world history-AP, yearbook.

Graduation Requirements Advanced Placement courses, American government, American history, Bible, chemistry, computer technologies, economics, electives, English, foreign language, geography, government, health, history, mathematics, physical education (includes health), science, senior career experience, social studies (includes history), Spanish, world history. Community service is required.

Special Academic Programs 2 Advanced Placement exams for which test preparation is offered; honors section; independent study; study at local college for college credit; academic accommodation for the gifted.

College Admission Counseling 27 students graduated in 2016; all went to college, including Georgia Institute of Technology; Kennesaw State University; Truett McConnell University; University of West Georgia; Valdosta State University. Mean SAT critical reading: 461, mean SAT math: 504, mean SAT writing: 516, mean combined SAT: 1481. 11% scored over 600 on SAT critical reading, 17% scored over 600 on SAT math, 17% scored over 600 on SAT writing, 17% scored over 1800 on combined SAT, 25% scored over 26 on composite ACT.

Student Life Upper grades have uniform requirement, student council, honor system. Discipline rests primarily with faculty. Attendance at religious services is required.

Summer Programs Remediation programs offered; held on campus; accepts boys and girls; not open to students from other schools. 5 students usually enrolled. 2017 schedule: June to June. Application deadline: June.

Tuition and Aid Day student tuition: $10,200. Tuition installment plan (monthly payment plans). Need-based scholarship grants available.

Admissions Traditional secondary-level entrance grade is 9. Admissions testing and any standardized test required. Deadline for receipt of application materials: none. Application fee required: $125. On-campus interview recommended.

Athletics Interscholastic: baseball (boys), basketball (b,g), cheering (g), cross-country running (b,g), soccer (b,g), softball (g), strength & conditioning (b,g), track and field (b,g), weight training (b,g); intramural: football (b). 1 PE instructor.

Computers Computers are regularly used in all academic, business applications, computer applications, newspaper, yearbook classes. Computer network features include on-campus library services, Internet access, wireless campus network, Internet filtering or blocking technology. Computer access in designated common areas is available to students. Students grades are available online. The school has a published electronic and media policy.

Contact Mrs. Sheila I. Langford, Assistant Principal. 770-382-9488. Fax: 770-606-9884. E-mail: tgriffith@excelca.org. Website: www.excelca.org

EXPLORATIONS ACADEMY

PO Box 3014
Bellingham, Washington 98227

Head of School: Abram Dickerson

General Information Coeducational day and distance learning college-preparatory, general academic, experiential education, and international field study expeditions school. Grades 9–12. Founded: 1995. Setting: small town. Nearest major city is Vancouver, BC, Canada. 1-acre campus. 1 building on campus. Approved or accredited by Northwest Accreditation Commission, Northwest Association of Independent Schools, and Northwest Association of Schools and Colleges. Total enrollment: 35. Upper school average class size: 10. Upper school faculty-student ratio: 1:7. There are 177 required school days per year for Upper School students. Upper School students typically attend 5 days per week. The average school day consists of 6 hours.

Upper School Student Profile Grade 9: 2 students (2 girls); Grade 10: 8 students (8 boys); Grade 11: 6 students (3 boys, 3 girls); Grade 12: 4 students (2 boys, 2 girls).

Faculty School total: 11. In upper school: 5 men, 3 women; 3 have advanced degrees.

Subjects Offered Agriculture, American literature, anatomy and physiology, anthropology, archaeology, art, boat building, botany, calculus, carpentry, chemistry, Chinese, computer graphics, computer programming, conflict resolution, construction, creative writing, desktop publishing, drawing, earth science, ecology, environmental science, first aid, gardening, gender issues, geology, government, health, horticulture, human relations, journalism, Latin American studies, leadership, marine biology, media, meteorology, microbiology, music, music history, painting, philosophy, photography, physical education, physics, poetry, political science, printmaking, psychology, sculpture, sexuality, short story, Spanish, technology, theater design and production, video film production, world cultures, world geography, world history, world literature, writing.

Graduation Requirements Arts and fine arts (art, music, dance, drama), computer science, English, foreign language, human relations, lab science, mathematics, occupational education, physical education (includes health), science, social sciences, social studies (includes history), U.S. government and politics, Washington State and Northwest History, world history, one term of self-designed interdisciplinary studies, one month-long international study/service expedition. Community service is required.

Special Academic Programs Advanced Placement exam preparation; honors section; accelerated programs; independent study; term-away projects; academic accommodation for the gifted.

College Admission Counseling 8 students graduated in 2016; 5 went to college, including Berklee College of Music; The Evergreen State College; University of Washington; Western Washington University. Other: 1 went to work, 2 had other specific plans.

Student Life Upper grades have student council, honor system. Discipline rests equally with students and faculty.

Summer Programs Enrichment, advancement, art/fine arts, rigorous outdoor training, computer instruction programs offered; session focuses on experiential learning; held both on and off campus; accepts boys and girls; open to students from other schools. 12 students usually enrolled. 2017 schedule: July 8 to August 16. Application deadline: none.

Tuition and Aid Day student tuition: $8000–$16,000. Tuition installment plan (monthly payment plans, individually arranged payment plans, school's own payment plan). Merit scholarship grants, need-based scholarship grants, need-based loans, low-interest loans with deferred payment available. In 2016–17, 48% of upper-school students received aid. Total amount of financial aid awarded in 2016–17: $200,000.

Admissions Traditional secondary-level entrance grade is 9. For fall 2016, 25 students applied for upper-level admission, 20 were accepted, 20 enrolled. Non-standardized placement tests required. Deadline for receipt of application materials: none. Application fee required: $35. Interview recommended.

Athletics 3 PE instructors.

Computers Computers are regularly used in animation, art, English, French, graphics, mathematics, media production, publications, SAT preparation, science, writing, yearbook classes. Computer resources include online commercial services, Internet access, wireless campus network. Computer access in designated common areas is available to students. The school has a published electronic and media policy.

Contact Kathy Winkle, Connections Coordinator. 360-671-8085. Fax: 360-671-2521. E-mail: info@explorationsacademy.org.
Website: http://www.ExplorationsAcademy.org

EZELL-HARDING CHRISTIAN SCHOOL

574 Bell Road
Antioch, Tennessee 37013

Head of School: Mrs. Belvia Pruitt

General Information Coeducational day college-preparatory, religious studies, and STEM school, affiliated with Church of Christ. Grades PK–12. Founded: 1973. Setting: suburban. Nearest major city is Nashville. 30-acre campus. 1 building on campus. Approved or accredited by National Christian School Association and Southern Association of Colleges and Schools. Endowment: $100,000. Total enrollment: 431. Upper school average class size: 17. Upper school faculty-student ratio: 1:9. There are 176 required school days per year for Upper School students. Upper School students typically attend 5 days per week. The average school day consists of 7 hours.

Upper School Student Profile Grade 9: 22 students (11 boys, 11 girls); Grade 10: 38 students (24 boys, 14 girls); Grade 11: 48 students (24 boys, 24 girls); Grade 12: 45 students (18 boys, 27 girls). 25% of students are members of Church of Christ.

Faculty School total: 21. In upper school: 10 men, 11 women; 16 have advanced degrees.

Subjects Offered ACT preparation, advanced biology, advanced chemistry, advanced math, Advanced Placement courses, algebra, American history, American history-AP, anatomy and physiology, art, band, Bible, biology, biotechnology, calculus, calculus-AP, chemistry, chorus, computer applications, economics, English literature and composition-AP, European history-AP, fitness, geography, geometry, government, grammar, keyboarding, physical science, pre-calculus, psychology, science, Spanish, statistics-AP, trigonometry, weight training, wellness, world history.

Graduation Requirements All academic, American government, American history, arts and fine arts (art, music, dance, drama), Bible, chemistry, computer literacy, computer science, computer skills, economics, electives, English, foreign language, geography, health and wellness, keyboarding, mathematics, physical education (includes health), religion (includes Bible studies and theology), science, social studies (includes history), Spanish, technology, typing. Community service is required.

Special Academic Programs 5 Advanced Placement exams for which test preparation is offered; honors section; independent study; study at local college for college credit.

College Admission Counseling 37 students graduated in 2016; 36 went to college, including Freed-Hardeman University; Lipscomb University; Middle Tennessee State University; Tennessee Technological University; The University of Tennessee; The University of Tennessee at Chattanooga. Other: 1 had other specific plans. Median composite ACT: 24, 34% scored over 26 on composite ACT.

Student Life Upper grades have uniform requirement, student council. Discipline rests primarily with faculty.

Tuition and Aid Day student tuition: $9000. Tuition installment plan (The Tuition Plan, monthly payment plans). Need-based scholarship grants available. In 2016–17, 30% of upper-school students received aid. Total amount of financial aid awarded in 2016–17: $136,000.

Admissions Traditional secondary-level entrance grade is 9. For fall 2016, 10 students applied for upper-level admission, 7 were accepted, 5 enrolled. MAT 7 Metropolitan Achievement Test, TOEFL or SLEP or writing sample required. Deadline for receipt of application materials: none. Application fee required: $75. On-campus interview recommended.

Athletics Interscholastic: baseball (boys), basketball (b,g), bowling (b,g), cheering (g), cross-country running (b,g), drill team (g), football (b), golf (b,g), soccer (b,g), softball (g), tennis (b,g), track and field (b,g), volleyball (g). 1 PE instructor, 6 coaches, 1 athletic trainer.

Computers Computers are regularly used in all academic classes. Computer network features include on-campus library services, Internet access, wireless campus network, Internet filtering or blocking technology. Student e-mail accounts are available to students. Students grades are available online. The school has a published electronic and media policy.

Contact Mrs. Lisa Phillips, Admissions Officer. 615-367-0532 Ext. 109. Fax: 615-399-8747. E-mail: lphillips@ezellharding.com. Website: www.ezellharding.com

FAIRFIELD COLLEGE PREPARATORY SCHOOL

1073 North Benson Road
Fairfield, Connecticut 06824-5157

Head of School: Rev. John J. Hanwell, SJ

General Information Boys' day college-preparatory, arts, religious studies, and technology school, affiliated with Roman Catholic Church. Grades 9–12. Founded: 1942. Setting: suburban. Nearest major city is Bridgeport. 220-acre campus. 4 buildings on campus. Approved or accredited by Jesuit Secondary Education Association, New England Association of Schools and Colleges, and Connecticut Department of Education. Member of National Association of Independent Schools. Endowment: $17 million. Total enrollment: 901. Upper school average class size: 21. Upper school faculty-student ratio: 1:18. There are 182 required school days per year for Upper School students. Upper School students typically attend 5 days per week. The average school day consists of 5 hours and 50 minutes.

Upper School Student Profile Grade 9: 249 students (249 boys); Grade 10: 211 students (211 boys); Grade 11: 222 students (222 boys); Grade 12: 219 students (219 boys). 68% of students are Roman Catholic.

Faculty School total: 55. In upper school: 33 men, 22 women; 49 have advanced degrees.

Subjects Offered Advanced Placement courses, algebra, American Civil War, American government, American history, American history-AP, American literature, American literature-AP, art, Asian studies, band, biology, biology-AP, British literature, British literature-AP, calculus, calculus-AP, career exploration, chemistry, chemistry-AP, choir, chorus, Christian education, Christian ethics, Christian scripture, Christian studies, Christianity, civil rights, Civil War, college admission preparation, college planning, community service, computer education, computer literacy, computer science, constitutional history of U.S., constitutional law, creative writing, drama, drama workshop, drawing and design, driver education, economics, English, English literature, English literature and composition-AP, English literature-AP, English-AP, environmental science, ethical decision making, ethics and responsibility, European history, European history-AP, expository writing, fine arts, French, French language-AP, French literature-AP, French-AP, geometry, government-AP, grammar, graphics, guidance, history, history of religion, history of the Catholic Church, honors algebra, honors English, honors geometry, honors U.S. history, introduction to theater, jazz band, journalism, language and composition, language arts, language structure, Latin, Latin-AP, Life of Christ, literary magazine, mathematics, Middle East, modern European history-AP, moral theology, music, musical productions, musical theater, physics, physics-AP, pre-calculus, religion, remedial study skills, SAT preparation, science, social justice, social studies, sociology, Spanish, Spanish language-AP, Spanish-AP, student government, studio art, symphonic band, technical drawing, theater, theater arts, theology, trigonometry, U.S. constitutional history, U.S. history-AP, United States government-AP, values and decisions, visual and performing arts, visual arts, Web site design, Western civilization, wind ensemble, word processing, world history, world literature, world religions, world religions, world studies, World War I, World War II, writing.

Graduation Requirements Arts and fine arts (art, music, dance, drama), computer science, English, foreign language, mathematics, religion (includes Bible studies and theology), science, social studies (includes history), senior comprehensive exercises. Community service is required.

Special Academic Programs Advanced Placement exam preparation; honors section; study at local college for college credit.

College Admission Counseling 201 students graduated in 2015; 193 went to college, including College of the Holy Cross; Loyola University Maryland; Saint Joseph's University; University of Connecticut; University of Notre Dame; Villanova University. Other: 8 entered a postgraduate year. Mean SAT critical reading: 588, mean SAT math: 604, mean SAT writing: 594, mean combined SAT: 1786.

Student Life Upper grades have specified standards of dress, student council. Discipline rests primarily with faculty. Attendance at religious services is required.

Tuition and Aid Day student tuition: $18,675. Tuition installment plan (FACTS Tuition Payment Plan). Need-based scholarship grants available. In 2015–16, 29% of upper-school students received aid. Total amount of financial aid awarded in 2015–16: $2,163,000.

Admissions Traditional secondary-level entrance grade is 9. For fall 2015, 481 students applied for upper-level admission, 249 enrolled. High School Placement Test required. Deadline for receipt of application materials: December 1. Application fee required: $60.

Athletics Interscholastic: baseball, basketball, bowling, crew, cross-country running, diving, fencing, football, golf, ice hockey, indoor track & field, lacrosse, rugby, sailing, skiing (downhill), soccer, strength & conditioning, swimming and diving, tennis, track and field, weight training, winter (indoor) track, wrestling; intramural: alpine skiing, basketball, bicycling, fitness, flag football, mountain biking, skiing (downhill), strength & conditioning, table tennis, weight lifting, weight training, whiffle ball. 33 coaches, 2 athletic trainers.

Computers Computers are regularly used in art, English, foreign language, history, mathematics, science, technology, theology classes. Computer network features include on-campus library services, online commercial services, Internet access, Internet filtering or blocking technology. Student e-mail accounts are available to students. Students grades are available online. The school has a published electronic and media policy.

Contact Mr. Andrew M. Davenport, Admissions Counselor. 203-254-4210. Fax: 203-254-4108. E-mail: adavenport@fairfieldprep.org. Website: www.fairfieldprep.org

FAITH CHRISTIAN HIGH SCHOOL

3105 Colusa Highway
Yuba City, California 95993

Head of School: Mr. Stephen Finlay

General Information Coeducational day college-preparatory and religious studies school, affiliated with Christian faith. Grades 9–12. Founded: 1975. Setting: small town. Nearest major city is Sacramento. 10-acre campus. 4 buildings on campus. Approved or accredited by Association of Christian Schools International, Western Association of Schools and Colleges, and California Department of Education. Total enrollment: 77. Upper school average class size: 25. Upper school faculty-student ratio:

1:9. There are 175 required school days per year for Upper School students. Upper School students typically attend 5 days per week. The average school day consists of 5 hours and 30 minutes.

Upper School Student Profile Grade 9: 16 students (6 boys, 10 girls); Grade 10: 21 students (13 boys, 8 girls); Grade 11: 21 students (13 boys, 8 girls); Grade 12: 17 students (7 boys, 10 girls). 85% of students are Christian faith.

Faculty School total: 14. In upper school: 9 men, 5 women; 4 have advanced degrees.

Subjects Offered Algebra, anatomy and physiology, arts, Bible, biology, biology-AP, British literature, calculus-AP, chemistry, civics, computer science, computer studies, concert band, drama, economics, English, English composition, English literature, English-AP, geography, geometry, government, health, honors English, physical education, physical science, pre-calculus, senior project, Spanish, U.S. history, world geography, world history, yearbook.

Graduation Requirements Algebra, Bible, biology, civics, economics, English, geometry, health, physical science, senior project, U.S. history, world geography, world history.

Special Academic Programs Advanced Placement exam preparation; study at local college for college credit.

College Admission Counseling 17 students graduated in 2016; all went to college, including California State University, Northridge; Grand Canyon University; Oregon State University; Penn State University Park; Sonoma State University; University of Portland. Median SAT critical reading: 580, median SAT math: 540, median SAT writing: 550, median combined SAT: 1640, median composite ACT: 20. 30% scored over 600 on SAT critical reading, 20% scored over 600 on SAT math, 30% scored over 600 on SAT writing, 30% scored over 1800 on combined SAT, 25% scored over 26 on composite ACT.

Student Life Upper grades have specified standards of dress, student council, honor system. Discipline rests primarily with faculty. Attendance at religious services is required.

Tuition and Aid Day student tuition: $9630. Tuition installment plan (monthly payment plans). Tuition reduction for siblings, need-based scholarship grants available. In 2016–17, 30% of upper-school students received aid. Total amount of financial aid awarded in 2016–17: $50,000.

Admissions Traditional secondary-level entrance grade is 9. For fall 2016, 14 students applied for upper-level admission, 14 were accepted, 14 enrolled. Achievement tests required. Deadline for receipt of application materials: none. Application fee required: $50. On-campus interview recommended.

Athletics Interscholastic: baseball (boys), basketball (b,g), cheering (g), soccer (b), softball (g), volleyball (g); coed interscholastic: cross-country running, golf, pillo polo, riflery, ropes courses, rugby. 2 PE instructors, 7 coaches.

Computers Computers are regularly used in all academic classes. Computer network features include on-campus library services, Internet access, Internet filtering or blocking technology. Students grades are available online. The school has a published electronic and media policy.

Contact Mrs. Cindy Reimers, Secretary. 530-674-5474. Fax: 530-674-0194. E-mail: creimers@fcs-k12.org. Website: www.fcs-k12.org

FAITH CHRISTIAN SCHOOL

7464 E Main St
Mesa, Arizona 85207

Head of School: Mr. Dick Buckingham

General Information Coeducational day college-preparatory and general academic school, affiliated with Christian faith. Grades K–12. Founded: 1988. Setting: suburban. 1 building on campus. Approved or accredited by Association of Christian Schools International, Christian Schools International, and North Central Association of Colleges and Schools. Upper school average class size: 20. Upper school faculty-student ratio: 1:15. There are 185 required school days per year for Upper School students. Upper School students typically attend 5 days per week. The average school day consists of 6 hours and 20 minutes.

Upper School Student Profile 90% of students are Christian.

Faculty School total: 14. In upper school: 4 men, 3 women; 4 have advanced degrees.

Subjects Offered Acting, algebra, American government, American history, American literature, ancient world history, art, athletics, band, Basic programming, basketball, Bible, Bible studies, biology, British literature, calculus, chemistry, chorus, Christian and Hebrew scripture, Christian doctrine, Christian ethics, Christian testament, civics/free enterprise, college admission preparation, computer applications, computer education, consumer mathematics, debate, drama, economics, English, general math, government, Greek, guitar, math applications, New Testament, physical education, physics, pre-algebra, pre-calculus, senior seminar, senior thesis, Spanish, U.S. history, volleyball, world cultures, world religions, yearbook.

College Admission Counseling 14 students graduated in 2016; all went to college, including Arizona State University at the Tempe campus; Grand Canyon University.

Student Life Upper grades have uniform requirement, student council. Discipline rests primarily with faculty. Attendance at religious services is required.

Tuition and Aid Day student tuition: $7900. Tuition installment plan (FACTS Tuition Payment Plan). Tuition reduction for siblings, need-based scholarship grants available.

Admissions Traditional secondary-level entrance grade is 9. Deadline for receipt of application materials: none. Application fee required: $250.

Athletics Interscholastic: basketball (boys, girls), cross-country running (b), soccer (b,g), volleyball (g). 2 PE instructors, 2 coaches.

Computers Computers are regularly used in computer applications, keyboarding, word processing, yearbook classes. Computer network features include Internet access, Internet filtering or blocking technology. Students grades are available online.

Contact Admissions. 480-833-1983. Fax: 480-361-2075. E-mail: admissions@faith-christian.org. Website: www.faith-christian.org

FAITH LUTHERAN HIGH SCHOOL

2015 South Hualapai Way
Las Vegas, Nevada 89117-6949

Head of School: Dr. Steven J. Buuck

General Information Coeducational day college-preparatory and law, STEM school, affiliated with Lutheran Church–Missouri Synod. Grades 6–12. Founded: 1979. Setting: suburban. 49-acre campus. 5 buildings on campus. Approved or accredited by Association of Christian Schools International and Nevada Department of Education. Endowment: $1.9 million. Total enrollment: 1,572. Upper school average class size: 21. Upper school faculty-student ratio: 1:17. There are 180 required school days per year for Upper School students. Upper School students typically attend 5 days per week. The average school day consists of 7 hours.

Upper School Student Profile Grade 6: 258 students (121 boys, 137 girls); Grade 7: 268 students (147 boys, 121 girls); Grade 8: 314 students (170 boys, 144 girls); Grade 9: 261 students (140 boys, 121 girls); Grade 10: 264 students (140 boys, 124 girls); Grade 11: 234 students (119 boys, 115 girls); Grade 12: 196 students (93 boys, 103 girls). 19% of students are Lutheran Church–Missouri Synod.

Faculty School total: 113. In upper school: 31 men, 45 women; 71 have advanced degrees.

Subjects Offered Advanced Placement courses, algebra, American history, art, biology, chemistry, computer science, earth science, English, fine arts, fitness, geometry, German, health, mathematics, music, physical education, physical science, religion, SAT/ACT preparation, science, social studies, Spanish.

Graduation Requirements American history, arts and fine arts (art, music, dance, drama), computer science, English, foreign language, mathematics, physical education (includes health), religion (includes Bible studies and theology), science, social studies (includes history), community service.

Special Academic Programs 7 Advanced Placement exams for which test preparation is offered; honors section; independent study; study at local college for college credit; programs in general development for dyslexic students.

College Admission Counseling 220 students graduated in 2016; 217 went to college, including Grand Canyon University; Northern Arizona University; University of Nevada, Las Vegas; University of Nevada, Reno. Other: 3 went to work. Median SAT critical reading: 534, median SAT math: 534, median SAT writing: 537, median combined SAT: 1605, median composite ACT: 24. 25% scored over 600 on SAT critical reading, 25% scored over 600 on SAT math, 20% scored over 600 on SAT writing, 23% scored over 1800 on combined SAT, 30% scored over 26 on composite ACT.

Student Life Upper grades have uniform requirement, student council. Discipline rests primarily with faculty. Attendance at religious services is required.

Summer Programs Remediation programs offered; held on campus; accepts boys and girls; not open to students from other schools. 125 students usually enrolled.

Tuition and Aid Day student tuition: $11,500. Tuition installment plan (SMART Tuition Payment Plan, monthly payment plans). Tuition reduction for siblings, need-based scholarship grants available. In 2016–17, 13% of upper-school students received aid. Total amount of financial aid awarded in 2016–17: $635,000.

Admissions Traditional secondary-level entrance grade is 9. For fall 2016, 161 students applied for upper-level admission, 151 were accepted, 145 enrolled. High School Placement Test and Stanford 9 required. Deadline for receipt of application materials: none. Application fee required: $350. Interview recommended.

Athletics Interscholastic: aerobics/dance (girls), aquatics (b,g), baseball (b), basketball (b,g), cheering (g), cross-country running (b,g), dance team (g), football (b), golf (b,g), lacrosse (b,g), soccer (b,g), softball (g), swimming and diving (b,g), tennis (b,g), track and field (b,g), volleyball (g), wrestling (b); intramural: strength & conditioning (b,g), weight training (b,g); coed interscholastic: strength & conditioning; coed intramural: skiing (downhill), snowboarding, ultimate Frisbee. 7 PE instructors, 26 coaches, 1 athletic trainer.

Computers Computers are regularly used in keyboarding, yearbook classes. Computer network features include on-campus library services, online commercial services, Internet access, wireless campus network, Internet filtering or blocking technology. Student e-mail accounts and computer access in designated common areas are available to students. Students grades are available online. The school has a published electronic and media policy.

Contact Mr. Joel Arnold, Director of Admissions. 702-804-4413. Fax: 702-562-7728. E-mail: arnoldj@flhsemail.org. Website: www.faithlutheranlv.org

FALMOUTH ACADEMY

7 Highfield Drive
Falmouth, Massachusetts 02540

Head of School: Mr. Stephen A. Duffy

General Information Coeducational day college-preparatory, arts, and liberal arts, college prep school. Grades 7–12. Founded: 1976. Setting: small town. Nearest major city is Boston. 34-acre campus. 3 buildings on campus. Approved or accredited by Association of Independent Schools in New England, New England Association of Schools and Colleges, and Massachusetts Department of Education. Member of National Association of Independent Schools and Secondary School Admission Test Board. Endowment: $6.5 million. Total enrollment: 200. Upper school average class size: 12. Upper school faculty-student ratio: 1:4. There are 170 required school days per year for Upper School students. Upper School students typically attend 5 days per week. The average school day consists of 6 hours and 35 minutes.

Upper School Student Profile Grade 9: 32 students (15 boys, 17 girls); Grade 10: 38 students (19 boys, 19 girls); Grade 11: 32 students (16 boys, 16 girls); Grade 12: 28 students (14 boys, 14 girls).

Faculty School total: 40. In upper school: 11 men, 22 women; 23 have advanced degrees.

Subjects Offered Advanced biology, advanced chemistry, advanced math, algebra, all academic, American culture, American history, American literature, art, Basic programming, biology, calculus, ceramics, character education, chemistry, choral music, creative writing, DNA science lab, drama, drama performance, drawing and design, earth science, ecology, English, English literature, environmental science, European history, expository writing, film, fine arts, French, French as a second language, gardening, geography, geology, geometry, German, grammar, health, history, humanities, independent study, instrumental music, jazz band, journalism, Latin, literary magazine, mathematics, music, orchestra, painting, participation in sports, photo shop, photography, physical education, physical science, physics, play/screen writing, pre-calculus, reading/study skills, SAT preparation, science, science project, science research, sculpture, social studies, speech and oral interpretations, statistics, student government, student teaching, studio art, study skills, theater, theater design and production, theater production, trigonometry, U.S. history, wellness, woodworking, world affairs, world civilizations, world history, world literature, writing.

Graduation Requirements American history, art, arts and fine arts (art, music, dance, drama), chemistry, classical studies, electives, English, foreign language, history, mathematics, science, world history.

Special Academic Programs 5 Advanced Placement exams for which test preparation is offered; independent study; term-away projects; study abroad.

College Admission Counseling 26 students graduated in 2016; all went to college, including Johns Hopkins University; Marist College; Tufts University; University of Massachusetts Amherst; Wellesley College; Yale University. Mean SAT critical reading: 679, mean SAT math: 656, mean SAT writing: 660.

Student Life Upper grades have specified standards of dress, student council, honor system. Discipline rests primarily with faculty.

Tuition and Aid Day student tuition: $28,990. Tuition installment plan (TADS installment plan, school administered payment plan). Merit scholarship grants, need-based scholarship grants, need-based loans available. In 2016–17, 50% of upper-school students received aid; total upper school merit-scholarship money awarded: $6000. Total amount of financial aid awarded in 2016–17: $1,300,000.

Admissions Traditional secondary-level entrance grade is 9. For fall 2016, 36 students applied for upper-level admission, 26 were accepted, 21 enrolled. ISEE, SSAT or TOEFL required. Deadline for receipt of application materials: February 15. Application fee required: $65. On-campus interview recommended.

Athletics Interscholastic: basketball (boys, girls), lacrosse (b,g), soccer (b,g). 1 PE instructor, 2 coaches, 1 athletic trainer.

Computers Computers are regularly used in design, English, foreign language, humanities, mathematics, science classes. Computer network features include on-campus library services, Internet access, wireless campus network, Internet filtering or blocking technology. Student e-mail accounts are available to students. The school has a published electronic and media policy.

Contact Ms. Karen A. Loder, Director of Admission and Enrollment Management. 508-457-9696 Ext. 236. Fax: 508-457-4112. E-mail: kloder@falmouthacademy.org. Website: www.falmouthacademy.org

FATHER DUENAS MEMORIAL SCHOOL

Mangilao
PO Box FD
Hagatna, Guam 96910

Head of School: Mr. Tony Thompson

General Information Boys' day college-preparatory and College Preparatory school, affiliated with Roman Catholic Church. Grades 9–12. Founded: 1948. Setting: rural. 9 buildings on campus. Approved or accredited by The College Board, Western Association of Schools and Colleges, Western Catholic Education Association, and Guam Department of Education. Member of Secondary School Admission Test Board. Total enrollment: 435. Upper school average class size: 25. Upper school faculty-student ratio: 1:25. There are 180 required school days per year for Upper School students. Upper School students typically attend 5 days per week. The average school day consists of 7 hours.

Upper School Student Profile Grade 9: 102 students (102 boys); Grade 10: 86 students (86 boys); Grade 11: 130 students (130 boys); Grade 12: 119 students (119 boys). 70% of students are Roman Catholic.

Faculty School total: 35. In upper school: 17 men, 18 women; 10 have advanced degrees.

Subjects Offered Microeconomics-AP, naval science, psychology-AP.

Special Academic Programs Advanced Placement exam preparation; study at local college for college credit.

College Admission Counseling 101 students graduated in 2016; 90 went to college, including Chaminade University of Honolulu; Saint Mary's College of California; Seattle University; University of Guam; University of Portland; University of San Francisco. Other: 5 went to work, 4 entered military service, 1 had other specific plans.

Student Life Upper grades have uniform requirement, student council, honor system. Discipline rests primarily with faculty. Attendance at religious services is required.

Summer Programs Remediation programs offered; held on campus; accepts boys and girls; open to students from other schools. 15 students usually enrolled. 2017 schedule: June 1 to July 7.

Tuition and Aid Day student tuition: $8000. Tuition reduction for siblings, merit scholarship grants, need-based scholarship grants available.

Admissions Traditional secondary-level entrance grade is 9. Otis-Lennon Mental Ability Test, Reading for Understanding and WRAT required. Deadline for receipt of application materials: May 30. Application fee required: $45.

Athletics Interscholastic: baseball, basketball, canoeing/kayaking, cross-country running, drill team, football, golf, JROTC drill, paddling, rugby, soccer, tennis, track and field, volleyball, wrestling; intramural: basketball, Frisbee, indoor soccer, table tennis, ultimate Frisbee, volleyball. 4 PE instructors, 30 coaches.

Computers Computer network features include on-campus library services, online commercial services, Internet access, wireless campus network, Internet filtering or blocking technology. Student e-mail accounts are available to students. Students grades are available online. The school has a published electronic and media policy.

Contact Mrs. Angela Thompson, Registrar. 671-734-2261. Fax: 671-734-5738. E-mail: iperez@fatherduenas.com. Website: www.fatherduenas.com

FATHER LOPEZ HIGH SCHOOL

3918 LPGA Boulevard
Daytona Beach, Florida 32124

Head of School: Dr. Michael J. Coury

General Information Coeducational day college-preparatory and religious studies school, affiliated with Roman Catholic Church. Grades 9–12. Founded: 1959. Setting: suburban. 90-acre campus. 7 buildings on campus. Approved or accredited by National Catholic Education Association, Southern Association of Colleges and Schools, and Florida Department of Education. Total enrollment: 474. Upper school average class size: 16. Upper school faculty-student ratio: 1:14. There are 181 required school days per year for Upper School students. Upper School students typically attend 5 days per week. The average school day consists of 7 hours.

Upper School Student Profile Grade 9: 123 students (67 boys, 56 girls); Grade 10: 149 students (75 boys, 74 girls); Grade 11: 124 students (59 boys, 65 girls); Grade 12: 93 students (39 boys, 54 girls). 67% of students are Roman Catholic.

Faculty School total: 34. In upper school: 10 men, 24 women; 18 have advanced degrees.

Subjects Offered 3-dimensional art, 3-dimensional design, ACT preparation, advanced biology, advanced chemistry, advanced math, Advanced Placement courses, advanced studio art-AP, aerobics, algebra, American history, American history-AP, American literature, anatomy and physiology, applied skills, art, art-AP, athletic training, audio visual/media, basketball, biology, biology-AP, British literature, broadcast journalism, calculus, calculus-AP, Catholic belief and practice, chemistry, chemistry-AP, Chinese, Christian and Hebrew scripture, Christian studies, church history, classical Greek literature, college writing, communication skills, computer applications, computer art, computer graphics, computer skills, computer technology certification, computer-aided design, consumer mathematics, creative writing, critical writing, culinary arts, dance, dance performance, death and loss, design, digital art, digital photography, drama, drama performance, dramatic arts, drawing, economics, English, English as a foreign language, English literature, English literature and composition-AP, environmental science-AP, ESL, film, film and literature, filmmaking, French, French-AP, geometry, global studies, government, grammar, graphic design, guitar, health education, honors algebra, honors English, honors geometry, honors U.S. history, honors world history, human geography - AP, journalism, marine science, mathematics, moral and social development, philosophy, photography, physical education, physical science, physics, physics-AP, poetry, pre-calculus, psychology, psychology-AP, SAT/ACT preparation, senior science survey, senior seminar, senior thesis, social justice, sociology, Spanish, Spanish language-AP, Spanish-AP, speech, statistics, studio art-AP, television, theology, U.S. government and politics-AP, U.S. history, U.S. history-AP, video film production, Web site design, weight training, weightlifting, world geography, world history, world history-AP, world religions, writing, yearbook.

Graduation Requirements Algebra, American history, American literature, arts, arts and fine arts (art, music, dance, drama), biology, British literature, chemistry, economics, electives, English, English literature, foreign language, geometry, health and wellness, mathematics, physical education (includes health), physics, science, theology, U.S. government, world history, 100 hours of community service.

Special Academic Programs 13 Advanced Placement exams for which test preparation is offered; honors section; study at local college for college credit; remedial reading and/or remedial writing; remedial math; ESL (24 students enrolled).

College Admission Counseling 91 students graduated in 2016; 90 went to college, including Embry-Riddle Aeronautical University–Daytona; Florida State University; Stetson University; Tallahassee Community College; University of Florida; University of North Florida. Other: 1 entered military service. Mean SAT critical reading: 495, mean SAT math: 518, mean SAT writing: 494, mean composite ACT: 22. 13% scored over 600 on SAT critical reading, 25% scored over 600 on SAT math, 18% scored over 600 on SAT writing, 17% scored over 1800 on combined SAT.

Student Life Upper grades have uniform requirement, student council, honor system. Discipline rests primarily with faculty. Attendance at religious services is required.

Tuition and Aid Day student tuition: $10,500. Tuition installment plan (FACTS Tuition Payment Plan). Tuition reduction for siblings, merit scholarship grants, need-based scholarship grants, tiered tuition rate based on income available. In 2016–17, 62% of upper-school students received aid. Total amount of financial aid awarded in 2016–17: $1,230,000.

Admissions Traditional secondary-level entrance grade is 9. For fall 2016, 156 students applied for upper-level admission, 143 were accepted, 120 enrolled. High School Placement Test required. Deadline for receipt of application materials: none. Application fee required: $50.

Athletics Interscholastic: baseball (boys), basketball (b,g), cross-country running (b,g), football (b), golf (b,g), lacrosse (b,g), soccer (b,g), softball (g), swimming and diving (b,g), tennis (b,g), track and field (b,g), volleyball (g), weight lifting (b,g); coed intramural: cheering, dance team, table tennis, weight training. 2 PE instructors, 24 coaches, 1 athletic trainer.

Computers Computers are regularly used in all academic, art, computer applications, graphic design, media production, photography, video film production, yearbook classes. Computer network features include Internet access, wireless campus network, Internet filtering or blocking technology. Student e-mail accounts and computer access in designated common areas are available to students. Students grades are available online. The school has a published electronic and media policy.

Contact Mrs. Carmen Rivera, Admissions Coordinator. 386-253-5213 Ext. 325. Fax: 386-252-6101. E-mail: crivera@fatherlopez.org. Website: www.fatherlopez.org

FATHER RYAN HIGH SCHOOL

700 Norwood Drive
Nashville, Tennessee 37204

Head of School: Mr. Jim McIntyre

General Information Coeducational day college-preparatory, arts, and religious studies school, affiliated with Roman Catholic Church. Grades 9–12. Founded: 1925. Setting: suburban. 40-acre campus. 9 buildings on campus. Approved or accredited by National Catholic Education Association, Southern Association of Colleges and Schools, Southern Association of Independent Schools, Tennessee Association of Independent Schools, and The College Board. Endowment: $5 million. Total enrollment: 948. Upper school average class size: 20. Upper school faculty-student ratio: 1:12. There are 180 required school days per year for Upper School students. Upper School students typically attend 5 days per week. The average school day consists of 7 hours and 10 minutes.

Upper School Student Profile Grade 9: 254 students (149 boys, 105 girls); Grade 10: 240 students (141 boys, 99 girls); Grade 11: 227 students (134 boys, 93 girls); Grade 12: 227 students (132 boys, 95 girls). 90% of students are Roman Catholic.

Faculty School total: 84. In upper school: 43 men, 41 women; 48 have advanced degrees.

Subjects Offered 3-dimensional design, Advanced Placement courses, aerobics, algebra, American government, American history, American history-AP, American literature, anatomy, art, art history, art-AP, Bible studies, biology, British literature, calculus, calculus-AP, Catholic belief and practice, chemistry, chemistry-AP, Chinese, Chinese studies, chorus, church history, college counseling, college planning, college writing, computer programming, computer science, computer studies, dance, dance performance, drama, drama performance, driver education, economics, English, English literature, English-AP, European history, European history-AP, film studies, French, French-AP, geography, geometry, government-AP, government/civics, grammar, health, history, honors geometry, honors U.S. history, journalism, Latin, mathematics, music, physical education, physics, physics-AP, physiology, psychology, psychology-AP, religion, SAT preparation, science, Shakespeare, social studies, Spanish, Spanish-AP, speech, statistics-AP, theater, theater production, theology, trigonometry, U.S. government and politics-AP, Web site design, wind ensemble, world history, world literature, world religions, writing.

Graduation Requirements Arts and fine arts (art, music, dance, drama), computer science, English, foreign language, health education, mathematics, physical education (includes health), religion (includes Bible studies and theology), science, social studies (includes history), service hours required each year.

Special Academic Programs 27 Advanced Placement exams for which test preparation is offered; honors section; academic accommodation for the gifted, the musically talented, and the artistically talented; programs in English, mathematics for dyslexic students.

College Admission Counseling 211 students graduated in 2015; all went to college, including Belmont University; Middle Tennessee State University; Tennessee Technological University; The University of Tennessee; The University of Tennessee at Chattanooga; Western Kentucky University. Median SAT critical reading: 553, median SAT math: 524, median composite ACT: 24. 20% scored over 26 on composite ACT.

Student Life Upper grades have uniform requirement, student council. Discipline rests primarily with faculty. Attendance at religious services is required.

Tuition and Aid Day student tuition: $13,275. Tuition installment plan (FACTS Tuition Payment Plan, individually arranged payment plans). Tuition reduction for siblings, need-based scholarship grants available. In 2014–15, 13% of upper-school students received aid. Total amount of financial aid awarded in 2014–15: $550,000.

Admissions Traditional secondary-level entrance grade is 9. For fall 2015, 347 students applied for upper-level admission, 278 were accepted, 251 enrolled. High School Placement Test required. Deadline for receipt of application materials: none. Application fee required: $85. On-campus interview required.

Athletics Interscholastic: aquatics (boys, girls), baseball (b), basketball (b,g), bowling (b,g), cheering (g), cross-country running (b,g), dance (b,g), dance squad (b), dance team (g), diving (b,g), football (b), golf (b,g), ice hockey (b), lacrosse (b,g), modern dance (g), power lifting (b), soccer (b,g), softball (g), Special Olympics (b,g), strength & conditioning (b,g), swimming and diving (b,g), tennis (b,g), track and field (b,g), volleyball (g), weight lifting (b,g), weight training (b,g), wrestling (b); intramural: fishing (b,g), indoor soccer (b,g), physical fitness (b,g). 1 athletic trainer.

Computers Computers are regularly used in all classes. Computer network features include on-campus library services, online commercial services, Internet access, wireless campus network, Internet filtering or blocking technology. Computer access in designated common areas is available to students. Students grades are available online. The school has a published electronic and media policy.

Contact Mrs. Marisol Preston, Director of Admission. 615-383-4200. Fax: 615-783-0264. E-mail: prestonm@fatherryan.org. Website: www.fatherryan.org

FATHER YERMO HIGH SCHOOL

250 Washington Street
El Paso, Texas 79905

Head of School: Sr. Laura Karina Tapia

General Information Coeducational day college-preparatory school, affiliated with Roman Catholic Church. Grades 9–12. Distance learning grades 11–12. Setting: urban. 2 buildings on campus. Approved or accredited by Southern Association of Colleges and Schools, Texas Catholic Conference, and Texas Department of Education. Endowment: 1 million. Upper school average class size: 17. There are 180 required school days per year for Upper School students. Upper School students typically attend 5 days per week. The average school day consists of 6 hours and 30 minutes.

Upper School Student Profile 99% of students are Roman Catholic.

Faculty School total: 15. In upper school: 7 men, 8 women; 6 have advanced degrees.

Subjects Offered Algebra, American literature, anatomy and physiology, art history, biology, British literature, calculus, Catholic belief and practice, chaplaincy, cheerleading, chemistry, choir, college admission preparation, college counseling, community service, criminal justice, earth science, economics, electives, English composition, English literature, European literature, French as a second language, geometry, health science, history of the Catholic Church, honors English, honors geometry, honors U.S. history, honors world history, human anatomy, human biology, law studies, Life of Christ, mathematical modeling, mathematics, medieval literature, Mexican literature, modern Western civilization, moral theology, New Testament, newspaper, non-Western literature, participation in sports, photojournalism, physical education, physics, prayer/spirituality, pre-calculus, reading, religious education, research skills, SAT/ACT preparation, science, service learning/internship, Shakespeare, social justice, Spanish, speech communications, student publications, studio art, study skills, technical writing, theater, theology, U.S. government and politics, U.S. history, visual arts, voice ensemble, volleyball, Western literature, world geography, world history, world literature, writing, yearbook.

Graduation Requirements American government, American history, arts and fine arts (art, music, dance, drama), chemistry, communication skills, economics, electives, English, foreign language, geography, health, mathematics, New Testament, physical education (includes health), reading, religion (includes Bible studies and theology), research skills, science, social justice, study skills, theology, world history, writing.

Special Academic Programs Honors section; accelerated programs; study at local college for college credit; programs in general development for dyslexic students; ESL.

College Admission Counseling 47 students graduated in 2016; all went to college, including El Paso Community College; New Mexico State University; The University of Texas at Austin; The University of Texas at El Paso.

Student Life Upper grades have uniform requirement, student council. Discipline rests primarily with faculty. Attendance at religious services is required.

Tuition and Aid Day student tuition: $4100. Tuition installment plan (FACTS Tuition Payment Plan). Tuition reduction for siblings, need-based scholarship grants, paying campus jobs available.

Admissions Traditional secondary-level entrance grade is 9. High School Placement Test (closed version) from Scholastic Testing Service required. Deadline for receipt of application materials: August 1. No application fee required. Interview recommended.

Athletics Interscholastic: basketball (boys, girls), volleyball (b,g); coed interscholastic: cheering, soccer. 1 PE instructor, 4 coaches.

Computers Computers are regularly used in all academic, journalism, library, newspaper, photojournalism, research skills, yearbook classes. Computer network features include on-campus library services, Internet access, wireless campus network, Internet filtering or blocking technology. Campus intranet, student e-mail accounts, and computer access in designated common areas are available to students. Students grades are available online. The school has a published electronic and media policy.

Contact 915-533-3185.

FAYETTEVILLE ACADEMY

3200 Cliffdale Road
Fayetteville, North Carolina 28303

Head of School: Mr. Ray J. Quesnel

General Information Coeducational day college-preparatory and college preparatory school. Grades PK–12. Founded: 1970. Setting: suburban. 30-acre campus 10 buildings on campus. Approved or accredited by North Carolina Association of Independent Schools, Southern Association of Colleges and Schools, Southern Association of Independent Schools, The College Board, and North Carolina Department of Education. Member of National Association of Independent Schools. Endowment: $604,473. Total enrollment: 370. Upper school average class size: 14. Upper school faculty-student ratio: 1:14. There are 177 required school days per year for Upper School students. Upper School students typically attend 5 days per week. The average school day consists of 6 hours and 55 minutes.

Upper School Student Profile Grade 6: 14 students (8 boys, 6 girls); Grade 7: 30 students (15 boys, 15 girls); Grade 8: 26 students (17 boys, 9 girls); Grade 9: 25 students (9 boys, 16 girls); Grade 10: 39 students (28 boys, 11 girls); Grade 11: 31 students (19 boys, 12 girls); Grade 12: 39 students (17 boys, 22 girls).

Faculty School total: 49. In upper school: 6 men, 15 women; 23 have advanced degrees.

Subjects Offered Algebra, American history, American literature, anatomy, art, band, biology, biology-AP, calculus, calculus-AP, chemistry, chemistry-AP, chorus, communications, ecology, English, English language and composition-AP, English literature, English literature-AP, European history, European history-AP, geography, geometry, government/civics, history, honors geometry, mathematics, music, physical education, physics, physiology, pre-calculus, psychology, science, social studies, Spanish, Spanish-AP, statistics-AP, trigonometry, typing, U.S. history-AP, weight training, world history, world history-AP, yearbook.

Graduation Requirements American history, arts and fine arts (art, music, dance, drama), English, foreign language, history, lab science, mathematics, physical education (includes health), science, senior projects.

Special Academic Programs Advanced Placement exam preparation; honors section; independent study; study at local college for college credit.

College Admission Counseling 31 students graduated in 2016; all went to college, including Arizona State University at the Tempe campus; Meredith College; North Carolina State University; Samford University; The University of North Carolina at Chapel Hill; Wake Forest University. Median SAT critical reading: 550, median SAT math: 575, median SAT writing: 535, median combined SAT: 1670, median composite ACT: 24. 23% scored over 600 on SAT critical reading, 30% scored over 600 on SAT math, 23% scored over 600 on SAT writing, 30% scored over 1800 on combined SAT, 39% scored over 26 on composite ACT.

Student Life Upper grades have specified standards of dress, student council, honor system. Discipline rests primarily with faculty.

Tuition and Aid Day student tuition: $9960–$14,790. Tuition installment plan (monthly payment plans, payment in full, 3 payment plan). Need-based scholarship grants available. In 2016–17, 30% of upper-school students received aid. Total amount of financial aid awarded in 2016–17: $562,297.

Admissions Traditional secondary-level entrance grade is 9. For fall 2016, 35 students applied for upper-level admission, 28 were accepted, 22 enrolled. Admissions testing, ERB, SSAT or TOEFL required. Deadline for receipt of application materials: none. Application fee required: $75. On-campus interview required.

Athletics Interscholastic: baseball (boys), basketball (b,g), cheering (g), cross-country running (b,g), soccer (b,g), softball (g), tennis (b,g), track and field (b,g), volleyball (g); coed interscholastic: golf, swimming and diving. 2 PE instructors, 10 coaches, 1 athletic trainer.

Computers Computers are regularly used in all classes. Computer network features include on-campus library services, online commercial services, Internet access, wireless campus network. Computer access in designated common areas is available to students. Students grades are available online. The school has a published electronic and media policy.

Contact Ms. Barbara E. Lambert, Director of Admissions. 910-868-5131 Ext. 3311. Fax: 910-868-7351. E-mail: blambert@fayettevilleacademy.com. Website: www.fayettevilleacademy.com

FAY SCHOOL

Southborough, Massachusetts
See Junior Boarding Schools section.

THE FESSENDEN SCHOOL

West Newton, Massachusetts
See Junior Boarding Schools section.

THE FIRST ACADEMY

2667 Bruton Boulevard
Orlando, Florida 32805

Head of School: Dr. Steve D. Whitaker

General Information Coeducational day college-preparatory, arts, religious studies, technology, and Apple Distinguished Program School school, affiliated with Baptist Church. Grades K4–12. Founded: 1986. Setting: suburban. 140-acre campus. 1 building on campus. Approved or accredited by Association of Christian Schools International, Association of Independent Schools of Florida, Southern Association of Colleges and Schools, Southern Association of Independent Schools, and Florida Department of Education. Member of National Association of Independent Schools and Secondary School Admission Test Board. Endowment: $2.5 million. Total enrollment: 990. Upper school average class size: 15. Upper school faculty-student ratio: 1:13. There are 180 required school days per year for Upper School students. Upper School students typically attend 5 days per week. The average school day consists of 6 hours and 30 minutes.

Upper School Student Profile Grade 9: 94 students (41 boys, 53 girls); Grade 10: 111 students (50 boys, 61 girls); Grade 11: 110 students (64 boys, 46 girls); Grade 12: 95 students (48 boys, 47 girls). 100% of students are Baptist.

Faculty School total: 90. In upper school: 17 men, 17 women; 14 have advanced degrees.

Subjects Offered Advanced biology, advanced chemistry, advanced computer applications, advanced math, Advanced Placement courses, advanced TOEFL/grammar, advertising design, aerospace education, aerospace science, algebra, alternative physical education, American biography, American democracy, American foreign policy, American government, American history, American history-AP, American legal systems, American literature, American literature-AP, American politics in film, American sign language, American studies, analysis, analysis of data, analytic geometry, anatomy, ancient world history, art, art-AP, athletics, audio visual/media, band, Bible, Bible studies, biology, biology-AP, broadcasting, calculus, calculus-AP, chemistry, chemistry-AP, choir, Christian doctrine, Christian ethics, Christian testament, comparative government and politics, composition, computer programming, computer science, creative writing, drama, economics, economics and history, electives, English, English composition, English literature, English literature-AP, English-AP, ethics, European history, European history-AP, expository writing, fine arts, genetics, geometry, government, grammar, health, history, history-AP, honors algebra, honors English, honors geometry, honors U.S. history, honors world history, integrated mathematics, journalism, keyboarding, Latin, life skills, literature, literature-AP, marine biology, mathematics, media communications, music, newspaper, physical education, physical science, physics, politics, pottery, pre-algebra, pre-calculus, psychology, psychology-AP, religion, SAT/ACT preparation, science, social sciences, social studies, Spanish, Spanish-AP, speech, speech and debate, theater, trigonometry, U.S. government, U.S. government and politics-AP, world history, world history-AP, world literature, writing, yearbook.

Graduation Requirements Arts and fine arts (art, music, dance, drama), computer science, English, foreign language, mathematics, physical education (includes health), religion (includes Bible studies and theology), science, social sciences, social studies (includes history), 5 Christian study courses.

Special Academic Programs Advanced Placement exam preparation; honors section; study at local college for college credit.

College Admission Counseling 121 students graduated in 2016; 120 went to college, including Auburn University at Montgomery; Clemson University; Florida State University; Samford University; University of Central Florida; University of Florida. Other: 1 entered military service. Mean SAT critical reading: 550, mean SAT math: 558, mean SAT writing: 550, mean combined SAT: 1658, mean composite ACT: 24. 32% scored over 600 on SAT critical reading, 24% scored over 600 on SAT math, 32% scored over 600 on SAT writing, 25% scored over 1800 on combined SAT, 30% scored over 26 on composite ACT.

Student Life Upper grades have uniform requirement, student council, honor system. Discipline rests primarily with faculty. Attendance at religious services is required.

Summer Programs Enrichment, advancement, sports, art/fine arts programs offered; session focuses on academics and athletic camps; held on campus; accepts boys and girls; open to students from other schools. 200 students usually enrolled. 2017 schedule: June 1 to July 31. Application deadline: March 1.

Tuition and Aid Day student tuition: $17,000. Tuition installment plan (SMART Tuition Payment Plan). Need-based scholarship grants available.

Admissions Traditional secondary-level entrance grade is 9. CTBS, Stanford Achievement Test, any other standardized test, ERB, ERB (CTP-Verbal, Quantitative) and TerraNova required. Deadline for receipt of application materials: none. Application fee required: $155. On-campus interview recommended.

Athletics Interscholastic: aerobics (boys, girls), aerobics/dance (b,g), aquatics (b,g), backpacking (b), baseball (b), basketball (b,g), cheering (g), cross-country running (b,g), dance team (b,g), diving (b,g), flag football (b), football (b), golf (b,g), lacrosse (b,g), physical fitness (b,g), physical training (b,g), power lifting (b,g), running (b,g), soccer (b,g), softball (g), strength & conditioning (b,g), swimming and diving (b,g), tennis (b,g), track and field (b,g), volleyball (b,g), weight lifting (b), wrestling (b), yoga (b,g). 6 PE instructors, 18 coaches, 1 athletic trainer.

Computers Computers are regularly used in all classes. Computer network features include on-campus library services, Internet access, wireless campus network, Internet filtering or blocking technology. Campus intranet and student e-mail accounts are available to students. Students grades are available online. The school has a published electronic and media policy.

Contact Kristi Summers, Assistant Director of Admissions. 407-206-8818. Fax: 407-206-8700. E-mail: kristisummers@thefirstacademy.org.
Website: http://www.TheFirstAcademy.org

FIRST BAPTIST ACADEMY

PO Box 868
Dallas, Texas 75221

Head of School: Mr. Jason Lovvorn

General Information Coeducational day college-preparatory, arts, religious studies, and technology school, affiliated with Baptist Church, Southern Baptist Convention. Grades PK–12. Founded: 1972. Setting: urban. 1 building on campus. Approved or accredited by Accreditation Commission of the Texas Association of Baptist Schools, Association of Christian Schools International, and Texas Department of Education. Total enrollment: 200. Upper school average class size: 15. Upper school faculty-student ratio: 1:8. There are 175 required school days per year for Upper School students. Upper School students typically attend 5 days per week. The average school day consists of 7 hours.

Upper School Student Profile 50% of students are Baptist, Southern Baptist Convention.

Faculty School total: 33.

Subjects Offered Algebra, American history, architecture, Bible, biology, calculus, calculus-AP, chemistry, choir, computer skills, concert band, desktop publishing, drawing, economics, English, English literature-AP, English-AP, fine arts, geometry, government-AP, history, math analysis, photography, physics, pre-calculus, Spanish, speech and debate, theater arts, world history.

Graduation Requirements Algebra, American history, arts and fine arts (art, music, dance, drama), Basic programming, Bible studies, biology, chemistry, economics, electives, English, foreign language, government, history, keyboarding, mathematics, physical education (includes health), physics, science, U.S. history, world geography, service hours are required for graduation. Community service is required.

Special Academic Programs 4 Advanced Placement exams for which test preparation is offered; honors section.

College Admission Counseling Colleges students went to include Baylor University; Texas A&M University; Texas Tech University; The University of Texas at Austin; University of Mississippi; University of Oklahoma.

Student Life Upper grades have uniform requirement, student council, honor system. Discipline rests primarily with faculty. Attendance at religious services is required.

Tuition and Aid Day student tuition: $13,950. Tuition installment plan (FACTS Tuition Payment Plan). Need-based scholarship grants available.

Admissions Traditional secondary-level entrance grade is 9. ERB (grade level), ISEE or Stanford Achievement Test required. Deadline for receipt of application materials: none. Application fee required: $100. Interview required.

Athletics Interscholastic: baseball (boys), basketball (b,g), cheering (g), drill team (g), football (b), golf (b,g), softball (g), strength & conditioning (b,g), swimming and diving (b,g), tennis (b,g), track and field (b,g), volleyball (g), wrestling (b). 1 PE instructor, 25 coaches.

Computers Computers are regularly used in computer applications, desktop publishing, yearbook classes. Computer resources include on-campus library services, Internet access. Students grades are available online. The school has a published electronic and media policy.

Contact Elizabeth Gore, Director of Admissions and Marketing. 214-969-7861. Fax: 214-969-7797. E-mail: egore@firstdallas.org. Website: www.fbacademy.com

FIRST PRESBYTERIAN DAY SCHOOL

5671 Calvin Drive
Macon, Georgia 31210

Head of School: Mr. Gregg E. Thompson

General Information Coeducational boarding and day college-preparatory, arts, and STEM school, affiliated with Presbyterian Church in America. Boarding grades 9–12, day grades PK–12. Founded: 1970. Setting: suburban. Nearest major city is Atlanta. Students are housed in coed dormitories. 140-acre campus. 7 buildings on campus. Approved or accredited by Council of Accreditation and School Improvement, Georgia Independent School Association, Southern Association of Colleges and Schools, Southern Association of Independent Schools, and Georgia Department of Education. Endowment: $4.2 million. Total enrollment: 962. Upper school average class size: 18. Upper school faculty-student ratio: 1:8. There are 180 required school days per year for Upper School students. Upper School students typically attend 5 days per week. The average school day consists of 7 hours.

Upper School Student Profile Grade 9: 85 students (45 boys, 40 girls); Grade 10: 102 students (55 boys, 47 girls); Grade 11: 96 students (47 boys, 49 girls); Grade 12: 100 students (50 boys, 50 girls). 3% of students are boarding students. 97% are state residents. 1 state is represented in upper school student body. 3% are international students. International students from China, Japan, Spain, and Viet Nam. 15% of students are Presbyterian Church in America.

Faculty School total: 103. In upper school: 29 men, 29 women; 46 have advanced degrees; 3 reside on campus.

Subjects Offered 3-dimensional art, 3-dimensional design, accounting, advanced biology, advanced chemistry, Advanced Placement courses, advanced studio art-AP, algebra, American literature, anatomy and physiology, art, art appreciation, art-AP, band, Bible, biology, biology-AP, British literature, calculus-AP, chemistry, chemistry-AP, chorus, comparative religion, computer applications, computer programming, computer programming-AP, computer science, computer science-AP, dance, debate, economics, English, English language and composition-AP, English literature and composition-AP, family living, French, geometry, government, government-AP, honors algebra, honors English, honors geometry, journalism, Latin, Latin-AP, logic, model United Nations, modern European history, music appreciation, physical science, physics, physics-AP, pre-calculus, psychology, Spanish, statistics, studio art-AP, theater, U.S. government and politics-AP, U.S. history, U.S. history-AP, world history.

Graduation Requirements Arts and fine arts (art, music, dance, drama), Bible, computer skills, electives, English, foreign language, mathematics, physical education (includes health), religion (includes Bible studies and theology), science, social studies (includes history), service to distressed populations.

Special Academic Programs 18 Advanced Placement exams for which test preparation is offered; honors section; study at local college for college credit; study abroad; ESL (13 students enrolled).

College Admission Counseling 92 students graduated in 2016; all went to college, including Auburn University; Georgia College & State University; Georgia Institute of Technology; Mercer University; The University of Alabama; University of Georgia. 35% scored over 600 on SAT critical reading, 47% scored over 600 on SAT math, 38% scored over 600 on SAT writing, 43% scored over 1800 on combined SAT, 36% scored over 26 on composite ACT.

Student Life Upper grades have uniform requirement, student council, honor system. Discipline rests primarily with faculty. Attendance at religious services is required.

Summer Programs Remediation, enrichment, sports, art/fine arts, computer instruction programs offered; session focuses on reading and study skills, mathematics enrichment, science, sports, recreation; held on campus; accepts boys and girls; open to students from other schools. 200 students usually enrolled. 2017 schedule: June 10 to July 30. Application deadline: May 15.

Tuition and Aid Day student tuition: $13,820. Tuition installment plan (monthly payment plans). Merit scholarship grants, need-based scholarship grants available. In 2016–17, 40% of upper-school students received aid; total upper-school merit-scholarship money awarded: $28,000. Total amount of financial aid awarded in 2016–17: $874,000.

Admissions Traditional secondary-level entrance grade is 9. CTP, English proficiency, ISEE, Math Placement Exam or writing sample required. Deadline for receipt of application materials: February 1. Application fee required: $50. Interview required.

Athletics Interscholastic: baseball (boys), basketball (b,g), cheering (g), cross-country running (b,g), dance (b,g), dance team (g), football (b), golf (b,g), gymnastics (g), lacrosse (b), skeet shooting (b,g), soccer (b,g), softball (g), swimming and diving (b,g), tennis (b,g), track and field (b,g), volleyball (g), wrestling (b,g); intramural: cheering (g), football (b), indoor soccer (b,g), soccer (b,g), strength & conditioning (b,g), weight training (b,g); coed intramural: cross-country running. 3 PE instructors, 6 coaches, 1 athletic trainer.

Computers Computers are regularly used in all classes. Computer network features include on-campus library services, online commercial services, Internet access, wireless campus network, Internet filtering or blocking technology, students issued convertible tablet PC. Campus intranet, student e-mail accounts, and computer access in designated common areas are available to students. Students grades are available online. The school has a published electronic and media policy.

Contact Mrs. Cheri Frame, Director of Admissions. 478-477-6505 Ext. 107. Fax: 478-477-2804. E-mail: admissions@fpdmacon.org. Website: www.fpdmacon.org

FLINT HILL SCHOOL

3320 Jermantown Road
Oakton, Virginia 22124
Head of School: Mr. John Thomas

General Information Coeducational day college-preparatory, arts, technology, and athletics, community service school. Grades JK–12. Founded: 1956. Setting: suburban. Nearest major city is Washington, DC. 45-acre campus. 1 building on campus. Approved or accredited by Virginia Association of Independent Schools and Virginia Department of Education. Member of National Association of Independent Schools and Secondary School Admission Test Board. Endowment: $2.3 million. Total enrollment: 1,086. Upper school average class size: 12. Upper school faculty-student ratio: 1:7. There are 168 required school days per year for Upper School students. Upper School students typically attend 5 days per week. The average school day consists of 6 hours and 30 minutes.

Upper School Student Profile Grade 9: 135 students (68 boys, 67 girls); Grade 10: 132 students (64 boys, 68 girls); Grade 11: 139 students (76 boys, 63 girls); Grade 12: 123 students (62 boys, 61 girls).

Faculty School total: 161. In upper school: 29 men, 43 women; 53 have advanced degrees.

Subjects Offered 20th century history, advanced chemistry, algebra, anatomy, art, ballet, biology, biology-AP, British literature, calculus, calculus-AP, ceramics, chemistry, chemistry-AP, Chinese, choir, choral music, chorus, civil rights, community service, computer animation, computer graphics, computer programming, computer science-AP, concert band, concert choir, creative writing, digital imaging, discrete mathematics, drama, drawing, drawing and design, earth science, economics-AP, English, English literature, English literature and composition-AP, English-AP, environmental science, environmental science-AP, environmental studies, European civilization, European history, fine arts, French, French language-AP, French literature-AP, geometry, government-AP, history, history of music, honors English, improvisation, jazz band, jazz dance, Latin, Latin American studies, Latin-AP, macro/microeconomics-AP, marine science, modern European history-AP, music, music history, music theory, music theory-AP, orchestra, ornithology, photography, physical education, physics, physics-AP, physiology, playwriting, pre-calculus, psychology, psychology-AP, science, sculpture, senior project, Shakespeare, short story, Spanish, Spanish-AP, statistics-AP, studio art, study skills, symphonic band, theater, trigonometry, U.S. history, U.S. history-AP, world religions.

Graduation Requirements Arts and fine arts (art, music, dance, drama), athletics, English, foreign language, history, mathematics, physical education (includes health), science, senior project. Community service is required.

Special Academic Programs 23 Advanced Placement exams for which test preparation is offered; honors section; academic accommodation for the musically talented and the artistically talented.

College Admission Counseling 137 students graduated in 2015; all went to college, including Duke University; Elon University; James Madison University; The College of William and Mary; University of Virginia; Virginia Polytechnic Institute and State University. Median SAT critical reading: 580, median SAT math: 620, median SAT writing: 590, median combined SAT: 1790, median composite ACT: 27. 44% scored over 600 on SAT critical reading, 56% scored over 600 on SAT math, 48% scored over 600 on SAT writing, 48% scored over 1800 on combined SAT, 56% scored over 26 on composite ACT.

Student Life Upper grades have specified standards of dress, student council, honor system. Discipline rests primarily with faculty.

Tuition and Aid Day student tuition: $37,280. Tuition installment plan (Insured Tuition Payment Plan, FACTS Tuition Payment Plan, monthly payment plans, one payment, two payments, or ten payments). Need-based scholarship grants available. In 2015–16, 17% of upper-school students received aid. Total amount of financial aid awarded in 2015–16: $2,089,701.

Admissions Traditional secondary-level entrance grade is 9. For fall 2015, 296 students applied for upper-level admission, 189 were accepted, 100 enrolled. PSAT, SAT, SSAT or Wechsler Intelligence Scale for Children required. Deadline for receipt of application materials: January 23. Application fee required: $50. On-campus interview required.

Athletics Interscholastic: aerobics/dance (girls), baseball (b), basketball (b,g), cross-country running (b,g), dance (g), dance team (g), diving (b,g), field hockey (g), football (b), lacrosse (b,g), self defense (g), soccer (b,g), softball (g), swimming and diving (b,g), tennis (b,g), track and field (b,g), volleyball (g); coed interscholastic: golf, hockey, ice hockey, independent competitive sports, physical fitness, running, strength & conditioning, yoga; coed intramural: aerobics/dance, canoeing/kayaking, climbing, dance, fitness, modern dance, mountaineering, outdoor activities, outdoor education, physical fitness, physical training, strength & conditioning, wall climbing, weight training, winter soccer. 16 coaches, 2 athletic trainers.

Computers Computers are regularly used in all academic classes. Computer network features include on-campus library services, online commercial services, Internet access, wireless campus network, Internet filtering or blocking technology. Campus intranet, student e-mail accounts, and computer access in designated common areas are available to students. Students grades are available online. The school has a published electronic and media policy.

Contact Ms. Lisa Knight, Director of Admission and Financial Aid. 703-584-2300. Fax: 703-242-0718. E-mail: lknight@flinthill.org. Website: www.flinthill.org

FLINTRIDGE PREPARATORY SCHOOL

4543 Crown Avenue
La Canada Flintridge, California 91011
Head of School: Mr. Peter H. Bachmann

General Information Coeducational day college-preparatory school. Grades 7–12. Founded: 1933. Setting: suburban. Nearest major city is Los Angeles. 7-acre campus. 8 buildings on campus. Approved or accredited by California Association of Independent Schools, The College Board, and Western Association of Schools and Colleges. Member of National Association of Independent Schools. Total enrollment: 500. Upper school average class size: 14. Upper school faculty-student ratio: 1:8. Upper School students typically attend 5 days per week. The average school day consists of 6 hours and 20 minutes.

Faculty School total: 67. In upper school: 38 men, 29 women; 47 have advanced degrees.

Subjects Offered Algebra, American history, American literature, analysis and differential calculus, anatomy and physiology, art, art history, art history-AP, art-AP, Basic programming, Bible as literature, biology, biology-AP, British literature-AP, business applications, calculus, calculus-AP, ceramics, chemistry, chemistry-AP, choral music, college counseling, computer literacy, computer programming, creative writing, dance, drama, earth science, economics, English, English literature-AP, environmental studies, European history, expository writing, fine arts, French, French language-AP, geography, geometry, government/civics, grammar, great books, history, jazz band, Latin, mathematics, music, photography, physical education, physics, physics-AP, psychology, science, social studies, Spanish, Spanish literature-AP, Spanish-AP, statistics, statistics-AP, theater, trigonometry, U.S. government and politics-AP, U.S. history-AP, world history, world literature, writing.

Graduation Requirements Arts and fine arts (art, music, dance, drama), English, foreign language, mathematics, science, social studies (includes history).

Special Academic Programs 18 Advanced Placement exams for which test preparation is offered; honors section; independent study.

College Admission Counseling 96 students graduated in 2016; all went to college, including Loyola Marymount University; Occidental College; University of California, Berkeley; University of California, Los Angeles; University of Southern California. Mean SAT critical reading: 702, mean SAT math: 696, mean SAT writing: 704, mean combined SAT: 2102.

Student Life Upper grades have specified standards of dress, student council, honor system. Discipline rests equally with students and faculty.

Summer Programs Remediation, enrichment, advancement, sports, art/fine arts, computer instruction programs offered; session focuses on academic enrichment/advancement, fine arts, and athletics; held on campus; accepts boys and girls; open to students from other schools. 300 students usually enrolled. 2017 schedule: June 23 to August 1. Application deadline: June 23.

Tuition and Aid Day student tuition: $34,200. Tuition installment plan (FACTS Tuition Payment Plan, Tuition Management Systems). Need-based scholarship grants available. In 2016–17, 25% of upper-school students received aid. Total amount of financial aid awarded in 2016–17: $2,286,100.

Admissions Traditional secondary-level entrance grade is 9. ISEE required. Deadline for receipt of application materials: January 15. Application fee required: $100. On-campus interview required.

Athletics Interscholastic: aquatics (boys, girls), baseball (b), basketball (b,g), cheering (g), cross-country running (b,g), diving (b,g), football (b), soccer (b,g), softball (g), swimming and diving (b,g), tennis (b,g), track and field (b,g), volleyball (b,g), water polo (b,g), winter soccer (b,g); coed interscholastic: golf. 4 PE instructors, 41 coaches, 1 athletic trainer.

Computers Computers are regularly used in all academic, foreign language, mathematics, photography, science classes. Computer network features include on-campus library services, online commercial services, Internet access, wireless campus network, Internet filtering or blocking technology. Campus intranet, student e-mail accounts, and computer access in designated common areas are available to students. Students grades are available online. The school has a published electronic and media policy.

Contact Ms. Dana Valentino, Admissions Assistant. 818-949-5514. Fax: 818-952-6247. E-mail: dvalentino@flintridgeprep.org. Website: www.flintridgeprep.org

FLINTRIDGE SACRED HEART ACADEMY

440 Saint Katherine Drive
La Canada Flintridge, California 91011
Head of School: Sr. Carolyn McCormack, OP

General Information Girls' boarding and day college-preparatory and arts school, affiliated with Roman Catholic Church. Grades 9–12. Founded: 1931. Setting: suburban. Nearest major city is Los Angeles. Students are housed in single-sex dormitories. 41-acre campus. 12 buildings on campus. Approved or accredited by California Association of Independent Schools, National Catholic Education Association, The Association of Boarding Schools, Western Association of Schools and Colleges, and California Department of Education. Member of National Association of Independent Schools and Secondary School Admission Test Board. Endowment: $6 million. Total enrollment: 406. Upper school average class size: 18. Upper school faculty-student ratio: 1:8. There are 180 required school days per year for Upper School students. Upper School students typically attend 5 days per week. The average school day consists of 6 hours.

Upper School Student Profile Grade 9: 99 students (99 girls); Grade 10: 100 students (100 girls); Grade 11: 100 students (100 girls); Grade 12: 93 students (93 girls). 12% of students are boarding students. 93% are state residents. 3 states are represented in upper school student body. 10% are international students. International students from Canada, China, Japan, Republic of Korea, Russian Federation, and Thailand; 5 other countries represented in student body. 60% of students are Roman Catholic.

Faculty School total: 41. In upper school: 11 men, 26 women; 27 have advanced degrees; 4 reside on campus.

Subjects Offered Algebra, American government, American history, American history-AP, American literature, American politics in film, analytic geometry, anatomy and physiology, art, art history, art history-AP, ASB Leadership, astronomy, biology, biology-AP, calculus, calculus-AP, cell biology, chemistry, chorus, community service, computer applications, dance, drama, driver education, economics, English, English-AP, ensembles, ESL, ethics, French, French-AP, geology, geometry, government/civics, health, honors algebra, honors geometry, journalism, keyboarding, marine biology, oceanography, organic chemistry, physical education, physics, piano, pre-calculus, psychology, religion, Spanish, Spanish-AP, stagecraft, studio art-AP, theater, theology, trigonometry, U.S. government and politics-AP, world history, yearbook.

Graduation Requirements Arts and fine arts (art, music, dance, drama), computer science, English, foreign language, mathematics, physical education (includes health), religion (includes Bible studies and theology), science, social studies (includes history). Community service is required.

Special Academic Programs 16 Advanced Placement exams for which test preparation is offered; honors section.

College Admission Counseling 98 students graduated in 2016; all went to college, including California Polytechnic State University, San Luis Obispo; University of California, Los Angeles; University of California, San Diego; University of California, Santa Cruz; University of San Diego; University of Southern California.

Student Life Upper grades have uniform requirement, student council, honor system. Discipline rests primarily with faculty. Attendance at religious services is required.

Summer Programs Enrichment, advancement, ESL, sports, art/fine arts, computer instruction programs offered; held on campus; accepts girls; not open to students from other schools. 75 students usually enrolled. 2017 schedule: June 28 to July 23. Application deadline: June 28.

Tuition and Aid Day student tuition: $22,500; 7-day tuition and room/board: $52,400. Guaranteed tuition plan. Tuition installment plan (The Tuition Plan, FACTS Tuition Payment Plan, 2-payment plan). Merit scholarship grants, need-based scholarship grants available. In 2016–17, 40% of upper-school students received aid; total upper-school merit-scholarship money awarded: $48,000. Total amount of financial aid awarded in 2016–17: $558,450.

Admissions Traditional secondary-level entrance grade is 9. For fall 2016, 212 students applied for upper-level admission, 110 were accepted, 99 enrolled. High School Placement Test, SSAT or TOEFL required. Deadline for receipt of application materials: January 12. Application fee required: $155. Interview recommended.

Athletics Interscholastic: aerobics/dance, aquatics, ballet, basketball, cross-country running, dance, diving, equestrian sports, golf, modern dance, outdoor activities, physical fitness, physical training, running, soccer, softball, swimming and diving, tennis, track and field, volleyball, water polo; intramural: aquatics, basketball, golf, soccer, softball, swimming and diving, volleyball. 2 PE instructors, 29 coaches.

Computers Computers are regularly used in college planning, creative writing, current events, economics, English, health, history, independent study, journalism, Latin, library, library skills, mathematics, media, newspaper, philosophy, photojournalism, psychology, religious studies, science, social sciences, social studies, Spanish, speech, study skills, technology, typing, yearbook classes. Computer network features include on-campus library services, online commercial services, Internet access, wireless campus network, Internet filtering or blocking technology, TologNet. Students grades are available online. The school has a published electronic and media policy.

Contact Claudia Guillen, Admissions Associate. 626-685-8333. Fax: 626-685-8520. E-mail: admissions@fsha.org. Website: www.fsha.org

FONTBONNE ACADEMY

930 Brook Road
Milton, Massachusetts 02186

Head of School: Maura Spignesi

General Information Girls' day college-preparatory school, affiliated with Roman Catholic Church. Grades 9–12. Founded: 1954. Setting: suburban. Nearest major city is Boston. 6-acre campus. 1 building on campus. Approved or accredited by Association of Independent Schools in New England, New England Association of Schools and Colleges, and Massachusetts Department of Education. Total enrollment: 335. Upper school average class size: 18. Upper school faculty-student ratio: 1:8. There are 180 required school days per year for Upper School students. Upper School students typically attend 5 days per week. The average school day consists of 6 hours and 15 minutes.

Upper School Student Profile Grade 9: 58 students (58 girls); Grade 10: 83 students (83 girls); Grade 11: 91 students (91 girls); Grade 12: 81 students (81 girls). 72% of students are Roman Catholic.

Faculty School total: 40. In upper school: 6 men, 32 women; 35 have advanced degrees.

Subjects Offered 20th century American writers, advanced computer applications, Advanced Placement courses, advanced studio art-AP, algebra, American history, American history-AP, American literature, analytic geometry, applied music, art, art-AP, biology, biology-AP, British literature (honors), calculus-AP, career/college preparation, Catholic belief and practice, chemistry, choral music, chorus, church history, college admission preparation, college counseling, computer music, computer programming, conceptual physics, ecology, environmental systems, electronic music, English, English literature, English-AP, fine arts, French, French-AP, geometry, guidance, health, instrumental music, integrated mathematics, jazz ensemble, Latin, law and the legal system, library research, literature by women, media communications, physical education, physics, physiology, pre-calculus, research skills, science, social justice, social studies, Spanish, Spanish-AP, theater production, theology, trigonometry, U.S. history-AP, vocal jazz, women's literature, world history.

Graduation Requirements Arts and fine arts (art, music, dance, drama), English, foreign language, guidance, health, mathematics, physical education (includes health), science, theology, U.S. history, world history, 100 hours of community service.

Special Academic Programs Advanced Placement exam preparation; honors section; independent study; study at local college for college credit.

College Admission Counseling 93 students graduated in 2016; all went to college, including Fairfield University; Merrimack College; Providence College; Stonehill College; University of Massachusetts Amherst; University of Vermont.

Student Life Upper grades have uniform requirement, student council, honor system. Discipline rests primarily with faculty. Attendance at religious services is required.

Summer Programs Enrichment, sports, art/fine arts, computer instruction programs offered; held on campus; accepts boys and girls; open to students from other schools. 130 students usually enrolled. 2017 schedule: July 10 to August 15. Application deadline: none.

Tuition and Aid Day student tuition: $16,200. Tuition installment plan (FACTS Tuition Payment Plan). Merit scholarship grants, need-based scholarship grants, tuition reduction for daughters of employees, work-study positions available.

Admissions Traditional secondary-level entrance grade is 9. Archdiocese of Boston High School entrance exam provided by STS, High School Placement Test or standardized test scores required. Deadline for receipt of application materials: December 15. Application fee required: $35.

Athletics Interscholastic: basketball, cheering, cross-country running, golf, hockey, ice hockey, indoor track, indoor track & field, lacrosse, soccer, softball, tennis, track and field, volleyball, winter (indoor) track; intramural: aerobics/Nautilus, alpine skiing, archery, basketball, dance, field hockey, fitness, fitness walking, flag football, gymnastics, lacrosse, physical fitness, physical training, skiing (downhill), snowboarding, strength & conditioning, weight training, yoga. 2 PE instructors, 27 coaches, 3 athletic trainers.

Computers Computers are regularly used in all classes. Computer network features include on-campus library services, online commercial services, Internet access, wireless campus network, Internet filtering or blocking technology. Student e-mail accounts and computer access in designated common areas are available to students. Students grades are available online. The school has a published electronic and media policy.

Contact Christin Schow, Director of Admissions. 617-615-3014. Fax: 617-696-7688. E-mail: admissions@fontbonneacademy.org. Website: www.fontbonneacademy.org

FONTBONNE HALL ACADEMY

9901 Shore Road
Brooklyn, New York 11209

Head of School: Mary Ann Spicijaric

General Information Girls' day college-preparatory school, affiliated with Roman Catholic Church. Grades 9–12. Founded: 1937. Setting: urban. Nearest major city is New York. 5 buildings on campus. Approved or accredited by Middle States Association of Colleges and Schools, New York State Board of Regents, and New York Department of Education. Total enrollment: 486. Upper school average class size: 18. Upper school faculty-student ratio: 1:13. There are 180 required school days per year for Upper School students. Upper School students typically attend 5 days per week. The average school day consists of 6 hours and 30 minutes.

Upper School Student Profile Grade 9: 101 students (101 girls); Grade 10: 132 students (132 girls); Grade 11: 125 students (125 girls); Grade 12: 128 students (128 girls). 90% of students are Roman Catholic.

Faculty School total: 39. In upper school: 3 men, 36 women; 37 have advanced degrees.

Subjects Offered Advanced chemistry, algebra, American literature-AP, anatomy and physiology, anthropology, art, biology-AP, calculus, calculus-AP, chemistry, chorus, computer multimedia, computers, earth science, economics, English, forensics, genetics, government, health, history-AP, Italian, Latin, marine science, mathematics, music, photography, physical education, physics, religion, Spanish, Spanish language-AP, U.S. history, world geography, world history.

Graduation Requirements Algebra, American government, American history, American literature, art, biology, British literature, chemistry, college counseling, college writing, computer applications, economics, electives, English, European civilization, foreign language, geometry, government, guidance, Internet research, lab science, music, physical education (includes health), religion (includes Bible studies and theology), science, world civilizations, Board of Regents requirements, 60 hours of service.

Special Academic Programs Advanced Placement exam preparation; honors section; study at local college for college credit; academic accommodation for the gifted, the musically talented, and the artistically talented.

College Admission Counseling 132 students graduated in 2016; all went to college, including Columbia University; Fordham University; Georgetown University; Manhattan College; New York University; The Catholic University of America. Median SAT critical reading: 560, median SAT math: 550, median SAT writing: 640, median combined SAT: 1750.

Student Life Upper grades have uniform requirement, student council. Discipline rests primarily with faculty. Attendance at religious services is required.

Summer Programs Sports programs offered; session focuses on sports clinics; held on campus; accepts girls; open to students from other schools. 50 students usually enrolled. 2017 schedule: August 1 to August 12. Application deadline: June 27.

Tuition and Aid Day student tuition: $8100. Tuition installment plan (monthly payment plans, 3 payments per year). Tuition reduction for siblings, merit scholarship grants, service scholarships available. In 2016–17, 20% of upper-school students received aid; total upper-school merit-scholarship money awarded: $100,000. Total amount of financial aid awarded in 2016–17: $121,500.

Admissions Traditional secondary-level entrance grade is 9. For fall 2016, 437 students applied for upper-level admission, 356 were accepted, 214 enrolled. Diocesan Entrance Exam required. Deadline for receipt of application materials: February 4. Application fee required: $250.

Athletics Interscholastic: aquatics, baseball, basketball, cheering, cross-country running, dance, dance squad, drill team, fishing, golf, running, soccer, softball, swimming and diving, tennis, track and field, volleyball. 2 PE instructors, 23 coaches.

Computers Computers are regularly used in all academic classes. Computer network features include on-campus library services, Internet access, wireless campus network, Internet filtering or blocking technology. Campus intranet and computer access in designated common areas are available to students. The school has a published electronic and media policy.

Contact Victoria Adamo, Director of Admissions. 718-748-2244. Fax: 718-439-0784. E-mail: vadamo@fontbonne.org. Website: www.fontbonne.org

FORDHAM PREPARATORY SCHOOL

441 East Fordham Road
Bronx, New York 10458-5175

Head of School: Rev. Christopher Devron, SJ

General Information Boys' day college-preparatory school, affiliated with Roman Catholic Church. Grades 9–12. Founded: 1841. Setting: urban. Nearest major city is New York. 5-acre campus. 2 buildings on campus. Approved or accredited by Jesuit Secondary Education Association, Middle States Association of Colleges and Schools, National Catholic Education Association, New York State Association of Independent Schools, and New York Department of Education. Member of National Association of Independent Schools. Endowment: $34 million. Total enrollment: 985. Upper school average class size: 22. Upper school faculty-student ratio: 1:12. There are 157 required school days per year for Upper School students. Upper School students typically attend 5 days per week. The average school day consists of 6 hours.

Upper School Student Profile Grade 9: 262 students (262 boys); Grade 10: 257 students (257 boys); Grade 11: 281 students (281 boys); Grade 12: 215 students (215 boys). 79% of students are Roman Catholic.

Faculty School total: 87. In upper school: 61 men, 26 women; 75 have advanced degrees.

Subjects Offered Advanced chemistry, American history, American history-AP, American literature, Ancient Greek, Arabic, architectural drawing, art history-AP, biochemistry, biology, biology-AP, calculus, calculus-AP, chemistry, chemistry-AP, Chinese, computer graphics, computer programming, creative writing, drama, economics, English, English language and composition-AP, English literature-AP, European history-AP, forensics, French, geometry, German, global studies, government and politics-AP, graphic design, health, Italian, Latin, Latin-AP, macroeconomics-AP, media communications, meteorology, modern history, music, physical education, physics, physics-AP, pre-calculus, religious studies, short story, Spanish, Spanish language-AP, Spanish literature-AP, statistics-AP, studio art, studio art-AP, trigonometry, world history-AP.

Graduation Requirements Arts and fine arts (art, music, dance, drama), English, foreign language, mathematics, physical education (includes health), religious studies, science, social studies (includes history), service requirement each year enrolled.

Special Academic Programs 17 Advanced Placement exams for which test preparation is offered; honors section; study at local college for college credit; study abroad.

College Admission Counseling 209 students graduated in 2016; 206 went to college, including Boston College; College of the Holy Cross; Fordham University;

Georgetown University; New York University; Providence College. Other: 3 went to work. Mean SAT critical reading: 598, mean SAT math: 589, mean SAT writing: 592, mean combined SAT: 1779, mean composite ACT: 28.

Student Life Upper grades have specified standards of dress. Discipline rests primarily with faculty. Attendance at religious services is required.

Tuition and Aid Day student tuition: $18,960. Tuition installment plan (monthly payment plans). Merit scholarship grants, need-based scholarship grants available. In 2016–17, 45% of upper-school students received aid; total upper-school merit-scholarship money awarded: $50,000. Total amount of financial aid awarded in 2016–17: $3,600,000.

Admissions Traditional secondary-level entrance grade is 9. For fall 2016, 1,049 students applied for upper-level admission, 705 were accepted, 262 enrolled. Cooperative Entrance Exam (McGraw-Hill), Diocesan Entrance Exam, High School Placement Test, ISEE, SSAT, STS or STS, Diocese Test required. Deadline for receipt of application materials: December 15. No application fee required.

Athletics Interscholastic: baseball, basketball, bowling, crew, cross-country running, diving, football, golf, ice hockey, indoor track, lacrosse, rugby, soccer, swimming and diving, tennis, track and field, volleyball, winter (indoor) track, wrestling; intramural: basketball, canoeing/kayaking, fitness, Frisbee, hiking/backpacking, outdoor activities, skiing (downhill), soccer, strength & conditioning, weight lifting, weight training. 2 PE instructors, 16 coaches.

Computers Computers are regularly used in all classes. Computer network features include on-campus library services, online commercial services, Internet access, wireless campus network, Internet filtering or blocking technology, Rosetta Stone. Student e-mail accounts and computer access in designated common areas are available to students. Students grades are available online. The school has a published electronic and media policy.

Contact Mr. Bradley J. Serton, Director of Admissions. 718-584-8367 Ext. 212. Fax: 718-367-7598. E-mail: admissions@fordhamprep.org. Website: www.fordhamprep.org

FOREST LAKE ACADEMY

500 Education Loop
Apopka, Florida 32703

Head of School: Mr. Frank Jones

General Information Coeducational boarding and day and distance learning college-preparatory school, affiliated with Seventh-day Adventists, Seventh-day Adventist Church. Grades 9–12. Distance learning grades 9–12. Founded: 1918. Setting: suburban. Nearest major city is Orlando. Students are housed in single-sex dormitories. 175-acre campus. 6 buildings on campus. Approved or accredited by CITA (Commission on International and Trans-Regional Accreditation), Middle States Association of Colleges and Schools, National Council for Private School Accreditation, and Florida Department of Education. Total enrollment: 397. Upper school average class size: 22. Upper school faculty-student ratio: 1:15. There are 179 required school days per year for Upper School students. Upper School students typically attend 5 days per week. The average school day consists of 6 hours.

Upper School Student Profile 8% of students are boarding students. 84% are state residents. 13 states are represented in upper school student body. 1% are international students. International students from Argentina, Brazil, China, Japan, Republic of Korea, and Spain. 95% of students are Seventh-day Adventists, Seventh-day Adventists.

Faculty School total: 32. In upper school: 20 men, 12 women; 15 have advanced degrees; 4 reside on campus.

Subjects Offered Algebra, American government, American literature, art, band, bell choir, Bible studies, biology, calculus, chemistry, choir, church history, computer applications, desktop publishing, digital photography, economics, English, environmental science, geometry, health, honors algebra, honors English, honors geometry, honors world history, integrated mathematics, life management skills, physical science, physics, play production, pre-calculus, psychology, SAT preparation, senior project, Spanish, statistics, strings, swimming, tennis, U.S. history, video film production, world geography, world history, world literature, writing, yearbook.

Graduation Requirements Algebra, American government, American literature, arts and fine arts (art, music, dance, drama), Bible studies, biology, chemistry, computer applications, computer science, economics, English, environmental science, fitness, foreign language, geometry, health education, life management skills, physical education (includes health), physical science, pre-calculus, religion (includes Bible studies and theology), science, social studies (includes history), Spanish, statistics, U.S. history, world history, world literature, writing, 25 hours of community service activity for each year enrolled.

Special Academic Programs Honors section; study at local college for college credit; ESL (12 students enrolled).

College Admission Counseling 94 students graduated in 2016; 93 went to college, including Adventist University of Health Sciences; Andrews University; Oakwood University; Seminole State College of Florida; Southern Adventist University; University of Central Florida. Other: 1 had other specific plans.

Student Life Upper grades have uniform requirement, student council, honor system. Discipline rests primarily with faculty.

Summer Programs ESL programs offered; held on campus; accepts boys and girls; open to students from other schools. 200 students usually enrolled. 2017 schedule: June to July. Application deadline: none.

Tuition and Aid Day student tuition: $12,610; 7-day tuition and room/board: $24,400. Tuition installment plan (FACTS Tuition Payment Plan, monthly payment plans, individually arranged payment plans). Merit scholarship grants, need-based scholarship grants, paying campus jobs available. In 2016–17, 37% of upper-school students received aid; total upper-school merit-scholarship money awarded: $75,000. Total amount of financial aid awarded in 2016–17: $347,000.

Admissions Traditional secondary-level entrance grade is 9. WRAT required. Deadline for receipt of application materials: none. Application fee required: $75. Interview recommended.

Athletics Interscholastic: basketball (boys, girls), golf (b), volleyball (g); intramural: golf (b); coed interscholastic: aquatics, life saving, physical fitness, strength & conditioning, tennis; coed intramural: basketball, flag football, floor hockey, indoor hockey, indoor soccer, soccer, tennis, volleyball. 2 PE instructors, 1 coach.

Computers Computers are regularly used in desktop publishing, photography, Web site design, writing, yearbook classes. Computer resources include on-campus library services, Internet access, wireless campus network, Internet filtering or blocking technology, financial aid and grant search programs for college. Campus intranet, student e-mail accounts, and computer access in designated common areas are available to students. Students grades are available online. The school has a published electronic and media policy.

Contact Mrs. Claudia Dure C. Osorio, Director of Student Records. 407-862-8411 Ext. 743. Fax: 407-862-7050. E-mail: osorioc@forestlake.org. Website: www.forestlakeacademy.org

FORSYTH COUNTRY DAY SCHOOL

5501 Shallowford Road
PO Box 549
Lewisville, North Carolina 27023-0549

Head of School: Mr. Gardner Barrier

General Information Coeducational day college-preparatory school. Grades PK–12. Founded: 1970. Setting: suburban. Nearest major city is Winston-Salem. 80-acre campus. 7 buildings on campus. Approved or accredited by North Carolina Association of Independent Schools, Southern Association of Colleges and Schools, Southern Association of Independent Schools, The College Board, and North Carolina Department of Education. Member of National Association of Independent Schools. Endowment: $13 million. Total enrollment: 702. Upper school average class size: 15. Upper school faculty-student ratio: 1:12. There are 175 required school days per year for Upper School students. Upper School students typically attend 5 days per week. The average school day consists of 6 hours.

Upper School Student Profile Grade 9: 40 students (23 boys, 17 girls); Grade 10: 57 students (23 boys, 34 girls); Grade 11: 70 students (40 boys, 30 girls); Grade 12: 76 students (42 boys, 34 girls).

Faculty School total: 175. In upper school: 18 men, 29 women; 24 have advanced degrees.

Subjects Offered Advanced Placement courses, advanced studio art-AP, algebra, American history, American history-AP, American literature, art, astronomy, biology, calculus, calculus-AP, ceramics, chemistry, Chinese studies, community service, computer math, computer programming, computer science, creative writing, digital art, drama, English, English literature, European history, fine arts, foreign policy, French, freshman seminar, geometry, grammar, health, history, history of science, humanities, international relations, Japanese studies, journalism, Latin, Mandarin, mathematics, Middle Eastern history, music, photography, physical education, physics, psychology, SAT/ACT preparation, science, social studies, Spanish, statistics-AP, theater, yearbook.

Graduation Requirements Arts and fine arts (art, music, dance, drama), English, foreign language, history, mathematics, physical education (includes health), physical fitness, science. Community service is required.

Special Academic Programs 18 Advanced Placement exams for which test preparation is offered; honors section; academic accommodation for the gifted; programs in English, general development for dyslexic students; ESL (7 students enrolled).

College Admission Counseling 74 students graduated in 2016; all went to college, including Duke University; Elon University; North Carolina State University; The University of North Carolina at Chapel Hill; The University of North Carolina Wilmington; Wake Forest University. Median SAT critical reading: 600, median SAT math: 615. 70% scored over 600 on SAT critical reading, 68% scored over 600 on SAT math.

Student Life Upper grades have specified standards of dress, student council, honor system. Discipline rests equally with students and faculty.

Tuition and Aid Day student tuition: $21,518. Tuition installment plan (Insured Tuition Payment Plan, monthly payment plans). Merit scholarship grants, need-based scholarship grants available. In 2016–17, 28% of upper-school students received aid; total upper-school merit-scholarship money awarded: $88,882. Total amount of financial aid awarded in 2016–17: $890,296.

Admissions Traditional secondary-level entrance grade is 9. For fall 2016, 84 students applied for upper-level admission, 46 were accepted, 33 enrolled. ERB CTP IV, WRAT

and writing sample required. Deadline for receipt of application materials: none. Application fee required: $100. On-campus interview recommended.

Athletics Interscholastic: baseball (boys), basketball (b,g), cheering (g), cross-country running (b,g), field hockey (g), golf (b,g), lacrosse (b,g), physical fitness (b,g), soccer (b,g), softball (g), tennis (b,g), track and field (b,g), volleyball (g), wrestling (b); coed interscholastic: swimming and diving; coed intramural: sailing. 4 PE instructors, 4 coaches, 2 athletic trainers.

Computers Computers are regularly used in art, English, foreign language, history, mathematics, music, science classes. Computer network features include on-campus library services, online commercial services, Internet access, wireless campus network, Internet filtering or blocking technology. Campus intranet, student e-mail accounts, and computer access in designated common areas are available to students. Students grades are available online. The school has a published electronic and media policy.

Contact Ashley H. Verwoerdt, Director of Admission. 336-945-3151 Ext. 313. Fax: 336-945-2907. E-mail: ashleyverwoerdt@fcds.org. Website: www.fcds.org

FORT WORTH CHRISTIAN SCHOOL

6200 Holiday Lane
North Richland Hills, Texas 76180

Head of School: Mr. Kenneth Cheeseman

General Information Coeducational day college-preparatory school. Grades PK–12. Founded: 1958. Setting: suburban. 40-acre campus. 6 buildings on campus. Approved or accredited by National Christian School Association, Southern Association of Colleges and Schools, Texas Private School Accreditation Commission, and Texas Department of Education. Endowment: $600,000. Total enrollment: 835. Upper school average class size: 17. Upper school faculty-student ratio: 1:14. There are 175 required school days per year for Upper School students. Upper School students typically attend 5 days per week. The average school day consists of 6 hours and 40 minutes.

Faculty School total: 108. In upper school: 12 men, 21 women; 12 have advanced degrees.

Subjects Offered Advanced Placement courses, African drumming, algebra, anatomy and physiology, art, band, Bible studies, biology, biology-AP, calculus, calculus-AP, chemistry, chemistry-AP, chorus, computer applications, computer information systems, computer science-AP, drama, economics, economics and history, economics-AP, English, English language and composition-AP, English literature and composition-AP, ethics, family studies, geometry, golf, government, government/civics, Latin, physical education, physics, pre-calculus, robotics, SAT/ACT preparation, Spanish, strings, theater arts, U.S. history, U.S. history-AP, video, world geography, world history, world history-AP, yearbook.

Graduation Requirements Arts and fine arts (art, music, dance, drama), business skills (includes word processing), computer science, electives, English, foreign language, history, mathematics, physical education (includes health), religion (includes Bible studies and theology), science, social sciences, social studies (includes history), world geography, community service hours.

Special Academic Programs 12 Advanced Placement exams for which test preparation is offered; honors section; independent study; study at local college for college credit.

College Admission Counseling 89 students graduated in 2016; all went to college, including Abilene Christian University; Baylor University; Harding University; Oklahoma State University; Texas A&M University; University of North Texas. Mean SAT critical reading: 511, mean SAT math: 538, mean SAT writing: 506, mean combined SAT: 1555, mean composite ACT: 24. 49% scored over 600 on SAT critical reading, 59% scored over 600 on SAT math, 46% scored over 600 on SAT writing, 21% scored over 1800 on combined SAT, 37% scored over 26 on composite ACT.

Student Life Upper grades have uniform requirement, student council, honor system. Discipline rests primarily with faculty.

Tuition and Aid Day student tuition: $12,600. Tuition installment plan (FACTS Tuition Payment Plan, monthly payment plans). Tuition reduction for siblings, need-based scholarship grants, tuition reduction for children of faculty and staff available. In 2016–17, 13% of upper-school students received aid. Total amount of financial aid awarded in 2016–17: $111,000.

Admissions Traditional secondary-level entrance grade is 9. Stanford Achievement Test required. Deadline for receipt of application materials: none. Application fee required: $100. On-campus interview required.

Athletics Interscholastic: baseball (boys), basketball (b,g), cheering (g), cross-country running (b,g), football (b), golf (b,g), physical fitness (b,g), physical training (b,g), rodeo (b,g), running (b,g), soccer (b,g), softball (g), strength & conditioning (b,g), swimming and diving (b,g), tennis (b,g), track and field (b,g), volleyball (g). 8 coaches, 1 athletic trainer.

Computers Computers are regularly used in computer applications, desktop publishing, independent study, media production, newspaper, technology, word processing, yearbook classes. Computer network features include on-campus library services, Internet access, wireless campus network, Internet filtering or blocking technology, online courses. Student e-mail accounts and computer access in designated common areas are available to students. Students grades are available online. The school has a published electronic and media policy.

Contact Mrs. Shirley Atkinson, Director of Admissions. 817-520-6561. Fax: 817-281-7063. E-mail: satkinson@fwc.org. Website: www.fwc.org

FORT WORTH COUNTRY DAY SCHOOL

4200 Country Day Lane
Fort Worth, Texas 76109-4299

Head of School: Eric V. Lombardi

General Information Coeducational day and distance learning college-preparatory, arts, and Athletics school. Grades K–12. Distance learning grades 11–12. Founded: 1962. Setting: suburban. 104-acre campus. 14 buildings on campus. Approved or accredited by Independent Schools Association of the Southwest. Member of National Association of Independent Schools. Endowment: $39.8 million. Total enrollment: 1,110. Upper school average class size: 13. Upper school faculty-student ratio: 1:10. There are 175 required school days per year for Upper School students. Upper School students typically attend 5 days per week. The average school day consists of 8 hours.

Upper School Student Profile Grade 9: 99 students (54 boys, 45 girls); Grade 10: 99 students (50 boys, 49 girls); Grade 11: 102 students (48 boys, 54 girls); Grade 12: 100 students (48 boys, 52 girls).

Faculty School total: 147. In upper school: 17 men, 25 women; 28 have advanced degrees.

Subjects Offered Acting, advanced biology, advanced chemistry, advanced math, Advanced Placement courses, advanced studio art-AP, American government, American literature-AP, art education, art history-AP, arts, athletic training, athletics, ballet, band, Basic programming, biology-AP, calculus-AP, career/college preparation, character education, cheerleading, chemistry-AP, choir, choral music, classical language, classical studies, college admission preparation, college awareness, college counseling, college placement, college planning, community service, computer literacy, computers, concert band, concert bell choir, concert choir, creative dance, creative drama, creative thinking, critical thinking, critical writing, dance performance, dramatic arts, drawing and design, economics and history, economics-AP, electives, English composition, English language and composition-AP, English language-AP, English literature and composition-AP, English literature-AP, English-AP, English/composition-AP, fitness, foreign language, French as a second language, government, government-AP, health and wellness, health education, history-AP, honors English, independent study, language-AP, literature and composition-AP, music theater, musical productions, musical theater dance, newspaper, painting, participation in sports, photojournalism, physics-AP, play production, portfolio art, pre-calculus, psychology-AP, publications, set design, softball, stage design, strings, studio art, swimming, tennis, theater arts, U.S. government, U.S. history, U.S. history-AP, visual and performing arts, vocal ensemble, volleyball, yearbook.

Graduation Requirements Algebra, American government, arts and fine arts (art, music, dance, drama), biology, English, foreign language, lab science, mathematics, physical education (includes health), science, social studies (includes history), participation in athletics, completion of a two-year College Counseling Course, Community Service Requirement. Community service is required.

Special Academic Programs 22 Advanced Placement exams for which test preparation is offered; honors section; independent study; academic accommodation for the gifted, the musically talented, and the artistically talented.

College Admission Counseling 84 students graduated in 2016; all went to college, including Southern Methodist University; Texas A&M University; Texas Christian University; The University of Texas at Arlington; The University of Texas at Austin; University of Oklahoma. Median SAT critical reading: 620, median SAT math: 615, median SAT writing: 620, median combined SAT: 1850, median composite ACT: 28. 63% scored over 600 on SAT critical reading, 56% scored over 600 on SAT math, 56% scored over 600 on SAT writing, 57% scored over 1800 on combined SAT, 79% scored over 26 on composite ACT.

Student Life Upper grades have uniform requirement, student council, honor system. Discipline rests equally with students and faculty.

Summer Programs Remediation, enrichment, sports, art/fine arts, computer instruction programs offered; session focuses on athletics, arts, STEM, STEAM,; held on campus; accepts boys and girls; open to students from other schools. 1,200 students usually enrolled. 2017 schedule: May 30 to August 5. Application deadline: May 30.

Tuition and Aid Day student tuition: $22,000. Tuition installment plan (monthly payment plans, individually arranged payment plans). Merit scholarship grants, need-based scholarship grants, Malone Scholars Program, Betty Reese Memorial, Vicki and Edward P. Bass Scholarship, Reilly Breakthrough Scholarship, Joey Pollard Memorial Scholarship, Joann Chandler Thompson Memorial Scholarship available. In 2016–17, 20% of upper-school students received aid; total upper-school merit-scholarship money awarded: $8,000,000. Total amount of financial aid awarded in 2016–17: $1,087,387.

Admissions Traditional secondary-level entrance grade is 9. For fall 2016, 60 students applied for upper-level admission, 32 were accepted, 22 enrolled. Deadline for receipt of application materials: March 4. Application fee required: $100. On-campus interview recommended.

Athletics Interscholastic: ballet (boys, girls), baseball (b), basketball (b,g), cheering (g), cross-country running (b,g), dance (b,g), field hockey (g), football (b), golf (b,g), lacrosse (b), outdoor activities (b,g), outdoor adventure (b,g), outdoor education (b,g), outdoor recreation (b,g), outdoors (b,g), physical fitness (b,g), physical training (b,g), soccer (b,g), softball (g), strength & conditioning (b,g), swimming and diving (b,g), tennis (b,g), track and field (b,g), volleyball (b,g), weight training (b,g), winter soccer (b,g), wrestling (b); coed interscholastic: ballet, basketball, cross-country running, dance, dance team, fitness, golf, independent competitive sports, outdoor activities, outdoor adventure, outdoor education, outdoor recreation, outdoors, physical fitness, physical training, ropes courses, soccer, strength & conditioning, swimming and diving, tennis, track and field, volleyball, weight training. 10 PE instructors, 10 coaches, 2 athletic trainers.

Computers Computers are regularly used in all classes. Computer network features include on-campus library services, online commercial services, Internet access, wireless campus network, Internet filtering or blocking technology, Malone Schools Online Network. Campus intranet, student e-mail accounts, and computer access in designated common areas are available to students. Students grades are available online. The school has a published electronic and media policy.

Contact Yolanda Espinoza, Admission Associate. 817-302-3209. Fax: 817-377-3425. E-mail: yolanda.espinoza@fwcd.com. Website: www.fwcd.org

FOUNDATION ACADEMY

15304 Tilden Road
Winter Garden, Florida 34787

Head of School: Mr. David Buckles

General Information Coeducational day college-preparatory, arts, and Foundation Academy offers excellent programs in Fine Arts school, affiliated with Christian faith. Grades 7–12. Founded: 1958. Setting: suburban. Nearest major city is Orlando. 70-acre campus. 5 buildings on campus. Approved or accredited by Association of Christian Schools International, Southern Association of Colleges and Schools, and Florida Department of Education. Total enrollment: 677. Upper school average class size: 17. Upper school faculty-student ratio: 1:9. There are 180 required school days per year for Upper School students. Upper School students typically attend 5 days per week. The average school day consists of 7 hours and 20 minutes.

Upper School Student Profile Grade 7: 61 students (46 boys, 15 girls); Grade 8: 74 students (39 boys, 35 girls); Grade 9: 63 students (35 boys, 28 girls); Grade 10: 59 students (37 boys, 22 girls); Grade 11: 64 students (37 boys, 27 girls); Grade 12: 62 students (34 boys, 28 girls). 90% of students are Christian.

Faculty School total: 44. In upper school: 10 men, 34 women; 13 have advanced degrees.

Subjects Offered Advanced math, Advanced Placement courses, advanced studio art-AP, algebra, American government, American literature, anatomy and physiology, art, band, Bible, biology, biology-AP, business law, business mathematics, calculus, calculus-AP, career/college preparation, chemistry, chemistry-AP, choir, Christian education, college admission preparation, communication skills, computer processing, drama, ecology, economics and history, English, English composition, English language-AP, English literature, English literature-AP, environmental science, environmental science-AP, geometry, government, health and wellness, health education, history-AP, honors algebra, honors English, honors geometry, honors U.S. history, honors world history, human anatomy, human biology, human geography - AP, journalism, life science, marine biology, personal fitness, photography, physical education, physical fitness, pre-algebra, pre-calculus, SAT preparation, SAT/ACT preparation, science, science project, Spanish, speech, speech and debate, speech communications, sports conditioning, statistics, statistics-AP, studio art-AP, U.S. government and politics-AP, U.S. history, weight training, weightlifting, yearbook.

Graduation Requirements Algebra, American government, American history, American literature, arts and fine arts (art, music, dance, drama), Bible, Bible studies, biology, chemistry, economics and history, English, English composition, English literature, geography, geometry, government, health and wellness, history, languages, pre-calculus, science, U.S. history.

Special Academic Programs Advanced Placement exam preparation; honors section; study at local college for college credit; programs in English, mathematics for dyslexic students.

College Admission Counseling 41 students graduated in 2016; all went to college, including Lakehead University; Southeastern University; University of Central Florida; University of Florida; Valencia College. Mean SAT critical reading: 501, mean SAT math: 479, mean SAT writing: 483, mean combined SAT: 1462, mean composite ACT: 21. 14% scored over 26 on composite ACT.

Student Life Upper grades have uniform requirement, student council. Discipline rests primarily with faculty. Attendance at religious services is required.

Summer Programs Remediation, enrichment, sports, art/fine arts programs offered; session focuses on sports camps, art, drama, academic; held on campus; accepts boys and girls; open to students from other schools. 100 students usually enrolled. 2017 schedule: June 1 to July 31.

Tuition and Aid Day student tuition: $11,250–$11,790. Tuition installment plan (FACTS Tuition Payment Plan). Tuition reduction for siblings, need-based scholarship grants available. In 2016–17, 20% of upper-school students received aid. Total amount of financial aid awarded in 2016–17: $200,000.

Admissions Traditional secondary-level entrance grade is 9. For fall 2016, 101 students applied for upper-level admission, 76 were accepted, 62 enrolled. Admissions testing, Gates MacGinite Reading Tests, Math Placement Exam, Wide Range Achievement Test and writing sample required. Deadline for receipt of application materials: none. Application fee required: $150. Interview recommended.

Athletics Interscholastic: baseball (boys), basketball (b,g), cheering (g), cross-country running (b,g), football (b), golf (b,g), soccer (b,g), softball (g), tennis (b,g), track and field (b,g), volleyball (g), winter soccer (b,g). 2 PE instructors, 1 athletic trainer.

Computers Computers are regularly used in career exploration, college planning, computer applications, health, independent study, keyboarding, mathematics, music, SAT preparation, word processing, writing, yearbook classes. Computer network features include Internet access, wireless campus network, Internet filtering or blocking technology. Campus intranet and student e-mail accounts are available to students. Students grades are available online.

Contact Mrs. Michelle Campbell, Admissions Director. 407-877-2744 Ext. 106. Fax: 407-877-1985. E-mail: michelle.campbell@foundationacademy.net.
Website: www.foundationacademy.net

FOUNTAIN VALLEY SCHOOL OF COLORADO

6155 Fountain Valley School Road
Colorado Springs, Colorado 80911

Head of School: Mr. William V. Webb

General Information Coeducational boarding and day college-preparatory, arts, and global education school. Grades 9–12. Founded: 1930. Setting: suburban. Students are housed in single-sex dormitories. 1,100-acre campus. 42 buildings on campus. Approved or accredited by Association of Colorado Independent Schools, The Association of Boarding Schools, and Colorado Department of Education. Member of National Association of Independent Schools and Secondary School Admission Test Board. Endowment: $36 million. Total enrollment: 236. Upper school average class size: 11. Upper school faculty-student ratio: 1:5. There are 155 required school days per year for Upper School students. Upper School students typically attend 5 days per week. The average school day consists of 9 hours and 15 minutes.

Upper School Student Profile Grade 9: 37 students (17 boys, 20 girls); Grade 10: 62 students (34 boys, 28 girls); Grade 11: 69 students (40 boys, 29 girls); Grade 12: 62 students (28 boys, 34 girls). 66% of students are boarding students. 50% are state residents. 21 states are represented in upper school student body. 26% are international students. International students from China, Finland, Japan, Republic of Korea, Saudi Arabia, and United States; 12 other countries represented in student body.

Faculty School total: 38. In upper school: 18 men, 20 women; 28 have advanced degrees; 25 reside on campus.

Subjects Offered 3-dimensional art, 3-dimensional design, ACT preparation, advanced chemistry, Advanced Placement courses, advanced studio art-AP, algebra, American history, American history-AP, American literature, band, biology, biology-AP, British literature, calculus, calculus-AP, ceramics, chamber groups, chemistry, chemistry-AP, college counseling, Colorado ecology, composition, computer applications, computer multimedia, computer programming, computer programming-AP, creative writing, drama, English, English literature and composition-AP, environmental science-AP, ESL, fiction, film and literature, French, French language-AP, geology, geometry, global issues, honors algebra, honors English, honors geometry, instrumental music, jewelry making, literature, Mandarin, music theory, musical productions, outdoor education, photography, physics, physics-AP, pre-calculus, probability and statistics, senior project, senior seminar, Shakespeare, Shakespearean histories, short story, Spanish, Spanish language-AP, statistics-AP, strings, student government, student publications, studio art, studio art-AP, U.S. government and politics-AP, visual and performing arts, vocal ensemble, wilderness education, wind ensemble, world history, world history-AP, world literature, writing.

Graduation Requirements Arts and fine arts (art, music, dance, drama), computer science, English, foreign language, history, mathematics, physical education (includes health), science, social studies (includes history), senior seminar. Community service is required.

Special Academic Programs 20 Advanced Placement exams for which test preparation is offered; honors section; independent study; study abroad; ESL (17 students enrolled).

College Admission Counseling 63 students graduated in 2016; 56 went to college, including Case Western Reserve University; Colorado State University; Connecticut College; New York University; The Colorado College; University of Colorado Boulder. Other: 7 had other specific plans.

Student Life Upper grades have specified standards of dress, student council, honor system. Discipline rests equally with students and faculty.

Tuition and Aid Day student tuition: $28,200; 7-day tuition and room/board: $52,700. Tuition installment plan (Key Tuition Payment Plan, monthly payment plans, individually arranged payment plans). Merit scholarship grants, need-based scholarship grants available. In 2016–17, 43% of upper-school students received aid. Total amount of financial aid awarded in 2016–17: $2,354,978.

Admissions Traditional secondary-level entrance grade is 9. For fall 2016, 225 students applied for upper-level admission, 150 were accepted, 96 enrolled. SSAT or TOEFL required. Deadline for receipt of application materials: February 1. Application fee required: $50. Interview recommended.

Athletics Interscholastic: basketball (boys, girls), bicycling (b,g), cross-country running (b,g), diving (g), hockey (b), ice hockey (b), lacrosse (b), mountain biking (b,g), rock climbing (b,g), soccer (b,g), swimming and diving (g), tennis (b,g), track and field (b,g), volleyball (b,g), wall climbing (b,g), winter soccer (g); coed interscholastic: climbing, equestrian sports, horseback riding, independent competitive sports, mountain biking, rock climbing, rodeo, skiing (downhill), snowboarding, telemark skiing, wall climbing; coed intramural: alpine skiing, backpacking, bicycling, climbing, equestrian sports, fitness, hiking/backpacking, horseback riding, mountain biking,

mountaineering, outdoor activities, outdoor adventure, outdoor education, outdoor recreation, outdoor skills, outdoors, physical fitness, rock climbing, skiing (downhill), snowboarding, strength & conditioning, table tennis, telemark skiing, tennis, wall climbing, weight lifting, weight training, wilderness, wilderness survival. 2 coaches, 1 athletic trainer.

Computers Computers are regularly used in all academic, college planning, multimedia, news writing, photography, publications, yearbook classes. Computer network features include on-campus library services, online commercial services, Internet access, wireless campus network, Internet filtering or blocking technology, live webcasts of select athletic events. Campus intranet, student e-mail accounts, and computer access in designated common areas are available to students. Students grades are available online. The school has a published electronic and media policy.

Contact Mrs. Kila McCann, Director of Admission and Financial Aid. 719-390-7035 Ext. 297. Fax: 719-390-7762. E-mail: kmccann@fvs.edu. Website: www.fvs.edu

FOWLERS ACADEMY

PO Box 921
Guaynabo, Puerto Rico 00970-0921

Head of School: Mr. Jared Ramos

General Information Coeducational day general academic, music, martial arts, and graphic art design, robotics school; primarily serves underachievers. Grades 7–12. Founded: 1986. Setting: urban. 2-acre campus. 2 buildings on campus. Approved or accredited by Comisión Acreditadora de Instituciones Educativas and Puerto Rico Department of Education. Languages of instruction: English and Spanish. Total enrollment: 71. Upper school average class size: 15. Upper school faculty-student ratio: 1:15. There are 160 required school days per year for Upper School students. Upper School students typically attend 5 days per week. The average school day consists of 6 hours and 50 minutes.

Upper School Student Profile Grade 7: 8 students (6 boys, 2 girls); Grade 8: 13 students (11 boys, 2 girls); Grade 9: 14 students (11 boys, 3 girls); Grade 10: 12 students (8 boys, 4 girls); Grade 11: 14 students (9 boys, 5 girls); Grade 12: 6 students (5 boys, 1 girl).

Faculty School total: 8. In upper school: 6 men, 2 women; 3 have advanced degrees.

Subjects Offered Algebra.

Graduation Requirements Algebra, ancient world history, biology, chemistry, Christian education, computer science, electives, English, ethics, geometry, physical education (includes health), physical science, physics, pre-college orientation, Puerto Rican history, Spanish, U.S. history, world history.

Special Academic Programs Accelerated programs; ESL (67 students enrolled).

College Admission Counseling 14 students graduated in 2016; all went to college, including University of Puerto Rico, Mayagüez Campus; University of Puerto Rico, Río Piedras Campus. Other: 13 entered a postgraduate year.

Student Life Upper grades have uniform requirement, honor system. Discipline rests primarily with faculty.

Summer Programs Remediation, enrichment, advancement, ESL programs offered; session focuses on academic courses and remediation; held on campus; accepts boys and girls; open to students from other schools. 35 students usually enrolled. 2017 schedule: June 1 to June 29. Application deadline: May 31.

Tuition and Aid Day student tuition: $6300. Tuition installment plan (monthly payment plans, individually arranged payment plans). Tuition reduction for siblings, need-based scholarship grants available. In 2016–17, 18% of upper-school students received aid; total upper-school merit-scholarship money awarded: $56,000. Total amount of financial aid awarded in 2016–17: $32,000.

Admissions Traditional secondary-level entrance grade is 9. For fall 2016, 4 students applied for upper-level admission, 4 were accepted, 4 enrolled. Achievement tests or psychoeducational evaluation required. Deadline for receipt of application materials: none. No application fee required. On-campus interview recommended.

Athletics Intramural: basketball (boys, girls), volleyball (b,g); coed intramural: archery, basketball, cooperative games, martial arts, physical fitness, table tennis, volleyball. 1 PE instructor.

Computers Computers are regularly used in computer applications, English, graphic arts, graphic design, keyboarding, mathematics, religious studies, science, Spanish classes. Computer resources include Internet access, Internet filtering or blocking technology. Computer access in designated common areas is available to students.

Contact Mrs. Lynette Ammacher de Montes, Dean of Students. 787-787-1350. Fax: 787-789-0055. E-mail: academiafowler@gmail.com.
Website: www.academiafowler.com/

FOXCROFT SCHOOL

22407 Foxhound Lane
P.O. Box 5555
Middleburg, Virginia 20118

Head of School: Mrs. Catherine S. McGehee

General Information Girls' boarding and day college-preparatory, STEM/STEAM, Exceptional Proficiency, and specializing in how girls learn best school. Grades 9–PG. Founded: 1914. Setting: rural. Nearest major city is Washington, DC. Students are housed in single-sex dormitories. 500-acre campus. 32 buildings on campus. Approved or accredited by The Association of Boarding Schools, The College Board, Virginia Association of Independent Schools, and Virginia Department of Education. Member of National Association of Independent Schools and Secondary School Admission Test Board. Endowment: $71 million. Total enrollment: 167. Upper school average class size: 12. Upper school faculty-student ratio: 1:6. There are 185 required school days per year for Upper School students. Upper School students typically attend 5 days per week. The average school day consists of 7 hours and 15 minutes.

Upper School Student Profile Grade 9: 34 students (34 girls); Grade 10: 47 students (47 girls); Grade 11: 36 students (36 girls); Grade 12: 34 students (34 girls). 74% of students are boarding students. 44% are state residents. 18 states are represented in upper school student body. 24% are international students. International students from China, Jamaica, Mexico, Republic of Korea, Switzerland, and Viet Nam; 7 other countries represented in student body.

Faculty School total: 25. In upper school: 6 men, 17 women; 17 have advanced degrees; 17 reside on campus.

Subjects Offered 3-dimensional art, acting, advanced biology, advanced chemistry, advanced computer applications, Advanced Placement courses, advanced TOEFL/grammar, algebra, American government, American history, American history-AP, American literature, anatomy and physiology, ancient world history, architecture, art, art history, arts, astronomy, athletic training, athletics, basketball, biology, biology-AP, British literature, calculus, calculus-AP, cell biology, ceramics, character education, chemistry, chemistry-AP, choir, chorus, college admission preparation, college counseling, college placement, community garden, community service, comparative religion, competitive science projects, composition-AP, computer graphics, computer programming-AP, computer science, computer science-AP, conceptual physics, conservation, constitutional law, creative dance, creative drama, creative writing, current events, dance, debate, digital photography, discrete mathematics, drama, drama performance, dramatic arts, drawing and design, economics, economics-AP, electives, engineering, English, English composition, English language-AP, English literature, English literature and composition-AP, English literature-AP, environmental science, environmental science-AP, equestrian sports, equitation, ESL, ethics, European civilization, European history, European literature, experiential education, expository writing, fine arts, fitness, food and nutrition, French, French as a second language, French language-AP, French literature-AP, French-AP, general science, geology, geometry, grammar, guitar, health and wellness, health education, history, human anatomy, human geography - AP, humanities, independent study, lab science, language-AP, languages, Latin, leadership, library, literature and composition-AP, macroeconomics-AP, mathematics, mathematics-AP, meditation, microbiology, microeconomics-AP, model United Nations, music, music theory, neuroscience, news writing, nutrition, outdoor education, painting, participation in sports, performing arts, photography, physical education, physics, physics-AP, piano, poetry, portfolio art, post-calculus, pottery, pre-calculus, probability and statistics, production, public speaking, publications, robotics, SAT preparation, SAT/ACT preparation, science and technology, sculpture, senior project, senior seminar, senior thesis, Shakespeare, social studies, softball, Spanish, Spanish language-AP, Spanish literature, Spanish literature-AP, Spanish-AP, sports, statistics-AP, student government, studio art, study skills, technology, tennis, The 20th Century, theater, theater arts, theater production, trigonometry, U.S. history, U.S. history-AP, visual and performing arts, vocal ensemble, vocal music, voice, voice ensemble, volleyball, wellness, women in literature, world cultures, world history-AP, world literature, writing, yearbook, yoga.

Graduation Requirements American history, arts and fine arts (art, music, dance, drama), English, foreign language, history, humanities, mathematics, physical education (includes health), science, senior thesis if student is not enrolled in AP English.

Special Academic Programs 11 Advanced Placement exams for which test preparation is offered; independent study; term-away projects; study abroad; academic accommodation for the gifted, the musically talented, and the artistically talented; ESL (25 students enrolled).

College Admission Counseling 47 students graduated in 2016; all went to college, including Boston University; High Point University; New York University; The College of William and Mary; University of Virginia; Virginia Polytechnic Institute and State University. Mean SAT critical reading: 562, mean SAT math: 557, mean SAT writing: 565, mean combined SAT: 1684, mean composite ACT: 25.

Student Life Upper grades have specified standards of dress, student council, honor system. Discipline rests equally with students and faculty.

Tuition and Aid Day student tuition: $43,760; 7-day tuition and room/board: $51,900. Tuition installment plan (Insured Tuition Payment Plan, Tuition Management Systems Plan (Monthly Payment Plan)). Merit scholarship grants, need-based scholarship grants, merit-based scholarship grants are offered to prospective 9th grade students available. In 2016–17, 33% of upper-school students received aid; total upper-school merit-scholarship money awarded: $31,000. Total amount of financial aid awarded in 2016–17: $1,589,890.

Admissions Traditional secondary-level entrance grade is 9. For fall 2016, 171 students applied for upper-level admission, 105 were accepted, 48 enrolled. SSAT or TOEFL required. Deadline for receipt of application materials: February 1. Application fee required: $75. On-campus interview recommended.

Athletics Interscholastic: basketball, cross-country running, dressage, equestrian sports, field hockey, horseback riding, lacrosse, running, soccer, softball, tennis, volleyball; intramural: aerobics, aerobics/dance, basketball, bicycling, climbing, combined training, dance, dance team, dressage, equestrian sports, field hockey, fitness, hiking/backpacking, horseback riding, independent competitive sports, indoor soccer, indoor track, lacrosse, modern dance, outdoor activities, outdoor recreation, physical fitness, physical training, rock climbing, ropes courses, running, soccer, softball, squash, strength & conditioning, swimming and diving, table tennis, tennis, volleyball, walking, weight lifting, weight training, winter walking, yoga. 3 coaches, 1 athletic trainer.

Computers Computers are regularly used in all classes. Computer resources include on-campus library services, online commercial services, Internet access, wireless campus network, Internet filtering or blocking technology. Campus intranet, student e-mail accounts, and computer access in designated common areas are available to students. Students grades are available online. The school has a published electronic and media policy.

Contact Mrs. Gina B. Finn, Director of Admission and Financial Aid. 540-687-4340. E-mail: gina.finn@foxcroft.org. Website: www.foxcroft.org

FRANKLIN ACADEMY

East Haddam, Connecticut
See Special Needs Schools section

FRANKLIN ROAD ACADEMY

4700 Franklin Road
Nashville, Tennessee 37220

Head of School: Mr. Sean Casey

General Information Coeducational day college-preparatory, arts, religious studies, and technology school; primarily serves students with learning disabilities and ASPIRE—Student Learning Services Program. Grades PK–12. Founded: 1971. Setting: suburban. 57-acre campus. 5 buildings on campus. Approved or accredited by Southern Association of Colleges and Schools, Southern Association of Independent Schools, and Tennessee Department of Education. Member of National Association of Independent Schools. Total enrollment: 720. Upper school average class size: 15. Upper school faculty-student ratio: 1:7. There are 185 required school days per year for Upper School students. Upper School students typically attend 5 days per week. The average school day consists of 6 hours and 30 minutes.

Upper School Student Profile Grade 9: 67 students (33 boys, 34 girls); Grade 10: 67 students (34 boys, 33 girls); Grade 11: 63 students (31 boys, 32 girls); Grade 12: 67 students (33 boys, 34 girls).

Faculty School total: 105. In upper school: 21 men, 14 women; 24 have advanced degrees.

Subjects Offered ACT preparation, advanced chemistry, Advanced Placement courses, algebra, American history, American literature, anatomy and physiology, art, art-AP, band, baseball, basketball, Bible, Bible studies, biology, biology-AP, calculus, calculus-AP, chemistry, chemistry-AP, choral music, Civil War, college counseling, computer education, computer music, computer programming, computer science, current events, dance, drama, dramatic arts, economics, economics and history, electronic music, English, English language-AP, English literature, English literature-AP, environmental science, European history, European history-AP, fine arts, French, French language-AP, French literature-AP, geometry, government/civics, grammar, history, history-AP, honors algebra, honors English, honors geometry, honors U.S. history, human anatomy, jazz band, keyboarding, Latin, Latin-AP, Life of Christ, mathematics, mathematics-AP, model United Nations, music, music theory, personal development, physical education, physics, physics-AP, pottery, pre-calculus, SAT preparation, SAT/ACT preparation, science, social sciences, social studies, Spanish, Spanish language-AP, Spanish literature-AP, speech, statistics, statistics-AP, student government, student publications, technical theater, theater, theater production, track and field, trigonometry, U.S. history, U.S. history-AP, vocal music, volleyball, weight training, world history, world literature, wrestling, writing.

Graduation Requirements Algebra, arts and fine arts (art, music, dance, drama), computer science, English, foreign language, mathematics, physical education (includes health), religion (includes Bible studies and theology), science, social studies (includes history), community service hours required for graduation. Community service is required.

Special Academic Programs Advanced Placement exam preparation; honors section; independent study; term-away projects; academic accommodation for the gifted, the musically talented, and the artistically talented; programs in general development for dyslexic students.

College Admission Counseling 63 students graduated in 2015; all went to college, including Belmont University; DePaul University; Mississippi State University; The University of Alabama; The University of Tennessee; The University of Tennessee at Chattanooga. 45% scored over 600 on SAT critical reading, 55% scored over 600 on SAT math, 55% scored over 26 on composite ACT.

Student Life Upper grades have uniform requirement, student council, honor system. Discipline rests primarily with faculty.

Tuition and Aid Day student tuition: $19,320. Tuition installment plan (Insured Tuition Payment Plan, FACTS Tuition Payment Plan, individually arranged payment plans). Need-based scholarship grants available. In 2015–16, 20% of upper-school students received aid. Total amount of financial aid awarded in 2015–16: $500,000.

Admissions Traditional secondary-level entrance grade is 9. Admissions testing, ISEE and writing sample required. Deadline for receipt of application materials: none. Application fee required: $40. On-campus interview required.

Athletics Interscholastic: baseball (boys), basketball (b,g), bowling (b,g), cheering (g), cross-country running (b,g), dance (g), diving (b,g), football (b), golf (b,g), hockey (b), ice hockey (b), soccer (b,g), softball (g), swimming and diving (b,g), tennis (b,g), track and field (b,g), volleyball (g), wrestling (b); intramural: aerobics/dance (g), physical fitness (b,g), physical training (b,g), power lifting (b), strength & conditioning (b,g); coed intramural: aerobics/dance. 2 PE instructors, 2 coaches, 1 athletic trainer.

Computers Computers are regularly used in art, Bible studies, college planning, creative writing, economics, English, foreign language, French, history, journalism, keyboarding, Latin, library skills, literary magazine, mathematics, music, religious studies, science, social sciences, Spanish, technology, theater, theater arts, Web site design, writing, yearbook classes. Computer network features include on-campus library services, online commercial services, Internet access, wireless campus network, Internet filtering or blocking technology, networked instructional software. Campus intranet, student e-mail accounts, and computer access in designated common areas are available to students. Students grades are available online. The school has a published electronic and media policy.

Contact Mrs. Courtney Williamson, Director of Admissions. 615-832-8845. Fax: 615-834-8845. E-mail: williamsonc@franklinroadacademy.com. Website: www.franklinroadacademy.com

FRASER ACADEMY

Vancouver, British Columbia, Canada
See Special Needs Schools section.

FREDERICKSBURG ACADEMY

10800 Academy Drive
Fredericksburg, Virginia 22408-1931

Head of School: Ms. Karen A. Moschetto

General Information Coeducational day college-preparatory, arts, and technology school. Grades PK–12. Founded: 1992. Setting: suburban. Nearest major city is Washington, DC. 45-acre campus. 3 buildings on campus. Approved or accredited by Virginia Association of Independent Specialized Education Facilities and Virginia Department of Education. Member of National Association of Independent Schools. Endowment: $61,400. Total enrollment: 357. Upper school average class size: 12. Upper school faculty-student ratio: 1:7. There are 173 required school days per year for Upper School students. Upper School students typically attend 5 days per week. The average school day consists of 6 hours and 20 minutes.

Upper School Student Profile Grade 6: 20 students (10 boys, 10 girls); Grade 7: 37 students (17 boys, 20 girls); Grade 8: 32 students (22 boys, 10 girls); Grade 9: 24 students (17 boys, 7 girls); Grade 10: 33 students (14 boys, 19 girls); Grade 11: 30 students (14 boys, 16 girls); Grade 12: 10 students (6 boys, 4 girls).

Faculty School total: 43. In upper school: 7 men, 10 women; 9 have advanced degrees.

Subjects Offered Advanced Placement courses, advanced studio art-AP, algebra, American government, American history, American history-AP, American literature-AP, anatomy and physiology, art, art-AP, band, biology, biology-AP, British literature, British literature (honors), calculus, calculus-AP, chemistry, Chesapeake Bay studies, choral music, chorus, classical civilization, classics, computer science, computer skills, computer tools, concert band, creative writing, critical thinking, cultural arts, drama, earth science, English, English literature, English-AP, expository writing, fine arts, foreign language, French, geometry, health, health education, history, history-AP, instrumental music, journalism, language arts, Latin, Latin History, life science, mathematics, music, music history, newspaper, oral communications, orchestra, physical education, physics, probability and statistics, programming, reading, Roman civilization, science, senior seminar, Shakespeare, social studies, Spanish, studio art, studio art-AP, technical writing, technology, trigonometry, U.S. history, U.S. history-AP, world geography, world history, world literature, writing, writing workshop, yearbook.

Graduation Requirements Arts, electives, English, foreign language, history, lab science, mathematics, independent exhibit-research project and presentation.

Special Academic Programs Advanced Placement exam preparation; independent study.

College Admission Counseling 19 students graduated in 2015; all went to college, including Denison University; George Mason University; Purdue University; The College of William and Mary; University of Virginia; Virginia Polytechnic Institute and State University. Median combined SAT: 1700, median composite ACT: 24. 26% scored over 1800 on combined SAT, 26% scored over 26 on composite ACT.

Student Life Upper grades have specified standards of dress, student council, honor system. Discipline rests equally with students and faculty.

Tuition and Aid Day student tuition: $21,270. Tuition installment plan (FACTS Tuition Payment Plan). Merit scholarship grants, need-based scholarship grants available. In 2015–16, 39% of upper-school students received aid; total upper-school merit-scholarship money awarded: $107,010. Total amount of financial aid awarded in 2015–16: $366,400.

Admissions Traditional secondary-level entrance grade is 9. For fall 2015, 25 students applied for upper-level admission, 10 were accepted, 7 enrolled. Admissions testing required. Deadline for receipt of application materials: none. Application fee required: $50. Interview required.

Athletics Interscholastic: basketball (boys, girls), cross-country running (b,g), field hockey (g), lacrosse (b,g), soccer (b,g), swimming and diving (b,g), tennis (b,g); coed interscholastic: aquatics, fitness, physical training. 6 coaches.

Computers Computers are regularly used in English, foreign language, French, history, journalism, Latin, mathematics, newspaper, publications, science, Spanish, writing, yearbook classes. Computer network features include on-campus library services, online commercial services, Internet access, wireless campus network, Internet filtering or blocking technology, syllabi and assignments online. Student e-mail accounts are available to students. Students grades are available online. The school has a published electronic and media policy.

Contact Mrs. Marnie Schattgen, Assistant Director of Admission. 540-898-0020 Ext. 228. Fax: 540-898-0440. E-mail: mschattgen@fredericksburgacademy.org. Website: www.fredericksburgacademy.org

FREDERICTON CHRISTIAN ACADEMY

778 MacLaren Ave
Fredericton, New Brunswick E3A 5J8, Canada

Head of School: Mr. Jonathan McAloon

General Information Coeducational day and distance learning college-preparatory, general academic, arts, religious studies, and technology school, affiliated with Baptist Church, Evangelical Christian Church; primarily serves students with learning disabilities. Grades 1–12. Distance learning grades 8–12. Founded: 1979. Setting: suburban. 5-acre campus. 1 building on campus. Approved or accredited by Association of Christian Schools International and New Brunswick Department of Education. Language of instruction: English. Total enrollment: 156. Upper school average class size: 15. Upper school faculty-student ratio: 1:14. Upper School students typically attend 5 days per week. The average school day consists of 7 hours.

Upper School Student Profile Grade 6: 12 students (6 boys, 6 girls); Grade 7: 9 students (2 boys, 7 girls); Grade 8: 11 students (5 boys, 6 girls); Grade 9: 7 students (6 boys, 1 girl); Grade 10: 21 students (10 boys, 11 girls); Grade 11: 17 students (9 boys, 8 girls); Grade 12: 17 students (8 boys, 9 girls). 30% of students are Baptist, members of Evangelical Christian Church.

Faculty School total: 13. In upper school: 4 men, 4 women; 1 has an advanced degree.

Subjects Offered All academic.

Special Academic Programs Accelerated programs; independent study; study at local college for college credit; academic accommodation for the gifted; remedial reading and/or remedial writing; remedial math; ESL (10 students enrolled).

College Admission Counseling 15 students graduated in 2015; 13 went to college. Other: 2 went to work.

Student Life Upper grades have specified standards of dress, student council, honor system. Discipline rests primarily with faculty. Attendance at religious services is required.

Tuition and Aid Tuition installment plan (monthly payment plans, individually arranged payment plans). Tuition reduction for siblings, bursaries, need-based scholarship grants available. In 2015–16, 10% of upper-school students received aid.

Admissions Traditional secondary-level entrance grade is 10. For fall 2015, 10 students applied for upper-level admission, 9 were accepted, 9 enrolled. Deadline for receipt of application materials: August 15. Application fee required: CAN$50. Interview required.

Athletics Interscholastic: basketball (boys, girls), cross-country running (b,g), soccer (b,g); intramural: aerobics/dance (b,g), badminton (b,g), ball hockey (b,g), basketball (b,g), soccer (b,g); coed intramural: aerobics/dance, badminton, ball hockey, soccer.

Computers Computer resources include Internet access, wireless campus network. Student e-mail accounts are available to students. Students grades are available online.

Contact Mrs. Sandra Amos, Administrator. 506-458-9379. Fax: 506-458-8702. E-mail: office@fcae.ca. Website: https://www.fcae.ca/

FRENCH-AMERICAN SCHOOL OF NEW YORK

525 Fenimore Road
Mamaroneck, New York 10543

Head of School: Mr. Joël Peinado

General Information Coeducational day college-preparatory school. Grades N–12. Founded: 1980. Setting: suburban. Nearest major city is White Plains. 1 building on campus. Approved or accredited by New York State Association of Independent Schools and New York Department of Education. Member of National Association of Independent Schools. Languages of instruction: English and French. Total enrollment: 842. Upper school average class size: 17. Upper school faculty-student ratio: 1:5. There are 168 required school days per year for Upper School students. Upper School students typically attend 5 days per week. The average school day consists of 8 hours and 30 minutes.

Upper School Student Profile Grade 9: 54 students (28 boys, 26 girls); Grade 10: 52 students (25 boys, 27 girls); Grade 11: 55 students (26 boys, 29 girls); Grade 12: 75 students (38 boys, 37 girls).

Faculty School total: 99. In upper school: 18 men, 32 women; 32 have advanced degrees.

Subjects Offered Algebra, American history, American literature, art, biology, choir, civics, computer applications, computer multimedia, current events, earth science, ecology, economics, English, European history, expository writing, French, French language-AP, French literature-AP, French studies, geometry, German, government, health, Latin, mathematics, multimedia, music, newspaper, philosophy, physical education, physics, physics-AP, public speaking, science, social studies, Spanish, Spanish language-AP, world history, world literature, writing, yearbook.

Graduation Requirements 20th century history, algebra, American history, biology, calculus, chemistry, civics, computer studies, current events, English, European history, foreign language, French, geography, geology, geometry, mathematics, music, philosophy, physical education (includes health), physics, pre-algebra, pre-calculus, research seminar, social studies (includes history). Community service is required.

Special Academic Programs Advanced Placement exam preparation; honors section; ESL (60 students enrolled).

College Admission Counseling 38 students graduated in 2016; all went to college, including McGill University. Mean SAT critical reading: 649, mean SAT math: 660, mean SAT writing: 637. 78% scored over 600 on SAT critical reading, 89% scored over 600 on SAT math, 78% scored over 600 on SAT writing, 81% scored over 1800 on combined SAT.

Student Life Upper grades have specified standards of dress, student council. Discipline rests primarily with faculty.

Tuition and Aid Day student tuition: $27,500–$31,900. Tuition installment plan (Academic Management Services Plan, monthly payment plans). Need-based scholarship grants available. In 2016–17, 5% of upper-school students received aid. Total amount of financial aid awarded in 2016–17: $259,955.

Admissions Traditional secondary-level entrance grade is 9. For fall 2016, 147 students applied for upper-level admission, 100 were accepted, 79 enrolled. English, French, and math proficiency required. Deadline for receipt of application materials: none. Application fee required: $150. On-campus interview recommended.

Athletics Interscholastic: baseball (boys), basketball (b,g), cross-country running (b,g), rugby (b,g), running (b,g), soccer (b,g), softball (g), tennis (b,g), coed intramural: fencing. 4 PE instructors, 4 coaches, 1 athletic trainer.

Computers Computers are regularly used in art, English, foreign language, French, history, mathematics, music, publications, science, social studies classes. Computer network features include on-campus library services, Internet access, Internet filtering or blocking technology, laptop use (in certain classes), Chromebooks, iPad program in seventh and eighth grade. Student e-mail accounts are available to students. The school has a published electronic and media policy.

Contact Mr. Clyde Javois, Director of Admissions. 914-250-0400. Fax: 914-940-2214. E-mail: cjavois@fasny.org. Website: www.fasny.org

FRESNO CHRISTIAN SCHOOLS

7200 North Cedar Avenue
Fresno, California 93720

Head of School: Mr. Jeremy Brown

General Information Coeducational day college-preparatory school, affiliated with Protestant-Evangelical faith. Grades K–12. Founded: 1977. Setting: suburban. 27-acre campus. 4 buildings on campus. Approved or accredited by Association of Christian Schools International, Western Association of Schools and Colleges, and California Department of Education. Endowment: $200,000. Total enrollment: 464. Upper school average class size: 20. Upper school faculty-student ratio: 1:10. There are 176 required school days per year for Upper School students. Upper School students typically attend 5 days per week. The average school day consists of 5 hours and 20 minutes.

Upper School Student Profile Grade 9: 36 students (18 boys, 18 girls); Grade 10: 39 students (20 boys, 19 girls); Grade 11: 49 students (29 boys, 20 girls); Grade 12: 52 students (22 boys, 30 girls). 90% of students are Protestant-Evangelical faith.

Faculty School total: 26. In upper school: 8 men, 9 women; 5 have advanced degrees.

Subjects Offered Advanced Placement courses, algebra, alternative physical education, American government, American history, American history-AP, art, athletics, band, baseball, basketball, Bible, Bible studies, biology, biology-AP, British literature, calculus-AP, cheerleading, chemistry, Chinese, choir, choral music, Christian education, civics, composition-AP, concert band, concert choir, drama, drama performance, economics, economics and history, English, English language and composition-AP, English literature and composition-AP, English-AP, ensembles, European history-AP, geometry, golf, home economics, honors algebra, honors English, honors geometry, humanities, jazz band, journalism, leadership, marching band, mathematics, mathematics-AP, physical education, physical science, physics, pre-calculus, softball, Spanish, sports, statistics-AP, student government, tennis, track and field, trigonometry, U.S. history, video film production, vocal music, volleyball, woodworking, work experience, world history, yearbook.

Graduation Requirements Arts and fine arts (art, music, dance, drama), electives, English, mathematics, physical education (includes health), religion (includes Bible

studies and theology), science, social studies (includes history), 4 years of Biblical Studies classes, 3 years of physical education.

Special Academic Programs 7 Advanced Placement exams for which test preparation is offered; honors section; independent study; study at local college for college credit; remedial reading and/or remedial writing; remedial math; special instructional classes for students with learning disabilities.

College Admission Counseling 53 students graduated in 2016; 51 went to college, including California State University, Fresno; Fresno City College. Other: 1 went to work, 1 entered military service, 2 had other specific plans. Mean SAT critical reading: 494, mean SAT math: 513, mean SAT writing: 479, mean combined SAT: 1486, mean composite ACT: 24.

Student Life Upper grades have specified standards of dress, student council, honor system. Discipline rests primarily with faculty. Attendance at religious services is required.

Tuition and Aid Day student tuition: $8275. Tuition installment plan (monthly payment plans, individually arranged payment plans). Tuition reduction for siblings, merit scholarship grants, need-based scholarship grants available. In 2016–17, 29% of upper-school students received aid; total upper-school merit-scholarship money awarded: $27,984. Total amount of financial aid awarded in 2016–17: $262,944.

Admissions Traditional secondary-level entrance grade is 9. Stanford Achievement Test required. Deadline for receipt of application materials: none. Application fee required: $100. Interview required.

Athletics Interscholastic: baseball (boys), basketball (b,g), cheering (g), cross-country running (b,g), drill team (g), football (b), soccer (b,g), softball (g), strength & conditioning (b,g), tennis (b,g), track and field (b,g), volleyball (g), weight training (b,g); coed interscholastic: golf, physical training; coed intramural: archery, martial arts, outdoor recreation, volleyball. 2 PE instructors, 16 coaches.

Computers Computers are regularly used in media production, publications, yearbook classes. Computer network features include on-campus library services, online commercial services, Internet access, wireless campus network, Internet filtering or blocking technology. Computer access in designated common areas is available to students. Students grades are available online. The school has a published electronic and media policy.

Contact Mrs. Kerry Roberts, Registrar. 559-299-1695 Ext. 102. Fax: 559-299-1051. E-mail: kroberts@fresnochristian.com. Website: www.fresnochristian.com

FRIENDS ACADEMY

270 Duck Pond Road
Locust Valley, New York 11560

Head of School: Andrea Kelly

General Information Coeducational day college-preparatory school, affiliated with Society of Friends. Grades N–12. Founded: 1876. Setting: suburban. Nearest major city is New York. 65-acre campus. 8 buildings on campus. Approved or accredited by New York State Association of Independent Schools and New York Department of Education. Member of National Association of Independent Schools and Secondary School Admission Test Board. Endowment: $30 million. Total enrollment: 781. Upper school average class size: 15. Upper school faculty-student ratio: 1:7. There are 165 required school days per year for Upper School students. Upper School students typically attend 5 days per week. The average school day consists of 7 hours and 15 minutes.

Upper School Student Profile Grade 9: 95 students (51 boys, 44 girls); Grade 10: 98 students (53 boys, 45 girls); Grade 11: 95 students (46 boys, 49 girls); Grade 12: 93 students (37 boys, 56 girls). 1% of students are members of Society of Friends.

Faculty School total: 100. In upper school: 25 men, 75 women; 87 have advanced degrees.

Subjects Offered Advanced Placement courses, African studies, algebra, American history, American literature, art, art history, Bible studies, biology, calculus, ceramics, chemistry, community service, computer literacy, computer programming, computer science, creative writing, drama, driver education, English, English literature, environmental science, ethics, European history, expository writing, fine arts, French, geography, geometry, grammar, Greek, health, history, Italian, Latin, logic, mathematics, mechanical drawing, music, outdoor education, photography, physical education, physics, psychology, religion, science, social sciences, social studies, Spanish, speech, theater, trigonometry, Western civilization, world literature, writing.

Graduation Requirements Arts and fine arts (art, music, dance, drama), computer literacy, English, foreign language, mathematics, outdoor education, physical education (includes health), religion (includes Bible studies and theology), science, social sciences, social studies (includes history), speech, participation in on-campus work crew program, independent service program. Community service is required.

Special Academic Programs 18 Advanced Placement exams for which test preparation is offered; honors section; independent study; remedial reading and/or remedial writing; remedial math.

College Admission Counseling 95 students graduated in 2016; all went to college, including Bentley University; Boston College; Dartmouth College; Duke University; Tufts University; University of Miami.

Student Life Upper grades have specified standards of dress, student council, honor system. Discipline rests equally with students and faculty. Attendance at religious services is required.

Summer Programs Art/fine arts programs offered; session focuses on arts and sports; held both on and off campus; accepts boys and girls; open to students from other schools. 500 students usually enrolled. 2017 schedule: June 26 to August 18.

Tuition and Aid Day student tuition: $32,800. Tuition installment plan (Insured Tuition Payment Plan, monthly payment plans). Need-based scholarship grants, Quaker grants, tuition remission for children of faculty and staff available. In 2016–17, 20% of upper-school students received aid.

Admissions Traditional secondary-level entrance grade is 9. For fall 2016, 112 students applied for upper-level admission, 46 were accepted, 36 enrolled. SSAT required. Deadline for receipt of application materials: January 18. Application fee required: $55. Interview recommended.

Athletics Interscholastic: baseball (boys), basketball (b,g), crew (b,g), cross-country running (b,g), field hockey (g), fitness (b,g), football (b), golf (b,g), ice hockey (b), indoor track & field (b,g), lacrosse (b,g), soccer (b,g), softball (g), tennis (b,g), track and field (b,g), winter (indoor) track (b,g); coed interscholastic: squash; coed intramural: dance, volleyball. 9 PE instructors, 4 coaches, 1 athletic trainer.

Computers Computers are regularly used in English, mathematics, science, technology classes. Computer network features include on-campus library services, online commercial services, Internet access, wireless campus network, Internet filtering or blocking technology, Chromebook program for lower and middle school students, iPads in lower school. Campus intranet, student e-mail accounts, and computer access in designated common areas are available to students. Students grades are available online. The school has a published electronic and media policy.

Contact Joanna Kim, Associate Director of Admissions. 516-393-4244. Fax: 516-465-1718. E-mail: joanna_kim@fa.org. Website: www.fa.org

FRIENDS' CENTRAL SCHOOL

1101 City Avenue
Wynnewood, Pennsylvania 19096

Head of School: Craig N. Sellers

General Information Coeducational day college-preparatory school, affiliated with Society of Friends. Grades N–12. Founded: 1845. Setting: suburban. Nearest major city is Philadelphia. 23-acre campus. 7 buildings on campus. Approved or accredited by Pennsylvania Department of Education. Member of National Association of Independent Schools and Secondary School Admission Test Board. Endowment: $25 million. Total enrollment: 788. Upper school average class size: 18. Upper school faculty-student ratio: 1:8. There are 170 required school days per year for Upper School students. Upper School students typically attend 5 days per week. The average school day consists of 6 hours and 40 minutes.

Upper School Student Profile Grade 9: 83 students (44 boys, 39 girls); Grade 10: 95 students (48 boys, 47 girls); Grade 11: 102 students (51 boys, 51 girls); Grade 12: 98 students (50 boys, 48 girls). 3% of students are members of Society of Friends.

Faculty School total: 115. In upper school: 22 men, 23 women; 34 have advanced degrees.

Subjects Offered Advanced biology, advanced chemistry, advanced math, algebra, American history, American literature, architecture, art history, Bible, biology, botany, calculus, ceramics, chemistry, chorus, computer applications, computer multimedia, computer programming, computer-aided design, conflict resolution, digital photography, drama, English, equality and freedom, film studies, French, geometry, German, health education, instrumental music, international relations, jazz band, Latin, life skills, media studies, modern European history, modern history, music history, music theory, philosophy, photography, physical education, physical science, physics, pre-calculus, psychology, Quakerism and ethics, senior project, sexuality, Spanish, statistics, studio art, study skills, Western literature, women in world history, woodworking, world history, writing workshop.

Graduation Requirements Arts and fine arts (art, music, dance, drama), English, foreign language, mathematics, science, service learning/internship, U.S. history, world cultures.

Special Academic Programs Independent study; term-away projects; study abroad.

College Admission Counseling 95 students graduated in 2015; all went to college, including Brown University; Bucknell University; Syracuse University; The George Washington University; University of Pennsylvania; Washington University in St. Louis. Mean SAT critical reading: 642, mean SAT math: 638, mean SAT writing: 640.

Student Life Upper grades have specified standards of dress, student council, honor system. Discipline rests primarily with faculty. Attendance at religious services is required.

Tuition and Aid Day student tuition: $17,000–$32,800. Tuition installment plan (FACTS Tuition Payment Plan, monthly payment plans, Higher Education Service, Inc). Need-based scholarship grants available. In 2015–16, 36% of upper-school students received aid. Total amount of financial aid awarded in 2015–16: $2,581,380.

Admissions Traditional secondary-level entrance grade is 9. For fall 2015, 211 students applied for upper-level admission, 95 were accepted, 44 enrolled. ISEE, SSAT or Wechsler Intelligence Scale for Children required. Deadline for receipt of application materials: January 8. Application fee required: $50. On-campus interview required.

Athletics Interscholastic: aquatics (boys, girls), baseball (b), basketball (b,g), cross-country running (b,g), field hockey (g), indoor track (b,g), lacrosse (g), soccer (b,g), softball (g), tennis (b,g), track and field (b,g), winter (indoor) track (b,g), wrestling (b,g); coed interscholastic: golf, squash, water polo; coed intramural: aerobics,

aerobics/dance, aerobics/Nautilus, cheering, dance, fitness, flag football, life saving, table tennis. 8 PE instructors, 10 coaches, 1 athletic trainer.

Computers Computers are regularly used in college planning, foreign language, French, health, information technology, introduction to technology, Latin, mathematics, publishing, science, Spanish, technology, Web site design, yearbook classes. Computer network features include on-campus library services, online commercial services, Internet access, wireless campus network, Internet filtering or blocking technology, Intranet collaboration. Campus intranet, student e-mail accounts, and computer access in designated common areas are available to students. Students grades are available online. The school has a published electronic and media policy.

Contact Dr. Susan Robinson, Director of Enrollment Management. 610-645-5032. Fax: 610-658-5644. E-mail: admission@friendscentral.org. Website: www.friendscentral.org

FRIENDSHIP CHRISTIAN SCHOOL

5400 Coles Ferry Pike
Lebanon, Tennessee 37087

Head of School: Mr. Jon Shoulders

General Information Coeducational day college-preparatory, arts, business, religious studies, technology, and dual enrollment school, affiliated with Christian faith. Grades PK–12. Founded: 1973. Setting: rural. Nearest major city is Nashville. 50-acre campus. 6 buildings on campus. Approved or accredited by National Christian School Association, Southern Association of Colleges and Schools, and Tennessee Department of Education. Member of National Association of Independent Schools. Total enrollment: 539. Upper school average class size: 20. Upper school faculty-student ratio: 1:15. There are 175 required school days per year for Upper School students. Upper School students typically attend 5 days per week. The average school day consists of 6 hours and 35 minutes.

Upper School Student Profile Grade 9: 56 students (34 boys, 22 girls); Grade 10: 57 students (31 boys, 26 girls); Grade 11: 50 students (27 boys, 23 girls); Grade 12: 63 students (35 boys, 28 girls). 80% of students are Christian faith.

Faculty School total: 50. In upper school: 9 men, 12 women; 18 have advanced degrees.

Subjects Offered Accounting, ACT preparation, advanced biology, advanced chemistry, advanced math, Advanced Placement courses, agriculture, algebra, American government, anatomy and physiology, Ancient Greek, art, athletic training, backpacking, band, Bible, Bible studies, biology, bowling, British literature (honors), business applications, calculus, calculus-AP, chemistry, choral music, chorus, college placement, college planning, computers, creative writing, drama, driver education, earth science, economics, English, English-AP, environmental science, geometry, honors algebra, honors English, honors geometry, Internet, journalism, keyboarding, mathematics, modern history, physical education, physical science, physics, physiology, pre-algebra, psychology, science project, science research, Spanish, speech, swimming, trigonometry, U.S. constitutional history, U.S. government, U.S. history, U.S. history-AP, U.S. Presidents, weight training, wellness, world geography, world history, yearbook.

Graduation Requirements ACT preparation, advanced chemistry, advanced math, Advanced Placement courses, algebra, American government, American history, American history-AP, applied arts, arts and fine arts (art, music, dance, drama), Bible, biology, chemistry, chemistry-AP, ecology, English language and composition-AP, English literature-AP, English-AP, foreign language, French, honors U.S. history, keyboarding, physical education (includes health), physics, pre-calculus, U.S. government and politics-AP, U.S. history-AP, weight training.

Special Academic Programs Advanced Placement exam preparation; honors section; study at local college for college credit.

College Admission Counseling 55 students graduated in 2015; 54 went to college, including Cumberland University; Lipscomb University; Tennessee Technological University; The University of Tennessee; The University of Tennessee at Chattanooga; United States Naval Academy. Other: 1 entered military service. Mean composite ACT: 25. 50% scored over 26 on composite ACT.

Student Life Upper grades have uniform requirement, student council, honor system. Discipline rests primarily with faculty.

Tuition and Aid Day student tuition: $9120. Tuition installment plan (FACTS Tuition Payment Plan). Tuition reduction for siblings, need-based scholarship grants, paying campus jobs available. In 2015–16, 2% of upper-school students received aid. Total amount of financial aid awarded in 2015–16: $5000.

Admissions Traditional secondary-level entrance grade is 9. For fall 2015, 25 students applied for upper-level admission, 19 were accepted, 19 enrolled. Otis-Lennon School Ability Test required. Deadline for receipt of application materials: none. Application fee required: $75. Interview recommended.

Athletics Interscholastic: baseball (boys), basketball (b,g), cheering (g), football (b), golf (b,g), physical fitness (b,g); coed interscholastic: bowling, cross-country running, golf, physical fitness. 2 PE instructors, 13 coaches, 1 athletic trainer.

Computers Computers are regularly used in accounting, all academic, business, college planning, creative writing, journalism, keyboarding, library, media, multimedia, newspaper, reading, remedial study skills, science, typing classes. Computer network features include on-campus library services, online commercial services, Internet access, wireless campus network, Internet filtering or blocking technology. Student e-mail accounts and computer access in designated common areas are available to students. Students grades are available online. The school has a published electronic and media policy.

Contact Terresia Williams, Director of Admissions. 615-449-1573 Ext. 207. Fax: 615-449-2769. E-mail: twilliams@friendshipchristian.org.
Website: www.friendshipchristian.org

FRIENDS SELECT SCHOOL

17th & Benjamin Franklin Parkway

Philadelphia, Pennsylvania 19103-1284

Head of School: Ms. Michael Gary

General Information Coeducational day college-preparatory school, affiliated with Society of Friends. Grades PK–12. Founded: 1689. Setting: urban. 1-acre campus. 2 buildings on campus. Approved or accredited by Pennsylvania Association of Independent Schools. Member of National Association of Independent Schools and Secondary School Admission Test Board. Endowment: $10 million. Total enrollment: 558. Upper school average class size: 15. Upper school faculty-student ratio: 1:15. There are 167 required school days per year for Upper School students. Upper School students typically attend 5 days per week. The average school day consists of 6 hours and 20 minutes.

Upper School Student Profile 5% of students are members of Society of Friends.

Faculty School total: 83. In upper school: 12 men, 23 women; 27 have advanced degrees.

Subjects Offered 20th century American writers, 3-dimensional art, algebra, American history, American literature, art, art history, biology, calculus, chemistry, computer math, computer programming, computer science, creative writing, drama, drawing, earth science, ecology, economics, electronics, English, English literature, ethics, European history, expository writing, fine arts, French, geography, geology, geometry, government/civics, grammar, health, history, Italian, Latin, marine biology, mathematics, music, photography, physical education, physics, religion, science, sculpture, social studies, Spanish, statistics, theater, trigonometry, world history, world literature, writing.

Graduation Requirements Arts and fine arts (art, music, dance, drama), English, foreign language, history, mathematics, physical education (includes health), religion (includes Bible studies and theology), science, senior project, social studies (includes history), junior internship.

Special Academic Programs Advanced Placement exam preparation; independent study; academic accommodation for the musically talented and the artistically talented; ESL (10 students enrolled).

College Admission Counseling Colleges students went to include Cornell University; Drexel University; New York University; School of the Art Institute of Chicago; The George Washington University; University of Pittsburgh.

Student Life Upper grades have student council. Discipline rests primarily with faculty. Attendance at religious services is required.

Summer Programs Remediation, enrichment, advancement, art/fine arts, computer instruction programs offered; session focuses on enrichment and advancement; held on campus; accepts boys and girls; open to students from other schools. 50 students usually enrolled. 2017 schedule: June 27 to August 5. Application deadline: June 6.

Tuition and Aid Day student tuition: $34,000. Tuition installment plan (10-month payment plan, 2-payment plan). Tuition reduction for siblings, need-based scholarship grants, need-based loans, K-12 Family Education Loan Program (SLM Financial Group), AchieverLoans (Key Education Resources), tuition reduction for 3-plus siblings from same family, 5% reduction for children of alumni/alumnae available. In 2016–17, 43% of upper-school students received aid. Total amount of financial aid awarded in 2016–17: $888,000.

Admissions Traditional secondary-level entrance grade is 9. ERB CTP IV, ISEE, PSAT and SAT for applicants to grade 11 and 12, SSAT or WISC or WAIS required. Deadline for receipt of application materials: none. Application fee required: $65. On-campus interview recommended.

Athletics Interscholastic: baseball (boys), basketball (b,g), crew (b,g), cross-country running (b,g), field hockey (g), soccer (b,g), softball (g); coed interscholastic: crew, cross-country running, swimming and diving, tennis. 3 PE instructors, 28 coaches, 1 athletic trainer.

Computers Computers are regularly used in all academic, English, foreign language, mathematics, science classes. Computer network features include on-campus library services, online commercial services, Internet access, online learning center. Campus intranet, student e-mail accounts, and computer access in designated common areas are available to students. The school has a published electronic and media policy.

Contact Annemiek Young, Director of Admission and Enrollment Management. 215-561-5900 Ext. 102. Fax: 215-864-2979. E-mail: annemieky@friends-select.org. Website: www.friends-select.org

THE FRISCH SCHOOL

120 West Century Road
Paramus, New Jersey 07652

Head of School: Rabbi Eli Ciner

General Information Coeducational day college-preparatory and Judaic studies, music, and engineering school, affiliated with Jewish faith. Grades 9–12. Founded: 1971. Setting: suburban. Nearest major city is New York, NY. 8-acre campus. 1 building on campus. Approved or accredited by Middle States Association of Colleges and Schools and New Jersey Department of Education. Languages of instruction: English and Hebrew. Total enrollment: 500. Upper school average class size: 20. Upper school faculty-student ratio: 1:7. There are 158 required school days per year for Upper School students. Upper School students typically attend 5 days per week. The average school day consists of 9 hours and 15 minutes.

Upper School Student Profile Grade 9: 199 students (99 boys, 100 girls); Grade 10: 180 students (90 boys, 90 girls); Grade 11: 158 students (86 boys, 72 girls); Grade 12: 161 students (92 boys, 69 girls). 100% of students are Jewish.

Faculty School total: 93. In upper school: 46 men, 47 women; 70 have advanced degrees.

Subjects Offered American history-AP, anatomy, art, art appreciation, biology, biology-AP, chemistry, chemistry-AP, computer applications, computer science-AP, creative writing, economics-AP, English, English-AP, expository writing, finite math, French, health, Jewish history, Jewish studies, Latin, law, mathematics, philosophy, physical education, physics, physics-AP, physiology, psychology-AP, public speaking, rhetoric, social studies, Spanish, statistics-AP, U.S. government and politics-AP.

Graduation Requirements English, foreign language, mathematics, physical education (includes health), religion (includes Bible studies and theology), science, social studies (includes history).

Special Academic Programs Advanced Placement exam preparation; honors section; independent study; remedial reading and/or remedial writing; remedial math; programs in English for dyslexic students; special instructional classes for deaf students, blind students.

College Admission Counseling 137 students graduated in 2016; 135 went to college, including Brandeis University; Columbia University; New York University; University of Pennsylvania; Yeshiva University. Other: 2 entered military service. 75% scored over 600 on SAT critical reading, 78% scored over 600 on SAT math.

Student Life Upper grades have specified standards of dress, student council. Discipline rests primarily with faculty. Attendance at religious services is required.

Tuition and Aid Tuition installment plan (The Tuition Plan, monthly payment plans). Need-based scholarship grants available.

Admissions Traditional secondary-level entrance grade is 9. Traditional secondary-level entrance age is 13. For fall 2016, 342 students applied for upper-level admission, 270 were accepted. Board of Jewish Education Entrance Exam required. Deadline for receipt of application materials: December 12. Application fee required: $150. On-campus interview recommended.

Athletics Interscholastic: aquatics (girls), basketball (b,g), dance (g), dance team (g), fencing (b,g), floor hockey (b), football (b), hockey (b), indoor hockey (b), jogging (b,g), soccer (b), softball (b,g), swimming and diving (g), tennis (b,g), track and field (b,g), volleyball (g), weight lifting (b), weight training (b), wrestling (b), yoga (g); intramural: ballet (g), basketball (b,g), dance (g), dance team (g), fencing (b,g), floor hockey (b), hockey (b), jogging (b,g), swimming and diving (g), volleyball (g), weight lifting (b), weight training (b), wrestling (b), yoga (g); coed interscholastic: jogging, physical fitness, running, soccer, softball, tennis, track and field, walking; coed intramural: physical fitness, running, soccer, softball, tennis, track and field, walking. 7 PE instructors, 9 coaches.

Computers Computers are regularly used in all academic, college planning, library classes. Computer network features include on-campus library services, Internet access, wireless campus network, Internet filtering or blocking technology. Campus intranet, student e-mail accounts, and computer access in designated common areas are available to students. Students grades are available online. The school has a published electronic and media policy.

Contact Mrs. Barbara Kessler, Registrar. 201-267-9100 Ext. 201. Fax: 201-261-9340. E-mail: barbara.kessler@frisch.org. Website: www.frisch.org

FRONT RANGE CHRISTIAN HIGH SCHOOL

6637 West Ottawa Avenue
Littleton, Colorado 80128

Head of School: David Cooper

General Information Coeducational day college-preparatory, general academic, and science, math, language arts, media, Spanish school, affiliated with Christian faith. Grades PK–12. Founded: 1994. Setting: suburban. Nearest major city is Denver. 23-acre campus. 3 buildings on campus. Approved or accredited by Association of Christian Schools International, North Central Association of Colleges and Schools, Northwest Accreditation Commission, Southern Association of Colleges and Schools, and Colorado Department of Education. Total enrollment: 437. Upper school average class size: 13. Upper school faculty-student ratio: 1:12. There are 175 required school days per year for Upper School students. Upper School students typically attend 5 days per week. The average school day consists of 7 hours and 20 minutes.

Upper School Student Profile Grade 9: 38 students (14 boys, 24 girls); Grade 10: 39 students (21 boys, 18 girls); Grade 11: 44 students (27 boys, 17 girls); Grade 12: 48 students (24 boys, 24 girls). 99% of students are Christian.

Faculty School total: 24. In upper school: 13 men, 16 women; 14 have advanced degrees.

Subjects Offered ACT preparation, acting, advanced biology, advanced math, Advanced Placement courses, algebra, American history, American literature, anatomy and physiology, ancient world history, art, athletics, band, baseball, basketball, Bible, biology, biology-AP, British literature, calculus, career and personal planning, career/college preparation, chemistry, choir, Christian doctrine, Christian scripture, composition, drama, drama performance, earth science, electives, foreign language, forensics, geometry, golf, grammar, guitar, health education, home economics, honors algebra, honors English, honors U.S. history, honors world history, junior and senior seminars, lab science, language arts, leadership and service, Life of Christ, literature and composition-AP, music, musical productions, participation in sports, performing arts, photojournalism, physical education, physical fitness, physics, pre-calculus, probability and statistics, psychology, Spanish, speech, speech and oral interpretations, sports, statistics, trigonometry, video and animation, video film production, visual arts, vocal ensemble, volleyball, world religions, yearbook.

Graduation Requirements Algebra, career planning, college planning, history, language arts, science, Spanish, speech, participation in annual Spring Practicum, participation in monthly service projects (called GO!).

Special Academic Programs 5 Advanced Placement exams for which test preparation is offered; honors section; study at local college for college credit; academic accommodation for the gifted; remedial reading and/or remedial writing; remedial math; programs in English, mathematics, general development for dyslexic students.

College Admission Counseling 49 students graduated in 2016; 45 went to college, including Bethel College; Colorado Christian University; Dordt College; Grand Canyon University. Other: 1 went to work, 1 entered military service, 2 had other specific plans. Median SAT critical reading: 460, median SAT math: 590, median SAT writing: 490, median combined SAT: 1560, median composite ACT: 23. 8% scored over 600 on SAT critical reading, 48% scored over 600 on SAT math, 4% scored over 600 on SAT writing, 30% scored over 26 on composite ACT.

Student Life Upper grades have specified standards of dress, student council, honor system. Discipline rests primarily with faculty. Attendance at religious services is required.

Summer Programs Remediation, enrichment, sports, art/fine arts programs offered; session focuses on keeping students ready for academics and competition over the long break; held on campus; accepts boys and girls; open to students from other schools. 50 students usually enrolled. 2017 schedule: June to August.

Tuition and Aid Day student tuition: $10,300. Tuition installment plan (FACTS Tuition Payment Plan). Merit scholarship grants, need-based scholarship grants, employee discount available. In 2016–17, 25% of upper-school students received aid; total upper-school merit-scholarship money awarded: $4000. Total amount of financial aid awarded in 2016–17: $181,000.

Admissions Traditional secondary-level entrance grade is 7. For fall 2016, 122 students applied for upper-level admission, 113 were accepted, 218 enrolled. Essay and Math Placement Exam required. Deadline for receipt of application materials: none. Application fee required: $50. Interview recommended.

Athletics Interscholastic: baseball (boys), basketball (b,g), football (b), golf (b), soccer (b,g), volleyball (g); intramural: basketball (b,g), cheering (g), golf (g), volleyball (g); coed interscholastic: cross-country running, track and field; coed intramural: aerobics, bicycling, combined training, dance, fitness, modern dance, mountain biking, outdoor recreation, outdoor skills, physical fitness, physical training, rock climbing, skiing (downhill), snowboarding, weight training. 2 PE instructors, 23 coaches.

Computers Computers are regularly used in all academic, basic skills, introduction to technology, media arts, multimedia, yearbook classes. Computer network features include Internet access, wireless campus network, Internet filtering or blocking technology, RenWeb parents and student access, 1:1 iPad program, Moodle for classrooms. Campus intranet, student e-mail accounts, and computer access in designated common areas are available to students. Students grades are available online. The school has a published electronic and media policy.

Contact Mrs. Jeannette King, Admissions Manager. 303-531-4522. Fax: 720-922-3296. E-mail: admissions@frcs.org. Website: www.frcs.org

FUQUA SCHOOL

605 Fuqua Drive
PO Box 328
Farmville, Virginia 23901

Head of School: Mr. John H. Melton

General Information Coeducational day college-preparatory, arts, vocational, and technology school. Grades PK–12. Founded: 1993. Setting: small town. Nearest major city is Richmond. 65-acre campus. 19 buildings on campus. Approved or accredited by Southern Association of Colleges and Schools, Virginia Association of Independent Schools, and Virginia Department of Education. Member of National Association of Independent Schools and Secondary School Admission Test Board. Endowment: $6 million. Total enrollment: 379. Upper school average class size: 15. Upper school faculty-student ratio: 1:7. There are 180 required school days per year for Upper School

students. Upper School students typically attend 5 days per week. The average school day consists of 6 hours.

Upper School Student Profile Grade 9: 40 students (20 boys, 20 girls); Grade 10: 44 students (24 boys, 20 girls); Grade 11: 28 students (13 boys, 15 girls); Grade 12: 39 students (20 boys, 19 girls).

Faculty School total: 42. In upper school: 10 men, 11 women; 6 have advanced degrees.

Graduation Requirements Arts and fine arts (art, music, dance, drama), communications, composition, computer information systems, driver education, English, fitness, foreign language, grammar, health education, mathematics, physical education (includes health), science, social studies (includes history), 40 community service hours (or 10 per years of enrollment in upper school). Community service is required.

Special Academic Programs Advanced Placement exam preparation; honors section; accelerated programs; independent study; study at local college for college credit; academic accommodation for the gifted; ESL (6 students enrolled).

College Admission Counseling 29 students graduated in 2016; 26 went to college, including Hampden-Sydney College; James Madison University; Longwood University; The College of William and Mary; University of Virginia; Virginia Polytechnic Institute and State University. Other: 2 went to work, 1 entered military service. Median SAT critical reading: 530, median SAT math: 520, median SAT writing: 520, median combined SAT: 1610, median composite ACT: 23. 25% scored over 600 on SAT critical reading, 35% scored over 600 on SAT math, 38% scored over 600 on SAT writing, 38% scored over 1800 on combined SAT, 40% scored over 26 on composite ACT.

Student Life Upper grades have specified standards of dress, student council, honor system. Discipline rests primarily with faculty.

Summer Programs Enrichment, sports, art/fine arts programs offered; session focuses on sports and sports skills, arts, enrichment; held on campus; accepts boys and girls; open to students from other schools. 75 students usually enrolled. 2017 schedule: June 15 to July 31. Application deadline: May 15.

Tuition and Aid Day student tuition: $8470. Tuition installment plan (Insured Tuition Payment Plan, FACTS Tuition Payment Plan, monthly payment plans, individually arranged payment plans). Tuition reduction for siblings, merit scholarship grants, need-based scholarship grants available. In 2016–17, 40% of upper-school students received aid; total upper-school merit-scholarship money awarded: $7000. Total amount of financial aid awarded in 2016–17: $67,636.

Admissions Traditional secondary-level entrance grade is 9. For fall 2016, 32 students applied for upper-level admission, 30 were accepted, 30 enrolled. Brigance Test of Basic Skills, non-standardized placement tests or SLEP for foreign students required. Deadline for receipt of application materials: none. Application fee required: $125. On-campus interview recommended.

Athletics Interscholastic: baseball (boys), basketball (b,g), cheering (g), football (b), lacrosse (b,g), softball (g), tennis (g), volleyball (g); coed interscholastic: cross-country running, golf, soccer, swimming and diving, track and field; coed intramural: basketball. 4 PE instructors, 38 coaches, 1 athletic trainer.

Computers Computers are regularly used in all academic, SAT preparation, yearbook classes. Computer network features include on-campus library services, online commercial services, Internet access, wireless campus network, Internet filtering or blocking technology. Student e-mail accounts and computer access in designated common areas are available to students. The school has a published electronic and media policy.

Contact Mrs. Christy M. Murphy, Director of Admissions. 434-392-4131 Ext. 273. Fax: 434-392-5062. E-mail: murphycm@fuquaschool.com. Website: http://www.FuquaSchool.com

GABRIEL RICHARD CATHOLIC HIGH SCHOOL

15325 Pennsylvania Road
Riverview, Michigan 48193

Head of School: Mr. Joseph J. Whalen

General Information Coeducational day college-preparatory school, affiliated with Roman Catholic Church. Grades 9–12. Founded: 1965. Setting: suburban. Nearest major city is Detroit. 23-acre campus. 1 building on campus. Approved or accredited by North Central Association of Colleges and Schools and Michigan Department of Education. Total enrollment: 323. Upper school average class size: 17. Upper school faculty-student ratio: 1:17. There are 180 required school days per year for Upper School students. Upper School students typically attend 5 days per week. The average school day consists of 7 hours and 5 minutes.

Upper School Student Profile Grade 9: 98 students (52 boys, 46 girls); Grade 10: 68 students (37 boys, 31 girls); Grade 11: 77 students (41 boys, 36 girls); Grade 12: 80 students (44 boys, 36 girls); Postgraduate: 323 students (174 boys, 149 girls). 90% of students are Roman Catholic.

Faculty School total: 18. In upper school: 4 men, 14 women; 13 have advanced degrees.

Subjects Offered 1 1/2 elective credits, 20th century American writers, 20th century history, 20th century world history, accounting, acting, advanced chemistry, advanced math, Advanced Placement courses, advanced studio art-AP, algebra, American Civil War, American democracy, American government, American history, American history-AP, American literature, American literature-AP, anatomy, anatomy and physiology, ancient history, ancient world history, animal science, art, band, basic language skills, biology, biology-AP, British literature (honors), business law, calculus, calculus-AP, campus ministry, Catholic belief and practice, ceramics, chemistry, chemistry-AP, Christian doctrine, Christian education, Christian scripture, Christian testament, Christianity, church history, Civil War, civil war history, clayworking, college planning, communications, comparative politics, comparative religion, constitutional history of U.S., constitutional law, digital art, digital photography, drama, drawing, earth science, economics, English literature, English-AP, environmental science, European history-AP, family living, forensics, French, general science, geography, geometry, government, government-AP, health, history, history of the Catholic Church, history-AP, honors algebra, honors English, human anatomy, humanities, lab science, logic, New Testament, participation in sports, peace and justice, peer ministry, photography, physical fitness, physics, physics-AP, portfolio art, psychology-AP, publications, research, senior composition, sociology, Spanish, speech, sports, studio art-AP, theater arts, U.S. government and politics-AP, U.S. history, U.S. history-AP, United States government-AP, weight training, zoology.

Graduation Requirements Arts and fine arts (art, music, dance, drama), English, mathematics, physical education (includes health), science, social studies (includes history), speech, theology.

Special Academic Programs Advanced Placement exam preparation; honors section; independent study.

College Admission Counseling 79 students graduated in 2016; all went to college, including Eastern Michigan University; Grand Valley State University; Michigan State University; University of Michigan; Wayne State University. Median composite ACT: 22. 22% scored over 26 on composite ACT.

Student Life Upper grades have uniform requirement, student council, honor system. Discipline rests primarily with faculty. Attendance at religious services is required.

Tuition and Aid Day student tuition: $6550. Tuition installment plan (The Tuition Plan, Academic Management Services Plan). Tuition reduction for siblings, merit scholarship grants, need-based scholarship grants available.

Admissions Traditional secondary-level entrance grade is 9. For fall 2016, 98 students applied for upper-level admission, 98 were accepted, 98 enrolled. High School Placement Test required. Deadline for receipt of application materials: none. Application fee required: $100. On-campus interview required.

Athletics Interscholastic: baseball (boys), basketball (b,g), cheering (g), cross-country running (b,g), football (b), ice hockey (b), soccer (b,g), softball (g), tennis (b,g), track and field (b,g), volleyball (g), wrestling (b); coed interscholastic: bowling, equestrian sports, figure skating, golf. 1 PE instructor.

Computers Computers are regularly used in digital applications, research skills, speech classes. Computer network features include on-campus library services, Internet access, Internet filtering or blocking technology. Computer access in designated common areas is available to students. Students grades are available online.

Contact Mr. Joseph J. Whalen, Principal. 734-284-1875. Fax: 734-284-9304. E-mail: whalenj@gabrielrichard.org. Website: www.gabrielrichard.org

THE GALLOWAY SCHOOL

215 West Wieuca Road NW
Atlanta, Georgia 30342

Head of School: Suzanna Jemsby

General Information Coeducational day college-preparatory school. Grades P3–12. Founded: 1969. Setting: suburban. 8-acre campus. 5 buildings on campus. Approved or accredited by Academy of Orton-Gillingham Practitioners and Educators, Georgia Independent School Association, Southern Association of Colleges and Schools, Southern Association of Independent Schools, and Georgia Department of Education. Member of National Association of Independent Schools and Secondary School Admission Test Board. Endowment: $18.3 million. Total enrollment: 750. Upper school average class size: 12. Upper school faculty-student ratio: 1:12. There are 170 required school days per year for Upper School students. Upper School students typically attend 5 days per week. The average school day consists of 7 hours.

Upper School Student Profile Grade 6: 55 students (26 boys, 29 girls); Grade 7: 64 students (29 boys, 35 girls); Grade 8: 61 students (23 boys, 38 girls); Grade 9: 62 students (33 boys, 29 girls); Grade 10: 74 students (35 boys, 39 girls); Grade 11: 69 students (34 boys, 35 girls); Grade 12: 63 students (26 boys, 37 girls).

Faculty School total: 112. In upper school: 16 men, 22 women; 31 have advanced degrees.

Subjects Offered Entrepreneurship, environmental science-AP, European history-AP, French studies, speech and debate.

Graduation Requirements Arts and fine arts (art, music, dance, drama), computers, electives, English, foreign language, health and wellness, mathematics, science, social studies (includes history).

Special Academic Programs Advanced Placement exam preparation; accelerated programs; independent study; term-away projects; study at local college for college credit; academic accommodation for the gifted, the musically talented, and the artistically talented.

College Admission Counseling 64 students graduated in 2016; all went to college, including Brown University; Emory University; Furman University; Georgia Institute of Technology; University of Colorado Boulder; University of Georgia. Median SAT

critical reading: 637, median SAT math: 624, median SAT writing: 636, median combined SAT: 1897, median composite ACT: 28. 67% scored over 600 on SAT critical reading, 57% scored over 600 on SAT math, 63% scored over 600 on SAT writing, 67% scored over 1800 on combined SAT, 70% scored over 26 on composite ACT.

Student Life Upper grades have student council, honor system. Discipline rests primarily with faculty.

Summer Programs Remediation, enrichment, advancement, sports, art/fine arts, computer instruction programs offered; session focuses on enrichment; held both on and off campus; accepts boys and girls; open to students from other schools. 55 students usually enrolled. 2017 schedule: June 5 to August 5. Application deadline: May 31.

Tuition and Aid Day student tuition: $25,900. Tuition installment plan (FACTS Tuition Payment Plan, 50/50 twice a year payments, payroll deductions, special arrangements provided to families based upon their circumstances). Need-based scholarship grants available. In 2016–17, 16% of upper-school students received aid. Total amount of financial aid awarded in 2016–17: $820,778.

Admissions Traditional secondary-level entrance grade is 9. For fall 2016, 123 students applied for upper-level admission, 57 were accepted, 24 enrolled. Admissions testing and SSAT required. Deadline for receipt of application materials: January 31. Application fee required: $85. On-campus interview required.

Athletics Interscholastic: baseball (boys), basketball (b,g), golf (b,g), soccer (b,g), softball (g), swimming and diving (b,g), tennis (b,g), track and field (b,g), volleyball (g); coed interscholastic: cross-country running, ultimate Frisbee. 1 PE instructor, 3 coaches, 1 athletic trainer.

Computers Computers are regularly used in art, desktop publishing, drawing and design, English, graphic arts, information technology, introduction to technology, journalism, keyboarding, literary magazine, mathematics, multimedia, music, newspaper, photography, publishing, research skills, science, technology, theater, Web site design, yearbook classes. Computer network features include on-campus library services, online commercial services, Internet access, wireless campus network, Internet filtering or blocking technology, print sharing. Campus intranet, student e-mail accounts, and computer access in designated common areas are available to students. Students grades are available online. The school has a published electronic and media policy.

Contact Elizabeth King, Director of Admissions. 404-252-8389 Ext. 106. Fax: 404-252-7770. E-mail: e.king@gallowayschool.org. Website: www.gallowayschool.org

GANN ACADEMY (THE NEW JEWISH HIGH SCHOOL OF GREATER BOSTON)

333 Forest Street
Waltham, Massachusetts 02452

Head of School: Rabbi Marc A. Baker

General Information Coeducational day college-preparatory and religious studies school, affiliated with Jewish faith. Grades 9–12. Founded: 1997. Setting: suburban. Nearest major city is Boston. 20-acre campus. 2 buildings on campus. Approved or accredited by Association of Independent Schools in New England, New England Association of Schools and Colleges, and Massachusetts Department of Education. Member of National Association of Independent Schools. Endowment: $6.9 million. Total enrollment: 277. Upper school average class size: 14. Upper school faculty-student ratio: 1:5. There are 165 required school days per year for Upper School students. Upper School students typically attend 5 days per week. The average school day consists of 8 hours.

Upper School Student Profile Grade 9: 72 students (36 boys, 36 girls); Grade 10: 76 students (39 boys, 37 girls); Grade 11: 69 students (33 boys, 36 girls); Grade 12: 71 students (34 boys, 37 girls). 100% of students are Jewish.

Faculty School total: 51. In upper school: 20 men, 31 women; 43 have advanced degrees.

Subjects Offered Advanced Placement courses, algebra, American history-AP, American literature-AP, art history, arts, Bible as literature, biology, calculus, calculus-AP, chemistry, computer science, creative arts, creative writing, drama, English, geometry, health and wellness, Hebrew, history, Holocaust, Jewish history, Judaic studies, Mandarin, modern dance, music, photography, physics, pre-calculus, Rabbinic literature, robotics, Spanish.

Graduation Requirements American history, art, arts, athletics, Bible as literature, English, health, Hebrew, history, Judaic studies, mathematics, science.

Special Academic Programs Advanced Placement exam preparation; study abroad.

College Admission Counseling 67 students graduated in 2016; all went to college, including Boston University; Brandeis University; Brown University; Princeton University; Syracuse University; The George Washington University. Median SAT critical reading: 650, median SAT math: 660, median SAT writing: 670, median combined SAT: 1985, median composite ACT: 27. 70.7% scored over 600 on SAT critical reading, 65.9% scored over 600 on SAT math, 75.6% scored over 600 on SAT writing, 73.2% scored over 1800 on combined SAT, 57.9% scored over 26 on composite ACT.

Student Life Upper grades have specified standards of dress, student council, honor system. Discipline rests primarily with faculty. Attendance at religious services is required.

Tuition and Aid Day student tuition: $39,000. Guaranteed tuition plan. Tuition installment plan (FACTS Tuition Payment Plan). Need-based scholarship grants, Pioneer Program, Professional Partner Program, Within Reach Program available. In 2016–17, 51% of upper-school students received aid. Total amount of financial aid awarded in 2016–17: $2,300,000.

Admissions Traditional secondary-level entrance grade is 9. For fall 2016, 138 students applied for upper-level admission, 125 were accepted, 83 enrolled. SSAT required. Deadline for receipt of application materials: January 17. Application fee required: $100. On-campus interview recommended.

Athletics Interscholastic: baseball (boys), basketball (b,g), lacrosse (b,g), soccer (b,g), softball (g), tennis (b,g), volleyball (g); intramural: dance team (g); coed interscholastic: cross-country running, ultimate Frisbee; coed intramural: basketball, fitness, golf, martial arts, modern dance, running, table tennis, tennis, ultimate Frisbee, volleyball, yoga. 30 coaches, 1 athletic trainer.

Computers Computers are regularly used in all classes. Computer network features include on-campus library services, Internet access, wireless campus network, Internet filtering or blocking technology, computer lab. Campus intranet, student e-mail accounts, and computer access in designated common areas are available to students. Students grades are available online. The school has a published electronic and media policy.

Contact Farrah Rubenstein, Director of Enrollment Management. 781-642-6800. Fax: 781-642-6805. E-mail: frubenstein@gannacademy.org.
Website: www.gannacademy.org/

GARRISON FOREST SCHOOL

300 Garrison Forest Road
Owings Mills, Maryland 21117

Head of School: Dr. Kimberley J. Roberts

General Information Girls' boarding and day (coeducational in lower grades) college-preparatory, arts, technology, and Women in Science & Engineering (WISE) school. Boarding girls grades 8–12, day boys grades N–PK, day girls grades N–12. Founded: 1910. Setting: suburban. Nearest major city is Baltimore. Students are housed in single-sex dormitories. 110-acre campus. 18 buildings on campus. Approved or accredited by Association of Independent Maryland Schools, Middle States Association of Colleges and Schools, The Association of Boarding Schools, and Maryland Department of Education. Member of National Association of Independent Schools and Secondary School Admission Test Board. Endowment: $42 million. Total enrollment: 614. Upper school average class size: 14. Upper school faculty-student ratio: 1:8. There are 173 required school days per year for Upper School students. Upper School students typically attend 5 days per week. The average school day consists of 7 hours.

Upper School Student Profile Grade 9: 76 students (76 girls); Grade 10: 68 students (68 girls); Grade 11: 58 students (58 girls); Grade 12: 78 students (78 girls). 26% of students are boarding students. 85% are state residents. 11 states are represented in upper school student body. 12% are international students. International students from British Virgin Islands, China, Germany, Mexico, Republic of Korea, and Spain; 6 other countries represented in student body.

Faculty School total: 86. In upper school: 5 men, 38 women; 35 have advanced degrees; 22 reside on campus.

Subjects Offered 3-dimensional art, 3-dimensional design, advanced chemistry, advanced math, algebra, American foreign policy, American government, American history, American history-AP, American literature, anatomy, ancient world history, animation, applied music, art, art history, art history-AP, arts and crafts, biology, calculus, calculus-AP, ceramics, chemistry, chemistry-AP, Chinese, Chinese studies, choral music, college counseling, college placement, college planning, computer science, computer skills, creative writing, dance, decision making skills, design, desktop publishing, digital applications, digital art, digital imaging, digital photography, drama, drawing, ecology, English, English composition, English literature, English-AP, environmental science-AP, environmental studies, equestrian sports, equine science, equitation, ESL, ethics, film studies, filmmaking, fine arts, French, French language-AP, French-AP, geometry, health and safety, health and wellness, history-AP, jewelry making, Latin, Latin-AP, leadership and service, life skills, mathematics, music, musical productions, painting, peace studies, peer counseling, philosophy, photography, physical education, physics, physics-AP, play production, portfolio art, pre-calculus, psychology-AP, public policy, public policy issues and action, public service, public speaking, publications, science, science project, science research, sculpture, social justice, Spanish, Spanish language-AP, Spanish-AP, sports, stage design, statistics, student government, study skills, technological applications, technology, technology/design, theater, trigonometry, U.S. history-AP, values and decisions, voice ensemble, world history, writing, yearbook.

Graduation Requirements Arts and fine arts (art, music, dance, drama), decision making skills, English, foreign language, mathematics, physical education (includes health), science, social studies (includes history).

Special Academic Programs 12 Advanced Placement exams for which test preparation is offered; honors section; independent study; term-away projects; academic accommodation for the gifted, the musically talented, and the artistically talented; ESL (22 students enrolled).

College Admission Counseling 68 students graduated in 2015; all went to college, including Boston University; Columbia University; Johns Hopkins University;

University of Maryland, College Park; University of South Carolina; University of Virginia. 50% scored over 600 on SAT critical reading, 50% scored over 600 on SAT math, 50% scored over 600 on SAT writing, 50% scored over 26 on composite ACT.

Student Life Upper grades have uniform requirement, student council, honor system. Discipline rests equally with students and faculty.

Tuition and Aid Day student tuition: $27,810; 7-day tuition and room/board: $52,540. Tuition installment plan (FACTS Tuition Payment Plan). Merit scholarship grants, need-based scholarship grants, merit-based Legacy Scholarship available. In 2015–16, 34% of upper-school students received aid; total upper-school merit-scholarship money awarded: $20,000. Total amount of financial aid awarded in 2015–16: $377,600.

Admissions Traditional secondary-level entrance grade is 9. For fall 2015, 174 students applied for upper-level admission, 86 were accepted, 36 enrolled. Admissions testing, ISEE, SSAT, TOEFL or WISC-R or WISC-III required. Deadline for receipt of application materials: December 11. Application fee required: $50. Interview required.

Athletics Interscholastic: badminton, basketball, cross-country running, equestrian sports, field hockey, golf, horseback riding, indoor soccer, indoor track, lacrosse, polo, soccer, softball, tennis, track and field, winter (indoor) track, winter soccer; intramural: aerobics, aerobics/dance, bowling, dance, fitness, horseback riding, modern dance, physical fitness, squash, strength & conditioning, volleyball, yoga. 5 PE instructors, 12 coaches, 1 athletic trainer.

Computers Computers are regularly used in animation, art, college planning, design, desktop publishing, digital applications, English, ESL, foreign language, French, history, humanities, literary magazine, mathematics, newspaper, photography, publications, science, Spanish, study skills, technology, word processing, writing, yearbook classes. Computer network features include on-campus library services, Internet access, wireless campus network, Internet filtering or blocking technology, Moodle. Student e-mail accounts and computer access in designated common areas are available to students. Students grades are available online. The school has a published electronic and media policy.

Contact Ms. Alison C. Greer, Director of Admission. 410-559-3110. Fax: 410-363-8441. E-mail: admission@gfs.org. Website: www.gfs.org

GASTON DAY SCHOOL

2001 Gaston Day School Road
Gastonia, North Carolina 28056

Head of School: Dr. Richard E. Rankin

General Information Coeducational day college-preparatory and arts school. Grades PS–12. Founded: 1967. Setting: suburban. Nearest major city is Charlotte. 60-acre campus. 4 buildings on campus. Approved or accredited by North Carolina Association of Independent Schools, Southern Association of Colleges and Schools, Southern Association of Independent Schools, and North Carolina Department of Education. Member of National Association of Independent Schools. Endowment: $2.3 million. Total enrollment: 481. Upper school average class size: 12. Upper school faculty-student ratio: 1:13. There are 169 required school days per year for Upper School students. Upper School students typically attend 5 days per week. The average school day consists of 7 hours and 15 minutes.

Upper School Student Profile Grade 9: 33 students (9 boys, 24 girls); Grade 10: 39 students (21 boys, 18 girls); Grade 11: 33 students (11 boys, 22 girls); Grade 12: 40 students (16 boys, 24 girls).

Faculty School total: 53. In upper school: 8 men, 12 women; 12 have advanced degrees.

Subjects Offered Advanced chemistry, Advanced Placement courses, advanced studio art-AP, algebra, American history-AP, American literature, anatomy and physiology, art, band, biology, biology-AP, British literature, British literature (honors), calculus-AP, chemistry, chemistry-AP, choral music, chorus, concert choir, creative writing, drama, English language and composition-AP, English language-AP, English literature and composition-AP, environmental science, environmental science-AP, film and literature, fine arts, French, general science, geometry, government/civics, honors algebra, honors English, honors geometry, honors U.S. history, honors world history, jazz band, journalism, learning lab, physics, pre-calculus, senior internship, Spanish, Spanish-AP, statistics-AP, student government, studio art-AP, study skills, U.S. government, U.S. history, U.S. history-AP, United States government-AP, visual arts, weight training, world literature, yearbook.

Graduation Requirements Arts and fine arts (art, music, dance, drama), electives, English, foreign language, mathematics, physical education (includes health), science, social studies (includes history), 25 hours of community service per year, seniors must complete a senior project.

Special Academic Programs Advanced Placement exam preparation; honors section; independent study; academic accommodation for the gifted; ESL (4 students enrolled).

College Admission Counseling 36 students graduated in 2016; all went to college, including Appalachian State University; Clemson University; High Point University; North Carolina State University; The University of North Carolina at Chapel Hill; Wake Forest University. Mean SAT critical reading: 590, mean SAT math: 605, mean SAT writing: 605, mean combined SAT: 1765, mean composite ACT: 25.

Student Life Upper grades have specified standards of dress, student council, honor system. Discipline rests primarily with faculty.

Summer Programs Remediation, enrichment, advancement, sports, art/fine arts, computer instruction programs offered; session focuses on academic enrichment, advancement in sports and arts; held on campus; accepts boys and girls; open to students from other schools. 300 students usually enrolled. 2017 schedule: June 5 to August 11.

Tuition and Aid Day student tuition: $15,450. Tuition installment plan (monthly payment plans, individually arranged payment plans). Merit scholarship grants, need-based scholarship grants available. In 2016–17, 52% of upper-school students received aid; total upper-school merit-scholarship money awarded: $106,700. Total amount of financial aid awarded in 2016–17: $203,858.

Admissions Traditional secondary-level entrance grade is 9. For fall 2016, 46 students applied for upper-level admission, 34 were accepted, 19 enrolled. ACT, ISEE, PSAT or SAT required. Deadline for receipt of application materials: none. Application fee required: $75. On-campus interview required.

Athletics Interscholastic: baseball (boys), basketball (b,g), cheering (g), cross-country running (b,g), golf (b,g), soccer (b,g), swimming and diving (b,g), tennis (b,g), track and field (b,g), volleyball (g); intramural: fitness (b,g); coed intramural: crew, rowing. 2 PE instructors, 7 coaches, 1 athletic trainer.

Computers Computers are regularly used in art, English, foreign language, history, journalism, mathematics, newspaper, science, yearbook classes. Computer network features include on-campus library services, online commercial services, Internet access, wireless campus network, Internet filtering or blocking technology, iPads issued to each middle and upper school student. Student e-mail accounts and computer access in designated common areas are available to students. Students grades are available online. The school has a published electronic and media policy.

Contact Mr. Davidson R. Hobson, Director of Admission. 704-864-7744 Ext. 174. Fax: 704-865-3813. E-mail: dhobson@gastonday.org. Website: www.gastonday.org

GEM STATE ACADEMY

16115 Montana Avenue
Caldwell, Idaho 83607

Head of School: Mr. Marvin Thorman

General Information Coeducational boarding and day and distance learning college-preparatory school, affiliated with Seventh-day Adventist Church. Ungraded, ages 14–18. Founded: 1918. Setting: suburban. Nearest major city is Boise. Students are housed in single-sex dormitories. 4 buildings on campus. Approved or accredited by National Council for Private School Accreditation, Northwest Accreditation Commission, and Idaho Department of Education. Total enrollment: 55. Upper school average class size: 15. Upper school faculty-student ratio: 1:6. There are 180 required school days per year for Upper School students. Upper School students typically attend 5 days per week. The average school day consists of 7 hours.

Upper School Student Profile Grade 9: 24 students (9 boys, 15 girls); Grade 10: 17 students (7 boys, 10 girls); Grade 11: 16 students (8 boys, 8 girls); Grade 12: 13 students (8 boys, 5 girls). 37% of students are boarding students. 84% are state residents. 7 states are represented in upper school student body. 1% are international students. International students from Republic of Korea.

Faculty School total: 10. In upper school: 6 men, 4 women; 4 have advanced degrees; 5 reside on campus.

Graduation Requirements Computer education, U.S. government, U.S. history, senior project.

Special Academic Programs Advanced Placement exam preparation; study at local college for college credit.

College Admission Counseling 15 students graduated in 2016; they went to Boise State University; Pacific Union College; Southern Adventist University; Walla Walla University. Other: 1 went to work.

Student Life Upper grades have specified standards of dress, student council, honor system. Discipline rests primarily with faculty. Attendance at religious services is required.

Tuition and Aid Day student tuition: $10,000; 5-day tuition and room/board: $14,260; 7-day tuition and room/board: $16,000. Tuition installment plan (FACTS Tuition Payment Plan, monthly payment plans, individually arranged payment plans). Tuition reduction for siblings, merit scholarship grants, need-based scholarship grants, paying campus jobs available.

Admissions Traditional secondary-level entrance grade is 9. TOEFL or SLEP required. Deadline for receipt of application materials: none. No application fee required.

Athletics Interscholastic: basketball (boys, girls), flag football (b), touch football (b), volleyball (g); intramural: basketball (b,g), flag football (b,g), floor hockey (b,g), soccer (b,g), softball (b,g), volleyball (b,g); coed intramural: softball, volleyball. 1 PE instructor.

Computers Computer network features include on-campus library services, online commercial services, Internet access, Internet filtering or blocking technology. Student e-mail accounts are available to students. Students grades are available online. The school has a published electronic and media policy.

Contact Mrs. Karen Davies, Registrar. 208-459-1627 Ext. 110. Fax: 208-454-9079. E-mail: kdavies@gemstate.org. Website: www.gemstate.org

GEORGE SCHOOL

1690 Newtown Langhorne Road
PO Box 4460
Newtown, Pennsylvania 18940

Head of School: Nancy O. Starmer

General Information Coeducational boarding and day college-preparatory, arts, religious studies, and International Baccalaureate school, affiliated with Society of Friends. Grades 9–12. Founded: 1893. Setting: suburban. Nearest major city is Philadelphia. Students are housed in single-sex dormitories. 265-acre campus. 19 buildings on campus. Approved or accredited by Friends Council on Education, International Baccalaureate Organization, Middle States Association of Colleges and Schools, The Association of Boarding Schools, The College Board, and Pennsylvania Department of Education. Member of National Association of Independent Schools and Secondary School Admission Test Board. Endowment: $150.6 million. Total enrollment: 540. Upper school average class size: 14. Upper school faculty-student ratio: 1:7. There are 165 required school days per year for Upper School students. Upper School students typically attend 5 days per week. The average school day consists of 6 hours.

Upper School Student Profile Grade 9: 112 students (54 boys, 58 girls), Grade 10: 142 students (74 boys, 68 girls); Grade 11: 142 students (73 boys, 69 girls); Grade 12: 144 students (80 boys, 64 girls). 53% of students are boarding students. 49% are state residents. 22 states are represented in upper school student body. 24% are international students. International students from China, Mexico, Republic of Korea, Taiwan, United Kingdom, and Viet Nam; 46 other countries represented in student body. 12% of students are members of Society of Friends.

Faculty School total: 80. In upper school: 32 men, 48 women; 57 have advanced degrees; 53 reside on campus.

Subjects Offered 3-dimensional art, acting, advanced biology, advanced chemistry, advanced math, Advanced Placement courses, advanced studio art-AP, African American history, African-American history, algebra, American history, American history-AP, American literature, analysis, analysis and differential calculus, ancient world history, art, art-AP, arts, Asian history, astronomy, athletic training, athletics, biology, biology-AP, calculus, calculus-AP, cell biology, ceramics, chemistry, chemistry-AP, Chinese, choral music, classical language, clayworking, community service, composition, computer science, computer science-AP, conceptual physics, creative arts, dance, dance performance, desktop publishing, digital imaging, drama, drama performance, drawing, driver education, economics-AP, electives, English, English as a foreign language, English composition, English language and composition-AP, English language-AP, English literature, English literature and composition-AP, English literature-AP, English-AP, English/composition-AP, ensembles, environmental science, environmental systems, equality and freedom, ESL, fine arts, foreign language, French, French as a second language, French language-AP, French literature-AP, French-AP, functions, gardening, general science, geography, geometry, global studies, health, health and wellness, health education, history, history-AP, honors algebra, honors English, honors geometry, honors U.S. history, honors world history, horticulture, human geography - AP, inorganic chemistry, instrumental music, International Baccalaureate courses, jazz band, jazz ensemble, journalism, lab science, language, language and composition, language-AP, languages, Latin, Latin-AP, life science, literature, literature and composition-AP, literature-AP, management information systems, Mandarin, marine science, mathematics, mathematics-AP, microcomputer technology applications, microeconomics-AP, modern dance, modern European history, modern history, modern languages, modern world history, music, music performance, musical productions, musical theater, newspaper, non-Western literature, orchestra, painting, peace and justice, peace education, peace studies, performing arts, photography, physical education, physical fitness, physics, physics-AP, portfolio art, pre-calculus, probability and statistics, programming, publications, Quakerism and ethics, religion, religious studies, robotics, science, sculpture, set design, Spanish, Spanish language-AP, Spanish literature, Spanish literature-AP, Spanish-AP, stage design, stagecraft, statistics, statistics-AP, studio art, studio art-AP, theater, theater arts, theory of knowledge, trigonometry, U.S. history, U.S. history-AP, video, video film production, visual arts, vocal ensemble, vocal music, wellness, Western religions, wind ensemble, woodworking, work camp program, world civilizations, world history, world literature, world religions, world religions, writing, yearbook, yoga.

Graduation Requirements Arts and fine arts (art, music, dance, drama), English, foreign language, geometry, mathematics, performing arts, religion (includes Bible studies and theology), science, social studies (includes history), 65 hours of community service.

Special Academic Programs International Baccalaureate program; Advanced Placement exam preparation; honors section; ESL (16 students enrolled).

College Admission Counseling 135 students graduated in 2015; 134 went to college, including Drexel University; Elon University; New York University; Temple University; University of Colorado Boulder; Vassar College. Other: 1 had other specific plans. Mean SAT critical reading: 625, mean SAT math: 621, mean SAT writing: 609, mean combined SAT: 1855, mean composite ACT: 27. 66% scored over 600 on SAT critical reading, 58% scored over 600 on SAT math, 56% scored over 600 on SAT writing, 61% scored over 1800 on combined SAT, 67% scored over 26 on composite ACT.

Student Life Upper grades have specified standards of dress, student council, honor system. Discipline rests equally with students and faculty. Attendance at religious services is required.

Tuition and Aid Day student tuition: $36,975; 7-day tuition and room/board: $54,600. Tuition installment plan (monthly payment plans, individually arranged payment plans). Merit scholarship grants, need-based scholarship grants available. In 2015–16, 50% of upper-school students received aid; total upper-school merit-scholarship money awarded: $225,000. Total amount of financial aid awarded in 2015–16: $8,500,000.

Admissions Traditional secondary-level entrance grade is 9. For fall 2015, 709 students applied for upper-level admission, 324 were accepted, 152 enrolled. ERB, SSAT or TOEFL or SLEP required. Deadline for receipt of application materials: February 1. Application fee required: $60. Interview required.

Athletics Interscholastic: baseball (boys), basketball (b,g), cross-country running (b,g), field hockey (g), football (b), hockey (g), lacrosse (b,g), soccer (b,g), softball (g), swimming and diving (b,g), tennis (b,g), track and field (b,g), volleyball (g), wrestling (b,g); coed interscholastic: cheering, equestrian sports, golf, horseback riding, indoor track, modern dance, winter (indoor) track; coed intramural: aerobics/dance, dance, horseback riding, strength & conditioning, yoga. 5 PE instructors, 5 coaches, 1 athletic trainer.

Computers Computers are regularly used in English, ESL, foreign language, history, mathematics, newspaper, photography, science, yearbook classes. Computer network features include on-campus library services, online commercial services, Internet access, wireless campus network, Internet filtering or blocking technology. Campus intranet, student e-mail accounts, and computer access in designated common areas are available to students. Students grades are available online. The school has a published electronic and media policy.

Contact Monica Isserman, Admission Services Coordinator. 215-579-6548. Fax: 215-579-6549. E-mail: misserman@georgeschool.org. Website: www.georgeschool.org

GEORGE STEVENS ACADEMY

23 Union Street
Blue Hill, Maine 04614

Head of School: Mr. Timothy Seeley

General Information Coeducational boarding and day college-preparatory, general academic, arts, business, vocational, and technology school. Grades 9–12. Founded: 1803. Setting: small town. Nearest major city is Bangor. Students are housed in single-sex dormitories and host family homes. 315-acre campus. 7 buildings on campus. Approved or accredited by Independent Schools of Northern New England, New England Association of Schools and Colleges, The Association of Boarding Schools, The College Board, and Maine Department of Education. Member of National Association of Independent Schools and Secondary School Admission Test Board. Endowment: $7.3 million. Total enrollment: 325. Upper school average class size: 15. Upper school faculty-student ratio: 1:9. There are 175 required school days per year for Upper School students. Upper School students typically attend 5 days per week. The average school day consists of 6 hours and 30 minutes.

Upper School Student Profile Grade 9: 71 students (46 boys, 25 girls); Grade 10: 76 students (31 boys, 45 girls); Grade 11: 75 students (37 boys, 38 girls); Grade 12: 92 students (47 boys, 45 girls). 15% of students are boarding students. 86% are state residents. 1 state is represented in upper school student body. 14% are international students. International students from China, Jamaica, Republic of Korea, Rwanda, Thailand, and Viet Nam.

Faculty School total: 38. In upper school: 1 man, 19 women; 29 have advanced degrees; 4 reside on campus.

Subjects Offered Transportation technology.

Graduation Requirements Arts and fine arts (art, music, dance, drama), electives, English, history, mathematics, physical education (includes health), science, social sciences, U.S. history, senior debate.

Special Academic Programs 9 Advanced Placement exams for which test preparation is offered; honors section; accelerated programs; independent study; term-away projects; study at local college for college credit; study abroad; academic accommodation for the gifted, the musically talented, and the artistically talented; remedial reading and/or remedial writing; remedial math; special instructional classes for deaf students, blind students; ESL (27 students enrolled).

College Admission Counseling 76 students graduated in 2016; 58 went to college, including Colby College; Eastern Maine Community College; Husson University; Thomas College; University of Maine; University of Maine at Machias. Other: 4 went to work, 14 had other specific plans. Mean SAT critical reading: 535, mean SAT math: 519, mean SAT writing: 517. 31% scored over 600 on SAT critical reading, 23% scored over 600 on SAT math, 26% scored over 600 on SAT writing, 26% scored over 1800 on combined SAT.

Student Life Upper grades have specified standards of dress, student council. Discipline rests primarily with faculty.

Tuition and Aid Day student tuition: $11,300; 7-day tuition and room/board: $43,500. Tuition installment plan (monthly payment plans, individually arranged payment plans). Need-based scholarship grants available. In 2016–17, 1% of upper-school students received aid. Total amount of financial aid awarded in 2016–17: $100,000.

Admissions Traditional secondary-level entrance grade is 9. International English Language Test, SSAT, TAP or TOEFL or SLEP required. Deadline for receipt of application materials: none. Application fee required: $75. Interview required.

Athletics Interscholastic: baseball (boys), basketball (b,g), cheering (b,g), cross-country running (b,g), golf (b,g), independent competitive sports (b,g), running (b,g), sailing (b,g), soccer (b,g), softball (g), swimming and diving (b,g), tennis (b,g), track and field (b,g), volleyball (g), wrestling (b); coed interscholastic: indoor track; coed intramural: backpacking, bocce, canoeing/kayaking, croquet, dance, dance team, fitness, fitness walking, flag football, floor hockey, Frisbee, hiking/backpacking, jogging, kayaking, modern dance, ocean paddling, outdoor activities, outdoor adventure, outdoor education, outdoor recreation, outdoor skills, paddle tennis, physical fitness, physical training, running, sailing, skateboarding, skiing (cross-country), skiing (downhill), snowboarding, snowshoeing, strength & conditioning, table tennis, ultimate Frisbee, volleyball, walking, weight lifting, weight training, wilderness, winter walking, yoga. 2 PE instructors, 26 coaches.

Computers Computers are regularly used in all classes. Computer network features include on-campus library services, online commercial services, internet access, wireless campus network, internet filtering or blocking technology, all students receive a MacBook Air laptop to work on. Student e-mail accounts and computer access in designated common areas are available to students. Students grades are available online. The school has a published electronic and media policy.

Contact Mr. Cameron McDonald, Director of Admissions. 207-374-2808 Ext. 126. Fax: 207-374-2982. E-mail: c.mcdonald@georgestevens.info.
Website: www.georgestevensacademy.org

GEORGE WALTON ACADEMY

One Bulldog Drive
Monroe, Georgia 30655

Head of School: Mr. William M. Nicholson

General Information Coeducational day college-preparatory, arts, and technology school. Grades K4–12. Founded: 1969. Setting: small town. Nearest major city is Atlanta. 63-acre campus. 12 buildings on campus. Approved or accredited by Georgia Independent School Association, Southern Association of Colleges and Schools, Southern Association of Independent Schools, and Georgia Department of Education. Total enrollment: 850. Upper school average class size: 17. Upper school faculty-student ratio: 1:12. There are 180 required school days per year for Upper School students. Upper School students typically attend 5 days per week. The average school day consists of 6 hours and 45 minutes.

Upper School Student Profile Grade 9: 75 students (45 boys, 30 girls); Grade 10: 71 students (36 boys, 35 girls); Grade 11: 92 students (44 boys, 48 girls); Grade 12: 78 students (41 boys, 37 girls).

Faculty School total: 85. In upper school: 15 men, 38 women; 20 have advanced degrees.

Subjects Offered Algebra, American history, American literature, anatomy, art, art history, Bible studies, biology, calculus, chemistry, creative writing, drama, economics, English, English literature, environmental science, European history, fine arts, geography, geometry, government/civics, grammar, health, history, journalism, Latin, mathematics, music, photography, physical education, physics, psychology, science, social sciences, social studies, sociology, Spanish, trigonometry, world history, world literature, writing.

Graduation Requirements Arts and fine arts (art, music, dance, drama), composition, English, foreign language, mathematics, physical education (includes health), science, social sciences, social studies (includes history), all students must be accepted to a college or university to graduate.

Special Academic Programs 13 Advanced Placement exams for which test preparation is offered; honors section; academic accommodation for the gifted, the musically talented, and the artistically talented.

College Admission Counseling 68 students graduated in 2015; all went to college, including Georgia College & State University; Georgia Institute of Technology; Georgia Southern University; Georgia State University; University of Georgia; University of North Georgia. Median combined SAT: 1720.

Student Life Upper grades have uniform requirement, student council, honor system. Discipline rests primarily with faculty.

Tuition and Aid Day student tuition: $10,485. Tuition installment plan (monthly payment plans). Tuition reduction for siblings, need-based scholarship grants available. In 2015–16, 1% of upper-school students received aid.

Admissions Traditional secondary-level entrance grade is 9. ACT, CAT 5, CTBS, Stanford Achievement Test, any other standardized test, Otis-Lennon, Stanford Achievement Test, PSAT or SAT required. Deadline for receipt of application materials: none. Application fee required: $175. On-campus interview recommended.

Athletics Interscholastic: aquatics (boys, girls), baseball (b), basketball (b,g), cheering (g), cross-country running (b,g), dance squad (g), drill team (g), football (b), golf (b), physical fitness (b,g), soccer (b,g), softball (g), swimming and diving (b,g), tennis (b,g), track and field (b,g), volleyball (g), weight lifting (b), weight training (b,g), wrestling (b); coed interscholastic: equestrian sports. 3 PE instructors, 8 coaches.

Computers Computers are regularly used in all academic classes. Computer network features include on-campus library services, online commercial services, Internet access, wireless campus network, Internet filtering or blocking technology. Student e-mail accounts and computer access in designated common areas are available to students. Students grades are available online. The school has a published electronic and media policy.

Contact Ms. Cari Bailey, Director of Admissions. 770-207-5172 Ext. 254. Fax: 770-267-4023. E-mail: cbailey@gwa.com. Website: www.gwa.com

GILMAN SCHOOL

5407 Roland Avenue
Baltimore, Maryland 21210

Head of School: Mr. Henry P.A. Smyth

General Information Boys' day college-preparatory school. Grades K–12. Founded: 1897. Setting: suburban. 68-acre campus. 6 buildings on campus. Approved or accredited by Association of Independent Maryland Schools and Maryland Department of Education. Member of National Association of Independent Schools and Secondary School Admission Test Board. Endowment: $110 million. Total enrollment: 1,017. Upper school average class size: 16. Upper school faculty-student ratio: 1:7. There are 172 required school days per year for Upper School students. Upper School students typically attend 5 days per week. The average school day consists of 9 hours.

Upper School Student Profile Grade 6: 74 students (74 boys); Grade 7: 80 students (80 boys); Grade 8: 91 students (91 boys); Grade 9: 119 students (119 boys); Grade 10: 118 students (118 boys); Grade 11: 120 students (120 boys); Grade 12: 109 students (109 boys).

Faculty School total: 147. In upper school: 59 men, 9 women; 57 have advanced degrees.

Subjects Offered Advanced Placement courses, advanced studio art-AP, algebra, American history, American literature, anatomy, Arabic, architectural drawing, art, art history, biology, calculus, chemistry, Chinese, community service, computer math, computer programming, computer science, creative writing, drafting, drama, ecology, economics, English, English literature, environmental science, European history, expository writing, fine arts, French, geometry, German, government/civics, Greek, history, industrial arts, Latin, mathematics, mechanical drawing, music, photography, physical education, physics, physiology, religion, Russian, science, social studies, Spanish, speech, statistics, theater, trigonometry, writing.

Graduation Requirements Art history, athletics, English, foreign language, history, mathematics, music appreciation, religion (includes Bible studies and theology), science, senior project.

Special Academic Programs 30 Advanced Placement exams for which test preparation is offered; honors section; independent study; term-away projects; academic accommodation for the gifted, the musically talented, and the artistically talented.

College Admission Counseling 114 students graduated in 2016; 113 went to college, including Harvard University; Johns Hopkins University; Princeton University; University of Maryland, College Park; University of Virginia. Other: 1 entered a postgraduate year. Mean SAT critical reading: 638, mean SAT math: 660, mean SAT writing: 637.

Student Life Upper grades have specified standards of dress, student council, honor system. Discipline rests equally with students and faculty.

Summer Programs Remediation, enrichment, advancement, sports, art/fine arts, rigorous outdoor training, computer instruction programs offered; session focuses on remediation and enrichment; held on campus; accepts boys and girls; open to students from other schools. 250 students usually enrolled. 2017 schedule: June 18 to July 26. Application deadline: June 18.

Tuition and Aid Day student tuition: $28,110. Tuition installment plan (Insured Tuition Payment Plan, FACTS Tuition Payment Plan, monthly payment plans). Need-based scholarship grants, need-based loans available. In 2016–17, 25% of upper-school students received aid. Total amount of financial aid awarded in 2016–17: $1,839,100.

Admissions Traditional secondary-level entrance grade is 9. For fall 2016, 164 students applied for upper-level admission, 70 were accepted, 47 enrolled. ISEE required. Deadline for receipt of application materials: December 16. Application fee required: $50. On-campus interview recommended.

Athletics Interscholastic: baseball, basketball, cross-country running, football, golf, ice hockey, indoor track, lacrosse, soccer, squash, swimming and diving, tennis, track and field, volleyball, water polo, winter (indoor) track, wrestling; intramural: basketball, bicycling, climbing, cross-country running, fitness, flag football, Frisbee, golf, physical fitness, rugby, table tennis, tennis, touch football, weight lifting. 3 PE instructors, 2 athletic trainers.

Computers Computers are regularly used in all academic, computer applications, design, digital applications classes. Computer network features include on-campus library services, Internet access, wireless campus network, Internet filtering or blocking technology. Campus intranet, student e-mail accounts, and computer access in designated common areas are available to students. Students grades are available online. The school has a published electronic and media policy.

Contact Ashley Metzbower, Admissions Associate. 410-323-7169. Fax: 410-864-2825. E-mail: ametzbower@gilman.edu. Website: www.gilman.edu

GILMOUR ACADEMY

34001 Cedar Road
Gates Mills, Ohio 44040-9356

Head of School: Kathleen C. Kenny

General Information Coeducational boarding and day and distance learning college-preparatory school, affiliated with Roman Catholic Church. Boarding grades 7–12, day grades PK–12. Distance learning grades 9–12. Founded: 1946. Setting: suburban. Nearest major city is Cleveland. Students are housed in single-sex by floor dormitories and boy's wing and girl's wing dormitory. 144-acre campus. 15 buildings on campus. Approved or accredited by Independent Schools Association of the Central States, Midwest Association of Boarding Schools, National Catholic Education Association, The Association of Boarding Schools, and Ohio Department of Education. Member of National Association of Independent Schools and Secondary School Admission Test Board. Endowment: $30 million. Total enrollment: 656. Upper school average class size: 15. Upper school faculty-student ratio: 1:9. There are 169 required school days per year for Upper School students. Upper School students typically attend 5 days per week. The average school day consists of 7 hours and 20 minutes.

Upper School Student Profile Grade 6: 20 students (11 boys, 9 girls); Grade 7: 31 students (18 boys, 13 girls); Grade 8: 32 students (17 boys, 15 girls); Grade 9: 89 students (46 boys, 43 girls); Grade 10: 109 students (56 boys, 53 girls); Grade 11: 124 students (64 boys, 60 girls); Grade 12: 102 students (60 boys, 42 girls). 15% of students are boarding students. 86% are state residents. 14 states are represented in upper school student body. 8% are international students. International students from Canada, China, Finland, Republic of Korea, and Switzerland. 80% of students are Roman Catholic.

Faculty School total: 73. In upper school: 34 men, 39 women; 58 have advanced degrees; 4 reside on campus.

Subjects Offered Advanced Placement courses, advanced studio art-AP, algebra, American government, American history, American literature, anatomy and physiology, architecture, art, audio visual/media, band, Bible, biology, biology-AP, British literature, broadcast journalism, calculus, calculus-AP, ceramics, chemistry, chemistry-AP, chorus, community service, computer programming, computer science, computer science-AP, constitutional law, creative writing, drama, drawing, economics, economics and history, English, English literature, English-AP, ensembles, entrepreneurship, ethics, European history, European history-AP, fashion, fine arts, forensics, French, French as a second language, French language-AP, French-AP, functions, genetics, geometry, geometry with art applications, government, government-AP, government/civics, health, history, history of rock and roll, independent study, jazz ensemble, journalism, Latin, Latin-AP, law, leadership, literature and composition-AP, Mandarin, mathematics, mathematics-AP, model United Nations, modern European history-AP, music, music theory-AP, musical productions, mythology, oceanography, oil painting, painting, photography, physical education, physical fitness, physics, physics-AP, pre-algebra, pre-calculus, programming, religion, religious studies, robotics, SAT/ACT preparation, science, social studies, Spanish, Spanish language-AP, speech, speech and debate, sports medicine, statistics-AP, student government, student publications, studio art, studio art-AP, swimming, theater, trigonometry, U.S. government, U.S. government and politics-AP, U.S. history, U.S. history-AP, weight training, work-study, world history, world history-AP, writing, writing workshop, yearbook.

Graduation Requirements Arts and fine arts (art, music, dance, drama), English, foreign language, mathematics, physical education (includes health), religion (includes Bible studies and theology), science, social studies (includes history), speech, senior project, community service. Community service is required.

Special Academic Programs 14 Advanced Placement exams for which test preparation is offered; accelerated programs; independent study; study at local college for college credit; academic accommodation for the gifted, the musically talented, and the artistically talented.

College Admission Counseling 115 students graduated in 2016; 103 went to college, including Case Western Reserve University; John Carroll University; Miami University; The Ohio State University; University of Cincinnati; University of Kentucky. Other: 2 went to work, 10 had other specific plans. Median SAT critical reading: 580, median SAT math: 560, median SAT writing: 560, median combined SAT: 1700, median composite ACT: 26. 44% scored over 600 on SAT critical reading, 43% scored over 600 on SAT math, 38% scored over 600 on SAT writing, 40% scored over 1800 on combined SAT, 50% scored over 26 on composite ACT.

Student Life Upper grades have specified standards of dress, student council, honor system. Discipline rests equally with students and faculty. Attendance at religious services is required.

Summer Programs Enrichment, advancement, sports programs offered; session focuses on academic enrichment; held both on and off campus; accepts boys and girls; open to students from other schools. 75 students usually enrolled. 2017 schedule: June 5 to August 5. Application deadline: none.

Tuition and Aid Day student tuition: $8400–$29,950; 7-day tuition and room/board: $42,500–$44,200. Tuition installment plan (SMART Tuition Payment Plan, monthly payment plans). Tuition reduction for siblings, merit scholarship grants, need-based scholarship grants, need-based loans, paying campus jobs, endowed scholarships with criteria specified by donors available. In 2016–17, 50% of upper-school students received aid; total upper-school merit-scholarship money awarded: $843,500. Total amount of financial aid awarded in 2016–17: $4,539,858.

Admissions Traditional secondary-level entrance grade is 9. ACT, ACT-Explore, ISEE, PSAT, SAT, SSAT or TOEFL required. Deadline for receipt of application materials: none. No application fee required. Interview required.

Athletics Interscholastic: baseball (boys), basketball (b,g), cross-country running (b,g), diving (g), football (b), hockey (b,g), ice hockey (b,g), lacrosse (b,g), running (b,g), soccer (b,g), softball (g), swimming and diving (b,g), tennis (b,g), track and field (b,g), volleyball (g); intramural: cheering (g), indoor soccer (b,g); coed interscholastic: figure skating, golf, indoor track, indoor track & field, winter (indoor) track; coed intramural: aerobics, alpine skiing, aquatics, basketball, bowling, broomball, figure skating, fitness, golf, ice skating, indoor track, paddle tennis, physical fitness, physical training, skiing (downhill), snowboarding, soccer, strength & conditioning, swimming and diving, tennis, volleyball, weight training, winter (indoor) track, winter soccer. 2 PE instructors, 16 coaches, 2 athletic trainers.

Computers Computers are regularly used in all academic classes. Computer network features include on-campus library services, online commercial services, Internet access, wireless campus network, Internet filtering or blocking technology. Campus intranet, student e-mail accounts, and computer access in designated common areas are available to students. Students grades are available online. The school has a published electronic and media policy.

Contact Jeanne Tippen, Admission Administrative Assistant. 440-473-8050. Fax: 440-473-8010. E-mail: admission@gilmour.org. Website: www.gilmour.org

GIRARD COLLEGE

2101 South College Avenue
Philadelphia, Pennsylvania 19121-4857

Head of School: Mr. Clarence D. Armbrister

General Information Coeducational boarding college-preparatory and general academic school. Grades 1–12. Founded: 1848. Setting: urban. Students are housed in single-sex by floor dormitories. 43-acre campus. 10 buildings on campus. Approved or accredited by Middle States Association of Colleges and Schools, The Association of Boarding Schools, and Pennsylvania Department of Education. Member of National Association of Independent Schools. Endowment: $450 million. Total enrollment: 270. Upper school average class size: 17. Upper school faculty-student ratio: 1:16. There are 180 required school days per year for Upper School students. Upper School students typically attend 5 days per week. The average school day consists of 6 hours and 30 minutes.

Upper School Student Profile Grade 6: 28 students (12 boys, 16 girls); Grade 7: 29 students (15 boys, 14 girls); Grade 8: 28 students (12 boys, 16 girls); Grade 9: 38 students (19 boys, 19 girls); Grade 10: 31 students (10 boys, 21 girls); Grade 11: 18 students (8 boys, 10 girls); Grade 12: 10 students (4 boys, 6 girls). 100% of students are boarding students. 92% are state residents. 7 states are represented in upper school student body.

Faculty School total: 60. In upper school: 9 men, 10 women; 9 have advanced degrees; 25 reside on campus.

Subjects Offered Algebra, American history, American literature, anatomy, art, biology, calculus, chemistry, choir, college counseling, community service, computer literacy, earth science, English, English literature, European history, French, geometry, government/civics, health, honors algebra, honors English, honors geometry, honors U.S. history, instrumental music, jazz band, life management skills, mathematics, multicultural studies, music appreciation, physical education, physics, poetry, pre-calculus, SAT preparation, senior project, social studies, sociology, Spanish, video film production, world cultures.

Graduation Requirements American politics in film, art, senior project, social sciences.

Special Academic Programs 1 Advanced Placement exam for which test preparation is offered; honors section; study at local college for college credit.

College Admission Counseling 26 students graduated in 2016; all went to college, including Community College of Philadelphia; La Salle University; Penn State University Park; Temple University; University of Pennsylvania; University of Pittsburgh.

Student Life Upper grades have uniform requirement, student council, honor system. Discipline rests primarily with faculty.

Summer Programs Enrichment, sports, art/fine arts, computer instruction programs offered; held on campus; accepts boys and girls; open to students from other schools. 500 students usually enrolled. 2017 schedule: June 26 to August 4. Application deadline: February 27.

Tuition and Aid Guaranteed tuition plan. Tuition installment plan (full scholarships awarded if admission requirements are met). Full scholarships awarded if admission requirements are met available. In 2016–17, 100% of upper-school students received aid; total upper-school merit-scholarship money awarded: $18,000,000.

Admissions Traditional secondary-level entrance grade is 9. For fall 2016, 251 students applied for upper-level admission, 71 were accepted, 37 enrolled. ISEE, SSAT, Wechsler Intelligence Scale for Children or Wide Range Achievement Test required. Deadline for receipt of application materials: none. Application fee required: $50. On-campus interview recommended.

Athletics Interscholastic: baseball (boys), basketball (b,g), cross-country running (b,g), soccer (b,g), softball (g), track and field (b,g); intramural: aquatics (b,g), strength & conditioning (b,g), swimming and diving (b,g), yoga (b,g); coed intramural: dance, fitness, flag football, jogging, jump rope, outdoor activities, outdoor adventure, physical fitness, running, touch football, walking. 2 PE instructors, 8 coaches.

Computers Computers are regularly used in college planning, English, foreign language, history, library, mathematics, newspaper, reading, research skills, SAT preparation, science, social studies, study skills, word processing, writing, yearbook classes. Computer network features include on-campus library services, Internet access, wireless campus network, Internet filtering or blocking technology, TEC Center (Technology, Education, Collaboration). Student e-mail accounts are available to students. The school has a published electronic and media policy.

Contact Admissions. 215-787-2621. Fax: 215-787-4402. E-mail: admissions@ girardcollege.edu. Website: www.girardcollege.edu

GLADES DAY SCHOOL

400 Gator Boulevard
Belle Glade, Florida 33430

Head of School: Mrs. Amie Pitts

General Information Coeducational day college-preparatory, general academic, vocational, and agriscience school; primarily serves students with learning disabilities. Grades PK–12. Distance learning grades 7–12. Founded: 1965. Setting: small town. Nearest major city is West Palm Beach. 21-acre campus. 4 buildings on campus. Approved or accredited by Florida Council of Independent Schools and Florida Department of Education. Total enrollment: 289. Upper school average class size: 15. Upper school faculty-student ratio: 1:7. There are 175 required school days per year for Upper School students. Upper School students typically attend 5 days per week. The average school day consists of 6 hours and 35 minutes.

Upper School Student Profile Grade 9: 23 students (14 boys, 9 girls); Grade 10: 27 students (17 boys, 10 girls); Grade 11: 27 students (15 boys, 12 girls); Grade 12: 39 students (22 boys, 17 girls).

Faculty School total: 18. In upper school: 7 men, 11 women; 3 have advanced degrees.

Subjects Offered ACT preparation, agriculture, algebra, American government, American history, American literature, anatomy, ancient history, art, Bible studies, biology, biology-AP, calculus, calculus-AP, chemistry, computer applications, computer skills, computer technologies, earth science, economics, English, English language and composition-AP, English literature, English literature and composition-AP, environmental science, European history, general math, geometry, government and politics-AP, grammar, health, health education, human geography - AP, journalism, keyboarding, literature and composition-AP, macroeconomics-AP, marine biology, modern world history, music performance, physical education, pre-calculus, SAT/ACT preparation, Spanish, Spanish-AP, trigonometry, U.S. government and politics-AP, U.S. history, U.S. history-AP, weightlifting, world geography, world history, world history-AP, yearbook.

Graduation Requirements Algebra, American government, American history, American literature, anatomy, ancient world history, arts and fine arts (art, music, dance, drama), biology, calculus, chemistry, computer applications, economics, electives, English, English composition, English literature, geometry, health, health education, macroeconomics-AP, marine biology, modern world history, physical education (includes health), physical fitness, physical science, physics, pre-calculus, Spanish, U.S. history, world geography, world history.

Special Academic Programs 8 Advanced Placement exams for which test preparation is offered; honors section; independent study; study at local college for college credit; programs in general development for dyslexic students.

College Admission Counseling 28 students graduated in 2016; 23 went to college, including Florida Gulf Coast University; Palm Beach State College; Santa Fe College; Tallahassee Community College; University of Central Florida; University of Florida. Other: 5 went to work.

Student Life Upper grades have uniform requirement, student council, honor system. Discipline rests primarily with faculty.

Summer Programs Remediation programs offered; session focuses on remediation; held on campus; accepts boys and girls; not open to students from other schools. 7 students usually enrolled. 2017 schedule: June 7 to July 15. Application deadline: June 4.

Tuition and Aid Day student tuition: $6900–$8750. Tuition installment plan (FACTS Tuition Payment Plan, monthly payment plans, individually arranged payment plans). Tuition reduction for siblings, need-based scholarship grants available. In 2016–17, 10% of upper-school students received aid.

Admissions Traditional secondary-level entrance grade is 9. For fall 2016, 10 students applied for upper-level admission, 8 were accepted, 8 enrolled. Deadline for receipt of application materials: none. Application fee required: $400. On-campus interview recommended.

Athletics Interscholastic: baseball (boys), basketball (b,g), cheering (g), football (b), soccer (b,g), softball (g), track and field (b,g), volleyball (g); intramural: strength & conditioning (b,g), weight training (b,g). 2 PE instructors, 2 coaches, 1 athletic trainer.

Computers Computers are regularly used in English, journalism, mathematics, newspaper, science, Spanish, word processing, yearbook classes. Computer network features include on-campus library services, Internet access, wireless campus network. Campus intranet and student e-mail accounts are available to students. Students grades are available online. The school has a published electronic and media policy.

Contact Mrs. Rachael Lewis, High School Secretary. 561-996-6769 Ext. 10. Fax: 561-992-9274. E-mail: rlewis@gladesdayschool.com. Website: www.gladesdayschool.com

GLENELG COUNTRY SCHOOL

12793 Folly Quarter Road
Ellicott City, Maryland 21042

Head of School: Mr. Gregory J. Ventre

General Information Coeducational day college-preparatory school. Grades PK–12. Founded: 1954. Setting: suburban. Nearest major city is Baltimore. 90-acre campus. 1 building on campus. Approved or accredited by Association of Colorado Independent Schools, Association of Independent Maryland Schools, Middle States Association of Colleges and Schools, and Maryland Department of Education. Member of National Association of Independent Schools. Endowment: $1 million. Total enrollment: 751. Upper school average class size: 15. Upper school faculty-student ratio: 1:6. There are 175 required school days per year for Upper School students. Upper School students typically attend 5 days per week. The average school day consists of 7 hours.

Upper School Student Profile Grade 9: 79 students (43 boys, 36 girls); Grade 10: 86 students (42 boys, 44 girls); Grade 11: 78 students (37 boys, 41 girls); Grade 12: 81 students (39 boys, 42 girls).

Faculty School total. 119. In upper school: 25 men, 22 women; 42 have advanced degrees.

Subjects Offered 3 dimensional art, 3-dimensional design, advanced biology, advanced computer applications, advanced math, Advanced Placement courses, advanced studio art-AP, African American studies, algebra, American history, American literature, American literature-AP, American sign language, American studies, analysis, anatomy and physiology, Ancient Greek, ancient history, art, art history, astronomy, athletics, band, basketball, biology, biology-AP, broadcast journalism, business studies, calculus, calculus-AP, character education, chemistry, chemistry-AP, Chinese, Chinese studies, choir, chorus, college counseling, college planning, community garden, community service, computer applications, computer programming, computer science, computer science-AP, CPR, creative writing, digital photography, drama, dramatic arts, economics-AP, English, English literature, English literature-AP, English-AP, environmental science-AP, equestrian sports, European history, expository writing, forensics, French, French literature-AP, French-AP, geometry, golf, history, honors geometry, honors U.S. history, humanities, integrative seminar, interdisciplinary studies, internship, interpersonal skills, introduction to theater, Islamic studies, Latin, Latin-AP, leadership education training, Mandarin, mathematics, modern world history, photography, physical education, physical science, physics, physics-AP, pre-calculus, psychology, publications, radio broadcasting, research seminar, science, senior project, senior thesis, social studies, Spanish, Spanish language-AP, Spanish literature-AP, Spanish-AP, stagecraft, statistics, studio art, theater, travel, trigonometry, video, volleyball, Web site design, Western civilization, Western literature, world affairs, wrestling, yearbook.

Graduation Requirements Civics, English, foreign language, integrative seminar, mathematics, physical education (includes health), science, social studies (includes history), participation in Civic Leadership program, 25 hours of community service per year.

Special Academic Programs 18 Advanced Placement exams for which test preparation is offered; honors section; independent study; academic accommodation for the gifted.

College Admission Counseling 81 students graduated in 2016; 68 went to college, including Roanoke College; University of Maryland, College Park; Wake Forest University. Mean SAT critical reading: 600, mean SAT math: 627, mean SAT writing: 610, mean combined SAT: 1837, mean composite ACT: 25. 51% scored over 600 on SAT critical reading, 55% scored over 600 on SAT math, 56% scored over 600 on SAT writing, 57% scored over 1800 on combined SAT, 45% scored over 26 on composite ACT.

Student Life Upper grades have uniform requirement, student council, honor system. Discipline rests equally with students and faculty.

Summer Programs Sports programs offered; session focuses on athletics and CIT (Counselor-In-Training) programs; held on campus; accepts boys and girls; open to students from other schools. 350 students usually enrolled. 2017 schedule: June 19 to July 28. Application deadline: May 31.

Tuition and Aid Day student tuition: $27,700. Tuition installment plan (monthly payment plans, individually arranged payment plans, 2-payment plan). Merit scholarship grants, need-based scholarship grants available. In 2016–17, 45% of upper-school students received aid; total upper-school merit-scholarship money awarded: $300,000. Total amount of financial aid awarded in 2016–17: $2,500,000.

Admissions Traditional secondary-level entrance grade is 9. For fall 2016, 82 students applied for upper-level admission, 65 were accepted, 47 enrolled. ISEE, PSAT or SAT for applicants to grade 11 and 12, SSAT or TOEFL required. Deadline for receipt of application materials: January 15. Application fee required: $75. On-campus interview recommended.

Athletics Interscholastic: baseball (boys), basketball (b,g), cross-country running (b,g), field hockey (g), golf (b,g), ice hockey (b), indoor soccer (g), indoor track (b,g), lacrosse (b,g), soccer (b,g), tennis (b,g), volleyball (g), winter soccer (g), wrestling (b); coed interscholastic: equestrian sports, golf, ice hockey, strength & conditioning; coed intramural: aerobics, aerobics/dance, dance, fitness, flag football, Frisbee, physical fitness, physical training, skiing (downhill), strength & conditioning, ultimate Frisbee, weight training, yoga. 5 PE instructors, 12 coaches, 1 athletic trainer.

Computers Computers are regularly used in all academic classes. Computer network features include on-campus library services, Internet access, wireless campus network. Campus intranet, student e-mail accounts, and computer access in designated common areas are available to students. Students grades are available online. The school has a published electronic and media policy.

Contact Mrs. Karen K. Wootton, Director of Admission and Financial Aid. 410-531-7346 Ext. 2203. Fax: 410-531-7363. E-mail: wootton@glenelg.org. Website: www.glenelg.org

THE GLENHOLME SCHOOL, DEVEREUX CONNECTICUT

Washington, Connecticut
See Special Needs Schools section.

GONZAGA COLLEGE HIGH SCHOOL

19 Eye Street NW
Washington, District of Columbia 20001

Head of School: Mr. Thomas K. Every II

General Information Boys' day college-preparatory school, affiliated with Roman Catholic Church. Grades 9–12. Founded: 1821. Setting: urban. 1-acre campus. 9 buildings on campus. Approved or accredited by Association of Independent Schools of Greater Washington, Jesuit Secondary Education Association, Middle States Association of Colleges and Schools, and District of Columbia Department of Education. Member of National Association of Independent Schools. Endowment: $9.1 million. Total enrollment: 962. Upper school average class size: 21. Upper school faculty-student ratio: 1:13. There are 165 required school days per year for Upper School students. Upper School students typically attend 5 days per week. The average school day consists of 6 hours and 35 minutes.

Upper School Student Profile Grade 9: 246 students (246 boys); Grade 10: 246 students (246 boys); Grade 11: 237 students (237 boys); Grade 12: 231 students (231 boys). 85% of students are Roman Catholic.

Faculty School total: 76. In upper school: 50 men, 26 women; 59 have advanced degrees.

Subjects Offered Acting, Advanced Placement courses, African-American literature, algebra, American history, American literature, applied music, art, band, biology, broadcasting, calculus, calculus-AP, Catholic belief and practice, chemistry, chemistry-AP, Chinese, choir, choral music, Christian and Hebrew scripture, Christian ethics, Christian scripture, communications, community service, computer applications, computer math, computer programming, computer science, concert band, concert choir, creative writing, earth science, economics, economics-AP, English, English literature, English literature and composition-AP, English literature-AP, English-AP, environmental science-AP, ethics, ethics and responsibility, European history, European history-AP, expository writing, film appreciation, film studies, fine arts, French, French-AP, functions, geometry, government, government/civics, grammar, Greek, health, health education, history, honors algebra, honors English, honors geometry, human geography - AP, independent study, Irish literature, jazz ensemble, Latin, Latin-AP, mathematics, media communications, music, musicianship, orchestra, philosophy, photography, physical education, physics, physics-AP, piano, poetry, political science, political systems, psychology, psychology-AP, religion, science, social justice, social sciences, social studies, Spanish, Spanish-AP, statistics, statistics-AP, studio art-AP, symphonic band, theology, trigonometry, U.S. government and politics-AP, Web site design, world history, world literature.

Graduation Requirements Arts and fine arts (art, music, dance, drama), English, ethics, foreign language, mathematics, physical education (includes health), religion (includes Bible studies and theology), science, social justice, social sciences, social studies (includes history). Community service is required.

Special Academic Programs Advanced Placement exam preparation; honors section; independent study.

College Admission Counseling 238 students graduated in 2016; 236 went to college, including James Madison University; University of Maryland, College Park; University of Michigan; University of South Carolina; University of Virginia; Virginia Polytechnic Institute and State University. Other: 2 had other specific plans.

Student Life Upper grades have specified standards of dress, student council, honor system. Discipline rests primarily with faculty. Attendance at religious services is required.

Summer Programs Remediation, enrichment programs offered; session focuses on new student remediation, enrichment, and SAT preparation; held on campus; accepts boys and girls; open to students from other schools. 200 students usually enrolled. 2017 schedule: June to July. Application deadline: June 1.

Tuition and Aid Day student tuition: $21,475. Tuition installment plan (Insured Tuition Payment Plan, monthly payment plans). Merit scholarship grants, need-based scholarship grants available. In 2016–17, 33% of upper-school students received aid;

total upper-school merit-scholarship money awarded: $100,000. Total amount of financial aid awarded in 2016–17: $2,900,000.

Admissions Traditional secondary-level entrance grade is 9. For fall 2016, 660 students applied for upper-level admission, 315 were accepted, 246 enrolled. High School Placement Test required. Deadline for receipt of application materials: December 9. Application fee required: $35.

Athletics Interscholastic: baseball, basketball, crew, cross-country running, diving, football, golf, ice hockey, indoor track & field, lacrosse, rugby, soccer, squash, swimming and diving, tennis, track and field, water polo, winter (indoor) track, wrestling; intramural: basketball, fencing, fitness, football, physical training, skiing (downhill), strength & conditioning, table tennis, weight lifting, whiffle ball. 2 PE instructors, 30 coaches, 2 athletic trainers.

Computers Computers are regularly used in all classes. Computer network features include on-campus library services, Internet access, wireless campus network. Campus intranet and student e-mail accounts are available to students. Students grades are available online. The school has a published electronic and media policy.

Contact Mr. Andrew C. Battaile, Dean of Admissions and Financial Aid. 202-336-7101. Fax: 202-454-1188. E-mail: abattaile@gonzaga.org. Website: www.gonzaga.org

GOOD HOPE COUNTRY DAY SCHOOL

RR #1, Box 6199
Kingshill, Virgin Islands 00850-9807

Head of School: Mr. Kari Loya

General Information Coeducational day college-preparatory school. Grades N–12. Founded: 1964. Setting: rural. Nearest major city is Christiansted, U.S. Virgin Islands. 34-acre campus. 6 buildings on campus. Approved or accredited by Middle States Association of Colleges and Schools, North Central Association of Colleges and Schools, and Virgin Islands Department of Education. Member of National Association of Independent Schools. Endowment: $574,000. Total enrollment: 360. Upper school average class size: 14. Upper school faculty-student ratio: 1:12. Upper School students typically attend 5 days per week. The average school day consists of 7 hours.

Upper School Student Profile Grade 9: 34 students (18 boys, 16 girls); Grade 10: 31 students (11 boys, 20 girls); Grade 11: 26 students (14 boys, 12 girls); Grade 12: 38 students (21 boys, 17 girls).

Faculty School total: 51. In upper school: 6 men, 17 women; 20 have advanced degrees.

Subjects Offered Algebra, American history, American literature, art, art history, arts, band, biology, calculus, ceramics, chemistry, chorus, community service, computer programming, computer science, creative writing, current events, dance, drama, earth science, ecology, economics, electronics, English, English literature, film, fine arts, French, geometry, government/civics, health, history, journalism, keyboarding, marine biology, mathematics, music, Native American studies, photography, physical education, physical science, physics, pre-calculus, psychology, public speaking, science, social studies, sociology, Spanish, statistics, swimming, theater, trigonometry, world history.

Graduation Requirements Arts and fine arts (art, music, dance, drama), computer science, English, foreign language, mathematics, physical education (includes health), science, social studies (includes history), swimming, typing. Community service is required.

Special Academic Programs Advanced Placement exam preparation.

College Admission Counseling Colleges students went to include Michigan Technological University; University of Pennsylvania; University of Pittsburgh; Vassar College. Median SAT critical reading: 520, median SAT math: 540, median composite ACT: 22. 35% scored over 600 on SAT critical reading, 25% scored over 600 on SAT math, 19% scored over 26 on composite ACT.

Student Life Upper grades have specified standards of dress, student council, honor system. Discipline rests primarily with faculty.

Tuition and Aid Day student tuition: $14,000. Tuition installment plan (monthly payment plans, individually arranged payment plans, semiannual and annual payment plans). Merit scholarship grants, need-based scholarship grants available. In 2016–17, 41% of upper-school students received aid; total upper-school merit-scholarship money awarded: $24,250. Total amount of financial aid awarded in 2016–17: $311,550.

Admissions Traditional secondary-level entrance grade is 9. For fall 2016, 96 students applied for upper-level admission, 11 were accepted, 20 enrolled. Essay and Test of Achievement and Proficiency required. Deadline for receipt of application materials: none. Application fee required: $200. On-campus interview required.

Athletics Interscholastic: baseball (boys), basketball (b,g), football (b), softball (g), tennis (b,g), volleyball (b,g); intramural: volleyball (b,g); coed interscholastic: aerobics, aquatics, basketball, cross-country running, sailing, soccer; coed intramural: basketball, soccer, ultimate Frisbee. 3 PE instructors, 3 coaches.

Computers Computers are regularly used in all academic, art, foreign language classes. Computer network features include on-campus library services, online commercial services, Internet access. The school has a published electronic and media policy.

Contact Mrs. Alma V. Castro-Nieves, Registrar. 340-778-1974 Ext. 2108. Fax: 340-779-3331. E-mail: acastronieves@ghcds.org. Website: www.ghcds.org/

THE GOVERNOR FRENCH ACADEMY

219 West Main Street
Belleville, Illinois 62220-1537

Head of School: Mr. Phillip E. Paeltz

General Information Coeducational boarding and day college-preparatory school. Boarding grades 9–12, day grades K–12. Founded: 1983. Setting: urban. Nearest major city is St. Louis, MO. Students are housed in homes of local families. 3 buildings on campus. Approved or accredited by North Central Association of Colleges and Schools and Illinois Department of Education. Endowment: $100,000. Total enrollment: 155. Upper school average class size: 15. Upper school faculty-student ratio: 1:6. There are 176 required school days per year for Upper School students. Upper School students typically attend 5 days per week. The average school day consists of 6 hours and 45 minutes.

Upper School Student Profile Grade 9: 8 students (6 boys, 2 girls); Grade 10: 10 students (4 boys, 6 girls); Grade 11: 11 students (6 boys, 5 girls); Grade 12: 9 students (3 boys, 6 girls).

Faculty School total: 13. In upper school: 3 men, 4 women; 4 have advanced degrees.

Subjects Offered Algebra, American history, American literature, biology, biology-AP, calculus, chemistry, creative writing, ecology, economics, engineering, English, English literature, environmental science, European history, expository writing, geometry, government/civics, history, mathematics, physical education, physics, psychology, science, social sciences, statistics, theater arts, trigonometry, world history, world literature.

Graduation Requirements English, foreign language, history, mathematics, science, social sciences, vote of faculty.

Special Academic Programs 10 Advanced Placement exams for which test preparation is offered; accelerated programs; independent study; study at local college for college credit; academic accommodation for the gifted; programs in English for dyslexic students; ESL (35 students enrolled).

College Admission Counseling 6 students graduated in 2016; all went to college, including Colorado State University; Saint Louis University; South Dakota School of Mines and Technology; Southern Illinois University Edwardsville; University of Chicago; University of Missouri. Median composite ACT: 26. 50% scored over 26 on composite ACT.

Student Life Upper grades have uniform requirement, student council, honor system. Discipline rests primarily with faculty.

Summer Programs Remediation, enrichment, advancement programs offered; session focuses on academics; held on campus; accepts boys and girls; open to students from other schools. 25 students usually enrolled. 2017 schedule: June 14 to July 28. Application deadline: none.

Tuition and Aid Day student tuition: $5940; 7-day tuition and room/board: $22,200. Tuition installment plan (monthly payment plans). Tuition reduction for siblings available.

Admissions Traditional secondary-level entrance grade is 9. For fall 2016, 15 students applied for upper-level admission, 12 were accepted, 9 enrolled. School placement exam required. Deadline for receipt of application materials: none. No application fee required. On-campus interview required.

Athletics Interscholastic: basketball (boys, girls), swimming and diving (g), volleyball (b,g); coed interscholastic: cross-country running; coed intramural: independent competitive sports, softball.

Computers Computers are regularly used in computer applications, science, yearbook classes. Computer network features include Internet access, wireless campus network, Internet filtering or blocking technology. Computer access in designated common areas is available to students. The school has a published electronic and media policy.

Contact Mrs. Nicole M. Barcinas, Dean of Admissions and Development. 618-233-7542. Fax: 618-233-0541. E-mail: admiss@governorfrench.com. Website: www.governorfrench.com

THE GOVERNOR'S ACADEMY

1 Elm Street
Byfield, Massachusetts 01922

Head of School: Dr. Peter H. Quimby

General Information Coeducational boarding and day college-preparatory and arts school. Grades 9–12. Founded: 1763. Setting: rural. Nearest major city is Boston. Students are housed in single-sex dormitories. 460-acre campus. 48 buildings on campus. Approved or accredited by Association of Independent Schools in New England, New England Association of Schools and Colleges, The Association of Boarding Schools, and Massachusetts Department of Education. Member of National Association of Independent Schools and Secondary School Admission Test Board. Endowment: $70 million. Total enrollment: 405. Upper school average class size: 12. Upper school faculty-student ratio: 1:5. There are 158 required school days per year for Upper School students. Upper School students typically attend 5 days per week. The average school day consists of 9 hours.

Upper School Student Profile Grade 9: 93 students (51 boys, 42 girls); Grade 10: 102 students (51 boys, 51 girls); Grade 11: 105 students (56 boys, 49 girls); Grade 12: 105 students (57 boys, 48 girls). 65% of students are boarding students. 50% are state residents. 23 states are represented in upper school student body. 14% are international students. International students from Canada, China, Republic of Korea, Thailand, United States, and Viet Nam; 17 other countries represented in student body.

Faculty School total: 82. In upper school: 46 men, 36 women; 54 have advanced degrees; 60 reside on campus.

Subjects Offered Advanced chemistry, algebra, American history, American history-AP, American literature, anatomy, art, band, biology, biology-AP, calculus-AP, ceramics, chemistry, chemistry-AP, Chinese, chorus, civics, computer graphics, computer math, computer programming, computer science, computer science-AP, constitutional law, creative writing, dance, drama, driver education, ecology, economics, economics-AP, English language-AP, English literature, English literature and composition-AP, environmental science, ESL, European history, European history-AP, expository writing, filmmaking, fine arts, French, French-AP, geometry, German, health, history, Holocaust and other genocides, honors algebra, jazz band, Latin, Latin-AP, marine biology, marine science, mathematics, Middle Eastern history, modern European history, modern European history-AP, music, music history, music theory, photography, physics, physics-AP, psychology, religion, science, social studies, Spanish, Spanish language-AP, Spanish literature-AP, statistics-AP, studio art-AP, theater, trigonometry, visual and performing arts, women in society, women's studies, writing.

Graduation Requirements Arts and fine arts (art, music, dance, drama), English, foreign language, history, mathematics, science, 100 hours of community service. Community service is required.

Special Academic Programs 27 Advanced Placement exams for which test preparation is offered; honors section; independent study; term-away projects; study abroad.

College Admission Counseling 103 students graduated in 2016; 102 went to college, including Colby College; Cornell University; Massachusetts Institute of Technology; New York University; Rochester Institute of Technology; Tufts University. Other: 1 entered a postgraduate year. Mean SAT critical reading: 602, mean SAT math: 633, mean SAT writing: 603, mean combined SAT: 1829. 38% scored over 600 on SAT critical reading, 50% scored over 600 on SAT math, 42% scored over 600 on SAT writing, 42% scored over 1800 on combined SAT.

Student Life Upper grades have specified standards of dress, student council. Discipline rests primarily with faculty.

Tuition and Aid Day student tuition: $44,500; 7-day tuition and room/board: $55,900. Tuition installment plan (Insured Tuition Payment Plan, FACTS Tuition Payment Plan, monthly payment plans). Need-based scholarship grants available. In 2016–17, 29% of upper-school students received aid. Total amount of financial aid awarded in 2016–17: $4,400,000.

Admissions Traditional secondary-level entrance grade is 9. For fall 2016, 978 students applied for upper-level admission, 228 were accepted, 116 enrolled. ISEE, SSAT or TOEFL required. Deadline for receipt of application materials: January 31. Application fee required: $60. Interview recommended.

Athletics Interscholastic: alpine skiing (boys, girls), baseball (b), basketball (b,g), cross-country running (b,g), field hockey (g), football (b), ice hockey (b,g), indoor track & field (b,g), lacrosse (b,g), skiing (downhill) (b,g), soccer (b,g), softball (g), tennis (b,g), track and field (b,g), volleyball (g), winter (indoor) track (b,g), wrestling (b,g); intramural: dance (g); coed interscholastic: golf; coed intramural: aerobics/dance, alpine skiing, dance, outdoor activities, outdoor recreation, tennis, yoga. 2 athletic trainers.

Computers Computers are regularly used in all classes. Computer network features include on-campus library services, online commercial services, Internet access, wireless campus network, Internet filtering or blocking technology, laptop sign-out in student center and library, Moodle Web site for teachers and students to share course data, events, and discussions. Campus intranet, student e-mail accounts, and computer access in designated common areas are available to students. Students grades are available online. The school has a published electronic and media policy.

Contact Michael Kinnealey, Director of Admission, Director of Financial Aid. 978-499-3120. Fax: 978-462-1278. E-mail: admissions@govsacademy.org. Website: www.thegovernorsacademy.org

THE GOW SCHOOL

South Wales, New York
See Special Needs Schools section.

GRACE BAPTIST ACADEMY

7815 Shallowford Road
Chattanooga, Tennessee 37421

Head of School: Mr. Matthew Pollock

General Information Coeducational day college-preparatory and religious studies school, affiliated with Baptist Church. Grades K4–12. Founded: 1985. Setting: suburban. 2 buildings on campus. Approved or accredited by Association of Christian Schools International, Southern Association of Colleges and Schools, and Tennessee Department of Education. Total enrollment: 469. Upper school average class size: 18. Upper school faculty-student ratio: 1:12. Upper School students typically attend 5 days per week. The average school day consists of 7 hours.

Upper School Student Profile Grade 6: 39 students (15 boys, 24 girls); Grade 7: 45 students (22 boys, 23 girls); Grade 8: 32 students (13 boys, 19 girls); Grade 9: 26 students (8 boys, 18 girls); Grade 10: 44 students (24 boys, 20 girls); Grade 11: 25 students (14 boys, 11 girls); Grade 12: 40 students (18 boys, 22 girls). 75% of students are Baptist.

Faculty School total: 30. In upper school: 14 men, 15 women; 10 have advanced degrees.

Subjects Offered Advanced biology, advanced computer applications, advanced math, Advanced Placement courses, algebra, American government, American history, American literature, art, band, Bible, Bible studies, biology, calculus, calculus-AP, career exploration, career/college preparation, chemistry, choir, Christian doctrine, Christian ethics, Christian testament, computer applications, consumer mathematics, drama performance, dramatic arts, economics, English, English composition, English literature, fitness, general math, general science, geometry, global studies, health, health and safety, honors English, honors world history, keyboarding, language arts, mathematics, music, New Testament, painting, personal finance, physical education, physical fitness, physics, pre-algebra, pre-calculus, senior internship, senior project, Spanish, speech, state history, statistics-AP, study skills, U.S. government and politics, U.S. history, U.S. history-AP, weight training, world geography, world religions, yearbook.

Graduation Requirements Algebra, American government, American history, arts and fine arts (art, music, dance, drama), Bible, biology, chemistry, economics, electives, English, English literature, foreign language, geography, geometry, global studies, government, health and wellness, mathematics, New Testament, oral communications, physical education (includes health), science, senior project, senior thesis, Spanish, speech, trigonometry, U.S. government, U.S. history, visual and performing arts, world geography, 1 credit of Biblical studies for every year at our school.

Special Academic Programs 2 Advanced Placement exams for which test preparation is offered; honors section; study at local college for college credit; remedial math; programs in general development for dyslexic students; special instructional classes for blind students.

College Admission Counseling 32 students graduated in 2016; 31 went to college, including Chattanooga State Community College; Middle Tennessee State University; Tennessee Technological University; The University of Tennessee; The University of Tennessee at Chattanooga. Other: 1 entered military service. Mean combined SAT: 1350, mean composite ACT: 23. 100% scored over 600 on SAT critical reading, 100% scored over 600 on SAT math, 100% scored over 600 on SAT writing, 45% scored over 26 on composite ACT.

Student Life Upper grades have uniform requirement, student council, honor system. Discipline rests primarily with faculty. Attendance at religious services is required.

Tuition and Aid Tuition installment plan (FACTS Tuition Payment Plan, monthly payment plans, individually arranged payment plans, bank draft). Tuition reduction for siblings, need based scholarship grants available.

Admissions Traditional secondary-level entrance grade is 9. Kaufman Test of Educational Achievement or latest standardized score from previous school required. Deadline for receipt of application materials: none. Application fee required: $50. On-campus interview recommended.

Athletics Interscholastic: baseball (boys), basketball (b,g), cheering (g), cross-country running (b,g), drill team (g), football (b), soccer (b,g), softball (g), tennis (b,g), track and field (b,g), volleyball (g), weight training (b,g); intramural: weight lifting (b), weight training (b); coed interscholastic: golf, running; coed intramural: physical training, strength & conditioning. 2 PE instructors, 5 coaches, 1 athletic trainer.

Computers Computers are regularly used in all academic, career education, career exploration, college planning, computer applications, keyboarding, mathematics, programming, science, senior seminar, video film production, yearbook classes. Computer network features include on-campus library services, Internet access, wireless campus network, Internet filtering or blocking technology, 1:1 iPad provided to students 5th grade and up. Student e-mail accounts and computer access in designated common areas are available to students. Students grades are available online. The school has a published electronic and media policy.

Contact Miss Taylor Walker, Advancement. 423-892-8224 Ext. 202. Fax: 423-892-1194. E-mail: twalker@mygracechatt.org. Website: www.gracechatt.org

GRACE CHRISTIAN SCHOOL

12407 Pintail Street
Anchorage, Alaska 99516

Head of School: Mr. Randy Karlberg

General Information Coeducational day college-preparatory school, affiliated with Christian faith. Grades K–12. Founded: 1980. Setting: urban. 7-acre campus. 1 building on campus. Approved or accredited by Association of Christian Schools International, Northwest Accreditation Commission, and Northwest Association of Schools and Colleges. Total enrollment: 532. Upper school average class size: 15. Upper school faculty-student ratio: 1:15. There are 170 required school days per year for Upper School students. Upper School students typically attend 5 days per week. The average school day consists of 6 hours and 50 minutes.

Upper School Student Profile Grade 7: 36 students (21 boys, 15 girls); Grade 8: 47 students (19 boys, 28 girls); Grade 9: 49 students (30 boys, 19 girls); Grade 10: 49

students (24 boys, 25 girls); Grade 11: 41 students (16 boys, 25 girls); Grade 12: 42 students (23 boys, 19 girls). 99% of students are Christian faith.

Faculty School total: 45. In upper school: 12 men, 15 women; 12 have advanced degrees.

Subjects Offered Algebra, American government, American history, American history-AP, art, astronomy, Bible, biology, biology-AP, calculus-AP, chemistry, chemistry-AP, choir, computer science, computer skills, computer technologies, creative writing, drama, economics, English, English language and composition-AP, English literature and composition-AP, English literature-AP, English/composition-AP, film, fine arts, geology, geometry, government-AP, health, leadership and service, literature, media, meteorology, music theory-AP, oceanography, physical education, physical science, physics, psychology, publications, science, social studies, Spanish, speech, trigonometry, U.S. history, U.S. history-AP, weightlifting, world history, yearbook.

Graduation Requirements Algebra, American government, American history, American literature, arts and fine arts (art, music, dance, drama), biology, British literature, consumer economics, electives, English, English composition, English literature, geometry, health, literary genres, literature, mathematics, physical education (includes health), physical science, practical arts, science, U.S. history, world history, one year of Bible for every year attending, Old Testament survey in 9th grade, 10th grade—New Testament survey, 11th grade—Life and Times of Christ/Marriage and Family, 12th grade—Defending Your Faith/Understanding the Times.

Special Academic Programs Advanced Placement exam preparation.

College Admission Counseling 37 students graduated in 2016; 34 went to college, including Dartmouth College; Montana State University; Point Loma Nazarene University; University of Alaska Anchorage; University of Alaska Fairbanks; Westmont College. Other: 2 went to work, 1 had other specific plans. Mean SAT critical reading: 552, mean SAT math: 512, mean SAT writing: 502, mean combined SAT: 1566, mean composite ACT: 23. 58% scored over 600 on SAT critical reading, 38% scored over 600 on SAT math, 26% scored over 26 on composite ACT.

Student Life Upper grades have specified standards of dress, student council, honor system. Discipline rests primarily with faculty. Attendance at religious services is required.

Tuition and Aid Day student tuition: $9500. Tuition installment plan (FACTS Tuition Payment Plan). Tuition reduction for siblings, need-based scholarship grants available. In 2016–17, 15% of upper-school students received aid. Total amount of financial aid awarded in 2016–17: $200,000.

Admissions Traditional secondary-level entrance grade is 9. For fall 2016, 41 students applied for upper-level admission, 30 were accepted, 29 enrolled. Math and English placement tests, school's own exam or Stanford Achievement Test required. Deadline for receipt of application materials: none. Application fee required: $350. Interview recommended.

Athletics Interscholastic: basketball (boys, girls), cheering (g), cross-country running (b,g), skiing (cross-country) (b,g), soccer (b,g), track and field (b,g), volleyball (g), wrestling (b). 2 PE instructors, 30 coaches, 1 athletic trainer.

Computers Computers are regularly used in computer applications, media, publications, technology, yearbook classes. Computer network features include on-campus library services, online commercial services, Internet access, wireless campus network, Internet filtering or blocking technology. Students grades are available online.

Contact Mrs. Karen Jones, Director of Admissions. 907-345-4814. Fax: 907-644-2260. E-mail: admissions@gracechristianalaska.org.
Website: www.gracechristianalaska.org

GRACE CHRISTIAN SCHOOL

50 Kirkdale Road
Charlottetown, Prince Edward Island C1E 1N6, Canada

Head of School: Mr. Jason Biech

General Information Coeducational day college-preparatory and technology school, affiliated with Baptist Church. Grades JK–12. Founded: 1980. Setting: small town. 6-acre campus. 1 building on campus. Approved or accredited by Association of Christian Schools International and Prince Edward Island Department of Education. Language of instruction: English. Endowment: CAN$50,000. Total enrollment: 124. Upper school average class size: 12. Upper school faculty-student ratio: 1:12. There are 190 required school days per year for Upper School students. Upper School students typically attend 5 days per week. The average school day consists of 6 hours.

Upper School Student Profile Grade 10: 21 students (13 boys, 8 girls); Grade 11: 10 students (1 boy, 9 girls); Grade 12: 12 students (3 boys, 9 girls). 10% of students are Baptist.

Faculty School total: 23. In upper school: 4 men, 8 women; 6 have advanced degrees.

Subjects Offered Accounting, American literature, American literature-AP, Bible, biology, British literature, business technology, Canadian history, chemistry, computer science.

Graduation Requirements Bible, English, language, mathematics, Christian ethics.

Special Academic Programs 2 Advanced Placement exams for which test preparation is offered; programs in general development for dyslexic students; ESL (55 students enrolled).

College Admission Counseling 11 students graduated in 2016; all went to college, including Acadia University.

Student Life Upper grades have specified standards of dress, student council. Discipline rests primarily with faculty. Attendance at religious services is required.

Tuition and Aid Day student tuition: CAN$5000. Tuition installment plan (monthly payment plans). Tuition reduction for siblings, bursaries available. In 2016–17, 5% of upper-school students received aid. Total amount of financial aid awarded in 2016–17: CAN$20,000.

Admissions Traditional secondary-level entrance grade is 10. For fall 2016, 11 students applied for upper-level admission, 11 were accepted, 11 enrolled. ESL required. Deadline for receipt of application materials: August 15. Application fee required: CAN$250. On-campus interview recommended.

Athletics Interscholastic: badminton (boys, girls), basketball (b,g), cheering (g), cross-country running (b,g), golf (b,g), soccer (b,g), track and field (b,g), volleyball (b,g); coed intramural: alpine skiing, basketball, floor hockey, indoor soccer, running, soccer, volleyball.

Computers Computers are regularly used in all classes. Computer network features include Internet access, wireless campus network. Student e-mail accounts and computer access in designated common areas are available to students. Students grades are available online. The school has a published electronic and media policy.

Contact Mr. Jason Biech, Administrator. 902-628-1668 Ext. 223. Fax: 902-628-1668. E-mail: principal@gcspei.ca. Website: www.gracechristianschool.ca/

THE GRAUER SCHOOL

1500 South El Camino Real
Encinitas, California 92024

Head of School: Dr. Stuart Robert Grauer

General Information Coeducational day college-preparatory school. Grades 7–12. Founded: 1991. Setting: suburban. Nearest major city is San Diego. 6-acre campus. 2 buildings on campus. Approved or accredited by Western Association of Schools and Colleges and California Department of Education. Member of National Association of Independent Schools. Endowment: $500,000. Total enrollment: 164. Upper school average class size: 12. Upper school faculty-student ratio: 1:7. There are 178 required school days per year for Upper School students. Upper School students typically attend 5 days per week. The average school day consists of 6 hours and 30 minutes.

Faculty School total: 31. In upper school: 14 men, 17 women; 20 have advanced degrees.

Subjects Offered ACT preparation, advanced biology, advanced chemistry, advanced math, algebra, alternative physical education, American government, American history, American sign language, anatomy and physiology, ancient history, applied music, art, art appreciation, art history, ASB Leadership, athletic training, audio visual/media, basketball, biology, business mathematics, calculus, character education, chemistry, Chinese, choir, civics, classical music, college admission preparation, college planning, community service, computer applications, computer education, computer multimedia, computers, creative writing, culinary arts, drama, dramatic arts, economics, English literature, environmental education, experiential education, film studies, filmmaking, fitness, French, gardening, geography, geometry, global studies, health, high adventure outdoor program, honors algebra, honors English, honors geometry, honors U.S. history, honors world history, Japanese, keyboarding, leadership and service, marine science, multimedia, music, music appreciation, music performance, outdoor education, peace studies, personal fitness, photo shop, photography, physical education, physics, pre-algebra, pre-calculus, religion, religion and culture, robotics, Spanish, speech and debate, studio art, study skills, surfing, tennis, theater arts, trigonometry, U.S. government, U.S. history, U.S. literature, world geography, world history, world religions.

Graduation Requirements Economics, electives, English, experiential education, foreign language, geography, health, mathematics, physical education (includes health), science, senior project, U.S. government, U.S. history, visual and performing arts, world history, world religions, expeditionary learning in the field and 50 hours community service, all students graduate with distinction in a subject of their choice. Community service is required.

Special Academic Programs Honors section; independent study; study abroad; academic accommodation for the gifted, the musically talented, and the artistically talented; ESL (9 students enrolled).

College Admission Counseling 30 students graduated in 2016; all went to college, including Lewis & Clark College; University of San Diego. Median SAT critical reading: 600, median SAT math: 560, median SAT writing: 600, median combined SAT: 1760, median composite ACT: 27.

Student Life Upper grades have specified standards of dress, student council, honor system. Discipline rests equally with students and faculty.

Summer Programs Remediation, enrichment, advancement, ESL, sports, art/fine arts, rigorous outdoor training, computer instruction programs offered; session focuses on academics and enrichment; held on campus; accepts boys and girls; open to students from other schools. 60 students usually enrolled.

Tuition and Aid Day student tuition: $24,000–$26,000. Tuition installment plan (individually arranged payment plans, 3 payment plans). Need-based scholarship grants available. In 2016–17, 14% of upper-school students received aid. Total amount of financial aid awarded in 2016–17: $160,877.

Admissions Traditional secondary-level entrance grade is 9. Deadline for receipt of application materials: February 3. Application fee required: $100. Interview recommended.

Athletics Interscholastic: baseball (boys), basketball (b,g), field hockey (g), football (b), golf (b,g), indoor soccer (b,g), lacrosse (b,g), soccer (b,g), softball (g), tennis (b,g), volleyball (b,g), water polo (b,g); intramural: soccer (b,g); coed interscholastic: archery, cross-country running, flag football, gymnastics, indoor soccer, surfing, swimming and diving, tennis, track and field, wrestling; coed intramural: basketball, cross-country running, flag football, independent competitive sports, outdoor activities, outdoor adventure, outdoor education, outdoor recreation, outdoor skills, outdoors, skateboarding, soccer, surfing, tennis, track and field. 5 PE instructors.

Computers Computers are regularly used in all classes. Computer network features include Internet access, wireless campus network, Internet filtering or blocking technology, online text books, online portfolios, all students required to have computers. Campus intranet, student e-mail accounts, and computer access in designated common areas are available to students. Students grades are available online. The school has a published electronic and media policy.

Contact Mrs. Olivia Kleinrath, Senior Admissions Associate. 760-274-2116. Fax: 760-944-6784. E-mail: admissions@grauerschool.com.

Website: www.grauerschool.com

GREATER ATLANTA CHRISTIAN SCHOOLS

1575 Indian Trail Road
Norcross, Georgia 30093

Head of School: Dr. David Fincher

General Information Coeducational day college-preparatory and arts school, affiliated with Christian faith, Christian faith. Boys grades P4–12, girls grades P3–12. Founded: 1961. Setting: suburban. Nearest major city is Atlanta. 88-acre campus. 22 buildings on campus. Approved or accredited by Georgia Independent School Association, National Christian School Association, Southern Association of Colleges and Schools, Southern Association of Independent Schools, The College Board, and Georgia Department of Education. Member of National Association of Independent Schools and Secondary School Admission Test Board. Endowment: $28.5 million. Total enrollment: 1,815. Upper school average class size: 18. Upper school faculty-student ratio: 1:13. There are 180 required school days per year for Upper School students. Upper School students typically attend 5 days per week. The average school day consists of 6 hours and 10 minutes.

Upper School Student Profile Grade 9: 204 students (106 boys, 98 girls); Grade 10: 203 students (103 boys, 100 girls); Grade 11: 175 students (103 boys, 72 girls); Grade 12: 195 students (103 boys, 92 girls). 97% of students are Christian, Christian.

Faculty School total: 150. In upper school: 39 men, 27 women; 42 have advanced degrees.

Subjects Offered 3-dimensional art, accounting, Advanced Placement courses, advanced studio art-AP, advertising design, algebra, American government, American history, American history-AP, American literature, American literature-AP, analysis, anatomy, anatomy and physiology, applied music, art, art appreciation, art history, art-AP, astronomy, audio visual/media, ballet, band, Basic programming, Bible, biology, biology-AP, British literature, British literature (honors), broadcast journalism, business, calculus, calculus-AP, chamber groups, chemistry, chemistry-AP, Chinese, choir, choral music, chorus, Christian education, Christian scripture, church history, comparative religion, composition, computer applications, computer literacy, computer math, computer programming, computer science-AP, concert choir, dance, dance performance, drama, dramatic arts, economics-AP, English language and composition-AP, English language-AP, English literature and composition-AP, English literature-AP, environmental science, environmental science-AP, environmental studies, ethics, European history, European history-AP, expository writing, foreign language, French, French as a second language, French-AP, geometry, government-AP, government/civics-AP, graphic design, health, home economics, honors English, human geography - AP, jazz band, journalism, language arts, Latin, Latin-AP, literature-AP, Mandarin, marching band, mathematics-AP, music appreciation, music theory-AP, music-AP, musical theater, newspaper, orchestra, painting, personal finance, philosophy, photography, physics, physics-AP, physiology, pre-calculus, psychology-AP, religion, SAT preparation, sculpture, sociology, Spanish, Spanish-AP, speech, speech communications, statistics, statistics-AP, studio art-AP, symphonic band, theology, trigonometry, U.S. history, U.S. history-AP, video, video film production, visual arts, Web site design, world history-AP, world literature, yearbook.

Graduation Requirements Art, English, foreign language, mathematics, physical education (includes health), religion (includes Bible studies and theology), religious studies, science, social sciences, social studies (includes history), one year of Bible for each year of attendance.

Special Academic Programs 23 Advanced Placement exams for which test preparation is offered; honors section; study abroad; academic accommodation for the gifted, the musically talented, and the artistically talented.

College Admission Counseling 178 students graduated in 2016; all went to college, including Auburn University; Georgia Institute of Technology; Samford University; The University of Alabama; University of Georgia; University of Mississippi. Median SAT critical reading: 566, median SAT math: 581, median SAT writing: 568, median combined SAT: 1715, median composite ACT: 26.

Student Life Upper grades have uniform requirement, student council, honor system. Discipline rests primarily with faculty. Attendance at religious services is required.

Summer Programs Enrichment, sports, art/fine arts programs offered; session focuses on recreation; held on campus; accepts boys and girls; open to students from other schools. 150 students usually enrolled. 2017 schedule: June 1 to August 1. Application deadline: May 1.

Tuition and Aid Day student tuition: $20,100. Tuition installment plan (monthly payment plans, quarterly payment plan). Need-based scholarship grants available. In 2016–17, 30% of upper-school students received aid.

Admissions Traditional secondary-level entrance grade is 9. ERB (grade level), OLSAT and English Exam or SSAT required. Deadline for receipt of application materials: none. Application fee required: $90. On-campus interview recommended.

Athletics Interscholastic: baseball (boys), dance team (g), flag football (b), football (b), golf (b,g), lacrosse (b,g), soccer (b,g), softball (g), tennis (b,g), volleyball (g), wrestling (b); intramural: aerobics (g), aerobics/dance (g), ballet (g), cheering (g), combined training (b,g), dance (g), physical fitness (b,g), strength & conditioning (b,g), weight lifting (b), weight training (b,g); coed interscholastic: aquatics, basketball, cross-country running, diving, swimming and diving, track and field, water polo; coed intramural: Frisbee. 5 PE instructors, 10 coaches, 2 athletic trainers.

Computers Computers are regularly used in all academic, college planning classes. Computer network features include on-campus library services, online commercial services, Internet access, wireless campus network, Internet filtering or blocking technology. Campus intranet is available to students. Students grades are available online. The school has a published electronic and media policy.

Contact Mrs. Mary Helen Bryant, Director of Admissions and Enrollment. 770-243-2274. Fax: 770-243-2227. E-mail: mbryant@greateratlantachristian.org.
Website: www.greateratlantachristian.org

GREAT LAKES CHRISTIAN HIGH SCHOOL

4875 King Street
Beamsville, Ontario L0R 1B6, Canada

Head of School: Mr. Don Rose

General Information Coeducational boarding and day college-preparatory, general academic, arts, religious studies, technology, and ESL school, affiliated with Church of Christ. Grades 9–12. Founded: 1952. Setting: small town. Nearest major city is St. Catharines, Canada. Students are housed in single-sex dormitories. 8 acre campus. 6 buildings on campus. Approved or accredited by Ontario Ministry of Education and Ontario Department of Education. Language of instruction: English. Endowment: CAN$500,000. Total enrollment: 124. Upper school average class size: 22. Upper school faculty-student ratio: 1:8. There are 252 required school days per year for Upper School students. Upper School students typically attend 5 days per week. The average school day consists of 6 hours and 10 minutes.

Upper School Student Profile Grade 9: 26 students (13 boys, 13 girls); Grade 10: 23 students (14 boys, 9 girls); Grade 11: 25 students (15 boys, 10 girls); Grade 12: 50 students (26 boys, 24 girls). 45% of students are boarding students. 40% are province residents. 7 provinces are represented in upper school student body. 60% are international students International students from China, Hong Kong, Nigeria, Republic of Korea, Taiwan, and United States; 2 other countries represented in student body. 40% of students are members of Church of Christ.

Faculty School total: 14. In upper school: 8 men, 6 women; 4 have advanced degrees; 2 reside on campus.

Subjects Offered Society.

Graduation Requirements 20th century history, advanced math, art, Bible, business, Canadian geography, Canadian history, Canadian literature, career planning, civics, computer information systems, conceptual physics, critical thinking, current events, economics, English, English composition, English literature, French as a second language, geography, mathematics, physical education (includes health), science, society challenge and change, world geography, world history.

Special Academic Programs Independent study; ESL (20 students enrolled).

College Admission Counseling 48 students graduated in 2016; 44 went to college, including Carleton University; McMaster University; University of Ottawa; University of Toronto; University of Waterloo; Wilfrid Laurier University. Other: 4 went to work.

Student Life Upper grades have uniform requirement, student council, honor system. Discipline rests primarily with faculty. Attendance at religious services is required.

Summer Programs Enrichment, rigorous outdoor training programs offered; session focuses on skill levels improvement; held on campus; accepts boys and girls; not open to students from other schools. 6 students usually enrolled. 2017 schedule: June 19 to August 31. Application deadline: May 8.

Tuition and Aid Day student tuition: CAN$8800; 5-day tuition and room/board: CAN$15,200; 7-day tuition and room/board: CAN$17,500. Tuition installment plan (monthly payment plans, individually arranged payment plans). Tuition reduction for siblings, bursaries, merit scholarship grants, need-based scholarship grants, need-based loans, middle-income loans, paying campus jobs available. In 2016–17, 55% of upper-school students received aid; total upper-school merit-scholarship money awarded: CAN$8000. Total amount of financial aid awarded in 2016–17: CAN$225,000.

Admissions Traditional secondary-level entrance grade is 9. For fall 2016, 134 students applied for upper-level admission, 126 were accepted, 124 enrolled. CAT and

SLEP required. Deadline for receipt of application materials: none. Application fee required: CAN$100. Interview recommended.

Athletics Interscholastic: badminton (boys, girls), basketball (b,g), cross-country running (b,g), golf (b), ice hockey (b,g), soccer (b,g), tennis (b,g), track and field (b,g), volleyball (b,g); intramural: aerobics (g), badminton (b,g), basketball (b,g), cooperative games (b,g), Cosom hockey (b,g), fitness (b,g), ice hockey (b,g), indoor hockey (b,g), indoor soccer (b,g), lacrosse (b,g), soccer (b,g), softball (b,g), table tennis (b,g), tennis (b,g), volleyball (b,g); coed interscholastic: badminton, tennis; coed intramural: badminton, ball hockey, baseball, basketball, cooperative games, Cosom hockey, floor hockey, hockey, indoor soccer, lacrosse, table tennis, tennis, volleyball. 2 PE instructors, 2 coaches.

Computers Computers are regularly used in accounting, business, computer applications, introduction to technology, technology, typing classes. Computer network features include on-campus library services, Internet access, wireless campus network, Internet filtering or blocking technology, Edsby system. Campus intranet and computer access in designated common areas are available to students. Students grades are available online. The school has a published electronic and media policy.

Contact Mrs. Ingrid Kielstra, Director of Domestic Admissions. 905-563-5374 Ext. 212. Fax: 905-563-0818. E-mail: study@glchs.on.ca. Website: www.glchs.on.ca

GREENFIELD SCHOOL

3351 NC Hwy 42 W
Wilson, North Carolina 27893

Head of School: Mrs. Beth Peters

General Information Coeducational day and distance learning college-preparatory school. Grades PS–12. Distance learning grades 11–12. Founded: 1969. Setting: small town. Nearest major city is Raleigh. 61-acre campus. 9 buildings on campus. Approved or accredited by Academy of Orton-Gillingham Practitioners and Educators, Southern Association of Colleges and Schools, and North Carolina Department of Education. Member of National Association of Independent Schools. Total enrollment: 250. Upper school average class size: 17. Upper school faculty-student ratio: 1:3. There are 178 required school days per year for Upper School students. Upper School students typically attend 5 days per week. The average school day consists of 6 hours and 45 minutes.

Upper School Student Profile Grade 6: 26 students (14 boys, 12 girls); Grade 7: 22 students (6 boys, 16 girls); Grade 8: 17 students (9 boys, 8 girls); Grade 9: 19 students (12 boys, 7 girls); Grade 10: 16 students (10 boys, 6 girls); Grade 11: 20 students (15 boys, 5 girls); Grade 12: 17 students (8 boys, 9 girls).

Faculty School total: 56. In upper school: 9 men, 16 women; 13 have advanced degrees.

Subjects Offered Advanced computer applications, advanced math, Advanced Placement courses, algebra, American history, American literature, ancient world history, art, athletics, biology, British literature, calculus, calculus-AP, chemistry, chorus, college awareness, community service, computer applications, computer education, computer graphics, computer information systems, computer math, computer multimedia, computer processing, computer programming, computer programming-AP, computer science, computer skills, computer technologies, desktop publishing, drama, earth science, economics, electives, English, English literature, fine arts, foreign language, geography, geometry, government/civics, grammar, health, history, honors algebra, honors English, honors geometry, honors world history, keyboarding, language arts, mathematics, music, physical education, physical science, physics, pre-algebra, pre-calculus, SAT preparation, science, social studies, Spanish, sports conditioning, trigonometry, Web site design, world geography, world history, writing, yearbook.

Graduation Requirements Arts and fine arts (art, music, dance, drama), computer science, English, foreign language, mathematics, physical education (includes health), science, social studies (includes history). Community service is required.

Special Academic Programs 5 Advanced Placement exams for which test preparation is offered; honors section; independent study; academic accommodation for the gifted; remedial reading and/or remedial writing; remedial math; programs in English, general development for dyslexic students.

College Admission Counseling 20 students graduated in 2016; all went to college, including Appalachian State University; East Carolina University; Meredith College; North Carolina State University; The University of North Carolina at Chapel Hill. Median SAT critical reading: 520, median SAT math: 510, median SAT writing: 500, median combined SAT: 1540, median composite ACT: 23. 18% scored over 600 on SAT critical reading, 24% scored over 600 on SAT math, 29% scored over 600 on SAT writing, 24% scored over 1800 on combined SAT, 38% scored over 26 on composite ACT.

Student Life Upper grades have specified standards of dress, student council, honor system. Discipline rests primarily with faculty.

Tuition and Aid Day student tuition: $5330–$10,659. Tuition installment plan (monthly payment plans). Tuition reduction for siblings, merit scholarship grants, need-based scholarship grants available. In 2016–17, 20% of upper-school students received aid; total upper-school merit-scholarship money awarded: $30,000. Total amount of financial aid awarded in 2016–17: $28,500.

Admissions Traditional secondary-level entrance grade is 9. For fall 2016, 15 students applied for upper-level admission, 12 were accepted, 7 enrolled. OLSAT, ERB required.

Deadline for receipt of application materials: none. Application fee required: $100. On-campus interview recommended.

Athletics Interscholastic: baseball (boys), basketball (b,g), cheering (g), cross-country running (b,g), golf (b), soccer (b,g), tennis (b,g), volleyball (g); coed interscholastic: golf. 3 PE instructors, 11 coaches.

Computers Computers are regularly used in all academic classes. Computer resources include on-campus library services, Internet access, wireless campus network, Internet filtering or blocking technology. Computer access in designated common areas is available to students. Students grades are available online. The school has a published electronic and media policy.

Contact Robin Hauser, Director of Advancement. 252-237-8046. Fax: 252-237-1825. E-mail: hauserr@greenfieldschool.org. Website: www.greenfieldschool.org

GREEN FIELDS COUNTRY DAY SCHOOL

6000 North Camino de la Tierra
Tucson, Arizona 85741

Head of School: Rebecca Cordier

General Information Coeducational day college-preparatory and arts school. Grades K–12. Distance learning grades 3–12. Founded: 1933. Setting: suburban. 22-acre campus. 15 buildings on campus. Approved or accredited by Arizona Association of Independent Schools. Member of National Association of Independent Schools. Total enrollment: 105. Upper school average class size: 12. Upper school faculty-student ratio: 1:5. There are 175 required school days per year for Upper School students. Upper School students typically attend 5 days per week. The average school day consists of 6 hours and 20 minutes.

Upper School Student Profile Grade 6: 10 students (1 boy, 9 girls); Grade 7: 9 students (1 boy, 8 girls); Grade 8: 5 students (2 boys, 3 girls); Grade 9: 13 students (8 boys, 5 girls); Grade 10: 9 students (3 boys, 6 girls); Grade 11: 10 students (3 boys, 7 girls); Grade 12: 12 students (5 boys, 7 girls).

Faculty School total: 21. In upper school: 4 men, 10 women; 10 have advanced degrees.

Subjects Offered 3-dimensional art, ACT preparation, advanced chemistry, advanced computer applications, advanced math, Advanced Placement courses, advanced studio art-AP, algebra, American government, American history, American history-AP, American literature, anatomy and physiology, art, art-AP, Basic programming, basketball, biology, biology-AP, British literature (honors), British literature-AP, calculus, calculus-AP, ceramics, chemistry, chorus, civics, classical Greek literature, clayworking, college counseling, college placement, computer math, computer programming, computer science, conceptual physics, creative drama, cultural geography, digital art, digital photography, drama, drama performance, drawing, earth science, East European studies, English, English as a foreign language, English literature and composition-AP, environmental science-AP, European history, European history-AP, expository writing, fine arts, French, French language-AP, French literature-AP, French-AP, geography, geometry, government and politics-AP, government-AP, grammar, humanities, independent study, journalism, modern European history, music theater, music theory, musical theater, newspaper, photojournalism, physical education, physics, play production, political science, pre-algebra, pre-calculus, probability, probability and statistics, SAT preparation, science project, senior project, Shakespeare, social studies, Spanish, Spanish language-AP, Spanish-AP, sports conditioning, statistics, studio art-AP, theater arts, trigonometry, U.S. government, U.S. government and politics-AP, U.S. history, U.S. history-AP, visual arts, Web site design, weight training, world history, writing, writing, yearbook.

Graduation Requirements Advanced math, algebra, American history, American literature, arts and fine arts (art, music, dance, drama), biology, chemistry, computer skills, electives, English, English literature, foreign language, geometry, mathematics, physical education (includes health), science, social studies (includes history), world history, writing.

Special Academic Programs Advanced Placement exam preparation; independent study; study abroad; ESL (2 students enrolled).

College Admission Counseling 7 students graduated in 2016; 6 went to college, including Connecticut College; Northern Arizona University; Syracuse University; The University of Arizona.

Student Life Upper grades have specified standards of dress, student council, honor system. Discipline rests primarily with faculty.

Tuition and Aid Day student tuition: $14,600. Tuition installment plan (SMART Tuition Payment Plan, individually arranged payment plans, semester payment plan). Merit scholarship grants, need-based scholarship grants available. In 2016–17, 40% of upper-school students received aid.

Admissions Traditional secondary-level entrance grade is 9. For fall 2016, 10 students applied for upper-level admission, 7 were accepted, 7 enrolled. Achievement tests or Achievement/Aptitude/Writing required. Deadline for receipt of application materials: none. Application fee required: $50. On-campus interview required.

Athletics Interscholastic: aquatics (girls), basketball (b,g), cross-country running (b,g), swimming and diving (g), tennis (b), volleyball (b,g); intramural: triathlon (b,g); coed interscholastic: flag football, physical fitness, physical training, running, soccer, track and field, winter soccer; coed intramural: ball hockey, kickball, rock climbing, tennis, yoga. 1 PE instructor, 8 coaches.

Computers Computers are regularly used in English, foreign language, mathematics, newspaper, science, yearbook classes. Computer network features include on-campus library services, online commercial services, Internet access, wireless campus network, Internet filtering or blocking technology. Campus intranet, student e-mail accounts, and computer access in designated common areas are available to students. Students grades are available online. The school has a published electronic and media policy.

Contact Andre Boudy, Director of Admission. 520-297-2288 Ext. 7106. Fax: 520-618-2599. E-mail: aboudy@greenfields.org. Website: www.greenfields.org

GREENHILL SCHOOL

4141 Spring Valley Road
Addison, Texas 75001

Head of School: Scott A. Griggs

General Information Coeducational day college-preparatory school. Grades PK–12. Founded: 1950. Setting: suburban. Nearest major city is Dallas. 78-acre campus. 8 buildings on campus. Approved or accredited by Independent Schools Association of the Southwest and Texas Department of Education. Member of National Association of Independent Schools and Secondary School Admission Test Board. Endowment: $32.8 million. Total enrollment: 1,280. Upper school average class size: 16. Upper school faculty-student ratio: 1:7. Upper School students typically attend 5 days per week. The average school day consists of 7 hours and 45 minutes.

Upper School Student Profile Grade 9: 114 students (56 boys, 58 girls); Grade 10: 114 students (59 boys, 55 girls); Grade 11: 121 students (55 boys, 66 girls); Grade 12: 113 students (58 boys, 55 girls).

Faculty School total: 169. In upper school: 45 men, 37 women; 52 have advanced degrees.

Subjects Offered Algebra, American history, American literature, art, art history, biology, calculus, ceramics, chemistry, Chinese, computer programming, computer science, creative writing, dance, drama, ecology, economics, English, English literature, European history, fine arts, French, geometry, government/civics, health, history, journalism, Latin, mathematics, music, philosophy, photography, physical education, physics, robotics, science, social studies, Spanish, speech, theater, trigonometry, wellness.

Graduation Requirements Arts and fine arts (art, music, dance, drama), classical language, computer studies, English, history, mathematics, modern languages, physical education (includes health), science. Community service is required.

Special Academic Programs Advanced Placement exam preparation; honors section; independent study; term-away projects; study abroad.

College Admission Counseling 118 students graduated in 2016; all went to college, including Boston University; Emory University; Southern Methodist University; The University of Texas at Austin; Tulane University; Vanderbilt University.

Student Life Upper grades have specified standards of dress, student council, honor system. Discipline rests primarily with faculty.

Summer Programs Enrichment, sports, art/fine arts, computer instruction programs offered; session focuses on enrichment and sports; held on campus; accepts boys and girls; open to students from other schools. 1,300 students usually enrolled. 2017 schedule: May 30 to August 11. Application deadline: none.

Tuition and Aid Day student tuition: $29,100. Need-based scholarship grants available. In 2016–17, 18% of upper-school students received aid. Total amount of financial aid awarded in 2016–17: $1,812,250.

Admissions Traditional secondary-level entrance grade is 9. For fall 2016, 197 students applied for upper-level admission, 86 were accepted, 56 enrolled. ISEE required. Deadline for receipt of application materials: January 6. Application fee required: $175. Interview required.

Athletics Interscholastic: aquatics (boys, girls), baseball (b), basketball (b,g), cross-country running (b,g), field hockey (g), football (b), golf (b,g), lacrosse (b,g), running (b,g), soccer (b,g), softball (g), swimming and diving (b,g), tennis (b,g), track and field (b,g), volleyball (b,g), winter soccer (b,g); intramural: baseball (b), basketball (b,g), field hockey (g), fitness (b,g), football (b), lacrosse (b,g), physical fitness (b,g), running (b,g), soccer (b,g), softball (g), strength & conditioning (b,g), swimming and diving (b,g), tennis (b,g), track and field (b,g), volleyball (b,g), weight lifting (b,g), winter soccer (b,g); coed interscholastic: cheering; coed intramural: aquatics, ballet, cross-country running, dance, fitness, Frisbee, golf, physical fitness, running, soccer, strength & conditioning, swimming and diving, tennis, track and field, ultimate Frisbee, volleyball, weight lifting, weight training, winter soccer, yoga. 15 PE instructors, 4 athletic trainers.

Computers Computers are regularly used in graphic arts, journalism classes. Computer network features include on-campus library services, online commercial services, Internet access, wireless campus network, Internet filtering or blocking technology. Campus intranet, student e-mail accounts, and computer access in designated common areas are available to students. Students grades are available online. The school has a published electronic and media policy.

Contact Sarah Markhovsky, Director of Admission. 972-628-5910. Fax: 972-404-8217. E-mail: admission@greenhill.org. Website: www.greenhill.org

GREENHILLS SCHOOL

850 Greenhills Drive
Ann Arbor, Michigan 48105

Head of School: Carl J. Pelofsky

General Information Coeducational day college-preparatory and arts school. Grades 6–12. Founded: 1968. Setting: urban. Nearest major city is Detroit. 30-acre campus. 1 building on campus. Approved or accredited by Independent Schools Association of the Central States and Michigan Department of Education. Member of National Association of Independent Schools and Secondary School Admission Test Board. Endowment: $8 million. Total enrollment: 574. Upper school average class size: 16. Upper school faculty-student ratio: 1:8. There are 165 required school days per year for Upper School students. Upper School students typically attend 5 days per week. The average school day consists of 7 hours.

Upper School Student Profile Grade 9: 87 students (41 boys, 46 girls); Grade 10: 85 students (42 boys, 43 girls); Grade 11: 80 students (43 boys, 37 girls); Grade 12: 88 students (43 boys, 45 girls).

Faculty School total: 69. In upper school: 26 men, 43 women; 54 have advanced degrees.

Subjects Offered 3-dimensional art, advanced chemistry, Advanced Placement courses, African-American literature, algebra, American history, American literature, ancient history, art, astronomy, biology, calculus, calculus-AP, ceramics, chemistry, Chinese, Chinese studies, chorus, community service, creative writing, discrete mathematics, drama, drawing, economics, economics and history, English, English literature, ethics, European history, expository writing, fine arts, French, geometry, government, health, history, jazz, journalism, Latin, mathematics, music, orchestra, painting, photography, physical education, physical science, physics, science, social studies, Spanish, theater, trigonometry, world history, world literature, writing.

Graduation Requirements Arts and fine arts (art, music, dance, drama), English, foreign language, mathematics, physical education (includes health), science, social studies (includes history), senior project. Community service is required.

Special Academic Programs Advanced Placement exam preparation; honors section; independent study; programs in English, mathematics for dyslexic students; special instructional classes for blind students.

College Admission Counseling 74 students graduated in 2016; all went to college, including Brown University; Johns Hopkins University; Michigan State University; Stanford University; The College of Wooster; University of Michigan. Mean SAT critical reading: 645, mean SAT math: 650, mean SAT writing: 653, mean combined SAT: 1948, mean composite ACT: 28.

Student Life Upper grades have specified standards of dress, student council. Discipline rests equally with students and faculty.

Tuition and Aid Day student tuition: $21,120. Tuition installment plan (SMART Tuition Payment Plan, monthly payment plans). Need-based scholarship grants available. In 2016–17, 18% of upper-school students received aid. Total amount of financial aid awarded in 2016–17: $10,011,500.

Admissions Traditional secondary-level entrance grade is 9. For fall 2016, 87 students applied for upper-level admission, 49 were accepted, 34 enrolled. SSAT or TOEFL required. Deadline for receipt of application materials: none. Application fee required: $50. Interview required.

Athletics Interscholastic: baseball (boys), basketball (b,g), cross-country running (b,g), field hockey (g), golf (b,g), ice hockey (b), lacrosse (b), soccer (b,g), softball (g), tennis (b,g), track and field (b,g), volleyball (g); intramural: basketball (b,g), cross-country running (b,g), field hockey (g), soccer (b,g); coed interscholastic: swimming and diving; coed intramural: hiking/backpacking, horseback riding, outdoor activities, outdoor education, physical fitness. 3 PE instructors, 36 coaches, 1 athletic trainer.

Computers Computers are regularly used in all academic classes. Computer network features include on-campus library services, online commercial services, Internet access, wireless campus network, Internet filtering or blocking technology. Campus intranet, student e-mail accounts, and computer access in designated common areas are available to students. Students grades are available online. The school has a published electronic and media policy.

Contact Betsy Ellsworth, Director of Admission and Financial Aid. 734-205-4061. Fax: 734-205-4056. E-mail: admission@greenhillsschool.org. Website: www.greenhillsschool.org

GREEN MEADOW WALDORF SCHOOL

307 Hungry Hollow Road
Chestnut Ridge, New York 10977

Head of School: Bill Pernice

General Information Coeducational day college-preparatory, general academic, arts, and Waldorf Education school. Grades N–12. Founded: 1950. Setting: suburban. Nearest major city is New York. 11-acre campus. 3 buildings on campus. Approved or accredited by Association of Waldorf Schools of North America, New York State Association of Independent Schools, and New York Department of Education. Total enrollment: 375. Upper school average class size: 20. Upper school faculty-student ratio: 1:9. There are 171 required school days per year for Upper School students. Upper School students typically attend 5 days per week. The average school day consists of 7 hours.

Upper School Student Profile Grade 9: 8 students (5 boys, 3 girls); Grade 10: 22 students (6 boys, 16 girls); Grade 11: 22 students (11 boys, 11 girls); Grade 12: 22 students (7 boys, 15 girls). 10% of students are boarding students. 6 states are represented in upper school student body. 10% are international students. International students from Argentina, Canada, China, and Germany; 2 other countries represented in student body.

Faculty School total: 60. In upper school: 8 men, 12 women; 11 have advanced degrees.

Subjects Offered 20th century American writers, 20th century history, 20th century physics, 20th century world history, 3-dimensional art, 3-dimensional design, ACT preparation, acting, adolescent issues, African American history, African history, African literature, African-American history, African-American literature, agriculture, algebra, American Civil War, American government, American history, American literature, analytic geometry, anatomy, anatomy and physiology, ancient history, ancient world history, ancient/medieval philosophy, applied arts, applied music, architecture, art, art history, arts, Bible studies, biology, botany, calculus, chemistry, computer math, computer science, creative writing, dance, drama, earth science, English, English literature, ethics, European history, expository writing, fine arts, French, geography, geology, geometry, German, government/civics, grammar, health, history, history of ideas, history of science, logic, marine biology, mathematics, music, orchestra, philosophy, physical education, physics, physiology, poetry, Russian literature, science, sculpture, social studies, Spanish, speech, theater, trigonometry, woodworking, world history, world literature, writing, zoology.

Graduation Requirements Arts and fine arts (art, music, dance, drama), English, foreign language, mathematics, physical education (includes health), science, social studies (includes history).

Special Academic Programs Independent study; term-away projects; study abroad; remedial reading and/or remedial writing; remedial math; programs in English, general development for dyslexic students; ESL (12 students enrolled).

College Admission Counseling 30 students graduated in 2016; 28 went to college, including Brandeis University; Cornell University; Eugene Lang College of Liberal Arts; Fordham University; Hampshire College; Northeastern University. Other: 2 went to work. 31% scored over 600 on SAT critical reading, 27% scored over 600 on SAT math.

Student Life Upper grades have specified standards of dress, student council, honor system. Discipline rests primarily with faculty.

Tuition and Aid Day student tuition: $25,150. Guaranteed tuition plan. Tuition installment plan (Insured Tuition Payment Plan, monthly payment plans). Tuition reduction for siblings, merit scholarship grants, need-based scholarship grants available. In 2016–17, 35% of upper-school students received aid.

Admissions Traditional secondary-level entrance grade is 9. Deadline for receipt of application materials: none. Application fee required: $50. Interview recommended.

Athletics Interscholastic: baseball (boys), basketball (b,g), running (g), softball (g), tennis (g), volleyball (g); intramural: basketball (b,g); coed interscholastic: Circus, cooperative games, cross-country running, equestrian sports, horseback riding, outdoor activities, outdoor adventure, outdoor education, outdoor recreation, outdoor skills, outdoors, physical fitness, running, tennis, volleyball, wilderness, wilderness survival; coed intramural: cooperative games, cross-country running, running, volleyball. 2 PE instructors, 5 coaches.

Computers Computers are regularly used in mathematics classes. Computer resources include Internet access, wireless campus network, Internet filtering or blocking technology. Computer access in designated common areas is available to students. Students grades are available online. The school has a published electronic and media policy.

Contact Melissa McDonagh, Director of Admissions, Grades 1-12. 845-356-2514 Ext. 302. Fax: 845-371-2358. E-mail: mmcdonagh@gmws.org. Website: www.gmws.org

GREENWOOD LABORATORY SCHOOL

901 South National Avenue
Springfield, Missouri 65897

Head of School: Dr. Janice Duncan

General Information Coeducational day college-preparatory and STEM school. Grades K–12. Founded: 1908. Setting: urban. 3-acre campus. 1 building on campus. Approved or accredited by North Central Association of Colleges and Schools and Missouri Department of Education. Endowment: $355,045. Total enrollment: 339. Upper school average class size: 20. Upper school faculty-student ratio: 1:22. There are 160 required school days per year for Upper School students. Upper School students typically attend 5 days per week. The average school day consists of 6 hours and 15 minutes.

Upper School Student Profile Grade 6: 22 students (9 boys, 13 girls); Grade 7: 37 students (20 boys, 17 girls); Grade 8: 30 students (14 boys, 16 girls); Grade 9: 24 students (12 boys, 12 girls); Grade 10: 32 students (20 boys, 12 girls); Grade 11: 27 students (14 boys, 13 girls); Grade 12: 40 students (24 boys, 16 girls).

Faculty School total: 21. In upper school: 11 men, 10 women; 20 have advanced degrees.

Subjects Offered English, fine arts, foreign language, health, instrumental music, mathematics, physical education, science, social studies, state government, vocal music.

Graduation Requirements American government, American history, athletics, CPR, electives, finance, foreign language, geography, health, leadership and service, senior seminar, students have to pass a Graduation Exhibition and achieve Public Affairs Merits.

Special Academic Programs Independent study; study at local college for college credit; study abroad.

College Admission Counseling 32 students graduated in 2016; 30 went to college, including University of Arkansas; University of Missouri. Other: 2 went to work. Mean composite ACT: 26. 57% scored over 26 on composite ACT.

Student Life Upper grades have specified standards of dress, student council. Discipline rests primarily with faculty.

Tuition and Aid Day student tuition: $6500. Tuition installment plan (individually arranged payment plans, single payment plan). Need-based scholarship grants, tuition reduction for children of fulltime employees available. In 2016–17, 10% of upper-school students received aid. Total amount of financial aid awarded in 2016–17: $75,000.

Admissions Traditional secondary-level entrance grade is 9. For fall 2016, 52 students applied for upper-level admission, 25 were accepted, 22 enrolled. Achievement tests, ACT, ACT-Explore or PSAT required. Deadline for receipt of application materials: none. Application fee required: $50. On-campus interview required.

Athletics Interscholastic: basketball (boys, girls), golf (b,g), soccer (b,g), swimming and diving (b,g), tennis (b,g); coed interscholastic: cheering, cross-country running, physical fitness, track and field. 3 PE instructors, 7 coaches.

Computers Computers are regularly used in English, French, history, science, Spanish, yearbook classes. Computer network features include on-campus library services, Internet access, wireless campus network. Student e-mail accounts and computer access in designated common areas are available to students. Students grades are available online. The school has a published electronic and media policy.

Contact Ms. Jeni Hopkins, Counselor. 417-836-7667. Fax: 417-836-8449. E-mail: Jenihopkins@missouristate.edu.
Website: www.education.missouristate.edu/greenwood

THE GREENWOOD SCHOOL

Putney, Vermont
See Junior Boarding Schools section.

GRIER SCHOOL

PO Box 308
Tyrone, Pennsylvania 16686-0308

Head of School: Mrs. Gina Borst

General Information Girls' boarding and day college-preparatory, arts, and art, theatre, music, dance, and horseback riding school. Boarding grades 7–PG, day grades 7–12. Distance learning grade NA. Founded: 1853. Setting: rural. Nearest major city is Pittsburgh. Students are housed in single-sex dormitories. 300-acre campus. 20 buildings on campus. Approved or accredited by Middle States Association of Colleges and Schools and Pennsylvania Department of Education. Member of National Association of Independent Schools and Secondary School Admission Test Board. Endowment: $23 million. Total enrollment: 309. Upper school average class size: 9. Upper school faculty-student ratio: 1:6. There are 160 required school days per year for Upper School students. Upper School students typically attend 5 days per week. The average school day consists of 8 hours and 43 minutes.

Upper School Student Profile Grade 7: 11 students (11 girls); Grade 8: 41 students (41 girls); Grade 9: 53 students (53 girls); Grade 10: 61 students (61 girls); Grade 11: 85 students (85 girls); Grade 12: 65 students (65 girls). 85% of students are boarding students. 21% are state residents. 22 states are represented in upper school student body. 50% are international students. International students from Bermuda, China, Mexico, Russian Federation, Turkey, and Viet Nam; 8 other countries represented in student body.

Faculty School total: 63. In upper school: 19 men, 44 women; 54 have advanced degrees; 47 reside on campus.

Subjects Offered 20th century history, 20th century world history, acting, advanced biology, advanced chemistry, advanced computer applications, Advanced Placement courses, advanced studio art-AP, advanced TOEFL/grammar, algebra, all academic, American government, American history, American history-AP, American literature, anatomy, anatomy and physiology, ancient world history, animal science, art, art history, art history-AP, art-AP, arts and crafts, ballet, ballet technique, batik, biology, biology-AP, British literature, British literature (honors), calculus, calculus-AP, ceramics, chemistry, chemistry-AP, Chinese, choir, choreography, clayworking, college admission preparation, college counseling, college planning, computer applications, computer graphics, computer literacy, computer programming, computer science, computer science-AP, conceptual physics, concert band, consumer mathematics, costumes and make-up, creative arts, creative writing, criminal justice, criminology, dance, dance performance, digital art, digital photography, directing, drama, drama performance, dramatic arts, drawing, drawing and design, earth and space science, earth science, ecology, ecology, environmental systems, economics, economics and history, economics-AP, English, English as a foreign language, English composition, English literature, English literature and composition-AP, English literature-AP, environmental science, environmental science-AP, environmental studies, equestrian sports, equine science, equitation, ESL, European history, European history-AP, European literature, fabric arts, fashion, fencing, fiber arts, filmmaking, finance, fine arts, fitness, foreign language, French, French language-AP, French-AP, geometry, global issues, global studies, government and politics-AP, government-AP, government/civics-AP, graphic arts, graphic design, guitar, health and wellness, history, history-AP, honors English, honors geometry, honors U.S. history, honors world history, human anatomy, human biology, instrumental music, international relations, introduction to theater, jazz band, jazz dance, jazz ensemble, jewelry making, journalism, lab science, learning strategies, library, library skills, life science, literature and composition-AP, literature-AP, macro/microeconomics-AP, macroeconomics-AP, marine biology, marine ecology, marine science, mathematics, mathematics-AP, microeconomics, microeconomics-AP, model United Nations, modern dance, modern European history, modern European history-AP, music, music performance, music technology, music theater, music theory, music theory-AP, music-AP, musical theater, musical theater dance, newspaper, oil painting, organic chemistry, painting, performing arts, personal finance, personal money management, philosophy, photography, physical education, physical fitness, physical science, physics, physics-AP, physiology, piano, portfolio art, pre-algebra, pre-calculus, printmaking, probability and statistics, psychology, psychology-AP, public speaking, reading/study skills, robotics, SAT/ACT preparation, science, set design, sewing, Shakespeare, social psychology, social studies, Spanish, Spanish language-AP, Spanish-AP, speech, stage design, stagecraft, statistics-AP, student government, studio art, studio art AP, study skills, symphonic band, tap dance, theater, theater arts, theater production, TOEFL preparation, trigonometry, typing, U.S. government, U.S. history, U.S. history-AP, U.S. literature, United Nations and international issues, United States government-AP, video, video film production, visual and performing arts, vocal ensemble, vocal music, voice, voice ensemble, weaving, women's studies, world cultures, world history, world history-AP, world literature, world studies, writing, writing, writing workshop, yearbook, yoga.

Graduation Requirements Arts and fine arts (art, music, dance, drama), English, foreign language, mathematics, physical education (includes health), science, social sciences, social studies (includes history).

Special Academic Programs 20 Advanced Placement exams for which test preparation is offered; honors section; academic accommodation for the gifted, the musically talented, and the artistically talented; remedial reading and/or remedial writing; remedial math; programs in English, mathematics, general development for dyslexic students; special instructional classes for blind students, our learning skills, student support, and counseling programs offer daytime and evening support to students, who struggle with learning or emotional challenges; ESL (43 students enrolled).

College Admission Counseling 56 students graduated in 2016; 53 went to college, including Boston University; Fashion Institute of Technology; Parsons School of Design; Penn State University Park; University of California, Berkeley; University of California, San Diego. Other: 3 had other specific plans. Median SAT critical reading: 600, median SAT math: 680, median SAT writing: 620, median combined SAT: 1900, median composite ACT: 24. 50% scored over 600 on SAT critical reading, 73% scored over 600 on SAT math, 54% scored over 600 on SAT writing, 59% scored over 1800 on combined SAT, 45% scored over 26 on composite ACT.

Student Life Upper grades have specified standards of dress, student council, honor system. Discipline rests primarily with faculty.

Summer Programs Enrichment, ESL, sports, art/fine arts programs offered; session focuses on recreation and ESL; held on campus; accepts girls; open to students from other schools. 100 students usually enrolled. 2017 schedule: June 26 to September 7 Application deadline: none.

Tuition and Aid Day student tuition: $18,000; 7-day tuition and room/board: $50,500. Tuition installment plan (individually arranged payment plans). Tuition reduction for siblings, merit scholarship grants, need-based scholarship grants, need-based loans, paying campus jobs available. In 2016–17, 51% of upper-school students received aid; total upper-school merit-scholarship money awarded: $800,000. Total amount of financial aid awarded in 2016–17: $2,000,000.

Admissions Traditional secondary-level entrance grade is 9. For fall 2016, 350 students applied for upper-level admission, 210 were accepted, 123 enrolled. SSAT or WISC III required. Deadline for receipt of application materials: none. Application fee required: $50. Interview recommended.

Athletics Interscholastic: basketball, dance, equestrian sports, fencing, skiing (downhill), soccer, tennis, volleyball; intramural: aerobics, aerobics/dance, aquatics, archery, badminton, ballet, basketball, bicycling, bowling, canoeing/kayaking, cheering, dance, dressage, equestrian sports, fencing, figure skating, fitness, fitness walking, golf, gymnastics, hiking/backpacking, horseback riding, jogging, jump rope, kayaking, martial arts, modern dance, mountain biking, nordic skiing, outdoor adventure, outdoor recreation, paddle tennis, physical fitness, physical training, ropes courses, running, scuba diving, skiing (cross-country), skiing (downhill), snowboarding, soccer, swimming and diving, tennis, volleyball, walking, weight training, yoga. 3 PE instructors, 3 coaches, 3 athletic trainers.

Computers Computers are regularly used in all classes. Computer network features include on-campus library services, Internet access, wireless campus network, Internet filtering or blocking technology, common cloud-based desktop. Campus intranet and student e-mail accounts are available to students. Students grades are available online. The school has a published electronic and media policy.

Contact Mrs. Jennifer D. Neely, Admissions Director. 814-684-3000 Ext. 7006. Fax: 814-684-2177. E-mail: admissions@grier.org. Website: www.grier.org

See Display on next page and Close-Up on page 598.

GRIGGS INTERNATIONAL ACADEMY

12501 Old Columbia Pike
Silver Spring, Maryland 20904-6600

Head of School: Ms. LaRonda Forsey

General Information Coeducational day and distance learning college-preparatory and general academic school, affiliated with Association of Seventh-day Adventist Schools and Colleges. Grades PK–12. Distance learning grades K–12. Founded: 1909. Setting: suburban. Nearest major city is Washington, DC. 1 building on campus. Approved or accredited by Board of Regents, General Conference of Seventh-day Adventists, Middle States Association of Colleges and Schools, Southern Association of Colleges and Schools, and Maryland Department of Education. Total enrollment: 1,559. Upper school faculty-student ratio: 1:21.

Upper School Student Profile 60% of students are Association of Seventh-day Adventist Schools and Colleges.

Faculty School total: 30. In upper school: 7 men, 19 women; 24 have advanced degrees.

Subjects Offered Accounting, algebra, American government, American history, American literature, art appreciation, art history, arts, Bible studies, biology, business skills, chemistry, digital photography, earth science, English, English literature, fine arts, food science, French, geography, geometry, government/civics, health, Holocaust, home economics, keyboarding, mathematics, Microsoft, music appreciation, physical education, physical science, physics, pre-algebra, science, social studies, Spanish, word processing, world history, writing.

Graduation Requirements American government, arts and fine arts (art, music, dance, drama), computer literacy, electives, English, health, history, language, mathematics, physical education (includes health), religion (includes Bible studies and theology), science, social studies (includes history), Spanish, requirements for standard diploma differ. Community service is required.

Special Academic Programs Accelerated programs; independent study; study at local college for college credit.

College Admission Counseling 192 students graduated in 2016; they went to Andrews University; Loma Linda University; Southern Adventist University; Towson University; University of Maryland, Baltimore County; Washington Adventist University.

Student Life Upper grades have honor system. Discipline rests primarily with faculty.

Summer Programs Remediation, enrichment programs offered; held on campus; accepts boys and girls; open to students from other schools.

Tuition and Aid Day student tuition: $2000–$3000. Tuition installment plan (monthly payment plans, individually arranged payment plans).

Admissions Stanford Achievement Test required. Deadline for receipt of application materials: none. Application fee required: $100.

Computers Computers are regularly used in computer applications, keyboarding, photography, Spanish, typing classes. Students grades are available online.

Contact Ms. Gabriela Melgar, Enrollment Coordinator. 269-471-6529. Fax: 301-680-5157. E-mail: enrollgia@andrews.edu. Website: www.griggs.edu

GROTON SCHOOL

Box 991
Farmers Row
Groton, Massachusetts 01450

Head of School: Temba B. Maqubela

General Information Coeducational boarding and day college-preparatory, arts, and religious studies school, affiliated with Episcopal Church. Grades 8–12. Founded: 1884. Setting: rural. Nearest major city is Boston. Students are housed in single-sex dormitories. 410-acre campus. 17 buildings on campus. Approved or accredited by Association of Independent Schools in New England, New England Association of Schools and Colleges, and The Association of Boarding Schools. Member of National Association of Independent Schools and Secondary School Admission Test Board. Endowment: $350 million. Total enrollment: 380. Upper school average class size: 12. Upper school faculty-student ratio: 1:5. There are 182 required school days per year for Upper School students. Upper School students typically attend 6 days per week. The average school day consists of 6 hours and 30 minutes.

Upper School Student Profile Grade 8: 26 students (15 boys, 11 girls); Grade 9: 84 students (43 boys, 41 girls); Grade 10: 94 students (52 boys, 42 girls); Grade 11: 92 students (44 boys, 48 girls); Grade 12: 84 students (40 boys, 44 girls). 84% of students are boarding students. 32% are state residents. 33 states are represented in upper school student body. 15% are international students. International students from Canada, China, Hong Kong, Mexico, Republic of Korea, and South Africa; 11 other countries represented in student body.

Faculty School total: 69. In upper school: 40 men, 29 women; 52 have advanced degrees; 58 reside on campus.

Subjects Offered Advanced chemistry, advanced math, Advanced Placement courses, algebra, American literature, American literature-AP, analytic geometry, Ancient Greek, ancient world history, archaeology, art, art history, art history-AP, Bible studies, biology, biology-AP, botany, Buddhism, calculus, calculus-AP, cell biology, Central and Eastern European history, ceramics, chemistry, chemistry-AP, Chinese, choir, choral music, civil rights, Civil War, civil war history, classical Greek literature, classical language, classics, composition, composition-AP, creative writing, dance, discrete mathematics, drawing, earth science, ecology, environmental systems, economics, English, English composition, English-AP, environmental science, environmental science-AP, environmental studies, ethics, ethics and responsibility, European history, European history-AP, expository writing, fine arts, fractal geometry, French, French language-AP, French literature-AP, geography, geometry, government, grammar, Greek, health, history, Holocaust, honors algebra, honors English, honors geometry, honors U.S. history, honors world history, independent study, lab science, language-AP, Latin, Latin-AP, linear algebra, literature, literature and composition-AP, mathematics, mathematics-AP, modern European history, modern European history-AP, modern history, modern languages, modern world history, music, music history, music theory, music theory-AP, organic biochemistry, painting, philosophy, photo shop, photography, physical science, physics, physics-AP, pre-algebra, pre-calculus, psychology, religion, religious education, religious studies, science, Shakespeare, social sciences, Spanish, Spanish language-AP, Spanish literature, Spanish literature-AP, sports medicine, statistics, studio art, studio art-AP, theology, trigonometry, U.S. constitutional history, U.S. government, U.S. government and politics, U.S. government and politics-AP, U.S. history, U.S. history-AP, vocal music, Western civilization, wood lab, woodworking, world history, world history-AP, writing.

Graduation Requirements Arts and fine arts (art, music, dance, drama), classical language, English, foreign language, mathematics, religious studies, science, social studies (includes history).

Special Academic Programs 13 Advanced Placement exams for which test preparation is offered; honors section; term-away projects; study abroad; academic accommodation for the gifted, the musically talented, and the artistically talented.

College Admission Counseling 88 students graduated in 2015; 86 went to college, including Bowdoin College; Brown University; Dartmouth College; Georgetown University; Harvard University; Yale University. Other: 2 had other specific plans. Median SAT critical reading: 710, median SAT math: 700, median SAT writing: 710, median combined SAT: 2110, median composite ACT: 31. 87% scored over 600 on SAT critical reading, 91% scored over 600 on SAT math, 92% scored over 600 on SAT writing, 92% scored over 1800 on combined SAT, 86% scored over 26 on composite ACT.

Student Life Upper grades have specified standards of dress, student council, honor system. Discipline rests equally with students and faculty. Attendance at religious services is required.

Tuition and Aid Day student tuition: $43,990; 7-day tuition and room/board: $56,700. Tuition installment plan (Insured Tuition Payment Plan, Key Tuition Payment Plan, monthly payment plans, individually arranged payment plans). Need-based scholarship grants, Key Education Resources available. In 2015–16, 39% of upper-school students received aid. Total amount of financial aid awarded in 2015–16: $6,200,000.

Admissions Traditional secondary-level entrance grade is 9. For fall 2015, 1,560 students applied for upper-level admission, 158 were accepted, 98 enrolled. ISEE, SSAT or TOEFL required. Deadline for receipt of application materials: January 15. Application fee required: $50. Interview required.

Athletics Interscholastic: baseball (boys), basketball (b,g), crew (b,g), cross-country running (b,g), field hockey (g), Fives (b,g), football (b), hockey (b,g), ice hockey (b,g), lacrosse (b,g), rowing (b,g), soccer (b,g), squash (b,g), tennis (b,g); intramural: self defense (g); weight training (b,g); coed intramural: aerobics/dance, alpine skiing, dance, fitness, Fives, Frisbee, golf, ice skating, modern dance, nordic skiing, outdoor activities, physical training, running, skeet shooting, skiing (cross-country), skiing (downhill), snowboarding, strength & conditioning, swimming and diving, track and field, trap and skeet, ultimate Frisbee, yoga. 2 coaches, 1 athletic trainer.

Computers Computers are regularly used in all academic classes. Computer network features include on-campus library services, Internet access, wireless campus network, Internet filtering or blocking technology, campus-wide wireless environment. Campus intranet and student e-mail accounts are available to students. Students grades are available online. The school has a published electronic and media policy.

Contact Mr. Ian Gracey, Director of Admission. 978-448-7510. Fax: 978-448-9623. E-mail: igracey@groton.org. Website: www.groton.org

GUAMANI PRIVATE SCHOOL

PO Box 3000
Guayama, Puerto Rico 00785

Head of School: Mr. Eduardo Delgado

General Information Coeducational day college-preparatory school. Grades 1–12. Founded: 1914. Setting: urban. Nearest major city is Caguas. 1-acre campus. 1 building on campus. Approved or accredited by Middle States Association of Colleges and Schools and Puerto Rico Department of Education. Total enrollment: 606. Upper school average class size: 20. Upper school faculty-student ratio: 1:13. There are 102 required school days per year for Upper School students. Upper School students typically attend 5 days per week. The average school day consists of 1 hours and 45 minutes.

Faculty School total: 32. In upper school: 10 men, 10 women; 3 have advanced degrees.

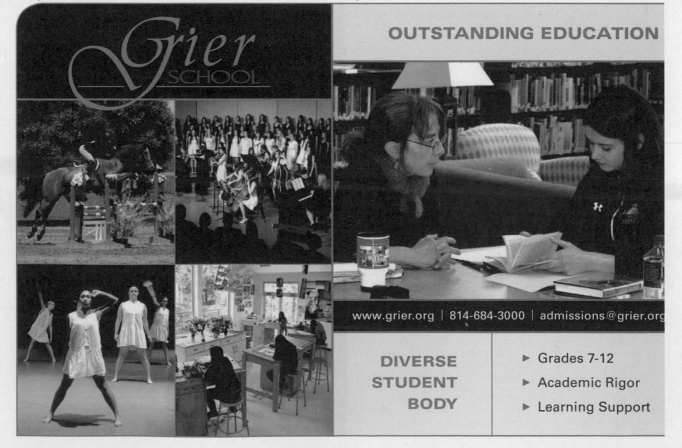

Subjects Offered Advanced math, Advanced Placement courses, algebra, American government, American history, analysis and differential calculus, chemistry, civics, pre-algebra, pre-calculus, science project, science research, social sciences, social studies, sociology, Spanish, Spanish language-AP, U.S. literature, visual arts, world geography, world history.

Graduation Requirements Mathematics, science, social sciences, Spanish, acceptance into a college or university. Community service is required.

Special Academic Programs Advanced Placement exam preparation; honors section; independent study.

College Admission Counseling 72 students graduated in 2016; 62 went to college, including Embry-Riddle Aeronautical University–Daytona; Syracuse University; University of Puerto Rico, Mayagüez Campus; University of Puerto Rico, Río Piedras Campus; University of Puerto Rico in Cayey. Other: 23 entered a postgraduate year.

Student Life Upper grades have uniform requirement, student council, honor system. Discipline rests primarily with faculty.

Summer Programs Remediation, ESL programs offered; held on campus; accepts boys and girls; open to students from other schools. 30 students usually enrolled. 2017 schedule: June 1 to June 30. Application deadline: May 27.

Admissions Traditional secondary-level entrance grade is 9. Traditional secondary-level entrance age is 12. For fall 2016, 30 students applied for upper-level admission, 21 were accepted, 20 enrolled. School's own test or Test of Achievement and Proficiency required. Deadline for receipt of application materials: none. Application fee required: $45. Interview required.

Athletics Interscholastic: aerobics/dance (girls), basketball (b,g), cheering (g), dance squad (g), volleyball (b,g); coed interscholastic: dance team. 3 PE instructors, 2 coaches.

Computers Computers are regularly used in aviation, English, mathematics, science, social sciences, Spanish, word processing classes. Computer resources include on-campus library services, Internet access, wireless campus network, Internet filtering or blocking technology. The school has a published electronic and media policy.

Contact Mrs. Digna Torres, Secretary. 787-864-6880 Ext. 20. Fax: 787-866-4947. Website: www.guamani.com

GULLIVER PREPARATORY SCHOOL

6575 North Kendall Drive
Miami, Florida 33156

Head of School: Mr. Frank Steel

General Information Coeducational day college-preparatory, arts, business, International Baccalaureate, architectural design, and law/litigation,Biomedical sciences,engineering,architecture school. Grades PK–12. Founded: 1926. Setting: suburban. 11 buildings on campus. Approved or accredited by CITA (Commission on International and Trans-Regional Accreditation), Florida Council of Independent Schools, Southern Association of Colleges and Schools, Southern Association of Independent Schools, and Florida Department of Education. Member of National Association of Independent Schools and Secondary School Admission Test Board. Total enrollment: 2,014. Upper school average class size: 14. Upper school faculty-student ratio: 1:8. There are 172 required school days per year for Upper School students. Upper School students typically attend 5 days per week.

Upper School Student Profile Grade 6: 168 students (97 boys, 71 girls); Grade 7: 171 students (95 boys, 76 girls); Grade 8: 157 students (83 boys, 74 girls); Grade 9: 215 students (113 boys, 102 girls); Grade 10: 245 students (122 boys, 123 girls); Grade 11: 278 students (145 boys, 133 girls); Grade 12: 248 students (125 boys, 123 girls).

Faculty School total: 102. In upper school: 49 men, 53 women; 71 have advanced degrees.

Subjects Offered Algebra, American history, American literature, anatomy, architectural drawing, architecture, art, art history, biology, calculus, ceramics, chemistry, college admission preparation, college writing, computer animation, computer applications, computer processing, computer programming, computer programming-AP, computer science, computer science-AP, computer skills, computer studies, concert band, concert choir, creative writing, dance, desktop publishing, drafting, drama, economics, engineering, English, English literature, European history, fine arts, French, geometry, government/civics, history, Italian, keyboarding, Latin, marine biology, mathematics, mechanical drawing, music, newspaper, physical education, physics, psychology, science, social studies, Spanish, speech, statistics, theater, trigonometry, video, world history, world literature, yearbook, zoology.

Graduation Requirements Arts and fine arts (art, music, dance, drama), computer science, English, foreign language, mathematics, physical education (includes health), science, social studies (includes history). Community service is required.

Special Academic Programs International Baccalaureate program; Advanced Placement exam preparation; honors section; study at local college for college credit; academic accommodation for the gifted, the musically talented, and the artistically talented.

College Admission Counseling 194 students graduated in 2016; all went to college, including Boston University; Florida International University; New York University; The George Washington University; University of Florida; University of Miami. Median SAT critical reading: 564, median SAT math: 579, median SAT writing: 573, median combined SAT: 1716, median composite ACT: 25. 29% scored over 600 on SAT critical reading, 39% scored over 600 on SAT math, 35% scored over 600 on

SAT writing, 36% scored over 1800 on combined SAT, 24% scored over 26 on composite ACT.

Student Life Upper grades have uniform requirement, student council, honor system. Discipline rests primarily with faculty.

Summer Programs Remediation, enrichment, advancement, sports, art/fine arts, rigorous outdoor training, computer instruction programs offered; session focuses on Enrichment, reinforcement and advancement in academics and athletics; held on campus; accepts boys and girls; open to students from other schools. 1,000 students usually enrolled. 2017 schedule: June 6 to July 15. Application deadline: May 20.

Tuition and Aid Day student tuition: $32,270–$36,840. Tuition installment plan (monthly payment plans, school's own tuition recovery plan). Tuition reduction for siblings, merit scholarship grants, need-based scholarship grants, family discounts are $500 for three students; $900 for four students; or $1,300 for five or more students. Tuition disounts for children of faculty and staff, dependent upon years of service, etc. available.

Admissions Traditional secondary-level entrance grade is 9. For fall 2016, 340 students applied for upper-level admission, 242 were accepted, 134 enrolled. School's own exam and SSAT required. Deadline for receipt of application materials: February 17. Application fee required: $100. Interview required.

Athletics Interscholastic: aerobics/Nautilus (girls), baseball (b), basketball (b,g), cross-country running (b,g), dance (g), dance squad (g), dance team (g), diving (b,g), football (b), golf (b,g), gymnastics (b,g), lacrosse (b,g), physical training (b,g), running (b,g), soccer (b,g), softball (g), swimming and diving (b,g), tennis (b,g), track and field (b,g), volleyball (g), water polo (b,g); intramural: boxing (b,g), weight training (g); coed interscholastic: aerobics, bowling, cheering, modern dance, sailing, yoga; coed intramural: aerobics/dance, aerobics/Nautilus, badminton, dance, dance squad, dance team, fitness, flag football, Frisbee, kickball, modern dance, netball, physical fitness, running, strength & conditioning, touch football, yoga. 5 PE instructors, 66 coaches, 2 athletic trainers.

Computers Computers are regularly used in architecture, art, college planning, drafting, English, graphic arts, graphic design, keyboarding, newspaper, programming, science, technology, word processing, yearbook classes. Computer network features include on-campus library services, online commercial services, Internet access, wireless campus network, Internet filtering or blocking technology, modified laptop program, SmartBoards and Audio enhancement systems. Student e-mail accounts and computer access in designated common areas are available to students. Students grades are available online. The school has a published electronic and media policy.

Contact Carol A. Bowen, Director of Admission. 305-666-7937 Ext. 1408. Fax: 305-665-3791. E-mail: bowc@gulliverschools.org. Website: www.gulliverschools.org

THE GUNNERY

99 Green Hill Road
Washington, Connecticut 06793

Head of School: Peter W.E. Becker

General Information Coeducational boarding and day college-preparatory, outdoor education, and character development school. Boarding grades 9–PG, day grades 9–12. Founded: 1850. Setting: rural. Nearest major city is Hartford. Students are housed in single-sex dormitories. 220-acre campus. 27 buildings on campus. Approved or accredited by Connecticut Association of Independent Schools, Headmasters' Conference, National Commission of Accreditation of Special Education Services, New England Association of Schools and Colleges, The Association of Boarding Schools, The College Board, and Connecticut Department of Education. Member of National Association of Independent Schools and Secondary School Admission Test Board. Endowment: $22 million. Total enrollment: 287. Upper school average class size: 12. Upper school faculty-student ratio: 1:6. Upper School students typically attend 6 days per week.

Upper School Student Profile Grade 9: 48 students (23 boys, 25 girls); Grade 10: 69 students (39 boys, 30 girls); Grade 11: 94 students (46 boys, 48 girls); Grade 12: 81 students (52 boys, 29 girls); Postgraduate: 6 students (5 boys, 1 girl). 68% of students are boarding students. 49% are state residents. 21 states are represented in upper school student body. 20% are international students. International students from Canada, China, Czech Republic, Germany, Republic of Korea, and Spain; 15 other countries represented in student body.

Faculty School total: 57. In upper school: 30 men, 25 women; 40 have advanced degrees; 52 reside on campus.

Subjects Offered Advanced chemistry, algebra, American history, American history-AP, American literature, anatomy, art, art history, biology, calculus, ceramics, chemistry, computer graphics, computer math, computer programming, computer science, creative writing, drama, drawing, earth science, economics, economics-AP, English, English language-AP, English literature, English literature-AP, environmental science, environmental studies, ESL, ethics, ethics and responsibility, European history, European history-AP, expository writing, fine arts, French, geometry, government/civics, grammar, health, history, history of rock and roll, honors algebra, honors English, honors geometry, human development, instruments, marine biology, mathematics, modern European history-AP, music, music composition, mythology, painting, photography, physical education, physical science, physics, physics-AP, physiology, political science, pottery, pre-calculus, psychology, public speaking, science, social studies, sociology, Spanish, Spanish language-AP, Spanish literature-AP, speech, studio art, theater, trigonometry, U.S. history-AP, values and decisions, voice, world history, world literature, writing.

Graduation Requirements Arts and fine arts (art, music, dance, drama), English, ethics and responsibility, foreign language, history, human development, mathematics, physical education (includes health), public speaking, science, speech, Senior Service Program—civic duty, leadership, and responsibilty, LEADS Program—four year character development.

Special Academic Programs Advanced Placement exam preparation; honors section; independent study; term-away projects; study abroad; academic accommodation for the gifted, the musically talented, and the artistically talented; remedial reading and/or remedial writing; remedial math; ESL (5 students enrolled).

College Admission Counseling 84 students graduated in 2016; 82 went to college, including Boston University; Hobart and William Smith Colleges; New York University; Northeastern University; United States Naval Academy; University of Wisconsin–Madison. Other: 2 had other specific plans.

Student Life Upper grades have specified standards of dress, student council, honor system. Discipline rests equally with students and faculty.

Summer Programs Sports programs offered; session focuses on Crew, Field Hockey and Soccer programs; held both on and off campus; accepts boys and girls; open to students from other schools. 40 students usually enrolled. 2017 schedule: July 1 to August 15. Application deadline: March 15.

Tuition and Aid Day student tuition: $41,650; 7-day tuition and room/board: $57,000. Tuition installment plan (Insured Tuition Payment Plan, monthly payment plans). Merit scholarship grants, need-based scholarship grants, need-based loans available. In 2016–17, 45% of upper-school students received aid. Total amount of financial aid awarded in 2016–17: $3,500,000.

Admissions Traditional secondary-level entrance grade is 9. For fall 2016, 476 students applied for upper-level admission, 312 were accepted, 123 enrolled. ACT, PSAT or SAT or SSAT required. Deadline for receipt of application materials: January 15. Application fee required: $50. On-campus interview required.

Athletics Interscholastic: baseball (boys), basketball (b,g), crew (b,g), cross-country running (b,g), field hockey (g), football (b), hockey (b,g), ice hockey (b,g), lacrosse (b,g), skiing (downhill) (b,g), soccer (b,g), softball (g), strength & conditioning (b,g), tennis (b,g); intramural: yoga (g); coed interscholastic: alpine skiing, Frisbee, golf; coed intramural: ballet, dance, dance team, fitness, Frisbee, outdoor education, ultimate Frisbee, yoga. 2 coaches, 1 athletic trainer.

Computers Computers are regularly used in art, basic skills, college planning, computer applications, English, foreign language, freshman foundations, graphic arts, history, independent study, library, library skills, literary magazine, mathematics, music, photography, SAT preparation, science, yearbook classes. Computer network features include on-campus library services, Internet access, wireless campus network. Campus intranet and student e-mail accounts are available to students. Students grades are available online. The school has a published electronic and media policy.

Contact Sara Lynn Leavenworth, Director of Admissions. 860-868-7334. Fax: 860-868-1614. E-mail: admissions@gunnery.org. Website: www.gunnery.org

THE GUNSTON SCHOOL

911 Gunston Road
PO Box 200
Centreville, Maryland 21617

Head of School: Mr. John A. Lewis, IV

General Information Coeducational day college-preparatory school. Grades 9–12. Founded: 1911. Setting: rural. Nearest major city is Annapolis. 35-acre campus. 4 buildings on campus. Approved or accredited by Accreditation Commission of the Texas Association of Baptist Schools and Maryland Department of Education. Member of National Association of Independent Schools and Secondary School Admission Test Board. Endowment: $1 million. Total enrollment: 182. Upper school average class size: 11. Upper school faculty-student ratio: 1:6. There are 175 required school days per year for Upper School students. Upper School students typically attend 5 days per week. The average school day consists of 8 hours.

Upper School Student Profile Grade 9: 43 students (23 boys, 20 girls); Grade 10: 57 students (27 boys, 30 girls); Grade 11: 46 students (23 boys, 23 girls); Grade 12: 43 students (23 boys, 20 girls).

Faculty School total: 27. In upper school: 14 men, 13 women; 17 have advanced degrees.

Subjects Offered Ideas, macroeconomics-AP, marine biology, modern European history-AP, robotics.

Graduation Requirements Arts and fine arts (art, music, dance, drama), athletics, computer science, English, foreign language, history, mathematics, science, social sciences, wellness. Community service is required.

Special Academic Programs 12 Advanced Placement exams for which test preparation is offered; honors section; independent study; term-away projects; study at local college for college credit; study abroad; academic accommodation for the gifted, the musically talented, and the artistically talented; ESL (32 students enrolled).

College Admission Counseling 39 students graduated in 2016; all went to college, including Dickinson College; Lehigh University; St. Mary's College of Maryland; University of Maryland, College Park; Virginia Polytechnic Institute and State

University; Washington College. Mean SAT critical reading: 575, mean SAT math: 528, mean SAT writing: 546, mean combined SAT: 1649.

Student Life Upper grades have specified standards of dress, student council, honor system. Discipline rests primarily with faculty.

Summer Programs Enrichment, advancement, sports, computer instruction programs offered; session focuses on student activities for ages 6-18; held on campus; accepts boys and girls; open to students from other schools. 300 students usually enrolled. 2017 schedule: June 13 to August 19. Application deadline: none.

Tuition and Aid Day student tuition: $24,460. Tuition installment plan (monthly payment plans, individually arranged payment plans). Merit scholarship grants, need-based scholarship grants available. In 2016–17, 70% of upper-school students received aid; total upper-school merit-scholarship money awarded: $12,000. Total amount of financial aid awarded in 2016–17: $1,400,000.

Admissions Traditional secondary-level entrance grade is 9. For fall 2016, 90 students applied for upper-level admission, 78 were accepted, 55 enrolled. ISEE, SSAT or TOEFL or SLEP required. Deadline for receipt of application materials: none. Application fee required: $50. On-campus interview recommended.

Athletics Interscholastic: basketball (boys, girls), field hockey (g), lacrosse (b,g), soccer (b,g), tennis (b,g); intramural: independent competitive sports (b,g), tennis (b,g); coed interscholastic: crew, sailing, tennis; coed intramural: fitness, independent competitive sports, strength & conditioning, tennis, weight training. 8 coaches.

Computers Computers are regularly used in all academic classes. Computer network features include on-campus library services, Internet access, wireless campus network, Internet filtering or blocking technology. Campus intranet, student e-mail accounts, and computer access in designated common areas are available to students.

Contact David Henry, Director of Admission and Financial Aid. 410-758-0620. Fax: 410-758-0628. E-mail: dhenry@gunston.org. Website: www.gunston.org

HALES FRANCISCAN HIGH SCHOOL

4930 South Cottage Grove Avenue
Chicago, Illinois 60615

Head of School: Mrs. Nichole Jackson

General Information Boys' day college-preparatory, general academic, arts, business, religious studies, and technology school, affiliated with Roman Catholic Church. Grades 9–12. Founded: 1962. Setting: urban. 4-acre campus. 2 buildings on campus. Approved or accredited by National Catholic Education Association, North Central Association of Colleges and Schools, and Illinois Department of Education. Total enrollment: 45. Upper school average class size: 8. Upper school faculty-student ratio: 1:8. Upper School students typically attend 5 days per week. The average school day consists of 7 hours and 15 minutes.

Upper School Student Profile Grade 9: 12 students (12 boys); Grade 10: 11 students (11 boys); Grade 11: 6 students (6 boys); Grade 12: 16 students (16 boys). 100% of students are Roman Catholic.

Faculty School total: 7. In upper school: 7 men; 5 have advanced degrees.

Subjects Offered Advanced computer applications, Advanced Placement courses, African-American history, African-American literature, algebra, American government, American literature, art, Bible studies, biology, biology-AP, business skills, calculus-AP, chemistry, community service, computer science, English, fine arts, geography, health, literature, mathematics, physical education, physics, pre-calculus, religion, SAT/ACT preparation, science, social sciences, social studies, speech, trigonometry, word processing, world history, writing.

Graduation Requirements Arts and fine arts (art, music, dance, drama), business skills (includes word processing), computer science, English, foreign language, mathematics, physical education (includes health), religion (includes Bible studies and theology), science, social sciences, social studies (includes history). Community service is required.

Special Academic Programs International Baccalaureate program; academic accommodation for the gifted.

College Admission Counseling 55 students graduated in 2015; 45 went to college, including Chicago State University; Earlham College; Eastern Michigan University; University of California, Berkeley; University of Chicago; University of Illinois at Urbana–Champaign. Other: 2 went to work, 8 had other specific plans. Median composite ACT: 17. 1% scored over 26 on composite ACT.

Student Life Upper grades have uniform requirement, student council, honor system. Discipline rests equally with students and faculty. Attendance at religious services is required.

Tuition and Aid Day student tuition: $7500. Tuition installment plan (SMART Tuition Payment Plan, monthly payment plans, individually arranged payment plans). Tuition reduction for siblings, merit scholarship grants, need-based scholarship grants, paying campus jobs available. In 2015–16, 95% of upper-school students received aid; total upper-school merit-scholarship money awarded: $25,000. Total amount of financial aid awarded in 2015–16: $1,500,000.

Admissions Traditional secondary-level entrance grade is 9. For fall 2015, 45 students applied for upper-level admission, 20 were accepted, 12 enrolled. Academic Profile Tests and TerraNova required. Deadline for receipt of application materials: none. No application fee required. On-campus interview required.

Athletics Interscholastic: baseball, basketball, football, indoor track, indoor track & field, strength & conditioning, track and field, weight lifting, weight training;

intramural: basketball, flag football, strength & conditioning, touch football, weight lifting, weight training; coed interscholastic: cheering. 1 PE instructor, 19 coaches, 1 athletic trainer.

Computers Computers are regularly used in basic skills, business education, business skills, introduction to technology, library skills, publications classes. Computer network features include on-campus library services, online commercial services, Internet access, wireless campus network. Student e-mail accounts are available to students. Students grades are available online.

Contact Mr. Daniel Szymanski, Business Manager. 773-285-8400. Fax: 773-285-7025. E-mail: daniel.szymanski@halesfranciscan.org.
Website: www.halesfranciscanhs.org

HALSTROM ACADEMY

8484 Wilshire Blvd., Ste. 220
Beverly Hills, California 90211
Head of School: Ms. Chanel Grant

General Information Coeducational day and distance learning college-preparatory and general academic school; primarily serves underachievers, students with learning disabilities, individuals with Attention Deficit Disorder, dyslexic students, students with mild learning disabilities, and students with social anxiety. Grades 6–12. Distance learning grades 6–12. Founded: 1985. Setting: urban. Nearest major city is Los Angeles. 1 building on campus. Approved or accredited by Western Association of Schools and Colleges and California Department of Education. Upper school average class size: 1. Upper school faculty-student ratio: 1:1. The average school day consists of 4 hours.

Faculty School total: 6. In upper school: 3 men, 3 women; 2 have advanced degrees.

Subjects Offered Algebra, American government, American history, American history-AP, American literature, American sign language, anatomy and physiology, anthropology, art appreciation, arts, arts appreciation, biology, biology-AP, British literature, business mathematics, calculus, calculus-AP, career/college preparation, chemistry, chemistry-AP, computer applications, contemporary issues, cultural geography, economics, economics-AP, English, English composition, English language and composition-AP, English language-AP, English literature-AP, English/composition-AP, fine arts, foreign language, French, geometry, government and politics-AP, health, history, Latin, mathematics, microeconomics-AP, music theory, physical education, physics, pre-calculus, psychology, psychology-AP, science, social sciences, Spanish, Spanish language-AP, Spanish literature, Spanish literature-AP, statistics-AP, trigonometry, U.S. government, U.S. government and politics, U.S. government and politics-AP, U.S. history, U.S. history-AP, world history, world history-AP, writing, yearbook.

Graduation Requirements Arts and fine arts (art, music, dance, drama), English, foreign language, mathematics, personal development, physical education (includes health), science, social sciences, portfolio presentation, proficiency exams, volunteer credit hours. Community service is required.

Special Academic Programs Advanced Placement exam preparation; honors section; accelerated programs; study at local college for college credit; academic accommodation for the gifted, the musically talented, and the artistically talented; remedial reading and/or remedial writing; remedial math; programs in English, mathematics, general development for dyslexic students; special instructional classes for students with mild learning disabilities and Attention Deficit Disorder, social anxiety.

Student Life Upper grades have specified standards of dress, student council, honor system. Discipline rests equally with students and faculty.

Summer Programs Remediation, enrichment, advancement, art/fine arts programs offered; session focuses on advancement and remedial academic work; held both on and off campus; accepts boys and girls; open to students from other schools. 130 students usually enrolled. 2017 schedule: June 6 to August 19. Application deadline: June 1.

Tuition and Aid Tuition installment plan (monthly payment plans, individually arranged payment plans). Tuition reduction for siblings available.

Admissions Traditional secondary-level entrance grade is 10. For fall 2016, 9 students applied for upper-level admission, 9 were accepted, 9 enrolled. English language and Math Placement Exam required. Deadline for receipt of application materials: none. No application fee required. On-campus interview required.

Computers Computers are regularly used in art, English, foreign language, history, mathematics, social studies classes. Computer network features include Internet access, wireless campus network, Internet filtering or blocking technology. Student e-mail accounts and computer access in designated common areas are available to students. Students grades are available online. The school has a published electronic and media policy.

HALSTROM ACADEMY

705 Palomar Airport Rd., Ste. 350
Calsbad, California 92011
Head of School: Ms. Patrizia Zary

General Information Coeducational day and distance learning college-preparatory and general academic school; primarily serves students with learning disabilities, individuals with Attention Deficit Disorder, individuals with emotional and behavioral problems, dyslexic students, and students with social anxiety. Grades 6–12. Distance learning grades 6–12. Founded: 1985. Setting: suburban. Nearest major city is San Diego. 1 building on campus. Approved or accredited by Western Association of Schools and Colleges and California Department of Education. Total enrollment: 51. Upper school average class size: 1. Upper school faculty-student ratio: 1:1. The average school day consists of 4 hours.

Faculty School total: 9. In upper school: 4 men, 5 women; 4 have advanced degrees.

Subjects Offered Algebra, American literature, American sign language, anatomy and physiology, art appreciation, arts, arts appreciation, astronomy, biology, biology-AP, British literature, business mathematics, calculus, calculus-AP, career/college preparation, chemistry, chemistry-AP, computer applications, contemporary issues, cultural geography, economics, English, English composition, English language and composition-AP, English literature, English literature and composition-AP, fine arts, French, geology, geometry, German, health, honors algebra, honors English, honors U.S. history, honors world history, Latin, literature, macroeconomics-AP, Mandarin, mathematics, microeconomics-AP, physical education, physics, physics-AP, pre-calculus, psychology, psychology-AP, social studies, Spanish, Spanish language-AP, Spanish literature-AP, speech and debate, statistics, statistics-AP, trigonometry, U.S. government, U.S. government and politics-AP, U.S. history, U.S. history-AP, world history, world history-AP, writing.

Graduation Requirements Arts and fine arts (art, music, dance, drama), English, foreign language, mathematics, personal development, physical education (includes health), science, social sciences, portfolio presentation, proficiency exams, volunteer credit hours. Community service is required.

Special Academic Programs Advanced Placement exam preparation; honors section; accelerated programs; independent study; study at local college for college credit; academic accommodation for the gifted, the musically talented, and the artistically talented; remedial reading and/or remedial writing; remedial math; programs in English, mathematics, general development for dyslexic students; special instructional classes for mild learning disabilities, social anxiety.

College Admission Counseling 10 students graduated in 2016; 9 went to college, including Drexel University; Loyola Marymount University; Portland State University; University of Southern California. Other: 1 went to work.

Student Life Upper grades have specified standards of dress, student council, honor system. Discipline rests equally with students and faculty.

Summer Programs Remediation, enrichment, advancement, art/fine arts programs offered; session focuses on advancement and remedial academic work; held both on and off campus; accepts boys and girls; open to students from other schools. 130 students usually enrolled. 2017 schedule: June 6 to August 19. Application deadline: June 1.

Tuition and Aid Tuition installment plan (monthly payment plans, individually arranged payment plans). Tuition reduction for siblings available.

Admissions Traditional secondary-level entrance grade is 9. For fall 2016, 41 students applied for upper-level admission, 41 were accepted, 41 enrolled. English language and Math Placement Exam required. Deadline for receipt of application materials: none. Application fee required. On-campus interview required.

Computers Computers are regularly used in art, English, foreign language, history, mathematics, science classes. Computer network features include Internet access, wireless campus network, Internet filtering or blocking technology. Computer access in designated common areas is available to students. Students grades are available online. The school has a published electronic and media policy.

HALSTROM ACADEMY

19638 Stevens Creek Blvd., Suite 230
Cupertino, California 95014
Head of School: Ms. Linda White

General Information Coeducational day and distance learning college-preparatory and general academic school; primarily serves underachievers, students with learning disabilities, individuals with Attention Deficit Disorder, dyslexic students, students with mild learning disabilities, and students with social anxiety. Grades 6–12. Distance learning grades 6–12. Founded: 1985. Setting: suburban. 1 building on campus. Approved or accredited by Western Association of Schools and Colleges and California Department of Education. Total enrollment: 19. Upper school average class size: 1. Upper school faculty-student ratio: 1:1. The average school day consists of 4 hours.

Faculty School total: 5. In upper school: 3 men, 2 women; 2 have advanced degrees.

Subjects Offered Algebra, American government, American literature, anatomy and physiology, art appreciation, arts, arts appreciation, astronomy, biology, biology-AP, British literature, business mathematics, calculus, calculus-AP, career/college preparation, chemistry, chemistry-AP, computer applications, contemporary issues, creative writing, cultural geography, drawing, economics, English, English composition, English language and composition-AP, English literature, English literature and composition-AP, European history, European history-AP, fine arts, French, geology, geometry, German, health, history, honors algebra, honors English, honors geometry, honors U.S. history, honors world history, journalism, Latin, macroeconomics-AP, Mandarin, mathematics, microeconomics-AP, music theory, photography, physical education, physics, physics-AP, pre-calculus, psychology, psychology-AP, robotics, social sciences, social studies, Spanish, Spanish language-AP, Spanish literature-AP, speech and debate, statistics, statistics-AP, trigonometry, U.S.

government, U.S. government and politics-AP, U.S. history, U.S. history-AP, world history, world history-AP, writing.

Graduation Requirements Arts and fine arts (art, music, dance, drama), English, foreign language, mathematics, personal development, physical education (includes health), science, social sciences, portfolio presentation, proficiency exams, volunteer credit hours. Community service is required.

Special Academic Programs Advanced Placement exam preparation; honors section; accelerated programs; study at local college for college credit; academic accommodation for the gifted, the musically talented, and the artistically talented; remedial reading and/or remedial writing; remedial math; programs in English, mathematics, general development for dyslexic students; special instructional classes for mild learning disabilities, social anxiety.

College Admission Counseling 1 student graduated in 2016. Other: 1 entered military service.

Student Life Upper grades have specified standards of dress, student council, honor system. Discipline rests equally with students and faculty.

Summer Programs Remediation, enrichment, advancement, art/fine arts programs offered; session focuses on Advancement and remedial academic work; held both on and off campus; accepts boys and girls; open to students from other schools. 130 students usually enrolled. 2017 schedule: June 6 to August 19. Application deadline: June 1.

Tuition and Aid Tuition installment plan (monthly payment plans, individually arranged payment plans). Tuition reduction for siblings available.

Admissions Traditional secondary-level entrance grade is 10. For fall 2016, 16 students applied for upper-level admission, 16 were accepted, 16 enrolled. English language and Math Placement Exam required. Deadline for receipt of application materials: none. Application fee required. On-campus interview required.

Computers Computers are regularly used in art, English, foreign language, history, mathematics, science classes. Computer network features include Internet access, wireless campus network, Internet filtering or blocking technology. Student e-mail accounts and computer access in designated common areas are available to students. Students grades are available online. The school has a published electronic and media policy.

HALSTROM ACADEMY

2100 Main St., Ste. 260
Huntington Beach, California 92648

Head of School: Ms. Jasmine Broderick

General Information Coeducational day and distance learning college-preparatory and general academic school; primarily serves underachievers, students with learning disabilities, individuals with Attention Deficit Disorder, dyslexic students, students with mild learning disabilities, and students with social anxiety. Grades 6–12. Distance learning grades 6–12. Founded: 1985. Setting: suburban. 1 building on campus. Approved or accredited by Western Association of Schools and Colleges and California Department of Education. Total enrollment: 32. Upper school average class size: 1. Upper school faculty-student ratio: 1:1. The average school day consists of 4 hours.

Faculty School total: 9. In upper school: 5 men, 4 women; 4 have advanced degrees.

Subjects Offered Algebra, American literature, anatomy and physiology, anthropology, art appreciation, arts, astronomy, biology, biology-AP, British literature, business mathematics, calculus, calculus-AP, career/college preparation, chemistry, computer applications, contemporary issues, creative writing, cultural geography, drawing, economics, English, English language and composition-AP, English literature, English literature and composition-AP, English literature-AP, English/composition-AP, European history-AP, fine arts, French, geology, geometry, German, government and politics-AP, health, history, honors algebra, honors English, honors geometry, honors U.S. history, honors world history, journalism, Latin, macroeconomics-AP, Mandarin, mathematics, microeconomics-AP, music theory, physical education, physics, physics-AP, pre-calculus, psychology, psychology-AP, robotics, science, social sciences, Spanish, Spanish language-AP, Spanish literature-AP, speech and debate, statistics, statistics-AP, trigonometry, U.S. government, U.S. government and politics-AP, U.S. history, world history, world history-AP, writing.

Graduation Requirements Arts and fine arts (art, music, dance, drama), English, foreign language, mathematics, personal development, physical education (includes health), science, social sciences, portfolio presentation, proficiency exams, volunteer credit hours. Community service is required.

Special Academic Programs Advanced Placement exam preparation; honors section; accelerated programs; study at local college for college credit; academic accommodation for the gifted, the musically talented, and the artistically talented; remedial reading and/or remedial writing; remedial math; programs in English, mathematics, general development for dyslexic students; special instructional classes for students with mild learning disabilities and Attention Deficit Disorder, social anxiety.

College Admission Counseling 10 students graduated in 2016; 7 went to college, including California State University, Long Beach; The University of Arizona; University of California, Davis; University of Washington. Other: 3 had other specific plans.

Student Life Upper grades have specified standards of dress, student council, honor system. Discipline rests equally with students and faculty.

Summer Programs Remediation, enrichment, advancement, art/fine arts programs offered; held both on and off campus; accepts boys and girls; open to students from other schools. 130 students usually enrolled. 2017 schedule: June 6 to August 19. Application deadline: June 1.

Tuition and Aid Tuition installment plan (monthly payment plans, individually arranged payment plans). Tuition reduction for siblings available.

Admissions Traditional secondary-level entrance grade is 10. For fall 2016, 21 students applied for upper-level admission, 21 were accepted, 21 enrolled. English language and Math Placement Exam required. Deadline for receipt of application materials: none. Application fee required. On-campus interview required.

Computers Computers are regularly used in art, English, foreign language, history, mathematics, science classes. Computer network features include Internet access, wireless campus network, Internet filtering or blocking technology. Student e-mail accounts and computer access in designated common areas are available to students. Students grades are available online. The school has a published electronic and media policy.

HALSTROM ACADEMY

2302 Martin St., Ste. 100, Colton Plaza
Irvine, California 92612

Head of School: Ms. June Tseng

General Information Coeducational day and distance learning college-preparatory and general academic school; primarily serves underachievers, students with learning disabilities, individuals with Attention Deficit Disorder, dyslexic students, students with mild learning disabilities, and students with social anxiety. Grades 6–12. Distance learning grades 6–12. Founded: 1985. Setting: suburban. 1 building on campus. Approved or accredited by Western Association of Schools and Colleges and California Department of Education. Total enrollment: 31. Upper school average class size: 1. Upper school faculty-student ratio: 1:1. The average school day consists of 4 hours.

Faculty School total: 6. In upper school: 3 men, 3 women; 2 have advanced degrees.

Subjects Offered Anthropology, art appreciation, arts, arts appreciation, astronomy, biology, biology-AP, British literature, business mathematics, calculus, career/college preparation, chemistry, chemistry-AP, computer applications, contemporary issues, creative writing, cultural geography, drawing, economics, English, English composition, English language and composition-AP, English literature, English literature and composition-AP, European history-AP, fine arts, French, geology, geometry, German, government and politics-AP, health, history, honors algebra, honors English, honors geometry, honors U.S. history, honors world history, journalism, Latin, Mandarin, mathematics, music theory, physical education, physics, pre-calculus, psychology, psychology-AP, robotics, science, social sciences, social studies, Spanish, speech and debate, statistics, statistics-AP, trigonometry, U.S. government, U.S. government and politics-AP, U.S. history, world history, world history-AP, writing, yearbook.

Graduation Requirements Arts and fine arts (art, music, dance, drama), English, foreign language, mathematics, personal development, physical education (includes health), science, social sciences, portfolio presentation, proficiency exams, volunteer credit hours. Community service is required.

Special Academic Programs Advanced Placement exam preparation; honors section; accelerated programs; study at local college for college credit; academic accommodation for the gifted, the musically talented, and the artistically talented; remedial reading and/or remedial writing; remedial math; programs in English, mathematics, general development for dyslexic students; special instructional classes for students with mild learning disabilities and Attention Deficit Disorder, social anxiety.

College Admission Counseling 8 students graduated in 2016; 7 went to college, including New York University; University of San Diego. Other: 1 had other specific plans.

Student Life Upper grades have specified standards of dress, student council, honor system. Discipline rests equally with students and faculty.

Summer Programs Remediation, enrichment, advancement, art/fine arts programs offered; held both on and off campus; accepts boys and girls; open to students from other schools. 130 students usually enrolled. 2017 schedule: June 6 to August 19. Application deadline: June 1.

Tuition and Aid Tuition installment plan (monthly payment plans, individually arranged payment plans). Tuition reduction for siblings available.

Admissions Traditional secondary-level entrance grade is 10. For fall 2016, 26 students applied for upper-level admission, 26 were accepted, 26 enrolled. English language and Math Placement Exam required. Deadline for receipt of application materials: none. Application fee required. On-campus interview required.

Computers Computers are regularly used in art, English, foreign language, history, mathematics, science classes. Computer network features include Internet access, wireless campus network, Internet filtering or blocking technology. Student e-mail accounts and computer access in designated common areas are available to students. Students grades are available online. The school has a published electronic and media policy.

HALSTROM ACADEMY

12300 Wilshire Blvd., Ste.110
Los Angeles, California 90025

Head of School: Mr. Kelly Bishop

General Information Coeducational day and distance learning college-preparatory and general academic school; primarily serves underachievers, students with learning disabilities, individuals with Attention Deficit Disorder, dyslexic students, students with mild learning disabilities, and students with social anxiety. Grades 6–12. Distance learning grades 6–12. Founded: 1985. Setting: urban. 1 building on campus. Approved or accredited by Western Association of Schools and Colleges and California Department of Education. Total enrollment: 13. Upper school average class size: 1. Upper school faculty-student ratio: 1:1. The average school day consists of 4 hours.
Faculty School total: 12. In upper school: 8 men, 4 women; 4 have advanced degrees.
Subjects Offered Anthropology, arts appreciation, astronomy, biology, biology-AP, chemistry, chemistry-AP, creative writing, cultural geography, drawing, English language and composition-AP, English literature, English literature and composition-AP, European history-AP, geology, German, government and politics-AP, honors algebra, honors English, honors geometry, honors U.S. history, honors world history, journalism, Mandarin, music theory, physics, psychology, psychology-AP, robotics, speech and debate, statistics, statistics-AP, tropical biology, U.S. government, U.S. government and politics-AP, U.S. history, world history, world history-AP, writing, yearbook.
Graduation Requirements Social sciences, portfolio presentation, proficiency exams, volunteer credit hours.
Special Academic Programs Advanced Placement exam preparation; honors section; accelerated programs; study at local college for college credit; academic accommodation for the gifted, the musically talented, and the artistically talented; remedial reading and/or remedial writing; remedial math; programs in English, mathematics, general development for dyslexic students; special instructional classes for students with mild learning disabilities and Attention Deficit Disorder, social anxiety.
College Admission Counseling 6 students graduated in 2016; 4 went to college, including California State University, Northridge; Loyola Marymount University; San Diego State University; Santa Monica College; Tulane University. Other: 2 had other specific plans.
Student Life Upper grades have specified standards of dress, student council, honor system. Discipline rests equally with students and faculty.
Summer Programs Enrichment, advancement, art/fine arts programs offered; session focuses on advancement and remedial academic work; held both on and off campus; accepts boys and girls; open to students from other schools. 130 students usually enrolled. 2017 schedule: June 6 to August. Application deadline: June 1.
Tuition and Aid Tuition installment plan (monthly payment plans, individually arranged payment plans). Tuition reduction for siblings available.
Admissions For fall 2016, 20 students applied for upper-level admission, 20 were accepted, 20 enrolled. English language and Math Placement Exam required. Deadline for receipt of application materials: none. Application fee required. On-campus interview required.
Computers Computers are regularly used in English, foreign language, history, mathematics, science classes. Computer network features include Internet access, wireless campus network, Internet filtering or blocking technology. Student e-mail accounts and computer access in designated common areas are available to students. Students grades are available online. The school has a published electronic and media policy.

HALSTROM ACADEMY

2101 Rosecrans Avenue, Ste. 1225
Manhattan Beach, California 90245

Head of School: Ms. Chanel Grant

General Information Coeducational day and distance learning college-preparatory and general academic school; primarily serves underachievers, students with learning disabilities, individuals with Attention Deficit Disorder, dyslexic students, students with mild learning disabilities, and students with social anxiety. Grades 6–12. Distance learning grades 6–12. Founded: 1985. Setting: suburban. 1 building on campus. Approved or accredited by Western Association of Schools and Colleges and California Department of Education. Total enrollment: 20. Upper school average class size: 1. Upper school faculty-student ratio: 1:1. The average school day consists of 4 hours.
Faculty School total: 9. In upper school: 4 men, 5 women; 3 have advanced degrees.
Subjects Offered American literature, American sign language, arts appreciation, biology-AP, calculus, calculus-AP, chemistry-AP, creative writing, cultural geography, drawing, English language and composition-AP, English literature, English literature and composition-AP, English literature-AP, English/composition-AP, European history-AP, fine arts, French, geology, geometry, German, health, history, honors algebra, honors English, honors geometry, honors U.S. history, honors world history, Latin, macroeconomics-AP, Mandarin, mathematics, microeconomics-AP, music theory, physical education, physics, pre-calculus, psychology, psychology-AP, robotics, science, social sciences, social studies, Spanish, Spanish language-AP, Spanish literature-AP, speech and debate, statistics, statistics-AP, trigonometry, U.S.

government, U.S. government and politics, U.S. history, world history, world history-AP, writing.
Graduation Requirements English, foreign language, mathematics, personal development, physical education (includes health), science, social sciences, portfolio presentation, proficiency exams, volunteer credit hours. Community service is required.
Special Academic Programs Advanced Placement exam preparation; honors section; accelerated programs; study at local college for college credit; academic accommodation for the gifted, the musically talented, and the artistically talented; remedial reading and/or remedial writing; remedial math; programs in English, mathematics, general development for dyslexic students; special instructional classes for students with mild learning disabilities and Attention Deficit Disorder, social anxiety.
College Admission Counseling 7 students graduated in 2016; all went to college, including California State Polytechnic University, Pomona; University of California, Riverside; University of California, San Diego; University of the Pacific.
Student Life Upper grades have specified standards of dress, student council, honor system. Discipline rests equally with students and faculty.
Summer Programs Remediation, enrichment, advancement, art/fine arts programs offered; session focuses on advancement and remedial academic work; held both on and off campus; accepts boys and girls; open to students from other schools. 130 students usually enrolled. 2017 schedule: June 6 to August 19. Application deadline: June 1.
Tuition and Aid Tuition installment plan (monthly payment plans, individually arranged payment plans). Tuition reduction for siblings available.
Admissions Traditional secondary-level entrance grade is 10. For fall 2016, 29 students applied for upper-level admission, 29 were accepted, 29 enrolled. English language and Math Placement Exam required. Deadline for receipt of application materials: none. Application fee required. On-campus interview required.
Computers Computers are regularly used in art, English, foreign language, history, mathematics, science classes. Computer network features include Internet access, wireless campus network, Internet filtering or blocking technology. Student e-mail accounts and computer access in designated common areas are available to students. Students grades are available online. The school has a published electronic and media policy.

HALSTROM ACADEMY

26440 La Alameda, Suite 350
Mission Viejo, California 92691-6319

Head of School: Ms. June Tseng

General Information Coeducational day and distance learning college-preparatory and general academic school; primarily serves students with learning disabilities, individuals with Attention Deficit Disorder, individuals with emotional and behavioral problems, students with mild learning disabilities, and students with social anxiety. Grades 6–12. Distance learning grades 6–12. Founded: 1985. Setting: suburban. 1 building on campus. Approved or accredited by Western Association of Schools and Colleges and California Department of Education. Upper school average class size: 1. Upper school faculty-student ratio: 1:1. The average school day consists of 4 hours.
Faculty School total: 16. In upper school: 8 men, 8 women; 5 have advanced degrees.
Subjects Offered ACT preparation, Advanced Placement courses, algebra, American history, anatomy, anthropology, art appreciation, arts appreciation, astronomy, biology, biology-AP, business mathematics, business skills, calculus, calculus-AP, chemistry, chemistry-AP, community service, computer applications, computer science, consumer mathematics, creative writing, cultural geography, drawing, earth science, economics, English, English language and composition-AP, English literature, English literature and composition-AP, European history-AP, French, geography, geology, geometry, German, government, honors algebra, honors English, honors geometry, honors U.S. history, honors world history, journalism, Latin, life science, macroeconomics-AP, Mandarin, mathematics, microeconomics-AP, music appreciation, music theory, physical education, physics, physiology, pre-algebra, pre-calculus, psychology, psychology-AP, robotics, science, social sciences, social studies, Spanish, speech and debate, statistics, statistics-AP, trigonometry, U.S. government and politics-AP, world history, world history-AP, writing, yearbook.
Graduation Requirements Arts and fine arts (art, music, dance, drama), foreign language, mathematics, personal development, physical education (includes health), science, social sciences, portfolio presentation, proficiency exams, volunteer credit hours. Community service is required.
Special Academic Programs Advanced Placement exam preparation; honors section; accelerated programs; study at local college for college credit; academic accommodation for the gifted, the musically talented, and the artistically talented; remedial reading and/or remedial writing; remedial math; programs in English, mathematics, general development for dyslexic students; special instructional classes for students with mild learning disabilities and Attention Deficit Disorder.
College Admission Counseling 19 students graduated in 2016; 17 went to college, including Concordia University Irvine; Humboldt State University; The University of Arizona; University of Washington; Washington State University. Other: 2 went to work.
Student Life Upper grades have specified standards of dress, student council, honor system. Discipline rests equally with students and faculty.

Summer Programs Remediation, enrichment, advancement, art/fine arts programs offered; session focuses on Acceleration and remediation; held both on and off campus; accepts boys and girls; open to students from other schools. 130 students usually enrolled. 2017 schedule: June 6 to August 19. Application deadline: June 1.

Tuition and Aid Tuition installment plan (monthly payment plans, individually arranged payment plans). Tuition reduction for siblings available.

Admissions Traditional secondary-level entrance grade is 10. For fall 2016, 44 students applied for upper-level admission, 44 were accepted, 44 enrolled. English language and Math Placement Exam required. Deadline for receipt of application materials: none. Application fee required. On-campus interview required.

Computers Computers are regularly used in English, foreign language, history, mathematics, science classes. Computer network features include Internet access, wireless campus network, Internet filtering or blocking technology. Student e-mail accounts and computer access in designated common areas are available to students. Students grades are available online. The school has a published electronic and media policy.

Contact 949-348-0608. Website: www.halstromacademy.org

HALSTROM ACADEMY

3111 N. Tustin St., Ste. 240
Orange, California 92865

Head of School: Ms. Mary Donielson

General Information Coeducational day and distance learning college-preparatory and general academic school; primarily serves underachievers, students with learning disabilities, individuals with Attention Deficit Disorder, dyslexic students, students with mild learning disabilities, and students with social anxiety. Grades 6–12. Distance learning grades 6–12. Founded: 1985. Setting: suburban. 1 building on campus. Approved or accredited by Western Association of Schools and Colleges and California Department of Education. Upper school average class size: 1. Upper school faculty-student ratio: 1:1. The average school day consists of 4 hours.

Faculty School total: 8. In upper school: 5 men, 3 women; 3 have advanced degrees.

Subjects Offered Algebra, American history-AP, American literature, American sign language, anatomy and physiology, art appreciation, arts, arts appreciation, biology, British literature, business mathematics, calculus, calculus-AP, career/college preparation, chemistry, chemistry-AP, computer applications, contemporary issues, cultural geography, drawing, economics, economics-AP, English, English composition, English language and composition-AP, English literature, English literature and composition-AP, fine arts, French, geometry, German, health, history, honors algebra, honors English, honors geometry, honors U.S. history, honors world history, journalism, Latin, macroeconomics-AP, Mandarin, mathematics, mathematics-AP, microeconomics-AP, music appreciation, music theory, painting, physical education, physics, physics-AP, pre-calculus, psychology, psychology-AP, robotics, science, social issues, social sciences, social studies, Spanish, Spanish language-AP, Spanish literature-AP, speech and debate, statistics, statistics-AP, trigonometry, U.S. government, U.S. government and politics-AP, U.S. history, U.S. history-AP, world geography, world history, world history-AP, world literature, writing.

Graduation Requirements Arts and fine arts (art, music, dance, drama), English, foreign language, mathematics, personal development, physical education (includes health), science, social sciences, portfolio presentation, proficiency exams, volunteer credit hours. Community service is required.

Special Academic Programs Advanced Placement exam preparation; honors section; accelerated programs; study at local college for college credit; academic accommodation for the gifted, the musically talented, and the artistically talented; remedial reading and/or remedial writing; remedial math; programs in English, mathematics, general development for dyslexic students.

College Admission Counseling 16 students graduated in 2016; 10 went to college, including California State Polytechnic University, Pomona; California State University, Fullerton; Oregon State University; San Francisco State University. Other: 1 entered military service.

Student Life Upper grades have specified standards of dress, student council, honor system. Discipline rests equally with students and faculty.

Summer Programs Remediation, enrichment, advancement, art/fine arts programs offered; session focuses on advancement and remedial academic work; held both on and off campus; accepts boys and girls; open to students from other schools. 130 students usually enrolled. 2017 schedule: June 6 to August 19. Application deadline: June 1.

Tuition and Aid Tuition installment plan (monthly payment plans, individually arranged payment plans). Tuition reduction for siblings available.

Admissions Traditional secondary-level entrance grade is 10. For fall 2016, 22 students applied for upper-level admission, 22 were accepted, 22 enrolled. English language and Math Placement Exam required. Deadline for receipt of application materials: none. Application fee required. On-campus interview required.

Computers Computers are regularly used in art, English, foreign language, history, mathematics, science classes. Computer network features include Internet access, wireless campus network, Internet filtering or blocking technology. Student e-mail accounts and computer access in designated common areas are available to students. Students grades are available online. The school has a published electronic and media policy.

HALSTROM ACADEMY

35 N. Lake Ave., Ste. 250
Pasadena, California 91101

Head of School: Ms. Ani Zeneian

General Information Coeducational day and distance learning college-preparatory and general academic school; primarily serves underachievers, students with learning disabilities, individuals with Attention Deficit Disorder, dyslexic students, students with mild learning disabilities, and students with social anxiety. Grades 6–12. Distance learning grades 6–12. Founded: 1985. Setting: urban. 1 building on campus. Approved or accredited by Western Association of Schools and Colleges and California Department of Education. Total enrollment: 27. Upper school average class size: 1. Upper school faculty-student ratio: 1:1. The average school day consists of 4 hours.

Faculty School total: 8. In upper school: 2 men, 6 women; 3 have advanced degrees.

Subjects Offered Algebra, American government, American literature, American sign language, anatomy and physiology, anthropology, art appreciation, arts, arts appreciation, astronomy, biology, biology-AP, British literature, business mathematics, calculus, calculus-AP, career/college preparation, chemistry, chemistry-AP, computer applications, contemporary issues, creative writing, cultural geography, economics, English composition, English language and composition-AP, English literature, English literature and composition-AP, English literature-AP, English/composition-AP, fiber arts, French, geology, geometry, German, health, history, honors algebra, honors English, honors geometry, honors U.S. history, honors world history, journalism, Latin, macroeconomics-AP, Mandarin, mathematics, microeconomics-AP, music theory, physical education, physics, pre-calculus, robotics, science, short story, social sciences, social studies, Spanish, Spanish language-AP, Spanish literature-AP, speech and debate, statistics, statistics-AP, trigonometry, U.S. government, U.S. government and politics-AP, U.S. history, U.S. history-AP, world history, world history-AP, writing, yearbook.

Graduation Requirements Arts and fine arts (art, music, dance, drama), English, foreign language, mathematics, personal development, physical education (includes health), science, social sciences, portfolio presentation, proficiency exams, volunteer credit hours. Community service is required.

Special Academic Programs Advanced Placement exam preparation; honors section; accelerated programs; study at local college for college credit; academic accommodation for the gifted, the musically talented, and the artistically talented; remedial reading and/or remedial writing; remedial math; programs in English, mathematics, general development for dyslexic students; special instructional classes for students with mild learning disabilities and Attention Deficit Disorder, social anxiety.

College Admission Counseling 7 students graduated in 2016; 6 went to college, including Pacific Lutheran University; University of California, Santa Barbara. Other: 1 had other specific plans.

Student Life Upper grades have specified standards of dress, student council, honor system. Discipline rests equally with students and faculty.

Summer Programs Remediation, enrichment, advancement, art/fine arts programs offered; session focuses on Advancement and remedial academic work; held both on and off campus; accepts boys and girls; open to students from other schools. 2017 schedule: June 6 to August 19. Application deadline: June 1.

Tuition and Aid Tuition installment plan (monthly payment plans, individually arranged payment plans). Tuition reduction for siblings available.

Admissions Traditional secondary-level entrance grade is 10. For fall 2016, 21 students applied for upper-level admission, 21 were accepted, 21 enrolled. English language and Math Placement Exam required. Deadline for receipt of application materials: none. Application fee required. On-campus interview required.

Computers Computers are regularly used in art, English, foreign language, history, mathematics, science classes. Computer network features include Internet access, wireless campus network, Internet filtering or blocking technology. Student e-mail accounts and computer access in designated common areas are available to students. Students grades are available online. The school has a published electronic and media policy.

HALSTROM ACADEMY

9915 Mira Mesa Boulevard
Suite 210
San Diego, California 92131

Head of School: Ms. Janee Johnson

General Information Coeducational day and distance learning college-preparatory and general academic school; primarily serves underachievers, students with learning disabilities, individuals with Attention Deficit Disorder, dyslexic students, students with mild learning disabilities, and students with social anxiety. Grades 6–12. Distance learning grades 6–12. Founded: 1985. Setting: urban. 1 building on campus. Approved or accredited by Western Association of Schools and Colleges and California Department of Education. Upper school average class size: 1. Upper school faculty-student ratio: 1:1. The average school day consists of 4 hours.

Faculty School total: 12. In upper school: 6 men, 6 women; 5 have advanced degrees.

Subjects Offered Algebra, American literature, anatomy and physiology, anthropology, art appreciation, arts, arts appreciation, astronomy, biology, biology-AP, British literature, business mathematics, calculus, career/college preparation, chemistry,

chemistry-AP, computer applications, contemporary issues, creative writing, cultural geography, drawing, economics, English, English composition, English language and composition-AP, English literature, English literature and composition-AP, European history-AP, fine arts, French, geology, geometry, German, government and politics-AP, health, honors algebra, honors English, honors geometry, honors U.S. history, honors world history, journalism, macroeconomics-AP, Mandarin, mathematics, microeconomics-AP, music theory, physical education, physics, pre-calculus, psychology, psychology-AP, robotics, social studies, Spanish, speech and debate, statistics, statistics-AP, trigonometry, U.S. government, U.S. government and politics-AP, U.S. history, world history, world history-AP, writing, yearbook.

Graduation Requirements Arts and fine arts (art, music, dance, drama), English, foreign language, mathematics, personal development, physical education (includes health), science, social sciences, portfolio presentation, proficiency exams, volunteer credit hours. Community service is required.

Special Academic Programs Advanced Placement exam preparation; honors section; accelerated programs; study at local college for college credit; academic accommodation for the gifted, the musically talented, and the artistically talented; remedial reading and/or remedial writing; remedial math; programs in English, mathematics, general development for dyslexic students; special instructional classes for students with mild learning disabilities and Attention Deficit Disorder.

College Admission Counseling 3 students graduated in 2016; all went to college, including California Polytechnic State University, San Luis Obispo.

Student Life Upper grades have honor system. Discipline rests equally with students and faculty.

Summer Programs Remediation, enrichment, advancement, art/fine arts, computer instruction programs offered; session focuses on advancement and remedial academic work; held both on and off campus; accepts boys and girls; open to students from other schools. 130 students usually enrolled. 2017 schedule: June 6 to August 19. Application deadline: June 1.

Tuition and Aid Tuition installment plan (monthly payment plans, individually arranged payment plans). Tuition reduction for siblings available.

Admissions Traditional secondary-level entrance grade is 10. For fall 2016, 36 students applied for upper-level admission, 36 were accepted, 36 enrolled. English language and Math Placement Exam required. Deadline for receipt of application materials: none. Application fee required. On-campus interview required.

Computers Computers are regularly used in art, English, foreign language, history, mathematics, science classes. Computer network features include Internet access, wireless campus network, Internet filtering or blocking technology. Computer access in designated common areas is available to students. Students grades are available online. The school has a published electronic and media policy.

Contact Lorena Moreno, Administrative Assistant. 866-814-4354. Fax: 858-549-6292. E-mail: sandiego@futures.edu. Website: www.halstromacademy.org

HALSTROM ACADEMY

1840 Gateway Dr., Ste. 100
San Mateo, California 94404

Head of School: Ms. Jayne Cho

General Information Coeducational day and distance learning college-preparatory and general academic school; primarily serves underachievers, students with learning disabilities, individuals with Attention Deficit Disorder, dyslexic students, students with mild learning disabilities, and students with social anxiety. Grades 6–12. Distance learning grades 6–12. Founded: 1985. Setting: suburban. 1 building on campus. Approved or accredited by Western Association of Schools and Colleges and California Department of Education. Total enrollment: 11. Upper school average class size: 1. Upper school faculty-student ratio: 1:1. The average school day consists of 4 hours.

Faculty School total: 4. In upper school: 2 men, 2 women; 1 has an advanced degree.

Subjects Offered Algebra, American literature, anatomy and physiology, anthropology, art appreciation, arts, arts appreciation, astronomy, biology, biology-AP, British literature, business mathematics, calculus, career/college preparation, chemistry, chemistry-AP, computer applications, contemporary issues, creative writing, cultural geography, drawing, economics, English, English composition, English language and composition-AP, English literature, English literature and composition-AP, European history-AP, fine arts, French, geology, geometry, German, health, history, honors algebra, honors English, honors geometry, honors U.S. history, honors world history, journalism, Latin, macroeconomics-AP, Mandarin, mathematics, music theory, physical education, physics, physics-AP, pre-calculus, psychology, psychology-AP, robotics, social sciences, social studies, Spanish, speech and debate, statistics, statistics-AP, trigonometry, U.S. government, U.S. government and politics-AP, U.S. history, world history, world history-AP, writing, yearbook.

Graduation Requirements Sculpture, social sciences, portfolio presentation, proficiency exams, volunteer credit hours.

Special Academic Programs Advanced Placement exam preparation; honors section; accelerated programs; study at local college for college credit; academic accommodation for the gifted, the musically talented, and the artistically talented; remedial reading and/or remedial writing; remedial math; programs in English, mathematics, general development for dyslexic students; special instructional classes for students with mild learning disabilities and Attention Deficit Disorder, social anxiety.

College Admission Counseling 1 student graduated in 2016 and went to San Francisco State University.

Student Life Upper grades have specified standards of dress, student council, honor system. Discipline rests equally with students and faculty.

Summer Programs Remediation, enrichment, advancement, art/fine arts programs offered; session focuses on Advancement and remedial academic work; held both on and off campus; accepts boys and girls; open to students from other schools. 130 students usually enrolled. 2017 schedule: June 6 to August 19. Application deadline: June 1.

Tuition and Aid Tuition installment plan (monthly payment plans, individually arranged payment plans). Tuition reduction for siblings available.

Admissions Traditional secondary-level entrance grade is 10. For fall 2016, 14 students applied for upper-level admission, 14 were accepted, 14 enrolled. English language and Math Placement Exam required. Deadline for receipt of application materials: none. Application fee required. On-campus interview required.

Computers Computers are regularly used in art, English, foreign language, history, mathematics, science classes. Computer network features include Internet access, wireless campus network, Internet filtering or blocking technology. Student e-mail accounts and computer access in designated common areas are available to students. Students grades are available online. The school has a published electronic and media policy.

HALSTROM ACADEMY

101 Ygnacio Valley Road
Suite 345
Walnut Creek, California 94596

Head of School: Ms. Carol Rupp

General Information Coeducational day and distance learning college-preparatory and general academic school; primarily serves underachievers, students with learning disabilities, individuals with Attention Deficit Disorder, and dyslexic students. Grades 6–12. Distance learning grades 6–12. Founded: 1985. Setting: suburban. 1 building on campus. Approved or accredited by Western Association of Schools and Colleges and California Department of Education. Total enrollment: 12. Upper school average class size: 1. Upper school faculty-student ratio: 1:1. The average school day consists of 4 hours.

Faculty School total: 6. In upper school: 2 men, 4 women; 2 have advanced degrees.

Subjects Offered Algebra, American literature, anatomy and physiology, art appreciation, arts, biology, British literature, business mathematics, calculus, career/college preparation, chemistry, computer applications, contemporary issues, economics, English, fine arts, French, geometry, health, history, Latin, mathematics, physical education, physics, pre-calculus, science, social sciences, social studies, Spanish, trigonometry, U.S. government, U.S. history, world history.

Graduation Requirements Arts and fine arts (art, music, dance, drama), English, foreign language, mathematics, personal development, physical education (includes health), science, social sciences, portfolio presentation, proficiency exams, volunteer credit hours. Community service is required.

Special Academic Programs Advanced Placement exam preparation; honors section; accelerated programs; study at local college for college credit; academic accommodation for the gifted, the musically talented, and the artistically talented; remedial reading and/or remedial writing; remedial math; programs in English, mathematics, general development for dyslexic students; special instructional classes for students with mild learning disabilities and Attention Deficit Disorder, social anxiety.

College Admission Counseling 3 students graduated in 2016; all went to college, including California Polytechnic State University, San Luis Obispo; Mount Saint Mary's University; University of Oregon.

Student Life Upper grades have specified standards of dress, student council, honor system. Discipline rests equally with students and faculty.

Summer Programs Remediation, enrichment, advancement, art/fine arts programs offered; session focuses on advancement and remedial academic work; held both on and off campus; accepts boys and girls; open to students from other schools. 130 students usually enrolled. 2017 schedule: June 6 to August 19. Application deadline: June 1.

Tuition and Aid Tuition installment plan (monthly payment plans, individually arranged payment plans). Tuition reduction for siblings available.

Admissions Traditional secondary-level entrance grade is 10. For fall 2016, 18 students applied for upper-level admission, 18 were accepted, 18 enrolled. English language and Math Placement Exam required. Deadline for receipt of application materials: none. Application fee required. On-campus interview required.

Computers Computers are regularly used in English, foreign language, history, mathematics, science classes. Computer resources include Internet access, wireless campus network, Internet filtering or blocking technology. Student e-mail accounts and computer access in designated common areas are available to students. Students grades are available online. The school has a published electronic and media policy.

HALSTROM ACADEMY

30700 Russell Ranch Rd., Ste. 180
Westlake Village, California 91362

Head of School: Mr. Michael Radka

General Information Coeducational day and distance learning college-preparatory and general academic school; primarily serves underachievers, students with learning disabilities, individuals with Attention Deficit Disorder, dyslexic students, and students with social anxiety. Grades 6–12. Distance learning grades 6–12. Founded: 1985. Setting: suburban. 1 building on campus. Approved or accredited by Western Association of Schools and Colleges and California Department of Education. Upper school average class size: 1. Upper school faculty-student ratio: 1:1. The average school day consists of 4 hours.

Faculty School total: 11. In upper school: 4 men, 7 women; 5 have advanced degrees.

Subjects Offered Algebra, American government, American history-AP, American literature, American sign language, art appreciation, arts, arts appreciation, astronomy, biology, biology-AP, British literature, business mathematics, calculus, calculus-AP, career/college preparation, chemistry, chemistry-AP, computer applications, contemporary issues, creative writing, cultural geography, drawing, economics, economics-AP, English, English composition, English language and composition-AP, English literature, English literature and composition-AP, fine arts, French, geology, geometry, German, health, honors algebra, honors English, honors geometry, honors U.S. history, honors world history, journalism, Latin, literature, macroeconomics-AP, Mandarin, mathematics, microeconomics-AP, music theory, physical education, physics, physics-AP, pre-calculus, psychology, psychology-AP, robotics, science, social sciences, social studies, sociology, Spanish, Spanish language-AP, Spanish literature-AP, speech and debate, statistics, statistics-AP, trigonometry, U.S. government, U.S. government and politics, U.S. government and politics-AP, U.S. history, U.S. history-AP, world history, world history-AP, world literature, writing, yearbook.

Graduation Requirements Arts and fine arts (art, music, dance, drama), English, foreign language, mathematics, personal development, physical education (includes health), science, social sciences, portfolio presentation, proficiency exams, volunteer credit hours. Community service is required.

Special Academic Programs Advanced Placement exam preparation; honors section; accelerated programs; study at local college for college credit; academic accommodation for the gifted, the musically talented, and the artistically talented; remedial reading and/or remedial writing; programs in English, mathematics, general development for dyslexic students; special instructional classes for mild learning disabilities, social anxiety.

College Admission Counseling 8 students graduated in 2016; 7 went to college, including California State University, Northridge; University of California, Santa Barbara; University of Oregon. Other: 1 had other specific plans.

Student Life Upper grades have specified standards of dress, student council, honor system. Discipline rests equally with students and faculty.

Summer Programs Remediation, enrichment, advancement, art/fine arts programs offered; held both on and off campus; accepts boys and girls; open to students from other schools. 130 students usually enrolled. 2017 schedule: June 6 to August 19. Application deadline: June 1.

Tuition and Aid Tuition installment plan (monthly payment plans, individually arranged payment plans). Tuition reduction for siblings available.

Admissions Traditional secondary-level entrance grade is 10. For fall 2016, 30 students applied for upper-level admission, 30 were accepted, 30 enrolled. English language and Math Placement Exam required. Deadline for receipt of application materials: none. Application fee required. On-campus interview required.

Computers Computers are regularly used in art, English, foreign language, history, mathematics, science classes. Computer network features include Internet access, wireless campus network, Internet filtering or blocking technology. Student e-mail accounts and computer access in designated common areas are available to students. Students grades are available online. The school has a published electronic and media policy.

HALSTROM ACADEMY

21800 Oxnard St., Ste. 270
Woodland Hills, California 91367

Head of School: Mr. Joseph Harper

General Information Coeducational day and distance learning college-preparatory and general academic school; primarily serves underachievers, students with learning disabilities, individuals with Attention Deficit Disorder, dyslexic students, students with mild learning disabilities, and students with social anxiety. Grades 6–12. Distance learning grades 6–12. Founded: 1985. Setting: suburban. 1 building on campus. Approved or accredited by Western Association of Schools and Colleges and California Department of Education. Total enrollment: 40. Upper school average class size: 1. Upper school faculty-student ratio: 1:1. The average school day consists of 4 hours.

Faculty School total: 12. In upper school: 5 men, 7 women; 4 have advanced degrees.

Subjects Offered Algebra, American literature, anatomy and physiology, anthropology, art appreciation, arts, arts appreciation, astronomy, biology, biology-AP, British literature, business mathematics, calculus, career/college preparation, chemistry, chemistry-AP, computer applications, contemporary issues, creative writing, cultural

geography, drawing, economics, English, English language and composition-AP, English literature, English literature and composition-AP, European history-AP, fine arts, French, geology, geometry, German, government and politics-AP, health, history, honors algebra, honors English, honors geometry, honors U.S. history, honors world history, journalism, Latin, macroeconomics-AP, Mandarin, mathematics, microeconomics-AP, music theory, physical education, physics, pre-calculus, robotics, science, social sciences, social studies, Spanish, speech and debate, statistics, statistics-AP, trigonometry, U.S. government, U.S. government and politics-AP, U.S. history, world history, world history-AP, writing, yearbook.

Graduation Requirements Arts and fine arts (art, music, dance, drama), English, foreign language, mathematics, personal development, physical education (includes health), science, social sciences, portfolio presentation, proficiency exams, volunteer credit hours. Community service is required.

Special Academic Programs Advanced Placement exam preparation; honors section; accelerated programs; study at local college for college credit; academic accommodation for the gifted, the musically talented, and the artistically talented; remedial reading and/or remedial writing; remedial math; programs in English, mathematics, general development for dyslexic students; special instructional classes for mild learning disabilities, social anxiety.

College Admission Counseling 9 students graduated in 2016; 8 went to college, including California State University, Fresno; New York University; Pace University; Pepperdine University; University of California, Santa Cruz; Willamette University. Other: 1 had other specific plans.

Student Life Upper grades have specified standards of dress, student council, honor system. Discipline rests equally with students and faculty.

Summer Programs Remediation, enrichment, advancement, art/fine arts programs offered; session focuses on advancement and remedial academic work; held both on and off campus; accepts boys and girls; open to students from other schools. 130 students usually enrolled. 2017 schedule: June 6 to August 19. Application deadline: June 1.

Tuition and Aid Tuition installment plan (monthly payment plans, individually arranged payment plans). Tuition reduction for siblings available.

Admissions Traditional secondary-level entrance grade is 10. For fall 2016, 44 students applied for upper-level admission, 44 were accepted, 44 enrolled. English language and Math Placement Exam required. Deadline for receipt of application materials: none. No application fee required. On-campus interview required.

Computers Computers are regularly used in art, English, foreign language, history, mathematics, science classes. Computer network features include Internet access, wireless campus network, Internet filtering or blocking technology. Student e-mail accounts and computer access in designated common areas are available to students. Students grades are available online. The school has a published electronic and media policy.

HAMMOND SCHOOL

854 Galway Lane
Columbia, South Carolina 29209

Head of School: Mr. Christopher B. Angel

General Information Coeducational day college-preparatory, arts, and technology school. Grades PK–12. Founded: 1966. Setting: suburban. 108-acre campus. 20 buildings on campus. Approved or accredited by New England Association of Schools and Colleges, South Carolina Independent School Association, Southern Association of Colleges and Schools, Southern Association of Independent Schools, and South Carolina Department of Education. Member of National Association of Independent Schools and Secondary School Admission Test Board. Endowment: $2 million. Total enrollment: 898. Upper school average class size: 15. Upper school faculty-student ratio: 1:9. There are 180 required school days per year for Upper School students. Upper School students typically attend 5 days per week. The average school day consists of 7 hours and 20 minutes.

Upper School Student Profile Grade 9: 67 students (26 boys, 41 girls); Grade 10: 74 students (38 boys, 36 girls); Grade 11: 76 students (45 boys, 31 girls); Grade 12: 84 students (47 boys, 37 girls).

Faculty School total: 112. In upper school: 22 men, 22 women; 24 have advanced degrees.

Subjects Offered Advanced Placement courses, African American history, algebra, American government, American history, American literature, art, art history, biology, calculus, chemistry, choir, chorus, computer programming, computer science, creative writing, drama, earth science, economics, electives, English, English literature, European history, film studies, finite math, French, geometry, government/civics, history, journalism, Latin, mathematics, music, physical education, physics, science, social studies, Spanish, speech, trigonometry, world history, world literature.

Graduation Requirements Arts and fine arts (art, music, dance, drama), English, foreign language, mathematics, physical education (includes health), science, social studies (includes history).

Special Academic Programs Advanced Placement exam preparation; honors section; independent study; study abroad; academic accommodation for the gifted, the musically talented, and the artistically talented; remedial reading and/or remedial writing; programs in English, mathematics, general development for dyslexic students; ESL (15 students enrolled).

College Admission Counseling 71 students graduated in 2016; all went to college, including Clemson University; Furman University; University of Georgia; University of South Carolina; Washington and Lee University; Wofford College. Mean SAT critical reading: 585, mean SAT math: 612, mean SAT writing: 586, mean combined SAT: 1783, mean composite ACT: 27. 45% scored over 600 on SAT critical reading, 55% scored over 600 on SAT math, 45% scored over 600 on SAT writing, 55% scored over 26 on composite ACT.

Student Life Upper grades have uniform requirement, student council, honor system. Discipline rests primarily with faculty.

Summer Programs Enrichment, advancement, sports, art/fine arts, computer instruction programs offered; session focuses on enrichment; held both on and off campus; accepts boys and girls; open to students from other schools. 700 students usually enrolled. 2017 schedule: June 1 to July 31. Application deadline: June 1.

Tuition and Aid Day student tuition: $17,497. Tuition installment plan (Insured Tuition Payment Plan). Merit scholarship grants, need-based scholarship grants available. In 2016–17, 23% of upper-school students received aid; total upper-school merit-scholarship money awarded: $91,000. Total amount of financial aid awarded in 2016–17: $1,400,000.

Admissions Traditional secondary-level entrance grade is 9. For fall 2016, 37 students applied for upper-level admission, 28 were accepted, 22 enrolled. ACT, any standardized test, ISEE, PSAT or SSAT required. Deadline for receipt of application materials: none. Application fee required: $75. On-campus interview required.

Athletics Interscholastic: backpacking (boys, girls), ballet (b,g), baseball (b), basketball (b,g), canoeing/kayaking (b,g), cheering (b,g), climbing (b,g), combined training (b,g), cross-country running (b,g), dance (b,g), dance squad (g), equestrian sports (b,g), fitness (b,g), football (b), golf (b,g), hiking/backpacking (b,g), horseback riding (b,g), kayaking (b,g), lacrosse (b), physical fitness (b,g), physical training (b,g), pom squad (g), rafting (b,g), rappelling (b,g), rock climbing (b,g), ropes courses (b,g), running (b,g), skeet shooting (b,g), soccer (b,g), softball (b,g), strength & conditioning (b,g), swimming and diving (b,g), tennis (b,g), track and field (b,g), trap and skeet (b,g), ultimate Frisbee (b,g), volleyball (g), wall climbing (b,g), weight lifting (b,g), weight training (b,g), wilderness (b,g), wrestling (b); coed interscholastic: aerobics/dance, aquatics, ballet, cheering, cross-country running, dance, equestrian sports, golf, horseback riding, outdoor activities, physical fitness, physical training, pom squad, skeet shooting, soccer, trap and skeet, ultimate Frisbee. 1 PE instructor, 73 coaches, 2 athletic trainers.

Computers Computers are regularly used in all classes. Computer network features include on-campus library services, online commercial services, Internet access, wireless campus network, Internet filtering or blocking technology. Campus intranet and student e-mail accounts are available to students. Students grades are available online. The school has a published electronic and media policy.

Contact Mrs. Carson O. McQueen, Admission Counselor. 803-776-0295 Ext. 1039. Fax: 803-776-0122. E-mail: cmcqueen@hammondschool.org. Website: www.hammondschool.org

HAMPSHIRE COUNTRY SCHOOL

Rindge, New Hampshire
See Junior Boarding Schools section.

HAMPTON ROADS ACADEMY

739 Academy Lane
Newport News, Virginia 23602

Head of School: Mr. Peter Mertz

General Information Coeducational day college-preparatory school. Grades JK–12. Founded: 1959. Setting: suburban. 52-acre campus. 4 buildings on campus. Approved or accredited by Virginia Association of Independent Schools and Virginia Department of Education. Member of National Association of Independent Schools. Total enrollment: 606. Upper school average class size: 14. Upper school faculty-student ratio: 1:10. Upper School students typically attend 5 days per week. The average school day consists of 6 hours and 30 minutes.

Upper School Student Profile Grade 9: 50 students (25 boys, 25 girls); Grade 10: 72 students (37 boys, 35 girls); Grade 11: 64 students (34 boys, 30 girls); Grade 12: 64 students (34 boys, 30 girls).

Faculty School total: 70. In upper school: 13 men, 17 women; 19 have advanced degrees.

Subjects Offered Algebra, American history, American literature, anatomy, art, biology, calculus, ceramics, chemistry, creative writing, drama, earth science, economics, English, English literature, European history, expository writing, fine arts, French, geography, geometry, government/civics, grammar, health, history, Latin, mathematics, music, photography, physical education, physics, physiology, science, social studies, Spanish, speech, statistics, theater, trigonometry, world history, world literature, writing.

Graduation Requirements Arts and fine arts (art, music, dance, drama), English, foreign language, mathematics, physical education (includes health), science, social

studies (includes history), community service, senior project. Community service is required.

Special Academic Programs 19 Advanced Placement exams for which test preparation is offered; honors section; independent study; ESL (10 students enrolled).

College Admission Counseling 65 students graduated in 2016; all went to college, including Hampden-Sydney College; James Madison University; Old Dominion University; The College of William and Mary; University of Virginia; Virginia Polytechnic Institute and State University. Median SAT critical reading: 600, median SAT math: 600, median SAT writing: 600, median combined SAT: 1800, median composite ACT: 22. 60% scored over 600 on SAT critical reading, 54% scored over 600 on SAT math, 56% scored over 600 on SAT writing, 57% scored over 1800 on combined SAT, 36% scored over 26 on composite ACT.

Student Life Upper grades have specified standards of dress, student council, honor system. Discipline rests primarily with faculty.

Tuition and Aid Day student tuition: $17,700. Tuition installment plan (SMART Tuition Payment Plan). Need-based scholarship grants available. In 2016–17, 20% of upper-school students received aid. Total amount of financial aid awarded in 2016–17: $600,000.

Admissions Traditional secondary-level entrance grade is 9. For fall 2016, 54 students applied for upper-level admission, 35 were accepted, 29 enrolled. ERB, school's own test and writing sample required. Deadline for receipt of application materials: none. Application fee required: $75. On-campus interview recommended.

Athletics Interscholastic: ball hockey (girls), baseball (b), basketball (b,g), cheering (g), cross-country running (b,g), equestrian sports (b,g), field hockey (g), football (b), golf (b,g), lacrosse (b), physical training (b,g), running (b,g), sailing (b,g), soccer (b,g), softball (g), swimming and diving (b,g), tennis (b,g), track and field (b,g), volleyball (g), weight training (b,g); intramural: hiking/backpacking (b,g), outdoor adventure (b,g), outdoor education (b,g), outdoor recreation (b,g), outdoor skills (b,g), outdoors (b,g), strength & conditioning (b,g); coed interscholastic: aquatics, cheering, equestrian sports, running; coed intramural: archery, equestrian sports, fitness, hiking/backpacking, outdoor adventure, outdoor education, outdoor recreation, outdoor skills, outdoors, paddle tennis, physical fitness, physical training, ropes courses, strength & conditioning, table tennis, ultimate Frisbee, weight training. 3 PE instructors, 44 coaches, 1 athletic trainer.

Computers Computers are regularly used in English, history, mathematics, music, science, social sciences, social studies, technology, writing, writing, yearbook classes. Computer network features include on-campus library services, online commercial services, Internet access, wireless campus network, Internet filtering or blocking technology. Student e-mail accounts and computer access in designated common areas are available to students. Students grades are available online. The school has a published electronic and media policy.

Contact Michelle Ford, Admission Associate. 757-884-9148. Fax: 757-884-9137. E-mail: admissions@hra.org. Website: www.hra.org

HARDING ACADEMY

Box 10775, Harding University
1529 East Park Avenue
Searcy, Arkansas 72149

Head of School: Mr. James Simmons

General Information Coeducational boarding and day college-preparatory school, affiliated with Church of Christ. Boarding boys grades 10–12, day boys grades K–12, day girls grades K–12. Founded: 1924. Setting: small town. Nearest major city is Little Rock. Students are housed in single-sex dormitories. 15-acre campus. 1 building on campus. Approved or accredited by Arkansas Nonpublic School Accrediting Association, National Christian School Association, North Central Association of Colleges and Schools, and Arkansas Department of Education. Total enrollment: 598. Upper school average class size: 25. Upper school faculty-student ratio: 1:11. There are 180 required school days per year for Upper School students. Upper School students typically attend 5 days per week. The average school day consists of 7 hours and 25 minutes.

Upper School Student Profile Grade 7: 44 students (23 boys, 21 girls); Grade 8: 57 students (29 boys, 28 girls); Grade 9: 49 students (25 boys, 24 girls); Grade 10: 66 students (35 boys, 31 girls); Grade 11: 67 students (32 boys, 35 girls); Grade 12: 44 students (21 boys, 23 girls). 4% of students are boarding students. 96% are state residents. 1 state is represented in upper school student body. 4% are international students. International students from China, Indonesia, United States, and Viet Nam. 80% of students are members of Church of Christ.

Faculty School total: 58. In upper school: 19 men, 15 women; 20 have advanced degrees; 1 resides on campus.

Subjects Offered Baseball, basketball, earth science, family and consumer science, fitness, food and nutrition, golf, softball, tennis, track and field, volleyball, yearbook.

Special Academic Programs Advanced Placement exam preparation; study at local college for college credit.

College Admission Counseling 53 students graduated in 2016; 50 went to college, including Arkansas State University; Harding University; Lipscomb University; University of Arkansas. Other: 1 went to work, 2 had other specific plans. Median composite ACT: 25.

Student Life Upper grades have specified standards of dress, student council, honor system. Discipline rests primarily with faculty. Attendance at religious services is required.

Tuition and Aid Tuition installment plan (monthly payment plans). Tuition reduction for siblings, need-based scholarship grants available.

Admissions Traditional secondary-level entrance grade is 7. Any standardized test or TOEFL required. Deadline for receipt of application materials: none. Application fee required: $50. Interview recommended.

Athletics Interscholastic: baseball (boys), basketball (b,g), cheering (g), cross-country running (b,g), football (b), golf (b,g), softball (g), swimming and diving (b), tennis (b,g), track and field (b,g), volleyball (g). 4 PE instructors, 10 coaches, 1 athletic trainer.

Computers Computers are regularly used in all academic classes. Computer network features include on-campus library services, Internet access, wireless campus network, Internet filtering or blocking technology. Student e-mail accounts are available to students. Students grades are available online. The school has a published electronic and media policy.

Contact Dr. Darren Mathews, High School Principal. 501-279-7201. Fax: 501-279-7213. E-mail: dmathews@harding.edu. Website: www.academy.harding.edu/

HARGRAVE MILITARY ACADEMY

200 Military Drive
Chatham, Virginia 24531

Head of School: Brig. Gen. Don Broome, USA (Ret.)

General Information Boys' boarding and day college-preparatory, general academic, arts, religious studies, bilingual studies, technology, academic postgraduate, leadership and ethics, and military school, affiliated with Baptist General Association of Virginia. Grades 7–PG. Founded: 1909. Setting: small town. Nearest major city is Danville. Students are housed in single-sex dormitories. 214-acre campus. 29 buildings on campus. Approved or accredited by Southern Association of Colleges and Schools, The Association of Boarding Schools, and Virginia Association of Independent Schools. Member of National Association of Independent Schools. Endowment: $3.5 million. Total enrollment: 230. Upper school average class size: 11. Upper school faculty-student ratio: 1:12. Upper School students typically attend 5 days per week.

Upper School Student Profile 24 states are represented in upper school student body. 20% of students are Baptist General Association of Virginia.

Faculty School total: 30. In upper school: 17 men, 13 women; 7 have advanced degrees; 6 reside on campus.

Subjects Offered Advanced biology, advanced chemistry, advanced math, Advanced Placement courses, algebra, American government, American history, American literature, art, astronomy, Bible studies, biology, calculus, chemistry, creative writing, debate, English, English literature, environmental science, ESL, functions, geometry, government/civics, health, history, journalism, leadership, leadership and service, leadership education training, Mandarin, mathematics, media production, physical education, physics, psychology, reading, religion, SAT/ACT preparation, science, social studies, sociology, Spanish, speech, study skills, TOEFL preparation, trigonometry.

Graduation Requirements English, foreign language, mathematics, physical education (includes health), religion (includes Bible studies and theology), science, social studies (includes history).

Special Academic Programs Advanced Placement exam preparation; honors section; independent study; study at local college for college credit; remedial reading and/or remedial writing; remedial math; programs in general development for dyslexic students; special instructional classes for students with Attention Deficit Disorder; ESL (8 students enrolled).

College Admission Counseling 62 students graduated in 2015; all went to college, including Hampden-Sydney College; The University of North Carolina at Charlotte; United States Military Academy; Virginia Military Institute; Virginia Polytechnic Institute and State University.

Student Life Upper grades have uniform requirement, student council, honor system. Discipline rests equally with students and faculty. Attendance at religious services is required.

Tuition and Aid Day student tuition: $12,900; 5-day tuition and room/board: $30,800; 7-day tuition and room/board: $30,800. Guaranteed tuition plan. Tuition installment plan (monthly payment plans, individually arranged payment plans). Tuition reduction for siblings, merit scholarship grants, need-based scholarship grants, need-based loans, Sallie Mae loans available. In 2015–16, 35% of upper-school students received aid; total upper-school merit-scholarship money awarded: $52,000. Total amount of financial aid awarded in 2015–16: $525,000.

Admissions Traditional secondary-level entrance grade is 10. Math and English placement tests required. Deadline for receipt of application materials: none. Application fee required: $75. Interview recommended.

Athletics Interscholastic: aquatics, baseball, basketball, cross-country running, football, golf, independent competitive sports, lacrosse, marksmanship, riflery, soccer, swimming and diving, tennis, track and field, wrestling; intramural: aquatics, billiards, canoeing/kayaking, climbing, cross-country running, drill team, fishing, fitness, fitness walking, hiking/backpacking, independent competitive sports, jogging, jump rope, kayaking, lacrosse, life saving, marksmanship, mountaineering, Nautilus, outdoor activities, outdoor adventure, outdoor recreation, paint ball, physical fitness, physical training, power lifting, rappelling, riflery, rock climbing, ropes courses, running, scuba

diving, skeet shooting, skiing (downhill), strength & conditioning, swimming and diving, table tennis, tennis, trap and skeet, walking, water polo, weight lifting, weight training. 1 PE instructor, 10 coaches, 1 athletic trainer.

Computers Computers are regularly used in all academic, photography classes. Computer network features include on-campus library services, online commercial services, Internet access, wireless campus network, Internet filtering or blocking technology. Campus intranet, student e-mail accounts, and computer access in designated common areas are available to students. Students grades are available online. The school has a published electronic and media policy.

Contact Mr. Thomas Messinger, Director of Admissions. 800-432-2480. Fax: 434-432-3129. E-mail: admissions@hargrave.edu. Website: www.hargrave.edu

THE HARKER SCHOOL

500 Saratoga Avenue
San Jose, California 95129

Head of School: Christopher Nikoloff

General Information Coeducational day college-preparatory and gifted students school. Grades K–12. Founded: 1893. Setting: urban. 16-acre campus. 7 buildings on campus. Approved or accredited by California Association of Independent Schools, Western Association of Schools and Colleges, and California Department of Education. Member of National Association of Independent Schools. Total enrollment: 1,911. Upper school average class size: 18. Upper school faculty-student ratio: 1:10. Upper School students typically attend 5 days per week. The average school day consists of 7 hours and 13 minutes.

Upper School Student Profile Grade 9: 198 students (98 boys, 100 girls); Grade 10: 199 students (95 boys, 104 girls); Grade 11: 192 students (93 boys, 99 girls); Grade 12: 190 students (93 boys, 97 girls).

Faculty School total: 222. In upper school: 43 men, 47 women; 69 have advanced degrees.

Subjects Offered 20th century American writers, acting, advanced math, algebra, American literature, anatomy and physiology, architecture, art history, art history-AP, Asian history, astronomy, baseball, basketball, biology, biology-AP, biotechnology, British literature, British literature (honors), calculus-AP, ceramics, cheerleading, chemistry, chemistry-AP, choreography, classical studies, college counseling, community service, computer science-AP, dance, dance performance, debate, digital photography, discrete mathematics, drawing, ecology, economics, electronics, engineering, English literature and composition-AP, English literature-AP, environmental science-AP, ethics, European history-AP, evolution, expository writing, film and literature, fitness, forensics, French, French language-AP, French literature-AP, geometry, golf, graphic arts, graphic design, great books, history of dance, Holocaust seminar, honors algebra, honors geometry, human geography - AP, Japanese, Japanese literature, jazz band, journalism, Latin, Latin-AP, linear algebra, literary magazine, Mandarin, medieval literature, mentorship program, music appreciation, music theory-AP, newspaper, orchestra, organic chemistry, painting, photography, physics, physics-AP, play production, poetry, political thought, pre-calculus, programming, psychology, psychology-AP, public policy, public speaking, research, robotics, scene study, sculpture, Shakespeare, softball, Spanish, Spanish language-AP, Spanish literature-AP, statistics, statistics-AP, stone carving, student government, studio art-AP, study skills, swimming, technical theater, tennis, theater arts, theater history, track and field, trigonometry, U.S. government and politics-AP, U.S. history, U.S. history-AP, video and animation, visual arts, vocal ensemble, volleyball, water polo, weight training, Western philosophy, world history, world history-AP, world religions, wrestling, yearbook, yoga.

Graduation Requirements Arts and fine arts (art, music, dance, drama), biology, chemistry, computer science, English, foreign language, mathematics, physical education (includes health), physics, public speaking, U.S. history, world history, 30 total hours of community service, one year arts survey theater, dance, music or visual arts.

Special Academic Programs Advanced Placement exam preparation; honors section; independent study; academic accommodation for the gifted.

College Admission Counseling 187 students graduated in 2016; all went to college, including Cornell University; Stanford University; University of California, Berkeley; University of Chicago; University of Southern California; Yale University. Mean SAT critical reading: 710, mean SAT math: 736, mean SAT writing: 736.

Student Life Upper grades have specified standards of dress, student council, honor system. Discipline rests primarily with faculty.

Summer Programs Enrichment, advancement, ESL, sports programs offered; session focuses on academics, sports, enrichment, research; held both on and off campus; accepts boys and girls; open to students from other schools. 1,112 students usually enrolled. 2017 schedule: June 19 to July 28.

Tuition and Aid Day student tuition: $43,693. Need-based scholarship grants available. In 2016–17, 10% of upper-school students received aid.

Admissions Traditional secondary-level entrance grade is 9. ERB CTP IV, essay, ISEE or SSAT required. Deadline for receipt of application materials: January 12. Application fee required: $100. Interview required.

Athletics Interscholastic: baseball (boys), basketball (b,g), cross-country running (b,g), football (b), golf (b,g), lacrosse (g), soccer (b,g), softball (g), swimming and diving (b,g), tennis (b,g), track and field (b,g), volleyball (b,g), water polo (b,g); coed interscholastic: cheering, wrestling; coed intramural: acrobics/dance, dance, fencing, fitness, physical fitness, tennis, yoga. 4 PE instructors, 27 coaches, 1 athletic trainer.

Computers Computers are regularly used in all academic, business, college planning, graphic arts, newspaper, yearbook classes. Computer network features include on-campus library services, online commercial services, Internet access, wireless campus network, Internet filtering or blocking technology, ProQuest, Gale Group, InfoTrac, Facts On File. Campus intranet and student e-mail accounts are available to students. The school has a published electronic and media policy.

Contact Christianne Marra, Assistant to the Director of Admission. 408-249-2510. Fax: 408-984-2325. E-mail: christianne.marra@harker.org. Website: www.harker.org

THE HARLEY SCHOOL

1981 Clover Street
Rochester, New York 14618

Head of School: Mr. Ward J. Ghory

General Information Coeducational day college-preparatory school. Grades N–12. Founded: 1917. Setting: suburban. 25-acre campus. 5 buildings on campus. Approved or accredited by National Independent Private Schools Association and New York State Association of Independent Schools. Member of National Association of Independent Schools. Endowment: $10.4 million. Total enrollment: 537. Upper school average class size: 8. Upper school faculty-student ratio: 1:8. There are 180 required school days per year for Upper School students. Upper School students typically attend 5 days per week. The average school day consists of 6 hours and 50 minutes.

Upper School Student Profile Grade 9: 48 students (21 boys, 27 girls); Grade 10: 45 students (18 boys, 27 girls); Grade 11: 46 students (21 boys, 25 girls); Grade 12: 47 students (17 boys, 30 girls).

Faculty School total: 90. In upper school: 14 men, 14 women; 28 have advanced degrees.

Subjects Offered 3-dimensional art, Advanced Placement courses, algebra, American history, anthropology, art, art history, art-AP, band, biology, calculus, calculus-AP, ceramics, chamber groups, chemistry, Chinese, choir, chorus, community service, comparative government and politics-AP, computer graphics, computer math, computer programming, computer science, creative writing, debate, desktop publishing, drama, drawing, driver education, economics-AP, English, English language and composition-AP, English literature, environmental science, ethics, European history, expository writing, film, fine arts, foreign language, French, gardening, geometry, graphic arts, Greek, health, jazz band, language-AP, Latin, mathematics, multimedia, music, music theory, orchestra, organic gardening, outdoor education, photography, physical education, physics, psychology, SAT preparation, science, Shakespeare, social studies, Spanish, speech, student government, study skills, theater, theater arts, theater production, U.S. history-AP, voice, world history, writing, yoga.

Graduation Requirements Arts and fine arts (art, music, dance, drama), computer science, English, foreign language, health education, internship, mathematics, physical education (includes health), science, social studies (includes history), sports, participation in team sports, community service, senior internship. Community service is required.

Special Academic Programs 17 Advanced Placement exams for which test preparation is offered.

College Admission Counseling 47 students graduated in 2016, all went to college, including Case Western Reserve University; Cornell University; Ithaca College; Rochester Institute of Technology; University of Rochester; Wellesley College. Mean SAT critical reading: 630, mean SAT math: 635, mean SAT writing: 590.

Student Life Upper grades have student council, honor system. Discipline rests primarily with faculty.

Summer Programs Remediation, enrichment, sports, art/fine arts, computer instruction programs offered; session focuses on summer Nursery, day camp, outdoor skills, swimming, tennis, writing, college prep; held both on and off campus; accepts boys and girls; open to students from other schools. 150 students usually enrolled. 2017 schedule: June 12 to August 18. Application deadline: May 1.

Tuition and Aid Day student tuition: $19,770–$25,400. Tuition installment plan (Insured Tuition Payment Plan, monthly payment plans, 2-payment plan, prepaid discount plan, quarterly plan). Tuition reduction for siblings, need-based scholarship grants available. In 2016–17, 50% of upper-school students received aid.

Admissions Traditional secondary-level entrance grade is 9. For fall 2016, 34 students applied for upper-level admission, 15 were accepted, 12 enrolled. Essay and Math Placement Exam required. Deadline for receipt of application materials: none. Application fee required: $75. On-campus interview recommended.

Athletics Interscholastic: baseball (boys), basketball (b,g), bowling (b,g), golf (b), skiing (downhill) (b,g), soccer (b,g), softball (b,g), swimming and diving (b,g), tennis (b,g), track and field (b,g), volleyball (b,g); coed interscholastic: cross-country running, outdoor education, running, yoga. 3 PE instructors, 11 coaches.

Computers Computers are regularly used in all academic, art classes. Computer network features include Internet access, wireless campus network. The school has a published electronic and media policy.

Contact Mrs. Ivone Foisy, Director of Advancement and Admissions. 585-442-1770 Ext. 1112. Fax: 585-442-5758. E-mail: ifoisy@harleyschool.org. Website: www.harleyschool.org

THE HARPETH HALL SCHOOL

3801 Hobbs Road
PO Box 150207
Nashville, Tennessee 37215-0207

Head of School: Dr. Stephanie Balmer

General Information Girls' day college-preparatory school. Grades 5–12. Founded: 1951. Setting: suburban. 45-acre campus. 7 buildings on campus. Approved or accredited by Southern Association of Colleges and Schools, Southern Association of Independent Schools, and Tennessee Association of Independent Schools. Member of National Association of Independent Schools. Endowment: $39.3 million. Total enrollment: 690. Upper school average class size: 16. Upper school faculty-student ratio: 1:8. There are 180 required school days per year for Upper School students. Upper School students typically attend 5 days per week. The average school day consists of 6 hours.

Upper School Student Profile Grade 9: 100 students (100 girls); Grade 10: 99 students (99 girls); Grade 11: 100 students (100 girls); Grade 12: 103 students (103 girls).

Faculty In upper school: 53 have advanced degrees.

Subjects Offered Advanced Placement courses, algebra, American government, American history, American history-AP, American literature, art, art history, art history-AP, athletics, audio visual/media, biology, biology-AP, calculus, chamber groups, chemistry, chemistry-AP, Chinese, choir, choral music, college admission preparation, college counseling, comparative politics, computer math, computer programming, computer science, conceptual physics, contemporary issues, creative writing, dance, digital art, drama, ecology, English, English literature, environmental science, environmental studies, European history, European history-AP, expository writing, fine arts, French, French language-AP, French literature-AP, functions, geometry, government/civics, grammar, health, history, honors algebra, honors English, Latin, Latin-AP, life skills, Mandarin, mathematics, media arts, music, photography, physical education, physics, physics-AP, probability and statistics, psychology, science, social sciences, social studies, Spanish, Spanish language-AP, Spanish literature-AP, speech, statistics-AP, studio art-AP, theater, theater arts, trigonometry, video, world history, world history-AP, world literature, writing.

Graduation Requirements Arts and fine arts (art, music, dance, drama), electives, English, foreign language, mathematics, physical education (includes health), science, social sciences, participation in Winterim program each year.

Special Academic Programs Advanced Placement exam preparation; honors section; independent study; term-away projects; study abroad; academic accommodation for the gifted, the musically talented, and the artistically talented.

College Admission Counseling 103 students graduated in 2016; all went to college, including Auburn University; Southern Methodist University; Texas Christian University; The University of Alabama; The University of Tennessee; University of Virginia. Other: 2 had other specific plans.

Student Life Upper grades have uniform requirement, student council, honor system. Discipline rests primarily with faculty.

Summer Programs Enrichment, sports, art/fine arts, computer instruction programs offered; session focuses on enrichment classes and sports; held on campus; accepts girls; open to students from other schools. 2017 schedule: June 5 to July 28. Application deadline: none.

Tuition and Aid Day student tuition: $26,240. Tuition installment plan (monthly payment plans, individually arranged payment plans, Tuition Management Systems Plan). Need-based scholarship grants available. In 2016–17, 16% of upper-school students received aid.

Admissions Traditional secondary-level entrance grade is 9. For fall 2016, 76 students applied for upper-level admission, 23 enrolled. ISEE required. Deadline for receipt of application materials: January 20. Application fee required: $50. Interview recommended.

Athletics Interscholastic: aquatics, basketball, bowling, crew, cross-country running, diving, golf, lacrosse, running, soccer, softball, swimming and diving, tennis, track and field, volleyball; intramural: aerobics/dance, cheering, climbing, cooperative games, dance, fitness, flag football, jogging, modern dance, outdoor activities, outdoor adventure, outdoor education, outdoor recreation, outdoor skills, physical training, rock climbing, self defense, strength & conditioning, ultimate Frisbee, walking, wall climbing, weight training, yoga; coed intramural: riflery. 4 PE instructors, 50 coaches, 1 athletic trainer.

Computers Computers are regularly used in all academic classes. Computer network features include on-campus library services, online commercial services, Internet access, wireless campus network, Internet filtering or blocking technology. Campus intranet and student e-mail accounts are available to students. Students grades are available online. The school has a published electronic and media policy.

Contact Mrs. Sandy Binkley, Admission Coordinator. 615-346-0126. Fax: 615-647-0724. E-mail: binkley@harpethhall.org. Website: www.harpethhall.org

HARRELLS CHRISTIAN ACADEMY

360 Tomahawk Highway
PO Box 88
Harrells, North Carolina 28444

Head of School: Mr. Kevin M. Kunst

General Information Coeducational day college-preparatory school, affiliated with Christian faith. Grades K–12. Founded: 1969. Setting: rural. Nearest major city is Wilmington. 52-acre campus. 7 buildings on campus. Approved or accredited by Southern Association of Colleges and Schools, Southern Association of Independent Schools, and North Carolina Department of Education. Total enrollment: 363. Upper school average class size: 13. Upper school faculty-student ratio: 1:8. There are 178 required school days per year for Upper School students. Upper School students typically attend 5 days per week. The average school day consists of 5 hours and 23 minutes.

Upper School Student Profile Grade 9: 32 students (17 boys, 15 girls); Grade 10: 28 students (16 boys, 12 girls); Grade 11: 34 students (22 boys, 12 girls); Grade 12: 35 students (22 boys, 13 girls). 96% of students are Christian.

Faculty School total: 18. In upper school: 5 men, 12 women; 5 have advanced degrees.

Subjects Offered Algebra, animal science, art, art education, biology, biology-AP, calculus, ceramics, chemistry, chemistry-AP, civil rights, computer art, drawing, earth science, English, English language and composition-AP, English literature, English literature and composition-AP, environmental science-AP, French, government/civics, history, journalism, mathematics, painting, physical education, psychology-AP, religion, social studies, Spanish, U.S. history-AP, weightlifting, world history-AP, yearbook.

Graduation Requirements Biology, computer applications, electives, English, environmental science, foreign language, mathematics, physical education (includes health), physical science, religious studies, science, social studies (includes history).

Special Academic Programs 5 Advanced Placement exams for which test preparation is offered; honors section; study at local college for college credit; programs in English, mathematics, general development for dyslexic students.

College Admission Counseling 42 students graduated in 2016; 39 went to college, including East Carolina University; Embry-Riddle Aeronautical University–Daytona; Meredith College; North Carolina State University; The University of North Carolina Wilmington; Whitworth University. Other: 1 went to work, 2 had other specific plans. Median SAT critical reading: 510, median SAT math: 500, median SAT writing: 500, median combined SAT: 1510, median composite ACT: 22. 19% scored over 600 on SAT critical reading, 22% scored over 600 on SAT math, 16% scored over 600 on SAT writing, 19% scored over 1800 on combined SAT, 19% scored over 26 on composite ACT.

Student Life Upper grades have specified standards of dress, honor system. Discipline rests primarily with faculty. Attendance at religious services is required.

Tuition and Aid Day student tuition: $8690. Tuition installment plan (SMART Tuition Payment Plan). Tuition reduction for siblings, need-based scholarship grants available. In 2016–17, 16% of upper-school students received aid.

Admissions Traditional secondary-level entrance grade is 9. For fall 2016, 22 students applied for upper-level admission, 19 were accepted, 16 enrolled. Achievement tests required. Deadline for receipt of application materials: none. Application fee required: $75. On-campus interview required.

Athletics Interscholastic: baseball (boys), basketball (b,g), cheering (g), football (b), soccer (b,g), softball (g), tennis (g), volleyball (g); coed interscholastic: golf. 1 PE instructor, 1 coach.

Computers Computers are regularly used in art, English, journalism, yearbook classes. Computer resources include Internet access, wireless campus network, Internet filtering or blocking technology. Students grades are available online. The school has a published electronic and media policy.

Contact Mrs. Susan Frederick, Administrative Assistant. 910-532-4575 Ext. 221. Fax: 910-532-2958. E-mail: sfrederick@harrellsca.com. Website: www.harrellschristianacademy.com

HARVARD-WESTLAKE SCHOOL

3700 Coldwater Canyon
Studio City, California 91604

Head of School: Richard B. Commons

General Information Coeducational day college-preparatory school. Grades 7–12. Founded: 1989. Setting: urban. Nearest major city is Los Angeles. 26-acre campus. 12 buildings on campus. Approved or accredited by Western Association of Schools and Colleges. Member of National Association of Independent Schools. Endowment: $78 million. Total enrollment: 1,592. Upper school average class size: 16. Upper school faculty-student ratio: 1:8. Upper School students typically attend 5 days per week. The average school day consists of 6 hours and 35 minutes.

Upper School Student Profile Grade 9: 288 students (159 boys, 129 girls); Grade 10: 298 students (154 boys, 144 girls); Grade 11: 284 students (159 boys, 125 girls); Grade 12: 290 students (155 boys, 135 girls).

Faculty School total: 122. In upper school: 72 men, 50 women; 85 have advanced degrees.

Subjects Offered 3-dimensional art, advanced studio art-AP, algebra, American history, American history-AP, American literature, American literature-AP, anatomy, architecture, art, art history, art history-AP, art-AP, Asian studies, astronomy, biology, biology-AP, calculus, calculus-AP, ceramics, chemistry, chemistry-AP, Chinese, choreography, chorus, classics, community service, comparative government and politics-AP, composition-AP, computer animation, computer programming, computer science, computer science-AP, creative writing, dance, dance performance, drama, drawing, economics, economics-AP, electronics, English, English language and composition-AP, English language-AP, English literature, English literature and composition-AP, English literature-AP, environmental science, environmental science-AP, European history, expository writing, film, film studies, fine arts, French, French language-AP, French literature-AP, French-AP, geography, geology, geometry, government and politics-AP, government-AP, government/civics, grammar, health, human development, human geography - AP, Japanese, jazz, jazz band, journalism, Latin, Latin-AP, law and the legal system, logic, macro/microeconomics-AP, Mandarin, mathematics, music, music history, music theory-AP, oceanography, orchestra, painting, photography, physical education, physics, physics-AP, physiology, political science, pre-calculus, psychology, Russian, science, senior project, Shakespeare, social studies, Spanish, Spanish language-AP, Spanish literature-AP, Spanish-AP, statistics, statistics-AP, studio art-AP, technical theater, theater, trigonometry, U.S. government and politics-AP, U.S. history, U.S. history-AP, video, women's studies, world history, world history-AP, world literature, yearbook, zoology.

Graduation Requirements English, foreign language, history, human development, mathematics, performing arts, physical education (includes health), science, technical skills, visual arts. Community service is required.

Special Academic Programs 30 Advanced Placement exams for which test preparation is offered; honors section; independent study; term-away projects; study abroad; academic accommodation for the gifted, the musically talented, and the artistically talented.

College Admission Counseling 283 students graduated in 2016; 281 went to college, including Brown University; Harvard University; New York University; University of Michigan; University of Pennsylvania; University of Southern California. Other: 2 had other specific plans. Mean SAT critical reading: 700, mean SAT math: 716, mean SAT writing: 720. 93% scored over 600 on SAT critical reading, 95% scored over 600 on SAT math, 93% scored over 600 on SAT writing, 93% scored over 1800 on combined SAT, 93% scored over 26 on composite ACT.

Student Life Upper grades have specified standards of dress, student council, honor system. Discipline rests primarily with faculty.

Summer Programs Enrichment, sports, art/fine arts, rigorous outdoor training, computer instruction programs offered; session focuses on enrichment and sports; held on campus; accepts boys and girls; open to students from other schools. 1,392 students usually enrolled. 2017 schedule: June 12 to July 28. Application deadline: none.

Tuition and Aid Day student tuition: $35,900. Tuition installment plan (monthly payment plans, semi-annual payment plan, quad-annual payment plan, monthly plan). Need-based scholarship grants available. In 2016–17, 20% of upper-school students received aid. Total amount of financial aid awarded in 2016–17: $6,859,500.

Admissions Traditional secondary-level entrance grade is 9. For fall 2016, 573 students applied for upper-level admission, 139 were accepted, 101 enrolled. ISEE required. Deadline for receipt of application materials: January 15. Application fee required: $200. On-campus interview required.

Athletics Interscholastic: baseball (boys), basketball (b,g), cross-country running (b,g), field hockey (g), football (b), golf (b,g), gymnastics (g), lacrosse (b), soccer (b,g), softball (g), swimming and diving (b,g), tennis (b,g), track and field (b,g), volleyball (b,g), water polo (b,g), wrestling (b); coed interscholastic: diving, equestrian sports, fencing, martial arts. 6 PE instructors, 32 coaches, 4 athletic trainers.

Computers Computers are regularly used in art, English, foreign language, history, mathematics, music, science classes. Computer resources include on-campus library services, Internet access, wireless campus network, 1:1 laptop program, music composition and editing, foreign language lab, science lab. Campus intranet, student e-mail accounts, and computer access in designated common areas are available to students. Students grades are available online. The school has a published electronic and media policy.

Contact Elizabeth Gregory, Director of Admission. 310-274-7281. Fax: 310-288-3212. E-mail: egregory@hw.com. Website: www.hw.com

THE HARVEY SCHOOL

260 Jay Street
Katonah, New York 10536

Head of School: Mr. William Knauer

General Information Coeducational boarding and day and distance learning college-preparatory school. Boarding grades 9–12, day grades 6–12. Distance learning grades 6–12. Founded: 1916. Setting: small town. Students are housed in single-sex dormitories and Five-day boarding. 125-acre campus. 14 buildings on campus. Approved or accredited by New York State Association of Independent Schools. Member of National Association of Independent Schools. Endowment: $3 million. Total enrollment: 365. Upper school average class size: 10. Upper school faculty-student ratio: 1:6. There are 165 required school days per year for Upper School students. Upper School students typically attend 5 days per week. The average school day consists of 8 hours and 50 minutes.

Upper School Student Profile Grade 9: 53 students (36 boys, 17 girls); Grade 10: 79 students (46 boys, 33 girls); Grade 11: 70 students (41 boys, 29 girls); Grade 12: 72 students (38 boys, 34 girls). 10% of students are boarding students. 75% are state residents. 3 states are represented in upper school student body. 7% are international students. International students from China, France, Samoa, and Taiwan.

Faculty School total: 64. In upper school: 28 men, 24 women; 31 have advanced degrees; 24 reside on campus.

Subjects Offered 3-dimensional design, algebra, American history, American literature, art, art history, biology, calculus, ceramics, chemistry, composition-AP, computer programming-AP, creative writing, drama, English, English literature, European history, expository writing, fine arts, general science, geology, geometry, government/civics, grammar, history, Japanese, Latin, mathematics, music, photography, physics, religion, science, social studies, Spanish, theater, trigonometry, world history, writing.

Graduation Requirements Arts and fine arts (art, music, dance, drama), computer literacy, English, foreign language, mathematics, science, social sciences, social studies (includes history).

Special Academic Programs 10 Advanced Placement exams for which test preparation is offered; honors section; independent study.

College Admission Counseling 68 students graduated in 2016; all went to college, including Barnard College; Bentley University; Cornell University; Quinnipiac University; University of Connecticut; Villanova University.

Student Life Upper grades have specified standards of dress, student council. Discipline rests primarily with faculty.

Summer Programs Remediation, advancement programs offered; session focuses on online academic course; held both on and off campus; held at via distance learning; accepts boys and girls; open to students from other schools. 2017 schedule: June 20 to August 10. Application deadline: May 1.

Tuition and Aid Day student tuition: $33,150–$36,150; 5-day tuition and room/board: $42,850–$44,150. Tuition installment plan (FACTS Tuition Payment Plan, individually arranged payment plans). Need-based scholarship grants available. In 2016–17, 26% of upper-school students received aid. Total amount of financial aid awarded in 2016–17: $2,080,000.

Admissions Traditional secondary-level entrance grade is 9. For fall 2016, 168 students applied for upper-level admission, 95 were accepted, 50 enrolled. Deadline for receipt of application materials: none. Application fee required: $50. Interview required.

Athletics Interscholastic: baseball (boys), basketball (b,g), football (b), ice hockey (b), lacrosse (b,g), rugby (b), soccer (b,g), softball (g), tennis (b,g), volleyball (g); coed interscholastic: cross-country running, weight lifting, yoga; coed intramural: aerobics, dance, figure skating, fitness, fitness walking, Frisbee, golf, modern dance, strength & conditioning, tai chi, yoga. 20 coaches, 1 athletic trainer.

Computers Computers are regularly used in English, foreign language, history, mathematics, science classes. Computer network features include on-campus library services, online commercial services, Internet access. The school has a published electronic and media policy.

Contact Mr. William Porter, Director of Admissions. 914-232-3161 Ext. 113. Fax: 914-232-6034. E-mail: wporter@harveyschool.org. Website: www.harveyschool.org

HATHAWAY BROWN SCHOOL

19600 North Park Boulevard
Shaker Heights, Ohio 44122

Head of School: H. William Christ

General Information Coeducational day (boys' only in lower grades) college-preparatory, arts, business, and technology school. Boys grade PS, girls grades PS–12. Founded: 1876. Setting: suburban. Nearest major city is Cleveland. 16-acre campus. 1 building on campus. Approved or accredited by Independent Schools Association of the Central States, Ohio Association of Independent Schools, and Ohio Department of Education. Member of National Association of Independent Schools. Endowment: $53.5 million. Total enrollment: 848. Upper school average class size: 18. Upper school faculty-student ratio: 1:8. There are 186 required school days per year for Upper School students. Upper School students typically attend 5 days per week. The average school day consists of 7 hours and 17 minutes.

Upper School Student Profile Grade 9: 96 students (96 girls); Grade 10: 108 students (108 girls); Grade 11: 96 students (96 girls); Grade 12: 85 students (85 girls).

Faculty School total: 143. In upper school: 19 men, 48 women; 37 have advanced degrees.

Subjects Offered Advanced Placement courses, algebra, American history, American literature, anatomy, art, art history, biology, biology-AP, calculus, ceramics, chemistry, chemistry-AP, communications, community service, computer math, computer programming, computer science, creative writing, dance, drama, economics, engineering, English, English literature, environmental science, ethics, European history, expository writing, fine arts, French, geography, geometry, government/civics, graphic design, health, history, international relations, journalism, Latin, mathematics, microbiology, music, outdoor education, photography, physical education, physics, physics-AP, physiology, psychology, research seminar, science, social studies, Spanish,

statistics, statistics-AP, theater, trigonometry, U.S. history, U.S. history-AP, woodworking, world history, writing.

Graduation Requirements Arts and fine arts (art, music, dance, drama), computer applications, computer science, English, foreign language, history, mathematics, physical education (includes health), science, senior speech, senior project.

Special Academic Programs 16 Advanced Placement exams for which test preparation is offered; honors section; independent study; term-away projects; study at local college for college credit; study abroad; academic accommodation for the gifted and the musically talented; remedial reading and/or remedial writing; remedial math; programs in general development for dyslexic students; special instructional classes for deaf students.

College Admission Counseling 85 students graduated in 2015; all went to college, including Bates College; Brown University; Columbia College; Miami University; Yale University. Mean SAT critical reading: 633, mean SAT math: 631, mean SAT writing: 653, mean combined SAT: 1917.

Student Life Upper grades have specified standards of dress, student council, honor system. Discipline rests equally with students and faculty.

Tuition and Aid Day student tuition: $26,100–$27,400. Tuition installment plan (Academic Management Services Plan, Key Tuition Payment Plan). Merit scholarship grants, need-based scholarship grants available. In 2015–16, 30% of upper-school students received aid. Total amount of financial aid awarded in 2015–16: $3,100,000.

Admissions Traditional secondary-level entrance grade is 9. For fall 2015, 150 students applied for upper-level admission, 40 enrolled. ISEE required. Deadline for receipt of application materials: none. Application fee required: $35. Interview required.

Athletics Interscholastic: basketball, cross-country running, diving, field hockey, golf, indoor track & field, lacrosse, soccer, softball, swimming and diving, tennis, track and field, volleyball; intramural: modern dance, outdoor adventure, physical fitness, physical training, ropes courses, strength & conditioning. 6 PE instructors, 22 coaches, 1 athletic trainer.

Computers Computers are regularly used in all academic classes. Computer network features include on-campus library services, online commercial services, Internet access, wireless campus network, Internet filtering or blocking technology. Student e-mail accounts and computer access in designated common areas are available to students. The school has a published electronic and media policy.

Contact Tina Reifsnyder, Admission Coordinator. 216-320-8767. Fax: 216-371-1501. E-mail: treifsnyder@hb.edu. Website: www.hb.edu

THE HAVERFORD SCHOOL

450 Lancaster Avenue
Haverford, Pennsylvania 19041

Head of School: Dr. John A. Nagl

General Information Boys' day college-preparatory school. Grades PK–12. Founded: 1884. Setting: suburban. Nearest major city is Philadelphia. 30-acre campus. 7 buildings on campus. Approved or accredited by Middle States Association of Colleges and Schools, Pennsylvania Association of Independent Schools, and Pennsylvania Department of Education. Member of National Association of Independent Schools and Secondary School Admission Test Board. Endowment: $69.5 million. Total enrollment: 977. Upper school average class size: 16. Upper school faculty-student ratio: 1:8. There are 169 required school days per year for Upper School students. Upper School students typically attend 5 days per week. The average school day consists of 6 hours and 43 minutes.

Upper School Student Profile Grade 6: 70 students (70 boys); Grade 7: 73 students (73 boys); Grade 8: 89 students (89 boys); Grade 9: 116 students (116 boys); Grade 10: 107 students (107 boys); Grade 11: 104 students (104 boys); Grade 12: 108 students (108 boys).

Faculty School total: 117. In upper school: 34 men, 19 women; 34 have advanced degrees.

Subjects Offered 3-dimensional art, 3-dimensional design, acting, advanced biology, advanced chemistry, advanced math, African drumming, algebra, all academic, Ancient Greek, ancient world history, art, biology, calculus, chemistry, Chinese, clayworking, engineering, geometry, Latin, modern world history, physical education, physics, Spanish, theater, U.S. history, video and animation, visual and performing arts, world history.

Graduation Requirements Arts and fine arts (art, music, dance, drama), English, foreign language, mathematics, physical education (includes health), science, social studies (includes history).

Special Academic Programs Honors section; independent study; term-away projects; study abroad; academic accommodation for the gifted; remedial reading and/or remedial writing; remedial math.

College Admission Counseling 103 students graduated in 2016; all went to college, including Boston College; Bucknell University; Gettysburg College; University of Pennsylvania; University of Virginia; Villanova University. Median SAT critical reading: 640, median SAT math: 660, median SAT writing: 650, median combined SAT: 1950, median composite ACT: 29. 71% scored over 600 on SAT critical reading, 72% scored over 600 on SAT math, 62% scored over 600 on SAT writing, 68% scored over 1800 on combined SAT, 76% scored over 26 on composite ACT.

Student Life Upper grades have uniform requirement, student council, honor system. Discipline rests equally with students and faculty.

Tuition and Aid Day student tuition: $37,500. Tuition installment plan (Insured Tuition Payment Plan, monthly payment plans, individually arranged payment plans). Need-based scholarship grants available. In 2016–17, 32% of upper-school students received aid. Total amount of financial aid awarded in 2016–17: $3,438,700.

Admissions Traditional secondary-level entrance grade is 9. For fall 2016, 156 students applied for upper-level admission, 75 were accepted, 45 enrolled. ISEE, SSAT or Wechsler Intelligence Scale for Children required. Deadline for receipt of application materials: none. Application fee required: $40. Interview recommended.

Athletics Interscholastic: aquatics, baseball, basketball, crew, cross-country running, football, golf, ice hockey, indoor track, lacrosse, rowing, soccer, squash, swimming and diving, tennis, track and field, ultimate Frisbee, water polo, winter (indoor) track, wrestling; intramural: fitness, physical fitness, physical training, strength & conditioning, weight training. 1 PE instructor, 80 coaches, 3 athletic trainers.

Computers Computers are regularly used in art, English, history, mathematics, music, science classes. Computer network features include on-campus library services, online commercial services, Internet access, wireless campus network, Internet filtering or blocking technology. Campus intranet, student e-mail accounts, and computer access in designated common areas are available to students. Students grades are available online. The school has a published electronic and media policy.

Contact Mr. Brian McBride, Associate Headmaster for External Affairs and Enrollment Management. 610-642-3020 Ext. 1435. Fax: 610-642-8724. E-mail: bmcbride@haverford.org. Website: www.haverford.org

HAWAII BAPTIST ACADEMY

2429 Pali Highway
Honolulu, Hawaii 96817

Head of School: Mr. Ronald Shiira

General Information Coeducational day college-preparatory and Christian education school, affiliated with Southern Baptist Convention. Grades K–12. Founded: 1949. Setting: urban. 13-acre campus. 5 buildings on campus. Approved or accredited by Association of Christian Schools International and Western Association of Schools and Colleges. Member of National Association of Independent Schools and Secondary School Admission Test Board. Endowment: $5.1 million. Total enrollment: 1,060. Upper school average class size: 18. Upper school faculty-student ratio: 1:10. There are 176 required school days per year for Upper School students. Upper School students typically attend 5 days per week. The average school day consists of 6 hours.

Upper School Student Profile Grade 9: 114 students (52 boys, 62 girls); Grade 10: 117 students (48 boys, 69 girls); Grade 11: 113 students (56 boys, 57 girls); Grade 12: 112 students (51 boys, 61 girls). 12% of students are Southern Baptist Convention.

Faculty School total: 89. In upper school: 20 men, 25 women; 23 have advanced degrees.

Subjects Offered All academic, choir.

Graduation Requirements Algebra, ancient history, arts and fine arts (art, music, dance, drama), Bible studies, biology, communication skills, computer applications, economics, English, foreign language, mathematics, physical education (includes health), political science, social studies (includes history), U.S. history, world history, Bible.

Special Academic Programs 9 Advanced Placement exams for which test preparation is offered; independent study.

College Admission Counseling 110 students graduated in 2016; all went to college, including Creighton University; Oregon State University; University of Hawaii at Manoa; University of Portland; University of San Francisco; University of Washington. Mean SAT critical reading: 619, mean SAT math: 642, mean composite ACT: 26.

Student Life Upper grades have uniform requirement, student council. Discipline rests primarily with faculty. Attendance at religious services is required.

Summer Programs Remediation, enrichment, sports, art/fine arts, computer instruction programs offered; session focuses on academic/social preparation for entrance to regular school, instruction/remediation, and personal growth; held both on and off campus; accepts boys and girls; open to students from other schools. 320 students usually enrolled. 2017 schedule: June 15 to July 11. Application deadline: April 28.

Tuition and Aid Day student tuition: $15,800. Guaranteed tuition plan. Tuition installment plan (Insured Tuition Payment Plan, FACTS Tuition Payment Plan). Need-based scholarship grants available. In 2016–17, 21% of upper-school students received aid. Total amount of financial aid awarded in 2016–17: $476,525.

Admissions Traditional secondary-level entrance grade is 9. For fall 2016, 50 students applied for upper-level admission, 48 were accepted, 27 enrolled. Achievement tests and SSAT required. Deadline for receipt of application materials: December 31. Application fee required: $75. On-campus interview required.

Athletics Interscholastic: aquatics (boys, girls), baseball (b), basketball (b,g), bowling (b,g), canoeing/kayaking (b,g), cheering (g), cross-country running (b,g), diving (b,g), football (b), golf (b,g), judo (b,g), kayaking (b,g), riflery (b,g), soccer (b,g), softball (g), swimming and diving (b,g), tennis (b,g), track and field (b,g), volleyball (b,g), water polo (b,g), wrestling (b,g); coed interscholastic: canoeing/kayaking, cheering, golf, sailing. 3 PE instructors, 30 coaches, 2 athletic trainers.

Computers Computers are regularly used in all academic, college planning, digital applications, graphic design, journalism, keyboarding, media production, newspaper, video film production, word processing, yearbook classes. Computer network features include on-campus library services, online commercial services, Internet access, wireless campus network, Internet filtering or blocking technology, one-to-one iPads. Campus intranet, student e-mail accounts, and computer access in designated common areas are available to students. Students grades are available online. The school has a published electronic and media policy.

Contact Mrs. Katherine Lee, Director of Admissions. 808-595-7585. Fax: 808-564-0332. E-mail: klee@hba.net. Website: www.hba.net

HAWAI`I PREPARATORY ACADEMY

65-1692 Kohala Mountain Road
Kamuela, Hawaii 96743-8476

Head of School: Mr. Robert McKendry Jr.

General Information Coeducational boarding and day college-preparatory school. Boarding grades 9–PG, day grades K–12. Founded: 1949. Setting: small town. Nearest major city is Kona. Students are housed in coed dormitories and single-sex dormitories. 220-acre campus. 22 buildings on campus. Approved or accredited by The Association of Boarding Schools and Western Association of Schools and Colleges. Member of National Association of Independent Schools and Secondary School Admission Test Board. Endowment: $43.1 million. Total enrollment: 628. Upper school average class size: 15. Upper school faculty-student ratio: 1:12. There are 163 required school days per year for Upper School students. Upper School students typically attend 5 days per week. The average school day consists of 8 hours.

Upper School Student Profile Grade 9: 77 students (33 boys, 44 girls); Grade 10: 93 students (53 boys, 40 girls); Grade 11: 122 students (60 boys, 62 girls); Grade 12: 110 students (57 boys, 53 girls); Postgraduate: 1 student (1 boy). 50% of students are boarding students. 60% are state residents. 17 states are represented in upper school student body. 23% are international students. International students from Christmas Island, Ghana, Jamaica, Jersey, Kenya, and Republic of Moldova; 18 other countries represented in student body.

Faculty School total: 66. In upper school: 21 men, 20 women; 32 have advanced degrees; 22 reside on campus.

Subjects Offered 3-dimensional art, advanced computer applications, Advanced Placement courses, algebra, American literature, art history-AP, astronomy, band, biology, biology-AP, calculus, calculus-AP, ceramics, chemistry, chemistry-AP, choir, comparative government and politics-AP, composition-AP, computer literacy, computer programming, creative writing, digital photography, drama, drama performance, drawing, driver education, economics, English, environmental science, environmental science-AP, ethnic studies, film, fine arts, forensics, geology, geometry, Hawaiian history, Hawaiian language, honors world history, human geography - AP, instrumental music, Japanese, literary genres, literature-AP, Mandarin, marine biology, marine science, math applications, music theater, orchestra, photography, physical education, physical science, physics, physics-AP, pre-calculus, probability and statistics, psychology, psychology-AP, robotics, science research, Spanish, statistics, statistics-AP, strings, studio art, theater arts, theater production, trigonometry, U.S. history, U.S. history-AP, video film production, visual arts, vocal music, Web site design, woodworking, world cultures, world history, world literature, yearbook.

Graduation Requirements Arts and fine arts (art, music, dance, drama), electives, English, mathematics, modern languages, science, social studies (includes history), sports, technology.

Special Academic Programs 17 Advanced Placement exams for which test preparation is offered; honors section; independent study; study at local college for college credit; ESL (25 students enrolled).

College Admission Counseling 97 students graduated in 2016; all went to college, including Brandeis University; Dartmouth College; Northern Arizona University; Seattle University; Stanford University; University of Hawaii at Manoa. Median SAT critical reading: 530, median SAT math: 560, median SAT writing: 540, median combined SAT: 1620, median composite ACT: 24. 36% scored over 600 on SAT critical reading, 39% scored over 600 on SAT math, 27% scored over 600 on SAT writing, 29% scored over 1800 on combined SAT, 35% scored over 26 on composite ACT.

Student Life Upper grades have specified standards of dress, student council, honor system. Discipline rests equally with students and faculty.

Summer Programs Enrichment, ESL, sports, art/fine arts, computer instruction programs offered; session focuses on academic enrichment; held on campus; accepts boys and girls; open to students from other schools. 100 students usually enrolled. 2017 schedule: June 26 to July 21. Application deadline: April 15.

Tuition and Aid Day student tuition: $24,800; 5-day tuition and room/board: $44,300; 7-day tuition and room/board: $49,000. Tuition installment plan (monthly payment plans, prepayment plan, 2-payment plan, 4-payment plan). Merit scholarship grants, need-based scholarship grants, Hawaii residential boarding grants, merit-based scholarship (75% demonstrated need to apply) available. In 2016–17, 50% of upper-school students received aid; total upper-school merit-scholarship money awarded: $600,000. Total amount of financial aid awarded in 2016–17: $3,651,310.

Admissions Traditional secondary-level entrance grade is 9. For fall 2016, 207 students applied for upper-level admission, 148 were accepted, 92 enrolled. Any standardized test, ISEE or SSAT required. Deadline for receipt of application materials: February 8. Application fee required: $50. Interview required.

Athletics Interscholastic: baseball (boys), basketball (b,g), cross-country running (b,g), ocean paddling (b,g), soccer (b,g), softball (g), swimming and diving (b,g), tennis (b,g), track and field (b,g), volleyball (b,g), water polo (g), wrestling (b,g); intramural: baseball (b); coed interscholastic: canoeing/kayaking, cheering, diving, dressage, football, golf, horseback riding; coed intramural: archery, badminton, basketball, dance, dressage, golf, hockey, horseback riding, lacrosse, life saving, outdoor adventure, outdoor recreation, polo, rugby, scuba diving, soccer, strength & conditioning, surfing, swimming and diving, tennis, ultimate Frisbee, volleyball, weight lifting, yoga. 1 PE instructor, 5 coaches, 1 athletic trainer.

Computers Computers are regularly used in computer applications, digital applications, science, video film production, yearbook classes. Computer network features include on-campus library services, online commercial services, Internet access, wireless campus network, Internet filtering or blocking technology. Campus intranet, student e-mail accounts, and computer access in designated common areas are available to students. Students grades are available online. The school has a published electronic and media policy.

Contact Mr. Joshua D. Clark, Director of Admission. 808-881-4074. Fax: 808-881-4003. E-mail: admissions@hpa.edu. Website: www.hpa.edu/

HAWKEN SCHOOL

12465 County Line Road
PO Box 8002
Gates Mills, Ohio 44040-8002

Head of School: D. Scott Looney

General Information Coeducational day college-preparatory, arts, business, STEMM (Science, Technology, Engineering, Math, Medicine), and experiential and service learning school. Grades PS–12. Founded: 1915. Setting: suburban. Nearest major city is Cleveland. 325-acre campus. 5 buildings on campus. Approved or accredited by Ohio Association of Independent Schools and Ohio Department of Education. Member of National Association of Independent Schools. Endowment: $54 million. Total enrollment: 1,011. Upper school average class size: 15. Upper school faculty-student ratio: 1:9. There are 176 required school days per year for Upper School students. Upper School students typically attend 5 days per week. The average school day consists of 5 hours and 54 minutes.

Upper School Student Profile Grade 9: 112 students (68 boys, 44 girls); Grade 10: 111 students (57 boys, 54 girls); Grade 11: 118 students (61 boys, 57 girls); Grade 12: 92 students (50 boys, 42 girls).

Faculty School total: 143. In upper school: 29 men, 31 women; 43 have advanced degrees.

Subjects Offered 20th century world history, accounting, acting, advanced chemistry, advanced math, Advanced Placement courses, advanced studio art-AP, African-American literature, algebra, American Civil War, American history, American history-AP, American literature, animal science, art, art appreciation, art history, band, Bible as literature, biology, business, calculus, calculus-AP, ceramics, chemistry, chemistry-AP, Chinese, choir, choral music, chorus, Civil War, classical Greek literature, creative dance, creative writing, dance, dance performance, drama, drawing, ecology, economics, economics and history, engineering, English, English literature, English-AP, entrepreneurship, environmental science-AP, ethics, European history, experiential education, field ecology, film, film studies, fine arts, first aid, French, French studies, French-AP, geography, geometry, government/civics, graphic design, health, history, Holocaust and other genocides, humanities, improvisation, Latin, Latin-AP, mathematics, mathematics-AP, music, music theory, outdoor education, painting, performing arts, philosophy, photography, physical education, physics, physics-AP, physiology, poetry, probability and statistics, science, science research, sculpture, senior project, service learning/internship, social sciences, social studies, Spanish, Spanish literature-AP, speech, statistics-AP, strings, studio art-AP, swimming, theater, theater arts, theater design and production, theater production, trigonometry, U.S. history, U.S. history-AP, world history, world literature, World War I, World War II, writing.

Graduation Requirements Arts and fine arts (art, music, dance, drama), computer science, English, foreign language, history, mathematics, physical education (includes health), science. Community service is required.

Special Academic Programs 16 Advanced Placement exams for which test preparation is offered; honors section; accelerated programs; independent study; term-away projects; study abroad.

College Admission Counseling 90 students graduated in 2016; all went to college, including Case Western Reserve University; Miami University; The College of Wooster; The George Washington University; The Ohio State University; Washington University in St. Louis. Median SAT critical reading: 635, median SAT math: 641, median SAT writing: 647, median combined SAT: 1913, median composite ACT: 28. 58% scored over 600 on SAT critical reading, 69% scored over 600 on SAT math, 61% scored over 600 on SAT writing, 64% scored over 1800 on combined SAT, 70% scored over 26 on composite ACT.

Student Life Upper grades have specified standards of dress, student council, honor system. Discipline rests equally with students and faculty.

Summer Programs Remediation, enrichment, advancement, computer instruction programs offered; session focuses on credit, review, preview, and enrichment in English, math, computer studies, and health; held on campus; accepts boys and girls; open to students from other schools. 133 students usually enrolled. 2017 schedule: June 5 to August 18. Application deadline: May 15.

Tuition and Aid Day student tuition: $23,115–$25,570. Tuition installment plan (Key Tuition Payment Plan, individually arranged payment plans, installment payment plan (60 percent by 8/15 and 40 percent by 1/15), AchieverLoans (Key Education Resources)). Merit scholarship grants, need-based scholarship grants, need-based loans available. In 2016–17, 37% of upper-school students received aid; total upper-school merit-scholarship money awarded: $162,000. Total amount of financial aid awarded in 2016–17: $5,102,962.

Admissions Traditional secondary-level entrance grade is 9. For fall 2016, 128 students applied for upper-level admission, 91 were accepted, 60 enrolled. ISEE required. Deadline for receipt of application materials: December 15. Application fee required: $50. On-campus interview required.

Athletics Interscholastic: baseball (boys), basketball (b,g), cross-country running (b,g), diving (b,g), field hockey (g), football (b), golf (b,g), lacrosse (b,g), soccer (b,g), softball (g), swimming and diving (b,g), tennis (b,g), track and field (b,g), wrestling (b); intramural: basketball (b); coed intramural: dance, life saving, outdoor skills. 3 PE instructors, 33 coaches, 1 athletic trainer.

Computers Computers are regularly used in all classes. Computer network features include on-campus library services, Internet access, wireless campus network, Internet filtering or blocking technology. Campus intranet and student e-mail accounts are available to students. Students grades are available online. The school has a published electronic and media policy.

Contact Heather Willis Daly, Assistant Head of School for Enrollment Management. 440-423-2955. Fax: 440-423-2994. E-mail: hdaly@hawken.edu. Website: www.hawken.edu/

HAWTHORNE CHRISTIAN ACADEMY

2000 Route 208
Hawthorne, New Jersey 07506

Head of School: Mr. David Seidman

General Information Coeducational day college-preparatory, religious studies, music, and missions school, affiliated with Christian faith. Grades PS–12. Distance learning grades 9–12. Founded: 1981. Setting: suburban. Nearest major city is New York, NY. 22-acre campus. 4 buildings on campus. Approved or accredited by Association of Christian Schools International, Middle States Association of Colleges and Schools, and New Jersey Department of Education. Endowment: $500,000. Total enrollment: 482. Upper school average class size: 20. Upper school faculty-student ratio: 1:7. There are 180 required school days per year for Upper School students. Upper School students typically attend 5 days per week. The average school day consists of 6 hours and 40 minutes.

Upper School Student Profile Grade 9: 35 students (17 boys, 18 girls); Grade 10: 32 students (21 boys, 11 girls); Grade 11: 43 students (23 boys, 20 girls); Grade 12: 27 students (19 boys, 8 girls). 100% of students are Christian faith.

Faculty School total: 47. In upper school: 10 men, 12 women; 12 have advanced degrees.

Subjects Offered 3-dimensional art, 3-dimensional design, ACT preparation, advanced math, American government, American history, American history-AP, American legal systems, American literature, anatomy, ancient history, art education, Bible studies, career/college preparation, ceramics, Christian and Hebrew scripture, Christian doctrine, Christian education, Christian scripture, Christian studies, Christian testament, Christianity, church history, communication skills, computer applications, computer science, computer science-AP, drawing, drawing and design, English-AP, foundations of civilization, freshman seminar, general math, government and politics-AP, government-AP, health and wellness, health education, history, history of music, history of the Americas, history-AP, human anatomy, language arts, law studies, Life of Christ, literature-AP, mechanics of writing, money management, New Testament, novels, nutrition, painting, physical fitness, portfolio art, probability and statistics, scripture, statistics, technical drawing, U.S. government and politics, United States government-AP, vocal music, water color painting.

Graduation Requirements Algebra, American government, Bible, biology, English literature, English literature-AP, geometry, intro to computers, physical science, pre-calculus, U.S. government, U.S. history, U.S. history-AP, Christian service hours, Apologetics and Current Issues, specified number of Academic Elective Courses.

Special Academic Programs 5 Advanced Placement exams for which test preparation is offered.

College Admission Counseling 36 students graduated in 2016; all went to college, including Bergen Community College; Caldwell University; Liberty University; New Jersey Institute of Technology. Median SAT critical reading: 580, median SAT math: 550, median SAT writing: 560, median combined SAT: 1120, median composite ACT: 23. 34% scored over 600 on SAT critical reading, 25% scored over 600 on SAT math, 31.2% scored over 600 on SAT writing, 37.5% scored over 1800 on combined SAT, 14% scored over 26 on composite ACT.

Student Life Upper grades have specified standards of dress, student council. Discipline rests primarily with faculty. Attendance at religious services is required.

Tuition and Aid Day student tuition: $12,700. Tuition installment plan (FACTS Tuition Payment Plan, monthly payment plans). Tuition reduction for siblings, merit scholarship grants, need-based scholarship grants, pastoral discounts, teacher/employee discounts available. In 2016–17, 30% of upper-school students received aid; total upper-school merit-scholarship money awarded: $26,500. Total amount of financial aid awarded in 2016–17: $175,000.

Admissions Traditional secondary-level entrance grade is 9. For fall 2016, 12 students applied for upper-level admission, 9 were accepted, 9 enrolled. Admissions testing, BASIS, Math Placement Exam or Otis-Lennon School Ability Test required. Deadline for receipt of application materials: none. Application fee required: $100. On-campus interview recommended.

Athletics Interscholastic: baseball (boys), basketball (b,g), soccer (b,g), softball (g), volleyball (g); coed interscholastic: bowling, cross-country running, independent competitive sports, track and field; coed intramural: strength & conditioning. 2 PE instructors.

Computers Computers are regularly used in all academic classes. Computer network features include on-campus library services, Internet access, wireless campus network, Internet filtering or blocking technology. Campus intranet and student e-mail accounts are available to students. Students grades are available online.

Contact Mrs. Judith De Boer, Admissions Coordinator. 973-423-3331 Ext. 261. Fax: 973-238-1718. E-mail: judith.deboer@hca.org. Website: www.hca.org/

HEBREW ACADEMY

14401 Willow Lane
Huntington Beach, California 92647

Head of School: Dr. Bryn Harari

General Information Girls' boarding and coeducational day college-preparatory, general academic, and Judaic Studies school, affiliated with Jewish faith. Boarding girls grades 9–12, day boys grades N–8, day girls grades N–12. Founded: 1969. Setting: suburban. Students are housed in coed dormitories. 11-acre campus. 11 buildings on campus. Approved or accredited by Accrediting Commission for Schools and Western Association of Schools and Colleges. Total enrollment: 257. Upper school average class size: 10. Upper school faculty-student ratio: 1:4. There are 176 required school days per year for Upper School students. Upper School students typically attend 5 days per week. The average school day consists of 7 hours and 30 minutes.

Upper School Student Profile Grade 9: 7 students (7 girls); Grade 10: 5 students (5 girls); Grade 11: 9 students (9 girls); Grade 12: 5 students (5 girls). 100% of students are Jewish.

Faculty School total: 41. In upper school: 6 men, 12 women; 2 have advanced degrees.

Subjects Offered 3-dimensional art, advanced studio art-AP, algebra, American government, American history, American literature, art history, Bible studies, biology, calculus, chemistry, community service, consumer mathematics, earth science, economics, English, English language and composition-AP, English literature, geography, geometry, government/civics, grammar, Hebrew, history, Jewish history, life science, mathematics, physical education, physics, physiology, pre-algebra, pre-calculus, psychology, religion, SAT preparation, science, senior project, social sciences, social studies, statistics-AP, theology, U.S. government, visual arts, Web site design, world cultures, world history, writing, yearbook.

Graduation Requirements Art, computer science, English, foreign language, Judaic studies, mathematics, physical education (includes health), religion (includes Bible studies and theology), science, social sciences, social studies (includes history), students are required to take both Judaic Studies and General Studies courses to graduate with dual diploma.

Special Academic Programs International Baccalaureate program; 5 Advanced Placement exams for which test preparation is offered; honors section; accelerated programs; independent study; academic accommodation for the gifted; remedial reading and/or remedial writing; remedial math; programs in general development for dyslexic students.

Student Life Upper grades have uniform requirement, student council. Discipline rests primarily with faculty. Attendance at religious services is required.

Tuition and Aid Day student tuition: $14,400–$16,600; 7-day tuition and room/board: $21,400–$21,600. Guaranteed tuition plan. Tuition installment plan (monthly payment plans, individually arranged payment plans). Tuition reduction for siblings, need-based scholarship grants available. In 2016–17, 30% of upper-school students received aid. Total amount of financial aid awarded in 2016–17: $30,000.

Admissions Traditional secondary-level entrance grade is 9. For fall 2016, 8 students applied for upper-level admission, 5 were accepted, 5 enrolled. Admissions testing and school placement exam required. Deadline for receipt of application materials: none. Application fee required: $100. On-campus interview recommended.

Athletics Interscholastic: aerobics/dance, aerobics/Nautilus, aquatics (b), archery (b), badminton, baseball (b), basketball (b), dance, jogging (b), physical fitness (b), soccer (b), softball (b), swimming and diving (b), volleyball; intramural: basketball. 2 PE instructors, 1 coach.

Computers Computers are regularly used in all academic, drawing and design, English, foreign language, science, technology classes. Computer network features include on-campus library services, online commercial services, Internet access, wireless campus network, Internet filtering or blocking technology, classroom smart boards, iPads. Campus intranet, student e-mail accounts, and computer access in

designated common areas are available to students. Students grades are available online. The school has a published electronic and media policy.

Contact Mrs. Nelli Greenspan, Enrollment Manager. 714-898-0051 Ext. 284. Fax: 714-898-0633. E-mail: nelli@hacds.org. Website: www.hebrewacademyhb.com

HEBREW ACADEMY OF THE FIVE TOWNS & ROCKAWAY

635 Central Avenue
Cedarhurst, New York 11516

Head of School: Ms. Naomi Lippman

General Information Coeducational day college-preparatory, arts, business, and religious studies school, affiliated with Jewish faith. Grades 9–12. Founded: 1978. Setting: suburban. Nearest major city is New York. 1 building on campus. Approved or accredited by Middle States Association of Colleges and Schools, The College Board, and New York Department of Education. Languages of instruction: English and Hebrew. Total enrollment: 388. Upper school average class size: 20. The average school day consists of 9 hours and 15 minutes.

Upper School Student Profile 100% of students are Jewish.

Faculty School total: 60.

Subjects Offered Advanced Placement courses, arts, English, fine arts, foreign language, Jewish studies, Judaic studies, mathematics, physical education, religion, science, social sciences, social studies.

Graduation Requirements Arts and fine arts (art, music, dance, drama), English, foreign language, Judaic studies, mathematics, physical education (includes health), religion (includes Bible studies and theology), science, social sciences, social studies (includes history), community service requirement.

Special Academic Programs 11 Advanced Placement exams for which test preparation is offered; honors section; independent study; study abroad; academic accommodation for the artistically talented.

College Admission Counseling 82 students graduated in 2015; all went to college, including Binghamton University, State University of New York; Columbia University; Cornell University; New York University; Queens College of the City University of New York; Yeshiva University. Median SAT critical reading: 590, median SAT math: 610, median SAT writing: 570. 48% scored over 600 on SAT critical reading, 56% scored over 600 on SAT math, 41% scored over 600 on SAT writing.

Student Life Upper grades have specified standards of dress, student council, honor system. Discipline rests primarily with faculty. Attendance at religious services is required.

Tuition and Aid Tuition installment plan (monthly payment plans, individually arranged payment plans). Need-based scholarship grants available.

Admissions Traditional secondary-level entrance grade is 9. Board of Jewish Education Entrance Exam required. Deadline for receipt of application materials: March 15. Application fee required. On-campus interview required.

Athletics Interscholastic: baseball (boys, girls), basketball (b,g), field hockey (b), softball (b,g), tennis (b,g), volleyball (g); coed intramural: skiing (downhill). 2 PE instructors, 8 coaches.

Computers Computers are regularly used in computer applications classes. Computer resources include on-campus library services, online commercial services, Internet access, Internet filtering or blocking technology. Student e-mail accounts are available to students. Students grades are available online. The school has a published electronic and media policy.

Contact Ms. Naomi Lippman, Principal, General Studies. 516-569-3807. Fax: 516-374-5761. Website: www.haftr.org

HEBRON ACADEMY

PO Box 309
Hebron, Maine 04238

Head of School: Mr. Dan J. Marchetti

General Information Coeducational boarding and day college-preparatory, arts, public speaking, and honors and AP Courses school. Boarding grades 9–PG, day grades 6–PG. Founded: 1804. Setting: rural. Nearest major city is Portland. Students are housed in single-sex dormitories. 1,500-acre campus. 22 buildings on campus. Approved or accredited by Independent Schools of Northern New England, New England Association of Schools and Colleges, The Association of Boarding Schools, and Maine Department of Education. Member of National Association of Independent Schools and Secondary School Admission Test Board. Endowment: $14 million. Total enrollment: 268. Upper school average class size: 12. Upper school faculty-student ratio: 1:7. There are 175 required school days per year for Upper School students. Upper School students typically attend 5 days per week. The average school day consists of 5 hours and 45 minutes.

Upper School Student Profile Grade 9: 25 students (16 boys, 9 girls); Grade 10: 57 students (32 boys, 25 girls); Grade 11: 63 students (48 boys, 15 girls); Grade 12: 70 students (40 boys, 30 girls); Postgraduate: 19 students (18 boys, 1 girl). 75% of students are boarding students. 43% are state residents. 15 states are represented in upper school student body. 40% are international students. International students from China,

Germany, India, Japan, Mexico, and Spain; 21 other countries represented in student body.

Faculty School total: 44. In upper school: 19 men, 22 women; 16 have advanced degrees; 28 reside on campus.

Subjects Offered Algebra, anatomy and physiology, art, art-AP, biology, business studies, calculus, calculus-AP, chemistry, chemistry-AP, college counseling, composition, composition-AP, computer multimedia, computer programming, computer science, computer studies, current events, digital photography, drama, drawing, drawing and design, English, environmental science, ESL, ethics, French, functions, geology, geometry, health and wellness, history, independent study, international relations, jazz, Latin, leadership, Mandarin, music, music theory, painting, personal fitness, photography, physics, piano, portfolio art, pottery, programming, psychology, sculpture, Spanish, studio art, U.S. history, wilderness education, world history, world religions.

Graduation Requirements Algebra, art, biology, chemistry, English, foreign language, geometry, U.S. history.

Special Academic Programs Advanced Placement exam preparation; honors section; independent study; academic accommodation for the gifted, the musically talented, and the artistically talented; programs in general development for dyslexic students; ESL (35 students enrolled).

College Admission Counseling 62 students graduated in 2016; 58 went to college, including Bates College, Elmira College; Husson University; New England College; University of New Hampshire; University of Vermont. Other: 1 entered a postgraduate year, 3 had other specific plans.

Student Life Upper grades have specified standards of dress, student council, honor system. Discipline rests primarily with faculty.

Summer Programs ESL programs offered; session focuses on English immersion; held on campus; accepts boys and girls; open to students from other schools. 20 students usually enrolled. 2017 schedule: August 10 to August 30. Application deadline: May 15.

Tuition and Aid Day student tuition: $31,600; 7-day tuition and room/board: $57,200. Tuition installment plan (Insured Tuition Payment Plan, FACTS Tuition Payment Plan, monthly payment plans). Merit scholarship grants, need-based scholarship grants, prepGATE loans available. In 2016–17, 60% of upper-school students received aid; total upper-school merit-scholarship money awarded: $250,000. Total amount of financial aid awarded in 2016–17: $2,000,000.

Admissions Traditional secondary-level entrance grade is 9. For fall 2016, 323 students applied for upper-level admission, 249 were accepted, 108 enrolled. PSAT or SAT for applicants to grade 11 and 12, SSAT or TOEFL or SLEP required. Deadline for receipt of application materials: February 1. Application fee required: $50. Interview required.

Athletics Interscholastic: alpine skiing (boys, girls), baseball (b), basketball (b,g), cross-country running (b,g), field hockey (g), football (b), ice hockey (b,g), lacrosse (b,g), mountain biking (b,g), outdoor education (b,g), outdoor skills (b,g), physical fitness (b,g), running (b,g), skiing (downhill) (b,g), snowboarding (b,g), soccer (b,g), softball (b,g), tennis (b,g), track and field (b,g), wall climbing (b,g); coed interscholastic: fitness, golf; coed intramural: aerobics/dance, broomball, canoeing/kayaking, dance, fitness, Frisbee, outdoor activities, outdoor education, outdoor skills, rock climbing, roller hockey, squash, yoga.

Computers Computers are regularly used in art, ESL, graphic design, introduction to technology, mathematics, media production, research skills, science, writing, yearbook classes. Computer network features include on-campus library services, online commercial services, Internet access, wireless campus network, Internet filtering or blocking technology. Campus intranet, student e-mail accounts, and computer access in designated common areas are available to students. Students grades are available online. The school has a published electronic and media policy.

Contact Mrs. Jennifer J. Ridley, Director of Admissions. 207-966-2100 Ext. 233. Fax: 207-966-1111. E-mail: admissions@hebronacademy.org. Website: www.hebronacademy.org

THE HEIGHTS SCHOOL

10400 Seven Locks Road
Potomac, Maryland 20854

Head of School: Mr. Alvaro J. de Vicente

General Information Boys' day college-preparatory and religious studies school, affiliated with Roman Catholic Church. Grades 3–12. Founded: 1969. Setting: suburban. Nearest major city is Washington, DC. 20-acre campus. 5 buildings on campus. Approved or accredited by Association of Independent Maryland Schools, Association of Independent Schools of Greater Washington, and Maryland Department of Education. Member of National Association of Independent Schools and Secondary School Admission Test Board. Total enrollment: 538. Upper school average class size: 16. Upper school faculty-student ratio: 1:7. There are 173 required school days per year for Upper School students. Upper School students typically attend 5 days per week. The average school day consists of 6 hours and 45 minutes.

Upper School Student Profile Grade 6: 59 students (59 boys); Grade 7: 60 students (60 boys); Grade 8: 54 students (54 boys); Grade 9: 70 students (70 boys); Grade 10: 66 students (66 boys); Grade 11: 60 students (60 boys); Grade 12: 59 students (59 boys). 90% of students are Roman Catholic.

Faculty School total: 64. In upper school: 64 men; 35 have advanced degrees.

Subjects Offered Algebra, American history, American literature, American literature-AP, Ancient Greek, art history-AP, bioethics, biology, biology-AP, calculus, calculus-AP, chemistry, chemistry-AP, chorus, computer programming, computer science, drama, economics, economics-AP, English, English literature, ethics, European history, European history-AP, geology, geometry, government-AP, history, Latin, Latin-AP, macro/microeconomics-AP, macroeconomics-AP, mathematics, medieval history, music, philosophy, physical education, physics, physics-AP, post-calculus, religion, science, Spanish, Spanish language-AP, Spanish literature-AP, statistics-AP, studio art-AP, trigonometry, world literature, World War II, writing.

Graduation Requirements Athletics, electives, English, foreign language, history, mathematics, religion (includes Bible studies and theology), science.

Special Academic Programs Advanced Placement exam preparation; independent study; academic accommodation for the gifted, the musically talented, and the artistically talented.

College Admission Counseling 59 students graduated in 2015; 54 went to college, including The Catholic University of America; University of Dallas; University of Maryland, College Park; University of Notre Dame; University of Virginia; Virginia Polytechnic Institute and State University. Other: 1 went to work, 3 had other specific plans.

Student Life Upper grades have specified standards of dress, student council. Discipline rests primarily with faculty.

Tuition and Aid Tuition installment plan (FACTS Tuition Payment Plan, monthly payment plans). Need-based scholarship grants available. In 2015–16, 45% of upper-school students received aid. Total amount of financial aid awarded in 2015–16: $1,000,000.

Admissions Traditional secondary-level entrance grade is 9. For fall 2015, 89 students applied for upper-level admission, 46 were accepted, 25 enrolled. High School Placement Test or SSAT required. Deadline for receipt of application materials: January 25. Application fee required: $50. On-campus interview required.

Athletics Interscholastic: aquatics, baseball, basketball, cross-country running, diving, golf, lacrosse, rugby, soccer, squash, swimming and diving, tennis, track and field, wrestling; intramural: archery, basketball, cross-country running, rock climbing, skateboarding. 2 PE instructors, 1 athletic trainer.

Computers Computers are regularly used in computer applications, journalism, library skills, newspaper, programming, yearbook classes. Computer network features include on-campus library services, online commercial services, Internet access, wireless campus network, Internet filtering or blocking technology. Computer access in designated common areas is available to students.

Contact Mr. George Che Martin, Admissions Associate. 301-765-2093. Fax: 301-365-4303. E-mail: gmartin@heights.edu. Website: www.heights.edu

HERITAGE ACADEMY

11 New Orleans Road
Hilton Head Island, South Carolina 29928

Head of School: Gloria Sprouse

General Information Coeducational boarding and day college-preparatory school. Grades 5–PG. Founded: 1993. Setting: small town. Nearest major city is Savannah, GA. Students are housed in single-sex condos. 3-acre campus. 1 building on campus. Approved or accredited by South Carolina Independent School Association, Southern Association of Colleges and Schools, and South Carolina Department of Education. Total enrollment: 116. Upper school average class size: 9. Upper school faculty-student ratio: 1:9. There are 175 required school days per year for Upper School students. Upper School students typically attend 5 days per week. The average school day consists of 4 hours and 30 minutes.

Upper School Student Profile Grade 6: 5 students (4 boys, 1 girl); Grade 7: 3 students (2 boys, 1 girl); Grade 8: 5 students (4 boys, 1 girl); Grade 9: 15 students (7 boys, 8 girls); Grade 10: 22 students (17 boys, 5 girls); Grade 11: 32 students (25 boys, 7 girls); Grade 12: 29 students (18 boys, 11 girls); Postgraduate: 1 student (1 boy). 59% of students are boarding students. 32% are state residents. 18 states are represented in upper school student body. 47% are international students. International students from Brazil, China, India, Japan, Mexico, and Thailand; 19 other countries represented in student body.

Faculty School total: 19. In upper school: 3 men, 13 women; 1 resides on campus.

Special Academic Programs Advanced Placement exam preparation; honors section; academic accommodation for the gifted; ESL (15 students enrolled).

College Admission Counseling 36 students graduated in 2015; 35 went to college, including Arizona State University at the Tempe campus; Indiana University Bloomington; The University of North Carolina at Chapel Hill; University of South Carolina; University of Washington; University of Wisconsin–Madison. Other: 1 entered a postgraduate year.

Student Life Upper grades have specified standards of dress, student council, honor system. Discipline rests primarily with faculty.

Tuition and Aid Day student tuition: $16,600; 7-day tuition and room/board: $35,900. Tuition installment plan (individually arranged payment plans). Tuition reduction for siblings, need-based scholarship grants available.

Admissions Deadline for receipt of application materials: none. Application fee required: $195. Interview recommended.

Athletics Interscholastic: golf (boys, girls).

Computers Computers are regularly used in all classes. Computer resources include Internet access, wireless campus network. Computer access in designated common areas is available to students. Students grades are available online.

Contact Tina Sprouse, Director of Admissions. 843-842-8600 Ext. 1. Fax: 843-842-9620. E-mail: tina.sprouse@heritagehhi.com. Website: www.heritagehhi.com

HERITAGE HALL

1800 Northwest 122nd Street
Oklahoma City, Oklahoma 73120-9524

Head of School: Guy A. Bramble

General Information Coeducational day college-preparatory, arts, and technology school. Grades PS–12. Founded: 1969. Setting: suburban. 97-acre campus. 3 buildings on campus. Approved or accredited by Independent Schools Association of the Southwest and Oklahoma Department of Education. Member of National Association of Independent Schools and Secondary School Admission Test Board. Endowment: $1.4 million. Total enrollment: 924. Upper school average class size: 16. Upper school faculty-student ratio: 1:16. There are 180 required school days per year for Upper School students. Upper School students typically attend 5 days per week. The average school day consists of 7 hours.

Faculty School total: 127. In upper school: 13 men, 30 women; 27 have advanced degrees.

Subjects Offered Advanced chemistry, algebra, American history, American literature, art, art history, biology, calculus, ceramics, chemistry, community service, computer science, debate, drama, drawing, earth science, economics, English, English language and composition-AP, English literature, entrepreneurship, environmental science, ethics, European history, European history-AP, film, film and literature, foreign language, French, French language-AP, French-AP, general science, geography, geometry, government-AP, government/civics, grammar, history, history-AP, honors algebra, honors U.S. history, honors world history, human anatomy, independent study, journalism, Latin, leadership and service, literature and composition-AP, Mandarin, mathematics, minority studies, modern European history-AP, music, music theory, musical productions, newspaper, participation in sports, personal finance, photography, physical education, physics, physics-AP, play production, poetry, pre-calculus, psychology, psychology-AP, science, social studies, Spanish, Spanish-AP, speech, stagecraft, technical writing, technological applications, trigonometry, U.S. history, visual and performing arts, Western civilization, world history, world history-AP, world literature, writing, yearbook.

Graduation Requirements Arts and fine arts (art, music, dance, drama), athletics, computer education, computer literacy, English, foreign language, mathematics, physical education (includes health), science, social studies (includes history), speech, 32 hours of documented community service each year in grades 9 through 12.

Special Academic Programs Advanced Placement exam preparation; honors section; independent study; academic accommodation for the gifted, the musically talented, and the artistically talented; programs in English, mathematics, general development for dyslexic students.

College Admission Counseling 92 students graduated in 2016; all went to college, including Oklahoma State University; Southern Methodist University; Texas Christian University; University of Oklahoma; University of Oklahoma. Mean SAT critical reading: 649, mean SAT math: 634, mean SAT writing: 627, mean composite ACT: 26.

Student Life Upper grades have specified standards of dress, student council, honor system. Discipline rests equally with students and faculty.

Summer Programs Remediation, enrichment, sports, art/fine arts, computer instruction programs offered; session focuses on arts, athletics, and academics; held on campus; accepts boys and girls; open to students from other schools. 416 students usually enrolled. 2017 schedule: June 4 to July 27.

Tuition and Aid Day student tuition: $14,120–$18,860. Tuition installment plan (Insured Tuition Payment Plan, monthly payment plans). Merit scholarship grants, need-based scholarship grants, need-based loans available. In 2016–17, 22% of upper-school students received aid. Total amount of financial aid awarded in 2016–17: $600,000.

Admissions Traditional secondary-level entrance grade is 9. For fall 2016, 55 students applied for upper-level admission, 32 were accepted, 24 enrolled. ERB CTP (level F), ERB CTP IV, essay, Math Placement Exam, WISC-III and Woodcock-Johnson and writing sample required. Deadline for receipt of application materials: none. Application fee required: $60.

Athletics Interscholastic: baseball (boys), basketball (b,g), cheering (g), cross-country running (b,g), field hockey (g), fitness (b,g), football (b), golf (b,g), physical fitness (b,g), soccer (b,g), softball (g), strength & conditioning (b,g), swimming and diving (b,g), tennis (b,g), track and field (b,g), volleyball (g), weight training (b,g), wrestling (b); intramural: Frisbee (b); coed intramural: bowling, rowing. 6 PE instructors, 40 coaches, 1 athletic trainer.

Computers Computers are regularly used in art, college planning, computer applications, desktop publishing, English, ESL, foreign language, library, mathematics, multimedia, newspaper, programming, publishing, SAT preparation, science, speech, Web site design, word processing, writing, yearbook classes. Computer network features include on-campus library services, online commercial services, Internet access, wireless campus network, Internet filtering or blocking technology, homework

assignments and test schedules available online. Campus intranet and computer access in designated common areas are available to students. Students grades are available online. The school has a published electronic and media policy.

Contact Genifer Ring, Director of Advancement. 405-749-3009. Fax: 405-751-7372. E-mail: gring@heritagehall.com. Website: www.heritagehall.com

THE HEWITT SCHOOL

45 East 75th Street
New York, New York 10021

Head of School: Ms. Tara Christie Kinsey

General Information Girls' day college-preparatory school. Grades K–12. Founded: 1920. Setting: urban. 1 building on campus. Approved or accredited by National Independent Private Schools Association, New York State Association of Independent Schools, and New York Department of Education. Member of National Association of Independent Schools and Secondary School Admission Test Board. Total enrollment: 517. Upper school average class size: 15. Upper school faculty-student ratio: 1:7. There are 158 required school days per year for Upper School students. Upper School students typically attend 5 days per week. The average school day consists of 7 hours.

Upper School Student Profile Grade 9: 38 students (38 girls); Grade 10: 31 students (31 girls); Grade 11: 39 students (39 girls); Grade 12: 31 students (31 girls).

Faculty School total: 88. In upper school: 12 men, 28 women; 24 have advanced degrees.

Subjects Offered Algebra, American history, American literature, anatomy and physiology, art, biology, calculus, chemistry, computers, drama, earth science, English, English literature, European history, fine arts, French, genetics, geometry, history, Latin, mathematics, music, photography, physical education, physics, pre-calculus, science, Spanish, world history.

Graduation Requirements Art, creative arts, English, foreign language, health and wellness, history, Latin, mathematics, physical education (includes health), science, social justice, technology, world history.

Special Academic Programs Advanced Placement exam preparation; honors section; independent study; term-away projects; study abroad.

College Admission Counseling 22 students graduated in 2016; all went to college, including Barnard College; Cornell University; New York University; Syracuse University; University of Michigan; University of Pennsylvania.

Student Life Upper grades have uniform requirement, student council, honor system. Discipline rests primarily with faculty.

Tuition and Aid Day student tuition: $46,700. Tuition installment plan (Insured Tuition Payment Plan, Key Tuition Payment Plan, monthly payment plans, individually arranged payment plans). Need-based scholarship grants available. In 2016–17, 22% of upper-school students received aid. Total amount of financial aid awarded in 2016–17: $3,241,816.

Admissions Traditional secondary-level entrance grade is 9. For fall 2016, 71 students applied for upper-level admission, 17 were accepted, 9 enrolled. ERB, ISEE or SSAT or WISC III required. Deadline for receipt of application materials: December 1. Application fee required: $75. On-campus interview recommended.

Athletics Interscholastic: badminton, basketball, cross-country running, soccer, squash, swimming and diving, tennis, track and field, volleyball; intramural: badminton, basketball, crew, cross-country running, fitness, independent competitive sports, lacrosse, soccer, strength & conditioning, swimming and diving, tennis, track and field, volleyball, weight training. 4 PE instructors.

Computers Computers are regularly used in all academic, architecture, art, English, foreign language, history, humanities, mathematics, music, science classes. Computer network features include on-campus library services, online commercial services, Internet access, wireless campus network, Internet filtering or blocking technology. Campus intranet, student e-mail accounts, and computer access in designated common areas are available to students. The school has a published electronic and media policy.

Contact Ms. Amy Jablonski, Director of Admissions. 212-994-2599. Fax: 212-472-7531. E-mail: AJablonski@hewittschool.org. Website: www.hewittschool.org

HIGHROAD ACADEMY

46641 Chilliwack Central Road
Chilliwack, British Columbia V2P 1K3, Canada

Head of School: Mr. Stuart Morris

General Information Coeducational day college-preparatory school. Grades K–12. Founded: 1978. Setting: small town. Nearest major city is Vancouver, Canada. 45-acre campus. 1 building on campus. Approved or accredited by Christian Schools International and British Columbia Department of Education. Language of instruction: English. Total enrollment: 427. Upper school average class size: 25. Upper school faculty-student ratio: 1:13. Upper School students typically attend 5 days per week. The average school day consists of 5 hours.

Upper School Student Profile Grade 6: 31 students (17 boys, 14 girls); Grade 7: 16 students (3 boys, 13 girls); Grade 8: 31 students (14 boys, 17 girls); Grade 9: 33 students (18 boys, 15 girls); Grade 10: 25 students (8 boys, 17 girls); Grade 11: 44 students (26 boys, 18 girls); Grade 12: 35 students (16 boys, 19 girls).

Faculty School total: 29. In upper school: 7 men, 7 women.

Graduation Requirements Bible.

Special Academic Programs Independent study; study at local college for college credit; ESL (28 students enrolled).

College Admission Counseling 34 students graduated in 2016; 20 went to college, including Simon Fraser University; The University of British Columbia. Other: 14 went to work, 11 entered a postgraduate year.

Student Life Upper grades have uniform requirement, student council, honor system. Discipline rests primarily with faculty. Attendance at religious services is required.

Tuition and Aid Tuition installment plan (monthly payment plans).

Admissions Traditional secondary-level entrance grade is 10. Deadline for receipt of application materials: none. Application fee required: CAN$100. Interview required.

Athletics 1 PE instructor, 8 coaches.

Computers Computer network features include Internet access, wireless campus network, Internet filtering or blocking technology. Computer access in designated common areas is available to students. Students grades are available online.

Contact Mrs. Denise Kraubner, Office Manager. 604-792-4680. Fax: 604-792-2465. E-mail: dkraubner@highroadacademy.com. Website: www.highroadacademy.com

THE HILL CENTER, DURHAM ACADEMY

Durham, North Carolina
See Special Needs Schools section.

HILLCREST CHRISTIAN SCHOOL

384 Erbes Road
Thousand Oaks, California 91362

Head of School: Mrs. Kathy Horan

General Information Coeducational day college-preparatory school, affiliated with Christian faith. Grades K–12. Founded: 1977. Setting: suburban. 4-acre campus. 7 buildings on campus. Approved or accredited by Association of Christian Schools International, Western Association of Schools and Colleges, and California Department of Education. Total enrollment: 263. Upper school average class size: 15. Upper school faculty-student ratio: 1:8. There are 179 required school days per year for Upper School students. Upper School students typically attend 5 days per week. The average school day consists of 6 hours and 30 minutes.

Upper School Student Profile Grade 6: 23 students (14 boys, 9 girls); Grade 7: 19 students (11 boys, 8 girls); Grade 8: 25 students (13 boys, 12 girls); Grade 9: 12 students (7 boys, 5 girls); Grade 10: 16 students (5 boys, 11 girls); Grade 11: 19 students (5 boys, 14 girls); Grade 12: 21 students (13 boys, 8 girls). 90% of students are Christian faith.

Faculty School total: 18. In upper school: 4 men, 10 women; 4 have advanced degrees.

Subjects Offered Advanced Placement courses, algebra, American history-AP, American literature, anatomy and physiology, art, Bible, biology, British literature, British literature (honors), business mathematics, calculus, calculus-AP, cheerleading, chemistry, Christian doctrine, Christian ethics, computer skills, computers, drama, earth science, economics, film studies, French, geometry, health, Hebrew scripture, home economics, honors English, honors U.S. history, honors world history, introduction to literature, keyboarding, life science, marine biology, physical education, physics, pre-algebra, pre-calculus, Spanish, trigonometry, U.S. government, U.S. government and politics-AP, U.S. history, U.S. history-AP, United States government-AP, world history, world literature, yearbook.

Graduation Requirements Algebra, American literature, Bible, biology, British literature, chemistry, economics, electives, English, foreign language, geometry, introduction to literature, mathematics, physical education (includes health), physical science, U.S. government, U.S. history, world history, world literature, 20 hours of community service each year.

Special Academic Programs 3 Advanced Placement exams for which test preparation is offered; honors section; independent study; ESL (3 students enrolled).

College Admission Counseling 22 students graduated in 2016; 19 went to college, including Abilene Christian University; Azusa Pacific University; Biola University; University of California, Irvine; University of California, San Diego; University of Washington. Other: 3 had other specific plans. Median SAT critical reading: 540, median SAT math: 630, median SAT writing: 560, median combined SAT: 577, median composite ACT: 23. 15% scored over 600 on SAT critical reading, 54% scored over 600 on SAT math, 46% scored over 600 on SAT writing, 15% scored over 1800 on combined SAT, 14% scored over 26 on composite ACT.

Student Life Upper grades have uniform requirement, student council, honor system. Discipline rests primarily with faculty. Attendance at religious services is required.

Tuition and Aid Day student tuition: $8180–$10,515. Tuition installment plan (FACTS Tuition Payment Plan). Need-based scholarship grants, tuition reduction for families of full-time pastors, tuition reduction for children of faculty and staff, loyalty discount for returning families available. In 2016–17, 10% of upper-school students received aid. Total amount of financial aid awarded in 2016–17: $12,700.

Admissions Traditional secondary-level entrance grade is 9. For fall 2016, 11 students applied for upper-level admission, 10 were accepted, 9 enrolled. Admissions testing or Stanford Diagnostic Test required. Deadline for receipt of application materials: none. Application fee required: $150. On-campus interview recommended.

Athletics Interscholastic: baseball (boys), basketball (b,g), cheering (g), football (b), volleyball (g); coed interscholastic: cross-country running, golf. 2 PE instructors, 4 coaches.

Computers Computers are regularly used in all classes. Computer resources include on-campus library services, Internet access, wireless campus network, Internet filtering or blocking technology, computer lab, school issued iPads in high school. Computer access in designated common areas is available to students. Students grades are available online. The school has a published electronic and media policy.

Contact Mrs. Gail Matheson, Office Manager. 805-497-7501 Ext. 200. Fax: 805-494-9355. E-mail: gmatheson@hillcrestcs.org. Website: www.hillcrestcs.org

HILLSIDE SCHOOL

Marlborough, Massachusetts
See Junior Boarding Schools section.

HO'ALA SCHOOL

1067A California Avenue
Wahiawa, Hawaii 96786

Head of School: Linda Perry

General Information Coeducational day college-preparatory, arts, and service learning school. Grades K–12. Founded: 1986. Setting: rural. Nearest major city is Honolulu. 1-acre campus. 1 building on campus. Approved or accredited by Western Association of Schools and Colleges and Hawaii Department of Education. Total enrollment: 93. Upper school average class size: 7. Upper school faculty-student ratio: 1:5. There are 183 required school days per year for Upper School students. Upper School students typically attend 5 days per week. The average school day consists of 5 hours and 30 minutes.

Upper School Student Profile Grade 6: 4 students (1 boy, 3 girls); Grade 7: 8 students (6 boys, 2 girls); Grade 8: 4 students (3 boys, 1 girl); Grade 9: 8 students (4 boys, 4 girls); Grade 10: 3 students (1 boy, 2 girls); Grade 11: 2 students (1 boy, 1 girl); Grade 12: 7 students (3 boys, 4 girls).

Faculty School total: 12. In upper school: 2 men, 4 women; 3 have advanced degrees.

Subjects Offered 1 1/2 elective credits, 20th century history, 20th century physics, 20th century world history, advanced biology, advanced chemistry, advanced computer applications, advanced math, Advanced Placement courses, advanced studio art-AP, algebra, alternative physical education, American Civil War, American government, American history, American history-AP, American literature, American literature-AP, analytic geometry, anthropology, art, art appreciation, art education, art history, art history-AP, athletics, basketball, biology, biology-AP, bowling, calculus, calculus-AP, character education, chemistry, chemistry-AP, civics, Civil War, civil war history, college admission preparation, college awareness, college counseling, college placement, college planning, college writing, community service, composition, composition-AP, computer applications, contemporary art, creative arts, creative dance, creative drama, creative thinking, creative writing, dance, drama, drama performance, drawing, drawing and design, English, English composition, English language and composition-AP, English language-AP, English literature and composition-AP, English literature-AP, English-AP, English/composition-AP, environmental science, environmental studies, fine arts, foreign language, general science, geometry, government/civics, government/civics-AP, grammar, guidance, Hawaiian history, health, health and safety, health and wellness, health education, history, home economics, honors algebra, honors English, honors geometry, honors U.S. history, honors world history, Internet, Internet research, lab science, language, language and composition, language-AP, life management skills, life skills, marine biology, marine science, mathematics-AP, mentorship program, modern dance, modern history, painting, personal and social education, physical education, physics, physics-AP, post-calculus, pre-algebra, pre-calculus, pre-college orientation, SAT/ACT preparation, science, scuba diving, senior career experience, senior project, service learning/internship, sewing, social sciences, social studies, Spanish, Spanish language-AP, Spanish-AP, student government, student teaching, studio art-AP, study skills, theater arts, volleyball, world geography, world governments, world history, world history-AP, writing, yearbook.

Special Academic Programs Advanced Placement exam preparation; honors section; academic accommodation for the gifted and the artistically talented; remedial reading and/or remedial writing; remedial math; programs in general development for dyslexic students.

College Admission Counseling 7 students graduated in 2016; all went to college, including University of Hawaii at Hilo; University of Hawaii at Manoa.

Student Life Upper grades have uniform requirement, student council, honor system. Discipline rests primarily with faculty.

Tuition and Aid Day student tuition: $10,262. Tuition installment plan (monthly payment plans, individually arranged payment plans). Tuition reduction for siblings, merit scholarship grants, need-based scholarship grants available. In 2016–17, 30% of upper-school students received aid. Total amount of financial aid awarded in 2016–17: $21,600.

Admissions Traditional secondary-level entrance grade is 9. For fall 2016, 12 students applied for upper-level admission, 10 were accepted, 10 enrolled. Admissions testing,

High School Placement Test, school's own exam and writing sample required. Deadline for receipt of application materials: none. Application fee required: $50. On-campus interview recommended.

Athletics Interscholastic: basketball (boys), cross-country running (b,g), golf (b), physical fitness (b), swimming and diving (b,g), track and field (b,g), volleyball (g), weight training (b); intramural: basketball (b). 5 PE instructors, 1 coach.

Computers Computers are regularly used in college planning, computer applications, English, health, history, keyboarding, lab/keyboard, mentorship program, science, Web site design, yearbook classes. Computer network features include wireless campus network. Students grades are available online.

Contact Mickie Hettema, Admissions Clerk. 808-621-1898. Fax: 808-622-3615. E-mail: Mickie@hoalaschool.org. Website: www.hoalaschool.org/

THE HOCKADAY SCHOOL

11600 Welch Road
Dallas, Texas 75229-2999
Head of School: Liza Lee

General Information Girls' boarding and day and distance learning college-preparatory, arts, and technology school. Boarding grades 8–12, day grades PK–12. Distance learning grades 9–12. Founded: 1913. Setting: suburban. Students are housed in single-sex dormitories. 88-acre campus. 12 buildings on campus. Approved or accredited by Independent Schools Association of the Southwest and Southern Association of Independent Schools. Member of National Association of Independent Schools and Secondary School Admission Test Board. Endowment: $145 million. Total enrollment: 1,096. Upper school average class size: 15. Upper school faculty-student ratio: 1:10. There are 160 required school days per year for Upper School students. Upper School students typically attend 5 days per week. The average school day consists of 6 hours and 40 minutes.

Upper School Student Profile 15% of students are boarding students. 91% are state residents. 5 states are represented in upper school student body. 9% are international students. International students from Canada, China, Mexico, Republic of Korea, Saudi Arabia, and Taiwan; 6 other countries represented in student body.

Faculty School total: 128. In upper school: 38 men, 90 women; 92 have advanced degrees; 4 reside on campus.

Subjects Offered Acting, advanced math, advanced studio art-AP, algebra, American history, American history-AP, American literature, analytic geometry, anatomy, applied arts, applied music, art history, astronomy, athletics, audio visual/media, ballet, basketball, biology, biology-AP, body human, British literature, broadcast journalism, broadcasting, Broadway dance, calculus, calculus-AP, cell biology, ceramics, chemistry, chemistry-AP, college counseling, comparative religion, computer applications, computer science, computer science-AP, concert choir, consumer economics, CPR, creative writing, current events, dance, dance performance, debate, digital art, digital imaging, digital music, digital photography, directing, discrete mathematics, drawing and design, ecology, environmental systems, economics-AP, English, English literature, English literature and composition-AP, English-AP, environmental science, environmental science-AP, ESL, fencing, fine arts, finite math, first aid, French, French language-AP, French literature-AP, genetics, geometry, guitar, health, health and wellness, honors English, humanities, information technology, interdisciplinary studies, journalism, Latin, Latin-AP, madrigals, Mandarin, microbiology, modern European history-AP, newspaper, non-Western literature, orchestra, philosophy, photography, physical education, physical fitness, physics, physics-AP, piano, pre-calculus, printmaking, probability and statistics, psychology, psychology-AP, self-defense, senior internship, set design, short story, Spanish, Spanish language-AP, Spanish literature-AP, stagecraft, studio art, studio art-AP, swimming, technology, tennis, track and field, U.S. government, U.S. history, U.S. history-AP, voice, volleyball, Web site design, wellness, world history, yearbook.

Graduation Requirements Algebra, American literature, art history, audio visual/media, biology-AP, chemistry, computer literacy, computer skills, English, English literature, geometry, history of music, information technology, languages, physical education (includes health), physics, senior project, U.S. government, U.S. history, world history, one semester of History of Art and Music, 60 hours of community service.

Special Academic Programs Advanced Placement exam preparation; honors section; independent study; term-away projects; domestic exchange program; study abroad; programs in English, mathematics, general development for dyslexic students; ESL (12 students enrolled).

College Admission Counseling 123 students graduated in 2016; all went to college, including Harvard University; Massachusetts Institute of Technology; Southern Methodist University; Stanford University; The University of Texas at Austin; Yale University. Mean SAT critical reading: 700, mean SAT math: 695, mean SAT writing: 705.

Student Life Upper grades have uniform requirement, student council, honor system. Discipline rests primarily with faculty.

Summer Programs Enrichment, advancement, ESL, sports, art/fine arts, computer instruction programs offered; session focuses on enrichment; held on campus; accepts boys and girls; open to students from other schools. 1,200 students usually enrolled. 2017 schedule: June 7 to July 18. Application deadline: March 1.

Tuition and Aid Day student tuition: $24,040–$29,375; 7-day tuition and room/board: $52,828–$54,191. Need-based scholarship grants, need-based financial aid available. In 2016–17, 18% of upper-school students received aid. Total amount of financial aid awarded in 2016–17: $3,400,000.

Admissions Traditional secondary-level entrance grade is 9. For fall 2016, 239 students applied for upper-level admission, 70 were accepted, 44 enrolled. Admissions testing required. Deadline for receipt of application materials: none. Application fee required: $175. Interview required.

Athletics Interscholastic: basketball (girls), crew (g), cross-country running (g), fencing (g), field hockey (g), golf (g), independent competitive sports (g), jogging (g), lacrosse (g), rowing (g), running (g), soccer (g), softball (g), swimming and diving (g), tennis (g), track and field (g), volleyball (g), winter soccer (g); intramural: aerobics (g), aerobics/dance (g), aquatics (g), archery (g), ballet (g), basketball (g), cheering (g), cooperative games (g), dance (g), fitness (g), independent competitive sports (g), jogging (g), life saving (g), martial arts (g), modern dance (g), outdoor skills (g), physical fitness (g), physical training (g), project adventure (g), racquetball (g), ropes courses (g), running (g), self defense (g), strength & conditioning (g), swimming and diving (g), tennis (g), track and field (g), ultimate Frisbee (g), volleyball (g), weight lifting (g), weight training (g), yoga (g). 13 PE instructors, 9 coaches, 3 athletic trainers.

Computers Computers are regularly used in animation, art, computer applications, creative writing, dance, engineering, English, French, health, history, humanities, information technology, introduction to technology, journalism, Latin, mathematics, media, media production, media services, multimedia, music, newspaper, photography, photojournalism, psychology, publications, publishing, science, Spanish, technology, Web site design, yearbook classes. Computer network features include on-campus library services, online commercial services, Internet access, wireless campus network, Internet filtering or blocking technology. Campus intranet, student e-mail accounts, and computer access in designated common areas are available to students. Students grades are available online. The school has a published electronic and media policy.

Contact Maryanna Phipps, Director of Admission. 214-363-6311. Fax: 214-265-1649. E-mail: admissions@hockaday.org. Website: www.hockaday.org

HOLLAND HALL

5666 East 81st Street
Tulsa, Oklahoma 74137-2099
Head of School: J.P. Culley

General Information Coeducational day college-preparatory, arts, religious studies, and technology school, affiliated with Episcopal Church. Grades PK–12. Founded: 1922. Setting: suburban. 162-acre campus. 5 buildings on campus. Approved or accredited by National Association of Episcopal Schools and Oklahoma Department of Education. Member of National Association of Independent Schools. Endowment: $68 million. Total enrollment: 995. Upper school average class size: 13. Upper school faculty-student ratio: 1:9. There are 172 required school days per year for Upper School students. Upper School students typically attend 5 days per week. The average school day consists of 6 hours and 52 minutes.

Upper School Student Profile Grade 6: 77 students (32 boys, 45 girls); Grade 7: 63 students (31 boys, 32 girls); Grade 8: 64 students (36 boys, 28 girls); Grade 9: 77 students (40 boys, 37 girls); Grade 10: 90 students (44 boys, 46 girls); Grade 11: 95 students (55 boys, 40 girls); Grade 12: 71 students (38 boys, 33 girls). 7% of students are members of Episcopal Church.

Faculty School total: 93. In upper school: 23 men, 19 women; 28 have advanced degrees.

Subjects Offered Algebra, American history, American studies, art, biology, calculus, calculus-AP, ceramics, chemistry, chemistry-AP, Chinese, computer programming, computer science, creative writing, dance, drama, driver education, ecology, economics, English, English literature, ethics, fine arts, French, geology, geometry, government/civics, history, journalism, Latin, leadership, mathematics, music, photography, physical education, physics, religion, science, social studies, Spanish, statistics-AP, theater, trigonometry, writing.

Graduation Requirements Arts and fine arts (art, music, dance, drama), English, foreign language, mathematics, physical education (includes health), religion (includes Bible studies and theology), science, social studies (includes history), senior intern program, 9th/12th grade wellness, college seminar.

Special Academic Programs Advanced Placement exam preparation; honors section; independent study; study at local college for college credit; study abroad; academic accommodation for the gifted, the musically talented, and the artistically talented.

College Admission Counseling 72 students graduated in 2016; 71 went to college, including Oklahoma State University; Southern Methodist University; The University of Tulsa; University of Oklahoma. Other: 1 entered a postgraduate year. Median combined SAT: 1366, median composite ACT: 28.

Student Life Upper grades have uniform requirement, student council, honor system. Discipline rests equally with students and faculty. Attendance at religious services is required.

Summer Programs Enrichment, advancement, sports, art/fine arts, computer instruction programs offered; session focuses on academic enrichment; held on campus; accepts boys and girls; open to students from other schools. 830 students usually enrolled. 2017 schedule: June 5 to August 4. Application deadline: July 28.

Tuition and Aid Day student tuition: $19,325. Tuition installment plan (monthly payment plans, individually arranged payment plans, school's own payment plan). Merit scholarship grants, need-based scholarship grants available. In 2016–17, 28% of upper-school students received aid; total upper-school merit-scholarship money awarded: $154,900. Total amount of financial aid awarded in 2016–17: $928,525.

Admissions Traditional secondary-level entrance grade is 9. Admissions testing and ISEE required. Deadline for receipt of application materials: none. Application fee required: $25. On-campus interview recommended.

Athletics Interscholastic: baseball (boys), basketball (b,g), cheering (g), cross-country running (b,g), field hockey (g), football (b), golf (b,g), modern dance (b,g), soccer (b,g), softball (g), tennis (b,g), track and field (b,g), volleyball (g), wrestling (b); intramural: aerobics (b,g), dance (b,g), modern dance (b,g), soccer (b,g); coed interscholastic: cheering, crew, modern dance, physical training, strength & conditioning, yoga; coed intramural: fitness, modern dance, physical training, soccer, weight lifting. 39 coaches, 1 athletic trainer.

Computers Computers are regularly used in art, English, foreign language, history, journalism, library, mathematics, science, yearbook classes. Computer network features include on-campus library services, online commercial services, Internet access, wireless campus network, Internet filtering or blocking technology. Student e-mail accounts and computer access in designated common areas are available to students. Students grades are available online. The school has a published electronic and media policy.

Contact Olivia Martin, Director of Admission and Financial Aid. 918-481-1111 Ext. 4740. Fax: 918-481-1145. E-mail: omartin@hollandhall.org. Website: www.hollandhall.org

HOLY CROSS HIGH SCHOOL

587 Oronoke Road
Waterbury, Connecticut 06708

Head of School: Mrs. Margaret Leger

General Information Coeducational day college-preparatory school, affiliated with Roman Catholic Church. Grades 9–12. Founded: 1968. Setting: suburban. 37-acre campus. 1 building on campus. Approved or accredited by National Catholic Education Association, New England Association of Schools and Colleges, and Connecticut Department of Education. Total enrollment: 489. Upper school average class size: 20. Upper school faculty-student ratio: 1:11. There are 160 required school days per year for Upper School students. Upper School students typically attend 5 days per week. The average school day consists of 6 hours.

Upper School Student Profile Grade 9: 86 students (52 boys, 34 girls); Grade 10: 119 students (61 boys, 58 girls); Grade 11: 121 students (58 boys, 63 girls); Grade 12: 111 students (58 boys, 53 girls). 70% of students are Roman Catholic.

Faculty School total: 60. In upper school: 28 men, 32 women; 37 have advanced degrees.

Subjects Offered Advanced biology, advanced math, Advanced Placement courses, advanced studio art-AP, algebra, American history, American history-AP, American literature, American literature-AP, American studies, anatomy, anatomy and physiology, art, art-AP, arts, band, Basic programming, biology, biology-AP, British literature, British literature-AP, business, business law, calculus, calculus-AP, campus ministry, Catholic belief and practice, chamber groups, chemistry, chemistry-AP, choir, computer applications, computer programming, computer science, concert band, concert choir, CPR, creative writing, drama, driver education, economics, economics and history, English, English literature, English-AP, environmental science, French, geometry, history, mathematics, music, physical education, physics, physiology, psychology, religion, science, social studies, Spanish, statistics, theater, theology, trigonometry, word processing, world history, world literature.

Graduation Requirements English, foreign language, mathematics, physical education (includes health), religion (includes Bible studies and theology), science, social studies (includes history).

Special Academic Programs Advanced Placement exam preparation; honors section; independent study; study at local college for college credit.

College Admission Counseling 151 students graduated in 2016; 144 went to college, including Naugatuck Valley Community College; Quinnipiac University; Southern Connecticut State University; University of Connecticut; University of Hartford; Western Connecticut State University. Other: 1 went to work, 1 entered military service.

Student Life Upper grades have specified standards of dress, student council. Discipline rests primarily with faculty. Attendance at religious services is required.

Summer Programs Sports, art/fine arts programs offered; session focuses on basketball, volleyball, theatre; held on campus; accepts boys and girls; open to students from other schools.

Tuition and Aid Day student tuition: $12,950. Tuition installment plan (monthly payment plans, individually arranged payment plans, Tuition Management Systems (TMS)). Merit scholarship grants, need-based scholarship grants available. In 2016–17, 30% of upper-school students received aid; total upper-school merit-scholarship money awarded: $135,000. Total amount of financial aid awarded in 2016–17: $650,000.

Admissions Traditional secondary-level entrance grade is 9. ETS HSPT (closed) required. Deadline for receipt of application materials: none. Application fee required: $25.

Athletics Interscholastic: baseball (boys), basketball (b,g), cheering (g), cross-country running (b,g), dance team (g), diving (b,g), football (b), golf (b,g), gymnastics (g), lacrosse (b,g), soccer (b,g), softball (g), swimming and diving (b,g), tennis (b,g), track and field (b,g), volleyball (g), winter (indoor) track (b,g), wrestling (b); intramural: basketball (b), skiing (downhill) (b,g), weight lifting (b); coed intramural: bowling, table tennis, ultimate Frisbee, yoga. 3 PE instructors, 22 coaches, 1 athletic trainer.

Computers Computers are regularly used in accounting, business, computer applications, creative writing, English, foreign language, French, history, mathematics, music technology, psychology, religious studies, science, social sciences, social studies, Spanish, technology, theology, Web site design, word processing, writing, writing, yearbook classes. Computer network features include on-campus library services, online commercial services, Internet access, wireless campus network. Campus intranet and computer access in designated common areas are available to students. Students grades are available online.

Contact Mrs. Terri Ann Parks, Director of Admissions. 203-757-9248. Fax: 203-757-3423. E-mail: tparks@holycrosshs-ct.com. Website: www.holycrosshs-ct.com

HOLY CROSS REGIONAL CATHOLIC SCHOOL

2125 Langhorne Road
Lynchburg, Virginia 24501-1449

Head of School: Ms. Mary Sherry

General Information Coeducational day college-preparatory, religious studies, and STEAM school, affiliated with Roman Catholic Church. Grades PK–12. Founded: 1879. Setting: small town. 1 building on campus. Approved or accredited by National Catholic Education Association, Southern Association of Colleges and Schools, and Virginia Department of Education. Upper school average class size: 14. Upper school faculty-student ratio: 1:7. There are 183 required school days per year for Upper School students. Upper School students typically attend 5 days per week. The average school day consists of 7 hours and 3 minutes.

Upper School Student Profile Grade 6: 14 students (6 boys, 8 girls); Grade 7: 17 students (8 boys, 9 girls); Grade 8: 11 students (5 boys, 6 girls); Grade 9: 18 students (8 boys, 10 girls); Grade 10: 10 students (4 boys, 6 girls); Grade 11: 8 students (6 boys, 2 girls); Grade 12: 19 students (9 boys, 10 girls). 62% of students are Roman Catholic.

Faculty School total: 24. In upper school: 3 men, 8 women; 4 have advanced degrees.

Subjects Offered Advanced biology, advanced chemistry, advanced math, Advanced Placement courses, algebra, all academic, American government, American history, biology, British literature, British literature-AP, calculus-AP, chemistry, composition-AP, dramatic arts, earth science, English literature and composition-AP, government-AP, health science, honors English, honors geometry, honors U.S. history, honors world history, Latin, physics, pre-algebra, pre-calculus, psychology, religious studies, Spanish, U.S. and Virginia government-AP.

Graduation Requirements Community service hour requirements.

Special Academic Programs Independent study; study at local college for college credit.

College Admission Counseling 13 students graduated in 2015; all went to college, including Christopher Newport University; Elon University; Stony Brook University; State University of New York, Virginia Military Institute; Virginia Polytechnic Institute and State University; Washington and Lee University. Mean SAT critical reading: 567, mean SAT math: 574, mean SAT writing: 559.

Student Life Upper grades have uniform requirement, student council, honor system. Discipline rests primarily with faculty. Attendance at religious services is required.

Tuition and Aid Tuition installment plan (FACTS Tuition Payment Plan). Tuition reduction for siblings available.

Admissions Traditional secondary-level entrance grade is 9. For fall 2015, 12 students applied for upper-level admission, 11 were accepted, 11 enrolled. TOEFL required. Deadline for receipt of application materials: none. Application fee required: $50. Interview required.

Athletics Interscholastic: baseball (boys), basketball (b,g), soccer (b), tennis (g), volleyball (g); coed interscholastic: golf. 1 PE instructor, 11 coaches.

Computers Computers are regularly used in computer applications, writing, yearbook classes. Computer network features include Internet access, Internet filtering or blocking technology. Student e-mail accounts are available to students. Students grades are available online. The school has a published electronic and media policy.

Contact Ms. Catherine Chapman Mosley, Director of School Relations and Advancement. 434-847-5436. Fax: 434-847-4156. E-mail: cmosley@hcfaculty.com. Website: http://hcrs-va.org/

HOLY CROSS SCHOOL

5500 Paris Avenue
New Orleans, Louisiana 70122

Head of School: Mr. Charles DiGange

General Information Boys' day college-preparatory school, affiliated with Roman Catholic Church. Grades PK–12. Founded: 1849. Setting: suburban. 20-acre campus. 5 buildings on campus. Approved or accredited by National Catholic Education Association, Southern Association of Colleges and Schools, and Louisiana Department of Education. Total enrollment: 1,140. Upper school average class size: 21. Upper school faculty-student ratio: 1:12. There are 184 required school days per year for Upper School students. Upper School students typically attend 5 days per week. The average school day consists of 6 hours and 35 minutes.

Upper School Student Profile Grade 6: 94 students (94 boys); Grade 7: 84 students (84 boys); Grade 8: 141 students (141 boys); Grade 9: 144 students (144 boys); Grade 10: 155 students (155 boys); Grade 11: 150 students (150 boys); Grade 12: 160 students (160 boys). 80% of students are Roman Catholic.

Faculty School total: 87. In upper school: 50 men, 32 women; 42 have advanced degrees.

Graduation Requirements Community service requirement.

Special Academic Programs 14 Advanced Placement exams for which test preparation is offered; honors section; study at local college for college credit; academic accommodation for the gifted, the musically talented, and the artistically talented.

College Admission Counseling 142 students graduated in 2016; 140 went to college, including Louisiana State University and Agricultural & Mechanical College; Loyola University New Orleans; St. Edward's University; Tulane University; University of Louisiana at Lafayette; University of Southern Mississippi. Other: 2 entered military service. Median composite ACT: 23. 35% scored over 26 on composite ACT.

Student Life Upper grades have uniform requirement, student council, honor system. Discipline rests primarily with faculty. Attendance at religious services is required.

Summer Programs Remediation, enrichment, sports, art/fine arts, computer instruction programs offered; session focuses on enrichment; held on campus; accepts boys; not open to students from other schools. 75 students usually enrolled. 2017 schedule: July 14 to July 28. Application deadline: May 31.

Tuition and Aid Day student tuition: $8000. Tuition installment plan (monthly payment plans). Tuition reduction for siblings, merit scholarship grants, need-based scholarship grants, paying campus jobs available. In 2016–17, 5% of upper-school students received aid; total upper-school merit-scholarship money awarded: $50,000.

Admissions Traditional secondary-level entrance grade is 8. For fall 2016, 350 students applied for upper-level admission, 235 were accepted, 210 enrolled. ACT-Explore, High School Placement Test, High School Placement Test (closed version) from Scholastic Testing Service or Iowa Subtests required. Deadline for receipt of application materials: November 15. Application fee required: $20. On-campus interview recommended.

Athletics Interscholastic: baseball, basketball, bowling, cheering, cross-country running, football, golf, indoor track, indoor track & field, power lifting, soccer, swimming and diving, tennis, wrestling; intramural: baseball, basketball, bicycling, fishing, flag football, football, Frisbee, lacrosse, martial arts, physical training, rugby, sailing, skateboarding, soccer, softball, strength & conditioning, ultimate Frisbee, volleyball, weight training. 10 PE instructors, 38 coaches, 2 athletic trainers.

Computers Computers are regularly used in all classes. Computer network features include on-campus library services, online commercial services, Internet access, wireless campus network, Internet filtering or blocking technology. Student e-mail accounts and computer access in designated common areas are available to students. Students grades are available online. The school has a published electronic and media policy.

Contact Mr. Brian Kitchen, Director of Admissions. 504-942-3100. Fax: 504-284-3424. E-mail: bkitchen@holycrosstigers.com. Website: www.holycrosstigers.com

HOLY GHOST PREPARATORY SCHOOL

2429 Bristol Pike
Bensalem, Pennsylvania 19020

Head of School: Mr. Gregory J. Geruson

General Information Boys' day college-preparatory school, affiliated with Roman Catholic Church. Grades 9–12. Founded: 1897. Setting: suburban. Nearest major city is Philadelphia. 53-acre campus. 5 buildings on campus. Approved or accredited by Middle States Association of Colleges and Schools, National Catholic Education Association, Pennsylvania Association of Independent Schools, and Pennsylvania Department of Education. Member of National Association of Independent Schools. Endowment: $3 million. Total enrollment: 467. Upper school average class size: 18. Upper school faculty-student ratio: 1:11. Upper School students typically attend 5 days per week. The average school day consists of 6 hours and 30 minutes.

Upper School Student Profile Grade 9: 126 students (126 boys); Grade 10: 125 students (125 boys); Grade 11: 117 students (117 boys); Grade 12: 117 students (117 boys). 94% of students are Roman Catholic.

Faculty School total: 50. In upper school: 32 men, 18 women; 36 have advanced degrees.

Subjects Offered 3-dimensional art, Advanced Placement courses, advanced studio art-AP, algebra, American government, American history, American history-AP, American literature, analysis, anatomy and physiology, art, Bible, biology, biology-AP, calculus, calculus-AP, campus ministry, career/college preparation, careers, ceremonies of life, chemistry, Chinese history, choral music, church history, college admission preparation, college counseling, communication arts, communication skills, computer programming-AP, computer science, computer science-AP, creative writing, drama performance, earth science, economics, English, English language and composition-AP, English literature, English literature and composition-AP, environmental science,

European history, European history-AP, film, fine arts, French, French language-AP, geometry, government and politics-AP, government/civics, health, history, journalism, language-AP, Latin, Latin-AP, mathematics, modern European history-AP, music, music theory-AP, oral communications, physical education, physics, public speaking, religion, science, sexuality, social studies, Spanish, Spanish language-AP, Spanish-AP, speech, statistics, trigonometry, U.S. history-AP, United States government-AP, world cultures, world history, world history-AP, world literature, writing, yearbook.

Graduation Requirements Arts and fine arts (art, music, dance, drama), computer science, English, foreign language, mathematics, physical education (includes health), religion (includes Bible studies and theology), science, social studies (includes history), summer reading. Community service is required.

Special Academic Programs Advanced Placement exam preparation; honors section; independent study; study abroad.

College Admission Counseling 121 students graduated in 2016; all went to college, including Boston College; Duquesne University; Penn State University Park; Saint Joseph's University; University of Pennsylvania; Villanova University. Median SAT critical reading: 610, median SAT math: 640.

Student Life Upper grades have specified standards of dress, student council, honor system. Discipline rests primarily with faculty.

Summer Programs Enrichment, advancement, sports, computer instruction programs offered; session focuses on entrance exam preparation; held on campus; accepts boys and girls; open to students from other schools. 100 students usually enrolled. 2017 schedule: June 22 to July 24. Application deadline: June 15.

Tuition and Aid Day student tuition: $21,500. Tuition installment plan (monthly payment plans, quarterly and semi-annual payment plans). Merit scholarship grants, need-based scholarship grants, music scholarships, minority scholarships, art scholarships available. In 2016–17, 40% of upper-school students received aid; total upper-school merit-scholarship money awarded: $750,000. Total amount of financial aid awarded in 2016–17: $750,000.

Admissions Traditional secondary-level entrance grade is 9. For fall 2016, 250 students applied for upper-level admission, 158 were accepted, 126 enrolled. High School Placement Test (closed version) from Scholastic Testing Service required. Deadline for receipt of application materials: none. Application fee required: $60. On-campus interview recommended.

Athletics Interscholastic: baseball, basketball, bowling, cross-country running, golf, ice hockey, indoor track & field, lacrosse, rowing, soccer, Special Olympics, swimming and diving, tennis, track and field; intramural: basketball, fitness walking, flag football, football, Frisbee, soccer, street hockey, tennis, ultimate Frisbee. 10 coaches, 1 athletic trainer.

Computers Computers are regularly used in college planning, English, foreign language, mathematics, programming, publications, science, speech, yearbook classes. Computer network features include on-campus library services, online commercial services, Internet access, wireless campus network, Internet filtering or blocking technology. Student e-mail accounts are available to students. The school has a published electronic and media policy.

Contact Mr. Ryan T. Abramson, Director of Admissions. 215-639-0811. Fax: 215-639-4225. E-mail: admissions@holyghostprep.org. Website: www.holyghostprep.org

HOLY INNOCENTS' EPISCOPAL SCHOOL

805 Mount Vernon Highway NW
Atlanta, Georgia 30327

Head of School: Mr. Paul A. Barton

General Information Coeducational day college-preparatory school, affiliated with Episcopal Church. Grades PS–12. Founded: 1959. Setting: suburban. 42-acre campus. 4 buildings on campus. Approved or accredited by Georgia Independent School Association, National Association of Episcopal Schools, Southern Association of Colleges and Schools, and Georgia Department of Education. Member of National Association of Independent Schools and Secondary School Admission Test Board. Endowment: $17 million. Total enrollment: 1,360. Upper school average class size: 14. Upper school faculty-student ratio: 1:7. There are 173 required school days per year for Upper School students. Upper School students typically attend 5 days per week. The average school day consists of 7 hours and 15 minutes.

Upper School Student Profile 22% of students are members of Episcopal Church.

Faculty School total: 180. In upper school: 29 men, 32 women; 45 have advanced degrees.

Subjects Offered 3-dimensional art, 3-dimensional design, advanced biology, advanced chemistry, advanced math, Advanced Placement courses, advanced studio art-AP, algebra, American government, American history, American history-AP, American literature, American literature-AP, anatomy and physiology, ancient world history, applied music, art, art-AP, athletics, band, baseball, basketball, Bible, Bible studies, biology, biology-AP, calculus, calculus-AP, cheerleading, chemistry, chemistry-AP, choir, choral music, chorus, college counseling, college placement, community service, composition, computer animation, computer education, computer graphics, computer resources, computer science-AP, concert band, concert choir, creative writing, drama, drama performance, drawing and design, earth science, economics, electives, English, English composition, English language-AP, English literature, English literature-AP, English-AP, environmental studies, ethics, European history, European history-AP, fine arts, French, French language-AP, French-AP, geometry, golf, government, government and politics-AP, government/civics, Greek, guidance, health and wellness, history, honors algebra, honors English, honors geometry, honors U.S. history, honors world history, human geography - AP, Jewish history, Jewish studies, language arts, Latin, Latin-AP, mathematics, New Testament, orchestra, peer counseling, performing arts, personal finance, photography, physical education, physics, physics-AP, pre-calculus, psychology, religion, religious studies, SAT preparation, SAT/ACT preparation, science, science project, sex education, social studies, Spanish, Spanish language-AP, speech and debate, sports, study skills, swimming, U.S. history, U.S. history-AP, visual arts, world history, writing workshop, yearbook.

Graduation Requirements American history, arts and fine arts (art, music, dance, drama), electives, English, foreign language, history, mathematics, physical education (includes health), physical fitness, religion (includes Bible studies and theology), science, world history, 15 hours of community service each year, plus additional hours for NHS students.

Special Academic Programs Advanced Placement exam preparation; honors section; term-away projects; study abroad; academic accommodation for the gifted, the musically talented, and the artistically talented.

College Admission Counseling 124 students graduated in 2016; all went to college, including Auburn University; Georgia Institute of Technology; Southern Methodist University; The University of Alabama; University of Georgia; Wake Forest University. Median SAT critical reading: 600, median SAT math: 620, median SAT writing: 620, median combined SAT: 1825, median composite ACT: 28. 56% scored over 600 on SAT critical reading, 61% scored over 600 on SAT math, 58% scored over 600 on SAT writing, 57% scored over 1800 on combined SAT, 67% scored over 26 on composite ACT.

Student Life Upper grades have uniform requirement, student council, honor system. Discipline rests equally with students and faculty. Attendance at religious services is required.

Summer Programs Remediation, enrichment, advancement, sports, art/fine arts, computer instruction programs offered; session focuses on athletics, fine arts, and academics; held on campus; accepts boys and girls; open to students from other schools. 725 students usually enrolled. 2017 schedule: June 5 to July 14. Application deadline: May 1.

Tuition and Aid Day student tuition: $9760–$25,520. Tuition installment plan (Insured Tuition Payment Plan, FACTS Tuition Payment Plan, monthly payment plans). Need-based scholarship grants available. In 2016–17, 13% of upper-school students received aid. Total amount of financial aid awarded in 2016–17: $1,465,280.

Admissions Traditional secondary-level entrance grade is 9. For fall 2016, 116 students applied for upper-level admission, 59 were accepted, 33 enrolled. Essay, ISEE, mathematics proficiency exam, PSAT and SAT for applicants to grade 11 and 12, school's own test, SSAT and WISC III or other aptitude measures; standardized achievement test required. Deadline for receipt of application materials: February 1. Application fee required: $95. Interview required.

Athletics Interscholastic: baseball (boys), basketball (b,g), cheering (g), cross-country running (b,g), equestrian sports (g), football (b), golf (b,g), lacrosse (b,g), physical fitness (b,g), physical training (b,g), soccer (b,g), softball (g), swimming and diving (b,g), tennis (b,g), track and field (b,g), volleyball (g), wrestling (b); intramural: combined training (b,g), fitness (b,g), ultimate Frisbee (b); coed intramural: combined training, fitness. 9 PE instructors, 112 coaches, 3 athletic trainers.

Computers Computers are regularly used in all academic classes. Computer network features include on-campus library services, online commercial services, Internet access, wireless campus network, Internet filtering or blocking technology, 1.1 student laptops (grades 5-12), iPad carts, three computer labs. Campus intranet, student e-mail accounts, and computer access in designated common areas are available to students. Students grades are available online. The school has a published electronic and media policy.

Contact Mr. Chris Pomar, Assistant Head of School for Enrollment and Planning. 404-255-4026 Ext. 203. Fax: 404-847-1156. E-mail: chris.pomar@hies.org. Website: www.hies.org

HOLY NAMES ACADEMY

728 21st Avenue East
Seattle, Washington 98112

Head of School: Elizabeth Swift

General Information Girls' day college-preparatory school, affiliated with Roman Catholic Church. Grades 9–12. Founded: 1880. Setting: urban. 1 building on campus. Approved or accredited by Northwest Association of Independent Schools and Washington Department of Education. Member of National Association of Independent Schools. Upper school average class size: 14. Upper school faculty-student ratio: 1:14. There are 180 required school days per year for Upper School students. Upper School students typically attend 5 days per week. The average school day consists of 6 hours.

Upper School Student Profile 74% of students are Roman Catholic.

Faculty School total: 52. In upper school: 10 men, 42 women; 46 have advanced degrees.

College Admission Counseling 160 students graduated in 2015; all went to college.

Student Life Upper grades have specified standards of dress. Attendance at religious services is required.

Tuition and Aid Day student tuition: $14,856. Financial aid available to upper-school students. In 2015–16, 31% of upper-school students received aid.

Admissions Traditional secondary-level entrance grade is 9. TerraNova required. Deadline for receipt of application materials: January 11. Application fee required: $30. **Contact** 206-323-4272. Website: www.holynames-sea.org

HOLY SAVIOR MENARD CATHOLIC HIGH SCHOOL

4603 Coliseum Boulevard
Alexandria, Louisiana 71303

Head of School: Mr. Joel Desselle

General Information Coeducational day college-preparatory school, affiliated with Roman Catholic Church. Grades 7–12. Founded: 1930. Setting: suburban. 5-acre campus. 5 buildings on campus. Approved or accredited by National Catholic Education Association, Southern Association of Colleges and Schools, The College Board, and Louisiana Department of Education. Total enrollment: 510. Upper school average class size: 20. Upper school faculty-student ratio: 1:14. There are 178 required school days per year for Upper School students. Upper School students typically attend 5 days per week. The average school day consists of 7 hours and 15 minutes.

Upper School Student Profile Grade 9: 96 students (49 boys, 47 girls); Grade 10: 107 students (60 boys, 47 girls); Grade 11: 69 students (30 boys, 39 girls); Grade 12: 78 students (38 boys, 40 girls). 79% of students are Roman Catholic.

Faculty School total: 38. In upper school: 10 men, 22 women; 13 have advanced degrees.

Subjects Offered Advanced math, algebra, American history, anatomy and physiology, art, athletics, biology, biology-AP, British literature, British literature (honors), calculus-AP, campus ministry, Catholic belief and practice, cheerleading, chemistry, civics/free enterprise, computer applications, computer science, digital photography, English, English composition, English literature, English literature-AP, fine arts, French, general science, geometry, health, honors algebra, honors English, honors geometry, honors U.S. history, honors world history, journalism, language arts, law studies, moral reasoning, New Testament, newspaper, philosophy, physical education, physical science, physics, pre-algebra, pre-calculus, psychology, publications, reading/study skills, religion, sociology, Spanish, speech, world geography, world history, yearbook.

Graduation Requirements Algebra, American history, arts and fine arts (art, music, dance, drama), biology, chemistry, civics/free enterprise, computer applications, English, foreign language, geometry, physical science, religion (includes Bible studies and theology), world history, 27 credits required.

Special Academic Programs 4 Advanced Placement exams for which test preparation is offered; honors section; independent study; study at local college for college credit; domestic exchange program.

College Admission Counseling 64 students graduated in 2016; 61 went to college, including Louisiana State University and Agricultural & Mechanical College; Louisiana Tech University; Northwestern State University of Louisiana; University of Louisiana at Lafayette; University of New Orleans. Other: 3 went to work, 1 entered military service, 2 entered a postgraduate year, 1 had other specific plans. Mean composite ACT: 24. 20% scored over 26 on composite ACT.

Student Life Upper grades have uniform requirement, student council, honor system. Discipline rests primarily with faculty. Attendance at religious services is required.

Tuition and Aid Day student tuition: $6300. Tuition installment plan (FACTS Tuition Payment Plan, monthly payment plans, individually arranged payment plans). Tuition reduction for siblings, merit scholarship grants, need-based scholarship grants available. In 2016–17, 12% of upper-school students received aid; total upper-school merit-scholarship money awarded: $5000. Total amount of financial aid awarded in 2016–17: $150,000.

Admissions Traditional secondary-level entrance grade is 9. For fall 2016, 38 students applied for upper-level admission, 38 were accepted, 38 enrolled. ACT or CTBS, Stanford Achievement Test, any other standardized test required. Deadline for receipt of application materials: March 15. Application fee required: $500. On-campus interview required.

Athletics Interscholastic: baseball (boys), basketball (b,g), cheering (g), cross-country running (b,g), danceline (g), fishing (b,g), football (b), golf (b,g), power lifting (b,g), running (b,g), soccer (b,g), softball (g), tennis (b,g), track and field (b,g); intramural: paddle tennis (b,g); coed interscholastic: swimming and diving; coed intramural: paddle tennis. 3 PE instructors, 3 coaches.

Computers Computers are regularly used in computer applications, English, journalism, mathematics, photography, publications, science, Web site design classes. Computer network features include on-campus library services, Internet access, wireless campus network, Internet filtering or blocking technology. Computer access in designated common areas is available to students. Students grades are available online.

Contact Mrs. Paula Morley, Guidance Secretary. 318-445-8233. Fax: 318-448-8170. E-mail: ameadows@holysaviormenard.com. Website: www.holysaviormenard.com

HOLY TRINITY DIOCESAN HIGH SCHOOL

98 Cherry Lane
Hicksville, New York 11801

Head of School: Ms. Kathleen Moran

General Information Coeducational day college-preparatory school, affiliated with Roman Catholic Church. Grades 9–12. Founded: 1967. Setting: suburban. Nearest major city is New York. 1 building on campus. Approved or accredited by Middle States Association of Colleges and Schools, National Council for Private School Accreditation, New York State Board of Regents, The College Board, and New York Department of Education. Total enrollment: 1,003. Upper school average class size: 32. Upper school faculty-student ratio: 1:17. There are 180 required school days per year for Upper School students. Upper School students typically attend 5 days per week. The average school day consists of 6 hours and 30 minutes.

Upper School Student Profile Grade 9: 191 students (92 boys, 99 girls); Grade 10: 225 students (102 boys, 123 girls); Grade 11: 218 students (103 boys, 115 girls); Grade 12: 263 students (113 boys, 150 girls). 90% of students are Roman Catholic.

Faculty School total: 61. In upper school: 25 men, 36 women; 66 have advanced degrees.

Subjects Offered Accounting, advanced math, Advanced Placement courses, American government, American history, American history-AP, American literature, American literature-AP, anatomy and physiology, architectural drawing, art, band, biology, biology-AP, British literature, British literature (honors), calculus, calculus-AP, campus ministry, ceramics, chemistry, chemistry-AP, chorus, Christian scripture, Christian studies, Christian testament, comparative religion, composition, concert band, criminology, critical studies in film, dance, desktop publishing, earth science, economics, English, English composition, English language and composition-AP, English literature, English literature-AP, environmental science, food and nutrition, French, government and politics-AP, health, honors English, honors U.S. history, honors world history, intro to computers, jazz theory, keyboarding, literature and composition-AP, mathematics, music, performing arts, physical education, physics, physics-AP, pre-calculus, public speaking, religion, Spanish, Spanish language-AP, stagecraft, statistics, theater arts, theology, U.S. government and politics, U.S. government and politics-AP, U.S. history, U.S. history-AP, world wide web design.

Graduation Requirements Arts and fine arts (art, music, dance, drama), economics, English, foreign language, mathematics, physical education (includes health), religion (includes Bible studies and theology), science, U.S. government and politics.

Special Academic Programs Advanced Placement exam preparation; honors section; study at local college for college credit.

College Admission Counseling 283 students graduated in 2016; 280 went to college, including Adelphi University; Hofstra University; Nassau Community College; State University of New York College at Cortland; Stony Brook University, State University of New York. Other: 1 went to work, 2 entered military service. Mean SAT critical reading: 494, mean SAT math: 492, mean SAT writing: 484.

Student Life Upper grades have uniform requirement, student council. Discipline rests primarily with faculty.

Tuition and Aid Day student tuition: $9950. Tuition installment plan (monthly payment plans, individually arranged payment plans, 10-month tuition plan, 3-payment plan). Merit scholarship grants, need-based scholarship grants available. In 2016–17, 8% of upper-school students received aid.

Admissions Traditional secondary-level entrance grade is 9. Catholic High School Entrance Examination required. Deadline for receipt of application materials: none. Application fee required: $50.

Athletics Interscholastic: badminton (girls), baseball (b), basketball (b,g), cheering (g), cross-country running (b,g), dance team (g), football (b), gymnastics (g), indoor track (b,g), lacrosse (b,g), soccer (b,g), softball (g), swimming and diving (b,g), tennis (b,g), track and field (b,g), volleyball (b,g), weight lifting (b), weight training (b), winter (indoor) track (b,g), wrestling (b); intramural: physical training (b), weight training (b); coed interscholastic: bowling, fitness, golf; coed intramural: modern dance. 3 PE instructors, 1 athletic trainer.

Computers Computers are regularly used in college planning, computer applications, desktop publishing, drawing and design, economics, English, foreign language, graphic design, history, journalism, library, music technology, newspaper, occupational education, programming, research skills, SAT preparation, science, social studies, theater, Web site design, writing, yearbook classes. Computer network features include on-campus library services, Internet access, wireless campus network, Internet filtering or blocking technology. Student e-mail accounts and computer access in designated common areas are available to students. Students grades are available online. The school has a published electronic and media policy.

Contact Admissions. 516-433-2900. Fax: 516-433-2827. E-mail: hths98@holytrinityhs.org. Website: www.holytrinityhs.org

HOLY TRINITY HIGH SCHOOL

1443 West Division Street
Chicago, Illinois 60642

Head of School: Mr. Timothy M. Bopp

General Information Coeducational day college-preparatory, technology, and business, STEM school, affiliated with Roman Catholic Church. Grades 9–12.

Founded: 1910. Setting: urban. 1 building on campus. Approved or accredited by North Central Association of Colleges and Schools and Illinois Department of Education. Endowment: $2 million. Total enrollment: 331. Upper school average class size: 18. Upper school faculty-student ratio: 1:11. There are 180 required school days per year for Upper School students. Upper School students typically attend 5 days per week. The average school day consists of 6 hours and 52 minutes.

Upper School Student Profile Grade 9: 78 students (38 boys, 40 girls); Grade 10: 101 students (50 boys, 51 girls); Grade 11: 85 students (45 boys, 40 girls); Grade 12: 65 students (32 boys, 33 girls). 50% of students are Roman Catholic.

Faculty School total: 28. In upper school: 13 men, 15 women; 17 have advanced degrees.

Subjects Offered ACT preparation, advanced biology, advanced chemistry, advanced computer applications, advanced studio art-AP, algebra, American government, American literature, anatomy, animation, art, Basic programming, Bible, biology, British literature, British literature (honors), British literature-AP, business, calculus, calculus-AP, career planning, career/college preparation, Catholic belief and practice, ceramics, chemistry, church history, college counseling, college planning, computer applications, computer science, concert band, critical studies in film, discrete mathematics, dramatic arts, earth science, economics, English, English literature, environmental science, film, French studies, freshman foundations, geography, government/civics, government/civics-AP, health and wellness, health education, Holocaust, honors algebra, honors English, honors geometry, honors U.S. history, honors world history, junior and senior seminars, lab science, New Testament, pre-calculus, psychology, public speaking, publications, SAT/ACT preparation, Spanish, Spanish language-AP, technology, trigonometry, U.S. history, work experience, world geography, world history, world literature, world religions, yearbook.

Graduation Requirements Business, English, mathematics, modern languages, physical education (includes health), religion (includes Bible studies and theology), science, social studies (includes history), visual and performing arts.

Special Academic Programs 6 Advanced Placement exams for which test preparation is offered; honors section; study at local college for college credit; remedial reading and/or remedial writing; ESL (25 students enrolled).

College Admission Counseling 82 students graduated in 2016; 78 went to college, including Knox College; Northeastern Illinois University; Northern Illinois University; Triton College; Western Illinois University. Other: 2 went to work, 1 entered military service, 1 entered a postgraduate year.

Student Life Upper grades have uniform requirement, student council, honor system. Discipline rests equally with students and faculty. Attendance at religious services is required.

Tuition and Aid Day student tuition: $7925. Tuition installment plan (SMART Tuition Payment Plan, monthly payment plans). Tuition reduction for siblings, merit scholarship grants, need-based scholarship grants available. In 2016–17, 85% of upper-school students received aid; total upper-school merit-scholarship money awarded: $125,000. Total amount of financial aid awarded in 2016–17: $600,000.

Admissions Traditional secondary-level entrance grade is 9. High School Placement Test required. Deadline for receipt of application materials: none. No application fee required. Interview required.

Athletics Interscholastic: baseball (boys), basketball (b,g), soccer (b,g), softball (g), volleyball (b,g); coed interscholastic: cheering, cross-country running, flag football, track and field; coed intramural: dance, dance team, fitness, physical fitness, weight lifting. 2 PE instructors, 6 coaches.

Computers Computers are regularly used in animation, business education, business skills, college planning, keyboarding classes. Computer network features include on-campus library services, online commercial services, Internet access, wireless campus network, Internet filtering or blocking technology. Student e-mail accounts and computer access in designated common areas are available to students. Students grades are available online. The school has a published electronic and media policy.

Contact Ms. Carla Rubalcava, Director of Enrollment Management. 773-278-4212 Ext. 3023. Fax: 773-278-0144. E-mail: crubalcava@holytrinity-hs.org. Website: www.holytrinity-hs.org

HOLY TRINITY SCHOOL

11300 Bayview Avenue
Richmond Hill, Ontario L4S 1L4, Canada

Head of School: Mr. Barry Hughes

General Information Coeducational day college-preparatory school, affiliated with Roman Catholic Church, Anglican Church of Canada. Grades JK–12. Founded: 1981. Setting: suburban. 37-acre campus. 1 building on campus. Approved or accredited by Canadian Association of Independent Schools, Conference of Independent Schools of Ontario, and Ontario Department of Education. Affiliate member of National Association of Independent Schools; member of Secondary School Admission Test Board. Language of instruction: English. Endowment: CAN$9 million. Total enrollment: 750. Upper school average class size: 22. Upper school faculty-student ratio: 1:17. Upper School students typically attend 5 days per week. The average school day consists of 6 hours.

Upper School Student Profile Grade 9: 88 students (44 boys, 44 girls); Grade 10: 88 students (44 boys, 44 girls); Grade 11: 80 students (45 boys, 35 girls); Grade 12: 88

students (44 boys, 44 girls). 30% of students are Roman Catholic, members of Anglican Church of Canada.

Faculty School total: 85. In upper school: 30 men, 20 women; 25 have advanced degrees.

Graduation Requirements English, French, mathematics, physical education (includes health), science, senior humanities.

Special Academic Programs 8 Advanced Placement exams for which test preparation is offered.

College Admission Counseling 110 students graduated in 2016; all went to college, including McMaster University; Queen's University at Kingston; The University of Western Ontario; University of Toronto; University of Waterloo.

Student Life Upper grades have uniform requirement, student council, honor system. Discipline rests primarily with faculty. Attendance at religious services is required.

Summer Programs Enrichment, sports, art/fine arts, computer instruction programs offered; held on campus; accepts boys and girls; open to students from other schools. 400 students usually enrolled. 2017 schedule: June 26 to July 30.

Tuition and Aid Day student tuition: CAN$27,000. Bursaries, need-based scholarship grants available. In 2016–17, 5% of upper-school students received aid. Total amount of financial aid awarded in 2016–17: CAN$50,000.

Admissions Traditional secondary-level entrance grade is 9. For fall 2016, 110 students applied for upper-level admission, 40 were accepted, 35 enrolled. CAT required. Deadline for receipt of application materials: December 1. Application fee required: CAN$125. On-campus interview recommended.

Athletics Interscholastic: badminton (boys, girls), baseball (b,g), basketball (b,g), cross-country running (g), field hockey (g), fitness (b,g), golf (b,g), hockey (b), ice hockey (b), indoor track (b,g), indoor track & field (b,g), outdoor education (b,g), outdoor recreation (b,g), rugby (b,g), soccer (b,g), softball (b,g), squash (b,g), tennis (b,g), track and field (b,g), ultimate Frisbee (b,g), volleyball (b,g); intramural: table tennis (b,g); coed interscholastic: badminton, Frisbee, ultimate Frisbee; coed intramural: floor hockey, horseback riding, street hockey, table tennis. 5 PE instructors, 50 coaches, 1 athletic trainer.

Computers Computers are regularly used in all classes. Computer network features include on-campus library services, Internet access, wireless campus network, Internet filtering or blocking technology. Campus intranet, student e-mail accounts, and computer access in designated common areas are available to students. Students grades are available online. The school has a published electronic and media policy.

Contact Mrs. Jennifer Gibbons, Admission Coordinator. 905-737-1115 Ext. 1. Fax: 905-737-5187. E-mail: jgibbons@hts.on.ca. Website: www.hts.on.ca

HOOSAC SCHOOL

PO Box 9
Hoosick, New York 12089

Head of School: Dean S. Foster

General Information Coeducational boarding and day college-preparatory and arts school, affiliated with Episcopal Church. Grades 8–PG. Founded: 1889. Setting: rural. Nearest major city is Albany. Students are housed in single-sex dormitories. 350-acre campus. 16 buildings on campus. Approved or accredited by Middle States Association of Colleges and Schools, National Association of Episcopal Schools, New York State Board of Regents, The Association of Boarding Schools, and New York Department of Education. Member of National Association of Independent Schools and Secondary School Admission Test Board. Endowment: $1.5 million. Total enrollment: 125. Upper school average class size: 8. Upper school faculty-student ratio: 1:5. Upper School students typically attend 6 days per week. The average school day consists of 6 hours and 15 minutes.

Upper School Student Profile Grade 8: 7 students (5 boys, 2 girls); Grade 9: 20 students (10 boys, 10 girls); Grade 10: 23 students (16 boys, 7 girls); Grade 11: 29 students (17 boys, 12 girls); Grade 12: 41 students (29 boys, 12 girls); Postgraduate: 7 students (5 boys, 2 girls). 90% of students are boarding students. 31% are state residents. 17 states are represented in upper school student body. 35% are international students. International students from Canada, China, Serbia and Montenegro, South Africa, Turkey, and United States; 9 other countries represented in student body. 10% of students are members of Episcopal Church.

Faculty School total: 24. In upper school: 14 men, 9 women; 15 have advanced degrees; 15 reside on campus.

Subjects Offered Advertising design, algebra, American history, American literature, art, art history, astronomy, biology, British literature, calculus, calculus-AP, ceramics, chemistry, choral music, computer science, creative writing, criminology, dance, drama, driver education, earth science, English, English literature, English-AP, ESL, ethics, European history, expository writing, fine arts, French, French as a second language, geometry, government/civics, grammar, history, history-AP, Latin, marketing, mathematics, music, photography, physical education, physics, science, social studies, speech communications, theater, world history, world literature, writing.

Graduation Requirements Arts and fine arts (art, music, dance, drama), computer literacy, English, ethics, foreign language, mathematics, physical education (includes health), science, social studies (includes history), ethics, public speaking.

Special Academic Programs 7 Advanced Placement exams for which test preparation is offered; honors section; accelerated programs; independent study; study at local college for college credit; academic accommodation for the musically talented

and the artistically talented; remedial reading and/or remedial writing; remedial math; programs in English, mathematics, general development for dyslexic students; ESL (25 students enrolled).

College Admission Counseling 45 students graduated in 2016; all went to college, including Bentley University; Cornell University; Gettysburg College; University of California, Berkeley; University of Michigan; Wake Forest University. Mean combined SAT: 1500.

Student Life Upper grades have specified standards of dress, student council, honor system. Discipline rests primarily with faculty. Attendance at religious services is required.

Summer Programs ESL programs offered; session focuses on ESL; held on campus; accepts boys and girls; open to students from other schools. 35 students usually enrolled. 2017 schedule: June 24 to July 22.

Tuition and Aid Day student tuition: $18,500; 7-day tuition and room/board: $49,000. Tuition installment plan (Academic Management Services Plan, Key Tuition Payment Plan, monthly payment plans, individually arranged payment plans). Merit scholarship grants, need-based scholarship grants available. In 2016–17, 35% of upper-school students received aid. Total amount of financial aid awarded in 2016–17: $625,000.

Admissions Traditional secondary-level entrance grade is 9. For fall 2016, 198 students applied for upper-level admission, 108 were accepted, 102 enrolled. Deadline for receipt of application materials: none. Application fee required: $75. On-campus interview recommended.

Athletics Interscholastic: baseball (boys), basketball (b,g), cross-country running (b,g), ice hockey (b), lacrosse (b,g); intramural: bicycling (b,g), flag football (b,g), floor hockey (b,g); coed intramural: aerobics/dance, alpine skiing, aquatics, backpacking, ball hockey, bowling, broomball, canoeing/kayaking, cooperative games, cross-country running, dance, deck hockey, fishing, freestyle skiing, golf, hiking/backpacking, indoor hockey, indoor soccer, life saving, mountain biking, outdoor activities, outdoor recreation, outdoor skills, physical fitness, physical training, weight training, whiffle ball, yoga. 1 PE instructor, 2 coaches.

Computers Computers are regularly used in computer applications, journalism, literary magazine, media arts, media production, multimedia, news writing, newspaper, photography, photojournalism classes. Computer network features include on-campus library services, Internet access, wireless campus network, Internet filtering or blocking technology, Naviance. Campus intranet, student e-mail accounts, and computer access in designated common areas are available to students. Students grades are available online. The school has a published electronic and media policy.

Contact John Harniman, Director of Admission. 518-686-7331. Fax: 518-686-3370. E-mail: jharniman@hoosac.org. Website: www.hoosac.com

HOPE CHRISTIAN SCHOOL

PO Box 235
Champion, Alberta T0L 0R0, Canada

Head of School: Mr. Dale Anger

General Information Coeducational day and distance learning college-preparatory and general academic school, affiliated with Evangelical Free Church of America. Grades 1–12. Distance learning grades 1–12. Founded: 1980. Setting: small town. Nearest major city is Lethbridge, Canada. 1-acre campus. 2 buildings on campus. Approved or accredited by Alberta Department of Education. Language of instruction: English. Total enrollment: 24. Upper school average class size: 10. Upper school faculty-student ratio: 1:12. There are 160 required school days per year for Upper School students. Upper School students typically attend 4 days per week. The average school day consists of 6 hours and 45 minutes.

Upper School Student Profile Grade 6: 2 students (1 boy, 1 girl); Grade 7: 4 students (1 boy, 3 girls); Grade 9: 1 student (1 girl); Grade 10: 1 student (1 girl).

Faculty School total: 4. In upper school: 2 men.

Subjects Offered All academic.

Student Life Upper grades have uniform requirement, student council. Discipline rests primarily with faculty. Attendance at religious services is required.

Admissions For fall 2016, 3 students applied for upper-level admission, 3 were accepted, 3 enrolled. Placement test required. Deadline for receipt of application materials: none. No application fee required. Interview required.

Computers Computer resources include Internet filtering or blocking technology. Campus intranet and computer access in designated common areas are available to students. Students grades are available online.

Contact Mr. Dale Anger, Principal. 403-897-3019 Ext. 1. Fax: 403-897-2392. E-mail: principal@hopechristianschool.ca. Website: www.hopechristianschool.ca

HORIZON CHRISTIAN SCHOOL

1889 Belmont Drive
Hood River, Oregon 97031

Head of School: Mr. Ken Block

General Information Coeducational day college-preparatory school. Grades 9–12. Distance learning grades 11–12. Setting: small town. Nearest major city is Portland.

8.5-acre campus. 1 building on campus. Approved or accredited by Association of Christian Schools International and Oregon Department of Education. Upper school average class size: 18. There are 166 required school days per year for Upper School students. Upper School students typically attend 5 days per week. The average school day consists of 5 hours and 50 minutes.

Upper School Student Profile Grade 6: 12 students (7 boys, 5 girls); Grade 7: 7 students (4 boys, 3 girls); Grade 8: 20 students (13 boys, 7 girls); Grade 9: 10 students (6 boys, 4 girls); Grade 10: 15 students (11 boys, 4 girls); Grade 11: 19 students (8 boys, 11 girls); Grade 12: 26 students (15 boys, 11 girls).

Faculty School total: 12. In upper school: 7 men, 5 women; 5 have advanced degrees.

Subjects Offered All academic.

Graduation Requirements American government, American history, arts and fine arts (art, music, dance, drama), chemistry, composition, computer skills, economics, electives, finance, foreign language, geography, government, literature seminar, mathematics, physical education (includes health), religion (includes Bible studies and theology), science.

Special Academic Programs Study at local college for college credit.

College Admission Counseling 16 students graduated in 2016; 14 went to college, including Cabrillo College; Concordia University Wisconsin; Denison University; Dordt College; Grand Canyon University. Other: 1 entered military service, 1 had other specific plans.

Student Life Upper grades have specified standards of dress, student council, honor system. Discipline rests primarily with faculty.

Tuition and Aid Day student tuition: $8385. Tuition installment plan (monthly payment plans, individually arranged payment plans). Tuition reduction for siblings, need-based scholarship grants available. In 2016–17, 42% of upper-school students received aid.

Admissions Traditional secondary-level entrance grade is 9. For fall 2016, 3 students applied for upper-level admission, 3 were accepted, 3 enrolled. Any standardized test required. Application fee required: $100. Interview recommended.

Athletics Interscholastic: basketball (boys, girls), soccer (b); coed interscholastic: golf, soccer, track and field. 1 PE instructor, 1 athletic trainer.

Computers Computers are regularly used in all academic classes. Computer network features include on-campus library services, Internet access, wireless campus network, Internet filtering or blocking technology. Campus intranet and computer access in designated common areas are available to students. Students grades are available online. The school has a published electronic and media policy.

Contact 541-387-3200. Fax: 541-386-3651.
Website: www.horizonchristianschool.org/

THE HOTCHKISS SCHOOL

11 Interlaken Road
Lakeville, Connecticut 06039

Head of School: Mr. Craig W. Bradley

General Information Coeducational boarding and day college-preparatory school. Grades 9–PG. Founded: 1891. Setting: rural. Nearest major city is Hartford. Students are housed in single-sex dormitories. 827-acre campus. 80 buildings on campus. Approved or accredited by Connecticut Association of Independent Schools, New England Association of Schools and Colleges, The Association of Boarding Schools, and Connecticut Department of Education. Member of National Association of Independent Schools and Secondary School Admission Test Board. Endowment: $444.1 million. Total enrollment: 598. Upper school average class size: 12. Upper school faculty-student ratio: 1:5. There are 172 required school days per year for Upper School students. Upper School students typically attend 6 days per week. The average school day consists of 6 hours and 50 minutes.

Upper School Student Profile Grade 9: 127 students (69 boys, 58 girls); Grade 10: 166 students (77 boys, 89 girls); Grade 11: 161 students (70 boys, 91 girls); Grade 12: 165 students (86 boys, 79 girls); Postgraduate: 10 students (7 boys, 3 girls).

Faculty School total: 152. In upper school: 77 men, 75 women; 86 have advanced degrees; 94 reside on campus.

Subjects Offered 3-dimensional design, acting, advanced math, Advanced Placement courses, advanced studio art-AP, African studies, algebra, American history, American history-AP, American literature, anatomy, anatomy and physiology, Ancient Greek, ancient history, architecture, art, art history-AP, astronomy, ballet, Bible, bioethics, bioethics, DNA and culture, biology, biology-AP, calculus, calculus-AP, ceramics, chemistry, chemistry-AP, China/Japan history, Chinese, chorus, classics, college counseling, comparative government and politics-AP, comparative politics, computer programming, computer science, computer science-AP, conceptual physics, constitutional history of U.S., creative writing, dance, digital photography, discrete mathematics, drama, drawing, economics, economics-AP, English, English-AP, environmental science, environmental science-AP, ethics, European history, European history-AP, expository writing, fine arts, French, French language-AP, French literature-AP, geometry, German, Greek, history of music, Holocaust, humanities, independent study, jazz dance, jazz ensemble, Latin, Latin American history, Latin-AP, limnology, mathematics, Middle East, music, music history, music technology, music theory, music theory-AP, musical productions, non-Western literature, orchestra, organic chemistry, philosophy, photography, physics, physics-AP, playwriting, pre-calculus, public

speaking, religion, science, Spanish, Spanish language-AP, Spanish literature-AP, statistics-AP, studio art, theater, trigonometry, video, voice, world literature, writing.

Graduation Requirements American history, arts and fine arts (art, music, dance, drama), English, foreign language, mathematics, science.

Special Academic Programs Advanced Placement exam preparation; honors section; independent study; term-away projects; study abroad; academic accommodation for the gifted, the musically talented, and the artistically talented.

College Admission Counseling 168 students graduated in 2016; all went to college, including Cornell University; Georgetown University; Harvard University; New York University; University of Chicago; Yale University.

Student Life Upper grades have specified standards of dress, student council. Discipline rests equally with students and faculty.

Summer Programs Enrichment, art/fine arts, computer instruction programs offered; session focuses on academic enrichment; held on campus; accepts boys and girls; open to students from other schools. 215 students usually enrolled. 2017 schedule: July 2 to July 30. Application deadline: none.

Tuition and Aid Day student tuition: $48,080; 7-day tuition and room/board: $56,545. Tuition installment plan (monthly payment plans). Need-based scholarship grants, need-based loans available. In 2016–17, 34% of upper-school students received aid. Total amount of financial aid awarded in 2016–17: $9,412,766.

Admissions Traditional secondary-level entrance grade is 9. For fall 2016, 1,782 students applied for upper-level admission, 338 were accepted, 189 enrolled. ACT, ISEE, PSAT, SAT, or ACT for applicants to grade 11 and 12, SSAT or TOEFL required. Deadline for receipt of application materials: January 15. Application fee required: $70. On-campus interview required.

Athletics Interscholastic: baseball (boys), basketball (b,g), cross-country running (b,g), diving (b,g), field hockey (g), football (b), golf (b,g), ice hockey (b,g), lacrosse (b,g), soccer (b,g), softball (g), squash (b,g), swimming and diving (b,g), tennis (b,g), touch football (b), track and field (b,g), volleyball (g), water polo (b), wrestling (b); coed interscholastic: Frisbee, sailing, ultimate Frisbee; coed intramural: aerobics, aerobics/Nautilus, ballet, basketball, canoeing/kayaking, climbing, combined training, dance, drill team, fitness, fitness walking, Frisbee, golf, hiking/backpacking, ice hockey, jogging, Nautilus, outdoor education, paddle tennis, physical fitness, physical training, rock climbing, running, squash, strength & conditioning, tennis, ultimate Frisbee, volleyball, walking, wall climbing, water polo, weight lifting, yoga. 2 coaches, 2 athletic trainers.

Computers Computers are regularly used in all academic classes. Computer network features include on-campus library services, online commercial services, Internet access, wireless campus network, Internet filtering or blocking technology. Campus intranet, student e-mail accounts, and computer access in designated common areas are available to students. Students grades are available online. The school has a published electronic and media policy.

Contact 860-435-2591. Website: www.hotchkiss.org

HOUGHTON ACADEMY

9790 Thayer Street
Houghton, New York 14744

Head of School: Mr. John Nelson

General Information Coeducational boarding and day college-preparatory school, affiliated with Christian faith. Grades 7–12. Founded: 1883. Setting: rural. Nearest major city is Buffalo. Students are housed in single-sex dormitories and staff house, townhouse. 25-acre campus. 6 buildings on campus. Approved or accredited by Association of Christian Schools International, Middle States Association of Colleges and Schools, and New York Department of Education. Member of National Association of Independent Schools and Secondary School Admission Test Board. Endowment: $90,000. Total enrollment: 124. Upper school average class size: 16. Upper school faculty-student ratio: 1:7. There are 176 required school days per year for Upper School students. Upper School students typically attend 5 days per week. The average school day consists of 6 hours and 30 minutes.

Upper School Student Profile Grade 9: 24 students (9 boys, 15 girls); Grade 10: 22 students (11 boys, 11 girls); Grade 11: 38 students (22 boys, 16 girls); Grade 12: 24 students (13 boys, 11 girls). 55% of students are boarding students. 45% are state residents. 3 states are represented in upper school student body. 52% are international students. International students from Cameroon, China, Nigeria, Republic of Korea, and Rwanda; 6 other countries represented in student body. 50% of students are Christian.

Faculty School total: 20. In upper school: 11 men, 9 women; 14 have advanced degrees; 2 reside on campus.

Subjects Offered Algebra, American history, American literature, art, band, Bible, Bible studies, biology, business, calculus, chemistry, chorus, community service, computer science, creative writing, desktop publishing, earth science, economics, English, English literature, environmental science, ESL, ethics, fine arts, geography, geometry, government/civics, grammar, history, mathematics, music, photography, physical education, physics, physics-AP, public policy, public service, science, social sciences, social studies, Spanish, speech, trigonometry, word processing, world history, writing.

Graduation Requirements Arts and fine arts (art, music, dance, drama), Bible, electives, English, mathematics, physical education (includes health), science, social studies (includes history).

Special Academic Programs 5 Advanced Placement exams for which test preparation is offered; honors section; independent study; study at local college for college credit; ESL (13 students enrolled).

College Admission Counseling 37 students graduated in 2016; 36 went to college, including Gonzaga University; Hofstra University; Houghton College; Northeastern University; Rutgers University–Newark; University at Buffalo, the State University of New York. Other: 1 went to work.

Student Life Upper grades have uniform requirement, student council. Discipline rests primarily with faculty. Attendance at religious services is required.

Tuition and Aid Day student tuition: $6310; 7-day tuition and room/board: $30,735. Tuition installment plan (FACTS Tuition Payment Plan). Need-based scholarship grants available. In 2016–17, 35% of upper-school students received aid. Total amount of financial aid awarded in 2016–17: $95,000.

Admissions Traditional secondary-level entrance grade is 9. For fall 2016, 82 students applied for upper-level admission, 42 were accepted, 32 enrolled. PSAT or SAT, SSAT or TOEFL required. Deadline for receipt of application materials: February 10. Application fee required: $100. Interview recommended.

Athletics Interscholastic: basketball (boys, girls), cheering (g), soccer (b), volleyball (g); intramural: badminton (b,g), basketball (b,g), floor hockey (b,g), golf (b,g), indoor soccer (b,g), paddle tennis (b,g), racquetball (b,g), skiing (downhill) (b,g), soccer (b,g), table tennis (b,g), tennis (b,g), volleyball (b,g); coed interscholastic: golf, track and field; coed intramural: badminton, golf, indoor soccer, paddle tennis, skiing (downhill), softball, table tennis, tennis, volleyball. 1 PE instructor, 1 athletic trainer.

Computers Computers are regularly used in accounting, Bible studies, college planning, English, graphic design, keyboarding, mathematics, multimedia, SAT preparation, science, word processing, yearbook classes. Computer network features include on-campus library services, Internet access, wireless campus network, Internet filtering or blocking technology, electronic access to Houghton College Library holdings. Student e-mail accounts are available to students. Students grades are available online. The school has a published electronic and media policy.

Contact Mrs. Sandy Merrill, Admission Coordinator. 585-567-8115. Fax: 585-567-8048. E-mail: admissions@houghton.academy. Website: www.houghtonacademy.org

HOUSTON ACADEMY

901 Buena Vista Drive
Dothan, Alabama 36303

Head of School: Dr. Scott P. Phillipps

General Information Coeducational day college-preparatory, arts, and technology school. Grades P3–12. Founded: 1970. Setting: small town. Nearest major city is Montgomery. 19-acre campus. 5 buildings on campus. Approved or accredited by Southern Association of Colleges and Schools, Southern Association of Independent Schools, and The College Board. Member of National Association of Independent Schools. Endowment: $700,000. Total enrollment: 621. Upper school average class size: 18. Upper school faculty-student ratio: 1:13. There are 175 required school days per year for Upper School students. Upper School students typically attend 5 days per week. The average school day consists of 7 hours and 15 minutes.

Upper School Student Profile Grade 6: 49 students (24 boys, 25 girls); Grade 7: 67 students (33 boys, 34 girls); Grade 8: 55 students (29 boys, 26 girls); Grade 9: 52 students (33 boys, 19 girls); Grade 10: 64 students (37 boys, 27 girls); Grade 11: 56 students (31 boys, 25 girls); Grade 12: 51 students (25 boys, 26 girls).

Faculty School total: 60. In upper school: 12 men, 22 women; 17 have advanced degrees.

Subjects Offered 20th century history, advanced chemistry, advanced computer applications, advanced math, Advanced Placement courses, algebra, American government, American history, American history-AP, American literature, analysis and differential calculus, art, Basic programming, biology, calculus, calculus-AP, career/college preparation, chemistry, chemistry-AP, chorus, communication skills, composition-AP, computer education, computer information systems, computer programming-AP, computer science, drama, driver education, earth and space science, earth science, economics, English, English composition, English language and composition-AP, English literature and composition-AP, European history, foreign language, French, French-AP, geography, geometry, German, German-AP, government/civics, history, history-AP, honors algebra, honors English, honors geometry, honors U.S. history, human anatomy, jazz band, journalism, Latin, Latin-AP, marching band, math review, mathematics, mathematics-AP, music, music theory-AP, physical education, physics, physics-AP, psychology, reading/study skills, SAT/ACT preparation, science, senior internship, social studies, Spanish, Spanish language-AP, theater, trigonometry, U.S. government, U.S. history-AP, United Nations and international issues, video communication, world history.

Graduation Requirements English, foreign language, mathematics, physical education (includes health), science, social studies (includes history).

Special Academic Programs Advanced Placement exam preparation; honors section; academic accommodation for the gifted and the musically talented; programs in general development for dyslexic students.

College Admission Counseling 38 students graduated in 2015; all went to college, including Auburn University; Birmingham-Southern College; The University of Alabama; The University of Alabama at Birmingham; Vanderbilt University.

Student Life Upper grades have uniform requirement, student council, honor system. Discipline rests primarily with faculty.

Tuition and Aid Day student tuition: $10,365–$10,700. Guaranteed tuition plan. Tuition installment plan (SMART Tuition Payment Plan, monthly payment plans, two-payment plan). Merit scholarship grants, need-based scholarship grants available. In 2015–16, 30% of upper-school students received aid; total upper-school merit-scholarship money awarded: $152,637. Total amount of financial aid awarded in 2015–16: $408,049.

Admissions Traditional secondary-level entrance grade is 7. For fall 2015, 23 students applied for upper-level admission, 21 were accepted, 20 enrolled. OLSAT, Stanford Achievement Test required. Deadline for receipt of application materials: none. Application fee required: $75. On-campus interview required.

Athletics Interscholastic: baseball (boys), basketball (b,g), bowling (b,g), cross-country running (b,g), football (b), golf (b,g), soccer (b,g), softball (g), tennis (b,g), volleyball (g); intramural: cheering (g), dance team (g). 2 PE instructors, 5 coaches, 1 athletic trainer.

Computers Computers are regularly used in all academic classes. Computer network features include on-campus library services, Internet access, Internet filtering or blocking technology. Campus intranet, student e-mail accounts, and computer access in designated common areas are available to students. The school has a published electronic and media policy.

Contact Mrs. Leanne M. Todd, Director of Admissions. 334-794-4106. Fax: 334-793-4053. E-mail: toddl@houstonacademy.com. Website: www.houstonacademy.com

THE HOWARD SCHOOL

Atlanta, Georgia
See Special Needs Schools section.

THE HUDSON SCHOOL

601 Park Avenue
Hoboken, New Jersey 07030

Head of School: Mrs. Suellen F. Newman

General Information Coeducational day college-preparatory, arts, and music, theater, foreign languages school. Grades 5–12. Founded: 1978. Setting: urban. Nearest major city is New York, NY. 1 building on campus. Approved or accredited by Middle States Association of Colleges and Schools, New Jersey Association of Independent Schools, and New Jersey Department of Education. Member of National Association of Independent Schools. Endowment: $2.5 million. Total enrollment: 187. Upper school average class size: 18. Upper school faculty student ratio: 1:4. There are 175 required school days per year for Upper School students. Upper School students typically attend 5 days per week. The average school day consists of 7 hours.

Upper School Student Profile Grade 9: 20 students (6 boys, 14 girls); Grade 10: 17 students (6 boys, 11 girls); Grade 11: 17 students (4 boys, 13 girls); Grade 12: 14 students (8 boys, 6 girls).

Faculty School total: 50. In upper school: 11 men, 19 women; 19 have advanced degrees.

Subjects Offered 3-dimensional design, acting, advanced biology, advanced chemistry, advanced math, Advanced Placement courses, advanced studio art-AP, African drumming, algebra, American literature, American sign language, analysis of data, Ancient Greek, art, art and culture, art history, art history-AP, art-AP, athletics, biology, biology-AP, British literature, calculus, calculus-AP, chamber groups, chemistry, chemistry-AP, Chinese, chorus, community service, computer graphics, computer science, computers, contemporary issues, creative writing, dance, electives, English, English literature, English-AP, environmental education, ESL, ethics, film, French, geometry, German, German literature, guitar, health, history of music, HTML design, humanities, instrumental music, Japanese, jazz band, language arts, Latin, learning strategies, Mandarin, mathematical modeling, mathematics, music, music history, performing arts, personal finance, personal money management, photo shop, photography, physical education, physics, poetry, post-calculus, pre-algebra, pre-calculus, psychology, public speaking, reading/study skills, robotics, Russian, science, science fiction, sculpture, senior project, senior seminar, skills for success, social justice, social sciences, Spanish, statistics, studio art, theater, trigonometry, U.S. history, visual arts, voice, world civilizations, world cultures, world geography, world governments, world history, world literature, writing, yoga.

Graduation Requirements American history, art, art history, biology, chemistry, computer science, English, foreign language, Latin, mathematics, music history, personal finance, physical education (includes health), physics, science, world history. Community service is required.

Special Academic Programs Advanced Placement exam preparation; honors section; accelerated programs; independent study; study at local college for college credit; study abroad; academic accommodation for the gifted, the musically talented, and the artistically talented; remedial reading and/or remedial writing; remedial math; ESL (3 students enrolled).

College Admission Counseling 24 students graduated in 2015; 23 went to college, including Bard College; Drexel University; Franklin & Marshall College; Northeastern University; Rutgers University–New Brunswick; University of Vermont. Other: 1 had other specific plans. Median SAT critical reading: 590, median SAT math: 590, median SAT writing: 600, median combined SAT: 1780. Mean composite ACT: 29. 37% scored over 600 on SAT critical reading, 32% scored over 600 on SAT math, 47% scored over 600 on SAT writing, 37% scored over 1800 on combined SAT, 86% scored over 26 on composite ACT.

Student Life Upper grades have student council, honor system. Discipline rests primarily with faculty.

Tuition and Aid Day student tuition: $18,510. Tuition installment plan (monthly payment plans, individually arranged payment plans, semiannual and annual payment plans, quarterly by special arrangement). Need-based scholarship grants available. In 2015–16, 36% of upper-school students received aid. Total amount of financial aid awarded in 2015–16: $308,710.

Admissions Traditional secondary-level entrance grade is 9. For fall 2015, 53 students applied for upper-level admission, 38 were accepted, 15 enrolled. ERB, ISEE or SSAT required. Deadline for receipt of application materials: December 31. Application fee required: $60. On-campus interview required.

Athletics Interscholastic: basketball (boys, girls), soccer (b,g), softball (g); coed interscholastic: track and field; coed intramural: aerobics/dance, dance, fencing, modern dance, outdoor education, physical fitness, yoga. 2 PE instructors, 4 coaches.

Computers Computers are regularly used in business education, college planning, creative writing, desktop publishing, ESL, English, ethics, French, history, humanities, mathematics, music, newspaper, philosophy, photography, photojournalism, programming, publications, Spanish, technology, theater, Web site design, word processing, writing, yearbook classes. Computer network features include on-campus library services, Internet access, wireless campus network, Internet filtering or blocking technology, Chrome books provided to students, free of charge. Campus intranet, student e-mail accounts, and computer access in designated common areas are available to students. Students grades are available online. The school has a published electronic and media policy.

Contact Mrs. Janet F. Wright, Admissions Assistant. 201-659-8335 Ext. 326. Fax: 201-222-3669. E-mail: admissions@thehudsonschool.org.
Website: www.thehudsonschool.org

THE HUN SCHOOL OF PRINCETON

176 Edgerstoune Road
Princeton, New Jersey 08540

Head of School: Mr. Jonathan Brougham

General Information Coeducational boarding and day college-preparatory school. Boarding grades 9–PG, day grades 6–PG. Founded: 1914. Setting: suburban. Nearest major city is New York, NY. Students are housed in single-sex dormitories. 45-acre campus. 7 buildings on campus. Approved or accredited by Middle States Association of Colleges and Schools, New England Association of Schools and Colleges, New Jersey Association of Independent Schools, New Jersey Department of Education, The Association of Boarding Schools, and New Jersey Department of Education. Member of National Association of Independent Schools and Secondary School Admission Test Board. Endowment: $20 million. Total enrollment: 630. Upper school average class size: 15. Upper school faculty-student ratio: 1:8. Upper School students typically attend 5 days per week.

Upper School Student Profile Grade 9: 131 students (74 boys, 57 girls); Grade 10: 118 students (67 boys, 51 girls); Grade 11: 140 students (79 boys, 61 girls); Grade 12: 142 students (74 boys, 68 girls); Postgraduate: 14 students (12 boys, 2 girls). 35% of students are boarding students. 18 states are represented in upper school student body. 13% are international students. International students from Brazil, China, Democratic People's Republic of Korea, Guatemala, Nigeria, and United Kingdom; 24 other countries represented in student body.

Faculty School total: 117. In upper school: 60 men, 57 women; 52 have advanced degrees; 29 reside on campus.

Subjects Offered 3-dimensional art, 3-dimensional design, advanced computer applications, Advanced Placement courses, advanced TOEFL/grammar, algebra, American government, American history, American history-AP, American literature, anatomy, architectural drawing, architecture, art, art history, art history-AP, astrophysics, biology, biology-AP, calculus, calculus-AP, ceramics, chemistry, chemistry-AP, chorus, community service, computer programming, computer science, drama, driver education, economics, engineering, English, English-AP, ESL, European history, fine arts, forensics, French, French-AP, geometry, government/civics, health, history, interdisciplinary studies, jazz band, Latin, Latin-AP, marine biology, mathematics, mechanical drawing, music, photography, physical education, physics, physics-AP, physiology, public speaking, science, social studies, Spanish, Spanish-AP, statistics-AP, television, theater, trigonometry, U.S. history-AP, video, video film production, world history.

Graduation Requirements Arts and fine arts (art, music, dance, drama), computer science, English, foreign language, health, history, mathematics, science, 10-20 hours of community service per year, extracurricular activities.

Special Academic Programs Advanced Placement exam preparation; honors section; academic accommodation for the gifted; programs in general development for dyslexic students; ESL (25 students enrolled).

College Admission Counseling 151 students graduated in 2016; all went to college, including Boston University; Hobart and William Smith Colleges; Princeton

University; Syracuse University; The George Washington University; Villanova University. Median SAT critical reading: 590, median SAT math: 620, median SAT writing: 610, median composite ACT: 27.

Student Life Upper grades have specified standards of dress, student council, honor system. Discipline rests equally with students and faculty.

Summer Programs Remediation, enrichment, advancement, ESL, sports, art/fine arts, computer instruction programs offered; session focuses on make-up courses, enrichment, SAT and TOEFL preparation; held on campus; accepts boys and girls; open to students from other schools. 110 students usually enrolled. 2017 schedule: June 28 to July 23. Application deadline: none.

Tuition and Aid Day student tuition: $39,000; 7-day tuition and room/board: $56,700. Tuition installment plan (Insured Tuition Payment Plan, Academic Management Services Plan, FACTS Tuition Payment Plan, individually arranged payment plans, some customized plans are available). Need-based scholarship grants, prepGATE loans available. In 2016–17, 37% of upper-school students received aid. Total amount of financial aid awarded in 2016–17: $4,600,000.

Admissions Traditional secondary-level entrance grade is 9. For fall 2016, 900 students applied for upper-level admission, 350 were accepted, 198 enrolled. International English Language Test, ISEE, PSAT or SAT for applicants to grade 11 and 12, SSAT or TOEFL required. Deadline for receipt of application materials: January 31. Application fee required: $75. Interview recommended.

Athletics Interscholastic: baseball (boys), basketball (b,g), crew (b,g), cross-country running (b,g), fencing (b,g), field hockey (g), football (b), lacrosse (b,g), soccer (b,g), softball (g), tennis (b,g); intramural: dance squad (g), soccer (b,g), weight training (b,g); coed interscholastic: golf, ice hockey, swimming and diving, track and field; coed intramural: aerobics/dance, aerobics/Nautilus, ballet, basketball, cross-country running, dance, fitness, flag football, Frisbee, jogging, Nautilus, paint ball, physical fitness, running, skiing (downhill), strength & conditioning, touch football, ultimate Frisbee, volleyball, weight lifting. 3 coaches, 2 athletic trainers.

Computers Computers are regularly used in all academic classes. Computer network features include on-campus library services, online commercial services, Internet access, wireless campus network, Internet filtering or blocking technology. Campus intranet, student e-mail accounts, and computer access in designated common areas are available to students. Students grades are available online. The school has a published electronic and media policy.

Contact Mr. Steven C. Bristol, Assistant Headmaster for Enrollment Management and Strategic Planning. 609-921-7600. Fax: 609-279-9398. E-mail: admiss@hunschool.org.
Website: www.hunschool.org

HUNTINGTON-SURREY SCHOOL

5206 Balcones Drive
Austin, Texas 78731

Head of School: Dr. Light Bailey German

General Information Coeducational day college-preparatory and writing school. Grades 9–12. Founded: 1973. Setting: urban. 1 building on campus. Approved or accredited by Southern Association of Colleges and Schools, The College Board, and Texas Department of Education. Total enrollment: 36. Upper school average class size: 6. Upper school faculty-student ratio: 1:2. There are 160 required school days per year for Upper School students. Upper School students typically attend 5 days per week. The average school day consists of 4 hours and 50 minutes.

Upper School Student Profile Grade 9: 4 students (3 boys, 1 girl); Grade 10: 9 students (8 boys, 1 girl); Grade 11: 8 students (3 boys, 5 girls); Grade 12: 8 students (5 boys, 3 girls).

Faculty School total: 18. In upper school: 7 men, 11 women; 11 have advanced degrees.

Subjects Offered Algebra, art, biology, calculus, chemistry, college planning, comparative religion, creative drama, discrete mathematics, drama, ecology, environmental systems, English, French, geometry, German, history, Latin, literature, math analysis, math review, mathematics, philosophy, physical science, physics, portfolio art, pre-algebra, pre-calculus, senior science survey, social studies, Spanish, student publications, study skills, theater arts, trigonometry, U.S. history, work-study, world history, writing, yearbook, yoga.

Graduation Requirements American literature, biology, British literature, economics, foreign language, mathematics, science, U.S. government, U.S. history, world history, world literature, writing, senior research project, school exit examinations: assertion with proof essay exam and mathematical competency exam, senior advisory course.

Special Academic Programs Accelerated programs; academic accommodation for the gifted.

College Admission Counseling 13 students graduated in 2016; all went to college, including Eckerd College; Hampshire College; Sam Houston State University; Southwestern University; St. Edward's University; Stephen F. Austin State University. Median SAT critical reading: 580, median SAT math: 530, median SAT writing: 610, median combined SAT: 1720. 25% scored over 600 on SAT critical reading, 33% scored over 600 on SAT math, 50% scored over 600 on SAT writing, 33% scored over 1800 on combined SAT.

Student Life Upper grades have student council, honor system. Discipline rests primarily with faculty.

Summer Programs Remediation, enrichment, advancement programs offered; session focuses on one-on-one teaching or small classes, college preparation; held both on and off campus; accepts boys and girls; open to students from other schools. 12 students usually enrolled. 2017 schedule: June 5 to July 28. Application deadline: May 1.

Tuition and Aid Day student tuition: $1350. Tuition installment plan (monthly payment plans).

Admissions Traditional secondary-level entrance grade is 9. For fall 2016, 12 students applied for upper-level admission, 9 were accepted, 9 enrolled. Deadline for receipt of application materials: none. No application fee required. On-campus interview recommended.

Athletics Coed Intramural: yoga. 1 PE instructor.

Computers Computers are regularly used in science, study skills, writing classes. Computer resources include study hall computers and printers (available for student use). Computer access in designated common areas is available to students.

Contact Ms. Johni Walker-Little, Assistant Director. 512-478-4743. Fax: 512-457-0235. Website: www.huntingtonsurrey.com

HYDE PARK BAPTIST SCHOOL

3901 Speedway
Austin, Texas 78751

Head of School: Mr. Bob Liverman

General Information Coeducational day college-preparatory, arts, business, religious studies, and technology school, affiliated with Baptist Church. Grades PK–12. Founded: 1968. Setting: urban. 60-acre campus. 1 building on campus. Approved or accredited by Accreditation Commission of the Texas Association of Baptist Schools, Southern Association of Colleges and Schools, Texas Private School Accreditation Commission, and Texas Department of Education. Endowment: $236,500. Total enrollment: 599. Upper school average class size: 18. Upper school faculty-student ratio: 1:12. There are 175 required school days per year for Upper School students. Upper School students typically attend 5 days per week. The average school day consists of 7 hours and 20 minutes.

Upper School Student Profile Grade 9: 61 students (37 boys, 24 girls); Grade 10: 75 students (39 boys, 36 girls); Grade 11: 72 students (36 boys, 36 girls); Grade 12: 78 students (49 boys, 29 girls). 10% of students are Baptist.

Faculty School total: 35. In upper school: 10 men, 24 women; 9 have advanced degrees.

Subjects Offered Algebra, anatomy and physiology, art, athletics, Bible, Bible studies, biology, biology-AP, calculus, calculus-AP, cheerleading, chemistry, chemistry-AP, choir, choral music, Christian doctrine, Christian education, Christian ethics, Christian studies, college writing, communication skills, computer information systems, computer technologies, creative writing, digital photography, drama performance, earth science, economics, economics-AP, English, English language and composition-AP, English literature and composition-AP, English literature-AP, English-AP, environmental science, ESL, film and literature, French, geometry, government/civics, health, honors algebra, honors English, honors geometry, honors U.S. history, honors world history, internship, keyboarding, Latin, Latin-AP, macroeconomics-AP, marine biology, microeconomics-AP, musical productions, personal money management, physical education, physics, physics-AP, pre-algebra, pre-calculus, psychology, public speaking, SAT preparation, science, sign language, sociology, Spanish, Spanish-AP, speech, statistics-AP, study skills, theater, theater arts, U.S. government, U.S. government and politics-AP, U.S. history, U.S. history-AP, world geography, world history, writing, yearbook.

Graduation Requirements Arts and fine arts (art, music, dance, drama), Bible studies, computer science, electives, English, foreign language, mathematics, physical education (includes health), public speaking, religion (includes Bible studies and theology), science, social studies (includes history), speech, sports, 15 hours of community service per year.

Special Academic Programs Advanced Placement exam preparation; honors section; independent study.

College Admission Counseling 70 students graduated in 2016; 69 went to college, including Baylor University; Texas A&M University; Texas Christian University; Texas State University; The University of Texas at Austin. Other: 1 went to work. Mean SAT critical reading: 564, mean SAT math: 582, mean SAT writing: 570, mean combined SAT: 1696, mean composite ACT: 24. 36% scored over 600 on SAT critical reading, 41% scored over 600 on SAT math, 31% scored over 600 on SAT writing, 25% scored over 26 on composite ACT.

Student Life Upper grades have specified standards of dress, student council, honor system. Discipline rests primarily with faculty. Attendance at religious services is required.

Tuition and Aid Day student tuition: $15,800. Tuition installment plan (SMART Tuition Payment Plan, monthly payment plans). Tuition reduction for siblings, merit scholarship grants, need-based scholarship grants available. In 2016–17, 14% of upper-school students received aid; total upper-school merit-scholarship money awarded: $5000. Total amount of financial aid awarded in 2016–17: $145,250.

Admissions Traditional secondary-level entrance grade is 9. For fall 2016, 77 students applied for upper-level admission, 60 were accepted, 55 enrolled. ISEE required.

Deadline for receipt of application materials: none. Application fee required: $150. On-campus interview recommended.

Athletics Interscholastic: baseball (boys), basketball (b,g), cheering (g), cross-country running (b,g), dance squad (g), dance team (g), drill team (g), football (b), golf (b,g), soccer (b,g), softball (g), strength & conditioning (b,g), tennis (b,g), track and field (b,g), volleyball (g). 1 PE instructor, 8 coaches, 1 athletic trainer.

Computers Computers are regularly used in business applications, computer applications, desktop publishing, keyboarding, multimedia, technology, Web site design, word processing, yearbook classes. Computer network features include on-campus library services, online commercial services, Internet access, wireless campus network, Internet filtering or blocking technology. Students grades are available online. The school has a published electronic and media policy.

Contact Mrs. Lisa Thomas, Director of Admissions, High School. 512-465-8333. Fax: 512-827-2020. E-mail: lthomas@hp-schools.org. Website: www.hp-schools.org

HYDE SCHOOL

PO Box 237
150 Route 169
Woodstock, Connecticut 06281

Head of School: Bob Felt

General Information Coeducational boarding and day college-preparatory, general academic, and leadership school. Grades 9–12. Founded: 1996. Setting: rural. Nearest major city is Providence, RI. Students are housed in coed dormitories. 120-acre campus. 7 buildings on campus. Approved or accredited by Association of Independent Schools in New England, Connecticut Association of Independent Schools, New England Association of Schools and Colleges, The Association of Boarding Schools, and Connecticut Department of Education. Member of National Association of Independent Schools. Endowment: $8 million. Total enrollment: 151. Upper school average class size: 6. Upper school faculty-student ratio: 1:6. There are 222 required school days per year for Upper School students. Upper School students typically attend 6 days per week. The average school day consists of 6 hours and 30 minutes.

Upper School Student Profile Grade 9: 12 students (8 boys, 4 girls); Grade 10: 25 students (18 boys, 7 girls); Grade 11: 54 students (38 boys, 16 girls); Grade 12: 58 students (40 boys, 18 girls); Postgraduate: 2 students (2 boys). 98% of students are boarding students. 24% are state residents. 21 states are represented in upper school student body. 27% are international students. International students from Brazil, China, Rwanda, Serbia and Montenegro, Sri Lanka, and Syrian Arab Republic; 1 other country represented in student body.

Faculty School total: 23. In upper school: 15 men, 8 women; 11 have advanced degrees, all reside on campus.

Subjects Offered 20th century history, advanced chemistry, Advanced Placement courses, algebra, athletics, biology, calculus, calculus-AP, character education, chemistry, English, English language and composition-AP, English language-AP, English literature, environmental science-AP, ethics, geometry, global issues, independent study, media arts, physics, pre-calculus, Spanish, Spanish-AP, sports, U.S. history, U.S. history-AP, wilderness education, wilderness experience.

Graduation Requirements Electives, English, foreign language, mathematics, science, social studies (includes history). Hyde's graduation requirements embody academic achievement and character development. Character growth is determined through an intense 40-hour, evaluation process involving all members of the senior class and faculty. All students make a speech at graduation representing their principles.

Special Academic Programs 5 Advanced Placement exams for which test preparation is offered; honors section; independent study; remedial reading and/or remedial writing; remedial math; ESL (26 students enrolled).

College Admission Counseling 55 students graduated in 2016; 53 went to college, including Boston University; Drexel University; Eastern Connecticut State University; Rutgers University–New Brunswick; University of Illinois at Urbana–Champaign; Wheaton College. Other: 2 entered a postgraduate year. Median SAT critical reading: 488, median SAT math: 536, median SAT writing: 481, median combined SAT: 1505, median composite ACT: 20.

Student Life Upper grades have specified standards of dress, honor system. Discipline rests equally with students and faculty.

Summer Programs Remediation, enrichment, advancement, ESL, sports, art/fine arts, rigorous outdoor training programs offered; session focuses on orientation for the fall and summer enrichment; held both on and off campus; accepts boys and girls; open to students from other schools. 50 students usually enrolled. 2017 schedule: June 5 to August 31. Application deadline: June 5.

Tuition and Aid Day student tuition: $28,500; 5-day tuition and room/board: $53,500; 7-day tuition and room/board: $53,500. Tuition installment plan (monthly payment plans, individually arranged payment plans). Tuition reduction for siblings, need-based scholarship grants available. In 2016–17, 30% of upper-school students received aid. Total amount of financial aid awarded in 2016–17: $258,000.

Admissions Traditional secondary-level entrance grade is 11. For fall 2016, 151 students applied for upper-level admission, 106 were accepted, 94 enrolled. Deadline for receipt of application materials: none. Application fee required: $100. Interview required.

Athletics Interscholastic: basketball (boys, girls), cross-country running (b,g), football (b), lacrosse (b,g), soccer (b,g), tennis (b,g), track and field (b,g), wrestling (b); coed interscholastic: equestrian sports, ropes courses, winter (indoor) track, wrestling; coed intramural: backpacking, canoeing/kayaking, climbing, dance team, hiking/backpacking, outdoor activities, outdoor adventure, outdoor skills, rafting, ropes courses, wilderness. 2 athletic trainers.

Computers Computers are regularly used in art, design, digital applications, drawing and design, graphic design classes. Computer network features include on-campus library services, online commercial services, Internet access, wireless campus network, Internet filtering or blocking technology. Student e-mail accounts and computer access in designated common areas are available to students. Students grades are available online. The school has a published electronic and media policy.

Contact Holly Thompson, Director of Admission. 860-963-4721. Fax: 860-928-0612. E-mail: hthompson@hyde.edu. Website: www.hyde.edu

HYDE SCHOOL

616 High Street
Bath, Maine 04530

Head of School: Laura Gauld

General Information Coeducational boarding and day college-preparatory, general academic, and leadership school. Grades 9–12. Founded: 1966. Setting: small town. Nearest major city is Portland. Students are housed in coed dormitories. 145-acre campus. 32 buildings on campus. Approved or accredited by Association of Independent Schools in New England, Independent Schools of Northern New England, New England Association of Schools and Colleges, and The Association of Boarding Schools. Member of National Association of Independent Schools. Endowment: $16.5 million. Total enrollment: 150. Upper school average class size: 7. Upper school faculty-student ratio: 1:6. There are 191 required school days per year for Upper School students. Upper School students typically attend 6 days per week. The average school day consists of 7 hours.

Upper School Student Profile Grade 9: 7 students (3 boys, 4 girls); Grade 10: 20 students (15 boys, 5 girls); Grade 11: 52 students (38 boys, 14 girls); Grade 12: 46 students (24 boys, 22 girls); Postgraduate: 4 students (3 boys, 1 girl). 99% of students are boarding students. 21% are state residents. 27 states are represented in upper school student body. 21% are international students. International students from Brazil, British Indian Ocean Territory, China, Christmas Island, Denmark, and Sri Lanka; 1 other country represented in student body.

Faculty School total: 23. In upper school: 12 men, 7 women; 16 have advanced degrees; 21 reside on campus.

Subjects Offered 20th century history, 3-dimensional design, acting, advanced biology, advanced chemistry, advanced math, Advanced Placement courses, advanced studio art-AP, advanced TOEFL/grammar, algebra, American government, American history, American history-AP, American literature-AP, ancient history, art, backpacking, band, biology, biology-AP, calculus, calculus-AP, chemistry, chemistry-AP, Chinese, college admission preparation, college counseling, college placement, college planning, college writing, communication skills, communications, comparative government and politics, comparative government and politics-AP, composition-AP, creative writing, early childhood, economics, English, European history, geometry, government, history, music, physical education, physics-AP, pre-calculus, public policy, religion and culture, Spanish, statistics, technical theater, U.S. history, U.S. history-AP.

Graduation Requirements Electives, English, foreign language, history, mathematics, science, Hyde's graduation requirements embody academic achievement and character development. Character growth is determined through an intense 40-hour, evaluation process involving all members of the senior class and faculty. All students make a speech at graduation representing their principles.

Special Academic Programs Advanced Placement exam preparation; honors section; independent study; study at local college for college credit; academic accommodation for the gifted, the musically talented, and the artistically talented; remedial reading and/or remedial writing; remedial math; programs in English, mathematics, general development for dyslexic students; ESL (18 students enrolled).

College Admission Counseling 53 students graduated in 2016; 51 went to college, including Brandeis University; Columbia University; Cornell University; Stanford University; Tufts University; United States Military Academy. Other: 1 went to work, 1 entered military service. Mean SAT critical reading: 530, mean SAT math: 520, mean SAT writing: 520, mean combined SAT: 1570, mean composite ACT: 21. 25% scored over 600 on SAT critical reading, 17% scored over 600 on SAT math, 14% scored over 600 on SAT writing, 18% scored over 1800 on combined SAT, 16% scored over 26 on composite ACT.

Student Life Upper grades have specified standards of dress, student council, honor system. Discipline rests equally with students and faculty.

Summer Programs Remediation, enrichment, advancement, ESL, sports, art/fine arts, rigorous outdoor training, computer instruction programs offered; session focuses on to offer a unique summer experience for teens; held both on and off campus; accepts boys and girls; open to students from other schools. 50 students usually enrolled. 2017 schedule: June 5 to August 31. Application deadline: June 5.

Tuition and Aid Day student tuition: $28,500; 5-day tuition and room/board: $53,500; 7-day tuition and room/board: $53,500. Tuition installment plan (The Tuition Plan, individually arranged payment plans). Tuition reduction for siblings, merit scholarship grants, need-based scholarship grants available. In 2016–17, 33% of upper-school students received aid. Total amount of financial aid awarded in 2016–17: $1,300,000.

Admissions Traditional secondary-level entrance grade is 9. For fall 2016, 137 students applied for upper-level admission, 83 were accepted, 68 enrolled. Deadline for receipt of application materials: none. Application fee required: $100. Interview required.

Athletics Interscholastic: basketball (boys, girls), crew (b,g), cross-country running (b,g), dance team (g), field hockey (g), football (b), lacrosse (b,g), rowing (b), soccer (b,g), swimming and diving (b,g), tennis (b,g), track and field (b,g), ultimate Frisbee (b); coed interscholastic: aerobics, aerobics/dance, aerobics/Nautilus, aquatics, climbing, dance, equestrian sports, hiking/backpacking, indoor track, nordic skiing, rock climbing, ropes courses, wrestling; coed intramural: hiking/backpacking, kayaking, life saving, outdoor adventure, outdoor skills, physical fitness, physical training, project adventure, ropes courses, skateboarding, skiing (downhill), snowshoeing, strength & conditioning, ultimate Frisbee, walking, weight lifting, weight training, wilderness, wilderness survival. 1 coach, 1 athletic trainer.

Computers Computers are regularly used in graphic design, video film production classes. Computer network features include on-campus library services, online commercial services, Internet access, wireless campus network, Internet filtering or blocking technology. Student e-mail accounts are available to students. Students grades are available online. The school has a published electronic and media policy.

Contact Wanda Smith, Admission Assistant. 207-443-7101. Fax: 207-442-9346. E-mail: wsmith@hyde.edu. Website: www.hyde.edu

HYMAN BRAND HEBREW ACADEMY OF GREATER KANSAS CITY

5801 West 115th Street
Overland Park, Kansas 66211

Head of School: Mr. Howard Haas

General Information Coeducational day college-preparatory and general academic school, affiliated with Jewish faith. Grades K–12. Founded: 1966. Setting: suburban. Nearest major city is Kansas City, MO. 32-acre campus. 1 building on campus. Approved or accredited by Independent Schools Association of the Central States. Languages of instruction: English and Hebrew. Endowment: $8.9 million. Total enrollment: 232. Upper school average class size: 11. Upper school faculty-student ratio: 1:5. There are 178 required school days per year for Upper School students. Upper School students typically attend 5 days per week. The average school day consists of 7 hours and 45 minutes.

Upper School Student Profile Grade 9: 12 students (6 boys, 6 girls); Grade 10: 11 students (9 boys, 2 girls); Grade 11: 14 students (4 boys, 10 girls); Grade 12: 4 students (1 boy, 3 girls). 100% of students are Jewish.

Faculty School total: 42. In upper school: 12 men, 10 women; 17 have advanced degrees.

Subjects Offered 3-dimensional design, algebra, American government, American history, American history-AP, American literature, anatomy and physiology, art, art history, Bible studies, biology, British literature, calculus-AP, chemistry, community service, computer applications, computer science, digital art, economics, English, English language and composition-AP, English literature, English literature and composition-AP, environmental science, ethics, European history, fine arts, geometry, health, Hebrew, Hebrew scripture, Holocaust seminar, Jewish studies, marine biology, model United Nations, physical education, physics, statistics-AP, Talmud, technology/design, trigonometry, U.S. government and politics-AP, U.S. history, U.S. history-AP, world history, world literature, yearbook.

Graduation Requirements Arts and fine arts (art, music, dance, drama), English, foreign language, mathematics, physical education (includes health), religion (includes Bible studies and theology), science, social studies (includes history). Community service is required.

Special Academic Programs 6 Advanced Placement exams for which test preparation is offered; honors section; independent study; study at local college for college credit; academic accommodation for the gifted.

College Admission Counseling 11 students graduated in 2016; all went to college, including Bradley University; The University of Kansas; Tulane University; University of Maryland, College Park; University of Richmond; Washington University in St. Louis. Median composite ACT: 28. 80% scored over 26 on composite ACT.

Student Life Upper grades have specified standards of dress, student council. Discipline rests primarily with faculty. Attendance at religious services is required.

Tuition and Aid Day student tuition: $9300. Tuition installment plan (FACTS Tuition Payment Plan). Need-based scholarship grants available. In 2016–17, 46% of upper-school students received aid. Total amount of financial aid awarded in 2016–17: $97,107.

Admissions Traditional secondary-level entrance grade is 9. For fall 2016, 2 students applied for upper-level admission, 2 were accepted, 2 enrolled. Any standardized test, latest standardized score from previous school, standardized test scores or writing sample required. Deadline for receipt of application materials: none. Application fee required: $50.

Athletics Interscholastic: basketball (boys, girls), soccer (b,g), tennis (b,g); coed interscholastic: cross-country running. 2 PE instructors, 6 coaches.

Computers Computers are regularly used in computer applications, desktop publishing, digital applications, economics, English, foreign language, humanities, journalism, mathematics, newspaper, psychology, religious studies, science, social studies, writing, yearbook classes. Computer network features include on-campus library services, Internet access, wireless campus network, Internet filtering or blocking technology. Student e-mail accounts and computer access in designated common areas are available to students. Students grades are available online. The school has a published electronic and media policy.

Contact Mrs. Tamara Lawson Schuster, Director of Admissions. 913-327-8135. Fax: 913-327-8180. E-mail: tschuster@hbha.edu. Website: www.hbha.edu

ILLIANA CHRISTIAN HIGH SCHOOL

2261 Indiana Avenue

Lansing, Illinois 60438

Head of School: Peter Boonstra

General Information Coeducational day college-preparatory, general academic, arts, business, vocational, and religious studies school, affiliated with Reformed Church in America; primarily serves students with learning disabilities, individuals with Attention Deficit Disorder, individuals with emotional and behavioral problems, dyslexic students, and IEP & 504 Plans. Grades 9–12. Founded: 1945. Setting: suburban. Nearest major city is Chicago. 15-acre campus. 1 building on campus. Approved or accredited by Association of Christian Schools International, North Central Association of Colleges and Schools, and Illinois Department of Education. Endowment: $17 million. Total enrollment: 520. Upper school average class size: 21. Upper school faculty-student ratio: 1:18. Upper School students typically attend 5 days per week. The average school day consists of 7 hours and 10 minutes.

Upper School Student Profile Grade 9: 155 students (87 boys, 68 girls); Grade 10: 187 students (97 boys, 90 girls); Grade 11: 170 students (92 boys, 78 girls); Grade 12: 163 students (75 boys, 88 girls). 70% of students are Reformed Church in America.

Faculty School total: 41. In upper school: 20 men, 21 women; 32 have advanced degrees.

Subjects Offered Algebra, American history, American literature, art, arts, Bible studies, biology, botany, business, business skills, calculus, ceramics, chemistry, computer programming, computer science, drama, earth science, economics, English, environmental science, European history, expository writing, fine arts, geometry, German, government/civics, history, home economics, industrial arts, journalism, mathematics, music, physical education, physics, psychology, social studies, sociology, Spanish, theater, typing, world history, world literature, zoology.

Graduation Requirements Arts and fine arts (art, music, dance, drama), business skills (includes word processing), English, foreign language, mathematics, physical education (includes health), practical arts, religion (includes Bible studies and theology), science, social studies (includes history).

Special Academic Programs Advanced Placement exam preparation; honors section; remedial reading and/or remedial writing; remedial math; programs in English, mathematics for dyslexic students.

College Admission Counseling 110 went to college, including Calvin College; Dordt College; Hope College; Olivet Nazarene University; Purdue University; Trinity Christian College. Other: 9 went to work, 1 entered military service.

Student Life Upper grades have specified standards of dress, student council. Discipline rests primarily with faculty. Attendance at religious services is required.

Summer Programs Sports, art/fine arts programs offered; session focuses on educational and recreational programs; held on campus; accepts boys and girls; open to students from other schools. 100 students usually enrolled. 2017 schedule: June 9 to July 18. Application deadline: none.

Tuition and Aid Day student tuition: $8780. Tuition installment plan (monthly payment plans). Need-based scholarship grants available.

Admissions Traditional secondary-level entrance grade is 9. ACT-Explore required. Deadline for receipt of application materials: none. No application fee required. On-campus interview required.

Athletics Interscholastic: baseball (boys), basketball (b,g), cheering (g), cross-country running (b,g), golf (b), indoor track & field (b,g), soccer (b,g), softball (g), tennis (b,g), track and field (b,g), volleyball (b,g), wrestling (b); coed intramural: bowling. 3 PE instructors, 37 coaches, 1 athletic trainer.

Computers Computers are regularly used in business applications, drawing and design, information technology classes. Computer network features include on-campus library services, online commercial services, Internet access. Students grades are available online. The school has a published electronic and media policy.

Contact Elly Makowski, Admissions Counselor. 708-474-0515 Ext. 49. Fax: 708-474-0581. E-mail: elly.makowski@illianachristian.org. Website: www.illianachristian.org/

IMMACULATA HIGH SCHOOL

600 Shawnee

Leavenworth, Kansas 66048

Head of School: Mr. Richard V. Geraci

General Information Coeducational day college-preparatory, religious studies, and technology school, affiliated with Roman Catholic Church. Grades 7–12. Founded: 1924. Setting: suburban. Nearest major city is Kansas City. 2-acre campus. 1 building on campus. Approved or accredited by National Catholic Education Association, North Central Association of Colleges and Schools, and Kansas Department of Education. Total enrollment: 74. Upper school average class size: 10. Upper school faculty-student ratio: 1:9. There are 171 required school days per year for Upper School students. Upper School students typically attend 5 days per week. The average school day consists of 7 hours and 30 minutes.

Upper School Student Profile 82% of students are Roman Catholic.

Faculty School total: 15. In upper school: 6 men, 9 women; 7 have advanced degrees.

Special Academic Programs Honors section; study at local college for college credit.

College Admission Counseling 26 students graduated in 2016; 24 went to college, including Johnson County Community College. 33% scored over 26 on composite ACT

Student Life Upper grades have uniform requirement, student council. Discipline rests primarily with faculty. Attendance at religious services is required.

Admissions Traditional secondary-level entrance grade is 9. ACT, ACT-Explore or Scholastic Achievement Test required. Deadline for receipt of application materials: none. Application fee required: $150. Interview recommended.

Athletics Interscholastic: baseball (boys), basketball (b,g), cheering (g), dance team (g), football (b), golf (b), power lifting (b,g), soccer (b,g), softball (g), swimming and diving (b), tennis (b,g), track and field (b,g), volleyball (g), wrestling (b). 2 PE instructors, 6 coaches.

Computers Computers are regularly used in all classes. Computer network features include on-campus library services, Internet access, wireless campus network, Internet filtering or blocking technology. Campus intranet and student e-mail accounts are available to students. Students grades are available online.

Contact Ms. Lisa Forge, Academic Advisor. 913-682-3900. Fax: 913-682-9036. E-mail: lisa.forge@leavenworthcatholicschools.org.
Website: www.leavenworthcatholicschools.org

IMMACULATA HIGH SCHOOL

240 Mountain Avenue

Somerville, New Jersey 08876

Head of School: Mrs. Jean Kline

General Information Coeducational day college-preparatory school, affiliated with Roman Catholic Church. Grades 9–12. Founded: 1962. Setting: suburban. 19-acre campus. 3 buildings on campus. Approved or accredited by New Jersey Department of Education and New Jersey Department of Education. Total enrollment: 690. Upper school average class size: 22. Upper school faculty-student ratio: 1:13. There are 180 required school days per year for Upper School students. Upper School students typically attend 5 days per week. The average school day consists of 6 hours and 30 minutes.

Upper School Student Profile Grade 9: 124 students (66 boys, 58 girls); Grade 10: 133 students (72 boys, 61 girls); Grade 11: 113 students (70 boys, 43 girls); Grade 12: 128 students (68 boys, 60 girls). 92% of students are Roman Catholic.

Faculty School total: 71. In upper school: 20 men, 51 women; 28 have advanced degrees.

Subjects Offered American government, American history-AP, American literature-AP, art history, art-AP, band, biology-AP, business education, campus ministry, ceramics, choral music, digital art, digital photography, economics, engineering, English language-AP, English literature and composition-AP, food and nutrition, French, pre-calculus, Shakespeare, Spanish.

Graduation Requirements Algebra, American literature, biology, British literature, geometry, physics, U.S. history.

Special Academic Programs Advanced Placement exam preparation; honors section; academic accommodation for the musically talented.

College Admission Counseling 135 students graduated in 2016; 134 went to college, including Loyola University Maryland; Penn State University Park; Rutgers University–New Brunswick; Saint Joseph's University; Seton Hall University; The University of Scranton. Other: 1 entered military service. Mean SAT critical reading: 538, mean SAT math: 550.

Student Life Upper grades have uniform requirement. Discipline rests primarily with faculty. Attendance at religious services is required.

Tuition and Aid Day student tuition: $13,500. Tuition installment plan (FACTS Tuition Payment Plan). Need-based scholarship grants available.

Admissions Traditional secondary-level entrance grade is 9. For fall 2016, 225 students applied for upper-level admission, 175 were accepted, 135 enrolled. High School Placement Test required. Deadline for receipt of application materials: December 31. Application fee required: $150. On-campus interview required.

Athletics Interscholastic: baseball (boys), basketball (b,g), cheering (g), cross-country running (b,g), football (b), lacrosse (b,g), soccer (b,g), softball (g), tennis (b,g), volleyball (g); coed interscholastic: bowling, golf, swimming and diving. 4 PE instructors, 50 coaches, 1 athletic trainer.

Computers Computers are regularly used in all academic classes. Computer network features include on-campus library services, online commercial services, internet access, wireless campus network, internet filtering or blocking technology, all students issued Chromebooks for school and home use. Student e-mail accounts and computer access in designated common areas are available to students. Students grades are available online. The school has a published electronic and media policy.

Contact Mr. Joseph Conry, Assistant Principal/Academic Dean. 908-722-0200 Ext. 118. Fax: 908-218-7765. E-mail: jconry@immaculatahighschool.org. Website: www.immaculatahighschool.org

IMMACULATA-LA SALLE HIGH SCHOOL

3601 South Miami Avenue
Miami, Florida 33133

Head of School: Sr. Kim Keraitis, FMA

General Information Coeducational day college-preparatory, arts, business, religious studies, and technology school, affiliated with Roman Catholic Church. Grades 9–12. Founded: 1958. Setting: urban. 13-acre campus. 7 buildings on campus. Approved or accredited by Southern Association of Colleges and Schools and Florida Department of Education. Endowment: $109,345. Total enrollment: 832. Upper school average class size: 18. Upper school faculty-student ratio: 1:18. There are 180 required school days per year for Upper School students. Upper School students typically attend 5 days per week. The average school day consists of 6 hours and 30 minutes.

Upper School Student Profile Grade 9: 207 students (62 boys, 145 girls); Grade 10: 224 students (84 boys, 140 girls); Grade 11: 226 students (99 boys, 127 girls); Grade 12: 197 students (80 boys, 117 girls). 93% of students are Roman Catholic.

Faculty School total: 58. In upper school: 23 men, 35 women; 36 have advanced degrees.

Subjects Offered 3-dimensional art, algebra, American government, American history, American history-AP, analytic geometry, anatomy, anatomy and physiology, art, band, Bible studies, biology, business technology, calculus, chemistry, chemistry-AP, Chinese, chorus, church history, comparative government and politics-AP, computer science, computer technology certification, creative writing, critical thinking, desktop publishing, digital photography, drama, driver education, economics, electronics, emerging technology, engineering, English, English language and composition-AP, English literature and composition-AP, environmental science-AP, ethics, European history-AP, filmmaking, finance, fine arts, first aid, French, French language-AP, geometry, government and politics-AP, government/civics, graphic design, health, health and wellness, history, honors algebra, honors English, honors geometry, honors U.S. history, honors world history, keyboarding, marine biology, mathematics, music appreciation, physical education, physics, psychology, religion, science, social studies, sociology, Spanish, U.S. government, U.S. government and politics-AP, U.S. history, U.S. history-AP, video film production, weight training, world history, world religions, yearbook.

Graduation Requirements Arts and fine arts (art, music, dance, drama), business skills (includes word processing), English, foreign language, geometry, mathematics, physical education (includes health), religion (includes Bible studies and theology), science, social studies (includes history), 100 hours of community service.

Special Academic Programs Advanced Placement exam preparation; honors section; independent study; study at local college for college credit.

College Admission Counseling 178 students graduated in 2016; all went to college, including Florida International University; Florida State University; Miami Dade College; New York University; University of Florida; University of Miami. Median SAT critical reading: 500, median SAT math: 500, median SAT writing: 500, median combined SAT: 1500, median composite ACT: 22. 14% scored over 600 on SAT critical reading, 16% scored over 600 on SAT math, 17% scored over 600 on SAT writing, 14% scored over 1800 on combined SAT, 19% scored over 26 on composite ACT.

Student Life Upper grades have uniform requirement, student council, honor system. Discipline rests equally with students and faculty. Attendance at religious services is required.

Summer Programs Remediation, enrichment, advancement programs offered; session focuses on remediation and advancement; held on campus; accepts boys and girls; open to students from other schools. 158 students usually enrolled. 2017 schedule: June 19 to July 14. Application deadline: June 12.

Tuition and Aid Day student tuition: $15,000. Tuition installment plan (FACTS Tuition Payment Plan, monthly payment plans). Merit scholarship grants, paying campus jobs available. In 2016–17, 18% of upper-school students received aid. Total amount of financial aid awarded in 2016–17: $455,000.

Admissions Traditional secondary-level entrance grade is 9. For fall 2016, 405 students applied for upper-level admission, 298 were accepted, 264 enrolled. Catholic High School Entrance Examination and High School Placement Test (closed version) from Scholastic Testing Service required. Deadline for receipt of application materials: none. Application fee required: $50. On-campus interview required.

Athletics Interscholastic: aerobics/dance (girls), baseball (b), basketball (b,g), cheering (g), cross-country running (b,g), dance team (g), football (b), golf (b,g), lacrosse (b), soccer (b,g), softball (g), swimming and diving (b,g), tennis (b,g), track and field (b,g), volleyball (b,g), weight training (b,g), winter soccer (b,g); coed intramural: physical fitness. 1 PE instructor, 12 coaches, 1 athletic trainer.

Computers Computers are regularly used in business, business applications, economics, French, health, history, journalism, mathematics, programming, psychology, religion, science, technology, video film production, word processing, yearbook classes. Computer network features include on-campus library services, online commercial services, Internet access, wireless campus network, Internet filtering or blocking technology. Campus intranet and student e-mail accounts are available to students. Students grades are available online. The school has a published electronic and media policy.

Contact Ms. Wendy Vargas, Admissions Director. 305-854-2334 Ext. 130. Fax: 305-858-5971. E-mail: admissions@ilsroyals.com. Website: www.ilsroyals.com

IMMACULATE CONCEPTION HIGH SCHOOL

258 South Main Street
Lodi, New Jersey 07644-2199

Head of School: Mr. Joseph Robert Azzolino

General Information Girls' day college-preparatory, arts, business, and religious studies school, affiliated with Roman Catholic Church. Ungraded, ages 14–18. Distance learning grades 11–12. Founded: 1915. Setting: suburban. Nearest major city is New York, NY. 3-acre campus. 1 building on campus. Approved or accredited by Middle States Association of Colleges and Schools and New Jersey Department of Education. Upper school average class size: 18. Upper school faculty-student ratio: 1:11. There are 185 required school days per year for Upper School students. Upper School students typically attend 5 days per week. The average school day consists of 6 hours and 20 minutes.

Upper School Student Profile Grade 9: 49 students (49 girls); Grade 10: 52 students (52 girls); Grade 11: 56 students (56 girls); Grade 12: 48 students (48 girls). 85% of students are Roman Catholic.

Faculty School total: 22. In upper school: 6 men, 16 women; 20 have advanced degrees.

Subjects Offered Advanced math, algebra, American government, American history, American history-AP, American literature, anatomy and physiology, art, Bible studies, biology, British literature, character education, chemistry, communications, computer graphics, computer skills, driver education, English, French, genetics, geometry, health and safety, honors algebra, honors English, honors geometry, honors U.S. history, lab science, musical productions, organic chemistry, performing arts, photography, physical education, physical science, pre-calculus, psychology, religious education, social psychology, Spanish, women in society, world cultures, writing.

Graduation Requirements American history, art, business, chemistry, college counseling, communications, creative writing, driver education, lab science, religious studies, service requirement.

Special Academic Programs Honors section; study at local college for college credit; ESL (2 students enrolled).

College Admission Counseling 56 students graduated in 2016; all went to college, including Bergen Community College; Felician University; Montclair State University; Ramapo College of New Jersey; Seton Hall University; William Paterson University of New Jersey. Mean SAT critical reading: 535, mean SAT math: 505, mean SAT writing: 545, mean combined SAT: 1585, mean composite ACT: 20. 3% scored over 600 on SAT critical reading, 2% scored over 600 on SAT math, 5% scored over 600 on SAT writing, 1% scored over 26 on composite ACT.

Student Life Upper grades have uniform requirement, student council. Discipline rests primarily with faculty. Attendance at religious services is required.

Summer Programs Remediation, enrichment, advancement programs offered; session focuses on Jump Start Program for incoming freshmen; held on campus; accepts girls; not open to students from other schools. 15 students usually enrolled. 2017 schedule: July 11 to July 28. Application deadline: May 20.

Tuition and Aid Day student tuition: $10,985. Tuition installment plan (FACTS Tuition Payment Plan, annual payment plan). Tuition reduction for siblings, merit scholarship grants, need-based scholarship grants available. In 2016–17, 45% of upper-school students received aid; total upper-school merit-scholarship money awarded: $36,500. Total amount of financial aid awarded in 2016–17: $165,000.

Admissions Traditional secondary-level entrance grade is 9. For fall 2016, 220 students applied for upper-level admission, 218 were accepted, 54 enrolled. Cooperative Entrance Exam (McGraw-Hill) required. Deadline for receipt of application materials: none. No application fee required. On-campus interview required.

Athletics Interscholastic: basketball, cheering, cross-country running, dance team, indoor track, indoor track & field, soccer, softball, swimming and diving, tennis, track and field, volleyball; intramural: basketball, fitness, fitness walking, floor hockey, physical fitness, physical training, tennis, volleyball, walking. 2 PE instructors, 12 coaches, 1 athletic trainer.

Computers Computer network features include Internet access, wireless campus network, Internet filtering or blocking technology. Campus intranet and student e-mail accounts are available to students. Students grades are available online. The school has a published electronic and media policy.

Contact Ms. Nicole Mineo, Director of Enrollment Management. 973-773-2665. Fax: 973-614-0893. E-mail: nmineo@ichslodi.org. Website: www.ichslodi.org

IMMACULATE HEART ACADEMY

500 Van Emburgh Avenue
Washington Township, New Jersey 07676

Head of School: Ms. Patricia Molloy

General Information Girls' day college-preparatory school, affiliated with Roman Catholic Church. Grades 9–12. Founded: 1960. Setting: suburban. Nearest major city is Paramus. 1 building on campus. Approved or accredited by New Jersey Association of Independent Schools and New Jersey Department of Education. Total enrollment: 830. Upper school average class size: 23. Upper school faculty-student ratio: 1:11. The average school day consists of 6 hours and 5 minutes.

Upper School Student Profile 90% of students are Roman Catholic.

Faculty School total: 70. In upper school: 11 men, 81 women; 52 have advanced degrees.

Subjects Offered All academic.

Graduation Requirements Christian service requirement.

Special Academic Programs Honors section; study at local college for college credit.

College Admission Counseling 200 students graduated in 2016; all went to college, including Fairfield University; Fordham University; Loyola University Maryland; Quinnipiac University; The University of Scranton; University of Delaware.

Student Life Upper grades have uniform requirement, student council, honor system. Discipline rests primarily with faculty. Attendance at religious services is required.

Tuition and Aid Day student tuition: $14,800. Tuition installment plan (monthly payment plans). Tuition reduction for siblings, merit scholarship grants, need-based scholarship grants available.

Admissions Traditional secondary-level entrance grade is 9. Newark or Paterson Diocesan Test required. Deadline for receipt of application materials: December 1. No application fee required.

Athletics Interscholastic: alpine skiing, basketball, bowling, cheering, cross-country running, dance team, ice hockey, indoor track & field, lacrosse, skiing (downhill), soccer, softball, tennis, track and field, volleyball. 5 PE instructors, 20 coaches, 2 athletic trainers.

Computers Computers are regularly used in all academic classes. Computer network features include on-campus library services, online commercial services, Internet access, wireless campus network, Internet filtering or blocking technology. Campus intranet, student e-mail accounts, and computer access in designated common areas are available to students. Students grades are available online. The school has a published electronic and media policy.

Contact 201-445-6800. Fax: 201-445-7416.

IMMACULATE HEART HIGH SCHOOL AND MIDDLE SCHOOL

5515 Franklin Avenue
Los Angeles, California 90028-5999

Head of School: Ms. Virginia Hurst

General Information Girls' day college-preparatory school, affiliated with Roman Catholic Church. Grades 6–12. Founded: 1906. Setting: urban. 5-acre campus. 7 buildings on campus. Approved or accredited by California Association of Independent Schools, Western Association of Schools and Colleges, and California Department of Education. Upper school average class size: 18. Upper school faculty-student ratio: 1:17.

Faculty School total: 45. In upper school: 36 have advanced degrees.

Subjects Offered Advanced biology, advanced chemistry, advanced computer applications, advanced math, Advanced Placement courses, advanced studio art-AP, algebra, American history-AP, ancient world history, art history-AP, ASB Leadership, athletics, biology-AP, British literature, British literature (honors), British literature-AP, calculus-AP, chemistry, chemistry-AP, chorus, Christian and Hebrew scripture, Christian testament, church history, college planning, computer graphics, computer programming, creative writing, dance, debate, drama, drama performance, drama workshop, dramatic arts, economics, English, English language-AP, English literature-AP, European history, European history-AP, French, French-AP, geometry, health and wellness, health education, history-AP, honors algebra, honors English, honors geometry, honors U.S. history, honors world history, journalism, marine biology, physics, physics-AP, physiology, pre-calculus, printmaking, probability and statistics, psychology-AP, robotics, Shakespeare, Spanish, Spanish language-AP, Spanish literature-AP, speech and debate, sports conditioning, statistics, statistics-AP, theology, U.S. history, U.S. history-AP, visual and performing arts, visual arts, women in literature, women spirituality and faith, world civilizations, writing workshop, yearbook.

Special Academic Programs Advanced Placement exam preparation; honors section; independent study.

Student Life Upper grades have uniform requirement, student council, honor system. Discipline rests primarily with faculty. Attendance at religious services is required.

Tuition and Aid Tuition installment plan (The Tuition Plan). Merit scholarship grants, need-based scholarship grants available.

Admissions High School Placement Test or High School Placement Test (closed version) from Scholastic Testing Service required. Deadline for receipt of application materials: January 8. Application fee required: $75. On-campus interview required.

Athletics Interscholastic: basketball, cheering, cross-country running, equestrian sports, soccer, softball, swimming and diving, track and field, volleyball, yoga.

Computers Computers are regularly used in all academic classes. Computer network features include Internet access, wireless campus network, Internet filtering or blocking technology. Campus intranet and student e-mail accounts are available to students. Students grades are available online.

Contact Ms. Jennie Lee, Director of Admissions. 323-461-3651 Ext. 240. Fax: 323-462-0610. E-mail: jlee@immaculateheart.org. Website: www.immaculateheart.org

INCARNATE WORD ACADEMY

609 Crawford
Houston, Texas 77002-3668

Head of School: Ms. Mary Aamodt

General Information Girls' day college-preparatory and leadership school, affiliated with Roman Catholic Church. Grades 9–12. Founded: 1873. Setting: urban. 1 building on campus. Approved or accredited by Southern Association of Colleges and Schools, Texas Catholic Conference, Texas Education Agency, and Texas Department of Education. Total enrollment: 272. Upper school average class size: 16. Upper school faculty-student ratio: 1:11. There are 180 required school days per year for Upper School students. Upper School students typically attend 5 days per week. The average school day consists of 7 hours and 20 minutes.

Upper School Student Profile Grade 9: 100 students (100 girls); Grade 10: 84 students (84 girls); Grade 11: 82 students (82 girls); Grade 12: 70 students (70 girls). 85% of students are Roman Catholic.

Faculty School total: 39. In upper school: 9 men, 30 women; 23 have advanced degrees.

Subjects Offered Algebra, American government, American history, American history-AP, American literature, American literature-AP, art, biology, biology-AP, British literature, British literature-AP, calculus, chemistry, chemistry-AP, choir, concert choir, dance, drama, English composition, English literature, English literature and composition-AP, English literature-AP, English-AP, English/composition-AP, environmental science-AP, forensics, French, government and politics-AP, government-AP, health, history-AP, honors algebra, honors English, honors geometry, honors U.S. history, honors world history, Latin, Latin-AP, leadership and service, leadership education training, literature and composition-AP, literature-AP, microeconomics, microeconomics-AP, modern dance, newspaper, physical education, physics, pre-calculus, psychology, publications, SAT/ACT preparation, social studies, Spanish, Spanish language-AP, Spanish literature-AP, Spanish-AP, theater arts, theater production, theology, trigonometry, U.S. government and politics, U.S. government and politics-AP, U.S. history, U.S. history-AP, U.S. literature, United States government-AP, video and animation, Web site design, world geography, world history, world literature, world religions, world studies, world wide web design, World-Wide-Web publishing, yearbook.

Graduation Requirements 75 hours of community service.

Special Academic Programs Advanced Placement exam preparation; honors section; study at local college for college credit.

College Admission Counseling 69 students graduated in 2016; all went to college, including Baylor University; Texas A&M University; The University of Texas at Austin; University of Houston.

Student Life Upper grades have uniform requirement, student council, honor system. Discipline rests primarily with faculty. Attendance at religious services is required.

Summer Programs Enrichment, sports programs offered; session focuses on sports conditioning camp; held both on and off campus; accepts girls; open to students from other schools. 100 students usually enrolled.

Tuition and Aid Day student tuition: $12,500. Tuition installment plan (monthly payment plans). Merit scholarship grants, need-based scholarship grants, paying campus jobs available. In 2016–17, 30% of upper-school students received aid.

Admissions Traditional secondary-level entrance grade is 9. For fall 2016, 250 students applied for upper-level admission, 200 were accepted, 100 enrolled. High School Placement Test (closed version) from Scholastic Testing Service or ISEE required. Deadline for receipt of application materials: January 15. Application fee required: $75. Interview recommended.

Athletics Interscholastic: basketball, cheering, cross-country running, dance, dance team, golf, running, soccer, softball, track and field, volleyball; intramural: fitness, physical fitness. 1 PE instructor, 11 coaches, 1 athletic trainer.

Computers Computers are regularly used in all classes. Computer network features include on-campus library services, online commercial services, Internet access, wireless campus network, Internet filtering or blocking technology, 1:1 iPad program. Student e-mail accounts and computer access in designated common areas are available to students. Students grades are available online. The school has a published electronic and media policy.

Contact Ms. Kate O'Brien, Director of Admissions. 713-227-3637 Ext. 117. Fax: 713-227-1014. E-mail: kobrien@incarnateword.org. Website: www.incarnateword.org

INDEPENDENT SCHOOL

8317 East Douglas
Wichita, Kansas 67207

Head of School: Dr. Milt Dougherty

General Information Coeducational day college-preparatory school. Grades PK–12. Founded: 1980. Setting: urban. 22-acre campus. 2 buildings on campus. Approved or accredited by Independent Schools Association of the Central States. Total enrollment: 538. Upper school average class size: 12. Upper school faculty-student ratio: 1:7. There are 160 required school days per year for Upper School students. Upper School students typically attend 5 days per week. The average school day consists of 6 hours.

Upper School Student Profile Grade 9: 46 students (23 boys, 23 girls); Grade 10: 44 students (22 boys, 22 girls); Grade 11: 40 students (21 boys, 19 girls); Grade 12: 51 students (31 boys, 20 girls).

Faculty School total: 60. In upper school: 14 men, 15 women; 18 have advanced degrees.

Subjects Offered 3-dimensional art, advanced chemistry, advanced math, Advanced Placement courses, algebra, American government, American history, American history-AP, American literature, anatomy and physiology, art, art history, astronomy, biology, biology-AP, British literature, British literature (honors), business law, calculus, calculus-AP, ceramics, chemistry, chemistry-AP, choir, choral music, computer applications, computer art, computer programming, concert band, creative writing, debate, drama, driver education, economics, engineering, English literature-AP, film and new technologies, foreign language, forensics, geometry, government, graphic design, health, health and wellness, journalism, Latin, Latin American literature, madrigals, music, music theory, music theory-AP, music-AP, newspaper, physics, physics-AP, psychology, psychology-AP, Spanish, Spanish-AP, statistics-AP, theater, theater arts, trigonometry, U.S. government and politics-AP, Web site design, weight training, yearbook, zoology.

Graduation Requirements Algebra, American government, American history, American literature, arts and fine arts (art, music, dance, drama), biology, British literature, chemistry, computer applications, computer literacy, English, foreign language, geography, geometry, humanities, physical education (includes health), world history, world literature, 50 hours of community service.

Special Academic Programs 14 Advanced Placement exams for which test preparation is offered; honors section; independent study; study at local college for college credit; academic accommodation for the gifted, the musically talented, and the artistically talented.

College Admission Counseling 53 students graduated in 2016; all went to college, including Colorado State University; Oklahoma State University; Savannah College of Art and Design; Texas A&M University; The University of Kansas; Wichita State University. Median SAT critical reading: 106, median SAT math: 581, median SAT writing: 592, median combined SAT: 1187, median composite ACT: 25. 57% scored over 600 on SAT critical reading, 50% scored over 600 on SAT math, 50% scored over 600 on SAT writing, 50% scored over 1800 on combined SAT, 46% scored over 26 on composite ACT.

Student Life Upper grades have specified standards of dress, student council, honor system. Discipline rests primarily with faculty.

Summer Programs Enrichment, advancement, sports, art/fine arts, computer instruction programs offered; held on campus; accepts boys and girls; open to students from other schools. 391 students usually enrolled. 2017 schedule: May 20 to August 15.

Tuition and Aid Day student tuition: $11,400. Tuition installment plan (monthly payment plans). Need-based scholarship grants available. In 2016–17, 25% of upper-school students received aid.

Admissions Traditional secondary-level entrance grade is 9. For fall 2016, 30 students applied for upper-level admission, 27 were accepted, 21 enrolled. Admissions testing, non-standardized placement tests and Otis-Lennon Ability or Stanford Achievement Test required. Deadline for receipt of application materials: none. Application fee required: $40. Interview recommended.

Athletics Interscholastic: baseball (boys), basketball (b,g), bowling (b,g), cheering (g), cross-country running (b,g), dance team (g), football (b), golf (b,g), soccer (b,g), softball (g), strength & conditioning (b,g), swimming and diving (b,g), tennis (b,g), track and field (b,g), volleyball (g), weight training (b,g), wrestling (b); coed interscholastic: strength & conditioning, weight training. 2 PE instructors, 5 coaches, 1 athletic trainer.

Computers Computers are regularly used in art, college planning, economics, English, humanities, introduction to technology, library, literary magazine, mathematics, newspaper, photography, publications, Web site design, yearbook classes. Computer network features include on-campus library services, Internet access, wireless campus network, Internet filtering or blocking technology, homework online. Student e-mail accounts and computer access in designated common areas are available to students. Students grades are available online. The school has a published electronic and media policy.

Contact Andrea Gartman, Director of Admissions. 316-686-0152 Ext. 406. Fax: 316-686-3918. E-mail: andrea.gartman@theindependentschool.com. Website: www.theindependentschool.com

INDIAN CREEK SCHOOL

Lower, Middle Schools: 680 Evergreen Road
Upper School-1130 Anne Chambers Way
Crownsville, Maryland 21032

Head of School: Dr. Rick Branson

General Information Coeducational day college-preparatory school. Grades PK–12. Founded: 1973. Setting: suburban. Nearest major city is Annapolis. 114-acre campus. 3 buildings on campus. Approved or accredited by Association of Independent Maryland Schools, National Independent Private Schools Association, and Maryland Department of Education. Member of National Association of Independent Schools. Endowment: $35 million. Total enrollment: 621. Upper school average class size: 16. Upper school faculty-student ratio: 1:7. There are 179 required school days per year for Upper School students. Upper School students typically attend 5 days per week. The average school day consists of 8 hours.

Upper School Student Profile Grade 9: 58 students (28 boys, 30 girls); Grade 10: 57 students (30 boys, 27 girls); Grade 11: 65 students (36 boys, 29 girls); Grade 12: 48 students (24 boys, 24 girls).

Faculty School total: 94. In upper school: 13 men, 23 women; 23 have advanced degrees.

Special Academic Programs 18 Advanced Placement exams for which test preparation is offered; independent study; academic accommodation for the gifted; remedial reading and/or remedial writing.

College Admission Counseling 49 students graduated in 2015; all went to college.

Student Life Upper grades have uniform requirement, student council. Discipline rests primarily with faculty.

Tuition and Aid Day student tuition: $8000–$22,800. Tuition installment plan (Insured Tuition Payment Plan, SMART Tuition Payment Plan, monthly payment plans, individually arranged payment plans). Merit scholarship grants, need-based scholarship grants available. In 2015–16, 22% of upper-school students received aid.

Admissions Traditional secondary-level entrance grade is 9. Math and English placement tests or writing sample required. Deadline for receipt of application materials: none. Application fee required: $50. Interview required.

Athletics Interscholastic: basketball (boys, girls), cross-country running (b,g), field hockey (g), lacrosse (b,g), soccer (b,g); intramural: baseball (b); coed interscholastic: dressage, equestrian sports, golf, horseback riding, sailing, tennis; coed intramural: aerobics/dance, aquatics, dance, martial arts, weight training, yoga. 15 coaches, 1 athletic trainer.

Computers Computers are regularly used in all academic classes. Computer network features include on-campus library services, online commercial services, Internet access, wireless campus network, Internet filtering or blocking technology. Campus intranet, student e-mail accounts, and computer access in designated common areas are available to students. Students grades are available online. The school has a published electronic and media policy.

Contact Ms. Melissa Haber, Director of Admission for Lower and Middle Schools. 410-923-3660. Fax: 410-923-0670. E-mail: mhaber@indiancreekschool.org. Website: www.indiancreekschool.org

INDIAN SPRINGS SCHOOL

190 Woodward Drive
Indian Springs, Alabama 35124

Head of School: Dr. Sharon Howell

General Information Coeducational boarding and day college-preparatory school. Grades 8–12. Founded: 1952. Setting: suburban. Nearest major city is Birmingham. Students are housed in single-sex dormitories. 350-acre campus. 38 buildings on campus. Approved or accredited by Southern Association of Colleges and Schools, Southern Association of Independent Schools, The Association of Boarding Schools, and Alabama Department of Education. Member of National Association of Independent Schools and Secondary School Admission Test Board. Endowment: $18 million. Total enrollment: 299. Upper school average class size: 12. Upper school faculty-student ratio: 1:8. There are 175 required school days per year for Upper School students. Upper School students typically attend 5 days per week. The average school day consists of 6 hours and 20 minutes.

Upper School Student Profile Grade 8: 34 students (23 boys, 11 girls); Grade 9: 67 students (35 boys, 32 girls); Grade 10: 72 students (35 boys, 37 girls); Grade 11: 76 students (31 boys, 45 girls); Grade 12: 60 students (34 boys, 26 girls). 28% of students are boarding students. 75% are state residents. 13 states are represented in upper school student body. 15% are international students. International students from Bulgaria, China, Ethiopia, Germany, Republic of Korea, and Singapore.

Faculty School total: 43. In upper school: 20 men, 21 women; 34 have advanced degrees; 23 reside on campus.

Subjects Offered Advanced Placement courses, algebra, American history, American literature, art, art history, astronomy, athletics, biology, biology-AP, calculus, calculus-AP, ceramics, chemistry, chemistry-AP, Chinese, computer applications, computer multimedia, concert choir, constitutional law, contemporary issues, creative writing, drama, economics, economics-AP, English, English literature, English-AP, environmental science-AP, European history, expository writing, film studies, fine arts, French, French-AP, geology, geometry, government-AP, government/civics, history, jazz, jazz ensemble, keyboarding, Latin, Latin-AP, mathematics, music, painting, philosophy, photo shop, physical education, physical fitness, physics, play production, pre-calculus, science, Shakespeare, social studies, Spanish, Spanish-AP, statistics-AP, theater, trigonometry, U.S. government and politics-AP, world history, world literature, world religions, writing, yearbook.

Graduation Requirements Arts and fine arts (art, music, dance, drama), English, foreign language, mathematics, physical education (includes health), science, social studies (includes history), art or music history.

Special Academic Programs Advanced Placement exam preparation; independent study; academic accommodation for the gifted and the musically talented.

College Admission Counseling 67 students graduated in 2016; all went to college, including Auburn University; Birmingham-Southern College; Emory University; Johns Hopkins University; The University of Alabama; The University of Alabama at Birmingham. Median SAT critical reading: 650, median SAT math: 625, median SAT writing: 640, median combined SAT: 1895, median composite ACT: 30. 85% scored over 600 on SAT critical reading, 64% scored over 600 on SAT math, 76% scored over 600 on SAT writing, 74% scored over 1800 on combined SAT, 83% scored over 26 on composite ACT.

Student Life Upper grades have student council, honor system. Discipline rests equally with students and faculty.

Summer Programs Remediation, enrichment, sports, art/fine arts programs offered; session focuses on middle school students; held on campus; accepts boys and girls, open to students from other schools. 2017 schedule: June 16 to August 3. Application deadline: June 1.

Tuition and Aid Day student tuition: $21,250; 7-day tuition and room/board: $46,200. Tuition installment plan (FACTS Tuition Payment Plan, monthly payment plans, individually arranged payment plans). Need-based scholarship grants available. In 2016–17, 34% of upper-school students received aid. Total amount of financial aid awarded in 2016–17: $1,615,000.

Admissions Traditional secondary-level entrance grade is 9. For fall 2016, 197 students applied for upper-level admission, 105 were accepted, 85 enrolled. SSAT or TOEFL required. Deadline for receipt of application materials: January 15. Application fee required: $75. Interview recommended.

Athletics Interscholastic: baseball (boys), basketball (b,g), soccer (b,g), softball (g), tennis (b,g), volleyball (g); intramural: basketball (b,g), flag football (b), soccer (b,g); coed interscholastic: cross-country running, golf, ultimate Frisbee; coed intramural: aerobics, aerobics/Nautilus, outdoor activities, paint ball, physical fitness, strength & conditioning, table tennis, ultimate Frisbee, yoga. 2 PE instructors, 5 coaches, 1 athletic trainer.

Computers Computers are regularly used in all academic classes. Computer network features include on-campus library services, online commercial services, Internet access, wireless campus network, Internet filtering or blocking technology. Campus intranet, student e-mail accounts, and computer access in designated common areas are available to students. Students grades are available online.

Contact Mrs. Christine Copeland, Assistant Director of Admission and Financial Aid. 205-332-0582. Fax: 205-988-3797. E-mail: ccopeland@indiansprings.org. Website: www.indiansprings.org

INSTITUT MONTE ROSA

57 Av. de Chillon
Montreux 1820, Switzerland

Head of School: Mr. Bernhard Gademann

General Information Coeducational boarding and day college-preparatory, business, and Languages school. Grades 7–12. Distance learning grades 7–12. Founded: 1874. Setting: small town. Students are housed in coed dormitories. 6-hectare campus. 2 buildings on campus. Approved or accredited by Swiss Federation of Private Schools. Member of European Council of International Schools. Languages of instruction: English and French. Upper school average class size: 6. Upper school faculty-student ratio: 1:4.

Special Academic Programs Advanced Placement exam preparation; programs in English, mathematics, general development for dyslexic students; ESL.

Student Life Upper grades have specified standards of dress, honor system. Discipline rests equally with students and faculty.

Summer Programs ESL, sports programs offered; session focuses on languages; held on campus; accepts boys and girls; open to students from other schools. 100 students usually enrolled. 2017 schedule: June 21 to August 23.

Admissions Math and English placement tests required. Deadline for receipt of application materials: none. Application fee required: 800 Swiss francs. Interview required.

Athletics Coed Intramural: aerobics/dance, alpine skiing, aquatics, archery, badminton, basketball, bicycling, canoeing/kayaking, dance, equestrian sports, fitness, football, freestyle skiing, golf, gymnastics, handball, horseback riding, ice hockey, ice skating, indoor soccer, kayaking, modern dance, mountain biking, mountaineering, outdoor activities, outdoor education, outdoor recreation, paddling, physical fitness, physical training, rafting, skiing (cross-country), skiing (downhill), snowboarding, soccer, swimming and diving, tennis, water skiing.

Computers Computer resources include Internet access, wireless campus network, Internet filtering or blocking technology.

INTERNATIONAL COLLEGE SPAIN

Calle Vereda Norte, #3
La Moraleja
Madrid 28109, Spain

Head of School: Mr. Andreas Swoboda

General Information Coeducational day college-preparatory, arts, bilingual studies, technology, and Many languages school. Grades K–12. Founded: 1980. Setting: suburban. 3-hectare campus. 4 buildings on campus. Approved or accredited by Council of International Schools, European Council of International Schools, International Baccalaureate Organization, and New England Association of Schools and Colleges. Member of European Council of International Schools. Language of instruction: English. Total enrollment: 709. Upper school average class size: 18. Upper school faculty-student ratio: 1:9. There are 176 required school days per year for Upper School students. Upper School students typically attend 5 days per week. The average school day consists of 6 hours.

Upper School Student Profile Grade 6: 56 students (27 boys, 29 girls); Grade 7: 73 students (41 boys, 32 girls); Grade 8: 63 students (40 boys, 23 girls); Grade 9: 76 students (42 boys, 34 girls); Grade 10: 70 students (27 boys, 43 girls); Grade 11: 70 students (39 boys, 31 girls); Grade 12: 60 students (28 boys, 32 girls).

Faculty School total. 123. In upper school: 32 men, 32 women; 27 have advanced degrees.

Subjects Offered 20th century history, ACT preparation, acting, advanced biology, advanced chemistry, Danish.

Graduation Requirements English, foreign language, mathematics, science, social sciences, social studies (includes history), 90% minimum attendance, minimum average effort grade of satisfactory. Community service is required.

Special Academic Programs International Baccalaureate program; programs in English, mathematics, general development for dyslexic students; ESL (45 students enrolled).

College Admission Counseling 64 students graduated in 2016; 56 went to college, including Boston University; Duke University; Georgetown University; Northeastern University; Saint Louis University; University of Chicago. Other: 1 entered military service, 8 had other specific plans.

Student Life Upper grades have specified standards of dress, student council. Discipline rests equally with students and faculty.

Tuition and Aid Day student tuition: €17,603. Tuition reduction for siblings, bursaries, merit scholarship grants, need-based scholarship grants available. In 2016–17, 1% of upper-school students received aid; total upper-school merit-scholarship money awarded: €17,600. Total amount of financial aid awarded in 2016–17: €17,600.

Admissions Traditional secondary-level entrance age is 11. Admissions testing and math and English placement tests required. Deadline for receipt of application materials: none. Application fee required: €650. On-campus interview recommended.

Athletics Interscholastic: basketball (boys, girls), cross-country running (b,g), soccer (b,g), volleyball (b,g); intramural: aerobics/dance (b,g), badminton (b,g), ballet (b,g), field hockey (b,g), gymnastics (b,g), physical fitness (b,g), soccer (b,g), softball (b,g), swimming and diving (b,g), table tennis (b,g), tennis (b,g), volleyball (b,g); coed interscholastic: track and field; coed intramural: alpine skiing, dance, fencing, golf, horseback riding, judo, martial arts, modern dance, skiing (downhill), snowboarding. 3 PE instructors, 5 coaches.

Computers Computers are regularly used in art, career education, career exploration, college planning, economics, English, ESL, information technology, mathematics, science classes. Computer network features include on-campus library services, online commercial services, Internet access, wireless campus network, Internet filtering or blocking technology. Campus intranet, student e-mail accounts, and computer access in designated common areas are available to students. Students grades are available online. The school has a published electronic and media policy.

Contact Mrs. Aurora López Martín, Admissions Manager. 34-916502398. E-mail: admissions@icsmadrid.org. Website: www.icsmadrid.org

INTERNATIONAL HIGH SCHOOL

150 Oak Street
San Francisco, California 94102

Head of School: Ms. Melinda Bihn

General Information Coeducational day college-preparatory and philosophy school. Grades PK–12. Founded: 1962. Setting: urban. 3-acre campus. 3 buildings on campus. Approved or accredited by California Association of Independent Schools, Council of International Schools, French Ministry of Education, International Baccalaureate Organization, Western Association of Schools and Colleges, and California Department of Education. Member of National Association of Independent Schools, Secondary School Admission Test Board, and European Council of International Schools. Languages of instruction: English and French. Endowment: $6 million. Total enrollment: 1,077. Upper school average class size: 17. Upper school faculty-student ratio: 1:10. There are 165 required school days per year for Upper School students. Upper School students typically attend 5 days per week. The average school day consists of 7 hours.

Upper School Student Profile Grade 9: 96 students (41 boys, 55 girls); Grade 10: 94 students (42 boys, 52 girls); Grade 11: 98 students (40 boys, 58 girls); Grade 12: 92 students (43 boys, 49 girls).

Faculty School total: 139. In upper school: 33 men, 30 women; 35 have advanced degrees.

Subjects Offered Advanced chemistry, advanced math, algebra, American history, American literature, art, biology, calculus, chemistry, community service, current events, drama, earth science, economics, English, English literature, environmental science, ESL, European history, fine arts, French, geography, geometry, German, government/civics, history, International Baccalaureate courses, Mandarin, mathematics, music, philosophy, physical education, physics, psychology, science, social studies, Spanish, theater, theory of knowledge, trigonometry, world history, world literature, writing.

Graduation Requirements Arts and fine arts (art, music, dance, drama), English, foreign language, International Baccalaureate courses, mathematics, physical education (includes health), science, social studies (includes history), theory of knowledge, extended essay, 150 hours of CAS.

Special Academic Programs International Baccalaureate program; honors section; independent study; term-away projects; study abroad; academic accommodation for the gifted, the musically talented, and the artistically talented; ESL (8 students enrolled).

College Admission Counseling 72 students graduated in 2016; all went to college, including Carnegie Mellon University; Stanford University; The University of British Columbia; University of California, Santa Barbara; University of Chicago; University of Washington. Mean SAT critical reading: 638, mean SAT math: 632, mean SAT writing: 633, mean composite ACT: 30.

Student Life Upper grades have student council. Discipline rests primarily with faculty.

Tuition and Aid Day student tuition: $38,320. Tuition installment plan (FACTS Tuition Payment Plan). Need-based scholarship grants, French bourse available. In 2016–17, 25% of upper-school students received aid. Total amount of financial aid awarded in 2016–17: $748,000.

Admissions Traditional secondary-level entrance grade is 9. For fall 2016, 224 students applied for upper-level admission, 146 were accepted, 47 enrolled. ISEE, SSAT or writing sample required. Deadline for receipt of application materials: January 12. Application fee required: $100. Interview recommended.

Athletics Interscholastic: baseball (boys, girls), basketball (b,g), soccer (b,g), volleyball (b,g); intramural: baseball (b), basketball (b,g), soccer (b,g), tennis (b,g), volleyball (b,g); coed interscholastic: badminton, cross-country running, sailing, swimming and diving, tennis, track and field; coed intramural: badminton, cross-country running, fencing, outdoor activities, outdoor adventure, physical fitness, physical training, sailing, swimming and diving, track and field. 4 PE instructors, 8 coaches, 2 athletic trainers.

Computers Computers are regularly used in all academic classes. Computer network features include on-campus library services, online commercial services, Internet access, wireless campus network, iPad program for all high school students. Campus intranet, student e-mail accounts, and computer access in designated common areas are available to students. Students grades are available online. The school has a published electronic and media policy.

Contact Ms. Erin Cronin, Associate Director of Admission. 415-558-2093. Fax: 415-558-2085. E-mail: erinc@internationalsf.org. Website: www.internationalsf.org

INTERNATIONAL SCHOOL BANGKOK

39/7 Soi Nichada Thani, Samakee Road
Pakkret 11120, Thailand

Head of School: Dr. Andrew Davies

General Information Coeducational day college-preparatory, arts, and technology school. Grades PK–12. Founded: 1951. Setting: suburban. Nearest major city is Bangkok, Thailand. 37-acre campus. 2 buildings on campus. Approved or accredited by International Baccalaureate Organization, Ministry of Education (Thailand), and Western Association of Schools and Colleges. Affiliate member of National Association of Independent Schools. Language of instruction: English. Total enrollment: 1,946. Upper school average class size: 18. Upper school faculty-student ratio: 1:10. There are 182 required school days per year for Upper School students. Upper School students typically attend 5 days per week. The average school day consists of 6 hours.

Faculty School total: 242. In upper school: 57 men, 37 women; 74 have advanced degrees.

Subjects Offered 3-dimensional design, algebra, American history, American literature, art, art history, biology, business, business education, business studies, calculus, calculus-AP, chemistry, choir, computer science, concert band, creative writing, dance, drama, drawing, drawing and design, Dutch, earth science, ecology, economics, economics and history, electives, English, English literature, environmental education, environmental science, environmental studies, ESL, European history, expository writing, fine arts, French, French studies, geography, geology, geometry, German, government/civics, health, history, humanities, industrial arts, Japanese, journalism, language arts, languages, mathematics, music, performing arts, photography, physical education, physics, psychology, reading, robotics, science, social

studies, sociology, Spanish, speech, statistics, Thai, theater, theory of knowledge, trigonometry, world history, world literature, writing.

Graduation Requirements Arts and fine arts (art, music, dance, drama), electives, English, health, mathematics, physical education (includes health), science, social studies (includes history), theory of knowledge, community service hours, Senior Seminar, Global Citizenship Week, Thailand and Southeast Asia course. Community service is required.

Special Academic Programs International Baccalaureate program; Advanced Placement exam preparation; ESL.

College Admission Counseling 178 students graduated in 2015; all went to college, including Boston University; Northeastern University; Penn State University Park; Syracuse University; University of California, Davis; University of Illinois at Urbana–Champaign. Mean SAT critical reading: 575, mean SAT math: 655, mean SAT writing: 592, mean combined SAT: 1822, mean composite ACT: 25.

Student Life Upper grades have uniform requirement, student council, honor system. Discipline rests primarily with faculty.

Tuition and Aid Day student tuition: 869,000 Thai bahts. Tuition installment plan (individually arranged payment plans).

Admissions Math and English placement tests and school's own exam required. Deadline for receipt of application materials: none. Application fee required: 4500 Thai bahts. On-campus interview required.

Athletics Interscholastic: aquatics (boys, girls), badminton (b,g), basketball (b,g), cross-country running (b,g), dance (b,g), rugby (b,g), running (b,g), soccer (b,g), softball (b,g), swimming and diving (b,g), tennis (b,g), track and field (b,g), volleyball (b,g); intramural: aquatics (b,g), badminton (b,g), basketball (b,g), cross-country running (b,g), dance (b,g), fencing (b), rugby (b,g), running (b,g), soccer (b,g), softball (b,g), swimming and diving (b,g), tennis (b,g), track and field (b,g), volleyball (b,g); coed interscholastic: dance team. 5 PE instructors.

Computers Computers are regularly used in all academic classes. Computer network features include on-campus library services, Internet access, wireless campus network, Internet filtering or blocking technology. Campus intranet, student e-mail accounts, and computer access in designated common areas are available to students. Students grades are available online. The school has a published electronic and media policy.

Contact Ms. Wendy Van Bramer, Admissions Director. 662-963-5800. Fax: 662-960-4103. E-mail: register@isb.ac.th. Website: www.isb.ac.th

INTERNATIONAL SCHOOL HAMBURG

Hemmingstedter Weg 130
Hamburg 22609, Germany

Head of School: Mr. Andrew Cross

General Information Coeducational day college-preparatory school. Grades PK–12. Founded: 1957. Setting: suburban. 3-acre campus. 1 building on campus. Approved or accredited by Council of International Schools and New England Association of Schools and Colleges. Member of European Council of International Schools. Language of instruction: English. Total enrollment: 755. Upper school average class size: 20. Upper school faculty-student ratio: 1:8. Upper School students typically attend 5 days per week. The average school day consists of 6 hours.

Upper School Student Profile Grade 9: 69 students (43 boys, 26 girls); Grade 10: 51 students (29 boys, 22 girls); Grade 11: 46 students (25 boys, 21 girls); Grade 12: 47 students (22 boys, 25 girls).

Faculty School total: 90. In upper school: 47 men, 25 women; 40 have advanced degrees.

Subjects Offered 20th century world history, 3-dimensional art, 3-dimensional design, advanced chemistry, art, biology, chemistry, computer math, drama, English, ESL, European history, fine arts, French, geography, German, history, mathematics, model United Nations, music, photography, physical education, physics, science, social studies, Spanish, theater, theory of knowledge, world history.

Graduation Requirements All academic, arts and fine arts (art, music, dance, drama), English, foreign language, mathematics, physical education (includes health), science, social studies (includes history).

Special Academic Programs International Baccalaureate program; programs in English, mathematics for dyslexic students; ESL (80 students enrolled).

College Admission Counseling 64 students graduated in 2016; 58 went to college, including Boston University; Columbia University; McGill University; Yale University. Other: 3 had other specific plans.

Student Life Upper grades have student council. Discipline rests primarily with faculty.

Tuition and Aid Day student tuition: €15,440–€19,230. Tuition installment plan (2-payment plan). Financial aid available to upper-school students. In 2016–17, 1% of upper-school students received aid.

Admissions Traditional secondary-level entrance grade is 9. For fall 2016, 60 students applied for upper-level admission, 60 were accepted, 59 enrolled. ACT, CTBS, Stanford Achievement Test, any other standardized test or PSAT and SAT for applicants to grade 11 and 12 required. Deadline for receipt of application materials: none. Application fee required: €100. On-campus interview required.

Athletics Interscholastic: badminton (boys, girls), basketball (b,g), canoeing/kayaking (b,g), climbing (b,g), cross-country running (b,g), floor hockey (b,g), football (b,g), indoor hockey (b,g), indoor soccer (b,g), netball (b,g), physical training (b,g), rowing (b,g), running (b,g), sailing (b,g), soccer (b,g), tennis (b,g), track and field (b,g), volleyball (b,g); intramural: basketball (b,g), cross-country running (b,g), field hockey (b,g), football (b,g), soccer (b,g), tennis (b,g), track and field (b,g), volleyball (b,g); coed interscholastic: badminton, canoeing/kayaking, climbing, cross-country running, floor hockey, football, indoor hockey, indoor soccer, netball, running, sailing, soccer, tennis, track and field, volleyball; coed intramural: cross-country running, football, soccer, tennis, track and field, volleyball. 6 PE instructors, 4 coaches.

Computers Computers are regularly used in business studies, English, ESL, foreign language, French, geography, history, humanities, library, mathematics, music, science, Spanish, yearbook classes. Computer network features include on-campus library services, online commercial services, Internet access, wireless campus network, Internet filtering or blocking technology. Campus intranet and student e-mail accounts are available to students. Students grades are available online. The school has a published electronic and media policy.

Contact Catherine Bissonnet, Director of Admissions. 49-40-800050-133. Fax: 49-40-881-1405. E-mail: cbissonnet@ishamburg.org. Website: www.ishamburg.org

INTERNATIONAL SCHOOL MANILA

University Parkway
Fort Bonifacio
1634 Taguig City, Philippines
Head of School: David Toze

General Information Coeducational day college-preparatory school. Grades PS–12. Founded: 1920. Setting: urban. Nearest major city is Manila, Philippines. 7-hectare campus. 1 building on campus. Approved or accredited by Council of International Schools and Western Association of Schools and Colleges. Affiliate member of National Association of Independent Schools; member of Secondary School Admission Test Board. Language of instruction: English. Endowment: $2 million. Total enrollment: 2,194. Upper school average class size: 16. Upper school faculty-student ratio: 1:9. There are 180 required school days per year for Upper School students. Upper School students typically attend 5 days per week. The average school day consists of 5 hours and 50 minutes.

Upper School Student Profile Grade 6: 167 students (88 boys, 79 girls); Grade 7: 179 students (88 boys, 91 girls); Grade 8: 193 students (104 boys, 89 girls); Grade 9: 208 students (104 boys, 104 girls); Grade 10: 194 students (100 boys, 94 girls); Grade 11: 191 students (87 boys, 104 girls); Grade 12: 178 students (90 boys, 88 girls).

Faculty School total: 220. In upper school: 47 men, 39 women; 60 have advanced degrees.

Subjects Offered Acting, anthropology, art, athletic training, band, Basic programming, biology, business, calculus-AP, chemistry, Chinese, choir, college admission preparation, college awareness, college counseling, college placement, college planning, computer applications, computer graphics, computer literacy, computer multimedia, computer programming, computer science, creative writing, critical writing, dance, desktop publishing, digital photography, economics, economics and history, English, environmental science, ESL, film, filmmaking, foreign language, French, French as a second language, general science, geography, graphic design, health, health and wellness, health education, information technology, integrated mathematics, International Baccalaureate courses, international relations, Japanese, Japanese as Second Language, jazz band, leadership, math applications, math methods, mathematics, media studies, music, orchestra, parenting, peer counseling, personal fitness, Philippine culture, physical science, physics, political science, pre-calculus, programming, psychology, reading/study skills, remedial study skills, research, service learning/internship, sex education, Spanish, theater, theater arts, theory of knowledge, track and field, U.S. history, U.S. history-AP, video film production, visual and performing arts, visual arts, weight fitness, weight training, world history, world religions, writing.

Special Academic Programs International Baccalaureate program; Advanced Placement exam preparation; honors section; accelerated programs; independent study; academic accommodation for the gifted, the musically talented, and the artistically talented; remedial reading and/or remedial writing; remedial math; programs in English, mathematics, general development for dyslexic students; special instructional classes for deaf students, The Self-Contained Classroom is for students with significant learning needs, which may include intellectual o; ESL (212 students enrolled).

College Admission Counseling 187 students graduated in 2016; all went to college, including McGill University; New York University; The University of British Columbia; University of California, Berkeley; University of Toronto. Mean SAT critical reading: 604, mean SAT math: 646, mean SAT writing: 613, mean combined SAT: 1863, mean composite ACT: 27.

Student Life Upper grades have uniform requirement, student council, honor system. Discipline rests primarily with faculty.

Summer Programs ESL, sports, art/fine arts programs offered; session focuses on ESL, Sports, Arts, Communication, College Bootcamps,; held both on and off campus; accepts boys and girls; open to students from other schools. 80 students usually enrolled. 2017 schedule: June 13 to June 23. Application deadline: May.

Tuition and Aid Day student tuition: $24,000. Tuition installment plan (monthly payment plans, individually arranged payment plans, quarterly payment plan). Scholarships for low-income local students available.

Admissions Traditional secondary-level entrance grade is 9. For fall 2016, 120 students applied for upper-level admission, 74 were accepted, 74 enrolled. Iowa Tests of Basic Skills required. Deadline for receipt of application materials: none. Application fee required: $450. On-campus interview recommended.

Athletics Interscholastic: badminton (boys, girls), basketball (b,g), cheering (g), cross-country running (b,g), golf (b,g), gymnastics (b,g), martial arts (b,g), rugby (b,g), soccer (b,g), softball (b,g), swimming and diving (b,g), table tennis (b,g), tennis (b,g), track and field (b,g), volleyball (b,g), wall climbing (b,g); intramural: rugby (b,g), wall climbing (b,g), water polo (b,g); coed interscholastic: dance, wall climbing; coed intramural: volleyball, wall climbing. 5 PE instructors, 10 coaches.

Computers Computers are regularly used in art, English, foreign language, history, mathematics, music, science classes. Computer network features include on-campus library services, online commercial services, Internet access, wireless campus network, Internet filtering or blocking technology. Campus intranet, student e-mail accounts, and computer access in designated common areas are available to students. Students grades are available online. The school has a published electronic and media policy.

Contact Stephanie Hagedorn, Director of Admissions and Advancement. 63-2-840-8488. Fax: 63-2-840-8489. E-mail: admissions@ismanila.org. Website: www.ismanila.org

THE INTERNATIONAL SCHOOL OF ABERDEEN

Pitfodels House
North Deeside Road
Pitfodels, Cults
Aberdeen AB15 9PN, United Kingdom
Head of School: Dr. Daniel A. Hovde

General Information Coeducational day college-preparatory and general academic school. Grades PK–12. Founded: 1972. Setting: suburban. 14-acre campus. 1 building on campus. Approved or accredited by Council of International Schools and Middle States Association of Colleges and Schools. Member of European Council of International Schools. Language of instruction: English. Total enrollment: 439. Upper school average class size: 18. Upper school faculty-student ratio: 1:5. There are 170 required school days per year for Upper School students. Upper School students typically attend 5 days per week. The average school day consists of 5 hours.

Upper School Student Profile Grade 6: 26 students (13 boys, 13 girls); Grade 7: 29 students (19 boys, 10 girls); Grade 8: 21 students (14 boys, 7 girls); Grade 9: 23 students (12 boys, 11 girls); Grade 10: 14 students (7 boys, 7 girls); Grade 11: 23 students (14 boys, 9 girls); Grade 12: 21 students (8 boys, 13 girls).

Faculty School total: 55. In upper school: 18 men, 20 women; 30 have advanced degrees.

Subjects Offered Algebra, art, band, biology, chemistry, choir, computer applications, desktop publishing, drama, Dutch, earth science, ecology, environmental systems, economics, English, ESL, fitness, French, French as a second language, geography, geometry, health education, history, information technology, language arts, library studies, mathematics, model United Nations, music, music composition, music performance, performing arts, physical education, physics, science, social studies, Spanish, technical theater.

Graduation Requirements Arts and fine arts (art, music, dance, drama), computer science, electives, English, foreign language, mathematics, physical education (includes health), science, social studies (includes history).

Special Academic Programs International Baccalaureate program; independent study; programs in English, mathematics, general development for dyslexic students; ESL (35 students enrolled).

College Admission Counseling 34 students graduated in 2016; 33 went to college, including Baylor University; Columbia College Chicago; Georgia Institute of Technology; Texas A&M University; University of Colorado Boulder; University of Oregon. Other: 1 had other specific plans.

Student Life Upper grades have student council, honor system. Discipline rests primarily with faculty.

Summer Programs Sports, art/fine arts, computer instruction programs offered; held on campus; accepts boys and girls; open to students from other schools. 2017 schedule: July to August. Application deadline: March.

Tuition and Aid Day student tuition: £9760–£10,935. Tuition installment plan (monthly payment plans, individually arranged payment plans). Bursaries, merit scholarship grants, need-based scholarship grants available.

Admissions Admissions testing or English for Non-native Speakers required. Deadline for receipt of application materials: none. Application fee required: £500. On-campus interview recommended.

Athletics Interscholastic: badminton (boys, girls), ball hockey (b,g), basketball (b,g), football (b,g), golf (b,g), soccer (b,g), volleyball (b,g); intramural: aerobics (g), aerobics/dance (g), badminton (b,g), ball hockey (b,g), ballet (b,g), baseball (b), basketball (b,g), Circus (b,g), climbing (b,g), football (b,g), handball (b,g), hockey (b,g), lacrosse (b,g), soccer (b,g), softball (b,g), table tennis (b,g), track and field (b,g), ultimate Frisbee (b,g), unicycling (b,g), volleyball (b,g); coed interscholastic: aquatics, archery, badminton, ball hockey, basketball, canoeing/kayaking, Circus, climbing, combined training, cross-country running, field hockey, fitness, kayaking, lacrosse, physical fitness, physical training, roller blading, roller skating, running, skateboarding, softball, swimming and diving, table tennis, tennis, track and field, wall climbing; coed intramural: aquatics, archery, badminton, ball hockey, basketball, canoeing/kayaking, Circus, climbing, combined training, croquet, cross-country running, fencing, fitness, Frisbee, gymnastics, indoor hockey, juggling, jump rope, kayaking, lacrosse, life saving, martial arts, outdoor activities, outdoor adventure, outdoor education, outdoor recreation, outdoor skills, physical fitness, physical training, roller blading, roller hockey, roller skating, running, skateboarding, soccer, softball, swimming and diving, table tennis, tennis, triathlon, ultimate Frisbee, wall climbing. 5 PE instructors, 10 coaches.

Computers Computers are regularly used in all academic, English, foreign language, mathematics, science classes. Computer network features include on-campus library services, Internet access, wireless campus network, Internet filtering or blocking technology. Campus intranet, student e-mail accounts, and computer access in designated common areas are available to students. Students grades are available online. The school has a published electronic and media policy.

Contact Mrs. Sheila Sibley, Admissions. 44-1224 730300. Fax: 44-1224 865558. E-mail: admissions@isa.aberdeen.sch.uk. Website: www.isa.aberdeen.sch.uk

INTERNATIONAL SCHOOL OF AMSTERDAM

Sportlaan 45
Amstelveen 1185 TB, Netherlands

Head of School: Dr. Ed Greene

General Information Coeducational day college-preparatory school. Grades PS–12. Founded: 1964. Setting: suburban. Nearest major city is Amsterdam, Netherlands. 1-acre campus. 3 buildings on campus. Approved or accredited by Council of International Schools, European Council of International Schools, and New England Association of Schools and Colleges. Member of European Council of International Schools. Language of instruction: English. Total enrollment: 1,327. Upper school average class size: 20. Upper school faculty-student ratio: 1:13. There are 177 required school days per year for Upper School students. Upper School students typically attend 5 days per week. The average school day consists of 7 hours.

Upper School Student Profile Grade 6: 100 students (49 boys, 51 girls); Grade 7: 100 students (47 boys, 53 girls); Grade 8: 99 students (50 boys, 49 girls); Grade 9: 93 students (45 boys, 48 girls); Grade 10: 98 students (47 boys, 51 girls); Grade 11: 96 students (43 boys, 53 girls); Grade 12: 74 students (42 boys, 32 girls).

Faculty School total: 237. In upper school: 43 men, 61 women; 45 have advanced degrees.

Subjects Offered Addiction, advanced math, algebra, American literature, art, biology, calculus, chemistry, community service, computer programming, computer science, drama, Dutch, economics, English, English literature, ESL, European history, film, food science, French, geography, geometry, history, Japanese, Mandarin, mathematics, music, photography, physical education, physics, science, social sciences, social studies, Spanish, technology, theater, theory of knowledge, trigonometry, world history, world literature.

Graduation Requirements Arts, computer science, English, foreign language, mathematics, physical education (includes health), science, social sciences, social studies (includes history). Community service is required.

Special Academic Programs International Baccalaureate program; independent study; academic accommodation for the gifted and the artistically talented; remedial reading and/or remedial writing; remedial math; programs in English, mathematics, general development for dyslexic students; ESL (45 students enrolled).

College Admission Counseling 65 students graduated in 2016; 60 went to college. Other: 5 had other specific plans. Median SAT critical reading: 645, median SAT math: 680, median SAT writing: 630, median combined SAT: 1920. Mean composite ACT: 29. 44% scored over 600 on SAT critical reading, 67% scored over 600 on SAT math, 670% scored over 600 on SAT writing, 61% scored over 1800 on combined SAT, 100% scored over 26 on composite ACT.

Student Life Upper grades have specified standards of dress, student council, honor system. Discipline rests primarily with faculty.

Tuition and Aid Day student tuition: €22,925–€23,575. Tuition installment plan (monthly payment plans, individually arranged payment plans).

Admissions Traditional secondary-level entrance grade is 9. For fall 2016, 287 students applied for upper-level admission, 112 were accepted, 82 enrolled. Deadline for receipt of application materials: none. Application fee required: €250. On-campus interview required.

Athletics Interscholastic: basketball (boys, girls), soccer (b,g), softball (b,g), swimming and diving (b,g), tennis (b,g), track and field (b,g), volleyball (g); coed intramural: aerobics, aerobics/dance, badminton, basketball, cricket, cross-country running, fitness, golf, handball, hockey, rugby, running, soccer, softball, tennis, track and field, volleyball. 16 PE instructors, 20 coaches, 14 athletic trainers.

Computers Computers are regularly used in all classes. Computer network features include on-campus library services, online commercial services, Internet access, wireless campus network, Internet filtering or blocking technology. Campus intranet and student e-mail accounts are available to students.

Contact Julia True, Admissions and Advancement Director. 31-20-347-1111. Fax: 31-20-347-1105. E-mail: admissions@isa.nl. Website: www.isa.nl

INTERNATIONAL SCHOOL OF BRUSSELS

19 Kattenberg
Brussels 1170, Belgium

Head of School: Mr. Lee Fertig

General Information Coeducational day college-preparatory school. Grades N–13. Founded: 1951. Setting: suburban. 40-acre campus. 2 buildings on campus. Approved or accredited by Middle States Association of Colleges and Schools. Affiliate member of National Association of Independent Schools; member of European Council of International Schools. Language of instruction: English. Endowment: €32,500. Total enrollment: 1,387. Upper school average class size: 20. Upper school faculty-student ratio: 1:10. Upper School students typically attend 5 days per week.

Upper School Student Profile Grade 10: 144 students (82 boys, 62 girls); Grade 11: 166 students (90 boys, 76 girls); Grade 12: 164 students (80 boys, 84 girls); Grade 13: 2 students (2 boys).

Faculty School total: 205. In upper school: 30 men, 35 women; 18 have advanced degrees.

Subjects Offered Advanced Placement courses, algebra, American history, American literature, anthropology, art, biology, business mathematics, calculus, chemistry, chorus, computer programming, computer science, creative writing, drama, ecology, English, English literature, environmental science, ESL, European history, expository writing, fine arts, French, geometry, grammar, graphic arts, health, history, instrumental music, Japanese, journalism, mathematics, orchestra, philosophy, physical education, physics, science, social sciences, social studies, Spanish, speech, statistics, theater, theory of knowledge, trigonometry, world history, world literature, writing.

Graduation Requirements Arts and fine arts (art, music, dance, drama), computer science, English, foreign language, mathematics, science, social sciences, social studies (includes history).

Special Academic Programs International Baccalaureate program; Advanced Placement exam preparation; honors section; academic accommodation for the gifted, the musically talented, and the artistically talented; remedial reading and/or remedial writing; remedial math; programs in English, mathematics, general development for dyslexic students; special instructional classes for students with cognitive impairment and those with a range of learning differences; ESL.

College Admission Counseling 152 students graduated in 2016.

Student Life Upper grades have student council, honor system. Discipline rests primarily with faculty.

Summer Programs Remediation, ESL, sports, art/fine arts, computer instruction programs offered; session focuses on mix of fun activities and academics; held on campus; accepts boys and girls; open to students from other schools. 442 students usually enrolled. 2017 schedule: June 24 to July 21.

Tuition and Aid Day student tuition: €36,150. Tuition installment plan (monthly payment plans, individually arranged payment plans). Need-based scholarship grants available. In 2016–17, 3% of upper-school students received aid. Total amount of financial aid awarded in 2016–17: €395,232.

Admissions Traditional secondary-level entrance grade is 10. English for Non-native Speakers or Math Placement Exam required. Deadline for receipt of application materials: none. Application fee required: €2000. On-campus interview required.

Athletics Interscholastic: baseball (boys), basketball (b,g), cross-country running (b,g), field hockey (g), football (b), golf (b,g), rugby (b), soccer (b,g), softball (g), swimming and diving (b,g), tennis (b,g), track and field (b,g), volleyball (b,g); intramural: climbing (b,g), gymnastics (b,g); coed intramural: dance.

Computers Computers are regularly used in all classes. Computer network features include on-campus library services, online commercial services, Internet access, wireless campus network, Internet filtering or blocking technology. Campus intranet and student e-mail accounts are available to students. Students grades are available online.

Contact Mr. Robin Berting, Admissions Manager. 32-2-6614224. Fax: 32-2-6614213. E-mail: bertingr@isb.be. Website: www.isb.be

INTERNATIONAL SCHOOL OF KENYA, LTD.

PO Box 14103
Nairobi, Kenya

Head of School: Mr. David Henry

General Information Coeducational day college-preparatory and International Baccalaureate, ESL school. Grades PK–PG. Distance learning grades 9–12. Founded: 1976. Setting: suburban. 40-acre campus. 7 buildings on campus. Approved or accredited by Commission on Secondary Schools, Middle States Association of Colleges and Schools, and state department of education. Member of European Council of International Schools. Language of instruction: English. Upper school average class size: 22. There are 182 required school days per year for Upper School students. Upper School students typically attend 5 days per week. The average school day consists of 7 hours.

Upper School Student Profile Grade 6: 61 students (30 boys, 31 girls); Grade 7: 77 students (30 boys, 47 girls); Grade 8: 82 students (41 boys, 41 girls); Grade 9: 98 students (48 boys, 50 girls); Grade 10: 65 students (30 boys, 35 girls); Grade 11: 74 students (31 boys, 43 girls); Grade 12: 98 students (46 boys, 52 girls).

Faculty School total: 128. In upper school: 23 men, 18 women; 31 have advanced degrees.

Subjects Offered African studies, algebra, American history, American literature, anthropology, art, art history, arts, biology, calculus, chemistry, computer graphics, computer science, creative writing, drama, earth science, economics, English, English literature, ESL, European history, expository writing, fine arts, French, geography, geometry, government/civics, health, history, information technology, journalism, mathematics, multimedia, music, physical education, physics, psychology, religion, science, social studies, sociology, Spanish, theater, theory of knowledge, trigonometry, world history, world literature.

Graduation Requirements CAS, Inter Cultural Trip.

Special Academic Programs International Baccalaureate program; Advanced Placement exam preparation; honors section; independent study; term-away projects; remedial reading and/or remedial writing; remedial math; programs in English, mathematics, general development for dyslexic students; ESL (55 students enrolled).

College Admission Counseling 77 students graduated in 2016; 65 went to college, including Brown University, Cardiff University, Durham University, Edinburgh University, Loughborough University, The University of British Columbia. Other: 2 went to work, 10 had other specific plans. Mean SAT critical reading: 579, mean SAT math: 636, mean SAT writing: 588. 55% scored over 600 on SAT critical reading, 45% scored over 600 on SAT math, 48% scored over 1800 on combined SAT, 52% scored over 26 on composite ACT.

Student Life Upper grades have student council, honor system. Discipline rests primarily with faculty.

Tuition and Aid Day student tuition: $14,510–$27,820. Tuition installment plan (individually arranged payment plans, bi yearly payment plan). Bursaries, merit scholarship grants, need-based scholarship grants available. In 2016–17, 1% of upper-school students received aid; total upper-school merit-scholarship money awarded: $1500. Total amount of financial aid awarded in 2016–17: $179,342.

Admissions Traditional secondary-level entrance grade is 8. For fall 2016, 75 students applied for upper-level admission, 53 were accepted, 53 enrolled. Deadline for receipt of application materials: none. Application fee required: 375 Kenyan shillings. On-campus interview recommended.

Athletics Interscholastic: aquatics (boys, girls), basketball (b,g), cross-country running (b,g), diving (b,g), field hockey (b,g), golf (b,g), hockey (b,g), rugby (b,g), running (b,g), soccer (b,g), swimming and diving (b,g), tennis (b,g), track and field (b,g), volleyball (b,g); intramural: triathlon (b,g), weight lifting (b); coed intramural: softball. 2 PE instructors.

Computers Computer network features include on-campus library services, Internet access, wireless campus network, Internet filtering or blocking technology. Student e-mail accounts and computer access in designated common areas are available to students. Students grades are available online. The school has a published electronic and media policy.

Contact Dr. Robert Blanchard, High School Principal. 254-20 209 1308/9. E-mail: rblanchard@isk.ac.ke.

THE INTERNATIONAL SCHOOL OF LONDON

139 Gunnersbury Avenue

London W3 8LG, United Kingdom

Head of School: Mr. Andy Atkinson

General Information Coeducational day college-preparatory school. Grades PK–12. Founded: 1972. Setting: urban. 2 buildings on campus. Approved or accredited by Council of International Schools. Member of European Council of International Schools. Language of instruction: English. Total enrollment: 340. Upper school average class size: 18. Upper school faculty-student ratio: 1:8. There are 178 required school days per year for Upper School students. Upper School students typically attend 5 days per week. The average school day consists of 7 hours and 30 minutes.

Upper School Student Profile Grade 11: 30 students (15 boys, 15 girls); Grade 12: 30 students (15 boys, 15 girls).

Faculty School total: 120. In upper school: 15 men, 16 women; 21 have advanced degrees.

Subjects Offered Art, economics, English, French, geography, history, languages, mathematics, music, physical education, science, social sciences, Spanish, world affairs.

Graduation Requirements Foreign language, mathematics, science, social sciences. Community service is required.

Special Academic Programs International Baccalaureate program; ESL (56 students enrolled).

College Admission Counseling 31 students graduated in 2016; all went to college.

Student Life Upper grades have student council. Discipline rests primarily with faculty.

Tuition and Aid Day student tuition: £18,600–£25,450. Need-based scholarship grants available. In 2016–17, 3% of upper-school students received aid.

Admissions For fall 2016, 10 students applied for upper-level admission, 10 were accepted, 7 enrolled. Deadline for receipt of application materials: July 30. Application fee required: £200. Interview required.

Athletics Interscholastic: badminton (boys, girls), basketball (b,g), soccer (b), tennis (b,g), volleyball (b,g), winter soccer (b,g); intramural: badminton (b,g), running (b,g), softball (b,g), swimming and diving (b,g), table tennis (b,g), tennis (b,g), volleyball (b,g), winter soccer (b,g); coed interscholastic: soccer; coed intramural: fitness, outdoor activities, softball, swimming and diving, table tennis, tennis. 3 PE instructors, 2 coaches.

Computers Computers are regularly used in art, design, drawing and design, economics, English, foreign language, French, French as a second language, geography, graphic arts, history, mathematics, music, psychology, science, Spanish, yearbook classes. Computer network features include on-campus library services, Internet access, wireless campus network, Internet filtering or blocking technology. Student e-mail accounts are available to students. The school has a published electronic and media policy.

Contact Mr. Yoel Gordon, Head of Admissions. 20-8992-5823. Fax: 44-8993-7012. E-mail: ygordon@isllondon.org. Website: www.isllondon.org

INTERNATIONAL SCHOOL OF LUXEMBOURG

36 Boulevard Pierre Dupong

L-1430 Luxembourg, Luxembourg

Head of School: Mrs. Nicki Crush

General Information Coeducational day college-preparatory, arts, bilingual studies, technology, and global issues and awareness school. Grades PK–12. Founded: 1963. Setting: suburban. Nearest major city is Luxembourg City, Luxembourg. 3-acre campus. 2 buildings on campus. Approved or accredited by Council of International Schools, International Baccalaureate Organization, and Middle States Association of Colleges and Schools. Affiliate member of National Association of Independent Schools; member of European Council of International Schools. Language of instruction: English. Total enrollment: 1,356. Upper school average class size: 18. Upper school faculty-student ratio: 1:8. There are 186 required school days per year for Upper School students. The average school day consists of 8 hours.

Upper School Student Profile Grade 6: 108 students (61 boys, 47 girls), Grade 7: 108 students (57 boys, 51 girls); Grade 8: 113 students (61 boys, 52 girls); Grade 9: 100 students (44 boys, 56 girls); Grade 10: 102 students (56 boys, 46 girls); Grade 11: 101 students (52 boys, 49 girls); Grade 12: 92 students (50 boys, 42 girls).

Faculty School total: 153. In upper school: 58 men, 95 women; 70 have advanced degrees.

Subjects Offered Advanced math, algebra, art, art history, biology, chemistry, computers, drama, earth science, English, English literature, ESL, European history, French, geography, geometry, German, health, history, International Baccalaureate courses, mathematics, music, physical education, physics, science, social studies, study skills, theory of knowledge, trigonometry, world history, world literature.

Graduation Requirements English, foreign language, mathematics, physical education (includes health), science, social studies (includes history). Community service is required.

Special Academic Programs International Baccalaureate program; ESL (165 students enrolled).

College Admission Counseling 74 students graduated in 2015; 67 went to college, including McGill University; Northeastern University; University of Victoria; Worcester Polytechnic Institute. Other: 7 had other specific plans. Median SAT critical reading: 570, median SAT math: 610, median SAT writing: 570, median combined SAT: 1770, median composite ACT: 26. 41% scored over 600 on SAT critical reading, 59% scored over 600 on SAT math, 38% scored over 600 on SAT writing, 44% scored over 1800 on combined SAT, 83% scored over 26 on composite ACT.

Student Life Upper grades have student council, honor system. Discipline rests primarily with faculty.

Tuition and Aid Day student tuition: €18,765.

Admissions For fall 2015, 131 students applied for upper-level admission, 75 were accepted, 60 enrolled. Admissions testing and math and English placement tests required. Deadline for receipt of application materials: none. Application fee required: €300. On-campus interview required.

Athletics Interscholastic: baseball (boys), basketball (b,g), soccer (b,g), swimming and diving (b,g), tennis (b,g), track and field (b,g), volleyball (g); intramural: basketball (b,g), soccer (b,g), track and field (b,g), volleyball (g); coed interscholastic: golf, rugby, skiing (downhill), soccer; coed intramural: badminton, fitness, gymnastics, modern dance, Nautilus, physical fitness, strength & conditioning, swimming and diving, triathlon, weight training. 5 PE instructors.

Computers Computers are regularly used in all academic classes. Computer network features include on-campus library services, Internet access, wireless campus network, Internet filtering or blocking technology. Student e-mail accounts are available to students. Students grades are available online. The school has a published electronic and media policy.

Contact Mrs. Henriette Rosenkvist, Head of Admissions. 352-260440. E-mail: admissions@islux.lu. Website: www.islux.lu

INTERNATIONAL SCHOOL OF PORT-OF-SPAIN

1 International Drive
Westmoorings, Trinidad and Tobago

Head of School: Mr. Jeffrey Latham

General Information Coeducational day college-preparatory and general academic school; primarily serves students with learning disabilities, individuals with Attention Deficit Disorder, and individuals with emotional and behavioral problems. Grades PK–12. Founded: 1994. Setting: suburban. Nearest major city is Port of Spain, Trinidad and Tobago. 3-acre campus. 1 building on campus. Approved or accredited by International Baccalaureate Organization and Southern Association of Colleges and Schools. Language of instruction: English. Total enrollment: 466. Upper school average class size: 12. Upper school faculty-student ratio: 1:12. There are 183 required school days per year for Upper School students. Upper School students typically attend 5 days per week. The average school day consists of 5 hours and 45 minutes.

Upper School Student Profile Grade 9: 25 students (10 boys, 15 girls); Grade 10: 36 students (13 boys, 23 girls); Grade 11: 45 students (25 boys, 20 girls); Grade 12: 37 students (17 boys, 20 girls).

Faculty School total: 33. In upper school: 14 men, 19 women; 24 have advanced degrees.

Subjects Offered Advanced Placement courses, algebra, American history, American history-AP, ancient world history, art, biology, biology-AP, calculus-AP, chemistry, chemistry-AP, computer literacy, computers, contemporary studies, dance, drama, economics, English, English literature and composition-AP, environmental science, French, geometry, human geography - AP, leadership, model United Nations, modern world history, music, physical education, physics, physics-AP, pre-calculus, psychology-AP, Spanish, Spanish language-AP, statistics-AP, studio art-AP, theater arts, theater production, U.S. history, video film production.

Graduation Requirements Algebra, ancient world history, biology, English, foreign language, geometry, mathematics, modern world history, physical education (includes health), physical science, science, technology.

Special Academic Programs Advanced Placement exam preparation; academic accommodation for the gifted; remedial reading and/or remedial writing; remedial math; ESL (1 student enrolled).

College Admission Counseling 51 students graduated in 2016; 34 went to college, including Boston University; Ryerson University; The University of Western Ontario; University of Florida; University of Miami; University of Toronto. Other: 2 went to work, 6 had other specific plans.

Student Life Upper grades have uniform requirement, student council, honor system. Discipline rests primarily with faculty.

Tuition and Aid Day student tuition: $18,734. Merit scholarship grants, need-based scholarship grants available. In 2016–17, 10% of upper-school students received aid; total upper-school merit-scholarship money awarded: $42,000. Total amount of financial aid awarded in 2016–17: $42,000.

Admissions Traditional secondary-level entrance grade is 9. For fall 2016, 33 students applied for upper-level admission, 31 were accepted, 23 enrolled. Math Placement Exam and writing sample required. Deadline for receipt of application materials: none. Application fee required: $100. On-campus interview required.

Athletics Coed Interscholastic: basketball, rugby, soccer, volleyball; coed intramural: archery, baseball, basketball, cheering, cricket, dance, martial arts, rugby, soccer, softball, ultimate Frisbee, volleyball. 3 PE instructors, 1 coach.

Computers Computers are regularly used in all classes. Computer network features include on-campus library services, online commercial services, Internet access. Student e-mail accounts are available to students. The school has a published electronic and media policy.

Contact Mrs. Jackie Fung-Kee-Fung, Director of Admission, Communication & Marketing. 868-632-4591 Ext. 411. Fax: 868-632-4033.
E-mail: jfungkeefung@isps.edu.tt. Website: www.isps.edu.tt

INTERNATIONAL SCHOOL OF ZUG AND LUZERN (ISZL)

Walterswil
Baar 6340, Switzerland

Head of School: Dominic Currer

General Information Coeducational day college-preparatory, International Baccalaureate (PYP, MYP, DP), and Advanced Placement school. Founded: 1961. Setting: small town. Nearest major city is Zurich, Switzerland. 5-hectare campus. 1 building on campus. Approved or accredited by International Baccalaureate Organization, New England Association of Schools and Colleges, and The College Board. Member of European Council of International Schools. Language of instruction: English. Total enrollment: 1,189. Upper school average class size: 18. Upper school faculty-student ratio: 1:6. There are 180 required school days per year for Upper School students. Upper School students typically attend 5 days per week. The average school day consists of 7 hours.

Faculty School total: 200. In upper school: 16 men, 28 women.

Subjects Offered Art, art history-AP, biology, biology-AP, calculus-AP, chemistry, chemistry-AP, computer graphics, computer science-AP, dance, drama, English, English language and composition-AP, English literature and composition-AP, environmental science-AP, ESL, European history-AP, French, French language-AP, German, German-AP, human geography - AP, humanities, integrated mathematics, integrated science, macro/microeconomics-AP, music, physical education, physics, physics-AP, pre-calculus, studio art-AP, technology/design.

Graduation Requirements Art, art history-AP, biology-AP, calculus-AP, chemistry-AP, choir, college counseling, computer programming-AP, computer science-AP, computers, dance, drama, economics-AP, English, English language-AP, English literature-AP, environmental science-AP, ESL, European history-AP, foreign language, French, French language-AP, German, German-AP, health education, human geography - AP, International Baccalaureate courses, lab science, macro/microeconomics-AP, macroeconomics-AP, mathematics, model United Nations, modern European history-AP, music, physical education (includes health), physics-AP, pre-calculus, SAT/ACT preparation, social sciences, Spanish, studio art-AP, yearbook. Community service is required.

Special Academic Programs International Baccalaureate program; Advanced Placement exam preparation; accelerated programs; independent study; ESL (40 students enrolled).

College Admission Counseling 33 students graduated in 2015; 26 went to college, including Pace University; Pepperdine University; Stanford University; Villanova University; Yale University. Other: 3 entered a postgraduate year, 4 had other specific plans.

Student Life Upper grades have specified standards of dress, student council. Discipline rests primarily with faculty.

Tuition and Aid Day student tuition: 21,500 Swiss francs–32,000 Swiss francs. Tuition installment plan (monthly payment plans, individually arranged payment plans, semester payment plan). Discounts for children of staff and reciprocal arrangements with international primary school available.

Admissions English for Non-native Speakers or math and English placement tests required. Deadline for receipt of application materials: none. Application fee required: 5000 Swiss francs. Interview recommended.

Athletics Interscholastic: aerobics/dance (girls), alpine skiing (b,g), basketball (b,g), cross-country running (b,g), golf (b,g), indoor soccer (b,g), rugby (b), skiing (downhill) (b,g), soccer (b,g), swimming and diving (b,g), track and field (b,g), volleyball (b,g); intramural: alpine skiing (b,g), basketball (b,g), cross-country running (b,g), indoor soccer (b,g), soccer (b,g), track and field (b,g); coed interscholastic: canoeing/kayaking, climbing, softball; coed intramural: aerobics/dance, backpacking, badminton, ball hockey, bicycling, canoeing/kayaking, climbing, dance, field hockey, golf, hiking/backpacking, ice skating, kayaking, martial arts, mountain biking, outdoor activities, outdoor education, racquetball, rowing, running, sailing, skiing (downhill), snowboarding, soccer, softball, swimming and diving, tennis, walking, winter walking. 2 PE instructors, 2 coaches, 2 athletic trainers.

Computers Computers are regularly used in college planning classes. Computer network features include Internet access, Internet filtering or blocking technology. Campus intranet, student e-mail accounts, and computer access in designated common areas are available to students. The school has a published electronic and media policy.

Contact Urs Kappeler, Business Director. 41-41-768 2950. Fax: 41-41-768 2951.
E-mail: urs.kappeler@iszl.ch. Website: www.iszl.ch

ISIDORE NEWMAN SCHOOL

1903 Jefferson Avenue
New Orleans, Louisiana 70115

Head of School: Dr. Dale M. Smith

General Information Coeducational day college-preparatory school. Grades PK–12. Founded: 1903. Setting: urban. 11-acre campus. 10 buildings on campus. Approved or accredited by Independent Schools Association of the Southwest and Louisiana Department of Education. Member of National Association of Independent Schools and Secondary School Admission Test Board. Endowment: $3.3 million. Total enrollment: 1,005. Upper school average class size: 16. Upper school faculty-student ratio: 1:17. There are 175 required school days per year for Upper School students. Upper School students typically attend 5 days per week. The average school day consists of 7 hours and 50 minutes.

Subjects Offered Advanced computer applications, Advanced Placement courses, algebra, American history, American history-AP, American literature, anatomy, art, art history, biology, biology-AP, calculus, calculus-AP, ceramics, chemistry, Chinese, choral music, chorus, civics, communications, computer science-AP, dance, drama, English, English literature, environmental science, European history-AP, film, film history, fine arts, French, French language-AP, French literature-AP, French-AP, genetics, geometry, government/civics, history, human development, humanities, Latin, Latin-AP, mathematics, modern European history, modern European history-AP, music, music theory, peer counseling, photojournalism, physical education, physics, physics-AP, physiology, science, sculpture, social studies, Spanish, Spanish language-AP, Spanish literature-AP, speech, statistics-AP, technical theater, theater, trigonometry, U.S. government and politics-AP, U.S. history, U.S. history-AP, world history.

Graduation Requirements Arts and fine arts (art, music, dance, drama), computer science, English, foreign language, mathematics, physical education (includes health), science, social studies (includes history), speech, senior Capstone Elective–one class each semester of senior year.

Special Academic Programs Advanced Placement exam preparation; honors section; independent study; term-away projects.

Student Life Upper grades have specified standards of dress, student council, honor system. Discipline rests equally with students and faculty.

Tuition and Aid Tuition installment plan (Sallie Mae tuition loans). Need-based scholarship grants, Sallie Mae loans available.

Admissions Traditional secondary-level entrance grade is 9. ERB (CTP-Verbal, Quantitative), ERB CTP III, independent norms, Individual IQ, Achievement and behavior rating scale, ISEE, school's own test and writing sample required. Deadline for receipt of application materials: none. Application fee required: $50. Interview required.

Athletics Interscholastic: aquatics (boys, girls), baseball (b), basketball (b,g), cross-country running (b,g), football (b), golf (b,g), gymnastics (b,g), indoor track & field (b), soccer (b,g), softball (g), swimming and diving (b,g), tennis (b,g), track and field (b,g), volleyball (g); coed interscholastic: cheering. 2 athletic trainers.

Computers Computers are regularly used in all academic classes. Computer network features include on-campus library services, online commercial services, Internet access, wireless campus network, Internet filtering or blocking technology. Campus intranet and student e-mail accounts are available to students. Students grades are available online. The school has a published electronic and media policy.

Contact Mrs. Kenley Breckenridge, Admission Coordinator. 504-896-6323. Fax: 504-896-8597. E-mail: kenleybreckenridge@newmanschool.org Website: www.newmanschool.org

ISTANBUL INTERNATIONAL COMMUNITY SCHOOL

Buyukcekmece Karaagac Mahallesi 51. Sokak
Buyukcekmece
Istanbul 34500, Turkey

Head of School: Ms. Jane Thompson

General Information Coeducational day college-preparatory, general academic, and International Baccalaureate school. Grades 1–12. Founded: 1911. Setting: rural. 16-hectare campus. 4 buildings on campus. Approved or accredited by Council of International Schools, International Baccalaureate Organization, New England Association of Schools and Colleges, and The College Board. Affiliate member of National Association of Independent Schools; member of European Council of International Schools. Language of instruction: English. Endowment: $7 million. Total enrollment: 619. Upper school average class size: 20. Upper school faculty-student ratio: 1:9. There are 178 required school days per year for Upper School students. Upper School students typically attend 5 days per week. The average school day consists of 5 hours and 30 minutes.

Upper School Student Profile Grade 7: 48 students (19 boys, 29 girls); Grade 8: 58 students (29 boys, 29 girls); Grade 9: 43 students (27 boys, 16 girls); Grade 10: 56 students (30 boys, 26 girls); Grade 11: 45 students (28 boys, 17 girls); Grade 12: 40 students (24 boys, 16 girls).

Faculty School total: 77. In upper school: 16 men, 11 women; 24 have advanced degrees.

Graduation Requirements International Baccalaureate courses.

Special Academic Programs International Baccalaureate program; independent study; academic accommodation for the gifted; remedial reading and/or remedial writing; remedial math; programs in English, general development for dyslexic students; ESL (60 students enrolled).

College Admission Counseling 30 students graduated in 2016; all went to college, including Georgetown University; Michigan State University; Northeastern Illinois University; Parsons School of Design; University of California, Los Angeles; University of Michigan. Mean SAT critical reading: 570, mean SAT math: 620, mean SAT writing: 600.

Student Life Upper grades have student council, honor system. Discipline rests primarily with faculty.

Tuition and Aid Day student tuition: $15,175–$30,350. Tuition installment plan (individually arranged payment plans).

Admissions For fall 2016, 46 students applied for upper-level admission, 44 were accepted, 44 enrolled. Comprehensive educational evaluation, English proficiency, school's own test or writing sample required. Application fee required: $1100. Interview required.

Athletics Interscholastic: badminton (boys, girls), basketball (b,g), cross-country running (b,g), equestrian sports (b,g), soccer (b,g), softball (b,g), table tennis (b,g), tennis (b,g), volleyball (b,g); intramural: basketball (b,g), cross-country running (b,g), soccer (b,g), softball (b,g), tennis (b,g), volleyball (b,g); coed interscholastic: aquatics, badminton, ballet, cross-country running, horseback riding, table tennis, tennis; coed intramural: tennis. 3 PE instructors, 20 coaches.

Computers Computers are regularly used in all academic classes. Computer network features include on-campus library services, online commercial services, Internet access, wireless campus network, Internet filtering or blocking technology, 1:1 laptop program in grades 6-12 (student purchases/owns), 2:1 laptop program in grades 2-5, iPads for Preschool-Grade 1. Campus intranet, student e-mail accounts, and computer access in designated common areas are available to students. Students grades are available online. The school has a published electronic and media policy.

Contact Mrs. Suzan Gurkan, Director of Admissions. 90-212-857-8264 Ext. 215. Fax: 90-212-857-8270. E-mail: admissions@iics.k12.tr. Website: www.iics.k12.tr

JACK M. BARRACK HEBREW ACADEMY

272 South Bryn Mawr Avenue
Bryn Mawr, Pennsylvania 19010

Head of School: Mrs. Sharon P. Levin

General Information Coeducational day college-preparatory, bilingual studies, and technology school, affiliated with Jewish faith. Grades 6–12. Founded: 1946. Setting: suburban. Nearest major city is Philadelphia. 35-acre campus. 2 buildings on campus. Approved or accredited by Middle States Association of Colleges and Schools, Pennsylvania Association of Independent Schools, and Pennsylvania Department of Education. Member of National Association of Independent Schools. Languages of instruction: English and Hebrew. Endowment: $3.2 million. Total enrollment: 274. Upper school average class size: 16. Upper school faculty-student ratio: 1:15. There are 168 required school days per year for Upper School students. Upper School students typically attend 5 days per week. The average school day consists of 7 hours.

Upper School Student Profile Grade 9: 60 students (23 boys, 37 girls); Grade 10: 55 students (20 boys, 35 girls); Grade 11: 42 students (23 boys, 19 girls); Grade 12: 50 students (22 boys, 28 girls). 100% of students are Jewish.

Faculty School total: 70. In upper school: 23 men, 34 women; 47 have advanced degrees.

Subjects Offered Algebra, American history, American literature, art, astronomy, Bible studies, biology, calculus, chemistry, community service, computer math, computer programming, computer science, creative writing, earth science, English, English literature, environmental science, environmental science-AP, ethics, European history, French, geometry, government/civics, grammar, health, Hebrew, history, Jewish studies, Latin, mathematics, music, physical education, physics, public speaking, religion, science, social studies, Spanish, trigonometry, world history, writing.

Graduation Requirements English, foreign language, mathematics, physical education (includes health), religion (includes Bible studies and theology), science, social studies (includes history), senior community service project&-150 hours in the senior year.

Special Academic Programs 8 Advanced Placement exams for which test preparation is offered; accelerated programs; independent study; term-away projects; study at local college for college credit; study abroad; academic accommodation for the gifted; remedial reading and/or remedial writing; remedial math; special instructional classes for deaf students.

College Admission Counseling 63 students graduated in 2016; all went to college, including Brandeis University; Columbia University; Muhlenberg College; The George Washington University; University of Maryland, College Park; University of Pennsylvania.

Student Life Upper grades have specified standards of dress, student council, honor system. Discipline rests primarily with faculty.

Tuition and Aid Day student tuition: $31,750–$32,500. Tuition installment plan (FACTS Tuition Payment Plan, monthly payment plans, individually arranged payment plans). Tuition reduction for siblings, merit scholarship grants, need-based scholarship grants available.

Admissions Traditional secondary-level entrance grade is 9. For fall 2016, 37 students applied for upper-level admission, 30 were accepted, 19 enrolled. ISEE required. Deadline for receipt of application materials: none. Application fee required: $75. On-campus interview required.

Athletics Interscholastic: baseball (boys), basketball (b,g), soccer (b,g), softball (g), tennis (b,g), track and field (g); intramural: basketball (b,g), field hockey (b,g), lacrosse (g), running (b,g), soccer (b,g), squash (g), track and field (g), volleyball (b,g); coed interscholastic: cross-country running, soccer, swimming and diving. 4 PE instructors, 17 coaches.

Computers Computers are regularly used in drawing and design, engineering, media arts classes. Computer network features include on-campus library services, online commercial services, Internet access, wireless campus network, Internet filtering or blocking technology. Campus intranet, student e-mail accounts, and computer access in designated common areas are available to students. Students grades are available online. The school has a published electronic and media policy.

Contact Jennifer Groen, Director of Admission and Strategic Engagement. 610-922-2350. Fax: 610-922-2301. E-mail: jgroen@jbha.org. Website: www.jbha.org

JACKSON CHRISTIAN SCHOOL

832 Country Club Lane
Jackson, Tennessee 38305

Head of School: Dr. Mark Benton

General Information Coeducational day college-preparatory, arts, religious studies, bilingual studies, and technology school, affiliated with Church of Christ. Grades JK–12. Founded: 1976. Setting: suburban. 30-acre campus. 6 buildings on campus.

Approved or accredited by National Christian School Association, Southern Association of Colleges and Schools, and Tennessee Department of Education. Endowment: $875,000. Total enrollment: 857. Upper school average class size: 19. Upper school faculty-student ratio: 1:19. There are 180 required school days per year for Upper School students. Upper School students typically attend 5 days per week. The average school day consists of 6 hours.

Upper School Student Profile Grade 6: 86 students (39 boys, 47 girls); Grade 7: 72 students (41 boys, 31 girls); Grade 8: 58 students (30 boys, 28 girls); Grade 9: 79 students (40 boys, 39 girls); Grade 10: 60 students (28 boys, 32 girls); Grade 11: 77 students (38 boys, 39 girls); Grade 12: 70 students (40 boys, 30 girls). 34% of students are members of Church of Christ.

Faculty School total: 65. In upper school: 14 men, 24 women; 13 have advanced degrees.

Subjects Offered Advanced chemistry, advanced computer applications, algebra, American government, American history, anatomy and physiology, art, baseball, basketball, Bible, Bible studies, biology, calculus, chemistry, choir, chorus, current events, ecology, economics, English, English composition, geometry, government, government/civics, honors English, journalism, keyboarding, life science, physical education, physical science, physics, pre-calculus, psychology, Spanish, state history, theater, theater arts, trigonometry, U.S. government, U.S. history, world geography, world history.

Graduation Requirements 20th century world history, arts and fine arts (art, music, dance, drama), English, foreign language, mathematics, physical education (includes health), religion (includes Bible studies and theology), science, social studies (includes history), must take the ACT test.

Special Academic Programs Honors section; study at local college for college credit; programs in English, mathematics for dyslexic students.

College Admission Counseling 68 students graduated in 2015; 66 went to college, including Freed-Hardeman University; Harding University; Jackson State Community College; The University of Tennessee at Chattanooga; Union University. Other: 2 went to work. Median composite ACT: 24. 35% scored over 26 on composite ACT.

Student Life Upper grades have uniform requirement, student council, honor system. Discipline rests primarily with faculty.

Tuition and Aid Day student tuition: $7200. Tuition installment plan (FACTS Tuition Payment Plan, monthly payment plans, individually arranged payment plans, quarterly payment plan, semester payment plan, pay-in-full discount). Tuition reduction for siblings, need-based scholarship grants available. In 2015–16, 15% of upper-school students received aid. Total amount of financial aid awarded in 2015–16: $15,218.

Admissions Traditional secondary-level entrance grade is 9. For fall 2015, 40 students applied for upper-level admission, 32 were accepted, 31 enrolled. Math and English placement tests required. Deadline for receipt of application materials: none. Application fee required: $100. Interview required.

Athletics Interscholastic: baseball (boys), basketball (b,g), cheering (g), cross-country running (b,g), football (b), golf (b,g), soccer (b,g), softball (g), tennis (b,g), track and field (b,g); coed interscholastic: cheering. 3 PE instructors, 10 coaches.

Computers Computers are regularly used in business applications, computer applications, desktop publishing, library, multimedia, programming, science, Web site design classes. Computer network features include online commercial services, Internet access, wireless campus network, Internet filtering or blocking technology. Campus intranet, student e-mail accounts, and computer access in designated common areas are available to students. Students grades are available online. The school has a published electronic and media policy.

Contact Jill Joiner, Director of Admissions. 731-300-4578. Fax: 731-664-5763. E-mail: jill.joiner@jcseagles.org. Website: www.jcseagles.org

JACKSON PREPARATORY SCHOOL

3100 Lakeland Drive
Jackson, Mississippi 39232

Head of School: Dr. Jason L. Walton

General Information Coeducational day college-preparatory school. Grades 6–12. Founded: 1970. Setting: urban. 74-acre campus. 6 buildings on campus. Approved or accredited by Mississippi Private School Association, Southern Association of Colleges and Schools, Southern Association of Independent Schools, and The College Board. Member of National Association of Independent Schools. Endowment: $993,373. Total enrollment: 836. Upper school average class size: 17. Upper school faculty-student ratio: 1:13. There are 176 required school days per year for Upper School students. Upper School students typically attend 5 days per week. The average school day consists of 6 hours and 45 minutes.

Upper School Student Profile Grade 10: 146 students (79 boys, 67 girls); Grade 11: 138 students (70 boys, 68 girls); Grade 12: 124 students (54 boys, 70 girls).

Faculty School total: 90. In upper school: 26 men, 49 women; 42 have advanced degrees.

Subjects Offered Accounting, ACT preparation, advanced biology, advanced chemistry, advanced computer applications, advanced math, Advanced Placement courses, algebra, American government, American history, American history-AP, American literature, art, Asian studies, Bible as literature, biology, biology-AP, British literature, calculus, calculus-AP, chemistry, chemistry-AP, choral music, civics, classical studies, computer science, creative writing, debate, discrete mathematics, drama, driver education, earth science, economics, engineering, English, English literature, English literature-AP, equestrian sports, European history, film, fine arts, finite math, French, geography, geometry, government-AP, government/civics, grammar, graphic design, Greek, Greek culture, history, honors algebra, honors English, honors geometry, journalism, Latin, Latin-AP, law and the legal system, Mandarin, mathematics, media arts, media communications, music, physical education, physics, physics-AP, pre-algebra, pre-calculus, science, social studies, Spanish, student publications, studio art-AP, trigonometry, U.S. government, U.S. government and politics-AP, U.S. history, U.S. history-AP, woodworking, world history, world literature.

Graduation Requirements Arts and fine arts (art, music, dance, drama), computer applications, English, foreign language, mathematics, science, social studies (includes history).

Special Academic Programs Advanced Placement exam preparation; honors section; academic accommodation for the gifted, the musically talented, and the artistically talented; programs in English, mathematics, general development for dyslexic students.

College Admission Counseling 129 students graduated in 2016; all went to college, including Louisiana State University in Shreveport; Mississippi College; Mississippi State University; Southern Methodist University; The University of Alabama; University of Mississippi. Mean SAT critical reading: 611, mean SAT math: 620, mean SAT writing: 598, mean composite ACT: 26. 48% scored over 26 on composite ACT.

Student Life Upper grades have uniform requirement, student council, honor system. Discipline rests primarily with faculty.

Summer Programs Remediation, enrichment, art/fine arts, computer instruction programs offered; session focuses on enrichment; held on campus; accepts boys and girls; open to students from other schools. 200 students usually enrolled. 2017 schedule: June 6 to July 15. Application deadline: May 1.

Tuition and Aid Day student tuition: $13,224. Tuition installment plan (monthly payment plans). Need-based scholarship grants available. In 2016–17, 12% of upper-school students received aid. Total amount of financial aid awarded in 2016–17: $210,000.

Admissions Traditional secondary-level entrance grade is 10. For fall 2016, 32 students applied for upper-level admission, 21 were accepted, 21 enrolled. Non-standardized placement tests and OLSAT, Stanford Achievement Test required. Deadline for receipt of application materials: none. Application fee required: $50. Interview required.

Athletics Interscholastic: archery (boys, girls), baseball (b), basketball (b,g), cheering (g), cross-country running (b,g), dance team (g), equestrian sports (b,g), fly fishing (b,g), football (b), Frisbee (b), soccer (b,g), softball (g), swimming and diving (b,g), tennis (b,g), track and field (b,g), ultimate Frisbee (b), volleyball (g); intramural: basketball (b,g), Frisbee (b), pom squad (g), soccer (b,g), volleyball (b,g); coed interscholastic: archery, cheering, equestrian sports, fly fishing, golf, marksmanship, riflery, skeet shooting; coed intramural: equestrian sports, skeet shooting. 4 coaches.

Computers Computers are regularly used in all classes. Computer network features include on-campus library services, online commercial services, Internet access, Electric Library, EBSCOhost®, GaleNet, Grolier Online, NewsBank, online subscription services. The school has a published electronic and media policy.

Contact Mrs. Tracie Mallard, Director of Admission. 601-932-8106 Ext. 1. Fax: 601-936-4068. E-mail: tmallard@jacksonprep.net. Website: www.jacksonprep.net

JEAN AND SAMUEL FRANKEL JEWISH ACADEMY OF METROPOLITAN DETROIT

6600 West Maple Road
West Bloomfield, Michigan 48322

Head of School: Rabbi Azaryah Cohen

General Information Coeducational day college-preparatory school, affiliated with International Church of the Foursquare Gospel. Grades 9–12. Founded: 2000. Setting: suburban. Nearest major city is West Bloomfield-Metro Detroit. 1 building on campus. Approved or accredited by Independent Schools Association of the Central States and Michigan Department of Education. Member of National Association of Independent Schools. Languages of instruction: English and Hebrew. Upper school average class size: 13. The average school day consists of 8 hours.

Upper School Student Profile Grade 9: 60 students (30 boys, 30 girls); Grade 10: 60 students (30 boys, 30 girls); Grade 11: 60 students (30 boys, 30 girls); Grade 12: 60 students (30 boys, 30 girls). 100% of students are International Church of the Foursquare Gospel.

Faculty In upper school: 30 have advanced degrees.

Special Academic Programs Advanced Placement exam preparation; honors section; study abroad; academic accommodation for the gifted; remedial reading and/or remedial writing; remedial math; special instructional classes for deaf students, blind students.

College Admission Counseling 56 went to college, including Michigan State University; University of Michigan–Dearborn.

Student Life Upper grades have specified standards of dress, student council, honor system. Discipline rests primarily with faculty. Attendance at religious services is required.

Tuition and Aid Day student tuition: $21,000. Tuition reduction for siblings, need-based scholarship grants available.

Admissions Traditional secondary-level entrance grade is 9. High School Placement Test required. Deadline for receipt of application materials: January 30. Application fee required: $100. Interview required.

Athletics 2 PE instructors, 8 coaches.

Computers Computer network features include on-campus library services, online commercial services, Internet access, wireless campus network, all students are given issued an iPad. Campus intranet and student e-mail accounts are available to students. Students grades are available online. The school has a published electronic and media policy.

Contact Lisa Gilan, Director of Admissions. 248-592-5263. Fax: 248-592-0022. E-mail: lgilan@frankelja.org. Website: www.frankelja.org/

JESUIT COLLEGE PREPARATORY SCHOOL

12345 Inwood Road
Dallas, Texas 75244

Head of School: Mr. Tom Garrison

General Information Boys' day college preparatory school, affiliated with Roman Catholic Church (Jesuit order). Grades 9–12. Founded: 1942. Setting: suburban 28-acre campus. 2 buildings on campus. Approved or accredited by Jesuit Secondary Education Association, Southern Association of Colleges and Schools, and Texas Department of Education. Endowment: $25.6 million. Total enrollment: 1,107. Upper school average class size: 17. Upper school faculty-student ratio: 1:11. There are 190 required school days per year for Upper School students. Upper School students typically attend 5 days per week. The average school day consists of 6 hours.

Upper School Student Profile Grade 9: 285 students (285 boys); Grade 10: 284 students (284 boys); Grade 11: 271 students (271 boys); Grade 12: 268 students (268 boys). 80% of students are Roman Catholic Church (Jesuit order).

Faculty School total: 115. In upper school: 85 men, 30 women, 56 have advanced degrees.

Subjects Offered Advanced chemistry, advanced computer applications, advanced math, American literature-AP, American studies, art, art appreciation, art-AP, arts, band, Bible, biology, biology-AP, British literature, British literature-AP, calculus, calculus-AP, Catholic belief and practice, ceramics, chemistry, chemistry-AP, choir, Christian ethics, church history, civics, college counseling, community service, composition, composition-AP, computer applications, computer graphics, computer science, computer science-AP, contemporary issues, discrete mathematics, drama, drama performance, drama workshop, drawing, drawing and design, driver education, earth science, economics, economics-AP, English, English composition, English language and composition-AP, English language-AP, English literature, English literature and composition-AP, English literature-AP, English AP, English/composition-AP, ethical decision making, European history, fine arts, French, French-AP, general science, geometry, government, government-AP, grammar, guitar, health, history, history-AP, honors algebra, honors English, honors geometry, honors U.S. history, honors world history, instrumental music, jazz band, journalism, Latin, literature and composition-AP, marching band, mathematics, mathematics-AP, microcomputer technology applications, music, music appreciation, musical productions, orchestra, peace and justice, peer ministry, performing arts, physical education, physics, physics-AP, pottery, prayer/spirituality, pre-calculus, psychology, public speaking, publications, religion, scripture, social studies, Spanish, Spanish language-AP, Spanish literature-AP, Spanish-AP, speech, speech and debate, speech and oral interpretation, statistics, student government, student publications, studio art, studio art-AP, symphonic band, theater, theology, U.S. government, U.S. government and politics-AP, U.S. history, U.S. history-AP, U.S. literature, world history, world history-AP.

Graduation Requirements Arts and fine arts (art, music, dance, drama), computer science, English, foreign language, mathematics, physical education (includes health), science, social studies (includes history), theology. Community service is required.

Special Academic Programs 18 Advanced Placement exams for which test preparation is offered; honors section; independent study; study at local college for college credit.

College Admission Counseling 256 students graduated in 2016; 254 went to college, including Saint Louis University; Southern Methodist University; Texas A&M University; Texas Christian University; The University of Alabama; The University of Texas at Austin. Other: 2 had other specific plans. Mean SAT critical reading: 598, mean SAT math: 618, mean SAT writing: 595.

Student Life Upper grades have specified standards of dress, student council, honor system. Discipline rests primarily with faculty. Attendance at religious services is required.

Summer Programs Remediation, enrichment, advancement, sports, art/fine arts, computer instruction programs offered; session focuses on youth recreation; held on campus; accepts boys and girls; open to students from other schools. 800 students usually enrolled. 2017 schedule: June 15 to July 10. Application deadline: May 30.

Tuition and Aid Day student tuition: $17,200. Tuition installment plan (FACTS Tuition Payment Plan). Merit scholarship grants, need-based scholarship grants, paying campus jobs available. In 2016–17, 25% of upper-school students received aid; total upper-school merit-scholarship money awarded: $56,000. Total amount of financial aid awarded in 2016–17: $1,233,850.

Admissions Traditional secondary-level entrance grade is 9. For fall 2016, 525 students applied for upper-level admission, 326 were accepted, 285 enrolled. ISEE required. Deadline for receipt of application materials: January 13. Application fee required: $100. On-campus interview recommended.

Athletics Interscholastic: baseball, basketball, bowling, crew, cross-country running, diving, fencing, football, golf, ice hockey, lacrosse, power lifting, rugby, soccer, swimming and diving, tennis, track and field, volleyball, water polo, wrestling; intramural: basketball, bicycling, broomball, flagball, floor hockey, indoor soccer, ultimate Frisbee, volleyball; coed interscholastic: cheering, drill team. 6 PE instructors, 30 coaches, 2 athletic trainers.

Computers Computers are regularly used in college planning, desktop publishing, digital applications, engineering, English, foreign language, graphic design, graphics, humanities, introduction to technology, journalism, literary magazine, mathematics, media production, multimedia, newspaper, programming, publications, science, social studies, technology, video film production, Web site design, writing, yearbook classes. Computer network features include on-campus library services, online commercial services, Internet access, wireless campus network, Internet filtering or blocking technology. Campus intranet, student e-mail accounts, and computer access in designated common areas are available to students. Students grades are available online. The school has a published electronic and media policy.

Contact Mrs. Maureen Miramontes, Admissions Assistant. 972-387-8700 Ext 453. Fax: 972-980-0707. E-mail: mmiramontes@jesuitcp.org. Website: www.jesuitcp.org

JESUIT HIGH SCHOOL OF TAMPA

4701 North Himes Avenue
Tampa, Florida 33614-6694

Head of School: Mr. Barry Neuburger

General Information Boys' day college-preparatory school, affiliated with Roman Catholic Church. Grades 9–12. Founded: 1899. Setting: urban. 40-acre campus. 9 buildings on campus. Approved or accredited by Jesuit Secondary Education Association, National Catholic Education Association, Southern Association of Colleges and Schools, and Florida Department of Education. Total enrollment: 775. Upper school average class size: 20. Upper school faculty-student ratio: 1:12. There are 180 required school days per year for Upper School students. Upper School students typically attend 5 days per week. The average school day consists of 7 hours and 23 minutes.

Upper School Student Profile Grade 9: 223 students (223 boys); Grade 10: 191 students (191 boys); Grade 11: 197 students (197 boys); Grade 12: 175 students (175 boys). 79% of students are Roman Catholic.

Faculty School total: 66. In upper school: 48 men, 18 women; 45 have advanced degrees.

Subjects Offered Algebra, American foreign policy, American government, American history, analytic geometry, anatomy, ancient world history, art, biology, biology-AP, calculus, calculus-AP, chemistry, chemistry-AP, chorus, computer programming, computer science, computer science-AP, economics, engineering, English, English language and composition-AP, English literature and composition-AP, environmental science, ethics, European history-AP, French, geometry, health, human geography - AP, journalism, Latin, Latin-AP, marine biology, music, physical education, physics, physics-AP, physiology, pre-calculus, psychology-AP, Spanish, Spanish language-AP, speech, statistics-AP, studio art AP, theology, trigonometry, U.S. government and politics-AP, U.S. history-AP, world history, world history-AP.

Graduation Requirements Arts and fine arts (art, music, dance, drama), English, foreign language, mathematics, physical education (includes health), science, social studies (includes history), theology, 150 hours of community service.

Special Academic Programs 16 Advanced Placement exams for which test preparation is offered; honors section.

College Admission Counseling 189 students graduated in 2016; all went to college, including Florida Gulf Coast University; Florida State University; University of Central Florida; University of Florida; University of Mississippi; University of South Florida. Median SAT critical reading: 600, median SAT math: 620, median SAT writing: 600, median combined SAT: 1800, median composite ACT: 26. 54% scored over 600 on SAT critical reading, 59% scored over 600 on SAT math, 51% scored over 600 on SAT writing, 51% scored over 1800 on combined SAT, 60% scored over 26 on composite ACT.

Student Life Upper grades have specified standards of dress, student council. Discipline rests primarily with faculty. Attendance at religious services is required.

Summer Programs Enrichment programs offered; session focuses on Enrichment; held on campus; accepts boys; not open to students from other schools. 75 students usually enrolled. 2017 schedule: June 12 to July 14.

Tuition and Aid Day student tuition: $14,975. Tuition installment plan (FACTS Tuition Payment Plan). Merit scholarship grants, need-based scholarship grants available. In 2016–17, 25% of upper-school students received aid; total upper-school merit-scholarship money awarded: $44,925. Total amount of financial aid awarded in 2016–17: $1,655,648.

Admissions Traditional secondary-level entrance grade is 9. For fall 2016, 397 students applied for upper-level admission, 259 were accepted, 223 enrolled. High School Placement Test (closed version) from Scholastic Testing Service required. Deadline for receipt of application materials: January 6. Application fee required: $50.

Athletics Interscholastic: baseball, basketball, bowling, cross-country running, football, golf, ice hockey, lacrosse, soccer, swimming and diving, tennis, track and field, wrestling; intramural: basketball, football, Frisbee, kickball, ultimate Frisbee, volleyball. 1 PE instructor, 4 coaches, 1 athletic trainer.

Computers Computers are regularly used in all academic classes. Computer network features include on-campus library services, online commercial services, Internet access, wireless campus network, Internet filtering or blocking technology, 1:1 iPad program, Learning Management Systems—Canvas. Campus intranet, student e-mail accounts, and computer access in designated common areas are available to students. Students grades are available online. The school has a published electronic and media policy.

Contact Mr. Steve Matesich, Director of Admissions. 813-877-5344 Ext. 715. Fax: 813-872-1853. E-mail: smatesich@jesuittampa.org. Website: www.jesuittampa.org

JEWISH COMMUNITY HIGH SCHOOL OF THE BAY

1835 Ellis Street
San Francisco, California 94115

Head of School: Rabbi Howard Ruben

General Information Coeducational day college-preparatory, arts, and religious studies school, affiliated with Jewish faith. Founded: 2001. Setting: urban. 1 building on campus. Approved or accredited by California Association of Independent Schools, Western Association of Schools and Colleges, and California Department of Education. Member of National Association of Independent Schools and Secondary School Admission Test Board. Languages of instruction: English, Hebrew, and Spanish. Upper school average class size: 14. The average school day consists of 6 hours.

Upper School Student Profile 100% of students are Jewish.

Special Academic Programs Advanced Placement exam preparation; honors section.

Student Life Upper grades have specified standards of dress, student council. Discipline rests primarily with faculty. Attendance at religious services is required.

Admissions Deadline for receipt of application materials: January 14. Application fee required: $90. On-campus interview recommended.

Athletics Interscholastic: basketball (boys, girls), soccer (b,g), volleyball (g); coed interscholastic: baseball, cross-country running, swimming and diving, tennis; coed intramural: dance team, ultimate Frisbee, yoga.

Computers Computer resources include on-campus library services, online commercial services, Internet access, wireless campus network, Internet filtering or blocking technology. Campus intranet, student e-mail accounts, and computer access in designated common areas are available to students. Students grades are available online. The school has a published electronic and media policy.

Contact Michelle Kushnir, Admissions Assistant. 415-345-9777 Ext. 112. Fax: 415-345-1888. E-mail: rbuonaiuto@jchsofthebay.org. Website: www.jchsofthebay.org/

JOHN BURROUGHS SCHOOL

755 South Price Road
St. Louis, Missouri 63124

Head of School: Andy Abbott

General Information Coeducational day college-preparatory school. Grades 7–12. Founded: 1923. Setting: suburban. 49-acre campus. 7 buildings on campus. Approved or accredited by Independent Schools Association of the Central States. Member of National Association of Independent Schools and Secondary School Admission Test Board. Endowment: $45.6 million. Total enrollment: 600. Upper school average class size: 13. Upper school faculty-student ratio: 1:7. There are 165 required school days per year for Upper School students. Upper School students typically attend 5 days per week. The average school day consists of 8 hours.

Upper School Student Profile Grade 9: 102 students (51 boys, 51 girls); Grade 10: 101 students (50 boys, 51 girls); Grade 11: 96 students (47 boys, 49 girls); Grade 12: 101 students (51 boys, 50 girls).

Faculty School total: 122. In upper school: 48 men, 60 women; 84 have advanced degrees.

Subjects Offered Acting, Advanced Placement courses, African American history, algebra, American history, American literature, Ancient Greek, ancient world history, applied arts, architectural drawing, art, art history, bioethics, biology, biology-AP, calculus, calculus-AP, ceramics, chemistry, chemistry-AP, Chinese, choral music, chorus, classical language, community service, computer science, computer skills, computer-aided design, creative writing, dance, debate, drama, earth science, ecology, economics, engineering, English, English literature, environmental science, environmental systems, expository writing, fine arts, finite math, foreign language, French, French language-AP, gardening, geology, geometry, German, global issues, global studies, Greek, Greek culture, health, history, home economics, honors English, industrial arts, jazz, jazz band, keyboarding, lab science, Latin, Latin-AP, mathematics, mechanical drawing, model United Nations, music, orchestra, organic chemistry, photography, physical education, physics-AP, poetry, pre-algebra, pre-calculus, probability and statistics, public speaking, reading/study skills, Russian, science, social sciences, social studies, Spanish, Spanish-AP, speech and debate, statistics, trigonometry, vocal music, word processing, world civilizations, world history, world literature, world religions, writing.

Graduation Requirements American history, arts and fine arts (art, music, dance, drama), English, foreign language, history, mathematics, performing arts, physical education (includes health), science, world history, senior May project, sophomore Diversity seminar, freshman health.

Special Academic Programs 9 Advanced Placement exams for which test preparation is offered; honors section; independent study.

College Admission Counseling 102 students graduated in 2016; all went to college, including Columbia University; New York University; Southern Methodist University; The George Washington University; Washington University in St. Louis; Yale University. Median SAT critical reading: 700, median SAT math: 740, median SAT writing: 710, median combined SAT: 2150, median composite ACT: 33. 93% scored over 600 on SAT critical reading, 91% scored over 600 on SAT math, 91% scored over 600 on SAT writing, 91% scored over 1800 on combined SAT, 95% scored over 26 on composite ACT.

Student Life Upper grades have student council, honor system. Discipline rests equally with students and faculty.

Tuition and Aid Day student tuition: $26,600. Tuition installment plan (monthly payment plans). Need-based scholarship grants, need-based loans available. In 2016–17, 22% of upper-school students received aid. Total amount of financial aid awarded in 2016–17: $2,527,400.

Admissions Traditional secondary-level entrance grade is 9. For fall 2016, 88 students applied for upper-level admission, 15 were accepted, 10 enrolled. SSAT required. Deadline for receipt of application materials: December 16. Application fee required: $40. On-campus interview recommended.

Athletics Interscholastic: baseball (boys), basketball (b,g), cheering (b,g), cross-country running (b,g), dance (b,g), dance squad (b,g), diving (b,g), field hockey (g), fitness (b,g), football (b), golf (b,g), ice hockey (b), independent competitive sports (b,g), lacrosse (b,g), modern dance (b,g), outdoor education (b,g), physical fitness (b,g), physical training (b,g), soccer (b,g), strength & conditioning (b,g), swimming and diving (b,g), tennis (b,g), track and field (b,g), volleyball (g), water polo (b), wrestling (b), yoga (b,g); coed interscholastic: baseball, cheering, dance, dance squad, fitness, football, ice hockey, independent competitive sports, modern dance, outdoor education, physical fitness, physical training, strength & conditioning, water polo, wrestling, yoga. 46 coaches, 1 athletic trainer.

Computers Computers are regularly used in all academic, animation, architecture, art, basic skills, cabinet making, classics, college planning, current events, desktop publishing, digital applications, drafting, drawing and design, economics, engineering, English, foreign language, French, French as a second language, health, history, humanities, independent study, industrial technology, journalism, keyboarding, lab/keyboard, library, library skills, literary magazine, mathematics, media production, multimedia, music, music technology, news writing, newspaper, photography, photojournalism, programming, publications, reading, remedial study skills, research skills, science, senior seminar, social sciences, social studies, Spanish, speech, study skills, technical drawing, technology, theater, typing, video film production, Web site design, woodworking, word processing, writing, writing, yearbook classes. Computer network features include on-campus library services, online commercial services, Internet access, wireless campus network, access to Google Apps, access to necessary curricular software, iPad/laptop check out from library. Campus intranet, student e-mail accounts, and computer access in designated common areas are available to students. The school has a published electronic and media policy.

Contact Caroline LaVigne, Director of Admissions and Tuition Aid. 314-993-4040. Fax: 314-567-2896. E-mail: clavigne@jburroughs.org. Website: www.jburroughs.org

THE JOHN DEWEY ACADEMY

Great Barrington, Massachusetts
See Special Needs Schools section.

JOHN F. KENNEDY CATHOLIC HIGH SCHOOL

500 Woods Mill Road
Manchester, Missouri 63011

Head of School: Fr. Richard Wosman

General Information Coeducational day college-preparatory, religious studies, and technology school, affiliated with Roman Catholic Church. Grades 9–12. Founded: 1968. Setting: suburban. Nearest major city is St. Louis. 26-acre campus. 2 buildings on campus. Approved or accredited by New England Association of Schools and Colleges, North Central Association of Colleges and Schools, and Missouri Department of Education. Total enrollment: 255. Upper school average class size: 20. Upper school faculty-student ratio: 1:10. Upper School students typically attend 5 days per week. The average school day consists of 7 hours.

Upper School Student Profile Grade 9: 51 students (20 boys, 31 girls); Grade 10: 59 students (19 boys, 40 girls); Grade 11: 76 students (37 boys, 39 girls); Grade 12: 69 students (30 boys, 39 girls). 96% of students are Roman Catholic.

Faculty School total: 41. In upper school: 14 men, 27 women; 15 have advanced degrees.

Special Academic Programs 4 Advanced Placement exams for which test preparation is offered; honors section.

College Admission Counseling 82 students graduated in 2015; 81 went to college. Other: 1 entered military service. Mean composite ACT: 24.

Student Life Upper grades have uniform requirement, student council, honor system. Discipline rests primarily with faculty. Attendance at religious services is required.

Tuition and Aid Day student tuition: $12,000. Tuition installment plan (FACTS Tuition Payment Plan, monthly payment plans, individually arranged payment plans). Tuition reduction for siblings, merit scholarship grants, need-based scholarship grants, paying campus jobs available. In 2015–16, 35% of upper-school students received aid.

Admissions Traditional secondary-level entrance grade is 9. For fall 2015, 67 students applied for upper-level admission, 66 were accepted, 55 enrolled. Deadline for receipt of application materials: none. No application fee required. On-campus interview recommended.

Athletics Interscholastic: baseball (boys), basketball (b,g), cheering (g), cross-country running (b,g), dance squad (g), dance team (g), diving (b,g), football (b), pom squad (g), soccer (b,g), softball (g), swimming and diving (g), tennis (b,g), track and field (b,g), volleyball (g); coed interscholastic: golf.

Computers Computer network features include on-campus library services, Internet access, wireless campus network, Internet filtering or blocking technology, every student receives a personal lap top computer. Campus intranet, student e-mail accounts, and computer access in designated common areas are available to students. Students grades are available online.

Contact Mr. Mark Clynes, Director of Enrollment. 636-227-5900 Ext. 104. Fax: 636-227-0298. E-mail: mclynes@kennedycatholic.net. Website: www.kennedycatholic.net

JOHN HANCOCK ACADEMY

PO Drawer E

Sparta, Georgia 31087

Head of School: Mr. Steve James

General Information Coeducational day college-preparatory, general academic, arts, religious studies, and technology school, affiliated with Baptist Church, United Methodist Church. Grades K–12. Founded: 1966. Setting: rural. Nearest major city is Macon. 1 building on campus. Approved or accredited by Georgia Accrediting Commission, Georgia Independent School Association, and Georgia Department of Education. Total enrollment: 150. Upper school average class size: 10. Upper school faculty-student ratio: 1:10. There are 180 required school days per year for Upper School students. Upper School students typically attend 5 days per week. The average school day consists of 8 hours.

Upper School Student Profile Grade 9: 20 students (9 boys, 11 girls); Grade 10: 8 students (5 boys, 3 girls); Grade 11: 14 students (10 boys, 4 girls); Grade 12: 8 students (6 boys, 2 girls). 80% of students are Baptist, United Methodist Church.

Faculty School total: 18. In upper school: 2 men, 4 women; 2 have advanced degrees.

Subjects Offered Advanced math, algebra, American government, American history, American literature, anatomy, art history, Bible, biology, botany, chemistry, computer applications, data processing, earth science, economics, English, English literature, environmental science, general math, geography, geometry, government, health, history, journalism, keyboarding, language arts, physical education, physical science, physics, pre algebra, science, social studies, Spanish, state history, statistics, trigonometry, U.S. government, U.S. history, Web site design, weight training, world geography, world history, yearbook.

Special Academic Programs International Baccalaureate program; honors section; independent study; study at local college for college credit.

College Admission Counseling 13 students graduated in 2015; 5 went to college, including Georgia Southern University; University of Georgia.

Student Life Upper grades have specified standards of dress, student council, honor system. Discipline rests primarily with faculty.

Tuition and Aid Day student tuition: $4400. Tuition installment plan (monthly payment plans, individually arranged payment plans). Tuition reduction for siblings available.

Admissions Traditional secondary-level entrance grade is 9. ACT, any standardized test, OLSAT, Stanford Achievement Test, Otis-Lennon Ability or Stanford Achievement Test, PSAT or SAT required. Deadline for receipt of application materials: none. Application fee required: $100. Interview required.

Athletics Interscholastic: baseball (boys), basketball (b,g), cheering (g), football (b), running (b,g), softball (g), tennis (b,g), track and field (b,g), volleyball (g), weight lifting (b,g); coed interscholastic: physical fitness. 2 PE instructors, 5 coaches.

Computers Computers are regularly used in keyboarding, Web site design, yearbook classes. Computer network features include Internet access.

Contact Ms. Nancy Roach, Secretary. 706-444-6470. Fax: 706-444-6933. E-mail: johnhancockad@bellsouth.net. Website: www.johnhancockacademy.com/

JOHN PAUL II CATHOLIC HIGH SCHOOL

5100 Terrebone Drive

Tallahassee, Florida 32311-7848

Head of School: Mr. Tommy Bridges

General Information Coeducational day college-preparatory, general academic, and religious studies school, affiliated with Roman Catholic Church. Grades 9–12. Founded: 2001. Setting: suburban. 37-acre campus. 3 buildings on campus. Approved or accredited by American Association of Christian Schools, Association of Christian Schools International, Association of Independent Schools of Florida, and Florida Department of Education. Total enrollment: 169. Upper school average class size: 15. Upper school faculty-student ratio: 1:12. There are 180 required school days per year for Upper School students. Upper School students typically attend 5 days per week. The average school day consists of 7 hours and 12 minutes.

Upper School Student Profile Grade 9: 35 students (19 boys, 16 girls); Grade 10: 41 students (24 boys, 17 girls); Grade 11: 51 students (27 boys, 24 girls); Grade 12: 41 students (22 boys, 19 girls). 75% of students are Roman Catholic.

Faculty School total: 22. In upper school: 9 men, 12 women; 14 have advanced degrees.

Subjects Offered All academic, Bible, English language and composition-AP, English literature and composition-AP, history of the Catholic Church, Latin, music, Spanish, Spanish language-AP, strings, world history-AP.

Graduation Requirements Algebra, American government, American history, biology, Christian doctrine, economics, English, fitness, foreign language, health, world history.

Special Academic Programs 12 Advanced Placement exams for which test preparation is offered; honors section; study at local college for college credit.

College Admission Counseling 43 students graduated in 2015; 42 went to college, including Florida State University; Tallahassee Community College; The University of North Carolina at Chapel Hill; University of Florida; University of South Florida. Other: 1 entered military service. Mean SAT critical reading: 559, mean SAT math: 544, mean SAT writing: 535. 50% scored over 600 on SAT critical reading, 48% scored over 600 on SAT math, 45% scored over 600 on SAT writing.

Student Life Upper grades have uniform requirement, student council. Discipline rests primarily with faculty. Attendance at religious services is required.

Tuition and Aid Day student tuition: $12,000. Tuition installment plan (SMART Tuition Payment Plan, monthly payment plans, individually arranged payment plans). Need-based scholarship grants available. In 2015–16, 40% of upper-school students received aid.

Admissions Traditional secondary-level entrance grade is 9. High School Placement Test or High School Placement Test (closed version) from Scholastic Testing Service required. Deadline for receipt of application materials: none. Application fee required: $250. On-campus interview recommended.

Athletics Interscholastic: baseball (boys), basketball (b,g), cross-country running (b,g), football (b), golf (b,g), soccer (b,g), softball (g), tennis (b,g), track and field (b,g), volleyball (g), weight training (b,g). 1 PE instructor, 14 coaches, 1 athletic trainer.

Computers Computers are regularly used in all academic, drawing and design, technology classes. Computer network features include on-campus library services, Internet access, wireless campus network, Internet filtering or blocking technology. Campus intranet and student e-mail accounts are available to students. Students grades are available online. The school has a published electronic and media policy.

Contact Mrs. Sharon Strohl, Office Administrator. 850-201-5744. Fax: 850-205-3299. E-mail: sstrohl@jpiichs.org. Website: www.jpiichs.org

JOSEPHINUM ACADEMY

1501 North Oakley Boulevard

Chicago, Illinois 60622

Head of School: Mrs. Mary Rose Guerin

General Information Girls' day college-preparatory school, affiliated with Roman Catholic Church. Grades 9–12. Founded: 1890. Setting: urban. 2-acre campus. 1 building on campus. Approved or accredited by International Baccalaureate Organization, National Catholic Education Association, Network of Sacred Heart Schools, North Central Association of Colleges and Schools, and Illinois Department of Education. Total enrollment: 200. Upper school average class size: 18. Upper school faculty-student ratio: 1:10. There are 176 required school days per year for Upper School students. Upper School students typically attend 5 days per week. The average school day consists of 7 hours and 30 minutes.

Upper School Student Profile Grade 9: 48 students (48 girls); Grade 10: 58 students (58 girls); Grade 11: 54 students (54 girls); Grade 12: 39 students (39 girls). 50% of students are Roman Catholic.

Faculty School total: 24. In upper school: 6 men, 14 women; 16 have advanced degrees.

Subjects Offered ACT preparation, acting, advanced biology, advanced chemistry, Advanced Placement courses, algebra, American literature, applied arts, art, athletics, basketball, biology, biology-AP, business education, calculus-AP, campus ministry, Catholic belief and practice, chemistry, Christian studies, civics, college admission preparation, college awareness, college counseling, college placement, college planning, community garden, community service, computer education, constitutional history of U.S., consumer economics, consumer education, current events, drama, drama performance, electives, English, English literature-AP, English-AP, environmental science, fitness, foreign language, French, French as a second language, freshman seminar, geometry, global issues, global studies, health, health and wellness, history of the Americas, honors English, honors geometry, honors U.S. history, honors world history, Life of Christ, literature by women, modern history, moral theology, peer counseling, performing arts, physical education, physical science, physics, pre-calculus, religious studies, research seminar, senior project, senior thesis, Shakespeare, social justice, softball, Spanish, Spanish literature, Spanish-AP, speech, U.S. history, volleyball, water color painting, women's literature, women's studies, world history, world literature, world religions, world religions, writing, yearbook.

Graduation Requirements Algebra, arts and fine arts (art, music, dance, drama), biology, college admission preparation, computer science, consumer education, English, foreign language, health, mathematics, physical education (includes health), religion (includes Bible studies and theology), science, social sciences, social studies (includes history), technology, senior Capstone project, portfolio projects. Community service is required.

Special Academic Programs 6 Advanced Placement exams for which test preparation is offered; honors section; domestic exchange program (with Network of Sacred Heart Schools); study abroad.

College Admission Counseling 55 students graduated in 2016; 50 went to college, including Carleton College; DePaul University; Grand Valley State University; Loyola University Chicago; University of Illinois at Chicago; University of Illinois at Urbana–Champaign. Other: 5 had other specific plans.

Student Life Upper grades have uniform requirement, student council, honor system. Discipline rests primarily with faculty. Attendance at religious services is required.

Summer Programs Remediation, enrichment, sports, art/fine arts, computer instruction programs offered; session focuses on community service and educational advancement; held both on and off campus; accepts girls; not open to students from other schools. 40 students usually enrolled.

Tuition and Aid Day student tuition: $8720. Tuition installment plan (FACTS Tuition Payment Plan, monthly payment plans, individually arranged payment plans). Merit scholarship grants, need-based scholarship grants available. In 2016–17, 89% of upper-school students received aid.

Admissions Traditional secondary-level entrance grade is 9. Catholic High School Entrance Examination required. Deadline for receipt of application materials: none. No application fee required. Interview required.

Athletics Interscholastic: basketball, soccer, softball, volleyball; intramural: aerobics/dance, ballet, dance team, fitness, football, track and field, weight training. 2 PE instructors, 5 coaches.

Computers Computers are regularly used in all academic classes. Computer network features include on-campus library services, Internet access, wireless campus network, Internet filtering or blocking technology, Chromebooks. Campus intranet, student e-mail accounts, and computer access in designated common areas are available to students. Students grades are available online. The school has a published electronic and media policy.

Contact Mrs. Stephanie Castrounis, Director of Admissions. 773-276-1261 Ext. 234. Fax: 773-292-3963. E-mail: stephanie.castrounis@josephinum.org. Website: www.josephinum.org

THE JOURNEYS SCHOOL OF TETON SCIENCE SCHOOL

700 Coyote Canyon Road
Jackson, Wyoming 83001

Head of School: Nancy Lang

General Information Coeducational day college-preparatory school. Grades K–12. Founded: 2001. Setting: rural. 800-acre campus. 1 building on campus. Approved or accredited by International Baccalaureate Organization, Northwest Association of Independent Schools, and Wyoming Department of Education. Member of National Association of Independent Schools. Endowment: $12 million. Total enrollment: 159. Upper school average class size: 10. Upper school faculty-student ratio: 1:7. There are 175 required school days per year for Upper School students. Upper School students typically attend 5 days per week. The average school day consists of 7 hours and 45 minutes.

Upper School Student Profile Grade 6: 17 students (9 boys, 8 girls); Grade 7: 15 students (9 boys, 6 girls); Grade 8: 17 students (8 boys, 9 girls); Grade 9: 13 students (7 boys, 6 girls); Grade 10: 9 students (4 boys, 5 girls); Grade 11: 8 students (6 boys, 2 girls); Grade 12: 9 students (4 boys, 5 girls).

Faculty School total: 40. In upper school: 8 men, 11 women; 13 have advanced degrees.

Subjects Offered International Baccalaureate courses.

Graduation Requirements International Baccalaureate courses.

Special Academic Programs International Baccalaureate program; academic accommodation for the gifted.

College Admission Counseling 10 students graduated in 2016; all went to college.

Student Life Upper grades have student council. Discipline rests equally with students and faculty.

Tuition and Aid Day student tuition: $22,600. Tuition installment plan (monthly payment plans, individually arranged payment plans). Need-based scholarship grants available. In 2016–17, 43% of upper-school students received aid. Total amount of financial aid awarded in 2016–17: $240,150.

Admissions Deadline for receipt of application materials: none. Application fee required: $50. Interview recommended.

Athletics Interscholastic: aerobics/dance (girls), alpine skiing (b,g), aquatics (g), baseball (b), basketball (b,g), cheering (g), cross-country running (b,g), dance (g), football (b), gymnastics (g), ice hockey (b,g), indoor track & field (g), lacrosse (b,g), martial arts (b,g), nordic skiing (b,g), soccer (b,g), swimming and diving (g), tennis (b,g), volleyball (g); intramural: dressage (g), equestrian sports (g), freestyle skiing (b,g), horseback riding (g), lacrosse (b,g), snowboarding (b,g); coed interscholastic: backpacking, skiing (cross-country), skiing (downhill), track and field; coed intramural: climbing, soccer, wall climbing. 1 PE instructor.

Computers Computer network features include Internet access, wireless campus network, Internet filtering or blocking technology. Campus intranet and student e-mail accounts are available to students. Students grades are available online.

Contact Warren Samuels, Director of Admissions. 307-732-7745. Fax: 307-733-3340. E-mail: warren.samuels@journeysschool.org. Website: www.tetonscience.org/journeys-school/home

JUDGE MEMORIAL CATHOLIC HIGH SCHOOL

650 South 1100 East
Salt Lake City, Utah 84102

Head of School: Mr. Patrick Lambert

General Information Coeducational day college-preparatory school, affiliated with Roman Catholic Church. Grades 9–12. Founded: 1921. Setting: urban. Approved or accredited by Western Association of Schools and Colleges, Western Catholic Education Association, and Utah Department of Education. Upper school average class size: 20.

Upper School Student Profile 60% of students are Roman Catholic.

Special Academic Programs Advanced Placement exam preparation; honors section.

Student Life Upper grades have uniform requirement, student council. Discipline rests primarily with faculty. Attendance at religious services is required.

Tuition and Aid Tuition installment plan (FACTS Tuition Payment Plan).

Admissions Application fee required.

Athletics Interscholastic: baseball (boys), basketball (b,g), bowling (b,g), cheering (g), cross-country running (b,g), football (b), golf (b,g), lacrosse (b,g), running (b,g), soccer (b,g), softball (g), swimming and diving (b), tennis (b,g), track and field (b,g), volleyball (g); coed interscholastic: hockey, ice hockey.

Contact Mrs. Suzanne Rainwater, Director of Admissions. 801-363-8895. Fax: 801-517-2190. E-mail: srainwater@judgememorial.com. Website: www.judgememorial.com/

THE JUDGE ROTENBERG EDUCATIONAL CENTER

Canton, Massachusetts
See Special Needs Schools section.

JUNIPERO SERRA HIGH SCHOOL

451 West 20th Avenue
San Mateo, California 94403-1385

Head of School: Mr. Lars Lund

General Information Boys' day college-preparatory school, affiliated with Roman Catholic Church. Grades 9–12. Founded: 1944. Setting: suburban. Nearest major city is San Francisco. 13-acre campus. 9 buildings on campus. Approved or accredited by Western Association of Schools and Colleges and Western Catholic Education Association. Endowment: $9.4 million. Total enrollment: 881. Upper school average class size: 23. Upper school faculty-student ratio: 1:15. There are 180 required school days per year for Upper School students. Upper School students typically attend 5 days per week. The average school day consists of 6 hours and 35 minutes.

Upper School Student Profile Grade 9: 215 students (215 boys); Grade 10: 239 students (239 boys); Grade 11: 227 students (227 boys); Grade 12: 179 students (179 boys). 65% of students are Roman Catholic.

Faculty School total: 57. In upper school: 56 men, 25 women; 61 have advanced degrees.

Subjects Offered Advanced biology, advanced chemistry, advanced computer applications, advanced math, Advanced Placement courses, algebra, American history, American history-AP, American literature, analytic geometry, architectural drawing, architecture, art, art history-AP, athletic training, athletics, band, biology, biology-AP, business, business communications, calculus, calculus-AP, ceramics, chemistry, chemistry-AP, Chinese, chorus, church history, college admission preparation, college counseling, college placement, college planning, college writing, community service, computer programming, computer programming-AP, computer science, concert band, creative writing, dance, drama, dramatic arts, driver education, ecology, environmental systems, economics, English, English language-AP, English literature, English literature-AP, English-AP, ethics, European history, film appreciation, fine arts, French, French language-AP, French-AP, geography, geometry, German, government/civics, grammar, health education, history, honors algebra, honors English, honors geometry, honors world history, instrumental music, jazz band, journalism, keyboarding, leadership and service, library skills, Mandarin, marketing, mathematics, music, musical productions, newspaper, performing arts, photography, physical education, physics, physics-AP, pre-calculus, psychology, psychology-AP, publications, religious studies, SAT preparation, science, social justice, social sciences, social studies, Spanish, Spanish language-AP, Spanish-AP, speech, sports conditioning, statistics, statistics-AP, student government, theater, trigonometry, U.S. government, U.S. government and politics, U.S. government and politics-AP, U.S. history, U.S. history-AP, visual and performing arts, world history, writing.

Graduation Requirements All academic, arts and fine arts (art, music, dance, drama), computer science, English, foreign language, literature, mathematics, physical education (includes health), political systems, religion (includes Bible studies and theology), science, social sciences, social studies (includes history), 80 hours of community service. Community service is required.

Special Academic Programs 19 Advanced Placement exams for which test preparation is offered; honors section, study at local college for college credit.

College Admission Counseling 209 students graduated in 2016; 205 went to college, including California Polytechnic State University, San Luis Obispo; Loyola Marymount University; Santa Clara University; The University of Arizona; University of California, Davis; University of California, San Diego. Other: 2 went to work, 2 had other specific plans.

Student Life Upper grades have specified standards of dress, student council, honor system. Discipline rests primarily with faculty. Attendance at religious services is required.

Summer Programs Remediation, enrichment, advancement, sports, art/fine arts, computer instruction programs offered; session focuses on enrichment and remediation; held on campus; accepts boys and girls; open to students from other schools. 480 students usually enrolled. 2017 schedule: June 13 to July 15. Application deadline: June 9.

Tuition and Aid Day student tuition: $20,465. Tuition installment plan (monthly payment plans, semester payment plan, annual payment plan, direct debit plan). Merit scholarship grants, need-based scholarship grants available. In 2016–17, 30% of upper-school students received aid; total upper-school merit-scholarship money awarded: $65,000. Total amount of financial aid awarded in 2016–17: $2,400,000.

Admissions Traditional secondary-level entrance grade is 9. For fall 2016, 440 students applied for upper-level admission, 325 were accepted, 220 enrolled. High School Placement Test required. Deadline for receipt of application materials: January 9. Application fee required: $95. On-campus interview recommended.

Athletics Interscholastic: baseball, basketball, crew, cross-country running, diving, football, golf, lacrosse, rowing, soccer, swimming and diving, tennis, track and field, volleyball, water polo, wrestling; intramural: basketball, bicycling, bowling, fishing, fitness, mountain biking, physical training, rock climbing, soccer, softball, strength & conditioning, surfing, touch football, weight lifting, weight training. 1 PE instructor, 48 coaches, 1 athletic trainer.

Computers Computers are regularly used in all academic classes. Computer network features include on-campus library services, Internet access, wireless campus network, Internet filtering or blocking technology. Campus intranet and student e-mail accounts are available to students. Students grades are available online. The school has a published electronic and media policy.

Contact Mr. Carl Dos Remedios, Director of Admissions. 650-345-8242 Ext. 117. Fax: 650-573-6638. E-mail: cdosremedios@serrahs.com. Website: www.serrahs.com

KALAMAZOO CHRISTIAN HIGH SCHOOL

2121 Stadium Drive
Kalamazoo, Michigan 49008-1692

Head of School: Mr. Bartel James Huizenga

General Information Coeducational day college-preparatory and general academic school. Grades 9–12. Founded: 1877. Setting: urban. 2-acre campus. 1 building on campus. Approved or accredited by Christian Schools International, North Central Association of Colleges and Schools, and Michigan Department of Education. Endowment: $1 million. Upper school average class size: 22. Upper school faculty-student ratio: 1:12. There are 174 required school days per year for Upper School students. Upper School students typically attend 5 days per week. The average school day consists of 6 hours and 45 minutes.

Upper School Student Profile Grade 9: 63 students (39 boys, 24 girls); Grade 10: 44 students (24 boys, 20 girls); Grade 11: 65 students (30 boys, 35 girls); Grade 12: 60 students (30 boys, 30 girls).

Faculty School total: 20. In upper school: 14 men, 6 women; 10 have advanced degrees.

Graduation Requirements 50 hours of community service.

Special Academic Programs Advanced Placement exam preparation; honors section; study at local college for college credit; academic accommodation for the gifted.

College Admission Counseling 52 students graduated in 2016; 50 went to college, including Calvin College; Grand Valley State University; Hope College; University of Michigan; Western Michigan University. Other: 2 went to work, 1 entered military service. Median composite ACT: 23. 27% scored over 26 on composite ACT.

Student Life Upper grades have specified standards of dress, student council, honor system. Discipline rests primarily with faculty.

Tuition and Aid Day student tuition: $8480. Tuition installment plan (FACTS Tuition Payment Plan, monthly payment plans, individually arranged payment plans). Tuition reduction for siblings, need-based scholarship grants available. In 2016–17, 50% of upper-school students received aid.

Admissions Traditional secondary-level entrance grade is 9. ACT or any standardized test required. Deadline for receipt of application materials: none. Application fee required: $150. Interview recommended.

Athletics Interscholastic: baseball (boys), basketball (b,g), bowling (b,g), cheering (g), cross-country running (b,g), football (b), golf (b,g), hockey (b), physical fitness (b,g), soccer (b,g), softball (g), strength & conditioning (b,g), tennis (b,g), track and field (b,g), volleyball (g), weight lifting (b,g), weight training (b,g). 2 PE instructors, 32 coaches, 1 athletic trainer.

Computers Computers are regularly used in accounting, business, business applications, business skills, data processing, graphic arts, graphic design, keyboarding, lab/keyboard classes. Computer network features include on-campus library services, online commercial services, Internet access, wireless campus network. Campus intranet and student e-mail accounts are available to students. Students grades are available online. The school has a published electronic and media policy.

Contact Mr. Bartel James Huizenga, Principal. 269-381-2250 Ext. 114. Fax: 269-381-0319. E-mail: bhuizenga@kcsa.org. Website: www.kcsa.org

KAOHSIUNG AMERICAN SCHOOL

35 Sheng-Li Road
Tzuo Yind District
Kaohsiung City 813, Taiwan

Head of School: Dr. Thomas Farrell

General Information Coeducational day college-preparatory and MYP, IB school. Grades PK–12. Founded: 1989. Setting: urban. 6-acre campus. 1 building on campus. Approved or accredited by East Asia Regional Council of Schools and Western Association of Schools and Colleges. Language of instruction: English. Total enrollment: 290. Upper school average class size: 20. Upper school faculty-student ratio: 1:8. There are 182 required school days per year for Upper School students. Upper School students typically attend 5 days per week. The average school day consists of 7 hours.

Upper School Student Profile Grade 9: 69 students (34 boys, 35 girls); Grade 10: 77 students (38 boys, 39 girls); Grade 11: 86 students (46 boys, 40 girls); Grade 12: 75 students (34 boys, 41 girls)

Faculty School total: 70. In upper school: 29 men, 75 women; 41 have advanced degrees.

Subjects Offered Algebra, American history, art, basketball, biology, calculus, chemistry, Chinese, Chinese literature, choir, college admission preparation, college counselling, college placement, college planning, community service, computer applications, computer education, computer science, creative writing, critical thinking, drama, dramatic arts, earth science, East Asian history, economics, electives, English, ESL, general science, geometry, guidance, history, information technology, instrumental music, Japanese, lab science, language arts, library research, library skills, mathematics, model United Nations, music, music appreciation, physical education, physical science, physics, pottery, pre-algebra, pre-calculus, publications, reading, SAT preparation, science, senior project, social sciences, social studies, softball, Spanish, student government, student publications, technology, U.S. history, volleyball, yearbook.

Graduation Requirements Arts and fine arts (art, music, dance, drama), computer science, English, foreign language, mathematics, physical education (includes health), science, senior project, social studies (includes history).

Special Academic Programs Advanced Placement exam preparation; ESL (60 students enrolled)

College Admission Counseling 59 students graduated in 2016; 58 went to college, including New York University; University of California, Berkeley; University of California, Irvine; University of California, Los Angeles; University of California, Riverside; University of Washington. Other: 1 had other specific plans. Mean SAT critical reading: 506, mean SAT math: 623, mean SAT writing: 522.

Student Life Upper grades have student council. Discipline rests equally with students and faculty.

Tuition and Aid Day student tuition: 1922 Taiwan dollars. Tuition reduction for siblings available.

Admissions Traditional secondary-level entrance grade is 9. For fall 2016, 60 students applied for upper-level admission, 60 were accepted, 52 enrolled. Achievement tests or admissions testing required. Deadline for receipt of application materials: none. No application fee required. On-campus interview required.

Athletics Interscholastic: soccer (boys, girls), softball (b,g), synchronized swimming (b,g), volleyball (b,g); intramural: cheering (g), dance team (g), table tennis (b,g), weight training (b); coed interscholastic: basketball, cross-country running; coed intramural: aquatics, fitness, flag football, Frisbee, physical fitness, physical training, soccer, softball, synchronized swimming, tennis, ultimate Frisbee, volleyball. 5 PE instructors, 1 athletic trainer.

Computers Computers are regularly used in art, English, history, science classes. Computer network features include online commercial services, Internet access, wireless campus network. Campus intranet and student e-mail accounts are available to students. The school has a published electronic and media policy.

Contact Lisa Fang, Admission Officer. 886-7-583-0112. Fax: 886-7-582-4536. E-mail: lfang@kas.kh.edu.tw. Website: www.kas.kh.edu.tw/

KAUAI CHRISTIAN ACADEMY

PO Box 1121
4000 Kilauea Road
Kilauea, Hawaii 96754

Head of School: Daniel A. Plunkett

General Information Coeducational day college-preparatory, general academic, and religious studies school, affiliated with Protestant-Evangelical faith. Grades PS–12. Founded: 1973. Setting: rural. Nearest major city is Lihue. 10-acre campus. 3 buildings on campus. Approved or accredited by American Association of Christian Schools and Hawaii Department of Education. Total enrollment: 79. Upper school average class size: 8. Upper school faculty-student ratio: 1:8. There are 181 required school days per year for Upper School students. Upper School students typically attend 5 days per week. The average school day consists of 6 hours and 30 minutes.

Upper School Student Profile Grade 7: 3 students (2 boys, 1 girl); Grade 8: 3 students (2 boys, 1 girl); Grade 9: 3 students (3 girls); Grade 10: 1 student (1 girl); Grade 11: 2 students (2 boys); Grade 12: 3 students (3 girls). 75% of students are Protestant-Evangelical faith.

Faculty School total: 12. In upper school: 3 men, 5 women; 1 has an advanced degree.

Subjects Offered Advanced math, agriculture, algebra, American government, American history, ancient history, art, arts, athletics, Basic programming, Bible, Bible as literature, Bible studies, biology, botany, calculus, chemistry, Christian and Hebrew scripture, economics, economics-AP, electives, English, English literature, English literature and composition-AP, family living, geography, geometry, government, history, Latin, music, physical science, pre-algebra, speech, world geography, world history.

Graduation Requirements Arts and fine arts (art, music, dance, drama), computer science, English, Latin, mathematics, science, social studies (includes history), speech, one year of Bible for each year enrolled.

Special Academic Programs Accelerated programs; independent study; remedial reading and/or remedial writing; remedial math.

College Admission Counseling 2 students graduated in 2016; all went to college, including Belmont University; Liberty University. Median SAT critical reading: 570, median SAT math: 530, median SAT writing: 550, median combined SAT: 1705, median composite ACT: 27. 50% scored over 600 on SAT critical reading, 50% scored over 600 on SAT writing.

Student Life Upper grades have specified standards of dress, honor system. Discipline rests primarily with faculty.

Tuition and Aid Day student tuition: $6300. Tuition installment plan (monthly payment plans, 10-month payment plan). Tuition reduction for siblings, need-based scholarship grants, paying campus jobs available. In 2016–17, 40% of upper-school students received aid. Total amount of financial aid awarded in 2016–17: $40,000.

Admissions Traditional secondary-level entrance grade is 7. For fall 2016, 12 students applied for upper-level admission, 12 were accepted, 12 enrolled. Cognitive Abilities Test, Iowa Test of Educational Development or OLSAT, Stanford Achievement Test required. Deadline for receipt of application materials: none. Application fee required: $100. Interview recommended.

Athletics Interscholastic: cross-country running (boys, girls), golf (b,g), track and field (b,g). 1 PE instructor, 1 coach.

Computers Computers are regularly used in computer applications, typing classes. Computer network features include Internet access, wireless campus network, Internet filtering or blocking technology. Campus intranet and computer access in designated common areas are available to students.

Contact Daniel A. Plunkett, Principal. 808-828-0047. Fax: 808-828-1850. E-mail: dplunkett@kcaschool.net. Website: www.kcaschool.net

KEIO ACADEMY OF NEW YORK

3 College Road
Purchase, New York 10577

General Information Coeducational boarding and day college-preparatory school. Grades 9–12. Founded: 1990. Setting: suburban. Nearest major city is White Plains. Students are housed in single-sex dormitories. 27-acre campus. 5 buildings on campus. Approved or accredited by Ministry of Education, Japan, New York State Association of Independent Schools, and New York Department of Education. Languages of instruction: English and Japanese. Total enrollment: 316. Upper school average class size: 20.

Subjects Offered Advanced Placement courses, art, Chinese, computer science, English, ESL, fine arts, French, general science, health, Japanese, Japanese as Second Language, mathematics, music, physical education, science, social studies, Spanish.

Graduation Requirements Arts and fine arts (art, music, dance, drama), computer science, English, health, Japanese, mathematics, physical education (includes health), science, social studies (includes history).

Special Academic Programs Advanced Placement exam preparation; honors section; study at local college for college credit; domestic exchange program; ESL.

Student Life Upper grades have specified standards of dress, student council. Discipline rests primarily with faculty.

Summer Programs Session focuses on Japanese and English Language and Culture; held both on and off campus; accepts boys and girls; open to students from other schools. 70 students usually enrolled. 2017 schedule: July 23 to August 5.

Tuition and Aid Need-based scholarship grants available.

Admissions School's own exam required. Deadline for receipt of application materials: none. Application fee required. Interview recommended.

Athletics Interscholastic: baseball (boys), basketball (b,g), cross-country running (b,g), golf (b), judo (b), lacrosse (g), martial arts (b,g), rugby (b), soccer (b,g), softball (g), street hockey (b), swimming and diving (b,g), tennis (b,g), volleyball (g); intramural: basketball (b,g), floor hockey (b,g), indoor soccer (b,g), martial arts (b,g), soccer (b,g), tennis (b,g), volleyball (b,g); coed intramural: table tennis, ultimate Frisbee, walking, wall climbing.

Computers Computers are regularly used in computer applications, English, mathematics, social sciences classes. Computer network features include on-campus library services, Internet access, wireless campus network, Internet filtering or blocking technology. Campus intranet, student e-mail accounts, and computer access in designated common areas are available to students. Students grades are available online. The school has a published electronic and media policy.

Contact 914-694-4825. Fax: 914-694-4830. Website: www.keio.edu

KENT DENVER SCHOOL

4000 East Quincy Avenue
Englewood, Colorado 80113

Head of School: Dr. Randal Harrington

General Information Coeducational day college-preparatory school. Grades 6–12. Founded: 1922. Setting: suburban. Nearest major city is Denver. 220-acre campus. 6 buildings on campus. Approved or accredited by Association of Colorado Independent Schools and Colorado Department of Education. Member of National Association of Independent Schools and Secondary School Admission Test Board. Endowment: $52.3 million. Total enrollment: 698. Upper school average class size: 13. Upper school faculty-student ratio: 1:13. There are 172 required school days per year for Upper School students. Upper School students typically attend 5 days per week. The average school day consists of 7 hours.

Upper School Student Profile Grade 6: 68 students (37 boys, 31 girls); Grade 7: 73 students (38 boys, 35 girls); Grade 8: 80 students (42 boys, 38 girls); Grade 9: 122 students (58 boys, 64 girls); Grade 10: 121 students (61 boys, 60 girls); Grade 11: 116 students (63 boys, 53 girls); Grade 12: 116 students (59 boys, 57 girls).

Faculty School total: 84. In upper school: 32 men, 30 women; 41 have advanced degrees.

Subjects Offered 20th century history, acting, advanced biology, advanced chemistry, advanced math, Advanced Placement courses, African-American literature, algebra, American history, American history-AP, American literature, art, art education, art history, art history-AP, Asian studies, band, biology, biology-AP, business, calculus, calculus-AP, career education internship, ceramics, chemistry, chemistry-AP, Chinese, choir, clayworking, college counseling, community service, computer math, computer programming, computer programming-AP, computer science, creative writing, digital applications, digital art, digital photography, drama, earth science, economics, economics and history, economics-AP, electives, English, English language-AP, English literature, English literature and composition-AP, ensembles, environmental science, equality and freedom, European history, European history-AP, fine arts, foreign language, French, French as a second language, French language-AP, French literature-AP, French-AP, general math, general science, genetics, geography, geology, geometry, government/civics, grammar, guitar, health and wellness, history, history-AP, human development, independent study, jazz band, Latin, Mandarin, mathematics, music, music performance, mythology, photography, physical education, physics, pre-calculus, science, social studies, Spanish, Spanish language-AP, Spanish literature-AP, statistics, studio art-AP, theater, Web site design, world history, world literature, writing.

Graduation Requirements Arts and fine arts (art, music, dance, drama), English, foreign language, history, internship, mathematics, participation in sports, science, world history, Career Internship Experience. Community service is required.

Special Academic Programs 20 Advanced Placement exams for which test preparation is offered; honors section; independent study; programs in general development for dyslexic students.

College Admission Counseling 114 students graduated in 2016; 113 went to college, including Emory University; Miami University; Middlebury College;

University of Colorado Boulder; University of Michigan; University of Southern California. Other: 1 had other specific plans. Mean SAT critical reading: 646, mean SAT math: 649, mean SAT writing: 652, mean composite ACT: 30. 75% scored over 600 on SAT critical reading, 74% scored over 600 on SAT math, 80% scored over 600 on SAT writing, 80% scored over 26 on composite ACT.

Student Life Upper grades have specified standards of dress, student council. Discipline rests equally with students and faculty.

Summer Programs Enrichment, sports, art/fine arts, computer instruction programs offered; session focuses on skill-building, arts, enrichment, athletics; held on campus; accepts boys and girls; open to students from other schools. 1,750 students usually enrolled. 2017 schedule: June 12 to July 28. Application deadline: none.

Tuition and Aid Day student tuition: $26,270. Tuition installment plan (Insured Tuition Payment Plan, FACTS Tuition Payment Plan, monthly payment plans). Need-based scholarship grants available. In 2016–17, 23% of upper-school students received aid. Total amount of financial aid awarded in 2016–17: $2,400,000.

Admissions Traditional secondary-level entrance grade is 9. For fall 2016, 186 students applied for upper-level admission, 76 were accepted, 57 enrolled. ISEE or SSAT required. Deadline for receipt of application materials: January 31. Application fee required: $60. Interview required.

Athletics Interscholastic: baseball (boys), basketball (b,g), cross-country running (b,g), field hockey (g), football (b), golf (b,g), hockey (b), ice hockey (b), lacrosse (b,g), soccer (b,g), swimming and diving (g), tennis (b,g), track and field (b,g), volleyball (g); coed interscholastic: independent competitive sports; coed intramural: bicycling, canoeing/kayaking, fitness, mountain biking, outdoor adventure, outdoor education, outdoor skills, physical fitness, physical training, strength & conditioning, weight lifting, yoga. 2 PE instructors, 17 coaches, 2 athletic trainers.

Computers Computers are regularly used in all classes. Computer network features include on-campus library services, online commercial services, Internet access, wireless campus network, Internet filtering or blocking technology. Student e-mail accounts and computer access in designated common areas are available to students. Students grades are available online. The school has a published electronic and media policy.

Contact Susan Green, Admission Office Manager. 303-770-7660 Ext. 237. Fax: 303-770-1398. E-mail: sgreen@kentdenver.org. Website: www.kentdenver.org

KENT SCHOOL

PO Box 2006
Kent, Connecticut 06757

Head of School: Rev. Richardson W. Schell

General Information Coeducational boarding and day college-preparatory, pre-engineering, and aviation, eEntrepreneurship, manufacturing school, affiliated with Episcopal Church. Grades 9–PG. Founded: 1906. Setting: small town. Nearest major city is New York, NY. Students are housed in coed dormitories. 1,200-acre campus. 17 buildings on campus. Approved or accredited by Association of Independent Schools in New England, Connecticut Association of Independent Schools, National Association of Episcopal Schools, New England Association of Schools and Colleges, New York State Association of Independent Schools, The Association of Boarding Schools, and Connecticut Department of Education. Member of National Association of Independent Schools and Secondary School Admission Test Board. Endowment: $80 million. Total enrollment: 570. Upper school average class size: 12. Upper school faculty-student ratio: 1:7. Upper School students typically attend 6 days per week. The average school day consists of 7 hours.

Upper School Student Profile Grade 9: 93 students (56 boys, 37 girls); Grade 10: 137 students (78 boys, 59 girls); Grade 11: 152 students (73 boys, 79 girls); Grade 12: 163 students (95 boys, 68 girls); Postgraduate: 27 students (21 boys, 6 girls). 92% of students are boarding students. 22% are state residents. 32 states are represented in upper school student body. 30% are international students. International students from Canada, China, Hong Kong, Republic of Korea, Russian Federation, and Thailand; 34 other countries represented in student body.

Faculty School total: 73. In upper school: 43 men, 30 women; 55 have advanced degrees; 66 reside on campus.

Subjects Offered Advanced math, advanced studio art-AP, African-American history, algebra, American history, American history-AP, American literature, architecture, art, art history-AP, Asian history, astronomy, aviation, Bible studies, biology, biology-AP, biotechnology, business skills, calculus, calculus-AP, ceramics, chemistry, chemistry-AP, Chinese, classical Greek literature, classical studies, composition-AP, computer math, computer programming, computer science, computer science-AP, computer-aided design, design, digital imaging, drama, ecology, economics, engineering, English, English literature, English literature-AP, entrepreneurship, environmental science-AP, environmental studies, European history, European history-AP, expository writing, fine arts, French, French language-AP, French literature-AP, genetics, geology, geometry, German, German-AP, government and politics-AP, Greek, history, Latin, Latin American history, Latin-AP, law and the legal system, mathematics, meteorology, Middle Eastern history, modern European history-AP, music, music theory-AP, photography, physical education, physics, physics-AP, probability and statistics, psychology-AP, religion, science, sculpture, social studies, Spanish, Spanish language-AP, Spanish literature-AP, statistics-AP, theater, theology, trigonometry, U.S. government and politics-AP, world geography, world history, world literature.

Graduation Requirements American history, art, arts and fine arts (art, music, dance, drama), English, foreign language, history, mathematics, music, religion (includes Bible studies and theology), science, theology, U.S. history, New Student Seminar for all freshmen and new sophomores.

Special Academic Programs 26 Advanced Placement exams for which test preparation is offered; honors section; independent study; academic accommodation for the gifted, the musically talented, and the artistically talented; ESL (7 students enrolled).

College Admission Counseling 171 students graduated in 2016; 168 went to college, including Boston University; Carnegie Mellon University; Colgate University; Cornell University; Princeton University; St. Lawrence University. Other: 1 entered a postgraduate year, 2 had other specific plans. Median SAT critical reading: 600, median SAT math: 620, median SAT writing: 590, median combined SAT: 1805, median composite ACT: 28. 53% scored over 600 on SAT critical reading, 57% scored over 600 on SAT math, 45% scored over 600 on SAT writing, 51% scored over 1800 on combined SAT, 61% scored over 26 on composite ACT.

Student Life Upper grades have specified standards of dress, student council, honor system. Discipline rests equally with students and faculty. Attendance at religious services is required.

Summer Programs Enrichment, computer instruction programs offered; session focuses on Summer Educational Experience at Kent; held on campus; accepts boys and girls; open to students from other schools. 65 students usually enrolled. 2017 schedule: June 5 to July 21. Application deadline: June 2.

Tuition and Aid Day student tuition: $46,300; 7-day tuition and room/board: $58,450. Tuition installment plan (Key Tuition Payment Plan, FACTS Tuition Payment Plan, monthly payment plans, individually arranged payment plans). Merit scholarship grants, need-based scholarship grants, need-based loans available. In 2016–17, 42% of upper-school students received aid; total upper-school merit-scholarship money awarded: $1,627,300. Total amount of financial aid awarded in 2016–17: $8,400,000.

Admissions Traditional secondary-level entrance grade is 9. For fall 2016, 1,372 students applied for upper-level admission, 567 were accepted, 198 enrolled. ACT, PSAT or SAT for applicants to grade 11 and 12, SSAT or TOEFL required. Deadline for receipt of application materials: January 15. Application fee required: $85. Interview recommended.

Athletics Interscholastic: baseball (boys), basketball (b,g), crew (b,g), cross-country running (b,g), diving (b,g), field hockey (g), football (b), golf (b,g), hockey (b,g), ice hockey (b,g), lacrosse (b,g), rowing (b,g), soccer (b,g), softball (g), squash (b,g), swimming and diving (b,g), tennis (b,g); intramural: basketball (b), crew (b,g), rowing (b,g); coed interscholastic: crew, dressage, equestrian sports, golf, horseback riding; coed intramural: aerobics/dance, aerobics/Nautilus, alpine skiing, aquatics, ballet, basketball, bicycling, combined training, crew, dance, dressage, equestrian sports, figure skating, fitness, hockey, horseback riding, ice skating, life saving, modern dance, mountain biking, physical fitness, physical training, ropes courses, sailing, skiing (downhill), snowboarding, soccer, squash, strength & conditioning, swimming and diving, tennis, ultimate Frisbee, weight training, yoga. 2 athletic trainers.

Computers Computers are regularly used in all academic, journalism, newspaper, yearbook classes. Computer network features include on-campus library services, online commercial services, Internet access, wireless campus network, students have online storage for schoolwork, Adobe Creative Suite, Autodesk, Solidworks, Mathcad, and Microsoft Office software for all students. Campus intranet, student e-mail accounts, and computer access in designated common areas are available to students. The school has a published electronic and media policy.

Contact Mrs. Sarah Gleason Ross, Assistant Head of School for Enrollment. 860-927-6111. Fax: 860-927-6109. E-mail: admissions@kent-school.edu. Website: www.kent-school.edu

KENTUCKY COUNTRY DAY SCHOOL

4100 Springdale Road
Louisville, Kentucky 40241

Head of School: Mr. Bradley E. Lyman

General Information Coeducational day college-preparatory, arts, technology, and honors program, independent study school. Grades JK–12. Founded: 1972. Setting: suburban. 85-acre campus. 3 buildings on campus. Approved or accredited by Independent Schools Association of the Central States. Member of National Association of Independent Schools. Endowment: $10.3 million. Total enrollment: 914. Upper school average class size: 16. Upper school faculty-student ratio: 1:7. There are 170 required school days per year for Upper School students. Upper School students typically attend 5 days per week. The average school day consists of 7 hours and 5 minutes.

Faculty School total: 125. In upper school: 19 men, 21 women; 36 have advanced degrees.

Subjects Offered Algebra, American history, American literature, art, biology, calculus, ceramics, chemistry, choral music, communications, computer math, computer programming, computer science, drama, economics, English, English literature, European history, fine arts, French, geology, geometry, government/civics, history, humanities, instrumental music, Latin, law, mathematics, multimedia, music, physical education, physics, play production, psychology, psychology-AP, science, sculpture, senior internship, senior project, social sciences, social studies, Spanish,

Spanish language-AP, speech, stagecraft, statistics, studio art-AP, technical theater, theater, trigonometry, U.S. government and politics-AP, U.S. history-AP.

Graduation Requirements Arts and fine arts (art, music, dance, drama), communications, English, foreign language, mathematics, physical education (includes health), science, social studies (includes history).

Special Academic Programs 20 Advanced Placement exams for which test preparation is offered; honors section; independent study; term-away projects; study abroad; academic accommodation for the gifted, the musically talented, and the artistically talented.

College Admission Counseling 67 students graduated in 2015; 66 went to college, including Brown University; Indiana University Bloomington; Miami University; University of Cincinnati; University of Kentucky; University of Louisville. Other: 1 had other specific plans. Median SAT critical reading: 610, median SAT math: 640, median SAT writing: 640, median combined SAT: 1900, median composite ACT: 27. 58% scored over 600 on SAT critical reading, 58% scored over 600 on SAT math, 58% scored over 600 on SAT writing, 64% scored over 1800 on combined SAT, 58% scored over 26 on composite ACT.

Student Life Upper grades have specified standards of dress, student council, honor system. Discipline rests equally with students and faculty.

Tuition and Aid Day student tuition: $19,950. Tuition installment plan (FACTS Tuition Payment Plan). Merit scholarship grants, need-based scholarship grants available. In 2015–16, 24% of upper-school students received aid; total upper-school merit-scholarship money awarded: $63,610.

Admissions Traditional secondary-level entrance grade is 9. For fall 2015, 58 students applied for upper-level admission, 36 were accepted, 26 enrolled. ERB Reading and Math required. Deadline for receipt of application materials: none. Application fee required: $75. On-campus interview required.

Athletics Interscholastic: baseball (boys), basketball (b,g), cross-country running (b,g), diving (b,g), field hockey (g), football (b), golf (b,g), lacrosse (b,g), soccer (b,g), softball (g), swimming and diving (b,g), tennis (b,g), track and field (b,g), volleyball (g), winter (indoor) track (b,g); coed interscholastic: weight training; coed intramural: bowling, project adventure, ropes courses, weight lifting. 8 PE instructors, 86 coaches, 1 athletic trainer.

Computers Computers are regularly used in all classes. Computer network features include on-campus library services, online commercial services, Internet access, wireless campus network, Internet filtering or blocking technology. Campus intranet and student e-mail accounts are available to students. Students grades are available online. The school has a published electronic and media policy.

Contact Mr. Jeff Holbrook, Director of Admissions. 502-814-4375. Fax: 502-814-4381. E-mail: admissions@kcd.org. Website: www.kcd.org

THE KEY SCHOOL

534 Hillsmere Drive
Annapolis, Maryland 21403

Head of School: Matthew Nespole

General Information Coeducational day college-preparatory and outdoor education school. Grades PK–12. Founded: 1958. Setting: suburban. Nearest major city is Washington, DC. 15-acre campus. 10 buildings on campus. Approved or accredited by Association of Independent Maryland Schools and Maryland Department of Education. Member of National Association of Independent Schools. Endowment: $11 million. Total enrollment: 630. Upper school average class size: 14. Upper school faculty-student ratio: 1:7. There are 173 required school days per year for Upper School students. Upper School students typically attend 5 days per week. The average school day consists of 7 hours and 20 minutes.

Upper School Student Profile Grade 9: 60 students (33 boys, 27 girls); Grade 10: 49 students (19 boys, 30 girls); Grade 11: 52 students (24 boys, 28 girls); Grade 12: 49 students (22 boys, 27 girls).

Faculty School total: 109. In upper school: 16 men, 24 women; 25 have advanced degrees.

Subjects Offered Acting, advanced biology, advanced chemistry, advanced math, algebra, American studies, ancient history, art, art history, biology, calculus, ceramics, chemistry, Chesapeake Bay studies, choir, computer education, computer literacy, computer science, computer skills, conceptual physics, creative writing, dance, digital art, digital photography, drama, drama performance, drawing, economics, English, English literature, European history, fine arts, French, geometry, journalism, Latin, literature by women, music, photography, physical education, physics, physiology, playwriting, pre-calculus, printmaking, Russian literature, sculpture, Shakespeare, Spanish, Spanish literature, statistics, studio art, theater, theater production, trigonometry.

Graduation Requirements Arts and fine arts (art, music, dance, drama), English, foreign language, history, mathematics, performing arts, physical education (includes health), science.

Special Academic Programs Advanced Placement exam preparation; honors section; independent study; academic accommodation for the gifted.

College Admission Counseling 47 students graduated in 2016; all went to college, including American University; College of Charleston; New York University; Smith

College; University of Maryland, College Park; University of South Carolina. Other: 2 had other specific plans.

Student Life Upper grades have specified standards of dress, student council. Discipline rests equally with students and faculty.

Summer Programs Remediation, enrichment, sports, art/fine arts, rigorous outdoor training, computer instruction programs offered; held both on and off campus; accepts boys and girls; open to students from other schools. 1,000 students usually enrolled. 2017 schedule: June 20 to August 11.

Tuition and Aid Day student tuition: $26,985. Tuition installment plan (FACTS Tuition Payment Plan, monthly payment plans, Tuition Refund Plan (TRP)). Tuition reduction for siblings, need-based scholarship grants available. In 2016–17, 25% of upper-school students received aid. Total amount of financial aid awarded in 2016–17: $667,300.

Admissions Traditional secondary-level entrance grade is 9. For fall 2016, 47 students applied for upper-level admission, 32 were accepted, 20 enrolled. ISEE, PSAT and SAT for applicants to grade 11 and 12 or SAT for students entering as juniors required. Deadline for receipt of application materials: January 23. Application fee required: $55. On-campus interview recommended.

Athletics Interscholastic: baseball (boys), basketball (b,g), field hockey (g), indoor soccer (g), lacrosse (b,g), soccer (b,g), volleyball (g); intramural: field hockey (g), lacrosse (b,g); coed interscholastic: baseball, cross-country running, equestrian sports, golf, sailing, swimming and diving, tennis; coed intramural: backpacking, basketball, canoeing/kayaking, climbing, cooperative games, dance, fitness, fitness walking, golf, hiking/backpacking, kayaking, kickball, modern dance, Newcombe ball, outdoor activities, project adventure, roller blading, running. 1 PE instructor, 44 coaches, 1 athletic trainer.

Computers Computers are regularly used in all academic classes. Computer network features include on-campus library services, online commercial services, Internet access, wireless campus network, online supplementary course materials. Campus intranet, student e-mail accounts, and computer access in designated common areas are available to students. Students grades are available online. The school has a published electronic and media policy.

Contact Tom Rossini, Director of Enrollment and Outreach. 410-263-9231 Ext. 1226. Fax: 410-280-5516. E-mail: trossini@keyschool.org. Website: www.keyschool.org

THE KEYSTONE SCHOOL

920 Central Road
Bloomsburg, Pennsylvania 17815

Head of School: Erica Rhone

General Information Distance learning only college-preparatory, general academic, arts, business, technology, and Distance Learning and Online Learning school. Distance learning grades 6–12. Founded: 1995. Setting: small town. Nearest major city is Harrisburg. Approved or accredited by Middle States Association of Colleges and Schools, Northwest Accreditation Commission, and Pennsylvania Department of Education. Total enrollment: 12,000.

Faculty School total: 100. In upper school: 40 men, 60 women.

Subjects Offered Advanced Placement courses, algebra, alternative physical education, American government, American history, American literature, art and culture, art appreciation, biology, British literature, business law, career and personal planning, chemistry, civics, composition, computer applications, computer technologies, consumer law, contemporary math, creative writing, earth science, economics, English, English composition, English literature, environmental science, fitness, foreign language, general math, geography, government, grammar, health, health education, history, independent study, intro to computers, lab science, life skills, marketing, math review, mathematics, microcomputer technology applications, music, music appreciation, physical science, physics, pre-algebra, pre-calculus, psychology, science, skills for success, social studies, sociology, trigonometry, wellness, work experience, world arts, writing.

Graduation Requirements Algebra, art, electives, English, health, mathematics, science, social sciences, 21 total credits required for graduation with a minimum of 5 coming from Keystone.

Special Academic Programs Accelerated programs; independent study; study at local college for college credit; academic accommodation for the gifted, the musically talented, and the artistically talented.

Student Life Upper grades have student council, honor system. Discipline rests equally with students and faculty.

Tuition and Aid Tuition installment plan (monthly payment plans). Tuition reduction for siblings available.

Admissions Deadline for receipt of application materials: none. No application fee required.

Computers Computers are regularly used in all classes. Computer resources include on-campus library services, Internet access, Internet filtering or blocking technology. Students grades are available online. The school has a published electronic and media policy.

Contact Elizabeth Letteer, Student Admissions Supervisor. 570-784-5220 Ext. 5512. Fax: 570-784-2129. E-mail: eletteer@keystonehighschool.com. Website: www.keystoneschoolonline.com

KEYSTONE SCHOOL

119 East Craig Place
San Antonio, Texas 78212-3497

Head of School: Mr. Brian Yager

General Information Coeducational day college-preparatory and accelerated curriculum school. Grades PK–12. Founded: 1948. Setting: urban. 3-acre campus. 12 buildings on campus. Approved or accredited by Independent Schools Association of the Southwest and Texas Department of Education. Member of National Association of Independent Schools. Endowment: $920,000. Total enrollment: 425. Upper school average class size: 16. Upper school faculty-student ratio: 1:10. Upper School students typically attend 5 days per week. The average school day consists of 7 hours and 15 minutes.

Upper School Student Profile Grade 9: 39 students (17 boys, 22 girls); Grade 10: 36 students (19 boys, 17 girls); Grade 11: 32 students (13 boys, 19 girls); Grade 12: 31 students (21 boys, 10 girls).

Faculty School total: 49. In upper school: 10 men, 11 women; 14 have advanced degrees.

Subjects Offered Advanced Placement courses, algebra, American history, American history-AP, anatomy and physiology, biology, biology-AP, calculus-AP, chemistry, chemistry-AP, civics, community service, computer science-AP, creative writing, digital imaging, English, English language and composition-AP, English literature and composition-AP, English-AP, environmental science-AP, European history-AP, French, French language-AP, French-AP, geometry, health, history, history-AP, mathematics, performing arts, photojournalism, physical education, physics, physics-AP, political science, psychology, science, social studies, Spanish, Spanish literature-AP, Spanish-AP, statistics-AP, studio art, theater, theater arts, U.S. history-AP, world history.

Graduation Requirements Arts and fine arts (art, music, dance, drama), English, foreign language, mathematics, physical education (includes health), science, social studies (includes history), 4 Advanced Placement courses. Community service is required.

Special Academic Programs Advanced Placement exam preparation; honors section; academic accommodation for the gifted.

College Admission Counseling 36 students graduated in 2015; 35 went to college, including Georgia Institute of Technology; Stanford University; The University of Texas at Austin; University of Southern California; Vanderbilt University; Washington University in St. Louis. Other: 1 had other specific plans. Mean SAT critical reading: 689, mean SAT math: 679, mean SAT writing: 694, mean combined SAT: 2062, mean composite ACT: 31.

Student Life Upper grades have student council. Discipline rests primarily with faculty.

Tuition and Aid Day student tuition: $17,535–$18,620. Tuition installment plan (monthly payment plans). Need-based scholarship grants available. In 2015–16, 15% of upper-school students received aid.

Admissions Traditional secondary-level entrance grade is 9. For fall 2015, 23 students applied for upper-level admission, 11 were accepted, 10 enrolled. ISEE, standardized test scores and writing sample required. Deadline for receipt of application materials: none. Application fee required: $50. On-campus interview required.

Athletics Interscholastic: basketball (boys, girls), golf (b,g), softball (g), tennis (b,g), volleyball (g); coed interscholastic: cross-country running, soccer; coed intramural: outdoor education. 3 PE instructors, 4 coaches.

Computers Computer network features include on-campus library services, online commercial services, Internet access, wireless campus network, Internet filtering or blocking technology, ProQuest Platinum. Computer access in designated common areas is available to students. Students grades are available online. The school has a published electronic and media policy.

Contact Mrs. Zina Wormley, Director of Admissions and Financial Aid. 210-735-4022. Fax: 210-732-4905. E-mail: zwormley@keystoneschool.org. Website: www.keystoneschool.org

KILDONAN SCHOOL

Amenia, New York
See Special Needs Schools section.

KIMBALL UNION ACADEMY

PO Box 188
7 Campus Center
Meriden, New Hampshire 03770

Head of School: Mr. Michael J. Schafer

General Information Coeducational boarding and day college-preparatory, arts, environmental science, and Global Scholar school. Grades 9–PG. Founded: 1813. Setting: small town. Nearest major city is Boston, MA. Students are housed in single-sex dormitories. 1,300-acre campus. 32 buildings on campus. Approved or accredited by Association of Independent Schools in New England, New England Association of Schools and Colleges, and New Hampshire Department of Education. Member of National Association of Independent Schools and Secondary School Admission Test Board. Endowment: $23 million. Total enrollment: 345. Upper school average class size: 12. Upper school faculty-student ratio: 1:6. There are 184 required school days per year for Upper School students. Upper School students typically attend 6 days per week. The average school day consists of 5 hours and 8 minutes.

Upper School Student Profile Grade 9: 55 students (29 boys, 26 girls); Grade 10: 76 students (40 boys, 36 girls); Grade 11: 105 students (59 boys, 46 girls); Grade 12: 95 students (50 boys, 45 girls); Postgraduate: 5 students (5 boys). 75% of students are boarding students. 25% are state residents. 28 states are represented in upper school student body. 22% are international students. International students from Canada, China, Hong Kong, Republic of Korea, Russian Federation, and Viet Nam; 24 other countries represented in student body.

Faculty School total: 55. In upper school: 31 men, 24 women; 35 have advanced degrees; 38 reside on campus.

Subjects Offered 3-dimensional design, acting, Advanced Placement courses, algebra, American history, American literature, anatomy, anthropology, architecture, art, art history, art history-AP, biology, biology-AP, calculus, calculus-AP, ceramics, chemistry, chemistry-AP, composition-AP, computer programming, creative writing, dance, digital photography, drama, driver education, English, English language and composition-AP, English literature, English literature and composition-AP, English-AP, environmental science, environmental science-AP, environmental studies, European history, fine arts, French, French language-AP, French literature-AP, geology, geometry, government/civics, grammar, health, history, history-AP, honors English, honors geometry, human geography - AP, independent study, international relations, jazz band, jazz ensemble, language-AP, Latin, Latin-AP, Mandarin, mathematical modeling, mathematics, modern European history-AP, modern world history, music, music history, music theory, music theory-AP, peer counseling, photo shop, photography, physics, physics-AP, physiology, playwriting, pottery, probability and statistics, programming, psychology, public speaking, science, social studies, Spanish, Spanish-AP, stagecraft, statistics-AP, student publications, studio art, studio art-AP, theater, theater arts, theater design and production, trigonometry, U.S. government, U.S. history, U.S. history-AP, video film production, visual arts, woodworking, world history, world literature, writing.

Graduation Requirements Art, English, foreign language, history, mathematics, science.

Special Academic Programs 19 Advanced Placement exams for which test preparation is offered; honors section; independent study; term away projects, study abroad; programs in English, mathematics, general development for dyslexic students.

College Admission Counseling 97 students graduated in 2016; 91 went to college, including Elon University; St. Lawrence University. Other: 6 had other specific plans. Median SAT critical reading: 570, median SAT math: 610, median SAT writing: 560, median combined SAT: 1740, median composite ACT: 26. 33% scored over 600 on SAT critical reading, 54% scored over 600 on SAT math, 40% scored over 600 on SAT writing, 37% scored over 1800 on combined SAT, 44% scored over 26 on composite ACT.

Student Life Upper grades have specified standards of dress, student council, honor system. Discipline rests equally with students and faculty.

Summer Programs Enrichment, sports programs offered; session focuses on Girl's Leadership Camp, Nike Running Camp; held on campus; accepts boys and girls; open to students from other schools. 200 students usually enrolled. 2017 schedule: July 2 to July 30. Application deadline: April 15.

Tuition and Aid Day student tuition: $36,200; 7-day tuition and room/board: $58,200. Tuition installment plan (Insured Tuition Payment Plan, Academic Management Services Plan, Key Tuition Payment Plan, monthly payment plans). Merit scholarship grants, need-based scholarship grants, merit scholarship program available. In 2016–17, 38% of upper-school students received aid. Total amount of financial aid awarded in 2016–17: $3,201,052.

Admissions Traditional secondary-level entrance grade is 9. For fall 2016, 628 students applied for upper-level admission, 280 were accepted, 125 enrolled. ACT, PSAT or SAT, SSAT or TOEFL required. Deadline for receipt of application materials: January 15. Application fee required: $100. Interview required.

Athletics Interscholastic: alpine skiing (boys, girls), baseball (b), basketball (b,g), cross-country running (b,g), equestrian sports (b,g), field hockey (g), freestyle skiing (b,g), golf (b,g), hockey (b,g), horseback riding (b,g), ice hockey (b,g), lacrosse (b,g), nordic skiing (b,g), rugby (b), running (b,g), skiing (cross-country) (b,g), skiing (downhill) (b,g), snowboarding (b,g), soccer (b,g), softball (g), swimming and diving (b,g), tennis (b,g); coed interscholastic: bicycling, combined training, mountain biking; coed intramural: aerobics/dance, alpine skiing, backpacking, canoeing/kayaking, combined training, dance, equestrian sports, fitness, freestyle skiing, hiking/backpacking, modern dance, outdoor activities, physical fitness, rock climbing, squash, strength & conditioning, surfing, weight lifting, yoga. 6 coaches, 2 athletic trainers.

Computers Computers are regularly used in architecture, computer applications, literary magazine, theater arts, woodworking classes. Computer network features include on-campus library services, Internet access, wireless campus network, Internet filtering or blocking technology, computer music studio/audio recording, 1-to-1 laptop program, iPad program for all students. Campus intranet, student e-mail accounts, and computer access in designated common areas are available to students. Students grades are available online. The school has a published electronic and media policy.

Contact Mr. Rich Ryerson, Director of Admissions. 603-469-2100. Fax: 603-469-2041. E-mail: admissions@kua.org. Website: www.kua.org

KIMBERTON WALDORF SCHOOL

PO Box 350
410 West Seven Stars Road
Kimberton, Pennsylvania 19442

Head of School: Kevin Hughes

General Information Coeducational day college-preparatory school. Grades PK–12. Founded: 1941. Setting: rural. Nearest major city is Philadelphia. 430-acre campus. 3 buildings on campus. Approved or accredited by Association of Waldorf Schools of North America and Middle States Association of Colleges and Schools. Member of National Association of Independent Schools. Endowment: $2 million. Total enrollment: 306. Upper school average class size: 18. Upper school faculty-student ratio: 1:7. Upper School students typically attend 5 days per week. The average school day consists of 7 hours and 15 minutes.

Upper School Student Profile Grade 9: 20 students (9 boys, 11 girls); Grade 10: 14 students (6 boys, 8 girls); Grade 11: 16 students (7 boys, 9 girls); Grade 12: 14 students (6 boys, 8 girls).

Faculty School total: 40. In upper school: 18 men, 13 women; 15 have advanced degrees.

Subjects Offered Algebra, American history, American literature, anatomy, architecture, art, art history, astronomy, biology, botany, calculus, ceramics, chemistry, community service, creative writing, drama, earth science, English, English literature, environmental science, European history, expository writing, fine arts, gardening, geology, geometry, German, government/civics, grammar, health, history, history of ideas, history of science, mathematics, music, music history, physical education, physics, physiology, science, social studies, Spanish, speech, theater, trigonometry, world history, world literature, writing, zoology.

Graduation Requirements 20th century history, African history, agriculture, algebra, American Civil War, American government, American literature, ancient world history, art history, biology, botany, career education internship, Civil War, drama, East Asian history, English, European history, eurythmy, fiber arts, foreign language, geology, geometry, inorganic chemistry, mathematics, modern world history, organic chemistry, painting, physical education (includes health), physics, physiology, poetry, Russian literature, U.S. history, woodworking. Community service is required.

Special Academic Programs Honors section; independent study; term-away projects; domestic exchange program; study abroad.

College Admission Counseling 22 students graduated in 2016; 19 went to college, including Dickinson College; Eckerd College; Hampshire College; Penn State University Park; Temple University; West Chester University of Pennsylvania. Other: 1 went to work, 2 had other specific plans. 29% scored over 600 on SAT critical reading, 29% scored over 600 on SAT writing.

Student Life Upper grades have specified standards of dress, student council. Discipline rests primarily with faculty.

Tuition and Aid Day student tuition: $17,810. Tuition installment plan (monthly payment plans, individually arranged payment plans, biannual payment plan). Tuition reduction for siblings, need-based scholarship grants available. In 2016–17, 25% of upper-school students received aid. Total amount of financial aid awarded in 2016–17: $164,250.

Admissions Traditional secondary-level entrance grade is 9. For fall 2016, 5 students applied for upper-level admission, 5 were accepted, 3 enrolled. School placement exam required. Deadline for receipt of application materials: none. Application fee required: $50. On-campus interview required.

Athletics Interscholastic: basketball (boys, girls), cross-country running (b,g), field hockey (g), hiking/backpacking (b,g), lacrosse (b,g), soccer (b), tennis (b,g), volleyball (b,g); intramural: outdoor activities (b,g), rock climbing (b,g), ropes courses (b,g); coed interscholastic: hiking/backpacking, volleyball; coed intramural: outdoor activities, rock climbing, ropes courses. 3 PE instructors, 8 coaches.

Computers Computer resources include on-campus library services, Internet access, Internet filtering or blocking technology. The school has a published electronic and media policy.

Contact Tammi Stein, Admissions Coordinator. 610-933-3635 Ext. 108. Fax: 610-935-6985. E-mail: admissions@kimberton.org. Website: www.kimberton.org

KING SCHOOL

1450 Newfield Avenue
Stamford, Connecticut 06905

Head of School: Thomas B. Main

General Information Coeducational day college-preparatory, global studies distinction, language distinction, and independent study school. Grades PK–12. Founded: 1865. Setting: suburban. Nearest major city is New York, NY. 40-acre campus. 3 buildings on campus. Approved or accredited by Connecticut Association of Independent Schools and New England Association of Schools and Colleges. Member of National Association of Independent Schools. Endowment: $25 million. Total enrollment: 674. Upper school average class size: 13. Upper school faculty-student ratio: 1:8. There are 164 required school days per year for Upper School students. Upper School students typically attend 5 days per week. The average school day consists of 7 hours.

Upper School Student Profile Grade 9: 81 students (39 boys, 42 girls); Grade 10: 91 students (44 boys, 47 girls); Grade 11: 88 students (45 boys, 43 girls); Grade 12: 87 students (45 boys, 42 girls).

Faculty School total: 97. In upper school: 28 men, 35 women; 55 have advanced degrees.

Subjects Offered Acting, advanced chemistry, advanced computer applications, advanced math, Advanced Placement courses, algebra, American history, ancient history, ancient world history, ancient/medieval philosophy, anthropology, archaeology, art, biology, calculus, calculus-AP, chemistry, chemistry-AP, Chinese, choral music, college counseling, college planning, computer multimedia, computer programming, computer science-AP, digital photography, economics, economics-AP, English, English language and composition-AP, English literature, English literature-AP, environmental studies, ethics, European history, European history-AP, fine arts, French, French language-AP, general science, geometry, global studies, government, history, honors algebra, honors geometry, honors U.S. history, honors world history, independent study, life skills, literature and composition-AP, macroeconomics-AP, mathematics, microeconomics-AP, model United Nations, modern European history-AP, modern languages, music theory-AP, musical productions, musical theater, oceanography, performing arts, philosophy, physics, physics-AP, play production, pre-calculus, psychology, public speaking, robotics, SAT preparation, SAT/ACT preparation, social studies, Spanish, Spanish language-AP, Spanish literature, Spanish literature-AP, statistics, statistics-AP, student government, student publications, studio art, theater arts, trigonometry, U.S. history-AP, U.S. literature, world history, world religions.

Graduation Requirements Art, arts and fine arts (art, music, dance, drama), English, ethics, foreign language, history, life skills, mathematics, science, sports, participation in one theater performance before graduation.

Special Academic Programs 17 Advanced Placement exams for which test preparation is offered; honors section; independent study; academic accommodation for the gifted, the musically talented, and the artistically talented.

College Admission Counseling 88 students graduated in 2016; 86 went to college, including Gettysburg College; Miami University; Syracuse University; University of Pennsylvania; Villanova University; Williams College. Other: 1 entered a postgraduate year, 1 had other specific plans. Median SAT critical reading: 605, median SAT math: 600, median SAT writing: 605, median combined SAT: 1820, median composite ACT: 28. 52% scored over 600 on SAT critical reading, 50% scored over 600 on SAT math, 46% scored over 600 on SAT writing, 50% scored over 1800 on combined SAT, 58% scored over 26 on composite ACT.

Student Life Upper grades have specified standards of dress, student council, honor system. Discipline rests primarily with faculty.

Summer Programs Remediation, enrichment, advancement, sports, art/fine arts, computer instruction programs offered; session focuses on academics (grades 6-12), enrichment (elementary school), and sports (grades 4-8) enrichment; held on campus; accepts boys and girls; open to students from other schools. 364 students usually enrolled. 2017 schedule: June 26 to August 4. Application deadline: June 9.

Tuition and Aid Day student tuition: $41,550. Tuition installment plan (Key Tuition Payment Plan). Need-based scholarship grants available. In 2016–17, 14% of upper-school students received aid. Total amount of financial aid awarded in 2016–17: $1,465,073.

Admissions Traditional secondary-level entrance grade is 9. For fall 2016, 201 students applied for upper-level admission, 74 were accepted, 35 enrolled. ISEE, school's own test or SSAT required. Deadline for receipt of application materials: January 1. Application fee required: $75. On-campus interview required.

Athletics Interscholastic: baseball (boys), basketball (b,g), crew (b,g), cross-country running (b,g), field hockey (g), football (b), golf (b,g), ice hockey (b), independent competitive sports (b,g), lacrosse (b,g), soccer (b,g), softball (g), squash (b,g), tennis (b,g), volleyball (g); intramural: dance (g), physical training (b,g); coed interscholastic: independent competitive sports; coed intramural: aerobics/dance, dance, fitness, physical training, strength & conditioning, weight lifting, weight training. 4 PE instructors, 27 coaches, 2 athletic trainers.

Computers Computers are regularly used in college planning, economics, English, ethics, foreign language, French, history, mathematics, science, technology, video film production, writing, yearbook classes. Computer network features include on-campus library services, online commercial services, Internet access, wireless campus network, Internet filtering or blocking technology. Campus intranet, student e-mail accounts, and computer access in designated common areas are available to students. The school has a published electronic and media policy.

Contact Nina Newman, Director of Admission and Financial Aid. 203-322-3496 Ext. 352. Fax: 203-505-6288. E-mail: nnewman@kingschoolct.org. Website: www.klht.org

THE KING'S CHRISTIAN HIGH SCHOOL

5 Carnegie Plaza
Cherry Hill, New Jersey 08003-1020

Head of School: Mr. James Duff

General Information Coeducational day and distance learning college-preparatory school. Grades P3–12. Distance learning grades 6–12. Founded: 1946. Setting: suburban. Nearest major city is Philadelphia, PA. 11-acre campus. 1 building on campus. Approved or accredited by American Association of Christian Schools, Association of Christian Schools International, Middle States Association of Colleges and Schools, and New Jersey Department of Education. Total enrollment: 311. Upper school average class size: 18. Upper school faculty-student ratio: 1:6. There are 180 required school days per year for Upper School students. Upper School students typically attend 5 days per week. The average school day consists of 6 hours and 30 minutes.

Upper School Student Profile Grade 6: 17 students (6 boys, 11 girls); Grade 7: 14 students (6 boys, 8 girls); Grade 8: 25 students (18 boys, 7 girls); Grade 9: 39 students (20 boys, 19 girls); Grade 10: 26 students (17 boys, 9 girls); Grade 11: 29 students (19 boys, 10 girls); Grade 12: 37 students (20 boys, 17 girls).

Faculty School total: 43. In upper school: 13 men, 14 women; 7 have advanced degrees.

Subjects Offered Advanced Placement courses, algebra, American literature, anatomy and physiology, art, art appreciation, band, bell choir, Bible, Bible studies, biology, biology-AP, British literature, calculus, calculus-AP, career and personal planning, career education, career/college preparation, chemistry, choir, Christian ethics, church history, college admission preparation, composition, computer education, computer graphics, computer skills, concert band, concert bell choir, concert choir, consumer mathematics, drama, economics, English literature, environmental science, ESL, fine arts, foreign language, general math, geometry, government-AP, handbells, health and safety, health and wellness, health education, honors algebra, honors English, honors geometry, honors U.S. history, instrumental music, jazz band, language arts, Life of Christ, marine science, music appreciation, music theory, New Testament, physical education, physics, SAT preparation, SAT/ACT preparation, Shakespeare, Spanish, speech, study skills, U.S. government, U.S. history, vocal ensemble, Web site design, world cultures, world history, yearbook.

Graduation Requirements Algebra, art history, arts and fine arts (art, music, dance, drama), Bible, biology, British literature, career education, career technology, chemistry, Christian ethics, church history, computer technologies, economics, English composition, English literature, ethics, human biology, Life of Christ, music, physical education (includes health), physical science, public speaking, SAT preparation, senior project, Spanish, study skills, U.S. government, U.S. history, world literature, writing, required volunteer service hours each year for grades 6–12.

Special Academic Programs 7 Advanced Placement exams for which test preparation is offered; honors section; independent study; study at local college for college credit; academic accommodation for the gifted, the musically talented, and the artistically talented; programs in English, mathematics, general development for dyslexic students; special instructional classes for students with learning disabilities, Attention Deficit Disorder; ESL (35 students enrolled).

College Admission Counseling 24 students graduated in 2016; all went to college, including Cedarville University; Eastern University; Liberty University; Rutgers University–New Brunswick. Mean SAT critical reading: 540, mean SAT math: 515, mean SAT writing: 522, mean combined SAT: 1577. 21% scored over 600 on SAT critical reading, 18% scored over 600 on SAT math, 15% scored over 600 on SAT writing.

Student Life Upper grades have specified standards of dress, student council, honor system. Discipline rests primarily with faculty. Attendance at religious services is required.

Summer Programs Remediation, enrichment, advancement, ESL, sports programs offered; session focuses on summer school programs; held both on and off campus; accepts boys and girls; open to students from other schools, 10 students usually enrolled. 2017 schedule: June 27 to August 26. Application deadline: June 21.

Tuition and Aid Day student tuition: $9136. Tuition installment plan (FACTS Tuition Payment Plan, annual and semi-annual payments). Tuition reduction for siblings, merit scholarship grants, need-based scholarship grants, military discount, Ministry Discount available. In 2016–17, 46% of upper-school students received aid.

Admissions Traditional secondary-level entrance grade is 9. Any standardized test, PSAT and SAT for applicants to grade 11 and 12 or writing sample required. Deadline for receipt of application materials: none. Application fee required: $100. On-campus interview recommended.

Athletics Interscholastic: baseball (boys), basketball (b,g), cross-country running (b,g), physical fitness (b,g), soccer (b,g), softball (g), tennis (b,g), track and field (b,g); intramural: basketball (b), flag football (b), golf (b,g). 2 PE instructors, 6 coaches.

Computers Computers are regularly used in career education, current events, desktop publishing, economics, foreign language, graphic design, library, library skills, mathematics, Web site design, writing, yearbook classes. Computer network features include on-campus library services, Internet access, wireless campus network, Internet filtering or blocking technology, Chromebooks. Campus intranet and computer access in designated common areas are available to students. Students grades are available online. The school has a published electronic and media policy.

Contact Mrs. Mimi Magill, Director of Admissions and Development. 856-489-6720 Ext. 228. Fax: 856-489-6727. E-mail: mmagill@tkcs.org. Website: www.tkcs.org

KING'S-EDGEHILL SCHOOL

254 College Road
Windsor, Nova Scotia B0N 2T0, Canada

Head of School: Mr. Joseph Seagram

General Information Coeducational boarding and day college-preparatory school. Grades 6–12. Founded: 1788. Setting: small town. Nearest major city is Halifax, Canada. Students are housed in single-sex dormitories. 65-acre campus. 17 buildings on campus. Approved or accredited by Canadian Association of Independent Schools and Nova Scotia Department of Education. Language of instruction: English. Total enrollment: 332. Upper school average class size: 15. Upper school faculty-student ratio: 1:10. Upper School students typically attend 5 days per week. The average school day consists of 7 hours.

Upper School Student Profile Grade 10: 76 students (44 boys, 32 girls); Grade 11: 85 students (46 boys, 39 girls); Grade 12: 66 students (33 boys, 33 girls). 68% of students are boarding students. 55% are province residents. 13 provinces are represented in upper school student body. 30% are international students. International students from China, Germany, Hong Kong, Mexico, Taiwan, and United States; 15 other countries represented in student body.

Faculty School total: 49. In upper school: 22 men, 23 women; 15 have advanced degrees; 22 reside on campus.

Subjects Offered Art, biology, calculus, chemistry, current events, drama, economics, English, French, geography, geology, history, mathematics, music, physics, political science, religion, science, social sciences, social studies, theater, theory of knowledge, world history.

Graduation Requirements English, foreign language, mathematics, science, social sciences, social studies (includes history).

Special Academic Programs International Baccalaureate program; honors section; term-away projects; study abroad; academic accommodation for the gifted; ESL (45 students enrolled).

College Admission Counseling 70 students graduated in 2016; all went to college, including Dalhousie University; McGill University; Queen's University at Kingston; The University of British Columbia; The University of Western Ontario; University of Toronto.

Student Life Upper grades have uniform requirement, student council, honor system. Discipline rests primarily with faculty.

Tuition and Aid Day student tuition: CAN$16,850; 7-day tuition and room/board: CAN$39,600. Tuition installment plan (monthly payment plans, individually arranged payment plans). Bursaries, merit scholarship grants available. In 2016–17, 35% of upper-school students received aid; total upper-school merit-scholarship money awarded: CAN$200,000. Total amount of financial aid awarded in 2016–17: CAN$900,000.

Admissions Traditional secondary-level entrance grade is 10. OLSAT and English Exam required. Deadline for receipt of application materials: none. Application fee required: CAN$100. Interview recommended.

Athletics Interscholastic: alpine skiing (boys, girls), aquatics (b,g), badminton (b,g), baseball (b,g), basketball (b,g), biathlon (b,g), bicycling (b,g), cross-country running (b,g), equestrian sports (b,g), fitness (b,g), Frisbee (b,g), golf (b,g), ice hockey (b,g), outdoor recreation (b,g), outdoor skills (b,g), physical fitness (b,g), rugby (b,g), skiing (cross-country) (b,g), skiing (downhill) (b,g), snowboarding (b,g), soccer (b,g), softball (b,g), table tennis (b,g), tennis (b,g), track and field (b,g), ultimate Frisbee (b,g), volleyball (b,g), weight lifting (b,g), wrestling (b,g); intramural: basketball (b,g), bicycling (b,g), cross-country running (b,g), golf (b,g), rugby (b,g), skiing (cross-country) (b,g), skiing (downhill) (b,g), snowboarding (b,g), soccer (b,g), softball (b,g), table tennis (b,g), tennis (b,g), track and field (b,g), weight lifting (b,g), yoga (b,g); coed interscholastic: aerobics/dance, alpine skiing, aquatics, backpacking, bicycling, curling, equestrian sports, fitness, Frisbee, outdoor recreation, outdoor skills, physical fitness, table tennis; coed intramural: bowling, curling, field hockey, table tennis, yoga. 40 coaches.

Computers Computers are regularly used in computer applications, English, foreign language, mathematics, music, science classes. Computer network features include on-campus library services, online commercial services, Internet access, Internet filtering or blocking technology. Campus intranet, student e-mail accounts, and computer access in designated common areas are available to students.

Contact Mr. Chris B. Strickey, Director of Admission. 902-798-2278. Fax: 902-798-2105. E-mail: strickey@kes.ns.ca. Website: www.kes.ns.ca

KINGSWAY COLLEGE

1200 Leland Road
Oshawa, Ontario L1K 2H4, Canada

Head of School: Mr. Lee Richards

General Information Coeducational boarding and day college-preparatory, general academic, arts, business, religious studies, bilingual studies, and technology school, affiliated with Seventh-day Adventists. Grades 9–12. Founded: 1903. Setting: small town. Nearest major city is Toronto, Canada. Students are housed in single-sex dormitories. 100-acre campus. 9 buildings on campus. Approved or accredited by Ontario Ministry of Education and Ontario Department of Education. Language of instruction: English. Endowment: CAN$1.6 million. Total enrollment: 214. Upper school average class size: 13. Upper school faculty-student ratio: 1:13. There are 180 required school days per year for Upper School students. Upper School students typically attend 5 days per week. The average school day consists of 5 hours and 50 minutes.

Upper School Student Profile Grade 9: 48 students (23 boys, 25 girls); Grade 10: 47 students (28 boys, 19 girls); Grade 11: 53 students (31 boys, 22 girls); Grade 12: 66 students (32 boys, 34 girls). 60% of students are boarding students. 65% are province residents. 5 provinces are represented in upper school student body. 33% are international students. International students from Bermuda, China, Germany, Republic of Korea, Ukraine, and United States; 1 other country represented in student body. 67% of students are Seventh-day Adventists.

Faculty School total: 17. In upper school: 10 men, 7 women; 5 have advanced degrees; 1 resides on campus.

Subjects Offered Accounting, advanced chemistry, advanced computer applications, advanced math, algebra, American history, anthropology, band, biology, business studies, calculus, Canadian geography, Canadian history, Canadian law, career education, ceramics, chemistry, choir, civics, computer applications, computer information systems, computer programming, computer studies, concert band, English, English literature, ESL, French, healthful living, information processing, intro to computers, music, music performance, physical education, physics, psychology, religious education, science, sociology, study skills, U.S. history, visual arts, work-study, world civilizations, world religions.

Graduation Requirements Art, Canadian geography, Canadian history, careers, civics, English, French, mathematics, physical education (includes health), science, all students must take one religion course per year.

Special Academic Programs ESL (63 students enrolled).

College Admission Counseling 48 students graduated in 2015; 45 went to college, including Andrews University; Southern Adventist University; University of Toronto; Walla Walla University. Other: 3 went to work.

Student Life Upper grades have specified standards of dress, student council. Discipline rests primarily with faculty.

Tuition and Aid Day student tuition: CAN$9350; 7-day tuition and room/board: CAN$15,600. Tuition installment plan (monthly payment plans, individually arranged payment plans). Tuition reduction for siblings, merit scholarship grants, need-based scholarship grants, paying campus jobs available. In 2015–16, 30% of upper-school students received aid; total upper-school merit-scholarship money awarded: CAN$5000. Total amount of financial aid awarded in 2015–16: CAN$250,000.

Admissions Traditional secondary-level entrance grade is 9. For fall 2015, 220 students applied for upper-level admission, 215 were accepted, 214 enrolled. Deadline for receipt of application materials: none. No application fee required. Interview recommended.

Athletics Interscholastic: basketball (boys, girls); intramural: basketball (b,g), flag football (b,g), floor hockey (b,g), ice hockey (b,g), racquetball (b,g), soccer (b,g), softball (b,g), volleyball (b,g); coed interscholastic: backpacking; coed intramural: badminton, canoeing/kayaking, gymnastics, hiking/backpacking, roller skating, skiing (downhill), snowboarding, volleyball. 1 PE instructor, 3 coaches.

Computers Computers are regularly used in accounting, business, career education, computer applications, data processing, English, ESL, history, programming, science, social sciences, yearbook classes. Computer network features include Internet access, wireless campus network, Internet filtering or blocking technology. Student e-mail accounts and computer access in designated common areas are available to students. Students grades are available online. The school has a published electronic and media policy.

Contact Mrs. Jessika Lopez, Communications Assistant. 905-433-1144 Ext. 211. Fax: 905-433-1156. E-mail: admissions@kingswaycollege.on.ca. Website: www.kingswaycollege.on.ca

KINGSWOOD-OXFORD SCHOOL

170 Kingswood Road
West Hartford, Connecticut 06119-1430

Head of School: Mr. Dennis Bisgaard

General Information Coeducational day college-preparatory school. Grades 6–12. Founded: 1909. Setting: suburban. Nearest major city is Hartford. 30-acre campus. 11 buildings on campus. Approved or accredited by Connecticut Association of Independent Schools, New England Association of Schools and Colleges, and Connecticut Department of Education. Member of National Association of Independent Schools and Secondary School Admission Test Board. Endowment: $29.9 million. Total enrollment: 507. Upper school average class size: 12. Upper school faculty-student ratio: 1:8. There are 172 required school days per year for Upper School students. Upper School students typically attend 5 days per week. The average school day consists of 7 hours.

Upper School Student Profile Grade 9: 88 students (56 boys, 32 girls); Grade 10: 83 students (42 boys, 41 girls); Grade 11: 89 students (54 boys, 35 girls); Grade 12: 79 students (38 boys, 41 girls).

Faculty School total: 53. In upper school: 27 men, 26 women; 33 have advanced degrees.

Subjects Offered Algebra, American history, American literature, art, art history-AP, band, biology, biology-AP, calculus, calculus-AP, chemistry, chemistry-AP, Chinese, Chinese studies, chorus, composition-AP, computer science, computer science-AP, concert band, concert choir, creative writing, digital music, digital photography, dramatic arts, drawing, economics, economics-AP, English, English language-AP, English literature, English literature-AP, environmental science, fine arts, forensics, French, French language-AP, geography, geometry, government/civics, jazz band, jazz ensemble, journalism, Latin, Latin-AP, marine biology, mathematics, media, music, orchestra, photography, physics, physics-AP, political science, public speaking, social

studies, Spanish, Spanish language-AP, Spanish-AP, statistics, statistics-AP, theater, U.S. history-AP, visual arts, world history, world literature, writing.

Graduation Requirements Computer science, English, foreign language, mathematics, performing arts, science, social studies (includes history), technology, visual arts, participation on athletic teams, senior thesis in English, 30 hours of community service. Community service is required.

Special Academic Programs 17 Advanced Placement exams for which test preparation is offered; honors section; independent study; term-away projects; study at local college for college credit.

College Admission Counseling 96 students graduated in 2016; all went to college, including Boston University; Elon University; Marist College; New York University; Trinity College; University of Connecticut. Mean SAT critical reading: 622, mean SAT math: 616, mean SAT writing: 613, mean combined SAT: 1851, mean composite ACT: 27.

Student Life Upper grades have specified standards of dress, student council, honor system. Discipline rests equally with students and faculty.

Summer Programs Advancement, sports, art/fine arts programs offered; session focuses on academics, sports, and arts; held on campus; accepts boys and girls; open to students from other schools. 45 students usually enrolled.

Tuition and Aid Day student tuition: $37,500. Tuition installment plan (SMART Tuition Payment Plan). Merit scholarship grants, need-based scholarship grants available. In 2016–17, 43% of upper-school students received aid; total upper-school merit-scholarship money awarded: $276,500. Total amount of financial aid awarded in 2016–17: $2,300,000.

Admissions Traditional secondary-level entrance grade is 9. For fall 2016, 212 students applied for upper-level admission, 129 were accepted, 43 enrolled. SSAT required. Deadline for receipt of application materials: February 1. Application fee required: $55. On-campus interview recommended.

Athletics Interscholastic: baseball (boys), basketball (b,g), cross-country running (b,g), diving (b,g), field hockey (g), football (b), ice hockey (b,g), lacrosse (b,g), soccer (b,g), softball (g), squash (b,g), strength & conditioning (b,g), swimming and diving (b,g), tennis (b,g), track and field (b,g), volleyball (g); intramural: basketball (b,g), ice hockey (b), soccer (b,g), yoga (g); coed interscholastic: golf; coed intramural: strength & conditioning. 9 coaches, 2 athletic trainers.

Computers Computers are regularly used in English, foreign language, history, mathematics, music technology, photography, science classes. Computer resources include on-campus library services, Internet access, wireless campus network. Student e-mail accounts and computer access in designated common areas are available to students. Students grades are available online. The school has a published electronic and media policy.

Contact Ms. Sharon N. Gaskin, Director of Enrollment Management. 860-727-5000. Fax: 860-236-3651. E-mail: gaskin.s@kingswoodoxford.org. Website: www.kingswoodoxford.org

THE KISKI SCHOOL

1888 Brett Lane
Saltsburg, Pennsylvania 15681

Head of School: Mr. Christopher A. Brueningsen

General Information Boys' boarding and day and distance learning college-preparatory and liberal arts and sciences school. Boarding grades 9–PG, day grades 9–12. Distance learning grades 9–12. Founded: 1888. Setting: rural. Nearest major city is Pittsburgh. Students are housed in single-sex dormitories. 350-acre campus. 42 buildings on campus. Approved or accredited by Middle States Association of Colleges and Schools, Pennsylvania Association of Independent Schools, The Association of Boarding Schools, and Pennsylvania Department of Education. Member of National Association of Independent Schools and Secondary School Admission Test Board. Endowment: $10 million. Total enrollment: 200. Upper school average class size: 10. Upper school faculty-student ratio: 1:7. There are 140 required school days per year for Upper School students. Upper School students typically attend 5 days per week. The average school day consists of 6 hours and 30 minutes.

Upper School Student Profile Grade 9: 42 students (42 boys); Grade 10: 40 students (40 boys); Grade 11: 51 students (51 boys); Grade 12: 63 students (63 boys); Postgraduate: 10 students (10 boys). 97% of students are boarding students. 45% are state residents. 21 states are represented in upper school student body. 25% are international students. International students from Brazil, China, Japan, Mexico, Republic of Korea, and Spain; 4 other countries represented in student body.

Faculty School total: 42. In upper school: 34 men, 8 women; 18 have advanced degrees; 38 reside on campus.

Subjects Offered Advanced chemistry, advanced math, algebra, American history-AP, analytic geometry, art, art history, biology, calculus, calculus-AP, ceramics, chemistry, chorus, computer programming, computer science, drama, drama performance, earth science, economics and history, English, English language-AP, English literature, ESL, European history, European history-AP, fine arts, foreign policy, French, French literature-AP, French-AP, geology, geometry, health, history, introduction to theater, music, organic chemistry, physics, physics-AP, political thought, pre-calculus, probability and statistics, psychology, SAT/ACT preparation, senior project, Spanish, speech and debate, The 20th Century, theater arts, theater production, trigonometry, U.S. history, U.S. history-AP, U.S. literature, wellness, world history, writing.

Graduation Requirements Arts and fine arts (art, music, dance, drama), English, ethics, foreign language, lab science, mathematics, personal development, physical education (includes health), social studies (includes history), senior research paper.

Special Academic Programs Advanced Placement exam preparation; honors section; academic accommodation for the gifted; ESL (15 students enrolled).

College Admission Counseling 51 students graduated in 2016; all went to college, including Carnegie Mellon University; Duquesne University; Johns Hopkins University; Muhlenberg College; Penn State University Park; United States Naval Academy. Mean SAT critical reading: 512, mean SAT math: 577, mean SAT writing: 529. 7% scored over 600 on SAT critical reading, 17% scored over 600 on SAT math, 5% scored over 600 on SAT writing.

Student Life Upper grades have specified standards of dress, student council, honor system. Discipline rests primarily with faculty.

Summer Programs Sports programs offered; session focuses on golf and other sports; held on campus; accepts boys and girls; open to students from other schools. 2017 schedule: July 2 to August 15. Application deadline: June 15.

Tuition and Aid Day student tuition: $32,100; 7-day tuition and room/board: $54,900. Tuition installment plan (Key Tuition Payment Plan, FACTS Tuition Payment Plan). Merit scholarship grants, need-based scholarship grants available. Total upper-school merit-scholarship money awarded for 2016–17: $164,700. Total amount of financial aid awarded in 2016–17: $4,085,095.

Admissions Traditional secondary-level entrance grade is 9. For fall 2016, 185 students applied for upper-level admission, 129 were accepted, 77 enrolled. ISEE or SSAT required. Deadline for receipt of application materials: none. Application fee required: $50. Interview required.

Athletics Interscholastic: baseball, basketball, cross-country running, diving, football, golf, hockey, ice hockey, lacrosse, soccer, swimming and diving, tennis, track and field, wrestling; intramural: alpine skiing, basketball, canoeing/kayaking, fishing, fitness, fitness walking, flag football, fly fishing, Frisbee, golf, hiking/backpacking, indoor track & field, jogging, martial arts, mountain biking, outdoor activities, outdoor recreation, paint ball, physical training, power lifting, rafting, skiing (downhill), snowboarding, strength & conditioning, swimming and diving, table tennis, ultimate Frisbee, weight lifting, weight training. 2 PE instructors, 24 coaches, 1 athletic trainer.

Computers Computers are regularly used in computer applications, economics, English, ESL, French, history, library skills, life skills, mathematics, psychology, science classes. Computer network features include on-campus library services, online commercial services, Internet access, wireless campus network, Internet filtering or blocking technology. Campus intranet and student e-mail accounts are available to students. Students grades are available online. The school has a published electronic and media policy.

Contact Mr. William W. Ellis, Assistant Headmaster for Enrollment Management. 724-639-3586 Ext. 237. Fax: 724-639-8467. E-mail: bill.ellis@kiski.org. Website: www.kiski.org

THE KNOX SCHOOL

541 Long Beach Road
St. James, New York 11780

Head of School: Ms. Kristen B. Tillona

General Information Coeducational boarding and day college-preparatory, arts, bilingual studies, and technology school. Grades 6–12. Founded: 1904. Setting: suburban. Students are housed in single-sex dormitories. 48-acre campus. 12 buildings on campus. Approved or accredited by Middle States Association of Colleges and Schools, New York State Association of Independent Schools, New York State Board of Regents, The Association of Boarding Schools, and New York Department of Education. Member of National Association of Independent Schools. Endowment: $5 million. Total enrollment: 150. Upper school average class size: 12. Upper school faculty-student ratio: 1:5. Upper School students typically attend 5 days per week.

Upper School Student Profile Grade 6: 6 students (3 boys, 3 girls); Grade 7: 13 students (8 boys, 5 girls); Grade 8: 10 students (5 boys, 5 girls); Grade 9: 28 students (16 boys, 12 girls); Grade 10: 34 students (11 boys, 23 girls); Grade 11: 27 students (14 boys, 13 girls); Grade 12: 27 students (15 boys, 12 girls). 50% of students are boarding students. 47% are state residents. 5 states are represented in upper school student body. 53% are international students. International students from China, Greece, Republic of Korea, Russian Federation, Spain, and Taiwan; 10 other countries represented in student body.

Faculty School total: 37. In upper school: 12 men, 20 women; 14 have advanced degrees; 20 reside on campus.

Subjects Offered 20th century history, algebra, American literature, art history, biology, biology-AP, British literature, calculus, calculus-AP, ceramics, chemistry, chemistry-AP, computer art, computer science, creative writing, earth science, economics, English, English composition, environmental science, ESL, European history, French, geometry, government, health and wellness, Latin, music, music history, photo shop, photography, physics, physics-AP, pre-algebra, pre-calculus, psychology, robotics, Spanish, studio art, theater, U.S. history, vocal music, world history, world literature.

Graduation Requirements Art, computer education, electives, English, foreign language, health, history, lab science, mathematics, senior project, community service.

Special Academic Programs Advanced Placement exam preparation; honors section; independent study; study at local college for college credit; study abroad; academic accommodation for the gifted; ESL (32 students enrolled).

College Admission Counseling 36 students graduated in 2015; 35 went to college, including Boston University; New York University; Syracuse University; The George Washington University; University of Connecticut; University of Maryland, College Park. Other: 1 had other specific plans.

Student Life Upper grades have uniform requirement, student council, honor system. Discipline rests primarily with faculty.

Tuition and Aid Day student tuition: $10,500; 5-day tuition and room/board: $34,500; 7-day tuition and room/board: $45,000. Tuition installment plan (SMART Tuition Payment Plan, individually arranged payment plans). Need-based scholarship grants available. In 2015–16, 25% of upper-school students received aid. Total amount of financial aid awarded in 2015–16: $400,000.

Admissions Traditional secondary-level entrance grade is 9. For fall 2015, 200 students applied for upper-level admission, 133 were accepted, 62 enrolled. ERB, PSAT, SAT, or ACT for applicants to grade 11 and 12, SSAT, TOEFL or TOEFL Junior required. Deadline for receipt of application materials: February 15. Application fee required: $75. Interview required.

Athletics Interscholastic: aerobics/dance (boys, girls), baseball (b), basketball (b,g), soccer (b), softball (g), tennis (b,g), volleyball (g); coed interscholastic: crew, cross-country running, equestrian sports, fencing, golf, horseback riding, soccer; coed intramural: bowling, combined training, dance, dressage, equestrian sports, fitness, golf, horseback riding, outdoor activities, physical training, yoga. 19 coaches.

Computers Computers are regularly used in computer applications, graphic arts, graphic design classes. Computer network features include on-campus library services, Internet access, wireless campus network. Computer access in designated common areas is available to students. Students grades are available online. The school has a published electronic and media policy.

Contact Ms. Brileigh I. Pinkney, Associate Dean of Admission. 631-686-1600 Ext. 413. Fax: 631-686-1650. E-mail: bpinkney@knoxschool.org.
Website: www.knoxschool.org

KOLBE-CATHEDRAL HIGH SCHOOL

33 Calhoun Place
Bridgeport, Connecticut 06604

Head of School: Mrs. Jo-Anne Jakab

General Information Coeducational day college-preparatory school, affiliated with Roman Catholic Church. Grades 9–12. Founded: 1963. Setting: urban. 2 buildings on campus. Approved or accredited by National Catholic Education Association, New England Association of Schools and Colleges, and Connecticut Department of Education. Upper school average class size: 20. Upper school faculty-student ratio: 1:18. There are 180 required school days per year for Upper School students. Upper School students typically attend 5 days per week. The average school day consists of 6 hours and 5 minutes.

Upper School Student Profile Grade 9: 77 students (40 boys, 37 girls); Grade 10: 80 students (39 boys, 41 girls); Grade 11: 76 students (41 boys, 35 girls); Grade 12: 75 students (36 boys, 39 girls). 55% of students are Roman Catholic.

Faculty School total: 18. In upper school: 13 men, 15 women; 28 have advanced degrees.

Subjects Offered Advanced biology, African American studies, algebra, American government, American history, American history-AP, American literature, art, biology, British literature, British literature (honors), calculus, chemistry, communications, computer literacy, contemporary history, crafts, creative writing, democracy in America, earth science, engineering, English, English language and composition-AP, English literature, environmental science, French, geography, geometry, health and wellness, history, honors algebra, honors English, honors geometry, honors U.S. history, honors world history, music, nutrition, painting, personal finance, physics, pre-calculus, psychology, religion, Spanish, theology, U.S. history, U.S. history-AP, Western civilization, world geography, world history.

Graduation Requirements American history, chemistry, foreign language, health and wellness, New Testament.

Special Academic Programs Honors section; study at local college for college credit; remedial math.

College Admission Counseling 72 students graduated in 2016; all went to college, including Fairfield University; Southern Connecticut State University; University of Connecticut; Western Connecticut State University.

Student Life Upper grades have uniform requirement. Discipline rests primarily with faculty. Attendance at religious services is required.

Tuition and Aid Day student tuition: $8500. Tuition installment plan (SMART Tuition Payment Plan). Merit scholarship grants, need-based scholarship grants available. In 2016–17, 85% of upper-school students received aid.

Admissions Traditional secondary-level entrance grade is 9. For fall 2016, 90 students applied for upper-level admission, 80 were accepted, 77 enrolled. High School Placement Test (closed version) from Scholastic Testing Service or STS - Educational

Development Series required. Deadline for receipt of application materials: none. Application fee required: $50. Interview recommended.

Athletics Interscholastic: baseball (boys), basketball (b,g), cheering (g), soccer (b,g), softball (g), volleyball (b,g). 2 PE instructors, 16 coaches.

Computers Computers are regularly used in college planning, computer applications, creative writing, desktop publishing, foreign language, music technology, SAT preparation, Web site design, yearbook classes. Computer network features include Internet access, wireless campus network, Internet filtering or blocking technology. Computer access in designated common areas is available to students. Students grades are available online. The school has a published electronic and media policy.

Contact Mrs. Maria Prim, Secretary. 203-335-2554. Fax: 203-335-2556. E-mail: Maria@kolbecaths.org. Website: www.kolbecaths.org

THE LAB SCHOOL OF WASHINGTON

Washington, District of Columbia
See Special Needs Schools section.

LA CHEIM SCHOOL

Antioch, California
See Special Needs Schools section.

LA GRANGE ACADEMY

1501 Vernon Road
La Grange, Georgia 30240

Head of School: Mr. Carl Parke

General Information Coeducational day college-preparatory school. Ungraded, ages 3–18. Founded: 1970. Setting: small town. Nearest major city is Atlanta. 15-acre campus. 4 buildings on campus. Approved or accredited by Georgia Independent School Association, Southern Association of Colleges and Schools, Southern Association of Independent Schools, and Georgia Department of Education. Member of National Association of Independent Schools. Total enrollment: 215. Upper school average class size: 15. Upper school faculty-student ratio: 1:16. There are 186 required school days per year for Upper School students. Upper School students typically attend 5 days per week. The average school day consists of 8 hours.

Upper School Student Profile Grade 9: 14 students (4 boys, 10 girls); Grade 10: 8 students (3 boys, 5 girls); Grade 11: 15 students (5 boys, 10 girls); Grade 12: 15 students (6 boys, 9 girls).

Faculty School total: 31. In upper school: 6 men, 7 women; 9 have advanced degrees.

Subjects Offered Advanced Placement courses, algebra, American history, American history-AP, American literature, anatomy, art, art history, biology, biology-AP, British literature, business, calculus, calculus-AP, chemistry, chemistry-AP, chorus, computer science, driver education, earth science, economics, English, English language and composition-AP, English literature, English literature and composition-AP, environmental science, environmental science-AP, expository writing, geography, geometry, government/civics, grammar, health, health education, history, instrumental music, Latin, mathematics, music, physical education, physics, political science, science, social studies, Spanish, trigonometry, world history, world literature.

Graduation Requirements English, foreign language, mathematics, physical education (includes health), science, social studies (includes history).

Special Academic Programs Advanced Placement exam preparation; honors section; independent study; academic accommodation for the gifted, the musically talented, and the artistically talented.

College Admission Counseling 19 students graduated in 2016; all went to college, including Armstrong State University; Auburn University; Georgia College & State University; LaGrange College; University of Georgia; University of West Georgia. Median SAT critical reading: 518, median SAT math: 540, median SAT writing: 517.

Student Life Upper grades have specified standards of dress, student council, honor system. Discipline rests primarily with faculty.

Tuition and Aid Tuition installment plan (monthly payment plans, quarterly payment plan). Merit scholarship grants, need-based scholarship grants, funded scholarships for specific groups or individuals available. In 2016–17, 20% of upper-school students received aid; total upper-school merit-scholarship money awarded: $25,000. Total amount of financial aid awarded in 2016–17: $159,411.

Admissions School's own exam required. Deadline for receipt of application materials: none. Application fee required: $50. On-campus interview required.

Athletics Interscholastic: baseball (boys), basketball (b,g), cheering (g), riflery (b,g), soccer (b,g), softball (g), tennis (b,g), weight training (b,g); coed interscholastic: tennis. 3 PE instructors, 8 coaches.

Computers Computers are regularly used in all classes. Computer network features include on-campus library services, Internet access, wireless campus network, Internet filtering or blocking technology. Campus intranet and computer access in designated common areas are available to students. Students grades are available online. The school has a published electronic and media policy.

Contact Mrs. Fayedra Mumme, Director of Admissions. 706-882-8097. Fax: 706-882-8640. E-mail: FayedraMumme@lagrangeacademy.org. Website: www.lagrangeacademy.org

LA JOLLA COUNTRY DAY SCHOOL

9490 Genesee Avenue
La Jolla, California 92037

Head of School: Dr. Gary Krahn

General Information Coeducational day college-preparatory, arts, and technology school. Grades N–12. Founded: 1926. Setting: suburban. Nearest major city is San Diego. 24-acre campus. 8 buildings on campus. Approved or accredited by California Association of Independent Schools, Western Association of Schools and Colleges, and California Department of Education. Member of National Association of Independent Schools and Secondary School Admission Test Board. Endowment: $24. Total enrollment: 1,118. Upper school average class size: 16. Upper school faculty-student ratio: 1:16. There are 171 required school days per year for Upper School students. Upper School students typically attend 5 days per week. The average school day consists of 7 hours.

Upper School Student Profile Grade 9: 106 students (57 boys, 49 girls); Grade 10: 118 students (60 boys, 58 girls); Grade 11: 117 students (68 boys, 49 girls); Grade 12: 118 students (55 boys, 63 girls).

Faculty School total: 146. In upper school: 20 men, 20 women; 31 have advanced degrees.

Subjects Offered Advanced studio art-AP, algebra, art, art history-AP, art-AP, ASB Leadership, astronomy, athletic training, band, baseball, basketball, biology, biology-AP, calculus, calculus-AP, ceramics, chemistry, chemistry-AP, choir, choral music, chorus, college counseling, community service, computer graphics, conceptual physics, concert band, creative writing, dance, dance performance, digital photography, drama, economics, English, English literature, English literature and composition-AP, English-AP, environmental science, European history, European history-AP, experiential education, film studies, French, French language-AP, French-AP, freshman seminar, geometry, golf, government, government and politics-AP, government-AP, history-AP, honors algebra, honors geometry, independent study, instrumental music, journalism, linear algebra, madrigals, Mandarin, marine biology, modern European history-AP, music appreciation, music theory, music theory-AP, music-AP, neuroscience, performing arts, photography, physical education, physics, physics-AP, portfolio art, pre-calculus, programming, psychology, psychology-AP, Spanish, Spanish language-AP, Spanish literature-AP, Spanish-AP, speech, statistics-AP, strings, studio art, studio art-AP, technical theater, theater, theater arts, theater history, theater production, U.S. history-AP, world cultures, writing.

Graduation Requirements Arts and fine arts (art, music, dance, drama), English, foreign language, mathematics, performing arts, physical education (includes health), science, senior project, social sciences, speech, 40 hours of community service.

Special Academic Programs Advanced Placement exam preparation; honors section; study abroad.

College Admission Counseling 128 students graduated in 2015; 126 went to college, including Chapman University; The George Washington University; Tulane University; University of California, Berkeley; University of San Diego; University of Southern California. Other: 2 had other specific plans. Median SAT critical reading: 600, median SAT math: 630, median SAT writing: 620, median composite ACT: 29. 48% scored over 600 on SAT critical reading, 61% scored over 600 on SAT math, 57% scored over 600 on SAT writing, 68% scored over 26 on composite ACT.

Student Life Upper grades have specified standards of dress, student council. Discipline rests equally with students and faculty.

Tuition and Aid Day student tuition: $30,920. Tuition installment plan (FACTS Tuition Payment Plan, monthly payment plans). Need-based scholarship grants available. In 2014–15, 25% of upper-school students received aid. Total amount of financial aid awarded in 2014–15: $2,285,386.

Admissions Traditional secondary-level entrance grade is 9. ERB (grade level), ISEE, TerraNova or writing sample required. Deadline for receipt of application materials: January 30. Application fee required: $125. On-campus interview required.

Athletics Interscholastic: aquatics (boys, girls), baseball (b), basketball (b,g), cross-country running (b,g), dance squad (g), fencing (b,g), football (b), golf (b,g), lacrosse (b,g), soccer (b,g), softball (g), surfing (b,g), swimming and diving (b,g), tennis (b,g), track and field (b,g), volleyball (g), water polo (b,g); intramural: independent competitive sports (b,g); coed interscholastic: cheering, rock climbing, strength & conditioning, ultimate Frisbee; coed intramural: outdoor education, snowboarding. 1 PE instructor, 5 coaches, 1 athletic trainer.

Computers Computers are regularly used in art, English, French, history, mathematics, science, Spanish, technology classes. Computer network features include on-campus library services, online commercial services, Internet access, wireless campus network, Internet filtering or blocking technology, email connection from home. Student e-mail accounts are available to students. The school has a published electronic and media policy.

Contact Ms. Inez Odom, Director of Admission. 858-453-3440 Ext. 273. Fax: 858-453-8210. E-mail: Iodom@ljcds.org. Website: www.ljcds.org

LAKEFIELD COLLEGE SCHOOL

4391 County Road #29
Lakefield, Ontario K0L 2H0, Canada

Head of School: Mr. Struan Robertson

General Information Coeducational boarding and day and distance learning college-preparatory, arts, and athletics, music, outdoor education school, affiliated with Church of England (Anglican). Grades 9–12. Distance learning grades 9–12. Founded: 1879. Setting: small town. Nearest major city is Toronto, Canada. Students are housed in single-sex dormitories. 315-acre campus. 27 buildings on campus. Approved or accredited by Canadian Association of Independent Schools, The Association of Boarding Schools, and Ontario Department of Education. Affiliate member of National Association of Independent Schools; member of Secondary School Admission Test Board. Language of instruction: English. Endowment: CAN$30.5 million. Total enrollment: 365. Upper school average class size: 16. Upper school faculty-student ratio: 1:7. There are 195 required school days per year for Upper School students. Upper School students typically attend 6 days per week. The average school day consists of 5 hours.

Upper School Student Profile Grade 9: 55 students (28 boys, 27 girls); Grade 10: 96 students (49 boys, 47 girls); Grade 11: 105 students (58 boys, 47 girls); Grade 12: 109 students (53 boys, 56 girls). 70% of students are boarding students. 59% are province residents. 16 provinces are represented in upper school student body. 32% are international students. International students from Barbados, Bermuda, China, Democratic People's Republic of Korea, Germany, and Mexico; 27 other countries represented in student body.

Faculty School total: 53. In upper school: 27 men, 22 women; 12 have advanced degrees; 25 reside on campus.

Subjects Offered Algebra, art, art history, biology, calculus, chemistry, computer science, creative writing, drama, earth science, economics, English, English literature, environmental science, fine arts, French, geography, geometry, government/civics, health, history, kinesiology, mathematics, music, outdoor education, physical education, physics, science, social studies, sociology, Spanish, theater, trigonometry, vocal music, world history, world literature.

Graduation Requirements English, foreign language, mathematics, physical education (includes health), science, social studies (includes history).

Special Academic Programs 8 Advanced Placement exams for which test preparation is offered; term-away projects; study abroad.

College Admission Counseling 103 students graduated in 2015; 98 went to college, including McGill University; Ryerson University; The University of Western Ontario; Trent University; University of Ottawa; University of Toronto. Other: 5 had other specific plans.

Student Life Upper grades have uniform requirement, student council, honor system. Discipline rests equally with students and faculty.

Tuition and Aid Day student tuition: CAN$30,200; 7-day tuition and room/board: CAN$53,950. Tuition installment plan (Insured Tuition Payment Plan, monthly payment plans, individually arranged payment plans, 3-payment plans or custom payment plans if req'd). Bursaries, merit scholarship grants, need-based scholarship grants available. In 2015–16, 25% of upper-school students received aid; total upper-school merit-scholarship money awarded: CAN$40,000. Total amount of financial aid awarded in 2015–16: CAN$180,000.

Admissions Traditional secondary-level entrance grade is 9. For fall 2015, 225 students applied for upper-level admission, 193 were accepted, 140 enrolled. Otis-Lennon School Ability Test or SSAT required. Deadline for receipt of application materials: none. Application fee required: CAN$100. Interview required.

Athletics Interscholastic: alpine skiing (boys, girls), baseball (b), basketball (g), crew (b,g), cross-country running (b,g), field hockey (g), hockey (b,g), ice hockey (b,g), nordic skiing (b,g), outdoor education (b,g), physical fitness (b,g), rock climbing (b,g), ropes courses (b,g), rowing (b,g), rugby (b,g), skiing (cross-country) (b,g), skiing (downhill) (b,g), snowboarding (b,g), soccer (b,g), softball (b), tennis (b), track and field (b,g), volleyball (g); intramural: aerobics/dance (g), basketball (b,g), cross-country running (b,g), fitness (b,g), running (b,g), skiing (cross-country) (b,g), tennis (b,g); coed interscholastic: alpine skiing, badminton, cross-country running, dressage, equestrian sports, Frisbee, hockey, horseback riding, ice hockey, nordic skiing, outdoor education, physical fitness, rock climbing, sailboarding, sailing, skiing (cross-country), skiing (downhill), snowboarding, tennis, track and field, ultimate Frisbee, wall climbing, windsurfing; coed intramural: basketball, canoeing/kayaking, climbing, cross-country running, dance, dance team, equestrian sports, fitness, ice hockey, kayaking, running, sailboarding, sailing, skiing (cross-country), skiing (downhill), softball, tennis, weight training, windsurfing, yoga.

Computers Computers are regularly used in all classes. Computer network features include on-campus library services, online commercial services, Internet access, wireless campus network, Internet filtering or blocking technology. Campus intranet, student e-mail accounts, and computer access in designated common areas are available to students. Students grades are available online. The school has a published electronic and media policy.

Contact Mrs. Barbara M. Rutherford, Assistant Director of Admissions. 705-652-3324 Ext. 345. Fax: 705-652-6320. E-mail: admissions@lcs.on.ca. Website: www.lcs.on.ca

LAKE FOREST ACADEMY

1500 West Kennedy Road
Lake Forest, Illinois 60045

Head of School: Dr. John Strudwick

General Information Coeducational boarding and day college-preparatory school. Grades 9–12. Founded: 1857. Setting: suburban. Nearest major city is Chicago. Students are housed in single-sex dormitories. 160-acre campus. 21 buildings on campus. Approved or accredited by Independent Schools Association of the Central States and Illinois Department of Education. Member of National Association of Independent Schools and Secondary School Admission Test Board. Endowment: $30 million. Total enrollment: 391. Upper school average class size: 12. Upper school faculty-student ratio: 1:7. Upper School students typically attend 5 days per week. The average school day consists of 7 hours.

Upper School Student Profile Grade 9: 80 students (48 boys, 32 girls); Grade 10: 104 students (56 boys, 48 girls); Grade 11: 108 students (60 boys, 48 girls); Grade 12: 94 students (52 boys, 42 girls); Postgraduate: 5 students (4 boys, 1 girl). 50% of students are boarding students. 71% are state residents. 20 states are represented in upper school student body. 30% are international students. International students from Cape Verde, Christmas Island, Ghana, Republic of Moldova, Tajikistan, and Togo; 30 other countries represented in student body.

Faculty School total: 69. In upper school: 36 men, 33 women; 46 have advanced degrees; 53 reside on campus.

Subjects Offered 20th century history, 20th century world history, 3-dimensional art, 3-dimensional design, acting, advanced chemistry, advanced computer applications, advanced math, Advanced Placement courses, advanced studio art-AP, algebra, American government, American history, American history-AP, American literature, American literature-AP, American studies, anatomy and physiology, anthropology, applied arts, applied music, art, art appreciation, art education, art history, art history-AP, art-AP, astronomy, bioethics, bioethics, DNA and culture, biology, biology-AP, calculus, calculus-AP, ceramics, chemistry, chemistry-AP, Chinese, choir, choral music, chorus, cinematography, comparative government and politics-AP, computer applications, computer graphics, computer information systems, computer programming, computer science, computer science-AP, creative writing, drama, ecology, English, English literature, environmental science, ESL, fine arts, French, geometry, health and wellness, history, journalism, Latin, Latin American literature, Latin-AP, literature and composition-AP, mathematics, music, mythology, photography, physics, poetry, pre-calculus, science, Shakespeare, social studies, Spanish, speech, statistics-AP, theater, U.S. government and politics-AP, world history.

Graduation Requirements Arts and fine arts (art, music, dance, drama), athletics, English, foreign language, mathematics, science, social studies (includes history). Community service is required.

Special Academic Programs Advanced Placement exam preparation; honors section; independent study; study abroad; academic accommodation for the gifted, the musically talented, and the artistically talented; ESL (25 students enrolled).

College Admission Counseling 105 students graduated in 2016; all went to college, including Duke University; Miami University; Northwestern University; University of Illinois at Urbana–Champaign; University of Michigan. Mean SAT critical reading: 580, mean SAT math: 640, mean SAT writing: 590, mean combined SAT: 1800, mean composite ACT: 27.

Student Life Upper grades have specified standards of dress, student council, honor system. Discipline rests equally with students and faculty.

Summer Programs ESL programs offered; session focuses on ESL; held on campus; accepts boys and girls; open to students from other schools. 85 students usually enrolled. 2017 schedule: July 13 to August 15. Application deadline: June 1.

Tuition and Aid Day student tuition: $31,000; 7-day tuition and room/board: $42,000. Tuition installment plan (FACTS Tuition Payment Plan). Merit scholarship grants, need-based scholarship grants available. In 2016–17, 30% of upper-school students received aid. Total amount of financial aid awarded in 2016–17: $3,100,000.

Admissions Traditional secondary-level entrance grade is 9. For fall 2016, 463 students applied for upper-level admission, 197 were accepted, 124 enrolled. SSAT or TOEFL required. Deadline for receipt of application materials: February 1. Application fee required: $50. On-campus interview required.

Athletics Interscholastic: baseball (boys), basketball (b,g), cross-country running (b,g), field hockey (g), football (b), ice hockey (b,g), soccer (b,g), softball (g), swimming and diving (b,g), tennis (b,g), track and field (b,g), volleyball (b,g), wrestling (b); intramural: lacrosse (b,g); coed interscholastic: cheering, golf; coed intramural: bowling, dance, dance squad, fitness, martial arts, racquetball, sailing, squash, water polo, weight training, yoga. 3 coaches, 1 athletic trainer.

Computers Computers are regularly used in English, foreign language, history, mathematics, science classes. Computer network features include on-campus library services, online commercial services, Internet access, wireless campus network, Internet filtering or blocking technology, Apple TV, Smart Boards in classrooms, iPads. Campus intranet, student e-mail accounts, and computer access in designated common areas are available to students. Students grades are available online. The school has a published electronic and media policy.

Contact Ms. Grace Everett, Admissions Office. 847-615-3267. Fax: 847-295-8149. E-mail: admissions@lfanet.org. Website: www.lfanet.org

LAKEHILL PREPARATORY SCHOOL

2720 Hillside Drive

Dallas, Texas 75214

Head of School: Mr. Roger L. Perry

General Information Coeducational day college-preparatory school. Grades K–12. Founded: 1971. Setting: urban. 23-acre campus. 4 buildings on campus. Approved or accredited by Texas Private School Accreditation Commission, The College Board, and Texas Department of Education. Member of National Association of Independent Schools. Endowment: $300,000. Total enrollment: 405. Upper school average class size: 15. Upper school faculty-student ratio: 1:10. There are 175 required school days per year for Upper School students. Upper School students typically attend 5 days per week. The average school day consists of 7 hours and 30 minutes.

Upper School Student Profile Grade 9: 33 students (16 boys, 17 girls); Grade 10: 31 students (17 boys, 14 girls); Grade 11: 23 students (14 boys, 9 girls); Grade 12: 33 students (17 boys, 16 girls).

Faculty School total: 44. In upper school: 9 men, 13 women; 18 have advanced degrees.

Subjects Offered Acting, advanced chemistry, advanced computer applications, advanced math, Advanced Placement courses, advanced studio art-AP, African studies, algebra, American government, American history, American history-AP, American literature, art, art history, art-AP, biology, biology-AP, British literature-AP, broadcast journalism, Buddhism, calculus, calculus-AP, career and personal planning, career education internship, cheerleading, chemistry, cinematography, college counseling, computer math, computer programming, computer programming-AP, computer science, computer science-AP, computer technology certification, digital photography, drama, earth science, economics, English, English language and composition-AP, English literature, environmental science-AP, European history, French, French language-AP, geography, geometry, government/civics, grammar, health, history, journalism, Latin, mathematics, music, music theater, physical education, physics, psychology, public speaking, publications, science, senior career experience, Shakespeare, social sciences, social studies, Spanish, Spanish language-AP, Spanish literature-AP, speech, statistics, theater, trigonometry, Western civilization, world history, world literature, writing, yearbook, yoga.

Graduation Requirements Arts and fine arts (art, music, dance, drama), computer science, electives, English, foreign language, mathematics, physical education (includes health), science, social studies (includes history), senior internship program.

Special Academic Programs 14 Advanced Placement exams for which test preparation is offered; honors section; independent study; study abroad.

College Admission Counseling 26 students graduated in 2016; all went to college, including Indiana University Bloomington; Rice University; Rose-Hulman Institute of Technology; Texas A&M University; The University of Texas at Austin; University of Southern California. Median SAT critical reading: 570, median SAT math: 615, median SAT writing: 553, median combined SAT: 1738, median composite ACT: 25.

Student Life Upper grades have specified standards of dress, student council, honor system. Discipline rests primarily with faculty.

Summer Programs Enrichment, sports, art/fine arts, computer instruction programs offered; session focuses on enrichment; held on campus; accepts boys and girls; open to students from other schools. 300 students usually enrolled. 2017 schedule: June 5 to August 4. Application deadline: May 15.

Tuition and Aid Day student tuition: $20,700. Tuition installment plan (monthly payment plans). Tuition reduction for siblings, need-based scholarship grants available. In 2016–17, 19% of upper-school students received aid.

Admissions Traditional secondary-level entrance grade is 9. ERB CTP IV, ISEE or Stanford Achievement Test required. Deadline for receipt of application materials: January 13. Application fee required: $100. On-campus interview required.

Athletics Interscholastic: baseball (boys), basketball (b,g), cheering (g), crew (b,g), cross-country running (b,g), football (b), golf (b,g), rock climbing (b,g), rowing (b,g), running (b,g), softball (g), strength & conditioning (b,g), swimming and diving (b,g), tennis (b,g), track and field (b,g), volleyball (g), weight training (b,g); coed interscholastic: soccer, swimming and diving, tennis; coed intramural: bowling. 3 PE instructors, 12 coaches, 1 athletic trainer.

Computers Computers are regularly used in all academic, art, college planning, creative writing, English, graphic design, journalism, mathematics, science, speech, Web site design, word processing, writing, yearbook classes. Computer network features include on-campus library services, online commercial services, Internet access, wireless campus network, Internet filtering or blocking technology. Student e-mail accounts and computer access in designated common areas are available to students. Students grades are available online. The school has a published electronic and media policy.

Contact Ms. Lisa Bracken, Director of Admission. 214-826-2931. Fax: 214-826-4623. E-mail: lbracken@lakehillprep.org. Website: www.lakehillprep.org

LAKELAND CHRISTIAN ACADEMY

1093 South 250 East

Winona Lake, Indiana 46590

Head of School: Mrs. Joy Lavender

General Information Coeducational day college-preparatory, arts, and religious studies school, affiliated with Christian faith; primarily serves students with learning disabilities and individuals with Attention Deficit Disorder. Grades 7–12. Founded: 1974. Setting: small town. Nearest major city is Fort Wayne. 40-acre campus. 1 building on campus. Approved or accredited by Association of Christian Schools International and North Central Association of Colleges and Schools. Endowment: $750,000. Total enrollment: 149. Upper school average class size: 102. Upper school faculty-student ratio: 1:14. There are 180 required school days per year for Upper School students. Upper School students typically attend 5 days per week. The average school day consists of 7 hours and 20 minutes.

Upper School Student Profile Grade 9: 22 students (12 boys, 10 girls); Grade 10: 30 students (16 boys, 14 girls); Grade 11: 34 students (21 boys, 13 girls); Grade 12: 16 students (10 boys, 6 girls). 100% of students are Christian.

Faculty School total: 15. In upper school: 3 men, 13 women; 7 have advanced degrees.

Subjects Offered ACT preparation, acting, advanced biology, advanced chemistry, advanced math, algebra, American government, American history, analysis and differential calculus, analytic geometry, anatomy, art, band, baseball, Basic programming, basketball, Bible, biology, calculus, career and personal planning, chemistry, choir, computer applications, computer education, consumer economics, consumer education, consumer mathematics, CPR, desktop publishing, economics, electives, English, English literature, food science, government, grammar, health education, history, human anatomy, human biology, keyboarding, mathematics, physical fitness, physics, poetry, pre-algebra, pre-calculus, psychology, Shakespeare, Spanish, speech, U.S. government, U.S. history, world geography.

Graduation Requirements Anatomy, anatomy and physiology, ancient world history, arts and fine arts (art, music, dance, drama), Basic programming, Bible, biochemistry, biology, calculus, character education, chemistry, civil war history, college planning, composition, constitutional law, consumer economics, desktop publishing, earth science, economics, electives, English, foreign language, geography, geometry, government, health, keyboarding, mathematics, physical education (includes health), physical science, physics, pre-algebra, pre-calculus, publications, religion (includes Bible studies and theology), science, Spanish, speech, U.S. government, U.S. history.

Special Academic Programs Honors section; accelerated programs; independent study; study at local college for college credit; academic accommodation for the gifted; remedial reading and/or remedial writing; remedial math; programs in general development for dyslexic students; special instructional classes for Joshua Class is for students who will not be earning an academic diploma. Adjusted academics and life skills.

College Admission Counseling 14 students graduated in 2016; 13 went to college, including Indiana University–Purdue University Fort Wayne; Indiana University Bloomington. Other: 1 went to work, 1 had other specific plans.

Student Life Upper grades have specified standards of dress, student council, honor system. Discipline rests primarily with faculty. Attendance at religious services is required.

Tuition and Aid Day student tuition: $7600. Tuition installment plan (monthly payment plans, individually arranged payment plans). Tuition reduction for siblings, need-based scholarship grants available. In 2016–17, 10% of upper-school students received aid. Total amount of financial aid awarded in 2016–17: $60,000.

Admissions Traditional secondary-level entrance grade is 9. For fall 2016, 25 students applied for upper-level admission, 24 were accepted, 24 enrolled. ACT, CTBS, Stanford Achievement Test, any other standardized test, latest standardized score from previous school, PSAT, PSAT and SAT for applicants to grade 11 and 12, SAT or Stanford Achievement Test required. Deadline for receipt of application materials: none. Application fee required: $75. On-campus interview recommended.

Athletics Interscholastic: basketball (boys, girls), cheering (g), soccer (b,g), softball (g), track and field (b,g), volleyball (g); intramural: basketball (b,g), physical training (b); coed interscholastic: baseball, soccer, track and field. 1 PE instructor, 12 coaches.

Computers Computers are regularly used in all academic classes. Computer network features include on-campus library services, online commercial services, Internet access, wireless campus network, Internet filtering or blocking technology. Campus intranet, student e-mail accounts, and computer access in designated common areas are available to students. Students grades are available online. The school has a published electronic and media policy.

Contact Joy Lavender, Administrator. 574-267-7265. Fax: 574-267-5687. E-mail: jlavender@lcacougars.com. Website: www.lcacougars.com

LAKE MARY PREPARATORY SCHOOL

650 Rantoul Lane

Lake Mary, Florida 32746

Head of School: Mr. Jack Delman

General Information Coeducational boarding and day and distance learning college-preparatory, arts, and technology school. Boarding grades 7–12, day grades PK–12.

Founded: 1999. Setting: suburban. Nearest major city is Orlando. Students are housed in coed dormitories. 48-acre campus. 1 building on campus. Approved or accredited by Florida Council of Independent Schools, Southern Association of Colleges and Schools, Southern Association of Independent Schools, and Florida Department of Education. Member of National Association of Independent Schools. Total enrollment: 550. Upper school average class size: 15. Upper school faculty-student ratio: 1:15. There are 180 required school days per year for Upper School students. Upper School students typically attend 5 days per week. The average school day consists of 7 hours and 30 minutes.

Upper School Student Profile Grade 6: 30 students (15 boys, 15 girls); Grade 7: 53 students (27 boys, 26 girls); Grade 8: 46 students (24 boys, 22 girls); Grade 9: 40 students (25 boys, 15 girls); Grade 10: 72 students (40 boys, 32 girls); Grade 11: 60 students (35 boys, 25 girls); Grade 12: 65 students (45 boys, 20 girls). 10% of students are boarding students. 83% are state residents. 5 states are represented in upper school student body. 10% are international students. International students from British Indian Ocean Territory, Christmas Island, Jamaica, Portugal, Turkmenistan, and Wallis and Futuna Islands; 10 other countries represented in student body.

Faculty School total: 62. In upper school: 18 men, 21 women; 13 have advanced degrees; 8 reside on campus.

Subjects Offered All academic.

Special Academic Programs Advanced Placement exam preparation; honors section; independent study; study abroad; academic accommodation for the gifted, the musically talented, and the artistically talented; ESL (48 students enrolled).

College Admission Counseling 64 students graduated in 2016; all went to college, including Florida State University; Stetson University; The University of Alabama at Birmingham; University of Central Florida; University of Florida; University of North Florida. Median SAT critical reading: 500, median SAT math: 550, median SAT writing: 500, median combined SAT: 1550, median composite ACT: 23.

Student Life Upper grades have uniform requirement, student council, honor system. Discipline rests primarily with faculty.

Summer Programs Remediation, enrichment, advancement programs offered; session focuses on enrichment activities; held on campus; accepts boys and girls; open to students from other schools. 250 students usually enrolled. 2017 schedule: June 1 to August 15. Application deadline: June 1.

Tuition and Aid Day student tuition: $15,200; 7-day tuition and room/board: $49,500. Tuition installment plan (monthly payment plans). Tuition reduction for siblings, merit scholarship grants, need-based scholarship grants available. In 2016–17, 10% of upper-school students received aid.

Admissions Traditional secondary-level entrance grade is 9. ERB (grade level), ISEE, Secondary Level English Proficiency or skills for ESL students required. Deadline for receipt of application materials: none. Application fee required: $100. On-campus interview recommended.

Athletics Interscholastic: aquatics (boys, girls), archery (b,g), baseball (b), basketball (b,g), bowling (b,g), cheering (g), cross-country running (b,g), dance (b,g), dance squad (b,g), dance team (b,g), diving (b,g), flag football (b,g), football (b), golf (b,g), lacrosse (b,g), power lifting (b,g), soccer (b,g), softball (g), swimming and diving (b,g), tennis (b,g), track and field (b,g), volleyball (g), weight lifting (b,g), winter soccer (b,g); intramural: flag football (b,g); coed intramural: yoga. 4 PE instructors, 25 coaches, 1 athletic trainer.

Computers Computers are regularly used in all academic classes. Computer network features include on-campus library services, Internet access, wireless campus network, Internet filtering or blocking technology. Campus intranet and student e-mail accounts are available to students. Students grades are available online. The school has a published electronic and media policy.

Contact Mrs. Angel Nguyen, Director of Admissions and Marketing. 407-805-0095 Ext. 207. Fax: 407-322-3872. E-mail: angel.nguyen@lakemaryprep.com. Website: www.lakemaryprep.com/podium/default.aspx?t=134873

LAKE RIDGE ACADEMY

37501 Center Ridge Road
North Ridgeville, Ohio 44039

Head of School: Mrs. Carol L. Klimas

General Information Coeducational day college-preparatory, arts, global citizenship, and scientific research school. Grades K–12. Founded: 1963. Setting: suburban. Nearest major city is Cleveland. 93-acre campus. 8 buildings on campus. Approved or accredited by Independent Schools Association of the Central States and Ohio Department of Education. Member of National Association of Independent Schools. Total enrollment: 339. Upper school average class size: 12. Upper school faculty-student ratio: 1:8. There are 172 required school days per year for Upper School students. Upper School students typically attend 5 days per week. The average school day consists of 6 hours.

Upper School Student Profile Grade 9: 41 students (20 boys, 21 girls); Grade 10: 34 students (18 boys, 16 girls); Grade 11: 55 students (23 boys, 32 girls); Grade 12: 40 students (15 boys, 25 girls).

Faculty School total: 60. In upper school: 15 men, 17 women; 24 have advanced degrees.

Subjects Offered Advanced Placement courses, advanced studio art-AP, African-American literature, engineering, English literature and composition-AP, interactive media.

Graduation Requirements Arts and fine arts (art, music, dance, drama), English, ethics, foreign language, mathematics, physical education (includes health), science, social studies (includes history), U.S. history.

Special Academic Programs Advanced Placement exam preparation; honors section; independent study; study at local college for college credit; academic accommodation for the gifted, the musically talented, and the artistically talented; programs in general development for dyslexic students; special instructional classes for deaf students; ESL (8 students enrolled).

College Admission Counseling 51 students graduated in 2016; all went to college, including American University; Miami University; Oberlin College; Smith College; The College of Wooster; University of Miami. Mean SAT critical reading: 580, mean SAT math: 630, mean SAT writing: 570, mean composite ACT: 26. 60% scored over 600 on SAT critical reading, 65% scored over 600 on SAT math, 40% scored over 600 on SAT writing, 50% scored over 1800 on combined SAT, 50% scored over 26 on composite ACT.

Student Life Upper grades have student council, honor system. Discipline rests primarily with faculty.

Summer Programs Remediation, enrichment, advancement, sports, art/fine arts, computer instruction programs offered; session focuses on academics, arts, athletics; held both on and off campus; accepts boys and girls; open to students from other schools. 180 students usually enrolled. 2017 schedule: June 5 to July 14. Application deadline: June 1.

Tuition and Aid Day student tuition: $24,420–$27,100. Tuition installment plan (The Tuition Plan, Insured Tuition Payment Plan, monthly payment plans, individually arranged payment plans). Tuition reduction for siblings, merit scholarship grants, need-based scholarship grants available.

Admissions Traditional secondary-level entrance grade is 9. For fall 2016, 72 students applied for upper-level admission, 47 were accepted, 27 enrolled. CTBS, OLSAT, essay, ISEE, mathematics proficiency exam, school's own exam, TOEFL or SLEP and writing sample required. Deadline for receipt of application materials: none. Application fee required: $45. Interview required.

Athletics Interscholastic: baseball (boys), basketball (b,g), cross-country running (b,g), golf (b,g), indoor track & field (b), soccer (b,g), tennis (b,g), track and field (b,g), volleyball (g), winter (indoor) track (b); intramural: indoor soccer (b,g), lacrosse (g), strength & conditioning (b,g); coed intramural: indoor soccer, outdoor adventure, outdoor recreation, physical fitness, physical training, strength & conditioning, ultimate Frisbee, weight lifting, weight training. 2 PE instructors, 12 coaches, 1 athletic trainer.

Computers Computers are regularly used in engineering, graphic arts, photography classes. Computer network features include on-campus library services, online commercial services, Internet access, wireless campus network, Internet filtering or blocking technology. Campus intranet, student e-mail accounts, and computer access in designated common areas are available to students. Students grades are available online. The school has a published electronic and media policy.

Contact Laura Coufalik, Admission Officer. 440-327-1175 Ext. 103. Fax: 440-327-3641. E-mail: admission@lakeridgeacademy.org. Website: www.lakeridgeacademy.org

LAKEVIEW ACADEMY

796 Lakeview Drive
Gainesville, Georgia 30501

Head of School: Dr. John Kennedy

General Information Coeducational day college-preparatory, arts, and technology school. Ungraded, ages 3–19. Distance learning grades K3–12. Founded: 1970. Setting: suburban. Nearest major city is Atlanta. 88-acre campus. 5 buildings on campus. Approved or accredited by Georgia Independent School Association, Southern Association of Colleges and Schools, and Southern Association of Independent Schools. Member of National Association of Independent Schools. Endowment: $1 million. Total enrollment: 598. Upper school average class size: 15. Upper school faculty-student ratio: 1:8. There are 175 required school days per year for Upper School students. Upper School students typically attend 5 days per week. The average school day consists of 8 hours.

Upper School Student Profile Grade 6: 35 students (21 boys, 14 girls); Grade 7: 47 students (26 boys, 21 girls); Grade 8: 47 students (29 boys, 18 girls); Grade 9: 61 students (33 boys, 28 girls); Grade 10: 57 students (25 boys, 32 girls); Grade 11: 56 students (28 boys, 28 girls); Grade 12: 63 students (39 boys, 24 girls).

Faculty School total: 119. In upper school: 15 men, 15 women; 16 have advanced degrees.

Subjects Offered 3-dimensional art, Advanced Placement courses, American history-AP, American literature-AP, art-AP, choir, college counseling, computer programming-AP, computer skills, digital photography, drama performance, dramatic arts, early childhood, English language-AP, English literature-AP, environmental science-AP, fitness, health, history of religion, honors U.S. history, musical productions, musical theater, physical fitness, Spanish-AP, statistics-AP, studio art, theater production, U.S. government, U.S. history, weight training, yoga.

Graduation Requirements Algebra, American literature, art, arts, biology, economics, government, U.S. government, U.S. history, world studies, 60 hours of community service.

Special Academic Programs 9 Advanced Placement exams for which test preparation is offered; honors section; independent study; study at local college for college credit; academic accommodation for the gifted, the musically talented, and the artistically talented; remedial reading and/or remedial writing; remedial math; programs in English, mathematics, general development for dyslexic students.

College Admission Counseling 53 students graduated in 2016; 52 went to college, including Clemson University; Georgia Institute of Technology; The University of Alabama; University of Georgia; University of Mississippi; University of North Georgia. Other: 1 entered military service. Median SAT critical reading: 535, median SAT math: 570, median SAT writing: 545, median combined SAT: 1660, median composite ACT: 25. 28% scored over 600 on SAT critical reading, 34% scored over 600 on SAT math, 24% scored over 600 on SAT writing, 24% scored over 1800 on combined SAT, 47% scored over 26 on composite ACT.

Student Life Upper grades have uniform requirement, student council, honor system. Discipline rests equally with students and faculty.

Summer Programs Enrichment, advancement, sports, art/fine arts, computer instruction programs offered; session focuses on instructional, fun summer activity camps; held on campus; accepts boys and girls; open to students from other schools. 350 students usually enrolled. 2017 schedule: June 5 to July 31. Application deadline: June 5.

Tuition and Aid Day student tuition: $8532–$16,560. Tuition installment plan (monthly payment plans, biannual payment plan). Tuition reduction for siblings, merit scholarship grants, need-based scholarship grants available.

Admissions Traditional secondary-level entrance grade is 9. For fall 2016, 24 students applied for upper-level admission, 21 were accepted, 21 enrolled. Deadline for receipt of application materials: none. Application fee required: $75. On-campus interview required.

Athletics Interscholastic: baseball (boys), basketball (b,g), cheering (g), football (b), soccer (b,g), tennis (b,g), volleyball (g); intramural: yoga (g); coed interscholastic: cross-country running, golf, riflery, skeet shooting, strength & conditioning, synchronized swimming, trap and skeet; coed intramural: aerobics/Nautilus, hiking/backpacking, physical fitness, physical training, synchronized swimming, weight training. 5 PE instructors, 5 coaches.

Computers Computers are regularly used in all classes. Computer network features include on-campus library services, Internet access, wireless campus network, Internet filtering or blocking technology, all Middle and Upper School students have a laptop computer equipped with wireless Internet access. Campus intranet and student e-mail accounts are available to students. Students grades are available online. The school has a published electronic and media policy.

Contact Mrs. kim Cottrell, Officer of Admission. 770-531-2602. Fax: 770-531-2647. E-mail: kim.cottrell@lakeviewacademy.org. Website: www.lakeviewacademy.com

LA LUMIERE SCHOOL

6801 North Wilhelm Road
La Porte, Indiana 46350

Head of School: Mr. Adam Kronk

General Information Coeducational boarding and day college-preparatory school, affiliated with Roman Catholic Church. Boarding grades 9–PG, day grades 9–12. Founded: 1963. Setting: rural. Nearest major city is Chicago, IL. Students are housed in single-sex dormitories. 190-acre campus. 22 buildings on campus. Approved or accredited by Midwest Association of Boarding Schools, North Central Association of Colleges and Schools, and The Association of Boarding Schools. Member of National Association of Independent Schools. Total enrollment: 230. Upper school average class size: 11. Upper school faculty-student ratio: 1:7. There are 174 required school days per year for Upper School students. Upper School students typically attend 5 days per week. The average school day consists of 7 hours and 30 minutes.

Upper School Student Profile Grade 9: 41 students (25 boys, 16 girls); Grade 10: 59 students (27 boys, 32 girls); Grade 11: 64 students (38 boys, 26 girls); Grade 12: 61 students (31 boys, 30 girls). 38% of students are boarding students. 8 states are represented in upper school student body. 25% are international students. International students from Australia, China, Czech Republic, Hong Kong, Mexico, and Viet Nam; 5 other countries represented in student body. 20% of students are Roman Catholic.

Faculty School total: 34. In upper school: 20 men, 14 women; 60 have advanced degrees; 28 reside on campus.

Subjects Offered Acting, advanced biology, advanced chemistry, advanced computer applications, Advanced Placement courses, algebra, American government, American history, American history-AP, American literature, anatomy and physiology, applied music, art, art history, band, Basic programming, Bible, Bible as literature, Bible studies, biochemistry, biology, biology-AP, British literature, calculus, chemistry, Chinese, choir, Christian and Hebrew scripture, Christian studies, college counseling, communications, comparative government and politics, comparative government and politics-AP, computer programming, computer programming-AP, conceptual physics, concert choir, contemporary issues, creative writing, current events, debate, desktop publishing, digital photography, drama, drama performance, drama workshop, economics, economics-AP, English, English as a foreign language, English

composition, English literature, English literature-AP, English-AP, entrepreneurship, environmental geography, environmental science, environmental science-AP, environmental studies, equality and freedom, equestrian sports, ESL, ethical decision making, ethics, ethics and responsibility, fine arts, finite math, fitness, foreign language, French, French as a second language, freshman seminar, geography, geometry, government, government and politics-AP, government-AP, government/civics, graphic design, health, health and safety, health and wellness, health education, Hebrew scripture, history, history-AP, human anatomy, human biology, independent study, instrumental music, international relations, introduction to literature, jazz band, jazz ensemble, language and composition, Latin, leadership, literature, literature-AP, marine biology, marine science, marine studies, moral reasoning, multicultural literature, music, music theory, New Testament, non-Western literature, oceanography, participation in sports, philosophy, photography, physics, physics-AP, physiology, portfolio art, pre-calculus, programming, psychology, psychology-AP, public speaking, SAT/ACT preparation, Spanish, Spanish literature, Spanish-AP, speech, speech and debate, sports, statistics, statistics-AP, studio art, study skills, theology, trigonometry, U.S. government, U.S. government and politics-AP, U.S. history, U.S. history-AP, U.S. literature, Web site design, world history, world literature, world religions, writing, writing, yearbook.

Graduation Requirements American government, American literature, arts and fine arts (art, music, dance, drama), Bible as literature, British literature, economics, electives, English, English composition, English literature, ethics, foreign language, health education, leadership, mathematics, science, social studies (includes history), U.S. history, world history.

Special Academic Programs Advanced Placement exam preparation; honors section; independent study; study at local college for college credit; academic accommodation for the gifted and the artistically talented; ESL (16 students enrolled).

College Admission Counseling 55 students graduated in 2016; all went to college, including Indiana University Bloomington; Loyola University Chicago; Marquette University; Purdue University; University of California, Los Angeles; University of Notre Dame. Mean SAT critical reading: 556, mean SAT math: 583, mean SAT writing: 549, mean combined SAT: 1689, mean composite ACT: 26. 50% scored over 26 on composite ACT.

Student Life Upper grades have uniform requirement, student council. Discipline rests primarily with faculty.

Summer Programs Enrichment, advancement, ESL, sports programs offered; session focuses on academics; held both on and off campus; accepts boys and girls; open to students from other schools.

Tuition and Aid Day student tuition: $14,550; 7-day tuition and room/board: $43,500. Tuition installment plan (FACTS Tuition Payment Plan, individually arranged payment plans). Merit scholarship grants, need-based scholarship grants available. In 2016–17, 27% of upper-school students received aid. Total amount of financial aid awarded in 2016–17: $988,830.

Admissions Traditional secondary-level entrance grade is 9. For fall 2016, 170 students applied for upper-level admission, 120 were accepted, 62 enrolled. SSAT or TOEFL required. Deadline for receipt of application materials: none. Application fee required: $50. Interview required.

Athletics Interscholastic: baseball (boys), basketball (b,g), cheering (b), crew (b,g), fitness (b,g), football (b), golf (b,g), independent competitive sports (b,g), lacrosse (b), soccer (b,g), track and field (b,g), volleyball (b); coed intramural: cross-country running. 10 coaches, 1 athletic trainer.

Computers Computers are regularly used in all academic, college planning, creative writing, programming, yearbook classes. Computer network features include on-campus library services, Internet access, wireless campus network, Internet filtering or blocking technology. Campus intranet, student e-mail accounts, and computer access in designated common areas are available to students. Students grades are available online. The school has a published electronic and media policy.

Contact Ms. Amanda M. Pietrzak, Advancement Associate. 219-326-7450. Fax: 219-325-3185. E-mail: apietrzak@lalumiere.org. Website: www.lalumiere.org

LANCASTER CATHOLIC HIGH SCHOOL

650 Juliette Avenue
Lancaster, Pennsylvania 17601

Head of School: Terry J. Klugh

General Information Coeducational day college-preparatory school, affiliated with Roman Catholic Church. Grades 9–12. Founded: 1929. Setting: small town. 1 building on campus. Approved or accredited by Middle States Association of Colleges and Schools, National Catholic Education Association, and Pennsylvania Department of Education. Total enrollment: 630. Upper school average class size: 25. There are 180 required school days per year for Upper School students. Upper School students typically attend 5 days per week. The average school day consists of 6 hours and 56 minutes.

Upper School Student Profile 85% of students are Roman Catholic.

Special Academic Programs Advanced Placement exam preparation; honors section; study at local college for college credit; academic accommodation for the gifted, the musically talented, and the artistically talented; remedial reading and/or remedial writing.

College Admission Counseling 146 students graduated in 2016.

Student Life Upper grades have uniform requirement, student council, honor system. Discipline rests primarily with faculty. Attendance at religious services is required.

Admissions Traditional secondary-level entrance grade is 9. No application fee required.

Athletics Interscholastic: aerobics/dance (girls), aquatics (b,g), ballet (g), baseball (b), basketball (b,g), bowling (b,g), cheering (g), cross-country running (b,g), dance (g), dance team (g), field hockey (g), flag football (g), football (b), golf (b), indoor track & field (b,g), lacrosse (b,g), modern dance (g), soccer (b,g), softball (g), swimming and diving (b,g), table tennis (b,g), tennis (b,g), track and field (b,g), volleyball (g), winter (indoor) track (b,g).

Computers Computer resources include Internet access, wireless campus network, Internet filtering or blocking technology. Students grades are available online. The school has a published electronic and media policy.

Contact Kyla Hockley, Admissions Counselor. 717-509-0313. Fax: 717-509-0312. E-mail: khockley@lchsyes.org. Website: www.lchsyes.org/

LANCASTER MENNONITE HIGH SCHOOL

2176 Lincoln Highway East

Lancaster, Pennsylvania 17602

Head of School: Mr. Elvin Kennel

General Information Coeducational boarding and day college-preparatory, general academic, arts, religious studies, and agriculture school, affiliated with Mennonite Church. Boarding grades 9–12, day grades 6–12. Founded: 1942. Setting: suburban. Nearest major city is Philadelphia. Students are housed in single-sex by floor dormitories and single-sex by wings. 100-acre campus. 10 buildings on campus. Approved or accredited by Mennonite Education Agency, Mennonite Schools Council, and Pennsylvania Department of Education. Endowment: $12 million. Total enrollment: 1,393. Upper school average class size: 18. Upper school faculty-student ratio: 1:15. There are 182 required school days per year for Upper School students. Upper School students typically attend 5 days per week. The average school day consists of 6 hours and 30 minutes.

Upper School Student Profile Grade 9: 126 students (59 boys, 67 girls); Grade 10: 144 students (63 boys, 81 girls); Grade 11: 152 students (72 boys, 80 girls); Grade 12: 170 students (93 boys, 77 girls). 8% of students are boarding students. 89% are state residents. 4 states are represented in upper school student body. 11% are international students. International students from China, Ethiopia, Hong Kong, Republic of Korea, Taiwan, and Viet Nam; 20 other countries represented in student body. 20% of students are Mennonite.

Faculty School total: 77. In upper school: 38 men, 37 women; 50 have advanced degrees; 6 reside on campus.

Subjects Offered 1 1/2 elective credits, 3-dimensional art, 3-dimensional design, accounting, advanced biology, advanced chemistry, advanced math, Advanced Placement courses, agriculture, American government, American history, American history-AP, art appreciation, athletics, band, baseball, basketball, bell choir, Bible, Bible as literature, Bible studies, biology, biology-AP, bowling, business, business mathematics, calculus, calculus-AP, career experience, career exploration, career/college preparation, chemistry, chemistry-AP, Chinese, choir, chorus, Christian doctrine, Christian education, Christian scripture, Christian studies, church history, communications, community service, comparative government and politics, comparative government and politics-AP, concert band, concert choir, creative writing, culinary arts, drama, drawing, driver education, ecology, electives, English, English composition, English language and composition-AP, entrepreneurship, environmental science, ESL, European history, family and consumer science, family living, family studies, fashion, foods, foreign language, French, German, guitar, health education, history, human development, instrumental music, jazz band, language arts, Life of Christ, literary magazine, literature-AP, music, music appreciation, music composition, music performance, music theory, music-AP, musical productions, newspaper, orchestra, painting, parent/child development, participation in sports, performing arts, photography, physical education, physics, physics-AP, psychology, psychology-AP, public speaking, science, senior project, small engine repair, sociology, softball, Spanish, Spanish language-AP, statistics, statistics-AP, strings, student government, student publications, tennis, track and field, U.S. history, U.S. history-AP, U.S. literature, visual and performing arts, visual arts, voice, volleyball, weight training, welding, wind ensemble, wind instruments, woodworking, world history, world history-AP, writing.

Graduation Requirements Creative arts, English, health education, mathematics, science, social studies (includes history), theology, a certain amount of credits are needed in various academic areas.

Special Academic Programs 13 Advanced Placement exams for which test preparation is offered; honors section; independent study; study at local college for college credit; academic accommodation for the musically talented; remedial reading and/or remedial writing; remedial math; special instructional classes for deaf students, blind students; ESL (40 students enrolled).

College Admission Counseling 170 students graduated in 2016; 127 went to college, including Drexel University; Eastern Mennonite University; Messiah College; Millersville University of Pennsylvania; Penn State University Park. Other: 29 went to work, 14 had other specific plans.

Student Life Upper grades have specified standards of dress, student council. Discipline rests primarily with faculty. Attendance at religious services is required.

Summer Programs Enrichment, sports, art/fine arts programs offered; held on campus; accepts boys and girls; open to students from other schools. 200 students usually enrolled. 2017 schedule: June to August. Application deadline: none.

Tuition and Aid Day student tuition: $8448; 5-day tuition and room/board: $15,008; 7-day tuition and room/board: $18,948. Tuition installment plan (monthly payment plans). Tuition reduction for siblings, merit scholarship grants, need-based scholarship grants, paying campus jobs available. In 2016–17, 40% of upper-school students received aid; total upper-school merit-scholarship money awarded: $20,000. Total amount of financial aid awarded in 2016–17: $3,000,000.

Admissions Traditional secondary-level entrance grade is 9. For fall 2016, 112 students applied for upper-level admission, 112 were accepted, 112 enrolled. Deadline for receipt of application materials: none. Application fee required: $100. Interview required.

Athletics Interscholastic: ball hockey (girls), baseball (b), basketball (b,g), cross-country running (b,g), field hockey (g), football (b), golf (b), lacrosse (b), soccer (b,g), softball (g), tennis (b,g), track and field (b,g), volleyball (b,g); coed interscholastic: baseball, bowling. 4 PE instructors, 20 coaches, 1 athletic trainer.

Computers Computers are regularly used in all academic classes. Computer network features include on-campus library services, Internet access, wireless campus network, Internet filtering or blocking technology. Campus intranet and student e-mail accounts are available to students. Students grades are available online. The school has a published electronic and media policy.

Contact Christy L. Horst, Director of Admissions. 717-509-4459 Ext. 312. Fax: 717-299-0823. E-mail: horstcl@lancastermennonite.org. Website: www.lancastermennonite.org

LANDMARK CHRISTIAN ACADEMY

6502 Johnsontown Road

Louisville, Kentucky 40272

Head of School: Mr. Monte L. Ashworth

General Information Coeducational day college-preparatory and religious studies school, affiliated with Baptist Church. Grades K4–12. Founded: 1978. Setting: suburban. 5-acre campus. 1 building on campus. Approved or accredited by American Association of Christian Schools. Total enrollment: 144. Upper school average class size: 8. Upper school faculty-student ratio: 1:6. There are 177 required school days per year for Upper School students. Upper School students typically attend 5 days per week. The average school day consists of 6 hours and 50 minutes.

Upper School Student Profile Grade 9: 5 students (4 boys, 1 girl); Grade 10: 11 students (7 boys, 4 girls); Grade 11: 5 students (1 boy, 4 girls); Grade 12: 5 students (2 boys, 3 girls). 80% of students are Baptist.

Faculty School total: 16. In upper school: 5 men, 4 women; 2 have advanced degrees.

Subjects Offered Advanced math, algebra, American history, American literature, analytic geometry, ancient history, ancient world history, Bible, biology, business mathematics, chemistry, choir, computer technologies, consumer economics, consumer mathematics, economics, English composition, English literature, general science, geography, geometry, grammar, health, history, home economics, keyboarding, modern history, physical education, physics, pre-algebra, pre-calculus, speech, trigonometry, world geography, world history.

Graduation Requirements Bible, computers, English, foreign language, history, mathematics, science, social sciences.

College Admission Counseling 10 students graduated in 2015; 8 went to college, including Indiana University Bloomington; Jefferson Community and Technical College; University of Louisville. Other: 1 went to work, 1 had other specific plans. Mean composite ACT: 22.

Student Life Upper grades have uniform requirement. Discipline rests primarily with faculty.

Tuition and Aid Day student tuition: $3500. Tuition installment plan (FACTS Tuition Payment Plan). Tuition reduction for siblings available.

Admissions Traditional secondary-level entrance grade is 9. For fall 2015, 3 students applied for upper-level admission, 3 were accepted, 3 enrolled. Math and English placement tests required. Deadline for receipt of application materials: none. Application fee required: $275. On-campus interview required.

Athletics Interscholastic: basketball (boys), soccer (b), track and field (b,g), volleyball (g). 1 PE instructor, 3 coaches.

Computers Computers are regularly used in computer applications, keyboarding, Spanish classes. The school has a published electronic and media policy.

Contact Mrs. Gloria G. Hope, School Secretary. 502-933-3000 Ext. 2. Fax: 502-933-5179. E-mail: LCAinfo@libcky.com. Website: www.lcaky.com/main.html

LANDMARK CHRISTIAN SCHOOL

50 SE Broad Street
Fairburn, Georgia 30213

Head of School: Mr. Mike Titus

General Information Coeducational day college-preparatory school, affiliated with Christian faith, Christian faith. Grades K4–12. Founded: 1989. Setting: suburban. Nearest major city is Atlanta. 62-acre campus. 4 buildings on campus. Approved or accredited by Association of Christian Schools International, Southern Association of Colleges and Schools, and Georgia Department of Education. Total enrollment: 807. Upper school average class size: 16. Upper school faculty-student ratio: 1:12. There are 177 required school days per year for Upper School students. Upper School students typically attend 5 days per week. The average school day consists of 7 hours and 15 minutes.

Upper School Student Profile Grade 9: 66 students (25 boys, 41 girls); Grade 10: 81 students (43 boys, 38 girls); Grade 11: 65 students (37 boys, 28 girls); Grade 12: 65 students (31 boys, 34 girls). 100% of students are Christian faith, Christian faith.

Faculty School total: 85. In upper school: 15 men, 34 women; 12 have advanced degrees.

Subjects Offered Advanced biology, advanced chemistry, advanced math, Advanced Placement courses, advanced studio art-AP, algebra, American government, American history, American literature-AP, anatomy and physiology, art, art-AP, athletic training, band, baseball, basketball, Bible, Bible studies, biology, biology-AP, British literature-AP, calculus, calculus-AP, chamber groups, cheerleading, chemistry, chemistry-AP, choral music, chorus, Christian studies, communications, composition, computer literacy, computer skills, computer technologies, computers, concert band, concert choir, drama, drama performance, economics, electives, English, English language and composition-AP, English literature, English literature-AP, English-AP, fine arts, foreign language, forensics, geometry, golf, government/civics-AP, health, health and wellness, history, history-AP, honors algebra, honors English, honors geometry, honors U.S. history, human anatomy, human biology, instrumental music, keyboarding, leadership education training, marine biology, music, music appreciation, music theater, physics, physics-AP, physiology, pre-calculus, social studies, Spanish, Spanish language-AP, Spanish-AP, speech, sports medicine, statistics, swimming, tennis, theater arts, U.S. history, U.S. history-AP, vocal ensemble, volleyball, weight training, writing, yearbook.

Graduation Requirements American government, American history, American literature, arts and fine arts (art, music, dance, drama), Bible, biology, British literature, chemistry, economics, electives, foreign language, geometry, language and composition, personal fitness, physical education (includes health), pre-calculus, world history, world literature, Bible.

Special Academic Programs 9 Advanced Placement exams for which test preparation is offered; honors section; study at local college for college credit.

College Admission Counseling 61 students graduated in 2016; all went to college, including Auburn University; Georgia Institute of Technology; Mercer University; Samford University; University of Georgia. Median SAT critical reading: 540, median SAT math: 540, median SAT writing: 540, median combined SAT: 1620, median composite ACT: 24. 27% scored over 600 on SAT critical reading, 26% scored over 600 on SAT math, 26% scored over 600 on SAT writing, 25% scored over 1800 on combined SAT, 35% scored over 26 on composite ACT.

Student Life Upper grades have specified standards of dress, student council, honor system. Discipline rests primarily with faculty. Attendance at religious services is required.

Summer Programs Remediation, enrichment, sports, art/fine arts, computer instruction programs offered; held on campus; accepts boys and girls; not open to students from other schools. 60 students usually enrolled. 2017 schedule: June to August.

Tuition and Aid Day student tuition: $4900–$15,375. Tuition installment plan (monthly payment plans). Need-based scholarship grants, Georgia Goal available. In 2016–17, 20% of upper-school students received aid.

Admissions Traditional secondary-level entrance grade is 9. For fall 2016, 50 students applied for upper-level admission, 25 were accepted, 18 enrolled. School placement exam required. Deadline for receipt of application materials: February 13. Application fee required: $200. On-campus interview recommended.

Athletics Interscholastic: baseball (boys), basketball (b,g), cheering (g), cross-country running (b,g), football (b), golf (b,g), physical training (b,g), soccer (b,g), softball (g), strength & conditioning (b,g), swimming and diving (b,g), tennis (b,g), track and field (b,g), volleyball (g), weight lifting (b,g), wrestling (b); coed intramural: yoga. 5 PE instructors, 49 coaches, 2 athletic trainers.

Computers Computers are regularly used in all academic, art, basic skills, Bible studies, career technology, college planning, computer applications, creative writing, current events, data processing, design, digital applications, engineering, English, foreign language, French, geography, graphic arts, graphic design, history, information technology, introduction to technology, journalism, keyboarding, lab/keyboard, library, library science, life skills, mathematics, media services, multimedia, news writing, newspaper, photography, photojournalism, publications, reading, religion, science, social studies, Spanish, technology, typing, word processing, writing, writing, yearbook classes. Computer network features include on-campus library services, Internet access, wireless campus network, Internet filtering or blocking technology, class assignments available online. Computer access in designated common areas is available to students.

Students grades are available online. The school has a published electronic and media policy.

Contact Mrs. Renee Chastain, Assistant to the Director of Admission. 770-692-6753. Fax: 770-969-6551. E-mail: admissions@landmark-cs.org. Website: www.landmarkchristianschool.org

LANDMARK EAST SCHOOL

Wolfville, Nova Scotia, Canada
See Special Needs Schools section.

LANDMARK SCHOOL

Prides Crossing, Massachusetts
See Special Needs Schools section.

LANDON SCHOOL

6101 Wilson Lane
Bethesda, Maryland 20817

Head of School: Mr. Jim Neill

General Information Boys' day college-preparatory, arts, technology, and music school. Grades 3–12. Founded: 1929. Setting: suburban. Nearest major city is Washington, DC. 75-acre campus. 13 buildings on campus. Approved or accredited by Association of Independent Maryland Schools, Middle States Association of Colleges and Schools, and Maryland Department of Education. Member of National Association of Independent Schools. Endowment: $10.5 million. Total enrollment: 681. Upper school average class size: 12. Upper school faculty-student ratio: 1:6. There are 170 required school days per year for Upper School students. Upper School students typically attend 5 days per week. The average school day consists of 7 hours and 10 minutes.

Upper School Student Profile Grade 9: 99 students (99 boys); Grade 10: 76 students (76 boys); Grade 11: 78 students (78 boys); Grade 12: 87 students (87 boys).

Faculty School total: 108. In upper school: 42 men, 12 women; 35 have advanced degrees.

Subjects Offered Acting, algebra, American Civil War, American foreign policy, American history, American literature, American studies, art, art history-AP, biology, biology-AP, calculus, calculus-AP, ceramics, chemistry, chemistry-AP, Chinese, Chinese history, classics, computer science, computer science-AP, conceptual physics, constitutional law, creative writing, digital art, drama, drawing, earth science, economics-AP, engineering, English, English literature, environmental science-AP, environmental studies, ethics, European history, expository writing, fine arts, foreign policy, forensics, French, French language-AP, French literature-AP, French studies, freshman foundations, geography, geology, geometry, government/civics, grammar, handbells, health, history, humanities, international relations, jazz band, journalism, justice seminar, Latin, mathematics, meteorology, Middle Eastern history, music, music history, music theory, music theory-AP, oceanography, painting, performing arts, photography, photojournalism, physical education, physics, physics-AP, pre-calculus, science, sculpture, senior project, Shakespeare, social studies, Spanish, Spanish language-AP, Spanish literature, statistics-AP, strings, technological applications, theater, trigonometry, typing, U.S. history, U.S. history-AP, world history, world literature, writing.

Graduation Requirements American Civil War, American government, arts and fine arts (art, music, dance, drama), biology, chemistry, English, ethics, foreign language, government, humanities, mathematics, music, physical education (includes health), pre-calculus, science, social studies (includes history), Independent Senior Project, 2-year arts requirement.

Special Academic Programs Advanced Placement exam preparation; honors section; independent study; term-away projects; study abroad.

College Admission Counseling 73 students graduated in 2016; all went to college, including Boston College; Bucknell University; Davidson College; University of Maryland, College Park; University of Virginia; Washington and Lee University. Mean SAT critical reading: 627, mean SAT math: 664, mean SAT writing: 622, mean combined SAT: 1913, mean composite ACT: 28.

Student Life Upper grades have specified standards of dress, student council, honor system. Discipline rests equally with students and faculty.

Summer Programs Remediation, enrichment, advancement, sports, art/fine arts, computer instruction programs offered; session focuses on enrichment, music, studio arts for middle and upper grades; advancement, remediation, travel for upper grades; held both on and off campus; accepts boys and girls; open to students from other schools. 200 students usually enrolled. 2017 schedule: June 12 to August 25. Application deadline: none.

Tuition and Aid Day student tuition: $36,430–$38,500. Tuition installment plan (FACTS Tuition Payment Plan, monthly payment plans). Need-based scholarship grants, 50% tuition remission for children of faculty available. In 2016–17, 25% of upper-school students received aid. Total amount of financial aid awarded in 2016–17: $3,723,217.

Admissions Traditional secondary-level entrance grade is 9. ISEE or SSAT required. Deadline for receipt of application materials: January 13. Application fee required: $75. On-campus interview required.

Athletics Interscholastic: baseball, basketball, cross-country running, diving, fencing, football, golf, ice hockey, lacrosse, riflery, rugby, soccer, squash, strength & conditioning, swimming and diving, tennis, track and field, ultimate Frisbee, water polo, winter (indoor) track, wrestling; intramural: basketball, Frisbee, physical fitness, physical training, sailing, strength & conditioning, tennis, ultimate Frisbee, weight training. 13 coaches, 2 athletic trainers.

Computers Computers are regularly used in art, computer applications, photojournalism, technology classes. Computer network features include on-campus library services, online commercial services, Internet access, wireless campus network, Internet filtering or blocking technology, password-accessed Web portals. Campus intranet, student e-mail accounts, and computer access in designated common areas are available to students. Students grades are available online. The school has a published electronic and media policy.

Contact Mr. Len Armstrong Jr., Assistant Head of School for Enrollment, Admissions and Community. 301-320-1069. Fax: 301-320-1133. E-mail: len_armstrong@landon.net. Website: www.landon.net

LANSDALE CATHOLIC HIGH SCHOOL

700 Lansdale Avenue
Lansdale, Pennsylvania 19446-2995

Head of School: Mrs. Rita McGovern

General Information Coeducational day and distance learning college-preparatory and general academic school, affiliated with Roman Catholic Church. Grades 9–12. Distance learning grades 9–12. Founded: 1949. Setting: suburban. Nearest major city is Philadelphia. 33-acre campus. 1 building on campus. Approved or accredited by Middle States Association of Colleges and Schools, National Catholic Education Association, and Pennsylvania Department of Education. Total enrollment: 703. Upper school average class size: 30. Upper school faculty-student ratio: 1:21. There are 190 required school days per year for Upper School students. Upper School students typically attend 5 days per week. The average school day consists of 6 hours and 45 minutes.

Upper School Student Profile Grade 9: 175 students (92 boys, 83 girls); Grade 10: 177 students (78 boys, 99 girls); Grade 11: 191 students (96 boys, 95 girls); Grade 12: 181 students (85 boys, 96 girls). 91% of students are Roman Catholic.

Faculty School total: 36. In upper school: 12 men, 23 women; 17 have advanced degrees.

Subjects Offered Algebra, American government, American history, American history-AP, American literature, art, art history-AP, art-AP, band, biology-AP, business law, calculus, calculus-AP, career education, career planning, career/college preparation, Catholic belief and practice, chemistry, Chinese, choir, chorus, church history, college counseling, college placement, college planning, composition-AP, computer education, computer programming, drama, English language and composition-AP, English literature and composition-AP, English literature-AP, English/composition-AP, environmental science, European history, European history-AP, French, government-AP, health education, Italian, Latin, mathematics-AP, physical fitness, physical science, physics, pre-calculus, SAT/ACT preparation, Spanish, statistics, statistics-AP, student government, studio art, studio art-AP, The 20th Century, trigonometry, U.S. government and politics, U.S. government and politics-AP, U.S. history, U.S. history-AP, United States government-AP, Western civilization.

Graduation Requirements 30 hour service requirement by the middle of junior year.

Special Academic Programs 17 Advanced Placement exams for which test preparation is offered; honors section; study at local college for college credit; remedial reading and/or remedial writing; remedial math.

College Admission Counseling 184 students graduated in 2016; 182 went to college, including La Salle University; Penn State University Park; Saint Joseph's University; Temple University; West Chester University of Pennsylvania. Other: 1 went to work, 1 entered military service. Mean SAT critical reading: 512, mean SAT math: 540, mean SAT writing: 510.

Student Life Upper grades have uniform requirement, student council, honor system. Discipline rests primarily with faculty. Attendance at religious services is required.

Summer Programs Remediation, enrichment, advancement, sports, art/fine arts programs offered; held on campus; accepts boys and girls; open to students from other schools. 100 students usually enrolled. 2017 schedule: June 19 to August 1. Application deadline: June 19.

Tuition and Aid Day student tuition: $7800. Tuition installment plan (SMART Tuition Payment Plan). Tuition reduction for siblings, merit scholarship grants, need-based scholarship grants, TAP Program available. In 2016–17, 20% of upper-school students received aid; total upper-school merit-scholarship money awarded: $70,000. Total amount of financial aid awarded in 2016–17: $125,000.

Admissions Traditional secondary-level entrance grade is 9. Deadline for receipt of application materials: none. Application fee required: $150. Interview recommended.

Athletics Interscholastic: baseball (boys), basketball (b,g), cheering (g), cross-country running (b,g), dance squad (b,g), field hockey (g), football (b), golf (b,g), ice hockey (b,g), lacrosse (b,g), soccer (b,g), softball (g), swimming and diving (b,g), tennis (b,g), track and field (b,g), volleyball (g), winter (indoor) track (b,g); intramural: flag football

(b), ice hockey (b,g); coed interscholastic: diving, indoor track, indoor track & field; coed intramural: yoga. 1 PE instructor, 1 athletic trainer.

Computers Computers are regularly used in all classes. Computer network features include on-campus library services, online commercial services, Internet access, wireless campus network, Internet filtering or blocking technology. Computer access in designated common areas is available to students. Students grades are available online. The school has a published electronic and media policy.

Contact Mr. James Casey, President. 215-362-6160 Ext. 133. Fax: 215-362-5746. E-mail: jcasey@lansdalecatholic.com. Website: www.lansdalecatholic.com

LA PIETRA–HAWAII SCHOOL FOR GIRLS

2933 Poni Moi Road
Honolulu, Hawaii 96815

Head of School: Mrs. Mahina Eleneki Hugo

General Information Girls' day college-preparatory school. Grades 6–12. Founded: 1962. Setting: suburban. 6-acre campus. 15 buildings on campus. Approved or accredited by Western Association of Schools and Colleges. Member of National Association of Independent Schools and Secondary School Admission Test Board. Total enrollment: 247. Upper school average class size: 7. Upper school faculty-student ratio: 1:7. There are 285 required school days per year for Upper School students. Upper School students typically attend 5 days per week. The average school day consists of 6 hours.

Upper School Student Profile Grade 9: 28 students (28 girls); Grade 10: 34 students (34 girls); Grade 11: 18 students (18 girls); Grade 12: 29 students (29 girls).

Faculty School total: 25. In upper school: 4 men, 19 women; 13 have advanced degrees.

Subjects Offered Advanced Placement courses, algebra, American history, American literature, art, art history, biology, calculus, ceramics, chemistry, creative writing, drama, earth science, ecology, English, English literature, ethics, ethics and responsibility, European history, expository writing, fine arts, French, geography, geometry, grammar, health, history, mathematics, music, photography, physical education, physics, physiology, psychology, science, social studies, Spanish, theater, trigonometry, world history, writing.

Graduation Requirements American government, arts and fine arts (art, music, dance, drama), English, foreign language, mathematics, physical education (includes health), science, social studies (includes history), independent project.

Special Academic Programs Advanced Placement exam preparation; honors section; independent study; remedial reading and/or remedial writing; remedial math.

College Admission Counseling 21 students graduated in 2016; all went to college, including University of Hawaii at Manoa.

Student Life Upper grades have uniform requirement, student council, honor system. Discipline rests primarily with faculty.

Tuition and Aid Day student tuition: $18,900. Tuition installment plan (monthly payment plans, individually arranged payment plans, tuition insurance). Need-based scholarship grants available. In 2016–17, 50% of upper-school students received aid. Total amount of financial aid awarded in 2016–17: $406,000.

Admissions Traditional secondary-level entrance grade is 9. SSAT required. Deadline for receipt of application materials: none. Application fee required: $50. Interview recommended.

Athletics Interscholastic: basketball, bowling, canoeing/kayaking, cheering, cross-country running, diving, equestrian sports, golf, gymnastics, judo, kayaking, ocean paddling, paddling, riflery, sailing, soccer, softball, swimming and diving, synchronized swimming, tennis, track and field, volleyball, water polo, wrestling. 2 PE instructors.

Computers Computers are regularly used in all academic, art classes. Computer network features include on-campus library services, online commercial services, Internet access, wireless campus network, Internet filtering or blocking technology. Student e-mail accounts are available to students. Students grades are available online. The school has a published electronic and media policy.

Contact Mrs. Megan Meyer, Director of Admissions. 808-922-2744. Fax: 808-923-4514. E-mail: mmeyer@lapietra.edu. Website: www.lapietra.edu

LA SALLE ACADEMY

612 Academy Avenue
Providence, Rhode Island 02908

Head of School: Br. Thomas Gerrow, FSC

General Information Coeducational day college-preparatory school, affiliated with Christian Churches and Churches of Christ. Grades 6–12. Founded: 1871. Setting: urban. 40-acre campus. 5 buildings on campus. Approved or accredited by New England Association of Schools and Colleges. Member of National Association of Independent Schools. Total enrollment: 1,462. Upper school average class size: 20. Upper school faculty-student ratio: 1:11. There are 185 required school days per year for Upper School students. Upper School students typically attend 5 days per week. The average school day consists of 6 hours and 30 minutes.

Upper School Student Profile 76% of students are Christian Churches and Churches of Christ.

Faculty School total: 142. In upper school: 81 men, 58 women; 119 have advanced degrees.

Subjects Offered Algebra, American history, American literature, anatomy, art, astronomy, biology, business, calculus, ceramics, chemistry, community service, computer programming, computer science, creative writing, dance, drama, drawing, economics, electronics, engineering, English, English literature, environmental science, ESL, film, fine arts, French, geology, geometry, history, Italian, journalism, law, mathematics, microbiology, music, painting, photography, physical education, physical science, physics, physiology, psychology, religion, science, social studies, sociology, Spanish, statistics, theater, trigonometry, world history, world literature, writing.

Graduation Requirements Arts and fine arts (art, music, dance, drama), computer science, English, foreign language, mathematics, physical education (includes health), religion (includes Bible studies and theology), science, social studies (includes history). Community service is required.

Special Academic Programs Advanced Placement exam preparation; honors section; study at local college for college credit; academic accommodation for the gifted, the musically talented, and the artistically talented.

College Admission Counseling 334 students graduated in 2016; 331 went to college, including Boston College; Brown University; Harvard University; United States Military Academy; University of Rhode Island; Yale University. Other: 2 went to work, 1 entered military service.

Student Life Upper grades have uniform requirement, student council, honor system. Discipline rests equally with students and faculty.

Summer Programs Enrichment, sports, art/fine arts, computer instruction programs offered; held on campus; accepts boys and girls; open to students from other schools. 80 students usually enrolled.

Tuition and Aid Day student tuition: $14,100. Tuition installment plan (FACTS Tuition Payment Plan). Merit scholarship grants, need-based scholarship grants available. In 2016–17, 37% of upper-school students received aid; total upper-school merit-scholarship money awarded: $600,000. Total amount of financial aid awarded in 2016–17: $2,200,000.

Admissions Traditional secondary-level entrance grade is 9. For fall 2016, 850 students applied for upper-level admission, 400 were accepted, 350 enrolled. STS and STS, Diocese Test required. Deadline for receipt of application materials: December 31. Application fee required: $50.

Athletics Interscholastic: baseball (boys), basketball (b,g), cross-country running (b,g), field hockey (g), football (b), golf (b,g), gymnastics (b,g), ice hockey (b,g), lacrosse (b,g), sailing (b,g), soccer (b,g), softball (g), swimming and diving (b,g), tennis (b,g), track and field (b,g), volleyball (b,g), wrestling (b,g); coed intramural: fencing, modern dance, physical fitness, physical training, table tennis, touch football, volleyball, walking, whiffle ball. 5 PE instructors, 61 coaches, 4 athletic trainers.

Computers Computers are regularly used in English, foreign language, history, mathematics, music, science classes. Computer network features include on-campus library services, online commercial services, Internet access. Student e-mail accounts are available to students. Students grades are available online. The school has a published electronic and media policy.

Contact Mr. George Aldrich, Director of Admissions and Public Relations. 401-351-7750 Ext. 122. Fax: 401-444-1782. E-mail: galdrich@lasalle-academy.org. Website: www.lasalle-academy.org

LA SALLE HIGH SCHOOL

3880 East Sierra Madre Boulevard
Pasadena, California 91107-1996

Head of School: Mrs. Courtney Kassakhian

General Information Coeducational day college-preparatory and arts school, affiliated with Roman Catholic Church. Grades 9–12. Founded: 1956. Setting: suburban. Nearest major city is Los Angeles. 10-acre campus. 3 buildings on campus. Approved or accredited by Western Association of Schools and Colleges, Western Catholic Education Association, and California Department of Education. Member of National Association of Independent Schools. Total enrollment: 650. Upper school average class size: 24. Upper school faculty-student ratio: 1:11. There are 180 required school days per year for Upper School students. Upper School students typically attend 5 days per week. The average school day consists of 6 hours and 30 minutes.

Upper School Student Profile Grade 9: 173 students (88 boys, 85 girls); Grade 10: 169 students (87 boys, 82 girls); Grade 11: 153 students (90 boys, 63 girls); Grade 12: 157 students (89 boys, 68 girls). 63% of students are Roman Catholic.

Faculty School total: 65. In upper school: 37 men, 28 women; 50 have advanced degrees.

Subjects Offered Education.

Graduation Requirements Algebra, American literature, biology, Christian doctrine, civics, English composition, geometry, integrated mathematics, macroeconomics-AP, religious studies, U.S. history.

Special Academic Programs 15 Advanced Placement exams for which test preparation is offered; honors section.

College Admission Counseling 160 students graduated in 2016; all went to college, including California State University, Northridge; Saint Mary's College of California; University of California, Berkeley; University of California, Los Angeles; University of Colorado Boulder; University of Southern California. Median SAT

critical reading: 550, median SAT math: 570, median SAT writing: 540, median combined SAT: 1660, median composite ACT: 24. 33% scored over 600 on SAT critical reading, 31% scored over 600 on SAT math, 37% scored over 600 on SAT writing, 32% scored over 1800 on combined SAT, 31% scored over 26 on composite ACT.

Student Life Upper grades have uniform requirement, student council, honor system. Discipline rests primarily with faculty. Attendance at religious services is required.

Summer Programs Remediation, enrichment, advancement, sports, art/fine arts, computer instruction programs offered; session focuses on academics and sports camps; held on campus; accepts boys and girls; open to students from other schools. 475 students usually enrolled. 2017 schedule: June 19 to July 20. Application deadline: June 2.

Tuition and Aid Day student tuition: $18,780. Tuition installment plan (monthly payment plans, annual and biannual; ACH Payments recommended). Merit scholarship grants, need-based scholarship grants, San Miguel Program for exceptional Catholic students under the poverty level available. In 2016–17, 38% of upper-school students received aid; total upper-school merit-scholarship money awarded: $350,500. Total amount of financial aid awarded in 2016–17: $2,100,250.

Admissions Traditional secondary-level entrance grade is 9. For fall 2016, 414 students applied for upper-level admission, 335 were accepted, 172 enrolled. High School Placement Test required. Deadline for receipt of application materials: January 13. Application fee required: $85. On-campus interview recommended.

Athletics Interscholastic: aerobics/dance (boys, girls), baseball (b), basketball (b,g), cross-country running (b,g), dance team (g), equestrian sports (g), football (b), golf (b,g), soccer (b,g), softball (g), swimming and diving (b,g), tennis (b,g), track and field (b,g), volleyball (b,g), water polo (b,g), weight lifting (b); intramural: basketball (b,g), dance team (g), flag football (b), touch football (b); coed interscholastic: aerobics/dance, cheering, physical fitness, weight training; coed intramural: dance, fitness, Frisbee, physical fitness, weight training. 4 PE instructors, 68 coaches, 2 athletic trainers.

Computers Computers are regularly used in all classes. Computer network features include on-campus library services, Internet access, wireless campus network, Internet filtering or blocking technology. Campus intranet and student e-mail accounts are available to students. Students grades are available online. The school has a published electronic and media policy.

Contact Mr. Nathan Housman, Assistant Director of Admissions. 626-696-4365. Fax: 626-696-4411. E-mail: nhousman@lasallehs.org. Website: www.lasallehs.org

LA SALLE INSTITUTE

174 Williams Road
Troy, New York 12180

Head of School: Dr. Paul D. Fallon

General Information Boys' day college-preparatory, religious studies, technology, and military school, affiliated with Roman Catholic Church. Grades 6–12. Founded: 1850. Setting: suburban. Nearest major city is Albany. 25-acre campus. 1 building on campus. Approved or accredited by Christian Brothers Association, Middle States Association of Colleges and Schools, and New York Department of Education. Endowment: $2 million. Total enrollment: 440. Upper school average class size: 15. Upper school faculty-student ratio: 1:10. The average school day consists of 6 hours and 30 minutes.

Upper School Student Profile Grade 9: 80 students (80 boys); Grade 10: 75 students (75 boys); Grade 11: 73 students (73 boys); Grade 12: 72 students (72 boys). 65% of students are Roman Catholic.

Faculty School total: 47. In upper school: 29 men, 17 women; 25 have advanced degrees.

Subjects Offered Advanced chemistry, advanced math, algebra, American history, American literature, anatomy, art, band, biology, biology-AP, business, calculus, campus ministry, career education, Catholic belief and practice, chemistry, chorus, college counseling, computer programming, computer resources, computer science, computer skills, computer studies, concert band, drama, driver education, earth science, economics, economics and history, English, English literature, English literature and composition-AP, environmental studies, European history, fine arts, French, French language-AP, geometry, government and politics-AP, government/civics, grammar, health education, history, jazz band, JROTC or LEAD (Leadership Education and Development), logic, mathematics, mathematics-AP, military science, music, philosophy, physical education, physics, physiology, pre-calculus, public speaking, religion, science, social studies, Spanish, Spanish-AP, theater, trigonometry, typing, U.S. government and politics-AP, U.S. history-AP, world history, world literature, writing.

Graduation Requirements Successfully pass all senior subjects and take SAT/ACT, annual service requirement.

Special Academic Programs Advanced Placement exam preparation; honors section; study at local college for college credit; academic accommodation for the musically talented; remedial reading and/or remedial writing; remedial math; programs in English, mathematics, general development for dyslexic students; special instructional classes for deaf students, blind students; ESL (14 students enrolled).

College Admission Counseling 70 students graduated in 2016; 68 went to college, including American International College; Buffalo State College, State University of New York; Manhattan College; Rensselaer Polytechnic Institute; Saint Anselm College;

Siena College. Other: 2 entered military service. Mean SAT critical reading: 560, mean SAT math: 570, mean SAT writing: 540, mean combined SAT: 1670, mean composite ACT: 25.

Student Life Upper grades have uniform requirement, student council, honor system. Discipline rests primarily with faculty. Attendance at religious services is required.

Tuition and Aid Tuition installment plan (FACTS Tuition Payment Plan, monthly payment plans, 3-payment plan). Tuition reduction for siblings, merit scholarship grants, need-based scholarship grants, paying campus jobs available. In 2016–17, 70% of upper-school students received aid.

Admissions Traditional secondary-level entrance grade is 9. Essay and placement test required. Deadline for receipt of application materials: none. No application fee required. On-campus interview required.

Athletics Interscholastic: alpine skiing, baseball, basketball, bowling, cross-country running, drill team, football, golf, ice hockey, indoor track, indoor track & field, JROTC drill, lacrosse, soccer, tennis, track and field, winter (indoor) track, wrestling; intramural: basketball, flag football, paint ball, skiing (downhill), snowboarding, strength & conditioning, table tennis, weight lifting. 3 PE instructors, 1 athletic trainer.

Computers Computers are regularly used in accounting, career technology, college planning, economics, English, graphic design, introduction to technology, journalism, keyboarding, library, literary magazine, mathematics, media production, newspaper, publications, SAT preparation, science, typing, yearbook classes. Computer network features include on-campus library services, online commercial services, Internet access. The school has a published electronic and media policy.

Contact Mr. Shane T. Hendry, Admissions Coordinator. 518-283-2500 Ext. 263. Fax: 518-283-6265. E-mail: shendry@lasalleinstitute.org. Website: www.lasalleinstitute.org

LA SIERRA ACADEMY

4900 Golden Avenue
Riverside, California 92505

Head of School: Mr. Walter W. Lancaster II

General Information Distance learning only college-preparatory, technology, Science, and Math school, affiliated with Seventh-day Adventist Church. Distance learning grades 1–12. Founded: 1922. Setting: suburban. 11 buildings on campus. Approved or accredited by Western Association of Schools and Colleges and California Department of Education. Endowment: $667,000. Upper school average class size: 20. Upper school faculty-student ratio: 1:14. There are 180 required school days per year for Upper School students. Upper School students typically attend 5 days per week. The average school day consists of 6 hours.

Upper School Student Profile 40% of students are boarding students. 84% are state residents. 16% are international students. International students from China and Mexico; 3 other countries represented in student body. 65% of students are Seventh-day Adventists.

Faculty School total: 42. In upper school: 9 men, 9 women; 16 have advanced degrees.

Subjects Offered 20th century history, 20th century world history, advanced biology, advanced chemistry, advanced math, Advanced Placement courses, advanced TOEFL/grammar, algebra, American culture, American government, American history, American literature, American literature-AP, analysis of data, anatomy, applied arts, art, ASB Leadership, athletics, audio visual/media, band, baseball, basic language skills, basketball, Bible, Bible studies, biology, biology-AP, biotechnology, British literature, broadcast journalism, broadcasting, calculus, calculus-AP, campus ministry, career and personal planning, career education, career/college preparation, chaplaincy, chemistry, choir, choral music, Christian doctrine, Christian education, Christian ethics, Christian scripture, Christian studies, Christian testament, Christianity, church history, cinematography, college admission preparation, college awareness, college counseling, college writing, community service, comparative religion, composition-AP, computer education, computer literacy, computer skills, concert band, conservation, critical thinking, culinary arts, data analysis, drama, English as a foreign language, English language and composition-AP, English language-AP, English literature, English-AP, English/composition-AP, ensembles, expository writing, freshman foundations, geometry, government, guidance, health education, healthful living, history, history of music, history-AP, Internet, lab science, language arts, library, Microsoft, music appreciation, physical education, physics, pre-algebra, publishing, reading/study skills, religion, religious education, remedial study skills, robotics, SAT/ACT preparation, scuba diving, softball, Spanish, sports, statistics, student government, study skills, trigonometry, U.S. government and politics-AP, U.S. history-AP, video film production, vocal music, wind ensemble, world history, world history-AP, world religions, writing workshop.

Graduation Requirements American government, American history, applied arts, arts and fine arts (art, music, dance, drama), career education, computer skills, electives, English, foreign language, freshman seminar, government, health, physical education (includes health), religion (includes Bible studies and theology), science, world history. Community service is required.

Special Academic Programs Study at local college for college credit; academic accommodation for the gifted, the musically talented, and the artistically talented; remedial math; ESL (25 students enrolled).

College Admission Counseling 70 students graduated in 2016; 63 went to college, including La Sierra University; Pacific Union College; University of California, Davis;

University of California, Irvine; University of California, Riverside; Walla Walla University. Other: 5 went to work, 2 entered military service.

Student Life Upper grades have uniform requirement, student council. Discipline rests primarily with faculty.

Summer Programs Remediation, enrichment programs offered; session focuses on Advancement and remediation plus recreation and ACT/SAT Prep; held on campus; accepts boys and girls; open to students from other schools. 35 students usually enrolled. 2017 schedule: July 11 to July 28. Application deadline: July 4.

Tuition and Aid Day student tuition: $8000–$8300; 7-day tuition and room/board: $31,000–$34,000. Tuition installment plan (monthly payment plans, individually arranged payment plans, 10 month and 11 month payment plans). Tuition reduction for siblings, merit scholarship grants, need-based scholarship grants, paying campus jobs available. In 2016–17, 50% of upper-school students received aid.

Admissions Traditional secondary-level entrance grade is 9. School placement exam, skills for ESL students, TOEFL or TOEFL Junior required. Deadline for receipt of application materials: April 28. Application fee required: $250. On-campus interview required.

Athletics Interscholastic: baseball (boys), basketball (b,g), cross-country running (b,g), softball (g), track and field (b,g), volleyball (b,g); coed interscholastic: outdoor education, scuba diving, soccer; coed intramural: ultimate Frisbee. 3 PE instructors, 10 coaches.

Computers Computers are regularly used in all classes. Computer network features include Internet access, wireless campus network, Internet filtering or blocking technology. Campus intranet, student e-mail accounts, and computer access in designated common areas are available to students. Students grades are available online. The school has a published electronic and media policy.

Contact Mrs. Michele McKinstry, Enrollment Coordinator. 951-351-1445 Ext. 217. Fax: 951-689-3708. E-mail: mmckinstry@lsak12.com. Website: www.lsak12.com

LAURALTON HALL

200 High Street
Milford, Connecticut 06460

Head of School: Dr. Antoinette Iadarola

General Information Girls' day college-preparatory school, affiliated with Roman Catholic Church. Grades 9–12. Founded: 1905. Setting: suburban. Nearest major city is New Haven. 30-acre campus. 5 buildings on campus. Approved or accredited by Connecticut Association of Independent Schools, Mercy Secondary Education Association, New England Association of Schools and Colleges, and Connecticut Department of Education. Member of National Association of Independent Schools. Total enrollment: 467. Upper school average class size: 15. Upper school faculty-student ratio: 1:9. There are 165 required school days per year for Upper School students. Upper School students typically attend 5 days per week. The average school day consists of 6 hours and 15 minutes.

Upper School Student Profile Grade 9: 107 students (107 girls); Grade 10: 112 students (112 girls); Grade 11: 108 students (108 girls); Grade 12: 129 students (129 girls). 76% of students are Roman Catholic.

Faculty School total: 49. In upper school: 7 men, 42 women; 29 have advanced degrees.

Graduation Requirements Arts and fine arts (art, music, dance, drama), English, foreign language, mathematics, physical education (includes health), religion (includes Bible studies and theology), science, social studies (includes history). Community service is required.

Special Academic Programs Honors section; study at local college for college credit.

College Admission Counseling 108 students graduated in 2016; 106 went to college, including Fairfield University; Fordham University; Loyola University Maryland; Tufts University; University of Connecticut; Villanova University. Other: 1 entered a postgraduate year, 1 had other specific plans. Mean SAT critical reading: 548, mean SAT math: 539, mean SAT writing: 565.

Student Life Upper grades have uniform requirement, student council, honor system. Discipline rests primarily with faculty. Attendance at religious services is required.

Tuition and Aid Day student tuition: $19,685. Tuition installment plan (FACTS Tuition Payment Plan, 1- and 2-payment plans). Tuition reduction for siblings, merit scholarship grants, need-based scholarship grants available. In 2016–17, 27% of upper-school students received aid; total upper-school merit-scholarship money awarded: $741,700. Total amount of financial aid awarded in 2016–17: $534,630.

Admissions Traditional secondary-level entrance grade is 9. High School Placement Test required. Deadline for receipt of application materials: none. Application fee required: $60.

Athletics Interscholastic: basketball, cheering, cross-country running, diving, field hockey, golf, gymnastics, ice hockey, indoor track, lacrosse, running, skiing (downhill), soccer, softball, swimming and diving, tennis, track and field, volleyball; intramural: basketball. 1 PE instructor, 27 coaches, 1 athletic trainer.

Computers Computers are regularly used in mathematics classes. Computer network features include on-campus library services, online commercial services, Internet access, wireless campus network, Internet filtering or blocking technology. Campus intranet, student e-mail accounts, and computer access in designated common areas are

available to students. Students grades are available online. The school has a published electronic and media policy.

Contact Kathleen Shine, Director of Enrollment Management. 203-877-2786 Ext. 125. Fax: 203-876-9760. E-mail: kshine@lauraltonhall.org.

Website: www.lauraltonhall.org

THE LAUREATE ACADEMY

Winnipeg, Manitoba, Canada
See Special Needs Schools section.

LAUREL SCHOOL

One Lyman Circle
Shaker Heights, Ohio 44122

Head of School: Ann V. Klotz

General Information Coeducational day (boys' only in lower grades) college-preparatory school. Boys grades PS–PK, girls grades PS–12. Founded: 1896. Setting: suburban. Nearest major city is Cleveland. 11-acre campus. 1 building on campus. Approved or accredited by Independent Schools Association of the Central States, Ohio Association of Independent Schools, and Ohio Department of Education. Member of National Association of Independent Schools. Endowment: $50.1 million. Total enrollment: 640. Upper school average class size: 14. Upper school faculty-student ratio: 1:8. Upper School students typically attend 5 days per week. The average school day consists of 7 hours and 18 minutes.

Upper School Student Profile Grade 9: 65 students (65 girls); Grade 10: 73 students (73 girls); Grade 11: 69 students (69 girls); Grade 12: 65 students (65 girls).

Faculty School total: 86. In upper school: 13 men, 24 women; 29 have advanced degrees.

Subjects Offered Algebra, American history, American literature, American literature-AP, anatomy and physiology, art, art history-AP, astronomy, biology, biology-AP, biotechnology, calculus, calculus-AP, ceramics, chemistry, chemistry-AP, choir, choreography, classical studies, classics, community service, computer art, computer multimedia, computer science, creative writing, discrete mathematics, drama, drawing, driver education, earth science, engineering, English, English literature, English-AP, environmental science, European history, European history-AP, experiential education, expository writing, fine arts, forensics, French, French-AP, geography, geology, geometry, government-AP, grammar, health, history, honors algebra, honors English, honors geometry, honors U.S. history, independent study, Latin, Latin-AP, mathematics, music, music theory, orchestra, painting, photography, physical education, physics, physics-AP, pre-calculus, probability and statistics, science, sculpture, senior project, social studies, Spanish, Spanish language-AP, Spanish literature, Spanish literature-AP, Spanish-AP, speech, studio art, studio art-AP, technical theater, theater, trigonometry, U.S. history-AP, world history, writing.

Graduation Requirements Arts and fine arts (art, music, dance, drama), English, foreign language, history, mathematics, physical education (includes health), science, speech, 10-minute speech on a subject of choice to the entire Upper School student body and faculty. Community service is required.

Special Academic Programs Advanced Placement exam preparation; honors section; independent study; term-away projects; study at local college for college credit; study abroad; academic accommodation for the gifted, the musically talented, and the artistically talented.

College Admission Counseling 67 students graduated in 2015; all went to college, including Case Western Reserve University; Purdue University; Syracuse University; Tulane University; University of Cincinnati; Washington University in St. Louis. Mean SAT critical reading: 612, mean SAT math: 609, mean SAT writing: 628, mean composite ACT: 26.

Student Life Upper grades have uniform requirement, student council, honor system. Discipline rests primarily with faculty.

Tuition and Aid Day student tuition: $27,750. Tuition installment plan (monthly payment plans, individually arranged payment plans). Tuition reduction for siblings, merit scholarship grants, need-based scholarship grants available. In 2015–16, 57% of upper-school students received aid; total upper-school merit-scholarship money awarded: $307,500. Total amount of financial aid awarded in 2015–16: $1,875,460.

Admissions Traditional secondary-level entrance grade is 9. For fall 2015, 86 students applied for upper-level admission, 66 were accepted, 30 enrolled. Deadline for receipt of application materials: none. Application fee required: $40. On-campus interview required.

Athletics Interscholastic: basketball, cross-country running, field hockey, golf, lacrosse, soccer, softball, strength & conditioning, swimming and diving, tennis, track and field, volleyball; intramural: basketball, field hockey, lacrosse, soccer, softball, swimming and diving, tennis, volleyball. 26 coaches, 1 athletic trainer.

Computers Computers are regularly used in all academic classes. Computer network features include on-campus library services, Internet access, wireless campus network, Internet filtering or blocking technology. Campus intranet, student e-mail accounts, and computer access in designated common areas are available to students.

Contact Kathryn Purcell, Assistant Head of School - Enrollment Management. 216-464-0946. Fax: 216-464-1446. E-mail: kPurcell@LaurelSchool.org.

Website: www.laurelschool.org

LAUREL SPRINGS SCHOOL

302 West El Paseo Road
Ojai, California 93023

Head of School: Darby Carr

General Information Distance learning only college-preparatory and distance learning school. Distance learning grades K–12. Founded: 1991. Setting: small town. Nearest major city is LOS ANGELES. Approved or accredited by Southern Association of Colleges and Schools, Western Association of Schools and Colleges, and California Department of Education. Total enrollment: 1,529. Upper school average class size: 1. Upper school faculty-student ratio: 1:1. The average school day consists of 6 hours.

Upper School Student Profile Grade 9: 178 students (87 boys, 91 girls); Grade 10: 249 students (118 boys, 131 girls); Grade 11: 260 students (124 boys, 136 girls); Grade 12: 189 students (91 boys, 98 girls).

Faculty School total: 86. In upper school: 13 men, 73 women; 63 have advanced degrees.

Subjects Offered Algebra, American literature, art appreciation, art history, biology, biology-AP, British literature, British literature (honors), calculus, calculus-AP, career/college preparation, cartooning/animation, chemistry, chemistry-AP, college admission preparation, college counseling, driver education, earth science, economics, electives, English composition, English language and composition-AP, English literature and composition-AP, environmental education, environmental studies, French, French-AP, geometry, German, health, history of music, honors algebra, honors English, honors geometry, honors U.S. history, honors world history, Latin, macroeconomics-AP, Mandarin, microeconomics-AP, music history, mythology, photo shop, physical education, physics, physics-AP, pre-calculus, psychology, psychology-AP, SAT/ACT preparation, Shakespeare, sociology, Spanish, Spanish language-AP, statistics-AP, trigonometry, U.S. government, U.S. government and politics-AP, U.S. history, U.S. history-AP, world cultures, world history, world literature.

Graduation Requirements Arts and fine arts (art, music, dance, drama), electives, English, foreign language, mathematics, physical education (includes health), science, social studies (includes history).

Special Academic Programs Advanced Placement exam preparation; honors section; accelerated programs; independent study; term-away projects; academic accommodation for the gifted, the musically talented, and the artistically talented; remedial reading and/or remedial writing; remedial math; programs in English, mathematics, general development for dyslexic students; special instructional classes for students needing customized learning options.

College Admission Counseling 102 students graduated in 2016; 94 went to college, including Middle Tennessee State University; New York University; Purdue University; University of California, Los Angeles; University of California, Santa Barbara; University of Southern California. Other: 8 had other specific plans. Mean SAT critical reading: 562, mean SAT math: 519, mean SAT writing: 547, mean composite ACT: 23.

Student Life Upper grades have student council, honor system. Discipline rests equally with students and faculty.

Summer Programs Enrichment, advancement, art/fine arts, computer instruction programs offered; session focuses on accelerated classes; held off campus; held at individual homes of enrolled students; accepts boys and girls; open to students from other schools. Application deadline: none.

Tuition and Aid Tuition installment plan (monthly payment plans, individually arranged payment plans). Tuition reduction for siblings, need-based scholarship grants available.

Admissions Traditional secondary-level entrance grade is 9. Deadline for receipt of application materials: none. Application fee required: $250.

Computers Computers are regularly used in art, economics, English, foreign language, geography, health, history, independent study, information technology, language development, life skills, mathematics, psychology, SAT preparation, science, social studies, writing classes. Computer network features include on-campus library services, Internet access, 100 online courses. Students grades are available online.

Contact Admissions. 800-377-5890 Ext. 5502. Fax: 805-646-0186.
E-mail: afuller@laurelsprings.com. Website: www.laurelsprings.com

LAURINBURG INSTITUTE

125 Mcgirts Bridge Road
Laurinburg, North Carolina 28353

Head of School: Mr. Frank H. McDuffie Jr.

General Information Coeducational boarding and day college-preparatory school. Grades 9–PG. Distance learning grades 9–12. Founded: 1904. Setting: rural. Nearest major city is Fayetteville. Students are housed in single-sex dormitories and Cottage. 55-acre campus. 11 buildings on campus. Approved or accredited by National Private School Accreditation Alliance and North Carolina Department of Education. Upper school average class size: 10. Upper school faculty-student ratio: 1:10. There are 180 required school days per year for Upper School students. Upper School students typically attend 6 days per week. The average school day consists of 6 hours and 30 minutes.

Upper School Student Profile Grade 12: 10 students (10 boys). 100% are state residents. 1 state is represented in upper school student body.

Faculty School total: 3. In upper school: 2 men, 1 woman; all have advanced degrees.

Subjects Offered Algebra, American history, American literature, biology, chemistry, creative writing, earth science, English, English literature, European history, French, geometry, physical education, social studies, Spanish, trigonometry, typing, world history.

Special Academic Programs Remedial reading and/or remedial writing; remedial math.

Student Life Upper grades have uniform requirement, student council. Discipline rests primarily with faculty.

Summer Programs Remediation, enrichment, advancement programs offered; session focuses on academics; held on campus; accepts boys and girls; open to students from other schools. 5 students usually enrolled. 2017 schedule: June to July. Application deadline: May 21.

Tuition and Aid Day student tuition: $1600; 7-day tuition and room/board: $16,000. Guaranteed tuition plan. Tuition installment plan (monthly payment plans). Tuition reduction for siblings, need-based scholarship grants available. In 2016–17, 90% of upper-school students received aid.

Admissions Traditional secondary-level entrance grade is 12. For fall 2016, 10 students applied for upper-level admission, 10 were accepted, 10 enrolled. Deadline for receipt of application materials: none. Application fee required: $125. Interview required.

Athletics Interscholastic: basketball, cross-country running, track and field; intramural: basketball, cross-country running, swimming and diving. 1 coach.

Computers Computers are regularly used in all academic classes. Computer resources include Internet access, Internet filtering or blocking technology. Campus intranet and computer access in designated common areas are available to students. The school has a published electronic and media policy.

Contact Mrs. Cynthia R. McDuffie, Director of Records Management. 910-276-0684. Fax: 910-276-2948. E-mail: lcscmcduffie@yahoo.com. Website: www.laurinburginstitute.org

LAWRENCE SCHOOL

Sagamore Hills, Ohio

See Special Needs Schools section.

THE LAWRENCEVILLE SCHOOL

PO Box 6008
2500 Main Street
Lawrenceville, New Jersey 08648

Head of School: Stephen S. Murray

General Information Coeducational boarding and day college-preparatory and business school. Grades 9–PG. Founded: 1810. Setting: suburban. Nearest major city is Philadelphia, PA. Students are housed in single-sex dormitories. 700-acre campus. 120 buildings on campus. Approved or accredited by Middle States Association of Colleges and Schools, New Jersey Association of Independent Schools, The Association of Boarding Schools, and New Jersey Department of Education. Member of National Association of Independent Schools and Secondary School Admission Test Board. Endowment: $403 million. Total enrollment: 815. Upper school average class size: 12. Upper school faculty-student ratio: 1:8. There are 169 required school days per year for Upper School students. Upper School students typically attend 6 days per week. The average school day consists of 7 hours.

Upper School Student Profile Grade 9: 154 students (76 boys, 78 girls); Grade 10: 220 students (114 boys, 106 girls); Grade 11: 223 students (116 boys, 107 girls); Grade 12: 211 students (109 boys, 102 girls); Postgraduate: 15 students (15 boys). 67% of students are boarding students. 42% are state residents. 32 states are represented in upper school student body. 14% are international students. International students from Cayman Islands, China, Hong Kong, Mexico, Republic of Korea, and Viet Nam; 32 other countries represented in student body.

Faculty In upper school: 73 men, 50 women; 91 have advanced degrees; 140 reside on campus.

Subjects Offered Acting, advanced chemistry, advanced computer applications, Advanced Placement courses, advanced studio art-AP, African-American literature, algebra, American Civil War, American foreign policy, American government, American history, American history-AP, American literature, American studies, architecture, art, art history, art history-AP, art-AP, arts, Asian history, astronomy, Basic programming, Bible, Bible studies, biochemistry, bioethics, bioethics, DNA and culture, biology, biology-AP, Buddhism, calculus, calculus-AP, Central and Eastern European history, ceramics, chamber groups, chemistry, chemistry-AP, China/Japan history, Chinese, Chinese studies, choir, chorus, Christian studies, Civil War, civil war history, classical Greek literature, classical language, comparative government and politics, conceptual physics, constitutional history of U.S., contemporary women writers, critical writing, dance, data analysis, design, digital applications, digital art, drama, dramatic arts, drawing, drawing and design, driver education, Eastern religion and philosophy, ecology, environmental systems, economics, economics-AP, electronic music, English, English literature, English literature-AP, English/composition-AP,

environmental science, environmental studies, ethics, European history, European literature, evolution, fiction, field ecology, film and new technologies, film appreciation, film studies, filmmaking, food science, foreign language, foreign policy, French, French language-AP, French studies, geometry, global science, health and wellness, Hebrew scripture, historical foundations for arts, history of China and Japan, Holocaust, honors geometry, honors U.S. history, human biology, humanities, independent study, instruments, interdisciplinary studies, introduction to literature, introduction to theater, Irish literature, Irish studies, Islamic studies, Japanese history, jazz, Jewish studies, journalism, Latin, linear algebra, literature, macro/microeconomics-AP, medieval literature, Middle East, Middle Eastern history, nature study, non-Western societies, orchestra, organic chemistry, painting, participation in sports, personal development, philosophy, photography, physics, physics-AP, physiology, poetry, pre-calculus, printmaking, probability and statistics, programming, research seminar, robotics, Russian history, science, senior project, set design, Shakespeare, short story, Southern literature, Spanish, Spanish language-AP, Spanish literature, studio art, the Presidency, the Sixties, theater, theater arts, U.S. constitutional history, U.S. government, U.S. government and politics, U.S. history, Vietnam War, visual arts, water color painting, women in world history, world religions, world religions, writing, Zen Buddhism.

Graduation Requirements Arts and fine arts (art, music, dance, drama), English, foreign language, history, interdisciplinary studies, mathematics, religion (includes Bible studies and theology), science, social studies (includes history). Community service is required.

Special Academic Programs Honors section; independent study; term-away projects; study at local college for college credit; study abroad.

College Admission Counseling 231 students graduated in 2016; 228 went to college, including Brown University; Georgetown University; Princeton University; University of Michigan; Williams College; Yale University. Other: 2 entered a postgraduate year, 1 had other specific plans. Mean SAT critical reading: 700, mean SAT math: 714, mean SAT writing: 710, mean combined SAT: 2124, mean composite ACT: 30.

Student Life Upper grades have specified standards of dress, student council, honor system. Discipline rests equally with students and faculty.

Tuition and Aid Day student tuition: $49,510; 7-day tuition and room/board: $59,860. Tuition installment plan (FACTS Tuition Payment Plan, monthly payment plans, one, two, and nine month installment plans are available). Merit scholarship grants, need-based scholarship grants available. In 2016–17, 29% of upper-school students received aid; total upper-school merit-scholarship money awarded: $239,000. Total amount of financial aid awarded in 2016–17: $11,533,470.

Admissions Traditional secondary-level entrance grade is 9. For fall 2016, 1,919 students applied for upper-level admission, 375 were accepted, 249 enrolled. ISEE, PSAT and SAT for applicants to grade 11 and 12, SSAT or TOEFL or SLEP required. Deadline for receipt of application materials: January 15. Application fee required: $50. Interview recommended.

Athletics Interscholastic: baseball (boys), basketball (b,g), crew (b,g), cross-country running (b,g), fencing (b,g), field hockey (g), football (b), golf (b,g), hockey (b,g), ice hockey (b,g), indoor track (b,g), indoor track & field (b,g), lacrosse (b,g), rowing (b,g), soccer (b,g), softball (g), squash (b,g), swimming and diving (b,g), tennis (b,g), track and field (b,g), volleyball (b,g), water polo (b,g), winter (indoor) track (b,g); intramural: basketball (b,g), Frisbee (g), handball (b,g), team handball (b,g), ultimate Frisbee (g), weight lifting (b,g), weight training (b,g); coed interscholastic: wrestling; coed intramural: aerobics/dance, backpacking, bicycling, broomball, canoeing/kayaking, climbing, cricket, dance, fitness, hiking/backpacking, ice skating, kayaking, modern dance, Nautilus, outdoor activities, physical fitness, physical training, rock climbing, ropes courses, squash, strength & conditioning, wall climbing, yoga. 32 coaches, 5 athletic trainers.

Computers Computers are regularly used in art, English, foreign language, mathematics, music, science, technology classes. Computer resources include on-campus library services, online commercial services, Internet access, wireless campus network, Internet filtering or blocking technology. Campus intranet, student e-mail accounts, and computer access in designated common areas are available to students. Students grades are available online. The school has a published electronic and media policy.

Contact Tom Sheppard, Dean of Admission and Financial Aid. 800-735-2030. Fax: 609-895-2217. E-mail: admission@lawrenceville.org. Website: www.lawrenceville.org

See Display on previous page and Close-Up on page 600.

LAWRENCE WOODMERE ACADEMY

336 Woodmere Boulevard
Woodmere, New York 11598-2066

Head of School: Mr. Alan Bernstein

General Information Coeducational day college-preparatory school. Grades PK–12. Founded: 1894. Setting: suburban. Nearest major city is New York. 8-acre campus. 3 buildings on campus. Approved or accredited by New York State Association of Independent Schools and New York Department of Education. Member of National Association of Independent Schools and Secondary School Admission Test Board. Total enrollment: 356. Upper school average class size: 13. Upper school faculty-student ratio: 1:6.

Faculty School total: 75. In upper school: 14 men, 16 women; 30 have advanced degrees.

Subjects Offered Advanced Placement courses, college admission preparation, community service, computer applications, drama, health education, humanities, interdisciplinary studies, mathematics, modern languages, physical education, science, science research, social sciences, visual and performing arts.

Graduation Requirements Arts, computer science, English, foreign language, mathematics, physical education (includes health), science, social sciences, social studies (includes history), college seminars, fine arts rotation (creative writing, drama, studio art). Community service is required.

Special Academic Programs Advanced Placement exam preparation; honors section; independent study; ESL (25 students enrolled).

College Admission Counseling 32 students graduated in 2016; all went to college, including New York University; Quinnipiac University; Savannah College of Art and Design; The University of Arizona; University of Maryland, College Park; University of Wisconsin–Madison. Median SAT critical reading: 600. 50% scored over 600 on SAT critical reading, 56% scored over 600 on SAT math.

Student Life Upper grades have specified standards of dress, student council, honor system. Discipline rests primarily with faculty.

Tuition and Aid Day student tuition: $35,000. Tuition installment plan (Insured Tuition Payment Plan, Academic Management Services Plan, monthly payment plans, individually arranged payment plans). Tuition reduction for siblings, merit scholarship grants, need-based scholarship grants, need-based loans available. In 2016–17, 22% of upper-school students received aid.

Admissions Traditional secondary-level entrance grade is 9. SSAT and writing sample required. Deadline for receipt of application materials: February 3. Application fee required: $75. Interview required.

Athletics Interscholastic: baseball (boys), basketball (b,g), cheering (g), cross-country running (b,g), golf (b,g), soccer (b,g), softball (g), tennis (b,g), volleyball (g); intramural: basketball (b,g), soccer (b,g), softball (b,g), volleyball (b,g); coed interscholastic: cross-country running, golf. 4 PE instructors, 8 coaches.

Computers Computers are regularly used in art, English, foreign language, history, mathematics, SAT preparation, science, technical drawing, word processing, yearbook classes. Computer network features include on-campus library services, Internet access, wireless campus network, Internet filtering or blocking technology.

Contact Trish Hughes, Admissions Associate. 516-394-1827. Fax: 516-374-2002. E-mail: thughes@lawrencewoodmere.org. Website: www.lawrencewoodmere.org

LEE ACADEMY

415 Lee Drive
Clarksdale, Mississippi 38614

Head of School: Tommy Gunn

General Information Coeducational day college-preparatory, arts, and business school. Grades 1–12. Founded: 1970. Setting: small town. Nearest major city is Memphis, TN. 4 buildings on campus. Approved or accredited by Mississippi Private School Association, Southern Association of Colleges and Schools, and Mississippi Department of Education. Total enrollment: 321. Upper school average class size: 22. Upper school faculty-student ratio: 1:20. There are 185 required school days per year for Upper School students. Upper School students typically attend 5 days per week. The average school day consists of 6 hours and 30 minutes.

Upper School Student Profile Grade 6: 9 students (5 boys, 4 girls); Grade 7: 41 students (21 boys, 20 girls); Grade 8: 40 students (17 boys, 23 girls); Grade 9: 33 students (17 boys, 16 girls); Grade 10: 31 students (15 boys, 16 girls); Grade 11: 42 students (21 boys, 21 girls); Grade 12: 40 students (24 boys, 16 girls).

Faculty School total: 45. In upper school: 3 men, 15 women; 8 have advanced degrees.

Subjects Offered ACT preparation, acting, American government, American history, ancient world history, art, athletics, baseball, basketball, Bible, biology, bookkeeping, business, business law, calculus, cheerleading, chemistry, choral music, computer applications, earth and space science, earth science, English, English composition, English literature, foreign language, geography, geometry, guidance, health, Spanish, U.S. history, writing workshop, yearbook.

Graduation Requirements Math methods.

College Admission Counseling 41 students graduated in 2015; all went to college, including Mississippi State University; University of Mississippi.

Student Life Upper grades have uniform requirement, student council. Discipline rests primarily with faculty.

Tuition and Aid Day student tuition: $5500. Tuition installment plan (monthly payment plans). Tuition reduction for siblings, need-based scholarship grants available. In 2015–16, 15% of upper-school students received aid. Total amount of financial aid awarded in 2015–16: $35,000.

Admissions Traditional secondary-level entrance grade is 9. For fall 2015, 80 students applied for upper-level admission, 80 were accepted, 80 enrolled. 3-R Achievement Test required. Deadline for receipt of application materials: February 28. No application fee required.

Athletics Interscholastic: baseball (boys), basketball (b), cheering (g), football (b); coed interscholastic: cross-country running, golf, soccer. 2 PE instructors, 5 coaches.

Computers Computer resources include on-campus library services. Computer access in designated common areas is available to students. Students grades are available online.

Contact Beverly Antici, Counselor. 662-627-7891. Fax: 662-627-7896. E-mail: leeoffice@acbleone.net. Website: www.leeacademycolts.com/

THE LEELANAU SCHOOL

Glen Arbor, Michigan
See Special Needs Schools section.

LEHIGH VALLEY CHRISTIAN HIGH SCHOOL

3436 Winchester Road
Allentown, Pennsylvania 18104

Head of School: Mr. Robert Walsh

General Information Coeducational day college-preparatory, general academic, and arts school. Grades 9–12. Founded: 1988. Setting: urban. 2-acre campus. 1 building on campus. Approved or accredited by Association of Christian Schools International, Middle States Association of Colleges and Schools, and Pennsylvania Department of Education. Endowment: $17,387. Total enrollment: 53. Upper school average class size: 15. Upper school faculty-student ratio: 1:5. There are 40 required school days per year for Upper School students. Upper School students typically attend 5 days per week. The average school day consists of 6 hours and 43 minutes.

Upper School Student Profile Grade 9: 5 students (5 boys); Grade 10: 7 students (4 boys, 3 girls); Grade 11: 18 students (9 boys, 9 girls); Grade 12: 10 students (7 boys, 3 girls).

Faculty School total: 5. In upper school: 3 men, 2 women; 3 have advanced degrees.

Subjects Offered Accounting, Advanced Placement courses, algebra, American history, ancient world history, art, Bible, biology, calculus-AP, chemistry, chorus, English, geometry, health, history, physical education, physical science, pre-calculus, Spanish, U.S. history, Western civilization.

Graduation Requirements Algebra, American history, American literature, art, Bible, Bible studies, biology, British literature, choir, civics, English, foreign language, geometry, mathematics, physical education (includes health), science, social sciences, Western civilization, general lifestyle not harmful to the testimony of the school as a Christian institution, minimum one year of full-time enrollment in LVCH or another Christian high school.

Special Academic Programs Advanced Placement exam preparation; honors section; accelerated programs; independent study; study at local college for college credit; programs in English, mathematics, general development for dyslexic students; special instructional classes for students needing learning support.

College Admission Counseling 7 students graduated in 2016; all went to college, including Albright College; Lehigh University; Liberty University; Moravian College; Penn State University Park; Temple University. Mean SAT critical reading: 552, mean SAT math: 564, mean SAT writing: 531, mean combined SAT: 1647.

Student Life Upper grades have specified standards of dress, student council. Discipline rests primarily with faculty.

Tuition and Aid Day student tuition: $7800. Tuition installment plan (FACTS Tuition Payment Plan, individually arranged payment plans). Tuition reduction for siblings, need-based scholarship grants available. In 2016–17, 24% of upper-school students received aid. Total amount of financial aid awarded in 2016–17: $17,387.

Admissions Traditional secondary-level entrance grade is 9. For fall 2016, 8 students applied for upper-level admission, 8 were accepted, 8 enrolled. Achievement tests, Gates MacGinite Reading Tests or Wide Range Achievement Test required. Deadline for receipt of application materials: none. Application fee required: $200. On-campus interview required.

Athletics Interscholastic: baseball (boys), basketball (b,g), soccer (b,g), track and field (b,g), volleyball (g); coed intramural: fitness walking. 1 PE instructor.

Computers Computers are regularly used in accounting, business, college planning, computer applications, creative writing, ESL, foreign language, history, science, social sciences, social studies, Spanish, writing, yearbook classes. Computer network features include on-campus library services, Internet access, wireless campus network, Internet filtering or blocking technology. Campus intranet, student e-mail accounts, and computer access in designated common areas are available to students. Students grades are available online. The school has a published electronic and media policy.

Contact Mrs. Deanna Gehman, Director of Admissions. 610-351-9144 Ext. 102. Fax: 610-351-9187. E-mail: d.gehman@lvchs.org. Website: www.lvchs.org

LEHMAN HIGH SCHOOL

2400 Saint Mary Avenue
Sidney, Ohio 45365

Head of School: Mrs. Denise Stauffer

General Information Coeducational day and distance learning college-preparatory, arts, business, and religious studies school, affiliated with Roman Catholic Church. Grades 9–12. Distance learning grades 10–12. Founded: 1970. Setting: small town. Nearest major city is Dayton. 50-acre campus. 1 building on campus. Approved or accredited by North Central Association of Colleges and Schools, Ohio Catholic Schools Accreditation Association (OCSAA), and Ohio Department of Education. Endowment: $600,000. Total enrollment: 202. Upper school average class size: 15. Upper school faculty-student ratio: 1:15. There are 178 required school days per year for Upper School students. Upper School students typically attend 5 days per week. The average school day consists of 7 hours.

Upper School Student Profile Grade 9: 62 students (28 boys, 34 girls); Grade 10: 55 students (27 boys, 28 girls); Grade 11: 45 students (22 boys, 23 girls); Grade 12: 40 students (16 boys, 24 girls). 93% of students are Roman Catholic.

Faculty School total: 18. In upper school: 8 men, 10 women; 9 have advanced degrees.

Subjects Offered Accounting, algebra, American government, American literature, anatomy and physiology, art, art history, biology, biology-AP, British literature, British literature (honors), business, calculus, calculus-AP, ceramics, chemistry, chemistry-AP, choir, computer applications, concert band, drafting, earth science, English, English literature and composition-AP, environmental science, geography, geometry, government, government-AP, health education, history of the Catholic Church, integrated science, intro to computers, Latin, moral theology, newspaper, painting, peace and justice, physical education, physics, pre-algebra, pre-calculus, psychology, sociology, Spanish, studio art, U.S. history, vocal music, weight fitness, world history, yearbook.

Graduation Requirements Biology, business, computer applications, electives, English composition, English literature, health education, mathematics, physical education (includes health), physical science, religion (includes Bible studies and theology), U.S. government, U.S. history, must attend a senior retreat.

Special Academic Programs Advanced Placement exam preparation; honors section; independent study; study at local college for college credit.

College Admission Counseling 47 students graduated in 2015; 44 went to college, including Bowling Green State University; Miami University; The Ohio State University; University of Cincinnati; University of Dayton; Wright State University. Other: 3 went to work. Median SAT critical reading: 656, median SAT math: 616, median SAT writing: 593, median combined SAT: 1960. Mean composite ACT: 24. 66.6% scored over 600 on SAT critical reading, 66.6% scored over 600 on SAT math, 66.6% scored over 600 on SAT writing, 66.6% scored over 1800 on combined SAT, 21% scored over 26 on composite ACT.

Student Life Upper grades have uniform requirement, student council, honor system. Discipline rests primarily with faculty. Attendance at religious services is required.

Tuition and Aid Day student tuition: $7400. Tuition installment plan (FACTS Tuition Payment Plan). Tuition reduction for siblings, need-based scholarship grants available. In 2015–16, 44% of upper-school students received aid. Total amount of financial aid awarded in 2015–16: $353,850.

Admissions Traditional secondary-level entrance grade is 9. Achievement tests or any standardized test required. Deadline for receipt of application materials: none. Application fee required: $100. Interview recommended.

Athletics Interscholastic: baseball (boys), basketball (b,g), cheering (g), cross-country running (b,g), football (b), golf (b), soccer (b,g), softball (g), swimming and diving (b,g), tennis (b,g), track and field (b,g), volleyball (g), wrestling (b); intramural: strength & conditioning (b,g); coed intramural: indoor track. 1 PE instructor, 35 coaches, 1 athletic trainer.

Computers Computers are regularly used in accounting, computer applications, drafting, newspaper, science, yearbook classes. Computer resources include on-campus library services, Internet access, wireless campus network, Internet filtering or blocking technology. Students grades are available online. The school has a published electronic and media policy.

Contact Mrs. Denise Stauffer, Principal/CEO. 937-498-1161 Ext. 115. Fax: 937-492-9877. E-mail: d.stauffer@lehmancatholic.com. Website: www.lehmancatholic.com/

LE LYCÉE FRANCAIS DE LOS ANGELES

3261 Overland Avenue
Los Angeles, California 90034-3589

Head of School: Mrs. Clara-Lisa Kabbaz

General Information Coeducational day college-preparatory, general academic, Classic French Baccalaureate Exam, and Franco-American Bacc Exam in association w/The College Board school. Grades PS–12. Founded: 1964. Setting: suburban. Nearest major city is Beverly Hills. 2-acre campus. 1 building on campus. Approved or accredited by French Ministry of Education, Western Association of Schools and Colleges, and California Department of Education. Member of National Association of Independent Schools. Languages of instruction: English and French. Endowment: $100 million. Total enrollment: 819. Upper school average class size: 17. Upper school faculty-student ratio: 1:4. There are 171 required school days per year for Upper School students. Upper School students typically attend 5 days per week. The average school day consists of 7 hours and 45 minutes.

Upper School Student Profile Grade 6: 65 students (30 boys, 35 girls); Grade 7: 45 students (24 boys, 21 girls); Grade 8: 50 students (24 boys, 26 girls); Grade 9: 43 students (18 boys, 25 girls); Grade 10: 57 students (28 boys, 29 girls); Grade 11: 58 students (30 boys, 28 girls); Grade 12: 40 students (23 boys, 17 girls).

Faculty School total: 105. In upper school: 29 men, 25 women; 38 have advanced degrees.

Subjects Offered 3-dimensional art, acting, advanced biology, advanced chemistry, advanced math, Advanced Placement courses, advanced studio art-AP, algebra, American government, American history, American history-AP, American literature, American literature-AP, analysis, Ancient Greek, ancient world history, applied arts, art, art history, art-AP, arts, athletics, ballet, band, basketball, biology, biology-AP, calculus, calculus-AP, chemistry, chemistry-AP, choir, civics, classical civilization, classical Greek literature, classical music, college admission preparation, college counseling, college writing, computer music, computer science, computer skills, computer technologies, creative arts, creative writing, dance, drama, earth science, economics, English, English language and composition-AP, English literature, environmental science, ESL, European history, expository writing, fencing, fine arts, French, French as a second language, French language-AP, French studies, gardening, geography, geometry, German, government/civics, grammar, history, Latin, Mandarin, mathematics, microeconomics-AP, music, philosophy, physical education, physics, pre-calculus, SAT preparation, science, social sciences, social studies, Spanish, sports, statistics, theater, theater arts, trigonometry, U.S. history, volleyball, world history, world literature, writing.

Graduation Requirements Arts and fine arts (art, music, dance, drama), electives, English, French, mathematics, physical education (includes health), science, U.S. history, world history.

Special Academic Programs International Baccalaureate program; 19 Advanced Placement exams for which test preparation is offered; honors section; remedial reading and/or remedial writing; remedial math; ESL (10 students enrolled).

College Admission Counseling 51 students graduated in 2016; all went to college, including Concordia University Irvine; Loyola Marymount University; McGill University; New York University; University of California, Los Angeles; University of Southern California. Median SAT critical reading: 620, median SAT math: 650, median SAT writing: 660, median combined SAT: 1930, median composite ACT: 27. 63.8% scored over 600 on SAT critical reading, 69.4% scored over 600 on SAT math, 77.7% scored over 600 on SAT writing, 72.2% scored over 1800 on combined SAT, 63.6% scored over 26 on composite ACT.

Student Life Upper grades have uniform requirement, student council, honor system. Discipline rests primarily with faculty.

Summer Programs Enrichment, advancement, sports, art/fine arts, computer instruction programs offered; session focuses on social activities, sports, foreign languages, SAT prep; held both on and off campus; accepts boys and girls; open to students from other schools. 222 students usually enrolled. 2017 schedule: June 26 to July 28. Application deadline: May 15.

Tuition and Aid Day student tuition: $28,000. Tuition installment plan (Insured Tuition Payment Plan, individually arranged payment plans). Merit scholarship grants, need-based scholarship grants available. In 2016–17, 15% of upper-school students received aid. Total amount of financial aid awarded in 2016–17: $225,080.

Admissions Traditional secondary-level entrance grade is 9. For fall 2016, 44 students applied for upper-level admission, 43 were accepted, 28 enrolled. International English Language Test, international math and English tests, ISEE, school's own exam, SSAT or TOEFL required. Deadline for receipt of application materials: none. Application fee required: $200. Interview required.

Athletics Interscholastic: basketball (boys, girls); intramural: ballet (b,g), basketball (b,g); coed interscholastic: basketball, soccer, tennis, volleyball; coed intramural: archery, ballet, basketball, fencing, fitness, gymnastics, handball, indoor soccer, kickball, life saving, martial arts, modern dance, physical fitness, rock climbing, self defense, soccer, softball, swimming and diving, table tennis, tennis, touch football, track and field, ultimate Frisbee, volleyball. 6 PE instructors, 4 coaches, 1 athletic trainer.

Computers Computers are regularly used in art, computer applications, English, ESL, foreign language, French, French as a second language, geography, history, introduction to technology, keyboarding, lab/keyboard, library, mathematics, media, SAT preparation, science, social studies, technology, typing, word processing, writing, yearbook classes. Computer network features include on-campus library services, Internet access, wireless campus network, Internet filtering or blocking technology, homework is available online/attendance, Student Information System online, libraries/Internet café/computer labs. Computer access in designated common areas is available to students. Students grades are available online.

Contact Mme. Sophie Darmon, Director of Admissions. 310-836-3464 Ext. 315. Fax: 310-558-8069. E-mail: admissions@lyceela.org. Website: http://www.LyceeLA.org

LEXINGTON CATHOLIC HIGH SCHOOL

2250 Clays Mill Road
Lexington, Kentucky 40503-1797

Head of School: Dr. Steven Angelucci

General Information Coeducational day college-preparatory and religious studies school, affiliated with Roman Catholic Church. Grades 9–12. Founded: 1823. Setting: urban. 7-acre campus. 3 buildings on campus. Approved or accredited by National Catholic Education Association, Southern Association of Colleges and Schools, and Kentucky Department of Education. Endowment: $500,000. Total enrollment: 874. Upper school average class size: 20. Upper school faculty-student ratio: 1:13. There are 177 required school days per year for Upper School students. Upper School students typically attend 5 days per week. The average school day consists of 7 hours and 15 minutes.

Upper School Student Profile Grade 9: 244 students (127 boys, 117 girls); Grade 10: 226 students (127 boys, 99 girls); Grade 11: 199 students (103 boys, 96 girls); Grade 12: 205 students (96 boys, 109 girls). 74% of students are Roman Catholic.

Faculty School total: 67. In upper school: 34 men, 33 women; 48 have advanced degrees.

Subjects Offered Accounting, advanced chemistry, Advanced Placement courses, advanced studio art-AP, algebra, American government, American history, American history-AP, American literature, anatomy and physiology, art, astronomy, band, Bible as literature, biology, biology-AP, British literature, British literature (honors), calculus, calculus-AP, Catholic belief and practice, ceramics, chemistry, chemistry-AP, choral music, Christian and Hebrew scripture, church history, comparative religion, computer applications, computer programming, creative writing, drama, economics, English-AP, ethics, film, French, French-AP, geography, geology, geometry, government and politics-AP, health, history of the Catholic Church, honors English, honors geometry, honors U.S. history, honors world history, humanities, introduction to literature, Latin, Latin-AP, physical education, physics, psychology, religious studies, sociology, Spanish, Spanish language-AP, U.S. government, U.S. government and politics-AP, U.S. history, U.S. history-AP, world history, world literature.

Graduation Requirements American history, American literature, arts and fine arts (art, music, dance, drama), biology, British literature, Catholic belief and practice, chemistry, church history, computer applications, English, foreign language, mathematics, physical education (includes health), religion (includes Bible studies and theology), science, U.S. government, U.S. government and politics, U.S. history, world history.

Special Academic Programs 18 Advanced Placement exams for which test preparation is offered; honors section.

College Admission Counseling 193 students graduated in 2015; 188 went to college, including University of Kentucky. Other: 2 went to work, 1 entered military service, 1 entered a postgraduate year. Mean SAT critical reading: 592, mean SAT math: 604, mean SAT writing: 552, mean composite ACT: 25. 59% scored over 26 on composite ACT.

Student Life Upper grades have uniform requirement, student council, honor system. Discipline rests primarily with faculty. Attendance at religious services is required.

Tuition and Aid Day student tuition: $8745. Tuition installment plan (monthly payment plans, individually arranged payment plans). Merit scholarship grants, need-based scholarship grants available. In 2015–16, 18% of upper-school students received aid; total upper-school merit-scholarship money awarded: $5000. Total amount of financial aid awarded in 2015–16: $650,000.

Admissions Traditional secondary-level entrance grade is 9. For fall 2015, 250 students applied for upper-level admission, 248 were accepted, 244 enrolled. Scholastic Testing Service High School Placement Test required. Deadline for receipt of application materials: none. Application fee required: $275.

Athletics Interscholastic: baseball (boys), basketball (b,g), cheering (g), cross-country running (b,g), dance team (g), diving (b,g), football (b), golf (b,g), soccer (b,g), softball (g), swimming and diving (b,g), tennis (b,g), track and field (b,g), volleyball (g); intramural: badminton (b,g), basketball (b,g), flag football (g), lacrosse (b), physical training (b,g); coed interscholastic: bowling, ultimate Frisbee; coed intramural: outdoor activities. 3 PE instructors, 2 athletic trainers.

Computers Computers are regularly used in all academic classes. Computer network features include on-campus library services, Internet access, wireless campus network, Internet filtering or blocking technology. Computer access in designated common areas is available to students. Students grades are available online. The school has a published electronic and media policy.

Contact Ms. Mindy Towles, Admissions Director. 859-277-7183 Ext. 231. Fax: 859-276-5086. E-mail: mtowles@lexingtoncatholic.com. Website: www.lexingtoncatholic.com

LEXINGTON CHRISTIAN ACADEMY

450 West Reynolds Road
Lexington, Kentucky 40503

Head of School: Rick Burslem

General Information Coeducational day college-preparatory and College preparatory school. Grades PK–12. Founded: 1989. Setting: suburban. 1 building on campus. Approved or accredited by Southern Association of Colleges and Schools and Kentucky Department of Education. Total enrollment: 1,445. Upper school average class size: 18. Upper school faculty-student ratio: 1:16. There are 178 required school days per year for Upper School students. Upper School students typically attend 5 days per week. The average school day consists of 6 hours and 40 minutes.

Subjects Offered 3-dimensional art, accounting, acting, advanced biology, advanced chemistry, advanced computer applications, advanced math, Advanced Placement courses, advanced studio art-AP, algebra, American government, American history, American history-AP, American literature-AP, analysis and differential calculus, anatomy and physiology, art, art-AP, band, Basic programming, Bible, biology, biology-AP, business law, calculus, calculus-AP, chemistry, choir, chorus, Christian education, Christian studies, Christian testament, computer applications, computer programming-AP, computer science-AP, concert band, digital art, digital imaging, drama, drawing, drawing and design, economics, economics-AP, electives, engineering, English, English language and composition-AP, English language-AP, English literature and composition-AP, English-AP, English/composition-AP, foreign language, French, French-AP, general math, geometry, government-AP, graphic arts, health and wellness, honors English, honors geometry, honors world history, Life of Christ, macro/microeconomics-AP, marketing, mathematics, money management, music theory-AP, personal finance, physical education, physics-AP, pre-algebra, printmaking, psychology, sculpture, Spanish, speech, speech and debate, statistics, U.S. government, U.S. history, Web site design, Western civilization.

Graduation Requirements Electives, English, foreign language, health, humanities, mathematics, physical education (includes health), religion (includes Bible studies and theology), science, social studies (includes history), speech.

Special Academic Programs Advanced Placement exam preparation; honors section; study at local college for college credit.

College Admission Counseling 96 students graduated in 2016; 93 went to college, including Asbury University; Eastern Kentucky University; Samford University; University of Kentucky; University of South Carolina; Western Kentucky University. Other: 3 had other specific plans. Median composite ACT: 26.

Student Life Upper grades have specified standards of dress, student council. Discipline rests primarily with faculty.

Tuition and Aid Day student tuition: $10,598. Tuition installment plan (FACTS Tuition Payment Plan). Need-based loans available.

Admissions Traditional secondary-level entrance grade is 9. ISEE required. Deadline for receipt of application materials: August 1. Application fee required: $50. Interview recommended.

Athletics Interscholastic: archery (boys, girls), baseball (b), basketball (b,g), cheering (g), cross-country running (b,g), dance team (g), diving (b,g), football (b), golf (b,g), soccer (b,g), softball (g), swimming and diving (b,g), tennis (b,g), track and field (b,g), volleyball (g), wrestling (b); intramural: cheering (g), flag football (g), lacrosse (b).

Computers Computers are regularly used in all classes. Computer network features include on-campus library services, online commercial services, Internet access, wireless campus network, Internet filtering or blocking technology. Campus intranet and student e-mail accounts are available to students. Students grades are available online. The school has a published electronic and media policy.

Contact Mrs. Lesley Sizemore-Hardin, Director of Admissions. 859-422-5733. Fax: 859-422-5783. E-mail: lhardin@lexingtonchristian.org. Website: www.lexingtonchristian.org

LEXINGTON CHRISTIAN ACADEMY

48 Bartlett Avenue
Lexington, Massachusetts 02420

Head of School: Mr. Timothy Russell

General Information Coeducational boarding and day college-preparatory school. Boarding grades 9–12, day grades 6–12. Founded: 1946. Setting: suburban. Nearest major city is Boston. Students are housed in single-sex by floor dormitories. 36-acre campus. 2 buildings on campus. Approved or accredited by Association of Christian Schools International, Association of Independent Schools in New England, Christian Schools International, New England Association of Schools and Colleges, and Massachusetts Department of Education. Member of National Association of Independent Schools and Secondary School Admission Test Board. Endowment: $3.6 million. Total enrollment: 317. Upper school average class size: 16. Upper school faculty-student ratio: 1:11. There are 168 required school days per year for Upper School students. Upper School students typically attend 5 days per week. The average school day consists of 7 hours.

Upper School Student Profile Grade 6: 27 students (12 boys, 15 girls); Grade 7: 37 students (20 boys, 17 girls); Grade 8: 31 students (17 boys, 14 girls); Grade 9: 58 students (27 boys, 31 girls); Grade 10: 43 students (21 boys, 22 girls); Grade 11: 57 students (30 boys, 27 girls); Grade 12: 53 students (24 boys, 29 girls). 18% of students are boarding students. 88% are state residents. 4 states are represented in upper school student body. 10% are international students. International students from China, Japan, and Republic of Korea; 10 other countries represented in student body.

Faculty School total: 42. In upper school: 21 men, 21 women; 36 have advanced degrees; 1 resides on campus.

Subjects Offered 3-dimensional art, acting, advanced studio art-AP, American history, American literature-AP, anatomy and physiology, ancient world history, architecture, athletics, Bible, British literature (honors), calculus, ceramics, college placement, concert choir, drawing and design, ethics, French as a second language, health education, stained glass, statistics-AP, strings, U.S. government and politics-AP, vocal music, yearbook.

Graduation Requirements Algebra, American literature, ancient world history, Bible, Bible studies, biology, British history, British literature, college admission preparation, college planning, English literature, European history, European literature, geometry, health, lab science, physics, SAT preparation, service learning/internship, U.S. history, senior internship (3-week work experience in career of student's choice, including a journal of the experience), Academics in Action (participation each year in one week of special courses).

Special Academic Programs Advanced Placement exam preparation; honors section; independent study; term-away projects; study at local college for college credit; ESL (4 students enrolled).

College Admission Counseling 71 students graduated in 2016; all went to college, including Boston University; Furman University; Gordon College; Northeastern University; Wheaton College.

Student Life Upper grades have specified standards of dress, student council. Discipline rests primarily with faculty.

Summer Programs Enrichment, sports programs offered; session focuses on day camp activities, sports camps; held on campus; accepts boys and girls; open to students from other schools.

Tuition and Aid Day student tuition: $24,300–$28,100; 5-day tuition and room/board: $38,100; 7-day tuition and room/board: $57,660–$61,860. Tuition installment plan (SMART Tuition Payment Plan, Tuition Management Systems). Merit scholarship grants, need-based scholarship grants available. In 2016–17, 56% of upper-school students received aid; total upper-school merit-scholarship money awarded: $223,973. Total amount of financial aid awarded in 2016–17: $739,135.

Admissions Traditional secondary-level entrance grade is 9. For fall 2016, 181 students applied for upper-level admission, 123 were accepted, 71 enrolled. Deadline for receipt of application materials: February 1. Application fee required: $50. Interview recommended.

Athletics Interscholastic: baseball (boys), basketball (b,g), cross-country running (b,g), field hockey (g), lacrosse (b,g), physical training (b,g), soccer (b,g), softball (g), wrestling (b); intramural: basketball (b,g), gymnastics (b,g), lacrosse (b,g), physical training (b,g), soccer (b,g), tennis (b,g), volleyball (b,g), wrestling (b); coed interscholastic: golf; coed intramural: fitness, outdoor activities, rock climbing, skiing (downhill), snowboarding, strength & conditioning, touch football, ultimate Frisbee, volleyball, wall climbing. 2 PE instructors, 10 coaches, 2 athletic trainers.

Computers Computers are regularly used in all academic classes. Computer network features include on-campus library services, online commercial services, Internet access, wireless campus network, Internet filtering or blocking technology. Campus intranet, student e-mail accounts, and computer access in designated common areas are available to students. Students grades are available online. The school has a published electronic and media policy.

Contact Mrs. Cynthia Torjesen, Director of Admission. 781-862-7850 Ext. 152. Fax: 781-863-8503. E-mail: cindy.torjesen@lca.edu. Website: www.lca.edu

LEYSIN AMERICAN SCHOOL IN SWITZERLAND

Belle Epoque Campus
Chemin de la Source 3
Leysin 1854, Switzerland

Head of School: Dr. Marc-Frédéric Ott

General Information Coeducational boarding college-preparatory school. Grades 7–PG. Founded: 1961. Setting: small town. Nearest major city is Geneva, Switzerland. Students are housed in coed dormitories. 14 buildings on campus. Approved or accredited by International Baccalaureate Organization, New England Association of Schools and Colleges, Swiss Federation of Private Schools, and The Association of Boarding Schools. Member of Secondary School Admission Test Board. Language of instruction: English. Total enrollment: 340. Upper school average class size: 12. Upper school faculty-student ratio: 1:8. There are 180 required school days per year for Upper School students. Upper School students typically attend 5 days per week. The average school day consists of 5 hours and 55 minutes.

Upper School Student Profile Grade 7: 7 students (4 boys, 3 girls); Grade 8: 11 students (6 boys, 5 girls); Grade 9: 32 students (20 boys, 12 girls); Grade 10: 86 students (46 boys, 40 girls); Grade 11: 84 students (42 boys, 42 girls); Grade 12: 96 students (50 boys, 46 girls); Postgraduate: 3 students (2 boys, 1 girl). 100% of students are boarding students. 98% are international students. International students from Brazil, China, Mexico, Russian Federation, Spain, and United States; 55 other countries represented in student body.

Faculty School total: 72. In upper school: 40 men, 32 women; 42 have advanced degrees; 67 reside on campus.

Subjects Offered Algebra, American history, American literature, ancient history, art, band, biology, business, business studies, calculus, calculus-AP, chemistry, chorus, college counseling, computer programming, computer science, computer technologies, creative arts, current events, dance, drama, ecology, environmental systems, economics, English, English literature, ensembles, ESL, European history, fine arts, fitness, French, French studies, geometry, German, health education, history, history of the Americas, humanities, information technology, International Baccalaureate courses, intro to computers, journalism, language arts, math analysis, math methods, mathematics, mathematics-AP, model United Nations, modern languages, music, music appreciation, performing arts, physical education, physical science, physics, piano, pre-algebra, pre-calculus, psychology, SAT preparation, science, social sciences, social studies, Spanish, Spanish literature, stagecraft, studio art, study skills, theater, theory of knowledge, TOEFL preparation, trigonometry, United Nations and international issues, weightlifting, world history, yearbook.

Graduation Requirements Arts and fine arts (art, music, dance, drama), computer science, English, foreign language, mathematics, physical education (includes health), science, senior humanities, social studies (includes history), Swiss and European cultural trip reports.

Special Academic Programs International Baccalaureate program; honors section; independent study; study abroad; academic accommodation for the gifted, the musically talented, and the artistically talented; ESL (110 students enrolled).

College Admission Counseling 96 students graduated in 2016; 93 went to college, including Boston University; Mount Holyoke College; New York University; Northeastern University; The University of Texas at Austin; University of Virginia.

Other: 2 entered a postgraduate year, 1 had other specific plans. Mean SAT critical reading: 496, mean SAT math: 548, mean SAT writing: 509.

Student Life Upper grades have specified standards of dress, student council, honor system. Discipline rests equally with students and faculty.

Summer Programs Remediation, enrichment, advancement, ESL, sports, art/fine arts, rigorous outdoor training, computer instruction programs offered; session focuses on enrichment, theater, music, leadership, European travel, English language; held on campus; accepts boys and girls; open to students from other schools. 250 students usually enrolled. 2017 schedule: June 26 to August 13. Application deadline: none.

Tuition and Aid 5-day tuition and room/board: 51,000 Swiss francs; 7-day tuition and room/board: 85,000 Swiss francs. Tuition installment plan (individually arranged payment plans, corporate payment plan). Tuition reduction for siblings, bursaries, merit scholarship grants, need-based scholarship grants, paying campus jobs available. In 2016–17, 10% of upper-school students received aid; total upper-school merit-scholarship money awarded: 250,000 Swiss francs. Total amount of financial aid awarded in 2016–17: 600,000 Swiss francs.

Admissions Traditional secondary-level entrance grade is 10. Achievement/Aptitude/Writing or essay required. Deadline for receipt of application materials: none. Application fee required: 1500 Swiss francs. Interview required.

Athletics Interscholastic: alpine skiing (boys, girls), basketball (b,g), hockey (b), ice hockey (b), soccer (b,g), tennis (b,g), volleyball (b,g); intramural: basketball (b,g), soccer (b,g), tennis (b,g), volleyball (b,g); coed interscholastic: bicycling, cross-country running, equestrian sports, golf, skiing (cross-country), skiing (downhill), snowboarding, squash, swimming and diving, track and field; coed intramural: aerobics, aerobics/dance, alpine skiing, backpacking, ball hockey, ballet, bicycling, canoeing/kayaking, climbing, cross-country running, curling, dance, dance team, equestrian sports, figure skating, fitness, flag football, floor hockey, freestyle skiing, golf, hiking/backpacking, horseback riding, indoor hockey, indoor soccer, jogging, juggling, martial arts, mountain biking, mountaineering, nordic skiing, outdoor activities, outdoor adventure, outdoor education, outdoor recreation, paddle tennis, paint ball, physical fitness, physical training, rafting, rappelling, rock climbing, ropes courses, running, sailing, skiing (cross-country), skiing (downhill), snowboarding, snowshoeing, squash, street hockey, strength & conditioning, swimming and diving, table tennis, track and field, unicycling, walking, wall climbing, weight lifting, weight training, yoga. 1 PE instructor, 2 athletic trainers.

Computers Computers are regularly used in all classes. Computer network features include on-campus library services, online commercial services, Internet access, wireless campus network, Internet filtering or blocking technology. Campus intranet and student e-mail accounts are available to students. Students grades are available online. The school has a published electronic and media policy.

Contact Mrs. Danka Perrauld, Admissions Office Manager. 024-431-4888. E-mail: admissions@las.ch. Website: www.las.ch

LIBERTY CHRISTIAN HIGH SCHOOL

3782 Churn Creek Road
Redding, California 96002

Head of School: Mr. Tom L. Adams

General Information Coeducational day college-preparatory school, affiliated with American Baptist Churches in the U.S.A. Grades PK–12. Founded: 1965. Setting: small town. 4-acre campus. 2 buildings on campus. Approved or accredited by Association of Christian Schools International and Western Association of Schools and Colleges. Upper school average class size: 13. Upper school faculty-student ratio: 1:5. There are 180 required school days per year for Upper School students. Upper School students typically attend 5 days per week. The average school day consists of 6 hours.

Upper School Student Profile Grade 6: 6 students (4 boys, 2 girls); Grade 7: 5 students (1 boy, 4 girls); Grade 8: 8 students (4 boys, 4 girls); Grade 9: 14 students (8 boys, 6 girls); Grade 10: 11 students (7 boys, 4 girls); Grade 11: 9 students (7 boys, 2 girls); Grade 12: 15 students (6 boys, 9 girls). 25% of students are American Baptist Churches in the U.S.A.

Faculty School total: 11. In upper school: 7 men, 4 women; 2 have advanced degrees.

Subjects Offered Algebra, art, biology, drama, economics, English, geometry, global studies, government, health, integrated science, mathematics, pre-algebra, U.S. history.

Graduation Requirements American government, American history, chemistry, economics, English, foreign language, geography, mathematics, physical education (includes health), science, world history, Bible.

Special Academic Programs Domestic exchange program.

College Admission Counseling 9 students graduated in 2016; 8 went to college. Other: 1 entered military service.

Student Life Upper grades have specified standards of dress, student council. Discipline rests primarily with faculty. Attendance at religious services is required.

Tuition and Aid Day student tuition: $5561. Tuition installment plan (monthly payment plans, individually arranged payment plans). Tuition reduction for siblings, need-based scholarship grants available. In 2016–17, 25% of upper-school students received aid.

Admissions Deadline for receipt of application materials: August 15. No application fee required. Interview recommended.

Athletics Interscholastic: baseball (boys), basketball (b,g), golf (b,g), softball (g), volleyball (g), winter soccer (b,g); coed interscholastic: winter soccer. 1 PE instructor, 1 coach.

Computers Computer network features include on-campus library services, Internet access, wireless campus network, Internet filtering or blocking technology. Campus intranet and student e-mail accounts are available to students. Students grades are available online.

Contact 530-222-2232. Website: www.libertychristianredding.com

LIBERTY CHRISTIAN SCHOOL

7661 Warner Avenue
Huntington Beach, California 92647

Head of School: Mr. David Whitmire

General Information Coeducational day college-preparatory and religious studies school, affiliated with Baptist Church. Grades K–12. Distance learning grades 8–12. Founded: 1970. Setting: suburban. Nearest major city is Los Angeles. 5-acre campus. 4 buildings on campus. Approved or accredited by Accrediting Commission for Schools, Western Association of Schools and Colleges, and California Department of Education. Total enrollment: 112. Upper school average class size: 7. Upper school faculty-student ratio: 1:6. There are 180 required school days per year for Upper School students. Upper School students typically attend 5 days per week. The average school day consists of 6 hours and 30 minutes.

Upper School Student Profile Grade 6: 7 students (3 boys, 4 girls); Grade 7: 6 students (5 boys, 1 girl); Grade 8: 14 students (11 boys, 3 girls); Grade 9: 4 students (2 boys, 2 girls); Grade 10: 10 students (5 boys, 5 girls); Grade 11: 4 students (2 boys, 2 girls); Grade 12: 8 students (4 boys, 4 girls). 50% of students are Baptist.

Faculty School total: 18. In upper school: 6 men, 8 women; 1 has an advanced degree.

Subjects Offered Algebra, all academic, American history, American literature, analytic geometry, ancient world history, applied arts, applied music, athletics, bell choir, biology, calculus, character education, chemistry, choir, Christian doctrine, college admission preparation, college counseling, computer science, computer skills, concert bell choir, consumer economics, consumer mathematics, cultural geography, drama, earth and space science, earth science, economics, electives, English, English composition, English literature, film history, fine arts, foreign language, general science, geography, geometry, government, grammar, handbells, health, history, history of music, honors English, internship, lab science, library assistant, Life of Christ, life science, mathematics, media, modern Western civilization, modern world history, moral and social development, music theory, musical productions, personal fitness, physical fitness, physical science, physics, play production, portfolio writing, pre-algebra, pre-calculus, pre-college orientation, reading/study skills, religious studies, science, senior project, social sciences, Spanish, Spanish-AP, sports, stage design, student government, U.S. government, U.S. history, visual and performing arts, weight training, world geography, yearbook.

Graduation Requirements World cultures.

Special Academic Programs Honors section; independent study; academic accommodation for the gifted; remedial reading and/or remedial writing; remedial math.

College Admission Counseling 12 students graduated in 2016; all went to college, including California State University, Long Beach; Grand Canyon University; Orange Coast College.

Student Life Upper grades have specified standards of dress, student council, honor system. Discipline rests primarily with faculty.

Tuition and Aid Day student tuition: $6600. Tuition installment plan (SMART Tuition Payment Plan). Need-based scholarship grants available. In 2016–17, 60% of upper-school students received aid. Total amount of financial aid awarded in 2016–17: $20,000.

Admissions Deadline for receipt of application materials: none. Application fee required: $400. On-campus interview recommended.

Athletics Interscholastic: basketball (boys, girls), flag football (b), softball (g), volleyball (b,g). 1 PE instructor, 1 coach.

Computers Computers are regularly used in computer applications, media, yearbook classes. Computer network features include Internet access, wireless campus network. Computer access in designated common areas is available to students. Students grades are available online. The school has a published electronic and media policy.

Contact Mrs. LeighAnne Lockerbie, Registrar. 714-842-5992. Fax: 714-848-7484. E-mail: info@libertychristian.org. Website: www.libertychristian.org

LINCOLN ACADEMY

81 Academy Hill
Newcastle, Maine 04553

Head of School: Mr. David B. Sturdevant

General Information Coeducational boarding and day college-preparatory, general academic, arts, technology, Advanced Placement, and world languages school; primarily serves students with learning disabilities, individuals with Attention Deficit Disorder, and dyslexic students. Grades 9–12. Founded: 1801. Setting: small town. Nearest major city is Portland. Students are housed in single-sex by floor dormitories.

100-acre campus. 7 buildings on campus. Approved or accredited by Independent Schools of Northern New England, New England Association of Schools and Colleges, The Association of Boarding Schools, and Maine Department of Education. Member of National Association of Independent Schools and Secondary School Admission Test Board. Endowment: $7 million. Total enrollment: 588. Upper school average class size: 18. Upper school faculty-student ratio: 1:11. There are 176 required school days per year for Upper School students. Upper School students typically attend 5 days per week. The average school day consists of 6 hours and 40 minutes.

Upper School Student Profile Grade 9: 131 students (75 boys, 56 girls); Grade 10: 145 students (80 boys, 65 girls); Grade 11: 153 students (89 boys, 64 girls); Grade 12: 140 students (68 boys, 72 girls). 15% of students are boarding students. 85% are state residents. 2 states are represented in upper school student body. 15% are international students. International students from China, Germany, Mexico, Republic of Korea, Spain, and Viet Nam; 13 other countries represented in student body.

Faculty School total: 63. In upper school: 22 men, 32 women; 31 have advanced degrees; 12 reside on campus.

Subjects Offered Architectural drawing, career education internship, chamber groups, choral music, communications, computer science-AP, English language and composition-AP, English literature and composition-AP, ESL, fencing, French language-AP, Japanese, macro/microeconomics-AP, maritime history, media communications, mentorship program, metal fabrication technology, musical theater, Native American history, SAT/ACT preparation, senior career experience, statistics-AP, technical education, U.S. history-AP, vocational-technical courses, weight training, world religions.

Graduation Requirements Creative arts, emerging technology, visual and performing arts, work experience, job shadow experiences, community service.

Special Academic Programs 16 Advanced Placement exams for which test preparation is offered; honors section; independent study; study at local college for college credit; study abroad; academic accommodation for the gifted, the musically talented, and the artistically talented; remedial reading and/or remedial writing; remedial math; ESL (40 students enrolled).

College Admission Counseling 148 students graduated in 2016; 102 went to college, including Saint Joseph's College of Maine; Southern Maine Community College; University of Maine; University of Maine at Farmington; University of New Hampshire; Wheaton College. Other: 43 went to work, 3 entered military service, 104 entered a postgraduate year, 46 had other specific plans.

Student Life Upper grades have specified standards of dress, student council. Discipline rests primarily with faculty.

Summer Programs ESL, art/fine arts programs offered; session focuses on English immersion, cultural experience; held on campus; accepts boys and girls; open to students from other schools. 2017 schedule: August 15 to August 31.

Tuition and Aid Day student tuition: $10,740; 7-day tuition and room/board: $44,500. Tuition reduction for siblings, need-based scholarship grants available. In 2016–17, 5% of upper-school students received aid. Total amount of financial aid awarded in 2016–17: $600,000.

Admissions Traditional secondary-level entrance grade is 9. For fall 2016, 104 students applied for upper-level admission, 73 were accepted, 43 enrolled. CTBS or ERB, ERB CTP IV, International English Language Test, PSAT, SSAT, TOEFL or TOEFL Junior required. Deadline for receipt of application materials: none. Application fee required: $50. Interview required.

Athletics Interscholastic: baseball (boys), basketball (b,g), cheering (g), cross-country running (b,g), field hockey (b,g), golf (b,g), lacrosse (b,g), soccer (b,g), softball (g), swimming and diving (b,g), tennis (b,g), track and field (b,g), wrestling (b,g); intramural: self defense (g); coed interscholastic: Indoor track, Special Olympics, winter (indoor) track; coed intramural: canoeing/kayaking, fencing, fly fishing, hiking/backpacking, indoor soccer, mountain biking, nordic skiing, outdoor activities, outdoor adventure, physical fitness, physical training, sailing, scuba diving, skiing (cross-country), skiing (downhill), snowboarding, table tennis, ultimate Frisbee, weight lifting, weight training. 3 PE instructors, 16 coaches, 1 athletic trainer.

Computers Computers are regularly used in all classes. Computer network features include on-campus library services, online commercial services, Internet access, wireless campus network. Campus intranet, student e-mail accounts, and computer access in designated common areas are available to students. Students grades are available online. The school has a published electronic and media policy.

Contact Ms. Sheryl Stearns, Director of Enrollment and Marketing. 207-563-3596 Ext. 108. Fax: 207-563-1067. E-mail: stearns@lincolnacademy.org.

Website: www.lincolnacademy.org

LINCOLN SCHOOL

301 Butler Avenue
Providence, Rhode Island 02906-5556

Head of School: Suzanne Fogarty

General Information Coeducational day (boys' only in lower grades) college-preparatory school. Boys grades N–PK, girls grades N–12. Founded: 1884. Setting: urban. 46-acre campus. 5 buildings on campus. Approved or accredited by Association of Independent Schools in New England, Friends Council on Education, New England Association of Schools and Colleges, and Rhode Island Department of Education. Member of National Association of Independent Schools and Secondary School

Admission Test Board. Endowment: $8 million. Total enrollment: 350. Upper school average class size: 13. Upper school faculty-student ratio: 1:4. Upper School students typically attend 5 days per week. The average school day consists of 7 hours and 13 minutes.

Upper School Student Profile Grade 9: 40 students (40 girls); Grade 10: 58 students (58 girls); Grade 11: 30 students (30 girls); Grade 12: 41 students (41 girls).

Faculty School total: 75. In upper school: 11 men, 35 women; 24 have advanced degrees.

Subjects Offered All academic, statistics, study skills, technology, U.S. history, visual and performing arts, visual arts, visual literacy, world cultures, writing.

Graduation Requirements College planning, public speaking, Quakerism and ethics, senior service trip.

Special Academic Programs Advanced Placement exam preparation; honors section; independent study; term-away projects; study at local college for college credit; study abroad; programs in general development for dyslexic students.

College Admission Counseling 41 students graduated in 2016; all went to college, including Brown University; Elon University; Providence College; University of Rhode Island. Median SAT critical reading: 580, median SAT math: 575, median SAT writing: 593.

Student Life Upper grades have uniform requirement, student council, honor system. Discipline rests equally with students and faculty.

Tuition and Aid Day student tuition: $33,700. Tuition installment plan (FACTS Tuition Payment Plan, Tuition Management Systems Plan). Merit scholarship grants, need-based scholarship grants available. In 2016–17, 40% of upper-school students received aid; total upper-school merit-scholarship money awarded: $60,000. Total amount of financial aid awarded in 2016–17: $2,000,000.

Admissions Traditional secondary-level entrance grade is 9. For fall 2016, 72 students applied for upper-level admission, 40 were accepted, 26 enrolled. ISEE or SSAT required. Deadline for receipt of application materials: February 15. Application fee required: $50. On-campus interview required.

Athletics Interscholastic: basketball, crew, cross-country running, field hockey, lacrosse, soccer, squash, swimming and diving, tennis. 3 PE instructors, 17 coaches, 1 athletic trainer.

Computers Computers are regularly used in college planning, technology classes. Computer network features include on-campus library services, Internet access, wireless campus network, Internet filtering or blocking technology. Student e-mail accounts and computer access in designated common areas are available to students. The school has a published electronic and media policy.

Contact Mrs. Diane Mota, Admission Office Administrative Assistant. 401-331-9696 Ext. 3157. Fax: 401-751-6670. E-mail: dmota@lincolnschool.org.

Website: www.lincolnschool.org

THE LINDEN SCHOOL

10 Rosehill Avenue
Toronto, Ontario M4T 1G5, Canada

Head of School: Ms. Janice Gladstone

General Information Girls' day college-preparatory, arts, technology, humanities, and science school. Grades JK–12. Founded: 1993. Setting: urban. 1 building on campus. Approved or accredited by Ontario Department of Education. Language of instruction: English. Total enrollment: 121. Upper school average class size: 12. Upper school faculty-student ratio: 1.5. There are 180 required school days per year for Upper School students. Upper School students typically attend 5 days per week. The average school day consists of 7 hours.

Upper School Student Profile Grade 9: 13 students (13 girls); Grade 10: 10 students (10 girls); Grade 11: 10 students (10 girls); Grade 12: 9 students (9 girls).

Faculty School total: 30. In upper school: 3 men, 26 women; 10 have advanced degrees.

Subjects Offered Algebra, biology, calculus, chemistry, computer science, dramatic arts, English, English literature, French, geography, geometry, history, information technology, Latin, physics, Spanish, visual arts, writing workshop.

Graduation Requirements Canadian geography, Canadian history, career education, English, French, mathematics, science and technology, Ontario Secondary School Diploma requirements.

Special Academic Programs Advanced Placement exam preparation; honors section; independent study; academic accommodation for the gifted.

College Admission Counseling 12 students graduated in 2016; all went to college, including Dalhousie University; Ryerson University; The University of British Columbia; University of Toronto; University of Waterloo; York University. Other: 12 entered a postgraduate year.

Student Life Upper grades have honor system. Discipline rests equally with students and faculty.

Tuition and Aid Day student tuition: CAN$14,000–CAN$19,400. Tuition installment plan (monthly payment plans, individually arranged payment plans). Tuition reduction for siblings, bursaries, merit scholarship grants, need-based scholarship grants available. In 2016–17, 20% of upper-school students received aid; total upper-school merit-scholarship money awarded: CAN$150,000. Total amount of financial aid awarded in 2016–17: CAN$150,000.

Admissions Traditional secondary-level entrance grade is 9. School's own test required. Deadline for receipt of application materials: none. Application fee required: CAN$100. Interview recommended.

Athletics Interscholastic: cross-country running, dance, fitness, fitness walking, flag football, floor hockey, indoor hockey, indoor soccer, running, track and field, ultimate Frisbee, volleyball; intramural: alpine skiing, backpacking, badminton, ball hockey, baseball, basketball, boxing, canoeing/kayaking, climbing, combined training, cooperative games, cross-country running, dance, fitness, floor hockey, Frisbee, hiking/backpacking, ice skating, indoor hockey, indoor soccer, kickball, modern dance, outdoor activities, physical fitness, rock climbing, ropes courses, running, skiing (cross-country), skiing (downhill), snowboarding, soccer, track and field, ultimate Frisbee, volleyball, yoga. 2 PE instructors.

Computers Computers are regularly used in all classes. Computer network features include on-campus library services, Internet access, wireless campus network, Internet filtering or blocking technology. Student e-mail accounts and computer access in designated common areas are available to students. The school has a published electronic and media policy.

Contact Ms. Jean Geary, Admissions Coordinator. 416-966-4406. Fax: 416-966-9736. E-mail: admissions@lindenschool.ca. Website: www.lindenschool.ca

LINFIELD CHRISTIAN SCHOOL

31950 Pauba Road
Temecula, California 92592

Head of School: Drake Charles

General Information Coeducational day college-preparatory, arts, vocational, religious studies, technology, STEAM, and biomedical school, affiliated with Christian faith. Grades JK–12. Founded: 1936. Setting: suburban. Nearest major city is San Diego. 105-acre campus. 6 buildings on campus. Approved or accredited by Association of Christian Schools International, Western Association of Schools and Colleges, and California Department of Education. Total enrollment: 757. Upper school average class size: 19. Upper school faculty-student ratio: 1:13. There are 171 required school days per year for Upper School students. Upper School students typically attend 5 days per week. The average school day consists of 5 hours and 55 minutes.

Upper School Student Profile Grade 6: 62 students (29 boys, 33 girls); Grade 7: 63 students (30 boys, 33 girls); Grade 8: 76 students (43 boys, 33 girls); Grade 9: 102 students (52 boys, 50 girls); Grade 10: 98 students (45 boys, 53 girls); Grade 11: 103 students (49 boys, 54 girls); Grade 12: 92 students (45 boys, 47 girls). 70% of students are Christian faith.

Faculty School total: 64. In upper school: 10 men, 15 women; 8 have advanced degrees.

Subjects Offered Advanced biology, advanced chemistry, advanced math, Advanced Placement courses, advanced studio art-AP, algebra, American history-AP, American sign language, anatomy and physiology, art, ASB Leadership, athletics, band, Bible, biology, calculus-AP, career/college preparation, chemistry, chemistry-AP, choir, Christian doctrine, Christian ethics, Christian studies, Christianity, college counseling, computers, economics, English, English-AP, European history-AP, film, filmmaking, French, freshman foundations, general science, geometry, government, government-AP, health, physical education, physics, pre-calculus, public policy, senior seminar, service learning/internship, Spanish, Spanish-AP, speech and debate, sports medicine, studio art-AP, theater, U.S. history, U.S. history-AP, world history, world religions, yearbook.

Graduation Requirements Arts and fine arts (art, music, dance, drama), computer science, economics, English, foreign language, freshman foundations, government, mathematics, physical education (includes health), religion (includes Bible studies and theology), science, senior seminar, social sciences, social studies (includes history), speech and debate. Community service is required.

Special Academic Programs 12 Advanced Placement exams for which test preparation is offered; honors section; academic accommodation for the gifted.

College Admission Counseling 85 students graduated in 2016; 84 went to college, including California State University, San Marcos; Pepperdine University; San Diego State University; University of California, San Diego; University of Colorado Boulder. Other: 1 had other specific plans. Mean SAT critical reading: 511, mean SAT math: 617, mean SAT writing: 528, mean combined SAT: 1656.

Student Life Upper grades have uniform requirement, student council, honor system. Discipline rests primarily with faculty. Attendance at religious services is required.

Tuition and Aid Day student tuition: $10,920. Tuition installment plan (monthly payment plans, two pay plan, One pay plan). Merit scholarship grants, need-based scholarship grants available. In 2016–17, 30% of upper-school students received aid.

Admissions Traditional secondary-level entrance grade is 9. For fall 2016, 322 students applied for upper-level admission, 253 were accepted, 181 enrolled. OLSAT, Stanford Achievement Test, Stanford Achievement Test, TerraNova or writing sample required. Deadline for receipt of application materials: none. Application fee required: $75. On-campus interview required.

Athletics Interscholastic: baseball (boys), basketball (b,g), cheering (g), cross-country running (b,g), football (b), lacrosse (b), soccer (b,g), softball (g), tennis (b,g), track and field (b,g), volleyball (g); intramural: volleyball (g); coed interscholastic: equestrian sports, golf; coed intramural: cross-country running, flag football. 3 PE instructors, 16 coaches, 1 athletic trainer.

Computers Computers are regularly used in computer applications, French, keyboarding, media production, science, senior seminar, yearbook classes. Computer network features include on-campus library services, online commercial services, Internet access, wireless campus network, Internet filtering or blocking technology. Campus intranet, student e-mail accounts, and computer access in designated common areas are available to students. Students grades are available online. The school has a published electronic and media policy.

Contact Mrs. Bria Hyink, Admissions Assistant. 951-676-8111 Ext. 1402. Fax: 951-695-1291. E-mail: bhyink@linfield.com. Website: www.linfield.com

LITTLE KESWICK SCHOOL

Keswick, Virginia
See Special Needs Schools section.

LIVINGSTONE ADVENTIST ACADEMY

5771 Fruitland Road NE
Salem, Oregon 97317

Head of School: Mr. Joel Reyes

General Information Coeducational day college-preparatory and choir, hand bells, robotics, yearbook, gardening school, affiliated with Seventh-day Adventist Church. Grades K–12. Founded: 1898. Setting: rural. 20-acre campus. 9 buildings on campus. Approved or accredited by National Council for Private School Accreditation and Oregon Department of Education. Upper school average class size: 20. Upper school faculty-student ratio: 1:12. There are 178 required school days per year for Upper School students. Upper School students typically attend 5 days per week. The average school day consists of 6 hours and 45 minutes.

Upper School Student Profile Grade 6: 12 students (7 boys, 5 girls); Grade 7: 10 students (5 boys, 5 girls); Grade 8: 14 students (6 boys, 8 girls); Grade 9: 17 students (8 boys, 9 girls); Grade 10: 13 students (6 boys, 7 girls); Grade 11: 17 students (8 boys, 9 girls); Grade 12: 14 students (9 boys, 5 girls). 98% of students are Seventh-day Adventists.

Faculty School total: 13. In upper school: 3 men, 2 women; 2 have advanced degrees.

Student Life Upper grades have specified standards of dress, student council, honor system. Discipline rests primarily with faculty.

Tuition and Aid Day student tuition: $7860. Tuition installment plan (monthly payment plans, semester plan, full payment plan). Need-based scholarship grants available.

Admissions Traditional secondary-level entrance grade is 9. For fall 2016, 67 students applied for upper-level admission, 61 were accepted, 61 enrolled. Application fee required: $50. On-campus interview recommended.

Athletics Interscholastic: basketball (boys, girls), volleyball (g); coed interscholastic: soccer, wilderness. 1 PE instructor, 2 coaches.

Contact Mrs. Pam Naylor, Office Manager. 503-363-9408. Fax: 503-363-5721. E-mail: pnaylor@laaonline.org. Website: www.laaonline.org

LONG ISLAND LUTHERAN MIDDLE AND HIGH SCHOOL

131 Brookville Road
Brookville, New York 11545-3399

Head of School: Dr. Andrew Gove

General Information Coeducational day college-preparatory school, affiliated with Lutheran Church. Boarding grades 8–12, day grades 6–12. Founded: 1960. Setting: suburban. Nearest major city is New York. Students are housed in single-sex dormitories. 32-acre campus. 6 buildings on campus. Approved or accredited by Evangelical Lutheran Church in America, Middle States Association of Colleges and Schools, US Department of State, and New York Department of Education. Member of National Association of Independent Schools. Endowment: $6.5 million. Total enrollment: 590. Upper school average class size: 18. Upper school faculty-student ratio: 1:9. There are 160 required school days per year for Upper School students. Upper School students typically attend 5 days per week. The average school day consists of 6 hours and 30 minutes.

Upper School Student Profile Grade 9: 118 students (57 boys, 61 girls); Grade 10: 98 students (46 boys, 52 girls); Grade 11: 94 students (49 boys, 45 girls); Grade 12: 103 students (52 boys, 51 girls). 8% of students are boarding students. 89% are state residents. 1 state is represented in upper school student body. 11% are international students. International students from China, Egypt, and Lithuania. 25% of students are Lutheran.

Faculty School total: 58. In upper school: 21 men, 29 women; 47 have advanced degrees; 8 reside on campus.

Graduation Requirements Arts and fine arts (art, music, dance, drama), business studies, English, foreign language, mathematics, physical education (includes health), religion (includes Bible studies and theology), science, social studies (includes history).

Special Academic Programs 14 Advanced Placement exams for which test preparation is offered; honors section; term-away projects.

College Admission Counseling 100 students graduated in 2016; all went to college, including Binghamton University, State University of New York; Fordham University; Hofstra University; New York University; Penn State University Park; Susquehanna University. Mean SAT critical reading: 572, mean SAT math: 564, mean SAT writing: 595, mean combined SAT: 1731, mean composite ACT: 24. 25% scored over 26 on composite ACT.

Student Life Upper grades have uniform requirement, student council, honor system. Discipline rests primarily with faculty. Attendance at religious services is required.

Summer Programs Sports, art/fine arts, computer instruction programs offered; session focuses on sports, recreation, and education; held both on and off campus; accepts boys and girls; open to students from other schools. 4,000 students usually enrolled. 2017 schedule: June 30 to August 22. Application deadline: January 1.

Tuition and Aid Day student tuition: $10,925–$12,945; 7-day tuition and room/board: $56,000. Tuition installment plan (monthly payment plans, school's own payment plan). Tuition reduction for siblings, merit scholarship grants, need-based scholarship grants available. In 2016–17, 25% of upper-school students received aid; total upper-school merit-scholarship money awarded: $28,000. Total amount of financial aid awarded in 2016–17: $420,000.

Admissions Traditional secondary-level entrance grade is 9. For fall 2016, 138 students applied for upper-level admission, 86 were accepted, 56 enrolled. Cognitive Abilities Test, Math Placement Exam and writing sample required. Deadline for receipt of application materials: none. Application fee required: $100. On-campus interview required.

Athletics Interscholastic: baseball (boys, girls), basketball (b), cheering (g), dance team (g), football (b), lacrosse (b,g), roller hockey (b), soccer (b,g), softball (g), tennis (b,g), volleyball (g), wrestling (b); intramural: dance team (g), flag football (b), horseback riding (b,g); coed interscholastic: cross-country running, golf, running, track and field; coed intramural: bowling, equestrian sports, physical training, skiing (downhill), winter (indoor) track. 3 PE instructors, 30 coaches.

Computers Computers are regularly used in accounting, art, business, business skills, English, graphic design, history, journalism, library skills, mathematics, science classes. Computer network features include on-campus library services, Internet access, wireless campus network, Internet filtering or blocking technology, 1:1 student iPad program required for all students. Student e-mail accounts and computer access in designated common areas are available to students. Students grades are available online. The school has a published electronic and media policy.

Contact Sarah Thompson, Director of Admissions. 516-626-1700 Ext. 546. Fax: 516-622-7459. E-mail: sarah.thompson@luhi.org. Website: www.luhi.org

LONG TRAIL SCHOOL

1045 Kirby Hollow Road
Dorset, Vermont 05251-9776

Head of School: Mr. Steven Dear

General Information Coeducational day college-preparatory and arts school. Grades 6–12. Founded: 1975. Setting: rural. Nearest major city is Rutland. 14-acre campus. 1 building on campus. Approved or accredited by International Baccalaureate Organization, New England Association of Schools and Colleges, and Vermont Department of Education. Member of National Association of Independent Schools. Endowment: $4.5 million. Total enrollment: 155. Upper school average class size: 10. Upper school faculty-student ratio: 1:8. There are 175 required school days per year for Upper School students. Upper School students typically attend 5 days per week. The average school day consists of 7 hours.

Upper School Student Profile Grade 6: 12 students (4 boys, 8 girls); Grade 7: 35 students (20 boys, 15 girls); Grade 8: 27 students (9 boys, 18 girls); Grade 9: 30 students (16 boys, 14 girls); Grade 10: 31 students (15 boys, 16 girls); Grade 11: 26 students (14 boys, 12 girls); Grade 12: 22 students (11 boys, 11 girls).

Faculty School total: 32. In upper school: 10 men, 22 women; 16 have advanced degrees.

Subjects Offered 20th century world history, acting, advanced biology, advanced TOEFL/grammar, algebra, American history, American literature, American literature-AP, art, band, biology, calculus, calculus-AP, chemistry, chorus, computer information systems, conceptual physics, concert band, drama, drawing, earth science, economics, English, English literature, English literature-AP, environmental science, environmental science-AP, French, geography, geometry, government/civics, history, mathematics, model United Nations, music, physical education, physical science, physics, political science, pre-algebra, pre-calculus, probability and statistics, psychology, psychology-AP, science, social studies, Spanish, statistics, statistics-AP, technical theater, theater, trigonometry, U.S. history, U.S. history-AP, world history, world literature, writing.

Graduation Requirements Arts and fine arts (art, music, dance, drama), computer science, English, foreign language, mathematics, physical education (includes health), science, social studies (includes history), brief graduation ceremony speech. Community service is required.

Special Academic Programs International Baccalaureate program; honors section; independent study; study at local college for college credit; programs in English, mathematics, general development for dyslexic students; ESL (8 students enrolled).

College Admission Counseling 23 students graduated in 2016; 22 went to college, including Brown University; Michigan State University; Princeton University; Syracuse University; University of Vermont; Wheaton College. Other: 1 went to work. Median SAT critical reading: 590, median SAT math: 590, median SAT writing: 540, median composite ACT: 27. 50% scored over 600 on SAT critical reading, 45% scored over 600 on SAT math, 25% scored over 600 on SAT writing, 35% scored over 1800 on combined SAT, 58% scored over 26 on composite ACT.

Student Life Upper grades have specified standards of dress, student council, honor system. Discipline rests equally with students and faculty.

Tuition and Aid Day student tuition: $17,986. Tuition installment plan (monthly payment plans, individually arranged payment plans, TADS Financial Management). Merit scholarship grants, need-based scholarship grants available. In 2016–17, 25% of upper-school students received aid; total upper-school merit-scholarship money awarded: $9000. Total amount of financial aid awarded in 2016–17: $99,599.

Admissions Traditional secondary-level entrance grade is 9. For fall 2016, 20 students applied for upper-level admission, 13 were accepted, 9 enrolled. Admissions testing, essay or WRAT required. Deadline for receipt of application materials: none. Application fee required: $35. On-campus interview recommended.

Athletics Interscholastic: baseball (boys), basketball (b,g), climbing (b,g), soccer (b,g), softball (g); coed interscholastic: alpine skiing, cross-country running, dance team, freestyle skiing, golf, rock climbing, skiing (downhill), snowboarding; coed intramural: aerobics/dance, alpine skiing, basketball, bicycling, climbing, dance, equestrian sports, fitness walking, fly fishing, freestyle skiing, Frisbee, golf, hiking/backpacking, ice skating, indoor soccer, mountain biking, nordic skiing, rock climbing, skiing (downhill), snowboarding, tennis, touch football, ultimate Frisbee, weight lifting. 1 PE instructor, 8 coaches.

Computers Computers are regularly used in art, English, foreign language, history, library, mathematics, music, science, technology, yearbook classes. Computer network features include on-campus library services, online commercial services, Internet access, wireless campus network, Internet filtering or blocking technology. Campus intranet and student e-mail accounts are available to students. Students grades are available online. The school has a published electronic and media policy.

Contact Ms. Kim Murphy, Admissions Coordinator. 802-867-5717 Ext. 191. Fax: 802-867-0147. E-mail: applylts@longtrailschool.org. Website: www.longtrailschool.org

LOUDOUN SCHOOL FOR THE GIFTED

44675 Cape Ct., #105
Ashburn, Virginia 20147

Head of School: Dr. Deep Sran

General Information Coeducational day college-preparatory school. Grades 6–12. Founded: 2008. Setting: suburban. .3-acre campus. 1 building on campus. Approved or accredited by Southern Association of Colleges and Schools and Virginia Department of Education. Member of National Association of Independent Schools. Total enrollment: 35. Upper school average class size: 6. Upper school faculty-student ratio: 1:3. There are 180 required school days per year for Upper School students. Upper School students typically attend 5 days per week. The average school day consists of 7 hours and 15 minutes.

Upper School Student Profile Grade 9: 11 students (5 boys, 6 girls); Grade 10: 6 students (4 boys, 2 girls); Grade 11: 5 students (3 boys, 2 girls); Grade 12: 9 students (2 boys, 7 girls).

Faculty School total: 12. In upper school: 6 men, 6 women; 8 have advanced degrees.

Subjects Offered All academic.

Special Academic Programs Advanced Placement exam preparation; honors section; accelerated programs; independent study; academic accommodation for the gifted.

College Admission Counseling 3 students graduated in 2016; all went to college, including American University; James Madison University; The College of William and Mary.

Student Life Upper grades have student council. Discipline rests primarily with faculty.

Tuition and Aid Day student tuition: $27,600. Tuition installment plan (SMART Tuition Payment Plan, monthly payment plans, individually arranged payment plans).

Admissions Traditional secondary-level entrance grade is 9. Stanford Binet or WISC or WAIS required. Deadline for receipt of application materials: none. No application fee required. On-campus interview recommended.

Athletics 1 PE instructor.

Computers Computers are regularly used in all classes. Computer network features include Internet access, wireless campus network, Internet filtering or blocking technology. Student e-mail accounts and computer access in designated common areas are available to students. Students grades are available online. The school has a published electronic and media policy.

Contact Susan Talbott, Executive Director. 703-956-5020. E-mail: stalbott@idealschools.org. Website: www.loudounschool.org

LOUISVILLE COLLEGIATE SCHOOL

2427 Glenmary Avenue
Louisville, Kentucky 40204

Head of School: Dr. James Calleroz White

General Information Coeducational day college-preparatory and arts school. Grades JK–12. Founded: 1915. Setting: urban. 11-acre campus. 2 buildings on campus. Member of National Association of Independent Schools and Secondary School Admission Test Board. Endowment: $5.7 million. Total enrollment: 676. Upper school average class size: 15. Upper school faculty-student ratio: 1:7. The average school day consists of 7 hours.

Faculty School total: 80. In upper school: 12 men, 10 women; 20 have advanced degrees.

Subjects Offered Algebra, American history, American literature, ancient history, art, art history, biology, calculus, chemistry, Chinese, chorus, community service, composition, computer science, creative writing, discrete mathematics, drama, economics, English, English literature, ensembles, environmental science, European history, fine arts, French, geometry, German, history, mathematics, media, music, music history, physical education, physics, physiology, pre-calculus, science, social studies, Spanish, statistics, studio art, theater, trigonometry, world history, world literature, writing.

Graduation Requirements Arts and fine arts (art, music, dance, drama), English, foreign language, mathematics, physical education (includes health), science, social studies (includes history), senior symposium in leadership and service, individual and class service projects, senior speech.

Special Academic Programs Advanced Placement exam preparation; honors section; independent study; term-away projects; study abroad.

College Admission Counseling 56 students graduated in 2016; all went to college, including Miami University; Northwestern University; University of Louisville; Vanderbilt University; Wake Forest University. Median SAT critical reading: 602, median SAT math: 662, median SAT writing: 629, median composite ACT: 28.

Student Life Upper grades have uniform requirement, student council, honor system. Discipline rests equally with students and faculty.

Summer Programs Enrichment, advancement, sports, art/fine arts, computer instruction programs offered; session focuses on educational enrichment and sports; held both on and off campus; accepts boys and girls; open to students from other schools. 350 students usually enrolled. 2017 schedule: June 1 to July 31. Application deadline: none.

Tuition and Aid Day student tuition: $22,800. Tuition installment plan (The Tuition Plan, monthly payment plans, individually arranged payment plans). Merit scholarship grants, need-based scholarship grants available. In 2016–17, 31% of upper-school students received aid.

Admissions Traditional secondary-level entrance grade is 9. School's own exam and SSAT required. Deadline for receipt of application materials: none. Application fee required: $50.

Athletics Interscholastic: basketball (boys, girls), crew (g), cross-country running (b,g), field hockey (g), golf (b,g), indoor track (b,g), lacrosse (b,g), rowing (b,g), soccer (b,g), softball (g), strength & conditioning (b,g), swimming and diving (b,g), tennis (b,g), track and field (b,g), winter (indoor) track (b,g); intramural: basketball (b,g), soccer (b,g), tennis (b,g); coed interscholastic: soccer, strength & conditioning; coed intramural: soccer. 4 PE instructors, 60 coaches, 1 athletic trainer.

Computers Computers are regularly used in art, English, foreign language, history, mathematics, science classes. Computer network features include on-campus library services, online commercial services, Internet access, wireless campus network, Internet filtering or blocking technology. Student e-mail accounts and computer access in designated common areas are available to students. Students grades are available online. The school has a published electronic and media policy.

Contact Lynne Age, Admission Office Coordinator. 502-479-0378. Fax: 502-454-0549. E-mail: lage@loucol.com. Website: www.loucol.com

LOUISVILLE HIGH SCHOOL

22300 Mulholland Drive
Woodland Hills, California 91364

Head of School: Mrs. Kathleen Vercillo

General Information Girls' day college-preparatory school, affiliated with Roman Catholic Church. Grades 9–12. Founded: 1960. Setting: suburban. Nearest major city is Tarzana. 17-acre campus. 7 buildings on campus. Approved or accredited by National Catholic Education Association, Western Association of Schools and Colleges, Western Catholic Education Association, and California Department of Education. Total enrollment: 337. Upper school average class size: 25. Upper school faculty-student ratio: 1:25. There are 180 required school days per year for Upper School students. Upper School students typically attend 5 days per week. The average school day consists of 6 hours.

Upper School Student Profile Grade 9: 112 students (112 girls); Grade 10: 75 students (75 girls); Grade 11: 76 students (76 girls); Grade 12: 108 students (108 girls). 71% of students are Roman Catholic.

Faculty School total: 35. In upper school: 5 men, 30 women; 26 have advanced degrees.

Subjects Offered 3-dimensional art, Advanced Placement courses, advanced studio art-AP, algebra, American history, American history-AP, American literature, American literature-AP, anatomy, art, art-AP, Bible studies, biology, calculus, calculus-AP, campus ministry, ceramics, chemistry, choir, chorus, computer science, creative writing, dance, drama, economics, English, English language-AP, English literature, English literature-AP, English-AP, environmental science, environmental science-AP, European history, European history-AP, fine arts, French, French language-AP, French-AP, geography, geometry, government-AP, government/civics, government/civics-AP, grammar, health, history, honors algebra, honors English, honors geometry, journalism, law, mathematics, media production, music, photography, physical education, physics, physics-AP, physiology, probability and statistics, psychology, religion, science, social sciences, social studies, Spanish, Spanish language-AP, Spanish-AP, speech, studio art-AP, technical theater, theater, theater production, trigonometry, U.S. history-AP, video film production, Web site design, world geography, world history, world history-AP, world literature, yoga.

Graduation Requirements Arts and fine arts (art, music, dance, drama), biology, chemistry, computer science, economics, English, foreign language, health, health education, mathematics, performing arts, physical education (includes health), religion (includes Bible studies and theology), science, social sciences, social studies (includes history), U.S. government, U.S. history, visual arts, world history. Community service is required.

Special Academic Programs Advanced Placement exam preparation; independent study.

College Admission Counseling 81 students graduated in 2016; all went to college, including Boston College; California State University, Northridge; Georgetown University; Loyola Marymount University; Oregon State University; University of California, Berkeley.

Student Life Upper grades have uniform requirement, student council, honor system. Discipline rests equally with students and faculty. Attendance at religious services is required.

Summer Programs Sports programs offered; session focuses on skill development; held both on and off campus; accepts girls; open to students from other schools. 200 students usually enrolled. 2017 schedule: June 17 to August 4. Application deadline: May 26.

Tuition and Aid Day student tuition: $16,100. Tuition installment plan (FACTS Tuition Payment Plan). Merit scholarship grants, need-based scholarship grants available. In 2016–17, 40% of upper-school students received aid; total upper-school merit-scholarship money awarded: $93,000. Total amount of financial aid awarded in 2016–17: $690,000.

Admissions Traditional secondary-level entrance grade is 9. For fall 2016, 160 students applied for upper-level admission, 152 were accepted, 112 enrolled. High School Placement Test required. Deadline for receipt of application materials: January 27. Application fee required: $110. On-campus interview recommended.

Athletics Interscholastic: basketball, cross-country running, equestrian sports, field hockey, golf, lacrosse, sand volleyball, soccer, softball, swimming and diving, tennis, track and field, volleyball, water polo; intramural: fitness walking, table tennis, tennis, yoga. 2 PE instructors, 23 coaches, 1 athletic trainer.

Computers Computers are regularly used in all academic, college planning, computer applications, creative writing, economics, English, foreign language, French, graphic design, health, journalism, library, literary magazine, mathematics, media, media production, photography, religion, religious studies, science, social studies, Spanish, speech, technology, yearbook classes. Computer network features include on-campus library services, online commercial services, Internet access, wireless campus network, Internet filtering or blocking technology. Student e-mail accounts and computer access in designated common areas are available to students. Students grades are available online. The school has a published electronic and media policy.

Contact Ms. Murphy Grimaldi, Admissions Associate. 818-346-8812. Fax: 818-346-9483. E-mail: mgrimaldi@louisvillehs.org. Website: www.louisvillehs.org

THE LOVETT SCHOOL

4075 Paces Ferry Road NW
Atlanta, Georgia 30327

Head of School: William S. Peebles

General Information Coeducational day college-preparatory school, affiliated with Christian faith. Grades K–12. Founded: 1926. Setting: suburban. 100-acre campus. 8 buildings on campus. Approved or accredited by Southern Association of Colleges and Schools, Southern Association of Independent Schools, and Georgia Department of Education. Member of National Association of Independent Schools and Secondary School Admission Test Board. Endowment: $70.4 million. Total enrollment: 1,673. Upper school average class size: 13. Upper school faculty-student ratio: 1:8. There are 180 required school days per year for Upper School students. Upper School students typically attend 5 days per week. The average school day consists of 8 hours.

Upper School Student Profile Grade 9: 179 students (94 boys, 85 girls); Grade 10: 173 students (87 boys, 86 girls); Grade 11: 158 students (71 boys, 87 girls); Grade 12: 162 students (85 boys, 77 girls).

Faculty School total: 241. In upper school: 41 men, 48 women; 48 have advanced degrees.

Subjects Offered Advanced chemistry, advanced computer applications, advanced math, Advanced Placement courses, African American history, African history, African literature, African-American literature, algebra, American government, American history, American history-AP, American legal systems, American literature, ancient history, ancient world history, architecture, art, art history, Asian history, Asian studies, band, biology, botany, calculus, calculus-AP, career and personal planning, career/college preparation, ceramics, character education, chemistry, chorus, computer art, computer education, computer graphics, computer programming, computer science, creative writing, dance, debate, drama, driver education, earth science, ecology, economics, electronic music, English, English literature, English literature-AP, English-AP, environmental science, ethics, European history, fiction, film history, fine arts, French, French language-AP, French literature-AP, French studies, French-AP, gender issues, genetics, geometry, German, history, human development, jazz dance, journalism, Latin, Latin-AP, leadership, marine biology, mathematics, medieval history, music theory, music theory-AP, newspaper, orchestra, painting, philosophy, photography, physical education, physics, portfolio art, pre-calculus, public speaking, religion, robotics, science, sculpture, social studies, Spanish, Spanish language-AP, Spanish literature-AP, speech, statistics, technical theater, theater, theater arts, trigonometry, U.S. government and politics-AP, video, Western civilization, Western philosophy, world cultures, world history, world literature, world religions, writing workshop, yearbook, zoology.

Graduation Requirements Algebra, American studies, arts and fine arts (art, music, dance, drama), biology, electives, English, foreign language, geometry, history, mathematics, physical education (includes health), religion (includes Bible studies and theology), science, Western civilization.

Special Academic Programs Advanced Placement exam preparation; honors section; independent study; term-away projects; study abroad.

College Admission Counseling 159 students graduated in 2016; all went to college, including Auburn University; Georgia Institute of Technology; Southern Methodist University; University of Georgia; University of Mississippi; University of Virginia.

Student Life Upper grades have uniform requirement, student council, honor system. Discipline rests primarily with faculty. Attendance at religious services is required.

Summer Programs Remediation, enrichment, advancement, art/fine arts, computer instruction programs offered; session focuses on academic course work; held both on and off campus; accepts boys and girls; open to students from other schools. 450 students usually enrolled. 2017 schedule: June 5 to July 14. Application deadline: January 18.

Tuition and Aid Day student tuition: $22,520–$26,650. Tuition installment plan (individually arranged payment plans, 1/2 paid in July and 1/2 paid in November). Need-based scholarship grants available. In 2016–17, 17% of upper-school students received aid. Total amount of financial aid awarded in 2016–17: $1,760,366.

Admissions Traditional secondary-level entrance grade is 9. For fall 2016, 128 students applied for upper-level admission, 25 were accepted, 13 enrolled. SSAT required. Deadline for receipt of application materials: January 14. Application fee required: $75. On-campus interview recommended.

Athletics Interscholastic: baseball (boys), basketball (b,g), cheering (g), cross-country running (b,g), football (b), golf (b,g), gymnastics (g), lacrosse (b,g), soccer (b,g), softball (g), swimming and diving (b,g), tennis (b,g), track and field (b,g), volleyball (g), wrestling (b); intramural: aerobics/dance (g), ballet (g), dance (g), in-line hockey (b), modern dance (g); coed intramural: backpacking, bicycling, bowling, canoeing/kayaking, climbing, equestrian sports, fitness, flag football, Frisbee, hiking/backpacking, kayaking, mountain biking, outdoor activities, physical fitness, physical training, rappelling, rock climbing, strength & conditioning, ultimate Frisbee, wall climbing, weight lifting, weight training, yoga. 3 PE instructors, 51 coaches, 4 athletic trainers.

Computers Computers are regularly used in all academic classes. Computer network features include on-campus library services, online commercial services, Internet access, wireless campus network, Internet filtering or blocking technology, central file storage. Student e-mail accounts and computer access in designated common areas are available to students. Students grades are available online.

Contact Mrs. Janie Beck, Director of Admission and Enrollment Management. 404-262-3032. Fax: 404-479-8463. E-mail: janie.beck@lovett.org. Website: www.lovett.org

LOWER CANADA COLLEGE

4090 Royal Avenue
Montreal, Quebec H4A 2M5, Canada

Head of School: Mr. Christopher Shannon

General Information Coeducational day college-preparatory and mathematics and science school. Grades K–12. Founded: 1861. Setting: urban. 7-acre campus. 3 buildings on campus. Approved or accredited by International Baccalaureate Organization and Quebec Department of Education. Affiliate member of National Association of Independent Schools; member of Secondary School Admission Test Board. Languages of instruction: English and French. Endowment: CAN$4.4 million. Total enrollment: 775. Upper school average class size: 22. Upper school faculty-student ratio: 1:22.

Upper School Student Profile Grade 9: 93 students (61 boys, 32 girls); Grade 10: 88 students (52 boys, 36 girls); Grade 11: 99 students (49 boys, 50 girls); Grade 12: 52 students (26 boys, 26 girls).

Faculty School total: 87. In upper school: 31 men, 17 women; 20 have advanced degrees.

Subjects Offered Accounting, advanced chemistry, advanced computer applications, advanced math, Advanced Placement courses, algebra, American history, ancient history, ancient world history, ancient/medieval philosophy, art, art history, biology, biology-AP, broadcast journalism, calculus, calculus-AP, Canadian geography, Canadian history, Canadian literature, career/college preparation, chemistry, chemistry-AP, cinematography, college admission preparation, college counseling, community service, computer graphics, computer math, computer multimedia, computer science, computer studies, concert band, creative writing, current events, desktop publishing, drama, earth science, ecology, economics, English, English literature, English-AP, environmental science, ethics, European history, expository writing, filmmaking, fine arts, finite math, French, French language-AP, general science, geography, health, health education, history, independent study, leadership, linear algebra, mathematics, media, music, North American literature, philosophy, physical education, physical fitness, physical science, physics, political science, pre-calculus, psychology, public speaking, robotics, SAT preparation, science, Shakespeare, social sciences, social studies, Spanish, Spanish-AP, theater, video film production, world geography, world history.

Graduation Requirements English, French, mathematics, science, social studies (includes history), overall average of 70%. Community service is required.

Special Academic Programs Advanced Placement exam preparation; honors section; independent study; domestic exchange program; remedial reading and/or remedial writing; remedial math.

College Admission Counseling 104 students graduated in 2016; all went to college, including Acadia University; Mount Allison University; Queen's University at Kingston; The University of British Columbia; The University of Western Ontario; University of Toronto.

Student Life Upper grades have uniform requirement, student council, honor system. Discipline rests equally with students and faculty.

Tuition and Aid Day student tuition: CAN$21,000. Tuition installment plan (monthly payment plans, individually arranged payment plans). Bursaries, merit scholarship grants, need-based scholarship grants, need-based loans available. In 2016–17, 15% of upper-school students received aid; total upper-school merit-scholarship money awarded: CAN$145,500. Total amount of financial aid awarded in 2016–17: CAN$327,845.

Admissions For fall 2016, 284 students applied for upper-level admission, 149 were accepted, 99 enrolled. School's own exam, SLEP, SSAT or TOEFL required. Deadline for receipt of application materials: none. Application fee required: CAN$50. On-campus interview recommended.

Athletics Interscholastic: badminton (boys, girls), baseball (b), basketball (b,g), cross-country running (b,g), football (b,g), hockey (b,g), ice hockey (b,g), indoor track & field (b,g), rugby (b,g), running (b,g), skiing (cross-country) (b,g), soccer (b,g), swimming and diving (b,g), tennis (b,g), touch football (b,g), track and field (b,g), volleyball (b,g); intramural: dance (g), football (b,g); coed interscholastic: aquatics, baseball, cross-country running, curling, football, golf, hockey, ice hockey, martial arts, skiing (cross-country), table tennis; coed intramural: aerobics, aerobics/dance, aerobics/Nautilus, aquatics, archery, backpacking, badminton, baseball, basketball, bowling, broomball, climbing, cooperative games, custom hockey, cross-country running, curling, fencing, field hockey, fitness, fitness walking, floor hockey, Frisbee, golf, gymnastics, handball, hiking/backpacking, hockey, ice hockey, ice skating, indoor track & field, judo, life saving, martial arts, outdoor activities, outdoor education, physical fitness, physical training, rappelling, rock climbing, rugby, running, self defense, skiing (cross-country), snowshoeing, soccer, softball, strength & conditioning, swimming and diving, table tennis, tennis, touch football, track and field, ultimate Frisbee, volleyball, wall climbing, weight training. 5 PE instructors, 8 coaches.

Computers Computers are regularly used in animation, basic skills, creative writing, current events, data processing, design, English, French, French as a second language, geography, graphic arts, graphic design, graphics, independent study, mathematics, multimedia, science, technology classes. Computer network features include on-campus library services, Internet access, Internet filtering or blocking technology, audio/video production, DVD production.

Contact Ms. Andrea Burdman, Admission Officer. 514-482-0951 Ext. 237. Fax: 514-482-0195. E-mail: aburdman@lcc.ca. Website: www.lcc.ca

LOYOLA-BLAKEFIELD

PO Box 6819
Baltimore, Maryland 21285-6819

Head of School: Mr. Anthony I. Day

General Information Boys' day college-preparatory, arts, religious studies, and technology school, affiliated with Roman Catholic Church. Grades 6–12. Founded: 1852. Setting: suburban. 60-acre campus. 6 buildings on campus. Approved or accredited by Association of Independent Maryland Schools. Endowment: $24.7 million. Total enrollment: 956. Upper school average class size: 17. Upper school faculty-student ratio: 1:10. There are 175 required school days per year for Upper

School students. Upper School students typically attend 5 days per week. The average school day consists of 7 hours.

Upper School Student Profile Grade 9: 178 students (178 boys); Grade 10: 194 students (194 boys); Grade 11: 180 students (180 boys); Grade 12: 168 students (168 boys). 77% of students are Roman Catholic.

Faculty School total: 91. In upper school: 51 men, 23 women; 65 have advanced degrees.

Subjects Offered Acting, Advanced Placement courses, African American history, algebra, American government, American literature, American literature-AP, architecture, art, art history, band, biology, biology-AP, biotechnology, British literature, British literature (honors), calculus, calculus-AP, chemistry, chemistry-AP, chorus, civil war history, composition, composition-AP, computer graphics, computer programming, computer science, conceptual physics, concert band, drawing, driver education, economics, engineering, English, English language-AP, English literature-AP, film studies, fine arts, forensics, German-AP, government and politics-AP, Greek, history, history of music, honors algebra, honors English, honors geometry, instrumental music, Italian, jazz ensemble, journalism, Latin, Latin-AP, marine science, mathematics, music history, music theory-AP, oil painting, painting, photography, physical education, physics, physics-AP, poetry, pre-calculus, psychology, religion, Roman civilization, science, Spanish, Spanish language-AP, statistics-AP, theater production, U.S. government and politics-AP, U.S. history, U.S. history-AP, voice ensemble, world religions, world wide web design.

Graduation Requirements Arts and fine arts (art, music, dance, drama), computer science, English, foreign language, mathematics, physical education (includes health), religion (includes Bible studies and theology), science, social studies (includes history), 40 hours of Christian service.

Special Academic Programs 20 Advanced Placement exams for which test preparation is offered; honors section; academic accommodation for the gifted, the musically talented, and the artistically talented; programs in English, mathematics, general development for dyslexic students.

College Admission Counseling 177 students graduated in 2016; 176 went to college, including Georgetown University; Loyola University Maryland; Salisbury University; Towson University; University of Maryland, Baltimore County; University of Maryland, College Park. Other: 1 had other specific plans. Median SAT critical reading: 590, median SAT math: 600, median SAT writing: 570, median combined SAT: 1740, median composite ACT: 26. 47% scored over 600 on SAT critical reading, 52% scored over 600 on SAT math, 34% scored over 600 on SAT writing, 41% scored over 1800 on combined SAT, 53% scored over 26 on composite ACT.

Student Life Upper grades have specified standards of dress, student council, honor system. Discipline rests primarily with faculty. Attendance at religious services is required.

Summer Programs Remediation, enrichment, advancement, sports, art/fine arts, computer instruction programs offered; held on campus; accepts boys and girls; open to students from other schools. 900 students usually enrolled. 2017 schedule: June 12 to August 4. Application deadline: none.

Tuition and Aid Day student tuition: $19,700. Tuition installment plan (FACTS Tuition Payment Plan). Merit scholarship grants, need-based scholarship grants available. In 2016–17, 46% of upper-school students received aid; total upper-school merit-scholarship money awarded: $623,800. Total amount of financial aid awarded in 2016–17: $2,510,301.

Admissions Traditional secondary-level entrance grade is 9. For fall 2016, 337 students applied for upper-level admission, 260 were accepted, 101 enrolled. High School Placement Test or ISEE required. Deadline for receipt of application materials: December 15. Application fee required: $50. On-campus interview required.

Athletics Interscholastic: baseball, basketball, cross-country running, diving, football, golf, ice hockey, indoor track & field, lacrosse, rugby, soccer, squash, swimming and diving, tennis, track and field, volleyball, water polo, winter (indoor) track, wrestling; intramural: basketball, flag football, indoor soccer, lacrosse, rock climbing, ultimate Frisbee. 5 PE instructors, 40 coaches, 1 athletic trainer.

Computers Computers are regularly used in all classes. Computer network features include on-campus library services, online commercial services, Internet access, wireless campus network, Internet filtering or blocking technology. Campus intranet, student e-mail accounts, and computer access in designated common areas are available to students. Students grades are available online. The school has a published electronic and media policy.

Contact Ms. Paddy M. London, Admissions Assistant. 443-841-3680. Fax: 443-841-3105. E-mail: plondon@loyolablakefield.org. Website: www.loyolablakefield.org

LOYOLA COLLEGE PREP

921 Jordan Street
Shreveport, Louisiana 71101

Head of School: Mr. John H. LeBlanc

General Information Coeducational day college-preparatory and strong college preparatory curriculum with emphasis on AP school, affiliated with Roman Catholic Church. Grades 9–12. Founded: 1902. Setting: urban. 13-acre campus. 3 buildings on campus. Approved or accredited by Southern Association of Colleges and Schools, Southern Association of Independent Schools, and Louisiana Department of Education. Endowment: $1.2 million. Total enrollment: 375. Upper school average class size: 18.

Upper school faculty-student ratio: 1:12. There are 178 required school days per year for Upper School students. Upper School students typically attend 5 days per week. The average school day consists of 7 hours.

Upper School Student Profile Grade 9: 130 students (66 boys, 64 girls); Grade 10: 112 students (56 boys, 56 girls); Grade 11: 108 students (44 boys, 64 girls); Grade 12: 113 students (56 boys, 57 girls). 41% of students are Roman Catholic.

Faculty School total: 37. In upper school: 16 men, 21 women; 19 have advanced degrees.

Subjects Offered Acting, advanced biology, advanced chemistry, advanced math, Advanced Placement courses, alternative physical education, American history-AP, American literature, American literature-AP, analytic geometry, art appreciation, athletics, audio visual/media, baseball, Basic programming, basketball, biology-AP, British literature, British literature-AP, broadcast journalism, calculus-AP, campus ministry, Catholic belief and practice, choir, Christian doctrine, Christian ethics, civics/free enterprise, classical music, composition-AP, computer multimedia, computer programming, creative drama, critical studies in film, English language and composition-AP, English language-AP, English literature and composition-AP, English literature-AP, English/composition-AP, environmental science, ethics, European history-AP, fencing, film, film studies, fine arts, French language-AP, French studies, French-AP, government and politics-AP, government-AP, honors algebra, honors English, honors geometry, honors world history, literature and composition-AP, moral theology, newspaper, psychology-AP, public speaking, softball, Spanish language-AP, Spanish-AP, sports, sports team management, U.S. government and politics-AP, U.S. history-AP, world history-AP, yearbook.

Graduation Requirements Computer science, economics, English, foreign language, mathematics, physical education (includes health), religion (includes Bible studies and theology), science, social studies (includes history), speech, study skills, students must complete 100 hours of service before graduation. Community service is required.

Special Academic Programs Advanced Placement exam preparation; honors section; independent study; study at local college for college credit; special instructional classes for each instructor makes 504 accommodations for each learning difference noted per child.

College Admission Counseling 90 students graduated in 2016; 89 went to college, including Centenary College of Louisiana; Louisiana State University and Agricultural & Mechanical College; Louisiana State University in Shreveport; Louisiana Tech University; Northwestern State University of Louisiana; University of Arkansas. Other: 1 entered military service. Mean composite ACT: 26. 53% scored over 26 on composite ACT.

Student Life Upper grades have uniform requirement, student council, honor system. Discipline rests primarily with faculty. Attendance at religious services is required.

Tuition and Aid Day student tuition: $9200. Guaranteed tuition plan. Tuition installment plan (monthly payment plans, individually arranged payment plans, quarterly and semi-annual payment plans). Merit scholarship grants, need-based scholarship grants available. In 2016–17, 22% of upper-school students received aid. Total amount of financial aid awarded in 2016–17: $133,300.

Admissions Traditional secondary-level entrance grade is 9. For fall 2016, 145 students applied for upper-level admission, 132 were accepted, 130 enrolled. ACT, admissions testing or PSAT required. Deadline for receipt of application materials: none. No application fee required. On-campus interview recommended.

Athletics Interscholastic: aquatics (boys, girls), baseball (b), basketball (b,g), bowling (b,g), cheering (g), cross-country running (b,g), danceline (g), fencing (b,g), football (b), golf (b,g), jogging (b,g), lacrosse (b,g), soccer (b,g), softball (g), tennis (b,g), track and field (b,g), volleyball (g), wrestling (b); coed interscholastic: fishing. 3 PE instructors, 3 coaches, 1 athletic trainer.

Computers Computers are regularly used in all classes. Computer network features include on-campus library services, online commercial services, Internet access, wireless campus network, Internet filtering or blocking technology, 1:1 iPad school. Student e-mail accounts and computer access in designated common areas are available to students. Students grades are available online. The school has a published electronic and media policy.

Contact Mrs. Mary Beth Fox, Director of Admissions. 318-226-6296. Fax: 318-221-2678. E-mail: mfox@loyolaprep.org. Website: www.loyolaprep.org

LUSTRE CHRISTIAN HIGH SCHOOL

294 Lustre Rd.
Lustre, Montana 59225

Head of School: Wes Young

General Information Coeducational boarding and day college-preparatory and general academic school, affiliated with Assemblies of God. Grades 9–12. Founded: 1948. Setting: rural. Nearest major city is Glasgow. Students are housed in single-sex dormitories. 20-acre campus. 1 building on campus. Approved or accredited by Association of Christian Schools International and Montana Department of Education. Endowment: $220,000. Total enrollment: 40. Upper school average class size: 7. Upper school faculty-student ratio: 1:4. There are 180 required school days per year for Upper School students. Upper School students typically attend 5 days per week. The average school day consists of 6 hours and 58 minutes.

Upper School Student Profile Grade 9: 6 students (2 boys, 4 girls); Grade 10: 5 students (2 boys, 3 girls); Grade 11: 6 students (3 boys, 3 girls); Grade 12: 3 students (2 boys, 1 girl). 20% of students are boarding students. 80% are state residents. 3 states are represented in upper school student body. 10% are international students. International students from Ethiopia and Italy; 2 other countries represented in student body. 60% of students are Assemblies of God.

Faculty School total: 7. In upper school: 4 men, 3 women; 1 has an advanced degree; 5 reside on campus.

Subjects Offered Algebra, American literature, band, Bible studies, biology, British literature, chemistry, choir, Christian studies, computer science, computers, current events, English, fine arts, foreign language, geometry, health, journalism, mathematics, physical education, physical science, pre-calculus, religion, science, social sciences, social studies, U.S. government, U.S. history, world history.

Graduation Requirements Arts and fine arts (art, music, dance, drama), Bible, computer science, English, mathematics, physical education (includes health), science, social studies (includes history), senior chapel message (as part of senior Bible program).

College Admission Counseling 11 students graduated in 2016; 10 went to college, including Montana State University. Other: 1 went to work, 1 entered military service.

Student Life Upper grades have specified standards of dress, student council. Discipline rests primarily with faculty. Attendance at religious services is required.

Tuition and Aid Day student tuition: $3200; 7-day tuition and room/board: $9600. Tuition installment plan (monthly payment plans, individually arranged payment plans). Need-based scholarship grants available. In 2016–17, 20% of upper-school students received aid.

Admissions Traditional secondary-level entrance grade is 9. For fall 2016, 16 students applied for upper-level admission, 13 were accepted, 10 enrolled. ITBS achievement test, PSAT, SLEP for foreign students or TOEFL or SLEP required. Deadline for receipt of application materials: none. No application fee required. Interview required.

Athletics Interscholastic: basketball (boys, girls), football (b), track and field (b,g), volleyball (g). 1 PE instructor, 3 coaches.

Computers Computers are regularly used in Bible studies, English, history, journalism, mathematics, religious studies, science, yearbook classes. Computer network features include on-campus library services, Internet access, wireless campus network, Internet filtering or blocking technology. Student e-mail accounts and computer access in designated common areas are available to students. Students grades are available online.

Contact Wes Young, Principal. 406-392-5735. Fax: 406-392-5765. E-mail: wyoung@nemont.net. Website: www.lustrechristian.org

LUTHERAN HIGH NORTH

1130 West 34th Street
Houston, Texas 77018

Head of School: Mr. Dana Gerard

General Information Coeducational day college-preparatory school, affiliated with Lutheran Church–Missouri Synod. Grades 9–12. Founded: 1982. Setting: urban. 10-acre campus. 3 buildings on campus. Approved or accredited by National Lutheran School Accreditation, Southern Association of Colleges and Schools, Texas Education Agency, and Texas Private School Accreditation Commission. Endowment: $1.5 million. Total enrollment: 295. Upper school average class size: 25. Upper school faculty-student ratio: 1:22. Upper School students typically attend 5 days per week. The average school day consists of 7 hours and 21 minutes.

Upper School Student Profile Grade 9: 30 students (20 boys, 10 girls); Grade 10: 34 students (17 boys, 17 girls); Grade 11: 47 students (28 boys, 19 girls); Grade 12: 37 students (17 boys, 20 girls). 50% of students are Lutheran Church–Missouri Synod.

Faculty School total: 18. In upper school: 8 men, 10 women; 10 have advanced degrees.

Graduation Requirements Algebra, anatomy and physiology, art education, arts and fine arts (art, music, dance, drama), computer science, economics, electives, English, foreign language, geography, geometry, government, human biology, mathematics, physical education (includes health), public speaking, religion (includes Bible studies and theology), science, social studies (includes history), U.S. history, world history, Distinguished Diploma students must have an additional credit in foreign language, 2 1/2 credits electives, 5 credits honors work, and 4 advanced measures with approved college courses with A or B.

Special Academic Programs Advanced Placement exam preparation; honors section; independent study; study at local college for college credit; programs in English, mathematics for dyslexic students.

College Admission Counseling 29 students graduated in 2016; 27 went to college, including Sam Houston State University; Texas A&M University; The University of Texas at Austin; The University of Texas at San Antonio; University of Houston. Other: 2 went to work. Mean SAT writing: 522, mean combined SAT: 1370, mean composite ACT: 25.

Student Life Upper grades have uniform requirement, student council, honor system. Discipline rests primarily with faculty. Attendance at religious services is required.

Summer Programs Enrichment, sports, art/fine arts, computer instruction programs offered; session focuses on sports and music; held on campus; accepts boys and girls;

open to students from other schools. 125 students usually enrolled. 2017 schedule: June 1 to July 31. Application deadline: May 31.

Tuition and Aid Day student tuition: $15,000–$20,000. Tuition installment plan (FACTS Tuition Payment Plan, special tuition arrangements-full, half, semester or monthly). Tuition reduction for siblings, merit scholarship grants, need-based scholarship grants available. In 2016–17, 60% of upper-school students received aid; total upper-school merit-scholarship money awarded: $20,000. Total amount of financial aid awarded in 2016–17: $175,000.

Admissions Traditional secondary-level entrance grade is 9. For fall 2016, 66 students applied for upper-level admission, 60 were accepted, 43 enrolled. Any standardized test and ISEE required. Deadline for receipt of application materials: none. Application fee required: $100. On-campus interview required.

Athletics Interscholastic: baseball (boys), basketball (b,g), football (b), soccer (b,g), softball (g), volleyball (g), winter soccer (b,g); coed interscholastic: cheering, cross-country running, golf, physical fitness, physical training, strength & conditioning, track and field, weight lifting, weight training; coed intramural: tennis, yoga. 1 PE instructor, 10 coaches.

Computers Computers are regularly used in current events, desktop publishing, drafting, English, graphic arts, graphic design, information technology, journalism, keyboarding, media arts, multimedia, news writing, publications, publishing, research skills, Spanish, theology, Web site design, word processing, writing, yearbook classes. Computer network features include on-campus library services, Internet access, wireless campus network, Internet filtering or blocking technology. Student e-mail accounts and computer access in designated common areas are available to students. Students grades are available online. The school has a published electronic and media policy.

Contact Ms. Kendra Benson, Director of Admissions. 713-880-3131 Ext. 330. Fax: 713-880-5447. E-mail: kendra.benson@lhnlions.org. Website: www.lutheranhighnorth.org

LUTHERAN HIGH SCHOOL

3201 West Arizona Avenue
Denver, Colorado 80219

Head of School: Mr. Daniel Gehrke

General Information Coeducational day college-preparatory, arts, religious studies, technology, and STEM school, affiliated with Lutheran Church–Missouri Synod. Grades 9–12. Founded: 1955. Setting: suburban. 22-acre campus. 1 building on campus. Approved or accredited by National Lutheran School Accreditation, North Central Association of Colleges and Schools, Southern Association of Colleges and Schools, and Colorado Department of Education. Total enrollment: 182. Upper school average class size: 20. Upper school faculty student ratio: 1:20. There are 175 required school days per year for Upper School students. Upper School students typically attend 5 days per week. The average school day consists of 7 hours.

Upper School Student Profile Grade 9: 158 students (89 boys, 69 girls); Grade 10: 95 students (55 boys, 40 girls); Grade 11: 108 students (65 boys, 43 girls); Grade 12: 108 students (61 boys, 47 girls). 20% of students are Lutheran Church–Missouri Synod.

Faculty School total: 40. In upper school: 23 men, 16 women; 13 have advanced degrees.

Subjects Offered 1 1/2 elective credits, 20th century history, 20th century world history, advanced biology, advanced chemistry, advanced math, Advanced Placement courses, algebra, American Civil War, American foreign policy, American government, American history, American history-AP, American literature, American literature-AP, anatomy and physiology, applied music, art, astrophysics, band, baseball, basketball, Bible, biochemistry, biology, British literature, British literature (honors), business, business mathematics, calculus, calculus-AP, campus ministry, career and personal planning, career education internship, career planning, career/college preparation, ceramics, chamber groups, cheerleading, chemistry, Chinese, choir, chorus, Christian doctrine, Christian education, college counseling, college planning, college writing, communications, composition-AP, computer art, computer graphics, computer processing, computer programming, computer science, concert band, concert choir, consumer mathematics, creative writing, engineering, English, English language and composition-AP, English literature, ensembles, fashion, fine arts, geography, geometry, government, government-AP, graphic design, health and wellness, honors geometry, honors U.S. history, honors world history, inorganic chemistry, introduction to literature, literature, marine biology, mathematics, microbiology, music theory, New Testament, participation in sports, personal fitness, photography, physical education, physical fitness, physics, pre-calculus, programming, psychology, public speaking, reading, religion, robotics, SAT/ACT preparation, science, social sciences, social studies, Spanish, speech, student government, technology, theater, track and field, trigonometry, U.S. government, video film production, volleyball, Web site design, weight training, women spirituality and faith, women's health, world civilizations, yearbook, zoology.

Graduation Requirements Algebra, arts and fine arts (art, music, dance, drama), biology, computer applications, electives, English, English composition, English literature, mathematics, physical education (includes health), science, social sciences, social studies (includes history), religion class for each year enrolled.

Special Academic Programs Advanced Placement exam preparation; honors section; independent study; study at local college for college credit; academic accommodation for the gifted and the artistically talented; remedial reading and/or remedial writing; programs in general development for dyslexic students; special instructional classes for resource class for students are IEP or 504; ESL (12 students enrolled).

College Admission Counseling 81 students graduated in 2016; 79 went to college, including Colorado Christian University; Colorado State University; Concordia University, Nebraska; Grand Canyon University; Texas A&M University; University of Northern Colorado. Other: 1 went to work, 1 entered military service. Mean composite ACT: 25.

Student Life Upper grades have specified standards of dress, student council, honor system. Discipline rests primarily with faculty.

Tuition and Aid Day student tuition: $10,400. Tuition installment plan (monthly payment plans, individually arranged payment plans). Need-based scholarship grants available. In 2016–17, 50% of upper-school students received aid. Total amount of financial aid awarded in 2016–17: $1,000,000.

Admissions Traditional secondary-level entrance grade is 9. For fall 2016, 254 students applied for upper-level admission, 210 were accepted, 160 enrolled. High School Placement Test required. Deadline for receipt of application materials: none. Application fee required: $50. On-campus interview required.

Athletics Interscholastic: baseball (boys), basketball (b,g), cross-country running (b,g), football (b), golf (b,g), lacrosse (b), soccer (b,g), tennis (g), track and field (b,g), volleyball (g). 3 PE instructors, 16 coaches, 1 athletic trainer.

Computers Computers are regularly used in all classes. Computer network features include on-campus library services, online commercial services, Internet access, wireless campus network, Internet filtering or blocking technology. Student e-mail accounts and computer access in designated common areas are available to students. Students grades are available online. The school has a published electronic and media policy.

Contact Mrs. Hannah Buchholz, Admissions Director. 303-841-5551 Ext. 203. Fax: 303-934-0455. E-mail: hannah.buchholz@lhsparker.org.

LUTHERAN HIGH SCHOOL

12411 Wornall Road
Kansas City, Missouri 64145-1736

Head of School: Dr. Cary Stelmachowicz

General Information Coeducational day college-preparatory and general academic school, affiliated with Lutheran Church–Missouri Synod. Grades 9–12. Founded: 1980. Setting: suburban. 29-acre campus. 1 building on campus. Approved or accredited by Missouri Independent School Association, National Lutheran School Accreditation, North Central Association of Colleges and Schools, and Missouri Department of Education. Endowment: $97,000. Total enrollment: 128. Upper school average class size: 15. Upper school faculty-student ratio: 1:11. There are 172 required school days per year for Upper School students. Upper School students typically attend 5 days per week. The average school day consists of 6 hours and 45 minutes.

Upper School Student Profile Grade 9: 37 students (15 boys, 22 girls); Grade 10: 31 students (14 boys, 17 girls); Grade 11: 28 students (13 boys, 15 girls); Grade 12: 41 students (13 boys, 28 girls). 80% of students are Lutheran Church–Missouri Synod.

Faculty School total: 15. In upper school: 7 men, 8 women; 5 have advanced degrees.

Subjects Offered Advanced math, algebra, American government, American literature, analysis, analytic geometry, anatomy and physiology, ancient world history, applied music, art, athletics, baseball, basketball, Bible studies, biology, biology-AP, calculus, cheerleading, chemistry, choir, Christian doctrine, Christian education, Christian ethics, Christian scripture, Christianity, church history, college counseling, communication skills, comparative religion, composition, contemporary art, earth science, English composition, English literature, geometry, government, graphic arts, health education, history, history of religion, instrumental music, Internet, Internet research, introduction to literature, keyboarding, Life of Christ, math analysis, New Testament, photography, physical education, physical science, physics, pre-algebra, psychology, sociology, Spanish, speech and oral interpretations, state history, statistics, student government, tennis, theater, theater production, track and field, trigonometry, U.S. government, volleyball, weightlifting.

Graduation Requirements Algebra, American government, American history, American literature, analytic geometry, art, arts and fine arts (art, music, dance, drama), Bible studies, biology, British literature, calculus, chemistry, church history, electives, geometry, health education, math analysis, modern world history, trigonometry, U.S. history.

Special Academic Programs Independent study; study at local college for college credit; academic accommodation for the artistically talented; remedial math.

College Admission Counseling 32 students graduated in 2016; 30 went to college, including Concordia University, Nebraska; Johnson County Community College; Kansas State University; Missouri State University; University of Arkansas; University of Missouri. Other: 1 went to work, 1 entered military service. Mean SAT critical reading: 550, mean SAT math: 480, mean composite ACT: 24. 50% scored over 600 on SAT critical reading, 50% scored over 600 on SAT math, 25% scored over 26 on composite ACT.

Student Life Upper grades have specified standards of dress, student council, honor system. Discipline rests primarily with faculty. Attendance at religious services is required.

Tuition and Aid Day student tuition: $8750–$11,000. Tuition installment plan (monthly payment plans, individually arranged payment plans). Tuition reduction for siblings, merit scholarship grants, need-based scholarship grants available. In 2016–17, 45% of upper-school students received aid; total upper-school merit-scholarship money awarded: $10,000. Total amount of financial aid awarded in 2016–17: $153,000.

Admissions Traditional secondary-level entrance grade is 9. For fall 2016, 137 students applied for upper-level admission, 137 were accepted, 137 enrolled. High School Placement Test or SLEP for foreign students required. Deadline for receipt of application materials: none. Application fee required: $275. On-campus interview required.

Athletics Interscholastic: baseball (boys), basketball (b,g), cheering (g), cross-country running (b,g), dance (g), dance team (g), fitness (b,g), golf (b), physical training (b,g), soccer (b,g), tennis (b,g), track and field (b,g), volleyball (g), weight lifting (b,g), weight training (b,g); intramural: flag football (b,g), floor hockey (b,g), gatorball (b,g), physical fitness (b,g); coed intramural: basketball, bowling, gatorball, golf, gymnastics, physical fitness, softball, touch football, volleyball, weight training. 2 coaches.

Computers Computers are regularly used in all academic, creative writing, publishing, Web site design, writing, yearbook classes. Computer network features include on-campus library services, Internet access, wireless campus network, Internet filtering or blocking technology. Campus intranet, student e-mail accounts, and computer access in designated common areas are available to students. Students grades are available online. The school has a published electronic and media policy.

Contact Mrs. Paula Meier, Registrar. 816-241-5478. Fax: 816-876-2069. E-mail: pmeier@lhskc.com. Website: www.lhskc.com/

LUTHERAN HIGH SCHOOL NORTH

5401 Lucas Hunt Road
St. Louis, Missouri 63121

Head of School: Mr. Timothy Brackman

General Information Coeducational day college-preparatory, arts, business, religious studies, bilingual studies, and technology school, affiliated with Lutheran Church–Missouri Synod. Grades 9–12. Founded: 1946. Setting: urban. 47-acre campus. 1 building on campus. Approved or accredited by Lutheran School Accreditation Commission, National Lutheran School Accreditation, North Central Association of Colleges and Schools, and Missouri Department of Education. Endowment: $6.8 million. Total enrollment: 286. Upper school average class size: 19. Upper school faculty-student ratio: 1:14. There are 178 required school days per year for Upper School students. Upper School students typically attend 5 days per week. The average school day consists of 6 hours and 20 minutes.

Upper School Student Profile Grade 9: 78 students (45 boys, 33 girls); Grade 10: 60 students (35 boys, 25 girls); Grade 11: 74 students (38 boys, 36 girls); Grade 12: 74 students (41 boys, 33 girls). 49% of students are Lutheran Church–Missouri Synod.

Faculty School total: 30. In upper school: 16 men, 14 women; 27 have advanced degrees.

Subjects Offered Accounting, advanced chemistry, Advanced Placement courses, algebra, American history, American history-AP, American literature, anatomy, art, Bible studies, biology, business, business law, business skills, calculus, calculus-AP, ceramics, chemistry, child development, choir, Christian doctrine, Christian education, Christian ethics, Christian scripture, Christian studies, Christianity, church history, computer applications, computer multimedia, computer science, concert band, concert choir, data analysis, design, drawing, drawing and design, economics, English, English composition, English literature, English literature-AP, entrepreneurship, European history, family and consumer science, fashion, fine arts, finite math, food and nutrition, foods, French, geography, geometry, government, government/civics, health education, history, human anatomy, keyboarding, literature-AP, Mandarin, marketing, mathematics, media studies, multimedia design, music, organic chemistry, painting, physical education, physics, physiology, practical arts, pre-calculus, printmaking, probability and statistics, psychology, religion, research, science, social studies, society and culture, Spanish, speech, statistics, student publications, theology, U.S. government, U.S. history-AP, world geography, world history, world literature, world religions, writing.

Graduation Requirements American history, arts and fine arts (art, music, dance, drama), English, mathematics, physical education (includes health), practical arts, religion (includes Bible studies and theology), science, social studies (includes history), Saved to Serve (community service hours).

Special Academic Programs Advanced Placement exam preparation; honors section; independent study; study at local college for college credit.

College Admission Counseling 76 students graduated in 2015; 75 went to college, including Missouri State University; Saint Louis University; Truman State University; University of Missouri; University of Missouri–St. Louis. Other: 1 entered military service. 50% scored over 26 on composite ACT.

Student Life Upper grades have uniform requirement, student council, honor system. Discipline rests primarily with faculty. Attendance at religious services is required.

Tuition and Aid Day student tuition: $10,500–$11,750. Tuition installment plan (FACTS Tuition Payment Plan, monthly payment plans, individually arranged payment plans, semester payment plan, full-year payment plan with discount). Tuition reduction for siblings, merit scholarship grants, need-based scholarship grants available. In 2015–

16, 72% of upper-school students received aid; total upper-school merit-scholarship money awarded: $22,000. Total amount of financial aid awarded in 2015–16: $820,000.

Admissions Traditional secondary-level entrance grade is 9. For fall 2015, 139 students applied for upper-level admission, 129 were accepted, 98 enrolled. School's own test required. Deadline for receipt of application materials: none. Application fee required: $250. Interview required.

Athletics Interscholastic: baseball (boys), basketball (b,g), cheering (g), cross-country running (b,g), dance squad (g), dance team (g), football (b), golf (b), pom squad (g), soccer (b,g), softball (g), swimming and diving (g), tennis (b,g), track and field (b,g), volleyball (g), wrestling (b); coed interscholastic: table tennis. 2 PE instructors, 15 coaches, 1 athletic trainer.

Computers Computers are regularly used in art, business education, English, history, mathematics, science, social studies, yearbook classes. Computer network features include on-campus library services, Internet access, wireless campus network, Internet filtering or blocking technology, Internet college work program. Campus intranet, student e-mail accounts, and computer access in designated common areas are available to students. Students grades are available online. The school has a published electronic and media policy.

Contact Karen Kersten, Records Clerk. 314-389-3100 Ext. 2934. Fax: 314-389-3103. E-mail: kkersten@lhsnstl.org. Website: www.lhsnstl.org

LUTHERAN HIGH SCHOOL NORTHWEST

1000 Bagley Avenue
Rochester Hills, Michigan 48309

Head of School: Mr. Paul Looker

General Information Coeducational day college-preparatory and religious studies school, affiliated with Lutheran Church–Missouri Synod. Grades 9–12. Founded: 1978. Setting: suburban. Nearest major city is Detroit. 30-acre campus. 1 building on campus. Approved or accredited by Lutheran School Accreditation Commission, North Central Association of Colleges and Schools, and Michigan Department of Education. Endowment: $1 million. Total enrollment: 177. Upper school average class size: 25. Upper school faculty-student ratio: 1:15. There are 185 required school days per year for Upper School students. Upper School students typically attend 5 days per week. The average school day consists of 7 hours and 20 minutes.

Upper School Student Profile Grade 9: 77 students (43 boys, 34 girls); Grade 10: 57 students (32 boys, 25 girls); Grade 11: 79 students (36 boys, 43 girls); Grade 12: 66 students (41 boys, 25 girls). 70% of students are Lutheran Church–Missouri Synod.

Faculty School total: 18. In upper school: 11 men, 7 women; 11 have advanced degrees.

Subjects Offered Accounting, advanced chemistry, algebra, American history, American history-AP, art, audio visual/media, band, Basic programming, biology, biology-AP, bookkeeping, business, business applications, business mathematics, calculus, ceramics, chemistry, choral music, chorus, Christian doctrine, Christian scripture, computer education, computer science, conceptual physics, concert band, concert choir, desktop publishing, drawing, drawing and design, Eastern world civilizations, economics, English, English language and composition-AP, English literature and composition-AP, English-AP, environmental science, geography, geometry, German, government/civics, graphic arts, health, law, mathematics, music, painting, physical education, physical science, physics-AP, psychology, Spanish, statistics-AP, theology, trigonometry, U.S. government and politics-AP, world history.

Graduation Requirements Arts and fine arts (art, music, dance, drama), English, mathematics, physical education (includes health), religion (includes Bible studies and theology), science, social sciences, social studies (includes history). Community service is required.

Special Academic Programs 6 Advanced Placement exams for which test preparation is offered; honors section; independent study; study at local college for college credit.

College Admission Counseling 77 students graduated in 2016; 68 went to college, including Central Michigan University; Concordia University Chicago; Grand Valley State University; Michigan State University; Oakland University; Western Michigan University. Other: 3 went to work, 6 entered military service. Median composite ACT: 23. 27% scored over 26 on composite ACT.

Student Life Upper grades have specified standards of dress, student council. Discipline rests primarily with faculty.

Tuition and Aid Day student tuition: $7550. Tuition installment plan (SMART Tuition Payment Plan). Merit scholarship grants, need-based scholarship grants available. In 2016–17, 2% of upper-school students received aid; total upper-school merit-scholarship money awarded: $20,000. Total amount of financial aid awarded in 2016–17: $20,000.

Admissions Traditional secondary-level entrance grade is 9. For fall 2016, 79 students applied for upper-level admission, 79 were accepted, 77 enrolled. High School Placement Test required. Deadline for receipt of application materials: none. Application fee required: $350. On-campus interview required.

Athletics Interscholastic: baseball (boys), basketball (b,g), cheering (g), cross-country running (b,g), dance team (g), football (b), golf (b,g), hockey (b), soccer (b,g), softball (g), track and field (b,g), volleyball (g), wrestling (b); intramural: indoor soccer (b,g); coed interscholastic: bowling; coed intramural: badminton, fitness, physical fitness, physical training, tennis, weight training. 1 PE instructor.

Computers Computers are regularly used in keyboarding, media, research skills, word processing, yearbook classes. Computer network features include Internet access, wireless campus network, Internet filtering or blocking technology. Student e-mail accounts are available to students. Students grades are available online. The school has a published electronic and media policy.

Contact Mr. Joseph Lower, Admissions Director. 248-852-6677. Fax: 248-852-2667. E-mail: jlower@lhsa.com. Website: www.lhnw.lhsa.com

LUTHERAN HIGH SCHOOL OF INDIANAPOLIS

5555 South Arlington Avenue
Indianapolis, Indiana 46237-2366

Head of School: Mr. Michael Brandt

General Information Coeducational day college-preparatory and general academic school, affiliated with Lutheran Church–Missouri Synod. Grades 9–12. Founded: 1976. Setting: suburban. 14-acre campus. 1 building on campus. Approved or accredited by National Lutheran School Accreditation, North Central Association of Colleges and Schools, and Indiana Department of Education. Endowment: $600,000. Total enrollment: 216. Upper school average class size: 18. Upper school faculty-student ratio: 1:15. There are 180 required school days per year for Upper School students. Upper School students typically attend 5 days per week. The average school day consists of 7 hours and 15 minutes.

Upper School Student Profile Grade 9: 74 students (38 boys, 36 girls); Grade 10: 62 students (38 boys, 24 girls); Grade 11: 56 students (29 boys, 27 girls); Grade 12: 59 students (41 boys, 18 girls). 64% of students are Lutheran Church–Missouri Synod.

Faculty School total: 17. In upper school: 12 men, 5 women; 15 have advanced degrees.

Subjects Offered 3-dimensional art, Advanced Placement courses, advanced studio art-AP, algebra, American government, American history, American history-AP, American literature-AP, American sign language, anatomy, anatomy and physiology, art, art-AP, band, biology, biology-AP, calculus, calculus-AP, career experience, ceramics, chemistry, chemistry-AP, choir, chorus, Christian ethics, Christian scripture, Christian testament, college placement, computer information systems, computer programming, concert band, current events, desktop publishing, discrete mathematics, earth science, economics, English, English composition, English literature and composition-AP, English literature-AP, English-AP, ethics, etymology, geography, geometry, German, health and wellness, history-AP, honors algebra, humanities, integrated physics, math review, music theory, music theory-AP, New Testament, physical education, physical fitness, physics, physics-AP, piano, pre-calculus, psychology, reading/study skills, sociology, Spanish, Spanish language-AP, Spanish-AP, speech, statistics, studio art, U.S. government, U.S. history-AP, world history, world religions.

Graduation Requirements Arts and fine arts (art, music, dance, drama), biology, chemistry, Christian doctrine, Christian ethics, computer applications, economics, foreign language, geography, health and wellness, integrated physics, literature and composition-AP, New Testament, physical education (includes health), U.S. government, U.S. history, world religions.

Special Academic Programs 6 Advanced Placement exams for which test preparation is offered; honors section; independent study; study at local college for college credit; remedial reading and/or remedial writing; remedial math.

College Admission Counseling 59 students graduated in 2016; 58 went to college, including Ball State University; Indiana University Purdue University Indianapolis; Indiana University Bloomington; Ivy Tech Community College–Central Indiana; Purdue University. Other: 1 went to work. Mean SAT critical reading: 515, mean SAT math: 550, mean SAT writing: 502, mean combined SAT: 1567, mean composite ACT: 23.

Student Life Upper grades have uniform requirement, student council. Discipline rests primarily with faculty. Attendance at religious services is required.

Tuition and Aid Day student tuition: $10,400. Tuition installment plan (FACTS Tuition Payment Plan, monthly payment plans, in full, by semester, or through 12-month payment plan). Tuition reduction for siblings, need-based scholarship grants, paying campus jobs, Church worker discount, Church Association member discount available. In 2016–17, 86% of upper-school students received aid. Total amount of financial aid awarded in 2016–17: $207,000.

Admissions Traditional secondary-level entrance grade is 9. For fall 2016, 102 students applied for upper-level admission, 90 were accepted, 87 enrolled. Math Placement Exam or SCAT required. Deadline for receipt of application materials: none. Application fee required: $200. On-campus interview recommended.

Athletics Interscholastic: baseball (boys), basketball (b,g), cross-country running (b,g), football (b), golf (b,g), soccer (b,g), softball (g), strength & conditioning (b,g), tennis (b,g), track and field (b,g), volleyball (b,g), weight lifting (b,g), weight training (b,g), wrestling (b); intramural: basketball (b,g), volleyball (b); coed interscholastic: cheering, physical fitness, weight training; coed intramural: bowling, fishing, football. 2 PE instructors, 22 coaches.

Computers Computers are regularly used in all academic classes. Computer network features include online commercial services, Internet access, wireless campus network, Internet filtering or blocking technology. Computer access in designated common areas is available to students. Students grades are available online. The school has a published electronic and media policy.

Contact Mrs. Deidre Barnett, Director of Admissions. 317-787-5474 Ext. 218. Fax: 317-787-2794. E-mail: admissions@lhsi.org. Website: www.lhsi.org

LUTHERAN HIGH SCHOOL OF SAN DIEGO

810 Buena Vista Way
Chula Vista, California 91910-6853

Head of School: Mr. Carlos Peralta

General Information Coeducational day college-preparatory school, affiliated with Lutheran Church–Missouri Synod. Grades 9–12. Founded: 1975. Setting: urban. Nearest major city is San Diego. 9-acre campus. 6 buildings on campus. Approved or accredited by National Lutheran School Accreditation, Western Association of Schools and Colleges, and California Department of Education. Total enrollment: 101. Upper school average class size: 12. Upper school faculty-student ratio: 1:12. There are 180 required school days per year for Upper School students. Upper School students typically attend 5 days per week. The average school day consists of 6 hours and 30 minutes.

Upper School Student Profile Grade 9: 18 students (11 boys, 7 girls); Grade 10: 18 students (9 boys, 9 girls); Grade 11: 25 students (15 boys, 10 girls); Grade 12: 35 students (21 boys, 14 girls). 25% of students are Lutheran Church–Missouri Synod.

Faculty School total: 12. In upper school: 4 men, 8 women; 5 have advanced degrees.

Subjects Offered Acting, Advanced Placement courses, algebra, American government, American history, American literature, analytic geometry, anatomy, anatomy and physiology, applied arts, applied music, art, ASB Leadership, athletics, band, baseball, basketball, bell choir, Bible, biology, calculus, calculus-AP, chemistry, choir, choral music, Christian education, Christian ethics, Christianity, civil rights, comparative religion, computer education, computer information systems, computer literacy, computer multimedia, computer technologies, concert bell choir, concert choir, creative writing, drama, drama performance, driver education, economics, electives, English, English-AP, ethics, French, general science, geometry, government, guitar, health education, history, lab science, leadership, Life of Christ, multimedia, music, music performance, music technology, musical productions, musical theater, New Testament, performing arts, physical education, physical fitness, physics, pre-calculus, reading/study skills, religion, science, scripture, set design, softball, Spanish, sports, stage design, student government, student publications, studio art, study skills, theology, U.S. government, U.S. government and politics, United States government-AP, vocal music, weight training, world history, world religions, world religions, yearbook.

Graduation Requirements Algebra, arts and fine arts (art, music, dance, drama), electives, English, foreign language, history, mathematics, physical education (includes health), religion (includes Bible studies and theology), science, social studies (includes history).

Special Academic Programs Advanced Placement exam preparation; independent study; ESL (10 students enrolled).

College Admission Counseling 33 students graduated in 2016; 30 went to college, including Grand Canyon University; Grossmont College. Other: 3 had other specific plans. Mean SAT critical reading: 630, mean SAT math: 674, mean SAT writing: 652, mean combined SAT: 1956.

Student Life Upper grades have uniform requirement, student council, honor system. Discipline rests primarily with faculty. Attendance at religious services is required.

Tuition and Aid Day student tuition: $9500. Tuition installment plan (monthly payment plans, individually arranged payment plans, Simply Giving—Thrivent Financial for Lutherans, Tuition Solution). Tuition reduction for siblings, merit scholarship grants, need-based scholarship grants available. In 2016–17, 21% of upper-school students received aid; total upper-school merit-scholarship money awarded: $2000. Total amount of financial aid awarded in 2016–17: $121,935.

Admissions Traditional secondary-level entrance grade is 9. For fall 2016, 96 students applied for upper-level admission, 96 were accepted, 96 enrolled. Admissions testing required. Application fee required: $250. Interview required.

Athletics Interscholastic: baseball (boys), basketball (b,g), cross-country running (b,g), football (b), softball (g), volleyball (b,g). 1 PE instructor, 10 coaches, 1 athletic trainer.

Computers Computers are regularly used in all classes. Computer network features include on-campus library services, Internet access, wireless campus network, Internet filtering or blocking technology. Campus intranet and student e-mail accounts are available to students. Students grades are available online. The school has a published electronic and media policy.

Contact Mrs. Debbie Heien, Office Manager. 619-262-4444 Ext. 120. Fax: 619-872-0974. E-mail: debbie.heien@lhssd.org. Website: www.lutheranhighsandiego.org

LUTHERAN HIGH SCHOOL WEST

3850 Linden Road
Rocky River, Ohio 44116-4099

Head of School: Dale Wolfgram

General Information Coeducational day college-preparatory and general academic school, affiliated with Lutheran Church. Grades 9–12. Distance learning grade 8. Founded: 1948. Setting: suburban. Nearest major city is Cleveland. 17-acre campus. 1 building on campus. Approved or accredited by North Central Association of Colleges and Schools. Endowment: $8.1 million. Total enrollment: 460. Upper school average class size: 22. Upper school faculty-student ratio: 1:14. There are 178 required school days per year for Upper School students. Upper School students typically attend 5 days per week. The average school day consists of 6 hours and 55 minutes.

Upper School Student Profile Grade 9: 128 students (68 boys, 60 girls); Grade 10: 102 students (50 boys, 52 girls); Grade 11: 97 students (48 boys, 49 girls); Grade 12: 107 students (53 boys, 54 girls). 62% of students are Lutheran.

Faculty School total: 34. In upper school: 17 men, 17 women; 18 have advanced degrees.

Subjects Offered Accounting, advanced chemistry, Advanced Placement courses, algebra, American history, American history-AP, American literature, art, art history, arts, Bible studies, biology, biology-AP, business, business applications, business education, business law, business skills, calculus, chemistry, chemistry-AP, choir, Christian doctrine, Christian ethics, cinematography, college planning, computer programming, computer science, concert band, construction, creative writing, digital art, drafting, economics, engineering, English, English literature, English-AP, entrepreneurship, environmental science, ethics, European history, expository writing, family living, fine arts, foreign language, geography, geometry, German, German-AP, government, government-AP, government/civics, grammar, health, health education, history, home economics, honors English, human anatomy, industrial arts, intro to computers, Latin, marching band, mathematics, mechanical drawing, music, New Testament, personal finance, personal fitness, physical education, physical science, physics, psychology, religion, science, sewing, shop, social studies, Spanish, speech, speech and debate, technology, theology, trigonometry, typing, U.S. government, U.S. history, U.S. history-AP, weight training, world civilizations, world history, world literature, writing.

Graduation Requirements Arts and fine arts (art, music, dance, drama), business skills (includes word processing), English, foreign language, mathematics, physical education (includes health), religion (includes Bible studies and theology), science, social studies (includes history), religion and speech.

Special Academic Programs Advanced Placement exam preparation; honors section; accelerated programs; independent study; study at local college for college credit; academic accommodation for the musically talented; remedial reading and/or remedial writing; remedial math.

College Admission Counseling 105 students graduated in 2016; 102 went to college, including Cleveland State University; Kent State University; Miami University; The College of Wooster; The Ohio State University. Other: 1 went to work, 2 entered military service. 25% scored over 26 on composite ACT.

Student Life Upper grades have specified standards of dress, student council. Discipline rests primarily with faculty. Attendance at religious services is required.

Tuition and Aid Day student tuition: $10,120. Tuition installment plan (FACTS Tuition Payment Plan). Tuition reduction for siblings, merit scholarship grants, need-based scholarship grants available. In 2016–17, 80% of upper-school students received aid; total upper-school merit-scholarship money awarded: $40,000. Total amount of financial aid awarded in 2016–17: $1,100,000.

Admissions Traditional secondary-level entrance grade is 9. High School Placement Test (closed version) from Scholastic Testing Service, math and English placement tests or SLEP for foreign students required. Deadline for receipt of application materials: none. Application fee required: $100. On-campus interview recommended.

Athletics Interscholastic: baseball (boys), basketball (b,g), bowling (b), cross-country running (b,g), drill team (g), football (b), golf (b,g), lacrosse (b), soccer (b,g), softball (g), track and field (b,g), volleyball (g), winter (indoor) track (b,g), wrestling (b); intramural: basketball (b,g), power lifting (b,g), softball (b,g); coed intramural: badminton, skiing (downhill), snowboarding, volleyball. 3 PE instructors, 26 coaches, 1 athletic trainer.

Computers Computers are regularly used in art, business studies, computer applications, desktop publishing, English, history, journalism, mathematics, multimedia, science, word processing, yearbook classes. Computer network features include on-campus library services, Internet access, wireless campus network, Internet filtering or blocking technology, whole school wireless access. Campus intranet, student e-mail accounts, and computer access in designated common areas are available to students. Students grades are available online. The school has a published electronic and media policy.

Contact Hyldee Hess, Recruitment Coordinator. 440-333-1660 Ext. 563. Fax: 440-333-1729. E-mail: hhesst@lutheranwest.com.

LUTHER COLLEGE HIGH SCHOOL

1500 Royal Street
Regina, Saskatchewan S4T 5A5, Canada

Head of School: Dr. Mark Anderson

General Information Coeducational boarding and day college-preparatory, general academic, International Baccalaureate, and ESL school, affiliated with Lutheran Church. Grades 9–12. Founded: 1913. Setting: urban. Nearest major city is Winnipeg, MB, Canada. Students are housed in coed dormitories. 27-acre campus. 7 buildings on campus. Approved or accredited by Canadian Association of Independent Schools and Saskatchewan Department of Education. Language of instruction: English. Endowment: CAN$600,000. Total enrollment: 440. Upper school average class size: 23. Upper school faculty-student ratio: 1:17. There are 190 required school days per year for Upper School students. Upper School students typically attend 5 days per week. The average school day consists of 7 hours.

Upper School Student Profile 14% of students are boarding students. 86% are province residents. 2 provinces are represented in upper school student body. 14% are international students. International students from China, Hong Kong, Mexico, Nigeria, Togo, and Viet Nam; 6 other countries represented in student body. 22% of students are Lutheran.

Faculty School total: 36. In upper school: 19 men, 17 women; 7 have advanced degrees; 1 resides on campus.

Subjects Offered Band, biology, calculus, chemistry, choir, Christian ethics, computer science, drama, English, ESL, French, German, handbells, history, information processing, International Baccalaureate courses, Latin, mathematics, music, orchestra, physical fitness, physics, psychology, science, video film production.

Graduation Requirements Christian ethics, English, mathematics, science, social studies (includes history), Christian Ethics.

Special Academic Programs International Baccalaureate program; independent study; study abroad; academic accommodation for the gifted; ESL (30 students enrolled).

College Admission Counseling 91 students graduated in 2016; 75 went to college, including McGill University; University of Alberta; University of Calgary; University of Regina; University of Saskatchewan. Other: 16 went to work. 40% scored over 600 on SAT critical reading, 40% scored over 600 on SAT math, 40% scored over 600 on SAT writing, 20% scored over 1800 on combined SAT.

Student Life Upper grades have specified standards of dress. Discipline rests primarily with faculty. Attendance at religious services is required.

Tuition and Aid Day student tuition: CAN$7050–CAN$18,170; 7-day tuition and room/board: CAN$18,440–CAN$29,560. Tuition installment plan (monthly payment plans, individually arranged payment plans). Tuition reduction for siblings, bursaries, merit scholarship grants, need-based scholarship grants available. In 2016–17, 20% of upper-school students received aid; total upper-school merit-scholarship money awarded: CAN$30,000. Total amount of financial aid awarded in 2016–17: CAN$165,000.

Admissions Traditional secondary-level entrance grade is 9. For fall 2016, 184 students applied for upper-level admission, 174 were accepted, 164 enrolled. English entrance exam required. Deadline for receipt of application materials: March 1. Application fee required: CAN$400.

Athletics Interscholastic: badminton (boys, girls), baseball (b), basketball (b,g), bicycling (b,g), cross-country running (b,g), curling (b,g), football (b), golf (b,g), hockey (b,g), pom squad (g), soccer (b,g), softball (g), volleyball (g); intramural: soccer (b,g), volleyball (g); coed interscholastic: badminton, cheering, curling, pom squad, track and field, ultimate Frisbee; coed intramural: outdoor education, running, table tennis, weight lifting, yoga. 2 PE instructors, 28 coaches, 2 athletic trainers.

Computers Computers are regularly used in basic skills, business classes. Computer network features include on-campus library services, Internet access, wireless campus network, Internet filtering or blocking technology. Student e-mail accounts and computer access in designated common areas are available to students. Students grades are available online.

Contact Ms. Jacqueline Wanner, Registrar. 306-791-9154. Fax: 306-359-6962. E-mail: lutherhs@luthercollege.edu. Website: www.luthercollege.edu

LYCÉE CLAUDEL

1635 Promenade Riverside
Ottawa, Ontario K1G 0E5, Canada

Head of School: Mme. Pascale Garrec

General Information Coeducational day and distance learning college-preparatory and general academic school. Grades 1–12. Founded: 1962. Setting: urban. 2-hectare campus. 1 building on campus. Approved or accredited by French Ministry of Education. Language of instruction: French. Endowment: CAN$9 million. Total enrollment: 1,010. Upper school average class size: 24. Upper school faculty-student ratio: 1:10. There are 174 required school days per year for Upper School students. Upper School students typically attend 5 days per week. The average school day consists of 7 hours.

Faculty School total: 52. In upper school: 25 men, 27 women.

Subjects Offered 20th century world history, advanced biology, advanced chemistry, advanced math, Advanced Placement courses, algebra, all academic, anatomy, anatomy and physiology, ancient world history, applied arts, applied music, art and culture, art history, arts, arts and crafts, audio visual/media, band, biology, botany, calculus, Canadian geography, Canadian history, Canadian literature, chemistry, cinematography, classics, composition, computer education, computer technologies, consumer economics, current history, drawing, ecology, ecology, environmental systems, economics, economics and history, English, English composition, English language and composition-AP, English language-AP, English literature, English literature-AP, English-AP, equality and freedom, ESL, European civilization, European history, experimental science, film and literature, fitness, foreign language, French, French as a second language, French studies, general math, general science, geography, geology, geometry, grammar, gymnastics, health and safety, health education, history, human anatomy, human biology, human issues, human sexuality, lab science, language-AP, Latin, Latin History, literacy, literature and composition-AP, literature-AP, math analysis, math applications, mathematics, music, music history, music performance,

oral communications, oral expression, organic chemistry, painting, philosophy, physical education, physics, political economy, reading, reading/study skills, science, science and technology, science project, social education, society, society and culture, sports, technology.

Special Academic Programs Advanced Placement exam preparation; ESL (50 students enrolled).

College Admission Counseling 86 students graduated in 2015; they went to Carleton University; McGill University; Queen's University at Kingston; University of Ottawa; University of Toronto; University of Waterloo. Other: 86 entered a postgraduate year.

Student Life Upper grades have specified standards of dress, student council, honor system. Discipline rests primarily with faculty.

Tuition and Aid Day student tuition: CAN$10,441. Tuition installment plan (monthly payment plans). Bursaries available.

Admissions For fall 2015, 250 students applied for upper-level admission, 200 were accepted, 150 enrolled. Admissions testing required. Deadline for receipt of application materials: June 15. Application fee required: CAN$120. Interview required.

Athletics Interscholastic: badminton (boys, girls), basketball (b), biathlon (b,g), cross-country running (b,g), golf (b), judo (b,g), skiing (downhill) (b), snowboarding (b), soccer (b,g), speedskating (g), track and field (b,g), volleyball (b,g); intramural: cross-country running (b,g), soccer (b,g); coed interscholastic: skiing (cross-country); coed intramural: badminton, basketball, fitness, gymnastics, handball, indoor soccer, indoor track, indoor track & field, jogging, judo, martial arts, Nautilus, physical fitness, physical training, running, soccer, strength & conditioning, swimming and diving, table tennis, tennis, track and field, volleyball, yoga. 4 PE instructors.

Computers Computers are regularly used in computer applications, English, ESL, foreign language, French, French as a second language, geography, graphic arts, graphic design, graphics, history, introduction to technology, mathematics, media, media arts, media production, multimedia, music, photography, programming, science, Spanish, technology, video film production, Web site design classes. Computer network features include on-campus library services, Internet access, wireless campus network. Campus intranet and student e-mail accounts are available to students. The school has a published electronic and media policy.

Contact Mme. Carla Khazzaka, Registrar. 613-733-8522 Ext. 606. Fax: 613-733-3782. E-mail: secretariat.lycee@claudel.org. Website: www.claudel.org/?lang=en

LYCÉE FRANÇAIS LA PÉROUSE

755 Ashbury Street
San Francisco, California 94117

Head of School: Philippe Legendre

General Information Coeducational day college-preparatory school. Grades PK–12. Founded: 1967. Setting: urban. 2 buildings on campus. Approved or accredited by California Association of Independent Schools, Western Association of Schools and Colleges, and California Department of Education. Member of National Association of Independent Schools. Language of instruction: French. Upper school average class size: 20. Upper school faculty-student ratio: 1:20. Upper School students typically attend 5 days per week. The average school day consists of 7 hours.

Subjects Offered Art, biology, English literature, geology.

Graduation Requirements Lycée students can prepare for and complete the French Baccalauréat which prepares them for entrance to either American or French universities.

Special Academic Programs ESL.

College Admission Counseling 47 students graduated in 2016; 44 went to college, including McGill University; University of California, Berkeley; University of California, Los Angeles; University of California, Santa Barbara. Other: 3 had other specific plans. Median SAT critical reading: 642, median SAT math: 620, median SAT writing: 641, median combined SAT: 1903, median composite ACT: 29. 57.5% scored over 600 on SAT critical reading, 55% scored over 600 on SAT math, 50% scored over 600 on SAT writing, 50% scored over 1800 on combined SAT, 67% scored over 26 on composite ACT.

Student Life Upper grades have student council. Discipline rests equally with students and faculty.

Tuition and Aid Day student tuition: $27,790. Tuition installment plan (SMART Tuition Payment Plan, FACTS Tuition Payment Plan). Tuition reduction for siblings, bursaries, need-based scholarship grants available. In 2016–17, 20% of upper-school students received aid.

Admissions Traditional secondary-level entrance grade is 9. For fall 2016, 350 students applied for upper-level admission, 200 were accepted, 180 enrolled. Deadline for receipt of application materials: January 15. Application fee required: $100. On-campus interview recommended.

Athletics 2 PE instructors.

Computers Computer network features include Internet access, Internet filtering or blocking technology. Campus intranet and student e-mail accounts are available to students. Students grades are available online. The school has a published electronic and media policy.

Contact Mathieu Verloove, Admissions Assistant. 415-661-5232 Ext. 2704. Fax: 415-661-0246. E-mail: mverloove@lelycee.org. Website: www.lelycee.org

THE LYCÉE INTERNATIONAL, AMERICAN SECTION

2 bis rue du Fer-à-Cheval
C.S. 40118
Saint-Germain-en-Laye Cedex 78105, France

Head of School: Mr. Scot Hicks

General Information Coeducational day college-preparatory and bilingual studies school. Grades PK–12. Founded: 1952. Setting: suburban. Nearest major city is Paris, France. 10-acre campus. 6 buildings on campus. Approved or accredited by AdvancED French Ministry of Education, and The College Board. Member of European Council of International Schools. Languages of instruction: English and French. Total enrollment: 705. Upper school average class size: 20. Upper school faculty-student ratio: 1:18. Upper School students typically attend 5 days per week. The average school day consists of 8 hours and 30 minutes.

Upper School Student Profile Grade 10: 63 students (27 boys, 36 girls); Grade 11: 54 students (19 boys, 35 girls); Grade 12: 55 students (19 boys, 36 girls).

Faculty School total: 20. In upper school: 5 men, 3 women; 7 have advanced degrees.

Subjects Offered Algebra, American history, American literature, art, biology, botany, calculus, chemistry, computer math, computer programming, computer science, drama, Dutch, economics, English, English literature, English-AP, European history, French, geography, geometry, German, grammar, Greek, health, history, Italian, Latin, mathematics, music, philosophy, physical education, physics, Russian, science, social sciences, social studies, Spanish, statistics, theater, trigonometry, world history, world literature, writing, zoology.

Graduation Requirements English, foreign language, French, mathematics, philosophy, physical education (includes health), science, social sciences, social studies (includes history), examination (French Baccalaureate with International option).

Special Academic Programs Advanced Placement exam preparation; honors section.

College Admission Counseling 58 students graduated in 2016; 56 went to college, including Brown University; Northeastern University; Stanford University; Swarthmore College; The University of North Carolina at Chapel Hill; Trinity College. Other: 2 had other specific plans. 73.4% scored over 600 on SAT critical reading, 73.4% scored over 600 on SAT math.

Student Life Upper grades have student council. Discipline rests primarily with faculty.

Tuition and Aid Day student tuition: €5149–€10,155. Tuition installment plan (monthly payment plans). Tuition reduction for siblings, need-based scholarship grants available. In 2016–17, 5% of upper-school students received aid. Total amount of financial aid awarded in 2016–17: €30,000.

Admissions Traditional secondary-level entrance grade is 10. For fall 2016, 42 students applied for upper-level admission, 3 were accepted, 3 enrolled. Admissions testing required. Deadline for receipt of application materials: none. Application fee required: €250. On-campus interview recommended.

Athletics Intramural: badminton (boys, girls), basketball (b,g), climbing (b,g), judo (b), rugby (b), soccer (b,g), tennis (b,g), track and field (b,g), volleyball (b,g), wall climbing (b,g); coed interscholastic: aerobics, aerobics/dance, badminton, basketball, climbing, cross-country running, dance, handball, judo, rugby, soccer, volleyball, wall climbing; coed intramural: swimming and diving, table tennis. 9 PE instructors.

Computers Computers are regularly used in English, foreign language, mathematics, technology classes. Computer resources include on-campus library services, Internet access, Internet filtering or blocking technology. Student e-mail accounts and computer access in designated common areas are available to students. Students grades are available online.

Contact Ms. Lisa Stephans Morvan, Director of Admissions. 33-1-34-51-90-92. Fax: 33-1 30 87 00 49. E-mail: admissions@americansection.org. Website: www.americansection.org

LYCÉE INTERNATIONALE DE BOSTON/INTERNATIONAL SCHOOL OF BOSTON

45 Matignon Road
Cambridge, Massachusetts 02140

Head of School: Mr. Richard Ulffers

General Information Coeducational day college-preparatory school. Grades PK–12. Founded: 1962. Setting: urban. Nearest major city is Boston. 5-acre campus. 2 buildings on campus. Approved or accredited by Association of Independent Schools in New England, French Ministry of Education, International Baccalaureate Organization, New England Association of Schools and Colleges, and Massachusetts Department of Education. Member of National Association of Independent Schools. Languages of instruction: English and French. Endowment: $50,000. Total enrollment: 567. Upper school average class size: 10. Upper school faculty-student ratio: 1:6. There are 169 required school days per year for Upper School students. Upper School students typically attend 5 days per week. The average school day consists of 7 hours and 30 minutes.

Upper School Student Profile Grade 9: 37 students (20 boys, 17 girls); Grade 10: 32 students (16 boys, 16 girls); Grade 11: 31 students (15 boys, 16 girls); Grade 12: 35 students (20 boys, 15 girls).

Faculty School total: 100. In upper school: 7 men, 20 women; 18 have advanced degrees.

Graduation Requirements French Baccalaureate requirements, International Baccalaureate requirements.

Special Academic Programs International Baccalaureate program; accelerated programs; independent study; ESL (50 students enrolled).

College Admission Counseling 44 students graduated in 2016; all went to college, including Boston University; Columbia University; Massachusetts Institute of Technology; McGill University; Penn State University Park; The George Washington University. Mean SAT critical reading: 621, mean SAT math: 619, mean SAT writing: 620.

Student Life Upper grades have specified standards of dress, student council. Discipline rests primarily with faculty.

Tuition and Aid Day student tuition: $30,660. Tuition installment plan (monthly payment plans, individually arranged payment plans). Bursaries, need-based scholarship grants available.

Admissions Traditional secondary-level entrance grade is 9. Placement test or PSAT or SAT required. Deadline for receipt of application materials: none. Application fee required: $2000. Interview recommended.

Athletics Coed Interscholastic: aerobics/dance, archery, badminton, basketball, bicycling, fencing, fitness, gymnastics, handball, indoor track, martial arts, soccer, table tennis, tennis, volleyball; coed intramural: basketball, fencing, handball, martial arts, outdoors, soccer, table tennis. 2 PE instructors, 10 coaches.

Computers Computers are regularly used in mathematics, science classes. Computer network features include on-campus library services, Internet access, wireless campus network, Internet filtering or blocking technology. Campus intranet, student e-mail accounts, and computer access in designated common areas are available to students. Students grades are available online. The school has a published electronic and media policy.

Contact Mrs. Kelly Herrity, Director of Admissions and Enrollment Management. 617-499-1459. Fax: 617-234-0064. E-mail: admissions@isbos.org. Website: www.isbos.org

LYDIA PATTERSON INSTITUTE

517 South Florence Street
El Paso, Texas 79901-2998

Head of School: Mr. Ernesto Morales

General Information Coeducational day college-preparatory, arts, religious studies, and technology school, affiliated with United Methodist Church. Grades 7–12. Distance learning grade 0. Founded: 1913. Setting: urban. 1-acre campus. 2 buildings on campus. Approved or accredited by Southern Association of Colleges and Schools, University Senate of United Methodist Church, and Texas Department of Education. Languages of instruction: English and Spanish. Endowment: $50,000. Total enrollment: 399. Upper school average class size: 70. Upper school faculty-student ratio: 1:20. There are 183 required school days per year for Upper School students. Upper School students typically attend 5 days per week. The average school day consists of 6 hours and 55 minutes.

Upper School Student Profile Grade 9: 40 students (21 boys, 19 girls); Grade 10: 49 students (24 boys, 25 girls); Grade 11: 56 students (24 boys, 32 girls); Grade 12: 86 students (39 boys, 47 girls). 2% of students are United Methodist Church.

Faculty School total: 26. In upper school: 16 men, 10 women; 5 have advanced degrees.

Subjects Offered Computer science, economics, English, fine arts, foreign language, health, mathematics, physical education, religion, U.S. government, U.S. history, world geography, world history.

Graduation Requirements Arts and fine arts (art, music, dance, drama), computer science, economics, English, foreign language, mathematics, physical education (includes health), religion (includes Bible studies and theology), science, U.S. government, U.S. history, world history, world geography, Religion.

Special Academic Programs International Baccalaureate program; Advanced Placement exam preparation; honors section; accelerated programs; independent study; study at local college for college credit; remedial reading and/or remedial writing.

College Admission Counseling 82 students graduated in 2016; 79 went to college, including El Paso Community College; MacMurray College; The University of Texas at El Paso. Other: 3 went to work. Median SAT critical reading: 400, median SAT math: 401, median SAT writing: 380, median combined SAT: 1170. 23% scored over 26 on composite ACT.

Student Life Upper grades have uniform requirement, student council, honor system. Discipline rests equally with students and faculty. Attendance at religious services is required.

Summer Programs Remediation, advancement programs offered; session focuses on advancement; held on campus; accepts boys and girls; open to students from other schools. 165 students usually enrolled. 2017 schedule: May 31 to July 5. Application deadline: May 27.

Tuition and Aid Day student tuition: $2430. Tuition installment plan (monthly payment plans). Need-based scholarship grants available. In 2016–17, 30% of upper-school students received aid. Total amount of financial aid awarded in 2016–17: $15,795.

Admissions Traditional secondary-level entrance grade is 9. Achievement tests, ACT, Iowa Tests of Basic Skills, PSAT or PSAT, SAT, or ACT for applicants to grade 11 and 12 required. Deadline for receipt of application materials: none. No application fee required.

Athletics Interscholastic: basketball (boys, girls), cross-country running (b,g), dance (b), soccer (b,g), track and field (b,g), volleyball (b,g), weight lifting (b,g); intramural: baseball (b), basketball (b,g), dance (b), soccer (b,g), track and field (b,g), volleyball (b,g); coed interscholastic: dance team. 2 PE instructors, 4 coaches.

Computers Computers are regularly used in art, basic skills, Bible studies, career education, college planning, computer applications, creative writing, desktop publishing, economics, English, ethics, foreign language, French, geography, health, history, information technology, journalism, library, mathematics, news writing, reading, religious studies, SAT preparation, Spanish, speech, Web site design, writing classes. Computer network features include on-campus library services, online commercial services, Internet access, wireless campus network, Internet filtering or blocking technology. Campus intranet and student e-mail accounts are available to students.

Contact Ms. Monica Irene Rueda, School Counselor. 915-533-8286 Ext. 29. Fax: 915-533-5236. E-mail: m.rueda@lpi-elp.org. Website: www.lydiapattersoninstitute.org

LYMAN WARD MILITARY ACADEMY

PO Drawer 550
174 Ward Circle
Camp Hill, Alabama 36850-0550

Head of School: Col. Roy W. Berwick

General Information Boys' boarding and distance learning college-preparatory, vocational, and military school, affiliated with Christian faith; primarily serves underachievers and individuals with Attention Deficit Disorder. Grades 6–12. Distance learning grades 11–12. Founded: 1898. Setting: small town. Nearest major city is Birmingham. Students are housed in single-sex dormitories. 300-acre campus. 23 buildings on campus. Approved or accredited by Southern Association of Colleges and Schools and Alabama Department of Education. Member of National Association of Independent Schools. Total enrollment: 115. Upper school average class size: 15. Upper school faculty-student ratio: 1:15. There are 185 required school days per year for Upper School students. Upper School students typically attend 5 days per week. The average school day consists of 7 hours.

Upper School Student Profile Grade 9: 20 students (20 boys); Grade 10: 20 students (20 boys); Grade 11: 20 students (20 boys); Grade 12: 25 students (25 boys). 98% of students are boarding students. 50% are state residents. 15 states are represented in upper school student body. 1% are international students. International students from Bermuda, China, Guatemala, Guinea, and Mexico. 85% of students are Christian faith.

Faculty School total: 14. In upper school: 8 men, 4 women; 6 have advanced degrees; 2 reside on campus.

Subjects Offered Advanced Placement courses, algebra, band, biology, chemistry, computers, economics, English, geometry, government, health, JROTC, physical science, physiology, pre-algebra, pre-calculus, reading, Spanish, trigonometry, U.S. history, world history.

Special Academic Programs Advanced Placement exam preparation; honors section; study at local college for college credit; remedial reading and/or remedial writing; remedial math

College Admission Counseling 18 students graduated in 2015; 15 went to college, including Auburn University; Jacksonville State University; Marion Military Institute; The University of Alabama; Troy University. Other: 3 entered military service. 5% scored over 600 on SAT critical reading, 5% scored over 600 on SAT math, 5% scored over 26 on composite ACT.

Student Life Upper grades have uniform requirement, student council, honor system. Discipline rests primarily with faculty. Attendance at religious services is required.

Tuition and Aid Day student tuition: $8990; 7-day tuition and room/board: $21,000. Tuition installment plan (monthly payment plans, individually arranged payment plans). Tuition reduction for siblings, merit scholarship grants, need-based scholarship grants available. In 2015–16, 15% of upper-school students received aid. Total amount of financial aid awarded in 2015–16: $100,000.

Admissions Traditional secondary-level entrance grade is 9. Star-9 required. Deadline for receipt of application materials: none. Application fee required: $250. Interview recommended.

Athletics Interscholastic: baseball, basketball, cross-country running, drill team, football, JROTC drill, marksmanship, riflery, soccer, weight training; intramural: aquatics, archery, basketball, billiards, canoeing/kayaking, cross-country running, drill team, fishing, fitness, flag football, football, Frisbee, hiking/backpacking, JROTC drill, life saving, marksmanship, outdoor activities, outdoor adventure, outdoor recreation, outdoor skills, paint ball, physical fitness, physical training, project adventure, rafting, rappelling, riflery, ropes courses, running, skiing (downhill), soccer, softball, strength & conditioning, swimming and diving, table tennis, tennis, ultimate Frisbee, volleyball, weight lifting. 2 PE instructors, 5 coaches, 1 athletic trainer.

Computers Computers are regularly used in keyboarding classes. Computer resources include on-campus library services, Internet access, Internet filtering or blocking

technology. Student e-mail accounts are available to students. The school has a published electronic and media policy.

Contact Maj. Joe C. Watson, Assistant to the President/Admissions. 256-392-8614. Fax: 256-896-4661. E-mail: info@lwma.org. Website: www.lwma.org

LYNDON INSTITUTE

PO Box 127
College Road
Lyndon Center, Vermont 05850-0127

Head of School: Mr. Daren M. Houck

General Information Coeducational boarding and day college-preparatory, general academic, arts, vocational, and ESL school. Grades 9–12. Founded: 1867. Setting: small town. Nearest major city is Burlington. Students are housed in single-sex dormitories. 150-acre campus. 27 buildings on campus. Approved or accredited by Independent Schools of Northern New England, New England Association of Schools and Colleges, The Association of Boarding Schools, and Vermont Department of Education. Endowment: $8 million. Upper school average class size: 15. Upper school faculty-student ratio: 1:10. There are 178 required school days per year for Upper School students. Upper School students typically attend 5 days per week. The average school day consists of 6 hours.

Upper School Student Profile Grade 9: 145 students (62 boys, 83 girls); Grade 10: 158 students (84 boys, 74 girls); Grade 11: 143 students (78 boys, 65 girls); Grade 12: 180 students (91 boys, 89 girls). 14% of students are boarding students. 91% are state residents. 9% are international students. International students from China; 19 other countries represented in student body.

Faculty School total: 68. In upper school: 36 men, 32 women; 20 have advanced degrees; 3 reside on campus.

Subjects Offered 3-dimensional art, accounting, advanced chemistry, advanced math, algebra, American literature, ancient world history, animal science, art, auto mechanics, band, Basic programming, biology, bookmaking, business, business education, business mathematics, business technology, calculus, chemistry, chemistry-AP, chorus, college counseling, computer applications, computer graphics, computer information systems, computer science, computer skills, computer technologies, computer-aided design, concert band, consumer economics, creative writing, desktop publishing, drafting, drawing, driver education, economics, English, English language and composition-AP, English literature, entrepreneurship, environmental science, European history, family and consumer science, fashion, fine arts, French, general math, geography, geometry, graphic design, health, history, honors algebra, honors English, honors U.S. history, honors world history, industrial arts, information processing, information technology, instrumental music, jazz ensemble, keyboarding, Latin, literary magazine, mathematics, metalworking, music, music theory, philosophy, photography, physical education, physics, printmaking, science, social studies, Spanish, street law, studio art, studio art-AP, theater, theater arts, trigonometry, U.S. history, woodworking, word processing, world cultures, world history, writing.

Graduation Requirements Arts and fine arts (art, music, dance, drama), electives, English, health education, mathematics, physical education (includes health), science, social studies (includes history), U.S. history.

Special Academic Programs Advanced Placement exam preparation; honors section; independent study; study at local college for college credit; remedial reading and/or remedial writing; remedial math; ESL (50 students enrolled).

College Admission Counseling 148 students graduated in 2016; 117 went to college, including Purdue University; Saint Michael's College; University of Vermont. Other: 19 went to work, 7 entered military service, 1 entered a postgraduate year, 4 had other specific plans.

Student Life Upper grades have specified standards of dress, student council. Discipline rests primarily with faculty.

Tuition and Aid Day student tuition: $14,004; 5-day tuition and room/board: $31,930; 7-day tuition and room/board: $44,700. Tuition installment plan (monthly payment plans, individually arranged payment plans). Need-based scholarship grants, prepGATE loans available. In 2016–17, 2% of upper-school students received aid.

Admissions Traditional secondary-level entrance grade is 9. International English Language Test, SSAT, ERB, PSAT, SAT, PLAN or ACT or TOEFL or SLEP required. Deadline for receipt of application materials: March 31. Application fee required: $50. Interview recommended.

Athletics Interscholastic: alpine skiing (boys, girls), baseball (b), basketball (b,g), cross-country running (b,g), field hockey (g), golf (b,g), ice hockey (b), nordic skiing (b,g), running (b,g), skiing (cross-country) (b,g), skiing (downhill) (b,g), soccer (b,g), softball (g), track and field (b,g), ultimate Frisbee (b,g); intramural: ballet (g), dance (b,g), volleyball (b,g); coed interscholastic: cheering, football, ice hockey, outdoor activities; coed intramural: aerobics/dance, bicycling, bowling, dance, dance team, equestrian sports, fitness walking, indoor soccer, indoor track, marksmanship, martial arts, modern dance, mountain biking, riflery, weight lifting. 2 PE instructors, 26 coaches, 2 athletic trainers.

Computers Computers are regularly used in architecture, business, business applications, business education, business skills, desktop publishing, drafting, engineering, graphic design, information technology, keyboarding, literary magazine, publishing, SAT preparation, science, technical drawing, technology, word processing, yearbook classes. Computer resources include on-campus library services, Internet access, Internet filtering or blocking technology, Big Chalk eLibrary, Vermont Online Library, NewsBank. Student e-mail accounts and computer access in designated common areas are available to students. Students grades are available online. The school has a published electronic and media policy.

Contact Tiaan van der Linde, Director of Admissions. 802-535-3700. Fax: 802-626-6138. E-mail: admissions@lyndoninstitute.org.
Website: http://www.LyndonInstitute.org

MA'AYANOT YESHIVA HIGH SCHOOL FOR GIRLS OF BERGEN COUNTY

1650 Palisade Avenue
Teaneck, New Jersey 07666

Head of School: Mrs. Rivka Kahan

General Information Girls' day college-preparatory, arts, religious studies, and technology school; affiliated with Jewish faith. Grades 9–12. Founded: 1995. Setting: suburban. 1 building on campus. Approved or accredited by Middle States Association of Colleges and Schools and New Jersey Department of Education. Languages of instruction: English and Hebrew. Total enrollment: 221. Upper school average class size: 22. Upper school faculty-student ratio: 1:6. There are 165 required school days per year for Upper School students. Upper School students typically attend 5 days per week. The average school day consists of 9 hours and 15 minutes.

Upper School Student Profile Grade 9: 82 students (82 girls); Grade 10: 77 students (77 girls); Grade 11: 70 students (70 girls); Grade 12: 60 students (60 girls). 100% of students are Jewish.

Faculty School total: 51. In upper school: 9 men, 46 women; 40 have advanced degrees.

Subjects Offered 20th century history, 20th century world history, acting, advanced biology, advanced chemistry, advanced math, Advanced Placement courses, advanced studio art-AP, algebra, American culture, American government, American history, American history-AP, American literature, American literature-AP, American sign language, ancient world history, applied music, Arabic, audio visual/media, Basic programming, Bible, Bible studies, biology, biology-AP, British literature, calculus, calculus-AP, chemistry, chemistry-AP, college counseling, college writing, computer programming, computer science-AP, computer skills, conceptual physics, CPR, creative writing, current events, debate, desktop publishing, drama performance, engineering, English literature and composition-AP, food and nutrition, geometry, government, government and politics-AP, graphic design, health education, Hebrew, Hebrew scripture, history, Holocaust studies, honors algebra, honors English, Israeli studies, Jewish history, Jewish studies, Judaic studies, lab science, language and composition, literature, model United Nations, music theory, nutrition, physical education, physics, physics-AP, pre-calculus, psychology-AP, public speaking, senior internship, sign language, Spanish, speech, statistics-AP, studio art-AP, Talmud, the Sixties, U.S. government, U.S. government and politics, United States government-AP, world history, writing.

Graduation Requirements Algebra, American government, American history, art, biology, chemistry, CPR, English, foreign language, geometry, Hebrew, history, Judaic studies, mathematics, physical education (includes health), physics, science, senior internship, technology, world history.

Special Academic Programs Advanced Placement exam preparation; honors section.

College Admission Counseling 89 students graduated in 2016; all went to college, including Barnard College; Binghamton University, State University of New York; Brandeis University; Queens College of the City University of New York; Rutgers University–Newark; Yeshiva University. Mean SAT critical reading: 611, mean SAT math: 606, mean SAT writing: 619, mean combined SAT: 1836, mean composite ACT: 25.

Student Life Upper grades have specified standards of dress, student council. Discipline rests primarily with faculty. Attendance at religious services is required.

Tuition and Aid Day student tuition: $22,585. Tuition installment plan (FACTS Tuition Payment Plan). Need-based scholarship grants available. In 2016–17, 40% of upper-school students received aid. Total amount of financial aid awarded in 2016–17: $1,446,363.

Admissions Traditional secondary-level entrance grade is 9. For fall 2016, 165 students applied for upper-level admission, 152 were accepted, 83 enrolled. Board of Jewish Education Entrance Exam and school's own test required. Deadline for receipt of application materials: none. Application fee required: $150. On-campus interview recommended.

Athletics Interscholastic: basketball, cross-country running, floor hockey, hockey, indoor hockey, indoor soccer, running, soccer, softball, swimming and diving, tennis, track and field, volleyball; intramural: dance, dance team, self defense, yoga. 3 PE instructors, 14 coaches.

Computers Computers are regularly used in all academic classes. Computer network features include on-campus library services, Internet access, wireless campus network, Internet filtering or blocking technology, students grades 9-11 are issued a school iPad. Campus intranet, student e-mail accounts, and computer access in designated common areas are available to students. Students grades are available online.

Contact Mrs. Nina Bieler, Director of Admissions. 201-833-4307 Ext. 255. Fax: 201-833-0816. E-mail: admissions@maayanot.org.

THE MADEIRA SCHOOL

8328 Georgetown Pike
McLean, Virginia 22102-1200

Head of School: Ms. Pilar Cabeza de Vaca

General Information Girls' boarding and day college-preparatory, arts, and technology school; primarily serves students with learning disabilities, individuals with Attention Deficit Disorder, individuals with emotional and behavioral problems, and dyslexic students. Grades 9–12. Founded: 1906. Setting: suburban. Nearest major city is Washington, DC. Students are housed in single-sex dormitories. 376-acre campus. 34 buildings on campus. Approved or accredited by Association of Independent Schools of Greater Washington, The Association of Boarding Schools, and Virginia Department of Education. Member of National Association of Independent Schools and Secondary School Admission Test Board. Endowment: $63.4 million. Total enrollment: 308. Upper school average class size: 12. Upper school faculty-student ratio: 1:10. There are 170 required school days per year for Upper School students. Upper School students typically attend 5 days per week. The average school day consists of 7 hours and 15 minutes.

Upper School Student Profile Grade 9: 76 students (76 girls); Grade 10: 88 students (88 girls); Grade 11: 81 students (81 girls); Grade 12: 70 students (70 girls). 54% of students are boarding students. 51% are state residents. 21 states are represented in upper school student body. 18% are international students. International students from China, Jamaica, Mexico, Nigeria, Republic of Korea, and United Arab Emirates; 7 other countries represented in student body.

Faculty School total: 38. In upper school: 7 men, 27 women; 28 have advanced degrees; 15 reside on campus.

Subjects Offered Acting, advanced biology, advanced math, Advanced Placement courses, algebra, American literature, ancient history, Arabic, art history-AP, Asian literature, ballet, Basic programming, basketball, biology, biology-AP, British literature, calculus, calculus-AP, career/college preparation, ceramics, chamber groups, character education, chemistry, chemistry-AP, Chinese, chorus, college counseling, comparative religion, computer programming, computer science-AP, conceptual physics, CPR, dance, digital photography, English, English composition, English language and composition-AP, English literature, English-AP, environmental science, equestrian sports, equitation, ESL, ethics, European history, European history-AP, expository writing, Farsi, filmmaking, fine arts, forensics, French, French language-AP, geometry, global issues, grammar, graphic design, health, health and wellness, history, jazz dance, junior and senior seminars, Latin, Latin-AP, leadership education training, linear algebra, literature seminar, madrigals, mathematics, media literacy, Middle Eastern history, modern civilization, modern world history, music, musical productions, mythology, orchestra, performing arts, photography, physical education, physics, physics-AP, politics, pre-calculus, public speaking, science, science and technology, sex education, Spanish, Spanish language-AP, sports, statistics, statistics-AP, student government, student publications, studio art, study skills, swimming, technical theater, theater, theater arts, trigonometry, U.S. government and politics-AP, U.S. history, U.S. history-AP, visual and performing arts, world civilizations, world history, world history-AP, world religions, writing, yearbook, yoga.

Graduation Requirements Arts and fine arts (art, music, dance, drama), English, foreign language, history, life management skills, mathematics, physical education (includes health), science, co-curriculum program (off-campus internship program). Community service is required.

Special Academic Programs Advanced Placement exam preparation; independent study; term-away projects; special instructional classes for deaf students; ESL (25 students enrolled).

College Admission Counseling 84 students graduated in 2015; 83 went to college, including Colgate University; New York University; The College of William and Mary; University of Pennsylvania; University of Virginia; Virginia Polytechnic Institute and State University. Other: 1 had other specific plans.

Student Life Upper grades have specified standards of dress, student council, honor system. Discipline rests equally with students and faculty.

Tuition and Aid Day student tuition: $42,461; 7-day tuition and room/board: $56,191. Tuition installment plan (Insured Tuition Payment Plan, FACTS Tuition Payment Plan, monthly payment plans). Merit scholarship grants, need-based scholarship grants, need-based loans, middle-income loans available. In 2015–16, 30% of upper-school students received aid; total upper-school merit-scholarship money awarded: $230,000. Total amount of financial aid awarded in 2015–16: $3,043,151.

Admissions Traditional secondary-level entrance grade is 9. For fall 2015, 388 students applied for upper-level admission, 227 were accepted, 104 enrolled. ISEE, PSAT, SAT, or ACT for applicants to grade 11 and 12, SSAT or TOEFL required. Deadline for receipt of application materials: January 31. Application fee required: $70. Interview required.

Athletics Interscholastic: basketball, cross-country running, dance, equestrian sports, field hockey, fitness, horseback riding, independent competitive sports, indoor track, lacrosse, martial arts, soccer, softball, squash, strength & conditioning, swimming and diving, tennis, track and field, volleyball, winter soccer; intramural: dance, weight training, yoga. 1 PE instructor, 20 coaches, 1 athletic trainer.

Computers Computers are regularly used in art, English, foreign language, history, mathematics, science classes. Computer network features include on-campus library services, online commercial services, Internet access, wireless campus network, Internet filtering or blocking technology, campus interactive network. Campus intranet, student e-mail accounts, and computer access in designated common areas are available to students. Students grades are available online. The school has a published electronic and media policy.

Contact Ms. Mary Herridge, Director of Enrollment Management. 703-556-8273. Fax: 703-821-2845. E-mail: admission@madeira.org. Website: www.madeira.org

MADISON ACADEMY

325 Slaughter Road
Madison, Alabama 35758

Head of School: Dr. Barry F. Kirkland

General Information Coeducational day college-preparatory school, affiliated with Christian Churches and Churches of Christ. Grades PS–12. Founded: 1955. Setting: suburban. Nearest major city is Huntsville. 160-acre campus. 3 buildings on campus. Approved or accredited by National Christian School Association and Southern Association of Colleges and Schools. Endowment: $2 million. Total enrollment: 850. Upper school average class size: 20. Upper school faculty-student ratio: 1:13. There are 180 required school days per year for Upper School students. Upper School students typically attend 5 days per week. The average school day consists of 6 hours.

Upper School Student Profile 35% of students are Christian Churches and Churches of Christ.

Faculty School total: 35. In upper school: 14 men, 20 women; 14 have advanced degrees.

Subjects Offered 20th century American writers, ACT preparation, advanced chemistry, Advanced Placement courses, advanced studio art-AP, American literature-AP, arts and crafts, athletic training, career and personal planning, career experience, career/college preparation, communications, engineering, finance, guidance, honors algebra, honors English, honors geometry, leadership, photojournalism, reading/study skills, statistics, yearbook.

Graduation Requirements Government, social sciences, social studies (includes history), four years of English, math, science, social science, and Bible, 1 credit of physical education, .5 credit of health.

Special Academic Programs Honors section; independent study; study at local college for college credit.

College Admission Counseling 70 students graduated in 2016; 67 went to college, including Auburn University; Freed-Hardeman University; Harding University; Lipscomb University; The University of Alabama; University of South Alabama. Other: 2 went to work, 1 entered military service. Mean composite ACT: 25. 40% scored over 26 on composite ACT.

Student Life Upper grades have uniform requirement, student council, honor system. Discipline rests primarily with faculty. Attendance at religious services is required.

Tuition and Aid Day student tuition: $8340. Tuition installment plan (FACTS Tuition Payment Plan). Tuition reduction for siblings, need-based scholarship grants available. In 2016–17, 10% of upper-school students received aid. Total amount of financial aid awarded in 2016–17: $84,000.

Admissions Traditional secondary-level entrance grade is 9. For fall 2016, 91 students applied for upper-level admission, 67 were accepted, 66 enrolled. Wide Range Achievement Test required. Deadline for receipt of application materials: none. Application fee required: $75. On-campus interview recommended.

Athletics Interscholastic: baseball (boys), basketball (b,g), cheering (g), cross-country running (b,g), football (b), golf (b,g), soccer (b,g), softball (g), swimming and diving (b,g), tennis (b,g), track and field (b,g), volleyball (g), winter (indoor) track (b,g). 3 PE instructors, 36 coaches, 1 athletic trainer.

Computers Computers are regularly used in Bible studies, career exploration, computer applications, engineering, history, journalism, keyboarding, reading, research skills, social sciences, technology, writing, yearbook classes. Computer network features include on-campus library services, Internet access, wireless campus network, Internet filtering or blocking technology. Student e-mail accounts are available to students. Students grades are available online. The school has a published electronic and media policy.

Contact Dr. Terry Davis, Principal. 256-469-6400. Fax: 256-649-6408. E-mail: tdavis@macademy.org. Website: www.macademy.org

MAGNOLIA HEIGHTS SCHOOL

One Chiefs Drive
Senatobia, Mississippi 38668

Head of School: Dr. Marvin Lishman

General Information Coeducational day college-preparatory and technology school, affiliated with Christian faith. Grades PK–12. Founded: 1970. Setting: rural. Nearest major city is Memphis, TN. 35-acre campus. 5 buildings on campus. Approved or accredited by Mississippi Private School Association, Southern Association of Colleges and Schools, Southern Association of Independent Schools, and Mississippi Department of Education. Endowment: $250,000. Total enrollment: 685. Upper school average class size: 20. Upper school faculty-student ratio: 1:12. There are 180 required school days per year for Upper School students. Upper School students typically attend 5 days per week. The average school day consists of 7 hours and 15 minutes.

Upper School Student Profile Grade 6: 39 students (20 boys, 19 girls); Grade 7: 47 students (25 boys, 22 girls); Grade 8: 50 students (27 boys, 23 girls); Grade 9: 58 students (32 boys, 26 girls); Grade 10: 61 students (30 boys, 31 girls); Grade 11: 54 students (32 boys, 22 girls); Grade 12: 54 students (25 boys, 29 girls). 90% of students are Christian.

Faculty School total: 35. In upper school: 10 men, 20 women; 10 have advanced degrees.

Subjects Offered ACT preparation, anatomy and physiology, baseball, basketball, business mathematics, cheerleading, golf, government, honors algebra, Latin, personal finance, softball, tennis, yearbook.

Special Academic Programs Honors section; study at local college for college credit.

College Admission Counseling 52 students graduated in 2016; 51 went to college, including Christian Brothers University; Delta State University; Mississippi College; Mississippi State University; University of Arkansas; University of Mississippi. Other: 1 entered military service. Median composite ACT: 22. 15% scored over 26 on composite ACT.

Student Life Upper grades have uniform requirement, student council. Discipline rests primarily with faculty.

Tuition and Aid Day student tuition: $6300. Tuition installment plan (FACTS Tuition Payment Plan, monthly payment plans). Need-based scholarship grants available. In 2016–17, 3% of upper-school students received aid.

Admissions Traditional secondary-level entrance grade is 9. For fall 2016, 60 students applied for upper-level admission, 53 were accepted, 42 enrolled. TOEFL required. Deadline for receipt of application materials: none. Application fee required: $200. Interview recommended.

Athletics Interscholastic: baseball (boys), basketball (b,g), cheering (g), football (b), golf (b,g), soccer (b,g), softball (g), tennis (b,g), track and field (b,g). 1 PE instructor, 3 coaches.

Computers Computers are regularly used in all classes. Computer network features include online commercial services, Internet access, wireless campus network, Internet filtering or blocking technology. Campus intranet and student e-mail accounts are available to students. Students grades are available online. The school has a published electronic and media policy.

Contact Mrs. Allison Burris, Director of Advancement. 662-562-4491 Ext. 16. Fax: 662-562-0386. E-mail: allison.burris@magnoliaheights.com. Website: www.magnoliaheights.com

MAINE CENTRAL INSTITUTE

295 Main Street
Pittsfield, Maine 04967

General Information Coeducational boarding and day college-preparatory, general academic, arts, vocational, bilingual studies, technology, humanities, and mathematics, the sciences school. Grades 9–PG. Founded: 1866. Setting: small town. Nearest major city is Portland. Students are housed in single-sex dormitories and honors dorm is coed. 23-acre campus. 19 buildings on campus. Approved or accredited by Independent Schools of Northern New England, New England Association of Schools and Colleges, The Association of Boarding Schools, and Maine Department of Education. Member of National Association of Independent Schools and Secondary School Admission Test Board. Endowment: $5 million. Total enrollment: 455. Upper school average class size: 16. Upper school faculty-student ratio: 1:14. There are 175 required school days per year for Upper School students. Upper School students typically attend 5 days per week. The average school day consists of 7 hours and 15 minutes.

See Display on next page and Close-Up on page 602.

MALDEN CATHOLIC HIGH SCHOOL

99 Crystal Street
Malden, Massachusetts 02148

Head of School: Mr. Thomas J. Doherty III

General Information Boys' day college-preparatory and technology school, affiliated with Roman Catholic Church; primarily serves students with learning disabilities and individuals with Attention Deficit Disorder. Grades 9–12. Founded: 1932. Setting: urban. Nearest major city is Boston. 15-acre campus. 1 building on campus. Approved or accredited by National Catholic Education Association, New England Association of Schools and Colleges, and Massachusetts Department of Education. Member of National Association of Independent Schools. Endowment: $3 million. Total enrollment: 562. Upper school average class size: 23. Upper school faculty-student ratio: 1:13. There are 168 required school days per year for Upper School students. Upper School students typically attend 5 days per week. The average school day consists of 6 hours.

Upper School Student Profile Grade 9: 121 students (121 boys); Grade 10: 156 students (156 boys); Grade 11: 143 students (143 boys); Grade 12: 142 students (142 boys). 85% of students are Roman Catholic.

Faculty School total: 60. In upper school: 34 men, 10 women; 49 have advanced degrees.

Subjects Offered 20th century history, 3-dimensional art, accounting, advanced chemistry, advanced math, Advanced Placement courses, algebra, American government, American history-AP, American literature, ancient world history, art, art appreciation, art history, Asian history, athletics, basic language skills, Bible studies, biology, British literature, British literature (honors), British literature-AP, business, calculus-AP, campus ministry, Chinese history, Christian and Hebrew scripture, Christian testament, college admission preparation, community service, computer programming, computer skills, desktop publishing, English language and composition-AP, English-AP, European history, European history-AP, fine arts, foreign language, French, French language-AP, genetics, geometry, global studies, government, health and safety, honors algebra, honors English, honors geometry, honors U.S. history, honors world history, independent study, integrated science, language arts, leadership and service, library studies, marine biology, marine science, math analysis, modern European history, music appreciation, physical education, psychology, religion, SAT preparation, Spanish, Spanish language-AP, studio art, the Sixties, U.S. history, U.S. history-AP, world history, world history-AP.

Graduation Requirements Algebra, American literature, arts and fine arts (art, music, dance, drama), biology, British literature, Catholic belief and practice, chemistry, computer skills, foreign language, geometry, global studies, mathematics, physical education (includes health), religion (includes Bible studies and theology), science, social studies (includes history), Christian service.

Special Academic Programs 12 Advanced Placement exams for which test preparation is offered; honors section; independent study; ESL (40 students enrolled).

College Admission Counseling 137 students graduated in 2016; 124 went to college, including Assumption College; Boston College; Boston University; Merrimack College; Saint Anselm College; University of Massachusetts Amherst. Other: 2 went to work, 2 entered military service, 9 entered a postgraduate year. Mean SAT critical reading: 542, mean SAT math: 545, mean SAT writing: 533, mean composite ACT: 25.

Student Life Upper grades have specified standards of dress, student council, honor system. Discipline rests primarily with faculty. Attendance at religious services is required.

Tuition and Aid Day student tuition: $15,500. Tuition installment plan (FACTS Tuition Payment Plan). Merit scholarship grants, need-based scholarship grants available. In 2016–17, 65% of upper-school students received aid; total upper-school merit-scholarship money awarded: $623,500. Total amount of financial aid awarded in 2016–17: $1,105,973.

Admissions Traditional secondary-level entrance grade is 9. For fall 2016, 275 students applied for upper-level admission, 260 were accepted, 121 enrolled. Archdiocese of Boston High School entrance exam provided by STS required. Deadline for receipt of application materials: December 15. No application fee required. Interview recommended.

Athletics Interscholastic: baseball, basketball, cross-country running, football, golf, hockey, ice hockey, indoor track, indoor track & field, lacrosse, rugby, soccer, swimming and diving, tennis, track and field, winter (indoor) track, wrestling; intramural: alpine skiing, badminton, ball hockey, basketball, fitness, flag football, floor hockey, Frisbee, jogging, lacrosse, life saving, nordic skiing, physical fitness, physical training, power lifting, skiing (downhill), snowboarding, strength & conditioning, table tennis, weight lifting, weight training. 1 PE instructor, 46 coaches, 1 athletic trainer.

Computers Computers are regularly used in all academic, basic skills, business applications, business studies, design, desktop publishing, graphic arts, graphic design, graphics, information technology, journalism, library, library skills, multimedia, news writing, photography, photojournalism, religion, study skills, technology, theology, Web site design, word processing classes. Computer network features include on-campus library services, online commercial services, Internet access, wireless campus network, Internet filtering or blocking technology. Student e-mail accounts are available to students. Students grades are available online. The school has a published electronic and media policy.

Contact Mr. Matthew O'Neil, Associate Director of Admissions. 781-475-5308. Fax: 781-397-0573. E-mail: oneilm@maldencatholic.org. Website: www.maldencatholic.org

MALVERN PREPARATORY SCHOOL

418 South Warren Avenue
Malvern, Pennsylvania 19355-2707

Head of School: Mr. Christian M. Talbot

General Information Boys' day college-preparatory school, affiliated with Roman Catholic Church. Grades 6–12. Founded: 1842. Setting: suburban. Nearest major city is Philadelphia. 104-acre campus. 16 buildings on campus. Approved or accredited by Pennsylvania Association of Independent Schools and Pennsylvania Department of Education. Member of National Association of Independent Schools. Total enrollment: 654. Upper school average class size: 15. Upper school faculty-student ratio: 1:9. There are 180 required school days per year for Upper School students. Upper School students typically attend 5 days per week. The average school day consists of 7 hours.

Upper School Student Profile Grade 9: 132 students (132 boys); Grade 10: 132 students (132 boys); Grade 11: 125 students (125 boys); Grade 12: 122 students (122 boys). 85% of students are Roman Catholic.

Faculty School total: 74. In upper school: 54 men, 20 women; 51 have advanced degrees.

Subjects Offered Algebra, American history, American literature, art, Bible studies, biology, calculus, ceramics, chemistry, Chinese, computer math, computer programming, computer science, concert band, creative writing, data analysis, drama, earth science, ecology, economics, English, English literature, environmental science, ethics, European history, expository writing, fine arts, French, geography, geometry, government/civics, grammar, health, history, jazz band, journalism, logic, Mandarin, mathematics, music, music performance, music theory, philosophy, photography, physical education, physics, printmaking, religion, science, sculpture, social sciences, social studies, sociology, Spanish, speech, sports medicine, studio art, theater, theology, trigonometry, world history, world literature, writing.

Graduation Requirements Arts and fine arts (art, music, dance, drama), computer science, English, foreign language, mathematics, physical education (includes health), religion (includes Bible studies and theology), science, senior career experience, social sciences, social studies (includes history). Community service is required.

Special Academic Programs Advanced Placement exam preparation; honors section; independent study; study at local college for college credit; study abroad.

College Admission Counseling 115 students graduated in 2016; 114 went to college, including Georgetown University; Penn State University Park; Saint Joseph's University; University of Notre Dame; University of Pennsylvania; Villanova University. Other: 1 had other specific plans.

Student Life Upper grades have specified standards of dress, student council, honor system. Discipline rests primarily with faculty.

Summer Programs Remediation, enrichment, advancement, sports, art/fine arts, computer instruction programs offered; session focuses on academics; held on campus; accepts boys and girls; open to students from other schools. 2017 schedule: June 21 to July 30. Application deadline: none.

Tuition and Aid Day student tuition: $31,975. Tuition installment plan (Insured Tuition Payment Plan, Bryn Mawr Trust Loan Program). Merit scholarship grants, need-based scholarship grants available. In 2016–17, 25% of upper-school students received aid.

Admissions Traditional secondary-level entrance grade is 9. Admissions testing required. Deadline for receipt of application materials: none. Application fee required: $35. On-campus interview required.

Athletics Interscholastic: aquatics, baseball, basketball, crew, cross-country running, diving, football, golf, ice hockey, indoor track, indoor track & field, lacrosse, rowing, rugby, soccer, squash, strength & conditioning, swimming and diving, tennis, track and field, water polo, weight lifting, weight training, winter (indoor) track, wrestling. 3 PE instructors, 40 coaches, 2 athletic trainers.

Computers Computers are regularly used in all academic classes. Computer network features include on-campus library services, online commercial services, Internet access, wireless campus network, Internet filtering or blocking technology. Campus intranet, student e-mail accounts, and computer access in designated common areas are available to students. Students grades are available online. The school has a published electronic and media policy.

Contact Mr. Sean Kenney, Director of Admissions. 484-595-1181. Fax: 484-595-1104. E-mail: admissions@malvernprep.org. Website: www.malvernprep.org

MANHATTAN CHRISTIAN HIGH SCHOOL

8000 Churchill Road
Manhattan, Montana 59741

Head of School: Mr. Patrick J. De Jong

General Information Coeducational day and distance learning college-preparatory and general academic school, affiliated with Calvinist faith; primarily serves students with learning disabilities, individuals with Attention Deficit Disorder, individuals with emotional and behavioral problems, and dyslexic students. Grades PK–12. Distance learning grades 9–12. Founded: 1907. Setting: rural. Nearest major city is Bozeman. 25-acre campus. 1 building on campus. Approved or accredited by Christian Schools International and Montana Department of Education. Endowment: $5.5 million. Total enrollment: 304. Upper school average class size: 23. Upper school faculty-student ratio: 1:11. There are 178 required school days per year for Upper School students. Upper School students typically attend 5 days per week. The average school day consists of 6 hours and 19 minutes.

Upper School Student Profile Grade 6: 19 students (8 boys, 11 girls); Grade 7: 22 students (9 boys, 13 girls); Grade 8: 22 students (14 boys, 8 girls); Grade 9: 27 students (12 boys, 15 girls); Grade 10: 27 students (13 boys, 14 girls); Grade 11: 20 students (13 boys, 7 girls); Grade 12: 19 students (10 boys, 9 girls). 35% of students are Calvinist.

Faculty School total: 23. In upper school: 4 men, 5 women; 3 have advanced degrees.

Subjects Offered Art, Bible studies, business, community service, English, general science, mathematics, music, physical education, senior project, social studies, Spanish.

Graduation Requirements Arts and fine arts (art, music, dance, drama), business skills (includes word processing), English, mathematics, physical education (includes health), religion (includes Bible studies and theology), science, senior project, social studies (includes history), speech. Community service is required.

Special Academic Programs Advanced Placement exam preparation; honors section; independent study; study at local college for college credit; remedial reading and/or remedial writing; remedial math; programs in English, mathematics, general development for dyslexic students.

College Admission Counseling 19 students graduated in 2016; 14 went to college, including Azusa Pacific University; Dordt College; Montana State University; Oklahoma State University; The University of Montana Western. Other: 4 went to work. Mean composite ACT: 24.

Student Life Upper grades have specified standards of dress, student council, honor system. Discipline rests primarily with faculty. Attendance at religious services is required.

Tuition and Aid Day student tuition: $9400. Tuition installment plan (monthly payment plans, individually arranged payment plans). Tuition reduction for siblings, need-based scholarship grants available. In 2016–17, 98% of upper-school students received aid. Total amount of financial aid awarded in 2016–17: $50,000.

Admissions Traditional secondary-level entrance grade is 9. For fall 2016, 10 students applied for upper-level admission, 10 were accepted, 10 enrolled. Academic Profile Tests or any standardized test required. Deadline for receipt of application materials: none. Application fee required: $50. On-campus interview recommended.

Athletics Interscholastic: basketball (boys, girls), cheering (b,g), cross-country running (b,g), football (b), golf (b,g), horseback riding (g), marksmanship (g), rodeo (b,g), track and field (b,g), volleyball (g). 2 PE instructors, 6 coaches, 2 athletic trainers.

Computers Computers are regularly used in art, business, English, religious studies, science, senior seminar, social studies classes. Computer network features include on-campus library services, online commercial services, Internet access, wireless campus network, Internet filtering or blocking technology. Student e-mail accounts and computer access in designated common areas are available to students. Students grades are available online. The school has a published electronic and media policy.

Contact Mrs. Gloria Veltkamp, Admissions Director. 406-282-7261. Fax: 406-282-7701. E-mail: gveltkamp@manhattanchristian.org.
Website: www.manhattanchristian.org

MAPLEBROOK SCHOOL

Amenia, New York
See Special Needs Schools section.

MARANATHA HIGH SCHOOL

169 South Saint John Avenue
Pasadena, California 91105

Head of School: Dr. Steven Sherman

General Information Coeducational day college-preparatory, religious studies, and performing arts school, affiliated with Christian faith. Grades 9–12. Founded: 1965. Setting: urban. 9-acre campus. 4 buildings on campus. Approved or accredited by Association of Christian Schools International, Western Association of Schools and Colleges, and California Department of Education. Member of National Association of Independent Schools. Total enrollment: 680. Upper school average class size: 20. Upper school faculty-student ratio: 1:13. There are 178 required school days per year for Upper School students. Upper School students typically attend 5 days per week. The average school day consists of 7 hours and 5 minutes.

Upper School Student Profile 90% of students are Christian faith.

Faculty School total: 48. In upper school: 20 men, 28 women; 29 have advanced degrees.

Subjects Offered Computer science, philosophy.

Graduation Requirements English, foreign language, history, life science, mathematics, performing arts, physical education (includes health), physical science, theology, visual arts, theology must be taken every year student attends school, 10-20 service hours are required each year. Community service is required.

Special Academic Programs 16 Advanced Placement exams for which test preparation is offered; honors section; study at local college for college credit; academic accommodation for the artistically talented; remedial reading and/or remedial writing; remedial math; special instructional classes for students with learning difficulties and Attention Deficit Disorder.

College Admission Counseling 165 students graduated in 2016; 162 went to college, including Azusa Pacific University; University of California, Los Angeles. Other: 1 entered military service, 2 had other specific plans. Median SAT critical reading: 553, median SAT math: 560, median SAT writing: 546.

Student Life Upper grades have uniform requirement, student council, honor system. Discipline rests primarily with faculty. Attendance at religious services is required.

Summer Programs Remediation, enrichment, advancement, sports, art/fine arts programs offered; session focuses on science and math; held on campus; accepts boys and girls; open to students from other schools. 140 students usually enrolled. 2017 schedule: June 12 to July 21. Application deadline: May 15.

Tuition and Aid Day student tuition: $18,375. Tuition installment plan (SMART Tuition Payment Plan, monthly payment plans). Merit scholarship grants, need-based scholarship grants available. In 2016–17, 30% of upper-school students received aid.

Admissions Traditional secondary-level entrance grade is 9. ISEE required. Deadline for receipt of application materials: none. Application fee required: $75. On-campus interview recommended.

Athletics Interscholastic: baseball (boys), basketball (b,g), cheering (b,g), cross-country running (b,g), diving (b,g), football (b), soccer (b,g), softball (g), swimming and diving (b,g), tennis (b,g), track and field (b,g), volleyball (b,g); coed interscholastic: cheering, dance team, equestrian sports, golf; coed intramural: Frisbee, hiking/backpacking, kayaking, outdoor activities, outdoor adventure, outdoor skills. 2 PE instructors, 42 coaches, 1 athletic trainer.

Computers Computers are regularly used in college planning, freshman foundations, graphic design, library, photography, research skills, yearbook classes. Computer network features include on-campus library services, online commercial services, Internet access, wireless campus network, Internet filtering or blocking technology, eLibrary, 1:1: iPad program. Campus intranet, student e-mail accounts, and computer access in designated common areas are available to students. Students grades are available online. The school has a published electronic and media policy.

Contact Mrs. Rachel Ponton, Admissions Coordinator. 626-817-4021. Fax: 626-817-4040. E-mail: r_ponton@mhs-hs.org. Website: www.maranatha-hs.org

MARIANAPOLIS PREPARATORY SCHOOL

PO Box 304
26 Chase Road
Thompson, Connecticut 06277-0304

Head of School: Mr. Joseph C. Hanrahan

General Information Coeducational boarding and day and distance learning college-preparatory and ESL school, affiliated with Roman Catholic Church. Grades 9–PG. Distance learning grades 9–12. Founded: 1926. Setting: small town. Nearest major city is Boston, MA. Students are housed in single-sex dormitories. 150-acre campus. 10 buildings on campus. Approved or accredited by Association of Independent Schools in New England, Connecticut Association of Independent Schools, New England Association of Schools and Colleges, The Association of Boarding Schools, and Connecticut Department of Education. Member of National Association of Independent Schools and Secondary School Admission Test Board. Total enrollment: 400. Upper school average class size: 12. Upper school faculty-student ratio: 1:7.

Upper School Student Profile Grade 9: 95 students (43 boys, 52 girls); Grade 10: 98 students (45 boys, 53 girls); Grade 11: 111 students (51 boys, 60 girls); Grade 12: 93 students (50 boys, 43 girls); Postgraduate: 3 students (3 boys). 43% of students are boarding students. 25% are state residents. 10 states are represented in upper school student body. 30% are international students. International students from Canada, China, Mexico, Republic of Korea, Taiwan, and Viet Nam; 14 other countries represented in student body.

Faculty School total: 55. In upper school: 27 men, 28 women; 28 have advanced degrees; 36 reside on campus.

Subjects Offered Advanced Placement courses, advanced studio art-AP, algebra, American government, American literature, architecture, art, astronomy, Bible as literature, Bible studies, biology, biology-AP, bookmaking, business, calculus, calculus-AP, chemistry, chemistry-AP, Chinese, choir, chorus, Christian and Hebrew scripture, Christian doctrine, Christian ethics, church history, classical language, comparative religion, composition, composition-AP, computer programming, computer science, conceptual physics, contemporary studies, creative writing, dance, dance performance, digital photography, drawing, drawing and design, economics, English, English composition, English language and composition-AP, English literature, English literature and composition-AP, English literature-AP, English-AP, English/composition-AP, ensembles, environmental science, ESL, ethics, etymology, fine arts, French, geometry, global studies, government, government/civics, guitar, history, honors algebra, honors English, honors geometry, human biology, journalism, literary genres, Mandarin, mathematics, modern European history, modern European history-AP, moral theology, music, music performance, music technology, music theory, painting, photography, physics, physics-AP, piano, pre-calculus, printmaking, probability and statistics, programming, psychology, religion, science, sculpture, social justice, social studies, sociology, Spanish, Spanish-AP, statistics, statistics-AP, theology, trigonometry, U.S. history, U.S. history-AP, Web site design, world history, world history-AP, world literature, world religions.

Graduation Requirements Arts and fine arts (art, music, dance, drama), computer science, electives, English, foreign language, history, mathematics, science, theology.

Special Academic Programs Advanced Placement exam preparation; honors section; independent study; ESL (90 students enrolled).

College Admission Counseling 89 students graduated in 2016; 88 went to college, including Boston University; College of the Holy Cross; Michigan State University; Quinnipiac University; Salve Regina University; University of Massachusetts Amherst. Other: 1 entered a postgraduate year.

Student Life Upper grades have specified standards of dress, student council. Discipline rests equally with students and faculty. Attendance at religious services is required.

Summer Programs Remediation, enrichment, advancement, ESL programs offered; held off campus; held at online; accepts boys and girls; open to students from other schools. 45 students usually enrolled. 2017 schedule: June 29 to August 9. Application deadline: June 15.

Tuition and Aid Day student tuition: $16,234; 7-day tuition and room/board: $50,014. Tuition installment plan (SMART Tuition Payment Plan, monthly payment plans, individually arranged payment plans). Merit scholarship grants, need-based

scholarship grants, tuition reduction for Diocese of Norwich affiliation available. In 2016–17, 43% of upper-school students received aid.

Admissions Traditional secondary-level entrance grade is 9. Common entrance examinations, International English Language Test, PSAT, SAT, SSAT, TOEFL, TOEFL Junior or TOEFL or SLEP required. Deadline for receipt of application materials: January 15. Application fee required: $100. Interview recommended.

Athletics Interscholastic: baseball (boys), basketball (b,g), crew (b,g), cross-country running (b,g), lacrosse (b,g), soccer (b,g), softball (g), tennis (b,g), volleyball (g); intramural: basketball (b,g), dance (g), modern dance (g); coed interscholastic: badminton, Frisbee, golf, gymnastics, horseback riding, indoor track & field, running, skiing (cross-country), skiing (downhill), swimming and diving, track and field, ultimate Frisbee, winter (indoor) track, wrestling; coed intramural: aerobics/dance, alpine skiing, ballet, cross-country running, dance, equestrian sports, flag football, Frisbee, horseback riding, independent competitive sports, jogging, judo, martial arts, modern dance, ropes courses, skiing (cross-country), skiing (downhill), snowboarding, snowshoeing, strength & conditioning, table tennis, tai chi, tennis, ultimate Frisbee, volleyball, weight lifting, weight training, yoga. 1 coach, 1 athletic trainer.

Computers Computers are regularly used in all academic, ESL classes. Computer network features include online commercial services, Internet access, wireless campus network, Internet filtering or blocking technology. Student e-mail accounts are available to students. Students grades are available online. The school has a published electronic and media policy.

Contact Mr. Ray Cross, Director of Admission. 860-923-9245. Fax: 860-923-3730. E-mail: rcross@marianapolis.org. Website: www.marianapolis.org

MARIAN CENTRAL CATHOLIC HIGH SCHOOL

1001 McHenry Avenue
Woodstock, Illinois 60098

Head of School: Ms. Debra Novy

General Information Coeducational day college-preparatory, arts, business, religious studies, and technology school, affiliated with Roman Catholic Church. Grades 9–12. Founded: 1959. Setting: suburban. 42-acre campus. 1 building on campus. Approved or accredited by National Catholic Education Association, North Central Association of Colleges and Schools, and Illinois Department of Education. Endowment: $1.7 million. Total enrollment: 687. Upper school average class size: 19. Upper school faculty-student ratio: 1:19. There are 176 required school days per year for Upper School students. Upper School students typically attend 5 days per week. The average school day consists of 6 hours and 25 minutes.

Upper School Student Profile Grade 9: 182 students (105 boys, 77 girls); Grade 10: 163 students (73 boys, 90 girls); Grade 11: 173 students (81 boys, 92 girls); Grade 12: 175 students (84 boys, 91 girls). 91.5% of students are Roman Catholic.

Faculty School total: 37. In upper school: 16 men, 21 women; 23 have advanced degrees.

Subjects Offered Accounting, advanced biology, advanced chemistry, advanced math, Advanced Placement courses, algebra, American government, anatomy and physiology, art, band, biology, biology-AP, business law, calculus, calculus-AP, chemistry, chemistry-AP, chorus, comparative government and politics-AP, composition, computer applications, consumer economics, cultural geography, desktop publishing, engineering, English, English composition, English language and composition-AP, English literature and composition-AP, English literature-AP, first aid, French, general science, geography, geometry, global issues, health, honors algebra, honors English, honors geometry, integrated science, macroeconomics-AP, marketing, photo shop, physical education, physical science, physics, physics-AP, pre-calculus, psychology, psychology-AP, publications, Spanish, speech, statistics-AP, theater, theology, U.S. government and politics-AP, U.S. history, U.S. history-AP, Web site design, world history, world history-AP.

Graduation Requirements Art, biology, consumer economics, electives, English, first aid, foreign language, government, health, mathematics, music, physical education (includes health), science, theology, U.S. history.

Special Academic Programs 10 Advanced Placement exams for which test preparation is offered; honors section; academic accommodation for the gifted; remedial reading and/or remedial writing; remedial math; special instructional classes for deaf students.

College Admission Counseling 158 students graduated in 2016; 156 went to college, including Indiana University Bloomington; Loyola University Chicago; Marquette University; The University of Iowa; University of Illinois at Urbana–Champaign; University of Wisconsin–Madison. Other: 2 entered military service. Mean composite ACT: 25. 47% scored over 26 on composite ACT.

Student Life Upper grades have uniform requirement, student council. Discipline rests primarily with faculty. Attendance at religious services is required.

Summer Programs Enrichment, sports, art/fine arts, computer instruction programs offered; session focuses on sports camps, study skills, art, band, chorus, media/technology, Model United Nations; held on campus; accepts boys and girls; open to students from other schools. 2017 schedule: June to August.

Tuition and Aid Day student tuition: $6255–$8375. Tuition installment plan (monthly payment plans, quarterly payment plan, semester payment plans, yearly payment plans). Tuition reduction for siblings, need-based scholarship grants, paying campus jobs available. In 2016–17, 17% of upper-school students received aid. Total amount of financial aid awarded in 2016–17: $288,816.

Admissions Traditional secondary-level entrance grade is 9. High School Placement Test (closed version) from Scholastic Testing Service required. Deadline for receipt of application materials: none. No application fee required.

Athletics Interscholastic: baseball (boys), basketball (b,g), cheering (g), climbing (g), dance team (g), football (b), soccer (b,g), softball (g), tennis (b,g), volleyball (g), wrestling (b); coed interscholastic: cross-country running, fencing, fishing, golf, track and field; coed intramural: floor hockey. 3 PE instructors, 68 coaches, 1 athletic trainer.

Computers Computers are regularly used in computer applications, desktop publishing, photography, publications, Web site design classes. Computer network features include Internet access, wireless campus network, Internet filtering or blocking technology. Campus intranet and computer access in designated common areas are available to students. Students grades are available online. The school has a published electronic and media policy.

Contact Mr. Michael Maloney, Director of Admissions. 815-338-4220 Ext. 108. Fax: 815-338-4253. E-mail: mmaloney@marian.com. Website: www.marian.com

MARIAN HIGH SCHOOL

1311 South Logan Street
Mishawaka, Indiana 46544

Head of School: Mark Kirzeder

General Information Coeducational day college-preparatory, arts, business, vocational, religious studies, bilingual studies, and technology school, affiliated with Roman Catholic Church. Grades 9–12. Founded: 1965. Setting: suburban. 72-acre campus. 1 building on campus. Approved or accredited by North Central Association of Colleges and Schools, The College Board, and Indiana Department of Education. Total enrollment: 690. Upper school average class size: 27. Upper school faculty-student ratio: 1:24. There are 180 required school days per year for Upper School students. Upper School students typically attend 5 days per week. The average school day consists of 6 hours and 30 minutes.

Upper School Student Profile 83% of students are Roman Catholic.

Faculty School total: 48. In upper school: 18 men, 30 women; 22 have advanced degrees.

Subjects Offered 20th century history, 20th century physics, 20th century world history, 3-dimensional art, 3-dimensional design, accounting, acting, advanced chemistry, advanced computer applications, advanced math, algebra, alternative physical education, American government, American literature, analysis and differential calculus, analytic geometry, anatomy, ancient world history, art, art history, arts and crafts, arts appreciation, business law, calculus, Catholic belief and practice, chemistry, drama, drawing, drawing and design, economics, English composition, English literature-AP, environmental science, environmental studies, environmental systems, family and consumer science, family living, fashion, fine arts, food and nutrition, foods, French, French language-AP, general business, general math, geography, geometry, German, government and politics-AP, government-AP, government/civics, guidance, health, histology, honors world history, independent living, integrated science, keyboarding, Latin, Life of Christ, media, media arts, moral theology, music, music appreciation, nutrition, physics, physics-AP, pre-algebra, pre-calculus, psychology, religion, scripture, senior project, sewing, sociology, Spanish, Spanish language-AP, Spanish-AP, study skills, theology, U.S. government and politics-AP, U.S. history, U.S. history-AP, visual arts, vocal music, Western civilization.

Graduation Requirements Algebra, American government, American history, analytic geometry, arts and fine arts (art, music, dance, drama), biology, chemistry, computer information systems, computer skills, economics, English, English composition, English literature, French, keyboarding, languages, mathematics, science, scripture, writing, four years of theology.

Special Academic Programs Advanced Placement exam preparation; study at local college for college credit; remedial reading and/or remedial writing; remedial math.

College Admission Counseling 162 students graduated in 2015; 155 went to college, including Ball State University; DePaul University; Indiana University–Purdue University Fort Wayne; Indiana University Bloomington; Purdue University; University of Notre Dame. Other: 4 went to work, 1 entered military service, 2 had other specific plans. Mean SAT critical reading: 542, mean SAT math: 541, mean SAT writing: 537, mean composite ACT: 23.

Student Life Upper grades have specified standards of dress, student council, honor system. Discipline rests equally with students and faculty. Attendance at religious services is required.

Tuition and Aid Day student tuition: $5575–$6575. Tuition installment plan (The Tuition Plan, FACTS Tuition Payment Plan, individually arranged payment plans). Tuition reduction for siblings, need-based loans available. In 2015–16, 45% of upper-school students received aid. Total amount of financial aid awarded in 2015–16: $350,000.

Admissions Traditional secondary-level entrance grade is 9. For fall 2015, 210 students applied for upper-level admission, 210 were accepted, 199 enrolled. High School Placement Test, Math Placement Exam or placement test required. Deadline for receipt of application materials: September 9. Application fee required: $100. Interview required.

Athletics Interscholastic: aerobics/dance (girls), aquatics (b,g), baseball (b), basketball (b,g), cheering (b,g), Cosom hockey (b), cross-country running (b,g), dance team (g), diving (b,g), flag football (g), football (b), golf (b,g), gymnastics (g), hockey (b), ice hockey (b), indoor hockey (b), lacrosse (b,g), power lifting (b,g), rugby (b), soccer (b,g), softball (g), swimming and diving (b,g), tennis (b,g), track and field (b,g), volleyball (g), weight training (b,g), wrestling (b,g); intramural: basketball (b), flag football (g), pom squad (g); coed interscholastic: cheering, wrestling; coed intramural: alpine skiing, bowling. 2 PE instructors, 42 coaches, 1 athletic trainer.

Computers Computers are regularly used in business education, business skills, career education, commercial art, economics, foreign language, graphic arts, history, library, media arts, occupational education, publications, religion, yearbook classes. Computer network features include on-campus library services, online commercial services, Internet access, Internet filtering or blocking technology. Students grades are available online. The school has a published electronic and media policy.

Contact Mary Kay Dance, Director of Admissions and Public Relations. 574-259-5257 Ext. 319. Fax: 574-258-7668. E-mail: mdance@marianhs.org. Website: www.marianhs.org/

MARIAN HIGH SCHOOL

273 Union Avenue
Framingham, Massachusetts 01702

Head of School: Mr. John J. Ermilio

General Information Coeducational day college-preparatory school, affiliated with Roman Catholic Church. Grades 9–12. Founded: 1956. Setting: urban. Nearest major city is Boston. 2-acre campus. 1 building on campus. Approved or accredited by Massachusetts Department of Education, National Catholic Education Association, New England Association of Schools and Colleges, and Massachusetts Department of Education. Endowment: $500,000. Total enrollment: 260. Upper school average class size: 17. Upper school faculty-student ratio: 1:17. There are 172 required school days per year for Upper School students. Upper School students typically attend 5 days per week. The average school day consists of 6 hours and 30 minutes.

Upper School Student Profile Grade 9: 53 students (22 boys, 31 girls); Grade 10: 48 students (16 boys, 32 girls); Grade 11: 84 students (42 boys, 42 girls); Grade 12: 67 students (34 boys, 33 girls). 47% of students are Roman Catholic.

Faculty School total: 23. In upper school: 14 men, 9 women; 22 have advanced degrees.

Subjects Offered 1968.

Graduation Requirements Arts and fine arts (art, music, dance, drama), English, foreign language, mathematics, religion (includes Bible studies and theology), science, U.S. history, world history, 4 years of religious studies.

Special Academic Programs Advanced Placement exam preparation; honors section; study at local college for college credit; ESL (35 students enrolled).

College Admission Counseling 67 students graduated in 2016; 66 went to college, including Boston University; College of the Holy Cross; Framingham State University; Providence College; Sacred Heart University; University of Massachusetts Amherst. Other: 1 went to work. 5% scored over 600 on SAT critical reading, 5% scored over 600 on SAT math, 5% scored over 600 on SAT writing, 5% scored over 1800 on combined SAT, 2% scored over 26 on composite ACT.

Student Life Upper grades have uniform requirement, student council. Discipline rests primarily with faculty. Attendance at religious services is required.

Tuition and Aid Day student tuition: $10,400. Tuition installment plan (FACTS Tuition Payment Plan). Merit scholarship grants, need-based scholarship grants available. In 2016–17, 36% of upper-school students received aid; total upper-school merit-scholarship money awarded: $58,000. Total amount of financial aid awarded in 2016–17: $600,000.

Admissions Traditional secondary-level entrance grade is 9. For fall 2016, 75 students applied for upper-level admission, 71 were accepted, 64 enrolled. High School Placement Test required. Deadline for receipt of application materials: January 15. No application fee required. Interview recommended.

Athletics Interscholastic: baseball (boys), basketball (b,g), cross-country running (b,g), field hockey (g), football (b), hockey (b), ice hockey (b), lacrosse (b,g), soccer (b,g), softball (g), tennis (g), track and field (b,g), volleyball (g), winter (indoor) track (b,g); coed interscholastic: cheering, dance, golf, indoor track. 15 coaches, 1 athletic trainer.

Computers Computers are regularly used in all classes. Computer network features include on-campus library services, online commercial services, Internet access, wireless campus network, Internet filtering or blocking technology, iPads. Campus intranet, student e-mail accounts, and computer access in designated common areas are available to students. Students grades are available online. The school has a published electronic and media policy.

Contact Ms. Jamie Gaudet, Director of Admissions. 508-875-7646 Ext. 203. Fax: 508-875-0838. E-mail: admissions@marianhigh.org. Website: www.marianhigh.org

MARIN ACADEMY

1600 Mission Avenue

San Rafael, California 94901-1859

Head of School: Travis Brownley

General Information Coeducational day college-preparatory and outdoor education program school. Grades 9–12. Founded: 1971. Setting: suburban. Nearest major city is San Francisco. 10-acre campus. 12 buildings on campus. Approved or accredited by California Association of Independent Schools, The College Board, and Western Association of Schools and Colleges. Member of National Association of Independent Schools and Secondary School Admission Test Board. Endowment: $13 million. Total enrollment: 406. Upper school average class size: 15. Upper school faculty-student ratio: 1:9. There are 180 required school days per year for Upper School students. Upper School students typically attend 5 days per week. The average school day consists of 6 hours and 45 minutes.

Upper School Student Profile Grade 9: 111 students (52 boys, 59 girls); Grade 10: 96 students (42 boys, 54 girls); Grade 11: 104 students (55 boys, 49 girls); Grade 12: 99 students (47 boys, 52 girls).

Faculty School total: 55. In upper school: 23 men, 32 women; 38 have advanced degrees.

Subjects Offered 20th century history, 20th century world history, 3-dimensional art, acting, adolescent issues, African history, algebra, American culture, American foreign policy, American government, American history, American literature, American minority experience, American studies, ancient world history, art, Asian history, Asian literature, biology, British literature (honors), calculus, ceramics, chemistry, college counseling, community service, creative writing, dance, digital imaging, digital photography, English, English literature, environmental science, European history, fine arts, French, geology, geometry, government/civics, health, history, honors U.S. history, human development, Islamic history, Islamic studies, Japanese, journalism, Mandarin, mathematics, music, oceanography, photography, physical education, physics, pre-calculus, science, social studies, Spanish, theater, trigonometry, world cultures, world history-AP.

Graduation Requirements Arts and fine arts (art, music, dance, drama), English, foreign language, health and wellness, health education, mathematics, physical education (includes health), science, social studies (includes history), annual one-week experiential education course. Community service is required.

Special Academic Programs 13 Advanced Placement exams for which test preparation is offered; honors section; independent study; term-away projects; study at local college for college credit; study abroad; academic accommodation for the gifted, the musically talented, and the artistically talented.

College Admission Counseling 107 students graduated in 2016; all went to college, including Middlebury College; Santa Clara University; Stanford University; The Colorado College; Tufts University; University of California, Santa Cruz. Median SAT critical reading: 730, median SAT math: 720, median SAT writing: 710, median combined SAT: 2200, median composite ACT: 33.

Student Life Upper grades have student council, honor system. Discipline rests primarily with faculty.

Summer Programs Art/fine arts programs offered; held on campus; accepts boys and girls; open to students from other schools. 40 students usually enrolled. 2017 schedule: June 15 to July 15. Application deadline: February 1.

Tuition and Aid Day student tuition: $42,100. Tuition installment plan (Tuition Management Systems (TMS)). Need-based scholarship grants available. In 2016–17, 22% of upper-school students received aid. Total amount of financial aid awarded in 2016–17: $2,900,000.

Admissions Traditional secondary-level entrance grade is 9. For fall 2016, 474 students applied for upper-level admission, 183 were accepted, 119 enrolled. ISEE or SSAT required. Deadline for receipt of application materials: January 16. Application fee required: $100. On-campus interview recommended.

Athletics Interscholastic: aquatics (boys, girls), backpacking (b,g), baseball (b), basketball (b,g), bicycling (b,g), climbing (b,g), combined training (b,g), cross-country running (b,g), fencing (b,g), golf (b,g), independent competitive sports (b,g), lacrosse (b), mountain biking (b,g), soccer (b,g), swimming and diving (b,g), tennis (b,g), track and field (b,g), volleyball (g), water polo (b,g), wilderness (b,g); coed interscholastic: dance, golf; coed intramural: bicycling, climbing, fitness, flag football, Frisbee, hiking/backpacking, kayaking, martial arts, Nautilus, outdoor adventure, outdoor education, outdoor skills, physical fitness, rock climbing, scuba diving, ultimate Frisbee. 28 coaches, 1 athletic trainer.

Computers Computers are regularly used in art, English, foreign language, history, library skills, mathematics, music, photography, science, yearbook classes. Computer network features include on-campus library services, online commercial services, Internet access, wireless campus network, multimedia hardware and production applications. Student e-mail accounts and computer access in designated common areas are available to students. The school has a published electronic and media policy.

Contact Trent Nutting, Director of Admissions and Financial Aid. 415-453-4550 Ext. 216. Fax: 415-453-8905. E-mail: tnutting@ma.org. Website: www.ma.org

MARINE MILITARY ACADEMY

320 Iwo Jima Boulevard

Harlingen, Texas 78550

Head of School: Col. R Glenn Hill, USMC-Ret.

General Information Boys' boarding college-preparatory, general academic, and military school; primarily serves underachievers. Grades 8–PG. Founded: 1965. Setting: small town. Students are housed in single-sex dormitories. 142-acre campus. 43 buildings on campus. Approved or accredited by Military High School and College Association, Southern Association of Colleges and Schools, Southern Association of Independent Schools, and Texas Department of Education. Member of National Association of Independent Schools. Endowment: $18 million. Total enrollment: 262. Upper school average class size: 11. Upper school faculty-student ratio: 1:13. The average school day consists of 6 hours.

Upper School Student Profile Grade 8: 18 students (18 boys); Grade 9: 43 students (43 boys); Grade 10: 55 students (55 boys); Grade 11: 81 students (81 boys); Grade 12: 51 students (51 boys); Postgraduate: 4 students (4 boys). 100% of students are boarding students. 31% are state residents. 23 states are represented in upper school student body. 39% are international students. International students from Christmas Island, Micronesia, Niue, Rwanda, Tajikistan, and Viet Nam; 5 other countries represented in student body.

Faculty School total: 34. In upper school: 17 men, 17 women; 16 have advanced degrees; 24 reside on campus.

Subjects Offered Aerospace science, algebra, American history, band, biology, calculus, calculus-AP, chemistry, computer programming, computer science, economics, English, environmental science, geography, geometry, government/civics, history, journalism, JROTC, keyboarding, mathematics, military science, physics, physics-AP, political science, SAT preparation, science, social sciences, social studies, Spanish, Spanish-AP, speech, world history.

Graduation Requirements Business skills (includes word processing), computer science, English, foreign language, mathematics, military science, physical education (includes health), science, social sciences, social studies (includes history).

Special Academic Programs Advanced Placement exam preparation; honors section; study at local college for college credit; academic accommodation for the gifted; remedial reading and/or remedial writing; remedial math; ESL (45 students enrolled).

College Admission Counseling 58 students graduated in 2016; 57 went to college, including Texas A&M University; Texas Tech University; The Citadel, The Military College of South Carolina; United States Military Academy; United States Naval Academy; Virginia Military Institute. Other: 1 entered military service, 1 entered a postgraduate year. Median SAT critical reading: 470, median SAT math: 470, median SAT writing: 440, median combined SAT: 1400, median composite ACT: 20. 17% scored over 600 on SAT critical reading, 20% scored over 600 on SAT math, 12% scored over 600 on SAT writing, 12% scored over 1800 on combined SAT, 18% scored over 26 on composite ACT.

Student Life Upper grades have uniform requirement, student council, honor system. Discipline rests equally with students and faculty.

Summer Programs ESL, sports, rigorous outdoor training programs offered; session focuses on leadership training; held on campus; accepts boys; open to students from other schools. 360 students usually enrolled. 2017 schedule: July 1 to July 29. Application deadline: none.

Tuition and Aid 7-day tuition and room/board: $36,750. Tuition installment plan (FACTS Tuition Payment Plan, monthly payment plans, individually arranged payment plans, Chief Financial Officer authorization required). Tuition reduction for siblings, merit scholarship grants, need-based scholarship grants, parent Active Duty Military Discount, referral reward discount available. In 2016–17, 40% of upper-school students received aid. Total amount of financial aid awarded in 2016–17: $1,000,000.

Admissions Traditional secondary-level entrance grade is 9. For fall 2016, 193 students applied for upper-level admission, 146 were accepted, 112 enrolled. Deadline for receipt of application materials: none. Application fee required: $100.

Athletics Interscholastic: baseball, basketball, bicycling, boxing, cross-country running, diving, drill team, football, golf, JROTC drill, marksmanship, physical fitness, riflery, running, soccer, swimming and diving, tennis, track and field, winter soccer; intramural: baseball, basketball, boxing, climbing, fitness, flag football, football, judo, kickball, martial arts, outdoor activities, outdoor adventure, paint ball, physical fitness, physical training, power lifting, racquetball, rappelling, rock climbing, running, sailing, scuba diving, soccer, softball, swimming and diving, track and field, volleyball, wall climbing, weight lifting, weight training. 15 coaches, 1 athletic trainer.

Computers Computers are regularly used in English, foreign language, mathematics, science, yearbook classes. Computer network features include on-campus library services, online commercial services, Internet access, Internet filtering or blocking technology. Student e-mail accounts and computer access in designated common areas are available to students. Students grades are available online. The school has a published electronic and media policy.

Contact Mrs. Jay Perez, Assistant Admissions Director. 956-423-6006 Ext. 251. Fax: 956-421-9273. E-mail: admissions@mma-tx.org. Website: www.mma-tx.org

MARION ACADEMY

1820 Prier Drive
Marion, Alabama 36756

Head of School: Mr. Benjamin Catlin Miller

General Information Coeducational day college-preparatory and general academic school. Grades K–12. Founded: 1987. Setting: small town. Nearest major city is Tuscaloosa. 5-acre campus. 1 building on campus. Approved or accredited by Southern Association of Colleges and Schools and Alabama Department of Education. Total enrollment: 53. Upper school average class size: 8. Upper school faculty-student ratio: 1:8. There are 180 required school days per year for Upper School students. Upper School students typically attend 5 days per week. The average school day consists of 6 hours and 30 minutes.

Upper School Student Profile Grade 6: 2 students (2 boys); Grade 7: 7 students (3 boys, 4 girls); Grade 8: 7 students (4 boys, 3 girls); Grade 9: 5 students (3 boys, 2 girls); Grade 10: 7 students (4 boys, 3 girls); Grade 11: 5 students (3 boys, 2 girls); Grade 12: 4 students (3 boys, 1 girl).

Faculty School total: 20. In upper school: 4 men, 6 women; 2 have advanced degrees.

Subjects Offered 20th century history, 20th century world history, advanced computer applications, advanced math, Alabama history and geography, algebra, American government, anatomy and physiology, art, athletics, basic language skills, Bible studies, biology, cheerleading, college planning, creative writing, drama, earth science, economics, English language and composition-AP, English language-AP, English literature, English literature and composition-AP, foreign language, general math, geography, government, grammar, health education, history, honors algebra, honors English, human anatomy, Internet, language, language and composition, language arts, library, math applications, math methods, math review, mathematics, mathematics-AP, physical education, SAT/ACT preparation, speech, U.S. government, U.S. history.

Graduation Requirements American government, chemistry, English, Spanish.

College Admission Counseling 5 students graduated in 2016; all went to college, including Marion Military Institute.

Student Life Upper grades have specified standards of dress, student council, honor system. Discipline rests primarily with faculty.

Tuition and Aid Guaranteed tuition plan. Tuition reduction for siblings available.

Admissions Traditional secondary-level entrance grade is 9. For fall 2016, 5 students applied for upper-level admission, 5 were accepted, 5 enrolled. Iowa Tests of Basic Skills required. Deadline for receipt of application materials: none. Application fee required: $150. On-campus interview required.

Athletics Interscholastic: baseball (boys), basketball (b,g), cheering (g), cross-country running (b,g), football (b), softball (g), track and field (b,g), volleyball (g); coed interscholastic: track and field. 1 PE instructor, 2 coaches.

Computers Computers are regularly used in career education, library skills classes. Computer network features include Internet access. Student e-mail accounts are available to students. Students grades are available online.

Contact Mrs. Margaret S. Hallmon, Secretary. 334-683-8204. Fax: 334-683-4938. E-mail: marionacademy@hotmail.com. Website: www.marion-academy.com

MARIST HIGH SCHOOL

4200 West 115th Street
Chicago, Illinois 60655-4306

Head of School: Br. Hank Hammer, FMS

General Information Coeducational day college-preparatory and business school, affiliated with Roman Catholic Church. Grades 9–12. Founded: 1963. Setting: suburban. 55-acre campus. 1 building on campus. Approved or accredited by National Catholic Education Association, National Council for Nonpublic Schools, and Illinois Department of Education. Total enrollment: 1,703. Upper school average class size: 27. Upper school faculty-student ratio: 1:18. There are 180 required school days per year for Upper School students. Upper School students typically attend 5 days per week. The average school day consists of 6 hours and 35 minutes.

Upper School Student Profile 93% of students are Roman Catholic.

Faculty School total: 107. In upper school: 61 men, 46 women; 81 have advanced degrees.

Subjects Offered Accounting, algebra, American legal systems, anatomy, architecture, art, art history-AP, band, biology, biology-AP, business mathematics, calculus, calculus-AP, chemistry, chemistry-AP, chorus, computer graphics, computer science, computer science-AP, creative writing, drafting, drawing, economics, English, English language and composition-AP, English literature and composition-AP, English-AP, entrepreneurship, environmental science, film and literature, film studies, forensics, French, French language-AP, French-AP, geometry, information technology, Italian, journalism, macro/microeconomics-AP, music appreciation, painting, peer counseling, philosophy, physics, physics-AP, pottery, psychology, psychology-AP, reading, religious studies, rhetoric, senior humanities, Spanish, Spanish language-AP, Spanish literature-AP, Spanish-AP, studio art, studio art-AP, U.S. government and politics-AP, U.S. history, U.S. history-AP, Web site design, wellness, Western civilization, world geography.

Graduation Requirements Electives, English, foreign language, mathematics, performing arts, physical education (includes health), religion (includes Bible studies and theology), science, social studies (includes history), technology, visual arts.

Special Academic Programs 21 Advanced Placement exams for which test preparation is offered; honors section; study at local college for college credit; study abroad; academic accommodation for the gifted, the musically talented, and the artistically talented; remedial reading and/or remedial writing; remedial math.

College Admission Counseling 416 students graduated in 2016; 410 went to college, including Illinois State University; Loyola University Chicago; Marquette University; Purdue University; The University of Iowa; University of Illinois at Urbana–Champaign. Other: 3 went to work, 3 entered military service. Mean composite ACT: 24.

Student Life Upper grades have uniform requirement, student council, honor system. Discipline rests primarily with faculty. Attendance at religious services is required.

Summer Programs Remediation, advancement programs offered; held on campus; accepts boys and girls; open to students from other schools. 350 students usually enrolled. 2017 schedule: June 1 to July 24.

Tuition and Aid Day student tuition: $11,000. Tuition installment plan (monthly payment plans, individually arranged payment plans). Tuition reduction for siblings, merit scholarship grants, need-based scholarship grants, paying campus jobs available. In 2016–17, 33% of upper-school students received aid.

Admissions Traditional secondary-level entrance grade is 9. High School Placement Test required. Deadline for receipt of application materials: January 10. Application fee required: $200.

Athletics Interscholastic: baseball (boys), basketball (b,g), bowling (b,g), boxing (b), cheering (g), cross-country running (b,g), dance team (g), football (b), golf (b,g), indoor track (b,g), indoor track & field (b,g), lacrosse (b,g), pom squad (b), rugby (b), soccer (b,g), softball (g), swimming and diving (g), tennis (b,g), track and field (b,g), volleyball (b,g), wrestling (b); intramural: basketball (b,g), boxing (b), field hockey (g), flag football (b,g), volleyball (b,g); coed interscholastic: billiards, fishing, Frisbee, ice hockey; coed intramural: bicycling, bowling, dance, fencing, Frisbee, judo, skiing (downhill), table tennis, volleyball. 3 PE instructors, 5 coaches, 2 athletic trainers.

Computers Computers are regularly used in architecture, business, computer applications, digital applications, drafting, drawing and design, engineering, graphic arts, graphic design, media, newspaper, photography, programming, Web site design, yearbook classes. Computer network features include on-campus library services, online commercial services, Internet access, wireless campus network, Internet filtering or blocking technology. Marist is a 1:1 school iPad school. Student e-mail accounts and computer access in designated common areas are available to students. Students grades are available online. The school has a published electronic and media policy.

Contact Mrs. Alex Brown, Director of Admissions. 773-881-5300 Ext. 5330. Fax: 773-881-0595. E-mail: alex@marist.net. Website: www.marist.net

MARIST SCHOOL

3790 Ashford-Dunwoody Road NE
Atlanta, Georgia 30319-1899

Head of School: Rev. Joel M Konzen, SM

General Information Coeducational day college-preparatory school, affiliated with Roman Catholic Church. Grades 7–12. Founded: 1901. Setting: suburban. 77-acre campus. 18 buildings on campus. Approved or accredited by Southern Association of Colleges and Schools, Southern Association of Independent Schools, and Georgia Department of Education. Member of National Association of Independent Schools. Endowment: $21 million. Total enrollment: 1,088. Upper school average class size: 18. Upper school faculty-student ratio: 1:11. There are 174 required school days per year for Upper School students. Upper School students typically attend 5 days per week. The average school day consists of 6 hours.

Upper School Student Profile Grade 7: 148 students (74 boys, 74 girls); Grade 8: 149 students (71 boys, 78 girls); Grade 9: 207 students (108 boys, 99 girls); Grade 10: 202 students (103 boys, 99 girls); Grade 11: 188 students (90 boys, 98 girls); Grade 12: 194 students (97 boys, 97 girls). 75% of students are Roman Catholic.

Faculty School total: 101. In upper school: 45 men, 39 women; 88 have advanced degrees.

Subjects Offered Algebra, American history, American literature, ancient history, art, art history, biology, business skills, calculus, ceramics, chemistry, community service, computer programming, computer science, creative writing, dance, drama, driver education, economics, English, English literature, European history, fine arts, French, general science, geography, geology, geometry, German, government/civics, health, history, humanities, journalism, Latin, mathematics, music, peace and justice, philosophy, photography, physical education, physics, religion, science, social studies, Spanish, speech, statistics, studio art, theater, theology, world history, world literature, world religions, writing.

Graduation Requirements Arts and fine arts (art, music, dance, drama), business skills (includes word processing), computer science, English, foreign language, mathematics, physical education (includes health), religion (includes Bible studies and theology), science, social studies (includes history), community service requirements in all grades. Community service is required.

Special Academic Programs 22 Advanced Placement exams for which test preparation is offered; honors section; independent study.

College Admission Counseling 187 students graduated in 2016; all went to college, including Auburn University; Georgia Institute of Technology; Louisiana State University and Agricultural & Mechanical College; University of Georgia; University of Mississippi. 52% scored over 600 on SAT critical reading, 62% scored over 600 on SAT math, 60% scored over 600 on SAT writing, 60% scored over 1800 on combined SAT, 65% scored over 26 on composite ACT.

Student Life Upper grades have uniform requirement, student council, honor system. Discipline rests primarily with faculty. Attendance at religious services is required.

Summer Programs Enrichment, sports, art/fine arts programs offered; held on campus; accepts boys and girls; open to students from other schools. 2017 schedule: June 19 to June 30.

Tuition and Aid Day student tuition: $18,650. Tuition installment plan (SMART Tuition Payment Plan, monthly payment plans). Need-based scholarship grants available. In 2016–17, 18% of upper-school students received aid. Total amount of financial aid awarded in 2016–17: $2,000,000.

Admissions Traditional secondary-level entrance grade is 9. For fall 2016, 297 students applied for upper-level admission, 89 were accepted, 61 enrolled. SSAT required. Deadline for receipt of application materials: January 30. Application fee required: $75. On-campus interview recommended.

Athletics Interscholastic: baseball (boys), basketball (b,g), cheering (g), cross-country running (b,g), diving (b,g), football (b), golf (b,g), lacrosse (b,g), soccer (b,g), softball (g), swimming and diving (b,g), tennis (b,g), track and field (b,g), volleyball (g), wrestling (b); coed interscholastic: drill team; coed intramural: ultimate Frisbee. 7 PE instructors.

Computers Computers are regularly used in accounting, business applications, computer applications, drawing and design, English, foreign language, mathematics, music, science classes. Computer network features include on-campus library services, online commercial services, Internet access, wireless campus network, Internet filtering or blocking technology, one-to-one computing program, dedicated technical support Web site, on-site technology training. Student e-mail accounts and computer access in designated common areas are available to students. Students grades are available online. The school has a published electronic and media policy.

Contact Mr. Jim Byrne, Director of Admissions. 770-936-2214. Fax: 770-457-8402. E-mail: admissions@marist.com. Website: www.marist.com

MARLBOROUGH SCHOOL

250 South Rossmore Avenue
Los Angeles, California 90004

Head of School: Dr. Priscilla G. Sands

General Information Girls' day college-preparatory school. Grades 7–12. Founded: 1889. Setting: urban. 4.5-acre campus. 5 buildings on campus. Approved or accredited by California Association of Independent Schools, The College Board, Western Association of Schools and Colleges, and California Department of Education. Member of National Association of Independent Schools and Secondary School Admission Test Board. Endowment: $45.5 million. Total enrollment: 530. Upper school average class size: 12. Upper school faculty-student ratio: 1:8. Upper School students typically attend 5 days per week. The average school day consists of 6 hours and 20 minutes.

Upper School Student Profile Grade 10: 107 students (107 girls); Grade 11: 89 students (89 girls); Grade 12: 84 students (84 girls).

Faculty School total: 75.

Subjects Offered Acting, Advanced Placement courses, advanced studio art-AP, African-American literature, algebra, all academic, American history, American history-AP, American literature, American studies, anatomy and physiology, architecture, art history, art history-AP, astronomy, athletic training, ballet technique, biology, biology-AP, calculus, calculus-AP, ceramics, chemistry, chemistry-AP, Chinese history, choral music, choreography, community service, computer programming, creative writing, dance, digital art, drawing, earth systems analysis, economics, English, English literature, English literature and composition-AP, environmental science, environmental science-AP, European history, European history-AP, French, French language-AP, gender issues, geometry, global studies, health, Hispanic literature, instrumental music, internship, journalism, Latin, Latin American literature, Latin-AP, linear algebra, Mandarin, metalworking, modern world history, music theory, newspaper, painting, photography, physical education, physics, physics-AP, political thought, psychology, research, robotics, Russian literature, sculpture, self-defense, social sciences, Spanish, Spanish language-AP, statistics, statistics-AP, studio art-AP, theater, trigonometry, U.S. history, U.S. history-AP, video and animation, world history, world history-AP, world literature, yearbook, yoga.

Graduation Requirements Arts and fine arts (art, music, dance, drama), English, foreign language, history, mathematics, physical education (includes health), science, social sciences.

Special Academic Programs 21 Advanced Placement exams for which test preparation is offered; honors section; independent study.

College Admission Counseling 80 students graduated in 2016; all went to college, including Brown University; Princeton University; Stanford University; University of Michigan; University of Pennsylvania; University of Southern California. Median SAT critical reading: 715, median SAT math: 675, median SAT writing: 730, median composite ACT: 32.

Student Life Upper grades have uniform requirement, student council, honor system. Discipline rests equally with students and faculty.

Tuition and Aid Day student tuition: $37,950. Tuition installment plan (FACTS Tuition Payment Plan, monthly payment plans). Need-based scholarship grants available. In 2016–17, 19% of upper-school students received aid.

Admissions ISEE, PSAT or SAT for applicants to grade 11 and 12 and SSAT required. Deadline for receipt of application materials: January 5. Application fee required: $150. On-campus interview recommended.

Athletics Interscholastic: aquatics, basketball, cross-country running, equestrian sports, golf, independent competitive sports, lacrosse, soccer, softball, swimming and diving, tennis, track and field, volleyball, water polo. 7 PE instructors, 31 coaches, 1 athletic trainer.

Computers Computers are regularly used in all academic classes. Computer network features include on-campus library services, online commercial services, Internet access, wireless campus network, Internet filtering or blocking technology, videoconferencing. Student e-mail accounts are available to students. Students grades are available online. The school has a published electronic and media policy.

Contact Ms. Jeanette Woo Chitjian, Director of Enrollment Management. 323-964-8450. Fax: 323-933-0542. E-mail: jeanette.woochitjian@marlborough.org. Website: www.marlborough.org

MARQUETTE UNIVERSITY HIGH SCHOOL

3401 West Wisconsin Avenue
Milwaukee, Wisconsin 53208

Head of School: Mr. Jeff Monday

General Information Boys' day college-preparatory school, affiliated with Roman Catholic Church. Grades 9–12. Founded: 1857. Setting: urban. 1 building on campus. Approved or accredited by National Catholic Education Association, North Central Association of Colleges and Schools, and Wisconsin Department of Education. Total enrollment: 1,074. Upper school average class size: 22. Upper school faculty-student ratio: 1:13. Upper School students typically attend 5 days per week. The average school day consists of 8 hours and 10 minutes.

Upper School Student Profile Grade 9: 264 students (264 boys); Grade 10: 289 students (289 boys); Grade 11: 272 students (272 boys); Grade 12: 249 students (249 boys). 85% of students are Roman Catholic.

Faculty School total: 80. In upper school: 55 men, 25 women; 62 have advanced degrees.

Subjects Offered Algebra, American history, American literature, architectural drawing, architecture, art, art-AP, Bible studies, biology, biology-AP, calculus, calculus-AP, ceramics, chemistry, chemistry-AP, choral music, computer math, computer programming, computer science, computer science-AP, creative writing, drama, driver education, economics, English, English language-AP, English literature, English literature-AP, ethics, European history, European history-AP, expository writing, geography, geometry, German, government/civics, grammar, graphic design, health, history, jazz band, Latin, Latin-AP, macroeconomics-AP, mathematics, microeconomics-AP, music, philosophy, photography, physical education, physics, psychology, psychology-AP, religion, social studies, sociology, Spanish, Spanish language-AP, statistics-AP, studio art-AP, theology, trigonometry, U.S. government and politics-AP, U.S. history-AP, world history, world literature, World War I, World War II, writing.

Graduation Requirements Arts and fine arts (art, music, dance, drama), English, foreign language, mathematics, science, social studies (includes history), theology, retreats, community service hours. Community service is required.

Special Academic Programs Advanced Placement exam preparation; honors section.

College Admission Counseling 248 students graduated in 2015; 246 went to college, including Marquette University; Saint Louis University; University of Wisconsin–Madison; University of Wisconsin–Milwaukee; Xavier University. Other: 2 entered military service. Median composite ACT: 27. Mean SAT critical reading: 670, mean SAT math: 690.

Student Life Upper grades have specified standards of dress, student council, honor system. Discipline rests primarily with faculty.

Tuition and Aid Day student tuition: $11,970. Tuition installment plan (SMART Tuition Payment Plan, monthly payment plans, prepaid tuition loan program). Need-based scholarship grants, state-sponsored voucher program available. In 2015–16, 41% of upper-school students received aid. Total amount of financial aid awarded in 2015–16: $2,400,000.

Admissions Traditional secondary-level entrance grade is 9. Essay and STS - Educational Development Series required. Deadline for receipt of application materials: November 1. Application fee required: $25.

Athletics Interscholastic: baseball, basketball, cross-country running, diving, fitness, football, golf, hockey, ice hockey, indoor track, indoor track & field, lacrosse, physical fitness, physical training, power lifting, rugby, sailing, skiing (downhill), soccer, strength & conditioning, swimming and diving, tennis, track and field, volleyball, weight lifting, weight training, wrestling; intramural: basketball, bowling, soccer, softball, volleyball.

Computers Computers are regularly used in architecture, college planning, creative writing, data processing, desktop publishing, economics, English, graphic design, literary magazine, mathematics, music, newspaper, research skills, stock market, Web site design, word processing, writing, yearbook classes. Computer network features include on-campus library services, online commercial services, Internet access, Internet filtering or blocking technology, university and county library systems link. Student e-mail accounts are available to students.

Contact Mr. Sean O'Brien, Director of Admissions. 414-933-7220 Ext. 3046. Fax: 414-933-3086. E-mail: admissions@muhs.edu. Website: www.muhs.edu

MARSHALL SCHOOL

1215 Rice Lake Road
Duluth, Minnesota 55811

Head of School: Kevin Breen

General Information Coeducational day college-preparatory school. Boarding grades 9–12, day grades 4–12. Founded: 1904. Setting: suburban. Nearest major city is Minneapolis. Students are housed in coed dormitories. 40-acre campus. 1 building on campus. Approved or accredited by Independent Schools Association of the Central States and Independent Schools Council (UK). Member of National Association of Independent Schools. Endowment: $5 million. Total enrollment: 446. Upper school average class size: 18. Upper school faculty-student ratio: 1:9. There are 166 required school days per year for Upper School students. Upper School students typically attend 5 days per week. The average school day consists of 7 hours.

Upper School Student Profile Grade 9: 67 students (31 boys, 36 girls); Grade 10: 81 students (43 boys, 38 girls); Grade 11: 76 students (38 boys, 38 girls); Grade 12: 59 students (35 boys, 24 girls). 10% of students are boarding students. 9% are state residents. 2 states are represented in upper school student body. 11% are international students. International students from Belgium, China, Colombia, Democratic People's Republic of Korea, and Viet Nam.

Faculty School total: 44. In upper school: 14 men, 16 women; 18 have advanced degrees.

Subjects Offered Algebra, American history, American literature, anatomy, art, biology, calculus, calculus-AP, chemistry, community service, computer science, computer science-AP, creative writing, drama, earth science, English, English literature, English literature-AP, environmental science, European history, expository writing, fine arts, French, French-AP, geography, geometry, German, government/civics, health, history, law, mathematics, music, outdoor education, physical education, physics, poetry, religion, science, social studies, Spanish, Spanish-AP, speech, theater, theology, trigonometry, vocal music, weight training, world geography, world history, world literature, world religions, writing, writing, yearbook.

Graduation Requirements Arts and fine arts (art, music, dance, drama), computer science, English, foreign language, mathematics, outdoor education, physical education (includes health), religion (includes Bible studies and theology), science, social studies (includes history). Community service is required.

Special Academic Programs 10 Advanced Placement exams for which test preparation is offered; honors section; independent study; study at local college for college credit; study abroad; academic accommodation for the gifted; remedial reading and/or remedial writing; remedial math; programs in English, mathematics, general development for dyslexic students; special instructional classes for deaf students.

College Admission Counseling 62 students graduated in 2016; 57 went to college, including University of Minnesota, Twin Cities Campus. Other: 5 entered a postgraduate year, 2 had other specific plans. Median SAT critical reading: 638, median SAT math: 624, median SAT writing: 604, median combined SAT: 1866, median composite ACT: 26.

Student Life Upper grades have student council, honor system. Discipline rests equally with students and faculty.

Summer Programs Enrichment, advancement, sports, art/fine arts, computer instruction programs offered; session focuses on enrichment and study skills; held on campus; accepts boys and girls; open to students from other schools. 300 students usually enrolled. 2017 schedule: June to August 18. Application deadline: June.

Tuition and Aid Day student tuition: $17,600. Tuition installment plan (Insured Tuition Payment Plan, monthly payment plans). Need-based scholarship grants, paying campus jobs available. In 2016–17, 45% of upper-school students received aid. Total amount of financial aid awarded in 2016–17: $1,800,000.

Admissions Traditional secondary-level entrance grade is 9. For fall 2016, 65 students applied for upper-level admission, 55 were accepted, 39 enrolled. ERB required. Deadline for receipt of application materials: none. No application fee required. Interview required.

Athletics Interscholastic: alpine skiing (boys, girls), baseball (b), basketball (b,g), cross-country running (b,g), dance (g), dance squad (g), dance team (g), danceline (g), football (b), golf (b,g), hockey (b,g), ice hockey (b,g), nordic skiing (b,g), skiing (cross-country) (b,g), skiing (downhill) (b,g), soccer (b,g), softball (g), tennis (b,g), track and field (b,g), volleyball (g); coed intramural: outdoor activities, outdoor adventure, outdoor education, outdoor recreation, outdoors, physical fitness, physical training. 3 PE instructors, 43 coaches, 1 athletic trainer.

Computers Computers are regularly used in English, foreign language, history, mathematics, science classes. Computer network features include on-campus library services, online commercial services, Internet access, wireless campus network, Internet filtering or blocking technology. Campus intranet, student e-mail accounts, and computer access in designated common areas are available to students. Students grades are available online. The school has a published electronic and media policy.

Contact Joe Wicklund, Director of Enrollment. 218-727-7266 Ext. 111. Fax: 218-727-1569. E-mail: joe.wicklund@marshallschool.org. Website: www.marshallschool.org

MARS HILL BIBLE SCHOOL

698 Cox Creek Parkway
Florence, Alabama 35630

Head of School: Mr. Dexter Rutherford

General Information Coeducational day college-preparatory, arts, and religious studies school, affiliated with Church of Christ. Grades K–12. Founded: 1947. Setting: suburban. Nearest major city is Huntsville. 80-acre campus. 7 buildings on campus. Approved or accredited by National Christian School Association and Southern Association of Colleges and Schools. Endowment: $2.7 million. Total enrollment: 525. Upper school average class size: 22. Upper school faculty-student ratio: 1:14. There are 180 required school days per year for Upper School students. Upper School students typically attend 5 days per week. The average school day consists of 7 hours.

Upper School Student Profile Grade 9: 45 students (23 boys, 22 girls); Grade 10: 35 students (20 boys, 15 girls); Grade 11: 38 students (24 boys, 14 girls); Grade 12: 51 students (18 boys, 33 girls). 81% of students are members of Church of Christ.

Faculty School total: 42. In upper school: 11 men, 12 women; 14 have advanced degrees.

Subjects Offered ACT preparation, algebra, American government, American literature, anatomy and physiology, ancient world history, band, Bible studies, biology, biology-AP, calculus, calculus-AP, chemistry, chorus, computer literacy, computer programming, computer science, concert band, concert choir, debate, drama, drama performance, driver education, ecology, economics, English, English composition, English literature, English literature and composition-AP, forensics, geometry, health, honors English, human anatomy, Internet research, jazz band, Life of Christ, marine biology, musical productions, physical education, physical science, physics, pre-algebra, pre-calculus, Spanish, speech, speech and debate, student government, student publications, U.S. history, Western civilization, word processing, world geography, world history, yearbook.

Graduation Requirements Algebra, American government, American history, American literature, ancient world history, art, Bible, biology, chemistry, college writing, computer applications, computer literacy, economics, English composition, foreign language, geometry, health and wellness, introduction to literature, mathematics, physical education (includes health), physical science, science, social studies (includes history). Community service is required.

Special Academic Programs Special instructional classes for students with learning disabilities, Attention Deficit Disorder, and dyslexia.

College Admission Counseling 38 students graduated in 2015; all went to college, including Auburn University; Freed-Hardeman University; Harding University; The University of Alabama; The University of Alabama at Birmingham; University of North Alabama.

Student Life Upper grades have specified standards of dress, student council. Discipline rests primarily with faculty. Attendance at religious services is required.

Tuition and Aid Day student tuition: $6867. Tuition installment plan (FACTS Tuition Payment Plan, monthly payment plans). Tuition reduction for siblings, need-based scholarship grants available. In 2015–16, 20% of upper-school students received aid. Total amount of financial aid awarded in 2015–16: $160,000.

Admissions For fall 2015, 10 students applied for upper-level admission, 9 were accepted, 9 enrolled. Achievement tests, ACT-Explore or PSAT required. Deadline for receipt of application materials: none. Application fee required: $100. Interview required.

Athletics Interscholastic: baseball (boys), basketball (b,g), cheering (g), cross-country running (b,g), football (b), golf (b,g), soccer (b,g), softball (g), tennis (b,g), track and field (b,g), volleyball (g); intramural: basketball (b,g). 3 PE instructors, 7 coaches.

Computers Computers are regularly used in all academic, Bible studies, English, history, remedial study skills, yearbook classes. Computer network features include on-campus library services, online commercial services, Internet access, wireless campus network, Internet filtering or blocking technology. Campus intranet and computer access in designated common areas are available to students. Students grades are available online. The school has a published electronic and media policy.

Contact Mrs. Jeannie Garrett, Director of Admissions. 256-767-1203 Ext. 2005. Fax: 256-767-6304. E-mail: jgarrett@mhbs.org. Website: www.mhbs.org

MARTIN LUTHER HIGH SCHOOL

60-02 Maspeth Avenue
Maspeth, New York 11378

Head of School: Mr. Randy Gast

General Information Coeducational day college-preparatory school, affiliated with Lutheran Church. Grades 6–12. Founded: 1960. Setting: urban. Nearest major city is New York. 1-acre campus. 1 building on campus. Approved or accredited by Middle States Association of Colleges and Schools and New York Department of Education.

Total enrollment: 225. Upper school average class size: 22. Upper school faculty-student ratio: 1:12.

Upper School Student Profile Grade 6: 6 students (2 boys, 4 girls); Grade 7: 3 students (1 boy, 2 girls); Grade 8: 8 students (3 boys, 5 girls); Grade 9: 38 students (23 boys, 15 girls); Grade 10: 52 students (25 boys, 27 girls); Grade 11: 43 students (29 boys, 14 girls); Grade 12: 65 students (43 boys, 22 girls). 16% of students are Lutheran.

Faculty School total: 21. In upper school: 8 men, 11 women; 11 have advanced degrees.

Subjects Offered Algebra, American history, art, Bible studies, biology, business, business skills, calculus, calculus-AP, chemistry, chemistry-AP, computer programming, computer science, drama, driver education, earth science, economics, English, English literature, English literature-AP, environmental science-AP, ethics, European history, fine arts, French, geography, geometry, German, government/civics, grammar, health, history, journalism, marine biology, mathematics, music, philosophy, photography, physical education, physics, psychology, religion, science, social studies, Spanish, Spanish-AP, speech, theater, theology, trigonometry, U.S. history-AP, world history.

Graduation Requirements 1 1/2 elective credits, arts and fine arts (art, music, dance, drama), computer applications, English, foreign language, health, mathematics, physical education (includes health), religion (includes Bible studies and theology), science, social studies (includes history), service hours.

Special Academic Programs Advanced Placement exam preparation; honors section; independent study; study at local college for college credit; programs in general development for dyslexic students; ESL (46 students enrolled).

College Admission Counseling 51 students graduated in 2016; 54 went to college, including John Jay College of Criminal Justice of the City University of New York; Queens College of the City University of New York; St. Francis College; St. John's University; St. Joseph's College, New York; Stony Brook University, State University of New York. Other: 1 went to work, 1 entered military service. Mean SAT critical reading: 482, mean SAT math: 511, mean SAT writing: 473.

Student Life Upper grades have uniform requirement, student council. Discipline rests primarily with faculty. Attendance at religious services is required.

Summer Programs Remediation, computer instruction programs offered; held on campus; accepts boys and girls; open to students from other schools. 70 students usually enrolled. 2017 schedule: July 2 to August 16. Application deadline: none.

Tuition and Aid Day student tuition: $8450. Tuition installment plan (SMART Tuition Payment Plan, monthly payment plans, quarterly payment plan, one payment plan). Tuition reduction for siblings, merit scholarship grants, need-based scholarship grants available. In 2016–17, 50% of upper-school students received aid; total upper-school merit-scholarship money awarded: $40,800. Total amount of financial aid awarded in 2016–17: $1,955,670.

Admissions Traditional secondary-level entrance grade is 9. Deadline for receipt of application materials: none. Application fee required: $50. On-campus interview required.

Athletics Interscholastic: baseball (boys), basketball (b,g), cross-country running (b,g), fitness (b,g), soccer (b), softball (g), tennis (b,g), track and field (b,g), volleyball (g), wrestling (b,g); intramural: basketball (b,g), cross-country running (b,g), floor hockey (b,g), indoor hockey (b,g), soccer (b,g), weight lifting (b,g), wrestling (b); coed interscholastic: cross-country running, fitness, soccer; coed intramural: archery, badminton, cross-country running, fitness, handball, paddle tennis, racquetball, track and field, volleyball, wrestling. 2 PE instructors, 15 coaches.

Computers Computers are regularly used in business education, career education, Christian doctrine, computer applications, desktop publishing, history, keyboarding, newspaper, SAT preparation, Spanish, Web site design, yearbook classes. Computer resources include on-campus library services, Internet access. Student e-mail accounts are available to students. Students grades are available online.

Contact Ms. Patricia Dee, Administrative Asst. 718-894-4000 Ext. 122. Fax: 718-894-1469. E-mail: pdee@martinluthernyc.org. Website: www.martinluthernyc.org

THE MARVELWOOD SCHOOL

476 Skiff Mountain Road
PO Box 3001
Kent, Connecticut 06757-3001

Head of School: Mr. Arthur Goodearl

General Information Coeducational boarding and day college-preparatory, arts, technology, field science, and community service, ESL school. Grades 9–12. Founded: 1956. Setting: rural. Nearest major city is Danbury. Students are housed in single-sex dormitories. 83-acre campus. 5 buildings on campus. Approved or accredited by Association for Experiential Education, Association of Independent Schools in New England, Connecticut Association of Independent Schools, New England Association of Schools and Colleges, The Association of Boarding Schools, and Connecticut Department of Education. Member of National Association of Independent Schools and Secondary School Admission Test Board. Endowment: $2.1 million. Total enrollment: 172. Upper school average class size: 10. Upper school faculty-student ratio: 1:4. There are 188 required school days per year for Upper School students. Upper School students typically attend 6 days per week. The average school day consists of 6 hours and 40 minutes.

Upper School Student Profile Grade 9: 21 students (13 boys, 8 girls); Grade 10: 35 students (21 boys, 14 girls); Grade 11: 48 students (30 boys, 18 girls); Grade 12: 45 students (26 boys, 19 girls); Postgraduate: 1 student (1 boy). 94% of students are boarding students. 30% are state residents. 14 states are represented in upper school student body. 28% are international students. International students from China, Hong Kong, Japan, Mexico, Venezuela, and Viet Nam; 7 other countries represented in student body.

Faculty School total: 49. In upper school: 20 men, 29 women; 24 have advanced degrees; 35 reside on campus.

Subjects Offered 3-dimensional art, ACT preparation, acting, advanced chemistry, advanced studio art-AP, American history-AP, analysis and differential calculus, animal behavior, applied music, arts, audio visual/media, calculus-AP, digital photography, drama performance, drama workshop, economics-AP, environmental science, ethology, film and literature, fitness, freshman seminar, functions, history of jazz, Korean literature, limnology.

Graduation Requirements Arts and fine arts (art, music, dance, drama), English, foreign language, mathematics, science, social studies (includes history), senior service project, weekly community service program.

Special Academic Programs 11 Advanced Placement exams for which test preparation is offered; honors section; independent study; remedial reading and/or remedial writing; remedial math; programs in English, mathematics, general development for dyslexic students; ESL (24 students enrolled).

College Admission Counseling 63 students graduated in 2016; 61 went to college, including California State University, Los Angeles; New York University; Pace University; Penn State University Park; Syracuse University; University of Connecticut. Other: 1 went to work, 1 entered military service. Median SAT critical reading: 458, median SAT math: 424, median SAT writing: 458.

Student Life Upper grades have specified standards of dress, student council, honor system. Discipline rests equally with students and faculty.

Summer Programs Remediation, enrichment, ESL, art/fine arts programs offered; session focuses on enrichment; held on campus; accepts boys and girls; open to students from other schools. 25 students usually enrolled. 2017 schedule: July 3 to July 31. Application deadline: March 1.

Tuition and Aid Day student tuition: $36,000; 7-day tuition and room/board: $55,900. Tuition installment plan (Insured Tuition Payment Plan, Academic Management Services Plan, SMART Tuition Payment Plan, individually arranged payment plans). Need-based scholarship grants available. In 2016–17, 24% of upper-school students received aid. Total amount of financial aid awarded in 2016–17: $1,250,000.

Admissions Traditional secondary-level entrance grade is 9. Traditional secondary-level entrance age is 14. For fall 2016, 151 students applied for upper-level admission, 94 were accepted, 67 enrolled. SSAT or WISC III required. Deadline for receipt of application materials: none. Application fee required: $50. Interview recommended.

Athletics Interscholastic: baseball (boys), basketball (b,g), cross-country running (b,g), lacrosse (b), soccer (b,g), softball (g), tennis (b,g), volleyball (g), wrestling (b); coed interscholastic: alpine skiing, Frisbee, golf, hockey, ice hockey, lacrosse, skiing (downhill), ultimate Frisbee, wrestling; coed intramural: backpacking, bicycling, canoeing/kayaking, climbing, dance, equestrian sports, fishing, fitness, hiking/backpacking, horseback riding, ice skating, kayaking, mountain biking, mountaineering, nordic skiing, outdoor activities, outdoor adventure, outdoor education, outdoor skills, physical training, rappelling, rock climbing, ropes courses, skiing (downhill), snowboarding, strength & conditioning, weight training, wilderness, wildernessways, yoga. 1 coach, 1 athletic trainer.

Computers Computers are regularly used in data processing, desktop publishing, ESL, introduction to technology, programming, yearbook classes. Computer network features include on-campus library services, Internet access, wireless campus network, Internet filtering or blocking technology. Campus intranet, student e-mail accounts, and computer access in designated common areas are available to students. Students grades are available online. The school has a published electronic and media policy.

Contact Mrs. Maureen Smith, Associate Director of Admission. 860-927-0047 Ext. 1005. Fax: 860-927-0021. E-mail: maureen.smith@marvelwood.org. Website: www.marvelwood.org

MARY HELP OF CHRISTIANS ACADEMY

659 Belmont Avenue
North Haledon, New Jersey 07508

Head of School: Sr. Marisa DeRose, FMA

General Information Girls' day college-preparatory and health care studies school, affiliated with Roman Catholic Church. Grades 9–12. Founded: 1940. Setting: suburban. Nearest major city is Paterson. 16-acre campus. 6 buildings on campus. Approved or accredited by Middle States Association of Colleges and Schools, National Catholic Education Association, and New Jersey Department of Education. Total enrollment: 342. Upper school average class size: 20. Upper school faculty-student ratio: 1:8. There are 180 required school days per year for Upper School students. Upper School students typically attend 5 days per week. The average school day consists of 7 hours.

Upper School Student Profile Grade 9: 42 students (42 girls); Grade 10: 29 students (29 girls); Grade 11: 43 students (43 girls); Grade 12: 50 students (50 girls). 89% of students are Roman Catholic.

Faculty School total: 30. In upper school: 5 men, 25 women; 15 have advanced degrees.

Subjects Offered 3-dimensional art, acting, American history, American history-AP, American sign language, animal behavior, astronomy, French as a second language, freshman seminar, internship, Italian, leadership and service, SAT/ACT preparation.

Graduation Requirements Algebra, American literature, arts and fine arts (art, music, dance, drama), biology, British literature, Catholic belief and practice, Christian and Hebrew scripture, Christian doctrine, computer applications, computers, general science, geometry, health and safety, history of the Catholic Church, literature, mathematics, moral theology, theology, world literature, 80 hours of service performed with a nonprofit community organization.

Special Academic Programs Advanced Placement exam preparation; honors section; independent study; study at local college for college credit; remedial reading and/or remedial writing; remedial math; special instructional classes for students with moderate learning disabilities.

College Admission Counseling 42 students graduated in 2016; all went to college, including Dartmouth College; Fairleigh Dickinson University, College at Florham; Montclair State University; Princeton University; Rutgers University–New Brunswick; William Paterson University of New Jersey.

Student Life Upper grades have uniform requirement, student council, honor system. Discipline rests primarily with faculty. Attendance at religious services is required.

Summer Programs Remediation, advancement, sports programs offered; session focuses on mathematics advancement, remediation in mathematics, language arts for incoming freshmen, honors biology; held on campus; accepts girls; not open to students from other schools. 30 students usually enrolled. 2017 schedule: June 26 to July 28. Application deadline: May 15.

Tuition and Aid Day student tuition: $10,900. Tuition installment plan (FACTS Tuition Payment Plan, individually arranged payment plans). Tuition reduction for siblings, merit scholarship grants, need-based scholarship grants available. In 2016–17, 40% of upper-school students received aid; total upper-school merit-scholarship money awarded: $93,500. Total amount of financial aid awarded in 2016–17: $311,100.

Admissions Traditional secondary-level entrance grade is 9. For fall 2016, 148 students applied for upper-level admission, 140 were accepted, 42 enrolled. Cooperative Entrance Exam (McGraw-Hill) or school placement exam required. Deadline for receipt of application materials: none. Application fee required: $20. Interview required.

Athletics Interscholastic: basketball, bowling, cheering, dance team, soccer, softball, tennis, volleyball; intramural: aquatics, basketball, cheering, dance team, fitness, volleyball. 1 PE instructor, 7 coaches, 1 athletic trainer.

Computers Computers are regularly used in accounting, English, graphic arts, graphics, journalism, publications, religion, SAT preparation, science, Spanish, video film production, Web site design, word processing, yearbook classes. Computer network features include on-campus library services, online commercial services, Internet access, wireless campus network, Internet filtering or blocking technology, EBSCOhost, Kurzweil 3000 (assistive reading software). Campus intranet and student e-mail accounts are available to students. Students grades are available online. The school has a published electronic and media policy.

Contact Mrs. Katie Caufield, Admissions Director. 973-790-6200 Ext. 148. Fax: 973-790-6125. E-mail: admissions@maryhelp.org. Website: www.maryhelp.org

MARY INSTITUTE AND ST. LOUIS COUNTRY DAY SCHOOL (MICDS)

101 North Warson Road
St. Louis, Missouri 63124

Head of School: Lisa Lyle

General Information Coeducational day college-preparatory school. Grades JK–12. Founded: 1859. Setting: suburban. 100-acre campus. 9 buildings on campus. Approved or accredited by Missouri Department of Education. Member of National Association of Independent Schools and Secondary School Admission Test Board. Endowment: $99.9 million. Total enrollment: 1,250. Upper school average class size: 15. Upper school faculty-student ratio: 1:8. There are 170 required school days per year for Upper School students. Upper School students typically attend 5 days per week. The average school day consists of 7 hours and 15 minutes.

Upper School Student Profile Grade 9: 167 students (82 boys, 85 girls); Grade 10: 154 students (77 boys, 77 girls); Grade 11: 160 students (74 boys, 86 girls); Grade 12: 161 students (75 boys, 86 girls).

Faculty School total: 150. In upper school: 36 men, 26 women; 50 have advanced degrees.

Subjects Offered 20th century world history, 3-dimensional design, acting, American Civil War, analytic geometry, anatomy and physiology, animal behavior, architecture, art history-AP, astronomy, biology-AP, biotechnology, calculus, calculus-AP, ceramics, chemistry-AP, Chinese, computer science-AP, concert choir, contemporary issues, creative writing, design, digital art, digital photography, discrete mathematics, drawing, economics, English, environmental science, environmental science-AP, European

history-AP, filmmaking, forensics, French, French language-AP, genetics, German, global issues, graphic design, independent study, instrumental music, integrated mathematics, integrated science, Irish literature, kinesiology, lab science, Latin, Latin-AP, literary genres, literature, macroeconomics-AP, marine biology, marine studies, methods of research, music theory-AP, music-AP, neuroscience, painting, personal finance, physics-AP, pre-calculus, programming, psychology-AP, public speaking, research seminar, science research, sculpture, Spanish, Spanish language-AP, sports medicine, statistics, statistics-AP, studio art-AP, theater arts, U.S. government and politics-AP, U.S. history, U.S. history-AP, urban studies, visual and performing arts, world history.

Graduation Requirements Arts and fine arts (art, music, dance, drama), English, foreign language, mathematics, physical education (includes health), science, social studies (includes history). Community service is required.

Special Academic Programs Advanced Placement exam preparation; honors section; independent study; term-away projects; study abroad; academic accommodation for the gifted.

College Admission Counseling 164 students graduated in 2016; all went to college, including Princeton University; Southern Methodist University; Tulane University; University of Missouri; University of Southern California; Washington University in St. Louis. Median SAT critical reading: 650, median SAT math: 635, median SAT writing: 660, median combined SAT: 1930, median composite ACT: 29.

Student Life Upper grades have specified standards of dress, student council, honor system. Discipline rests equally with students and faculty.

Summer Programs Remediation, enrichment, advancement, sports, art/fine arts, rigorous outdoor training, computer instruction programs offered; session focuses on conditioning/training; held on campus; accepts boys and girls; open to students from other schools. 200 students usually enrolled. 2017 schedule: June 13 to July 26. Application deadline: January 15.

Tuition and Aid Day student tuition: $26,500. Tuition installment plan (FACTS Tuition Payment Plan, monthly plan through FACTS Management, Your Tuition Solution (Loan), credit card payment). Merit scholarship grants, need-based scholarship grants available. In 2016–17, 23% of upper-school students received aid; total upper-school merit-scholarship money awarded: $100,000. Total amount of financial aid awarded in 2016–17: $2,587,645.

Admissions Traditional secondary-level entrance grade is 9. For fall 2016, 109 students applied for upper-level admission, 53 were accepted, 43 enrolled. ISEE, SSAT or TOEFL or SLEP required. Deadline for receipt of application materials: January 17. Application fee required: $40. Interview recommended.

Athletics Interscholastic: baseball (boys), basketball (b,g), cheering (g), cross-country running (b,g), dance (b,g), diving (b,g), field hockey (g), fitness (b,g), football (b), golf (b,g), ice hockey (b), lacrosse (b,g), soccer (b,g), squash (b,g), swimming and diving (b,g), tennis (b,g), track and field (b,g), volleyball (g), water polo (b), wrestling (b); intramural: fitness (b,g), independent competitive sports (b,g), jogging (b,g), modern dance (b,g), physical fitness (b,g), physical training (b,g), strength & conditioning (b,g), weight training (b,g); coed interscholastic: bicycling, dance, fitness, water polo, wrestling; coed intramural: dressage, fitness, independent competitive sports, modern dance, physical fitness, physical training, strength & conditioning, weight training. 2 athletic trainers.

Computers Computers are regularly used in all classes. Computer network features include on-campus library services, online commercial services, Internet access, wireless campus network, Internet filtering or blocking technology. Campus intranet, student e-mail accounts, and computer access in designated common areas are available to students. Students grades are available online. The school has a published electronic and media policy.

Contact Peggy B. Laramie, Director of Admission and Financial Aid. 314-995-7367. Fax: 314-872-3257. E-mail: plaramie@micds.org. Website: www.micds.org/home

THE MARY LOUIS ACADEMY

176-21 Wexford Terrace
Jamaica Estates, New York 11432-2926

Head of School: Sr. Kathleen M. McKinney, CSJ, EdD

General Information Girls' day college-preparatory, religious studies, and college preparatory school, affiliated with Roman Catholic Church. Grades 9–12. Founded: 1936. Setting: suburban. Nearest major city is New York. 5-acre campus. 8 buildings on campus. Approved or accredited by Middle States Association of Colleges and Schools, National Catholic Education Association, New York Department of Education, New York State Board of Regents, and New York Department of Education. Endowment: $15 million. Total enrollment: 782. Upper school average class size: 25. Upper school faculty-student ratio: 1:13. There are 180 required school days per year for Upper School students. Upper School students typically attend 5 days per week. The average school day consists of 6 hours and 30 minutes.

Upper School Student Profile Grade 9: 214 students (214 girls); Grade 10: 147 students (147 girls); Grade 11: 167 students (167 girls); Grade 12: 202 students (202 girls). 74.5% of students are Roman Catholic.

Faculty School total: 68. In upper school: 14 men, 54 women; 66 have advanced degrees.

Subjects Offered 20th century American writers, 20th century history, 20th century physics, 20th century world history, 3-dimensional art, 3-dimensional design, advanced biology, advanced chemistry, advanced computer applications, advanced math, Advanced Placement courses, advanced studio art-AP, algebra, American Civil War, American culture, American democracy, American foreign policy, American government, American history, American history-AP, American legal systems, American literature, American literature-AP, American studies, analysis and differential calculus, anatomy, anatomy and physiology, ancient history, ancient world history, ancient/medieval philosophy, animation, anthropology, applied arts, applied music, art, art and culture, art appreciation, art education, art history, art history-AP, art in New York, art-AP, astronomy, athletics, audio visual/media, Basic programming, Bible, Bible studies, biology, biology-AP, British history, British literature, British literature (honors), British literature-AP, business communications, business law, business skills, calculus, calculus-AP, campus ministry, career and personal planning, career exploration, career/college preparation, Catholic belief and practice, chemistry, chemistry-AP, Christian doctrine, Christian ethics, Christian scripture, Christian testament, church history, Civil War, civil war history, classical civilization, classical language, classical music, college admission preparation, college counseling, college placement, college planning, college writing, communication arts, community service, composition, computer animation, computer applications, computer art, computer education, computer graphics, computer information systems, computer literacy, computer programming, computer programming-AP, computer science, computer science-AP, computer skills, computer studies, conflict resolution, constitutional history of U.S., contemporary women writers, creative dance, criminal justice, criminology, cultural geography, current events, current history, digital art, drawing, driver education, earth science, ecology, ecology, environmental systems, economics, economics and history, engineering, English, English composition, English literature, English literature and composition-AP, environmental science, ethics and responsibility, European history, European literature, family studies, female experience in America, fine arts, first aid, forensics, French, government, government/civics, graphic arts, graphic design, guidance, health and wellness, health education, health science, healthful living, heritage of American Women, history, history of music, history of religion, history of the Americas, history of the Catholic Church, history-AP, honors algebra, honors English, honors geometry, honors U.S. history, honors world history, human biology, human development, instrumental music, integrated mathematics, integrated physics, integrated science, Italian, jazz, journalism, language-AP, Latin, Latin-AP, law, leadership, leadership and service, leadership education training, library research, library science, life management skills, life skills, literary magazine, literature, literature by women, literature-AP, mathematics, mathematics-AP, mechanics of writing, medieval history, mentorship program, microbiology, modern European history, modern European history-AP, music, music history, music performance, music theory, music theory-AP, music-AP, New Testament, nutrition, painting, performing arts, personal money management, physical education, physical science, physics, physics-AP, piano, poetry, political science, pre-calculus, psychology, psychology-AP, religion, robotics, SAT preparation, SAT/ACT preparation, science, science and technology, sculpture, social studies, sociology, Spanish, Spanish-AP, speech and debate, statistics, statistics-AP, studio art, studio art-AP, theater arts, theology, U.S. government and politics-AP, U.S. history, U.S. history-AP, U.S. literature, visual and performing arts, visual arts, vocal ensemble, vocal music, voice, volleyball, wind instruments, women in literature, women in society, women in the classical world, women in world history, women spirituality and faith, women's health, women's literature, women's studies, world history, world history-AP, world literature, world studies, yearbook.

Graduation Requirements Arts and fine arts (art, music, dance, drama), English, foreign language, mathematics, music, physical education (includes health), religion (includes Bible studies and theology), science, social studies (includes history), technology, community service project, Regents Diploma.

Special Academic Programs 17 Advanced Placement exams for which test preparation is offered; honors section; study at local college for college credit; study abroad; academic accommodation for the gifted, the musically talented, and the artistically talented; programs in general development for dyslexic students.

College Admission Counseling 202 students graduated in 2016; all went to college, including Adelphi University; Cornell University; Hofstra University; Hunter College of the City University of New York; Rensselaer Polytechnic Institute; St. John's University.

Student Life Upper grades have uniform requirement, student council. Discipline rests primarily with faculty. Attendance at religious services is required.

Summer Programs Remediation, enrichment, sports, art/fine arts, computer instruction programs offered; session focuses on Regents Competency Test preparation, athletic camps, junior high student enrichment; held on campus; accepts boys and girls; open to students from other schools. 250 students usually enrolled. 2017 schedule: July 1 to August 30. Application deadline: June 30.

Tuition and Aid Day student tuition: $8600. Tuition installment plan (monthly payment plans, quarterly payment plan, tuition in full (yearly)). Tuition reduction for siblings, merit scholarship grants, need-based scholarship grants available. In 2016–17, 50% of upper-school students received aid; total upper-school merit-scholarship money awarded: $2,400,000. Total amount of financial aid awarded in 2016–17: $615,000.

Admissions Traditional secondary-level entrance grade is 9. For fall 2016, 807 students applied for upper-level admission, 504 were accepted, 214 enrolled. Catholic High School Entrance Examination or school's own exam required. Deadline for receipt of application materials: February 1. Application fee required: $450. On-campus interview recommended.

Athletics Interscholastic: aerobics, aerobics/dance, archery, badminton, basketball, billiards, bowling, cheering, cross-country running, dance, dance team, golf, gymnastics, indoor track, indoor track & field, lacrosse, physical fitness, physical training, running, self defense, soccer, softball, strength & conditioning, swimming and diving, tennis, track and field, volleyball, weight training, winter (indoor) track, yoga; intramural: basketball, billiards, fitness, physical fitness, physical training, self defense, soccer, softball, strength & conditioning, swimming and diving, tennis, track and field, volleyball, weight training, yoga. 4 PE instructors, 32 coaches, 3 athletic trainers.

Computers Computers are regularly used in career exploration, college planning, English, foreign language, graphic design, history, library skills, literary magazine, mathematics, music, newspaper, science classes. Computer network features include on-campus library services, online commercial services, Internet access, wireless campus network, Internet filtering or blocking technology, iPads provided to all students. Campus intranet and student e-mail accounts are available to students. Students grades are available online. The school has a published electronic and media policy.

Contact Sr. Lorraine A. O'Neill, CSJ, Administrative Secretary. 718-297-2120 Ext. 228. Fax: 718-739-0037. E-mail: sloneill@tmla.org. Website: www.tmla.org

MARYMOUNT HIGH SCHOOL

10643 Sunset Boulevard
Los Angeles, California 90077

Head of School: Ms. Jacqueline Landry

General Information Girls' day college-preparatory, arts, technology, and STEAM, Theology school, affiliated with Roman Catholic Church. Grades 9–12. Distance learning grade 12. Founded: 1923. Setting: suburban. 5-acre campus. 6 buildings on campus. Approved or accredited by Canadian Association of Independent Schools, Western Association of Schools and Colleges, Western Catholic Education Association, and California Department of Education. Member of National Association of Independent Schools. Endowment: $11.9 million. Total enrollment: 396. Upper school average class size: 14. Upper school faculty-student ratio: 1:7. There are 170 required school days per year for Upper School students. Upper School students typically attend 5 days per week. The average school day consists of 6 hours and 15 minutes.

Upper School Student Profile Grade 9: 123 students (123 girls); Grade 10: 91 students (91 girls); Grade 11: 97 students (97 girls); Grade 12: 99 students (99 girls). 64% of students are Roman Catholic.

Faculty School total: 57. In upper school: 14 men, 43 women; 47 have advanced degrees.

Subjects Offered Acting, advanced biology, advanced chemistry, advanced math, Advanced Placement courses, advanced studio art-AP, aerobics, African literature, African-American literature, algebra, American culture, American government, American history, American history-AP, American legal systems, American literature, American literature-AP, anatomy, anatomy and physiology, art, art history, art history-AP, art-AP, athletics, basketball, biology, biology-AP, British literature, calculus, calculus-AP, ceramics, chemistry, chemistry-AP, choir, Christian testament, community service, computer literacy, computer science, contemporary issues, dance, death and loss, design, drama, drawing, ecology, economics, English, English literature, environmental science, environmental science-AP, ethics, fencing, film, fine arts, French, French-AP, gender and religion, geography, geometry, government/civics, Hebrew scripture, human development, Japanese literature, jazz ensemble, journalism, language and composition, literary magazine, literature, literature-AP, music, musical productions, oceanography, painting, peace studies, performing arts, photography, physical education, physics, physiology, pre-calculus, printmaking, psychology, religion, religious studies, robotics, science, self-defense, service learning/internship, social justice, social studies, softball, Spanish, Spanish language-AP, Spanish literature-AP, speech, swimming, theology, trigonometry, U.S. government and politics-AP, U.S. history, U.S. history-AP, vocal music, volleyball, women's studies, world religions, writing.

Graduation Requirements Arts and fine arts (art, music, dance, drama), English, foreign language, mathematics, performing arts, physical education (includes health), religion (includes Bible studies and theology), science, social studies (includes history).

Special Academic Programs 18 Advanced Placement exams for which test preparation is offered; honors section; independent study.

College Admission Counseling 100 students graduated in 2016; 99 went to college, including New York University; Stanford University; University of California, Berkeley; University of Notre Dame; University of Southern California; University of Wisconsin–Madison. Other: 1 had other specific plans. Mean SAT critical reading: 668, mean SAT math: 637, mean SAT writing: 694, mean combined SAT: 1999, mean composite ACT: 29.

Student Life Upper grades have uniform requirement, student council, honor system. Discipline rests equally with students and faculty. Attendance at religious services is required.

Summer Programs Remediation, enrichment, advancement, sports, art/fine arts, computer instruction programs offered; session focuses on enrichment, advancement; held on campus; accepts girls; open to students from other schools. 100 students usually enrolled. 2017 schedule: June 19 to July 21. Application deadline: June 5.

Tuition and Aid Day student tuition: $33,000–$33,600. Tuition installment plan (FACTS Tuition Payment Plan). Merit scholarship grants, need-based scholarship grants available. In 2016–17, 25% of upper-school students received aid; total upper-school merit-scholarship money awarded: $20,000. Total amount of financial aid awarded in 2016–17: $1,320,000.

Admissions Traditional secondary-level entrance grade is 9. ISEE required. Deadline for receipt of application materials: December 15. Application fee required: $100. On-campus interview recommended.

Athletics Interscholastic: basketball, cross-country running, equestrian sports, golf, rowing, soccer, softball, swimming and diving, tennis, track and field, volleyball, water polo; intramural: aerobics, aerobics/dance, archery, crew, dance, fitness, physical fitness, self defense, strength & conditioning. 1 PE instructor, 35 coaches, 1 athletic trainer.

Computers Computers are regularly used in all academic classes. Computer network features include on-campus library services, online commercial services, Internet access, wireless campus network, Internet filtering or blocking technology, one-to-one student laptop program, access to UCLA Library, Loyola Marymount University Library, 14 independent high school libraries. Campus intranet, student e-mail accounts, and computer access in designated common areas are available to students. Students grades are available online. The school has a published electronic and media policy.

Contact Ms. Patti Lemlein, Director of Admission. 310-472-1205 Ext. 220. Fax: 310-440-4316. E-mail: plemlein@mhs-la.org. Website: www.mhs-la.org

MARYMOUNT SCHOOL OF NEW YORK

1026 Fifth Avenue
New York, New York 10028

Head of School: Mrs. Concepcion Alvar, EdD

General Information Coeducational day (boys' only in lower grades) college-preparatory school, affiliated with Roman Catholic Church. Boys grades N–PK, girls grades N–12. Founded: 1926. Setting: urban. 3 buildings on campus. Approved or accredited by New York State Association of Independent Schools. Member of National Association of Independent Schools. Endowment: $8 million. Total enrollment: 744. Upper school average class size: 15. Upper school faculty-student ratio: 1:5. There are 166 required school days per year for Upper School students. Upper School students typically attend 5 days per week. The average school day consists of 7 hours.

Upper School Student Profile Grade 9: 71 students (71 girls); Grade 10: 63 students (63 girls); Grade 11: 58 students (58 girls); Grade 12: 55 students (55 girls). 69% of students are Roman Catholic.

Faculty School total: 134. In upper school: 14 men, 32 women; 41 have advanced degrees.

Subjects Offered Advanced studio art-AP, algebra, American history, American history-AP, American literature, art, art history, art-AP, astronomy, bell choir, Bible studies, biology, biology-AP, British literature-AP, calculus, chemistry, chemistry-AP, chorus, community service, computer science, computer science-AP, contemporary history, dance, digital applications, DNA research, economics, English, English literature, English literature-AP, ethics, European history, European history-AP, fine arts, fitness, French, French literature-AP, French-AP, geometry, Greek, health, information design technology, integrated technology fundamentals, Latin, Latin-AP, mathematics, music, music history, physical education, physics, political science, religion, science, Spanish, speech, statistics, studio art, studio art-AP, technological applications, technology, theater history, trigonometry, world history, world literature, writing.

Graduation Requirements American history, arts and fine arts (art, music, dance, drama), computer science, English, foreign language, health, history, mathematics, physical education (includes health), religion (includes Bible studies and theology), science, senior internship, speech, world history, senior internships, senior seminars, Class XII retreat. Community service is required.

Special Academic Programs Advanced Placement exam preparation; honors section; study abroad; academic accommodation for the gifted.

College Admission Counseling 56 students graduated in 2016; all went to college, including Boston College; Boston University; Fordham University; New York University; Tulane University; University of Pennsylvania. Mean SAT critical reading: 636, mean SAT math: 624, mean SAT writing: 663.

Student Life Upper grades have uniform requirement, student council, honor system. Discipline rests primarily with faculty. Attendance at religious services is required.

Summer Programs Enrichment, advancement, sports programs offered; session focuses on internships, preseason sports, community service; held both on and off campus; accepts girls; not open to students from other schools. 60 students usually enrolled. 2017 schedule: June 14 to August 31.

Tuition and Aid Day student tuition: $47,085. Tuition installment plan (Key Tuition Payment Plan, individually arranged payment plans). Need-based scholarship grants available. In 2016–17, 21% of upper-school students received aid. Total amount of financial aid awarded in 2016–17: $3,000,000.

Admissions Traditional secondary-level entrance grade is 9. ISEE or SSAT required. Deadline for receipt of application materials: November 30. Application fee required: $70. On-campus interview recommended.

Athletics Interscholastic: aerobics, badminton, basketball, bicycling, cross-country running, dance, fencing, field hockey, fitness, jogging, lacrosse, modern dance, physical fitness, soccer, softball, swimming and diving, tennis, track and field, volleyball, yoga; intramural: aerobics, badminton, basketball, bicycling, crew, cross-country running, dance, fitness, jogging, lacrosse, martial arts, modern dance, outdoor adventure, physical fitness, soccer, softball, volleyball, yoga. 3 PE instructors, 18 coaches, 1 athletic trainer.

Computers Computers are regularly used in all classes. Computer network features include on-campus library services, online commercial services, Internet access, wireless campus network, Internet filtering or blocking technology. Campus intranet, student e-mail accounts, and computer access in designated common areas are available to students. Students grades are available online. The school has a published electronic and media policy.

Contact Ms. Carolyn Booth, Director of Admissions. 212-744-4486 Ext. 8152. Fax: 212-744-0716. E-mail: cbooth@marymountnyc.org. Website: www.marymountnyc.org

See Display on next page and Close-Up on page 604.

MARYVALE PREPARATORY SCHOOL

11300 Falls Road
Brooklandville, Maryland 21022

Head of School: Tracey H. Ford

General Information Girls' day college-preparatory school, affiliated with Roman Catholic Church. Grades 6–12. Founded: 1945. Setting: suburban. Nearest major city is Baltimore. 113-acre campus. 4 buildings on campus. Approved or accredited by Association of Independent Maryland Schools, Middle States Association of Colleges and Schools, National Catholic Education Association, and Maryland Department of Education. Member of National Association of Independent Schools. Total enrollment: 362. Upper school average class size: 15. Upper school faculty-student ratio: 1:8. Upper School students typically attend 5 days per week. The average school day consists of 6 hours.

Upper School Student Profile Grade 6: 31 students (31 girls); Grade 7: 36 students (36 girls); Grade 8: 39 students (39 girls); Grade 9: 91 students (91 girls); Grade 10: 77 students (77 girls); Grade 11: 70 students (70 girls); Grade 12: 72 students (72 girls).

Faculty School total: 53. In upper school: 8 men, 37 women; 32 have advanced degrees.

Subjects Offered American history-AP, art and culture, computer science-AP, creative writing, economics-AP, electives, English language and composition-AP, English literature and composition-AP, environmental science, French language AP, graphic design, health science, history-AP, leadership, modern world history, music composition, peer ministry, photography, physics-AP, playwriting, religious education, robotics, Spanish language-AP, statistics-AP, studio art-AP, technology, theater production, U.S. government and politics-AP, world history-AP.

Graduation Requirements Electives, theology, 70 hours of community service.

Special Academic Programs Advanced Placement exam preparation; honors section; accelerated programs; study at local college for college credit.

College Admission Counseling 64 students graduated in 2016; all went to college, including Drexel University; Fordham University; Temple University; Towson University; University of Maryland, Baltimore County; University of Maryland, College Park.

Student Life Upper grades have uniform requirement, student council, honor system. Discipline rests equally with students and faculty. Attendance at religious services is required.

Summer Programs Enrichment, sports, art/fine arts, computer instruction programs offered; held on campus; accepts girls; open to students from other schools. 2017 schedule: June 19 to July 20.

Tuition and Aid Day student tuition: $18,850. Tuition installment plan (FACTS Tuition Payment Plan). Bursaries, merit scholarship grants, need-based scholarship grants available.

Admissions Traditional secondary-level entrance grade is 9. ISEE required. Deadline for receipt of application materials: December 9. Application fee required: $50. On-campus interview required.

Athletics Interscholastic: badminton, basketball, cross-country running, field hockey, indoor soccer, indoor track & field, lacrosse, soccer, softball, swimming and diving, track and field, volleyball, winter (indoor) track, winter soccer. 3 PE instructors, 36 coaches, 1 athletic trainer.

Computers Computers are regularly used in all academic classes. Computer network features include on-campus library services, online commercial services, Internet access, wireless campus network, Internet filtering or blocking technology. Student e-mail accounts and computer access in designated common areas are available to students. Students grades are available online. The school has a published electronic and media policy.

Contact Sheryl Piron, Director of Admissions. 410-308-8531. E-mail: pirons@maryvale.com. Website: www.maryvale.com

MASSANUTTEN MILITARY ACADEMY

614 South Main Street
Woodstock, Virginia 22664

Head of School: Dr. David Skipper

General Information Coeducational boarding and day college-preparatory, STEM, and military school, affiliated with United Church of Christ. Grades 6–PG. Founded: 1899. Setting: small town. Nearest major city is Washington, DC. Students are housed in single-sex dormitories. 40-acre campus. 11 buildings on campus. Approved or accredited by Southern Association of Colleges and Schools, The Association of Boarding Schools, Virginia Association of Independent Schools, and Virginia Department of Education. Member of National Association of Independent Schools. Endowment: $13 million. Total enrollment: 99. Upper school average class size: 10. Upper school faculty-student ratio: 1:8. Upper School students typically attend 5 days per week.

Upper School Student Profile Grade 6: 1 student (1 girl); Grade 7: 4 students (3 boys, 1 girl); Grade 8: 3 students (1 boy, 2 girls); Grade 9: 12 students (6 boys, 6 girls); Grade 10: 19 students (14 boys, 5 girls); Grade 11: 27 students (19 boys, 8 girls); Grade 12: 25 students (15 boys, 10 girls); Postgraduate: 15 students (15 boys). 99% of students are boarding students. 15% are state residents. 17 states are represented in upper school student body. 30% are international students. International students from China, Egypt, Kuwait, Nigeria, Saudi Arabia, and Viet Nam; 4 other countries represented in student body.

Faculty School total: 27. In upper school: 19 men, 8 women; 8 have advanced degrees; 13 reside on campus.

Subjects Offered Algebra, American history, American literature, art, art appreciation, band, biology, calculus, character education, chemistry, computer applications, earth science, English, English literature, ESL, French, geometry, government/civics, grammar, health, history, Internet research, intro to computers, introduction to literature, JROTC, leadership, mathematics, music, news writing, physical education, physical science, physics, pre-calculus, Russian, SAT/ACT preparation, science, social sciences, social studies, Spanish, U.S. history, world history, world literature.

Graduation Requirements Arts and fine arts (art, music, dance, drama), computer applications, English, foreign language, JROTC, mathematics, physical education (includes health), science, social studies (includes history), one year of JROTC for each year enrolled.

Special Academic Programs Advanced Placement exam preparation; honors section; independent study; study at local college for college credit; remedial reading and/or remedial writing; remedial math; ESL (20 students enrolled).

College Admission Counseling 25 students graduated in 2016; they went to George Mason University; Mary Baldwin University; Radford University; The Citadel, The Military College of South Carolina; University of Georgia; Virginia Polytechnic Institute and State University. Other: 1 entered military service.

Student Life Upper grades have uniform requirement, student council, honor system. Discipline rests equally with students and faculty.

Summer Programs Remediation, advancement, ESL, sports, art/fine arts, computer instruction programs offered; session focuses on academics, JROTC program, leadership; held on campus; accepts boys and girls; open to students from other schools. 90 students usually enrolled. 2017 schedule: July 1 to July 30. Application deadline: June 30.

Tuition and Aid Day student tuition: $8800; 5-day tuition and room/board: $30,000; 7-day tuition and room/board: $34,000. Tuition installment plan (FACTS Tuition Payment Plan, monthly payment plans, individually arranged payment plans). Tuition reduction for siblings, merit scholarship grants, need-based scholarship grants, need-based loans, middle-income loans, USS Education Loan Program, PLATO Loans, legacy discounts available.

Admissions Traditional secondary-level entrance grade is 10. For fall 2016, 140 students applied for upper-level admission, 110 were accepted, 60 enrolled. Deadline for receipt of application materials: none. Application fee required: $50. Interview required.

Athletics Interscholastic: baseball (boys), basketball (b,g), cross-country running (b,g), fitness (b,g), football (b), independent competitive sports (b,g), softball (g), strength & conditioning (b), track and field (b,g), volleyball (g); coed interscholastic: drill team, JROTC drill, lacrosse, marksmanship, pistol, riflery, soccer, tennis, wrestling; coed intramural: billiards, canoeing/kayaking, cheering, cross-country running, kickball, outdoor activities, outdoor adventure, outdoor education, outdoor recreation, outdoor skills, outdoors, paddle tennis, physical fitness, physical training, power lifting, rafting, rappelling, running, skiing (downhill), snowboarding, snowshoeing, strength & conditioning, table tennis, tennis, walking, weight lifting, weight training, whiffle ball. 1 PE instructor, 5 coaches, 1 athletic trainer.

Computers Computers are regularly used in all academic, business applications, business skills, business studies, computer applications, journalism, JROTC, SAT preparation, yearbook classes. Computer network features include on-campus library services, Internet access, wireless campus network, Internet filtering or blocking technology. Computer access in designated common areas is available to students. Students grades are available online. The school has a published electronic and media policy.

Contact Mr. Murali Sinnathamby, Director of Admissions. 877-466-6222. Fax: 540-459-5421. E-mail: admissions@militaryschool.com. Website: www.militaryschool.com

THE MASTERS SCHOOL

49 Clinton Avenue
Dobbs Ferry, New York 10522

Head of School: Laura Danforth

General Information Coeducational boarding and day college-preparatory, arts, and technology school. Boarding grades 9–12, day grades 5–12. Founded: 1877. Setting: suburban. Nearest major city is New York. Students are housed in single-sex dormitories. 100-acre campus. 15 buildings on campus. Approved or accredited by Middle States Association of Colleges and Schools, The Association of Boarding Schools, and New York Department of Education. Member of National Association of Independent Schools and Secondary School Admission Test Board. Endowment: $45 million. Total enrollment: 665. Upper school average class size: 14. Upper school faculty-student ratio: 1:7. Upper School students typically attend 5 days per week. The average school day consists of 6 hours.

Upper School Student Profile Grade 9: 113 students (55 boys, 58 girls); Grade 10: 127 students (65 boys, 62 girls); Grade 11: 130 students (65 boys, 65 girls); Grade 12: 120 students (60 boys, 60 girls). 40% of students are boarding students. 50% are state residents. 20 states are represented in upper school student body. 18% are international students. International students from Canada, China, Germany, Republic of Korea, Russian Federation, and Switzerland; 29 other countries represented in student body.

Faculty School total: 99. In upper school: 45 men, 50 women; 76 have advanced degrees, 60 reside on campus.

Subjects Offered Acting, algebra, American history, American literature, art history, biology, biology-AP, calculus, calculus-AP, ceramics, chemistry, chemistry-AP, computer math, computer programming, computer science, creative writing, dance, drama, driver education, earth science, electronics, English, English language-AP, English literature, English literature-AP, environmental science, ESL, ethics, European history, European history-AP, expository writing, fine arts, French, French language-AP, French literature-AP, geography, geometry, grammar, health, health and wellness, health education, jazz, jazz band, journalism, Latin, Latin-AP, mathematics, meteorology, music, music theory-AP, performing arts, photography, physical education, physics, physics-AP, pre-calculus, religion, science, senior thesis, social studies, Spanish, Spanish language-AP, Spanish literature-AP, speech, statistics, statistics-AP, studio art, studio art-AP, theater, trigonometry, U.S. history, U.S. history-AP, world history, world literature, world religions, writing, yearbook, yoga.

Graduation Requirements Arts and fine arts (art, music, dance, drama), computer science, English, foreign language, health, mathematics, physical education (includes health), public speaking, science, U.S. history, world history, world religions.

Special Academic Programs 19 Advanced Placement exams for which test preparation is offered; honors section; independent study; term-away projects; study at local college for college credit; study abroad; academic accommodation for the gifted, the musically talented, and the artistically talented; ESL (18 students enrolled).

College Admission Counseling 112 students graduated in 2015; all went to college, including Boston University; Cornell University; Middlebury College; New York University; University of Chicago; Williams College. Mean SAT critical reading: 660, mean SAT math: 660, mean SAT writing: 680, mean combined SAT: 2000. 61% scored over 600 on SAT critical reading, 57% scored over 600 on SAT math, 68% scored over 600 on SAT writing, 58% scored over 1800 on combined SAT.

Student Life Upper grades have specified standards of dress, student council, honor system. Discipline rests equally with students and faculty.

Tuition and Aid Day student tuition: $41,110; 7-day tuition and room/board: $57,810. Tuition installment plan (Insured Tuition Payment Plan, monthly payment plans, individually arranged payment plans). Need-based scholarship grants available. In 2015–16, 25% of upper-school students received aid. Total amount of financial aid awarded in 2015–16: $50,400,000.

Admissions Traditional secondary-level entrance grade is 9. For fall 2015, 610 students applied for upper-level admission, 215 were accepted, 102 enrolled. ISEE, SSAT or TOEFL required. Deadline for receipt of application materials: February 1. Application fee required: $75. Interview required.

Athletics Interscholastic: baseball (boys), basketball (b,g), cross-country running (b,g), fencing (b,g), field hockey (g), lacrosse (b,g), soccer (b,g), softball (g), squash (b,g), tennis (b,g), volleyball (g); intramural: fencing (b,g), squash (b,g), swimming and diving (b,g); coed interscholastic: dance, dance team, golf, indoor track, swimming and diving, track and field; coed intramural: aerobics, aerobics/dance, aerobics/Nautilus, combined training, dance squad, dance team, fitness, Frisbee, martial arts, modern dance, outdoor activities, physical fitness, physical training, strength & conditioning, ultimate Frisbee, weight lifting, weight training, yoga. 2 PE instructors, 13 coaches, 1 athletic trainer.

Computers Computers are regularly used in computer applications, English, foreign language, graphic arts, graphic design, history, mathematics, newspaper, photography, programming, publications, science, senior seminar, study skills, video film production, Web site design, writing, yearbook classes. Computer network features include on-campus library services, online commercial services, Internet access, wireless campus network, Internet filtering or blocking technology. Campus intranet, student e-mail accounts, and computer access in designated common areas are available to students. The school has a published electronic and media policy.

Contact Office of Admission. 914-479-6420. Fax: 914-693-7295.
E-mail: admission@mastersny.org. Website: www.mastersny.org

MATER DEI HIGH SCHOOL

900 North Mater Dei Drive
Breese, Illinois 62230

Head of School: Mr. Dennis Litteken Sr.

General Information Coeducational day college-preparatory school, affiliated with Roman Catholic Church. Founded: 1954. Setting: small town. Nearest major city is St. Louis, MO. 55-acre campus. 1 building on campus. Approved or accredited by National Christian School Association, North Central Association of Colleges and Schools, and Illinois Department of Education. Endowment: $3 million. Total enrollment: 414. Upper school average class size: 18. Upper school faculty-student ratio: 1:18. There are 178 required school days per year for Upper School students. Upper School students typically attend 5 days per week. The average school day consists of 6 hours and 35 minutes.

Upper School Student Profile Grade 9: 93 students (44 boys, 49 girls); Grade 10: 90 students (47 boys, 43 girls); Grade 11: 119 students (58 boys, 61 girls); Grade 12: 112 students (58 boys, 54 girls). 99% of students are Roman Catholic.

Faculty School total: 43. In upper school: 18 men, 21 women; 22 have advanced degrees.

Graduation Requirements Algebra.

Special Academic Programs Advanced Placement exam preparation; honors section; academic accommodation for the gifted, remedial reading and/or remedial writing; remedial math.

College Admission Counseling 117 students graduated in 2016; 115 went to college, including Saint Louis University; Southern Illinois University Edwardsville; University of Illinois at Urbana–Champaign. Other: 1 went to work, 1 entered military service. Median composite ACT: 24. 35% scored over 26 on composite ACT.

Student Life Upper grades have uniform requirement, student council, honor system. Discipline rests primarily with faculty. Attendance at religious services is required.

Tuition and Aid Day student tuition: $5000. Tuition installment plan (SMART Tuition Payment Plan, monthly payment plans). Tuition reduction for siblings, need-based scholarship grants available. In 2016–17, 51% of upper-school students received aid. Total amount of financial aid awarded in 2016–17: $120,000.

Admissions Traditional secondary-level entrance grade is 9. For fall 2016, 95 students applied for upper-level admission, 93 were accepted, 93 enrolled. Explore required. Deadline for receipt of application materials: February 27. Application fee required: $50.

Athletics Interscholastic: baseball (boys), basketball (b), cheering (g), dance team (g), football (b), golf (b,g), volleyball (g), wrestling (b); intramural: weight lifting (h), weight training (b,g); coed interscholastic: bowling, fishing. 2 PE instructors, 15 coaches, 1 athletic trainer.

Computers Computer network features include on-campus library services, Internet access, wireless campus network, Internet filtering or blocking technology. Campus intranet and student e-mail accounts are available to students. Students grades are available online. The school has a published electronic and media policy.

Contact Mrs. Donna Goetz, Guidance Director. 618-526-7216. Fax: 618-526-8310.
E-mail: dgoetz@materdeiknights.org. Website: www.materdeiknights.org

MATER DEI PREP

538 Church Street
New Monmouth, New Jersey 07748

Head of School: Mr. James Joseph Hauenstein

General Information Coeducational day college-preparatory and dual enrollment coursework/coillege advantage school, affiliated with Roman Catholic Church. Grades 9–12. Setting: suburban. Nearest major city is New York, NY. 60-acre campus. 3 buildings on campus. Approved or accredited by Middle States Association of Colleges and Schools and National Catholic Education Association. Upper school average class size: 15. There are 182 required school days per year for Upper School students. Upper School students typically attend 5 days per week. The average school day consists of 6 hours and 25 minutes.

Upper School Student Profile Grade 9: 71 students (44 boys, 27 girls); Grade 10: 49 students (34 boys, 15 girls); Grade 11: 114 students (61 boys, 53 girls); Grade 12: 88 students (45 boys, 43 girls). 67% of students are Roman Catholic.

Faculty School total: 35. In upper school: 15 men, 20 women.

Subjects Offered Acting, advanced biology, advanced chemistry, advanced math, Advanced Placement courses, algebra, American government, American history-AP, analysis and differential calculus, ancient world history, art, bioethics, biology, British literature, broadcast journalism, calculus, calculus-AP, Catholic belief and practice, chemistry, choral music, college writing, computer applications, computer graphics, computer literacy, CPR, criminal justice, dance, ecology, environmental systems, English literature-AP, environmental science, environmental science-AP, family living, film and literature, fine arts, foreign language, French, freshman seminar, geometry, health, history, history of rock and roll, Holocaust, honors algebra, honors English, honors geometry, honors U.S. history, human sexuality, Italian, journalism, lab science, marine biology, media communications, painting, peace education, performing arts, photography, physical education, physics, piano, play production, pre-calculus, probability, probability and statistics, psychology, religion, SAT preparation, sculpture, service learning/internship, sex education, Spanish, state history, statistics, technology, theater arts, TOEFL preparation, U.S. history, U.S. history-AP, United Nations and international issues, Vietnam history, word processing, world civilizations, world history-AP, world religions, yearbook.

Graduation Requirements Art, career education, chemistry, CPR, English, finance, French, health education, mathematics, science, Spanish, technology, world history, required hours of community service.

Special Academic Programs Honors section; independent study; study at local college for college credit; academic accommodation for the gifted; remedial reading and/or remedial writing; remedial math; programs in English, mathematics, general development for dyslexic students; special instructional classes for provide for 1 period a year of study skill supports delendent on ISP/504; ESL (8 students enrolled).

College Admission Counseling 105 students graduated in 2016; 104 went to college, including Marist College; Rowan University; Saint Joseph's University; The College of New Jersey; The University of Scranton; University of Delaware. Other: 1 entered a postgraduate year. Mean SAT critical reading: 533, mean SAT math: 538, mean SAT writing: 530.

Student Life Upper grades have specified standards of dress, student council, honor system. Discipline rests primarily with faculty. Attendance at religious services is required.

Tuition and Aid Day student tuition: $12,200. Tuition installment plan (SMART Tuition Payment Plan, FACTS Tuition Payment Plan). Merit scholarship grants, need-based scholarship grants available.

Admissions Traditional secondary-level entrance grade is 9. For fall 2016, 114 students applied for upper-level admission, 108 were accepted, 71 enrolled. ACT required. Deadline for receipt of application materials: December 9. No application fee required. On-campus interview required.

Athletics Interscholastic: baseball (boys), basketball (b,g), cheering (g), cross-country running (b,g), dance (b,g), field hockey (g), football (b), golf (b,g), ice hockey (b,g), indoor track (b,g), lacrosse (g), softball (g), strength & conditioning (b,g), tennis (b,g), track and field (b,g), winter (indoor) track (b,g). 3 PE instructors, 44 coaches, 1 athletic trainer.

Computers Computer network features include Internet access, wireless campus network, Internet filtering or blocking technology. Student e-mail accounts are available to students. Students grades are available online. The school has a published electronic and media policy.

Contact Mrs. Kathleen Daly, Director of Admission and Advancement. 732-671-9100. Fax: 732-671-9214. E-mail: kdaly@materdeiprep.org. Website: www.materdeihs.org

MATIGNON HIGH SCHOOL

One Matignon Road
Cambridge, Massachusetts 02140

Head of School: Mr. Timothy M. Welsh

General Information Coeducational day college-preparatory, arts, business, technology, and STEM school, affiliated with Roman Catholic Church. Grades 9–12. Distance learning grades 11–12. Founded: 1945. Setting: suburban. Nearest major city is Boston. 10-acre campus. 3 buildings on campus. Approved or accredited by Massachusetts Department of Education, National Catholic Education Association, New England Association of Schools and Colleges, The College Board, and Massachusetts Department of Education. Endowment: $150,000. Total enrollment: 462. Upper school average class size: 18. Upper school faculty-student ratio: 1:18. There are 180 required school days per year for Upper School students. Upper School students typically attend 5 days per week. The average school day consists of 7 hours.

Upper School Student Profile Grade 9: 89 students (43 boys, 46 girls); Grade 10: 116 students (44 boys, 72 girls); Grade 11: 107 students (50 boys, 57 girls); Grade 12: 107 students (50 boys, 57 girls). 70% of students are Roman Catholic.

Faculty School total: 36. In upper school: 13 men, 23 women; 25 have advanced degrees.

Subjects Offered Accounting, Advanced Placement courses, advanced studio art-AP, algebra, American history, American literature, anatomy and physiology, art, art history, biology, biology-AP, calculus, chemistry, Christian and Hebrew scripture, community service, computer science, drawing and design, English, English literature, English-AP, fine arts, French, French language-AP, French-AP, freshman seminar, geometry, grammar, graphic design, health, Hebrew scripture, history, honors algebra, honors geometry, honors U.S. history, honors world history, Latin, Latin-AP, law, mathematics, physical education, physics, physics-AP, pre-calculus, psychology, psychology-AP, religion, SAT preparation, science, social justice, social sciences, social studies, Spanish, Spanish-AP, studio art, studio art-AP, theology, trigonometry, U.S. history, U.S. history-AP, world history, world history-AP, writing.

Graduation Requirements 20th century history, accounting, Advanced Placement courses, algebra, anatomy and physiology, electives, English, English-AP, foreign language, French-AP, geometry, health education, honors algebra, honors English, honors geometry, honors world history, law, mathematics, physical education (includes health), psychology-AP, religious studies, science, social studies (includes history), Spanish-AP, U.S. history, U.S. history-AP, world cultures, Christian service, 45 hours of community service (before junior year).

Special Academic Programs Advanced Placement exam preparation; honors section; independent study; study at local college for college credit; study abroad; ESL (18 students enrolled).

College Admission Counseling 118 students graduated in 2016; 116 went to college, including Boston University; Merrimack College; Northeastern University; Stonehill College; University of Massachusetts Amherst; University of Massachusetts Boston. Other: 1 entered military service, 1 entered a postgraduate year. Mean SAT critical reading: 510, mean SAT math: 540, mean SAT writing: 520, mean combined SAT: 1320. 21% scored over 600 on SAT critical reading, 23% scored over 600 on SAT math, 14% scored over 600 on SAT writing, 20% scored over 1800 on combined SAT, 35% scored over 26 on composite ACT.

Student Life Upper grades have uniform requirement, student council, honor system. Discipline rests primarily with faculty. Attendance at religious services is required.

Summer Programs Remediation, enrichment programs offered; session focuses on remediation/makeup and enrichment; held on campus; accepts boys and girls; open to students from other schools. 50 students usually enrolled. 2017 schedule: June 19 to July 14. Application deadline: June 16.

Tuition and Aid Day student tuition: $10,450. Tuition installment plan (FACTS Tuition Payment Plan). Merit scholarship grants, need-based scholarship grants available. In 2016–17, 50% of upper-school students received aid; total upper-school merit-scholarship money awarded: $475,000. Total amount of financial aid awarded in 2016–17: $600,000.

Admissions Traditional secondary-level entrance grade is 9. For fall 2016, 420 students applied for upper-level admission, 325 were accepted, 109 enrolled. Archdiocese of Boston High School entrance exam provided by STS, SSAT or TOEFL or SLEP required. Deadline for receipt of application materials: none. No application fee required. On-campus interview recommended.

Athletics Interscholastic: baseball (boys), basketball (b,g), cheering (g), football (b), ice hockey (b,g), lacrosse (b,g), soccer (b,g), softball (g), tennis (b,g), volleyball (g); intramural: aerobics/dance (b,g), dance (b,g), dance squad (b,g), dance team (b,g), Frisbee (b,g), physical training (b,g), strength & conditioning (b,g), weight lifting (b,g), weight training (b,g); coed interscholastic: cross-country running, golf, swimming and diving, track and field; coed intramural: table tennis, yoga. 1 PE instructor, 20 coaches, 1 athletic trainer.

Computers Computers are regularly used in all academic classes. Computer network features include on-campus library services, Internet access, wireless campus network, Internet filtering or blocking technology, all academic homework is provided online. Student e-mail accounts and computer access in designated common areas are available to students. Students grades are available online. The school has a published electronic and media policy.

Contact Mr. Joseph A. DiSarcina, Principal. 617-876-1212 Ext. 14. Fax: 617-661-3905. E-mail: jdisarcina@matignon.org. Website: www.matignon.org

MAUI PREPARATORY ACADEMY

5095 Napilihau Street, #109B
PMB #186
Lahaina, Hawaii 96761

Head of School: Dr. Jonathan L. Silver

General Information Coeducational boarding and day college-preparatory, arts, technology, and project-based 21st Century Skills school. Boarding grades 9–12, day grades PK–12. Founded: 2005. Setting: small town. Students are housed in coed dormitories. 22-acre campus. 7 buildings on campus. Approved or accredited by Western Association of Schools and Colleges and Hawaii Department of Education. Member of National Association of Independent Schools. Total enrollment: 187. Upper school average class size: 15. Upper school faculty-student ratio: 1:4. There are 177 required school days per year for Upper School students. Upper School students typically attend 5 days per week. The average school day consists of 7 hours.

Upper School Student Profile Grade 6: 17 students (7 boys, 10 girls); Grade 7: 12 students (8 boys, 4 girls); Grade 8: 17 students (4 boys, 13 girls); Grade 9: 10 students (4 boys, 6 girls); Grade 10: 14 students (6 boys, 8 girls); Grade 11: 26 students (11 boys, 15 girls); Grade 12: 12 students (6 boys, 6 girls). 15% of students are boarding students. 75% are state residents. 2 states are represented in upper school student body. 25% are international students. International students from Brazil, Canada, China, France, Germany, and Japan.

Faculty School total: 22. In upper school: 7 men, 7 women; 10 have advanced degrees; 2 reside on campus.

Subjects Offered Art, biology, calculus, chemistry, English, environmental science, foreign language, health, history, marine science, mathematics, physics, social studies, technology.

Graduation Requirements 1 1/2 elective credits, algebra, all academic, art, athletics, biology, calculus-AP, chemistry, college planning, English, foreign language, geometry, physics-AP, science project, 25 hours of community service per year, two varsity teams per year.

Special Academic Programs Advanced Placement exam preparation; independent study; study at local college for college credit; ESL (8 students enrolled).

College Admission Counseling 11 students graduated in 2015; 8 went to college, including Chapman University; Lehigh University; The George Washington University; University of Hawaii at Manoa; University of San Diego; William Paterson University of New Jersey. Other: 3 went to work. Median SAT critical reading: 520, median SAT math: 510, median SAT writing: 490, median combined SAT: 1510. 11% scored over

600 on SAT critical reading, 11% scored over 600 on SAT math, 11% scored over 600 on SAT writing, 11% scored over 1800 on combined SAT.

Student Life Upper grades have uniform requirement, student council, honor system. Discipline rests primarily with faculty.

Tuition and Aid Day student tuition: $17,350; 7-day tuition and room/board: $32,400. Tuition installment plan (Insured Tuition Payment Plan, monthly payment plans, TADS Tuition Payment Plan). Tuition reduction for siblings, merit scholarship grants, need-based scholarship grants available. In 2015–16, 40% of upper-school students received aid; total upper-school merit-scholarship money awarded: $212,801. Total amount of financial aid awarded in 2015–16: $261,776.

Admissions Traditional secondary-level entrance grade is 9. For fall 2015, 24 students applied for upper-level admission, 21 were accepted, 13 enrolled. CTP, ERB Mathematics and TOEFL required. Deadline for receipt of application materials: March 30. Application fee required: $125. Interview required.

Athletics Interscholastic: aquatics (boys, girls), canoeing/kayaking (b,g), cross-country running (b,g), diving (b,g), golf (b,g), independent competitive sports (b,g), ocean paddling (b,g), surfing (b,g), swimming and diving (b,g), tennis (b,g), track and field (b,g), volleyball (g); intramural: basketball (b,g), surfing (b,g); coed interscholastic: ocean paddling; coed intramural: basketball, cross-country running, flag football, golf, surfing. 1 PE instructor, 9 coaches.

Computers Computers are regularly used in all classes. Computer network features include on-campus library services, Internet access, wireless campus network. Campus intranet and student e-mail accounts are available to students. Students grades are available online. The school has a published electronic and media policy.

Contact Mrs. Cathi Minami, Director of Advancement. 808-665-9966. Fax: 808-665-1075. E-mail: cminami@mauiprep.org. Website: www.mauiprep.org

MAUMEE VALLEY COUNTRY DAY SCHOOL

1715 South Reynolds Road
Toledo, Ohio 43614-1499

Head of School: Mr. Gary Boehm

General Information Coeducational boarding and day college-preparatory and global studies school. Boarding grades 9–12, day grades P3–12. Founded: 1884. Setting: suburban. Students are housed in coed dormitories. 72-acre campus. 4 buildings on campus. Approved or accredited by Independent Schools Association of the Central States, Ohio Association of Independent Schools, The Association of Boarding Schools, and Ohio Department of Education. Member of National Association of Independent Schools. Endowment: $8 million. Total enrollment: 532. Upper school average class size: 14. Upper school faculty-student ratio: 1:9. Upper School students typically attend 5 days per week. The average school day consists of 7 hours.

Upper School Student Profile Grade 9: 51 students (25 boys, 26 girls); Grade 10: 60 students (30 boys, 30 girls); Grade 11: 63 students (31 boys, 32 girls); Grade 12: 41 students (21 boys, 20 girls). 20% of students are boarding students. 80% are state residents. 1 state is represented in upper school student body. 20% are international students. International students from China, Japan, Mexico, Poland, Sweden, and Viet Nam; 8 other countries represented in student body.

Faculty School total: 62. In upper school: 12 men, 10 women; 21 have advanced degrees.

Subjects Offered Algebra, American government, American history, anthropology, art, biology, biology-AP, calculus-AP, chemistry, Chinese, choir, computer graphics, computer science, creative writing, design, drama, earth science, ecology, English, environmental science, European history, expository writing, fine arts, geology, geometry, government/civics, grammar, health, history, human development, humanities, mathematics, microbiology, music, physical education, physics, science, social studies, Spanish, Spanish-AP, speech, statistics, statistics-AP, theater, trigonometry, women's studies, world history.

Graduation Requirements American government, arts and fine arts (art, music, dance, drama), English, foreign language, mathematics, physical education (includes health), science, social studies (includes history). Community service is required.

Special Academic Programs Advanced Placement exam preparation; honors section; independent study; term-away projects; study at local college for college credit; domestic exchange program (with The Athenian School, The Network Program Schools); study abroad; academic accommodation for the gifted, the musically talented, and the artistically talented; ESL (43 students enrolled).

College Admission Counseling 54 students graduated in 2016; all went to college, including Bowling Green State University; Case Western Reserve University; Ohio Wesleyan University; The Ohio State University; The University of Toledo; University of Michigan. Mean SAT critical reading: 634, mean SAT math: 632, mean SAT writing: 621, mean combined SAT: 1887, mean composite ACT: 28. 50% scored over 600 on SAT critical reading, 50% scored over 600 on SAT math.

Student Life Upper grades have student council, honor system. Discipline rests equally with students and faculty.

Summer Programs Enrichment, ESL, sports, art/fine arts, computer instruction programs offered; session focuses on day camp, sports camps, ESL camp; held on campus; accepts boys and girls; open to students from other schools. 300 students usually enrolled. 2017 schedule: June 15 to August 15. Application deadline: June 3.

Tuition and Aid Day student tuition: $18,500–$19,500; 7-day tuition and room/board: $42,450. Tuition installment plan (FACTS Tuition Payment Plan, monthly payment plans, individually arranged payment plans). Merit scholarship grants, need-based scholarship grants available. In 2016–17, 50% of upper-school students received aid; total upper-school merit-scholarship money awarded: $136,000. Total amount of financial aid awarded in 2016–17: $454,900.

Admissions Traditional secondary-level entrance grade is 9. For fall 2016, 99 students applied for upper-level admission, 52 were accepted, 33 enrolled. OLSAT, ERB, Otis-Lennon and 2 sections of ERB, SSAT, TOEFL or writing sample required. Deadline for receipt of application materials: none. Application fee required: $50. On-campus interview required.

Athletics Interscholastic: baseball (boys), basketball (b,g), cheering (b,g), cross-country running (b,g), field hockey (g), golf (b,g), lacrosse (g), soccer (b,g), tennis (b,g), track and field (b,g); intramural: indoor soccer (g), lacrosse (g); coed intramural: strength & conditioning, weight training. 3 PE instructors, 10 coaches, 1 athletic trainer.

Computers Computers are regularly used in English, foreign language, graphic design, history, information technology, library skills, literary magazine, mathematics, music, newspaper, science, yearbook classes. Computer network features include on-campus library services, online commercial services, Internet access, wireless campus network, Internet filtering or blocking technology. Student e-mail accounts are available to students. Students grades are available online. The school has a published electronic and media policy.

Contact Sarah Bigenho, Associate Director of Admission. 419-381-1313 Ext. 105. Fax: 419-381-1314. E-mail: sbigenho@mvcds.org. Website: www.mvcds.org

MAUR HILL-MOUNT ACADEMY

1000 Green Street
Atchison, Kansas 66002

Head of School: Mr. Phil Baniewicz

General Information Coeducational boarding and day college-preparatory, English as a Second language, and STEM school, affiliated with Roman Catholic Church. Grades 9–12. Founded: 1863. Setting: small town. Nearest major city is Kansas City, MO. Students are housed in single-sex dormitories. 90-acre campus. 7 buildings on campus. Approved or accredited by National Catholic Education Association, North Central Association of Colleges and Schools, The Association of Boarding Schools, and Kansas Department of Education. Member of Secondary School Admission Test Board. Total enrollment: 195. Upper school average class size: 15. Upper school faculty-student ratio: 1:9. There are 179 required school days per year for Upper School students. Upper School students typically attend 5 days per week. The average school day consists of 6 hours and 30 minutes.

Upper School Student Profile Grade 9: 50 students (26 boys, 24 girls); Grade 10: 53 students (27 boys, 26 girls); Grade 11: 52 students (27 boys, 25 girls); Grade 12: 50 students (24 boys, 26 girls). 44% of students are boarding students. 50% are state residents. 13 states are represented in upper school student body. 30% are international students. International students from China, Mexico, Nigeria, Republic of Korea, Spain, and Viet Nam; 11 other countries represented in student body. 60% of students are Roman Catholic.

Faculty School total: 21. In upper school: 13 men, 8 women; 11 have advanced degrees; 2 reside on campus.

Subjects Offered Algebra, American history, American literature, anatomy, art, Bible studies, biology, botany, calculus, calculus-AP, chemistry, computer science, drama, economics, English, English literature, ESL, fine arts, geography, geometry, government/civics, grammar, health, history, journalism, mathematics, music, photography, physical education, physics, physiology, psychology, religion, science, social sciences, social studies, sociology, Spanish, speech, theater, theology, trigonometry, typing, world history, world literature, writing.

Graduation Requirements Arts and fine arts (art, music, dance, drama), business skills (includes word processing), computer science, English, foreign language, mathematics, physical education (includes health), religion (includes Bible studies and theology), science, social sciences, social studies (includes history).

Special Academic Programs Advanced Placement exam preparation; honors section; study at local college for college credit; academic accommodation for the gifted; special instructional classes for students with Attention Deficit Disorder; ESL (15 students enrolled).

College Admission Counseling 53 students graduated in 2016; 52 went to college, including Benedictine College; Kansas State University; Penn State University Park; The University of Kansas; The University of Texas at Austin. Other: 1 went to work.

Student Life Upper grades have uniform requirement, student council, honor system. Discipline rests primarily with faculty. Attendance at religious services is required.

Summer Programs ESL programs offered; session focuses on activities camp, ESL program; held on campus; accepts boys and girls; open to students from other schools. 17 students usually enrolled. 2017 schedule: July 5 to August 5. Application deadline: June 1.

Tuition and Aid 5-day tuition and room/board: $21,250; 7-day tuition and room/board: $22,750. Tuition installment plan (monthly payment plans, individually arranged payment plans, Sallie Mae). Tuition reduction for siblings, merit scholarship grants, need-based scholarship grants, need-based loans, paying campus jobs available. In 2016–17, 40% of upper-school students received aid.

Admissions Traditional secondary-level entrance grade is 9. For fall 2016, 152 students applied for upper-level admission, 79 were accepted, 71 enrolled. ACT, ACT-

Explore, any standardized test, High School Placement Test, SAT or SSAT required. Deadline for receipt of application materials: none. Application fee required: $50. Interview recommended.

Athletics Interscholastic: aquatics (girls), baseball (b), basketball (b,g), cheering (g), cross-country running (b,g), dance (g), dance squad (g), dance team (g), drill team (g), football (b), soccer (b), softball (g), swimming and diving (b,g), tennis (b,g), track and field (b,g), volleyball (g); intramural: boxing (b), field hockey (b), fitness (b), flag football (b), floor hockey (b), football (b), running (b,g), skateboarding (b), skiing (downhill) (b,g), soccer (b,g), strength & conditioning (b,g), swimming and diving (b,g), touch football (b), track and field (b,g), weight lifting (b,g), weight training (b,g); coed interscholastic: bowling, golf, physical fitness, physical training, running, soccer, wrestling; coed intramural: baseball, basketball, Nautilus, physical fitness, physical training, roller blading, table tennis, tennis, volleyball, walking. 7 coaches, 1 athletic trainer.

Computers Computer network features include on-campus library services, Internet access, wireless campus network, Internet filtering or blocking technology. Student e-mail accounts are available to students. Students grades are available online. The school has a published electronic and media policy.

Contact Mr. Deke Nolan, Director of Admission. 913-367-5482 Ext. 110. Fax: 913-367-5096. E-mail: admissions@mh-ma.com. Website: www.mh-ma.com

MAYER LUTHERAN HIGH SCHOOL

305 5th Street NE
Mayer, Minnesota 55360

Head of School: Joel Philip Landskroener

General Information Coeducational day college-preparatory and STEM (Science, Technology, Engineering, and Math) school, affiliated with Lutheran Church–Missouri Synod. Grades 9–12. Founded: 1961. Setting: small town. Nearest major city is Minneapolis. 54-acre campus. 3 buildings on campus. Approved or accredited by National Lutheran School Accreditation, North Central Association of Colleges and Schools, and Minnesota Department of Education. Endowment: $600,000. Total enrollment: 252. Upper school average class size: 17. Upper school faculty-student ratio: 1:14. There are 174 required school days per year for Upper School students. Upper School students typically attend 5 days per week. The average school day consists of 5 hours and 15 minutes.

Upper School Student Profile Grade 9: 59 students (35 boys, 24 girls); Grade 10: 39 students (22 boys, 17 girls); Grade 11: 41 students (19 boys, 22 girls); Grade 12: 46 students (20 boys, 26 girls). 4% of students are boarding students. 96% are state residents. 1 state is represented in upper school student body. 4% are international students. International students from United States; 4 other countries represented in student body. 75% of students are Lutheran Church–Missouri Synod.

Faculty School total: 20. In upper school: 11 men, 9 women; 5 have advanced degrees.

Subjects Offered 1 1/2 elective credits, algebra, American history, American history-AP, art, band, biology, ceramics, chemistry, choir, computer science, drawing, earth science, English, environmental science, fine arts, geometry, health, history, music, music appreciation, painting, physical education, physical science, physics, pre-calculus, psychology, religion, science, sculpture, Spanish, world geography, writing.

Graduation Requirements Arts and fine arts (art, music, dance, drama), computer science, English, foreign language, mathematics, physical education (includes health), religion (includes Bible studies and theology), science, social sciences, social studies (includes history).

Special Academic Programs 2 Advanced Placement exams for which test preparation is offered; honors section; accelerated programs; independent study; study at local college for college credit; academic accommodation for the gifted and the musically talented; remedial reading and/or remedial writing; remedial math; programs in English, mathematics for dyslexic students.

College Admission Counseling 46 students graduated in 2016; 44 went to college, including Minnesota State University Mankato; North Dakota State University; St. Cloud State University; University of Minnesota, Duluth; University of Minnesota, Twin Cities Campus; University of St. Thomas. Other: 2 went to work, 3 entered military service. Median composite ACT: 26. 53% scored over 26 on composite ACT.

Student Life Upper grades have specified standards of dress. Discipline rests primarily with faculty. Attendance at religious services is required.

Summer Programs Enrichment, advancement, art/fine arts, computer instruction programs offered; held on campus; accepts boys and girls; open to students from other schools. 80 students usually enrolled. 2017 schedule: June 7 to August 6. Application deadline: June 1.

Tuition and Aid Day student tuition: $9925. Tuition installment plan (monthly payment plans, individually arranged payment plans, guaranteed tuition pre-payment plan). Need-based scholarship grants, Timothy Scholarship, non-Lutherans only available. In 2016–17, 40% of upper-school students received aid. Total amount of financial aid awarded in 2016–17: $280,000.

Admissions Traditional secondary-level entrance grade is 9. For fall 2016, 66 students applied for upper-level admission, 59 were accepted, 59 enrolled. TOEFL or writing sample required. Deadline for receipt of application materials: August 1. Application fee required: $25. Interview recommended.

Athletics Interscholastic: baseball (boys), basketball (b,g), cross-country running (b,g), dance (g), dance squad (g), dance team (g), danceline (g), football (b), golf (b,g),

soccer (g), softball (g), track and field (b,g), volleyball (g); intramural: weight lifting (b,g); coed interscholastic: bowling, trap and skeet. 1 PE instructor, 8 coaches, 1 athletic trainer.

Computers Computers are regularly used in all classes. Computer network features include on-campus library services, online commercial services, Internet access, wireless campus network, Internet filtering or blocking technology. Computer access in designated common areas is available to students. Students grades are available online. The school has a published electronic and media policy.

Contact Dan D. Perrel, Director of Enrollment. 952-657-2251 Ext. 1011. Fax: 952-657-2344. E-mail: dan.perrel@mayerlutheran.org. Website: www.lhsmayer.org

THE McCALLIE SCHOOL

500 Dodds Avenue
Chattanooga, Tennessee 37404

Head of School: Mr. A. Lee Burns III

General Information Boys' boarding and day college-preparatory school. Boarding grades 9–12, day grades 6–12. Founded: 1905. Setting: suburban. Nearest major city is Atlanta, GA. Students are housed in single-sex dormitories. 110-acre campus. 19 buildings on campus. Approved or accredited by Southern Association of Colleges and Schools, Southern Association of Independent Schools, Tennessee Association of Independent Schools, The Association of Boarding Schools, and Tennessee Department of Education. Member of National Association of Independent Schools and Secondary School Admission Test Board. Endowment: $98 million. Total enrollment: 913. Upper school average class size: 14. Upper school faculty-student ratio: 1:8. Upper School students typically attend 5 days per week. The average school day consists of 6 hours and 30 minutes.

Upper School Student Profile Grade 9: 164 students (164 boys); Grade 10: 163 students (163 boys); Grade 11: 171 students (171 boys); Grade 12: 158 students (158 boys). 35% of students are boarding students. 24 states are represented in upper school student body. 8% are international students. International students from Bahamas, China, Finland, Jamaica, Mexico, and Republic of Korea; 2 other countries represented in student body.

Faculty School total: 140. In upper school: 93 men, 15 women; 76 have advanced degrees; 58 reside on campus.

Subjects Offered Advanced biology, advanced chemistry, Advanced Placement courses, advanced studio art-AP, African-American history, American history-AP, Ancient Greek, animation, band, biology-AP, business, calculus-AP, chemistry-AP, chorus, college admission preparation, computer science-AP, concert band, concert bell choir, English literature and composition-AP, environmental science-AP, epic literature, European history-AP, filmmaking, geography, German-AP, history of rock and roll, Italian, Latin-AP, leadership, linear algebra, macro/microeconomics-AP, marine biology, marketing, Middle Eastern history, modern European history-AP, modern world history, physics-AP, play/screen writing, pre-calculus, psychology, SAT/ACT preparation, Spanish language-AP, statistics, statistics-AP, strings, symphonic band, technology/design, The 20th Century, video film production, world history-AP, writing workshop.

Graduation Requirements Arts and fine arts (art, music, dance, drama), English, foreign language, mathematics, physical education (includes health), public speaking, religion (includes Bible studies and theology), science, social sciences, social studies (includes history).

Special Academic Programs Advanced Placement exam preparation; honors section; independent study; study abroad; academic accommodation for the gifted.

College Admission Counseling 169 students graduated in 2016; all went to college, including Georgia Institute of Technology; North Carolina State University; The University of North Carolina at Chapel Hill; The University of Tennessee; University of Georgia; Vanderbilt University. Mean SAT critical reading: 615, mean SAT math: 635, mean composite ACT: 28.

Student Life Upper grades have specified standards of dress, student council, honor system. Discipline rests equally with students and faculty.

Summer Programs Enrichment, advancement, sports, rigorous outdoor training programs offered; session focuses on introduction to McCallie School with special emphasis on fun and participation; held on campus; accepts boys; open to students from other schools. 2,500 students usually enrolled. 2017 schedule: June 1 to August 1.

Tuition and Aid Day student tuition: $18,795; 7-day tuition and room/board: $36,850. Tuition installment plan (Insured Tuition Payment Plan, monthly payment plans, individually arranged payment plans). Merit scholarship grants, need-based scholarship grants, need-based loans available. In 2016–17, 38% of upper-school students received aid; total upper-school merit-scholarship money awarded: $850,000. Total amount of financial aid awarded in 2016–17: $3,500,000.

Admissions Traditional secondary-level entrance grade is 9. ISEE or SSAT required. Deadline for receipt of application materials: March 1. Application fee required: $50. On-campus interview required.

Athletics Interscholastic: baseball, basketball, bowling, climbing, crew, cross-country running, diving, football, golf, indoor track, indoor track & field, lacrosse, physical training, rock climbing, rowing, skeet shooting, soccer, swimming and diving, tennis, track and field, trap and skeet, ultimate Frisbee, wall climbing, wrestling; intramural: backpacking, baseball, basketball, bicycling, billiards, bowling, canoeing/kayaking, climbing, fencing, fishing, fitness, flag football, fly fishing, football, Frisbee, golf, hiking/backpacking, indoor soccer, juggling, kayaking, lacrosse, martial arts, mountain biking, mountaineering, outdoor activities, paint ball, physical fitness, physical training, power lifting, racquetball, rappelling, rock climbing, ropes courses, scuba diving, soccer, softball, strength & conditioning, swimming and diving, table tennis, tennis, touch football, ultimate Frisbee, volleyball, wall climbing, water polo, weight lifting, weight training, whiffle ball, wilderness, wilderness survival, wrestling, yoga; coed interscholastic: cheering. 10 coaches, 3 athletic trainers.

Computers Computers are regularly used in history, programming, religion classes. Computer network features include on-campus library services, online commercial services, Internet access, wireless campus network, Internet filtering or blocking technology. Campus intranet, student e-mail accounts, and computer access in designated common areas are available to students. Students grades are available online. The school has a published electronic and media policy.

Contact Mr. Hank Bramblet, Director of Boarding Admission. 423-624-8300. Fax: 423-493-5426. E-mail: admission@mccallie.org. Website: www.mccallie.org

McDONOGH SCHOOL

8600 McDonogh Road
Owings Mills, Maryland 21117-0380

Head of School: Charles W. Britton

General Information Coeducational boarding and day college-preparatory school. Boarding grades 9–12, day grades PK–12. Founded: 1873. Setting: suburban. Nearest major city is Baltimore. Students are housed in single-sex dormitories. 800-acre campus. 46 buildings on campus. Approved or accredited by Association of Independent Maryland Schools. Member of National Association of Independent Schools and Secondary School Admission Test Board. Endowment: $89 million. Total enrollment: 1,350. Upper school average class size: 15. Upper school faculty-student ratio: 1:9. There are 175 required school days per year for Upper School students. Upper School students typically attend 5 days per week. The average school day consists of 6 hours and 10 minutes.

Upper School Student Profile Grade 6: 114 students (60 boys, 54 girls); Grade 7: 98 students (53 boys, 45 girls); Grade 8: 118 students (63 boys, 55 girls); Grade 9: 159 students (87 boys, 72 girls); Grade 10: 155 students (85 boys, 70 girls); Grade 11: 146 students (77 boys, 69 girls); Grade 12: 143 students (73 boys, 70 girls).

Faculty School total: 177. In upper school: 37 men, 51 women; 60 have advanced degrees; 37 reside on campus.

Subjects Offered 20th century American writers, acting, Advanced Placement courses, African history, African literature, African-American studies, algebra, American history, American history-AP, American literature, American literature-AP, anatomy, art, art history, art-AP, Asian studies, band, biology, biology-AP, botany, calculus, calculus-AP, ceramics, chemistry, chemistry-AP, Chesapeake Bay studies, classical Greek literature, composition-AP, computer animation, computer graphics, computer music, computer programming, computer science, computer science-AP, concert band, concert choir, creative writing, dance, drama, drawing, ecology, economics, economics-AP, electives, engineering, English, English composition, English literature, English literature and composition-AP, English literature-AP, English-AP, English/composition-AP, environmental science, environmental science-AP, ethics, European history, film, film and literature, fine arts, fitness, foreign language, French, French language-AP, French literature-AP, French-AP, genetics, geology, geometry, German, German-AP, government and politics-AP, government-AP, government/civics, health and wellness, history, history-AP, honors algebra, honors English, honors geometry, honors U.S. history, honors world history, jazz band, jazz dance, journalism, language-AP, languages, Latin, Latin American literature, linguistics, literature and composition-AP, literature by women, marine biology, mathematics, Middle Eastern history, music, music theory, music theory-AP, oceanography, photography, physical education, physical fitness, physics, poetry, pre-calculus, psychology, religion, Russian history, science, senior project, set design, Shakespeare, short story, Spanish, Spanish language-AP, Spanish literature, Spanish literature-AP, Spanish-AP, speech, speech communications, statistics-AP, tap dance, theater, trigonometry, U.S. government and politics-AP, U.S. history, U.S. history-AP, video, visual arts, Web site design, woodworking, world history, world history-AP, world religions, world wide web design, writing workshop, yearbook.

Graduation Requirements Arts and fine arts (art, music, dance, drama), English, foreign language, mathematics, physical education (includes health), science, senior project, social studies (includes history). Community service is required.

Special Academic Programs Advanced Placement exam preparation; honors section; independent study; term-away projects.

College Admission Counseling 145 students graduated in 2016; all went to college. Mean SAT critical reading: 615, mean SAT math: 628, mean SAT writing: 606, mean combined SAT: 1850, mean composite ACT: 27.

Student Life Upper grades have uniform requirement, student council, honor system. Discipline rests primarily with faculty.

Summer Programs Enrichment, ESL, sports, art/fine arts, computer instruction programs offered; session focuses on recreation and sports camps; held both on and off campus; accepts boys and girls; open to students from other schools. 1,700 students usually enrolled. 2017 schedule: June 20 to July 29. Application deadline: May 1.

Tuition and Aid Day student tuition: $28,120; 5-day tuition and room/board: $37,790. Tuition installment plan (Key Tuition Payment Plan, monthly payment plans, individually arranged payment plans). Need-based scholarship grants available. In 2016–17, 28% of upper-school students received aid. Total amount of financial aid awarded in 2016–17: $3,340,390.

Admissions Traditional secondary-level entrance grade is 9. For fall 2016, 377 students applied for upper-level admission, 75 were accepted, 51 enrolled. ISEE required. Deadline for receipt of application materials: December 4. Application fee required: $55. On-campus interview required.

Athletics Interscholastic: aquatics (boys, girls), baseball (b), basketball (b,g), cross-country running (b,g), equestrian sports (b,g), field hockey (g), football (b), golf (b,g), indoor track & field (b,g), lacrosse (b,g), soccer (b,g), softball (g), swimming and diving (b,g), tennis (b,g), volleyball (g), water polo (b,g), winter (indoor) track (b,g), wrestling (b); coed interscholastic: cheering, equestrian sports, horseback riding, indoor track & field, squash, track and field; coed intramural: badminton, ballet, dance, fencing, fitness, squash, ultimate Frisbee. 14 PE instructors, 92 coaches, 2 athletic trainers.

Computers Computers are regularly used in all classes. Computer network features include on-campus library services, online commercial services, Internet access, wireless campus network, Internet filtering or blocking technology. Campus intranet, student e-mail accounts, and computer access in designated common areas are available to students. Students grades are available online. The school has a published electronic and media policy.

Contact Steve Birdsall, Director of Enrollment Management. 443-544-7021. Fax: 443-544-7030. E-mail: sbirdsall@mcdonogh.org. Website: www.mcdonogh.org

THE McLEAN SCHOOL OF MARYLAND, INC.

8224 Lochinver Lane
Potomac, Maryland 20854

Head of School: Mr. Michael Saxenian

General Information Coeducational day college-preparatory and Latin, American Sign Language, robotics school. Grades K–12. Founded: 1954. Setting: suburban. Nearest major city is Washington, DC. 10-acre campus. 1 building on campus. Approved or accredited by Association of Independent Maryland Schools and Maryland Department of Education. Member of National Association of Independent Schools. Total enrollment: 355. Upper school average class size: 7. Upper school faculty-student ratio: 1:9. There are 175 required school days per year for Upper School students. Upper School students typically attend 5 days per week. The average school day consists of 7 hours.

Upper School Student Profile Grade 9: 50 students (29 boys, 21 girls); Grade 10: 33 students (18 boys, 15 girls); Grade 11: 31 students (19 boys, 12 girls); Grade 12: 36 students (21 boys, 15 girls).

Faculty School total: 90. In upper school: 10 men, 10 women; 12 have advanced degrees.

Subjects Offered Advanced Placement courses, all academic, American sign language, Latin, robotics, Spanish.

Graduation Requirements Art, English, foreign language, history, humanities, literature, mathematics, physical education (includes health), science, 40 hours of community services.

Special Academic Programs 9 Advanced Placement exams for which test preparation is offered; honors section; independent study; study at local college for college credit; domestic exchange program; academic accommodation for the gifted; remedial reading and/or remedial writing; remedial math; programs in English, mathematics for dyslexic students.

College Admission Counseling 25 students graduated in 2016; all went to college, including American University; Berklee College of Music; Brandeis University; Duke University; Smith College; Tulane University. Median SAT critical reading: 594, median SAT math: 567, median SAT writing: 566.

Student Life Upper grades have uniform requirement, student council, honor system. Discipline rests equally with students and faculty.

Summer Programs Remediation, enrichment, advancement programs offered; session focuses on academic and recreational; held on campus; accepts boys and girls; open to students from other schools. 350 students usually enrolled. 2017 schedule: June 19 to August 14. Application deadline: none.

Tuition and Aid Day student tuition: $29,990–$41,990. Tuition installment plan (monthly payment plans). Need-based scholarship grants available.

Admissions WISC or WAIS and Woodcock-Johnson required. Deadline for receipt of application materials: none. Application fee required. Interview required.

Athletics Interscholastic: basketball (boys, girls), cross-country running (b,g), fitness (b,g), lacrosse (b), soccer (b,g), softball (b), track and field (b,g), volleyball (g), wrestling (b,g). 4 PE instructors, 8 coaches, 1 athletic trainer.

Computers Computers are regularly used in all classes. Computer network features include on-campus library services, online commercial services, Internet access, wireless campus network. Campus intranet and student e-mail accounts are available to students. Students grades are available online.

Contact Ms. Cathy Patterson, Director of Admission. 240-395-0698. Fax: 301-299-1639. E-mail: cpatterson@mcleanschool.org. Website: www.mcleanschool.org

THE MEADOWS SCHOOL

8601 Scholar Lane
Las Vegas, Nevada 89128-7302

Head of School: Mr. Jeremy B. Gregersen

General Information Coeducational day college-preparatory and debate, foreign languages, science school. Grades PK–12. Founded: 1981. Setting: suburban. 40-acre campus. 11 buildings on campus. Approved or accredited by Northwest Association of Independent Schools and Nevada Department of Education. Member of National Association of Independent Schools and Secondary School Admission Test Board. Endowment: $15.9 million. Total enrollment: 871. Upper school average class size: 12. Upper school faculty-student ratio: 1:11. There are 181 required school days per year for Upper School students. Upper School students typically attend 5 days per week. The average school day consists of 7 hours.

Upper School Student Profile Grade 9: 64 students (34 boys, 30 girls); Grade 10: 58 students (27 boys, 31 girls); Grade 11: 59 students (28 boys, 31 girls); Grade 12: 66 students (26 boys, 40 girls).

Faculty School total: 92. In upper school: 21 men, 20 women; 33 have advanced degrees.

Subjects Offered Acting, Advanced Placement courses, advanced studio art-AP, anatomy and physiology, Ancient Greek, anthropology, art history-AP, band, banking, biology, biology-AP, calculus, calculus-AP, chemistry, chemistry-AP, chorus, composition, constitutional law, dance, economics, English language and composition-AP, English literature and composition-AP, European history, European history-AP, film studies, filmmaking, finance, forensics, French, French-AP, genetics, geometry, honors English, honors geometry, honors U.S. history, honors world history, human anatomy, instrumental music, international relations, journalism, keyboarding, language and composition, Latin, Latin-AP, literary genres, literature, military history, money management, music theater, music theory-AP, musical theater dance, philosophy, photography, physics, physics-AP, policy and value, pre-calculus, psychology-AP, religion, social justice, Spanish, Spanish language-AP, Spanish literature, Spanish literature-AP, Spanish-AP, sports medicine, statistics, statistics-AP, strings, studio art, studio art-AP, technical theater, technology, theater production, trigonometry, U.S. government, U.S. government and politics-AP, U.S. history, U.S. history-AP, world history, world history-AP, yearbook.

Graduation Requirements American literature, ancient world history, art, biology, English, English composition, English literature, European history, foreign language, geometry, mathematics, physical education (includes health), physics, pre-calculus, science, social studies (includes history), technical skills, U.S. government, U.S. history, seniors have a 24-hour per semester community service requirement, grades 9-11 have a 16-hour per semester community service requirement.

Special Academic Programs 26 Advanced Placement exams for which test preparation is offered; honors section; academic accommodation for the gifted, the musically talented, and the artistically talented.

College Admission Counseling 60 students graduated in 2016; all went to college, including Boston University; The University of Arizona; University of California, Los Angeles; University of Nevada, Las Vegas; University of Nevada, Reno; University of Southern California. Median SAT critical reading: 640, median SAT math: 670, median SAT writing: 670, median combined SAT: 1980, median composite ACT: 29. 70% scored over 600 on SAT critical reading, 86% scored over 600 on SAT math, 88% scored over 600 on SAT writing, 88% scored over 1800 on combined SAT, 79% scored over 26 on composite ACT.

Student Life Upper grades have uniform requirement, student council, honor system. Discipline rests equally with students and faculty.

Summer Programs Enrichment, sports, art/fine arts programs offered; session focuses on enrichment; held on campus; accepts boys and girls; open to students from other schools. 50 students usually enrolled. 2017 schedule: May 30 to July 1. Application deadline: May 28.

Tuition and Aid Day student tuition: $23,375. Tuition installment plan (Insured Tuition Payment Plan, monthly payment plans, individually arranged payment plans, 2-payment plan, 70% by July 15 and 30% by February 15, 10 monthly payment plan using electronic withdrawal only). Need-based scholarship grants available. In 2016–17, 12% of upper-school students received aid. Total amount of financial aid awarded in 2016–17: $486,845.

Admissions Traditional secondary-level entrance grade is 9. For fall 2016, 82 students applied for upper-level admission, 39 were accepted, 19 enrolled. ERB, ISEE, PSAT or SSAT required. Deadline for receipt of application materials: none. Application fee required: $100. On-campus interview recommended.

Athletics Interscholastic: baseball (boys), basketball (b,g), bowling (b,g), cheering (g), cross-country running (b,g), football (b), softball (g), tennis (b,g), track and field (b,g), volleyball (g); coed interscholastic: golf, soccer. 1 athletic trainer.

Computers Computers are regularly used in all academic, art, college planning, desktop publishing, economics, English, foreign language, French, geography, graphic design, history, independent study, introduction to technology, journalism, library, mathematics, music, news writing, photography, photojournalism, programming, publications, publishing, science, speech, technology, yearbook classes. Computer network features include on-campus library services, online commercial services, Internet access, wireless campus network, Internet filtering or blocking technology, SmartBoards in all classrooms, 5 iPad carts, 6 laptop carts, 10 Chromebooks carts, course syllabus and homework available online. Campus intranet, student e-mail accounts, and computer access in designated common areas are available to students. Students grades are available online. The school has a published electronic and media policy.

Contact Mrs. Laura Ommen, Admissions Coordinator/Office of Advancement. 702-254-1610 Ext. 5928. Fax: 702-363-5298. E-mail: lommen@themeadowsschool.org. Website: http://www.themeadowsschool.org

MEMORIAL HALL SCHOOL

2501 Central Parkway Ste A-19
Houston, Texas 77092

Head of School: Mrs. Kimberly Aurich Taylor

General Information Coeducational day college-preparatory, general academic, and bilingual studies school. Grades 6–12. Founded: 1966. Setting: urban. 1 building on campus. Approved or accredited by Southern Association of Colleges and Schools, Southern Association of Independent Schools, Texas Education Agency, and Texas Department of Education. Total enrollment: 91. Upper school average class size: 14. Upper school faculty-student ratio: 1:14. Upper School students typically attend 4 days per week. The average school day consists of 7 hours and 30 minutes.

Faculty School total: 11. In upper school: 2 men, 9 women; 3 have advanced degrees.

Subjects Offered Algebra, American history, art, biology, business mathematics, business skills, chemistry, computer science, economics, English, ESL, fine arts, geography, geometry, government/civics, health, history, journalism, mathematics, physical education, physics, psychology, science, social sciences, social studies, sociology, Spanish, trigonometry, world history.

Graduation Requirements Arts and crafts, arts and fine arts (art, music, dance, drama), business skills (includes word processing), computer science, English, foreign language, mathematics, physical education (includes health), science, social sciences, social studies (includes history), community service, foreign credit accepted upon completion.

Special Academic Programs Study at local college for college credit; remedial reading and/or remedial writing; remedial math; programs in English, mathematics, general development for dyslexic students; special instructional classes for students with learning disabilities, Attention Deficit Disorder, and dyslexia; ESL (85 students enrolled).

College Admission Counseling 24 students graduated in 2015; 22 went to college, including Houston Community College; Sam Houston State University; St. Thomas University; Texas A&M University; The University of Texas at Austin; University of Houston. Other: 2 went to work.

Student Life Upper grades have uniform requirement, student council, honor system. Discipline rests equally with students and faculty.

Tuition and Aid Day student tuition: $13,700. Tuition installment plan (monthly payment plans, individually arranged payment plans). Tuition reduction for siblings available. In 2015–16, 5% of upper-school students received aid.

Admissions Traditional secondary-level entrance grade is 9. Deadline for receipt of application materials: none. Application fee required: $300. Interview required.

Athletics Interscholastic: aerobics (boys, girls), aerobics/dance (b,g), bowling (b,g), fitness (b,g), fitness walking (b,g), jump rope (b,g), paddle tennis (b,g), yoga (b,g); coed interscholastic: bowling, paddle tennis; coed intramural: dance, outdoor activities, physical fitness. 2 PE instructors.

Computers Computers are regularly used in all academic, basic skills, foreign language classes. Computer resources include wireless campus network. Campus intranet is available to students. The school has a published electronic and media policy.

Contact Mrs. Kimberly Aurich Taylor, Director. 713-688-5566. Fax: 713-956-9751. E-mail: memhallsch@aol.com. Website: www.memorialhall.org

MEMPHIS CATHOLIC HIGH SCHOOL AND MIDDLE SCHOOL

61 North McLean Boulevard
Memphis, Tennessee 38104-2644

Head of School: Mr. Kevin Alexander Kimberly

General Information Coeducational day college-preparatory and religious studies school, affiliated with Roman Catholic Church. Grades 7–12. Founded: 1954. Setting: urban. 4-acre campus. 1 building on campus. Approved or accredited by Southern Association of Colleges and Schools and Tennessee Department of Education. Total enrollment: 275. Upper school average class size: 18. Upper school faculty-student ratio: 1:15. There are 200 required school days per year for Upper School students. Upper School students typically attend 5 days per week. The average school day consists of 7 hours and 40 minutes.

Upper School Student Profile 30% of students are Roman Catholic.

Faculty School total: 23. In upper school: 12 men, 10 women; 10 have advanced degrees.

Subjects Offered ACT preparation, all academic.

Graduation Requirements Acceptance into a four-year college or university (whether or not a student chooses to attend), Four years/credits of Theology, Two 1/2 credits of ACT Prep.

Special Academic Programs Honors section.

College Admission Counseling 35 students graduated in 2016; all went to college, including Austin Peay State University; Christian Brothers University; Mississippi State University; Spring Hill College; University of Memphis; Xavier University of Louisiana.

Student Life Upper grades have uniform requirement, student council, honor system. Discipline rests primarily with faculty. Attendance at religious services is required.

Tuition and Aid Tuition installment plan (SMART Tuition Payment Plan). Tuition reduction for siblings, merit scholarship grants, need-based scholarship grants, paying campus jobs available. In 2016–17, 100% of upper-school students received aid.

Admissions Traditional secondary-level entrance grade is 9. High School Placement Test required. Deadline for receipt of application materials: none. Application fee required: $30. On-campus interview recommended.

Athletics Interscholastic: baseball (boys), basketball (b,g), cross-country running (b,g), football (b), golf (b,g), soccer (b,g), softball (g), track and field (b,g), volleyball (b,g); coed interscholastic: cheering, physical fitness. 2 PE instructors, 2 coaches.

Computers Computers are regularly used in all academic classes. Computer network features include Internet access, wireless campus network, Internet filtering or blocking technology. Student e-mail accounts and computer access in designated common areas are available to students. Students grades are available online. The school has a published electronic and media policy.

Contact Mrs. Debra Robinson, Vice Principal. 901-276-1221 Ext. 15. Fax: 901-725-1447. E-mail: drobinson@memphiscatholic.org. Website: www.memphiscatholic.org

MEMPHIS UNIVERSITY SCHOOL

6191 Park Avenue
Memphis, Tennessee 38119-5399

Head of School: Mr. Ellis L. Haguewood

General Information Boys' day college-preparatory school. Grades 7–12. Founded: 1893. Setting: suburban. 94-acre campus. 8 buildings on campus. Approved or accredited by Southern Association of Colleges and Schools and Southern Association of Independent Schools. Member of National Association of Independent Schools. Endowment: $33.1 million. Total enrollment: 633. Upper school average class size: 15. Upper school faculty-student ratio: 1:8. There are 176 required school days per year for Upper School students. Upper School students typically attend 5 days per week. The average school day consists of 7 hours.

Upper School Student Profile Grade 9: 126 students (126 boys); Grade 10: 99 students (99 boys); Grade 11: 105 students (105 boys); Grade 12: 107 students (107 boys).

Faculty School total: 78. In upper school: 44 men, 14 women; 53 have advanced degrees.

Subjects Offered 3-dimensional art, 3-dimensional design, advanced biology, advanced chemistry, advanced math, Advanced Placement courses, African literature, American history, American history-AP, analysis and differential calculus, analysis of data, analytic geometry, baseball, Basic programming, basketball, Bible studies, bowling, business applications, choir, chorus, cinematography, classics, college admission preparation, college planning, communication skills, community service, computer art, computer literacy, computer music, computer resources, computer studies, concert band, film, film appreciation, film history, fitness, French language-AP, French-AP, general science, geology, golf, government/civics-AP, graphics, guitar, health and wellness, Hispanic literature, history-AP, honors English, honors geometry, honors U.S. history, illustration, instrumental music, Internet research, introduction to digital multitrack recording techniques, Irish literature, jazz band, language, language-AP, Latin-AP, leadership and service, learning strategies, library research, literary magazine, literature and composition-AP, literature-AP, math applications, media production, mentorship program, microbiology, model United Nations, modern European history-AP, modern politics, modern Western civilization, music history, music technology, music theory-AP, musical theater, New Testament, newspaper, nutrition, oral communications, orchestra, painting, peer counseling, photography, piano, play production, printmaking, publishing, research, robotics, SAT/ACT preparation, science research, set design, Shakespeare, short story, social psychology, Spanish language-AP, Spanish literature-AP, speech, sports, sports team management, stagecraft, statistics, statistics-AP, student government, technical theater, theater arts, track and field, transition mathematics, U.S. government, U.S. government and politics-AP, U.S. literature, video film production, vocal ensemble, weight training, wellness, wrestling, writing, yearbook.

Graduation Requirements Arts and fine arts (art, music, dance, drama), English, foreign language, mathematics, physical education (includes health), religion (includes Bible studies and theology), science, social sciences, social studies (includes history).

Special Academic Programs 18 Advanced Placement exams for which test preparation is offered; honors section; independent study; term-away projects; study abroad; academic accommodation for the gifted, the musically talented, and the artistically talented; remedial reading and/or remedial writing; remedial math.

College Admission Counseling 109 students graduated in 2016; all went to college, including Rhodes College; The University of Alabama in Huntsville; The University of North Carolina at Chapel Hill; The University of Tennessee; University of Mississippi; Vanderbilt University. Mean SAT critical reading: 616, mean SAT math: 631, mean SAT writing: 615, mean combined SAT: 1862, mean composite ACT: 30. 64% scored over 600 on SAT critical reading, 64% scored over 600 on SAT math, 58%

scored over 600 on SAT writing, 62% scored over 1800 on combined SAT, 87% scored over 26 on composite ACT.

Student Life Upper grades have specified standards of dress, student council, honor system. Discipline rests equally with students and faculty.

Summer Programs Remediation, enrichment, advancement, sports, art/fine arts, computer instruction programs offered; session focuses on academics and athletics; held on campus; accepts boys; open to students from other schools. 460 students usually enrolled. 2017 schedule: June 5 to July 28. Application deadline: none.

Tuition and Aid Day student tuition: $20,350. Tuition installment plan (FACTS Tuition Payment Plan, monthly payment plans). Need-based scholarship grants available. In 2016–17, 30% of upper-school students received aid. Total amount of financial aid awarded in 2016–17: $2,500,000.

Admissions Traditional secondary-level entrance grade is 9. For fall 2016, 57 students applied for upper-level admission, 50 were accepted, 37 enrolled. ISEE required. Deadline for receipt of application materials: December 10. Application fee required: $50. On-campus interview recommended.

Athletics Interscholastic: baseball, basketball, cross-country running, fencing, football, golf, lacrosse, soccer, swimming and diving, tennis, track and field, trap and skeet, water polo, weight training, wrestling; intramural: basketball, table tennis. 5 PE instructors, 41 coaches, 2 athletic trainers.

Computers Computers are regularly used in design, desktop publishing, independent study, literary magazine, multimedia, photography, theater arts, writing classes. Computer network features include on-campus library services, online commercial services, Internet access, wireless campus network, Internet filtering or blocking technology, online learning-management system. Campus intranet, student e-mail accounts, and computer access in designated common areas are available to students. Students grades are available online. The school has a published electronic and media policy.

Contact Mrs. Peggy E. Williamson, Director of Admissions. 901-260-1349. Fax: 901-260-1301. E-mail: peggy.williamson@musowls.org. Website: www.musowls.org

MENLO SCHOOL

50 Valparaiso Avenue
Atherton, California 94027

Head of School: Mr. Than Healy

General Information Coeducational day college-preparatory school. Grades 6–12. Founded: 1915. Setting: suburban. Nearest major city is San Jose. 35-acre campus. 23 buildings on campus. Approved or accredited by California Association of Independent Schools, Western Association of Schools and Colleges, and California Department of Education. Member of National Association of Independent Schools. Endowment: $37.7 million. Total enrollment: 795. Upper school average class size: 10. Upper school faculty-student ratio: 1:10. There are 170 required school days per year for Upper School students. Upper School students typically attend 5 days per week. The average school day consists of 6 hours and 30 minutes.

Faculty School total: 111. In upper school: 34 men, 39 women; 58 have advanced degrees.

Subjects Offered 20th century American writers, advanced biology, advanced chemistry, advanced computer applications, advanced math, algebra, American history, American history-AP, American literature, American literature-AP, analytic geometry, anatomy and physiology, ancient world history, art, art history, art-AP, Asian studies, biology, biology-AP, British literature-AP, calculus, calculus-AP, chemistry, chemistry-AP, chorus, computer graphics, computer literacy, computer multimedia, computer programming, computer science, computer science-AP, creative writing, dance, debate, drama, earth science, economics, economics-AP, engineering, English, English language and composition-AP, English literature, English literature-AP, English-AP, environmental science, ethics, European history, European history-AP, film studies, fine arts, French, French as a second language, French language-AP, French literature-AP, French-AP, freshman seminar, geometry, government and politics-AP, history, honors English, honors geometry, honors U.S. history, intro to computers, Japanese, jazz band, jazz dance, jazz ensemble, journalism, Latin, Latin-AP, law, literature-AP, Mandarin, mathematics, mathematics-AP, methods of research, modern European history, modern world history, multimedia, music, music theory, music theory-AP, music-AP, musical productions, newspaper, orchestra, performing arts, philosophy, photography, physical education, physics, physics-AP, play production, poetry, pre-calculus, rhetoric, robotics, science, science fiction, science research, senior project, Shakespeare, society and culture, Spanish, Spanish language-AP, Spanish literature-AP, Spanish-AP, statistics, statistics-AP, student government, student publications, studio art, studio art-AP, swimming, U.S. government and politics-AP, U.S. history-AP, video film production, wellness, women's literature, world history, world religions, writing, yearbook.

Graduation Requirements Arts and fine arts (art, music, dance, drama), English, foreign language, mathematics, physical education (includes health), science, social studies (includes history), Freshman seminar, Knight School, senior project (3-week project at the end of senior year). Community service is required.

Special Academic Programs Advanced Placement exam preparation; honors section; independent study.

College Admission Counseling 145 students graduated in 2016; all went to college, including Dartmouth College; Duke University; Harvard University; Stanford University; University of California, Berkeley; University of Southern California.

Other: 1 entered a postgraduate year. Median SAT critical reading: 680, median SAT math: 710, median SAT writing: 710. 74% scored over 600 on SAT critical reading, 79% scored over 600 on SAT math, 77% scored over 600 on SAT writing, 81% scored over 1800 on combined SAT, 90% scored over 26 on composite ACT.

Student Life Upper grades have student council. Discipline rests equally with students and faculty.

Summer Programs Enrichment programs offered; session focuses on academic enrichment; held on campus; accepts boys and girls; open to students from other schools. 70 students usually enrolled. 2017 schedule: June 15 to July 2. Application deadline: April 30.

Tuition and Aid Day student tuition: $42,830. Tuition installment plan (Key Tuition Payment Plan). Need-based scholarship grants, paying campus jobs available. In 2016–17, 20% of upper-school students received aid. Total amount of financial aid awarded in 2016–17: $5,600,000.

Admissions Traditional secondary-level entrance grade is 9. For fall 2016, 462 students applied for upper-level admission, 98 were accepted, 76 enrolled. ISEE, SSAT or TOEFL required. Deadline for receipt of application materials: January 12. Application fee required: $90. On-campus interview required.

Athletics Interscholastic: aerobics/dance (girls), baseball (b), basketball (b,g), cross-country running (b,g), dance (g), football (b), golf (b,g), lacrosse (b,g), soccer (b,g), softball (g), swimming and diving (b,g), tennis (b,g), track and field (b,g), volleyball (b,g), water polo (b,g); coed interscholastic: aerobics/dance, dance, martial arts, yoga. 67 coaches, 2 athletic trainers.

Computers Computers are regularly used in English, foreign language, history, journalism, mathematics, media arts, multimedia, newspaper, science, yearbook classes. Computer network features include on-campus library services, online commercial services, Internet access, wireless campus network, Internet filtering or blocking technology. Student e-mail accounts and computer access in designated common areas are available to students.

Contact Ms. Melanie Rossi, Admissions Assistant. 650-330-2000 Ext. 2435. E-mail: melanie.rossi@menloschool.org. Website: www.menloschool.org

MERCERSBURG ACADEMY

300 East Seminary Street
Mercersburg, Pennsylvania 17236

Head of School: Mrs. Katherine M. Titus

General Information Coeducational boarding and day college-preparatory school. Boarding grades 9–PG, day grades 9–11. Founded: 1893. Setting: small town. Nearest major city is Washington, DC. Students are housed in single-sex dormitories. 300-acre campus. 30 buildings on campus. Approved or accredited by Middle States Association of Colleges and Schools and Pennsylvania Department of Education. Member of National Association of Independent Schools and Secondary School Admission Test Board. Endowment: $244 million. Total enrollment: 430. Upper school average class size: 12. Upper school faculty-student ratio: 1:5. Upper School students typically attend 5 days per week. The average school day consists of 7 hours.

Upper School Student Profile Grade 9: 71 students (38 boys, 33 girls); Grade 10: 123 students (69 boys, 54 girls); Grade 11: 122 students (56 boys, 66 girls); Grade 12: 108 students (56 boys, 52 girls); Postgraduate: 18 students (10 boys, 8 girls). 85% of students are boarding students. 27% are state residents. 28 states are represented in upper school student body. 23% are international students. International students from China, Germany, Ghana, Republic of Korea, Spain, and Viet Nam; 45 other countries represented in student body.

Faculty School total: 104. In upper school: 64 men, 33 women; 75 have advanced degrees; 60 reside on campus.

Subjects Offered 20th century American writers, 20th century world history, 3-dimensional art, 3-dimensional design, ACT preparation, acting, advanced biology, advanced chemistry, advanced computer applications, advanced math, Advanced Placement courses, advanced studio art-AP, advertising design, African American history, African dance, African drumming, algebra, American Civil War, American history, American history-AP, American literature, American literature-AP, anatomy, anatomy and physiology, aquatics, art, art history, art history-AP, art-AP, Asian history, astronomy, audio visual/media, backpacking, ballet, ballet technique, band, baseball, Basic programming, basketball, Bible as literature, biology, biology-AP, botany, British literature-AP, Buddhism, calculus, calculus-AP, ceramics, chemistry, chemistry-AP, Chinese, choral music, chorus, comparative government and politics-AP, computer graphics, computer math, computer programming-AP, computer science, computer science-AP, concert band, creative writing, dance, digital art, drama, drawing, economics-AP, English, English literature, English literature and composition-AP, environmental science-AP, ethics, European history, European history-AP, film and literature, film studies, fine arts, French, French language-AP, French literature-AP, genetics, geometry, German, German-AP, government and politics-AP, health, history, history of music, honors algebra, honors English, honors geometry, honors U.S. history, honors world history, humanities, interdisciplinary studies, Islamic studies, jazz band, jazz dance, jazz ensemble, journalism, lab science, Latin, Latin-AP, mathematics, modern European history-AP, music, music composition, music history, musical theater dance, orchestra, painting, personal fitness, physical education, physical science, physics, physics-AP, poetry, public speaking, religion, robotics, SAT preparation, science, sculpture, social studies, Spanish, Spanish language-AP, speech, stagecraft,

statistics-AP, strings, studio art, swimming, tennis, theater, theater design and production, travel, trigonometry, U.S. constitutional history, U.S. government, U.S. government and politics, U.S. government and politics-AP, U.S. history, U.S. history-AP, U.S. literature, United States government-AP, vocal music, world history, world history-AP, world literature, yoga.

Graduation Requirements Arts and fine arts (art, music, dance, drama), English, foreign language, history, mathematics, physical education (includes health), religion (includes Bible studies and theology), science, participation in sports, performing arts, or other activities.

Special Academic Programs Advanced Placement exam preparation; honors section; independent study; term-away projects; study abroad; academic accommodation for the gifted, the musically talented, and the artistically talented.

College Admission Counseling 127 students graduated in 2016; all went to college, including Boston University; Bucknell University; Georgetown University; Northwestern University; United States Naval Academy; University of Pennsylvania.

Student Life Upper grades have specified standards of dress, student council, honor system. Discipline rests primarily with students.

Summer Programs Enrichment, ESL, sports, art/fine arts, rigorous outdoor training programs offered; session focuses on enrichment; held on campus; accepts boys and girls; open to students from other schools. 1,500 students usually enrolled. 2017 schedule: June 10 to August 22. Application deadline: none.

Tuition and Aid Day student tuition: $39,050; 7-day tuition and room/board: $56,350. Tuition installment plan (Insured Tuition Payment Plan, Key Tuition Payment Plan, monthly payment plans). Merit scholarship grants, need-based scholarship grants, need-based loans available. In 2016–17, 50% of upper-school students received aid; total upper-school merit-scholarship money awarded: $1,138,175. Total amount of financial aid awarded in 2016–17: $6,178,725.

Admissions Traditional secondary-level entrance grade is 9. For fall 2016, 689 students applied for upper-level admission, 289 were accepted, 155 enrolled. ACT, PSAT and SAT for applicants to grade 11 and 12, SAT, SSAT or TOEFL required. Deadline for receipt of application materials: January 15. Application fee required: $50. On-campus interview recommended.

Athletics Interscholastic: baseball (boys), basketball (b,g), cross-country running (b,g), diving (b,g), field hockey (g), football (b), lacrosse (b,g), running (b,g), soccer (b,g), softball (g), squash (b,g), swimming and diving (b,g), tennis (b,g), track and field (b,g), volleyball (g), winter (indoor) track (b,g), wrestling (b); coed interscholastic: alpine skiing, golf; coed intramural: aerobics/dance, alpine skiing, backpacking, ballet, bicycling, canoeing/kayaking, climbing, dance, equestrian sports, fitness, freestyle skiing, Frisbee, golf, hiking/backpacking, horseback riding, kayaking, martial arts, modern dance, mountain biking, outdoor activities, outdoor adventure, outdoor education, outdoor recreation, outdoor skills, outdoors, paddling, physical fitness, physical training, rafting, rappelling, rock climbing, skiing (downhill), snowboarding, strength & conditioning, table tennis, ultimate Frisbee, wall climbing, weight lifting, weight training, wilderness survival, yoga. 4 PE instructors, 24 coaches, 2 athletic trainers.

Computers Computers are regularly used in art, English, foreign language, history, mathematics, music, science classes. Computer network features include on-campus library services, online commercial services, Internet access, wireless campus network. Student e-mail accounts and computer access in designated common areas are available to students. The school has a published electronic and media policy.

Contact Mr. Quentin R. McDowell, Assistant Head of School for Enrollment. 717-328-6173. Fax: 717-328-6319. E-mail: admission@mercersburg.edu. Website: www.mercersburg.edu

MERCHISTON CASTLE SCHOOL

Colinton
Edinburgh EH13 0PU, United Kingdom

Head of School: Mr. Andrew R. Hunter

General Information Boys' boarding and day college-preparatory, arts, religious studies, and technology school. Ungraded, ages 8–18. Founded: 1833. Setting: small town. Students are housed in single-sex dormitories. 100-acre campus. 11 buildings on campus. Approved or accredited by Boarding Schools Association (UK) and Independent Schools Council (UK). Language of instruction: English. Upper school average class size: 9. Upper school faculty-student ratio: 1:7. The average school day consists of 9 hours.

Upper School Student Profile 70% of students are boarding students.

Faculty School total: 82. In upper school: 41 men, 38 women; 32 have advanced degrees; 30 reside on campus.

Subjects Offered Algebra, art, biology, calculus, career education, chemistry, Chinese, computer science, creative writing, design, drama, Dutch, economics, electronics, English, English as a foreign language, English literature, European history, French, geography, geometry, German, government/civics, grammar, history, Italian, Japanese, Latin, Mandarin, mathematics, music, physical education, physics, political thought, politics, Portuguese, religion, Russian, science, social studies, Spanish, trigonometry, world history.

Graduation Requirements Any three A-level courses.

Special Academic Programs Independent study; term-away projects; study at local college for college credit; study abroad; academic accommodation for the gifted, the musically talented, and the artistically talented; remedial reading and/or remedial writing; remedial math; programs in English, mathematics, general development for dyslexic students; special instructional classes for deaf students, blind students; ESL.

Student Life Upper grades have specified standards of dress, student council, honor system. Discipline rests equally with students and faculty.

Tuition and Aid Day student tuition: £4700–£7570; 5-day tuition and room/board: £6180–£6495; 7-day tuition and room/board: £6550–£10,220. Tuition reduction for siblings, bursaries available.

Admissions Traditional secondary-level entrance grade is 9. Traditional secondary-level entrance age is 13. Achievement/Aptitude/Writing, common entrance examinations and school's own exam required. Deadline for receipt of application materials: none. Application fee required: £100. Interview recommended.

Athletics Interscholastic: badminton (boys), ball hockey (b), basketball (b), boxing (b), cricket (b), cross-country running (b), curling (b), fencing (b), Fives (b), football (b), freestyle skiing (b), golf (b), hockey (b), indoor soccer (b), riflery (b), rugby (b), sailing (b), scuba diving (b), skiing (cross-country) (b), skiing (downhill) (b), soccer (b), squash (b), swimming and diving (b), table tennis (b), tennis (b), track and field (b), wall climbing (b); intramural: archery (b), badminton (b), ball hockey (b), basketball (b), bicycling (b), boxing (b), canoeing/kayaking (b), climbing (b), cricket (b), cross-country running (b), curling (b), diving (b), fencing (b), Fives (b), football (b), freestyle skiing (b), golf (b), gymnastics (b), hockey (b), indoor soccer (b), jogging (b), judo (b), life saving (b), marksmanship (b), martial arts (b), mountain biking (b), outdoor activities (b), outdoor education (b), outdoor skills (b), physical fitness (b), riflery (b), rock climbing (b), rugby (b), sailing (b), scuba diving (b), skiing (cross-country) (b), skiing (downhill) (b), soccer (b), squash (b), strength & conditioning (b), swimming and diving (b), table tennis (b), tennis (b), track and field (b), volleyball (b), wall climbing (b). 4 PE instructors, 2 coaches.

Computers Computers are regularly used in all academic, design, music classes. Computer network features include Internet access, wireless campus network, Internet filtering or blocking technology. Campus intranet, student e-mail accounts, and computer access in designated common areas are available to students. The school has a published electronic and media policy.

Contact Mrs. Kay Wilson, Admissions Manager. 44-131-312-2201. Fax: 44-131-312-2201. E-mail: admissions@merchiston.co.uk. Website: www.merchiston.co.uk

MERCY HIGH SCHOOL

1740 Randolph Road
Middletown, Connecticut 06457-5155

Head of School: Sr. Mary McCarthy, RSM

General Information Girls' day college-preparatory, arts, and religious studies school, affiliated with Roman Catholic Church. Grades 9–12. Distance learning grades 9–12. Founded: 1963. Setting: rural. Nearest major city is Hartford. 26-acre campus. 1 building on campus. Approved or accredited by National Catholic Education Association, New England Association of Schools and Colleges, and Connecticut Department of Education. Total enrollment: 573. Upper school average class size: 21. Upper school faculty-student ratio: 1:13. There are 172 required school days per year for Upper School students. Upper School students typically attend 5 days per week. The average school day consists of 6 hours and 30 minutes.

Upper School Student Profile Grade 9: 135 students (135 girls); Grade 10: 134 students (134 girls); Grade 11: 125 students (125 girls); Grade 12: 139 students (139 girls). 78% of students are Roman Catholic.

Faculty School total: 45. In upper school: 9 men, 36 women; 40 have advanced degrees.

Subjects Offered Computer science, computer science-AP, digital music.

Graduation Requirements Civics, computer applications, technology, U.S. history, 100 hours of community service.

Special Academic Programs 16 Advanced Placement exams for which test preparation is offered; honors section; independent study; study at local college for college credit.

College Admission Counseling 158 students graduated in 2016; 156 went to college, including Assumption College; Central Connecticut State University; Fairfield University; Quinnipiac University; University of Connecticut; University of Vermont. Other: 1 entered a postgraduate year, 1 had other specific plans. Median SAT critical reading: 530, median SAT math: 500, median SAT writing: 525, median combined SAT: 1565, median composite ACT: 23. 21% scored over 600 on SAT critical reading, 22% scored over 600 on SAT math, 25% scored over 600 on SAT writing, 18% scored over 1800 on combined SAT, 29% scored over 26 on composite ACT.

Student Life Upper grades have uniform requirement, student council. Discipline rests primarily with faculty. Attendance at religious services is required.

Tuition and Aid Day student tuition: $13,000–$13,500. Tuition installment plan (FACTS Tuition Payment Plan, individually arranged payment plans). Tuition reduction for siblings, merit scholarship grants, need-based scholarship grants available.

Admissions Traditional secondary-level entrance grade is 9. For fall 2016, 284 students applied for upper-level admission, 254 were accepted, 158 enrolled. High School Placement Test (closed version) from Scholastic Testing Service required. Deadline for receipt of application materials: none. Application fee required: $50.

Athletics Interscholastic: basketball, cheering, cross-country running, diving, field hockey, gatorball (b), golf, gymnastics, ice hockey, indoor track, lacrosse, soccer,

softball, swimming and diving, tennis, track and field, volleyball, winter (indoor) track. 1 PE instructor, 33 coaches, 1 athletic trainer.

Computers Computers are regularly used in all classes. Computer network features include on-campus library services, Internet access, wireless campus network, Internet filtering or blocking technology. Campus intranet, student e-mail accounts, and computer access in designated common areas are available to students. Students grades are available online.

Contact Mrs. Diane Santostefano, Director of Admissions. 860-346-6659 Ext. 115. Fax: 860-344-9887. E-mail: dsantostefano@mercyhigh.com. Website: www.mercyhigh.com

MERCY HIGH SCHOOL

29300 West Eleven Mile Road
Farmington Hills, Michigan 48336-1409

Head of School: Dr. Cheryl Delaney Kreger

General Information Girls' day college-preparatory, arts, religious studies, and technology school, affiliated with Roman Catholic Church. Grades 9–12. Founded: 1945. Setting: suburban. Nearest major city is Detroit. 25-acre campus. 1 building on campus. Approved or accredited by Mercy Secondary Education Association, North Central Association of Colleges and Schools, Southern Association of Colleges and Schools, and Michigan Department of Education. Endowment: $7 million. Upper school average class size: 25. Upper school faculty-student ratio: 1:15. There are 195 required school days per year for Upper School students. Upper School students typically attend 5 days per week. The average school day consists of 6 hours and 37 minutes.

Upper School Student Profile Grade 9: 197 students (197 girls); Grade 10: 153 students (153 girls); Grade 11: 174 students (174 girls); Grade 12: 206 students (206 girls). 80% of students are Roman Catholic.

Faculty School total: 48. In upper school: 14 men, 34 women; 40 have advanced degrees.

Subjects Offered 20th century American writers, acting, advanced biology, advanced chemistry, advanced computer applications, advanced math, Advanced Placement courses, advanced studio art-AP, algebra, American government, American history, American history-AP, American literature, American literature-AP, anatomy, anatomy and physiology, art, art education, arts, athletics, Bible as literature, Bible studies, biology, biology-AP, British literature, broadcasting, business, business skills, calculus, calculus-AP, Catholic belief and practice, ceramics, chemistry, chemistry-AP, child development, Chinese, choral music, Christian testament, Christianity, community service, computer art, computer literacy, computer science, contemporary issues, creative writing, critical studies in film, design, drama, dramatic arts, drawing and design, economics, English, English literature, English literature and composition-AP, entrepreneurship, European history, expository writing, film and literature, fine arts, foreign language, French, French language-AP, French-AP, geometry, government and politics-AP, government/civics, health, health education, history, history-AP, home economics, honors algebra, honors English, honors geometry, honors U.S. history, human anatomy, journalism, Latin, life skills, literature by women, mathematics, media, microbiology, music, musical theater, orchestra, performing arts, personal fitness, photography, physical education, physics, poetry, pre-algebra, pre-calculus, psychology, relationships, religion, religious studies, science, Shakespeare, short story, social psychology, social studies, sociology, Spanish, Spanish language-AP, speech, speech and debate, speech and oral interpretations, stage design, statistics, student government, student publications, technology/design, theater, theology, trigonometry, U.S. government, U.S. government and politics, U.S. government and politics-AP, U.S. history, U.S. history-AP, United States government-AP, video and animation, video film production, visual and performing arts, vocal music, women's literature, world history, world literature, writing.

Graduation Requirements Arts and fine arts (art, music, dance, drama), computer science, English, mathematics, physical education (includes health), religion (includes Bible studies and theology), science, social studies (includes history), speech. Community service is required.

Special Academic Programs Advanced Placement exam preparation; honors section; independent study; study at local college for college credit.

College Admission Counseling 207 students graduated in 2016; all went to college, including Central Michigan University; Grand Valley State University; Michigan State University; University of Detroit Mercy; University of Michigan; Wayne State University. Mean composite ACT: 25, 30% scored over 26 on composite ACT.

Student Life Upper grades have uniform requirement, student council, honor system. Discipline rests primarily with faculty. Attendance at religious services is required.

Summer Programs Remediation, enrichment programs offered; session focuses on reading, mathematics, and grammar; held on campus; accepts boys and girls; open to students from other schools. 80 students usually enrolled.

Tuition and Aid Day student tuition: $5745. Tuition installment plan (monthly payment plans, individually arranged payment plans, 4-payment ($500 deposit) plan). Tuition reduction for siblings, paying campus jobs, need-based financial aid available. In 2016–17, 11% of upper-school students received aid. Total amount of financial aid awarded in 2016–17: $60,000.

Admissions Traditional secondary-level entrance grade is 9. High School Placement Test required. Deadline for receipt of application materials: none. Application fee required: $50. On-campus interview required.

Athletics Interscholastic: basketball, bowling, cross-country running, dance team, diving, equestrian sports, field hockey, figure skating, golf, ice hockey, lacrosse, skiing (downhill), soccer, softball, swimming and diving, tennis, track and field, volleyball. 2 PE instructors, 40 coaches, 1 athletic trainer.

Computers Computers are regularly used in all classes. Computer network features include on-campus library services, online commercial services, Internet access, wireless campus network, Internet filtering or blocking technology. Student e-mail accounts are available to students. Students grades are available online. The school has a published electronic and media policy.

Contact Kelly Stirling McSweeney, Admissions Director. 248-476-2484. Fax: 248-476-3691. E-mail: admissions@mhsmi.org. Website: www.mhsmi.org

MERCYHURST PREPARATORY SCHOOL

538 East Grandview Boulevard
Erie, Pennsylvania 16504-2697

Head of School: Mrs. Deborah A. Laughlin

General Information Coeducational day college-preparatory, arts, religious studies, technology, and International Baccalaureate level classes school, affiliated with Roman Catholic Church. Grades 9–12. Founded: 1926. Setting: urban. Students are housed in single-sex by floor dormitories. 7-acre campus. 1 building on campus. Approved or accredited by International Baccalaureate Organization, Middle States Association of Colleges and Schools, and Pennsylvania Department of Education. Total enrollment: 545. Upper school average class size: 23. Upper school faculty-student ratio: 1:14. There are 180 required school days per year for Upper School students. Upper School students typically attend 5 days per week. The average school day consists of 6 hours and 45 minutes.

Upper School Student Profile Grade 9: 111 students (47 boys, 64 girls); Grade 10: 139 students (58 boys, 81 girls); Grade 11: 153 students (66 boys, 87 girls); Grade 12: 142 students (49 boys, 93 girls). 22% of students are boarding students. 99% are state residents. 2 states are represented in upper school student body. 22% are international students. International students from China, Egypt, Italy, Kyrgyzstan, Serbia and Montenegro, and Viet Nam; 2 other countries represented in student body. 61% of students are Roman Catholic.

Faculty School total: 50. In upper school: 16 men, 34 women; 20 have advanced degrees.

Subjects Offered Accounting, advanced biology, advanced chemistry, advanced math, algebra, American Civil War, American government, American history, American literature, analysis and differential calculus, analysis of data, analytic geometry, anatomy and physiology, anthropology, art, art appreciation, art education, art history, arts, astronomy, athletic training, ballet, biology, British literature, British literature (honors), business skills, calculus, campus ministry, career exploration, ceramics, chemistry, chorus, Christian ethics, communications, community service, computer applications, computer programming, computer science, creative arts, dance, digital photography, drama, drama performance, drawing, drawing and design, earth science, English, English literature, environmental science, ethics, European history, expository writing, fine arts, French, geology, geometry, government/civics, guitar, health, Hebrew scripture, history, humanities, Internet, journalism, leadership, mathematics, multimedia, music, music appreciation, music history, music theory-AP, musical productions, orchestra, painting, photography, physical education, physics, physiology, piano, psychology, public speaking, publications, reading/study skills, religion, SAT preparation, SAT/ACT preparation, science, senior internship, set design, social studies, Spanish, speech, speech and debate, study skills, tap dance, technical theater, technology/design, theater, theater arts, theology, theory of knowledge, trigonometry, U.S. government, U.S. history, visual and performing arts, weight fitness, weightlifting, word processing, world cultures, world history, writing, yearbook.

Graduation Requirements Arts and fine arts (art, music, dance, drama), arts appreciation, business skills (includes word processing), computer science, creative arts, English, foreign language, health and wellness, mathematics, physical education (includes health), public speaking, religion (includes Bible studies and theology), science, social studies (includes history), technological applications, 25 service hours per year.

Special Academic Programs International Baccalaureate program; honors section; independent study; study at local college for college credit; academic accommodation for the gifted, the musically talented, and the artistically talented; remedial reading and/or remedial writing; remedial math; ESL (45 students enrolled).

College Admission Counseling 148 students graduated in 2016; 146 went to college, including Edinboro University of Pennsylvania; Gannon University; Indiana University of Pennsylvania; John Carroll University; Mercyhurst University; Penn State University Park. Other: 2 went to work. Median SAT critical reading: 535.

Student Life Upper grades have uniform requirement, student council, honor system. Discipline rests primarily with faculty. Attendance at religious services is required.

Summer Programs Remediation, enrichment, advancement, art/fine arts, computer instruction programs offered; session focuses on enrichment; held on campus; accepts boys and girls; open to students from other schools. 130 students usually enrolled. 2017 schedule: June 18 to August 10. Application deadline: June 1.

Tuition and Aid Day student tuition: $7300. Tuition installment plan (FACTS Tuition Payment Plan). Merit scholarship grants, need-based scholarship grants, creative arts scholarships, alumni scholarships, endowment scholarships available. In 2016–17, 51% of upper-school students received aid; total upper-school merit-scholarship money awarded: $89,950. Total amount of financial aid awarded in 2016–17: $578,050.

Admissions Traditional secondary-level entrance grade is 9. For fall 2016, 200 students applied for upper-level admission, 185 were accepted, 111 enrolled. Achievement tests, ACT, High School Placement Test or Iowa Tests of Basic Skills required. Deadline for receipt of application materials: none. Application fee required: $10.

Athletics Interscholastic: ballet (girls), baseball (b), basketball (b,g), bowling (g), cheering (g), crew (b,g), cross-country running (b,g), football (b), golf (b,g), modern dance (g), rowing (b,g), skiing (downhill) (g), soccer (b,g), softball (g), swimming and diving (b,g), tennis (b,g), track and field (b,g), volleyball (g); coed interscholastic: tennis, weight training; coed intramural: weight lifting, weight training. 2 PE instructors, 40 coaches, 1 athletic trainer.

Computers Computers are regularly used in all academic, college planning, data processing, design, desktop publishing, English, foreign language, graphic design, history, journalism, mathematics, media, newspaper, photography, photojournalism, programming, publications, publishing, SAT preparation, science, typing, Web site design, word processing, writing, yearbook classes. Computer network features include on-campus library services, online commercial services, Internet access, wireless campus network, Internet filtering or blocking technology. Campus intranet, student e-mail accounts, and computer access in designated common areas are available to students. Students grades are available online. The school has a published electronic and media policy.

Contact Mrs. Marcia E. DiTullio, Administrative Assistant. 814-824-2323. Fax: 814-824-2116. E-mail: mditullio@mpslakers.com. Website: www.mpslakers.com

MERION MERCY ACADEMY

511 Montgomery Avenue
Merion Station, Pennsylvania 19066

Head of School: Sr. Barbara Buckley

General Information Girls' day college-preparatory and arts school, affiliated with Roman Catholic Church. Grades 9–12. Founded: 1884. Setting: suburban. Nearest major city is Philadelphia. 35-acre campus. 7 buildings on campus. Approved or accredited by Middle States Association of Colleges and Schools, North Central Association of Colleges and Schools, and Pennsylvania Association of Independent Schools. Member of National Association of Independent Schools. Total enrollment: 484. Upper school average class size: 17. Upper school faculty-student ratio: 1:9. The average school day consists of 6 hours and 7 minutes.

Upper School Student Profile Grade 9: 110 students (110 girls); Grade 10: 103 students (103 girls); Grade 11: 123 students (123 girls); Grade 12: 124 students (124 girls). 90% of students are Roman Catholic.

Faculty School total: 53. In upper school: 6 men, 47 women; 41 have advanced degrees.

Subjects Offered Algebra, American history, American literature, art, art history, biology, business, calculus, chemistry, computer programming, creative writing, drama, economics, English, English literature, environmental science, European history, fine arts, French, geometry, government/civics, grammar, health, history, journalism, Latin, mathematics, music, music history, physical education, physics, physiology, psychology, religion, science, social studies, Spanish, speech, theater, theology, trigonometry, women's studies, world history, world literature, writing.

Graduation Requirements Arts and fine arts (art, music, dance, drama), English, foreign language, mathematics, physical education (includes health), religion (includes Bible studies and theology), science, social studies (includes history).

Special Academic Programs Advanced Placement exam preparation; honors section; study at local college for college credit; academic accommodation for the gifted, the musically talented, and the artistically talented; remedial reading and/or remedial writing; remedial math.

College Admission Counseling 127 students graduated in 2016; all went to college, including Fordham University; Loyola University Maryland; Penn State University Park; Saint Joseph's University; Temple University; West Chester University of Pennsylvania. Mean SAT critical reading: 577, mean SAT math: 565, mean SAT writing: 587, mean combined SAT: 1729.

Student Life Upper grades have uniform requirement, student council, honor system. Discipline rests primarily with faculty. Attendance at religious services is required.

Summer Programs Enrichment, advancement, sports, art/fine arts programs offered; session focuses on enrichment; held on campus; accepts boys and girls; open to students from other schools. 150 students usually enrolled. 2017 schedule: June 13 to August 5. Application deadline: May 10.

Tuition and Aid Day student tuition: $17,800. Tuition installment plan (The Tuition Plan, monthly payment plans, two equal payments plan, one entire payment, 10 payments July-April). Tuition reduction for siblings, merit scholarship grants, need-based scholarship grants, alumnae, Mercy, art and music scholarships available. In 2016–17, 45% of upper-school students received aid.

Admissions Traditional secondary-level entrance grade is 9. For fall 2016, 259 students applied for upper-level admission, 252 were accepted, 110 enrolled. High

School Placement Test required. Deadline for receipt of application materials: November 11. Application fee required: $60. On-campus interview required.

Athletics Interscholastic: basketball, crew, cross-country running, dance team, field hockey, golf, lacrosse, soccer, softball, swimming and diving, tennis, track and field, volleyball, winter (indoor) track; intramural: basketball, dance, tennis. 2 PE instructors, 19 coaches, 1 athletic trainer.

Computers Computers are regularly used in all academic classes. Computer network features include on-campus library services, online commercial services, Internet access, wireless campus network, Internet filtering or blocking technology. Student e-mail accounts and computer access in designated common areas are available to students. Students grades are available online. The school has a published electronic and media policy.

Contact Eileen Killeen, Director of Admissions. 610-664-6655 Ext. 116. Fax: 610-664-6322. E-mail: ekilleen@merion-mercy.com. Website: www.merion-mercy.com

MESA GRANDE SEVENTH-DAY ACADEMY

975 Fremont Street
Calimesa, California 92320

Head of School: Alfred J. Riddle

General Information Coeducational day college-preparatory and religious studies school, affiliated with Seventh-day Adventist Church. Grades K–12. Founded: 1928. Setting: rural. Nearest major city is San Bernardino. 14-acre campus. 3 buildings on campus. Approved or accredited by Western Association of Schools and Colleges and California Department of Education. Endowment: $650,000. Total enrollment: 252. Upper school average class size: 27. Upper school faculty-student ratio: 1:10. There are 180 required school days per year for Upper School students. Upper School students typically attend 5 days per week. The average school day consists of 8 hours.

Upper School Student Profile Grade 9: 17 students (5 boys, 12 girls); Grade 10: 14 students (11 boys, 3 girls); Grade 11: 26 students (14 boys, 12 girls); Grade 12: 28 students (16 boys, 12 girls). 85% of students are Seventh-day Adventists.

Faculty School total: 12. In upper school: 5 men, 7 women; 7 have advanced degrees.

Subjects Offered Algebra, American literature, arts, ASB Leadership, auto mechanics, bell choir, biology, British literature, career education, chemistry, choral music, community service, composition, computer applications, computer-aided design, computers, concert choir, desktop publishing, drama, economics, economics and history, English, English composition, family living, fine arts, geometry, government/civics, graphic arts, handbells, health, instrumental music, keyboarding, lab science, marine biology, mathematics, music composition, music theory, physical education, physical science, physics, pre-calculus, relationships, religion, religious education, science, social sciences, social studies, Spanish, U.S. government, U.S. history, video film production, world history, world literature, yearbook.

Graduation Requirements Algebra, biology, British literature, computer education, computer literacy, computer skills, computer technologies, English composition, family living, health, industrial technology, modern languages, physical fitness, physical science, physics, religious studies, technical skills, world history, work experience, community service.

Special Academic Programs Remedial math; ESL (10 students enrolled).

College Admission Counseling 19 students graduated in 2016; all went to college, including La Sierra University; Pacific Union College; Penn State University Park; Southwestern Adventist University; University of California, Los Angeles; Walla Walla University.

Student Life Upper grades have uniform requirement, student council, honor system. Discipline rests primarily with faculty. Attendance at religious services is required.

Summer Programs Sports programs offered; session focuses on sports; held both on and off campus; accepts boys and girls; open to students from other schools. 50 students usually enrolled. 2017 schedule: June 12 to August 3. Application deadline: May 5.

Tuition and Aid Day student tuition: $8915. Tuition installment plan (monthly payment plans, individually arranged payment plans). Tuition reduction for siblings, need-based scholarship grants, need-based loans, middle-income loans available. In 2016–17, 30% of upper-school students received aid. Total amount of financial aid awarded in 2016–17: $35,000.

Admissions Traditional secondary-level entrance grade is 9. For fall 2016, 30 students applied for upper-level admission, 28 were accepted, 28 enrolled. ESL required. Deadline for receipt of application materials: none. Application fee required: $50. On-campus interview recommended.

Athletics Interscholastic: baseball (boys), basketball (b,g), flag football (b,g), softball (g), volleyball (b,g); coed interscholastic: cross-country running, golf, physical fitness, weight lifting, weight training. 2 PE instructors, 10 coaches, 2 athletic trainers.

Computers Computers are regularly used in art, design, graphic design, science, technical drawing, technology, typing, video film production, writing, yearbook classes. Computer network features include on-campus library services, online commercial services, Internet access, wireless campus network, Internet filtering or blocking technology. Student e-mail accounts and computer access in designated common areas are available to students. Students grades are available online. The school has a published electronic and media policy.

Contact Lois M. Myhre, Admissions Office. 909-795-1112 Ext. 257. Fax: 909-795-1653. E-mail: lois.myhre@mgak-12.org. Website: www.mesagrandeacademy.org

MIAMI COUNTRY DAY SCHOOL

601 Northeast 107th Street
Miami, Florida 33161

Head of School: Dr. John P. Davies

General Information Coeducational day college-preparatory school. Grades PK–12. Founded: 1938. Setting: suburban. 22-acre campus. 6 buildings on campus. Approved or accredited by Florida Council of Independent Schools, Missouri Independent School Association, Southern Association of Colleges and Schools, Southern Association of Independent Schools, The College Board, and Florida Department of Education. Member of National Association of Independent Schools and Secondary School Admission Test Board. Endowment: $4.5 million. Total enrollment: 1,250. Upper school average class size: 18. Upper school faculty-student ratio: 1:10. There are 179 required school days per year for Upper School students. Upper School students typically attend 5 days per week. The average school day consists of 6 hours and 15 minutes.

Upper School Student Profile Grade 9: 115 students (54 boys, 61 girls); Grade 10: 117 students (60 boys, 57 girls); Grade 11: 97 students (52 boys, 45 girls); Grade 12: 88 students (43 boys, 45 girls).

Faculty School total: 90. In upper school: 28 men, 32 women; 48 have advanced degrees.

Subjects Offered Advanced Placement courses, African-American studies, algebra, American history, American history-AP, American literature, ancient history, art, art history, backpacking, band, biology, calculus, calculus-AP, ceramics, chemistry, community service, composition, computer programming, computer science, conflict resolution, creative writing, design, desktop publishing, DNA science lab, drama, drawing, economics, English, English language and composition-AP, English literature, English literature-AP, environmental science-AP, ESL, European history, film, film and literature, fine arts, French, geography, geometry, government/civics, health, instrumental music, jewelry making, journalism, law, life management skills, literature, marine biology, mathematics, music theory, orchestra, painting, philosophy, photography, physical education, physical science, physics, physics-AP, post-calculus, psychology, public speaking, religion, science, sculpture, social sciences, social studies, Spanish, Spanish language-AP, Spanish literature-AP, theater, trigonometry, U.S. government and politics-AP, video film production, world history, world literature, writing, yearbook.

Graduation Requirements Arts and fine arts (art, music, dance, drama), computer science, electives, English, foreign language, mathematics, philosophy, physical education (includes health), science, social studies (includes history), speech and debate, 100 hours of community service.

Special Academic Programs 24 Advanced Placement exams for which test preparation is offered; honors section; independent study; study at local college for college credit; ESL (9 students enrolled).

College Admission Counseling 97 students graduated in 2015; all went to college, including American University; Boston University; Duke University; Florida State University; University of Florida; University of Miami. Median SAT critical reading: 630, median SAT math: 660, median SAT writing: 630.

Student Life Upper grades have uniform requirement, student council, honor system. Discipline rests equally with students and faculty.

Tuition and Aid Day student tuition: $29,904. Need-based scholarship grants available. In 2015–16, 21% of upper-school students received aid. Total amount of financial aid awarded in 2015–16: $3,100,000.

Admissions Traditional secondary-level entrance grade is 9. For fall 2015, 161 students applied for upper-level admission, 49 were accepted, 30 enrolled. ISEE or PSAT and SAT for applicants to grade 11 and 12 required. Deadline for receipt of application materials: January 29. Application fee required: $100. Interview required.

Athletics Interscholastic: baseball (boys), basketball (b,g), cheering (g), cross-country running (b,g), football (b), golf (b,g), lacrosse (b), soccer (b,g), softball (g), swimming and diving (b,g), tennis (b,g), track and field (b,g), volleyball (g), water polo (b,g), yoga (b,g); intramural: baseball (b), basketball (b,g), cheering (g), cross-country running (b,g), dance (g), lacrosse (b), volleyball (b), yoga (g); coed intramural: flag football, modern dance, outdoor education, outdoor skills, physical fitness, physical training, soccer, strength & conditioning, weight training. 3 PE instructors, 24 coaches, 1 athletic trainer.

Computers Computers are regularly used in all academic, graphic design, journalism, media, research skills, Web site design, yearbook classes. Computer network features include on-campus library services, online commercial services, Internet access, wireless campus network, Internet filtering or blocking technology, Google Drive. Student e-mail accounts and computer access in designated common areas are available to students. Students grades are available online. The school has a published electronic and media policy.

Contact Ingrid Palmisano, Director of Admission and Financial Aid. 305-779-7230. Fax: 305-397-0370. E-mail: admissions@miamicountryday.org. Website: www.miamicountryday.org

THE MIAMI VALLEY SCHOOL

5151 Denise Drive
Dayton, Ohio 45429

Head of School: Jay Scheurle

General Information Coeducational day college-preparatory school. Grades PK–12. Founded: 1964. Setting: suburban. 22-acre campus. 1 building on campus. Approved or accredited by Independent Schools Association of the Central States, Ohio Association of Independent Schools, and Ohio Department of Education. Member of National Association of Independent Schools. Endowment: $64 million. Total enrollment: 474. Upper school average class size: 14. Upper school faculty-student ratio: 1:8. There are 180 required school days per year for Upper School students. Upper School students typically attend 5 days per week. The average school day consists of 7 hours and 20 minutes.

Upper School Student Profile Grade 9: 41 students (17 boys, 24 girls); Grade 10: 46 students (30 boys, 16 girls); Grade 11: 52 students (32 boys, 20 girls); Grade 12: 49 students (21 boys, 28 girls).

Faculty School total: 63. In upper school: 11 men, 13 women; 19 have advanced degrees.

Subjects Offered Advanced Placement courses, algebra, American history, American literature, anatomy, art, art history, biology, calculus, ceramics, chemistry, Chinese, Chinese history, choir, college admission preparation, college counseling, community service, computer programming, computer science, creative writing, criminal justice, drama, earth science, Eastern world civilizations, ecology, economics, English, English literature, environmental science, ESL, European history, fine arts, French, gardening, gender issues, genetics, geology, geometry, government/civics, grammar, health, history, human issues, instrumental music, jazz, jazz band, journalism, Latin, Mandarin, marine biology, mathematics, microbiology, model United Nations, modern European history-AP, music, philosophy, photography, physical education, physics, physiology, pottery, pre-algebra, pre-calculus, religion, science, social sciences, social studies, Spanish, speech, statistics, theater, trigonometry, woodworking, word processing, world civilizations, world history, world literature, writing, yearbook.

Graduation Requirements Alternative physical education, arts and fine arts (art, music, dance, drama), English, foreign language, mathematics, science, social sciences, social studies (includes history), immersion term, community service. Community service is required.

Special Academic Programs Advanced Placement exam preparation; honors section; independent study; term-away projects; study at local college for college credit; study abroad; academic accommodation for the gifted, the musically talented, and the artistically talented; ESL (9 students enrolled).

College Admission Counseling 48 students graduated in 2016; all went to college, including Miami University; New York University; Rhodes College; The Ohio State University; University of Dayton; Wright State University. Median SAT critical reading: 610, median SAT math: 625, median SAT writing: 575, median combined SAT: 1760, median composite ACT: 27. 56% scored over 600 on SAT critical reading, 63% scored over 600 on SAT math, 44% scored over 600 on SAT writing, 47% scored over 1800 on combined SAT, 52% scored over 26 on composite ACT.

Student Life Upper grades have specified standards of dress, student council, honor system. Discipline rests primarily with faculty.

Summer Programs Remediation, enrichment, ESL, art/fine arts, rigorous outdoor training programs offered; session focuses on general summer day camp; held on campus; accepts boys and girls; open to students from other schools. 200 students usually enrolled. 2017 schedule: June 13 to July 28.

Tuition and Aid Day student tuition: $20,220. Tuition installment plan (FACTS Tuition Payment Plan). Merit scholarship grants, need-based scholarship grants available. In 2016–17, 40% of upper-school students received aid; total upper-school merit-scholarship money awarded: $118,850. Total amount of financial aid awarded in 2016–17: $1,070,670.

Admissions Traditional secondary-level entrance grade is 9. For fall 2016, 26 students applied for upper-level admission, 17 were accepted, 14 enrolled. Achievement/Aptitude/Writing, school's own test, SSAT, Stanford Achievement Test, Otis-Lennon School Ability Test, TOEFL or SLEP or writing sample required. Deadline for receipt of application materials: none. Application fee required: $125. On-campus interview recommended.

Athletics Interscholastic: basketball (boys, girls), cheering (g), lacrosse (b,g), soccer (b,g), strength & conditioning (b,g), tennis (b,g), track and field (b,g), volleyball (g), weight training (b,g); intramural: squash (b); coed interscholastic: bowling, cross-country running, golf, swimming and diving; coed intramural: crew. 1 PE instructor, 17 coaches, 1 athletic trainer.

Computers Computers are regularly used in literary magazine, mathematics, media production, multimedia, music technology, newspaper, photography, programming, science, social sciences, technology, yearbook classes. Computer network features include on-campus library services, online commercial services, Internet access, wireless campus network, Internet filtering or blocking technology. Campus intranet and student e-mail accounts are available to students. Students grades are available online. The school has a published electronic and media policy.

Contact Susan Strong, Director of Enrollment and Financial Aid. 937-434-4444 Ext. 230. Fax: 937-434-1033. E-mail: susan.strong@mvschool.com. Website: www.mvschool.com

MIDDLESEX SCHOOL

1400 Lowell Road
Concord, Massachusetts 01742

Head of School: Kathleen C. Giles

General Information Coeducational boarding and day college-preparatory school. Grades 9–12. Founded: 1901. Setting: suburban. Nearest major city is Boston. Students are housed in coed dormitories. 350-acre campus. 31 buildings on campus. Approved or accredited by New England Association of Schools and Colleges. Member of National Association of Independent Schools and Secondary School Admission Test Board. Endowment: $244 million. Total enrollment: 384. Upper school average class size: 12. Upper school faculty-student ratio: 1:4. There are 180 required school days per year for Upper School students. Upper School students typically attend 6 days per week. The average school day consists of 7 hours and 15 minutes.

Upper School Student Profile Grade 9: 86 students (41 boys, 45 girls); Grade 10: 101 students (49 boys, 52 girls); Grade 11: 107 students (54 boys, 53 girls); Grade 12: 100 students (52 boys, 48 girls). 69% of students are boarding students. 45% are state residents. 30 states are represented in upper school student body. 12% are international students. International students from Canada, China, Jamaica, Nigeria, Republic of Korea, and Viet Nam; 9 other countries represented in student body.

Faculty School total: 73. In upper school: 53 men, 41 women; 66 have advanced degrees; 61 reside on campus.

Subjects Offered Acting, advanced biology, advanced chemistry, advanced computer applications, Advanced Placement courses, advanced studio art-AP, African American history, African history, African-American history, algebra, American literature, analytic geometry, art, art history, art history-AP, art-AP, Asian literature, astronomy, biology, biology-AP, British literature, calculus, calculus-AP, ceramics, chemistry, chemistry-AP, Chinese, classical Greek literature, computer programming, computer programming-AP, computer science, computer science-AP, creative writing, discrete mathematics, DNA, drama, economics, economics-AP, English, English literature, English literature and composition-AP, environmental science, environmental science-AP, ethics, European history, European history-AP, finite math, forensics, French, French language-AP, French literature-AP, geometry, Greek, history, history of jazz, Holocaust studies, independent study, jazz band, Latin, Latin American history, marine studies, mathematics, media, meditation, Middle East, Middle Eastern history, model United Nations, music, music theory, music theory-AP, philosophy, photography, physics, physics-AP, political science, religion, Shakespeare, Spanish, Spanish language-AP, Spanish literature-AP, statistics, statistics-AP, studio art-AP, theater, trigonometry, U.S. government and politics-AP, U.S. history, U.S. history-AP, video film production, Vietnam history, Vietnam War, vocal ensemble, women in world history, woodworking, world history, writing, writing workshop.

Graduation Requirements Algebra, American history, analytic geometry, art, arts, English, English literature and composition-AP, European history, foreign language, geometry, mathematics, science, sports, trigonometry, U.S. history, world history, writing, each senior completes a hand-carved wooden plaque. Students also attend mindfullness classes, writing workshops, and a math/science/computer science problem solving initiative.

Special Academic Programs 23 Advanced Placement exams for which test preparation is offered; honors section; independent study; academic accommodation for the gifted.

College Admission Counseling 93 students graduated in 2016; 92 went to college, including Columbia University; Dartmouth College; Georgetown University; Harvard University; University of Chicago; Vanderbilt University. Other: 1 entered a postgraduate year. Median composite ACT: 30. Mean SAT critical reading: 704, mean SAT math: 702, mean SAT writing: 702, mean combined SAT: 2106. 96% scored over 600 on SAT critical reading, 99% scored over 600 on SAT math, 97% scored over 600 on SAT writing, 95% scored over 1800 on combined SAT, 85% scored over 26 on composite ACT.

Student Life Upper grades have specified standards of dress, student council, honor system. Discipline rests primarily with faculty.

Tuition and Aid Day student tuition: $46,200; 7-day tuition and room/board: $58,020. Guaranteed tuition plan. Tuition installment plan (Insured Tuition Payment Plan, monthly payment plans, semiannual payment plan). Need-based scholarship grants available. In 2016–17, 35% of upper-school students received aid. Total amount of financial aid awarded in 2016–17: $5,800,000.

Admissions Traditional secondary-level entrance grade is 9. For fall 2016, 1,173 students applied for upper-level admission, 216 were accepted, 113 enrolled. ISEE, SSAT or TOEFL required. Deadline for receipt of application materials: January 31. Application fee required: $60. On-campus interview required.

Athletics Interscholastic: alpine skiing (boys, girls), baseball (b), basketball (b,g), crew (b,g), cross-country running (b,g), field hockey (g), football (b), ice hockey (b,g), lacrosse (b,g), skiing (downhill) (b,g), soccer (b,g), squash (b,g), tennis (b,g), volleyball (g), wrestling (b); coed interscholastic: dance, golf, track and field; coed intramural: dance, fitness, physical training, squash, strength & conditioning, yoga. 1 PE instructor, 23 coaches, 2 athletic trainers.

Computers Computers are regularly used in all classes. Computer network features include on-campus library services, online commercial services, Internet access, wireless campus network, Internet filtering or blocking technology. Campus intranet, student e-mail accounts, and computer access in designated common areas are available to students. Students grades are available online. The school has a published electronic and media policy.

Contact Douglas C. Price, Dean of Admissions and Financial Aid. 978-371-6527. Fax: 978-402-1400. E-mail: dprice@mxschool.edu. Website: www.mxschool.edu

MIDDLE TENNESSEE CHRISTIAN SCHOOL

100 East MTCS Road
Murfreesboro, Tennessee 37129

Head of School: Dr. Phil Ellenburg

General Information Coeducational day college-preparatory, arts, religious studies, and technology school, affiliated with Church of Christ. Grades PK–12. Founded: 1962. Setting: suburban. Nearest major city is Nashville. 37-acre campus. 3 buildings on campus. Approved or accredited by National Christian School Association, Southern Association of Colleges and Schools, Southern Association of Independent Schools, and Tennessee Department of Education. Member of National Association of Independent Schools. Total enrollment: 668. Upper school average class size: 18. Upper school faculty-student ratio: 1:18. There are 175 required school days per year for Upper School students. Upper School students typically attend 5 days per week. The average school day consists of 7 hours and 15 minutes.

Upper School Student Profile Grade 9: 63 students (30 boys, 33 girls); Grade 10: 63 students (37 boys, 26 girls); Grade 11: 55 students (33 boys, 22 girls); Grade 12: 51 students (31 boys, 20 girls). 49% of students are members of Church of Christ.

Faculty School total: 50. In upper school: 15 men, 15 women; 20 have advanced degrees.

Subjects Offered ACT preparation, advanced math, algebra, American history, American history-AP, American literature, anatomy, art, band, Bible, biology, biology-AP, calculus, chemistry, chorus, computer applications, computer technologies, driver education, economics, electives, English, French, geometry, integrated mathematics, keyboarding, physics, pre-algebra, pre-calculus, Spanish, speech, U.S. government, U.S. history, wellness, yearbook.

Graduation Requirements Algebra, arts, Bible, biology, chemistry, computer applications, economics, electives, English, French, geometry, keyboarding, physical science, pre-algebra, Spanish, speech, U.S. government, U.S. history, wellness, world history.

Special Academic Programs 3 Advanced Placement exams for which test preparation is offered; honors section; study at local college for college credit.

College Admission Counseling 57 students graduated in 2015; 55 went to college, including Freed-Hardeman University; Harding University; Lipscomb University; Middle Tennessee State University; Tennessee Technological University; The University of Tennessee at Chattanooga. Other: 1 went to work, 1 entered military service. Mean composite ACT: 24. 24% scored over 26 on composite ACT.

Student Life Upper grades have specified standards of dress, student council, honor system. Discipline rests primarily with faculty. Attendance at religious services is required.

Tuition and Aid Day student tuition: $8480. Tuition installment plan (monthly payment plans, individually arranged payment plans). Tuition reduction for siblings, need-based scholarship grants available.

Admissions Traditional secondary-level entrance grade is 9. For fall 2015, 31 students applied for upper-level admission, 26 were accepted, 21 enrolled. Achievement tests and OLSAT/Stanford required. Deadline for receipt of application materials: none. Application fee required: $75. Interview required.

Athletics Interscholastic: baseball (boys), basketball (b,g), bowling (b,g), cheering (g), cross-country running (b,g), football (b), golf (b), skeet shooting (b,g), soccer (b,g), softball (g), tennis (b,g), trap and skeet (b,g), volleyball (g). 2 PE instructors.

Computers Computers are regularly used in engineering, keyboarding, mathematics, science, writing, yearbook classes. Computer network features include on-campus library services, Internet access, wireless campus network, Internet filtering or blocking technology. Student e-mail accounts and computer access in designated common areas are available to students. Students grades are available online. The school has a published electronic and media policy.

Contact Mrs. Monica Helton, Admissions and Public Relations. 615-893-0601 Ext. 15. Fax: 615-895-8815. E-mail: monicahelton@mtcscougars.org. Website: www.mtcscougars.org

MIDLAND SCHOOL

PO Box 8
5100 Figueroa Mountain Road
Los Olivos, California 93441

Head of School: Mr. Christopher Barnes

General Information Coeducational boarding college-preparatory and environmental studies school. Grades 9–12. Founded: 1932. Setting: rural. Nearest major city is Santa Barbara. Students are housed in single-sex cabins. 2,860-acre campus. 15 buildings on campus. Approved or accredited by California Association of Independent Schools, The Association of Boarding Schools, Western Association of Schools and Colleges, and California Department of Education. Member of National Association of Independent Schools and Secondary School Admission Test Board. Endowment: $17 million. Total enrollment: 81. Upper school average class size: 10. Upper school faculty-student ratio: 1:4. There are 180 required school days per year for Upper School students. Upper School students typically attend 6 days per week. The average school day consists of 6 hours and 45 minutes.

Upper School Student Profile Grade 9: 14 students (7 boys, 7 girls); Grade 10: 21 students (10 boys, 11 girls); Grade 11: 25 students (9 boys, 16 girls); Grade 12: 21 students (11 boys, 10 girls). 100% of students are boarding students. 70% are state residents. 10 states are represented in upper school student body. 16% are international students. International students from China, Japan, and Mexico.

Faculty School total: 22. In upper school: 11 men, 9 women; 10 have advanced degrees; 18 reside on campus.

Subjects Offered 3-dimensional art, advanced chemistry, advanced math, agroecology, algebra, American history, American literature, American studies, anthropology, backpacking, basketball, biology, ceramics, character education, chemistry, clayworking, community service, composition, creative writing, drama, economics, environmental education, environmental studies, equestrian sports, foreign language, gardening, geology, geometry, health education, human sexuality, hydrology, integrated science, land and ranch management, leadership, literature by women, metalworking, music, painting, physics, pre-calculus, senior project, senior seminar, senior thesis, Spanish, Spanish literature, statistics, U.S. history, volleyball, wilderness education, wilderness experience, world studies.

Graduation Requirements Arts and fine arts (art, music, dance, drama), English, foreign language, history, mathematics, science, senior thesis.

Special Academic Programs 9 Advanced Placement exams for which test preparation is offered; honors section; independent study.

College Admission Counseling 20 students graduated in 2016; 19 went to college, including California Polytechnic State University, San Luis Obispo; Harvard University; Harvey Mudd College; Montana State University; Oberlin College; Wellesley College. Other: 1 had other specific plans. Mean SAT critical reading: 584, mean SAT math: 587, mean SAT writing: 559, mean combined SAT: 1697, mean composite ACT: 29.

Student Life Upper grades have student council. Discipline rests equally with students and faculty.

Tuition and Aid 7-day tuition and room/board: $49,900. Tuition installment plan (monthly payment plans, Your Tuition Solution, Tuition Management Systems). Need-based scholarship grants available. In 2016–17, 49% of upper-school students received aid. Total amount of financial aid awarded in 2016–17: $1,500,000.

Admissions Traditional secondary-level entrance grade is 9. For fall 2016, 77 students applied for upper-level admission, 57 were accepted, 27 enrolled. ISEE, SSAT or TOEFL required. Deadline for receipt of application materials: February 15. Application fee required: $50. On-campus interview recommended.

Athletics Interscholastic: basketball (boys, girls), cross-country running (b,g), soccer (b,g), softball (g), volleyball (b,g); intramural: table tennis (b,g); coed intramural: backpacking, equestrian sports, fitness, hiking/backpacking, horseback riding, mountain biking, outdoor adventure, outdoor skills, physical fitness, strength & conditioning, yoga.

Computers Computer network features include on-campus library services, online commercial services, Internet access, Internet filtering or blocking technology. Student e-mail accounts and computer access in designated common areas are available to students. The school has a published electronic and media policy.

Contact Tim Weir, Director of Admission. 805-688-5114 Ext. 114. Fax: 805-686-2470. E-mail: tweir@midland-school.org. Website: www.midland-school.org

MID-PACIFIC INSTITUTE

2445 Kaala Street
Honolulu, Hawaii 96822-2299

Head of School: Dr. Paul Turnbull

General Information Coeducational day college-preparatory, arts, and International Baccalaureate school. Grades K–12. Founded: 1908. Setting: urban. 42-acre campus. 37 buildings on campus. Approved or accredited by International Baccalaureate Organization and Western Association of Schools and Colleges. Member of National Association of Independent Schools and Secondary School Admission Test Board. Total enrollment: 1,556. Upper school average class size: 20. Upper school faculty-student ratio: 1:20. Upper School students typically attend 5 days per week. The average school day consists of 7 hours and 15 minutes.

Faculty School total: 150. In upper school: 25 have advanced degrees.

Subjects Offered Algebra, American history, American literature, art, art history, astronomy, ballet, band, biology, business skills, calculus, career education, ceramics, chemistry, computer programming, computer science, creative writing, dance, debate, drama, drawing, economics, English, English literature, ESL, film, fine arts, first aid, French, general science, geography, geometry, Hawaiian history, health, history, instrumental music, Japanese, Latin, law, mathematics, oceanography, oral communications, painting, philosophy, photography, physical education, physics, printmaking, psychology, religion, science, sculpture, social sciences, social studies, Spanish, speech, swimming, swimming competency, technological applications, technology, theater, video, weight training, world history, world literature, writing.

Graduation Requirements Arts and fine arts (art, music, dance, drama), business skills (includes word processing), career education, computer science, English, foreign language, mathematics, oral communications, physical education (includes health), religion (includes Bible studies and theology), science, social sciences, social studies (includes history), speech, swimming competency.

Special Academic Programs International Baccalaureate program; Advanced Placement exam preparation; honors section; study at local college for college credit; academic accommodation for the gifted, the musically talented, and the artistically talented; ESL (55 students enrolled).

College Admission Counseling 200 students graduated in 2016; all went to college, including Oregon State University; Pacific University; University of Hawaii at Manoa; University of Oregon; University of Washington.

Student Life Upper grades have specified standards of dress, student council, honor system. Discipline rests primarily with faculty.

Summer Programs Remediation, enrichment, ESL, art/fine arts, computer instruction programs offered; session focuses on physical fitness and skills; held on campus; accepts boys and girls; open to students from other schools. 1,200 students usually enrolled. 2017 schedule: June 5 to July 26. Application deadline: April 5.

Tuition and Aid Day student tuition: $22,100. Tuition installment plan (FACTS Tuition Payment Plan, monthly payment plans, semiannual payment plan). Merit scholarship grants, need-based scholarship grants, paying campus jobs, tuition reduction for children of employees available. In 2016–17, 17% of upper-school students received aid.

Admissions Traditional secondary-level entrance grade is 9. For fall 2016, 700 students applied for upper-level admission, 220 were accepted, 150 enrolled. SAT, SSAT and TOEFL required. Deadline for receipt of application materials: December 1. Application fee required: $125. On-campus interview required.

Athletics Interscholastic: aquatics (boys, girls), baseball (b), basketball (b,g), bowling (b,g), canoeing/kayaking (b,g), cheering (g), cross-country running (b,g), football (b), golf (b,g), gymnastics (g), independent competitive sports (b,g), kayaking (b,g), ocean paddling (b,g), physical fitness (b,g), physical training (b,g), riflery (b,g), soccer (b,g), softball (g), strength & conditioning (b,g), surfing (b,g), swimming and diving (b,g), tennis (b,g), track and field (b,g), volleyball (b,g), water polo (b,g), wrestling (b,g); intramural: badminton (b,g), weight lifting (b,g), weight training (b,g); coed interscholastic: fitness, modern dance; coed intramural: badminton. 7 PE instructors, 50 coaches, 3 athletic trainers.

Computers Computers are regularly used in English, foreign language, history, mathematics, media arts, science classes. Computer network features include on-campus library services, online commercial services, Internet access, wireless campus network, Internet filtering or blocking technology, one-to-one iPad program. Campus intranet, student e-mail accounts, and computer access in designated common areas are available to students. Students grades are available online. The school has a published electronic and media policy.

Contact Ms. Lani Corrie, Admissions Assistant. 808-973-5005. Fax: 808-973-5099. E-mail: admissions@midpac.edu. Website: www.midpac.edu

MILLBROOK SCHOOL

131 Millbrook School Road
Millbrook, New York 12545

Head of School: Mr. Drew Casertano

General Information Coeducational boarding and day college-preparatory, environmental stewardship, and community service school. Grades 9–12. Founded: 1931. Setting: rural. Nearest major city is New York. Students are housed in single-sex dormitories. 800-acre campus. 42 buildings on campus. Approved or accredited by New York State Association of Independent Schools, The Association of Boarding Schools, and New York Department of Education. Member of National Association of Independent Schools and Secondary School Admission Test Board. Endowment: $34 million. Total enrollment: 294. Upper school average class size: 14. Upper school faculty-student ratio: 1:5. There are 180 required school days per year for Upper School students. Upper School students typically attend 6 days per week. The average school day consists of 7 hours.

Upper School Student Profile Grade 9: 56 students (27 boys, 29 girls); Grade 10: 78 students (34 boys, 44 girls); Grade 11: 91 students (47 boys, 44 girls); Grade 12: 85 students (42 boys, 43 girls); Postgraduate: 3 students (2 boys, 1 girl). 83% of students are boarding students. 40% are state residents. 24 states are represented in upper school student body. 15% are international students. International students from China, Germany, Ghana, Guatemala, Russian Federation, and Viet Nam; 13 other countries represented in student body.

Faculty School total: 62. In upper school: 30 men, 32 women; 40 have advanced degrees; 55 reside on campus.

Subjects Offered 20th century American writers, 20th century history, 20th century world history, 3-dimensional design, ACT preparation, acting, adolescent issues, advanced biology, advanced chemistry, advanced math, Advanced Placement courses, advanced studio art-AP, aesthetics, algebra, American history, American literature, anatomy, ancient history, ancient world history, animal behavior, animal science, anthropology, art, art history, astronomy, biology, calculus, calculus-AP, ceramics, chemistry, Chinese, choral music, choreography, college counseling, college planning, computer programming, constitutional history of U.S., constitutional law, creative writing, dance, dance performance, digital photography, drama, drama performance, dramatic arts, drawing, ecology, ecology, environmental systems, economics, English, English language and composition-AP, English language-AP, English literature, English literature and composition-AP, English literature-AP, English-AP, environmental science, environmental studies, European history, fine arts, forensics, French, French language-AP, French literature-AP, French-AP, geography, geometry, global studies, guitar, health and wellness, history, honors English, honors geometry, human biology, human development, independent study, instrumental music, jazz band, jazz ensemble, journalism, Latin, literature-AP, Mandarin, mathematics, mathematics-AP, medieval history, Middle Eastern history, music, music appreciation, music history, music theater, musical theater, painting, philosophy, photography, physics, piano, playwriting, playwriting and directing, poetry, pottery, pre-calculus, printmaking, psychology, public speaking, SAT preparation, science, science research, senior project, senior thesis, social sciences, social studies, Spanish, Spanish language-AP, Spanish literature-AP, Spanish-AP, statistics, statistics-AP, student publications, studio art, study skills, technical theater, theater, trigonometry, U.S. history, video, vocal ensemble, voice, world history, yearbook.

Graduation Requirements American history, art, biology, English, foreign language, history, mathematics, science, visual and performing arts, biology.

Special Academic Programs 9 Advanced Placement exams for which test preparation is offered; honors section; independent study; term-away projects; study abroad.

College Admission Counseling 83 students graduated in 2016; 77 went to college, including Dickinson College; Elon University; Hamilton College; Hobart and William Smith Colleges; New York University; Skidmore College. Other: 1 entered a postgraduate year, 5 had other specific plans. Mean SAT critical reading: 570, mean SAT math: 584, mean SAT writing: 570, mean combined SAT: 1724, mean composite ACT: 25. 30% scored over 600 on SAT critical reading, 40% scored over 600 on SAT math, 30% scored over 600 on SAT writing, 30% scored over 1800 on combined SAT, 30% scored over 26 on composite ACT.

Student Life Upper grades have specified standards of dress, student council. Discipline rests equally with students and faculty.

Tuition and Aid Day student tuition: $43,575; 7-day tuition and room/board: $57,750. Tuition installment plan (SMART Tuition Payment Plan). Need-based scholarship grants, need-based loans available. In 2016–17, 29% of upper-school students received aid. Total amount of financial aid awarded in 2016–17: $3,496,436.

Admissions Traditional secondary-level entrance grade is 9. For fall 2016, 580 students applied for upper-level admission, 238 were accepted, 113 enrolled. ACT, ISEE, PSAT or SAT for applicants to grade 11 and 12, SSAT, TOEFL or writing sample required. Deadline for receipt of application materials: January 15. Application fee required: $50. Interview recommended.

Athletics Interscholastic: baseball (boys), basketball (b,g), cross-country running (b,g), field hockey (g), football (b), ice hockey (b,g), lacrosse (b,g), soccer (b,g), softball (g), squash (b,g), tennis (b,g), volleyball (g); coed interscholastic: golf, track and field; coed intramural: aerobics/dance, aerobics/Nautilus, alpine skiing, badminton, ballet, bicycling, dance, equestrian sports, fitness, hiking/backpacking, horseback riding, modern dance, outdoor adventure, outdoor education, physical training, running, skiing (downhill), snowboarding, strength & conditioning, weight training, yoga. 2 coaches, 1 athletic trainer.

Computers Computers are regularly used in art, college planning, creative writing, foreign language, French, history, journalism, literary magazine, mathematics, newspaper, photography, psychology, SAT preparation, science, Spanish, study skills, video film production, writing, yearbook classes. Computer network features include on-campus library services, online commercial services, Internet access, wireless campus network, Internet filtering or blocking technology. Campus intranet, student e-mail accounts, and computer access in designated common areas are available to students. Students grades are available online. The school has a published electronic and media policy.

Contact Mrs. Wendy Greenfield, Admission Office Assistant. 845-677-8261 Ext. 138. Fax: 845-677-1265. E-mail: admissions@millbrook.org. Website: www.millbrook.org

MILL SPRINGS ACADEMY

Alpharetta, Georgia
See Special Needs Schools section.

MILTON ACADEMY

170 Centre Street
Milton, Massachusetts 02186

Head of School: Todd Bland

General Information Coeducational boarding and day college-preparatory school. Boarding grades 9–12, day grades K–12. Founded: 1798. Setting: suburban. Nearest major city is Boston. Students are housed in single-sex dormitories. 125-acre campus. 25 buildings on campus. Approved or accredited by Association of Independent Schools in New England, New England Association of Schools and Colleges, The Association of Boarding Schools, and Massachusetts Department of Education. Member of National Association of Independent Schools and Secondary School Admission Test Board. Endowment: $244 million. Total enrollment: 1,000. Upper school average class size: 14. Upper school faculty-student ratio: 1:5. There are 162 required school days per year for Upper School students. Upper School students typically attend 5 days per week. The average school day consists of 7 hours.

Upper School Student Profile 50% of students are boarding students. 28% are state residents. 26 states are represented in upper school student body. 14% are international students. International students from China, Jamaica, Mexico, Nigeria, Republic of Korea, and Russian Federation; 17 other countries represented in student body.

Faculty School total: 139. In upper school: 66 men, 73 women; 104 have advanced degrees; 111 reside on campus.

Subjects Offered Algebra, American history, American literature, anatomy, architecture, art, art history, astronomy, biology, calculus, ceramics, chemistry, Chinese, computer math, computer programming, computer science, creative writing, current events, dance, drama, earth science, economics, English, English literature, ethics, European history, expository writing, fine arts, French, geography, geometry, government/civics, grammar, Greek, health, history, Latin, mathematics, music, philosophy, photography, physical education, physics, physiology, psychology, religion, science, social studies, sociology, Spanish, speech, statistics, theater, trigonometry, world history, world literature, writing.

Graduation Requirements Arts and fine arts (art, music, dance, drama), current events, English, foreign language, leadership, mathematics, physical education (includes health), public speaking, science, social studies (includes history).

Special Academic Programs Advanced Placement exam preparation; honors section; independent study, term-away projects; study abroad; academic accommodation for the gifted, the musically talented, and the artistically talented.

College Admission Counseling 178 students graduated in 2016; all went to college, including Boston College; Brown University; Columbia University; Harvard University; University of Chicago; Wesleyan University. Mean SAT critical reading: 690, mean SAT math: 660, mean composite ACT: 30.

Student Life Upper grades have student council, honor system. Discipline rests equally with students and faculty.

Tuition and Aid Day student tuition: $45,490; 7-day tuition and room/board: $55,410. Tuition installment plan (The Tuition Management Systems (TMS)). Need-based scholarship grants available. In 2016–17, 35% of upper-school students received aid. Total amount of financial aid awarded in 2016–17: $9,900,000.

Admissions Traditional secondary-level entrance grade is 9. For fall 2016, 1,700 students applied for upper-level admission, 280 were accepted, 150 enrolled. Deadline for receipt of application materials: January 15. Application fee required: $50. Interview recommended.

Athletics Interscholastic: baseball (boys), basketball (b,g), cross-country running (b,g), field hockey (g), football (b), ice hockey (b,g), lacrosse (b,g), soccer (b,g), softball (g), squash (b,g), tennis (b,g), track and field (b,g), volleyball (g); intramural: basketball (b,g), soccer (b,g), strength & conditioning (b,g); coed interscholastic: alpine skiing, diving, golf, sailing, skiing (downhill), swimming and diving, wrestling; coed intramural: climbing, outdoor activities, outdoor education, project adventure, rock climbing, skiing (downhill), squash, tennis, ultimate Frisbee, yoga. 6 PE instructors, 107 coaches, 3 athletic trainers.

Computers Computers are regularly used in all classes. Computer network features include on-campus library services, online commercial services, Internet access, wireless campus network, Internet filtering or blocking technology. Student e-mail accounts and computer access in designated common areas are available to students.

Contact Mrs. Patricia Finn, Database Manager. 617-898-2227. Fax: 617-898-1701. E-mail: admissions@milton.edu. Website: www.milton.edu

MILTON HERSHEY SCHOOL

PO Box 830
Hershey, Pennsylvania 17033-0830

Head of School: Mr. Peter Gurt

General Information Coeducational boarding college-preparatory and general academic school, affiliated with Protestant faith. Grades PK–12. Founded: 1909. Setting: rural. Nearest major city is Harrisburg. Students are housed in student homes of 8 to 10 students. 4,200-acre campus. 9 buildings on campus. Approved or accredited by Middle States Association of Colleges and Schools, Pennsylvania Association of Independent Schools, and The Association of Boarding Schools. Member of National Association of Independent Schools. Total enrollment: 2,012. Upper school average class size: 15. Upper school faculty-student ratio: 1:15.

Upper School Student Profile Grade 9: 242 students (118 boys, 124 girls); Grade 10: 249 students (130 boys, 119 girls); Grade 11: 219 students (109 boys, 110 girls); Grade 12: 233 students (113 boys, 120 girls). 100% of students are boarding students. 77% are state residents. 31 states are represented in upper school student body.

Faculty School total: 147. In upper school: 32 men, 27 women; 19 have advanced degrees.

Subjects Offered Agriculture, algebra, American history, American literature, art, art history, arts, auto mechanics, biology, business, business education, Canadian literature, carpentry, chemistry, communications, computer applications, computer education, computer graphics, computer information systems, computer literacy, computer math, computer music, computer science, computer technologies, computer-aided design, computers, construction, creative writing, drafting, drama, driver education, earth

science, ecology, economics, English, English literature, environmental science, European history, fine arts, French, geography, geometry, German, government/civics, graphic arts, health, history, home economics, horticulture, journalism, keyboarding, mathematics, music, physical education, physics, science, social sciences, social studies, Spanish, speech, statistics, technology, theater, trigonometry, typing, vocational-technical courses, world history, writing.

Graduation Requirements American government, American history, applied skills, social sciences.

Special Academic Programs Advanced Placement exam preparation; honors section; independent study; study at local college for college credit; study abroad; academic accommodation for the musically talented and the artistically talented; remedial reading and/or remedial writing; remedial math.

College Admission Counseling 202 students graduated in 2016; 145 went to college, including Susquehanna University; Temple University. Other: 32 went to work, 6 entered military service, 14 entered a postgraduate year. 9% scored over 600 on SAT critical reading, 8% scored over 600 on SAT math, 6% scored over 26 on composite ACT.

Student Life Upper grades have specified standards of dress, student council. Discipline rests primarily with faculty. Attendance at religious services is required.

Summer Programs Remediation, enrichment, advancement, art/fine arts, computer instruction programs offered; session focuses on academics, career preparation, and life skills; held both on and off campus; accepts boys and girls; not open to students from other schools. 486 students usually enrolled. 2017 schedule: June 12 to August 20. Application deadline: April 1.

Tuition and Aid School's endowment covers all costs for all students available. In 2016–17, 100% of upper-school students received aid.

Admissions Traditional secondary-level entrance grade is 9. Achievement tests or admissions testing required. Deadline for receipt of application materials: none. No application fee required. On-campus interview required.

Athletics Interscholastic: baseball (boys), basketball (b,g), cheering (g), cross-country running (b,g), diving (b,g), field hockey (g), football (b), soccer (b), softball (g), swimming and diving (b,g), track and field (b,g), wrestling (b); intramural: baseball (b,g), basketball (b,g), field hockey (g), football (b), ice hockey (b), soccer (b), softball (b,g), swimming and diving (b,g), track and field (b,g), wrestling (b). 4 PE instructors, 3 coaches, 1 athletic trainer.

Computers Computers are regularly used in all classes. Computer network features include on-campus library services, online commercial services, Internet access, Media on Demand, video conferencing, laptop computers (for all high school students).

Contact 717-520-2000. Website: www.mhskids.org

See Display on next page and Close-Up on page 606.

MISS EDGAR'S AND MISS CRAMP'S SCHOOL

525 Mount Pleasant Avenue
Montreal, Quebec H3Y 3H6, Canada

Head of School: Ms. Lynn L'esperance Claude

General Information Girls' day college-preparatory school. Grades K–11. Founded: 1909. Setting: urban 4-acre campus. 1 building on campus. Approved or accredited by Quebec Association of Independent Schools and Quebec Department of Education. Affiliate member of National Association of Independent Schools; member of Secondary School Admission Test Board. Languages of instruction: English and French. Total enrollment: 320. Upper school average class size: 19. Upper school faculty-student ratio: 1:9. There are 180 required school days per year for Upper School students. Upper School students typically attend 5 days per week. The average school day consists of 5 hours.

Upper School Student Profile Grade 9: 41 students (41 girls); Grade 10: 38 students (38 girls); Grade 11: 29 students (29 girls).

Faculty School total: 40. In upper school: 4 men, 14 women; 8 have advanced degrees.

Subjects Offered Art, art history, biology, calculus, career exploration, chemistry, computer science, creative writing, drama, ecology, economics, English, environmental science, European history, French, geography, history, mathematics, media, music, physical education, physics, science, social studies, Spanish, theater, women's studies, world history.

Graduation Requirements English, foreign language, mathematics, science, social studies (includes history).

Special Academic Programs 2 Advanced Placement exams for which test preparation is offered; honors section.

College Admission Counseling 41 students graduated in 2016; all went to college, including Lower Canada College.

Student Life Upper grades have uniform requirement, student council, honor system. Discipline rests primarily with faculty.

Tuition and Aid Day student tuition: CAN$18,500. Tuition installment plan (individually arranged payment plans). Bursaries, merit scholarship grants available. In 2016–17, 18% of upper-school students received aid; total upper-school merit-scholarship money awarded: CAN$80,000. Total amount of financial aid awarded in 2016–17: CAN$135,000.

Admissions Traditional secondary-level entrance grade is 9. For fall 2016, 20 students applied for upper-level admission, 12 were accepted, 5 enrolled. CCAT, SSAT or writing sample required. Deadline for receipt of application materials: none. Application fee required: CAN$50. On-campus interview required.

Athletics Interscholastic: badminton, basketball, cross-country running, golf, hockey, ice hockey, running, soccer, swimming and diving, tennis, touch football, track and field, volleyball; intramural: badminton, baseball, basketball, crew, cross-country running, curling, dance, field hockey, gymnastics, ice hockey, outdoor adventure, outdoor education, outdoor skills, physical fitness, rugby, running, skiing (cross-country), soccer, softball, touch football, track and field, volleyball. 3 PE instructors, 11 coaches.

Computers Computers are regularly used in art, English, French, history, newspaper, writing, yearbook classes. Computer network features include on-campus library services, Internet access, wireless campus network, Internet filtering or blocking technology. Campus intranet, student e-mail accounts, and computer access in designated common areas are available to students. The school has a published electronic and media policy.

Contact Ms. Julie Beaulieu, Admissions Coordinator. 514-935-6357 Ext. 254. Fax: 514-935-1099. E-mail: beaulieuj@ecs.qc.ca. Website: www.ecs.qc.ca

MISS HALL'S SCHOOL

492 Holmes Road
Pittsfield, Massachusetts 01201

Head of School: Ms. Julia Nakano Heaton

General Information Girls' boarding and day college-preparatory, arts, technology, community service, and leadership development school. Grades 9–PG. Founded: 1898. Setting: suburban. Nearest major city is Albany, NY. Students are housed in single-sex dormitories. 80-acre campus. 11 buildings on campus. Approved or accredited by Association of Independent Schools in New England, New England Association of Schools and Colleges, The Association of Boarding Schools, The College Board, and Massachusetts Department of Education. Member of National Association of Independent Schools and Secondary School Admission Test Board. Endowment: $19 million. Total enrollment: 214. Upper school average class size: 10. Upper school faculty-student ratio: 1:6. There are 157 required school days per year for Upper School students. Upper School students typically attend 5 days per week. The average school day consists of 6 hours.

Upper School Student Profile Grade 9: 48 students (48 girls); Grade 10: 52 students (52 girls); Grade 11: 52 students (52 girls); Grade 12: 62 students (62 girls). 68% of students are boarding students. 34% are state residents. 18 states are represented in upper school student body. 34% are international students. International students from Bhutan, China, Japan, Republic of Korea, Rwanda, and Vietnam; 23 other countries represented in student body.

Faculty School total: 36. In upper school: 8 men, 28 women; 25 have advanced degrees; 16 reside on campus.

Subjects Offered 20th century history, 3-dimensional art, acting, advanced biology, advanced chemistry, advanced math, Advanced Placement courses, advanced studio art-AP, African-American literature, algebra, American government, American history, American literature, anatomy, art, art history, athletics, biology, business skills, calculus, career exploration, ceramics, chamber groups, character education, chemistry, Chinese, college counseling, community service, computer science, CPR, creative writing, dance, drama, drawing, driver education, ecology, economics, English, English literature, English-AP, ensembles, entrepreneurship, environmental education, environmental science, environmental science-AP, ESL, ethics, ethics and responsibility, European history, European history-AP, expressive arts, fashion, field ecology, fine arts, forensics, French, French-AP, gardening, geometry, government/civics, Greek culture, health, history, human geography - AP, human sexuality, Italian history, Latin, leadership and service, mathematics, media literacy, music, music history, painting, photography, physics, physiology, political science, psychology, robotics, science, senior internship, service learning/internship, social studies, sociology, Spanish, theater, trigonometry, world cultures, world history.

Graduation Requirements Arts, arts and fine arts (art, music, dance, drama), English, foreign language, history, mathematics, physical education (includes health), science. Community service is required.

Special Academic Programs Advanced Placement exam preparation; honors section; independent study; term-away projects; academic accommodation for the gifted, the musically talented, and the artistically talented; programs in English, mathematics for dyslexic students; special instructional classes for students with mild learning disabilities and Attention Deficit Disorder; ESL (20 students enrolled).

College Admission Counseling 62 students graduated in 2015; all went to college.

Student Life Upper grades have specified standards of dress, student council, honor system. Discipline rests equally with students and faculty.

Tuition and Aid Day student tuition: $33,430; 7-day tuition and room/board: $55,105. Tuition installment plan (Insured Tuition Payment Plan, Academic Management Services Plan, Key Tuition Payment Plan, monthly payment plans, individually arranged payment plans). Merit scholarship grants, need-based scholarship grants available. In 2015–16, 50% of upper-school students received aid; total upper-school merit-scholarship money awarded: $275,000. Total amount of financial aid awarded in 2015–16: $3,000,000.

Admissions Traditional secondary-level entrance grade is 9. For fall 2015, 299 students applied for upper-level admission, 152 were accepted, 74 enrolled. PSAT, SAT, SSAT or TOEFL required. Deadline for receipt of application materials: February 1. Application fee required: $75. Interview required.

Athletics Interscholastic: alpine skiing, basketball, cross-country running, equestrian sports, golf, lacrosse, skiing (downhill), soccer, softball, tennis, volleyball; intramural:

aerobics, aerobics/dance, alpine skiing, dance, equestrian sports, fitness, fitness walking, golf, gymnastics, horseback riding, jogging, modern dance, outdoor activities, outdoor education, physical fitness, ropes courses, running, skiing (cross-country), skiing (downhill), snowboarding, swimming and diving, tennis, volleyball, walking, wall climbing, wilderness, yoga. 10 coaches, 1 athletic trainer.

Computers Computers are regularly used in computer applications, English, foreign language, history, mathematics, music, newspaper, photography, science, yearbook classes. Computer network features include on-campus library services, online commercial services, Internet access, wireless campus network, Internet filtering or blocking technology. Campus intranet, student e-mail accounts, and computer access in designated common areas are available to students. Students grades are available online. The school has a published electronic and media policy.

Contact Ms. Julie Bradley, Director of Admission. 413-499-1300. Fax: 413-448-2994. E-mail: info@misshalls.org. Website: www.misshalls.org

MISSOURI MILITARY ACADEMY

204 Grand Avenue
Mexico, Missouri 65265

Head of School: Mr. Charles A. McGeorge

General Information Boys' boarding and day college-preparatory, technology, ESL, military science, and military school, affiliated with Christian faith. Boarding grades 6–PG, day grades 6–12. Founded: 1889. Setting: small town. Nearest major city is St. Louis. Students are housed in single-sex dormitories. 288-acre campus. 19 buildings on campus. Approved or accredited by Independent Schools Association of the Central States and The Association of Boarding Schools. Member of National Association of Independent Schools and Secondary School Admission Test Board. Endowment: $39 million. Total enrollment: 228. Upper school average class size: 10. Upper school faculty-student ratio: 1:11. There are 180 required school days per year for Upper School students. Upper School students typically attend 5 days per week. The average school day consists of 5 hours and 50 minutes.

Upper School Student Profile Grade 9: 34 students (34 boys); Grade 10: 38 students (38 boys); Grade 11: 53 students (53 boys); Grade 12: 65 students (65 boys); Postgraduate: 1 student (1 boy). 99% of students are boarding students. 20% are state residents. 30 states are represented in upper school student body. 40% are international students. International students from China, Mexico, Mongolia, Republic of Korea, Russian Federation, and Taiwan; 13 other countries represented in student body.

Faculty School total: 47. In upper school: 27 men, 8 women; 27 have advanced degrees; 5 reside on campus.

Subjects Offered Algebra, American literature, art, biology, broadcasting, business, business skills, calculus, chemistry, computer science, drama, economics, English, ESL, fine arts, French, geography, geometry, government/civics, history, honors algebra, honors English, honors U.S. history, humanities, instrumental music, Internet, jazz band, journalism, JROTC or LEAD (Leadership Education and Development), keyboarding, languages, Latin American studies, leadership, literary magazine, marching band, mathematics, military science, music, newspaper, physical education, physical science, physics, physics-AP, psychology, science, social studies, sociology, Spanish, speech, statistics, student government, student publications, swimming, theater, track and field, typing, U.S. government, U.S. history, vocal ensemble, vocal music, world history, wrestling, writing, yearbook.

Graduation Requirements Arts and fine arts (art, music, dance, drama), business skills (includes word processing), computer science, English, foreign language, JROTC, mathematics, physical education (includes health), science, social studies (includes history), 20 hours of community service per school year.

Special Academic Programs 9 Advanced Placement exams for which test preparation is offered; honors section; independent study; study at local college for college credit; academic accommodation for the gifted, the musically talented, and the artistically talented; remedial reading and/or remedial writing; remedial math; special instructional classes for students with Attention Deficit Disorder; ESL (33 students enrolled).

College Admission Counseling 67 students graduated in 2015; all went to college, including Texas A&M University; The University of Texas at Austin; University of California, Berkeley; University of Miami; University of Missouri; Washington University in St. Louis. Median SAT critical reading: 467, median SAT math: 547, median combined SAT: 1016, median composite ACT: 21.

Student Life Upper grades have uniform requirement, student council, honor system. Discipline rests equally with students and faculty. Attendance at religious services is required.

Tuition and Aid Day student tuition: $9100; 7-day tuition and room/board: $34,700. Tuition installment plan (individually arranged payment plans, school's own payment plan). Tuition reduction for siblings, merit scholarship grants, need-based scholarship grants, need-based loans available. In 2015–16, 42% of upper-school students received aid; total upper-school merit-scholarship money awarded: $25,000. Total amount of financial aid awarded in 2015–16: $1,200,000.

Admissions Traditional secondary-level entrance grade is 9. For fall 2015, 252 students applied for upper-level admission, 158 were accepted, 100 enrolled. SSAT or TOEFL or SLEP required. Deadline for receipt of application materials: none. Application fee required: $25. Interview required.

Athletics Interscholastic: baseball, basketball, cross-country running, drill team, football, golf, JROTC drill, lacrosse, marksmanship, outdoor activities, riflery, rugby, soccer, swimming and diving, tennis, track and field, weight training, wrestling; intramural: aquatics, basketball, canoeing/kayaking, equestrian sports, fishing, fitness, fitness walking, flag football, horseback riding, indoor track, marksmanship, martial arts, outdoor activities, outdoor recreation, outdoor skills, paint ball, physical fitness, physical training, rappelling, riflery, roller blading, ropes courses, running, soccer, softball, strength & conditioning, swimming and diving, table tennis, tennis, touch football, track and field, volleyball, weight lifting, weight training, winter (indoor) track, wrestling. 12 coaches, 1 athletic trainer.

Computers Computers are regularly used in business, English, history, journalism, library, mathematics, newspaper, science, yearbook classes. Computer network features include on-campus library services, online commercial services, Internet access, wireless campus network, Internet filtering or blocking technology. Campus intranet, student e-mail accounts, and computer access in designated common areas are available to students. Students grades are available online. The school has a published electronic and media policy.

Contact Mrs. Michele Schulte, Enrollment Office Coordinator. 573-581-1776 Ext. 321. Fax: 573-581-0081. E-mail: michele.schulte@missourimilitaryacademy.com. Website: www.MissouriMilitaryAcademy.org

MISS PORTER'S SCHOOL

60 Main Street
Farmington, Connecticut 06032

Head of School: Dr. Katherine G. Windsor

General Information Girls' boarding and day college-preparatory and arts school. Grades 9–12. Founded: 1843. Setting: suburban. Nearest major city is Hartford. Students are housed in single-sex dormitories. 50-acre campus. 56 buildings on campus. Approved or accredited by Connecticut Association of Independent Schools, New England Association of Schools and Colleges, and Connecticut Department of Education. Member of National Association of Independent Schools and Secondary School Admission Test Board. Endowment: $111 million. Total enrollment: 323. Upper school average class size: 10. Upper school faculty-student ratio: 1:6. There are 166 required school days per year for Upper School students. Upper School students typically attend 5 days per week. The average school day consists of 7 hours and 20 minutes.

Upper School Student Profile Grade 9: 78 students (78 girls); Grade 10: 81 students (81 girls); Grade 11: 85 students (85 girls); Grade 12: 81 students (81 girls). 66% of students are boarding students. 54% are state residents. 24 states are represented in upper school student body. 17% are international students. International students from China, Mexico, and Republic of Korea; 15 other countries represented in student body.

Faculty School total: 51. In upper school: 12 men, 39 women; 38 have advanced degrees; 34 reside on campus.

Subjects Offered Acting, advanced chemistry, advanced computer applications, advanced math, Advanced Placement courses, advanced studio art-AP, African history, algebra, American history, American literature, anatomy and physiology, aquatics, area studies, art, art history-AP, arts, astronomy, athletics, ballet, biology, biology-AP, British literature, calculus, calculus-AP, career/college preparation, ceramics, chemistry, chemistry-AP, Chinese, Chinese history, classical language, college counseling, college planning, community service, computer applications, computer graphics, computer programming, computer science, concert choir, creative writing, dance, dance performance, desktop publishing, drama, drama performance, economics, economics and history, engineering, English, English literature, environmental science, environmental science-AP, ethical decision making, European history, European history-AP, experiential education, expository writing, fitness, foreign language, forensics, French, French language-AP, French literature-AP, geometry, global issues, golf, graphic design, health and wellness, healthful living, history, honors geometry, human rights, international relations, intro to computers, Japanese history, jazz, jazz band, jewelry making, languages, Latin, Latin American literature, Latin-AP, leadership, mathematics, Middle Eastern history, model United Nations, modern dance, modern European history-AP, multicultural literature, music, music history, music performance, music theory, participation in sports, performing arts, personal finance, photography, physics, physics-AP, pre-calculus, printmaking, psychology, public speaking, science, Shakespeare, social studies, Spanish, Spanish language-AP, Spanish literature-AP, sports, squash, statistics, statistics-AP, student government, studio art, studio art-AP, swimming, swimming test, tennis, textiles, theater, trigonometry, U.S. history, U.S. history-AP, video film production, visual arts, vocal music, Web site design, Western civilization, writing, yoga.

Graduation Requirements Arts and fine arts (art, music, dance, drama), athletics, computer science, English, experiential education, foreign language, leadership, mathematics, science, social studies (includes history), online course. Community service is required.

Special Academic Programs 26 Advanced Placement exams for which test preparation is offered; honors section; independent study; term-away projects; domestic exchange program; study abroad; academic accommodation for the gifted, the musically talented, and the artistically talented.

College Admission Counseling 81 students graduated in 2016; all went to college, including Bard College; Boston University; Georgetown University; Middlebury College; New York University; University of Michigan. Median SAT critical reading: 630, median SAT math: 610, median SAT writing: 650, median combined SAT: 1880, median composite ACT: 26. 67% scored over 600 on SAT critical reading, 56% scored over 600 on SAT math, 71% scored over 600 on SAT writing, 63% scored over 1800 on combined SAT, 61% scored over 26 on composite ACT.

Student Life Upper grades have specified standards of dress, student council, honor system. Discipline rests equally with students and faculty.

Summer Programs Enrichment, advancement, ESL programs offered; session focuses on for middle school girls: Model UN, leadership, STEAM and CHAT (an English immersion program); held on campus; accepts girls; open to students from other schools. 100 students usually enrolled. 2017 schedule: July 9 to July 29. Application deadline: none.

Tuition and Aid Day student tuition: $45,660; 7-day tuition and room/board: $56,700. Tuition installment plan (monthly payment plans, individually arranged payment plans). Merit scholarship grants, need-based scholarship grants available. In 2016–17, 34% of upper-school students received aid. Total amount of financial aid awarded in 2016–17: $3,900,000.

Admissions Traditional secondary-level entrance grade is 9. For fall 2016, 460 students applied for upper-level admission, 184 were accepted, 100 enrolled. ISEE, PSAT and SAT for applicants to grade 11 and 12, SSAT or TOEFL required. Deadline for receipt of application materials: January 15. Application fee required: $65. Interview required.

Athletics Interscholastic: alpine skiing, badminton, basketball, crew, cross-country running, dance, diving, equestrian sports, field hockey, Frisbee, golf, horseback riding, independent competitive sports, lacrosse, rowing, running, skiing (downhill), soccer, softball, squash, swimming and diving, tennis, track and field, ultimate Frisbee, volleyball; intramural: aerobics, aerobics/Nautilus, ballet, climbing, dance, equestrian sports, fitness, horseback riding, jogging, life saving, martial arts, modern dance, outdoor adventure, outdoor recreation, physical fitness, physical training, rock climbing, running, self defense, skiing (downhill), snowboarding, squash, strength & conditioning, swimming and diving, tennis, wall climbing, weight training, yoga.

Computers Computers are regularly used in all classes. Computer network features include on-campus library services, online commercial services, Internet access, wireless campus network, Internet filtering or blocking technology, online courses. Campus intranet, student e-mail accounts, and computer access in designated common areas are available to students. Students grades are available online. The school has a published electronic and media policy.

Contact Kimberly M. Mount, Director of Admission and Financial Aid. 860-409-3530. Fax: 860-409-3531. E-mail: kim_mount@missporters.org. Website: www.porters.org.

MMI PREPARATORY SCHOOL

154 Centre Street
Freeland, Pennsylvania 18224

Head of School: Mr. D. Scott Wiggins

General Information Coeducational day college-preparatory, arts, and technology school. Grades 6–12. Founded: 1879. Setting: small town. Nearest major city is Hazleton. 20-acre campus. 1 building on campus. Approved or accredited by Middle States Association of Colleges and Schools and Pennsylvania Department of Education. Member of National Association of Independent Schools. Endowment: $22 million. Total enrollment: 252. Upper school average class size: 16. Upper school faculty-student ratio: 1:13. There are 177 required school days per year for Upper School students. Upper School students typically attend 5 days per week. The average school day consists of 6 hours and 30 minutes.

Upper School Student Profile Grade 9: 32 students (18 boys, 14 girls); Grade 10: 44 students (22 boys, 22 girls); Grade 11: 40 students (22 boys, 18 girls); Grade 12: 42 students (24 boys, 18 girls).

Faculty School total: 23. In upper school: 10 men, 13 women; 17 have advanced degrees.

Subjects Offered 3-dimensional art, algebra, American history, American history-AP, American literature, anthropology, art, art-AP, biology, biology-AP, calculus, chemistry, chemistry-AP, Chinese, Chinese studies, college planning, computer programming, computer programming-AP, computer science, creative writing, earth science, economics, English, English language and composition-AP, English literature, English literature and composition-AP, environmental science, European history, European history-AP, expository writing, fine arts, geography, geometry, German, government/civics, grammar, health, history, keyboarding, Latin, marine biology, mathematics, music, physical education, physics, physics-AP, physiology, psychology, science, social studies, Spanish, speech, statistics, trigonometry, world history, world literature.

Graduation Requirements Analysis and differential calculus, arts and fine arts (art, music, dance, drama), college counseling, computer science, consumer education, economics, English, foreign language, mathematics, physical education (includes health), science, social studies (includes history), speech, independent research project presentation every spring, public speaking assembly project every year.

Special Academic Programs 10 Advanced Placement exams for which test preparation is offered; honors section.

College Admission Counseling 32 students graduated in 2016; all went to college, including Immaculata University; McDaniel College; Penn State University Park; Temple University; The University of Scranton; University of Pittsburgh. Median SAT critical reading: 580, median SAT math: 610, median SAT writing: 585, median combined SAT: 1775, median composite ACT: 28.

Student Life Upper grades have specified standards of dress, student council. Discipline rests primarily with faculty.

Tuition and Aid Day student tuition: $14,025. Tuition installment plan (FACTS Tuition Payment Plan, monthly payment plans). Merit scholarship grants, need-based scholarship grants, paying campus jobs available. In 2016–17, 57% of upper-school students received aid; total upper-school merit-scholarship money awarded: $104,000. Total amount of financial aid awarded in 2016–17: $666,170.

Admissions Traditional secondary-level entrance grade is 9. For fall 2016, 27 students applied for upper-level admission, 18 were accepted, 14 enrolled. Cognitive Abilities Test and Iowa Tests of Basic Skills required. Deadline for receipt of application materials: none. No application fee required. On-campus interview recommended.

Athletics Interscholastic: baseball (boys), basketball (b,g), cross-country running (b,g), soccer (b,g), softball (g), tennis (b,g), volleyball (g); intramural: bowling (b,g); coed interscholastic: golf; coed intramural: skiing (downhill), snowboarding. 2 PE instructors, 15 coaches, 1 athletic trainer.

Computers Computers are regularly used in all academic classes. Computer network features include on-campus library services, Internet access, wireless campus network, Internet filtering or blocking technology. Computer access in designated common areas is available to students. Students grades are available online. The school has a published electronic and media policy.

Contact Marcianna Hosier, Director of Admissions and Marketing. 570-636-1108 Ext. 136. Fax: 570-636-0742. E-mail: mhosier@mmiprep.org. Website: www.mmiprep.org

THE MONARCH SCHOOL

Houston, Texas
See Special Needs Schools section.

MONCTON WESLEYAN ACADEMY

945 St. George Boulevard
Moncton, New Brunswick E1E 2C9, Canada

Head of School: Mr. Willie Brownlee

General Information Coeducational day college-preparatory and science and math school, affiliated with Wesleyan Church. Grades K–12. Setting: urban. Students are housed in no housing or dorms. 5-acre campus. 1 building on campus. Approved or accredited by Association of Christian Schools International. Language of instruction: English. Upper school average class size: 44. There are 180 required school days per year for Upper School students. Upper School students typically attend 5 days per week. The average school day consists of 6 hours and 30 minutes.

Upper School Student Profile Grade 6: 7 students (4 boys, 3 girls); Grade 7: 22 students (11 boys, 11 girls); Grade 8: 14 students (8 boys, 6 girls); Grade 9: 8 students (2 boys, 6 girls); Grade 10: 16 students (8 boys, 8 girls); Grade 11: 9 students (3 boys, 6 girls); Grade 12: 11 students (6 boys, 5 girls). 40% of students are members of Wesleyan Church.

Faculty School total: 16. In upper school: 2 men, 5 women; 1 has an advanced degree.

Subjects Offered All academic.

Graduation Requirements Canadian history, English, French, mathematics, physical education (includes health), science.

Special Academic Programs ESL (3 students enrolled).

College Admission Counseling 15 students graduated in 2016; 13 went to college, including Dalhousie University. Other: 2 went to work.

Student Life Upper grades have specified standards of dress, student council, honor system. Discipline rests primarily with faculty.

Tuition and Aid Day student tuition: CAN$4805. Tuition installment plan (monthly payment plans). Need-based scholarship grants, staff tuition discount available. In 2016–17, 25% of upper-school students received aid. Total amount of financial aid awarded in 2016–17: CAN$84,200.

Admissions Traditional secondary-level entrance grade is 9. Traditional secondary-level entrance age is 15. For fall 2016, 6 students applied for upper-level admission, 6 were accepted, 6 enrolled. Deadline for receipt of application materials: August 1. Application fee required: CAN$50. On-campus interview recommended.

Athletics Interscholastic: badminton (boys, girls), basketball (b,g), cross-country running (b,g), soccer (b,g); intramural: badminton (b,g), soccer (b,g). 3 PE instructors, 5 coaches.

Computers Computers are regularly used in all academic classes. Computer resources include Internet access, wireless campus network. Computer access in designated common areas is available to students.

Contact 506-855-5405. Fax: 506-857-9016.

MONSIGNOR BONNER AND ARCHBISHOP PRENDERGAST CATHOLIC HIGH SCHOOL

403 North Lansdowne Avenue
Drexel Hill, Pennsylvania 19026-1196

Head of School: Mr. James Strandberg

General Information Boys' day college-preparatory school, affiliated with Roman Catholic Church; primarily serves students with learning disabilities. Grades 9–12. Founded: 1953. Setting: suburban. Nearest major city is Philadelphia. 41-acre campus. 1 building on campus. Approved or accredited by Middle States Association of Colleges and Schools and Pennsylvania Department of Education. Total enrollment: 901. Upper school average class size: 26. Upper school faculty-student ratio: 1:22. There are 180 required school days per year for Upper School students. Upper School students typically attend 5 days per week. The average school day consists of 6 hours and 40 minutes.

Upper School Student Profile 75% of students are Roman Catholic.

Faculty School total: 48. In upper school: 29 men, 19 women; 28 have advanced degrees.

Subjects Offered Aerobics.

Graduation Requirements Service project.

Special Academic Programs Advanced Placement exam preparation; honors section; remedial reading and/or remedial writing; remedial math; special instructional classes for deaf students, blind students.

College Admission Counseling 206 students graduated in 2016; 204 went to college, including Penn State University Park; Temple University; Villanova University; West Chester University of Pennsylvania. Other: 2 went to work.

Student Life Upper grades have uniform requirement, student council. Discipline rests primarily with faculty. Attendance at religious services is required.

Summer Programs Remediation, enrichment programs offered; session focuses on mathematics, English, technology; held on campus; accepts boys; not open to students from other schools. 2017 schedule: June to July. Application deadline: June 1.

Tuition and Aid Day student tuition: $8550. Tuition installment plan (monthly payment plans). Merit scholarship grants, need-based scholarship grants, grants based upon need available.

Admissions Traditional secondary-level entrance grade is 9. High School Placement Test required. Deadline for receipt of application materials: none. No application fee required.

Athletics Interscholastic: ball hockey, baseball, basketball (g), bowling (g), cheering (g), crew, cross-country running (g), dance squad (g), dance team (g), field hockey (g), football, golf (g), hockey, ice hockey, in-line hockey, indoor track & field (g), lacrosse (g), rowing (g), rugby, soccer (g), softball (g), strength & conditioning, swimming and diving (g), tennis (g), weight training, intramural: basketball, billiards, paddle tennis, touch football, ultimate Frisbee. 3 PE instructors, 1 athletic trainer.

Computers Computers are regularly used in all classes. Computer network features include Internet access, Internet filtering or blocking technology. Students grades are available online.

Contact 610-259-0280. Fax: 610-259-1630. Website: www.bonnerhigh.com

MONSIGNOR EDWARD PACE HIGH SCHOOL

15600 NW 32nd Avenue
Miami Gardens, Florida 33054

Head of School: Mrs. Ana M. Garcia

General Information Coeducational boarding and day and distance learning college-preparatory and STEM, Law Studies, Communications, Visual and Performing Art school, affiliated with Roman Catholic Church. Grades 9–12. Founded: 1961. Setting: urban. Nearest major city is Miami. 44-acre campus. 11 buildings on campus. Approved or accredited by National Catholic Education Association, Southern Association of Colleges and Schools, and Florida Department of Education. Total enrollment: 817. Upper school average class size: 19. Upper school faculty-student ratio: 1:19. There are 180 required school days per year for Upper School students. Upper School students typically attend 5 days per week. The average school day consists of 6 hours and 23 minutes.

Upper School Student Profile Grade 9: 205 students (107 boys, 98 girls); Grade 10: 221 students (107 boys, 114 girls); Grade 11: 201 students (106 boys, 95 girls); Grade 12: 223 students (118 boys, 105 girls). 80% of students are Roman Catholic.

Faculty School total: 60. In upper school: 31 men, 29 women; 41 have advanced degrees.

Subjects Offered All academic.

Graduation Requirements College admission preparation, religion (includes Bible studies and theology).

Special Academic Programs Advanced Placement exam preparation; honors section; study at local college for college credit; study abroad.

College Admission Counseling 195 students graduated in 2016; 190 went to college, including Barry University; Florida International University; Miami Dade College; St. Thomas University; University of Florida; University of Miami. Other: 1 went to work, 4 had other specific plans.

Student Life Upper grades have uniform requirement, student council. Discipline rests primarily with faculty. Attendance at religious services is required.

Summer Programs Remediation, enrichment, sports, computer instruction programs offered; session focuses on enrichment; held on campus; accepts boys and girls; open to students from other schools. 250 students usually enrolled. 2017 schedule: June 19 to July 14. Application deadline: June 1.

Tuition and Aid Day student tuition: $11,325–$11,575. Tuition installment plan (FACTS Tuition Payment Plan, monthly payment plans). Tuition reduction for siblings, need-based scholarship grants available.

Admissions Traditional secondary-level entrance grade is 9. High School Placement Test required. Deadline for receipt of application materials: February 28. Application fee required: $50. On-campus interview required.

Athletics Interscholastic: baseball (boys), basketball (b,g), cheering (g), cross-country running (b,g), dance (g), danceline (g), flag football (g), football (b), golf (b,g), soccer (b,g), softball (g), swimming and diving (b,g), table tennis (b,g), tennis (b,g), track and field (b,g), volleyball (b,g), wrestling (b); coed interscholastic: fishing. 2 PE instructors, 21 coaches, 1 athletic trainer.

Computers Computers are regularly used in all academic classes. Computer network features include Internet access, wireless campus network, Internet filtering or blocking technology, 1:1 iPad program. Campus intranet, student e-mail accounts, and computer access in designated common areas are available to students. Students grades are available online. The school has a published electronic and media policy.

Contact Mrs. Maria Garcia, Admissions Representative. 305-623-7223 Ext. 342. Fax: 305-521-0185. E-mail: mgarcia@pacehs.com. Website: www.pacehs.com

MONTCLAIR KIMBERLEY ACADEMY

201 Valley Road
Montclair, New Jersey 07042

Head of School: Mr. Thomas W. Nammack

General Information Coeducational day college-preparatory school. Grades PK–12. Founded: 1887. Setting: suburban. Nearest major city is New York, NY. 28-acre campus. 1 building on campus. Approved or accredited by Middle States Association of Colleges and Schools and New Jersey Association of Independent Schools. Member of National Association of Independent Schools and Secondary School Admission Test Board. Endowment: $12 million. Total enrollment: 990. Upper school average class size: 12. Upper school faculty-student ratio: 1:6. There are 163 required school days per year for Upper School students. Upper School students typically attend 5 days per week. The average school day consists of 6 hours and 30 minutes.

Upper School Student Profile Grade 6: 72 students (43 boys, 29 girls); Grade 7: 93 students (46 boys, 47 girls); Grade 8: 93 students (53 boys, 40 girls); Grade 9: 111 students (59 boys, 52 girls); Grade 10: 102 students (55 boys, 47 girls); Grade 11: 107 students (55 boys, 52 girls); Grade 12: 100 students (50 boys, 50 girls).

Faculty School total: 74. In upper school: 41 men, 33 women; 60 have advanced degrees.

Subjects Offered Acting, advanced chemistry, advanced math, algebra, American history, American literature, architecture, art, astronomy, biology, biology-AP, British literature, calculus, calculus-AP, chemistry, chemistry-AP, Chinese, chorus, communications, concert band, creative writing, dance, digital photography, drama, driver education, ecology, economics, economics-AP, English, English literature, environmental science, ethics, European history, expository writing, fine arts, French, French language-AP, French literature-AP, geometry, government/civics, health, history, Latin, mathematics, music, photography, physical education, physics, physics-AP, post-calculus, Spanish, Spanish language-AP, Spanish literature-AP, statistics-AP, theater, trigonometry, world history, world literature, world wide web design, writing.

Graduation Requirements Art, arts and fine arts (art, music, dance, drama), English, foreign language, history, mathematics, music, physical education (includes health), science, swimming, citizenship. Community service is required.

Special Academic Programs Advanced Placement exam preparation; honors section; independent study; term-away projects; study abroad; academic accommodation for the gifted.

College Admission Counseling 106 students graduated in 2016; all went to college, including Boston College; Lehigh University; New York University; University of Pennsylvania; Villanova University; Wesleyan University. Other: 1 entered a postgraduate year. Mean SAT critical reading: 630, mean SAT math: 647. 60% scored over 600 on SAT critical reading, 65% scored over 600 on SAT math.

Student Life Upper grades have specified standards of dress, student council, honor system. Discipline rests equally with students and faculty.

Summer Programs Enrichment, advancement, sports, art/fine arts, computer instruction programs offered; held on campus; accepts boys and girls; open to students from other schools. 250 students usually enrolled. 2017 schedule: June 27 to August 5. Application deadline: none.

Tuition and Aid Day student tuition: $34,400. Tuition installment plan (Insured Tuition Payment Plan, monthly payment plans, individually arranged payment plans). Need-based scholarship grants available. In 2016–17, 15% of upper-school students received aid. Total amount of financial aid awarded in 2016–17: $1,222,000.

Admissions Traditional secondary-level entrance grade is 9. For fall 2016, 177 students applied for upper-level admission, 67 were accepted, 37 enrolled. ISEE or

SSAT required. Deadline for receipt of application materials: December 16. Application fee required: $50. On-campus interview recommended.

Athletics Interscholastic: baseball (boys), basketball (b,g), cheering (g), cross-country running (b,g), dance (b,g), dance team (b,g), fencing (b,g), field hockey (g), football (b), ice hockey (b), lacrosse (b,g), outdoor activities (b,g), physical fitness (b,g), soccer (b,g), softball (g), swimming and diving (b,g), tennis (b,g), track and field (b,g), volleyball (g), winter (indoor) track (b,g); coed interscholastic: golf. 5 PE instructors, 9 coaches, 2 athletic trainers.

Computers Computers are regularly used in architecture classes. Computer network features include on-campus library services, online commercial services, Internet access, wireless campus network, Internet filtering or blocking technology, 1:1 laptop school, community Intranet. Campus intranet and student e-mail accounts are available to students. The school has a published electronic and media policy.

Contact Alyson Waldman, Director of Admissions and Financial Aid. 973-509-7930. Fax: 973-509-4526. E-mail: awaldman@mka.org. Website: www.mka.org

MONTEREY BAY ACADEMY

783 San Andreas Road
La Selva Beach, California 95076-1907

Head of School: Mr. Jeffrey M. Deming

General Information Coeducational boarding and day college-preparatory school, affiliated with Seventh-day Adventist Church. Grades 9–12. Founded: 1949. Setting: rural. Nearest major city is San Jose. Students are housed in single-sex dormitories. 379-acre campus. 8 buildings on campus. Approved or accredited by Western Association of Schools and Colleges and California Department of Education. Total enrollment: 181. Upper school average class size: 20. Upper school faculty-student ratio: 1:13. There are 180 required school days per year for Upper School students. Upper School students typically attend 5 days per week. The average school day consists of 7 hours.

Upper School Student Profile Grade 9: 34 students (17 boys, 17 girls); Grade 10: 51 students (24 boys, 27 girls); Grade 11: 64 students (33 boys, 31 girls); Grade 12: 51 students (30 boys, 21 girls). 80% of students are boarding students. 65% are state residents. 10 states are represented in upper school student body. 30% are international students. International students from China, Colombia, Ethiopia, and Japan; 4 other countries represented in student body. 75% of students are Seventh-day Adventists.

Faculty School total: 17. In upper school: 13 men, 4 women; 7 have advanced degrees; all reside on campus.

Subjects Offered Accounting, Advanced Placement courses, algebra, American literature, biology, calculus, chemistry, choir, Christianity, computer applications, computer literacy, drama, economics, English, English literature and composition-AP, geometry, graphics, health, instrumental music, marine biology, photography, physical education, physical science, physics, physiology, pre-algebra, pre-calculus, religion, Spanish, technology, U.S. government, U.S. history, U.S. history-AP, voice, weight training, woodworking, world history.

Graduation Requirements Algebra, American literature, arts and fine arts (art, music, dance, drama), biology, computer applications, computer literacy, electives, English, English composition, English literature, geometry, health, keyboarding, mathematics, physical education (includes health), physics, religion (includes Bible studies and theology), science, social studies (includes history), U.S. government, U.S. history, work experience, religious studies for each year in a Seventh-day Adventist School.

Special Academic Programs Advanced Placement exam preparation; ESL (21 students enrolled).

College Admission Counseling 57 students graduated in 2016; 54 went to college, including La Sierra University; Pacific Union College; Southern Adventist University; Walla Walla University. Other: 1 went to work, 2 had other specific plans. Mean SAT critical reading: 515, mean SAT math: 555, mean SAT writing: 513, mean combined SAT: 1583, mean composite ACT: 23. 15% scored over 600 on SAT critical reading, 33% scored over 600 on SAT math, 15% scored over 600 on SAT writing, 19% scored over 1800 on combined SAT, 19% scored over 26 on composite ACT.

Student Life Upper grades have specified standards of dress, student council. Discipline rests primarily with faculty. Attendance at religious services is required.

Tuition and Aid Day student tuition: $9630–$11,860; 7-day tuition and room/board: $16,000–$30,000. Tuition installment plan (monthly payment plans). Need-based scholarship grants, paying campus jobs available. In 2016–17, 30% of upper-school students received aid. Total amount of financial aid awarded in 2016–17: $240,000.

Admissions Traditional secondary-level entrance grade is 9. For fall 2016, 220 students applied for upper-level admission, 218 were accepted, 201 enrolled. ITBS achievement test or TOEFL required. Deadline for receipt of application materials: July 15. Application fee required: $50. Interview required.

Athletics Interscholastic: basketball (boys, girls), flag football (b,g), volleyball (b,g); intramural: basketball (b,g), flag football (b,g), volleyball (b,g); coed interscholastic: soccer, softball; coed intramural: soccer, softball. 1 PE instructor, 10 coaches.

Computers Computers are regularly used in accounting, computer applications, English, keyboarding, mathematics, religious studies, science, yearbook classes. Computer network features include Internet access, Internet filtering or blocking technology. Computer access in designated common areas is available to students.

Students grades are available online. The school has a published electronic and media policy.

Contact Mr. Kevin Bowen, Director of Marketing and Recruitment. 831-728-1481 Ext. 1221. Fax: 831-728-1485. E-mail: info@montereybayacademy.org. Website: www.montereybayacademy.org

MONTGOMERY BELL ACADEMY

4001 Harding Road
Nashville, Tennessee 37205

Head of School: Bradford Gioia

General Information Boys' day college-preparatory school. Grades 7–12. Founded: 1867. Setting: urban. 43-acre campus. 13 buildings on campus. Approved or accredited by Southern Association of Colleges and Schools, Southern Association of Independent Schools, and Tennessee Association of Independent Schools. Member of National Association of Independent Schools and Secondary School Admission Test Board. Endowment: $63 million. Total enrollment: 752. Upper school average class size: 14. Upper school faculty-student ratio: 1:7. There are 180 required school days per year for Upper School students. Upper School students typically attend 5 days per week. The average school day consists of 7 hours and 20 minutes.

Upper School Student Profile Grade 9: 133 students (133 boys); Grade 10: 125 students (125 boys); Grade 11: 133 students (133 boys); Grade 12: 124 students (124 boys).

Faculty School total: 101. In upper school: 58 men, 12 women; 50 have advanced degrees.

Subjects Offered Advanced Placement courses, algebra, American history, American history-AP, American literature, American literature-AP, art, art history, art history-AP, biology, biology-AP, calculus, calculus-AP, chemistry, chemistry-AP, Chinese, computer programming, computer science, computer science-AP, drama, earth science, economics, English, English literature, environmental science-AP, European history, European history-AP, fine arts, French, French language-AP, French literature-AP, French-AP, geography, geology, geometry, German, German-AP, government/civics, grammar, Greek, history, Latin, Latin-AP, mathematics, music, music history, music theory, music theory-AP, physical education, physics, physics-AP, science, social studies, Spanish, Spanish-AP, speech, statistics, statistics-AP, theater, trigonometry, U.S. government and politics-AP, U.S. history-AP, world history, world history-AP, writing.

Graduation Requirements Arts and fine arts (art, music, dance, drama), English, foreign language, mathematics, physical education (includes health), science, social studies (includes history).

Special Academic Programs Advanced Placement exam preparation; honors section; term-away projects; domestic exchange program; study abroad.

College Admission Counseling 127 students graduated in 2016; all went to college, including Rhodes College; Southern Methodist University; The University of Tennessee; Tulane University; University of Mississippi; Vanderbilt University. Mean combined SAT: 1888, mean composite ACT: 28.

Student Life Upper grades have specified standards of dress, student council, honor system. Discipline rests primarily with faculty.

Summer Programs Remediation, enrichment, sports, art/fine arts, rigorous outdoor training, computer instruction programs offered; session focuses on academics and athletics; held both on and off campus; accepts boys and girls; open to students from other schools. 3,100 students usually enrolled. 2017 schedule: June 1 to July 31.

Tuition and Aid Day student tuition: $25,200. Tuition installment plan (monthly payment plans, Dewar Tuition Refund Plan). Need-based scholarship grants available. In 2016–17, 22% of upper-school students received aid. Total amount of financial aid awarded in 2016–17: $2,150,000.

Admissions Traditional secondary-level entrance grade is 9. For fall 2016, 61 students applied for upper-level admission, 30 were accepted, 26 enrolled. ISEE required. Deadline for receipt of application materials: February 1. Application fee required: $50. Interview recommended.

Athletics Interscholastic: baseball, basketball, bowling, crew, cross-country running, diving, football, Frisbee, golf, hockey, ice hockey, lacrosse, riflery, rock climbing, rowing, soccer, swimming and diving, tennis, track and field, ultimate Frisbee, wrestling; intramural: backpacking, baseball, basketball, cheering, climbing, crew, cricket, fencing, flag football, football, Frisbee, hiking/backpacking, independent competitive sports, outdoor activities, paddle tennis, running, soccer, strength & conditioning, table tennis, track and field, weight training, wilderness, yoga. 2 PE instructors, 4 coaches, 2 athletic trainers.

Computers Computers are regularly used in all academic classes. Computer network features include on-campus library services, online commercial services, Internet access, wireless campus network, Internet filtering or blocking technology. Student e-mail accounts and computer access in designated common areas are available to students. Students grades are available online. The school has a published electronic and media policy.

Contact Mr. Greg Ferrell, Director, Admission and Financial Aid. 615-369-5311. Fax: 615-369-5316. E-mail: greg.ferrell@montgomerybell.edu. Website: www.montgomerybell.edu

MONTROSE SCHOOL

29 North Street
Medfield, Massachusetts 02052

Head of School: Dr. Karen E. Bohlin

General Information Girls' day college-preparatory school, affiliated with Roman Catholic Church. Grades 6–12. Founded: 1979. Setting: suburban. Nearest major city is Boston. 14-acre campus. 3 buildings on campus. Approved or accredited by Association of Independent Schools in New England and New England Association of Schools and Colleges. Member of National Association of Independent Schools and Secondary School Admission Test Board. Total enrollment: 217. Upper school average class size: 15. Upper school faculty-student ratio: 1:5. There are 169 required school days per year for Upper School students. Upper School students typically attend 5 days per week. The average school day consists of 7 hours and 20 minutes.

Upper School Student Profile 71% of students are Roman Catholic.

Faculty School total: 35. In upper school: 27 women; 20 have advanced degrees.

Subjects Offered 20th century American writers, 20th century history, advanced biology, advanced math, Advanced Placement courses, algebra, American history-AP, American literature, anatomy and physiology, art, biology, biology-AP, British literature, calculus-AP, chemistry, chorus, church history, comparative politics, composition-AP, computer science, computers, drama, English-AP, French, geometry, Latin-AP, Life of Christ, medieval/Renaissance history, modern European history, moral theology, music, physical education, physics, physics-AP, pre-calculus, religion, social doctrine, Spanish, Spanish language-AP, speech, studio art, studio art-AP, trigonometry, U.S. history, world history, world literature.

Graduation Requirements Arts and fine arts (art, music, dance, drama), English, foreign language, mathematics, physical education (includes health), religion (includes Bible studies and theology), science, social studies (includes history).

Special Academic Programs 8 Advanced Placement exams for which test preparation is offered; honors section; independent study; study abroad.

College Admission Counseling 40 students graduated in 2016; all went to college, including Boston College; College of the Holy Cross; Emmanuel College; Fairfield University; Stonehill College; Worcester Polytechnic Institute. Mean SAT critical reading: 622, mean SAT math: 597, mean SAT writing: 634.

Student Life Upper grades have uniform requirement, student council, honor system. Discipline rests primarily with faculty.

Summer Programs Remediation, enrichment, sports, art/fine arts programs offered; held both on and off campus; accepts girls; open to students from other schools. 80 students usually enrolled. Application deadline: June 1.

Tuition and Aid Day student tuition: $27,020. Tuition installment plan (SMART Tuition Payment Plan). Merit scholarship grants, need-based scholarship grants, need-based tuition assistance available. In 2016–17, 39% of upper-school students received aid. Total amount of financial aid awarded in 2016–17: $500,000.

Admissions Traditional secondary-level entrance grade is 9. Admissions testing, essay, ISEE or SSAT required. Deadline for receipt of application materials: January 31. Application fee required: $50. On-campus interview recommended.

Athletics Interscholastic: basketball, cross-country running, field hockey, golf, lacrosse, soccer, softball, volleyball; intramural: dance, fitness, life saving, physical fitness, physical training, skiing (downhill), strength & conditioning. 1 PE instructor, 7 coaches, 1 athletic trainer.

Computers Computers are regularly used in English, foreign language, French, history, newspaper, philosophy, religion, Spanish, theology classes. Computer network features include on-campus library services, Internet access, wireless campus network, Internet filtering or blocking technology, laptop carts, BYOD device program. Campus intranet and student e-mail accounts are available to students. The school has a published electronic and media policy.

Contact Mrs. Sarah McGowan, Associate Director of Admissions. 508-359-2423 Ext. 315. Fax: 508-359-2597. E-mail: smcgowan@montroseschool.org. Website: www.montroseschool.org

MOORESTOWN FRIENDS SCHOOL

110 East Main Street
Moorestown, New Jersey 08057

Head of School: Mr. Laurence Van Meter

General Information Coeducational day college-preparatory school, affiliated with Society of Friends. Grades PS–12. Founded: 1785. Setting: suburban. Nearest major city is Philadelphia, PA. 48-acre campus. 9 buildings on campus. Approved or accredited by Friends Council on Education, Middle States Association of Colleges and Schools, New Jersey Association of Independent Schools, and New Jersey Department of Education. Member of National Association of Independent Schools. Endowment: $11 million. Total enrollment: 730. Upper school average class size: 14. Upper school faculty-student ratio: 1:7. There are 170 required school days per year for Upper School students. Upper School students typically attend 5 days per week. The average school day consists of 7 hours and 10 minutes.

Upper School Student Profile Grade 9: 76 students (39 boys, 37 girls); Grade 10: 70 students (33 boys, 37 girls); Grade 11: 77 students (37 boys, 40 girls); Grade 12: 77 students (36 boys, 41 girls). 3% of students are members of Society of Friends.

Faculty School total: 100. In upper school: 20 men, 26 women; 35 have advanced degrees.

Subjects Offered Algebra, American history, American literature, art, art history, biology, calculus, ceramics, chemistry, Chinese, community service, computer programming, computer science, creative writing, drama, driver education, earth science, economics, English, English literature, environmental science, ethics, European history, expository writing, finance, fine arts, French, geometry, government/civics, grammar, health, history, mathematics, music, philosophy, photography, physical education, physics, psychology, religion, science, social studies, Spanish, theater, trigonometry, world history, writing.

Graduation Requirements Arts and fine arts (art, music, dance, drama), English, foreign language, history, mathematics, physical education (includes health), science, senior project, social studies (includes history). Community service is required.

Special Academic Programs Advanced Placement exam preparation; honors section; independent study; term-away projects; study abroad.

College Admission Counseling 76 students graduated in 2016; all went to college, including Cornell University; Lehigh University; Muhlenberg College; Princeton University; Rutgers University–New Brunswick; The George Washington University. Mean SAT critical reading: 630, mean SAT math: 628, mean SAT writing: 628, mean combined SAT: 1886.

Student Life Upper grades have specified standards of dress, student council, honor system. Discipline rests primarily with faculty. Attendance at religious services is required.

Summer Programs Enrichment, advancement, art/fine arts programs offered; session focuses on academic courses for acceleration, enrichment experiences in video/audio, mock trial, and robotics; held on campus; accepts boys and girls; open to students from other schools. 300 students usually enrolled. 2017 schedule: June 26 to August 24.

Tuition and Aid Day student tuition: $28,650. Tuition installment plan (Academic Management Services Plan, Tuition Refund Plan). Tuition reduction for siblings, merit scholarship grants, need-based scholarship grants, need-based loans, tuition reduction for children of faculty and staff available. In 2016–17, 24% of upper-school students received aid; total upper-school merit-scholarship money awarded: $12,500. Total amount of financial aid awarded in 2016–17: $1,784,855.

Admissions Traditional secondary-level entrance grade is 9. For fall 2016, 101 students applied for upper-level admission, 57 were accepted, 40 enrolled. ERB CTP required. Deadline for receipt of application materials: January 8. Application fee required: $45. On-campus interview required.

Athletics Interscholastic: baseball (boys), basketball (b,g), crew (b,g), cross-country running (b,g), fencing (b,g), field hockey (g), independent competitive sports (b,g), lacrosse (b,g), physical training (b,g), soccer (b,g), swimming and diving (b,g), tennis (b,g); intramural: floor hockey (b), roller hockey (b), street hockey (b), weight training (b,g); coed interscholastic: golf; coed intramural: ultimate Frisbee. 5 PE instructors, 23 coaches, 1 athletic trainer.

Computers Computers are regularly used in English, foreign language, mathematics, media production, music, newspaper, photography, publications, religion, science, social studies, video film production, yearbook classes. Computer network features include on-campus library services, Internet access, wireless campus network, Internet filtering or blocking technology, campus portal. Campus intranet, student e-mail accounts, and computer access in designated common areas are available to students. Students grades are available online. The school has a published electronic and media policy.

Contact Rachel Tilney, Director of Admissions and Financial Aid. 856-914-4426. Fax: 856-235-6684. E-mail: rtilney@mfriends.org. Website: www.mfriends.org

MOOSEHEART HIGH SCHOOL

255 James J. Davis Drive
Mooseheart, Illinois 60539

Head of School: Dr. Jeffrey Scott Szymczak

General Information Coeducational boarding and day college-preparatory, general academic, vocational, automotive; commercial music; cosmetology, and business and computers; and Family Consumer Science school; primarily serves underachievers, individuals with Attention Deficit Disorder, and Other Health Impaired. Grades K–12. Founded: 1913. Setting: small town. Nearest major city is Aurora. Students are housed in coed dormitories and family homes. 1,000-acre campus. 40 buildings on campus. Approved or accredited by North Central Association of Colleges and Schools and Illinois Department of Education. Endowment: $2 million. Total enrollment: 199. Upper school average class size: 13. Upper school faculty-student ratio: 1:6. There are 176 required school days per year for Upper School students. Upper School students typically attend 5 days per week. The average school day consists of 6 hours and 45 minutes.

Upper School Student Profile Grade 6: 11 students (9 boys, 2 girls); Grade 7: 12 students (9 boys, 3 girls); Grade 8: 21 students (10 boys, 11 girls); Grade 9: 19 students (10 boys, 9 girls); Grade 10: 26 students (16 boys, 10 girls); Grade 11: 32 students (18 boys, 14 girls); Grade 12: 19 students (11 boys, 8 girls). 100% of students are boarding students. 50% are state residents. 24 states are represented in upper school student body. 9% are international students. International students from Algeria, Egypt, Haiti, Rwanda, and Sudan.

Faculty School total: 45. In upper school: 9 men, 11 women; 6 have advanced degrees.

Subjects Offered Algebra, American government, American history, applied music, auto mechanics, biology, business education, business law, career and personal planning, chemistry, child development, computer education, concert band, consumer education, ESL, geometry, government, language arts, mathematics, music technology, NJROTC, pre-algebra, religious education, vocational arts, world geography.

Graduation Requirements American government, CPR, electives, English, health, mathematics, NJROTC, religion (includes Bible studies and theology), senior seminar, vocational arts, vocational class and NJROTC required.

Special Academic Programs Advanced Placement exam preparation; independent study; remedial reading and/or remedial writing; remedial math; ESL (23 students enrolled).

College Admission Counseling 30 students graduated in 2016; 22 went to college, including Illinois State University; University of Illinois at Chicago; University of Illinois at Urbana–Champaign; University of Memphis; Waubonsee Community College; Western Illinois University. Other: 6 went to work, 2 entered military service. Median composite ACT: 19. 10% scored over 26 on composite ACT.

Student Life Upper grades have specified standards of dress, student council, honor system. Discipline rests primarily with faculty.

Summer Programs Remediation, sports programs offered; session focuses on Credit recovery; held both on and off campus; accepts boys and girls; not open to students from other schools. 75 students usually enrolled. 2017 schedule: June 12 to July 21. Application deadline: May 1.

Tuition and Aid Tuition installment plan (no cost to attend if need documented, Social Security and Child Support payments may be required).

Admissions Traditional secondary-level entrance grade is 9. Latest standardized score from previous school, mathematics proficiency exam or writing sample required. Deadline for receipt of application materials: none. No application fee required. Interview required.

Athletics Interscholastic: basketball (boys, girls), cross-country running (g), drill team (b,g), football (b), indoor track & field (b,g), track and field (b,g), volleyball (g), wrestling (b); intramural: aerobics (b), aerobics/dance (g), fitness (b,g); coed interscholastic: flag football, JROTC drill, marksmanship, rugby; coed intramural: horseback riding, strength & conditioning. 2 PE instructors, 12 coaches.

Computers Computers are regularly used in business education, computer applications, music technology, vocational-technical courses, word processing classes. Computer network features include on-campus library services, online commercial services, Internet access, wireless campus network, Internet filtering or blocking technology, 1:1 computers (Surface Pro 4). Campus intranet and computer access in designated common areas are available to students. Students grades are available online. The school has a published electronic and media policy.

Contact Kyle Rife, Director of Admission. 630-906-3631 Ext. 3631. Fax: 630-906-3634 Ext. 3634. E-mail: krife@mooseheart.org.

Website: www.mooseheart.org/Academic.asp

MORAVIAN ACADEMY

4313 Green Pond Road
Bethlehem, Pennsylvania 18020

Head of School: Jeffrey Zemsky

General Information Coeducational day college-preparatory school, affiliated with Moravian Church. Grades PS–12. Founded: 1742. Setting: rural. Nearest major city is Philadelphia. 120-acre campus. 10 buildings on campus. Approved or accredited by Middle States Association of Colleges and Schools, Pennsylvania Association of Independent Schools, and Pennsylvania Department of Education. Member of National Association of Independent Schools and Secondary School Admission Test Board. Endowment: $14.3 million. Total enrollment: 734. Upper school average class size: 15. Upper school faculty-student ratio: 1:7. There are 173 required school days per year for Upper School students. Upper School students typically attend 5 days per week. The average school day consists of 7 hours and 15 minutes.

Upper School Student Profile Grade 9: 75 students (48 boys, 27 girls); Grade 10: 84 students (44 boys, 40 girls); Grade 11: 80 students (44 boys, 36 girls); Grade 12: 71 students (40 boys, 31 girls).

Faculty School total: 102. In upper school: 19 men, 25 women; 39 have advanced degrees.

Subjects Offered Acting, advanced biology, advanced chemistry, Advanced Placement courses, algebra, American history, American history-AP, anatomy and physiology, ancient history, ancient world history, art, bell choir, biology, biology-AP, calculus, calculus-AP, ceramics, chemistry, chemistry-AP, Chinese, Chinese history, community service, drama, drawing, driver education, ecology, economics, English, English language-AP, English literature-AP, environmental science, environmental science-AP, ethics, European history, European history-AP, film, fine arts, French, French language-AP, geometry, government, health, history, honors geometry, Latin American history, mathematics, Middle East, music, painting, photography, physical education, physics, physics-AP, playwriting, poetry, probability and statistics, religion, science, short story, Spanish, Spanish language-AP, statistics, statistics-AP, theater, trigonometry, U.S. history-AP, woodworking, world history, world literature, Zen Buddhism, zoology.

Graduation Requirements Arts and fine arts (art, music, dance, drama), comedy, English, foreign language, mathematics, physical education (includes health), religion (includes Bible studies and theology), science, social studies (includes history), service project.

Special Academic Programs 13 Advanced Placement exams for which test preparation is offered; honors section; independent study; study at local college for college credit.

College Admission Counseling 80 students graduated in 2016; all went to college, including American University; Lafayette College; Lehigh University; Penn State University Park; Tufts University; University of Rochester. Median SAT critical reading: 600, median SAT math: 620, median SAT writing: 590, median combined SAT: 1820, median composite ACT: 28. 55% scored over 600 on SAT critical reading, 60% scored over 600 on SAT math, 52% scored over 600 on SAT writing, 54% scored over 1800 on combined SAT, 72% scored over 26 on composite ACT.

Student Life Upper grades have specified standards of dress, student council. Discipline rests equally with students and faculty. Attendance at religious services is required.

Summer Programs Enrichment, sports, art/fine arts programs offered; session focuses on enrichment; held on campus; accepts boys and girls; open to students from other schools. 2017 schedule: June 12 to August 4.

Tuition and Aid Day student tuition: $27,330. Tuition installment plan (monthly payment plans). Need-based scholarship grants available. In 2016–17, 30% of upper-school students received aid. Total amount of financial aid awarded in 2016–17: $1,400,000.

Admissions Traditional secondary-level entrance grade is 9. For fall 2016, 58 students applied for upper-level admission, 49 were accepted, 35 enrolled. ERB and Otis-Lennon School Ability Test required. Deadline for receipt of application materials: none. Application fee required: $65. On-campus interview required.

Athletics Interscholastic: baseball (boys), basketball (b,g), field hockey (g), football (b), lacrosse (b,g), soccer (b,g), softball (g), tennis (b,g), track and field (b,g), volleyball (g), wrestling (b); coed interscholastic: cross-country running, golf, swimming and diving; coed intramural: outdoor education. 3 PE instructors, 15 coaches, 1 athletic trainer.

Computers Computers are regularly used in all academic, art, English, foreign language, history, mathematics, music, science classes. Computer resources include on-campus library services, Internet access, wireless campus network, Internet filtering or blocking technology, 1:1 program using MacBook Air computers. Student e-mail accounts and computer access in designated common areas are available to students. The school has a published electronic and media policy.

Contact Daniel Axford, Director of Upper School Admissions. 610-691-1600. Fax: 610-691-3354. E-mail: daxford@moravianacademy.org.

Website: www.moravianacademy.org

MOREAU CATHOLIC HIGH SCHOOL

27170 Mission Boulevard
Hayward, California 94544

Head of School: Mr. Terry Lee

General Information Coeducational day college-preparatory and STEM school, affiliated with Roman Catholic Church. Grades 9–12. Founded: 1965. Setting: suburban. Nearest major city is San Francisco. 14-acre campus. 6 buildings on campus. Approved or accredited by National Catholic Education Association, Western Association of Schools and Colleges, Western Catholic Education Association, and California Department of Education. Total enrollment: 945. Upper school average class size: 24. Upper school faculty-student ratio: 1:18. There are 186 required school days per year for Upper School students. Upper School students typically attend 5 days per week. The average school day consists of 6 hours and 35 minutes.

Upper School Student Profile Grade 9: 232 students (122 boys, 110 girls); Grade 10: 261 students (140 boys, 121 girls); Grade 11: 250 students (124 boys, 126 girls); Grade 12: 202 students (90 boys, 112 girls). 63% of students are Roman Catholic.

Faculty School total: 65. In upper school: 32 men, 28 women; 30 have advanced degrees.

Subjects Offered Advanced Placement courses, algebra, American Civil War, American history, American legal systems, American literature, anatomy, art, ASB Leadership, athletics, Bible as literature, biology, biology-AP, business, business law, calculus, calculus-AP, campus ministry, ceramics, cheerleading, chemistry, choral music, Christian ethics, Christian scripture, Christianity, church history, community service, computer education, computer programming, computer science, concert band, drama, drama performance, economics, engineering, English, English literature, English/composition-AP, ethics, ethics and responsibility, European history, expository writing, fine arts, French, French-AP, geometry, government-AP, government/civics, grammar, health, health education, history, history of the Catholic Church, honors algebra, honors English, honors geometry, honors U.S. history, honors world history, human biology, instrumental music, jazz band, jazz ensemble, journalism, marching band, mathematics, media studies, moral theology, music, music appreciation, newspaper, physical education, physics, physics-AP, physiology, psychology, religion, science, sculpture, social sciences, social studies, Spanish, Spanish language-AP, speech, sports medicine, sports science, student government, student publications, symphonic band, theater, theology, trigonometry, U.S. government, U.S. government and politics-AP, U.S. history, U.S. history-AP, weight training, world history, world literature, writing, yearbook.

Graduation Requirements Arts and fine arts (art, music, dance, drama), English, foreign language, mathematics, physical education (includes health), religion (includes Bible studies and theology), science, social sciences, social studies (includes history). Community service is required.

Special Academic Programs Advanced Placement exam preparation; honors section; special instructional classes for Saints and Scholars program for students with documented learning disabilities who require accommodations; ESL.

College Admission Counseling 239 students graduated in 2016; 235 went to college, including California State University, East Bay; San Francisco State University; Sonoma State University; University of California, Berkeley; University of California, Riverside; University of California, Santa Cruz. Other: 2 went to work, 2 had other specific plans. Mean SAT critical reading: 514, mean SAT math: 537, mean SAT writing: 531, mean composite ACT: 24.

Student Life Upper grades have specified standards of dress, student council, honor system. Discipline rests primarily with faculty. Attendance at religious services is required.

Summer Programs Remediation, enrichment, sports programs offered; session focuses on enrichment and remediation; held on campus; accepts boys and girls; open to students from other schools. 120 students usually enrolled. 2017 schedule: June 12 to July 20. Application deadline: June 9.

Tuition and Aid Day student tuition: $17,986. Tuition installment plan (FACTS Tuition Payment Plan, monthly payment plans). Merit scholarship grants, need-based scholarship grants available. In 2016–17, 35% of upper-school students received aid. Total amount of financial aid awarded in 2016–17: $2,100,000.

Admissions Traditional secondary-level entrance grade is 9. Scholastic Testing Service High School Placement Test required. Deadline for receipt of application materials: December 30. Application fee required: $110. On-campus interview recommended.

Athletics Interscholastic: aquatics (boys, girls), badminton (b,g), baseball (b), basketball (b,g), cheering (g), cross-country running (b,g), dance squad (g), football (b), golf (b,g), soccer (b,g), softball (g), swimming and diving (b,g), tennis (b,g), track and field (b,g), volleyball (b,g), water polo (b,g); intramural: lacrosse (g); coed interscholastic: aerobics/dance, modern dance; coed intramural: strength & conditioning. 4 PE instructors, 87 coaches, 1 athletic trainer.

Computers Computers are regularly used in career exploration, college planning, English, foreign language, history, journalism, mathematics, newspaper, religious studies, science, Spanish, technology, theology, writing, yearbook classes. Computer network features include on-campus library services, online commercial services, Internet access, wireless campus network, PowerSchool grade program, 1:1 student laptop program, laptop included in tuition. Campus intranet, student e-mail accounts, and computer access in designated common areas are available to students. Students grades are available online. The school has a published electronic and media policy.

Contact Claudia Briones, Admission Coordinator. 510-881-4320. Fax: 510-582-8405. E-mail: admissions@moreaucatholic.org. Website: www.moreaucatholic.org

MORRIS CATHOLIC HIGH SCHOOL

200 Morris Avenue
Denville, New Jersey 07834

Head of School: Mr. Robert Stickles

General Information Coeducational day college-preparatory school, affiliated with Roman Catholic Church. Grades 9–12. Setting: suburban. 32-acre campus. 1 building on campus. Approved or accredited by New Jersey Department of Education. Upper school average class size: 18. Upper school faculty-student ratio: 1:11. There are 180 required school days per year for Upper School students. Upper School students typically attend 5 days per week. The average school day consists of 6 hours and 40 minutes.

Upper School Student Profile 80% of students are Roman Catholic.

Special Academic Programs Honors section; study at local college for college credit.

Student Life Upper grades have uniform requirement, student council, honor system. Discipline rests primarily with faculty. Attendance at religious services is required.

Admissions Interview recommended.

Athletics Interscholastic: baseball (boys), basketball (b,g), cheering (g), cross-country running (b,g), fencing (b,g), football (b), indoor track (b,g), lacrosse (b,g), soccer (b,g), softball (g), track and field (b,g), volleyball (g), winter (indoor) track (b,g), wrestling (b).

Computers Computer resources include wireless campus network. Campus intranet and student e-mail accounts are available to students. Students grades are available online.

Contact Mrs. Maureen Costello, Director of Admissions. 973-627-6674 Ext. 132. Fax: 973-627-7351. E-mail: mcostello@morriscatholic.org.
Website: www.morriscatholic.org

MOTHER MCAULEY HIGH SCHOOL

3737 West 99th Street
Chicago, Illinois 60655-3133

Head of School: Ms. Eileen O'Reilly

General Information Girls' day college-preparatory school, affiliated with Roman Catholic Church. Grades 9–12. Founded: 1846. Setting: urban. 21-acre campus. 2 buildings on campus. Approved or accredited by Mercy Secondary Education Association, National Catholic Education Association, North Central Association of Colleges and Schools, The College Board, and Illinois Department of Education. Endowment: $2 million. Total enrollment: 1,027. Upper school average class size: 25. Upper school faculty-student ratio: 1:13. There are 180 required school days per year for Upper School students. Upper School students typically attend 5 days per week. The average school day consists of 6 hours and 30 minutes.

Upper School Student Profile Grade 9: 231 students (231 girls); Grade 10: 241 students (241 girls); Grade 11: 232 students (232 girls); Grade 12: 271 students (271 girls). 87% of students are Roman Catholic.

Faculty School total: 92. In upper school: 12 men, 80 women; 56 have advanced degrees.

Subjects Offered ACT preparation, advanced studio art-AP, anatomy and physiology, art history, art history-AP, biology, biology-AP, calculus, calculus-AP, ceramics, chemistry-AP, child development, chorus, college counseling, comparative government and politics-AP, composition-AP, CPR, English, English language and composition-AP, English literature, English literature and composition-AP, European history-AP, first aid, French, French-AP, general science, geography, geometry, global issues, government/civics-AP, graphic design, honors algebra, honors English, honors geometry, honors U.S. history, honors world history, introduction to theater, journalism, Latin, Latin-AP, marching band, media literacy, music appreciation, newspaper, orchestra, painting, photography, physical education, physics, physics-AP, play production, Spanish, Spanish-AP, speech, studio art, studio art-AP, theater, theology, U.S. history, U.S. history-AP, U.S. literature, Web site design, wind ensemble, women's studies, world history, world history-AP, yearbook.

Graduation Requirements Art history, arts and fine arts (art, music, dance, drama), English, foreign language, lab science, language, mathematics, music, physical education (includes health), science, social sciences, social studies (includes history), theology.

Special Academic Programs 16 Advanced Placement exams for which test preparation is offered; honors section; study at local college for college credit.

College Admission Counseling 271 students graduated in 2016; all went to college, including Eastern Illinois University; Illinois State University; Loyola University Chicago; University of Illinois at Chicago; University of Illinois at Urbana–Champaign. Mean composite ACT: 23.

Student Life Upper grades have uniform requirement, student council. Discipline rests primarily with faculty. Attendance at religious services is required.

Summer Programs Remediation, enrichment, advancement, sports, art/fine arts, computer instruction programs offered; session focuses on academics; held on campus; accepts girls; open to students from other schools. 200 students usually enrolled. 2017 schedule: June 12 to July 20. Application deadline: June 1.

Tuition and Aid Day student tuition: $11,100. Tuition installment plan (monthly payment plans, individually arranged payment plans). Tuition reduction for siblings, need-based scholarship grants, paying campus jobs available. In 2016–17, 61% of upper-school students received aid; total upper-school merit-scholarship money awarded: $30,000. Total amount of financial aid awarded in 2016–17: $1,000,000.

Admissions Traditional secondary-level entrance grade is 9. For fall 2016, 361 students applied for upper-level admission, 312 were accepted, 231 enrolled. High School Placement Test required. Deadline for receipt of application materials: May 1. Application fee required: $300.

Athletics Interscholastic: basketball, bowling, cross-country running, dance team, diving, golf, independent competitive sports, lacrosse, sailing, soccer, softball, swimming and diving, tennis, track and field, volleyball, water polo; intramural: aerobics, basketball, bowling, flag football, Frisbee, softball, touch football, ultimate Frisbee, volleyball. 3 PE instructors, 20 coaches, 1 athletic trainer.

Computers Computers are regularly used in all classes. Computer network features include on-campus library services, Internet access, wireless campus network, Internet filtering or blocking technology, 1:1 iPad program for all students. Student e-mail accounts and computer access in designated common areas are available to students. Students grades are available online. The school has a published electronic and media policy.

Contact Mrs. Kathryn Klyczek, Director of Admissions and Financial Aid. 773-881-6534. Fax: 773-881-6515. E-mail: kklyczek@mothermcauley.org.
Website: www.mothermcauley.org

MOUNDS PARK ACADEMY

2051 Larpenteur Avenue East
Maplewood, Minnesota 55109

Head of School: Dr. William Hudson

General Information Coeducational day college-preparatory, arts, bilingual studies, and technology school. Grades PK–12. Founded: 1982. Setting: suburban. Nearest major city is St. Paul. 32-acre campus. 1 building on campus. Approved or accredited by Independent Schools Association of the Central States, Middle States Association of Colleges and Schools, and Minnesota Department of Education. Member of National Association of Independent Schools. Endowment: $6 million. Total enrollment: 480. Upper school average class size: 16. Upper school faculty-student ratio: 1:9. There are 175 required school days per year for Upper School students. Upper School students typically attend 5 days per week. The average school day consists of 6 hours and 40 minutes.

Upper School Student Profile Grade 9: 52 students (25 boys, 27 girls); Grade 10: 55 students (27 boys, 28 girls); Grade 11: 55 students (27 boys, 28 girls); Grade 12: 57 students (27 boys, 30 girls).

Faculty School total: 76. In upper school: 11 men, 23 women; 16 have advanced degrees.

Subjects Offered Algebra, American history, American literature, anatomy, area studies, art, biology, calculus, ceramics, chemistry, chorus, contemporary women writers, creative writing, debate, design, drama, drawing, economics, English literature, fine arts, French, geometry, health, history, independent study, instrumental music, law, literature, mathematics, media, men's studies, multicultural literature, music, painting, photography, physical education, physical science, physics, physiology, psychology, public policy issues and action, science, senior seminar, social sciences, social studies, Spanish, speech, statistics, theater, trigonometry, vocal music, Western civilization, world literature, writing.

Graduation Requirements Arts and fine arts (art, music, dance, drama), English, foreign language, health education, mathematics, physical education (includes health), science, senior seminar, social studies (includes history), senior performance. Community service is required.

Special Academic Programs 6 Advanced Placement exams for which test preparation is offered; honors section; independent study; study at local college for college credit; programs in general development for dyslexic students; ESL (8 students enrolled).

College Admission Counseling 40 students graduated in 2015; all went to college, including Harvard University; Rice University; St. Olaf College; University of Minnesota, Twin Cities Campus; University of St. Thomas; University of Wisconsin–Madison. Mean SAT critical reading: 628, mean SAT math: 613, mean SAT writing: 607, mean combined SAT: 1848, mean composite ACT: 28.

Student Life Upper grades have specified standards of dress, student council, honor system. Discipline rests equally with students and faculty.

Tuition and Aid Day student tuition: $23,900. Tuition installment plan (monthly payment plans, 2-payment plan, 3-payment plan, 4-payment plan, 8-payment plan). Need-based scholarship grants, Malone Scholarship for qualified applicants available. In 2015–16, 30% of upper-school students received aid. Total amount of financial aid awarded in 2015–16: $1,000,000.

Admissions Traditional secondary-level entrance grade is 9. For fall 2015, 50 students applied for upper-level admission, 40 were accepted, 19 enrolled. Writing sample required. Deadline for receipt of application materials: March 1. Application fee required: $50. Interview required.

Athletics Interscholastic: baseball (boys), basketball (b,g), cross-country running (b,g), dance team (g), equestrian sports (g), football (b), golf (b,g), hockey (b), nordic skiing (b,g), skiing (cross-country) (b,g), soccer (b,g), softball (g), swimming and diving (g), tennis (b,g), track and field (b,g), volleyball (g). 4 PE instructors, 20 coaches.

Computers Computers are regularly used in English, foreign language, mathematics, science, social studies classes. Computer network features include on-campus library services, online commercial services, Internet access, wireless campus network, Internet filtering or blocking technology. Student e-mail accounts are available to students. Students grades are available online. The school has a published electronic and media policy.

Contact Craig Dodson, Director of Admission. 651-748-5577. Fax: 651-748-5534. E-mail: cdodson@moundsparkacademy.org. Website: www.moundsparkacademy.org

MOUNTAIN VIEW ACADEMY

360 South Shoreline Boulevard
Mountain View, California 94041

Head of School: Mr. Gerald Corson

General Information Coeducational day college-preparatory school, affiliated with Seventh-day Adventist Church. Grades 9–12. Founded: 1923. Setting: urban. Nearest major city is San Jose. 3-acre campus. 4 buildings on campus. Approved or accredited by Western Association of Schools and Colleges and California Department of Education. Total enrollment: 150. Upper school average class size: 20. Upper school faculty-student ratio: 1:12. There are 180 required school days per year for Upper School students. Upper School students typically attend 5 days per week. The average school day consists of 7 hours.

Upper School Student Profile Grade 9: 28 students (16 boys, 12 girls); Grade 10: 36 students (19 boys, 17 girls); Grade 11: 33 students (17 boys, 16 girls); Grade 12: 36 students (19 boys, 17 girls). 70% of students are Seventh-day Adventists.

Faculty School total: 14. In upper school: 8 men, 6 women; 8 have advanced degrees.

Graduation Requirements Algebra, American government, American history, arts and fine arts (art, music, dance, drama), biology, computer literacy, economics,

electives, English, English composition, English literature, foreign language, geometry, health, home economics, religion (includes Bible studies and theology), world history, 25 hours of community service per year.

Special Academic Programs Advanced Placement exam preparation; honors section; accelerated programs; remedial reading and/or remedial writing; remedial math.

College Admission Counseling 36 students graduated in 2016; all went to college, including De Anza College; La Sierra University; Pacific Union College; San Jose State University; University of California, Davis; University of California, Los Angeles.

Student Life Upper grades have specified standards of dress, student council, honor system. Discipline rests primarily with faculty.

Tuition and Aid Day student tuition: $15,831–$20,102. Tuition installment plan (monthly payment plans). Merit scholarship grants, need-based scholarship grants, paying campus jobs available. In 2016–17, 35% of upper-school students received aid; total upper-school merit-scholarship money awarded: $20,000. Total amount of financial aid awarded in 2016–17: $65,000.

Admissions Traditional secondary-level entrance grade is 9. For fall 2016, 150 students applied for upper-level admission, 134 were accepted, 134 enrolled. High School Placement Test (closed version) from Scholastic Testing Service or ITBS achievement test required. Deadline for receipt of application materials: March 1. No application fee required. Interview recommended.

Athletics Interscholastic: basketball (boys, girls), flag football (b,g), soccer (b,g), softball (b,g), volleyball (b,g); intramural: basketball (b,g), flag football (b,g), softball (b,g), volleyball (b,g). 1 PE instructor, 3 coaches.

Computers Computers are regularly used in all classes. Computer network features include on-campus library services, Internet access, wireless campus network, Internet filtering or blocking technology. Campus intranet, student e-mail accounts, and computer access in designated common areas are available to students. Students grades are available online. The school has a published electronic and media policy.

Contact Alyce Schales, Registrar. 650-967-2324 Ext. 6654. Fax: 650-967-6886. E-mail: registrar@mtnviewacademy.org. Website: www.mtnviewacademy.org

MOUNTAIN VIEW CHRISTIAN HIGH SCHOOL

3900 East Bonanza Road
Las Vegas, Nevada 89110

Head of School: Dr. Crystal Van Kempen-McClanahan

General Information Coeducational day college-preparatory, culinary arts, and technology school, affiliated with Assemblies of God. Grades K–12. Founded: 1983. Setting: urban. 20-acre campus. 3 buildings on campus. Approved or accredited by Association of Christian Schools International and Northwest Association of Schools and Colleges. Total enrollment: 631. Upper school average class size: 25. Upper school faculty-student ratio: 1:8. There are 180 required school days per year for Upper School students. Upper School students typically attend 5 days per week. The average school day consists of 6 hours and 45 minutes.

Upper School Student Profile Grade 6: 10 students (7 boys, 3 girls); Grade 7: 16 students (9 boys, 7 girls); Grade 8: 17 students (8 boys, 9 girls); Grade 9: 17 students (13 boys, 4 girls); Grade 10: 10 students (6 boys, 4 girls); Grade 11: 22 students (9 boys, 13 girls); Grade 12: 15 students (7 boys, 8 girls). 20% of students are Assemblies of God.

Faculty School total: 21. In upper school: 7 men, 10 women; 5 have advanced degrees.

Subjects Offered Art, cheerleading, college counseling, community service, computer literacy, culinary arts, leadership, media production, photography, psychology, reading/study skills, weight training, yearbook.

Graduation Requirements Bible, computer literacy, computers, economics, health, history, social studies (includes history).

Special Academic Programs Honors section; study at local college for college credit; academic accommodation for the gifted, the musically talented, and the artistically talented; remedial reading and/or remedial writing.

College Admission Counseling 27 students graduated in 2016; 20 went to college, including Evangel University; Grand Canyon University; University of Nevada, Las Vegas; University of Nevada, Reno. Other: 5 went to work, 2 entered military service. Mean SAT critical reading: 490, mean SAT math: 491, mean composite ACT: 24. 10% scored over 600 on SAT critical reading, 10% scored over 600 on SAT math.

Student Life Upper grades have uniform requirement, student council, honor system. Discipline rests primarily with faculty. Attendance at religious services is required.

Tuition and Aid Day student tuition: $8850. Tuition installment plan (monthly payment plans). Tuition reduction for siblings, need-based scholarship grants, Nevada State Treasury Department offers Nevada residents educational savings account available.

Admissions Traditional secondary-level entrance grade is 9. Scholastic Achievement Test or school's own test required. Deadline for receipt of application materials: none. Application fee required: $350. Interview recommended.

Athletics Interscholastic: baseball (boys), basketball (b,g), football (b), golf (b,g), softball (g), volleyball (g); intramural: basketball (b,g), volleyball (g); coed interscholastic: cheering, physical fitness; coed intramural: cheering, fitness, flag football, physical fitness, strength & conditioning, weight training. 1 PE instructor, 4 coaches.

Computers Computers are regularly used in computer applications, media production classes. Computer resources include on-campus library services, Internet access, wireless campus network, Internet filtering or blocking technology. Student e-mail accounts are available to students. Students grades are available online. The school has a published electronic and media policy.

Contact Dannette Kirk, Director of Admissions. 702-452-1300. Fax: 702-452-9006. E-mail: dlkirk@mvcs.net. Website: www.mvcs.net

MOUNT CARMEL ACADEMY

7027 Milne Boulevard
New Orleans, Louisiana 70124

Head of School: Ms. Beth Ann Simno

General Information Girls' day college-preparatory school, affiliated with Roman Catholic Church. Grades 8–12. Approved or accredited by Louisiana Department of Education. Total enrollment: 1,081. Upper school average class size: 15.

Upper School Student Profile 96% of students are Roman Catholic.

Subjects Offered Accounting, acting, advanced math, Advanced Placement courses, algebra, American history-AP, art, biology, calculus, calculus-AP, ceramics, chemistry, choir, civics, composition-AP, computer applications, computer science, contemporary issues, economics, English, English-AP, family and consumer science, fine arts, food and nutrition, French, geometry, interior design, Latin, law studies, mathematics, music theater, philosophy, physical education, physics, play production, psychology, sculpture, Spanish, speech, television, theology, world geography, world literature.

Graduation Requirements Computer applications, computer technologies, English, family and consumer science, foreign language, mathematics, physical education (includes health), science, social studies (includes history), theology.

Special Academic Programs Advanced Placement exam preparation; honors section; study at local college for college credit; academic accommodation for the artistically talented.

College Admission Counseling Colleges students went to include Louisiana State University and Agricultural & Mechanical College; Loyola University New Orleans; University of Georgia; University of New Orleans; University of Southern Mississippi.

Student Life Attendance at religious services is required.

Summer Programs Remediation, enrichment, advancement, sports, art/fine arts, computer instruction programs offered; held on campus; accepts girls; open to students from other schools. 300 students usually enrolled. 2017 schedule: June 5 to June 30. Application deadline: May 5.

Tuition and Aid Tuition installment plan (monthly payment plans, individually arranged payment plans). Merit scholarship grants, need-based scholarship grants, paying campus jobs available.

Admissions Traditional secondary-level entrance grade is 9. Achievement tests required. Application fee required: $30. Interview required.

Athletics Interscholastic: basketball, cheering, cross-country running, dance, dance squad, dance team, drill team, golf, indoor track & field, physical fitness, physical training, sailing, softball, tennis, track and field, volleyball, winter (indoor) track, winter soccer; intramural: aerobics/dance, basketball, flag football.

Computers Computers are regularly used in all classes. Computer network features include on-campus library services, Internet access.

Contact Mrs. Jeanne Rachuba, Director of Admissions. 504-2887630. Fax: 504-2887629. E-mail: jrachuba@mcacubs.org. Website: www.mtcarmelcubs.org

MOUNT DORA CHRISTIAN ACADEMY

301 West 13th Avenue
Mount Dora, Florida 32757

Head of School: Dr. Brad Moser

General Information Coeducational day college-preparatory and general academic school, affiliated with Church of Christ. Grades PK–12. Founded: 1945. Setting: small town. Nearest major city is Orlando. 70-acre campus. 10 buildings on campus. Approved or accredited by National Christian School Association, Southern Association of Colleges and Schools, and Florida Department of Education. Total enrollment: 557. Upper school average class size: 20. Upper school faculty-student ratio: 1:12. There are 180 required school days per year for Upper School students. Upper School students typically attend 5 days per week. The average school day consists of 6 hours and 30 minutes.

Upper School Student Profile Grade 6: 55 students (32 boys, 23 girls); Grade 7: 41 students (22 boys, 19 girls); Grade 8: 38 students (22 boys, 16 girls); Grade 9: 56 students (35 boys, 21 girls); Grade 10: 47 students (23 boys, 24 girls); Grade 11: 45 students (26 boys, 19 girls); Grade 12: 44 students (29 boys, 15 girls). 20% of students are members of Church of Christ.

Faculty School total: 46. In upper school: 13 men, 16 women; 11 have advanced degrees.

Subjects Offered 3-dimensional art, algebra, American government, American history, anatomy and physiology, art, band, Bible, biology, calculus-AP, career technology, ceramics, chemistry, civics, computer science-AP, computer skills, consumer mathematics, creative writing, drawing, earth and space science, economics,

English, English language-AP, English literature-AP, English-AP, environmental science, geography, geometry, government, health, honors algebra, honors English, honors geometry, honors world history, human geography - AP, journalism, leadership and service, life science, life skills, marine science, mathematics, media, music history, painting, photography, physical education, physical science, physics, physiology, pre-algebra, pre-calculus, probability and statistics, robotics, sculpture, Spanish, speech, statistics, studio art, technology, technology/design, television, theater, trigonometry, U.S. history, U.S. history-AP, video communication, video film production, weight training, world history, zoology.

Graduation Requirements Advanced biology, advanced math, algebra, American government, American history, American literature-AP, art history, arts and fine arts (art, music, dance, drama), Bible, biology, chemistry, economics, electives, English, foreign language, lab science, life skills, physical education (includes health), physical science, world history, 100 hours of community service.

Special Academic Programs 4 Advanced Placement exams for which test preparation is offered; honors section; independent study; study at local college for college credit.

College Admission Counseling 47 students graduated in 2016; 41 went to college, including Boston University; Harding University; Lipscomb University; Seminole State College of Florida; The University of Alabama. Other: 2 went to work, 2 entered a postgraduate year, 2 had other specific plans.

Student Life Upper grades have specified standards of dress, student council. Discipline rests primarily with faculty. Attendance at religious services is required.

Summer Programs Remediation programs offered; session focuses on math; held on campus; accepts boys and girls; not open to students from other schools. 5 students usually enrolled. 2017 schedule: June 5 to June 20.

Tuition and Aid Day student tuition: $8831–$9790. Tuition installment plan (FACTS Tuition Payment Plan). Tuition reduction for siblings, need-based scholarship grants, discount for members of the Churches of Christ available. In 2016–17, 30% of upper-school students received aid.

Admissions Traditional secondary-level entrance grade is 9. For fall 2016, 57 students applied for upper-level admission, 47 were accepted, 43 enrolled. School placement exam required. Deadline for receipt of application materials: none. Application fee required: $125. On-campus interview required.

Athletics Interscholastic: baseball (boys), basketball (b,g), bowling (b,g), cheering (g), cross-country running (b,g), fitness (b,g), football (b), golf (b,g), physical fitness (b,g), softball (g), tennis (b,g), track and field (b,g), volleyball (g), weight training (b,g). 3 coaches.

Computers Computers are regularly used in all academic, independent study, journalism, library, mathematics, publications, reading, video film production, Web site design, yearbook classes. Computer network features include on-campus library services, Internet access, wireless campus network, Internet filtering or blocking technology, NetClassroom communication for students and parents, desktop monitoring and manage software, Accelerated Reader Access. Campus intranet, student e-mail accounts, and computer access in designated common areas are available to students. Students grades are available online. The school has a published electronic and media policy.

Contact Natalie Yawn, Admissions Director. 352-383-2155 Ext. 261. Fax: 352-383-0098. E-mail: natalie.yawn@mdcacademy.org. Website: www.mdcacademy.org

MOUNT MERCY ACADEMY

88 Red Jacket Parkway
Buffalo, New York 14220

Head of School: Mrs. Margaret Staszak

General Information Girls' day college-preparatory, arts, and business school, affiliated with Roman Catholic Church. Grades 9–12. Founded: 1904. Setting: urban. 1-acre campus. 2 buildings on campus. Approved or accredited by Mercy Secondary Education Association, Middle States Association of Colleges and Schools, National Catholic Education Association, New York Department of Education, New York State Board of Regents, The College Board, and New York Department of Education. Total enrollment: 229. Upper school average class size: 20. Upper school faculty-student ratio: 1:20. There are 180 required school days per year for Upper School students. Upper School students typically attend 5 days per week. The average school day consists of 6 hours and 45 minutes.

Upper School Student Profile Grade 9: 60 students (60 girls); Grade 10: 57 students (57 girls); Grade 11: 66 students (66 girls); Grade 12: 54 students (54 girls). 97% of students are Roman Catholic.

Faculty School total: 30. In upper school: 6 men, 24 women; 23 have advanced degrees.

Subjects Offered 1 1/2 elective credits, accounting, ACT preparation, Advanced Placement courses, advanced studio art-AP, American government, American history-AP, American literature-AP, anatomy and physiology, biology-AP, business law, calculus-AP, chemistry, chorus, concert bell choir, digital photography, drawing and design, earth science, economics, electives, English language and composition-AP, English literature, English literature and composition-AP, European history-AP, film and literature, foreign language, geometry, global studies, handbells, health, Holocaust, honors English, human biology, keyboarding, Latin, leadership and service, learning lab, madrigals, mathematics, painting, personal finance, physics, piano, portfolio art, psychology-AP, Spanish, statistics-AP, theology, U.S. history-AP, world history-AP.

Special Academic Programs Advanced Placement exam preparation; honors section; independent study; remedial math.

College Admission Counseling 58 students graduated in 2016; all went to college.

Student Life Upper grades have uniform requirement, student council, honor system. Discipline rests equally with students and faculty. Attendance at religious services is required.

Summer Programs Remediation, enrichment programs offered; session focuses on Regents review; held on campus; accepts boys and girls; open to students from other schools. 100 students usually enrolled. 2017 schedule: August 10 to August 18. Application deadline: July 31.

Tuition and Aid Day student tuition: $9450. Tuition installment plan (FACTS Tuition Payment Plan). Tuition reduction for siblings, merit scholarship grants, need-based scholarship grants, paying campus jobs available.

Admissions Traditional secondary-level entrance grade is 9. For fall 2016, 245 students applied for upper-level admission, 245 were accepted, 237 enrolled. Admissions testing and High School Placement Test (closed version) from Scholastic Testing Service required. Deadline for receipt of application materials: none. Application fee required. On-campus interview required.

Athletics Interscholastic: basketball, bowling, cheering, crew, cross-country running, golf, hockey, lacrosse, skiing (downhill), soccer, softball, tennis, volleyball. 1 PE instructor, 13 coaches.

Computers Computers are regularly used in all academic classes. Computer network features include on-campus library services, Internet access, wireless campus network, Internet filtering or blocking technology. Campus intranet, student e-mail accounts, and computer access in designated common areas are available to students. Students grades are available online. The school has a published electronic and media policy.

Contact Mrs. Jeanne Burvid, Counseling Center Assistant. 716-825-8796 Ext. 201. Fax: 716-825-0976. E-mail: jburvid@mtmercy.org. Website: www.mtmercy.org

MOUNT NOTRE DAME HIGH SCHOOL

711 East Columbia Avenue
Cincinnati, Ohio 45215

Head of School: Mrs. Judy Back Gerwe '78

General Information Girls' day college-preparatory school, affiliated with Roman Catholic Church. Grades 9–12. Founded: 1860. Setting: suburban. 1 building on campus. Approved or accredited by North Central Association of Colleges and Schools, Ohio Catholic Schools Accreditation Association (OCSAA), and Ohio Department of Education. Upper school average class size: 19. Upper school faculty-student ratio: 1:15. There are 180 required school days per year for Upper School students. Upper School students typically attend 5 days per week. The average school day consists of 6 hours and 30 minutes.

Upper School Student Profile Grade 9: 149 students (149 girls); Grade 10: 182 students (182 girls); Grade 11: 166 students (166 girls); Grade 12: 152 students (152 girls). 85% of students are Roman Catholic.

Faculty In upper school: 8 men, 52 women; 42 have advanced degrees.

Special Academic Programs International Baccalaureate program; 20 Advanced Placement exams for which test preparation is offered; honors section; independent study; study at local college for college credit; study abroad.

College Admission Counseling 190 students graduated in 2016; 188 went to college. Other: 2 went to work. Median composite ACT: 25. Mean SAT critical reading: 577, mean SAT math: 543, mean SAT writing: 572.

Student Life Upper grades have uniform requirement, student council, honor system. Discipline rests primarily with faculty. Attendance at religious services is required.

Tuition and Aid Day student tuition: $11,995. Tuition installment plan (FACTS Tuition Payment Plan). Tuition reduction for siblings, merit scholarship grants, need-based scholarship grants available. In 2016–17, 40% of upper-school students received aid.

Admissions Traditional secondary-level entrance grade is 9. High School Placement Test required. Deadline for receipt of application materials: none. Application fee required: $30.

Computers Computer network features include on-campus library services, Internet access, wireless campus network, Internet filtering or blocking technology, submitting homework, taking exams. Campus intranet, student e-mail accounts, and computer access in designated common areas are available to students. Students grades are available online. The school has a published electronic and media policy.

Contact Mrs. Donna Groene, Director of Admissions. 513-821-3044 Ext. 164. Fax: 513-821-6068. E-mail: dgroene@mndhs.org. Website: www.mndhs.org

MOUNT ST. AGNES ACADEMY

Cedar Avenue/Dundonald Street
Hamilton HM09, Bermuda

Head of School: Susan Moench

General Information Coeducational day college-preparatory and general academic school, affiliated with Roman Catholic Church. Grades K–12. Distance learning grades 7–12. Founded: 1890. Setting: small town. 1 building on campus. Approved or accredited by National Catholic Education Association and state department of education. Language of instruction: English. Upper school average class size: 20. Upper school faculty-student ratio: 1:10. There are 184 required school days per year for Upper School students. Upper School students typically attend 5 days per week. The average school day consists of 6 hours.

Upper School Student Profile Grade 6: 38 students (22 boys, 16 girls); Grade 7: 40 students (19 boys, 21 girls); Grade 8: 20 students (9 boys, 11 girls); Grade 9: 27 students (16 boys, 11 girls); Grade 10: 30 students (11 boys, 19 girls); Grade 11: 27 students (11 boys, 16 girls); Grade 12: 27 students (14 boys, 13 girls). 75% of students are Roman Catholic.

Faculty School total: 34. In upper school: 11 men, 4 women; 5 have advanced degrees.

Subjects Offered All academic.

Graduation Requirements Arts and fine arts (art, music, dance, drama), computer science, English, foreign language, mathematics, physical education (includes health), religion (includes Bible studies and theology), science, social studies (includes history), Students must meet the graduation requirements of Alberta Education. Community service is required.

Special Academic Programs Advanced Placement exam preparation; independent study; academic accommodation for the gifted; remedial reading and/or remedial writing; remedial math.

College Admission Counseling 33 students graduated in 2016; 28 went to college, including Acadia University; Dalhousie University; Mount Saint Vincent University; Queen's University at Kingston; Saint Mary's University; St. Francis Xavier University. Other: 5 went to work. Median SAT critical reading: 460, median SAT math: 500. 9.5% scored over 600 on SAT critical reading.

Student Life Upper grades have uniform requirement, student council, honor system. Discipline rests primarily with faculty. Attendance at religious services is required.

Tuition and Aid Day student tuition: $17,000–$18,000. Tuition installment plan (monthly payment plans, individually arranged payment plans). Need-based scholarship grants available. In 2016–17, 4% of upper-school students received aid. Total amount of financial aid awarded in 2016–17: $20,000.

Admissions Traditional secondary-level entrance grade is 9. For fall 2016, 10 students applied for upper-level admission, 10 were accepted, 10 enrolled. Deadline for receipt of application materials: none. Application fee required: 50 Bermuda dollars. On-campus interview recommended.

Athletics Interscholastic: badminton (boys, girls), basketball (b,g), cross-country running (b,g), football (b), netball (g), rugby (b,g), sailing (b,g), scooter football (b), volleyball (b,g); intramural: badminton (b,g), bowling (b,g), cross-country running (b,g), golf (b,g), softball (b,g), volleyball (b,g); coed intramural: volleyball. 2 PE instructors, 6 coaches.

Computers Computers are regularly used in all classes. Computer network features include on-campus library services, Internet access, Internet filtering or blocking technology. Student e-mail accounts and computer access in designated common areas are available to students. Students grades are available online. The school has a published electronic and media policy.

Contact Margaret DiGiacomo, Assistant Principal. 441-292-4134 Ext. 1901. Fax: 441-295-7265. E-mail: mdigiacomo@msa.bm.

MOUNT SAINT CHARLES ACADEMY

800 Logee Street
Woonsocket, Rhode Island 02895-5599

Head of School: Mr. Herve E. Richer Jr.

General Information Coeducational day college-preparatory school, affiliated with Roman Catholic Church. Grades 6–12. Founded: 1924. Setting: suburban. Nearest major city is Providence. 22-acre campus. 2 buildings on campus. Approved or accredited by New England Association of Schools and Colleges and Rhode Island Department of Education. Total enrollment: 627. Upper school average class size: 25. Upper school faculty-student ratio: 1:14. There are 180 required school days per year for Upper School students. Upper School students typically attend 5 days per week. The average school day consists of 6 hours and 15 minutes.

Upper School Student Profile Grade 6: 34 students (13 boys, 21 girls); Grade 7: 42 students (25 boys, 17 girls); Grade 8: 62 students (36 boys, 26 girls); Grade 9: 109 students (50 boys, 59 girls); Grade 10: 110 students (40 boys, 70 girls); Grade 11: 134 students (58 boys, 76 girls); Grade 12: 130 students (51 boys, 79 girls). 85% of students are Roman Catholic.

Faculty School total: 54. In upper school: 27 men, 27 women; 34 have advanced degrees.

Subjects Offered Government-AP, graphic design, health and wellness, sociology, Spanish-AP.

Graduation Requirements Arts and fine arts (art, music, dance, drama), computer science, English, foreign language, mathematics, physical education (includes health), religion (includes Bible studies and theology), science, social studies (includes history).

Special Academic Programs 13 Advanced Placement exams for which test preparation is offered; honors section.

College Admission Counseling 113 students graduated in 2016; 112 went to college. Other: 1 had other specific plans.

Student Life Upper grades have uniform requirement, student council, honor system. Discipline rests primarily with faculty. Attendance at religious services is required.

Summer Programs Sports, art/fine arts programs offered; session focuses on fine arts, soccer, hockey, basketball, baseball, volleyball; held on campus; accepts boys and girls; open to students from other schools. 350 students usually enrolled. 2017 schedule: July to August. Application deadline: none.

Tuition and Aid Day student tuition: $13,350. Tuition installment plan (FACTS Tuition Payment Plan, full payment discount plan). Need-based scholarship grants available. In 2016–17, 38% of upper-school students received aid. Total amount of financial aid awarded in 2016–17: $750,000.

Admissions Traditional secondary-level entrance grade is 9. For fall 2016, 150 students applied for upper-level admission, 100 were accepted, 70 enrolled. SAS, STS-HSPT or Scholastic Testing Service High School Placement Test required. Deadline for receipt of application materials: none. Application fee required: $30.

Athletics Interscholastic: baseball (boys), basketball (b,g), cross-country running (b,g), gymnastics (g), ice hockey (b,g), indoor track (b,g), lacrosse (b,g), soccer (b,g), softball (g), swimming and diving (b,g), tennis (b,g), track and field (b,g), volleyball (b,g), winter (indoor) track (b,g); intramural: aerobics/dance (g), basketball (b,g), dance (g); coed interscholastic: cheering, golf; coed intramural: billiards, bowling, dance team, equestrian sports, flag football, indoor soccer, lacrosse, physical training, soccer, strength & conditioning, touch football. 3 PE instructors, 15 coaches, 1 athletic trainer.

Computers Computers are regularly used in all classes. Computer network features include on-campus library services, online commercial services, Internet access, wireless campus network, Internet filtering or blocking technology. Campus intranet, student e-mail accounts, and computer access in designated common areas are available to students. Students grades are available online. The school has a published electronic and media policy.

Contact Joseph J. O'Neill Jr., Director of Admissions / Registrar. 401-769-0310 Ext. 137. Fax: 401-762-2327. E-mail: oneillj@mtstcharles.org. Website: www.mountsaintcharles.org

MOUNT SAINT JOSEPH ACADEMY

120 West Wissahickon Avenue
Flourtown, Pennsylvania 19031

Head of School: Sr. Kathleen Brabson, SSJ

General Information Girls' day college-preparatory, arts, business, and technology school, affiliated with Roman Catholic Church. Grades 9–12. Founded: 1858. Setting: suburban. Nearest major city is Philadelphia. 78-acre campus. 1 building on campus. Approved or accredited by Middle States Association of Colleges and Schools, Missouri Independent School Association, National Catholic Education Association, and Pennsylvania Department of Education. Member of National Association of Independent Schools. Endowment: $4 million. Total enrollment: 531. Upper school average class size: 19. Upper school faculty-student ratio: 1:10. There are 180 required school days per year for Upper School students. Upper School students typically attend 5 days per week. The average school day consists of 6 hours and 45 minutes.

Upper School Student Profile Grade 9: 122 students (122 girls); Grade 10: 139 students (139 girls); Grade 11: 137 students (137 girls); Grade 12: 133 students (133 girls). 91% of students are Roman Catholic.

Faculty School total: 63. In upper school: 15 men, 47 women; 49 have advanced degrees.

Graduation Requirements Arts and fine arts (art, music, dance, drama), computer science, English, foreign language, mathematics, physical education (includes health), religion (includes Bible studies and theology), science, social studies (includes history).

Special Academic Programs 13 Advanced Placement exams for which test preparation is offered; honors section; independent study; study at local college for college credit; academic accommodation for the gifted, the musically talented, and the artistically talented.

College Admission Counseling 142 students graduated in 2015; all went to college, including Drexel University; Fordham University; Loyola University Maryland; Penn State University Park; Temple University; Villanova University. Mean SAT critical reading: 632, mean SAT math: 610, mean SAT writing: 655, mean combined SAT: 1897. 60% scored over 600 on SAT critical reading, 57% scored over 600 on SAT math, 68% scored over 600 on SAT writing, 60% scored over 1800 on combined SAT.

Student Life Upper grades have uniform requirement, student council, honor system. Discipline rests primarily with faculty. Attendance at religious services is required.

Tuition and Aid Day student tuition: $17,350. Tuition installment plan (Higher Education Service, Inc, semester payment plan). Tuition reduction for siblings, merit scholarship grants, need-based scholarship grants available. In 2015–16, 26% of upper-school students received aid; total upper-school merit-scholarship money awarded: $398,900. Total amount of financial aid awarded in 2015–16: $699,113.

Admissions Traditional secondary-level entrance grade is 9. For fall 2015, 248 students applied for upper-level admission. High School Placement Test, SAS, STS-HSPT or school's own test required. Deadline for receipt of application materials: October 30. Application fee required: $75.

Athletics Interscholastic: basketball, crew, cross-country running, diving, field hockey, golf, indoor track, lacrosse, soccer, softball, swimming and diving, tennis, track and field, volleyball. 2 PE instructors, 24 coaches, 1 athletic trainer.

Computers Computers are regularly used in art, business studies, career exploration, college planning, commercial art, computer applications, desktop publishing, English, foreign language, graphic design, history, mathematics, music, science, theater arts, writing, writing, yearbook classes. Computer network features include on-campus library services, online commercial services, Internet access, wireless campus network, Internet filtering or blocking technology, video conferencing, SmartBoards, iPads. Campus intranet, student e-mail accounts, and computer access in designated common areas are available to students. Students grades are available online. The school has a published electronic and media policy.

Contact Ms. Carol Finney, Director of Admissions. 215-233-9133. Fax: 215-233-5887. E-mail: cfinney@msjacad.org. Website: www.msjacad.org

MOUNT VERNON PRESBYTERIAN SCHOOL

471 Mt. Vernon Highway NE
Atlanta, Georgia 30328

Head of School: Dr. Brett Jacobsen

General Information Coeducational day college-preparatory and design thinking school, affiliated with Christian faith. Grades PK–12. Distance learning grades 9–12. Founded: 1972. Setting: suburban. 37-acre campus. 4 buildings on campus. Approved or accredited by Southern Association of Colleges and Schools, Southern Association of Independent Schools, and Georgia Department of Education. Member of National Association of Independent Schools and Secondary School Admission Test Board. Total enrollment: 932. Upper school average class size: 15. Upper school faculty-student ratio: 1:12. There are 175 required school days per year for Upper School students. Upper School students typically attend 5 days per week. The average school day consists of 7 hours.

Upper School Student Profile Grade 6: 77 students (45 boys, 32 girls); Grade 7: 100 students (52 boys, 48 girls); Grade 8: 78 students (44 boys, 34 girls); Grade 9: 84 students (49 boys, 35 girls); Grade 10: 78 students (40 boys, 38 girls); Grade 11: 80 students (40 boys, 40 girls); Grade 12: 78 students (47 boys, 31 girls). 85% of students are Christian faith.

Faculty School total: 140. In upper school: 24 men, 23 women; 38 have advanced degrees.

Subjects Offered All academic.

Graduation Requirements College admission preparation.

Special Academic Programs Advanced Placement exam preparation; honors section; term-away projects; domestic exchange program; study abroad; programs in English, mathematics, general development for dyslexic students; ESL (5 students enrolled).

College Admission Counseling 61 students graduated in 2016; all went to college, including Georgia Institute of Technology; University of Georgia.

Student Life Upper grades have uniform requirement, student council, honor system. Discipline rests primarily with faculty. Attendance at religious services is required.

Summer Programs Remediation, enrichment, advancement, sports programs offered; session focuses on advancement; held on campus; accepts boys and girls; not open to students from other schools. 100 students usually enrolled. 2017 schedule: June 6 to August 5. Application deadline: May 1.

Tuition and Aid Day student tuition: $19,030–$21,010. Guaranteed tuition plan. Tuition installment plan (monthly payment plans). Need-based scholarship grants available. In 2016–17, 24% of upper-school students received aid.

Admissions Traditional secondary-level entrance grade is 9. ISEE, SSAT and Wechsler Intelligence Scale for Children required. Deadline for receipt of application materials: February 1. Application fee required: $100. On-campus interview required.

Athletics Interscholastic: baseball (boys), basketball (b,g), cheering (g), dance (b,g), fitness (b,g), football (b,g), lacrosse (b,g), modern dance (b,g), physical fitness (b,g), physical training (b,g), soccer (b,g), softball (g), volleyball (g), wrestling (b), yoga (b); intramural: baseball (b), basketball (b,g), cheering (g), dance squad (g), dance team (g), flag football (b), football (b,g), jogging (b,g), running (b,g), soccer (b,g), softball (g); coed interscholastic: basketball, cross-country running, dance, diving, fitness, football, golf, lacrosse, modern dance, physical fitness, physical training, swimming and diving, tennis, track and field, weight lifting, weight training; coed intramural: basketball, football, golf, jogging, running, soccer, tennis, track and field, volleyball.

Computers Computers are regularly used in all academic classes. Computer network features include on-campus library services, online commercial services, Internet access, wireless campus network, Internet filtering or blocking technology. Student e-mail accounts and computer access in designated common areas are available to students. Students grades are available online. The school has a published electronic and media policy.

Contact Kirsten Beard, Chief Admissions Officer. 404-252-3448 Ext. 2401. Fax: 404-252-8300. E-mail: kbeard@mountvernonschool.org. Website: www.mountvernonschool.org/

NAMPA CHRISTIAN SCHOOLS

11920 W. Flamingo Ave.
Nampa, Idaho 83651

Head of School: Dr. Greg Wiles

General Information Coeducational day college-preparatory, general academic, and religious studies school, affiliated with Christian faith. Grades PK–12. Distance learning grades 9–12. Founded: 1959. Setting: suburban. Nearest major city is Boise. 17-acre campus. 1 building on campus. Approved or accredited by Association of Christian Schools International and Idaho Department of Education. Endowment: $1.2 million. Total enrollment: 586. Upper school average class size: 18. Upper school faculty-student ratio: 1:13. There are 172 required school days per year for Upper School students. Upper School students typically attend 5 days per week. The average school day consists of 5 hours and 51 minutes.

Upper School Student Profile Grade 9: 44 students (20 boys, 24 girls); Grade 10: 40 students (23 boys, 17 girls); Grade 11: 58 students (17 boys, 41 girls); Grade 12: 50 students (24 boys, 26 girls). 100% of students are Christian.

Faculty School total: 15. In upper school: 7 men, 8 women; 8 have advanced degrees.

Subjects Offered Bible, biology-AP, calculus-AP, chemistry-AP, Christian doctrine, Christian education, Christian ethics, Christian scripture, Christian studies, Christian testament, Christianity, early childhood, economics-AP, English composition, English-AP, fitness, French, home economics, human biology, math analysis, physical science, physics-AP, Spanish language-AP, technology, U.S. government and politics-AP, U.S. history, U.S. history-AP, U.S. literature, world literature.

Graduation Requirements Economics, English, mathematics, physical education (includes health), reading, religion (includes Bible studies and theology), science, social sciences, speech.

Special Academic Programs Honors section; independent study; study at local college for college credit.

College Admission Counseling 49 students graduated in 2016; 42 went to college, including Boise State University; George Fox University; Liberty University; Northwest Nazarene University; Seattle Pacific University; The College of Idaho. Other: 8 went to work, 1 entered a postgraduate year, 8 had other specific plans. Median SAT critical reading: 370, median SAT math: 300, median SAT writing: 380, median combined SAT: 1390, median composite ACT: 23. 15% scored over 600 on SAT critical reading, 26% scored over 600 on SAT math, 7% scored over 600 on SAT writing, 10% scored over 1800 on combined SAT, 18% scored over 26 on composite ACT.

Student Life Upper grades have specified standards of dress, student council. Discipline rests primarily with faculty. Attendance at religious services is required.

Tuition and Aid Day student tuition: $6270. Tuition installment plan (FACTS Tuition Payment Plan, monthly payment plans, individually arranged payment plans). Tuition reduction for siblings, need-based scholarship grants available. In 2016–17, 42% of upper-school students received aid. Total amount of financial aid awarded in 2016–17: $37,786.

Admissions Traditional secondary-level entrance grade is 9. Deadline for receipt of application materials: none. Application fee required: $25. Interview recommended.

Athletics Interscholastic: baseball (boys), basketball (b,g), cheering (g), cross-country running (b,g), football (b), softball (g), volleyball (g); coed interscholastic: alpine skiing, fitness, freestyle skiing, golf, skiing (downhill), track and field. 1 PE instructor, 24 coaches, 1 athletic trainer.

Computers Computers are regularly used in all academic classes. Computer network features include on-campus library services, Internet access, wireless campus network, Internet filtering or blocking technology. Student e-mail accounts and computer access in designated common areas are available to students. Students grades are available online. The school has a published electronic and media policy.

Contact Tracie Johanson, Registrar. 208-475-1711. Fax: 208-466-8452. E-mail: tjohanson@nampachristianschools.com.
Website: www.nampachristianschools.com

NASHVILLE CHRISTIAN SCHOOL

7555 Sawyer Brown Road
Nashville, Tennessee 37221

Head of School: Mrs. Connie Jo Shelton

General Information Coeducational day college-preparatory, arts, and religious studies school, affiliated with Christian faith. Grades K–12. Founded: 1971. Setting: suburban. 45-acre campus. 2 buildings on campus. Approved or accredited by National Christian School Association, North Central Association of Colleges and Schools, Southern Association of Colleges and Schools, and Tennessee Department of Education. Total enrollment: 467. Upper school average class size: 18. Upper school faculty-student ratio: 1:18. There are 176 required school days per year for Upper School students. Upper School students typically attend 5 days per week. The average school day consists of 7 hours and 15 minutes.

Upper School Student Profile Grade 6: 49 students (26 boys, 23 girls); Grade 7: 34 students (19 boys, 15 girls); Grade 8: 30 students (12 boys, 18 girls); Grade 9: 63 students (45 boys, 18 girls); Grade 10: 44 students (36 boys, 8 girls); Grade 11: 64 students (34 boys, 30 girls); Grade 12: 62 students (41 boys, 21 girls). 90% of students are Christian.

Faculty School total: 44. In upper school: 11 men, 14 women; 15 have advanced degrees.

Subjects Offered Advanced Placement courses, algebra, American history, art, Bible, Bible studies, biology, calculus, chemistry, chorus, computer science, economics, English, fine arts, general science, geometry, government/civics, health, journalism, keyboarding, Latin, Mandarin, mathematics, music, physical education, physical science, physics, pre-algebra, pre-calculus, science, social sciences, social studies, Spanish, speech.

Graduation Requirements American history, American history-AP, arts and fine arts (art, music, dance, drama), Bible, computer science, English, foreign language, mathematics, physical education (includes health), science, social sciences, social studies (includes history).

Special Academic Programs Advanced Placement exam preparation; honors section; independent study; study at local college for college credit; remedial reading and/or remedial writing; remedial math; programs in English, mathematics, general development for dyslexic students; special instructional classes for students with Attention Deficit Disorder.

College Admission Counseling 48 students graduated in 2015; 45 went to college, including Freed-Hardeman University; The University of Tennessee; The University of Tennessee at Chattanooga; The University of Tennessee at Martin; University of Mississippi; Western Kentucky University. Other: 2 went to work, 1 entered military service.

Student Life Upper grades have uniform requirement, student council, honor system. Discipline rests primarily with faculty. Attendance at religious services is required.

Tuition and Aid Day student tuition: $7790. Guaranteed tuition plan. Tuition installment plan (FACTS Tuition Payment Plan). Tuition reduction for siblings, need-based scholarship grants, paying campus jobs available. In 2015–16, 3% of upper-school students received aid. Total amount of financial aid awarded in 2015–16: $3000.

Admissions Traditional secondary-level entrance grade is 9. For fall 2015, 52 students applied for upper-level admission, 37 were accepted, 35 enrolled. Stanford Diagnostic Test required. Deadline for receipt of application materials: none. Application fee required: $100. Interview required.

Athletics Interscholastic: baseball (boys), basketball (b,g), bowling (b,g), cheering (g), cross-country running (b,g), football (b), golf (b,g), riflery (b,g), soccer (b,g), softball (g), strength & conditioning (b,g), track and field (b,g), volleyball (g), weight lifting (b,g), weight training (b,g), wrestling (b); intramural: aerobics/dance (g); coed interscholastic: fitness, physical fitness, physical training, soccer; coed intramural: archery. 2 PE instructors, 6 coaches, 1 athletic trainer.

Computers Computers are regularly used in all academic classes. Computer network features include on-campus library services, Internet access, wireless campus network, Internet filtering or blocking technology. Student e-mail accounts and computer access in designated common areas are available to students. Students grades are available online. The school has a published electronic and media policy.

Contact Mrs. Wendy Paszek, Admissions Coordinator. 615-356-5600 Ext. 162. Fax: 615-352-1324. E-mail: paszekw@nashvillechristian.org.
Website: www.nashvillechristian.org/

NATIONAL CATHEDRAL SCHOOL

3612 Woodley Road NW
Washington, District of Columbia 20016-5000

Head of School: Mrs. Kathleen O'Neill Jamieson

General Information Girls' day college-preparatory school, affiliated with Episcopal Church. Grades 4–12. Founded: 1900. Setting: urban. 59-acre campus. 7 buildings on campus. Approved or accredited by Association of Independent Maryland Schools, Association of Independent Schools of Greater Washington, Middle States Association of Colleges and Schools, National Association of Episcopal Schools, and District of Columbia Department of Education. Member of National Association of Independent Schools and Secondary School Admission Test Board. Endowment: $19 million. Total enrollment: 590. Upper school average class size: 14. Upper school faculty-student ratio: 1:7.

Upper School Student Profile Grade 9: 93 students (93 girls); Grade 10: 74 students (74 girls); Grade 11: 73 students (73 girls); Grade 12: 73 students (73 girls).

Faculty School total: 101. In upper school: 11 men, 34 women; 36 have advanced degrees.

Subjects Offered Advanced Placement courses, African American history, African-American literature, algebra, American history, American literature, art, art history, art history-AP, biology, calculus, ceramics, chemistry, Chinese, community service, computer programming, computer science, creative writing, dance, drama, earth science, economics, English, English literature, ethics, European history, expository writing, fine arts, French, geography, geometry, government/civics, Greek, history, Japanese, Latin, mathematics, music, photography, physical education, physics, political science, psychology, public speaking, religion, science, social studies, Spanish, statistics, theater, trigonometry, world history, writing.

Graduation Requirements Arts and fine arts (art, music, dance, drama), English, foreign language, mathematics, physical education (includes health), religion (includes Bible studies and theology), science, social studies (includes history). Community service is required.

Special Academic Programs 17 Advanced Placement exams for which test preparation is offered; honors section; independent study; term-away projects; study abroad; academic accommodation for the gifted.

College Admission Counseling 73 students graduated in 2015; all went to college, including Brown University; Dartmouth College; Princeton University; Stanford University; University of Pennsylvania; Yale University. Mean SAT critical reading: 718, mean SAT math: 698, mean SAT writing: 724.

Student Life Upper grades have specified standards of dress, student council, honor system. Discipline rests equally with students and faculty. Attendance at religious services is required.

Tuition and Aid Day student tuition: $38,850. Tuition installment plan (FACTS Tuition Payment Plan). Need-based scholarship grants available. In 2015–16, 22% of upper-school students received aid. Total amount of financial aid awarded in 2015–16: $1,604,156.

Admissions Traditional secondary-level entrance grade is 9. For fall 2015, 111 students applied for upper-level admission, 60 were accepted, 32 enrolled. ISEE or SSAT required. Deadline for receipt of application materials: January 15. Application fee required: $75. Interview required.

Athletics Interscholastic: basketball, crew, dance team, field hockey, ice hockey, indoor soccer, indoor track, indoor track & field, lacrosse, Nautilus, rowing, soccer, softball, tennis, track and field, volleyball, winter (indoor) track; intramural: aerobics, aerobics/dance, aerobics/Nautilus, backpacking, ballet, canoeing/kayaking, climbing, dance, fitness, hiking/backpacking, independent competitive sports, kayaking, modern dance, mountain biking, outdoor adventure, physical fitness, rafting, rappelling, rock climbing, strength & conditioning, weight lifting, weight training, yoga; coed interscholastic: cross-country running, diving, swimming and diving. 11 PE instructors, 11 coaches, 1 athletic trainer.

Computers Computers are regularly used in art, English, foreign language, mathematics, multimedia, science classes. Computer network features include on-campus library services, online commercial services, Internet access, wireless campus network, Internet filtering or blocking technology. Student e-mail accounts and computer access in designated common areas are available to students. The school has a published electronic and media policy.

Contact Ms. Elizabeth Wilson, Admission Assistant. 202-537-6374. Fax: 202-537-2382. E-mail: ncs_admissions@cathedral.org. Website: www.ncs.cathedral.org

NAZARETH ACADEMY

1209 West Ogden Avenue
LaGrange Park, Illinois 60526

Head of School: Mrs. Deborah A. Tracy

General Information Coeducational day college-preparatory school, affiliated with Roman Catholic Church. Grades 9–12. Founded: 1900. Setting: suburban. Nearest major city is Chicago. 20-acre campus. 4 buildings on campus. Approved or accredited by North Central Association of Colleges and Schools, The College Board, and Illinois Department of Education. Total enrollment: 763. Upper school average class size: 24. Upper school faculty-student ratio: 1:17. There are 180 required school days per year for Upper School students. Upper School students typically attend 5 days per week. The average school day consists of 7 hours.

Upper School Student Profile Grade 9: 206 students (105 boys, 101 girls); Grade 10: 216 students (104 boys, 112 girls); Grade 11: 172 students (95 boys, 77 girls); Grade 12: 190 students (81 boys, 109 girls). 85% of students are Roman Catholic.

Faculty School total: 49. In upper school: 19 men, 30 women; 46 have advanced degrees.

Subjects Offered Acting, algebra, American government, American literature, art, biology, biology-AP, calculus-AP, chemistry, chemistry-AP, Chinese, computer programming, computer science-AP, concert band, concert choir, creative writing, drawing and design, economics, English, English language and composition-AP, English literature and composition-AP, environmental science, French, geometry, health, Italian, photography, physical education, physics, physics-AP, pre-calculus, psychology, religion, scripture, Spanish, speech, studio art, theater, trigonometry, U.S. history, U.S. history-AP, wind ensemble, world history, world literature, world religions.

Graduation Requirements Advanced math, algebra, American literature, arts and fine arts (art, music, dance, drama), biology, chemistry, church history, English, foreign language, geometry, physical education (includes health), physics, religion (includes Bible studies and theology), scripture, U.S. history, Western civilization, world literature, world religions, world studies, service hours, off-campus retreat for juniors.

Special Academic Programs 12 Advanced Placement exams for which test preparation is offered; honors section; study at local college for college credit.

College Admission Counseling 184 students graduated in 2016; 183 went to college, including Loyola University Chicago; Marquette University; Northwestern University; University of Illinois at Chicago; University of Illinois at Urbana–Champaign; University of Notre Dame. Other: 1 entered military service. Median composite ACT: 25. 40% scored over 26 on composite ACT.

Student Life Upper grades have uniform requirement, student council, honor system. Discipline rests primarily with faculty. Attendance at religious services is required.

Summer Programs Enrichment, advancement, sports, art/fine arts programs offered; session focuses on athletic camps and academic enrichment; held on campus; accepts boys and girls; open to students from other schools.

Tuition and Aid Day student tuition: $12,770. Tuition installment plan (monthly payment plans). Tuition reduction for siblings, merit scholarship grants, need-based scholarship grants available. In 2016–17, 22% of upper-school students received aid; total upper-school merit-scholarship money awarded: $60,000. Total amount of financial aid awarded in 2016–17: $300,000.

Admissions Traditional secondary-level entrance grade is 9. For fall 2016, 310 students applied for upper-level admission, 206 enrolled. High School Placement Test or TOEFL required. Deadline for receipt of application materials: June 30. No application fee required. Interview recommended.

Athletics Interscholastic: baseball (boys), basketball (b,g), cheering (g), cross-country running (b,g), football (b), golf (b,g), lacrosse (b,g), soccer (b,g), softball (g), tennis (b,g), track and field (b,g), volleyball (b,g), wrestling (b); intramural: weight training (b,g); coed interscholastic: hockey. 1 PE instructor, 2 coaches, 1 athletic trainer.

Computers Computers are regularly used in all academic classes. Computer network features include on-campus library services, Internet access, wireless campus network, Internet filtering or blocking technology. Student e-mail accounts and computer access in designated common areas are available to students. Students grades are available online. The school has a published electronic and media policy.

Contact Mr. John Bonk, Recruitment Director. 708-387-8538. Fax: 708-354-0109. E-mail: jbonk@nazarethacademy.com. Website: www.nazarethacademy.com

NEBRASKA CHRISTIAN SCHOOLS

1847 Inskip Avenue
Central City, Nebraska 68826

Head of School: Mr. Josh Cumpston

General Information Coeducational boarding and day college-preparatory school, affiliated with Protestant-Evangelical faith. Boarding grades 7–12, day grades K–12. Founded: 1959. Setting: rural. Nearest major city is Lincoln. Students are housed in single-sex dormitories. 27-acre campus. 8 buildings on campus. Approved or accredited by Association of Christian Schools International and Nebraska Department of Education. Total enrollment: 201. Upper school average class size: 15. Upper school faculty-student ratio: 1:10. There are 155 required school days per year for Upper School students. Upper School students typically attend 4 days per week. The average school day consists of 8 hours and 5 minutes.

Upper School Student Profile Grade 6: 10 students (5 boys, 5 girls); Grade 7: 17 students (10 boys, 7 girls); Grade 8: 13 students (8 boys, 5 girls); Grade 9: 27 students (11 boys, 16 girls); Grade 10: 35 students (17 boys, 18 girls); Grade 11: 34 students (18 boys, 16 girls); Grade 12: 34 students (15 boys, 19 girls). 27% of students are boarding students. 78% are state residents. 1 state is represented in upper school student body. 22% are international students. International students from China, Democratic People's Republic of Korea, Kenya, Taiwan, Thailand, and Viet Nam. 85% of students are Protestant-Evangelical faith.

Faculty School total: 23. In upper school: 13 men, 7 women; 4 have advanced degrees; 4 reside on campus.

Subjects Offered Accounting, ACT preparation, advanced math, algebra, American government, American history, American literature, anatomy and physiology, ancient world history, art, band, Bible, biology, botany, business, business law, calculus, chemistry, choir, Christian doctrine, Christian ethics, Christian studies, composition, computer applications, computer programming, concert band, consumer mathematics, creation science, desktop publishing, economics, economics and history, English, English composition, ESL, family living, fitness, general math, geography, geometry, health and safety, history, keyboarding, lab science, language arts, Life of Christ, life science, literature, mathematics, music, music theory, physical education, physical fitness, physical science, physics, pre-calculus, SAT preparation, SAT/ACT preparation, science, science project, social studies, Spanish, speech, trigonometry, U.S. government, vocal ensemble, vocal music, Web site design, word processing, world geography, world history, writing, yearbook.

Graduation Requirements Algebra, American government, American history, American literature, art, arts and fine arts (art, music, dance, drama), Bible, biology, calculus-AP, chemistry, Christian doctrine, economics, English, family living, geometry, history, keyboarding, Life of Christ, music, physical education (includes health), physical science, public speaking, Spanish, vocal music, world history.

Special Academic Programs Independent study; study at local college for college credit; ESL (26 students enrolled).

College Admission Counseling 35 students graduated in 2016; 33 went to college, including South Dakota School of Mines and Technology; University of Illinois at Urbana–Champaign; University of Nebraska–Lincoln; University of Nebraska at Kearney; University of Nebraska at Omaha; University of Wisconsin–Madison. Other: 2 went to work, 1 entered military service. Median composite ACT: 22. 55% scored over 26 on composite ACT.

Student Life Upper grades have specified standards of dress, student council, honor system. Discipline rests primarily with faculty. Attendance at religious services is required.

Tuition and Aid Day student tuition: $5000; 5-day tuition and room/board: $8000; 7-day tuition and room/board: $28,000. Guaranteed tuition plan. Tuition installment plan

(FACTS Tuition Payment Plan, individually arranged payment plans). Tuition reduction for siblings, merit scholarship grants, need-based scholarship grants available. In 2016–17, 26% of upper-school students received aid; total upper-school merit-scholarship money awarded: $100,000. Total amount of financial aid awarded in 2016–17: $140,000.

Admissions Traditional secondary-level entrance grade is 9. For fall 2016, 43 students applied for upper-level admission, 35 were accepted, 35 enrolled. SLEP for foreign students or TOEFL or SLEP required. Deadline for receipt of application materials: none. Application fee required: $100. Interview recommended.

Athletics Interscholastic: basketball (boys, girls), cross-country running (b,g), football (b), soccer (b,g), track and field (b,g), volleyball (g), wrestling (b). 3 PE instructors, 7 coaches.

Computers Computers are regularly used in business applications, desktop publishing, drafting, Web site design, yearbook classes. Computer network features include Internet access, wireless campus network, Internet filtering or blocking technology. Students grades are available online.

Contact Mr. Gib Killion, Director, International Programs. 308-946-3836. Fax: 308-946-3837. E-mail: gkillion@nebraskachristian.org. Website: www.nebraskachristian.org

NERINX HALL

530 East Lockwood Avenue
Webster Groves, Missouri 63119

Head of School: Mr. John Gabriel

General Information Girls' day college-preparatory school, affiliated with Roman Catholic Church. Grades 9–12. Founded: 1924. Setting: suburban. Nearest major city is St. Louis. 7-acre campus. 4 buildings on campus. Approved or accredited by National Catholic Education Association, North Central Association of Colleges and Schools, and Missouri Department of Education. Endowment: $6 million. Total enrollment: 597. Upper school average class size: 19. Upper school faculty-student ratio: 1:9. There are 176 required school days per year for Upper School students. Upper School students typically attend 5 days per week. The average school day consists of 6 hours and 25 minutes.

Upper School Student Profile Grade 9: 153 students (153 girls); Grade 10: 166 students (166 girls); Grade 11: 160 students (160 girls); Grade 12: 116 students (116 girls). 86% of students are Roman Catholic.

Faculty School total: 55. In upper school: 14 men, 41 women; 48 have advanced degrees.

Subjects Offered Accounting, acting, advanced math, American government, American history, American literature, anatomy, anthropology, art, art-AP, astronomy, athletics, biology, biology-AP, business, calculus, ceramics, chemistry, computer applications, computer graphics, computer science, conceptual physics, creative writing, death and loss, drawing and design, Eastern world civilizations, economics, English composition, English literature, English literature-AP, environmental science, film appreciation, French, French-AP, gender issues, geology, German, graphics, health, history, Holocaust, honors algebra, honors English, honors geometry, honors U.S. history, instrumental music, jazz band, keyboarding, lab science, Latin, Latin-AP, Mandarin, media, Middle East, model United Nations, multimedia, orchestra, painting, performing arts, personal finance, physics, pre-calculus, psychology, religious education, science and technology, Spanish, Spanish-AP, theology, Web site design, world history-AP, world religions.

Graduation Requirements Algebra, arts and fine arts (art, music, dance, drama), biology, computer applications, computer science, English, foreign language, geometry, mathematics, physical education (includes health), physical fitness, physics, science, social studies (includes history), theology, U.S. government and politics, U.S. history, U.S. literature, world history, writing. Community service is required.

Special Academic Programs 11 Advanced Placement exams for which test preparation is offered; honors section; study at local college for college credit.

College Admission Counseling 149 students graduated in 2016; all went to college, including Loyola University Chicago; Missouri State University; Saint Louis University; Truman State University; University of Dayton; University of Missouri. Median composite ACT: 27. 64% scored over 26 on composite ACT.

Student Life Upper grades have uniform requirement, student council, honor system. Discipline rests primarily with faculty. Attendance at religious services is required.

Summer Programs Advancement, art/fine arts, computer instruction programs offered; session focuses on advancement; held on campus; accepts girls; not open to students from other schools. 175 students usually enrolled.

Tuition and Aid Day student tuition: $13,600. Tuition installment plan (SMART Tuition Payment Plan, monthly payment plans). Tuition reduction for siblings, merit scholarship grants, need-based scholarship grants, paying campus jobs available. In 2016–17, 33% of upper-school students received aid; total upper-school merit-scholarship money awarded: $187,000. Total amount of financial aid awarded in 2016–17: $987,386.

Admissions Traditional secondary-level entrance grade is 9. For fall 2016, 183 students applied for upper-level admission, 167 were accepted, 153 enrolled. Any standardized test or CTBS (or similar from their school) required. Deadline for receipt of application materials: November 16. Application fee required: $10. On-campus interview required.

Athletics Interscholastic: basketball, cross-country running, diving, field hockey, golf, lacrosse, racquetball, soccer, softball, swimming and diving, tennis, track and field, volleyball. 3 PE instructors, 25 coaches, 1 athletic trainer.

Computers Computers are regularly used in graphics, humanities, keyboarding, mathematics, science, speech, writing, writing classes. Computer network features include on-campus library services, Internet access, wireless campus network, Internet filtering or blocking technology. Student e-mail accounts are available to students. Students grades are available online. The school has a published electronic and media policy.

Contact Ms. Monica Sullivan, Admissions. 314-968-1505 Ext. 115. Fax: 314-962-6556. E-mail: msullivan@nerinxhs.org. Website: www.nerinxhs.org

NEUCHATEL JUNIOR COLLEGE

Cret-Taconnet 4
Neuchâtel 2002, Switzerland

Head of School: Mr. William S. Boyer

General Information Coeducational boarding college-preparatory and international development school. Grade 12. Founded: 1956. Setting: urban. Nearest major city is Berne, Switzerland. Students are housed in homestay. 1-acre campus. 3 buildings on campus. Approved or accredited by Canadian Association of Independent Schools, Canadian Educational Standards Institute, and state department of education. Affiliate member of National Association of Independent Schools. Languages of instruction: English and French. Endowment: CAN$550,000. Total enrollment: 62. Upper school average class size: 15. Upper school faculty-student ratio: 1:10. There are 168 required school days per year for Upper School students. Upper School students typically attend 5 days per week. The average school day consists of 6 hours and 50 minutes.

Upper School Student Profile Grade 12: 45 students (12 boys, 33 girls); Postgraduate: 17 students (10 boys, 7 girls). 100% of students are boarding students. 7 states are represented in upper school student body. 9% are international students. International students from Belgium, Canada, Italy, Lithuania, Switzerland, and United States.

Faculty School total: 7. In upper school: 3 men, 4 women; 2 have advanced degrees; 1 resides on campus.

Subjects Offered 20th century world history, advanced chemistry, advanced math, Advanced Placement courses, advanced studio art-AP, algebra, analysis and differential calculus, ancient history, applied arts, art, art history, art history-AP, athletics, biology, biology-AP, British history, business, business mathematics, calculus, calculus-AP, Canadian history, Canadian law, Canadian literature, career and personal planning, Central and Eastern European history, chemistry, chemistry-AP, classical civilization, classical studies, community service, comparative government and politics-AP, comparative political systems-AP, comparative politics, critical thinking, debate, decision making skills, drama, drama performance, dramatic arts, earth science, economics, economics-AP, electives, English, English composition, English language and composition-AP, English literature, English literature-AP, environmental science, environmental studies, European civilization, European history, European history-AP, finite math, French as a second language, French language-AP, French literature-AP, German-AP, government and politics-AP, guidance, history-AP, human geography - AP, independent study, Internet research, law, media studies, model United Nations, modern European history-AP, performing arts, personal and social education, personal finance, physical fitness, physics, physics-AP, portfolio art, public speaking, SAT/ACT preparation, society, politics and law, studio art-AP, United Nations and international issues, visual arts, world history-AP, world issues.

Graduation Requirements English, minimum of 6 senior year university prep level courses.

Special Academic Programs 8 Advanced Placement exams for which test preparation is offered; study abroad; academic accommodation for the gifted, the musically talented, and the artistically talented.

College Admission Counseling 73 students graduated in 2016; 71 went to college, including Dalhousie University; McGill University; Queen's University at Kingston; The University of Western Ontario; University of Guelph; University of Toronto. Other: 1 entered military service, 1 had other specific plans.

Student Life Upper grades have specified standards of dress, student council, honor system. Discipline rests primarily with faculty.

Tuition and Aid 7-day tuition and room/board: 29,000 Swiss francs–54,500 Swiss francs. Guaranteed tuition plan. Tuition installment plan (individually arranged payment plans). Tuition reduction for siblings, bursaries, merit scholarship grants available. In 2016–17, 16% of upper-school students received aid; total upper-school merit-scholarship money awarded: CAN$2000. Total amount of financial aid awarded in 2016–17: CAN$393,000.

Admissions Traditional secondary-level entrance grade is 12. For fall 2016, 79 students applied for upper-level admission, 79 were accepted, 62 enrolled. Deadline for receipt of application materials: February 10. Application fee required: CAN$175. Interview required.

Athletics Interscholastic: field hockey (boys, girls), rugby (b,g), soccer (b,g), volleyball (b,g); intramural: hockey (b,g), ice hockey (b,g), indoor hockey (b,g), rugby (b,g), soccer (b,g); coed interscholastic: alpine skiing, aquatics, badminton, cross-country running, golf, skiing (downhill), snowboarding, swimming and diving; coed intramural: alpine skiing, aquatics, backpacking, basketball, bicycling, cross-country running, curling, equestrian sports, fitness, floor hockey, golf, hiking/backpacking, horseback riding, jogging, nordic skiing, outdoor activities, outdoor adventure, outdoor recreation, physical fitness, rafting, sailing, skiing (cross-country), skiing (downhill), snowboarding, snowshoeing, table tennis, tennis, ultimate Frisbee, volleyball, yoga.

Computers Computers are regularly used in all classes. Computer network features include on-campus library services, Internet access, wireless campus network, e-books for math and science courses. Campus intranet, student e-mail accounts, and computer access in designated common areas are available to students. The school has a published electronic and media policy.

Contact Mrs. Brenda Neil, Director of Admission. 416-368-8169 Ext. 222. Fax: 416-368-0956. E-mail: admissions@neuchatel.org. Website: www.njc.ch

NEWARK ACADEMY

91 South Orange Avenue
Livingston, New Jersey 07039-4989

Head of School: M. Donald M. Austin

General Information Coeducational day college-preparatory, arts, technology, and International Baccalaureate school. Grades 6–12. Founded: 1774. Setting: suburban. Nearest major city is Morristown. 68-acre campus. 1 building on campus. Approved or accredited by Middle States Association of Colleges and Schools and New Jersey Department of Education. Member of National Association of Independent Schools and Secondary School Admission Test Board. Endowment: $25 million. Total enrollment: 580. Upper school average class size: 13. Upper school faculty-student ratio: 1:12. There are 165 required school days per year for Upper School students. Upper School students typically attend 5 days per week. The average school day consists of 6 hours.

Upper School Student Profile Grade 9: 104 students (45 boys, 59 girls); Grade 10: 104 students (55 boys, 49 girls); Grade 11: 102 students (54 boys, 48 girls); Grade 12: 93 students (48 boys, 45 girls).

Faculty School total: 75. In upper school: 32 men, 35 women; 67 have advanced degrees.

Subjects Offered Accounting, acting, advanced biology, advanced chemistry, advanced computer applications, advanced math, Advanced Placement courses, advanced studio art-AP, algebra, American history, American literature, anatomy, art, art history, arts, biology, botany, calculus, ceramics, chemistry, chorus, community service, computer programming, computer science, creative writing, drama, driver education, ecology, economics, English, English literature, European history, film studies, filmmaking, finance, fine arts, French, geometry, government/civics, grammar, health, history, history-AP, Holocaust studies, honors algebra, honors geometry, humanities, International Baccalaureate courses, jazz band, leadership, Mandarin, mathematics, mechanical drawing, model United Nations, modern dance, money management, music, musical theater, newspaper, oil painting, participation in sports, peer counseling, philosophy, physical education, physical science, physics, play production, playwriting and directing, poetry, political science, pottery, pre-algebra, pre-calculus, probability and statistics, SAT/ACT preparation, science, Spanish, theater, theory of knowledge, trigonometry, world history, world literature, writing.

Graduation Requirements Arts and fine arts (art, music, dance, drama), computer science, English, foreign language, mathematics, physical education (includes health), science, social studies (includes history), 40-hour senior service project, community service.

Special Academic Programs International Baccalaureate program; 5 Advanced Placement exams for which test preparation is offered; honors section; accelerated programs; independent study; term-away projects; study abroad; academic accommodation for the gifted, the musically talented, and the artistically talented.

College Admission Counseling 101 students graduated in 2015; all went to college, including Cornell University; Georgetown University; Harvard University; New York University; The George Washington University; University of Pennsylvania. Median SAT critical reading: 697, median SAT math: 688, median SAT writing: 703, median combined SAT: 2088, median composite ACT: 30.

Student Life Upper grades have specified standards of dress, student council, honor system. Discipline rests primarily with faculty.

Tuition and Aid Day student tuition: $34,760. Tuition installment plan (Insured Tuition Payment Plan, Key Tuition Payment Plan, monthly payment plans). Need-based scholarship grants available. In 2015–16, 17% of upper-school students received aid. Total amount of financial aid awarded in 2015–16: $1,729,521.

Admissions Traditional secondary-level entrance grade is 9. For fall 2015, 574 students applied for upper-level admission, 94 were accepted, 52 enrolled. ISEE or SSAT required. Deadline for receipt of application materials: December 7. Application fee required: $75. On-campus interview required.

Athletics Interscholastic: baseball (boys), basketball (b,g), cross-country running (b,g), fencing (b,g), field hockey (g), football (b), golf (b,g), lacrosse (b,g), running (b,g), skiing (downhill) (b,g), soccer (b,g), softball (g), swimming and diving (b,g), tennis (b,g), track and field (b,g), volleyball (g), wrestling (b); intramural: aerobics/dance (b,g), aerobics/Nautilus (b,g), baseball (b), basketball (b,g), bicycling (b,g), cross-country running (b,g), dance (b,g), dance team (b,g), field hockey (g), fitness (b,g), football (b), golf (b,g), hockey (b), ice hockey (b), lacrosse (b,g), modern dance (b,g), soccer (b,g), softball (g), swimming and diving (b,g), tennis (b,g), track and field (b,g), volleyball (g), weight lifting (b,g), wrestling (b), yoga (b,g); coed intramural: aerobics/dance, aerobics/Nautilus, bicycling, cricket, dance, dance team,

fitness, modern dance, mountain biking, skiing (downhill), table tennis, ultimate Frisbee, weight lifting, yoga. 5 PE instructors, 10 coaches, 1 athletic trainer.

Computers Computers are regularly used in all academic classes. Computer network features include on-campus library services, online commercial services, Internet access, wireless campus network, Internet filtering or blocking technology. Campus intranet and student e-mail accounts are available to students. Students grades are available online. The school has a published electronic and media policy.

Contact Mrs. Dana Pomykala, Admission Office Manager. 973-992-7000 Ext. 323. Fax: 973-488-0040. E-mail: dpomykala@newarka.edu. Website: www.newarka.edu

NEW COVENANT ACADEMY

3304 South Cox Road
Springfield, Missouri 65807

Head of School: Mr. Matt Searson

General Information Coeducational day college-preparatory and science, math, foreign language, language arts school, affiliated with Christian faith. Grades JK–12. Founded: 1979. Setting: suburban. 27-acre campus. 1 building on campus. Approved or accredited by Association of Christian Schools International and North Central Association of Colleges and Schools. Total enrollment: 478. Upper school faculty-student ratio: 1:10. There are 167 required school days per year for Upper School students. Upper School students typically attend 5 days per week. The average school day consists of 7 hours and 30 minutes.

Upper School Student Profile 99% of students are Christian.

Faculty School total: 30. In upper school: 7 men, 7 women.

Subjects Offered Advanced math, algebra, American government, American history, American literature, anatomy and physiology, ancient world history, art, athletics, Bible, biology, British literature, business, calculus, chemistry, Christianity, comparative government and politics, computer processing, computer technologies, computers, concert choir, economics, English, English composition, geology, geometry, health, history, independent study, Life of Christ, literature, mathematics, music appreciation, New Testament, oceanography, physical education, physics, pre-algebra, robotics, science, scripture, Spanish, trigonometry, world history, yearbook.

Special Academic Programs Study at local college for college credit.

College Admission Counseling 22 students graduated in 2016.

Student Life Upper grades have specified standards of dress, student council, honor system. Discipline rests primarily with faculty. Attendance at religious services is required.

Tuition and Aid Tuition installment plan (monthly payment plans, individually arranged payment plans). Need-based scholarship grants available.

Admissions Otis-Lennon School Ability Test, Stanford Achievement Test or TOEFL Junior required. Deadline for receipt of application materials: none. Application fee required: $50. Interview recommended.

Athletics Interscholastic: baseball (boys, girls), basketball (b,g), cheering (g), cross-country running (b,g), golf (b), soccer (b,g), swimming and diving (g), track and field (b,g), volleyball (g); intramural: basketball (b,g), soccer (b,g); coed interscholastic: golf. 1 PE instructor, 11 coaches.

Computers Computers are regularly used in computer applications, journalism, technology, word processing, yearbook classes. Computer network features include Internet access, wireless campus network, Internet filtering or blocking technology. Student e-mail accounts and computer access in designated common areas are available to students. Students grades are available online.

Contact Mrs. Delana Reynolds, Admissions Officer. 417-887-9848 Ext. 403. Fax: 417-887-2419. E-mail: dreynolds@newcovenant.net. Website: www.newcovenant.net

NEW INTERNATIONAL SCHOOL OF THAILAND

36 Sukhumvit Soi 15
Bangkok 10110, Thailand

Head of School: Brett Penny

General Information Coeducational day college-preparatory and bilingual studies school. Grades N–12. Founded: 1992. Setting: urban. 9-acre campus. 9 buildings on campus. Approved or accredited by Ministry of Education (Thailand). Language of instruction: English. Total enrollment: 1,319. Upper school average class size: 22. Upper school faculty-student ratio: 1:8. There are 182 required school days per year for Upper School students. Upper School students typically attend 5 days per week. The average school day consists of 5 hours and 30 minutes.

Upper School Student Profile Grade 6: 95 students (46 boys, 49 girls); Grade 7: 98 students (56 boys, 42 girls); Grade 8: 97 students (42 boys, 55 girls); Grade 9: 88 students (52 boys, 36 girls); Grade 10: 98 students (51 boys, 47 girls); Grade 11: 96 students (53 boys, 43 girls); Grade 12: 73 students (30 boys, 43 girls).

Faculty School total: 112. In upper school: 43 men, 52 women.

Subjects Offered Art, biology, business, chemistry, community service, computer science, drama, economics, English, environmental systems, fine arts, French, geography, Hindi, history, information technology, Japanese, Korean, life skills, literature, Mandarin, mathematics, music, physical education, physics, psychology, science, social sciences, social studies, Spanish, technology, Thai, theater, theory of knowledge.

Graduation Requirements Arts and fine arts (art, music, dance, drama), computer science, English, foreign language, mathematics, physical education (includes health), science, social sciences, social studies (includes history), theory of knowledge, extended essay. Community service is required.

Special Academic Programs International Baccalaureate program; remedial reading and/or remedial writing; remedial math; ESL (124 students enrolled).

College Admission Counseling 43 students graduated in 2016; all went to college, including Amherst College; Babson College; Clark University; Grinnell College; Hawai`i Pacific University; Massachusetts Institute of Technology.

Student Life Upper grades have uniform requirement, student council. Discipline rests primarily with faculty.

Summer Programs Remediation, enrichment, ESL, sports programs offered; session focuses on language acquisition and enrichment; held on campus; accepts boys and girls; open to students from other schools. 180 students usually enrolled. 2017 schedule: June to July. Application deadline: June 1.

Tuition and Aid Day student tuition: 237,000 Thai bahts–476,800 Thai bahts. Tuition installment plan (individually arranged payment plans). Bursaries available.

Admissions Admissions testing required. Deadline for receipt of application materials: none. Application fee required: 4000 Thai bahts. On-campus interview required.

Athletics Interscholastic: baseball (boys, girls), basketball (b,g), bowling (b), cricket (b), football (b), physical fitness (b,g), rappelling (b,g), rugby (b), scuba diving (b,g), soccer (b,g), softball (b,g), tennis (b,g), volleyball (b,g), wilderness survival (b,g); intramural: basketball (b,g), cricket (b,g), physical fitness (b,g), roller blading (b,g), soccer (b,g), softball (b,g), volleyball (b,g); coed interscholastic: physical fitness, rappelling, scuba diving, wilderness survival; coed intramural: physical fitness, roller blading. 5 PE instructors, 5 coaches.

Computers Computers are regularly used in English, music classes. Computer network features include on-campus library services, Internet access, Internet filtering or blocking technology. The school has a published electronic and media policy.

Contact Yvonne Trisynthia, Director of Admissions. 66-(0)2 017 5888 Ext. 1102. Fax: 66-(0)2 253 3800. E-mail: admissions@nist.ac.th. Website: www.nist.ac.th/

NEW ROADS SCHOOL

3131 Olympic Boulevard
Santa Monica, California 90404

Head of School: Luthern Williams

General Information Coeducational day college-preparatory school. Grades K–12. Founded: 1995. Setting: urban. 2-acre campus. 9 buildings on campus. Approved or accredited by California Association of Independent Schools, New England Association of Schools and Colleges, and Western Association of Schools and Colleges. Member of National Association of Independent Schools. Total enrollment: 615. Upper school average class size: 20. Upper school faculty-student ratio: 1:11.

Student Life Upper grades have student council, honor system. Discipline rests primarily with faculty.

Summer Programs Enrichment, sports, art/fine arts programs offered; held on campus; accepts boys and girls; open to students from other schools.

Tuition and Aid Day student tuition: $33,160. Tuition installment plan (monthly payment plans). Need-based scholarship grants available. In 2016–17, 49% of upper-school students received aid. Total amount of financial aid awarded in 2016–17: $4,800,000.

Admissions Traditional secondary-level entrance grade is 9. ISEE required. Deadline for receipt of application materials: December 12. Application fee required: $125. Interview required.

Athletics Interscholastic: baseball (boys), basketball (b,g), cross-country running (b,g), golf (b), soccer (b,g), swimming and diving (b,g), tennis (b,g), track and field (b,g), volleyball (b,g); intramural: drill team (g); coed intramural: flag football. 2 PE instructors, 25 coaches.

Contact Admissions Office. 310-828-5582. Fax: 310-828-2582. E-mail: admissions@newroads.org. Website: www.newroads.org/

NEWTON COUNTRY DAY SCHOOL OF THE SACRED HEART

785 Centre Street
Newton, Massachusetts 02458

Head of School: Barbara Rogers, RSCJ

General Information Girls' day college-preparatory, arts, religious studies, and science, math, and history school, affiliated with Roman Catholic Church. Grades 5–12. Founded: 1880. Setting: suburban. Nearest major city is Boston. 20-acre campus. 7 buildings on campus. Approved or accredited by Association of Independent Schools in New England, Network of Sacred Heart Schools, New England Association of Schools and Colleges, and Massachusetts Department of Education. Member of National Association of Independent Schools and Secondary School Admission Test Board. Endowment: $18.9 million. Total enrollment: 409. Upper school average class size: 15.

Upper school faculty-student ratio: 1:7. Upper School students typically attend 5 days per week. The average school day consists of 8 hours.

Upper School Student Profile Grade 9: 61 students (61 girls); Grade 10: 50 students (50 girls); Grade 11: 63 students (63 girls); Grade 12: 64 students (64 girls). 70% of students are Roman Catholic.

Faculty School total: 74. In upper school: 20 men, 37 women; 45 have advanced degrees.

Subjects Offered African American history, algebra, American history, American history-AP, American literature, anatomy, art, art history, art-AP, biology, biology-AP, calculus, calculus-AP, chemistry, chemistry-AP, Chinese, community service, comparative government and politics, comparative government and politics-AP, creative writing, dance, drama, earth science, economics, English, English language-AP, English literature, English literature-AP, environmental science, environmental science-AP, European history-AP, expository writing, French, French language-AP, geography, geometry, government/civics, grammar, history, Latin, Latin-AP, mathematics, music, music theory, photography, physical education, physics, physics-AP, physiology, psychology, public speaking, religion, science, social sciences, social studies, Spanish, Spanish language-AP, Spanish literature-AP, statistics, statistics-AP, technology, theater, theology, trigonometry, U.S. government and politics-AP, world history, world literature, writing.

Graduation Requirements Arts and fine arts (art, music, dance, drama), English, foreign language, mathematics, physical education (includes health), religion (includes Bible studies and theology), science, senior project, social sciences, social studies (includes history), senior project. Community service is required.

Special Academic Programs 21 Advanced Placement exams for which test preparation is offered; honors section; independent study; term-away projects; study at local college for college credit; domestic exchange program (with Network of Sacred Heart Schools); study abroad.

College Admission Counseling 66 students graduated in 2016; all went to college, including Boston College; College of the Holy Cross; Georgetown University; Harvard University; Johns Hopkins University; Villanova University.

Student Life Upper grades have specified standards of dress, student council, honor system. Discipline rests equally with students and faculty. Attendance at religious services is required.

Summer Programs Sports programs offered; session focuses on athletics; held on campus; accepts girls; open to students from other schools. 80 students usually enrolled. 2017 schedule: June to July. Application deadline: June 1.

Tuition and Aid Day student tuition: $46,450. Tuition installment plan (Academic Management Services Plan, monthly payment plans). Need-based scholarship grants available. In 2016–17, 22% of upper-school students received aid. Total amount of financial aid awarded in 2016–17: $1,080,000.

Admissions Traditional secondary-level entrance grade is 9. For fall 2016, 63 students applied for upper-level admission, 27 were accepted, 17 enrolled. ISEE or SSAT required. Deadline for receipt of application materials: January 15. Application fee required: $50. On-campus interview recommended.

Athletics Interscholastic: basketball, crew, cross-country running, dance team, field hockey, golf, ice hockey, lacrosse, sailing, soccer, softball, squash, tennis, volleyball; intramural: aerobics, aerobics/dance, ballet, basketball, cooperative games, crew, cross-country running, dance, dance team, fitness, flag football, modern dance, outdoor adventure, outdoor education, outdoor recreation, outdoor skills, physical fitness, physical training, soccer, softball, swimming and diving, tennis, volleyball, yoga. 1 PE instructor, 1 coach, 1 athletic trainer.

Computers Computers are regularly used in all academic classes. Computer network features include on-campus library services, online commercial services, Internet access, wireless campus network, Internet filtering or blocking technology. Student e-mail accounts are available to students. The school has a published electronic and media policy.

Contact Ms. Clare Martin, Director of Admissions. 617-244-4246. Fax: 617-965-5313. E-mail: cmartin@newtoncountryday.org. Website: www.newtoncountryday.org

NEWTON'S GROVE SCHOOL

1 City View Drive
Toronto, Ontario M9W 5A5, Canada

Head of School: Mrs. Gabrielle Bush

General Information Coeducational day college-preparatory, science, humanities, and math school. Grades JK–12. Founded: 1977. Setting: urban. 1 building on campus. Approved or accredited by Ontario Ministry of Education and Ontario Department of Education. Language of instruction: English. Total enrollment: 249. Upper school average class size: 18. Upper school faculty-student ratio: 1:18. There are 192 required school days per year for Upper School students. Upper School students typically attend 5 days per week. The average school day consists of 6 hours and 30 minutes.

Upper School Student Profile Grade 9: 17 students (10 boys, 7 girls); Grade 10: 29 students (21 boys, 8 girls); Grade 11: 36 students (22 boys, 14 girls); Grade 12: 28 students (14 boys, 14 girls).

Faculty School total: 35. In upper school: 8 men, 6 women; 2 have advanced degrees.

Subjects Offered Exercise science.

Graduation Requirements English, Ontario Ministry of Education requirements.

Special Academic Programs 2 Advanced Placement exams for which test preparation is offered; ESL (15 students enrolled).

College Admission Counseling 33 students graduated in 2016; all went to college, including McMaster University; Ryerson University; University of Guelph; University of Toronto; University of Waterloo; York University.

Student Life Upper grades have uniform requirement, student council, honor system. Discipline rests primarily with faculty.

Summer Programs Remediation, enrichment, advancement, ESL, sports, art/fine arts, computer instruction programs offered; session focuses on academics; held on campus; accepts boys and girls; open to students from other schools. 100 students usually enrolled. 2017 schedule: July 6 to July 31. Application deadline: June 25.

Tuition and Aid Day student tuition: CAN$14,800. Tuition installment plan (individually arranged payment plans, MPS Payment Plan). Tuition reduction for siblings, early payment discount available.

Admissions Traditional secondary-level entrance grade is 9. For fall 2016, 25 students applied for upper-level admission, 25 were accepted, 25 enrolled. Admissions testing required. Deadline for receipt of application materials: October 31. No application fee required. Interview required.

Athletics Interscholastic: aquatics (boys, girls), ball hockey (b,g), baseball (b,g), basketball (b,g), flag football (b,g), football (b), golf (b), indoor track & field (b,g), running (b,g), soccer (b,g), swimming and diving (b,g), track and field (b,g), volleyball (b,g); intramural: basketball (b,g), flag football (b,g), floor hockey (b,g), Frisbee (b,g), indoor hockey (b,g), physical fitness (b,g), rhythmic gymnastics (b,g), running (b,g), soccer (b,g), swimming and diving (b,g), touch football (b,g), track and field (b,g), ultimate Frisbee (b,g), volleyball (b,g), winter (indoor) track (b,g), winter soccer (b,g); coed interscholastic: aquatics, badminton, bowling, cross-country running, field hockey, flag football, Frisbee, track and field; coed intramural: badminton, ball hockey, baseball, basketball, bowling, cooperative games, cricket, cross-country running, flag football, tennis, track and field. 2 PE instructors.

Computers Computers are regularly used in accounting, business, design classes. Computer resources include Internet access, Internet filtering or blocking technology. Student e-mail accounts are available to students. The school has a published electronic and media policy.

Contact Mrs. Gabrielle Bush, Director. 416-745-1328. Fax: 416-745-4168. E-mail: info@newtonsgroveschool.com. Website: www.newtonsgroveschool.com

NEW YORK MILITARY ACADEMY

78 Academy Avenue
Cornwall-on-Hudson, New York 12520

Head of School: Ms. Jie Zhang

General Information Coeducational boarding and day college-preparatory, Junior ROTC, ESL, and military school, affiliated with Anglican Church of Canada. Grades 8–12. Founded: 1889. Setting: small town. Nearest major city is New York. Students are housed in coed dormitories. 140-acre campus. 11 buildings on campus. Approved or accredited by Middle States Association of Colleges and Schools, New York State Association of Independent Schools, The Association of Boarding Schools, and New York Department of Education. Member of National Association of Independent Schools and Secondary School Admission Test Board. Endowment: $2.6 million. Total enrollment: 141. Upper school faculty-student ratio: 1:8. There are 189 required school days per year for Upper School students. Upper School students typically attend 5 days per week. The average school day consists of 6 hours and 30 minutes.

Upper School Student Profile Grade 9: 17 students (13 boys, 4 girls); Grade 10: 28 students (22 boys, 6 girls); Grade 11: 38 students (31 boys, 7 girls); Grade 12: 41 students (29 boys, 12 girls); Grade 13: 124 students (95 boys, 29 girls).

Faculty School total: 15. In upper school: 8 men, 7 women; 14 have advanced degrees; all reside on campus.

Subjects Offered Algebra, American history, American history-AP, art, biology, business mathematics, chemistry, computer literacy, criminology, earth science, economics, English, English-AP, environmental science, geography, geometry, government, health, JROTC, physical science, physics, pre-calculus, social studies, Spanish, trigonometry, world history.

Graduation Requirements American history, art, biology, calculus, chemistry, computer science, economics, English, English composition, English literature, foreign language, global studies, government, JROTC or LEAD (Leadership Education and Development), mathematics, physical education (includes health), science, trigonometry. Community service is required.

Special Academic Programs International Baccalaureate program; 9 Advanced Placement exams for which test preparation is offered; honors section; study at local college for college credit; ESL (12 students enrolled).

College Admission Counseling 40 students graduated in 2016; 38 went to college, including American University; Boston University; Drexel University; Embry-Riddle Aeronautical University–Daytona; Stony Brook University; State University of New York; United States Military Academy. Other: 2 had other specific plans.

Student Life Upper grades have uniform requirement, student council, honor system. Discipline rests primarily with faculty. Attendance at religious services is required.

Tuition and Aid Day student tuition: $13,890; 7-day tuition and room/board: $36,190. Tuition installment plan (individually arranged payment plans). Tuition reduction for siblings, merit scholarship grants, need-based scholarship grants, Sallie

Mae loans available. In 2016–17, 74% of upper-school students received aid; total upper-school merit-scholarship money awarded: $36,000. Total amount of financial aid awarded in 2016–17: $355,000.

Admissions Traditional secondary-level entrance grade is 10. For fall 2016, 51 students applied for upper-level admission, 42 were accepted, 36 enrolled. California Achievement Test, Cooperative Entrance Exam (McGraw-Hill), Iowa Tests of Basic Skills, Otis-Lennon School Ability Test, PSAT and SAT for applicants to grade 11 and 12, SLEP, SSAT, Stanford Achievement Test or TOEFL required. Deadline for receipt of application materials: none. Application fee required: $100. On-campus interview required.

Athletics Interscholastic: baseball (boys), basketball (b,g), football (b), ice hockey (b), lacrosse (b), soccer (b), softball (g), volleyball (g), wrestling (b); intramural: hockey (b); coed interscholastic: cross-country running, drill team, fencing, golf, JROTC drill, marksmanship, martial arts, paint ball, project adventure, riflery, tennis, track and field, weight lifting; coed intramural: dance, dance team, equestrian sports, handball, martial arts. 1 PE instructor, 1 coach, 1 athletic trainer.

Computers Computers are regularly used in all academic classes. Computer network features include on-campus library services, Internet access, Internet filtering or blocking technology. Student e-mail accounts are available to students. Students grades are available online. The school has a published electronic and media policy.

Contact John J. Dolan, Admissions Director. 845-534-3710 Ext. 4272. Fax: 845-534-7699. E-mail: admissions@nyma.org. Website: www.nyma.org

NIAGARA CATHOLIC JR. /SR. HIGH SCHOOL

520 66th Street
Niagara Falls, New York 14304

Head of School: Robert Cluckey

General Information Coeducational day college-preparatory and arts school, affiliated with Christian faith. Grades 7–12. Setting: urban. Nearest major city is Buffalo. 15-acre campus. 2 buildings on campus. Approved or accredited by Middle States Association of Colleges and Schools and New York Department of Education. Upper school average class size: 28. There are 185 required school days per year for Upper School students. Upper School students typically attend 5 days per week. The average school day consists of 7 hours.

Upper School Student Profile 70% of students are Christian.

Faculty School total: 25. In upper school: 12 men, 25 women; 15 have advanced degrees.

Special Academic Programs Honors section; domestic exchange program.

College Admission Counseling 35 students graduated in 2016; 32 went to college, including Buffalo State College, State University of New York; Niagara County Community College; Niagara University. Other: 2 went to work, 1 entered military service.

Student Life Upper grades have uniform requirement, student council, honor system. Discipline rests primarily with faculty. Attendance at religious services is required.

Tuition and Aid Day student tuition: $8400. Tuition installment plan (FACTS Tuition Payment Plan, monthly payment plans, individually arranged payment plans). Tuition reduction for siblings, merit scholarship grants, need-based scholarship grants, paying campus jobs available. In 2016–17, 80% of upper-school students received aid.

Admissions No application fee required. On-campus interview required.

Athletics Interscholastic: baseball (boys), basketball (b,g), cheering (g), football (b), golf (b), hockey (b), soccer (b,g), softball (g), tennis (b,g), volleyball (g).

Computers Computer resources include on-campus library services, Internet access, wireless campus network. Student e-mail accounts are available to students. Students grades are available online.

Contact 716-283-8771. Fax: 716-283-8774.
Website: www.niagaracatholic.org/index.php

NIAGARA CHRISTIAN COMMUNITY OF SCHOOLS

2619 Niagara Boulevard
Fort Erie, Ontario L2A 5M4, Canada

Head of School: Mr. Mark Thiessen

General Information Coeducational boarding and day college-preparatory, general academic, and ESL school, affiliated with Brethren in Christ Church. Grades 9–12. Founded: 1932. Setting: rural. Nearest major city is Niagara Falls, Canada. Students are housed in single-sex dormitories. 121-acre campus. 16 buildings on campus. Approved or accredited by Ontario Department of Education. Language of instruction: English. Total enrollment: 205. Upper school average class size: 18. Upper school faculty-student ratio: 1:18. There are 170 required school days per year for Upper School students. Upper School students typically attend 5 days per week. The average school day consists of 6 hours.

Upper School Student Profile Grade 9: 30 students (17 boys, 13 girls); Grade 10: 35 students (18 boys, 17 girls); Grade 11: 63 students (29 boys, 34 girls); Grade 12: 84 students (50 boys, 34 girls). 80% of students are boarding students. 30% are province residents. 5 provinces are represented in upper school student body. 70% are international students. International students from Brazil, China, Hong Kong, Japan,

Mexico, and Nigeria; 4 other countries represented in student body. 35% of students are Brethren in Christ Church.

Faculty School total: 27. In upper school: 10 men, 17 women; 2 have advanced degrees.

Subjects Offered Accounting, advanced chemistry, advanced math, algebra, analysis and differential calculus, analytic geometry, anthropology, art, art history, athletics, Bible, biology, business, business applications, business education, business mathematics, business technology, calculus, Canadian geography, Canadian history, Canadian literature, career education, chemistry, choir, civics, computer applications, computer programming, concert choir, data processing, early childhood, economics, English, English literature, exercise science, family studies, French as a second language, general math, geography, geometry, guidance, health education, history, information technology, instrumental music, integrated science, international affairs, leadership education training, Life of Christ, mathematics, media studies, modern world history, music, parenting, physical education, physics, politics, pre-calculus, science, Spanish, world history, world issues, writing, writing.

Special Academic Programs Academic accommodation for the gifted; special instructional classes for students with learning disabilities; ESL (100 students enrolled).

College Admission Counseling 73 students graduated in 2016; 70 went to college, including McMaster University; Queen's University at Kingston; University of Guelph; University of Ottawa; University of Toronto; University of Waterloo. Other: 2 went to work, 70 entered a postgraduate year.

Student Life Upper grades have uniform requirement, student council, honor system. Discipline rests primarily with faculty. Attendance at religious services is required.

Summer Programs ESL programs offered; session focuses on ESL; held on campus; accepts boys and girls; open to students from other schools. 160 students usually enrolled. 2017 schedule: July 14 to August 30. Application deadline: none.

Tuition and Aid Day student tuition: CAN$9050; 5-day tuition and room/board: CAN$29,895; 7-day tuition and room/board: CAN$38,840. Tuition installment plan (monthly payment plans, individually arranged payment plans, quarterly payment plan). Tuition reduction for siblings, bursaries, merit scholarship grants, need-based scholarship grants, paying campus jobs available. In 2016–17, 10% of upper-school students received aid; total upper-school merit-scholarship money awarded: CAN$50,000. Total amount of financial aid awarded in 2016–17: CAN$400,000.

Admissions Traditional secondary-level entrance grade is 9. For fall 2016, 210 students applied for upper-level admission, 150 were accepted, 150 enrolled. Admissions testing and English proficiency required. Deadline for receipt of application materials: none. Application fee required: CAN$100. Interview required.

Athletics Interscholastic: aquatics (boys, girls), badminton (b,g), baseball (g), basketball (b,g), cross-country running (b,g), golf (b), soccer (b,g), softball (g), track and field (b,g), volleyball (b,g); coed interscholastic: badminton, swimming and diving; coed intramural: aerobics, alpine skiing, ball hockey, canoeing/kayaking, fitness, fitness walking, floor hockey, skiing (downhill). 2 PE instructors.

Computers Computers are regularly used in accounting, all academic, business, data processing, economics, ESL, mathematics, science, yearbook classes. Computer network features include on-campus library services, Internet access, wireless campus network, Internet filtering or blocking technology. Computer access in designated common areas is available to students. Students grades are available online. The school has a published electronic and media policy.

Contact Mrs. Lesley Burrison, Enrolment Specialist. 905-871-6980. Fax: 905-871-9260. E-mail: enrol@niagaracc.com. Website: www.niagaracc.com

NOBLE ACADEMY

Greensboro, North Carolina
See Special Needs Schools section.

NOBLE AND GREENOUGH SCHOOL

10 Campus Drive
Dedham, Massachusetts 02026-4099

Head of School: Mr. Robert P. Henderson Jr.

General Information Coeducational boarding and day college-preparatory school. Boarding grades 9–12, day grades 7–12. Founded: 1866. Setting: suburban. Nearest major city is Boston. Students are housed in coed dormitories and 5-day boarding. 187-acre campus. 12 buildings on campus. Approved or accredited by New England Association of Schools and Colleges and Massachusetts Department of Education. Member of National Association of Independent Schools and Secondary School Admission Test Board. Endowment: $122 million. Total enrollment: 615. Upper school average class size: 14. Upper school faculty-student ratio: 1:7. There are 162 required school days per year for Upper School students. Upper School students typically attend 5 days per week. The average school day consists of 7 hours and 5 minutes.

Upper School Student Profile Grade 9: 117 students (63 boys, 54 girls); Grade 10: 133 students (67 boys, 66 girls); Grade 11: 117 students (53 boys, 64 girls); Grade 12: 129 students (67 boys, 62 girls). 8% of students are boarding students. 100% are state residents. 1 state is represented in upper school student body. International students from United States.

Faculty School total: 127. In upper school: 61 men, 66 women; 36 reside on campus.

Subjects Offered 20th century history, Advanced Placement courses, African-American literature, algebra, American history, American literature, anatomy, ancient history, art, art history, astronomy, biology, calculus, ceramics, chemistry, community service, computer programming, computer science, concert band, creative writing, drama, drawing, earth science, ecology, economics, English, English literature, environmental science, ethics, European history, expository writing, fine arts, French, genetics, geography, geometry, government/civics, grammar, health, history, independent study, Japanese, journalism, Latin, Latin American history, marine biology, mathematics, music, painting, philosophy, photography, physics, physiology, printmaking, psychology, Roman civilization, science, senior internship, senior project, social studies, Spanish, speech, statistics, theater, trigonometry, Vietnam, world history, world literature, writing.

Graduation Requirements Arts and fine arts (art, music, dance, drama), computer science, English, foreign language, mathematics, performing arts, physical education (includes health), science, social studies (includes history), 80 hours of community service must be completed.

Special Academic Programs Advanced Placement exam preparation; honors section; independent study; term-away projects; study abroad; academic accommodation for the gifted, the musically talented, and the artistically talented.

College Admission Counseling 129 students graduated in 2016; all went to college, including Boston College; Brown University; Colby College; Dartmouth College; Harvard University. 82% scored over 600 on SAT critical reading, 81% scored over 600 on SAT math, 83% scored over 600 on SAT writing, 87% scored over 1800 on combined SAT, 79% scored over 26 on composite ACT.

Student Life Upper grades have specified standards of dress, student council, honor system. Discipline rests equally with students and faculty.

Tuition and Aid Day student tuition: $46,250; 5-day tuition and room/board: $52,050. Tuition installment plan (FACTS Tuition Payment Plan, Tuition Management Systems). Need-based scholarship grants available. In 2016–17, 24% of upper-school students received aid. Total amount of financial aid awarded in 2016–17: $3,985,500.

Admissions Traditional secondary-level entrance grade is 9. For fall 2016, 603 students applied for upper-level admission, 109 were accepted, 69 enrolled. ISEE or SSAT required. Deadline for receipt of application materials: January 15. Application fee required: $60. On-campus interview recommended.

Athletics Interscholastic: baseball (boys), basketball (b,g), crew (b,g), cross-country running (b,g), dance (b,g), field hockey (g), football (b), golf (b), hockey (b,g), outdoor adventure (b,g), sailing (b,g), skiing (cross-country) (b,g), soccer (b,g), softball (b,g), squash (b,g), strength & conditioning (b,g), tennis (b,g), volleyball (g), wrestling (b); coed intramural: aerobics/dance, dance. 12 coaches, 2 athletic trainers.

Computers Computers are regularly used in English, foreign language, history, journalism, Latin, mathematics, music, science classes. Computer network features include on-campus library services, online commercial services, Internet access, Internet filtering or blocking technology, NoblesNet (first class email and bulletin board with electronic conferencing capability), wireless iBooks. Campus intranet, student e-mail accounts, and computer access in designated common areas are available to students. The school has a published electronic and media policy.

Contact Ms. Brooke Asnis, Director of Admission. 781-320-7100. Fax: 781-320-1329. E-mail: admission@nobles.edu. Website: www.nobles.edu

THE NORA SCHOOL

955 Sligo Avenue
Silver Spring, Maryland 20910

Head of School: David E. Mullen

General Information Coeducational day college-preparatory school. Grades 9–12. Founded: 1964. Setting: urban. Nearest major city is Washington, DC. 1-acre campus. 1 building on campus. Approved or accredited by Association of Independent Maryland Schools, Association of Independent Schools of Greater Washington, Middle States Association of Colleges and Schools, and Maryland Department of Education. Member of National Association of Independent Schools. Endowment: $250,000. Total enrollment: 66. Upper school average class size: 8. Upper school faculty-student ratio: 1:5. There are 175 required school days per year for Upper School students. Upper School students typically attend 5 days per week. The average school day consists of 5 hours and 35 minutes.

Upper School Student Profile Grade 9: 12 students (6 boys, 6 girls); Grade 10: 13 students (7 boys, 6 girls); Grade 11: 19 students (14 boys, 5 girls); Grade 12: 19 students (7 boys, 12 girls).

Faculty School total: 14. In upper school: 7 men, 7 women; 11 have advanced degrees.

Subjects Offered College counseling, electronic music, film studies, freshman seminar, journalism, Latin, music, strategies for success, study skills, the comic tradition, yoga.

Graduation Requirements Arts and fine arts (art, music, dance, drama), English, foreign language, lab science, mathematics, personal fitness, science, social studies (includes history), sports, U.S. history, wilderness education, writing, graduation portfolio, team sport (1). Community service is required.

Special Academic Programs Independent study; term-away projects; study at local college for college credit; academic accommodation for the gifted and the artistically talented; remedial reading and/or remedial writing; remedial math; programs in English, mathematics, general development for dyslexic students; special instructional classes for students with Attention Deficit Disorder and learning disabilities, students who have been unsuccessful in a traditional learning environment.

College Admission Counseling 17 students graduated in 2016; all went to college, including Bard College; Dickinson College; Goucher College; Guilford College; Loyola University Maryland; University of Vermont.

Student Life Upper grades have student council. Discipline rests primarily with faculty.

Tuition and Aid Day student tuition: $28,500. Tuition installment plan (monthly payment plans). Need-based scholarship grants, Black Student Fund, Latino Student Fund, Washington Scholarship Fund available. In 2016–17, 24% of upper-school students received aid. Total amount of financial aid awarded in 2016–17: $177,000.

Admissions Traditional secondary-level entrance grade is 9. For fall 2016, 70 students applied for upper-level admission, 67 were accepted, 65 enrolled. Writing sample required. Deadline for receipt of application materials: none. Application fee required: $75. On-campus interview recommended.

Athletics Interscholastic: basketball (boys, girls); intramural: cheering (g); coed interscholastic: soccer, softball; coed intramural: alpine skiing, backpacking, bicycling, bowling, canoeing/kayaking, climbing, cooperative games, dance, Frisbee, hiking/backpacking, kayaking, life saving, outdoor activities, outdoor adventure, rafting, rock climbing, ropes courses, running, skiing (downhill), table tennis, volleyball, wilderness, winter walking, yoga. 2 coaches.

Computers Computers are regularly used in all classes. Computer network features include on-campus library services, online commercial services, Internet access, wireless campus network, Internet filtering or blocking technology. Computer access in designated common areas is available to students. Students grades are available online. The school has a published electronic and media policy.

Contact Marcia D. Miller, Director of Admissions. 301-495-6672. Fax: 301-495-7829. E-mail: marcia@nora-school.org. Website: www.nora-school.org

NORMAN HOWARD SCHOOL

Rochester, New York
See Special Needs Schools section.

THE NORTH BROWARD PREPARATORY UPPER SCHOOL

7600 Lyons Road
Coconut Creek, Florida 33073

Head of School: Elise R. Ecoff

General Information Coeducational boarding and day college-preparatory, technology, and STEAM, IB Diploma school. Boarding grades 6–12, day grades PK–12. Founded: 1957. Setting: suburban. Nearest major city is Boca Raton. Students are housed in single-sex dormitories. 75-acre campus. 11 buildings on campus. Approved or accredited by Florida Council of Independent Schools, Southern Association of Colleges and Schools, and Florida Department of Education. Member of National Association of Independent Schools and Secondary School Admission Test Board. Total enrollment: 1,550. Upper school average class size: 18. Upper school faculty-student ratio: 1:18. There are 172 required school days per year for Upper School students. Upper School students typically attend 5 days per week. The average school day consists of 6 hours and 20 minutes.

Upper School Student Profile Grade 6: 95 students (46 boys, 49 girls); Grade 7: 114 students (66 boys, 48 girls); Grade 8: 133 students (87 boys, 46 girls); Grade 9: 225 students (120 boys, 105 girls); Grade 10: 244 students (143 boys, 101 girls); Grade 11: 246 students (148 boys, 98 girls); Grade 12: 241 students (131 boys, 110 girls). 30% of students are boarding students. 85% are state residents. 3 states are represented in upper school student body. 30% are international students. International students from Brazil, China, Italy, Russian Federation, United States, and Venezuela; 30 other countries represented in student body.

Faculty School total: 110. In upper school: 37 men, 73 women; 73 have advanced degrees.

Subjects Offered Algebra, American history-AP, analysis and differential calculus, analytic geometry, ancient world history, art, art history, audio visual/media, Basic programming, biology, biology-AP, British literature, broadcast journalism, business, calculus, calculus-AP, chemistry, chemistry-AP, choir, choral music, college counseling, computer applications, computer graphics, computer programming, computer programming-AP, computers, concert band, concert choir, contemporary women writers, drama workshop, dramatic arts, ecology, environmental systems, economics, English, English composition, English literature, English literature and composition-AP, environmental science, environmental science-AP, ESL, European history, European history-AP, forensics, French, French language-AP, French literature-AP, geometry, guitar, honors algebra, honors English, honors geometry, honors U.S. history, honors world history, jazz band, jazz dance, jazz ensemble, keyboarding, Latin, model United Nations, modern European history, modern European history-AP, music, music appreciation, performing arts, physical education, physical fitness, physics-AP, psychology-AP, robotics, SAT preparation, Shakespeare, skills for success, sociology, Spanish, Spanish language-AP, Spanish literature, Spanish literature-AP, U.S. government, U.S. government and politics-AP, U.S. history, U.S. literature, wind ensemble, wind instruments, women in literature, world history-AP.

Graduation Requirements Algebra, American history, American literature, biology, calculus, chemistry, computer applications, electives, English, European history, foreign language, geometry, mathematics, performing arts, physical education (includes health), physics, social studies (includes history), technology, U.S. government, U.S. literature, world cultures. Community service is required.

Special Academic Programs International Baccalaureate program; Advanced Placement exam preparation; honors section; independent study; study at local college for college credit; academic accommodation for the gifted, the musically talented, and the artistically talented; remedial reading and/or remedial writing; remedial math; programs in English, mathematics, general development for dyslexic students; ESL (80 students enrolled).

College Admission Counseling 240 students graduated in 2016; all went to college, including Florida Atlantic University; Florida International University; Florida State University; Indiana University Bloomington; University of Florida; University of Miami. Mean SAT critical reading: 522, mean SAT math: 570, mean SAT writing: 526.

Student Life Upper grades have uniform requirement, student council, honor system. Discipline rests primarily with faculty.

Summer Programs Remediation, enrichment, advancement, sports, art/fine arts, computer instruction programs offered; session focuses on enrichment; held on campus; accepts boys and girls; open to students from other schools. 200 students usually enrolled. 2017 schedule: June 12.

Tuition and Aid Tuition installment plan (monthly payment plans). Tuition reduction for siblings, merit scholarship grants, need-based scholarship grants available. In 2016–17, 22% of upper-school students received aid.

Admissions Traditional secondary-level entrance grade is 9. Any standardized test, SSAT or writing sample required. Deadline for receipt of application materials: none. Application fee required: $150. Interview recommended.

Athletics Interscholastic: aerobics/dance (boys, girls), aquatics (b,g), baseball (b), basketball (b,g), cross-country running (b,g), dance (g), dance squad (g), dance team (g), flag football (g), football (b), golf (b,g), hockey (b,g), ice hockey (b,g), lacrosse (b,g), physical fitness (b,g), soccer (b,g), softball (g), swimming and diving (b,g), tennis (b,g), track and field (b,g), volleyball (g), water polo (b,g), winter soccer (b,g); intramural: ballet (b,g), equestrian sports (b,g), horseback riding (b,g), weight training (b,g); coed interscholastic: aerobics/dance, aquatics, cheering, cross country running, dance, dressage, fencing, golf, hockey, ice hockey, physical fitness; coed intramural: aerobics/dance, ballet, basketball, equestrian sports, flag football, horseback riding, scuba diving, strength & conditioning, weight training. 4 PE instructors, 18 coaches, 1 athletic trainer.

Computers Computers are regularly used in all academic classes. Computer network features include on-campus library services, online commercial services, Internet access, wireless campus network, Internet filtering or blocking technology. Campus intranet, student e-mail accounts, and computer access in designated common areas are available to students. Students grades are available online. The school has a published electronic and media policy.

Contact Jackie Fagan, Director of Admissions. 954-247-0011 Ext. 303. Fax: 954-247-0012. E-mail: faganj@nbps.org. Website: www.nbps.org

NORTH CENTRAL TEXAS ACADEMY

3846 North Highway 144
Granbury, Texas 76048

Head of School: Mrs. Amanda Schwausch

General Information Coeducational boarding and day and distance learning college-preparatory, arts, and agriculture/FFA/equestrian school. Grades PK–12. Founded: 1975. Setting: rural. Nearest major city is Dallas. Students are housed in single-sex residences. 500-acre campus. 1 building on campus. Approved or accredited by Association of Christian Schools International, Southern Association of Colleges and Schools, and The Association of Boarding Schools. Member of National Association of Independent Schools. Total enrollment: 175. Upper school average class size: 8. Upper school faculty-student ratio: 1:7. There are 186 required school days per year for Upper School students. Upper School students typically attend 5 days per week. The average school day consists of 6 hours and 30 minutes.

Upper School Student Profile 70% of students are boarding students. 70% are state residents. 8 states are represented in upper school student body. 15% are international students. International students from Brazil, China, Ethiopia, Mexico, Nigeria, and Serbia and Montenegro; 6 other countries represented in student body.

Faculty School total: 38. In upper school: 9 men, 22 women; 8 have advanced degrees; 10 reside on campus.

Subjects Offered 1 1/2 elective credits.

Special Academic Programs Honors section; independent study; study at local college for college credit; academic accommodation for the gifted, the musically talented, and the artistically talented; ESL (15 students enrolled).

College Admission Counseling 22 students graduated in 2016; all went to college, including Hardin-Simmons University; Southwestern University; Texas A&M University; Texas Christian University; Texas Wesleyan University; The University of Texas at Austin.

Student Life Upper grades have uniform requirement, student council, honor system. Discipline rests primarily with faculty.

Summer Programs Remediation, enrichment, ESL, sports, art/fine arts programs offered; session focuses on enrichment; held on campus; accepts boys and girls; not open to students from other schools. 90 students usually enrolled. 2017 schedule: June 6 to July 15.

Tuition and Aid Day student tuition: $8800; 7-day tuition and room/board: $49,000. Tuition installment plan (monthly payment plans, individually arranged payment plans). Tuition reduction for siblings, need-based scholarship grants available. In 2016–17, 90% of upper-school students received aid.

Admissions Traditional secondary-level entrance grade is 10. Achievement tests, English for Non-native Speakers, Stanford Achievement Test or writing sample required. Deadline for receipt of application materials: none. Application fee required: $95. Interview recommended.

Athletics Interscholastic: baseball (boys), basketball (b,g), cheering (g), cross-country running (b,g), football (b), golf (b,g), horseback riding (b,g), outdoor education (b,g), physical fitness (b,g), running (b,g), soccer (g), softball (g), strength & conditioning (b,g), tennis (b,g), track and field (b,g), volleyball (g), weight training (b,g). 2 PE instructors, 4 coaches.

Computers Computers are regularly used in computer applications, creative writing, desktop publishing, English, journalism, library, newspaper, yearbook classes. Computer resources include on-campus library services, Internet access, wireless campus network, Internet filtering or blocking technology. Computer access in designated common areas is available to students. Students grades are available online.

Contact Mr. Todd Shipman, President/Chief Financial Officer. 254-897-4822. Fax: 254-897-7650. E-mail: todd@northcentraltexasacademy.org. Website: http://www.NorthCentralTexasAcademy.org

NORTH CLACKAMAS CHRISTIAN SCHOOL

19575 Sebastian Way
Oregon City, Oregon 97045

Head of School: Mr. Tim Tutty

General Information Coeducational day college-preparatory, arts, religious studies, bilingual studies, and technology school, affiliated with Christian faith. Grades PK–12. Founded: 1973. Setting: suburban. Nearest major city is Portland. 5-acre campus. 3 buildings on campus. Approved or accredited by Association of Christian Schools International, Northwest Accreditation Commission, and Oregon Department of Education. Total enrollment: 258. Upper school average class size: 22. Upper school faculty-student ratio: 1:20. There are 168 required school days per year for Upper School students. Upper School students typically attend 5 days per week. The average school day consists of 7 hours.

Upper School Student Profile Grade 6: 28 students (17 boys, 11 girls); Grade 7: 14 students (9 boys, 5 girls); Grade 8: 19 students (9 boys, 10 girls); Grade 9: 16 students (6 boys, 10 girls); Grade 10: 18 students (11 boys, 7 girls); Grade 11: 15 students (7 boys, 8 girls); Grade 12: 14 students (7 boys, 7 girls). 100% of students are Christian faith.

Faculty School total: 22. In upper school: 4 men, 7 women; 7 have advanced degrees.

Subjects Offered Art, ASB Leadership, band, basketball, Bible, Bible studies, biology, calculus, calligraphy, chemistry, choir, computer skills, economics, electives, English, government, honors U.S. history, library, mathematics, meteorology, music, physical fitness, physics, pre-calculus, publications, SAT/ACT preparation, science, Spanish, speech, track and field, U.S. history, U.S. history-AP, volleyball, world geography, writing, yearbook.

Graduation Requirements Arts and fine arts (art, music, dance, drama), Bible, electives, English, foreign language, health, leadership, mathematics, physical education (includes health), science, social sciences, speech.

College Admission Counseling 15 students graduated in 2015; 12 went to college, including Corban University; George Fox University; LeTourneau University; Oregon State University; University of Oregon; University of Portland. Other: 1 went to work, 2 had other specific plans.

Student Life Upper grades have specified standards of dress, student council, honor system. Discipline rests primarily with faculty. Attendance at religious services is required.

Tuition and Aid Day student tuition: $6693. Tuition installment plan (monthly payment plans, individually arranged payment plans). Tuition reduction for siblings, need-based scholarship grants available. In 2015–16, 25% of upper-school students received aid.

Admissions Traditional secondary-level entrance grade is 9. Terra Nova-CTB required. Deadline for receipt of application materials: none. Application fee required: $100. On-campus interview required.

Athletics Interscholastic: basketball (boys, girls), cross-country running (b,g), track and field (b,g), volleyball (g); intramural: basketball (b,g), cross-country running (b,g), track and field (b,g), volleyball (g); coed interscholastic: soccer; coed intramural: soccer. 1 PE instructor, 10 coaches.

Computers Computers are regularly used in all academic, Bible studies, writing classes. Computer resources include on-campus library services, Internet access, Internet filtering or blocking technology. Computer access in designated common areas is available to students. Students grades are available online.

Contact Mrs. Julie Gatewood, Office Manager. 503-655-5961 Ext. 100. Fax: 503-655-4875. E-mail: julie_gatewood@ncchristianschool.com. Website: www.ncchristianschool.com

NORTH COUNTRY SCHOOL

Lake Placid, New York
See Junior Boarding Schools section.

NORTHFIELD MOUNT HERMON SCHOOL

One Lamplighter Way
Mount Hermon, Massachusetts 01354

Head of School: Peter B. Fayroian

General Information Coeducational boarding and day college-preparatory and College Model Academic Program (CMAP) school. Grades 9–PG. Founded: 1879. Setting: rural. Nearest major city is Hartford, CT. Students are housed in single-sex dormitories. 1,353-acre campus. 73 buildings on campus. Approved or accredited by Association of Independent Schools in New England, New England Association of Schools and Colleges, The Association of Boarding Schools, and Massachusetts Department of Education. Member of National Association of Independent Schools and Secondary School Admission Test Board. Endowment: $120 million. Total enrollment: 650. Upper school average class size: 11. Upper school faculty-student ratio: 1:6. There are 165 required school days per year for Upper School students. Upper School students typically attend 5 days per week. The average school day consists of 8 hours.

Upper School Student Profile Grade 9: 113 students (61 boys, 52 girls); Grade 10: 156 students (79 boys, 77 girls); Grade 11: 187 students (93 boys, 94 girls); Grade 12: 171 students (92 boys, 79 girls); Postgraduate: 24 students (18 boys, 6 girls). 81% of students are boarding students. 25% are state residents. 34 states are represented in upper school student body. 23% are international students. International students from China, Hong Kong, Japan, Republic of Korea, Saudi Arabia, and Viet Nam; 53 other countries represented in student body.

Faculty School total: 102. In upper school: 53 men, 49 women; 70 have advanced degrees; 100 reside on campus.

Subjects Offered 3-dimensional art, 3-dimensional design, acting, advanced biology, advanced chemistry, Advanced Placement courses, aerobics, algebra, American history, American history-AP, American literature, American literature-AP, analytic geometry, anatomy, anatomy and physiology, ancient history, applied music, Arabic, art, art-AP, arts, astronomy, athletics, ballet, band, baseball, Basic programming, basketball, Bible, bioethics, biology, biology-AP, botany, broadcasting, calculus, calculus-AP, campus ministry, cell biology, ceramics, chamber groups, chemistry, chemistry-AP, Chinese, Chinese literature, choir, choral music, choreography, chorus, Christian doctrine, Christianity, Civil War, collage and assemblage, college admission preparation, college counseling, community service, computer programming-AP, computers, concert band, concert choir, creative writing, dance, dance performance, debate, digital imaging, digital music, digital photography, drama, drama performance, drama workshop, dramatic arts, drawing, driver education, earth science, East Asian history, economics, economics-AP, electives, English, English composition, English language and composition-AP, English language-AP, English literature and composition-AP, English-AP, English/composition-AP, ensembles, environmental science, environmental science-AP, environmental studies, epic literature, equality and freedom, ESL, ESL, ethics, European history, European history-AP, European literature, expository writing, fiction, film, film and literature, film history, film studies, fine arts, fitness, foreign language, foreign policy, French, French language-AP, French literature-AP, French-AP, functions, general science, genetics, geology, geometry, global issues, global studies, golf, government, graphic design, great books, guitar, Harlem Renaissance, health, health and wellness, health education, history, history of jazz, history of music, history of religion, history-AP, honors algebra, honors English, honors geometry, honors U.S. history, honors world history, human anatomy, humanities, independent study, instrumental music, instruments, introduction to literature, introduction to theater, jazz, jazz band, jewelry making, journalism, language-AP, languages, Latin, Latin American studies, Latin-AP, life science, linear algebra, literary magazine, literature, literature and composition-AP, literature seminar, literature-AP, macro/microeconomics-AP, Mandarin, martial arts, mathematics, mathematics-AP, mechanics of writing, media arts, meditation, microeconomics, Middle East, model United Nations, modern dance, modern European history, modern European history-AP, modern history, modern Western civilization, modern world history, music, music history, music performance, music theater, music theory, music theory-AP, music-AP, musical productions, musical theater, musicianship, New Testament, news writing, newspaper, non-Western literature, non-Western societies, North American literature, novels, oral communications, oral expression, orchestra, outdoor education, painting, performing arts, philosophy, photography, physical education, physical fitness, physical science, physics, physics-AP, physiology, piano, play production, playwriting, playwriting and directing, poetry, political science, portfolio art, pottery, pre-calculus, printmaking, programming, psychology-AP, public speaking, publications, radio broadcasting, religion, religion and culture, religious studies, research skills, robotics, Russian studies, SAT preparation, SAT/ACT preparation, science, science research, scripture, sculpture, Shakespeare, short story, social justice, social studies, society, politics and law, Spanish, Spanish language-AP, Spanish literature, Spanish literature-

AP, Spanish-AP, speech, speech and debate, stage design, stagecraft, statistics, statistics-AP, strings, student government, student publications, studio art, studio art-AP, study skills, swimming, tennis, The 20th Century, theater, theater arts, theater design and production, theater production, topics in dramatic literature, track and field, travel, trigonometry, Turkish history, U.S. government, U.S. government and politics, U.S. history, U.S. history-AP, U.S. literature, United States government-AP, video, video film production, visual and performing arts, visual arts, vocal ensemble, vocal music, voice ensemble, volleyball, Western religions, wilderness experience, wind ensemble, women's literature, work experience, work-study, world cultures, world governments, world history, world issues, world literature, world religions, world religions, world studies, wrestling, writing, writing, writing workshop, yearbook, yoga.

Graduation Requirements Arts and fine arts (art, music, dance, drama), English, foreign language, mathematics, physical education (includes health), religion (includes Bible studies and theology), science, social studies (includes history), participation in work program, diversity and social justice.

Special Academic Programs Advanced Placement exam preparation; honors section; independent study; term-away projects; study abroad; academic accommodation for the gifted, the musically talented, and the artistically talented; ESL (14 students enrolled).

College Admission Counseling 200 students graduated in 2016; 193 went to college, including Boston University; New York University; Northeastern University; Trinity College; United States Naval Academy; Wesleyan University. Other: 1 entered a postgraduate year, 6 had other specific plans.

Student Life Upper grades have specified standards of dress, student council, honor system. Discipline rests primarily with faculty.

Summer Programs Remediation, enrichment, advancement, ESL, sports, art/fine arts programs offered; session focuses on intense academic preparation; held on campus; accepts boys and girls; open to students from other schools. 2017 schedule: July 1 to August 5.

Tuition and Aid Day student tuition: $40,500; 7-day tuition and room/board: $59,500. Tuition installment plan (SMART Tuition Payment Plan, monthly payment plans, Tuition Pay 10-Month). Need-based scholarship grants, need-based loans available. In 2016–17, 31% of upper-school students received aid. Total amount of financial aid awarded in 2016–17: $9,400,000.

Admissions Traditional secondary-level entrance grade is 9. For fall 2016, 1,601 students applied for upper-level admission, 241 enrolled. ACT, ISEE, PSAT, SAT, SSAT or TOEFL required. Deadline for receipt of application materials: February 1. Application fee required: $50. On-campus interview recommended.

Athletics Interscholastic: alpine skiing (boys, girls), aquatics (b,g), baseball (b), basketball (b,g), canoeing/kayaking (b,g), crew (b,g), cross-country running (b,g), field hockey (g), Frisbee (b,g), golf (b,g), hockey (b,g), ice hockey (b,g), lacrosse (b,g), nordic skiing (b,g), skiing (cross-country) (b,g), skiing (downhill) (b,g), soccer (b,g), softball (b,g), swimming and diving (b,g), tennis (b,g), track and field (b,g), ultimate Frisbee (b,g), volleyball (b,g), wrestling (b,g); intramural: aerobics/dance (b,g); coed interscholastic: ballet, dance, golf, modern dance, outdoor activities, swimming and diving; coed intramural: aerobics, aerobics/dance, alpine skiing, aquatics, backpacking, badminton, ballet, basketball, bicycling, canoeing/kayaking, climbing, dance, dance team, fencing, fitness, flag football, Frisbee, hiking/backpacking, kayaking, lacrosse, martial arts, modern dance, mountain biking, nordic skiing, outdoor activities, outdoor education, outdoor recreation, physical fitness, physical training, rock climbing, running, sailing, skiing (cross-country), skiing (downhill), snowboarding, snowshoeing, soccer, softball, strength & conditioning, ultimate Frisbee, volleyball, weight training, yoga. 3 PE instructors, 2 athletic trainers.

Computers Computers are regularly used in all academic classes. Computer network features include on-campus library services, online commercial services, Internet access, wireless campus network, Internet filtering or blocking technology. Campus intranet, student e-mail accounts, and computer access in designated common areas are available to students. Students grades are available online. The school has a published electronic and media policy.

Contact Office of Admission. 413-498-3227. Fax: 413-498-3152. E-mail: admission@nmhschool.org. Website: www.nmhschool.org

NORTHPOINT CHRISTIAN SCHOOL

7400 Getwell Road
Southaven, Mississippi 38672

Head of School: Mr. David H. Manley

General Information Coeducational day college preparatory and chorus and band school, affiliated with Christian faith. Grades PK–12. Founded: 1972. Setting: suburban. Nearest major city is Memphis, TN. 61-acre campus. 4 buildings on campus. Approved or accredited by Southern Association of Colleges and Schools and Southern Association of Independent Schools. Member of National Association of Independent Schools. Total enrollment: 1,084. Upper school average class size: 21. Upper school faculty-student ratio: 1:13. There are 176 required school days per year for Upper School students. Upper School students typically attend 5 days per week. The average school day consists of 7 hours and 5 minutes.

Upper School Student Profile Grade 7: 77 students (38 boys, 39 girls); Grade 8: 89 students (48 boys, 41 girls); Grade 9: 68 students (29 boys, 39 girls); Grade 10: 83

students (35 boys, 48 girls); Grade 11: 80 students (42 boys, 38 girls); Grade 12: 64 students (31 boys, 33 girls). 90% of students are Christian.

Faculty School total: 101. In upper school: 17 men, 31 women; 18 have advanced degrees.

Subjects Offered ACT preparation, architectural drawing, etymology, food and nutrition, honors algebra, honors English, honors geometry, human anatomy, human biology, integrated physics, lab/keyboard, life science, marching band, mathematics, music appreciation, physics-AP, pre-calculus, science, sewing, sports, student government, study skills, technical drawing, track and field, trigonometry, U.S. history, weightlifting, world geography.

Graduation Requirements 20th century world history, advanced math, algebra, anatomy and physiology, Bible, Christian studies, education, electives, geometry, government, physics, religion (includes Bible studies and theology), U.S. government and politics-AP.

Special Academic Programs 5 Advanced Placement exams for which test preparation is offered; honors section; academic accommodation for the gifted; remedial reading and/or remedial writing; remedial math; programs in English, mathematics, general development for dyslexic students.

College Admission Counseling 60 students graduated in 2016; all went to college, including Belmont University; Mississippi College; Mississippi State University; University of Memphis; University of Mississippi; Vanderbilt University. Mean composite ACT: 26, 32% scored over 26 on composite ACT.

Student Life Upper grades have uniform requirement, student council, honor system. Discipline rests primarily with faculty. Attendance at religious services is required.

Tuition and Aid Day student tuition: $8625–$9675. Tuition installment plan (SMART Tuition Payment Plan). Tuition reduction for siblings, need-based scholarship grants available. In 2016–17, 15% of upper-school students received aid. Total amount of financial aid awarded in 2016–17: $70,000.

Admissions Traditional secondary-level entrance grade is 9. For fall 2016, 57 students applied for upper-level admission, 57 were accepted, 50 enrolled. Admissions testing, Individual IQ, math and English placement tests and Math Placement Exam required. Deadline for receipt of application materials: none. Application fee required: $225. On-campus interview required.

Athletics Interscholastic: baseball (boys), basketball (b,g), cheering (g), combined training (b), cross-country running (b,g), drill team (g), football (b), golf (b,g), soccer (b,g), softball (g), strength & conditioning (b,g), swimming and diving (b,g), tennis (b,g), track and field (b,g), volleyball (g), weight lifting (b,g), weight training (b,g). 1 PE instructor, 15 coaches, 2 athletic trainers.

Computers Computers are regularly used in English, foreign language, geography, lab/keyboard, social studies, technology, typing classes. Computer network features include on-campus library services, Internet access, wireless campus network, Internet filtering or blocking technology. Student e-mail accounts and computer access in designated common areas are available to students. Students grades are available online. The school has a published electronic and media policy.

Contact Mrs. Sheila Sheron, Director of Admission. 662-349-5127. Fax: 662-349-4962. E-mail: ssheron@ncstrojans.com. Website: www.ncstrojans.com/

NORTH SHORE COUNTRY DAY SCHOOL

310 Green Bay Road
Winnetka, Illinois 60093-4094

Head of School: Dr. Tom Flemma

General Information Coeducational day college-preparatory and global education school. Grades PK–12. Founded: 1919. Setting: suburban. Nearest major city is Chicago. 16-acre campus. 6 buildings on campus. Approved or accredited by Independent Schools Association of the Central States and Illinois Department of Education. Member of National Association of Independent Schools and Secondary School Admission Test Board. Endowment: $23 million. Total enrollment: 525. Upper school average class size: 14. Upper school faculty-student ratio: 1:7. There are 174 required school days per year for Upper School students. Upper School students typically attend 5 days per week. The average school day consists of 6 hours and 30 minutes.

Upper School Student Profile Grade 6: 40 students (18 boys, 22 girls); Grade 7: 43 students (24 boys, 19 girls); Grade 8: 42 students (15 boys, 27 girls); Grade 9: 62 students (32 boys, 30 girls); Grade 10: 54 students (30 boys, 24 girls); Grade 11: 60 students (28 boys, 32 girls); Grade 12: 52 students (24 boys, 28 girls).

Faculty School total: 75. In upper school: 12 men, 21 women; 20 have advanced degrees.

Subjects Offered Algebra, American history, American literature, anatomy and physiology, art, Asian studies, biology, biology-AP, calculus, calculus-AP, ceramics, chemistry, chemistry-AP, creative writing, drama, earth science, ecology, economics, English, English literature, English-AP, European history, expository writing, fine arts, French, French-AP, geography, geometry, government/civics, grammar, journalism, Mandarin, mathematics, music, photography, physical education, physics, physics-AP, printmaking, science, social studies, Spanish, Spanish-AP, speech, statistics, statistics-AP, technology, theater, trigonometry, U.S. history-AP, world history, world literature, writing.

Graduation Requirements Arts and fine arts (art, music, dance, drama), English, foreign language, mathematics, physical education (includes health), physical fitness, science, service learning/internship, social studies (includes history), technology, one stage performance in four years, completion of senior service project in May, completion of one-week community service project in four years.

Special Academic Programs Advanced Placement exam preparation; independent study; term-away projects; study at local college for college credit; study abroad.

College Admission Counseling 48 students graduated in 2016; all went to college, including Northwestern University; University of Chicago; University of Michigan; Vanderbilt University. Mean composite ACT: 31.

Student Life Upper grades have specified standards of dress, student council, honor system. Discipline rests primarily with faculty.

Tuition and Aid Day student tuition: $12,350–$30,550. Tuition installment plan (Insured Tuition Payment Plan, Key Tuition Payment Plan, monthly payment plans, individually arranged payment plans, trimester payment plan). Merit scholarship grants, need-based scholarship grants, need-based loans, middle-income loans available. In 2016–17, 20% of upper-school students received aid. Total amount of financial aid awarded in 2016–17: $1,750,000.

Admissions Traditional secondary-level entrance grade is 9. ISEE, SSAT, SSAT or WISC III or writing sample required. Deadline for receipt of application materials: February 1. Application fee required: $75. On-campus interview recommended.

Athletics Interscholastic: baseball (boys), basketball (b,g), cross-country running (b,g), field hockey (g), football (b), golf (b,g), indoor track & field (b,g), soccer (b,g), tennis (b,g), track and field (b,g), volleyball (g), winter (indoor) track (b,g); intramural: physical training (b,g), weight lifting (b,g); coed intramural: dance, sailing. 4 PE instructors, 24 coaches, 1 athletic trainer.

Computers Computers are regularly used in all academic classes. Computer network features include on-campus library services, online commercial services, Internet access, wireless campus network, Internet filtering or blocking technology, 1-1 iPad program for grades 6-12. Campus intranet and student e-mail accounts are available to students. Students grades are available online. The school has a published electronic and media policy.

Contact Ms. Mullery Doar, Associate Director of Admissions. 847-881-8887. Fax: 847-446-0675. E-mail: lodonohoe@nscds.org. Website: www.nscds.org

NORTHSIDE CHRISTIAN SCHOOL

7777 62nd Avenue North
St. Petersburg, Florida 33709

Head of School: Mrs. Donald James

General Information Coeducational day college-preparatory school, affiliated with Baptist Church. Grades PS–12. Founded: 1971. Setting: urban. 28-acre campus. 3 buildings on campus. Approved or accredited by Association of Christian Schools International, Scottish Education Department, Southern Association of Colleges and Schools, and Florida Department of Education. Endowment: $50,000. Total enrollment: 877. Upper school average class size: 18. Upper school faculty-student ratio: 1:11. There are 180 required school days per year for Upper School students. Upper School students typically attend 5 days per week. The average school day consists of 7 hours and 10 minutes.

Upper School Student Profile 25% of students are Baptist.

Faculty School total: 62. In upper school: 10 men, 24 women; 19 have advanced degrees.

Subjects Offered 3-dimensional art, Advanced Placement courses, algebra, American government, American history, American history-AP, anatomy and physiology, band, Bible studies, biology, business mathematics, calculus-AP, chamber groups, chemistry, chemistry-AP, chorus, Christian education, communication skills, computer applications, computer information systems, computer multimedia, computers, drama, economics, economics and history, English, English literature and composition-AP, English-AP, eurythmics (guard), fine arts, fitness, foreign language, French, general science, geometry, health, health education, jazz band, journalism, keyboarding, language arts, marine biology, marine science, mathematics, mathematics-AP, music, music appreciation, music theory, physical education, physical science, physics, pre-algebra, pre-calculus, psychology, Spanish, Spanish literature, speech, sports, study skills, track and field, U.S. history, volleyball, weight fitness, weight training, world history, world religions, yearbook.

Graduation Requirements Arts and fine arts (art, music, dance, drama), business skills (includes word processing), computer science, English, foreign language, mathematics, physical education (includes health), religion (includes Bible studies and theology), science, social sciences, social studies (includes history), SAT and ACT testing. Community service is required.

Special Academic Programs Advanced Placement exam preparation; honors section; academic accommodation for the gifted; programs in English, mathematics, general development for dyslexic students.

College Admission Counseling 64 students graduated in 2016; 62 went to college, including Florida Gulf Coast University; Florida State University; Southeastern University; St. Petersburg College; University of Florida; University of South Florida. Other: 1 went to work, 1 entered military service. Mean SAT critical reading: 538, mean SAT math: 529, mean composite ACT: 23. 25% scored over 600 on SAT critical reading, 25% scored over 600 on SAT math.

Student Life Upper grades have uniform requirement, student council. Discipline rests primarily with faculty.

Summer Programs Sports, art/fine arts, computer instruction programs offered; held on campus; accepts boys and girls; not open to students from other schools. 70 students usually enrolled. 2017 schedule: June 1 to August 1. Application deadline: May 31.

Tuition and Aid Day student tuition: $10,000. Tuition installment plan (monthly payment plans). Need-based scholarship grants available. In 2016–17, 20% of upper-school students received aid.

Admissions Traditional secondary-level entrance grade is 9. For fall 2016, 81 students applied for upper-level admission, 63 were accepted, 55 enrolled. ACT required. Deadline for receipt of application materials: none. Application fee required: $100. Interview recommended.

Athletics Interscholastic: baseball (boys), basketball (b,g), cheering (g), cross-country running (b,g), diving (b,g), drill team (g), football (b), golf (b,g), soccer (b,g), softball (g), swimming and diving (b,g), tennis (b,g), track and field (b,g), volleyball (g), wrestling (b); intramural: basketball (b,g), climbing (b,g), fishing (b,g), fitness (b,g), flag football (b,g), rock climbing (b,g), weight training (b,g). 3 PE instructors, 4 coaches, 1 athletic trainer.

Computers Computers are regularly used in business, desktop publishing, ESL, library, mathematics, newspaper, science, typing, word processing, yearbook classes. Computer network features include on-campus library services, Internet access, wireless campus network, Internet filtering or blocking technology. Campus intranet and student e-mail accounts are available to students. Students grades are available online. The school has a published electronic and media policy.

Contact Mrs. Tessa Madasz, Director of Development and Enrollment. 727-541-7593 Ext. 247. Fax: 727-546-5836. E-mail: tessa.madasz@ncsschools.com. Website: www.nck12.com

NORTH TORONTO CHRISTIAN SCHOOL

255 Yorkland Boulevard
Toronto, Ontario M2J 1S3, Canada

Head of School: Mr. Allen Schenk

General Information Coeducational day college-preparatory school, affiliated with Protestant-Evangelical faith. Grades JK–12. Founded: 1981. Setting: urban. 6-acre campus. 1 building on campus. Approved or accredited by Association of Christian Schools International and Ontario Department of Education. Language of instruction: English. Total enrollment: 407. Upper school average class size: 25. Upper school faculty-student ratio: 1:15. There are 184 required school days per year for Upper School students. Upper School students typically attend 5 days per week. The average school day consists of 6 hours.

Upper School Student Profile 80% of students are Protestant-Evangelical faith.

Faculty School total: 17. In upper school: 8 men, 9 women; 8 have advanced degrees.

Subjects Offered Accounting, biology, business, calculus, Canadian geography, Canadian law, career exploration, chemistry, civics, computer applications, discrete mathematics, English, French, functions, geography, geometry, healthful living, information technology, instrumental music, marketing, physics, visual arts, world history, world issues, world religions.

Graduation Requirements 40 hours of community service, successful completion of the Ontario Secondary School Literacy Test.

Special Academic Programs Independent study; ESL (17 students enrolled).

College Admission Counseling 36 students graduated in 2016; 35 went to college, including McMaster University; Queen's University at Kingston; Ryerson University; The University of Western Ontario; University of Toronto; York University. Other: 1 had other specific plans.

Student Life Upper grades have uniform requirement. Discipline rests primarily with faculty. Attendance at religious services is required.

Summer Programs ESL programs offered; held on campus; accepts boys and girls; open to students from other schools. 15 students usually enrolled. 2017 schedule: August 3 to August 28. Application deadline: August 3.

Tuition and Aid Day student tuition: CAN$8856. Tuition installment plan (monthly payment plans, individually arranged payment plans). Tuition reduction for siblings available.

Admissions Traditional secondary-level entrance grade is 9. Deadline for receipt of application materials: none. Application fee required: CAN$150. Interview recommended.

Athletics Interscholastic: rugby (girls); coed interscholastic: aquatics, badminton, ball hockey, basketball, cross-country running, golf, soccer, softball, squash, swimming and diving, table tennis, tennis, track and field, volleyball; coed intramural: alpine skiing, canoeing/kayaking, diving, fitness, floor hockey, judo, kayaking, outdoor education, outdoor skills, street hockey, water polo. 5 PE instructors.

Computers Computers are regularly used in business applications, information technology, introduction to technology, keyboarding, mathematics, programming, science, typing, word processing classes. Computer network features include Internet access, Internet filtering or blocking technology. The school has a published electronic and media policy.

Contact Mr. Gordon Cooke, Administrator. 416-491-7667 Ext. 223. Fax: 416-491-3806. E-mail: gcooke@ntcs.on.ca. Website: www.ntcs.on.ca

NORTHWEST ACADEMY

1130 Southwest Main Street
Portland, Oregon 97205

Head of School: Scott Kerman

General Information Coeducational day college-preparatory school. Grades 6–12. Founded: 1996. Setting: urban. 5 buildings on campus. Approved or accredited by Northwest Association of Independent Schools and Oregon Department of Education. Member of National Association of Independent Schools. Total enrollment: 211. Upper school average class size: 15. Upper school faculty-student ratio: 1:5. Upper School students typically attend 5 days per week. The average school day consists of 7 hours and 30 minutes.

Upper School Student Profile Grade 6: 36 students (11 boys, 25 girls); Grade 7: 37 students (15 boys, 22 girls); Grade 8: 40 students (19 boys, 21 girls); Grade 9: 25 students (12 boys, 13 girls); Grade 10: 22 students (13 boys, 9 girls); Grade 11: 27 students (17 boys, 10 girls); Grade 12: 26 students (9 boys, 17 girls).

Faculty School total: 42. In upper school: 14 men, 20 women; 21 have advanced degrees.

Subjects Offered 20th century history, acting, algebra, anatomy and physiology, animation, art history, ballet, biology, calculus, career/college preparation, chemistry, comparative government and politics, comparative politics, comparative religion, computer animation, computer literacy, computer music, creative writing, critical thinking, dance performance, desktop publishing, digital art, drama workshop, drawing, earth and space science, ecology, environmental systems, English literature, European civilization, film studies, French, geometry, history of music, human anatomy, humanities, illustration, independent study, internship, introduction to digital multitrack recording techniques, jazz band, jazz dance, jazz ensemble, journalism, keyboarding, media arts, medieval/Renaissance history, multimedia design, music composition, music history, music performance, musical theater, painting, photo shop, physics, play/screen writing, political systems, pre-calculus, printmaking, senior thesis, Shakespeare, social sciences, Spanish, student publications, tap dance, theater, trigonometry, U.S. government and politics, U.S. history, video film production, visual arts, vocal ensemble, vocal jazz, world cultures, world history, world wide web design, writing, yearbook, yoga.

Graduation Requirements Senior thesis, 4 years of English/humanities, senior thesis seminar, 3 years of both math and science, 2 years of foreign language, 7 units of credit of arts electives, community service, computer literacy, physical education.

Special Academic Programs Independent study; study at local college for college credit.

College Admission Counseling 15 students graduated in 2016; 14 went to college, including Beloit College; Chapman University; Emory University; Pitzer College; Sarah Lawrence College; University of Chicago. Other: 1 went to work. Mean SAT critical reading: 649, mean SAT math: 572, mean combined SAT: 1282. 100% scored over 600 on SAT critical reading, 52% scored over 600 on SAT math.

Student Life Upper grades have student council, honor system. Discipline rests primarily with faculty.

Tuition and Aid Day student tuition: $20,500. Tuition installment plan (FACTS Tuition Payment Plan). Need-based scholarship grants available. In 2016–17, 20% of upper-school students received aid. Total amount of financial aid awarded in 2016–17: $500,000.

Admissions Traditional secondary-level entrance grade is 9. For fall 2016, 27 students applied for upper-level admission, 23 were accepted, 12 enrolled. Admissions testing, placement test and writing sample required. Deadline for receipt of application materials: January 29. Application fee required: $100. Interview required.

Athletics Coed Intramural: aerobics, aerobics/dance, artistic gym, ballet, combined training, cooperative games, dance, dance squad, fitness, modern dance, outdoor activities, yoga.

Computers Computers are regularly used in all academic, yearbook classes. Computer network features include Internet access, wireless campus network, film and audio editing, sound design, animation, Flash. Campus intranet, student e-mail accounts, and computer access in designated common areas are available to students. Students grades are available online. The school has a published electronic and media policy.

Contact Lainie Keslin Ettinger, Director of Admissions and Marketing. 503-223-3367 Ext. 104. Fax: 503-402-1043. E-mail: lettinger@nwacademy.org. Website: www.nwacademy.org

NORTHWEST CATHOLIC HIGH SCHOOL

29 Wampanoag Drive
West Hartford, Connecticut 06117

Head of School: Mr. David Eustis

General Information Coeducational day college-preparatory school, affiliated with Roman Catholic Church. Grades 9–12. Founded: 1961. Setting: suburban. Nearest major city is Hartford. 1 building on campus. Approved or accredited by New England Association of Schools and Colleges and Connecticut Department of Education. Total enrollment: 587. Upper school average class size: 17. Upper school faculty-student ratio: 1:12. There are 180 required school days per year for Upper School students.

Upper School students typically attend 5 days per week. The average school day consists of 6 hours and 18 minutes.

Upper School Student Profile Grade 9: 140 students (70 boys, 70 girls); Grade 10: 146 students (80 boys, 66 girls); Grade 11: 122 students (64 boys, 58 girls); Grade 12: 161 students (72 boys, 89 girls). 79% of students are Roman Catholic.

Faculty School total: 51. In upper school: 18 men, 33 women; 37 have advanced degrees.

Subjects Offered Biology-AP, calculus-AP, chemistry-AP, computer science-AP, English language and composition-AP, English literature and composition-AP, French language-AP, Latin-AP, music theory-AP, physics-AP, Spanish-AP, statistics-AP, studio art-AP, U.S. government and politics-AP, U.S. history-AP.

Graduation Requirements Arts and fine arts (art, music, dance, drama), English, foreign language, health education, leadership and service, mathematics, physical education (includes health), religion (includes Bible studies and theology), science, social studies (includes history), 25 hours of community service.

Special Academic Programs 15 Advanced Placement exams for which test preparation is offered; honors section; study at local college for college credit.

College Admission Counseling 147 students graduated in 2016; 140 went to college, including Boston College; Central Connecticut State University; Keene State College; Quinnipiac University; University of Connecticut; University of Hartford. Other: 3 went to work, 1 entered military service, 1 entered a postgraduate year, 2 had other specific plans. Mean SAT critical reading: 576, mean SAT math: 584, mean SAT writing: 571.

Student Life Upper grades have uniform requirement, student council, honor system. Discipline rests primarily with faculty. Attendance at religious services is required.

Tuition and Aid Day student tuition: $14,300. Tuition installment plan (monthly payment plans). Tuition reduction for siblings, merit scholarship grants, need-based scholarship grants available. Total upper-school merit-scholarship money awarded for 2016–17: $90,000. Total amount of financial aid awarded in 2016–17: $2,034,000.

Admissions Traditional secondary-level entrance grade is 9. High School Placement Test required. Deadline for receipt of application materials: March 1. Application fee required: $25.

Athletics Interscholastic: baseball (boys), basketball (b,g), cross-country running (b,g), field hockey (g), golf (b,g), ice hockey (b,g), indoor track & field (b,g), lacrosse (b,g), soccer (b,g), softball (g), tennis (b,g), track and field (b,g), volleyball (g), winter (indoor) track (b,g); intramural: basketball (b,g); coed interscholastic: cheering, diving, football, swimming and diving; coed intramural: canoeing/kayaking, climbing, fitness, flag football, hiking/backpacking, indoor soccer, outdoor adventure, rappelling, rock climbing, skiing (downhill), snowboarding, snowshoeing, strength & conditioning, ultimate Frisbee, weight training, whiffle ball. 1 PE instructor, 1 athletic trainer.

Computers Computers are regularly used in all academic classes. Computer network features include on-campus library services, Internet access, wireless campus network, Internet filtering or blocking technology, many software programs, 1:1 iPad program. Student e-mail accounts and computer access in designated common areas are available to students. Students grades are available online. The school has a published electronic and media policy.

Contact Mrs. Nancy Scully Bannon, Director of Admissions. 860-236-4221 Ext. 124. Fax: 860-570-0080. E-mail: nbannon@nwcath.org. Website: www.northwestcatholic.org

THE NORTHWEST SCHOOL

1415 Summit Avenue
Seattle, Washington 98122

Head of School: Mike McGill

General Information Coeducational boarding and day college-preparatory and ESL school. Boarding grades 9–12, day grades 6–12. Founded: 1978. Setting: urban. Students are housed in single-sex by floor dormitories. 1-acre campus. 4 buildings on campus. Approved or accredited by Washington Department of Education. Member of National Association of Independent Schools. Endowment: $8 million. Total enrollment: 506. Upper school average class size: 17. Upper school faculty-student ratio: 1:9. There are 168 required school days per year for Upper School students. Upper School students typically attend 5 days per week. The average school day consists of 7 hours and 20 minutes.

Upper School Student Profile Grade 9: 90 students (44 boys, 46 girls); Grade 10: 88 students (44 boys, 44 girls); Grade 11: 93 students (36 boys, 57 girls); Grade 12: 79 students (38 boys, 41 girls). 15% of students are boarding students. 84% are state residents. 2 states are represented in upper school student body. 20% are international students. International students from China, Japan, Republic of Korea, Russian Federation, Taiwan, and Viet Nam; 6 other countries represented in student body.

Faculty School total: 74. In upper school: 27 men, 47 women; 55 have advanced degrees.

Subjects Offered Advanced chemistry, algebra, astronomy, biology, calculus, ceramics, chemistry, Chinese, chorus, computer skills, contemporary problems, dance, drama, drawing, earth science, English, evolution, fiber arts, film, fine arts, French, geometry, health, history, humanities, illustration, improvisation, jazz dance, jazz ensemble, journalism, life science, literature, math analysis, mathematics, mentorship program, musical theater, orchestra, outdoor education, painting, performing arts, philosophy, photography, physical education, physical science, physics, play production, pre-algebra, pre-calculus, printmaking, Spanish, statistics, strings, textiles, theater, trigonometry, U.S. government and politics, U.S. history, visual arts, Washington State and Northwest History, water color painting, wilderness education, world history, writing.

Graduation Requirements English, foreign language, history, humanities, mathematics, physical education (includes health), science, senior project, social studies (includes history), visual and performing arts, participation in environmental maintenance program.

Special Academic Programs Term-away projects; ESL (44 students enrolled).

College Admission Counseling 77 students graduated in 2016; 72 went to college, including Boston University; The Colorado College; University of Colorado Boulder; University of Southern California; University of Washington; Wesleyan University. Other: 5 had other specific plans.

Student Life Upper grades have honor system. Discipline rests primarily with faculty.

Summer Programs Enrichment, ESL, sports, art/fine arts, computer instruction programs offered; session focuses on global connections with international students; held on campus; accepts boys and girls; open to students from other schools. 350 students usually enrolled. 2017 schedule: July 10 to August 18. Application deadline: June 1.

Tuition and Aid Day student tuition: $35,025–$39,620; 7-day tuition and room/board: $51,235–$55,830. Tuition installment plan (school's own payment plan). Need-based scholarship grants available. In 2016–17, 14% of upper-school students received aid. Total amount of financial aid awarded in 2016–17: $1,380,220.

Admissions Traditional secondary-level entrance grade is 9. For fall 2016, 255 students applied for upper-level admission, 119 were accepted, 48 enrolled. Deadline for receipt of application materials: January 12. Application fee required: $70. On-campus interview required.

Athletics Interscholastic: basketball (boys, girls), cross-country running (b,g), soccer (b,g), track and field (b,g), ultimate Frisbee (b,g), volleyball (g); coed intramural: fitness, hiking/backpacking, outdoor education, physical fitness, physical training, rock climbing, ropes courses, skiing (cross-country), skiing (downhill), snowboarding. 2 PE instructors, 30 coaches.

Computers Computers are regularly used in art, English, ESL, foreign language, graphic design, health, history, humanities, journalism, library, mathematics, music, science, social studies, theater, video film production, writing, yearbook classes. Computer network features include on-campus library services, Internet access, wireless campus network, ProQuest, ABC-Cleo, JSTOR, eLibrary, CultureGrams, World Conflicts and Online Encyclopedias. Student e-mail accounts and computer access in designated common areas are available to students. Students grades are available online. The school has a published electronic and media policy.

Contact Douglas Leek, Director of Admissions and Enrollment Management. 206-682-7309. Fax: 206-467-7353. E-mail: douglas.leek@northwestschool.org. Website: www.northwestschool.org

NORTHWEST YESHIVA HIGH SCHOOL

5017 90th Avenue Southeast
Mercer Island, Washington 98040

Head of School: Rabbi Bernie Fox

General Information Coeducational day college-preparatory and religious studies school, affiliated with Jewish faith. Grades 9–12. Founded: 1974. Setting: suburban. Nearest major city is Seattle. 2-acre campus. 3 buildings on campus. Approved or accredited by Northwest Association of Schools and Colleges and Washington Department of Education. Languages of instruction: English, Hebrew, and Spanish. Endowment: $1.2 million. Total enrollment: 60. Upper school average class size: 12. Upper school faculty-student ratio: 1:4. There are 180 required school days per year for Upper School students. Upper School students typically attend 5 days per week. The average school day consists of 8 hours.

Upper School Student Profile Grade 9: 22 students (11 boys, 11 girls); Grade 10: 14 students (7 boys, 7 girls); Grade 11: 18 students (8 boys, 10 girls); Grade 12: 5 students (2 boys, 3 girls). 100% of students are Jewish.

Faculty School total: 22. In upper school: 12 men, 10 women; 18 have advanced degrees.

Subjects Offered 20th century history, algebra, American legal systems, art, art history, biology, calculus, chemistry, college admission preparation, college counseling, drama, economics, English, film appreciation, fine arts, geometry, Hebrew, Hebrew scripture, integrated mathematics, Jewish history, Judaic studies, lab science, language arts, modern Western civilization, newspaper, philosophy, physical education, physics, prayer/spirituality, pre-algebra, pre-calculus, psychology, Rabbinic literature, religious studies, Spanish, Talmud, U.S. government, U.S. history, U.S. literature, Western civilization, world history, writing, yearbook.

Graduation Requirements Advanced math, arts and fine arts (art, music, dance, drama), biology, conceptual physics, Hebrew, integrated mathematics, Judaic studies, language arts, physics, Spanish, Talmud, U.S. government, U.S. history, world history. Community service is required.

Special Academic Programs Honors section; independent study; study at local college for college credit; academic accommodation for the gifted; remedial reading and/or remedial writing; remedial math; special instructional classes for deaf students, blind students; ESL (2 students enrolled).

College Admission Counseling 22 students graduated in 2015; 16 went to college, including American University; Brandeis University; University of Washington; Yeshiva University. Other: 6 had other specific plans. Median SAT critical reading: 620, median SAT math: 620, median SAT writing: 630, median combined SAT: 1870. 53% scored over 600 on SAT critical reading, 67% scored over 600 on SAT math, 60% scored over 600 on SAT writing, 53% scored over 1800 on combined SAT.

Student Life Upper grades have specified standards of dress, student council, honor system. Discipline rests primarily with faculty. Attendance at religious services is required.

Tuition and Aid Day student tuition: $17,940. Tuition installment plan (monthly payment plans, individually arranged payment plans). Need-based scholarship grants available. In 2015–16, 50% of upper-school students received aid. Total amount of financial aid awarded in 2015–16: $348,936.

Admissions Traditional secondary-level entrance grade is 9. For fall 2015, 22 students applied for upper-level admission, 22 were accepted, 22 enrolled. Deadline for receipt of application materials: none. Application fee required: $100. Interview required.

Athletics Interscholastic: basketball (boys, girls), crew (b,g), cross-country running (b,g), golf (b,g), volleyball (g); coed interscholastic: cross-country running, softball. 5 PE instructors, 5 coaches.

Computers Computers are regularly used in all classes. Computer network features include Internet access, wireless campus network, Internet filtering or blocking technology. Student e-mail accounts are available to students. Students grades are available online.

Contact Mr. Ian Weiner, Director of Student Services. 206-232-5272. Fax: 206-232-2711. E-mail: iw@nyhs.net. Website: www.nyhs.net

NORTH YARMOUTH ACADEMY

148 Main Street
Yarmouth, Maine 04096

Head of School: Mr. Benjamin Jackson

General Information Coeducational day college-preparatory, Distinction Diplomas in music/entrepreneurship, and STEM, global citizenship school. Grades PK–12. Founded: 1814. Setting: suburban. Nearest major city is Portland. 25-acre campus. 9 buildings on campus. Approved or accredited by Association of Independent Schools in New England, Independent Schools of Northern New England, New England Association of Schools and Colleges, and Maine Department of Education. Member of National Association of Independent Schools and Secondary School Admission Test Board. Total enrollment: 345. Upper school average class size: 15. Upper school faculty-student ratio: 1:6. There are 165 required school days per year for Upper School students. Upper School students typically attend 5 days per week. The average school day consists of 6 hours and 45 minutes.

Upper School Student Profile Grade 9: 33 students (16 boys, 17 girls); Grade 10: 37 students (24 boys, 13 girls); Grade 11: 27 students (16 boys, 11 girls); Grade 12: 40 students (24 boys, 16 girls).

Faculty School total: 51. In upper school: 9 men, 16 women; 15 have advanced degrees.

Subjects Offered Algebra, American government, American history, American history-AP, ancient world history, art, art history-AP, art-AP, biology-AP, calculus-AP, chemistry, chorus, classical language, college counseling, composition-AP, computer graphics, contemporary issues, drama, drawing and design, earth science, English, English composition, English literature, English literature and composition-AP, English-AP, environmental science-AP, European history, European history-AP, experiential education, fine arts, French, French-AP, genetics, geometry, history, instrumental music, jazz, language-AP, Latin, Latin-AP, Mandarin, mathematical modeling, mathematics, meditation, model United Nations, modern European history, modern European history-AP, music, music theory-AP, music-AP, painting, photography, physical education, physical science, physics, physics-AP, pottery, pre-algebra, pre-calculus, psychology, science, senior project, social issues, social studies, society challenge and change, Spanish, Spanish-AP, speech and debate, statistics, statistics-AP, student publications, studio art, studio art-AP, study skills, technology, theater, trigonometry, U.S. government and politics-AP, U.S. history, U.S. history-AP, visual and performing arts, vocal music, world history.

Graduation Requirements Arts and fine arts (art, music, dance, drama), English, foreign language, history, mathematics, science, senior project, speech, two-week volunteer senior service project, senior speech, participation in athletics or performing arts program each season (3).

Special Academic Programs 17 Advanced Placement exams for which test preparation is offered; honors section; independent study; study abroad.

College Admission Counseling 43 students graduated in 2016; 40 went to college, including Boston College; Johns Hopkins University; Pratt Institute. Other: 3 entered a postgraduate year.

Student Life Upper grades have specified standards of dress, student council, honor system. Discipline rests equally with students and faculty.

Tuition and Aid Day student tuition: $27,850. Tuition installment plan (Insured Tuition Payment Plan, monthly payment plans). Need-based scholarship grants available. In 2016–17, 40% of upper-school students received aid. Total amount of financial aid awarded in 2016–17: $900,000.

Admissions Traditional secondary-level entrance grade is 9. School placement exam or SSAT required. Deadline for receipt of application materials: February 1. Application fee required: $50. Interview recommended.

Athletics Interscholastic: baseball (boys), basketball (b,g), cross-country running (b,g), field hockey (g), golf (b,g), ice hockey (b,g), independent competitive sports (b,g), indoor track (b,g), indoor track & field (b,g), lacrosse (b,g), physical training (b,g), sailing (b,g), soccer (b,g), strength & conditioning (b,g), swimming and diving (b,g), tennis (b,g), track and field (b,g), volleyball (g), weight lifting (b,g), weight training (b,g). 1 PE instructor, 17 coaches, 1 athletic trainer.

Computers Computers are regularly used in English, foreign language, graphic design, history, mathematics, science, technology classes. Computer network features include on-campus library services, Internet access, wireless campus network, Internet filtering or blocking technology. Campus intranet, student e-mail accounts, and computer access in designated common areas are available to students. The school has a published electronic and media policy.

Contact Mr. Tyler Walsh, Assistant Director of Admission. 207-846-2376. E-mail: admission@nya.org. Website: www.nya.org

THE NORWICH FREE ACADEMY

305 Broadway
Norwich, Connecticut 06360

Head of School: Mr. David J. Klein

General Information Coeducational day college-preparatory, general academic, and arts school. Grades 9–12. Founded: 1856. Setting: suburban. 15-acre campus. 11 buildings on campus. Approved or accredited by New England Association of Schools and Colleges and Connecticut Department of Education. Member of National Association of Independent Schools. Total enrollment: 2,280. Upper school average class size: 24. Upper school faculty-student ratio: 1:13. There are 181 required school days per year for Upper School students. Upper School students typically attend 5 days per week. The average school day consists of 7 hours.

Upper School Student Profile Grade 9: 589 students (305 boys, 284 girls); Grade 10: 563 students (270 boys, 293 girls); Grade 11: 578 students (287 boys, 291 girls); Grade 12: 608 students (272 boys, 336 girls).

Faculty School total: 171. In upper school: 60 men, 111 women.

Subjects Offered 3-dimensional art, 3-dimensional design, accounting, advanced biology, advanced chemistry, advanced computer applications, advanced math, Advanced Placement courses, advanced studio art-AP, advanced TOEFL/grammar, algebra, American history, American history-AP, American literature, American sign language, anatomy and physiology, Arabic, architectural drawing, art, art history-AP, audio visual/media, band, biology, biology-AP, biotechnology, British literature, British literature-AP, business technology, calculus-AP, chemistry, chemistry-AP, child development, Chinese, choir, choral music, chorus, civics, classical language, clayworking, composition-AP, computer science-AP, computer-aided design, consumer mathematics, creative writing, culinary arts, dance, digital photography, discrete mathematics, drafting, drama, drawing, drawing and design, early childhood, economics, economics-AP, English language and composition-AP, English language-AP, English literature, English literature and composition AP, English literature-AP, environmental science, environmental science-AP, ESL, European history-AP, exercise science, family and consumer science, finance, food and nutrition, foods, forensics, French, French language-AP, French studies, geometry, government/civics, graphic design, Greek, health, health and wellness, human anatomy, integrated science, international foods, Italian, jazz band, jazz dance, journalism, kinesiology, Latin, Latin-AP, marching band, marine biology, marketing, metalworking, microeconomics-AP, modern European history-AP, modern history, music theory, oceanography, personal finance, photo shop, photography, physical education, physical fitness, physics, physics-AP, piano, political science, politics, pre-calculus, printmaking, probability and statistics, psychology, psychology-AP, public speaking, Spanish language-AP, speech, speech communications, sports science, television, U.S. history, U.S. history-AP, visual arts, vocal ensemble, woodworking, zoology.

Graduation Requirements Art, electives, English, foreign language, health, mathematics, physical education (includes health), science, social studies (includes history), vocational arts.

Special Academic Programs 20 Advanced Placement exams for which test preparation is offered; honors section; study at local college for college credit; remedial reading and/or remedial writing; remedial math; special instructional classes for students with learning disabilities, Attention Deficit Disorder, emotional and behavioral problems, and dyslexia; ESL (90 students enrolled).

College Admission Counseling 518 students graduated in 2016; 394 went to college, including Central Connecticut State University; Eastern Connecticut State University; Southern Connecticut State University; University of Connecticut; University of New Hampshire; University of Rhode Island. Other: 33 went to work, 11 entered military service, 14 entered a postgraduate year, 66 had other specific plans. Mean SAT critical reading: 498, mean SAT math: 490, mean SAT writing: 491, mean composite ACT: 23.

Student Life Upper grades have specified standards of dress, student council, honor system. Discipline rests primarily with faculty.

Summer Programs Remediation, enrichment, ESL, sports programs offered; held on campus; accepts boys and girls; not open to students from other schools. 250 students usually enrolled. 2017 schedule: June 26 to July 21. Application deadline: June 1.

Tuition and Aid Day student tuition: $13,038.

Admissions Traditional secondary-level entrance grade is 9. Deadline for receipt of application materials: none. No application fee required. Interview required.

Athletics Interscholastic: baseball (boys), basketball (b,g), cheering (b,g), cross-country running (b,g), fencing (b,g), field hockey (g), football (b), golf (b,g), gymnastics (g), hockey (b), ice hockey (b), indoor track (b,g), indoor track & field (b,g), lacrosse (b,g), running (b,g), soccer (b,g), softball (b,g), Special Olympics (b,g), swimming and diving (b,g), tennis (b,g), track and field (b,g), volleyball (b,g), winter (indoor) track (b,g), wrestling (b); intramural: skiing (downhill) (b,g), snowboarding (b); coed interscholastic: drill team; coed intramural: dance, dance team, physical fitness, physical training, power lifting, skateboarding, snowboarding, strength & conditioning, weight lifting, weight training. 6 PE instructors, 25 coaches, 5 athletic trainers.

Computers Computers are regularly used in accounting, art, business, business education, career exploration, college planning, computer applications, drafting, engineering, graphic arts, keyboarding, music technology, programming, video film production, word processing classes. Computer network features include on-campus library services, Internet access, wireless campus network, Internet filtering or blocking technology. Student e-mail accounts are available to students. Students grades are available online. The school has a published electronic and media policy.

Contact Mr. John Iovino, Director of Student Affairs. 860-425-5510. Fax: 860-889-7124. E-mail: iovinoj@nfaschool.org. Website: www.nfaschool.org

NOTRE DAME-CATHEDRAL LATIN SCHOOL

13000 Auburn Road
Chardon, Ohio 44024

Head of School: Mr. Joseph Waler

General Information Coeducational day college-preparatory and STEM school, affiliated with Roman Catholic Church. Grades 9–12. Founded: 1988. Setting: suburban. Nearest major city is Cleveland. 75-acre campus. 2 buildings on campus. Approved or accredited by National Catholic Education Association, North Central Association of Colleges and Schools, and Ohio Department of Education. Total enrollment: 678. Upper school average class size: 18. Upper school faculty-student ratio: 1:14. There are 180 required school days per year for Upper School students. Upper School students typically attend 5 days per week. The average school day consists of 6 hours and 50 minutes.

Upper School Student Profile 89% of students are Roman Catholic.

Faculty School total: 59.

Subjects Offered Accounting, acting, advanced biology, advanced chemistry, Advanced Placement courses, algebra, American history, American literature, anatomy, art, band, biology, business, calculus, ceramics, chemistry, Chinese, choir, community service, computer programming, computer science-AP, creative writing, desktop publishing, drawing, economics, electronic research, English, English literature, English literature-AP, environmental science, family and consumer science, film studies, fine arts, forensics, French, geography, geometry, government-AP, government/civics, health, health and wellness, health education, history, home economics, honors algebra, honors English, honors U.S. history, honors world history, human anatomy, independent living, journalism, keyboarding, mathematics, music, music theory, photography, physical education, physical science, physics, physics-AP, physiology, pre-calculus, psychology, religion, science, social studies, sociology, Spanish, speech, statistics, statistics-AP, studio art, studio art-AP, theology, trigonometry, U.S. government, world affairs, world history, world literature.

Graduation Requirements All academic.

Special Academic Programs Advanced Placement exam preparation; honors section; study at local college for college credit; academic accommodation for the gifted; ESL (5 students enrolled).

College Admission Counseling Colleges students went to include John Carroll University; Miami University; Ohio University; The Ohio State University; University of Cincinnati; University of Dayton.

Student Life Upper grades have uniform requirement, student council, honor system. Discipline rests primarily with faculty. Attendance at religious services is required.

Summer Programs Enrichment, advancement, sports, art/fine arts programs offered; held on campus; accepts boys and girls; open to students from other schools. 2017 schedule: June 1 to August 1. Application deadline: June 1.

Tuition and Aid Day student tuition: $11,800. Tuition installment plan (FACTS Tuition Payment Plan). Merit scholarship grants, need-based scholarship grants available. In 2016–17, 50% of upper-school students received aid.

Admissions Otis-Lennon School Ability Test required. Deadline for receipt of application materials: none. No application fee required.

Athletics Interscholastic: baseball (boys), basketball (b,g), bowling (b,g), cheering (g), cross-country running (b,g), dance team (g), drill team (g), football (b), golf (b,g), gymnastics (g), lacrosse (b,g), physical fitness (b,g), physical training (b,g), soccer (b,g), softball (g), swimming and diving (b,g), tennis (b,g), track and field (b,g), volleyball (b,g), wrestling (b); intramural: skiing (downhill) (b,g), snowboarding (b,g), strength & conditioning (b,g), table tennis (b,g), weight training (b,g); coed interscholastic: diving, gymnastics, hockey, ice hockey, indoor track & field, physical fitness, physical training, winter (indoor) track; coed intramural: skiing (downhill), snowboarding, strength & conditioning, table tennis, ultimate Frisbee. 3 PE instructors, 60 coaches, 1 athletic trainer.

Computers Computers are regularly used in all classes. Computer network features include on-campus library services, online commercial services, Internet access, wireless campus network. Campus intranet and student e-mail accounts are available to students. Students grades are available online. The school has a published electronic and media policy.

Contact Mr. Michael Suso, Director of Admissions. 440-279-1088. Fax: 440-286-7199. E-mail: michael.suso@ndcl.org. Website: www.ndcl.org

NOTRE DAME HIGH SCHOOL

1540 Ralston Avenue
Belmont, California 94002-1995

Head of School: Ms. Maryann Osmond

General Information Girls' day college-preparatory, arts, religious studies, technology, and visual and performing arts school, affiliated with Roman Catholic Church; primarily serves students with learning disabilities, individuals with Attention Deficit Disorder, and dyslexic students. Grades 9–12. Founded: 1851. Setting: suburban. Nearest major city is San Francisco. 11-acre campus. 1 building on campus. Approved or accredited by Western Association of Schools and Colleges, Western Catholic Education Association, and California Department of Education. Member of National Association of Independent Schools. Total enrollment: 450. Upper school average class size: 23. Upper school faculty-student ratio: 1:14. There are 180 required school days per year for Upper School students. Upper School students typically attend 5 days per week. The average school day consists of 6 hours.

Upper School Student Profile Grade 9: 115 students (115 girls); Grade 10: 110 students (110 girls); Grade 11: 100 students (100 girls); Grade 12: 125 students (125 girls). 66% of students are Roman Catholic.

Faculty School total: 45. In upper school: 12 men, 33 women; 37 have advanced degrees.

Subjects Offered Advanced chemistry, advanced computer applications, advanced math, Advanced Placement courses, advanced studio art-AP, algebra, American government, American history, American literature, art, art history, art history-AP, art-AP, band, bioethics, biology, biology-AP, British literature, British literature-AP, calculus, calculus-AP, chemistry, chemistry-AP, choir, choral music, chorus, Christian and Hebrew scripture, church history, computer applications, computer literacy, computer science, creative writing, dance, decision making skills, digital photography, driver education, economics, economics and history, economics-AP, English, English literature, English literature-AP, environmental science, ethics, European history, French, French language-AP, geometry, government and politics-AP, government-AP, health, Hebrew scripture, history, honors English, honors geometry, honors U.S. history, honors world history, integrated science, jazz band, journalism, leadership, leadership and service, modern world history, moral reasoning, newspaper, orchestra, photography, physical education, physical science, physics, physics-AP, pre-calculus, psychology, relationships, religion, science, sculpture, self-defense, social justice, social sciences, Spanish, Spanish language-AP, Spanish-AP, sports conditioning, sports medicine, studio art-AP, television, trigonometry, U.S. government, U.S. government and politics-AP, U.S. history-AP, video film production, weight training, world history, world literature, world religions, yearbook.

Graduation Requirements Arts and fine arts (art, music, dance, drama), English, foreign language, mathematics, physical education (includes health), religion (includes Bible studies and theology), science, social sciences, social studies (includes history), 80 hours community service.

Special Academic Programs 12 Advanced Placement exams for which test preparation is offered; honors section; independent study; study at local college for college credit; special instructional classes for deaf students, blind students, students with learning differences.

College Admission Counseling 100 students graduated in 2015; all went to college, including Loyola Marymount University; Santa Clara University; University of California, Davis; University of California, Santa Barbara; University of Oregon; University of Southern California. Mean SAT critical reading: 543, mean SAT math: 533, mean SAT writing: 558.

Student Life Upper grades have uniform requirement, student council, honor system. Discipline rests primarily with faculty. Attendance at religious services is required.

Tuition and Aid Day student tuition: $20,440. Tuition installment plan (FACTS Tuition Payment Plan, individually arranged payment plans). Merit scholarship grants, need-based scholarship grants available. In 2014–15, 24% of upper-school students received aid; total upper-school merit-scholarship money awarded: $200,000. Total amount of financial aid awarded in 2014–15: $10,000,000.

Admissions Traditional secondary-level entrance grade is 9. For fall 2015, 250 students applied for upper-level admission, 225 were accepted, 115 enrolled. High School Placement Test (closed version) from Scholastic Testing Service and writing sample required. Deadline for receipt of application materials: January 8. Application fee required: $110. On-campus interview required.

Athletics Interscholastic: aquatics, basketball, cheering, cross-country running, dance, dance team, golf, modern dance, physical fitness, physical training, pom squad,

running, soccer, softball, strength & conditioning, swimming and diving, tennis, track and field, volleyball, water polo, weight training, yoga; intramural: cheering, touch football, ultimate Frisbee. 1 PE instructor, 33 coaches, 2 athletic trainers.

Computers Computers are regularly used in college planning, creative writing, English, foreign language, health, history, independent study, journalism, mathematics, media production, newspaper, photography, publishing, religious studies, SAT preparation, science, social studies, video film production, yearbook classes. Computer network features include on-campus library services, Internet access, wireless campus network, Internet filtering or blocking technology. Student e-mail accounts and computer access in designated common areas are available to students. Students grades are available online. The school has a published electronic and media policy.

Contact Mrs. Wendy Bell, Associate Director of Admissions. 650-595-1913 Ext. 310. Fax: 650-595-2116. E-mail: wbell@ndhsb.org. Website: www.ndhsb.org

NOTRE DAME HIGH SCHOOL

7085 Brockton Avenue
Riverside, California 92506

Head of School: Mr. Matthew M. Luttringer

General Information Coeducational day college-preparatory, arts, and technology school, affiliated with Roman Catholic Church; primarily serves individuals with Attention Deficit Disorder. Grades 9–12. Founded: 1956. Setting: small town. Nearest major city is Los Angeles. 4-acre campus. 7 buildings on campus. Approved or accredited by Western Association of Schools and Colleges, Western Catholic Education Association, and California Department of Education. Endowment: $10,000. Total enrollment: 629. Upper school average class size: 20. Upper school faculty-student ratio: 1:19. There are 181 required school days per year for Upper School students. Upper School students typically attend 5 days per week. The average school day consists of 7 hours and 5 minutes.

Upper School Student Profile Grade 9: 223 students (116 boys, 107 girls); Grade 10: 151 students (69 boys, 82 girls); Grade 11: 117 students (59 boys, 58 girls); Grade 12: 138 students (76 boys, 62 girls). 86% of students are Roman Catholic.

Faculty School total: 39. In upper school: 23 men, 16 women; 35 have advanced degrees.

Subjects Offered Advanced computer applications, advanced math, algebra, anatomy and physiology, ancient world history, art, ASB Leadership, audio visual/media, Basic programming, biology, British literature, British literature (honors), business law, calculus, campus ministry, Catholic belief and practice, chemistry, choir, choral music, church history, comparative religion, composition-AP, computer education, computer programming, computer programming-AP, computers, consumer mathematics, drama, drama performance, driver education, economics, economics-AP, English literature and composition-AP, fine arts, finite math, foreign language, French, geometry, government, health, history, history of the Catholic Church, honors algebra, honors English, honors geometry, honors U.S. history, humanities, independent study, intro to computers, journalism, keyboarding, martial arts, moral theology, music history, musical productions, peer ministry, philosophy, physical education, physical science, physics, play production, pre-algebra, pre-calculus, psychology, psychology-AP, public speaking, religion, science, scripture, Shakespeare, social sciences, social studies, sociology, Spanish, speech, sports conditioning, sports team management, stage design, student government, student publications, study skills, theology, training, trigonometry, U.S. government, U.S. government and politics-AP, U.S. history, U.S. history-AP, U.S. literature, video, weight training, word processing, work experience, world history, world literature, yearbook.

Graduation Requirements 100 hours of community service, ACRE Catholic Test.

Special Academic Programs Advanced Placement exam preparation; honors section; independent study; study at local college for college credit; ESL (26 students enrolled).

College Admission Counseling 126 students graduated in 2016; 122 went to college, including Cornell University; Loyola Marymount University; Northwestern University; University of California, Los Angeles; University of California, Riverside; University of Notre Dame. Other: 2 went to work, 2 entered military service. Median SAT critical reading: 500, median SAT math: 470. 13% scored over 600 on SAT critical reading, 16% scored over 600 on SAT math.

Student Life Upper grades have uniform requirement, student council. Discipline rests primarily with faculty. Attendance at religious services is required.

Summer Programs Remediation, enrichment, advancement, sports, art/fine arts programs offered; session focuses on remediation and advancement; held on campus; accepts boys and girls; open to students from other schools. 300 students usually enrolled. 2017 schedule: June 19 to July 28. Application deadline: May 20.

Tuition and Aid Day student tuition: $7500–$16,000. Tuition installment plan (Insured Tuition Payment Plan, FACTS Tuition Payment Plan, monthly payment plans, individually arranged payment plans, discounts for annual and semi-annual payments). Tuition reduction for siblings, need-based scholarship grants available. In 2016–17, 11% of upper-school students received aid. Total amount of financial aid awarded in 2016–17: $120,000.

Admissions Traditional secondary-level entrance grade is 9. For fall 2016, 275 students applied for upper-level admission, 238 were accepted, 212 enrolled. High School Placement Test required. Deadline for receipt of application materials: none. Application fee required: $130. On-campus interview recommended.

Athletics Interscholastic: baseball (boys), basketball (b,g), cheering (g), cross-country running (b,g), football (b), golf (b,g), soccer (b,g), softball (g), swimming and diving (b,g), tennis (b,g), track and field (b,g), volleyball (b,g), wrestling (b); coed interscholastic: cross-country running, equestrian sports, weight lifting. 3 PE instructors, 15 coaches, 1 athletic trainer.

Computers Computers are regularly used in journalism, newspaper, video film production, yearbook classes. Computer resources include on-campus library services, Internet access, wireless campus network, Internet filtering or blocking technology, iPad school. Campus intranet and computer access in designated common areas are available to students. Students grades are available online. The school has a published electronic and media policy.

Contact Ms. Beverly A. Wilson, Director of Tuition and Enrollment. 951-275-5861. Fax: 951-781-9020. E-mail: bwilson@ndhsriverside.org.

Website: www.notredameriverside.org

NOTRE DAME HIGH SCHOOL

596 South Second Street
San Jose, California 95112

Head of School: Mrs. Mary Elizabeth Riley

General Information Girls' day college-preparatory school, affiliated with Roman Catholic Church. Grades 9–12. Founded: 1851. Setting: urban. 2-acre campus. 4 buildings on campus. Approved or accredited by Western Association of Schools and Colleges, Western Catholic Education Association, and California Department of Education. Endowment: $8.8 million. Total enrollment: 631. Upper school average class size: 24. Upper school faculty-student ratio: 1:11. There are 180 required school days per year for Upper School students. Upper School students typically attend 5 days per week. The average school day consists of 6 hours and 55 minutes.

Upper School Student Profile Grade 9: 165 students (165 girls); Grade 10: 160 students (160 girls); Grade 11: 167 students (167 girls); Grade 12: 147 students (147 girls). 48% of students are Roman Catholic.

Faculty School total: 62. In upper school: 7 men, 54 women; 52 have advanced degrees.

Subjects Offered Advanced biology, advanced chemistry, Advanced Placement courses, algebra, art, ASB Leadership, athletics, band, Basic programming, biology, biology-AP, biotechnology, calculus-AP, campus ministry, ceramics, chemistry, chorus, Christian and Hebrew scripture, college admission preparation, computer programming, computer science, creative writing, dance, decision making skills, digital photography, drama, drama performance, economics, English, English language and composition-AP, English literature, English literature and composition-AP, environmental science-AP, film and literature, fine arts, French, French language-AP, French literature-AP, geography, geometry, global studies, government/civics, healthful living, honors algebra, honors English, honors geometry, honors U.S. history, honors world history, journalism, library research, library skills, mathematics, modern world history, moral and social development, musical theater, painting, peer counseling, peer ministry, philosophy, photography, physical education, physical fitness, physics, post-calculus, pre-calculus, psychology, psychology-AP, public speaking, religion, research skills, robotics, science, service learning/internship, social justice, social psychology, social studies, Spanish, Spanish language-AP, Spanish literature-AP, speech and debate, statistics, study skills, theater, trigonometry, U.S. government, U.S. government and politics-AP, U.S. history, U.S. history-AP, video film production, Web site design, women in society, world history, world history-AP, world religions, yearbook.

Graduation Requirements Arts and fine arts (art, music, dance, drama), English, foreign language, mathematics, physical education (includes health), religion (includes Bible studies and theology), science, social studies (includes history), community service learning program.

Special Academic Programs 11 Advanced Placement exams for which test preparation is offered; honors section; independent study; study at local college for college credit.

College Admission Counseling 149 students graduated in 2016; 147 went to college, including San Jose State University; Santa Clara University; Seattle University; University of California, Berkeley; University of San Francisco; University of Southern California. Other: 1 entered military service, 1 had other specific plans. Mean SAT critical reading: 598, mean SAT math: 584, mean SAT writing: 600. 46% scored over 600 on SAT critical reading, 46% scored over 600 on SAT math, 50% scored over 600 on SAT writing.

Student Life Upper grades have uniform requirement, student council, honor system. Discipline rests primarily with faculty. Attendance at religious services is required.

Summer Programs Remediation, enrichment, advancement programs offered; session focuses on enrichment/advancement; held on campus; accepts boys and girls; open to students from other schools. 130 students usually enrolled. 2017 schedule: June to July. Application deadline: May.

Tuition and Aid Day student tuition: $16,960. Tuition installment plan (FACTS Tuition Payment Plan, annual payment plan, 2-payment plan). Merit scholarship grants, need-based scholarship grants, individual sponsored grants available. In 2016–17, 24% of upper-school students received aid; total upper-school merit-scholarship money awarded: $8000. Total amount of financial aid awarded in 2016–17: $1,200,000.

Admissions Traditional secondary-level entrance grade is 9. For fall 2016, 432 students applied for upper-level admission, 327 were accepted, 165 enrolled. High School Placement Test required. Deadline for receipt of application materials: January 11. Application fee required: $100.

Athletics Interscholastic: basketball, cross-country running, golf, lacrosse, soccer, softball, swimming and diving, tennis, track and field, volleyball; intramural: badminton, basketball, cheering, volleyball. 2 PE instructors, 25 coaches, 2 athletic trainers.

Computers Computers are regularly used in all academic, computer applications, English, foreign language, graphic design, history, journalism, mathematics, religious studies, science, social studies, Web site design, yearbook classes. Computer network features include on-campus library services, online commercial services, Internet access, wireless campus network, Internet filtering or blocking technology. Student e-mail accounts are available to students. Students grades are available online. The school has a published electronic and media policy.

Contact Ms. Susana Garcia, Vice Principal, Enrollment and Public Relations. 408-294-1113 Ext. 2159. Fax: 408-293-9779. E-mail: sgarcia@ndsj.org.

Website: www.ndsj.org

NOTRE DAME HIGH SCHOOL

910 North Eastern Avenue
Crowley, Louisiana 70526

Head of School: Mrs. Cindy Istre

General Information Coeducational day college-preparatory, arts, vocational, religious studies, and technology school, affiliated with Roman Catholic Church. Grades 9–12. Founded: 1967. Setting: small town. Nearest major city is Lafayette. 10-acre campus. 7 buildings on campus. Approved or accredited by Southern Association of Colleges and Schools and Louisiana Department of Education. Total enrollment: 450. Upper school average class size: 25. Upper school faculty-student ratio: 1:25. There are 178 required school days per year for Upper School students. Upper School students typically attend 5 days per week. The average school day consists of 7 hours and 15 minutes.

Upper School Student Profile 99% of students are Roman Catholic.

Faculty School total: 38. In upper school: 13 men, 25 women; 9 have advanced degrees.

Subjects Offered Accounting, adolescent issues, advanced math, agriculture, algebra, American history, anatomy and physiology, ancient world history, art, athletics, baseball, basketball, biology, calculus, chemistry, civics/free enterprise, computer applications, computer technologies, dance, drama, driver education, early childhood, English, environmental science, family and consumer science, fine arts, food and nutrition, French, geometry, health education, honors algebra, honors English, honors geometry, honors U.S. history, honors world history, keyboarding, physical education, physical science, physics, pre-calculus, psychology, publications, religion, softball, Spanish, speech, study skills, swimming, tennis, theater, track and field, U.S. history, volleyball, world history, yearbook.

Special Academic Programs Honors section; independent study; study at local college for college credit; academic accommodation for the gifted.

College Admission Counseling 108 students graduated in 2015; 104 went to college, including Louisiana State University and Agricultural & Mechanical College; Louisiana State University at Eunice; University of Louisiana at Lafayette. Other: 3 went to work, 1 entered military service.

Student Life Upper grades have uniform requirement, student council. Discipline rests primarily with faculty. Attendance at religious services is required.

Tuition and Aid Tuition installment plan (The Tuition Plan, monthly payment plans). Tuition reduction for siblings available.

Admissions ACT or Explore required. Deadline for receipt of application materials: none. No application fee required. Interview required.

Athletics Interscholastic: baseball (boys), basketball (b,g), cheering (g), cross-country running (b,g), dance squad (g), football (b), softball (g), tennis (b,g), track and field (b,g), volleyball (g); coed interscholastic: drill team, golf, soccer, swimming and diving. 12 coaches, 2 athletic trainers.

Computers Computers are regularly used in computer applications, English classes. Computer network features include on-campus library services, Internet access, Internet filtering or blocking technology. Students grades are available online.

Contact Mr. Nolan Theriot, Dean of Students. 337-783-3519. Fax: 337-788-2115. Website: www.ndpios.com

NOTRE DAME HIGH SCHOOL

320 East Ripa Avenue
St. Louis, Missouri 63125-2897

Head of School: Dr. Meghan Bohac

General Information Girls' day college-preparatory, arts, business, religious studies, bilingual studies, and technology school, affiliated with Roman Catholic Church; primarily serves students with learning disabilities, individuals with Attention Deficit Disorder, individuals with emotional and behavioral problems, and dyslexic students. Grades 9–12. Founded: 1934. Setting: suburban. 40-acre campus. 3 buildings on campus. Approved or accredited by North Central Association of Colleges and Schools and Missouri Department of Education. Total enrollment: 205. Upper school average class size: 16. Upper school faculty-student ratio: 1:12. There are 180 required school days per year for Upper School students. Upper School students typically attend 5 days per week. The average school day consists of 7 hours.

Upper School Student Profile Grade 9: 55 students (55 girls); Grade 10: 50 students (50 girls); Grade 11: 49 students (49 girls); Grade 12: 51 students (51 girls). 89% of students are Roman Catholic.

Faculty School total: 44. In upper school: 8 men, 36 women; 20 have advanced degrees.

Subjects Offered 3-dimensional art, ACT preparation, acting, advanced biology, advanced chemistry, advanced math, African-American literature, algebra, American history, American history-AP, American literature, analytic geometry, anatomy and physiology, applied music, art, arts, basketball, Bible studies, biology, botany, British literature, broadcast journalism, business, business education, business law, calculus, calculus-AP, career/college preparation, ceramics, chemistry, chemistry-AP, child development, Chinese, choir, choral music, choreography, chorus, Christian and Hebrew scripture, Christian education, Christian ethics, Christian scripture, Christian studies, Christian testament, Christianity, church history, civics, civil rights, Civil War, civil war history, college admission preparation, college counseling, college placement, college planning, college writing, communication arts, communication skills, communications, community service, composition-AP, computer applications, computer art, computer education, computer graphics, computer literacy, computer multimedia, computer programming, computer science, computer skills, computer technologies, concert choir, constitutional history of U.S., contemporary issues, costumes and make-up, creative writing, culinary arts, dance, death and loss, debate, developmental language skills, developmental math, digital art, digital imaging, digital photography, drama, drama workshop, drawing, drawing and design, early childhood, earth science, ecology, economics, economics and history, English, English literature, English literature and composition-AP, English literature-AP, environmental geography, environmental science, ethics, European history, exercise science, expository writing, fabric arts, family and consumer science, family living, family studies, fashion, fiction, film and literature, finance, fine arts, food and nutrition, foods, foreign language, forensics, French as a second language, freshman seminar, gardening, general science, geography, geology, geometry, global studies, government, government and politics-AP, government/civics, grammar, graphic design, guidance, health, health education, health enhancement, health science, histology, historical research, history, history of architecture, history-AP, home economics, honors English, honors U.S. history, human sexuality, independent study, interdisciplinary studies, intro to computers, journalism, keyboarding, law, leadership, leadership and service, library, library research, library skills, literary genres, marketing, mathematics, media literacy, music, music appreciation, music for dance, music theater, musical productions, musical theater, musical theater dance, newspaper, novels, nutrition, oral communications, parent/child development, participation in sports, peace education, peer ministry, performing arts, personal finance, photography, physical education, physics, playwriting and directing, practical arts, pre-calculus, public speaking, reading/study skills, religion, religious education, religious studies, science, science and technology, sculpture, senior seminar, social studies, society, politics and law, sociology, softball, sophomore skills, Spanish, Spanish-AP, speech, speech and debate, sports, stage design, statistics, student government, study skills, theater, theater arts, trigonometry, typing, U.S. government, U.S. government and politics, U.S. history, U.S. history-AP, vocal music, volleyball, wind ensemble, world civilizations, world cultures, world geography, world governments, world history, world history-AP, world literature, world religions, world religions, world studies, writing, writing, yearbook, zoology.

Graduation Requirements Arts and fine arts (art, music, dance, drama), athletics, business skills (includes word processing), computer science, English, mathematics, physical education (includes health), religion (includes Bible studies and theology), science, social studies (includes history), service hour requirement. Community service is required.

Special Academic Programs Advanced Placement exam preparation; honors section; accelerated programs; independent study; study at local college for college credit; academic accommodation for the gifted, the musically talented, and the artistically talented; remedial reading and/or remedial writing; remedial math; programs in English, mathematics, general development for dyslexic students.

College Admission Counseling 61 students graduated in 2015; all went to college, including Fontbonne University; Missouri State University; Rockhurst University; St. Louis Community College at Meramec; University of Missouri; Webster University.

Student Life Upper grades have uniform requirement, student council, honor system. Discipline rests primarily with faculty. Attendance at religious services is required.

Tuition and Aid Day student tuition: $11,300. Tuition installment plan (FACTS Tuition Payment Plan, monthly payment plans, individually arranged payment plans, quarterly payment plan). Tuition reduction for siblings, merit scholarship grants, need-based scholarship grants, tuition reduction for children of faculty and staff, reciprocal tuition agreement consortium, tuition reduction for local Emergency Responders available. In 2015–16, 31% of upper-school students received aid; total upper-school merit-scholarship money awarded: $10,000.

Admissions Traditional secondary-level entrance grade is 9. Any standardized test or Iowa Tests of Basic Skills required. Deadline for receipt of application materials: none. No application fee required. Interview required.

Athletics Interscholastic: basketball, cheering, cross-country running, diving, field hockey, golf, lacrosse, racquetball, soccer, softball, swimming and diving, tennis, track

and field, volleyball; intramural: aerobics/dance, cheering, cross-country running, dance, fitness, flag football, modern dance, walking. 2 PE instructors, 9 coaches, 1 athletic trainer.

Computers Computers are regularly used in business skills, English, journalism, mathematics, newspaper, writing, yearbook classes. Computer network features include on-campus library services, online commercial services, Internet access, wireless campus network, Internet filtering or blocking technology. Campus intranet, student e-mail accounts, and computer access in designated common areas are available to students. Students grades are available online. The school has a published electronic and media policy.

Contact Ms. Katie Mallette, Director of Admissions. 314-544-1015 Ext. 1104. Fax: 314-544-8003. E-mail: mallk@ndhs.net. Website: www.ndhs.net

NOTRE DAME HIGH SCHOOL

601 Lawrence Road
Lawrenceville, New Jersey 08648

Head of School: Mr. Barry Edward Breen and Ms. Mary Liz Ivins

General Information Coeducational day college-preparatory school, affiliated with Roman Catholic Church. Grades 9–12. Distance learning grades 11–12. Founded: 1957. Setting: suburban. Nearest major city is Trenton. 100-acre campus. 1 building on campus. Approved or accredited by National Catholic Education Association and New Jersey Department of Education. Total enrollment: 1,292. Upper school average class size: 22. Upper school faculty-student ratio: 1:15. There are 180 required school days per year for Upper School students. Upper School students typically attend 5 days per week. The average school day consists of 6 hours and 30 minutes.

Upper School Student Profile Grade 9: 280 students (135 boys, 145 girls); Grade 10: 333 students (185 boys, 148 girls); Grade 11: 271 students (125 boys, 146 girls); Grade 12: 352 students (175 boys, 177 girls). 80% of students are Roman Catholic.

Faculty School total: 89. In upper school: 32 men, 57 women; 40 have advanced degrees.

Subjects Offered 20th century history, 3-dimensional art, 3-dimensional design, accounting, acting, advanced chemistry, advanced computer applications, advanced math, Advanced Placement courses, algebra, American government, American literature, ancient world history, applied music, art, art and culture, art-AP, athletics, Basic programming, Bible studies, biology, biology-AP, British literature, business, business applications, business studies, calculus, calculus-AP, campus ministry, Catholic belief and practice, ceramics, chemistry, chemistry-AP, choir, chorus, Christian doctrine, community service, comparative religion, computer applications, computer science, concert band, concert choir, constitutional law, contemporary issues, creative writing, dance, dance performance, digital music, discrete mathematics, drama, driver education, ecology, environmental systems, economics, economics-AP, English, English composition, English language and composition-AP, English literature and composition-AP, English literature-AP, environmental science-AP, etymology, European history-AP, exercise science, film appreciation, film studies, filmmaking, finance, first aid, French, French-AP, geometry, German, German literature, government-AP, health education, honors algebra, honors English, honors world history, independent study, Italian, Japanese, jazz band, journalism, kinesiology, language-AP, Latin, law, law and the legal system, leadership and service, leadership education training, literature and composition-AP, literature-AP, macro/microeconomics-AP, madrigals, Mandarin, math review, media communications, media literacy, music theory, newspaper, orchestra, painting, peer counseling, peer ministry, personal finance, philosophy, photography, physical education, physics, physics-AP, piano, portfolio art, pottery, pre-algebra, pre-calculus, probability and statistics, psychology, psychology-AP, public speaking, reading/study skills, religion, religion and culture, robotics, Russian, SAT preparation, scripture, senior internship, senior project, service learning/internship, sociology, Spanish, Spanish literature, Spanish-AP, speech and debate, sports medicine, statistics-AP, strings, studio art-AP, U.S. government, U.S. government and politics-AP, U.S. history, U.S. history-AP, U.S. literature, United States government-AP, Web site design, weight training, women spirituality and faith, world history, world literature, writing.

Graduation Requirements Biology, English, foreign language, integrated technology fundamentals, lab science, mathematics, physical education (includes health), religion (includes Bible studies and theology), U.S. history, world history. Community service is required.

Special Academic Programs 15 Advanced Placement exams for which test preparation is offered; honors section; independent study; study at local college for college credit; remedial reading and/or remedial writing; remedial math; ESL (29 students enrolled).

College Admission Counseling 337 students graduated in 2016; 330 went to college, including Penn State University Park; Rowan University; Rutgers University–New Brunswick; Saint Joseph's University; The College of New Jersey; University of Delaware. Other: 3 went to work, 4 entered military service. Mean SAT critical reading: 547, mean SAT math: 567, mean SAT writing: 552, mean combined SAT: 1666.

Student Life Upper grades have uniform requirement, student council, honor system. Discipline rests primarily with faculty. Attendance at religious services is required.

Summer Programs Enrichment, advancement, sports, art/fine arts, computer instruction programs offered; session focuses on sports, arts, academic and writing camps, college application seminar; held on campus; accepts boys and girls; open to students from other schools. 775 students usually enrolled. 2017 schedule: July 5 to August 18. Application deadline: June 21.

Tuition and Aid Day student tuition: $13,025. Tuition reduction for siblings, need-based scholarship grants available. In 2016–17, 19% of upper-school students received aid. Total amount of financial aid awarded in 2016–17: $720,000.

Admissions Traditional secondary-level entrance grade is 9. For fall 2016, 525 students applied for upper-level admission, 420 were accepted, 280 enrolled. Scholastic Testing Service High School Placement Test required. Deadline for receipt of application materials: December 2. Application fee required: $50. On-campus interview recommended.

Athletics Interscholastic: baseball (boys), basketball (b,g), cheering (g), crew (b,g), cross-country running (b,g), dance (g), field hockey (g), football (b), golf (b,g), ice hockey (b), indoor track (b,g), lacrosse (b,g), soccer (b,g), softball (g), swimming and diving (b,g), tennis (b,g), track and field (b,g), volleyball (g), winter (indoor) track (b,g), wrestling (b); intramural: touch football (g), volleyball (b,g); coed interscholastic: cheering, dance, diving, fitness, strength & conditioning; coed intramural: bocce, Frisbee, outdoor activities, outdoor recreation, physical fitness, ultimate Frisbee, volleyball, weight lifting, weight training. 8 PE instructors, 97 coaches, 1 athletic trainer.

Computers Computers are regularly used in all academic classes. Computer network features include on-campus library services, online commercial services, Internet access, wireless campus network, Internet filtering or blocking technology. Campus intranet, student e-mail accounts, and computer access in designated common areas are available to students. Students grades are available online. The school has a published electronic and media policy.

Contact Mr. Joseph Petitto, Interim Director of Enrollment Management. 609-882-7900 Ext. 183. Fax: 609-882-6599. E-mail: admissions@ndnj.org.
Website: www.ndnj.org

NOTRE DAME HIGH SCHOOL

1400 Maple Avenue
Elmira, New York 14904

Head of School: Sr. Mary Walter Hickey

General Information Coeducational day college-preparatory school, affiliated with Roman Catholic Church. Grades 7–12. Founded: 1954. Setting: suburban. Nearest major city is Binghamton. 30-acre campus. 1 building on campus. Approved or accredited by Mercy Secondary Education Association, Middle States Association of Colleges and Schools, National Catholic Education Association, and New York Department of Education. Member of Secondary School Admission Test Board. Total enrollment: 373. Upper school average class size: 20. Upper school faculty-student ratio: 1:15. There are 180 required school days per year for Upper School students. Upper School students typically attend 5 days per week. The average school day consists of 5 hours and 30 minutes.

Upper School Student Profile Grade 7: 49 students (26 boys, 23 girls); Grade 8: 51 students (22 boys, 29 girls); Grade 9: 67 students (38 boys, 29 girls); Grade 10: 64 students (31 boys, 33 girls); Grade 11: 71 students (41 boys, 30 girls); Grade 12: 92 students (59 boys, 33 girls). 80% of students are Roman Catholic.

Faculty School total: 35. In upper school: 13 men, 22 women; 19 have advanced degrees.

Subjects Offered Art, arts, band, biology, calculus, ceramics, chemistry, chemistry-AP, Chinese, choir, computer literacy, creative writing, drama, drawing, earth science, English, English-AP, fine arts, government/civics, health, human development, mathematics, multimedia, music history, music theory, painting, physical education, physics, portfolio art, pre-calculus, psychology, public speaking, religion, science, social studies, Spanish, studio art, theology.

Graduation Requirements Arts and fine arts (art, music, dance, drama), English, language, mathematics, physical education (includes health), religion (includes Bible studies and theology), science, social studies (includes history).

Special Academic Programs Advanced Placement exam preparation; honors section; study at local college for college credit; academic accommodation for the gifted and the artistically talented; remedial reading and/or remedial writing; remedial math.

College Admission Counseling 55 students graduated in 2016; 54 went to college, including Cornell University; Harvard University; Rochester Institute of Technology; The Catholic University of America; University of Notre Dame. Other: 1 entered military service. Median SAT critical reading: 563, median SAT math: 582, median SAT writing: 547, median composite ACT: 26.

Student Life Upper grades have uniform requirement, student council. Discipline rests primarily with faculty. Attendance at religious services is required.

Tuition and Aid Day student tuition: $8975. Tuition installment plan (FACTS Tuition Payment Plan, local bank-arranged plan). Tuition reduction for siblings, merit scholarship grants, need-based scholarship grants available. In 2016–17, 60% of upper-school students received aid; total upper-school merit-scholarship money awarded: $2000. Total amount of financial aid awarded in 2016–17: $600,000.

Admissions Traditional secondary-level entrance grade is 9. Scholastic Testing Service High School Placement Test required. Deadline for receipt of application materials: none. Application fee required: $100. Interview recommended.

Athletics Interscholastic: baseball (boys), basketball (b,g), bowling (b,g), cross-country running (b,g), football (b), golf (b), lacrosse (b), soccer (b,g), softball (g),

swimming and diving (b,g), tennis (b,g), track and field (b,g). 3 PE instructors, 27 coaches, 1 athletic trainer.

Computers Computer network features include on-campus library services, Internet access, wireless campus network, Internet filtering or blocking technology. Campus intranet, student e-mail accounts, and computer access in designated common areas are available to students. Students grades are available online. The school has a published electronic and media policy.

Contact Mrs. Michelle Barkley, Director of Public Relations and Marketing. 607-734-2267 Ext. 321. Fax: 607-737-8903. E-mail: barkleym@notredamehighschool.com. Website: www.notredamehighschool.com

NOTRE DAME HIGH SCHOOL

2701 Vermont Avenue
Chattanooga, Tennessee 37404

Head of School: Mr. George D. Valadie

General Information Coeducational day college-preparatory and Microsoft IT Academy Certification school, affiliated with Roman Catholic Church. Grades 9–12. Founded: 1876. Setting: urban. 22-acre campus. 3 buildings on campus. Approved or accredited by Southern Association of Colleges and Schools and Tennessee Department of Education. Endowment: $750,000. Total enrollment: 423. Upper school average class size: 20. Upper school faculty-student ratio: 1:10. There are 180 required school days per year for Upper School students. Upper School students typically attend 5 days per week. The average school day consists of 5 hours and 50 minutes.

Upper School Student Profile Grade 9: 113 students (53 boys, 60 girls); Grade 10: 115 students (58 boys, 57 girls); Grade 11: 99 students (43 boys, 56 girls); Grade 12: 96 students (42 boys, 54 girls). 77% of students are Roman Catholic.

Faculty School total: 39. In upper school: 15 men, 24 women; 25 have advanced degrees.

Subjects Offered 3-dimensional art, ACT preparation, Advanced Placement courses, algebra, American history-AP, American literature, anatomy, anatomy and physiology, art-AP, band, biology, biology-AP, British literature, calculus, Catholic belief and practice, chemistry, choir, civics, conceptual physics, creative dance, drama, economics, electives, English composition, English literature, English-AP, environmental science-AP, European history-AP, foreign language, French, geometry, German, government, government/civics, health and wellness, history-AP, honors algebra, honors English, honors geometry, honors U.S. history, honors world history, Latin, physics, public speaking, religion, Spanish, U.S. government and politics-AP, weight training, wellness, world geography, world history, world history-AP, writing, yoga.

Graduation Requirements American history, arts and fine arts (art, music, dance, drama), chemistry, economics, English, finance, foreign language, four units of summer reading, geography, health and wellness, mathematics, physical education (includes health), religion (includes Bible studies and theology), social studies (includes history), technology, world history.

Special Academic Programs Advanced Placement exam preparation; honors section; independent study; study at local college for college credit.

College Admission Counseling 96 students graduated in 2016; 95 went to college, including Auburn University; Middle Tennessee State University; The University of Tennessee; The University of Tennessee at Chattanooga; University of Georgia. Other: 1 went to work.

Student Life Upper grades have uniform requirement, student council, honor system. Discipline rests primarily with faculty. Attendance at religious services is required.

Tuition and Aid Day student tuition: $11,862–$15,565. Tuition installment plan (Insured Tuition Payment Plan, FACTS Tuition Payment Plan, monthly payment plans, individually arranged payment plans). Tuition reduction for siblings, need-based scholarship grants available. In 2016–17, 30% of upper-school students received aid. Total amount of financial aid awarded in 2016–17: $1,600,000.

Admissions Traditional secondary-level entrance grade is 9. ACT-Explore or High School Placement Test required. Deadline for receipt of application materials: none. Application fee required: $125. On-campus interview recommended.

Athletics Interscholastic: aerobics/dance (girls), baseball (b), basketball (b,g), bowling (b,g), cross-country running (b,g), dance (g), dance squad (g), dance team (g), diving (b,g), football (b), golf (b,g), modern dance (g), physical training (b,g), running (b,g), soccer (b,g), softball (g), swimming and diving (b,g), tennis (b,g), track and field (b,g), volleyball (g), weight training (b,g), wrestling (b); intramural: aerobics/dance (b,g), cheering (g), indoor soccer (b), indoor track (b,g), lacrosse (b,g); coed interscholastic: cheering, climbing, yoga; coed intramural: backpacking, canoeing/kayaking, climbing, crew, hiking/backpacking, kayaking, mountaineering, outdoors, rafting, rappelling, rock climbing, rowing, skiing (downhill), snowboarding, wall climbing. 3 PE instructors, 43 coaches, 1 athletic trainer.

Computers Computers are regularly used in information technology classes. Computer network features include on-campus library services, Internet access, wireless campus network, Internet filtering or blocking technology, language software labs, Microsoft IT Academy Training. Student e-mail accounts and computer access in designated common areas are available to students. Students grades are available online. The school has a published electronic and media policy.

Contact Ms. Laura Goodhard, Admissions Director. 423-624-4618 Ext. 1004. Fax: 423-624-4621. E-mail: admissions@myndhs.com. Website: www.myndhs.com

NOTRE DAME JUNIOR/SENIOR HIGH SCHOOL

60 Spangenburg Avenue
East Stroudsburg, Pennsylvania 18301-2799

Head of School: Mr. Jeffrey Neill Lyons

General Information Coeducational day college-preparatory school, affiliated with Roman Catholic Church. Grades 7–12. Founded: 1967. Setting: suburban. 40-acre campus. 4 buildings on campus. Approved or accredited by Middle States Association of Colleges and Schools, National Catholic Education Association, and Pennsylvania Department of Education. Total enrollment: 317. Upper school average class size: 25. Upper school faculty-student ratio: 1:15. There are 180 required school days per year for Upper School students. Upper School students typically attend 5 days per week. The average school day consists of 6 hours and 30 minutes.

Upper School Student Profile Grade 7: 46 students (21 boys, 25 girls); Grade 8: 32 students (10 boys, 22 girls); Grade 9: 53 students (26 boys, 27 girls); Grade 10: 59 students (34 boys, 25 girls); Grade 11: 46 students (19 boys, 27 girls); Grade 12: 52 students (20 boys, 32 girls). 75% of students are Roman Catholic.

Faculty School total: 24. In upper school: 8 men, 16 women; 14 have advanced degrees.

Graduation Requirements Lab/keyboard, mathematics, moral theology, physical education (includes health), physical science, religion (includes Bible studies and theology), senior project, U.S. history, U.S. literature, word processing, world cultures, world religions.

Special Academic Programs Advanced Placement exam preparation; honors section; study at local college for college credit.

College Admission Counseling 72 students graduated in 2016; 69 went to college, including Marywood University; Mount St. Mary's University; Penn State University Park; Saint Joseph's University; Temple University; The University of Scranton. Other: 1 went to work, 1 entered military service, 1 entered a postgraduate year. Median SAT critical reading: 500, median SAT math: 460, median SAT writing: 500, median combined SAT: 1460. 10% scored over 600 on SAT critical reading, 15% scored over 600 on SAT math, 10% scored over 600 on SAT writing, 25% scored over 1800 on combined SAT.

Student Life Upper grades have uniform requirement, student council. Discipline rests primarily with faculty. Attendance at religious services is required.

Tuition and Aid Tuition installment plan (FACTS Tuition Payment Plan). Tuition reduction for siblings, need-based scholarship grants available. In 2016–17, 35% of upper-school students received aid.

Admissions Traditional secondary-level entrance grade is 7. Achievement tests or TerraNova required. Deadline for receipt of application materials: May 1. No application fee required. Interview required.

Athletics Interscholastic: baseball (boys), basketball (b,g), field hockey (g), soccer (b,g), softball (g), tennis (b,g); coed interscholastic: golf, soccer; coed intramural: cross-country running, strength & conditioning. 2 PE instructors, 15 coaches, 1 athletic trainer.

Computers Computer network features include on-campus library services, Internet access, Internet filtering or blocking technology. The school has a published electronic and media policy.

Contact Mr. Jeffrey Neill Lyons, Principal. 570-421-0466. Fax: 570-476-0629. E-mail: principal@ndhigh.org. Website: www.ndhigh.org

OAK GROVE LUTHERAN SCHOOL

124 North Terrace
Fargo, North Dakota 58102

Head of School: Mike Slette

General Information Coeducational day college-preparatory, general academic, arts, business, vocational, religious studies, technology, and music school, affiliated with Evangelical Lutheran Church in America; primarily serves We can serve a limited amount of special needs. We only have one Paraprofessional. Grades K–12. Founded: 1906. Setting: suburban. Nearest major city is Minneapolis, MN. 5.3-acre campus. 5 buildings on campus. Approved or accredited by North Central Association of Colleges and Schools and North Dakota Department of Education. Endowment: $4.5 million. Total enrollment: 430. Upper school average class size: 17. Upper school faculty-student ratio: 1:10. There are 175 required school days per year for Upper School students. Upper School students typically attend 5 days per week. The average school day consists of 5 hours and 50 minutes.

Upper School Student Profile 75% of students are Evangelical Lutheran Church in America.

Faculty School total: 19. In upper school: 9 men, 10 women; 6 have advanced degrees.

Subjects Offered Accounting, algebra, American history, American literature, art, band, Bible studies, biology, British literature, business law, business skills, calculus, chemistry, chorus, civics, computer programming, computer science, consumer mathematics, driver education, Eastern world civilizations, economics, English, ensembles, family studies, food science, geography, geometry, German, government, health, history, keyboarding, mathematics, music appreciation, nutrition, physical education, physical science, physics, pre-calculus, psychology, religion, science, social sciences, social studies, sociology, Spanish, speech, textiles, trigonometry, weight training, world affairs, world cultures, world history.

Graduation Requirements Business skills (includes word processing), English, mathematics, physical education (includes health), religion (includes Bible studies and theology), science, social sciences, social studies (includes history).

Special Academic Programs Advanced Placement exam preparation; honors section; independent study; study at local college for college credit; study abroad; academic accommodation for the gifted and the musically talented; remedial reading and/or remedial writing; remedial math; programs in English, mathematics, general development for dyslexic students; special instructional classes for students with learning disabilities, Attention Deficit Disorder; ESL (15 students enrolled).

College Admission Counseling 40 students graduated in 2016; all went to college, including North Dakota State University; South Dakota State University; University of North Dakota.

Student Life Upper grades have specified standards of dress, student council, honor system. Discipline rests equally with students and faculty. Attendance at religious services is required.

Summer Programs Enrichment, sports, art/fine arts programs offered; held on campus; accepts boys and girls; open to students from other schools. 150 students usually enrolled.

Tuition and Aid Day student tuition: $9110. Tuition installment plan (FACTS Tuition Payment Plan). Tuition reduction for siblings, merit scholarship grants, need-based scholarship grants, paying campus jobs, work-study tuition reduction plan available. In 2016–17, 46% of upper-school students received aid; total upper-school merit-scholarship money awarded: $13,150. Total amount of financial aid awarded in 2016–17: $241,144.

Admissions Traditional secondary-level entrance grade is 9. Achievement tests, ACT, Iowa Test, CTBS, or TAP, PSAT or SAT, Stanford Achievement Test, TOEFL or Woodcock-Johnson required. Deadline for receipt of application materials: none. Application fee required: $200. Interview recommended.

Athletics Interscholastic: aquatics (boys, girls), baseball (b), basketball (b,g), cross-country running (b,g), diving (b,g), football (b), golf (b,g), ice hockey (b,g), physical training (b,g), soccer (b,g), softball (g), swimming and diving (b,g), tennis (b,g), track and field (b,g), volleyball (g); coed intramural: billiards, table tennis. 2 PE instructors, 2 coaches, 1 athletic trainer.

Computers Computers are regularly used in business, college planning, English, history, independent study, library skills, mathematics, religious studies, science classes. Computer network features include on-campus library services, online commercial services, Internet access, wireless campus network, Internet filtering or blocking technology. Campus intranet, student e-mail accounts, and computer access in designated common areas are available to students. Students grades are available online. The school has a published electronic and media policy.

Contact Deb Lackmann, Director of Admissions. 701-373-7114. Fax: 701-297-1993. E-mail: deb.lackmann@oakgrovelutheran.com. Website: www.oakgrovelutheran.com

OAK GROVE SCHOOL

220 West Lomita Avenue
Ojai, California 93023

Head of School: Mr. Willem Zwart

General Information Coeducational boarding and day college-preparatory school. Boarding grades 9–12, day grades PK–12. Founded: 1975. Setting: small town. Nearest major city is Los Angeles. Students are housed in single-sex by floor dormitories. 150-acre campus. 6 buildings on campus. Approved or accredited by California Association of Independent Schools, The Association of Boarding Schools, Western Association of Schools and Colleges, and California Department of Education. Member of National Association of Independent Schools and Secondary School Admission Test Board. Endowment: $450,000. Total enrollment: 227. Upper school average class size: 15. Upper school faculty-student ratio: 1:7. There are 170 required school days per year for Upper School students. Upper School students typically attend 5 days per week. The average school day consists of 8 hours and 30 minutes.

Upper School Student Profile 25% of students are boarding students. 83% are state residents. 2 states are represented in upper school student body. 23% are international students. International students from China, India, Japan, Mexico, Republic of Korea, and Wallis and Futuna Islands.

Faculty School total: 35. In upper school: 6 men, 6 women; 8 have advanced degrees; 3 reside on campus.

Subjects Offered Algebra, American history, American literature, anatomy, art, art history, biology, calculus, ceramics, chemistry, communications, community service, comparative religion, computer science, drama, earth science, economics, English, English literature, ethics, film and new technologies, fine arts, gardening, geography, geometry, global studies, history, horticulture, human development, inquiry into relationship, mathematics, music, permaculture, photography, physical education, physics, relationships, religion and culture, science, social studies, Spanish, studio art, theater, world cultures, world history, world literature.

Graduation Requirements Algebra, American history, arts and fine arts (art, music, dance, drama), backpacking, biology, chemistry, college admission preparation, comparative religion, economics and history, English, ethics and responsibility, foreign language, geometry, mathematics, science, social studies (includes history), Spanish, world religions, participation in camping and travel programs and sports, one year of visual and performing arts. Community service is required.

Special Academic Programs 3 Advanced Placement exams for which test preparation is offered; honors section; independent study; ESL (8 students enrolled).

College Admission Counseling 15 students graduated in 2016; 14 went to college, including Claremont McKenna College; Cornish College of the Arts; New York University; Oregon State University; University of California, Davis; Westmont College. Other: 1 had other specific plans. Mean SAT critical reading: 627, mean SAT math: 580, mean SAT writing: 617. 57% scored over 600 on SAT critical reading, 28% scored over 600 on SAT math, 42% scored over 600 on SAT writing.

Student Life Upper grades have student council, honor system. Discipline rests equally with students and faculty.

Summer Programs ESL programs offered; held on campus; accepts boys and girls; open to students from other schools. 15 students usually enrolled. 2017 schedule: July to August. Application deadline: June 1.

Tuition and Aid Day student tuition: $19,276; 7-day tuition and room/board: $44,656. Tuition installment plan (FACTS Tuition Payment Plan, annual and semiannual payment plans). Need-based scholarship grants, African-American scholarships, art scholarships, Kinetic Learner scholarships available. In 2016–17, 40% of upper-school students received aid. Total amount of financial aid awarded in 2016–17: $80,000.

Admissions Traditional secondary-level entrance grade is 9. For fall 2016, 60 students applied for upper-level admission, 21 were accepted, 10 enrolled. SSAT or TOEFL or SLEP required. Deadline for receipt of application materials: none. Application fee required: $50. On-campus interview required.

Athletics Interscholastic: soccer (boys, girls), volleyball (b,g); intramural: equestrian sports (b,g), soccer (b,g), volleyball (b,g); coed intramural: backpacking, fitness, hiking/backpacking, outdoor activities, outdoor education, outdoor skills, physical fitness, ropes courses, skiing (downhill), table tennis, tennis, wilderness. 1 PE instructor, 3 coaches.

Computers Computers are regularly used in art, ESL, graphic arts, history, independent study, library, mathematics, multimedia, photography, SAT preparation, science, technology, typing, writing, yearbook classes. Computer network features include on-campus library services, online commercial services, Internet access, wireless campus network, Internet filtering or blocking technology. Computer access in designated common areas is available to students. Students grades are available online.

Contact Andy Gilman, Director of Admissions and Outreach. 805-646-8236 Ext. 109. Fax: 805-646-6509. E-mail: enroll@oakgroveschool.org.

Website: www.oakgroveschool.org

OAK HILL SCHOOL

86397 Eldon Schafer Drive
Eugene, Oregon 97405-9647

Head of School: Bob Sarkisian

General Information Coeducational day college-preparatory, arts, and technology school. Grades K–12. Founded: 1994. Setting: small town. 72-acre campus. 2 buildings on campus. Approved or accredited by Northwest Accreditation Commission, Northwest Association of Independent Schools, Northwest Association of Schools and Colleges, and Oregon Department of Education. Member of National Association of Independent Schools. Endowment: $100,000. Total enrollment: 151. Upper school average class size: 13. Upper school faculty-student ratio: 1:10. There are 177 required school days per year for Upper School students. Upper School students typically attend 5 days per week. The average school day consists of 7 hours.

Faculty School total: 26. In upper school: 6 men, 7 women; 10 have advanced degrees.

Subjects Offered Acting, advanced math, algebra, American literature, analytic geometry, anatomy, art, arts, band, calculus-AP, ceramics, chemistry, comparative government and politics, composition, computer education, drama performance, drawing and design, economics, English composition, English literature, English literature-AP, fitness, French, geometry, health education, history, independent study, Mandarin, outdoor education, physical education, pre-calculus, probability and statistics, Spanish, Spanish language-AP, Spanish literature-AP, speech communications, theater arts, U.S. government and politics, U.S. history, world history, writing.

Graduation Requirements Algebra, American government, American history, arts, computer skills, economics, English, English composition, foreign language, French, lab science, mathematics, physical education (includes health), science, Spanish, world history, 70 community service hours.

Special Academic Programs Advanced Placement exam preparation; honors section; academic accommodation for the gifted; ESL (13 students enrolled).

College Admission Counseling 6 students graduated in 2015; all went to college, including Oregon State University; Pomona College; Savannah College of Art and Design; Southern Oregon University; University of California, Berkeley; University of Oregon. Median SAT critical reading: 547, median SAT math: 612, median SAT writing: 547. 28% scored over 600 on SAT critical reading, 27% scored over 600 on SAT math, 28% scored over 600 on SAT writing.

Student Life Upper grades have specified standards of dress, student council, honor system. Discipline rests equally with students and faculty.

Tuition and Aid Day student tuition: $5000–$16,600. Tuition installment plan (monthly payment plans). Merit scholarship grants, need-based scholarship grants available. In 2015–16, 51% of upper-school students received aid; total upper-school

merit-scholarship money awarded: $12,000. Total amount of financial aid awarded in 2015–16: $106,000.

Admissions Traditional secondary-level entrance grade is 9. Admissions testing or comprehensive educational evaluation required. Deadline for receipt of application materials: none. Application fee required: $100. Interview required.

Athletics Interscholastic: basketball (boys), volleyball (g); intramural: basketball (g), indoor soccer (b), volleyball (g); coed interscholastic: backpacking, canoeing/kayaking, cooperative games, cross-country running, fitness, hiking/backpacking, indoor track & field, juggling, kickball, outdoor skills, ropes courses, running, snowshoeing, touch football, track and field, wilderness survival; coed intramural: golf, outdoor education, physical training, strength & conditioning. 2 PE instructors, 1 coach.

Computers Computers are regularly used in desktop publishing, graphic arts, graphic design, information technology, introduction to technology, multimedia, publications, technology, video film production, Web site design, writing classes. Computer network features include Internet access, wireless campus network, Internet filtering or blocking technology, online homework calendars for each upper school class. Campus intranet, student e-mail accounts, and computer access in designated common areas are available to students. The school has a published electronic and media policy.

Contact James Pearson, Admissions Director. 541-744-0954 Ext. 105. Fax: 541-741-6968. E-mail: jpearson@oakhillschool.net. Website: www.oakhillschool.com

OAKLAND SCHOOL

Troy, Virginia
See Special Needs Schools section.

OAK RIDGE MILITARY ACADEMY

2317 Oak Ridge Road
PO Box 498
Oak Ridge, North Carolina 27310

Head of School: Mr. John Haynes

General Information Coeducational boarding and day college-preparatory, leadership, and military school. Grades 7–12. Founded: 1852. Setting: small town. Nearest major city is Greensboro. Students are housed in coed dormitories. 101-acre campus. 22 buildings on campus. Approved or accredited by Southern Association of Colleges and Schools, Southern Association of Independent Schools, and North Carolina Department of Education. Member of National Association of Independent Schools. Total enrollment: 65. Upper school average class size: 7. Upper school faculty-student ratio: 1:11. Upper School students typically attend 5 days per week. The average school day consists of 7 hours.

Upper School Student Profile 88% of students are boarding students. 34% are state residents. 26 states are represented in upper school student body. 20% are international students. International students from Angola, Belize, China, Hong Kong, Mexico, and United States; 2 other countries represented in student body.

Faculty School total: 25. In upper school: 12 men, 13 women; 8 have advanced degrees; 9 reside on campus.

Subjects Offered Algebra, American history, American literature, biology, calculus, chemistry, college writing, computer math, computer science, creative writing, driver education, earth science, English, English literature, environmental science, ESL, French, geometry, German, government/civics, grammar, health, JROTC, JROTC or LEAD (Leadership Education and Development), mathematics, military science, music, physical education, physics, SAT preparation, science, social studies, Spanish, trigonometry, world history, writing.

Graduation Requirements Computer science, English, foreign language, mathematics, physical education (includes health), ROTC, SAT preparation, science, social studies (includes history), writing, complete three college applications, 20 hours of community service.

Special Academic Programs Honors section; accelerated programs; study at local college for college credit; academic accommodation for the gifted; special instructional classes for students with Attention Deficit Disorder and Attention Deficit Hyperactivity Disorder; ESL (6 students enrolled).

College Admission Counseling 28 students graduated in 2016; 27 went to college, including Appalachian State University; East Carolina University; North Carolina State University; The Citadel, The Military College of South Carolina; The University of North Carolina at Chapel Hill; The University of North Carolina at Charlotte. Other: 1 entered military service.

Student Life Upper grades have uniform requirement, student council, honor system. Discipline rests equally with students and faculty.

Summer Programs Remediation, enrichment, advancement, ESL, rigorous outdoor training programs offered; session focuses on leadership, adventure, academics, confidence building; held both on and off campus; accepts boys and girls; open to students from other schools. 200 students usually enrolled. 2017 schedule: June 24 to August 5. Application deadline: June 1.

Tuition and Aid Day student tuition: $12,815; 7-day tuition and room/board: $29,000. Tuition installment plan (Key Tuition Payment Plan, SMART Tuition Payment Plan, monthly payment plans). Tuition reduction for siblings, merit scholarship grants, USS Education Loan Program available. In 2016–17, 24% of upper-school students received aid.

Admissions Traditional secondary-level entrance grade is 10. Deadline for receipt of application materials: none. Application fee required: $200. Interview recommended.

Athletics Interscholastic: baseball (boys), basketball (b,g), football (b), golf (b), soccer (b,g), swimming and diving (b,g), tennis (b), track and field (b,g), volleyball (g), wrestling (b); intramural: basketball (b,g), flag football (b), outdoor adventure (b,g), paint ball (b,g), rappelling (b,g), scuba diving (b,g), skydiving (b,g), strength & conditioning (b,g), weight lifting (b,g); coed interscholastic: cross-country running, drill team, JROTC drill, marksmanship, riflery, swimming and diving, track and field; coed intramural: outdoor adventure, paint ball, pistol, rappelling, scuba diving, skydiving, softball, strength & conditioning, weight lifting. 1 PE instructor, 10 coaches, 1 athletic trainer.

Computers Computers are regularly used in English, mathematics, science classes. Computer resources include on-campus library services, Internet access. The school has a published electronic and media policy.

Contact Mr. Bob Lipke, Director of Admissions. 336-643-4131 Ext. 196. Fax: 336-643-1797. E-mail: blipke@ormila.com. Website: www.oakridgemilitary.com

THE OAKRIDGE SCHOOL

5900 West Pioneer Parkway
Arlington, Texas 76013-2899

Head of School: Mr. Jonathan Kellam

General Information Coeducational day college-preparatory and arts school. Grades PS–12. Founded: 1979. Setting: suburban. 100-acre campus. 12 buildings on campus. Approved or accredited by Independent Schools Association of the Southwest and Texas Department of Education. Member of National Association of Independent Schools. Endowment: $700,000. Total enrollment: 869. Upper school average class size: 16. Upper school faculty-student ratio: 1:11. There are 171 required school days per year for Upper School students. Upper School students typically attend 5 days per week. The average school day consists of 7 hours.

Upper School Student Profile Grade 6: 64 students (33 boys, 31 girls); Grade 7: 70 students (34 boys, 36 girls); Grade 8: 72 students (35 boys, 37 girls); Grade 9: 82 students (41 boys, 41 girls); Grade 10: 75 students (38 boys, 37 girls); Grade 11: 83 students (36 boys, 47 girls); Grade 12: 74 students (42 boys, 32 girls).

Faculty School total: 82. In upper school: 12 men, 14 women; 26 have advanced degrees.

Subjects Offered 3-dimensional art, acting, Advanced Placement courses, advanced studio art-AP, algebra, American history, American history-AP, American literature, anatomy, ancient world history, anthropology, archaeology, art, art history-AP, athletics, biology, British literature, calculus, calculus-AP, chemistry, chemistry-AP, Chinese, choir, choral music, college admission preparation, college counseling, college writing, community service, comparative religion, composition-AP, computer art, computer graphics, computer literacy, computer multimedia, computer science-AP, concert choir, creative writing, current events, desktop publishing, digital applications, digital art, digital imaging, digital photography, discrete mathematics, drama, drama performance, drama workshop, dramatic arts, drawing, drawing and design, economics, economics and history, English, English language and composition-AP, English literature and composition-AP, environmental science-AP, European civilization, European history-AP, expository writing, film and literature, fine arts, fractal geometry, French, French language-AP, French-AP, geometry, golf, government, government and politics-AP, government-AP, government/civics, graphic arts, graphic design, graphics, honors algebra, honors English, honors geometry, honors world history, human biology, independent study, language and composition, language arts, literature and composition-AP, modern European history-AP, modern world history, music theory, music theory-AP, musical productions, physics, physics-AP, play production, poetry, portfolio art, portfolio writing, pre-algebra, pre-calculus, probability and statistics, programming, public service, public speaking, reading/study skills, SAT preparation, SAT/ACT preparation, Spanish, Spanish-AP, strings, theater, track and field, U.S. government, U.S. government and politics, U.S. government and politics-AP, U.S. history, U.S. history-AP, United States government-AP, video, video communication, video film production, visual and performing arts, voice, voice ensemble, Web site design, weightlifting, world history.

Graduation Requirements Arts and fine arts (art, music, dance, drama), English, foreign language, mathematics, physical education (includes health), science, social studies (includes history), participation in six seasons of athletics, 60 hours of community service. Community service is required.

Special Academic Programs 21 Advanced Placement exams for which test preparation is offered; honors section; independent study; study at local college for college credit; study abroad; academic accommodation for the gifted, the musically talented, and the artistically talented.

College Admission Counseling 80 students graduated in 2016; all went to college, including Austin College; Oklahoma State University; Texas A&M University; Texas Christian University; The University of Texas at Austin; Vassar College. Mean SAT critical reading: 600, mean SAT math: 619, mean SAT writing: 595, mean combined SAT: 1814, mean composite ACT: 27.

Student Life Upper grades have uniform requirement, student council, honor system. Discipline rests primarily with faculty.

Summer Programs Remediation, enrichment, advancement, sports, art/fine arts, rigorous outdoor training, computer instruction programs offered; session focuses on enrichment; held both on and off campus; accepts boys and girls; open to students from other schools. 317 students usually enrolled. 2017 schedule: June 10 to July 19. Application deadline: none.

Tuition and Aid Day student tuition: $21,520. Tuition installment plan (FACTS Tuition Payment Plan, early discount option). Need-based scholarship grants available. In 2016–17, 22% of upper-school students received aid. Total amount of financial aid awarded in 2016–17: $523,375.

Admissions Traditional secondary-level entrance grade is 9. ERB Reading and Math, ISEE, Otis-Lennon School Ability Test or SSAT, ERB, PSAT, SAT, PLAN or ACT required. Deadline for receipt of application materials: March 1. Application fee required: $75. Interview required.

Athletics Interscholastic: baseball (boys), basketball (b,g), cheering (b,g), cross-country running (b,g), equestrian sports (b,g), field hockey (g), football (b), golf (b,g), physical fitness (b,g), physical training (b,g), power lifting (b), soccer (b,g), softball (g), strength & conditioning (b,g), swimming and diving (b,g), tennis (b,g), track and field (b,g), volleyball (g), weight lifting (b), wrestling (b); intramural: equestrian sports (b,g), fitness (b,g), physical fitness (b,g), physical training (b,g), strength & conditioning (b,g), weight lifting (b), weight training (b); coed interscholastic: horseback riding; coed intramural: archery, horseback riding, outdoor activities, outdoor education, sailing. 7 PE instructors, 10 coaches, 2 athletic trainers.

Computers Computers are regularly used in art, English, foreign language, history, mathematics, programming, science, stock market, technology, video film production, Web site design, writing, yearbook classes. Computer network features include on-campus library services, online commercial services, Internet access, wireless campus network, Internet filtering or blocking technology. Campus intranet, student e-mail accounts, and computer access in designated common areas are available to students. Students grades are available online. The school has a published electronic and media policy.

Contact Mrs. Amy Wilson, Interim Director of Admissions. 817-451-4994 Ext. 2708. Fax: 817-457-6681. E-mail: awilson@theoakridgeschool.org. Website: www.theoakridgeschool.org

OJAI VALLEY SCHOOL

723 El Paseo Road
Ojai, California 93023

Head of School: Mr. Michael J. Hall-Mounsey

General Information Coeducational boarding and day college-preparatory school; primarily serves students with learning disabilities, individuals with Attention Deficit Disorder, and dyslexic students. Boarding grades 3–12, day grades PK–12. Founded: 1911. Setting: rural. Nearest major city is Los Angeles. Students are housed in coed dormitories. 200-acre campus. 13 buildings on campus. Approved or accredited by California Association of Independent Schools, The Association of Boarding Schools, Western Association of Schools and Colleges, and California Department of Education. Member of National Association of Independent Schools and Secondary School Admission Test Board. Endowment: $1 million. Total enrollment: 288. Upper school average class size: 12. Upper school faculty-student ratio: 1:6.

Upper School Student Profile Grade 9: 24 students (15 boys, 9 girls); Grade 10: 31 students (12 boys, 19 girls); Grade 11: 24 students (14 boys, 10 girls); Grade 12: 30 students (19 boys, 11 girls).

Faculty School total: 54. In upper school: 11 men, 12 women; 10 have advanced degrees; 10 reside on campus.

Subjects Offered 20th century history, algebra, American history, American literature, art, art history, biology, biology-AP, calculus-AP, chemistry, chemistry-AP, community service, computer science, conceptual physics, creative writing, drama, ecology, economics, English, English literature, English-AP, environmental science, equestrian sports, ESL, fine arts, geography, geometry, government/civics, grammar, history, honors English, humanities, independent study, mathematics, music, music theory-AP, photography, physical education, physics, psychology, science, social studies, Spanish, Spanish-AP, speech, statistics, studio art, studio art-AP, theater, trigonometry, wilderness education, world history, writing.

Graduation Requirements Arts and fine arts (art, music, dance, drama), economics, English, foreign language, government, mathematics, science, social studies (includes history).

Special Academic Programs 11 Advanced Placement exams for which test preparation is offered; honors section; accelerated programs; independent study; study abroad; academic accommodation for the gifted and the artistically talented; remedial reading and/or remedial writing; remedial math; ESL (12 students enrolled).

College Admission Counseling 23 students graduated in 2016; all went to college, including Boston University; Johns Hopkins University; New York University; University of California, Riverside; University of California, Santa Barbara. Median SAT critical reading: 540, median SAT math: 625, median SAT writing: 585, median combined SAT: 1750. 25% scored over 600 on SAT math.

Student Life Upper grades have specified standards of dress, student council, honor system. Discipline rests equally with students and faculty.

Summer Programs Remediation, enrichment, advancement, ESL, art/fine arts, computer instruction programs offered; session focuses on academic and course credit;

held on campus; accepts boys and girls; open to students from other schools. 300 students usually enrolled. 2017 schedule: June 24 to August 2. Application deadline: none.

Tuition and Aid Day student tuition: $19,500; 7-day tuition and room/board: $47,950. Tuition installment plan (individually arranged payment plans). Need-based scholarship grants, need-based loans available. In 2016–17, 15% of upper-school students received aid. Total amount of financial aid awarded in 2016–17: $347,360.

Admissions Traditional secondary-level entrance grade is 9. For fall 2016, 150 students applied for upper-level admission, 65 were accepted, 32 enrolled. Any standardized test, SSAT or TOEFL required. Deadline for receipt of application materials: none. Application fee required: $50. Interview required.

Athletics Interscholastic: baseball (boys), basketball (b,g), cross-country running (b,g), dressage (b,g), football (b), lacrosse (b,g), soccer (b,g), volleyball (b,g); coed interscholastic: equestrian sports, golf, track and field; coed intramural: backpacking, basketball, bicycling, climbing, cross-country running, equestrian sports, fencing, fitness, fitness walking, golf, hiking/backpacking, horseback riding, kayaking, martial arts, mountain biking, outdoor education, physical fitness, rappelling, rock climbing, ropes courses, surfing, swimming and diving, weight training, yoga. 2 PE instructors, 2 coaches, 2 athletic trainers.

Computers Computers are regularly used in economics, English, ESL, geography, history, humanities, journalism, mathematics, music, photography, SAT preparation, science, social sciences, yearbook classes. Computer resources include on-campus library services, online commercial services, Internet access, wireless campus network, Internet filtering or blocking technology. The school has a published electronic and media policy.

Contact Ms. Tracy Wilson, Director of Admission. 805-646-1423. Fax: 805-646-0362. E-mail: admission@ovs.org. Website: www.ovs.org

OLDENBURG ACADEMY

1 Twister Circle
P.O. Box 200
Oldenburg, Indiana 47036

Head of School: Ms. Diane H. Laake

General Information Coeducational day college-preparatory and arts school, affiliated with Roman Catholic Church. Grades 9–12. Founded: 1852. Setting: small town. Nearest major city is Cincinnati, OH. 23-acre campus. 3 buildings on campus. Approved or accredited by American Association of Christian Schools, North Central Association of Colleges and Schools, and Indiana Department of Education. Total enrollment: 198. Upper school average class size: 15. Upper school faculty-student ratio: 1:12. There are 180 required school days per year for Upper School students. The average school day consists of 7 hours.

Upper School Student Profile Grade 9: 54 students (27 boys, 27 girls); Grade 10: 54 students (17 boys, 37 girls); Grade 11: 41 students (23 boys, 18 girls); Grade 12: 59 students (29 boys, 30 girls). 80% of students are Roman Catholic.

Faculty School total: 17. In upper school: 7 men, 10 women; 14 have advanced degrees.

Subjects Offered 3-dimensional art, advanced biology, advanced chemistry, advanced math, Advanced Placement courses, advanced studio art-AP, algebra, anatomy and physiology, applied arts, applied music, art, art-AP, arts appreciation, biology, biology-AP, business, calculus-AP, campus ministry, career education internship, chemistry-AP, choir, church history, composition-AP, creative writing, digital art, engineering, English language and composition-AP, English literature, English literature and composition-AP, entrepreneurship, finite math, foreign language, German-AP, graphic arts, honors U.S. history, marketing, music composition, music theater, music theory-AP, New Testament, painting, personal finance, photography, physics, probability and statistics, public speaking, SAT/ACT preparation, sociology, studio art-AP, U.S. history, U.S. history-AP, vocal ensemble, voice.

Graduation Requirements 40 hours of community service.

Special Academic Programs Advanced Placement exam preparation; honors section; study at local college for college credit; study abroad; ESL (4 students enrolled).

College Admission Counseling Colleges students went to include Indiana University Bloomington; Purdue University; University of Cincinnati.

Student Life Upper grades have uniform requirement, student council, honor system. Discipline rests primarily with faculty. Attendance at religious services is required.

Tuition and Aid Day student tuition: $7925. Tuition installment plan (FACTS Tuition Payment Plan). Tuition reduction for siblings, merit scholarship grants, need-based scholarship grants available. In 2016–17, 57% of upper-school students received aid; total upper-school merit-scholarship money awarded: $25,000. Total amount of financial aid awarded in 2016–17: $65,000.

Admissions Traditional secondary-level entrance grade is 9. High School Placement Test (closed version) from Scholastic Testing Service required. Deadline for receipt of application materials: none. Application fee required: $350. Interview recommended.

Athletics Interscholastic: baseball (boys), basketball (b,g), cheering (g), cross-country running (b,g), dance (b,g), dance team (g), football (b), physical fitness (b,g), soccer (b,g), softball (g), swimming and diving (b,g), tennis (b,g), track and field (b,g),

volleyball (g), weight lifting (b,g), weight training (b,g). 1 PE instructor, 9 coaches, 1 athletic trainer.

Computers Computers are regularly used in all academic classes. Computer network features include on-campus library services, Internet access, wireless campus network, Internet filtering or blocking technology, one-to-one student iPad program. Campus intranet, student e-mail accounts, and computer access in designated common areas are available to students. Students grades are available online. The school has a published electronic and media policy.

Contact Mr. Brian McFee, Principal. 812-934-4440 Ext. 223. Fax: 812-934-4838. E-mail: bmcfee@oldenburgacademy.org. Website: www.oldenburgacademy.org/

THE O'NEAL SCHOOL

3300 Airport Road
PO Box 290
Southern Pines, North Carolina 28388-0290

Head of School: Mr. John Elmore

General Information Coeducational day college-preparatory school. Grades PK–12. Founded: 1971. Setting: small town. Nearest major city is Raleigh. 40-acre campus. 3 buildings on campus. Approved or accredited by North Carolina Association of Independent Schools, Southern Association of Colleges and Schools, Southern Association of Independent Schools, and North Carolina Department of Education. Member of National Association of Independent Schools. Endowment: $1.1 million. Total enrollment: 411. Upper school average class size: 15. Upper school faculty-student ratio: 1:8. There are 175 required school days per year for Upper School students. Upper School students typically attend 5 days per week. The average school day consists of 6 hours and 15 minutes.

Upper School Student Profile Grade 9: 36 students (14 boys, 22 girls); Grade 10: 49 students (23 boys, 26 girls); Grade 11: 29 students (12 boys, 17 girls); Grade 12: 38 students (15 boys, 23 girls).

Faculty School total: 56. In upper school: 6 men, 12 women; 7 have advanced degrees.

Subjects Offered Algebra, American history, American literature, art, art history, art history-AP, biology, biology-AP, calculus-AP, chemistry, community service, computer science, drama, economics, English, English language-AP, English literature, English literature-AP, environmental science, environmental science-AP, European history, European history-AP, expository writing, film, filmmaking, fine arts, French, geometry, government-AP, mathematics, photography, physical education, physics-AP, pottery, pre-calculus, robotics, science, social studies, Spanish, statistics-AP, U.S. history-AP, world history, world literature, yearbook.

Graduation Requirements Arts and fine arts (art, music, dance, drama), English, foreign language, mathematics, physical education (includes health), science, social studies (includes history), 36 hours of community service.

Special Academic Programs 13 Advanced Placement exams for which test preparation is offered; independent study; study at local college for college credit.

College Admission Counseling 32 students graduated in 2016; all went to college, including East Carolina University; The University of North Carolina at Chapel Hill; The University of North Carolina at Charlotte; The University of North Carolina at Greensboro; Washington and Lee University; Wellesley College. Other: 2 had other specific plans. Median SAT critical reading: 570, median SAT math: 540, median SAT writing: 555, median combined SAT: 1665. Mean composite ACT: 24. 27% scored over 600 on SAT critical reading, 31% scored over 600 on SAT math, 31% scored over 600 on SAT writing, 27% scored over 1800 on combined SAT, 26% scored over 26 on composite ACT.

Student Life Upper grades have specified standards of dress, student council, honor system. Discipline rests primarily with faculty.

Tuition and Aid Day student tuition: $16,990. Tuition installment plan (Insured Tuition Payment Plan, monthly payment plans, individually arranged payment plans). Merit scholarship grants, need-based scholarship grants available. In 2016–17, 38% of upper-school students received aid; total upper-school merit-scholarship money awarded: $38,223. Total amount of financial aid awarded in 2016–17: $423,937.

Admissions Traditional secondary-level entrance grade is 9. For fall 2016, 29 students applied for upper-level admission, 27 were accepted, 24 enrolled. Admissions testing, essay, OLSAT, Stanford Achievement Test, PSAT and SAT for applicants to grade 11 and 12, WRAT or writing sample required. Deadline for receipt of application materials: none. Application fee required: $100. On-campus interview recommended.

Athletics Interscholastic: baseball (boys), basketball (b,g), cross-country running (b,g), soccer (b,g), swimming and diving (b,g), tennis (b,g), track and field (b,g), volleyball (g); coed interscholastic: cheering, golf. 2 PE instructors, 2 coaches, 1 athletic trainer.

Computers Computers are regularly used in all academic classes. Computer network features include on-campus library services, Internet access, wireless campus network, Internet filtering or blocking technology, EBSCO, World Book Online. Student e-mail accounts and computer access in designated common areas are available to students. The school has a published electronic and media policy.

Contact Mrs. Olivia Webb, Director of Admissions and Financial Aid. 910-692-6920 Ext. 103. Fax: 910-692-6930. E-mail: owebb@onealschool.org. Website: www.onealschool.org

ONEIDA BAPTIST INSTITUTE

11 Mulberry Street
Oneida, Kentucky 40972

Head of School: Mr. Larry A. Gritton Jr.

General Information Coeducational boarding and day college-preparatory, general academic, arts, vocational, religious studies, and agriculture school, affiliated with Southern Baptist Convention. Grades 6–12. Founded: 1899. Setting: rural. Nearest major city is Lexington. Students are housed in coed dormitories. 200-acre campus. 15 buildings on campus. Approved or accredited by The Kentucky Non-Public School Commission, The National Non-Public School Commission, and Kentucky Department of Education. Endowment: $28 million. Total enrollment: 320. Upper school average class size: 11. Upper school faculty-student ratio: 1:11. There are 170 required school days per year for Upper School students. Upper School students typically attend 5 days per week. The average school day consists of 6 hours.

Upper School Student Profile Grade 9: 44 students (18 boys, 26 girls); Grade 10: 38 students (21 boys, 17 girls); Grade 11: 72 students (43 boys, 29 girls); Grade 12: 57 students (28 boys, 29 girls). 82% of students are boarding students. 41% are state residents. 27 states are represented in upper school student body. 30% are international students. International students from China, Ethiopia, Haiti, Nigeria, Republic of Korea, and Thailand; 17 other countries represented in student body. 25% of students are Southern Baptist Convention.

Faculty School total: 40. In upper school: 15 men, 16 women; 12 have advanced degrees; 36 reside on campus.

Subjects Offered Agriculture, algebra, anatomy, band, Bible, biology, biology-AP, calculus-AP, careers, chemistry, child development, choir, commercial art, computer skills, culinary arts, English, English-AP, ESL, European history-AP, fashion, French, geography, geometry, government, government-AP, health, integrated mathematics, language arts, leadership, life skills, literature, mathematics, media production, music appreciation, physical education, physical science, piano, psychology, sociology, Spanish, stagecraft, U.S. history, U.S. history-AP, United States government-AP, vocal ensemble, world history, zoology.

Graduation Requirements Arts and fine arts (art, music, dance, drama), Bible, computer literacy, English, foreign language, mathematics, physical education (includes health), science, social studies (includes history), Bible class, 20 service hours.

Special Academic Programs 6 Advanced Placement exams for which test preparation is offered; honors section; study at local college for college credit; remedial reading and/or remedial writing; remedial math; ESL (17 students enrolled).

College Admission Counseling 55 students graduated in 2016; 48 went to college, including Alice Lloyd College; Asbury University; Bluegrass Community and Technical College; Eastern Kentucky University; University of Kentucky; University of Pikeville. Other: 5 went to work, 2 entered military service.

Student Life Upper grades have specified standards of dress. Discipline rests primarily with faculty. Attendance at religious services is required.

Summer Programs Remediation, enrichment, advancement programs offered; session focuses on remediation and make-up courses; held on campus; accepts boys and girls; open to students from other schools. 125 students usually enrolled. 2017 schedule: May 22 to June 23. Application deadline: June 1.

Tuition and Aid 7-day tuition and room/board: $6750–$14,000. Tuition installment plan (monthly payment plans). Need-based scholarship grants available. In 2016–17, 100% of upper-school students received aid.

Admissions Traditional secondary-level entrance grade is 9. Deadline for receipt of application materials: none. Application fee required: $50. On-campus interview required.

Athletics Interscholastic: baseball (boys), basketball (b,g), cheering (g), cross-country running (b,g), golf (b,g), soccer (b,g), softball (g), swimming and diving (b,g), tennis (b,g), track and field (b,g), volleyball (g). 2 PE instructors.

Computers Computers are regularly used in commercial art, media production, technology, yearbook classes. Computer resources include Internet access, Internet filtering or blocking technology. Student e-mail accounts are available to students. The school has a published electronic and media policy.

Contact Admissions. 606-847-4111 Ext. 233. Fax: 606-847-4496. E-mail: admissions@oneidaschool.org. Website: www.oneidaschool.org

ORANGEBURG PREPARATORY SCHOOLS, INC.

2651 North Road
Orangeburg, South Carolina 29118

Head of School: Dr. Brian Newsome

General Information Coeducational day college-preparatory and arts school. Grades K4–12. Founded: 1986. Setting: small town. Nearest major city is Columbia. 40-acre campus. 7 buildings on campus. Approved or accredited by South Carolina Independent School Association, Southern Association of Colleges and Schools, and South Carolina Department of Education. Endowment: $500,000. Total enrollment: 678. Upper school average class size: 20. Upper school faculty-student ratio: 1:12. Upper School students typically attend 5 days per week. The average school day consists of 6 hours and 40 minutes.

Upper School Student Profile Grade 9: 63 students (35 boys, 28 girls); Grade 10: 49 students (26 boys, 23 girls); Grade 11: 40 students (18 boys, 22 girls); Grade 12: 38 students (15 boys, 23 girls).

Faculty School total: 30. In upper school: 9 men, 20 women; 10 have advanced degrees.

Subjects Offered Acting, advanced chemistry, advanced computer applications, advanced math, algebra, American government, American history, American literature-AP, analysis and differential calculus, analytic geometry, anatomy and physiology, ancient world history, applied arts, art, automated accounting, baseball, Basic programming, basketball, biology, British literature, British literature-AP, calculus-AP, career/college preparation, cheerleading, chemistry, chemistry-AP, choral music, civics, college admission preparation, college counseling, college placement, college planning, composition, computer studies, desktop publishing, English literature and composition-AP, fencing, forensics, four units of summer reading, French, golf, government, grammar, history, honors algebra, honors English, honors geometry, honors U.S. history, honors world history, Internet, introduction to theater, musical theater, physical education, physical fitness, physical science, physics, pre-algebra, pre-calculus, probability and statistics, psychology, SAT preparation, senior composition, softball, Spanish, speech and debate, speech and oral interpretations, tennis, theater, track and field, U.S. history-AP, volleyball, weight training.

Graduation Requirements Algebra, American government, American history, American literature, analytic geometry, biology, British literature, chemistry, computer studies, economics, English literature, foreign language.

Special Academic Programs Advanced Placement exam preparation; honors section; independent study; study at local college for college credit; ESL (10 students enrolled).

College Admission Counseling 48 students graduated in 2015; all went to college, including Clemson University; College of Charleston; Presbyterian College; The Citadel, The Military College of South Carolina; University of South Carolina; Wofford College.

Student Life Upper grades have specified standards of dress, student council, honor system. Discipline rests primarily with faculty.

Tuition and Aid Day student tuition: $4428–$5880. Tuition installment plan (monthly payment plans). Tuition reduction for siblings, merit scholarship grants, need-based scholarship grants available. In 2015–16, 6% of upper-school students received aid; total upper-school merit-scholarship money awarded: $6600. Total amount of financial aid awarded in 2015–16: $20,370.

Admissions Traditional secondary-level entrance grade is 9. For fall 2015, 7 students applied for upper-level admission, 7 were accepted, 7 enrolled. Achievement tests, PSAT and SAT for applicants to grade 11 and 12 or Stanford Achievement Test required. Deadline for receipt of application materials: none. Application fee required: $150. Interview recommended.

Athletics Interscholastic: baseball (boys), basketball (b,g), cheering (g), softball (g), track and field (b,g), volleyball (g); coed interscholastic: cross-country running, golf, soccer; coed intramural: archery, badminton, cooperative games, fencing, fitness, physical fitness, physical training, strength & conditioning. 3 PE instructors, 8 coaches, 1 athletic trainer.

Computers Computers are regularly used in all classes. Computer network features include on-campus library services, online commercial services, Internet access, wireless campus network, Internet filtering or blocking technology. Campus intranet is available to students. Students grades are available online. The school has a published electronic and media policy.

Contact 803-534-7970. Fax: 803-535-2190.
Website: http://www.orangeburgprep.com/

ORANGEWOOD ADVENTIST ACADEMY

13732 Clinton Street
Garden Grove, California 92843

Head of School: Ms. Elizabeth Munoz Beard

General Information Coeducational day college-preparatory, arts, and religious studies school, affiliated with Seventh-day Adventist Church. Grades PK–12. Founded: 1956. Setting: urban. Nearest major city is Anaheim. 11-acre campus. 6 buildings on campus. Approved or accredited by Board of Regents, General Conference of Seventh-day Adventists, Western Association of Schools and Colleges, and California Department of Education. Total enrollment: 261. Upper school average class size: 24. Upper school faculty-student ratio: 1:10. There are 180 required school days per year for Upper School students. Upper School students typically attend 5 days per week. The average school day consists of 7 hours.

Upper School Student Profile Grade 9: 22 students (9 boys, 13 girls); Grade 10: 25 students (11 boys, 14 girls); Grade 11: 22 students (13 boys, 9 girls); Grade 12: 26 students (16 boys, 10 girls). 80% of students are Seventh-day Adventists.

Faculty School total: 20. In upper school: 4 men, 7 women; 4 have advanced degrees.

Subjects Offered Algebra, American literature, American literature-AP, art, arts, band, biology, calculus, calculus-AP, career education, chemistry, choir, computer science, computers, concert bell choir, drama, English, family studies, fine arts, geometry, government, health, journalism, life skills, mathematics, physical education, physical science, physics, pre-calculus, religion, science, social studies, Spanish, statistics-AP, typing, U.S. government, U.S. history, U.S. history-AP, world history, yearbook.

Graduation Requirements Arts and fine arts (art, music, dance, drama), business skills (includes word processing), career education, computer science, economics, English, foreign language, government, health, mathematics, physical education (includes health), religion (includes Bible studies and theology), science, social studies (includes history), work experience, community service.

Special Academic Programs Advanced Placement exam preparation; honors section.

College Admission Counseling 24 students graduated in 2016; 22 went to college, including California State University; La Sierra University; Loma Linda University. Other: 1 went to work, 1 had other specific plans.

Student Life Upper grades have uniform requirement, student council, honor system. Discipline rests primarily with faculty. Attendance at religious services is required.

Summer Programs Sports programs offered; session focuses on volleyball and basketball; held on campus; accepts boys and girls; open to students from other schools. 50 students usually enrolled.

Tuition and Aid Day student tuition: $11,155. Tuition installment plan (monthly payment plans). Tuition reduction for siblings, merit scholarship grants, need-based scholarship grants, paying campus jobs available. In 2016–17, 52% of upper-school students received aid; total upper-school merit-scholarship money awarded: $150,000. Total amount of financial aid awarded in 2016–17: $200,000.

Admissions Traditional secondary-level entrance grade is 9. TOEFL required. Deadline for receipt of application materials: none. Application fee required: $250. Interview recommended.

Athletics Interscholastic: basketball (boys, girls), cheering (g), flag football (b), soccer (b), softball (g), volleyball (b,g); intramural: basketball (b,g), flag football (b), softball (g), volleyball (b,g); coed interscholastic: badminton, fitness, golf, physical fitness, running, soccer; coed intramural: golf, gymnastics, running. 1 PE instructor, 5 coaches.

Computers Computers are regularly used in accounting, all academic, art, Bible studies, business applications, career education, college planning, computer applications, economics, English, geography, health, independent study, introduction to technology, journalism, keyboarding, mathematics, media production, music, newspaper, photography, photojournalism, religion, SAT preparation, science, social sciences, study skills, typing, word processing, writing, yearbook classes. Computer network features include on-campus library services, online commercial services, Internet access, wireless campus network, Internet filtering or blocking technology. Students grades are available online. The school has a published electronic and media policy.

Contact Mrs. Aime Cuevas, Vice Principal and Registrar. 714-534-4694 Ext. 207. Fax: 714-534-5931. E-mail: acuevas@orangewoodacademy.com. Website: www.orangewoodacademy.com

ORANGEWOOD CHRISTIAN SCHOOL

1300 West Maitland Boulevard
Maitland, Florida 32751

Head of School: Donald M. Larson, PhD

General Information Coeducational day college-preparatory, arts, religious studies, and technology school, affiliated with Presbyterian Church, Christian faith. Grades K4–12. Founded: 1980. Setting: suburban. Nearest major city is Orlando. 8-acre campus. 2 buildings on campus. Approved or accredited by Association of Christian Schools International, Christian Schools of Florida, National Council for Private School Accreditation, and Southern Association of Colleges and Schools. Total enrollment: 732. Upper school average class size: 14. Upper school faculty-student ratio: 1:11. The average school day consists of 7 hours.

Upper School Student Profile 100% of students are Presbyterian, Christian.

Faculty School total: 65. In upper school: 18 have advanced degrees.

Subjects Offered Advanced Placement courses, algebra, American culture, American government, American history, American history-AP, anatomy and physiology, art, art-AP, astronomy, Bible, biology, biology-AP, calculus-AP, career exploration, ceramics, chemistry, choir, commercial art, computer applications, computer graphics, creative writing, drama, drawing, economics, English, English language and composition-AP, English literature and composition-AP, environmental science, foreign language, geometry, graphic design, honors algebra, honors English, honors geometry, honors U.S. history, honors world history, Latin, life management skills, marine science, meteorology, oceanography, painting, personal fitness, photography, physics, physics-AP, pre-calculus, psychology, SAT preparation, sculpture, senior seminar, Spanish, Spanish language-AP, speech, studio art-AP, television, trigonometry, weight training, world geography, world history, world religions, yearbook.

Graduation Requirements Algebra, American government, American history, arts and fine arts (art, music, dance, drama), Bible, biology, computer applications, economics, electives, English, foreign language, life management skills, mathematics, personal fitness, physical education (includes health), science, senior seminar, world history.

Special Academic Programs Advanced Placement exam preparation; honors section; accelerated programs; independent study; study at local college for college credit.

College Admission Counseling 68 students graduated in 2015; 67 went to college, including Covenant College; Florida State University; Palm Beach Atlantic University; University of Central Florida; University of Florida; University of North Florida. Median SAT critical reading: 550, median SAT math: 550, median SAT writing: 525. 32% scored over 600 on SAT critical reading, 27% scored over 600 on SAT math, 22% scored over 600 on SAT writing.

Student Life Upper grades have specified standards of dress, student council, honor system. Discipline rests primarily with faculty. Attendance at religious services is required.

Tuition and Aid Tuition installment plan (SMART Tuition Payment Plan, 4% discount if paid in full). Tuition reduction for siblings, need-based scholarship grants available. In 2015–16, 11% of upper-school students received aid. Total amount of financial aid awarded in 2015–16: $124,000.

Admissions Traditional secondary-level entrance grade is 9. Admissions testing and ISEE required. Deadline for receipt of application materials: none. Application fee required: $125. Interview required.

Athletics Interscholastic: baseball (boys), basketball (b,g), cheering (g), cross-country running (b,g), flag football (b), football (b), golf (b,g), lacrosse (b,g), physical fitness (b,g), physical training (b,g), soccer (b,g), strength & conditioning (b,g), tennis (b,g), track and field (b,g), volleyball (g), weight lifting (b,g), weight training (b,g); intramural: yoga (g); coed intramural: bowling, fishing, sailing, table tennis, ultimate Frisbee. 2 PE instructors, 8 coaches, 2 athletic trainers

Computers Computers are regularly used in all classes. Computer network features include on-campus library services, Internet access, wireless campus network, Internet filtering or blocking technology. Campus intranet, student e-mail accounts, and computer access in designated common areas are available to students. Students grades are available online. The school has a published electronic and media policy.

Contact Mrs. Joyce McDonald, Director of Admissions. 407-339-0223. Fax: 407-339-4148. E-mail: jmcdonald@ocsrams.org. Website: www.ocsrams.org

ORATORY PREPARATORY SCHOOL

1 Beverly Road
Summit, New Jersey 07901

Head of School: Mr. Robert Costello

General Information Boys' day college-preparatory school, affiliated with Roman Catholic Church. Grades 7–12. Founded: 1907. Setting: suburban. Nearest major city is Newark. 10-acre campus. 2 buildings on campus. Approved or accredited by Middle States Association of Colleges and Schools, National Catholic Education Association, New Jersey Association of Independent Schools, and New Jersey Department of Education. Endowment: $2 million. Total enrollment: 359. Upper school average class size: 14. Upper school faculty-student ratio: 1:9. There are 170 required school days per year for Upper School students. Upper School students typically attend 5 days per week. The average school day consists of 6 hours and 35 minutes.

Upper School Student Profile Grade 7: 26 students (26 boys); Grade 8: 16 students (16 boys); Grade 9: 86 students (86 boys); Grade 10: 91 students (91 boys); Grade 11: 73 students (73 boys); Grade 12: 67 students (67 boys). 72% of students are Roman Catholic.

Faculty School total: 40. In upper school: 25 men, 15 women; 18 have advanced degrees.

Subjects Offered Algebra, American history, American literature, art, art-AP, biology, British literature, calculus, chemistry, computer applications, computer math, computer programming, computer science, conceptual physics, creative writing, economics, English, English literature, English-AP, expository writing, finite math, first aid, foreign language, geography, geometry, grammar, health, history, history-AP, honors algebra, honors English, honors geometry, honors U.S. history, honors world history, journalism, language-AP, Latin, mathematics, mathematics-AP, media, music appreciation, philosophy, physical education, physics, pre-algebra, probability, religion, rhetoric, science, social sciences, social studies, sociology, Spanish, statistics, theology, trigonometry, U.S. history, U.S. history-AP, world cultures, world geography, world history, world history-AP, world literature, writing.

Graduation Requirements English, foreign language, mathematics, physical education (includes health), religion (includes Bible studies and theology), science, social sciences, social studies (includes history). Community service is required.

Special Academic Programs Advanced Placement exam preparation; honors section; independent study; study at local college for college credit.

College Admission Counseling 66 students graduated in 2015; all went to college, including Boston College; Bucknell University; Fairfield University; Fairleigh Dickinson University, College at Florham; University of Pennsylvania; Villanova University. Mean SAT critical reading: 616, mean SAT math: 608, mean SAT writing: 615, mean composite ACT: 27.

Student Life Upper grades have specified standards of dress, student council, honor system. Discipline rests primarily with faculty. Attendance at religious services is required.

Tuition and Aid Day student tuition: $19,650. Tuition installment plan (monthly payment plans, individually arranged payment plans). Merit scholarship grants, need-based scholarship grants available. In 2015–16, 41% of upper-school students received aid; total upper-school merit-scholarship money awarded: $381,300. Total amount of financial aid awarded in 2015–16: $542,300.

Admissions Traditional secondary-level entrance grade is 9. For fall 2015, 196 students applied for upper-level admission, 172 were accepted, 84 enrolled. Admissions testing or independent norms required. Deadline for receipt of application materials: none. Application fee required: $50. On-campus interview required.

Athletics Interscholastic: baseball, basketball, bowling, cross-country running, fencing, golf, hockey, ice hockey, indoor track, indoor track & field, lacrosse, soccer, swimming and diving, tennis, track and field, winter (indoor) track; intramural: basketball, combined training, fishing, flag football, football, Frisbee, kickball, physical training, skiing (downhill), snowboarding, strength & conditioning, tennis, ultimate Frisbee, volleyball. 3 PE instructors, 12 coaches, 1 athletic trainer.

Computers Computers are regularly used in English, foreign language, history, Latin, mathematics, religious studies, science, Spanish, technology, yearbook classes. Computer network features include on-campus library services, online commercial services, Internet access, wireless campus network, Internet filtering or blocking technology, laptop program, wireless campus network. Student e-mail accounts are available to students. Students grades are available online. The school has a published electronic and media policy.

Contact Mr. Thomas R. Boniello, Director of Admissions. 908-273-5771 Ext. 11. Fax: 908-273-1554. E-mail: admissions@oratoryprep.org. Website: www.oratoryprep.org

OREGON EPISCOPAL SCHOOL

6300 Southwest Nicol Road
Portland, Oregon 97223-7566

Head of School: Mrs. Mo Copeland

General Information Coeducational boarding and day college-preparatory and science school, affiliated with Episcopal Church. Boarding grades 9–12, day grades PK–12. Founded: 1869. Setting: suburban. Students are housed in single-sex dormitories. 59-acre campus. 9 buildings on campus. Approved or accredited by National Association of Episcopal Schools, Northwest Association of Independent Schools, and Oregon Department of Education. Member of National Association of Independent Schools and Secondary School Admission Test Board. Endowment: $19.8 million. Total enrollment: 870. Upper school average class size: 16. Upper school faculty-student ratio: 1:7. There are 175 required school days per year for Upper School students. Upper School students typically attend 5 days per week. The average school day consists of 7 hours.

Upper School Student Profile Grade 9: 83 students (42 boys, 41 girls); Grade 10: 78 students (33 boys, 45 girls); Grade 11: 81 students (38 boys, 43 girls); Grade 12: 68 students (30 boys, 38 girls); Postgraduate: 2 students (2 boys). 18% of students are boarding students. 82% are state residents. 5 states are represented in upper school student body. 15% are international students. International students from Chad, China, Hong Kong, Republic of Korea, Taiwan, and Viet Nam; 3 other countries represented in student body. 10% of students are members of Episcopal Church.

Faculty School total: 120. In upper school: 22 men, 27 women; 40 have advanced degrees; 6 reside on campus.

Subjects Offered Acting, advanced biology, advanced chemistry, advanced math, Advanced Placement courses, algebra, American Civil War, American government, American history, American literature, American studies, anatomy and physiology, Ancient Greek, ancient history, ancient/medieval philosophy, animation, Arabic studies, art, Asian history, astronomy, athletic training, athletics, backpacking, Basic programming, biology, Buddhism, calculus-AP, ceramics, chemistry, Chinese, chorus, Christian studies, Christianity, college counseling, college planning, college writing, community service, computer graphics, computer science, computer science-AP, constitutional law, creative writing, debate, discrete mathematics, drama, drawing, East Asian history, ecology, electronics, engineering, English, English literature, environmental science, ESL, European history, fencing, film, film and literature, filmmaking, fine arts, finite math, foreign language, foreign policy, French, French language-AP, French-AP, freshman seminar, functions, geology, geometry, graphic arts, graphic design, graphics, health, health and wellness, history, human anatomy, human relations, human sexuality, humanities, independent study, international affairs, international relations, jazz band, jazz ensemble, journalism, literature, marine biology, marine ecology, mathematics, mathematics-AP, microbiology, model United Nations, music, music history, music technology, musical productions, musical theater, newspaper, painting, personal finance, personal fitness, philosophy, photography, photojournalism, physical education, physical fitness, physics, playwriting and directing, poetry, pre-algebra, pre-calculus, religion, religion and culture, research, science, science project, science research, service learning/internship, sex education, sexuality, Shakespeare, social studies, Spanish, Spanish language-AP, Spanish literature, Spanish-AP, speech, stagecraft, statistics, statistics-AP, tennis, theater, theater design and production, track and field, trigonometry, U.S. history, urban studies, video and animation, video film production, visual arts, vocal ensemble, vocal music, weight training, weightlifting, wellness, wilderness education, wilderness experience, world history, world literature, world religions, world religions, yearbook, yoga.

Graduation Requirements Arts and fine arts (art, music, dance, drama), electives, English, foreign language, health education, humanities, mathematics, philosophy, physical education (includes health), religion (includes Bible studies and theology), science, service learning/internship, U.S. history, Service learning.

Special Academic Programs Advanced Placement exam preparation; honors section; independent study; term-away projects; study abroad; academic accommodation for the gifted; ESL (9 students enrolled).

College Admission Counseling 80 students graduated in 2016; 75 went to college, including Carleton College; Grinnell College; Massachusetts Institute of Technology; Stanford University; Washington University in St. Louis; Whitman College. Other: 1 entered a postgraduate year, 4 had other specific plans. Mean SAT critical reading: 670, mean SAT math: 669, mean SAT writing: 659, mean combined SAT: 2000, mean composite ACT: 30. 85% scored over 1800 on combined SAT, 82% scored over 26 on composite ACT.

Student Life Upper grades have specified standards of dress, student council. Discipline rests equally with students and faculty. Attendance at religious services is required.

Summer Programs Remediation, enrichment, advancement, sports, art/fine arts, computer instruction programs offered; session focuses on a variety of academic, sports, and artistic enrichment programs; held both on and off campus; accepts boys and girls; open to students from other schools. 2,500 students usually enrolled. 2017 schedule: June 19 to August 25. Application deadline: June 19.

Tuition and Aid Day student tuition: $30,700; 7-day tuition and room/board: $58,600. Tuition installment plan (monthly payment plans). Need-based scholarship grants available. In 2016–17, 16% of upper-school students received aid. Total amount of financial aid awarded in 2016–17: $1,051,590.

Admissions Traditional secondary-level entrance grade is 9. For fall 2016, 256 students applied for upper-level admission, 71 were accepted, 35 enrolled. SSAT or TOEFL required. Deadline for receipt of application materials: January 26. Application fee required: $75. On-campus interview recommended.

Athletics Interscholastic: alpine skiing (boys, girls), basketball (b,g), cross-country running (b,g), fencing (b,g), golf (b,g), independent competitive sports (b,g), lacrosse (b,g), running (b,g), skiing (downhill) (b,g), soccer (b,g), tennis (b,g), track and field (b,g), volleyball (g); intramural: backpacking (b,g), hiking/backpacking (b,g), outdoor activities (b,g), outdoor adventure (b,g), outdoor education (b,g), outdoor recreation (b,g), outdoor skills (b,g), outdoors (b,g), rafting (b,g), rock climbing (b,g), ropes courses (b,g), running (b,g), snowboarding (b,g), strength & conditioning (b,g), walking (b,g), weight lifting (b,g), weight training (b,g), wilderness (b,g), wilderness survival (b,g), wildernessways (b,g), yoga (b,g); coed interscholastic: running; coed intramural: backpacking, hiking/backpacking, outdoor activities, outdoor adventure, outdoor education, outdoor recreation, outdoor skills, outdoors, physical fitness, physical training, rafting, rock climbing, ropes courses, running, strength & conditioning, walking, weight lifting, weight training, wilderness, wilderness survival, wildernessways. 2 PE instructors, 79 coaches, 1 athletic trainer.

Computers Computers are regularly used in all academic classes. Computer network features include on-campus library services, online commercial services, Internet access, wireless campus network, Internet filtering or blocking technology, one-to-one laptop program. Campus intranet, student e-mail accounts, and computer access in designated common areas are available to students. Students grades are available online. The school has a published electronic and media policy.

Contact Ms. Molly Mulkey, Admissions Administrative Assistant. 503-768-3115. Fax: 503-768-3140. E-mail: admit@oes.edu. Website: www.oes.edu

ORINDA ACADEMY

19 Altarinda Road
Orinda, California 94563-2602

Head of School: Ron Graydon

General Information Coeducational day college-preparatory and general academic school. Grades 8–12. Founded: 1982. Setting: suburban. Nearest major city is Walnut Creek. 1-acre campus. 2 buildings on campus. Approved or accredited by East Bay Independent Schools Association, The College Board, and Western Association of Schools and Colleges. Total enrollment: 78. Upper school average class size: 8. Upper school faculty-student ratio: 1:8. There are 180 required school days per year for Upper School students. Upper School students typically attend 5 days per week. The average school day consists of 6 hours and 30 minutes.

Upper School Student Profile Grade 8: 5 students (4 boys, 1 girl); Grade 9: 11 students (6 boys, 5 girls); Grade 10: 16 students (10 boys, 6 girls); Grade 11: 23 students (14 boys, 9 girls); Grade 12: 17 students (12 boys, 5 girls).

Faculty School total: 18. In upper school: 6 men, 12 women; 9 have advanced degrees.

Subjects Offered Algebra, American history, American literature, American sign language, art, basketball, biology, calculus, chemistry, community service, computer graphics, computer multimedia, computer music, contemporary issues, creative writing, dance, drama, earth science, economics, English, English literature, English literature and composition-AP, ensembles, environmental science, European history, film history, fine arts, French, geography, geometry, government/civics, health, history, history of music, introduction to theater, journalism, mathematics, music, music performance, musical productions, performing arts, physical education, physics, science, social studies, Spanish, Spanish language-AP, theater, trigonometry, visual arts, yearbook.

Graduation Requirements Algebra, biology, civics, geometry, trigonometry, U.S. history, visual and performing arts.

Special Academic Programs 2 Advanced Placement exams for which test preparation is offered; honors section; accelerated programs; academic accommodation for the gifted; ESL (15 students enrolled).

College Admission Counseling 23 students graduated in 2016; 20 went to college, including Cornell University; Landmark College; Penn State University Park; Stanford University; University of Redlands; Whitman College. Other: 1 went to work, 2 had other specific plans. Mean SAT critical reading: 512, mean SAT math: 510, mean SAT writing: 510, mean combined SAT: 1532, mean composite ACT: 20. 29% scored over 600 on SAT critical reading, 35% scored over 600 on SAT math, 29% scored over 600 on SAT writing, 24% scored over 1800 on combined SAT, 22% scored over 26 on composite ACT.

Student Life Upper grades have specified standards of dress, student council, honor system. Discipline rests primarily with faculty.

Summer Programs Remediation, enrichment, advancement programs offered; session focuses on academics; held on campus; accepts boys and girls; open to students from other schools. 30 students usually enrolled. 2017 schedule: June 19 to August 11. Application deadline: none.

Tuition and Aid Day student tuition: $35,980. Tuition installment plan (FACTS Tuition Payment Plan). Tuition reduction for siblings, need-based scholarship grants available. In 2016–17, 25% of upper-school students received aid. Total amount of financial aid awarded in 2016–17: $400,000.

Admissions Traditional secondary-level entrance grade is 9. For fall 2016, 70 students applied for upper-level admission, 42 were accepted, 21 enrolled. Any standardized test, ISEE, SSAT or Star-9 required. Deadline for receipt of application materials: January 15. Application fee required: $75. On-campus interview required.

Athletics Coed Interscholastic: basketball, cheering, soccer; coed intramural: badminton, dance, soccer, weight training, yoga. 1 PE instructor, 1 coach.

Computers Computers are regularly used in all classes. Computer network features include Internet access, wireless campus network, Internet filtering or blocking technology, Homework Portal. Student e-mail accounts are available to students. Students grades are available online. The school has a published electronic and media policy.

Contact Ron Graydon, Director of Admissions. 925-254-7553. Fax: 925-254-4768. E-mail: ron@orindaacademy.org. Website: www.orindaacademy.org

THE ORME SCHOOL

HC 63, Box 3040
1000
Mayer, Arizona 86333

Head of School: Mr. Bruce Sanborn

General Information Coeducational boarding and day college-preparatory, ESL, and horsemanship school; primarily serves individuals with Attention Deficit Disorder and dyslexic students. Grades 8–PG. Founded: 1929. Setting: rural. Nearest major city is Phoenix. Students are housed in single-sex dormitories. 360-acre campus. 30 buildings on campus. Approved or accredited by Arizona Association of Independent Schools, North Central Association of Colleges and Schools, The Association of Boarding Schools, and Arizona Department of Education. Member of National Association of Independent Schools and Secondary School Admission Test Board. Endowment: $2 million. Total enrollment: 75. Upper school average class size: 12. Upper school faculty-student ratio: 1:6. There are 179 required school days per year for Upper School students. Upper School students typically attend 5 days per week. The average school day consists of 7 hours.

Upper School Student Profile Grade 8: 9 students (3 boys, 6 girls); Grade 9: 14 students (7 boys, 7 girls); Grade 10: 16 students (8 boys, 8 girls); Grade 11: 39 students (19 boys, 20 girls); Grade 12: 41 students (24 boys, 17 girls); Postgraduate: 2 students (1 boy, 1 girl). 99% of students are boarding students. 25% are state residents. 10 states are represented in upper school student body. 40% are international students. International students from Brazil, China, Ethiopia, Germany, Italy, and Viet Nam; 14 other countries represented in student body.

Faculty School total: 20. In upper school: 10 men, 10 women; 15 have advanced degrees; all reside on campus.

Subjects Offered 3-dimensional art, ACT preparation, advanced biology, advanced chemistry, advanced math, Advanced Placement courses, advanced TOEFL/grammar, agriculture, algebra, American history, American history-AP, American literature, American literature-AP, ancient world history, art, art history, astronomy, band, biology, British literature (honors), calculus, calculus-AP, ceramics, chemistry, choir, college admission preparation, college counseling, college placement, college planning, community service, computer programming, computer resources, computer science, creative writing, culinary arts, drama, drama performance, ecology, English, English language and composition-AP, English language-AP, English literature, English literature and composition-AP, English literature-AP, environmental science, equine science, European history, European history-AP, fine arts, French, geography, geology, geometry, government, government-AP, grammar, graphic design, guitar, history, history of music, history-AP, honors English, honors U.S. history, humanities, instrumental music, Latin, mathematics, music, performing arts, photography, physics, physics-AP, psychology, science, social sciences, social studies, Spanish, statistics-AP,

student government, theater, trigonometry, U.S. history, U.S. history-AP, weightlifting, world cultures, world history, world literature, writing.

Graduation Requirements Advanced Placement courses, arts and fine arts (art, music, dance, drama), computer science, English, equine science, ESL, foreign language, humanities, mathematics, science, social sciences, social studies (includes history), students must participate annually in Caravan and the Fine Arts Festival. All students also take "sustainability". Community service is required.

Special Academic Programs 8 Advanced Placement exams for which test preparation is offered; independent study; ESL (10 students enrolled).

College Admission Counseling 18 students graduated in 2016; all went to college, including Arizona State University at the Tempe campus; Boston University; Carleton College; Cornell University; Dartmouth College; Northern Arizona University. Mean SAT critical reading: 513, mean SAT math: 586, mean SAT writing: 495, mean combined SAT: 1530, mean composite ACT: 21. 19% scored over 600 on SAT critical reading, 12% scored over 1800 on combined SAT, 9% scored over 26 on composite ACT.

Student Life Upper grades have specified standards of dress, honor system. Discipline rests equally with students and faculty.

Summer Programs Remediation, enrichment, advancement, ESL, sports, rigorous outdoor training programs offered; session focuses on enrichment; held both on and off campus; accepts boys and girls; open to students from other schools. 50 students usually enrolled. 2017 schedule: June 27 to July 25. Application deadline: June 1.

Tuition and Aid Day student tuition: $12,000; 5-day tuition and room/board: $46,000; 7-day tuition and room/board: $46,000. Tuition installment plan (individually arranged payment plans). Need-based scholarship grants available. In 2016–17, 60% of upper-school students received aid. Total amount of financial aid awarded in 2016–17: $1,200,000.

Admissions Traditional secondary-level entrance grade is 8. For fall 2016, 91 students applied for upper-level admission, 66 were accepted, 50 enrolled. ACT, PSAT and SAT for applicants to grade 11 and 12, SSAT, standardized test scores, TOEFL or SLEP or writing sample required. Deadline for receipt of application materials: none. No application fee required. On-campus interview recommended.

Athletics Interscholastic: baseball (boys), basketball (b,g), cross-country running (b,g), equestrian sports (b,g), football (b), pom squad (g), rodeo (b,g), running (b,g), softball (g), tennis (b,g), track and field (b,g), volleyball (g); intramural: aerobics/dance (g), fitness (b,g), physical training (b,g), rappelling (b,g), rock climbing (b,g), rodeo (b,g), strength & conditioning (b,g), wall climbing (b,g), weight lifting (b,g), weight training (b,g), wilderness (b,g), wilderness survival (b,g), wrestling (b); coed interscholastic: aquatics, dressage, equestrian sports, horseback riding, rodeo, soccer, swimming and diving; coed intramural: alpine skiing, aquatics, archery, backpacking, bicycling, billiards, canoeing/kayaking, climbing, fishing, fitness, fitness walking, fly fishing, freestyle skiing, Frisbee, hiking/backpacking, horseback riding, ice skating, life saving, marksmanship, mountain biking, mountaineering, nordic skiing, outdoor activities, outdoor adventure, outdoor recreation, outdoor skills, outdoors, paddle tennis, physical training, power lifting, rappelling, rock climbing, rodeo, ropes courses, skiing (cross-country), skiing (downhill), snowboarding, soccer, strength & conditioning, table tennis, tennis, ultimate Frisbee, volleyball, walking, wall climbing, weight lifting, weight training, wilderness, wilderness survival, yoga. 1 coach.

Computers Computers are regularly used in all academic classes. Computer network features include on-campus library services, Internet access, wireless campus network, Internet filtering or blocking technology. Campus intranet, student e-mail accounts, and computer access in designated common areas are available to students. Students grades are available online. The school has a published electronic and media policy.

Contact Mrs. Jessica Calmes, Associate Director of Advancement. 928-632-1564. Fax: 928-632-7605. E-mail: admissions@ormeschool.org.
Website: www.ormeschool.org

OUR LADY OF GOOD COUNSEL HIGH SCHOOL

17301 Old Vic Boulevard
Olney, Maryland 20832

Head of School: Dr. Paul G. Barker, EdD

General Information Coeducational day college-preparatory, arts, religious studies, technology, International Baccalaureate, and STEM program school, affiliated with Roman Catholic Church. Grades 9–12. Founded: 1958. Setting: suburban. Nearest major city is Washington, DC. 52-acre campus. 1 building on campus. Approved or accredited by Middle States Association of Colleges and Schools and Maryland Department of Education. Member of National Association of Independent Schools. Total enrollment: 1,240. Upper school average class size: 22. Upper school faculty-student ratio: 1:13. There are 185 required school days per year for Upper School students. Upper School students typically attend 5 days per week. The average school day consists of 6 hours and 45 minutes.

Upper School Student Profile Grade 9: 307 students (144 boys, 163 girls); Grade 10: 327 students (157 boys, 170 girls); Grade 11: 317 students (162 boys, 155 girls); Grade 12: 298 students (161 boys, 137 girls). 70% of students are Roman Catholic.

Faculty School total: 86. In upper school: 48 men, 38 women; 61 have advanced degrees.

Subjects Offered 20th century world history, accounting, algebra, American history, American history-AP, American literature, American literature-AP, art, art history, athletic training, Bible studies, biology, biology-AP, business law, business skills, calculus, calculus-AP, chemistry, chemistry-AP, choral music, college admission preparation, comparative government and politics-AP, composition-AP, computer applications, computer math, computer programming, computer science, creative writing, drama, economics, economics-AP, English, English literature, English literature and composition-AP, environmental science, ethics, European history, European history-AP, fine arts, French, French language-AP, general science, geometry, government/civics, health, health education, history, HTML design, International Baccalaureate courses, keyboarding, Latin, Latin American history, mathematics, music, music performance, physical education, physics, programming, psychology, religion, science, social sciences, social studies, Spanish, Spanish language-AP, speech, trigonometry, typing, world history, world literature.

Graduation Requirements All academic, service requirements for each grade.

Special Academic Programs International Baccalaureate program; 18 Advanced Placement exams for which test preparation is offered; honors section; academic accommodation for the gifted; remedial reading and/or remedial writing; programs in English, mathematics for dyslexic students; special instructional classes for students with learning disabilities (Ryken Program).

College Admission Counseling 282 students graduated in 2015; all went to college, including Towson University; University of Dayton; University of Maryland, College Park; University of South Carolina; University of Virginia; Virginia Polytechnic Institute and State University.

Student Life Upper grades have uniform requirement, student council, honor system. Discipline rests primarily with faculty. Attendance at religious services is required.

Tuition and Aid Day student tuition: $19,500. Tuition installment plan (FACTS Tuition Payment Plan). Merit scholarship grants, need-based scholarship grants available. In 2015–16, 25% of upper-school students received aid; total upper-school merit-scholarship money awarded: $500,000. Total amount of financial aid awarded in 2015–16: $2,000,000.

Admissions Traditional secondary-level entrance grade is 9. For fall 2015, 704 students applied for upper-level admission, 477 were accepted, 307 enrolled. High School Placement Test required. Deadline for receipt of application materials: December 11. Application fee required: $50. On-campus interview required.

Athletics Interscholastic: baseball (boys), basketball (b,g), cheering (g), cross-country running (b,g), dance squad (g), dance team (g), diving (b,g), dressage (g), equestrian sports (b,g), field hockey (g), football (b), indoor track & field (b,g), lacrosse (b,g), pom squad (g), rugby (b), soccer (b,g), softball (g), swimming and diving (b,g), tennis (b,g), track and field (b,g), volleyball (g); intramural: basketball (b,g), equestrian sports (g), softball (b); coed interscholastic: aquatics, golf, ice hockey, indoor track & field, winter (indoor) track, wrestling; coed intramural: aerobics, aerobics/dance, martial arts, physical training, skiing (downhill), strength & conditioning, weight training. 5 PE instructors, 73 coaches, 3 athletic trainers.

Computers Computers are regularly used in all academic classes. Computer network features include on-campus library services, online commercial services, Internet access, wireless campus network, Internet filtering or blocking technology. Student e-mail accounts are available to students. Students grades are available online. The school has a published electronic and media policy.

Contact Emmy McNamara, Assistant Director of Admissions. 240-283-3235. Fax: 240-283-3250. E-mail: admissions@olgchs.org. Website: www.olgchs.org

OUR LADY OF MERCY ACADEMY

1001 Main Road
Newfield, New Jersey 08344

Head of School: Sr. Grace Marie Scandale

General Information Girls' day college-preparatory, arts, business, religious studies, bilingual studies, and technology school, affiliated with Roman Catholic Church. Grades 9–12. Founded: 1962. Setting: rural. Nearest major city is Vineland. 58-acre campus. 2 buildings on campus. Approved or accredited by Middle States Association of Colleges and Schools and National Catholic Education Association. Endowment: $255,000. Total enrollment: 128. Upper school average class size: 20. Upper school faculty-student ratio: 1:11. There are 180 required school days per year for Upper School students. Upper School students typically attend 5 days per week. The average school day consists of 6 hours and 30 minutes.

Upper School Student Profile Grade 9: 44 students (44 girls); Grade 10: 28 students (28 girls); Grade 11: 20 students (20 girls); Grade 12: 35 students (35 girls); Postgraduate: 128 students (128 girls). 90% of students are Roman Catholic.

Faculty School total: 20. In upper school: 20 women; 10 have advanced degrees.

Subjects Offered Algebra, American history, American literature, art, biology, botany, British literature (honors), career and personal planning, Catholic belief and practice, chemistry, choral music, chorus, Christian ethics, Christian scripture, Christian testament, Christianity, college counseling, computer technologies, CPR, current events, death and loss, driver education, electronic publishing, English literature, first aid, food and nutrition, French, graphic design, honors algebra, honors geometry, Middle Eastern history, physics, pre-calculus, probability and statistics, psychology, publications, religion, social justice, sociology, technology, Western civilization.

Graduation Requirements Algebra, biology, chemistry, English, geometry, physical education (includes health), religion (includes Bible studies and theology), religious studies, technology, U.S. history, Western civilization.

Special Academic Programs 1 Advanced Placement exam for which test preparation is offered; honors section; study at local college for college credit.

College Admission Counseling 43 students graduated in 2015; 25 went to college, including Rutgers University–New Brunswick; Saint Joseph's University; Seton Hall University.

Student Life Upper grades have uniform requirement, student council, honor system. Discipline rests primarily with faculty. Attendance at religious services is required.

Tuition and Aid Day student tuition: $10,950. Tuition installment plan (SMART Tuition Payment Plan, monthly payment plans, individually arranged payment plans). Tuition reduction for siblings, merit scholarship grants, need-based scholarship grants, paying campus jobs available. In 2015–16, 15% of upper-school students received aid; total upper-school merit-scholarship money awarded: $34,500. Total amount of financial aid awarded in 2015–16: $35,000.

Admissions Traditional secondary-level entrance grade is 9. For fall 2015, 52 students applied for upper-level admission, 52 were accepted, 44 enrolled. High School Placement Test (closed version) from Scholastic Testing Service required. Deadline for receipt of application materials: none. Application fee required: $200.

Athletics Interscholastic: basketball, cheering, crew, lacrosse, soccer, softball, strength & conditioning, swimming and diving, tennis, track and field, volleyball; intramural: badminton, basketball, flag football, golf, gymnastics, physical fitness, soccer, softball, synchronized swimming, volleyball. 2 PE instructors, 12 coaches, 1 athletic trainer.

Computers Computers are regularly used in all academic, career exploration, college planning, creative writing, graphic design, graphics, library, library skills, photography, publications, research skills, technology, typing, Web site design, word processing, yearbook classes. Computer network features include on-campus library services, Internet access, wireless campus network, Internet filtering or blocking technology. Computer access in designated common areas is available to students. Students grades are available online. The school has a published electronic and media policy.

Contact Mrs. Natalie Cusick, Secretary. 856-697-2008 Ext. 120. Fax: 856-697-2887. E-mail: ncusick@olmanj.org. Website: www.olmanj.org

OUT-OF-DOOR-ACADEMY

5950 Deer Drive
Sarasota, Florida 34240

Head of School: Mr. David Mahler

General Information Coeducational day college-preparatory school. Grades PK–12. Founded: 1924. Setting: suburban. Nearest major city is Tampa. 85-acre campus. 10 buildings on campus. Approved or accredited by Florida Council of Independent Schools and National Independent Private Schools Association. Member of National Association of Independent Schools. Endowment: $16 million. Total enrollment: 723. Upper school average class size: 16. Upper school faculty-student ratio: 1:7. There are 172 required school days per year for Upper School students. Upper School students typically attend 5 days per week. The average school day consists of 7 hours.

Upper School Student Profile Grade 9: 83 students (50 boys, 33 girls); Grade 10: 68 students (34 boys, 34 girls); Grade 11: 77 students (43 boys, 34 girls); Grade 12: 46 students (22 boys, 24 girls).

Faculty School total: 88. In upper school: 13 men, 23 women; 20 have advanced degrees.

Subjects Offered Advanced Placement courses, advanced studio art-AP, algebra, American history-AP, art history, biology, biology-AP, British literature, calculus, calculus-AP, chemistry, chemistry-AP, college counseling, computers, drama, drama performance, dramatic arts, English, English composition, English language and composition-AP, English literature, English literature and composition-AP, English-AP, European history-AP, expository writing, French, French language-AP, geometry, graphic design, health and wellness, history-AP, honors algebra, honors geometry, Latin, Latin-AP, literature, literature and composition-AP, music, newspaper, photography, portfolio art, robotics, Spanish, Spanish language-AP, studio art, studio art-AP, U.S. government, U.S. history, U.S. history-AP, women's studies, world cultures, world literature, world studies, yearbook, zoology.

Graduation Requirements Arts and fine arts (art, music, dance, drama), electives, English, foreign language, health, history, mathematics, performing arts, personal fitness, science. Community service is required.

Special Academic Programs 21 Advanced Placement exams for which test preparation is offered; honors section; independent study.

College Admission Counseling 61 students graduated in 2015; 60 went to college, including Duke University; Florida State University; New York University; Rollins College; Stanford University; University of Florida. Mean SAT critical reading: 611, mean SAT math: 611, mean SAT writing: 612, mean combined SAT: 1222.

Student Life Upper grades have specified standards of dress, student council, honor system. Discipline rests equally with students and faculty.

Tuition and Aid Day student tuition: $19,700. Tuition installment plan (FACTS Tuition Payment Plan). Need-based scholarship grants, faculty/staff tuition remission available. In 2015–16, 30% of upper-school students received aid. Total amount of financial aid awarded in 2015–16: $1,133,313.

Admissions Traditional secondary-level entrance grade is 9. For fall 2015, 90 students applied for upper-level admission, 47 were accepted, 34 enrolled. ERB or SSAT required. Deadline for receipt of application materials: March 1. Application fee required: $100. Interview required.

Athletics Interscholastic: baseball (boys), basketball (b,g), cheering (g), cross-country running (b,g), football (b), golf (h,g), independent competitive sports (b,g), lacrosse (b,g), soccer (b,g), softball (g), swimming and diving (b,g), tennis (b,g), track and field (b,g), volleyball (g); intramural: fitness (b,g); coed interscholastic: sailing; coed intramural: physical fitness, physical training, strength & conditioning, weight training. 4 PE instructors, 35 coaches, 1 athletic trainer.

Computers Computers are regularly used in all academic, computer applications, English, foreign language, French, graphic design, history, Latin, mathematics, newspaper, science, senior seminar, social studies, Spanish, yearbook classes. Computer network features include on-campus library services, online commercial services, Internet access, wireless campus network, Internet filtering or blocking technology, digital video production. Campus intranet, student e-mail accounts, and computer access in designated common areas are available to students. Students grades are available online. The school has a published electronic and media policy.

Contact Mr. Michael Salmon, Director of Middle and Upper School Admissions. 941-554-5955. Fax: 941-907-1251. E-mail: msalmon@oda.edu. Website: www.oda.edu

THE OXFORD ACADEMY

1393 Boston Post Road
Westbrook, Connecticut 06498-0685

Head of School: Mr. Philip B. Cocchiola

General Information Boys' boarding college-preparatory, general academic, arts, bilingual studies, and ESL school; primarily serves students with learning disabilities and individuals with Attention Deficit Disorder. Grades 9–PG. Founded: 1906. Setting: small town. Nearest major city is New Haven. Students are housed in single-sex dormitories. 13-acre campus. 8 buildings on campus. Approved or accredited by Connecticut Association of Independent Schools, New England Association of Schools and Colleges, The Association of Boarding Schools, and Connecticut Department of Education. Member of National Association of Independent Schools and Secondary School Admission Test Board. Endowment: $250,000. Total enrollment: 45. Upper school average class size: 1. Upper school faculty-student ratio: 1:1. There are 150 required school days per year for Upper School students. Upper School students typically attend 5 days per week. The average school day consists of 7 hours.

Upper School Student Profile Grade 9: 3 students (3 boys); Grade 10: 10 students (10 boys); Grade 11: 17 students (17 boys); Grade 12: 14 students (14 boys); Grade 13: 1 student (1 boy). 100% of students are boarding students. 22% are state residents. 11 states are represented in upper school student body. 28% are international students. International students from China, Egypt, India, Rwanda, Saudi Arabia, and Turks and Caicos Islands; 1 other country represented in student body.

Faculty School total: 22. In upper school: 13 men, 7 women; 12 have advanced degrees; 11 reside on campus.

Subjects Offered Algebra, American history, American history-AP, American literature, anatomy, art, astronomy, biology, biology-AP, botany, calculus, calculus-AP, chemistry, chemistry-AP, creative writing, drawing, earth science, ecology, economics, English, English as a foreign language, English literature, English literature-AP, environmental science, ESL, European history, expository writing, French, geography, geology, geometry, government/civics, grammar, history, Latin, marine biology, mathematics, oceanography, paleontology, philosophy, physical education, physics, physiology, psychology, science, social studies, sociology, Spanish, study skills, trigonometry, world history, world literature, writing, zoology.

Graduation Requirements English, foreign language, mathematics, science, social studies (includes history). Community service is required.

Special Academic Programs Advanced Placement exam preparation; honors section; accelerated programs; independent study; academic accommodation for the gifted; remedial reading and/or remedial writing; remedial math; ESL (10 students enrolled).

College Admission Counseling 11 students graduated in 2015; all went to college. 20% scored over 600 on SAT critical reading, 20% scored over 600 on SAT math, 20% scored over 600 on SAT writing.

Student Life Upper grades have specified standards of dress, student council, honor system. Discipline rests equally with students and faculty.

Tuition and Aid 5-day tuition and room/board: $50,000; 7-day tuition and room/board: $58,600. Guaranteed tuition plan. Tuition installment plan (individually arranged payment plans). Tuition reduction for siblings, need-based scholarship grants available. In 2015–16, 17% of upper-school students received aid.

Admissions For fall 2015, 33 students applied for upper-level admission, 30 were accepted, 15 enrolled. English proficiency, psychoeducational evaluation, TOEFL, Wechsler Individual Achievement Test or WISC-III and Woodcock-Johnson required. Deadline for receipt of application materials: none. Application fee required: $65. Interview required.

Athletics Interscholastic: basketball, soccer, tennis; intramural: alpine skiing, badminton, baseball, basketball, bicycling, bowling, cross-country running, fishing, fitness, flag football, floor hockey, Frisbee, golf, hiking/backpacking, kickball, lacrosse, outdoor activities, paint ball, physical fitness, running, sailing, skiing (downhill), snowboarding, soccer, strength & conditioning, table tennis, tennis, ultimate Frisbee, weight lifting, weight training, whiffle ball.

Computers Computers are regularly used in mathematics classes. Computer network features include on-campus library services, online commercial services, Internet access, wireless campus network, Internet filtering or blocking technology. Student e-mail accounts and computer access in designated common areas are available to students. The school has a published electronic and media policy.

Contact Ms. Hilary L. Holmes, Assistant Director of Admissions. 860-399-6247 Ext. 100. Fax: 860-399-5555. E-mail: admissions@oxfordacademy.net. Website: www.oxfordacademy.net

PACE ACADEMY

966 West Paces Ferry Road NW
Atlanta, Georgia 30327

Head of School: Mr. Frederick G. Assaf

General Information Coeducational day college-preparatory and global leadership school. Grades K–12. Founded: 1958. Setting: suburban. 57-acre campus. 7 buildings on campus. Approved or accredited by Southern Association of Colleges and Schools and Southern Association of Independent Schools. Member of National Association of Independent Schools and Secondary School Admission Test Board. Endowment: $50.6 million. Total enrollment: 1,015. Upper school average class size: 12. Upper school faculty-student ratio: 1:7. There are 180 required school days per year for Upper School students. Upper School students typically attend 5 days per week. The average school day consists of 6 hours and 50 minutes.

Upper School Student Profile Grade 9: 118 students (63 boys, 55 girls); Grade 10: 121 students (60 boys, 61 girls); Grade 11: 115 students (57 boys, 58 girls); Grade 12: 105 students (55 boys, 50 girls).

Faculty School total: 178. In upper school: 32 men, 37 women; 53 have advanced degrees.

Subjects Offered Acting, adolescent issues, advanced math, advanced studio art-AP, algebra, American history, American history-AP, American literature, ancient world history, architectural drawing, art, art history, art history-AP, arts, band, biology, biology-AP, British literature, British literature (honors), calculus, calculus-AP, ceramics, chemistry, chemistry-AP, Chinese history, chorus, community service, comparative government and politics-AP, comparative politics, computer science-AP, computer skills, creative writing, debate, digital imaging, digital photography, directing, drawing, earth science, economics, English, English literature, English-AP, environmental science-AP, European history, fine arts, French, French language-AP, geometry, history, honors English, honors geometry, honors U.S. history, honors world history, Japanese history, keyboarding, Latin, Latin-AP, leadership education training, mathematics, modern European history-AP, music history, music theory-AP, painting, photography, physical education, physics, physics-AP, political science, pre-algebra, psychology, public speaking, religion, science, social sciences, Spanish, Spanish language-AP, stagecraft, statistics-AP, student publications, trigonometry, world history, world literature, yearbook.

Graduation Requirements Arts and fine arts (art, music, dance, drama), English, foreign language, mathematics, physical education (includes health), science, social sciences, social studies (includes history), 40 hours of community service, one semester of public speaking.

Special Academic Programs 17 Advanced Placement exams for which test preparation is offered; honors section; independent study; term-away projects; study abroad; academic accommodation for the gifted, the musically talented, and the artistically talented.

College Admission Counseling 108 students graduated in 2016; all went to college, including Auburn University; Elon University; Georgia Institute of Technology; The University of Alabama; University of Georgia; University of Pennsylvania. Mean combined SAT: 1282, mean composite ACT: 29.

Student Life Upper grades have specified standards of dress, student council, honor system. Discipline rests primarily with students.

Summer Programs Remediation, enrichment, advancement, sports, art/fine arts, computer instruction programs offered; session focuses on traditional day camp with specialty academic, activity, and athletic camps; held on campus; accepts boys and girls; open to students from other schools. 1,200 students usually enrolled. 2017 schedule: June 1 to July 30.

Tuition and Aid Day student tuition: $26,180. Tuition installment plan (FACTS Tuition Payment Plan). Need-based scholarship grants available. In 2016–17, 12% of upper-school students received aid.

Admissions Traditional secondary-level entrance grade is 9. SSAT required. Deadline for receipt of application materials: February 1. Application fee required: $95. Interview recommended.

Athletics Interscholastic: baseball (boys), basketball (b,g), cheering (g), cross-country running (b,g), diving (b,g), fitness (b,g), football (b), golf (b,g), gymnastics (g), lacrosse (b,g), soccer (b,g), softball (g), swimming and diving (b,g), tennis (b,g), track and field (b,g), volleyball (g), wrestling (b); intramural: squash (b), water polo (b); coed interscholastic: physical training, strength & conditioning; coed intramural: equestrian sports, flag football, mountain biking, ultimate Frisbee.

Computers Computers are regularly used in all classes. Computer network features include on-campus library services, online commercial services, Internet access, wireless campus network, Internet filtering or blocking technology, classroom SmartBoards and ActivBoards, student laptop/iPad loaner program. Campus intranet, student e-mail accounts, and computer access in designated common areas are available to students. Students grades are available online. The school has a published electronic and media policy.

Contact Mrs. Ashley Stafford, Admissions Database Manager. 404-240-7412. Fax: 404-240-9124. E-mail: ashley.stafford@paceacademy.org.

Website: www.paceacademy.org

PACE/BRANTLEY HALL HIGH SCHOOL

Longwood, Florida
See Special Needs Schools section.

PACIFIC CREST COMMUNITY SCHOOL

116 Northeast 29th Street
Portland, Oregon 97232

Head of School: Jenny Osborne

General Information Coeducational day college-preparatory and arts school. Grades 6–12. Founded: 1993. Setting: urban. 1 building on campus. Approved or accredited by Northwest Accreditation Commission, Northwest Association of Schools and Colleges, and Oregon Department of Education. Total enrollment: 95. Upper school average class size: 10. Upper school faculty-student ratio: 1:9. There are 180 required school days per year for Upper School students. Upper School students typically attend 5 days per week. The average school day consists of 6 hours.

Faculty School total: 14. In upper school: 6 men, 8 women; 11 have advanced degrees.

Subjects Offered Acting, advanced math, African drumming, algebra, American government, American history, American literature, animal behavior, anthropology, art history, Asian history, bioethics, botany, calculus, cell biology, chemistry, civil war history, comparative religion, computer applications, creative writing, cultural criticism, current events, drama, drawing, ecology, economics, English literature, entomology, ethics, European history, filmmaking, foreign language, geometry, government, health, history of mathematics, HTML design, Japanese studies, linear algebra, literature by women, logic, marine biology, medieval history, Pacific Island studies, personal finance, philosophy, physical education, physics, play/screen writing, pre-algebra, pre-calculus, printmaking, probability and statistics, psychology, public speaking, SAT preparation, science fiction, senior seminar, service learning/internship, set design, Shakespeare, short story, sociology, Spanish, stage design, theater arts, U.S. government, U.S. history, visual literacy, Web site design, women's literature, writing.

Graduation Requirements Senior seminar/dissertation.

Special Academic Programs Independent study; study at local college for college credit; academic accommodation for the gifted.

College Admission Counseling 16 students graduated in 2015; 13 went to college. Other: 3 had other specific plans.

Student Life Discipline rests equally with students and faculty.

Tuition and Aid Day student tuition: $13,000. Tuition installment plan (FACTS Tuition Payment Plan, monthly payment plans). Need-based scholarship grants available. In 2015–16, 15% of upper-school students received aid. Total amount of financial aid awarded in 2015–16: $60,000.

Admissions Traditional secondary-level entrance grade is 9. For fall 2015, 22 students applied for upper-level admission, 19 were accepted, 19 enrolled. Deadline for receipt of application materials: March 1. Application fee required: $100. Interview required.

Athletics Coed Intramural: basketball, bicycling, bowling, canoeing/kayaking, hiking/backpacking, outdoor adventure, outdoor education, outdoor skills, rock climbing, running, skiing (cross-country). 2 PE instructors.

Computers Computers are regularly used in all academic classes. Computer network features include Internet access, wireless campus network. Student e-mail accounts are available to students.

Contact Jenny Osborne, Director. 503-234-2826. Fax: 503-234-3186. E-mail: Jenny@pcrest.org. Website: www.pcrest.org

PACIFIC LUTHERAN HIGH SCHOOL

2814 Manhattan Beach Blvd.
Gardena, California 90249

Head of School: Mr. Lucas Michael Fitzgerald

General Information Coeducational day college-preparatory and general academic school, affiliated with Lutheran Church–Missouri Synod; primarily serves underachievers. Grades 9–12. Founded: 1997. Setting: suburban. Nearest major city is Los Angeles. 2-acre campus. 1 building on campus. Approved or accredited by Western Association of Schools and Colleges and California Department of Education. Upper school average class size: 15. Upper school faculty-student ratio: 1:10. There are 181 required school days per year for Upper School students. Upper School students typically attend 5 days per week. The average school day consists of 6 hours and 30 minutes.

Upper School Student Profile Grade 7: 13 students (6 boys, 7 girls); Grade 8: 5 students (2 boys, 3 girls); Grade 9: 16 students (9 boys, 7 girls); Grade 10: 22 students (12 boys, 10 girls); Grade 11: 28 students (16 boys, 12 girls); Grade 12: 23 students (10 boys, 13 girls). 15% of students are Lutheran Church–Missouri Synod.

Faculty School total: 14. In upper school: 8 men, 7 women; 6 have advanced degrees.

Subjects Offered 1 1/2 elective credits, 1968, 3-dimensional art, 3-dimensional design, accounting, ACT preparation, acting, addiction, ADL skills, advanced biology, advanced chemistry, advanced computer applications, advanced studio art-AP, advanced TOEFL/grammar, advertising design, aerobics, aerospace education, aerospace science, aesthetics, African American history, African American studies, African dance, African drumming, African history, African literature, African studies.

Graduation Requirements Students are required to take four years of theology courses.

Special Academic Programs International Baccalaureate program; Advanced Placement exam preparation; academic accommodation for the gifted; remedial reading and/or remedial writing; ESL (17 students enrolled).

College Admission Counseling 26 students graduated in 2016; 23 went to college. Other: 3 went to work.

Student Life Upper grades have specified standards of dress, student council, honor system. Discipline rests equally with students and faculty.

Summer Programs Remediation, enrichment, sports programs offered; session focuses on remedial and enrichment work in English and the sciences; held on campus; accepts boys and girls; open to students from other schools. 7 students usually enrolled. 2017 schedule: July 6 to August 21.

Tuition and Aid Day student tuition: $7000. Tuition installment plan (monthly payment plans, individually arranged payment plans). Tuition reduction for siblings, merit scholarship grants, need-based scholarship grants, middle-income loans, we work with families to arrange payment plans where/if necessary available. In 2016–17, 50% of upper-school students received aid; total upper-school merit-scholarship money awarded: $10,000. Total amount of financial aid awarded in 2016–17: $20,000.

Admissions Traditional secondary-level entrance grade is 9. Iowa Test of Educational Development required. Deadline for receipt of application materials: none. Application fee required: $50. Interview required.

Athletics Interscholastic: basketball (boys, girls), football (b), volleyball (b,g); coed interscholastic: baseball, cheering, cross-country running, golf, winter soccer; coed intramural: flag football, outdoor activities, outdoor education, outdoor recreation, ropes courses, strength & conditioning, touch football. 1 PE instructor, 4 coaches.

Computers Computer network features include Internet access, wireless campus network, Internet filtering or blocking technology. Students grades are available online.

Contact Mrs. Heidi Kerpan, Office Manager. 310-538-6863 Ext. 1000. Fax: 310-510-6761. E-mail: pacificlutheranhigh@gmail.com.

Website: www.pacificlutheranhigh.com/

THE PACKER COLLEGIATE INSTITUTE

170 Joralemon Street
Brooklyn, New York 11201

Head of School: Dr. Bruce L. Dennis

General Information Coeducational day college-preparatory school. Grades PK–12. Founded: 1845. Setting: urban. Nearest major city is New York. 5 buildings on campus. Approved or accredited by New York State Association of Independent Schools and New York Department of Education. Member of National Association of Independent Schools and Secondary School Admission Test Board. Endowment: $16 million. Total enrollment: 941. Upper school average class size: 15. Upper school faculty-student ratio: 1:7.

Upper School Student Profile Grade 9: 66 students (34 boys, 32 girls); Grade 10: 87 students (45 boys, 42 girls); Grade 11: 70 students (36 boys, 34 girls); Grade 12: 83 students (38 boys, 45 girls).

Faculty School total: 149. In upper school: 27 men, 42 women; 48 have advanced degrees.

Subjects Offered African literature, algebra, American history, American literature, art, art history, biology, calculus, chemistry, community service, computer math, computer programming, computer science, creative writing, dance, drama, English, English literature, ethics, European history, expository writing, fine arts, French, geometry, government/civics, health, history, Latin, music, philosophy, photography, physical education, physics, science, sociology, Spanish, theater, trigonometry, women's studies, world history, world literature.

Graduation Requirements Arts and fine arts (art, music, dance, drama), English, foreign language, mathematics, physical education (includes health), science, social studies (includes history). Community service is required.

Special Academic Programs Honors section; independent study; term-away projects; study at local college for college credit; study abroad.

College Admission Counseling 90 students graduated in 2016; all went to college, including Brown University; Skidmore College; Wesleyan College; Williams College; Yale University.

Student Life Upper grades have student council. Discipline rests equally with students and faculty.

Tuition and Aid Day student tuition: $40,000. Tuition installment plan (monthly payment plans). Need-based scholarship grants available. In 2016–17, 30% of upper-school students received aid. Total amount of financial aid awarded in 2016–17: $7,400,000.

Admissions Traditional secondary-level entrance grade is 9. For fall 2016, 400 students applied for upper-level admission, 80 were accepted, 35 enrolled. ISEE or

SSAT required. Deadline for receipt of application materials: December 1. Application fee required: $60. On-campus interview required.

Athletics Interscholastic: baseball (boys), basketball (b,g), cross-country running (b,g), dance (b,g). 10 PE instructors, 4 coaches, 2 athletic trainers.

Computers Computers are regularly used in mathematics, science, writing classes. Computer network features include on-campus library services, online commercial services, Internet access, laptop program (grades 6-12).

Contact Sara Goin, Admissions Coordinator. 718-250-0385. Fax: 718-875-1363. E-mail: sgoin@packer.edu. Website: www.packer.edu

PADUA ACADEMY

905 North Broom Street

Wilmington, Delaware 19806

Head of School: Mrs. Cindy Hayes Mann

General Information Girls' day college-preparatory, general academic, arts, business, religious studies, and technology school, affiliated with Roman Catholic Church. Grades 9–12. Founded: 1954. Setting: urban. 2 buildings on campus. Approved or accredited by Middle States Association of Colleges and Schools and Delaware Department of Education. Member of Secondary School Admission Test Board. Endowment: $1 million. Total enrollment: 600. Upper school average class size: 23. Upper school faculty-student ratio: 1:11. There are 180 required school days per year for Upper School students. Upper School students typically attend 5 days per week. The average school day consists of 5 hours and 50 minutes.

Upper School Student Profile Grade 9: 150 students (150 girls); Grade 10: 150 students (150 girls); Grade 11: 150 students (150 girls); Grade 12: 150 students (150 girls). 80% of students are Roman Catholic.

Faculty School total: 57. In upper school: 18 men, 39 women; 42 have advanced degrees.

Subjects Offered Advanced Placement courses, algebra, American history, American literature, anatomy, art, art history, biology, business, calculus, chemistry, computer programming, computer science, English, English literature, environmental science, European history, fine arts, French, geometry, government/civics, health, history, home economics, Italian, mathematics, physical education, physics, religion, science, social studies, Spanish, statistics, theology, trigonometry, world history, world literature.

Graduation Requirements Arts and fine arts (art, music, dance, drama), electives, English, foreign language, mathematics, physical education (includes health), religion (includes Bible studies and theology), science, social studies (includes history). Community service is required.

Special Academic Programs Advanced Placement exam preparation; honors section; study at local college for college credit.

College Admission Counseling 154 students graduated in 2015; 153 went to college, including Cabrini University; Saint Joseph's University; University of Delaware; West Chester University of Pennsylvania; Widener University. Other: 1 went to work. Mean SAT critical reading: 550, mean SAT math: 510, mean SAT writing: 550, mean combined SAT: 1610.

Student Life Upper grades have uniform requirement, student council, honor system. Discipline rests primarily with faculty. Attendance at religious services is required.

Tuition and Aid Day student tuition: $6797. Tuition installment plan (monthly payment plans). Tuition reduction for siblings, merit scholarship grants, need-based scholarship grants available. In 2015–16, 25% of upper-school students received aid; total upper-school merit-scholarship money awarded: $50,000. Total amount of financial aid awarded in 2015–16: $500,000.

Admissions Traditional secondary-level entrance grade is 9. For fall 2015, 250 students applied for upper-level admission, 180 were accepted, 154 enrolled. High School Placement Test (closed version) from Scholastic Testing Service required. Deadline for receipt of application materials: July 1. Application fee required: $100. On-campus interview recommended.

Athletics Interscholastic: aerobics/dance, basketball, cross-country running, dance squad, diving, field hockey, golf, indoor track, soccer, softball, swimming and diving, track and field, volleyball, winter (indoor) track; intramural: bowling, volleyball. 3 PE instructors, 10 coaches, 1 athletic trainer.

Computers Computers are regularly used in business studies, career exploration, Christian doctrine, college planning, desktop publishing, foreign language, health, library science, library skills, literary magazine, newspaper, psychology, religious studies, SAT preparation, social studies, yearbook classes. Computer network features include on-campus library services, Internet access, wireless campus network. Student e-mail accounts are available to students. Students grades are available online. The school has a published electronic and media policy.

Contact Ms. Shana L. Maguire, Director of Admission. 302-421-3765. Fax: 302-421-3763. E-mail: smaguire@paduaacademy.org. Website: www.paduaacademy.org

PADUA FRANCISCAN HIGH SCHOOL

6740 State Road

Parma, Ohio 44134-4598

Head of School: Mr. David Stec

General Information Coeducational day college-preparatory, arts, business, and MedTrack (advanced science & healthcare program) school, affiliated with Roman Catholic Church. Grades 9–12. Founded: 1961. Setting: suburban. Nearest major city is Cleveland. 34-acre campus. 1 building on campus. Approved or accredited by North Central Association of Colleges and Schools, Ohio Catholic Schools Accreditation Association (OCSAA), and Ohio Department of Education. Endowment: $3 million. Total enrollment: 773. Upper school average class size: 23. Upper school faculty-student ratio: 1:12. There are 179 required school days per year for Upper School students. Upper School students typically attend 5 days per week. The average school day consists of 6 hours and 30 minutes.

Upper School Student Profile Grade 9: 195 students (97 boys, 98 girls); Grade 10: 186 students (101 boys, 85 girls); Grade 11: 224 students (102 boys, 122 girls); Grade 12: 185 students (90 boys, 95 girls). 85% of students are Roman Catholic.

Faculty School total: 55. In upper school: 23 men, 34 women; 33 have advanced degrees.

Subjects Offered Accounting, algebra, American government, art appreciation, biology-AP, business, calculus-AP, chemistry, child development, Christian ethics, church history, computers, concert band, concert choir, consumer economics, current events, design, drawing, earth science, economics, English, English language-AP, ensembles, fitness, food and nutrition, French, French-AP, geography, geometry, German, German-AP, honors algebra, honors English, honors geometry, honors U.S. history, integrated science, interior design, Italian, Latin, Latin-AP, marching band, marketing, math analysis, music appreciation, music theory, orchestra, painting, photography, physics, pre-calculus, programming, psychology, social issues, social justice, sociology, Spanish, Spanish-AP, stagecraft, symphonic band, theater, trigonometry, U.S. history, U.S. history-AP, world cultures, world history.

Graduation Requirements Arts and fine arts (art, music, dance, drama), computer science, English, foreign language, lab science, mathematics, physical education (includes health), social studies (includes history), theology, four years of service projects.

Special Academic Programs Advanced Placement exam preparation; honors section; study at local college for college credit; remedial reading and/or remedial writing; remedial math; programs in English, mathematics for dyslexic students; special instructional classes for students with learning disabilities.

College Admission Counseling 183 students graduated in 2016; 179 went to college, including Cleveland State University; John Carroll University; Kent State University; Miami University; The University of Akron. Other: 3 went to work, 1 entered military service. Mean SAT critical reading: 510, mean SAT math: 533, mean SAT writing: 518, mean combined SAT: 1581, mean composite ACT: 23. 25% scored over 600 on SAT critical reading, 23% scored over 600 on SAT math, 28% scored over 600 on SAT writing, 37% scored over 26 on composite ACT.

Student Life Upper grades have uniform requirement, student council, honor system. Discipline rests primarily with faculty. Attendance at religious services is required.

Summer Programs Enrichment, sports, art/fine arts, computer instruction programs offered; session focuses on introducing students to school, programs, coaches, and other students; PE for credit; held on campus; accepts boys and girls; open to students from other schools. 175 students usually enrolled. 2017 schedule: June 8 to June 12. Application deadline: May 29.

Tuition and Aid Day student tuition: $9985. Tuition installment plan (monthly payment plans, individually arranged payment plans). Tuition reduction for siblings, merit scholarship grants, need-based scholarship grants, paying campus jobs, early payment discount, music scholarships available. In 2016–17, 45% of upper-school students received aid; total upper-school merit-scholarship money awarded: $415,000. Total amount of financial aid awarded in 2016–17: $540,000.

Admissions Traditional secondary-level entrance grade is 9. For fall 2016, 235 students applied for upper-level admission, 200 were accepted, 195 enrolled. High School Placement Test, STS or STS, Diocese Test required. Deadline for receipt of application materials: January 31. Application fee required: $50.

Athletics Interscholastic: aquatics (boys, girls), baseball (b), basketball (b,g), bowling (b,g), cheering (g), combined training (b,g), cross-country running (b,g), dance team (g), diving (b,g), football (b), golf (b,g), gymnastics (g), ice hockey (b), lacrosse (b), physical fitness (b,g), soccer (b,g), softball (g), strength & conditioning (b,g), swimming and diving (b,g), tennis (b,g), track and field (b,g), volleyball (g), wrestling (b); intramural: basketball (b), flag football (b), football (b), golf (g), power lifting (b), touch football (b), weight lifting (b), weight training (b,g), winter soccer (b), yoga (b); coed interscholastic: figure skating, fitness; coed intramural: alpine skiing, freestyle skiing, skiing (downhill), snowboarding, wilderness, wilderness survival, wildernessways. 3 PE instructors, 30 coaches, 5 athletic trainers.

Computers Computers are regularly used in all academic classes. Computer network features include on-campus library services, online commercial services, Internet access, wireless campus network, Internet filtering or blocking technology, all students received a Chromebook for 2016-17. Student e-mail accounts and computer access in designated common areas are available to students. Students grades are available online. The school has a published electronic and media policy.

Contact Mrs. Ann Marie Frattare, Admissions Coordinator. 440-845-2444 Ext. 184. Fax: 888-372-4033. E-mail: afrattare@paduafranciscan.com. Website: www.paduafranciscan.com

THE PAIDEIA SCHOOL

1509 Ponce de Leon Avenue
Atlanta, Georgia 30307

Head of School: Paul F. Bianchi

General Information Coeducational day college-preparatory, arts, technology, STEAM, including research internships at local universities, and urban agriculture school. Grades PK–12. Founded: 1971. Setting: urban. 28-acre campus. 13 buildings on campus. Approved or accredited by Georgia Independent School Association, Southern Association of Colleges and Schools, Southern Association of Independent Schools, and Georgia Department of Education. Member of National Association of Independent Schools. Endowment: $15.5 million. Total enrollment: 991. Upper school average class size: 14. Upper school faculty-student ratio: 1:9. There are 177 required school days per year for Upper School students. Upper School students typically attend 5 days per week. The average school day consists of 5 hours.

Upper School Student Profile Grade 9: 115 students (52 boys, 63 girls); Grade 10: 106 students (57 boys, 49 girls); Grade 11: 109 students (43 boys, 66 girls); Grade 12: 104 students (47 boys, 57 girls).

Faculty School total: 148. In upper school: 27 men, 41 women; 61 have advanced degrees.

Subjects Offered 20th century American writers, 20th century history, 3-dimensional art, 3-dimensional design, acting, advanced biology, advanced chemistry, advanced computer applications, advanced math, Advanced Placement courses, African drumming, African-American history, African-American literature, agriculture, algebra, American culture, American government, American literature, anatomy, anatomy and physiology, art, art history, Asian history, Asian studies, athletic training, auto mechanics, bioethics, biology, biology-AP, calculus, calculus-AP, ceramics, chemistry, chemistry-AP, chorus, community service, comparative religion, computer programming, computer science, creative writing, data analysis, digital art, digital photography, discrete mathematics, drama, drama performance, drama workshop, dramatic arts, drawing, ecology, environmental systems, economics, English, English literature, environmental science, ethics, expository writing, film, film and literature, film studies, filmmaking, fine arts, forensics, French, French studies, gardening, geography, geology, geometry, government/civics, health, health and wellness, history, humanities, jazz band, jewelry making, journalism, literary magazine, literature, mathematics, medieval history, music theory, Native American studies, newspaper, orchestra, peer counseling, photography, physical education, physics, physics-AP, play production, playwriting and directing, poetry, pre-calculus, psychology, Shakespeare, social studies, Spanish, Spanish literature, speech, stage design, statistics, statistics-AP, studio art, theater, theater arts, theater design and production, trigonometry, U.S. history, Web site design, weight training, women's health, women's studies, world civilizations, world history, world literature, writing, yearbook.

Graduation Requirements American history, arts and fine arts (art, music, dance, drama), English, ethics, foreign language, healthful living, mathematics, physical education (includes health), science, social studies (includes history), 60 hours of community service with local non-profit agency. Community service is required.

Special Academic Programs 6 Advanced Placement exams for which test preparation is offered; honors section; independent study.

College Admission Counseling 103 students graduated in 2016; 101 went to college, including Emory University; Georgia Institute of Technology; Georgia State University; Oberlin College; Tulane University; University of Georgia. Other: 1 went to work, 1 had other specific plans.

Student Life Upper grades have student council, honor system. Discipline rests equally with students and faculty.

Tuition and Aid Day student tuition: $23,214. Need-based scholarship grants, need-based tuition assistance available. In 2016–17, 22% of upper-school students received aid. Total amount of financial aid awarded in 2016–17: $1,481,011.

Admissions Traditional secondary-level entrance grade is 9. Deadline for receipt of application materials: February 1. Application fee required: $75. On-campus interview recommended.

Athletics Interscholastic: baseball (boys), basketball (b,g), cross-country running (b,g), diving (b,g), golf (b,g), soccer (b,g), softball (g), swimming and diving (b,g), tennis (b,g), track and field (b,g), ultimate Frisbee (b,g), volleyball (g); coed intramural: basketball, bicycling, bocce, flag football, horseshoes, kickball, running, soccer, softball, ultimate Frisbee, volleyball. 1 PE instructor, 15 coaches, 1 athletic trainer.

Computers Computers are regularly used in all classes. Computer network features include on-campus library services, online commercial services, Internet access, wireless campus network, Internet filtering or blocking technology, technology specialist program, computer borrowing program for students, all students have iPads. Campus intranet, student e-mail accounts, and computer access in designated common areas are available to students. The school has a published electronic and media policy.

Contact Becki Veal, Admissions assistant. 404-270-2312. Fax: 404-270-2666. E-mail: admissions@paideiaschool.org. Website: www.paideiaschool.org

PALMA SCHOOL

919 Iverson Street
Salinas, California 93901

Head of School: Br. Patrick D. Dunne, CFC

General Information Boys' day college-preparatory school, affiliated with Roman Catholic Church. Grades 7–12. Founded: 1951. Setting: suburban. 25-acre campus. 16 buildings on campus. Approved or accredited by Western Association of Schools and Colleges, Western Catholic Education Association, and California Department of Education. Endowment: $800,000. Total enrollment: 428. Upper school average class size: 25. Upper school faculty-student ratio: 1:15. Upper School students typically attend 5 days per week. The average school day consists of 6 hours.

Upper School Student Profile Grade 9: 109 students (109 boys); Grade 10: 79 students (79 boys); Grade 11: 81 students (81 boys); Grade 12: 84 students (84 boys). 69% of students are Roman Catholic.

Faculty School total: 28. In upper school: 23 men, 5 women; 19 have advanced degrees.

Subjects Offered Agriculture, algebra, American history, American literature, anatomy, art, art history, band, biology, biology-AP, business, calculus, calculus-AP, chemistry, Chinese, Christian and Hebrew scripture, church history, civics, community service, computer applications, computer art, computer math, computer multimedia, computer programming, computer programming-AP, computer science, computer-aided design, creative writing, debate, digital art, driver education, earth science, economics, English, English language and composition-AP, English language-AP, English literature, English literature and composition-AP, English literature-AP, English/composition-AP, ethics, European history, European history-AP, expository writing, film, film studies, fine arts, finite math, French, geography, geometry, government and politics-AP, government/civics, grammar, health, health education, history, honors algebra, honors geometry, jazz, jazz ensemble, journalism, Latin, mathematics, music, oceanography, participation in sports, physical education, physical science, physics, physics-AP, pre-algebra, pre-calculus, psychology, religion, SAT/ACT preparation, science, social studies, Spanish, Spanish language-AP, Spanish-AP, speech, statistics-AP, student government, studio art-AP, study skills, symphonic band, theology, trigonometry, typing, U.S. government and politics-AP, U.S. history-AP, United States government-AP, video film production, world history, world history-AP, world literature, world religions, world religions, writing, yearbook.

Graduation Requirements Advanced biology, arts and fine arts (art, music, dance, drama), chemistry, English, foreign language, mathematics, physical education (includes health), religion (includes Bible studies and theology), science, social studies (includes history), religious retreat (7th-12th grades), 60 hours of community service, must take the ACT College Entrance Exam.

Special Academic Programs Advanced Placement exam preparation; honors section; academic accommodation for the gifted; remedial reading and/or remedial writing; remedial math.

College Admission Counseling 97 students graduated in 2016; 96 went to college, including California Polytechnic State University, San Luis Obispo; California State University, Fresno; California State University, Monterey Bay; Saint Mary's College of California; Santa Clara University; University of California, Davis. Other: 1 went to work, 2 entered military service.

Student Life Upper grades have specified standards of dress, student council, honor system. Discipline rests primarily with faculty. Attendance at religious services is required.

Summer Programs Remediation, enrichment, advancement, sports, art/fine arts, rigorous outdoor training, computer instruction programs offered; session focuses on remediation, advancement, and enrichment; held on campus; accepts boys and girls; open to students from other schools. 150 students usually enrolled. 2017 schedule: June 12 to July 14. Application deadline: May 1.

Tuition and Aid Day student tuition: $14,000. Tuition installment plan (Insured Tuition Payment Plan, monthly payment plans, 2-payment plan). Merit scholarship grants, need-based scholarship grants available. In 2016–17, 15% of upper-school students received aid. Total amount of financial aid awarded in 2016–17: $700,000.

Admissions Traditional secondary-level entrance grade is 9. For fall 2016, 54 students applied for upper-level admission, 47 were accepted, 33 enrolled. ETS high school placement exam and ETS HSPT (closed) required. Deadline for receipt of application materials: none. Application fee required: $75. On-campus interview required.

Athletics Interscholastic: baseball, basketball, cross-country running, field hockey, football, golf, mountain biking, soccer, swimming and diving, tennis, track and field, volleyball, water polo, winter soccer, wrestling; intramural: basketball, bicycling, indoor soccer, kayaking, mountain biking, physical training, power lifting, skiing (downhill), snowboarding, strength & conditioning, ultimate Frisbee, weight lifting, weight training, whiffle ball. 5 PE instructors, 15 coaches, 1 athletic trainer.

Computers Computers are regularly used in art, economics, English, foreign language, history, mathematics, multimedia, music, newspaper, photography, science, social sciences, video film production, writing, yearbook classes. Computer network features include on-campus library services, online commercial services, Internet access, wireless campus network, Internet filtering or blocking technology. Campus intranet, student e-mail accounts, and computer access in designated common areas are available to students. Students grades are available online. The school has a published electronic and media policy.

Contact Mr. Raul Rico, Director of Admissions. 831-422-6391. Fax: 831-422-5065. E-mail: rico@palmahschool.org. Website: www.palmaschool.org

PALO ALTO PREPARATORY SCHOOL

2462 Wyandotte Street
Mountain View, California 94043

Head of School: Christopher Morley Keck

General Information Coeducational day and distance learning college-preparatory and arts school; primarily serves students with learning disabilities, individuals with Attention Deficit Disorder, individuals with emotional and behavioral problems, and dyslexic students. Grades 8–12. Distance learning grades 9–12. Founded: 1986. Setting: suburban. 1 building on campus. Approved or accredited by Western Association of Schools and Colleges and California Department of Education. Total enrollment: 75. Upper school average class size: 8. Upper school faculty-student ratio: 1:8. There are 180 required school days per year for Upper School students. Upper School students typically attend 5 days per week. The average school day consists of 6 hours.

Upper School Student Profile Grade 8: 2 students (2 boys); Grade 9: 16 students (11 boys, 5 girls); Grade 10: 19 students (13 boys, 6 girls); Grade 11: 14 students (9 boys, 5 girls); Grade 12: 24 students (16 boys, 8 girls).

Faculty School total: 14. In upper school: 7 men, 4 women; 5 have advanced degrees.

Subjects Offered 20th century world history, African American history, African American studies, algebra, American government, American history, American history-AP, American sign language, applied arts, applied music, art, ASB Leadership, biology, calculus, chemistry, chemistry-AP, civics, computer art, digital art, economics, English, English composition, English literature, environmental science, geometry, government, health, marine biology, modern civilization, music, music performance, pre-algebra, senior project, Spanish, study skills.

Graduation Requirements African American history, art, biology, economics, English, geometry, government, health, senior project, U.S. history, world civilizations.

Special Academic Programs 3 Advanced Placement exams for which test preparation is offered; honors section; accelerated programs; independent study; term-away projects; study at local college for college credit; study abroad; programs in English, mathematics for dyslexic students.

College Admission Counseling 15 students graduated in 2015; 13 went to college, including California Polytechnic State University; San Luis Obispo; California State University Channel Islands; Lewis & Clark College; The Evergreen State College; University of California, Davis; University of California, Santa Cruz. Other: 1 went to work, 1 had other specific plans.

Student Life Upper grades have specified standards of dress, student council, honor system. Discipline rests primarily with faculty.

Tuition and Aid Day student tuition: $27,500. Tuition installment plan (SMART Tuition Payment Plan). Need-based scholarship grants available. In 2015–16, 1% of upper-school students received aid.

Admissions Traditional secondary-level entrance grade is 9. Deadline for receipt of application materials: none. No application fee required. On-campus interview required.

Computers Computers are regularly used in all classes. Computer network features include Internet access, wireless campus network, Internet filtering or blocking technology. Campus intranet, student e-mail accounts, and computer access in designated common areas are available to students. Students grades are available online. The school has a published electronic and media policy.

Contact Lisa Olearn-Keck, Dean of Students. 650-493-7071 Ext. 102. Fax: 650-493-7073. E-mail: lisa@paloaltoprep.com. Website: www.paloaltoprep.com

PARADISE ADVENTIST ACADEMY

5699 Academy Drive
PO Box 2169
Paradise, California 95969

Head of School: Mr. Monte Nystrom

General Information Coeducational day college-preparatory school, affiliated with Seventh-day Adventists. Grades K–12. Founded: 1908. Setting: small town. Nearest major city is Sacramento. 12-acre campus. 6 buildings on campus. Approved or accredited by Board of Regents, General Conference of Seventh-day Adventists, Western Association of Schools and Colleges, and California Department of Education. Endowment: $200,000. Total enrollment: 143. Upper school average class size: 16. Upper school faculty-student ratio: 1:8. There are 180 required school days per year for Upper School students. Upper School students typically attend 5 days per week. The average school day consists of 8 hours and 5 minutes.

Upper School Student Profile Grade 6: 9 students (6 boys, 3 girls); Grade 7: 14 students (8 boys, 6 girls); Grade 8: 21 students (14 boys, 7 girls); Grade 9: 16 students (11 boys, 5 girls); Grade 10: 16 students (8 boys, 8 girls); Grade 11: 11 students (9 boys, 2 girls); Grade 12: 10 students (3 boys, 7 girls). 80% of students are Seventh-day Adventists.

Faculty School total: 15. In upper school: 7 men, 3 women; 3 have advanced degrees.

Subjects Offered 20th century world history, accounting, advanced biology, advanced computer applications, advanced math, algebra, American government,

American history, band, basketball, Bible, biology, career education, chemistry, choir, computer applications, computers, drama, earth science, English, geometry, health, keyboarding, military history, physical education, physical science, physics, pre-algebra, pre-calculus, Spanish, U.S. government, U.S. history, volleyball, weight training, weightlifting, world history, yearbook.

Graduation Requirements Advanced computer applications, algebra, American government, American history, arts and fine arts (art, music, dance, drama), Bible, biology, career and personal planning, career education, chemistry, computer literacy, electives, English, keyboarding, languages, life skills, physical education (includes health), physics, Spanish, world history, 25 hours of community service per year of attendance, 20 credits of fine arts, 10 credits of religion for each year of attendance.

Special Academic Programs Accelerated programs; independent study.

College Admission Counseling 14 students graduated in 2016; all went to college, including California State University, Chico; Pacific Union College; Walla Walla University. Median SAT critical reading: 640, median SAT math: 580, median SAT writing: 580, median combined SAT: 1790. 67% scored over 600 on SAT critical reading, 44% scored over 600 on SAT math, 44% scored over 600 on SAT writing, 29% scored over 1800 on combined SAT, 33% scored over 26 on composite ACT.

Student Life Upper grades have specified standards of dress, student council. Discipline rests primarily with faculty. Attendance at religious services is required.

Tuition and Aid Day student tuition: $7540–$9230. Tuition installment plan (monthly payment plans, individually arranged payment plans, full year or semester payments, 10 or 12 month plan, automatic bank withdrawal). Tuition reduction for siblings, merit scholarship grants, need-based scholarship grants, paying campus jobs available. In 2016–17, 25% of upper-school students received aid. Total amount of financial aid awarded in 2016–17: $30,000.

Admissions Traditional secondary-level entrance grade is 9. For fall 2016, 8 students applied for upper-level admission, 8 were accepted, 8 enrolled. 3-R Achievement Test, achievement tests, ACT, any standardized test, comprehensive educational evaluation, Iowa Test of Educational Development, Iowa Test, CTBS, or TAP, PSAT or SAT or TOEFL or SLEP required. Deadline for receipt of application materials: none. Application fee required: $50. Interview recommended.

Athletics Interscholastic: basketball (boys, girls), volleyball (g); coed interscholastic: soccer. 1 PE instructor, 4 coaches.

Computers Computers are regularly used in all academic, career education, career exploration, computer applications, creative writing, English, Web site design, word processing, yearbook classes. Computer network features include on-campus library services, Internet access, wireless campus network, Internet filtering or blocking technology. Campus intranet, student e-mail accounts, and computer access in designated common areas are available to students. Students grades are available online. The school has a published electronic and media policy.

Contact Mrs. Brenda Muth, Registrar. 530-877-6540 Ext. 3010. Fax: 530-877-0870. E-mail: bmuth@mypaa.net. Website: www.mypaa.net

THE PARK SCHOOL OF BALTIMORE

2425 Old Court Road
Baltimore, Maryland 21208

Head of School: Mr. Daniel Paradis

General Information Coeducational day college-preparatory school. Grades PK–12. Founded: 1912. Setting: suburban. 100-acre campus. 4 buildings on campus. Approved or accredited by Association of Independent Maryland Schools and Maryland Department of Education. Member of National Association of Independent Schools. Endowment: $35.0 million. Total enrollment: 788. Upper school average class size: 15. Upper school faculty-student ratio: 1:7. There are 173 required school days per year for Upper School students. Upper School students typically attend 5 days per week. The average school day consists of 7 hours.

Upper School Student Profile Grade 9: 83 students (42 boys, 41 girls); Grade 10: 93 students (48 boys, 45 girls); Grade 11: 86 students (42 boys, 44 girls); Grade 12: 82 students (43 boys, 39 girls).

Faculty School total: 116. In upper school: 28 men, 24 women; 42 have advanced degrees.

Subjects Offered 20th century world history, 3-dimensional art, acting, advanced chemistry, advanced math, African studies, anatomy, anatomy and physiology, animal behavior, anthropology, architectural drawing, art history, astronomy, audio visual/media, biochemistry, bioethics, DNA and culture, biology, British literature, calculus, ceramics, chemistry, Chinese, Chinese history, Chinese literature, choir, choral music, computer animation, computer programming, criminal justice, criminology, debate, design, digital art, digital music, digital photography, discrete mathematics, drama workshop, drawing, drawing and design, ecology, economics, economics and history, engineering, English, English composition, English literature, environmental science, equality and freedom, ethics, etymology, European history, film studies, filmmaking, forensics, French, French studies, functions, Greek drama, health education, human sexuality, illustration, independent study, Irish literature, Islamic studies, jazz ensemble, jewelry making, keyboarding, literature by women, madrigals, mathematics, Middle East, modern languages, modern world history, multicultural studies, music composition, music performance, musical theater, organic chemistry, painting, photography, physical education, physics, playwriting and directing, poetry, printmaking, publications, sculpture, senior project, set design, Shakespeare, social justice, Spanish, Spanish literature, statistics, studio art, theater, theater arts, U.S. history, visual and performing arts, vocal ensemble, Web site design, women in literature, woodworking, world religions, World War II, World-Wide-Web publishing, writing, writing workshop.

Graduation Requirements American history, art, English, foreign language, history, human sexuality, mathematics, modern languages, physical education (includes health), science, world history.

Special Academic Programs Advanced Placement exam preparation; independent study; term-away projects; study abroad; academic accommodation for the gifted, the musically talented, and the artistically talented.

College Admission Counseling 69 students graduated in 2016; all went to college, including Case Western Reserve University; Emory University; Johns Hopkins University; Lafayette College; University of Maryland, College Park; Washington University in St. Louis.

Student Life Upper grades have student council, honor system. Discipline rests equally with students and faculty.

Summer Programs Sports, art/fine arts, computer instruction programs offered; held both on and off campus; accepts boys and girls; open to students from other schools. 340 students usually enrolled. 2017 schedule: June 19 to August 4.

Tuition and Aid Day student tuition: $29,620. Tuition installment plan (The Tuition Plan, Insured Tuition Payment Plan, FACTS Tuition Payment Plan, monthly payment plans). Need-based scholarship grants available. In 2016–17, 32% of upper-school students received aid. Total amount of financial aid awarded in 2016–17: $2,084,995.

Admissions Traditional secondary-level entrance grade is 9. For fall 2016, 100 students applied for upper-level admission, 63 were accepted, 37 enrolled. ISEE, latest standardized score from previous school, OLSAT, Stanford Achievement Test, OLSAT/Stanford, Otis-Lennon School Ability Test/writing sample, Otis-Lennon, Stanford Achievement Test or Stanford Achievement Test, Otis-Lennon required. Deadline for receipt of application materials: January 1. Application fee required: $50. On-campus interview required.

Athletics Interscholastic: baseball (boys), basketball (b,g), cross-country running (b,g), field hockey (g), golf (b), indoor soccer (g), lacrosse (b,g), soccer (b,g), softball (g), tennis (b,g), winter soccer (g); coed interscholastic: squash; coed intramural: climbing, strength & conditioning, ultimate Frisbee, wall climbing, yoga. 3 PE instructors, 19 coaches, 1 athletic trainer.

Computers Computers are regularly used in art, computer applications, creative writing, desktop publishing, English, foreign language, French, graphic design, history, journalism, library skills, mathematics, media production, music, music technology, news writing, newspaper, photography, photojournalism, programming, publications, science, Spanish, theater, theater arts, video film production, woodworking, writing, writing, yearbook classes. Computer network features include on-campus library services, online commercial services, Internet access, wireless campus network, Internet filtering or blocking technology, access to course materials and assignments through school and faculty Web pages and wikis, discounted software purchase plan. Campus intranet, student e-mail accounts, and computer access in designated common areas are available to students. Students grades are available online. The school has a published electronic and media policy.

Contact Rachel Hockett, Administrative Assistant. 410-339-4130. Fax: 410-339-4127. E-mail: admission@parkschool.net. Website: www.parkschool.net

THE PARK SCHOOL OF BUFFALO

4625 Harlem Road
Snyder, New York 14226

Head of School: Christopher J. Lauricella

General Information Coeducational boarding and day college-preparatory, arts, and technology school. Boarding grades 9–12, day grades PK–12. Founded: 1912. Setting: suburban. Nearest major city is Buffalo. Students are housed in host families. 34-acre campus. 9 buildings on campus. Approved or accredited by New York Department of Education, New York State Association of Independent Schools, and New York Department of Education. Member of National Association of Independent Schools. Endowment: $2 million. Total enrollment: 298. Upper school average class size: 16. Upper school faculty-student ratio: 1:8. There are 167 required school days per year for Upper School students. Upper School students typically attend 5 days per week. The average school day consists of 7 hours.

Upper School Student Profile Grade 9: 35 students (19 boys, 16 girls); Grade 10: 33 students (20 boys, 13 girls); Grade 11: 31 students (12 boys, 19 girls); Grade 12: 27 students (9 boys, 18 girls).

Faculty School total: 42. In upper school: 14 men, 12 women; 20 have advanced degrees.

Subjects Offered Advanced Placement courses, advanced studio art-AP, African-American studies, algebra, American history, American history-AP, American literature, American literature-AP, anatomy and physiology, art, band, biology, biology-AP, calculus, calculus-AP, career/college preparation, ceramics, chemistry, choral music, chorus, clayworking, college admission preparation, college counseling, college writing, community service, computer applications, computer education, computer literacy, computer programming, computer skills, computer-aided design, concert choir, creative arts, creative thinking, critical thinking, critical writing, current events, drama, drama performance, dramatic arts, drawing, earth science, East Asian history,

economics, engineering, English, English literature, English/composition-AP, environmental science, environmental studies, ESL, experiential education, expository writing, film and literature, fine arts, foreign language, forensics, French, French language-AP, French studies, French-AP, freshman seminar, gardening, gender issues, geometry, government/civics, health, health education, history, history-AP, Holocaust and other genocides, honors English, honors geometry, honors U.S. history, honors world history, instrumental music, intro to computers, junior and senior seminars, language arts, literature and composition-AP, marine biology, media, media production, metalworking, music, music history, musical productions, orchestra, organic chemistry, outdoor education, performing arts, photography, physical education, physical fitness, physics, piano, pre-algebra, pre-calculus, probability and statistics, senior project, senior seminar, senior thesis, sophomore skills, Spanish, Spanish language-AP, Spanish-AP, statistics, studio art-AP, trigonometry, U.S. government and politics-AP, woodworking, world history, yearbook, yoga.

Graduation Requirements Arts and fine arts (art, music, dance, drama), computer science, English, foreign language, mathematics, physical education (includes health), science, senior project, senior thesis, social sciences, social studies (includes history). Community service is required.

Special Academic Programs Advanced Placement exam preparation; honors section; accelerated programs; independent study; study at local college for college credit; study abroad; academic accommodation for the gifted; ESL (10 students enrolled).

College Admission Counseling 35 students graduated in 2016; 31 went to college, including Nazareth College of Rochester; State University of New York at Fredonia; State University of New York College at Geneseo. Other: 2 went to work, 1 entered a postgraduate year, 1 had other specific plans. Median SAT critical reading: 550, median SAT math: 530, median SAT writing: 540, median combined SAT: 1620, median composite ACT: 22. 30% scored over 600 on SAT critical reading, 30% scored over 600 on SAT math, 23% scored over 600 on SAT writing, 20% scored over 1800 on combined SAT, 23% scored over 26 on composite ACT.

Student Life Upper grades have specified standards of dress, student council, honor system. Discipline rests equally with students and faculty.

Summer Programs Enrichment, advancement, ESL, sports, art/fine arts programs offered; session focuses on recreational day camp, basketball camps, soccer camp, ESL, summer scholars; held on campus; accepts boys and girls; open to students from other schools. 385 students usually enrolled. 2017 schedule: July 3 to August 25. Application deadline: February 24.

Tuition and Aid Day student tuition: $21,450–$22,530; 7-day tuition and room/board: $42,000. Tuition installment plan (Insured Tuition Payment Plan, FACTS Tuition Payment Plan, monthly payment plans). Tuition reduction for siblings, merit scholarship grants, need-based scholarship grants available. In 2016–17, 48% of upper-school students received aid; total upper-school merit-scholarship money awarded: $173,382. Total amount of financial aid awarded in 2016–17: $533,061.

Admissions Traditional secondary-level entrance grade is 9. For fall 2016, 52 students applied for upper-level admission, 47 were accepted, 35 enrolled. ERB Reading and Math, Otis-Lennon School Ability Test or TOEFL required. Deadline for receipt of application materials: none. Application fee required: $50. Interview required.

Athletics Interscholastic: basketball (boys, girls), bowling (b,g), golf (b), lacrosse (b), soccer (b,g), tennis (b,g); coed interscholastic: bowling, soccer; coed intramural: bicycling, cooperative games, cross-country running, fitness, flag football, floor hockey, Frisbee, hiking/backpacking, indoor soccer, outdoor activities, outdoor adventure, outdoor education, outdoor recreation, outdoor skills, outdoors, physical fitness, ropes courses, running, skiing (downhill), snowboarding, snowshoeing, soccer, strength & conditioning, weight lifting, weight training, winter walking, yoga. 2 PE instructors, 30 coaches.

Computers Computers are regularly used in business, career education, creative writing, current events, data processing, English, graphic arts, independent study, keyboarding, library skills, mathematics, media, media arts, media production, media services, music technology, newspaper, photography, science, technical drawing, technology, typing, Web site design, word processing, yearbook classes. Computer network features include on-campus library services, online commercial services, Internet access, wireless campus network, Internet filtering or blocking technology, Dragon Naturally Speaking. Campus intranet, student e-mail accounts, and computer access in designated common areas are available to students. Students grades are available online. The school has a published electronic and media policy.

Contact Marnie Cerrato, Director of Enrollment Management. 716-839-1242 Ext. 107. Fax: 716-408-9511. E-mail: mcerrato@theparkschool.org. Website: www.theparkschool.org

PARKVIEW ADVENTIST ACADEMY

6940 University Drive
Lacombe, Alberta T4L 2E7, Canada

Head of School: Ms. Angie Bishop

General Information Coeducational boarding and day college-preparatory, general academic, arts, vocational, religious studies, and technology school, affiliated with Seventh-day Adventist Church. Grades 10–12. Founded: 1907. Setting: small town. Nearest major city is Edmonton, Canada. Students are housed in single-sex by floor dormitories. 160-acre campus. 11 buildings on campus. Approved or accredited by

National Council for Private School Accreditation and Alberta Department of Education. Language of instruction: English. Endowment: CAN$10 million. Upper school average class size: 20. Upper school faculty-student ratio: 1:10. There are 188 required school days per year for Upper School students. Upper School students typically attend 5 days per week. The average school day consists of 5 hours and 50 minutes.

Upper School Student Profile Grade 10: 30 students (15 boys, 15 girls); Grade 11: 32 students (17 boys, 15 girls); Grade 12: 45 students (24 boys, 21 girls). 40% of students are boarding students. 70% are province residents. 4 provinces are represented in upper school student body. 1% are international students. International students from China and Rwanda; 3 other countries represented in student body. 80% of students are Seventh-day Adventists.

Faculty School total: 9. In upper school: 3 men, 6 women; 2 have advanced degrees; 1 resides on campus.

Subjects Offered Advanced math, art, arts, band, biology, career and technology systems, chemistry, choir, choral music, English, fine arts, foods, French, home economics, industrial arts, instrumental music, language arts, mathematics, mechanics, metalworking, music, photography, physical education, physics, religion, religious studies, science, social sciences, social studies, welding, woodworking.

Graduation Requirements Computer processing, keyboarding, physical education (includes health), word processing.

Special Academic Programs ESL.

College Admission Counseling 36 went to college. Other: 3 went to work.

Student Life Upper grades have specified standards of dress, student council, honor system. Discipline rests primarily with faculty. Attendance at religious services is required.

Tuition and Aid Day student tuition: CAN$7500; 7-day tuition and room/board: CAN$14,000. Tuition installment plan (monthly payment plans, individually arranged payment plans). Tuition reduction for siblings, merit scholarship grants available.

Admissions Traditional secondary-level entrance grade is 10. Deadline for receipt of application materials: none. Application fee required: CAN$20. Interview required.

Athletics Interscholastic: aquatics (boys), basketball (b,g), hockey (b), soccer (b), volleyball (b,g); intramural: basketball (b,g), football (b), softball (g), volleyball (b,g); coed interscholastic: baseball, basketball, soccer; coed intramural: baseball, basketball. 1 PE instructor, 3 coaches.

Computers Computer network features include on-campus library services, Internet access, wireless campus network, Internet filtering or blocking technology. Student e-mail accounts are available to students. Students grades are available online. The school has a published electronic and media policy.

Contact Mr. Rodney Jamieson, Vice Principal. 403-782-3381 Ext. 4111. Fax: 866-931-2652. E-mail: rjamieso@paa.ca. Website: http://www.paa.ca/

PARKVIEW BAPTIST SCHOOL

5750 Parkview Church Road
Baton Rouge, Louisiana 70816

Head of School: Ben D. Haindel

General Information Coeducational day college-preparatory school, affiliated with Baptist Church. Founded: 1981. Setting: urban. 21-acre campus. 2 buildings on campus. Approved or accredited by Southern Association of Colleges and Schools, Southern Association of Independent Schools, and Louisiana Department of Education. Member of National Association of Independent Schools and Secondary School Admission Test Board. Upper school average class size: 22. Upper school faculty-student ratio: 1:21. There are 175 required school days per year for Upper School students. The average school day consists of 8 hours.

Upper School Student Profile 30% of students are Baptist.

Faculty School total: 40. In upper school: 10 have advanced degrees.

Student Life Upper grades have uniform requirement, honor system. Discipline rests primarily with faculty. Attendance at religious services is required.

Tuition and Aid Day student tuition: $8960. Tuition installment plan (FACTS Tuition Payment Plan). Tuition reduction for siblings, need-based scholarship grants available.

Admissions ISEE required. Deadline for receipt of application materials: none. Application fee required: $150. Interview required.

Contact Cindy K. Harrison, Admissions Coordinator. 225-291-2500 Ext. 104. Fax: 225-293-4135. E-mail: admissions@Parkviewbaptist.com. Website: www.parkviewbaptist.com/

THE PATHWAY SCHOOL

Jeffersonville, Pennsylvania
See Special Needs Schools section.

PATTEN ACADEMY OF CHRISTIAN EDUCATION

2430 Coolidge Avenue
Oakland, California 94601

Head of School: Dr. Sharon Anderson

General Information Coeducational day college-preparatory, arts, religious studies, and bilingual studies school, affiliated with Christian faith. Grades K–12. Founded: 1944. Setting: urban. Nearest major city is San Francisco. 3 buildings on campus. Approved or accredited by Association of Christian Schools International, Western Association of Schools and Colleges, and California Department of Education. Total enrollment: 119. Upper school average class size: 14. Upper school faculty-student ratio: 1:8. There are 175 required school days per year for Upper School students. Upper School students typically attend 5 days per week. The average school day consists of 6 hours and 45 minutes.

Upper School Student Profile Grade 9: 12 students (3 boys, 9 girls); Grade 10: 17 students (7 boys, 10 girls); Grade 11: 12 students (9 boys, 3 girls); Grade 12: 13 students (7 boys, 6 girls). 14% of students are Christian faith.

Faculty School total: 16. In upper school: 6 men, 1 woman; 5 have advanced degrees.

Subjects Offered Algebra, American literature, band, Bible studies, biology, chemistry, choir, community service, computer science, economics, English, English literature, fine arts, geometry, health, instrumental music, introduction to literature, language arts, life skills, mathematics, music, physical education, physical science, physics, piano, pre-calculus, religion, science, sign language, social studies, Spanish, statistics, strings, U.S. government, U.S. history, vocal music, world geography, world history, world literature, writing.

Graduation Requirements Arts and fine arts (art, music, dance, drama), English, environmental science, foreign language, mathematics, science, social studies (includes history). Community service is required.

College Admission Counseling 7 students graduated in 2015; 5 went to college, including California State University, East Bay; University of California, Davis; University of California, Riverside. Other: 1 went to work, 1 had other specific plans.

Student Life Upper grades have uniform requirement, student council, honor system. Discipline rests primarily with faculty. Attendance at religious services is required.

Tuition and Aid Day student tuition: $5999. Tuition installment plan (monthly payment plans). Tuition reduction for siblings, need-based scholarship grants available. In 2015–16, 22% of upper-school students received aid. Total amount of financial aid awarded in 2015–16: $22,650.

Admissions Traditional secondary-level entrance grade is 9. For fall 2015, 13 students applied for upper-level admission, 13 were accepted, 13 enrolled. Deadline for receipt of application materials: none. Application fee required: $50. On-campus interview required.

Athletics Interscholastic: basketball (boys, girls), cross-country running (b), track and field (b,g), volleyball (b,g). 1 PE instructor.

Computers Computers are regularly used in all academic classes. Computer network features include Internet access.

Contact Mrs. Sharon Moncher, Coordinator. 510-533-3121. E-mail: smoncher@pattenceca.org. Website: pattenacademy.org

PEDDIE SCHOOL

201 South Main Street
Hightstown, New Jersey 08520

Head of School: Peter Quinn

General Information Coeducational boarding and day college-preparatory school. Grades 9–PG. Founded: 1864. Setting: small town. Nearest major city is Princeton. Students are housed in single-sex dormitories. 280-acre campus. 54 buildings on campus. Approved or accredited by Middle States Association of Colleges and Schools, New Jersey Association of Independent Schools, The Association of Boarding Schools, and New Jersey Department of Education. Member of National Association of Independent Schools and Secondary School Admission Test Board. Endowment: $326.7 million. Total enrollment: 542. Upper school average class size: 12. Upper school faculty-student ratio: 1:6. There are 180 required school days per year for Upper School students. Upper School students typically attend 6 days per week. The average school day consists of 7 hours.

Upper School Student Profile Grade 9: 106 students (56 boys, 50 girls); Grade 10: 138 students (73 boys, 65 girls); Grade 11: 144 students (78 boys, 66 girls); Grade 12: 141 students (61 boys, 80 girls); Postgraduate: 13 students (10 boys, 3 girls). 62% of students are boarding students. 29 states are represented in upper school student body. 17% are international students.

Faculty School total: 84. In upper school: 43 men, 36 women; 74 have advanced degrees; 72 reside on campus.

Subjects Offered Acting, African studies, algebra, American history, American literature, American studies, anatomy, architecture, art, art history, art history-AP, Asian studies, astronomy, Bible studies, biology, biology-AP, calculus, calculus-AP, chemistry, Chinese, comedy, comparative religion, computer programming, computer science, creative writing, debate, digital imaging, DNA, DNA science lab, drama, earth science, ecology, economics, English, English literature, environmental science, environmental science-AP, European history, European history-AP, expository writing, film history, fine arts, forensics, French, French language-AP, French literature-AP, geometry, global issues, global science, government/civics, health, history, information technology, Latin, Latin-AP, mathematics, Middle East, music, music theory-AP, neuroscience, philosophy, photography, physical education, physics, physics-AP, psychology, psychology-AP, robotics, science, Shakespeare, social studies, Spanish, Spanish language-AP, Spanish literature-AP, speech, statistics, statistics-AP, studio art-AP, theater, trigonometry, U.S. history, U.S. history-AP, video film production, world history, world literature, World War I, World War II, writing.

Graduation Requirements Arts and fine arts (art, music, dance, drama), computer science, English, foreign language, history, mathematics, physical education (includes health), science. Community service is required.

Special Academic Programs 18 Advanced Placement exams for which test preparation is offered; honors section; independent study; term-away projects; study abroad.

College Admission Counseling 140 students graduated in 2016; all went to college, including Carnegie Mellon University; Cornell University; Johns Hopkins University; New York University; The George Washington University; United States Naval Academy. Mean SAT critical reading: 616, mean SAT math: 646, mean SAT writing: 622, mean combined SAT: 1844, mean composite ACT: 27.

Student Life Upper grades have specified standards of dress, student council. Discipline rests primarily with faculty.

Summer Programs Enrichment, advancement, sports, art/fine arts, computer instruction programs offered; session focuses on enrichment; held on campus; accepts boys and girls; open to students from other schools. 175 students usually enrolled. 2017 schedule: June 29 to August 7. Application deadline: none.

Tuition and Aid Day student tuition: $47,000; 7-day tuition and room/board: $56,100. Tuition installment plan (Academic Management Services Plan, individually arranged payment plans). Merit scholarship grants, need-based scholarship grants, need-based loans available. In 2016–17, 36% of upper-school students received aid; total upper-school merit-scholarship money awarded: $70,000. Total amount of financial aid awarded in 2016–17: $7,000,000.

Admissions Traditional secondary-level entrance grade is 9. For fall 2016, 1,480 students applied for upper-level admission, 325 were accepted, 171 enrolled. ISEE or SSAT required. Deadline for receipt of application materials: January 15. Application fee required: $50. Interview required.

Athletics Interscholastic: aquatics (boys, girls), baseball (b), basketball (b,g), crew (b,g), cross-country running (b,g), field hockey (g), football (b), golf (b,g), indoor track & field (b,g), lacrosse (b,g), soccer (b,g), softball (g), swimming and diving (b,g), tennis (b,g), track and field (b,g), winter (indoor) track (b,g), wrestling (b); intramural: fitness (b,g), strength & conditioning (b,g), weight lifting (b,g), weight training (b,g), yoga (b,g); coed intramural: bicycling, dance, physical fitness, physical training, softball. 9 coaches, 3 athletic trainers.

Computers Computers are regularly used in all academic, English, foreign language, history, mathematics, science classes. Computer network features include on-campus library services, online commercial services, Internet access, wireless campus network, Internet filtering or blocking technology, NewsBank, Britannica, GaleNet, Electric Library. Student e-mail accounts are available to students. Students grades are available online. The school has a published electronic and media policy.

Contact Molly Dunne, Director of Admission and Financial Aid. 609-944-7501. Fax: 609-944-7901. E-mail: admission@peddie.org. Website: www.peddie.org

THE PEMBROKE HILL SCHOOL

400 West 51st Street
Kansas City, Missouri 64112

Head of School: Dr. Steven J. Bellis

General Information Coeducational day college-preparatory and arts school. Grades PS–12. Founded: 1910. Setting: urban. 36-acre campus. 8 buildings on campus. Approved or accredited by Independent Schools Association of the Central States, The College Board, and Missouri Department of Education. Member of National Association of Independent Schools. Endowment: $37.5 million. Total enrollment: 1,188. Upper school average class size: 15. Upper school faculty-student ratio: 1:11. Upper School students typically attend 5 days per week. The average school day consists of 7 hours.

Upper School Student Profile Grade 9: 111 students (73 boys, 38 girls); Grade 10: 109 students (64 boys, 45 girls); Grade 11: 109 students (60 boys, 49 girls); Grade 12: 107 students (47 boys, 60 girls).

Faculty School total: 129. In upper school: 25 men, 37 women; 42 have advanced degrees.

Subjects Offered Advanced Placement courses, advanced studio art-AP, algebra, American history, American literature, art, art history, biology, calculus, ceramics, chemistry, choir, computer programming, computer science-AP, creative writing, debate, drama, economics, electronic imagery, English, English literature, European history, fine arts, French, geometry, government/civics, independent study, journalism, Latin, mathematics, metalworking, microbiology, music, photography, physical education, physics, physiology, poetry, programming, psychology, science, social studies, Spanish, speech, statistics, theater, Web site design, world history, world literature, writing, yearbook.

Graduation Requirements Arts and fine arts (art, music, dance, drama), English, foreign language, mathematics, physical education (includes health), science, social studies (includes history). Community service is required.

Special Academic Programs Advanced Placement exam preparation; honors section; independent study; term-away projects; study abroad; academic accommodation for the gifted, the musically talented, and the artistically talented.

College Admission Counseling 92 students graduated in 2016; 91 went to college, including Dartmouth College; Southern Methodist University; The University of Kansas; University of Southern California; Yale University. Other: 1 had other specific plans. Mean SAT critical reading: 645, mean SAT math: 633, mean SAT writing: 648, mean composite ACT: 27. 81% scored over 600 on SAT critical reading, 67% scored over 600 on SAT math, 79% scored over 600 on SAT writing, 80% scored over 26 on composite ACT.

Student Life Upper grades have specified standards of dress, student council. Discipline rests primarily with faculty.

Summer Programs Enrichment, advancement, sports, art/fine arts, computer instruction programs offered; session focuses on enrichment; held on campus; accepts boys and girls; open to students from other schools. 1,075 students usually enrolled. 2017 schedule: June 5 to August 11. Application deadline: none.

Tuition and Aid Day student tuition: $15,375. Tuition installment plan (monthly payment plans, 2-payment plan, 1-payment plan). Merit scholarship grants, need-based scholarship grants, need-based loans available. In 2016–17, 18% of upper-school students received aid; total upper-school merit-scholarship money awarded: $23,500. Total amount of financial aid awarded in 2016–17: $466,410.

Admissions Traditional secondary-level entrance grade is 9. For fall 2016, 65 students applied for upper-level admission, 54 were accepted, 33 enrolled. ITBS achievement test and Otis-Lennon School Ability Test required. Deadline for receipt of application materials: January 14. Application fee required: $40. Interview required.

Athletics Interscholastic: baseball (boys), basketball (b,g), cheering (g), cross-country running (b,g), dance (g), dance team (g), diving (b,g), field hockey (g), football (b), golf (b,g), independent competitive sports (b,g), indoor track & field (b,g), soccer (b,g), swimming and diving (b,g), tennis (b,g), track and field (b,g), volleyball (g), wrestling (b); coed interscholastic: cheering. 4 PE instructors, 20 coaches, 1 athletic trainer.

Computers Computers are regularly used in all academic classes. Computer network features include on-campus library services, online commercial services, Internet access, Internet filtering or blocking technology. The school has a published electronic and media policy.

Contact Laura Linn, Director of Admissions and Financial Aid. 816-936-1230. Fax: 816-936-1238. E-mail: llinn@pembrokehill.org. Website: www.pembrokehill.org

PENINSULA CATHOLIC HIGH SCHOOL

600 Harpersville Road
Newport News, Virginia 23601-1813

Head of School: Mrs. Janine C. Franklin

General Information Coeducational day college-preparatory school, affiliated with Roman Catholic Church. Grades 8–12. Distance learning grades 8–12. Founded: 1903. Setting: suburban. Nearest major city is Newport News/Norfolk. 15-acre campus. 1 building on campus. Approved or accredited by National Catholic Education Association, Southern Association of Colleges and Schools, and Virginia Department of Education. Total enrollment: 305. Upper school average class size: 11. Upper school faculty-student ratio: 1:11. There are 183 required school days per year for Upper School students. Upper School students typically attend 5 days per week. The average school day consists of 7 hours.

Upper School Student Profile Grade 8: 26 students (12 boys, 14 girls); Grade 9: 101 students (48 boys, 53 girls); Grade 10: 66 students (25 boys, 41 girls); Grade 11: 79 students (39 boys, 40 girls); Grade 12: 66 students (28 boys, 38 girls). 68% of students are Roman Catholic.

Faculty School total: 29. In upper school: 10 men, 18 women; 20 have advanced degrees.

Subjects Offered 20th century American writers, 20th century history, 20th century world history, acting, advanced biology, advanced chemistry, advanced math, Advanced Placement courses, advanced studio art-AP, algebra, American Civil War, American foreign policy, American government, American history, American history-AP, American literature, American literature-AP, analysis and differential calculus, anatomy and physiology, applied arts, applied music, art, art-AP, athletic training, athletics, band, baseball, basketball, Bible as literature, Bible studies, biology, biology-AP, bowling, business, business applications, calculus, calculus-AP, campus ministry, career and personal planning, career/college preparation, ceramics, chaplaincy, chemistry, chemistry-AP, choir, Christian ethics, Christian testament, church history, civics, college admission preparation, college placement, college planning, college writing, concert band, CPR, digital photography, drama, driver education, earth science, economics, English, English as a foreign language, English composition, English language and composition-AP, English language-AP, English literature, English literature and composition-AP, English-AP, European history, European history-AP, fine arts, foreign language, forensics, French, geography, geology, geometry, German, government, government-AP, health education, history, history of the Catholic Church, history-AP, honors algebra, honors English, honors geometry, honors U.S. history, honors world history, keyboarding, macro/microeconomics-AP, marketing, mathematics-AP, microeconomics-AP, personal finance, photography, physical education, physics, physics-AP, play production, playwriting and directing, pre-calculus, psychology, public speaking, religion, SAT preparation, senior project, set design, Spanish, Spanish language-AP, speech and debate, stage design, statistics-AP, student government, studio art, studio art-AP, technical theater, tennis, theater, theater arts, theology, track and field, trigonometry, U.S. government, U.S. government and politics-AP, U.S. history, U.S. history-AP, video film production, volleyball, world history-AP, wrestling, writing, yearbook.

Graduation Requirements Arts and fine arts (art, music, dance, drama), English, foreign language, mathematics, physical education (includes health), religion (includes Bible studies and theology), science, social studies (includes history).

Special Academic Programs Advanced Placement exam preparation; honors section; independent study; academic accommodation for the gifted; programs in English, mathematics, general development for dyslexic students; ESL (8 students enrolled).

College Admission Counseling 66 students graduated in 2016; 65 went to college, including James Madison University; Old Dominion University; The College of William and Mary; University of Virginia; Virginia Commonwealth University; Virginia Polytechnic Institute and State University. Other: 1 went to work, 1 entered military service.

Student Life Upper grades have uniform requirement, student council, honor system. Discipline rests primarily with faculty. Attendance at religious services is required.

Tuition and Aid Day student tuition: $11,600. Tuition installment plan (FACTS Tuition Payment Plan). Tuition reduction for siblings, need-based scholarship grants, earned income tax credit scholarships, McMahon Pareter Scholarships, Named Scholarships available. In 2016–17, 25% of upper-school students received aid. Total amount of financial aid awarded in 2016–17: $378,000.

Admissions Traditional secondary-level entrance grade is 9. High School Placement Test (closed version) from Scholastic Testing Service or placement test required. Deadline for receipt of application materials: none. Application fee required: $100. Interview recommended.

Athletics Interscholastic: baseball (boys), basketball (b,g), cross-country running (b,g), soccer (b,g), softball (g), swimming and diving (b,g), tennis (b,g), track and field (b,g), volleyball (b,g), wrestling (b); coed interscholastic: cheering, golf; coed intramural: bowling. 2 PE instructors, 4 coaches, 1 athletic trainer.

Computers Computers are regularly used in journalism, programming, yearbook classes. Computer network features include on-campus library services, online commercial services, Internet access, wireless campus network, Internet filtering or blocking technology, 1:1 technology gives every student a Chromebook, Digital Learning Days, Google Apps for Education school. Campus intranet, student e-mail accounts, and computer access in designated common areas are available to students. Students grades are available online. The school has a published electronic and media policy.

Contact Mrs. Sharon Hyland, Enrollment Coordinator. 757-596-7247 Ext. 110. Fax: 757-591-9718. E-mail: shyland@peninsulacatholic.com.
Website: www.peninsulacatholic.com

THE PENNINGTON SCHOOL

112 West Delaware Avenue
Pennington, New Jersey 08534-1601

Head of School: Dr. William S. Hawkey

General Information Coeducational boarding and day college-preparatory, 20 AP classes, and certificate programs in applied science and global studies school, affiliated with Methodist Church; primarily serves students with learning disabilities and dyslexic students. Ungraded, ages 11–19. Founded: 1838. Setting: suburban. Nearest major city is Philadelphia, PA. Students are housed in coed dormitories. 54-acre campus. 17 buildings on campus. Approved or accredited by Middle States Association of Colleges and Schools, National Independent Private Schools Association, New Jersey Association of Independent Schools, The Association of Boarding Schools, The College Board, University Senate of United Methodist Church, and New Jersey Department of Education. Member of National Association of Independent Schools and Secondary School Admission Test Board. Endowment: $35 million. Total enrollment: 500. Upper school average class size: 12. Upper school faculty-student ratio: 1:6. There are 180 required school days per year for Upper School students. Upper School students typically attend 5 days per week. The average school day consists of 7 hours.

Upper School Student Profile Grade 9: 91 students (45 boys, 46 girls); Grade 10: 103 students (47 boys, 56 girls); Grade 11: 113 students (56 boys, 57 girls); Grade 12: 102 students (47 boys, 55 girls). 30% of students are boarding students. 85% are state residents. 7 states are represented in upper school student body. 12% are international students. International students from Brazil, China, Finland, Germany, Nigeria, and Republic of Korea; 24 other countries represented in student body. 5% of students are Methodist.

Faculty School total: 87. In upper school: 31 men, 38 women; 55 have advanced degrees; 50 reside on campus.

Subjects Offered Advanced studio art-AP, advanced TOEFL/grammar, African-American history, algebra, American history, American literature, anatomy, anatomy and physiology, art, bioethics, DNA and culture, biology, British literature-AP, calculus-AP, cheerleading, chemistry, chemistry-AP, Chinese, chorus, computer applications, computer skills, drama, economics, English, English literature, English literature-AP, English-AP, environmental science, ESL, fine arts, forensics, French, French language-AP, genetics, geometry, German, government and politics-AP, Greek, Greek culture, health, history-AP, honors algebra, honors English, honors geometry, honors U.S. history, jazz ensemble, Latin, macroeconomics-AP, music, music history, music theory, organic chemistry, photography, physics, physics-AP, pottery, pre-calculus, psychology, public speaking, religion, robotics, senior internship, Spanish, Spanish literature, Spanish-AP, stage design, stagecraft, technical theater, U.S. government and politics-AP, Web site design, weight training, world history, world history-AP.

Graduation Requirements Algebra, American history, arts and fine arts (art, music, dance, drama), athletics, biology, chemistry, computer education, English, foreign language, geometry, health education, public speaking, religion (includes Bible studies and theology), religion and culture, world history.

Special Academic Programs 20 Advanced Placement exams for which test preparation is offered; honors section; independent study; term-away projects; study at local college for college credit; study abroad; academic accommodation for the gifted; programs in English, mathematics, general development for dyslexic students; special instructional classes for students with LD enroll through our Cervone Center for Learning and receive individualized support; ESL (7 students enrolled).

College Admission Counseling 105 students graduated in 2016; 10 went to college, including Boston University; Lafayette College; Syracuse University; The George Washington University; University of California, San Diego; University of Chicago. Mean combined SAT: 1700, mean composite ACT: 27. 85% scored over 26 on composite ACT.

Student Life Upper grades have specified standards of dress, student council, honor system. Discipline rests primarily with faculty. Attendance at religious services is required.

Summer Programs Enrichment, sports, art/fine arts programs offered; session focuses on enrichment; held on campus; accepts boys and girls; open to students from other schools. 300 students usually enrolled. 2017 schedule: June 29 to August 6. Application deadline: none.

Tuition and Aid Day student tuition: $34,300–$36,300; 7-day tuition and room/board: $53,950. Tuition installment plan (monthly payment plans). Merit scholarship grants, need-based scholarship grants available. In 2016–17, 28% of upper-school students received aid; total upper-school merit-scholarship money awarded: $30,000. Total amount of financial aid awarded in 2016–17: $4,000,000.

Admissions Traditional secondary-level entrance grade is 9. For fall 2016, 721 students applied for upper-level admission, 272 were accepted, 127 enrolled. SSAT or TOEFL required. Deadline for receipt of application materials: February 1. Application fee required: $50. Interview recommended.

Athletics Interscholastic: baseball (boys), basketball (b,g), cheering (g), field hockey (g), flag football (b), football (b), ice hockey (b), softball (g); intramural: aquatics (b,g), bowling (b,g), coed interscholastic: cross-country running, golf, indoor track, lacrosse, soccer, swimming and diving, tennis, track and field, water polo, weight training, winter (indoor) track; coed intramural: badminton, bicycling, dance team, fitness, physical training, strength & conditioning, volleyball, weight training, winter soccer, yoga. 3 coaches, 2 athletic trainers.

Computers Computers are regularly used in art, college planning, computer applications, creative writing, current events, data processing, desktop publishing, drawing and design, economics, English, ESL, ethics, foreign language, French, graphic design, health, history, library, literary magazine, mathematics, music, newspaper, photography, psychology, religious studies, research skills, science, Spanish, technology, theater, video film production, word processing, writing, yearbook classes. Computer network features include on-campus library services, online commercial services, Internet access, wireless campus network, Internet filtering or blocking technology, one to one iPad program; iPads are issued to each student and are included in tuition. Campus intranet, student e-mail accounts, and computer access in designated common areas are available to students. Students grades are available online. The school has a published electronic and media policy.

Contact Ms. Lynn Zahn, Assistant Director of Admission and Financial Aid. 609-737-6128. Fax: 609-730-1405. E-mail: lzahn@pennington.org.
Website: www.pennington.org

PENSACOLA CATHOLIC HIGH SCHOOL

3043 West Scott Street
Pensacola, Florida 32505

Head of School: Sr. Kierstin Martin

General Information Coeducational day college-preparatory and technology school, affiliated with Roman Catholic Church. Grades 9–12. Founded: 1941. Setting: urban. 25-acre campus. 5 buildings on campus. Approved or accredited by Southern Association of Colleges and Schools. Total enrollment: 599. Upper school average class size: 25. Upper school faculty-student ratio: 1:18. There are 180 required school days per year for Upper School students. Upper School students typically attend 5 days per week. The average school day consists of 7 hours.

Upper School Student Profile Grade 9: 187 students (108 boys, 79 girls); Grade 10: 180 students (99 boys, 81 girls); Grade 11: 134 students (70 boys, 64 girls); Grade 12: 129 students (77 boys, 52 girls). 60% of students are Roman Catholic.

Faculty School total: 50. In upper school: 15 men, 35 women; 15 have advanced degrees.

Subjects Offered 20th century world history, advanced computer applications.

Graduation Requirements American literature, art, art appreciation, biology, computer literacy, English, four units of summer reading, health education, mathematics, music, personal fitness, physical education (includes health), religion (includes Bible studies and theology), science, social studies (includes history), sociology, U.S. history, world geography, students must have earned 26 credits in order to graduate, and many of those credits are specific to specific courses. Community service is required.

Special Academic Programs Advanced Placement exam preparation; honors section; independent study; study at local college for college credit; special instructional classes for deaf students, blind students.

College Admission Counseling 146 students graduated in 2016; 144 went to college, including Florida State University; Mississippi State University; Pensacola State College; The University of Alabama; University of Florida. Other: 2 entered military service. Mean SAT critical reading: 536, mean SAT math: 521, mean SAT writing: 526, mean combined SAT: 1583, mean composite ACT: 23.

Student Life Upper grades have specified standards of dress, student council. Discipline rests primarily with faculty. Attendance at religious services is required.

Summer Programs Remediation, enrichment programs offered; session focuses on religion courses, enrichment, and study skills; held both on and off campus; accepts boys and girls; not open to students from other schools. 20 students usually enrolled. 2017 schedule: June 1 to August 1. Application deadline: June 1.

Tuition and Aid Guaranteed tuition plan. Tuition installment plan (FACTS Tuition Payment Plan, individually arranged payment plans). Tuition reduction for siblings, need-based scholarship grants available.

Admissions Traditional secondary-level entrance grade is 9. Educational Development Series required. Deadline for receipt of application materials: none. Application fee required: $175. On-campus interview required.

Athletics Interscholastic: baseball (boys), basketball (b,g), cheering (b,g), cross-country running (b,g), dance squad (g), dance team (g), football (b), golf (b,g), lacrosse (b,g), soccer (b,g), softball (g), swimming and diving (b,g), tennis (b,g), track and field (b,g), volleyball (g), weight lifting (b); coed interscholastic: physical fitness.

Computers Computers are regularly used in all academic classes. Computer network features include on-campus library services, online commercial services, Internet access, wireless campus network, Internet filtering or blocking technology. Campus intranet, student e-mail accounts, and computer access in designated common areas are available to students. Students grades are available online. The school has a published electronic and media policy.

Contact Ms. Mary Kyte, Junior and Senior Advisor. 850-436-6400 Ext. 120. Fax: 850-436-6405. E-mail: mkyte@pensacolachs.org. Website: www.pensacolachs.org

PEOPLES CHRISTIAN ACADEMY

245 Renfrew Drive
Markham, Ontario L3R 6G3, Canada

Head of School: Mr. Alex Abdulnour

General Information Coeducational day college-preparatory school, affiliated with Evangelical faith. Grades JK–12. Founded: 1971. Setting: suburban. Nearest major city is Toronto, Canada. 5-acre campus. 1 building on campus. Approved or accredited by Association of Christian Schools International, Christian Schools International, Ontario Ministry of Education, and Ontario Department of Education. Language of instruction: English. Endowment: CAN$15,000. Total enrollment: 376. Upper school average class size: 20. Upper school faculty-student ratio: 1:10. There are 194 required school days per year for Upper School students. Upper School students typically attend 5 days per week. The average school day consists of 7 hours.

Upper School Student Profile Grade 9: 21 students (15 boys, 6 girls); Grade 10: 33 students (15 boys, 18 girls); Grade 11: 22 students (11 boys, 11 girls); Grade 12: 28 students (11 boys, 17 girls). 85% of students are members of Evangelical faith.

Faculty School total: 39. In upper school: 7 men, 10 women; 8 have advanced degrees.

Subjects Offered Accounting, Bible, biology, calculus, Canadian geography, Canadian history, Canadian law, careers, chemistry, civics, discrete mathematics, dramatic arts, economics, English, exercise science, family studies, French, functions, geography, geometry, health education, healthful living, ideas, information technology, instrumental music, journalism, keyboarding, literature, mathematics, media arts, organizational studies, philosophy, physical education, physics, psychology, science, sociology, visual arts, vocal music, world history, world religions, writing.

Graduation Requirements Arts, Canadian geography, Canadian history, careers, civics, English, French as a second language, mathematics, physical education (includes health), science, must complete Bible course curriculum for all grades.

Special Academic Programs Advanced Placement exam preparation; independent study.

College Admission Counseling 29 students graduated in 2016; 27 went to college, including McMaster University; The University of Western Ontario; University of Guelph; University of Toronto; Wilfrid Laurier University; York University. Other: 2 had other specific plans.

Student Life Upper grades have uniform requirement, student council, honor system. Discipline rests primarily with faculty. Attendance at religious services is required.

Tuition and Aid Day student tuition: CAN$7590–CAN$10,120. Tuition installment plan (monthly payment plans). Tuition reduction for siblings, bursaries, need-based scholarship grants, alumni scholarships, prepayment tuition reduction available. In 2016–17, 2% of upper-school students received aid. Total amount of financial aid awarded in 2016–17: CAN$30,000.

Admissions Traditional secondary-level entrance grade is 9. For fall 2016, 15 students applied for upper-level admission, 15 were accepted, 15 enrolled. CTBS (or similar from their school) required. Deadline for receipt of application materials: none. Application fee required: CAN$150. Interview recommended.

Athletics Interscholastic: badminton (boys, girls), baseball (b,g), basketball (b,g), cross-country running (b,g), Frisbee (b,g), running (b,g), track and field (b,g), ultimate Frisbee (b,g), volleyball (b,g); intramural: badminton (b,g), basketball (b,g), cross-country running (b,g), floor hockey (b,g), running (b,g), weight training (b,g); coed interscholastic: badminton, baseball, basketball, cross-country running, Frisbee, running, track and field, ultimate Frisbee; coed intramural: badminton, basketball, cross-country running, floor hockey, running, volleyball, weight training. 2 PE instructors.

Computers Computers are regularly used in business studies, drawing and design, graphics, information technology, introduction to technology, journalism, mathematics, yearbook classes. Computer network features include Internet access, Internet filtering or blocking technology. The school has a published electronic and media policy.

Contact Admissions. 416-733-2010 Ext. 204. Fax: 416-733-2011.
E-mail: admissions@pca.ca. Website: www.pca.ca

PERKINS SCHOOL FOR THE BLIND

Watertown, Massachusetts
See Special Needs Schools section.

PERKIOMEN SCHOOL

200 Seminary Street
Pennsburg, Pennsylvania 18073

Head of School: Mr. Mark A. Devey

General Information Coeducational boarding and day college-preparatory and entrepreneurism school. Grades 6–PG. Founded: 1875. Setting: small town. Nearest major city is Philadelphia. Students are housed in single-sex dormitories. 172-acre campus. 25 buildings on campus. Approved or accredited by Middle States Association of Colleges and Schools. Member of National Association of Independent Schools and Secondary School Admission Test Board. Endowment: $7 million. Total enrollment: 350. Upper school average class size: 11. Upper school faculty-student ratio: 1:7. There are 180 required school days per year for Upper School students. Upper School students typically attend 5 days per week. The average school day consists of 6 hours and 50 minutes.

Upper School Student Profile Grade 9: 56 students (36 boys, 20 girls); Grade 10: 89 students (52 boys, 37 girls); Grade 11: 78 students (47 boys, 31 girls); Grade 12: 79 students (48 boys, 31 girls); Postgraduate: 1 student (1 boy). 10 states are represented in upper school student body.

Subjects Offered All academic.

Graduation Requirements Arts and fine arts (art, music, dance, drama), computer studies, English, foreign language, mathematics, religion (includes Bible studies and theology), science, social studies (includes history). Community service is required.

Special Academic Programs Advanced Placement exam preparation; honors section; independent study; programs in English, mathematics for dyslexic students; ESL.

College Admission Counseling 85 students graduated in 2016; all went to college.

Student Life Upper grades have uniform requirement, student council, honor system. Discipline rests primarily with faculty.

Summer Programs Enrichment, ESL, sports, art/fine arts, computer instruction programs offered; held on campus; accepts boys and girls; open to students from other schools.

Tuition and Aid Day student tuition: $31,500; 7-day tuition and room/board: $55,400. Tuition installment plan (monthly payment plans). Merit scholarship grants, need-based scholarship grants available.

Admissions Traditional secondary-level entrance grade is 9. SSAT or TOEFL required. Deadline for receipt of application materials: February 1. Application fee required: $50. Interview recommended.

Athletics Interscholastic: baseball (boys), basketball (b,g), football (b), lacrosse (b,g), soccer (b,g), softball (g), tennis (b,g), volleyball (g); coed interscholastic: badminton, boxing, cross-country running, golf, strength & conditioning, track and field, winter (indoor) track; coed intramural: backpacking, dance, Frisbee, indoor soccer, table tennis.

Computers Computers are regularly used in all academic classes. Computer network features include on-campus library services, online commercial services, Internet access, wireless campus network, Internet filtering or blocking technology. Campus intranet, student e-mail accounts, and computer access in designated common areas are available to students. The school has a published electronic and media policy.

Contact Ms. Abby P. Moser, Director of Admissions and Financial Aid. 215-679-9511. Fax: 215-679-5202. E-mail: amoser@perkiomen.org.
Website: www.perkiomen.org

THE PHELPS SCHOOL

583 Sugartown Road
Malvern, Pennsylvania 19355

Head of School: Mr. Daniel E. Knopp

General Information Boys' boarding and day college-preparatory, Academic Support Program (ASP), and ESL program school. Grades 6–PG. Founded: 1946. Setting: suburban. Nearest major city is Philadelphia. Students are housed in single-sex dormitories. 70-acre campus. 18 buildings on campus. Approved or accredited by Middle States Association of Colleges and Schools, Pennsylvania Association of Independent Schools, and Pennsylvania Department of Education. Member of National Association of Independent Schools and Secondary School Admission Test Board. Endowment: $1.1 million. Total enrollment: 97. Upper school average class size: 7. Upper school faculty-student ratio: 1:4. There are 160 required school days per year for Upper School students. Upper School students typically attend 5 days per week. The average school day consists of 7 hours.

Upper School Student Profile Grade 6: 2 students (2 boys); Grade 7: 5 students (5 boys); Grade 8: 7 students (7 boys); Grade 9: 17 students (17 boys); Grade 10: 17 students (17 boys); Grade 11: 24 students (24 boys); Grade 12: 23 students (23 boys); Postgraduate: 3 students (3 boys). 81% of students are boarding students. 32% are state residents. 10 states are represented in upper school student body. 40% are international students. International students from China, Egypt, Saudi Arabia, South Africa, Spain, and Turkey; 12 other countries represented in student body.

Faculty School total: 23. In upper school: 12 men, 8 women; 9 have advanced degrees; 16 reside on campus.

Subjects Offered Advanced Placement courses, algebra, American government, American history, American literature, art, athletics, baseball, basketball, biology, biology-AP, bowling, British literature, calculus, calculus-AP, career/college preparation, chemistry, chemistry-AP, college admission preparation, college counseling, college planning, computer science, computer technologies, culinary arts, current events, earth science, English, English literature and composition-AP, English literature-AP, environmental science, environmental science-AP, ESL, ESL, ethics, film appreciation, finance, fitness, gardening, general math, general science, geography, geometry, golf, health, history, history-AP, information technology, learning strategies, life science, mathematics, music, participation in sports, personal finance, photography, physical education, physical science, physics, physics-AP, pre-algebra, pre-calculus, psychology, psychology-AP, public speaking, reading, reading/study skills, robotics, SAT preparation, science, sociology, Spanish, Spanish language-AP, Spanish-AP, sports, statistics, statistics-AP, student government, studio art, study skills, tennis, TOEFL preparation, U.S. government and politics-AP, U.S. history-AP, weight fitness, woodworking, world geography, world history, world history-AP, wrestling, writing, writing workshop, yearbook.

Graduation Requirements Electives, English, health, mathematics, physical education (includes health), science, social studies (includes history). Community service is required.

Special Academic Programs Advanced Placement exam preparation; independent study; academic accommodation for the gifted; remedial reading and/or remedial writing; remedial math; programs in English, mathematics, general development for dyslexic students; special instructional classes for Academic Support (ASP); ESL (24 students enrolled).

College Admission Counseling 30 students graduated in 2016; 28 went to college, including Drexel University; Ithaca College; Michigan State University; Penn State University Park; Saint Joseph's University; Temple University. Other: 1 went to work.

Student Life Upper grades have uniform requirement, student council, honor system. Discipline rests primarily with faculty.

Tuition and Aid Day student tuition: $26,700; 5-day tuition and room/board: $48,200; 7-day tuition and room/board: $48,200. Tuition installment plan (FACTS Tuition Payment Plan). Merit scholarship grants, need-based scholarship grants available. In 2016–17, 45% of upper-school students received aid. Total amount of financial aid awarded in 2016–17: $1,100,000.

Admissions Deadline for receipt of application materials: none. Application fee required: $50. Interview recommended.

Athletics Interscholastic: baseball, basketball, cross-country running, golf, lacrosse, soccer, tennis, wrestling; intramural: bowling, cooperative games, fitness, Frisbee, golf, indoor soccer, jump rope, outdoor activities, outdoor adventure, outdoor education, outdoor recreation, outdoor skills, paint ball, physical fitness, street hockey, strength & conditioning, table tennis, weight lifting, weight training, whiffle ball, winter soccer. 2 PE instructors, 16 coaches, 3 athletic trainers.

Computers Computers are regularly used in all academic classes. Computer network features include Internet access, wireless campus network, Internet filtering or blocking technology, all students are provided a Chromebook with the option to buy. Campus intranet, student e-mail accounts, and computer access in designated common areas are available to students. Students grades are available online. The school has a published electronic and media policy.

Contact Mrs. Lisa Ballard, Admissions Associate. 610-644-1754. Fax: 610-644-6679. E-mail: admis@thephelpsschool.org. Website: www.thephelpsschool.org

PHILADELPHIA-MONTGOMERY CHRISTIAN ACADEMY

35 Hillcrest Avenue
Erdenheim, Pennsylvania 19038

Head of School: Mr. Donald B. Beebe

General Information Coeducational day college-preparatory and Bible school. Grades K–12. Founded: 1943. Setting: suburban. Nearest major city is Philadelphia. 1-acre campus. 1 building on campus. Approved or accredited by Association of Christian Schools International, Christian Schools International, and Middle States Association of Colleges and Schools. Endowment: $150,205. Total enrollment: 252. Upper school average class size: 15. Upper school faculty-student ratio: 1:10. There are 178 required school days per year for Upper School students. Upper School students typically attend 5 days per week. The average school day consists of 6 hours and 50 minutes.

Upper School Student Profile Grade 9: 21 students (10 boys, 11 girls); Grade 10: 40 students (19 boys, 21 girls); Grade 11: 22 students (13 boys, 9 girls); Grade 12: 24 students (10 boys, 14 girls).

Faculty School total: 31. In upper school: 9 men, 6 women; 7 have advanced degrees.

Subjects Offered Algebra, American history, American literature, art, art history, biology, calculus, ceramics, chemistry, creative writing, drama, English, English literature, ethics, European history, fine arts, French, geography, geometry, German, government/civics, grammar, health, history, mathematics, music, physical education, physics, religion, science, social studies, sociology, Spanish, theater, trigonometry, typing, world history, writing.

Graduation Requirements American government, arts and fine arts (art, music, dance, drama), Bible, English, languages, mathematics, physical education (includes health), science, social studies (includes history), 4 years of Bible instruction are required to graduate if student attends from grades 9-12.

Special Academic Programs 4 Advanced Placement exams for which test preparation is offered; honors section; academic accommodation for the gifted, the musically talented, and the artistically talented; ESL (12 students enrolled).

College Admission Counseling 38 students graduated in 2016; 37 went to college, including Liberty University; Montgomery County Community College; Penn State University Park; Temple University; West Chester University of Pennsylvania. Other: 1 entered military service.

Student Life Upper grades have uniform requirement, student council. Discipline rests primarily with faculty.

Tuition and Aid Day student tuition: $14,085. Tuition installment plan (FACTS Tuition Payment Plan). Tuition reduction for siblings, need based scholarship grants available. In 2016–17, 100% of upper-school students received aid. Total amount of financial aid awarded in 2016–17: $650,000.

Admissions Traditional secondary-level entrance grade is 9. For fall 2016, 33 students applied for upper-level admission, 28 were accepted, 22 enrolled. Brigance Test of Basic Skills or Iowa Tests of Basic Skills required. Deadline for receipt of application materials: none. Application fee required: $100. On-campus interview recommended.

Athletics Interscholastic: baseball (boys), basketball (b,g), soccer (b,g), softball (b,g), tennis (g), track and field (b,g), wrestling (b); coed interscholastic: cross-country running; coed intramural: tennis. 2 PE instructors, 6 coaches, 2 athletic trainers.

Computers Computers are regularly used in art, Bible studies, Christian doctrine, creative writing, drawing and design, English, ESL, foreign language, graphic design, history, life skills, mathematics, music, religious studies, research skills, science, Spanish, theater, theater arts, theology, yearbook classes. Computer network features include on-campus library services, Internet access, wireless campus network, Internet filtering or blocking technology, online college search. Campus intranet, student e-mail accounts, and computer access in designated common areas are available to students. Students grades are available online. The school has a published electronic and media policy.

Contact Mr. Phil VanVeldhuizen, Admissions and Marketing Manager. 215-233-0782 Ext. 408. Fax: 215-233-0829. E-mail: admissions@phil-mont.com. Website: www.phil-mont.com

PHILLIPS ACADEMY (ANDOVER)

180 Main Street
Andover, Massachusetts 01810-4161

Head of School: John G. Palfrey Jr.

General Information Coeducational boarding and day college-preparatory school. Grades 9–PG. Founded: 1778. Setting: suburban. Nearest major city is Boston. Students are housed in single-sex dormitories and 9th graders housed separately from other students. 500-acre campus. 160 buildings on campus. Approved or accredited by New England Association of Schools and Colleges and The Association of Boarding Schools. Member of National Association of Independent Schools and Secondary School Admission Test Board. Endowment: $1 billion. Total enrollment: 1,131. Upper school average class size: 13. Upper school faculty-student ratio: 1:5. There are 154 required school days per year for Upper School students. Upper School students typically attend 5 days per week. The average school day consists of 7 hours.

Upper School Student Profile Grade 9: 228 students (110 boys, 118 girls); Grade 10: 300 students (150 boys, 150 girls); Grade 11: 284 students (139 boys, 145 girls);

Grade 12: 289 students (144 boys, 145 girls); Postgraduate: 30 students (20 boys, 10 girls). 74% of students are boarding students. 40% are state residents. 45 states are represented in upper school student body. 10% are international students. International students from Canada, China, Hong Kong, Republic of Korea, Thailand, and United Kingdom; 39 other countries represented in student body.

Faculty School total: 217. In upper school: 103 men, 114 women; 181 have advanced degrees; 185 reside on campus.

Subjects Offered Algebra, American history, American literature, ancient history, animal behavior, animation, architecture, art, art history, astronomy, band, Bible studies, biology, calculus, ceramics, chamber groups, chemistry, Chinese, chorus, computer graphics, computer programming, computer science, creative writing, dance, drama, drawing, ecology, economics, English, English literature, environmental science, ethics, European history, expository writing, film, fine arts, French, geology, geometry, German, government/civics, grammar, Greek, health, history, international relations, Japanese, jazz, Latin, Latin American studies, life issues, literature, mathematics, Middle Eastern history, music, mythology, oceanography, painting, philosophy, photography, physical education, physics, physiology, printmaking, psychology, religion, Russian, Russian studies, science, sculpture, social sciences, social studies, sociology, Spanish, speech, swimming, theater, trigonometry, video, world history, writing.

Graduation Requirements Arts and fine arts (art, music, dance, drama), English, foreign language, history, life issues, mathematics, philosophy, physical education (includes health), religion (includes Bible studies and theology), science, social sciences, swimming test.

Special Academic Programs Advanced Placement exam preparation; honors section; independent study; term-away projects; study abroad; academic accommodation for the gifted, the musically talented, and the artistically talented; programs in English, mathematics, general development for dyslexic students; special instructional classes for deaf students, blind students.

College Admission Counseling 328 students graduated in 2015; 324 went to college, including Boston College; Cornell University; Harvard University; Stanford University; University of Chicago; University of Pennsylvania. Other: 4 had other specific plans. Mean SAT critical reading: 703, mean SAT math: 714, mean SAT writing: 695.

Student Life Upper grades have student council, honor system. Discipline rests primarily with faculty.

Tuition and Aid Day student tuition: $39,100; 7-day tuition and room/board: $50,300. Tuition installment plan (individually arranged payment plans, The Andover Plan). Need-based scholarship grants available. In 2015–16, 47% of upper-school students received aid. Total amount of financial aid awarded in 2015–16: $20,195,000.

Admissions For fall 2015, 3,040 students applied for upper-level admission, 436 were accepted, 365 enrolled. ISEE or SSAT required. Deadline for receipt of application materials: February 1. Application fee required: $40. Interview required.

Athletics Interscholastic: baseball (boys), basketball (b,g), bicycling (b,g), crew (b,g), cross-country running (b,g), diving (b,g), field hockey (g), football (b), golf (b,g), ice hockey (b,g), indoor track & field (b,g), lacrosse (b,g), nordic skiing (b,g), skiing (cross-country) (b,g), soccer (b,g), softball (g), squash (b,g), swimming and diving (b,g), tennis (b,g), track and field (b,g), volleyball (b,g), water polo (b,g), winter (indoor) track (b,g); intramural: aerobics/dance (b,g), backpacking (b,g), basketball (b,g), crew (b,g), martial arts (b,g), physical fitness (b,g), physical training (b,g); coed interscholastic: bicycling, Frisbee, golf, ultimate Frisbee, wrestling; coed intramural: badminton, ballet, canoeing/kayaking, cheering, cross-country running, dance, fencing, fitness, fitness walking, hiking/backpacking, martial arts, modern dance, outdoor adventure, outdoor education, physical fitness, physical training, rappelling, rock climbing, ropes courses, soccer, softball, strength & conditioning, tennis, wall climbing. 7 PE instructors, 25 coaches, 3 athletic trainers.

Computers Computers are regularly used in animation, architecture, art, classics, computer applications, digital applications, English, foreign language, history, mathematics, music, photography, psychology, religious studies, science, theater, video film production classes. Computer network features include on-campus library services, online commercial services, Internet access, wireless campus network. Campus intranet and student e-mail accounts are available to students. Students grades are available online. The school has a published electronic and media policy.

Contact Jim Ventre, Dean of Admission and Director of Financial Aid. 978-749-4050. Fax: 978-749-4068. E-mail: admissions@andover.edu. Website: www.andover.edu

PHOENIX CHRISTIAN PREPARATORY SCHOOL

1751 West Indian School Road
Phoenix, Arizona 85015

Head of School: Mr. Joe Bradley

General Information Coeducational day college-preparatory, general academic, arts, religious studies, technology, and AP/honors school. Grades PS–12. Founded: 1949. Setting: urban. 22-acre campus. 10 buildings on campus. Approved or accredited by Association of Christian Schools International, North Central Association of Colleges and Schools, and Arizona Department of Education. Total enrollment: 385. Upper school average class size: 20. Upper school faculty-student ratio: 1:11. There are 179 required school days per year for Upper School students. Upper School students

typically attend 5 days per week. The average school day consists of 6 hours and 40 minutes.

Upper School Student Profile Grade 9: 54 students (29 boys, 25 girls); Grade 10: 50 students (24 boys, 26 girls); Grade 11: 61 students (37 boys, 24 girls); Grade 12: 49 students (23 boys, 26 girls).

Faculty School total: 30. In upper school: 12 men, 8 women; 16 have advanced degrees.

Subjects Offered Advanced computer applications, algebra, American literature, American literature-AP, anatomy, art, arts, band, Bible, biology, biology-AP, calculus, calculus-AP, career and personal planning, chemistry, choir, choral music, computer applications, computers, creative writing, drama, drama performance, drawing, economics, English, English literature, English literature-AP, English-AP, film studies, forensics, geometry, government, government-AP, Greek, instrumental music, instruments, integrated science, intro to computers, language-AP, literature, literature-AP, marching band, photography, physical education, physics, piano, pre-algebra, pre-calculus, psychology, religious education, sociology, Spanish, Spanish language-AP, sports medicine, statistics, student government, study skills, U.S. government, U.S. history, U.S. history-AP, Web site design, world history, world studies, yearbook.

Graduation Requirements Advanced math, Advanced Placement courses, algebra, American literature, arts and fine arts (art, music, dance, drama), biology, British literature, chemistry, computer education, economics, electives, English, English composition, English literature, foreign language, geometry, government, integrated science, mathematics, pre-calculus, religious studies, science, social studies (includes history), study skills, U.S. history, world history, world literature, a Bible class must be taken every semester while attending.

Special Academic Programs 7 Advanced Placement exams for which test preparation is offered; honors section; accelerated programs; independent study; study at local college for college credit; academic accommodation for the gifted; remedial reading and/or remedial writing; remedial math; ESL (20 students enrolled).

College Admission Counseling 53 students graduated in 2016; 50 went to college, including Arizona State University at the Tempe campus; Drexel University; Glendale Community College; Grand Canyon University; The University of Arizona; The University of Arizona. Other: 3 went to work. Mean SAT critical reading: 548, mean SAT math: 575, mean composite ACT: 24.

Student Life Upper grades have uniform requirement, student council, honor system. Discipline rests primarily with faculty.

Summer Programs Remediation, advancement, sports programs offered; session focuses on advance education, redemption, refine skills; held on campus; accepts boys and girls; open to students from other schools. 60 students usually enrolled. 2017 schedule: June 5 to July 15. Application deadline: May 15.

Tuition and Aid Day student tuition: $9643. Tuition installment plan (FACTS Tuition Payment Plan, monthly payment plans, individually arranged payment plans). Tuition reduction for siblings, need-based scholarship grants, allow families to use state tax credits available. In 2016–17, 75% of upper-school students received aid.

Admissions Traditional secondary-level entrance grade is 9. For fall 2016, 87 students applied for upper-level admission, 84 were accepted, 84 enrolled. Achievement tests, any standardized test or placement test required. Deadline for receipt of application materials: none. Application fee required: $100. On-campus interview recommended.

Athletics Interscholastic: baseball (boys), basketball (b,g), cheering (g), football (b), softball (g), volleyball (g), wrestling (b); intramural: flag football (g), volleyball (b); coed interscholastic: cross-country running, golf, soccer, tennis, track and field, winter soccer. 1 PE instructor, 25 coaches, 1 athletic trainer.

Computers Computers are regularly used in career exploration, college planning, computer applications, keyboarding, library, media services, Web site design, yearbook classes. Computer network features include on-campus library services, Internet access, wireless campus network, Internet filtering or blocking technology. Student e-mail accounts and computer access in designated common areas are available to students. Students grades are available online. The school has a published electronic and media policy.

Contact Mrs. Gretchen Janes, Admissions Director. 602-265-4707 Ext. 270. Fax: 602-277-7170. E-mail: gjanes@phoenixchristian.org. Website: www.phoenixchristian.org

PHOENIX COUNTRY DAY SCHOOL

3901 East Stanford Drive
Paradise Valley, Arizona 85253

Head of School: Mr. Andrew Rodin

General Information Coeducational day college-preparatory, performing and studio arts, extensive athletics, and community service, global citizenship, and travel school. Grades PK–12. Founded: 1961. Setting: suburban. Nearest major city is Phoenix. 40-acre campus. 9 buildings on campus. Approved or accredited by Independent Schools Association of the Southwest, National Independent Private Schools Association, and Arizona Department of Education. Member of National Association of Independent Schools. Endowment: $20 million. Total enrollment: 750. Upper school average class size: 15. Upper school faculty-student ratio: 1:8. There are 173 required school days per year for Upper School students. Upper School students typically attend 5 days per week. The average school day consists of 5 hours.

Faculty School total: 110. In upper school: 17 men, 13 women; 26 have advanced degrees.

Subjects Offered Acting, advanced biology, advanced chemistry, advanced math, Advanced Placement courses, African-American literature, algebra, American government, American history, American history-AP, American literature, anatomy, anatomy and physiology, anthropology, art, art history, art history-AP, astronomy, band, baseball, basketball, biology, biology-AP, British literature, calculus, calculus-AP, ceramics, chemistry, chemistry-AP, Chinese, Chinese studies, choir, chorus, computer programming, computer science, creative writing, digital photography, directing, discrete mathematics, drawing, ecology, English, English composition, English literature, environmental science, environmental science-AP, ethics, European history, evolution, fine arts, French, French-AP, geography, geology, geometry, government/civics, history, Holocaust studies, jazz band, journalism, Latin, Latin American literature, Latin-AP, literature, Mandarin, marine biology, mathematics, music, oceanography, orchestra, painting, photography, physical education, physics, physics-AP, physiology, pre-calculus, probability and statistics, psychology, scene study, science, Shakespeare, social sciences, social studies, Spanish, Spanish-AP, speech, statistics, statistics-AP, theater, theater arts, trigonometry, world history, world literature, world religions.

Graduation Requirements Advanced biology, American history, American literature, ancient world history, arts and fine arts (art, music, dance, drama), biology, chemistry, English, foreign language, mathematics, physical education (includes health), physics, science, U.S. history, Western civilization, world history, 40 hours of community service.

Special Academic Programs 15 Advanced Placement exams for which test preparation is offered; honors section; independent study; study abroad.

College Admission Counseling 63 students graduated in 2016; all went to college, including Arizona State University at the Tempe campus; Harvard University; Massachusetts Institute of Technology; New York University; Southern Methodist University; University of Southern California. Median SAT critical reading: 670, median SAT math: 680, median SAT writing: 690, median combined SAT: 2010, median composite ACT: 29. 77% scored over 600 on SAT critical reading, 86% scored over 600 on SAT math, 86% scored over 600 on SAT writing, 86% scored over 1800 on combined SAT, 78% scored over 26 on composite ACT.

Student Life Upper grades have specified standards of dress, student council, honor system. Discipline rests primarily with faculty.

Summer Programs Enrichment, advancement, sports, art/fine arts, computer instruction programs offered; session focuses on academics/sports camp/arts program; held on campus; accepts boys and girls; open to students from other schools. 500 students usually enrolled. 2017 schedule: June 4 to July 13. Application deadline: none.

Tuition and Aid Day student tuition: $24,000. Tuition installment plan (Insured Tuition Payment Plan, monthly payment plans, individually arranged payment plans, 10 months, quarterly, semiannual, and yearly payment plans). Need-based scholarship grants available. In 2016–17, 21% of upper-school students received aid. Total amount of financial aid awarded in 2016–17: $1,016,600.

Admissions Traditional secondary-level entrance grade is 9. For fall 2016, 90 students applied for upper-level admission, 30 were accepted, 18 enrolled. Achievement/Aptitude/Writing, ERB CTP IV, Math Placement Exam, Otis-Lennon IQ or writing sample required. Deadline for receipt of application materials: February 1. Application fee required: $75. Interview required.

Athletics Interscholastic: aquatics (boys, girls), baseball (b), basketball (b,g), cheering (g), cross-country running (b,g), dance squad (b,g), diving (b,g), flag football (b), golf (b,g), lacrosse (b,g), soccer (b,g), softball (g), winter soccer (g); intramural: archery (b,g), badminton (b,g), basketball (b,g), cross-country running (b,g), lacrosse (b,g), outdoor activities (b,g), outdoor adventure (b,g), outdoor education (b,g), outdoor recreation (b,g), physical fitness (b,g), softball (g), strength & conditioning (b,g), yoga (b,g); coed interscholastic: cheering, diving, swimming and diving, tennis, volleyball; coed intramural: basketball, climbing, cross-country running, dance, flag football, golf, hiking/backpacking, running, soccer, swimming and diving, tennis, volleyball, weight lifting, winter soccer. 5 PE instructors, 23 coaches, 1 athletic trainer.

Computers Computers are regularly used in art, college planning, creative writing, data processing, desktop publishing, economics, engineering, English, foreign language, French, history, humanities, independent study, information technology, keyboarding, library, library skills, literary magazine, mathematics, news writing, newspaper, photography, programming, publications, research skills, science, social sciences, social studies, Spanish, stock market, Web site design, writing, yearbook classes. Computer network features include on-campus library services, online commercial services, Internet access, wireless campus network, Internet filtering or blocking technology. Campus intranet, student e-mail accounts, and computer access in designated common areas are available to students. Students grades are available online. The school has a published electronic and media policy.

Contact Kaitlan Cady, Admissions Counselor. 602-955-8200 Ext. 2255. Fax: 602-381-4554. E-mail: kaitlan.cady@pcds.org. Website: www.pcds.org

PICKENS ACADEMY

225 Ray Bass Road
Carrollton, Alabama 35447

Head of School: Mr. Brach White

General Information Coeducational day college-preparatory, general academic, and technology school. Grades K4–12. Founded: 1970. Setting: rural. Nearest major city is Tuscaloosa. 3 buildings on campus. Approved or accredited by Southern Association of Colleges and Schools, distance education, and Alabama Department of Education. Total enrollment: 267. Upper school average class size: 25. Upper school faculty-student ratio: 1:20. There are 180 required school days per year for Upper School students. Upper School students typically attend 5 days per week. The average school day consists of 7 hours.

Upper School Student Profile Grade 7: 25 students (11 boys, 14 girls); Grade 8: 28 students (11 boys, 17 girls); Grade 9: 15 students (7 boys, 8 girls); Grade 10: 26 students (13 boys, 13 girls); Grade 11: 19 students (7 boys, 12 girls); Grade 12: 34 students (15 boys, 19 girls).

Faculty School total: 21. In upper school: 5 men, 16 women; 8 have advanced degrees.

Subjects Offered 20th century history, 20th century world history, advanced chemistry, advanced computer applications, advanced math, Alabama history and geography, algebra, American democracy, American government, American history, American literature, anatomy and physiology, ancient history, ancient world history, applied music, art, band, baseball, basketball, biology, British literature, business mathematics, calculus, career/college preparation, cheerleading, chemistry, civics, college admission preparation, composition, computer literacy, consumer economics, CPR, creative writing, desktop publishing, economics, English composition, English literature, environmental science, family and consumer science, French, geography, government, grammar, health education, history, keyboarding, land management, leadership education training, library assistant, Microsoft, music, music appreciation, physical education, physical science, physics, research skills, science, student government, trigonometry, U.S. government and politics, Web site design, weight training, weightlifting.

Graduation Requirements 20th century world history, advanced math, American government, American history, anatomy and physiology, calculus, economics, English, English composition, English literature, physics, research skills, trigonometry.

Special Academic Programs Study at local college for college credit.

College Admission Counseling 24 students graduated in 2015; 17 went to college, including Auburn University; Mississippi State University; The University of Alabama. Other: 1 went to work, 1 entered military service. Median composite ACT: 21. 4% scored over 26 on composite ACT.

Student Life Upper grades have specified standards of dress, student council. Discipline rests primarily with faculty.

Tuition and Aid Day student tuition: $3000. Guaranteed tuition plan. Tuition installment plan (Insured Tuition Payment Plan, monthly payment plans).

Admissions Traditional secondary-level entrance grade is 9. PSAT or Stanford Achievement Test, Otis-Lennon School Ability Test required. Deadline for receipt of application materials: none. No application fee required. On-campus interview required.

Athletics Interscholastic: baseball (boys), basketball (b,g), cheering (g), cross-country running (b,g), danceline (g), football (b), golf (b,g), softball (g), volleyball (g), weight lifting (b,g); coed interscholastic: tennis, track and field. 1 PE instructor, 2 coaches.

Computers Computers are regularly used in all academic classes. Computer network features include on-campus library services, Internet access, Internet filtering or blocking technology. Student e-mail accounts are available to students. Students grades are available online. The school has a published electronic and media policy.

Contact Admissions. 205-367-8144. Fax: 205-367-8145. Website: www.pickensacademy.com

PICKERING COLLEGE

16945 Bayview Avenue
Newmarket, Ontario L3Y 4X2, Canada

Head of School: Mr. Peter C. Sturrup

General Information Coeducational boarding and day college-preparatory, film studies and radio station, and leadership school. Boarding grades 7–12, day grades JK–12. Founded: 1842. Setting: suburban. Nearest major city is Toronto, Canada. Students are housed in single-sex dormitories. 42-acre campus. 6 buildings on campus. Approved or accredited by Canadian Association of Independent Schools, Canadian Educational Standards Institute, National Independent Private Schools Association, Ontario Ministry of Education, The Association of Boarding Schools, and Ontario Department of Education. Affiliate member of National Association of Independent Schools; member of Secondary School Admission Test Board. Language of instruction: English. Total enrollment: 423. Upper school average class size: 18. Upper school faculty-student ratio: 1:8. There are 164 required school days per year for Upper School students. Upper School students typically attend 5 days per week. The average school day consists of 8 hours.

Upper School Student Profile 43% of students are boarding students. 57% are province residents. 1 province is represented in upper school student body. 43% are international students. International students from China, Germany, Japan, Mexico, Republic of Korea, and Ukraine; 16 other countries represented in student body.

Faculty School total: 51. In upper school: 12 men, 20 women; 8 have advanced degrees; 16 reside on campus.

Subjects Offered Algebra, art, art history, biology, business, business skills, business studies, calculus, Canadian geography, Canadian history, careers, chemistry, community service, computer applications, computer multimedia, computer programming, computer science, concert band, creative writing, drama, dramatic arts, economics, English, English composition, English literature, entrepreneurship, environmental science, experiential education, family studies, filmmaking, fine arts, finite math, French, geography, geometry, government/civics, guitar, health, health education, history, instrumental music, jazz band, law, leadership, literature, mathematics, media studies, music, physical education, physics, politics, science, social sciences, social studies, theater, video film production, visual arts, vocal music, world history.

Graduation Requirements English, 60 hours of community service completed over 4 years before graduation.

Special Academic Programs Advanced Placement exam preparation; independent study; programs in general development for dyslexic students; ESL (44 students enrolled).

College Admission Counseling 65 students graduated in 2016; 3 went to college, including Queen's University at Kingston; Ryerson University; The University of Western Ontario; University of Guelph; University of Toronto; University of Waterloo. Other: 1 entered military service, 59 entered a postgraduate year, 2 had other specific plans.

Student Life Upper grades have uniform requirement, student council, honor system. Discipline rests equally with students and faculty.

Summer Programs ESL programs offered; session focuses on ESL summer camp; held on campus; accepts boys and girls; open to students from other schools. 70 students usually enrolled. 2017 schedule: June 26 to August 19. Application deadline: May 1.

Tuition and Aid Day student tuition: CAN$19,130–CAN$23,000; 7-day tuition and room/board: CAN$47,700–CAN$49,930. Tuition installment plan (Insured Tuition Payment Plan, monthly payment plans). Tuition reduction for siblings, bursaries, merit scholarship grants, need-based scholarship grants available. In 2016–17, 4% of upper-school students received aid; total upper-school merit-scholarship money awarded: CAN$13,000. Total amount of financial aid awarded in 2016–17: CAN$125,000.

Admissions Traditional secondary-level entrance grade is 9. For fall 2016, 109 students applied for upper-level admission, 52 enrolled. CAT, International English Language Test, SLEP for foreign students or TOEFL required. Deadline for receipt of application materials: none. Application fee required: CAN$200. Interview required.

Athletics Interscholastic: basketball (boys, girls), cross-country running (b,g), figure skating (b,g), hockey (b), ice hockey (b), rugby (b,g), skiing (downhill) (b,g), snowboarding (b,g), soccer (b,g), softball (b,g), swimming and diving (b,g), tennis (b,g), track and field (b,g), volleyball (b,g); intramural: figure skating (b,g), outdoor activities (b,g), outdoor adventure (b,g), outdoor recreation (b,g), paddle tennis (b,g), physical training (b,g), running (b,g), skiing (downhill) (b,g), soccer (b,g), strength & conditioning (b,g), swimming and diving (b,g), tennis (b,g), track and field (b,g), volleyball (b,g); coed interscholastic: alpine skiing, aquatics, cross-country running, figure skating, freestyle skiing, hockey, ice hockey, mountain biking, skiing (downhill), snowboarding, soccer, swimming and diving, tennis, track and field; coed intramural: aerobics/dance, badminton, climbing, cooperative games, curling, dance squad, equestrian sports, figure skating, fitness, fitness walking, floor hockey, Frisbee, hockey, horseback riding, indoor soccer, mountain biking, nordic skiing, outdoor adventure, outdoor education, paint ball, rock climbing, skiing (downhill), soccer, strength & conditioning, swimming and diving, table tennis, tennis, touch football, track and field, volleyball, wall climbing, wilderness survival, yoga. 4 PE instructors, 4 coaches, 2 athletic trainers.

Computers Computers are regularly used in all classes. Computer network features include on-campus library services, Internet access, wireless campus network, Internet filtering or blocking technology. Campus intranet and student e-mail accounts are available to students. The school has a published electronic and media policy.

Contact Mrs. Susan Hundert, Admission Associate, Day and North American Boarding. 905-895-1700 Ext. 259. Fax: 905-895-1306. E-mail: admission@pickeringcollege.on.ca. Website: www.pickeringcollege.on.ca

PIEDMONT ACADEMY

PO Box 231
126 Highway 212 West
Monticello, Georgia 31064

Head of School: Mr. Tony Tanner

General Information Coeducational day college-preparatory, arts, business, vocational, religious studies, bilingual studies, and technology school, affiliated with Protestant faith. Grades 1–12. Founded: 1970. Setting: rural. Nearest major city is Macon. 22-acre campus. 8 buildings on campus. Approved or accredited by Georgia Accrediting Commission, Georgia Independent School Association, and Southern Association of Independent Schools. Total enrollment: 259. Upper school average class size: 13. Upper school faculty-student ratio: 1:13. There are 180 required school days per year for Upper School students. Upper School students typically attend 5 days per week. The average school day consists of 7 hours.

Upper School Student Profile Grade 6: 26 students (12 boys, 14 girls); Grade 7: 18 students (8 boys, 10 girls); Grade 8: 20 students (12 boys, 8 girls); Grade 9: 30 students (10 boys, 20 girls); Grade 10: 32 students (15 boys, 17 girls); Grade 11: 27 students (15 boys, 12 girls); Grade 12: 29 students (16 boys, 13 girls). 98% of students are Protestant.

Faculty School total: 31. In upper school: 6 men, 15 women; 15 have advanced degrees.

Subjects Offered Advanced chemistry, advanced computer applications, advanced math, algebra, American government, American history, American history-AP, anatomy and physiology, band, biology, business law, calculus, calculus-AP, chemistry, chemistry-AP, civics, computer science, computer science-AP, computers, concert band, concert choir, consumer economics, consumer law, economics, English, English-AP, geometry, government and politics-AP, government-AP, government/civics, grammar, health education, honors algebra, honors English, honors geometry, Internet, intro to computers, keyboarding, language arts, leadership and service, literature, mathematics, performing arts, personal finance, physical fitness, physical science, physics, pre-calculus, science, sociology, Spanish, student government, wind instruments, world history, yearbook.

Graduation Requirements Algebra, American government, American literature, biology, calculus, chemistry, civics, English composition, English literature, geometry, government, grammar, history, keyboarding, mathematics, physical education (includes health), physical science, science, Spanish.

Special Academic Programs Study at local college for college credit.

College Admission Counseling 33 went to college, including Georgia Institute of Technology; Georgia Perimeter College; University of Georgia; University of North Georgia. Other: 33 entered a postgraduate year.

Student Life Upper grades have uniform requirement, student council, honor system. Discipline rests primarily with faculty.

Tuition and Aid Day student tuition: $6730–$6910. Guaranteed tuition plan. Tuition installment plan (monthly payment plans, individually arranged payment plans, APOGEE School Choice Scholarship, Financial Assistance (Grant)). Tuition reduction for siblings, need-based scholarship grants available. In 2015–16, 8% of upper-school students received aid. Total amount of financial aid awarded in 2015–16: $30,000.

Admissions Traditional secondary-level entrance grade is 9. For fall 2015, 30 students applied for upper-level admission, 23 were accepted, 23 enrolled. Cognitive Abilities Test, OLSAT, Stanford Achievement Test or WAIS, WICS required. Deadline for receipt of application materials: none. Application fee required: $75. Interview required.

Athletics Interscholastic: baseball (boys), basketball (b,g), cheering (b,g), fitness (b,g), flag football (b,g), football (b), golf (b,g), power lifting (b,g); coed interscholastic: cross-country running, skeet shooting; coed intramural: cross-country running, flag football. 6 PE instructors, 14 coaches, 1 athletic trainer.

Computers Computers are regularly used in all academic classes. Computer network features include on-campus library services, online commercial services, Internet access, wireless campus network, Internet filtering or blocking technology. Campus intranet is available to students. Students grades are available online. The school has a published electronic and media policy.

Contact Judy M. Nelson, Director of Admissions/Public and Alumni Relations. 706-468-8818 Ext. 304. Fax: 706-468-2409. E-mail: judy_nelson@piedmontacademy.com. Website: www.piedmontacademy.com

PINECREST ACADEMY

955 Peachtree Parkway
Cumming, Georgia 30041

Head of School: Fr. David Steffy, LC

General Information Coeducational day college-preparatory school, affiliated with Roman Catholic Church. Grades PK–12. Founded: 1993. Setting: suburban. Nearest major city is Atlanta. 79-acre campus. 3 buildings on campus. Approved or accredited by Southern Association of Colleges and Schools, Southern Association of Independent Schools, and Georgia Department of Education. Member of Secondary School Admission Test Board. Total enrollment: 807. Upper school average class size: 16. Upper school faculty-student ratio: 1:8. There are 180 required school days per year for Upper School students. Upper School students typically attend 5 days per week. The average school day consists of 7 hours and 30 minutes.

Upper School Student Profile Grade 9: 81 students (53 boys, 28 girls); Grade 10: 76 students (36 boys, 40 girls); Grade 11: 76 students (33 boys, 43 girls); Grade 12: 73 students (37 boys, 36 girls). 79% of students are Roman Catholic.

Faculty School total: 80. In upper school: 18 men, 18 women; 13 have advanced degrees.

Subjects Offered 3-dimensional art, 3-dimensional design, advanced biology, advanced chemistry, advanced math, Advanced Placement courses, advanced studio art-AP, algebra, American history, American history-AP, American literature, anatomy and physiology, ancient world history, art, art history-AP, art-AP, arts, band, biology, biology-AP, British literature, British literature-AP, calculus, calculus-AP, career/college preparation, chemistry, chemistry-AP, chorus, Christian ethics, composition, composition-AP, computer science-AP, concert band, creative writing, debate, digital imaging, digital photography, drama, drama performance, dramatic arts, drawing, drawing and design, economics, electives, engineering, English, English composition, English language and composition-AP, English language-AP, English literature, English literature and composition-AP, English literature-AP, English-AP, English/composition-AP, environmental science, European history-AP, geometry, government and politics-AP, health education, history of the Catholic Church, history-AP, honors algebra, honors English, honors geometry, honors U.S. history, honors world history, journalism, language, language and composition, language arts, language-AP, languages, Latin, Latin-AP, leadership and service, Life of Christ, literature and composition-AP, macroeconomics-AP, microeconomics-AP, modern world history, music, music theory-AP, painting, personal fitness, philosophy, physical education, physics, physics-AP, play production, pre-algebra, pre-calculus, psychology, psychology-AP, SAT preparation, SAT/ACT preparation, science, scripture, sculpture, Spanish, Spanish language-AP, Spanish literature, Spanish literature-AP, Spanish-AP, speech and debate, statistics, statistics-AP, studio art, studio art-AP, symphonic band, technology, theater arts, theology, U.S. government, U.S. government and politics, U.S. government and politics-AP, U.S. history, U.S. history-AP, United States government-AP, weight fitness, weight training, weightlifting, world history, world history-AP, world literature, yearbook.

Graduation Requirements Arts and fine arts (art, music, dance, drama), electives, English, foreign language, health, mathematics, physical education (includes health), science, social studies (includes history), technology, theology, service hours.

Special Academic Programs 17 Advanced Placement exams for which test preparation is offered; honors section.

College Admission Counseling 66 students graduated in 2016; 62 went to college, including Auburn University; Georgia College & State University; Georgia Institute of Technology; Georgia Southern University; Kennesaw State University; University of Georgia. Other: 4 had other specific plans. Median SAT critical reading: 560, median SAT math: 600, median SAT writing: 650, median combined SAT: 1880, median composite ACT: 26. 35% scored over 600 on SAT critical reading, 41% scored over 600 on SAT math, 41% scored over 600 on SAT writing, 37% scored over 1800 on combined SAT, 44% scored over 26 on composite ACT.

Student Life Upper grades have uniform requirement, student council, honor system. Discipline rests primarily with faculty. Attendance at religious services is required.

Summer Programs Advancement programs offered; session focuses on math programs; held on campus; accepts boys and girls; not open to students from other schools. 10 students usually enrolled.

Tuition and Aid Day student tuition: $15,950. Tuition installment plan (monthly payment plans). Tuition reduction for siblings, need-based scholarship grants available.

Admissions Traditional secondary-level entrance grade is 9. For fall 2016, 42 students applied for upper-level admission, 38 were accepted, 31 enrolled. Admissions testing, Individual IQ, Achievement and behavior rating scale, PSAT or SAT for applicants to grade 11 and 12, psychoeducational evaluation, school's own exam, SSAT, SSAT or WISC III or TOEFL required. Deadline for receipt of application materials: none. Application fee required: $150. On-campus interview recommended.

Athletics Interscholastic: baseball (boys), basketball (b,g), cheering (g), cross-country running (b,g), fencing (b,g), football (b), golf (b), lacrosse (b,g), soccer (b,g), swimming and diving (b,g), tennis (b,g), volleyball (g), wrestling (b); coed interscholastic: cross-country running, fencing, swimming and diving, tennis. 2 PE instructors.

Computers Computers are regularly used in all classes. Computer network features include on-campus library services, online commercial services, Internet access, wireless campus network, Internet filtering or blocking technology, homework is available online. Campus intranet and student e-mail accounts are available to students. Students grades are available online. The school has a published electronic and media policy.

Contact Ms. Melissa McWaters, Admissions Coordinator. 770-888-4477 Ext. 245. Fax: 770-888-0404. E-mail: mmcwaters@pinecrestacademy.org. Website: www.pinecrestacademy.org/

PINE TREE ACADEMY

67 Pownal Road
Freeport, Maine 04032

Head of School: Mr. Brendan Krueger

General Information Coeducational boarding and day college-preparatory and general academic school, affiliated with Seventh-day Adventist Church. Boarding grades 9–12, day grades K–12. Founded: 1961. Setting: small town. Nearest major city is Portland. Students are housed in single-sex dormitories. 80-acre campus. 4 buildings on campus. Approved or accredited by Middle States Association of Colleges and Schools, National Council for Private School Accreditation, and Maine Department of Education. Total enrollment: 121. Upper school average class size: 15. Upper school faculty-student ratio: 1:6. There are 180 required school days per year for Upper School students. Upper School students typically attend 5 days per week. The average school day consists of 7 hours.

Upper School Student Profile Grade 9: 17 students (11 boys, 6 girls); Grade 10: 12 students (6 boys, 6 girls); Grade 11: 17 students (7 boys, 10 girls); Grade 12: 15 students (9 boys, 6 girls). 32% of students are boarding students. 87% are state residents. 4 states are represented in upper school student body. International students from United States, United States, and United States. 80% of students are Seventh-day Adventists.

Faculty School total: 14. In upper school: 6 men, 8 women; 5 have advanced degrees; 4 reside on campus.

Subjects Offered Algebra, American government, American history, American literature, ancient world history, archaeology, art, auto mechanics, band, basketball, bell choir, Bible, Bible studies, biology, British literature, calculus, chemistry, choir, church history, composition, computer science, concert band, concert bell choir, concert choir, driver education, earth science, economics, French, general math, geometry, German, government, health, instruments, keyboarding, Life of Christ, music, personal finance, personal fitness, physical education, physics, piano, pre-algebra, pre-calculus, Spanish, voice, woodworking, world history, world religions, yearbook.

Graduation Requirements American government, American history, arts and fine arts (art, music, dance, drama), business, chemistry, computer science, economics, English, foreign language, health education, mathematics, music, physical education (includes health), religion (includes Bible studies and theology), science, social studies (includes history), technology, world history.

Special Academic Programs Accelerated programs; independent study.

College Admission Counseling 15 students graduated in 2016; 13 went to college, including Andrews University; Pacific Union College; Southern Adventist University; Southwestern Adventist University; University of Maine at Farmington; Walla Walla University. Other: 1 went to work, 1 entered military service. Median SAT critical reading: 595, median SAT math: 485, median SAT writing: 555, median combined SAT: 1660, median composite ACT: 27. 50% scored over 600 on SAT critical reading, 17% scored over 600 on SAT writing.

Student Life Upper grades have uniform requirement, student council, honor system. Discipline rests primarily with faculty. Attendance at religious services is required.

Tuition and Aid Tuition installment plan (FACTS Tuition Payment Plan). Tuition reduction for siblings, need-based scholarship grants, paying campus jobs available. In 2016–17, 25% of upper-school students received aid.

Admissions Traditional secondary-level entrance grade is 9. Iowa Test of Educational Development or Iowa Tests of Basic Skills required. Deadline for receipt of application materials: none. Application fee required: $25. Interview required.

Athletics Interscholastic: basketball (boys, girls), soccer (b,g). 2 PE instructors.

Computers Computers are regularly used in all academic classes. Computer resources include Internet access, Internet filtering or blocking technology. Student e-mail accounts and computer access in designated common areas are available to students. Students grades are available online. The school has a published electronic and media policy.

Contact Mrs. Barb Glover, Office Manager. 207-865-4747. Fax: 207-865-1768. E-mail: bglover@pinetreeacademy.org. Website: www.pinetreeacademy.org

PINEWOOD PREPARATORY SCHOOL

1114 Orangeburg Road
Summerville, South Carolina 29483

Head of School: Mr. Steve Mandell

General Information Coeducational day college-preparatory school. Grades PS–12. Founded: 1952. Setting: suburban. Nearest major city is Charleston. 43-acre campus. 9 buildings on campus. Approved or accredited by South Carolina Independent School Association, Southern Association of Colleges and Schools, Southern Association of Independent Schools, and South Carolina Department of Education. Member of National Association of Independent Schools. Endowment: $1 million. Total enrollment: 675. Upper school average class size: 15. Upper school faculty-student ratio: 1:12. There are 175 required school days per year for Upper School students. Upper School students typically attend 5 days per week. The average school day consists of 7 hours and 20 minutes.

Upper School Student Profile Grade 6: 65 students (32 boys, 33 girls); Grade 7: 53 students (26 boys, 27 girls); Grade 8: 36 students (18 boys, 18 girls); Grade 9: 61 students (31 boys, 30 girls); Grade 10: 50 students (25 boys, 25 girls); Grade 11: 66 students (33 boys, 33 girls); Grade 12: 64 students (32 boys, 32 girls).

Faculty School total: 90. In upper school: 14 men, 22 women; 23 have advanced degrees.

Graduation Requirements Community service hour requirement, leadership program completion.

Special Academic Programs Advanced Placement exam preparation; honors section; independent study; study at local college for college credit; domestic exchange program; academic accommodation for the gifted; ESL (13 students enrolled).

College Admission Counseling 71 students graduated in 2016; 70 went to college, including Charleston Southern University; Clemson University; College of Charleston; Furman University; University of South Carolina. Other: 1 entered military service. Median SAT critical reading: 530, median SAT math: 550, median SAT writing: 520, median combined SAT: 1600, median composite ACT: 23. 25% scored over 600 on SAT critical reading, 21% scored over 600 on SAT math, 20% scored over 600 on SAT writing, 28% scored over 1800 on combined SAT, 25% scored over 26 on composite ACT.

Student Life Upper grades have specified standards of dress, student council, honor system. Discipline rests primarily with faculty.

Tuition and Aid Day student tuition: $9200–$11,920. Tuition installment plan (monthly payment plans, two payments per year, 4 payments per year). Tuition reduction for siblings, need-based scholarship grants available. In 2016–17, 45% of upper-school students received aid.

Admissions Traditional secondary-level entrance grade is 9. For fall 2016, 76 students applied for upper-level admission, 62 were accepted, 57 enrolled. Admissions testing or Stanford Achievement Test required. Application fee required: $75. On-campus interview recommended.

Athletics Interscholastic: aquatics (boys, girls), baseball (b), basketball (b,g), cheering (b,g), cross-country running (b,g), football (b,g), golf (b,g), skeet shooting (b,g), soccer (b,g), strength & conditioning (b,g), swimming and diving (b,g), tennis (b,g), track and field (b,g), trap and skeet (b,g), volleyball (g), wrestling (b,g); intramural: dance team (b,g), flag football (b), lacrosse (g), running (b,g); coed intramural: aerobics, aerobics/dance, running. 4 PE instructors.

Computers Computers are regularly used in all academic classes. Computer network features include on-campus library services, Internet access, wireless campus network, Internet filtering or blocking technology, Chromebooks, iPads. Campus intranet, student e-mail accounts, and computer access in designated common areas are available to students. Students grades are available online. The school has a published electronic and media policy.

Contact Mrs. Nicole Bailey, Director of Admissions. 843-873-1643 Ext. 1. Fax: 843-821-4257. E-mail: nbailey@pinewoodprep.com. Website: www.pinewoodprep.com/

THE PINGREE SCHOOL

537 Highland Street
South Hamilton, Massachusetts 01982

Head of School: Dr. Timothy M. Johnson

General Information Coeducational day college-preparatory school. Grades 9–12. Founded: 1961. Setting: suburban. Nearest major city is Boston. 100-acre campus. 3 buildings on campus. Approved or accredited by Association of Independent Schools in New England, National Independent Private Schools Association, and New England Association of Schools and Colleges. Member of National Association of Independent Schools and Secondary School Admission Test Board. Endowment: $11 million. Total enrollment: 364. Upper school average class size: 15. Upper school faculty-student ratio: 1:6. There are 162 required school days per year for Upper School students. Upper School students typically attend 5 days per week. The average school day consists of 8 hours.

Upper School Student Profile Grade 9: 89 students (44 boys, 45 girls); Grade 10: 114 students (54 boys, 60 girls); Grade 11: 81 students (40 boys, 41 girls); Grade 12: 91 students (38 boys, 53 girls).

Faculty School total: 58. In upper school: 27 men, 29 women; 48 have advanced degrees.

Subjects Offered Algebra, American history, American literature, American studies, art, art history, astronomy, biology, calculus, ceramics, chemistry, computer programming, computer science, creative writing, dance, drama, driver education, earth science, ecology, economics, engineering, English, English literature, European history, fine arts, French, geometry, history, Latin, mathematics, music, oceanography, philosophy, photography, physics, psychology, Russian literature, science, social studies, Spanish, theater, trigonometry, writing.

Graduation Requirements Arts and fine arts (art, music, dance, drama), English, foreign language, mathematics, science, social studies (includes history), senior projects.

Special Academic Programs Advanced Placement exam preparation; honors section; independent study; term-away projects.

College Admission Counseling 87 students graduated in 2016; all went to college, including Boston University; Brown University; Connecticut College; Cornell University; Northeastern University; University of Rochester. Median SAT critical reading: 630, median SAT math: 620, median SAT writing: 600, median combined SAT: 1800, median composite ACT: 27. 52% scored over 600 on SAT critical reading, 60% scored over 600 on SAT math, 50% scored over 600 on SAT writing, 52% scored over 1800 on combined SAT, 55% scored over 26 on composite ACT.

Student Life Upper grades have specified standards of dress, student council, honor system. Discipline rests equally with students and faculty.

Tuition and Aid Day student tuition: $42,500. Tuition installment plan (FACTS Tuition Payment Plan). Merit scholarship grants, need-based scholarship grants, need-based loans available. In 2016–17, 38% of upper-school students received aid; total upper-school merit-scholarship money awarded: $150,000. Total amount of financial aid awarded in 2016–17: $3,200,000.

Admissions Traditional secondary-level entrance grade is 9. For fall 2016, 375 students applied for upper-level admission, 202 were accepted, 106 enrolled. ISEE or SSAT required. Deadline for receipt of application materials: January 15. Application fee required: $50. On-campus interview recommended.

Athletics Interscholastic: baseball (boys), basketball (b,g), crew (b,g), cross-country running (b,g), field hockey (g), football (b), golf (b,g), ice hockey (b,g), lacrosse (b,g), running (b,g), soccer (b,g), softball (g), swimming and diving (b,g), tennis (b,g), volleyball (g); coed interscholastic: Frisbee, sailing, ultimate Frisbee; coed intramural: dance, fitness, golf, hiking/backpacking, modern dance, mountaineering, outdoor adventure, outdoor education, outdoor skills, physical fitness, physical training, skiing (downhill), strength & conditioning, weight lifting, weight training, wilderness. 24 coaches, 2 athletic trainers.

Computers Computers are regularly used in college planning, computer applications, desktop publishing, digital applications, drawing and design, English, foreign language, graphic arts, graphic design, independent study, information technology, mathematics, programming, publications, science, technology, Web site design, word processing, writing, yearbook classes. Computer network features include on-campus library services, online commercial services, Internet access, wireless campus network, Internet filtering or blocking technology. Campus intranet, student e-mail accounts, and

computer access in designated common areas are available to students. Students grades are available online. The school has a published electronic and media policy.

Contact Ms. Kate Frost, Admission Office Coordinator. 978-468-4415 Ext. 262. Fax: 978-468-3758. E-mail: kfrost@pingree.org. Website: www.pingree.org

THE PINGRY SCHOOL

Martinsville Road
131 Martinsville Road
Basking Ridge, New Jersey 07920

Head of School: Mr. Nathaniel Conard

General Information Coeducational day college-preparatory school. Grades K–12. Founded: 1861. Setting: suburban. Nearest major city is New York, NY. 240-acre campus. 2 buildings on campus. Approved or accredited by Middle States Association of Colleges and Schools, New Jersey Association of Independent Schools, and New Jersey Department of Education. Member of National Association of Independent Schools and Secondary School Admission Test Board. Endowment: $80 million. Total enrollment: 1,116. Upper school average class size: 13. Upper school faculty-student ratio: 1:7. There are 168 required school days per year for Upper School students. Upper School students typically attend 5 days per week. The average school day consists of 6 hours and 15 minutes.

Upper School Student Profile Grade 9: 148 students (74 boys, 74 girls); Grade 10: 141 students (76 boys, 65 girls); Grade 11: 139 students (81 boys, 58 girls); Grade 12: 129 students (62 boys, 67 girls).

Faculty School total: 120. In upper school: 47 men, 37 women; 61 have advanced degrees.

Subjects Offered Algebra, American literature, analysis, analysis and differential calculus, anatomy, architecture, art, art history-AP, biology, biology-AP, brass choir, calculus, chemistry, chemistry-AP, Chinese, clayworking, comparative cultures, computer science-AP, creative writing, drafting, drama, driver education, English, ethics, European literature, filmmaking, French, French-AP, geometry, German, German-AP, Greek drama, health, jazz band, jewelry making, Latin, literature by women, macro/microeconomics-AP, macroeconomics-AP, modern European history, music theory, mythology, orchestra, painting, peer counseling, photography, physics, physics-AP, physiology, psychology, psychology-AP, sculpture, Shakespeare, Spanish, Spanish-AP, studio art-AP, trigonometry, U.S. government and politics-AP, U.S. history-AP, wind ensemble, world literature, yearbook.

Graduation Requirements Arts and fine arts (art, music, dance, drama), English, foreign language, mathematics, physical education (includes health), science, social studies (includes history). Community service is required.

Special Academic Programs 20 Advanced Placement exams for which test preparation is offered; honors section; independent study; term-away projects; study abroad; academic accommodation for the gifted.

College Admission Counseling 142 students graduated in 2016; all went to college, including Boston University; Columbia University; Cornell University; Northwestern University; University of Notre Dame; University of Pennsylvania. Mean SAT critical reading: 681, mean SAT math: 696, mean SAT writing: 695, mean composite ACT: 30.

Student Life Upper grades have specified standards of dress, student council, honor system. Discipline rests equally with students and faculty.

Summer Programs Enrichment, sports programs offered; session focuses on enrichment, writing, and study skills; held on campus; accepts boys and girls; open to students from other schools. 30 students usually enrolled. 2017 schedule: June 27 to August 12.

Tuition and Aid Day student tuition: $31,504–$37,062. Tuition installment plan (individually arranged payment plans, My Tuition Solutions). Need-based scholarship grants available. In 2016–17, 15% of upper-school students received aid. Total amount of financial aid awarded in 2016–17: $2,711,787.

Admissions Traditional secondary-level entrance grade is 9. For fall 2016, 316 students applied for upper-level admission, 81 were accepted, 60 enrolled. ERB, ISEE, SSAT or Wechsler Intelligence Scale for Children required. Deadline for receipt of application materials: January 1. Application fee required: $75. On-campus interview required.

Athletics Interscholastic: alpine skiing (boys, girls), baseball (b), basketball (b,g), cross-country running (b,g), fencing (b,g), field hockey (g), football (b), golf (b,g), ice hockey (b,g), indoor track & field (b,g), lacrosse (b,g), skiing (downhill) (b,g), soccer (b,g), softball (g), squash (b,g), swimming and diving (b,g), tennis (b,g), track and field (b,g), wrestling (b); intramural: fitness (b,g), yoga (b,g); coed interscholastic: dance, physical fitness, physical training, water polo. 3 PE instructors, 15 coaches, 1 athletic trainer.

Computers Computers are regularly used in all academic classes. Computer network features include on-campus library services, online commercial services, Internet access, wireless campus network, Internet filtering or blocking technology. Campus intranet, student e-mail accounts, and computer access in designated common areas are available to students. The school has a published electronic and media policy.

Contact Ms. Lorian Morales, Admission Coordinator. 908-647-5555 Ext. 1221. Fax: 908-647-4395. E-mail: lmorales@pingry.org. Website: www.pingry.org

PIONEER VALLEY CHRISTIAN ACADEMY

965 Plumtree Road
Springfield, Massachusetts 01119

Head of School: Mr. Timothy L. Duff

General Information Coeducational day college-preparatory, religious studies, bilingual studies, and technology school. Grades PS–12. Founded: 1972. Setting: suburban. 25-acre campus. 1 building on campus. Approved or accredited by American Association of Christian Schools, New England Association of Schools and Colleges, and Massachusetts Department of Education. Total enrollment: 293. Upper school average class size: 18. Upper school faculty-student ratio: 1:10. There are 181 required school days per year for Upper School students. Upper School students typically attend 5 days per week. The average school day consists of 6 hours and 40 minutes.

Upper School Student Profile Grade 9: 24 students (16 boys, 8 girls); Grade 10: 33 students (19 boys, 14 girls); Grade 11: 19 students (11 boys, 8 girls); Grade 12: 20 students (12 boys, 8 girls).

Faculty School total: 30. In upper school: 6 men, 10 women; 7 have advanced degrees.

Subjects Offered Advanced math, algebra, American literature, American literature-AP, anatomy and physiology, art, art history, athletics, baseball, basketball, Bible, British literature, calculus, calculus-AP, chemistry, Christian education, concert choir, drama, electives, English, English literature-AP, English-AP, geography, geometry, history, honors English, human biology, microeconomics-AP, music, New Testament, personal money management, physical education, physical science, physics, pre-algebra, pre-calculus, sewing, sociology, Spanish, sports, stained glass, statistics, technology, tennis, U.S. history, volleyball, weight training, world history, yearbook.

Graduation Requirements Algebra, American literature, arts and fine arts (art, music, dance, drama), Bible, biology, British literature, English, foreign language, mathematics, New Testament, physical education (includes health), physical science, religion (includes Bible studies and theology), science, social studies (includes history), sociology, U.S. history, world history, Christian/community service hours.

Special Academic Programs Advanced Placement exam preparation; honors section; remedial reading and/or remedial writing; remedial math; programs in English, mathematics, general development for dyslexic students; special instructional classes for students with learning disabilities, Attention Deficit Disorder, and dyslexia.

College Admission Counseling 22 students graduated in 2016; 21 went to college, including Holyoke Community College; Liberty University; University of Massachusetts Amherst; University of Massachusetts Boston; Western New England University. Other: 1 went to work. Median SAT critical reading: 530, median SAT math: 470, median SAT writing: 470.

Student Life Upper grades have uniform requirement, honor system. Discipline rests primarily with faculty.

Tuition and Aid Day student tuition: $12,800. Tuition installment plan (FACTS Tuition Payment Plan, individually arranged payment plans, Electronic Funds Transfer, weekly, biweekly, monthly). Need-based scholarship grants, need-based financial aid and scholarship available. In 2016–17, 49% of upper-school students received aid. Total amount of financial aid awarded in 2016–17: $217,115.

Admissions Traditional secondary-level entrance grade is 9. For fall 2016, 21 students applied for upper-level admission, 21 were accepted, 20 enrolled. Admissions testing required. Deadline for receipt of application materials: none. Application fee required: $100. On-campus interview recommended.

Athletics Interscholastic: baseball (boys), basketball (b,g), soccer (b), tennis (b,g), volleyball (g); coed intramural: combined training, physical fitness, power lifting, weight lifting. 2 PE instructors, 8 coaches.

Computers Computers are regularly used in all academic classes. Computer network features include Internet access, Internet filtering or blocking technology, homework assignments available online. Students grades are available online.

Contact Mrs. Denise Richards, Director of Admissions. 413-782-8031. Fax: 413-782-8033. E-mail: drichards@pvcama.org. Website: www.pvcama.org

PIUS X HIGH SCHOOL

6000 A Street
Lincoln, Nebraska 68510

Head of School: Fr. James J. Meysenburg

General Information Coeducational day college-preparatory, general academic, and religious studies school, affiliated with Roman Catholic Church; primarily serves students with learning disabilities, individuals with Attention Deficit Disorder, and individuals with emotional and behavioral problems. Grades 9–12. Founded: 1956. Setting: urban. 30-acre campus. 1 building on campus. Approved or accredited by North Central Association of Colleges and Schools, Western Catholic Education Association, and Nebraska Department of Education. Upper school average class size: 26. Upper school faculty-student ratio: 1:23. There are 182 required school days per year for Upper School students. Upper School students typically attend 5 days per week. The average school day consists of 6 hours.

Upper School Student Profile Grade 9: 319 students (154 boys, 165 girls); Grade 10: 324 students (154 boys, 170 girls); Grade 11: 311 students (155 boys, 156 girls); Grade 12: 267 students (140 boys, 127 girls). 97.5% of students are Roman Catholic.

Faculty School total: 81. In upper school: 40 men, 41 women; 51 have advanced degrees.

Subjects Offered Accounting, acting, advanced chemistry, advanced computer applications, advanced math, algebra, American government, American literature, anatomy, applied arts, applied music, architectural drawing, art, art appreciation, art history, Bible studies, biology, biology-AP, British literature, business, business law, calculus, calculus-AP, carpentry, Catholic belief and practice, chemistry, chemistry-AP, choir, choral music, civics, comparative government and politics-AP, comparative religion, composition, computer applications, computer graphics, computer literacy, concert band, concert choir, drafting, drama, drawing, drawing and design, English, English composition, English literature, English literature-AP, family living, fitness, food and nutrition, French, general math, geography, government and politics-AP, government-AP, graphic design, health, history of music, history of the Catholic Church, human anatomy, industrial arts, instrumental music, integrated science, interior design, jazz band, journalism, keyboarding, literature-AP, marching band, marketing, mechanical drawing, moral theology, music appreciation, personal money management, photography, physical education, physical science, physics, physics-AP, play production, pre-algebra, pre-calculus, psychology, religion, small engine repair, social justice, Spanish, speech and debate, stage design, student publications, studio art, symphonic band, textiles, U.S. government and politics-AP, U.S. history, U.S. history-AP, vocal music, world geography, world history, yearbook.

Graduation Requirements Arts and fine arts (art, music, dance, drama), civics, computer literacy, electives, English, geography, mathematics, physical education (includes health), religion (includes Bible studies and theology), science, speech communications, U.S. history, world history, senior service requirement, all-school retreat attendance.

Special Academic Programs 13 Advanced Placement exams for which test preparation is offered; independent study; study at local college for college credit; remedial reading and/or remedial writing; remedial math.

College Admission Counseling 269 students graduated in 2015; 251 went to college, including Benedictine College; Creighton University; University of Nebraska–Lincoln; University of Nebraska at Kearney; University of Nebraska at Omaha; Wesleyan University. Other: 2 went to work, 5 entered military service, 1 entered a postgraduate year, 6 had other specific plans. Mean SAT critical reading: 628, mean SAT math: 622, mean SAT writing: 610, mean composite ACT: 24. 64% scored over 600 on SAT critical reading, 61% scored over 600 on SAT math, 54% scored over 600 on SAT writing, 32% scored over 26 on composite ACT.

Student Life Upper grades have uniform requirement, student council. Discipline rests primarily with faculty. Attendance at religious services is required.

Tuition and Aid Day student tuition: $1500. Guaranteed tuition plan. Tuition installment plan (monthly payment plans, individually arranged payment plans). Need-based scholarship grants available. In 2015–16, 5% of upper-school students received aid. Total amount of financial aid awarded in 2015–16: $10,000.

Admissions Traditional secondary-level entrance grade is 9. Deadline for receipt of application materials: none. Application fee required: $70.

Athletics Interscholastic: baseball (boys), basketball (b,g), cheering (g), cross-country running (b,g), dance team (g), drill team (g), football (b), golf (b,g), soccer (b,g), softball (g), swimming and diving (b,g), tennis (b,g), track and field (b,g), volleyball (g), wrestling (b); intramural: running (g); coed interscholastic: weight training; coed intramural: basketball, bowling, running. 4 PE instructors, 2 coaches, 1 athletic trainer.

Computers Computers are regularly used in accounting, business, business applications, business education, business skills, business studies, computer applications, creative writing, drafting, journalism, multimedia, Web site design, yearbook classes. Computer network features include on-campus library services, Internet access, wireless campus network, Internet filtering or blocking technology. Computer access in designated common areas is available to students. Students grades are available online. The school has a published electronic and media policy.

Contact Mrs. Jan Frayser, Director of Guidance. 402-488-0931. Fax: 402-488-1061. E-mail: jan.frayser@piusx.net. Website: www.piusx.net

PLUMSTEAD CHRISTIAN SCHOOL

P.O. Box 216
5765 Old Easton Road
Plumsteadville, Pennsylvania 18949

Head of School: Mr. Patrick Fitzpatrick

General Information Coeducational day college-preparatory and Bible studies school. Grades K–12. Setting: suburban. Nearest major city is Philadelphia. 47-acre campus. 1 building on campus. Approved or accredited by Association of Christian Schools International, Middle States Association of Colleges and Schools, and Pennsylvania Department of Education. Upper school average class size: 15. There are 180 required school days per year for Upper School students. Upper School students typically attend 5 days per week. The average school day consists of 7 hours.

Upper School Student Profile Grade 6: 18 students (8 boys, 10 girls); Grade 7: 17 students (11 boys, 6 girls); Grade 8: 16 students (10 boys, 6 girls); Grade 9: 20 students (11 boys, 9 girls); Grade 10: 33 students (22 boys, 11 girls); Grade 11: 34 students (24 boys, 10 girls); Grade 12: 31 students (19 boys, 12 girls).

Faculty School total: 30. In upper school: 9 men, 10 women; 6 have advanced degrees.

Subjects Offered 20th century history, 20th century physics, 20th century world history, 3-dimensional art, acting, advanced biology, advanced chemistry, advanced computer applications, advanced math, Advanced Placement courses, algebra, American history, American history-AP, American literature-AP, analytic geometry, art, athletics, band, baseball, bell choir, Bible, Bible studies, biology, biology-AP, calculus, calculus-AP, choir, choral music, Christian doctrine, Christian education, Christian ethics, Christian scripture, computer studies, computers, drama, drama performance, drawing, economics, English, English literature, English literature-AP, English-AP, fine arts, general science, geometry, health, history-AP, human biology, lab science, library, mathematics-AP, physics, prayer/spirituality, pre-algebra, pre-calculus, scripture, senior project, softball, Spanish, sports, statistics, statistics-AP, student government, technology, tennis, U.S. constitutional history, U.S. government, U.S. history-AP, wind instruments, world history-AP, writing, yearbook.

Special Academic Programs Accelerated programs; independent study; term-away projects; study at local college for college credit; academic accommodation for the gifted; remedial reading and/or remedial writing; remedial math.

College Admission Counseling 38 students graduated in 2016; 36 went to college, including Grove City College; Liberty University; Messiah College; Rensselaer Polytechnic Institute; Taylor University; Wheaton College. Other: 2 entered military service, 1 entered a postgraduate year.

Student Life Upper grades have uniform requirement, student council, honor system. Discipline rests equally with students and faculty.

Admissions Traditional secondary-level entrance grade is 9. Traditional secondary-level entrance age is 15. For fall 2016, 24 students applied for upper-level admission, 22 were accepted, 22 enrolled. Achievement tests, school placement exam or school's own test required. Deadline for receipt of application materials: June 30. Application fee required: $200. On-campus interview required.

Athletics Interscholastic: baseball (boys), basketball (b,g), dance team (g), field hockey (g), softball (g), tennis (g); intramural: basketball (b,g), field hockey (g), softball (g), tennis (g); coed interscholastic: basketball, track and field; coed intramural: basketball, track and field.

Computers Computers are regularly used in all classes. Computer network features include Internet filtering or blocking technology. Campus intranet, student e-mail accounts, and computer access in designated common areas are available to students. Students grades are available online. The school has a published electronic and media policy.

Contact Mrs. Laurie Meyer, Admissions Director. 215-766-8073 Ext. 203. Fax: 215-766-2033. E-mail: lmeyer@plumsteadchristian.org. Website: www.plumsteadchristian.org

POLYTECHNIC SCHOOL

1030 East California Boulevard
Pasadena, California 91106-4099

Head of School: Mr. John Bracker

General Information Coeducational day college-preparatory school. Grades K–12. Founded: 1907. Setting: suburban. 15-acre campus. 7 buildings on campus. Approved or accredited by California Association of Independent Schools, The College Board, Western Association of Schools and Colleges, and California Department of Education. Member of National Association of Independent Schools. Endowment: $61.7 million. Total enrollment: 858. Upper school average class size: 15. Upper School students typically attend 5 days per week. The average school day consists of 6 hours and 30 minutes.

Upper School Student Profile Grade 6: 66 students (35 boys, 31 girls); Grade 7: 77 students (43 boys, 34 girls); Grade 8: 74 students (36 boys, 38 girls); Grade 9: 96 students (48 boys, 48 girls); Grade 10: 95 students (50 boys, 45 girls); Grade 11: 90 students (52 boys, 38 girls); Grade 12: 102 students (54 boys, 48 girls).

Faculty School total: 57. In upper school: 21 men, 36 women; 40 have advanced degrees.

Subjects Offered Acting, algebra, American history, American history-AP, analytic geometry, art history, athletics, audio visual/media, Basic programming, batik, biology, biology-AP, calculus, calculus-AP, ceramics, chamber groups, chemistry, chemistry-AP, choral music, communications, computer art, computer science, constitutional law, data analysis, drama, drama performance, drawing, East Asian history, economics, English, English language and composition-AP, English literature and composition-AP, ensembles, ethics, filmmaking, French, French literature-AP, functions, geometry, guitar, improvisation, jazz dance, jazz ensemble, Latin, Latin-AP, madrigals, math analysis, mathematical modeling, music history, music theory, musical productions, musical theater, orchestra, painting, photography, physical science, physics, physics-AP, Roman civilization, sculpture, silk screening, society, Spanish, Spanish literature-AP, statistics, tap dance, technical theater, theater, theater design and production, theater history, trigonometry, U.S. government and politics, U.S. history-AP, Vietnam War, visual arts, Western civilization, woodworking, world cultures, world religions.

Special Academic Programs 12 Advanced Placement exams for which test preparation is offered; honors section; independent study; study abroad.

College Admission Counseling 87 students graduated in 2016; all went to college, including Brown University; Duke University; Loyola Marymount University; New York University; Stanford University; University of Southern California. 81% scored over 600 on SAT critical reading, 81% scored over 600 on SAT math, 83% scored over 600 on SAT writing, 78% scored over 1800 on combined SAT, 87% scored over 26 on composite ACT.

Student Life Upper grades have specified standards of dress, student council, honor system. Discipline rests equally with students and faculty.

Summer Programs Remediation, enrichment, advancement, art/fine arts, computer instruction programs offered; session focuses on For students to have a fun and balanced summer experience; held on campus; accepts boys and girls; open to students from other schools. 685 students usually enrolled. 2017 schedule: June 19 to July 28. Application deadline: May 1.

Tuition and Aid Day student tuition: $34,800. Tuition installment plan (monthly payment plans). Need-based scholarship grants available. In 2016–17, 26% of upper-school students received aid. Total amount of financial aid awarded in 2016–17: $2,219,233.

Admissions Traditional secondary-level entrance grade is 9. For fall 2016, 264 students applied for upper-level admission, 35 were accepted, 27 enrolled. ISEE required. Deadline for receipt of application materials: January 13. Application fee required: $100. Interview required.

Athletics Interscholastic: aquatics (boys, girls), baseball (b), basketball (b,g), cross-country running (b,g), diving (b,g), football (b), golf (b,g), soccer (b,g), softball (g), swimming and diving (b,g), tennis (b,g), track and field (b,g), volleyball (b,g), water polo (b,g); coed interscholastic: badminton, dance team, equestrian sports, fencing, outdoor education, physical fitness, physical training, strength & conditioning, weight lifting, weight training, yoga. 6 PE instructors, 58 coaches, 2 athletic trainers.

Computers Computers are regularly used in all classes. Computer network features include on-campus library services, Internet access, wireless campus network, Internet filtering or blocking technology, Bring Your Own Device program, faculty web pages, library resources online, Global Online Academy. Student e-mail accounts are available to students. Students grades are available online. The school has a published electronic and media policy.

Contact Ms. Sally Jeanne McKenna, Director of Admission. 626-396-6300. Fax: 626-396-6591. E-mail: sjmckenna@polytechnic.org. Website: www.polytechnic.org

POPE FRANCIS HIGH SCHOOL

134 Springfield Street
Chicopee, Massachusetts 01013

Head of School: Dr. Thomas Y. McDowell

General Information Coeducational day college-preparatory, arts, business, and religious studies school, affiliated with Roman Catholic Church. Grades 9–12. Founded: 1963. Setting: urban. Nearest major city is Springfield. 1 building on campus. Approved or accredited by International Baccalaureate Organization, Massachusetts Department of Education, National Catholic Education Association, New England Association of Schools and Colleges, and Massachusetts Department of Education. Total enrollment: 245. Upper school average class size: 15. Upper school faculty-student ratio: 1:10. There are 180 required school days per year for Upper School students. Upper School students typically attend 5 days per week. The average school day consists of 6 hours.

Upper School Student Profile Grade 9: 68 students (36 boys, 32 girls); Grade 10: 102 students (55 boys, 47 girls); Grade 11: 85 students (46 boys, 39 girls); Grade 12: 112 students (50 boys, 62 girls). 77% of students are Roman Catholic.

Faculty School total: 36. In upper school: 15 men, 26 women; 23 have advanced degrees.

Subjects Offered Advanced biology, advanced math, algebra, American literature, American literature-AP, art, biology, calculus, calculus-AP, Catholic belief and practice, chemistry, English, English literature, environmental science, forensics, French, geometry, Latin, literature-AP, moral theology, multimedia design, physics, pottery, pre-calculus, psychology, social sciences, Spanish, studio art, The 20th Century, U.S. history, U.S. history-AP, Web site design, world civilizations, world history, world religions.

Graduation Requirements Electives, English, foreign language, mathematics, religion (includes Bible studies and theology), science, social studies (includes history), U.S. literature, community service hours at each grade level, English research paper at each level, senior internship program.

Special Academic Programs 5 Advanced Placement exams for which test preparation is offered; honors section; independent study; study at local college for college credit; ESL.

College Admission Counseling Colleges students went to include Bryant University; Elms College; Holyoke Community College; Merrimack College; Siena College; Western New England University.

Student Life Upper grades have uniform requirement, student council. Discipline rests primarily with faculty. Attendance at religious services is required.

Summer Programs Enrichment programs offered; session focuses on study skills, essay writing, SAT prep, Algebra review; held on campus; accepts boys and girls; not open to students from other schools. 25 students usually enrolled. 2017 schedule: July 30 to August 17. Application deadline: July 2.

Tuition and Aid Day student tuition: $8800. Tuition installment plan (FACTS Tuition Payment Plan, Your Tuition Solution Loan Program (YTS)). Need-based scholarship grants available. In 2016–17, 32% of upper-school students received aid. Total amount of financial aid awarded in 2016–17: $150,000.

Admissions Traditional secondary-level entrance grade is 9. Scholastic Testing Service High School Placement Test required. Deadline for receipt of application materials: none. Application fee required: $50. Interview required.

Athletics Interscholastic: baseball (boys), basketball (b,g), cross-country running (b,g), ice hockey (b), indoor track (b,g), lacrosse (b,g), rugby (g), soccer (b,g), softball (g), winter (indoor) track (b,g); coed interscholastic: dance, golf, hiking/backpacking, juggling, outdoor adventure, swimming and diving, tennis. 10 coaches.

Computers Computers are regularly used in multimedia classes. Computer network features include on-campus library services, Internet access, Internet filtering or blocking technology. Campus intranet and student e-mail accounts are available to students. Students grades are available online. The school has a published electronic and media policy.

Contact Mrs. Ann M. Rivers, Director of Admissions. 413-331-2480 Ext. 1132. Fax: 413-331-2708. E-mail: arivers@popefrancishigh.org.
Website: www.holyokecatholichigh.org

POPE JOHN PAUL II HIGH SCHOOL

1901 Jaguar Drive
Slidell, Louisiana 70461-0000
Head of School: Mrs. Martha M. Mundine

General Information Coeducational day college-preparatory, arts, and religious studies school, affiliated with Roman Catholic Church. Grades 8–12. Founded: 1980. Setting: suburban. Nearest major city is New Orleans. 2 buildings on campus. Approved or accredited by National Catholic Education Association, Southern Association of Colleges and Schools, and Louisiana Department of Education. Total enrollment: 346. Upper school average class size: 24. Upper school faculty-student ratio: 1:11. Upper School students typically attend 5 days per week. The average school day consists of 7 hours and 15 minutes.

Upper School Student Profile 97% of students are Roman Catholic.

Special Academic Programs Advanced Placement exam preparation; honors section; study at local college for college credit.

College Admission Counseling 78 students graduated in 2015; 76 went to college. Other: 1 went to work, 1 entered military service.

Student Life Upper grades have uniform requirement, student council, honor system. Discipline rests primarily with faculty. Attendance at religious services is required.

Tuition and Aid Need-based scholarship grants available. In 2015–16, 18% of upper-school students received aid.

Admissions Traditional secondary-level entrance grade is 8. Deadline for receipt of application materials: none. Application fee required: $300. Interview required.

Athletics Interscholastic: aerobics/dance (girls), baseball (b), dance team (g), football (b), softball (g), volleyball (g); coed interscholastic: basketball, cheering, cross-country running, fitness, golf, physical fitness, power lifting, soccer, strength & conditioning, swimming and diving, tennis, track and field.

Computers Computer network features include on-campus library services, Internet access, wireless campus network, Internet filtering or blocking technology. Campus intranet and student e-mail accounts are available to students. Students grades are available online. The school has a published electronic and media policy.

Contact Ms. Lise Bremond, Assistant Principal. 504-649-0914. Fax: 504-649-5494. E-mail: lbremond@pjp.org. Website: www.pjp.org

POPE JOHN XXIII REGIONAL HIGH SCHOOL

28 Andover Road
Sparta, New Jersey 07871
Head of School: Mr. Thomas J. Costello

General Information Coeducational day college-preparatory school. Grades 8–12. Founded: 1956. Setting: suburban. Nearest major city is New York, NY. 15-acre campus. 1 building on campus. Approved or accredited by New Jersey Department of Education. Total enrollment: 953. Upper school average class size: 20. Upper school faculty-student ratio: 1:12. There are 180 required school days per year for Upper School students. Upper School students typically attend 5 days per week. The average school day consists of 5 hours and 42 minutes.

Upper School Student Profile Grade 8: 111 students (54 boys, 57 girls); Grade 9: 191 students (108 boys, 83 girls); Grade 10: 182 students (100 boys, 82 girls); Grade 11: 199 students (119 boys, 80 girls); Grade 12: 209 students (113 boys, 96 girls).

Faculty School total: 98. In upper school: 50 men, 48 women; 32 have advanced degrees.

Subjects Offered Advanced chemistry, advanced computer applications, advanced math, Advanced Placement courses, algebra, American literature, American studies, anatomy and physiology, art, biology, biology-AP, British literature, business, business law, calculus, calculus-AP, chemistry, chemistry-AP, choral music, computer science, computer science-AP, conceptual physics, concert choir, earth science, economics, English, English language-AP, English literature, English literature and composition-AP, environmental science, environmental science-AP, European history-AP, fine arts, French, French-AP, geometry, German, global issues, government and politics-AP, graphic arts, health and safety, history-AP, honors algebra, honors English, honors

geometry, honors U.S. history, honors world history, human geography - AP, Italian, Japanese, jazz band, journalism, lab science, Latin, macroeconomics-AP, microeconomics-AP, modern politics, music theory, physical education, physics, physics-AP, pre-calculus, psychology, psychology-AP, reading/study skills, robotics, Spanish, Spanish language-AP, statistics, statistics-AP, theater arts, theology, U.S. government, U.S. government and politics-AP, U.S. history, U.S. history-AP, world cultures, world history-AP, zoology.

Graduation Requirements Arts and fine arts (art, music, dance, drama), English, foreign language, health and safety, mathematics, science, social studies (includes history), theology, 60 hours of community service (15 hours per year).

Special Academic Programs 22 Advanced Placement exams for which test preparation is offered; honors section.

College Admission Counseling 194 students graduated in 2016; 200 went to college, including Marist College; Ramapo College of New Jersey; Rowan University; Stevens Institute of Technology; Susquehanna University; University of Delaware. Other: 1 went to work, 4 entered a postgraduate year. Mean SAT critical reading: 550, mean SAT math: 560, mean SAT writing: 540, mean combined SAT: 1650.

Student Life Upper grades have uniform requirement, student council. Discipline rests primarily with faculty.

Tuition and Aid Day student tuition: $15,000. Guaranteed tuition plan. Tuition installment plan (FACTS Tuition Payment Plan). Need-based scholarship grants available.

Admissions Traditional secondary-level entrance grade is 9. CTB/McGraw-Hill/Macmillan Co-op Test, Math Placement Exam, placement test and writing sample required. Deadline for receipt of application materials: none. No application fee required. Interview required.

Athletics Interscholastic: baseball (boys), basketball (b,g), cheering (g), cross-country running (b,g), field hockey (g), football (b), ice hockey (b), indoor track & field (b,g), lacrosse (b,g), running (b,g), skiing (downhill) (b,g), softball (g), swimming and diving (b,g), tennis (b,g), track and field (b,g), volleyball (b,g), winter (indoor) track (b,g), wrestling (b); coed interscholastic: golf.

Computers Computers are regularly used in all academic classes. Computer network features include Internet access, wireless campus network, Internet filtering or blocking technology, Naviance Succeed. Computer access in designated common areas is available to students. Students grades are available online. The school has a published electronic and media policy.

Contact Mrs. Anne Kaiser, Administrative Assistant for Admissions. 973-729-6125 Ext. 255. Fax: 973-729-4536. E-mail: annekaiser@popejohn.org.
Website: www.popejohn.org

PORTLEDGE SCHOOL

355 Duck Pond Road
Locust Valley, New York 11560
Head of School: Mr. Simon Owen Williams

General Information Coeducational day college-preparatory school. Grades N–12. Founded: 1965. Setting: suburban. Nearest major city is New York. 62-acre campus. 8 buildings on campus. Approved or accredited by New York State Association of Independent Schools, New York State Board of Regents, and New York Department of Education. Member of National Association of Independent Schools and Secondary School Admission Test Board. Endowment: $2.5 million. Total enrollment: 475. Upper school average class size: 14. Upper school faculty-student ratio: 1:8. There are 170 required school days per year for Upper School students. Upper School students typically attend 5 days per week. The average school day consists of 6 hours and 55 minutes.

Upper School Student Profile Grade 6: 32 students (16 boys, 16 girls); Grade 7: 32 students (16 boys, 16 girls); Grade 8: 48 students (25 boys, 23 girls); Grade 9: 52 students (26 boys, 26 girls); Grade 10: 58 students (29 boys, 29 girls); Grade 11: 54 students (25 boys, 29 girls); Grade 12: 54 students (28 boys, 26 girls).

Faculty School total: 83. In upper school: 19 men, 18 women; 21 have advanced degrees.

Subjects Offered 3-dimensional art, advanced biology, advanced chemistry, advanced computer applications, advanced math, Advanced Placement courses, advanced studio art-AP, algebra, American history, American history-AP, American literature, American literature-AP, ancient history, architectural drawing, architecture, art, art appreciation, art history, art-AP, Basic programming, biology, calculus, calculus-AP, ceramics, chemistry, chemistry-AP, chorus, community service, computer programming, computer science, computers, creative writing, digital music, drama, drama workshop, driver education, earth science, economics, English, English literature, English literature-AP, environmental science, European history, expository writing, fine arts, foreign language, French, French-AP, geography, geometry, government/civics, grammar, graphic design, health, health education, history, honors algebra, honors English, honors geometry, honors U.S. history, independent study, instrumental music, jazz ensemble, journalism, keyboarding, Mandarin, mathematics, music, Native American history, photography, physical education, physics, psychology, public policy, public service, public speaking, science, senior project, social sciences, social studies, sociology, Spanish, Spanish-AP, theater, trigonometry, U.S. history-AP, world history.

Graduation Requirements Arts and fine arts (art, music, dance, drama), computer science, English, foreign language, mathematics, performing arts, physical education (includes health), public speaking, science, senior project, social sciences, social studies (includes history). Community service is required.

Special Academic Programs Honors section; independent study; term-away projects; study abroad; academic accommodation for the gifted, the musically talented, and the artistically talented; ESL (10 students enrolled).

College Admission Counseling 55 students graduated in 2016; all went to college. Median SAT critical reading: 580, median SAT math: 610, median SAT writing: 590, median composite ACT: 28.

Student Life Upper grades have specified standards of dress, student council, honor system. Discipline rests equally with students and faculty.

Summer Programs Enrichment, sports, art/fine arts, computer instruction programs offered; session focuses on chess, computers, tennis, field hockey, lacrosse, soccer; held on campus; accepts boys and girls; open to students from other schools. 300 students usually enrolled. 2017 schedule: June 21 to August 21.

Tuition and Aid Day student tuition: $29,950. Tuition installment plan (Tuition Management Systems). Tuition reduction for siblings, need-based scholarship grants available. In 2016–17, 26% of upper-school students received aid.

Admissions Traditional secondary-level entrance grade is 9. For fall 2016, 225 students applied for upper-level admission, 102 enrolled. SSAT required. Deadline for receipt of application materials: February 5. Application fee required: $75. On-campus interview required.

Athletics Interscholastic: baseball (boys), basketball (b,g), fencing (b,g), flag football (b), hockey (b,g), ice hockey (b,g), lacrosse (b,g), soccer (b,g), softball (g), tennis (b,g); intramural: ballet (g), cheering (g), tennis (g); coed interscholastic: cross-country running, golf, squash; coed intramural: yoga. 3 PE instructors, 3 coaches, 1 athletic trainer.

Computers Computers are regularly used in art, English, foreign language, history, mathematics, music, science classes. Computer network features include on-campus library services, online commercial services, Internet access, wireless campus network, Internet filtering or blocking technology. Student e-mail accounts and computer access in designated common areas are available to students. Students grades are available online. The school has a published electronic and media policy.

Contact Mr. Michael Coope, Director of Admissions. 516-750-3203. Fax: 516-674-7063. E-mail: mcoope@portledge.org. Website: www.portledge.org

PORTSMOUTH ABBEY SCHOOL

285 Cory's Lane
Portsmouth, Rhode Island 02871

Head of School: Mr. Daniel McDonough

General Information Coeducational boarding and day college-preparatory school, affiliated with Roman Catholic Church. Grades 9–12. Founded: 1926. Setting: small town. Nearest major city is Providence. Students are housed in single-sex dormitories. 525-acre campus. 36 buildings on campus. Approved or accredited by Association of Independent Schools in New England, National Independent Private Schools Association, New England Association of Schools and Colleges, and The Association of Boarding Schools. Member of National Association of Independent Schools and Secondary School Admission Test Board. Endowment: $46 million. Total enrollment: 354. Upper school average class size: 13. Upper school faculty-student ratio: 1:7. There are 180 required school days per year for Upper School students. Upper School students typically attend 6 days per week. The average school day consists of 7 hours.

Upper School Student Profile Grade 9: 84 students (41 boys, 43 girls); Grade 10: 87 students (47 boys, 40 girls); Grade 11: 86 students (46 boys, 40 girls); Grade 12: 97 students (53 boys, 44 girls). 70% of students are boarding students. 35% are state residents. 24 states are represented in upper school student body. 16% are international students. International students from China, Dominican Republic, Guatemala, Republic of Korea, Spain, and Trinidad and Tobago; 15 other countries represented in student body. 60% of students are Roman Catholic.

Faculty School total: 79. In upper school: 31 men, 19 women; 40 have advanced degrees; 58 reside on campus.

Subjects Offered Algebra, American literature, art, art history, art history-AP, art-AP, biology, biology-AP, calculus, calculus-AP, chemistry, chemistry-AP, Chinese, Christian doctrine, Christian ethics, computer programming-AP, computer science, computer science-AP, creative writing, drama, drama workshop, economics, English, English language and composition-AP, English literature, English literature and composition-AP, fine arts, French, French language-AP, French literature-AP, geometry, government/civics, Greek, health, history, history-AP, humanities, international relations, Latin, Latin-AP, Mandarin, marine biology, mathematics, mathematics-AP, modern European history-AP, music, music composition, music theory, music theory-AP, philosophy, photography, physics, physics-AP, physiology, political science, religion, science, social sciences, Spanish, Spanish language-AP, Spanish literature-AP, statistics-AP, studio art-AP, theater, theology, trigonometry, U.S. history, U.S. history-AP, world history, writing workshop.

Graduation Requirements Arts and fine arts (art, music, dance, drama), English, foreign language, history, Latin, mathematics, religion (includes Bible studies and theology), science, humanities.

Special Academic Programs 17 Advanced Placement exams for which test preparation is offered; honors section; independent study; study abroad; academic accommodation for the gifted.

College Admission Counseling 118 students graduated in 2015; all went to college, including Boston College; Brown University; Georgetown University; New York University; Northeastern University; The George Washington University. Mean SAT critical reading: 618, mean SAT math: 616, mean SAT writing: 619, mean combined SAT: 1853.

Student Life Upper grades have specified standards of dress, student council, honor system. Discipline rests primarily with faculty. Attendance at religious services is required.

Tuition and Aid Day student tuition: $35,860; 7-day tuition and room/board: $54,630. Tuition installment plan (FACTS Tuition Payment Plan, monthly payment plans). Merit scholarship grants, need-based scholarship grants available. In 2015–16, 36% of upper-school students received aid; total upper-school merit-scholarship money awarded: $300,000. Total amount of financial aid awarded in 2015–16: $4,000,000.

Admissions Traditional secondary-level entrance grade is 9. For fall 2015, 550 students applied for upper-level admission, 208 were accepted, 114 enrolled. PSAT or SAT for applicants to grade 11 and 12, SSAT and TOEFL required. Deadline for receipt of application materials: January 31. Application fee required: $50. Interview required.

Athletics Interscholastic: baseball (boys), basketball (b,g), cross-country running (b,g), field hockey (g), football (b), golf (b,g), ice hockey (b,g), lacrosse (b,g), soccer (b,g), softball (g), squash (b,g), swimming and diving (b,g), tennis (b,g), track and field (b,g), wrestling (g); coed interscholastic: cross-country running, sailing, swimming and diving, track and field; coed intramural: ballet, dance, equestrian sports, fitness, horseback riding, modern dance, strength & conditioning, weight training. 1 athletic trainer.

Computers Computer network features include on-campus library services, online commercial services, Internet access, wireless campus network. Campus intranet and student e-mail accounts are available to students. Students grades are available online.

Contact Mrs. Ann Motta, Admissions Coordinator. 401-643-1248. Fax: 401-643-1355. E-mail: admissions@portsmouthabbey.org. Website: www.portsmouthabbey.org

PORTSMOUTH CHRISTIAN ACADEMY

20 Seaborne Drive
Dover, New Hampshire 03820

Head of School: Dr. John Engstrom

General Information Coeducational day college-preparatory and science/mathematics/fine arts school, affiliated with Christian faith. Grades K–12. Founded: 1979. Setting: rural. Nearest major city is Portsmouth. 50-acre campus. 2 buildings on campus. Approved or accredited by Association of Christian Schools International, New England Association of Schools and Colleges, and New Hampshire Department of Education. Total enrollment: 551. Upper school average class size: 16. Upper school faculty-student ratio: 1:9. There are 180 required school days per year for Upper School students. Upper School students typically attend 5 days per week. The average school day consists of 7 hours and 10 minutes.

Upper School Student Profile 70% of students are Christian faith.

Faculty School total: 55. In upper school: 13 men, 9 women; 16 have advanced degrees.

Subjects Offered 3-dimensional art, 3-dimensional design, ACT preparation, advanced chemistry, advanced math, Advanced Placement courses, advanced studio art-AP, algebra, American history, American literature, American literature-AP, anatomy and physiology, art, art education, art history, art history-AP, athletic training, athletics, band, baseball, basketball, Bible, biology, British literature, calculus, calculus-AP, chemistry, chemistry-AP, choir, choral music, chorus, Christian doctrine, Christian ethics, Christian studies, Christianity, church history, civics, college admission preparation, college awareness, college counseling, college placement, college planning, college writing, comparative religion, composition, computer applications, computer-aided design, debate, digital photography, drama, drama performance, drama workshop, drawing, drawing and design, economics, economics and history, English, English as a foreign language, English composition, English language and composition-AP, English literature and composition-AP, English literature-AP, English-AP, European history, film and literature, foreign language, French, French language-AP, geometry, government, government/civics, guitar, health and wellness, honors algebra, honors English, honors geometry, honors world history, human anatomy, instrumental music, integrated physics, jazz band, lab science, literature, literature and composition-AP, literature-AP, logic, rhetoric, and debate, marine science, mathematics, modern European history, music, musical productions, musical theater, New Testament, performing arts, photography, physics, physics-AP, pre-calculus, rhetoric, SAT preparation, SAT/ACT preparation, Shakespeare, Spanish, Spanish language-AP, Spanish-AP, student government, symphonic band, theater arts, theology, U.S. history, U.S. history-AP, world history, World War II, writing, writing workshop, yearbook.

Graduation Requirements Arts and fine arts (art, music, dance, drama), Bible, electives, English, foreign language, mathematics, physical education (includes health), science, social sciences, 1 Bible course for each year of Upper School attendance, service hours, participate in athletics.

Special Academic Programs 15 Advanced Placement exams for which test preparation is offered; honors section; accelerated programs; independent study; study at local college for college credit; academic accommodation for the gifted and the musically talented; programs in English, general development for dyslexic students; special instructional classes for deaf students, blind students, students with Attention Deficit Disorder and Dyslexia; ESL (15 students enrolled).

College Admission Counseling 45 students graduated in 2016; 44 went to college, including Boston College; Boston University; New York University; Penn State University Park; University of New Hampshire; Villanova University. Other: 1 entered military service. Mean SAT critical reading: 585, mean SAT math: 576, mean SAT writing: 579.

Student Life Upper grades have specified standards of dress, student council, honor system. Discipline rests primarily with faculty.

Summer Programs Remediation, enrichment, ESL, sports, art/fine arts programs offered; session focuses on soccer, basketball, and volleyball; ESL, instrumental, enrichment, remediation; held on campus; accepts boys and girls; open to students from other schools. 100 students usually enrolled. 2017 schedule: June 13 to August 19. Application deadline: May 15.

Tuition and Aid Day student tuition: $11,250–$22,000. Tuition installment plan (SMART Tuition Payment Plan, monthly payment plans). Need-based scholarship grants, Tuition Assistance available. In 2016–17, 32% of upper-school students received aid. Total amount of financial aid awarded in 2016–17: $225,000.

Admissions Traditional secondary-level entrance grade is 9. Achievement tests, PSAT or SAT, PSAT or SAT for applicants to grade 11 and 12, SAT, standardized test scores, Stanford Achievement Test, Test of Achievement and Proficiency, TOEFL or writing sample required. Deadline for receipt of application materials: none. Application fee required: $100. On-campus interview recommended.

Athletics Interscholastic: baseball (boys), basketball (b,g), cross-country running (b,g), gymnastics (g), horseback riding (g), indoor track & field (b,g), skiing (downhill) (b), soccer (b,g), softball (g), swimming and diving (g), tennis (b,g), track and field (b,g), triathlon (b), volleyball (g), winter (indoor) track (b,g); intramural: bicycling (b,g), golf (b,g), skiing (cross-country) (b,g), skiing (downhill) (b,g), snowboarding (b,g), table tennis (b,g), tennis (b,g); coed interscholastic: cross-country running, fitness, indoor track & field, track and field, winter (indoor) track; coed intramural: alpine skiing, bicycling, skiing (cross-country), skiing (downhill), snowboarding, table tennis, tennis. 1 PE instructor, 14 coaches.

Computers Computers are regularly used in college planning, graphic design, library, SAT preparation, yearbook classes. Computer network features include on-campus library services, online commercial services, Internet access, wireless campus network, Internet filtering or blocking technology. Student e-mail accounts and computer access in designated common areas are available to students. Students grades are available online. The school has a published electronic and media policy.

Contact Elaina Russo, Director of Admissions. 603-742-3617. Fax: 603-750-0490. E-mail: Admissions@pcaschool.org. Website: www.pcaschool.org

THE POTOMAC SCHOOL

1301 Potomac School Road
McLean, Virginia 22101

Head of School: John Kowalik

General Information Coeducational day college-preparatory and liberal arts, arts, athletics, and character education school. Grades K–12. Founded: 1904. Setting: suburban. Nearest major city is Washington, DC. 90-acre campus. Approved or accredited by Association of Independent Schools of Greater Washington and Virginia Association of Independent Schools. Member of National Association of Independent Schools and Secondary School Admission Test Board. Endowment: $36 million. Total enrollment: 1,032. Upper school average class size: 14. Upper school faculty-student ratio: 1:6.

Upper School Student Profile Grade 9: 113 students (52 boys, 61 girls); Grade 10: 118 students (62 boys, 56 girls); Grade 11: 118 students (58 boys, 60 girls); Grade 12: 110 students (59 boys, 51 girls).

Faculty School total: 160. In upper school: 29 men, 43 women.

Subjects Offered 20th century world history, 3-dimensional art, acting, advanced computer applications, advanced math, Advanced Placement courses, advanced studio art-AP, African-American studies, algebra, American literature, anatomy and physiology, ancient world history, architecture, art, art history, band, biology, biology-AP, British literature, calculus, calculus-AP, ceramics, character education, chemistry, chemistry-AP, Chinese history, choral music, civil rights, community service, comparative religion, computer programming, computer programming-AP, computer science, creative writing, debate, directing, drama, drawing and design, economics and history, engineering, English, English literature, environmental science, European history, expository writing, fine arts, foreign policy, French, French language-AP, French literature-AP, French-AP, geometry, global studies, government, government/civics, handbells, history of music, independent study, jazz band, Latin, Latin American history, Latin-AP, leadership, literary magazine, mathematics, Middle Eastern history, model United Nations, modern European history, music, music composition, music history, music theory-AP, newspaper, painting, performing arts, photography, physical education, physics, physics-AP, portfolio art, pre-calculus, robotics, science, science and technology, sculpture, senior project, Shakespeare, short story, Spanish, Spanish language-AP, Spanish literature-AP, stagecraft, statistics-AP,

strings, student government, studio art-AP, theater arts, trigonometry, U.S. government and politics, U.S. history-AP, vocal music, yearbook.

Graduation Requirements American history, arts and fine arts (art, music, dance, drama), English, foreign language, history, mathematics, physical education (includes health), science, senior project, world history, month-long senior project.

Special Academic Programs Advanced Placement exam preparation; honors section; independent study.

College Admission Counseling 97 students graduated in 2016; 95 went to college, including Duke University; Elon University; The College of William and Mary; University of Chicago; University of Notre Dame; University of Virginia. Other: 2 entered a postgraduate year. Mean SAT critical reading: 670, mean SAT math: 684, mean SAT writing: 684.

Student Life Upper grades have specified standards of dress, student council, honor system. Discipline rests equally with students and faculty.

Tuition and Aid Day student tuition: $38,550. Tuition installment plan (Insured Tuition Payment Plan, FACTS Tuition Payment Plan, monthly payment plans). Need-based scholarship grants available. In 2016–17, 18% of upper-school students received aid.

Admissions Traditional secondary-level entrance grade is 9. ISEE or SSAT required. Deadline for receipt of application materials: January 6. Application fee required: $65. Interview recommended.

Athletics Interscholastic: baseball (boys), basketball (b,g), cross-country running (b,g), field hockey (g), football (b), lacrosse (b,g), soccer (b,g), softball (g), squash (b,g), tennis (b,g), track and field (b,g), volleyball (g), wrestling (b); intramural: independent competitive sports (b,g); coed interscholastic: golf, ice hockey, indoor track & field, swimming and diving, winter (indoor) track; coed intramural: dance, fitness, physical fitness, physical training, sailing, strength & conditioning, weight training, yoga. 5 PE instructors, 60 coaches, 2 athletic trainers.

Computers Computers are regularly used in all academic, computer applications, independent study, literary magazine, newspaper, photography, programming, yearbook classes. Computer network features include on-campus library services, online commercial services, Internet access, wireless campus network, Internet filtering or blocking technology, eBooks. Campus intranet, student e-mail accounts, and computer access in designated common areas are available to students. Students grades are available online. The school has a published electronic and media policy.

Contact Ellen Fitzpatrick, Admission Services Coordinator. 703-749-6313. Fax: 703-356-1764. E-mail: admission@potomacschool.org. Website: www.potomacschool.org

POUGHKEEPSIE DAY SCHOOL

260 Boardman Road
Poughkeepsie, New York 12603

Head of School: Benedict Chant

General Information Coeducational day college-preparatory, arts, and technology school. Grades PK–12. Founded: 1934. Setting: suburban. Nearest major city is New York. 35-acre campus. 2 buildings on campus. Approved or accredited by New York State Association of Independent Schools and New York Department of Education. Member of National Association of Independent Schools. Endowment: $4.1 million. Total enrollment: 264. Upper school average class size: 12. Upper school faculty-student ratio: 1:7. There are 165 required school days per year for Upper School students. Upper School students typically attend 5 days per week. The average school day consists of 7 hours.

Upper School Student Profile Grade 9: 30 students (14 boys, 16 girls); Grade 10: 24 students (13 boys, 11 girls); Grade 11: 22 students (10 boys, 12 girls); Grade 12: 30 students (14 boys, 16 girls).

Faculty School total: 45. In upper school: 9 men, 11 women; 10 have advanced degrees.

Subjects Offered 3-dimensional art, acting, advanced math, Advanced Placement courses, African drumming, algebra, American literature, American literature-AP, analysis and differential calculus, analytic geometry, anatomy, anatomy and physiology, ancient history, ancient world history, art history, arts, Basic programming, bioethics, biology, calculus, calculus-AP, chamber groups, chemistry, collage and assemblage, college admission preparation, college planning, community service, computer programming, computer science, computer-aided design, conflict resolution, contemporary art, creative arts, creative drama, creative writing, decision making skills, desktop publishing, digital art, digital music, digital photography, discrete mathematics, drama, drama performance, drawing, ecology, economics, English, English literature, English literature-AP, English-AP, ensembles, European civilization, European history, fiction, filmmaking, fine arts, French, French language-AP, French-AP, geology, geometry, guitar, history, Holocaust and other genocides, Holocaust studies, independent study, instrumental music, integrated arts, interdisciplinary studies, Islamic studies, jazz band, jazz ensemble, lab science, leadership, life saving, life skills, linear algebra, literary magazine, literature, literature-AP, mathematics, modern European history, multicultural literature, multicultural studies, music, music appreciation, music composition, music performance, music theory, music theory-AP, musical productions, oil painting, painting, peer counseling, performing arts, photography, physical education, physical science, physics, physiology, play production, playwriting and directing, pre-calculus, printmaking, probability and statistics, religion and culture, SAT preparation, science, senior internship, service learning/internship, social issues, social studies, Spanish, Spanish language-AP, Spanish-AP, stained glass, statistics, strings, studio art, theater arts, theater production, trigonometry, U.S. history, video film production, visual arts, voice ensemble, Western civilization, wind ensemble, writing workshop, yearbook, zoology.

Graduation Requirements Algebra, arts, biology, chemistry, college planning, electives, English, English literature, foreign language, geometry, interdisciplinary studies, life skills, mathematics, music, performing arts, physical education (includes health), physics, physiology, pre-calculus, SAT preparation, senior internship, senior thesis, trigonometry, visual arts, four-week off-campus senior internship. Community service is required.

Special Academic Programs 10 Advanced Placement exams for which test preparation is offered; honors section; independent study; term-away projects; study at local college for college credit; academic accommodation for the gifted, the musically talented, and the artistically talented; ESL (17 students enrolled).

College Admission Counseling 38 students graduated in 2016; all went to college, including Earlham College; Hobart and William Smith Colleges; Ithaca College; Johns Hopkins University; Rensselaer Polytechnic Institute; Rhode Island School of Design. Mean SAT critical reading: 653, mean SAT math: 620, mean SAT writing: 637, mean combined SAT: 1910. 90% scored over 600 on SAT critical reading, 90% scored over 600 on SAT math, 90% scored over 600 on SAT writing, 90% scored over 1800 on combined SAT.

Student Life Upper grades have student council, honor system. Discipline rests primarily with faculty.

Summer Programs Enrichment, art/fine arts programs offered; session focuses on visual and performing arts, enrichment, jazz; held on campus; accepts boys and girls; open to students from other schools. 200 students usually enrolled. 2017 schedule: June 15 to August 21. Application deadline: June 1.

Tuition and Aid Day student tuition: $26,220. Tuition installment plan (FACTS Tuition Payment Plan, The Tuition Refund Plan). Need-based scholarship grants, tuition reduction for children of full-time faculty and staff available. In 2016–17, 43% of upper-school students received aid. Total amount of financial aid awarded in 2016–17: $550,000.

Admissions Traditional secondary-level entrance grade is 9. For fall 2016, 35 students applied for upper-level admission, 24 were accepted, 13 enrolled. School's own exam required. Deadline for receipt of application materials: none. Application fee required: $50. On-campus interview required.

Athletics Interscholastic: baseball (boys), basketball (b,g), cross-country running (b,g), soccer (b,g), softball (g), volleyball (g); intramural: basketball (b,g), softball (g); coed interscholastic: cross-country running, Frisbee, soccer, ultimate Frisbee; coed intramural: alpine skiing, basketball, cooperative games, cross-country running, dance, fitness, fitness walking, Frisbee, hiking/backpacking, jogging, life saving, outdoor education, outdoor skills, outdoors, skiing (downhill), snowboarding, soccer, ultimate Frisbee, volleyball, walking, yoga. 2 PE instructors, 12 coaches.

Computers Computers are regularly used in all academic, college planning, desktop publishing, journalism, library skills, literary magazine, media, music, newspaper, photography, photojournalism, programming, SAT preparation, video film production, Web site design, yearbook classes. Computer network features include on-campus library services, online commercial services, Internet access, wireless campus network, EBSCOhost, Maps101, Web Feet Guides, Gale databases, ProQuest, unitedstreaming, Britannica Online, World Book Online, Grolier Online. Campus intranet, student e-mail accounts, and computer access in designated common areas are available to students. Students grades are available online. The school has a published electronic and media policy.

Contact Tammy Reilly, Director of Admissions. 845-462-7600 Ext. 201. Fax: 845-746-2686. E-mail: treilly@poughkeepsieday.org. Website: www.poughkeepsieday.org/

POWERS CATHOLIC HIGH SCHOOL

1505 West Court Street
Flint, Michigan 48503

Head of School: Mrs. Sally Bartos

General Information Coeducational day college-preparatory school, affiliated with Roman Catholic Church. Grades 9–12. Founded: 1970. Setting: urban. 80-acre campus. 1 building on campus. Approved or accredited by National Catholic Education Association, North Central Association of Colleges and Schools, and Michigan Department of Education. Endowment: $3 million. Total enrollment: 605. Upper school average class size: 25. Upper school faculty-student ratio: 1:18. There are 188 required school days per year for Upper School students. Upper School students typically attend 5 days per week. The average school day consists of 6 hours and 51 minutes.

Upper School Student Profile Grade 9: 165 students (81 boys, 84 girls); Grade 10: 179 students (91 boys, 88 girls); Grade 11: 191 students (107 boys, 84 girls); Grade 12: 138 students (65 boys, 73 girls). 80% of students are Roman Catholic.

Faculty School total: 37. In upper school: 17 men, 19 women; 26 have advanced degrees.

Subjects Offered Art, art-AP, biology, biology-AP, calculus-AP, ceramics, chemistry, choir, computer skills, concert band, drafting, economics, English, English literature and composition-AP, European history-AP, French, geometry, government, government-AP, health, honors algebra, honors English, honors geometry, integrated science, interdisciplinary studies, macroeconomics-AP, marching band, math analysis,

math applications, mechanical drawing, physics, pre-algebra, pre-calculus, psychology, psychology-AP, public speaking, religion, social justice, Spanish, state history, studio art-AP, theology, trigonometry, U.S. history, wind ensemble, world geography, world history, world religions, yearbook.

Graduation Requirements American history, English, French, government, health, mathematics, science, Spanish, theology, world history, 40 hours of community service (5 hours for each semester in attendance at Powers).

Special Academic Programs 7 Advanced Placement exams for which test preparation is offered; honors section; study at local college for college credit; remedial reading and/or remedial writing; remedial math.

College Admission Counseling 138 students graduated in 2016; 133 went to college, including Central Michigan University; Grand Valley State University; Hope College; Michigan State University; Saginaw Valley State University; University of Michigan. Other: 2 entered military service, 3 had other specific plans. Mean composite ACT: 23.

Student Life Upper grades have uniform requirement, student council. Discipline rests primarily with faculty. Attendance at religious services is required.

Tuition and Aid Day student tuition: $9165. Tuition installment plan (SMART Tuition Payment Plan). Tuition reduction for siblings, need-based scholarship grants available. In 2016–17, 50% of upper-school students received aid. Total amount of financial aid awarded in 2016–17: $400,000.

Admissions Traditional secondary-level entrance grade is 9. ACT-Explore or admissions testing required. Deadline for receipt of application materials: none. Application fee required: $100. Interview required.

Athletics Interscholastic: baseball (boys), basketball (b,g), bowling (b,g), cheering (g), cross-country running (b,g), dance squad (g), dance team (g), diving (b,g), football (b), golf (b,g), ice hockey (b), lacrosse (b,g), skiing (downhill) (b,g), soccer (b,g), softball (g), swimming and diving (b,g), tennis (b,g), track and field (b,g), volleyball (g), wrestling (b); coed interscholastic: indoor track, power lifting, skeet shooting, strength & conditioning, weight lifting; coed intramural: ultimate Frisbee, weight training. 1 PE instructor.

Computers Computers are regularly used in accounting, business applications, drafting, graphic design, keyboarding, yearbook classes. Computer network features include on-campus library services, Internet access, wireless campus network, Internet filtering or blocking technology. Computer access in designated common areas is available to students. Students grades are available online. The school has a published electronic and media policy.

Contact Mr. Brian Sheeran, Athletic Director. 810-591-4741. Fax: 810-591-1794. E-mail: bsheeran@powerscatholic.org. Website: www.powerscatholic.org/

PRESBYTERIAN PAN AMERICAN SCHOOL

PO Box 1578
223 North FM Road 772
Kingsville, Texas 78364-1578

Head of School: Dr. Doug Dalglish

General Information Coeducational boarding and day and distance learning college-preparatory, career, Human Anatomy & Physiology, Intro. To Business, and Principles of Engineering school, affiliated with Presbyterian Church. Grades 9–12. Distance learning grades 9–12. Founded: 1912. Setting: rural. Nearest major city is Corpus Christi. Students are housed in single-sex dormitories. 670-acre campus. 23 buildings on campus. Approved or accredited by Southern Association of Colleges and Schools, Texas Private School Accreditation Commission, and Texas Department of Education. Endowment: $9.4 million. Total enrollment: 168. Upper school average class size: 22. Upper school faculty-student ratio: 1:10. There are 180 required school days per year for Upper School students. Upper School students typically attend 5 days per week. The average school day consists of 8 hours.

Upper School Student Profile Grade 9: 26 students (12 boys, 14 girls); Grade 10: 32 students (11 boys, 21 girls); Grade 11: 49 students (22 boys, 27 girls); Grade 12: 33 students (20 boys, 13 girls). 99% of students are boarding students. 1% are state residents. 1 state is represented in upper school student body. 99% are international students. International students from China, Colombia, Kenya, Mexico, Republic of Korea, and Rwanda; 5 other countries represented in student body. 34% of students are Presbyterian.

Faculty School total: 17. In upper school: 8 men, 9 women; 6 have advanced degrees; 2 reside on campus.

Subjects Offered Algebra, American history, American literature, anatomy and physiology, animal science, art, arts, Bible studies, biology, business, calculus, career exploration, chemistry, choir, communications, computer science, debate, economics, engineering, English, English literature, ESL, geography, geometry, government/civics, health, horticulture, journalism, literary genres, mathematical modeling, physical education, physics, pre-calculus, religion, Spanish, theater arts, U.S. history, world history, world literature, yearbook.

Graduation Requirements Algebra, arts and fine arts (art, music, dance, drama), Bible, biology, career/college preparation, chemistry, communications, economics, electives, English, ESL, foreign language, government, health, junior and senior seminars, mathematical modeling, physical education (includes health), physics, pre-calculus, science, social studies (includes history), U.S. history, world geography, world history, TOEFL score of 550, or SAT Reading of 550.

Special Academic Programs 3 Advanced Placement exams for which test preparation is offered; honors section; independent study; study at local college for college credit; ESL (39 students enrolled).

College Admission Counseling 47 students graduated in 2016; all went to college, including Schreiner University; Texas A&M University–Kingsville; The University of Texas at San Antonio. Median SAT critical reading: 420, median SAT math: 460, median SAT writing: 420. 4% scored over 600 on SAT critical reading, 5% scored over 600 on SAT math.

Student Life Upper grades have uniform requirement, student council, honor system. Discipline rests primarily with faculty. Attendance at religious services is required.

Tuition and Aid Day student tuition: $10,500; 7-day tuition and room/board: $19,000. Guaranteed tuition plan. Tuition installment plan (monthly payment plans, individually arranged payment plans, quarterly payment plan, semester payment plan). Tuition reduction for siblings, merit scholarship grants, need-based scholarship grants, need-based financial aid, discounts tied to enrollment referred by current student families available. In 2016–17, 94% of upper-school students received aid. Total amount of financial aid awarded in 2016–17: $1,342,850.

Admissions Traditional secondary-level entrance grade is 10. For fall 2016, 84 students applied for upper-level admission, 55 were accepted, 46 enrolled. Any standardized test, PSAT, SAT, or ACT for applicants to grade 11 and 12, TerraNova or TOEFL required. Deadline for receipt of application materials: none. Application fee required: $75. Interview required.

Athletics Interscholastic: baseball (boys), basketball (b,g), cheering (b,g), cross-country running (b,g), soccer (b,g), track and field (b,g), volleyball (g); intramural: billiards (b), jogging (b,g), life saving (b,g), paddle tennis (b,g), physical fitness (b,g), strength & conditioning (b,g), table tennis (b,g), tennis (b,g), volleyball (b), walking (b,g), winter walking (b,g); coed intramural: aquatics, fitness walking, jogging, life saving, paddle tennis, strength & conditioning, table tennis, volleyball, walking, winter walking. 1 PE instructor, 2 coaches.

Computers Computers are regularly used in all academic, art, Bible studies, business, career exploration, college planning, economics, engineering, English, ESL, geography, health, history, journalism, mathematics, publications, religion, SAT preparation, science, senior seminar, social sciences, theater arts, yearbook classes. Computer network features include on-campus library services, Internet access, wireless campus network, Internet filtering or blocking technology. Campus intranct, student e-mail accounts, and computer access in designated common areas are available to students. Students grades are available online. The school has a published electronic and media policy.

Contact Joe L. Garcia, Director of Admissions. 361-592-4307 Ext. 1004. Fax: 361-592-6126. E-mail: jlgarcia@ppas.org. Website: www.ppas.org

PRESTON HIGH SCHOOL

2780 Schurz Avenue
Bronx, New York 10465

Head of School: Mrs. Jane Grendell

General Information Girls' day college-preparatory school, affiliated with Roman Catholic Church. Grades 9–12. Founded: 1947. Setting: urban. Nearest major city is New York. 2-acre campus. 2 buildings on campus. Approved or accredited by Middle States Association of Colleges and Schools, New York Department of Education, New York State Board of Regents, and New York Department of Education. Total enrollment: 511. Upper school average class size: 25. Upper school faculty-student ratio: 1:10. There are 180 required school days per year for Upper School students. Upper School students typically attend 5 days per week. The average school day consists of 6 hours and 14 minutes.

Upper School Student Profile Grade 9: 130 students (130 girls); Grade 10: 118 students (118 girls); Grade 11: 104 students (104 girls); Grade 12: 144 students (144 girls). 70% of students are Roman Catholic.

Faculty School total: 50. In upper school: 16 men, 34 women; 35 have advanced degrees.

Subjects Offered 1 1/2 elective credits, advanced computer applications, advanced math, advanced studio art-AP, advertising design, algebra, American government, American history, American history-AP, American legal systems, American literature, anatomy, anatomy and physiology, art, art appreciation, art education, art history, art-AP, arts, athletic training, band, Basic programming, biology, biology-AP, British literature, British literature (honors), broadcast journalism, calculus, Catholic belief and practice, chamber groups, character education, chemistry, choir, Christian doctrine, civics, classical language, college admission preparation, college counseling, college planning, college writing, commercial art, communication skills, communications, community service, comparative religion, composition, computer animation, computer art, computer graphics, computer literacy, computer multimedia, computer processing, computer programming, computer skills, concert choir, constitutional law, consumer economics, consumer mathematics, creative drama, design, digital art, drama, drama workshop, dramatic arts, earth science, economics, economics and history, electives, English, English composition, English language and composition-AP, English language-AP, English literature, English literature and composition-AP, English literature-AP, English-AP, ensembles, film, film studies, fine arts, fitness, folk dance, forensics, gender and religion, gender issues, general science, geometry, global studies, government, government/civics, graphic arts, graphic design, guidance, health, health

education, Hispanic literature, history, history of the Catholic Church, history-AP, honors algebra, honors English, honors geometry, honors U.S. history, humanities, instruments, integrated mathematics, introduction to literature, introduction to theater, lab science, language, language arts, language-AP, Latin, law, law and the legal system, life science, literacy, literature, literature and composition-AP, literature-AP, marketing, mathematics, modern civilization, modern European history, modern history, modern languages, modern Western civilization, moral and social development, music, music appreciation, music performance, music theory, musical productions, musical theater dance, mythology, New Testament, peer ministry, personal fitness, philosophy, physical education, physical fitness, physical science, physics, physiology, play production, play/screen writing, portfolio art, pre-calculus, psychology, public speaking, reading, reading/study skills, religion, religion and culture, religious education, religious studies, SAT preparation, science, scripture, senior humanities, senior project, senior seminar, senior thesis, service learning/internship, social sciences, social studies, socioeconomic problems, sociology, Spanish, Spanish language-AP, Spanish literature, Spanish literature-AP, Spanish-AP, speech, speech and oral interpretations, speech communications, telecommunications, television, theater arts, theology, trigonometry, U.S. constitutional history, U.S. government, U.S. government and politics, U.S. history, U.S. history-AP, U.S. literature, video, video and animation, video communication, video film production, visual and performing arts, vocal ensemble, vocal music, voice, voice ensemble, weight fitness, weight training, Western civilization, Western literature, wilderness education, wind ensemble, women in society, women spirituality and faith, world history, world literature, world religions, world religions, writing, writing, writing workshop, yearbook.

Graduation Requirements All academic, American history, art, arts and fine arts (art, music, dance, drama), communications, computer skills, economics, electives, English, foreign language, government, health, independent study, mathematics, music, physical education (includes health), reading, religion (includes Bible studies and theology), science, social studies (includes history), theology, world history, students must complete an Independent Senior Project, students must complete service hours at home, at school and at an approved agency or site.

Special Academic Programs Advanced Placement exam preparation; honors section; independent study; study at local college for college credit.

College Admission Counseling 130 students graduated in 2016; 128 went to college, including Binghamton University, State University of New York; Iona College; Manhattan College; Pace University; St. John's University; Westchester Community College. Other: 1 entered a postgraduate year, 1 had other specific plans. Median SAT critical reading: 500, median SAT math: 500, median SAT writing: 470, median combined SAT: 1470. 11% scored over 600 on SAT critical reading, 9% scored over 600 on SAT math, 12% scored over 600 on SAT writing.

Student Life Upper grades have uniform requirement, student council, honor system. Discipline rests equally with students and faculty. Attendance at religious services is required.

Summer Programs Remediation, enrichment, advancement programs offered; session focuses on enrichment and advancement for incoming freshmen; held on campus; accepts girls; not open to students from other schools. 90 students usually enrolled. 2017 schedule: July 31 to August 11. Application deadline: June 23.

Tuition and Aid Day student tuition: $9820. Tuition installment plan (FACTS Tuition Payment Plan, monthly payment plans). Tuition reduction for siblings, merit scholarship grants, need-based scholarship grants available. In 2016–17, 25% of upper-school students received aid; total upper-school merit-scholarship money awarded: $625,000. Total amount of financial aid awarded in 2016–17: $510,000.

Admissions Traditional secondary-level entrance grade is 9. For fall 2016, 492 students applied for upper-level admission, 395 were accepted, 130 enrolled. Math, reading, and mental ability tests, New York Archdiocesan Cooperative Entrance Examination, school placement exam and writing sample required. Deadline for receipt of application materials: none. No application fee required.

Athletics Interscholastic: basketball, cheering, fitness, soccer, softball, volleyball; intramural: yoga. 2 PE instructors, 9 coaches.

Computers Computers are regularly used in all academic, graphic design, programming, video film production, Web site design, yearbook classes. Computer network features include on-campus library services, Internet access, Internet filtering or blocking technology. Students grades are available online. The school has a published electronic and media policy.

Contact Mrs. Cristina Fragale, Director of Admissions. 718-863-9134 Ext. 132. Fax: 718-863-6125. E-mail: cfragale@prestonhs.org. Website: www.prestonhs.org

PRESTONWOOD CHRISTIAN ACADEMY

6801 West Park Boulevard
Plano, Texas 75093

Head of School: Dr. Larry Taylor

General Information Coeducational day and distance learning college-preparatory and Bible courses school, affiliated with Southern Baptist Convention. Grades PK–12. Distance learning grades 6–12. Founded: 1997. Setting: suburban. Nearest major city is Dallas. 44-acre campus. 2 buildings on campus. Approved or accredited by Southern Association of Colleges and Schools and Texas Department of Education. Total enrollment: 1,551. Upper school average class size: 18. Upper school faculty-student ratio: 1:12. There are 172 required school days per year for Upper School students.

Upper School students typically attend 5 days per week. The average school day consists of 7 hours and 35 minutes.

Upper School Student Profile Grade 9: 133 students (67 boys, 66 girls); Grade 10: 129 students (75 boys, 54 girls); Grade 11: 126 students (66 boys, 60 girls); Grade 12: 119 students (61 boys, 58 girls). 66% of students are Southern Baptist Convention.

Faculty School total: 128. In upper school: 13 men, 25 women; 20 have advanced degrees.

Subjects Offered 20th century history, 20th century physics, advanced chemistry, advanced math, Advanced Placement courses, algebra, American history-AP, American literature, anatomy and physiology, art, art-AP, band, Bible, biology, biology-AP, British literature, calculus-AP, ceramics, chemistry, choir, Christian doctrine, computer applications, conceptual physics, debate, drama, drawing, economics, ethics, fine arts, fitness, geometry, government, government-AP, health, honors algebra, honors English, honors geometry, honors U.S. history, honors world history, internship, language-AP, leadership education training, learning lab, literature-AP, logic, multimedia, multimedia design, newspaper, painting, performing arts, personal fitness, philosophy, photo shop, physical fitness, physics, physics-AP, pre-calculus, printmaking, sculpture, service learning/internship, Spanish, Spanish-AP, speech, statistics, strings, student government, studio art, U.S. government and politics-AP, U.S. history, Web site design, Western literature, world history, world religions, yearbook.

Graduation Requirements 1 1/2 elective credits, algebra, arts and fine arts (art, music, dance, drama), Bible, biology, British literature, chemistry, Christian doctrine, computer applications, economics, English, English literature, ethics, foreign language, geometry, government, mathematics, philosophy, physical education (includes health), physics, speech, U.S. history, Western literature, world history, mission trip.

Special Academic Programs Advanced Placement exam preparation; honors section; academic accommodation for the gifted.

College Admission Counseling 130 students graduated in 2016; all went to college, including Baylor University; Oklahoma State University; Southern Methodist University; Texas A&M University; The University of Texas at Austin; University of Oklahoma. Median SAT critical reading: 560, median SAT math: 550, median SAT writing: 550, median combined SAT: 1540, median composite ACT: 24. 37% scored over 600 on SAT critical reading, 35% scored over 600 on SAT math, 31% scored over 600 on SAT writing, 47% scored over 1800 on combined SAT, 38% scored over 26 on composite ACT.

Student Life Upper grades have uniform requirement, student council, honor system. Discipline rests primarily with faculty. Attendance at religious services is required.

Summer Programs Remediation, enrichment, advancement, sports, art/fine arts, rigorous outdoor training, computer instruction programs offered; held on campus; accepts boys and girls; open to students from other schools. 800 students usually enrolled. 2017 schedule: June 1 to August 5. Application deadline: May 1.

Tuition and Aid Day student tuition: $19,276–$19,866. Tuition installment plan (FACTS Tuition Payment Plan, monthly payment plans, individually arranged payment plans). Tuition reduction for siblings, need-based scholarship grants available. In 2016–17, 21% of upper-school students received aid. Total amount of financial aid awarded in 2016–17: $734,381.

Admissions Traditional secondary-level entrance grade is 9. For fall 2016, 117 students applied for upper-level admission, 59 were accepted, 50 enrolled. ISEE or Stanford Achievement Test required. Deadline for receipt of application materials: none. Application fee required: $100. Interview recommended.

Athletics Interscholastic: baseball (boys), basketball (b,g), cheering (g), cross-country running (b,g), drill team (g), football (b), golf (b,g), soccer (b,g), softball (g), swimming and diving (b,g), tennis (b,g), track and field (b,g), volleyball (g). 7 PE instructors, 42 coaches.

Computers Computers are regularly used in all academic, technology classes. Computer network features include on-campus library services, Internet access, wireless campus network, Internet filtering or blocking technology. Student e-mail accounts are available to students. Students grades are available online. The school has a published electronic and media policy.

Contact Mrs. Allison P. Taylor, Admissions Assistant. 972-930-4010. Fax: 972-930-4008. E-mail: aptaylor@prestonwoodchristian.org.
Website: www.prestonwoodchristian.org

PROCTOR ACADEMY

PO Box 500
204 Main Street
Andover, New Hampshire 03216

Head of School: Mr. Michael Henriques

General Information Coeducational boarding and day college-preparatory, arts, environmental studies, and experiential learning programs school. Grades 9–12. Founded: 1848. Setting: small town. Nearest major city is Concord. Students are housed in single-sex dormitories. 3,000-acre campus. 46 buildings on campus. Approved or accredited by Association for Experiential Education, Association of Independent Schools in New England, Independent Schools of Northern New England, New England Association of Schools and Colleges, The Association of Boarding Schools, and New Hampshire Department of Education. Member of National Association of Independent Schools and Secondary School Admission Test Board. Endowment: $25 million. Total enrollment: 360. Upper school average class size: 12. Upper school

faculty-student ratio: 1:5. There are 175 required school days per year for Upper School students. Upper School students typically attend 6 days per week. The average school day consists of 5 hours and 45 minutes.

Upper School Student Profile Grade 9: 71 students (41 boys, 30 girls); Grade 10: 80 students (48 boys, 32 girls); Grade 11: 114 students (68 boys, 46 girls); Grade 12: 106 students (59 boys, 47 girls). 78% of students are boarding students. 26% are state residents. 28 states are represented in upper school student body. 9% are international students. International students from Canada, China, Italy, Mexico, Spain, and Viet Nam; 10 other countries represented in student body.

Faculty School total: 85. In upper school: 39 men, 46 women; 66 have advanced degrees; 55 reside on campus.

Subjects Offered Algebra, American history, American literature, art, art history, biology, boat building, calculus, ceramics, chemistry, computer math, computer programming, creative writing, drama, economics, English, English literature, environmental science, European history, fine arts, finite math, forestry, French, genetics, geometry, health, history, industrial arts, mathematics, Middle Eastern history, music, music history, music technology, Native American history, performing arts, photography, physical education, physics, piano, play/screen writing, poetry, political thought, probability and statistics, psychology, public speaking, publications, science, senior project, social sciences, Spanish, sports medicine, studio art, study skills, the Web, theater, theater history, U.S. government and politics-AP, U.S. history-AP, Vietnam history, voice, voice ensemble, wilderness experience, woodworking, world literature, writing, writing workshop.

Graduation Requirements Arts and fine arts (art, music, dance, drama), English, foreign language, mathematics, science, social sciences.

Special Academic Programs 14 Advanced Placement exams for which test preparation is offered; honors section; independent study; term-away projects; study at local college for college credit; study abroad; academic accommodation for the gifted; programs in general development for dyslexic students; ESL (9 students enrolled).

College Admission Counseling 96 students graduated in 2016; all went to college, including Denison University; Elon University; St. Lawrence University; Syracuse University; The George Washington University; University of New Hampshire. Mean SAT critical reading: 555, mean SAT math: 560, mean SAT writing: 545, mean combined SAT: 1660, mean composite ACT: 23. 20% scored over 600 on SAT critical reading, 24% scored over 600 on SAT math, 22% scored over 600 on SAT writing, 28% scored over 1800 on combined SAT, 24% scored over 26 on composite ACT.

Student Life Upper grades have student council, honor system. Discipline rests equally with students and faculty.

Tuition and Aid Day student tuition: $34,500; 7-day tuition and room/board: $57,200. Tuition installment plan (SMART Tuition Payment Plan). Need-based scholarship grants available. In 2016–17, 32% of upper-school students received aid. Total amount of financial aid awarded in 2016–17: $3,200,000.

Admissions Traditional secondary-level entrance grade is 9. For fall 2016, 708 students applied for upper-level admission, 253 were accepted, 121 enrolled. ISEE, PSAT or SAT for applicants to grade 11 and 12, SSAT, TOEFL or SLEP, WISC/Woodcock-Johnson or writing sample required. Deadline for receipt of application materials: February 1. Application fee required: $50. Interview recommended.

Athletics Interscholastic: alpine skiing (boys, girls), archery (b,g), baseball (b), basketball (b,g), bicycling (b,g), canoeing/kayaking (b,g), cross-country running (b,g), field hockey (g), football (b), hockey (b,g), ice hockey (b,g), lacrosse (b,g), nordic skiing (b,g); intramural: alpine skiing (b,g); coed interscholastic: crew, dance, freestyle skiing, golf, horseback riding, kayaking; coed intramural: aerobics/dance, aerobics/Nautilus, backpacking, ballet, broomball, canoeing/kayaking, climbing, combined training, dance, equestrian sports, fencing, fitness, Frisbee, hiking/backpacking, horseback riding, kayaking, martial arts, modern dance, mountain biking, mountaineering, outdoor activities, outdoor adventure, outdoor education, outdoor recreation, outdoor skills, outdoors, paint ball, rock climbing, yoga. 5 coaches, 2 athletic trainers.

Computers Computers are regularly used in all academic classes. Computer network features include on-campus library services, online commercial services, Internet access, wireless campus network, Internet filtering or blocking technology. Campus intranet and student e-mail accounts are available to students. Students grades are available online. The school has a published electronic and media policy.

Contact Lisa Wood, Admissions Office Coordinator. 603-735-6312. Fax: 603-735-6284. E-mail: woodli@proctoracademy.org. Website: www.proctoracademy.org

PROFESSIONAL CHILDREN'S SCHOOL

132 West 60th Street
New York, New York 10023

Head of School: Dr. James Dawson

General Information Coeducational day college-preparatory school. Grades 6–12. Founded: 1914. Setting: urban. 1 building on campus. Approved or accredited by New York State Association of Independent Schools. Member of National Association of Independent Schools. Endowment: $2.7 million. Total enrollment: 198. Upper school average class size: 16. Upper school faculty-student ratio: 1:8. There are 162 required school days per year for Upper School students. Upper School students typically attend 5 days per week. The average school day consists of 7 hours.

Upper School Student Profile Grade 6: 5 students (3 boys, 2 girls); Grade 7: 10 students (6 boys, 4 girls); Grade 8: 15 students (9 boys, 6 girls); Grade 9: 39 students (27 boys, 12 girls); Grade 10: 44 students (29 boys, 15 girls); Grade 11: 41 students (24 boys, 17 girls); Grade 12: 44 students (30 boys, 14 girls).

Faculty School total: 29. In upper school: 13 men, 12 women; 20 have advanced degrees.

Subjects Offered Advanced math, algebra, American government, American history, biology, calculus, chemistry, chorus, computer education, constitutional history of U.S., constitutional law, creative writing, drama, English, English literature, environmental science, ESL, foreign language, French, general math, geometry, health education, introduction to literature, keyboarding, library research, library skills, physical education, physics, pre-algebra, pre-calculus, Spanish, studio art, U.S. government, U.S. history.

Graduation Requirements Art, English, foreign language, health, history, mathematics, science.

Special Academic Programs ESL (35 students enrolled).

College Admission Counseling 52 students graduated in 2016; 37 went to college. Other: 3 went to work, 1 entered military service, 6 entered a postgraduate year, 5 had other specific plans.

Student Life Upper grades have student council, honor system. Discipline rests primarily with faculty.

Summer Programs Remediation, enrichment, advancement programs offered; held off campus; held at Online; accepts boys and girls; open to students from other schools. 20 students usually enrolled. 2017 schedule: June 25 to August 15. Application deadline: July 1.

Tuition and Aid Day student tuition: $38,300. Tuition installment plan (Tuition Management Systems). Need-based scholarship grants available. In 2016–17, 30% of upper-school students received aid. Total amount of financial aid awarded in 2016–17: $795,802.

Admissions Traditional secondary-level entrance grade is 9. For fall 2016, 85 students applied for upper-level admission, 75 were accepted, 55 enrolled. Deadline for receipt of application materials: none. Application fee required: $75. Interview required.

Athletics 1 PE instructor.

Computers Computers are regularly used in all academic classes. Computer network features include on-campus library services, Internet access, wireless campus network, Internet filtering or blocking technology. Student e-mail accounts and computer access in designated common areas are available to students. The school has a published electronic and media policy.

Contact Ms. Shari Honig, Director of Admissions. 212-582-3116 Ext. 112. Fax: 212-307-6542. E-mail: admissions@pcs-nyc.org. Website: www.pcs-nyc.org

THE PROUT SCHOOL

4640 Tower Hill Road
Wakefield, Rhode Island 02879

Head of School: Mr. David Estes

General Information Coeducational day college-preparatory, arts, religious studies, and technology school, affiliated with Roman Catholic Church. Grades 9–12. Founded: 1966. Setting: small town. Nearest major city is Providence. 25-acre campus. 1 building on campus. Approved or accredited by International Baccalaureate Organization, New England Association of Schools and Colleges, Rhode Island State Certified Resource Program, and Rhode Island Department of Education. Member of National Association of Independent Schools. Total enrollment: 500. Upper school average class size: 23. Upper school faculty-student ratio: 1:18. There are 182 required school days per year for Upper School students. Upper School students typically attend 5 days per week. The average school day consists of 6 hours and 30 minutes.

Upper School Student Profile 75% of students are Roman Catholic.

Faculty School total: 48. In upper school: 20 men, 28 women; 40 have advanced degrees.

Subjects Offered Acting, American literature, anatomy and physiology, art education, art history, athletic training, ballet, ballet technique, band, biology, calculus, chemistry, choir, chorus, Christian doctrine, Christian education, Christian ethics, Christian scripture, Christian studies, Christianity, church history, clayworking, college planning, college writing, community service, comparative religion, computer applications, computer art, computer education, computer graphics, computer multimedia, computer programming, computer science, computer skills, computer studies, contemporary history, contemporary issues, costumes and make-up, CPR, creative dance, creative drama, creative thinking, critical studies in film, critical writing, dance performance, drama performance, drama workshop, dramatic arts, drawing, drawing and design, earth science, economics, economics and history, English, English composition, English literature, environmental science, environmental studies, first aid, fitness, food and nutrition, foreign language, French, general science, government, graphic arts, graphic design, health, health and wellness, history, history of the Catholic Church, honors English, honors U.S. history, honors world history, human anatomy, instruments, introduction to theater, Italian, jazz band, keyboarding, lab science, language, language and composition, law and the legal system, life science, marine science, mathematics, modern history, music performance, music theater, musical theater, musical theater dance, oceanography, personal fitness, physical fitness, physics, play production, portfolio art, pre-calculus, public service, religion, religion

and culture, religious education, religious studies, scene study, science, science research, scripture, set design, Spanish, sports nutrition, stage and body movement, stage design, theater, theater arts, theater design and production, theater history, visual and performing arts, yearbook.

Graduation Requirements Computers, English, foreign language, health education, history, lab science, mathematics, oceanography, physical education (includes health), religion (includes Bible studies and theology), science.

Special Academic Programs International Baccalaureate program; Advanced Placement exam preparation; honors section.

College Admission Counseling 140 students graduated in 2015; 137 went to college, including Northeastern University; Providence College; Roger Williams University; University of New Hampshire; University of Rhode Island. Other: 1 entered a postgraduate year, 2 had other specific plans.

Student Life Upper grades have uniform requirement, student council, honor system. Discipline rests primarily with faculty. Attendance at religious services is required.

Tuition and Aid Day student tuition: $12,975. Tuition installment plan (FACTS Tuition Payment Plan). Tuition reduction for siblings, need-based scholarship grants available. In 2015–16, 35% of upper-school students received aid.

Admissions Traditional secondary-level entrance grade is 9. Admissions testing, essay and High School Placement Test required. Deadline for receipt of application materials: December 22. Application fee required: $45.

Athletics Interscholastic: baseball (boys), basketball (b,g), cheering (g), cross-country running (b,g), gymnastics (g), lacrosse (b,g), soccer (b,g), softball (g), swimming and diving (b,g), tennis (b,g), track and field (b,g), volleyball (g); intramural: dance (g), outdoor recreation (b,g); coed interscholastic: aquatics, golf, ice hockey; coed intramural: aerobics, aerobics/dance, ballet, bicycling, fitness, outdoor recreation, sailing, strength & conditioning, table tennis, weight lifting, weight training. 3 PE instructors, 14 coaches, 1 athletic trainer.

Computers Computers are regularly used in all academic classes. Computer network features include on-campus library services, Internet access, Internet filtering or blocking technology. Computer access in designated common areas is available to students. The school has a published electronic and media policy.

Contact Ms. Sharon DeLuca, Director of Admissions. 401-789-9262 Ext. 514. Fax: 401-782-2262. E-mail: sdeluca@theproutschool.org. Website: www.theproutschool.org

PROVIDENCE CATHOLIC SCHOOL, THE COLLEGE PREPARATORY SCHOOL FOR GIRLS GRADES 6-12

1215 North St. Mary's
San Antonio, Texas 78215-1787

Head of School: Ms. Alicia Garcia

General Information Girls' day college-preparatory, arts, and religious studies school, affiliated with Roman Catholic Church. Grades 6–12. Founded: 1951. Setting: urban. 3-acre campus. 4 buildings on campus. Approved or accredited by Southern Association of Colleges and Schools, Southern Association of Independent Schools, Texas Catholic Conference, and Texas Education Agency. Endowment: $500,000. Total enrollment: 301. Upper school average class size: 22. Upper school faculty-student ratio: 1:12. There are 186 required school days per year for Upper School students. Upper School students typically attend 5 days per week. The average school day consists of 7 hours.

Upper School Student Profile Grade 9: 37 students (37 girls); Grade 10: 49 students (49 girls); Grade 11: 53 students (53 girls); Grade 12: 44 students (44 girls). 80% of students are Roman Catholic.

Faculty School total: 30. In upper school: 6 men, 21 women; 20 have advanced degrees.

Subjects Offered Acting, advanced biology, advanced chemistry, advanced math, Advanced Placement courses, aerobics, algebra, American history, American history-AP, American literature, American literature-AP, anatomy, ancient world history, art, athletics, audio visual/media, band, biology, biology-AP, British literature, British literature-AP, broadcast journalism, broadcasting, calculus-AP, career education internship, Catholic belief and practice, cheerleading, chemistry, choir, choral music, church history, composition-AP, computer information systems, concert band, concert choir, conflict resolution, creative writing, dance, dance performance, desktop publishing, drama, drama performance, drama workshop, economics, English, English language and composition-AP, English language-AP, English literature, English literature and composition-AP, English literature-AP, English-AP, film, fitness, foreign language, French, geography, government, government and politics-AP, history, history-AP, human anatomy, jazz band, journalism, JROTC, JROTC or LEAD (Leadership Education and Development), Latin, law, leadership, literature and composition-AP, music theory, newspaper, peer ministry, personal fitness, photography, photojournalism, physical education, physical fitness, physical science, physics, play production, psychology, social justice, sociology, softball, Spanish, Spanish language-AP, Spanish-AP, speech, sports, statistics-AP, student government, student publications, swimming, swimming competency, tennis, Texas history, the Web, theater, theater arts, theater design and production, theater production, theology, track and field, U.S. government and politics, U.S. government and politics-AP, U.S. history, U.S. history-AP, volleyball, Web site design, world geography, world history, yearbook.

Graduation Requirements All academic, 100 hours of community service completed by grade 12, senior retreat participation.

Special Academic Programs International Baccalaureate program; 13 Advanced Placement exams for which test preparation is offered; honors section; independent study; study at local college for college credit.

College Admission Counseling 46 students graduated in 2015; all went to college, including St. Mary's University; Texas A&M University; The University of Texas at Austin; The University of Texas at San Antonio; University of the Incarnate Word.

Student Life Upper grades have uniform requirement, student council, honor system. Discipline rests primarily with faculty. Attendance at religious services is required.

Tuition and Aid Day student tuition: $7842. Tuition installment plan (FACTS Tuition Payment Plan, Middle School tuition $4,748). Tuition reduction for siblings, merit scholarship grants, need-based scholarship grants available. In 2015–16, 12% of upper-school students received aid; total upper-school merit-scholarship money awarded: $58,550. Total amount of financial aid awarded in 2015–16: $214,713.

Admissions Traditional secondary-level entrance grade is 9. For fall 2015, 51 students applied for upper-level admission, 43 were accepted, 43 enrolled. High School Placement Test or QUIC required. Deadline for receipt of application materials: none. No application fee required. On-campus interview recommended.

Athletics Interscholastic: aerobics, aerobics/dance, basketball, bowling, cheering, cross-country running, dance, dance team, JROTC drill, physical fitness, physical training, running, soccer, softball, tennis, track and field, volleyball, weight training, winter soccer; coed interscholastic: aquatics. 1 PE instructor, 7 coaches, 1 athletic trainer.

Computers Computers are regularly used in desktop publishing, journalism, newspaper, Web site design, yearbook classes. Computer network features include on-campus library services, online commercial services, Internet access, Internet filtering or blocking technology, online classrooms. Campus intranet and student e-mail accounts are available to students. Students grades are available online. The school has a published electronic and media policy.

Contact Mrs. Stephanie Takas-Mercer, Admissions Director. 210-224-6651 Ext. 210. Fax: 210-224-9242. E-mail: stakas-mercer@providencehs.net. Website: www.providencehs.net

PROVIDENCE COUNTRY DAY SCHOOL

660 Waterman Avenue
East Providence, Rhode Island 02914-1724

Head of School: Mr. Vince Watchorn

General Information Coeducational day college-preparatory school. Grades 6–12. Founded: 1923. Setting: suburban. Nearest major city is Providence. 31-acre campus. 6 buildings on campus. Approved or accredited by Association of Independent Schools in New England, New England Association of Schools and Colleges, The College Board, and Rhode Island Department of Education. Member of National Association of Independent Schools and Secondary School Admission Test Board. Endowment: $1.7 million. Total enrollment: 208. Upper school average class size: 12. Upper school faculty-student ratio: 1:8. There are 166 required school days per year for Upper School students. Upper School students typically attend 5 days per week. The average school day consists of 6 hours and 30 minutes.

Upper School Student Profile Grade 9: 38 students (21 boys, 17 girls); Grade 10: 46 students (28 boys, 18 girls); Grade 11: 46 students (28 boys, 18 girls); Grade 12: 45 students (32 boys, 13 girls).

Faculty School total: 35. In upper school: 12 men, 19 women; 20 have advanced degrees.

Subjects Offered 3-dimensional art, advanced biology, advanced chemistry, Advanced Placement courses, algebra, American government, American history, American history-AP, American literature, ancient history, art, art history-AP, Asian studies, band, Bible as literature, bioethics, biology, biology-AP, calculus, calculus-AP, ceramics, chemistry, choir, college counseling, computer science, conceptual physics, creative writing, drawing, electives, English, English literature, English literature-AP, environmental science, European history, European history-AP, evolution, fiction, fine arts, foreign language, forensics, geometry, government/civics, health, history, independent study, jazz ensemble, Latin, Latin American history, Latin-AP, leadership, literature seminar, mathematics, media production, medieval history, modern European history, modern world history, music, painting, participation in sports, performing arts, photography, physics, politics, portfolio art, pottery, pre-calculus, printmaking, public speaking, science, sculpture, senior internship, senior project, Shakespeare, social studies, Spanish, Spanish-AP, sports, studio art, theater, trigonometry, U.S. government and politics-AP, U.S. history-AP, visual and performing arts, visual arts, water color painting, wellness, Western literature, world history, world literature, writing, yearbook, yoga.

Graduation Requirements Arts and fine arts (art, music, dance, drama), English, foreign language, history, humanities, mathematics, performing arts, science, Senior Independent Project, community service, athletics.

Special Academic Programs 10 Advanced Placement exams for which test preparation is offered; honors section; independent study; term-away projects; study abroad; academic accommodation for the gifted, the musically talented, and the artistically talented.

College Admission Counseling 37 students graduated in 2016; all went to college, including American University; Boston University; Brown University; Providence College; University of Massachusetts Amherst; University of Vermont. Mean SAT critical reading: 559, mean SAT math: 570, mean SAT writing: 550, mean combined SAT: 1679, mean composite ACT: 24.

Student Life Upper grades have specified standards of dress, student council, honor system. Discipline rests equally with students and faculty.

Tuition and Aid Day student tuition: $30,400–$34,650. Tuition installment plan (FACTS Tuition Payment Plan, monthly payment plans, Tuition Refund Insurance). Merit scholarship grants, need-based scholarship grants available. In 2016–17, 45% of upper-school students received aid; total upper-school merit-scholarship money awarded: $138,600. Total amount of financial aid awarded in 2016–17: $2,294,300.

Admissions Traditional secondary-level entrance grade is 9. For fall 2016, 133 students applied for upper-level admission, 96 were accepted, 40 enrolled. ISEE or SSAT required. Deadline for receipt of application materials: February 1. Application fee required: $55. On-campus interview recommended.

Athletics Interscholastic: basketball (boys, girls), football (b), ice hockey (b), indoor track (b,g), lacrosse (b,g), soccer (b,g), tennis (b,g), volleyball (g), winter (indoor) track (b,g); coed interscholastic: baseball, cross-country running, golf, ice hockey, independent competitive sports, sailing, swimming and diving, track and field; coed intramural: physical fitness, rock climbing, strength & conditioning, weight training, yoga. 25 coaches, 1 athletic trainer.

Computers Computers are regularly used in art, English, foreign language, history, mathematics, science classes. Computer network features include on-campus library services, online commercial services, Internet access, wireless campus network, Internet filtering or blocking technology. Campus intranet, student e-mail accounts, and computer access in designated common areas are available to students. The school has a published electronic and media policy.

Contact Mr. Dave Provost, Director of Admissions and Financial Aid. 401-438-5170 Ext. 102. Fax: 401-435-4514. E-mail: provost@providencecountryday.org. Website: www.providencecountryday.org

PROVIDENCE DAY SCHOOL

5800 Sardis Road
Charlotte, North Carolina 28270

Head of School: Dr. Glyn Cowlishaw

General Information Coeducational day college-preparatory and global studies diploma program school. Grades PK–12. Founded: 1970. Setting: suburban. 44-acre campus. 18 buildings on campus. Approved or accredited by North Carolina Association of Independent Schools, Southern Association of Colleges and Schools, Southern Association of Independent Schools, and North Carolina Department of Education. Member of National Association of Independent Schools. Endowment: $10 million. Total enrollment: 1,580. Upper school average class size: 18. Upper school faculty-student ratio: 1:9. There are 176 required school days per year for Upper School students. Upper School students typically attend 5 days per week. The average school day consists of 7 hours and 10 minutes.

Upper School Student Profile Grade 9: 150 students (85 boys, 65 girls); Grade 10: 148 students (81 boys, 67 girls); Grade 11: 145 students (80 boys, 65 girls); Grade 12: 141 students (62 boys, 79 girls).

Faculty School total: 148. In upper school: 46 men, 34 women; 56 have advanced degrees.

Subjects Offered 3-dimensional design, accounting, African-American history, algebra, American history, American literature, art, art history-AP, Asian history, band, biology, biology-AP, calculus-AP, chemistry, chemistry-AP, chorus, Civil War, composition, computer graphics, computer programming, computer science, computer science-AP, drama, economics, English, English literature, English-AP, environmental science, environmental science-AP, fine arts, French, French-AP, geometry, German, German-AP, government-AP, government/civics, health, history, history-AP, instrumental music, international relations, journalism, Judaic studies, keyboarding, Latin, Latin-AP, literature, Mandarin, mathematics, music-AP, photography, physical education, physical science, physics, physics-AP, political science, pre-calculus, psychology, science, set design, social studies, Spanish, Spanish-AP, sports medicine, statistics-AP, theater, word processing, world history, writing, yearbook.

Graduation Requirements Arts and fine arts (art, music, dance, drama), computer science, English, foreign language, mathematics, physical education (includes health), science, social studies (includes history), Global Studies Diploma.

Special Academic Programs 24 Advanced Placement exams for which test preparation is offered; honors section; accelerated programs; study abroad; academic accommodation for the gifted, the musically talented, and the artistically talented.

College Admission Counseling 142 students graduated in 2016; all went to college, including Appalachian State University; Duke University; North Carolina State University; The University of North Carolina at Chapel Hill; Vanderbilt University; Wake Forest University. Median SAT critical reading: 650, median SAT math: 660, median SAT writing: 650, median combined SAT: 1960, median composite ACT: 28. 73% scored over 600 on SAT critical reading, 80% scored over 600 on SAT math, 71% scored over 600 on SAT writing, 73% scored over 1800 on combined SAT.

Student Life Upper grades have specified standards of dress, student council, honor system. Discipline rests equally with students and faculty.

Summer Programs Remediation, enrichment, advancement, sports, art/fine arts, computer instruction programs offered; session focuses on academics, enrichment; held both on and off campus; accepts boys and girls; open to students from other schools. 2,500 students usually enrolled. 2017 schedule: June 7 to August 6. Application deadline: none.

Tuition and Aid Day student tuition: $24,030. Tuition installment plan (Academic Management Services Plan, SMART Tuition Payment Plan, monthly payment plans). Need-based scholarship grants available. In 2016–17, 14% of upper-school students received aid. Total amount of financial aid awarded in 2016–17: $1,106,585.

Admissions Traditional secondary-level entrance grade is 9. For fall 2016, 165 students applied for upper-level admission, 63 were accepted, 46 enrolled. Cognitive Abilities Test, ERB CTP IV, ISEE, SSAT, ERB, PSAT, SAT, PLAN or ACT or Woodcock-Johnson Educational Evaluation, WISC III required. Deadline for receipt of application materials: January 15. Application fee required: $90. Interview recommended.

Athletics Interscholastic: aerobics/dance (girls), aquatics (b,g), baseball (b), basketball (b,g), cheering (g), cross-country running (b,g), dance squad (g), field hockey (g), football (b), golf (b,g), lacrosse (b,g), soccer (b,g), softball (g), swimming and diving (b,g), tennis (b,g), track and field (b,g), volleyball (g), wrestling (b); intramural: indoor hockey (b,g), indoor soccer (b,g), Newcombe ball (b,g), physical fitness (b,g), pillo polo (b,g), soccer (b,g), softball (b,g), strength & conditioning (b,g), volleyball (b,g); coed intramural: indoor hockey, indoor soccer, Newcombe ball, physical fitness, pillo polo, soccer, softball, strength & conditioning, tennis, volleyball. 4 PE instructors, 36 coaches, 2 athletic trainers.

Computers Computers are regularly used in English, mathematics, science, technology, word processing classes. Computer network features include on-campus library services, online commercial services, Internet access, wireless campus network, Internet filtering or blocking technology, wireless iBook lab available for individual student check-out, iPads. Student e-mail accounts and computer access in designated common areas are available to students. Students grades are available online. The school has a published electronic and media policy.

Contact Mrs. Carissa Goddard, Admissions Assistant. 704-887-7040. Fax: 704-887-7520. E-mail: carissa.goddard@providenceday.org. Website: www.providenceday.org

PROVIDENCE HIGH SCHOOL
511 South Buena Vista Street
Burbank, California 91505-4865

Head of School: Mr. Joe Sciuto

General Information Coeducational day college-preparatory, technology, medical, and cinema arts school, affiliated with Roman Catholic Church. Grades 9–12. Founded: 1955. Setting: urban. Nearest major city is Los Angeles. 4-acre campus. 7 buildings on campus. Approved or accredited by California Association of Independent Schools, National Catholic Education Association, Western Association of Schools and Colleges, Western Catholic Education Association, and California Department of Education. Endowment: $1.6 million. Total enrollment: 435. Upper school average class size: 17. Upper school faculty-student ratio: 1:9. There are 179 required school days per year for Upper School students. Upper School students typically attend 5 days per week. The average school day consists of 7 hours and 15 minutes.

Upper School Student Profile Grade 9: 110 students (45 boys, 65 girls); Grade 10: 99 students (51 boys, 48 girls); Grade 11: 122 students (54 boys, 68 girls); Grade 12: 103 students (42 boys, 61 girls). 69% of students are Roman Catholic.

Faculty School total: 52. In upper school: 24 men, 22 women; 31 have advanced degrees.

Subjects Offered 3-dimensional art, accounting, advanced computer applications, Advanced Placement courses, advanced studio art-AP, algebra, American history, American history-AP, American literature, American literature-AP, anatomy and physiology, ASB Leadership, athletics, audio visual/media, Basic programming, basketball, Bible studies, biology, biology-AP, biotechnology, British literature, British literature (honors), British literature-AP, business mathematics, calculus, calculus-AP, Catholic belief and practice, ceramics, chemistry, chemistry-AP, Chinese, choir, choral music, chorus, Christian and Hebrew scripture, community service, computer animation, computer art, computer programming, computer science, computer science-AP, digital photography, drama, economics, economics-AP, electives, English, English language and composition-AP, English literature, English literature and composition-AP, English literature-AP, environmental science, environmental science-AP, ethics, film, fine arts, food and nutrition, French, geometry, government and politics-AP, graphic arts, history, instruments, journalism, kinesiology, language-AP, Latin, law, leadership, macroeconomics-AP, Mandarin, mathematics, media studies, music, photography, physical education, physics, physics-AP, pre-calculus, psychology, psychology-AP, public speaking, religion, robotics, science, social justice, social studies, Spanish, Spanish language-AP, Spanish-AP, theater, trigonometry, U.S. government, U.S. government and politics-AP, U.S. history-AP, United States government-AP, video, video and animation, video film production, visual and performing arts, volleyball, world history, world history-AP, world religions, world religions, writing, yearbook, yoga.

Graduation Requirements Advanced math, American government, American history, American literature, art, biology, British literature, chemistry, comparative religion, computer science, economics, electives, English, foreign language,

mathematics, physical education (includes health), religion (includes Bible studies and theology), science, social studies (includes history), world history, world literature, completion of Christian Service Hours, completion of Senior Project.

Special Academic Programs 15 Advanced Placement exams for which test preparation is offered; honors section; academic accommodation for the musically talented and the artistically talented.

College Admission Counseling 102 students graduated in 2016; 99 went to college, including California State Polytechnic University, Pomona; California State University, Northridge; Loyola Marymount University; Mount Saint Mary's University; University of California, Irvine; University of California, Los Angeles. Other: 3 went to work.

Student Life Upper grades have uniform requirement, student council. Discipline rests equally with students and faculty. Attendance at religious services is required.

Summer Programs Remediation, enrichment, advancement, sports, art/fine arts, computer instruction programs offered; session focuses on enrichment, remediation, and extracurricular activities; held on campus; accepts boys and girls; open to students from other schools. 300 students usually enrolled. 2017 schedule: June 12 to July 14. Application deadline: June 12.

Tuition and Aid Day student tuition: $16,200. Tuition installment plan (SMART Tuition Payment Plan). Tuition reduction for siblings, merit scholarship grants, need-based scholarship grants available. In 2016–17, 44% of upper-school students received aid; total upper-school merit-scholarship money awarded: $214,000. Total amount of financial aid awarded in 2016–17: $942,250.

Admissions Traditional secondary-level entrance grade is 9. For fall 2016, 285 students applied for upper-level admission, 266 were accepted, 122 enrolled. Admissions testing, High School Placement Test and Math Placement Exam required. Deadline for receipt of application materials: January 13. Application fee required: $75. On-campus interview recommended.

Athletics Interscholastic: baseball (boys), basketball (b,g), cheering (g), cross-country running (b,g), equestrian sports (g), golf (b), soccer (b,g), softball (g), tennis (g), track and field (b,g), volleyball (b,g). 4 PE instructors, 25 coaches, 1 athletic trainer.

Computers Computers are regularly used in accounting, animation, computer applications, desktop publishing, digital applications, information technology, journalism, library, literary magazine, media, media production, newspaper, photography, programming, publications, video film production, Web site design, writing, yearbook classes. Computer network features include on-campus library services, online commercial services, Internet access, wireless campus network, Internet filtering or blocking technology, Adobe Creative Cloud 2015, Microsoft Office Suite 2016, campus Extranet portal. Campus intranet, student e-mail accounts, and computer access in designated common areas are available to students. Students grades are available online. The school has a published electronic and media policy.

Contact Mrs. Judy Egan Umeck, Director of Admissions. 818-846-8141 Ext. 14501. Fax: 818-843-8421. E-mail: judy.umeck@providencehigh.org. Website: www.providencehigh.org

PROVIDENCE SCHOOL
2701 Hodges Boulevard
Jacksonville, Florida 32224

Head of School: Mr. Don Barfield

General Information Coeducational day college preparatory school. Grades K–12. Founded: 1997. Setting: suburban. 1 building on campus. Approved or accredited by Association of Christian Schools International, Florida Council of Independent Schools, Southern Association of Colleges and Schools, and Florida Department of Education. Total enrollment: 1,170. Upper school average class size: 25. Upper school faculty-student ratio: 1:15.

Faculty School total: 49. In upper school: 22 men, 32 women; 28 have advanced degrees.

Subjects Offered 3-dimensional art, 3-dimensional design, ACT preparation, acting, advanced chemistry, advanced computer applications, advanced math, Advanced Placement courses, advanced studio art-AP, algebra, American government, American history, American history-AP, American legal systems, American literature, American literature-AP, analysis and differential calculus, anatomy and physiology, art, art-AP, athletic training, athletics, ballet, ballet technique, band, baseball, Basic programming, basketball, Bible, biology, biology-AP, British literature, British literature-AP, calculus-AP, career and personal planning, ceramics, character education, cheerleading, chemistry, chemistry-AP, choir, choral music, chorus, Christian education, Christian ethics, civics, civics/free enterprise, college admission preparation, college awareness, college counseling, college placement, college planning, college writing, composition, composition-AP, computer information systems, computer programming, computer-aided design, conceptual physics, concert band, concert bell choir, concert choir, constitutional history of U.S., constitutional law, CPR, dance, dance performance, death and loss, debate, digital imaging, digital photography, drama, dramatic arts, drawing, drawing and design, earth science, economics, English composition, English language and composition-AP, English literature and composition-AP, English-AP, English/composition-AP, European history-AP, first aid, fitness, foreign language, French, geography, geometry, government, government/civics, grammar, guidance, health, health and safety, health and wellness, health education, history, honors algebra, honors English, honors geometry, honors U.S. history, honors world history, human anatomy, human biology, intro to computers, jazz band, jazz dance, jazz ensemble, junior and senior seminars, language and composition, Latin, law and the legal system, law studies, leadership education training, Life of Christ, mathematics-AP, music theory, musical theater, musical theater dance, mythology, newspaper, novels, oceanography, oral expression, painting, peer counseling, performing arts, physical fitness, physical science, physics, physics-AP, poetry, portfolio art, pre-algebra, pre-calculus, probability and statistics, psychology, psychology-AP, reading, reading/study skills, religious studies, research, research and reference, research skills, robotics, SAT/ACT preparation, science, science project, science research, set design, Shakespeare, social skills, social studies, society, politics and law, sociology, Spanish, Spanish literature-AP, speech and debate, speech and oral interpretations, sports, stage design, stagecraft, student government, student publications, studio art-AP, study skills, tap dance, theater arts, theater design and production, track and field, U.S. government, U.S. history-AP, visual and performing arts, vocal music, Web authoring, Web site design, weight fitness, weight training, wind ensemble, world geography, world history-AP, wrestling, yearbook.

Special Academic Programs Advanced Placement exam preparation; honors section; study at local college for college credit.

College Admission Counseling Colleges students went to include Florida Atlantic University; Florida Institute of Technology; Florida State University; University of Central Florida; University of Florida; University of North Florida.

Student Life Upper grades have uniform requirement, student council, honor system. Discipline rests primarily with faculty. Attendance at religious services is required.

Summer Programs Remediation programs offered; held on campus; accepts boys and girls; not open to students from other schools. 25 students usually enrolled.

Tuition and Aid Tuition installment plan (FACTS Tuition Payment Plan). Tuition reduction for siblings, H.E.R.O.E.S. Scholarships through State of Florida available.

Admissions Traditional secondary-level entrance grade is 9. Achievement tests, OLSAT and English Exam and placement test required. Deadline for receipt of application materials: none. Application fee required: $100. On-campus interview required.

Athletics Interscholastic: aquatics (boys, girls), baseball (b), basketball (b,g), cheering (g), cross-country running (b,g), dance (b,g), dance team (b,g), football (b), golf (b,g), physical fitness (b,g), soccer (b,g), softball (g), strength & conditioning (b,g), tennis (b,g), volleyball (g). 3 PE instructors, 8 coaches, 1 athletic trainer.

Computers Computer resources include on-campus library services, online commercial services, Internet access, Internet filtering or blocking technology. Student e-mail accounts are available to students. The school has a published electronic and media policy.

Contact Mrs. Becky Grant, Director of Admissions. 904-223-5270 Ext. 1. Fax: 904-223-7837. E-mail: bgrant@prov.org. Website: www.prov.org

PUNAHOU SCHOOL

1601 Punahou Street
Honolulu, Hawaii 96822

Head of School: Dr. James K. Scott

General Information Coeducational day and distance learning college-preparatory and arts school. Grades K–12. Distance learning grades 9–12. Founded: 1841. Setting: urban. 76-acre campus. 21 buildings on campus. Approved or accredited by Western Association of Schools and Colleges. Member of National Association of Independent Schools and Secondary School Admission Test Board. Endowment: $231 million. Total enrollment: 3,768. Upper school average class size: 25. Upper school faculty-student ratio: 1:9. There are 169 required school days per year for Upper School students. Upper School students typically attend 5 days per week. The average school day consists of 8 hours.

Upper School Student Profile Grade 9: 431 students (211 boys, 220 girls); Grade 10: 430 students (211 boys, 219 girls); Grade 11: 433 students (216 boys, 217 girls); Grade 12: 426 students (204 boys, 222 girls).

Faculty School total: 355. In upper school: 61 men, 72 women; 108 have advanced degrees.

Subjects Offered 3-dimensional art, acting, advanced biology, advanced chemistry, advanced math, Advanced Placement courses, algebra, American history, American history-AP, American literature, American studies, anatomy and physiology, anthropology, art, Asian history, astronomy, athletic training, athletics, ballet, ballet technique, band, baseball, basketball, Bible as literature, bioethics, bioethics, DNA and culture, biology, biology-AP, biotechnology, bowling, business studies, calculus, calculus-AP, career/college preparation, ceramics, character education, cheerleading, chemistry, chemistry-AP, child development, Chinese, choir, choral music, chorus, clayworking, college admission preparation, college counseling, college planning, community garden, comparative government and politics, comparative religion, composition, computer programming, computer science, computer science-AP, computer studies, concert band, contemporary issues, CPR, creative writing, dance, dance performance, digital art, digital photography, drama, drama performance, drawing, driver education, economics, electives, engineering, English, English composition, English literature, environmental science, environmental science-AP, environmental studies, European civilization, European history, European history-AP, film and literature, filmmaking, foreign language, French, French language-AP, French-AP, gender issues, general science, geometry, glassblowing, government and politics-

AP, government-AP, graphic arts, graphic design, guitar, Hawaiian history, Hawaiian language, history, honors English, honors geometry, human issues, humanities, independent study, instruments, Japanese, jazz dance, jewelry making, journalism, JROTC, JROTC or LEAD (Leadership Education and Development), language-AP, law, literature, Mandarin, marching band, marine biology, marine science, marine studies, mathematics, mechanical drawing, medieval history, medieval/Renaissance history, microeconomics, money management, music, music theory, musical theater, musical theater dance, oceanography, organic chemistry, outdoor education, painting, peer counseling, photography, physical education, physics, physics-AP, piano, poetry, pottery, pre-calculus, psychology, psychology-AP, religion, robotics, SAT preparation, science fiction, sculpture, self-defense, Shakespeare, social studies, Spanish, Spanish language-AP, Spanish-AP, sports, sports psychology, stage design, statistics, statistics-AP, studio art, studio art-AP, swimming, symphonic band, tap dance, technical theater, tennis, theater, theater design and production, theater production, track and field, U.S. government, U.S. government and politics, U.S. government and politics-AP, U.S. history, U.S. history-AP, United States government-AP, video, video film production, volleyball, water polo, weight training, Western literature, wind ensemble, wind instruments, world civilizations, world history, world literature, writing, writing, yearbook, yoga.

Graduation Requirements Electives, English, foreign language, mathematics, physical education (includes health), science, social studies (includes history), visual and performing arts, seniors are required to take a Capstone course that combines economics and community service, one course with the Spiritual, Ethical, Community Responsibility (SECR) designation.

Special Academic Programs 17 Advanced Placement exams for which test preparation is offered; honors section; independent study; study abroad.

College Admission Counseling 431 students graduated in 2016; 427 went to college, including Chapman University; Santa Clara University; Seattle University; University of Hawaii at Manoa; University of Southern California; University of Washington. Other: 4 had other specific plans. Median SAT critical reading: 630, median SAT math: 660, median SAT writing: 640, median combined SAT: 1920. 55.8% scored over 600 on SAT critical reading, 77.8% scored over 600 on SAT math, 63.3% scored over 600 on SAT writing, 71.7% scored over 1800 on combined SAT.

Student Life Upper grades have specified standards of dress, student council. Discipline rests primarily with faculty.

Summer Programs Enrichment, advancement, sports, art/fine arts programs offered; session focuses on enrichment and graduation credit; held both on and off campus; accepts boys and girls; not open to students from other schools. 1,385 students usually enrolled. 2017 schedule: June 13 to July 21. Application deadline: April 7.

Tuition and Aid Day student tuition: $22,950. Tuition installment plan (monthly payment plans, semester payment plan, annual payment plan). Merit scholarship grants, need-based scholarship grants available. In 2016–17, 18% of upper-school students received aid; total upper-school merit-scholarship money awarded: $252,450. Total amount of financial aid awarded in 2016–17: $3,644,200.

Admissions Traditional secondary-level entrance grade is 9. For fall 2016, 315 students applied for upper-level admission, 134 were accepted, 86 enrolled. SAT and SSAT required. Deadline for receipt of application materials: November 15. Application fee required: $125. Interview recommended.

Athletics Interscholastic: baseball (boys), basketball (b,g), bowling (b,g), canoeing/kayaking (b,g), cheering (g), cross-country running (b,g), football (b), golf (b,g), judo (b,g), kayaking (b,g), paddling (b,g), riflery (b,g), sailing (b,g), soccer (b,g), softball (g), swimming and diving (b,g), tennis (b,g), track and field (b,g), volleyball (b,g), water polo (b,g), wrestling (b,g); coed interscholastic: canoeing/kayaking, paddling. 4 PE instructors, 294 coaches, 4 athletic trainers.

Computers Computers are regularly used in all academic classes. Computer network features include on-campus library services, online commercial services, Internet access, wireless campus network, Internet filtering or blocking technology. Campus intranet, student e-mail accounts, and computer access in designated common areas are available to students. Students grades are available online. The school has a published electronic and media policy.

Contact Mrs. Betsy S. Hata, Director of Admission and Financial Aid. 808-944-5714. Fax: 808-943-3602. E-mail: admission@punahou.edu. Website: www.punahou.edu

QUEEN MARGARET'S SCHOOL

660 Brownsey Avenue
Duncan, British Columbia V9L 1C2, Canada

Head of School: Mrs. Wilma Jamieson

General Information Girls' boarding and coeducational day college-preparatory, equestrian studies, and Advanced Placement (AP) school, affiliated with Anglican Church of Canada. Boarding girls grades 6–12, day boys grades PS–7, day girls grades PS–12. Founded: 1921. Setting: small town. Nearest major city is Victoria, Canada. Students are housed in single-sex dormitories. 27-acre campus. 9 buildings on campus. Approved or accredited by Canadian Association of Independent Schools, Canadian Educational Standards Institute, The Association of Boarding Schools, and British Columbia Department of Education. Affiliate member of National Association of Independent Schools; member of Secondary School Admission Test Board and Canadian Association of Independent Schools. Language of instruction: English. Endowment: CAN$500,000. Total enrollment: 339. Upper school average class size:

18. Upper school faculty-student ratio: 1:8. There are 168 required school days per year for Upper School students. Upper School students typically attend 5 days per week. The average school day consists of 7 hours.

Upper School Student Profile Grade 8: 18 students (18 girls); Grade 9: 29 students (29 girls); Grade 10: 38 students (38 girls); Grade 11: 36 students (36 girls); Grade 12: 24 students (24 girls). 59% of students are boarding students. 48% are province residents. 4 provinces are represented in upper school student body. 67% are international students. International students from Canada, China, Japan, Mexico, United States, and Viet Nam; 2 other countries represented in student body.

Faculty School total: 52. In upper school: 5 men, 19 women; 4 have advanced degrees; 3 reside on campus.

Subjects Offered Acting, advanced math, advanced studio art-AP, all academic, animal science, applied skills, art, athletics, band, biology, business education, business skills, calculus, calculus-AP, Canadian history, career and personal planning, career exploration, chemistry, Chinese, choir, chorus, college planning, communications, computer science, creative writing, diversity studies, drama, drama performance, dramatic arts, engineering, English, English language-AP, English literature, English-AP, environmental science-AP, equestrian sports, equine management, equine science, equitation, ESL, finance, fine arts, food and nutrition, French, French-AP, geography, grammar, guitar, health, history, home economics, information technology, instrumental music, international relations, international studies, Japanese, jazz ensemble, journalism, law, leadership, leadership and service, macroeconomics-AP, Mandarin, mathematics, media, media arts, music, music composition, music theory, outdoor education, photography, physical education, physics, science, social issues, social studies, society, politics and law, speech, sports, sports psychology, textiles, theater, visual arts, world history, writing, yearbook.

Graduation Requirements Applied skills, arts and fine arts (art, music, dance, drama), career and personal planning, English, language arts, life skills, mathematics, physical education (includes health), science, social studies (includes history). Community service is required.

Special Academic Programs Advanced Placement exam preparation; independent study; study at local college for college credit; academic accommodation for the gifted, the musically talented, and the artistically talented; ESL (31 students enrolled).

College Admission Counseling 33 students graduated in 2016; 31 went to college, including Fashion Institute of Technology; McGill University; Queen's University at Kingston; Simon Fraser University; University of Toronto; University of Victoria. Other: 1 went to work, 1 had other specific plans.

Student Life Upper grades have uniform requirement, student council, honor system. Discipline rests primarily with faculty. Attendance at religious services is required.

Summer Programs Enrichment, ESL, sports programs offered; session focuses on English 10-11 Courses & Equestrian Riding; held on campus; accepts boys and girls; open to students from other schools. 15 students usually enrolled. 2017 schedule: June 26 to August 25. Application deadline: April 7.

Tuition and Aid Day student tuition: CAN$11,650–CAN$13,900; 5-day tuition and room/board: CAN$38,200; 7-day tuition and room/board: CAN$44,600–CAN$59,900. Tuition installment plan (Insured Tuition Payment Plan, monthly payment plans, individually arranged payment plans). Tuition reduction for siblings, bursaries, merit scholarship grants, need-based scholarship grants, staff tuition discount available. In 2016–17, 33% of upper-school students received aid; total upper-school merit-scholarship money awarded: CAN$50,000. Total amount of financial aid awarded in 2016–17: CAN$150,000.

Admissions Traditional secondary-level entrance grade is 8. Deadline for receipt of application materials: none. Application fee required: CAN$250. Interview recommended.

Athletics Interscholastic: aquatics, badminton, basketball (b), cross-country running (b), dressage, equestrian sports (b), field hockey, golf, horseback riding (b), rowing, running (b), soccer (b), swimming and diving, track and field (b), volleyball (b); intramural: aerobics, aerobics/dance, cross-country running (b), modern dance, rugby (b), sailing, track and field (b), ultimate Frisbee, volleyball (b), yoga (b); coed intramural: aquatics, badminton, ball hockey, baseball, basketball, bowling, canoeing/kayaking, climbing, cooperative games, curling, dance, equestrian sports, field hockey, figure skating, fitness, flag football, floor hockey, Frisbee, golf, gymnastics, hiking/backpacking, hockey, horseback riding, kayaking, ocean paddling, outdoor activities, outdoor adventure, outdoor education, outdoor recreation, outdoor skills, outdoors, physical fitness, physical training, rock climbing, ropes courses, rounders, rugby, soccer, softball, street hockey, strength & conditioning, swimming and diving, touch football, walking, weight training. 1 PE instructor.

Computers Computers are regularly used in all academic, art, career education, career exploration, college planning, creative writing, English, ESL, French, information technology, introduction to technology, journalism, mathematics, media arts, media production, science, social sciences, technology classes. Computer network features include on-campus library services, Internet access, wireless campus network, Internet filtering or blocking technology. Campus intranet and student e-mail accounts are available to students. The school has a published electronic and media policy.

Contact Admissions Coordinator. 250-746-4185 Ext. 237. Fax: 250-746-4187. E-mail: admissions@qms.bc.ca. Website: www.qms.bc.ca

QUEEN OF PEACE HIGH SCHOOL
7659 South Linder Avenue
Burbank, Illinois 60459

Head of School: Mr. Hedi Belkaoui

General Information Girls' day college-preparatory school, affiliated with Roman Catholic Church. Grades 9–12. Founded: 1962. Setting: suburban. Nearest major city is Chicago. 1 building on campus. Approved or accredited by North Central Association of Colleges and Schools and Illinois Department of Education. Upper school average class size: 14. Upper school faculty-student ratio: 1:14. There are 183 required school days per year for Upper School students. Upper School students typically attend 5 days per week. The average school day consists of 7 hours and 46 minutes.

Upper School Student Profile 75% of students are Roman Catholic.

Faculty School total: 28. In upper school: 5 men, 20 women.

Student Life Upper grades have uniform requirement, student council, honor system. Discipline rests primarily with faculty. Attendance at religious services is required.

Admissions No application fee required.

Contact Ms. Alicia Erskine, Manager of Admissions and Recruitment. 708-496-4792. Fax: 708-458-5734. E-mail: erskinea@queenofpeacehs.org. Website: www.queenofpeacehs.org

QUIGLEY CATHOLIC HIGH SCHOOL
200 Quigley Drive
Baden, Pennsylvania 15005-1295

Head of School: Mrs. Rita McCormick

General Information Coeducational day college-preparatory school, affiliated with Roman Catholic Church. Grades 9–12. Founded: 1967. Setting: suburban. Nearest major city is Pittsburgh. 19-acre campus. 1 building on campus. Approved or accredited by Middle States Association of Colleges and Schools, National Catholic Education Association, and Pennsylvania Department of Education. Endowment: $2.5 million. Total enrollment: 203. Upper school average class size: 20. Upper school faculty-student ratio: 1:12. There are 180 required school days per year for Upper School students. Upper School students typically attend 5 days per week. The average school day consists of 6 hours and 30 minutes.

Upper School Student Profile Grade 9: 31 students (15 boys, 16 girls); Grade 10: 28 students (14 boys, 14 girls); Grade 11: 27 students (12 boys, 15 girls); Grade 12: 28 students (12 boys, 16 girls). 95% of students are Roman Catholic.

Faculty School total: 16. In upper school: 2 men, 14 women; 7 have advanced degrees.

Subjects Offered Advanced Placement courses, algebra, American government, American history-AP, American literature, anatomy and physiology, art, athletics, band, baseball, Basic programming, basketball, biology, bookbinding, bowling, British literature, British literature (honors), calculus, calculus-AP, campus ministry, ceramics, cheerleading, chemistry, choir, chorus, church history, composition-AP, computer programming, computer science, concert choir, debate, drawing, ecology, English-AP, European history-AP, French language-AP, geometry, government, guitar, health education, honors algebra, honors world history, library, physical education, physical science, physics, piano, play production, pottery, pre-algebra, pre-calculus, printmaking, religious education, SAT preparation, Spanish, speech and debate, sports, student government, studio art, trigonometry, yearbook.

Graduation Requirements Algebra, American government, American history, American history-AP, British literature, British literature (honors), chemistry, church history, computer science, English, English literature, European history, European history-AP, French, geometry, government, health, math review, music, physical science, physics, religion (includes Bible studies and theology), Spanish, U.S. history, 125 hours of service completed by end of senior year.

Special Academic Programs Advanced Placement exam preparation; honors section; study at local college for college credit.

College Admission Counseling 28 students graduated in 2016; 27 went to college, including Duquesne University; John Carroll University; Malone University; University of Pittsburgh. Other: 1 entered military service.

Student Life Upper grades have uniform requirement, student council, honor system. Discipline rests primarily with faculty. Attendance at religious services is required.

Tuition and Aid Day student tuition: $8350. Tuition installment plan (SMART Tuition Payment Plan, individually arranged payment plans, one-time payment in full). Tuition reduction for siblings, merit scholarship grants, need-based scholarship grants available. In 2016–17, 48% of upper-school students received aid; total upper-school merit-scholarship money awarded: $33,660. Total amount of financial aid awarded in 2016–17: $299,953.

Admissions Traditional secondary-level entrance grade is 9. For fall 2016, 35 students applied for upper-level admission, 35 were accepted, 30 enrolled. Iowa Test, CTBS, or TAP, Math Placement Exam or PSAT required. Deadline for receipt of application materials: none. Application fee required: $30.

Athletics Interscholastic: baseball (boys), basketball (b,g), bowling (b,g), cheering (g), cross-country running (b,g), golf (b), gymnastics (g), soccer (b,g), softball (g), swimming and diving (g), volleyball (g), winter soccer (g); intramural: aerobics (g); coed interscholastic: aquatics; coed intramural: artistic gym. 1 PE instructor, 11 coaches, 1 athletic trainer.

Computers Computers are regularly used in newspaper, programming, yearbook classes. Computer resources include on-campus library services, Internet access.
Contact Sr. Bridget Reilly, Director of Guidance. 724-869-2188. Fax: 724-869-3091. E-mail: reillyb@qchs.org. Website: www.qchs.org

QUINTE CHRISTIAN HIGH SCHOOL

138 Wallbridge-Loyalist Road
RR 2
Belleville, Ontario K8N 4Z2, Canada

Head of School: Mr. John VanderWindt

General Information Coeducational day college-preparatory, general academic, arts, vocational, religious studies, and technology school, affiliated with Protestant faith. Grades 9–12. Founded: 1977. Setting: suburban. Nearest major city is Toronto, Canada. 25-acre campus. 1 building on campus. Approved or accredited by Christian Schools International, Ontario Ministry of Education, and Ontario Department of Education. Language of instruction: English. Total enrollment: 148. Upper school average class size: 15. Upper school faculty-student ratio: 1:15. There are 176 required school days per year for Upper School students. Upper School students typically attend 5 days per week. The average school day consists of 6 hours and 10 minutes.
Upper School Student Profile 90% of students are Protestant.
Faculty School total: 16. In upper school: 7 men, 9 women; 2 have advanced degrees.
Subjects Offered Accounting, art, Bible, biology, calculus, careers, chemistry, Christian education, civics, computers, drama, English, English literature, ESL, French, geography, history, law, leadership education training, mathematics, mathematics-AP, media, music, peer counseling, physical education, physics, religious education, science, shop, society challenge and change, technical education, transportation technology, world issues, world religions.
Graduation Requirements Accounting, applied arts, careers, Christian education, civics, computers, English, French, geography, mathematics, physical education (includes health), religious education, science, social studies (includes history), world religions, Ontario Christian School diploma requirements.
Special Academic Programs Programs in English, mathematics for dyslexic students; special instructional classes for students with learning disabilities; ESL (10 students enrolled).
College Admission Counseling 35 students graduated in 2016; 30 went to college, including Queen's University at Kingston; Redeemer University College; University of Guelph; University of Ottawa; University of Toronto; University of Waterloo. Other: 3 went to work, 2 had other specific plans.
Student Life Upper grades have uniform requirement, student council, honor system. Discipline rests primarily with faculty. Attendance at religious services is required.
Tuition and Aid Day student tuition: CAN$14,100. Tuition installment plan (monthly payment plans, individually arranged payment plans). Tuition reduction for siblings, need-based scholarship grants available.
Admissions Traditional secondary-level entrance grade is 9. Deadline for receipt of application materials: March 31. Application fee required: CAN$500. On-campus interview required.
Athletics Interscholastic: badminton (boys, girls), basketball (b,g), cross-country running (b,g), curling (b,g), soccer (b,g), track and field (b,g), volleyball (b,g); coed interscholastic: badminton, curling; coed intramural: badminton, basketball, fitness walking, indoor soccer, physical training, volleyball. 3 PE instructors.
Computers Computers are regularly used in Bible studies, business, career education, English, ESL, French, graphic arts, mathematics, religious studies, science, technology classes. Computer network features include on-campus library services, Internet access, wireless campus network, Internet filtering or blocking technology, EDSBY for students and parents. Campus intranet, student e-mail accounts, and computer access in designated common areas are available to students. Students grades are available online. The school has a published electronic and media policy.
Contact Mrs. Sharon Siderius, Administrative Assistant. 613-968-7870. Fax: 613-968-7970. E-mail: admin@qchs.ca. Website: www.qchs.ca

RABUN GAP-NACOOCHEE SCHOOL

339 Nacoochee Drive
Rabun Gap, Georgia 30568

Head of School: Dr. Anthony Sgro

General Information Coeducational boarding and day college-preparatory, arts, ESL, and performing arts school, affiliated with Presbyterian Church. Boarding grades 7–12, day grades 5–12. Founded: 1903. Setting: rural. Nearest major city is Atlanta. Students are housed in single-sex dormitories. 1,400-acre campus. 14 buildings on campus. Approved or accredited by North Carolina Association of Independent Schools, Southern Association of Colleges and Schools, Southern Association of Independent Schools, The Association of Boarding Schools, and Georgia Department of Education. Member of National Association of Independent Schools and Secondary School Admission Test Board. Endowment: $50 million. Total enrollment: 423. Upper school average class size: 16. Upper school faculty-student ratio: 1:10. There are 172 required school days per year for Upper School students. Upper School students

typically attend 5 days per week. The average school day consists of 6 hours and 15 minutes.
Upper School Student Profile Grade 9: 69 students (39 boys, 30 girls); Grade 10: 81 students (44 boys, 37 girls); Grade 11: 93 students (46 boys, 47 girls); Grade 12: 76 students (44 boys, 32 girls). 63% of students are boarding students. 65% are state residents. 15 states are represented in upper school student body. 26% are international students. International students from Bahamas, China, Germany, Mexico, Republic of Korea, and Taiwan; 22 other countries represented in student body. 10% of students are Presbyterian.
Faculty School total: 54. In upper school: 19 men, 21 women; 26 have advanced degrees; 49 reside on campus.
Subjects Offered Advanced Placement courses, algebra, American literature, anatomy, ancient world history, art, art history, art history-AP, band, Bible studies, biology, biology-AP, botany, calculus-AP, chemistry, chemistry-AP, chorus, computer-aided design, creative writing, economics, English language-AP, English literature-AP, environmental science, environmental science-AP, ESL, European history-AP, French, French-AP, geography, geometry, government, government-AP, health, health education, history-AP, honors algebra, honors English, honors U.S. history, honors world history, industrial arts, journalism, life science, mathematics, modern European history-AP, modern world history, music, orchestra, physical education, physical science, physics, physics-AP, pre-algebra, pre-calculus, probability and statistics, psychology, science, Spanish, Spanish language-AP, Spanish-AP, studio art-AP, theater, U.S. government and politics-AP, U.S. history, U.S. history-AP, wind ensemble, world geography, world history, world literature, yearbook.
Graduation Requirements Algebra, ancient world history, arts and fine arts (art, music, dance, drama), biology, chemistry, English, foreign language, geometry, mathematics, modern world history, physical education (includes health), physics, religion (includes Bible studies and theology), science, social studies (includes history), U.S. history, participation in Intersession/G.A.P. week, science symposium, Project Eagle.
Special Academic Programs 12 Advanced Placement exams for which test preparation is offered; honors section; independent study; study abroad; ESL (16 students enrolled).
College Admission Counseling 75 students graduated in 2015; 72 went to college, including Berry College; Emory University; Georgia Institute of Technology; The University of North Carolina at Chapel Hill; Vanderbilt University. Other: 3 went to work. Mean SAT critical reading: 503, mean SAT math: 544, mean SAT writing: 506, mean combined SAT: 1553, mean composite ACT: 23.
Student Life Upper grades have uniform requirement, student council, honor system. Discipline rests equally with students and faculty. Attendance at religious services is required.
Tuition and Aid Day student tuition: $18,390; 7-day tuition and room/board: $46,610. Tuition installment plan (monthly payment plans, semester payment plan). Merit scholarship grants, need-based scholarship grants, tuition remission for children of faculty and staff available. In 2015–16, 76% of upper-school students received aid; total upper-school merit-scholarship money awarded: $300,000. Total amount of financial aid awarded in 2015–16: $5,000,000.
Admissions Traditional secondary-level entrance grade is 9. For fall 2015, 365 students applied for upper-level admission, 196 were accepted, 81 enrolled. ISEE, SSAT or TOEFL required. Deadline for receipt of application materials: February 5. Application fee required: $85. Interview required.
Athletics Interscholastic: baseball (boys), basketball (b,g), cross-country running (b,g), football (b), soccer (b,g), softball (g), swimming and diving (b,g), tennis (b,g), volleyball (g), wrestling (b); intramural: soccer (b,g), swimming and diving (b,g), tennis (b,g); coed interscholastic: Circus, dance team, golf, marksmanship, riflery, skeet shooting, tennis; coed intramural: aerobics/dance, backpacking, ballet, basketball, bicycling, canoeing/kayaking, Circus, climbing, combined training, dance, dance team, fitness, fitness walking, hiking/backpacking, kayaking, modern dance, mountain biking, Nautilus, outdoor activities, physical training, rafting, rock climbing, strength & conditioning, swimming and diving, tennis, triathlon, ultimate Frisbee, wall climbing, weight lifting, weight training, yoga. 1 PE instructor, 22 coaches, 1 athletic trainer.
Computers Computers are regularly used in English, library skills, literary magazine, technical drawing, theater arts, writing, yearbook classes. Computer network features include on-campus library services, online commercial services, Internet access, wireless campus network, Internet filtering or blocking technology, application and re-enrollment online services. Campus intranet, student e-mail accounts, and computer access in designated common areas are available to students. Students grades are available online. The school has a published electronic and media policy.
Contact Mrs. Kathy Watts, Admission Assistant. 706-746-7720. Fax: 706-746-7797. E-mail: kwatts@rabungap.org. Website: www.rabungap.org

RACINE LUTHERAN HIGH SCHOOL

251 Luedtke Avenue
Racine, Wisconsin 53405

Head of School: Mr. David S. Burgess

General Information Coeducational day college-preparatory and general academic school, affiliated with Lutheran Church–Missouri Synod. Founded: 1944. Setting: urban. Nearest major city is Milwaukee. 1 building on campus. Approved or accredited by North Central Association of Colleges and Schools and Wisconsin Department of Education. Upper school average class size: 15.

Upper School Student Profile 46% of students are Lutheran Church–Missouri Synod.

Faculty School total: 18. In upper school: 11 men, 7 women; 5 have advanced degrees.

Special Academic Programs 4 Advanced Placement exams for which test preparation is offered; study at local college for college credit.

Student Life Upper grades have specified standards of dress, student council, honor system. Discipline rests primarily with faculty.

Tuition and Aid Tuition installment plan (FACTS Tuition Payment Plan, monthly payment plans). Tuition reduction for siblings, merit scholarship grants, need-based scholarship grants, Government-funded school choice vouchers, Church grants available. In 2015–16, 75% of upper-school students received aid.

Admissions Deadline for receipt of application materials: none. No application fee required. Interview recommended.

Athletics Interscholastic: baseball (boys), basketball (b,g), cheering (b,g), football (b), golf (b), soccer (b,g), softball (g), strength & conditioning (b,g), track and field (b,g), trap and skeet (b,g), volleyball (b,g).

Contact Mrs. Susie Drummond, Director of Admissions. 262-637-6538. Fax: 262-637-6601. E-mail: sdrummond@racinelutheran.org. Website: www.racinelutheran.org/

RAMONA CONVENT SECONDARY SCHOOL

1701 West Ramona Road
Alhambra, California 91803-3080

Head of School: Ms. Mary E. Mansell

General Information Girls' day college-preparatory school, affiliated with Roman Catholic Church. Grades 9–12. Founded: 1889. Setting: suburban. Nearest major city is Los Angeles. 19-acre campus. 10 buildings on campus. Approved or accredited by Western Association of Schools and Colleges, Western Catholic Education Association, and California Department of Education. Endowment: $2 million. Upper school average class size: 22. Upper school faculty-student ratio: 1:9. There are 180 required school days per year for Upper School students. Upper School students typically attend 5 days per week. The average school day consists of 6 hours and 30 minutes.

Upper School Student Profile Grade 9: 65 students (65 girls); Grade 10: 60 students (60 girls); Grade 11: 65 students (65 girls); Grade 12: 60 students (60 girls). 80% of students are Roman Catholic.

Faculty School total: 31. In upper school: 7 men, 24 women; all have advanced degrees.

Subjects Offered Advanced Placement courses, advanced studio art-AP, algebra, American history, American literature, art history, Bible studies, biology, biology-AP, calculus, calculus-AP, ceramics, chemistry, chemistry-AP, computer programming, computer science, dance, drama, economics, English, English literature, environmental science, European history, European history-AP, fine arts, French, French-AP, geography, geometry, government/civics, grammar, graphic arts, health, history, honors English, honors geometry, mathematics, music, photography, physical education, physics, pre-calculus, religion, science, social sciences, social studies, Spanish, Spanish language-AP, Spanish literature-AP, speech, theater, theology, trigonometry, U.S. government and politics-AP, visual arts, word processing, world history, world literature.

Graduation Requirements Arts and fine arts (art, music, dance, drama), business skills (includes word processing), computer science, English, foreign language, mathematics, physical education (includes health), religion (includes Bible studies and theology), science, social studies (includes history), speech.

Special Academic Programs Advanced Placement exam preparation; honors section; independent study; study abroad; academic accommodation for the gifted, the musically talented, and the artistically talented.

College Admission Counseling 89 students graduated in 2016; all went to college, including California State University, Los Angeles; Loyola Marymount University; Mount Saint Mary's University; Pitzer College; University of California, Irvine; University of California, Los Angeles. Mean SAT critical reading: 532, mean SAT math: 511, mean SAT writing: 536.

Student Life Upper grades have uniform requirement, student council, honor system. Discipline rests primarily with faculty. Attendance at religious services is required.

Summer Programs Remediation, enrichment, advancement, sports, art/fine arts, computer instruction programs offered; session focuses on academics; held on campus; accepts boys and girls; open to students from other schools. 200 students usually enrolled. 2017 schedule: June 26 to July 21. Application deadline: June 1.

Tuition and Aid Day student tuition: $13,500. Tuition installment plan (monthly payment plans, quarterly and semester payment plans). Merit scholarship grants, need-based scholarship grants, paying campus jobs available. In 2016–17, 33% of upper-school students received aid; total upper-school merit-scholarship money awarded: $18,000. Total amount of financial aid awarded in 2016–17: $350,000.

Admissions Traditional secondary-level entrance grade is 9. High School Placement Test required. Deadline for receipt of application materials: January 25. Application fee required: $100. On-campus interview recommended.

Athletics Interscholastic: basketball, cross-country running, soccer, softball, swimming and diving, tennis, track and field, volleyball. 1 PE instructor, 9 coaches.

Computers Computers are regularly used in all academic classes. Computer network features include on-campus library services, Internet access, wireless campus network, Internet filtering or blocking technology. Student e-mail accounts and computer access in designated common areas are available to students. Students grades are available online. The school has a published electronic and media policy.

Contact Mrs. Veronica Fernandez, Associate Director of Enrollment and Public Relations. 626-282-4151 Ext. 168. Fax: 626-281-0797. E-mail: vfernandez@ramonaconvent.org. Website: www.ramonaconvent.org

RANDOLPH-MACON ACADEMY

200 Academy Drive
Front Royal, Virginia 22630

Head of School: Brig. Gen. David Wesley

General Information Coeducational boarding and day college-preparatory, Air Force Junior ROTC, ESL, and military school, affiliated with Methodist Church. Grades 6–PG. Founded: 1892. Setting: small town. Nearest major city is Washington, DC. Students are housed in coed dormitories. 135-acre campus. 9 buildings on campus. Approved or accredited by Southern Association of Colleges and Schools, The Association of Boarding Schools, University Senate of United Methodist Church, Virginia Association of Independent Schools, and Virginia Department of Education. Member of National Association of Independent Schools. Endowment: $6.7 million. Total enrollment: 293. Upper school average class size: 13. Upper school faculty-student ratio: 1:8. There are 180 required school days per year for Upper School students. Upper School students typically attend 5 days per week. The average school day consists of 7 hours.

Upper School Student Profile Grade 6: 9 students (6 boys, 3 girls); Grade 7: 14 students (12 boys, 2 girls); Grade 8: 26 students (17 boys, 9 girls); Grade 9: 53 students (36 boys, 17 girls); Grade 10: 51 students (31 boys, 20 girls); Grade 11: 77 students (55 boys, 22 girls); Grade 12: 61 students (41 boys, 20 girls); Postgraduate: 11 students (8 boys, 3 girls). 86% of students are boarding students. 35% are state residents. 157 states are represented in upper school student body. 38% are international students. International students from Angola, China, Hong Kong, Mongolia, Nigeria, and Viet Nam; 7 other countries represented in student body. 12.2% of students are Methodist.

Faculty School total: 41. In upper school: 21 men, 10 women; 24 have advanced degrees; 19 reside on campus.

Subjects Offered 20th century history, advanced biology, advanced chemistry, advanced math, Advanced Placement courses, aerospace science, algebra, American government, American history, American history-AP, American literature, American literature-AP, anatomy, anatomy and physiology, art, art history, art history-AP, arts, Asian history, athletics, aviation, band, Bible studies, biology, biology-AP, British literature, calculus, calculus-AP, career education, chemistry, chorus, college counseling, comparative religion, composition-AP, computer applications, computer literacy, conceptual physics, concert band, concert choir, critical thinking, desktop publishing, discrete mathematics, drama, English, English composition, English literature, English literature and composition-AP, English-AP, epic literature, ESL, flight instruction, geography, geometry, German, German-AP, government/civics, handbells, history, honors algebra, honors English, honors geometry, honors U.S. history, independent study, journalism, JROTC, keyboarding, life management skills, mathematics, music, music appreciation, New Testament, personal finance, personal fitness, photography, physical education, physics, physics-AP, physiology, pre-algebra, pre-calculus, psychology, religion, SAT preparation, science, senior seminar, Shakespeare, social studies, Spanish, Spanish literature-AP, speech and debate, statistics-AP, studio art, theater arts, trigonometry, U.S. government, U.S. history, world history, yearbook.

Graduation Requirements Aerospace science, arts and fine arts (art, music, dance, drama), computer science, English, foreign language, mathematics, physical education (includes health), religion (includes Bible studies and theology), science, social studies (includes history), Air Force Junior ROTC for each year student is enrolled.

Special Academic Programs Advanced Placement exam preparation; honors section; independent study; study at local college for college credit; academic accommodation for the gifted; ESL (21 students enrolled).

College Admission Counseling 75 students graduated in 2016; all went to college, including Arizona State University at the Tempe campus; George Mason University; Michigan State University; Penn State University Park; University of Virginia; Virginia Polytechnic Institute and State University. Mean SAT critical reading: 505, mean SAT math: 544, mean SAT writing: 496, mean composite ACT: 23.

Student Life Upper grades have uniform requirement, student council, honor system. Discipline rests equally with students and faculty. Attendance at religious services is required.

Summer Programs Remediation, enrichment, advancement, ESL, art/fine arts, computer instruction programs offered; session focuses on remediation, new courses, ESL, flight, college counseling; held on campus; accepts boys and girls; open to students from other schools. 180 students usually enrolled. 2017 schedule: July 2 to July 28. Application deadline: June 30.

Tuition and Aid Day student tuition: $19,146; 7-day tuition and room/board: $37,409. Tuition installment plan (monthly payment plans, 2-payment plan). Tuition reduction for siblings, merit scholarship grants, need-based scholarship grants, paying campus jobs, Methodist Church scholarships available. In 2016–17, 37% of upper-school students received aid; total upper-school merit-scholarship money awarded: $276,598. Total amount of financial aid awarded in 2016–17: $940,455.

Admissions Traditional secondary-level entrance grade is 9. For fall 2016, 141 students applied for upper-level admission, 120 were accepted, 88 enrolled. Any standardized test or SSAT required. Deadline for receipt of application materials: none. Application fee required: $75. Interview recommended.

Athletics Interscholastic: baseball (boys), basketball (b,g), cross-country running (b,g), football (b,g), lacrosse (b), soccer (b,g), softball (g), swimming and diving (b,g), tennis (b,g), track and field (b,g), volleyball (b,g), wrestling (b,g); intramural: basketball (b,g), horseback riding (g), independent competitive sports (b,g), soccer (b,g), softball (g), strength & conditioning (b,g), swimming and diving (b,g), tennis (b,g), track and field (b,g), volleyball (b,g); coed interscholastic: cheering, drill team, golf, JROTC drill; coed intramural: golf, horseback riding, indoor soccer, jogging, JROTC drill, outdoor activities, outdoor recreation, physical fitness, soccer, strength & conditioning, swimming and diving, table tennis, volleyball, weight lifting, weight training. 2 PE instructors, 1 athletic trainer.

Computers Computers are regularly used in aerospace science, aviation, English, ESL, foreign language, independent study, mathematics, science, yearbook classes. Computer network features include on-campus library services, online commercial services, Internet access, wireless campus network, Internet filtering or blocking technology. Campus intranet and student e-mail accounts are available to students. Students grades are available online. The school has a published electronic and media policy.

Contact Ms. Jonni Mahr, Admission Assistant. 540-636-5484. Fax: 540-636-5419. E-mail: jmahr@rma.edu. Website: www.rma.edu

RANDOLPH SCHOOL

1005 Drake Avenue SE
Huntsville, Alabama 35802

Head of School: Mr. James E. Rainey Jr.

General Information Coeducational day college-preparatory and arts school. Grades K–12. Founded: 1959. Setting: suburban. 67-acre campus. 3 buildings on campus. Approved or accredited by Southern Association of Colleges and Schools, Southern Association of Independent Schools, and The College Board. Member of National Association of Independent Schools. Endowment: $16 million. Total enrollment: 969. Upper school average class size: 13. Upper school faculty-student ratio: 1:10. There are 182 required school days per year for Upper School students. Upper School students typically attend 5 days per week. The average school day consists of 7 hours.

Upper School Student Profile Grade 9: 95 students (40 boys, 55 girls); Grade 10: 94 students (45 boys, 49 girls); Grade 11: 86 students (39 boys, 47 girls); Grade 12: 101 students (50 boys, 51 girls).

Faculty School total: 140. In upper school: 18 men, 22 women; 32 have advanced degrees.

Subjects Offered 3-dimensional art, acting, algebra, American history, American history-AP, American literature, anatomy, art, art-AP, band, biology, biology-AP, calculus, calculus-AP, ceramics, chemistry, chemistry-AP, comparative government and politics-AP, computer math, concert choir, creative writing, drama, drama workshop, economics, English, English literature, English-AP, environmental science, European history, European history-AP, film appreciation, filmmaking, fine arts, French, French-AP, geometry, history, journalism, Latin, marine biology, mathematics, music, music theory-AP, physical education, physics, physics-AP, physiology, psychology, science, social studies, Southern literature, Spanish, Spanish-AP, speech, stage design, stagecraft, student publications, studio art-AP, theater, trigonometry, U.S. government and politics-AP, U.S. history-AP, world history, world history-AP, world literature, writing, yearbook.

Graduation Requirements Algebra, arts and fine arts (art, music, dance, drama), biology, chemistry, English, foreign language, geometry, health, literature, mathematics, science, social studies (includes history), U.S. history, world history.

Special Academic Programs 12 Advanced Placement exams for which test preparation is offered; honors section; independent study; study at local college for college credit.

College Admission Counseling 91 students graduated in 2015; 89 went to college, including Auburn University; Birmingham-Southern College; Emory University; Oxford College; Samford University; Texas Christian University; The University of Alabama. Other: 2 had other specific plans. Mean SAT critical reading: 575, mean SAT math: 581, mean SAT writing: 584, mean combined SAT: 1741, mean composite ACT: 28. 38% scored over 600 on SAT critical reading, 41% scored over 600 on SAT math, 46% scored over 600 on SAT writing, 41% scored over 1800 on combined SAT, 40% scored over 26 on composite ACT.

Student Life Upper grades have specified standards of dress, student council, honor system. Discipline rests equally with students and faculty.

Tuition and Aid Day student tuition: $13,890–$18,990. Tuition installment plan (Insured Tuition Payment Plan, 2- and 10-month payment plans). Need-based scholarship grants, middle-income loans available. In 2014–15, 9% of upper-school students received aid. Total amount of financial aid awarded in 2014–15: $258,240.

Admissions Traditional secondary-level entrance grade is 9. For fall 2015, 30 students applied for upper-level admission, 24 were accepted, 21 enrolled. ISEE, PSAT and SAT for applicants to grade 11 and 12, SSAT or writing sample required. Deadline for receipt

of application materials: none. No application fee required. On-campus interview required.

Athletics Interscholastic: baseball (boys), basketball (b,g), bowling (b,g), cheering (g), cross-country running (b,g), diving (b,g), football (b), golf (b,g), indoor track & field (b,g), physical fitness (b,g), physical training (b,g), soccer (b,g), softball (g), swimming and diving (b,g), tennis (b,g), track and field (b,g), volleyball (g), winter (indoor) track (b,g); coed interscholastic: diving. 2 PE instructors, 19 coaches, 2 athletic trainers.

Computers Computers are regularly used in all academic classes. Computer network features include on-campus library services, online commercial services, Internet access, wireless campus network, Internet filtering or blocking technology, laptops, netbooks, iPads. Campus intranet, student e-mail accounts, and computer access in designated common areas are available to students. Students grades are available online. The school has a published electronic and media policy.

Contact Glynn Below, Director of Admissions. 256-799-6104. Fax: 256-881-1784. E-mail: gbelow@randolphschool.net. Website: www.randolphschool.net

RANSOM EVERGLADES SCHOOL

3575 Main Highway
Miami, Florida 33133

Head of School: Mrs. Stephanie G. Townsend

General Information Coeducational day college-preparatory school. Grades 6–12. Founded: 1903. Setting: suburban. 11-acre campus. 19 buildings on campus. Approved or accredited by Southern Association of Colleges and Schools, Southern Association of Independent Schools, and Florida Department of Education. Member of National Association of Independent Schools and Secondary School Admission Test Board. Endowment: $28.7 million. Total enrollment: 1,085. Upper school average class size: 14. Upper school faculty-student ratio: 1:9. There are 172 required school days per year for Upper School students. Upper School students typically attend 5 days per week. The average school day consists of 5 hours and 40 minutes.

Upper School Student Profile Grade 9: 156 students (82 boys, 74 girls); Grade 10: 150 students (85 boys, 65 girls); Grade 11: 159 students (84 boys, 75 girls); Grade 12: 147 students (75 boys, 72 girls).

Faculty School total: 112. In upper school: 28 men, 26 women; 42 have advanced degrees.

Subjects Offered Advanced Placement courses, algebra, American history, American history-AP, American literature, anatomy and physiology, art, art history, art history-AP, Asian studies, astronomy, band, biology, calculus, calculus-AP, ceramics, chemistry, chemistry-AP, Chinese, choir, chorus, college counseling, comparative government and politics-AP, computer math, computer programming, computer science, computer science-AP, computer-aided design, concert band, creative writing, dance, dance performance, debate, digital photography, drama, earth science, ecology, economics, economics-AP, engineering, English, English literature, English literature and composition-AP, English-AP, environmental science, environmental science-AP, environmental studies, ethical decision making, ethics, ethics and responsibility, European history, European history-AP, experiential education, fine arts, French, French language-AP, French-AP, geography, geology, geometry, government and politics-AP, government/civics, grammar, graphic design, guitar, health, health and wellness, history, history-AP, human anatomy, interdisciplinary studies, jazz ensemble, journalism, macro/microeconomics-AP, macroeconomics-AP, Mandarin, marine biology, mathematics, mathematics-AP, music, music theory, music theory-AP, music-AP, mythology, philosophy, photography, physical education, physics, physics-AP, probability and statistics, psychology, psychology-AP, robotics, science, sculpture, social studies, sociology, Spanish, Spanish language-AP, Spanish literature-AP, speech, speech and debate, statistics, statistics-AP, strings, theater, theory of knowledge, trigonometry, U.S. government and politics-AP, U.S. history, U.S. history-AP, world history, world history-AP, world literature, writing, yearbook.

Graduation Requirements Electives.

Special Academic Programs 26 Advanced Placement exams for which test preparation is offered; honors section.

College Admission Counseling 146 students graduated in 2016; all went to college, including Cornell University; Tufts University; Tulane University; University of Florida; University of Miami; Washington University in St. Louis. Median SAT critical reading: 670, median SAT math: 680, median SAT writing: 680, median combined SAT: 2030, median composite ACT: 32. 86% scored over 600 on SAT critical reading, 93% scored over 600 on SAT math, 88% scored over 600 on SAT writing, 84% scored over 1800 on combined SAT, 91% scored over 26 on composite ACT.

Student Life Upper grades have specified standards of dress, student council, honor system. Discipline rests primarily with faculty.

Summer Programs Enrichment, advancement, computer instruction programs offered; session focuses on enrichment to reinforce basic skills and advancement for credit; held on campus; accepts boys and girls; open to students from other schools. 90 students usually enrolled. 2017 schedule: June 20 to July 29. Application deadline: May 29.

Tuition and Aid Day student tuition: $35,450. Tuition installment plan (monthly payment plans, 60%/40% payment plan). Need-based scholarship grants available. In 2016–17, 18% of upper-school students received aid. Total amount of financial aid awarded in 2016–17: $4,123,309.

Admissions Traditional secondary-level entrance grade is 9. For fall 2016, 103 students applied for upper-level admission, 18 were accepted, 15 enrolled. SSAT required. Deadline for receipt of application materials: December 1. Application fee required: $100. On-campus interview recommended.

Athletics Interscholastic: baseball (boys), basketball (b,g), canoeing/kayaking (b,g), cheering (g), crew (b,g), cross-country running (b,g), dance (g), dance team (g), football (b), golf (b,g), kayaking (b,g), lacrosse (b,g), physical training (b,g), sailing (b,g), soccer (b,g), softball (g), swimming and diving (b,g), tennis (b,g), track and field (b,g), volleyball (b,g), water polo (b,g), wrestling (b); coed interscholastic: crew, kayaking, sailing. 6 PE instructors, 77 coaches, 3 athletic trainers.

Computers Computers are regularly used in all classes. Computer network features include on-campus library services, online commercial services, Internet access, wireless campus network, Internet filtering or blocking technology. Student e-mail accounts and computer access in designated common areas are available to students. Students grades are available online. The school has a published electronic and media policy.

Contact Amy Sayfie Zichella, Director of Admission. 305-250-6875. Fax: 305-854-1846. E-mail: asayfie@ransomeverglades.org. Website: www.ransomeverglades.org

RAVENSCROFT SCHOOL

7409 Falls of the Neuse Road
Raleigh, North Carolina 27615

Head of School: Mrs. Doreen C. Kelly

General Information Coeducational day college-preparatory school. Grades PK–12. Founded: 1862. Setting: suburban. 127-acre campus. 13 buildings on campus. Approved or accredited by Southern Association of Colleges and Schools, Southern Association of Independent Schools, and North Carolina Department of Education. Member of National Association of Independent Schools. Endowment: $15 million. Total enrollment: 1,169. Upper school average class size: 13. Upper school faculty-student ratio: 1:8. There are 176 required school days per year for Upper School students. Upper School students typically attend 5 days per week. The average school day consists of 7 hours and 30 minutes.

Upper School Student Profile Grade 6: 98 students (55 boys, 43 girls); Grade 7: 102 students (41 boys, 61 girls); Grade 8: 113 students (62 boys, 51 girls); Grade 9: 121 students (69 boys, 52 girls); Grade 10: 125 students (67 boys, 58 girls); Grade 11: 112 students (57 boys, 55 girls); Grade 12: 110 students (58 boys, 52 girls).

Faculty School total: 156. In upper school: 28 men, 26 women; 42 have advanced degrees.

Subjects Offered Advanced Placement courses, algebra, American history, American literature, anatomy, art, art history, astronomy, biology, biotechnology, calculus, chemistry, computer programming, computer science, discrete mathematics, drama, economics, engineering, English, English literature, environmental science, environmental science-AP, European history, expository writing, fine arts, French, geometry, government/civics, health, history, journalism, Latin, mathematics, music, photography, physical education, physics, psychology, science, social sciences, social studies, Spanish, speech, sports medicine, stagecraft, statistics-AP, theater, world history, writing.

Graduation Requirements Arts and fine arts (art, music, dance, drama), composition, English, foreign language, mathematics, physical education (includes health), science, social sciences, social studies (includes history). Community service is required.

Special Academic Programs 24 Advanced Placement exams for which test preparation is offered; honors section; independent study; term-away projects; study at local college for college credit; study abroad; academic accommodation for the gifted, the musically talented, and the artistically talented.

College Admission Counseling 111 students graduated in 2016; all went to college, including Appalachian State University; Duke University; East Carolina University; Elon University; North Carolina State University; The University of North Carolina at Chapel Hill. Median SAT critical reading: 600, median SAT math: 650, median SAT writing: 640, median combined SAT: 1890, median composite ACT: 29. 57% scored over 600 on SAT critical reading, 67% scored over 600 on SAT math, 58% scored over 600 on SAT writing, 60% scored over 1800 on combined SAT, 66% scored over 26 on composite ACT.

Student Life Upper grades have specified standards of dress, student council, honor system. Discipline rests equally with students and faculty.

Summer Programs Enrichment, advancement, sports, art/fine arts, computer instruction programs offered; session focuses on enrichment; held on campus; accepts boys and girls; open to students from other schools. 2,000 students usually enrolled. 2017 schedule: June 12 to August 11. Application deadline: April 5.

Tuition and Aid Day student tuition: $22,650. Tuition installment plan (FACTS Tuition Payment Plan, individually arranged payment plans). Merit scholarship grants, need-based scholarship grants, need-based loans available. In 2016–17, 20% of upper-school students received aid.

Admissions Traditional secondary-level entrance grade is 9. For fall 2016, 141 students applied for upper-level admission, 86 were accepted, 59 enrolled. ERB and SSAT required. Deadline for receipt of application materials: none. Application fee required: $70. On-campus interview recommended.

Athletics Interscholastic: baseball (boys), basketball (b,g), cheering (g), cross-country running (b,g), dance squad (g), field hockey (g), fitness (b,g), football (b), golf (b,g), lacrosse (b,g), physical fitness (b,g), physical training (b,g), soccer (b,g), softball (g), strength & conditioning (b,g), swimming and diving (b,g), tennis (b,g), track and field (b,g), volleyball (g), weight training (b,g), wrestling (b); intramural: baseball (b), basketball (b,g), cheering (g), dance squad (g), dance team (g), football (b,g), lacrosse (b), soccer (b,g), softball (g), strength & conditioning (b,g), swimming and diving (b,g), tennis (b,g), track and field (b,g), volleyball (g), wrestling (b); coed interscholastic: aquatics, life saving. 10 PE instructors, 68 coaches, 2 athletic trainers.

Computers Computers are regularly used in economics, English, foreign language, history, mathematics, science, social studies, writing classes. Computer network features include on-campus library services, online commercial services, Internet access, wireless campus network, Internet filtering or blocking technology. Campus intranet, student e-mail accounts, and computer access in designated common areas are available to students. Students grades are available online. The school has a published electronic and media policy.

Contact Mrs. Toni V. Katen, Assistant to the Director of Admissions. 919-847-0900 Ext. 2227. Fax: 919-846-2371. E-mail: admissions@ravenscroft.org. Website: www.ravenscroft.org

REALMS OF INQUIRY

4998 S. Galleria Drive
Murray, Utah 84123

Head of School: Mr. Peter Westman

General Information Coeducational day college-preparatory, general academic, outdoor education, and project-based learning school. Grades 6–12. Founded: 1972. Setting: suburban. Nearest major city is Salt Lake City. 1 building on campus. Approved or accredited by Northwest Accreditation Commission and Northwest Association of Independent Schools. Languages of instruction: English and Spanish. Total enrollment: 32. Upper school average class size: 12. Upper school faculty-student ratio: 1:8. There are 180 required school days per year for Upper School students. Upper School students typically attend 5 days per week. The average school day consists of 6 hours and 15 minutes.

Upper School Student Profile Grade 6: 3 students (1 boy, 2 girls); Grade 7: 5 students (3 boys, 2 girls); Grade 8: 3 students (2 boys, 1 girl); Grade 9: 9 students (5 boys, 4 girls); Grade 10: 5 students (5 boys); Grade 11: 3 students (2 boys, 1 girl); Grade 12: 3 students (3 boys).

Faculty School total: 4. In upper school: 3 men, 1 woman; 2 have advanced degrees.

Subjects Offered Algebra, art, band, biology, calculus, chemistry, computer literacy, drama, earth science, English, geometry, history, life skills, outdoor education, photography, physical education, physics, pre-calculus, Spanish, writing.

Graduation Requirements Arts and fine arts (art, music, dance, drama), computer science, English, foreign language, mathematics, outdoor education, physical education (includes health), science, social sciences, social studies (includes history).

Special Academic Programs Accelerated programs; independent study; study at local college for college credit; study abroad; academic accommodation for the gifted, the musically talented, and the artistically talented; programs in English, mathematics, general development for dyslexic students.

College Admission Counseling 3 students graduated in 2016; 2 went to college, including Salt Lake Community College; University of Utah; Westminster College. Other: 1 went to work. Median SAT critical reading: 690, median SAT math: 640, median SAT writing: 670, median combined SAT: 2000, median composite ACT: 28. 100% scored over 600 on SAT critical reading, 100% scored over 600 on SAT math, 100% scored over 600 on SAT writing, 100% scored over 1800 on combined SAT, 100% scored over 26 on composite ACT.

Student Life Upper grades have specified standards of dress, student council, honor system. Discipline rests equally with students and faculty.

Tuition and Aid Day student tuition: $6500. Tuition installment plan (monthly payment plans, individually arranged payment plans). Tuition reduction for siblings, merit scholarship grants, need-based scholarship grants available. In 2016–17, 10% of upper-school students received aid; total upper-school merit-scholarship money awarded: $2200. Total amount of financial aid awarded in 2016–17: $10,000.

Admissions Traditional secondary-level entrance grade is 9. For fall 2016, 6 students applied for upper-level admission, 6 were accepted, 5 enrolled. Admissions testing, WISC-III and Woodcock-Johnson, WISC/Woodcock-Johnson or Woodcock-Johnson required. Deadline for receipt of application materials: none. Application fee required: $25. Interview recommended.

Athletics Coed Interscholastic: backpacking, bicycling, canoeing/kayaking, climbing, combined training, cooperative games, cross-country running, fishing, fitness, flag football, Frisbee, gymnastics, hiking/backpacking, kayaking, life saving, martial arts, mountain biking, mountaineering, nordic skiing, outdoor activities, outdoor adventure, outdoor education, outdoor recreation, outdoor skills, outdoors, paddling, physical fitness, physical training, project adventure, rafting, rappelling, rock climbing, running, skiing (cross-country), skiing (downhill), snowboarding, snowshoeing, strength & conditioning, swimming and diving, touch football, ultimate Frisbee, walking, wall climbing, weight lifting, weight training, wilderness, wilderness survival, wildernessways, winter walking, yoga.

Computers Computers are regularly used in all academic, career exploration, college planning, commercial art, computer applications, creative writing, current events, design, desktop publishing, digital applications, drafting, drawing and design, engineering, English, foreign language, graphic design, graphics, history, independent study, mathematics, media, media arts, media production, media services, music, photography, photojournalism, publishing, research skills, SAT preparation, science, social sciences, social studies classes. Computer network features include Internet access, wireless campus network. Computer access in designated common areas is available to students. Students grades are available online. The school has a published electronic and media policy.

Contact Karri Van Tongeren, Administrator. 801-467-5911. Fax: 801-590-7701. E-mail: frontdesk@realmsofinquiry.org. Website: www.realmsofinquiry.org

THE RECTORY SCHOOL

Pomfret, Connecticut
See Junior Boarding Schools section.

REDEEMER CHRISTIAN HIGH SCHOOL

82 Colonnade Road North
Ottawa, Ontario K2E 7L2, Canada

Head of School: Ms. Linda Delean

General Information Coeducational day college-preparatory and general academic school, affiliated with Protestant faith. Grades 9–12. Founded: 1975. Setting: urban. 2-acre campus. 1 building on campus. Approved or accredited by Christian Schools International, Ontario Ministry of Education, and Ontario Department of Education. Language of instruction: English. Total enrollment: 149. Upper school average class size: 20. Upper school faculty-student ratio: 1:10. There are 186 required school days per year for Upper School students. Upper School students typically attend 5 days per week. The average school day consists of 6 hours and 20 minutes.

Upper School Student Profile Grade 9: 30 students (12 boys, 18 girls); Grade 10: 27 students (8 boys, 19 girls); Grade 11: 44 students (18 boys, 26 girls); Grade 12: 44 students (18 boys, 26 girls). 90% of students are Protestant.

Faculty School total: 15. In upper school: 9 men, 6 women; 5 have advanced degrees.

Subjects Offered Accounting, acting, advanced biology, advanced chemistry, advanced math, algebra, analysis and differential calculus, applied music, art, athletic training, athletics, audio visual/media, band, Bible, biology, business, calculus, Canadian geography, Canadian history, Canadian literature, career and personal planning, carpentry, chemistry, choir, civics, creative writing, drama, English, French, geography, mathematics, media studies, music, music performance, science, social sciences, visual arts, woodworking, writing.

Graduation Requirements Graduating students must have proof they have completed a minimum of 60 volunteer hours in the community.

Student Life Upper grades have uniform requirement, student council, honor system. Discipline rests primarily with faculty. Attendance at religious services is required.

Tuition and Aid Day student tuition: CAN$7700–CAN$14,050. Tuition installment plan (monthly payment plans, individually arranged payment plans).

Admissions Traditional secondary-level entrance grade is 9. For fall 2016, 43 students applied for upper-level admission, 42 were accepted, 42 enrolled. Deadline for receipt of application materials: none. Application fee required: CAN$250. On-campus interview recommended.

Athletics Interscholastic: basketball (boys, girls), cross-country running (b,g), indoor track & field (b,g), soccer (b,g), track and field (b,g), volleyball (b,g); coed interscholastic: badminton, golf; coed intramural: ball hockey, basketball, curling, fitness, floor hockey, indoor soccer. 1 PE instructor.

Computers Computer network features include on-campus library services, Internet access, Internet filtering or blocking technology. The school has a published electronic and media policy.

Contact Ms. Mary Joustra, Office Administrator. 613-723-9262 Ext. 21. Fax: 613-723-9321. E-mail: info@rchs.on.ca. Website: www.rchs.on.ca

REDEMPTION CHRISTIAN ACADEMY

154 South Mountain Road
P.O. Box 183
Northfield, Massachusetts 01360

Head of School: Pastor John Massey Jr.

General Information Coeducational boarding and day college-preparatory, agricultural engineering, and career development school, affiliated with Pentecostal Church. Boarding grades 7–PG, day grades K–PG. Founded: 1979. Setting: rural. Nearest major city is Boston. Students are housed in single-sex dormitories. 100-acre campus. 6 buildings on campus. Approved or accredited by American Association of Christian Schools, Association of Christian Schools International, and Massachusetts Department of Education. Upper school average class size: 10. Upper school faculty-student ratio: 1:7. There are 180 required school days per year for Upper School

students. Upper School students typically attend 5 days per week. The average school day consists of 6 hours and 30 minutes.

Upper School Student Profile 100% of students are boarding students. 5% are state residents. 6 states are represented in upper school student body. 50% are international students. International students from Bahamas, Czech Republic, Dominican Republic, France, Jamaica, and Venezuela; 4 other countries represented in student body. 31% of students are Pentecostal.

Faculty School total: 8. In upper school: 4 men, 4 women; 3 have advanced degrees; 6 reside on campus.

Subjects Offered Advanced chemistry, Advanced Placement courses, American history-AP, American literature-AP, arts and crafts, athletics, biology-AP, calculus-AP, career/college preparation, chemistry-AP, CPR, English as a foreign language, gardening, nature study, ornithology, outdoor education, personal fitness, physical fitness, SAT/ACT preparation, U.S. history, volleyball, weight training, wilderness experience.

Graduation Requirements Art, English, foreign language, health science, keyboarding, mathematics, physical education (includes health), science, social studies (includes history).

Special Academic Programs 6 Advanced Placement exams for which test preparation is offered; accelerated programs; academic accommodation for the gifted; remedial reading and/or remedial writing; remedial math; programs in English, mathematics, general development for dyslexic students; special instructional classes for students with learning disabilities, Attention Deficit Disorder, emotional and behavioral problems, dyslexia; ESL (5 students enrolled).

College Admission Counseling 15 students graduated in 2016; 13 went to college. Other: 1 entered a postgraduate year, 1 had other specific plans.

Student Life Upper grades have uniform requirement, student council, honor system. Discipline rests primarily with faculty.

Summer Programs Remediation, enrichment, advancement, ESL, sports, art/fine arts, rigorous outdoor training programs offered; session focuses on program for new students, students seeking additional high school credits, and credit recovery; held on campus; accepts boys and girls; open to students from other schools. 2017 schedule: July 5 to August 12. Application deadline: none.

Tuition and Aid Day student tuition: $7000; 5-day tuition and room/board: $19,500; 7-day tuition and room/board: $24,500. Tuition installment plan (individually arranged payment plans, installment payment plan). Tuition reduction for siblings, merit scholarship grants, need-based scholarship grants, middle-income loans, work study, parent fundraiser program available.

Admissions Deadline for receipt of application materials: none. Application fee required: $50. Interview required.

Athletics Interscholastic: basketball (boys); intramural: aerobics (g), basketball (b,g), outdoor recreation (b,g), outdoor skills (b,g), physical fitness (b,g), soccer (b,g), table tennis (b,g), volleyball (b,g); coed intramural: archery. 2 PE instructors, 4 coaches, 1 athletic trainer.

Computers Computers are regularly used in English, social sciences classes. Computer network features include Internet access, wireless campus network, Internet filtering or blocking technology. Computer access in designated common areas is available to students. The school has a published electronic and media policy.

Contact Laura A. Holmes, Vice Principal. 413-722-1979 Ext. 108. Fax: 518-270-8039. E-mail: admissions@redemptionchristianacademy.org. Website: www.redemptionchristianacademy.org

REDWOOD CHRISTIAN SCHOOLS

4200 James Avenue
Castro Valley, California 94546

Head of School: Mr. Al Hearne II

General Information Coeducational day college-preparatory and college preparatory school. Grades K–12. Founded: 1970. Setting: urban. Nearest major city is Oakland. 10-acre campus. 11 buildings on campus. Approved or accredited by Association of Christian Schools International, Western Association of Schools and Colleges, and California Department of Education. Total enrollment: 650. Upper school average class size: 20. Upper school faculty-student ratio: 1:16. There are 175 required school days per year for Upper School students. Upper School students typically attend 5 days per week. The average school day consists of 6 hours and 50 minutes.

Upper School Student Profile Grade 9: 56 students (25 boys, 31 girls); Grade 10: 84 students (52 boys, 32 girls); Grade 11: 69 students (38 boys, 31 girls); Grade 12: 81 students (44 boys, 37 girls).

Faculty School total: 31. In upper school: 18 men, 13 women; 8 have advanced degrees.

Subjects Offered Advanced math, Advanced Placement courses, algebra, art, athletics, band, baseball, basketball, Bible studies, biology, calculus-AP, chemistry, choir, civics, computer literacy, concert band, creative writing, drama, drama performance, economics, English, English language and composition-AP, English literature and composition-AP, ensembles, European history-AP, fitness, geometry, honors English, keyboarding, macro/microeconomics-AP, physical education, physical science, physics, softball, Spanish, speech, track and field, trigonometry, U.S. government, U.S. history, vocal music, woodworking, world history, world history-AP, yearbook.

Graduation Requirements Arts and fine arts (art, music, dance, drama), Bible, computer literacy, electives, English, foreign language, mathematics, physical education (includes health), science, speech, world history.

Special Academic Programs Advanced Placement exam preparation; honors section; study at local college for college credit; remedial reading and/or remedial writing; remedial math; programs in English, mathematics, general development for dyslexic students.

College Admission Counseling 70 students graduated in 2016; 67 went to college, including California State University, East Bay; Pepperdine University; San Jose State University; University of California, Berkeley; University of California, Davis; University of California, Irvine. Other: 1 went to work, 1 entered military service, 1 had other specific plans. Median SAT critical reading: 560, median SAT math: 550, median SAT writing: 580, median combined SAT: 1730. 40% scored over 600 on SAT critical reading, 23% scored over 600 on SAT math, 40% scored over 600 on SAT writing, 34% scored over 1800 on combined SAT.

Student Life Upper grades have specified standards of dress, student council, honor system. Discipline rests primarily with faculty.

Tuition and Aid Day student tuition: $10,420–$26,995. Tuition installment plan (FACTS Tuition Payment Plan, monthly payment plans, individually arranged payment plans). Tuition reduction for siblings, need-based scholarship grants, paying campus jobs available. In 2016–17, 40% of upper-school students received aid. Total amount of financial aid awarded in 2016–17: $420,000.

Admissions Traditional secondary-level entrance grade is 9. For fall 2016, 179 students applied for upper-level admission, 123 were accepted, 81 enrolled. Stanford Achievement Test required. Deadline for receipt of application materials: none. Application fee required: $175. On-campus interview required.

Athletics Interscholastic: baseball (boys), basketball (b,g), cross-country running (b,g), soccer (b,g), softball (g), tennis (b,g), track and field (b,g), volleyball (b,g). 2 PE instructors, 1 coach.

Computers Computers are regularly used in computer applications, keyboarding, yearbook classes. Computer network features include on-campus library services, Internet access, wireless campus network, 1:1 iPad Initiative for grades 9-12. Campus intranet and student e-mail accounts are available to students. Students grades are available online. The school has a published electronic and media policy.

Contact Mrs. Deborah Wright, Administrative Assistant. 510-317-8990 Ext. 338. Fax: 510-278-4773. E-mail: deborahwright@rcs.edu. Website: www.rcs.edu

REGINA JUNIOR-SENIOR HIGH SCHOOL

2150 Rochester Avenue
Iowa City, Iowa 52245

Head of School: Glenn Plummer

General Information Coeducational day college-preparatory and religious studies school, affiliated with Roman Catholic Church. Grades 7–12. Founded: 1958. Setting: urban. 1 building on campus. Approved or accredited by National Catholic Education Association and Iowa Department of Education. Total enrollment: 902. Upper school average class size: 17. Upper school faculty-student ratio: 1:15. There are 180 required school days per year for Upper School students. Upper School students typically attend 5 days per week. The average school day consists of 6 hours.

Upper School Student Profile Grade 7: 71 students (40 boys, 31 girls); Grade 8: 70 students (35 boys, 35 girls); Grade 9: 51 students (29 boys, 22 girls); Grade 10: 63 students (27 boys, 36 girls); Grade 11: 74 students (41 boys, 33 girls); Grade 12: 53 students (25 boys, 28 girls). 90% of students are Roman Catholic.

Faculty School total: 40. In upper school: 14 men, 16 women; 11 have advanced degrees.

Subjects Offered Advanced Placement courses.

Graduation Requirements American government, American history, arts and fine arts (art, music, dance, drama), career/college preparation, CPR, economics, English, health, mathematics, physical education (includes health), science, senior seminar, speech, theology, world history.

Special Academic Programs Advanced Placement exam preparation; study at local college for college credit; ESL.

College Admission Counseling 58 students graduated in 2016; 57 went to college, including Iowa State University of Science and Technology; The University of Iowa; University of Northern Iowa. Other: 1 entered military service. Mean composite ACT: 25. 40% scored over 26 on composite ACT.

Student Life Upper grades have specified standards of dress, student council. Discipline rests primarily with faculty. Attendance at religious services is required.

Tuition and Aid Tuition installment plan (SMART Tuition Payment Plan). Tuition reduction for siblings, need-based scholarship grants available. In 2016–17, 25% of upper-school students received aid. Total amount of financial aid awarded in 2016–17: $325,000.

Admissions Traditional secondary-level entrance grade is 7. Deadline for receipt of application materials: none. Application fee required: $100. Interview required.

Athletics Interscholastic: baseball (boys), basketball (b,g), bowling (b,g), cross-country running (b,g), football (b), golf (b,g), soccer (b,g), track and field (b,g), volleyball (g), wrestling (b); coed interscholastic: dance team, strength & conditioning, weight training. 1 PE instructor, 1 athletic trainer.

Computers Computers are regularly used in all classes. Computer network features include Internet access, wireless campus network, Internet filtering or blocking technology. Student e-mail accounts are available to students. Students grades are available online. The school has a published electronic and media policy.

Contact Pam Schowalter, Director of Admissions. 319-499-9006. Fax: 319-337-4109. E-mail: pam.schowalter@regina.org. Website: https://regina.org/

REGIS HIGH SCHOOL

55 East 84th Street
New York, New York 10028-0884

Head of School: Dr. Gary J. Tocchet

General Information Boys' day college-preparatory school, affiliated with Roman Catholic Church. Grades 9–12. Founded: 1914. Setting: urban. 3-acre campus. 1 building on campus. Approved or accredited by Jesuit Secondary Education Association, Middle States Association of Colleges and Schools, and New York Department of Education. Total enrollment: 532. Upper school average class size: 15. Upper school faculty-student ratio: 1:15. There are 180 required school days per year for Upper School students. Upper School students typically attend 5 days per week. The average school day consists of 6 hours and 50 minutes.

Upper School Student Profile Grade 9: 136 students (136 boys); Grade 10: 131 students (131 boys); Grade 11: 134 students (134 boys); Grade 12: 131 students (131 boys). 100% of students are Roman Catholic.

Faculty School total: 54. In upper school: 35 men, 19 women; 48 have advanced degrees.

Subjects Offered Algebra, American history, American literature, art, art history, band, biology, calculus, chemistry, Chinese, computer programming, computer science, creative writing, drama, driver education, economics, English, English literature, ethics, European history, expository writing, film, French, geometry, German, health, history, Latin, mathematics, music, physical education, physics, psychology, social studies, Spanish, speech, statistics, theater, theology, trigonometry, writing.

Graduation Requirements Art, computer literacy, English, foreign language, history, mathematics, music, physical education (includes health), science, theology, Christian service program.

Special Academic Programs 14 Advanced Placement exams for which test preparation is offered; independent study; study abroad.

College Admission Counseling Colleges students went to include Boston College; Cornell University; Fordham University; Georgetown University; New York University; Northeastern University. Mean SAT critical reading: 721, mean SAT math: 722, mean SAT writing: 724, mean combined SAT: 2163.

Student Life Upper grades have specified standards of dress, student council. Discipline rests primarily with faculty. Attendance at religious services is required.

Tuition and Aid Tuition-free school available.

Admissions Traditional secondary-level entrance grade is 9. For fall 2015, 772 students applied for upper-level admission, 140 were accepted, 136 enrolled. Admissions testing required. Deadline for receipt of application materials: October 23. Application fee required: $85. On-campus interview required.

Athletics Interscholastic: baseball, basketball, cross-country running, fencing, floor hockey, indoor track & field, track and field, volleyball; intramural: baseball, basketball, cross-country running, floor hockey, indoor soccer. 2 PE instructors, 10 coaches.

Computers Computers are regularly used in all academic classes. Computer network features include on-campus library services, Internet access, wireless campus network, Internet filtering or blocking technology. Campus intranet, student e-mail accounts, and computer access in designated common areas are available to students.

Contact Mr. Eric P. DiMichele, Director of Admissions. 212-288-1100 Ext. 2057. Fax: 212-794-1221. E-mail: edimiche@regis.org. Website: www.regis.org

REGIS HIGH SCHOOL

550 West Regis Street
Stayton, Oregon 97383

Head of School: Mr. Rick Schindler

General Information Coeducational day college-preparatory and general academic school, affiliated with Roman Catholic Church. Grades 9–12. Founded: 1963. Setting: rural. Nearest major city is Salem. 35-acre campus. 3 buildings on campus. Approved or accredited by Western Catholic Education Association and Oregon Department of Education. Total enrollment: 189. Upper school average class size: 16. Upper school faculty-student ratio: 1:12. There are 276 required school days per year for Upper School students. Upper School students typically attend 5 days per week. The average school day consists of 5 hours and 50 minutes.

Upper School Student Profile Grade 9: 26 students (14 boys, 12 girls); Grade 10: 25 students (12 boys, 13 girls); Grade 11: 36 students (17 boys, 19 girls); Grade 12: 43 students (29 boys, 14 girls). 72% of students are Roman Catholic.

Faculty School total: 13. In upper school: 10 men, 3 women.

Subjects Offered Accounting, algebra, athletics, biology, business, Catholic belief and practice, chemistry, composition, computer science, English, fine arts, geometry, journalism, mathematics, music, physical education, physical science, physics, psychology, religion, science, social sciences, yearbook.

Graduation Requirements Arts and fine arts (art, music, dance, drama), business skills (includes word processing), computer science, English, mathematics, physical education (includes health), religion (includes Bible studies and theology), science, social sciences, social studies (includes history), 60 hours of Christian service.

Special Academic Programs Advanced Placement exam preparation; study at local college for college credit; remedial reading and/or remedial writing; remedial math; programs in general development for dyslexic students.

College Admission Counseling 42 students graduated in 2016; all went to college, including Chemeketa Community College; Oregon State University; University of Oregon; University of Portland; Western Oregon University.

Student Life Upper grades have specified standards of dress, student council, honor system. Discipline rests primarily with faculty. Attendance at religious services is required.

Tuition and Aid Day student tuition: $5450–$7450. Tuition installment plan (FACTS Tuition Payment Plan). Tuition reduction for siblings, merit scholarship grants, need-based scholarship grants available. In 2016–17, 45% of upper-school students received aid; total upper-school merit-scholarship money awarded: $8000.

Admissions Traditional secondary-level entrance grade is 9. STS and STS, Diocese Test required. Deadline for receipt of application materials: April 25. Application fee required: $175. Interview required.

Athletics Interscholastic: baseball (boys), basketball (b,g), cheering (g), cross-country running (b,g), football (b), golf (b), softball (g), track and field (b,g), volleyball (g); coed intramural: basketball, bowling, skiing (downhill), snowboarding, volleyball, weight lifting. 1 PE instructor, 5 coaches.

Computers Computers are regularly used in business, economics, English, history, journalism, keyboarding, library, mathematics, multimedia, newspaper, occupational education, publications, research skills, science, stock market, word processing, yearbook classes. Computer network features include online commercial services, Internet access, wireless campus network, Internet filtering or blocking technology, Chromebooks for every student. Student e-mail accounts are available to students. Students grades are available online. The school has a published electronic and media policy.

Contact Mrs. Gina Keudell, Office Manager. 503-769-2159. Fax: 503-769-1706. E-mail: office@regishighschool.net. Website: www.regishighschool.net

REGIS JESUIT HIGH SCHOOL, BOYS DIVISION

6400 South Lewiston Way
Aurora, Colorado 80016

Head of School: Mr. Alan Carruthers

General Information Boys' day college-preparatory and Jesuit pedagogical approach to all subject areas school, affiliated with Roman Catholic Church (Jesuit order). Grades 9–12. Founded: 1877. Setting: suburban. 64-acre campus. 3 buildings on campus. Approved or accredited by Jesuit Secondary Education Association, North Central Association of Colleges and Schools, and Colorado Department of Education. Member of National Association of Independent Schools. Endowment: $13 million. Total enrollment: 944. Upper school average class size: 26. Upper school faculty-student ratio: 1:12. There are 182 required school days per year for Upper School students. Upper School students typically attend 5 days per week. The average school day consists of 6 hours and 45 minutes.

Upper School Student Profile Grade 9: 250 students (250 boys); Grade 10: 248 students (248 boys); Grade 11: 234 students (234 boys); Grade 12: 198 students (198 boys). 70% of students are Roman Catholic Church (Jesuit order).

Faculty School total: 84. In upper school: 43 men, 25 women; 64 have advanced degrees.

Subjects Offered Algebra, American literature, anatomy, art, band, biology, British literature, calculus, chemistry, chorus, Colorado ecology, computer applications, computer graphics, computer literacy, computer programming, earth science, economics, English, English literature, fine arts, French, geography, geometry, history, integrated science, international relations, Latin, Mandarin, math analysis, mathematics, mechanical drawing, media studies, music, physical education, physics, physiology, programming, social studies, sociology, Spanish, speech, statistics, theater, theology, trigonometry, U.S. government, U.S. history, Western civilization, world history.

Graduation Requirements Arts and fine arts (art, music, dance, drama), communications, English, foreign language, mathematics, physical education (includes health), religion (includes Bible studies and theology), science, social sciences, social studies (includes history), technology, theology. Community service is required.

Special Academic Programs 19 Advanced Placement exams for which test preparation is offered; honors section; term-away projects; remedial reading and/or remedial writing; remedial math; programs in English, mathematics, general development for dyslexic students.

College Admission Counseling 231 students graduated in 2016; 223 went to college, including Colorado State University; Creighton University; Gonzaga University; Regis University; Santa Clara University; University of Colorado Boulder. Other: 2 entered military service, 7 had other specific plans. Mean SAT critical reading: 579, mean SAT math: 612, mean SAT writing: 599, mean composite ACT: 27.

Student Life Upper grades have specified standards of dress, student council, honor system. Discipline rests primarily with faculty. Attendance at religious services is required.

Summer Programs Remediation, enrichment, advancement, sports, art/fine arts, computer instruction programs offered; held on campus; accepts boys and girls; open to students from other schools. 75 students usually enrolled. 2017 schedule: June 1 to July 31.

Tuition and Aid Day student tuition: $15,475. Tuition installment plan (FACTS Tuition Payment Plan). Merit scholarship grants, need-based scholarship grants, work grant tuition exchange program available. In 2016–17, 25% of upper-school students received aid; total upper-school merit-scholarship money awarded: $15,000. Total amount of financial aid awarded in 2016–17: $1,900,000.

Admissions Traditional secondary-level entrance grade is 9. High School Placement Test required. Deadline for receipt of application materials: December 7. No application fee required.

Athletics Interscholastic: aquatics, baseball, basketball, cross-country running, diving, football, golf, ice hockey, lacrosse, rugby, soccer, swimming and diving, tennis, track and field, volleyball, wrestling; intramural: basketball, bicycling, bowling, golf, kickball, power lifting, rock climbing, rugby, self defense, skateboarding, soccer, Special Olympics (g), table tennis (g), ultimate Frisbee, volleyball, water polo, weight lifting, weight training, whiffle ball, yoga; coed intramural: climbing, fencing, rowing. 4 PE instructors, 75 coaches, 2 athletic trainers.

Computers Computers are regularly used in all academic classes. Computer network features include on-campus library services, online commercial services, Internet access, wireless campus network, Internet filtering or blocking technology. Campus intranet and student e-mail accounts are available to students. Students grades are available online. The school has a published electronic and media policy.

Contact Mr. Paul Muller, Director of Admissions. 303-269-8064. Fax: 303-766-2240. E-mail: pmuller@regisjesuit.com. Website: www.regisjesuit.com

REGIS JESUIT HIGH SCHOOL, GIRLS DIVISION

6300 South Lewiston Way
Aurora, Colorado 80016

Head of School: Ms. Gretchen M. Kessler

General Information Girls' day college-preparatory and Jesuit pedagogical approach to all subject areas school, affiliated with Roman Catholic Church (Jesuit order). Grades 9–12. Founded: 1877. Setting: suburban. 64-acre campus. 3 buildings on campus. Approved or accredited by Jesuit Secondary Education Association, North Central Association of Colleges and Schools, and Colorado Department of Education. Member of National Association of Independent Schools. Endowment: $13 million. Total enrollment: 738. Upper school average class size: 20. Upper school faculty-student ratio: 1:12. There are 182 required school days per year for Upper School students. Upper School students typically attend 5 days per week. The average school day consists of 6 hours and 45 minutes.

Upper School Student Profile Grade 9: 185 students (185 girls); Grade 10: 194 students (194 girls); Grade 11: 175 students (175 girls); Grade 12: 166 students (166 girls). 70% of students are Roman Catholic Church (Jesuit order).

Faculty School total: 65. In upper school: 20 men, 46 women; 53 have advanced degrees.

Subjects Offered ACT preparation, acting, advanced biology, advanced chemistry, advanced computer applications, advanced math, Advanced Placement courses, advanced studio art-AP, algebra, American government, American history, American history-AP, American literature, American literature-AP, American studies, analysis and differential calculus, analytic geometry, anatomy, anatomy and physiology, Ancient Greek, architecture, art, art-AP, athletic training, Basic programming, biology, biology-AP, British literature, British literature (honors), British literature-AP, broadcast journalism, business, calculus, calculus-AP, campus ministry, ceramics, chemistry, chemistry-AP, Chinese, choir, choral music, chorus, Christian doctrine, Christian ethics, Christian studies, Christianity, church history, classical studies, classics, communication skills, communications, community service, computer applications, computer art, computer graphics, concert band, dance, debate, drama, drama performance, earth science, English, English composition, English language and composition-AP, English language-AP, English literature, English literature and composition-AP, English literature-AP, English-AP, English/composition-AP, fine arts, French, French language-AP, geometry, history, Latin, Latin-AP, mathematics-AP, physics-AP, public speaking, religion, social studies, Spanish, Spanish language-AP, speech and debate, theater, yoga.

Graduation Requirements Arts and fine arts (art, music, dance, drama), communications, computer education, English, foreign language, mathematics, physical education (includes health), religious studies, science, social studies (includes history), technology, theology. Community service is required.

Special Academic Programs 19 Advanced Placement exams for which test preparation is offered; honors section; independent study; term-away projects; remedial reading and/or remedial writing; remedial math; programs in English, mathematics, general development for dyslexic students.

College Admission Counseling 179 students graduated in 2016; 176 went to college, including Colorado State University; Creighton University; Gonzaga University; Regis University; Santa Clara University; University of Colorado Boulder.

Other: 1 entered military service, 3 had other specific plans. Mean SAT critical reading: 553, mean SAT math: 535, mean SAT writing: 575, mean composite ACT: 26.

Student Life Upper grades have specified standards of dress, student council, honor system. Discipline rests primarily with faculty. Attendance at religious services is required.

Summer Programs Remediation, enrichment, advancement, sports, art/fine arts, computer instruction programs offered; held on campus; accepts boys and girls; open to students from other schools. 50 students usually enrolled. 2017 schedule: June 1 to July 31.

Tuition and Aid Day student tuition: $15,475. Tuition installment plan (FACTS Tuition Payment Plan). Merit scholarship grants, need-based scholarship grants, work grant tuition exchange program available. In 2016–17, 25% of upper-school students received aid; total upper-school merit-scholarship money awarded: $15,000. Total amount of financial aid awarded in 2016–17: $1,900,000.

Admissions Traditional secondary-level entrance grade is 9. High School Placement Test required. Deadline for receipt of application materials: December 7. No application fee required.

Athletics Interscholastic: aerobics/dance, aquatics, baseball, basketball, cheering, cross-country running, dance, dance team, field hockey, fitness, golf, modern dance, rugby, soccer, softball, swimming and diving, tennis, track and field, volleyball; intramural: basketball, golf, Special Olympics, table tennis, ultimate Frisbee, weight lifting, whiffle ball (b), yoga. 4 PE instructors, 40 coaches, 2 athletic trainers.

Computers Computers are regularly used in all academic classes. Computer network features include on-campus library services, Internet access, wireless campus network, Internet filtering or blocking technology. Campus intranet, student e-mail accounts, and computer access in designated common areas are available to students. Students grades are available online. The school has a published electronic and media policy.

Contact Ms. Patricia Long, Director of Admissions. 303-269-8164. Fax: 303-221-4772. E-mail: plong@regisjesuit.com. Website: www.regisjesuit.com

REJOICE CHRISTIAN SCHOOLS

12200 East 86th Street North
Owasso, Oklahoma 74055

Head of School: Dr. Craig D. Shaw

General Information Coeducational day college-preparatory school, affiliated with Free Will Baptist Church. Grades P3–12. Founded: 1992. Setting: suburban. Nearest major city is Tulsa. 1 building on campus. Approved or accredited by Association of Christian Schools International and Oklahoma Department of Education. Total enrollment: 873. Upper school average class size: 16. Upper school faculty-student ratio: 1:14. There are 175 required school days per year for Upper School students. The average school day consists of 7 hours.

Upper School Student Profile Grade 6: 57 students (28 boys, 29 girls); Grade 7: 48 students (26 boys, 22 girls); Grade 8: 58 students (31 boys, 27 girls); Grade 9: 52 students (34 boys, 18 girls); Grade 10: 47 students (25 boys, 22 girls); Grade 11: 51 students (26 boys, 25 girls); Grade 12: 44 students (24 boys, 20 girls). 30% of students are Free Will Baptist Church.

Faculty School total: 79. In upper school: 13 men, 24 women; 10 have advanced degrees.

Subjects Offered Advanced biology, advanced chemistry, Advanced Placement courses, algebra, American democracy, American government, American history, American history-AP, anatomy, anatomy and physiology, art, art appreciation, art education, art history, athletic training, athletics, band, basketball, Bible, Bible studies, biology, biology-AP, business, business education, calculus, calculus-AP, cheerleading, chemistry, chemistry-AP, choir, chorus, Christian education, civics, computer skills, electives, English, English language-AP, English literature and composition-AP, English literature-AP, English-AP, English/composition-AP, fitness, general business, general math, geography, geometry, golf, government, government and politics-AP, government-AP, government/civics, government/civics-AP, history, honors algebra, honors English, honors geometry, honors U.S. history, honors world history, journalism, language, language arts, library, mathematics, mathematics-AP, media, music, novels, physical education, physical fitness, physical science, pre-algebra, pre-calculus, Spanish, Spanish language-AP, speech, speech and debate, sports, sports conditioning, state history, technology, track and field, trigonometry, U.S. government, U.S. government and politics-AP, U.S. history, U.S. history-AP, weight training, world history, world history-AP, yearbook.

Special Academic Programs Honors section; study at local college for college credit.

College Admission Counseling 44 students graduated in 2016.

Student Life Upper grades have student council, honor system. Discipline rests primarily with faculty.

Tuition and Aid Tuition installment plan (SMART Tuition Payment Plan, monthly payment plans, annual payment plans, semi-annual payment plans). Need-based scholarship grants available.

Admissions PSAT, Stanford Achievement Test or TerraNova required. Deadline for receipt of application materials: none. Application fee required: $55. Interview recommended.

Athletics Interscholastic: baseball (boys), basketball (b,g), cheering (g), cross-country running (b,g), football (b), golf (b,g), physical fitness (b,g), physical training (b,g),

soccer (b,g), tennis (b,g), track and field (b,g), volleyball (g), weight training (b,g). 3 PE instructors, 11 coaches, 1 athletic trainer.

Computers Computers are regularly used in all academic classes. Computer network features include on-campus library services, Internet access, wireless campus network, Internet filtering or blocking technology, Chromebooks for all upper level students. Campus intranet and student e-mail accounts are available to students. Students grades are available online. The school has a published electronic and media policy.

Contact Mrs. Heather Koerner, District Registrar. 918-516-0048. Fax: 918-516-0299. E-mail: hkoerner@rejoiceschool.com. Website: www.rejoiceschool.com

RICE MEMORIAL HIGH SCHOOL

99 Proctor Avenue
South Burlington, Vermont 05403

Head of School: Dr. Laura Della Santa

General Information Coeducational day college-preparatory, arts, and religious studies school, affiliated with Roman Catholic Church. Grades 9–12. Founded: 1918. Setting: suburban. Nearest major city is Montreal, QC, Canada. 33-acre campus. 1 building on campus. Approved or accredited by New England Association of Schools and Colleges and Vermont Department of Education. Total enrollment: 461. Upper school average class size: 20. Upper school faculty-student ratio: 1:11. There are 175 required school days per year for Upper School students. Upper School students typically attend 5 days per week. The average school day consists of 6 hours and 30 minutes.

Upper School Student Profile Grade 9: 116 students (58 boys, 58 girls); Grade 10: 95 students (45 boys, 50 girls); Grade 11: 121 students (52 boys, 69 girls); Grade 12: 104 students (60 boys, 44 girls); Postgraduate: 2 students (2 boys). 65% of students are Roman Catholic.

Faculty School total: 35. In upper school: 17 men, 18 women; 19 have advanced degrees.

Subjects Offered 20th century history, 20th century world history, 3-dimensional design, accounting, advanced chemistry, advanced math, Advanced Placement courses, algebra, American government, American history, American history-AP, American literature, anatomy, anatomy and physiology, ancient world history, art, arts, athletics, band, baseball, basketball, Bible, Bible studies, biology, biology-AP, British literature, business, calculus, calculus-AP, campus ministry, career/college preparation, ceramics, chemistry, choir, choral music, chorus, college counseling, college writing, community service, composition-AP, concert band, creative writing, critical studies in film, drama, earth science, economics, English, English language and composition-AP, English literature, English literature-AP, English-AP, ethics, European history, filmmaking, fine arts, foreign language, French, freshman foundations, geometry, government and politics-AP, grammar, history, history of the Catholic Church, history-AP, honors algebra, honors English, honors geometry, honors world history, jazz band, jazz ensemble, journalism, Latin, mathematics, moral theology, music, musical theater, participation in sports, philosophy, photography, physical science, physics, pre-calculus, religion, religious education, science, scripture, senior project, social justice, social studies, Spanish, speech, student government, tennis, theology, track and field, trigonometry, U.S. government and politics-AP, U.S. history, U.S. history-AP, volleyball, world history, world literature, world religions, world studies, yearbook, yoga.

Graduation Requirements Arts and fine arts (art, music, dance, drama), English, foreign language, mathematics, physical education (includes health), religion (includes Bible studies and theology), science, social studies (includes history).

Special Academic Programs Advanced Placement exam preparation; honors section; study at local college for college credit; study abroad; academic accommodation for the gifted; remedial reading and/or remedial writing; remedial math.

College Admission Counseling 103 students graduated in 2016; 85 went to college, including Saint Michael's College; University of Vermont. Other: 3 entered a postgraduate year, 15 had other specific plans. Mean SAT critical reading: 518, mean SAT math: 514, mean SAT writing: 525, mean combined SAT: 1557, mean composite ACT: 24.

Student Life Upper grades have uniform requirement, student council, honor system. Discipline rests primarily with faculty. Attendance at religious services is required.

Tuition and Aid Day student tuition: $9630. Tuition installment plan (FACTS Tuition Payment Plan, monthly payment plans). Need-based scholarship grants available. In 2016–17, 65% of upper-school students received aid. Total amount of financial aid awarded in 2016–17: $650,000.

Admissions Traditional secondary-level entrance grade is 9. High School Placement Test required. Deadline for receipt of application materials: February 17. Application fee required: $150.

Athletics Interscholastic: baseball (boys), basketball (b,g), field hockey (g), football (b), ice hockey (b,g), lacrosse (b,g), soccer (b,g), softball (g), tennis (b,g), volleyball (g); coed interscholastic: alpine skiing, cross-country running, Frisbee, golf, indoor track & field, rowing, snowboarding, track and field, ultimate Frisbee; coed intramural: sailing, skiing (downhill), yoga. 50 coaches.

Computers Computers are regularly used in all academic classes. Computer resources include on-campus library services, online commercial services, Internet access,

wireless campus network, access to Saint Michael's College periodicals, Naviance. Student e-mail accounts are available to students. Students grades are available online.
Contact Ms. Christy Warner Bahrenburg, Director of Enrollment. 802-862-6521 Ext. 235. Fax: 802-864-9931. E-mail: bahrenburg@rmhsvt.org. Website: www.ricehs.org

RIDLEY COLLEGE

2 Ridley Road
St. Catharines, Ontario L2R7C3, Canada

Head of School: Mr. Edward Kidd

General Information Coeducational boarding and day college-preparatory, arts, and Science school, affiliated with Anglican Church of Canada. Boarding grades 5–PG, day grades JK–PG. Founded: 1889. Setting: suburban. Nearest major city is Buffalo, NY. Students are housed in coed dormitories and single-sex dormitories. 90-acre campus. 13 buildings on campus. Approved or accredited by Canadian Association of Independent Schools, Conference of Independent Schools of Ontario, International Baccalaureate Organization, The Association of Boarding Schools, and Ontario Department of Education. Affiliate member of National Association of Independent Schools; member of Secondary School Admission Test Board. Language of instruction: English. Endowment: CAN$30 million. Total enrollment: 649. Upper school average class size: 17. Upper school faculty-student ratio: 1:8. There are 232 required school days per year for Upper School students. Upper School students typically attend 6 days per week. The average school day consists of 6 hours.
Upper School Student Profile Grade 9: 38 students (13 boys, 25 girls); Grade 10: 62 students (36 boys, 26 girls); Grade 11: 110 students (61 boys, 49 girls); Grade 12: 123 students (75 boys, 48 girls); Postgraduate: 2 students (2 boys). 68% of students are boarding students. 56% are province residents. 15 provinces are represented in upper school student body. 30% are international students. International students from China, Germany, Mexico, Nigeria, Russian Federation, and United States; 38 other countries represented in student body. 20% of students are members of Anglican Church of Canada.
Faculty School total: 77. In upper school: 37 men, 40 women; 26 have advanced degrees; 40 reside on campus.
Subjects Offered Accounting, algebra, American history, anthropology, art, art history, biology, business mathematics, business skills, calculus, Canadian history, Canadian law, chemistry, computer multimedia, computer programming, computer science, creative writing, drafting, drama, dramatic arts, driver education, economics, English, English literature, environmental science, ESL, exercise science, finance, fine arts, French, geography, German, health education, health science, instrumental music, International Baccalaureate courses, kinesiology, Latin, Mandarin, mathematics, music, philosophy, physical education, physics, science, social sciences, social studies, Spanish, sports science, theater, world history, world religions, writing.
Graduation Requirements Arts and fine arts (art, music, dance, drama), business skills (includes word processing), English, foreign language, mathematics, physical education (includes health), science, social sciences, social studies (includes history), 40 Hours of Community Service.
Special Academic Programs International Baccalaureate program; honors section; independent study; study abroad; academic accommodation for the gifted, the musically talented, and the artistically talented; ESL (20 students enrolled).
College Admission Counseling 131 students graduated in 2016; 122 went to college, including Brock University; Carleton University; Queen's University at Kingston; The University of Western Ontario; University of Guelph; University of Toronto. Other: 9 had other specific plans.
Student Life Upper grades have uniform requirement, student council, honor system. Discipline rests primarily with faculty. Attendance at religious services is required.
Summer Programs ESL programs offered; session focuses on improvement of English language skills; held on campus; accepts boys and girls; open to students from other schools. 2017 schedule: August 1 to August 26. Application deadline: July 1.
Tuition and Aid Day student tuition: CAN$14,500–CAN$30,950; 5-day tuition and room/board: CAN$54,950; 7-day tuition and room/board: CAN$60,900. Tuition installment plan (monthly payment plans, individually arranged payment plans). Bursaries, merit scholarship grants, need-based scholarship grants, need-based loans available. In 2016–17, 33% of upper-school students received aid; total upper-school merit-scholarship money awarded: CAN$789,000. Total amount of financial aid awarded in 2016–17: CAN$1,800,000.
Admissions Traditional secondary-level entrance grade is 9. For fall 2016, 537 students applied for upper-level admission, 305 were accepted, 194 enrolled. Deadline for receipt of application materials: none. Application fee required: CAN$150. Interview required.
Athletics Interscholastic: artistic gym (girls), basketball (b,g), crew (b,g), cross-country running (b,g), field hockey (g), fitness walking (g), gymnastics (g), hockey (b,g), ice hockey (b,g), rowing (b,g), rugby (b,g), running (b,g), soccer (b,g), softball (b,g), squash (b,g), swimming and diving (b,g), tennis (b,g), track and field (b,g), volleyball (g); intramural: basketball (b,g), hockey (b,g), ice hockey (b,g), running (b,g); coed interscholastic: golf, tennis; coed intramural: aerobics, aerobics/dance, alpine skiing, aquatics, backpacking, badminton, ball hockey, baseball, bicycling, billiards, bowling, broomball, canoeing/kayaking, climbing, cooperative games, Cosom hockey, cross-country running, curling, dance, dance squad, dance team, drill team, equestrian sports, fencing, fitness, flag football, Frisbee, golf, hiking/backpacking, horseback riding, ice skating, indoor soccer, jogging, life saving, martial arts, modern dance, outdoor activities, outdoor education, outdoor recreation, outdoor skills, physical fitness, physical training, power lifting, racquetball, rock climbing, ropes courses, sailing, scuba diving, self defense, skiing (cross-country), skiing (downhill), snowboarding, snowshoeing, soccer, softball, squash, strength & conditioning, swimming and diving, table tennis, tennis, track and field, triathlon, ultimate Frisbee, volleyball, walking, wall climbing, weight lifting, weight training, wilderness survival, yoga. 8 coaches, 3 athletic trainers.
Computers Computers are regularly used in all academic classes. Computer network features include on-campus library services, online commercial services, Internet access, wireless campus network, Internet filtering or blocking technology. Student e-mail accounts and computer access in designated common areas are available to students. Students grades are available online. The school has a published electronic and media policy.
Contact Mrs. Stephanie Park, Admissions Administrative Assistant. 905-684-1889 Ext. 2207. Fax: 905-684-8875. E-mail: admissions@ridleycollege.com. Website: www.ridleycollege.com

RIVERDALE COUNTRY SCHOOL

5250 Fieldston Road
Bronx, New York 10471-2999

Head of School: Dominic A.A. Randolph

General Information Coeducational day college-preparatory school. Grades PK–12. Founded: 1907. Setting: suburban. Nearest major city is New York. 27-acre campus. 9 buildings on campus. Approved or accredited by New York State Association of Independent Schools and New York Department of Education. Member of National Association of Independent Schools and Secondary School Admission Test Board. Endowment: $48 million. Total enrollment: 1,150. Upper school average class size: 16. Upper school faculty-student ratio: 1:8. Upper School students typically attend 5 days per week.
Faculty School total: 185.
Subjects Offered Algebra, American literature, anatomy, art, art history, biology, calculus, ceramics, chemistry, community service, computer math, computer programming, computer science, creative writing, drama, driver education, earth science, ecology, economics, English, English literature, environmental science, European history, expository writing, fine arts, French, geology, geometry, government/civics, grammar, health, history, history of science, introduction to liberal studies, Japanese, journalism, Latin, Mandarin, marine biology, mathematics, music, oceanography, philosophy, photography, physical education, physics, psychology, science, social studies, Spanish, speech, statistics, theater, theory of knowledge, trigonometry, world history, writing.
Graduation Requirements American studies, arts and fine arts (art, music, dance, drama), computer science, English, foreign language, mathematics, physical education (includes health), science, social studies (includes history), integrated liberal studies. Community service is required.
Special Academic Programs Honors section; independent study; term-away projects; study abroad; academic accommodation for the gifted, the musically talented, and the artistically talented.
College Admission Counseling 120 students graduated in 2016; all went to college, including Columbia University; Cornell University; Dartmouth College; Harvard University; University of Pennsylvania; Wesleyan University.
Student Life Upper grades have student council, honor system. Discipline rests equally with students and faculty.
Summer Programs Enrichment programs offered; session focuses on science research, interdisciplinary programs; held both on and off campus; accepts boys and girls; open to students from other schools.
Tuition and Aid Day student tuition: $49,805. Tuition installment plan (monthly payment plans). Need-based scholarship grants available. In 2016–17, 20% of upper-school students received aid.
Admissions Traditional secondary-level entrance grade is 9. ISEE or SSAT required. Deadline for receipt of application materials: November 15. Application fee required: $60. On-campus interview recommended.
Athletics Interscholastic: baseball (boys), basketball (b,g), crew (b,g), field hockey (g), football (b), lacrosse (b,g), soccer (b,g), softball (g), tennis (b,g), volleyball (g); intramural: baseball (b), basketball (b,g), field hockey (g), football (b), lacrosse (b,g), soccer (b,g), softball (g), tennis (b,g), volleyball (g); coed interscholastic: cross-country running, fencing, golf, squash, swimming and diving, track and field, ultimate Frisbee, winter (indoor) track; coed intramural: cross-country running, dance, fencing, fitness, physical fitness, squash, swimming and diving, tennis, track and field, ultimate Frisbee, yoga. 7 PE instructors, 31 coaches, 1 athletic trainer.
Computers Computers are regularly used in art, English, foreign language, history, mathematics, music, science classes. Computer network features include on-campus library services, online commercial services, Internet access, wireless campus network, Internet filtering or blocking technology, off-campus email, off-campus library services. Student e-mail accounts and computer access in designated common areas are available to students. The school has a published electronic and media policy.
Contact Jenna Rogers King, Director of Admission and Enrollment. 718-519-2715. Fax: 718-519-2793. E-mail: jrking@riverdale.edu. Website: www.riverdale.edu

RIVERMONT COLLEGIATE

1821 Sunset Drive
Bettendorf, Iowa 52722

Head of School: Mr. C. Max Roach

General Information Coeducational day college-preparatory, arts, and technology school. Grades PS–12. Founded: 1884. Setting: suburban. Nearest major city is Davenport. Students are housed in Home stay program. 16-acre campus. 4 buildings on campus. Approved or accredited by Independent Schools Association of the Central States and Iowa Department of Education. Member of National Association of Independent Schools and Secondary School Admission Test Board. Endowment: $5 million. Total enrollment: 192. Upper school average class size: 9. Upper school faculty-student ratio: 1:2. Upper School students typically attend 5 days per week. The average school day consists of 7 hours and 10 minutes.

Faculty School total: 31. In upper school: 4 men, 14 women; 6 have advanced degrees.

Subjects Offered Acting, advanced chemistry, advanced math, Advanced Placement courses, algebra, animation, art, arts, band, basketball, biology, biology-AP, calculus, calculus-AP, character education, cheerleading, chemistry, chemistry-AP, Chinese, choir, choral music, chorus, college counseling, college writing, computer animation, computer graphics, computer multimedia, computer programming, computer science, concert band, concert choir, creative drama, creative writing, desktop publishing, digital photography, drama, drama performance, drama workshop, dramatic arts, drawing, drawing and design, earth science, economics, English, English language and composition-AP, English literature, English literature and composition-AP, English-AP, environmental science-AP, fine arts, foreign language, French, French language-AP, French literature-AP, French-AP, geography, geometry, global science, government/civics, guidance, health, health education, Hispanic literature, history, history-AP, honors algebra, honors English, HTML design, human biology, humanities, independent study, instrumental music, Latin, Latin American literature, life science, literature and composition-AP, macro/microeconomics-AP, mathematics, media, media arts, microeconomics, Middle East, model United Nations, multimedia, multimedia design, music, music theater, musical productions, musical theater, oral communications, performing arts, photography, physical education, physical fitness, physics, physics-AP, play production, pre-algebra, pre-calculus, probability and statistics, psychology, psychology-AP, public speaking, science, science project, science research, senior career experience, senior internship, senior project, service learning/internship, social studies, Spanish, Spanish language-AP, Spanish literature, Spanish literature-AP, Spanish-AP, speech, speech and debate, stage design, statistics-AP, studio art, symphonic band, theater, theater arts, theater design and production, theater production, U.S. government, U.S. government and politics, U.S. government and politics-AP, U.S. history, U.S. history-AP, United States government-AP, visual and performing arts, visual arts, vocal ensemble, voice, Web site design, wilderness education, wilderness experience, wind ensemble, wind instruments, world history, world history-AP, writing, yearbook.

Graduation Requirements Senior project/internship, junior service project.

Special Academic Programs Advanced Placement exam preparation; honors section; independent study; study at local college for college credit; academic accommodation for the gifted, the musically talented, and the artistically talented.

College Admission Counseling 11 students graduated in 2016; all went to college, including Cairn University; Case Western Reserve University; Pratt Institute; The University of Iowa; University of Illinois at Urbana–Champaign; University of Miami. Median SAT critical reading: 620, median SAT math: 600, median SAT writing: 600, median combined SAT: 1820, median composite ACT: 30.

Student Life Upper grades have specified standards of dress, student council, honor system. Discipline rests primarily with students.

Summer Programs Enrichment, advancement, sports, art/fine arts, computer instruction programs offered; session focuses on enrichment; held on campus; accepts boys and girls; open to students from other schools. 80 students usually enrolled. 2017 schedule: June 15 to August 8.

Tuition and Aid Day student tuition: $4500–$14,780. Tuition installment plan (Insured Tuition Payment Plan, monthly payment plans, individually arranged payment plans). Tuition reduction for siblings, need-based scholarship grants available. In 2016–17, 60% of upper-school students received aid.

Admissions Traditional secondary-level entrance grade is 9. Otis-Lennon Ability or Stanford Achievement Test, Otis-Lennon School Ability Test, Otis-Lennon School Ability Test, ERB CPT III, Otis-Lennon School Ability Test/writing sample, Otis-Lennon, Stanford Achievement Test, Wide Range Achievement Test or WRAT required. Deadline for receipt of application materials: none. Application fee required: $50. Interview required.

Athletics Interscholastic: basketball (boys, girls), cheering (g), cross-country running (b,g), running (b,g), track and field (b,g), volleyball (g); intramural: basketball (b,g), cheering (g), cross-country running (b,g), running (b,g), track and field (b,g), volleyball (g). 1 PE instructor, 4 coaches.

Computers Computers are regularly used in computer applications, English, science, technology, yearbook classes. Computer network features include on-campus library services, online commercial services, Internet access, wireless campus network, Internet filtering or blocking technology. Campus intranet and student e-mail accounts are available to students. Students grades are available online. The school has a published electronic and media policy.

Contact Mr. Phillip Dunbridge, Director of Enrollment Management and Communications. 563-359-1366 Ext. 302. Fax: 563-359-7576. E-mail: dunbridge@rvmt.org. Website: www.rvmt.org

RIVER OAKS BAPTIST SCHOOL

2300 Willowick
Houston, Texas 77027

Head of School: Mrs. Leanne Reynolds

General Information Coeducational day college-preparatory and character education school, affiliated with Baptist Church. Grades PK–8. Founded: 1955. Setting: urban. 12-acre campus. Approved or accredited by Accreditation Commission of the Texas Association of Baptist Schools and Texas Department of Education. Member of National Association of Independent Schools. Endowment: $30 million. Total enrollment: 732. Upper school faculty-student ratio: 1:16. There are 187 required school days per year for Upper School students. The average school day consists of 6 hours and 10 minutes.

Upper School Student Profile Grade 6: 80 students (40 boys, 40 girls); Grade 7: 80 students (40 boys, 40 girls); Grade 8: 80 students (40 boys, 40 girls). 11% of students are Baptist.

Faculty School total: 91. In upper school: 11 men, 31 women; 21 have advanced degrees.

Student Life Upper grades have uniform requirement, honor system. Discipline rests primarily with faculty. Attendance at religious services is required.

Tuition and Aid Tuition installment plan (monthly payment plans). Need-based scholarship grants available.

Admissions Individual IQ, ISEE and OLSAT, Stanford Achievement Test required. Deadline for receipt of application materials: December 10. Application fee required: $100. On-campus interview required.

Computers Computer network features include on-campus library services, wireless campus network, Internet filtering or blocking technology. Campus intranet and student e-mail accounts are available to students. Students grades are available online. The school has a published electronic and media policy.

Contact Mrs. Kristin Poe, Director of Admission. 713-623-6938 Ext. 263. Fax: 713-623-0650. E-mail: kpoe@robs.org. Website: www.robs.org

THE RIVERS SCHOOL

333 Winter Street
Weston, Massachusetts 02493-1040

Head of School: Mr. Edward V. Parsons

General Information Coeducational day college-preparatory and arts school. Grades 6–12. Founded: 1915. Setting: suburban. Nearest major city is Boston. 53-acre campus. 8 buildings on campus. Approved or accredited by Association of Independent Schools in New England and New England Association of Schools and Colleges. Member of National Association of Independent Schools and Secondary School Admission Test Board. Endowment: $22.3 million. Total enrollment: 490. Upper school average class size: 12. Upper school faculty-student ratio: 1:6. Upper School students typically attend 5 days per week. The average school day consists of 7 hours and 15 minutes.

Upper School Student Profile Grade 9: 94 students (53 boys, 41 girls); Grade 10: 88 students (43 boys, 45 girls); Grade 11: 95 students (43 boys, 52 girls); Grade 12: 90 students (50 boys, 40 girls).

Faculty School total: 86. In upper school: 43 men, 43 women; 56 have advanced degrees.

Subjects Offered Advanced Placement courses, algebra, American history, American literature, art, art history, art history-AP, astronomy, biochemistry, biology, biology-AP, calculus, calculus-AP, ceramics, chamber groups, chemistry, chemistry-AP, chorus, civil rights, Civil War, computer graphics, computer science, computer science-AP, creative writing, drama, earth science, economics-AP, English, English language and composition-AP, English literature, English literature and composition-AP, environmental science-AP, European history, expository writing, film studies, filmmaking, fine arts, French, French-AP, geography, geometry, history, Holocaust, jazz band, journalism, kinesiology, Latin, Latin-AP, Mandarin, mathematics, modern European history-AP, music, photography, physics, physics-AP, playwriting, science, Spanish, Spanish-AP, statistics-AP, the Presidency, theater, theater arts, trigonometry, U.S. history-AP, world history, world literature.

Graduation Requirements Algebra, art, biology, geometry, history, modern European history, U.S. history, visual and performing arts, Participation in athletics and the arts.

Special Academic Programs Advanced Placement exam preparation; honors section; independent study; study at local college for college credit.

College Admission Counseling 93 students graduated in 2016; all went to college, including Boston College; Colby College; Colgate University; Connecticut College; Tufts University; Yale University. Median SAT critical reading: 630, median SAT math: 660, median SAT writing: 650, median composite ACT: 31.

Student Life Upper grades have specified standards of dress, student council, honor system. Discipline rests equally with students and faculty.

Tuition and Aid Day student tuition: $45,590. Need-based scholarship grants available. In 2016–17, 27% of upper-school students received aid. Total amount of financial aid awarded in 2016–17: $3,727,504.

Admissions Traditional secondary-level entrance grade is 9. For fall 2016, 320 students applied for upper-level admission, 110 were accepted, 50 enrolled. ISEE or SSAT required. Deadline for receipt of application materials: January 15. Application fee required: $50. On-campus interview recommended.

Athletics Interscholastic: alpine skiing (boys, girls), baseball (b), basketball (b,g), cross-country running (b,g), field hockey (g), football (b), ice hockey (b,g), lacrosse (b,g), skiing (downhill) (b,g), soccer (b,g), softball (g), strength & conditioning (b,g), tennis (b,g), volleyball (g); intramural: basketball (b,g), tennis (g); coed interscholastic: fitness, golf, nordic skiing, physical training, track and field, weight lifting, weight training; coed intramural: strength & conditioning. 4 coaches, 2 athletic trainers.

Computers Computers are regularly used in art, English, foreign language, history, humanities, language development, mathematics, newspaper, publications, science, writing, yearbook classes. Computer network features include on-campus library services, online commercial services, Internet access, wireless campus network, Internet filtering or blocking technology. Campus intranet, student e-mail accounts, and computer access in designated common areas are available to students. Students grades are available online. The school has a published electronic and media policy.

Contact Ms. Gillian Lloyd, Director of Admissions. 781-235-9300 Ext. 251. Fax: 781-239-3614. E-mail: g.lloyd@rivers.org. Website: www.rivers.org

RIVERSTONE INTERNATIONAL SCHOOL

5521 Warm Springs Avenue
Boise, Idaho 83716

Head of School: Mr. Bob Carignan

General Information Coeducational day college-preparatory and International Baccalaureate Programmes school. Grades PS–12. Founded: 1997. Setting: suburban. 14-acre campus. 6 buildings on campus. Approved or accredited by International Baccalaureate Organization, Northwest Accreditation Commission, Northwest Association of Independent Schools, Northwest Association of Schools and Colleges, and Idaho Department of Education. Member of National Association of Independent Schools and Secondary School Admission Test Board. Endowment: $750,000. Total enrollment: 325. Upper school average class size: 12. Upper school faculty-student ratio: 1:5. There are 170 required school days per year for Upper School students. Upper School students typically attend 5 days per week. The average school day consists of 6 hours and 45 minutes.

Upper School Student Profile Grade 9: 28 students (11 boys, 17 girls); Grade 10: 14 students (5 boys, 9 girls); Grade 11: 34 students (17 boys, 17 girls); Grade 12: 27 students (14 boys, 13 girls).

Faculty School total: 45. In upper school: 6 men, 11 women; 12 have advanced degrees.

Subjects Offered International Baccalaureate courses.

Graduation Requirements Art, English, foreign language, history, mathematics, science.

Special Academic Programs International Baccalaureate program; study abroad; ESL (15 students enrolled).

College Admission Counseling 18 students graduated in 2015; 17 went to college, including Claremont McKenna College; Linfield College; Stanford University; University of Chicago; University of Southern California. Other: 1 had other specific plans. Mean SAT critical reading: 655, mean SAT math: 621, mean SAT writing: 617, mean combined SAT: 1832, mean composite ACT: 27.

Student Life Upper grades have specified standards of dress, student council, honor system. Discipline rests primarily with faculty.

Tuition and Aid Day student tuition: $17,120. Tuition installment plan (monthly payment plans). Need-based scholarship grants available. In 2015–16, 20% of upper-school students received aid.

Admissions Traditional secondary-level entrance grade is 9. For fall 2015, 21 students applied for upper-level admission, 18 were accepted, 15 enrolled. Deadline for receipt of application materials: none. Application fee required: $75. Interview required.

Athletics Interscholastic: basketball (boys, girls), volleyball (g); coed interscholastic: alpine skiing, nordic skiing, skiing (cross-country), skiing (downhill), snowboarding, soccer; coed intramural: backpacking, canoeing/kayaking, climbing, hiking/backpacking, kayaking, nordic skiing, outdoor activities, outdoor adventure, outdoor education, outdoor recreation, outdoor skills, outdoors, physical fitness, rafting, rock climbing, skiing (cross-country), skiing (downhill), snowboarding, snowshoeing, wilderness, yoga. 1 PE instructor, 10 coaches.

Computers Computers are regularly used in art, business, college planning, English, ESL, foreign language, French, history, humanities, lab/keyboard, mathematics, music, research skills, science, Spanish, technology, writing, yearbook classes. Computer network features include online commercial services, Internet access, wireless campus network. Campus intranet and student e-mail accounts are available to students. Students grades are available online. The school has a published electronic and media policy.

Contact Ms. Rachel Pusch, Director of Enrollment Management and Administration. 208-424-5000 Ext. 3. Fax: 208-424-0033. E-mail: rpusch@riverstoneschool.org. Website: www.riverstoneschool.org

ROCKHURST HIGH SCHOOL

9301 State Line Road
Kansas City, Missouri 64114-3299

Head of School: Rev. Terrence Baum

General Information Boys' day college-preparatory, arts, religious studies, and technology school, affiliated with Roman Catholic Church (Jesuit order). Grades 9–12. Founded: 1910. Setting: suburban. 36-acre campus. 3 buildings on campus. Approved or accredited by Jesuit Secondary Education Association, North Central Association of Colleges and Schools, and Missouri Department of Education. Member of National Association of Independent Schools. Endowment: $16.4 million. Upper school average class size: 22. Upper school faculty-student ratio: 1:12. There are 172 required school days per year for Upper School students. Upper School students typically attend 5 days per week. The average school day consists of 7 hours.

Upper School Student Profile Grade 9: 290 students (290 boys); Grade 10: 248 students (248 boys); Grade 11: 246 students (246 boys); Grade 12: 247 students (247 boys). 78.5% of students are Roman Catholic Church (Jesuit order).

Faculty School total: 83. In upper school: 69 men, 14 women; 62 have advanced degrees.

Subjects Offered Advanced biology, advanced chemistry, Advanced Placement courses, advanced studio art-AP, algebra, American government, American history, American history-AP, American literature, anatomy, art, biology, biology-AP, business, business law, calculus, ceramics, chemistry, chemistry-AP, Chinese, choir, Christian and Hebrew scripture, Christian scripture, Christian testament, church history, classical Greek literature, communication skills, computer literacy, computer math, computer programming, computer science, computer-aided design, concert band, creative writing, digital photography, drama, drawing and design, earth science, economics, English, English literature, English-AP, environmental science, European history, fine arts, foreign language, forensics, French, French studies, French-AP, freshman seminar, geography, geometry, government-AP, government/civics, Greek, history, history-AP, journalism, Latin, Latin-AP, learning strategies, literature-AP, Mandarin, math analysis, mathematics, mathematics-AP, music, New Testament, photography, physical education, physics, physics-AP, physiology, pottery, pre-calculus, public speaking, religion, science, service learning/internship, social studies, Spanish, Spanish language-AP, Spanish literature-AP, speech, speech and debate, studio art-AP, theater, theology, trigonometry, U.S. history-AP, world history-AP, world religions, yearbook.

Graduation Requirements Arts and fine arts (art, music, dance, drama), computer science, English, foreign language, mathematics, physical education (includes health), religion (includes Bible studies and theology), science, social studies (includes history), attendance at retreats, community service hours.

Special Academic Programs 16 Advanced Placement exams for which test preparation is offered; honors section; study at local college for college credit.

College Admission Counseling 247 students graduated in 2016; all went to college, including Creighton University; Kansas State University; Rockhurst University; Saint Louis University; The University of Kansas; University of Missouri. Mean SAT critical reading: 635, mean SAT math: 665, mean SAT writing: 626, mean combined SAT: 1926, mean composite ACT: 27.

Student Life Upper grades have specified standards of dress, student council. Discipline rests primarily with faculty. Attendance at religious services is required.

Summer Programs Remediation, enrichment, advancement, sports, art/fine arts, computer instruction programs offered; session focuses on transition to high school and enrichment; held on campus; accepts boys and girls; open to students from other schools. 1,000 students usually enrolled. 2017 schedule: June 5 to June 30. Application deadline: June 2.

Tuition and Aid Day student tuition: $12,300. Tuition installment plan (monthly payment plans, individually arranged payment plans). Merit scholarship grants, need-based scholarship grants, paying campus jobs available. In 2016–17, 40% of upper-school students received aid; total upper-school merit-scholarship money awarded: $39,000. Total amount of financial aid awarded in 2016–17: $2,200,000.

Admissions Traditional secondary-level entrance grade is 9. For fall 2016, 357 students applied for upper-level admission, 337 were accepted, 290 enrolled. High School Placement Test (closed version) from Scholastic Testing Service required. Deadline for receipt of application materials: December 15. No application fee required.

Athletics Interscholastic: baseball, basketball, cross-country running, diving, football, golf, ice hockey, lacrosse, soccer, swimming and diving, tennis, track and field, wrestling; intramural: basketball, football, juggling, outdoor activities, outdoor adventure, racquetball, soccer, softball, ultimate Frisbee, volleyball, weight lifting, weight training; coed intramural: self defense. 2 PE instructors, 21 coaches, 1 athletic trainer.

Computers Computers are regularly used in mathematics, science, technology classes. Computer network features include on-campus library services, online commercial services, Internet access, wireless campus network, Internet filtering or blocking technology, the majority of student textbooks are downloaded to their iPad. Campus intranet, student e-mail accounts, and computer access in designated common areas are available to students. Students grades are available online. The school has a published electronic and media policy.

Contact Mr. Jack Reichmeier, Director of Admission and Financial Aid. 816-363-2036 Ext. 558. Fax: 816-363-3764. E-mail: jreichme@rockhursths.edu. Website: www.rockhursths.edu

ROCKLAND COUNTRY DAY SCHOOL

34 Kings Highway
Congers, New York 10920-2253

Head of School: Ms. Kimberly A. Morcate

General Information Coeducational boarding and day college-preparatory and arts school. Boarding grades 8–12, day grades PK–12. Founded: 1959. Setting: suburban. Nearest major city is New York. Students are housed in coed dormitories. 22-acre campus. 5 buildings on campus. Approved or accredited by New York State Association of Independent Schools and New York Department of Education. Member of National Association of Independent Schools. Total enrollment: 117. Upper school average class size: 15. Upper school faculty-student ratio: 1:7. There are 166 required school days per year for Upper School students. Upper School students typically attend 5 days per week. The average school day consists of 7 hours and 30 minutes.

Upper School Student Profile Grade 9: 7 students (4 boys, 3 girls); Grade 10: 12 students (9 boys, 3 girls); Grade 11: 21 students (15 boys, 6 girls); Grade 12: 19 students (9 boys, 10 girls). 33% of students are boarding students. 45% are state residents. 3 states are represented in upper school student body. 55% are international students. International students from China and Republic of Korea; 2 other countries represented in student body.

Faculty School total: 25. In upper school: 4 men, 9 women; 12 have advanced degrees; 3 reside on campus.

Subjects Offered Advanced Placement courses, American history-AP, American literature-AP, art-AP.

Graduation Requirements Arts and fine arts (art, music, dance, drama), computer science, English, experiential education, foreign language, mathematics, music, physical education (includes health), science, social studies (includes history), WISE Program, off-campus senior independent senior project. Community service is required.

Special Academic Programs 15 Advanced Placement exams for which test preparation is offered; honors section; independent study; study at local college for college credit; academic accommodation for the gifted, the musically talented, and the artistically talented.

College Admission Counseling 21 students graduated in 2016; all went to college, including Boston University; Drexel University; Emerson College; Emory University; New York University; Oberlin College. Median SAT math: 560, median SAT writing: 460, median composite ACT: 25. Mean SAT critical reading: 480. 50% scored over 600 on SAT critical reading, 70% scored over 600 on SAT math, 60% scored over 600 on SAT writing, 60% scored over 1800 on combined SAT, 20% scored over 26 on composite ACT.

Student Life Upper grades have specified standards of dress, student council, honor system. Discipline rests primarily with faculty.

Tuition and Aid Day student tuition: $33,050; 7-day tuition and room/board: $54,050. Tuition installment plan (Insured Tuition Payment Plan, monthly payment plans, individually arranged payment plans, TADS). Tuition reduction for siblings, need-based scholarship grants available. In 2016–17, 22% of upper-school students received aid. Total amount of financial aid awarded in 2016–17: $371,140.

Admissions Traditional secondary-level entrance grade is 9. For fall 2016, 43 students applied for upper-level admission, 22 were accepted, 16 enrolled. Any standardized test and writing sample required. Deadline for receipt of application materials: none. Application fee required: $75. Interview recommended.

Athletics Interscholastic: basketball (boys, girls); coed interscholastic: aerobics/dance, field hockey, soccer; coed intramural: dance, golf, jogging, lacrosse, outdoor adventure, physical fitness, tennis, volleyball. 3 PE instructors, 2 coaches.

Computers Computers are regularly used in art, desktop publishing, English, foreign language, history, humanities, independent study, keyboarding, lab/keyboard, literary magazine, mathematics, music, newspaper, photography, research skills, SAT preparation, science, theater, video film production, word processing, writing, yearbook classes. Computer network features include online commercial services, Internet access, wireless campus network, Internet filtering or blocking technology, eLibrary. Computer access in designated common areas is available to students. Students grades are available online. The school has a published electronic and media policy.

Contact Ms. Tricia Mayer, Admissions Coordinator. 845-268-6802 Ext. 206. Fax: 845-268-4644. E-mail: tmayer@rocklandcds.org. Website: www.rocklandcds.org

ROCK POINT SCHOOL

1 Rock Point Road
Burlington, Vermont 05408

Head of School: C.J. Spirito

General Information Coeducational boarding and day college-preparatory and arts school, affiliated with Episcopal Church. Grades 9–12. Founded: 1928. Setting: small town. Students are housed in single-sex by floor dormitories. 130-acre campus. 1 building on campus. Approved or accredited by Association of Independent Schools in New England, Independent Schools of Northern New England, National Association of Episcopal Schools, New England Association of Schools and Colleges, The Association of Boarding Schools, and Vermont Department of Education. Member of National Association of Independent Schools. Endowment: $1.9 million. Total enrollment: 26. Upper school average class size: 8. Upper school faculty-student ratio: 1:5. There are 167 required school days per year for Upper School students. Upper School students typically attend 5 days per week. The average school day consists of 6 hours.

Upper School Student Profile Grade 9: 1 student (1 girl); Grade 10: 9 students (5 boys, 4 girls); Grade 11: 9 students (5 boys, 4 girls); Grade 12: 7 students (3 boys, 4 girls). 80% of students are boarding students. 15% are state residents. 10 states are represented in upper school student body. 7% of students are members of Episcopal Church.

Faculty School total: 10. In upper school: 3 men, 7 women; 6 have advanced degrees; 6 reside on campus.

Subjects Offered Acting, global studies, government/civics, physics.

Graduation Requirements Art, art history, English, history, mathematics, physical education (includes health), science. Community service is required.

Special Academic Programs Independent study; study at local college for college credit; academic accommodation for the gifted and the artistically talented; remedial math; programs in English, mathematics, general development for dyslexic students; special instructional classes for our school provides a curriculum for students who need structure and personal attention.

College Admission Counseling 7 students graduated in 2016; 5 went to college, including Brevard College; Goucher College; North Carolina State University. Other: 2 went to work.

Student Life Upper grades have specified standards of dress. Discipline rests primarily with faculty.

Summer Programs Remediation, art/fine arts programs offered; session focuses on explore outdoor education, earn credits, and have fun in Vermont; held both on and off campus; held at day trips outside into Burlington, Vermont, throughout the state, and beyond; accepts boys and girls; open to students from other schools. 10 students usually enrolled. 2017 schedule: July 5 to August 12. Application deadline: June 30.

Tuition and Aid Day student tuition: $28,400; 7-day tuition and room/board: $57,700. Tuition installment plan (individually arranged payment plans, deposit and two installment plan (September 1 and December 1), other specially created plans with a family). Need-based scholarship grants available. In 2016–17, 31% of upper-school students received aid. Total amount of financial aid awarded in 2016–17: $150,000.

Admissions Traditional secondary-level entrance grade is 10. Essay or writing sample required. Deadline for receipt of application materials: none. Application fee required: $50. On-campus interview required.

Athletics Coed Interscholastic: basketball, Frisbee, ultimate Frisbee; coed intramural: alpine skiing, backpacking, ball hockey, basketball, bicycling, billiards, bocce, broomball, canoeing/kayaking, climbing, cooperative games, fishing, fitness, fitness walking, floor hockey, Frisbee, hiking/backpacking, jogging, kickball, martial arts, nordic skiing, outdoor activities, outdoor adventure, outdoor recreation, physical fitness, physical training, rock climbing, ropes courses, running, skateboarding, skiing (downhill), snowboarding, soccer, softball, touch football, ultimate Frisbee, walking, weight lifting, winter walking, yoga. 5 PE instructors.

Computers Computers are regularly used in all academic, animation, art, college planning, creative writing, media, music, photography, video film production, word processing classes. Computer network features include Internet access, Internet filtering or blocking technology. Student e-mail accounts and computer access in designated common areas are available to students.

Contact Hillary Kramer, Director of Admissions. 802-863-1104 Ext. 12. Fax: 802-863-6628. E-mail: hkramer@rockpoint.org. Website: www.rockpoint.org

ROCKWAY MENNONITE COLLEGIATE

110 Doon Road
Kitchener, Ontario N2G 3C8, Canada

Head of School: Ms. Ann L. Schultz

General Information Coeducational boarding and day college-preparatory, arts, religious studies, and technology school, affiliated with Mennonite Church. Grades 7–12. Founded: 1945. Setting: suburban. Nearest major city is Toronto, Canada. Students are housed in host family homes. 14-acre campus. 7 buildings on campus. Approved or accredited by Mennonite Schools Council and Ontario Department of Education. Language of instruction: English. Endowment: CAN$735,000. Total enrollment: 265. Upper school average class size: 21. Upper school faculty-student ratio: 1:10. There are 194 required school days per year for Upper School students. Upper School students typically attend 5 days per week. The average school day consists of 6 hours.

Upper School Student Profile Grade 9: 50 students (25 boys, 25 girls); Grade 10: 37 students (21 boys, 16 girls); Grade 11: 62 students (33 boys, 29 girls); Grade 12: 71 students (34 boys, 37 girls). 40% of students are Mennonite.

Faculty School total: 35. In upper school: 12 men, 18 women; 8 have advanced degrees.

Subjects Offered Business, transportation technology.

Graduation Requirements Ontario Ministry of Education requirements, 2 credits in a language other than English, religious studies courses through grade 10.

Special Academic Programs Independent study; ESL (34 students enrolled).

College Admission Counseling 64 students graduated in 2016; 47 went to college, including Carleton University; The University of Western Ontario; University of Guelph; University of Toronto; University of Waterloo; Wilfrid Laurier University. Other: 13 went to work, 4 had other specific plans.

Student Life Upper grades have specified standards of dress, student council. Discipline rests primarily with faculty. Attendance at religious services is required.

Tuition and Aid Day student tuition: CAN\$15,120; 7-day tuition and room/board: CAN\$31,200. Tuition installment plan (monthly payment plans, individually arranged payment plans). Tuition reduction for siblings, bursaries, need-based scholarship grants, paying campus jobs available. In 2016–17, 20% of upper-school students received aid. Total amount of financial aid awarded in 2016–17: CAN\$191,200.

Admissions Traditional secondary-level entrance grade is 9. For fall 2016, 60 students applied for upper-level admission, 56 were accepted, 55 enrolled. Deadline for receipt of application materials: none. Application fee required: CAN\$200. Interview recommended.

Athletics Interscholastic: badminton (boys, girls), baseball (b,g), basketball (b,g), cross-country running (b,g), track and field (b,g), volleyball (b,g), wrestling (b,g); intramural: ball hockey (b,g), baseball (b,g), basketball (b,g), cooperative games (b,g), dance (b,g), flag football (b,g), flagball (b,g), floor hockey (b,g), indoor soccer (b,g), outdoor education (b,g), physical training (b,g), power lifting (b,g), rock climbing (b,g), rugby (b,g), soccer (b,g), strength & conditioning (b,g), volleyball (b,g); coed interscholastic: Frisbee; coed intramural: baseball, cooperative games, outdoor education, street hockey, table tennis, track and field. 3 PE instructors.

Computers Computers are regularly used in Bible studies, business, career technology, college planning, construction, drafting, English, geography, library, mathematics, religious studies, science, typing, Web site design, yearbook classes. Computer resources include on-campus library services, Internet access, wireless campus network. Campus intranet, student e-mail accounts, and computer access in designated common areas are available to students. The school has a published electronic and media policy.

Contact Mr. David J. Lobe, Director of Admissions and Recruitment. 519-743-5209 Ext. 3029. Fax: 519-743-5935. E-mail: admissions@rockway.ca. Website: www.rockway.ca

ROCKY MOUNT ACADEMY

1313 Avondale Avenue
Rocky Mount, North Carolina 27803

Head of School: Ms. Beth B. Covolo

General Information Coeducational day college-preparatory, arts, and math and Science school. Ungraded, ages 4–17. Founded: 1968. Setting: small town. Nearest major city is Raleigh. 48-acre campus. 9 buildings on campus. Approved or accredited by Southern Association of Colleges and Schools. Member of National Association of Independent Schools. Endowment: \$1 million. Total enrollment: 447. Upper school average class size: 9. Upper school faculty-student ratio: 1:6. There are 177 required school days per year for Upper School students. Upper School students typically attend 5 days per week. The average school day consists of 6 hours and 15 minutes.

Upper School Student Profile Grade 9: 35 students (20 boys, 15 girls); Grade 10: 44 students (24 boys, 20 girls); Grade 11: 31 students (19 boys, 12 girls); Grade 12: 34 students (14 boys, 20 girls).

Faculty School total: 48. In upper school: 10 men, 14 women; 11 have advanced degrees.

Subjects Offered 3-dimensional art, 3-dimensional design, acting, adolescent issues, advanced biology, advanced chemistry, advanced computer applications, advanced math, Advanced Placement courses, advanced studio art-AP, algebra, American culture, American government, American history, American history-AP, American literature, American literature-AP, analysis of data, analytic geometry, anatomy, art, art appreciation, art history, art-AP, astronomy, athletic training, athletics, baseball, biology, biology-AP, British history, British literature, calculus, calculus-AP, cell biology, Central and Eastern European history, ceramics, cheerleading, chemistry, chemistry-AP, choral music, civics, college admission preparation, college awareness, college counseling, college placement, college planning, communication skills, community service, comparative government and politics-AP, comparative religion, composition, computer education, computer literacy, computer skills, creative writing, criminal justice, critical thinking, critical writing, cultural arts, data analysis, digital photography, drama, drama performance, drama workshop, dramatic arts, drawing, earth science, ecology, ecology, environmental systems, economics, economics-AP, English, English literature, English literature and composition-AP, English literature-AP, English-AP, environmental science, environmental science-AP, European history, European history-AP, expository writing, finance, fine arts, first aid, fitness, foreign language, French, French studies, French-AP, geography, geology, geometry, global studies, golf, government and politics-AP, government-AP, government/civics, grammar, guitar, history, history-AP, honors algebra, honors English, honors geometry, honors U.S. history, honors world history, HTML design, human biology, human sexuality, humanities, intro to computers, keyboarding, Latin, literature and composition-AP, literature-AP, macro/microeconomics-AP, macroeconomics-AP, marine biology, marine ecology, marine studies, mathematics, mathematics-AP, media communications, microbiology, microeconomics, microeconomics-AP, model United Nations, modern European history, modern European history-AP, multimedia design, music appreciation, music composition, music performance, music technology, news writing, newspaper, North Carolina history, novels, oil painting, oral communications, participation in sports, personal finance, personal fitness, photo shop, photography, photojournalism, physical education, physical fitness, physical science, physics,

physics-AP, political science, portfolio art, pottery, pre-algebra, pre-calculus, probability, probability and statistics, psychology, psychology-AP, public speaking, publications, religion, research skills, SAT preparation, science, social sciences, social studies, softball, Spanish, sports, sports conditioning, sports medicine, statistics, statistics-AP, student government, studio art, studio art-AP, technology, theater, track and field, trigonometry, U.S. government and politics-AP, U.S. history, U.S. history-AP, United States government-AP, visual arts, vocational arts, volleyball, Web site design, weight training, weightlifting, Western religions, word processing, world cultures, world history, world history-AP, world literature, yearbook, zoology.

Graduation Requirements Arts and fine arts (art, music, dance, drama), career/college preparation, communications, computer science, English, foreign language, mathematics, physical education (includes health), public speaking, science, social studies (includes history), sports. Community service is required.

Special Academic Programs 13 Advanced Placement exams for which test preparation is offered; honors section; independent study; study at local college for college credit; study abroad; academic accommodation for the gifted; remedial reading and/or remedial writing; remedial math.

College Admission Counseling 33 students graduated in 2016; all went to college, including East Carolina University; Meredith College; North Carolina State University; The University of North Carolina at Chapel Hill; The University of North Carolina Wilmington; Wake Forest University. Median SAT critical reading: 545, median SAT math: 538, median SAT writing: 534, median combined SAT: 1616, median composite ACT: 22. 16.7% scored over 600 on SAT critical reading, 20% scored over 600 on SAT math, 23.3% scored over 600 on SAT writing, 20% scored over 1800 on combined SAT, 27.3% scored over 26 on composite ACT.

Student Life Upper grades have specified standards of dress, student council, honor system. Discipline rests primarily with faculty.

Summer Programs Enrichment, sports, art/fine arts, computer instruction programs offered; session focuses on enrichment; held on campus; accepts boys and girls; open to students from other schools. 40 students usually enrolled. 2017 schedule: May 30 to August 11. Application deadline: May 30.

Tuition and Aid Day student tuition: \$12,010–\$12,460. Tuition installment plan (monthly payment plans, individually arranged payment plans, 3-payment plan, full-year payment plan). Merit scholarship grants, need-based scholarship grants available. In 2016–17, 35% of upper-school students received aid; total upper-school merit-scholarship money awarded: \$66,480. Total amount of financial aid awarded in 2016–17: \$186,005.

Admissions Traditional secondary-level entrance grade is 9. For fall 2016, 15 students applied for upper-level admission, 11 were accepted, 11 enrolled. Admissions testing and QUIC required. Deadline for receipt of application materials: none. Application fee required: \$90. On-campus interview recommended.

Athletics Interscholastic: aquatics (boys, girls), baseball (b), basketball (b,g), cheering (g), cross-country running (b,g), football (b), golf (b,g), physical fitness (b,g), riflery (b,g), skeet shooting (b,g), soccer (b,g), softball (g), swimming and diving (b,g), tennis (b,g), track and field (b,g), volleyball (g); coed interscholastic: golf, physical fitness, riflery, skeet shooting, swimming and diving; coed intramural: table tennis, ultimate Frisbee. 3 PE instructors, 18 coaches, 1 athletic trainer.

Computers Computers are regularly used in all academic, English, foreign language, graphics, health, history, independent study, library, mathematics, news writing, photojournalism, reading, research skills, science, speech, technology, writing, yearbook classes. Computer network features include on-campus library services, Internet access, wireless campus network, Internet filtering or blocking technology, INET Library. Student e-mail accounts and computer access in designated common areas are available to students. Students grades are available online. The school has a published electronic and media policy.

Contact Mrs. Hadley Dempsey Gross, Director of Admissions. 252-443-4126 Ext. 224. Fax: 252-937-7922. E-mail: hgross@rmacademy.com. Website: www.rmacademy.com

THE ROEPER SCHOOL

41190 Woodward Avenue
Bloomfield Hills, Michigan 48304

Head of School: David Feldman

General Information Coeducational day college-preparatory and gifted education school. Grades PK–12. Founded: 1941. Setting: urban. Nearest major city is Birmingham. 1-acre campus. 1 building on campus. Approved or accredited by Independent Schools Association of the Central States. Member of National Association of Independent Schools. Endowment: \$7 million. Total enrollment: 579. Upper school average class size: 16. Upper school faculty-student ratio: 1:8. There are 165 required school days per year for Upper School students. Upper School students typically attend 5 days per week. The average school day consists of 7 hours and 10 minutes.

Upper School Student Profile Grade 9: 47 students (30 boys, 17 girls); Grade 10: 33 students (20 boys, 13 girls); Grade 11: 28 students (17 boys, 11 girls); Grade 12: 39 students (28 boys, 11 girls).

Faculty In upper school: 14 men, 20 women; 22 have advanced degrees.

Subjects Offered 20th century American writers, 20th century history, 3-dimensional art, acting, advanced biology, advanced chemistry, advanced math, Advanced

Placement courses, African-American history, African-American literature, algebra, American government, American history, American literature, anatomy, architecture, art, art history, athletics, audition methods, band, bioethics, biology, calculus, calculus-AP, cartooning/animation, ceramics, chamber groups, chemistry, chemistry-AP, Chinese, choir, choreography, communications, comparative government and politics, computer programming, concert band, constitutional law, costumes and make-up, creative writing, dance, debate, digital photography, drama, drawing and design, economics, English, English literature, English-AP, European history, European history-AP, film, fine arts, first aid, fitness, forensics, French, geometry, government, government/civics, graphic design, health, health education, history, independent study, jazz band, journalism, Latin, mathematics, model United Nations, music, music theory, musical theater, newspaper, philosophy, photography, physical education, physical fitness, physics, poetry, programming, science, senior project, social studies, Spanish, speech, stagecraft, statistics, strings, taxonomy, theater, trigonometry, world history, world literature, writing, yearbook.

Graduation Requirements Arts and fine arts (art, music, dance, drama), computer science, English, foreign language, government, health, mathematics, science, social studies (includes history).

Special Academic Programs 13 Advanced Placement exams for which test preparation is offered; independent study; academic accommodation for the gifted, the musically talented, and the artistically talented; programs in English, mathematics, general development for dyslexic students.

College Admission Counseling 37 students graduated in 2016; all went to college, including DePaul University; Johns Hopkins University; Michigan State University; New York University; Northwestern University; University of Michigan.

Student Life Upper grades have student council, honor system. Discipline rests primarily with faculty.

Summer Programs Art/fine arts programs offered; session focuses on theater; held on campus; accepts boys and girls; open to students from other schools. 75 students usually enrolled. 2017 schedule: June 19 to July 31.

Tuition and Aid Day student tuition: $27,050. Tuition installment plan (FACTS Tuition Payment Plan, individually arranged payment plans). Need-based scholarship grants available. In 2016–17, 40% of upper-school students received aid. Total amount of financial aid awarded in 2016–17: $60,000.

Admissions Traditional secondary-level entrance grade is 9. For fall 2016, 30 students applied for upper-level admission, 12 were accepted, 9 enrolled. Individual IQ and TOEFL or SLEP required. Deadline for receipt of application materials: none. Application fee required: $75. On-campus interview recommended.

Athletics Interscholastic: baseball (boys), basketball (b,g), cross-country running (b,g), golf (b,g), physical training (b,g), soccer (b,g), strength & conditioning (b,g), track and field (b,g), volleyball (g), weight lifting (b,g); intramural: indoor soccer (b,g); coed intramural: physical training, strength & conditioning, weight lifting. 3 PE instructors, 30 coaches.

Computers Computers are regularly used in college planning, creative writing, English, foreign language, French, graphic design, history, journalism, library, mathematics, news writing, photography, programming, publications, publishing, science, Spanish, video film production, writing, yearbook classes. Computer network features include on-campus library services, online commercial services, Internet access, wireless campus network. Student e-mail accounts and computer access in designated common areas are available to students. Students grades are available online.

Contact Lori Zinser, Director of Admissions. 248-203-7302. Fax: 248-203-7310. E-mail: lori.zinser@roeper.org. Website: www.roeper.org

ROLAND PARK COUNTRY SCHOOL

5204 Roland Avenue
Baltimore, Maryland 21210

Head of School: Mrs. Caroline Blatti

General Information Coeducational day (boys only in lower grades) and distance learning college-preparatory and STEM Certificate, World Languages Certificate school. Boys grade PS, girls grades PS–12. Distance learning grades 9–12. Founded: 1901. Setting: suburban. 21-acre campus. 1 building on campus. Approved or accredited by Association of Independent Maryland Schools. Member of National Association of Independent Schools and Secondary School Admission Test Board. Endowment: $56.6 million. Total enrollment: 644. Upper school average class size: 14. Upper school faculty-student ratio: 1:7. There are 177 required school days per year for Upper School students. Upper School students typically attend 5 days per week. The average school day consists of 7 hours and 45 minutes.

Upper School Student Profile Grade 6: 43 students (43 girls); Grade 7: 35 students (35 girls); Grade 8: 39 students (39 girls); Grade 9: 84 students (84 girls); Grade 10: 71 students (71 girls); Grade 11: 85 students (85 girls); Grade 12: 77 students (77 girls).

Faculty School total: 92. In upper school: 10 men, 41 women; 35 have advanced degrees.

Subjects Offered 3-dimensional art, advanced biology, advanced chemistry, advanced math, Advanced Placement courses, advanced studio art-AP, algebra, American history-AP, American literature, American literature-AP, anatomy, ancient world history, Arabic, archaeology, art, art history, art history-AP, astronomy, biology, biology-AP, calculus, calculus-AP, ceramics, chemistry, chemistry-AP, Chesapeake Bay

studies, Chinese, community service, computer programming, computer science, creative writing, dance, drama, ecology, economics, engineering, English, English language-AP, English literature, English literature-AP, English-AP, environmental science, environmental studies, European civilization, European history, European history-AP, French, French language-AP, French literature-AP, geometry, German, government/civics, Greek, health, integrated mathematics, Latin, music, philosophy, photography, physical education, physics, physiology, religion, Russian, science, social studies, Spanish, speech, statistics, theater, trigonometry, world history.

Graduation Requirements Adolescent issues, arts and fine arts (art, music, dance, drama), biology, chemistry, English, foreign language, history, mathematics, physical education (includes health), physics, public speaking, science. Community service is required.

Special Academic Programs Advanced Placement exam preparation; honors section; independent study; term-away projects; study abroad; ESL (5 students enrolled).

College Admission Counseling 80 students graduated in 2016; all went to college, including Elon University; New York University; Rhodes College; St. Mary's College of Maryland; University of Delaware; University of Maryland, College Park. Mean SAT critical reading: 576, mean SAT math: 574, mean SAT writing: 600, mean combined SAT: 1750, mean composite ACT: 24. 43% scored over 600 on SAT critical reading, 48% scored over 600 on SAT math, 49% scored over 600 on SAT writing, 46% scored over 1800 on combined SAT, 55% scored over 26 on composite ACT.

Student Life Upper grades have uniform requirement, student council, honor system. Discipline rests equally with students and faculty.

Tuition and Aid Day student tuition: $28,290. Tuition installment plan (FACTS Tuition Payment Plan, individually arranged payment plans). Need-based scholarship grants, paying campus jobs available. In 2016–17, 35% of upper-school students received aid. Total amount of financial aid awarded in 2016–17: $1,645,815.

Admissions Traditional secondary-level entrance grade is 9. For fall 2016, 112 students applied for upper-level admission, 68 were accepted, 36 enrolled. ISEE required. Deadline for receipt of application materials: December 16. Application fee required: $60. Interview recommended.

Athletics Interscholastic: badminton, basketball, crew, cross-country running, field hockey, golf, independent competitive sports, indoor soccer, indoor track, lacrosse, soccer, softball, squash, swimming and diving, tennis, track and field, volleyball, winter (indoor) track, winter soccer; intramural: dance, fitness, modern dance, outdoor education, physical fitness, rock climbing, strength & conditioning. 2 PE instructors, 38 coaches, 1 athletic trainer.

Computers Computers are regularly used in all classes. Computer network features include on-campus library services, online commercial services, Internet access, wireless campus network, Internet filtering or blocking technology, online database. Campus intranet, student e-mail accounts, and computer access in designated common areas are available to students. Students grades are available online. The school has a published electronic and media policy.

Contact Kathleen Curtis, Director of Admissions and Enrollment Management. 410-323-5500. Fax: 410-323-2164. E-mail: admissions@rpcs.org. Website: www.rpcs.org

ROLLING HILLS PREPARATORY SCHOOL

One Rolling Hills Prep Way
San Pedro, California 90732

Head of School: Peter McCormack

General Information Coeducational day college-preparatory school. Grades 6–12. Founded: 1981. Setting: suburban. Nearest major city is Los Angeles. 21 acre campus. 20 buildings on campus. Approved or accredited by California Association of Independent Schools, Western Association of Schools and Colleges, and California Department of Education. Member of National Association of Independent Schools. Endowment: $100,000. Total enrollment: 256. Upper school average class size: 17. Upper school faculty-student ratio: 1:9. There are 180 required school days per year for Upper School students. Upper School students typically attend 5 days per week. The average school day consists of 6 hours.

Upper School Student Profile Grade 9: 60 students (31 boys, 29 girls); Grade 10: 60 students (35 boys, 25 girls); Grade 11: 34 students (17 boys, 17 girls); Grade 12: 50 students (25 boys, 25 girls).

Faculty School total: 36. In upper school: 9 men, 20 women; 13 have advanced degrees.

Subjects Offered Algebra, American history, American literature, American sign language, anatomy, art, biology, calculus, ceramics, chemistry, Chinese, computer science, creative writing, drama, economics, English, English literature, European history, fine arts, French, geography, geometry, government/civics, history, mathematics, music, photography, physical education, physics, pre-calculus, psychology-AP, robotics, science, social studies, Spanish, speech, statistics, theater, trigonometry, world history.

Graduation Requirements Arts and fine arts (art, music, dance, drama), English, foreign language, mathematics, outdoor education, physical education (includes health), science, social studies (includes history), two-week senior internship, senior speech, outdoor education.

Special Academic Programs 10 Advanced Placement exams for which test preparation is offered; honors section; independent study; academic accommodation for the gifted; programs in general development for dyslexic students; ESL (25 students enrolled).

College Admission Counseling 35 students graduated in 2016; 34 went to college, including Carnegie Mellon University; Lewis & Clark College; University of California, Berkeley; University of California, Los Angeles; University of Southern California; University of Washington. Other: 1 had other specific plans. Mean SAT critical reading: 620, mean SAT math: 600, mean SAT writing: 610. 45% scored over 600 on SAT critical reading, 40% scored over 600 on SAT math, 45% scored over 600 on SAT writing, 20% scored over 1800 on combined SAT, 20% scored over 26 on composite ACT.

Student Life Upper grades have specified standards of dress, student council, honor system. Discipline rests primarily with faculty.

Summer Programs Enrichment, ESL, art/fine arts programs offered; session focuses on ELL, algebra, and photography; held on campus; accepts boys and girls; open to students from other schools. 30 students usually enrolled. 2017 schedule: June 25 to August 27. Application deadline: June 1.

Tuition and Aid Day student tuition: $28,600. Tuition installment plan (Insured Tuition Payment Plan, Key Tuition Payment Plan, monthly payment plans). Merit scholarship grants, need-based scholarship grants available. In 2016–17, 40% of upper-school students received aid. Total amount of financial aid awarded in 2016–17: $1,200,000.

Admissions Traditional secondary-level entrance grade is 9. For fall 2016, 80 students applied for upper-level admission, 60 were accepted, 50 enrolled. ISEE, TOEFL, TOEFL Junior or writing sample required. Deadline for receipt of application materials: none. Application fee required: $125. Interview required.

Athletics Interscholastic: baseball (boys), basketball (b,g), cheering (g), football (b), soccer (b,g), softball (g), track and field (g), volleyball (b,g); intramural: cheering (g), dance (g); coed interscholastic: cross-country running, golf, roller hockey, running, sailing, track and field; coed intramural: backpacking, climbing, fitness, hiking/backpacking, outdoor education, physical fitness, rock climbing, ropes courses. 4 PE instructors, 10 coaches, 1 athletic trainer.

Computers Computers are regularly used in English, foreign language, history, mathematics, photography, science classes. Computer network features include on-campus library services, Internet access, wireless campus network. Students grades are available online. The school has a published electronic and media policy.

Contact Ryan Tillson, Director of Admission. 310-791-1101 Ext. 148. Fax: 310-373-4931. E-mail: rtillson@rollinghillsprep.org. Website: www.rollinghillsprep.org

RON PETTIGREW CHRISTIAN SCHOOL

1761 110th Avenue
Dawson Creek, British Columbia V1G 4X4, Canada

Head of School: Phyllis L. Roch

General Information Coeducational day college-preparatory and general academic school. Grades K–12. Founded: 1989. Setting: small town. Nearest major city is Edmonton, AB, Canada. 1-acre campus. 1 building on campus. Approved or accredited by Association of Christian Schools International and British Columbia Department of Education. Language of instruction: English. Total enrollment: 88. Upper school average class size: 20. Upper school faculty-student ratio: 1:5. There are 178 required school days per year for Upper School students. Upper School students typically attend 5 days per week. The average school day consists of 5 hours and 45 minutes.

Faculty School total: 6. In upper school: 2 men, 4 women.

College Admission Counseling 2 students graduated in 2016. Other: 2 went to work.

Student Life Upper grades have uniform requirement, student council, honor system. Discipline rests primarily with faculty.

Admissions No application fee required. Interview required.

Computers Computer network features include Internet access, wireless campus network, Internet filtering or blocking technology.

Contact Connie J. Brett, Office Coordinator. 250-782-4580. Fax: 250-782-9805. E-mail: admin@rpschool.ca.

ROSATI-KAIN HIGH SCHOOL

4389 Lindell Boulevard
St. Louis, Missouri 63108

Head of School: Dr. Elizabeth Ann Goodwin

General Information Girls' day college-preparatory and arts school, affiliated with Roman Catholic Church. Grades 9–12. Founded: 1911. Setting: urban. Nearest major city is Saint Louis. Students are housed in No housing. 1 building on campus. Approved or accredited by Missouri Department of Education. Upper school average class size: 300. Upper school faculty-student ratio: 1:12. There are 180 required school days per year for Upper School students. Upper School students typically attend 5 days per week. The average school day consists of 6 hours and 45 minutes.

Upper School Student Profile Grade 9: 70 students (70 girls); Grade 10: 66 students (66 girls); Grade 11: 92 students (92 girls); Grade 12: 72 students (72 girls). 75% of students are Roman Catholic.

Faculty School total: 35. In upper school: 5 men, 30 women; 20 have advanced degrees.

Subjects Offered Accounting, advanced biology, advanced chemistry, advanced computer applications, advanced math, Advanced Placement courses, algebra, American government, American history, American history-AP, American literature, American literature-AP, analysis and differential calculus, ancient world history, art, art history, audio visual/media, biology, biology-AP, business skills, calculus, calculus-AP, career/college preparation, Catholic belief and practice, chemistry, chemistry-AP, chorus, Christianity, civics, college planning, communications, community service, comparative government and politics, comparative government and politics-AP, composition, composition-AP, computer applications, computer art, computer education, computer graphics, computer information systems, computer literacy, computer math, computer multimedia, computer processing, computer programming, computer programming-AP, computer science, computer science-AP, computer studies, concert band, constitutional history of U.S., contemporary art, CPR, creative arts, creative writing, debate, dramatic arts, drawing and design, ecology, ecology, environmental systems, economics, economics-AP, English language and composition-AP, English literature, English literature and composition-AP, English literature-AP, English/composition-AP, environmental education, environmental science, fine arts, French, French language-AP, French-AP, geometry, government and politics-AP, government/civics, government/civics-AP, graphic arts, graphic design, health and wellness, health education, history-AP, Holocaust and other genocides, humanities, language-AP, literature and composition-AP, literature-AP, mathematics-AP, media production, microeconomics, music, music appreciation, musical theater, nature study, news writing, newspaper, nutrition, personal finance, personal money management, photography, photojournalism, physical education, physical fitness, physics, physics-AP, play production, poetry, political science, portfolio art, pottery, pre-calculus, probability and statistics, psychology, public speaking, publications, reading/study skills, SAT/ACT preparation, sculpture, sociology, Spanish language-AP, sports, statistics, statistics-AP, student government, studio art, telecommunications and the Internet, theater arts, theater production, theology, trigonometry, U.S. government, U.S. government and politics, U.S. government and politics-AP, U.S. history, U.S. history-AP, United States government-AP, visual and performing arts, women's studies, world history-AP, writing, yearbook.

Special Academic Programs Advanced Placement exam preparation; independent study; study at local college for college credit; academic accommodation for the gifted, the musically talented, and the artistically talented; special instructional classes for deaf students, blind students.

College Admission Counseling 88 students graduated in 2015; all went to college, including Fontbonne University; Kansas State University; Loyola University Chicago; Mercer University; Stanford University; University of Missouri. Median composite ACT: 27.

Student Life Upper grades have specified standards of dress, student council, honor system. Discipline rests primarily with faculty. Attendance at religious services is required.

Tuition and Aid Day student tuition: $10,000. Tuition installment plan (FACTS Tuition Payment Plan, monthly payment plans, individually arranged payment plans). Tuition reduction for siblings, merit scholarship grants, need-based scholarship grants, paying campus jobs available. In 2015–16, 40% of upper-school students received aid; total upper-school merit-scholarship money awarded: $5000. Total amount of financial aid awarded in 2015–16: $100,000.

Admissions Traditional secondary-level entrance grade is 9. For fall 2015, 95 students applied for upper-level admission, 75 were accepted, 70 enrolled. Deadline for receipt of application materials: none. No application fee required. Interview recommended.

Athletics Interscholastic: aquatics, basketball, bocce, cheering, cross-country running, dance, dance team, field hockey, Frisbee, lacrosse, pom squad, soccer, softball, swimming and diving, tennis, track and field, ultimate Frisbee. 1 PE instructor, 10 coaches, 5 athletic trainers.

Computers Computers are regularly used in all classes. Computer network features include on-campus library services, online commercial services, Internet access, wireless campus network, Internet filtering or blocking technology, personal student laptops provided at no charge. Campus intranet, student e-mail accounts, and computer access in designated common areas are available to students. Students grades are available online. The school has a published electronic and media policy.

Contact Mrs. Laura A. Schulte, Director of Enrollment Management. 314-533-8513 Ext. 2215. Fax: 314-533-1618. E-mail: lschulte@rosati-kain.org. Website: www.rosati-kain.org/

ROSSEAU LAKE COLLEGE

1967 Bright Street
Rosseau, Ontario P0C 1J0, Canada

Head of School: Mr. Lance Postma

General Information Coeducational boarding and day college-preparatory, arts, business, technology, and outdoor education school. Grades 7–12. Founded: 1967. Setting: rural. Nearest major city is Toronto, Canada. Students are housed in single-sex dormitories. 53-acre campus. 13 buildings on campus. Approved or accredited by Canadian Association of Independent Schools, Canadian Educational Standards Institute, Ontario Ministry of Education, The Association of Boarding Schools, and

Ontario Department of Education. Languages of instruction: English and French. Endowment: CAN$100,000. Total enrollment: 84. Upper school average class size: 15. Upper school faculty-student ratio: 1:6. There are 176 required school days per year for Upper School students. Upper School students typically attend 5 days per week. The average school day consists of 7 hours and 30 minutes.

Upper School Student Profile Grade 7: 4 students (2 boys, 2 girls); Grade 8: 6 students (3 boys, 3 girls); Grade 9: 18 students (12 boys, 6 girls); Grade 10: 16 students (9 boys, 7 girls); Grade 11: 26 students (13 boys, 13 girls); Grade 12: 26 students (19 boys, 7 girls). 62% of students are boarding students. 54% are province residents. 3 provinces are represented in upper school student body. 46% are international students. International students from China, Japan, Mexico, and Taiwan; 7 other countries represented in student body.

Faculty School total: 16. In upper school: 7 men, 9 women; 3 have advanced degrees; 9 reside on campus.

Subjects Offered Accounting, algebra, art, art history, biology, business, calculus, Canadian law, career and personal planning, chemistry, civics, computer programming, computer science, data analysis, economics, English, entrepreneurship, ESL, European history, experiential education, fine arts, French, geography, geometry, health, history, information technology, marketing, mathematics, music, outdoor education, physical education, physics, political science, science, social sciences, trigonometry, visual arts, world governments, writing.

Graduation Requirements Arts and fine arts (art, music, dance, drama), business skills (includes word processing), career planning, civics, computer science, English, foreign language, mathematics, physical education (includes health), science, social studies (includes history).

Special Academic Programs Independent study; term-away projects; study abroad; ESL (30 students enrolled).

College Admission Counseling 19 students graduated in 2016; 18 went to college, including McMaster University; Queen's University at Kingston; The University of Western Ontario; University of Guelph; University of Toronto; York University. Other: 1 went to work.

Student Life Upper grades have uniform requirement, student council, honor system. Discipline rests equally with students and faculty.

Summer Programs Remediation, enrichment, advancement programs offered; session focuses on academics; held on campus; accepts boys and girls; open to students from other schools. 10 students usually enrolled. 2017 schedule: July 1 to July 30. Application deadline: June 15.

Tuition and Aid Day student tuition: CAN$18,800; 7-day tuition and room/board: CAN$47,500. Tuition installment plan (individually arranged payment plans). Bursaries, merit scholarship grants, need-based scholarship grants, high performance bursaries available. In 2016–17, 10% of upper-school students received aid; total upper-school merit-scholarship money awarded: CAN$40,000. Total amount of financial aid awarded in 2016–17: CAN$160,000.

Admissions Traditional secondary-level entrance grade is 9. For fall 2016, 69 students applied for upper-level admission, 42 were accepted, 42 enrolled. Admissions testing and English Composition Test for ESL students required. Deadline for receipt of application materials: none. Application fee required: CAN$300. Interview recommended.

Athletics Interscholastic: baseball (boys), basketball (b,g), cross-country running (b,g), field hockey (g), hockey (b), ice hockey (b), mountain biking (b,g), nordic skiing (b,g), rugby (b), running (b,g), skiing (cross-country) (b,g), snowboarding (b,g), soccer (b,g), softball (b), swimming and diving (b,g), tennis (b,g), track and field (b,g), volleyball (b,g); intramural: alpine skiing (b,g), baseball (b), basketball (b,g), cross-country running (b,g), field hockey (g), hockey (b,g), ice hockey (b,g), rugby (b), running (b,g), skiing (cross-country) (b,g), snowboarding (b,g); coed interscholastic: bicycling, canoeing/kayaking, climbing, golf, kayaking, mountain biking, nordic skiing, running, skiing (cross-country), skiing (downhill), snowboarding, softball, track and field; coed intramural: aerobics, aerobics/dance, aquatics, backpacking, ball hockey, baseball, basketball, bicycling, bowling, broomball, canoeing/kayaking, climbing, combined training, cooperative games, Cosom hockey, cross-country running, equestrian sports, fishing, fitness, fitness walking, flag football, floor hockey, freestyle skiing, Frisbee, golf, hiking/backpacking, horseback riding, indoor hockey, indoor soccer, jogging, kayaking, life saving, mountain biking, mountaineering, nordic skiing, outdoor activities, paddle tennis, paddling, physical fitness, physical training, rappelling, rock climbing, ropes courses, sailboarding, sailing, scuba diving, skateboarding, skiing (cross-country), skiing (downhill), snowboarding, snowshoeing, soccer, softball, squash, street hockey, strength & conditioning, swimming and diving, table tennis, tennis, track and field, triathlon, ultimate Frisbee, volleyball, walking, wall climbing, water skiing, weight lifting, weight training, wilderness, wilderness survival, wildernessways, windsurfing, winter walking, yoga. 2 PE instructors, 2 coaches.

Computers Computers are regularly used in animation, geography, graphic arts, information technology classes. Computer network features include on-campus library services, Internet access, wireless campus network, Internet filtering or blocking technology. Campus intranet, student e-mail accounts, and computer access in designated common areas are available to students. The school has a published electronic and media policy.

Contact Mr. Sharon Magor, Director of Enrollment Management. 705-732-4351 Ext. 12. Fax: 705-732-6319. E-mail: sharon.magor@rosseaulakecollege.com. Website: www.rosseaulakecollege.com

ROTHESAY NETHERWOOD SCHOOL

40 College Hill Road
Rothesay, New Brunswick E2E 5H1, Canada

Head of School: Mr. Paul McLellan

General Information Coeducational boarding and day college-preparatory and International Baccalaureate Diploma Program school. Grades 6–12. Founded: 1877. Setting: small town. Nearest major city is Saint John, Canada. Students are housed in single-sex dormitories. 200-acre campus. 26 buildings on campus. Approved or accredited by Canadian Association of Independent Schools, Conference of Independent Schools of Ontario, International Baccalaureate Organization, The Association of Boarding Schools, and New Brunswick Department of Education. Affiliate member of National Association of Independent Schools; member of Secondary School Admission Test Board. Languages of instruction: English and French. Endowment: CAN$7 million. Total enrollment: 271. Upper school average class size: 16. Upper school faculty-student ratio: 1:7. There are 176 required school days per year for Upper School students. Upper School students typically attend 5 days per week. The average school day consists of 7 hours and 45 minutes.

Upper School Student Profile Grade 9: 43 students (20 boys, 23 girls); Grade 10: 58 students (30 boys, 28 girls); Grade 11: 57 students (36 boys, 21 girls); Grade 12: 54 students (26 boys, 28 girls). 51% of students are boarding students. 61% are province residents. 8 provinces are represented in upper school student body. 25% are international students. International students from China, Germany, Mexico, Nigeria, Norway, and United States; 4 other countries represented in student body.

Faculty School total: 38. In upper school: 19 men, 19 women; 21 have advanced degrees; 35 reside on campus.

Subjects Offered Advanced biology, advanced chemistry, algebra, art, biology, Canadian history, chemistry, computer programming, CPR, digital art, drama, English, English literature, ESL, European history, fine arts, French, geography, geometry, health, history, information technology, International Baccalaureate courses, leadership, math applications, mathematics, music, outdoor education, physical education, physics, science, social studies, Spanish, theater arts, world history, writing.

Graduation Requirements Arts and fine arts (art, music, dance, drama), computer science, English, foreign language, mathematics, physical education (includes health), science, social sciences, social studies (includes history), International Baccalaureate Theory of Knowledge, IB designation CAS hours (creativity, action, service), Extended Essay, Outward Bound adventure.

Special Academic Programs International Baccalaureate program; honors section; independent study; term-away projects; study at local college for college credit; academic accommodation for the gifted, the musically talented, and the artistically talented; ESL (14 students enrolled).

College Admission Counseling 56 students graduated in 2016; 54 went to college, including Acadia University; Dalhousie University; Mount Allison University; Queen's University at Kingston; St. Francis Xavier University; University of Toronto. Other: 1 entered military service, 1 had other specific plans.

Student Life Upper grades have uniform requirement, student council, honor system. Discipline rests primarily with faculty.

Summer Programs ESL, sports programs offered; session focuses on preparing ESL students for high school and sports camps; held on campus; accepts boys and girls; open to students from other schools. 25 students usually enrolled. 2017 schedule: July 18 to August 5. Application deadline: May 31.

Tuition and Aid Day student tuition: CAN$21,480; 7-day tuition and room/board: CAN$35,550. Tuition installment plan (monthly payment plans, individually arranged payment plans). Tuition reduction for siblings, bursaries, merit scholarship grants, need-based scholarship grants available. In 2016–17, 34% of upper-school students received aid; total upper-school merit-scholarship money awarded: CAN$99,740. Total amount of financial aid awarded in 2016–17: CAN$1,029,195.

Admissions Traditional secondary-level entrance grade is 9. For fall 2016, 167 students applied for upper-level admission, 135 were accepted, 95 enrolled. Deadline for receipt of application materials: none. Application fee required: CAN$100. Interview recommended.

Athletics Interscholastic: basketball (boys, girls), crew (b,g), cross-country running (b,g), field hockey (g), golf (b,g), ice hockey (b,g), rowing (b,g), rugby (b,g), running (b,g), soccer (b,g), squash (b,g), tennis (b,g), track and field (b,g), volleyball (b,g); intramural: ballet (g), crew (b,g), cross-country running (b,g), Frisbee (g), gatorball (g), ice hockey (b,g), indoor soccer (b), squash (b,g), tennis (b,g), track and field (b,g), yoga (g); coed interscholastic: badminton, crew, cross-country running, ice hockey, rowing, tennis, track and field; coed intramural: aerobics, aerobics/dance, backpacking, badminton, bicycling, billiards, bowling, broomball, canoeing/kayaking, climbing, cooperative games, crew, cross-country running, fitness, fitness walking, floor hockey, Frisbee, hiking/backpacking, ice hockey, indoor soccer, jogging, kayaking, outdoor activities, outdoor education, physical fitness, physical training, rock climbing, running, skiing (cross-country), skiing (downhill), snowboarding, snowshoeing, squash, street hockey, strength & conditioning, tennis, track and field, ultimate Frisbee, volleyball, walking, wall climbing, weight training. 4 PE instructors, 1 athletic trainer.

Computers Computers are regularly used in all classes. Computer network features include on-campus library services, Internet access, wireless campus network, Internet filtering or blocking technology, Web site for each academic course, informative, interactive online community for parents, teachers, and students. Campus intranet and student e-mail accounts are available to students. Students grades are available online. The school has a published electronic and media policy.

Contact Mr. Patrick Nobbs, Director of Enrolment Management. 506-848-0859. Fax: 506-848-0851. E-mail: patrick.nobbs@rns.cc. Website: www.rns.cc

ROTTERDAM INTERNATIONAL SECONDARY SCHOOL, WOLFERT VAN BORSELEN

Bentincklaan 294
Rotterdam 3039 KK, Netherlands

Head of School: Ms. Jane Forrest

General Information Coeducational day college-preparatory and languages school. Grades 6–12. Founded: 1987. Setting: urban. 1 building on campus. Approved or accredited by Council of International Schools and New England Association of Schools and Colleges. Member of European Council of International Schools. Language of instruction: English. Total enrollment: 278. Upper school average class size: 15. Upper school faculty-student ratio: 1:10. There are 190 required school days per year for Upper School students. Upper School students typically attend 5 days per week. The average school day consists of 6 hours.

Upper School Student Profile Grade 6: 26 students (13 boys, 13 girls); Grade 7: 35 students (15 boys, 20 girls); Grade 8: 28 students (19 boys, 9 girls); Grade 9: 55 students (28 boys, 27 girls); Grade 10: 35 students (20 boys, 15 girls); Grade 11: 71 students (37 boys, 34 girls); Grade 12: 31 students (15 boys, 16 girls).

Faculty School total: 38. In upper school: 10 men, 20 women; 16 have advanced degrees.

Special Academic Programs International Baccalaureate program; academic accommodation for the gifted; programs in English, mathematics, general development for dyslexic students; ESL (59 students enrolled).

College Admission Counseling 34 students graduated in 2016; 32 went to college. Other: 2 had other specific plans.

Student Life Upper grades have student council. Discipline rests primarily with faculty.

Tuition and Aid Day student tuition: €6800–€8500. Tuition installment plan (monthly payment plans).

Admissions Traditional secondary-level entrance grade is 11. Admissions testing required. Deadline for receipt of application materials: none. Application fee required: €250. On-campus interview required.

Athletics Coed Interscholastic: basketball, soccer; coed intramural: baseball, basketball, bicycling, rugby, soccer, table tennis, track and field, volleyball. 2 PE instructors.

Computers Computers are regularly used in all academic classes. Computer network features include on-campus library services, online commercial services, Internet access, wireless campus network. Student e-mail accounts are available to students. Students grades are available online. The school has a published electronic and media policy.

Contact Cinzia Maffazioli, Admissions Officer. 31-10 890 7749. Fax: 31-10 8907755. E-mail: cmf@wolfert.nl. Website: www.wolfert.nl/riss/

ROUTT CATHOLIC HIGH SCHOOL

500 East College
Jacksonville, Illinois 62650

Head of School: Mr. Nicholas Roscetti

General Information Coeducational day college-preparatory, arts, business, and religious studies school, affiliated with Roman Catholic Church. Grades 9–12. Founded: 1902. Setting: small town. Nearest major city is Springfield. 3-acre campus. 1 building on campus. Approved or accredited by National Catholic Education Association and Illinois Department of Education. Total enrollment: 118. Upper school average class size: 15. Upper school faculty-student ratio: 1:8. There are 176 required school days per year for Upper School students. Upper School students typically attend 5 days per week. The average school day consists of 6 hours and 30 minutes.

Upper School Student Profile Grade 9: 44 students (24 boys, 20 girls); Grade 10: 32 students (15 boys, 17 girls); Grade 11: 30 students (14 boys, 16 girls); Grade 12: 26 students (7 boys, 19 girls). 75% of students are Roman Catholic.

Faculty School total: 16. In upper school: 7 men, 12 women; 5 have advanced degrees.

Subjects Offered 3-dimensional art, 3-dimensional design, advanced computer applications, Advanced Placement courses, algebra, American history, American history-AP, American literature-AP, analysis and differential calculus, anatomy and physiology, band, biology, botany, business skills, calculus, calculus-AP, Catholic belief and practice, chemistry, composition, computer education, drama, economics-AP, English, English literature-AP, environmental science, geography, geometry, government, health, history of the Catholic Church, Life of Christ, marketing, physical education, physics, psychology, public speaking, sociology, Spanish, U.S. history-AP, Web site design, world history, world religions, yearbook, zoology.

Graduation Requirements 1968, arts and fine arts (art, music, dance, drama), English, government, health education, keyboarding, mathematics, physical education (includes health), research skills, science, social studies (includes history), study skills, 15 community service hours per year (60 total).

Special Academic Programs 2 Advanced Placement exams for which test preparation is offered; honors section; study at local college for college credit; remedial reading and/or remedial writing; remedial math.

College Admission Counseling 30 students graduated in 2016; 27 went to college, including Hope College; Purdue University; Rose-Hulman Institute of Technology; Southeast Missouri State University. Other: 2 went to work, 1 entered military service, 1 had other specific plans. Median composite ACT: 24. 24% scored over 26 on composite ACT.

Student Life Upper grades have uniform requirement, student council, honor system. Discipline rests primarily with faculty. Attendance at religious services is required.

Tuition and Aid Day student tuition: $3700. Tuition installment plan (FACTS Tuition Payment Plan). Tuition reduction for siblings, merit scholarship grants, need-based scholarship grants available. In 2016–17, 44% of upper-school students received aid; total upper-school merit-scholarship money awarded: $3500.

Admissions Traditional secondary-level entrance grade is 9. Any standardized test or High School Placement Test (closed version) from Scholastic Testing Service required. Deadline for receipt of application materials: none. No application fee required. On-campus interview required.

Athletics Interscholastic: baseball (boys), basketball (b,g), cheering (g), football (b), golf (b,g), softball (g), swimming and diving (b,g), track and field (b,g), volleyball (g); coed intramural: bowling. 1 PE instructor, 10 coaches.

Computers Computers are regularly used in accounting, computer applications, desktop publishing, keyboarding, media production, photojournalism, programming, Web site design, word processing, yearbook classes. Computer network features include Internet access, Internet filtering or blocking technology. The school has a published electronic and media policy.

Contact Mrs. Betty Kuvinka, Development Director. 217-243-8563 Ext. 6. Fax: 217-243-3138. E-mail: bkuvinka@routtcatholic.com. Website: www.routtcatholic.com

ROWLAND HALL

843 South Lincoln Street
Salt Lake City, Utah 84102

Head of School: Mr. Alan C. Sparrow

General Information Coeducational day college-preparatory school. Grades PK–12. Founded: 1867. Setting: urban. 4-acre campus. 1 building on campus. Approved or accredited by Northwest Association of Independent Schools, Northwest Association of Schools and Colleges, The College Board, and Utah Department of Education. Member of National Association of Independent Schools. Endowment: $15 million. Total enrollment: 918. Upper school average class size: 16. Upper school faculty-student ratio: 1:7. There are 170 required school days per year for Upper School students. Upper School students typically attend 5 days per week. The average school day consists of 6 hours.

Upper School Student Profile Grade 9: 73 students (33 boys, 40 girls); Grade 10: 88 students (41 boys, 47 girls); Grade 11: 72 students (26 boys, 46 girls); Grade 12: 67 students (25 boys, 42 girls).

Faculty School total: 130. In upper school: 21 men, 22 women; 32 have advanced degrees.

Subjects Offered Adolescent issues, algebra, biology, biology-AP, calculus, calculus-AP, ceramics, chemistry, chemistry-AP, Chinese, chorus, computer graphics, creative writing, dance, debate, drama, English, English language and composition-AP, English literature and composition-AP, environmental science, ethics, European history-AP, French, geometry, graphic arts, graphic design, history, human development, jazz band, math applications, modern European history-AP, music theory, newspaper, orchestra, photography, physical education, physics, physics-AP, political science, pre-calculus, psychology-AP, Spanish, Spanish-AP, statistics-AP, studio art, studio art-AP, theater, trigonometry, U.S. history, U.S. history-AP, weight training, Western civilization, world cultures, world religions, yearbook.

Graduation Requirements American history, arts and fine arts (art, music, dance, drama), biology, chemistry, English, ethics, foreign language, health education, mathematics, physical education (includes health), physics, science, social studies (includes history), world religions.

Special Academic Programs 17 Advanced Placement exams for which test preparation is offered; honors section; independent study.

College Admission Counseling 69 students graduated in 2016; 68 went to college, including Boston College; California Polytechnic State University, San Luis Obispo; New York University; University of Southern California; University of Utah; Wesleyan University. Other: 1 had other specific plans. Median SAT critical reading: 630, median SAT math: 620, median SAT writing: 620, median combined SAT: 1870, median composite ACT: 29. 59% scored over 600 on SAT critical reading, 57% scored over 600 on SAT math, 51% scored over 600 on SAT writing, 56% scored over 1800 on combined SAT, 65% scored over 26 on composite ACT.

Student Life Upper grades have specified standards of dress, student council, honor system. Discipline rests equally with students and faculty.

Summer Programs Enrichment, advancement, sports, art/fine arts, computer instruction programs offered; session focuses on advancement and elective courses; held on campus; accepts boys and girls; open to students from other schools. 40 students usually enrolled. 2017 schedule: June 15 to August 14. Application deadline: none.

Tuition and Aid Day student tuition: $19,515. Tuition installment plan (monthly payment plans, individually arranged payment plans, 2-installment plan). Merit scholarship grants, need-based scholarship grants, ethnic/racial diversity scholarship grants, Malone Family Foundation academically talented/need-based scholarships available. In 2016–17, 20% of upper-school students received aid; total upper-school merit-scholarship money awarded: $37,500. Total amount of financial aid awarded in 2016–17: $867,697.

Admissions Traditional secondary-level entrance grade is 9. For fall 2016, 87 students applied for upper-level admission, 56 were accepted, 37 enrolled. ACT-Explore, ERB CTP IV, ISEE, PSAT, TOEFL or writing sample required. Deadline for receipt of application materials: March 1. Application fee required: $60. Interview required.

Athletics Interscholastic: alpine skiing (boys, girls), baseball (b), basketball (b,g), golf (b,g), skiing (downhill) (b,g), soccer (b,g), softball (g), swimming and diving (b,g), tennis (b,g), volleyball (g); intramural: skiing (downhill) (b,g); coed interscholastic: alpine skiing, cross-country running, dance, modern dance, skiing (downhill), track and field; coed intramural: climbing, deck hockey, hiking/backpacking, mountain biking, outdoor activities, outdoor education, physical fitness, physical training, rock climbing, ropes courses, skiing (cross-country), skiing (downhill), snowboarding, strength & conditioning, swimming and diving, telemark skiing, weight training, yoga. 6 PE instructors, 22 coaches, 1 athletic trainer.

Computers Computers are regularly used in desktop publishing, graphic design, yearbook classes. Computer network features include on-campus library services, Internet access, wireless campus network, Internet filtering or blocking technology, all students have their own laptop computer. Campus intranet, student e-mail accounts, and computer access in designated common areas are available to students. Students grades are available online. The school has a published electronic and media policy.

Contact Ms. Kathryn B. Gundersen, Director of Admission. 801-924-2950. Fax: 801-363-5521. E-mail: kathygundersen@rowlandhall.org. Website: www.rowlandhall.org

THE ROXBURY LATIN SCHOOL

101 St. Theresa Avenue

West Roxbury, Massachusetts 02132

Head of School: Mr. Kerry Paul Brennan

General Information Boys' day college-preparatory school. Grades 7–12. Founded: 1645. Setting: urban. Nearest major city is Boston. 117-acre campus. 10 buildings on campus. Approved or accredited by Association of Independent Schools in New England, Headmasters' Conference, and New England Association of Schools and Colleges. Member of National Association of Independent Schools and Secondary School Admission Test Board. Endowment: $135 million. Total enrollment: 303. Upper school average class size: 13. Upper school faculty-student ratio: 1:7. There are 155 required school days per year for Upper School students. Upper School students typically attend 5 days per week. The average school day consists of 6 hours and 30 minutes.

Upper School Student Profile Grade 7: 43 students (43 boys); Grade 8: 44 students (44 boys); Grade 9: 55 students (55 boys); Grade 10: 55 students (55 boys); Grade 11: 50 students (50 boys); Grade 12: 54 students (54 boys).

Faculty School total: 44. In upper school: 35 men, 9 women; 34 have advanced degrees.

Subjects Offered Advanced biology, advanced chemistry, advanced math, algebra, American Civil War, American government, American history, American literature, American studies, analysis, analytic geometry, Ancient Greek, ancient history, ancient world history, applied arts, art, art history, art history-AP, arts, biology, calculus, calculus-AP, chemistry, classical Greek literature, classical language, college counseling, college placement, computer science, computer science-AP, creative writing, design, drama, earth science, English, English literature, environmental science, European history, expository writing, fine arts, French, French language-AP, geometry, global studies, government/civics, grammar, history, Indian studies, Latin, Latin-AP, life science, macro/microeconomics-AP, mathematics, Middle East, model United Nations, modern European history-AP, music, music theory-AP, personal development, photography, physical education, physical science, physics, pre-algebra, science, senior project, Spanish, Spanish language-AP, Spanish-AP, statistics-AP, studio art, theater, trigonometry, U.S. history, visual arts, water color painting, Western civilization, world history, writing.

Graduation Requirements American history, arts, classical language, English, foreign language, history, Latin, mathematics, science, U.S. history, Western civilization, independent senior project.

Special Academic Programs 13 Advanced Placement exams for which test preparation is offered; honors section; independent study; study abroad; academic accommodation for the gifted, the musically talented, and the artistically talented.

College Admission Counseling 52 students graduated in 2016; all went to college, including Boston College; Bowdoin College; College of the Holy Cross; Dartmouth College; Harvard University; Yale University. Median SAT critical reading: 720, median SAT math: 720, median SAT writing: 750, median combined SAT: 2170. 96% scored over 600 on SAT critical reading, 96% scored over 600 on SAT math, 94% scored over 600 on SAT writing, 96% scored over 1800 on combined SAT.

Student Life Upper grades have specified standards of dress, student council, honor system. Discipline rests equally with students and faculty.

Summer Programs Enrichment, sports, computer instruction programs offered; held on campus; accepts boys and girls; open to students from other schools. 200 students usually enrolled. 2017 schedule: June 30 to July 31. Application deadline: none.

Tuition and Aid Day student tuition: $30,500. Tuition installment plan (Insured Tuition Payment Plan, Key Tuition Payment Plan, 2-payment plan). Need-based scholarship grants available. In 2016–17, 36% of upper-school students received aid. Total amount of financial aid awarded in 2016–17: $2,429,625.

Admissions Traditional secondary-level entrance grade is 7. For fall 2016, 494 students applied for upper-level admission, 63 were accepted, 54 enrolled. ISEE or SSAT required. Deadline for receipt of application materials: January 6. No application fee required. On-campus interview recommended.

Athletics Interscholastic: baseball, basketball, cross-country running, football, ice hockey, lacrosse, soccer, tennis, track and field, wrestling. 7 coaches, 1 athletic trainer.

Computers Computers are regularly used in all academic, desktop publishing, literary magazine, newspaper, yearbook classes. Computer network features include on-campus library services, online commercial services, Internet access, wireless campus network, Internet filtering or blocking technology, Campus intranet, student e-mail accounts, and computer access in designated common areas are available to students. The school has a published electronic and media policy.

Contact Ms. Lindsay Schuyler, Assistant Director of Admission. 617-325-4920. Fax: 617-325-3585. E-mail: admission@roxburylatin.org. Website: www.roxburylatin.org

ROYAL CANADIAN COLLEGE

8610 Ash Street

Vancouver, British Columbia V6P 3M2, Canada

Head of School: Mr. Howard H. Jiang

General Information Coeducational day college-preparatory and general academic school. Grades 8–12. Founded: 1989. Setting: suburban. 1-acre campus. 2 buildings on campus. Approved or accredited by British Columbia Department of Education. Language of instruction: English. Total enrollment: 149. Upper school average class size: 20. Upper school faculty-student ratio: 1:20. There are 197 required school days per year for Upper School students. Upper School students typically attend 5 days per week. The average school day consists of 5 hours and 30 minutes.

Upper School Student Profile Grade 11: 50 students (33 boys, 17 girls); Grade 12: 72 students (43 boys, 29 girls).

Faculty School total: 9. In upper school: 6 men, 3 women; 2 have advanced degrees.

Subjects Offered Applied skills, biology, business education, calculus, Canadian history, career planning, chemistry, communications, drama, economics, English, ESL, fine arts, general science, history, Mandarin, marketing, mathematics, physical education, physics, pre-calculus, social sciences, world history, writing.

Graduation Requirements Applied skills, arts and fine arts (art, music, dance, drama), career and personal planning, English, language arts, mathematics, science, social studies (includes history).

Special Academic Programs ESL (16 students enrolled).

College Admission Counseling 66 students graduated in 2016; 61 went to college, including McGill University; McMaster University; Simon Fraser University; The University of British Columbia; University of Miami; University of Toronto. Other: 5 had other specific plans.

Student Life Upper grades have student council, honor system. Discipline rests primarily with faculty.

Tuition and Aid Day student tuition: CAN$15,900. Merit scholarship grants available. In 2016–17, 4% of upper-school students received aid; total upper-school merit-scholarship money awarded: CAN$10,000. Total amount of financial aid awarded in 2016–17: CAN$18,000.

Admissions Traditional secondary-level entrance grade is 11. For fall 2016, 21 students applied for upper-level admission, 20 were accepted, 20 enrolled. English language required. Deadline for receipt of application materials: none. Application fee required: CAN$200. Interview recommended.

Athletics Intramural: badminton (boys, girls), baseball (b,g), basketball (b,g), Frisbee (b,g), soccer (b,g), table tennis (b,g), ultimate Frisbee (b,g), volleyball (b,g); coed intramural: badminton, baseball, Frisbee, soccer, table tennis, ultimate Frisbee, volleyball. 1 PE instructor.

Computers Computers are regularly used in career exploration, English, science, social studies classes. Computer network features include Internet access, Internet filtering or blocking technology. Computer access in designated common areas is available to students.

Contact Ms. Alice Syn, Admissions Manager. 604-738-2221. Fax: 604-738-2282. E-mail: alice.syn@royalcanadiancollege.com. Website: www.royalcanadiancollege.com

RUDOLF STEINER SCHOOL OF ANN ARBOR

2230 Pontiac Trail
Ann Arbor, Michigan 48105

Head of School: Ms. Sandra Greenstone

General Information Coeducational day college-preparatory and Waldorf Education school. Grades 9–12. Founded: 1980. Setting: suburban. 6-acre campus. 3 buildings on campus. Approved or accredited by Association of Waldorf Schools of North America and Michigan Department of Education. Member of National Association of Independent Schools. Total enrollment: 345. Upper school average class size: 20. Upper school faculty-student ratio: 1:10. There are 175 required school days per year for Upper School students. Upper School students typically attend 5 days per week. The average school day consists of 7 hours and 10 minutes.

Upper School Student Profile Grade 9: 23 students (11 boys, 12 girls); Grade 10: 30 students (14 boys, 16 girls); Grade 11: 23 students (7 boys, 16 girls); Grade 12: 29 students (15 boys, 14 girls).

Faculty School total: 41. In upper school: 12 men, 29 women; 15 have advanced degrees.

Subjects Offered All academic.

Special Academic Programs Study abroad; academic accommodation for the gifted; remedial reading and/or remedial writing; programs in English, mathematics, general development for dyslexic students; ESL (11 students enrolled).

College Admission Counseling 28 students graduated in 2016; 27 went to college, including Adrian College; Grand Valley State University; Kalamazoo College; Macalester College; Michigan State University; University of Michigan. Other: 1 went to work. Median SAT critical reading: 590, median SAT math: 540, median SAT writing: 580, median composite ACT: 25. 45% scored over 600 on SAT critical reading, 25% scored over 600 on SAT math, 55% scored over 600 on SAT writing, 25% scored over 1800 on combined SAT, 40% scored over 26 on composite ACT.

Student Life Discipline rests primarily with faculty.

Tuition and Aid Day student tuition: $18,150. Tuition installment plan (FACTS Tuition Payment Plan). Need-based scholarship grants available. In 2016–17, 40% of upper-school students received aid.

Admissions Traditional secondary-level entrance grade is 9. For fall 2016, 24 students applied for upper-level admission, 17 were accepted, 17 enrolled. Deadline for receipt of application materials: none. Application fee required: $60. Interview recommended.

Athletics Interscholastic: baseball (boys), basketball (b,g), ice hockey (b), lacrosse (b), soccer (b,g), volleyball (g); coed interscholastic: cross-country running, golf, running, tennis; coed intramural: backpacking, crew, freestyle skiing, hiking/backpacking, outdoor activities, outdoor adventure, outdoor education, outdoor recreation, outdoor skills, outdoors, rowing, skiing (downhill). 1 PE instructor, 8 coaches.

Computers Computers are regularly used in all academic classes. Computer resources include Internet access, Internet filtering or blocking technology. Computer access in designated common areas is available to students. The school has a published electronic and media policy.

Contact Dr. Sian Owen-Cruise, High School Coordinator. 734-669-9394 Ext. 12. Fax: 734-669-9394. E-mail: sowen-cruise@steinerschool.org. Website: www.steinerschool.org/

RUMSEY HALL SCHOOL

Washington Depot, Connecticut
See Junior Boarding Schools section.

RUNDLE COLLEGE

7375 17th Avenue SW
Calgary, Alberta T3H 3W5, Canada

Head of School: Mr. Jason Rogers

General Information Coeducational day college-preparatory, arts, business, bilingual studies, and technology school. Grades K–12. Founded: 1985. Setting: suburban. 20-acre campus. 1 building on campus. Approved or accredited by Canadian Association of Independent Schools and Alberta Department of Education. Member of Secondary School Admission Test Board. Language of instruction: English. Total enrollment: 811. Upper school average class size: 14. Upper school faculty-student ratio: 1:14. There are 187 required school days per year for Upper School students. Upper School students typically attend 5 days per week. The average school day consists of 7 hours.

Upper School Student Profile Grade 10: 84 students (37 boys, 47 girls); Grade 11: 94 students (46 boys, 48 girls); Grade 12: 78 students (41 boys, 37 girls).

Faculty School total: 45. In upper school: 14 men, 31 women; 15 have advanced degrees.

Subjects Offered Accounting, art, band, biology, calculus, chemistry, computer science, drama, English, French, general science, mathematics, physical education, physics, science, social studies, Spanish, theater.

Graduation Requirements Career and personal planning, English, mathematics, physical education (includes health), science, social sciences.

Special Academic Programs Honors section; study abroad.

College Admission Counseling 84 students graduated in 2016; 82 went to college, including Queen's University at Kingston; St. Francis Xavier University; The University of British Columbia; University of Alberta; University of Calgary; University of Victoria. Other: 1 went to work, 1 had other specific plans.

Student Life Upper grades have uniform requirement, student council, honor system. Discipline rests primarily with faculty.

Tuition and Aid Day student tuition: CAN$12,000. Tuition installment plan (monthly payment plans). Bursaries, merit scholarship grants available. In 2016–17, 1% of upper-school students received aid; total upper-school merit-scholarship money awarded: CAN$24,000. Total amount of financial aid awarded in 2016–17: CAN$90,000.

Admissions Traditional secondary-level entrance grade is 10. For fall 2016, 50 students applied for upper-level admission, 25 were accepted, 20 enrolled. Achievement tests and SSAT or WISC III required. Deadline for receipt of application materials: none. Application fee required: CAN$100. Interview required.

Athletics Interscholastic: badminton (boys, girls), basketball (b,g), cross-country running (b,g), curling (b,g), dance squad (b,g), flag football (b,g), floor hockey (b,g), football (b), golf (b,g), rugby (b,g), soccer (b,g), track and field (b,g), volleyball (b,g), wrestling (b,g); intramural: aerobics (g), badminton (b,g), dance (g), football (b); coed interscholastic: badminton, softball; coed intramural: badminton, baseball, basketball, cross-country running, flag football, football, lacrosse, outdoor recreation, skiing (downhill), soccer, table tennis, track and field, volleyball, weight lifting, wrestling. 4 PE instructors.

Computers Computers are regularly used in technology classes. Computer network features include Internet access, wireless campus network, Web page hosting, multimedia productions, streaming video student news. Student e-mail accounts and computer access in designated common areas are available to students. Students grades are available online. The school has a published electronic and media policy.

Contact Ms. Nicola Spencer, Director of Admissions. 403-291-3866 Ext. 106. Fax: 403-291-5458. E-mail: spencer@rundle.ab.ca. Website: www.rundle.ab.ca

RUTGERS PREPARATORY SCHOOL

1345 Easton Avenue
Somerset, New Jersey 08873

Head of School: Dr. Steven A. Loy

General Information Coeducational day college-preparatory school. Grades PK–12. Founded: 1766. Setting: suburban. Nearest major city is New York, NY. 41-acre campus. 8 buildings on campus. Approved or accredited by Council of International Schools and New Jersey Association of Independent Schools. Member of National Association of Independent Schools and Secondary School Admission Test Board. Total enrollment: 640. Upper school average class size: 14. Upper school faculty-student ratio: 1:7. There are 165 required school days per year for Upper School students. Upper School students typically attend 5 days per week. The average school day consists of 6 hours and 45 minutes.

Upper School Student Profile Grade 6: 25 students (12 boys, 13 girls); Grade 7: 46 students (30 boys, 16 girls); Grade 8: 59 students (29 boys, 30 girls); Grade 9: 88 students (51 boys, 37 girls); Grade 10: 94 students (53 boys, 41 girls); Grade 11: 105 students (63 boys, 42 girls); Grade 12: 93 students (44 boys, 49 girls).

Faculty School total: 98. In upper school: 23 men, 31 women; 41 have advanced degrees.

Subjects Offered 3-dimensional art, acting, advanced chemistry, advanced computer applications, Advanced Placement courses, algebra, American history, American history-AP, American literature, Arabic, architecture, art, art history, astronomy, band, baseball, basketball, biology, biology-AP, business mathematics, calculus, calculus-AP, career/college preparation, ceramics, chemistry, choir, classics, college admission preparation, college placement, comedy, community service, comparative religion, computer art, computer multimedia, computer programming, computer science, computer science-AP, creative arts, creative writing, digital photography, discrete mathematics, drama, driver education, economics, economics-AP, English, English literature, entrepreneurship, environmental science, European history, fine arts, foundations of civilization, French, French-AP, geometry, government/civics, health, health education, history, history-AP, Holocaust studies, independent study, Japanese, jazz ensemble, Latin, literary magazine, literature, literature-AP, marching band, mathematics, media, model United Nations, multimedia, multimedia design, music, mythology, peer counseling, photography, physical education, physical fitness, physical science, physics, physics-AP, poetry, post-calculus, pre-calculus, probability and statistics, psychology, psychology-AP, SAT/ACT preparation, scene study, science, science research, senior project, sex education, Shakespeare, social studies, softball, software design, Spanish, Spanish literature-AP, Spanish-AP, stage design, statistics, statistics-AP, swimming, tennis, theater, theater design and production, U.S. government and politics-AP, U.S. history-AP, United States government-AP, vocal music, volleyball, word processing, world history, world history-AP, wrestling, writing, yearbook.

Special Academic Programs 22 Advanced Placement exams for which test preparation is offered; honors section; independent study; term-away projects; academic accommodation for the gifted, the musically talented, and the artistically talented.

College Admission Counseling 91 students graduated in 2015; all went to college, including Bucknell University; Emory University; New York University; Northeastern University; Rutgers, The State University of New Jersey, Rutgers College; University of Michigan. Mean SAT critical reading: 608, mean SAT math: 647, mean SAT writing: 617, mean combined SAT: 1871, mean composite ACT: 26. 60.7% scored over 600 on SAT critical reading, 64% scored over 600 on SAT math, 65% scored over 600 on SAT writing.

Student Life Upper grades have specified standards of dress, student council, honor system. Discipline rests primarily with faculty.

Tuition and Aid Day student tuition: $34,000. Tuition installment plan (RPS Tuition Plan). Need-based financial aid available. In 2015–16, 31% of upper-school students received aid.

Admissions Iowa Tests of Basic Skills, ISEE or SSAT required. Deadline for receipt of application materials: none. Application fee required: $75. Interview required.

Athletics Interscholastic: baseball (boys), basketball (b,g), lacrosse (b,g), soccer (b,g), softball (g), tennis (b,g), volleyball (g), wrestling (b); intramural: dance team (g); coed interscholastic: cross-country running, golf, swimming and diving; coed intramural: croquet, dance, Frisbee, ice hockey, jogging, physical fitness, power lifting, strength & conditioning, ultimate Frisbee, wall climbing, weight training. 6 PE instructors, 9 coaches, 2 athletic trainers.

Computers Computers are regularly used in all academic, college planning, publications classes. Computer network features include on-campus library services, online commercial services, Internet access, wireless campus network, Internet filtering or blocking technology, laptops, iPads, iPad minis, Apple TV, Smartboards. Student e-mail accounts and computer access in designated common areas are available to students. The school has a published electronic and media policy.

Contact Audrey Forte, Admission Assistant. 732-545-5600 Ext. 261. Fax: 732-214-1819. E-mail: forte@rutgersprep.org. Website: www.rutgersprep.org

SACRAMENTO COUNTRY DAY SCHOOL

2636 Latham Drive
Sacramento, California 95864-7198

Head of School: Mr. Lee Thomsen

General Information Coeducational day college-preparatory school. Grades PK–12. Founded: 1964. Setting: suburban. 12-acre campus. 8 buildings on campus. Approved or accredited by California Association of Independent Schools and Western Association of Schools and Colleges. Member of National Association of Independent Schools. Endowment: $2.6 million. Total enrollment: 503. Upper school average class size: 10. Upper school faculty-student ratio: 1:9. There are 175 required school days per year for Upper School students. Upper School students typically attend 5 days per week. The average school day consists of 6 hours and 25 minutes.

Upper School Student Profile Grade 9: 32 students (15 boys, 17 girls); Grade 10: 38 students (16 boys, 22 girls); Grade 11: 29 students (14 boys, 15 girls); Grade 12: 29 students (15 boys, 14 girls).

Faculty School total: 68. In upper school: 12 men, 14 women; 20 have advanced degrees.

Subjects Offered Acting, algebra, American history, American literature, ancient history, ancient/medieval philosophy, art, art history, art history-AP, art-AP, band, biology, biology-AP, British literature, calculus, calculus-AP, ceramics, chamber groups, chemistry, chemistry-AP, community service, computer skills, computer technologies, concert band, creative writing, digital imaging, drama, drama performance, drawing, earth science, economics, English, English literature, European history, fine arts, French, French-AP, geography, geometry, government/civics, grammar, history, international relations, jazz band, journalism, language and composition, Latin, Latin-AP, mathematics, microeconomics, newspaper, nutrition, orchestra, physical education, physics, physics-AP, physiology, pre-calculus, public speaking, science, social studies, Spanish, Spanish-AP, speech, studio art, studio art-AP, technology/design, theater, trigonometry, U.S. history, U.S. history-AP, world history, world literature, writing.

Graduation Requirements Arts and fine arts (art, music, dance, drama), computer science, electives, English, foreign language, history, interdisciplinary studies, mathematics, physical education (includes health), science, Senior Seminars. Community service is required.

Special Academic Programs Advanced Placement exam preparation; honors section; independent study; study at local college for college credit.

College Admission Counseling 34 students graduated in 2016; all went to college, including California Polytechnic State University, San Luis Obispo; Dartmouth College; New York University; Stanford University; University of California, Berkeley; University of California, Santa Barbara. Median SAT critical reading: 645, median SAT math: 649, median SAT writing: 665, median combined SAT: 1959. 63% scored over 600 on SAT critical reading, 73% scored over 600 on SAT math, 80% scored over 600 on SAT writing, 70% scored over 1800 on combined SAT.

Student Life Upper grades have specified standards of dress, student council, honor system. Discipline rests primarily with faculty.

Summer Programs Enrichment, advancement, sports, art/fine arts, computer instruction programs offered; session focuses on Enrichment; held on campus; accepts boys and girls; open to students from other schools. 250 students usually enrolled. 2017 schedule: June 19 to July 28. Application deadline: June 19.

Tuition and Aid Day student tuition: $18,600–$24,200. Tuition installment plan (Insured Tuition Payment Plan, monthly payment plans, individually arranged payment plans). Need-based scholarship grants available. In 2016–17, 28% of upper-school students received aid. Total amount of financial aid awarded in 2016–17: $468,000.

Admissions Traditional secondary-level entrance grade is 9. For fall 2016, 44 students applied for upper-level admission, 24 were accepted, 18 enrolled. ERB, Otis-Lennon Mental Ability Test and writing sample required. Deadline for receipt of application materials: none. Application fee required: $125. On-campus interview required.

Athletics Interscholastic: baseball (boys), basketball (b,g), flag football (b), lacrosse (b), soccer (b,g), softball (g), swimming and diving (b,g), track and field (b,g), volleyball (b,g); coed interscholastic: cross-country running, golf, skiing (downhill), snowboarding, tennis. 3 PE instructors, 15 coaches.

Computers Computers are regularly used in all academic classes. Computer network features include on-campus library services, online commercial services, Internet access, wireless campus network, Internet filtering or blocking technology. Campus intranet and student e-mail accounts are available to students. The school has a published electronic and media policy.

Contact Lonna Bloedau, Director of Admission. 916-481-8811. Fax: 916-481-6016. E-mail: lbloedau@saccds.org. Website: www.saccds.org

SACRAMENTO WALDORF SCHOOL

3750 Bannister Road
Fair Oaks, California 95628

Head of School: Marcela Iglesias

General Information Coeducational day college-preparatory and general academic school. Grades PK–12. Founded: 1959. Setting: suburban. Nearest major city is Sacramento. 22-acre campus. 8 buildings on campus. Approved or accredited by Association of Waldorf Schools of North America, Western Association of Schools and Colleges, and California Department of Education. Member of National Association of Independent Schools. Endowment: $50,000. Total enrollment: 441. Upper school average class size: 25. Upper school faculty-student ratio: 1:6. There are 170 required school days per year for Upper School students. Upper School students typically attend 5 days per week. The average school day consists of 6 hours and 30 minutes.

Upper School Student Profile Grade 6: 22 students (14 boys, 8 girls); Grade 7: 29 students (11 boys, 18 girls); Grade 8: 25 students (9 boys, 16 girls); Grade 9: 37 students (20 boys, 17 girls); Grade 10: 45 students (23 boys, 22 girls); Grade 11: 36 students (16 boys, 20 girls); Grade 12: 38 students (19 boys, 19 girls).

Faculty School total: 52. In upper school: 11 men, 14 women; 11 have advanced degrees.

Subjects Offered 20th century American writers, 20th century history, 20th century world history, 3-dimensional art, acting, advanced math, algebra, American government, American history, American literature, anatomy, applied arts, applied music, architectural drawing, architecture, art, art history, arts, astronomy, bacteriology, band, biology, bookbinding, botany, British literature, calculus, calligraphy, career/college preparation, chemistry, choir, choral music, chorus, civics, classical Greek literature, college admission preparation, college awareness, college counseling, college placement, college planning, communication skills, community service, computer literacy, computer skills, concert choir, conflict resolution, crafts, creative arts, creative thinking, drama, drama performance, drama workshop, dramatic arts, drawing, electives, English, English composition, English literature, ensembles, European civilization, European history, European literature, eurythmy, expressive arts, liberal arts, fine arts, freshman seminar, gardening, general math, general science, geography, geology, geometry, German, government/civics, grammar, Greek drama, health, history, history of the Americas, human anatomy, human sexuality, language arts, literature, mathematics, medieval history, medieval literature, medieval/Renaissance history, multicultural studies, music, music appreciation, music performance, musical productions, mythology, orchestra, organic gardening, participation in sports, performing arts, physical education, physical science, physics, physiology, play production, pottery, pre-calculus, printmaking, projective geometry, Russian literature, science, sculpture, senior career experience, senior project, sex education, sexuality, Shakespeare, Shakespearean histories, social sciences, social studies, Spanish, speech, strings, student publications, theater, theater arts, theater design and production, theater production, theory of knowledge, trigonometry, U.S. government, U.S. history, U.S. literature, visual and performing arts, visual arts, vocal ensemble, vocal jazz, vocal music, woodworking, world arts, world civilizations, world cultures, world geography, world history, world literature, writing, writing, writing workshop, yearbook, zoology.

Graduation Requirements Algebra, American government, American history, anatomy and physiology, ancient world history, architecture, art history, arts and crafts, arts and fine arts (art, music, dance, drama), biochemistry, biology, bookbinding, botany, calligraphy, cell biology, ceramics, chemistry, civics, computer literacy, computer skills, English, foreign language, mathematics, physical education (includes health), science, senior project, social sciences, social studies (includes history), world history. Community service is required.

Special Academic Programs Independent study; term-away projects; study abroad.

College Admission Counseling 28 students graduated in 2016; 25 went to college, including Occidental College; Saint Mary's College of California; University of California, Berkeley; University of California, Santa Cruz; University of Puget Sound;

University of Redlands. Other: 1 went to work, 2 had other specific plans. Median SAT critical reading: 648, median SAT math: 580, median SAT writing: 590, median combined SAT: 1680, median composite ACT: 25. 40% scored over 600 on SAT critical reading, 40% scored over 600 on SAT math, 40% scored over 600 on SAT writing, 20% scored over 1800 on combined SAT.

Student Life Upper grades have specified standards of dress, student council. Discipline rests primarily with faculty.

Tuition and Aid Day student tuition: $10,950–$19,500. Tuition installment plan (Insured Tuition Payment Plan, monthly payment plans, semiannual and annual payment plans). Tuition reduction for siblings, need-based scholarship grants available. In 2016–17, 45% of upper-school students received aid. Total amount of financial aid awarded in 2016–17: $398,000.

Admissions Traditional secondary-level entrance grade is 9. For fall 2016, 43 students applied for upper-level admission, 35 were accepted, 29 enrolled. Math Placement Exam or TOEFL required. Deadline for receipt of application materials: none. Application fee required: $75. Interview recommended.

Athletics Interscholastic: baseball (boys), basketball (b,g), cross-country running (b,g), golf (b), soccer (b,g), volleyball (g); coed interscholastic: climbing, combined training, cooperative games, mountain biking, physical fitness, physical training, rock climbing, skiing (downhill), track and field, ultimate Frisbee, winter soccer. 1 PE instructor, 8 coaches.

Computers Computers are regularly used in college planning, independent study, introduction to technology, mathematics, photography, word processing, yearbook classes. Computer network features include Internet access, wireless campus network, Internet filtering or blocking technology, online college and career searches. Campus intranet and computer access in designated common areas are available to students. Students grades are available online. The school has a published electronic and media policy.

Contact Betsy Petering, Admissions Assistant. 916-860-2522. Fax: 916-961-3970. E-mail: bpetering@sacwaldorf.org. Website: www.sacwaldorf.org

SACRED HEART ACADEMY

3175 Lexington Road
Louisville, Kentucky 40206

Head of School: Ms. Mary Lee McCoy

General Information Girls' day college-preparatory, arts, business, religious studies, and technology school, affiliated with Roman Catholic Church. Grades 9–12. Founded: 1877. Setting: suburban. 46-acre campus. 2 buildings on campus. Approved or accredited by Southern Association of Colleges and Schools and Kentucky Department of Education. Upper school average class size: 21. Upper school faculty-student ratio: 1:15.

Upper School Student Profile 87% of students are Roman Catholic.

Faculty School total: 87. In upper school: 9 men, 78 women; 48 have advanced degrees.

Subjects Offered Algebra, American history, American literature, anatomy, art, art history, biology, business, calculus, ceramics, chemistry, computer graphics, computer programming, computer science, creative writing, drama, English, English literature, environmental science, ethics, European history, French, geography, geometry, government/civics, grammar, health, history, journalism, marketing, mathematics, music, nutrition, physical education, physics, physiology, psychology, religion, science, social studies, sociology, Spanish, speech, statistics, theater, theology, trigonometry, video, world history, writing.

Graduation Requirements Computer science, English, foreign language, mathematics, physical education (includes health), religion (includes Bible studies and theology), science, social studies (includes history).

Special Academic Programs Advanced Placement exam preparation; honors section; independent study; study at local college for college credit; academic accommodation for the gifted, the musically talented, and the artistically talented.

College Admission Counseling 211 students graduated in 2015; 100 went to college, including Bellarmine University; Miami University; Saint Louis University; University of Kentucky; University of Louisville; Xavier University.

Student Life Upper grades have uniform requirement, student council. Discipline rests primarily with faculty. Attendance at religious services is required.

Tuition and Aid Day student tuition: $5035. Merit scholarship grants, need-based scholarship grants, paying campus jobs available. In 2015–16, 86% of upper-school students received aid; total upper-school merit-scholarship money awarded: $10,500.

Admissions High School Placement Test required. Deadline for receipt of application materials: none. No application fee required. On-campus interview required.

Athletics Interscholastic: archery, basketball, cross-country running, diving, field hockey, golf, soccer, softball, swimming and diving, tennis, track and field, volleyball; intramural: basketball, volleyball. 1 PE instructor, 14 coaches, 1 athletic trainer.

Computers Computers are regularly used in English, mathematics classes. Computer network features include on-campus library services, Internet access, Internet filtering or blocking technology. Campus intranet, student e-mail accounts, and computer access in designated common areas are available to students. Students grades are available online. The school has a published electronic and media policy.

Contact Dean of Studies. 502-897-6097. Fax: 502-896-3935. Website: www.sacredheartschools.org

SACRED HEART ACADEMY

47 Cathedral Avenue
Hempstead, New York 11550

Head of School: Mrs. Kristin Lynch Graham

General Information Girls' day college-preparatory school, affiliated with Roman Catholic Church. Grades 9–12. Founded: 1949. Setting: suburban. Nearest major city is New York City. 3 buildings on campus. Approved or accredited by Middle States Association of Colleges and Schools, New York Department of Education, North Central Association of Colleges and Schools, and New York Department of Education. Upper school average class size: 15. Upper school faculty-student ratio: 1:15. Upper School students typically attend 5 days per week. The average school day consists of 6 hours and 30 minutes.

College Admission Counseling 211 students graduated in 2016; all went to college.

Student Life Upper grades have uniform requirement, student council, honor system. Discipline rests primarily with faculty. Attendance at religious services is required.

Contact Ms. Mary White, Director of Admissions. 516-483-7383 Ext. 207. Fax: 516-483-1016. E-mail: admissions@sacredheartacademyhempstead.org. Website: www.sacredheartacademyhempstead.org/

SACRED HEART/GRIFFIN HIGH SCHOOL

1200 West Washington
Springfield, Illinois 62702-4794

Head of School: Sr. Katherine O'Connor, OP

General Information Coeducational day college-preparatory school, affiliated with Roman Catholic Church. Grades 9–12. Founded: 1895. Setting: urban. 13-acre campus. 2 buildings on campus. Approved or accredited by National Catholic Education Association, North Central Association of Colleges and Schools, and Illinois Department of Education. Endowment: $12 million. Total enrollment: 725. Upper school average class size: 24. Upper school faculty-student ratio: 1:15. There are 176 required school days per year for Upper School students. Upper School students typically attend 5 days per week. The average school day consists of 7 hours.

Upper School Student Profile Grade 9: 153 students (78 boys, 75 girls); Grade 10: 168 students (81 boys, 87 girls); Grade 11: 168 students (82 boys, 86 girls); Grade 12: 154 students (84 boys, 70 girls). 88% of students are Roman Catholic.

Faculty School total: 49. In upper school: 23 men, 26 women; 26 have advanced degrees.

Subjects Offered Advanced biology.

Graduation Requirements 80 hours of service to community or approved organizations.

Special Academic Programs 9 Advanced Placement exams for which test preparation is offered; honors section; study at local college for college credit; academic accommodation for the gifted, the musically talented, and the artistically talented.

College Admission Counseling 185 students graduated in 2016; 181 went to college, including Bradley University; Saint Louis University; University of Illinois at Urbana–Champaign. Other: 1 went to work, 2 entered military service, 1 had other specific plans. Median composite ACT: 24.

Student Life Upper grades have uniform requirement, student council, honor system. Discipline rests primarily with faculty. Attendance at religious services is required.

Summer Programs Remediation, enrichment, advancement, sports programs offered; session focuses on physical education and health; held on campus; accepts boys and girls; open to students from other schools. 300 students usually enrolled. 2017 schedule: May 30 to June 30. Application deadline: April 15.

Tuition and Aid Day student tuition: $8225. Tuition installment plan (FACTS Tuition Payment Plan, monthly payment plans, individually arranged payment plans). Tuition reduction for siblings, merit scholarship grants, need-based scholarship grants available. In 2016–17, 40% of upper-school students received aid; total upper-school merit-scholarship money awarded: $16,000. Total amount of financial aid awarded in 2016–17: $556,298.

Admissions Traditional secondary-level entrance grade is 9. For fall 2016, 168 students applied for upper-level admission, 168 were accepted, 168 enrolled. Explore required. Deadline for receipt of application materials: none. Application fee required: $300. On-campus interview recommended.

Athletics Interscholastic: aquatics (boys, girls), baseball (b), basketball (b,g), cheering (g), cross-country running (b,g), diving (b,g), football (b), golf (b,g), hockey (b), pom squad (g), soccer (b,g), softball (g), swimming and diving (b,g), tennis (b,g), track and field (b,g), volleyball (g); intramural: basketball (b,g). 1 PE instructor, 3 coaches, 1 athletic trainer.

Computers Computers are regularly used in all academic classes. Computer network features include on-campus library services, Internet access, wireless campus network, Internet filtering or blocking technology. Students grades are available online. The school has a published electronic and media policy.

Contact Taylor Fishburn, Marketing/Communications. 217-787-9732. Fax: 217-726-9791. E-mail: Fishburn@shg.org. Website: www.shg.org

SACRED HEART HIGH SCHOOL

2111 Griffin Avenue
Los Angeles, California 90031

Head of School: Mr. Raymond Saborio

General Information Girls' day college-preparatory and general academic school, affiliated with Roman Catholic Church. Grades 9–12. Founded: 1907. Setting: urban. 1-acre campus. 2 buildings on campus. Approved or accredited by Western Association of Schools and Colleges, Western Catholic Education Association, and California Department of Education. Languages of instruction: English and Spanish. Total enrollment: 250. Upper school average class size: 25. Upper school faculty-student ratio: 1:25. There are 180 required school days per year for Upper School students. Upper School students typically attend 5 days per week. The average school day consists of 6 hours.

Upper School Student Profile Grade 9: 70 students (70 girls); Grade 10: 55 students (55 girls); Grade 11: 60 students (60 girls); Grade 12: 41 students (41 girls). 95% of students are Roman Catholic.

Faculty School total: 25. In upper school: 4 men, 21 women; 2 have advanced degrees.

Graduation Requirements Arts and fine arts (art, music, dance, drama), business skills (includes word processing), computer science, English, foreign language, mathematics, physical education (includes health), religion (includes Bible studies and theology), science, social studies (includes history). Community service is required.

Special Academic Programs 9 Advanced Placement exams for which test preparation is offered; honors section; independent study; study at local college for college credit; remedial reading and/or remedial writing; remedial math.

College Admission Counseling 41 students graduated in 2016; 40 went to college, including Brown University; California State University, Los Angeles; California State University, Northridge; Pepperdine University; University of California, Irvine; University of California, Los Angeles. Other: 1 entered military service.

Student Life Upper grades have uniform requirement, student council, honor system. Discipline rests primarily with faculty. Attendance at religious services is required.

Summer Programs Remediation, enrichment, advancement, computer instruction programs offered; held on campus; accepts girls; not open to students from other schools. 80 students usually enrolled. 2017 schedule: June 19 to July 21. Application deadline: June 1.

Tuition and Aid Day student tuition: $7300. Tuition installment plan (FACTS Tuition Payment Plan, monthly payment plans, individually arranged payment plans). Tuition reduction for siblings, merit scholarship grants, need based scholarship grants, paying campus jobs available. In 2016–17, 90% of upper-school students received aid. Total amount of financial aid awarded in 2016–17: $1,000,000.

Admissions Traditional secondary-level entrance grade is 9. For fall 2016, 150 students applied for upper-level admission, 120 were accepted, 70 enrolled. High School Placement Test (closed version) from Scholastic Testing Service required. Deadline for receipt of application materials: August 15. Application fee required: $25. On-campus interview recommended.

Athletics Interscholastic: basketball, cross-country running, soccer, softball, track and field, volleyball. 1 PE instructor, 6 coaches.

Computers Computers are regularly used in remedial study skills classes. Computer network features include on-campus library services, Internet access, wireless campus network, Internet filtering or blocking technology. Student e-mail accounts are available to students. Students grades are available online. The school has a published electronic and media policy.

Contact Ms. Jennifer Beltran, Admissions Coordinator. 323-225-2209. Fax: 323-225-5046. E-mail: admissions@shhsla.org. Website: www.shhsla.org

SACRED HEART HIGH SCHOOL

34 Convent Avenue
Yonkers, New York 10703

Head of School: Mrs. Karen K. Valenti-DeCecco

General Information Coeducational day college-preparatory school, affiliated with Roman Catholic Church. Grades 9–12. Founded: 1923. Setting: suburban. Nearest major city is New York. 5-acre campus. 3 buildings on campus. Approved or accredited by Middle States Association of Colleges and Schools, New York State Board of Regents, and New York Department of Education. Languages of instruction: French, Italian, and Spanish. Endowment: $150,000. Total enrollment: 401. Upper school average class size: 25. Upper school faculty-student ratio: 1:15. There are 180 required school days per year for Upper School students. The average school day consists of 7 hours and 8 minutes.

Upper School Student Profile 85% of students are Roman Catholic.

Faculty School total: 22. In upper school: 17 men, 5 women; 19 have advanced degrees.

Subjects Offered 20th century history, accounting, advanced chemistry, advanced math, algebra, American history, American history-AP, American literature, analytic geometry, ancient world history, applied arts, applied music, art, art history, Bible studies, biology, British literature, business law, business mathematics, calculus, calculus-AP, Catholic belief and practice, ceramics, chemistry, chemistry-AP, choir, Christian and Hebrew scripture, Christian doctrine, Christian ethics, Christian testament, church history, classical civilization, college counseling, computer animation, computer education, computer graphics, computer literacy, computers, criminal justice, critical studies in film, critical writing, desktop publishing, drama, earth science, Eastern world civilizations, ecology, economics, English, English language and composition-AP, English language-AP, English literature, English literature-AP, English-AP, environmental science, ethics, European history, female experience in America, fiction, film and literature, finance, fine arts, finite math, fitness, food and nutrition, general math, geometry, government, graphic arts, graphic design, health, heritage of American Women, Hispanic literature, honors English, honors geometry, honors U.S. history, honors world history, human anatomy, Italian, leadership, library skills, life management skills, linear algebra, literary magazine, literature by women, math analysis, math applications, mathematics, mathematics-AP, medieval history, moral reasoning, music appreciation, nutrition, oceanography, painting, physical education, physics, pottery, pre-algebra, pre-calculus, psychology, reading/study skills, SAT preparation, sociology, Spanish language-AP, Spanish literature-AP, sports medicine, stained glass, statistics, studio art, technology, trigonometry, U.S. government, Western civilization, women's studies.

Graduation Requirements Foreign language, religion (includes Bible studies and theology), Board of Regents requirements. Community service is required.

Special Academic Programs Advanced Placement exam preparation; honors section; study at local college for college credit.

College Admission Counseling 86 students graduated in 2016; 83 went to college, including Binghamton University, State University of New York; Fordham University; Iona College; Manhattan College; Pace University; State University of New York at Oswego. Other: 3 entered military service.

Student Life Upper grades have uniform requirement, student council, honor system. Discipline rests primarily with faculty. Attendance at religious services is required.

Tuition and Aid Day student tuition: $8500. Tuition installment plan (SMART Tuition Payment Plan, monthly payment plans). Merit scholarship grants available. In 2016–17, 15% of upper-school students received aid; total upper-school merit-scholarship money awarded: $20,000. Total amount of financial aid awarded in 2016–17: $25,000.

Admissions Traditional secondary-level entrance grade is 9. Catholic High School Entrance Examination required. Deadline for receipt of application materials: June 15. Application fee required: $150. On-campus interview recommended.

Athletics Interscholastic: baseball (boys), basketball (b,g), football (b), soccer (b), softball (g), volleyball (g); coed interscholastic: bowling; coed intramural: cheering, dance squad. 1 PE instructor, 10 coaches.

Computers Computers are regularly used in art, Bible studies, business education, Christian doctrine, computer applications, creative writing, economics, English, French as a second language, freshman foundations, health, history, life skills, psychology, religion, yearbook classes. Computer network features include on-campus library services, online commercial services, Internet access, wireless campus network, Internet filtering or blocking technology. Campus intranet, student e-mail accounts, and computer access in designated common areas are available to students. Students grades are available online. The school has a published electronic and media policy.

Contact Mrs. Karen K. Valenti-DeCecco, Principal. 914-965-3114. Fax: 914-965-4510. E-mail: admissions@sacredhearths.org. Website: www.sacredhearths.net

SADDLEBROOK PREPARATORY SCHOOL

5700 Saddlebrook Way
Wesley Chapel, Florida 33543

Head of School: Mr. Chris T. Wester

General Information Coeducational boarding and day college-preparatory school. Boarding grades 6–12, day grades 3–12. Founded: 1993. Setting: suburban. Nearest major city is Tampa. Students are housed in coed dormitories. 50-acre campus. 8 buildings on campus. Approved or accredited by Florida Council of Independent Schools, Southern Association of Colleges and Schools, and Florida Department of Education. Total enrollment: 80. Upper school average class size: 8. Upper school faculty-student ratio: 1:8. There are 175 required school days per year for Upper School students. Upper School students typically attend 5 days per week. The average school day consists of 7 hours and 15 minutes.

Upper School Student Profile Grade 9: 14 students (12 boys, 2 girls); Grade 10: 18 students (13 boys, 5 girls); Grade 11: 13 students (10 boys, 3 girls); Grade 12: 18 students (13 boys, 5 girls); Postgraduate: 3 students (3 boys).

Faculty School total: 12. In upper school: 2 men, 5 women; 5 have advanced degrees.

Subjects Offered Algebra, American government, American history, biology, calculus, chemistry, economics, English, French, geometry, marine biology, physical science, physics, pre-algebra, pre-calculus, probability and statistics, SAT preparation, Spanish, world geography, world history.

Graduation Requirements Algebra, American government, American history, biology, chemistry, economics, English, geometry, mathematics, physical education (includes health), physical science, science, social studies (includes history), world history.

Special Academic Programs Honors section; ESL (12 students enrolled).

College Admission Counseling 17 students graduated in 2016; all went to college, including Rice University; The University of Arizona; The University of Tampa; University of California, Los Angeles; University of Mississippi; Xavier University.

Student Life Upper grades have uniform requirement, student council, honor system. Discipline rests primarily with faculty.

Summer Programs Remediation, enrichment, advancement, ESL, sports, art/fine arts programs offered; session focuses on academics; held on campus; accepts boys and girls; open to students from other schools. 8 students usually enrolled. 2017 schedule: June 16 to August 18. Application deadline: May 25.

Tuition and Aid Day student tuition: $16,885; 7-day tuition and room/board: $32,885. Tuition installment plan (individually arranged payment plans). Tuition reduction for siblings available.

Admissions Traditional secondary-level entrance grade is 12. For fall 2016, 60 students applied for upper-level admission, 51 were accepted, 46 enrolled. Deadline for receipt of application materials: none. Application fee required: $50. Interview recommended.

Athletics 28 coaches, 3 athletic trainers.

Computers Computers are regularly used in English, foreign language, history, mathematics, science classes. Computer network features include on-campus library services, online commercial services, Internet access, wireless campus network, Internet filtering or blocking technology, RenWeb. Student e-mail accounts and computer access in designated common areas are available to students. Students grades are available online. The school has a published electronic and media policy.

Contact Ms. Donna Claggett, Administrative Manager. 813-907-4515. Fax: 813-991-4713. E-mail: dclaggett@saddlebrook.com. Website: www.saddlebrookprep.com

SAGE HILL SCHOOL

20402 Newport Coast Drive
Newport Coast, California 92657-0300

Head of School: Ms. Patricia Merz

General Information Coeducational day college-preparatory school. Grades 9–12. Founded: 2000. Setting: suburban. Nearest major city is Newport Beach. 30-acre campus. 7 buildings on campus. Approved or accredited by California Association of Independent Schools, Western Association of Schools and Colleges, and California Department of Education. Member of National Association of Independent Schools. Endowment: $16.2 million. Total enrollment: 521. Upper school average class size: 16. Upper school faculty-student ratio: 1:10. There are 162 required school days per year for Upper School students. Upper School students typically attend 5 days per week. The average school day consists of 6 hours and 20 minutes.

Upper School Student Profile Grade 9: 142 students (67 boys, 75 girls); Grade 10: 136 students (71 boys, 65 girls); Grade 11: 122 students (59 boys, 63 girls); Grade 12: 118 students (61 boys, 57 girls).

Faculty School total: 52. In upper school: 26 men, 25 women; 29 have advanced degrees.

Subjects Offered Advanced biology, advanced chemistry, advanced math, Advanced Placement courses, algebra, American history, American history-AP, art, athletics, biology, biology-AP, British literature, calculus, calculus-AP, ceramics, chemistry, chemistry-AP, Chinese, choral music, computer science-AP, dance, dance performance, digital art, economics-AP, engineering, English, English literature and composition-AP, English-AP, environmental science-AP, forensics, French, geometry, honors algebra, honors English, honors geometry, instrumental music, international relations, Latin, modern dance, modern world history, music, music theory-AP, physical science, physics-AP, pre-calculus, psychology, psychology-AP, science research, Spanish, Spanish-AP, statistics-AP, studio art-AP, theater, theater design and production, U.S. history, U.S. history-AP, United States government-AP, wind ensemble.

Graduation Requirements American history, art, arts, English, foreign language, history, languages, mathematics, physical education (includes health), science.

Special Academic Programs 20 Advanced Placement exams for which test preparation is offered; honors section; independent study; academic accommodation for the gifted, the musically talented, and the artistically talented.

College Admission Counseling 125 students graduated in 2016; all went to college, including Chapman University; New York University; Stanford University; University of California, Berkeley; University of California, Los Angeles; University of Southern California. Mean SAT critical reading: 653, mean SAT math: 676, mean SAT writing: 665, mean combined SAT: 1994, mean composite ACT: 30.

Student Life Upper grades have specified standards of dress, student council, honor system. Discipline rests equally with students and faculty.

Summer Programs Remediation, enrichment, advancement, sports, art/fine arts programs offered; session focuses on academics; held on campus; accepts boys and girls; open to students from other schools. 513 students usually enrolled. 2017 schedule: June to July.

Tuition and Aid Day student tuition: $35,960. Tuition installment plan (SMART Tuition Payment Plan, monthly payment plans). Need-based scholarship grants available. In 2016–17, 13% of upper-school students received aid. Total amount of financial aid awarded in 2016–17: $2,093,974.

Admissions Traditional secondary-level entrance grade is 9. ISEE required. Deadline for receipt of application materials: February 15. Application fee required: $100. On-campus interview recommended.

Athletics Interscholastic: baseball (boys), basketball (b,g), cross-country running (b,g), diving (b,g), football (b), golf (b,g), lacrosse (b,g), soccer (b,g), swimming and diving (b,g), tennis (b,g), track and field (b,g), volleyball (b,g), water polo (b);

intramural: sand volleyball (g); coed interscholastic: yoga; coed intramural: equestrian sports, strength & conditioning. 2 PE instructors, 51 coaches, 1 athletic trainer.

Computers Computers are regularly used in computer applications, digital applications, video film production classes. Computer network features include on-campus library services, online commercial services, Internet access, wireless campus network, Internet filtering or blocking technology. Student e-mail accounts and computer access in designated common areas are available to students. Students grades are available online. The school has a published electronic and media policy.

Contact Mrs. Tina McDaniel, Admission Coordinator. 949-219-1337. Fax: 949-219-1399. E-mail: mcdanielt@sagehillschool.org. Website: www.sagehillschool.org

SAGE RIDGE SCHOOL

2515 Crossbow Court
Reno, Nevada 89511

Head of School: Mr. Norm Colb

General Information Coeducational day college-preparatory, arts, and technology school. Grades 5–12. Founded: 1997. Setting: suburban. 44-acre campus. 2 buildings on campus. Approved or accredited by Northwest Association of Independent Schools and Nevada Department of Education. Member of National Association of Independent Schools. Total enrollment: 220. Upper school average class size: 15. Upper school faculty-student ratio: 1:8. There are 180 required school days per year for Upper School students. Upper School students typically attend 5 days per week. The average school day consists of 7 hours and 10 minutes.

Upper School Student Profile Grade 9: 21 students (11 boys, 10 girls); Grade 10: 18 students (9 boys, 9 girls); Grade 11: 31 students (17 boys, 14 girls); Grade 12: 28 students (13 boys, 15 girls).

Faculty School total: 32. In upper school: 8 men, 8 women; 9 have advanced degrees.

Subjects Offered Advanced chemistry, algebra, American history-AP, American literature, American literature-AP, analytic geometry, anatomy and physiology, ancient world history, art history, biology, biology-AP, British literature, British literature-AP, calculus, calculus-AP, ceramics, chemistry, choir, classical language, college counseling, conceptual physics, creative writing, debate, drama performance, electives, English language and composition-AP, English language-AP, English literature and composition-AP, English literature-AP, European history, European literature, foreign language, geometry, honors algebra, honors English, lab science, language-AP, Latin, Latin-AP, medieval history, modern European history, music history, music performance, music theory, outdoor education, philosophy, physical education, physical fitness, physics, playwriting and directing, poetry, pre-algebra, pre-calculus, probability and statistics, public speaking, senior internship, senior seminar, senior thesis, Spanish, Spanish language-AP, Spanish literature, Spanish literature-AP, Spanish-AP, statistics, studio art, studio art-AP, theater, theater arts, theater history, theory of knowledge, trigonometry, U.S. government and politics-AP, U.S. history, U.S. history-AP, Western literature, world history.

Graduation Requirements 20th century world history, algebra, American history, American literature, analytic geometry, ancient world history, art history, biology, British literature, chemistry, conceptual physics, English composition, European history, foreign language, history of music, modern European history, music, outdoor education, participation in sports, pre-calculus, public speaking, science, senior internship, senior thesis, speech, theater history, trigonometry, U.S. history, 15 hours of community service per year, senior thesis and senior internship, two mini-semester seminars per year.

Special Academic Programs 16 Advanced Placement exams for which test preparation is offered; honors section; independent study; ESL (5 students enrolled).

College Admission Counseling 14 students graduated in 2015; all went to college, including Boston College; Emory University; New York University; Stanford University; University of San Diego; University of Southern California. Mean SAT critical reading: 609, mean SAT math: 604, mean SAT writing: 644, mean combined SAT: 1857, mean composite ACT: 27.

Student Life Upper grades have uniform requirement, student council, honor system. Discipline rests equally with students and faculty.

Tuition and Aid Day student tuition: $20,300. Tuition installment plan (Insured Tuition Payment Plan). Need-based scholarship grants available. In 2015–16, 13% of upper-school students received aid. Total amount of financial aid awarded in 2015–16: $179,225.

Admissions Traditional secondary-level entrance grade is 9. ISEE required. Deadline for receipt of application materials: none. Application fee required: $50. Interview required.

Athletics Interscholastic: alpine skiing (boys, girls), basketball (b,g), cross-country running (b,g), golf (b), skiing (downhill) (b,g), track and field (b,g), volleyball (g), wrestling (b,g); intramural: alpine skiing (b,g), basketball (b,g), cross-country running (b,g), golf (b,g), skiing (downhill) (b,g), swimming and diving (b,g), track and field (b,g), volleyball (g); coed intramural: bicycling, Frisbee, lacrosse, outdoor education, ropes courses, soccer. 2 PE instructors, 13 coaches.

Computers Computers are regularly used in art, classics, college planning, current events, English, foreign language, history, humanities, independent study, Latin, literary magazine, mathematics, newspaper, publications, SAT preparation, science, senior seminar, social sciences, social studies, Spanish, speech, word processing, writing, yearbook classes. Computer network features include on-campus library services, online commercial services, Internet access, wireless campus network, Internet filtering or blocking technology. Student e-mail accounts are available to students. Students grades are available online. The school has a published electronic and media policy.

Contact Ms. Kendra Moore, Director of Admissions. 775-852-6222 Ext. 509. Fax: 775-852-6228. E-mail: kmoore@sageridge.org. Website: www.sageridge.org

SAINT AGNES ACADEMIC HIGH SCHOOL

13-20 124th Street

College Point, New York 11356

General Information Girls' day college-preparatory and general academic school, affiliated with Roman Catholic Church. Approved or accredited by New York Department of Education. Upper school average class size: 350.

Student Life Attendance at religious services is required.

Admissions Deadline for receipt of application materials: none. No application fee required.

Contact 718-353-6276. Fax: 718-353-6068. Website: http://www.stagneshs.org/

ST. AGNES ACADEMY

9000 Bellaire Boulevard

Houston, Texas 77036

Head of School: Sr. Jane Meyer

General Information Girls' day college-preparatory school, affiliated with Roman Catholic Church. Grades 9–12. Founded: 1906. Setting: urban. 33-acre campus. 3 buildings on campus. Approved or accredited by Southern Association of Colleges and Schools, Texas Catholic Conference, and Texas Department of Education. Endowment: $12 million. Total enrollment: 899. Upper school average class size: 19. Upper school faculty-student ratio: 1:12. There are 180 required school days per year for Upper School students. Upper School students typically attend 5 days per week. The average school day consists of 6 hours and 50 minutes.

Upper School Student Profile Grade 9: 239 students (239 girls); Grade 10: 228 students (228 girls); Grade 11: 228 students (228 girls); Grade 12: 226 students (226 girls). 72% of students are Roman Catholic.

Faculty School total: 104. In upper school: 21 men, 72 women; 62 have advanced degrees.

Subjects Offered Accounting, acting, advanced biology, advanced chemistry, advanced math, Advanced Placement courses, aerobics, algebra, American history, American history-AP, American literature, American literature-AP, anatomy and physiology, applied music, art, art history, athletics, band, biology, biology-AP, British literature-AP, business law, business skills, calculus, calculus-AP, chamber groups, chemistry, Chinese, choral music, community service, computer programming, computer science, computer science-AP, creative writing, dance, digital photography, drama, drawing, economics, English, English literature, environmental science-AP, European history, fine arts, fitness, French, geology, geometry, government-AP, government/civics, graphic design, health, health and wellness, history, integrated physics, journalism, keyboarding, Latin, marine biology, mathematics, music, philosophy, photography, physical education, physics, physiology, psychology, religion, science, social sciences, social studies, Spanish, speech, theater, theology, trigonometry, video film production, world history, world literature.

Graduation Requirements Advanced Placement courses, arts and fine arts (art, music, dance, drama), computer science, electives, English, foreign language, mathematics, physical education (includes health), religion (includes Bible studies and theology), science, social sciences, social studies (includes history), speech, 100 hours of community service.

Special Academic Programs Advanced Placement exam preparation; honors section; independent study.

College Admission Counseling 223 students graduated in 2016; 222 went to college, including Baylor University; Louisiana State University and Agricultural & Mechanical College; Texas A&M University; The University of Texas at Austin; The University of Texas at San Antonio. Other: 1 went to work. Mean SAT critical reading: 630, mean SAT math: 640, mean composite ACT: 29. 50% scored over 26 on composite ACT.

Student Life Upper grades have uniform requirement, student council, honor system. Discipline rests primarily with faculty. Attendance at religious services is required.

Summer Programs Remediation, art/fine arts, computer instruction programs offered; session focuses on remediation and elective credit; held on campus; accepts girls; not open to students from other schools. 100 students usually enrolled. 2017 schedule: June to June.

Tuition and Aid Day student tuition: $17,950. Tuition installment plan (plans arranged through local bank). Merit scholarship grants, need-based scholarship grants available. In 2016–17, 30% of upper-school students received aid; total upper-school merit-scholarship money awarded: $24,000. Total amount of financial aid awarded in 2016–17: $1,400,000.

Admissions Traditional secondary-level entrance grade is 9. For fall 2016, 563 students applied for upper-level admission, 311 were accepted, 239 enrolled. ISEE required. Deadline for receipt of application materials: December 15. Application fee required: $75.

Athletics Interscholastic: aquatics, basketball, cheering, cross-country running, dance team, diving, field hockey, golf, lacrosse, soccer, softball, swimming and diving, tennis, track and field, volleyball, water polo, winter soccer; intramural: badminton, floor hockey, strength & conditioning, volleyball, yoga. 6 PE instructors, 14 coaches, 1 athletic trainer.

Computers Computers are regularly used in all classes. Computer network features include on-campus library services, online commercial services, Internet access, wireless campus network, Internet filtering or blocking technology. Campus intranet and student e-mail accounts are available to students. Students grades are available online. The school has a published electronic and media policy.

Contact Maddy Echols, Associate Admission Director. 713-219-5400. Fax: 713-219-5499. E-mail: maddy.echols@st-agnes.org. Website: www.st-agnes.org

SAINT AGNES ACADEMY–ST. DOMINIC SCHOOL

4830 Walnut Grove Road

Memphis, Tennessee 38117

Head of School: Mr. Thomas G. Hood

General Information Coeducational day college-preparatory and music school, affiliated with Roman Catholic Church. Boys grades PK–8, girls grades PK–12. Founded: 1851. Setting: suburban. 25-acre campus. 3 buildings on campus. Approved or accredited by Southern Association of Colleges and Schools, distance education, and Tennessee Department of Education. Member of National Association of Independent Schools. Endowment: $6 million. Total enrollment: 847. Upper school average class size: 15. Upper school faculty-student ratio: 1:8. There are 178 required school days per year for Upper School students. Upper School students typically attend 5 days per week. The average school day consists of 7 hours and 15 minutes.

Upper School Student Profile Grade 9: 108 students (108 girls); Grade 10: 78 students (78 girls); Grade 11: 86 students (86 girls); Grade 12: 87 students (87 girls). 63% of students are Roman Catholic.

Faculty School total: 42. In upper school: 7 men, 35 women; 27 have advanced degrees.

Subjects Offered Advanced Placement courses, algebra, American history, anatomy, art, arts, biology, calculus-AP, chemistry, computer science, drama, English, environmental science, fine arts, French, German, government/civics, health, journalism, mathematics, music, physical education, physical science, physics, psychology, religion, science, social sciences, social studies, Spanish, theater, trigonometry, world history.

Graduation Requirements Arts and fine arts (art, music, dance, drama), computer science, English, etymology, foreign language, mathematics, physical education (includes health), religion (includes Bible studies and theology), science, social sciences, social studies (includes history).

Special Academic Programs Advanced Placement exam preparation; honors section; study at local college for college credit; academic accommodation for the gifted and the artistically talented.

College Admission Counseling 87 students graduated in 2016; all went to college, including Mississippi State University; The University of Tennessee; University of Arkansas; University of Mississippi. Median SAT critical reading: 580, median SAT math: 555, median composite ACT: 26.

Student Life Upper grades have uniform requirement, student council, honor system. Discipline rests primarily with faculty. Attendance at religious services is required.

Summer Programs Remediation, enrichment, computer instruction programs offered; held on campus; accepts boys and girls; open to students from other schools. 35 students usually enrolled. 2017 schedule: June 5 to July 28. Application deadline: April 30.

Tuition and Aid Day student tuition: $15,975. Tuition installment plan (Insured Tuition Payment Plan, FACTS Tuition Payment Plan, monthly payment plans, individually arranged payment plans, 2- or 8-payment plans). Merit scholarship grants, need-based scholarship grants available. In 2016–17, 37% of upper-school students received aid.

Admissions Traditional secondary-level entrance grade is 9. High School Placement Test and ISEE required. Deadline for receipt of application materials: none. Application fee required: $75. On-campus interview recommended.

Athletics Interscholastic: basketball, bowling, cheering, cross-country running, golf, lacrosse, soccer, softball, swimming and diving, tennis, track and field, trap and skeet, volleyball. 2 PE instructors, 5 coaches, 1 athletic trainer.

Computers Computers are regularly used in all classes. Computer network features include on-campus library services, Internet access, wireless campus network, Internet filtering or blocking technology. Campus intranet and student e-mail accounts are available to students. Students grades are available online.

Contact Mrs. Jean Skorupa-Moore, Director of Upper School Admissions. 901-435-5858. Fax: 901-435-5866. E-mail: jmoore@saa-sds.org. Website: www.saa-sds.org

ST. ALBANS SCHOOL

Mount Saint Alban
Washington, District of Columbia 20016

Head of School: Mr. Vance Wilson

General Information Boys' boarding and day college-preparatory school, affiliated with Episcopal Church. Boarding grades 9–12, day grades 4–12. Founded: 1909. Setting: urban. Students are housed in coed dormitories. 54-acre campus. 7 buildings on campus. Approved or accredited by Association of Independent Maryland Schools, Association of Independent Schools of Greater Washington, The Association of Boarding Schools, and District of Columbia Department of Education. Member of National Association of Independent Schools and Secondary School Admission Test Board. Endowment: $64.6 million. Total enrollment: 593. Upper school average class size: 13. Upper school faculty-student ratio: 1:7. There are 175 required school days per year for Upper School students. Upper School students typically attend 5 days per week. The average school day consists of 9 hours and 30 minutes.

Upper School Student Profile Grade 9: 84 students (84 boys); Grade 10: 82 students (82 boys); Grade 11: 80 students (80 boys); Grade 12: 77 students (77 boys). 9% of students are boarding students. 47% are state residents. 5 states are represented in upper school student body. 2% are international students. International students from China and Somalia; 2 other countries represented in student body. 20% of students are members of Episcopal Church.

Faculty School total: 80. In upper school: 49 men, 21 women; 45 have advanced degrees; 6 reside on campus.

Subjects Offered Advanced Placement courses, algebra, American history, American literature, Ancient Greek, art, art history, art history-AP, Bible studies, biology, biotechnology, calculus, ceramics, chemistry, Chinese, community service, computer math, computer programming, computer science, creative writing, dance, directing, drama, earth science, economics, engineering, English, English literature, ethics, European history, expository writing, filmmaking, fine arts, French, geography, geology, geometry, government/civics, Greek, history, Japanese, Latin, marine biology, mathematics, music, photography, physical education, physics, religion, science, sculpture, social studies, Spanish, speech, stagecraft, theater, zoology.

Graduation Requirements American history, ancient history, arts and fine arts (art, music, dance, drama), English, ethics, foreign language, mathematics, physical education (includes health), religious studies, science, participation in athletic program, participation in community service. Community service is required.

Special Academic Programs Advanced Placement exam preparation; honors section; independent study; term-away projects; study abroad.

College Admission Counseling 83 students graduated in 2016; all went to college, including Columbia University; Harvard University; Indiana University Bloomington; The George Washington University; University of Chicago; University of Miami. Other: 1 entered military service.

Student Life Upper grades have specified standards of dress, student council, honor system. Discipline rests equally with students and faculty. Attendance at religious services is required.

Summer Programs Remediation, enrichment, advancement, ESL, sports, art/fine arts, rigorous outdoor training, computer instruction programs offered; session focuses on academics, day camp, and sports camps; held on campus; accepts boys and girls; open to students from other schools. 1,500 students usually enrolled. 2017 schedule: June 8 to August 21. Application deadline: none.

Tuition and Aid Day student tuition: $42,484; 7-day tuition and room/board: $59,892. Tuition installment plan (Insured Tuition Payment Plan, monthly payment plans, individually arranged payment plans). Need-based scholarship grants, need-based loans available. In 2016–17, 24% of upper-school students received aid. Total amount of financial aid awarded in 2016–17: $4,034,535.

Admissions Traditional secondary-level entrance grade is 9. For fall 2016, 177 students applied for upper-level admission, 34 were accepted, 25 enrolled. Admissions testing, ISEE or SSAT required. Deadline for receipt of application materials: January 8. Application fee required: $80. Interview recommended.

Athletics Interscholastic: aquatics, baseball, basketball, canoeing/kayaking, climbing, crew, cross-country running, diving, football, golf, ice hockey, independent competitive sports, indoor soccer, indoor track, indoor track & field, kayaking, lacrosse, rappelling, rock climbing, soccer, swimming and diving, tennis, track and field, wall climbing, weight training, winter (indoor) track, winter soccer, wrestling; intramural: aquatics, basketball, combined training, dance, fitness, indoor soccer, outdoor activities, paddling, physical training, running, tennis, track and field, weight lifting, yoga. 5 coaches, 2 athletic trainers.

Computers Computers are regularly used in all academic, mathematics, programming, science classes. Computer network features include on-campus library services, online commercial services, Internet access, wireless campus network. Campus intranet and student e-mail accounts are available to students. The school has a published electronic and media policy.

Contact Ms. Lily Fardshisheh, Admissions and Financial Aid Coordinator. 202-537-6440. Fax: 202-537-2225. E-mail: lfardshisheh@stalbansschool.org.
Website: www.stalbansschool.org/

SAINT ALBERT JUNIOR-SENIOR HIGH SCHOOL

400 Gleason Avenue
Council Bluffs, Iowa 51503

Head of School: Mr. David M. Schweitzer

General Information Coeducational day college-preparatory school, affiliated with Roman Catholic Church. Boarding grades 6–12, day grades PK–12. Distance learning grades 6–12. Founded: 1963. Setting: suburban. Nearest major city is Omaha, NE. Students are housed in Host family arrangements for international students. 36-acre campus. 1 building on campus. Approved or accredited by North Central Association of Colleges and Schools and Iowa Department of Education. Endowment: $2.4 million. Total enrollment: 720. Upper school average class size: 20. Upper school faculty-student ratio: 1:11. There are 176 required school days per year for Upper School students. Upper School students typically attend 5 days per week. The average school day consists of 7 hours.

Upper School Student Profile Grade 6: 45 students (20 boys, 25 girls); Grade 7: 46 students (26 boys, 20 girls); Grade 8: 56 students (32 boys, 24 girls); Grade 9: 45 students (24 boys, 21 girls); Grade 10: 43 students (23 boys, 20 girls); Grade 11: 55 students (26 boys, 29 girls); Grade 12: 46 students (20 boys, 26 girls). 5% of students are boarding students. 90% are state residents. 2 states are represented in upper school student body. 5% are international students. International students from China, Germany, Mexico, Thailand, and Viet Nam. 85% of students are Roman Catholic.

Faculty School total: 32. In upper school: 12 men, 20 women; 20 have advanced degrees.

Subjects Offered All academic.

Graduation Requirements World religions, annual community service requirements for grades 9-12.

Special Academic Programs 9 Advanced Placement exams for which test preparation is offered; honors section; study at local college for college credit; academic accommodation for the gifted; remedial reading and/or remedial writing; remedial math; programs in English, mathematics for dyslexic students; special instructional classes for deaf students; ESL (26 students enrolled).

College Admission Counseling 50 students graduated in 2016; 47 went to college, including Iowa State University of Science and Technology; Northwest Missouri State University; The University of Iowa; University of Nebraska–Lincoln; University of Nebraska at Omaha; University of Northern Iowa. Other: 2 went to work, 1 entered military service. Median composite ACT: 23. 35% scored over 26 on composite ACT.

Student Life Upper grades have uniform requirement, student council. Discipline rests primarily with faculty. Attendance at religious services is required.

Summer Programs Remediation, sports programs offered; session focuses on learning recovery, dance, cheer, and athletic strength and conditioning; held on campus; accepts boys and girls; not open to students from other schools. 120 students usually enrolled. 2017 schedule: June 1 to August 15.

Tuition and Aid Day student tuition: $6400–$8200. Tuition installment plan (FACTS Tuition Payment Plan, monthly payment plans, individually arranged payment plans). Tuition reduction for siblings, merit scholarship grants, need-based scholarship grants, paying campus jobs, free and reducted meals for qualifying students available. In 2016–17, 35% of upper-school students received aid; total upper-school merit-scholarship money awarded: $17,500. Total amount of financial aid awarded in 2016–17: $390,000.

Admissions Traditional secondary-level entrance grade is 9. For fall 2016, 32 students applied for upper-level admission, 30 were accepted, 28 enrolled. Deadline for receipt of application materials: none. No application fee required. Interview recommended.

Athletics Interscholastic: baseball (boys), basketball (b,g), bowling (b,g), cheering (b,g), cross-country running (b,g), dance (g), dance squad (g), dance team (g), football (b), golf (b,g), soccer (b,g), softball (g), swimming and diving (b,g), tennis (b,g), track and field (b,g), wrestling (b). 2 PE instructors, 53 coaches, 1 athletic trainer.

Computers Computers are regularly used in all classes. Computer network features include on-campus library services, Internet access, wireless campus network, Internet filtering or blocking technology, laptop computers provided for 6-8th grade students, laptop computers provided in classrooms for grades 3-5, access to tablet computers provided in k-2nd grade. Campus intranet and student e-mail accounts are available to students. Students grades are available online. The school has a published electronic and media policy.

Contact Mrs. JoAnn Jensen, Director of Admissions and Community Relations. 712-328-2316 Ext. 310. Fax: 712-328-8316. E-mail: jensenj@saintalbertschools.org. Website: www.saintalbertschools.org/

ST. ANDREW'S EPISCOPAL SCHOOL

8804 Postoak Road
Potomac, Maryland 20854

Head of School: Mr. Robert Kosasky

General Information Coeducational day college-preparatory school, affiliated with Episcopal Church. Grades PS–12. Founded: 1978. Setting: suburban. Nearest major city is Washington, DC. 19-acre campus. 5 buildings on campus. Approved or accredited by Association of Independent Maryland Schools, Association of Independent Schools of Greater Washington, and National Association of Episcopal Schools. Member of National Association of Independent Schools and Secondary School Admission Test Board. Endowment: $10 million. Total enrollment: 553. Upper school average class size: 15. Upper school faculty-student ratio: 1:7. There are 172 required school days per year for Upper School students. Upper School students typically attend 5 days per week. The average school day consists of 6 hours and 40 minutes.

Upper School Student Profile Grade 6: 27 students (18 boys, 9 girls); Grade 7: 37 students (21 boys, 16 girls); Grade 8: 51 students (25 boys, 26 girls); Grade 9: 71 students (40 boys, 31 girls); Grade 10: 78 students (33 boys, 45 girls); Grade 11: 90 students (49 boys, 41 girls); Grade 12: 78 students (40 boys, 38 girls). 15% of students are members of Episcopal Church.

Faculty School total: 66. In upper school: 23 men, 24 women; 27 have advanced degrees.

Subjects Offered 20th century history, 3-dimensional art, 3-dimensional design, acting, Advanced Placement courses, advanced studio art-AP, algebra, American history, American literature, art, art history, art history-AP, art-AP, athletics, band, Bible, biology, biology-AP, British literature, calculus, calculus-AP, ceramics, chemistry, Chinese studies, chorus, civics, college counseling, composition-AP, computer animation, computer art, computer graphics, computer science, creative writing, dance, digital photography, drama, dramatic arts, earth science, English, English literature, English literature and composition-AP, English-AP, ethics, European history, fine arts, French, French language-AP, French literature-AP, geography, geometry, global studies, government/civics, guitar, health, history, instrumental music, jazz band, journalism, Latin, Latin American studies, Latin-AP, mathematics, modern European history, music, musical theater, newspaper, orchestra, organic biochemistry, painting, photography, physical education, physical science, physics, physics-AP, pre-algebra, pre-calculus, public speaking, religion, robotics, science, service learning/internship, Spanish, Spanish language-AP, Spanish literature-AP, Spanish-AP, sports, stage design, statistics, student publications, studio art, studio art-AP, theater, theater design and production, theology, trigonometry, U.S. history, U.S. history-AP, video, visual and performing arts, vocal music, world cultures, world history, world religions, writing, yearbook.

Graduation Requirements English, foreign language, history, mathematics, performing arts, physical education (includes health), religion (includes Bible studies and theology), science, senior thesis, visual arts. Community service is required.

Special Academic Programs Advanced Placement exam preparation; honors section; independent study; academic accommodation for the gifted; special instructional classes for deaf students.

College Admission Counseling 61 students graduated in 2016; all went to college, including Brown University; Cornell University; Dartmouth College; Georgetown University; Stanford University; Williams College.

Student Life Upper grades have specified standards of dress, student council, honor system. Discipline rests primarily with faculty. Attendance at religious services is required.

Summer Programs Enrichment, advancement, sports, art/fine arts, computer instruction programs offered; session focuses on advancement and enrichment; held both on and off campus; accepts boys and girls; open to students from other schools. 2,000 students usually enrolled. 2017 schedule: June 20 to August 5. Application deadline: none.

Tuition and Aid Day student tuition: $39,490. Tuition installment plan (FACTS Tuition Payment Plan, monthly payment plans). Need-based scholarship grants available. In 2016–17, 25% of upper-school students received aid. Total amount of financial aid awarded in 2016–17: $2,708,400.

Admissions Traditional secondary-level entrance grade is 9. ISEE or SSAT required. Deadline for receipt of application materials: January 13. Application fee required: $50. On-campus interview recommended.

Athletics Interscholastic: baseball (boys), basketball (b,g), cross-country running (b,g), lacrosse (b,g), soccer (b,g), softball (g), tennis (b,g), volleyball (g); coed interscholastic: equestrian sports, golf, indoor track & field, track and field, wrestling; coed intramural: dance, fitness, physical fitness, strength & conditioning, weight training, winter (indoor) track, yoga. 12 coaches, 1 athletic trainer.

Computers Computers are regularly used in all classes. Computer network features include on-campus library services, online commercial services, Internet access, wireless campus network, Internet filtering or blocking technology, one-to-one technology program. Campus intranet, student e-mail accounts, and computer access in designated common areas are available to students. Students grades are available online. The school has a published electronic and media policy.

Contact Mrs. Aileen Moodie, Associate Director of Admission/Admission Office Coordinator. 240-477-1700. Fax: 301-765-8912. E-mail: admission@saes.org. Website: www.saes.org

ST. ANDREW'S EPISCOPAL SCHOOL

370 Old Agency Road
Ridgeland, Mississippi 39157

Head of School: Dr. George D. Penick Jr.

General Information Coeducational day college-preparatory, arts, religious studies, technology, and global studies school, affiliated with Episcopal Church. Grades PK–12. Founded: 1947. Setting: suburban. Nearest major city is Jackson. 108-acre campus. 12 buildings on campus. Approved or accredited by National Association of Episcopal Schools, Southern Association of Colleges and Schools, and Southern Association of Independent Schools. Member of National Association of Independent Schools.

Endowment: $8 million. Total enrollment: 1,217. Upper school average class size: 18. Upper school faculty-student ratio: 1:9. Upper School students typically attend 5 days per week. The average school day consists of 7 hours and 30 minutes.

Upper School Student Profile Grade 9: 77 students (31 boys, 46 girls); Grade 10: 93 students (43 boys, 50 girls); Grade 11: 90 students (40 boys, 50 girls); Grade 12: 86 students (42 boys, 44 girls). 29% of students are members of Episcopal Church.

Faculty School total: 138. In upper school: 21 men, 23 women; 32 have advanced degrees.

Subjects Offered 3-dimensional design, algebra, American history, American literature, art, art history-AP, astronomy, biology, biology-AP, calculus, calculus-AP, chemistry, chemistry-AP, community service, computer programming, computers, creative writing, drama, driver education, engineering, English, English literature, English literature-AP, English-AP, European history, European literature, film, French, French language-AP, freshman seminar, geometry, government-AP, government/civics, grammar, history-AP, honors algebra, honors English, honors geometry, honors U.S. history, international studies, Latin, Latin-AP, literature-AP, Mandarin, mathematics, modern European history, music, physics, physics-AP, probability and statistics, psychology, Spanish, Spanish language-AP, speech, speech and debate, studio art-AP, theater arts, U.S. government and politics-AP, U.S. history-AP, visual arts, world history, world literature.

Graduation Requirements Arts and fine arts (art, music, dance, drama), English, foreign language, mathematics, science, social studies (includes history), speech, 100 community service hours. Community service is required.

Special Academic Programs Advanced Placement exam preparation; honors section; study abroad; academic accommodation for the gifted, the musically talented, and the artistically talented.

College Admission Counseling 85 students graduated in 2015; all went to college, including Harvard University; Millsaps College; Mississippi State University; Southern Methodist University; University of Mississippi; Vanderbilt University. Mean SAT critical reading: 657, mean SAT math: 626, mean SAT writing: 665, mean combined SAT: 1948, mean composite ACT: 30.

Student Life Upper grades have specified standards of dress, student council, honor system. Discipline rests equally with students and faculty. Attendance at religious services is required.

Tuition and Aid Day student tuition: $16,480. Tuition installment plan (monthly payment plans, individually arranged payment plans, semester payment plan). Tuition reduction for siblings, merit scholarship grants, need-based scholarship grants available. In 2015–16, 21% of upper-school students received aid; total upper-school merit-scholarship money awarded: $104,509. Total amount of financial aid awarded in 2015–16: $300,000.

Admissions Traditional secondary-level entrance grade is 9. For fall 2015, 38 students applied for upper-level admission, 30 were accepted, 23 enrolled. ERB Reading and Math, PSAT, SAT, or ACT for applicants to grade 11 and 12 or writing sample required. Deadline for receipt of application materials: none. Application fee required: $35. On-campus interview required.

Athletics Interscholastic: baseball (boys), basketball (b,g), bowling (b,g), cross-country running (b,g), dance squad (g), dance team (g), fitness (b,g), football (b), golf (b,g), lacrosse (b), power lifting (b,g), running (b,g), soccer (b,g), softball (g), swimming and diving (b,g), tennis (b,g), track and field (b,g), volleyball (g); coed interscholastic: archery, cheering, physical fitness, physical training, weight training, yoga; coed intramural: equestrian sports. 10 coaches.

Computers Computers are regularly used in all academic, college planning, geography, journalism, newspaper, theater, yearbook classes. Computer network features include on-campus library services, online commercial services, Internet access, wireless campus network, Internet filtering or blocking technology, laptop requirement for all students in grades 9 through 12. Student e-mail accounts and computer access in designated common areas are available to students. Students grades are available online. The school has a published electronic and media policy.

Contact Mrs. Mary Purvis, Director of Admissions. 601-853-6042. Fax: 601-853-6001. E-mail: purvism@gosaints.org. Website: www.gosaints.org

SAINT ANDREW'S EPISCOPAL SCHOOL

5901 West 31st Street
Austin, Texas 78705-1902

Head of School: Mr. Sean Murphy

General Information Coeducational day college-preparatory school, affiliated with Episcopal Church. Grades K–12. Founded: 1952. Setting: suburban. 140-acre campus. 10 buildings on campus. Approved or accredited by National Association of Episcopal Schools and Texas Department of Education. Member of National Association of Independent Schools and Secondary School Admission Test Board. Languages of instruction: English, Mandarin, and Spanish. Upper school average class size: 13. Upper school faculty-student ratio: 1:10.

Upper School Student Profile 30% of students are members of Episcopal Church.

College Admission Counseling 103 students graduated in 2016; all went to college.

Student Life Upper grades have specified standards of dress, student council, honor system. Discipline rests equally with students and faculty. Attendance at religious services is required.

Admissions Traditional secondary-level entrance grade is 9.
Contact Ms. Priscilla Lund, Director of Enrollment Management and Financial Aid. 512-299-9846. Fax: 512-892-3589. Website: www.sasaustin.org/default.aspx

ST. ANDREW'S REGIONAL HIGH SCHOOL

880 Mckenzie Avenue
Victoria, British Columbia V8X 3G5, Canada
Head of School: Mr. Andrew Keleher

General Information Coeducational day college-preparatory, general academic, and religious studies school, affiliated with Roman Catholic Church. Grades 8–12. Founded: 1983. Setting: urban. 2-acre campus. 1 building on campus. Approved or accredited by British Columbia Department of Education. Language of instruction: English. Total enrollment: 335. Upper school average class size: 24. Upper school faculty-student ratio: 1:14. There are 178 required school days per year for Upper School students. Upper School students typically attend 5 days per week. The average school day consists of 5 hours.
Upper School Student Profile 65% of students are Roman Catholic.
Faculty School total: 25. In upper school: 11 men, 13 women; 12 have advanced degrees.
Subjects Offered Advanced Placement courses, religious education.
Graduation Requirements Religious studies.
Special Academic Programs 2 Advanced Placement exams for which test preparation is offered; honors section.
College Admission Counseling 72 students graduated in 2015; 45 went to college, including University of Victoria. Other: 20 went to work, 7 had other specific plans.
Student Life Upper grades have uniform requirement, student council, honor system. Discipline rests primarily with faculty. Attendance at religious services is required.
Tuition and Aid Day student tuition: CAN$7608. Tuition installment plan (monthly payment plans). Tuition reduction for siblings, bursaries, merit scholarship grants available. In 2015–16, 15% of upper-school students received aid; total upper-school merit-scholarship money awarded: CAN$25,000. Total amount of financial aid awarded in 2015–16: CAN$100,000.
Admissions Traditional secondary-level entrance grade is 12. For fall 2015, 5 students applied for upper-level admission, 5 were accepted, 5 enrolled. Deadline for receipt of application materials: February 28. Application fee required: CAN$50. Interview required.
Athletics Interscholastic: badminton (boys, girls), basketball (b,g), cross-country running (b,g), golf (b), rowing (b,g), track and field (b,g), volleyball (b,g); intramural: basketball (b,g); coed interscholastic: aquatics, rowing, track and field; coed intramural: dance team, floor hockey, indoor soccer. 4 PE instructors, 2 coaches.
Computers Computers are regularly used in business education, computer applications, digital applications, photography classes. Computer resources include on-campus library services, Internet access, Internet filtering or blocking technology. Student e-mail accounts are available to students. The school has a published electronic and media policy.
Contact Mr. Ciaran McLaverty, Vice Principal. 250-479-1414. Fax: 250-479-5356. E-mail: cmclaverty@cisdv.bc.ca. Website: www.standrewshigh.ca/

ST. ANDREW'S SCHOOL

350 Noxontown Road
Middletown, Delaware 19709
Head of School: Daniel T. Roach

General Information Coeducational boarding college-preparatory, arts, religious studies, and technology school, affiliated with Episcopal Church. Grades 9–12. Founded: 1929. Setting: small town. Nearest major city is Wilmington. Students are housed in single-sex dormitories. 2,100-acre campus. 16 buildings on campus. Approved or accredited by Middle States Association of Colleges and Schools, National Association of Episcopal Schools, The Association of Boarding Schools, The College Board, and Delaware Department of Education. Member of National Association of Independent Schools and Secondary School Admission Test Board. Endowment: $190 million. Total enrollment: 310. Upper school average class size: 11. Upper school faculty-student ratio: 1:5. Upper School students typically attend 6 days per week.
Upper School Student Profile Grade 9: 66 students (34 boys, 32 girls); Grade 10: 83 students (41 boys, 42 girls); Grade 11: 84 students (41 boys, 43 girls); Grade 12: 77 students (42 boys, 35 girls). 100% of students are boarding students. 12% are state residents. 26 states are represented in upper school student body. 17% are international students. International students from Bermuda, China, India, Philippines, Republic of Korea, and Viet Nam; 10 other countries represented in student body. 30% of students are members of Episcopal Church.
Faculty School total: 70. In upper school: 35 men, 35 women; 57 have advanced degrees; all reside on campus.
Subjects Offered 20th century world history, acting, advanced chemistry, advanced math, algebra, American history, American literature, art, art history, art history-AP, Asian history, biology, calculus, calculus-AP, ceramics, chemistry, Chinese, choir, choral music, college counseling, comparative religion, computer literacy, computer programming, concert choir, creative writing, digital music, drama, drawing, driver

education, East Asian history, English, English literature, English literature-AP, environmental science, ethics, European history, European history-AP, film, film studies, fine arts, French, French literature-AP, geometry, Greek, history, honors geometry, improvisation, Islamic history, Latin, Latin-AP, mathematics, Middle Eastern history, modern European history, music, music theory, organic chemistry, painting, philosophy, photography, physics, physics-AP, poetry, pottery, psychology, religion, religious studies, science, science research, Spanish, Spanish literature-AP, speech, statistics-AP, theater, trigonometry, U.S. history, Western religions.
Graduation Requirements Arts and fine arts (art, music, dance, drama), English, foreign language, history, mathematics, religion (includes Bible studies and theology), science.
Special Academic Programs Honors section; independent study; academic accommodation for the gifted, the musically talented, and the artistically talented.
College Admission Counseling 70 students graduated in 2015; 68 went to college, including Davidson College; Duke University; Harvard University; New York University; Wesleyan University; Williams College. Other: 1 entered a postgraduate year, 1 had other specific plans. Mean SAT critical reading: 629, mean SAT math: 651, mean SAT writing: 625.
Student Life Upper grades have specified standards of dress, student council, honor system. Discipline rests equally with students and faculty. Attendance at religious services is required.
Tuition and Aid 7-day tuition and room/board: $55,500. Tuition installment plan (monthly payment plans). Need-based scholarship grants available. In 2015–16, 46% of upper-school students received aid. Total amount of financial aid awarded in 2015–16: $6,066,500.
Admissions Traditional secondary-level entrance grade is 9. For fall 2015, 546 students applied for upper-level admission, 148 were accepted, 90 enrolled. ISEE, SSAT or TOEFL required. Deadline for receipt of application materials: January 15. Application fee required: $60. On-campus interview required.
Athletics Interscholastic: aquatics (boys, girls), baseball (b), basketball (b,g), crew (b,g), cross-country running (b,g), field hockey (g), football (b), lacrosse (b,g), rowing (b,g), soccer (b,g), squash (b,g), swimming and diving (b,g), tennis (b,g), volleyball (g), wrestling (b); coed intramural: aerobics, aerobics/dance, canoeing/kayaking, dance, fencing, fishing, fitness, Frisbee, indoor soccer, kayaking, outdoors, paddle tennis, physical training, rowing, sailboarding, sailing, weight lifting, weight training, windsurfing, yoga. 1 athletic trainer.
Computers Computers are regularly used in English, foreign language, history, mathematics, science classes. Computer network features include on-campus library services, online commercial services, Internet access, wireless campus network, Internet filtering or blocking technology. Campus intranet, student e-mail accounts, and computer access in designated common areas are available to students. The school has a published electronic and media policy.
Contact Louisa H. Zendt, Director of Admission. 302-285-4230. Fax: 302-378-7120. E-mail: lzendt@standrews-de.org. Website: www.standrews-de.org

SAINT ANDREW'S SCHOOL

3900 Jog Road
Boca Raton, Florida 33434
Head of School: Dr. Jim Byer

General Information Coeducational boarding and day college-preparatory school, affiliated with Episcopal Church. Boarding grades 9–12, day grades JK–12. Founded: 1961. Setting: suburban. Nearest major city is West Palm Beach. Students are housed in coed dormitories. 81-acre campus. 18 buildings on campus. Approved or accredited by Florida Council of Independent Schools, Southern Association of Colleges and Schools, The Association of Boarding Schools, and Florida Department of Education. Member of National Association of Independent Schools and Secondary School Admission Test Board. Endowment: $16 million. Total enrollment: 1,285. Upper school average class size: 14. Upper school faculty-student ratio: 1:9. There are 180 required school days per year for Upper School students. Upper School students typically attend 5 days per week. The average school day consists of 7 hours and 30 minutes.
Upper School Student Profile Grade 9: 138 students (68 boys, 70 girls); Grade 10: 148 students (76 boys, 72 girls); Grade 11: 163 students (88 boys, 75 girls); Grade 12: 153 students (77 boys, 76 girls). 17% of students are boarding students. 82% are state residents. 7 states are represented in upper school student body. 12% are international students. International students from Bahamas, China, Germany, Russian Federation, Spain, and Viet Nam; 40 other countries represented in student body. 5% of students are members of Episcopal Church.
Faculty School total: 210. In upper school: 55 men, 75 women; 80 have advanced degrees; 38 reside on campus.
Subjects Offered Advanced studio art-AP, algebra, American history, American literature, American studies, anatomy, archaeology, art, art history, Bible studies, biology, biology-AP, calculus, calculus-AP, chemistry, chemistry-AP, Chinese, community service, computer math, computer programming, computer science, computer science-AP, creative writing, drafting, drama, earth science, ecology, economics, English, English literature, English-AP, environmental science, ethics, European history, expository writing, fine arts, French, French-AP, geography, geometry, German, German-AP, government/civics, grammar, history, journalism, Latin, marine biology, mathematics, music, photography, physical education, physics,

physics-AP, pre-calculus, psychology, science, social studies, Spanish, Spanish-AP, speech, statistics, theater, theology, trigonometry, U.S. history-AP, world history, world history-AP, world literature, writing.

Graduation Requirements Arts and fine arts (art, music, dance, drama), computer science, English, foreign language, mathematics, physical education (includes health), religion (includes Bible studies and theology), science, social studies (includes history), speech, visual and performing arts, participation in sports, community service hours. Community service is required.

Special Academic Programs 25 Advanced Placement exams for which test preparation is offered; honors section; study abroad; academic accommodation for the gifted; ESL (20 students enrolled).

College Admission Counseling 140 students graduated in 2016; all went to college, including Florida State University; The George Washington University; University of Florida; University of Miami; Vanderbilt University. Mean SAT critical reading: 608, mean SAT math: 624, mean SAT writing: 616, mean combined SAT: 1848, mean composite ACT: 27. 50% scored over 600 on SAT critical reading, 60% scored over 600 on SAT math, 57% scored over 600 on SAT writing, 59% scored over 1800 on combined SAT, 58% scored over 26 on composite ACT.

Student Life Upper grades have specified standards of dress, student council, honor system. Discipline rests primarily with faculty. Attendance at religious services is required.

Summer Programs Remediation, enrichment, advancement, ESL, sports, art/fine arts, computer instruction programs offered; session focuses on academics; held on campus; accepts boys and girls; open to students from other schools. 225 students usually enrolled. 2017 schedule: June 10 to July 20. Application deadline: none.

Tuition and Aid Day student tuition: $30,390; 7-day tuition and room/board: $53,230. Tuition installment plan (Insured Tuition Payment Plan, SMART Tuition Payment Plan, monthly payment plans, individually arranged payment plans). Merit scholarship grants, need-based scholarship grants available. In 2016–17, 15% of upper-school students received aid; total upper-school merit-scholarship money awarded: $220,000. Total amount of financial aid awarded in 2016–17: $3,000,000.

Admissions Traditional secondary-level entrance grade is 9. For fall 2016, 397 students applied for upper-level admission, 198 were accepted, 124 enrolled. SSAT and TOEFL or SLEP required. Deadline for receipt of application materials: February 1. Application fee required: $75. Interview required.

Athletics Interscholastic: baseball (boys), basketball (b,g), cheering (g), cross-country running (b,g), dance (b,g), danceline (g), diving (b,g), fitness (b,g), football (b), golf (b,g), ice hockey (b,g), lacrosse (b,g), soccer (b,g), softball (g), swimming and diving (b,g), tennis (b,g), track and field (b,g), volleyball (g), water polo (b,g), wrestling (b), yoga (b,g); intramural: weight lifting (b,g); coed interscholastic: bowling, water polo. 48 coaches.

Computers Computers are regularly used in college planning, English, foreign language, history, mathematics, science classes. Computer network features include on-campus library services, online commercial services, Internet access, wireless campus network, Internet filtering or blocking technology. Campus intranet, student e-mail accounts, and computer access in designated common areas are available to students. Students grades are available online. The school has a published electronic and media policy.

Contact Peter Kravchuk, Interim Director of Admission. 561-210-2020. Fax: 561-210-2027. E-mail: admission@saintandrews.net. Website: www.saintandrews.net

ST. ANDREW'S SCHOOL

601 Penn Waller Road
Savannah, Georgia 31410

Head of School: Dr. Kelley Waldron

General Information Coeducational day college-preparatory and technology school. Grades PK–12. Founded: 1947. Setting: suburban. 28-acre campus. 4 buildings on campus. Approved or accredited by Georgia Independent School Association, South Carolina Independent School Association, Southern Association of Colleges and Schools, and Southern Association of Independent Schools. Member of National Association of Independent Schools. Endowment: $400,000. Total enrollment: 457. Upper school average class size: 16. Upper school faculty-student ratio: 1:6. There are 180 required school days per year for Upper School students. Upper School students typically attend 5 days per week. The average school day consists of 7 hours and 25 minutes.

Upper School Student Profile Grade 9: 44 students (24 boys, 20 girls); Grade 10: 42 students (22 boys, 20 girls); Grade 11: 30 students (16 boys, 14 girls); Grade 12: 41 students (19 boys, 22 girls).

Faculty School total: 72. In upper school: 17 men, 8 women; 23 have advanced degrees.

Subjects Offered 3-dimensional design, acting, advanced biology, advanced chemistry, advanced math, advanced studio art-AP, advertising design, algebra, American government, American history, American legal systems, American literature, anatomy, animation, art, art history, arts, band, Basic programming, biology, calculus, chemistry, Chinese, choir, classical studies, communication skills, community service, computer art, computer programming, computer science, computer skills, computer-aided design, costumes and make-up, creative writing, current history, digital art, drafting, drama, drama performance, drama workshop, drawing, drawing and design,

earth science, economics, electives, English, English as a foreign language, English literature, environmental science, ESL, European history, fine arts, geography, geometry, government/civics, health, history, Mandarin, mathematics, music, physical education, physics, psychology, science, social studies, Spanish, theater, trigonometry, Web site design, world history.

Graduation Requirements Arts and fine arts (art, music, dance, drama), computer science, English, foreign language, mathematics, physical education (includes health), science, social studies (includes history), community service. Community service is required.

Special Academic Programs International Baccalaureate program; honors section; accelerated programs; independent study; study at local college for college credit; domestic exchange program; study abroad; academic accommodation for the gifted, the musically talented, and the artistically talented; remedial reading and/or remedial writing; remedial math; ESL (15 students enrolled).

College Admission Counseling 38 students graduated in 2016; all went to college, including Georgia Institute of Technology; Georgia Southern University; University of Georgia; University of Michigan; University of South Carolina; Wake Forest University.

Student Life Upper grades have specified standards of dress, student council, honor system. Discipline rests primarily with faculty.

Summer Programs Remediation, enrichment, sports, art/fine arts programs offered; session focuses on enrichment; held on campus; accepts boys and girls; open to students from other schools. 339 students usually enrolled. 2017 schedule: June 14 to July 30.

Tuition and Aid Day student tuition: $14,250. Tuition installment plan (monthly payment plans). Need-based scholarship grants, need-based grants available. In 2016–17, 30% of upper-school students received aid. Total amount of financial aid awarded in 2016–17: $150,000.

Admissions Traditional secondary-level entrance grade is 9. For fall 2016, 64 students applied for upper-level admission, 28 were accepted, 22 enrolled. Deadline for receipt of application materials: none. Application fee required: $150. Interview recommended.

Athletics Interscholastic: aerobics/dance (girls), baseball (b), basketball (b,g), cheering (g), cross-country running (b,g), dance team (g), football (b), golf (b,g), physical fitness (b,g), physical training (b,g), soccer (b,g), softball (g), strength & conditioning (b,g), swimming and diving (b,g), tennis (b,g), track and field (b,g), volleyball (g), weight lifting (b,g), weight training (b,g); intramural: basketball (b,g), cheering (b,g), cross-country running (b,g), football (b), golf (b), lacrosse (b), physical fitness (b,g), physical training (b,g), soccer (b,g), softball (g), swimming and diving (b,g), tennis (b,g), track and field (b,g), volleyball (g), weight lifting (b,g), weight training (b,g); coed interscholastic: cheering, cross-country running, physical fitness, physical training, weight lifting, weight training; coed intramural: physical fitness, physical training. 2 PE instructors, 3 coaches, 1 athletic trainer.

Computers Computers are regularly used in all classes. Computer network features include on-campus library services, online commercial services, Internet access, wireless campus network, Internet filtering or blocking technology. Campus intranet, student e-mail accounts, and computer access in designated common areas are available to students. Students grades are available online. The school has a published electronic and media policy.

Contact Mrs. Casey Awad, Director of Admissions. 912-897-4941 Ext. 402. Fax: 912-897-4943. E-mail: awadc@saintschool.com. Website: www.saintschool.com

ST. ANDREW'S SCHOOL

63 Federal Road
Barrington, Rhode Island 02806

Head of School: Mr. David Tinagero

General Information Coeducational boarding and day college-preparatory and arts school. Boarding grades 9–12, day grades 6–12. Founded: 1893. Setting: suburban. Nearest major city is Providence. Students are housed in single-sex dormitories. 100-acre campus. 33 buildings on campus. Approved or accredited by Massachusetts Department of Education, National Association of Episcopal Schools, New England Association of Schools and Colleges, Rhode Island State Certified Resource Progam, The Association of Boarding Schools, and Rhode Island Department of Education. Member of National Association of Independent Schools and Secondary School Admission Test Board. Endowment: $16.4 million. Total enrollment: 205. Upper school average class size: 10. Upper school faculty-student ratio: 1:5. There are 150 required school days per year for Upper School students. Upper School students typically attend 5 days per week. The average school day consists of 8 hours.

Upper School Student Profile Grade 9: 34 students (23 boys, 11 girls); Grade 10: 40 students (22 boys, 18 girls); Grade 11: 47 students (31 boys, 16 girls); Grade 12: 51 students (32 boys, 19 girls); Postgraduate: 3 students (3 boys). 31% of students are boarding students. 59% are state residents. 8 states are represented in upper school student body. 18% are international students. International students from China, India, Republic of Korea, South Africa, Taiwan, and United Kingdom; 2 other countries represented in student body.

Faculty School total: 42. In upper school: 14 men, 24 women; 25 have advanced degrees; 21 reside on campus.

Subjects Offered Advanced biology, Advanced Placement courses, algebra, American history, ancient history, art, astronomy, biology, calculus, calculus-AP, ceramics, chemistry, chorus, college counseling, computer applications, creative writing, digital applications, digital photography, drawing, English, environmental science, ESL, European history, French, geometry, human anatomy, humanities, jewelry making, lab science, music history, music theory, music theory-AP, oceanography, oral communications, physical education, physics, pre-calculus, printmaking, probability and statistics, remedial study skills, Spanish, stagecraft, statistics-AP, studio art, study skills, technical theater, theater, TOEFL preparation, trigonometry, water color painting, yearbook.

Graduation Requirements Arts and fine arts (art, music, dance, drama), English, mathematics, physical education (includes health), science, social studies (includes history), community service.

Special Academic Programs Advanced Placement exam preparation; honors section; independent study; remedial reading and/or remedial writing; programs in English for dyslexic students; special instructional classes for deaf students, blind students, students with mild language-based learning disabilities, students with attention/organizational issues (ADHD); ESL (24 students enrolled).

College Admission Counseling 47 students graduated in 2015; 44 went to college, including Bard College; Brandeis University; Emory University; Fordham University; Gettysburg College; Worcester Polytechnic Institute. Other: 3 went to work. Median SAT critical reading: 480, median SAT math: 520, median SAT writing: 490, median combined SAT: 1540, median composite ACT: 20. 10% scored over 600 on SAT critical reading, 21% scored over 600 on SAT math, 10% scored over 600 on SAT writing, 10% scored over 1800 on combined SAT.

Student Life Upper grades have specified standards of dress, student council. Discipline rests primarily with faculty.

Tuition and Aid Day student tuition: $35,500; 7-day tuition and room/board: $53,700. Tuition installment plan (Key Tuition Payment Plan). Need-based scholarship grants, need-based loans available. In 2015–16, 47% of upper-school students received aid. Total amount of financial aid awarded in 2015–16: $2,117,710.

Admissions Traditional secondary-level entrance grade is 9. For fall 2015, 291 students applied for upper-level admission, 137 were accepted, 52 enrolled. Any standardized test required. Deadline for receipt of application materials: January 15. Application fee required: $50. Interview required.

Athletics Interscholastic: basketball (boys, girls), cross-country running (b,g), golf (b), lacrosse (b,g), soccer (b,g), tennis (b,g); coed interscholastic: soccer; coed intramural: badminton, ball hockey, basketball, bicycling, billiards, bocce, cooperative games, croquet, dance, fitness, fitness walking, flag football, floor hockey, Frisbee, horseshoes, jogging, physical fitness, project adventure, ropes courses, running, soccer, strength & conditioning, tennis, touch football, ultimate Frisbee, walking, weight lifting, weight training, yoga. 1 PE instructor, 20 coaches, 1 athletic trainer.

Computers Computers are regularly used in all academic, computer applications, library skills, multimedia, photography, SAT preparation, yearbook classes. Computer network features include on-campus library services, Internet access, wireless campus network, Internet filtering or blocking technology, NetClassroom is available for parents and students. Campus intranet, student e-mail accounts, and computer access in designated common areas are available to students. Students grades are available online. The school has a published electronic and media policy.

Contact Kristel Dunphy, Associate Director to Admissions. 401-246-1230 Ext. 3053. Fax: 401-246-0510. E-mail: kdunphy@standrews-ri.org.

Website: www.standrews-ri.org

ST. ANDREW'S–SEWANEE SCHOOL

290 Quintard Road
Sewanee, Tennessee 37375-3000

Head of School: Mr. Karl J. Sjolund

General Information Coeducational boarding and day college-preparatory and arts school, affiliated with Episcopal Church. Boarding grades 9–12, day grades 6–12. Founded: 1868. Setting: small town. Nearest major city is Chattanooga. Students are housed in single-sex dormitories. 550-acre campus. 19 buildings on campus. Approved or accredited by National Association of Episcopal Schools, Southern Association of Colleges and Schools, Southern Association of Independent Schools, Tennessee Association of Independent Schools, The Association of Boarding Schools, and Tennessee Department of Education. Member of National Association of Independent Schools and Secondary School Admission Test Board. Endowment: $11.5 million. Total enrollment: 230. Upper school average class size: 16. Upper school faculty-student ratio: 1:6. There are 168 required school days per year for Upper School students. Upper School students typically attend 5 days per week. The average school day consists of 4 hours and 30 minutes.

Upper School Student Profile Grade 9: 49 students (27 boys, 22 girls); Grade 10: 33 students (22 boys, 11 girls); Grade 11: 50 students (24 boys, 26 girls); Grade 12: 44 students (18 boys, 26 girls). 44% of students are boarding students. 72% are state residents. 14 states are represented in upper school student body. 15% are international students. International students from China, Germany, Jamaica, Japan, Rwanda, and Spain; 4 other countries represented in student body. 31% of students are members of Episcopal Church.

Faculty School total: 37. In upper school: 14 men, 16 women; 17 have advanced degrees; 17 reside on campus.

Subjects Offered 20th century American writers, 20th century history, 20th century world history, 3-dimensional art, 3-dimensional design, acting, adolescent issues, advanced biology, advanced chemistry, advanced math, advanced TOEFL/grammar, aerobics, African history, African literature, African-American literature, algebra, American history, American literature, American studies, art, Asian history, Asian literature, band, biology, British literature, British literature (honors), calculus, chamber groups, chemistry, Chinese, choir, college counseling, community service, comparative religion, creative writing, drama, dramatic arts, ecology, English, English literature, environmental systems, ESL, European literature, filmmaking, fine arts, general science, geometry, history, humanities, Latin, Latin American literature, leadership, literature, mathematics, minority studies, music, philosophy, physical education, physics, poetry, pottery, pre-algebra, psychology, religion, religious studies, science, social studies, Southern literature, Spanish, statistics, theater, trigonometry, world history, World War I, World War II, wrestling, writing, writing workshop, yearbook, yoga.

Graduation Requirements Arts and fine arts (art, music, dance, drama), English, foreign language, mathematics, physical education (includes health), religion (includes Bible studies and theology), science, social studies (includes history), creedal statement. Community service is required.

Special Academic Programs 13 Advanced Placement exams for which test preparation is offered; independent study; term-away projects; study at local college for college credit; study abroad; academic accommodation for the gifted, the musically talented, and the artistically talented; remedial reading and/or remedial writing; remedial math; ESL (10 students enrolled).

College Admission Counseling 32 students graduated in 2016; all went to college, including Middlebury College; Sewanee: The University of the South; University of California, San Diego; University of Virginia; University of Washington; Warren Wilson College.

Student Life Upper grades have specified standards of dress, student council, honor system. Discipline rests equally with students and faculty. Attendance at religious services is required.

Summer Programs ESL, sports, art/fine arts, rigorous outdoor training programs offered; session focuses on sports, outdoor adventure, writing, chorale, ELL; held on campus; accepts boys and girls; open to students from other schools. 140 students usually enrolled. 2017 schedule: May 30 to July 15. Application deadline: May 25.

Tuition and Aid Day student tuition: $18,500; 7-day tuition and room/board: $45,000. Tuition installment plan (FACTS Tuition Payment Plan, monthly payment plans). Merit scholarship grants, need-based scholarship grants available. In 2016–17, 50% of upper-school students received aid; total upper-school merit-scholarship money awarded: $106,000. Total amount of financial aid awarded in 2016–17: $2,010,689.

Admissions Traditional secondary-level entrance grade is 9. For fall 2016, 133 students applied for upper-level admission, 110 were accepted, 64 enrolled. SLEP, TOEFL or writing sample required. Deadline for receipt of application materials: none. Application fee required: $50. On-campus interview required.

Athletics Interscholastic: baseball (boys), basketball (b,g), cross-country running (b,g), diving (b,g), football (b), soccer (b,g), swimming and diving (b,g), tennis (b,g), track and field (b,g), volleyball (g), wrestling (b,g); intramural: ballet (g); coed interscholastic: bicycling, climbing, cross-country running, diving, golf, mountain biking, swimming and diving, tennis, track and field; coed intramural: aerobics, aerobics/dance, backpacking, ballet, billiards, canoeing/kayaking, combined training, fitness, Frisbee, hiking/backpacking, independent competitive sports, kayaking, modern dance, mountaineering, outdoor activities, outdoor adventure, outdoor education, outdoor recreation, outdoor skills, outdoors, physical fitness, physical training, rafting, rock climbing, running, soccer, strength & conditioning, table tennis, ultimate Frisbee, walking, wall climbing, weight lifting, weight training, wilderness, wilderness survival, yoga. 8 coaches.

Computers Computers are regularly used in all academic, art, college planning, creative writing, design, desktop publishing, digital applications, English, foreign language, graphic arts, graphic design, history, humanities, introduction to technology, Latin, literary magazine, mathematics, religion, SAT preparation, science, Spanish, yearbook classes. Computer network features include on-campus library services, online commercial services, Internet access, wireless campus network, Internet filtering or blocking technology, access to University of the South technology facilities. Student e-mail accounts and computer access in designated common areas are available to students. Students grades are available online.

Contact Ms. Anneke Skidmore, Director of Admission and Financial Aid. 931-598-5651 Ext. 2117. Fax: 931-914-1222. E-mail: admissions@sasweb.org. Website: www.sasweb.org

ST. ANNE'S–BELFIELD SCHOOL

2132 Ivy Road
Charlottesville, Virginia 22903

Head of School: Mr. David S. Lourie

General Information Coeducational boarding and day college-preparatory, arts, religious studies, and ESL school, affiliated with Christian faith. Boarding grades 9–12, day grades PK–12. Founded: 1910. Setting: small town. Nearest major city is Washington, DC. Students are housed in coed dormitories. 49-acre campus. 6 buildings on campus. Approved or accredited by The Association of Boarding Schools, Virginia Association of Independent Schools, and Virginia Department of Education. Member of National Association of Independent Schools and Secondary School Admission Test

Board. Endowment: $31 million. Total enrollment: 910. Upper school average class size: 13. Upper school faculty-student ratio: 1:8. There are 180 required school days per year for Upper School students. Upper School students typically attend 5 days per week. The average school day consists of 7 hours and 30 minutes.

Upper School Student Profile Grade 9: 82 students (40 boys, 42 girls); Grade 10: 87 students (43 boys, 44 girls); Grade 11: 100 students (54 boys, 46 girls); Grade 12: 89 students (41 boys, 48 girls). 18% of students are boarding students. 87% are state residents. 7 states are represented in upper school student body. 9% are international students. International students from Azerbaijan, China, Ethiopia, Republic of Korea, Saint Kitts and Nevis, and South Africa; 22 other countries represented in student body.

Faculty School total: 111. In upper school: 16 men, 25 women; 35 have advanced degrees; 7 reside on campus.

Subjects Offered 1968, algebra, art, biology, biology-AP, calculus-AP, ceramics, chemistry, chemistry-AP, choir, conceptual physics, drama, economics, English, environmental science-AP, ESL, French, French language-AP, geometry, honors algebra, honors geometry, humanities, Latin, Latin-AP, modern European history-AP, modern world history, music theory, music theory-AP, orchestra, photography, physics, physics-AP, pre-calculus, religion, sculpture, Spanish, Spanish language-AP, statistics, statistics-AP, theology, trigonometry, U.S. history, U.S. history-AP, video, world history, writing workshop.

Graduation Requirements Art, English, foreign language, history, mathematics, physical education (includes health), religion (includes Bible studies and theology), science. Community service is required.

Special Academic Programs 14 Advanced Placement exams for which test preparation is offered; honors section; independent study; study at local college for college credit; ESL (12 students enrolled).

College Admission Counseling 358 students graduated in 2015; they went to James Madison University; Lynchburg College; The College of William and Mary; University of Mary Washington; University of Virginia; Virginia Commonwealth University. Other: 1 had other specific plans. Median SAT critical reading: 630, median SAT math: 620. Mean SAT writing: 622. 59% scored over 600 on SAT critical reading, 57% scored over 600 on SAT math, 68% scored over 600 on SAT writing, 72% scored over 1800 on combined SAT.

Student Life Upper grades have uniform requirement, student council, honor system. Discipline rests primarily with faculty. Attendance at religious services is required.

Tuition and Aid Day student tuition: $24,600; 5-day tuition and room/board: $40,500; 7-day tuition and room/board: $51,500. Tuition installment plan (Insured Tuition Payment Plan, FACTS Tuition Payment Plan, monthly payment plans). Need-based scholarship grants, need-based financial aid available. In 2015–16, 39% of upper-school students received aid. Total amount of financial aid awarded in 2015–16: $4,700,000.

Admissions Traditional secondary-level entrance grade is 9. For fall 2015, 213 students applied for upper-level admission, 81 were accepted, 53 enrolled. ERB verbal, ERB math, SSAT, TOEFL or writing sample required. Deadline for receipt of application materials: February 5. No application fee required. Interview required.

Athletics Interscholastic: baseball (boys), basketball (b,g), cross-country running (b,g), field hockey (g), football (b), golf (b,g), lacrosse (b,g), soccer (b,g), softball (g), squash (b,g), swimming and diving (b,g), tennis (b,g), track and field (b,g), volleyball (g), wrestling (b); coed interscholastic: cross-country running, golf, squash, swimming and diving, track and field; coed intramural: aerobics/dance, alpine skiing, dance, fitness, physical fitness, yoga. 6 PE instructors, 8 coaches, 2 athletic trainers.

Computers Computers are regularly used in all academic classes. Computer network features include on-campus library services, online commercial services, Internet access, wireless campus network. Student e-mail accounts and computer access in designated common areas are available to students. Students grades are available online. The school has a published electronic and media policy.

Contact Mr. Sintayehu Taye, Assistant Director of Admission for Grades 5-12. 434-296-5106. Fax: 434-979-1486. E-mail: staye@stab.org. Website: www.stab.org

SAINT ANTHONY HIGH SCHOOL

304 East Roadway Avenue
Effingham, Illinois 62401

Head of School: Mr. Greg Fearday

General Information Coeducational day college-preparatory and religious studies school, affiliated with Roman Catholic Church. Grades 9–12. Setting: small town. Nearest major city is St. Louis, MO. 1 building on campus. Approved or accredited by National Catholic Education Association, North Central Association of Colleges and Schools, and Illinois Department of Education. Total enrollment: 190. Upper school average class size: 20. Upper school faculty-student ratio: 1:10. There are 176 required school days per year for Upper School students. Upper School students typically attend 5 days per week. The average school day consists of 5 hours and 42 minutes.

Upper School Student Profile Grade 9: 55 students (23 boys, 32 girls); Grade 10: 51 students (25 boys, 26 girls); Grade 11: 57 students (29 boys, 28 girls); Grade 12: 42 students (23 boys, 19 girls). 97% of students are Roman Catholic.

Faculty School total: 21. In upper school: 6 men, 15 women; 8 have advanced degrees.

Subjects Offered Advanced math, algebra, American government, anatomy, art appreciation, band, biology, British literature, calculus-AP, career exploration, Catholic belief and practice, ceramics, chemistry, chorus, communications, composition,

computer applications, conceptual physics, concert band, consumer education, current events, earth science, English literature, English-AP, environmental science, finite math, general math, geography, geometry, health, microbiology, music appreciation, physical education, physical science, physics, pre-algebra, psychology, publications, Spanish, statistics-AP, U.S. history, world history, world wide web design.

Graduation Requirements American government, arts and fine arts (art, music, dance, drama), computer science, consumer education, English, mathematics, physical education (includes health), religion (includes Bible studies and theology), science, social sciences, speech, U.S. history, world history.

Special Academic Programs International Baccalaureate program; 3 Advanced Placement exams for which test preparation is offered; independent study; study at local college for college credit; remedial math; special instructional classes for deaf students.

College Admission Counseling 42 students graduated in 2016; 40 went to college, including Illinois State University; Southern Illinois University Edwardsville; University of Illinois at Urbana–Champaign; University of Missouri. Other: 1 went to work, 1 entered military service. Median composite ACT: 25.

Student Life Upper grades have uniform requirement, student council. Discipline rests primarily with faculty. Attendance at religious services is required.

Tuition and Aid Tuition installment plan (monthly payment plans). Need-based scholarship grants available.

Admissions Traditional secondary-level entrance grade is 9. Deadline for receipt of application materials: none. No application fee required.

Athletics Interscholastic: baseball (boys), basketball (b,g), cheering (g), dance team (g), fishing (b), golf (b,g), soccer (b,g), softball (g), tennis (b,g), track and field (b,g), volleyball (g); coed interscholastic: cross-country running. 1 PE instructor, 19 coaches.

Computers Computers are regularly used in business skills, publications, yearbook classes. Computer network features include on-campus library services, Internet access, Internet filtering or blocking technology. Student e-mail accounts are available to students. Students grades are available online. The school has a published electronic and media policy.

Contact Mr. Greg Fearday, Principal. 217-342-6969. Fax: 217-342-6997. E-mail: gfearday@stanthony.com. Website: www.stanthony.com

SAINT AUGUSTINE PREPARATORY SCHOOL

611 Cedar Avenue
PO Box 279
Richland, New Jersey 08350

Head of School: Rev. Donald F. Reilly, OSA

General Information Boys' day college-preparatory, arts, business, religious studies, bilingual studies, technology, and Experiential Learning, Service Learning, Job Shadowing school, affiliated with Roman Catholic Church. Grades 9–12. Founded: 1959. Setting: rural. Nearest major city is Vineland. 120-acre campus. 5 buildings on campus. Approved or accredited by Middle States Association of Colleges and Schools, National Catholic Education Association, New Jersey Association of Independent Schools, and New Jersey Department of Education. Member of National Association of Independent Schools. Endowment: $2 million. Total enrollment: 695. Upper school average class size: 17. Upper school faculty-student ratio: 1:12. There are 180 required school days per year for Upper School students. Upper School students typically attend 5 days per week. The average school day consists of 6 hours and 8 minutes.

Upper School Student Profile Grade 9: 150 students (150 boys); Grade 10: 187 students (187 boys); Grade 11: 195 students (195 boys); Grade 12: 150 students (150 boys). 78% of students are Roman Catholic.

Faculty School total: 63. In upper school: 48 men, 15 women; 36 have advanced degrees.

Subjects Offered Advanced biology, advanced math, algebra, anatomy, art history-AP, business law, business skills, campus ministry, career experience, career exploration, character education, Christian education, Christian scripture, Christian studies, Christian testament, Christianity, college awareness, college placement, communication arts, communication skills, communications, comparative government and politics-AP, comparative political systems-AP, computer education, computer graphics, computer information systems, computer literacy, computer programming-AP, computer skills, computer studies, constitutional law, creative arts, criminal justice.

Graduation Requirements Electives, English, foreign language, lab science, mathematics, religion (includes Bible studies and theology), science, service learning/internship, U.S. history, world cultures, social service project (approximately 100 hours), retreat experiences, third semester experiences (travel, hands-on learning).

Special Academic Programs 18 Advanced Placement exams for which test preparation is offered; honors section; independent study; term-away projects; study at local college for college credit; study abroad; academic accommodation for the gifted, the musically talented, and the artistically talented; programs in general development for dyslexic students; special instructional classes for deaf students, blind students.

College Admission Counseling 167 students graduated in 2016; all went to college, including Drexel University; La Salle University; Rowan University; Saint Joseph's University; University of Delaware; Villanova University. Mean SAT critical reading: 565, mean SAT math: 580, mean SAT writing: 550, mean combined SAT: 1695, mean composite ACT: 25. 34% scored over 600 on SAT critical reading, 46%

scored over 600 on SAT math, 33% scored over 600 on SAT writing, 32% scored over 1800 on combined SAT, 36% scored over 26 on composite ACT.

Student Life Upper grades have uniform requirement, student council, honor system. Discipline rests primarily with faculty. Attendance at religious services is required.

Summer Programs Enrichment, advancement, sports, art/fine arts, rigorous outdoor training programs offered; session focuses on academic enrichment, community relations, sports camps; held both on and off campus; accepts boys and girls; open to students from other schools. 700 students usually enrolled. 2017 schedule: July 1 to August 15. Application deadline: June 1.

Tuition and Aid Day student tuition: $17,350. Tuition installment plan (FACTS Tuition Payment Plan, individually arranged payment plans, credit card payment). Merit scholarship grants, need-based scholarship grants available. In 2016–17, 40% of upper-school students received aid; total upper-school merit-scholarship money awarded: $200,000. Total amount of financial aid awarded in 2016–17: $1,600,000.

Admissions Traditional secondary-level entrance grade is 9. For fall 2016, 275 students applied for upper-level admission, 230 were accepted, 150 enrolled. School's own exam required. Deadline for receipt of application materials: January 31. Application fee required: $75. On-campus interview required.

Athletics Interscholastic: baseball, basketball, bowling, crew, cross-country running, fencing, football, golf, ice hockey, indoor track, lacrosse, rowing, rugby, sailing, soccer, squash, surfing, swimming and diving, tennis, track and field, volleyball, winter (indoor) track, wrestling; intramural: basketball, flag football, physical training, soccer, ultimate Frisbee, volleyball, weight training. 2 PE instructors, 12 coaches, 1 athletic trainer.

Computers Computers are regularly used in all academic, art, career education, computer applications, design, photojournalism, SAT preparation classes. Computer network features include on-campus library services, online commercial services, Internet access, wireless campus network, Internet filtering or blocking technology, syllabus, current grades, and assignments available online for all courses. Student e-mail accounts and computer access in designated common areas are available to students. Students grades are available online. The school has a published electronic and media policy.

Contact Mr. Stephen Cappuccio, Dean of Enrollment Management. 856-697-2600 Ext. 112. Fax: 856-285-7108. E-mail: mr.cappuccio@hermits.com. Website: www.hermits.com

SAINT BASIL ACADEMY

711 Fox Chase Road
Jenkintown, Pennsylvania 19046

Head of School: Ms. Gwenda Coté

General Information Girls' day college-preparatory school, affiliated with Roman Catholic Church. Grades 9–12. Founded: 1931. Setting: suburban. Nearest major city is Philadelphia. 28-acre campus. 1 building on campus. Approved or accredited by Middle States Association of Colleges and Schools and Pennsylvania Department of Education. Endowment: $350,000. Total enrollment: 324. Upper school average class size: 18. Upper school faculty-student ratio: 1:10. There are 180 required school days per year for Upper School students. Upper School students typically attend 5 days per week. The average school day consists of 6 hours and 30 minutes.

Upper School Student Profile Grade 9: 71 students (71 girls); Grade 10: 83 students (83 girls); Grade 11: 79 students (79 girls); Grade 12: 91 students (91 girls). 96% of students are Roman Catholic.

Faculty School total: 36. In upper school: 9 men, 25 women; 22 have advanced degrees.

Subjects Offered Accounting, advanced biology, algebra, American history, American history-AP, American literature, anatomy, art, band, biology, British literature, business, calculus-AP, chemistry, Christian and Hebrew scripture, computer applications, concert choir, creative writing, desktop publishing, digital applications, economics, English, English language-AP, English literature, English literature-AP, ensembles, environmental science, European history, fine arts, French, French literature-AP, geometry, German, government/civics, guitar, health, Hebrew scripture, history, honors algebra, honors English, honors geometry, Italian, journalism, keyboarding, Latin, mathematics, music, physical education, physics, pre-calculus, probability and statistics, psychology, religion, religious studies, SAT preparation, science, Shakespeare, social studies, sociology, Spanish, Spanish literature-AP, Spanish-AP, statistics, trigonometry, U.S. government and politics-AP, U.S. history, U.S. history-AP, Ukrainian, world cultures, world history.

Graduation Requirements Arts and fine arts (art, music, dance, drama), English, foreign language, keyboarding, mathematics, physical education (includes health), religion (includes Bible studies and theology), science, social studies (includes history). Community service is required.

Special Academic Programs Advanced Placement exam preparation; honors section; study at local college for college credit.

College Admission Counseling 73 students graduated in 2016; all went to college, including Drexel University; La Salle University; Penn State University Park; Saint Joseph's University; Temple University; West Chester University of Pennsylvania. Mean SAT critical reading: 539, mean SAT math: 521, mean SAT writing: 548, mean combined SAT: 1726, mean composite ACT: 23.

Student Life Upper grades have uniform requirement, student council, honor system. Discipline rests primarily with faculty. Attendance at religious services is required.

Summer Programs Enrichment, sports programs offered; session focuses on sports camps, enrichment programs; held on campus; accepts girls; open to students from other schools. 50 students usually enrolled. 2017 schedule: June 15 to June 30. Application deadline: May 31.

Tuition and Aid Tuition installment plan (monthly payment plans, 2-installments (pay 1/2 tuition July 15, 1/2 tuition November 15), first installment due July 15 (3 months), 7 installments (pay Oct. 15-April 15)). Tuition reduction for siblings, merit scholarship grants, need-based scholarship grants, Ellis Grant for children of single parents living in Philadelphia, BLOCS scholarships and foundations available. In 2016–17, 20% of upper-school students received aid; total upper-school merit-scholarship money awarded: $193,925. Total amount of financial aid awarded in 2016–17: $268,175.

Admissions Traditional secondary-level entrance grade is 9. For fall 2016, 162 students applied for upper-level admission, 71 enrolled. High School Placement Test required. Deadline for receipt of application materials: October 24. Application fee required: $40.

Athletics Interscholastic: basketball, cheering, cross-country running, field hockey, indoor track, lacrosse, soccer, softball, tennis, track and field, volleyball, winter (indoor) track. 1 PE instructor, 25 coaches.

Computers Computers are regularly used in accounting, computer applications, creative writing, desktop publishing, digital applications, economics, journalism, keyboarding, science classes. Computer network features include Internet access, wireless campus network, Internet filtering or blocking technology, student accessible server storage space, on-campus and Web-based library services (catalog and book request). Student e-mail accounts are available to students. The school has a published electronic and media policy.

Contact Mrs. Kimberley Clearkin, Director of Admissions. 215-885-3771 Ext. 125. Fax: 215-885-4025. E-mail: kclearkin@stbasilacademy.org. Website: www.stbasilacademy.org

ST. BENEDICT AT AUBURNDALE

8250 Varnavas Drive
Cordova, Tennessee 38016

Head of School: Mrs. Sondra Morris

General Information Coeducational day college-preparatory school, affiliated with Roman Catholic Church. Grades 9–12. Founded: 1966. Setting: suburban. Nearest major city is Memphis. 40-acre campus. 1 building on campus. Approved or accredited by National Catholic Education Association, Southern Association of Colleges and Schools, and Tennessee Department of Education. Endowment: $200,000. Total enrollment: 945. Upper school average class size: 26. Upper school faculty-student ratio: 1:16. There are 186 required school days per year for Upper School students. Upper School students typically attend 5 days per week. The average school day consists of 7 hours and 15 minutes.

Upper School Student Profile Grade 9: 156 students (69 boys, 87 girls); Grade 10: 200 students (93 boys, 107 girls); Grade 11: 206 students (84 boys, 122 girls); Grade 12: 201 students (84 boys, 117 girls); Postgraduate: 763 students (330 boys, 433 girls). 85% of students are Roman Catholic.

Faculty School total: 58. In upper school: 25 men, 33 women; 40 have advanced degrees.

Subjects Offered Accounting, acting, algebra, American government, American history, American history-AP, American literature-AP, anatomy and physiology, applied music, art, art appreciation, art education, art history, art-AP, astronomy, band, biology, calculus, calculus-AP, Catholic belief and practice, chemistry, choir, choral music, choreography, chorus, church history, cinematography, clayworking, comparative religion, composition-AP, computer graphics, computer multimedia, computers, creative writing, dance, digital art, digital photography, drama, drama performance, drawing, driver education, ecology, economics, economics-AP, English, English language-AP, English literature-AP, English-AP, English/composition-AP, etymology, European history, film, filmmaking, fine arts, first aid, fitness, forensics, French, French-AP, general business, geometry, German, government, government-AP, graphic arts, graphic design, health and wellness, health education, history, history of the Catholic Church, history-AP, honors algebra, honors English, honors geometry, honors U.S. history, human anatomy, human biology, instrumental music, internship, jazz band, jazz dance, journalism, keyboarding, lab/keyboard, Latin, literature-AP, macroeconomics-AP, marketing, modern history, music appreciation, music history, music theory, newspaper, performing arts, personal finance, photography, physical education, physical science, physics, play production, pre-algebra, pre-calculus, psychology, religion, set design, sociology, Spanish, Spanish-AP, speech, sports conditioning, stage design, statistics-AP, student publications, U.S. government and politics-AP, U.S. history-AP, world geography, world history, yearbook.

Graduation Requirements Arts and fine arts (art, music, dance, drama), economics, English, foreign language, government, mathematics, physical education (includes health), religion (includes Bible studies and theology), science, social studies (includes history), technology, theology.

Special Academic Programs 10 Advanced Placement exams for which test preparation is offered; study at local college for college credit; academic accommodation for the gifted, the musically talented, and the artistically talented; remedial reading and/or remedial writing; remedial math; programs in English, mathematics, general development for dyslexic students; special instructional classes for students with diagnosed learning disabilities and Attention Deficit Disorder.

College Admission Counseling 232 students graduated in 2016; all went to college, including Christian Brothers University; Middle Tennessee State University; Mississippi State University; The University of Alabama; The University of Tennessee; University of Memphis. Mean SAT critical reading: 570, mean SAT math: 560, mean composite ACT: 24. 38% scored over 600 on SAT critical reading, 37% scored over 600 on SAT math, 30% scored over 26 on composite ACT.

Student Life Upper grades have uniform requirement, student council, honor system. Discipline rests primarily with faculty. Attendance at religious services is required.

Summer Programs Remediation, enrichment programs offered; session focuses on enrichment for math and language; held on campus; accepts boys and girls; not open to students from other schools. 30 students usually enrolled. 2017 schedule: July 5 to July 29. Application deadline: none.

Tuition and Aid Day student tuition: $10,320. Tuition installment plan (FACTS Tuition Payment Plan, monthly payment plans, individually arranged payment plans). Merit scholarship grants, need-based scholarship grants available. In 2016–17, 4% of upper-school students received aid; total upper-school merit-scholarship money awarded: $30,000. Total amount of financial aid awarded in 2016–17: $35,000.

Admissions Traditional secondary-level entrance grade is 9. For fall 2016, 170 students applied for upper level admission, 170 were accepted, 160 enrolled. High School Placement Test required. Deadline for receipt of application materials: none. Application fee required: $75. On-campus interview recommended.

Athletics Interscholastic: baseball (boys), basketball (b,g), bowling (b,g), cheering (g), cross-country running (b,g), dance (g), dance squad (g), dance team (g), football (b), Frisbee (b,g), golf (b,g), lacrosse (b,g), soccer (b,g), softball (g), strength & conditioning (b), swimming and diving (b,g), tennis (b,g), track and field (b,g), volleyball (g), weight lifting (b), weight training (b), wrestling (b); coed interscholastic: riflery, water polo; coed intramural: Frisbee. 4 PE instructors, 17 coaches, 1 athletic trainer.

Computers Computers are regularly used in all academic, art, business, commercial art, current events, dance, design, desktop publishing, economics, French, graphic arts, graphic design, health, history, journalism, lab/keyboard, Latin, mathematics, music, newspaper, photography, psychology, publications, religion, science, social sciences, social studies, Spanish, speech, study skills, technology, theater, theater arts, theology, Web site design, writing, yearbook classes. Computer network features include on-campus library services, Internet access, wireless campus network, Internet filtering or blocking technology. Campus intranet and student e-mail accounts are available to students. Students grades are available online. The school has a published electronic and media policy.

Contact Mrs. Terri Heath, Director of Admissions. 901-260-2873. Fax: 901-260-2850. E-mail: heatht@sbaeagles.org. Website: www.sbaeagles.org

ST. BERNARD HIGH SCHOOL

9100 Falmouth Avenue
Playa del Rey, California 90293-8299

Head of School: Dr. Patrick Lynch

General Information Coeducational day college-preparatory, arts, and religious studies school, affiliated with Roman Catholic Church. Grades 9–12. Founded: 1957. Setting: suburban. Nearest major city is Los Angeles. 14-acre campus. 5 buildings on campus. Approved or accredited by National Catholic Education Association, Western Association of Schools and Colleges, Western Catholic Education Association, and California Department of Education. Endowment: $1.2 million. Total enrollment: 260. Upper school average class size: 20. Upper school faculty-student ratio: 1:20.

Upper School Student Profile 65% of students are Roman Catholic.

Faculty School total: 20. In upper school: 9 men, 9 women; 14 have advanced degrees.

Subjects Offered Advanced math, algebra, American literature, American minority experience, ancient history, applied music, band, Bible, biology, biology-AP, British literature, British literature (honors), broadcasting, business law, calculus, campus ministry, Catholic belief and practice, chemistry, chemistry-AP, choir, choral music, Christian and Hebrew scripture, church history, college counseling, comparative religion, competitive science projects, computer literacy, concert band, concert choir, CPR, dance, drama, drawing and design, driver education, earth science, economics, economics-AP, English, English composition, English language and composition-AP, English literature-AP, entrepreneurship, ethics, European history, European history-AP, first aid, French, government, health, history of the Catholic Church, honors algebra, honors English, honors geometry, honors U.S. history, honors world history, human biology, instrumental music, introduction to theater, Life of Christ, literary magazine, marine biology, modern European history-AP, music appreciation, physics, play production, psychology, social sciences, Spanish, Spanish language-AP, speech, study skills, U.S. government, U.S. government and politics-AP, U.S. history, U.S. history-AP, yearbook.

Graduation Requirements 60 hours of community service.

Special Academic Programs Advanced Placement exam preparation; honors section; study at local college for college credit.

College Admission Counseling 65 students graduated in 2015; 62 went to college, including California State University, Dominguez Hills; California State University, Long Beach; California State University, Northridge; Loyola Marymount University; St. John's University; University of California, Los Angeles. Other: 3 went to work.

Student Life Upper grades have uniform requirement, student council, honor system. Discipline rests primarily with faculty. Attendance at religious services is required.

Tuition and Aid Day student tuition: $8435. Tuition installment plan (FACTS Tuition Payment Plan). Tuition reduction for siblings, merit scholarship grants, need-based scholarship grants, Catholic Education Foundation available. In 2014–15, 60% of upper-school students received aid.

Admissions Traditional secondary-level entrance grade is 9. Catholic High School Entrance Examination required. Deadline for receipt of application materials: January 16. Application fee required: $79. On-campus interview required.

Athletics Interscholastic: baseball (boys), basketball (b,g), cheering (g), cross-country running (b,g), dance team (g), football (b), golf (b), soccer (b,g), softball (g), track and field (b,g), volleyball (b,g), wrestling (b); coed interscholastic: aerobics/dance, basketball, cross-country running, dance, modern dance; coed intramural: aerobics/dance, bowling, dance, dance squad, jogging, physical fitness, strength & conditioning, surfing, weight training. 1 PE instructor, 15 coaches, 1 athletic trainer.

Computers Computers are regularly used in all classes. Computer network features include on-campus library services, Internet access, Internet filtering or blocking technology. The school has a published electronic and media policy

Contact Ms. Christina McCole, Director of Admissions. 310-823-4651 Ext. 113. Fax: 310-827-3365. E-mail: cmccole@stbernardhs.org. Website: www.stbernardhs.org

ST. BERNARD HIGH SCHOOL

1593 Norwich-New London Turnpike
Uncasville, Connecticut 06382

Head of School: Mr. Donald Macrino Sr.

General Information Coeducational day college-preparatory school, affiliated with Roman Catholic Church. Grades 6–12. Founded: 1956. Setting: suburban. Nearest major city is Hartford. 119-acre campus. 2 buildings on campus. Approved or accredited by New England Association of Schools and Colleges and Connecticut Department of Education. Member of National Association of Independent Schools. Endowment: $1 million. Total enrollment: 322. Upper school average class size: 19. Upper school faculty-student ratio: 1:10. There are 177 required school days per year for Upper School students. Upper School students typically attend 5 days per week. The average school day consists of 6 hours.

Upper School Student Profile Grade 6: 25 students (11 boys, 14 girls); Grade 7: 23 students (11 boys, 12 girls); Grade 8: 42 students (22 boys, 20 girls); Grade 9: 54 students (28 boys, 26 girls); Grade 10: 66 students (23 boys, 43 girls); Grade 11: 70 students (34 boys, 36 girls); Grade 12: 54 students (27 boys, 27 girls). 60% of students are Roman Catholic.

Faculty School total: 39. In upper school: 16 men, 23 women; 32 have advanced degrees.

Subjects Offered 3-dimensional art, accounting, acting, advanced biology, advanced chemistry, advanced computer applications, advanced math, Advanced Placement courses, advanced studio art-AP, algebra, American history, American history-AP, American literature, American literature-AP, analysis, analysis and differential calculus, analytic geometry, anatomy and physiology, art history-AP, art-AP, athletic training, band, biology, biology-AP, British literature, British literature (honors), British literature-AP, calculus, calculus-AP, chemistry, chemistry-AP, choir, Christian doctrine, Christian ethics, Christian scripture, church history, composition-AP, conceptual physics, concert band, concert choir, creative writing, design, drawing and design, economics, English, English language and composition-AP, English literature and composition-AP, environmental science, ESL, European history-AP, fine arts, forensics, French, French-AP, geometry, global issues, health, honors algebra, honors English, honors geometry, honors U.S. history, honors world history, integrated science, intro to computers, modern European history-AP, modern world history, moral theology, music, music theory, music theory-AP, music-AP, Native American studies, nutrition, organic chemistry, painting, peace and justice, peer counseling, peer ministry, performing arts, personal finance, personal fitness, philosophy, photography, physical education, physics, pottery, pre-algebra, pre-calculus, printmaking, psychology-AP, public speaking, religion and culture, religious studies, scripture, sociology, Spanish, Spanish-AP, sports conditioning, sports nutrition, statistics, street law, strings, studio art, studio art-AP, technology, theater arts, U.S. history, U.S. history-AP, world history.

Graduation Requirements Art, biology, chemistry, English, health education, history, intro to computers, mathematics, physical education (includes health), theology, U.S. history, world history, all students are required to complete 100 hours of community service prior to high school graduation.

Special Academic Programs Honors section; study at local college for college credit; ESL (16 students enrolled).

College Admission Counseling 74 students graduated in 2015; 72 went to college, including Providence College; Saint Michael's College; University of Connecticut; Worcester Polytechnic Institute. Other: 2 entered military service. Mean SAT critical reading: 550, mean SAT math: 526, mean SAT writing: 568, mean combined SAT: 1644. 10% scored over 1800 on combined SAT.

Student Life Upper grades have uniform requirement, student council, honor system. Discipline rests primarily with faculty. Attendance at religious services is required.

Tuition and Aid Day student tuition: $11,400. Tuition installment plan (SMART Tuition Payment Plan, FACTS Tuition Payment Plan, monthly payment plans, individually arranged payment plans). Tuition reduction for siblings, merit scholarship grants, need-based scholarship grants available. In 2014–15, 35% of upper-school students received aid; total upper-school merit-scholarship money awarded: $166,050. Total amount of financial aid awarded in 2014–15: $354,257.

Admissions Traditional secondary-level entrance grade is 9. For fall 2015, 136 students applied for upper-level admission, 120 were accepted, 110 enrolled. High School Placement Test (closed version) from Scholastic Testing Service and Scholastic Testing Service required. Deadline for receipt of application materials: January 15. Application fee required. On-campus interview recommended.

Athletics Interscholastic: baseball (boys), basketball (b,g), cheering (g), cross-country running (b,g), diving (b,g), fencing (b,g), football (b), golf (b,g), ice hockey (b), indoor track & field (b,g), lacrosse (b,g), physical fitness (b,g), soccer (b,g), softball (g), swimming and diving (b,g), tennis (b,g), track and field (b,g), wrestling (b,g); intramural: dance squad (g); coed interscholastic: cheering, cross-country running, fencing, golf, physical fitness, soccer, swimming and diving, wrestling; coed intramural: skiing (cross-country), skiing (downhill), snowboarding, strength & conditioning, volleyball, weight training. 2 PE instructors, 50 coaches, 1 athletic trainer.

Computers Computers are regularly used in computer applications, design classes. Computer resources include on-campus library services, Internet access, wireless campus network, Internet filtering or blocking technology. Campus intranet, student e-mail accounts, and computer access in designated common areas are available to students. Students grades are available online. The school has a published electronic and media policy.

Contact Mrs. Catherine Brown, Director of Admissions (Gr. 6-8) and International Programs. 860-848-1271 Ext. 102. Fax: 860-848-1274. E-mail: Admissions@Saint-Bernard.com. Website: www.saint-bernard.com

ST. BERNARD'S CATHOLIC SCHOOL

222 Dollison Street
Eureka, California 95501

Head of School: Mr. Paul Shanahan

General Information Coeducational boarding and day college-preparatory and religious studies school, affiliated with Roman Catholic Church. Boarding grades 8–12, day grades 7–12. Founded: 1912. Setting: small town. Nearest major city is San Francisco. Students are housed in single-sex by floor dormitories and coed dormitories. 5-acre campus. 4 buildings on campus. Approved or accredited by National Catholic Education Association, Western Association of Schools and Colleges, Western Catholic Education Association, and California Department of Education. Endowment: $63,000. Total enrollment: 231. Upper school average class size: 20. Upper school faculty-student ratio: 1:12. There are 180 required school days per year for Upper School students. Upper School students typically attend 5 days per week. The average school day consists of 6 hours.

Upper School Student Profile Grade 7: 22 students (13 boys, 9 girls); Grade 8: 18 students (4 boys, 14 girls); Grade 9: 48 students (33 boys, 15 girls); Grade 10: 44 students (24 boys, 20 girls); Grade 11: 58 students (36 boys, 22 girls); Grade 12: 50 students (29 boys, 21 girls). 15% of students are boarding students. 85% are state residents. 1 state is represented in upper school student body. 15% are international students. International students from China, Republic of Korea, and Viet Nam; 2 other countries represented in student body. 35% of students are Roman Catholic.

Faculty School total: 23. In upper school: 11 men, 12 women; 6 have advanced degrees; 2 reside on campus.

Subjects Offered Arts, community service, English, fine arts, mathematics, physical education, religion, science, social studies.

Graduation Requirements Arts and fine arts (art, music, dance, drama), English, foreign language, mathematics, physical education (includes health), science, social studies (includes history), theology, follow the University of California requirements (240 units). Community service is required.

Special Academic Programs Advanced Placement exam preparation; honors section; study at local college for college credit; remedial reading and/or remedial writing; remedial math; special instructional classes for students with learning disabilities.

College Admission Counseling 26 students graduated in 2016; 19 went to college, including California State University, Sacramento; College of the Redwoods; Humboldt State University; University of California, Berkeley; University of California, Davis; University of California, Santa Cruz. Other: 2 went to work, 1 entered military service. Median SAT critical reading: 500, median SAT math: 550, median SAT writing: 530, median composite ACT: 39.

Student Life Upper grades have specified standards of dress, student council. Discipline rests equally with students and faculty. Attendance at religious services is required.

Tuition and Aid Day student tuition: $6300. Tuition installment plan (monthly payment plans, individually arranged payment plans). Tuition reduction for siblings, merit scholarship grants, need-based scholarship grants, paying campus jobs available.

In 2016–17, 47% of upper-school students received aid; total upper-school merit-scholarship money awarded: $2500. Total amount of financial aid awarded in 2016–17: $55,000.

Admissions Traditional secondary-level entrance grade is 9. For fall 2016, 46 students applied for upper-level admission, 46 were accepted, 44 enrolled. Admissions testing or TOEFL required. Deadline for receipt of application materials: none. Application fee required: $40. On-campus interview recommended.

Athletics Interscholastic: baseball (boys), basketball (b,g), cheering (g), football (b), golf (b,g), soccer (b,g), softball (g), tennis (b,g), volleyball (g), wrestling (b); intramural: cheering (g); coed interscholastic: track and field, wrestling. 1 PE instructor, 15 coaches, 1 athletic trainer.

Computers Computers are regularly used in computer applications, graphic design, journalism, yearbook classes. Computer network features include on-campus library services, Internet access, wireless campus network, Internet filtering or blocking technology. Student e-mail accounts are available to students. Students grades are available online. The school has a published electronic and media policy.

Contact Stacy Kastler, Vice Principal. 707-443-2735 Ext. 114. Fax: 707-443-4723. E-mail: kastler@saintbernards.us. Website: www.saintbernards.us/

ST. BRENDAN HIGH SCHOOL

2950 Southwest 87th Avenue
Miami, Florida 33165-3295

Head of School: Mr. Jose Rodelgo-Bueno

General Information Coeducational day college-preparatory, general academic, arts, business, religious studies, bilingual studies, and technology school, affiliated with Roman Catholic Church. Grades 9–12. Founded: 1975. Setting: urban. 34-acre campus. 4 buildings on campus. Approved or accredited by Southern Association of Colleges and Schools and Florida Department of Education. Total enrollment: 1,145. Upper school average class size: 27. Upper school faculty-student ratio: 1:16. There are 180 required school days per year for Upper School students. Upper School students typically attend 5 days per week. The average school day consists of 6 hours and 45 minutes.

Upper School Student Profile 98% of students are Roman Catholic.

Faculty School total: 73. In upper school: 25 men, 47 women; 35 have advanced degrees.

Graduation Requirements Algebra, students must complete 100 learning community service hours in their four years of high school.

Special Academic Programs 10 Advanced Placement exams for which test preparation is offered; honors section; study at local college for college credit; academic accommodation for the gifted; remedial reading and/or remedial writing; remedial math.

College Admission Counseling 258 students graduated in 2015; all went to college, including Florida International University; Florida State University; Miami Dade College; University of Central Florida; University of Florida; University of Miami. Median SAT critical reading: 500, median SAT math: 490, median SAT writing: 500, median combined SAT: 1490, median composite ACT: 22. 12% scored over 600 on SAT critical reading, 10% scored over 600 on SAT math, 9% scored over 26 on composite ACT.

Student Life Upper grades have uniform requirement, student council, honor system. Discipline rests primarily with faculty. Attendance at religious services is required.

Tuition and Aid Tuition installment plan (FACTS Tuition Payment Plan, monthly payment plans). Tuition reduction for siblings, need-based scholarship grants, paying campus jobs available. In 2015–16, 23% of upper-school students received aid. Total amount of financial aid awarded in 2015–16: $266,000.

Admissions Traditional secondary-level entrance grade is 9. Catholic High School Entrance Examination or placement test required. Deadline for receipt of application materials: none. Application fee required: $50.

Athletics Interscholastic: baseball (boys), basketball (b,g), cheering (g), cross-country running (b,g), dance (g), dance team (g), lacrosse (b), physical fitness (b,g), physical training (b,g), soccer (b,g), softball (g), swimming and diving (b,g), tennis (b,g), track and field (b,g), volleyball (b,g). 1 PE instructor, 17 coaches, 1 athletic trainer.

Computers Computers are regularly used in business, computer applications, graphic design, mathematics, media arts, media production, newspaper, programming, reading, remedial study skills, research skills, science, speech, Web site design, word processing, yearbook classes. Computer network features include on-campus library services, Internet access, wireless campus network, Internet filtering or blocking technology, 1:1 iPad program. Campus intranet and computer access in designated common areas are available to students. Students grades are available online. The school has a published electronic and media policy.

Contact Melissa Ferrer. 305-223-5181 Ext. 578. Fax: 305-220-7434. E-mail: mferrer@stbhs.org. Website: www.stbrendanhigh.org

ST. CATHERINE'S ACADEMY

Anaheim, California
See Junior Boarding Schools section.

ST. CATHERINE'S SCHOOL

6001 Grove Avenue
Richmond, Virginia 23226

Head of School: Dr. Terrie Hale Scheckelhoff

General Information Girls' day college-preparatory school, affiliated with Episcopal Church. Grades JK–12. Founded: 1890. Setting: urban. Nearest major city is Washington, DC. 16-acre campus. 22 buildings on campus. Approved or accredited by National Association of Episcopal Schools, Virginia Association of Independent Schools, and Virginia Department of Education. Member of National Association of Independent Schools and Secondary School Admission Test Board. Endowment: $46 million. Total enrollment: 985. Upper school average class size: 16. Upper School students typically attend 5 days per week. The average school day consists of 7 hours and 30 minutes.

Upper School Student Profile Grade 6: 79 students (79 girls); Grade 7: 87 students (87 girls); Grade 8: 90 students (90 girls); Grade 9: 71 students (71 girls); Grade 10: 82 students (82 girls); Grade 11: 75 students (75 girls); Grade 12: 85 students (85 girls). 35.5% of students are members of Episcopal Church.

Subjects Offered Acting, adolescent issues, advanced chemistry, advanced computer applications, advanced math, algebra, American government, American history, American history-AP, American literature, ancient history, architecture, art, art and culture, art history, art history-AP, band, Bible, biology, British literature-AP, calculus, calculus-AP, ceramics, chamber groups, chemistry, chemistry-AP, Chinese, choir, choral music, choreography, chorus, comparative government and politics-AP, comparative religion, computer applications, computer math, computer programming, computer science, computer science-AP, constitutional law, creative writing, dance, dance performance, desktop publishing, drama, driver education, economics, economics-AP, English, English language and composition-AP, English literature, English literature and composition-AP, environmental science, environmental science-AP, ethics, ethics and responsibility, European history, expository writing, film and literature, fine arts, French, French language-AP, French literature-AP, gender issues, geography, geometry, government and politics-AP, government/civics, grammar, Greek, guitar, health and wellness, health education, history, history of jazz, honors algebra, honors English, honors geometry, independent study, Latin, Latin-AP, macro/microeconomics-AP, mathematics, modern dance, moral and social development, moral theology, music, music history, music theory, music theory-AP, orchestra, painting, performing arts, philosophy, photography, physical education, physical fitness, physics, physics-AP, playwriting and directing, portfolio art, post-calculus, pre-calculus, printmaking, regional literature, religion, rhetoric, robotics, science, sculpture, short story, social studies, Southern literature, Spanish, Spanish language-AP, Spanish literature, Spanish literature-AP, speech, speech communications, statistics, statistics-AP, theater, theater arts, theology, trigonometry, U.S. government and politics-AP, world cultures, world geography, world history, world literature, writing.

Graduation Requirements Arts and fine arts (art, music, dance, drama), computer science, English, foreign language, health, mathematics, physical education (includes health), religion (includes Bible studies and theology), science, social sciences, social studies (includes history), community service requirement.

Special Academic Programs 23 Advanced Placement exams for which test preparation is offered; honors section; independent study; term-away projects; study abroad.

College Admission Counseling 67 students graduated in 2015; all went to college, including James Madison University; The College of William and Mary; University of Virginia; Virginia Commonwealth University; Washington and Lee University. Median SAT critical reading: 600, median SAT math: 580, median SAT writing: 610, median combined SAT: 1800, median composite ACT: 25. 53% scored over 600 on SAT critical reading, 48% scored over 600 on SAT math, 59% scored over 600 on SAT writing, 53% scored over 1800 on combined SAT, 47% scored over 26 on composite ACT.

Student Life Upper grades have specified standards of dress, student council, honor system. Discipline rests equally with students and faculty. Attendance at religious services is required.

Tuition and Aid Day student tuition: $14,500–$24,980. Tuition installment plan (SMART Tuition Payment Plan, Tuition Management Systems Plan). Need-based scholarship grants available. In 2015–16, 23% of upper-school students received aid. Total amount of financial aid awarded in 2015–16: $917,330.

Admissions Traditional secondary-level entrance grade is 9. For fall 2015, 51 students applied for upper-level admission, 29 were accepted, 17 enrolled. Achievement tests, SSAT and Wechsler Intelligence Scale for Children required. Deadline for receipt of application materials: none. Application fee required: $50. On-campus interview required.

Athletics Interscholastic: basketball, cross-country running, diving, field hockey, golf, indoor track, indoor track & field, lacrosse, soccer, softball, squash, swimming and diving, tennis, track and field, volleyball, winter (indoor) track; intramural: aerobics, aerobics/dance, aerobics/Nautilus, aquatics, ballet, basketball, canoeing/kayaking, climbing, dance, equestrian sports, field hockey, golf, lacrosse, martial arts, modern dance, physical fitness, physical training, soccer, softball, strength & conditioning, swimming and diving, tennis, track and field, volleyball, weight lifting, weight training, wilderness, yoga; coed interscholastic: indoor track & field, track and field; coed intramural: aerobics/dance, backpacking, ballet, canoeing/kayaking, climbing, dance, modern dance, outdoor adventure, wilderness. 7 PE instructors, 87 coaches, 3 athletic trainers.

Computers Computers are regularly used in all classes. Computer network features include on-campus library services, online commercial services, Internet access, wireless campus network, Internet filtering or blocking technology. Campus intranet and student e-mail accounts are available to students. Students grades are available online. The school has a published electronic and media policy.

Contact Jennifer Cullinan, Director of Admissions. 804-288-2804. Fax: 804-285-8169. E-mail: jcullinan@st.catherines.org. Website: www.st.catherines.org

ST. CHRISTOPHER'S SCHOOL

711 St. Christopher's Road
Richmond, Virginia 23226

Head of School: Mr. Mason Lecky

General Information Boys' day college-preparatory school, affiliated with Episcopal Church. Grades JK–12. Founded: 1911. Setting: suburban. 60-acre campus. 9 buildings on campus. Approved or accredited by Virginia Association of Independent Schools. Member of National Association of Independent Schools and Secondary School Admission Test Board. Endowment: $60 million. Total enrollment: 1,006. Upper school average class size: 16. Upper school faculty-student ratio: 1:8. Upper School students typically attend 5 days per week. The average school day consists of 7 hours and 30 minutes.

Upper School Student Profile Grade 9: 87 students (87 boys); Grade 10: 88 students (88 boys); Grade 11: 83 students (83 boys); Grade 12: 78 students (78 boys). 50% of students are members of Episcopal Church.

Faculty School total: 170. In upper school: 32 men, 13 women; 34 have advanced degrees.

Subjects Offered Algebra, American history, American literature, ancient history, architecture, art, art history, astronomy, Bible studies, biology, calculus, ceramics, chemistry, Chinese, communications, community service, computer math, computer programming, computer science, creative thinking, creative writing, current events, dance, digital photography, drama, driver education, ecology, economics, English, English literature, environmental science, ethics, European history, expository writing, fine arts, French, geography, geology, geometry, government/civics, grammar, Greek, health, history, industrial arts, journalism, Latin, mathematics, music, philosophy, photography, physics, public speaking, religion, robotics, science, social studies, Spanish, speech, statistics, theater, theology, trigonometry, typing, video film production, woodworking, writing.

Graduation Requirements 1 1/2 elective credits, algebra, American literature, ancient history, biology, British literature, church history, English literature, European history, geometry, health, mathematics, physics, science, U.S. history, world history.

Special Academic Programs 23 Advanced Placement exams for which test preparation is offered; honors section; independent study; academic accommodation for the gifted, the musically talented, and the artistically talented.

College Admission Counseling 84 students graduated in 2016; all went to college, including James Madison University; The College of William and Mary; The University of North Carolina at Chapel Hill; University of Richmond; University of Virginia; Virginia Polytechnic Institute and State University.

Student Life Upper grades have specified standards of dress, student council, honor system. Discipline rests equally with students and faculty. Attendance at religious services is required.

Summer Programs Enrichment, advancement, sports, art/fine arts programs offered; session focuses on enrichment, sports, day camp, leadership; held on campus; accepts boys and girls; open to students from other schools. 500 students usually enrolled. 2017 schedule: June 20 to July 29. Application deadline: none.

Tuition and Aid Day student tuition: $26,350. Tuition installment plan (Academic Management Services Plan, monthly payment plans, individually arranged payment plans, Tuition Refund Plan). Need-based scholarship grants available. In 2016–17, 29% of upper-school students received aid. Total amount of financial aid awarded in 2016–17: $783,200.

Admissions Traditional secondary-level entrance grade is 9. For fall 2016, 70 students applied for upper-level admission, 31 were accepted, 22 enrolled. ERB (CTP-Verbal, Quantitative), Wechsler Intelligence Scale for Children or Wechsler Intelligence Scale for Children III required. Deadline for receipt of application materials: none. Application fee required: $50. On-campus interview required.

Athletics Interscholastic: baseball, basketball, bicycling, cross-country running, diving, football, golf, indoor soccer, indoor track & field, lacrosse, mountain biking, physical training, sailing, soccer, squash, strength & conditioning, swimming and diving, tennis, track and field, weight lifting, weight training, winter (indoor) track, wrestling; coed interscholastic: canoeing/kayaking, climbing, dance, outdoor adventure, rappelling. 6 coaches, 1 athletic trainer.

Computers Computers are regularly used in all classes. Computer network features include on-campus library services, online commercial services, Internet access, wireless campus network, Internet filtering or blocking technology. Campus intranet, student e-mail accounts, and computer access in designated common areas are available to students. Students grades are available online. The school has a published electronic and media policy.

Contact Cary C. Mauck, Director of Admissions. 804-282-3185 Ext. 2388. Fax: 804-673-6632. E-mail: mauckc@stcva.org. Website: www.stchristophers.com

ST. CLEMENT'S SCHOOL

21 St. Clements Avenue
Toronto, Ontario M4R 1G8, Canada

Head of School: Ms. Martha Perry

General Information Girls' day college-preparatory, arts, business, and technology school, affiliated with Anglican Church of Canada. Grades 1–12. Founded: 1901. Setting: urban. 1-acre campus. 1 building on campus. Approved or accredited by Canadian Educational Standards Institute and Ontario Department of Education. Affiliate member of National Association of Independent Schools; member of Secondary School Admission Test Board. Language of instruction: English. Total enrollment: 470. Upper school average class size: 16. Upper school faculty-student ratio: 1:7. Upper School students typically attend 5 days per week.

Subjects Offered Accounting, Advanced Placement courses, algebra, Ancient Greek, ancient world history, art, art history-AP, art-AP, band, biology, biology-AP, business, business studies, calculus, calculus-AP, Canadian geography, Canadian history, Canadian law, Canadian literature, career and personal planning, career education, character education, chemistry, chemistry-AP, civics, classics, college admission preparation, communication arts, computer science, creative writing, dance, data processing, design, drama, economics, economics-AP, English, English language-AP, English literature, English literature and composition-AP, environmental science, environmental science-AP, European history, European history-AP, exercise science, film studies, fine arts, finite math, French, French-AP, geography, geometry, grammar, graphic design, guidance, health, history, history-AP, human geography - AP, instrumental music, interdisciplinary studies, jazz ensemble, keyboarding, kinesiology, language and composition, language arts, Latin, Latin-AP, law, leadership and service, library, macro/microeconomics-AP, Mandarin, mathematics, modern Western civilization, music, music theory-AP, musical theater, philosophy, photography, physical education, physics, physics-AP, physiology, religion, science, social sciences, social studies, Spanish, Spanish-AP, statistics-AP, studio art-AP, theater, trigonometry, U.S. history-AP, Western civilization, world history, world issues, writing workshop.

Graduation Requirements Arts, business skills (includes word processing), career/college preparation, civics, computer science, English, foreign language, geography, mathematics, physical education (includes health), science, social studies (includes history).

Special Academic Programs 20 Advanced Placement exams for which test preparation is offered; independent study.

College Admission Counseling 64 students graduated in 2015; all went to college, including Dalhousie University; McGill University; Queen's University at Kingston; The University of British Columbia; The University of Western Ontario; University of Toronto.

Student Life Upper grades have uniform requirement, student council, honor system. Discipline rests equally with students and faculty. Attendance at religious services is required.

Tuition and Aid Day student tuition: CAN$26,675. Tuition installment plan (monthly payment plans). Bursaries, merit scholarship grants, need-based scholarship grants available. In 2015–16, 8% of upper-school students received aid.

Admissions SSAT required. Deadline for receipt of application materials: December 4. Application fee required: CAN$175. Interview required.

Athletics Interscholastic: alpine skiing, aquatics, badminton, basketball, cross-country running, dance, dance team, field hockey, golf, hockey, ice hockey, skiing (downhill), soccer, softball, tennis, track and field, volleyball; intramural: aerobics/dance, ballet, basketball, canoeing/kayaking, cooperative games, dance, dance team, fitness, floor hockey, jogging, life saving, outdoor education, running, table tennis, yoga. 5 PE instructors, 12 coaches.

Computers Computers are regularly used in all academic classes. Computer network features include on-campus library services, online commercial services, Internet access, wireless campus network, Internet filtering or blocking technology. Campus intranet, student e-mail accounts, and computer access in designated common areas are available to students. The school has a published electronic and media policy.

Contact Ms. Elena Holeton, Director of Admissions. 416-483-4414 Ext. 2227. Fax: 416-483-8242. E-mail: elena.holeton@scs.on.ca. Website: www.scs.on.ca

ST. CROIX SCHOOLS

1200 Oakdale Avenue
West St. Paul, Minnesota 55118

Head of School: Pres. Todd Russ

General Information Coeducational boarding and day college-preparatory, general academic, technology, ESL, and engineering school, affiliated with Wisconsin Evangelical Lutheran Synod. Grades 6–12. Founded: 1958. Setting: suburban. Nearest major city is St. Paul. Students are housed in coed dormitories. 30-acre campus. 4 buildings on campus. Approved or accredited by Minnesota Non-Public School Accrediting Association and Minnesota Department of Education. Endowment: $4.4 million. Total enrollment: 500. Upper school average class size: 19. Upper school faculty-student ratio: 1:13. There are 176 required school days per year for Upper School students. Upper School students typically attend 5 days per week. The average school day consists of 6 hours and 30 minutes.

Upper School Student Profile Grade 9: 110 students (52 boys, 58 girls); Grade 10: 110 students (57 boys, 53 girls); Grade 11: 110 students (56 boys, 54 girls); Grade 12: 110 students (53 boys, 57 girls). 30% of students are boarding students. 74% are state residents. 5 states are represented in upper school student body. 25% are international students. International students from Brazil, China, Japan, Kazakhstan, United States, and Viet Nam; 10 other countries represented in student body. 55% of students are Wisconsin Evangelical Lutheran Synod.

Faculty School total: 38. In upper school: 24 men, 11 women; 26 have advanced degrees; 5 reside on campus.

Subjects Offered Accounting, advanced biology, advanced chemistry, advanced math, Advanced Placement courses, algebra, American history, American literature, applied skills, art, band, Bible studies, biology, biology-AP, business skills, calculus, chemistry, choir, chorus, composition-AP, computer programming, computer programming-AP, computer science, drama, economics, engineering, English, English literature, English/composition-AP, environmental science, general science, geography, geology, geometry, German, home economics, keyboarding, Latin, literature, Mandarin, mathematics, music, physical education, physics, pre-algebra, reading, religion, science, social sciences, social studies, Spanish, speech, trigonometry, world history, writing.

Graduation Requirements Algebra, arts and fine arts (art, music, dance, drama), biology, chemistry, English, English composition, English literature, foreign language, geometry, government, grammar, literature, physical education (includes health), physics, religion (includes Bible studies and theology), science, social studies (includes history), speech, world geography.

Special Academic Programs 14 Advanced Placement exams for which test preparation is offered; honors section; independent study; academic accommodation for the gifted, the musically talented, and the artistically talented; remedial reading and/or remedial writing; remedial math; programs in English for dyslexic students; special instructional classes for students with learning disabilities; ESL (30 students enrolled).

College Admission Counseling 116 students graduated in 2016; 115 went to college, including Bethany Lutheran College; Cornell University; Martin Luther College; Minnesota State University Mankato; University of Minnesota, Twin Cities Campus; University of Wisconsin–Madison. Other: 1 went to work, 2 entered military service. Mean composite ACT: 25.

Student Life Upper grades have specified standards of dress, student council, honor system. Discipline rests equally with students and faculty.

Summer Programs ESL, sports programs offered; session focuses on ESL and activities, and a variety of sports camps; held on campus; accepts boys and girls; open to students from other schools. 80 students usually enrolled. 2017 schedule: July 15 to August 21. Application deadline: May 15.

Tuition and Aid 7-day tuition and room/board: $34,100. Merit scholarship grants, need-based scholarship grants available. In 2016–17, 40% of upper-school students received aid; total upper-school merit-scholarship money awarded: $80,000. Total amount of financial aid awarded in 2016–17: $850,000.

Admissions Traditional secondary-level entrance grade is 9. For fall 2016, 177 students applied for upper-level admission, 122 were accepted, 102 enrolled. Secondary Level English Proficiency or writing sample required. Deadline for receipt of application materials: none. Application fee required: $100. Interview required.

Athletics Interscholastic: baseball (boys), basketball (b,g), bowling (b,g), cheering (g), cross-country running (b,g), dance team (g), football (b), golf (b,g), hockey (b,g), ice hockey (b,g), lacrosse (b), soccer (b,g), softball (g), swimming and diving (b,g), tennis (b,g), track and field (b,g), volleyball (g), wrestling (b); intramural: badminton (b,g), basketball (b,g); coed interscholastic: riflery; coed intramural: alpine skiing, ball hockey, basketball, bowling, cheering, cross-country running, dance team, flag football, floor hockey, Frisbee, jogging, juggling, kickball, physical fitness, physical training, power lifting, skiing (downhill), snowboarding, softball, strength & conditioning, swimming and diving, table tennis, tennis, touch football, track and field, ultimate Frisbee, volleyball, weight lifting, weight training, whiffle ball. 3 PE instructors, 3 coaches, 2 athletic trainers.

Computers Computers are regularly used in accounting, computer applications, desktop publishing, economics, graphic design, keyboarding, media arts, media production, writing, yearbook classes. Computer network features include on-campus library services, online commercial services, Internet access, wireless campus network, Internet filtering or blocking technology. Student e-mail accounts and computer access in designated common areas are available to students. Students grades are available online. The school has a published electronic and media policy.

Contact Dr. Jeff Lemke, Admissions Director. 651-455-1521. Fax: 651-451-3968. E-mail: international@stcroixlutheran.org. Website: www.stcroixlutheran.org

SAINT DOMINIC ACADEMY

Bishop Joseph OSB Boulevard
121 Gracelawn Road
Auburn, Maine 04210

Head of School: Mr. Donald Fournier

General Information Coeducational day and distance learning college-preparatory, arts, business, and religious studies school, affiliated with Roman Catholic Church. Grades PK–12. Distance learning grades 11–12. Founded: 1941. Setting: suburban. 70-acre campus. 1 building on campus. Approved or accredited by Maine Department of

Education. Total enrollment: 571. Upper school average class size: 18. Upper school faculty-student ratio: 1:12. There are 175 required school days per year for Upper School students. Upper School students typically attend 5 days per week. The average school day consists of 6 hours and 15 minutes.

Upper School Student Profile 70% of students are Roman Catholic.

Faculty School total: 25. In upper school: 10 men, 15 women.

Subjects Offered Advanced Placement courses.

Special Academic Programs Advanced Placement exam preparation; honors section; independent study.

College Admission Counseling 63 students graduated in 2015; 60 went to college. Other: 1 went to work, 2 entered military service. Median SAT critical reading: 542, median SAT math: 534, median SAT writing: 524, median combined SAT: 1600.

Student Life Upper grades have specified standards of dress, student council, honor system. Discipline rests primarily with faculty. Attendance at religious services is required.

Tuition and Aid Day student tuition: $11,414. Tuition installment plan (FACTS Tuition Payment Plan). Merit scholarship grants, need-based scholarship grants available. In 2015–16, 55% of upper-school students received aid. Total amount of financial aid awarded in 2015–16: $600,000.

Admissions Traditional secondary-level entrance grade is 9. Scholastic Testing Service High School Placement Test required. Deadline for receipt of application materials: none. Application fee required: $50. Interview required.

Athletics Interscholastic: baseball (boys), basketball (b,g), field hockey (g), ice hockey (b,g), indoor track & field (b,g), soccer (b,g), softball (b,g), swimming and diving (b); coed interscholastic: alpine skiing, cheering, cross-country running, dance team, golf, nordic skiing. 1 PE instructor, 30 coaches, 1 athletic trainer.

Computers Computer network features include on-campus library services, online commercial services, Internet access, wireless campus network, Internet filtering or blocking technology. Campus intranet, student e-mail accounts, and computer access in designated common areas are available to students. Students grades are available online. The school has a published electronic and media policy.

Contact Ms. Marianne Pelletier, Director of Admissions. 207-782-6911 Ext. 2110. Fax: 207-795-6439. E-mail: Marianne.pelletier@portlanddiocese.org. Website: www.stdomsmaine.org

SAINT DOMINIC ACADEMY

2572 Kennedy Boulevard
Jersey City, New Jersey 07304

Head of School: Sarah Degnan-Moje

General Information Girls' day college-preparatory and arts school, affiliated with Roman Catholic Church. Grades 7–12. Distance learning grades 9–12. Founded: 1878. Setting: urban. Nearest major city is New York, NY. 2-acre campus. 1 building on campus. Approved or accredited by Middle States Association of Colleges and Schools, National Catholic Education Association, New Jersey Association of Independent Schools, and New Jersey Department of Education. Member of National Association of Independent Schools. Total enrollment: 451. Upper school average class size: 20. Upper school faculty-student ratio: 1:12. There are 180 required school days per year for Upper School students. Upper School students typically attend 5 days per week. The average school day consists of 6 hours and 5 minutes.

Upper School Student Profile Grade 7: 8 students (8 girls); Grade 8: 13 students (13 girls); Grade 9: 70 students (70 girls); Grade 10: 75 students (75 girls); Grade 11: 35 students (35 girls); Grade 12: 40 students (40 girls). 70% of students are Roman Catholic.

Faculty School total: 44. In upper school: 11 men, 32 women; 24 have advanced degrees.

Subjects Offered Accounting, advanced chemistry, algebra, American history, American literature, anatomy, art, art appreciation, art history, art history-AP, Bible studies, biology, business, business applications, business education, business skills, calculus, calculus-AP, chemistry, Chinese, collage and assemblage, college counseling, college placement, college writing, computer applications, computer education, computer literacy, computer math, computer processing, computer programming, computer science, CPR, creative writing, critical thinking, critical writing, drama, driver education, economics, English, English language and composition-AP, English literature, European history, fine arts, French, French language-AP, geometry, government/civics, health, history, history-AP, International Baccalaureate courses, Italian, keyboarding, Latin, mathematics, music, music performance, music theory, peer counseling, peer ministry, physical education, physics, physiology, psychology, psychology-AP, religion, science, social studies, sociology, Spanish, Spanish language-AP, theater, theology, trigonometry, women in literature, women's studies, world history, world literature, writing.

Graduation Requirements Arts and fine arts (art, music, dance, drama), business skills (includes word processing), computer science, English, foreign language, mathematics, physical education (includes health), religion (includes Bible studies and theology), science, social studies (includes history), 40 hours of community service, term paper.

Special Academic Programs International Baccalaureate program; Advanced Placement exam preparation; honors section; independent study; study at local college for college credit; remedial reading and/or remedial writing; remedial math.

College Admission Counseling 85 students graduated in 2016; all went to college, including New Jersey City University; New York University; Rutgers University–New Brunswick; Saint Peter's University; Saint Peter's University; Seton Hall University.

Student Life Upper grades have uniform requirement, student council, honor system. Discipline rests primarily with faculty. Attendance at religious services is required.

Summer Programs Remediation, enrichment, advancement, computer instruction programs offered; session focuses on preparing students for a successful high school career; held on campus; accepts girls; not open to students from other schools. 50 students usually enrolled. 2017 schedule: July 1 to July 31. Application deadline: June 1.

Tuition and Aid Day student tuition: $11,000. Tuition installment plan (SMART Tuition Payment Plan, FACTS Tuition Payment Plan, monthly payment plans, individually arranged payment plans, quarterly payment plan, semiannual payment plan). Tuition reduction for siblings, merit scholarship grants, need-based scholarship grants, paying campus jobs available. In 2016–17, 40% of upper-school students received aid.

Admissions Traditional secondary-level entrance grade is 9. For fall 2016, 300 students applied for upper-level admission, 150 were accepted, 70 enrolled. Cooperative Entrance Exam (McGraw-Hill) required. Deadline for receipt of application materials: January 6. No application fee required.

Athletics Interscholastic: basketball, cross-country running, dance team, diving, indoor track & field, outdoor activities, soccer, softball, swimming and diving, tennis, track and field; intramural: volleyball. 1 PE instructor, 18 coaches.

Computers Computers are regularly used in accounting, all academic, art, basic skills, business applications, business education, business skills, business studies, career education, career exploration, career technology, creative writing, economics, introduction to technology, keyboarding, programming classes. Computer network features include on-campus library services, Internet access, wireless campus network, Internet filtering or blocking technology. Campus intranet, student e-mail accounts, and computer access in designated common areas are available to students. Students grades are available online. The school has a published electronic and media policy.

Contact Mrs. Andrea Apruzzese, Director of Admissions. 201-434-5938 Ext. 14. Fax: 201-434-2603. E-mail: aapruzzese@stdominicacad.com. Website: www.stdominicacad.com

SAINT FRANCIS HIGH SCHOOL

200 Foothill Boulevard
La Canada Flintridge, California 91011

Head of School: Fr. Antonio Marti

General Information Boys' day college-preparatory and religious studies school, affiliated with Roman Catholic Church. Grades 9–12. Founded: 1946. Setting: suburban. Nearest major city is Los Angeles. 19-acre campus. 5 buildings on campus. Approved or accredited by Western Association of Schools and Colleges and Western Catholic Education Association. Total enrollment: 663. Upper school average class size: 28. Upper school faculty-student ratio: 1:12. There are 182 required school days per year for Upper School students. Upper School students typically attend 5 days per week. The average school day consists of 6 hours.

Upper School Student Profile Grade 9: 186 students (186 boys); Grade 10: 165 students (165 boys); Grade 11: 146 students (146 boys); Grade 12: 160 students (160 boys). 65% of students are Roman Catholic.

Faculty School total: 50. In upper school: 39 men, 11 women; 25 have advanced degrees.

Subjects Offered Acting, Advanced Placement courses, American history-AP, art, Bible studies, biology-AP, British literature, British literature (honors), calculus-AP, chemistry, chemistry-AP, chorus, Christian ethics, civics, comparative government and politics-AP, composition-AP, computer programming-AP, computer science-AP, computer skills, economics-AP, English, English language and composition-AP, English-AP, European history-AP, fine arts, foreign language, geometry, government and politics-AP, history, history of the Catholic Church, honors English, honors geometry, human geography - AP, kinesiology, Latin, Latin-AP, literature and composition-AP, macroeconomics-AP, mathematics, media production, physical education, physics-AP, pre-calculus, religion, science, social justice, social sciences, sociology, Spanish language-AP, statistics-AP, technology, U.S. history-AP, world geography, world religions, yearbook.

Graduation Requirements Arts and fine arts (art, music, dance, drama), English, foreign language, mathematics, physical education (includes health), religion (includes Bible studies and theology), science, social sciences, technology, Christian service hours, retreat each year of attendance. Community service is required.

Special Academic Programs Advanced Placement exam preparation; honors section; special instructional classes for directed study for students with learning challenges.

College Admission Counseling 163 students graduated in 2016; 161 went to college, including California State Polytechnic University, Pomona; California State University, Northridge; Loyola Marymount University; San Diego State University; University of California, Los Angeles; University of Southern California. Other: 2 entered military service. Mean SAT critical reading: 571, mean SAT math: 571, mean SAT writing: 553, mean composite ACT: 25.

Student Life Upper grades have specified standards of dress, student council. Discipline rests primarily with faculty. Attendance at religious services is required.

Summer Programs Remediation, enrichment, sports, art/fine arts, computer instruction programs offered; session focuses on remediation and enrichment; held on campus; accepts boys and girls; open to students from other schools. 400 students usually enrolled. 2017 schedule: June 19 to July 21. Application deadline: June 12.

Tuition and Aid Day student tuition: $15,000. Tuition installment plan (FACTS Tuition Payment Plan, monthly payment plans). Merit scholarship grants, need-based scholarship grants available. In 2016–17, 20% of upper-school students received aid; total upper-school merit-scholarship money awarded: $90,000. Total amount of financial aid awarded in 2016–17: $1,000,000.

Admissions Traditional secondary-level entrance grade is 9. For fall 2016, 350 students applied for upper-level admission, 220 were accepted, 186 enrolled. High School Placement Test required. Deadline for receipt of application materials: January 21. Application fee required: $75. On-campus interview recommended.

Athletics Interscholastic: baseball, basketball, cheering, cross-country running, football, golf, lacrosse, mountain biking, soccer, swimming and diving, tennis, track and field, volleyball, water polo. 3 PE instructors, 14 coaches, 2 athletic trainers.

Computers Computers are regularly used in all academic, yearbook classes. Computer network features include on-campus library services, Internet access, wireless campus network, Internet filtering or blocking technology, students purchase iPads. Students grades are available online. The school has a published electronic and media policy.

Contact Mrs. Betty Dowling, Registrar. 818-790-0325 Ext. 502. Fax: 818-790-5542. E-mail: dowlingb@sfhs.net. Website: www.sfhs.net

SAINT FRANCIS HIGH SCHOOL

1885 Miramonte Avenue
Mountain View, California 94040

Head of School: Mr. Simon Chiu

General Information Coeducational day college-preparatory, arts, religious studies, and technology school, affiliated with Roman Catholic Church, Roman Catholic Church. Grades 9–12. Founded: 1954. Setting: suburban. Nearest major city is San Jose. 25-acre campus. 10 buildings on campus. Approved or accredited by Western Association of Schools and Colleges and California Department of Education. Total enrollment: 1,761. Upper school average class size: 27. Upper school faculty-student ratio: 1:27. There are 180 required school days per year for Upper School students. Upper School students typically attend 5 days per week. The average school day consists of 6 hours and 30 minutes.

Upper School Student Profile Grade 9: 466 students (257 boys, 209 girls); Grade 10: 445 students (218 boys, 227 girls); Grade 11: 427 students (211 boys, 216 girls); Grade 12: 423 students (213 boys, 210 girls). 70% of students are Roman Catholic, Roman Catholic.

Faculty School total: 103. In upper school: 56 men, 47 women; 63 have advanced degrees.

Subjects Offered 20th century American writers, 3-dimensional design, algebra, American literature, analytic geometry, anatomy and physiology, band, biology, biology-AP, British literature, British literature (honors), business, calculus-AP, chemistry, chemistry-AP, Christianity, computer graphics, computer literacy, computer programming, computer science, computer science-AP, concert band, concert choir, contemporary issues, contemporary problems, creative writing, design, drama, drawing, economics, electronic music, English, English literature-AP, film and literature, French, French-AP, geography, geometry, German-AP, global science, graphics, health science, human biology, information technology, jazz band, jazz ensemble, journalism, music, oil painting, philosophy, physical education, physical science, pre-calculus, printmaking, psychology, religious studies, science fiction, social justice, Spanish, Spanish-AP, speech, speech communications, statistics, symphonic band, technology, trigonometry, U.S. government, U.S. government and politics-AP, U.S. history, U.S. history-AP, water color painting, world history, world religions.

Graduation Requirements Computer literacy, English, foreign language, human biology, mathematics, physical education (includes health), religious studies, science, social studies (includes history).

Special Academic Programs Advanced Placement exam preparation; honors section; study at local college for college credit.

College Admission Counseling 430 students graduated in 2015; 425 went to college, including Loyola Marymount University; Stanford University; University of California, Berkeley; University of California, Los Angeles; University of Southern California. Mean SAT critical reading: 711, mean SAT math: 743, mean SAT writing: 742.

Student Life Upper grades have specified standards of dress, student council, honor system. Discipline rests primarily with faculty. Attendance at religious services is required.

Tuition and Aid Day student tuition: $16,700. Tuition installment plan (SMART Tuition Payment Plan, monthly payment plans, individually arranged payment plans). Need-based scholarship grants, paying campus jobs available. In 2015–16, 18% of upper-school students received aid. Total amount of financial aid awarded in 2015–16: $3,000,000.

Admissions Traditional secondary-level entrance grade is 9. For fall 2015, 1,500 students applied for upper-level admission, 800 were accepted, 495 enrolled. High School Placement Test required. Deadline for receipt of application materials: December 11. Application fee required: $75. On-campus interview required.

Athletics Interscholastic: aquatics (boys, girls), baseball (b,g), basketball (b,g), cheering (g), cross-country running (b,g), dance squad (g), diving (b,g), drill team (b,g), field hockey (g), football (b), golf (b,g), gymnastics (g), ice hockey (b,g), lacrosse (b,g), soccer (b,g), softball (g), strength & conditioning (b,g), swimming and diving (b,g), track and field (b,g), volleyball (b,g), water polo (b,g), wrestling (b); intramural: cooperative games (b,g), flag football (b,g), indoor soccer (b,g), physical fitness (b,g), rugby (b,g), soccer (b,g), strength & conditioning (b,g), swimming and diving (b,g), table tennis (b,g), volleyball (b,g), whiffle ball (b,g); coed interscholastic: cheering, ice hockey, roller hockey; coed intramural: basketball, cooperative games, flag football, indoor soccer, soccer, volleyball, whiffle ball. 6 PE instructors, 51 coaches, 1 athletic trainer.

Computers Computers are regularly used in creative writing, current events, digital applications, graphic arts, graphic design, photography, publications classes. Computer network features include on-campus library services, Internet access, wireless campus network, Internet filtering or blocking technology. Campus intranet, student e-mail accounts, and computer access in designated common areas are available to students. Students grades are available online.

Contact Mr. Simon Raines, Director of Admissions. 650-968-1213 Ext. 213. Fax: 650-968-1706. E-mail: simonraines@sfhs.com. Website: www.sfhs.com

ST. FRANCIS HIGH SCHOOL

233 West Broadway
Louisville, Kentucky 40202

Head of School: Ms. Alexandra Schreiber Thurstone

General Information Coeducational day college-preparatory school. Grades 9–12. Founded: 1965. Setting: urban. 2-acre campus. 1 building on campus. Approved or accredited by Kentucky Department of Education. Member of National Association of Independent Schools. Endowment: $2.1 million. Total enrollment: 154. Upper school average class size: 12. Upper school faculty-student ratio: 1:7. There are 172 required school days per year for Upper School students. Upper School students typically attend 5 days per week. The average school day consists of 7 hours.

Upper School Student Profile Grade 9: 38 students (16 boys, 22 girls); Grade 10: 38 students (19 boys, 19 girls); Grade 11: 32 students (20 boys, 12 girls); Grade 12: 46 students (24 boys, 22 girls).

Faculty School total: 24. In upper school: 14 men, 10 women; 16 have advanced degrees.

Subjects Offered 20th century history, ACT preparation, Advanced Placement courses, algebra, American history, anatomy, ancient history, ancient world history, art, biology, biology-AP, calculus-AP, chemistry, chemistry-AP, Chinese, community service, constitutional law, creative writing, drama, drawing, English, English literature, English literature and composition-AP, English literature-AP, environmental science, environmental science-AP, European history, European history-AP, film studies, filmmaking, fine arts, finite math, French, French language-AP, French literature-AP, French-AP, gender issues, geometry, health, history-AP, law, medieval history, modern civilization, photography, physical education, physics, physics-AP, playwriting, pre-calculus, senior project, Spanish, Spanish language-AP, Spanish literature-AP, Spanish-AP, statistics, statistics-AP, The 20th Century, U.S. history-AP, video film production, world history, writing.

Graduation Requirements Arts and fine arts (art, music, dance, drama), English, foreign language, history, mathematics, physical education (includes health), science, social studies (includes history), senior project (year-long research project on a topic of student's choice). Community service is required.

Special Academic Programs Advanced Placement exam preparation; independent study; study abroad; academic accommodation for the gifted and the artistically talented.

College Admission Counseling 35 students graduated in 2016; all went to college.

Student Life Upper grades have student council. Discipline rests equally with students and faculty.

Tuition and Aid Day student tuition: $21,800. Tuition installment plan (Insured Tuition Payment Plan, FACTS Tuition Payment Plan, monthly payment plans). Merit scholarship grants, need-based scholarship grants, tuition remission for children of faculty and staff available. In 2016–17, 50% of upper-school students received aid.

Admissions Traditional secondary-level entrance grade is 9. For fall 2016, 47 students applied for upper-level admission, 42 were accepted, 39 enrolled. Deadline for receipt of application materials: January 15. Application fee required: $60. On-campus interview recommended.

Athletics Interscholastic: basketball (boys, girls), bowling (b,g), cross-country running (b,g), field hockey (g), tennis (b,g), track and field (b,g); intramural: indoor hockey (g), indoor soccer (b); coed interscholastic: golf, independent competitive sports, soccer, softball; coed intramural: bicycling, fitness, outdoor activities, skiing (cross-country), snowboarding, weight lifting, yoga. 1 PE instructor, 12 coaches.

Computers Computers are regularly used in all academic classes. Computer network features include Internet access, wireless campus network, word processing, publishing, and Web page programs. Student e-mail accounts and computer access in designated common areas are available to students. The school has a published electronic and media policy.

Contact Ms. Trisha Amirault, Director of Admissions. 502-736-1009. Fax: 502-736-1049. E-mail: tamirault@stfrancisschool.org. Website: www.stfrancisschool.org

ST. FRANCIS SCHOOL

13440 Cogburn Road
Milton, Georgia 30004

Head of School: Mr. Drew Buccellato

General Information Coeducational day college-preparatory, arts, technology, and science, tech, engineering, arts and mathematics (STEAM) school. Grades K–12. Founded: 1976. Setting: suburban. Nearest major city is Atlanta. 47-acre campus. 8 buildings on campus. Approved or accredited by Georgia Accrediting Commission, Georgia Independent School Association, Southern Association of Colleges and Schools, Southern Association of Independent Schools, and Georgia Department of Education. Endowment: $2 million. Total enrollment: 778. Upper school average class size: 14. Upper school faculty-student ratio: 1:14. There are 180 required school days per year for Upper School students. Upper School students typically attend 5 days per week. The average school day consists of 5 hours and 45 minutes.

Upper School Student Profile Grade 9: 78 students (40 boys, 38 girls); Grade 10: 74 students (44 boys, 30 girls); Grade 11: 69 students (38 boys, 31 girls); Grade 12: 95 students (60 boys, 35 girls).

Faculty School total: 40. In upper school: 15 men, 25 women; 22 have advanced degrees.

Subjects Offered 3-dimensional art, 3-dimensional design, acting, Advanced Placement courses, algebra, American literature, art-AP, arts, biology, British literature, calculus, character education, cheerleading, chemistry, chorus, Civil War, college counseling, computer processing, computer programming, computer science-AP, computers, drama, drawing, economics, engineering, English, English literature-AP, English-AP, environmental science, geography, geometry, government, graphic arts, graphic design, health, history-AP, honors algebra, honors English, honors geometry, honors U.S. history, honors world history, instrumental music, journalism, keyboarding, Latin, mathematics, newspaper, painting, performing arts, physical education, physical science, physics, play production, psychology, public speaking, SAT preparation, science, social studies, Spanish, studio art, studio art-AP, study skills, trigonometry, U.S. government, U.S. government and politics-AP, U.S. history, U.S. history-AP, word processing, world history, writing, yearbook.

Graduation Requirements Arts and fine arts (art, music, dance, drama), electives, English, foreign language, mathematics, physical education (includes health), science, social studies (includes history), technology, writing, community service hours.

Special Academic Programs Advanced Placement exam preparation; honors section; remedial reading and/or remedial writing; remedial math; special instructional classes for students with learning disabilities and Attention Deficit Disorder.

College Admission Counseling 61 students graduated in 2016; all went to college, including Georgia College & State University; Kennesaw State University; The University of Alabama; University of Georgia.

Student Life Upper grades have uniform requirement, student council, honor system. Discipline rests primarily with faculty.

Summer Programs Held on campus; accepts boys and girls; not open to students from other schools. 60 students usually enrolled.

Tuition and Aid Day student tuition: $20,000. Tuition installment plan (monthly payment plans). Tuition reduction for siblings, need-based scholarship grants available.

Admissions Traditional secondary-level entrance grade is 9. For fall 2016, 95 students applied for upper-level admission, 39 were accepted, 28 enrolled. School placement exam required. Deadline for receipt of application materials: March 4. Application fee required: $150. On-campus interview required.

Athletics Interscholastic: baseball (boys), basketball (b,g), cheering (g), cross-country running (b,g), equestrian sports (b,g), football (b), golf (b,g), horseback riding (b,g), physical fitness (b,g), soccer (b,g), softball (g), strength & conditioning (b,g), swimming and diving (b,g), tennis (b,g), track and field (b,g), volleyball (g), weight lifting (b,g), weight training (b,g), wrestling (b); intramural: equestrian sports (g), horseback riding (g); coed interscholastic: swimming and diving, tennis, track and field. 3 PE instructors, 6 coaches, 1 athletic trainer.

Computers Computers are regularly used in all classes. Computer network features include on-campus library services, online commercial services, Internet access, wireless campus network, Internet filtering or blocking technology. Campus intranet, student e-mail accounts, and computer access in designated common areas are available to students. Students grades are available online. The school has a published electronic and media policy.

Contact Mr. Brandon Bryan, High School Admissions. 678-339-9989 Ext. 33. Fax: 678-339-0473. E-mail: bbryan@sfschools.net.
Website: http://www.SaintFrancisSchools.com

ST. GEORGE'S INDEPENDENT SCHOOL

1880 Wolf River Road
Collierville, Tennessee 38017

Head of School: Mr. J. Ross Peters

General Information Coeducational day college-preparatory school, affiliated with Episcopal Church. Grades PK–12. Founded: 1959. Setting: suburban. Nearest major city is Memphis. 250-acre campus. 5 buildings on campus. Approved or accredited by National Association of Episcopal Schools, Southern Association of Colleges and Schools, and Southern Association of Independent Schools. Member of National Association of Independent Schools. Endowment: $7.1 million. Total enrollment: 1,188. Upper school average class size: 19. Upper school faculty-student ratio: 1:9. There are 175 required school days per year for Upper School students. Upper School students typically attend 5 days per week. The average school day consists of 6 hours and 45 minutes.

Faculty School total: 249. In upper school: 60 have advanced degrees.

Subjects Offered Algebra, band, biology, biology-AP, calculus, calculus-AP, chemistry, chemistry-AP, chorus, computer programming, drawing, English, English language and composition-AP, English literature and composition-AP, environmental science, European history-AP, film, French, French language-AP, global issues, global studies, government and politics-AP, government/civics, honors algebra, honors geometry, human anatomy, independent study, journalism, Latin, Latin-AP, Mandarin, painting, philosophy, photography, physics, physics-AP, pottery, pre-calculus, psychology, psychology-AP, religion, social justice, Spanish, Spanish language-AP, Spanish literature-AP, statistics-AP, theater, trigonometry, U.S. history, U.S. history-AP, visual arts, wellness, world history, world history-AP, writing, yearbook.

Graduation Requirements Art, electives, English, history, independent study, language, mathematics, religion (includes Bible studies and theology), science, wellness, Senior Independent Study.

Special Academic Programs 17 Advanced Placement exams for which test preparation is offered; honors section; independent study.

College Admission Counseling 108 students graduated in 2016; all went to college, including Mississippi State University; The University of Alabama; The University of Tennessee; The University of Tennessee at Chattanooga; University of Arkansas; University of Mississippi. Mean combined SAT: 1836.

Student Life Upper grades have specified standards of dress, student council, honor system. Discipline rests equally with students and faculty. Attendance at religious services is required.

Summer Programs Remediation, enrichment, advancement, sports, art/fine arts, computer instruction programs offered; session focuses on enrichment; held on campus; accepts boys and girls; open to students from other schools. 2017 schedule: June to August. Application deadline: June 1.

Tuition and Aid Day student tuition: $13,510–$19,500. Tuition installment plan (individually arranged payment plans, one payment per year, two payments per year, and four payments per year.). Need-based scholarship grants available. In 2016–17, 29% of upper-school students received aid. Total amount of financial aid awarded in 2016–17: $975,000.

Admissions Traditional secondary-level entrance grade is 9. Admissions testing or ISEE required. Deadline for receipt of application materials: none. Application fee required: $50. On-campus interview recommended.

Athletics Interscholastic: baseball (boys), basketball (b,g), cheering (g), cross-country running (b,g), football (b), lacrosse (b,g), soccer (b,g), softball (g), tennis (b,g), track and field (b,g), volleyball (g), wrestling (b); intramural: bowling (b); coed interscholastic: golf, swimming and diving, trap and skeet, water polo; coed intramural: equestrian sports.

Computers Computers are regularly used in all classes. Computer network features include on-campus library services, Internet access, wireless campus network, Internet filtering or blocking technology. Campus intranet, student e-mail accounts, and computer access in designated common areas are available to students. Students grades are available online. The school has a published electronic and media policy.

Contact Mrs. Olivia Hammond, Director of Admission. 901-261-2300. Fax: 901-261-2311. E-mail: ohammond@sgis.org. Website: www.sgis.org

ST. GEORGE'S SCHOOL

372 Purgatory Road
Middletown, Rhode Island 02842-5984

Head of School: Eric F. Peterson

General Information Coeducational boarding and day college-preparatory and marine sciences school, affiliated with Episcopal Church. Grades 9–12. Founded: 1896. Setting: suburban. Nearest major city is Providence. Students are housed in single-sex dormitories. 125-acre campus. 47 buildings on campus. Approved or accredited by Association of Independent Schools in New England, National Association of Episcopal Schools, New England Association of Schools and Colleges, The Association of Boarding Schools, and Rhode Island Department of Education. Member of National Association of Independent Schools and Secondary School Admission Test Board. Endowment: $120 million. Total enrollment: 370. Upper school average class size: 11.

Upper school faculty-student ratio: 1:6. Upper School students typically attend 6 days per week. The average school day consists of 6 hours and 50 minutes.

Upper School Student Profile Grade 9: 67 students (33 boys, 34 girls); Grade 10: 95 students (44 boys, 51 girls); Grade 11: 111 students (55 boys, 56 girls); Grade 12: 97 students (53 boys, 44 girls). 85% of students are boarding students. 20% are state residents. 31 states are represented in upper school student body. 15% are international students. International students from Bermuda, Canada, China, Mexico, Republic of Korea, and Singapore; 18 other countries represented in student body.

Faculty School total: 70. In upper school: 32 men, 37 women; 55 have advanced degrees; 65 reside on campus.

Subjects Offered 3-dimensional art, 3-dimensional design, acting, advanced biology, advanced chemistry, advanced computer applications, advanced math, Advanced Placement courses, advanced studio art-AP, African American history, African American studies, algebra, American history, American history-AP, American literature, American literature-AP, American studies, analytic geometry, architectural drawing, architecture, art, art history, art-AP, Asian studies, Bible, Bible as literature, Bible studies, biology, biology-AP, calculus, calculus-AP, ceramics, chemistry, chemistry-AP, Chinese, computer graphics, computer math, computer programming, computer science, computer science-AP, creative writing, dance, DNA, drama, dramatic arts, drawing, ecology, economics, economics-AP, English, English language and composition-AP, English literature, English literature-AP, environmental science, environmental science-AP, ethics, European history, European history-AP, expository writing, fine arts, French, French language-AP, geometry, global studies, government/civics, grammar, health, history, journalism, Latin, Latin-AP, law, logic, macro/microeconomics-AP, Mandarin, marine biology, mathematics, microbiology, music, music theory-AP, navigation, oceanography, philosophy, photography, physics, physics-AP, psychology, public speaking, religion, robotics, science, sculpture, social studies, Spanish, Spanish language-AP, Spanish literature-AP, statistics, studio art-AP, theater, theology, trigonometry, U.S. government and politics-AP, veterinary science, world history, world history-AP, world literature, writing.

Graduation Requirements Arts and fine arts (art, music, dance, drama), computer science, English, foreign language, mathematics, physical education (includes health), religion (includes Bible studies and theology), science, social studies (includes history).

Special Academic Programs Advanced Placement exam preparation; honors section; independent study; term-away projects; study abroad; academic accommodation for the gifted, the musically talented, and the artistically talented.

College Admission Counseling 92 students graduated in 2016; all went to college, including Columbia University; Dartmouth College; Georgetown University; Harvard University; Middlebury College; Wake Forest University. Mean SAT critical reading: 630, mean SAT math: 655, mean SAT writing: 630, mean combined SAT: 1915.

Student Life Upper grades have specified standards of dress, student council, honor system. Discipline rests primarily with faculty. Attendance at religious services is required.

Tuition and Aid Day student tuition: $39,900; 7-day tuition and room/board: $58,000. Tuition installment plan (Insured Tuition Payment Plan, monthly payment plans, individually arranged payment plans). Need-based scholarship grants, need-based loans, middle-income loans available. In 2016–17, 33% of upper-school students received aid. Total amount of financial aid awarded in 2016–17: $42,000,000.

Admissions Traditional secondary-level entrance grade is 9. For fall 2016, 800 students applied for upper-level admission, 210 were accepted, 101 enrolled. ISEE, PSAT, SSAT or TOEFL required. Deadline for receipt of application materials: February 1. Application fee required: $50. Interview recommended.

Athletics Interscholastic: baseball (boys), basketball (b,g), cross-country running (b,g), field hockey (g), football (b), hockey (b,g), ice hockey (b,g), lacrosse (b,g), sailing (b,g), soccer (b,g), softball (g), squash (b,g), swimming and diving (b,g), tennis (b,g), track and field (b,g); coed interscholastic: dance, golf, sailing; coed intramural: aerobics/dance, dance, modern dance, mountain biking, Nautilus, soccer, softball, squash, strength & conditioning. 3 coaches, 3 athletic trainers.

Computers Computers are regularly used in art, English, foreign language, history, mathematics, music, religion, science, theater classes. Computer network features include on-campus library services, online commercial services, Internet access, wireless campus network, Internet filtering or blocking technology, scanners, digital cameras, and access to printers. Campus intranet, student e-mail accounts, and computer access in designated common areas are available to students. Students grades are available online. The school has a published electronic and media policy.

Contact Ryan P. Mulhern, Director of Admission. 401-842-6600. Fax: 401-842-6696. E-mail: admission@stgeorges.edu. Website: www.stgeorges.edu

ST. GEORGE'S SCHOOL

4175 West 29th Avenue
Vancouver, British Columbia V6S 1V1, Canada

Head of School: Dr. Tom Matthews

General Information Boys' boarding and day college-preparatory school. Boarding grades 8–12, day grades 1–12. Founded: 1930. Setting: urban. Students are housed in single-sex dormitories. 27-acre campus. 2 buildings on campus. Approved or accredited by Canadian Association of Independent Schools, Northwest Association of Independent Schools, The Association of Boarding Schools, and British Columbia Department of Education. Affiliate member of National Association of Independent Schools; member of Secondary School Admission Test Board. Language of instruction: English. Endowment: CAN$22 million. Total enrollment: 1,150. Upper school average class size: 19. Upper school faculty-student ratio: 1:8. There are 157 required school days per year for Upper School students. Upper School students typically attend 5 days per week. The average school day consists of 6 hours.

Upper School Student Profile Grade 6: 76 students (76 boys); Grade 7: 92 students (92 boys); Grade 8: 141 students (141 boys); Grade 9: 151 students (151 boys); Grade 10: 163 students (163 boys); Grade 11: 159 students (159 boys); Grade 12: 157 students (157 boys). 18% of students are boarding students. 91% are province residents. 9 provinces are represented in upper school student body. 9% are international students. International students from China, Germany, Hong Kong, Jamaica, Mexico, and Viet Nam; 13 other countries represented in student body.

Faculty School total: 130. In upper school: 62 men, 31 women; 55 have advanced degrees; 15 reside on campus.

Subjects Offered Advanced chemistry, advanced computer applications, advanced math, algebra, analysis and differential calculus, applied arts, applied music, applied skills, architecture, art, art history, art history-AP, biology, biology-AP, business, business skills, calculus, calculus-AP, Canadian geography, Canadian history, Canadian literature, career and personal planning, ceramics, chemistry, chemistry-AP, comparative government and politics-AP, computer graphics, computer programming, computer programming-AP, computer science, computer science-AP, creative writing, critical thinking, debate, drama, drama performance, dramatic arts, earth science, economics, economics-AP, English, English literature, English literature-AP, environmental science, European history, expository writing, film, fine arts, French, French-AP, geography, geology, geometry, German, German-AP, government/civics, grammar, history, industrial arts, introduction to theater, Japanese, journalism, Latin, Latin-AP, law, library, Mandarin, mathematics, mathematics-AP, music, music-AP, performing arts, photography, physical education, physical fitness, physics, physics-AP, psychology, psychology-AP, science, social studies, society, politics and law, Spanish, Spanish-AP, speech and debate, studio art, studio art-AP, technical theater, theater, trigonometry, typing, U.S. history-AP, United States government-AP, Western civilization, world history, world literature, writing.

Graduation Requirements Arts and fine arts (art, music, dance, drama), business skills (includes word processing), career planning, English, foreign language, guidance, mathematics, physical education (includes health), science, social studies (includes history), volunteer/work experience.

Special Academic Programs Advanced Placement exam preparation; honors section; academic accommodation for the gifted; remedial reading and/or remedial writing.

College Admission Counseling 160 students graduated in 2016; all went to college, including McGill University; New York University; Queen's University at Kingston; The University of British Columbia; The University of Western Ontario; University of Toronto. Other: 1 entered military service, 100 entered a postgraduate year.

Student Life Upper grades have uniform requirement, student council, honor system. Discipline rests primarily with faculty.

Summer Programs Enrichment, ESL, sports, art/fine arts, computer instruction programs offered; session focuses on recreation and enrichment; held both on and off campus; accepts boys and girls; open to students from other schools. 1,000 students usually enrolled. 2017 schedule: July 1 to August 15. Application deadline: none.

Tuition and Aid Day student tuition: CAN$22,737–CAN$33,020; 7-day tuition and room/board: CAN$45,630–CAN$60,600. Tuition installment plan (monthly payment plans, individually arranged payment plans, term payment plan, one-time payment plan). Tuition reduction for siblings, bursaries, merit scholarship grants, need-based scholarship grants available. In 2016–17, 7% of upper-school students received aid; total upper-school merit-scholarship money awarded: CAN$250,000. Total amount of financial aid awarded in 2016–17: CAN$1,000,000.

Admissions Traditional secondary-level entrance grade is 8. For fall 2016, 549 students applied for upper-level admission, 213 were accepted, 195 enrolled. School's own exam and SSAT required. Deadline for receipt of application materials: February 1. Application fee required: CAN$250. Interview recommended.

Athletics Interscholastic: badminton, basketball, cricket, cross-country running, curling, field hockey, Frisbee, golf, hockey, ice hockey, rowing, rugby, soccer, squash, swimming and diving, table tennis, tennis, track and field, triathlon, ultimate Frisbee, volleyball, water polo; intramural: archery, badminton, ball hockey, basketball, bicycling, canoeing/kayaking, cross-country running, curling, fitness, flag football, floor hockey, freestyle skiing, golf, hiking/backpacking, ice hockey, jogging, kayaking, martial arts, outdoor education, outdoor recreation, physical fitness, rock climbing, rugby, running, sailing, scuba diving, skiing (downhill), snowboarding, soccer, softball, strength & conditioning, swimming and diving, table tennis, tennis, track and field, volleyball, water polo, weight training, yoga. 10 PE instructors, 3 coaches, 2 athletic trainers.

Computers Computers are regularly used in desktop publishing, history, information technology, mathematics, media, publications, science, technology classes. Computer network features include on-campus library services, online commercial services, Internet access, wireless campus network, Internet filtering or blocking technology. Campus intranet, student e-mail accounts, and computer access in designated common areas are available to students. Students grades are available online. The school has a published electronic and media policy.

Contact Mr. Gordon C. Allan, Director of Admissions. 604-221-3881. Fax: 604-221-3893. E-mail: gallan@stgeorges.bc.ca. Website: www.stgeorges.bc.ca

SAINT GERTRUDE HIGH SCHOOL

3215 Stuart Avenue
Richmond, Virginia 23221

Head of School: Mrs. Renata Rafferty

General Information Girls' day college-preparatory school, affiliated with Roman Catholic Church. Grades 9–12. Founded: 1922. Setting: urban. 1 building on campus. Approved or accredited by National Catholic Education Association, Southern Association of Colleges and Schools, Virginia Association of Independent Schools, and Virginia Department of Education. Member of National Association of Independent Schools. Total enrollment: 247. Upper school average class size: 15. Upper school faculty-student ratio: 1:9. There are 180 required school days per year for Upper School students. Upper School students typically attend 5 days per week. The average school day consists of 7 hours.

Upper School Student Profile Grade 9: 63 students (63 girls); Grade 10: 48 students (48 girls); Grade 11: 64 students (64 girls); Grade 12: 65 students (65 girls). 60% of students are Roman Catholic.

Faculty School total: 40. In upper school: 3 men, 33 women.

Subjects Offered Advanced Placement courses, algebra, American history, American history-AP, American literature, American literature-AP, anatomy, art, bell choir, Bible studies, biology, calculus, calculus-AP, ceramics, chemistry, chemistry-AP, chorus, church history, community service, computer science, computer technologies, drama, drawing, driver education, English, English language and composition-AP, English language-AP, English literature, English literature and composition-AP, environmental science, European history, expository writing, fine arts, French, geometry, government and politics-AP, government/civics, grammar, history, honors algebra, honors English, honors world history, humanities, keyboarding, Latin, mathematics, media, music, painting, physical education, physics, physics-AP, pre-calculus, probability and statistics, psychology, religion, science, social sciences, social studies, sociology, Spanish, Spanish literature, studio art-AP, theater, theology, trigonometry, U.S. government and politics-AP, world history, world literature, writing, yearbook.

Graduation Requirements Arts and fine arts (art, music, dance, drama), computer science, English, keyboarding, mathematics, physical education (includes health), religion (includes Bible studies and theology), science, social sciences, social studies (includes history), 4 years of theology. Community service is required.

Special Academic Programs Advanced Placement exam preparation; honors section.

College Admission Counseling 65 students graduated in 2016; all went to college, including James Madison University; The College of William and Mary; University of Virginia; Virginia Commonwealth University; Virginia Polytechnic Institute and State University.

Student Life Upper grades have uniform requirement, student council, honor system. Discipline rests equally with students and faculty. Attendance at religious services is required.

Summer Programs Sports, art/fine arts programs offered; held both on and off campus; accepts girls; open to students from other schools. 50 students usually enrolled. 2017 schedule: June to August. Application deadline: March.

Tuition and Aid Day student tuition: $16,800. Tuition installment plan (FACTS Tuition Payment Plan, monthly payment plans). Merit scholarship grants, need-based scholarship grants available. In 2016–17, 30% of upper-school students received aid.

Admissions Traditional secondary-level entrance grade is 9. For fall 2016, 114 students applied for upper-level admission, 101 were accepted, 63 enrolled. Admissions testing, latest standardized score from previous school, Otis-Lennon School Ability Test and writing sample required. Deadline for receipt of application materials: January 31. Application fee required: $50. On-campus interview recommended.

Athletics Interscholastic: basketball, cross-country running, field hockey, golf, indoor track, lacrosse, soccer, softball, swimming and diving, tennis, track and field, volleyball; coed interscholastic: swimming and diving, track and field. 1 PE instructor, 14 coaches, 1 athletic trainer.

Computers Computers are regularly used in all academic classes. Computer network features include on-campus library services, Internet access, wireless campus network, Internet filtering or blocking technology. Campus intranet, student e-mail accounts, and computer access in designated common areas are available to students. Students grades are available online. The school has a published electronic and media policy.

Contact Ms. Meredith McNamara, Director of Admission. 804-822-3955. Fax: 804-353-8929. E-mail: mmcnamara@saintgertrude.org. Website: www.saintgertrude.org

SAINT IGNATIUS COLLEGE PREP

1076 West Roosevelt Road
Chicago, Illinois 60608-1594

Head of School: Ms. Brianna Latko

General Information Coeducational day college-preparatory school, affiliated with Roman Catholic Church (Jesuit order). Grades 9–12. Founded: 1870. Setting: urban. 18-acre campus. 5 buildings on campus. Approved or accredited by Jesuit Secondary Education Association, National Catholic Education Association, North Central Association of Colleges and Schools, The College Board, and Illinois Department of Education. Total enrollment: 1,364. Upper school average class size: 24. Upper school faculty-student ratio: 1:14.

Upper School Student Profile Grade 9: 350 students (179 boys, 171 girls); Grade 10: 354 students (173 boys, 181 girls); Grade 11: 331 students (163 boys, 168 girls); Grade 12: 329 students (164 boys, 165 girls). 86% of students are Roman Catholic Church (Jesuit order).

Faculty School total: 129. In upper school: 73 men, 56 women; 95 have advanced degrees.

Subjects Offered Acting, African-American history, African-American literature, algebra, American culture, American literature, ancient history, art, band, biology-AP, calculus-AP, Catholic belief and practice, chemistry-AP, college writing, computer programming, computer programming-AP, concert choir, creative writing, dance, desktop publishing, earth science, economics, economics-AP, English, English-AP, environmental science, fiction, film studies, finite math, fitness, foreign policy, French, French literature-AP, French-AP, geometry, government and politics-AP, Greek, independent study, instrumental music, integrated mathematics, introduction to technology, Irish literature, journalism, Latin, Latin-AP, modern European history-AP, modern history, music, music appreciation, orchestra, personal development, photography, physical education, physics-AP, political science, pre-calculus, scripture, Shakespeare, Spanish, Spanish literature-AP, Spanish-AP, speech, statistics, statistics-AP, studio art, studio art-AP, trigonometry, U.S. government, U.S. history, U.S. history-AP, wind ensemble, women's literature, world history, world religions.

Graduation Requirements Algebra, art, arts and fine arts (art, music, dance, drama), creative writing, economics, English, ethics, geometry, health, integrated science, intro to computers, language, modern languages, music, physical education (includes health), pre-calculus, speech, trigonometry, U.S. government, U.S. history, world history, world religions, zoology. Community service is required.

Special Academic Programs Honors section; independent study; study at local college for college credit.

College Admission Counseling 309 students graduated in 2016; 306 went to college, including Boston College; Indiana University Bloomington; Marquette University; Miami University; University of Illinois at Urbana–Champaign; University of Notre Dame. Mean SAT critical reading: 602, mean SAT math: 601, mean composite ACT: 26. 53% scored over 600 on SAT critical reading, 55% scored over 600 on SAT math, 50% scored over 26 on composite ACT.

Student Life Upper grades have specified standards of dress, student council. Discipline rests primarily with faculty. Attendance at religious services is required.

Summer Programs Remediation, enrichment, sports, art/fine arts, computer instruction programs offered; held on campus; accepts boys and girls; open to students from other schools. 400 students usually enrolled. 2017 schedule: June 19 to July 28.

Tuition and Aid Tuition installment plan (annual plan, semester plan, quarterly plan, monthly plan). Need-based loans, paying campus jobs, alumni grants available. In 2016–17, 22% of upper-school students received aid. Total amount of financial aid awarded in 2016–17: $3,000,000.

Admissions Traditional secondary-level entrance grade is 9. For fall 2016, 815 students applied for upper-level admission, 481 were accepted, 350 enrolled. Scholastic Testing Service High School Placement Test and SLEP required. Deadline for receipt of application materials: March 15. Application fee required.

Athletics Interscholastic: baseball (boys), basketball (b,g), bowling (b,g), cheering (g), crew (b,g), cross-country running (b,g), dance (g), dance squad (g), dance team (g), diving (b,g), football (b), golf (b,g), ice hockey (b), indoor track & field (b,g), lacrosse (b,g), rowing (b,g), rugby (b), sailing (b,g), soccer (b,g), softball (g), swimming and diving (b,g), tennis (b,g), track and field (b,g), volleyball (b,g), water polo (b,g), wrestling (b); intramural: ball hockey (b,g), basketball (b,g), floor hockey (b,g), Frisbee (b,g), indoor hockey (b,g), indoor soccer (b,g), soccer (b,g), ultimate Frisbee (b,g), volleyball (b,g); coed interscholastic: aerobics/dance. 3 PE instructors, 85 coaches, 3 athletic trainers.

Computers Computers are regularly used in desktop publishing, French, keyboarding, newspaper, programming, Spanish, technology, Web site design classes. Computer network features include on-campus library services, online commercial services, Internet access, wireless campus network, Internet filtering or blocking technology. Students grades are available online. The school has a published electronic and media policy.

Contact 312-421-5900. Fax: 312-421-7124. Website: www.ignatius.org

SAINT JAMES SCHOOL

17641 College Road
Hagerstown, Maryland 21740

Head of School: Rev. Dr. D. Stuart Dunnan

General Information Coeducational boarding and day college-preparatory school, affiliated with Episcopal Church. Grades 8–12. Founded: 1842. Setting: rural. Nearest major city is Washington, DC. Students are housed in single-sex dormitories. 1,000-acre campus. 36 buildings on campus. Approved or accredited by Association of Independent Maryland Schools, Association of Independent Schools of Greater Washington, Middle States Association of Colleges and Schools, National Association of Episcopal Schools, The Association of Boarding Schools, and Maryland Department of Education. Member of National Association of Independent Schools and Secondary School Admission Test Board. Endowment: $25 million. Total enrollment: 237. Upper school average class size: 12. Upper school faculty-student ratio: 1:7. There are 180 required school days per year for Upper School students. Upper School students typically attend 5 days per week. The average school day consists of 6 hours and 30 minutes.

Upper School Student Profile Grade 8: 29 students (16 boys, 13 girls); Grade 9: 54 students (33 boys, 21 girls); Grade 10: 54 students (37 boys, 17 girls); Grade 11: 53 students (33 boys, 20 girls); Grade 12: 47 students (27 boys, 20 girls). 75% of students are boarding students. 40% are state residents. 17 states are represented in upper school student body. 22% are international students. International students from China, Ghana, Hong Kong, Mexico, Nigeria, and Republic of Korea; 12 other countries represented in student body. 38% of students are members of Episcopal Church.

Faculty School total: 31. In upper school: 17 men, 14 women; 16 have advanced degrees; all reside on campus.

Subjects Offered Algebra, American history-AP, American literature, ancient history, art, art history, art-AP, biology-AP, calculus-AP, chemistry, chemistry-AP, choir, community service, economics, English, English literature, environmental science, European history-AP, fine arts, French-AP, geography, geometry, government-AP, keyboarding, Latin-AP, mathematics, modern European history, music, music history, physical science, physics, physics-AP, political science, science, Spanish-AP, theology, voice, world literature, writing workshop.

Graduation Requirements Arts and fine arts (art, music, dance, drama), English, foreign language, history, mathematics, science. Community service is required.

Special Academic Programs 14 Advanced Placement exams for which test preparation is offered; honors section; academic accommodation for the musically talented.

College Admission Counseling 57 students graduated in 2015; all went to college, including Cornell University; Davidson College; Sewanee: The University of the South; The George Washington University; University of Virginia.

Student Life Upper grades have specified standards of dress, student council, honor system. Discipline rests equally with students and faculty. Attendance at religious services is required.

Tuition and Aid Day student tuition: $29,300; 7-day tuition and room/board: $44,000. Tuition installment plan (SMART Tuition Payment Plan, individually arranged payment plans). Need-based scholarship grants available. In 2015–16, 33% of upper-school students received aid. Total amount of financial aid awarded in 2015–16: $2,500,000.

Admissions Traditional secondary-level entrance grade is 9. For fall 2015, 300 students applied for upper-level admission, 110 were accepted, 80 enrolled. PSAT or SAT, SSAT or TOEFL required. Deadline for receipt of application materials: January 31. Application fee required: $65. Interview required.

Athletics Interscholastic: baseball (boys), basketball (b,g), cross-country running (b), field hockey (g), football (b), golf (b), lacrosse (b,g), soccer (b,g), softball (g), tennis (b,g), volleyball (g), wrestling (b); intramural: aerobics/dance (g), ballet (g), dance (g), modern dance (g), weight training (b,g); coed intramural: alpine skiing, fitness, indoor soccer, martial arts, physical fitness, skiing (downhill), snowboarding, strength & conditioning, weight training, winter (indoor) track. 2 coaches, 2 athletic trainers.

Computers Computers are regularly used in all academic classes. Computer network features include on-campus library services, online commercial services, Internet access, wireless campus network, Internet filtering or blocking technology. Student e-mail accounts are available to students. The school has a published electronic and media policy.

Contact Mrs. Karla R. McNamee, Admission Assistant. 301-733-9330. Fax: 301-739-1310. E-mail: admissions@stjames.edu. Website: www.stjames.edu

SAINT JOAN ANTIDA HIGH SCHOOL

1341 North Cass Street
Milwaukee, Wisconsin 53202

Head of School: Mr. Paul Gessner

General Information Girls' day college-preparatory, arts, business, religious studies, technology, and engineering school, affiliated with Roman Catholic Church. Grades 9–12. Founded: 1954. Setting: urban. 2 buildings on campus. Approved or accredited by International Baccalaureate Organization, North Central Association of Colleges and Schools, and Wisconsin Department of Education. Total enrollment: 163. Upper school average class size: 25. Upper school faculty-student ratio: 1:14. Upper School students typically attend 5 days per week.

Upper School Student Profile Grade 9: 66 students (66 girls); Grade 10: 26 students (26 girls); Grade 11: 40 students (40 girls); Grade 12: 31 students (31 girls). 50% of students are Roman Catholic.

Faculty School total: 20. In upper school: 4 men, 16 women; 9 have advanced degrees.

Subjects Offered Advanced biology, advanced chemistry, advanced math, algebra, architecture, art, Bible, biology, biotechnology, calculus, chemistry, Christianity, engineering, English, environmental science, geometry, global studies, health, history of the Americas, moral theology, physical education, physical fitness, pre-calculus, Spanish, theology, U.S. government, U.S. history, world history, world literature.

Graduation Requirements Algebra, American history, art, biology, chemistry, Christian studies, church history, composition, electives, engineering, English, English composition, English literature, geometry, history, literature, physical education (includes health), physics, religion (includes Bible studies and theology), science, Spanish, U.S. history, world history.

Special Academic Programs International Baccalaureate program; study at local college for college credit; remedial reading and/or remedial writing; remedial math.

College Admission Counseling 27 students graduated in 2015; 23 went to college, including Milwaukee Area Technical College; University of Wisconsin–Milwaukee. Other: 4 had other specific plans. Median composite ACT: 18.

Student Life Upper grades have uniform requirement, student council, honor system. Discipline rests primarily with faculty. Attendance at religious services is required.

Tuition and Aid Day student tuition: $7900. Tuition installment plan (SMART Tuition Payment Plan, monthly payment plans, individually arranged payment plans). Merit scholarship grants, need-based scholarship grants available. In 2015–16, 98% of upper-school students received aid.

Admissions Traditional secondary-level entrance grade is 9. For fall 2015, 150 students applied for upper-level admission, 120 were accepted, 118 enrolled. Admissions testing required. Deadline for receipt of application materials: none. No application fee required. On-campus interview required.

Athletics Interscholastic: cross-country running, soccer, volleyball. 1 PE instructor.

Computers Computers are regularly used in architecture, career exploration, college planning, engineering classes. Computer network features include on-campus library services, Internet access, wireless campus network, Internet filtering or blocking technology. Student e-mail accounts are available to students. Students grades are available online. The school has a published electronic and media policy.

Contact Ms. Mary Fowler, Front Desk Receptionist. 414-272-8423. Fax: 414-272-3135. Website: www.saintjoanantida.org/

SAINT JOHN BOSCO HIGH SCHOOL

13460 Bellflower Boulevard
Bellflower, California 90706

Head of School: Casey Yeazel

General Information Boys' day college-preparatory, religious studies, and entrepreneurship, bio-medical, sports medicine, engineering school, affiliated with Roman Catholic Church. Grades 9–12. Founded: 1940. Setting: suburban. Nearest major city is Los Angeles. Students are housed in Single sex dorms for international students with partner Cambridge Institute of International Education. 35-acre campus. 5 buildings on campus. Approved or accredited by Western Association of Schools and Colleges and California Department of Education. Member of National Association of Independent Schools. Total enrollment: 821. Upper school average class size: 25. Upper school faculty-student ratio: 1:25. There are 178 required school days per year for Upper School students. Upper School students typically attend 5 days per week. The average school day consists of 6 hours and 30 minutes.

Upper School Student Profile Grade 9: 232 students (232 boys); Grade 10: 222 students (222 boys); Grade 11: 193 students (193 boys); Grade 12: 188 students (188 boys). 1% of students are boarding students. 100% are state residents. 2 states are represented in upper school student body. 1% are international students. International students from China; 4 other countries represented in student body. 85% of students are Roman Catholic.

Faculty School total: 52. In upper school: 39 men, 13 women; 25 have advanced degrees.

Subjects Offered 3-dimensional art, 3-dimensional design, acting, advanced biology, advanced chemistry, advanced computer applications, advanced math, Advanced Placement courses, algebra, all academic, American government, American history, American history-AP, American literature, American literature-AP, anatomy and physiology, animation, art, art history, art history-AP, ASB Leadership, Bible studies, biology, biology-AP, British literature, British literature-AP, business, business education, business law, calculus-AP, cell biology, ceramics, chemistry, chemistry-AP, Christian and Hebrew scripture, Christian ethics, church history, civics, comparative government and politics-AP, comparative religion, composition-AP, computer animation, computer applications, concert band, cultural geography, debate, desktop publishing, drama, drawing, economics, electives, engineering, English as a foreign language, English language and composition-AP, English language-AP, English literature, English literature and composition-AP, English literature-AP, English-AP, English/composition-AP, entrepreneurship, environmental science, French, French language-AP, French literature-AP, French-AP, geometry, government, government and politics-AP, government-AP, health, history-AP, honors algebra, human geography -AP, instrumental music, jazz band, journalism, Latin, leadership, modern world history, moral theology, music appreciation, music theory, oceanography, painting, personal finance, photojournalism, physical education, physical science, physics, physics-AP, pre-calculus, psychology, religious studies, SAT/ACT preparation, social justice, Spanish, Spanish language-AP, Spanish literature-AP, Spanish-AP, speech and debate, trigonometry, U.S. government and politics, U.S. government and politics-AP, U.S. history, U.S. history-AP, United States government-AP, Web site design, world history, world history-AP, world literature, world religions.

Graduation Requirements American government, American history, art, arts and fine arts (art, music, dance, drama), computer science, English, foreign language, mathematics, physical education (includes health), religion (includes Bible studies and theology), science, social studies (includes history), community service.

Special Academic Programs 12 Advanced Placement exams for which test preparation is offered; study at local college for college credit; academic accommodation for the gifted, the musically talented, and the artistically talented; remedial reading and/or remedial writing; remedial math; ESL (30 students enrolled).

College Admission Counseling 182 students graduated in 2016; all went to college, including California State University, Fullerton; California State University, Long Beach; El Camino College; Long Beach City College; Loyola Marymount University; University of California, Los Angeles. Mean SAT critical reading: 480, mean SAT math: 490, mean SAT writing: 470, mean combined SAT: 1440, mean composite ACT: 22. 15% scored over 600 on SAT critical reading, 15% scored over 600 on SAT math, 15% scored over 600 on SAT writing, 25% scored over 26 on composite ACT.

Student Life Upper grades have specified standards of dress, student council. Discipline rests primarily with faculty. Attendance at religious services is required.

Summer Programs Remediation, enrichment, advancement, sports, art/fine arts, computer instruction programs offered; session focuses on Enrichment and Remediation; held on campus; accepts boys and girls; open to students from other schools. 400 students usually enrolled. 2017 schedule: June 19 to July 21. Application deadline: June 1.

Tuition and Aid Day student tuition: $13,500. Tuition installment plan (FACTS Tuition Payment Plan). Tuition reduction for siblings, merit scholarship grants, need-based scholarship grants available. In 2016–17, 40% of upper-school students received aid; total upper-school merit-scholarship money awarded: $100,000. Total amount of financial aid awarded in 2016–17: $1,368,000.

Admissions Traditional secondary-level entrance grade is 9. For fall 2016, 410 students applied for upper-level admission, 280 were accepted, 240 enrolled. STS and STS, Diocese Test required. Deadline for receipt of application materials: January 31. Application fee required: $50. On-campus interview recommended.

Athletics Interscholastic: baseball, basketball, cross-country running, football, golf, ice hockey, lacrosse, rugby, soccer, strength & conditioning, swimming and diving, tennis, track and field, volleyball, water polo, wrestling; intramural: flag football, football, soccer, softball, touch football. 4 PE instructors, 72 coaches, 1 athletic trainer.

Computers Computers are regularly used in computer applications, desktop publishing, graphic design classes. Computer network features include on-campus library services, online commercial services, Internet access, wireless campus network, Internet filtering or blocking technology. Student e-mail accounts and computer access in designated common areas are available to students. Students grades are available online. The school has a published electronic and media policy.

Contact Mr. Edgar Alonso, Admissions Director. 562-920-1734 Ext. 313. Fax: 562-867-5322. E-mail: eantonel@bosco.org. Website: www.bosco.org

ST. JOHN NEUMANN HIGH SCHOOL

3000 53rd Street SW
Naples, Florida 34116-8018

Head of School: Sr. Patricia Roche, FMA

General Information Coeducational day college-preparatory school, affiliated with Roman Catholic Church. Grades 9–12. Founded: 1980. Setting: suburban. 10-acre campus. 5 buildings on campus. Approved or accredited by Southern Association of Colleges and Schools and Florida Department of Education. Total enrollment: 213. Upper school average class size: 20. Upper school faculty-student ratio: 1:15. There are 182 required school days per year for Upper School students. Upper School students typically attend 5 days per week. The average school day consists of 6 hours and 45 minutes.

Upper School Student Profile Grade 9: 76 students (42 boys, 34 girls); Grade 10: 49 students (25 boys, 24 girls); Grade 11: 59 students (36 boys, 23 girls); Grade 12: 60 students (27 boys, 33 girls). 80% of students are Roman Catholic.

Faculty School total: 30. In upper school: 12 men, 18 women; 20 have advanced degrees.

Subjects Offered Athletics, Basic programming.

Graduation Requirements Arts and fine arts (art, music, dance, drama), English, foreign language, health, mathematics, physical education (includes health), science, social studies (includes history), theology, community service.

Special Academic Programs 11 Advanced Placement exams for which test preparation is offered; honors section; independent study; study at local college for college credit; academic accommodation for the gifted.

College Admission Counseling 62 students graduated in 2016; 59 went to college, including Auburn University; Florida Atlantic University; Florida State University; The University of Tampa; University of Central Florida; University of Florida. Other: 1 went to work, 1 entered a postgraduate year, 1 had other specific plans. Median SAT critical reading: 530, median SAT math: 530, median SAT writing: 500, median combined SAT: 1480, median composite ACT: 23. 25% scored over 600 on SAT critical reading, 25% scored over 600 on SAT math, 16% scored over 600 on SAT writing, 18% scored over 1800 on combined SAT, 23% scored over 26 on composite ACT.

Student Life Upper grades have uniform requirement, student council, honor system. Discipline rests primarily with faculty. Attendance at religious services is required.

Tuition and Aid Day student tuition: $11,250. Tuition installment plan (FACTS Tuition Payment Plan). Merit scholarship grants, need-based scholarship grants, Step Up for Students available. In 2016–17, 60% of upper-school students received aid; total upper-school merit-scholarship money awarded: $10,000. Total amount of financial aid awarded in 2016–17: $300,000.

Admissions Traditional secondary-level entrance grade is 9. For fall 2016, 114 students applied for upper-level admission, 100 were accepted, 95 enrolled. STS and STS, Diocese Test required. Deadline for receipt of application materials: January 20. Application fee required: $30. On-campus interview recommended.

Athletics Interscholastic: baseball (boys), basketball (b,g), cheering (g), cross-country running (b,g), football (b), golf (b,g), soccer (b,g), softball (g), strength & conditioning (b,g), swimming and diving (b,g), tennis (b,g), track and field (b,g), volleyball (g). 1 PE instructor, 14 coaches, 1 athletic trainer.

Computers Computers are regularly used in all classes. Computer network features include Internet access, wireless campus network, Internet filtering or blocking technology, iPads provided by school. Campus intranet, student e-mail accounts, and computer access in designated common areas are available to students. Students grades are available online. The school has a published electronic and media policy.

Contact Mrs. Betsi Jones, Director of Admissions. 239-455-3044 Ext. 201. Fax: 239-455-2966. E-mail: ejones@sjnceltics.org. Website: www.sjnceltics.org

ST. JOHN'S CATHOLIC PREP

3989 Buckeystown Pike
P.O. Box 909
Buckeystown, Maryland 21717

Head of School: Dr. Thomas Powell

General Information Coeducational day college-preparatory school, affiliated with Roman Catholic Church. Grades 9–12. Founded: 1829. Setting: rural. Nearest major city is Baltimore. 65-acre campus. 1 building on campus. Approved or accredited by Association of Independent Maryland Schools, Southern Association of Colleges and Schools, and Maryland Department of Education. Total enrollment: 260. Upper school average class size: 15. Upper school faculty-student ratio: 1:9. There are 181 required school days per year for Upper School students. Upper School students typically attend 5 days per week. The average school day consists of 6 hours and 45 minutes.

Upper School Student Profile Grade 9: 82 students (42 boys, 40 girls); Grade 10: 68 students (36 boys, 32 girls); Grade 11: 84 students (39 boys, 45 girls); Grade 12: 60 students (32 boys, 28 girls). 65% of students are Roman Catholic.

Faculty School total: 31. In upper school: 14 men, 17 women; 21 have advanced degrees.

Subjects Offered Advanced Placement courses.

Graduation Requirements English, foreign language, government, mathematics, science, theology, world history.

Special Academic Programs Advanced Placement exam preparation; honors section; study at local college for college credit.

College Admission Counseling 59 students graduated in 2016; all went to college, including High Point University; Salisbury University; Shepherd University; Temple University; University of Maryland, College Park; West Virginia University. Median SAT critical reading: 541, median SAT math: 565, median SAT writing: 530.

Student Life Upper grades have uniform requirement, honor system. Discipline rests primarily with faculty. Attendance at religious services is required.

Tuition and Aid Day student tuition: $15,785. Tuition installment plan (FACTS Tuition Payment Plan). Tuition reduction for siblings, merit scholarship grants, need-based scholarship grants available. In 2016–17, 50% of upper-school students received aid; total upper-school merit-scholarship money awarded: $20,000. Total amount of financial aid awarded in 2016–17: $800,000.

Admissions Traditional secondary-level entrance grade is 9. For fall 2016, 161 students applied for upper level admission, 153 were accepted, 106 enrolled. High School Placement Test (closed version) from Scholastic Testing Service required. Deadline for receipt of application materials: none. Application fee required: $105. On-campus interview recommended.

Athletics Interscholastic: baseball (boys), basketball (b,g), cheering (g), cross-country running (b,g), football (b), golf (b,g), lacrosse (b,g), soccer (b,g), softball (g), tennis (b,g), volleyball (g); coed interscholastic: indoor track & field, track and field. 1 PE instructor, 15 coaches, 1 athletic trainer.

Computers Computers are regularly used in all classes. Computer network features include on-campus library services, Internet access, wireless campus network. Student e-mail accounts are available to students. Students grades are available online.

Contact Mr. Michael W. Schultz, Executive Director of Advancement. 301-662-4210 Ext. 121. Fax: 301-892-6877. E-mail: mschultz@saintjohnsprep.org. Website: www.saintjohnsprep.org

ST. JOHN'S INTERNATIONAL

#300 1885 West Broadway
Vancouver, British Columbia V6J 1Y5, Canada

Head of School: Mr. Tobin Sheldon

General Information Coeducational day college-preparatory and sciences school. Grades 10–12. Founded: 1988. Setting: urban. 1 building on campus. Approved or accredited by British Columbia Department of Education. Language of instruction: English. Upper school average class size: 10. Upper school faculty-student ratio: 1:10.

There are 225 required school days per year for Upper School students. Upper School students typically attend 5 days per week. The average school day consists of 6 hours.

Upper School Student Profile Grade 10: 45 students (23 boys, 22 girls); Grade 11: 40 students (20 boys, 20 girls); Grade 12: 40 students (20 boys, 20 girls).

Faculty School total: 13. In upper school: 10 men, 3 women; 7 have advanced degrees.

Subjects Offered Biology, calculus, career education, chemistry, drama, earth science, economics, English, English as a foreign language, English composition, film, fine arts, Mandarin, mathematics, media arts, music, physical education, physics, science, social studies.

Graduation Requirements Arabic studies, arts and fine arts (art, music, dance, drama), career and personal planning, English, general science, language, math applications, mathematics, physical education (includes health), science, social studies (includes history).

Special Academic Programs ESL (40 students enrolled).

College Admission Counseling 28 students graduated in 2016; 23 went to college, including Simon Fraser University; The University of British Columbia; University of Alberta; University of Toronto; University of Waterloo. Other: 1 went to work, 2 entered a postgraduate year, 1 had other specific plans.

Student Life Upper grades have specified standards of dress, student council, honor system. Discipline rests primarily with faculty.

Summer Programs ESL programs offered; session focuses on ESL; held on campus; accepts boys and girls; open to students from other schools. 20 students usually enrolled.

Tuition and Aid Day student tuition: CAN$16,300.

Admissions Traditional secondary-level entrance grade is 10. For fall 2016, 40 students applied for upper-level admission, 35 were accepted, 30 enrolled. English for Non-native Speakers or English language required. Deadline for receipt of application materials: none. Application fee required: CAN$200.

Athletics 1 PE instructor.

Computers Computers are regularly used in all classes. Computer resources include Internet access, wireless campus network, open lab for assignments.

Contact Admissions Officer. 604-683-4572. Fax: 604-683-4579. E-mail: info@stjohnsis.com. Website: www.stjohnsis.com

ST. JOHN'S JESUIT HIGH SCHOOL

5901 Airport Highway
Toledo, Ohio 43615

Head of School: Rev. Jeff Putthoff, SJ

General Information Boys' day college-preparatory school, affiliated with Roman Catholic Church (Jesuit order). Grades 7–12. Founded: 1965. Setting: suburban. 54-acre campus. 1 building on campus. Approved or accredited by Ohio Department of Education. Endowment: $13 million. Total enrollment: 950. Upper school average class size: 26. Upper school faculty-student ratio: 1:14.

Upper School Student Profile Grade 9: 150 students (150 boys); Grade 10: 130 students (130 boys); Grade 11: 185 students (185 boys); Grade 12: 175 students (175 boys). 65% of students are Roman Catholic Church (Jesuit order).

Faculty School total: 61. In upper school: 45 men, 16 women; 38 have advanced degrees.

Subjects Offered Accounting, Advanced Placement courses, American history, American literature, art, biology, calculus, chemistry, computer programming, computer science, drama, drawing, ecology, economics, English, fine arts, French, German, government/civics, graphics, health, mathematics, music, music appreciation, painting, physical education, physics, religion, science, social studies, sociology, Spanish, theater, theology, world history.

Graduation Requirements Arts and fine arts (art, music, dance, drama), computer science, English, foreign language, mathematics, physical education (includes health), religion (includes Bible studies and theology), science, social studies (includes history), senior project, senior retreat, senior paper.

Special Academic Programs Advanced Placement exam preparation; honors section; study at local college for college credit; ESL (10 students enrolled).

College Admission Counseling 164 students graduated in 2016; 161 went to college, including Bowling Green State University; Miami University; The Ohio State University; The University of Toledo; University of Cincinnati; University of Dayton. Other: 2 went to work, 1 entered military service. Mean composite ACT: 25.

Student Life Upper grades have specified standards of dress, student council, honor system. Discipline rests primarily with faculty. Attendance at religious services is required.

Tuition and Aid Day student tuition: $5255. Tuition installment plan (The Tuition Plan, FACTS Tuition Payment Plan). Tuition reduction for siblings, merit scholarship grants, need-based scholarship grants, paying campus jobs available. In 2016–17, 68% of upper-school students received aid.

Admissions STS and STS, Diocese Test required. Deadline for receipt of application materials: February. No application fee required.

Athletics Interscholastic: baseball, basketball, bowling, cheering, crew, cross-country running, diving, football, golf, ice hockey, lacrosse, soccer, swimming and diving, tennis, track and field, wrestling; intramural: basketball, bowling, Frisbee.

Computers Computers are regularly used in college planning, English, foreign language, media production, music, newspaper, publications, science, technology, yearbook classes.

Contact 419-865-5743. Fax: 419-867-9695. Website: www.sjjtitans.org

ST. JOHN'S PREPARATORY SCHOOL

72 Spring Street
Danvers, Massachusetts 01923

Head of School: Edward P. Hardiman, PhD

General Information Boys' day college-preparatory school, affiliated with Roman Catholic Church. Grades 6–12. Founded: 1907. Setting: suburban. Nearest major city is Boston. 175-acre campus. 11 buildings on campus. Approved or accredited by Association of Independent Schools in New England, National Catholic Education Association, and New England Association of Schools and Colleges. Member of National Association of Independent Schools. Endowment: $17.8 million. Total enrollment: 1,450. Upper school average class size: 18. Upper school faculty-student ratio: 1:11. There are 161 required school days per year for Upper School students. Upper School students typically attend 5 days per week. The average school day consists of 6 hours and 9 minutes.

Upper School Student Profile Grade 6: 100 students (100 boys); Grade 7: 100 students (100 boys); Grade 8: 100 students (100 boys); Grade 9: 300 students (300 boys); Grade 10: 300 students (300 boys); Grade 11: 300 students (300 boys); Grade 12: 300 students (300 boys). 70% of students are Roman Catholic.

Faculty School total: 153. In upper school: 77 men, 40 women; 87 have advanced degrees.

Subjects Offered 3-dimensional art, acting, aerospace science, algebra, all academic, American history, American history-AP, American literature, American literature-AP, anatomy and physiology, art, band, biology, biology-AP, business, calculus, calculus-AP, ceramics, chemistry, chemistry-AP, Chinese, chorus, computer programming, computer science, computer science-AP, constitutional law, desktop publishing, drama, driver education, economics, economics-AP, English, English language-AP, English literature, environmental science, environmental studies, ethics, European history, European history-AP, geometry, German, German-AP, government/civics, Holocaust, human geography - AP, jazz ensemble, Latin, Latin-AP, law studies, mathematics, music, music technology, neuroscience, physical education, physics, physics-AP, psychology-AP, religion, robotics, science, sculpture, social studies, society, politics and law, Spanish, Spanish-AP, statistics, statistics-AP, studio art, technology, trigonometry, U.S. history-AP, video, world history, world religions.

Graduation Requirements Arts and fine arts (art, music, dance, drama), computer science, English, foreign language, mathematics, physical education (includes health), religion (includes Bible studies and theology), science, social studies (includes history).

Special Academic Programs Advanced Placement exam preparation; honors section; independent study.

College Admission Counseling 280 students graduated in 2016; 270 went to college, including Boston College; Northeastern University; Providence College; Syracuse University; University of Massachusetts Amherst; University of New Hampshire. Other: 4 entered a postgraduate year, 6 had other specific plans.

Student Life Upper grades have specified standards of dress, student council. Discipline rests primarily with faculty. Attendance at religious services is required.

Summer Programs Enrichment, advancement, sports, art/fine arts, computer instruction programs offered; session focuses on academic enrichment, study skills, arts, fitness; held on campus; accepts boys and girls; open to students from other schools.

Tuition and Aid Day student tuition: $21,955. Tuition installment plan (SMART Tuition Payment Plan). Merit scholarship grants, need-based scholarship grants available. In 2016–17, 31% of upper-school students received aid. Total amount of financial aid awarded in 2016–17: $4,000,000.

Admissions Traditional secondary-level entrance grade is 9. SSAT required. Deadline for receipt of application materials: December 15. Application fee required: $50. Interview required.

Athletics Interscholastic: alpine skiing, baseball, basketball, bicycling, crew, cross-country running, diving, fencing, football, Frisbee, golf, hockey, ice hockey, indoor track, lacrosse, mountain biking, rugby, sailing, skiing (downhill), soccer, swimming and diving, tennis, track and field, ultimate Frisbee, volleyball, water polo, winter (indoor) track, wrestling; intramural: baseball, basketball, bicycling, bocce, bowling, boxing, climbing, combined training, cooperative games, crew, fitness, flag football, floor hockey, Frisbee, golf, hiking/backpacking, ice hockey, judo, martial arts, mountain biking, Nautilus, outdoor adventure, physical fitness, power lifting, rowing, sailing, skiing (downhill), snowboarding, strength & conditioning, surfing, table tennis, tennis, touch football, ultimate Frisbee, volleyball, weight lifting, weight training, whiffle ball, yoga. 2 PE instructors, 90 coaches, 2 athletic trainers.

Computers Computers are regularly used in all academic, career exploration, college planning, research skills classes. Computer network features include on-campus library services, online commercial services, Internet access, wireless campus network, Internet filtering or blocking technology, 1:1 iPad program; high school program is family-owned and school-managed, access to 200 computer workstations. Campus intranet, student e-mail accounts, and computer access in designated common areas are

available to students. Students grades are available online. The school has a published electronic and media policy.

Contact Joan Spencer, Administrative Assistant. 978-624-1301. Fax: 978-624-1315. E-mail: jspencer@stjohnsprep.org. Website: www.stjohnsprep.org

SAINT JOHN'S PREPARATORY SCHOOL

Box 4000
2280 Watertower Road
Collegeville, Minnesota 56321

Head of School: Fr. Jonathan Licari, OSB

General Information Coeducational boarding and day college-preparatory, arts, religious studies, and bilingual studies school, affiliated with Roman Catholic Church. Boarding grades 9–PG, day grades 6–PG. Founded: 1857. Setting: rural. Nearest major city is Minneapolis/St. Paul. Students are housed in single-sex dormitories. 2,700-acre campus. 23 buildings on campus. Approved or accredited by Minnesota Department of Education. Member of National Association of Independent Schools. Endowment: $12.5 million. Total enrollment: 285. Upper school average class size: 15. Upper school faculty-student ratio: 1:10. There are 172 required school days per year for Upper School students. Upper School students typically attend 5 days per week. The average school day consists of 5 hours and 35 minutes.

Upper School Student Profile Grade 8: 34 students (18 boys, 16 girls); Grade 9: 40 students (19 boys, 21 girls); Grade 10: 72 students (35 boys, 37 girls); Grade 11: 52 students (25 boys, 27 girls); Grade 12: 47 students (25 boys, 22 girls). 33% of students are boarding students. 63% are state residents. 4 states are represented in upper school student body. 25% are international students. International students from Austria, China, Hong Kong, Mexico, Republic of Korea, and Taiwan; 14 other countries represented in student body. 50% of students are Roman Catholic.

Faculty School total: 34. In upper school: 18 men, 16 women; 24 have advanced degrees; 2 reside on campus.

Subjects Offered 3-dimensional design, advanced chemistry, Advanced Placement courses, algebra, American history, American literature, art, art history, band, Bible studies, biology, biology-AP, British literature, calculus, ceramics, chemistry, Chinese, choir, civics, conceptual physics, creative writing, current events, drawing, earth science, economics, English, English literature, English-AP, environmental science-AP, ESL, European history, fine arts, geometry, German, government/civics, health, history, International Baccalaureate courses, mathematics, music, orchestra, photography, physical education, physics, pre-calculus, religion, science, social studies, Spanish, speech, statistics, theology, trigonometry, world history, world literature, writing.

Graduation Requirements American literature, British literature, English, theology and the arts, world literature.

Special Academic Programs International Baccalaureate program; Advanced Placement exam preparation; honors section; independent study; term-away projects; study at local college for college credit; study abroad; ESL (23 students enrolled).

College Admission Counseling 71 students graduated in 2015; 69 went to college, including Babson College; Boston College; College of Saint Benedict; Penn State University Park; St. John's University; University of Minnesota, Twin Cities Campus. Other: 2 had other specific plans. Mean SAT critical reading: 559, mean SAT math: 660, mean SAT writing: 574, mean combined SAT: 1793, mean composite ACT: 27.

Student Life Upper grades have specified standards of dress, student council, honor system. Discipline rests primarily with faculty. Attendance at religious services is required.

Tuition and Aid Day student tuition: $15,448; 5-day tuition and room/board: $32,178; 7-day tuition and room/board: $35,945. Tuition installment plan (monthly payment plans, individually arranged payment plans, semester payment plan). Merit scholarship grants, need-based scholarship grants, paying campus jobs available. In 2015–16, 46% of upper-school students received aid; total upper-school merit-scholarship money awarded: $30,000. Total amount of financial aid awarded in 2015–16: $896,000.

Admissions Traditional secondary-level entrance grade is 9. For fall 2015, 127 students applied for upper-level admission, 85 were accepted, 56 enrolled. International English Language Test or TOEFL required. Deadline for receipt of application materials: none. Application fee required: $25. Interview required.

Athletics Interscholastic: alpine skiing (boys, girls), aquatics (g), baseball (b), basketball (b,g), cross-country running (b,g), diving (g), football (b), gymnastics (g), ice hockey (b,g), indoor track & field (b,g), nordic skiing (b,g), soccer (b,g), softball (g), swimming and diving (g), tennis (b,g), track and field (b,g); intramural: aerobics (g), aerobics/dance (g), dance (g), figure skating (g), golf (b,g), ice skating (g); coed intramural: bicycling, canoeing/kayaking, cross-country running, fitness, fitness walking, flag football, floor hockey, Frisbee, indoor soccer, mountain biking, nordic skiing, physical fitness, physical training, racquetball, rock climbing, roller blading, skiing (cross-country), skiing (downhill), soccer, strength & conditioning, swimming and diving, ultimate Frisbee, volleyball, walking, wall climbing, wallyball, weight lifting, weight training, winter (indoor) track, winter soccer, winter walking, yoga. 1 PE instructor, 21 coaches.

Computers Computers are regularly used in all academic, English, science classes. Computer network features include on-campus library services, Internet access, wireless campus network, Internet filtering or blocking technology. Campus intranet, student e-mail accounts, and computer access in designated common areas are available to students. Students grades are available online. The school has a published electronic and media policy.

Contact Mr. Jeremy Meyer, Assistant Director of Admissions. 320-363-3320. Fax: 320-363-3322. E-mail: jmeyer@sjprep.net. Website: www.sjprep.net

ST. JOHN'S-RAVENSCOURT SCHOOL

400 South Drive
Winnipeg, Manitoba R3T 3K5, Canada

Head of School: Mr. Jim Keefe

General Information Coeducational boarding and day college-preparatory, Advanced Placement (AP), and Reggio Amelia program school. Boarding grades 8–12, day grades K–12. Founded: 1820. Setting: suburban. Students are housed in single-sex dormitories. 23-acre campus. 6 buildings on campus. Approved or accredited by Canadian Association of Independent Schools, Canadian Educational Standards Institute, The Association of Boarding Schools, and Manitoba Department of Education. Affiliate member of National Association of Independent Schools; member of Secondary School Admission Test Board. Language of instruction: English. Endowment: CAN$8.3 million. Total enrollment: 822. Upper school average class size: 20. Upper school faculty-student ratio: 1:10. There are 172 required school days per year for Upper School students. Upper School students typically attend 5 days per week. The average school day consists of 6 hours.

Upper School Student Profile Grade 9: 96 students (49 boys, 47 girls); Grade 10: 88 students (53 boys, 35 girls); Grade 11: 100 students (60 boys, 40 girls); Grade 12: 89 students (47 boys, 42 girls). 7% of students are boarding students. 96% are province residents. 5 provinces are represented in upper school student body. 5% are international students. International students from Austria, Canada, China, Hong Kong, Mexico, and Ukraine; 2 other countries represented in student body.

Faculty School total: 78. In upper school: 25 men, 23 women; 16 have advanced degrees; 6 reside on campus.

Subjects Offered Advanced Placement courses, algebra, American history, animation, art, biology, biology-AP, calculus, calculus-AP, Canadian geography, Canadian history, chemistry, chemistry-AP, computer science, debate, drama, driver education, economics, English, English literature, European history, European history-AP, French, French-AP, geography, geometry, history, information technology, law, linear algebra, mathematics, music, physical education, physics, physics-AP, pre-calculus, psychology, psychology-AP, science, social studies, Spanish, theater, visual arts, Web site design, world issues.

Graduation Requirements Canadian geography, Canadian history, computer science, English, French, geography, history, mathematics, physical education (includes health), pre-calculus, science, social sciences.

Special Academic Programs Advanced Placement exam preparation; honors section; independent study; study at local college for college credit; ESL (35 students enrolled).

College Admission Counseling 100 students graduated in 2016; 98 went to college, including McGill University; Queen's University at Kingston; The University of British Columbia; The University of Western Ontario; University of Manitoba; University of Toronto.

Student Life Upper grades have uniform requirement, student council, honor system. Discipline rests equally with students and faculty.

Tuition and Aid Day student tuition: CAN$18,650; 7-day tuition and room/board: CAN$37,420–CAN$49,440. Tuition installment plan (monthly payment plans, individually arranged payment plans). Bursaries, merit scholarship grants available. In 2016–17, 21% of upper-school students received aid; total upper-school merit-scholarship money awarded: CAN$95,000. Total amount of financial aid awarded in 2016–17: CAN$262,250.

Admissions Traditional secondary-level entrance grade is 9. Traditional secondary-level entrance age is 14. For fall 2016, 72 students applied for upper-level admission, 47 were accepted, 39 enrolled. Otis-Lennon School Ability Test, school's own exam or TOEFL or SLEP required. Deadline for receipt of application materials: none. Application fee required: CAN$125. Interview recommended.

Athletics Interscholastic: aerobics (boys, girls), badminton (b,g), basketball (b,g), cross-country running (b,g), Frisbee (b,g), golf (b), hockey (b,g), ice hockey (b,g), indoor track (b,g), indoor track & field (b,g), lacrosse (b,g); intramural: badminton (b,g), basketball (b,g), cross-country running (b,g), dance (b,g), hockey (b,g); coed interscholastic: badminton, Frisbee, physical fitness; coed intramural: badminton, flag football, floor hockey. 6 PE instructors.

Computers Computers are regularly used in all classes. Computer network features include on-campus library services, Internet access, wireless campus network, Internet filtering or blocking technology, EBSCO. Campus intranet and student e-mail accounts are available to students. The school has a published electronic and media policy.

Contact Mr. Paul Prieur, Director of Admissions & Marketing. 204-477-2400. Fax: 204-477-2429. E-mail: admissions@sjr.mb.ca. Website: www.sjr.mb.ca

SAINT JOHN'S SCHOOL

911 North Marine Corps Drive
Tumon, Guam 96913

Head of School: Ms. Patricia Bennett

General Information Coeducational boarding and day college-preparatory and arts school, affiliated with Episcopal Church. Grades PK–12. Founded: 1962. Setting: urban. Nearest major city is Manila, Philippines. 17-acre campus. 7 buildings on campus. Approved or accredited by International Baccalaureate Organization, National Association of Episcopal Schools, The College Board, Western Association of Schools and Colleges, and Guam Department of Education. Member of National Association of Independent Schools. Endowment: $1.7 million. Total enrollment: 533. Upper school average class size: 15. Upper school faculty-student ratio: 1:12. There are 180 required school days per year for Upper School students. Upper School students typically attend 5 days per week. The average school day consists of 7 hours and 30 minutes.

Upper School Student Profile Grade 6: 34 students (16 boys, 18 girls); Grade 7: 45 students (27 boys, 18 girls); Grade 8: 31 students (18 boys, 13 girls); Grade 9: 42 students (17 boys, 25 girls); Grade 10: 54 students (32 boys, 22 girls); Grade 11: 54 students (28 boys, 26 girls); Grade 12: 39 students (21 boys, 18 girls). 10% of students are members of Episcopal Church.

Faculty School total: 70. In upper school: 9 men, 17 women; 13 have advanced degrees.

Subjects Offered Algebra, American government, American history, American literature, anatomy, ancient world history, art, art history, Asian history, biology, biotechnology, campus ministry, chemistry, Christian education, computer applications, computers, creative writing, current events, dance, drama, drawing and design, earth science, economics, English, environmental science, ethics, European history, film, geography, geometry, health, history of the Americas, honors algebra, honors geometry, human sexuality, International Baccalaureate courses, Japanese, journalism, language arts, library assistant, library skills, Life of Christ, life science, marine science, math methods, mathematics, modern languages, modern world history, music, mythology, nutrition, personal fitness, philosophy, physical education, physics, pre-algebra, reading, religion, science, social sciences, social studies, Spanish, speech, theory of knowledge, trigonometry, weight training, world history, yearbook.

Graduation Requirements Algebra, arts and fine arts (art, music, dance, drama), English, foreign language, geometry, mathematics, physical education (includes health), social sciences, theory of knowledge.

Special Academic Programs International Baccalaureate program; Advanced Placement exam preparation; honors section; ESL (38 students enrolled).

College Admission Counseling 41 students graduated in 2016; all went to college, including Hawai'i Pacific University; Santa Clara University; University of California, Santa Barbara; University of Pennsylvania; University of Portland; University of Southern California. 44% scored over 600 on SAT critical reading, 67% scored over 600 on SAT math, 48% scored over 600 on SAT writing, 75% scored over 26 on composite ACT.

Student Life Upper grades have uniform requirement, student council, honor system. Discipline rests primarily with faculty. Attendance at religious services is required.

Summer Programs Remediation, enrichment, advancement, ESL, sports, art/fine arts, computer instruction programs offered; session focuses on enrichment; held on campus; accepts boys and girls; open to students from other schools. 100 students usually enrolled. 2017 schedule: June 11 to July 29. Application deadline: May 31.

Tuition and Aid Day student tuition: $13,100; 7-day tuition and room/board: $27,500. Tuition installment plan (Insured Tuition Payment Plan, monthly payment plans). Tuition reduction for siblings, merit scholarship grants, need-based scholarship grants available. In 2016–17, 21% of upper-school students received aid; total upper-school merit-scholarship money awarded: $21,000. Total amount of financial aid awarded in 2016–17: $500,000.

Admissions Traditional secondary-level entrance grade is 9. For fall 2016, 35 students applied for upper-level admission, 32 were accepted, 32 enrolled. Admissions testing required. Deadline for receipt of application materials: none. Application fee required: $100. Interview required.

Athletics Interscholastic: basketball (boys, girls), cross-country running (b,g), golf (b,g), ocean paddling (b,g), paddling (b,g), rugby (b,g), soccer (b,g), softball (g), tennis (b,g), track and field (b,g), volleyball (b,g); intramural: fitness (b,g), ocean paddling (b,g), physical fitness (b,g); coed interscholastic: ocean paddling; coed intramural: basketball, kickball, ocean paddling, outdoor activities, outdoor recreation, physical fitness, soccer, softball, strength & conditioning, volleyball. 4 PE instructors, 12 coaches.

Computers Computers are regularly used in all classes. Computer network features include on-campus library services, Internet access, wireless campus network, Internet filtering or blocking technology. Computer access in designated common areas is available to students. Students grades are available online. The school has a published electronic and media policy.

Contact Mrs. Emily Caseres, Registrar. 671-646-8080 Ext. 221. Fax: 671-649-6791. E-mail: ecaseres@stjohnsguam.com. Website: www.stjohnsguam.com

SAINT JOSEPH ACADEMY

500 Las Flores Drive
San Marcos, California 92078

Head of School: Mr. Anthony Biese

General Information Coeducational day college-preparatory, arts, and religious studies school, affiliated with Roman Catholic Church. Grades K–12. Founded: 1995. Setting: suburban. Nearest major city is San Diego. 4-acre campus. 3 buildings on campus. Approved or accredited by Western Association of Schools and Colleges and California Department of Education. Total enrollment: 302. Upper school average class size: 15. Upper school faculty-student ratio: 1:15. There are 176 required school days per year for Upper School students. Upper School students typically attend 5 days per week. The average school day consists of 6 hours and 40 minutes.

Upper School Student Profile Grade 6: 24 students (13 boys, 11 girls); Grade 7: 28 students (10 boys, 18 girls); Grade 8: 23 students (10 boys, 13 girls); Grade 9: 13 students (10 boys, 3 girls); Grade 10: 16 students (9 boys, 7 girls); Grade 11: 14 students (3 boys, 11 girls); Grade 12: 17 students (7 boys, 10 girls). 96% of students are Roman Catholic.

Faculty School total: 23. In upper school: 7 men, 7 women; 7 have advanced degrees.

Subjects Offered Acting, Advanced Placement courses, algebra, all academic, American history-AP, American literature, American literature-AP, art history, art history-AP, ASB Leadership, athletics, Bible, biology, British literature, British literature-AP, calculus, calculus-AP, Catholic belief and practice, Christian ethics, church history, composition, composition-AP, economics, English composition, English language-AP, general math, geography, geometry, government/civics-AP, health, physical education, physics, physics-AP, Spanish, speech and debate, U.S. government and politics-AP, world history, world history-AP, yearbook.

Graduation Requirements Christian service hours.

Special Academic Programs 4 Advanced Placement exams for which test preparation is offered; honors section; independent study.

College Admission Counseling 14 students graduated in 2016; all went to college, including California State University, San Marcos; Palomar College; Point Loma Nazarene University; San Diego State University; The College of William and Mary; University of San Diego. Mean SAT critical reading: 564, mean SAT math: 537, mean SAT writing: 574, mean combined SAT: 1675. 30% scored over 600 on SAT critical reading, 10% scored over 600 on SAT math, 40% scored over 600 on SAT writing, 40% scored over 1800 on combined SAT.

Student Life Upper grades have uniform requirement, student council, honor system. Discipline rests primarily with faculty. Attendance at religious services is required.

Tuition and Aid Day student tuition: $9900. Tuition installment plan (FACTS Tuition Payment Plan, monthly payment plans). Tuition reduction for siblings, need-based scholarship grants, paying campus jobs available. In 2016–17, 42% of upper-school students received aid; total upper-school merit-scholarship money awarded: $10,000. Total amount of financial aid awarded in 2016–17: $95,848.

Admissions Traditional secondary-level entrance grade is 9. Traditional secondary-level entrance age is 14. For fall 2016, 12 students applied for upper-level admission, 10 were accepted, 9 enrolled. Catholic High School Entrance Examination required. Deadline for receipt of application materials: none. Application fee required: $60. On-campus interview required.

Athletics Interscholastic: basketball (boys, girls), football (b), volleyball (g); coed interscholastic: golf, track and field; coed intramural: snowboarding. 6 coaches.

Computers Computer network features include Internet access, wireless campus network, Internet filtering or blocking technology. Campus intranet and student e-mail accounts are available to students. Students grades are available online. The school has a published electronic and media policy.

Contact Mrs. Patti Terich, Business Manager. 760-305-8505 Ext. 1121. Fax: 760-305-8466. E-mail: pterich@saintjosephacademy.org. Website: www.saintjosephacademy.org

ST. JOSEPH ACADEMY

155 State Road 207
St. Augustine, Florida 32084

Head of School: Mr. Todd DeClemente

General Information Coeducational day college-preparatory school, affiliated with Roman Catholic Church. Grades 9–12. Founded: 1866. Setting: suburban. 34-acre campus. 13 buildings on campus. Approved or accredited by National Catholic Education Association, Southern Association of Colleges and Schools, and Florida Department of Education. Total enrollment: 318. Upper school average class size: 14. Upper school faculty-student ratio: 1:11. There are 180 required school days per year for Upper School students. Upper School students typically attend 5 days per week. The average school day consists of 6 hours and 40 minutes.

Upper School Student Profile Grade 9: 76 students (30 boys, 46 girls); Grade 10: 84 students (46 boys, 38 girls); Grade 11: 84 students (43 boys, 41 girls); Grade 12: 76 students (37 boys, 39 girls). 84% of students are Roman Catholic.

Faculty School total: 22. In upper school: 12 men, 10 women; 18 have advanced degrees.

Subjects Offered Advanced computer applications, advanced math, Advanced Placement courses, advanced studio art-AP, algebra, American government, American history, American sign language, anatomy and physiology, ancient world history, applied arts, art, art history, Bible studies, biology, calculus-AP, career education, career exploration, career planning, Catholic belief and practice, chemistry, Christianity, church history, clayworking, college counseling, college placement, college planning, community service, computer applications, computer education, computer skills, costumes and make-up, creative drama, drama, drama performance, drama workshop, drawing, English, English composition, English language-AP, environmental science, government, history of the Catholic Church, honors algebra, honors English, honors geometry, honors U.S. history, honors world history, integrated mathematics, Internet research, life management skills, marine biology, Microsoft, moral theology, peer ministry, personal fitness, physical education, physics, play production, portfolio art, pottery, pre-calculus, psychology, religious education, Shakespeare, Spanish, Spanish language-AP, Spanish literature-AP, theology, U.S. history, weight training.

Graduation Requirements Advanced Placement courses, American government, career/college preparation, Catholic belief and practice, college writing, computer literacy, dramatic arts, economics, English, environmental science, foreign language, government, mathematics, physical education (includes health), religion (includes Bible studies and theology), social studies (includes history), theology, world history.

Special Academic Programs Advanced Placement exam preparation; honors section; study at local college for college credit; academic accommodation for the gifted and the artistically talented; special instructional classes for students with Attention Deficit Disorder.

College Admission Counseling 76 students graduated in 2016; all went to college, including Florida Atlantic University; Florida State University; University of Central Florida; University of Florida; University of North Florida; University of South Florida. 25% scored over 1800 on combined SAT, 45% scored over 26 on composite ACT.

Student Life Upper grades have uniform requirement, student council, honor system. Discipline rests primarily with faculty. Attendance at religious services is required.

Summer Programs Sports, computer instruction programs offered; session focuses on football conditioning, weight training, basketball clinics and tournaments; held on campus; accepts boys and girls; not open to students from other schools. 104 students usually enrolled. 2017 schedule: June 1 to July 31.

Tuition and Aid Day student tuition: $8570–$9950. Tuition installment plan (FACTS Tuition Payment Plan). Tuition reduction for siblings, need-based scholarship grants available. In 2016–17, 41% of upper-school students received aid. Total amount of financial aid awarded in 2016–17: $120,000.

Admissions Traditional secondary-level entrance grade is 9. For fall 2016, 108 students applied for upper-level admission, 98 were accepted, 95 enrolled. High School Placement Test, Iowa Tests of Basic Skills, Iowa Tests of Basic Skills-Grades 7-8, Archdiocese HSEPT-Grade 9, PSAT or SAT required. Deadline for receipt of application materials: none. Application fee required: $600. On-campus interview recommended.

Athletics Interscholastic: baseball (boys), basketball (b,g), cheering (g), cross-country running (b,g), football (b), golf (b,g), physical fitness (b,g), physical training (b,g), soccer (b,g), softball (g), swimming and diving (b,g), tennis (b,g), track and field (b,g), volleyball (g), weight training (b), winter soccer (b,g); intramural: lacrosse (b,g). 2 PE instructors, 3 coaches, 1 athletic trainer.

Computers Computers are regularly used in all academic, animation, computer applications, media classes. Computer network features include on-campus library services, Internet access, wireless campus network, Internet filtering or blocking technology. Student e-mail accounts and computer access in designated common areas are available to students. Students grades are available online. The school has a published electronic and media policy.

Contact Mr. Patrick M. Keane, Director of Admissions. 904-824-0431 Ext. 305. Fax: 904-824-4412. E-mail: patrick.keane@sjaweb.org. Website: www.sjaweb.org

ST. JOSEPH HIGH SCHOOL

4120 Bradley Road
Santa Maria, California 93455

Head of School: Ms. Joanne Poloni

General Information Coeducational day college-preparatory and religious studies school, affiliated with Roman Catholic Church. Grades 9–12. Founded: 1964. Setting: suburban. 15-acre campus. 8 buildings on campus. Approved or accredited by Western Association of Schools and Colleges and Western Catholic Education Association. Endowment: $3.6 million. Total enrollment: 561. Upper school average class size: 25. Upper school faculty-student ratio: 1:19. There are 180 required school days per year for Upper School students. Upper School students typically attend 5 days per week. The average school day consists of 6 hours and 49 minutes.

Upper School Student Profile Grade 9: 100 students (54 boys, 46 girls); Grade 10: 105 students (57 boys, 48 girls); Grade 11: 100 students (60 boys, 40 girls); Grade 12: 91 students (54 boys, 37 girls). 66% of students are Roman Catholic.

Faculty School total: 28. In upper school: 11 men, 17 women; 20 have advanced degrees.

Graduation Requirements Arts and fine arts (art, music, dance, drama), Catholic belief and practice, Christian and Hebrew scripture, Christian doctrine, Christian ethics, church history, civics, communication arts, composition, computer skills, economics, English, English literature, ethics, foreign language, health, history, human biology, introduction to literature, keyboarding, language structure, life science, literature,

mathematics, religion (includes Bible studies and theology), science, U.S. government, Western civilization, world geography, 100 hours of service, 3 interim course credits.

Special Academic Programs Honors section; independent study; remedial reading and/or remedial writing; remedial math.

College Admission Counseling 97 students graduated in 2016; all went to college, including California Polytechnic State University, San Luis Obispo; California State University, Bakersfield; San Diego State University; Santa Clara University; University of California, Los Angeles. Mean SAT critical reading: 529, mean SAT math: 528, mean SAT writing: 528. 22% scored over 600 on SAT critical reading, 28% scored over 600 on SAT math, 22% scored over 600 on SAT writing.

Student Life Upper grades have specified standards of dress, student council. Discipline rests primarily with faculty. Attendance at religious services is required.

Summer Programs Remediation, advancement, sports programs offered; session focuses on Preparing incoming freshmen for high school; held on campus; accepts boys and girls; not open to students from other schools. 200 students usually enrolled. 2017 schedule: June 26 to July 21. Application deadline: June 20.

Tuition and Aid Day student tuition: $8350. Tuition installment plan (FACTS Tuition Payment Plan). Tuition reduction for siblings, merit scholarship grants, need-based scholarship grants, paying campus jobs available. In 2016–17, 50% of upper-school students received aid; total upper-school merit-scholarship money awarded: $20,000. Total amount of financial aid awarded in 2016–17: $525,000.

Admissions Traditional secondary-level entrance grade is 9. For fall 2016, 137 students applied for upper-level admission, 110 were accepted, 100 enrolled. High School Placement Test required. Deadline for receipt of application materials: February 3. Application fee required: $50. On-campus interview recommended.

Athletics Interscholastic: baseball (boys), basketball (b,g), cross-country running (b,g), football (b), golf (b,g), soccer (b,g), softball (g), swimming and diving (b,g), tennis (b,g), track and field (b,g), volleyball (b,g), water polo (b,g); intramural: dance team (g), flag football (g); coed interscholastic: cheering, wrestling. 3 PE instructors, 35 coaches, 1 athletic trainer.

Computers Computers are regularly used in all classes. Computer network features include on-campus library services, online commercial services, Internet access, wireless campus network, Internet filtering or blocking technology. Student e-mail accounts and computer access in designated common areas are available to students. Students grades are available online. The school has a published electronic and media policy.

Contact Ms. Jennifer Perez, Director of Admissions. 805-937-2038 Ext. 112. Fax: 805-937-4248. E-mail: jperez@sjhsknights.com. Website: www.sjhsknights.com

ST. JOSEPH HIGH SCHOOL

2320 Huntington Turnpike
Trumbull, Connecticut 06611

Head of School: Pres. William J. Fitzgerald, PhD

General Information Coeducational day college-preparatory, arts, business, and technology school, affiliated with Roman Catholic Church. Grades 9–12. Distance learning grades 11–12. Founded: 1962. Setting: suburban. Nearest major city is Bridgeport. 25-acre campus. 5 buildings on campus. Approved or accredited by New England Association of Schools and Colleges and Connecticut Department of Education. Upper school average class size: 22. Upper school faculty-student ratio: 1:12. There are 183 required school days per year for Upper School students. Upper School students typically attend 5 days per week. The average school day consists of 6 hours.

Upper School Student Profile Grade 9: 200 students (100 boys, 100 girls); Grade 10: 200 students (100 boys, 100 girls); Grade 11: 200 students (100 boys, 100 girls); Grade 12: 200 students (100 boys, 100 girls). 77% of students are Roman Catholic.

Faculty School total: 69. In upper school: 29 men, 40 women; all have advanced degrees.

Subjects Offered Advanced Placement courses, algebra, American government, American history, American history-AP, anatomy, art, art history, biology, biology-AP, business skills, calculus, calculus-AP, Catholic belief and practice, current events, design, dramatic arts, ecology, English, English literature, ESL, French, geometry, government, health, human anatomy, human biology, integrated science, Italian, journalism, microbiology, music, New Testament, personal finance, physical education, physics, pottery, pre-calculus, religion, religious studies, science, social sciences, social studies, Spanish, Spanish language-AP, Spanish-AP, trigonometry, U.S. government, U.S. history, U.S. history-AP, word processing.

Graduation Requirements College awareness.

Special Academic Programs 11 Advanced Placement exams for which test preparation is offered; honors section; study at local college for college credit; academic accommodation for the gifted; special instructional classes for students with learning disabilities and Attention Deficit Disorder; ESL (10 students enrolled).

College Admission Counseling 220 students graduated in 2016; 215 went to college, including Fairfield University; Providence College; Quinnipiac University; Sacred Heart University; Southern Connecticut State University; University of Connecticut. Other: 5 entered military service. Mean SAT critical reading: 529, mean SAT math: 520, mean SAT writing: 533, mean combined SAT: 1597, mean composite ACT: 22.

Student Life Upper grades have uniform requirement, student council. Discipline rests primarily with faculty. Attendance at religious services is required.

Summer Programs Remediation, enrichment, advancement, sports, art/fine arts, computer instruction programs offered; session focuses on academics, athletics, enrichment; held on campus; accepts boys and girls; open to students from other schools. 150 students usually enrolled. 2017 schedule: June 26 to August 20.

Tuition and Aid Day student tuition: $14,900. Tuition installment plan (FACTS Tuition Payment Plan, one lump sum payment with discount by June 1 or two payments by semester, payment plan through People's Bank). Tuition reduction for siblings, merit scholarship grants, need-based scholarship grants available. In 2016–17, 50% of upper-school students received aid; total upper-school merit-scholarship money awarded: $50,000. Total amount of financial aid awarded in 2016–17: $1,400,000.

Admissions Traditional secondary-level entrance grade is 9. For fall 2016, 500 students applied for upper-level admission, 430 were accepted, 223 enrolled. Deadline for receipt of application materials: November 19. Application fee required: $50.

Athletics Interscholastic: baseball (boys), basketball (b,g), cheering (g), cross-country running (b,g), diving (g), field hockey (g), football (b), gymnastics (g), hockey (b,g), ice hockey (b,g), indoor track (b,g), indoor track & field (b,g), lacrosse (b,g), softball (g), swimming and diving (b,g), tennis (b,g), track and field (b,g), volleyball (b,g), winter (indoor) track (b,g); coed interscholastic: bowling, golf. 2 PE instructors, 80 coaches, 2 athletic trainers.

Computers Computers are regularly used in all academic classes. Computer network features include on-campus library services, online commercial services, Internet access, wireless campus network, Internet filtering or blocking technology, Internet access throughout the building. Campus intranet, student e-mail accounts, and computer access in designated common areas are available to students. Students grades are available online. The school has a published electronic and media policy.

Contact Linda Lucy, Assistant Director of Admissions Operations. 203-378-9378 Ext. 455. Fax: 203-378-7306. E-mail: llucy@sjcadets.org. Website: www.sjcadets.org

SAINT JOSEPH HIGH SCHOOL

145 Plainfield Avenue
Metuchen, New Jersey 08840

Head of School: Mr. Justin J. Fleetwood

General Information Boys' day college-preparatory school, affiliated with Roman Catholic Church. Grades 9–12. Founded: 1961. Setting: suburban. Nearest major city is New York, NY. 68-acre campus. 8 buildings on campus. Approved or accredited by Middle States Association of Colleges and Schools and New Jersey Department of Education. Total enrollment: 683. Upper school average class size: 24. Upper school faculty-student ratio: 1:12. There are 178 required school days per year for Upper School students. Upper School students typically attend 5 days per week. The average school day consists of 6 hours and 20 minutes.

Upper School Student Profile Grade 9: 158 students (158 boys); Grade 10: 167 students (167 boys); Grade 11: 158 students (158 boys); Grade 12: 148 students (148 boys). 75% of students are Roman Catholic.

Faculty School total: 68. In upper school: 30 men, 20 women; 27 have advanced degrees.

Subjects Offered Acting, Advanced Placement courses, algebra, American Civil War, American government, American history, American literature, art, astronomy, biology, biology-AP, calculus, calculus-AP, campus ministry, career education, Catholic belief and practice, chemistry, chemistry-AP, Christian doctrine, Christian education, Christian ethics, Christian scripture, Christian studies, Christianity, church history, community service, computer animation, computer applications, computer programming, computer science, computer science-AP, constitutional law, desktop publishing, digital applications, digital imaging, digital photography, discrete mathematics, driver education, economics, economics and history, English, English literature, English-AP, European civilization, European history, European history-AP, film, forensics, French, French as a second language, French-AP, geometry, German, German literature, government and politics-AP, government/civics-AP, guitar, health, history, lab science, Latin, math methods, mathematics-AP, meteorology, music, personal finance, photography, physical education, physics, physics-AP, pre-calculus, probability, probability and statistics, public speaking, religion, SAT preparation, SAT/ACT preparation, social justice, social studies, Spanish, Spanish-AP, statistics, technical drawing, theology, U.S. government and politics-AP, U.S. history-AP, Web site design, world history, world literature, writing.

Graduation Requirements Arts and fine arts (art, music, dance, drama), career education, computer science, English, foreign language, lab science, mathematics, physical education (includes health), religion (includes Bible studies and theology), science, social studies (includes history). Community service is required.

Special Academic Programs 12 Advanced Placement exams for which test preparation is offered; honors section; independent study; study at local college for college credit; academic accommodation for the gifted.

College Admission Counseling 170 students graduated in 2016; all went to college, including Penn State University Park; Rutgers, The State University of New Jersey, Rutgers College; Stevens Institute of Technology; The Catholic University of America; University of Pittsburgh; Villanova University.

Student Life Upper grades have uniform requirement, student council, honor system. Discipline rests primarily with faculty. Attendance at religious services is required.

Summer Programs Remediation, enrichment, advancement, sports, computer instruction programs offered; session focuses on remediation and enrichment; held on campus; accepts boys and girls; open to students from other schools. 225 students usually enrolled. 2017 schedule: June 28 to July 26. Application deadline: June 1.

Tuition and Aid Day student tuition: $13,600. Tuition installment plan (FACTS Tuition Payment Plan, monthly payment plans). Merit scholarship grants, need-based scholarship grants available. In 2016–17, 16% of upper-school students received aid; total upper-school merit-scholarship money awarded: $350,000. Total amount of financial aid awarded in 2016–17: $750,000.

Admissions Traditional secondary-level entrance grade is 9. High School Placement Test required. Deadline for receipt of application materials: none. No application fee required. On-campus interview recommended.

Athletics Interscholastic: baseball, basketball, bowling, cross-country running, football, golf, ice hockey, indoor track & field, lacrosse, soccer, swimming and diving, tennis, track and field, volleyball, winter (indoor) track; intramural: crew, flag football, Frisbee, skiing (downhill), snowboarding, strength & conditioning, ultimate Frisbee, weight lifting, weight training. 3 PE instructors, 41 coaches, 1 athletic trainer.

Computers Computers are regularly used in animation, computer applications, desktop publishing, desktop publishing, ESL, drawing and design, graphic design, graphics, journalism, mathematics, news writing, newspaper, photography, publications, publishing, science, technical drawing, technology, Web site design, word processing, yearbook classes. Computer network features include on-campus library services, online commercial services, Internet access, wireless campus network, Internet filtering or blocking technology. Campus intranet, student e-mail accounts, and computer access in designated common areas are available to students. Students grades are available online. The school has a published electronic and media policy.

Contact Mr. Casey Ransone, Director of Admissions. 732-549-7600 Ext. 221. Fax: 732-549-0282. E-mail: admissions@stjoes.org. Website: www.stjoes.org

ST. JOSEPH HIGH SCHOOL

110 East Red River Street
Victoria, Texas 77901

Head of School: Mr. Thomas Maj

General Information Coeducational day college-preparatory school, affiliated with Roman Catholic Church. Grades 9–12. Founded: 1868. Setting: small town. Nearest major city is Houston. 12-acre campus. 10 buildings on campus. Approved or accredited by Southern Association of Colleges and Schools, Texas Catholic Conference, and Texas Department of Education. Endowment: $2 million. Total enrollment: 407. Upper school average class size: 18. Upper school faculty-student ratio: 1:14. Upper School students typically attend 5 days per week. The average school day consists of 7 hours.

Upper School Student Profile 65% of students are Roman Catholic.

Faculty School total: 27. In upper school: 11 men, 16 women; 16 have advanced degrees.

Special Academic Programs Advanced Placement exam preparation; honors section; independent study; study at local college for college credit.

College Admission Counseling 78 students graduated in 2016; 77 went to college, including St. Mary's University; Texas A&M University; Texas State University; Victoria College; Victoria College. Other: 1 entered military service.

Student Life Upper grades have specified standards of dress, student council, honor system. Discipline rests primarily with faculty. Attendance at religious services is required.

Summer Programs Sports programs offered; session focuses on strength and conditioning; held both on and off campus; accepts boys and girls; open to students from other schools. 85 students usually enrolled. 2017 schedule: June 5 to July 14.

Tuition and Aid Tuition installment plan (FACTS Tuition Payment Plan, monthly payment plans). Need-based scholarship grants available. In 2016–17, 45% of upper-school students received aid. Total amount of financial aid awarded in 2016–17: $320,000.

Admissions Traditional secondary-level entrance grade is 9. Deadline for receipt of application materials: none. Application fee required: $75.

Athletics Interscholastic: aquatics (boys, girls), baseball (b), basketball (b,g), cheering (g), cross-country running (b,g), dance (g), dance team (g), football (b), golf (b,g), power lifting (b,g), soccer (b,g), softball (g), strength & conditioning (b,g), swimming and diving (b,g), tennis (b,g), track and field (b,g), volleyball (g), weight training (b); coed interscholastic: fitness. 1 PE instructor, 20 coaches.

Computers Computers are regularly used in accounting, business applications, desktop publishing, English, foreign language, history, journalism, library, mathematics, science, technology, Web site design classes. Computer network features include on-campus library services, online commercial services, Internet access, wireless campus network. The school has a published electronic and media policy.

Contact Mrs. Jen Korinek, Admissions Coordinator. 361-573-2446 Ext. 217. Fax: 361-573-4221. E-mail: jkorinek@STJvictoria.com. Website: www.stjvictoria.com

SAINT JOSEPH REGIONAL HIGH SCHOOL

40 Chestnut Ridge Road
Montvale, New Jersey 07645

Head of School: Mr. Barry Donnelly

General Information Boys' day college-preparatory school, affiliated with Roman Catholic Church. Grades 9–12. Founded: 1962. Setting: suburban. Nearest major city is New York, NY. 33-acre campus. 1 building on campus. Approved or accredited by Middle States Association of Colleges and Schools and New Jersey Department of Education. Total enrollment: 516. Upper school average class size: 23. Upper school faculty-student ratio: 1:12. There are 176 required school days per year for Upper School students. Upper School students typically attend 5 days per week. The average school day consists of 6 hours.

Upper School Student Profile Grade 9: 146 students (146 boys); Grade 10: 121 students (121 boys); Grade 11: 123 students (123 boys); Grade 12: 126 students (126 boys).

Faculty School total: 38. In upper school: 28 men, 10 women; 27 have advanced degrees.

Subjects Offered Accounting, advanced chemistry, advanced math, Advanced Placement courses, algebra, American government, American history, American history-AP, American literature, anatomy, art, art appreciation, Bible studies, biology, biology-AP, British literature, calculus, calculus-AP, Catholic belief and practice, chemistry, chemistry-AP, Christian doctrine, church history, computer applications, computer science, driver education, economics, English, English-AP, European history-AP, French, geography, geometry, health education, honors algebra, honors English, honors geometry, honors U.S. history, honors world history, keyboarding, Latin, law, New Testament, physical education, physics, physics-AP, pre-calculus, psychology, religion, science, social studies, Spanish, Spanish-AP, studio art, The 20th Century, theology, U.S. government, U.S. history, U.S. history-AP, Western civilization, word processing, world cultures, world geography, world history.

Graduation Requirements All academic.

Special Academic Programs Advanced Placement exam preparation; honors section; study at local college for college credit.

College Admission Counseling 116 students graduated in 2016; all went to college, including Fairfield University; Iona College; Penn State University Park; Rutgers University–New Brunswick; The University of Scranton.

Student Life Upper grades have specified standards of dress, student council, honor system. Discipline rests primarily with faculty. Attendance at religious services is required.

Tuition and Aid Day student tuition: $13,100. Tuition installment plan (FACTS Tuition Payment Plan). Tuition reduction for siblings, merit scholarship grants, need-based scholarship grants, need-based loans available.

Admissions Traditional secondary-level entrance grade is 9. Cooperative Entrance Exam (McGraw-Hill) required. Deadline for receipt of application materials: none. No application fee required. Interview required.

Athletics Interscholastic: baseball, basketball, bowling, cross-country running, football, golf, hockey, ice hockey, indoor hockey, indoor track, indoor track & field, lacrosse, physical fitness, running, soccer, tennis, track and field, weight lifting, weight training, winter (indoor) track, wrestling; intramural: basketball, floor hockey, Frisbee, indoor soccer, skiing (downhill), strength & conditioning, ultimate Frisbee, volleyball. 2 athletic trainers.

Computers Computers are regularly used in accounting, all academic classes. Computer network features include on-campus library services, Internet access, wireless campus network, Internet filtering or blocking technology. Campus intranet, student e-mail accounts, and computer access in designated common areas are available to students. Students grades are available online. The school has a published electronic and media policy.

Contact Mr. Michael J. Doherty, Director of Admissions. 201-391-3300 Ext. 41. Fax: 201-391-8073. E-mail: dohertym@saintjosephregional.org. Website: www.saintjosephregional.org

ST. JOSEPH'S ACADEMY

3015 Broussard Street
Baton Rouge, Louisiana 70808

Head of School: Dr. Michele Lambert

General Information Girls' day college-preparatory, arts, religious studies, and technology school, affiliated with Roman Catholic Church. Grades 9–12. Founded: 1868. Setting: urban. 14-acre campus. 8 buildings on campus. Approved or accredited by National Catholic Education Association, Southern Association of Colleges and Schools, Southern Association of Independent Schools, and Louisiana Department of Education. Endowment: $2.5 million. Total enrollment: 1,070. Upper school average class size: 20. Upper school faculty-student ratio: 1:15. There are 178 required school days per year for Upper School students. Upper School students typically attend 5 days per week. The average school day consists of 7 hours and 20 minutes.

Upper School Student Profile Grade 9: 252 students (252 girls); Grade 10: 272 students (272 girls); Grade 11: 281 students (281 girls); Grade 12: 265 students (265 girls). 92.1% of students are Roman Catholic.

Faculty School total: 71. In upper school: 8 men, 63 women; 35 have advanced degrees.

Subjects Offered Accounting, acting, advanced biology, advanced chemistry, advanced computer applications, advanced math, Advanced Placement courses, algebra, American history, American history-AP, American literature, American literature-AP, analysis, analysis and differential calculus, art, art appreciation, art history-AP, band, Basic programming, biology, biology-AP, business law, calculus-AP, campus ministry, Catholic belief and practice, chemistry, child development, choir, choral music, chorus, Christian and Hebrew scripture, church history, civics, civics/free enterprise, computer applications, computer information systems, computer multimedia, computer programming, computer technologies, computer technology certification, CPR, critical studies in film, dance, desktop publishing, drama, drama performance, economics, English, English literature-AP, English-AP, environmental science, European history-AP, family and consumer science, film and literature, fine arts, foreign language, French, French as a second language, geometry, grammar, health, health and safety, health education, Hebrew scripture, honors algebra, honors English, honors geometry, human sexuality, independent study, information technology, Latin, marching band, media arts, media production, music, novels, physical education, physical fitness, physics, poetry, pre-calculus, public speaking, religion, research, Shakespeare, social justice, Spanish, speech, speech communications, technology, the Web, transition mathematics, U.S. history, U.S. history-AP, U.S. literature, visual arts, vocal ensemble, vocal music, Web authoring, Web site design, world history-AP.

Graduation Requirements Advanced math, algebra, American history, arts and fine arts (art, music, dance, drama), biology, chemistry, civics, computer applications, English, foreign language, geometry, physical education (includes health), physical science, physics, religion (includes Bible studies and theology), world history, service hours.

Special Academic Programs Advanced Placement exam preparation; honors section; independent study; study at local college for college credit.

College Admission Counseling 241 students graduated in 2015; 240 went to college, including Louisiana State University and Agricultural & Mechanical College; Louisiana Tech University; Southeastern Louisiana University; Spring Hill College; Tulane University; University of Louisiana at Lafayette. Other: 1 went to work. 66% scored over 26 on composite ACT.

Student Life Upper grades have uniform requirement, student council, honor system. Discipline rests primarily with faculty. Attendance at religious services is required.

Tuition and Aid Day student tuition: $10,330. Tuition installment plan (monthly debit plan). Need-based scholarship grants available. In 2015–16, 11% of upper-school students received aid. Total amount of financial aid awarded in 2015–16: $513,581.

Admissions Traditional secondary-level entrance grade is 9. ACT-Explore required. Deadline for receipt of application materials: November 20. Application fee required: $65. On-campus interview required.

Athletics Interscholastic: ballet, basketball, bowling, cheering, cross-country running, dance squad, golf, gymnastics, indoor track, physical fitness, physical training, running, soccer, softball, strength & conditioning, swimming and diving, tennis, track and field, volleyball, weight training, winter (indoor) track, winter soccer; coed intramural: volleyball. 6 PE instructors, 7 coaches, 1 athletic trainer.

Computers Computers are regularly used in all classes. Computer network features include on-campus library services, online commercial services, Internet access, wireless campus network, Internet filtering or blocking technology, administrative software/grading/scheduling. Campus intranet and student e-mail accounts are available to students. Students grades are available online. The school has a published electronic and media policy.

Contact Mrs. Sheri Gillio, Admissions Director. 225-388-2243 Fax: 225-344-5714. E-mail: gillios@sjabr.org. Website: www.sjabr.org

ST. JOSEPH'S CATHOLIC SCHOOL

100 St. Joseph's Drive
Greenville, South Carolina 29607

Head of School: Mr. Keith F. Kiser

General Information Coeducational day college-preparatory school, affiliated with Roman Catholic Church. Grades 6–12. Founded: 1993. Setting: suburban. 36-acre campus. 3 buildings on campus. Approved or accredited by South Carolina Independent School Association, Southern Association of Colleges and Schools, and South Carolina Department of Education. Total enrollment: 677. Upper school average class size: 17. Upper school faculty-student ratio: 1:10. There are 175 required school days per year for Upper School students. Upper School students typically attend 5 days per week. The average school day consists of 7 hours and 10 minutes.

Upper School Student Profile Grade 9: 122 students (59 boys, 63 girls); Grade 10: 114 students (55 boys, 59 girls); Grade 11: 101 students (52 boys, 49 girls); Grade 12: 100 students (46 boys, 54 girls). 68% of students are Roman Catholic.

Faculty School total: 57. In upper school: 24 men, 33 women; 29 have advanced degrees.

Subjects Offered Advanced Placement courses, algebra, American history, American literature, anatomy and physiology, ancient history, art, art history-AP, arts appreciation, astronomy, band, bioethics, biology, biology-AP, calculus, calculus-AP, chemistry, chemistry-AP, choral music, chorus, Christian doctrine, Christian ethics, church history, composition, computer applications, computer graphics, computer science, creative writing, dance, digital photography, directing, drama workshop, dramatic arts, drawing, economics, English language and composition-AP, English literature and composition-AP, ensembles, environmental science, European history, European history-AP, European literature, exercise science, film, film studies, fine arts, forensics, French, genetics, geometry, government, government-AP, honors algebra, honors English, honors geometry, honors U.S. history, human movement and its application to health, improvisation, instrumental music, keyboarding, Latin, literary magazine, literature, media, medieval/Renaissance history, moral theology, newspaper, organic chemistry, personal finance, physical education, physics, physics-AP, pre-algebra, pre-calculus, psychology, Shakespeare, Spanish, Spanish language-AP, Spanish-AP, speech, sports conditioning, statistics, statistics-AP, strings, theater arts, theater production, U.S. history, U.S. history-AP, yearbook.

Graduation Requirements American government, American history, chemistry, economics, foreign language, geography, theology, 65 hours of community service.

Special Academic Programs 14 Advanced Placement exams for which test preparation is offered; honors section; independent study.

College Admission Counseling 101 students graduated in 2016; all went to college, including Auburn University; Clemson University; College of Charleston; Furman University; University of South Carolina; Wofford College. Mean SAT critical reading: 599, mean SAT math: 599, mean SAT writing: 585, mean combined SAT: 1783, mean composite ACT: 27.

Student Life Upper grades have uniform requirement, student council, honor system. Discipline rests primarily with faculty. Attendance at religious services is required.

Summer Programs Enrichment, sports, art/fine arts programs offered; held on campus; accepts boys and girls; open to students from other schools. 216 students usually enrolled. 2017 schedule: June 1 to August 16.

Tuition and Aid Day student tuition: $12,770. Tuition installment plan (monthly payment plans, yearly payment plan, semiannual payment plan). Tuition reduction for siblings, merit scholarship grants, need-based scholarship grants, tuition reduction for staff available. In 2016–17, 37% of upper-school students received aid; total upper-school merit-scholarship money awarded: $51,000. Total amount of financial aid awarded in 2016–17: $805,000.

Admissions Traditional secondary-level entrance grade is 9. For fall 2016, 84 students applied for upper-level admission, 74 were accepted, 58 enrolled. Scholastic Testing Service High School Placement Test (open version) required. Deadline for receipt of application materials: none. Application fee required: $180. On-campus interview recommended.

Athletics Interscholastic: baseball (boys), basketball (b,g), cheering (g), cross-country running (b,g), football (b), golf (b), lacrosse (b,g), soccer (b,g), softball (g), swimming and diving (b,g), tennis (b,g), track and field (b,g), volleyball (g), wrestling (b); intramural: basketball (b,g), flag football (b), soccer (b,g), volleyball (g); coed interscholastic: golf. 1 PE instructor, 22 coaches, 1 athletic trainer.

Computers Computers are regularly used in computer applications, graphic design, photography, programming, yearbook classes. Computer network features include on-campus library services, Internet access, wireless campus network, Internet filtering or blocking technology. Student e-mail accounts and computer access in designated common areas are available to students. Students grades are available online. The school has a published electronic and media policy.

Contact Mrs. Barbara L. McGrath, Director of Admissions. 864-234-9009 Ext. 104. Fax: 864-234-5516. E-mail: bmcgrath@sjcatholicschool.org. Website: www.sjcatholicschool.org

ST. JOSEPH'S PREPARATORY SCHOOL

1733 Girard Avenue
Philadelphia, Pennsylvania 19130

Head of School: Rev. John W. Swope, SJ

General Information Boys' day college-preparatory school, affiliated with Roman Catholic Church. Grades 9–12. Founded: 1851. Setting: urban. 7-acre campus. 3 buildings on campus. Approved or accredited by Jesuit Secondary Education Association, Middle States Association of Colleges and Schools, and Pennsylvania Department of Education. Endowment: $16 million. Total enrollment: 890. Upper school average class size: 22. Upper school faculty-student ratio: 1:16. There are 180 required school days per year for Upper School students. Upper School students typically attend 5 days per week. The average school day consists of 6 hours.

Upper School Student Profile Grade 9: 256 students (256 boys); Grade 10: 196 students (196 boys); Grade 11: 223 students (223 boys); Grade 12: 227 students (227 boys). 85% of students are Roman Catholic.

Faculty School total: 80. In upper school: 60 men, 20 women; 75 have advanced degrees.

Subjects Offered Algebra, American history, American literature, anatomy, archaeology, art, biology, business, calculus, chemistry, classics, computer math, computer programming, computer science, earth science, economics, English, English literature, environmental science, ethics, European history, fine arts, French, geometry, German, government/civics, Greek, history, Latin, Mandarin, marine biology, mathematics, photography, physical education, physics, physiology, religion, robotics, science, social sciences, social studies, Spanish, speech, trigonometry, world history, world literature.

Graduation Requirements Arts and fine arts (art, music, dance, drama), classics, computer science, English, foreign language, mathematics, physical education (includes health), religion (includes Bible studies and theology), science, social sciences, social studies (includes history), Christian service hours in junior and senior year.

Special Academic Programs International Baccalaureate program; 15 Advanced Placement exams for which test preparation is offered; honors section; independent study; study at local college for college credit; study abroad; academic accommodation for the gifted, the musically talented, and the artistically talented.

College Admission Counseling 241 students graduated in 2016; all went to college, including Boston College; Drexel University; Penn State University Park; Saint Joseph's University; Temple University; The University of Alabama. Mean SAT critical reading: 615, mean SAT math: 623, mean SAT writing: 606, mean combined SAT: 1847. 57% scored over 600 on SAT critical reading, 67% scored over 600 on SAT math, 53% scored over 600 on SAT writing, 61% scored over 1800 on combined SAT.

Student Life Upper grades have specified standards of dress, student council. Discipline rests primarily with faculty. Attendance at religious services is required.

Summer Programs Remediation, enrichment, advancement, sports, art/fine arts, computer instruction programs offered; session focuses on pre-8th grade enrichment; held on campus; accepts boys and girls; open to students from other schools. 300 students usually enrolled. 2017 schedule: June 20 to July 15. Application deadline: none.

Tuition and Aid Day student tuition: $21,500. Tuition installment plan (monthly payment plans). Tuition reduction for siblings, merit scholarship grants, need-based scholarship grants, need-based loans, middle-income loans, paying campus jobs available. In 2016–17, 42% of upper-school students received aid; total upper-school merit-scholarship money awarded: $500,000. Total amount of financial aid awarded in 2016–17: $3,900,000.

Admissions Traditional secondary-level entrance grade is 9. For fall 2016, 600 students applied for upper-level admission, 360 were accepted, 256 enrolled. High School Placement Test or High School Placement Test (closed version) from Scholastic Testing Service required. Deadline for receipt of application materials: November 6. Application fee required: $50. On-campus interview recommended.

Athletics Interscholastic: baseball, basketball, bowling, crew, cross-country running, diving, football, Frisbee, golf, ice hockey, indoor track & field, lacrosse, rowing, rugby, running, soccer, squash, swimming and diving, tennis, track and field, ultimate Frisbee, volleyball, winter (indoor) track, wrestling; intramural: basketball, bicycling, climbing, fishing, flag football, handball, martial arts, paint ball, physical fitness, table tennis, team handball, volleyball, water polo. 35 coaches, 3 athletic trainers.

Computers Computers are regularly used in all academic classes. Computer network features include on-campus library services, online commercial services, Internet access, wireless campus network, Internet filtering or blocking technology, Chromebook-approved Helpdesk to repair all student machines. Campus intranet, student e-mail accounts, and computer access in designated common areas are available to students. Students grades are available online. The school has a published electronic and media policy.

Contact Mrs. Lorrie McKenna, Admission Counselor. 215-978-1954. Fax: 215-765-1710. E-mail: lmckenna@sjprep.org. Website: www.sjprep.org

ST. LAWRENCE SEMINARY HIGH SCHOOL

301 Church Street
Mount Calvary, Wisconsin 53057

Head of School: Fr. John Holly, OFMCAP

General Information Boys' boarding college-preparatory school, affiliated with Roman Catholic Church. Grades 9–12. Founded: 1860. Setting: rural. Nearest major city is Milwaukee. Students are housed in single-sex dormitories. 150-acre campus. 11 buildings on campus. Approved or accredited by National Catholic Education Association, North Central Association of Colleges and Schools, and Wisconsin Department of Education. Total enrollment: 203. Upper school average class size: 17. Upper school faculty-student ratio: 1:9. There are 167 required school days per year for Upper School students. Upper School students typically attend 5 days per week. The average school day consists of 7 hours and 45 minutes.

Upper School Student Profile Grade 9: 46 students (46 boys); Grade 10: 48 students (48 boys); Grade 11: 58 students (58 boys); Grade 12: 41 students (41 boys); Postgraduate: 193 students (193 boys). 100% of students are boarding students. 30% are state residents. 16 states are represented in upper school student body. 10% are international students. International students from Ghana, Italy, Republic of Korea, Saudi Arabia, United Arab Emirates, and Viet Nam. 100% of students are Roman Catholic.

Faculty School total: 23. In upper school: 19 men, 5 women; 12 have advanced degrees; 6 reside on campus.

Subjects Offered Accounting, advanced chemistry, advanced computer applications, advanced math, algebra, American government, American history, American literature, art, biology, business, business law, calculus, chemistry, classical studies, computer applications, computer science, economics, English, English literature, fine arts, geometry, German, government/civics, guidance, health, health and wellness, humanities, industrial arts, Latin, literary genres, mathematics, mechanical drawing, music, music appreciation, music theory, physical education, physics, pre-calculus, probability and statistics, psychology, religion, science, socioeconomic problems,

Spanish, theology, trigonometry, U.S. history, woodworking, world history, world literature, writing.

Graduation Requirements Arts and fine arts (art, music, dance, drama), business skills (includes word processing), computer science, English, foreign language, health education, humanities, mathematics, physical education (includes health), religion (includes Bible studies and theology), science, social studies (includes history), study skills, ministry hours.

Special Academic Programs Independent study; study at local college for college credit.

College Admission Counseling 46 students graduated in 2016; all went to college, including DePaul University; Millbrook School; University of Dallas; University of Illinois at Urbana–Champaign; University of Wisconsin–Madison; University of Wisconsin–Milwaukee. Median SAT critical reading: 550, median SAT math: 600, median SAT writing: 540, median combined SAT: 1630, median composite ACT: 23. 10% scored over 600 on SAT critical reading, 50% scored over 600 on SAT math, 20% scored over 600 on SAT writing, 30% scored over 1800 on combined SAT, 23% scored over 26 on composite ACT.

Student Life Upper grades have specified standards of dress, student council, honor system. Discipline rests primarily with faculty. Attendance at religious services is required.

Tuition and Aid 7-day tuition and room/board: $13,700. Tuition installment plan (SMART Tuition Payment Plan, monthly payment plans, individually arranged payment plans). Need-based scholarship grants available. In 2016–17, 73% of upper-school students received aid. Total amount of financial aid awarded in 2016–17: $778,110.

Admissions Traditional secondary-level entrance grade is 9. For fall 2016, 85 students applied for upper-level admission, 70 were accepted, 70 enrolled. 3-R Achievement Test and any standardized test required. Deadline for receipt of application materials: none. Application fee required: $300. Interview recommended.

Athletics Interscholastic: archery, baseball, basketball, cross-country running, soccer, tennis, track and field, wrestling; intramural: basketball, bicycling, billiards, bowling, flag football, floor hockey, Frisbee, handball, kickball, outdoor activities, outdoor recreation, physical fitness, physical training, racquetball, skiing (downhill), softball, table tennis, tennis, volleyball, wallyball, weight lifting, weight training, winter soccer. 3 PE instructors, 8 coaches, 1 athletic trainer.

Computers Computers are regularly used in computer applications, publications, writing classes. Computer network features include on-campus library services, Internet access, Internet filtering or blocking technology. Campus intranet, student e-mail accounts, and computer access in designated common areas are available to students. The school has a published electronic and media policy.

Contact Mrs. Deann Sippel, Administrative Assistant to Admissions. 920-753-7570. Fax: 920-753-7507. E-mail: dsippel@stlawrence.edu. Website: www.stlawrence.edu

ST. LOUIS UNIVERSITY HIGH SCHOOL

4970 Oakland Avenue
St. Louis, Missouri 63110

Head of School: Mr. David J. Laughlin

General Information Boys' day college-preparatory school, affiliated with Roman Catholic Church (Jesuit order). Grades 9–12. Founded: 1818. Setting: urban. 27-acre campus. 2 buildings on campus. Approved or accredited by Jesuit Secondary Education Association, North Central Association of Colleges and Schools, and Missouri Department of Education. Member of National Association of Independent Schools. Upper school average class size: 21. Upper school faculty-student ratio: 1:12. There are 167 required school days per year for Upper School students. Upper School students typically attend 5 days per week. The average school day consists of 7 hours and 10 minutes.

Upper School Student Profile 87% of students are Roman Catholic Church (Jesuit order).

Faculty School total: 95. In upper school: 70 men, 25 women; 90 have advanced degrees.

Special Academic Programs 20 Advanced Placement exams for which test preparation is offered; honors section; study at local college for college credit; study abroad.

College Admission Counseling 268 students graduated in 2015; 267 went to college, including Dalhousie University. Mean SAT critical reading: 659, mean SAT math: 686, mean SAT writing: 650, mean composite ACT: 30.

Student Life Upper grades have specified standards of dress, student council, honor system. Discipline rests primarily with faculty. Attendance at religious services is required.

Tuition and Aid Day student tuition: $15,400. Tuition installment plan (FACTS Tuition Payment Plan, quarterly, semi-annually). Need-based scholarship grants available. In 2015–16, 40% of upper-school students received aid. Total amount of financial aid awarded in 2015–16: $3,246,000.

Admissions Traditional secondary-level entrance grade is 9. For fall 2015, 320 students applied for upper-level admission, 286 were accepted, 260 enrolled. Scholastic Achievement Test required. Deadline for receipt of application materials: November 19. Application fee required: $7. Interview required.

Athletics Interscholastic: baseball, basketball, cross-country running, football, golf, ice hockey, in-line hockey, lacrosse, racquetball, riflery, rugby, soccer, swimming and diving, tennis, track and field, ultimate Frisbee, volleyball, water polo, wrestling; intramural: bicycling, billiards, bocce, Circus, climbing, dance, fishing, hiking/backpacking, juggling, outdoor adventure, table tennis, ultimate Frisbee, weight lifting. 58 coaches, 1 athletic trainer.

Computers Computer network features include on-campus library services, online commercial services, Internet access, wireless campus network, Internet filtering or blocking technology. Campus intranet, student e-mail accounts, and computer access in designated common areas are available to students. Students grades are available online. The school has a published electronic and media policy.

Contact Dr. John Moran, Principal. 314-531-0330 Ext. 2125.
E-mail: jmoran@sluh.org. Website: www.sluh.org

SAINT LUCY'S PRIORY HIGH SCHOOL

655 West Sierra Madre Avenue
Glendora, California 91741-1997

Head of School: Ms. Regina Giuliucci

General Information Girls' day college-preparatory school, affiliated with Roman Catholic Church. Grades 9–12. Founded: 1962. Setting: suburban. Nearest major city is Pasadena. 14-acre campus. 4 buildings on campus. Approved or accredited by Western Association of Schools and Colleges, Western Catholic Education Association, and California Department of Education. Member of National Association of Independent Schools. Endowment: $1.5 million. Total enrollment: 647. Upper school average class size: 17. Upper school faculty-student ratio: 1:17. There are 180 required school days per year for Upper School students. Upper School students typically attend 5 days per week. The average school day consists of 6 hours and 45 minutes.

Upper School Student Profile Grade 9: 166 students (166 girls); Grade 10: 151 students (151 girls); Grade 11: 152 students (152 girls); Grade 12: 178 students (178 girls). 78% of students are Roman Catholic.

Faculty School total: 36. In upper school: 5 men, 31 women; 22 have advanced degrees.

Graduation Requirements Arts and fine arts (art, music, dance, drama), English, foreign language, mathematics, physical education (includes health), religion (includes Bible studies and theology), science, social sciences, social studies (includes history).

Special Academic Programs Advanced Placement exam preparation; honors section.

College Admission Counseling 171 students graduated in 2016; all went to college, including Azusa Pacific University; California State Polytechnic University, Pomona; Loyola Marymount University; Mount Saint Mary's University; University of California, Irvine; University of California, Riverside. Mean SAT critical reading: 540, mean SAT math: 521, mean SAT writing: 548, mean composite ACT: 23. 40% scored over 600 on SAT critical reading, 20% scored over 600 on SAT math, 35% scored over 600 on SAT writing, 46% scored over 26 on composite ACT.

Student Life Upper grades have uniform requirement, student council. Discipline rests equally with students and faculty. Attendance at religious services is required.

Summer Programs Remediation programs offered; session focuses on remediation; held on campus; accepts girls; not open to students from other schools. 80 students usually enrolled. 2017 schedule: June 20 to July 15. Application deadline: June 1.

Tuition and Aid Day student tuition: $7800. Tuition installment plan (SMART Tuition Payment Plan, monthly payment plans, individually arranged payment plans, quarterly payment plan). Tuition reduction for siblings, merit scholarship grants, need-based scholarship grants available. In 2016–17, 5% of upper-school students received aid; total upper-school merit-scholarship money awarded: $3500. Total amount of financial aid awarded in 2016–17: $90,000.

Admissions Traditional secondary-level entrance grade is 9. Deadline for receipt of application materials: January 21. Application fee required: $75. On-campus interview required.

Athletics Interscholastic: basketball, cheering, cross-country running, dance, dance squad, dance team, drill team, equestrian sports, golf, horseback riding, soccer, softball, swimming and diving, tennis, track and field, volleyball, water polo; intramural: badminton, basketball, cheering, dance, dance squad, dance team, jogging, physical fitness, soccer, softball, yoga. 2 PE instructors, 36 coaches, 1 athletic trainer.

Computers Computer resources include Internet access, wireless campus network, Internet filtering or blocking technology. Campus intranet and computer access in designated common areas are available to students. Students grades are available online.

Contact Ms. Katie Rossi, Director of Public Relations and Enrollment. 909-297-6752. Fax: 626-335-4373. E-mail: krossi@stlucys.com. Website: www.stlucys.com

ST. LUKE'S SCHOOL

377 North Wilton Road
New Canaan, Connecticut 06840

Head of School: Mr. Mark C. Davis

General Information Coeducational day college-preparatory school. Grades 5–12. Founded: 1928. Setting: suburban. Nearest major city is New York, NY. 40-acre campus. 5 buildings on campus. Approved or accredited by Connecticut Association of Independent Schools, New England Association of Schools and Colleges, and Connecticut Department of Education. Member of National Association of Independent Schools. Endowment: $26 million. Upper school average class size: 11. Upper school faculty-student ratio: 1:8. There are 180 required school days per year for Upper School students. Upper School students typically attend 5 days per week. The average school day consists of 9 hours.

Upper School Student Profile Grade 9: 79 students (37 boys, 42 girls); Grade 10: 71 students (33 boys, 38 girls); Grade 11: 87 students (43 boys, 44 girls); Grade 12: 77 students (43 boys, 34 girls).

Faculty School total: 75. In upper school: 34 men, 28 women; 60 have advanced degrees.

Subjects Offered 20th century American writers, 20th century history, 20th century world history, acting, advanced chemistry, advanced computer applications, advanced math, Advanced Placement courses, advanced studio art-AP, African American studies, algebra, American Civil War, American foreign policy, American history, American literature, anatomy and physiology, Ancient Greek, ancient history, art, art history, biology, biology-AP, British literature (honors), calculus, calculus-AP, ceramics, chemistry, chemistry-AP, choral music, chorus, classical civilization, classical language, classical studies, classics, college counseling, community service, computer applications, computer art, computer education, computer graphics, computer information systems, computer math, computer programming, computer science, computer science-AP, concert band, creative writing, digital art, digital photography, discrete mathematics, drama, drawing, earth science, economics, engineering, English, English language and composition-AP, English literature, environmental science, environmental science-AP, European history, European history-AP, expository writing, fine arts, French, French-AP, geography, geometry, government and politics-AP, government/civics, grammar, health education, honors algebra, honors English, honors geometry, honors U.S. history, honors world history, human geography - AP, humanities, journalism, Latin, Latin-AP, leadership, literature and composition-AP, literature-AP, Mandarin, marine biology, marine science, mathematics, modern European history-AP, music, photography, physical education, physics, physics-AP, pre-calculus, psychology, religion and culture, robotics, Roman civilization, Roman culture, science, social sciences, social studies, Spanish, Spanish-AP, sports medicine, statistics, statistics-AP, studio art, studio art-AP, technical theater, the Sixties, theater, trigonometry, U.S. government and politics-AP, U.S. history, U.S. history-AP, Vietnam, Vietnam War, Western civilization, world history, world history-AP, writing, yearbook.

Graduation Requirements Arts and fine arts (art, music, dance, drama), computer science, English, foreign language, mathematics, music, science, social studies (includes history), 20 hours of community service per year.

Special Academic Programs Advanced Placement exam preparation; honors section; independent study; term-away projects; study abroad; academic accommodation for the gifted.

College Admission Counseling 66 students graduated in 2016; all went to college, including Bowdoin College; Elon University; Massachusetts Institute of Technology; Penn State University Park; Washington University in St. Louis; Wesleyan University. Median SAT critical reading: 620, median SAT math: 620, median SAT writing: 620, median composite ACT: 30. 66% scored over 600 on SAT critical reading, 59% scored over 600 on SAT math, 63% scored over 600 on SAT writing, 56% scored over 1800 on combined SAT, 85% scored over 26 on composite ACT.

Student Life Upper grades have specified standards of dress, student council, honor system. Discipline rests usually with students and faculty.

Summer Programs Enrichment, advancement, sports, art/fine arts, computer instruction programs offered; session focuses on enrichment; held on campus; accepts boys and girls; open to students from other schools. 500 students usually enrolled. 2017 schedule: June 19 to August 12. Application deadline: April 1.

Tuition and Aid Day student tuition: $38,840–$40,640. Tuition installment plan (The Tuition Plan, Insured Tuition Payment Plan, monthly payment plans). Need-based scholarship grants available. In 2016–17, 16% of upper-school students received aid. Total amount of financial aid awarded in 2016–17: $1,911,149.

Admissions Traditional secondary-level entrance grade is 9. For fall 2016, 220 students applied for upper-level admission, 62 were accepted, 35 enrolled. ISEE or SSAT required. Deadline for receipt of application materials: January 15. Application fee required: $75. On-campus interview recommended.

Athletics Interscholastic: baseball (boys), basketball (b,g), crew (b,g), cross-country running (b,g), field hockey (g), football (b), golf (b), hockey (b), lacrosse (b,g), soccer (b,g), softball (g), squash (b,g), tennis (b,g), volleyball (g); intramural: equestrian sports (g), fitness (b,g), physical training (b,g), skiing (downhill) (b,g); coed interscholastic: crew, cross-country running, golf, hockey, squash; coed intramural: bicycling, physical training, skiing (downhill), weight training. 2 PE instructors, 21 coaches, 2 athletic trainers.

Computers Computers are regularly used in all academic, art, college planning, design, English, foreign language, graphic design, library, mathematics, media, science, social sciences, technology, yearbook classes. Computer network features include on-campus library services, online commercial services, Internet access, wireless campus network, Internet filtering or blocking technology. Student e-mail accounts are available to students. Students grades are available online. The school has a published electronic and media policy.

Contact Ginny Bachman, Director of Admission and Financial Aid. 203-80-4833. Fax: 203-972-5353. E-mail: bachmanv@stlukesct.org. Website: www.stlukesct.org

ST. MARGARET'S SCHOOL

1080 Lucas Avenue
Victoria, British Columbia V8X 3P7, Canada

Head of School: Cathy Thornicroft

General Information Girls' boarding and day college-preparatory, general academic, arts, technology, and ESL school. Boarding grades 7–12, day grades JK–12. Founded: 1908. Setting: suburban. Students are housed in single-sex dormitories. 22-acre campus. 10 buildings on campus. Approved or accredited by Canadian Association of Independent Schools, The Association of Boarding Schools, and British Columbia Department of Education. Language of instruction: English. Total enrollment: 346. Upper school average class size: 18. Upper school faculty-student ratio: 1:8.

Upper School Student Profile Grade 6: 20 students (20 girls); Grade 7: 18 students (18 girls); Grade 8: 18 students (18 girls); Grade 9: 15 students (15 girls); Grade 10: 32 students (32 girls); Grade 11: 46 students (46 girls); Grade 12: 34 students (34 girls). 55% of students are boarding students. 45% are province residents. 6 provinces are represented in upper school student body. 55% are international students. International students from China, Hong Kong, Japan, Mexico, Republic of Korea, and Taiwan; 6 other countries represented in student body.

Faculty School total: 38. In upper school: 7 men, 30 women; 12 have advanced degrees.

Subjects Offered 1968, Advanced Placement courses, algebra, applied skills, art, biology, calculus, Canadian geography, Canadian history, career and personal planning, chemistry, Chinese, choir, communications, comparative civilizations, computer science, creative writing, dance, drama, English, English literature, ESL, fine arts, French, geography, history, information technology, Japanese, journalism, law, leadership, Mandarin, mathematics, music, music appreciation, outdoor education, performing arts, photography, physical education, physics, science, social studies, Spanish, theater, Western civilization, writing.

Graduation Requirements Applied skills, arts and fine arts (art, music, dance, drama), English, foreign language, mathematics, science, social studies (includes history).

Special Academic Programs 4 Advanced Placement exams for which test preparation is offered; ESL (38 students enrolled).

College Admission Counseling 44 students graduated in 2015; 42 went to college, including McGill University; Simon Fraser University; The University of British Columbia; University of Toronto; University of Victoria; University of Waterloo. Other: 2 had other specific plans.

Student Life Upper grades have uniform requirement, student council. Discipline rests primarily with faculty.

Tuition and Aid Day student tuition: CAN$6054–CAN$16,301; 7-day tuition and room/board: CAN$31,831–CAN$39,411. Tuition installment plan (Insured Tuition Payment Plan, monthly payment plans). Tuition reduction for siblings, bursaries, merit scholarship grants, need-based scholarship grants available. In 2015–16, 17% of upper-school students received aid; total upper-school merit-scholarship money awarded: CAN$30,000. Total amount of financial aid awarded in 2015–16: CAN$70,000.

Admissions Traditional secondary-level entrance grade is 7. For fall 2015, 115 students applied for upper-level admission, 97 were accepted, 92 enrolled. School's own exam required. Deadline for receipt of application materials: none. Application fee required: CAN$225. Interview required.

Athletics Interscholastic: aerobics/dance, aquatics, badminton, basketball, cross-country running, dance, field hockey, fitness, rowing, running, soccer, swimming and diving, synchronized swimming, track and field, volleyball; intramural: aerobics, aerobics/dance, alpine skiing, aquatics, backpacking, badminton, baseball, basketball, bicycling, canoeing/kayaking, climbing, cooperative games, cross-country running, dance, equestrian sports, field hockey, figure skating, fitness, floor hockey, Frisbee, golf, gymnastics, hiking/backpacking, horseback riding, ice skating, indoor soccer, jogging, jump rope, kayaking, martial arts, modern dance, mountain biking, ocean paddling, outdoor activities, paddle tennis, physical fitness, rock climbing, ropes courses, rugby, running, sailing, skiing (cross-country), skiing (downhill), snowboarding, soccer, softball, squash, strength & conditioning, surfing, swimming and diving, table tennis, tennis, track and field, ultimate Frisbee, volleyball, wallyball, weight training, wilderness, wilderness survival, yoga. 4 PE instructors, 10 coaches, 2 athletic trainers.

Computers Computers are regularly used in career exploration, English, ESL, foreign language, French, history, journalism, mathematics, science classes. Computer network features include Internet access, wireless campus network, Internet filtering or blocking technology. Student e-mail accounts and computer access in designated common areas are available to students.

Contact Ms. Kathy Charleson, Director of Admissions. 250-479-7171. Fax: 250-479-8976. E-mail: stmarg@stmarg.ca. Website: www.stmarg.ca

ST. MARK'S SCHOOL OF TEXAS

10600 Preston Road

Dallas, Texas 75230-4000

Head of School: Mr. David W. Dini

General Information Boys' day college-preparatory, arts, technology, and Advanced Placement school. Grades 1–12. Founded: 1906. Setting: urban. 40-acre campus. 13 buildings on campus. Approved or accredited by Independent Schools Association of the Southwest. Member of National Association of Independent Schools and Secondary School Admission Test Board. Endowment: $130 million. Total enrollment: 863. Upper school average class size: 14. Upper school faculty-student ratio: 1:8. There are 172 required school days per year for Upper School students. Upper School students typically attend 5 days per week. The average school day consists of 7 hours and 55 minutes.

Upper School Student Profile Grade 9: 99 students (99 boys); Grade 10: 93 students (93 boys); Grade 11: 92 students (92 boys); Grade 12: 88 students (88 boys).

Subjects Offered 3-dimensional art, acting, algebra, American history-AP, ancient world history, art, art history, astronomy, Basic programming, biology, biology-AP, calculus, calculus-AP, ceramics, chemistry, chemistry-AP, Chinese, choir, civil rights, community service, computer programming, computer science, computer science-AP, conceptual physics, concert band, creative drama, creative writing, debate, digital art, digital photography, directing, DNA science lab, drama, drama workshop, economics, economics-AP, English, English literature and composition-AP, English literature-AP, environmental science-AP, European history, European history-AP, film studies, fine arts, gender issues, geology, geometry, history, honors English, honors geometry, humanities, independent study, Japanese, journalism, Latin, Latin-AP, macroeconomics-AP, marine ecology, mathematics, microeconomics-AP, modern European history-AP, modern world history, music, oceanography, photography, physical education, physics, physics-AP, piano, science, science fiction, sculpture, senior project, Spanish, Spanish language-AP, Spanish literature-AP, statistics-AP, strings, theater, trigonometry, U.S. history, video film production, Web site design, woodworking, world history, world religions.

Graduation Requirements Arts and fine arts (art, music, dance, drama), English, foreign language, mathematics, physical education (includes health), science, social studies (includes history), senior exhibition. Community service is required.

Special Academic Programs Advanced Placement exam preparation; honors section; independent study; term-away projects; study abroad; academic accommodation for the gifted.

College Admission Counseling 91 students graduated in 2015; all went to college, including Dartmouth College; Georgetown University; Southern Methodist University; Texas A&M University; The University of Texas at Austin; University of Pennsylvania. Mean SAT critical reading: 699, mean SAT math: 724, mean SAT writing: 688, mean combined SAT: 2111, mean composite ACT: 32.

Student Life Upper grades have uniform requirement, student council, honor system. Discipline rests primarily with faculty. Attendance at religious services is required.

Tuition and Aid Day student tuition: $23,525. Tuition installment plan (Insured Tuition Payment Plan, individually arranged payment plans, financial aid student monthly payment plan). Need-based scholarship grants, tuition remission for sons of faculty and staff, need-based middle-income financial aid available. In 2015–16, 17% of upper-school students received aid. Total amount of financial aid awarded in 2015–16: $1,170,052.

Admissions Traditional secondary-level entrance grade is 9. For fall 2015, 100 students applied for upper-level admission, 17 were accepted, 14 enrolled. ISEE required. Deadline for receipt of application materials: January 5. Application fee required: $175. Interview required.

Athletics Interscholastic: backpacking, baseball, basketball, cheering, climbing, crew, cross-country running, diving, fencing, football, golf, hiking/backpacking, hockey, ice hockey, lacrosse, outdoor education, outdoor skills, physical fitness, physical training, soccer, strength & conditioning, swimming and diving, tennis, track and field, volleyball, wall climbing, water polo, weight training, wilderness, winter soccer, wrestling; intramural: basketball, bicycling, cooperative games, cross-country running, fitness, flag football, floor hockey, jump rope, kickball, lacrosse, physical fitness, physical training, soccer, softball, swimming and diving, table tennis, team handball, tennis, track and field, volleyball, water polo, weight training, winter soccer, wrestling. 11 PE instructors, 69 coaches, 2 athletic trainers.

Computers Computers are regularly used in English, foreign language, humanities, mathematics, science classes. Computer network features include on-campus library services, online commercial services, Internet access, wireless campus network, Internet filtering or blocking technology. Student e-mail accounts and computer access in designated common areas are available to students. Students grades are available online. The school has a published electronic and media policy.

Contact Mr. David P. Baker, Director of Admission and Financial Aid. 214-346-8171. Fax: 214-346-8701. E-mail: admission@smtexas.org. Website: www.smtexas.org

ST. MARTIN'S EPISCOPAL SCHOOL

225 Green Acres Road

Metairie, Louisiana 70003

Head of School: Merry Sorrells

General Information Coeducational day college-preparatory, arts, religious studies, bilingual studies, and technology school, affiliated with Episcopal Church. Grades PK–12. Founded: 1947. Setting: suburban. Nearest major city is New Orleans. 18-acre campus. 13 buildings on campus. Approved or accredited by Independent Schools Association of the Southwest, National Association of Episcopal Schools, Southwest Association of Episcopal Schools, The College Board, and Louisiana Department of Education. Member of National Association of Independent Schools. Endowment: $6.7 million. Total enrollment: 473. Upper school average class size: 15. Upper school faculty-student ratio: 1:6. There are 178 required school days per year for Upper School students. Upper School students typically attend 5 days per week. The average school day consists of 5 hours and 30 minutes.

Upper School Student Profile Grade 9: 45 students (23 boys, 22 girls); Grade 10: 40 students (22 boys, 18 girls); Grade 11: 42 students (28 boys, 14 girls); Grade 12: 47 students (28 boys, 19 girls). 11% of students are members of Episcopal Church.

Faculty School total: 87. In upper school: 9 men, 18 women; 23 have advanced degrees.

Subjects Offered Advanced chemistry, advanced math, Advanced Placement courses, advanced studio art-AP, algebra, American history, American history-AP, American literature, American literature-AP, art, art history, band, baseball, basketball, Bible studies, biology, biology-AP, calculus, calculus-AP, career education internship, career/college preparation, ceramics, cheerleading, chemistry, chemistry-AP, Chinese studies, chorus, civics, college counseling, community garden, community service, computer literacy, creative writing, current events, digital photography, drama, earth science, economics, economics and history, English, English as a foreign language, English composition, English language and composition-AP, English literature, English literature and composition-AP, English literature-AP, environmental science, ethics, European history-AP, fine arts, French, French-AP, geography, geology, geometry, grammar, history-AP, honors algebra, honors English, honors geometry, humanities, internship, journalism, lab science, Latin, Latin-AP, life management skills, life skills, literary magazine, Mandarin, mathematics, model United Nations, music, music appreciation, music-AP, musical productions, newspaper, philosophy, physical education, physics, pre-algebra, publications, religion, SAT preparation, science, scripture, senior internship, social studies, softball, Spanish, Spanish-AP, speech, statistics-AP, student government, studio art, studio art-AP, swimming, tennis, theater, theater design and production, theology, track and field, trigonometry, U.S. history-AP, volleyball, world history, world literature, world religions, writing.

Graduation Requirements Arts and fine arts (art, music, dance, drama), electives, English, foreign language, life skills, mathematics, physical education (includes health), religion (includes Bible studies and theology), science, senior internship, social studies (includes history), senior intern program, 50 hours of community service.

Special Academic Programs 12 Advanced Placement exams for which test preparation is offered; honors section; independent study; ESL (9 students enrolled).

College Admission Counseling 58 students graduated in 2015; 57 went to college, including Chapman University; Louisiana State University and Agricultural & Mechanical College; Savannah College of Art and Design; St. Edward's University; Texas A&M University; Texas Christian University. Median SAT critical reading: 560, median SAT math: 570, median SAT writing: 570, median combined SAT: 1740, median composite ACT: 26. 24% scored over 600 on SAT critical reading, 41% scored over 600 on SAT math, 32% scored over 600 on SAT writing, 32% scored over 1800 on combined SAT, 40% scored over 26 on composite ACT.

Student Life Upper grades have specified standards of dress, student council, honor system. Discipline rests primarily with faculty. Attendance at religious services is required.

Tuition and Aid Day student tuition: $19,950. Tuition installment plan (local bank-arranged plan). Merit scholarship grants, need-based scholarship grants available. In 2015–16, 47% of upper-school students received aid; total upper-school merit-scholarship money awarded: $239,042. Total amount of financial aid awarded in 2015–16: $349,973.

Admissions Traditional secondary-level entrance grade is 9. For fall 2015, 41 students applied for upper-level admission, 31 were accepted, 23 enrolled. Admissions testing, ISEE, Kaufman Test of Educational Achievement, math and English placement tests, WISC III or other aptitude measures; standardized achievement test or writing sample required. Deadline for receipt of application materials: none. Application fee required: $50. Interview required.

Athletics Interscholastic: baseball (boys), basketball (b,g), cheering (g), cross-country running (b,g), football (b), golf (b,g), soccer (b,g), softball (g), swimming and diving (b,g), tennis (b,g), track and field (b,g), volleyball (g), winter (indoor) track (b); intramural: basketball (b,g), lacrosse (b,g), ropes courses (b,g), soccer (b,g), swimming and diving (b,g), tennis (b,g), track and field (b,g), volleyball (g); coed intramural: project adventure. 2 PE instructors, 5 coaches, 1 athletic trainer.

Computers Computers are regularly used in all academic classes. Computer network features include on-campus library services, online commercial services, Internet access, wireless campus network, Internet filtering or blocking technology, vpn for teachers, staff, and students. Campus intranet, student e-mail accounts, and computer access in designated common areas are available to students. Students grades are available online. The school has a published electronic and media policy.

Contact Mrs. DeAnna Tillery, Admission Assistant. 504-736-9917. Fax: 504-736-8802. E-mail: deanna.tillery@stmsaints.com. Website: www.stmsaints.com

SAINT MARY OF THE ASSUMPTION HIGH SCHOOL

237 South Broad Street
Elizabeth, New Jersey 07202

Head of School: Mr. David Evans

General Information Coeducational day school, affiliated with Roman Catholic Church. Founded: 1930. Setting: urban. 1 building on campus. Approved or accredited by Middle States Association of Colleges and Schools, New England Association of Schools and Colleges, and New Jersey Department of Education. Member of National Association of Independent Schools. Upper school average class size: 20. Upper school faculty-student ratio: 1:13. There are 188 required school days per year for Upper School students. Upper School students typically attend 5 days per week. The average school day consists of 6 hours and 45 minutes.

Upper School Student Profile Grade 9: 42 students (25 boys, 17 girls); Grade 10: 52 students (35 boys, 17 girls); Grade 11: 63 students (42 boys, 21 girls); Grade 12: 52 students (31 boys, 21 girls). 40% of students are Roman Catholic.

Faculty In upper school: 8 men, 7 women.

Graduation Requirements American history, chemistry, driver education, English, religion (includes Bible studies and theology).

College Admission Counseling 48 students graduated in 2016; all went to college, including Fairleigh Dickinson University, College at Florham; Montclair State University; Saint Peter's University.

Student Life Upper grades have uniform requirement, student council, honor system. Discipline rests primarily with faculty.

Summer Programs Remediation programs offered; session focuses on Remediation; held on campus; accepts boys and girls; open to students from other schools. 40 students usually enrolled. 2017 schedule: July 5 to July 31. Application deadline: June 14.

Tuition and Aid Day student tuition: $8000. Tuition installment plan (SMART Tuition Payment Plan). Tuition reduction for siblings, merit scholarship grants, need-based scholarship grants available. In 2016–17, 92% of upper-school students received aid; total upper-school merit-scholarship money awarded: $360,000. Total amount of financial aid awarded in 2016–17: $360,000.

Admissions Traditional secondary-level entrance grade is 9. For fall 2016, 167 students applied for upper-level admission, 160 were accepted, 42 enrolled. Deadline for receipt of application materials: none. No application fee required. On-campus interview required.

Athletics Interscholastic: baseball (boys), basketball (b,g), soccer (b,g), softball (g); coed interscholastic: bowling, cheering, dance team. 1 PE instructor, 12 coaches.

Computers Computer resources include wireless campus network. Computer access in designated common areas is available to students. Students grades are available online.

Contact 908-352-4350. Fax: 908-352-2359. Website: www.stmaryhsnj.org

ST. MARY'S EPISCOPAL SCHOOL

60 Perkins Extended
Memphis, Tennessee 38117-3199

Head of School: Mr. Albert L. Throckmorton

General Information Girls' day college-preparatory, technology, and STEM (Science, Technology, Engineering, Math) school, affiliated with Episcopal Church. Grades PK–12. Distance learning grades 9–12. Founded: 1847. Setting: urban. 29-acre campus. 8 buildings on campus. Approved or accredited by National Association of Episcopal Schools, Southern Association of Colleges and Schools, Southern Association of Independent Schools, Tennessee Association of Independent Schools, The College Board, and Tennessee Department of Education. Member of National Association of Independent Schools. Endowment: $20.1 million. Total enrollment: 837. Upper school average class size: 12. Upper school faculty-student ratio: 1:9. There are 175 required school days per year for Upper School students. Upper School students typically attend 5 days per week. The average school day consists of 6 hours and 25 minutes.

Upper School Student Profile Grade 9: 60 students (60 girls); Grade 10: 64 students (64 girls); Grade 11: 65 students (65 girls); Grade 12: 64 students (64 girls). 12.3% of students are members of Episcopal Church.

Faculty School total: 110. In upper school: 5 men, 33 women; 32 have advanced degrees.

Subjects Offered Algebra, anatomy and physiology, art history, art history-AP, biology, biology-AP, calculus, calculus-AP, chamber groups, chemistry, chemistry-AP, choir, comparative religion, economics, English, English language and composition-AP, English literature and composition-AP, ethics, French, French-AP, geography, geometry, global issues, global studies, guitar, health, humanities, instrumental music, Latin, Latin-AP, Mandarin, microbiology, music theory-AP, performing arts, physical

education, physics, physics-AP, pre-calculus, psychology, religion, robotics, Spanish, Spanish-AP, speech, studio art, studio art-AP, technology, theater, U.S. government, U.S. history, U.S. history-AP, wind ensemble, world history, world history-AP.

Graduation Requirements 1 1/2 elective credits, algebra, American history, arts and fine arts (art, music, dance, drama), biology, calculus, chemistry, English, English language-AP, English literature-AP, foreign language, geometry, mathematics, physical education (includes health), physics, pre-calculus, religion (includes Bible studies and theology), social studies (includes history), U.S. history, world history, each student is required to complete one online class.

Special Academic Programs 16 Advanced Placement exams for which test preparation is offered; honors section; independent study; academic accommodation for the gifted, the musically talented, and the artistically talented.

College Admission Counseling 64 students graduated in 2016; all went to college, including Emory University; Northeastern University; Saint Louis University; Tulane University; University of California, Los Angeles; University of Mississippi. Median SAT critical reading: 630, median SAT math: 610, median SAT writing: 650, median combined SAT: 1900, median composite ACT: 30. 67% scored over 600 on SAT critical reading, 52% scored over 600 on SAT math, 79% scored over 600 on SAT writing, 65% scored over 1800 on combined SAT, 89% scored over 26 on composite ACT.

Student Life Upper grades have specified standards of dress, student council, honor system. Discipline rests primarily with faculty. Attendance at religious services is required.

Summer Programs Enrichment, sports programs offered; session focuses on summer enrichment, College Essay, Test Prep, Literature; held on campus; accepts boys and girls; open to students from other schools. 200 students usually enrolled. 2017 schedule: May 30 to August 11. Application deadline: none.

Tuition and Aid Day student tuition: $19,850. Tuition installment plan (Insured Tuition Payment Plan, FACTS Tuition Payment Plan, monthly payment plans, individually arranged payment plans, credit card payment). Need-based scholarship grants, tuition remission to faculty, staff, and clergy available. In 2016–17, 25% of upper-school students received aid. Total amount of financial aid awarded in 2016–17: $674,412.

Admissions Traditional secondary-level entrance grade is 9. For fall 2016, 30 students applied for upper-level admission, 28 were accepted, 19 enrolled. ISEE and writing sample required. Deadline for receipt of application materials: none. Application fee required: $75. On-campus interview recommended.

Athletics Interscholastic: basketball, bowling, cross-country running, fencing, golf, lacrosse, soccer, swimming and diving, tennis, track and field, trap and skeet, volleyball. 1 PE instructor, 15 coaches, 1 athletic trainer.

Computers Computers are regularly used in all academic classes. Computer network features include on-campus library services, Internet access, wireless campus network, Internet filtering or blocking technology, online database services for research available at school and at home. Campus intranet, student e-mail accounts, and computer access in designated common areas are available to students. Students grades are available online. The school has a published electronic and media policy.

Contact Ms. Nicole Hernandez, Director of Admission and Financial Aid. 901-537-1405. Fax: 901-685-1098. E-mail: nhernandez@stmarysschool.org. Website: www.stmarysschool.org

SAINT MARY'S HALL

9401 Starcrest Drive
San Antonio, Texas 78217

Head of School: Mr. Jonathan Eades

General Information Coeducational day college-preparatory school. Grades PK–12. Founded: 1879. Setting: suburban. 60-acre campus. 15 buildings on campus. Approved or accredited by Independent Schools Association of the Southwest. Member of National Association of Independent Schools. Endowment: $40 million. Total enrollment: 996. Upper school average class size: 15. Upper school faculty-student ratio: 1:6. There are 173 required school days per year for Upper School students. Upper School students typically attend 5 days per week. The average school day consists of 7 hours and 15 minutes.

Upper School Student Profile Grade 9: 97 students (46 boys, 51 girls); Grade 10: 106 students (56 boys, 50 girls); Grade 11: 90 students (47 boys, 43 girls); Grade 12: 94 students (41 boys, 53 girls).

Faculty School total: 56. In upper school: 28 men, 21 women; 38 have advanced degrees.

Subjects Offered 3-dimensional art, Advanced Placement courses, algebra, American history-AP, American literature, anatomy and physiology, art, art history, art history-AP, art-AP, athletic training, ballet, baseball, basketball, biology, biology-AP, British literature, calculus, calculus-AP, cell biology, ceramics, chemistry, chemistry-AP, choir, college counseling, composition, computer science, computer science-AP, concert choir, creative writing, dance, digital photography, directing, drama, drawing, drawing and design, economics, economics-AP, English language and composition-AP, English literature and composition-AP, environmental science-AP, European history, European history-AP, fitness, French, French language-AP, genetics, geology, geometry, golf, government/civics, great books, guitar, health, human geography - AP, jazz band, Latin, Latin-AP, literary magazine, marine biology, model United Nations, music theory, painting, photography, physical education, physics, physics-AP, piano, pre-calculus, religious studies, science research, sculpture, set design, softball, Spanish, Spanish language-AP, Spanish literature-AP, speech, statistics-AP, swimming, technical theater, tennis, track and field, U.S. history, voice, volleyball, Web site design, world geography, world history, world literature, world religions, yearbook, zoology.

Graduation Requirements Arts and fine arts (art, music, dance, drama), athletics, electives, English, foreign language, mathematics, physical education (includes health), science, social studies (includes history), 40 hours of community service.

Special Academic Programs 25 Advanced Placement exams for which test preparation is offered; honors section; independent study; study abroad.

College Admission Counseling 100 students graduated in 2016; 99 went to college, including Baylor University; Stanford University; Texas A&M University; The University of Texas at Austin; Trinity University; University of Richmond. Other: 1 had other specific plans. Median SAT critical reading: 647, median SAT math: 656, median SAT writing: 656, median combined SAT: 733. 67% scored over 600 on SAT critical reading, 69% scored over 600 on SAT math, 71% scored over 600 on SAT writing, 73% scored over 1800 on combined SAT, 70% scored over 26 on composite ACT.

Student Life Upper grades have uniform requirement, student council, honor system. Discipline rests primarily with faculty.

Summer Programs Enrichment, sports, art/fine arts, computer instruction programs offered; held on campus; accepts boys and girls; open to students from other schools. 837 students usually enrolled. 2017 schedule: June 5 to August 4. Application deadline: May 13.

Tuition and Aid Day student tuition: $24,510. Tuition installment plan (monthly payment plans, individually arranged payment plans, full-year payment plan, 2-payment plan, monthly payment plan). Merit scholarship grants, need-based scholarship grants available. In 2016–17, 22% of upper-school students received aid; total upper-school merit-scholarship money awarded: $382,320. Total amount of financial aid awarded in 2016–17: $621,990.

Admissions Traditional secondary-level entrance grade is 9. For fall 2016, 71 students applied for upper-level admission, 62 were accepted, 49 enrolled. ISEE required. Deadline for receipt of application materials: November 11. Application fee required: $50. On-campus interview recommended.

Athletics Interscholastic: ballet (boys, girls), baseball (b), basketball (b,g), cheering (g), dance (b,g), field hockey (g), fitness (b,g), football (b), golf (b,g), independent competitive sports (b,g), lacrosse (b), soccer (b,g), softball (g), volleyball (b,g); coed interscholastic: cross-country running, physical fitness, physical training, strength & conditioning, tennis, track and field, weight training. 14 coaches, 2 athletic trainers.

Computers Computers are regularly used in all academic, media arts classes. Computer network features include on-campus library services, Internet access, wireless campus network, Internet filtering or blocking technology, SmartBoards, Apple TV. Student e-mail accounts are available to students. Students grades are available online. The school has a published electronic and media policy.

Contact Mrs. Julie Hellmund, Director of Admission. 210-483-9234. Fax: 210-655-5211. E-mail: jhellmund@smhall.org. Website: www.smhall.org

SAINT MARY'S HIGH SCHOOL

2525 North Third Street
Phoenix, Arizona 85004

Head of School: Mrs. Suzanne M. Fessler

General Information Coeducational day college-preparatory, arts, and religious studies school, affiliated with Roman Catholic Church. Grades 9–12. Founded: 1917. Setting: urban. 6-acre campus. 5 buildings on campus. Approved or accredited by North Central Association of Colleges and Schools, Western Catholic Education Association, and Arizona Department of Education. Endowment: $1.5 million. Total enrollment: 541. Upper school average class size: 22. Upper school faculty-student ratio: 1:13. There are 180 required school days per year for Upper School students. Upper School students typically attend 5 days per week. The average school day consists of 6 hours and 45 minutes.

Upper School Student Profile Grade 9: 153 students (71 boys, 82 girls); Grade 10: 144 students (75 boys, 69 girls); Grade 11: 150 students (84 boys, 66 girls); Grade 12: 126 students (54 boys, 72 girls). 90% of students are Roman Catholic.

Faculty School total: 45. In upper school: 22 men, 23 women; 27 have advanced degrees.

Graduation Requirements Advanced math, algebra, American literature, anatomy and physiology, biology, British literature, Catholic belief and practice, Christian and Hebrew scripture, geometry, history of the Catholic Church, language and composition, physics, pre-calculus, trigonometry, world literature, 4 credits of history, 4 credits of Catholic Theology courses.

Special Academic Programs 5 Advanced Placement exams for which test preparation is offered; honors section; study at local college for college credit; remedial reading and/or remedial writing; remedial math.

College Admission Counseling 99 students graduated in 2016; 90 went to college, including Arizona State University at the Tempe campus; Benedictine University at Mesa; Grand Canyon University; Northern Arizona University; The University of Arizona. Other: 5 went to work, 4 entered military service, 90 entered a postgraduate year, 9 had other specific plans. Median composite ACT: 20. Mean SAT critical reading: 472, mean SAT math: 458, mean SAT writing: 453. 8% scored over 600 on

SAT critical reading, 9% scored over 600 on SAT math, 9% scored over 600 on SAT writing, 3% scored over 1800 on combined SAT, 1% scored over 26 on composite ACT.

Student Life Upper grades have uniform requirement, student council. Discipline rests primarily with faculty. Attendance at religious services is required.

Summer Programs Remediation, enrichment, advancement, sports, art/fine arts programs offered; session focuses on high school preparation for incoming freshmen and advancement for upper classmen; held on campus; accepts boys and girls; not open to students from other schools. 200 students usually enrolled. 2017 schedule: June 5 to June 30. Application deadline: May 12.

Tuition and Aid Day student tuition: $14,000. Tuition installment plan (monthly payment plans, individually arranged payment plans, quarterly and semester payment plans). Need-based scholarship grants, paying campus jobs available. In 2016–17, 80% of upper-school students received aid. Total amount of financial aid awarded in 2016–17: $3,800,000.

Admissions Traditional secondary-level entrance grade is 9. For fall 2016, 180 students applied for upper-level admission, 170 were accepted, 155 enrolled. High School Placement Test required. Deadline for receipt of application materials: none. Application fee required: $300. On-campus interview recommended.

Athletics Interscholastic: baseball (boys), basketball (b,g), cheering (g), football (b), golf (b,g), physical fitness (b,g), soccer (b,g), softball (g), strength & conditioning (b,g), tennis (b,g), volleyball (b,g), weight training (b,g), winter soccer (b,g); intramural: dance (g); coed interscholastic: cross-country running, physical fitness, strength & conditioning, swimming and diving, track and field, weight training. 2 PE instructors, 20 coaches, 1 athletic trainer.

Computers Computers are regularly used in digital applications, graphics, yearbook classes. Computer resources include on-campus library services, online commercial services, Internet access, wireless campus network, Internet filtering or blocking technology. Students grades are available online. The school has a published electronic and media policy.

Contact Ms. Allison Madigan, Director of Admissions. 602-251-2515. Fax: 602-251-2595. E-mail: amadigan@smknights.org. Website: www.smknights.org

ST. MARY'S HIGH SCHOOL

2501 East Yampa Street
Colorado Springs, Colorado 80909

Head of School: Mr. Jim Felice

General Information Coeducational day college-preparatory school, affiliated with Roman Catholic Church. Grades 9–12. Founded: 1885. Setting: urban. 5-acre campus. 4 buildings on campus. Approved or accredited by National Catholic Education Association, North Central Association of Colleges and Schools, and Colorado Department of Education. Total enrollment: 389. Upper school average class size: 15. Upper school faculty-student ratio: 1:11. There are 180 required school days per year for Upper School students. Upper School students typically attend 5 days per week. The average school day consists of 7 hours and 30 minutes.

Upper School Student Profile Grade 9: 65 students (30 boys, 35 girls); Grade 10: 56 students (25 boys, 31 girls); Grade 11: 61 students (30 boys, 31 girls); Grade 12: 70 students (34 boys, 36 girls). 70% of students are Roman Catholic.

Faculty School total: 31. In upper school: 14 men, 13 women; 22 have advanced degrees.

Subjects Offered Advanced Placement courses, advanced studio art-AP, advanced TOEFL/grammar, baseball, basketball, biology-AP, statistics-AP, student government, TOEFL preparation, track and field, transition mathematics, trigonometry, U.S. government and politics-AP, U.S. history, U.S. history-AP.

Graduation Requirements American history, biology, computer applications, geometry, religious studies, world geography, community service&-150 hours over 4 years, theology.

Special Academic Programs Advanced Placement exam preparation; honors section; independent study; study at local college for college credit; remedial math; programs in English, mathematics for dyslexic students.

College Admission Counseling 57 students graduated in 2016; 56 went to college, including Colorado School of Mines; Colorado State University; Creighton University; Gonzaga University; University of Colorado Boulder; University of Portland. Other: 1 entered military service, 56 entered a postgraduate year. Median SAT critical reading: 27, median SAT math: 25, median SAT writing: 27, median combined SAT: 26.

Student Life Upper grades have specified standards of dress, student council, honor system. Discipline rests primarily with faculty. Attendance at religious services is required.

Summer Programs Enrichment, advancement, computer instruction programs offered; session focuses on academics; held on campus; accepts boys and girls; not open to students from other schools. 100 students usually enrolled. 2017 schedule: June 6 to July 1. Application deadline: February 28.

Tuition and Aid Day student tuition: $9800. Tuition installment plan (SMART Tuition Payment Plan, monthly payments). Merit scholarship grants, need-based scholarship grants available. In 2016–17, 30% of upper-school students received aid; total upper-school merit-scholarship money awarded: $10,000. Total amount of financial aid awarded in 2016–17: $750,000.

Admissions Traditional secondary-level entrance grade is 9. For fall 2016, 80 students applied for upper-level admission, 68 were accepted, 65 enrolled. International English

Language Test, SLEP for foreign students and writing sample required. Deadline for receipt of application materials: February 15. Application fee required: $400. Interview recommended.

Athletics Interscholastic: baseball (boys), basketball (b,g), cheering (b,g), cross-country running (b,g), football (b), golf (b,g), lacrosse (b), soccer (b,g), softball (g), swimming and diving (g), tennis (g), track and field (b,g), volleyball (g). 1 PE instructor, 15 coaches, 2 athletic trainers.

Computers Computers are regularly used in architecture, business education, career exploration, college planning, creative writing, data processing, engineering, French, independent study, media production, music technology, philosophy, programming, Web site design classes. Computer network features include Internet access, wireless campus network, Internet filtering or blocking technology, JVLA courses. Campus intranet, student e-mail accounts, and computer access in designated common areas are available to students. Students grades are available online.

Contact Mrs. Robyn Cross, Director of Student Life. 719-635-7540 Ext. 16. Fax: 719-471-7623. E-mail: rcross@smhscs.org. Website: www.smhscs.org

ST. MARY'S PREPARATORY SCHOOL

3535 Indian Trail
Orchard Lake, Michigan 48324

Head of School: Cormac Lynn

General Information Boys' boarding and day college-preparatory school, affiliated with Roman Catholic Church. Grades 9–12. Founded: 1885. Setting: suburban. Nearest major city is Detroit. Students are housed in coed dormitories. 80-acre campus. 12 buildings on campus. Approved or accredited by Michigan Association of Non-Public Schools and Michigan Department of Education. Total enrollment: 540. Upper school average class size: 18. Upper school faculty-student ratio: 1:10. There are 185 required school days per year for Upper School students. Upper School students typically attend 5 days per week. The average school day consists of 7 hours.

Upper School Student Profile Grade 9: 133 students (133 boys); Grade 10: 137 students (137 boys); Grade 11: 126 students (126 boys); Grade 12: 127 students (127 boys). 15% of students are boarding students. 80% are state residents. 5 states are represented in upper school student body. 15% are international students. International students from China, Mexico, and United States. 80% of students are Roman Catholic.

Faculty School total: 58. In upper school: 43 men, 15 women; 20 have advanced degrees; 6 reside on campus.

Subjects Offered Advanced Placement courses, algebra, American government, American history, American literature, anatomy, art, astronomy, band, Bible studies, biology, broadcasting, business, business skills, calculus, calculus-AP, campus ministry, career experience, ceramics, chemistry, Chinese, computer programming, computer science, creative writing, drafting, driver education, earth science, ecology, economics, English, English literature, expository writing, fine arts, French, geometry, government/civics, grammar, graphic design, health, history, jazz band, journalism, law, mathematics, music technology, mythology, physical education, physics, Polish, psychology, religion, robotics, science, social sciences, social studies, Spanish, speech, theology, trigonometry, world history, world literature, writing.

Graduation Requirements Arts and fine arts (art, music, dance, drama), business skills (includes word processing), computer science, English, foreign language, mathematics, physical education (includes health), religion (includes Bible studies and theology), science, social sciences, social studies (includes history).

Special Academic Programs Advanced Placement exam preparation; honors section; study at local college for college credit; academic accommodation for the musically talented and the artistically talented; programs in general development for dyslexic students; special instructional classes for students with learning disabilities, Attention Deficit Disorder, and dyslexia; ESL (50 students enrolled).

College Admission Counseling 103 students graduated in 2016; 95 went to college, including Michigan State University; Oakland University; University of Michigan; Wayne State University; Western Michigan University; Western Michigan University. Other: 2 went to work, 1 entered military service, 5 had other specific plans. Median SAT critical reading: 503, median SAT math: 600, median SAT writing: 510, median combined SAT: 1613, median composite ACT: 24. 5% scored over 600 on SAT critical reading, 15% scored over 600 on SAT math, 40% scored over 26 on composite ACT.

Student Life Upper grades have specified standards of dress, student council, honor system. Discipline rests primarily with faculty. Attendance at religious services is required.

Summer Programs Sports programs offered; session focuses on football, basketball, and lacrosse, hockey; held on campus; accepts boys and girls; open to students from other schools. 400 students usually enrolled. 2017 schedule: June to August. Application deadline: June 1.

Tuition and Aid Day student tuition: $11,000; 5-day tuition and room/board: $20,000; 7-day tuition and room/board: $30,000. Tuition installment plan (SMART Tuition Payment Plan, individually arranged payment plans). Tuition reduction for siblings, merit scholarship grants, need-based scholarship grants available. In 2016–17, 80% of upper-school students received aid.

Admissions Traditional secondary-level entrance grade is 9. For fall 2016, 300 students applied for upper-level admission, 200 were accepted, 150 enrolled. STS, STS,

Diocese Test and TOEFL required. Deadline for receipt of application materials: none. Application fee required: $35. Interview required.

Athletics Interscholastic: alpine skiing, baseball, basketball, crew, cross-country running, football, freestyle skiing, golf, hockey, ice hockey, indoor track, indoor track & field, jogging, lacrosse, rowing, skiing (downhill), soccer, track and field, wrestling; intramural: aerobics/Nautilus, aquatics, basketball, bicycling, billiards, bowling, broomball, fitness, Frisbee, golf, hockey, ice hockey, ice skating, indoor hockey, indoor soccer, indoor track, jogging, lacrosse, mountain biking, Nautilus, physical fitness, physical training, rowing, running, skeet shooting, skiing (downhill), snowboarding, soccer, strength & conditioning, swimming and diving, table tennis, tennis, weight lifting, weight training, whiffle ball. 2 PE instructors, 25 coaches, 3 athletic trainers.

Computers Computers are regularly used in desktop publishing, drafting, engineering, yearbook classes. Computer network features include on-campus library services, Internet access, Internet filtering or blocking technology. Campus intranet and student e-mail accounts are available to students. Students grades are available online.

Contact Candace Knight, Dean of Admissions. 248-683-0514. Fax: 248-683-1740. E-mail: cknight@stmarysprep.com. Website: www.stmarysprep.com/

SAINT MARY'S SCHOOL

900 Hillsborough Street
Raleigh, North Carolina 27603-1689

Head of School: Dr. Monica M. Gillespie

General Information Girls' boarding and day college-preparatory, arts, religious studies, bilingual studies, and technology school, affiliated with Episcopal Church. Grades 9–12. Founded: 1842. Setting: urban. Students are housed in single-sex dormitories. 23-acre campus. 26 buildings on campus. Approved or accredited by National Association of Episcopal Schools, North Carolina Association of Independent Schools, Southern Association of Colleges and Schools, Southern Association of Independent Schools, and The Association of Boarding Schools. Member of National Association of Independent Schools and Secondary School Admission Test Board. Total enrollment: 262. Upper school average class size: 12. Upper school faculty-student ratio: 1:8. Upper School students typically attend 5 days per week. The average school day consists of 7 hours.

Upper School Student Profile Grade 9: 56 students (56 girls); Grade 10: 67 students (67 girls); Grade 11: 78 students (78 girls); Grade 12: 61 students (61 girls). 49% of students are boarding students. 78% are state residents. 12 states are represented in upper school student body. 11% are international students. International students from China, Nigeria, Poland, Republic of Korea, United Kingdom, and Viet Nam; 1 other country represented in student body.

Faculty School total: 40. In upper school: 10 men, 30 women; 30 have advanced degrees; 36 reside on campus.

Subjects Offered 3-dimensional art, acting, advanced chemistry, advanced math, Advanced Placement courses, algebra, American government, American history, American history-AP, American literature, anatomy, art, astronomy, athletics, ballet, biology, biology-AP, calculus, calculus-AP, ceramics, chemistry, chemistry-AP, choir, choral music, computer science, dance, drama, drama performance, drawing, drawing and design, earth science, ecology, English, English literature, English literature-AP, European history, French, French language-AP, geometry, government, government-AP, government/civics, honors English, honors geometry, honors U.S. history, honors world history, Latin, Latin-AP, mathematics, philosophy, physical education, physics, physics-AP, piano, psychology-AP, religion, senior project, Spanish, Spanish language-AP, speech, U.S. government and politics-AP, U.S. history, U.S. history-AP, Western civilization, world literature, yearbook, yoga.

Graduation Requirements Algebra, arts and fine arts (art, music, dance, drama), biology, electives, English, foreign language, geometry, government, physical education (includes health), physical science, religion (includes Bible studies and theology), social sciences, U.S. history, Western civilization.

Special Academic Programs Advanced Placement exam preparation; honors section; independent study; study at local college for college credit; study abroad; academic accommodation for the gifted, the musically talented, and the artistically talented.

College Admission Counseling 73 students graduated in 2015; all went to college.

Student Life Upper grades have specified standards of dress, student council, honor system. Discipline rests equally with students and faculty. Attendance at religious services is required.

Tuition and Aid Day student tuition: $24,850; 7-day tuition and room/board: $49,500. Tuition installment plan (FACTS Tuition Payment Plan, monthly payment plans). Merit scholarship grants, need-based scholarship grants available. In 2015–16, 32% of upper-school students received aid.

Admissions Traditional secondary-level entrance grade is 9. For fall 2015, 178 students applied for upper-level admission, 123 were accepted, 77 enrolled. SSAT and TOEFL required. Deadline for receipt of application materials: none. Application fee required: $100. Interview required.

Athletics Interscholastic: basketball, cross-country running, field hockey, golf, lacrosse, soccer, softball, swimming and diving, tennis, track and field, volleyball; intramural: ballet, dance, dance team, modern dance. 2 PE instructors, 32 coaches, 1 athletic trainer.

Computers Computers are regularly used in dance, English, foreign language, history, introduction to technology, mathematics, newspaper, publications, science, senior seminar, writing, yearbook classes. Computer network features include on-campus library services, online commercial services, Internet access, wireless campus network, Internet filtering or blocking technology. Campus intranet, student e-mail accounts, and computer access in designated common areas are available to students. Students grades are available online. The school has a published electronic and media policy.

Contact Mrs. Elizabeth Lynnes, Manager of Admission Systems and Data. 919-424-4003. Fax: 919-424-4122. E-mail: admission@sms.edu. Website: www.sms.edu

ST. MARY'S SCHOOL

816 Black Oak Drive
Medford, Oregon 97504-8504

Head of School: Mr. Frank Phillips

General Information Coeducational boarding and day college-preparatory, arts, religious studies, and ESL school, affiliated with Roman Catholic Church. Boarding grades 9–12, day grades 6–12. Founded: 1865. Setting: small town. Nearest major city is Eugene. Students are housed in single-sex dormitories. 24-acre campus. 9 buildings on campus. Approved or accredited by National Catholic Education Association, Northwest Accreditation Commission, Northwest Association of Independent Schools, Northwest Association of Schools and Colleges, Office for Standards in Education (OFSTED), and Oregon Department of Education. Member of National Association of Independent Schools. Total enrollment: 467. Upper school average class size: 20. Upper school faculty-student ratio: 1:10. There are 180 required school days per year for Upper School students. Upper School students typically attend 5 days per week. The average school day consists of 7 hours and 15 minutes.

Upper School Student Profile Grade 9: 78 students (44 boys, 34 girls); Grade 10: 88 students (50 boys, 38 girls); Grade 11: 68 students (38 boys, 30 girls); Grade 12: 88 students (52 boys, 36 girls). 15% of students are boarding students. 85% are state residents. 2 states are represented in upper school student body. 15% are international students. International students from China, Republic of Korea, and Thailand; 5 other countries represented in student body. 35% of students are Roman Catholic.

Faculty School total: 48. In upper school: 22 men, 26 women; 21 have advanced degrees; 2 reside on campus.

Subjects Offered Advanced Placement courses, advanced TOEFL/grammar, algebra, American history, American history-AP, American literature, ancient history, art, art history-AP, biology, biology-AP, calculus-AP, chamber groups, chemistry, chemistry-AP, chorus, community service, computer programming-AP, computer science, creative writing, drama, earth science, economics-AP, English, English-AP, environmental science-AP, ESL, ethics, European history, European history-AP, expository writing, fine arts, general science, geometry, German, government/civics, government/civics-AP, grammar, health, history, human geography - AP, instrumental music, jazz band, Latin, Latin-AP, mathematics, music theory-AP, physical education, physics, physics-AP, playwriting and directing, religion, science, social sciences, social studies, Spanish, Spanish-AP, speech, studio art-AP, trigonometry, world history, world literature, writing.

Graduation Requirements Arts and fine arts (art, music, dance, drama), electives, English, foreign language, mathematics, physical education (includes health), religion (includes Bible studies and theology), science, social sciences, social studies (includes history), 28 credits required for graduation, 100 hours of community service (25 each year in Upper School).

Special Academic Programs 24 Advanced Placement exams for which test preparation is offered; independent study; study at local college for college credit; academic accommodation for the gifted, the musically talented, and the artistically talented; ESL (60 students enrolled).

College Admission Counseling 76 students graduated in 2015; all went to college, including Oregon State University; Portland State University; Santa Clara University; University of Oregon; University of Portland; University of San Diego. Mean SAT critical reading: 603, mean SAT math: 565, mean SAT writing: 601, mean combined SAT: 1769, mean composite ACT: 25.

Student Life Upper grades have specified standards of dress, student council, honor system. Discipline rests equally with students and faculty. Attendance at religious services is required.

Tuition and Aid Tuition installment plan (monthly payment plans, annual payment plan). Need-based scholarship grants available. In 2015–16, 47% of upper-school students received aid. Total amount of financial aid awarded in 2015–16: $1,000,000.

Admissions Traditional secondary-level entrance grade is 9. PSAT required. Deadline for receipt of application materials: February 15. Application fee required: $50. Interview required.

Athletics Interscholastic: baseball (boys), basketball (b,g), combined training (b,g), cross-country running (b,g), football (b), golf (b,g), independent competitive sports (b,g), soccer (b,g), softball (g), swimming and diving (b,g), tennis (b,g), track and field (b,g), volleyball (g); intramural: alpine skiing (b,g), canoeing/kayaking (b,g), equestrian sports (b,g), flag football (g), hiking/backpacking (b,g); coed interscholastic: martial arts; coed intramural: backpacking, bicycling, fencing, fitness, floor hockey, kayaking,

outdoor activities, outdoor adventure, rafting, skiing (downhill), strength & conditioning, tennis, weight lifting. 2 PE instructors.

Computers Computers are regularly used in English, history, mathematics, science, speech classes. Computer network features include on-campus library services, online commercial services, Internet access, wireless campus network, Internet filtering or blocking technology, access to homework, daily bulletins, and teachers via email, WiFi. Campus intranet and computer access in designated common areas are available to students. Students grades are available online. The school has a published electronic and media policy.

Contact Ms. Rebecca Naumes Vega, Director of Admissions. 541-773-7877. Fax: 541-772-8973. E-mail: admissions@smschool.us. Website: www.smschool.us

SAINT MAUR INTERNATIONAL SCHOOL

83 Yamate-cho, Naka-ku
Yokohama 231-8654, Japan

Head of School: Mrs. Catherine Oslas Endo

General Information Coeducational day college-preparatory, general academic, arts, religious studies, and technology school, affiliated with Roman Catholic Church. Grades PK–12. Founded: 1872. Setting: urban. 1.1-hectare campus. 7 buildings on campus. Approved or accredited by Council of International Schools, East Asia Regional Council of Schools, International Baccalaureate Organization, Ministry of Education, Japan, and New England Association of Schools and Colleges. Language of instruction: English. Total enrollment: 446. Upper school average class size: 36. Upper school faculty-student ratio: 1:4. There are 175 required school days per year for Upper School students. Upper School students typically attend 5 days per week. The average school day consists of 5 hours and 30 minutes.

Upper School Student Profile Grade 9: 40 students (18 boys, 22 girls); Grade 10: 38 students (15 boys, 23 girls); Grade 11: 31 students (18 boys, 13 girls); Grade 12: 36 students (15 boys, 21 girls). 30% of students are Roman Catholic.

Faculty School total: 64. In upper school: 18 men, 15 women; 22 have advanced degrees.

Subjects Offered Algebra, art, biology, calculus, calculus-AP, chemistry, computer science, drama, drama performance, economics, English, fine arts, French, geography, geometry, Japanese, Japanese history, mathematics, modern Chinese history, modern European history, music, music performance, physical education, physics, psychology, religious studies, science, social studies, Spanish, theory of knowledge, TOEFL preparation, trigonometry, visual arts, world history.

Graduation Requirements Arts and fine arts (art, music, dance, drama), English, foreign language, mathematics, physical education (includes health), religion (includes Bible studies and theology), science, social studies (includes history).

Special Academic Programs International Baccalaureate program; 10 Advanced Placement exams for which test preparation is offered; independent study; academic accommodation for the gifted; remedial reading and/or remedial writing; ESL (16 students enrolled).

College Admission Counseling 36 students graduated in 2016; 35 went to college, including Imperial College London, McGill University, Northeastern University, University of Melbourne, University of Toronto, Yamanashi Gakuin University. Other: 1 had other specific plans. Mean SAT critical reading: 554, mean SAT math: 662, mean SAT writing: 554, mean combined SAT: 1790, mean composite ACT: 28. 33% scored over 600 on SAT critical reading, 82% scored over 600 on SAT math, 42% scored over 600 on SAT writing, 49% scored over 1800 on combined SAT.

Student Life Upper grades have uniform requirement, student council. Discipline rests primarily with faculty. Attendance at religious services is required.

Summer Programs Enrichment, advancement, ESL, sports, art/fine arts, computer instruction programs offered; session focuses on TOEFL and SAT preparation, pre-IB, math, technology; held both on and off campus; accepts boys and girls; open to students from other schools. 130 students usually enrolled. 2017 schedule: June 12 to July 7. Application deadline: May 15.

Tuition and Aid Day student tuition: ¥2,356,000. Tuition installment plan (tuition installment upon request).

Admissions For fall 2016, 37 students applied for upper-level admission, 28 were accepted, 18 enrolled. School's own test required. Deadline for receipt of application materials: none. Application fee required: ¥20,000. On-campus interview required.

Athletics Interscholastic: baseball (boys), basketball (b,g), cross-country running (b,g), soccer (b,g), volleyball (g); intramural: soccer (b); coed interscholastic: cross-country running, table tennis. 2 PE instructors.

Computers Computers are regularly used in art, computer applications, economics, English, foreign language, French, geography, independent study, mathematics, music, psychology, SAT preparation, science, social studies, Spanish, technology classes. Computer resources include on-campus library services, Internet access, wireless campus network, Internet filtering or blocking technology, checking out laptops. Campus intranet, student e-mail accounts, and computer access in designated common areas are available to students. Students grades are available online. The school has a published electronic and media policy.

Contact Mr. Richard B. Rucci, Director of Admissions. 81-(0) 45-641-5751. Fax: 81-(0) 45-641-6688. E-mail: rrucci@stmaur.ac.jp. Website: www.stmaur.ac.jp

ST. MICHAEL'S COLLEGE SCHOOL

1515 Bathurst Street
Toronto, Ontario M5P 3H4, Canada

Head of School: Fr. Jefferson Thomson, CSB

General Information Boys' day college-preparatory and religious studies school, affiliated with Roman Catholic Church. Grades 7–12. Founded: 1852. Setting: urban. 10-acre campus. 2 buildings on campus. Approved or accredited by Ontario Ministry of Education and Ontario Department of Education. Member of Secondary School Admission Test Board. Language of instruction: English. Total enrollment: 1,029. Upper school average class size: 24. Upper school faculty-student ratio: 1:16. There are 184 required school days per year for Upper School students. Upper School students typically attend 5 days per week. The average school day consists of 6 hours and 19 minutes.

Upper School Student Profile Grade 9: 212 students (212 boys); Grade 10: 193 students (193 boys); Grade 11: 208 students (208 boys); Grade 12: 211 students (211 boys). 90% of students are Roman Catholic.

Faculty School total: 70. In upper school: 62 men, 8 women; 20 have advanced degrees.

Subjects Offered Advanced Placement courses, all academic, American history, anatomy and physiology, ancient history, art, biology, calculus, calculus-AP, Canadian geography, Canadian history, Canadian law, Canadian literature, career and personal planning, career education, chemistry, civics, computer multimedia, economics, English, English composition, English literature, finite math, French, functions, geography, history, history-AP, Italian, Latin, leadership, mathematics, media arts, modern Western civilization, outdoor education, physical education, religion, robotics, science, Spanish, theology, world religions.

Graduation Requirements English, religion (includes Bible studies and theology), 20 hours of community service, 20 hours of Christian service must be completed over the 4 years of high school.

Special Academic Programs 3 Advanced Placement exams for which test preparation is offered.

College Admission Counseling 205 students graduated in 2015; 200 went to college, including Queen's University at Kingston; Ryerson University; The University of Western Ontario; University of Guelph; University of Toronto; York University. Other: 5 entered a postgraduate year.

Student Life Upper grades have uniform requirement, student council, honor system. Discipline rests primarily with faculty. Attendance at religious services is required.

Tuition and Aid Day student tuition: CAN$18,100. Tuition installment plan (monthly payment plans, individually arranged payment plans). Bursaries, merit scholarship grants, need-based scholarship grants available. In 2015–16, 15% of upper-school students received aid; total upper-school merit-scholarship money awarded: CAN$105,000. Total amount of financial aid awarded in 2015–16: CAN$1,800,000.

Admissions Traditional secondary-level entrance grade is 9. For fall 2015, 268 students applied for upper-level admission, 244 were accepted, 122 enrolled. SSAT required. Deadline for receipt of application materials: none. Application fee required: CAN$125.

Athletics Interscholastic: alpine skiing, aquatics, archery, badminton, baseball, basketball, cross-country running, football, golf, ice hockey, indoor track & field, lacrosse, mountain biking, nordic skiing, rugby, skiing (cross-country), skiing (downhill), snowboarding, soccer, softball, swimming and diving, tennis, track and field, volleyball; intramural: archery, badminton, ball hockey, basketball, fishing, fitness, flag football, ice hockey, indoor soccer, outdoor education, soccer, tennis, touch football. 2 athletic trainers.

Computers Computers are regularly used in all academic, media arts classes. Computer network features include on-campus library services, Internet access, wireless campus network, Internet filtering or blocking technology. Student e-mail accounts and computer access in designated common areas are available to students. The school has a published electronic and media policy.

Contact Ms. Marilyn Furgiuele, Admissions Assistant. 416-653-3180 Ext. 438. Fax: 416-653-7704. E-mail: furgiuele@smcsmail.com.
Website: www.stmichaelscollegeschool.com

ST. MICHAEL'S PREPARATORY SCHOOL OF THE NORBERTINE FATHERS

19292 El Toro Road
Silverado, California 92676-9710

Head of School: Rev. Victor J. Szczurek, OPRAEM

General Information Boys' boarding college-preparatory and religious studies school, affiliated with Roman Catholic Church. Grades 9–12. Distance learning grade 0. Founded: 1961. Setting: suburban. Nearest major city is Foothill Ranch. Students are housed in single-sex dormitories and Boys in 9th to 12 grade only. 35-acre campus. 4 buildings on campus. Approved or accredited by National Catholic Education Association, Western Association of Schools and Colleges, and California Department of Education. Total enrollment: 64. Upper school average class size: 12. Upper school faculty-student ratio: 1:3. There are 180 required school days per year for Upper School students. Upper School students typically attend 5 days per week. The average school day consists of 7 hours.

Upper School Student Profile Grade 9: 16 students (16 boys); Grade 10: 16 students (16 boys); Grade 11: 16 students (16 boys); Grade 12: 16 students (16 boys). 100% of students are boarding students. 95% are state residents. 50 states are represented in upper school student body. 5% are international students. International students from French Guiana, Mexico, Micronesia, Republic of Korea, Viet Nam, and Wallis and Futuna Islands. 98% of students are Roman Catholic.

Faculty School total: 24. In upper school: 24 men; 12 have advanced degrees; 12 reside on campus.

Subjects Offered ACT preparation, advanced biology, advanced chemistry, advanced math, Advanced Placement courses, algebra, American government, American history, American history-AP, American literature, American literature-AP, analysis and differential calculus, analytic geometry, anatomy, anatomy and physiology, ancient history, ancient world history, ancient/medieval philosophy, biology, biology-AP, British literature, British literature (honors), British literature-AP, calculus-AP, Catholic belief and practice, chemistry, chemistry-AP, chorus, college admission preparation, college counseling, conceptual physics, drawing, economics, economics and history, economics-AP, English, English composition, English literature, English literature-AP, ethics, ethics and responsibility, general science, geography, geometry, government-AP, government/civics, government/civics-AP, health, history, history-AP, honors algebra, honors English, honors geometry, honors U.S. history, honors world history, Latin, Latin-AP, marine biology, marine science, mathematics, medieval history, microeconomics-AP, modern European history, modern European history-AP, participation in sports, philosophy, physical education, physical fitness, physical science, physics, physics-AP, pre-calculus, religion, SAT/ACT preparation, science, social studies, theology, track and field, trigonometry, Western civilization, world history, world history-AP, world literature.

Graduation Requirements Arts and fine arts (art, music, dance, drama), English, foreign language, mathematics, physical education (includes health), religion (includes Bible studies and theology), science, social studies (includes history), Senior Matura.

Special Academic Programs Advanced Placement exam preparation; honors section; independent study; academic accommodation for the gifted; ESL (2 students enrolled).

College Admission Counseling 17 students graduated in 2016; all went to college, including California State University, Fullerton; California State University, Long Beach; Thomas Aquinas College; University of California, Davis; University of Dallas; University of Notre Dame. Median combined SAT: 1844, median composite ACT: 27. 100% scored over 26 on composite ACT.

Student Life Upper grades have uniform requirement, student council, honor system. Discipline rests primarily with faculty. Attendance at religious services is required.

Tuition and Aid 5-day tuition and room/board: $22,785. Tuition installment plan (FACTS Tuition Payment Plan, monthly payment plans, individually arranged payment plans). Need-based scholarship grants available. In 2016–17, 80% of upper-school students received aid. Total amount of financial aid awarded in 2016–17: $500,000.

Admissions Traditional secondary-level entrance grade is 9. High School Placement Test required. Deadline for receipt of application materials: none. Application fee required: $120. Interview recommended.

Athletics Interscholastic: baseball (boys), basketball (b), cross-country running (b), football (b), running (b), soccer (b), track and field (b); intramural: archery (b), bowling (b), outdoor activities (b), outdoor recreation (b), physical fitness (b), physical training (b), skateboarding (b), strength & conditioning (b), surfing (b), swimming and diving (b), table tennis (b), volleyball (b), weight lifting (b), weight training (b). 2 PE instructors, 7 coaches, 5 athletic trainers.

Computers Computers are regularly used in creative writing, English, history, Latin, religion, science, senior seminar, writing classes. Computer network features include on-campus library services, Internet access, Internet filtering or blocking technology. Campus intranet, student e-mail accounts, and computer access in designated common areas are available to students. Students grades are available online. The school has a published electronic and media policy.

Contact Mrs. Pamela M. Christian, School Secretary. 949-858-0222 Ext. 237. Fax: 949-858-7365. E-mail: admissions@stmichaelsprep.org.
Website: www.stmichaelsprep.org

ST. PATRICK CATHOLIC HIGH SCHOOL

18300 St. Patrick Road
Biloxi, Mississippi 39532

Head of School: Mrs. J. Renee McDaniel

General Information Coeducational day college-preparatory and religious studies school, affiliated with Roman Catholic Church; primarily serves dyslexic students. Grades 7–12. Founded: 2007. Setting: rural. 32-acre campus. 7 buildings on campus. Approved or accredited by Southern Association of Colleges and Schools and Mississippi Department of Education. Endowment: $400,000. Total enrollment: 441. Upper school average class size: 20. Upper school faculty-student ratio: 1:13. There are 180 required school days per year for Upper School students. Upper School students typically attend 5 days per week. The average school day consists of 6 hours and 45 minutes.

Upper School Student Profile Grade 7: 87 students (39 boys, 48 girls); Grade 8: 53 students (29 boys, 24 girls); Grade 9: 60 students (25 boys, 35 girls); Grade 10: 86 students (42 boys, 44 girls); Grade 11: 61 students (22 boys, 39 girls); Grade 12: 90

students (47 boys, 43 girls); Postgraduate: 440 students (204 boys, 236 girls). 80% of students are Roman Catholic.

Faculty School total: 37. In upper school: 14 men, 20 women; 16 have advanced degrees.

Subjects Offered Accounting, advanced chemistry, advanced computer applications, advanced math, Advanced Placement courses, algebra, American government, American history, American literature, analytic geometry, anatomy and physiology, art, athletics, band, baseball, Basic programming, basketball, biology, British literature, business applications, business law, calculus, calculus-AP, campus ministry, Catholic belief and practice, cheerleading, chemistry, chemistry-AP, choral music, Christian and Hebrew scripture, church history, civics, college counseling, college placement, college planning, composition-AP, computer applications, creative writing, desktop publishing, drama, driver education, earth science, economics, English, English literature and composition-AP, environmental science, French, geometry, global studies, health, humanities, introduction to theater, journalism, keyboarding, law, Life of Christ, marching band, marine biology, marine science, oral communications, physical education, physical science, pre-algebra, pre-calculus, probability and statistics, psychology, softball, Spanish, track and field, trigonometry, U.S. government, U.S. history, U.S. history-AP, volleyball, Web site design, weight fitness, weight training, weightlifting, wood processing, world geography, world history, yearbook.

Graduation Requirements Algebra, American history, American literature, art, biology, British literature, cell biology, chemistry, computer applications, English literature, foreign language, physical education (includes health), state history, U.S. government, U.S. history, world geography, world history, world literature, religion.

Special Academic Programs International Baccalaureate program; Advanced Placement exam preparation; independent study; study at local college for college credit; programs in general development for dyslexic students.

College Admission Counseling 70 students graduated in 2015; all went to college, including Louisiana State University and Agricultural & Mechanical College; Millsaps College; Mississippi State University; University of Mississippi; University of South Alabama; University of Southern Mississippi. Mean SAT critical reading: 647, mean SAT math: 623, mean SAT writing: 617, mean composite ACT: 24. 67% scored over 600 on SAT critical reading, 83% scored over 600 on SAT math, 67% scored over 600 on SAT writing, 37% scored over 26 on composite ACT.

Student Life Upper grades have uniform requirement, student council, honor system. Discipline rests primarily with faculty. Attendance at religious services is required.

Tuition and Aid Day student tuition: $7150. Tuition installment plan (monthly payments through local bank). Tuition reduction for siblings, need-based scholarship grants available. In 2015–16, 25% of upper-school students received aid. Total amount of financial aid awarded in 2015–16: $168,524.

Admissions Traditional secondary-level entrance grade is 7. For fall 2015, 443 students applied for upper-level admission, 443 were accepted, 441 enrolled. PSAT required. Deadline for receipt of application materials: none. No application fee required. Interview required.

Athletics Interscholastic: baseball (boys), basketball (b,g), cheering (g), cross-country running (b,g), dance team (g), football (b), golf (b,g), power lifting (b,g), soccer (b,g), softball (g), strength & conditioning (b), swimming and diving (b,g), tennis (b,g), track and field (b,g), volleyball (g), weight lifting (b,g), weight training (b,g); coed interscholastic: sailing; coed intramural: sailing. 2 PE instructors, 26 coaches, 1 athletic trainer.

Computers Computers are regularly used in accounting, business applications, business education, computer applications, desktop publishing, journalism, mathematics, newspaper, Web site design, word processing, yearbook classes. Computer network features include on-campus library services, Internet access, Internet filtering or blocking technology. Campus intranet and computer access in designated common areas are available to students. Students grades are available online. The school has a published electronic and media policy.

Contact Mrs. Theresa Whiteside, Records Clerk. 228-702-0500. Fax: 228-702-0511. E-mail: twhiteside@stpatrickhighschool.net. Website: www.stpatrickhighschool.net

SAINT PATRICK HIGH SCHOOL

5900 West Belmont Avenue
Chicago, Illinois 60634

Head of School: Dr. Joseph G. Schmidt

General Information Boys' day college-preparatory, arts, religious studies, entrepreneurship, and STEM (STEAM) school, affiliated with Roman Catholic Church. Grades 9–12. Founded: 1861. Setting: urban. 1 building on campus. Approved or accredited by Christian Brothers Association, National Catholic Education Association, North Central Association of Colleges and Schools, and Illinois Department of Education. Endowment: $5.5 million. Total enrollment: 648. Upper school average class size: 21. Upper school faculty-student ratio: 1:15. There are 180 required school days per year for Upper School students. Upper School students typically attend 5 days per week. The average school day consists of 7 hours.

Upper School Student Profile Grade 9: 175 students (175 boys); Grade 10: 145 students (145 boys); Grade 11: 185 students (185 boys); Grade 12: 150 students (150 boys). 75% of students are Roman Catholic.

Faculty School total: 52. In upper school: 39 men, 18 women; 38 have advanced degrees.

Subjects Offered 20th century history, accounting, ACT preparation, advanced biology, Advanced Placement courses, algebra, American democracy, American government, American history, American history-AP, American literature, anatomy, ancient history, art, art history, biology, business, business skills, calculus, chemistry, Chinese, chorus, computer graphics, computer science, creative writing, drama, driver education, ecology, economics, English, English as a foreign language, English literature, ethics, European history, fine arts, French, geography, geometry, government/civics, grammar, health, history, journalism, keyboarding, mathematics, music, physical education, physics, psychology, religion, science, social sciences, social studies, sociology, Spanish, speech, theater, trigonometry, word processing, world history, writing.

Graduation Requirements Arts and fine arts (art, music, dance, drama), business skills (includes word processing), computer science, English, foreign language, mathematics, physical education (includes health), religion (includes Bible studies and theology), science, service learning/internship, social sciences, social studies (includes history), participation in a retreat program. Community service is required.

Special Academic Programs Advanced Placement exam preparation; honors section; study at local college for college credit; remedial reading and/or remedial writing; remedial math.

College Admission Counseling 132 students graduated in 2016; 125 went to college, including Illinois State University; Lewis University; Loyola University Chicago; Marquette University; University of Illinois at Chicago; University of Illinois at Urbana–Champaign. Other: 6 went to work, 1 entered military service. Mean composite ACT: 21. 28% scored over 26 on composite ACT.

Student Life Upper grades have specified standards of dress, student council, honor system. Discipline rests primarily with faculty. Attendance at religious services is required.

Summer Programs Remediation, enrichment, advancement, sports, art/fine arts, computer instruction programs offered; session focuses on remediation and enrichment; held both on and off campus; accepts boys and girls; open to students from other schools. 160 students usually enrolled. 2017 schedule: June 19 to August 4. Application deadline: June 12.

Tuition and Aid Day student tuition: $11,250. Guaranteed tuition plan. Tuition installment plan (monthly payment plans, quarterly payment plan). Tuition reduction for siblings, merit scholarship grants, need-based scholarship grants, legacy (sons and grandsons of alumni), Archdiocese employee reduction, First Responder reduction available. In 2016–17, 53% of upper-school students received aid; total upper-school merit-scholarship money awarded: $240,000. Total amount of financial aid awarded in 2016–17: $1,600,000.

Admissions Traditional secondary-level entrance grade is 9. For fall 2016, 263 students applied for upper-level admission, 263 were accepted, 175 enrolled. ACT-Explore or any standardized test required. Deadline for receipt of application materials: none. No application fee required. On-campus interview required.

Athletics Interscholastic: baseball, basketball, bowling, cross-country running, diving, fishing, football, golf, ice hockey, indoor track & field, soccer, swimming and diving, tennis, track and field, volleyball, water polo, wrestling. 1 PE instructor, 2 coaches, 1 athletic trainer.

Computers Computers are regularly used in business, English, foreign language, geography, graphic arts, graphic design, graphics, history, information technology, introduction to technology, library skills, mathematics, media arts, media production, media services, newspaper, photojournalism, religion, remedial study skills, research skills, science, typing, word processing, yearbook classes. Computer network features include on-campus library services, online commercial services, Internet access, wireless campus network, Internet filtering or blocking technology, 1:1 iPad school. Student e-mail accounts and computer access in designated common areas are available to students. Students grades are available online. The school has a published electronic and media policy.

Contact Mike Fabrizio, Assistant Director of Admissions. 773-282-8844 Ext. 230. Fax: 773-282-2361. E-mail: mfabrizio@stpatrick.org. Website: www.stpatrick.org

ST. PATRICK'S REGIONAL SECONDARY

115 East 11th Avenue
Vancouver, British Columbia V5T 2C1, Canada

Head of School: Mr. Ralph J. Gabriele

General Information Coeducational day college-preparatory and general academic school, affiliated with Roman Catholic Church. Grades 8–12. Founded: 1923. Setting: urban. 2 buildings on campus. Approved or accredited by British Columbia Department of Education. Language of instruction: English. Total enrollment: 500. Upper school average class size: 25. There are 180 required school days per year for Upper School students. Upper School students typically attend 5 days per week. The average school day consists of 6 hours.

Upper School Student Profile Grade 8: 100 students (50 boys, 50 girls); Grade 9: 87 students (37 boys, 50 girls); Grade 10: 99 students (41 boys, 58 girls); Grade 11: 104 students (35 boys, 69 girls); Grade 12: 100 students (34 boys, 66 girls). 97% of students are Roman Catholic.

Faculty School total: 40. In upper school: 20 men, 20 women; 8 have advanced degrees.

Special Academic Programs Advanced Placement exam preparation; ESL (16 students enrolled).

College Admission Counseling 100 students graduated in 2016; all went to college.

Student Life Upper grades have uniform requirement. Discipline rests primarily with faculty. Attendance at religious services is required.

Tuition and Aid Guaranteed tuition plan. Tuition installment plan (monthly payment plans). Total amount of financial aid awarded in 2016–17: CAN$4000.

Admissions Application fee required: CAN$100. Interview required.

Athletics Interscholastic: basketball (boys, girls), dance squad (b,g), soccer (b,g), track and field (b,g), volleyball (g), wrestling (b,g); intramural: dance squad (b,g); coed interscholastic: dance squad; coed intramural: badminton, ball hockey, dance squad. 5 PE instructors, 5 coaches.

Computers The school has a published electronic and media policy.

Contact Mr. Ralph J. Gabriele, Principal. 604-874-6422. Fax: 604-874-5176. E-mail: administration@stpats.bc.ca. Website: www.stpats.bc.ca

ST. PAUL ACADEMY AND SUMMIT SCHOOL

1712 Randolph Avenue
St. Paul, Minnesota 55105

Head of School: Bryn S. Roberts

General Information Coeducational day college-preparatory school. Grades K–12. Founded: 1900. Setting: urban. 32-acre campus. 4 buildings on campus. Approved or accredited by Independent Schools Association of the Central States, National Independent Private Schools Association, and Minnesota Department of Education. Member of National Association of Independent Schools. Endowment: $42.3 million. Total enrollment: 918. Upper school average class size: 15. Upper school faculty-student ratio: 1:8. Upper School students typically attend 5 days per week.

Upper School Student Profile Grade 9: 109 students (55 boys, 54 girls); Grade 10: 101 students (52 boys, 49 girls); Grade 11: 113 students (59 boys, 54 girls); Grade 12: 96 students (42 boys, 54 girls).

Faculty School total: 109. In upper school: 19 men, 25 women; 36 have advanced degrees.

Subjects Offered Algebra, American literature, art, biology, calculus, ceramics, chemistry, Chinese, creative writing, current events, debate, drama, earth science, economics, English, English literature, European history, expository writing, fine arts, French, geometry, German, journalism, law and the legal system, marine biology, mathematics, multicultural studies, music, music theory, newspaper, photography, physical education, physics, psychology, science, senior project, Shakespeare, social psychology, social studies, sociology, space and physical sciences, Spanish, trigonometry, world history, world literature, world religions, yearbook.

Graduation Requirements Arts and fine arts (art, music, dance, drama), English, foreign language, mathematics, physical education (includes health), science, social studies (includes history), month-long senior project, senior speech.

Special Academic Programs Honors section; independent study; term-away projects; study abroad.

College Admission Counseling 89 students graduated in 2015; all went to college, including Carleton College; Northeastern University; St. Olaf College; University of Minnesota, Twin Cities Campus; University of Wisconsin–Madison. Median SAT critical reading: 640, median SAT math: 650, median SAT writing: 620, median combined SAT: 1870, median composite ACT: 30. 62% scored over 600 on SAT critical reading, 68% scored over 600 on SAT math, 57% scored over 600 on SAT writing, 64% scored over 1800 on combined SAT, 78% scored over 26 on composite ACT.

Student Life Upper grades have specified standards of dress, student council. Discipline rests equally with students and faculty.

Tuition and Aid Day student tuition: $27,500. Tuition installment plan (Insured Tuition Payment Plan, monthly payment plans). Need-based scholarship grants available. In 2015–16, 23% of upper-school students received aid. Total amount of financial aid awarded in 2015–16: $3,200,000.

Admissions Traditional secondary-level entrance grade is 9. For fall 2015, 82 students applied for upper-level admission, 46 were accepted, 32 enrolled. SSAT, ERB, PSAT, SAT, PLAN or ACT or writing sample required. Deadline for receipt of application materials: February 1. Application fee required: $75. Interview required.

Athletics Interscholastic: alpine skiing (boys, girls), baseball (b), basketball (b,g), cross-country running (b,g), dance team (g), diving (b,g), fencing (b,g), football (b), golf (b,g), ice hockey (b,g), lacrosse (g), skiing (cross-country) (b,g), skiing (downhill) (b,g), soccer (b,g), softball (g), swimming and diving (b,g), tennis (b,g), volleyball (g); intramural: outdoor adventure (b,g); coed interscholastic: strength & conditioning, track and field; coed intramural: hiking/backpacking, physical fitness, snowboarding, table tennis. 3 PE instructors, 90 coaches, 1 athletic trainer.

Computers Computers are regularly used in all academic classes. Computer network features include on-campus library services, online commercial services, Internet access, wireless campus network, Internet filtering or blocking technology, laptop program (beginning in grade 6). Student e-mail accounts and computer access in designated common areas are available to students. The school has a published electronic and media policy.

Contact Mrs. Heather Cameron Ploen, Director of Admission and Financial Aid. 651-698-2451. Fax: 651-698-6787. E-mail: hploen@spa.edu. Website: www.spa.edu

SAINT PAUL LUTHERAN HIGH SCHOOL

205 South Main Street
PO Box 719
Concordia, Missouri 64020

Head of School: Rev. Paul M. Mehl

General Information Coeducational boarding and day college-preparatory, general academic, and religious studies school, affiliated with Lutheran Church–Missouri Synod. Grades 9–12. Founded: 1883. Setting: small town. Nearest major city is Kansas City. Students are housed in single-sex dormitories. 50-acre campus. 9 buildings on campus. Approved or accredited by Lutheran School Accreditation Commission, Midwest Association of Boarding Schools, North Central Association of Colleges and Schools, and Missouri Department of Education. Endowment: $2.5 million. Total enrollment: 189. Upper school average class size: 25. Upper school faculty-student ratio: 1:9. There are 173 required school days per year for Upper School students. Upper School students typically attend 5 days per week. The average school day consists of 6 hours.

Upper School Student Profile Grade 9: 45 students (25 boys, 20 girls); Grade 10: 60 students (26 boys, 34 girls); Grade 11: 72 students (40 boys, 32 girls); Grade 12: 38 students (19 boys, 19 girls). 61% of students are boarding students. 43% are state residents. 15 states are represented in upper school student body. 33% are international students. International students from China, Hong Kong, Norway, Taiwan, United States, and Viet Nam; 11 other countries represented in student body. 60% of students are Lutheran Church–Missouri Synod.

Faculty School total: 21. In upper school: 12 men, 9 women; 10 have advanced degrees; 3 reside on campus.

Subjects Offered Accounting, ADL skills, advanced biology, algebra, American history, American literature, analytic geometry, art, athletic training, band, Bible studies, biology, business law, calculus, ceramics, chemistry, child development, chorus, Christian doctrine, church history, community service, comparative religion, composition, computer science, concert choir, creative writing, current events, drama, drawing, economics, English, English literature, ESL, family studies, freshman seminar, general science, geography, geometry, German, government/civics, health, human anatomy, music appreciation, music theory, novels, painting, physical education, physical science, physics, poetry, pre-algebra, psychology, religion, Shakespeare, sociology, Spanish, speech, statistics, theology, trigonometry, world history, world literature, writing.

Graduation Requirements Arts and fine arts (art, music, dance, drama), computer science, English, foreign language, mathematics, physical education (includes health), practical arts, religion (includes Bible studies and theology), science, social studies (includes history), 3.0 grade point average on a 4.0 scale for college preparatory students, above (national) average score on ACT or SAT. Community service is required.

Special Academic Programs International Baccalaureate program; independent study; study at local college for college credit.

College Admission Counseling 41 students graduated in 2016; 36 went to college, including Concordia University, Nebraska; Concordia University Irvine; University of Central Missouri; University of Missouri. Other: 2 went to work, 3 had other specific plans. Median SAT critical reading: 450, median SAT math: 650, median SAT writing: 490, median combined SAT: 1590, median composite ACT: 24. 15% scored over 600 on SAT critical reading, 66% scored over 600 on SAT math, 14% scored over 600 on SAT writing.

Student Life Upper grades have specified standards of dress, student council, honor system. Discipline rests primarily with faculty. Attendance at religious services is required.

Tuition and Aid Guaranteed tuition plan. Tuition installment plan (FACTS Tuition Payment Plan, monthly payment plans, individually arranged payment plans, lump sum payment discount plan). Tuition reduction for siblings, need-based scholarship grants, paying campus jobs, LCMS Grants for church vocation students, early bird tuition grants available. In 2016–17, 54% of upper-school students received aid. Total amount of financial aid awarded in 2016–17: $273,555.

Admissions Traditional secondary-level entrance grade is 9. For fall 2016, 108 students applied for upper-level admission, 108 were accepted, 101 enrolled. School placement exam or SLEP for foreign students required. Deadline for receipt of application materials: none. Application fee required. On-campus interview required.

Athletics Interscholastic: baseball (boys), basketball (b,g), cheering (g), cross-country running (b,g), football (b), golf (b,g), soccer (b,g), softball (g), track and field (b,g), volleyball (g); intramural: baseball (b), basketball (b,g), dance team (g), football (b), golf (b,g), jogging (b,g), physical training (b,g), roller blading (b,g), running (b,g), soccer (b,g), softball (g), strength & conditioning (b,g), tennis (b,g), volleyball (b,g), weight lifting (b,g); coed interscholastic: cross-country running, track and field; coed intramural: jogging, roller blading, running, soccer, table tennis, ultimate Frisbee. 2 PE instructors, 1 coach.

Computers Computers are regularly used in Christian doctrine, creative writing, data processing, English, freshman foundations, history, keyboarding, lab/keyboard, library skills, religious studies, speech, study skills, word processing, writing, writing classes. Computer resources include Internet access, wireless campus network. Students grades are available online. The school has a published electronic and media policy.

Contact Mr. Clint Colwell, Director of Recruitment. 660-463-2238 Ext. 245. Fax: 660-463-7621. E-mail: admissions@splhs.org. Website: www.splhs.org

ST. PAUL PREPARATORY SCHOOL

380 Jackson Street
Suite 100
Saint Paul, Minnesota 55101

Head of School: Mr. John Belpedio

General Information Coeducational day college-preparatory, general academic, arts, business, bilingual studies, technology, and Liberal Arts school. Grades 9–12. Founded: 2003. Setting: urban. Nearest major city is St. Paul. 2-acre campus. 1 building on campus. Approved or accredited by North Central Association of Colleges and Schools and Minnesota Department of Education. Total enrollment: 166. Upper school average class size: 13. Upper school faculty-student ratio: 1:12. There are 175 required school days per year for Upper School students. Upper School students typically attend 5 days per week. The average school day consists of 6 hours and 44 minutes.

Upper School Student Profile Grade 9: 1 student (1 girl); Grade 10: 27 students (16 boys, 11 girls); Grade 11: 40 students (21 boys, 19 girls); Grade 12: 98 students (53 boys, 45 girls).

Faculty School total: 19. In upper school: 9 men, 9 women; 9 have advanced degrees.

Subjects Offered Advanced Placement courses, algebra, American history, American literature, art, art history, aviation, biology, calculus, chemistry, chemistry-AP, Chinese, college admission preparation, composition, computer science, computer science-AP, creative writing, drama, drawing, economics, English as a foreign language, English composition, English literature and composition-AP, ESL, fitness, French, geography, geometry, guitar, health, internship, intro to computers, introduction to literature, life science, literature, music, music theory-AP, painting, physical education, physical fitness, physical science, physics, pre-calculus, psychology, robotics, SAT preparation, sociology, Spanish, Spanish literature, speech, statistics-AP, theater, U.S. history, U.S. history-AP, world history, world history-AP, world literature, writing, writing, writing workshop, yearbook.

Special Academic Programs International Baccalaureate program; 9 Advanced Placement exams for which test preparation is offered; honors section; accelerated programs; study at local college for college credit; study abroad; academic accommodation for the musically talented and the artistically talented; ESL (100 students enrolled).

College Admission Counseling 78 students graduated in 2015; 70 went to college, including Hamline University; University of Minnesota, Twin Cities Campus; University of St. Thomas. Other: 8 had other specific plans. Mean SAT critical reading: 494, mean SAT math: 476, mean SAT writing: 532, mean combined SAT: 1502, mean composite ACT: 23.

Student Life Upper grades have specified standards of dress, student council, honor system. Discipline rests equally with students and faculty.

Tuition and Aid Day student tuition: $10,500. Tuition installment plan (monthly payment plans, individually arranged payment plans, Admissions & Enrollment Financial Aid Assessment Tuition Management (TADS)). Merit scholarship grants, need-based scholarship grants available. In 2015–16, 60% of upper-school students received aid; total upper-school merit-scholarship money awarded: $4500. Total amount of financial aid awarded in 2015–16: $5500.

Admissions Traditional secondary-level entrance grade is 11. For fall 2015, 2,180 students applied for upper-level admission, 167 were accepted, 166 enrolled. Iowa Tests of Basic Skills, Stanford Achievement Test or TOEFL or SLEP required. Deadline for receipt of application materials: none. No application fee required. Interview required.

Athletics Interscholastic: basketball (boys, girls), soccer (b,g); coed interscholastic: track and field; coed intramural: badminton, Frisbee, table tennis, ultimate Frisbee, volleyball. 1 PE instructor, 4 coaches.

Computers Computers are regularly used in aviation, college planning, creative writing, English, ESL, foreign language, mathematics, SAT preparation, science, social sciences, Web site design, writing, yearbook classes. Computer network features include Internet access, wireless campus network, Internet filtering or blocking technology, PowerSchool Database Host. Computer access in designated common areas is available to students. Students grades are available online. The school has a published electronic and media policy.

Contact Annika Bowers, Admissions Director. 651-288-4610. Fax: 651-288-4616. E-mail: abowers@stpaulprep.org. Website: www.stpaulprep.org

ST. PAUL'S HIGH SCHOOL

2200 Grant Avenue
Winnipeg, Manitoba R3P 0P8, Canada

Head of School: Fr. Len Altilia, SJ

General Information Boys' day college-preparatory school, affiliated with Roman Catholic Church. Grades 9–12. Founded: 1926. Setting: suburban. 18-acre campus. 6 buildings on campus. Approved or accredited by Jesuit Secondary Education Association and Manitoba Department of Education. Language of instruction: English. Endowment: CAN$7.5 million. Total enrollment: 554. Upper school average class size: 25. Upper school faculty-student ratio: 1:14. There are 196 required school days per year for Upper School students. Upper School students typically attend 5 days per week. The average school day consists of 5 hours and 50 minutes.

Upper School Student Profile Grade 9: 148 students (148 boys); Grade 10: 131 students (131 boys); Grade 11: 141 students (141 boys); Grade 12: 140 students (140 boys). 68% of students are Roman Catholic.

Faculty School total: 44. In upper school: 32 men, 10 women; 19 have advanced degrees.

Subjects Offered Algebra, American history, art, biology, calculus, chemistry, classics, computer science, current events, economics, English, ethics, French, geography, geometry, history, law, mathematics, media, multimedia, multimedia design, music, Native American studies, physical education, physics, political science, psychology, religion, science, social studies, speech, theology, world wide web design.

Graduation Requirements English, mathematics, physical education (includes health), religion (includes Bible studies and theology), science, social studies (includes history), completion of Christian service program.

Special Academic Programs Advanced Placement exam preparation; honors section; remedial math.

College Admission Counseling 147 students graduated in 2016; 117 went to college, including McGill University; Queen's University at Kingston; The University of British Columbia; The University of Winnipeg; University of Manitoba; University of Toronto. Other: 30 had other specific plans.

Student Life Upper grades have specified standards of dress, student council, honor system. Discipline rests primarily with faculty. Attendance at religious services is required.

Summer Programs Sports programs offered; session focuses on sport skills and relationship building; held on campus; accepts boys; open to students from other schools. 80 students usually enrolled. 2017 schedule: August 19 to September 1.

Tuition and Aid Day student tuition: CAN$8550. Tuition installment plan (Insured Tuition Payment Plan, monthly payment plans, individually arranged payment plans). Bursaries, need-based loans available. In 2016–17, 14% of upper-school students received aid. Total amount of financial aid awarded in 2016–17: CAN$355,200.

Admissions Traditional secondary-level entrance grade is 9. Achievement tests, STS and STS, Diocese Test required. Deadline for receipt of application materials: February 1. Application fee required: CAN$100. On-campus interview required.

Athletics Interscholastic: badminton, basketball, cross-country running, curling, football, golf, ice hockey, indoor track, indoor track & field, rugby, soccer, track and field, ultimate Frisbee, volleyball, wrestling; intramural: badminton, basketball, curling, fitness, flag football, golf, physical fitness, physical training, skiing (downhill), strength & conditioning, table tennis, volleyball, weight training. 4 PE instructors, 1 athletic trainer.

Computers Computers are regularly used in French, French as a second language, geography, mathematics, multimedia, religious studies, science, Web site design classes. Computer network features include on-campus library services, online commercial services, Internet access, wireless campus network, Internet filtering or blocking technology. Campus intranet, student e-mail accounts, and computer access in designated common areas are available to students. Students grades are available online. The school has a published electronic and media policy.

Contact Mr. Bob Lewin, Principal. 204-831-2300. Fax: 204-831-2340. E-mail: blewin@stpauls.mb.ca. Website: www.stpauls.mb.ca

ST. PAUL'S SCHOOL

325 Pleasant Street
Concord, New Hampshire 03301-2591

Head of School: Mr. Michael G. Hirschfeld

General Information Coeducational boarding college-preparatory school, affiliated with Episcopal Church. Grades 9–12. Founded: 1856. Setting: suburban. Students are housed in single-sex dormitories. 2,000-acre campus. 88 buildings on campus. Approved or accredited by Association of Independent Schools in New England, National Association of Episcopal Schools, New England Association of Schools and Colleges, The Association of Boarding Schools, and New Hampshire Department of Education. Member of National Association of Independent Schools and Secondary School Admission Test Board. Endowment: $573 million. Total enrollment: 541. Upper school average class size: 11. Upper school faculty-student ratio: 1:5. There are 180 required school days per year for Upper School students. Upper School students typically attend 5 days per week. The average school day consists of 6 hours.

Upper School Student Profile Grade 9: 106 students (52 boys, 54 girls); Grade 10: 136 students (68 boys, 68 girls); Grade 11: 141 students (73 boys, 68 girls); Grade 12: 148 students (74 boys, 74 girls). 100% of students are boarding students. 11% are state residents. 38 states are represented in upper school student body. 18% are international students. International students from Canada, China, Democratic People's Republic of Korea, Hong Kong, Nigeria, and United Kingdom; 14 other countries represented in student body. 33% of students are members of Episcopal Church.

Faculty School total: 121. In upper school: 53 men, 44 women; 71 have advanced degrees; 111 reside on campus.

Subjects Offered 3-dimensional design, algebra, American history, American literature, applied arts, applied music, architecture, art, art history, astronomy, ballet, biology, calculus, ceramics, chemistry, Chinese, classical civilization, classical Greek literature, classical language, computer math, computer programming, computer science, creative writing, drama, driver education, ecology, English, English literature, environmental science, ethics, European history, fine arts, French, geometry, German, government/civics, grammar, Greek, health, history, humanities, independent study, instrumental music, Japanese, Latin, mathematics, music, photography, physical education, physics, religion, robotics, science, social studies, Spanish, speech, statistics, theater, trigonometry, writing.

Graduation Requirements Art, athletics, humanities, language, mathematics, music, religion (includes Bible studies and theology), science, residential life. Community service is required.

Special Academic Programs 9 Advanced Placement exams for which test preparation is offered; honors section; accelerated programs; independent study; term-away projects; study abroad; academic accommodation for the gifted, the musically talented, and the artistically talented.

College Admission Counseling 140 students graduated in 2016; 138 went to college, including Bowdoin College; Columbia University; Cornell University; Dartmouth College; Georgetown University; Stanford University. Other: 2 had other specific plans. Median SAT critical reading: 683, median SAT math: 683, median SAT writing: 681.

Student Life Upper grades have specified standards of dress, student council, honor system. Discipline rests primarily with faculty.

Summer Programs Enrichment programs offered; session focuses on enrichment for New Hampshire public high school juniors only; held on campus; accepts boys and girls; open to students from other schools. 245 students usually enrolled. 2017 schedule: June 23 to July 30. Application deadline: December 15.

Tuition and Aid 7-day tuition and room/board: $56,460. Tuition installment plan (Academic Management Services Plan, monthly payment plans). Need-based scholarship grants, tuition remission for children of faculty and staff available. In 2016–17, 40% of upper-school students received aid. Total amount of financial aid awarded in 2016–17: $11,200,000.

Admissions Traditional secondary-level entrance grade is 9. For fall 2016, 1,461 students applied for upper-level admission, 190 were accepted, 151 enrolled. SSAT required. Deadline for receipt of application materials: January 15. Application fee required: $75. Interview required.

Athletics Interscholastic: alpine skiing (boys, girls), baseball (b), basketball (b,g), crew (b,g), cross-country running (b,g), field hockey (g), football (b), ice hockey (b,g), lacrosse (b,g), nordic skiing (b,g), rowing (b,g), skiing (cross-country) (b,g), skiing (downhill) (b,g), soccer (b,g), softball (g), squash (b,g), tennis (b,g), track and field (b,g), volleyball (g), wrestling (b); intramural: crew (b,g), ice hockey (b,g), rowing (b,g), soccer (b,g); coed interscholastic: ballet; coed intramural: aerobics, aerobics/Nautilus, alpine skiing, backpacking, baseball, basketball, crew, equestrian sports, fitness, fly fishing, horseback riding, ice hockey, physical fitness, rowing, skeet shooting, skiing (cross-country), skiing (downhill), snowboarding, soccer, squash, tai chi, tennis, weight training, wrestling. 2 coaches, 2 athletic trainers.

Computers Computers are regularly used in English, foreign language, humanities, mathematics, science classes. Computer network features include on-campus library services, online commercial services, Internet access, wireless campus network, Internet filtering or blocking technology. Campus intranet, student e-mail accounts, and computer access in designated common areas are available to students. Students grades are available online. The school has a published electronic and media policy.

Contact Ms. Holly Foote, Assistant Director of Admission Operations. 603-229-4700. Fax: 603-229-4771. E-mail: admissions@sps.edu. Website: www.sps.edu

ST. PETER'S PREPARATORY SCHOOL

144 Grand Street
Jersey City, New Jersey 07302

Head of School: Rev. Kenneth J. Boller, SJ

General Information Boys' day college-preparatory, arts, technology, and music school, affiliated with Roman Catholic Church. Grades 9–12. Founded: 1872. Setting: urban. Nearest major city is New York, NY. 7-acre campus. 8 buildings on campus. Approved or accredited by Jesuit Secondary Education Association, Middle States Association of Colleges and Schools, New Jersey Association of Independent Schools, and New Jersey Department of Education. Member of National Association of Independent Schools. Endowment: $22.5 million. Total enrollment: 931. Upper school average class size: 22. Upper school faculty-student ratio: 1:12. There are 176 required school days per year for Upper School students. Upper School students typically attend 5 days per week. The average school day consists of 6 hours and 10 minutes.

Upper School Student Profile Grade 9: 260 students (260 boys); Grade 10: 248 students (248 boys); Grade 11: 234 students (234 boys); Grade 12: 189 students (189 boys). 78% of students are Roman Catholic.

Faculty School total: 77. In upper school: 52 men, 23 women; 60 have advanced degrees.

Subjects Offered Advanced Placement courses, algebra, American history, American history-AP, American legal systems, American literature, Ancient Greek, architecture, art, art history, biology, biology-AP, calculus, calculus-AP, ceramics, chemistry, chemistry-AP, choir, Christian ethics, community service, computer programming, computer science, concert band, creative writing, drawing, English, English language-AP, English literature, English literature-AP, European history, forensics, French, French language-AP, geometry, German, German-AP, government and politics-AP, health, history, human anatomy, Italian, jazz band, Latin, Latin-AP, Mandarin, mathematics, music, music theory, physical education, physics, religion, sculpture,

social justice, Spanish, Spanish language-AP, Spanish literature-AP, statistics, statistics-AP, studio art, theology, trigonometry, Web site design, world civilizations, world history, world literature, writing.

Graduation Requirements Algebra, American history, American literature, ancient world history, art, biology, British literature, chemistry, English, geometry, Latin, modern languages, music, physical education (includes health), physics, religion (includes Bible studies and theology), U.S. history, world civilizations, 20 hours of community service in freshman and sophomore years, 60 hours in the third (junior) year.

Special Academic Programs 18 Advanced Placement exams for which test preparation is offered; honors section; study at local college for college credit; study abroad.

College Admission Counseling 248 students graduated in 2015; all went to college, including Fordham University; Loyola University Maryland; New Jersey Institute of Technology; Rutgers, The State University of New Jersey, Rutgers College; Saint Peter's University; Seton Hall University. Median SAT critical reading: 576, median SAT math: 593. Mean SAT writing: 574, mean combined SAT: 1731. 44% scored over 600 on SAT critical reading, 48% scored over 600 on SAT math, 50% scored over 600 on SAT writing, 50% scored over 1800 on combined SAT.

Student Life Upper grades have specified standards of dress, student council. Discipline rests primarily with faculty.

Tuition and Aid Day student tuition: $15,150. Tuition installment plan (FACTS Tuition Payment Plan, monthly payment plans). Merit scholarship grants, need-based scholarship grants, paying campus jobs available. In 2015–16, 51% of upper-school students received aid; total upper-school merit-scholarship money awarded: $721,500. Total amount of financial aid awarded in 2015–16: $1,718,000.

Admissions Traditional secondary-level entrance grade is 9. For fall 2015, 960 students applied for upper-level admission, 449 were accepted, 264 enrolled. Cooperative Entrance Exam (McGraw-Hill) or SSAT required. Deadline for receipt of application materials: November 15. No application fee required.

Athletics Interscholastic: baseball, basketball, bowling, crew, cross-country running, diving, fencing, football, golf, ice hockey, indoor track, indoor track & field, lacrosse, rugby, soccer, swimming and diving, tennis, track and field, volleyball, water polo, winter (indoor) track, wrestling; intramural: basketball, flag football, Frisbee, handball, indoor soccer, outdoor recreation, team handball, touch football, ultimate Frisbee, whiffle ball. 4 PE instructors, 23 coaches, 1 athletic trainer.

Computers Computers are regularly used in all academic classes. Computer network features include on-campus library services, online commercial services, Internet access, wireless campus network, Internet filtering or blocking technology. Campus intranet and student e-mail accounts are available to students. Students grades are available online. The school has a published electronic and media policy.

Contact Mr. John T. Irvine, Director of Admissions. 201-547-6389. Fax: 201-547-2341. E-mail: Irvinej@spprep.org. Website: www.spprep.org

ST. PIUS X CATHOLIC HIGH SCHOOL

2674 Johnson Road NE
Atlanta, Georgia 30345

Head of School: Mr. Steve Spellman

General Information Coeducational day college-preparatory school, affiliated with Roman Catholic Church. Grades 9–12. Founded: 1958. Setting: suburban. 33-acre campus. 8 buildings on campus. Approved or accredited by National Catholic Education Association, Southern Association of Colleges and Schools, The College Board, and Georgia Department of Education. Member of Secondary School Admission Test Board. Total enrollment: 1,100. Upper school average class size: 21. Upper school faculty-student ratio: 1:12. There are 180 required school days per year for Upper School students. Upper School students typically attend 5 days per week. The average school day consists of 7 hours.

Upper School Student Profile Grade 9: 275 students (140 boys, 135 girls); Grade 10: 285 students (140 boys, 145 girls); Grade 11: 260 students (130 boys, 130 girls); Grade 12: 260 students (130 boys, 130 girls). 84% of students are Roman Catholic.

Faculty School total: 102. In upper school: 49 men, 52 women; 72 have advanced degrees.

Subjects Offered Accounting, algebra, American history, American literature, anatomy, art, band, biology, business, business law, calculus, ceramics, chemistry, chorus, computer programming, computer science, creative writing, current events, dance, drama, driver education, economics, English, English literature, European history, expository writing, forensics, French, geography, geometry, German, government/civics, health, history, instrumental music, journalism, Latin, mathematics, music, physical education, physical science, physics, physiology, psychology, religion, science, social studies, sociology, Spanish, speech, statistics, theater, trigonometry, world history, world literature.

Graduation Requirements American history, computer science, English, foreign language, mathematics, physical education (includes health), religion (includes Bible studies and theology), science, social studies (includes history), Works of Mercy.

Special Academic Programs 20 Advanced Placement exams for which test preparation is offered; honors section; special instructional classes for students with learning disabilities and Attention Deficit Disorder.

College Admission Counseling 260 students graduated in 2016; 258 went to college, including Emory University; Georgia Institute of Technology; Georgia State University; University of Georgia; University of Notre Dame. Other: 1 went to work, 1 had other specific plans. Median composite ACT: 26. 60% scored over 600 on SAT critical reading, 60% scored over 600 on SAT math, 50% scored over 26 on composite ACT.

Student Life Upper grades have uniform requirement, student council, honor system. Discipline rests equally with students and faculty. Attendance at religious services is required.

Summer Programs Enrichment, sports, art/fine arts programs offered; held on campus; accepts boys and girls; open to students from other schools. 500 students usually enrolled. 2017 schedule: June 3 to July 30.

Tuition and Aid Day student tuition: $12,700. Tuition installment plan (FACTS Tuition Payment Plan, monthly payment plans). Tuition reduction for siblings, need-based scholarship grants available. In 2016–17, 20% of upper-school students received aid. Total amount of financial aid awarded in 2016–17: $400,000.

Admissions Traditional secondary-level entrance grade is 9. For fall 2016, 525 students applied for upper-level admission, 300 were accepted, 275 enrolled. SSAT required. Deadline for receipt of application materials: February 1. Application fee required: $100.

Athletics Interscholastic: baseball (boys), basketball (b,g), cheering (b,g), cross-country running (b,g), dance (b), dance squad (g), dance team (g), diving (b,g), drill team (g), football (b), golf (b,g), lacrosse (b,g), soccer (b,g), softball (g), strength & conditioning (b,g), swimming and diving (b,g), tennis (b,g), track and field (b,g), volleyball (g), water polo (b,g), weight training (b,g), wrestling (b); coed interscholastic: sailing, water polo. 4 PE instructors, 35 coaches, 1 athletic trainer.

Computers Computers are regularly used in all academic classes. Computer network features include on-campus library services, online commercial services, Internet access, wireless campus network, Internet filtering or blocking technology. Campus intranet, student e-mail accounts, and computer access in designated common areas are available to students. Students grades are available online. The school has a published electronic and media policy.

Contact Terry Sides, Coordinator of Admissions. 404-636-0323 Ext. 291. Fax: 404-636-2118. E-mail: tsides@spx.org. Website: www.spx.org

ST. PIUS X HIGH SCHOOL

811 West Donovan Street
Houston, Texas 77091-5699

Head of School: Mrs. Carmen Garrett Armistead

General Information Coeducational day college-preparatory and STREAM school, affiliated with Roman Catholic Church. Grades 9–12. Distance learning grades 10–12. Founded: 1956. Setting: urban. 28-acre campus. 2 buildings on campus. Approved or accredited by Southern Association of Colleges and Schools, Texas Catholic Conference, and Texas Department of Education. Member of National Association of Independent Schools. Endowment: $4 million. Total enrollment: 682. Upper school average class size: 19. Upper school faculty-student ratio: 1:12. There are 180 required school days per year for Upper School students. Upper School students typically attend 5 days per week. The average school day consists of 7 hours.

Upper School Student Profile Grade 9: 141 students (79 boys, 62 girls); Grade 10: 166 students (102 boys, 64 girls); Grade 11: 180 students (102 boys, 78 girls); Grade 12: 103 students (95 boys, 8 girls). 60% of students are Roman Catholic.

Faculty School total: 53. In upper school: 23 men, 29 women; 45 have advanced degrees.

Subjects Offered Advanced chemistry, advanced computer applications, advanced math, Advanced Placement courses, algebra, American history-AP, American literature, art, band, biology, biology-AP, business law, calculus, calculus-AP, campus ministry, Catholic belief and practice, chemistry, choir, chorus, Christian ethics, church history, college counseling, communications, community service, computer applications, computer multimedia, computer programming, computer science-AP, earth and space science, economics, English language-AP, English literature-AP, environmental science, film history, fine arts, foreign language, French, geometry, graphic design, health, health education, history of the Catholic Church, honors geometry, honors world history, introduction to theater, jewelry making, language arts, Latin, Latin-AP, library assistant, marching band, modern world history, moral and social development, moral theology, musical productions, painting, personal finance, photography, physical education, physics, physics-AP, psychology, reading/study skills, SAT/ACT preparation, Shakespeare, social justice, Spanish, Spanish language-AP, Spanish-AP, speech, speech communications, stagecraft, student government, student publications, technical theater, theology, U.S. government, U.S. government and politics-AP, U.S. history, U.S. history-AP, Web site design, world history, world religions, world wide web design, yearbook.

Graduation Requirements Advanced math, Advanced Placement courses, algebra, American government, American history, ancient world history, arts and fine arts (art, music, dance, drama), athletic training, band, biology, biology-AP, British literature-AP, calculus-AP, chemistry, Christian education, communications, computer science-AP, concert band, concert bell choir, concert choir, dance performance, digital photography, drama performance, earth and space science, economics, economics-AP, electives, English, English language-AP, English literature-AP, environmental science, film history, foreign language, French studies, geometry, handbells, health, history-AP, honors algebra, honors English, honors geometry, honors U.S. history, honors world history, integrated physics, introduction to theater, jewelry making, Latin-AP, leadership and service, marching band, mathematics, moral and social development, New Testament, personal finance, physical education (includes health), physics, physics-AP, reading/study skills, religious education, science, Shakespeare, social issues, social justice, social studies (includes history), Spanish-AP, stagecraft, theater, theater arts, theater production, theology, U.S. history-AP, video film production, vocal music, voice ensemble, weight training, weightlifting, world history-AP, 2 years of foreign language or reading development, Christian service learning (100 hours of community service), 4 years of theology.

Special Academic Programs 10 Advanced Placement exams for which test preparation is offered; honors section; study at local college for college credit; academic accommodation for the gifted; remedial reading and/or remedial writing; remedial math; programs in English, mathematics, general development for dyslexic students.

College Admission Counseling 148 students graduated in 2016; 147 went to college, including Houston Baptist University; Sam Houston State University; Texas A&M University; Texas State University; The University of Texas at Austin; University of Houston. Other: 1 entered military service. Mean SAT critical reading: 512, mean SAT math: 505, mean SAT writing: 500, mean combined SAT: 1514, mean composite ACT: 23. 18% scored over 600 on SAT critical reading, 15% scored over 600 on SAT math, 17% scored over 600 on SAT writing, 16% scored over 1800 on combined SAT, 20% scored over 26 on composite ACT.

Student Life Upper grades have uniform requirement, student council, honor system. Discipline rests primarily with faculty. Attendance at religious services is required.

Summer Programs Remediation, enrichment, advancement, sports, art/fine arts, computer instruction programs offered; session focuses on enrichment and remediation, sports; held on campus; accepts boys and girls; open to students from other schools. 200 students usually enrolled. 2017 schedule: June 12 to July 31. Application deadline: May 1.

Tuition and Aid Day student tuition: $14,600. Tuition installment plan (monthly payment plans). Tuition reduction for siblings, merit scholarship grants, need-based scholarship grants available. In 2016–17, 24% of upper-school students received aid.

Admissions Traditional secondary-level entrance grade is 9. For fall 2016, 390 students applied for upper-level admission, 250 were accepted, 184 enrolled. Catholic High School Entrance Examination or ISEE required. Deadline for receipt of application materials: January 15. Application fee required: $50. Interview required.

Athletics Interscholastic: baseball (boys), basketball (b,g), cheering (g), cross-country running (b,g), dance squad (g), dance team (b,g), drill team (g), football (b), golf (b,g), lacrosse (b,g), rugby (b,g), soccer (b,g), softball (g), strength & conditioning (b,g), swimming and diving (b,g), tennis (b,g), track and field (b,g), volleyball (g), weight training (b,g), wrestling (b). 3 PE instructors, 25 coaches, 1 athletic trainer.

Computers Computers are regularly used in art, career exploration, career technology, college planning, current events, desktop publishing, drawing and design, graphic arts, graphic design, health, library skills, literary magazine, mathematics, multimedia, news writing, photography, photojournalism, publications, reading, remedial study skills, research skills, SAT preparation, science, social sciences, social studies, stock market, technology, theater, video film production, Web site design, yearbook classes. Computer network features include on-campus library services, Internet access, wireless campus network, Internet filtering or blocking technology, Learning Management System with online classrooms. Campus intranet, student e-mail accounts, and computer access in designated common areas are available to students. Students grades are available online. The school has a published electronic and media policy.

Contact Mrs. Kathryn Griep, Admissions Director. 713-692-3581 Ext. 159. Fax: 713-692-5725. E-mail: griepk@stpiusx.org. Website: www.stpiusx.org

ST. STANISLAUS COLLEGE

304 South Beach Boulevard
Bay St. Louis, Mississippi 39520

Head of School: Br. Barry Landry, SC

General Information Boys' boarding and day college-preparatory, business, religious studies, and ESL school, affiliated with Roman Catholic Church. Grades 7–12. Founded: 1854. Setting: small town. Nearest major city is New Orleans, LA. Students are housed in single-sex dormitories. 30-acre campus. 8 buildings on campus. Approved or accredited by National Catholic Education Association, Southern Association of Colleges and Schools, Southern Association of Independent Schools, and Mississippi Department of Education. Member of National Association of Independent Schools. Endowment: $5 million. Total enrollment: 352. Upper school average class size: 22. Upper school faculty-student ratio: 1:12. There are 180 required school days per year for Upper School students. Upper School students typically attend 5 days per week. The average school day consists of 6 hours and 23 minutes.

Upper School Student Profile Grade 9: 65 students (65 boys); Grade 10: 64 students (64 boys); Grade 11: 66 students (66 boys); Grade 12: 55 students (55 boys). 65% of students are Roman Catholic.

Faculty School total: 34. In upper school: 28 men, 6 women; 21 have advanced degrees; 8 reside on campus.

Subjects Offered Accounting, ACT preparation, advanced biology, advanced chemistry, advanced computer applications, advanced math, Advanced Placement courses, algebra, American history, American history-AP, American literature, anatomy, art, astronomy, biology, biology-AP, business, business education, business law, calculus, calculus-AP, campus ministry, ceramics, chemistry, chemistry-AP, computer programming, computer science, computer science-AP, creative writing, desktop publishing, drama, economics, economics and history, English, English language and composition-AP, English literature, English literature and composition-AP, environmental science, ESL, finance, French, French as a second language, genetics, geography, geology, geometry, government, government/civics, grammar, guidance, health, health education, history, journalism, law, marine biology, marine science, mathematics, music, music performance, physical education, physics, physics-AP, pre-calculus, psychology, psychology-AP, religion, science, scuba diving, short story, social sciences, social studies, sociology, Spanish, speech, swimming, symphonic band, theater, theater arts, theology, track and field, trigonometry, typing, U.S. history-AP, world history, world literature.

Graduation Requirements Arts and fine arts (art, music, dance, drama), computer science, English, foreign language, mathematics, physical education (includes health), religion (includes Bible studies and theology), science, social sciences, social studies (includes history), volunteer service hours are required.

Special Academic Programs 4 Advanced Placement exams for which test preparation is offered; honors section; study at local college for college credit; remedial reading and/or remedial writing; remedial math; special instructional classes for deaf students, blind students; ESL (7 students enrolled).

College Admission Counseling 59 students graduated in 2016; all went to college, including Loyola University New Orleans; Mississippi State University; Tulane University; University of Mississippi; University of Mississippi; University of New Orleans. Other: 1 entered military service. Median SAT critical reading: 520, median SAT math: 620, median SAT writing: 570, median composite ACT: 25. 40% scored over 600 on SAT critical reading, 50% scored over 600 on SAT math, 35% scored over 600 on SAT writing, 22% scored over 1800 on combined SAT, 45% scored over 26 on composite ACT.

Student Life Upper grades have uniform requirement, student council, honor system. Discipline rests primarily with faculty. Attendance at religious services is required.

Summer Programs ESL programs offered; session focuses on water sports summer camp and ESL, cultural summer camp; held both on and off campus; accepts boys and girls; open to students from other schools. 180 students usually enrolled. 2017 schedule: June 21 to July 18. Application deadline: none.

Tuition and Aid Day student tuition: $6290; 7-day tuition and room/board: $24,257. Tuition installment plan (monthly payment plans, individually arranged payment plans). Need-based scholarship grants, paying campus jobs available.

Admissions Traditional secondary-level entrance grade is 9. For fall 2016, 100 students applied for upper-level admission, 90 were accepted, 80 enrolled. Deadline for receipt of application materials: none. Application fee required: $100. Interview required.

Athletics Interscholastic: baseball, basketball, cross-country running, football, golf, power lifting, soccer, track and field; intramural: baseball, basketball, billiards, croquet, fishing, flag football, floor hockey, football, hiking/backpacking, jogging, outdoor activities, outdoor adventure, outdoor education, outdoor recreation, outdoor skills, outdoors, physical fitness, physical training, power lifting, scuba diving, swimming and diving, table tennis, tennis, touch football, volleyball, water polo, water skiing, weight lifting, weight training; coed interscholastic: cheering, sailing, swimming and diving, tennis. 5 PE instructors, 16 coaches, 1 athletic trainer.

Computers Computers are regularly used in accounting, English, mathematics, religion, SAT preparation, science, Spanish classes. Computer resources include on-campus library services, online commercial services, Internet access, wireless campus network, Internet filtering or blocking technology. Student e-mail accounts and computer access in designated common areas are available to students. Students grades are available online.

Contact Mr. Richard Gleber, Director of Admissions. 228-467-9057 Ext. 249. Fax: 228-466-2972. E-mail: richard@ststan.com. Website: www.ststan.com

SAINT STEPHEN'S EPISCOPAL SCHOOL

315 41st Street West
Bradenton, Florida 34209

Head of School: Janet S. Pullen

General Information Coeducational day college-preparatory and marine science school, affiliated with Episcopal Church. Grades PK–12. Founded: 1970. Setting: small town. Nearest major city is Tampa. 35-acre campus. 3 buildings on campus. Approved or accredited by Florida Council of Independent Schools, National Association of Episcopal Schools, Southern Association of Colleges and Schools, and Southern Association of Independent Schools. Member of National Association of Independent Schools. Endowment: $5.5 million. Total enrollment: 654. Upper school average class size: 15. Upper school faculty-student ratio: 1:11. There are 177 required school days per year for Upper School. Upper School students typically attend 5 days per week. The average school day consists of 7 hours.

Upper School Student Profile Grade 9: 62 students (32 boys, 30 girls); Grade 10: 54 students (26 boys, 28 girls); Grade 11: 73 students (38 boys, 35 girls); Grade 12: 70 students (34 boys, 36 girls); Postgraduate: 2 students (2 boys). 15% of students are members of Episcopal Church.

Faculty School total: 90. In upper school: 13 men, 18 women; 21 have advanced degrees.

Subjects Offered 3-dimensional art, Advanced Placement courses, advanced studio art-AP, algebra, American government, American history, American history-AP, American literature, art, art history, art history-AP, art-AP, astronomy, band, biology, biology-AP, British literature, broadcast journalism, calculus, calculus-AP, ceramics, chemistry, chemistry-AP, choir, chorus, community service, comparative religion, composition, composition-AP, computer programming, computer programming-AP, computer science, computer science-AP, conceptual physics, debate, digital art, digital photography, discrete mathematics, drama, economics, English, English language and composition-AP, English language-AP, English literature, English literature and composition-AP, English literature-AP, English-AP, environmental science-AP, European history, European history-AP, French, French language-AP, geometry, graphic design, humanities, international relations, journalism, Latin, Latin-AP, marine biology, marine science, music, newspaper, organic chemistry, painting, photography, physical education, physics, physics-AP, portfolio art, pre-calculus, probability and statistics, psychology, public speaking, science research, Spanish, Spanish language-AP, speech and debate, studio art, studio art-AP, trigonometry, U.S. history, U.S. history-AP, weight training, Western civilization, world history, world history-AP.

Graduation Requirements Arts and fine arts (art, music, dance, drama), electives, English, foreign language, mathematics, physical education (includes health), science, social studies (includes history), senior speech. Community service is required.

Special Academic Programs 17 Advanced Placement exams for which test preparation is offered; honors section.

College Admission Counseling 69 students graduated in 2016; all went to college, including Florida State University; University of Central Florida; University of Florida; University of Miami; University of South Florida. Mean SAT critical reading: 570, mean SAT math: 614, mean SAT writing: 579, mean composite ACT: 25. 39% scored over 600 on SAT critical reading, 56% scored over 600 on SAT math, 36% scored over 600 on SAT writing, 38% scored over 26 on composite ACT.

Student Life Upper grades have specified standards of dress, student council, honor system. Discipline rests primarily with faculty. Attendance at religious services is required.

Summer Programs Enrichment, advancement, sports, art/fine arts, computer instruction programs offered; session focuses on academic enrichment and sports; held on campus; accepts boys and girls; open to students from other schools. 500 students usually enrolled. 2017 schedule: June 10 to August 8. Application deadline: June 1.

Tuition and Aid Day student tuition: $21,500. Tuition installment plan (SMART Tuition Payment Plan, monthly payment plans). Need-based scholarship grants available. In 2016–17, 10% of upper-school students received aid.

Admissions Traditional secondary-level entrance grade is 9. For fall 2016, 37 students applied for upper-level admission, 34 were accepted, 34 enrolled. Otis-Lennon School Ability Test or TOEFL Junior required. Deadline for receipt of application materials: none. Application fee required: $100. Interview recommended.

Athletics Interscholastic: aerobics/dance (girls), aquatics (b,g), baseball (b), basketball (b,g), cheering (g), crew (b,g), cross-country running (b,g), dance (g), dance team (g), diving (b,g), football (b), golf (b,g), independent competitive sports (b,g), lacrosse (b,g), soccer (b,g), softball (g), swimming and diving (b,g), tennis (b,g), track and field (b,g), volleyball (g), winter soccer (b,g), wrestling (b); intramural: aerobics/dance (g), ballet (g), basketball (b,g), cheering (g), crew (b,g), cross-country running (b,g), dance (g), fitness (b,g), gymnastics (b,g), horseback riding (b,g), jogging (b,g), lacrosse (b,g), physical fitness (b,g), physical training (b,g), running (b,g), sailing (b,g), soccer (b,g), softball (b,g), strength & conditioning (b,g), tennis (b,g), track and field (b,g), volleyball (b,g), weight training (b,g), wrestling (b); coed intramural: yoga. 8 PE instructors, 15 coaches, 1 athletic trainer.

Computers Computers are regularly used in art, computer applications, foreign language, journalism, library, mathematics, media, science, social sciences, word processing, writing, yearbook classes. Computer network features include on-campus library services, online commercial services, Internet access, wireless campus network, Internet filtering or blocking technology, Microsoft Office, Google Docs. Student e-mail accounts and computer access in designated common areas are available to students. Students grades are available online. The school has a published electronic and media policy.

Contact Larry Jensen, Director of Admissions. 941-746-2121 Ext. 1568. Fax: 941-345-1237. E-mail: ljensen@saintstephens.org. Website: www.saintstephens.org

ST. STEPHEN'S EPISCOPAL SCHOOL

6500 St. Stephen's Drive
Austin, Texas 78746

Head of School: Mr. Chris Gunnin

General Information Coeducational boarding and day college-preparatory and theater focus school, affiliated with Episcopal Church. Boarding grades 8–12, day grades 6–12. Founded: 1950. Setting: suburban. Students are housed in single-sex dormitories. 370-acre campus. 45 buildings on campus. Approved or accredited by Independent Schools Association of the Southwest, National Association of Episcopal Schools, Southern Association of Colleges and Schools, The Association of Boarding Schools, and Texas Department of Education. Member of National Association of Independent Schools and Secondary School Admission Test Board. Endowment: $13 million. Total enrollment: 688. Upper school average class size: 17. Upper school faculty-student ratio: 1:8. There are 165 required school days per year for Upper School students. Upper School students typically attend 5 days per week. The average school day consists of 7 hours and 35 minutes.

Upper School Student Profile Grade 9: 121 students (60 boys, 61 girls); Grade 10: 121 students (55 boys, 66 girls); Grade 11: 116 students (60 boys, 56 girls); Grade 12: 123 students (65 boys, 58 girls). 35% of students are boarding students. 80% are state residents. 10 states are represented in upper school student body. 20% are international students. International students from China, Finland, Jamaica, Mexico, Nigeria, and Saudi Arabia; 13 other countries represented in student body. 18% of students are members of Episcopal Church.

Faculty School total: 98. In upper school: 40 men, 35 women; 45 have advanced degrees; 45 reside on campus.

Subjects Offered 3-dimensional design, acting, algebra, American history, American history-AP, anthropology, art, art history, astrophysics, ballet, band, biology, calculus, ceramics, chamber groups, chemistry, Chinese, choreography, classics, computer applications, computer math, computer science, computer studies, creative writing, directing, drama, English, English literature, environmental science, European history, fine arts, French, geology, geometry, government/civics, graphic design, history, jazz band, Latin, mathematics, music, musical theater, photography, physical education, physics, physics-AP, play/screen writing, pre-calculus, psychology, public policy issues and action, public speaking, religion, science, social studies, Spanish, theater arts, theology, video, world history, world literature.

Graduation Requirements Arts and fine arts (art, music, dance, drama), electives, English, foreign language, mathematics, physical education (includes health), religion (includes Bible studies and theology), science, social studies (includes history), community service requirement in middle and upper schools.

Special Academic Programs Advanced Placement exam preparation; honors section; independent study; study abroad.

College Admission Counseling 126 students graduated in 2016; all went to college, including Rice University; Texas A&M University; The University of Texas at Austin; Trinity University; University of Chicago; University of Colorado Boulder. Other: 2 entered military service. Mean SAT critical reading: 611, mean SAT math: 651, mean SAT writing: 631, mean combined SAT: 1893, mean composite ACT: 29.

Student Life Upper grades have specified standards of dress, student council. Discipline rests equally with students and faculty. Attendance at religious services is required.

Summer Programs Sports, art/fine arts programs offered; session focuses on soccer, tennis, travel abroad, foreign language/culture, fine arts, community service; held both on and off campus; accepts boys and girls; open to students from other schools. 120 students usually enrolled. 2017 schedule: June 1 to July 1. Application deadline: none.

Tuition and Aid Day student tuition: $24,750; 7-day tuition and room/board: $51,460. Tuition installment plan (individually arranged payment plans). Need-based scholarship grants available. In 2016–17, 12% of upper-school students received aid; total upper-school merit-scholarship money awarded: $10,000. Total amount of financial aid awarded in 2016–17: $2,460,000.

Admissions Traditional secondary-level entrance grade is 9. For fall 2016, 363 students applied for upper-level admission, 187 were accepted, 78 enrolled. ISEE or SSAT required. Deadline for receipt of application materials: January 25. Application fee required: $100. Interview recommended.

Athletics Interscholastic: baseball (boys), basketball (b,g), crew (b,g), cross-country running (b,g), field hockey (g), football (b), golf (b,g), lacrosse (b,g), running (b,g), soccer (b,g), softball (g), swimming and diving (b,g), tennis (b,g), track and field (b,g), volleyball (g), winter soccer (b,g); intramural: bicycling (b,g), climbing (b,g), combined training (b,g), dance (b,g), fitness (b,g), hiking/backpacking (b,g), independent competitive sports (b,g), indoor hockey (b,g), modern dance (b,g), mountain biking (b,g), mountaineering (b,g), outdoor adventure (b,g), outdoor education (b,g), paddle tennis (b,g), physical fitness (b,g), physical training (b,g), rappelling (b,g), rock climbing (b,g), ropes courses (b,g), strength & conditioning (b,g), surfing (b,g), wall climbing (b,g), weight training (b,g); coed interscholastic: aerobics/dance, badminton, bicycling, climbing, mountain biking. 2 PE instructors, 5 coaches, 2 athletic trainers.

Computers Computer network features include on-campus library services, online commercial services, Internet access, wireless campus network, Internet filtering or blocking technology, online schedules, syllabi, homework, examples, and links to information sources. Campus intranet, student e-mail accounts, and computer access in designated common areas are available to students. Students grades are available online. The school has a published electronic and media policy.

Contact Lawrence Sampleton, Associate Head for Enrollment Management. 512-327-1213 Ext. 210. Fax: 512-327-6771. E-mail: admission@sstx.org. Website: www.sstx.org

ST. STEPHEN'S INTERNATIONAL SCHOOL

998 Vipawadee Rangsit Road, Ladyao Chatuchak
Bangkok 10900, Thailand

Head of School: Mr. John Rolfe

General Information Coeducational day general academic school. Founded: 1995. 3 buildings on campus. Approved or accredited by Council of International Schools. Language of instruction: English. Upper school average class size: 25.

Faculty In upper school: 15 men, 20 women.

Special Academic Programs Programs in English for dyslexic students; ESL.

College Admission Counseling 12 students graduated in 2016; all went to college.

Student Life Upper grades have uniform requirement, student council, honor system. Discipline rests equally with students and faculty.

Admissions Application fee required: 5000 Thai bahts. Interview required.

Computers The school has a published electronic and media policy.

Contact Ms. Wanwimon Wipattarametheekul, Registrar. 662-5130270 Ext. 200. Fax: 662-9303307. E-mail: info@sis.edu. Website: www.sis.edu

ST. STEPHEN'S SCHOOL, ROME

Via Aventina 3
Rome 00153, Italy

Head of School: Mr. Eric J. Mayer

General Information Coeducational boarding and day college-preparatory and arts school. Grades 9–PG. Founded: 1964. Setting: urban. Students are housed in single-sex by floor dormitories. 2-acre campus. 2 buildings on campus. Approved or accredited by International Baccalaureate Organization, New England Association of Schools and Colleges, and US Department of State. Affiliate member of National Association of Independent Schools; member of European Council of International Schools. Language of instruction: English. Endowment: $6 million. Total enrollment: 287. Upper school average class size: 13. Upper school faculty-student ratio: 1:7. There are 175 required school days per year for Upper School students. Upper School students typically attend 5 days per week. The average school day consists of 7 hours.

Upper School Student Profile Grade 9: 62 students (34 boys, 28 girls); Grade 10: 71 students (36 boys, 35 girls); Grade 11: 85 students (35 boys, 50 girls); Grade 12: 77 students (34 boys, 43 girls). 15% of students are boarding students. 62% are international students. International students from Australia, China, France, Germany, United Kingdom, and United States; 34 other countries represented in student body.

Faculty School total: 54. In upper school: 16 men, 38 women; 45 have advanced degrees; 9 reside on campus.

Subjects Offered 20th century history, algebra, American literature, art history, biology, calculus, chemistry, chorus, classical studies, creative writing, dance, drama, drawing, economics, English, English literature, environmental systems, European history, French, geometry, health, instrumental music, Islamic studies, Italian, Latin, music theory, painting, photography, physical education, physics, pre-calculus, Roman civilization, sculpture, Spanish, theory of knowledge, trigonometry, world literature.

Graduation Requirements Arts and fine arts (art, music, dance, drama), English, foreign language, mathematics, physical education (includes health), science, social studies (includes history), senior research paper, computer proficiency examination, service project.

Special Academic Programs International Baccalaureate program; 9 Advanced Placement exams for which test preparation is offered; domestic exchange program (with Buckingham Browne & Nichols School, Choate Rosemary Hall).

College Admission Counseling 70 students graduated in 2016; all went to college, including Boston University; Northeastern University; Savannah College of Art and Design; Texas A&M University; University of California, Los Angeles; University of Chicago. Mean SAT critical reading: 608, mean SAT math: 607, mean SAT writing: 581, mean combined SAT: 1796. 50% scored over 600 on SAT critical reading, 50% scored over 600 on SAT math, 48% scored over 600 on SAT writing, 50% scored over 1800 on combined SAT, 20% scored over 26 on composite ACT.

Student Life Upper grades have student council. Discipline rests equally with students and faculty.

Summer Programs Remediation, enrichment, advancement, ESL, art/fine arts programs offered; session focuses on liberal arts/pre-college; held on campus; accepts boys and girls; open to students from other schools. 50 students usually enrolled. 2017 schedule: June 19 to August 4. Application deadline: May 19.

Tuition and Aid Day student tuition: €25,600–€26,100; 7-day tuition and room/board: €37,450–€37,950. Tuition installment plan (individually arranged payment plans). Tuition reduction for siblings, need-based scholarship grants available. In 2016–17, 15% of upper-school students received aid. Total amount of financial aid awarded in 2016–17: €530,000.

Admissions Traditional secondary-level entrance grade is 9. For fall 2016, 174 students applied for upper-level admission, 118 were accepted, 107 enrolled. School's own exam required. Deadline for receipt of application materials: January 30. Application fee required: €150. Interview recommended.

Athletics Interscholastic: basketball (boys, girls), soccer (b,g), volleyball (b,g); intramural: basketball (b,g), soccer (b,g), volleyball (b,g); coed interscholastic: tennis; coed intramural: dance, tennis, track and field, yoga. 1 PE instructor, 7 coaches.

Computers Computers are regularly used in English, foreign language, mathematics, photography, science, social studies classes. Computer network features include on-campus library services, Internet access, wireless campus network, Internet filtering or blocking technology, in-house technical assistance. Campus intranet, student e-mail accounts, and computer access in designated common areas are available to students. Students grades are available online. The school has a published electronic and media policy.

Contact Ms. Alex Perniciaro, Admissions Officer. 39-06-575-0605. Fax: 39-06-574-1941. E-mail: alex.perniciaro@sssrome.it. Website: www.sssrome.it

SAINT TERESA'S ACADEMY

5600 Main Street
Kansas City, Missouri 64113

Head of School: Mrs. Nan Tiehen Bone

General Information Girls' day college-preparatory school, affiliated with Roman Catholic Church. Grades 9–12. Founded: 1866. Setting: urban. 20-acre campus. 4 buildings on campus. Approved or accredited by National Catholic Education Association and North Central Association of Colleges and Schools. Endowment: $150,000. Total enrollment: 596. Upper school average class size: 21. Upper school faculty-student ratio: 1:12. There are 174 required school days per year for Upper School students. Upper School students typically attend 5 days per week. The average school day consists of 6 hours and 40 minutes.

Upper School Student Profile Grade 9: 148 students (148 girls); Grade 10: 162 students (162 girls); Grade 11: 127 students (127 girls); Grade 12: 152 students (152 girls). 87% of students are Roman Catholic.

Faculty School total: 55. In upper school: 11 men, 50 women; 42 have advanced degrees.

Subjects Offered Advanced biology, advanced chemistry, advanced math, algebra, American government, American history, American history-AP, American literature, American literature-AP, analysis, anatomy and physiology, art, astronomy, athletics, basketball, biology, biology-AP, botany, British literature, calculus, calculus-AP, career/college preparation, ceramics, chamber groups, chemistry, chemistry-AP, Chinese, choir, chorus, computer graphics, computer programming, computer science, computer science-AP, current events, dance, directing, drama, drawing, ecology, economics, English, English language and composition-AP, English language-AP, English literature, English literature and composition-AP, English literature-AP, environmental science-AP, European history, European history-AP, fiber arts, fitness, foreign language, forensics, French, French language-AP, French-AP, freshman seminar, geometry, golf, government-AP, graphic design, health, health and wellness, honors geometry, independent study, journalism, keyboarding, language arts, language-AP, Latin, Latin History, Latin-AP, literature and composition-AP, literature-AP, music theory-AP, music-AP, newspaper, painting, physical education, physics, piano, playwriting, portfolio art, pre-calculus, probability and statistics, psychology, psychology-AP, Shakespeare, social issues, social justice, social studies, sociology, softball, Spanish, Spanish language-AP, Spanish literature-AP, Spanish-AP, speech, speech and debate, speech communications, sports conditioning, sports performance development, stagecraft, student publications, substance abuse, swimming, technical theater, tennis, theater, theology and the arts, track and field, trigonometry, U.S. government, U.S. government and politics, U.S. government and politics-AP, U.S. history, U.S. history-AP, United States government-AP, volleyball, Western civilization, women in literature, women spirituality and faith, world geography, world history-AP, world religions, world religions, writing, writing, yearbook, yoga.

Graduation Requirements Arts and fine arts (art, music, dance, drama), computer science, electives, English, foreign language, mathematics, physical education (includes health), science, social studies (includes history), theology. Community service is required.

Special Academic Programs 10 Advanced Placement exams for which test preparation is offered; honors section; study at local college for college credit.

College Admission Counseling 152 students graduated in 2016; all went to college, including Kansas State University; Saint Louis University; The University of Kansas; University of Arkansas; University of Missouri. Mean SAT critical reading: 600, mean SAT math: 580, mean SAT writing: 610, mean combined SAT: 1780, mean composite ACT: 26.

Student Life Upper grades have uniform requirement, student council. Discipline rests primarily with faculty. Attendance at religious services is required.

Summer Programs Enrichment, advancement, sports, art/fine arts, computer instruction programs offered; session focuses on fine arts, sports, credit bearing courses, and enrichment summer school programs; held on campus; accepts girls; open to students from other schools. 135 students usually enrolled. 2017 schedule: June 5 to June 30. Application deadline: March 1.

Tuition and Aid Day student tuition: $12,090. Tuition installment plan (SMART Tuition Payment Plan). Tuition reduction for siblings, merit scholarship grants, need-based scholarship grants available. In 2016–17, 40% of upper-school students received aid; total upper-school merit-scholarship money awarded: $200,000. Total amount of financial aid awarded in 2016–17: $200,000.

Admissions Traditional secondary-level entrance grade is 9. For fall 2016, 181 students applied for upper-level admission, 155 were accepted, 148 enrolled. High School Placement Test (closed version) from Scholastic Testing Service and placement test required. Deadline for receipt of application materials: February 27. Application fee required: $350.

Athletics Interscholastic: aerobics/dance, basketball, cross-country running, dance team, diving, golf, lacrosse, soccer, softball, swimming and diving, tennis, track and field, volleyball; intramural: aerobics/dance, badminton, fitness, fitness walking, jogging, physical fitness, physical training, running, strength & conditioning, table tennis, volleyball, walking, weight lifting, weight training, yoga. 1 PE instructor, 25 coaches, 1 athletic trainer.

Computers Computers are regularly used in business education, creative writing, desktop publishing, graphic arts, graphic design, graphics, journalism, library, literary magazine, newspaper, photography, research skills, science, writing, yearbook classes.

Computer network features include on-campus library services, Internet access, wireless campus network, Internet filtering or blocking technology. Campus intranet and student e-mail accounts are available to students. Students grades are available online. The school has a published electronic and media policy.

Contact Mrs. Roseann Hudnall, Admissions Director. 816-501-0011 Ext. 135. Fax: 816-523-0232. E-mail: rhudnall@stteresasacademy.org. Website: www.stteresasacademy.org

SAINT THOMAS ACADEMY

949 Mendota Heights Road
Mendota Heights, Minnesota 55120

Head of School: Mr. Matthew C. Mohs

General Information Boys' day college-preparatory, leadership/Independent Military School, and military school, affiliated with Roman Catholic Church. Grades 7–12. Founded: 1885. Setting: suburban. Nearest major city is St. Paul. 88-acre campus. 6 buildings on campus. Approved or accredited by Minnesota Department of Education. Member of National Association of Independent Schools. Endowment: $21.7 million. Total enrollment: 671. Upper school average class size: 18. Upper school faculty-student ratio: 1:10. There are 174 required school days per year for Upper School students. Upper School students typically attend 5 days per week. The average school day consists of 7 hours.

Upper School Student Profile Grade 7: 43 students (43 boys); Grade 8: 60 students (60 boys); Grade 9: 100 students (100 boys); Grade 10: 142 students (142 boys); Grade 11: 119 students (119 boys); Grade 12: 133 students (133 boys). 80% of students are Roman Catholic.

Faculty School total: 58. In upper school: 34 men, 17 women; 43 have advanced degrees.

Subjects Offered ACT preparation, advanced biology, advanced math, Advanced Placement courses, algebra, American democracy, American government, American history, American history-AP, American literature, American literature-AP, American studies, art, art and culture, art appreciation, art history, band, biology, biology-AP, calculus, campus ministry, chemistry, Chinese, choir, Christian doctrine, Christian education, Christian ethics, Christian scripture, Christian studies, Christian testament, church history, civics, Civil War, college admission preparation, college awareness, college counseling, college placement, college planning, college writing, communication skills, community service, comparative government and politics, computer art, computer science, concert band, concert choir, consumer economics, CPR, creative writing, criminal justice, critical thinking, critical writing, digital art, drama, drawing, earth science, economics, economics-AP, English, English literature, English literature and composition-AP, environmental science, environmental science-AP, environmental studies, ethical decision making, ethics and responsibility, European civilization, European history, European literature, expository writing, fine arts, finite math, first aid, foreign language, foundations of civilization, fractal geometry, French, French language-AP, French-AP, general math, general science, geography, geology, geometry, global issues, government and politics-AP, government/civics, grammar, graphic arts, guitar, health, health and wellness, health education, history, history of the Catholic Church, Internet research, interpersonal skills, jazz ensemble, lab science, Latin, leadership, leadership and service, leadership education training, life management skills, Life of Christ, linear algebra, logic, rhetoric, and debate, macro/microeconomics-AP, marching band, mathematics, military science, music, peer counseling, personal growth, personal money management, photo shop, photography, physical education, physical fitness, physical science, physics, political science, political thought, pottery, prayer/spirituality, pre-algebra, pre-calculus, psychology, public service, public speaking, reading/study skills, religion, religion and culture, robotics, SAT preparation, SAT/ACT preparation, science, science project, scripture, senior project, Shakespeare, skills for success, social justice, social studies, Spanish, Spanish language-AP, Spanish literature, state government, state history, statistics, statistics-AP, study skills, swimming, trigonometry, United States government-AP, visual and performing arts, vocal ensemble, world history, world literature, writing.

Graduation Requirements Arts and fine arts (art, music, dance, drama), biology, English, foreign language, health education, leadership and service, mathematics, physical education (includes health), science, social studies (includes history), theology, U.S. history, 100 hours of community service in 12th grade.

Special Academic Programs 11 Advanced Placement exams for which test preparation is offered; honors section; independent study; study at local college for college credit.

College Admission Counseling 115 students graduated in 2016; 112 went to college, including Creighton University; Marquette University; Saint John's University; University of Minnesota, Twin Cities Campus; University of St. Thomas; University of Wisconsin–Madison. Other: 3 had other specific plans. Mean composite ACT: 28. 57% scored over 26 on composite ACT.

Student Life Upper grades have uniform requirement, student council, honor system. Discipline rests equally with students and faculty. Attendance at religious services is required.

Summer Programs Enrichment, sports, art/fine arts programs offered; session focuses on study and organizational strategies, time management, test preparation and orientation, writing skills; held on campus; accepts boys and girls; open to students from other schools. 250 students usually enrolled. 2017 schedule: June to August. Application deadline: June.

Tuition and Aid Day student tuition: $21,100. Tuition installment plan (SMART Tuition Payment Plan, monthly payment plans, individually arranged payment plans, quarterly payment plan). Merit scholarship grants, need-based scholarship grants available. In 2016–17, 40% of upper-school students received aid; total upper-school merit-scholarship money awarded: $250,000. Total amount of financial aid awarded in 2016–17: $2,800,000.

Admissions Traditional secondary-level entrance grade is 9. For fall 2016, 209 students applied for upper-level admission, 159 were accepted, 126 enrolled. Cognitive Abilities Test required. Deadline for receipt of application materials: none. No application fee required. On-campus interview required.

Athletics Interscholastic: alpine skiing, baseball, basketball, cross-country running, drill team, fitness, football, golf, hockey, ice hockey, lacrosse, marksmanship, nordic skiing, outdoor skills, physical fitness, riflery, skeet shooting, skiing (cross-country), skiing (downhill), soccer, swimming and diving, tennis, track and field, wrestling; intramural: basketball, bowling, football, hockey, physical training, strength & conditioning, table tennis, ultimate Frisbee, weight lifting, weight training. 3 PE instructors, 6 coaches, 1 athletic trainer.

Computers Computers are regularly used in all classes. Computer network features include on-campus library services, online commercial services, Internet access, wireless campus network, Internet filtering or blocking technology. Student e-mail accounts and computer access in designated common areas are available to students. Students grades are available online. The school has a published electronic and media policy.

Contact Mrs. Angi Aguirre, Admissions Assistant. 651-683-1515. Fax: 651-683-1576. E-mail: aaguirre@cadets.com. Website: www.cadets.com

ST. THOMAS AQUINAS HIGH SCHOOL

2801 Southwest 12th Street
Fort Lauderdale, Florida 33312-2999

Head of School: Dr. Denise Aloma

General Information Coeducational day college-preparatory, campus ministry, and college preparatory school, affiliated with Roman Catholic Church. Ungraded, ages 13–18. Founded: 1936. Setting: suburban. 24-acre campus. 23 buildings on campus. Approved or accredited by National Catholic Education Association, Southern Association of Colleges and Schools, and Florida Department of Education. Total enrollment: 2,171. Upper school average class size: 25. Upper school faculty-student ratio: 1:18. There are 180 required school days per year for Upper School students. Upper School students typically attend 5 days per week. The average school day consists of 6 hours and 30 minutes.

Upper School Student Profile Grade 9: 517 students (285 boys, 232 girls); Grade 10: 528 students (273 boys, 255 girls); Grade 11: 547 students (257 boys, 290 girls); Grade 12: 541 students (255 boys, 286 girls). 85% of students are Roman Catholic.

Faculty School total: 130. In upper school: 60 men, 70 women; 72 have advanced degrees.

Subjects Offered 20th century history, 20th century world history, 3-dimensional art, ACT preparation, acting, advanced biology, advanced chemistry, advanced computer applications, advanced math, Advanced Placement courses, advanced studio art-AP, aerobics, algebra, all academic, American government, American history, American history-AP, American literature, anatomy, anatomy and physiology, animation, art, art appreciation, art history, art history-AP, art-AP, athletics, audio visual/media, audition methods, ballet, baseball, Bible, biology, biology-AP, bowling, British literature, British literature (honors), British literature-AP, broadcast journalism, broadcasting, Broadway dance, calculus, calculus-AP, campus ministry, cartooning/animation, Catholic belief and practice, cheerleading, chemistry, chemistry-AP, Chinese, choir, choral music, choreography, chorus, Christian scripture, Christianity, church history, comparative government and politics-AP, comparative political systems-AP, composition-AP, computer applications, computer art, computer graphics, computer programming-AP, computer science, computer science-AP, computer skills, concert band, concert choir, creative dance, creative drama, debate, desktop publishing, digital art, digital imaging, directing, drama, drama performance, drama workshop, dramatic arts, drawing, drawing and design, driver education, earth science, economics, economics-AP, electives, English, English composition, English language and composition-AP, English language-AP, English literature, English literature and composition-AP, English literature-AP, English-AP, English/composition-AP, environmental science, environmental science-AP, environmental studies, ethics, European history, European history-AP, fiction, film, film and literature, film and new technologies, film appreciation, film history, fitness, food science, foreign language, forensics, French, French language-AP, French literature-AP, French-AP, general science, genetics, geography, geometry, government, government and politics-AP, government-AP, government/civics-AP, grammar, graphic arts, graphic design, health, health and safety, health and wellness, health education, health enhancement, health science, healthful living, Hispanic literature, history, history of drama, history-AP, Holocaust, honors algebra, honors English, honors geometry, honors U.S. history, honors world history, human anatomy, human geography - AP, instrumental music, Italian, Italian history, jazz, jazz band, jazz ensemble, jazz theory, journalism, keyboarding, lab science, language, language and composition, language arts, language-AP, Latin, Latin-AP, leadership, leadership and service, leadership education training, library skills, Life of Christ, literature, literature and composition-AP, literature-AP, macro/microeconomics-AP, macroeconomics-AP, marching band, marine biology, marine science, marine studies, mathematics, mathematics-AP, media, microeconomics, microeconomics-AP, model United Nations, modern dance, modern European history, modern European history-AP, music, music appreciation, music composition, music performance, music theory, musical theater, New Testament, news writing, newspaper, nutrition, oral communications, oral expression, orchestra, painting, peace and justice, peace education, peace studies, performing arts, photography, photojournalism, physical education, physical fitness, physical science, physics, physics-AP, play production, playwriting and directing, poetry, political systems, pottery, prayer/spirituality, pre-algebra, pre-calculus, probability, probability and statistics, psychology, psychology-AP, public speaking, publications, reading, religion, religion and culture, religious education, religious studies, robotics, SAT preparation, SAT/ACT preparation, science, science and technology, science project, science research, Shakespeare, Shakespearean histories, Spanish, Spanish language-AP, Spanish literature, Spanish literature-AP, Spanish-AP, speech, speech and debate, speech and oral interpretations, speech communications, sports team management, stage and body movement, stage design, stagecraft, statistics, statistics-AP, student government, student publications, studio art, study skills, swimming, technical theater, television, tennis, theater arts, theater design and production, theater history, theater production, theology, trigonometry, U.S. government, U.S. government and politics, U.S. government and politics-AP, U.S. history, U.S. history-AP, U.S. literature, U.S. Presidents, United States government-AP, vocal ensemble, vocal jazz, vocal music, voice, voice and diction, voice ensemble, volleyball, water color painting, water polo, weight training, weightlifting, Western civilization, women's studies, world history, world history-AP.

Graduation Requirements Arts and fine arts (art, music, dance, drama), computer science, electives, English, foreign language, health, mathematics, personal fitness, science, social sciences, theology, 25 service hours per yer.

Special Academic Programs Advanced Placement exam preparation; honors section; study at local college for college credit; remedial reading and/or remedial writing; remedial math.

College Admission Counseling 527 students graduated in 2016; 518 went to college, including Florida Atlantic University; Florida State University; University of Central Florida; University of Florida; University of Miami; University of North Florida. Other: 1 entered military service, 4 had other specific plans. Mean SAT critical reading: 550, mean SAT math: 550, mean SAT writing: 554, mean composite ACT: 23.

Student Life Upper grades have uniform requirement, honor system. Discipline rests primarily with faculty. Attendance at religious services is required.

Summer Programs Remediation, enrichment, art/fine arts, computer instruction programs offered; session focuses on enrichment; held on campus; accepts boys and girls; open to students from other schools. 800 students usually enrolled. 2017 schedule: June 12 to June 28. Application deadline: June 9.

Tuition and Aid Guaranteed tuition plan. Tuition installment plan (FACTS Tuition Payment Plan). Need-based scholarship grants available.

Admissions Traditional secondary-level entrance grade is 9. For fall 2016, 754 students applied for upper-level admission, 578 were accepted, 517 enrolled. High School Placement Test required. Deadline for receipt of application materials: none. Application fee required: $50. On-campus interview required.

Athletics Interscholastic: aerobics/dance (girls), baseball (b), basketball (b,g), bowling (b,g), cheering (g), cross-country running (b,g), dance (b,g), dance squad (g), dance team (g), diving (b,g), drill team (g), football (b), golf (b,g), lacrosse (b,g), physical fitness (b,g), running (b,g), sailing (b,g), soccer (b,g), softball (g), swimming and diving (b,g), tennis (b,g), track and field (b,g), volleyball (b,g), water polo (b,g), wrestling (b); intramural: dance team (g), danceline (g), drill team (g); coed interscholastic: ballet, bowling, hockey, ice hockey, indoor hockey, physical training; coed intramural: physical training, running. 1 PE instructor, 39 coaches, 1 athletic trainer.

Computers Computers are regularly used in all academic, data processing, desktop publishing, graphic arts, graphic design, graphics, journalism, keyboarding, lab/keyboard, media, media arts, media production, media services, news writing, newspaper, programming, publications, publishing, technology, video film production, Web site design, word processing classes. Computer network features include on-campus library services, online commercial services, Internet access, wireless campus network, Internet filtering or blocking technology. Campus intranet, student e-mail accounts, and computer access in designated common areas are available to students. Students grades are available online. The school has a published electronic and media policy.

Contact Admissions Office. 954-581-2127 Ext. 8623. Fax: 954-327-2193. E-mail: mary.facella@aquinas-sta.org. Website: www.aquinas-sta.org

SAINT THOMAS AQUINAS HIGH SCHOOL

11411 Pflumm Road
Overland Park, Kansas 66215-4816

Head of School: Dr. William P. Ford

General Information Coeducational day college-preparatory school, affiliated with Roman Catholic Church. Grades 9–12. Founded: 1988. Setting: suburban. Nearest major city is Kansas City, MO. 44-acre campus. 2 buildings on campus. Approved or accredited by National Catholic Education Association, North Central Association of

Colleges and Schools, and Kansas Department of Education. Total enrollment: 900. Upper school average class size: 24. Upper school faculty-student ratio: 1:14. There are 180 required school days per year for Upper School students. Upper School students typically attend 5 days per week. The average school day consists of 7 hours.

Upper School Student Profile Grade 9: 258 students (129 boys, 129 girls); Grade 10: 260 students (135 boys, 125 girls); Grade 11: 215 students (95 boys, 120 girls); Grade 12: 228 students (113 boys, 115 girls). 97% of students are Roman Catholic.

Faculty School total: 68. In upper school: 32 men, 36 women; 64 have advanced degrees.

Graduation Requirements Arts and fine arts (art, music, dance, drama), computer technologies, electives, English, Latin, mathematics, modern languages, physical education (includes health), science, social studies (includes history), speech, theology, service (one fourth credit each of 4 years).

Special Academic Programs Advanced Placement exam preparation; honors section; study at local college for college credit; academic accommodation for the gifted; remedial reading and/or remedial writing; remedial math.

College Admission Counseling 228 students graduated in 2016; 226 went to college, including Benedictine College; Kansas State University; The University of Kansas; University of Arkansas; University of Missouri; University of Notre Dame. Other: 2 entered military service. Mean SAT critical reading: 619, mean SAT math: 638, mean SAT writing: 603, mean composite ACT: 25. 37% scored over 26 on composite ACT.

Student Life Upper grades have uniform requirement, student council. Discipline rests primarily with faculty. Attendance at religious services is required.

Summer Programs Remediation, advancement, sports, computer instruction programs offered; session focuses on sports camps and selected academic coursework; held on campus; accepts boys and girls; open to students from other schools.

Tuition and Aid Day student tuition: $9000–$9900. Tuition installment plan (SMART Tuition Payment Plan). Tuition reduction for siblings, merit scholarship grants, need-based scholarship grants available. In 2016–17, 30% of upper-school students received aid. Total amount of financial aid awarded in 2016–17: $1,100,000.

Admissions Traditional secondary-level entrance grade is 9. High School Placement Test required. Deadline for receipt of application materials: none. Application fee required: $200. Interview required.

Athletics Interscholastic: baseball (boys), basketball (b,g), bowling (b,g), cross-country running (b,g), dance team (g), diving (b,g), football (b,g), golf (b,g), soccer (b,g), softball (g), swimming and diving (b,g), tennis (b,g), track and field (b,g), volleyball (g), wrestling (b); intramural: lacrosse (b,g), rugby (b); coed interscholastic: cheering; coed intramural: table tennis, ultimate Frisbee. 3 PE instructors, 1 athletic trainer.

Computers Computers are regularly used in all academic, computer applications, desktop publishing, programming, video film production, Web site design classes. Computer network features include on-campus library services, Internet access, wireless campus network, computer labs and laptop carts. Student e-mail accounts and computer access in designated common areas are available to students. Students grades are available online. The school has a published electronic and media policy.

Contact Mrs. Diane Pyle, Director of Admissions. 913-319-2423. Fax: 913-345-2319. E-mail: dpyle@stasaints.net. Website: www.stasaints.net

ST. THOMAS AQUINAS HIGH SCHOOL

197 Dover Point Road
Dover, New Hampshire 03820

Head of School: Mr. Kevin Collins

General Information Coeducational day college-preparatory school, affiliated with Roman Catholic Church. Grades 9–12. Founded: 1960. Setting: small town. Nearest major city is Boston, MA. 11-acre campus. 2 buildings on campus. Approved or accredited by New England Association of Schools and Colleges and New Hampshire Department of Education. Total enrollment: 526. Upper school average class size: 17. Upper school faculty-student ratio: 1:13. There are 186 required school days per year for Upper School students. Upper School students typically attend 5 days per week. The average school day consists of 6 hours and 25 minutes.

Subjects Offered 3-dimensional design, advanced math, algebra, American history-AP, American literature-AP, anatomy and physiology, biology, biology-AP, biotechnology, British literature, British literature (honors), calculus, calculus-AP, chemistry, chorus, Christian ethics, civics, concert band, drawing, economics, English, English language-AP, English literature-AP, environmental science-AP, French, geometry, government-AP, health education, honors algebra, honors English, honors geometry, honors U.S. history, international relations, introduction to technology, jazz band, Latin, marine biology, math applications, media arts, music appreciation, music theory, painting, physics, pre-calculus, psychology, public speaking, science, scripture, sculpture, social justice, sociology, Spanish, statistics-AP, studio art, theology, trigonometry, U.S. government and politics-AP, U.S. history, U.S. history-AP, Western civilization, world religions.

Graduation Requirements Arts and fine arts (art, music, dance, drama), Christian ethics, electives, English, foreign language, freshman seminar, mathematics, prayer/spirituality, science, scripture, social justice, social studies (includes history), theology, world religions, 40 hour community service requirement.

Special Academic Programs Advanced Placement exam preparation; honors section; independent study; ESL.

College Admission Counseling 130 students graduated in 2016; 123 went to college, including Emmanuel College; Endicott College; Husson University; Saint Michael's College; University of New Hampshire; Worcester Polytechnic Institute. Other: 2 entered military service, 1 entered a postgraduate year, 4 had other specific plans. Mean SAT critical reading: 583, mean SAT math: 560, mean SAT writing: 569, mean composite ACT: 25.

Student Life Upper grades have specified standards of dress, student council. Discipline rests with faculty. Attendance at religious services is required.

Tuition and Aid Day student tuition: $13,175. Tuition installment plan (annual, semiannual, and 10-month payment plans). Need-based scholarship grants available. In 2016–17, 33% of upper-school students received aid.

Admissions Traditional secondary-level entrance grade is 9. Scholastic Testing Service High School Placement Test or SSAT required. Deadline for receipt of application materials: December 19. Application fee required: $40.

Athletics Interscholastic: baseball (boys), basketball (b,g), cross-country running (b,g), field hockey (g), football (b), golf (b,g), ice hockey (b,g), lacrosse (b,g), skiing (downhill) (b,g), soccer (b,g), softball (g), swimming and diving (b,g), tennis (b,g), track and field (b,g), volleyball (g), winter (indoor) track (b,g); intramural: dance team (g). 51 coaches, 1 athletic trainer.

Computers Computers are regularly used in animation, design, introduction to technology, media arts, programming classes. Computer network features include on-campus library services, Internet access, wireless campus network. Student e-mail accounts and computer access in designated common areas are available to students. Students grades are available online.

Contact Mr. Keith Adams, Director of Admissions. 603-742-3206. Fax: 603-749-7822. E-mail: kadams@stalux.org. Website: www.stalux.org

ST. THOMAS CHOIR SCHOOL

New York, New York
See Junior Boarding Schools section.

SAINT THOMAS MORE CATHOLIC HIGH SCHOOL

450 East Farrel Road
Lafayette, Louisiana 70508

Head of School: Mrs. Kelley Leger

General Information Coeducational day college-preparatory school, affiliated with Roman Catholic Church. Grades 9–12. Founded: 1982. Setting: suburban. Nearest major city is Baton Rouge. 45-acre campus. 1 building on campus. Approved or accredited by National Catholic Education Association, Southern Association of Colleges and Schools, and Louisiana Department of Education. Endowment: $3.4 million. Total enrollment: 1,050. Upper school average class size: 24. Upper school faculty-student ratio: 1:12. There are 178 required school days per year for Upper School students. Upper School students typically attend 5 days per week. The average school day consists of 7 hours.

Upper School Student Profile Grade 9: 306 students (151 boys, 155 girls); Grade 10: 262 students (139 boys, 123 girls); Grade 11: 249 students (125 boys, 124 girls); Grade 12: 246 students (122 boys, 124 girls). 93% of students are Roman Catholic.

Faculty School total: 93. In upper school: 31 men, 62 women; 44 have advanced degrees.

Subjects Offered ACT preparation, advanced chemistry, advanced math, Advanced Placement courses, advanced studio art-AP, algebra, American history, anatomy and physiology, art, athletics, band, biology, business, calculus-AP, campus ministry, chemistry, chemistry-AP, chorus, civics/free enterprise, computer literacy, computer multimedia, computer science, computer skills, creative writing, debate, desktop publishing, drama, engineering, English, English language and composition-AP, English literature and composition-AP, environmental science, European history-AP, fitness, French, geography, geometry, health, honors algebra, honors English, honors U.S. history, honors world history, independent study, kinesiology, Latin, mathematics, newspaper, physical education, physical science, physics, play production, pre-calculus, probability and statistics, psychology, psychology-AP, public speaking, religion, sociology, Spanish, speech, speech and debate, studio art-AP, study skills, theater, trigonometry, U.S. government and politics-AP, U.S. history-AP, Web site design, weight training, world history, yearbook.

Graduation Requirements Arts and fine arts (art, music, dance, drama), business applications, English, French, mathematics, physical education (includes health), religion (includes Bible studies and theology), science, social studies (includes history), Spanish, world history.

Special Academic Programs 10 Advanced Placement exams for which test preparation is offered; honors section; independent study; study at local college for college credit; academic accommodation for the gifted; remedial reading and/or remedial writing; remedial math.

College Admission Counseling 265 students graduated in 2016; 262 went to college, including Louisiana State University and Agricultural & Mechanical College; Texas Christian University; Tulane University; University of Louisiana at Lafayette; University of Mississippi. Other: 2 went to work, 1 entered a postgraduate year. Median composite ACT: 24. 30% scored over 26 on composite ACT.

Student Life Upper grades have uniform requirement, student council, honor system. Discipline rests primarily with faculty. Attendance at religious services is required.

Tuition and Aid Day student tuition: $7437–$7637. Tuition installment plan (FACTS Tuition Payment Plan, monthly payment plans, individually arranged payment plans). Merit scholarship grants, need-based scholarship grants, paying campus jobs available. In 2016–17, 5% of upper-school students received aid; total upper-school merit-scholarship money awarded: $98,000. Total amount of financial aid awarded in 2016–17: $100,000.

Admissions Traditional secondary-level entrance grade is 9. For fall 2016, 380 students applied for upper-level admission, 339 were accepted, 329 enrolled. Achievement tests, ACT-Explore, any standardized test, Explore, High School Placement Test, latest standardized score from previous school and standardized test scores required. Deadline for receipt of application materials: none. No application fee required.

Athletics Interscholastic: aquatics (boys, girls), baseball (b), basketball (b,g), bowling (b,g), cheering (g), cross-country running (b,g), dance squad (g), dance team (g), football (b), golf (b), gymnastics (g), indoor track (b,g), indoor track & field (b,g), physical training (b,g), soccer (b,g), softball (g), strength & conditioning (b,g), tennis (b,g), track and field (b,g), volleyball (g), weight lifting (b,g), weight training (b,g), winter (indoor) track (b,g), wrestling (b); intramural: flag football (b,g), lacrosse (b); coed interscholastic: fishing, Special Olympics. 5 PE instructors, 5 coaches.

Computers Computers are regularly used in all academic, library classes. Computer network features include on-campus library services, online commercial services, Internet access, wireless campus network, Internet filtering or blocking technology, computer access in the library before and after school and during lunch. Campus intranet, student e-mail accounts, and computer access in designated common areas are available to students. Students grades are available online. The school has a published electronic and media policy.

Contact Mrs. Robyn Alfonso, Assistant Director of Admissions. 337-988-7779. Fax: 337-988-2911. E-mail: robyn.alfonso@stmcougars.net. Website: www.stmcougars.net

ST. TIMOTHY'S SCHOOL

8400 Greenspring Avenue
Stevenson, Maryland 21153

Head of School: Randy S. Stevens

General Information Girls' boarding and day college-preparatory, arts, and International Baccalaureate school, affiliated with Episcopal Church. Grades 9–12. Founded: 1882. Setting: suburban. Nearest major city is Baltimore. Students are housed in single-sex dormitories. 145 acre campus. 24 buildings on campus. Approved or accredited by Association of Independent Maryland Schools, International Baccalaureate Organization, Middle States Association of Colleges and Schools, National Association of Episcopal Schools, The Association of Boarding Schools, and Maryland Department of Education. Member of National Association of Independent Schools and Secondary School Admission Test Board. Endowment: $10 million. Total enrollment: 199. Upper school average class size: 12. Upper school faculty-student ratio: 1:6. There are 175 required school days per year for Upper School students. Upper School students typically attend 5 days per week. The average school day consists of 7 hours.

Upper School Student Profile Grade 9: 40 students (40 girls); Grade 10: 52 students (52 girls); Grade 11: 57 students (57 girls); Grade 12: 50 students (50 girls). 69% of students are boarding students. 37% are state residents. 20 states are represented in upper school student body. 31% are international students. International students from China, Germany, Ghana, Japan, Mexico, and Nigeria; 21 other countries represented in student body.

Faculty School total: 27. In upper school: 11 men, 15 women; 17 have advanced degrees; 22 reside on campus.

Subjects Offered Algebra, American literature, art, art history, bell choir, biology, British literature, calculus, chemistry, Chinese, choir, college counseling, comparative politics, creative writing, dance, drama, drama performance, drama workshop, economics, English, English composition, English literature, ESL, ethics, European history, fine arts, foreign language, French, geometry, history, integrated mathematics, International Baccalaureate courses, Mandarin, mathematics, modern dance, music, photography, physics, piano, SAT preparation, science, Spanish, U.S. history, world history, world literature, writing.

Graduation Requirements Arts and fine arts (art, music, dance, drama), English, foreign language, history, mathematics, physical education (includes health), science, Theory of Knowledge course, extended essay, Community, Action, and Service (CAS). Community service is required.

Special Academic Programs International Baccalaureate program; independent study; ESL (21 students enrolled).

College Admission Counseling 39 students graduated in 2015; all went to college, including Haverford College; Syracuse University; University of California, Los Angeles; University of Maryland, College Park; Wake Forest University.

Student Life Upper grades have uniform requirement, student council, honor system. Discipline rests equally with students and faculty. Attendance at religious services is required.

Tuition and Aid Day student tuition: $29,300; 7-day tuition and room/board: $51,800. Tuition installment plan (FACTS Tuition Payment Plan). Merit scholarship grants, need-based scholarship grants, need-based loans available. In 2015–16, 51% of upper-school students received aid; total upper-school merit-scholarship money awarded: $445,000. Total amount of financial aid awarded in 2015–16: $3,257,000.

Admissions Traditional secondary-level entrance grade is 9. For fall 2015, 229 students applied for upper-level admission, 121 were accepted, 65 enrolled. ISEE, SLEP for foreign students, SSAT or TOEFL required. Deadline for receipt of application materials: February 1. Application fee required: $50. Interview required.

Athletics Interscholastic: badminton, basketball, cross-country running, dressage, equestrian sports, field hockey, golf, horseback riding, ice hockey, indoor soccer, lacrosse, soccer, softball, squash, swimming and diving, tennis, volleyball; intramural: ballet, dance, dance squad, equestrian sports, horseback riding, modern dance, outdoor adventure, weight training, yoga. 8 coaches, 1 athletic trainer.

Computers Computers are regularly used in art, college planning, English, mathematics, publications, SAT preparation, science, yearbook classes. Computer network features include on-campus library services, online commercial services, Internet access, wireless campus network, Internet filtering or blocking technology. Student e-mail accounts are available to students. The school has a published electronic and media policy.

Contact Kimberly Coughlin, Director of Admissions. 410-486-7401. Fax: 410-486-1167. E-mail: kcoughlin@stt.org. Website: www.stt.org

SAINT URSULA ACADEMY

1339 East McMillan Street
Cincinnati, Ohio 45206

Head of School: Mr. Craig Maliborski

General Information Girls' day college-preparatory school, affiliated with Roman Catholic Church. Grades 9–12. Founded: 1910. Setting: urban. 10-acre campus. 6 buildings on campus. Approved or accredited by North Central Association of Colleges and Schools, Ohio Catholic Schools Accreditation Association (OCSAA), and Ohio Department of Education. Upper school average class size: 665. Upper school faculty-student ratio: 1:15.

Upper School Student Profile Grade 6: 665 students (665 girls). 90% of students are Roman Catholic.

Special Academic Programs Programs in English, mathematics for dyslexic students; special instructional classes for learning disabilities like ADHD and dyslexia.

College Admission Counseling 165 students graduated in 2016; all went to college.

Student Life Upper grades have uniform requirement, honor system. Attendance at religious services is required.

Tuition and Aid Day student tuition: $13,060. Tuition installment plan (FACTS Tuition Payment Plan). Merit scholarship grants, need-based scholarship grants, paying campus jobs available.

Admissions Traditional secondary-level entrance grade is 9. Deadline for receipt of application materials: November 19. No application fee required.

Computers Computer network features include on-campus library services, Internet access, wireless campus network, Internet filtering or blocking technology, one-to-one tablet PC program. Campus intranet and student e-mail accounts are available to students. Students grades are available online. The school has a published electronic and media policy.

Contact Ms. Michelle Dellecave, Director of Admissions. 513-961-3410 Ext. 183. Fax: 513-961-3856. E-mail: mdellecave@saintursula.org. Website: www.saintursula.org

SAINT URSULA ACADEMY

4025 Indian Road
Toledo, Ohio 43606

Head of School: Mrs. Mary Werner

General Information Girls' day college-preparatory, arts, business, religious studies, bilingual studies, technology, and college preparatory school, affiliated with Roman Catholic Church. Grades 6–12. Founded: 1854. Setting: suburban. 16-acre campus. 1 building on campus. Approved or accredited by National Catholic Education Association, North Central Association of Colleges and Schools, Ohio Catholic Schools Accreditation Association (OCSAA), and Ohio Department of Education. Total enrollment: 552. Upper school average class size: 17. Upper school faculty-student ratio: 1:10. There are 185 required school days per year for Upper School students. Upper School students typically attend 5 days per week. The average school day consists of 7 hours.

Upper School Student Profile Grade 6: 16 students (16 girls); Grade 7: 28 students (28 girls); Grade 8: 42 students (42 girls); Grade 9: 127 students (127 girls); Grade 10: 102 students (102 girls); Grade 11: 96 students (96 girls); Grade 12: 110 students (110 girls). 70% of students are Roman Catholic.

Faculty School total: 50. In upper school: 6 men, 44 women; 32 have advanced degrees.

Subjects Offered 3-dimensional art, accounting, ACT preparation, Advanced Placement courses, advanced studio art-AP, algebra, American government, American history, American history-AP, American literature, American literature-AP, anatomy, anatomy and physiology, art, art history-AP, art-AP, ballet, biology, biology-AP, British literature, British literature-AP, business law, calculus-AP, career exploration, Catholic belief and practice, ceramics, chemistry, chemistry-AP, choral music, choreography, chorus, church history, comparative government and politics-AP, comparative religion, composition-AP, computer applications, computer graphics, computer programming, computer science-AP, concert choir, dance, digital art, digital photography, drama, drawing, economics, electives, engineering, English language and composition-AP, English language-AP, English literature and composition-AP, English/composition-AP, fashion, female experience in America, film history, foreign language, French language-AP, geometry, government, government and politics-AP, graphic arts, health, history of the Catholic Church, honors algebra, honors English, honors geometry, honors world history, human geography - AP, instrumental music, Latin, Latin-AP, literature, literature and composition-AP, Mandarin, marketing, mathematics-AP, microeconomics, music, music theory-AP, New Testament, nutrition, orchestra, painting, personal finance, personal fitness, photography, physical education, physics, physiology, pre-calculus, printmaking, probability and statistics, psychology, psychology-AP, religion and culture, religious education, sculpture, single survival, social psychology, Spanish, Spanish language-AP, speech, statistics, statistics-AP, student publications, studio art-AP, symphonic band, theology, trigonometry, U.S. government and politics, U.S. government and politics-AP, U.S. history, U.S. history-AP, U.S. literature, United States government-AP, vocal music, women's health, women's studies, world wide web design, yearbook.

Graduation Requirements Arts and fine arts (art, music, dance, drama), computers, English, foreign language, mathematics, physical education (includes health), science, social studies (includes history), theology, community service, career exploration experience.

Special Academic Programs 15 Advanced Placement exams for which test preparation is offered; honors section; study at local college for college credit.

College Admission Counseling 131 students graduated in 2016; all went to college, including Bowling Green State University; Miami University; The Ohio State University; The University of Toledo; University of Cincinnati; University of Dayton. Mean SAT critical reading: 600, mean SAT math: 583, mean SAT writing: 575, mean composite ACT: 24. 40% scored over 600 on SAT critical reading, 25% scored over 600 on SAT math, 58% scored over 600 on SAT writing, 37% scored over 26 on composite ACT.

Student Life Upper grades have uniform requirement, student council, honor system. Discipline rests primarily with faculty. Attendance at religious services is required.

Summer Programs Enrichment, advancement, sports, art/fine arts, computer instruction programs offered; session focuses on athletics and academics; held both on and off campus; held at golf course; accepts girls; open to students from other schools. 300 students usually enrolled. 2017 schedule: June 6 to July 29. Application deadline: June 1.

Tuition and Aid Day student tuition: $10,400. Tuition installment plan (SMART Tuition Payment Plan). Tuition reduction for siblings, merit scholarship grants, need-based scholarship grants, paying campus jobs available. In 2016–17, 75% of upper-school students received aid; total upper-school merit-scholarship money awarded: $200,000. Total amount of financial aid awarded in 2016–17: $1,420,000.

Admissions Traditional secondary-level entrance grade is 9. High School Placement Test or placement test required. Deadline for receipt of application materials: none. No application fee required.

Athletics Interscholastic: aerobics/dance, ballet, basketball, bowling, cheering, crew, cross-country running, dance, dance squad, dance team, diving, drill team, equestrian sports, fencing, golf, gymnastics, independent competitive sports, lacrosse, modern dance, physical fitness, physical training, rowing, soccer, softball, swimming and diving, tennis, track and field, volleyball, water polo, weight training; intramural: archery, broomball, cooperative games, flag football, horseback riding, volleyball. 2 PE instructors, 32 coaches, 1 athletic trainer.

Computers Computers are regularly used in all classes. Computer network features include on-campus library services, online commercial services, Internet access, wireless campus network, Internet filtering or blocking technology. Campus intranet, student e-mail accounts, and computer access in designated common areas are available to students. Students grades are available online. The school has a published electronic and media policy.

Contact Mrs. Nichole Flores, Principal. 419-531-1693. Fax: 419-531-4575. E-mail: nflores@toledosua.org. Website: www.toledosua.org

SAINT VINCENT-SAINT MARY HIGH SCHOOL

15 North Maple Street
Akron, Ohio 44303-2394

Head of School: Mr. Thomas M. Carone

General Information Coeducational day college-preparatory, arts, business, vocational, religious studies, technology, and World Languages school, affiliated with Roman Catholic Church. Grades 9–12. Founded: 1972. Setting: urban. 10-acre campus. 4 buildings on campus. Approved or accredited by North Central Association of Colleges and Schools, Ohio Catholic Schools Accreditation Association (OCSAA), and Ohio Department of Education. Endowment: $11 million. Total enrollment: 686. Upper school average class size: 25. Upper school faculty-student ratio: 1:12. There are 172

required school days per year for Upper School students. Upper School students typically attend 5 days per week. The average school day consists of 7 hours.

Upper School Student Profile Grade 9: 130 students (68 boys, 62 girls); Grade 10: 190 students (105 boys, 85 girls); Grade 11: 156 students (76 boys, 80 girls); Grade 12: 177 students (96 boys, 81 girls). 66% of students are Roman Catholic.

Faculty School total: 50. In upper school: 20 men, 30 women; 37 have advanced degrees.

Subjects Offered British literature.

Graduation Requirements 100 Christian service hours.

Special Academic Programs Advanced Placement exam preparation; honors section; independent study; study at local college for college credit; study abroad; academic accommodation for the gifted; remedial reading and/or remedial writing; remedial math; programs in English, mathematics, general development for dyslexic students; special instructional classes for deaf students, blind students, vocational classes are offered for those with severe learning challenges. Fundamental classes are offered for those with mild learning challenges.

College Admission Counseling 151 students graduated in 2016; 146 went to college, including Bowling Green State University; Kent State University; Ohio University; The Ohio State University; The University of Akron; University of Dayton. Other: 3 went to work, 2 entered military service. Median combined SAT: 1670, median composite ACT: 24. 40% scored over 1800 on combined SAT, 32% scored over 26 on composite ACT.

Student Life Upper grades have uniform requirement, student council, honor system. Discipline rests primarily with faculty. Attendance at religious services is required.

Summer Programs Enrichment, sports programs offered; session focuses on Physical Education and Elective Courses; held both on and off campus; accepts boys and girls; not open to students from other schools. 180 students usually enrolled. 2017 schedule: June 5 to June 23. Application deadline: June 12.

Tuition and Aid Day student tuition: $10,150. Tuition installment plan (FACTS Tuition Payment Plan, monthly payment plans, Quarterly payment plan, Bi-annual payment plan). Tuition reduction for siblings, merit scholarship grants, need-based scholarship grants, State of Ohio Scholarships/Stipends, including: The EdChoice Scholarship, The Jon Peterson Special Needs Scholarship,, and the State of Ohio Autism Scholarship available. In 2016–17, 50% of upper-school students received aid; total upper-school merit-scholarship money awarded: $353,800. Total amount of financial aid awarded in 2016–17: $809,720.

Admissions Traditional secondary-level entrance grade is 9. For fall 2016, 987 students applied for upper-level admission, 790 were accepted, 653 enrolled. Deadline for receipt of application materials: none. No application fee required.

Athletics Interscholastic: baseball (boys), basketball (b,g), bowling (b,g), cross-country running (b,g), football (b), golf (b,g), gymnastics (g), lacrosse (b,g), soccer (b,g), softball (g), tennis (b,g), track and field (b,g), volleyball (b,g), winter (indoor) track (b,g), wrestling (b); coed interscholastic: cheering; coed intramural: dance, skiing (downhill), strength & conditioning, weight training. 2 PE instructors, 17 coaches, 2 athletic trainers.

Computers Computer network features include on-campus library services, online commercial services, internet access, wireless campus network, internet filtering or blocking technology, homework assignments are available online. All students are provided with a school-issued Chromebook. Fully digital library resources available including research databases and e-reference books, etc. Campus intranet, student e-mail accounts, and computer access in designated common areas are available to students. Students grades are available online. The school has a published electronic and media policy.

Contact Mrs. Joanne Wiseman, Director of Admissions. 330-253-9113 Ext. 115. Fax: 330-996-0000. E-mail: jwiseman@stvm.com. Website: www.stvm.com

SAINT XAVIER HIGH SCHOOL

1609 Poplar Level Road
Louisville, Kentucky 40217

Head of School: Dr. Perry Sangalli

General Information Boys' day college-preparatory, arts, business, religious studies, and technology school, affiliated with Roman Catholic Church. Grades 9–12. Founded: 1864. Setting: urban. 54-acre campus. 9 buildings on campus. Approved or accredited by Southern Association of Colleges and Schools, Southern Association of Independent Schools, and Kentucky Department of Education. Member of National Association of Independent Schools. Endowment: $21.1 million. Total enrollment: 1,334. Upper school average class size: 18. Upper school faculty-student ratio: 1:11. There are 170 required school days per year for Upper School students. Upper School students typically attend 5 days per week. The average school day consists of 5 hours and 15 minutes.

Upper School Student Profile Grade 9: 349 students (349 boys); Grade 10: 301 students (301 boys); Grade 11: 360 students (360 boys); Grade 12: 334 students (334 boys). 84% of students are Roman Catholic.

Faculty School total: 120. In upper school: 92 men, 28 women; 114 have advanced degrees.

Subjects Offered Accounting, acting, Advanced Placement courses, algebra, American government, anatomy and physiology, band, biology, business law, ceramics, chemistry, chorus, computer applications, computer programming, computer-aided design, creative writing, desktop publishing, drafting, economics, English, environmental science, fitness, French, geometry, German, global issues, health, humanities, journalism, keyboarding, mathematics, mechanical drawing, music, music history, music theory, philosophy, photography, physical education, physics, probability and statistics, psychology, reading, sculpture, sociology, Spanish, speech, theology, trigonometry, U.S. history, world civilizations, world geography, yearbook.

Graduation Requirements Arts and fine arts (art, music, dance, drama), electives, English, foreign language, mathematics, physical education (includes health), science, social studies (includes history), theology, U.S. history.

Special Academic Programs Advanced Placement exam preparation; honors section; independent study; study at local college for college credit; academic accommodation for the gifted, the musically talented, and the artistically talented; remedial reading and/or remedial writing; remedial math; programs in English, mathematics, general development for dyslexic students; special instructional classes for students with Attention Deficit Disorder, Attention Deficit Hyperactivity Disorder, dyslexia, central auditory processing disorder.

College Admission Counseling 311 students graduated in 2016; 309 went to college, including Bellarmine University; Miami University; University of Kentucky; University of Louisville; Western Kentucky University; Xavier University. Other: 2 entered military service. Mean SAT critical reading: 643, mean SAT math: 642, mean SAT writing: 638, mean combined SAT: 1923, mean composite ACT: 26.

Student Life Upper grades have specified standards of dress, student council. Discipline rests primarily with faculty. Attendance at religious services is required.

Tuition and Aid Tuition installment plan (FACTS Tuition Payment Plan). Merit scholarship grants, need-based scholarship grants, paying campus jobs available. In 2016–17, 34% of upper-school students received aid; total upper-school merit-scholarship money awarded: $200,000. Total amount of financial aid awarded in 2016–17: $2,100,000.

Admissions Traditional secondary-level entrance grade is 9. For fall 2016, 379 students applied for upper-level admission, 2 were accepted, 349 enrolled. Placement test required. Deadline for receipt of application materials: March 1. Application fee required: $100. On-campus interview recommended.

Athletics Interscholastic: aquatics, archery, baseball, basketball, bowling, cross-country running, diving, fishing, fitness, football, golf, hockey, ice hockey, indoor track & field, lacrosse, power lifting, running, soccer, strength & conditioning, swimming and diving, tennis, track and field, volleyball, water polo, weight lifting, weight training, wrestling; intramural: alpine skiing, backpacking, basketball, bicycling, billiards, bowling, cooperative games, fishing, flag football, football, Frisbee, golf, kickball, mountain biking, outdoor activities, outdoor adventure, outdoor education, outdoor recreation, scuba diving, skiing (downhill), snowboarding, soccer, table tennis, tennis, touch football, ultimate Frisbee, weight training. 3 PE instructors, 63 coaches, 1 athletic trainer.

Computers Computers are regularly used in all classes. Computer network features include on-campus library services, online commercial services, Internet access, wireless campus network, Internet filtering or blocking technology, one-to-one. Campus intranet, student e-mail accounts, and computer access in designated common areas are available to students. Students grades are available online. The school has a published electronic and media policy.

Contact Mr. Curt White, Director of Admissions. 502-637-2145. Fax: 502-634-2171. E-mail: cwhite@saintx.com. Website: www.saintx.com

SAINT XAVIER HIGH SCHOOL

600 North Bend Road
Cincinnati, Ohio 45224

Head of School: Rev. Timothy A. Howe, SJ

General Information Boys' day college-preparatory, arts, religious studies, technology, and service learning school, affiliated with Roman Catholic Church. Grades 9–12. Founded: 1831. Setting: suburban. 114-acre campus. 1 building on campus. Approved or accredited by Jesuit Secondary Education Association, North Central Association of Colleges and Schools, Ohio Catholic Schools Accreditation Association (OCSAA), and Ohio Department of Education. Endowment: $45 million. Total enrollment: 1,600. Upper school average class size: 25. Upper school faculty-student ratio: 1:15. There are 185 required school days per year for Upper School students. Upper School students typically attend 5 days per week. The average school day consists of 7 hours and 5 minutes.

Upper School Student Profile Grade 9: 411 students (411 boys); Grade 10: 409 students (409 boys); Grade 11: 382 students (382 boys); Grade 12: 392 students (392 boys). 80% of students are Roman Catholic.

Faculty School total: 132. In upper school: 88 men, 44 women; 88 have advanced degrees.

Subjects Offered Arts, biology, chemistry, Chinese, computer science, English, fine arts, French, German, Greek, health, Latin, mathematics, physical education, physics, religion, science, social studies, Spanish.

Graduation Requirements Arts and fine arts (art, music, dance, drama), computer science, English, foreign language, forensics, mathematics, physical education (includes health), religion (includes Bible studies and theology), science, social studies (includes history).

Special Academic Programs Advanced Placement exam preparation; independent study; term-away projects; study at local college for college credit.

College Admission Counseling 378 students graduated in 2015; 377 went to college, including Miami University; Saint Louis University; The Ohio State University; University of Cincinnati; University of Notre Dame; Xavier University. Other: 1 went to work. Median SAT critical reading: 630, median SAT math: 640, median composite ACT: 29. 64% scored over 600 on SAT critical reading, 72% scored over 600 on SAT math, 60% scored over 26 on composite ACT.

Student Life Upper grades have specified standards of dress, student council. Discipline rests primarily with faculty. Attendance at religious services is required.

Tuition and Aid Day student tuition: $13,870. Tuition installment plan (FACTS Tuition Payment Plan, monthly payment plans, individually arranged payment plans). Merit scholarship grants, need-based scholarship grants, paying campus jobs available. In 2015–16, 40% of upper-school students received aid; total upper-school merit-scholarship money awarded: $50,000. Total amount of financial aid awarded in 2015–16: $3,800,000.

Admissions Traditional secondary-level entrance grade is 9. For fall 2015, 800 students applied for upper-level admission, 450 were accepted, 390 enrolled. High School Placement Test required. Deadline for receipt of application materials: December 1. Application fee required: $30.

Athletics Interscholastic: baseball, basketball, bowling, cheering, crew, cross-country running, diving, football, golf, ice hockey, lacrosse, rugby, soccer, swimming and diving, tennis, track and field, volleyball, water polo, weight training, wrestling; intramural: basketball, football, golf, soccer, table tennis, tennis, volleyball. 3 PE instructors, 2 athletic trainers.

Computers Computers are regularly used in art, design, drawing and design, foreign language, graphic arts, graphic design, graphics, keyboarding, lab/keyboard, language development, library, programming, research skills, science classes. Computer network features include on-campus library services, online commercial services, Internet access, wireless campus network, Internet filtering or blocking technology. Campus intranet, student e-mail accounts, and computer access in designated common areas are available to students. Students grades are available online. The school has a published electronic and media policy.

Contact Mr. Roderick D. Hinton, Assistant Vice President and Director of Enrollment. 513-761-7815 Ext. 106. Fax: 513-761-3811. E-mail: rhinton@stxavier.org. Website: www.stxavier.org

SALEM ACADEMY

500 Salem Avenue
Winston-Salem, North Carolina 27101-0578

Head of School: Mrs. Lisa Pence

General Information Girls' boarding and day college-preparatory school, affiliated with Moravian Church. Grades 9–12. Founded: 1772. Setting: urban. Students are housed in single-sex dormitories. 60-acre campus. 4 buildings on campus. Approved or accredited by Southern Association of Colleges and Schools, The Association of Boarding Schools, and North Carolina Department of Education. Member of National Association of Independent Schools and Secondary School Admission Test Board. Endowment: $7 million. Total enrollment: 160. Upper school average class size: 10. Upper school faculty-student ratio: 1:7. There are 172 required school days per year for Upper School students. Upper School students typically attend 5 days per week. The average school day consists of 7 hours and 30 minutes.

Upper School Student Profile Grade 9: 31 students (31 girls); Grade 10: 39 students (39 girls); Grade 11: 44 students (44 girls), Grade 12: 38 students (38 girls). 60% of students are boarding students. 30% are state residents. 11 states are represented in upper school student body. 33% are international students. International students from China, Ghana, and Republic of Moldova; 3 other countries represented in student body. 4% of students are Moravian.

Faculty School total: 24. In upper school: 2 men, 22 women; 13 have advanced degrees; 3 reside on campus.

Subjects Offered Algebra, American history, art, biology, calculus, chemistry, dance, drama, economics, English, European history, fine arts, French, geometry, government/civics, Latin, mathematics, music, physical education, physics, pre-calculus, psychology, religion, science, social sciences, social studies, Spanish, theater, trigonometry, world history.

Graduation Requirements Arts and fine arts (art, music, dance, drama), English, foreign language, mathematics, physical education (includes health), religion (includes Bible studies and theology), science, social sciences, social studies (includes history), completion of January term.

Special Academic Programs 8 Advanced Placement exams for which test preparation is offered; honors section; term-away projects; study at local college for college credit; study abroad; programs in general development for dyslexic students; ESL (8 students enrolled).

College Admission Counseling 36 students graduated in 2016; all went to college, including New York University; Penn State University Park; The University of North Carolina at Chapel Hill; The University of North Carolina at Greensboro. Mean SAT critical reading: 575, mean SAT math: 631, mean SAT writing: 598, mean combined SAT: 1876.

Student Life Upper grades have specified standards of dress, student council, honor system. Discipline rests equally with students and faculty.

Tuition and Aid Day student tuition: $19,940; 7-day tuition and room/board: $40,490. Tuition installment plan (Key Tuition Payment Plan, monthly payment plans). Merit scholarship grants, need-based scholarship grants available. In 2016–17, 45% of upper-school students received aid; total upper-school merit-scholarship money awarded: $123,100. Total amount of financial aid awarded in 2016–17: $1,033,794.

Admissions Traditional secondary-level entrance grade is 9. For fall 2016, 160 students applied for upper-level admission, 85 were accepted, 65 enrolled. ACT, PSAT, SAT, SSAT or TOEFL required. Deadline for receipt of application materials: none. Application fee required: $50. Interview required.

Athletics Interscholastic: basketball, cross-country running, fencing, field hockey, golf, soccer, softball, swimming and diving, tennis, track and field, volleyball; intramural: aerobics/dance, archery, badminton, dance, fitness, flag football, floor hockey, golf, horseback riding, indoor hockey, indoor soccer, self defense. 2 PE instructors, 15 coaches, 1 athletic trainer.

Computers Computers are regularly used in all academic classes. Computer network features include on-campus library services, online commercial services, Internet access, wireless campus network. Student e-mail accounts and computer access in designated common areas are available to students. Students grades are available online.

Contact Jessica Rogers, Director of Admissions. 336-721-2643. Fax: 336-917-5340. E-mail: academy@salem.edu. Website: www.salemacademy.com

SALEM ACADEMY

942 Lancaster Drive NE
Salem, Oregon 97301

Head of School: Micah Powers

General Information Coeducational day college-preparatory, general academic, arts, and religious studies school, affiliated with Protestant-Evangelical faith. Grades K–12. Founded: 1945. Setting: suburban. 34-acre campus. 6 buildings on campus. Approved or accredited by Association of Christian Schools International and Oregon Department of Education. Total enrollment: 646. Upper school average class size: 20. Upper school faculty-student ratio: 1:14. Upper School students typically attend 5 days per week. The average school day consists of 7 hours and 15 minutes.

Upper School Student Profile 90% of students are Protestant-Evangelical faith.

Faculty School total: 51. In upper school: 11 men, 14 women; 16 have advanced degrees.

Subjects Offered Advanced chemistry, Advanced Placement courses, algebra, American history, American literature, American sign language, anatomy and physiology, art, astronomy, athletics, baseball, Bible, Bible studies, biology, business, calculus, ceramics, cheerleading, chemistry, choir, college writing, computer programming, computer science, drama, drama performance, economics, English, English literature, English literature and composition-AP, English literature-AP, ESL, foods, geography, geometry, government/civics, grammar, health, history, history-AP, home economics, honors English, industrial arts, mathematics, music, physical education, physical science, physics, psychology, religion, SAT preparation, science, social sciences, social studies, softball, Spanish, speech, track and field, typing, U.S. history-AP, vocal music, volleyball, weight training, world history, world literature, writing.

Graduation Requirements English, foreign language, mathematics, physical education (includes health), religion (includes Bible studies and theology), science, social sciences, social studies (includes history), one credit in biblical studies for each year attended, 10 hours of community service per year (high school).

Special Academic Programs 7 Advanced Placement exams for which test preparation is offered; honors section; independent study; study at local college for college credit; ESL (10 students enrolled).

College Admission Counseling 54 students graduated in 2016; 49 went to college, including Chemeketa Community College; Corban University; George Fox University; Grand Canyon University; Oregon State University; University of Oregon. Other: 1 entered military service, 4 had other specific plans. Mean SAT critical reading: 519, mean SAT math: 494, mean SAT writing: 490, mean combined SAT: 1498, mean composite ACT: 25.

Student Life Upper grades have specified standards of dress, student council, honor system. Discipline rests primarily with faculty.

Tuition and Aid Day student tuition: $7205–$7515. Tuition installment plan (FACTS Tuition Payment Plan). Tuition reduction for siblings, need-based scholarship grants available. In 2016–17, 33% of upper-school students received aid.

Admissions Traditional secondary-level entrance grade is 9. For fall 2016, 32 students applied for upper-level admission, 28 were accepted, 28 enrolled. Math Placement Exam, Reading for Understanding, school's own exam and writing sample required. Deadline for receipt of application materials: none. Application fee required: $50. Interview required.

Athletics Interscholastic: baseball (boys), basketball (b,g), cheering (g), cross-country running (b,g), football (b), golf (b,g), soccer (b,g), softball (g), track and field (b,g),

volleyball (g); coed interscholastic: equestrian sports, swimming and diving; coed intramural: jump rope, racquetball. 2 PE instructors, 36 coaches.

Computers Computers are regularly used in Bible studies, computer applications, English, history, photography, photojournalism, yearbook classes. Computer network features include on-campus library services, Internet access, wireless campus network, Internet filtering or blocking technology. Students grades are available online. The school has a published electronic and media policy.

Contact Mrs. Stephanie Jorgensen, Director of Admissions. 503-378-1219. Fax: 503-375-3522. E-mail: sjorgensen@salemacademy.org. Website: www.salemacademy.org

SALESIANUM SCHOOL

1801 North Broom Street
Wilmington, Delaware 19802-3891

Head of School: Rev. J. Christian Beretta, OSFS

General Information Boys' day college-preparatory school, affiliated with Roman Catholic Church. Grades 9–12. Founded: 1903. Setting: suburban. 22-acre campus. 1 building on campus. Approved or accredited by Middle States Association of Colleges and Schools and Delaware Department of Education. Total enrollment: 1,035. Upper school average class size: 20. Upper school faculty-student ratio: 1:12.

Upper School Student Profile Grade 9: 264 students (264 boys); Grade 10: 272 students (272 boys); Grade 11: 260 students (260 boys); Grade 12: 239 students (239 boys). 86% of students are Roman Catholic.

Faculty School total: 92. In upper school: 67 men, 25 women; 53 have advanced degrees.

Subjects Offered Algebra, American history, American history-AP, American literature, anatomy, architecture, art, art-AP, band, biology, biology-AP, business, business law, calculus, calculus-AP, career/college preparation, chemistry, chemistry-AP, chorus, community service, computer applications, computer programming, computer science, computer science-AP, drafting, driver education, ecology, economics, English, English literature, English-AP, ensembles, environmental science-AP, European history-AP, fine arts, foreign policy, French, French-AP, geometry, government/civics, health, journalism, Latin, law, literature, Mandarin, marketing, mathematics, physical education, physics, physics-AP, pre-calculus, psychology, psychology-AP, religion, science, social sciences, social studies, Spanish, Spanish-AP, statistics, statistics-AP, television, trigonometry, U.S. government and politics-AP, video, Western literature, world affairs, world history, world literature.

Graduation Requirements Arts and fine arts (art, music, dance, drama), college planning, computer science, driver education, electives, English, foreign language, mathematics, physical education (includes health), religion (includes Bible studies and theology), science, social sciences, social studies (includes history). Community service is required.

Special Academic Programs Advanced Placement exam preparation; honors section; independent study; study at local college for college credit; domestic exchange program (with Ursuline Academy, Padua Academy); academic accommodation for the gifted; remedial reading and/or remedial writing; remedial math.

College Admission Counseling 238 students graduated in 2015; 236 went to college, including Penn State University Park; Saint Joseph's University; University of Delaware; University of South Carolina; Villanova University. Other: 1 went to work, 1 entered military service.

Student Life Upper grades have specified standards of dress, student council. Discipline rests primarily with faculty. Attendance at religious services is required.

Tuition and Aid Day student tuition: $14,200. Tuition installment plan (Insured Tuition Payment Plan, monthly payment plans, semester payment plan, annual payment plan, monthly payment plan). Merit scholarship grants, need-based scholarship grants, paying campus jobs available. In 2015–16, 30% of upper-school students received aid; total upper-school merit-scholarship money awarded: $375,000. Total amount of financial aid awarded in 2015–16: $1,000,000.

Admissions Traditional secondary-level entrance grade is 9. Scholastic Testing Service High School Placement Test required. Deadline for receipt of application materials: November 20. Application fee required: $65. Interview recommended.

Athletics Interscholastic: baseball, basketball, cross-country running, diving, football, golf, ice hockey, lacrosse, rugby, soccer, swimming and diving, tennis, track and field, volleyball, wrestling; intramural: basketball, bowling, flag football, Frisbee, lacrosse, roller hockey, rowing, skateboarding, tennis, ultimate Frisbee, weight lifting. 4 PE instructors, 58 coaches, 1 athletic trainer.

Computers Computers are regularly used in architecture, college planning, drafting, English, foreign language, mathematics, science, social studies classes. Computer network features include on-campus library services, online commercial services, Internet access, wireless campus network, Internet filtering or blocking technology. Campus intranet, student e-mail accounts, and computer access in designated common areas are available to students. Students grades are available online. The school has a published electronic and media policy.

Contact Mrs. Barbara Palena, Admissions Associate. 302-654-2495 Ext. 148. Fax: 302-654-7767. E-mail: bpalena@salesianum.org. Website: www.salesianum.org

SALPOINTE CATHOLIC HIGH SCHOOL

1545 East Copper Street
Tucson, Arizona 85719-3199

Head of School: Mrs. Kay Sullivan

General Information Coeducational day college-preparatory, humanities, and STEM school, affiliated with Roman Catholic Church. Grades 9–12. Founded: 1950. Setting: urban. 40-acre campus. 12 buildings on campus. Approved or accredited by North Central Association of Colleges and Schools, Western Catholic Education Association, and Arizona Department of Education. Endowment: $3.9 million. Total enrollment: 1,093. Upper school average class size: 24. Upper school faculty-student ratio: 1:15. There are 180 required school days per year for Upper School students. Upper School students typically attend 5 days per week. The average school day consists of 6 hours and 50 minutes.

Upper School Student Profile Grade 9: 314 students (164 boys, 150 girls); Grade 10: 291 students (146 boys, 145 girls); Grade 11: 283 students (144 boys, 139 girls); Grade 12: 237 students (119 boys, 118 girls). 77% of students are Roman Catholic.

Faculty School total: 83. In upper school: 27 men, 49 women; 66 have advanced degrees.

Subjects Offered 3-dimensional art, 3-dimensional design, accounting, acting, advanced biology, advanced chemistry, advanced math, Advanced Placement courses, advanced studio art-AP, acrobics, algebra, American culture, American government, American history, American history-AP, American literature, American literature-AP, American studies, analysis and differential calculus, animation, art, art appreciation, art history, art history-AP, art-AP, arts, athletic training, athletics, band, Bible studies, biology, biology-AP, British literature, British literature (honors), business, calculus, calculus-AP, career and personal planning, career and technology systems, career technology, career/college preparation, Catholic belief and practice, ceramics, chemistry, chemistry-AP, choir, choral music, classics, comparative religion, composition, computer animation, computer art, computer programming, computer science, computer skills, computer-aided design, computers, concert band, concert choir, constitutional history of U.S., consumer economics, creative writing, dance, desktop publishing, digital art, digital photography, discrete mathematics, drama, drama performance, drawing and design, earth science, economics, electives, electronic publishing, engineering, English, English literature, English literature and composition-AP, English literature-AP, environmental science, environmental science-AP, European history, finance, fitness, French, French language-AP, French literature-AP, French-AP, geography, geometry, government, government and politics-AP, government/civics, history, honors algebra, honors English, honors geometry, honors U.S. history, humanities, instrumental music, jazz band, jazz ensemble, journalism, language arts, Latin, Latin-AP, law, leadership, leadership and service, learning lab, Life of Christ, literary magazine, macroeconomics-AP, marching band, marketing, music history, newspaper, non-Western literature, orchestra, painting, performing arts, personal fitness, photo shop, photography, photojournalism, physical fitness, physics, physics-AP, play production, politics, pottery, pre-algebra, pre-calculus, probability and statistics, programming, psychology, rhetoric, robotics, SAT/ACT preparation, scripture, sculpture, Shakespeare, social justice, space and physical sciences, Spanish, Spanish language-AP, Spanish literature, Spanish literature-AP, Spanish-AP, sports conditioning, sports medicine, statistics, statistics-AP, student government, student publications, studio art, studio art-AP, symphonic band, theater, theology, trigonometry, U.S. government and politics, U.S. history-AP, United States government-AP, visual and performing arts, visual arts, vocal music, voice ensemble, water color painting, weight fitness, weight training, weightlifting, world history, world history-AP, world literature, world religions, world studies, writing, writing workshop, yearbook.

Graduation Requirements Arts and fine arts (art, music, dance, drama), career and technology systems, English, exercise science, mathematics, modern languages, science, social studies (includes history), theology.

Special Academic Programs 18 Advanced Placement exams for which test preparation is offered; honors section; study at local college for college credit; remedial reading and/or remedial writing; remedial math; programs in English, mathematics, general development for dyslexic students.

College Admission Counseling 257 students graduated in 2016; 252 went to college, including Arizona State University at the Tempe campus; Grand Canyon University; Northern Arizona University; Pima Community College; The University of Arizona; University of San Diego. Other: 4 entered military service. Median SAT critical reading: 530, median SAT math: 510, median SAT writing: 500, median combined SAT: 1560, median composite ACT: 23. 24% scored over 600 on SAT critical reading, 22% scored over 600 on SAT math, 18% scored over 600 on SAT writing, 14% scored over 1800 on combined SAT, 28% scored over 26 on composite ACT.

Student Life Upper grades have specified standards of dress, student council, honor system. Discipline rests primarily with faculty. Attendance at religious services is required.

Summer Programs Remediation, enrichment, advancement, sports, computer instruction programs offered; session focuses on advancement, remediation, sports camps; held on campus; accepts boys and girls; open to students from other schools. 329 students usually enrolled. 2017 schedule: May 22 to June 29. Application deadline: May 18.

Tuition and Aid Day student tuition: $9200. Tuition installment plan (monthly payment plans, individually arranged payment plans). Merit scholarship grants, need-based scholarship grants, USS Education Loan Program available. In 2016–17, 52% of upper-school students received aid; total upper-school merit-scholarship money awarded: $62,000. Total amount of financial aid awarded in 2016–17: $1,848,925.

Admissions Traditional secondary-level entrance grade is 9. For fall 2016, 401 students applied for upper-level admission, 372 were accepted, 309 enrolled. High School Placement Test or TOEFL required. Deadline for receipt of application materials: none. Application fee required: $60. On-campus interview required.

Athletics Interscholastic: aerobics/dance (girls), baseball (b), basketball (b,g), cheering (g), cross-country running (b,g), dance team (g), diving (b,g), football (b), golf (b,g), lacrosse (b), soccer (b,g), softball (g), swimming and diving (b,g), tennis (b,g), track and field (b,g), volleyball (b,g), wrestling (b). 3 PE instructors, 110 coaches, 2 athletic trainers.

Computers Computers are regularly used in all academic classes. Computer network features include on-campus library services, Internet access, wireless campus network, Internet filtering or blocking technology. Campus intranet, student e-mail accounts, and computer access in designated common areas are available to students. Students grades are available online. The school has a published electronic and media policy.

Contact Mr. Michael Fisher, Director of Admission. 520-547-4460. Fax: 520-327-8477. E-mail: mfisher@salpointe.org. Website: www.salpointe.org

SAN DOMENICO SCHOOL

1500 Butterfield Road
San Anselmo, California 94960

Head of School: Ms. Cecily Stock

General Information Coeducational boarding and day college-preparatory, arts, religious studies, music, theater arts, dance, and social justice school, affiliated with Roman Catholic Church. Boarding grades 9–12, day grades K–12. Founded: 1850. Setting: suburban. Nearest major city is San Francisco. Students are housed in single-sex by floor dormitories. 515-acre campus. 4 buildings on campus. Approved or accredited by California Association of Independent Schools, New Jersey Association of Independent Schools, The Association of Boarding Schools, Western Association of Schools and Colleges, and Western Catholic Education Association. Member of National Association of Independent Schools. Endowment: $9 million. Total enrollment: 621. Upper school average class size: 12. Upper school faculty-student ratio: 1:5. There are 180 required school days per year for Upper School students. Upper School students typically attend 5 days per week. The average school day consists of 7 hours.

Upper School Student Profile Grade 6: 73 students (30 boys, 43 girls); Grade 7: 73 students (31 boys, 42 girls); Grade 8: 69 students (25 boys, 44 girls); Grade 9: 45 students (45 girls); Grade 10: 52 students (52 girls); Grade 11: 40 students (40 girls); Grade 12: 46 students (46 girls). 53% of students are boarding students. 57% are state residents. 2 states are represented in upper school student body. 43% are international students. International students from China, Hong Kong, Japan, Mexico, Republic of Korea, and Taiwan. 25% of students are Roman Catholic.

Faculty School total: 35. In upper school: 7 men, 28 women; 17 have advanced degrees; 7 reside on campus.

Subjects Offered Acting, advanced studio art-AP, algebra, American history, American literature, art, art history, biology, biology-AP, calculus, calculus-AP, ceramics, chemistry, chemistry-AP, community service, drama, English, English language and composition-AP, English literature, English literature-AP, environmental science, environmental science-AP, ESL, ethics, European history, expository writing, fine arts, geometry, government/civics, grammar, history, Mandarin, mathematics, modern world history, music, music composition, music theater, music theory, music theory-AP, musical productions, musicianship, photography, physical education, physics, physics-AP, psychology-AP, religion, science, social studies, sociology, Spanish, Spanish language-AP, statistics-AP, studio art-AP, theater, theology, trigonometry, U.S. history-AP, world history, world literature.

Graduation Requirements Arts and fine arts (art, music, dance, drama), English, foreign language, health, mathematics, physical education (includes health), religion (includes Bible studies and theology), science, social studies (includes history). Community service is required.

Special Academic Programs Advanced Placement exam preparation; honors section; independent study; study abroad; academic accommodation for the musically talented; ESL (18 students enrolled).

College Admission Counseling 30 students graduated in 2015; all went to college, including Boston University; California Polytechnic State University, San Luis Obispo; Lehigh University; Stanford University; The Juilliard School; University of California, Berkeley. Mean SAT critical reading: 584, mean SAT math: 606, mean SAT writing: 592, mean combined SAT: 1782, mean composite ACT: 29.

Student Life Upper grades have specified standards of dress, student council, honor system. Discipline rests primarily with faculty.

Tuition and Aid Day student tuition: $36,100; 7-day tuition and room/board: $52,600. Tuition installment plan (Insured Tuition Payment Plan, monthly payment plans). Need-based scholarship grants available. In 2015–16, 46% of upper-school students received aid. Total amount of financial aid awarded in 2015–16: $2,000,000.

Admissions Traditional secondary-level entrance grade is 9. For fall 2015, 155 students applied for upper-level admission, 103 were accepted, 54 enrolled. High School Placement Test, ISEE or SSAT required. Deadline for receipt of application materials: January 15. Application fee required: $100. Interview required.

Athletics Interscholastic: badminton (girls), basketball (b,g), cross-country running (b,g), equestrian sports (b,g), flag football (b,g), horseback riding (b,g), mountain biking (b,g), soccer (b,g), swimming and diving (b,g), tennis (b,g), volleyball (g); intramural: dance (g), golf (b,g), modern dance (g); coed interscholastic: cross-country running; coed intramural: dance, modern dance. 1 PE instructor, 5 coaches.

Computers Computers are regularly used in English, mathematics, science, social studies, yearbook classes. Computer network features include on-campus library services, online commercial services, Internet access, wireless campus network, Internet filtering or blocking technology. Student e-mail accounts are available to students. Students grades are available online. The school has a published electronic and media policy.

Contact Mr. Dan Babior, Director of Upper School Admissions and Marketing/Communications. 415-258-1905. Fax: 415-258-1906. E-mail: dbabior@sandomenico.org. Website: www.sandomenico.org/

SANDY SPRING FRIENDS SCHOOL

16923 Norwood Road
Sandy Spring, Maryland 20860

Head of School: Thomas R. Gibian

General Information Coeducational boarding and day college-preparatory, arts, and ESL school, affiliated with Society of Friends. Boarding grades 9–12, day grades PK–12. Founded: 1961. Setting: suburban. Nearest major city is Washington, DC. Students are housed in single-sex by floor dormitories. 140-acre campus. 15 buildings on campus. Approved or accredited by Association of Independent Maryland Schools, Association of Independent Schools of Greater Washington, Friends Council on Education, The Association of Boarding Schools, and Maryland Department of Education. Member of National Association of Independent Schools and Secondary School Admission Test Board. Endowment: $1.1 million. Total enrollment: 577. Upper school average class size: 14. Upper school faculty-student ratio: 1:8. There are 171 required school days per year for Upper School students. Upper School students typically attend 5 days per week. The average school day consists of 7 hours and 30 minutes.

Upper School Student Profile Grade 9: 61 students (34 boys, 27 girls); Grade 10: 71 students (41 boys, 30 girls); Grade 11: 82 students (44 boys, 38 girls); Grade 12: 71 students (41 boys, 30 girls). 31% of students are boarding students. 71% are state residents. 6 states are represented in upper student body. 24% are international students. International students from China, Thailand, and Viet Nam; 2 other countries represented in student body. 11% of students are members of Society of Friends.

Faculty School total: 68. In upper school: 12 men, 20 women; 22 have advanced degrees; 6 reside on campus.

Subjects Offered Algebra, American history, American literature, art, biology, British literature-AP, calculus, calculus-AP, ceramics, chemistry, chemistry-AP, choral music, creative writing, cultural geography, dance, dance performance, desktop publishing, drama, drawing, English, English as a foreign language, English literature and composition-AP, English literature-AP, environmental science-AP, ESL, ESL, French, French language-AP, geology, geometry, grammar, history, mathematics, music, music theory-AP, Native American history, painting, photography, physical education, physics, poetry, Quakerism and ethics, Russian literature, science, Spanish, Spanish language-AP, statistics-AP, trigonometry, U.S. history-AP, weaving, Western civilization, world literature.

Graduation Requirements Art, English, foreign language, history, mathematics, physical education (includes health), religion (includes Bible studies and theology), science. Community service is required.

Special Academic Programs 15 Advanced Placement exams for which test preparation is offered; honors section; independent study; academic accommodation for the gifted, the musically talented, and the artistically talented; ESL (25 students enrolled).

College Admission Counseling 72 students graduated in 2015; 70 went to college, including McDaniel College; Penn State University Park; Purdue University; St. Mary's College of Maryland; Syracuse University; Washington College. Other: 1 entered a postgraduate year, 1 had other specific plans. Median SAT critical reading: 580, median SAT math: 590, median SAT writing: 580, median combined SAT: 1750, median composite ACT: 24. 23% scored over 600 on SAT critical reading, 20% scored over 600 on SAT math, 19% scored over 600 on SAT writing, 23% scored over 1800 on combined SAT, 4% scored over 26 on composite ACT.

Student Life Upper grades have specified standards of dress, student council, honor system. Discipline rests equally with students and faculty. Attendance at religious services is required.

Tuition and Aid Day student tuition: $31,400; 5-day tuition and room/board: $46,225; 7-day tuition and room/board: $57,825. Tuition installment plan (FACTS Tuition Payment Plan). Need-based scholarship grants available. In 2015–16, 31% of upper-school students received aid. Total amount of financial aid awarded in 2015–16: $3,035,000.

Admissions Traditional secondary-level entrance grade is 9. For fall 2015, 198 students applied for upper-level admission, 106 were accepted, 57 enrolled. ISEE, PSAT, SSAT or TOEFL or SLEP required. Deadline for receipt of application materials: January 1. Application fee required: $75. Interview required.

Athletics Interscholastic: baseball (boys), basketball (b,g), cross-country running (b,g), ice hockey (b), lacrosse (b,g), soccer (b,g), softball (g), tennis (b,g), volleyball (g); coed interscholastic: cooperative games, golf, kickball, modern dance, running, track and field; coed intramural: basketball, cooperative games, dance, Frisbee, hiking/backpacking, jogging, outdoor activities, outdoor adventure, outdoor education, outdoor recreation, outdoor skills, outdoors, physical fitness, physical training, rappelling, rock climbing, ropes courses, running, skiing (downhill), snowboarding, strength & conditioning, table tennis, track and field, ultimate Frisbee, walking, wall climbing, weight lifting, weight training, wilderness, wilderness survival, wrestling, yoga. 5 PE instructors, 3 coaches, 1 athletic trainer.

Computers Computers are regularly used in all academic classes. Computer network features include on-campus library services, Internet access, wireless campus network. Student e-mail accounts and computer access in designated common areas are available to students. Students grades are available online.

Contact Tony McCudden, Director of Enrollment Management. 301-774-7455 Ext. 182. Fax: 301-576-8664. E-mail: tony.mccudden@ssfs.org. Website: www.ssfs.org

SAN FRANCISCO UNIVERSITY HIGH SCHOOL

3065 Jackson Street
San Francisco, California 94115

Head of School: Mrs. Julia Eells

General Information Coeducational day college-preparatory, community rngagement, and human development school. Grades 9–12. Founded: 1973. Setting: urban. 2-acre campus. 4 buildings on campus. Approved or accredited by California Association of Independent Schools, Western Association of Schools and Colleges, and California Department of Education. Member of National Association of Independent Schools and Secondary School Admission Test Board. Endowment: $27 million. Total enrollment: 403. Upper school average class size: 15. Upper school faculty-student ratio: 1:7.

Upper School Student Profile Grade 9: 104 students (51 boys, 53 girls); Grade 10: 104 students (52 boys, 52 girls); Grade 11: 100 students (49 boys, 51 girls); Grade 12: 95 students (45 boys, 50 girls).

Faculty School total: 53. In upper school: 28 men, 32 women; 50 have advanced degrees.

Subjects Offered 20th century physics, adolescent issues, advanced chemistry, advanced math, advanced studio art-AP, African American studies, African-American literature, algebra, American history, American literature, American literature-AP, analysis and differential calculus, anatomy, art, art history, Asian history, astronomy, band, Bible as literature, biochemistry, biology, calculus, calculus-AP, cell biology, ceramics, chamber groups, chemistry, chemistry-AP, chorus, clayworking, college counseling, community service, computer programming, computer science, creative writing, drawing, economics, economics and history, economics-AP, electronic music, English, English language and composition-AP, English literature, English literature-AP, environmental science, environmental science-AP, European history, European history-AP, film, fine arts, fractal geometry, French, French language-AP, French literature-AP, French-AP, genetics, geography, geometry, global issues, grammar, health education, instrumental music, introduction to theater, jazz band, jazz ensemble, Latin, Latin-AP, marine biology, mathematics, mathematics-AP, Mexican history, microbiology, music, music theory, music theory-AP, music-AP, musical productions, musical theater, orchestra, peer counseling, philosophy, photography, physical education, physics, physics-AP, physiology, pre-calculus, probability and statistics, psychology, science, senior internship, senior project, senior seminar, social studies, Spanish, Spanish language-AP, Spanish literature, Spanish literature-AP, Spanish-AP, studio art-AP, theater, trigonometry, U.S. government and politics-AP, U.S. history-AP, Western civilization, world history, world literature, writing.

Graduation Requirements American history-AP, art, English, foreign language, mathematics, physical education (includes health), science, social studies (includes history). Community service is required.

Special Academic Programs Advanced Placement exam preparation; honors section; independent study; term-away projects; domestic exchange program (with The Masters School); study abroad; academic accommodation for the gifted, the musically talented, and the artistically talented.

College Admission Counseling 95 students graduated in 2016; all went to college, including Amherst College; Columbia University; Harvard University; Stanford University; University of California, Berkeley; Yale University. Mean SAT critical reading: 720, mean SAT math: 710, mean SAT writing: 710.

Student Life Upper grades have student council, honor system. Discipline rests equally with students and faculty.

Tuition and Aid Day student tuition: $42,850. Tuition installment plan (SMART Tuition Payment Plan, monthly payment plans). Need-based scholarship grants available. In 2016–17, 23% of upper-school students received aid. Total amount of financial aid awarded in 2016–17: $2,600,000.

Admissions Traditional secondary-level entrance grade is 9. For fall 2016, 557 students applied for upper-level admission, 104 enrolled. ISEE, SSAT or TOEFL required. Deadline for receipt of application materials: January 12. Application fee required: $90. On-campus interview recommended.

Athletics Interscholastic: baseball (boys), basketball (b,g), cross-country running (b,g), fencing (b,g), field hockey (g), lacrosse (b), soccer (b,g), swimming and diving (b,g), tennis (b,g), track and field (b,g), volleyball (g); intramural: basketball (b,g), cross-country running (b,g), field hockey (g), lacrosse (b), soccer (b,g), strength & conditioning (b,g), volleyball (g); coed interscholastic: badminton; coed intramural: archery, bowling, canoeing/kayaking, climbing, crew, dance, fencing, fitness, golf, hiking/backpacking, outdoor education, yoga. 4 PE instructors, 43 coaches.

Computers Computers are regularly used in all academic classes. Computer network features include on-campus library services, online commercial services, Internet access, wireless campus network. Student e-mail accounts are available to students. Students grades are available online. The school has a published electronic and media policy.

Contact Admissions Assistant. 415-447-3100. Fax: 415-447-5801. E-mail: admissions@sfuhs.org. Website: www.sfuhs.org

SAN MARCOS BAPTIST ACADEMY

2801 Ranch Road Twelve
San Marcos, Texas 78666-9406

Head of School: Mr. Jimmie W. Scott

General Information Coeducational boarding and day and distance learning college-preparatory, learning skills, and ESL school, affiliated with Baptist Church. Boarding grades 7–12, day grades 6–12. Distance learning grades 6–12. Founded: 1907. Setting: small town. Nearest major city is Austin. Students are housed in single-sex dormitories. 220-acre campus. 10 buildings on campus. Approved or accredited by Accreditation Commission of the Texas Association of Baptist Schools, Southern Association of Colleges and Schools, The Association of Boarding Schools, and Texas Department of Education. Member of National Association of Independent Schools. Endowment: $6 million. Total enrollment: 270. Upper school average class size: 12. Upper school faculty-student ratio: 1:8. There are 180 required school days per year for Upper School students. Upper School students typically attend 5 days per week. The average school day consists of 7 hours and 40 minutes.

Upper School Student Profile Grade 9: 38 students (27 boys, 11 girls); Grade 10: 34 students (21 boys, 13 girls); Grade 11: 63 students (38 boys, 25 girls); Grade 12: 52 students (35 boys, 17 girls). 66% of students are boarding students. 52% are state residents. 6 states are represented in upper school student body. 46% are international students. International students from Angola, China, Hong Kong, Mexico, Taiwan, and Viet Nam; 9 other countries represented in student body. 10% of students are Baptist.

Faculty School total: 40. In upper school: 18 men, 22 women; 22 have advanced degrees; 3 reside on campus.

Subjects Offered Advanced math, Advanced Placement courses, algebra, American government, American history, American literature, analysis and differential calculus, analytic geometry, anatomy and physiology, ancient world history, applied arts, applied music, art, athletic training, athletics, band, baseball, Basic programming, basketball, Bible, Bible studies, biology, biology-AP, British literature, British literature (honors), British literature-AP, business applications, calculus, calculus-AP, career/college preparation, character education, cheerleading, chemistry, choir, Christian scripture, Christian testament, Christianity, civics, civics/free enterprise, clayworking, college admission preparation, college counseling, college planning, communication skills, community service, comparative religion, computer applications, computer information systems, computer programming, computer science, computers, concert band, concert choir, contemporary art, critical thinking, desktop publishing, digital photography, drama, drama performance, drama workshop, dramatic arts, drawing, driver education, earth and space science, earth science, economics, economics and history, English, English as a foreign language, English composition, English literature, English literature and composition-AP, English literature-AP, English-AP, family and consumer science, fine arts, foreign language, French, geography, geometry, golf, government/civics, grammar, guidance, health, health education, history, history of the Americas, honors algebra, honors geometry, honors U.S. history, honors world history, HTML design, human anatomy, human biology, instrumental music, instruments, intro to computers, introduction to theater, jazz band, journalism, JROTC, JROTC or LEAD (Leadership Education and Development), keyboarding, language and composition, language arts, Latin, leadership, leadership and service, leadership education training, learning strategies, library, library skills, library studies, Life of Christ, life skills, literature, literature and composition-AP, literature-AP, logic, mathematical modeling, mathematics, mathematics-AP, military science, music, music appreciation, music performance, music theory, musical productions, musical theater, musicianship, New Testament, news writing, newspaper, novels, painting, participation in sports, personal and social education, personal fitness, personal growth, photography, photojournalism, physical education, physical fitness, physical science, physics, piano, play production, pottery, prayer/spirituality, pre-calculus, psychology, public speaking, reading, reading/study skills, religion, religious education, remedial study skills, research skills, SAT preparation, SAT/ACT preparation, science, social skills, social studies, society and culture, sociology, softball, Spanish, speech, speech and debate, speech communications, sports, sports conditioning, sports performance development, sports team management, state government, state history, stock market, student government, student publications, study skills, swimming, tennis, Texas history, theater, theater arts, theater production, theology, TOEFL preparation, track and field, U.S. government, U.S. government and politics, U.S. history, U.S. literature, visual arts, vocal ensemble, vocal jazz, vocal music, voice, voice and diction, voice ensemble, volleyball, Web site design, weight training, weightlifting, Western civilization, world civilizations, world cultures, world geography, world history, world issues, world literature, world religions, world religions, world studies, world wide web design, yearbook.

Graduation Requirements Arts and fine arts (art, music, dance, drama), computer science, economics, electives, English, foreign language, government, JROTC or LEAD (Leadership Education and Development), mathematics, physical education (includes health), religion (includes Bible studies and theology), science, social studies (includes history), speech.

Special Academic Programs 6 Advanced Placement exams for which test preparation is offered; honors section; accelerated programs; independent study; study at local college for college credit; academic accommodation for the gifted, the musically talented, and the artistically talented; programs in English, mathematics, general development for dyslexic students; special instructional classes for students with Section 504 learning disabilities, Attention Deficit Disorder, and dyslexia; ESL (50 students enrolled).

College Admission Counseling 58 students graduated in 2016; 52 went to college, including Baylor University; Penn State University Park; Texas A&M University; Texas State University; The University of Texas at Arlington; The University of Texas at Austin. Other: 1 went to work, 2 had other specific plans. Median SAT critical reading: 480, median SAT math: 510, median SAT writing: 480, median combined SAT: 1470, median composite ACT: 21. 19% scored over 600 on SAT critical reading, 42% scored over 600 on SAT math, 19% scored over 600 on SAT writing, 17% scored over 1800 on combined SAT, 11% scored over 26 on composite ACT.

Student Life Upper grades have uniform requirement, student council, honor system. Discipline rests primarily with faculty. Attendance at religious services is required.

Tuition and Aid Day student tuition: $9900; 5-day tuition and room/board: $25,000; 7-day tuition and room/board: $33,000. Guaranteed tuition plan. Tuition installment plan (SMART Tuition Payment Plan, monthly payment plans, individually arranged payment plans). Need-based scholarship grants available. In 2016–17, 31% of upper-school students received aid. Total amount of financial aid awarded in 2016–17: $50,000.

Admissions Traditional secondary-level entrance grade is 9. For fall 2016, 100 students applied for upper-level admission, 85 were accepted, 58 enrolled. Deadline for receipt of application materials: none. Application fee required: $150. Interview required.

Athletics Interscholastic: baseball (boys), basketball (b,g), cross-country running (b,g), football (b), golf (b,g), JROTC drill (b,g), power lifting (b,g), riflery (b,g), softball (g), swimming and diving (b,g), tennis (b,g), track and field (b,g), volleyball (g), weight lifting (b,g); coed interscholastic: equestrian sports, flag football, marksmanship, soccer, winter soccer; coed intramural: cheering, Frisbee, horseback riding, ropes courses, table tennis, weight lifting, weight training. 3 PE instructors, 20 coaches, 1 athletic trainer.

Computers Computers are regularly used in all classes. Computer network features include on-campus library services, online commercial services, Internet access, wireless campus network, Internet filtering or blocking technology, 1:1 computer device program for high school students, tablet program for middle school students. Student e-mail accounts and computer access in designated common areas are available to students. Students grades are available online. The school has a published electronic and media policy.

Contact Mrs. Shelley Henry, Director of Admissions and Communications. 800-428-5120. Fax: 512-753-8031. E-mail: admissions@smabears.org. Website: www.smabears.org

SANTA CATALINA SCHOOL

1500 Mark Thomas Drive
Monterey, California 93940-5291

Head of School: Ms. Margaret "Meg" Bradley

General Information Girls' boarding and day college-preparatory, liberal arts, and marine ecology school, affiliated with Roman Catholic Church. Grades 9–12. Founded: 1950. Setting: small town. Nearest major city is San Francisco. Students are housed in single-sex dormitories. 36-acre campus. 24 buildings on campus. Approved or accredited by California Association of Independent Schools, National Catholic Education Association, The Association of Boarding Schools, The College Board, Western Association of Schools and Colleges, and California Department of Education. Member of National Association of Independent Schools and Secondary School Admission Test Board. Endowment: $29 million. Total enrollment: 244. Upper school average class size: 12. Upper school faculty-student ratio: 1:8. There are 184 required school days per year for Upper School students. Upper School students typically attend 5 days per week. The average school day consists of 6 hours and 50 minutes.

Upper School Student Profile Grade 9: 51 students (51 girls); Grade 10: 54 students (54 girls); Grade 11: 72 students (72 girls); Grade 12: 54 students (54 girls). 50% of students are boarding students. 79% are state residents. 9 states are represented in upper school student body. 16% are international students. International students from China, Hong Kong, Indonesia, Italy, Mexico, and Republic of Korea; 1 other country represented in student body. 43% of students are Roman Catholic.

Faculty School total: 35. In upper school: 13 men, 22 women; 27 have advanced degrees; 15 reside on campus.

Subjects Offered Algebra, American literature, art, art history-AP, ballet, biology, biology-AP, British literature, calculus, calculus-AP, ceramics, chemistry, chemistry-

AP, Chinese, choir, college counseling, computer science, computer technologies, conceptual physics, creative writing, dance, digital art, drama, drama performance, English, English language and composition-AP, English literature, English literature and composition-AP, ensembles, European history, finance, fine arts, French, French language-AP, geometry, global issues, honors algebra, honors English, honors geometry, human geography - AP, jazz dance, Latin, Latin-AP, macro/microeconomics-AP, Mandarin, marine ecology, marine science, media arts, music, music performance, music theory-AP, peace and justice, philosophy, photography, physical education, physics, physics-AP, pre-calculus, Spanish, Spanish language-AP, Spanish literature-AP, statistics, statistics-AP, studio art, studio art-AP, theater, theater arts, theater design and production, theology, trigonometry, U.S. history, U.S. history-AP, world history, world history-AP, world issues, world literature, world religions.

Graduation Requirements Arts, English, foreign language, history, lab science, mathematics, physical education (includes health), religious studies, science, history, religious studies, arts elective.

Special Academic Programs 21 Advanced Placement exams for which test preparation is offered; honors section; academic accommodation for the gifted, the musically talented, and the artistically talented.

College Admission Counseling 56 students graduated in 2016; all went to college, including Boston University; California Polytechnic State University, San Luis Obispo; University of California, Berkeley; University of Oregon; University of San Francisco; University of Southern California. Mean SAT critical reading: 580, mean SAT math: 599, mean SAT writing: 599, mean composite ACT: 28.

Student Life Upper grades have uniform requirement, student council, honor system. Discipline rests equally with students and faculty. Attendance at religious services is required.

Summer Programs Enrichment, sports, art/fine arts programs offered; session focuses on recreation and enrichment fun; held on campus; accepts girls; open to students from other schools. 210 students usually enrolled. 2017 schedule: June 18 to July 22. Application deadline: none.

Tuition and Aid Day student tuition: $34,000; 7-day tuition and room/board: $52,000. Need-based scholarship grants available. In 2016–17, 42% of upper-school students received aid. Total amount of financial aid awarded in 2016–17: $1,964,000.

Admissions Traditional secondary-level entrance grade is 9. For fall 2016, 175 students applied for upper-level admission, 110 were accepted, 62 enrolled. ISEE, SSAT or TOEFL required. Deadline for receipt of application materials: February 1. Application fee required: $75. On-campus interview recommended.

Athletics Interscholastic: basketball, cross-country running, diving, field hockey, golf, lacrosse, soccer, softball, swimming and diving, tennis, track and field, volleyball, water polo; intramural: ballet, canoeing/kayaking, dance, equestrian sports, fencing, fitness, horseback riding, kayaking, modern dance, ocean paddling, outdoor activities, physical fitness, rafting, rock climbing, sailing, self defense, strength & conditioning, surfing, weight training, yoga. 1 PE instructor, 26 coaches.

Computers Computers are regularly used in English, foreign language, mathematics, media arts, science, yearbook classes. Computer network features include on-campus library services, Internet access, wireless campus network, Internet filtering or blocking technology. Campus intranet, student e-mail accounts, and computer access in designated common areas are available to students. The school has a published electronic and media policy.

Contact Mrs. Jamie Buffington Browne '85, Director of Admission. 831-655-9356. Fax: 831-655-7535.
E-mail: admission@santacatalina.org. Website: www.santacatalina.org

SANTA FE PREPARATORY SCHOOL

1101 Camino de la Cruz Blanca
Santa Fe, New Mexico 87505

Head of School: Mr. James W. Leonard

General Information Coeducational day college-preparatory, arts, and community service school. Grades 7–12. Founded: 1961. Setting: suburban. 33-acre campus. 4 buildings on campus. Approved or accredited by Independent Schools Association of the Southwest and New Mexico Department of Education. Member of National Association of Independent Schools. Endowment: $14.6 million. Total enrollment: 317. Upper school average class size: 13. Upper school faculty-student ratio: 1:14. There are 171 required school days per year for Upper School students. Upper School students typically attend 5 days per week. The average school day consists of 6 hours and 23 minutes.

Upper School Student Profile Grade 9: 61 students (37 boys, 24 girls); Grade 10: 44 students (25 boys, 19 girls); Grade 11: 51 students (28 boys, 23 girls); Grade 12: 67 students (29 boys, 38 girls).

Faculty School total: 51. In upper school: 19 men, 20 women; 27 have advanced degrees.

Subjects Offered 3-dimensional art, advanced biology, Advanced Placement courses, American legal systems, American sign language, biochemistry, pre-algebra, printmaking, robotics, yearbook.

Graduation Requirements Arts and fine arts (art, music, dance, drama), computer science, English, foreign language, history, humanities, mathematics, physical education (includes health), science, social studies (includes history), senior seminar program. Community service is required.

Special Academic Programs 5 Advanced Placement exams for which test preparation is offered; honors section; independent study; term-away projects; study at local college for college credit; study abroad; academic accommodation for the gifted.

College Admission Counseling 48 students graduated in 2016; 46 went to college, including Montana State University Billings; New York University; Occidental College; The Colorado College; University of Denver; University of New Mexico. Other: 1 entered a postgraduate year, 1 had other specific plans. Median SAT critical reading: 620, median SAT math: 610, median SAT writing: 600, median combined SAT: 1850, median composite ACT: 28. 61% scored over 600 on SAT critical reading, 61% scored over 600 on SAT math, 54% scored over 600 on SAT writing, 61% scored over 1800 on combined SAT, 58% scored over 26 on composite ACT.

Student Life Upper grades have specified standards of dress, student council. Discipline rests equally with students and faculty.

Tuition and Aid Day student tuition: $18,906. Tuition installment plan (individually arranged payment plans, Tuition Management Systems Plan). Need-based scholarship grants, tuition remission for faculty available. In 2016–17, 40% of upper-school students received aid.

Admissions Traditional secondary-level entrance grade is 9. For fall 2016, 40 students applied for upper-level admission, 37 were accepted, 21 enrolled. Mathematics proficiency exam required. Deadline for receipt of application materials: none. Application fee required: $55. Interview required.

Athletics Interscholastic: aquatics (boys, girls), basketball (b,g), cross-country running (b,g), diving (b,g), fencing (b,g), lacrosse (b,g), soccer (b,g), swimming and diving (b,g), tennis (b,g), track and field (b,g), volleyball (g); intramural: basketball (b,g), cross-country running (b,g), football (b,g), Frisbee (b,g), handball (b,g), hiking/backpacking (b,g), martial arts (b,g), outdoor activities (b,g), soccer (b,g), tennis (b,g), track and field (b,g), ultimate Frisbee (b,g), volleyball (g); coed interscholastic: baseball; coed intramural: basketball, skiing (downhill), snowshoeing, swimming and diving. 1 PE instructor, 16 coaches, 1 athletic trainer.

Computers Computers are regularly used in current events, English, geography, graphic arts, history, humanities, journalism, library, literary magazine, mathematics, newspaper, photography, photojournalism, science, social sciences, writing, yearbook classes. Computer network features include on-campus library services, Internet access, wireless campus network, Internet filtering or blocking technology, On-line learning management system—Power Learning. Campus intranet, student e-mail accounts, and computer access in designated common areas are available to students. Students grades are available online. The school has a published electronic and media policy.

Contact Michael Multari, Director of Admissions. 505-982-1829 Ext. 1212. Fax: 505-982-2897. E-mail: mmultari@sfprep.org. Website: www.santafeprep.org

SANTA MARGARITA CATHOLIC HIGH SCHOOL

22062 Antonio Parkway
Rancho Santa Margarita, California 92688

Head of School: Mr. Ray Dunne

General Information Coeducational day college-preparatory, International Baccalaureate, and auxiliary studies program school, affiliated with Roman Catholic Church. Grades 9–12. Founded: 1987. Setting: suburban. 42-acre campus. 18 buildings on campus. Approved or accredited by International Baccalaureate Organization, National Catholic Education Association, Western Association of Schools and Colleges, Western Catholic Education Association, and California Department of Education. Total enrollment: 1,755. Upper school average class size: 28. Upper school faculty-student ratio: 1:14. There are 180 required school days per year for Upper School students. Upper School students typically attend 5 days per week. The average school day consists of 5 hours and 30 minutes.

Upper School Student Profile Grade 9: 430 students (218 boys, 212 girls); Grade 10: 465 students (225 boys, 240 girls); Grade 11: 413 students (179 boys, 234 girls); Grade 12: 426 students (203 boys, 223 girls). 61% of students are Roman Catholic.

Faculty School total: 128. In upper school: 67 have advanced degrees.

Subjects Offered Accounting, ACT preparation, advanced biology, advanced chemistry, advanced math, Advanced Placement courses, algebra, American Civil War, American government, American history, American history-AP, American literature, anatomy and physiology, art, art education, art history, art history-AP, art-AP, audio visual/media, Bible studies, biology, biology-AP, business communications, business studies, calculus, calculus-AP, campus ministry, career/college preparation, Catholic belief and practice, ceramics, chamber groups, chemistry, chemistry-AP, choir, chorus, Christian doctrine, Christian education, Christian studies, Christianity, cinematography, classical music, classical studies, community service, comparative government and politics, comparative government and politics-AP, comparative political systems-AP, comparative politics, comparative religion, composition, computer education, computer programming, computer science, computer science-AP, concert band, creative arts, current events, debate, drama, drawing, earth science, East European studies, economics, economics and history, economics-AP, English, English composition, English language-AP, English literature, English literature and composition-AP, English literature-AP, English-AP, English/composition-AP, environmental science, environmental science-AP, ethics, European civilization, European history, European history-AP, European literature, finance, fine arts, forensics, French, French language-AP, French literature-AP, French-AP, geography, geology, geometry, government and politics-AP, government-AP, government/civics, government/civics-AP, graphic arts, graphic design, health and wellness, health education, health science, history, history of religion, history of the Catholic Church, history-AP, honors algebra, honors English, honors geometry, honors U.S. history, honors world history, human biology, instrumental music, international relations, jazz band, jazz ensemble, journalism, language and composition, language arts, language-AP, Latin, Latin-AP, law studies, literature and composition-AP, literature-AP, macro/microeconomics-AP, macroeconomics-AP, marine biology, mathematics, mathematics-AP, microeconomics-AP, model United Nations, music, music theory-AP, musical theater, newspaper, nutrition, oceanography, orchestra, painting, philosophy, photography, physical science, physics, physics-AP, physiology, poetry, political science, politics, pre-algebra, pre-calculus, probability, probability and statistics, psychology, psychology-AP, public speaking, reading/study skills, religion, religious education, remedial/makeup course work, SAT preparation, SAT/ACT preparation, social studies, sociology, Spanish, Spanish language-AP, Spanish literature, Spanish literature-AP, Spanish-AP, speech, speech and debate, speech communications, sports, statistics, statistics-AP, student government, student publications, studio art, theater arts, trigonometry, U.S. government, U.S. government and politics, U.S. government and politics-AP, U.S. history, U.S. history-AP, United States government-AP, vocal music, weight training, world governments, world history, world history-AP, world issues, world literature, world religions, World War I, World War II, writing, yearbook.

Graduation Requirements Foreign language, health, science, social sciences.

Special Academic Programs International Baccalaureate program; 19 Advanced Placement exams for which test preparation is offered; honors section; independent study; study at local college for college credit; academic accommodation for the gifted, the musically talented, and the artistically talented; remedial reading and/or remedial writing; remedial math; programs in English, mathematics, general development for dyslexic students; special instructional classes for deaf students, blind students, students with learning disabilities, Attention Deficit Disorder, and dyslexia.

College Admission Counseling 424 students graduated in 2016; 420 went to college, including Arizona State University at the Tempe campus; Southern Methodist University; The University of Arizona; University of California, Irvine; University of Colorado Boulder; University of Oregon. Other: 1 went to work, 1 had other specific plans. Mean SAT critical reading: 568, mean SAT math: 577, mean SAT writing: 572, mean combined SAT: 1717, mean composite ACT: 27.

Student Life Upper grades have uniform requirement, student council, honor system. Discipline rests primarily with faculty. Attendance at religious services is required.

Summer Programs Remediation, enrichment, advancement, sports, art/fine arts, computer instruction programs offered; session focuses on enrichment; held on campus; accepts boys and girls; open to students from other schools. 1,272 students usually enrolled. 2017 schedule: June to July. Application deadline: none.

Tuition and Aid Day student tuition: $13,425. Tuition installment plan (monthly payment plans, annual payment, semi-annual). Tuition reduction for siblings, need-based scholarship grants available. In 2016–17, 20% of upper-school students received aid. Total amount of financial aid awarded in 2016–17: $1,500,000.

Admissions Traditional secondary-level entrance grade is 9. For fall 2016, 620 students applied for upper-level admission, 550 were accepted, 405 enrolled. High School Placement Test required. Deadline for receipt of application materials: none. Application fee required: $50.

Athletics Interscholastic: aerobics/dance (girls), aquatics (b,g), ballet (g), baseball (b), basketball (b,g), cheering (g), cross-country running (b,g), dance (b,g), dance squad (g), dance team (g), diving (b,g), dressage (b,g), drill team (g), equestrian sports (b,g), fitness (b,g), football (b), golf (b,g), hockey (b), ice hockey (b), in-line hockey (b), lacrosse (b,g), modern dance (g), physical fitness (b,g), physical training (b,g), power lifting (b), roller hockey (b), running (b,g), soccer (b,g), softball (g), surfing (b,g), swimming and diving (b,g), tennis (b,g), track and field (b,g), volleyball (b,g), water polo (b,g), wrestling (b); intramural: fitness (b,g), power lifting (b), running (b,g), self defense (b,g), weight lifting (b,g), weight training (b,g); coed interscholastic: aerobics/dance; coed intramural: dance, Special Olympics. 4 PE instructors, 27 coaches, 2 athletic trainers.

Computers Computers are regularly used in all academic classes. Computer network features include on-campus library services, online commercial services, Internet access, wireless campus network, Internet filtering or blocking technology, custom learning portal, Aeries, DyKnow, Windows 8 for Education. Campus intranet and student e-mail accounts are available to students. Students grades are available online. The school has a published electronic and media policy.

Contact Mr. Ron Blanc, Admissions Director. 949-766-6076. Fax: 949-766-6005. E-mail: admissions@smhs.org. Website: www.smhs.org

SAVANNAH CHRISTIAN PREPARATORY SCHOOL

PO Box 2848
Savannah, Georgia 31402-2848

Head of School: Dr. David Pitre

General Information Coeducational day college-preparatory school, affiliated with Christian faith. Grades PK–12. Founded: 1951. Setting: suburban. 236-acre campus. 6 buildings on campus. Approved or accredited by Georgia Independent School Association, Southern Association of Colleges and Schools, and Georgia Department of Education. Endowment: $1.1 million. Total enrollment: 1,227. Upper school average class size: 17. Upper school faculty-student ratio: 1:14. There are 180 required school

days per year for Upper School students. Upper School students typically attend 5 days per week. The average school day consists of 6 hours and 35 minutes.

Upper School Student Profile Grade 9: 129 students (68 boys, 61 girls); Grade 10: 118 students (61 boys, 57 girls); Grade 11: 126 students (75 boys, 51 girls); Grade 12: 104 students (42 boys, 62 girls). 95% of students are Christian faith.

Faculty School total: 125. In upper school: 10 men, 25 women; 26 have advanced degrees.

Subjects Offered 20th century history, accounting, advanced TOEFL/grammar, algebra, American Civil War, American history, American history-AP, art, astronomy, band, Bible, biology, botany, business law, calculus-AP, chemistry, chemistry-AP, chorus, Christian ethics, computer applications, computer-aided design, creative writing, design, drama, driver education, earth science, ecology, economics, English, English-AP, European history-AP, French, geometry, government/civics, graphic arts, health, marine biology, mathematics, mechanical drawing, music appreciation, physical education, physics, probability and statistics, psychology, science, social studies, sociology, Spanish, speech, technical theater, theater, trigonometry, typing, world history, yearbook.

Graduation Requirements Accounting, algebra, biology, chemistry, economics, English, foreign language, geometry, mathematics, physical education (includes health), religion (includes Bible studies and theology), science, social studies (includes history).

Special Academic Programs Advanced Placement exam preparation; honors section; study at local college for college credit.

College Admission Counseling 108 students graduated in 2015; 107 went to college, including Armstrong State University; Georgia College & State University; Georgia Southern University; University of Georgia; University of South Carolina; Valdosta State University. Other: 1 entered military service. Mean SAT critical reading: 545, mean SAT math: 551, mean SAT writing: 545, mean combined SAT: 1641, mean composite ACT: 24.

Student Life Upper grades have uniform requirement, student council, honor system. Discipline rests primarily with faculty.

Tuition and Aid Day student tuition: $8167. Tuition installment plan (monthly payment plans). Merit scholarship grants, need based scholarship grants available. In 2015–16, 15% of upper-school students received aid; total upper-school merit-scholarship money awarded: $35,000. Total amount of financial aid awarded in 2015–16: $110,000.

Admissions Traditional secondary-level entrance grade is 9. For fall 2015, 61 students applied for upper-level admission, 58 were accepted, 58 enrolled. Stanford Achievement Test and writing sample required. Deadline for receipt of application materials: none. Application fee required: $125.

Athletics Interscholastic: baseball (boys), basketball (b,g), cheering (g), cross-country running (b,g), dance team (g), football (b), golf (b,g), lacrosse (b,g), soccer (b,g), softball (g), tennis (b,g), track and field (b,g), volleyball (g), wrestling (b); coed intramural: sailing. 3 PE instructors, 3 coaches, 1 athletic trainer.

Computers Computers are regularly used in accounting, business applications, computer applications, English, graphic arts, history, science, word processing, yearbook classes. Computer network features include on-campus library services, Internet access, wireless campus network, Internet filtering or blocking technology. Computer access in designated common areas is available to students. Students grades are available online. The school has a published electronic and media policy.

Contact Mrs. Debbie Fairbanks, Director of Admissions. 912-721-2114. Fax: 912-234-0491. E-mail: dfairbanks@savcps.com. Website: www.savcps.com

THE SAVANNAH COUNTRY DAY SCHOOL

824 Stillwood Drive
Savannah, Georgia 31419-2643

Head of School: Mr. Kef Wilson

General Information Coeducational day college-preparatory, arts, and technology school. Grades PK–12. Founded: 1955. Setting: suburban. 65-acre campus. 11 buildings on campus. Approved or accredited by Georgia Independent School Association, Southern Association of Colleges and Schools, and Southern Association of Independent Schools. Member of National Association of Independent Schools. Endowment: $32.2 million. Total enrollment: 893. Upper school average class size: 6. Upper school faculty-student ratio: 1:6. There are 180 required school days per year for Upper School students. Upper School students typically attend 5 days per week. The average school day consists of 7 hours.

Faculty School total: 81. In upper school: 21 men, 18 women; 24 have advanced degrees.

Subjects Offered Advanced Placement courses, algebra, American history, American literature, analysis and differential calculus, anatomy and physiology, art, art history, biology, biology-AP, British literature-AP, calculus, calculus-AP, ceramics, chemistry, chemistry-AP, chorus, composition, computer education, computer science, dance, drama, drama performance, economics and history, English, English literature, English-AP, environmental science, environmental science-AP, European history, European history-AP, fine arts, French, geometry, government-AP, government/civics, guidance, health, honors algebra, honors English, honors geometry, honors U.S. history, honors world history, independent study, instrumental music, intro to computers, jazz band, language-AP, Latin, Latin-AP, music, photography, physical education, physics,

physics-AP, pre-calculus, public speaking, Spanish, Spanish language-AP, statistics, studio art-AP, theater, U.S. history-AP, world history, world history-AP, yearbook.

Graduation Requirements Arts and fine arts (art, music, dance, drama), English, foreign language, health education, history, mathematics, physical education (includes health), science, speech.

Special Academic Programs Advanced Placement exam preparation; honors section; independent study; study at local college for college credit; ESL.

College Admission Counseling 55 students graduated in 2015; 54 went to college. Other: 1 entered military service.

Student Life Upper grades have uniform requirement, student council, honor system. Discipline rests equally with students and faculty.

Tuition and Aid Tuition installment plan (Insured Tuition Payment Plan, FACTS Tuition Payment Plan, monthly payment plans, individually arranged payment plans). Need-based scholarship grants available.

Admissions Traditional secondary-level entrance grade is 9. ERB Reading and Math, Math Placement Exam, Otis-Lennon Mental Ability Test or writing sample required. Deadline for receipt of application materials: none. Application fee required: $175. Interview required.

Athletics Interscholastic: baseball (boys), basketball (b,g), cheering (g), cross-country running (b,g), football (b), golf (b,g), soccer (b,g), softball (g), tennis (b,g), track and field (b,g), volleyball (g); intramural: basketball (b,g), bocce (b,g), cheering (g), climbing (b,g), cross-country running (b,g), dance (b,g), outdoor adventure (b,g), outdoor education (b,g), physical training (b,g), power lifting (b,g), project adventure (b,g), ropes courses (b,g), strength & conditioning (b,g), track and field (b,g), volleyball (g), weight lifting (b,g), weight training (b,g); coed interscholastic: swimming and diving; coed intramural: archery, sailing, soccer, strength & conditioning. 6 PE instructors, 6 coaches, 2 athletic trainers.

Computers Computers are regularly used in college planning, creative writing, English, foreign language, history, library skills, mathematics, publications, publishing, research skills, SAT preparation, science, yearbook classes. Computer network features include on-campus library services, online commercial services, Internet access, wireless campus network, Internet filtering or blocking technology. Campus intranet and student e-mail accounts are available to students. The school has a published electronic and media policy.

Contact Mrs. Amy Pinckney, Assistant Director of Admissions. 912-961-8700. Fax: 912-920-7800. E-mail: pinckney@savcds.org. Website: www.savcds.org

SAYRE SCHOOL

194 North Limestone Street
Lexington, Kentucky 40507

Head of School: Mr. Stephen Manella

General Information Coeducational day college-preparatory, arts, technology, and concentrations in global studies and sustainability school. Grades PK–12. Founded: 1854. Setting: urban. 60-acre campus. 10 buildings on campus. Approved or accredited by Independent Schools Association of the Central States, National Council for Private School Accreditation, and Kentucky Department of Education. Member of National Association of Independent Schools. Endowment: $7 million. Total enrollment: 549. Upper school average class size: 16. Upper school faculty-student ratio: 1:8. There are 177 required school days per year for Upper School students. Upper School students typically attend 5 days per week. The average school day consists of 7 hours and 30 minutes.

Upper School Student Profile Grade 9: 48 students (24 boys, 24 girls); Grade 10: 70 students (31 boys, 39 girls); Grade 11: 63 students (35 boys, 28 girls); Grade 12: 64 students (35 boys, 29 girls).

Faculty School total: 34. In upper school: 12 men, 22 women; 24 have advanced degrees.

Subjects Offered 3-dimensional art, acting, Advanced Placement courses, algebra, American government, American history, American history-AP, American literature, American literature-AP, anatomy and physiology, ancient history, art, art history, biology, biology-AP, calculus, calculus-AP, chemistry, chemistry-AP, chorus, college counseling, community service, computer science, creative writing, drama, earth science, English, English literature, fine arts, French, geometry, government/civics, health, history, journalism, mathematics, music, photography, physical education, physics, public speaking, science, social studies, Spanish, speech, statistics, theater, U.S. constitutional history, world history, writing.

Graduation Requirements Arts and fine arts (art, music, dance, drama), computer science, creative writing, English, foreign language, mathematics, physical education (includes health), public speaking, science, social studies (includes history), senior project internship, senior seminars. Community service is required.

Special Academic Programs 13 Advanced Placement exams for which test preparation is offered; honors section; independent study; term-away projects; study at local college for college credit; academic accommodation for the gifted and the artistically talented; remedial reading and/or remedial writing; remedial math.

College Admission Counseling 67 students graduated in 2016; all went to college, including Loyola University Chicago; Middlebury College; University of Kentucky; University of Mississippi; Wake Forest University; Yale University.

Student Life Upper grades have specified standards of dress, student council, honor system. Discipline rests equally with students and faculty.

Tuition and Aid Day student tuition: $20,480–$22,050. Tuition installment plan (Insured Tuition Payment Plan, monthly payment plans, individually arranged payment plans). Need-based scholarship grants available. In 2016–17, 24% of upper-school students received aid. Total amount of financial aid awarded in 2016–17: $624,000.

Admissions Traditional secondary-level entrance grade is 9. Admissions testing, Math Placement Exam, PSAT and SAT for applicants to grade 11 and 12, school's own exam or writing sample required. Deadline for receipt of application materials: none. Application fee required: $75. On-campus interview required.

Athletics Interscholastic: baseball (boys), basketball (b,g), cheering (g), diving (b,g), golf (b,g), lacrosse (b), physical fitness (b,g), physical training (b,g), soccer (b,g), swimming and diving (b,g), tennis (b,g); coed interscholastic: cross-country running. 5 PE instructors, 10 coaches, 1 athletic trainer.

Computers Computers are regularly used in English, foreign language, history, mathematics, music, science classes. Computer network features include on-campus library services, online commercial services, Internet access, wireless campus network, Internet filtering or blocking technology. Student e-mail accounts are available to students. Students grades are available online. The school has a published electronic and media policy.

Contact Mr. Jeff Oldham, Director of Admission. 859-254-1361 Ext. 207. Fax: 859-254-5627. E-mail: joldham@sayreschool.org. Website: www.sayreschool.org

SCATTERGOOD FRIENDS SCHOOL

1951 Delta Avenue
West Branch, Iowa 52358-8507

Head of School: Mr. Thomas Weber

General Information Coeducational boarding and day college-preparatory, sustainable agriculture, and agriculture research school, affiliated with Society of Friends. Ungraded, ages 14–19. Founded: 1890. Setting: rural. Nearest major city is Iowa City. Students are housed in Single-gender/gender identity dorms. 126-acre campus. 15 buildings on campus. Approved or accredited by Friends Council on Education, Independent Schools Association of the Central States, The Association of Boarding Schools, and Iowa Department of Education. Member of National Association of Independent Schools. Endowment: $5.5 million. Total enrollment: 35. Upper school average class size: 10. Upper school faculty-student ratio: 1:3. There are 180 required school days per year for Upper School students. Upper School students typically attend 5 days per week. The average school day consists of 7 hours.

Upper School Student Profile Grade 9: 5 students (3 boys, 2 girls); Grade 10: 9 students (5 boys, 4 girls); Grade 11: 10 students (6 boys, 4 girls); Grade 12: 11 students (6 boys, 5 girls). 94% of students are boarding students. 29% are state residents. 12 states are represented in upper school student body. 26% are international students. International students from Afghanistan, China, Colombia, Ethiopia, Mexico, and Taiwan; 2 other countries represented in student body. 20% of students are members of Society of Friends.

Faculty School total: 14. In upper school: 9 men, 5 women; 7 have advanced degrees; 12 reside on campus.

Subjects Offered 3-dimensional art, advanced biology, agriculture, algebra, American democracy, American government, American history, animal husbandry, art, backpacking, biology, calculus, career/college preparation, ceramics, chemistry, college admission preparation, college counseling, college placement, college planning, college writing, community service, creative writing, critical thinking, digital art, drama, drama performance, drawing and design, ecology, environmental systems, environmental science, ESL, ethics, expository writing, fencing, fine arts, geometry, government/civics, history, independent study, Internet research, mathematics, organic gardening, photography, physics, poetry, portfolio writing, pottery, Quakerism and ethics, religion, research seminar, science, science project, science research, senior seminar, sex education, social justice, social studies, Spanish, sports conditioning, studio art, U.S. government, U.S. history, writing, writing workshop, yearbook, yoga.

Graduation Requirements Algebra, American history, biology, college counseling, English, foreign language, geometry, government, health and wellness, history, humanities, junior and senior seminars, physical education (includes health), physics, Quakerism and ethics, religious studies, science, senior thesis, U.S. government, U.S. history, world history, world literature, 30 hours of community service per year of attendance, 20-page senior research paper with a thesis defense presentation, acceptance to an accredited 4-year college or university.

Special Academic Programs Honors section; independent study; academic accommodation for the gifted; ESL (9 students enrolled).

College Admission Counseling 12 students graduated in 2016; 11 went to college, including Earlham College; Howard University; Luther College; Reed College; Syracuse University; Warren Wilson College. Other: 1 went to work.

Student Life Upper grades have specified standards of dress, student council. Discipline rests equally with students and faculty. Attendance at religious services is required.

Summer Programs Session focuses on organic farming; held on campus; accepts boys and girls; open to students from other schools. 5 students usually enrolled. 2017 schedule: June to August.

Tuition and Aid Day student tuition: $4588–$18,350; 5-day tuition and room/board: $7463–$29,850; 7-day tuition and room/board: $7463–$29,850. Tuition installment plan (monthly payment plans, individually arranged payment plans). Need-based scholarship grants, needs-based sliding scale tuition available. In 2016–17, 60% of upper-school students received aid. Total amount of financial aid awarded in 2016–17: $469,965.

Admissions Traditional secondary-level entrance grade is 9. Essay and Math Placement Exam required. Deadline for receipt of application materials: none. Application fee required: $65. Interview recommended.

Athletics Coed Interscholastic: basketball, cross-country running, fencing, soccer; coed intramural: archery, backpacking, bicycling, canoeing/kayaking, cooperative games, dance, fishing, fitness, fitness walking, Frisbee, hiking/backpacking, juggling, kayaking, martial arts, outdoor activities, outdoor recreation, outdoors, physical fitness, running, ultimate Frisbee, yoga.

Computers Computers are regularly used in all classes. Computer network features include on-campus library services, online commercial services, Internet access, wireless campus network, Internet filtering or blocking technology, 1-to-1 laptop program. Campus intranet, student e-mail accounts, and computer access in designated common areas are available to students. Students grades are available online.

Contact Ms. Alicia Taylor, Director of Admissions. 319-643-7628. Fax: 319-643-7485. E-mail: admissions@scattergood.org. Website: www.scattergood.org

SCHECK HILLEL COMMUNITY SCHOOL

19000 25th Avenue

North Miami Beach, Florida 33180

Head of School: Dr. Ezra Levy

General Information Coeducational day and distance learning college-preparatory, arts, religious studies, bilingual studies, and technology school, affiliated with Jewish faith; primarily serves students with learning disabilities and dyslexic students. Grades PK–12. Distance learning grades 9–12. Founded: 1970. Setting: suburban. 14-acre campus. 3 buildings on campus. Approved or accredited by Florida Department of Education. Member of National Association of Independent Schools and Secondary School Admission Test Board. Total enrollment: 1,045. Upper school average class size: 20. Upper school faculty-student ratio: 1:15. There are 180 required school days per year for Upper School students. Upper School students typically attend 5 days per week. The average school day consists of 8 hours.

Upper School Student Profile 100% of students are Jewish.

Faculty School total: 250.

Subjects Offered Studio art, studio art-AP, tennis, the Web, theater, track and field, U.S. government, U.S. government and politics-AP, U.S. history-AP, United States government-AP, Web site design, world history, world history-AP.

Graduation Requirements Jewish studies.

Special Academic Programs International Baccalaureate program; Advanced Placement exam preparation; honors section; study at local college for college credit; academic accommodation for the gifted and the artistically talented; remedial reading and/or remedial writing; remedial math; programs in English, mathematics, general development for dyslexic students; ESL (100 students enrolled).

College Admission Counseling 70 students graduated in 2015; all went to college, including Florida International University; Florida State University, University of Central Florida; University of Florida, University of Maryland, Baltimore County; University of Miami. Mean SAT critical reading: 577, mean SAT math: 612, mean SAT writing: 574, mean composite ACT: 24.

Student Life Upper grades have uniform requirement, student council, honor system. Discipline rests primarily with faculty. Attendance at religious services is required.

Tuition and Aid Day student tuition: $24,700–$30,000. Tuition installment plan (FACTS Tuition Payment Plan). Tuition reduction for siblings, merit scholarship grants, need-based scholarship grants available. In 2015–16, 25% of upper-school students received aid; total upper-school merit-scholarship money awarded: $100,000. Total amount of financial aid awarded in 2015–16: $1,000,000.

Admissions Traditional secondary-level entrance grade is 9. For fall 2015, 200 students applied for upper-level admission, 180 were accepted, 170 enrolled. SSAT required. Deadline for receipt of application materials: February 15. Application fee required: $200. Interview required.

Athletics Interscholastic: basketball (boys, girls), crew (b,g), cross-country running (b,g), fitness (b,g), flag football (b,g), football (b), golf (b,g), running (b,g), soccer (b,g), strength & conditioning (b,g), tennis (b,g), volleyball (b,g), winter soccer (b,g); coed interscholastic: crew, cross-country running, fitness, tennis. 10 PE instructors.

Computers Computer network features include on-campus library services, Internet access, Internet filtering or blocking technology. Campus intranet, student e-mail accounts, and computer access in designated common areas are available to students. Students grades are available online. The school has a published electronic and media policy.

Contact Mrs. Betty Salinas, Director of Admissions. 305-931-2831 Ext. 173. Fax: 305-932-7463. E-mail: salinas@ehillel.org. Website: www.hillel-nmb.org/

SCHOLAR'S HALL PREPARATORY SCHOOL

888 Trillium Drive

Kitchener, Ontario N2R 1K4, Canada

Head of School: Mr. Frederick T. Gore

General Information Coeducational day college-preparatory, general academic, arts, and business school. Grades JK–12. Founded: 1997. Setting: small town. Nearest major city is Toronto, Canada. 10-acre campus. 1 building on campus. Approved or accredited by Ontario Department of Education. Language of instruction: English. Total enrollment: 105. Upper school average class size: 15. Upper school faculty-student ratio: 1:10. There are 200 required school days per year for Upper School students. Upper School students typically attend 5 days per week. The average school day consists of 7 hours.

Upper School Student Profile Grade 6: 14 students (7 boys, 7 girls); Grade 7: 14 students (7 boys, 7 girls); Grade 8: 14 students (7 boys, 7 girls); Grade 9: 15 students (8 boys, 7 girls); Grade 10: 15 students (8 boys, 7 girls); Grade 11: 15 students (8 boys, 7 girls); Grade 12: 15 students (8 boys, 7 girls).

Faculty School total: 10. In upper school: 5 men, 5 women; 5 have advanced degrees.

Subjects Offered 20th century history, 20th century physics, accounting, acting, advanced biology, advanced chemistry, advanced computer applications, advanced math, algebra, all academic, analysis and differential calculus, anthropology, applied arts, art, art history, biology, business mathematics, calculus, Canadian geography, Canadian history, Canadian literature, career education, career planning, character education, chemistry, computer processing, computer science, computer technologies, consumer law, drama performance, economics, English, entrepreneurship, environmental science, family studies, finite math, functions, geography, government/civics, health education, history, history of rock and roll, humanities, integrated arts, language arts, law studies, marketing, martial arts, mathematics, media arts, media studies, music, physical education, physics, science, social sciences, society challenge and change, strategies for success, urban studies, world issues.

Special Academic Programs Academic accommodation for the gifted, the musically talented, and the artistically talented; remedial reading and/or remedial writing; remedial math; programs in English, mathematics, general development for dyslexic students; ESL (20 students enrolled).

College Admission Counseling 14 students graduated in 2016; 2 went to college, including McMaster University; Queen's University at Kingston; St. Francis Xavier University; The University of Western Ontario; University of Waterloo; Wilfrid Laurier University. Other: 1 entered military service, 11 entered a postgraduate year.

Student Life Upper grades have uniform requirement, student council, honor system. Discipline rests primarily with faculty.

Summer Programs Remediation, advancement, ESL, art/fine arts, computer instruction programs offered; session focuses on academics; held on campus; accepts boys and girls; open to students from other schools. 100 students usually enrolled. 2017 schedule: July 1 to August 30. Application deadline: May 30.

Tuition and Aid Day student tuition: CAN$11,900. Guaranteed tuition plan. Tuition installment plan (The Tuition Plan, monthly payment plans, individually arranged payment plans). Tuition reduction for siblings, bursaries available. In 2016–17, 10% of upper-school students received aid. Total amount of financial aid awarded in 2016–17: CAN$20,000.

Admissions Traditional secondary-level entrance grade is 9. For fall 2016, 50 students applied for upper-level admission, 50 were accepted, 50 enrolled. Woodcock-Johnson Educational Evaluation, WISC III required. Deadline for receipt of application materials: June 1. No application fee required. On-campus interview required.

Athletics Coed Interscholastic: badminton, ball hockey, baseball, basketball, cross-country running, fencing, fitness, fitness walking, flag football, floor hockey, Frisbee, golf, hockey, ice hockey, independent competitive sports, indoor hockey, martial arts, outdoor activities, outdoor education, physical fitness, self defense, soccer, softball, table tennis, volleyball; coed intramural: badminton, ball hockey, baseball, basketball, bowling, cross-country running, fencing, fitness, fitness walking, flag football, floor hockey, Frisbee, golf, hockey, ice hockey, indoor hockey, martial arts, outdoor activities, outdoor education, physical fitness, self defense, soccer, softball, table tennis, volleyball. 2 PE instructors.

Computers Computers are regularly used in all academic classes. Computer network features include Internet access, wireless campus network, Internet filtering or blocking technology. Campus intranet and computer access in designated common areas are available to students. The school has a published electronic and media policy.

Contact 519-888-6620. Fax: 519-884-0316. Website: www.scholarshall.com

SCHULE SCHLOSS SALEM

Schlossbezirk 1

Salem 88682, Germany

Head of School: Mr. Bernd Westermeyer

General Information Coeducational boarding and day college-preparatory, general academic, German Abitur, and International Baccalaureate school, affiliated with Advent Christian Church. Grades 5–12. Founded: 1920. Setting: small town. Nearest major city is Stuttgart, Germany. Students are housed in coed dormitories. 32-hectare campus. 14 buildings on campus. Approved or accredited by International Baccalaureate Organization. Member of European Council of International Schools.

Languages of instruction: English and German. Endowment: €45 million. Total enrollment: 675. Upper school average class size: 15. Upper school faculty-student ratio: 1:5. There are 200 required school days per year for Upper School students. Upper School students typically attend 6 days per week. The average school day consists of 6 hours.

Upper School Student Profile Grade 11: 130 students (67 boys, 63 girls); Grade 12: 157 students (81 boys, 76 girls); Grade 13: 161 students (86 boys, 75 girls).

Faculty School total: 125. In upper school: 35 men, 30 women; 60 have advanced degrees; 40 reside on campus.

Subjects Offered Art history, biology, chemistry, computer science, economics, English, ethics, French, geography, German, Greek, history, Latin, mathematics, music, philosophy, physical education, physics, political science, religion, Russian, science, Spanish, theater arts, visual arts.

Graduation Requirements Arts and fine arts (art, music, dance, drama), English, foreign language, German, mathematics, physical education (includes health), science, social sciences, theory of knowledge, 2 hours of community service per week, academic requirements vary depending upon academic program pursued.

Special Academic Programs International Baccalaureate program; independent study; term-away projects; domestic exchange program (with Bishop's College School, Sedbergh School, The Athenian School, Choate Rosemary Hall); study abroad; academic accommodation for the gifted, the musically talented, and the artistically talented; ESL.

College Admission Counseling 132 students graduated in 2016; 128 went to college, including Harvard University; University of Chicago.

Student Life Upper grades have student council. Discipline rests equally with students and faculty.

Summer Programs Enrichment, advancement, ESL, sports, art/fine arts programs offered; session focuses on language training in English and German; held on campus; accepts boys and girls; open to students from other schools. 65 students usually enrolled. 2017 schedule: July 25 to August 9. Application deadline: none.

Tuition and Aid Day student tuition: €12,000; 7-day tuition and room/board: €28,000. Guaranteed tuition plan. Tuition installment plan (monthly payment plans, individually arranged payment plans, trimester payment plan, annual payment plan). Tuition reduction for siblings, merit scholarship grants, need-based scholarship grants, need-based loans available. In 2016–17, 30% of upper-school students received aid; total upper-school merit-scholarship money awarded: €2,000,000.

Admissions School's own exam or school's own test required. Deadline for receipt of application materials: none. Application fee required: €1200. Interview required.

Athletics Interscholastic: basketball (boys, girls), field hockey (b,g), gymnastics (b,g), indoor hockey (b,g), rugby (b), volleyball (b,g); intramural: aerobics/dance (g); basketball (b,g), field hockey (b,g), gymnastics (b,g), indoor hockey (b,g), rowing (b,g), rugby (b), soccer (b,g), softball (b,g), track and field (b,g), ultimate Frisbee (b,g), volleyball (b,g); coed interscholastic: sailing, volleyball; coed intramural: alpine skiing, archery, backpacking, badminton, bicycling, canoeing/kayaking, Circus, climbing, cross-country running, equestrian sports, fitness, golf, handball, hiking/backpacking, horseback riding, independent competitive sports, jogging, kayaking, life saving, mountain biking, nordic skiing, outdoor activities, rock climbing, running, sailing, sea rescue, skiing (cross-country), skiing (downhill), snowboarding, snowshoeing, squash, strength & conditioning, swimming and diving, table tennis, tennis, volleyball, wall climbing, water polo, weight training, windsurfing, yoga. 7 PE instructors, 7 coaches.

Computers Computers are regularly used in economics classes. Computer network features include on-campus library services, Internet access, Internet filtering or blocking technology. The school has a published electronic and media policy.

Contact Ms. Dagmar Berger, Director of Admissions. 49-7553-919 Ext. 337. Fax: 49-7553-919 Ext. 303. E-mail: dagmar.berger@schule-schloss-salem.de. Website: www.salem-net.de

SCICORE ACADEMY

156 Maxwell Ave.
Hightstown, New Jersey 08520

Head of School: Arthur T. Poulos, PhD

General Information Coeducational day college-preparatory school. Grades K–12. Founded: 2002. Setting: small town. Nearest major city is Princeton. 5-acre campus. 1 building on campus. Approved or accredited by Middle States Association of Colleges and Schools. Total enrollment: 95. Upper school average class size: 11. Upper school faculty-student ratio: 1:7. There are 170 required school days per year for Upper School students. Upper School students typically attend 5 days per week. The average school day consists of 6 hours and 30 minutes.

Faculty School total: 16. In upper school: 8 men, 3 women; 5 have advanced degrees.

Subjects Offered Advanced biology, advanced chemistry, advanced math, algebra, American government, American history, American literature, anatomy and physiology, art, biology, biology-AP, biotechnology, British literature, calculus, chemistry, chemistry-AP, Chinese, choir, drama, electronics, English composition, French, history of science, lab science, logic, rhetoric, and debate, microcomputer technology applications, music appreciation, physics, pre-calculus, programming, public speaking, SAT preparation, science project, senior project, Spanish, speech and debate, U.S. history, Western civilization, world literature.

Graduation Requirements Advanced math, algebra, American government, American history, American literature, art, biology, British literature, chemistry, civics, computer programming, computer science, English, English composition, foreign language, geometry, lab science, logic, rhetoric, and debate, music, physical education (includes health), physics, programming, SAT preparation, science project, U.S. history, Western civilization, world literature, 4 years science including physics, 4 years mathematics, senior project, 4 years foreign language, statistics, math fair project.

Special Academic Programs 3 Advanced Placement exams for which test preparation is offered; honors section; independent study; academic accommodation for the gifted and the artistically talented; ESL (8 students enrolled).

College Admission Counseling 8 students graduated in 2016; all went to college, including Cornell University; Emory University, Oxford College; Rutgers University–New Brunswick; Tulane University.

Student Life Upper grades have uniform requirement, honor system. Discipline rests primarily with faculty.

Summer Programs Enrichment, advancement, computer instruction programs offered; session focuses on science, math, writing, and computer camps; held on campus; accepts boys and girls; open to students from other schools. 90 students usually enrolled. 2017 schedule: June 21 to August 20. Application deadline: none.

Tuition and Aid Day student tuition: $10,700. Tuition installment plan (monthly payment plans). Tuition reduction for siblings available.

Admissions Traditional secondary-level entrance grade is 9. Admissions testing required. Deadline for receipt of application materials: none. Application fee required: $50. Interview recommended.

Athletics Interscholastic: basketball (boys); intramural: aerobics/dance (g); coed interscholastic: cross-country running, golf, soccer, volleyball; coed intramural: cross-country running, equestrian sports, fencing, horseback riding. 2 PE instructors, 1 coach.

Computers Computers are regularly used in English, foreign language, French, programming, science, Spanish, yearbook classes. Computer resources include Internet access, wireless campus network. Student e-mail accounts and computer access in designated common areas are available to students. Students grades are available online. The school has a published electronic and media policy.

Contact Mrs. Danette N. Poulos, Vice Principal. 609-448-8950. Fax: 609-448-8952. E-mail: atpoulos@scicore.org. Website: www.scicore.org/

SCOTUS CENTRAL CATHOLIC HIGH SCHOOL

1554 18th Avenue
Columbus, Nebraska 68601-5132

Head of School: Mr. Jeff Ohnoutka

General Information Coeducational day college-preparatory school, affiliated with Roman Catholic Church. Grades 7–12. Founded: 1884. Setting: small town. Nearest major city is Omaha. 1-acre campus. 1 building on campus. Approved or accredited by National Catholic Education Association, North Central Association of Colleges and Schools, and Nebraska Department of Education. Endowment: $8.3 million. Total enrollment: 364. Upper school average class size: 20. Upper school faculty-student ratio: 1:13. There are 174 required school days per year for Upper School students. Upper School students typically attend 5 days per week. The average school day consists of 6 hours and 40 minutes.

Upper School Student Profile Grade 9: 49 students (24 boys, 25 girls); Grade 10: 68 students (37 boys, 31 girls); Grade 11: 65 students (33 boys, 32 girls); Grade 12: 65 students (35 boys, 30 girls). 95% of students are Roman Catholic.

Faculty School total: 30. In upper school: 8 men, 21 women; 7 have advanced degrees.

Subjects Offered Accounting, ACT preparation, advanced biology, advanced chemistry, advanced math, Advanced Placement courses, algebra, American government, American history, art, astronomy, band, Bible studies, biology, bookkeeping, calculus, calculus-AP, campus ministry, career and personal planning, career exploration, career/college preparation, Catholic belief and practice, character education, chemistry, child development, choir, choral music, chorus, community service, computer applications, computer multimedia, computer studies, computer technologies, concert band, concert choir, consumer economics, consumer mathematics, contemporary problems, CPR, current events, digital applications, drama, earth science, economics, English, English-AP, fabric arts, family and consumer science, fitness, food and nutrition, geography, government, guidance, health and safety, history, history-AP, human development, instrumental music, jazz band, jazz ensemble, journalism, keyboarding, life management skills, life skills, marching band, modern world history, personal fitness, physical education, physical science, physics, physiology, psychology, reading/study skills, sociology, Spanish, speech, speech and debate, speech communications, student publications, textiles, theater, U.S. history, vocal ensemble, voice, weight training, world history, yearbook.

Graduation Requirements Algebra, American government, American history, biology, chemistry, computer applications, electives, English, geometry, mathematics, modern history, physical education (includes health), religion (includes Bible studies and theology), Spanish, speech, U.S. history, world history, 80 hours of Living the Faith community/church/school service.

Special Academic Programs Study at local college for college credit; special instructional classes for IEP for students with learning disabilities.

College Admission Counseling 64 students graduated in 2016; 60 went to college, including Creighton University; South Dakota State University; University of

Nebraska–Lincoln; University of Nebraska at Kearney; University of Nebraska at Omaha; University of Notre Dame. Other: 1 went to work, 3 entered military service. Median composite ACT: 23. 42% scored over 26 on composite ACT.

Student Life Upper grades have uniform requirement, student council, honor system. Discipline rests primarily with faculty. Attendance at religious services is required.

Tuition and Aid Day student tuition: $2675–$2775. Tuition installment plan (monthly payment plans). Need-based scholarship grants, paying campus jobs available. In 2016–17, 26% of upper-school students received aid. Total amount of financial aid awarded in 2016–17: $176,709.

Admissions Traditional secondary-level entrance grade is 9. Deadline for receipt of application materials: none. No application fee required. Interview recommended.

Athletics Interscholastic: baseball (boys), basketball (b,g), cheering (g), cross-country running (b,g), football (b), golf (b,g), soccer (b,g), softball (g), swimming and diving (b,g), tennis (b,g), track and field (b,g), volleyball (g), wrestling (b). 3 PE instructors, 15 coaches, 2 athletic trainers.

Computers Computers are regularly used in business, computer applications, English, graphic design, history, journalism, keyboarding, lab/keyboard, news writing, newspaper, photography, publications, religion, social sciences, speech, technology, Web site design, word processing, writing, yearbook classes. Computer network features include on-campus library services, Internet access, wireless campus network, Internet filtering or blocking technology. Campus intranet, student e-mail accounts, and computer access in designated common areas are available to students. Students grades are available online. The school has a published electronic and media policy.

Contact Mrs. Pamela K. Weir, 7-12 Guidance Counselor. 402-564-7165 Ext. 121. Fax: 402-564-6004. E-mail: pweir@scotuscc.org. Website: www.scotuscc.org

SEABURY HALL

480 Olinda Road
Makawao, Hawaii 96768-9399

Head of School: Ms. Sarah Bakhiet

General Information Coeducational day college-preparatory and arts school, affiliated with Episcopal Church. Grades 6–12. Founded: 1964. Setting: rural. Nearest major city is Kahului. 65-acre campus. 8 buildings on campus. Approved or accredited by Western Association of Schools and Colleges. Member of National Association of Independent Schools and Secondary School Admission Test Board. Endowment: $37.9 million. Total enrollment: 455. Upper school average class size: 15. Upper school faculty-student ratio: 1:11. There are 175 required school days per year for Upper School students. Upper School students typically attend 5 days per week. The average school day consists of 7 hours and 30 minutes.

Upper School Student Profile Grade 9: 83 students (38 boys, 45 girls); Grade 10: 81 students (42 boys, 39 girls); Grade 11: 79 students (36 boys, 43 girls); Grade 12: 77 students (36 boys, 41 girls). 5% of students are members of Episcopal Church.

Faculty School total: 56. In upper school: 23 men, 15 women; 23 have advanced degrees.

Subjects Offered Acting, algebra, American history, American history-AP, American literature, American literature-AP, art, band, biology, biology-AP, calculus-AP, ceramics, chemistry, chorus, college counseling, college placement, college planning, community service, comparative religion, computer programming, dance, drawing, economics, engineering, English, English literature, ethics, European history-AP, expository writing, fine arts, geometry, global issues, government, Hawaiian history, Hawaiian language, history, Japanese, keyboarding, mathematics, mythology, painting, philosophy, physical education, physics, physics-AP, political science, pre-algebra, pre-calculus, religion, SAT preparation, science, set design, social studies, Spanish, Spanish-AP, speech, studio art-AP, yearbook.

Graduation Requirements Arts and fine arts (art, music, dance, drama), English, foreign language, mathematics, physical education (includes health), religion (includes Bible studies and theology), science, social studies (includes history), speech. Community service is required.

Special Academic Programs 13 Advanced Placement exams for which test preparation is offered; honors section; independent study; academic accommodation for the gifted.

College Admission Counseling 72 students graduated in 2016; 71 went to college, including California Polytechnic State University, San Luis Obispo; Chapman University; Colorado State University; Gonzaga University; University of Hawaii at Manoa; University of San Diego. Other: 1 had other specific plans. Mean SAT critical reading: 550, mean SAT math: 570, mean SAT writing: 565, mean combined SAT: 1685, mean composite ACT: 25.

Student Life Upper grades have specified standards of dress, student council, honor system. Discipline rests primarily with faculty.

Summer Programs Enrichment, sports, art/fine arts programs offered; session focuses on enrichment; held on campus; accepts boys and girls; open to students from other schools. 180 students usually enrolled. 2017 schedule: June 6 to July 8. Application deadline: June 6.

Tuition and Aid Day student tuition: $19,425. Tuition installment plan (FACTS Tuition Payment Plan). Need-based scholarship grants available. In 2016–17, 31% of upper-school students received aid. Total amount of financial aid awarded in 2016–17: $935,850.

Admissions Traditional secondary-level entrance grade is 9. For fall 2016, 92 students applied for upper-level admission, 63 were accepted, 46 enrolled. ERB CTP III, ISEE or SSAT required. Deadline for receipt of application materials: February 17. Application fee required: $75. Interview recommended.

Athletics Interscholastic: ballet (boys, girls), baseball (b), basketball (b,g), cross-country running (b,g), dance (g), diving (g), football (b), golf (b,g), independent competitive sports (b,g), modern dance (b,g), paddling (b,g), physical fitness (b,g), riflery (b,g), soccer (b,g), softball (g), surfing (b,g), swimming and diving (b,g), tennis (b,g), track and field (b,g), volleyball (b,g), water polo (g); intramural: basketball (b,g), fitness (b,g), strength & conditioning (b,g); coed interscholastic: dance, paddling, physical fitness; coed intramural: fitness, outdoor adventure, outdoor education, track and field, volleyball. 4 PE instructors, 12 coaches, 1 athletic trainer.

Computers Computers are regularly used in art, economics, English, foreign language, history, journalism, mathematics, newspaper, science, speech, yearbook classes. Computer network features include on-campus library services, online commercial services, Internet access, wireless campus network, Internet filtering or blocking technology. Campus intranet, student e-mail accounts, and computer access in designated common areas are available to students. Students grades are available online. The school has a published electronic and media policy.

Contact Elaine V. Nelson, Director of Admissions. 808-572-0807. Fax: 808-572-2042. E-mail: enelson@seaburyhall.org. Website: www.seaburyhall.org

SEACREST COUNTRY DAY SCHOOL

7100 Davis Boulevard
Naples, Florida 34104

Head of School: Dr. John Watson

General Information Coeducational day college-preparatory, arts, technology, and internships school. Grades 9–12. Founded: 1983. Setting: suburban. 40-acre campus. 3 buildings on campus. Approved or accredited by Florida Council of Independent Schools, Southern Association of Colleges and Schools, Southern Association of Independent Schools, and Florida Department of Education. Member of National Association of Independent Schools. Total enrollment: 399. Upper school average class size: 16. Upper school faculty-student ratio: 1:9. There are 180 required school days per year for Upper School students. Upper School students typically attend 5 days per week. The average school day consists of 7 hours and 45 minutes.

Upper School Student Profile Grade 6: 34 students (15 boys, 19 girls); Grade 7: 28 students (14 boys, 14 girls); Grade 8: 39 students (20 boys, 19 girls); Grade 9: 41 students (25 boys, 16 girls); Grade 10: 37 students (25 boys, 12 girls); Grade 11: 41 students (22 boys, 19 girls); Grade 12: 38 students (18 boys, 20 girls).

Faculty School total: 30. In upper school: 15 men, 14 women; 18 have advanced degrees.

Subjects Offered 3-dimensional art, 3-dimensional design, acting, advanced biology, advanced chemistry, advanced math, Advanced Placement courses, advanced studio art-AP, algebra, American government, American history, American literature, anatomy and physiology, athletics, band, baseball, Basic programming, basketball, Bible as literature, biology, biology-AP, calculus, calculus-AP, career/college preparation, ceramics, character education, chemistry, chemistry-AP, choir, chorus, college admission preparation, college counseling, college placement, college planning, college writing, composition, composition-AP, computer education, computer programming, concert band, conservation, creative thinking.

Graduation Requirements 120 volunteer hours, internship

Special Academic Programs Honors section; independent study; academic accommodation for the gifted, the musically talented, and the artistically talented.

College Admission Counseling 37 students graduated in 2016; all went to college. Mean SAT critical reading: 572, mean SAT math: 555, mean SAT writing: 591, mean composite ACT: 25.

Student Life Upper grades have specified standards of dress, student council, honor system. Discipline rests primarily with faculty.

Tuition and Aid Day student tuition: $22,580. Tuition installment plan (FACTS Tuition Payment Plan, monthly payment plans). Need-based scholarship grants available. In 2016–17, 44% of upper-school students received aid. Total amount of financial aid awarded in 2016–17: $880,234.

Admissions Traditional secondary-level entrance grade is 9. For fall 2016, 40 students applied for upper-level admission, 28 were accepted, 20 enrolled. Deadline for receipt of application materials: none. Application fee required: $75. Interview recommended.

Athletics Interscholastic: aquatics (boys, girls), baseball (b), basketball (b,g), cross-country running (b,g), diving (b,g), golf (b,g), soccer (b,g), softball (g), swimming and diving (b,g), tennis (b,g), track and field (b,g), volleyball (g); intramural: flag football (b); coed interscholastic: sailing; coed intramural: fishing, physical training, scuba diving, strength & conditioning, weight training. 2 PE instructors, 10 coaches, 1 athletic trainer.

Computers Computer network features include on-campus library services, online commercial services, Internet access, wireless campus network, Internet filtering or blocking technology. Campus intranet, student e-mail accounts, and computer access in designated common areas are available to students. The school has a published electronic and media policy.

Contact Mr. Ryan Jobe, Director of Enrollment Management. 239-793-1986. Fax: 239-793-1460. E-mail: rjobe@seacrest.org. Website: www.seacrest.org/

SEATTLE ACADEMY OF ARTS AND SCIENCES

1201 East Union Street
Seattle, Washington 98122

Head of School: Joe Puggelli

General Information Coeducational day college-preparatory school. Grades 6–12. Founded: 1983. Setting: urban. 3-acre campus. 6 buildings on campus. Approved or accredited by Northwest Association of Independent Schools and Washington Department of Education. Member of National Association of Independent Schools. Endowment: $15.3 million. Total enrollment: 764. Upper school average class size: 18. Upper school faculty-student ratio: 1:6. There are 170 required school days per year for Upper School students. Upper School students typically attend 5 days per week. The average school day consists of 6 hours and 45 minutes.

Upper School Student Profile Grade 9: 132 students (68 boys, 64 girls); Grade 10: 140 students (63 boys, 77 girls); Grade 11: 124 students (63 boys, 61 girls); Grade 12: 117 students (56 boys, 61 girls).

Faculty School total: 123. In upper school: 60 men, 63 women; 78 have advanced degrees.

Subjects Offered 20th century world history, 3-dimensional art, 3-dimensional design, acting, advanced biology, advanced chemistry, advanced math, algebra, all academic, American democracy, American government, American history, American literature, Asian studies, biology, biotechnology, calculus, chemistry, choir, civics, community service, dance, debate, drawing, economics, English, environmental systems, French, geometry, health, history, humanities, independent study, instrumental music, lab science, literature, Mandarin, marine science, math analysis, musical productions, painting, physical education, physics, printmaking, robotics, sculpture, Spanish, speech, stagecraft, statistics, visual arts, vocal music, world literature, yearbook.

Graduation Requirements Arts and fine arts (art, music, dance, drama), English, foreign language, history, mathematics, physical education (includes health), science, social studies (includes history). Community service is required.

Special Academic Programs Honors section; independent study; term-away projects; study abroad; academic accommodation for the gifted, the musically talented, and the artistically talented; remedial reading and/or remedial writing; remedial math; programs in English, mathematics, general development for dyslexic students.

College Admission Counseling 112 students graduated in 2016; 111 went to college, including Loyola Marymount University; Pitzer College; Seattle University; The University of British Columbia; University of Southern California; University of Washington. Other: 1 went to work. Mean SAT critical reading: 642, mean SAT math: 617, mean SAT writing: 6161, mean combined SAT: 1874, mean composite ACT: 27.

Student Life Upper grades have student council, honor system. Discipline rests equally with students and faculty.

Summer Programs Enrichment, sports, art/fine arts programs offered; held both on and off campus; accepts boys and girls; open to students from other schools. 100 students usually enrolled. 2017 schedule: June 12 to August 11. Application deadline: May 1.

Tuition and Aid Day student tuition: $32,382. Tuition installment plan (Academic Management Services Plan, monthly payment plans). Need-based scholarship grants available. In 2016–17, 20% of upper-school students received aid.

Admissions Traditional secondary-level entrance grade is 9. ISEE or SSAT required. Deadline for receipt of application materials: January 12. Application fee required: $100. On-campus interview required.

Athletics Interscholastic: basketball (boys, girls), cross-country running (b,g), Frisbee (b,g), golf (b,g), lacrosse (b,g), soccer (b,g), tennis (b,g), track and field (b,g), ultimate Frisbee (b,g), volleyball (g); coed interscholastic: dance, dance squad, dance team, wrestling; coed intramural: alpine skiing, backpacking, canoeing/kayaking, climbing, fitness, hiking/backpacking, kayaking, outdoor activities, outdoor recreation, paint ball, physical fitness, skiing (cross-country), skiing (downhill), snowboarding, snowshoeing, squash, weight training. 5 PE instructors, 30 coaches, 2 athletic trainers.

Computers Computers are regularly used in all academic, computer applications, English, foreign language, graphic design, history, mathematics, newspaper, science, speech, study skills, theater arts, video film production, Web site design, yearbook classes. Computer network features include on-campus library services, online commercial services, Internet access, wireless campus network, Internet filtering or blocking technology. Student e-mail accounts are available to students. Students grades are available online. The school has a published electronic and media policy.

Contact Jim Rupp, Admission Director. 206-324-7227. Fax: 206-323-6618. E-mail: jrupp@seattleacademy.org. Website: www.seattleacademy.org

SEATTLE LUTHERAN HIGH SCHOOL

4100 SW Genesee Street
Seattle, Washington 98116

Head of School: Dave Meyer

General Information Coeducational day college-preparatory, general academic, arts, and religious studies school, affiliated with Lutheran Church; primarily serves students with learning disabilities and dyslexic students. Grades 9–12. Founded: 1977. Setting: urban. 2-acre campus. 1 building on campus. Approved or accredited by Lutheran School Accreditation Commission, National Lutheran School Accreditation, Northwest Accreditation Commission, and Washington Department of Education. Endowment: $385,000. Total enrollment: 128. Upper school average class size: 18. Upper school faculty-student ratio: 1:9. There are 180 required school days per year for Upper School students. Upper School students typically attend 5 days per week. The average school day consists of 6 hours and 45 minutes.

Upper School Student Profile Grade 9: 27 students (17 boys, 10 girls); Grade 10: 37 students (26 boys, 11 girls); Grade 11: 28 students (15 boys, 13 girls); Grade 12: 36 students (21 boys, 15 girls). 20% of students are Lutheran.

Faculty School total: 16. In upper school: 8 men, 6 women; 5 have advanced degrees.

Subjects Offered 3-dimensional art, Advanced Placement courses, algebra, American government, American history, American history-AP, American literature, American sign language, art, art history, band, biology, boating, British literature (honors), British literature-AP, calculus, calculus-AP, ceramics, chemistry, choir, Christian doctrine, Christian education, Christian ethics, community service, design, drama, earth science, economics, English, English composition, English literature, ESL, French, geography, geometry, handbells, health, history, jazz band, journalism, keyboarding, life skills, newspaper, painting, physical education, physics, portfolio art, pre-algebra, pre-calculus, psychology, publications, religion, robotics, science, senior project, social sciences, social studies, Spanish, Spanish-AP, state history, student government, study skills, world cultures, world history, world literature.

Graduation Requirements American government, American history, arts and fine arts (art, music, dance, drama), biology, English, foreign language, keyboarding, life skills, mathematics, physical education (includes health), religion (includes Bible studies and theology), science, senior project, social sciences, world cultures. Community service is required.

Special Academic Programs 3 Advanced Placement exams for which test preparation is offered; honors section; independent study; remedial reading and/or remedial writing; remedial math; programs in English, mathematics, general development for dyslexic students; ESL (1 student enrolled).

College Admission Counseling 32 students graduated in 2015; 31 went to college, including Concordia University Irvine; Pacific Lutheran University; Seattle Pacific University; South Seattle College; University of Washington; Western Washington University. Other: 1 went to work.

Student Life Upper grades have specified standards of dress, student council, honor system. Discipline rests equally with students and faculty. Attendance at religious services is required.

Tuition and Aid Day student tuition: $8900. Tuition installment plan (SMART Tuition Payment Plan, monthly payment plans). Tuition reduction for siblings, merit scholarship grants, need-based scholarship grants, honors scholarship at entrance to incoming valedictorians of 8th grade class available. In 2015–16, 21% of upper-school students received aid; total upper-school merit-scholarship money awarded: $1000. Total amount of financial aid awarded in 2015–16: $92,710.

Admissions Traditional secondary-level entrance grade is 9. For fall 2015, 42 students applied for upper-level admission, 40 were accepted, 32 enrolled. School's own exam and TAP required. Deadline for receipt of application materials: February 12. Application fee required: $50. Interview required.

Athletics Interscholastic: baseball (boys), basketball (b,g), cheering (b,g), cross-country running (b,g), football (b), physical training (b,g), soccer (g), softball (g), strength & conditioning (b,g), tennis (g), track and field (b,g), volleyball (g), weight training (b,g); intramural: yoga (g); coed interscholastic: golf; coed intramural: fencing, fitness, sailing. 3 PE instructors, 25 coaches.

Computers Computers are regularly used in English, keyboarding, life skills, newspaper, publications, social sciences, study skills, yearbook classes. Computer network features include on-campus library services, Internet access, wireless campus network, Internet filtering or blocking technology. Computer access in designated common areas is available to students. Students grades are available online. The school has a published electronic and media policy.

Contact Rachel Bigliardi, Director of Admission. 206-937-7722 Ext. 18. Fax: 206-937-6781. E-mail: rbigliardi@seattlelutheran.org. Website: www.seattlelutheran.org

SECOND BAPTIST SCHOOL

6410 Woodway Drive
Houston, Texas 77057

Head of School: Dr. Jeff Williams

General Information Coeducational day college-preparatory school, affiliated with Baptist Church. Grades PK–12. Founded: 1946. Setting: suburban. 42-acre campus. 4 buildings on campus. Approved or accredited by Southern Association of Colleges and Schools, Texas Education Agency, and Texas Department of Education. Upper school average class size: 13. The average school day consists of 7 hours and 30 minutes.

Upper School Student Profile 65% of students are Baptist.

Faculty In upper school: 49 have advanced degrees.

Subjects Offered 3-dimensional art, Advanced Placement courses, algebra, American literature, anatomy and physiology, art, art-AP, band, Bible, biology, biology-AP, British literature, British literature-AP, broadcasting, calculus, calculus-AP, chemistry, chemistry-AP, choir, computer programming, computer programming-AP, computer science, computer science-AP, concert band, concert choir, debate, desktop publishing, drama, economics, English, English-AP, European history-AP, French, French language-AP, French literature-AP, geometry, government, health, honors algebra, honors geometry, jazz ensemble, journalism, Latin, marching band, music theory-AP, photography, physical education, physics, physics-AP, pre-calculus, Spanish, Spanish language-AP, Spanish literature-AP, speech, statistics-AP, U.S. history, U.S. history-AP, world geography, world history.

Graduation Requirements Arts and fine arts (art, music, dance, drama), Bible, computer science, economics, electives, English, foreign language, government, mathematics, physical education (includes health), science, social studies (includes history), speech.

Special Academic Programs Advanced Placement exam preparation; honors section; accelerated programs; independent study; term-away projects; study at local college for college credit; study abroad.

College Admission Counseling 81 students graduated in 2016; all went to college.

Student Life Upper grades have specified standards of dress, student council, honor system. Discipline rests primarily with faculty. Attendance at religious services is required.

Tuition and Aid Day student tuition: $13,116. Tuition installment plan (monthly payment plans). Merit scholarship grants, need-based scholarship grants available. In 2016–17, 20% of upper-school students received aid.

Admissions Traditional secondary-level entrance grade is 9. ISEE and writing sample required. Deadline for receipt of application materials: none. Application fee required: $100. Interview required.

Athletics Interscholastic: baseball (boys), basketball (b,g), cross-country running (b,g), diving (b,g), drill team (g), fitness (b,g), football (b), golf (b,g); coed interscholastic: cheering. 9 PE instructors, 37 coaches, 2 athletic trainers.

Computers Computers are regularly used in all academic classes. Computer network features include on-campus library services, online commercial services, Internet access, wireless campus network, Internet filtering or blocking technology, science student interactive programs and computer-based labs. The school has a published electronic and media policy.

Contact Mrs. Andrea Prothro, Director of Admissions. 713-365-2314. Fax: 713-365-2445. E-mail: aprothro@secondbaptistschool.org. Website: www.secondbaptistschool.org

SEDONA SKY ACADEMY

Rimrock, Arizona
See Special Needs Schools section.

SEISEN INTERNATIONAL SCHOOL

1-12-15 Yoga, Setagaya-ku
Tokyo 158-0097, Japan

Head of School: Ms. Colette Rogers

General Information Coeducational day (boys' only in lower grades) college-preparatory school, affiliated with Roman Catholic Church. Boys grade K, girls grades K–12. Distance learning grades 11–12. Founded: 1962. Setting: urban. Nearest major city is Tokyo, Japan, Japan. 1-hectare campus. 3 buildings on campus. Approved or accredited by Department of Defense Dependents Schools and New England Association of Schools and Colleges. Member of Secondary School Admission Test Board and European Council of International Schools. Language of instruction: English. Total enrollment: 646. Upper school average class size: 19. Upper school faculty-student ratio: 1:4. There are 172 required school days per year for Upper School students. Upper School students typically attend 5 days per week. The average school day consists of 6 hours.

Upper School Student Profile Grade 9: 50 students (50 girls); Grade 10: 37 students (37 girls); Grade 11: 34 students (34 girls); Grade 12: 52 students (52 girls). 12% of students are Roman Catholic.

Faculty School total: 93. In upper school: 21 men, 29 women; 26 have advanced degrees.

Subjects Offered 3-dimensional art, advanced biology, advanced chemistry, advanced math, algebra, art, Asian history, band, bell choir, biology, business, career planning, chemistry, Chinese, choir, college planning, computer graphics, computers, Danish, drama, economics, English, English literature, entrepreneurship, environmental studies, environmental systems, ESL, European history, experiential education, filmmaking, French, geography, geometry, health education, history, honors algebra, honors geometry, information technology, International Baccalaureate courses, Japanese, journalism, Korean, library, library science, math methods, mathematics, model United Nations, music, music composition, music performance, orchestra, painting, performing arts, personal and social education, physical education, physics, pottery, psychology, religion, robotics, science, social sciences, social studies, Spanish, speech, study skills, theory of knowledge, trigonometry, visual arts, world history, yearbook.

Graduation Requirements Arts and fine arts (art, music, dance, drama), electives, English, experiential education, foreign language, mathematics, modern languages, physical education (includes health), religion (includes Bible studies and theology), science, social studies (includes history).

Special Academic Programs International Baccalaureate program; honors section; independent study; remedial reading and/or remedial writing; remedial math; ESL (10 students enrolled).

College Admission Counseling 50 students graduated in 2016; all went to college, including Chapman University, Durham University, Keio University, School of the Art Institute of Chicago, University of British Columbia, University of Edinburgh. Median SAT critical reading: 580, median SAT math: 690, median SAT writing: 630, median combined SAT: 1900, median composite ACT: 28. 44% scored over 600 on SAT critical reading, 74% scored over 600 on SAT math, 59% scored over 600 on SAT writing, 52% scored over 1800 on combined SAT, 67% scored over 26 on composite ACT.

Student Life Upper grades have uniform requirement, student council, honor system. Discipline rests primarily with faculty.

Summer Programs Remediation, enrichment, advancement, ESL, sports, art/fine arts, computer instruction programs offered; session focuses on academic classes; held on campus; accepts boys and girls; open to students from other schools. 6 students usually enrolled. 2017 schedule: June 12 to June 30. Application deadline: May 1.

Tuition and Aid Day student tuition: ¥2,070,000. Tuition installment plan (monthly payment plans, individually arranged payment plans). Tuition reduction for siblings, need-based scholarship grants available. In 2016–17, 2% of upper-school students received aid. Total amount of financial aid awarded in 2016–17: ¥4,500,000.

Admissions Traditional secondary-level entrance grade is 9. For fall 2016, 26 students applied for upper-level admission, 12 were accepted, 6 enrolled. Admissions testing, mathematics proficiency exam, Reading for Understanding or writing sample required. Deadline for receipt of application materials: none. Application fee required: ¥20,000. Interview required.

Athletics Interscholastic: basketball, cross-country running, running, soccer, swimming and diving, tennis, track and field, volleyball, winter soccer; intramural: badminton, outdoor activities, running, soccer, table tennis, tennis. 3 PE instructors.

Computers Computers are regularly used in art, business studies, career education, college planning, economics, English, ESL, foreign language, French, graphic design, history, independent study, information technology, journalism, library science, mathematics, music, psychology, religion, science, Spanish, study skills, writing, yearbook classes. Computer network features include on-campus library services, online commercial services, Internet access, wireless campus network, Internet filtering or blocking technology. Campus intranet, student e-mail accounts, and computer access in designated common areas are available to students.

Contact Ms. Sung Hee Kim, Admissions and Student Records. 81-3-3704-2661 Ext. 1461. Fax: 81-3-3701-1033. E-mail: skim@seisen.com. Website: www.seisen.com

SERVITE HIGH SCHOOL

1952 West La Palma Avenue
Anaheim, California 92801-3595

Head of School: Mr. Michael P. Brennan

General Information Boys' day college-preparatory, arts, business, religious studies, and technology school, affiliated with Roman Catholic Church. Grades 9–12. Founded: 1958. Setting: suburban. 14-acre campus. 9 buildings on campus. Approved or accredited by Western Association of Schools and Colleges and Western Catholic Education Association. Total enrollment: 905. Upper school average class size: 23. Upper school faculty-student ratio: 1:15. There are 187 required school days per year for Upper School students. Upper School students typically attend 5 days per week. The average school day consists of 6 hours and 55 minutes.

Upper School Student Profile Grade 9: 236 students (236 boys); Grade 10: 238 students (238 boys); Grade 11: 224 students (224 boys); Grade 12: 207 students (207 boys). 80% of students are Roman Catholic.

Faculty School total: 60. In upper school: 36 men, 22 women; 50 have advanced degrees.

Subjects Offered Advanced Placement courses, algebra, American government, American history, American history-AP, American literature, anatomy, ancient world history, art, art history, art history-AP, band, biology, calculus, calculus-AP, Catholic belief and practice, chemistry, chemistry-AP, Christian and Hebrew scripture, Christianity, computer science, computer science-AP, drama, drawing, driver education, economics, economics-AP, English, English literature, English literature-AP, English-AP, European history, European history-AP, fine arts, French, general science, geometry, government/civics, guitar, health, health education, history, history of the Catholic Church, honors algebra, honors English, honors geometry, honors U.S. history, instrumental music, journalism, Latin, Latin-AP, mathematics, modern European history-AP, music, music appreciation, performing arts, philosophy, physical education, physical science, physics-AP, physiology, pre-calculus, religion, science, social studies, Spanish, Spanish-AP, studio art, theater, trigonometry, U.S. government and politics-AP, U.S. history, U.S. history-AP, word processing, world cultures.

Graduation Requirements ADL skills, algebra, ancient/medieval philosophy, arts and fine arts (art, music, dance, drama), biology, Catholic belief and practice, church history, English, English composition, English literature, foreign language, geometry, government, language, mathematics, moral theology, physical education (includes health), religion (includes Bible studies and theology), science, social studies (includes history), theology and the arts, U.S. history, 100 hours of Christian service.

Special Academic Programs Advanced Placement exam preparation; honors section; study at local college for college credit; study abroad; special instructional classes for deaf students, blind students.

College Admission Counseling 220 students graduated in 2015; all went to college. Mean SAT critical reading: 538, mean SAT math: 553, mean SAT writing: 522, mean composite ACT: 25.

Student Life Upper grades have specified standards of dress, student council, honor system. Discipline rests equally with students and faculty. Attendance at religious services is required.

Tuition and Aid Day student tuition: $15,275. Tuition installment plan (FACTS Tuition Payment Plan, monthly payment plans, individually arranged payment plans, paid in full or semester payments). Tuition reduction for siblings, merit scholarship grants, need-based scholarship grants, need-based loans, middle-income loans, paying campus jobs available. In 2015–16, 30% of upper-school students received aid; total upper-school merit-scholarship money awarded: $5000. Total amount of financial aid awarded in 2015–16: $1,500,000.

Admissions Traditional secondary-level entrance grade is 9. High School Placement Test or STS required. Deadline for receipt of application materials: January 29. Application fee required: $65. On-campus interview required.

Athletics Interscholastic: aquatics, baseball, basketball, cross-country running, football, golf, lacrosse, soccer, swimming and diving, tennis, track and field, volleyball, water polo, wrestling; intramural: ice hockey, rugby. 2 PE instructors, 101 coaches, 2 athletic trainers.

Computers Computers are regularly used in accounting, art, Bible studies, business, computer applications, economics, English, ethics, history, journalism, Latin, mathematics, music, philosophy, photojournalism, religion, science, social studies, Spanish, technology, theology, video film production, yearbook classes. Computer network features include on-campus library services, online commercial services, Internet access, wireless campus network, Internet filtering or blocking technology, student server profile account and data storage space, homework posting online. Campus intranet, student e-mail accounts, and computer access in designated common areas are available to students. Students grades are available online. The school has a published electronic and media policy.

Contact Mr. Chris Weir '97, Director of Admissions. 714-774-7575 Ext. 1170. Fax: 714-774-1404. E-mail: admissions@servitehs.org. Website: www.servitehs.org

accommodation for the gifted and the artistically talented; remedial reading and/or remedial writing; remedial math.

College Admission Counseling 45 students graduated in 2016; all went to college, including Binghamton University, State University of New York; Le Moyne College; St. Bonaventure University; The University of Scranton; University at Buffalo, the State University of New York. Mean SAT critical reading: 544, mean SAT math: 564, mean SAT writing: 534, mean composite ACT: 24.

Student Life Upper grades have uniform requirement, student council, honor system. Discipline rests primarily with faculty. Attendance at religious services is required.

Summer Programs Sports programs offered; session focuses on athletics; held on campus; accepts boys and girls; open to students from other schools. 200 students usually enrolled. 2017 schedule: July 5 to July 19. Application deadline: June 10.

Tuition and Aid Day student tuition: $6500. Tuition installment plan (monthly payment plans). Tuition reduction for siblings, merit scholarship grants, need-based scholarship grants available. In 2016–17, 40% of upper-school students received aid; total upper-school merit-scholarship money awarded: $10,000. Total amount of financial aid awarded in 2016–17: $200,000.

Admissions Traditional secondary-level entrance grade is 9. Deadline for receipt of application materials: none. Application fee required: $100. Interview required.

Athletics Interscholastic: baseball (boys), basketball (b,g), cross-country running (b,g), field hockey (g), football (b), ice hockey (b), indoor track & field (b,g), lacrosse (b,g), soccer (b,g), softball (g), swimming and diving (b,g), tennis (b,g), track and field (b,g), winter (indoor) track (b,g), wrestling (b); intramural: snowboarding (b,g), strength & conditioning (b,g), weight training (b,g); coed interscholastic: cheering, golf; coed intramural: alpine skiing. 2 PE instructors, 25 coaches, 2 athletic trainers.

Computers Computers are regularly used in business applications, computer applications, desktop publishing, economics, engineering, English, foreign language, history, keyboarding, Latin, mathematics, science, social studies, Spanish, technology, yearbook classes. Computer network features include on-campus library services, online commercial services, Internet access, wireless campus network, Internet filtering or blocking technology. Student e-mail accounts and computer access in designated common areas are available to students. The school has a published electronic and media policy.

Contact Mr. John Kiereck, Director of Admissions. 607-748-7423 Ext. 3. Fax: 607-474-9576. E-mail: jkiereck@syrdiocese.org. Website: www.setoncchs.com

SETON CATHOLIC CENTRAL HIGH SCHOOL

70 Seminary Avenue
Binghamton, New York 13905

Head of School: Mr. Matthew D. Martinkovic

General Information Coeducational day college-preparatory and cybersecurity school, affiliated with Roman Catholic Church. Grades 7–12. Founded: 1963. Setting: suburban. 4-acre campus. 1 building on campus. Approved or accredited by Middle States Association of Colleges and Schools, National Catholic Education Association, and New York Department of Education. Endowment: $1.5 million. Upper school average class size: 23. Upper school faculty-student ratio: 1:23. There are 185 required school days per year for Upper School students. Upper School students typically attend 5 days per week. The average school day consists of 6 hours and 45 minutes.

Upper School Student Profile Grade 7: 62 students (29 boys, 33 girls); Grade 8: 43 students (19 boys, 24 girls); Grade 9: 62 students (33 boys, 29 girls); Grade 10: 52 students (27 boys, 25 girls); Grade 11: 78 students (44 boys, 34 girls); Grade 12: 55 students (31 boys, 24 girls). 90% of students are Roman Catholic.

Faculty School total: 43. In upper school: 16 men, 19 women; 27 have advanced degrees.

Subjects Offered 3-dimensional design, accounting, advanced computer applications, Advanced Placement courses, advertising design, algebra, alternative physical education, American government, American history-AP, American legal systems, American literature, American literature-AP, ancient world history, applied music, architectural drawing, art-AP, band, Bible, biology, biology-AP, business, business law, business mathematics, calculus, calculus-AP, chemistry, chemistry-AP, chorus, Christian scripture, church history, comparative religion, computer applications, computer programming, computer programming-AP, creative drama, criminal justice, dramatic arts, economics, engineering, English, English language and composition-AP, English literature and composition-AP, entrepreneurship, environmental science, ethical decision making, ethics and responsibility, European history-AP, food and nutrition, foreign language, forensics, French, government/civics, guitar, health, honors English, honors geometry, instrumental music, integrated mathematics, keyboarding, Latin, Latin-AP, law and the legal system, literature and composition-AP, math applications, mathematics-AP, music theater, music theory, performing arts, photography, physical education, physics, physics-AP, pre-algebra, religion, social psychology, Spanish, Spanish-AP, studio art-AP, theater arts, theology, U.S. history, U.S. history-AP, wood processing, work-study, world history-AP, world religions.

Graduation Requirements Arts and fine arts (art, music, dance, drama), English, foreign language, mathematics, physical education (includes health), science, social studies (includes history), theology.

Special Academic Programs 18 Advanced Placement exams for which test preparation is offered; honors section; study at local college for college credit; academic

SETON CATHOLIC HIGH SCHOOL

1150 North Dobson Road
Chandler, Arizona 85224

Head of School: Patricia L. Collins

General Information Coeducational day college-preparatory and dual enrollment school, affiliated with Roman Catholic Church. Grades 9–12. Founded: 1954. Setting: suburban. Nearest major city is Phoenix. 32-acre campus. 11 buildings on campus. Approved or accredited by New England Association of Schools and Colleges, North Central Association of Colleges and Schools, Western Association of Schools and Colleges, Western Catholic Education Association, and Arizona Department of Education. Endowment: $342,000. Total enrollment: 563. Upper school average class size: 21. Upper school faculty-student ratio: 1:13. There are 182 required school days per year for Upper School students. Upper School students typically attend 5 days per week. The average school day consists of 6 hours and 55 minutes.

Upper School Student Profile Grade 9: 147 students (73 boys, 74 girls); Grade 10: 145 students (70 boys, 75 girls); Grade 11: 151 students (76 boys, 75 girls); Grade 12: 120 students (65 boys, 55 girls). 87% of students are Roman Catholic.

Faculty School total: 45. In upper school: 21 men, 24 women; 29 have advanced degrees.

Subjects Offered Aerobics, algebra, American government, American history, anatomy, art, athletic training, Basic programming, biology, biology-AP, calculus, chemistry, chemistry-AP, choir, Christian and Hebrew scripture, Christian scripture, church history, computer applications, dance, drama, drawing, economics, English, English-AP, European history-AP, fitness, foreign language, French, geometry, government, guitar, health, honors English, honors geometry, honors U.S. history, keyboarding, Latin, Latin-AP, personal fitness, photography, physics, pre-calculus, psychology, reading/study skills, religion, scripture, social justice, Spanish, Spanish-AP, study skills, television, theology, U.S. government, U.S. history, video film production, weight training, world history, world religions, yearbook.

Graduation Requirements Arts and fine arts (art, music, dance, drama), computer applications, computer literacy, English, foreign language, mathematics, physical education (includes health), religion (includes Bible studies and theology), science, social studies (includes history), study skills.

Special Academic Programs 11 Advanced Placement exams for which test preparation is offered; honors section.

College Admission Counseling 137 students graduated in 2016; 136 went to college, including Arizona State University at the Tempe campus; Northern Arizona University; The University of Arizona. Other: 1 had other specific plans. Mean SAT critical reading: 573, mean SAT math: 567, mean SAT writing: 543, mean composite ACT: 25. 26% scored over 600 on SAT critical reading, 31% scored over 600 on SAT math, 20% scored over 600 on SAT writing, 68% scored over 26 on composite ACT.

Student Life Upper grades have uniform requirement, student council, honor system. Discipline rests primarily with faculty. Attendance at religious services is required.

Summer Programs Enrichment, advancement, sports, art/fine arts programs offered; session focuses on academic support for incoming students, athletic camps, theatre camp; held on campus; accepts boys and girls; open to students from other schools. 60 students usually enrolled. 2017 schedule: June 1 to June 30. Application deadline: May 30.

Tuition and Aid Day student tuition: $13,690. Tuition installment plan (FACTS Tuition Payment Plan, monthly payment plans). Merit scholarship grants, need-based scholarship grants, Catholic Tuition Organization of Diocese of Phoenix available. In 2016–17, 50% of upper-school students received aid; total upper-school merit-scholarship money awarded: $44,000. Total amount of financial aid awarded in 2016–17: $705,000.

Admissions Traditional secondary-level entrance grade is 9. For fall 2016, 249 students applied for upper-level admission, 185 were accepted, 159 enrolled. Catholic High School Entrance Examination or Scholastic Testing Service High School Placement Test required. Deadline for receipt of application materials: January 31. Application fee required: $75. On-campus interview recommended.

Athletics Interscholastic: baseball (boys), basketball (b,g), cheering (g), cross-country running (b,g), dance squad (g), danceline (g), diving (b,g), football (b), golf (b,g), physical training (b,g), sand volleyball (b,g), soccer (b,g), softball (g), swimming and diving (b,g), tennis (b,g), track and field (b,g), volleyball (b,g), weight lifting (b,g), wrestling (b); coed interscholastic: aerobics/dance, dance, dance team, football, physical fitness, strength & conditioning, weight training. 2 PE instructors, 70 coaches, 1 athletic trainer.

Computers Computers are regularly used in all academic, religious studies, yearbook classes. Computer network features include on-campus library services, Internet access, wireless campus network, Internet filtering or blocking technology, Turnitin. Campus intranet and student e-mail accounts are available to students. Students grades are available online. The school has a published electronic and media policy.

Contact Mr. Brandon Harris, Director of Admissions. 480-963-1900 Ext. 2008. Fax: 480-963-1974. E-mail: bharris@setoncatholic.org. Website: www.setoncatholic.org

THE SEVEN HILLS SCHOOL

5400 Red Bank Road
Cincinnati, Ohio 45227

Head of School: Mr. Christopher P. Garten

General Information Coeducational day college-preparatory school. Grades PK–12. Founded: 1974. Setting: suburban. 35-acre campus. 16 buildings on campus. Approved or accredited by Ohio Association of Independent Schools and Ohio Department of Education. Member of National Association of Independent Schools and Secondary School Admission Test Board. Endowment: $31.6 million. Total enrollment: 1,017. Upper school average class size: 15. Upper school faculty-student ratio: 1:15. There are 180 required school days per year for Upper School students. Upper School students typically attend 5 days per week. The average school day consists of 7 hours and 5 minutes.

Upper School Student Profile Grade 9: 89 students (42 boys, 47 girls); Grade 10: 81 students (40 boys, 41 girls); Grade 11: 92 students (44 boys, 48 girls); Grade 12: 81 students (46 boys, 35 girls).

Faculty School total: 127. In upper school: 22 men, 28 women; 45 have advanced degrees.

Subjects Offered Acting, advanced computer applications, Advanced Placement courses, algebra, American history, American literature, ancient history, art, art history, biology, British literature, calculus, ceramics, chemistry, computer programming, computer science, economics, English, European history, fine arts, French, geometry, journalism, Latin, linear algebra, Mandarin, medieval/Renaissance history, modern political theory, music, physical education, physics, pre-calculus, psychology, Spanish, speech, theater, world history, world literature, writing.

Graduation Requirements Algebra, American history, arts and fine arts (art, music, dance, drama), biology, chemistry, computer science, English, foreign language, geometry, mathematics, performing arts, physical education (includes health), physics, science, U.S. history, U.S. literature, world history, completion of a personal challenge project, successfully pass writing competency exam, 30 hours of community service.

Special Academic Programs 16 Advanced Placement exams for which test preparation is offered; honors section; independent study; term-away projects; study abroad; academic accommodation for the gifted.

College Admission Counseling 85 students graduated in 2016; 84 went to college, including Carnegie Mellon University; Cornell University; Princeton University; University of Cincinnati; Vanderbilt University; Washington University in St. Louis. Other: 1 had other specific plans. Median SAT critical reading: 660, median SAT math: 660, median SAT writing: 680, median combined SAT: 2000, median composite ACT: 29. 86% scored over 600 on SAT critical reading, 73% scored over 600 on SAT math, 82% scored over 600 on SAT writing, 80% scored over 1800 on combined SAT, 83% scored over 26 on composite ACT.

Student Life Upper grades have specified standards of dress, student council. Discipline rests primarily with faculty.

Summer Programs Enrichment programs offered; session focuses on SAT review, sports clinics, acting workshop, and more; held on campus; accepts boys and girls; open to students from other schools. 400 students usually enrolled. 2017 schedule: June 19 to August 11. Application deadline: none.

Tuition and Aid Day student tuition: $23,240–$24,015. Tuition installment plan (monthly payment plans). Merit scholarship grants, need-based scholarship grants available. In 2016–17, 43% of upper-school students received aid; total upper-school merit-scholarship money awarded: $741,893. Total amount of financial aid awarded in 2016–17: $1,357,434.

Admissions Traditional secondary-level entrance grade is 9. For fall 2016, 57 students applied for upper-level admission, 46 were accepted, 20 enrolled. ISEE required. Deadline for receipt of application materials: November 22. Application fee required: $50. On-campus interview required.

Athletics Interscholastic: baseball (boys), basketball (b,g), bowling (b,g), cheering (g), cross-country running (b,g), golf (b), gymnastics (g), lacrosse (b,g), soccer (b,g), softball (g), swimming and diving (b,g), tennis (b,g), volleyball (g); coed interscholastic: track and field. 4 PE instructors, 32 coaches, 1 athletic trainer.

Computers Computers are regularly used in foreign language, mathematics, science classes. Computer network features include on-campus library services, online commercial services, Internet access, wireless campus network, Internet filtering or blocking technology. Student e-mail accounts and computer access in designated common areas are available to students. Students grades are available online. The school has a published electronic and media policy.

Contact Mrs. Janet S. Hill, Director of Admission and Financial Aid. 513-728-2405. Fax: 513-728-2409. E-mail: janet.hill@7hills.org. Website: http://www.7hills.org

SEVERN SCHOOL

201 Water Street
Severna Park, Maryland 21146

Head of School: Douglas H. Lagarde

General Information Coeducational day college-preparatory, arts, and technology school. Grades PS–12. Founded: 1914. Setting: suburban. Nearest major city is Annapolis. 19-acre campus. 8 buildings on campus. Approved or accredited by Association of Independent Maryland Schools and Maryland Department of Education. Member of National Association of Independent Schools and Secondary School Admission Test Board. Endowment: $11.3 million. Total enrollment: 843. Upper school average class size: 12. Upper school faculty-student ratio: 1:8. There are 175 required school days per year for Upper School students. Upper School students typically attend 5 days per week. The average school day consists of 6 hours and 35 minutes.

Upper School Student Profile Grade 9: 105 students (51 boys, 54 girls); Grade 10: 109 students (78 boys, 31 girls); Grade 11: 105 students (57 boys, 48 girls); Grade 12: 99 students (60 boys, 39 girls).

Faculty School total: 115. In upper school: 27 men, 30 women; 38 have advanced degrees.

Subjects Offered Algebra, American history, American literature, art, biology, calculus, ceramics, chemistry, community service, computer programming, computer science, CPR, creative writing, dance, desktop publishing, digital art, digital imaging, digital photography, discrete mathematics, drama, drama performance, dramatic arts, drawing, drawing and design, earth science, ecology, economics, economics-AP, English, English literature, environmental science, environmental systems, European civilization, European history, European history AP, expository writing, fine arts, forensics, French, French language-AP, French literature-AP, geometry, government/civics, grammar, graphic arts, health, history, journalism, Latin, marine biology, mathematics, multimedia, music, photography, physical education, physics, psychology, science, social studies, Spanish, speech, theater, trigonometry, world history, world literature, writing.

Graduation Requirements Arts and fine arts (art, music, dance, drama), computer science, CPR, English, foreign language, mathematics, physical education (includes health), science, social studies (includes history). Community service is required.

Special Academic Programs Advanced Placement exam preparation; honors section; independent study; study abroad; academic accommodation for the gifted, the musically talented, and the artistically talented.

College Admission Counseling 99 students graduated in 2015; 98 went to college, including Boston University; Elon University; Johns Hopkins University; The George Washington University; The University of Alabama; University of Maryland, College Park. Other: 1 entered a postgraduate year. Median SAT critical reading: 600, median SAT math: 630, median SAT writing: 620, median combined SAT: 1860, median composite ACT: 26. 47% scored over 600 on SAT critical reading, 56% scored over 600 on SAT math, 55% scored over 600 on SAT writing, 58% scored over 1800 on combined SAT, 47% scored over 26 on composite ACT.

Student Life Upper grades have uniform requirement, student council, honor system. Discipline rests primarily with faculty.

Tuition and Aid Day student tuition: $24,575. Tuition installment plan (FACTS Tuition Payment Plan). Need-based scholarship grants available. In 2015–16, 28% of upper-school students received aid. Total amount of financial aid awarded in 2015–16: $1,800,000.

Admissions Traditional secondary-level entrance grade is 9. For fall 2015, 131 students applied for upper-level admission, 70 were accepted, 45 enrolled. ISEE required. Deadline for receipt of application materials: January 19. Application fee required: $60. On-campus interview required.

Athletics Interscholastic: baseball (boys), basketball (b,g), combined training (b,g), field hockey (g), football (b), lacrosse (b,g), soccer (b,g), tennis (b,g), wrestling (b); coed interscholastic: cross-country running, dance, diving, fitness, golf, outdoor education, physical fitness, ropes courses, sailing, strength & conditioning, swimming and diving, track and field, weight training, yoga; coed intramural: aerobics/dance, ice hockey, outdoor adventure, paint ball. 4 PE instructors, 56 coaches, 2 athletic trainers.

Computers Computers are regularly used in all academic classes. Computer network features include on-campus library services, online commercial services, Internet access, wireless campus network, Internet filtering or blocking technology. Campus intranet, student e-mail accounts, and computer access in designated common areas are available to students. Students grades are available online. The school has a published electronic and media policy.

Contact Ellen Murray, Associate Director of Admissions. 410-647-7701 Ext. 2266. Fax: 410-544-9451. E-mail: e.murray@severnschool.com.
Website: www.severnschool.com

SEWICKLEY ACADEMY

315 Academy Avenue
Sewickley, Pennsylvania 15143

Head of School: Mr. Kolia J. O'Connor

General Information Coeducational day college-preparatory, arts, and technology school. Grades PK–12. Founded: 1838. Setting: suburban. Nearest major city is Pittsburgh. 30-acre campus. 10 buildings on campus. Approved or accredited by Pennsylvania Department of Education. Member of National Association of Independent Schools. Endowment: $31 million. Total enrollment: 657. Upper school average class size: 15. Upper school faculty-student ratio: 1:7. There are 167 required school days per year for Upper School students. Upper School students typically attend 5 days per week. The average school day consists of 7 hours.

Upper School Student Profile Grade 9: 72 students (40 boys, 32 girls); Grade 10: 59 students (30 boys, 29 girls); Grade 11: 70 students (39 boys, 31 girls); Grade 12: 66 students (31 boys, 35 girls).

Faculty School total: 106. In upper school: 28 men, 28 women; 32 have advanced degrees.

Subjects Offered Advanced chemistry, advanced studio art-AP, African studies, algebra, American history, American history-AP, American literature, American literature-AP, art, art-AP, astronomy, band, biology, biology-AP, calculus, calculus-AP, ceramics, chemistry, chemistry-AP, choral music, chorus, clayworking, computer applications, computer art, computer programming, computer science, computer science-AP, concert band, concert choir, contemporary issues, creative writing, dance, dance performance, digital art, drama, drama performance, drama workshop, drawing, driver education, economics, English, English literature, environmental science, ethics, European history, European history-AP, expository writing, fine arts, French, French language-AP, French literature-AP, geometry, German, German-AP, government/civics, health, health education, history, Italian, keyboarding, Mandarin, music, musical theater, performing arts, photography, physical education, physics, physics-AP, pre-calculus, psychology, psychology-AP, senior project, Spanish, Spanish literature, Spanish-AP, speech and debate, statistics, statistics-AP, studio art, theater, trigonometry, U.S. history-AP, U.S. literature, Vietnam War, world history, world literature, writing.

Graduation Requirements Arts and fine arts (art, music, dance, drama), English, foreign language, health education, mathematics, physical education (includes health), science, social studies (includes history), U.S. history, world cultures, world studies. Community service is required.

Special Academic Programs Advanced Placement exam preparation; honors section; independent study; term-away projects; study at local college for college credit; study abroad.

College Admission Counseling 77 students graduated in 2015; all went to college, including Carnegie Mellon University; New York University; Penn State University Park; University of Virginia; Virginia Polytechnic Institute and State University; Wake Forest University.

Student Life Upper grades have specified standards of dress, student council, honor system. Discipline rests equally with students and faculty.

Tuition and Aid Day student tuition: $25,705. Tuition installment plan (monthly payment plans). Need-based scholarship grants available.

Admissions Traditional secondary-level entrance grade is 9. ISEE or SSAT required. Deadline for receipt of application materials: February 8. Application fee required: $50. Interview required.

Athletics Interscholastic: baseball (boys), basketball (b,g), cross-country running (b,g), golf (b,g), ice hockey (b), lacrosse (b,g), physical fitness (b,g), soccer (b,g), softball (g), tennis (b,g); coed interscholastic: bowling, diving, field hockey, physical fitness, swimming and diving, track and field. 5 PE instructors, 5 coaches, 1 athletic trainer.

Computers Computers are regularly used in all academic classes. Computer network features include on-campus library services, online commercial services, Internet access, wireless campus network, Internet filtering or blocking technology. Campus intranet, student e-mail accounts, and computer access in designated common areas are available to students. The school has a published electronic and media policy.

Contact Ms. Wendy Berns, Admission Assistant. 412-741-2235. Fax: 412-741-1411. E-mail: wberns@sewickley.org. Website: www.sewickley.org

SHADY SIDE ACADEMY

423 Fox Chapel Road
Pittsburgh, Pennsylvania 15238

Head of School: Mr. Thomas Cangiano

General Information Coeducational boarding and day college-preparatory and requirements in the arts and athletics school. Boarding grades 9–12, day grades PK–12. Founded: 1883. Setting: suburban. Students are housed in coed dormitories. 130-acre campus. 26 buildings on campus. Approved or accredited by Middle States Association of Colleges and Schools, Pennsylvania Association of Independent Schools, and Pennsylvania Department of Education. Member of National Association of Independent Schools. Endowment: $54 million. Total enrollment: 945. Upper school average class size: 13. Upper school faculty-student ratio: 1:8. There are 172 required school days per year for Upper School students. Upper School students typically attend 5 days per week. The average school day consists of 8 hours and 15 minutes.

Upper School Student Profile Grade 9: 91 students (54 boys, 37 girls); Grade 10: 131 students (73 boys, 58 girls); Grade 11: 137 students (73 boys, 64 girls); Grade 12: 126 students (73 boys, 53 girls). 13% of students are boarding students. 93% are state residents. 9 states are represented in upper school student body. 4% are international students. International students from China, Germany, Hungary, India, South Africa, and United Arab Emirates.

Faculty School total: 116. In upper school: 31 men, 32 women; 48 have advanced degrees; 26 reside on campus.

Subjects Offered 3-dimensional art, advanced biology, advanced chemistry, advanced computer applications, advanced math, Advanced Placement courses, algebra, American history, American literature, architectural drawing, architecture, art, art history, band, biology, calculus, calculus-AP, ceramics, chemistry, Chinese, Chinese history, choir, college counseling, computer graphics, computer math, computer programming, computer science, computer science-AP, concert band, creative writing, drama, economics, English, English literature, environmental science, ethics, European history, expository writing, film and literature, fine arts, fractal geometry, French, French-AP, gender issues, geography, geometry, German, German-AP, health, history, introduction to theater, jazz ensemble, Latin, linear algebra, logic, mathematics, modern dance, music, music technology, musical theater, philosophy, photography, physical education, physics, pre-calculus, probability and statistics, religion and culture, science, senior project, social studies, Spanish, Spanish-AP, speech, statistics, studio art, technical theater, theater arts, trigonometry, world history, world literature, writing.

Graduation Requirements Art, athletics, computer science, English, foreign language, history, mathematics, physical education (includes health), science, participation in five seasons of athletics.

Special Academic Programs 6 Advanced Placement exams for which test preparation is offered; honors section; accelerated programs; independent study; term-away projects; study at local college for college credit; study abroad; academic accommodation for the gifted, the musically talented, and the artistically talented.

College Admission Counseling 128 students graduated in 2016; 125 went to college, including Bucknell University; Carnegie Mellon University; Elon University; Penn State University Park; University of Pennsylvania; University of Pittsburgh. Other: 3 had other specific plans. Median SAT critical reading: 625, median SAT math: 645, median SAT writing: 640, median combined SAT: 1915, median composite ACT: 28.

Student Life Upper grades have specified standards of dress, student council. Discipline rests primarily with faculty.

Summer Programs Remediation, enrichment, advancement, sports, art/fine arts, computer instruction programs offered; session focuses on academic and non-academic enrichment; held on campus; accepts boys and girls; open to students from other schools. 1,200 students usually enrolled. 2017 schedule: June 20 to July 29. Application deadline: none.

Tuition and Aid Day student tuition: $29,675; 5-day tuition and room/board: $42,675; 7-day tuition and room/board: $46,175. Tuition installment plan (monthly payment plans, Tuition Refund Plan available through Dewar's). Tuition reduction for siblings, merit scholarship grants, need-based scholarship grants available. In 2016–17, 18% of upper-school students received aid; total upper-school merit-scholarship money awarded: $81,000. Total amount of financial aid awarded in 2016–17: $2,951,630.

Admissions Traditional secondary-level entrance grade is 9. For fall 2016, 119 students applied for upper-level admission, 94 were accepted, 57 enrolled. International English Language Test, ISEE, SSAT or TOEFL required. Deadline for receipt of application materials: February 6. Application fee required: $50. Interview recommended.

Athletics Interscholastic: baseball (boys), basketball (b,g), cheering (g), crew (b,g), cross-country running (b,g), field hockey (g), football (b), golf (b,g), ice hockey (b,g), lacrosse (b,g), soccer (b,g), softball (g), squash (b,g), swimming and diving (b,g), tennis (b,g), track and field (b,g); intramural: volleyball (g); coed interscholastic: ultimate Frisbee; coed intramural: badminton, bowling, fitness, outdoor adventure, ultimate Frisbee, weight lifting. 1 PE instructor, 47 coaches, 2 athletic trainers.

Computers Computers are regularly used in all academic classes. Computer network features include on-campus library services, online commercial services, Internet access, wireless campus network, Internet filtering or blocking technology, report cards are available in the parent portal four times a year. Student e-mail accounts and computer access in designated common areas are available to students. The school has a published electronic and media policy.

Contact Mr. Robert Grandizio, Director of Admission. 412-968-3080. Fax: 412-968-3213. E-mail: rgrandizio@shadysideacademy.org. Website: www.shadysideacademy.org

SHANLEY HIGH SCHOOL

5600 25th Street South
Fargo, North Dakota 58104

Head of School: Mrs. Sarah Crary

General Information Coeducational day college-preparatory, arts, business, and religious studies school, affiliated with Roman Catholic Church. Grades 9–12. Distance learning grades 9–12. Founded: 1882. Setting: suburban. 1 building on campus. Approved or accredited by North Central Association of Colleges and Schools and North Dakota Department of Education. Total enrollment: 327. Upper school average class size: 20. Upper school faculty-student ratio: 1:14. There are 175 required school days per year for Upper School students. Upper School students typically attend 5 days per week. The average school day consists of 7 hours and 30 minutes.

Upper School Student Profile Grade 9: 93 students (46 boys, 47 girls); Grade 10: 82 students (45 boys, 37 girls); Grade 11: 80 students (36 boys, 44 girls); Grade 12: 72 students (45 boys, 27 girls). 90% of students are Roman Catholic.

Faculty School total: 24. In upper school: 10 men, 14 women; 12 have advanced degrees.

Subjects Offered Accounting, advanced chemistry, advanced math, Advanced Placement courses, algebra, American history, anatomy and physiology, art, band, biology, business applications, business law, calculus-AP, ceramics, chemistry, chemistry-AP, choir, computer applications, economics, English, English literature-AP, general math, geography, global issues, health, journalism, Latin, leadership, modern European history-AP, physical education, physics, pre-algebra, pre-calculus, psychology-AP, religion, science, social studies, U.S. government, U.S. history, world history.

Graduation Requirements All academic.

Special Academic Programs International Baccalaureate program; 5 Advanced Placement exams for which test preparation is offered; honors section; independent study; programs in English, mathematics, general development for dyslexic students.

College Admission Counseling 75 students graduated in 2016; 72 went to college, including Concordia College; North Dakota State University; University of Mary; University of North Dakota. Other: 2 went to work, 1 entered military service. Median composite ACT: 25.

Student Life Upper grades have uniform requirement, student council, honor system. Discipline rests primarily with faculty. Attendance at religious services is required.

Tuition and Aid Tuition installment plan (monthly payment plans). Tuition reduction for siblings, merit scholarship grants, need-based scholarship grants available. In 2016–17, 20% of upper-school students received aid.

Admissions Traditional secondary-level entrance grade is 9. For fall 2016, 29 students applied for upper-level admission, 29 were accepted, 29 enrolled. Deadline for receipt of application materials: none. Application fee required: $50. On-campus interview recommended.

Athletics Interscholastic: aquatics (boys, girls), baseball (b), basketball (b,g), cheering (g), cross-country running (b,g), diving (b,g), football (b), golf (b,g), hockey (b), ice hockey (b,g), softball (g), strength & conditioning (b,g), swimming and diving (b,g), synchronized swimming (b,g), tennis (b,g), track and field (b,g), volleyball (g), weight lifting (b,g), weight training (b,g).

Computers Computers are regularly used in all academic classes. Computer resources include on-campus library services, Internet access, wireless campus network, Internet filtering or blocking technology. Campus intranet and student e-mail accounts are available to students. Students grades are available online. The school has a published electronic and media policy.

Contact Ms. Lori K. Hager, Director of Admissions, Marketing and Recruitment. 701-893-3271. Fax: 701-356-0473. E-mail: lori.hager@jp2schools.org. Website: www.jp2schools.org

SHATTUCK-ST. MARY'S SCHOOL

1000 Shumway Avenue
PO Box 218
Faribault, Minnesota 55021

Head of School: Don MacMillian

General Information Coeducational boarding and day college-preparatory and bio-science, engineering, STEM education school, affiliated with Episcopal Church. Grades 6–PG. Founded: 1858. Setting: small town. Nearest major city is Minneapolis/St. Paul. Students are housed in single-sex dormitories. 250-acre campus. 12 buildings on campus. Approved or accredited by Independent Schools Association of the Central States and Minnesota Department of Education. Member of National Association of Independent Schools and Secondary School Admission Test Board. Endowment: $25 million. Total enrollment: 443. Upper school average class size: 11. Upper school faculty-student ratio: 1:8. There are 167 required school days per year for Upper School

students. Upper School students typically attend 5 days per week. The average school day consists of 7 hours.

Upper School Student Profile Grade 6: 7 students (4 boys, 3 girls); Grade 7: 11 students (7 boys, 4 girls); Grade 8: 23 students (13 boys, 10 girls); Grade 9: 91 students (49 boys, 42 girls); Grade 10: 117 students (61 boys, 56 girls); Grade 11: 144 students (78 boys, 66 girls); Grade 12: 126 students (66 boys, 60 girls); Postgraduate: 3 students (2 boys, 1 girl). 75% of students are boarding students. 25% are state residents. 44 states are represented in upper school student body. 32% are international students. International students from Canada, China, Hong Kong, Mexico, Republic of Korea, and Viet Nam; 26 other countries represented in student body. 10% of students are members of Episcopal Church.

Faculty School total: 70. In upper school: 33 men, 37 women; 42 have advanced degrees; 50 reside on campus.

Subjects Offered 3-dimensional art, 3-dimensional design, acting, sign language.

Graduation Requirements Arts and fine arts (art, music, dance, drama), English, foreign language, mathematics, religion (includes Bible studies and theology), science, social studies (includes history), 20 hours of community service per year.

Special Academic Programs 17 Advanced Placement exams for which test preparation is offered; honors section; independent study; academic accommodation for the gifted, the musically talented, and the artistically talented; remedial reading and/or remedial writing; remedial math; programs in English, mathematics, general development for dyslexic students; ESL (65 students enrolled).

College Admission Counseling 126 students graduated in 2016; 99 went to college, including Boston University; DePaul University; Drake University; Minnesota State University Mankato; Union College; University of Minnesota, Twin Cities Campus. Other: 4 entered a postgraduate year, 21 had other specific plans. Median SAT critical reading: 540, median SAT math: 560, median SAT writing: 530, median combined SAT: 1660, median composite ACT: 24. 23% scored over 600 on SAT critical reading, 37% scored over 600 on SAT math, 24% scored over 600 on SAT writing, 24% scored over 1800 on combined SAT, 25% scored over 26 on composite ACT.

Student Life Upper grades have uniform requirement, student council. Discipline rests primarily with faculty. Attendance at religious services is required.

Summer Programs ESL, sports, art/fine arts programs offered; session focuses on challenging, diversified instruction in the arts and athletics; ESL summer program; held on campus; accepts boys and girls; open to students from other schools. 150 students usually enrolled. 2017 schedule: June 1 to August 7. Application deadline: May 15.

Tuition and Aid Day student tuition: $31,175; 7-day tuition and room/board: $46,800. Tuition installment plan (Insured Tuition Payment Plan, monthly payment plans). Need-based scholarship grants available. In 2016–17, 52% of upper-school students received aid. Total amount of financial aid awarded in 2016–17: $5,200,000.

Admissions Traditional secondary-level entrance grade is 10. For fall 2016, 1,012 students applied for upper-level admission, 312 were accepted, 184 enrolled. Otis-Lennon School Ability Test required. Deadline for receipt of application materials: none. Application fee required: $75. Interview recommended.

Athletics Interscholastic: baseball (boys), basketball (b,g), golf (b,g), ice hockey (b,g), lacrosse (b,g), soccer (b,g), tennis (b,g), volleyball (g); intramural: drill team (b,g), weight training (b,g); coed interscholastic: figure skating, Frisbee, soccer, ultimate Frisbee; coed intramural: basketball, dance, dance team, Frisbee, jogging, modern dance, outdoor activities, outdoor recreation, ropes courses, strength & conditioning, table tennis, ultimate Frisbee, yoga. 39 coaches, 3 athletic trainers.

Computers Computers are regularly used in all academic classes. Computer network features include on-campus library services, Internet access, wireless campus network, Internet filtering or blocking technology. Campus intranet, student e-mail accounts, and computer access in designated common areas are available to students. Students grades are available online. The school has a published electronic and media policy.

Contact Mr. Kelly DeShane, Director of Enrollment Management. 800-421-2724. Fax: 507-333-1661. E-mail: admissions@s-sm.org. Website: www.s-sm.org

SHAWE MEMORIAL JUNIOR/SENIOR HIGH SCHOOL

201 West State Street
Madison, Indiana 47250-2899

Head of School: Mr. Steven J. Hesse

General Information Coeducational day college-preparatory, religious studies, and all of the core subjects as well as Engineering school, affiliated with Roman Catholic Church. Grades 7–12. Founded: 1954. Setting: small town. 30-acre campus. 1 building on campus. Approved or accredited by North Central Association of Colleges and Schools and Indiana Department of Education. Endowment: $4.2 million. Total enrollment: 342. Upper school average class size: 11. Upper school faculty-student ratio: 1:8. There are 180 required school days per year for Upper School students. Upper School students typically attend 5 days per week. The average school day consists of 7 hours and 15 minutes.

Upper School Student Profile Grade 9: 25 students (12 boys, 13 girls); Grade 10: 23 students (11 boys, 12 girls); Grade 11: 41 students (22 boys, 19 girls); Grade 12: 20 students (11 boys, 9 girls). 65% of students are Roman Catholic.

Faculty School total: 19. In upper school: 3 men, 16 women; 10 have advanced degrees.

Special Academic Programs International Baccalaureate program; 6 Advanced Placement exams for which test preparation is offered; honors section; independent study; study at local college for college credit; academic accommodation for the gifted; remedial reading and/or remedial writing; programs in general development for dyslexic students; special instructional classes for deaf students, some students with special needs can be accommodated on an individual basis; ESL (8 students enrolled).

College Admission Counseling 27 students graduated in 2016; 25 went to college. Other: 2 went to work. Mean SAT critical reading: 534, mean SAT math: 516, mean SAT writing: 515, mean combined SAT: 1565. 24% scored over 600 on SAT critical reading, 19% scored over 600 on SAT math, 27% scored over 600 on SAT writing.

Student Life Upper grades have uniform requirement, student council, honor system. Discipline rests primarily with faculty. Attendance at religious services is required.

Tuition and Aid Day student tuition: $5915. Tuition installment plan (The Tuition Plan, FACTS Tuition Payment Plan, monthly payment plans, individually arranged payment plans, multiple options). Tuition reduction for siblings, need-based scholarship grants, summer work program available. In 2016–17, 35% of upper-school students received aid; total upper-school merit-scholarship money awarded: $40,000. Total amount of financial aid awarded in 2016–17: $80,000.

Admissions Traditional secondary-level entrance grade is 9. Deadline for receipt of application materials: none. Application fee required: $160. On-campus interview recommended.

Athletics Interscholastic: baseball (boys), basketball (b,g), cheering (g), cross-country running (b,g), golf (b,g), soccer (b,g), softball (g), tennis (b,g), track and field (b,g), volleyball (g); coed interscholastic: archery. 2 PE instructors, 10 coaches, 1 athletic trainer.

Computers Computer network features include on-campus library services, Internet access, wireless campus network, Internet filtering or blocking technology, 1 to 1 Chromebook pilot program for 7th and 8th grade for the year 2016-17. Campus intranet and computer access in designated common areas are available to students. Students grades are available online.

Contact Mr. Philip J. Kahn, President. 812-273-5835 Ext. 245. Fax: 812-273-3427. E-mail: poppresident@popeace.org. Website: www.popeaceschools.org/

SHAWNIGAN LAKE SCHOOL

1975 Renfrew Road
Shawnigan Lake, British Columbia V0R 2W1, Canada

Head of School: Mr. David Robertson

General Information Coeducational boarding and day college-preparatory, athletics, leadership, citizenship, and entrepreneurship, and language studies school. Grades 8–12. Founded: 1916. Setting: rural. Nearest major city is Victoria, Canada. Students are housed in single-sex dormitories. 380-acre campus. 26 buildings on campus. Approved or accredited by British Columbia Independent Schools Association, Canadian Association of Independent Schools, The Association of Boarding Schools, Western Boarding Schools Association, and British Columbia Department of Education. Affiliate member of National Association of Independent Schools; member of Secondary School Admission Test Board. Language of instruction: English. Endowment: CAN$14 million. Total enrollment: 493. Upper school average class size: 16. Upper school faculty-student ratio: 1:8. There are 170 required school days per year for Upper School students. Upper School students typically attend 7 days per week. The average school day consists of 6 hours and 30 minutes.

Upper School Student Profile Grade 8: 33 students (19 boys, 14 girls); Grade 9: 74 students (46 boys, 28 girls); Grade 10: 124 students (66 boys, 58 girls); Grade 11: 127 students (74 boys, 53 girls); Grade 12: 136 students (79 boys, 57 girls). 85% of students are boarding students. 55% are province residents. 14 provinces are represented in upper school student body. 30% are international students. International students from China, Democratic People's Republic of Korea, Germany, Hong Kong, Mexico, and United States; 21 other countries represented in student body.

Faculty School total: 67. In upper school: 37 men, 30 women; 29 have advanced degrees; 32 reside on campus.

Subjects Offered Advanced Placement courses, advanced studio art-AP, algebra, art, art history, biology, biology-AP, business skills, calculus, calculus-AP, career and personal planning, ceramics, chemistry, chemistry-AP, choir, comparative civilizations, computer science, computer science-AP, creative writing, earth science, economics, economics and history, English, English language and composition-AP, English literature, English literature and composition-AP, English-AP, entrepreneurship, environmental science, European history, European history-AP, fine arts, French, French language-AP, French literature-AP, French-AP, geography, geometry, German-AP, history, human geography - AP, information technology, law, Mandarin, mathematics, media studies, music, philosophy, physical education, physics, physics-AP, robotics, science, social studies, Spanish, Spanish language-AP, sports science, study skills, theater, U.S. history-AP, woodworking, writing.

Graduation Requirements Arts and fine arts (art, music, dance, drama), career and personal planning, English, mathematics, physical education (includes health), science, social studies (includes history), graduation requirements are mandated by the BC Provincial Government and include English 12 plus 4 additional grade 12 courses, and 30 hours of work experience, refer to the curriculum courses to see the subject offerings.

Special Academic Programs Advanced Placement exam preparation; honors section; academic accommodation for the gifted; remedial reading and/or remedial writing; remedial math; programs in English, mathematics, general development for dyslexic students; ESL (36 students enrolled).

College Admission Counseling 135 students graduated in 2016; 120 went to college, including McGill University; Simon Fraser University; The University of British Columbia; University of Alberta; University of Toronto; University of Victoria. Other: 6 went to work, 4 entered military service, 5 had other specific plans. Mean SAT critical reading: 536, mean SAT math: 614, mean SAT writing: 508.

Student Life Upper grades have uniform requirement, student council, honor system. Discipline rests primarily with faculty.

Summer Programs Sports programs offered; session focuses on squash, ice hockey, rugby; held on campus; accepts boys and girls; open to students from other schools. 180 students usually enrolled. 2017 schedule: July 1 to July 31.

Tuition and Aid Day student tuition: CAN$23,800; 7-day tuition and room/board: CAN$44,200–CAN$58,300. Tuition installment plan (monthly payment plans). Tuition reduction for siblings, bursaries, merit scholarship grants available. In 2016–17, 25% of upper-school students received aid; total upper-school merit-scholarship money awarded: CAN$1,000,000. Total amount of financial aid awarded in 2016–17: CAN$1,500,000.

Admissions Traditional secondary-level entrance grade is 8. For fall 2016, 630 students applied for upper-level admission, 235 were accepted, 175 enrolled. English entrance exam and Math Placement Exam required. Deadline for receipt of application materials: none. Application fee required: CAN$200. Interview required.

Athletics Interscholastic: aquatics (boys, girls), basketball (b,g), crew (b,g), cross-country running (b,g), field hockey (g), golf (b,g), hockey (b,g), ice hockey (b,g), rowing (b,g), rugby (b,g), soccer (b,g), squash (b,g), tennis (b,g), volleyball (g); intramural: alpine skiing (b,g), ballet (g), basketball (b,g), crew (b,g), field hockey (g), figure skating (g), rowing (b,g), rugby (b,g), soccer (b,g), squash (b,g), strength & conditioning (b,g), tennis (b,g), volleyball (g), weight training (b,g), winter soccer (g); coed intramural: aerobics/dance, backpacking, badminton, canoeing/kayaking, climbing, cross-country running, dance, fitness, hiking/backpacking, jogging, kayaking, modern dance, nordic skiing, ocean paddling, outdoor activities, outdoor adventure, outdoor education, outdoor recreation, outdoor skills, outdoors, physical fitness, physical training, rock climbing, running, skiing (cross-country), skiing (downhill), snowboarding, snowshoeing, swimming and diving, track and field, triathlon, wilderness survival, yoga. 5 PE instructors, 5 coaches, 3 athletic trainers.

Computers Computers are regularly used in art, computer applications, creative writing, drawing and design, English, geography, graphic arts, human geography - AP, information technology, library, mathematics, music, music technology, programming, research skills, SAT preparation, science, social studies, video film production, writing, yearbook classes. Computer network features include on-campus library services, Internet access, wireless campus network, Internet filtering or blocking technology. Campus intranet and student e-mail accounts are available to students. Students grades are available online. The school has a published electronic and media policy.

Contact Mrs. Gaynor Samuel, Director of Admissions. 250-743-6207. Fax: 250-743-6280. E-mail: admissions@shawnigan.ca. Website: www.shawnigan.ca

SHELTON SCHOOL AND EVALUATION CENTER

Dallas, Texas
See Special Needs Schools section.

SHORECREST PREPARATORY SCHOOL

5101 First Street NE
Saint Petersburg, Florida 33703

Head of School: Mr. Michael A. Murphy

General Information Coeducational day college-preparatory, arts, and medical sciences, Global Scholars school. Grades PK–12. Founded: 1923. Setting: suburban. Nearest major city is Tampa. 28-acre campus. 3 buildings on campus. Approved or accredited by Florida Council of Independent Schools, Southern Association of Colleges and Schools, Southern Association of Independent Schools, The College Board, and Florida Department of Education. Member of National Association of Independent Schools and Secondary School Admission Test Board. Endowment: $4.1 million. Total enrollment: 940. Upper school average class size: 15. Upper school faculty-student ratio: 1:10. There are 175 required school days per year for Upper School students. Upper School students typically attend 5 days per week. The average school day consists of 6 hours and 45 minutes.

Upper School Student Profile Grade 9: 82 students (38 boys, 44 girls); Grade 10: 81 students (41 boys, 40 girls); Grade 11: 81 students (46 boys, 35 girls); Grade 12: 76 students (41 boys, 35 girls).

Faculty School total: 97. In upper school: 22 men, 14 women; 26 have advanced degrees.

Subjects Offered 3-dimensional design, algebra, American literature, anatomy and physiology, ancient history, animation, architecture, art, art history, art history-AP, band, biology, biology-AP, calculus, calculus-AP, chemistry, chemistry-AP, computer graphics, computer music, computer science, computer science-AP, conceptual physics, contemporary issues, creative writing, dance, digital imaging, drama, drawing and design, economics, economics-AP, English, English language-AP, English literature-AP, European history, European history-AP, fashion, film history, fine arts, fitness, French, French language-AP, French literature-AP, geometry, guitar, health, history of ideas, human geography - AP, humanities, journalism, macroeconomics-AP, marine biology, music, music theory-AP, musical productions, musical theater, philosophy, photography, physical education, physics, physics-AP, play/screen writing, political science, portfolio art, pre-calculus, probability and statistics, psychology, psychology-AP, social studies, Spanish, Spanish language-AP, studio art-AP, theater, trigonometry, U.S. history, U.S. history-AP, video film production, Web site design, weight training, Western civilization, world civilizations, world history, world history-AP, world literature, world religions, world studies, world wide web design, writing, yearbook.

Graduation Requirements Arts and fine arts (art, music, dance, drama), English, foreign language, health education, mathematics, science, social studies (includes history).

Special Academic Programs 22 Advanced Placement exams for which test preparation is offered; honors section; independent study; academic accommodation for the gifted.

College Admission Counseling 84 students graduated in 2016; 83 went to college, including Brown University; Florida Gulf Coast University; Florida State University; Northeastern University; The George Washington University; University of Florida. Other: 1 had other specific plans. Mean SAT critical reading: 584, mean SAT math: 612, mean SAT writing: 592, mean combined SAT: 1794, mean composite ACT: 28.

Student Life Upper grades have specified standards of dress, student council, honor system. Discipline rests primarily with faculty.

Summer Programs Enrichment, sports, art/fine arts programs offered; session focuses on arts, academic enrichment, athletics and recreational activities; held on campus; accepts boys and girls; open to students from other schools. 2017 schedule: June 5 to August 11.

Tuition and Aid Day student tuition: $21,770. Tuition installment plan (monthly payment plans, semiannual payment plan). Need-based scholarship grants available. In 2016–17, 19% of upper-school students received aid. Total amount of financial aid awarded in 2016–17: $739,305.

Admissions Traditional secondary-level entrance grade is 9. For fall 2016, 73 students applied for upper-level admission, 45 were accepted, 31 enrolled. ACT, ISEE, PSAT or SAT or SSAT required. Deadline for receipt of application materials: none. Application fee required: $75. Interview recommended.

Athletics Interscholastic: baseball (boys), basketball (b,g), cheering (g), cross-country running (b,g), diving (b,g), football (b), golf (b,g), soccer (b,g), softball (g), swimming and diving (b,g), tennis (b,g), track and field (b,g), volleyball (g); coed interscholastic: bowling, golf, sailing; coed intramural: climbing, dance, outdoor education, rock climbing. 4 PE instructors, 28 coaches, 1 athletic trainer.

Computers Computers are regularly used in all academic classes. Computer network features include on-campus library services, online commercial services, Internet access, wireless campus network, Internet filtering or blocking technology, Learning Management System. Campus intranet, student e-mail accounts, and computer access in designated common areas are available to students. Students grades are available online. The school has a published electronic and media policy.

Contact Dr. Jean Spencer Carnes, Director of Admissions. 727-456-7511. Fax: 727-527-4191. E-mail: admissions@shorecrest.org. Website: www.shorecrest.org

SHORELINE CHRISTIAN

2400 Northeast 147th Street
Shoreline, Washington 98155
Head of School: Mr. Timothy E. Visser

General Information Coeducational day college-preparatory and general academic school, affiliated with Presbyterian Church in America, Christian Reformed Church. Grades PS–12. Founded: 1952. Setting: suburban. Nearest major city is Seattle. 7-acre campus. 3 buildings on campus. Approved or accredited by Christian Schools International, Northwest Accreditation Commission, Northwest Association of Independent Schools, Northwest Association of Schools and Colleges, and Washington Department of Education. Total enrollment: 199. Upper school average class size: 15. Upper school faculty-student ratio: 1:8. There are 180 required school days per year for Upper School students. Upper School students typically attend 5 days per week. The average school day consists of 6 hours and 30 minutes.

Upper School Student Profile Grade 6: 16 students (8 boys, 8 girls); Grade 7: 8 students (2 boys, 6 girls); Grade 8: 11 students (2 boys, 9 girls); Grade 9: 11 students (5 boys, 6 girls); Grade 10: 12 students (7 boys, 5 girls); Grade 11: 11 students (8 boys, 3 girls); Grade 12: 11 students (6 boys, 5 girls). 100% of students are Presbyterian Church in America, members of Christian Reformed Church.

Faculty School total: 25. In upper school: 5 men, 6 women; 6 have advanced degrees.

Subjects Offered 20th century history, advanced math, Advanced Placement courses, algebra, American history, American literature, art, band, Bible, biology, British literature, calculus, calculus-AP, chemistry, choir, Christian doctrine, college writing, composition, computer applications, consumer education, current events, current history, drama, drawing, English, English composition, English literature, fine arts, geography, geometry, global studies, government, health, human anatomy, jazz band, keyboarding, language arts, life science, life skills, literature, mathematics, mathematics-AP, music appreciation, physical education, physical science, physics, pre-

calculus, psychology, sculpture, sociology, Spanish, speech, study skills, U.S. history, Washington State and Northwest History, weight training, Western civilization, world literature, world religions, yearbook.

Graduation Requirements American government, American literature, Bible, British literature, composition, electives, English, global issues, keyboarding, mathematics, occupational education, physical education (includes health), portfolio art, portfolio writing, science, social sciences, speech, U.S. history, Washington State and Northwest History, Western civilization, world literature, Bible.

Special Academic Programs Honors section; independent study; study at local college for college credit; remedial reading and/or remedial writing; programs in English for dyslexic students.

College Admission Counseling 13 students graduated in 2016; 10 went to college, including Edmonds Community College; Seattle Pacific University; University of Washington; Washington State University; Western Washington University; Whitworth University. Other: 3 went to work, 1 entered military service. Median SAT critical reading: 521, median SAT math: 512, median SAT writing: 528, median combined SAT: 1561, median composite ACT: 26. 32% scored over 600 on SAT critical reading, 28% scored over 600 on SAT math, 33% scored over 600 on SAT writing, 31% scored over 1800 on combined SAT, 67% scored over 26 on composite ACT.

Student Life Upper grades have specified standards of dress, student council, honor system. Discipline rests primarily with faculty. Attendance at religious services is required.

Tuition and Aid Day student tuition: $10,200–$11,975. Tuition installment plan (monthly payment plans, individually arranged payment plans, prepaid cash tuition discount, quarterly or semi-annual payment plans). Tuition reduction for siblings, need-based scholarship grants, discount for qualifying Pastor families, discount for staff available. In 2016–17, 30% of upper-school students received aid. Total amount of financial aid awarded in 2016–17: $170,000.

Admissions Traditional secondary-level entrance grade is 9. Deadline for receipt of application materials: none. Application fee required: $125. On-campus interview recommended.

Athletics Interscholastic: baseball (boys), basketball (b,g), soccer (b), volleyball (g); coed interscholastic: golf, soccer, track and field. 1 PE instructor, 17 coaches.

Computers Computers are regularly used in all academic, art, computer applications, library, music, occupational education, research skills, yearbook classes. Computer network features include on-campus library services, Internet access, wireless campus network, Internet filtering or blocking technology, Campus intranet, student e-mail accounts, and computer access in designated common areas are available to students. Students grades are available online. The school has a published electronic and media policy.

Contact Ms. Tassie DeMoney, Director of Development and Marketing. 206-364-7777 Ext. 312. Fax: 206-364-0349. E-mail: tdemoney@shorelinechristian.org. Website: www.shorelinechristian.org

THE SIENA SCHOOL

Silver Spring, Maryland
See Special Needs Schools section.

SIERRA CANYON SCHOOL

20801 Rinaldi Street
Chatsworth, California 91311
Head of School: Mr. Jim Skrumbis

General Information Coeducational day college-preparatory, 25 Advanced Placement courses and 36 Honors courses, and traditional liberal arts curriculum school. Founded: 1978. Setting: suburban. Nearest major city is Los Angeles. 42-acre campus. 6 buildings on campus. Approved or accredited by California Association of Independent Schools, Western Association of Schools and Colleges, and California Department of Education. Member of National Association of Independent Schools and Secondary School Admission Test Board. Total enrollment: 1,000. Upper school average class size: 14. Upper school faculty-student ratio: 1:10. There are 170 required school days per year for Upper School students. Upper School students typically attend 5 days per week. The average school day consists of 7 hours.

Faculty School total: 88. In upper school: 34 men, 17 women; 4700 have advanced degrees.

Subjects Offered 20th century history, 20th century world history, 3-dimensional art, 3-dimensional design, acting, advanced biology, advanced chemistry, advanced computer applications, advanced math, Advanced Placement courses, advanced studio art-AP, African-American history, algebra, American government, American history-AP, American literature-AP, anatomy and physiology, ancient world history, architecture, art history-AP, art-AP, band, calculus, calculus-AP, ceramics, chemistry, chemistry-AP, Chinese, choir, choreography, chorus, civil rights, Civil War, comparative government and politics-AP, computer programming, computer programming-AP, computer science, computer science-AP, conceptual physics, dance, debate, digital art, digital photography, drama, drama performance, drawing and design, economics, economics and history, economics-AP, electives, English, English language and composition-AP, English language-AP, English literature, English literature and composition-AP, English literature-AP, English-AP, English/composition-AP, environmental science, environmental science-AP, environmental studies, equality and freedom, ethics, ethics and responsibility, ethnic studies, European history-AP, experiential education, experimental science, film, filmmaking, fitness, foreign language, forensics, foundations of civilization, French, French as a second language, French language-AP, French literature-AP, French studies, French-AP, functions, geometry, global studies, government, government and politics-AP, government-AP, government/civics, government/civics-AP, grammar, graphic arts, health, history, history of architecture, history of rock and roll, history-AP, Holocaust, Holocaust and other genocides, Holocaust legacy, Holocaust seminar, Holocaust studies, honors algebra, honors English, honors geometry, honors U.S. history, honors world history, independent study, information technology, introduction to theater, journalism, lab science, language, language and composition, language arts, language-AP, languages, Latin, Latin-AP, leadership and service, life science, literature and composition-AP, literature seminar, literature-AP, logarithms, macro/microeconomics-AP, macroeconomics-AP, Mandarin, marketing, mathematics, mathematics-AP, modern European history, modern European history-AP, music, music theory, music theory-AP, musical theater, newspaper, orchestra, painting, performing arts, personal development, photography, physical education, physical fitness, physics, physics-AP, poetry, politics, pottery, pre-algebra, pre-calculus, programming, psychology, research seminar, Roman civilization, science, science research, sculpture, senior seminar, service learning/internship, Shakespeare, short story, Spanish language-AP, Spanish literature-AP, Spanish-AP, speech and debate, student government, student publications, studio art, studio art-AP, The 20th Century, theater arts, theater design and production, trigonometry, U.S. constitutional history, U.S. government, U.S. government and politics, U.S. government and politics-AP, U.S. history, U.S. history-AP, visual and performing arts, visual arts, vocal music, yoga.

Graduation Requirements Art, English, foreign language, history, language, mathematics, science, visual and performing arts, world history, students are required to take 4 years of English, 2 years of Science and Visual/Performing Arts (3 or more recommended), and 3 years of History (4 recommended), Math (minimum of Pre-Calculus recommended), and World Languages.

Special Academic Programs 23 Advanced Placement exams for which test preparation is offered; honors section; independent study; academic accommodation for the gifted, the musically talented, and the artistically talented.

College Admission Counseling 98 students graduated in 2016; all went to college, including New York University; The University of Arizona; University of California, Davis; University of California, Los Angeles; University of Southern California; University of Washington. Mean SAT critical reading: 573, mean SAT math: 598, mean SAT writing: 590, mean combined SAT: 1761, mean composite ACT: 27.

Student Life Upper grades have specified standards of dress, student council, honor system. Discipline rests primarily with faculty.

Tuition and Aid Day student tuition: $33,850. Tuition installment plan (SMART Tuition Payment Plan, single, two, four, and monthly (over 10 months) payment plans). Need-based scholarship grants available. In 2016–17, 38% of upper-school students received aid.

Admissions Traditional secondary-level entrance grade is 9. Admissions testing, ISEE or school placement exam required. Deadline for receipt of application materials: January 15. Application fee required: $150. On-campus interview recommended.

Athletics Interscholastic: baseball (boys), basketball (b,g), cheering (g), dance (g), dance squad (g), dance team (g), flag football (b), football (b), golf (b), lacrosse (b), modern dance (g), sand volleyball (g), soccer (b,g), softball (g), tennis (b), volleyball (g); coed interscholastic: cross-country running, dressage, equestrian sports, golf, swimming and diving, track and field. 4 PE instructors, 37 coaches, 2 athletic trainers.

Computers Computers are regularly used in all classes. Computer network features include on-campus library services, Internet access, wireless campus network, Internet filtering or blocking technology, iPads. Campus intranet, student e-mail accounts, and computer access in designated common areas are available to students. Students grades are available online. The school has a published electronic and media policy.

Contact 818-882-8121. Website: https://www.sierracanyonschool.org/

SIGNET CHRISTIAN SCHOOL

95 Jonesville Crescent
North York, Ontario M4A 1H2, Canada

Head of School: Mrs. Catherine Dume

General Information Coeducational day college-preparatory and science school. Grades JK–12. Founded: 1975. Setting: urban. Nearest major city is Toronto, Canada. 1-acre campus. 1 building on campus. Approved or accredited by Association of Christian Schools International and Ontario Department of Education. Language of instruction: English. Total enrollment: 30. Upper school average class size: 6. Upper school faculty-student ratio: 1:5. There are 176 required school days per year for Upper School students. Upper School students typically attend 5 days per week. The average school day consists of 6 hours and 30 minutes.

Upper School Student Profile Grade 9: 3 students (2 boys, 1 girl); Grade 10: 2 students (2 boys); Grade 11: 4 students (3 boys, 1 girl); Grade 12: 5 students (3 boys, 2 girls).

Faculty School total: 8. In upper school: 1 man, 3 women; 1 has an advanced degree.

Subjects Offered Biology, business studies, calculus, Canadian geography, Canadian history, career education, chemistry, civics, English, ESL, French as a second language, math analysis, math applications, physics, science, visual arts.

Graduation Requirements English, Ontario Ministry of Education requirements.

Special Academic Programs Independent study; ESL (3 students enrolled).

College Admission Counseling 3 students graduated in 2016; all went to college, including Ryerson University.

Student Life Upper grades have uniform requirement. Discipline rests primarily with faculty. Attendance at religious services is required.

Tuition and Aid Day student tuition: CAN$7000. Tuition installment plan (individually arranged payment plans). Tuition reduction for siblings available.

Admissions SLEP required. Deadline for receipt of application materials: none. No application fee required.

Athletics Coed Intramural: basketball, bowling, cross-country running, skiing (downhill), snowboarding, soccer, table tennis, track and field.

Computers Computers are regularly used in English, mathematics, technology classes. Computer network features include Internet access.

Contact Admissions. 416-750-7515. Fax: 416-750-7720.
E-mail: info@signetschool.ca. Website: www.signetschool.ca

SMITH SCHOOL

New York, New York
See Special Needs Schools section.

SMITHVILLE CHRISTIAN HIGH SCHOOL

Smithville Christian High School
6488 Smithville Townline Road
Smithville, Ontario L0R 2A0, Canada

Head of School: Mr. Ted W. Harris

General Information Coeducational day college-preparatory, general academic, arts, business, vocational, religious studies, bilingual studies, and technology school, affiliated with Christian faith, Christian faith. Grades 9–12. Founded: 1980. Setting: small town. Nearest major city is Hamilton, Canada. 4-acre campus. 1 building on campus. Approved or accredited by Christian Schools International, Ontario Ministry of Education, and Ontario Department of Education. Language of instruction: English. Endowment: CAN$500,000. Total enrollment: 220. Upper school average class size: 18. Upper school faculty-student ratio: 1:11. The average school day consists of 5 hours and 20 minutes.

Upper School Student Profile 95% of students are Christian, Christian.

Faculty School total: 18. In upper school: 12 men, 6 women; 7 have advanced degrees.

Subjects Offered 20th century history, accounting, advanced math, ancient history, arts, athletics, Bible, biology, business, calculus, Canadian geography, Canadian history, careers, chemistry, civics, computer applications, computer information systems, computer science, construction, data analysis, discrete mathematics, drama, dramatic arts, English, finance, fitness, food and nutrition, French, French as a second language, functions, general math, geography, geometry, health, health education, healthful living, history, instrumental music, integrated technology fundamentals, mathematics, media, parenting, personal finance, physical education, physics, science, society challenge and change, transportation technology, urban studies, visual arts, world geography, world history, writing.

Graduation Requirements Arts, Bible, Canadian geography, Canadian history, careers, civics, electives, English, French, mathematics, physical education (includes health), science, society challenge and change.

Special Academic Programs Independent study; remedial reading and/or remedial writing; remedial math; programs in English for dyslexic students; special instructional classes for students with learning disabilities, Attention Deficit Disorder, emotional and behavioral problems; ESL (20 students enrolled).

College Admission Counseling 65 students graduated in 2015; 55 went to college, including Calvin College; Carleton University; Dordt College; Redeemer University College; University of Toronto; University of Waterloo. Other: 5 went to work, 5 had other specific plans.

Student Life Upper grades have uniform requirement, student council, honor system. Discipline rests primarily with faculty.

Tuition and Aid Day student tuition: CAN$13,500. Tuition installment plan (monthly payment plans, individually arranged payment plans). Tuition reduction for siblings, bursaries, need-based scholarship grants available. In 2015–16, 25% of upper-school students received aid. Total amount of financial aid awarded in 2015–16: CAN$150,000.

Admissions Traditional secondary-level entrance grade is 9. Deadline for receipt of application materials: none. Application fee required: CAN$500. Interview recommended.

Athletics Interscholastic: badminton (boys, girls), basketball (b,g), cross-country running (b,g), soccer (b,g), track and field (b,g), volleyball (b,g); coed interscholastic: badminton; coed intramural: backpacking, ball hockey, basketball, floor hockey, hiking/backpacking, hockey, outdoor education, outdoor skills, winter soccer. 2 PE instructors, 10 coaches.

Computers Computers are regularly used in all academic, Bible studies, business education, college planning, construction, current events, data processing, design, drafting, English, geography, history, independent study, introduction to technology, keyboarding, library, occupational education, photography, reading, social sciences, social studies, technical drawing, word processing, writing, writing, yearbook classes. Computer network features include Internet access, wireless campus network, one-to-one program, starting September 2016, all incoming students will be issued a laptop. Student e-mail accounts are available to students. Students grades are available online. The school has a published electronic and media policy.

Contact Mr. Will Lammers, Director of Program. 905-957-3255. Fax: 905-957-3431. E-mail: wlammers@smithvillechristian.ca. Website: www.smithvillechristian.ca

SOLEBURY SCHOOL

6832 Phillips Mill Road
New Hope, Pennsylvania 18938-9682
Head of School: Mr. Thomas G. Wilschutz

General Information Coeducational boarding and day college-preparatory, arts, and technology school. Boarding grades 9–12, day grades 7–12. Founded: 1925. Setting: small town. Nearest major city is Philadelphia. Students are housed in single-sex dormitories. 90-acre campus. 25 buildings on campus. Approved or accredited by Pennsylvania Association of Independent Schools and Pennsylvania Department of Education. Member of National Association of Independent Schools and Secondary School Admission Test Board. Endowment: $6.2 million. Total enrollment: 223. Upper school average class size: 11. Upper school faculty-student ratio: 1:12. Upper School students typically attend 5 days per week. The average school day consists of 9 hours and 30 minutes.

Upper School Student Profile Grade 9: 46 students (27 boys, 19 girls); Grade 10: 53 students (31 boys, 22 girls); Grade 11: 56 students (31 boys, 25 girls); Grade 12: 50 students (25 boys, 25 girls). 35% of students are boarding students. 39% are state residents. 7 states are represented in upper school student body. 20% are international students. International students from China, Republic of Korea, Rwanda, South Africa, and Taiwan; 3 other countries represented in student body.

Faculty School total: 70. In upper school: 28 men, 21 women; 34 have advanced degrees; 24 reside on campus.

Subjects Offered 20th century world history, 3-dimensional art, 3-dimensional design, acting, advanced biology, advanced chemistry, advanced computer applications, advanced math, Advanced Placement courses, advanced studio art-AP, advanced TOEFL/grammar, algebra, American government, American history-AP, American studies, anatomy, anatomy and physiology, ancient history, anthropology, applied music, art, art education, art history, art history-AP, art-AP, astronomy, audio visual/media, biology, biology-AP, calculus, calculus-AP, ceramics, chemistry, chemistry-AP, chorus, comparative government and politics, comparative government and politics AP, computer art, computer education, computer graphics, computer math, computer music, computer programming, computer skills, computer-aided design, conceptual physics, concert choir, creative writing, criminal justice, current events, digital photography, drama, drawing, English, English-AP, environmental science-AP, ESL, ethics, fine arts, food and nutrition, forensics, fractal geometry, French, French-AP, geometry, government and politics-AP, health, honors geometry, jazz band, Middle East, music, painting, performing arts, photography, physical education, pre-algebra, pre-calculus, printmaking, psychology, public speaking, sculpture, senior project, Shakespeare, Spanish, Spanish-AP, statistics-AP, studio art, theater, theater design and production, trigonometry, U.S. government and politics-AP, U.S. history, world history, writing.

Graduation Requirements Art, computers, electives, English, foreign language, health, mathematics, science, social studies (includes history), 10 hours of community service per year.

Special Academic Programs 10 Advanced Placement exams for which test preparation is offered; honors section; independent study; term-away projects; academic accommodation for the gifted, the musically talented, and the artistically talented; remedial reading and/or remedial writing; remedial math; programs in English, general development for dyslexic students; ESL (26 students enrolled).

College Admission Counseling 53 students graduated in 2015; 51 went to college, including American University; Brown University; Dickinson College; Drexel University; Purdue University; The George Washington University. Other: 1 went to work, 1 entered a postgraduate year. Median SAT critical reading: 575, median SAT math: 560, median SAT writing: 575, median combined SAT: 1750, median composite ACT: 22. 37% scored over 600 on SAT critical reading, 37% scored over 600 on SAT math, 41% scored over 600 on SAT writing, 43% scored over 1800 on combined SAT, 32% scored over 26 on composite ACT.

Student Life Upper grades have student council. Discipline rests equally with students and faculty.

Tuition and Aid Day student tuition: $35,950; 7-day tuition and room/board: $51,995. Tuition installment plan (monthly payment plans). Merit scholarship grants, need-based scholarship grants available. In 2015–16, 40% of upper-school students received aid; total upper-school merit-scholarship money awarded: $117,500. Total amount of financial aid awarded in 2015–16: $1,975,000.

Admissions Traditional secondary-level entrance grade is 9. For fall 2015, 340 students applied for upper-level admission, 136 were accepted, 79 enrolled. ACT, any standardized test, International English Language Test, SSAT or TOEFL Junior required. Deadline for receipt of application materials: January 15. Application fee required: $50. Interview required.

Athletics Interscholastic: baseball (boys), basketball (b,g), field hockey (g), lacrosse (g), soccer (b,g), softball (g), wrestling (b); coed interscholastic: cross-country running, golf, tennis, track and field; coed intramural: bicycling, canoeing/kayaking, cheering, dance, dance team, fitness, fitness walking, hiking/backpacking, horseback riding, independent competitive sports, modern dance, outdoor activities, outdoor education, rock climbing, skiing (downhill), snowboarding, tennis, ultimate Frisbee, walking, wall climbing, weight lifting, weight training, yoga. 1 PE instructor, 1 coach, 2 athletic trainers.

Computers Computers are regularly used in art, college planning, English, ESL, foreign language, independent study, language development, literary magazine, mathematics, music, news writing, newspaper, research skills, science, social studies, technical drawing, theater, theater arts, video film production, yearbook classes. Computer network features include on-campus library services, online commercial services, Internet access, wireless campus network, Internet filtering or blocking technology, audio-visual room/library, mobile computer carts. Campus intranet, student e-mail accounts, and computer access in designated common areas are available to students. Students grades are available online. The school has a published electronic and media policy.

Contact Mr. Scott Eckstein, Director of Admission. 215-862-5261. Fax: 215-862-3366. E-mail: admissions@solebury.org. Website: www.solebury.org

SONOMA ACADEMY

2500 Farmers Lane
Santa Rosa, California 95404
Head of School: Janet Durgin

General Information Coeducational day college-preparatory and Environmental Leadership a Global Citizenship concentrations school. Grades 9–12. Founded: 1999. Setting: suburban. 34-acre campus. 4 buildings on campus. Approved or accredited by California Association of Independent Schools, Western Association of Schools and Colleges, and California Department of Education. Member of National Association of Independent Schools. Total enrollment: 284. Upper school average class size: 15. Upper school faculty-student ratio: 1:10. Upper School students typically attend 5 days per week. The average school day consists of 6 hours and 30 minutes.

Faculty School total: 35. In upper school: 13 men, 15 women; 22 have advanced degrees.

Subjects Offered 3-dimensional design, acting, advanced math, Advanced Placement courses, African studies, algebra, alternative physical education, American history, American literature, anatomy and physiology, art, art history, arts, athletic training, athletics, audio visual/media, baseball, Basic programming, basketball, biology, calculus, calculus-AP, chemistry, chemistry-AP, choir, college admission preparation, college awareness, college counseling, college placement, college planning, college writing, comparative cultures, computer programming, constitutional law, costumes and make-up, creative writing, digital photography, drama, drama performance, dramatic arts, drawing, East European studies, ecology, environmental systems, economics, economics and history, engineering, English, English language and composition-AP, English literature and composition-AP, English literature-AP, environmental education, environmental studies, equestrian sports, expository writing, fine arts, fitness, foreign language, forensics, French, genetics, geometry, health and wellness, historiography, history of rock and roll, honors algebra, honors geometry, instrumental music, international relations, journalism, literature, Mandarin, music history, Native American studies, oceanography, philosophy, physics, physics-AP, public speaking, Russian history, Shakespeare, Spanish, Spanish language-AP, sports, studio art, theater, theater arts, theater design and production, theater production, track and field, visual arts, weight training.

Graduation Requirements American history, art, chemistry, college admission preparation, college counseling, drama, English, foreign language, health and wellness, humanities, mathematics, physical education (includes health), science, participation in intersession each year; exploratory, Connections, senior speech.

Special Academic Programs 7 Advanced Placement exams for which test preparation is offered; honors section; independent study; study abroad.

College Admission Counseling 70 students graduated in 2016; 68 went to college, including Chapman University; Stanford University; University of Chicago; University of Washington. Other: 2 had other specific plans. Mean combined SAT: 1884.

Student Life Upper grades have specified standards of dress, student council, honor system. Discipline rests equally with students and faculty.

Tuition and Aid Day student tuition: $39,900. Tuition installment plan (Insured Tuition Payment Plan, monthly payment plans). Need-based scholarship grants, STEM scholarships, Davis Scholarship available. In 2016–17, 50% of upper-school students received aid. Total amount of financial aid awarded in 2016–17: $3,000,000.

Admissions Traditional secondary-level entrance grade is 9. SSAT required. Deadline for receipt of application materials: January 11. Application fee required: $90. On-campus interview recommended.

Athletics Interscholastic: baseball (boys), basketball (b,g), cross-country running (b,g), equestrian sports (b,g), lacrosse (b,g), soccer (b,g), tennis (b,g), track and field (b,g), volleyball (g); coed intramural: aerobics/dance, combined training, dance, fencing, fitness, flag football, Frisbee, kickball, martial arts, outdoor education, physical fitness, physical training, power lifting, rock climbing, softball, strength & conditioning, ultimate Frisbee, weight training, yoga.

Computers Computers are regularly used in all academic classes. Computer network features include on-campus library services, online commercial services, Internet access, wireless campus network, Internet filtering or blocking technology, digital technology center, broadcast studio. Campus intranet, student e-mail accounts, and computer access in designated common areas are available to students. Students grades are available online. The school has a published electronic and media policy.

Contact Sandy Stack, Director of Enrollment and Marketing. 707-545-1770. Fax: 707-636-2474. E-mail: sandy.stack@sonomaacademy.org.

Website: www.sonomaacademy.org/

SOUNDVIEW PREPARATORY SCHOOL

370 Underhill Avenue
Yorktown Heights, New York 10598

Head of School: W. Glyn Hearn

General Information Coeducational day college-preparatory, arts, and technology school. Grades 6–PG. Founded: 1989. Setting: suburban. Nearest major city is New York. 13-acre campus. 7 buildings on campus. Approved or accredited by New York Department of Education, New York State Association of Independent Schools, and New York Department of Education. Member of National Association of Independent Schools. Total enrollment: 70. Upper school average class size: 7. Upper school faculty-student ratio: 1:5. There are 164 required school days per year for Upper School students. Upper School students typically attend 5 days per week. The average school day consists of 6 hours and 47 minutes.

Upper School Student Profile Grade 9: 9 students (4 boys, 5 girls); Grade 10: 12 students (7 boys, 5 girls); Grade 11: 17 students (9 boys, 8 girls); Grade 12: 19 students (11 boys, 8 girls).

Faculty School total: 14. In upper school: 5 men, 9 women; 12 have advanced degrees.

Subjects Offered Advanced Placement courses, advanced studio art-AP, algebra, American history, American literature, art, art-AP, biology, calculus, calculus-AP, chemistry, chemistry-AP, computer science, computer science-AP, earth science, English, English literature, English-AP, environmental science, European history-AP, forensics, French, geometry, government-AP, health, Italian, Latin, mathematics, music, physical education, physics, physics-AP, pottery, psychology-AP, science, social studies, Spanish, study skills, U.S. history-AP, world history.

Graduation Requirements Art, electives, English, foreign language, health, history, mathematics, physical education (includes health), science.

Special Academic Programs 9 Advanced Placement exams for which test preparation is offered; honors section; accelerated programs; independent study; academic accommodation for the gifted, the musically talented, and the artistically talented; special instructional classes for students needing wheelchair accessibility.

College Admission Counseling 7 students graduated in 2015; 6 went to college, including Clark University; Curry College; Merrimack College; New York University. Other: 1 had other specific plans. Mean SAT critical reading: 610, mean SAT math: 619, mean SAT writing: 525, mean composite ACT: 26. 50% scored over 600 on SAT critical reading, 50% scored over 600 on SAT math, 50% scored over 600 on SAT writing.

Student Life Discipline rests primarily with faculty.

Tuition and Aid Day student tuition: $36,500–$38,000. Need-based scholarship grants available. In 2015–16, 30% of upper-school students received aid. Total amount of financial aid awarded in 2015–16: $569,000.

Admissions Traditional secondary-level entrance grade is 9. For fall 2015, 41 students applied for upper-level admission, 28 were accepted, 19 enrolled. Deadline for receipt of application materials: none. Application fee required: $50. On-campus interview required.

Athletics Interscholastic: basketball (boys, girls); coed interscholastic: bowling, soccer, ultimate Frisbee. 1 PE instructor, 1 coach.

Computers Computers are regularly used in all academic classes. Computer network features include Internet access, wireless campus network, Internet filtering or blocking technology. Campus intranet and student e-mail accounts are available to students. The school has a published electronic and media policy.

Contact Mary E. Ivanyi, Assistant Head. 914-962-2780. Fax: 914-302-2769. E-mail: mivanyi@soundviewprep.org. Website: www.soundviewprep.org

SOUTHERN ONTARIO COLLEGIATE

28 Rebecca Street
Hamilton, Ontario L8R 1B4, Canada

Head of School: Susan J. Woods

General Information Coeducational day college-preparatory school. Grades 9–12. Founded: 1980. Setting: urban. 1 building on campus. Approved or accredited by Ontario Ministry of Education and Ontario Department of Education. Language of instruction: English. Upper school average class size: 20. Upper school faculty-student

ratio: 1:15. Upper School students typically attend 5 days per week. The average school day consists of 8 hours and 45 minutes.

Faculty School total: 7. In upper school: 3 men, 3 women; 3 have advanced degrees.

Special Academic Programs ESL (15 students enrolled).

College Admission Counseling 50 students graduated in 2016; 5 went to college, including Penn State University Park. Other: 45 entered a postgraduate year.

Student Life Upper grades have uniform requirement, student council, honor system. Discipline rests primarily with faculty.

Tuition and Aid Guaranteed tuition plan.

Admissions Application fee required: CAN$150.

Computers Computers are regularly used in accounting, career education, computer applications classes. Computer resources include Internet access, wireless campus network, Internet filtering or blocking technology.

Contact Mrs. Maryam Yussuf, Admissions Officer. 905-546-1501. Fax: 866-875-2619. E-mail: admin@mysoc.ca. Website: www.mysoc.ca

SOUTHFIELD CHRISTIAN HIGH SCHOOL

28650 Lahser Road
Southfield, Michigan 48034-2099

Head of School: Mrs. Sue Hoffenbacher

General Information Coeducational day college-preparatory school, affiliated with Baptist Church. Grades PK–12. Founded: 1970. Setting: suburban. Nearest major city is Detroit. 28-acre campus. 1 building on campus. Approved or accredited by Association of Christian Schools International, Independent Schools Association of the Central States, North Central Association of Colleges and Schools, and Michigan Department of Education. Endowment: $1.5 million. Total enrollment: 588. Upper school average class size: 22. Upper school faculty-student ratio: 1:10. There are 180 required school days per year for Upper School students. Upper School students typically attend 5 days per week. The average school day consists of 7 hours.

Upper School Student Profile Grade 9: 49 students (25 boys, 24 girls); Grade 10: 46 students (26 boys, 20 girls); Grade 11: 39 students (15 boys, 24 girls); Grade 12: 50 students (19 boys, 31 girls). 30% of students are Baptist.

Faculty School total: 55. In upper school: 13 men, 16 women; 13 have advanced degrees.

Subjects Offered Accounting, Advanced Placement courses, algebra, American government, American history, American history-AP, American literature, American literature-AP, ancient world history, art, band, Bible, biology, biology-AP, British literature, calculus-AP, chemistry, chemistry-AP, choir, chorus, communication arts, composition-AP, computer applications, computer programming, conceptual physics, creative writing, drawing and design, economics, English language-AP, English literature and composition-AP, film and literature, French, geography, geometry, government, graphic design, health, instrumental music, Life of Christ, literature and composition-AP, Middle Eastern history, New Testament, organic chemistry, photography, physical education, physics-AP, pre-calculus, probability and statistics, Russian history, senior project, Spanish, speech and debate, U.S. history, vocal music, Web site design, world studies, yearbook.

Special Academic Programs Advanced Placement exam preparation; honors section; independent study.

College Admission Counseling 45 students graduated in 2016; all went to college, including Grand Valley State University; Hope College; Michigan State University; Oakland University; University of Michigan; Wheaton College. Median SAT critical reading: 460, median SAT math: 430, median SAT writing: 480, median composite ACT: 25. 25% scored over 26 on composite ACT.

Student Life Upper grades have uniform requirement, student council, honor system. Discipline rests primarily with faculty. Attendance at religious services is required.

Tuition and Aid Day student tuition: $9810. Tuition installment plan (FACTS Tuition Payment Plan). Tuition reduction for siblings, need-based scholarship grants available. In 2016–17, 10% of upper-school students received aid.

Admissions Traditional secondary-level entrance grade is 9. For fall 2016, 65 students applied for upper-level admission, 25 were accepted, 20 enrolled. Any standardized test required. Deadline for receipt of application materials: none. No application fee required. On-campus interview recommended.

Athletics Interscholastic: baseball (boys), basketball (b,g), cheering (g), cross-country running (b,g), football (b), soccer (b,g), softball (g), track and field (b,g), volleyball (g); coed interscholastic: golf; coed intramural: skiing (downhill), weight lifting. 1 PE instructor, 1 athletic trainer.

Computers Computers are regularly used in art, commercial art, computer applications, creative writing, drawing and design, graphic arts, graphic design, independent study, media production, programming, publishing, Web site design, writing, yearbook classes. Computer network features include on-campus library services, Internet access, wireless campus network, Internet filtering or blocking technology. Student e-mail accounts are available to students. Students grades are available online. The school has a published electronic and media policy.

Contact Mrs. Alisa Ruffin, High School Principal. 248-357-3660 Ext. 278. Fax: 248-357-5271. E-mail: aruffin@southfieldchristian.org.

Website: www.southfieldchristian.org

SOUTHWEST CHRISTIAN SCHOOL, INC.

6901 Altamesa Boulevard
Fort Worth, Texas 76123

Head of School: Dr. Shane Naterman

General Information Coeducational day college-preparatory, arts, religious studies, and technology school, affiliated with Christian faith. Grades PK–12. Founded: 1969. Setting: suburban. 39-acre campus. 3 buildings on campus. Approved or accredited by Southern Association of Colleges and Schools and Texas Department of Education. Member of National Association of Independent Schools. Total enrollment: 820. Upper school average class size: 15. Upper school faculty-student ratio: 1:10. There are 176 required school days per year for Upper School students. Upper School students typically attend 5 days per week. The average school day consists of 7 hours.

Faculty School total: 130. In upper school: 13 men, 35 women; 34 have advanced degrees.

Subjects Offered 1 1/2 elective credits, advanced math, algebra, American government, American literature, American literature-AP, anatomy and physiology, art, Bible studies, biology, biology-AP, British literature, British literature-AP, calculus, calculus-AP, chemistry, chemistry-AP, choir, drama, English, English literature-AP, English-AP, foreign language, French, geometry, government, history, honors algebra, honors English, honors geometry, honors U.S. history, honors world history, journalism, keyboarding, lab science, leadership, literature and composition-AP, physics, physics-AP, pre-algebra, pre-calculus, psychology, SAT preparation, Spanish, speech, technology, U.S. history, U.S. history-AP, Web site design.

Graduation Requirements 4 years of Bible courses.

Special Academic Programs Advanced Placement exam preparation; honors section; accelerated programs; study at local college for college credit; study abroad; academic accommodation for the gifted.

College Admission Counseling 77 students graduated in 2015.

Student Life Upper grades have uniform requirement, student council, honor system. Discipline rests primarily with faculty. Attendance at religious services is required.

Tuition and Aid Day student tuition: $10,275–$13,700. Tuition installment plan (FACTS Tuition Payment Plan). Need-based scholarship grants available. In 2015–16, 20% of upper-school students received aid. Total amount of financial aid awarded in 2015–16: $455,000.

Admissions Traditional secondary-level entrance grade is 9. Stanford 9 required. Deadline for receipt of application materials: none. No application fee required. Interview required.

Athletics Interscholastic: baseball (boys), basketball (b,g), cheering (g), cross-country running (b,g), dance (g), dance team (g), equestrian sports (b,g), football (b), golf (b,g), soccer (b,g), softball (g), track and field (b,g), volleyball (g), wrestling (b); intramural: physical training (b,g); coed interscholastic: aquatics, equestrian sports, paint ball, rodeo; coed intramural: aquatics, fitness, strength & conditioning, weight training. 2 PE instructors, 12 coaches, 1 athletic trainer.

Computers Computers are regularly used in all academic classes. Computer network features include on-campus library services, online commercial services, Internet access, wireless campus network, Internet filtering or blocking technology, computer carts for classroom use. Student e-mail accounts and computer access in designated common areas are available to students. Students grades are available online. The school has a published electronic and media policy.

Contact Mr. Travis Crow, Dean of Student Services. 817-294-9596 Ext. 207. Fax: 817-294-9603. E-mail: tcrow@southwestchristian.org.
Website: www.southwestchristian.org

SOUTHWESTERN ACADEMY

8800 East Ranch Campus Road
Rimrock, Arizona 86335

Head of School: Mr. Kenneth Veronda

General Information Coeducational boarding and day college-preparatory and general academic school. Grades 6–PG. Founded: 1924. Setting: suburban. Students are housed in single-sex dormitories. 8-acre campus. 24 buildings on campus. Approved or accredited by The Association of Boarding Schools, Western Association of Schools and Colleges, and Arizona Department of Education. Member of Secondary School Admission Test Board. Endowment: $10 million. Total enrollment: 1,161. Upper school average class size: 12. Upper school faculty-student ratio: 1:9. There are 184 required school days per year for Upper School students. Upper School students typically attend 5 days per week. The average school day consists of 8 hours.

Upper School Student Profile Grade 6: 5 students (3 boys, 2 girls); Grade 7: 4 students (2 boys, 2 girls); Grade 8: 5 students (5 boys); Grade 9: 14 students (9 boys, 5 girls); Grade 10: 39 students (23 boys, 16 girls); Grade 11: 44 students (24 boys, 20 girls); Grade 12: 32 students (25 boys, 7 girls). 98% of students are boarding students. 25% are state residents. 4 states are represented in upper school student body. 75% are international students. International students from China, Japan, Russian Federation, Taiwan, United States, and Viet Nam; 9 other countries represented in student body.

Faculty School total: 31. In upper school: 18 men, 13 women; 14 have advanced degrees; 6 reside on campus.

Subjects Offered Advanced math, Advanced Placement courses, algebra, American history, American literature, American literature-AP, art, art appreciation, art history, astronomy, biology, biology-AP, British literature, calculus, chemistry, earth science, ecology, economics, English, English composition, environmental education, environmental science, environmental studies, fashion, fine arts, general math, geometry, health, integrated science, math review, mathematics, music, music appreciation, outdoor education, physics, pre-algebra, Spanish, studio art, U.S. government, world cultures, yearbook.

Graduation Requirements Algebra, American government, American history, American literature, British literature, computer literacy, economics, electives, English, foreign language, geometry, lab science, mathematics, physical education (includes health), visual and performing arts, world cultures, 20 hours per school year of community service. Community service is required.

Special Academic Programs 12 Advanced Placement exams for which test preparation is offered; honors section; independent study; study at local college for college credit; academic accommodation for the musically talented and the artistically talented; ESL (65 students enrolled).

College Admission Counseling 36 students graduated in 2016; all went to college, including Arizona State University at the Tempe campus; California State University, Los Angeles; Marymount California University; University of California, Irvine; University of California, Los Angeles. Median SAT critical reading: 550, median SAT math: 700, median SAT writing: 550, median combined SAT: 1800.

Student Life Upper grades have specified standards of dress, student council, honor system. Discipline rests primarily with faculty.

Summer Programs Remediation, enrichment, advancement, ESL, art/fine arts, rigorous outdoor training programs offered; session focuses on academics and outdoor/environmental education; held on campus; accepts boys and girls; open to students from other schools. 60 students usually enrolled. 2017 schedule: June 12 to September 17. Application deadline: none.

Tuition and Aid Day student tuition: $19,750; 7-day tuition and room/board: $47,850. Tuition installment plan (monthly payment plans, individually arranged payment plans). Need-based scholarship grants available. In 2016–17, 30% of upper-school students received aid. Total amount of financial aid awarded in 2016–17: $240,000.

Admissions Traditional secondary-level entrance grade is 9. For fall 2016, 199 students applied for upper-level admission, 133 were accepted, 47 enrolled. English language, English proficiency, ESL, High School Placement Test, International English Language Test, international math and English tests, SLEP, SLEP for foreign students, TOEFL or writing sample required. Deadline for receipt of application materials: none. Application fee required: $100. Interview recommended.

Athletics Interscholastic: basketball (boys, girls), golf (b,g), volleyball (b,g); coed interscholastic: baseball, golf, soccer; coed intramural: alpine skiing, aquatics, archery, backpacking, badminton, baseball, basketball, bicycling, billiards, canoeing/kayaking, climbing, croquet, cross-country running, equestrian sports, fishing, fitness, fitness walking, flag football, flagball, Frisbee, golf, hiking/backpacking, horseback riding, horseshoes, mountain biking, outdoor activities, outdoor adventure, outdoor education, outdoor recreation, outdoor skills, outdoors, paint ball, physical fitness, rafting, rock climbing, ropes courses, running, skiing (cross-country), skiing (downhill), snowboarding, soccer, softball, swimming and diving, table tennis, tennis, touch football, track and field, volleyball, walking, weight lifting, weight training, wilderness. 1 PE instructor, 7 coaches.

Computers Computers are regularly used in all academic, animation, architecture, art, basic skills, career education, career exploration, classics, college planning, commercial art, computer applications, creative writing, current events, data processing, design, digital applications, drafting, drawing and design, economics, English, ESL, ethics, foreign language, geography, graphic arts, graphic design, graphics, health, historical foundations for arts, history, humanities, independent study, information technology, journalism, keyboarding, lab/keyboard, language development, learning cognition, library, life skills, literacy, literary magazine, mathematics, media, media arts, media production, media services, mentorship program, multimedia, music, music technology, news writing, newspaper, occupational education, philosophy, photography, photojournalism, programming, psychology, publications, publishing, reading, research skills, SAT preparation, science, senior seminar, social sciences, social studies, Spanish, speech, stock market, study skills, technical drawing, technology, theater, theater arts, typing, video film production, vocational-technical courses, Web site design, wilderness education, word processing, writing, writing, yearbook classes. Computer network features include on-campus library services, Internet access, wireless campus network, Internet filtering or blocking technology. Student e-mail accounts and computer access in designated common areas are available to students.

Contact Ms. Elena Lopez, Director of Admissions. 626-799-5010 Ext. 204. Fax: 626-799-0407. E-mail: elopez@southwesternacademy.edu.
Website: www.southwesternacademy.edu

SOUTHWESTERN ACADEMY

2800 Monterey Road
San Marino, California 91108

General Information Coeducational boarding and day college-preparatory, general academic, arts, and ESL school. Grades 6–PG. Founded: 1924. Setting: suburban. Nearest major city is Los Angeles. Students are housed in single-sex dormitories. 8-acre campus. 9 buildings on campus. Approved or accredited by The Association of

Boarding Schools, Western Association of Schools and Colleges, and California Department of Education. Member of Secondary School Admission Test Board. Endowment: $9 million. Total enrollment: 134. Upper school average class size: 12. Upper school faculty-student ratio: 1:6. There are 184 required school days per year for Upper School students. Upper School students typically attend 5 days per week. The average school day consists of 8 hours.

See Display below and Close-Up on page 608.

THE SPENCE SCHOOL

22 East 91st Street
New York, New York 10128-0657

Head of School: Ellanor (Bodie) N. Brizendine

General Information Girls' day college-preparatory, arts, and technology school. Grades K–12. Founded: 1892. Setting: urban. 2 buildings on campus. Approved or accredited by New York State Association of Independent Schools. Member of National Association of Independent Schools and Secondary School Admission Test Board. Total enrollment: 738. Upper school average class size: 16. Upper school faculty-student ratio: 1:7. There are 160 required school days per year for Upper School students. Upper School students typically attend 5 days per week. The average school day consists of 7 hours.

Upper School Student Profile Grade 6: 58 students (58 girls); Grade 7: 59 students (59 girls); Grade 8: 59 students (59 girls); Grade 9: 61 students (61 girls); Grade 10: 67 students (67 girls); Grade 11: 68 students (68 girls); Grade 12: 57 students (57 girls).

Faculty School total: 127. In upper school: 22 men, 59 women; 79 have advanced degrees.

Subjects Offered 20th century American writers, 20th century history, 20th century world history, 3-dimensional design, acting, addiction, advanced chemistry, advanced math, aerobics, African history, African literature, African-American literature, algebra, alternative physical education, American culture, American history, American literature, art, art and culture, art history, art-AP, Asian history, Asian literature, bioethics, bioethics, DNA and culture, biology, calculus, ceramics, chemistry, Chinese, Chinese history, Chinese literature, civil rights, college admission preparation, composition, computer programming, computer science, constitutional law, CPR, critical writing, dance, dance performance, design, digital imaging, digital photography, discrete mathematics, drama, drama performance, dramatic arts, drawing, earth science, economics, English, environmental science, equality and freedom, European history, exercise science, female experience in America, fiber arts, film studies, first aid, fitness, foreign language, French, geometry, global studies, health, health and wellness, history, instrumental music, Israeli studies, Japanese history, Japanese literature, Latin, Latin American history, Latin American literature, Latin American studies, linear algebra, literature, mathematics, media literacy, Middle East, modern European history, multimedia, music, music composition, music theory, non-Western literature, novels, painting, performing arts, photo shop, photography, physical education, physics, poetry, pre-algebra, printmaking, psychology, robotics, science, science research, sculpture, self-defense, Shakespeare, South African history, Spanish, Spanish literature, speech, statistics, technology, theater production, U.S. history, video film production, visual and performing arts, women's studies, world history, world religions, world studies, yoga.

Graduation Requirements Advanced math, algebra, American literature, art, biology, chemistry, computer science, dance, English, European history, foreign language, geometry, global studies, health, history, languages, music, non-Western societies, performing arts, physical education (includes health), physics, science, Shakespeare, speech, technology, U.S. history, visual and performing arts, visual arts, world religions, world studies.

Special Academic Programs 1 Advanced Placement exam for which test preparation is offered; independent study; term-away projects; domestic exchange program; study abroad; special instructional classes for Our resource centers and learning specialists accommodate our students with documented differences, We address such needs on an individual basis.

College Admission Counseling 54 students graduated in 2016; all went to college, including Columbia University; Cornell University; Georgetown University; Princeton University; University of Chicago; University of Pennsylvania. Median SAT critical reading: 730, median SAT math: 740, median SAT writing: 730, median combined SAT: 2210, median composite ACT: 31. 100% scored over 600 on SAT critical reading, 97% scored over 600 on SAT math, 90% scored over 600 on SAT writing, 96% scored over 1800 on combined SAT, 96% scored over 26 on composite ACT.

Student Life Upper grades have uniform requirement, student council. Discipline rests primarily with faculty.

Tuition and Aid Day student tuition: $47,410. Need-based scholarship grants available. In 2016–17, 23% of upper-school students received aid. Total amount of financial aid awarded in 2016–17: $2,260,164.

Admissions Traditional secondary-level entrance grade is 9. ISEE, school's own exam or SSAT required. Deadline for receipt of application materials: December 1. Application fee required: $65. On-campus interview recommended.

Athletics Interscholastic: badminton, basketball, cross-country running, field hockey, indoor track & field, lacrosse, soccer, softball, squash, swimming and diving, tennis, track and field, volleyball, winter (indoor) track. 9 PE instructors, 39 coaches, 2 athletic trainers.

Computers Computers are regularly used in all classes. Computer network features include on-campus library services, online commercial services, Internet access, wireless campus network, all classrooms equipped with Smart Boards. Campus intranet, student e-mail accounts, and computer access in designated common areas are available to students. The school has a published electronic and media policy.

Contact Susan Parker, Director of Admissions. 212-710-8140. Fax: 212-289-6025. E-mail: sparker@spenceschool.org. Website: www.spenceschool.org

SPRING CREEK ACADEMY

6000 Custer Road
Building 5
Plano, Texas 75023

Head of School: Matt Thomas

General Information Coeducational boarding and day and distance learning college-preparatory and general academic school. Grades 2–12. Founded: 1997. Setting: suburban. Nearest major city is Dallas. 3 buildings on campus. Approved or accredited by Southern Association of Colleges and Schools, Texas Education Agency, Texas Private School Accreditation Commission, and Texas Department of Education. Upper school average class size: 6. Upper school faculty-student ratio: 1:6. There are 180 required school days per year for Upper School students. Upper School students typically attend 5 days per week. The average school day consists of 3 hours.

Faculty School total: 20. In upper school: 6 men, 14 women; 12 have advanced degrees.

Special Academic Programs Advanced Placement exam preparation; honors section; study at local college for college credit.

College Admission Counseling 15 students graduated in 2015; all went to college.

Student Life Upper grades have specified standards of dress, student council, honor system. Discipline rests primarily with faculty.

Admissions Traditional secondary-level entrance grade is 9. Iowa Tests of Basic Skills required. Deadline for receipt of application materials: none. Application fee required: $750. On-campus interview recommended.

Computers Computer network features include Internet access, wireless campus network, Internet filtering or blocking technology. Student e-mail accounts and computer access in designated common areas are available to students. Students grades are available online. The school has a published electronic and media policy.

Contact 972-517-6730. Fax: 972-517-8750. Website: www.springcreekacademy.com/

SPRINGSIDE CHESTNUT HILL ACADEMY

500 West Willow Grove Avenue
Philadelphia, Pennsylvania 19118

Head of School: Dr. Stephen L. Druggan, EdD

General Information Coeducational day college-preparatory and science, math, entrepreneurism, engineering & robotics school. Grades PK–12. Founded: 1861. Setting: suburban. 62-acre campus. 4 buildings on campus. Approved or accredited by Pennsylvania Association of Independent Schools and Pennsylvania Department of Education. Member of National Association of Independent Schools and Secondary School Admission Test Board. Endowment: $42 million. Total enrollment: 1,059. Upper school average class size: 18. Upper school faculty-student ratio: 1:10. There are 172 required school days per year for Upper School students. Upper School students typically attend 5 days per week. The average school day consists of 7 hours and 15 minutes.

Upper School Student Profile Grade 9: 132 students (66 boys, 66 girls); Grade 10: 111 students (63 boys, 48 girls); Grade 11: 98 students (48 boys, 50 girls); Grade 12: 123 students (59 boys, 64 girls).

Faculty School total: 140. In upper school: 27 men, 42 women; 43 have advanced degrees.

Subjects Offered Advanced biology, advanced chemistry, advanced math, Advanced Placement courses, African studies, algebra, all academic, American history, architecture, art, art history, biology, biology-AP, calculus, calculus-AP, ceramics, chamber groups, chemistry, Chinese, choral music, college counseling, communications, community service, computer animation, computer programming, computer science, constitutional law, dance, dance performance, digital art, digital music, digital photography, drama, drawing and design, East Asian history, engineering, English, English literature, English-AP, entrepreneurship, environmental science, ethics and responsibility, European history, fine arts, forensics, French, French language-AP, gardening, geometry, handbells, health, independent study, international relations, jazz ensemble, Latin, Latin American studies, mathematics, Middle Eastern history, money management, music, oceanography, orchestra, painting, peer counseling, photography, physical education, physics, physics-AP, physiology, playwriting and directing, pre-calculus, printmaking, robotics, science, senior project, social studies, Spanish, Spanish-AP, statistics, statistics-AP, studio art, the Sixties, theater, trigonometry, U.S. government and politics-AP, U.S. history, U.S. history-AP, video, video and animation, video communication, video film production, weight reduction, woodworking, world history, world history-AP, World War II, writing, writing workshop, yearbook.

Graduation Requirements Art, arts, English, foreign language, health, history, humanities, mathematics, physical education (includes health), science, senior internship, senior project, sports, senior speech, senior project, Center for Entrepreneurial Leadership seminars.

Special Academic Programs 12 Advanced Placement exams for which test preparation is offered; honors section; independent study; term-away projects;

academic accommodation for the gifted, the musically talented, and the artistically talented.

College Admission Counseling 113 students graduated in 2016; 108 went to college, including Bucknell University; Penn State University Park; Stanford University; Syracuse University; The George Washington University; University of Pennsylvania. Other: 1 went to work, 1 entered a postgraduate year, 3 had other specific plans. Median SAT critical reading: 600, median SAT math: 610, median SAT writing: 610, median combined SAT: 1840, median composite ACT: 28. 45% scored over 600 on SAT critical reading, 48% scored over 600 on SAT math, 50% scored over 600 on SAT writing, 46% scored over 1800 on combined SAT, 52% scored over 26 on composite ACT.

Student Life Upper grades have specified standards of dress, student council, honor system. Discipline rests equally with students and faculty.

Summer Programs Enrichment, sports, computer instruction programs offered; session focuses on to offer a variety of interesting opportunities for kids of all ages and interests; held on campus; accepts boys and girls; open to students from other schools. 600 students usually enrolled. 2017 schedule: June 12 to August 18.

Tuition and Aid Day student tuition: $20,500–$34,975. Tuition installment plan (FACTS Tuition Payment Plan, monthly payment plans). Need-based scholarship grants available. In 2016–17, 48% of upper-school students received aid; total upper-school merit-scholarship money awarded: $8,800,000. Total amount of financial aid awarded in 2016–17: $4,500,000.

Admissions Traditional secondary-level entrance grade is 9. For fall 2016, 171 students applied for upper-level admission, 103 were accepted, 42 enrolled. ISEE or SSAT required. Application fee required: $50. On-campus interview required.

Athletics Interscholastic: baseball (boys), basketball (b,g), crew (b,g), cross-country running (b,g), field hockey (g), football (b), golf (b,g), ice hockey (b), independent competitive sports (b,g), indoor track & field (b,g), lacrosse (b,g), rowing (b,g), soccer (b,g), softball (g), squash (b,g), swimming and diving (b,g), table tennis (b,g), tennis (b,g), track and field (b,g), volleyball (g), winter (indoor) track (b,g), wrestling (b). 2 PE instructors, 57 coaches, 2 athletic trainers.

Computers Computers are regularly used in all classes. Computer network features include on-campus library services, online commercial services, Internet access, wireless campus network, Internet filtering or blocking technology, 1:1 school in grades 3-12, and 1:2 in PK-2, many faculty are 1+1 with iPads and laptops. Campus intranet, student e-mail accounts, and computer access in designated common areas are available to students. Students grades are available online. The school has a published electronic and media policy.

Contact Ms. Maggie Baker, Admissions Coordinator. 215-247-7007. E-mail: mbaker@sch.org. Website: www.sch.org

SPRINGWOOD SCHOOL

PO Box 1030, 1814 Cherry Drive
Lanett, Alabama 36863

Head of School: Mr. Rick Johnson

General Information Coeducational day school. Setting: rural. Nearest major city is Columbus, GA. 46-acre campus. 4 buildings on campus. Approved or accredited by Southern Association of Colleges and Schools, Southern Association of Independent Schools, and US Department of State. Upper school average class size: 15.

Faculty In upper school: 10 men, 10 women.

Special Academic Programs Honors section; independent study; study at local college for college credit.

College Admission Counseling 25 students graduated in 2016.

Student Life Upper grades have specified standards of dress, student council, honor system. Discipline rests primarily with faculty.

Athletics Interscholastic: baseball (boys), basketball (b,g), cheering (g), football (b), soccer (b), softball (g), tennis (b,g), track and field (b,g); coed interscholastic: cross-country running, field hockey, golf.

Computers Computers are regularly used in all classes. The school has a published electronic and media policy.

Contact Mrs. Ann Hixon, Director of Admissions, Development, Alumni Relations. 334-644-2123. Fax: 334-644-2194. E-mail: ahixon@springwoodschool.com. Website: www.springwoodschool.com

SQUAW VALLEY ACADEMY

235 Squaw Valley Road
Olympic Valley, California 96146

Head of School: Mr. Bill Grant

General Information Coeducational boarding and day college-preparatory school. Grades 9–12. Founded: 1978. Setting: rural. Nearest major city is Reno, NV. Students are housed in single-sex by floor dormitories and single-sex dormitories. 3-acre campus. 5 buildings on campus. Approved or accredited by National Independent Private Schools Association, Western Association of Schools and Colleges, and California Department of Education. Member of National Association of Independent Schools and Secondary School Admission Test Board. Total enrollment: 100. Upper school average class size: 8. Upper school faculty-student ratio: 1:8. There are 180 required school days per year for Upper School students. Upper School students typically attend 5 days per week. The average school day consists of 8 hours.

Upper School Student Profile 100% of students are boarding students. 60% are international students. International students from China, Indonesia, Japan, Mexico, Russian Federation, and Viet Nam.

Faculty School total: 12. In upper school: 9 men, 3 women; all have advanced degrees; 10 reside on campus.

Subjects Offered 3-dimensional art, ACT preparation, advanced biology, advanced chemistry, advanced math, Advanced Placement courses, advanced TOEFL/grammar, algebra, American democracy, American government, American history, American history-AP, American literature, American literature-AP, anatomy, applied arts, applied music, art, art education, art history, backpacking, band, biology, biology-AP, British literature, British literature (honors), calculus, calculus-AP, ceramics, chemistry, civics, college admission preparation, college counseling, college placement, college planning, college writing, computer science, computers, concert band, creative writing, drama, drawing, English, English literature, environmental science, expository writing, fine arts, French, geography, geometry, government-AP, government/civics, grammar, health, history, history-AP, instruments, Internet, Internet research, jazz, jazz ensemble, jewelry making, language-AP, linear algebra, literature-AP, martial arts, mathematics, mathematics-AP, music, music appreciation, music history, music performance, music theory, novels, outdoor education, photography, physical education, physics, physics-AP, poetry, pre-calculus, psychology, publications, research and reference, SAT preparation, SAT/ACT preparation, science, short story, social sciences, social studies, Spanish, Spanish-AP, strings, student government, student publications, studio art, surfing, swimming, TOEFL preparation, travel, trigonometry, typing, U.S. history, U.S. history-AP, United States government-AP, video, visual and performing arts, visual arts, vocal music, weight fitness, world history, world history-AP, writing, yearbook, yoga.

Graduation Requirements Arts and fine arts (art, music, dance, drama), college admission preparation, English, foreign language, mathematics, physical education (includes health), science, social sciences, participation in skiing and snowboarding, seniors must gain acceptance into a minimum of one (1) college or university.

Special Academic Programs 15 Advanced Placement exams for which test preparation is offered; honors section; accelerated programs; independent study; study at local college for college credit; academic accommodation for the gifted, the musically talented, and the artistically talented; programs in English, mathematics for dyslexic students; special instructional classes for students with ADD and dyslexia; ESL.

College Admission Counseling 21 students graduated in 2016; all went to college, including California Polytechnic State University, San Luis Obispo; Embry-Riddle Aeronautical University–Daytona; University of California, Berkeley; University of California, Davis; University of California, Davis; University of San Francisco. Median combined SAT: 1950, median composite ACT: 25.

Student Life Upper grades have specified standards of dress, student council, honor system. Discipline rests primarily with faculty.

Summer Programs Remediation, enrichment, advancement, ESL, sports, art/fine arts programs offered; session focuses on academics and mountain sports; held both on and off campus; accepts boys and girls; open to students from other schools. 25 students usually enrolled. 2017 schedule: July 2 to August 11. Application deadline: none.

Tuition and Aid 7-day tuition and room/board: $52,950. Tuition installment plan (individually arranged payment plans). Tuition reduction for siblings, merit scholarship grants, need-based scholarship grants available. In 2016–17, 10% of upper-school students received aid; total upper-school merit-scholarship money awarded: $175,000. Total amount of financial aid awarded in 2016–17: $175,000.

Admissions Traditional secondary-level entrance grade is 10. For fall 2016, 120 students applied for upper-level admission, 110 were accepted, 80 enrolled. Math Placement Exam and writing sample required. Deadline for receipt of application materials: none. Application fee required: $100. Interview required.

Athletics Interscholastic: alpine skiing (boys, girls), freestyle skiing (b,g), skiing (downhill) (b,g), snowboarding (b,g); intramural: aerobics (b,g), aerobics/Nautilus (b,g), alpine skiing (b,g), aquatics (b,g), backpacking (b,g), badminton (b,g), basketball (b,g), bicycling (b,g), billiards (b,g), blading (b,g), bowling (b,g), canoeing/kayaking (b,g), climbing (b,g), combined training (b,g), croquet (b,g), cross-country running (b,g), field hockey (b,g), fishing (b,g), fitness (b,g), fitness walking (b,g), flag football (b,g), freestyle skiing (b,g), Frisbee (b,g), golf (b,g), hiking/backpacking (b,g), horseback riding (b,g), jogging (b,g), kayaking (b,g), mountain biking (b,g), mountaineering (b,g), nordic skiing (b,g), outdoor activities (b,g), outdoor adventure (b,g), outdoor education (b,g), outdoor recreation (b,g), outdoor skills (b,g), outdoors (b,g), paddling (b,g), paint ball (b,g), physical fitness (b,g), physical training (b,g), rafting (b,g), rock climbing (b,g), ropes courses (b,g), running (b,g), self defense (b,g), skateboarding (b,g), skiing (cross-country) (b,g), skiing (downhill) (b,g), snowboarding (b,g), snowshoeing (b,g), strength & conditioning (b,g), swimming and diving (b,g), table tennis (b,g), telemark skiing (b,g), tennis (b,g), ultimate Frisbee (b,g), volleyball (b,g), walking (b,g), wall climbing (b,g), weight lifting (b,g), weight training (b,g), yoga (b,g); coed interscholastic: alpine skiing, freestyle skiing, skiing (downhill), snowboarding, soccer; coed intramural: aerobics, aerobics/Nautilus, alpine skiing, aquatics, backpacking, badminton, baseball, basketball, bicycling, billiards, blading, bowling, canoeing/kayaking, climbing, combined training, croquet, cross-country running, field hockey, fishing, fitness, fitness walking, flag football, freestyle skiing, Frisbee, golf, hiking/backpacking, horseback riding, jogging, kayaking, mountain

biking, mountaineering, nordic skiing, outdoor activities, outdoor adventure, outdoor education, outdoor recreation, outdoor skills, outdoors, paddling, paint ball, physical fitness, physical training, rafting, rock climbing, ropes courses, running, self defense, skateboarding, skiing (cross-country), skiing (downhill), snowboarding, snowshoeing, soccer, softball, strength & conditioning, swimming and diving, table tennis, telemark skiing, tennis, ultimate Frisbee, volleyball, walking, wall climbing, weight lifting, weight training, yoga.

Computers Computers are regularly used in all academic classes. Computer network features include on-campus library services, online commercial services, Internet access, wireless campus network, Internet filtering or blocking technology. Student e-mail accounts and computer access in designated common areas are available to students. Students grades are available online. The school has a published electronic and media policy.

Contact Adrienne Forbes, M.Ed., Director of International Admissions. 530-583-9393 Ext. 105. Fax: 530-581-1111. E-mail: aforbes@sva.org. Website: www.sva.org

STANSTEAD COLLEGE

450 Dufferin Street
Stanstead, Quebec J0B 3E0, Canada

Head of School: Mr. Michael Wolfe

General Information Coeducational boarding and day college-preparatory and bilingual studies school, affiliated with Christian faith. Grades 7–12. Founded: 1872. Setting: rural. Nearest major city is Montreal, Canada. Students are housed in single-sex dormitories. 720-acre campus. 10 buildings on campus. Approved or accredited by Canadian Association of Independent Schools, Canadian Educational Standards Institute, New England Association of Schools and Colleges, Quebec Association of Independent Schools, and Quebec Department of Education. Affiliate member of National Association of Independent Schools; member of Secondary School Admission Test Board. Language of instruction: English. Endowment: CAN$5 million. Total enrollment: 220. Upper school average class size: 12. Upper school faculty-student ratio: 1:8. There are 180 required school days per year for Upper School students. Upper School students typically attend 5 days per week. The average school day consists of 5 hours and 30 minutes.

Upper School Student Profile Grade 10: 52 students (24 boys, 28 girls); Grade 11: 47 students (28 boys, 19 girls); Grade 12: 58 students (41 boys, 17 girls). 75% of students are boarding students. 50% are province residents. 12 provinces are represented in upper school student body. 40% are international students. International students from China, Germany, Japan, Mexico, Saudi Arabia, and United States; 22 other countries represented in student body.

Faculty School total: 35. In upper school: 16 men, 14 women; 7 have advanced degrees; 20 reside on campus.

Subjects Offered Advanced Placement courses, algebra, art, athletic training, biology, calculus, career planning, chemistry, college admission preparation, college counseling, college placement, college planning, comparative politics, computer programming, computer science, drama, ecology, economics, English, English literature, environmental science, ESL, ethics, French, French as a second language, geography, geometry, history, mathematics, music, philosophy, physics, political science, psychology, science, social studies, sociology, statistics, technology, theater, trigonometry, world history.

Graduation Requirements English, foreign language, mathematics, science, social studies (includes history).

Special Academic Programs Advanced Placement exam preparation; honors section; independent study; study at local college for college credit; study abroad; special instructional classes for students with mild learning disorders; ESL (5 students enrolled).

College Admission Counseling 54 students graduated in 2015; 52 went to college, including Carleton University; Harvard University; McGill University; University of Ottawa; University of Toronto; University of Vermont. Other: 2 entered a postgraduate year.

Student Life Upper grades have uniform requirement, student council, honor system. Discipline rests primarily with faculty.

Tuition and Aid Day student tuition: CAN$19,990; 7-day tuition and room/board: CAN$44,300. Tuition installment plan (monthly payment plans, monthly or term payment plans). Tuition reduction for siblings, merit scholarship grants, need-based scholarship grants, need-based loans available. In 2015–16, 40% of upper-school students received aid; total upper-school merit-scholarship money awarded: CAN$200,000. Total amount of financial aid awarded in 2015–16: CAN$1,400,000.

Admissions Traditional secondary-level entrance grade is 10. OLSAT, Stanford Achievement Test or SSAT required. Deadline for receipt of application materials: none. Application fee required: CAN$50. Interview required.

Athletics Interscholastic: basketball (boys, girls), cross-country running (b,g), football (b), ice hockey (b,g), lacrosse (b), physical fitness (b,g), physical training (b,g), rugby (b,g), soccer (b,g), squash (b,g), strength & conditioning (b,g), swimming and diving (b,g), tennis (b,g), track and field (b,g); coed interscholastic: aquatics, curling, golf, skiing (cross-country); coed intramural: alpine skiing, archery, backpacking, badminton, basketball, broomball, canoeing/kayaking, dance, equestrian sports, fishing, fitness, freestyle skiing, hiking/backpacking, horseback riding, kayaking, life saving, nordic skiing, outdoor activities, outdoor education, outdoor recreation, outdoor skills, skiing (cross-country), skiing (downhill), snowboarding, softball, swimming and diving, track and field, volleyball, walking, weight training, yoga. 1 PE instructor, 3 coaches, 1 athletic trainer.

Computers Computers are regularly used in English, mathematics, science classes. Computer network features include on-campus library services, Internet access, wireless campus network, Internet filtering or blocking technology. Student e-mail accounts and computer access in designated common areas are available to students. The school has a published electronic and media policy.

Contact Joanne Tracy Carruthers, Director of Admissions. 819-876-2223. Fax: 819-876-5891. E-mail: admissions@stansteadcollege.com.
Website: www.stansteadcollege.com

THE STANWICH SCHOOL

257 Stanwich Road
Greenwich, Connecticut 06830

Head of School: Mr. Charles Sachs

General Information Coeducational day college-preparatory school. Grades PK–12. Founded: 1998. Setting: suburban. Nearest major city is Stamford. 40-acre campus. 2 buildings on campus. Approved or accredited by Association of Independent Schools in New England, Connecticut Association of Independent Schools, New England Association of Schools and Colleges, and Connecticut Department of Education. Member of National Association of Independent Schools and Secondary School Admission Test Board. Total enrollment: 345. Upper school average class size: 12. Upper school faculty-student ratio: 1:5. There are 163 required school days per year for Upper School students. Upper School students typically attend 5 days per week. The average school day consists of 7 hours.

Upper School Student Profile Grade 6: 41 students (28 boys, 13 girls); Grade 7: 36 students (21 boys, 15 girls); Grade 8: 34 students (22 boys, 12 girls); Grade 9: 17 students (9 boys, 8 girls); Grade 10: 14 students (8 boys, 6 girls); Grade 11: 14 students (6 boys, 8 girls); Grade 12: 13 students (5 boys, 8 girls).

Faculty School total: 60. In upper school: 18 men, 13 women; 30 have advanced degrees.

Subjects Offered American government, American history, American history-AP, American literature, American literature AP, American studies, applied arts, art, art-AP, athletics, band, baseball, basketball, bell choir, biology, biology-AP, British literature, British literature (honors), British literature-AP, calculus, calculus-AP, chemistry, chemistry-AP, choir, choral music, chorus, college admission preparation, college counseling, comparative government and politics-AP, composition, composition-AP, computer programming, computers, concert band, concert bell choir, CPR, debate, democracy in America, digital photography, drama, earth science, economics, economics AP, electives, English, English composition, English language and composition-AP, English language-AP, English literature, English literature and composition-AP, English literature-AP, English-AP, English/composition-AP, entrepreneurship, ethics and responsibility, European history, European literature, French, French language-AP, French-AP, general science, golf, government and politics-AP, government-AP, grammar, graphic arts, Greek culture, handbells, health, history, history-AP, honors algebra, honors English, honors geometry, instrumental music, instruments, internship, introduction to theater, jazz, jazz band, journalism, language arts, language-AP, languages, Latin, Latin-AP, leadership and service, life skills, linear algebra, literature, literature and composition-AP, literature seminar, marine biology, marine science, mathematics-AP, medieval history, modern European history, modern European history-AP, music, musical productions, musical theater, news writing, newspaper, painting, participation in sports, performing arts, photography, physical fitness, physics, piano, politics, probability and statistics, public speaking, reading/study skills, robotics, SAT preparation, SAT/ACT preparation, Shakespeare, Shakespearean histories, softball, Spanish, Spanish language-AP, Spanish-AP, squash, statistics-AP, student government, studio art, studio art-AP, study skills, tennis, theater, U.S. government and politics, U.S. government and politics-AP, U.S. history, U.S. history-AP, U.S. literature, visual and performing arts, voice, volleyball, writing, writing, yearbook.

Graduation Requirements American history, American literature, art, biology, British literature, calculus, chemistry, college counseling, computers, economics, English, geometry, government/civics, health, history, independent study, language, literature, mathematics, physics, public speaking, U.S. history, U.S. literature, Moral Leadership Program.

Special Academic Programs 12 Advanced Placement exams for which test preparation is offered; honors section; independent study; academic accommodation for the gifted, the musically talented, and the artistically talented; remedial reading and/or remedial writing; remedial math; programs in English, mathematics for dyslexic students.

College Admission Counseling 4 students graduated in 2016; all went to college, including Drew University; La Salle University; Wheaton College. Mean combined SAT: 1680, mean composite ACT: 26.

Student Life Upper grades have uniform requirement, student council, honor system. Discipline rests primarily with faculty.

Summer Programs Enrichment, art/fine arts programs offered; session focuses on theatre and film; study skills; held on campus; accepts boys and girls; not open to students from other schools. 20 students usually enrolled. 2017 schedule: June 15 to July 2. Application deadline: April 1.

Tuition and Aid Day student tuition: $30,450–$39,750. Tuition installment plan (Insured Tuition Payment Plan, monthly payment plans, individually arranged payment plans). Need-based scholarship grants available. In 2016–17, 30% of upper-school students received aid.

Admissions Traditional secondary-level entrance grade is 9. For fall 2016, 59 students applied for upper-level admission, 46 were accepted, 19 enrolled. Admissions testing, ERB (grade level), ERB CTP IV, ISEE, TOEFL, TOEFL Junior or writing sample required. Deadline for receipt of application materials: none. Application fee required: $80. Interview recommended.

Athletics Interscholastic: baseball (boys), basketball (b,g), field hockey (g), football (b), lacrosse (b), soccer (b,g), softball (g), volleyball (g); intramural: lacrosse (g), softball (g); coed interscholastic: cross-country running, golf, physical training, sailing, squash, tennis; coed intramural: dance, fencing, fitness, flag football, golf, ice hockey, physical fitness, rock climbing, running. 3 PE instructors, 10 coaches, 3 athletic trainers.

Computers Computers are regularly used in all academic, art, college planning, computer applications, data processing, design, economics, English, foreign language, French, graphic arts, graphic design, health, history, independent study, journalism, Latin, literacy, mathematics, music, news writing, newspaper, photography, programming, SAT preparation, science, Spanish, theater, video film production, writing, yearbook classes. Computer network features include on-campus library services, online commercial services, Internet access, wireless campus network, Internet filtering or blocking technology. Campus intranet, student e-mail accounts, and computer access in designated common areas are available to students. Students grades are available online. The school has a published electronic and media policy.

Contact Mrs. Jessie Drennen, Associate Director of Admissions. 203-542-0035. Fax: 203-542-0025. E-mail: jdrennen@stanwichschool.org.
Website: www.stanwichschool.org/

STAR PREP ACADEMY

1518 S. Robertson Blvd.
Los Angeles, California 90035

Head of School: Mr. Zahir Robb

General Information Coeducational day college-preparatory, arts, and zoology/life sciences school. Grades 6–12. Founded: 2003. Setting: suburban. 1 building on campus. Approved or accredited by Western Association of Schools and Colleges and California Department of Education. Upper school average class size: 6. Upper school faculty-student ratio: 1:7. There are 180 required school days per year for Upper School students. Upper School students typically attend 5 days per week. The average school day consists of 7 hours and 30 minutes.

Upper School Student Profile Grade 6: 4 students (2 boys, 2 girls); Grade 7: 4 students (2 boys, 2 girls); Grade 8: 9 students (7 boys, 2 girls); Grade 9: 4 students (1 boy, 3 girls); Grade 10: 9 students (7 boys, 2 girls); Grade 11: 9 students (6 boys, 3 girls); Grade 12: 7 students (5 boys, 2 girls).

Faculty School total: 11. In upper school: 5 men, 4 women; 7 have advanced degrees.

Subjects Offered 20th century history, 20th century world history, advanced math, Advanced Placement courses, algebra, American government, American literature, anatomy, animal behavior, animal husbandry, animal science, animation, art, ASB Leadership, Basic programming, biology, calculus, calculus-AP, civics, college admission preparation, college placement, college planning, computer science, creative writing, digital music, digital photography, drama, ecology, ecology, environmental systems, economics, economics and history, English, English composition, English language and composition-AP, English literature, English/composition-AP, environmental education, environmental science, environmental studies, fashion, film, film studies, filmmaking, fine arts, French as a second language, geography, geometry, global studies, government, honors English, honors U.S. history, Japanese, Japanese as Second Language, social studies, theater, U.S. history, video film production.

Graduation Requirements American government, American history, chemistry, economics, electives, foreign language, mathematics, science.

Special Academic Programs Honors section; accelerated programs; study at local college for college credit; academic accommodation for the gifted and the musically talented.

College Admission Counseling 6 students graduated in 2016; all went to college, including Beloit College; Loyola Marymount University; San Diego State University; University of California, Davis; University of California, Los Angeles. Median SAT critical reading: 650, median SAT math: 630, median SAT writing: 590, median combined SAT: 1870, median composite ACT: 30. 66% scored over 600 on SAT critical reading, 66% scored over 600 on SAT math, 66% scored over 600 on SAT writing, 83% scored over 1800 on combined SAT, 83% scored over 26 on composite ACT.

Student Life Upper grades have student council. Discipline rests primarily with faculty.

Tuition and Aid Day student tuition: $25,500. Guaranteed tuition plan. Tuition installment plan (monthly payment plans, individually arranged payment plans). Merit scholarship grants, need-based scholarship grants available. In 2016–17, 50% of upper-school students received aid; total upper-school merit-scholarship money awarded: $51,000. Total amount of financial aid awarded in 2016–17: $500,000.

Admissions Traditional secondary-level entrance grade is 9. For fall 2016, 24 students applied for upper-level admission, 8 were accepted, 5 enrolled. Deadline for receipt of application materials: January 30. Application fee required: $120. On-campus interview recommended.

Athletics 4 PE instructors.

Computers Computers are regularly used in mathematics classes. Computer resources include Internet access, wireless campus network, Internet filtering or blocking technology. Campus intranet, student e-mail accounts, and computer access in designated common areas are available to students. Students grades are available online. The school has a published electronic and media policy.

Contact Ms. Ali Hinds, Admissions/Marketing. 310-842-8808. E-mail: alih@starinc.org. Website: www.starprepacademy.org/

STEAMBOAT MOUNTAIN SCHOOL

42605 County Road 36
Steamboat Springs, Colorado 80487

Head of School: Meg Morse

General Information Coeducational boarding and day college-preparatory school. Grades 9–12. Founded: 1957. Setting: rural. Nearest major city is Denver. Students are housed in coed dormitories. 140-acre campus. 10 buildings on campus. Approved or accredited by Association of Colorado Independent Schools and Colorado Department of Education. Member of National Association of Independent Schools and Secondary School Admission Test Board. Endowment: $1 million. Upper school average class size: 8. Upper school faculty-student ratio: 1:8. There are 175 required school days per year for Upper School students. Upper School students typically attend 5 days per week. The average school day consists of 7 hours.

Upper School Student Profile Grade 9: 13 students (7 boys, 6 girls); Grade 10: 18 students (5 boys, 13 girls); Grade 11: 12 students (8 boys, 4 girls); Grade 12: 12 students (9 boys, 3 girls).

Faculty School total: 14. In upper school: 5 men, 9 women; 7 have advanced degrees; 11 reside on campus.

Subjects Offered 20th century history, algebra, American history, American literature, American studies, anatomy, art, art history, biology, calculus, chemistry, computer math, computer programming, computer science, creative writing, drama, economics, English, English literature, expository writing, film, fine arts, French, geography, geology, geometry, government/civics, grammar, mathematics, physical education, physics, science, social sciences, social studies, Spanish, theater, trigonometry, typing, world history, writing.

Graduation Requirements Algebra, arts and fine arts (art, music, dance, drama), chemistry, computer science, English, foreign language, geography, geometry, mathematics, physical education (includes health), science, social sciences, social studies (includes history), Western civilization, foreign travel program, competitive ski/snowboarding program, outdoor program.

Special Academic Programs Advanced Placement exam preparation; honors section; independent study; study abroad; academic accommodation for the gifted.

College Admission Counseling 9 students graduated in 2016; all went to college, including Colorado School of Mines; Colorado State University; Emory University; The George Washington University; University of Denver; University of Puget Sound.

Student Life Upper grades have student council, honor system. Discipline rests equally with students and faculty.

Tuition and Aid Day student tuition: $22,240; 7-day tuition and room/board: $42,075. Tuition installment plan (individually arranged payment plans, school's own payment plan). Merit scholarship grants, need-based scholarship grants available. In 2016–17, 45% of upper-school students received aid; total upper-school merit-scholarship money awarded: $10,000. Total amount of financial aid awarded in 2016–17: $220,000.

Admissions Traditional secondary-level entrance grade is 9. For fall 2016, 37 students applied for upper-level admission, 37 were accepted, 23 enrolled. Deadline for receipt of application materials: February. Application fee required: $100. Interview recommended.

Athletics Interscholastic: alpine skiing (boys, girls), biathlon (b,g), cheering (g), cross-country running (b,g), dance team (g), freestyle skiing (b,g), hockey (b,g), ice hockey (b,g), indoor hockey (b,g), mountain biking (b,g), mountaineering (b,g), nordic skiing (b,g), outdoor adventure (b,g), skiing (cross-country) (b,g), skiing (downhill) (b,g), snowboarding (b,g), soccer (b,g); intramural: backpacking (b,g), bicycling (b,g), ice hockey (b,g), independent competitive sports (b,g), indoor hockey (b,g), jogging (b,g), lacrosse (g), mountain biking (b,g), mountaineering (b,g), outdoor adventure (b,g), rock climbing (b,g), skiing (cross-country) (b,g), skiing (downhill) (b,g), snowboarding (b,g), soccer (b,g); coed interscholastic: alpine skiing, biathlon, climbing, cross-country running, freestyle skiing, ice hockey, indoor hockey, kayaking, mountain biking, mountaineering, nordic skiing, outdoor adventure, outdoor education, outdoor recreation, outdoor skills, rock climbing, skiing (cross-country), skiing (downhill), snowboarding, soccer, telemark skiing, wall climbing; coed intramural: aerobics, backpacking, badminton, bicycling, canoeing/kayaking, climbing, figure skating, fitness, flag football, Frisbee, golf, hiking/backpacking, horseback riding, ice hockey, independent competitive sports, indoor hockey, jogging, judo, juggling, kayaking, lacrosse, mountain biking, mountaineering, nordic skiing, outdoor adventure, outdoor education, outdoor recreation, outdoor skills, physical fitness, physical training, rafting,

rappelling, rock climbing, running, skateboarding, skiing (cross-country), skiing (downhill), snowboarding, snowshoeing, soccer, strength & conditioning, telemark skiing, volleyball, wall climbing, weight lifting, weight training, wilderness, wilderness survival, wildernessways, winter walking, yoga.

Computers Computers are regularly used in all academic classes. Computer network features include on-campus library services, online commercial services, Internet access, wireless campus network, Internet filtering or blocking technology. Campus intranet and student e-mail accounts are available to students. The school has a published electronic and media policy.

Contact Pearson Alspach, Director of Admissions. 970-879-1350 Ext. 18. Fax: 970-879-0506. E-mail: alspachp@steamboatmountainschoo.org. Website: www.steamboatmountainschool.org

STEPHEN T. BADIN HIGH SCHOOL

571 New London Road
Hamilton, Ohio 45013

Head of School: Mr. Brian Pendergest

General Information Coeducational day college-preparatory, general academic, arts, business, vocational, religious studies, and technology school, affiliated with Roman Catholic Church; primarily serves students with learning disabilities and individuals with Attention Deficit Disorder. Grades 9–12. Founded: 1966. Setting: urban. Nearest major city is Cincinnati. 22-acre campus. 2 buildings on campus. Approved or accredited by National Catholic Education Association and Ohio Department of Education. Endowment: $120,000. Total enrollment: 543. Upper school average class size: 22. Upper school faculty-student ratio: 1:19. There are 187 required school days per year for Upper School students. Upper School students typically attend 5 days per week. The average school day consists of 7 hours.

Upper School Student Profile Grade 9: 147 students (73 boys, 74 girls); Grade 10: 122 students (76 boys, 46 girls); Grade 11: 134 students (75 boys, 59 girls); Grade 12: 140 students (76 boys, 64 girls). 85% of students are Roman Catholic.

Faculty School total: 41. In upper school: 17 men, 24 women; 23 have advanced degrees.

Subjects Offered Accounting, algebra, American history, American literature, art, band, biology, British literature, calculus, calculus-AP, chemistry, chorus, computer programming, computer resources, consumer economics, economics, English, English literature, English-AP, French, geometry, government-AP, government/civics, history, integrated science, intro to computers, journalism, marketing, mathematics, music, music theory, physical education, physical science, physics, physiology, pre-calculus, publications, religion, science, social studies, Spanish, Web site design, Western literature, world history.

Graduation Requirements Computer science, English, mathematics, physical education (includes health), religion (includes Bible studies and theology), science, social studies (includes history), 15 hours of community service per year for seniors.

Special Academic Programs 8 Advanced Placement exams for which test preparation is offered; honors section; study at local college for college credit; study abroad; remedial reading and/or remedial writing; remedial math.

College Admission Counseling 119 students graduated in 2015; 118 went to college, including Miami University; Mount St. Joseph University; Ohio University; The Ohio State University; University of Cincinnati; Xavier University. Other: 1 entered military service. Median SAT critical reading: 526, median SAT math: 521, median SAT writing: 529, median combined SAT: 1574, median composite ACT: 24. 21% scored over 600 on SAT critical reading, 11% scored over 600 on SAT math, 16% scored over 600 on SAT writing, 20% scored over 1800 on combined SAT, 25% scored over 26 on composite ACT.

Student Life Upper grades have uniform requirement, student council. Discipline rests primarily with faculty. Attendance at religious services is required.

Tuition and Aid Day student tuition: $8840. Tuition installment plan (monthly payment plans, individually arranged payment plans, quarterly payment plan). Merit scholarship grants, need-based scholarship grants, paying campus jobs available. In 2015–16, 43% of upper-school students received aid; total upper-school merit-scholarship money awarded: $334,800. Total amount of financial aid awarded in 2015–16: $688,200.

Admissions Traditional secondary-level entrance grade is 9. Deadline for receipt of application materials: none. No application fee required. On-campus interview recommended.

Athletics Interscholastic: baseball (boys), basketball (b,g), bowling (b,g), cheering (g), diving (b,g), football (b), golf (b,g), gymnastics (g), soccer (b,g), softball (g), swimming and diving (b,g), tennis (b,g), volleyball (b,g). 1 PE instructor, 59 coaches, 1 athletic trainer.

Computers Computers are regularly used in all academic, mathematics, music, science, Web site design classes. Computer network features include on-campus library services, Internet access, wireless campus network, Internet filtering or blocking technology, scanners, travelling laptops, digital cameras. Campus intranet, student e-mail accounts, and computer access in designated common areas are available to students. Students grades are available online. The school has a published electronic and media policy.

Contact Mrs. Angie Gray, Director of Recruitment. 513-863-3993 Ext. 145. Fax: 513-785-2844. E-mail: agray@mail.badinhs.org. Website: http://www.badinhs.org/

STEVENSON SCHOOL

3152 Forest Lake Road
Pebble Beach, California 93953

Head of School: Dr. Kevin Hicks

General Information Coeducational boarding and day college-preparatory school. Boarding grades 9–12, day grades PK–12. Founded: 1952. Setting: suburban. Nearest major city is San Francisco. Students are housed in coed dormitories and single-sex by wing. 50-acre campus. 24 buildings on campus. Approved or accredited by Western Association of Schools and Colleges and California Department of Education. Member of National Association of Independent Schools and Secondary School Admission Test Board. Endowment: $32 million. Total enrollment: 747. Upper school average class size: 14. Upper school faculty-student ratio: 1:10. There are 160 required school days per year for Upper School students. Upper School students typically attend 5 days per week. The average school day consists of 6 hours and 30 minutes.

Upper School Student Profile Grade 9: 104 students (49 boys, 55 girls); Grade 10: 135 students (71 boys, 64 girls); Grade 11: 132 students (60 boys, 72 girls); Grade 12: 127 students (67 boys, 60 girls).

Faculty School total: 95. In upper school: 42 men, 20 women; 46 have advanced degrees; 38 reside on campus.

Subjects Offered 3-dimensional art, advanced chemistry, Advanced Placement courses, algebra, American history, American literature, American literature-AP, architecture, art, art history, art-AP, biology, biology-AP, broadcasting, calculus, calculus-AP, ceramics, chemistry, chemistry-AP, Chinese, computer programming, computer science, concert band, creative writing, dance, dance performance, drama, drama performance, drama workshop, dramatic arts, drawing, drawing and design, driver education, economics, economics-AP, English, English literature, English-AP, environmental science, environmental science-AP, ethics, European civilization, European history, expository writing, fine arts, French, French-AP, geometry, government/civics, grammar, history of ideas, history-AP, honors algebra, honors English, honors geometry, honors U.S. history, Japanese, jazz, jazz band, jazz ensemble, jazz theory, journalism, Latin, Latin-AP, macroeconomics-AP, marine biology, mathematics, mathematics-AP, microbiology, music, musical productions, musical theater, ornithology, photography, physical education, physics, physics-AP, portfolio art, pre-calculus, psychology, science, social studies, Spanish, Spanish-AP, speech, stage design, stagecraft, studio art-AP, tap dance, theater, trigonometry, U.S. history-AP, visual and performing arts, visual arts, vocal ensemble, wilderness education, wilderness experience, wind ensemble, world cultures, world history, world literature, world studies, writing, yearbook.

Graduation Requirements Arts and fine arts (art, music, dance, drama), athletics, English, foreign language, history, mathematics, science.

Special Academic Programs 23 Advanced Placement exams for which test preparation is offered; honors section; independent study; term-away projects; study abroad.

College Admission Counseling 135 students graduated in 2016; 128 went to college, including New York University; Northwestern University; Pepperdine University; The University of Arizona; University of California, Santa Barbara; University of Oregon. Other: 1 entered military service, 3 had other specific plans. Median SAT critical reading: 620, median SAT math: 640, median SAT writing: 610, median combined SAT: 1870. Mean composite ACT: 28. 59% scored over 600 on SAT critical reading, 60% scored over 600 on SAT math, 56% scored over 600 on SAT writing, 58% scored over 1800 on combined SAT.

Student Life Upper grades have specified standards of dress, student council, honor system. Discipline rests equally with students and faculty.

Summer Programs Enrichment, advancement, sports, art/fine arts programs offered; held on campus; accepts boys and girls; open to students from other schools. 140 students usually enrolled. 2017 schedule: June 26 to August 29. Application deadline: May 15.

Tuition and Aid Day student tuition: $36,200; 7-day tuition and room/board: $59,800. Tuition installment plan (Insured Tuition Payment Plan). Need-based scholarship grants available. In 2016–17, 35% of upper-school students received aid. Total amount of financial aid awarded in 2016–17: $3,475,000.

Admissions Traditional secondary-level entrance grade is 9. For fall 2016, 458 students applied for upper-level admission, 267 were accepted, 135 enrolled. ISEE, PSAT, SSAT, TOEFL or writing sample required. Deadline for receipt of application materials: February 1. Application fee required: $75. Interview required.

Athletics Interscholastic: baseball (boys), basketball (b,g), cross-country running (b,g), diving (b,g), field hockey (g), football (b), golf (b,g), lacrosse (b,g), sailing (b,g), soccer (b,g), softball (g), swimming and diving (b,g), tennis (b,g), track and field (b,g), volleyball (g), water polo (b,g); intramural: ballet (g), dance (b,g), golf (b,g), horseback riding (b,g), independent competitive sports (b,g), kayaking (b,g), modern dance (b,g), mountaineering (b,g), outdoor education (b,g), outdoors (b,g), rock climbing (b,g), strength & conditioning (b,g), table tennis (b,g), weight lifting (b,g), wilderness (b,g), yoga (b,g); coed interscholastic: sailing; coed intramural: backpacking, ballet, bicycling, climbing, dance, equestrian sports, fitness walking, hiking/backpacking, horseback riding, independent competitive sports, kayaking, modern dance, mountaineering, outdoor education, outdoors, rock climbing, sailing, softball, strength & conditioning, table tennis, weight lifting, weight training, wilderness, yoga. 30 coaches.

Computers Computers are regularly used in all classes. Computer network features include on-campus library services, online commercial services, Internet access, wireless campus network, Internet filtering or blocking technology. Campus intranet and student e-mail accounts are available to students. Students grades are available online. The school has a published electronic and media policy.

Contact Mrs. Melissa Schuette, Associate Director of Admission. 831-625-8309. Fax: 831-625-5208. E-mail: info@stevensonschool.org. Website: www.stevensonschool.org

ST LEONARDS SCHOOL AND SIXTH FORM COLLEGE

St. Andrews
Fife, Scotland KY16 9QJ, United Kingdom

Head of School: Dr. Michael Carslaw

General Information Coeducational boarding and day college-preparatory, general academic, arts, business, religious studies, bilingual studies, and technology school. Boarding grades 8–13, day grades 1–13. Founded: 1877. Setting: small town. Nearest major city is St, Andrews (Near Edinburgh), United Kingdom. Students are housed in single-sex dormitories. 26-acre campus. 8 buildings on campus. Approved or accredited by Boarding Schools Association (UK), Headmasters' Conference, Independent Schools Council (UK), International Baccalaureate Organization, and Scottish Education Department. Language of instruction: English. Total enrollment: 453. Upper school average class size: 16. Upper school faculty-student ratio: 1:9. The average school day consists of 8 hours.

Upper School Student Profile Grade 8: 39 students (18 boys, 21 girls); Grade 9: 33 students (14 boys, 19 girls); Grade 10: 40 students (17 boys, 23 girls); Grade 11: 45 students (19 boys, 26 girls); Grade 12: 73 students (38 boys, 35 girls); Grade 13: 53 students (27 boys, 26 girls). 65% of students are boarding students. 40% are international students. International students from Austria, China, Germany, Hong Kong, and Russian Federation; 11 other countries represented in student body.

Faculty In upper school: 21 men, 30 women; 9 have advanced degrees; 8 reside on campus.

Subjects Offered 20th century physics, 20th century world history, 3-dimensional art, 3-dimensional design, acting, adolescent issues, advanced chemistry, advanced computer applications, advanced math, advanced TOEFL/grammar, Ancient Greek, art, art history, arts, biology, British history, business, career and personal planning, chemistry, classics, computer literacy, computer skills, creative arts, design, drama, economics, English, English as a foreign language, European history, geography, German, Greek, history, humanities, Latin, mathematics, modern history, modern languages, music, personal and social education, physics, politics, psychology, religious studies, science, theater design and production, vocal ensemble, voice, wind ensemble, wind instruments, word processing, work experience, world geography, world history.

Special Academic Programs International Baccalaureate program; study at local college for college credit; academic accommodation for the gifted, the musically talented, and the artistically talented; programs in English, mathematics, general development for dyslexic students; ESL (25 students enrolled).

College Admission Counseling 56 students graduated in 2015; 54 went to college. Other: 2 had other specific plans.

Student Life Upper grades have specified standards of dress, student council, honor system. Discipline rests equally with students and faculty.

Tuition and Aid Day student tuition: £9297; 7-day tuition and room/board: £30,957. Tuition installment plan (monthly payment plans, individually arranged payment plans). Need-based scholarship grants available.

Admissions For fall 2015, 74 students applied for upper-level admission, 70 were accepted, 70 enrolled. School's own exam required. Deadline for receipt of application materials: none. Application fee required: £100. Interview required.

Athletics Interscholastic: cricket (boys), golf (b,g), hockey (b,g), lacrosse (g), netball (g), rugby (b), running (b,g), squash (b,g), swimming and diving (b,g), tennis (b,g); intramural: aerobics (g), aerobics/dance (g), ballet (g), cricket (b), football (b), lacrosse (g), netball (g), rounders (b,g), rugby (b), running (b,g), squash (b,g), tennis (b,g), yoga (g); coed interscholastic: alpine skiing, cross-country running, equestrian sports, freestyle skiing, golf, hockey, horseback riding, judo, physical fitness, rounders, running, skiing (downhill), squash, swimming and diving, tennis, track and field, winter soccer; coed intramural: alpine skiing, archery, backpacking, badminton, ball hockey, basketball, bicycling, canoeing/kayaking, climbing, cross-country running, dance, equestrian sports, fencing, field hockey, fitness, freestyle skiing, golf, gymnastics, hiking/backpacking, hockey, horseback riding, indoor hockey, indoor soccer, judo, kayaking, lacrosse, life saving, outdoor activities, physical fitness, rock climbing, rounders, running, sailing, self defense, skiing (downhill), soccer, squash, surfing, swimming and diving, table tennis, tennis, track and field, volleyball, wall climbing, weight training, wilderness survival, windsurfing, winter soccer. 4 PE instructors, 13 coaches.

Computers Computers are regularly used in art, career exploration, English, French, geography, history, information technology, language development, library skills, mathematics, music, research skills, Spanish, technical drawing classes. Computer network features include on-campus library services, Internet access, wireless campus network, Internet filtering or blocking technology. Campus intranet, student e-mail accounts, and computer access in designated common areas are available to students. The school has a published electronic and media policy.

Contact Dr. Caroline Routledge, Registrar. 44-1334-472126. Fax: 44-1334 476152. E-mail: info@stleonards-fife.org. Website: www.stleonards-fife.org/

STONE RIDGE SCHOOL OF THE SACRED HEART

9101 Rockville Pike
Bethesda, Maryland 20814

Head of School: Mrs. Catherine Ronan Karrels

General Information Coeducational day (boys' only in lower grades) college-preparatory, arts, religious studies, and technology school, affiliated with Roman Catholic Church. Boys grades PS–K, girls grades PS–12. Founded: 1923. Setting: suburban. Nearest major city is Washington, DC. 35-acre campus. 12 buildings on campus. Approved or accredited by Association of Independent Schools of Greater Washington, Middle States Association of Colleges and Schools, National Catholic Education Association, Network of Sacred Heart Schools, and Maryland Department of Education. Member of National Association of Independent Schools and Secondary School Admission Test Board. Endowment: $37 million. Total enrollment: 719. Upper school average class size: 15. Upper school faculty-student ratio: 1:7. Upper School students typically attend 5 days per week. The average school day consists of 5 hours and 20 minutes.

Upper School Student Profile 75% of students are Roman Catholic.

Faculty School total: 84. In upper school: 21 men, 35 women; 56 have advanced degrees.

Subjects Offered Advanced chemistry, advanced math, Advanced Placement courses, algebra, American history, American literature, art, art history, biochemistry, biology, ceramics, chemistry, chorus, community service, computer graphics, computer programming, computer science, creative writing, drama, economics, economics and history, English, English literature, environmental science, ethics, European history, film, fine arts, French, geometry, history, independent study, journalism, Latin, mathematics, media arts, microbiology, music, photography, physical science, physics, pre-calculus, religion, science, social studies, Spanish, theater, theology, trigonometry, women's studies, world history, world literature, world religions, writing.

Graduation Requirements Arts and fine arts (art, music, dance, drama), English, foreign language, mathematics, physical education (includes health), science, social studies (includes history), theology. Community service is required.

Special Academic Programs Advanced Placement exam preparation; honors section; independent study; term-away projects; domestic exchange program (with Network of Sacred Heart Schools); study abroad; academic accommodation for the gifted and the artistically talented.

College Admission Counseling 80 students graduated in 2015; all went to college, including Boston College; Elon University; Georgetown University; University of Maryland, College Park; University of Notre Dame; University of Virginia.

Student Life Upper grades have uniform requirement, student council, honor system. Discipline rests primarily with faculty. Attendance at religious services is required.

Tuition and Aid Day student tuition: $309,000. Tuition installment plan (Key Tuition Payment Plan, FACTS Tuition Payment Plan). Merit scholarship grants, need-based scholarship grants available. In 2015–16, 30% of upper-school students received aid; total upper-school merit-scholarship money awarded: $85,000. Total amount of financial aid awarded in 2015–16: $2,600,000.

Admissions Traditional secondary-level entrance grade is 9. ERB, SSAT or Wechsler Intelligence Scale for Children required. Deadline for receipt of application materials: December 4. Application fee required: $50. On-campus interview required.

Athletics Interscholastic: aquatics (girls), basketball (g), cross-country running (g), diving (g), field hockey (g), lacrosse (g), soccer (g), softball (g), swimming and diving (g), tennis (g), track and field (g), volleyball (g); intramural: aerobics (g), aerobics/dance (g), aerobics/Nautilus (g), aquatics (g), dance (g), equestrian sports (g), fitness (g), golf (g), ice hockey (g), independent competitive sports (g), modern dance (g), running (g), squash (g), synchronized swimming (g), wall climbing (g), weight training (g), yoga (g). 3 PE instructors, 28 coaches, 1 athletic trainer.

Computers Computers are regularly used in all academic classes. Computer network features include on-campus library services, online commercial services, Internet access, wireless campus network, Internet filtering or blocking technology. Campus intranet, student e-mail accounts, and computer access in designated common areas are available to students. Students grades are available online. The school has a published electronic and media policy.

Contact Ms. Mary Tobias, Director of Admission. 301-657-4322 Ext. 321. Fax: 301-657-4393. E-mail: admissions@stoneridgeschool.org. Website: www.stoneridgeschool.org

THE STONY BROOK SCHOOL

1 Chapman Parkway
Stony Brook, New York 11790

Head of School: Mr. Joshua Crane

General Information Coeducational boarding and day college-preparatory, arts, religious studies, technology, and STEM school, affiliated with Christian faith. Grades 7–12. Founded: 1922. Setting: suburban. Nearest major city is New York. Students are housed in single-sex dormitories. 55-acre campus. 15 buildings on campus. Approved or accredited by Middle States Association of Colleges and Schools, New York State Association of Independent Schools, The Association of Boarding Schools, and New York Department of Education. Member of National Association of Independent Schools and Secondary School Admission Test Board. Endowment: $14.5 million. Total enrollment: 360. Upper school average class size: 14. Upper school faculty-student ratio: 1:7. There are 156 required school days per year for Upper School students. Upper School students typically attend 5 days per week. The average school day consists of 7 hours and 15 minutes.

Upper School Student Profile Grade 9: 75 students (43 boys, 32 girls); Grade 10: 84 students (48 boys, 36 girls); Grade 11: 72 students (31 boys, 41 girls); Grade 12: 74 students (40 boys, 34 girls). 55% of students are boarding students. 62% are state residents. 7 states are represented in upper school student body. 33% are international students. International students from China, Germany, Nigeria, Russian Federation, South Africa, and Taiwan; 18 other countries represented in student body. 50% of students are Christian faith.

Faculty School total: 57. In upper school: 28 men, 29 women; 34 have advanced degrees; 45 reside on campus.

Subjects Offered 3-dimensional art, Advanced Placement courses, athletics, aviation, Christianity, college counseling, computer programming, digital photography, economics, European civilization, European literature, filmmaking, internship, jazz band, performing arts, robotics, theater production.

Graduation Requirements Algebra, Bible, European history, geometry, religion (includes Bible studies and theology), U.S. history. Community service is required.

Special Academic Programs Advanced Placement exam preparation; honors section; independent study; study at local college for college credit; ESL (20 students enrolled).

College Admission Counseling 66 students graduated in 2016; all went to college, including Boston College; Georgetown University; Johns Hopkins University; Loyola University Maryland; New York University; University of Delaware. Mean SAT critical reading: 600, mean SAT math: 611, mean SAT writing: 605, mean combined SAT: 1812.

Student Life Upper grades have specified standards of dress, student council, honor system. Discipline rests equally with students and faculty. Attendance at religious services is required.

Summer Programs Enrichment, sports, rigorous outdoor training, computer instruction programs offered; session focuses on Sports, Sailing, Outdoor Adventure, STEM, Marine Biology, Elementary Education; held both on and off campus; accepts boys and girls; open to students from other schools. 600 students usually enrolled. 2017 schedule: July 3 to August 11.

Tuition and Aid Day student tuition: $27,800; 5-day tuition and room/board: $43,900; 7-day tuition and room/board: $51,400. Tuition installment plan (FACTS Tuition Payment Plan, two payment plan). Need-based scholarship grants available. In 2016–17, 40% of upper-school students received aid.

Admissions Traditional secondary-level entrance grade is 9. For fall 2016, 364 students applied for upper-level admission, 117 were accepted, 72 enrolled. SSAT or TOEFL required. Deadline for receipt of application materials: none. Application fee required: $100. Interview recommended.

Athletics Interscholastic: baseball (boys), basketball (b,g), cross-country running (b,g), lacrosse (b,g), soccer (b,g), strength & conditioning (b,g), swimming and diving (b,g), tennis (b,g), track and field (b,g), volleyball (g), wrestling (b); coed interscholastic: badminton, golf, sailing; coed intramural: flag football, Frisbee, outdoor adventure, physical fitness, physical training, ultimate Frisbee, weight lifting. 1 PE instructor, 1 athletic trainer.

Computers Computers are regularly used in all academic, theater, video film production, yearbook classes. Computer network features include on-campus library services, Internet access, wireless campus network, Internet filtering or blocking technology. Campus intranet, student e-mail accounts, and computer access in designated common areas are available to students. Students grades are available online. The school has a published electronic and media policy.

Contact Mrs. Molly Shteierman, Admissions Counselor. 631-751-1800 Ext. 1. Fax: 631-751-4211. E-mail: admissions@stonybrookschool.org. Website: www.stonybrookschool.org

THE STORM KING SCHOOL

314 Mountain Road
Cornwall-on-Hudson, New York 12520-1899

Head of School: Mr. Jonathan W.R. Lamb

General Information Coeducational boarding and day college-preparatory school. Grades 8–PG. Founded: 1867. Setting: small town. Nearest major city is New York. Students are housed in coed dormitories. 47-acre campus. 24 buildings on campus. Approved or accredited by Middle States Association of Colleges and Schools, New York State Association of Independent Schools, The Association of Boarding Schools, and New York Department of Education. Member of National Association of Independent Schools and Secondary School Admission Test Board. Endowment: $1 million. Total enrollment: 167. Upper school average class size: 12. Upper school faculty-student ratio: 1:5. There are 170 required school days per year for Upper School students. Upper School students typically attend 5 days per week. The average school day consists of 7 hours and 52 minutes.

Upper School Student Profile Grade 8: 12 students (2 boys, 10 girls); Grade 9: 33 students (14 boys, 19 girls); Grade 10: 46 students (27 boys, 19 girls); Grade 11: 41 students (25 boys, 16 girls); Grade 12: 45 students (26 boys, 19 girls). 71% of students are boarding students. 34% are state residents. 5 states are represented in upper school student body. 57% are international students. International students from China, France, Mexico, Russian Federation, Spain, and Turkey; 19 other countries represented in student body.

Faculty School total: 38. In upper school: 18 men, 16 women; 22 have advanced degrees; 24 reside on campus.

Subjects Offered 20th century world history, 3-dimensional art, acting, Advanced Placement courses, advanced studio art-AP, advanced TOEFL/grammar, algebra, American history, American literature, American sign language, art, art and culture, art history, art history-AP, art-AP, astronomy, athletics, biology, biology-AP, British literature (honors), broadcasting, calculus, calculus-AP, ceramics, chemistry, Chinese, choir, choral music, chorus, college counseling, college placement, college planning, community service, computer graphics, computer programming, computer programming-AP, computer science, computer science-AP, creative writing, dance, dance performance, digital art, digital photography, drama, drama performance, drawing, drawing and design, earth science, economics, economics-AP, English, English language and composition-AP, English literature, English literature and composition-AP, English literature-AP, English-AP, environmental science, ESL, ESL, fencing, fine arts, foreign language, geometry, global studies, government/civics, guitar, health education, high adventure outdoor program, history, humanities, integrated mathematics, literacy, literature, macro/microeconomics-AP, macroeconomics-AP, Mandarin, mathematics, model United Nations, music, music composition, music theory-AP, musical productions, outdoor education, painting, performing arts, photography, physics, physics-AP, piano, pre-algebra, pre-calculus, psychology, psychology-AP, SAT preparation, SAT/ACT preparation, science, Spanish, stage design, stagecraft, statistics-AP, student government, studio art-AP, theater, theater design and production, U.S. history, video film production, visual and performing arts, voice, world history, world literature, writing, yearbook.

Graduation Requirements Art, biology, college counseling, English, foreign language, mathematics, performing arts, science, social studies (includes history), visual arts, at least two community service, outdoor adventure, and cultural experiences per year. Community service is required.

Special Academic Programs 10 Advanced Placement exams for which test preparation is offered; honors section; academic accommodation for the gifted, the musically talented, and the artistically talented; remedial reading and/or remedial writing; programs in English, mathematics, general development for dyslexic students; ESL (40 students enrolled).

College Admission Counseling 44 students graduated in 2016; 43 went to college, including Carnegie Mellon University; Cornell University; Marist College; Pace University; Parsons School of Design; Penn State University Park. Other: 1 had other specific plans. Median SAT critical reading: 430, median SAT math: 580, median SAT writing: 455, median combined SAT: 1425. Mean composite ACT: 23. 8% scored over 600 on SAT critical reading, 40% scored over 600 on SAT math, 15% scored over 600 on SAT writing, 34% scored over 1800 on combined SAT.

Student Life Upper grades have uniform requirement, student council, honor system. Discipline rests primarily with faculty.

Summer Programs ESL programs offered; session focuses on ESL and outdoor activities; held on campus; accepts boys and girls; open to students from other schools. 30 students usually enrolled. 2017 schedule: June 21 to August 6. Application deadline: April 1.

Tuition and Aid Day student tuition: $30,257; 7-day tuition and room/board: $56,642. Tuition installment plan (individually arranged payment plans). Need-based scholarship grants available. In 2016–17, 45% of upper-school students received aid. Total amount of financial aid awarded in 2016–17: $1,742,313.

Admissions Traditional secondary-level entrance grade is 9. For fall 2016, 166 students applied for upper-level admission, 118 were accepted, 52 enrolled. Academic Profile Tests, SSAT or WISC III or TOEFL or SLEP required. Deadline for receipt of application materials: none. Application fee required: $85. Interview required.

Athletics Interscholastic: baseball (boys), basketball (b,g), cross-country running (b,g), lacrosse (b,g), soccer (b,g), softball (g), tennis (b,g), volleyball (g), wrestling (b); intramural: physical fitness (b,g); coed interscholastic: crew, fencing, golf, mountain biking, rowing, running, skiing (downhill), snowboarding, ultimate Frisbee; coed intramural: aerobics/dance, alpine skiing, backpacking, badminton, ballet, bowling, canoeing/kayaking, climbing, dance, fitness, fitness walking, freestyle skiing, golf, hiking/backpacking, jogging, kayaking, modern dance, mountaineering, Nautilus, outdoor activities, outdoor adventure, outdoor education, outdoor recreation, outdoor skills, outdoors, paddle tennis, physical fitness, physical training, power lifting, project adventure, rappelling, rock climbing, ropes courses, sailing, skiing (cross-country), skiing (downhill), snowboarding, snowshoeing, strength & conditioning, table tennis, tennis, touch football, walking, wall climbing, weight lifting, weight training, wilderness, winter walking, yoga. 3 coaches, 1 athletic trainer.

Computers Computers are regularly used in all academic, art, college planning, computer applications, digital applications, drawing and design, economics, English, ESL, foreign language, graphic design, history, library skills, mathematics, media production, music technology, newspaper, photography, psychology, publications, video film production, writing, yearbook classes. Computer network features include on-campus library services, online commercial services, Internet access, wireless campus network, Internet filtering or blocking technology, parent/student/teacher communication portal, wireless internet throughout campus. Campus intranet, student e-mail accounts, and computer access in designated common areas are available to students. Students grades are available online. The school has a published electronic and media policy.

Contact Mr. Marek Pramuka, Director of Admissions and Marketing. 845-458-7542. Fax: 845-534-4128. E-mail: mpramuka@sks.org. Website: www.sks.org

STRATFORD ACADEMY

6010 Peake Road
Macon, Georgia 31220-3903

Head of School: Dr. Robert E. Veto

General Information Coeducational day college-preparatory school. Grades PK–12. Founded: 1960. Setting: suburban. Nearest major city is Atlanta. 70-acre campus. 5 buildings on campus. Approved or accredited by Georgia Independent School Association, Southern Association of Colleges and Schools, Southern Association of Independent Schools, and Georgia Department of Education. Member of National Association of Independent Schools. Endowment: $1 million. Total enrollment: 896. Upper school average class size: 17. Upper school faculty-student ratio: 1:13. There are 180 required school days per year for Upper School students. Upper School students typically attend 5 days per week. The average school day consists of 6 hours.

Faculty School total: 101. In upper school: 24 men, 23 women; 27 have advanced degrees.

Subjects Offered Advanced Placement courses, algebra, American history, American literature, anatomy, art, art history, art-AP, athletics, baseball, basketball, biology, biology-AP, calculus, calculus-AP, chemistry, chemistry-AP, community service, comparative government and politics-AP, computer programming, computer science, creative writing, drama, drama performance, driver education, earth science, economics, English, English literature, English literature-AP, English-AP, European history, European history-AP, expository writing, French, French-AP, geography, geometry, government/civics, grammar, history, history-AP, humanities, journalism, keyboarding, Latin, Latin-AP, Mandarin, mathematics, mathematics-AP, music, physical education, physical science, physics, pre-calculus, science, social sciences, social studies, sociology, Spanish, Spanish-AP, speech, speech and debate, theater, trigonometry, U.S. government and politics-AP, water color painting, world history, world literature, writing.

Graduation Requirements English, foreign language, math applications, mathematics, science, senior seminar, social sciences, social studies (includes history), community service. Community service is required.

Special Academic Programs Advanced Placement exam preparation; independent study; special instructional classes for students with learning disabilities, Attention Deficit Disorder, and dyslexia.

College Admission Counseling 72 students graduated in 2016; 74 went to college, including Auburn University; Georgia Institute of Technology; Georgia Southern University; Mercer University; University of Georgia; University of Virginia.

Student Life Upper grades have uniform requirement, student council, honor system. Discipline rests primarily with faculty.

Summer Programs Enrichment, sports, art/fine arts programs offered; held on campus; accepts boys and girls; open to students from other schools. 250 students usually enrolled.

Tuition and Aid Day student tuition: $15,035. Tuition installment plan (Insured Tuition Payment Plan, monthly payment plans, individually arranged payment plans). Merit scholarship grants, need-based scholarship grants available. Total upper-school merit-scholarship money awarded for 2016–17: $15,035.

Admissions Traditional secondary-level entrance grade is 9. ERB or Iowa Tests of Basic Skills required. Deadline for receipt of application materials: none. Application fee required: $50. On-campus interview required.

Athletics Interscholastic: aerobics (girls), aquatics (b,g), baseball (b), basketball (b,g), cheering (g), cross-country running (b,g), dance team (g), drill team (g), fitness (b,g), football (b), horseback riding (b,g), lacrosse (b,g), physical training (b,g), soccer (b,g), softball (g), tennis (b,g), track and field (b,g), volleyball (g), wrestling (b), yoga (g); coed interscholastic: badminton, equestrian sports, golf, skeet shooting. 9 PE instructors, 6 coaches, 2 athletic trainers.

Computers Computers are regularly used in art, creative writing, English, French, graphics, information technology, Spanish classes. Computer network features include on-campus library services, Internet access, wireless campus network. Student e-mail accounts and computer access in designated common areas are available to students. Students grades are available online. The school has a published electronic and media policy.

Contact Mrs. Lori Palmer, Director of Admissions. 478-477-8073 Ext. 203. Fax: 478-477-0299. E-mail: lori.palmer@stratford.org. Website: www.stratford.org

STRATTON MOUNTAIN SCHOOL

World Cup Circle
Stratton Mountain, Vermont 05155

Head of School: Christopher G. Kaltsas

General Information Coeducational boarding and day college-preparatory and Winter Sports Academy school. Grades 7–PG. Founded: 1972. Setting: rural. Nearest major city is Albany, NY. Students are housed in single-sex by floor dormitories and single-sex dormitories. 12-acre campus. 7 buildings on campus. Approved or accredited by National Christian School Association, New England Association of Schools and Colleges, and Vermont Department of Education. Member of National Association of Independent Schools. Endowment: $2.4 million. Total enrollment: 134. Upper school average class size: 10. Upper school faculty-student ratio: 1:7. There are 170 required school days per year for Upper School students. Upper School students typically attend 5 days per week. The average school day consists of 6 hours.

Upper School Student Profile Grade 9: 25 students (14 boys, 11 girls); Grade 10: 20 students (11 boys, 9 girls); Grade 11: 24 students (13 boys, 11 girls); Grade 12: 24 students (14 boys, 10 girls); Postgraduate: 11 students (9 boys, 2 girls). 55% of students are boarding students. 45% are state residents. 22 states are represented in upper school student body. 5% are international students. International students from Australia, Chile, Japan, Poland, Republic of Korea, and Turkey; 2 other countries represented in student body.

Faculty School total: 19. In upper school: 7 men, 12 women; 8 have advanced degrees; 9 reside on campus.

Subjects Offered Algebra, American history, American literature, art, biology, calculus, chemistry, computer science, English, English literature, environmental science, French, geography, geometry, grammar, health, history, journalism, mathematics, nutrition, physical education, physics, science, social studies, Spanish, world history.

Graduation Requirements Arts and fine arts (art, music, dance, drama), computer education, English, foreign language, health education, mathematics, science, social studies (includes history), superior competence in winter sports (skiing/snowboarding). Community service is required.

Special Academic Programs Honors section; independent study.

College Admission Counseling 28 students graduated in 2016; 19 went to college, including Bates College; Dartmouth College; Middlebury College; University of Colorado Boulder; University of New Hampshire; University of Vermont. Other: 9 entered a postgraduate year. Mean SAT critical reading: 637, mean SAT math: 633, mean combined SAT: 1270.

Student Life Upper grades have specified standards of dress, student council, honor system. Discipline rests primarily with faculty.

Tuition and Aid Day student tuition: $37,500; 7-day tuition and room/board: $51,500. Tuition installment plan (choice of one or two tuition installments plus advance deposit). Need-based scholarship grants, need-based loans available. In 2016–17, 45% of upper-school students received aid. Total amount of financial aid awarded in 2016–17: $760,000.

Admissions Traditional secondary-level entrance grade is 9. For fall 2016, 67 students applied for upper-level admission, 44 were accepted, 38 enrolled. Math Placement Exam required. Deadline for receipt of application materials: March 15. Application fee required: $100. On-campus interview required.

Athletics Interscholastic: alpine skiing (boys, girls), bicycling (b,g), cross-country running (b,g), freestyle skiing (b,g), golf (b,g), lacrosse (b,g), mountain biking (b,g), nordic skiing (b,g), skiing (cross-country) (b,g), skiing (downhill) (b,g), snowboarding (b,g), soccer (b,g), tennis (b,g); intramural: strength & conditioning (b,g), tennis (b,g), yoga (b,g); coed intramural: skateboarding, tennis, yoga. 24 coaches, 2 athletic trainers.

Computers Computers are regularly used in computer applications, graphic design, mathematics, media production, research skills, science, Web site design, yearbook classes. Computer network features include on-campus library services, online commercial services, Internet access, wireless campus network, Internet filtering or blocking technology. Campus intranet, student e-mail accounts, and computer access in designated common areas are available to students. Students grades are available online. The school has a published electronic and media policy.

Contact Ms. Kate Nolan, Director of Admissions. 802-856-1124. Fax: 802-297-0020. E-mail: knolan@gosms.org. Website: www.gosms.org

STUART HALL

235 West Frederick Street
PO Box 210
Staunton, Virginia 24401

Head of School: Mr. Mark H. Eastham

General Information Coeducational boarding and day college-preparatory school, affiliated with Episcopal Church. Boarding grades 8–12, day grades PK–12. Founded: 1844. Setting: small town. Nearest major city is Richmond. Students are housed in single-sex by floor dormitories and coed dormitories. 8-acre campus. 7 buildings on campus. Approved or accredited by National Association of Episcopal Schools, Virginia Association of Independent Schools, and Virginia Department of Education. Member of National Association of Independent Schools and Secondary School Admission Test Board. Endowment: $5.5 million. Total enrollment: 302. Upper school average class size: 12. Upper school faculty-student ratio: 1:8. There are 172 required school days per year for Upper School students. Upper School students typically attend 5 days per week. The average school day consists of 7 hours and 25 minutes.

Upper School Student Profile Grade 9: 27 students (13 boys, 14 girls); Grade 10: 29 students (16 boys, 13 girls); Grade 11: 43 students (15 boys, 28 girls); Grade 12: 29 students (8 boys, 21 girls). 60% of students are boarding students. 46% are state residents. 11 states are represented in upper school student body. 43% are international students. International students from China, Rwanda, and Viet Nam; 12 other countries represented in student body. 10% of students are members of Episcopal Church.

Faculty School total: 38. In upper school: 9 men, 14 women; 20 have advanced degrees; 15 reside on campus.

Subjects Offered Algebra, American literature, ancient world history, applied arts, applied music, art appreciation, art history, biology, biology-AP, British literature, calculus-AP, career education, career/college preparation, ceramics, chamber groups, chemistry, chemistry-AP, choir, choral music, chorus, civics, college counseling, composition, creative writing, drama, drama performance, dramatic arts, English, English composition, English language and composition-AP, English literature-AP, English-AP, entrepreneurship, environmental science, environmental science-AP, ESL, fine arts, French, geometry, grammar, guitar, health education, history of drama, history of music, history-AP, honors algebra, honors English, honors geometry, honors world history, instrumental music, lab science, language and composition, leadership, learning lab, mathematics, modern world history, music, music composition, music history, music performance, music theater, music theory, philosophy, photography, physical education, physical fitness, physics, piano, playwriting and directing, portfolio art, pre-algebra, pre-calculus, probability and statistics, religion, SAT preparation, science, social studies, Spanish, Spanish language-AP, Spanish-AP, stage and body movement, stage design, strings, student government, student publications, study skills, theater, theater arts, theater history, theater production, trigonometry, U.S. government, U.S. government and politics-AP, U.S. history, U.S. history-AP, visual and performing arts, visual arts, vocal ensemble, vocal music, voice, voice ensemble, world geography, world history, world history-AP, world literature, yearbook.

Graduation Requirements Arts and fine arts (art, music, dance, drama), English, foreign language, mathematics, philosophy, physical education (includes health), religion (includes Bible studies and theology), SAT preparation, science, social studies (includes history).

Special Academic Programs Advanced Placement exam preparation; honors section; study at local college for college credit; academic accommodation for the gifted, the musically talented, and the artistically talented; ESL (18 students enrolled).

College Admission Counseling 31 students graduated in 2016; all went to college, including James Madison University; Roanoke College; The College of William and Mary; University of Virginia; Virginia Commonwealth University; Virginia Polytechnic Institute and State University. Mean SAT critical reading: 577, mean SAT math: 567, mean SAT writing: 561.

Student Life Upper grades have specified standards of dress, student council, honor system. Discipline rests equally with students and faculty. Attendance at religious services is required.

Tuition and Aid Day student tuition: $15,100; 5-day tuition and room/board: $33,000; 7-day tuition and room/board: $48,000. Tuition installment plan (Insured Tuition Payment Plan, monthly payment plans, individually arranged payment plans). Merit scholarship grants, need-based scholarship grants available. In 2016–17, 40% of upper-school students received aid; total upper-school merit-scholarship money awarded: $30,000. Total amount of financial aid awarded in 2016–17: $1,400,000.

Admissions Traditional secondary-level entrance grade is 9. For fall 2016, 50 students applied for upper-level admission, 40 were accepted, 29 enrolled. SSAT, TOEFL Junior or TOEFL or SLEP required. Deadline for receipt of application materials: none. Application fee required: $65. On-campus interview required.

Athletics Interscholastic: basketball (boys, girls), cheering (g), golf (b,g), jogging (b,g), soccer (b,g), volleyball (g); intramural: cheering (g), skiing (downhill) (b,g), snowboarding (b,g); coed interscholastic: cross-country running, running, soccer; coed intramural: golf. 1 PE instructor, 1 coach.

Computers Computers are regularly used in all classes. Computer network features include on-campus library services, Internet access, wireless campus network, Internet filtering or blocking technology. Student e-mail accounts and computer access in designated common areas are available to students. Students grades are available online. The school has a published electronic and media policy.

Contact Ms. Alisa Loughlin, Enrollment Coordinator and Database Manager. 540-213-3726. Fax: 540-886-2275. E-mail: aloughlin@stuart-hall.org. Website: www.stuarthallschool.org

THE STUDY

3233 The Boulevard
Westmount, Montreal, Quebec H3Y 1S4, Canada

Head of School: Nancy Sweer

General Information Girls' day college-preparatory, arts, bilingual studies, technology, and science school. Grades K–11. Founded: 1915. Setting: urban. Nearest major city is Montreal, Canada. 2 buildings on campus. Approved or accredited by Canadian Association of Independent Schools, Quebec Association of Independent Schools, and Quebec Department of Education. Affiliate member of National

Association of Independent Schools. Languages of instruction: English and French. Endowment: CAN$8 million. Total enrollment: 327. Upper school average class size: 18. Upper school faculty-student ratio: 1:8. There are 180 required school days per year for Upper School students. Upper School students typically attend 5 days per week. The average school day consists of 7 hours.

Faculty School total: 60. In upper school: 1 man, 28 women; 8 have advanced degrees.

Subjects Offered Algebra, art, art history, arts appreciation, biology, chemistry, computer science, ecology, economics, English, entrepreneurship, environmental science, ethics, European history, French, gender issues, geography, geometry, history, Mandarin, mathematics, music, philosophy, physical education, physics, religion and culture, science, social studies, Spanish, stagecraft, technology, theater, world history.

Graduation Requirements English, ethics, foreign language, French, mathematics, physical education (includes health), science, social studies (includes history), technology. Community service is required.

Special Academic Programs Advanced Placement exam preparation; academic accommodation for the gifted.

Student Life Upper grades have uniform requirement, student council, honor system. Discipline rests primarily with faculty.

Tuition and Aid Day student tuition: CAN$17,285. Tuition installment plan (monthly payment plans, individually arranged payment plans, 2-payment plan). Tuition reduction for siblings, bursaries, merit scholarship grants, need-based scholarship grants available. In 2015–16, 15% of upper-school students received aid. Total amount of financial aid awarded in 2015–16: CAN$400,000.

Admissions Traditional secondary-level entrance grade is 7. Admissions testing, CAT, common entrance examinations, English, French, and math proficiency or school's own test required. Deadline for receipt of application materials: none. Application fee required: CAN$50. Interview required.

Athletics Interscholastic: alpine skiing, badminton, basketball, crew, cross-country running, flag football, golf, hockey, ice hockey, rowing, running, skiing (cross-country), soccer, swimming and diving, tennis, touch football, track and field, volleyball; intramural: aerobics, aerobics/dance, aerobics/Nautilus, aquatics, badminton, ballet, basketball, bicycling, cooperative games, dance, fitness, ice hockey, indoor hockey, jump rope, martial arts, outdoor activities, soccer, squash, swimming and diving, tennis, touch football, track and field, ultimate Frisbee, volleyball. 4 PE instructors, 8 coaches.

Computers Computers are regularly used in art, college planning, engineering, English, French, history, mathematics, photography, science, technology, video film production classes. Computer network features include on-campus library services, Internet access, wireless campus network, Internet filtering or blocking technology. Campus intranet, student e-mail accounts, and computer access in designated common areas are available to students. Students grades are available online. The school has a published electronic and media policy.

Contact Antonia Zannis, Deputy Head of School. 514-935-9352 Ext. 260. Fax: 514-935-1721. E-mail: admissions@thestudy.qc.ca. Website: www.thestudy.qc.ca

SUBIACO ACADEMY

405 North Subiaco Avenue
Subiaco, Arkansas 72865

Head of School: Mr. Matthew C. Stengel

General Information Boys' boarding and day college-preparatory, arts, business, religious studies, technology, and art and performing art school, affiliated with Roman Catholic Church. Grades 7–12. Founded: 1887. Setting: small town. Nearest major city is Fort Smith. Students are housed in single-sex dormitories. 100-acre campus. 10 buildings on campus. Approved or accredited by Arkansas Nonpublic School Accrediting Association, Independent Schools Association of the Central States, National Catholic Education Association, North Central Association of Colleges and Schools, The Association of Boarding Schools, and Arkansas Department of Education. Member of National Association of Independent Schools. Endowment: $3.5 million. Total enrollment: 199. Upper school average class size: 15. Upper school faculty-student ratio: 1:9. There are 179 required school days per year for Upper School students. Upper School students typically attend 5 days per week. The average school day consists of 6 hours and 25 minutes.

Upper School Student Profile Grade 7: 10 students (10 boys); Grade 8: 15 students (15 boys); Grade 9: 37 students (37 boys); Grade 10: 47 students (47 boys); Grade 11: 50 students (50 boys); Grade 12: 40 students (40 boys). 60% of students are boarding students. 57% are state residents. 18 states are represented in upper school student body. 17% are international students. International students from China, Mexico, Nigeria, Republic of Korea, Taiwan, and Viet Nam; 7 other countries represented in student body. 65% of students are Roman Catholic.

Faculty School total: 31. In upper school: 21 men, 10 women; 18 have advanced degrees; 9 reside on campus.

Subjects Offered Algebra, American history, American history-AP, art, art-AP, band, biology, biology-AP, broadcasting, calculus, calculus-AP, chemistry, chemistry-AP, choral music, chorus, Christian doctrine, Christian education, Christian scripture, Christian studies, Christian testament, church history, communications, computer art, computer science, drama, drama workshop, driver education, earth and space science, earth science, economics, English, English literature, English literature and composition-AP, English-AP, finance, fine arts, geography, geometry, government/civics, jazz ensemble, journalism, Latin, mathematics-AP, music, physical

education, physics, piano, psychology, religion, sociology, Spanish, speech, statistics-AP, Western civilization, world history.

Graduation Requirements American government, American history, art, arts and fine arts (art, music, dance, drama), college counseling, composition, creative writing, economics, English, foreign language, health, mathematics, physical education (includes health), religion (includes Bible studies and theology), science, social studies (includes history), Western civilization. Community service is required.

Special Academic Programs 8 Advanced Placement exams for which test preparation is offered; honors section; independent study; academic accommodation for the gifted, the musically talented, and the artistically talented; ESL (11 students enrolled).

College Admission Counseling 41 students graduated in 2016; all went to college, including Hendrix College; Penn State University Park; Rhodes College; Texas Christian University; University of Arkansas; University of Dallas. Median SAT critical reading: 543, median SAT math: 620, median SAT writing: 551, median combined SAT: 1714, median composite ACT: 26.

Student Life Upper grades have uniform requirement, student council, honor system. Discipline rests equally with students and faculty. Attendance at religious services is required.

Tuition and Aid Day student tuition: $7700; 5-day tuition and room/board: $21,800; 7-day tuition and room/board: $25,600. Tuition installment plan (FACTS Tuition Payment Plan, monthly payment plans, individually arranged payment plans). Need-based scholarship grants available. In 2016–17, 43% of upper-school students received aid. Total amount of financial aid awarded in 2016–17: $475,550.

Admissions Traditional secondary-level entrance grade is 9. For fall 2016, 70 students applied for upper-level admission, 54 were accepted, 46 enrolled. International English Language Test, OLSAT, Stanford Achievement Test or TOEFL required. Deadline for receipt of application materials: none. Application fee required: $50. On-campus interview recommended.

Athletics Interscholastic: baseball, basketball, cross-country running, football, golf, soccer, tennis, track and field; intramural: archery, backpacking, cross-country running, fishing, flag football, Frisbee, handball, hiking/backpacking, outdoor activities, outdoor adventure, outdoor recreation, outdoor skills, outdoors, physical fitness, sand volleyball, skateboarding, soccer. 1 PE instructor, 12 coaches.

Computers Computers are regularly used in art, Christian doctrine, commercial art, creative writing, desktop publishing, digital applications, drawing and design, economics, English, geography, graphic arts, history, journalism, keyboarding, literary magazine, mathematics, news writing, newspaper, photography, photojournalism, publications, religion, religious studies, SAT preparation, science, Spanish, stock market, video film production, word processing, writing, yearbook classes. Computer network features include on-campus library services, Internet access, wireless campus network, Internet filtering or blocking technology. Computer access in designated common areas is available to students. Students grades are available online. The school has a published electronic and media policy.

Contact Ms. Evelyn Bauer, Assistant Director of Admissions. 479-934-1034. Fax: 479-934-1033. E-mail: ebauer@subi.org. Website: http://www.SubiacoAcademy.us

THE SUDBURY VALLEY SCHOOL

2 Winch Street
Framingham, Massachusetts 01701

Head of School: Owen Harnish

General Information Coeducational day college-preparatory and general academic school. Grades PS–12. Founded: 1968. Setting: suburban. Nearest major city is Boston. 10-acre campus. 2 buildings on campus. Approved or accredited by Massachusetts Department of Education. Total enrollment: 160. Upper school faculty-student ratio: 1:16. There are 180 required school days per year for Upper School students. Upper School students typically attend 5 days per week. The average school day consists of 6 hours.

Faculty School total: 9. In upper school: 4 men, 5 women; 3 have advanced degrees.

Subjects Offered Algebra, American history, American literature, anatomy, anthropology, archaeology, art, art history, Bible studies, biology, botany, business, calculus, ceramics, chemistry, computer programming, computer science, creative writing, dance, drama, economics, English, English literature, ethics, European history, expository writing, French, geography, geometry, German, government/civics, grammar, Hebrew, history, history of ideas, history of science, home economics, Latin, mathematics, music, philosophy, photography, physical education, physics, physiology, psychology, religion, social studies, Spanish, speech, theater, trigonometry, typing, world history, world literature, writing.

Graduation Requirements Students must justify the proposition that they have developed the problem solving skill, the adaptability, and the abilities needed to function, independently in the world.

Special Academic Programs Independent study.

College Admission Counseling 6 students graduated in 2016; 4 went to college. Other: 2 went to work.

Student Life Upper grades have student council, honor system. Discipline rests equally with students and faculty.

Tuition and Aid Day student tuition: $8700. Tuition reduction for siblings available.

Admissions Deadline for receipt of application materials: none. Application fee required: $50. On-campus interview required.

Computers Computer network features include on-campus library services, Internet access. Student e-mail accounts are available to students. The school has a published electronic and media policy.

Contact Hanna Greenberg, Admissions Clerk. 508-877-3030. Fax: 508-788-0674. E-mail: office@sudval.org. Website: www.sudval.org

SUMMERFIELD WALDORF SCHOOL

655 Willowside Road
Santa Rosa, California 95401

Head of School: Mr. Bob Flagg

General Information Coeducational day college-preparatory, arts, and Waldorf curriculum school. Grades K–12. Founded: 1974. Setting: rural. 38-acre campus. 8 buildings on campus. Approved or accredited by Association of Waldorf Schools of North America, Western Association of Schools and Colleges, and California Department of Education. Total enrollment: 409. Upper school average class size: 28. Upper school faculty-student ratio: 1:7. Upper School students typically attend 5 days per week. The average school day consists of 7 hours.

Faculty School total: 23. In upper school: 11 men, 12 women; all have advanced degrees.

Subjects Offered Advanced chemistry, arts, history, humanities, literature, mathematics, music, science.

Graduation Requirements All academic, senior thesis project.

Special Academic Programs Honors section; study abroad.

College Admission Counseling 22 students graduated in 2015; 21 went to college, including Bennington College; Cornell University; Oberlin College; Sonoma State University; University of California, Davis; University of Redlands. Other: 1 went to work.

Student Life Upper grades have specified standards of dress, student council, honor system. Discipline rests primarily with faculty.

Tuition and Aid Day student tuition: $17,000. Tuition installment plan (FACTS Tuition Payment Plan, monthly payment plans). Tuition reduction for siblings, need-based scholarship grants available. In 2015–16, 40% of upper-school students received aid.

Admissions Traditional secondary-level entrance grade is 9. For fall 2015, 56 students applied for upper-level admission, 38 were accepted, 34 enrolled. Deadline for receipt of application materials: January 16. Application fee required: $75. On-campus interview required.

Athletics Interscholastic: basketball (boys, girls), soccer (b,g), volleyball (b,g); coed interscholastic: tennis. 5 PE instructors, 5 coaches.

Computers The school has a published electronic and media policy.

Contact Ms. Sallie Miller, Admissions Director. 707-575-7194 Ext. 102. Fax: 707-575-3217. E-mail: sallie@summerfieldwaldof.org. Website: http://www.summerfieldws.org/home/

THE SUMMIT COUNTRY DAY SCHOOL

2161 Grandin Road
Cincinnati, Ohio 45208-3300

Head of School: Mr. Rich Wilson

General Information Coeducational day college-preparatory school, affiliated with Roman Catholic Church. Grades PK–12. Founded: 1890. Setting: suburban. 24-acre campus. 4 buildings on campus. Approved or accredited by Independent Schools Association of the Central States, Ohio Association of Independent Schools, The College Board, and Ohio Department of Education. Member of National Association of Independent Schools. Endowment: $20 million. Total enrollment: 1,011. Upper school average class size: 16. Upper school faculty-student ratio: 1:9. There are 187 required school days per year for Upper School students. Upper School students typically attend 5 days per week. The average school day consists of 7 hours.

Upper School Student Profile Grade 9: 108 students (61 boys, 47 girls); Grade 10: 107 students (58 boys, 49 girls); Grade 11: 90 students (46 boys, 44 girls); Grade 12: 93 students (36 boys, 57 girls). 60% of students are Roman Catholic.

Faculty School total: 136. In upper school: 14 men, 23 women; 33 have advanced degrees.

Subjects Offered Advanced Placement courses, algebra, American history, American history-AP, American literature, anatomy and physiology, archaeology, art, biology, biology-AP, business law, calculus, calculus-AP, ceramics, chemistry, chemistry-AP, chorus, college admission preparation, college placement, community service, computer applications, computer science, computer science-AP, concert choir, critical studies in film, drama, economics, English, English literature, English-AP, environmental science, European history, European history-AP, fine arts, French, French-AP, geometry, government-AP, government/civics, grammar, graphic design, Greek, health, history, history of science, history-AP, Holocaust studies, language-AP, Latin, Latin-AP, leadership, leadership and service, leadership education training, literary magazine, mathematics, music, music theory-AP, music-AP, philosophy, physical education, physics, physics-AP, pre-calculus, psychology, psychology-AP, public speaking, religion, religious studies, science, senior career experience, service learning/internship, social studies, Spanish, Spanish language-AP, Spanish-AP, speech, speech communications, statistics-AP, student government, studio art, studio art-AP, study skills, theater, trigonometry, U.S. government and politics-AP, world history, world history-AP, world literature, world religions, writing.

Graduation Requirements Arts and fine arts (art, music, dance, drama), computer applications, computer science, English, foreign language, mathematics, physical education (includes health), religion (includes Bible studies and theology), science, social sciences, social studies (includes history), speech communications, junior year leadership course (one semester), junior year speech course, 40 hours of community service, senior search (2-week field experience in career of interest area).

Special Academic Programs 19 Advanced Placement exams for which test preparation is offered; honors section; independent study; study abroad; academic accommodation for the gifted and the artistically talented.

College Admission Counseling 98 students graduated in 2015; 97 went to college, including Boston College; Miami University; The Ohio State University; University of Cincinnati; University of Richmond; Vanderbilt University. Other: 1 entered a postgraduate year. Median SAT critical reading: 631, median SAT math: 609, median composite ACT: 28.

Student Life Upper grades have uniform requirement, student council, honor system. Discipline rests equally with students and faculty. Attendance at religious services is required.

Tuition and Aid Day student tuition: $19,825–$20,550. Tuition installment plan (Insured Tuition Payment Plan, monthly payment plans, individually arranged payment plans). Merit scholarship grants, need-based scholarship grants available. In 2015–16, 50% of upper-school students received aid.

Admissions Traditional secondary-level entrance grade is 9. For fall 2015, 285 students applied for upper-level admission, 173 were accepted, 50 enrolled. High School Placement Test or ISEE required. Deadline for receipt of application materials: December 15. Application fee required: $50. On-campus interview required.

Athletics Interscholastic: baseball (boys, girls), basketball (b,g), bowling (b,g), cheering (g), cross-country running (b,g), diving (b,g), field hockey (g), football (b), golf (b,g), lacrosse (b), soccer (b,g), softball (g), swimming and diving (b,g), tennis (b,g), track and field (b,g), volleyball (g), wrestling (b); intramural: dance team (g); coed interscholastic: weight lifting. 52 coaches, 1 athletic trainer.

Computers Computers are regularly used in all classes. Computer network features include on-campus library services, online commercial services, Internet access, wireless campus network, Internet filtering or blocking technology, mobile laptop computer lab, school-wide PORTAL/grades, Sketchpad, 8 full-text databases including Big Chalk, World Book, Children's Lit, SIRS, Biography Resource Center, Wilson Web, INFOhio, JSTOR. Campus intranet, student e-mail accounts, and computer access in designated common areas are available to students. Students grades are available online. The school has a published electronic and media policy.

Contact Mrs. Kelley Schiess, Assistant Head of School for Enrollment Management and Special Projects. 513-871-4700 Ext. 207. Fax: 513-533-5350. E-mail: schiess_k@summitcds.org. Website: www.summitcds.org

SUMMIT PREPARATORY SCHOOL

Kalispell, Montana
See Special Needs Schools section.

SUNRISE ACADEMY

Hurricane, Utah
See Special Needs Schools section.

SUNSHINE BIBLE ACADEMY

400 Sunshine Drive
Miller, South Dakota 57362-6821

Head of School: Mr. Jason Watson

General Information Coeducational boarding and day college-preparatory, general academic, arts, business, vocational, religious studies, bilingual studies, and technology school, affiliated with Christian faith. Boarding grades 8–12, day grades K–12. Founded: 1951. Setting: rural. Nearest major city is Pierre. Students are housed in single-sex dormitories. 160-acre campus. 6 buildings on campus. Approved or accredited by Association of Christian Schools International and South Dakota Department of Education. Total enrollment: 85. Upper school average class size: 28. Upper school faculty-student ratio: 1:9. There are 175 required school days per year for Upper School students. Upper School students typically attend 5 days per week. The average school day consists of 6 hours and 40 minutes.

Upper School Student Profile Grade 9: 16 students (8 boys, 8 girls); Grade 10: 15 students (5 boys, 10 girls); Grade 11: 17 students (7 boys, 10 girls); Grade 12: 10 students (4 boys, 6 girls). 91% of students are boarding students. 70% are state residents. 6 states are represented in upper school student body. 15% are international students. International students from Ethiopia and Republic of Korea; 2 other countries represented in student body. 100% of students are Christian faith.

Faculty School total: 15. In upper school: 8 men, 3 women; 4 have advanced degrees; all reside on campus.

Subjects Offered Accounting, advanced math, agriculture, algebra, American history, American literature, band, bell choir, Bible, Bible studies, biology, chemistry, choir, Christian doctrine, Christian ethics, computer science, creative writing, drama, drama performance, economics, English, English literature, ethics, fine arts, geography, geometry, government/civics, grammar, health, history, HTML design, journalism, mathematics, music, music appreciation, music composition, music history, music performance, newspaper, physical education, physics, science, social sciences, social studies, Spanish, speech, speech and oral interpretations, trigonometry, typing, U.S. government, U.S. history, vocal music, world geography, world history, writing, yearbook.

Graduation Requirements Arts and fine arts (art, music, dance, drama), Bible, computer science, English, mathematics, science, social sciences, social studies (includes history).

Special Academic Programs Independent study; study at local college for college credit; academic accommodation for the musically talented; remedial math.

College Admission Counseling 18 students graduated in 2015; 16 went to college, including Dordt College; South Dakota State University; The University of South Dakota; University of Sioux Falls. Other: 2 went to work. Median composite ACT: 23. 25% scored over 26 on composite ACT.

Student Life Upper grades have specified standards of dress, student council, honor system. Discipline rests primarily with faculty. Attendance at religious services is required.

Tuition and Aid Day student tuition: $5965; 5-day tuition and room/board: $8350; 7-day tuition and room/board: $8350. Tuition installment plan (monthly payment plans). Tuition reduction for siblings, need-based scholarship grants available. In 2015–16, 20% of upper-school students received aid. Total amount of financial aid awarded in 2015–16: $38,520.

Admissions Traditional secondary-level entrance grade is 9. For fall 2015, 32 students applied for upper-level admission, 31 were accepted, 27 enrolled. Deadline for receipt of application materials: none. Application fee required: $50. On-campus interview required.

Athletics Interscholastic: basketball (boys, girls), cheering (g), cross-country running (b,g), football (b), track and field (b,g), volleyball (g), wrestling (b); intramural: physical fitness (b,g), physical training (b,g), strength & conditioning (b,g), weight lifting (b,g), weight training (b,g). 1 PE instructor, 6 coaches.

Computers Computers are regularly used in art, journalism, newspaper, publications, publishing, research skills, speech, typing, Web site design, writing, yearbook classes. Computer resources include on-campus library services, Internet access, wireless campus network, Internet filtering or blocking technology. Student e-mail accounts are available to students.

Contact Mr. Wes McClure, Dean of Students. 605-853-3071 Ext. 227. Fax: 605-853-3072. E-mail: wes.mcclure@k12.sd.us. Website: www.sunshinebible.org

THE TAFT SCHOOL

110 Woodbury Road
Watertown, Connecticut 06795

Head of School: Mr. William R. MacMullen

General Information Coeducational boarding and day college-preparatory and humanities school. Grades 9–PG. Founded: 1890. Setting: small town. Nearest major city is Waterbury. Students are housed in coed dormitories. 226-acre campus. 20 buildings on campus. Approved or accredited by Missouri Independent School Association, New England Association of Schools and Colleges, The Association of Boarding Schools, The College Board, and Connecticut Department of Education. Member of National Association of Independent Schools and Secondary School Admission Test Board. Endowment: $236 million. Total enrollment: 594. Upper school average class size: 11. Upper school faculty-student ratio: 1:5. There are 176 required school days per year for Upper School students. Upper School students typically attend 6 days per week. The average school day consists of 7 hours.

Upper School Student Profile Grade 9: 108 students (51 boys, 57 girls); Grade 10: 150 students (75 boys, 75 girls); Grade 11: 157 students (77 boys, 80 girls); Grade 12: 178 students (89 boys, 89 girls).

Faculty School total: 126. In upper school: 68 men, 58 women; 91 have advanced degrees; 118 reside on campus.

Subjects Offered Acting, adolescent issues, advanced biology, advanced chemistry, advanced computer applications, advanced math, Advanced Placement courses, advanced studio art-AP, African-American literature, algebra, American history, American history-AP, American literature, anatomy, anatomy and physiology, animal behavior, architectural drawing, architecture, art, art history, art history-AP, astronomy, biology, biology-AP, calculus, calculus-AP, ceramics, chamber groups, character education, chemistry, chemistry-AP, Chinese, computer math, computer programming, computer science, computer science-AP, concert choir, creative writing, dance, design, digital imaging, drama, drawing, ecology, economics, economics-AP, English, English literature, English literature-AP, environmental science, environmental science-AP, ethics, European history, European history-AP, expository writing, film studies, fine arts, forensics, French, French language-AP, geography, geology, geometry, government-AP, government/civics, grammar, Greek, history, history of rock and roll,

history of science, honors algebra, honors English, honors geometry, human rights, humanities, Islamic studies, Japanese, jazz band, Latin, Mandarin, marine biology, mathematics, music, music theory-AP, philosophy, photography, physical education, physics, physics-AP, physiology, pre-calculus, psychology, religion, science, senior project, senior thesis, service learning/internship, sex education, South African history, Spanish, Spanish literature-AP, Spanish-AP, speech, statistics, statistics-AP, studio art-AP, theater, theology, trigonometry, U.S. government and politics-AP, U.S. history-AP, video film production, world history, world literature, writing, zoology.

Graduation Requirements American history, arts and fine arts (art, music, dance, drama), English, foreign language, mathematics, science, social studies (includes history), three semesters of arts.

Special Academic Programs 29 Advanced Placement exams for which test preparation is offered; honors section; independent study; term-away projects; study abroad; academic accommodation for the gifted, the musically talented, and the artistically talented.

College Admission Counseling 177 students graduated in 2016; 175 went to college, including Cornell University; Georgetown University; Middlebury College; Trinity College; Tufts University; University of Virginia. Other: 1 entered a postgraduate year, 1 had other specific plans. Mean SAT critical reading: 643, mean SAT math: 654, mean SAT writing: 648.

Student Life Upper grades have specified standards of dress, student council, honor system. Discipline rests equally with students and faculty.

Summer Programs Enrichment, ESL, sports, art/fine arts programs offered; session focuses on academic enrichment; held on campus; accepts boys and girls; open to students from other schools. 150 students usually enrolled. 2017 schedule: June 26 to July 30. Application deadline: none.

Tuition and Aid Day student tuition: $41,950; 7-day tuition and room/board: $56,550. Tuition installment plan (SMART Tuition Payment Plan). Need-based scholarship grants, need-based loans available. In 2016–17, 34% of upper-school students received aid. Total amount of financial aid awarded in 2016–17: $8,000,000.

Admissions Traditional secondary-level entrance grade is 9. For fall 2016, 1,670 students applied for upper-level admission, 350 were accepted, 195 enrolled. SSAT required. Deadline for receipt of application materials: January 15. Application fee required: $50. Interview recommended.

Athletics Interscholastic: alpine skiing (boys, girls), baseball (b), basketball (b,g), crew (b,g), cross-country running (b,g), field hockey (g), football (b), golf (b,g), hockey (b,g), ice hockey (b,g), lacrosse (b,g), rowing (b,g), soccer (b,g), softball (g), squash (b,g), tennis (b,g), track and field (b,g), ultimate Frisbee (b,g), volleyball (g), wrestling (b); coed interscholastic: dressage, equestrian sports, horseback riding; coed intramural: aerobics, aerobics/dance, ballet, basketball, climbing, cross-country running, dance, dressage, equestrian sports, figure skating, fitness, fitness walking, Frisbee, hockey, horseback riding, ice hockey, jogging, martial arts, modern dance, outdoor activities, physical fitness, rock climbing, rowing, running, sailing, self defense, soccer, squash, strength & conditioning, tennis, track and field, ultimate Frisbee, walking, wall climbing, weight lifting, weight training, yoga. 1 coach, 3 athletic trainers.

Computers Computers are regularly used in art, English, foreign language, geography, history, mathematics, music, science classes. Computer network features include on-campus library services, online commercial services, Internet access, wireless campus network, Internet filtering or blocking technology. Campus intranet, student e-mail accounts, and computer access in designated common areas are available to students. The school has a published electronic and media policy.

Contact Mr. Peter A. Frew, Director of Admissions. 860-945-7700. Fax: 860-945-7808. E-mail: admissions@taftschool.org. Website: www.taftschool.org

TAIPEI AMERICAN SCHOOL

800 Chung Shan North Road, Section 6
Taipei 11152, Taiwan

Head of School: Dr. Sharon Hennessy

General Information Coeducational day college-preparatory, fine and performing arts, STEAM, robotics, public speaking, and character education school. Grades PK–12. Founded: 1949. Setting: urban. 15-acre campus. 5 buildings on campus. Approved or accredited by International Baccalaureate Organization, US Department of State, and Western Association of Schools and Colleges. Affiliate member of National Association of Independent Schools. Language of instruction: English. Total enrollment: 2,323. Upper school average class size: 17. Upper school faculty-student ratio: 1:9. There are 180 required school days per year for Upper School students. Upper School students typically attend 5 days per week. The average school day consists of 6 hours and 40 minutes.

Upper School Student Profile Grade 9: 193 students (101 boys, 92 girls); Grade 10: 225 students (120 boys, 105 girls); Grade 11: 203 students (104 boys, 99 girls); Grade 12: 219 students (114 boys, 105 girls).

Faculty School total: 291. In upper school: 59 men, 48 women; 80 have advanced degrees.

Subjects Offered American history, American history-AP, Ancient Greek, art history, Chinese, Chinese history, film studies.

Graduation Requirements English, mathematics, modern languages, performing arts, physical education (includes health), public speaking, science, social studies (includes history).

Special Academic Programs International Baccalaureate program; 29 Advanced Placement exams for which test preparation is offered; honors section; ESL.

College Admission Counseling 217 students graduated in 2016; 212 went to college, including Boston University; Emory University; New York University; University of California, Irvine; University of Southern California; University of Toronto. Other: 1 entered military service, 4 had other specific plans. Mean SAT critical reading: 647, mean SAT math: 705, mean SAT writing: 664, mean combined SAT: 2015.

Student Life Upper grades have specified standards of dress, student council, honor system. Discipline rests primarily with faculty.

Summer Programs Remediation, enrichment, advancement, computer instruction programs offered; session focuses on internships, advancement, and make-up courses; honors math and science, robotics, writing, public speaking; held on campus; accepts boys and girls; open to students from other schools. 400 students usually enrolled. 2017 schedule: June 5 to July 30. Application deadline: May 1.

Tuition and Aid Day student tuition: 693,800 Taiwan dollars. Tuition installment plan (individually arranged payment plans).

Admissions For fall 2016, 109 students applied for upper-level admission, 64 were accepted, 54 enrolled. California Achievement Test, English for Non-native Speakers, ERB CTP IV, Iowa Tests of Basic Skills, ISEE, latest standardized score from previous school, PSAT, SAT, SSAT or Stanford Achievement Test required. Deadline for receipt of application materials: none. Application fee required: 10,000 Taiwan dollars.

Athletics Interscholastic: badminton (boys, girls), basketball (b,g), cross-country running (b,g), dance (b,g), golf (b,g), rugby (b,g), soccer (b,g), softball (b,g), swimming and diving (b,g), tennis (b,g), track and field (b,g), volleyball (b,g); intramural: basketball (b,g), cross-country running (b,g), soccer (b,g), softball (b,g), swimming and diving (b,g), tennis (b,g), volleyball (b,g). 6 PE instructors, 1 athletic trainer.

Computers Computers are regularly used in all academic classes. Computer network features include on-campus library services, online commercial services, Internet access, wireless campus network, Internet filtering or blocking technology. Campus intranet, student e-mail accounts, and computer access in designated common areas are available to students. Students grades are available online. The school has a published electronic and media policy.

Contact Dr. Winnie Tang, Director of Admissions. 886-2-2873-9900 Ext. 328. Fax: 886-2-2873-1641. E-mail: admissions@tas.edu.tw. Website: www.tas.edu.tw

TAKOMA ACADEMY

8120 Carroll Avenue
Takoma Park, Maryland 20912-7397

Head of School: Mrs. Carla Thrower

General Information Coeducational day college-preparatory school, affiliated with Seventh-day Adventist Church. Grades 9–12. Founded: 1904. Setting: suburban. 10-acre campus. 1 building on campus. Approved or accredited by Middle States Association of Colleges and Schools, National Council for Private School Accreditation, and Maryland Department of Education. Endowment: $400,000. Total enrollment: 226. Upper school average class size: 20. Upper school faculty-student ratio: 1:14. There are 180 required school days per year for Upper School students. Upper School students typically attend 4 days per week. The average school day consists of 8 hours and 25 minutes.

Upper School Student Profile Grade 9: 61 students (18 boys, 43 girls); Grade 10: 52 students (25 boys, 27 girls); Grade 11: 52 students (27 boys, 25 girls); Grade 12: 62 students (33 boys, 29 girls). 80% of students are Seventh-day Adventists.

Faculty School total: 17. In upper school: 6 men, 10 women; 9 have advanced degrees.

Graduation Requirements Applied arts, arts and fine arts (art, music, dance, drama), English, foreign language, health education, mathematics, physical education (includes health), religion (includes Bible studies and theology), science, social studies (includes history).

Special Academic Programs Advanced Placement exam preparation; honors section; study at local college for college credit; remedial reading and/or remedial writing; remedial math.

College Admission Counseling 56 students graduated in 2016; 55 went to college, including Andrews University; Oakwood University; Pacific Union College; Southern Adventist University; University of Maryland, College Park; Washington Adventist University. Other: 1 entered a postgraduate year.

Student Life Upper grades have uniform requirement, student council, honor system. Discipline rests primarily with faculty.

Summer Programs Remediation, enrichment programs offered; session focuses on Preparing students for the next grade level; held both on and off campus; accepts boys and girls; open to students from other schools. 65 students usually enrolled. 2017 schedule: June 5 to July 10.

Tuition and Aid Day student tuition: $13,832. Tuition installment plan (SMART Tuition Payment Plan). Tuition reduction for siblings, merit scholarship grants, need-based scholarship grants available.

Admissions Traditional secondary-level entrance grade is 9. Deadline for receipt of application materials: none. Application fee required: $125. On-campus interview recommended.

Athletics Interscholastic: basketball (boys, girls), soccer (b,g), volleyball (g); coed interscholastic: cross-country running, track and field, weight training. 1 PE instructor.

TAMPA PREPARATORY SCHOOL

727 West Cass Street
Tampa, Florida 33606

Head of School: Mr. Kevin M. Plummer

General Information Coeducational day college-preparatory, arts, and technology school. Grades 6–12. Founded: 1974. Setting: urban. 12-acre campus. 4 buildings on campus. Approved or accredited by Florida Council of Independent Schools, Southern Association of Colleges and Schools, Southern Association of Independent Schools, and Florida Department of Education. Member of National Association of Independent Schools and Secondary School Admission Test Board. Endowment: $10 million. Total enrollment: 650. Upper school average class size: 16. Upper school faculty-student ratio: 1:16. There are 180 required school days per year for Upper School students. Upper School students typically attend 5 days per week. The average school day consists of 6 hours and 40 minutes.

Upper School Student Profile Grade 6: 60 students (41 boys, 19 girls); Grade 7: 65 students (38 boys, 27 girls); Grade 8: 67 students (41 boys, 26 girls); Grade 9: 121 students (69 boys, 52 girls); Grade 10: 111 students (56 boys, 55 girls); Grade 11: 114 students (57 boys, 57 girls); Grade 12: 109 students (61 boys, 48 girls).

Faculty School total: 52. In upper school: 27 men, 25 women; 41 have advanced degrees.

Subjects Offered 3-dimensional design, Advanced Placement courses, aerospace science, computer science-AP, engineering, global studies, marine biology, music theater, music theory-AP, music-AP, orchestra, physics-AP, robotics, SAT preparation, Spanish literature-AP, speech and oral interpretations, sports medicine, statistics-AP, theater arts, TOEFL preparation, U.S. government and politics-AP, video and animation, video film production, world religions.

Graduation Requirements Arts and fine arts (art, music, dance, drama), English, foreign language, history, mathematics, physical education (includes health), science.

Special Academic Programs 21 Advanced Placement exams for which test preparation is offered; honors section; independent study; study abroad; academic accommodation for the gifted, the musically talented, and the artistically talented.

College Admission Counseling 110 students graduated in 2015; all went to college, including Elon University; Florida State University; Southern Methodist University; University of Central Florida; University of Florida.

Student Life Upper grades have specified standards of dress, student council, honor system. Discipline rests primarily with faculty.

Tuition and Aid Day student tuition: $20,090. Tuition installment plan (FACTS Tuition Payment Plan, monthly payment plans, individually arranged payment plans). Merit scholarship grants, need-based scholarship grants available. In 2015–16, 21% of upper-school students received aid; total upper-school merit-scholarship money awarded: $90,500. Total amount of financial aid awarded in 2015–16: $1,000,000.

Admissions Traditional secondary-level entrance grade is 9. For fall 2015, 273 students applied for upper-level admission, 175 were accepted, 153 enrolled. ISEE, PSAT or SAT for applicants to grade 11 and 12, SSAT, TOEFL or writing sample required. Deadline for receipt of application materials: February 15. Application fee required: $75. On-campus interview recommended.

Athletics Interscholastic: aquatics (boys, girls), baseball (b), basketball (b,g), bowling (b,g), crew (b,g), cross-country running (b,g), diving (b,g), golf (b,g), lacrosse (b), rowing (b,g), running (b,g), soccer (b,g), softball (g), swimming and diving (b,g), tennis (b,g), track and field (b,g), volleyball (b,g), wrestling (b). 4 PE instructors, 65 coaches, 2 athletic trainers.

Computers Computers are regularly used in aerospace science classes. Computer network features include on-campus library services, online commercial services, Internet access, wireless campus network, Internet filtering or blocking technology. Student e-mail accounts and computer access in designated common areas are available to students. Students grades are available online. The school has a published electronic and media policy.

Contact Mrs. Linda Y. Quinn, Admissions Assistant. 813-251-8481 Ext. 4011. Fax: 813-254-2106. E-mail: lquinn@tampaprep.org. Website: www.tampaprep.org

TANDEM FRIENDS SCHOOL

279 Tandem Lane
Charlottesville, Virginia 22902

Head of School: Edward Hollinger

General Information Coeducational day college-preparatory school. Grades 5–12. Founded: 1970. Setting: small town. Nearest major city is Richmond. 30-acre campus. 7 buildings on campus. Approved or accredited by Friends Council on Education and Virginia Association of Independent Schools. Member of National Association of

Independent Schools. Endowment: $3.3 million. Upper school average class size: 12. Upper school faculty-student ratio: 1:5. There are 180 required school days per year for Upper School students. Upper School students typically attend 5 days per week. The average school day consists of 7 hours.

Upper School Student Profile Grade 9: 20 students (9 boys, 11 girls); Grade 10: 25 students (12 boys, 13 girls); Grade 11: 29 students (12 boys, 17 girls); Grade 12: 24 students (11 boys, 13 girls).

Faculty School total: 35. In upper school: 9 men, 12 women; 15 have advanced degrees.

Subjects Offered Algebra, American literature, anatomy, art, bioethics, biology, biology-AP, calculus, calculus-AP, ceramics, chemistry, chemistry-AP, college counseling, computer applications, creative writing, cultural geography, discrete mathematics, drama, economics, economics and history, engineering, English, English-AP, environmental science-AP, expository writing, fine arts, French, French-AP, geometry, health and wellness, jazz ensemble, Latin, Latin-AP, marine biology, media studies, modern world history, music, musical productions, performing arts, photo shop, photography, physics, Quakerism and ethics, senior project, Spanish, Spanish-AP, statistics, statistics-AP, student government, student publications, studio art, theater, trigonometry, U.S. government, U.S. history, U.S. history-AP, weaving, world history, world literature, writing, yearbook.

Graduation Requirements Arts and fine arts (art, music, dance, drama), computer science, English, foreign language, government/civics, history, mathematics, science, senior year independent experiential learning project. Community service is required.

Special Academic Programs Advanced Placement exam preparation; independent study; academic accommodation for the gifted; remedial reading and/or remedial writing; remedial math; ESL (9 students enrolled).

College Admission Counseling 34 students graduated in 2016; 32 went to college, including Goucher College; New York University; Northwestern University; University of Virginia; Virginia Commonwealth University; Virginia Polytechnic Institute and State University. Other: 2 had other specific plans. Median SAT critical reading: 670, median SAT math: 605, median SAT writing: 620, median composite ACT: 28.

Student Life Upper grades have student council, honor system. Discipline rests equally with students and faculty.

Summer Programs Art/fine arts programs offered; session focuses on arts, grades K-8; held on campus; accepts boys and girls; open to students from other schools. 130 students usually enrolled. 2017 schedule: June 12 to July 21. Application deadline: May 1.

Tuition and Aid Day student tuition: $20,000–$22,000. Tuition installment plan (Insured Tuition Payment Plan, FACTS Tuition Payment Plan, monthly payment plans, individually arranged payment plans). Need-based scholarship grants, tuition remission for children of full-time faculty available. In 2016–17, 37% of upper-school students received aid.

Admissions Traditional secondary-level entrance grade is 9. Woodcock-Johnson required. Deadline for receipt of application materials: none. Application fee required: $50. Interview recommended.

Athletics Interscholastic: basketball (boys, girls), lacrosse (b,g), soccer (b,g), volleyball (g); coed interscholastic: cross-country running, fencing, outdoor education, outdoor skills, track and field; coed intramural: fencing. 2 PE instructors, 12 coaches, 1 athletic trainer.

Computers Computers are regularly used in all academic classes. Computer network features include on-campus library services, online commercial services, Internet access, wireless campus network, Internet filtering or blocking technology, virtual classroom, iPad and Chromebook program for grades 5-9. Student e-mail accounts and computer access in designated common areas are available to students. Students grades are available online. The school has a published electronic and media policy.

Contact Emily Robey Morrison, Director of Admissions. 434-951-9314. Fax: 434-296-1886. E-mail: emorrison@tandemfs.org. Website: www.tandemfs.org

TAPPLY BINET COLLEGE

245 Garner Road West
Ancaster, Ontario L9G 3K9, Canada

Head of School: Ms. Sue Davidson

General Information Coeducational day college-preparatory and general academic school. Grades 7–12. Founded: 1997. Setting: small town. Nearest major city is Hamilton, Canada. 1-acre campus. 1 building on campus. Approved or accredited by Ontario Ministry of Education and Ontario Department of Education. Language of instruction: English. Total enrollment: 17. Upper school average class size: 6. Upper school faculty-student ratio: 1:3.

Upper School Student Profile Grade 9: 2 students (1 boy, 1 girl); Grade 10: 3 students (2 boys, 1 girl); Grade 11: 2 students (1 boy, 1 girl); Grade 12: 10 students (7 boys, 3 girls).

Faculty School total: 6. In upper school: 1 man, 3 women; 3 have advanced degrees.

College Admission Counseling 4 students graduated in 2015; they went to Brock University; Trent University; Wilfrid Laurier University.

Student Life Upper grades have uniform requirement, student council, honor system. Discipline rests primarily with faculty.

Admissions Battery of testing done through outside agency required. Deadline for receipt of application materials: none. No application fee required.

Athletics Coed Interscholastic: aerobics/Nautilus. 1 PE instructor.

Contact Ms. Sue Davidson, Principal. 905-648-2737. Fax: 905-648-8762. E-mail: tapplybinetcollege@cogeco.net. Website: www.tapplybinetcollege.com

TASIS THE AMERICAN SCHOOL IN ENGLAND

Coldharbour Lane
Thorpe, Surrey TW20 8TE, United Kingdom

Head of School: Mr. David Hicks

General Information Coeducational boarding and day college-preparatory and arts school. Boarding grades 9–13, day grades N–13. Founded: 1976. Setting: rural. Nearest major city is London, United Kingdom. Students are housed in single-sex dormitories. 46-acre campus. 26 buildings on campus. Approved or accredited by Council of International Schools, International Baccalaureate Organization, New England Association of Schools and Colleges, Office for Standards in Education (OFSTED), and state department of education. Member of Secondary School Admission Test Board and European Council of International Schools. Language of instruction: English. Total enrollment: 750. Upper school average class size: 13. Upper school faculty-student ratio: 1:7. There are 172 required school days per year for Upper School students. Upper School students typically attend 5 days per week. The average school day consists of 5 hours and 45 minutes.

Upper School Student Profile Grade 9: 78 students (31 boys, 47 girls); Grade 10: 107 students (55 boys, 52 girls); Grade 11: 124 students (58 boys, 66 girls); Grade 12: 95 students (48 boys, 47 girls); Grade 13: 1 student (1 boy). 47% of students are boarding students. 47% are international students. International students from China, Germany, Italy, Russian Federation, Spain, and United States; 53 other countries represented in student body.

Faculty School total: 133. In upper school: 25 men, 31 women; 42 have advanced degrees; 14 reside on campus.

Subjects Offered French language AP, human geography AP.

Graduation Requirements History, lab science, science.

Special Academic Programs International Baccalaureate program; 15 Advanced Placement exams for which test preparation is offered; study abroad; academic accommodation for the gifted; remedial reading and/or remedial writing; ESL (53 students enrolled).

College Admission Counseling 98 students graduated in 2016; 90 went to college, including Barnard College; New York University; Northeastern University; Penn State University Park; University of California, San Diego; University of Southern California. Other: 8 had other specific plans.

Student Life Upper grades have uniform requirement, student council. Discipline rests primarily with faculty.

Summer Programs Remediation, enrichment, advancement, ESL, sports, art/fine arts, computer instruction programs offered; session focuses on ESL, academics, enrichment, and theater; held on campus; accepts boys and girls; open to students from other schools. 350 students usually enrolled. 2017 schedule: June 24 to August 5. Application deadline: none.

Tuition and Aid Day student tuition: £22,510; 7-day tuition and room/board: £39,500. Tuition installment plan (individually arranged payment plans). Need-based scholarship grants available. In 2016–17, 13% of upper-school students received aid. Total amount of financial aid awarded in 2016–17: £223,600.

Admissions TOEFL or SLEP required. Deadline for receipt of application materials: none. Application fee required: £125. Interview required.

Athletics Interscholastic: baseball (boys), basketball (b,g), cross-country running (b,g), lacrosse (b,g), rugby (b), soccer (b,g), softball (g), tennis (b,g), volleyball (b,g); intramural: aerobics (g), aerobics/dance (g), badminton (b,g), ballet (g), dance (g), dance team (g), field hockey (b,g), fitness (b,g), floor hockey (b,g), gymnastics (b,g), indoor soccer (b,g), lacrosse (b,g), physical fitness (b,g), physical training (b,g), rugby (b), running (b,g), soccer (b,g), softball (b,g), strength & conditioning (b,g), weight training (b,g), winter soccer (b,g); coed interscholastic: cheering, golf; coed intramural: basketball, bicycling, golf, gymnastics, horseback riding, indoor soccer, lacrosse, martial arts, modern dance, outdoor activities, outdoor adventure, strength & conditioning, swimming and diving, table tennis, tennis, track and field, ultimate Frisbee, volleyball, weight training, winter soccer, yoga. 2 PE instructors, 10 coaches, 1 athletic trainer.

Computers Computers are regularly used in all academic classes. Computer network features include on-campus library services, online commercial services, Internet access, wireless campus network, Internet filtering or blocking technology. Campus intranet, student e-mail accounts, and computer access in designated common areas are available to students. Students grades are available online. The school has a published electronic and media policy.

Contact Ms. Karen House, Director of Admissions and Enrollment Management. 44-1932-582316. E-mail: ukadmissions@tasisengland.org. Website: www.tasisengland.org

TASIS, THE AMERICAN SCHOOL IN SWITZERLAND

Via Collina d'Oro

Montagnola-Lugano CH-6926, Switzerland

Head of School: Dr. Lyle Rigg

General Information Coeducational boarding and day college-preparatory, arts, bilingual studies, and Global Service Program, academic travel program school. Boarding grades 6–PG, day grades PK–PG. Founded: 1956. Setting: small town. Nearest major city is Lugano, Switzerland. Students are housed in coed dormitories. 9-acre campus. 19 buildings on campus. Approved or accredited by New England Association of Schools and Colleges and Swiss Federation of Private Schools. Member of European Council of International Schools. Language of instruction: English. Total enrollment: 722. Upper school average class size: 13. Upper school faculty-student ratio: 1:6. There are 175 required school days per year for Upper School students. Upper School students typically attend 5 days per week. The average school day consists of 6 hours.

Upper School Student Profile 66% of students are boarding students. 82% are international students. International students from Brazil, China, Italy, Switzerland, Turkey, and United States; 54 other countries represented in student body.

Faculty School total: 67. In upper school: 34 men, 31 women; 51 have advanced degrees; 33 reside on campus.

Subjects Offered Advanced Placement courses, algebra, American history, American literature, ancient history, art, art history, art history-AP, biology, biology-AP, calculus, calculus-AP, ceramics, chemistry, chemistry-AP, digital photography, drama, economics, economics-AP, English, English language and composition-AP, English literature, English literature and composition-AP, environmental science, ESL, European history, European history-AP, fine arts, French, French language-AP, geography, geometry, German, German-AP, graphic design, health, history, international relations, Italian, mathematics, medieval/Renaissance history, music, photography, physical education, physics, science, social studies, Spanish, Spanish language-AP, theater, theory of knowledge, U.S. government, U.S. history-AP, world cultures, world history, world literature.

Graduation Requirements Arts, English, European history, foreign language, mathematics, science, senior humanities, sports, U.S. history. Community service is required.

Special Academic Programs International Baccalaureate program; Advanced Placement exam preparation; honors section; independent study; study abroad; academic accommodation for the gifted, the musically talented, and the artistically talented; programs in English, mathematics, general development for dyslexic students; ESL (150 students enrolled).

College Admission Counseling 123 students graduated in 2016; 121 went to college, including Boston University; Duke University; New York University; Northeastern University; University of California, Berkeley; University of California, Los Angeles. Other: 2 entered a postgraduate year.

Student Life Upper grades have uniform requirement, student council, honor system. Discipline rests equally with students and faculty.

Summer Programs Enrichment, advancement, ESL, sports, art/fine arts, rigorous outdoor training programs offered; session focuses on languages, sports, arts, outdoor adventure, travel; held both on and off campus; accepts boys and girls; open to students from other schools. 700 students usually enrolled. 2017 schedule: June 24 to August 12. Application deadline: none.

Tuition and Aid Day student tuition: 46,300 Swiss francs; 7-day tuition and room/board: 80,000 Swiss francs. Tuition installment plan (individually arranged payment plans). Need-based scholarship grants available. In 2016–17, 15% of upper-school students received aid.

Admissions TOEFL or SLEP required. Deadline for receipt of application materials: none. Application fee required: 300 Swiss francs. Interview recommended.

Athletics Interscholastic: alpine skiing (boys, girls), badminton (b,g), basketball (b,g), golf (b), rugby (b), soccer (b,g), swimming and diving (b,g), tennis (b,g), track and field (b,g), volleyball (b,g); intramural: basketball (b,g), rugby (b); coed interscholastic: skiing (downhill), softball, swimming and diving, track and field; coed intramural: aerobics, aerobics/dance, aerobics/Nautilus, badminton, basketball, climbing, combined training, cross-country running, dance, fitness, flag football, floor hockey, golf, horseback riding, indoor soccer, jogging, lacrosse, martial arts, modern dance, physical fitness, physical training, rock climbing, running, sailing, skiing (downhill), soccer, softball, squash, strength & conditioning, swimming and diving, tennis, ultimate Frisbee, volleyball, weight lifting, weight training. 3 PE instructors, 20 coaches.

Computers Computers are regularly used in art, English, ESL, foreign language, history, photography, science classes. Computer network features include on-campus library services, Internet access, wireless campus network, Internet filtering or blocking technology. Student e-mail accounts are available to students. Students grades are available online. The school has a published electronic and media policy.

Contact William E. Eichner, Director of Admissions. 41-91-960-5151. Fax: 41-91-993-2979. E-mail: admissions@tasis.ch. Website: www.tasis.com

THE TENNEY SCHOOL

3500 South Gessner

Houston, Texas 77063

Head of School: Mr. Michael E. Tenney

General Information Coeducational day college-preparatory and general academic school; primarily serves individuals with Attention Deficit Disorder. Grades 6–12. Founded: 1973. Setting: suburban. 2-acre campus. 1 building on campus. Approved or accredited by Southern Association of Colleges and Schools, Texas Private School Accreditation Commission, and Texas Department of Education. Total enrollment: 57. Upper school average class size: 1. Upper school faculty-student ratio: 1:2. There are 170 required school days per year for Upper School students. Upper School students typically attend 5 days per week. The average school day consists of 5 hours.

Upper School Student Profile Grade 6: 6 students (4 boys, 2 girls); Grade 7: 5 students (3 boys, 2 girls); Grade 8: 9 students (3 boys, 6 girls); Grade 9: 6 students (3 boys, 3 girls); Grade 10: 13 students (7 boys, 6 girls); Grade 11: 11 students (7 boys, 4 girls); Grade 12: 7 students (4 boys, 3 girls).

Faculty School total: 27. In upper school: 3 men, 24 women; 14 have advanced degrees.

Subjects Offered Accounting, algebra, American history, American literature, biology, British literature, business law, calculus, chemistry, computer programming, computer studies, creative writing, economics, English, fine arts, geometry, government, health, independent study, journalism, keyboarding, mathematics, microcomputer technology applications, physical education, physical science, physics, pre-calculus, psychology, science, social studies, sociology, Spanish, studio art, study skills, world geography, world history, world literature, yearbook.

Graduation Requirements American government, American history.

Special Academic Programs Advanced Placement exam preparation; honors section; academic accommodation for the gifted, the musically talented, and the artistically talented; remedial reading and/or remedial writing; remedial math; special instructional classes for deaf students; ESL (10 students enrolled).

College Admission Counseling 10 students graduated in 2016; all went to college, including Houston Baptist University; St. Thomas University; Texas A&M University; The University of Texas at Austin; University of Houston.

Student Life Upper grades have specified standards of dress. Discipline rests primarily with faculty.

Summer Programs Remediation, enrichment, advancement programs offered; session focuses on academic course work; held on campus; accepts boys and girls; open to students from other schools. 45 students usually enrolled. 2017 schedule: June 7 to June 30. Application deadline: June 1.

Tuition and Aid Day student tuition: $27,100.

Admissions Traditional secondary-level entrance grade is 9. For fall 2016, 38 students applied for upper-level admission, 33 were accepted, 29 enrolled. Naglieri Nonverbal School Ability Test, Otis-Lennon School Ability Test or Scholastic Achievement Test required. Deadline for receipt of application materials: none. Application fee required: $100. Interview recommended.

Athletics 1 PE instructor.

Computers Computers are regularly used in computer applications, creative writing, desktop publishing, English, foreign language, journalism, keyboarding, speech, word processing, yearbook classes. Computer network features include on-campus library services, Internet access, wireless campus network, Internet filtering or blocking technology. Campus intranet, student e-mail accounts, and computer access in designated common areas are available to students. Students grades are available online.

Contact Mr. Michael E. Tenney, Head of School. 713-783-6990. Fax: 713-783-0786. E-mail: mtenney@tenneyschool.com. Website: www.tenneyschool.com

TEURLINGS CATHOLIC HIGH SCHOOL

139 Teurlings Drive

Lafayette, Louisiana 70501-3832

Head of School: Mr. Michael Harrison Boyer

General Information Coeducational day college-preparatory and dual enrollment partnerships with local universities school, affiliated with Roman Catholic Church. Grades 9–12. Founded: 1955. Setting: urban. Nearest major city is Baton Rouge. 33-acre campus. 13 buildings on campus. Approved or accredited by Southern Association of Colleges and Schools and Louisiana Department of Education. Endowment: $140,000. Total enrollment: 779. Upper school average class size: 17. Upper school faculty-student ratio: 1:17. There are 179 required school days per year for Upper School students. Upper School students typically attend 5 days per week. The average school day consists of 5 hours and 50 minutes.

Upper School Student Profile Grade 9: 218 students (107 boys, 111 girls); Grade 10: 212 students (106 boys, 106 girls); Grade 11: 196 students (93 boys, 103 girls); Grade 12: 153 students (80 boys, 73 girls). 95% of students are Roman Catholic.

Faculty School total: 46. In upper school: 16 men, 28 women; 16 have advanced degrees.

Subjects Offered Acting, advanced math, algebra, American history, American literature, anatomy and physiology, art, biology, calculus, campus ministry, Catholic belief and practice, chemistry, civics/free enterprise, drama, English, environmental science, fine arts, French, geography, geometry, health, honors algebra, honors English, honors geometry, honors U.S. history, honors world history, interpersonal skills, physical education, physical science, physics, psychology, publications, sociology, Spanish, speech, sports medicine, theology, world history.

Graduation Requirements Advanced math, algebra, American history, American literature, biology, chemistry, civics, civics/free enterprise, electives, English, geometry, literature, physical education (includes health), physical science, theology, world geography, world history.

Special Academic Programs Honors section; study at local college for college credit.

College Admission Counseling 164 students graduated in 2016; 148 went to college, including Louisiana State University and Agricultural & Mechanical College; Louisiana State University at Eunice; Nicholls State University; Northwestern State University of Louisiana; Tulane University; University of Louisiana at Lafayette. Other: 13 went to work, 2 entered military service, 1 had other specific plans. Median composite ACT: 23. 22% scored over 26 on composite ACT.

Student Life Upper grades have uniform requirement, student council. Discipline rests equally with students and faculty. Attendance at religious services is required.

Tuition and Aid Day student tuition: $6400. Tuition installment plan (monthly payment plans). Need-based scholarship grants, paying campus jobs available. In 2016–17, 20% of upper-school students received aid. Total amount of financial aid awarded in 2016–17: $84,000.

Admissions Traditional secondary-level entrance grade is 9. For fall 2016, 286 students applied for upper-level admission, 275 were accepted, 275 enrolled. ACT, ACT-Explore, Explore, PSAT or Stanford Achievement Test required. Deadline for receipt of application materials: January 27. No application fee required.

Athletics Interscholastic: baseball (boys), basketball (b,g), bowling (b,g), cheering (g), cross-country running (b,g), dance team (g), football (b), golf (b,g), gymnastics (b,g), indoor track & field (b,g), soccer (b,g), softball (g), strength & conditioning (b,g), swimming and diving (b,g), tennis (b,g), track and field (b,g), volleyball (g), winter (indoor) track (b,g), wrestling (b); coed interscholastic: riflery, skeet shooting, trap and skeet; coed intramural: fishing. 3 coaches.

Computers Computers are regularly used in business applications, English, French, geography, history, mathematics, publications, science, Spanish, theater classes. Computer network features include on-campus library services, Internet access, wireless campus network, Internet filtering or blocking technology. Student e-mail accounts and computer access in designated common areas are available to students. Students grades are available online. The school has a published electronic and media policy.

Contact Mrs. Maria L. Hanes, Admissions Director. 337-235-5711 Ext. 128. Fax: 337-234-8057. E-mail: mhanes@tchs.net. Website: www.tchs.net

THE THACHER SCHOOL

5025 Thacher Road
Ojai, California 93023

Head of School: Mr. Michael K. Mulligan

General Information Coeducational boarding and day college-preparatory school. Grades 9–12. Founded: 1889. Setting: small town. Nearest major city is Santa Barbara. Students are housed in coed dormitories. 450-acre campus. 89 buildings on campus. Approved or accredited by California Association of Independent Schools, Georgia Association of Private Schools for Exceptional Children, National Independent Private Schools Association, The Association of Boarding Schools, Western Association of Schools and Colleges, and California Department of Education. Member of National Association of Independent Schools and Secondary School Admission Test Board. Endowment: $138.8 million. Total enrollment: 252. Upper school average class size: 11. Upper school faculty-student ratio: 1:5. Upper School students typically attend 5 days per week. The average school day consists of 7 hours.

Upper School Student Profile Grade 9: 61 students (30 boys, 31 girls); Grade 10: 71 students (34 boys, 37 girls); Grade 11: 62 students (30 boys, 32 girls); Grade 12: 66 students (33 boys, 33 girls).

Faculty School total: 51. In upper school: 27 men, 24 women; 33 have advanced degrees; 49 reside on campus.

Subjects Offered 3-dimensional art, ACT preparation, acting, advanced chemistry, advanced math, Advanced Placement courses, advanced studio art-AP, algebra, American history, American history-AP, American literature, art, art history, art history-AP, astronomy, biology, biology-AP, calculus, calculus-AP, ceramics, chemistry, chemistry-AP, Chinese, computer math, computer science, computer science-AP, conceptual physics, creative writing, dance, drama, ecology, economics, economics and history, electronic music, English, English literature, English literature-AP, English/composition-AP, environmental science, environmental science-AP, European history, European history-AP, film, fine arts, French, French language-AP, French literature-AP, geography, geometry, health, history, journalism, Latin, logic, marine biology, mathematics, music, music theory-AP, philosophy, photography, physical education, physics, physics-AP, psychology, religion, science, social studies, Spanish, Spanish language-AP, Spanish literature-AP, statistics, studio art-AP, theater, trigonometry, U.S. history-AP, world history, world literature, writing.

Graduation Requirements Arts and fine arts (art, music, dance, drama), English, foreign language, mathematics, physical education (includes health), science, social

studies (includes history), senior exhibition program (students choose an academic topic of interest and study it for one year, culminating in a school-wide presentation).

Special Academic Programs 17 Advanced Placement exams for which test preparation is offered; honors section; independent study; study abroad; academic accommodation for the gifted, the musically talented, and the artistically talented.

College Admission Counseling 62 students graduated in 2016; all went to college, including Claremont McKenna College; Duke University; Harvard University; New York University; University of Southern California; Yale University.

Student Life Upper grades have specified standards of dress, student council, honor system. Discipline rests equally with students and faculty.

Tuition and Aid Day student tuition: $36,800; 7-day tuition and room/board: $55,600. Tuition installment plan (monthly payment plans). Need-based scholarship grants available. In 2016–17, 28% of upper-school students received aid. Total amount of financial aid awarded in 2016–17: $2,818,894.

Admissions Traditional secondary-level entrance grade is 9. For fall 2016, 646 students applied for upper-level admission, 85 were accepted, 65 enrolled. ACT-Explore, ISEE, PSAT or SSAT required. Deadline for receipt of application materials: January 15. Application fee required: $75. On-campus interview recommended.

Athletics Interscholastic: baseball (boys), basketball (b,g), cross-country running (b,g), dance (b,g), football (b), lacrosse (b,g), soccer (b,g), tennis (b,g), track and field (b,g), volleyball (g); intramural: aerobics (b,g), backpacking (b,g), ballet (b,g), bicycling (b,g), canoeing/kayaking (b,g), climbing (b,g), dance (b,g), dance squad (b,g), horseback riding (b,g), outdoor activities (b,g), weight training (b,g), wilderness (b,g), wilderness survival (b,g), yoga (b,g); coed interscholastic: dance, equestrian sports; coed intramural: aerobics, backpacking, ballet, bicycling, bowling, canoeing/kayaking, climbing, dance, equestrian sports, fencing, Frisbee, golf, handball, hiking/backpacking, horseback riding, kayaking, modern dance, mountain biking, outdoor activities, paddle tennis, pistol, polo, Polocrosse, riflery, rock climbing, rodeo, skiing (downhill), surfing, trap and skeet, ultimate Frisbee, wall climbing, weight lifting, yoga. 18 coaches, 1 athletic trainer.

Computers Computers are regularly used in English, foreign language, history, mathematics, science classes. Computer network features include on-campus library services, online commercial services, Internet access, wireless campus network, Internet filtering or blocking technology. Campus intranet, student e-mail accounts, and computer access in designated common areas are available to students. Students grades are available online. The school has a published electronic and media policy.

Contact Ms. Yung Roman, Admission Office Manager. 805-640-3210. Fax: 805-640-9377. E-mail: yroman@thacher.org. Website: www.thacher.org

THINK GLOBAL SCHOOL

1562 First Avenue #205-3296
New York, New York 10028

Head of School: Mr. James Steckart

General Information Coeducational boarding college-preparatory and International Baccalaureate curriculum school. Grades 10–12. Founded: 2009. Setting: suburban. Students are housed in coed facilities in host city. Approved or accredited by International Baccalaureate Organization and Western Association of Schools and Colleges. Endowment: $50 million. Total enrollment: 44. Upper school average class size: 12. Upper school faculty-student ratio: 1:3. There are 193 required school days per year for Upper School students. Upper School students typically attend 5 days per week. The average school day consists of 6 hours and 45 minutes.

Upper School Student Profile Grade 10: 14 students (7 boys, 7 girls); Grade 11: 16 students (4 boys, 12 girls); Grade 12: 14 students (5 boys, 9 girls). 100% of students are boarding students. 10 states are represented in upper school student body. 100% are international students. International students from Bhutan, Ecuador, Germany, India, New Zealand, and South Africa; 15 other countries represented in student body.

Faculty School total: 14. In upper school: 7 men, 7 women; 10 have advanced degrees; 13 reside on campus.

Subjects Offered All academic.

Graduation Requirements International Baccalaureate courses.

Special Academic Programs International Baccalaureate program; study abroad.

College Admission Counseling 13 students graduated in 2015; 11 went to college, including Clark University; Columbia University; Georgetown University; Harvard University; New York University; Syracuse University. Other: 2 had other specific plans.

Student Life Upper grades have specified standards of dress, student council, honor system. Discipline rests equally with students and faculty.

Tuition and Aid 7-day tuition and room/board: $79,000. Tuition installment plan (monthly payment plans, individually arranged payment plans). Need-based scholarship grants available. In 2015–16, 90% of upper-school students received aid. Total amount of financial aid awarded in 2015–16: $2,649,200.

Admissions Traditional secondary-level entrance grade is 10. For fall 2015, 93 students applied for upper-level admission, 16 were accepted, 14 enrolled. Admissions testing or English proficiency required. Deadline for receipt of application materials: March 1. No application fee required. Interview required.

Athletics Coed Intramural: soccer.

Computers Computers are regularly used in all classes. Computer network features include Internet access, wireless campus network, Internet filtering or blocking technology, all students are provided with laptops, iPads, and phones. Campus intranet and student e-mail accounts are available to students. Students grades are available online. The school has a published electronic and media policy.

Contact Mrs. Melanie Anderson, Admissions Associate. 646-504-6924. E-mail: manderson@thinkglobalschool.org. Website: www.thinkglobalschool.org

THOMAS JEFFERSON SCHOOL

4100 South Lindbergh Boulevard
St. Louis, Missouri 63127

Head of School: Dr. Elizabeth L. Holekamp

General Information Coeducational boarding and day college-preparatory and classical liberal arts education school. Grades 7–PG. Founded: 1946. Setting: suburban. Students are housed in single-sex dormitories. 20-acre campus. 12 buildings on campus. Approved or accredited by Independent Schools Association of the Central States and The Association of Boarding Schools. Member of National Association of Independent Schools and Secondary School Admission Test Board. Endowment: $1.5 million. Total enrollment: 91. Upper school average class size: 14. Upper school faculty-student ratio: 1:7. There are 140 required school days per year for Upper School students. Upper School students typically attend 5 days per week. The average school day consists of 8 hours and 30 minutes.

Upper School Student Profile Grade 9: 17 students (10 boys, 7 girls); Grade 10: 12 students (7 boys, 5 girls); Grade 11: 15 students (12 boys, 3 girls); Grade 12: 14 students (8 boys, 6 girls). 45% of students are boarding students. 43% are state residents. 7 states are represented in upper school student body. 32% are international students. International students from Albania, China, Israel, Poland, Republic of Korea, and Tajikistan.

Faculty School total: 17. In upper school: 6 men, 7 women; 11 have advanced degrees; 1 resides on campus.

Subjects Offered Advanced Placement courses, algebra, American history-AP, ancient history, ancient world history, art, art history, biology, biology-AP, calculus, calculus-AP, ceramics, chemistry, chemistry-AP, dance, earth science, English, English language-AP, English literature-AP, ESL, fine arts, French, geography, geometry, government and politics-AP, government/civics, Greek, history, Homeric Greek, Italian, Latin, life science, mathematics, music, physical science, physics, physics-AP, science, social studies, trigonometry, U.S. history-AP, world history, world history-AP.

Graduation Requirements Art, arts and fine arts (art, music, dance, drama), English, foreign language, mathematics, science, social studies (includes history). Community service is required.

Special Academic Programs 10 Advanced Placement exams for which test preparation is offered; honors section; academic accommodation for the gifted; ESL (7 students enrolled).

College Admission Counseling 15 students graduated in 2016; all went to college, including Case Western Reserve University; New York University; Northwestern University; Pomona College; The University of Tampa; University of South Florida. Median SAT critical reading: 680, median SAT math: 700, median SAT writing: 680, median combined SAT: 2050, median composite ACT: 30. 80% scored over 600 on SAT critical reading, 90% scored over 600 on SAT math, 80% scored over 600 on SAT writing, 90% scored over 1800 on combined SAT, 95% scored over 26 on composite ACT.

Student Life Upper grades have specified standards of dress, student council, honor system. Discipline rests equally with students and faculty.

Tuition and Aid Day student tuition: $26,500; 5-day tuition and room/board: $44,350; 7-day tuition and room/board: $47,050. Tuition installment plan (SMART Tuition Payment Plan, monthly payment plans, individually arranged payment plans, Sallie Mae TuitionPay). Merit scholarship grants, need-based scholarship grants, paying campus jobs available. In 2016–17, 35% of upper-school students received aid; total upper-school merit-scholarship money awarded: $25,000. Total amount of financial aid awarded in 2016–17: $700,000.

Admissions Traditional secondary-level entrance grade is 9. For fall 2016, 37 students applied for upper-level admission, 17 were accepted, 11 enrolled. SSAT or TOEFL required. Deadline for receipt of application materials: January 17. Application fee required: $40. On-campus interview required.

Athletics Interscholastic: basketball (boys, girls), soccer (b,g), volleyball (b,g); intramural: basketball (b,g), soccer (b,g), volleyball (b,g); coed intramural: aerobics, aerobics/dance, dance, fitness, physical fitness, physical training, tennis, weight lifting, weight training, yoga.

Computers Computers are regularly used in foreign language, mathematics, science, yearbook classes. Computer network features include online commercial services, Internet access, wireless campus network, Internet filtering or blocking technology. Campus intranet, student e-mail accounts, and computer access in designated common areas are available to students. Students grades are available online. The school has a published electronic and media policy.

Contact Mr. Stephen Held, Director of Admissions. 314-843-4151 Ext. 2340. Fax: 314-843-3527. E-mail: admissions@tjs.org. Website: www.tjs.org

THORNTON ACADEMY

438 Main Street
Saco, Maine 04072

Head of School: Mr. Rene Menard

General Information Coeducational boarding and day college-preparatory, general academic, arts, technology, and Science/Engineering school. Grades 6–12. Founded: 1811. Setting: small town. Nearest major city is Boston, MA. Students are housed in single-sex dormitories and Homestay. 80-acre campus. 10 buildings on campus. Approved or accredited by New England Association of Schools and Colleges and Maine Department of Education. Member of National Association of Independent Schools and Secondary School Admission Test Board. Total enrollment: 1,503. Upper school average class size: 25. Upper school faculty-student ratio: 1:15. There are 175 required school days per year for Upper School students. Upper School students typically attend 5 days per week. The average school day consists of 7 hours.

Upper School Student Profile Grade 9: 352 students (181 boys, 171 girls); Grade 10: 359 students (188 boys, 171 girls); Grade 11: 366 students (198 boys, 168 girls); Grade 12: 356 students (186 boys, 170 girls). 10% of students are boarding students. 90% are state residents. 3 states are represented in upper school student body. 10% are international students. International students from China, Czech Republic, Spain, Ukraine, United States, and Viet Nam; 30 other countries represented in student body.

Faculty School total: 121. In upper school: 82 have advanced degrees; 25 reside on campus.

Subjects Offered 3-dimensional art, acting, advanced biology, advanced chemistry, advanced computer applications, advanced math, advanced studio art-AP, advanced TOEFL/grammar, American government, American history-AP, American literature-AP, Ancient Greek, Arabic, art education, art history, arts, astronomy, athletics, audio visual/media, baseball, basketball, biology-AP, business skills, calculus-AP, career education, career education internship, career experience, career planning, career/college preparation, ceramics, cheerleading, chemistry-AP, Chinese, choir, choreography, classical language, college admission preparation, college counseling, college planning, community service, composition-AP, computer applications, computer multimedia, computer music, computer programming-AP, computer science-AP, computer studies, computer-aided design, concert band, concert choir, creative dance, creative writing, cultural geography, dance performance, debate, design, digital art, digital photography, drama performance, dramatic arts, drawing, drawing and design, ecology, economics-AP, engineering, English as a foreign language, English composition, English language and composition-AP, English literature, English literature and composition-AP, English-AP, environmental science-AP, equestrian sports, European history-AP, exercise science, filmmaking, food and nutrition, four team activities, French language-AP, French-AP, German-AP, government and politics-AP, graphic design, health and wellness, history, history of jazz, Homeric Greek, human geography - AP, jazz band, Latin-AP, library, literature and composition-AP, macro/microeconomics-AP, Mandarin, marine biology, media production, model United Nations, modern dance, multimedia design, music history, music performance, music theory-AP, musical productions, musical theater, orchestra, physics-AP, piano, pre-algebra, pre-calculus, probability and statistics, psychology-AP, public speaking, radio broadcasting, robotics, SAT preparation, set design, softball, Spanish language-AP, Spanish-AP, statistics-AP, strings, studio art-AP, swimming, technology/design, tennis, TOEFL preparation, U.S. government, U.S. government and politics-AP, U.S. history, visual and performing arts, wind ensemble, writing, yearbook.

Special Academic Programs Advanced Placement exam preparation; honors section; accelerated programs; independent study; study at local college for college credit; academic accommodation for the gifted, the musically talented, and the artistically talented; remedial reading and/or remedial writing; remedial math; ESL.

Student Life Upper grades have student council, honor system. Discipline rests primarily with faculty.

Summer Programs ESL, sports, art/fine arts, computer instruction programs offered; held on campus; accepts boys and girls; open to students from other schools. 50 students usually enrolled. 2017 schedule: July to August. Application deadline: none.

Tuition and Aid Day student tuition: $12,500; 7-day tuition and room/board: $46,000. Tuition installment plan (FACTS Tuition Payment Plan, monthly payment plans). Merit scholarship grants, need-based scholarship grants available.

Admissions Traditional secondary-level entrance grade is 9. Deadline for receipt of application materials: none. Application fee required: $50. Interview recommended.

Athletics Interscholastic: baseball (boys), basketball (b,g), cheering (g), cross-country running (b,g), field hockey (g), football (b), ice hockey (b,g), indoor track & field (b,g), lacrosse (b,g), soccer (b,g), softball (g), tennis (b,g), track and field (b,g), volleyball (g), wrestling (b); coed interscholastic: golf, swimming and diving; coed intramural: aerobics/dance, bicycling, dance, equestrian sports, fishing, freestyle skiing, horseback riding, modern dance, mountain biking, outdoor activities, physical fitness, rafting, skiing (downhill), snowboarding.

Computers Computers are regularly used in all classes. Computer network features include on-campus library services, online commercial services, Internet access, wireless campus network, Internet filtering or blocking technology, 1:1 Student iPad Program, Students in grades 6-7 are assigned laptops. Student e-mail accounts and computer access in designated common areas are available to students. Students grades are available online. The school has a published electronic and media policy.

Contact Ms. Megan Theberge, Admissions Associate. 207-282-3361 Ext. 4221. Fax: 207-282-3508. E-mail: admissions@thorntonacademy.org. Website: www.thorntonacademy.org

TILTON SCHOOL

30 School Street
Tilton, New Hampshire 03276

Head of School: Peter Saliba

General Information Coeducational boarding and day college-preparatory school. Grades 9–PG. Founded: 1845. Setting: small town. Nearest major city is Concord. Students are housed in coed dormitories and single-sex dormitories. 150-acre campus. 30 buildings on campus. Approved or accredited by Association of Independent Schools in New England, Independent Schools of Northern New England, New England Association of Schools and Colleges, The Association of Boarding Schools, and New Hampshire Department of Education. Member of National Association of Independent Schools and Secondary School Admission Test Board. Endowment: $16.4 million. Total enrollment: 233. Upper school average class size: 12. Upper school faculty-student ratio: 1:7. There are 187 required school days per year for Upper School students. Upper School students typically attend 6 days per week. The average school day consists of 7 hours.

Upper School Student Profile Grade 9: 40 students (25 boys, 15 girls); Grade 10: 56 students (28 boys, 28 girls); Grade 11: 71 students (41 boys, 30 girls); Grade 12: 74 students (48 boys, 26 girls); Postgraduate: 16 students (13 boys, 3 girls). 75% of students are boarding students. 33% are state residents. 17 states are represented in upper school student body. 27% are international students. International students from Canada, China, Japan, Republic of Korea, Saudi Arabia, and Spain; 11 other countries represented in student body.

Faculty School total: 40. In upper school: 24 men, 16 women; 30 have advanced degrees; 34 reside on campus.

Subjects Offered Advanced chemistry, advanced math, advanced studio art-AP, advertising design, algebra, American history, American literature, anatomy and physiology, art, biology, biology-AP, calculus, calculus-AP, ceramics, chemistry, chemistry-AP, clayworking, college counseling, computer graphics, criminal justice, criminology, dance, digital art, drama, drawing, ecology, economics, English, English language and composition-AP, English literature-AP, ESL, European history, European history-AP, forensics, French, French literature-AP, French-AP, functions, geology, geometry, global studies, graphic arts, graphic design, guitar, honors algebra, honors English, honors geometry, independent study, integrated mathematics, integrated science, Japanese, leadership, music, music appreciation, music theory, musical productions, painting, photography, physics, physics-AP, politics, pre-calculus, psychology, psychology-AP, Russian, SAT preparation, sociology, Spanish, Spanish literature-AP, Spanish-AP, statistics, studio art, studio art-AP, theater, trigonometry, wilderness education, world cultures, world literature, world religions, yearbook.

Graduation Requirements American history, arts and fine arts (art, music, dance, drama), English, foreign language, history, lab science, mathematics, science, annual participation in Plus/5 (including activities in art and culture, athletics, community service, leadership, and outdoor experience).

Special Academic Programs 11 Advanced Placement exams for which test preparation is offered; honors section; independent study; remedial reading and/or remedial writing; remedial math; ESL (17 students enrolled).

College Admission Counseling 84 students graduated in 2016; 79 went to college, including Brandeis University, Bryant University, Gordon College, Indiana University Bloomington, Stonehill College, Suffolk University. Other: 1 entered military service, 1 entered a postgraduate year, 3 had other specific plans. Mean SAT critical reading: 499, mean SAT math: 569, mean SAT writing: 508, mean combined SAT: 1576.

Student Life Upper grades have specified standards of dress, student council, honor system. Discipline rests primarily with faculty.

Summer Programs Enrichment, advancement, ESL, sports, art/fine arts, computer instruction programs offered; held both on and off campus; accepts boys and girls; open to students from other schools. 300 students usually enrolled. 2017 schedule: June 20 to August 26. Application deadline: June 1.

Tuition and Aid Day student tuition: $32,875; 7-day tuition and room/board: $57,200. Tuition installment plan (FACTS Tuition Payment Plan, individually arranged payment plans). Merit scholarship grants, need-based scholarship grants, need-based loans available. In 2016–17, 60% of upper-school students received aid; total upper-school merit-scholarship money awarded: $88,500. Total amount of financial aid awarded in 2016–17: $4,100,000.

Admissions Traditional secondary-level entrance grade is 9. For fall 2016, 532 students applied for upper-level admission, 289 were accepted, 107 enrolled. ACT, PSAT, PSAT or SAT for applicants to grade 11 and 12, SAT, SLEP, SSAT, SSAT, ERB, PSAT, SAT, PLAN or ACT, TOEFL, TOEFL or SLEP, WAIS, WICS or writing sample required. Deadline for receipt of application materials: February 1. Application fee required: $50. Interview recommended.

Athletics Interscholastic: baseball (boys), basketball (b,g), field hockey (g), football (b), ice hockey (b,g), lacrosse (b,g), soccer (b,g), softball (g), tennis (b,g); coed interscholastic: alpine skiing, cross-country running, golf, mountain biking, skiing (downhill), snowboarding, weight lifting, weight training, wrestling; coed intramural: canoeing/kayaking, hiking/backpacking, outdoor activities, outdoor education, outdoor

skills, rock climbing, squash, strength & conditioning, wall climbing, weight training, wilderness survival. 7 coaches, 1 athletic trainer.

Computers Computers are regularly used in college planning, engineering, English, foreign language, graphic arts, history, mathematics, newspaper, photography, science, social sciences, technology, writing, yearbook classes. Computer network features include on-campus library services, online commercial services, Internet access, wireless campus network, Internet filtering or blocking technology, USB ports, Smart Media Readers. Campus intranet, student e-mail accounts, and computer access in designated common areas are available to students. Students grades are available online. The school has a published electronic and media policy.

Contact Sharon Trudel, Admissions Assistant. 603-286-1733. Fax: 603-286-1705. E-mail: admissions@tiltonschool.org. Website: www.tiltonschool.org

TIMOTHY CHRISTIAN HIGH SCHOOL

1061 South Prospect Avenue
Elmhurst, Illinois 60126

Head of School: Mr. Bradford Mitchell

General Information Coeducational day college-preparatory and general academic school, affiliated with Christian Reformed Church. Grades 9–12. Founded: 1911. Setting: suburban. Nearest major city is Chicago. 26-acre campus. 1 building on campus. Approved or accredited by North Central Association of Colleges and Schools and Illinois Department of Education. Total enrollment: 990. Upper school average class size: 20. Upper school faculty-student ratio: 1:10. There are 176 required school days per year for Upper School students. Upper School students typically attend 5 days per week. The average school day consists of 6 hours and 45 minutes.

Upper School Student Profile Grade 9: 84 students (51 boys, 33 girls); Grade 10: 94 students (51 boys, 43 girls); Grade 11: 81 students (46 boys, 35 girls); Grade 12: 84 students (41 boys, 43 girls).

Faculty School total: 30. In upper school: 16 men, 14 women; 18 have advanced degrees.

Subjects Offered Advanced math, algebra, American literature, anatomy and physiology, art, band, Bible, biology, biology-AP, British literature, business studies, calculus-AP, ceramics, chemistry, child development, choir, Christian doctrine, Christian ethics, church history, communication skills, community service, computer applications, computer-aided design, concert choir, desktop publishing, drawing and design, economics, electives, English, English literature-AP, expository writing, food and nutrition, geometry, health, home economics, honors algebra, honors geometry, human geography - AP, independent living, instrumental music, interior design, jazz ensemble, music, music appreciation, music theory, New Testament, oral communications, orchestra, parent/child development, photography, physical education, physics, physics-AP, pre-calculus, psychology, sewing, Spanish, Spanish language-AP, trigonometry, U.S. government, U.S. history, U.S. history-AP, United States government-AP, Western civilization, world literature.

Graduation Requirements Arts and fine arts (art, music, dance, drama), computer processing, computer skills, English, mathematics, physical education (includes health), religion (includes Bible studies and theology), religious studies, science, social studies (includes history), 8 day Winterim (Renew). Community service is required.

Special Academic Programs 7 Advanced Placement exams for which test preparation is offered; honors section; study at local college for college credit; remedial reading and/or remedial writing.

College Admission Counseling 95 students graduated in 2016; 90 went to college, including Calvin College; Olivet Nazarene University; Trinity Christian College; University of Illinois at Chicago; University of Illinois at Urbana–Champaign; Wheaton College. Other: 2 went to work, 3 entered military service. Mean composite ACT: 24.

Student Life Upper grades have specified standards of dress, student council, honor system. Discipline rests primarily with faculty. Attendance at religious services is required.

Summer Programs Advancement, sports, art/fine arts programs offered; session focuses on athletic and art camps for any student, along with 3 wk academic summer school program for TC students; held on campus; accepts boys and girls; open to students from other schools. 136 students usually enrolled. 2017 schedule: June 1 to August 1.

Tuition and Aid Day student tuition: $10,175–$25,000. Tuition installment plan (FACTS Tuition Payment Plan, FACTS is required unless paying the total tuition at once). Need-based scholarship grants, some need-based financial assistance available through school foundation available. In 2016–17, 13% of upper-school students received aid.

Admissions Traditional secondary-level entrance grade is 9. International English Language Test, Scholastic Testing Service High School Placement Test, school's own exam, TOEFL or TOEFL Junior required. Deadline for receipt of application materials: none. Application fee required: $50. On-campus interview required.

Athletics Interscholastic: baseball (boys), basketball (b,g), cross-country running (b,g), dance team (g), soccer (b,g), softball (g), tennis (b,g), track and field (b,g), volleyball (g); intramural: basketball (b), flag football (b); coed interscholastic: cheering, golf. 2 PE instructors.

Computers Computers are regularly used in business education, Christian doctrine, computer applications, engineering, English, foreign language, graphic design, human geography - AP, keyboarding, mathematics, science, Spanish, technology, theology, word processing, writing classes. Computer network features include on-campus library services, Internet access, wireless campus network, Internet filtering or blocking technology, iPads (one-to-one) included in tuition. Student e-mail accounts are available to students. Students grades are available online. The school has a published electronic and media policy.

Contact Mr. Dan Quist, Director of Admissions and Student Recruitment. 630-782-4043. Fax: 630-833-9238. E-mail: quist@timothychristian.com.
Website: www.timothychristian.com

TIMOTHY CHRISTIAN SCHOOL

2008 Ethel Road

Piscataway, New Jersey 08854

Head of School: Dr. Hubert Hartzler

General Information Coeducational day college-preparatory, arts, business, religious studies, bilingual studies, and technology school, affiliated with Christian faith. Grades PK–12. Founded: 1949. Setting: suburban. Nearest major city is New Brunswick. 25-acre campus. 7 buildings on campus. Approved or accredited by Association of Christian Schools International and Middle States Association of Colleges and Schools. Endowment: $76,000. Total enrollment: 465. Upper school average class size: 18. Upper school faculty-student ratio: 1:11. There are 175 required school days per year for Upper School students. Upper School students typically attend 5 days per week. The average school day consists of 6 hours and 30 minutes.

Upper School Student Profile Grade 9: 38 students (14 boys, 24 girls); Grade 10: 25 students (13 boys, 12 girls); Grade 11: 45 students (27 boys, 18 girls); Grade 12: 40 students (23 boys, 17 girls). 100% of students are Christian faith.

Faculty School total: 62. In upper school: 7 men, 10 women; 15 have advanced degrees.

Subjects Offered Accounting, acting, advanced biology, advanced chemistry, advanced computer applications, advanced math, Advanced Placement courses, advanced studio art-AP, advanced TOEFL/grammar, algebra, American government, American history, American history-AP, American literature, American literature-AP, American studies, art, band, Bible, Bible studies, biology, biology-AP, British literature, calculus, calculus-AP, chamber groups, chemistry, chemistry-AP, computer applications, computer programming, computer science, computer science-AP, concert choir, creative writing, critical thinking, debate, earth science, English, English language-AP, home economics, journalism, keyboarding, music, music theory, physics, pre-algebra, pre-calculus, programming, psychology, Spanish, technical theater, theater arts, trigonometry, woodworking, yearbook.

Graduation Requirements Algebra, American literature, Bible, Bible studies, biology, British literature, chemistry, composition, earth science, geometry, health, introduction to literature, physical education (includes health), trigonometry, U.S. history, world history, world literature, worldview studies.

Special Academic Programs 6 Advanced Placement exams for which test preparation is offered; honors section; independent study; study at local college for college credit; remedial reading and/or remedial writing; programs in English, mathematics, general development for dyslexic students; ESL (20 students enrolled).

College Admission Counseling 45 students graduated in 2015; they went to Gordon College; Liberty University; Messiah College; Rutgers University–New Brunswick; Virginia Polytechnic Institute and State University; Wheaton College. Median SAT critical reading: 556, median SAT math: 524.

Student Life Upper grades have uniform requirement, student council, honor system. Discipline rests primarily with faculty. Attendance at religious services is required.

Tuition and Aid Tuition installment plan (FACTS Tuition Payment Plan). Need-based scholarship grants available. In 2015–16, 30% of upper-school students received aid. Total amount of financial aid awarded in 2015–16: $100,000.

Admissions Traditional secondary-level entrance grade is 9. For fall 2015, 26 students applied for upper-level admission, 16 were accepted, 16 enrolled. Admissions testing, TerraNova and TOEFL required. Deadline for receipt of application materials: none. Application fee required: $95. On-campus interview required.

Athletics Interscholastic: baseball (boys), basketball (b,g), cheering (g), golf (b,g), soccer (b,g), softball (g), track and field (b,g), volleyball (g), weight training (b,g). 2 PE instructors, 20 coaches, 1 athletic trainer.

Computers Computers are regularly used in foreign language, yearbook classes. Computer network features include on-campus library services, Internet access, Internet filtering or blocking technology. Computer access in designated common areas is available to students. Students grades are available online. The school has a published electronic and media policy.

Contact Mrs. Ella Mendalski, Admissions Secretary. 732-985-0300 Ext. 613. Fax: 732-985-8008. E-mail: emendalski@timothychristian.org.
Website: www.timothychristian.org

TMI - THE EPISCOPAL SCHOOL OF TEXAS

20955 West Tejas Trail
San Antonio, Texas 78257

Head of School: Dr. John W. Cooper

General Information Coeducational boarding and day college-preparatory, military/leadership, and military school, affiliated with Episcopal Church. Boarding grades 8–12, day grades 6–12. Founded: 1893. Setting: suburban. Students are housed in single-sex dormitories. 82-acre campus. 18 buildings on campus. Approved or accredited by Independent Schools Association of the Southwest, Southwest Association of Episcopal Schools, and Texas Department of Education. Member of National Association of Independent Schools. Total enrollment: 472. Upper school average class size: 16. Upper school faculty-student ratio: 1:9. There are 168 required school days per year for Upper School students. Upper School students typically attend 5 days per week. The average school day consists of 6 hours and 5 minutes.

Upper School Student Profile Grade 6: 26 students (18 boys, 8 girls); Grade 7: 42 students (26 boys, 16 girls); Grade 8: 55 students (37 boys, 18 girls); Grade 9: 92 students (53 boys, 39 girls); Grade 10: 73 students (43 boys, 30 girls); Grade 11: 78 students (42 boys, 36 girls); Grade 12: 98 students (48 boys, 50 girls). 18% of students are boarding students. 93% are state residents. 3 states are represented in upper school student body. 6% are international students. International students from China, Mexico, Republic of Korea, and Saudi Arabia. 78% of students are members of Episcopal Church.

Faculty School total: 67. In upper school: 49 have advanced degrees; 18 reside on campus.

Subjects Offered 20th century history, acting, Advanced Placement courses, algebra, American Civil War, American history, American literature, anatomy and physiology, astronomy, athletics, biology, biology-AP, British literature, calculus, calculus-AP, ceramics, chemistry, chemistry-AP, choir, computer programming, computer science-AP, conceptual physics, earth science, economics, economics-AP, English, English literature, environmental science, environmental science-AP, fine arts, geometry, government, government-AP, history, JROTC, Latin, Latin-AP, literary magazine, meteorology, Middle East, military history, model United Nations, music, outdoor education, peer counseling, philosophy, photography, physical education, physics, physics-AP, playwriting, playwriting and directing, pre-algebra, pre-calculus, programming, psychology, psychology-AP, religion, robotics, set design, Spanish, Spanish language-AP, Spanish literature-AP, statistics, statistics-AP, studio art, studio art-AP, theater, theater arts, theater design and production, U.S. government and politics, U.S. history, video and animation, video film production, visual and performing arts, visual arts, vocal music, weight fitness, world history, world religions, writing, writing, yearbook.

Graduation Requirements Arts and fine arts (art, music, dance, drama), electives, English, foreign language, history, mathematics, philosophy, physical education (includes health), religion (includes Bible studies and theology), science, community service requirement, senior chapel talk.

Special Academic Programs Advanced Placement exam preparation; honors section; independent study; ESL.

College Admission Counseling 81 students graduated in 2016; 80 went to college, including Hofstra University; Northeastern University; Sewanee: The University of the South; Texas A&M University; The University of Texas at Austin; Trinity University. Other: 1 went to work, 1 entered military service.

Student Life Upper grades have uniform requirement, student council, honor system. Discipline rests equally with students and faculty. Attendance at religious services is required.

Summer Programs Enrichment, advancement, sports, art/fine arts, rigorous outdoor training programs offered; session focuses on academics, activities, sports and enrichment; held on campus; accepts boys and girls; open to students from other schools. 1,050 students usually enrolled. 2017 schedule: June 5 to July 28. Application deadline: May 1.

Tuition and Aid Day student tuition: $23,450; 5-day tuition and room/board: $42,425; 7-day tuition and room/board: $46,525. Tuition installment plan (FACTS Tuition Payment Plan). Merit scholarship grants, need-based scholarship grants available.

Admissions Traditional secondary-level entrance grade is 9. ERB, ISEE, PSAT or SAT, SSAT or TOEFL required. Deadline for receipt of application materials: none. Application fee required: $75. Interview required.

Athletics Interscholastic: baseball (boys), basketball (b,g), cheering (b,g), cross-country running (b,g), dance (g), fitness (b,g), football (b), golf (b,g), independent competitive sports (b,g), lacrosse (b,g), soccer (b,g), softball (g), strength & conditioning (b,g), swimming and diving (b,g), tennis (b,g), track and field (b,g), volleyball (g), weight training (b,g); coed interscholastic: JROTC drill, marksmanship, outdoor education, physical fitness, physical training, riflery, strength & conditioning.

Computers Computers are regularly used in digital applications, graphic arts, graphic design, graphics, journalism, language development, library, literary magazine, mathematics, media production, multimedia, newspaper, photography, programming, science, video film production, yearbook classes. Computer network features include on-campus library services, online commercial services, Internet access, wireless campus network, Internet filtering or blocking technology. Campus intranet, student e-mail accounts, and computer access in designated common areas are available to students. Students grades are available online. The school has a published electronic and media policy.

Contact Mr. Aaron Hawkins, Director of Admissions. 210-564-6152. Fax: 210-698-0715. E-mail: a.hawkins@tmi-sa.org. Website: www.tmi-sa.org

TOME SCHOOL

581 South Maryland Avenue
North East, Maryland 21901

Head of School: Christine Szymanski

General Information Coeducational day college-preparatory school. Grades K–12. Founded: 1889. Setting: small town. Nearest major city is Baltimore. 100-acre campus. 1 building on campus. Approved or accredited by Maryland Department of Education. Endowment: $3 million. Total enrollment: 480. Upper school average class size: 16. Upper school faculty-student ratio: 1:10. There are 170 required school days per year for Upper School students. Upper School students typically attend 5 days per week. The average school day consists of 6 hours and 35 minutes.

Upper School Student Profile Grade 9: 39 students (16 boys, 23 girls); Grade 10: 45 students (19 boys, 26 girls); Grade 11: 29 students (13 boys, 16 girls); Grade 12: 36 students (18 boys, 18 girls).

Faculty School total: 50. In upper school: 5 men, 10 women; 9 have advanced degrees.

Subjects Offered Advanced biology, algebra, American history, American literature, ancient history, ancient world history, biology, British literature (honors), calculus, chemistry, composition-AP, English, English language and composition-AP, English literature, English literature and composition-AP, environmental science, forensics, French, geometry, government/civics, grammar, history, mathematics, physical education, physics, pre-calculus, Spanish, statistics, world history, world literature.

Graduation Requirements English, foreign language, mathematics, science, social sciences, social studies (includes history), 4 credits in Literature, 4 credits in composition.

Special Academic Programs Advanced Placement exam preparation; honors section; study at local college for college credit.

College Admission Counseling 32 students graduated in 2015; 31 went to college, including Salisbury University; Towson University; University of Maryland, Baltimore County; University of Maryland, College Park; University of South Florida. Other: 1 entered military service. Median SAT critical reading: 620, median SAT math: 610, median SAT writing: 640, median combined SAT: 1870, median composite ACT: 26. 60% scored over 600 on SAT critical reading, 54% scored over 600 on SAT math, 79% scored over 600 on SAT writing, 53% scored over 26 on composite ACT.

Student Life Upper grades have uniform requirement, student council, honor system. Discipline rests primarily with faculty.

Tuition and Aid Day student tuition: $7500. Tuition installment plan (SMART Tuition Payment Plan). Merit scholarship grants, need-based scholarship grants available. In 2015–16, 30% of upper-school students received aid; total upper-school merit-scholarship money awarded: $25,000.

Admissions Traditional secondary-level entrance grade is 9. For fall 2015, 24 students applied for upper-level admission, 20 were accepted, 15 enrolled. Otis-Lennon School Ability Test and Stanford Achievement Test required. Deadline for receipt of application materials: none. Application fee required: $50. On-campus interview required.

Athletics Interscholastic: baseball (boys), basketball (b,g), field hockey (g), lacrosse (b), soccer (b,g), softball (g), tennis (b,g), volleyball (g); coed interscholastic: cheering, cross-country running, tennis; coed intramural: baseball, basketball, cross-country running, fitness walking, flag football, football, Frisbee, paddle tennis, speedball, table tennis, tennis, ultimate Frisbee, volleyball, weight lifting, yoga. 2 PE instructors, 12 coaches.

Computers Computers are regularly used in English, mathematics classes. Computer resources include on-campus library services, Internet access, wireless campus network, Internet filtering or blocking technology. Students grades are available online. The school has a published electronic and media policy.

Contact Christine Szymanski, Head of School. 410-287-2050. Fax: 410-287-8999. E-mail: c.szymanski@tomeschool.org. Website: www.tomeschool.org

TOWER HILL SCHOOL

2813 West 17th Street
Wilmington, Delaware 19806

Head of School: Mrs. Elizabeth Speers

General Information Coeducational day college-preparatory and arts school. Grades PS–12. Founded: 1919. Setting: suburban. Nearest major city is Philadelphia, PA. 44-acre campus. 4 buildings on campus. Approved or accredited by Middle States Association of Colleges and Schools, Pennsylvania Association of Independent Schools, and Delaware Department of Education. Member of National Association of Independent Schools and Secondary School Admission Test Board. Endowment: $34 million. Total enrollment: 703. Upper school average class size: 14. Upper school faculty-student ratio: 1:6. There are 162 required school days per year for Upper School

students. Upper School students typically attend 5 days per week. The average school day consists of 7 hours.

Upper School Student Profile Grade 9: 67 students (34 boys, 33 girls); Grade 10: 66 students (32 boys, 34 girls); Grade 11: 74 students (37 boys, 37 girls); Grade 12: 75 students (37 boys, 38 girls).

Faculty School total: 118. In upper school: 23 men, 23 women; 29 have advanced degrees.

Subjects Offered Acting, advanced biology, advanced chemistry, advanced computer applications, advanced math, advanced studio art-AP, algebra, American government, American literature, art, art history, astronomy, band, biology, British literature, calculus, calculus-AP, chemistry, chemistry-AP, China/Japan history, chorus, civil rights, community service, computer science, digital imaging, drama, drawing, driver education, economics, electives, engineering, English, English literature, English-AP, European history, film, fine arts, French, geometry, health and wellness, historical research, history, human anatomy, jazz band, Latin, Latin American literature, Mandarin, mathematics, music, music theory, painting, photography, physical science, physics, poetry, politics, pre-calculus, Roman culture, SAT preparation, science, set design, Shakespeare, social issues, social justice, Spanish, Spanish literature, statistics, strings, theater, theater design and production, U.S. constitutional history, U.S. history, U.S. history-AP, voice ensemble, woodworking, world history, writing, writing, yearbook.

Graduation Requirements Arts, athletics, English, foreign language, mathematics, science, social studies (includes history). Community service is required.

Special Academic Programs Advanced Placement exam preparation; honors section; independent study; academic accommodation for the gifted, the musically talented, and the artistically talented; special instructional classes for deaf students.

College Admission Counseling 60 students graduated in 2016; all went to college, including Johns Hopkins University; New York University; Sewanee: The University of the South; The University of Alabama; University of Delaware; University of Miami. Median SAT critical reading: 650, median SAT math: 660, median SAT writing: 640, median composite ACT: 30. 67% scored over 600 on SAT critical reading, 75% scored over 600 on SAT math, 60% scored over 600 on SAT writing, 71% scored over 1800 on combined SAT, 73% scored over 26 on composite ACT.

Student Life Upper grades have specified standards of dress, student council, honor system. Discipline rests equally with students and faculty.

Summer Programs Enrichment, sports programs offered; session focuses on sports camps; held on campus; accepts boys and girls; open to students from other schools. 60 students usually enrolled. 2017 schedule: June 19 to August 8. Application deadline: June 15.

Tuition and Aid Day student tuition: $28,400. Tuition installment plan (monthly payment plans, 60/40). Merit scholarship grants, need-based scholarship grants available. In 2016–17, 28% of upper-school students received aid; total upper-school merit-scholarship money awarded: $125,000. Total amount of financial aid awarded in 2016–17: $1,300,000.

Admissions Traditional secondary level entrance grade is 9. For fall 2016, 101 students applied for upper-level admission, 75 were accepted, 29 enrolled. ERB, ISEE, PSAT or SAT for applicants to grade 11 and 12, SSAT, TOEFL or writing sample required. Deadline for receipt of application materials: January 6. Application fee required: $40. On-campus interview recommended.

Athletics Interscholastic: baseball (boys), basketball (b,g), cross-country running (b,g), field hockey (g), football (b), indoor track (b,g), lacrosse (b,g), soccer (b,g), swimming and diving (b,g), tennis (b,g), track and field (b,g), volleyball (g), winter (indoor) track (b,g), wrestling (b); intramural: dance (g), fitness (g), physical fitness (g), self defense (g), yoga (g); coed interscholastic: golf, squash; coed intramural: aerobics/Nautilus, independent competitive sports, physical training, strength & conditioning, weight lifting. 27 coaches, 2 athletic trainers.

Computers Computers are regularly used in all academic classes. Computer network features include on-campus library services, Internet access, wireless campus network, Internet filtering or blocking technology. Campus intranet, student e-mail accounts, and computer access in designated common areas are available to students. Students grades are available online. The school has a published electronic and media policy.

Contact Mr. William R. Ushler, Associate Director of Admission. 302-657-8350 Ext. 221. Fax: 302-657-8377. E-mail: wushler@towerhill.org. Website: www.towerhill.org

TRADITIONAL LEARNING ACADEMY

1189 Rochester Avenue
Coquitlam, British Columbia V3K 2X3, Canada

Head of School: Mr. Martin Charles Postgate Dale

General Information Coeducational day college-preparatory and general academic school, affiliated with Roman Catholic Church. Grades K–12. Founded: 1991. Setting: suburban. Nearest major city is Vancouver, Canada. 4-acre campus. 1 building on campus. Approved or accredited by British Columbia Department of Education. Language of instruction: English. Total enrollment: 200. Upper school average class size: 10. Upper school faculty-student ratio: 1:10. There are 185 required school days per year for Upper School students. Upper School students typically attend 5 days per week. The average school day consists of 5 hours and 55 minutes.

Upper School Student Profile Grade 8: 17 students (7 boys, 10 girls); Grade 9: 5 students (3 boys, 2 girls); Grade 10: 9 students (7 boys, 2 girls); Grade 11: 7 students (3

boys, 4 girls); Grade 12: 8 students (6 boys, 2 girls). 85% of students are Roman Catholic.

Faculty School total: 17. In upper school: 6 men, 4 women; 2 have advanced degrees.

Subjects Offered 20th century world history, art, art education, athletic training, Bible studies, biology, British literature, calculus, Canadian geography, Canadian history, career planning, Catholic belief and practice, chaplaincy, chemistry, choir, choral music, Christian doctrine, college admission preparation, computer education, dance, drama performance, English, English literature, French, French as a second language, grammar, history, Latin, mathematics, oral expression, participation in sports, physical education, physics, play production, prayer/spirituality, pre-algebra, pre-calculus, religion, religious education, science, scripture, social studies, speech, vocal music.

Graduation Requirements High School students must take a full schedule of all the courses offered. In grades 11 & 12, some choice of subjects may be offered.

College Admission Counseling 3 students graduated in 2015; 2 went to college, including Simon Fraser University; The University of British Columbia. Other: 1 entered military service.

Student Life Upper grades have uniform requirement, honor system. Discipline rests equally with students and faculty. Attendance at religious services is required.

Tuition and Aid Day student tuition: CAN$4000. Tuition installment plan (monthly payment plans, individually arranged payment plans). Tuition reduction for siblings, bursaries, need-based scholarship grants available. In 2015–16, 90% of upper-school students received aid. Total amount of financial aid awarded in 2015–16: CAN$25,000.

Admissions Traditional secondary-level entrance grade is 8. For fall 2015, 10 students applied for upper-level admission, 10 were accepted, 10 enrolled. English entrance exam required. Deadline for receipt of application materials: none. Application fee required: CAN$50. On-campus interview required.

Athletics Interscholastic: basketball (boys, girls), floor hockey (b), soccer (b,g), softball (b,g), track and field (b,g), volleyball (b,g); intramural: basketball (b,g), floor hockey (b), volleyball (g); coed interscholastic: Frisbee, ultimate Frisbee; coed intramural: alpine skiing, badminton, canoeing/kayaking, dance, hiking/backpacking, kayaking, tennis, ultimate Frisbee. 1 PE instructor.

Computers Computers are regularly used in career education classes. Computer resources include Internet access, Internet filtering or blocking technology.

Contact Mrs. Rina Caan, Secretary. 604-931-7265. Fax: 604-931-3432. E-mail: tlaoffice@traditionallearning.com. Website: www.traditionallearning.com

TRAFALGAR CASTLE SCHOOL

401 Reynolds Street
Whitby, Ontario L1N 3W9, Canada

Head of School: Dr. Leanne Foster

General Information Girls' boarding and day college-preparatory, arts, technology, and robotics school. Boarding grades 7–12, day grades 5–12. Founded: 1874. Setting: small town. Nearest major city is Toronto, Canada. Students are housed in single-sex dormitories. 17-acre campus. 2 buildings on campus. Approved or accredited by Canadian Association of Independent Schools, Ontario Ministry of Education, and Ontario Department of Education. Affiliate member of National Association of Independent Schools. Language of instruction: English. Endowment: CAN$955,000. Total enrollment: 191. Upper school average class size: 15. Upper school faculty-student ratio: 1:18. There are 170 required school days per year for Upper School students. Upper School students typically attend 5 days per week. The average school day consists of 7 hours.

Upper School Student Profile Grade 9: 32 students (32 girls); Grade 10: 30 students (30 girls); Grade 11: 34 students (34 girls); Grade 12: 42 students (42 girls). 38% of students are boarding students. 70% are province residents. 2 provinces are represented in upper school student body. 30% are international students. International students from Canada, Canada, China, Hong Kong, Mexico, and Republic of Korea.

Faculty School total: 30. In upper school: 5 men, 16 women; 9 have advanced degrees; 6 reside on campus.

Subjects Offered All academic.

Graduation Requirements Arts and fine arts (art, music, dance, drama), business skills (includes word processing), computer science, English, foreign language, mathematics, physical education (includes health), science, social studies (includes history).

Special Academic Programs Advanced Placement exam preparation; honors section; independent study; term-away projects; academic accommodation for the gifted, the musically talented, and the artistically talented; special instructional classes for students with individualized education plan; ESL (20 students enrolled).

College Admission Counseling 36 students graduated in 2016; all went to college, including McGill University; The University of British Columbia; The University of Western Ontario; University of Guelph; University of Ottawa; University of Toronto. Other: 1 entered military service.

Student Life Upper grades have uniform requirement, student council. Discipline rests primarily with faculty.

Tuition and Aid Day student tuition: CAN$21,115–CAN$23,390; 5-day tuition and room/board: CAN$41,475; 7-day tuition and room/board: CAN$44,940. Tuition installment plan (monthly payment plans, individually arranged payment plans, early payment discounts). Tuition reduction for siblings, bursaries, merit scholarship grants,

need-based scholarship grants available. In 2016–17, 3% of upper-school students received aid; total upper-school merit-scholarship money awarded: CAN$16,000. Total amount of financial aid awarded in 2016–17: CAN$43,000.

Admissions Traditional secondary-level entrance grade is 9. For fall 2016, 95 students applied for upper-level admission, 81 were accepted, 70 enrolled. Cognitive Abilities Test required. Deadline for receipt of application materials: none. Application fee required: CAN$2500. Interview required.

Athletics Interscholastic: badminton, basketball, cross-country running, field hockey, independent competitive sports, soccer, softball, swimming and diving, synchronized swimming, tennis, track and field, volleyball; intramural: badminton, basketball, dance team, field hockey, fitness, fitness walking, outdoor activities, outdoor adventure, outdoor education, physical fitness, ropes courses, rowing, running, skiing (cross-country), skiing (downhill), snowboarding, soccer, softball, swimming and diving, synchronized swimming, tennis, track and field, volleyball, yoga. 2 PE instructors.

Computers Computers are regularly used in all academic classes. Computer network features include on-campus library services, Internet access, wireless campus network, Internet filtering or blocking technology. Campus intranet and student e-mail accounts are available to students. Students grades are available online. The school has a published electronic and media policy.

Contact Ms. Rhonda Daley, Director of Enrolment Management. 905-668-3358 Ext. 254. Fax: 905-668-4136. E-mail: daley.rhonda@trafalgarcastle.ca. Website: www.trafalgarcastle.ca

TREVOR DAY SCHOOL

312 East 95th Street
New York, New York 10128

Head of School: Scott R. Reisinger

General Information Coeducational day college-preparatory school. Grades PK–12. Founded: 1930. Setting: urban. 1 building on campus. Approved or accredited by New York State Association of Independent Schools and New York Department of Education. Member of National Association of Independent Schools and Secondary School Admission Test Board. Endowment: $19.3 million. Total enrollment: 795. Upper school average class size: 14. Upper school faculty-student ratio: 1:6. There are 178 required school days per year for Upper School students. Upper School students typically attend 5 days per week. The average school day consists of 6 hours and 45 minutes.

Upper School Student Profile Grade 12: 68 students (34 boys, 34 girls).

Faculty School total: 150. In upper school: 26 men, 36 women; 44 have advanced degrees.

Subjects Offered All academic, American literature, ancient world history, art, art history, Asian literature, Basic programming, biology, British literature, choreography, chorus, college counseling, community service, computer programming, computer science, computer studies, concert band, creative writing, dance, discrete mathematics, drama, drama performance, drawing, economics, English, English literature, environmental science, equality and freedom, ethics, European history, expository writing, film and literature, filmmaking, fine arts, foreign language, forensics, French, genetics, geometry, grammar, Harlem Renaissance, health, Hispanic literature, history, honors English, independent study, intro to computers, jazz ensemble, literary magazine, madrigals, mathematics, model United Nations, music, musical productions, newspaper, peer counseling, performing arts, photography, photojournalism, physical education, physics, play production, playwriting, poetry, pottery, pre-calculus, science, senior internship, Shakespeare, Shakespearean histories, social studies, Spanish, stained glass, statistics, statistics-AP, student government, studio art, technical theater, theater, U.S. history-AP, video, Web site design, wilderness education, world history, world literature, writing, yearbook.

Graduation Requirements Arts and fine arts (art, music, dance, drama), computer science, English, ethics, foreign language, mathematics, physical education (includes health), science, social studies (includes history), 80 hours of community service.

Special Academic Programs Advanced Placement exam preparation; honors section; independent study; term-away projects; study at local college for college credit; academic accommodation for the gifted, the musically talented, and the artistically talented.

College Admission Counseling 55 students graduated in 2016; all went to college, including New York University; Oberlin College; Rice University; University of Pennsylvania; Washington University in St. Louis; Wesleyan University.

Student Life Upper grades have student council. Discipline rests equally with students and faculty.

Tuition and Aid Day student tuition: $46,600. Tuition installment plan (FACTS Tuition Payment Plan). Need-based scholarship grants available. In 2016–17, 20% of upper-school students received aid. Total amount of financial aid awarded in 2016–17: $5,884,000.

Admissions Traditional secondary-level entrance grade is 9. ISEE, PSAT, SAT, or ACT for applicants to grade 11 and 12 or SSAT required. Deadline for receipt of application materials: January 4. Application fee required: $60. On-campus interview recommended.

Athletics Interscholastic: baseball (boys), basketball (b,g), cross-country running (b,g), indoor track (b,g), indoor track & field (b,g), soccer (b,g), softball (g), tennis (b,g), track and field (b,g), volleyball (g); coed interscholastic: dance, golf, modern dance, outdoor education.

Computers Computers are regularly used in art, English, foreign language, history, mathematics, music, science classes. Computer network features include on-campus library services, online commercial services, Internet access, wireless campus network, Internet filtering or blocking technology, personal portals with homework and schedules for each student. Campus intranet and student e-mail accounts are available to students. Students grades are available online. The school has a published electronic and media policy.

Contact Karyn Delay, Director of Middle and Upper School Admissions and Financial Aid. 212-426-3380. E-mail: kdelay@trevor.org. Website: www.trevor.org

TRI-CITY CHRISTIAN ACADEMY

2211 W Germann Road
Chandler, Arizona 85286

Head of School: Lauren Brady

General Information Coeducational day college-preparatory and music school, affiliated with Baptist Church. Grades K–12. Founded: 1971. Setting: suburban. Nearest major city is Phoenix. 13-acre campus. 1 building on campus. Approved or accredited by Association of Christian Schools International. Total enrollment: 276. Upper school average class size: 30. Upper school faculty-student ratio: 1:7. There are 174 required school days per year for Upper School students. Upper School students typically attend 5 days per week. The average school day consists of 7 hours and 5 minutes.

Upper School Student Profile Grade 9: 24 students (7 boys, 17 girls); Grade 10: 30 students (16 boys, 14 girls); Grade 11: 31 students (18 boys, 13 girls); Grade 12: 25 students (13 boys, 12 girls). 30% of students are Baptist.

Faculty School total: 24. In upper school: 8 men, 7 women; 4 have advanced degrees.

Subjects Offered 20th century history, 20th century world history, algebra, American government, American history, American literature, applied music, athletic training, athletics, band, basic language skills, basketball, bell choir, Bible, Bible studies, biology, brass choir, business mathematics, calculus, career and personal planning, career/college preparation, cheerleading, chemistry, choir, choral music, chorus, Christian doctrine, Christian education, Christian ethics, Christian scripture, civics, computer applications, computer studies, computers, concert choir, debate, drama, drama performance, dramatic arts, English, English composition, English literature, ESL, foreign language, geometry, government, journalism, keyboarding, library skills, public speaking, Spanish, strings, U.S. history, voice and diction, volleyball, wind instruments, world history, yearbook.

Special Academic Programs Honors section; independent study; study at local college for college credit; ESL (10 students enrolled).

College Admission Counseling 23 students graduated in 2016; all went to college, including Arizona State University at the Tempe campus; Bob Jones University; Grand Canyon University; Northern Arizona University; The University of Arizona. Median SAT critical reading: 520, median SAT math: 620, median SAT writing: 560, median combined SAT: 1750, median composite ACT: 28. 36% scored over 600 on SAT critical reading, 57% scored over 600 on SAT math, 36% scored over 600 on SAT writing, 36% scored over 1800 on combined SAT, 50% scored over 26 on composite ACT.

Student Life Upper grades have uniform requirement, student council, honor system. Discipline rests primarily with faculty.

Tuition and Aid Day student tuition: $6500. Tuition installment plan (monthly payment plans). Tuition reduction for siblings, tuition tax scholarships available. In 2016–17, 40% of upper-school students received aid. Total amount of financial aid awarded in 2016–17: $25,000.

Admissions Traditional secondary-level entrance grade is 11. For fall 2016, 18 students applied for upper-level admission, 18 were accepted, 18 enrolled. Deadline for receipt of application materials: none. Application fee required: $225. On-campus interview recommended.

Athletics Interscholastic: baseball (boys), basketball (b,g), soccer (b,g), volleyball (g); coed interscholastic: golf. 2 PE instructors.

Computers Computers are regularly used in ESL, foreign language classes. Computer resources include on-campus library services, Internet access. Students grades are available online.

Contact 480-245-7902. Fax: 480-245-7908. Website: www.tcawarriors.org

TRINITY ACADEMY

12345 East 21st Street North
Wichita, Kansas 67206

Head of School: Mr. J Matthew Brewer

General Information Coeducational day college-preparatory and religious studies school, affiliated with Christian faith. Grades K–12. Founded: 1994. Setting: suburban. 80-acre campus. 1 building on campus. Approved or accredited by Association of Christian Schools International and North Central Association of Colleges and Schools. Total enrollment: 279. Upper school average class size: 16. Upper school faculty-student ratio: 1:12. There are 176 required school days per year for Upper School

students. Upper School students typically attend 5 days per week. The average school day consists of 7 hours and 15 minutes.

Upper School Student Profile Grade 9: 90 students (44 boys, 46 girls); Grade 10: 86 students (42 boys, 44 girls); Grade 11: 79 students (37 boys, 42 girls); Grade 12: 80 students (39 boys, 41 girls). 100% of students are Christian faith.

Faculty School total: 36. In upper school: 21 men, 15 women; 20 have advanced degrees.

Subjects Offered Advanced chemistry, advanced computer applications, advanced math, algebra, anatomy and physiology, art, band, Bible, biology, business, calculus, chemistry, choir, Christian ethics, community service, computer applications, creative writing, debate, desktop publishing, economics, electives, English, entrepreneurship, environmental science, environmental studies, ethics, forensics, geometry, honors algebra, honors English, honors geometry, jazz band, lab science, madrigals, New Testament, newspaper, photography, physics, pottery, pre-calculus, psychology, SAT/ACT preparation, sociology, sophomore skills, Spanish, speech, sports conditioning, theater arts, U.S. government, U.S. history, world history, yearbook.

Graduation Requirements Advanced math, algebra, Bible, biology, chemistry, computer applications, English, geometry, mathematics, physics, pre-calculus, Spanish, U.S. government, U.S. history, world history.

Special Academic Programs Honors section; study at local college for college credit; academic accommodation for the gifted; programs in general development for dyslexic students.

College Admission Counseling 84 students graduated in 2016, 81 went to college, including Baylor University; John Brown University; Kansas State University; The University of Kansas. Other: 2 entered military service, 1 had other specific plans. Mean SAT critical reading: 570, mean SAT math: 600, mean SAT writing: 600, mean composite ACT: 26. 36% scored over 600 on SAT critical reading, 45% scored over 600 on SAT math, 45% scored over 600 on SAT writing, 39% scored over 26 on composite ACT.

Student Life Upper grades have uniform requirement, student council. Discipline rests primarily with faculty. Attendance at religious services is required.

Summer Programs Advancement, sports, art/fine arts programs offered; held on campus; accepts boys and girls; open to students from other schools. 50 students usually enrolled. 2017 schedule: June 2 to June 2. Application deadline: May 1.

Tuition and Aid Day student tuition: $10,750. Tuition installment plan (FACTS Tuition Payment Plan). Need-based scholarship grants available. In 2016–17, 30% of upper-school students received aid. Total amount of financial aid awarded in 2016–17: $500,000.

Admissions Traditional secondary-level entrance grade is 9. For fall 2016, 110 students applied for upper-level admission, 107 were accepted, 106 enrolled. Math, reading, and mental ability tests, mathematics proficiency exam, OLSAT, Stanford Achievement Test, TerraNova or writing sample required. Deadline for receipt of application materials: none. Application fee required: $125. On-campus interview recommended.

Athletics Interscholastic: aquatics (boys, girls), baseball (b), basketball (b,g), bowling (b), cheering (g), cross-country running (b,g), drill team (g), fitness (b,g), football (b), golf (b), physical training (b,g), soccer (b,g), softball (g), strength & conditioning (b,g), swimming and diving (b,g), tennis (b,g), track and field (b,g), volleyball (g), weight training (b,g). 2 PE instructors, 26 coaches, 1 athletic trainer.

Computers Computers are regularly used in business education, digital applications, engineering, journalism, media production, newspaper, photojournalism, programming, Web site design, yearbook classes. Computer resources include on-campus library services, Internet access, wireless campus network, Internet filtering or blocking technology. Student e-mail accounts and computer access in designated common areas are available to students. Students grades are available online. The school has a published electronic and media policy.

Contact Mrs. Ellie Kriwiel, Director of Admissions. 316-634-0909. Fax: 316-634-0928. E-mail: kriwiele@trinityacademy.org. Website: www.trinityacademy.org

TRINITY CATHOLIC HIGH SCHOOL

926 Newfield Avenue
Stamford, Connecticut 06905

Head of School: Mr. Anthony Pavia

General Information Coeducational day college-preparatory school, affiliated with Roman Catholic Church. Grades 9–12. Distance learning grades 11–12. Founded: 1956. Setting: suburban. 27-acre campus. 1 building on campus. Approved or accredited by New England Association of Schools and Colleges and Connecticut Department of Education. Total enrollment: 429. Upper school average class size: 24. Upper school faculty-student ratio: 1:13. There are 180 required school days per year for Upper School students. Upper School students typically attend 5 days per week. The average school day consists of 6 hours and 10 minutes.

Upper School Student Profile Grade 9: 100 students (58 boys, 42 girls); Grade 10: 105 students (59 boys, 46 girls); Grade 11: 87 students (50 boys, 37 girls); Grade 12: 124 students (64 boys, 60 girls). 60% of students are Roman Catholic.

Faculty School total: 31. In upper school: 13 men, 18 women; 23 have advanced degrees.

Subjects Offered Advanced Placement courses, algebra, American history, American history-AP, American literature, anatomy, anatomy and physiology, art, art appreciation, art history, arts, audio visual/media, Bible studies, biology, British literature, calculus, calculus-AP, Catholic belief and practice, chemistry, chemistry-AP, civics, community service, composition-AP, computer applications, computer art, computer literacy, computer science, conceptual physics, digital art, drawing, earth science, economics, engineering, English, English language and composition-AP, English language-AP, English literature, English literature-AP, environmental science, environmental studies, European civilization, European history, European history-AP, fine arts, foreign language, forensics, geography, geometry, government, government/civics, health, health and wellness, honors English, honors geometry, honors U.S. history, honors world history, language arts, law, math applications, mathematics, New Testament, painting, personal fitness, physical education, physical science, physics, physics-AP, pre-calculus, psychology, religion, religious education, social studies, sociology, Spanish, Spanish language-AP, Spanish-AP, speech, trigonometry, video, video film production, visual arts, vocational arts, word processing, world history, world literature, world studies, writing.

Graduation Requirements Arts and fine arts (art, music, dance, drama), computer science, English, foreign language, mathematics, physical education (includes health), religion (includes Bible studies and theology), science, social studies (includes history). Community service is required.

Special Academic Programs 9 Advanced Placement exams for which test preparation is offered; honors section; study at local college for college credit; ESL (15 students enrolled).

College Admission Counseling 102 students graduated in 2016; 96 went to college, including Fairfield University; High Point University; Iona College; University of Connecticut; University of Rhode Island; Western Connecticut State University. Other: 2 entered a postgraduate year, 4 had other specific plans. Mean SAT critical reading: 513, mean SAT math: 497, mean SAT writing: 524, mean combined SAT: 1534, mean composite ACT: 21. 15% scored over 600 on SAT critical reading, 24% scored over 600 on SAT math, 19% scored over 600 on SAT writing, 16% scored over 1800 on combined SAT, 14% scored over 26 on composite ACT.

Student Life Upper grades have uniform requirement, student council. Discipline rests primarily with faculty. Attendance at religious services is required.

Summer Programs Remediation programs offered; session focuses on remediation; held both on and off campus; accepts boys and girls; open to students from other schools. 40 students usually enrolled. 2017 schedule: June 26 to August 4. Application deadline: June 23.

Tuition and Aid Day student tuition: $13,560. Tuition installment plan (SMART Tuition Payment Plan, individually arranged payment plans). Tuition reduction for siblings, merit scholarship grants, need-based scholarship grants available. In 2016–17, 31% of upper-school students received aid; total upper-school merit-scholarship money awarded: $149,000. Total amount of financial aid awarded in 2016–17: $477,260.

Admissions Traditional secondary-level entrance grade is 9. For fall 2016, 165 students applied for upper-level admission, 157 were accepted, 100 enrolled. High School Placement Test required. Deadline for receipt of application materials: none. Application fee required: $50. On-campus interview required.

Athletics Interscholastic: baseball (boys), basketball (b,g), cheering (g), diving (g), football (b), ice hockey (b), lacrosse (b), soccer (b,g), softball (g), tennis (b,g), volleyball (g); coed interscholastic: cross-country running, golf; coed intramural: swimming and diving. 1 PE instructor, 11 coaches, 1 athletic trainer.

Computers Computers are regularly used in all classes. Computer network features include online commercial services, Internet access, wireless campus network, Internet filtering or blocking technology. Student e-mail accounts are available to students. Students grades are available online. The school has a published electronic and media policy.

Contact Mr. Jon DeBenedictis, Director of Admissions. 203-322-3401 Ext. 302. Fax: 203-322-5330. E-mail: jdebenedictis@trinitycatholic.org. Website: www.trinitycatholic.org

TRINITY COLLEGE SCHOOL

55 Deblaquire Street North
Port Hope, Ontario L1A 4K7, Canada

Head of School: Mr. Stuart K.C. Grainger

General Information Coeducational boarding and day college-preparatory and liberal arts school, affiliated with Anglican Church of Canada. Boarding grades 9–12, day grades 5–12. Founded: 1865. Setting: small town. Nearest major city is Toronto, Canada. Students are housed in single-sex dormitories. 100-acre campus. 15 buildings on campus. Approved or accredited by Canadian Association of Independent Schools, Conference of Independent Schools of Ontario, The Association of Boarding Schools, and Ontario Department of Education. Affiliate member of National Association of Independent Schools; member of Secondary School Admission Test Board. Language of instruction: English. Endowment: CAN$54.3 million. Total enrollment: 562. Upper school average class size: 16. Upper school faculty-student ratio: 1:8. There are 165 required school days per year for Upper School students. Upper School students typically attend 5 days per week. The average school day consists of 6 hours.

Upper School Student Profile Grade 9: 82 students (44 boys, 38 girls); Grade 10: 114 students (64 boys, 50 girls); Grade 11: 132 students (75 boys, 57 girls); Grade 12: 125 students (73 boys, 52 girls). 60% of students are boarding students. 41% are province residents. 8 provinces are represented in upper school student body. 48% are

international students. International students from Bermuda, Cayman Islands, China, Mexico, Nigeria, and Saudi Arabia; 30 other countries represented in student body. 25% of students are members of Anglican Church of Canada.

Faculty School total: 79. In upper school: 33 men, 28 women; 18 have advanced degrees; 13 reside on campus.

Subjects Offered Algebra, American history, art, art history-AP, astronomy, biology, biology-AP, calculus, calculus-AP, Canadian geography, Canadian history, Canadian law, career education, career/college preparation, chemistry, chemistry-AP, civics, classical civilization, community service, comparative government and politics-AP, computer programming, computer science, computer science-AP, creative writing, dramatic arts, earth science, economics, English, English language-AP, English literature, English literature-AP, environmental science, environmental science-AP, environmental studies, ESL, fine arts, finite math, French, French-AP, general science, geography, geometry, German, guidance, health education, history, human geography - AP, independent study, Latin, law, mathematics, microeconomics-AP, music, music theory-AP, outdoor education, philosophy, physical education, physics, physics-AP, political science, politics, research seminar, social justice, society challenge and change, Spanish, statistics-AP, studio art-AP, world history, world history-AP.

Graduation Requirements Arts, Canadian geography, Canadian history, civics, English, French, guidance, mathematics, physical education (includes health), science, social sciences, technology, minimum 40 hours of community service, provincial literacy test completion, addtional arts and language credits.

Special Academic Programs 16 Advanced Placement exams for which test preparation is offered; term-away projects; study abroad; ESL (27 students enrolled).

College Admission Counseling 127 students graduated in 2016; 12 went to college, including Queen's University at Kingston; St. Francis Xavier University; The University of Western Ontario; University of Toronto; University of Waterloo; Wilfrid Laurier University. Other: 7 had other specific plans. Mean SAT critical reading: 539, mean SAT math: 596, mean SAT writing: 552, mean combined SAT: 539.

Student Life Upper grades have uniform requirement, student council, honor system. Discipline rests primarily with faculty. Attendance at religious services is required.

Summer Programs Enrichment, advancement, ESL programs offered; session focuses on advancement through cultural enrichment; held both on and off campus; held at England; accepts boys and girls; open to students from other schools. 30 students usually enrolled. 2017 schedule: July 4 to July 26. Application deadline: May 1.

Tuition and Aid Day student tuition: CAN$22,950–CAN$31,850; 7-day tuition and room/board: CAN$38,950–CAN$56,950. Tuition installment plan (monthly payment plans, quarterly payment plan (domestic students only), three payment option (international students)). Bursaries, merit scholarship grants, need-based scholarship grants available. In 2016–17, 30% of upper-school students received aid; total upper-school merit-scholarship money awarded: CAN$156,100. Total amount of financial aid awarded in 2016–17: CAN$2,407,200.

Admissions Traditional secondary-level entrance grade is 9. For fall 2016, 309 students applied for upper-level admission, 272 were accepted, 176 enrolled. Otis-Lennon Ability or Stanford Achievement Test, SSAT or TOEFL required. Deadline for receipt of application materials: none. Application fee required: CAN$150. Interview required.

Athletics Interscholastic: baseball (boys), basketball (b,g), cricket (b), field hockey (g), football (b), ice hockey (b,g), rugby (b,g), soccer (b,g), squash (b,g), tennis (b,g), volleyball (g); coed interscholastic: alpine skiing, badminton, cross-country running, golf, nordic skiing, outdoor education, rowing, swimming and diving, track and field; coed intramural: aerobics, aerobics/dance, alpine skiing, badminton, basketball, canoeing/kayaking, cooperative games, cricket, cross-country running, dance, dance squad, fitness, golf, gymnastics, hiking/backpacking, horseback riding, ice hockey, skiing (downhill), snowboarding, soccer, softball, squash, strength & conditioning, swimming and diving, table tennis, tennis, ultimate Frisbee, weight lifting, weight training, yoga. 4 PE instructors, 5 coaches, 2 athletic trainers.

Computers Computers are regularly used in all academic classes. Computer network features include on-campus library services, Internet access, wireless campus network, Internet filtering or blocking technology. Campus intranet and student e-mail accounts are available to students. Students grades are available online. The school has a published electronic and media policy.

Contact Ms. Kathryn A. LaBranche, Director of Admissions. 905-885-3217 Ext. 1208. Fax: 905-885-7444. E-mail: admissions@tcs.on.ca. Website: www.tcs.on.ca

TRINITY EPISCOPAL SCHOOL

3850 Pittaway Drive
Richmond, Virginia 23235

Head of School: Mr. Robert A. Short

General Information Coeducational day college-preparatory and International Baccalaureate school, affiliated with Episcopal Church. Grades 8–12. Founded: 1972. Setting: suburban. 40-acre campus. 6 buildings on campus. Approved or accredited by International Baccalaureate Organization, National Association of Episcopal Schools, Virginia Association of Independent Schools, and Virginia Department of Education. Member of National Association of Independent Schools. Endowment: $300,000. Total enrollment: 495. Upper school average class size: 14. Upper school faculty-student ratio: 1:9. There are 180 required school days per year for Upper School students.

Upper School students typically attend 5 days per week. The average school day consists of 7 hours and 10 minutes.

Faculty School total: 60. In upper school: 30 have advanced degrees.

Subjects Offered 20th century history, 20th century world history, 3-dimensional art, Advanced Placement courses, advanced studio art-AP, algebra, American government, American history, American history-AP, American literature, American politics in film, anatomy, art, astronomy, band, Bible studies, biology, biology-AP, calculus, calculus-AP, chemistry, chemistry-AP, chorus, computer graphics, computer programming, computer science, concert band, concert choir, creative writing, digital music, drama, driver education, earth science, economics, English, English literature, English-AP, environmental science, European history, European history-AP, filmmaking, foreign policy, French, French-AP, geography, geology, geometry, German, German-AP, government-AP, government/civics, International Baccalaureate courses, jazz band, keyboarding, Latin, math analysis, mathematics, music, physics, physics-AP, pre-calculus, religion, science, social sciences, social studies, Southern literature, Spanish, studio art-AP, theater, theology, theory of knowledge, trigonometry, U.S. government and politics-AP, U.S. history-AP, Web site design, word processing, world history, world literature, world religions, writing.

Graduation Requirements Arts and fine arts (art, music, dance, drama), athletics, English, foreign language, mathematics, religion (includes Bible studies and theology), science, social studies (includes history), Junior Work Week. Community service is required.

Special Academic Programs International Baccalaureate program; 10 Advanced Placement exams for which test preparation is offered; honors section; independent study; academic accommodation for the gifted, the musically talented, and the artistically talented.

College Admission Counseling 116 students graduated in 2016; all went to college, including James Madison University; Longwood University; The College of William and Mary; University of Virginia; Virginia Commonwealth University; Virginia Polytechnic Institute and State University. Mean SAT critical reading: 583, mean SAT math: 574.

Student Life Upper grades have specified standards of dress, student council, honor system. Discipline rests equally with students and faculty. Attendance at religious services is required.

Summer Programs Enrichment, advancement, sports, art/fine arts, rigorous outdoor training, computer instruction programs offered; held on campus; accepts boys and girls; open to students from other schools. 250 students usually enrolled. 2017 schedule: June 1 to August 10. Application deadline: April 1.

Tuition and Aid Day student tuition: $22,800. Tuition installment plan (Insured Tuition Payment Plan, FACTS Tuition Payment Plan). Merit scholarship grants, need-based scholarship grants available. In 2016–17, 30% of upper-school students received aid.

Admissions Traditional secondary-level entrance grade is 9. Otis-Lennon, Stanford Achievement Test required. Deadline for receipt of application materials: February 10. Application fee required: $50. On-campus interview recommended.

Athletics Interscholastic: baseball (boys), basketball (b,g), cross-country running (b,g), field hockey (g), football (b), indoor soccer (b,g), lacrosse (b,g), soccer (b,g), softball (g), tennis (b,g), track and field (b,g), volleyball (b,g), winter soccer (b,g); coed interscholastic: aquatics, canoeing/kayaking, diving, golf, indoor track, kayaking, mountain biking, paddling, running, swimming and diving, winter (indoor) track; coed intramural: aerobics/dance, backpacking, canoeing/kayaking, climbing, dance, fitness, outdoor activities, outdoor adventure, outdoor education, outdoor recreation, outdoor skills, physical fitness, physical training, rappelling, rock climbing, scuba diving, strength & conditioning, table tennis, wall climbing, weight lifting, weight training, yoga. 1 PE instructor, 14 coaches, 2 athletic trainers.

Computers Computers are regularly used in animation, graphic design, library, library skills, music technology, photography, science, social studies, video film production, word processing, writing, yearbook classes. Computer network features include on-campus library services, online commercial services, Internet access, wireless campus network, Internet filtering or blocking technology, 1:1 Apple laptop program. Campus intranet and student e-mail accounts are available to students. Students grades are available online. The school has a published electronic and media policy.

Contact Mrs. Margie Snead, Director of Admission. 804-327-3151. Fax: 804-272-4652. E-mail: margiesnead@trinityes.org. Website: www.trinityes.org

TRINITY HIGH SCHOOL

4011 Shelbyville Road
Louisville, Kentucky 40207-9427

Head of School: Robert J. Mullen, EdD

General Information Boys' day college-preparatory school, affiliated with Roman Catholic Church. Grades 9–12. Founded: 1953. Setting: suburban. 110-acre campus. 11 buildings on campus. Approved or accredited by National Catholic Education Association, Southern Association of Colleges and Schools, Southern Association of Independent Schools, and Kentucky Department of Education. Member of National Association of Independent Schools. Endowment: $21 million. Total enrollment: 1,230. Upper school average class size: 19. Upper school faculty-student ratio: 1:12. There are 175 required school days per year for Upper School students. Upper School students typically attend 5 days per week. The average school day consists of 7 hours.

Upper School Student Profile Grade 9: 320 students (320 boys); Grade 10: 300 students (300 boys); Grade 11: 310 students (310 boys); Grade 12: 300 students (300 boys). 84% of students are Roman Catholic.

Faculty School total: 120. In upper school: 88 men, 30 women; 110 have advanced degrees.

Subjects Offered 20th century history, 3-dimensional art, accounting, acting, adolescent issues, advanced chemistry, advanced computer applications, advanced math, Advanced Placement courses, advanced studio art-AP, algebra, American Civil War, American democracy, American foreign policy, American government, American history, American history-AP, American literature, American literature-AP, analysis and differential calculus, analysis of data, anatomy and physiology, ancient history, ancient world history, applied arts, applied music, art, art and culture, art appreciation, art education, art history, art-AP, arts, arts appreciation, athletic training, athletics, band, banking, Basic programming, Bible as literature, biology, biology-AP, broadcasting, business, business education, business law, business mathematics, business studies, business technology, calculus, calculus-AP, campus ministry, career exploration, career planning, career/college preparation, cell biology, character education, cheerleading, chemistry, chemistry-AP, choir, choral music, chorus, Christian doctrine, Christian ethics, Christian scripture, church history, cinematography, civics, Civil War, classical civilization, classical Greek literature, classical music, college admission preparation, college awareness, college counseling, college placement, college planning, communication arts, communication skills, community service, comparative cultures, comparative government and politics, composition AP, computer animation, computer applications, computer art, computer education, computer graphics, computer information systems, computer literacy, computer math, computer multimedia, computer music, computer processing, computer programming, computer science, computer skills, computer studies, computer technologies, computer technology certification, computer tools, computers, concert band, concert choir, conflict resolution, constitutional law, contemporary art, CPR, creative writing, critical studies in film, critical thinking, critical writing, data analysis, data processing, death and loss, decision making skills, developmental math, digital photography, DNA research, drama, drama performance, drawing, drawing and design, earth and space science, earth science, ecology, economics, economics and history, economics-AP, English, English language and composition-AP, English literature, English-AP, environmental studies, European civilization, European history, evolution, family living, fencing, film, film studies, finite math, first aid, forensics, French, general science, geography, geometry, German, health, health science, Hebrew scripture, Holocaust studies, HTML design, humanities, independent study, information technology, instrumental music, integrated mathematics, interdisciplinary studies, Internet, jazz band, journalism, keyboarding, language arts, leadership and service, literature, literature-AP, martial arts, mathematics, modern civilization, moral and social development, multimedia design, music performance, musical theater, New Testament, news writing, newspaper, oil painting, painting, peace and justice, philosophy, photography, photojournalism, physical education, physical fitness, physical science, physics, physics-AP, post-calculus, pottery, pre-algebra, pre calculus, probability and statistics, programming, psychology, public speaking, religion, religious studies, Roman civilization, Romantic period literature, Russian history, SAT/ACT preparation, science, sculpture, senior seminar, social justice, social psychology, social sciences, social studies, sociology, software design, space and physical sciences, Spanish, Spanish literature, Spanish-AP, speech and debate, sports medicine, sports nutrition, stage design, stained glass, statistics, student government, student publications, technology, trigonometry, U.S. government and politics-AP, U.S. history-AP, video film production, Web site design, weight training, Western civilization, work-study, world civilizations, world history, world history-AP, yearbook.

Graduation Requirements ACT preparation, algebra, biology, chemistry, Christian and Hebrew scripture, Christian ethics, church history, civics, communication arts, computer education, English, English literature, European literature, foreign language, grammar, health and wellness, humanities, lab science, mathematics, physical education (includes health), physics, pre-calculus, reading, religion (includes Bible studies and theology), science, social justice, social studies (includes history), U.S. history, world geography, several elective offerings, must have taken the ACT. Community service is required.

Special Academic Programs Advanced Placement exam preparation; honors section; independent study; study at local college for college credit; study abroad; academic accommodation for the gifted, the musically talented, and the artistically talented; remedial reading and/or remedial writing; remedial math; programs in English, mathematics, general development for dyslexic students; special instructional classes for deaf students, blind students.

College Admission Counseling 292 students graduated in 2016; 289 went to college, including Bellarmine University; Eastern Kentucky University; Indiana University Bloomington; University of Dayton; University of Kentucky; University of Louisville. Other: 2 went to work, 1 entered military service. Mean combined SAT: 1817, mean composite ACT: 24.

Student Life Upper grades have specified standards of dress, student council, honor system. Discipline rests primarily with faculty. Attendance at religious services is required.

Summer Programs Remediation, enrichment, advancement, sports, art/fine arts, computer instruction programs offered; session focuses on academic advancement and enrichment/sports camps; held on campus; accepts boys; not open to students from other schools. 1,000 students usually enrolled. 2017 schedule: June 1 to August 3. Application deadline: May 15.

Tuition and Aid Day student tuition: $13,200. Guaranteed tuition plan. Tuition installment plan (FACTS Tuition Payment Plan). Merit scholarship grants, need-based scholarship grants, paying campus jobs available. In 2016–17, 44% of upper-school students received aid; total upper-school merit-scholarship money awarded: $120,000. Total amount of financial aid awarded in 2016–17: $2,800,000.

Admissions Traditional secondary-level entrance grade is 9. High School Placement Test required. Deadline for receipt of application materials: none. Application fee required: $75. On-campus interview recommended.

Athletics Interscholastic: archery, baseball, basketball, bicycling, bowling, cheering, crew, cross-country running, diving, fishing, football, golf, hockey, ice hockey, lacrosse, power lifting, rugby, soccer, swimming and diving, tennis, track and field, volleyball, weight lifting, wrestling; intramural: alpine skiing, basketball, bocce, climbing, cricket, fencing, fishing, flag football, freestyle skiing, Frisbee, golf, hiking/backpacking, judo, kickball, life saving, martial arts, mountain biking, outdoor adventure, paddle tennis, rock climbing, skiing (downhill), snowboarding, strength & conditioning, table tennis, ultimate Frisbee, volleyball, water polo, weight lifting, weight training; coed intramural: bowling. 5 PE instructors, 30 coaches, 3 athletic trainers.

Computers Computers are regularly used in all academic classes. Computer network features include on-campus library services, online commercial services, Internet access, wireless campus network, Internet filtering or blocking technology, free use of Office 365, cloud-based document storage. Campus intranet, student e-mail accounts, and computer access in designated common areas are available to students. Students grades are available online. The school has a published electronic and media policy.

Contact Mr. James Torra, Director of Admissions. 502-736-2120. Fax: 502-899-2052. E-mail: torra@thsrock.net. Website: www.trinityrocks.com

TRINITY HIGH SCHOOL

581 Bridge Street
Manchester, New Hampshire 03104

Head of School: Mr. Denis Mailloux

General Information Coeducational day college-preparatory, arts, religious studies, and technology school, affiliated with Roman Catholic Church. Grades 9–12. Founded: 1886. Setting: urban. Nearest major city is Boston, MA. 5-acre campus. 2 buildings on campus. Approved or accredited by National Catholic Education Association, New England Association of Schools and Colleges, and New Hampshire Department of Education. Total enrollment: 398. Upper school average class size: 15. Upper school faculty-student ratio: 1:12. There are 180 required school days per year for Upper School students. Upper School students typically attend 5 days per week. The average school day consists of 6 hours and 40 minutes.

Upper School Student Profile Grade 9: 91 students (46 boys, 45 girls); Grade 10: 85 students (38 boys, 47 girls); Grade 11: 110 students (65 boys, 45 girls); Grade 12: 112 students (63 boys, 49 girls). 80% of students are Roman Catholic.

Faculty School total: 34. In upper school: 20 men, 14 women; 25 have advanced degrees.

Subjects Offered 3-dimensional art, advanced biology, advanced math, Advanced Placement courses, algebra, American government, American history, American history-AP, American literature, analysis and anatomy and physiology, art, Bible studies, biology, calculus, calculus-AP, chemistry, computer science, driver education, English, English literature, English-AP, ethics, French, geometry, grammar, health, history, human development, journalism, Latin, mathematics, physical education, physics, psychology, psychology-AP, religion, science, social studies, sociology, Spanish, theology, trigonometry, U.S. history-AP, world history, world literature.

Special Academic Programs 5 Advanced Placement exams for which test preparation is offered; honors section; study at local college for college credit.

College Admission Counseling 101 students graduated in 2015; 95 went to college, including Boston University; Keene State College; Northeastern University; Saint Anselm College; Stonehill College; University of New Hampshire. Other: 4 went to work, 2 entered a postgraduate year.

Student Life Upper grades have specified standards of dress, student council, honor system. Discipline rests primarily with faculty. Attendance at religious services is required.

Tuition and Aid Day student tuition: $10,875. Tuition installment plan (FACTS Tuition Payment Plan). Need-based scholarship grants available. In 2015–16, 10% of upper-school students received aid.

Admissions Traditional secondary-level entrance grade is 9. STS required. Deadline for receipt of application materials: none. Application fee required: $50. Interview recommended.

Athletics Interscholastic: baseball (boys), basketball (b,g), cheering (g), crew (b,g), cross-country running (b,g), football (b), gymnastics (g), hockey (b), ice hockey (b), indoor track & field (b,g), lacrosse (b), skiing (cross-country) (b,g), skiing (downhill) (b,g), soccer (b,g), softball (g), swimming and diving (b,g), tennis (b,g), volleyball (g), winter (indoor) track (b,g), wrestling (b); coed interscholastic: alpine skiing, golf, track and field; coed intramural: gymnastics. 1 PE instructor, 25 coaches, 1 athletic trainer.

Computers Computers are regularly used in all academic, English, journalism, science, social sciences, yearbook classes. Computer network features include Internet

access, wireless campus network. Campus intranet and student e-mail accounts are available to students. Students grades are available online.

Contact Mr. Patrick Smith, Dean of Students and Director of Admissions. 603-668-2910 Ext. 218. Fax: 603-668-2913. E-mail: psmith@trinity-hs.org. Website: www.trinity-hs.org

TRINITY HIGH SCHOOL

12425 Granger Road
Garfield Heights, Ohio 44125

Head of School: Mrs. Linda Bacho

General Information Coeducational day college-preparatory, technical, and medical school, affiliated with Roman Catholic Church. Grades 9–12. Founded: 1926. Setting: suburban. Nearest major city is Cleveland. 26-acre campus. 3 buildings on campus. Approved or accredited by National Catholic Education Association, North Central Association of Colleges and Schools, Ohio Catholic Schools Accreditation Association (OCSAA), and Ohio Department of Education. Total enrollment: 327. Upper school average class size: 17. Upper school faculty-student ratio: 1:10. There are 199 required school days per year for Upper School students. Upper School students typically attend 5 days per week. The average school day consists of 7 hours.

Upper School Student Profile Grade 9: 93 students (25 boys, 68 girls); Grade 10: 67 students (30 boys, 37 girls); Grade 11: 87 students (43 boys, 44 girls); Grade 12: 73 students (35 boys, 38 girls). 73% of students are Roman Catholic.

Faculty School total: 30. In upper school: 10 men, 20 women; 16 have advanced degrees.

Subjects Offered 3-dimensional art, accounting, advanced biology, advanced chemistry, advanced computer applications, advanced math, Advanced Placement courses, advanced studio art-AP, algebra, American government, American history, American history-AP, American literature, analysis and differential calculus, anatomy and physiology, animation, art, athletics, automated accounting, band, Bible, Bible studies, biology, bookkeeping, British literature, British literature (honors), business applications, business skills, business technology, calculus-AP, campus ministry, career and personal planning, career education, career education internship, career experience, career exploration, career planning, career/college preparation, Catholic belief and practice, ceramics, chemistry, choir, Christian and Hebrew scripture, Christian doctrine, Christian ethics, Christian scripture, Christian testament, church history, college admission preparation, college awareness, college counseling, college placement, college planning, college writing, communication skills, community service, comparative religion, competitive science projects, computer animation, computer applications, computer art, computer education, computer graphics, computer information systems, computer multimedia, computer technologies, computer technology certification, computer-aided design, concert band, concert choir, consumer economics, creative writing, critical thinking, critical writing, culinary arts, digital applications, drama performance, drawing and design, earth science, economics and history, electives, English, English literature and composition-AP, environmental science, ethics, European history, food and nutrition, foods, foreign language, four units of summer reading, geometry, global studies, government-AP, graphic arts, graphic design, graphics, guidance, health education, honors algebra, honors English, honors geometry, human anatomy, human biology, instrumental music, integrated mathematics, Internet research, internship, lab science, library, life issues, Life of Christ, marching band, marine biology, Microsoft, moral theology, musical theater, neuroscience, oral communications, participation in sports, peace and justice, peer ministry, personal finance, photo shop, physical education, physics, play production, portfolio art, prayer/spirituality, pre-algebra, pre-calculus, psychology, public speaking, SAT/ACT preparation, speech, sports, studio art-AP, study skills, symphonic band, theology, U.S. government and politics-AP, video, video and animation, vocal ensemble, Web site design, wind ensemble, word processing, world history, yearbook.

Graduation Requirements Arts and fine arts (art, music, dance, drama), electives, English, government, human relations, mathematics, physical education (includes health), science, social studies (includes history), theology, Western civilization, service hours, internship.

Special Academic Programs Advanced Placement exam preparation; honors section; independent study; academic accommodation for the gifted and the artistically talented; remedial math; programs in English, mathematics, general development for dyslexic students.

College Admission Counseling 95 students graduated in 2016; 93 went to college, including John Carroll University; Kent State University; Miami University; Ohio University; The Ohio State University; University of Dayton. Other: 1 went to work, 1 entered military service. Median composite ACT: 21. 6% scored over 26 on composite ACT.

Student Life Upper grades have uniform requirement, student council. Discipline rests primarily with faculty. Attendance at religious services is required.

Summer Programs Enrichment, advancement, sports, art/fine arts programs offered; session focuses on recruitment; held both on and off campus; accepts boys and girls; open to students from other schools. 125 students usually enrolled. 2017 schedule: June 12 to June 30. Application deadline: May 30.

Tuition and Aid Day student tuition: $11,400. Guaranteed tuition plan. Tuition installment plan (individually arranged payment plans, private bank loans). Tuition reduction for siblings, need-based scholarship grants, middle-income loans, private bank loans available. In 2016–17, 25% of upper-school students received aid. Total amount of financial aid awarded in 2016–17: $150,000.

Admissions Traditional secondary-level entrance grade is 9. For fall 2016, 103 students applied for upper-school admission, 100 were accepted, 93 enrolled. Scholastic Testing Service High School Placement Test required. Deadline for receipt of application materials: none. Application fee required: $20. On-campus interview recommended.

Athletics Interscholastic: baseball (boys), basketball (b,g), cheering (g), cross-country running (b,g), danceline (g), football (b), soccer (b,g), softball (g), track and field (b,g), volleyball (g), wrestling (b); coed interscholastic: golf, indoor track & field; coed intramural: skiing (downhill), snowboarding. 1 PE instructor, 34 coaches, 1 athletic trainer.

Computers Computers are regularly used in all academic classes. Computer network features include on-campus library services, online commercial services, Internet access, wireless campus network, Internet filtering or blocking technology, network printing, personal storage on network, weekly email grade reports, electronic newsletters, remote access, school Web site, online homework tracking system. Student e-mail accounts and computer access in designated common areas are available to students. Students grades are available online. The school has a published electronic and media policy.

Contact Sr. Dian Majsterek, Administrative Assistant, Admissions and Marketing. 216-581-1061. Fax: 216-581-9348. E-mail: SisterDian@ths.org. Website: www.ths.org

TRINITY-PAWLING SCHOOL

700 Route 22
Pawling, New York 12564

Head of School: Mr. William W. Taylor

General Information Boys' boarding and day college-preparatory and language through enrichment, analysis, and development school, affiliated with Episcopal Church. Boarding grades 9–PG, day grades 7–PG. Founded: 1907. Setting: small town. Nearest major city is New York. Students are housed in single-sex dormitories. 140-acre campus. 31 buildings on campus. Approved or accredited by New York State Association of Independent Schools and New York Department of Education. Member of National Association of Independent Schools and Secondary School Admission Test Board. Endowment: $35 million. Total enrollment: 285. Upper school average class size: 12. Upper school faculty-student ratio: 1:8. There are 186 required school days per year for Upper School students. Upper School students typically attend 6 days per week. The average school day consists of 6 hours and 30 minutes.

Upper School Student Profile Grade 9: 37 students (37 boys); Grade 10: 50 students (50 boys); Grade 11: 83 students (83 boys); Grade 12: 87 students (87 boys); Postgraduate: 13 students (13 boys). 76% of students are boarding students. 42% are state residents. 23 states are represented in upper school student body. 28% are international students. International students from Canada, China, Hong Kong, Republic of Korea, Taiwan, and Viet Nam; 8 other countries represented in student body. 20% of students are members of Episcopal Church.

Faculty School total: 56. In upper school: 37 men, 19 women; 37 have advanced degrees; 52 reside on campus.

Subjects Offered Advanced Placement courses, advanced studio art-AP, algebra, American government, American history, American legal systems, American literature, American studies, anatomy, anatomy and physiology, architectural drawing, art, art history, art history-AP, Asian history, Asian studies, astronomy, Bible, biology, biology-AP, calculus, calculus-AP, ceramics, chemistry, chemistry-AP, choir, chorus, Christian ethics, civil rights, composition-AP, computer applications, computer information systems, computer math, computer music, computer programming, computer science, computer science-AP, computer technologies, constitutional history of U.S., data analysis, drafting, drama, drama performance, earth science, East Asian history, ecology, economics, economics-AP, English, English language-AP, English literature, English literature-AP, English-AP, English/composition-AP, environmental science, environmental science-AP, environmental studies, ESL, ethics, European history, European history-AP, fine arts, French, French language-AP, French studies, geology, geometry, government, government and politics-AP, government/civics, grammar, health science, history, honors algebra, honors English, honors geometry, honors U.S. history, honors world history, human anatomy, keyboarding, Latin, Latin American literature, Latin-AP, law and the legal system, literature, literature and composition-AP, Mandarin, mathematics, mechanical drawing, model United Nations, music, philosophy, photography, physical education, physics, physics-AP, physiology, political science, pre-calculus, probability and statistics, psychology, public speaking, reading/study skills, religion, religious education, religious studies, SAT preparation, science, Shakespeare, social justice, social sciences, social studies, Spanish, Spanish language-AP, Spanish literature-AP, statistics-AP, studio art, studio art-AP, study skills, theater, theology, trigonometry, U.S. government and politics, U.S. history, U.S. history-AP, Vietnam War, word processing, world history, writing, yearbook.

Graduation Requirements Arts and fine arts (art, music, dance, drama), English, foreign language, mathematics, religion (includes Bible studies and theology), science, social studies (includes history).

Special Academic Programs 17 Advanced Placement exams for which test preparation is offered; honors section; independent study; remedial reading and/or

remedial writing; programs in English for dyslexic students; ESL (44 students enrolled).

College Admission Counseling 81 students graduated in 2016; 80 went to college, including Cornell University; Elon University; Hobart and William Smith Colleges; Penn State University Park; Sewanee: The University of the South; University of Richmond. Other: 1 had other specific plans. Mean SAT critical reading: 580, mean SAT math: 570.

Student Life Upper grades have specified standards of dress, student council, honor system. Discipline rests equally with students and faculty. Attendance at religious services is required.

Tuition and Aid Day student tuition: $40,000; 7-day tuition and room/board: $56,500. Tuition installment plan (monthly payment plans, individually arranged payment plans, payment plans are arranged directly with the school business office). Need-based scholarship grants, need-based loans, middle-income loans, loans are arranged directly through the Your Tuition Solution Plan available. In 2016–17, 40% of upper-school students received aid. Total amount of financial aid awarded in 2016–17: $3,500,000.

Admissions Traditional secondary-level entrance grade is 9. For fall 2016, 368 students applied for upper-level admission, 183 were accepted, 94 enrolled. PSAT or SAT, SSAT, TOEFL, Wechsler Intelligence Scale for Children III or WISC-R required. Deadline for receipt of application materials: January 15. Application fee required: $50. On-campus interview recommended.

Athletics Interscholastic: alpine skiing, baseball, basketball, cross-country running, football, golf, hockey, ice hockey, lacrosse, ropes courses, skiing (downhill), soccer, squash, strength & conditioning, tennis, track and field, weight lifting, weight training, wrestling; intramural: alpine skiing, basketball, bicycling, climbing, fishing, fitness, floor hockey, Frisbee, golf, hiking/backpacking, mountain biking, outdoor education, outdoor recreation, physical training, polo, rock climbing, running, skiing (downhill), snowboarding, soccer, softball, squash, strength & conditioning, tennis, trap and skeet, ultimate Frisbee, wall climbing, weight lifting. 30 coaches, 2 athletic trainers.

Computers Computers are regularly used in English, history, mathematics, remedial study skills, science classes. Computer network features include on-campus library services, online commercial services, Internet access, wireless campus network, Internet filtering or blocking technology. Campus intranet, student e-mail accounts, and computer access in designated common areas are available to students. Students grades are available online. The school has a published electronic and media policy.

Contact Ms. Amy Heinrich, Admission Office Manager. 845-855-4825. Fax: 845-855-4827. E-mail: aheinrich@trinitypawling.org. Website: www.trinitypawling.org

TRINITY PREPARATORY SCHOOL

5700 Trinity Prep Lane
Winter Park, Florida 32792

Head of School: Byron M. Lawson Jr.

General Information Coeducational day college-preparatory, arts, and Malone Schools Online Network school, affiliated with Episcopal Church. Grades 6–12. Founded: 1966. Setting: suburban. Nearest major city is Orlando. 104-acre campus. 12 buildings on campus. Approved or accredited by Florida Council of Independent Schools and Florida Department of Education. Member of National Association of Independent Schools and Secondary School Admission Test Board. Total enrollment: 861. Upper school average class size: 18. Upper school faculty-student ratio: 1:12. There are 175 required school days per year for Upper School students. Upper School students typically attend 5 days per week. The average school day consists of 5 hours and 45 minutes.

Upper School Student Profile Grade 9: 131 students (65 boys, 66 girls); Grade 10: 129 students (66 boys, 63 girls); Grade 11: 129 students (74 boys, 55 girls); Grade 12: 127 students (72 boys, 55 girls). 7% of students are members of Episcopal Church.

Faculty School total: 75. In upper school: 23 men, 34 women; 34 have advanced degrees.

Subjects Offered 20th century American writers, 20th century world history, 3-dimensional art, advanced math, Advanced Placement courses, advanced studio art-AP, algebra, American history, American literature, anatomy, animal science, art, athletic training, audio visual/media, band, Basic programming, Bible, biology, biology-AP, calculus, calculus-AP, character education, chemistry, chemistry-AP, chorus, civics, comparative religion, computer graphics, computer multimedia, computer processing, computer programming, computer programming-AP, concert band, concert choir, creative writing, critical studies in film, digital photography, drama, drawing, economics, economics-AP, English, English language and composition-AP, English literature, English literature and composition-AP, environmental science, environmental science-AP, ethics, European history, European history-AP, filmmaking, fine arts, forensics, French, French language-AP, French literature-AP, geography, geometry, government and politics-AP, health, honors algebra, honors English, honors geometry, journalism, Latin, Latin-AP, life management skills, mathematics, music, music theory-AP, newspaper, painting, physical education, physics, physics-AP, portfolio art, pottery, pre-algebra, pre-calculus, probability and statistics, psychology, psychology-AP, robotics, science, sculpture, social studies, Spanish, Spanish language-AP, Spanish literature-AP, speech, strings, studio art-AP, theater, trigonometry, U.S. government and politics-AP, U.S. history-AP, weight training, world history, world wide web design, writing, yearbook.

Graduation Requirements 1 1/2 elective credits, arts and fine arts (art, music, dance, drama), computer science, electives, English, foreign language, life management skills, life skills, mathematics, physical education (includes health), science, social sciences, social studies (includes history).

Special Academic Programs 26 Advanced Placement exams for which test preparation is offered; honors section; independent study; study at local college for college credit; study abroad; academic accommodation for the gifted, the musically talented, and the artistically talented.

College Admission Counseling 130 students graduated in 2016; all went to college, including Emory University; Florida State University; Stanford University; The University of North Carolina at Chapel Hill; University of Central Florida; University of Florida.

Student Life Upper grades have specified standards of dress, student council, honor system. Discipline rests primarily with faculty. Attendance at religious services is required.

Summer Programs Remediation, enrichment, advancement, sports, art/fine arts, computer instruction programs offered; session focuses on enrichment; held on campus; accepts boys and girls; open to students from other schools. 300 students usually enrolled. 2017 schedule: June 12 to August 4. Application deadline: none.

Tuition and Aid Day student tuition: $20,200. Tuition installment plan (Insured Tuition Payment Plan, monthly payment plans, semiannual and annual payment plans). Need-based scholarship grants available. In 2016–17, 26% of upper-school students received aid. Total amount of financial aid awarded in 2016–17: $1,800,000.

Admissions Traditional secondary-level entrance grade is 9. For fall 2016, 74 students applied for upper-level admission, 41 were accepted, 29 enrolled. ISEE required. Deadline for receipt of application materials: February 10. Application fee required: $75. Interview recommended.

Athletics Interscholastic: aquatics (boys, girls), baseball (b), basketball (b,g), bowling (b,g), cheering (g), cross-country running (b,g), diving (b,g), fitness (b,g), football (b), golf (b,g), lacrosse (b,g), physical fitness (b,g), soccer (b,g), softball (g), strength & conditioning (b,g), swimming and diving (b,g), tennis (b,g), track and field (b,g), volleyball (g), weight lifting (b,g), weight training (b,g); intramural: ropes courses (b,g), strength & conditioning (b,g); coed intramural: fishing. 5 PE instructors, 48 coaches, 1 athletic trainer.

Computers Computers are regularly used in all academic classes. Computer network features include on-campus library services, online commercial services, Internet access, wireless campus network, Internet filtering or blocking technology. Student e-mail accounts and computer access in designated common areas are available to students. Students grades are available online. The school has a published electronic and media policy.

Contact Jackie Hewitt, Admission Associate. 407-671-4140. Fax: 407-671-6935. E-mail: inquire@trinityprep.org. Website: www.trinityprep.org

TRINITY SCHOOL OF TEXAS

215 Teague Street
Longview, Texas 75601

Head of School: Mr. Gary L. Whitwell

General Information Coeducational day college-preparatory, arts, religious studies, and technology school, affiliated with Episcopal Church. Grades PK–12. Founded: 1957. Setting: small town. Nearest major city is Dallas. 14-acre campus. 4 buildings on campus. Approved or accredited by National Association of Episcopal Schools, Southern Association of Colleges and Schools, Southwest Association of Episcopal Schools, and Texas Department of Education. Endowment: $315,000. Total enrollment: 265. Upper school average class size: 12. Upper school faculty-student ratio: 1:8. There are 174 required school days per year for Upper School students. Upper School students typically attend 5 days per week. The average school day consists of 6 hours and 20 minutes.

Upper School Student Profile Grade 9: 15 students (9 boys, 6 girls); Grade 10: 15 students (9 boys, 6 girls); Grade 11: 12 students (5 boys, 7 girls); Grade 12: 18 students (9 boys, 9 girls). 11% of students are members of Episcopal Church.

Faculty School total: 38. In upper school: 3 men, 13 women; 3 have advanced degrees.

Subjects Offered Advanced studio art-AP, algebra, American history, art, astronomy, athletics, biology, biology-AP, calculus, calculus-AP, Central and Eastern European history, character education, chemistry, chemistry-AP, choral music, college admission preparation, college writing, community service, computer applications, computer literacy, conflict resolution, creative writing, desktop publishing, digital photography, drama performance, earth science, economics, English-AP, environmental studies, European history-AP, geography, geometry, government, government/civics, grammar, health, junior and senior seminars, keyboarding, language and composition, language arts, leadership and service, library, life science, literature and composition-AP, mathematics, modern European history, modern Western civilization, modern world history, music, music performance, mythology, newspaper, participation in sports, personal finance, photography, photojournalism, physical education, physical fitness, physical science, physics, pre-algebra, pre-calculus, probability and statistics, psychology, psychology-AP, religious studies, research seminar, research skills, SAT preparation, SAT/ACT preparation, sociology, Spanish, Spanish language-AP, sports, statistics, student publications, studio art, Texas history, U.S. government, U.S. history, world geography, world history, world religions, yearbook.

Graduation Requirements Arts and fine arts (art, music, dance, drama), computers, English, government/civics, languages, mathematics, physical education (includes health), science, social sciences, speech, theology.

Special Academic Programs Advanced Placement exam preparation; accelerated programs; independent study; term-away projects; study at local college for college credit; study abroad; academic accommodation for the gifted, the musically talented, and the artistically talented; programs in English, mathematics for dyslexic students.

College Admission Counseling 18 students graduated in 2015; all went to college, including Louisiana State University and Agricultural & Mechanical College; Texas A&M University; The University of Texas at Austin. Median SAT critical reading: 530, median SAT math: 620, median SAT writing: 535, median combined SAT: 1690, median composite ACT: 23. 18% scored over 600 on SAT critical reading, 23% scored over 600 on SAT math, 13% scored over 600 on SAT writing, 42% scored over 26 on composite ACT.

Student Life Upper grades have specified standards of dress, student council, honor system. Discipline rests primarily with faculty. Attendance at religious services is required.

Tuition and Aid Day student tuition: $8500. Tuition installment plan (FACTS Tuition Payment Plan, monthly payment plans, individually arranged payment plans, semester payment plan). Merit scholarship grants, need-based scholarship grants available. In 2015–16, 22% of upper-school students received aid; total upper-school merit-scholarship money awarded: $650,000.

Admissions Traditional secondary-level entrance grade is 9. For fall 2015, 12 students applied for upper-level admission, 12 were accepted, 12 enrolled. Otis-Lennon, Stanford Achievement Test, PSAT or SAT for applicants to grade 11 and 12, Woodcock-Johnson Revised Achievement Test and writing sample required. Deadline for receipt of application materials: none. Application fee required: $850. On-campus interview required.

Athletics Interscholastic: baseball (boys), basketball (b,g), cheering (g), football (b), golf (b,g), physical fitness (b), power lifting (b), tennis (b,g), track and field (b,g), volleyball (g); intramural: football (b), physical fitness (b,g), tennis (b,g), volleyball (g); coed interscholastic: soccer; coed intramural: soccer, track and field, weight training. 2 PE instructors, 4 coaches.

Computers Computers are regularly used in college planning, computer applications, creative writing, English, geography, history, journalism, keyboarding, library, mathematics, newspaper, photography, photojournalism, psychology, publications, publishing, research skills, SAT preparation, science, senior seminar, Spanish, technology, writing, yearbook classes. Computer network features include on-campus library services, online commercial services, Internet access, Internet filtering or blocking technology. The school has a published electronic and media policy.

Contact Mrs. Cissy Abernathy, Director of Admission. 903-753-0612 Ext. 236. Fax: 903-753-4812. E-mail: cabernathy@trinityschooloftexas.com. Website: www.trinityschooloftexas.com

TUSCALOOSA ACADEMY

420 Rice Valley Road North
Tuscaloosa, Alabama 35406

Head of School: Dr. Isaac Espy

General Information Coeducational day college-preparatory, arts, bilingual studies, technology, and ESL school. Grades PK–12. Founded: 1967. Setting: suburban. Nearest major city is Birmingham. 35-acre campus. 2 buildings on campus. Approved or accredited by Southern Association of Colleges and Schools and Southern Association of Independent Schools. Member of National Association of Independent Schools. Total enrollment: 438. Upper school average class size: 15. Upper school faculty-student ratio: 1:15. There are 177 required school days per year for Upper School students. Upper School students typically attend 5 days per week. The average school day consists of 6 hours and 55 minutes.

Upper School Student Profile Grade 9: 38 students (17 boys, 21 girls); Grade 10: 35 students (24 boys, 11 girls); Grade 11: 39 students (18 boys, 21 girls); Grade 12: 42 students (26 boys, 16 girls).

Faculty School total: 56. In upper school: 10 men, 12 women; 11 have advanced degrees.

Subjects Offered ACT preparation, advanced math, Advanced Placement courses, algebra, American government, American history, American history-AP, American literature, American literature-AP, anatomy, art, art history, art-AP, baseball, basketball, biology, biology-AP, calculus, calculus-AP, cheerleading, chemistry, chemistry-AP, choir, choral music, chorus, college counseling, computer programming, computer science, computer studies, creative writing, drama, earth science, economics, English, English literature, English-AP, English/composition-AP, European history, expository writing, fine arts, French, French language-AP, French-AP, geography, geometry, German, golf, government-AP, government/civics, grammar, health, history, history-AP, journalism, Latin, Latin-AP, literature-AP, mathematics, mathematics-AP, music, physical education, pre-calculus, psychology, psychology-AP, SAT preparation, SAT/ACT preparation, science, senior thesis, social studies, sociology, softball, Spanish, Spanish language-AP, Spanish-AP, speech, sports conditioning, studio art, studio art-AP, theater, track and field, trigonometry, U.S. history-AP, world literature, yearbook.

Graduation Requirements Algebra, American government, American history, arts and fine arts (art, music, dance, drama), biology, chemistry, computer science, electives, English, foreign language, geometry, literature, mathematics, modern European history, physical education (includes health), physical science, pre-calculus, science, social studies (includes history), speech, U.S. history, 80 community service hours.

Special Academic Programs Advanced Placement exam preparation; honors section; independent study; study at local college for college credit; study abroad; academic accommodation for the gifted; ESL (81 students enrolled).

College Admission Counseling 31 students graduated in 2015; all went to college, including Auburn University; Birmingham-Southern College; Shelton State Community College; The University of Alabama; University of Mississippi.

Student Life Upper grades have specified standards of dress, student council, honor system. Discipline rests primarily with faculty.

Tuition and Aid Day student tuition: $7334–$9388. Guaranteed tuition plan. Tuition installment plan (Insured Tuition Payment Plan, monthly payment plans, semester payment plan, annual payment plan). Tuition reduction for siblings, need-based scholarship grants available. In 2015–16, 20% of upper-school students received aid. Total amount of financial aid awarded in 2015–16: $160,000.

Admissions Traditional secondary-level entrance grade is 9. For fall 2015, 27 students applied for upper-level admission, 24 were accepted, 16 enrolled. Any standardized test, Star-9 and writing sample required. Deadline for receipt of application materials: none. Application fee required: $100. Interview required.

Athletics Interscholastic: baseball (boys), basketball (b,g), cheering (g), cross-country running (b,g), dance team (g), football (b), golf (b,g), softball (g), strength & conditioning (b), tennis (b,g), track and field (b,g), volleyball (g), weight training (b); coed interscholastic: soccer. 1 PE instructor, 2 coaches, 6 athletic trainers.

Computers Computers are regularly used in journalism, keyboarding, yearbook classes. Computer network features include on-campus library services, online commercial services, Internet access, wireless campus network, Internet filtering or blocking technology, laptop program. Campus intranet, student e-mail accounts, and computer access in designated common areas are available to students. Students grades are available online. The school has a published electronic and media policy.

Contact Niccole Poole, Director of Admission. 205-758-4462 Ext. 202. Fax: 205-758-4418. E-mail: npoole@tuscaloosaacademy.org. Website: www.tuscaloosaacademy.org

TYLER STREET CHRISTIAN ACADEMY

915 West 9th Street
Dallas, Texas 75208

Head of School: Dr. Karen J. Egger

General Information Coeducational day college-preparatory, general academic, arts, religious studies, and technology school, affiliated with Christian faith. Boys grades P3–5, girls grades P3–1. Founded: 1972. Setting: urban. 5-acre campus. 2 buildings on campus. Approved or accredited by Association of Christian Schools International, Southern Association of Colleges and Schools, Texas Private School Accreditation Commission, and Texas Department of Education. Endowment: $45,000. Total enrollment: 161. Upper school average class size: 10. Upper school faculty-student ratio: 1:11. There are 176 required school days per year for Upper School students. Upper School students typically attend 5 days per week. The average school day consists of 7 hours and 40 minutes.

Upper School Student Profile Grade 9: 13 students (8 boys, 5 girls); Grade 10: 8 students (3 boys, 5 girls); Grade 11: 13 students (8 boys, 5 girls); Grade 12: 11 students (4 boys, 7 girls) 75% of students are Christian faith.

Faculty School total: 25. In upper school: 8 men, 8 women, 5 have advanced degrees.

Subjects Offered Advanced Placement courses, algebra, American government, American history, art, art appreciation, art history, arts and crafts, athletic training, ballet, band, bell choir, Bible studies, biology, British literature, British literature (honors), calculus, calculus-AP, cheerleading, chemistry, choir, choral music, Christian education, college admission preparation, college counseling, college planning, community service, composition, computer applications, computer literacy, computer skills, computer technologies, computer-aided design, concert band, concert bell choir, CPR, critical writing, economics, English literature, family living, freshman seminar, geography, geometry, government, grammar, guidance, health, history, Holocaust studies, honors algebra, honors English, honors geometry, human anatomy, human biology, integrated physics, keyboarding, lab science, lab/keyboard, leadership, leadership and service, literature, mathematics-AP, musical productions, physical education, physical science, physics, physiology, pre-calculus, religion, robotics, science, social studies, Spanish, speech communications, student government, track and field, U.S. government, U.S. history, U.S. literature, volleyball, weight training, world geography, world history, world literature, yearbook.

Graduation Requirements Algebra, American government, arts and fine arts (art, music, dance, drama), Bible, biology, calculus, chemistry, computer science, economics, English, geometry, physical education (includes health), physical science, physics, Spanish, speech communications, U.S. history, world geography, world history.

Special Academic Programs International Baccalaureate program; 1 Advanced Placement exam for which test preparation is offered; honors section; independent study; study at local college for college credit.

College Admission Counseling 11 students graduated in 2015; 9 went to college, including Baylor University; Prairie View A&M University; Texas A&M University-Commerce; University of North Texas. Other: 2 had other specific plans. Median composite ACT: 26.

Student Life Upper grades have uniform requirement, student council, honor system. Discipline rests primarily with faculty. Attendance at religious services is required.

Tuition and Aid Day student tuition: $8700. Tuition installment plan (FACTS Tuition Payment Plan). Merit scholarship grants, need-based scholarship grants available. In 2015–16, 80% of upper-school students received aid; total upper-school merit-scholarship money awarded: $2500. Total amount of financial aid awarded in 2015–16: $92,000.

Admissions Traditional secondary-level entrance grade is 9. Admissions testing, English entrance exam, mathematics proficiency exam and writing sample required. Deadline for receipt of application materials: none. Application fee required: $75. On-campus interview required.

Athletics Interscholastic: basketball (boys, girls), cheering (g), dance squad (b,g), football (b), independent competitive sports (b,g), life saving (b,g), physical training (b,g), strength & conditioning (b,g), track and field (b,g), volleyball (g), weight lifting (b,g), weight training (b,g); coed interscholastic: cooperative games, life saving, physical training. 1 PE instructor, 2 coaches.

Computers Computers are regularly used in business applications, business skills, career exploration, Christian doctrine, college planning, computer applications, data processing, desktop publishing, digital applications, engineering, graphic arts, information technology, introduction to technology, journalism, keyboarding, lab/keyboard, library, library skills, literacy, photojournalism, reading, technology, word processing, yearbook classes. Computer network features include on-campus library services, Internet access, wireless campus network, Internet filtering or blocking technology, on-campus library services for Accelerated Reader Program. Student e-mail accounts and computer access in designated common areas are available to students. Students grades are available online. The school has a published electronic and media policy.

Contact Mrs. Jennifer Pena, Registrar. 214-941-9717 Ext. 200. Fax: 214-941-0324. E-mail: jenniferpena@tsca.org. Website: www.tsca.org

UNITED MENNONITE EDUCATIONAL INSTITUTE

614 Mersca Road 6, RR 5
Leamington, Ontario N8H 3V8, Canada

Head of School: Mrs. Sonya A. Bedal

General Information Coeducational day college-preparatory, arts, religious studies, and technology school, affiliated with Mennonite Church. Grades 9–12. Founded: 1945. Setting: rural. Nearest major city is Windsor, Canada. 12 acre campus. 1 building on campus. Approved or accredited by Mennonite Education Agency, Mennonite Schools Council, and Ontario Department of Education. Language of instruction: English. Total enrollment: 48. Upper school average class size: 18. Upper school faculty-student ratio: 1:9. There are 194 required school days per year for Upper School students. Upper School students typically attend 5 days per week. The average school day consists of 6 hours.

Upper School Student Profile Grade 9: 22 students (11 boys, 11 girls); Grade 10: 15 students (5 boys, 10 girls); Grade 11: 19 students (8 boys, 11 girls); Grade 12: 18 students (7 boys, 11 girls). 65% of students are Mennonite.

Faculty School total: 8. In upper school: 4 men, 4 women.

Subjects Offered Acting, advanced chemistry, advanced math, algebra, American history, Bible, biology, career exploration, chemistry, choral music, Christian ethics, church history, civics, communication arts, computer technologies, English, French as a second language, instrumental music, introduction to theater, leadership and service, literacy, mathematics, philosophy, physical education, physics, religious studies, robotics, society challenge and change, theater arts.

Graduation Requirements Arts, Canadian geography, Canadian history, careers, civics, English, French, mathematics, physical education (includes health), science.

College Admission Counseling 7 students graduated in 2016; 6 went to college, including Canadian Mennonite University; Fanshawe College; Redeemer University College; St. Clair College; University of Guelph. Other: 1 had other specific plans.

Student Life Upper grades have specified standards of dress, student council. Discipline rests primarily with faculty. Attendance at religious services is required.

Tuition and Aid Day student tuition: CAN$7500. Tuition installment plan (monthly payment plans). Tuition reduction for siblings, bursaries, need-based scholarship grants, need-based loans available. In 2016–17, 23% of upper-school students received aid. Total amount of financial aid awarded in 2016–17: CAN$46,000.

Admissions Traditional secondary-level entrance grade is 9. For fall 2016, 22 students applied for upper-level admission, 22 were accepted, 22 enrolled. Deadline for receipt of application materials: none. Application fee required: CAN$200. Interview recommended.

Athletics Interscholastic: badminton (boys, girls), basketball (b,g), cross-country running (b,g), soccer (b), softball (g), track and field (b,g), volleyball (b,g); intramural: indoor hockey (b,g), indoor soccer (b,g), outdoor activities (b,g), soccer (b,g), track and field (b,g), volleyball (b,g); coed intramural: fitness, ultimate Frisbee, weight lifting, yoga.

Computers Computers are regularly used in all classes. Computer network features include Internet access, wireless campus network, Internet filtering or blocking technology. Computer access in designated common areas is available to students. Students grades are available online. The school has a published electronic and media policy.

Contact Ms. Chrissy Kelton, Admissions Director. 519-326 7448. Fax: 519-326 0278. E-mail: chrissy.kelton@umei.ca. Website: www.umei.ca

UNITED NATIONS INTERNATIONAL SCHOOL

24-50 Franklin D. Roosevelt Drive
New York, New York 10010-4046

Head of School: Ms. Jane Camblin

General Information Coeducational day college-preparatory, English Language Learners and Eight Mother Tongue programs, and International Baccalaureate, Eight 3rd Language Programs school. Grades PK–12. Founded: 1947. Setting: urban. 3-acre campus. 1 building on campus. Approved or accredited by Council of International Schools, International Baccalaureate Organization, and New York Department of Education. Member of National Association of Independent Schools and European Council of International Schools. Languages of instruction: English and Spanish. Endowment: $19 million. Total enrollment: 1,570. Upper school average class size: 12. Upper school faculty-student ratio: 1:6. There are 171 required school days per year for Upper School students. Upper School students typically attend 5 days per week. The average school day consists of 6 hours and 40 minutes.

Upper School Student Profile Grade 9: 126 students (61 boys, 65 girls); Grade 10: 118 students (60 boys, 58 girls); Grade 11: 122 students (60 boys, 62 girls); Grade 12: 121 students (60 boys, 61 girls).

Faculty School total: 221. In upper school: 51 men, 54 women; 83 have advanced degrees.

Subjects Offered 3-dimensional art, algebra, American history, American literature, American studies, anthropology, Arabic, art, biology, calculus, chemistry, Chinese, community service, computer applications, computer science, creative writing, drama, economics, English, English literature, ESL, European history, expository writing, film, film studies, fine arts, French, geometry, German, history, humanities, Italian, Japanese, journalism, languages, library, mathematics, media production, modern languages, music, philosophy, photography, physical education, physics, psychology, Russian, science, social sciences, social studies, Spanish, theater arts, theory of knowledge, United Nations and international issues, video, video and animation, video communication, video film production, world history, world literature, writing.

Graduation Requirements Art, electives, English, health and wellness, humanities, independent study, mathematics, modern languages, music, physical education (includes health), science, International Baccalaureate, Theory of Knowledge, extended essay, Creative Aesthetic Service, individual project. Community service is required.

Special Academic Programs International Baccalaureate program; honors section; independent study; academic accommodation for the gifted, the musically talented, and the artistically talented; ESL (185 students enrolled).

College Admission Counseling 113 students graduated in 2016; 111 went to college, including Emory University; Fordham University; Harvard University; McGill University; New York University; Northeastern University. Other: 2 entered military service. Median SAT critical reading: 620, median SAT math: 600, median SAT writing: 610, median combined SAT: 1830, median composite ACT: 27. 62% scored over 600 on SAT critical reading, 54% scored over 600 on SAT math, 63% scored over 600 on SAT writing, 60% scored over 1800 on combined SAT, 67% scored over 26 on composite ACT.

Student Life Upper grades have student council. Discipline rests primarily with faculty.

Summer Programs Enrichment, ESL, sports, art/fine arts, computer instruction programs offered; session focuses on recreational program for students 4 to 14 years old; held on campus; accepts boys and girls; open to students from other schools. 300 students usually enrolled. 2017 schedule: June 22 to July 31. Application deadline: May 15.

Tuition and Aid Day student tuition: $34,580–$38,500. Tuition installment plan (monthly payment plans). Need-based scholarship grants available. In 2016–17, 7% of upper-school students received aid.

Admissions Traditional secondary-level entrance grade is 9. ISEE, PSAT and SAT for applicants to grade 11 and 12 or SSAT required. Deadline for receipt of application materials: November 15. Application fee required: $75. On-campus interview recommended.

Athletics Interscholastic: baseball (boys), basketball (b,g), cross-country running (b,g), indoor track (b,g), indoor track & field (b,g), soccer (b,g), softball (g), track and field (b,g), volleyball (b,g); intramural: volleyball (b,g); coed interscholastic: swimming and diving; coed intramural: aerobics, aerobics/dance, aerobics/Nautilus, aquatics, badminton, ball hockey, basketball, canoeing/kayaking, climbing, cooperative games, cross-country running, dance, field hockey, fitness, flag football, floor hockey, gymnastics, handball, hiking/backpacking, independent competitive sports, indoor hockey, indoor soccer, indoor track, indoor track & field, jogging, jump rope, life saving, martial arts, modern dance, outdoor activities, physical fitness, physical training, rock climbing, ropes courses, rounders, running, soccer, softball, strength & conditioning, swimming and diving, table tennis, team handball, tennis, touch football,

track and field, volleyball, wall climbing, weight training. 10 PE instructors, 25 coaches.

Computers Computers are regularly used in all academic, animation, art, basic skills, career education, career exploration, career technology, college planning, computer applications, creative writing, current events, data processing, desktop publishing, desktop publishing, ESL, digital applications, drawing and design, economics, English, ESL, foreign language, French, French as a second language, graphic arts, graphic design, graphics, health, history, humanities, independent study, information technology, introduction to technology, journalism, keyboarding, lab/keyboard, learning cognition, library, library science, library skills, life skills, literacy, literary magazine, mathematics, media, media arts, media production, media services, multimedia, music, music technology, news writing, newspaper, philosophy, photography, photojournalism, programming, publications, publishing, research skills, science, social sciences, social studies, Spanish, study skills, technology, theater, theater arts, video film production, Web site design, writing, yearbook classes. Computer network features include on-campus library services, online commercial services, Internet access, wireless campus network, Internet filtering or blocking technology, media lab, TV studio, Web portal, film production, digital video streaming, digital video editing. Campus intranet, student e-mail accounts, and computer access in designated common areas are available to students. Students grades are available online. The school has a published electronic and media policy.

Contact Admissions Office. 212-584-3071. Fax: 212-685-5023. E-mail: admissions@unis.org. Website: www.unis.org

THE UNITED WORLD COLLEGE - USA

PO Box 248
State Road 65
Montezuma, New Mexico 87731

Head of School: Dr. Mukul Kumar

General Information Coeducational boarding college-preparatory, arts, bilingual studies, wilderness, search and rescue, conflict resolution, and service, science, humanities school. Grades 11–12. Founded: 1982. Setting: small town. Nearest major city is Santa Fe. Students are housed in single-sex dormitories. 320-acre campus. 20 buildings on campus. Approved or accredited by Independent Schools Association of the Southwest and New Mexico Department of Education. Member of National Association of Independent Schools. Endowment: $120 million. Upper school average class size: 15. Upper school faculty-student ratio: 1:9. There are 245 required school days per year for Upper School students. Upper School students typically attend 5 days per week. The average school day consists of 6 hours and 30 minutes.

Upper School Student Profile Grade 11: 118 students (48 boys, 70 girls); Grade 12: 111 students (57 boys, 54 girls). 100% of students are boarding students. 1% are state residents. 28 states are represented in upper school student body. 81% are international students. International students from China, Denmark, Germany, Mexico, Senegal, and Spain; 70 other countries represented in student body.

Faculty School total: 30. In upper school: 15 men, 15 women; 25 have advanced degrees; 18 reside on campus.

Subjects Offered Anthropology, art, biology, calculus, chemistry, community service, conflict resolution, economics, English, environmental geography, environmental science, environmental studies, environmental systems, fine arts, French, German, history, information technology, International Baccalaureate courses, mathematics, music, physics, science, social sciences, social studies, Spanish, theater arts, theory of knowledge, voice, voice and diction, voice ensemble, weight fitness, weight training, welding, Western civilization, wilderness education, wilderness experience, wind ensemble, wind instruments, women in literature, women in society, world affairs, world cultures, world history, world issues, world literature, world religions, world studies.

Graduation Requirements Arts and fine arts (art, music, dance, drama), biology, calculus, chemistry, economics, English literature, environmental geography, environmental systems, European history, foreign language, French, French as a second language, geography, German, German literature, history of the Americas, International Baccalaureate courses, literature, math methods, mathematics, music, music theory, organic chemistry, physics, post-calculus, pre-algebra, pre-calculus, research, science, senior thesis, Spanish, Spanish literature, statistics, studio art, theater, theater arts, theory of knowledge, visual arts, extended essay, independent research, theory of knowledge.

Special Academic Programs International Baccalaureate program; honors section; independent study; academic accommodation for the musically talented and the artistically talented; ESL (43 students enrolled).

College Admission Counseling 104 students graduated in 2015; 98 went to college, including Harvard University; Middlebury College; St. Lawrence University; Stanford University; University of Florida; Williams College. Other: 3 entered military service, 3 had other specific plans. 35% scored over 600 on SAT critical reading, 75% scored over 600 on SAT math, 50% scored over 600 on SAT writing, 50% scored over 1800 on combined SAT, 95% scored over 26 on composite ACT.

Student Life Upper grades have student council, honor system. Discipline rests equally with students and faculty.

Tuition and Aid 7-day tuition and room/board: $36,750. Guaranteed tuition plan. Tuition installment plan (all accepted U.S. students are awarded full merit scholarships, need-based aid available to all other students). Merit scholarship grants, need-based scholarship grants, full tuition merit scholarships awarded to all admitted U.S. citizens available. In 2015–16, 85% of upper-school students received aid; total upper-school merit-scholarship money awarded: $6,800,000. Total amount of financial aid awarded in 2015–16: $6,800,000.

Admissions Traditional secondary-level entrance grade is 11. For fall 2015, 486 students applied for upper-level admission, 52 were accepted, 52 enrolled. ACT, PSAT or SAT or PSAT, SAT, or ACT for applicants to grade 11 and 12 required. Deadline for receipt of application materials: November 5. No application fee required. Interview required.

Athletics Coed Intramural: aerobics, aerobics/dance, aerobics/Nautilus, alpine skiing, aquatics, backpacking, badminton, ballet, baseball, basketball, bicycling, billiards, canoeing/kayaking, climbing, combined training, cooperative games, cricket, cross-country running, dance, fitness, Frisbee, hiking/backpacking, jogging, modern dance, mountaineering, nordic skiing, outdoor activities, physical training, racquetball, rock climbing, ropes courses, running, sailing, skiing (cross-country), skiing (downhill), snowboarding, snowshoeing, soccer, softball, squash, strength & conditioning, swimming and diving, table tennis, tennis, ultimate Frisbee, volleyball, walking, weight lifting, weight training, wilderness, wilderness survival, yoga. 1 PE instructor, 12 athletic trainers.

Computers Computers are regularly used in art, English, ESL, foreign language, mathematics, music, science classes. Computer network features include on-campus library services, Internet access, wireless campus network, Internet filtering or blocking technology. Campus intranet, student e-mail accounts, and computer access in designated common areas are available to students. Students grades are available online.

Contact Ms. Kathy Gonzales, Assistant to the Director of Admission. 505-454-4245. Fax: 505-454-4294. E-mail: kathy.gonzales@uwc-usa.org. Website: www.uwc-usa.org

UNIVERSITY LAKE SCHOOL

4024 Nagawicka Road
Hartland, Wisconsin 53029

Head of School: Mr. Ronald Smyczek

General Information Coeducational day college-preparatory school. Grades PK–12. Founded: 1956. Setting: suburban. Nearest major city is Milwaukee. 180-acre campus. 4 buildings on campus. Member of National Association of Independent Schools. Endowment: $2.4 million. Total enrollment: 258. Upper school average class size: 12. Upper school faculty-student ratio: 1:9. Upper School students typically attend 5 days per week. The average school day consists of 3 hours and 20 minutes.

Upper School Student Profile Grade 6: 16 students (7 boys, 9 girls); Grade 7: 21 students (8 boys, 13 girls); Grade 8: 28 students (14 boys, 14 girls); Grade 9: 19 students (10 boys, 9 girls); Grade 10: 20 students (7 boys, 13 girls), Grade 11: 28 students (10 boys, 18 girls); Grade 12: 31 students (12 boys, 19 girls).

Faculty School total: 41. In upper school: 11 men, 4 women; 11 have advanced degrees.

Subjects Offered Advanced Placement courses, algebra, American history, American literature, art, biology, calculus, chemistry, cinematography, computer science, creative writing, design, drama, English, English literature, environmental science, fine arts, French, geometry, government/civics, journalism, mathematics, music, photography, physical education, physics, science, social studies, Spanish, speech, statistics, theater, Web site design, world history, world literature, writing.

Graduation Requirements Art, arts and fine arts (art, music, dance, drama), English, foreign language, health education, literature, mathematics, physical education (includes health), science, social studies (includes history).

Special Academic Programs Advanced Placement exam preparation; honors section; independent study; study at local college for college credit; academic accommodation for the gifted, the musically talented, and the artistically talented; remedial reading and/or remedial writing; remedial math; programs in English for dyslexic students; special instructional classes for blind students.

College Admission Counseling 12 students graduated in 2016; all went to college, including Auburn University; Columbia College Chicago; Furman University; University of Wisconsin–Madison. Median composite ACT: 28. 30% scored over 26 on composite ACT.

Student Life Upper grades have specified standards of dress, student council, honor system. Discipline rests equally with students and faculty.

Summer Programs Remediation, enrichment, advancement, sports, art/fine arts programs offered; session focuses on academics, arts, and athletics; held on campus; accepts boys and girls; open to students from other schools. 500 students usually enrolled. 2017 schedule: June 15 to August 7. Application deadline: none.

Tuition and Aid Day student tuition: $17,980. Tuition installment plan (Insured Tuition Payment Plan, FACTS Tuition Payment Plan, monthly payment plans, individually arranged payment plans). Merit scholarship grants, need-based scholarship grants available. In 2016–17, 37% of upper-school students received aid; total upper-school merit-scholarship money awarded: $80,000. Total amount of financial aid awarded in 2016–17: $272,000.

Admissions Traditional secondary-level entrance grade is 9. For fall 2016, 13 students applied for upper-level admission, 13 were accepted, 13 enrolled. Admissions testing, Kuhlmann-Anderson and Kuhlmann-Anderson Level G (for grades 7-9) or Level H (for

grades 10-12) required. Deadline for receipt of application materials: none. Application fee required: $25. On-campus interview recommended.

Athletics Interscholastic: basketball (boys, girls), field hockey (g), lacrosse (b), skiing (downhill) (b,g), soccer (b,g), tennis (b,g), volleyball (g); coed interscholastic: alpine skiing, aquatics, cross-country running, golf, ice hockey, swimming and diving; coed intramural: volleyball, wall climbing. 2 PE instructors, 7 coaches.

Computers Computers are regularly used in all academic classes. Computer network features include on-campus library services, Internet access, wireless campus network, Internet filtering or blocking technology. Campus intranet and student e-mail accounts are available to students. Students grades are available online. The school has a published electronic and media policy.

Contact Mrs. Deb Smith, Director of Admissions. 262-367-6011 Ext. 1455. Fax: 262-367-3146. E-mail: deb.smith@universitylake.org. Website: www.universitylake.org

UNIVERSITY OF CHICAGO LABORATORY SCHOOLS

1362 East 59th Street
Chicago, Illinois 60637

Head of School: Ms. Beth Harris

General Information Coeducational day college-preparatory school. Grades N–12. Founded: 1896. Setting: urban. 15-acre campus. 4 buildings on campus. Approved or accredited by North Central Association of Colleges and Schools and Illinois Department of Education. Member of National Association of Independent Schools. Endowment: $19.8 million. Total enrollment: 2,007. Upper school average class size: 15. Upper school faculty-student ratio: 1:10. There are 171 required school days per year for Upper School students. Upper School students typically attend 5 days per week. The average school day consists of 7 hours and 5 minutes.

Upper School Student Profile Grade 9: 156 students (78 boys, 78 girls); Grade 10: 125 students (59 boys, 66 girls); Grade 11: 126 students (57 boys, 69 girls); Grade 12: 124 students (55 boys, 69 girls).

Faculty School total: 254. In upper school: 32 men, 43 women; 66 have advanced degrees.

Subjects Offered Acting, advanced biology, advanced chemistry, African-American history, algebra, American history, art, art history, band, biology, calculus, calculus-AP, chemistry, Chinese, choir, community service, computer science, computer science-AP, CPR, creative writing, discrete mathematics, drama, drawing, driver education, English, English literature, European history, expository writing, fine arts, French, French-AP, geometry, German, German-AP, government/civics, Greek, history, Holocaust, honors geometry, jazz band, journalism, Latin, Mandarin, mathematics, modern European history, music, music theory, music theory-AP, newspaper, orchestra, painting, photography, photojournalism, physical education, physics, play production, post-calculus, science, sculpture, social studies, Spanish, Spanish language-AP, Spanish-AP, statistics, statistics-AP, studio art, theater, trigonometry, U.S. history, video film production, Web site design, Western civilization, world history, writing, yearbook.

Graduation Requirements Arts and fine arts (art, music, dance, drama), computer science, English, foreign language, mathematics, music, physical education (includes health), science, social studies (includes history). Community service is required.

Special Academic Programs 8 Advanced Placement exams for which test preparation is offered; accelerated programs; independent study; study at local college for college credit.

College Admission Counseling 129 students graduated in 2016; 127 went to college, including Bard College; New York University; Northwestern University; University of Chicago; University of Illinois at Urbana–Champaign; Yale University. Other: 2 had other specific plans. Median SAT critical reading: 686, median SAT math: 686, median SAT writing: 674, median combined SAT: 2046, median composite ACT: 30. 75% scored over 600 on SAT critical reading, 90% scored over 600 on SAT math, 84% scored over 600 on SAT writing, 85% scored over 1800 on combined SAT, 85% scored over 26 on composite ACT.

Student Life Upper grades have student council. Discipline rests primarily with faculty.

Summer Programs Enrichment, advancement, sports, computer instruction programs offered; session focuses on advancement of placement in courses; held on campus; accepts boys and girls; open to students from other schools. 125 students usually enrolled. 2017 schedule: June 19 to July 28. Application deadline: May 15.

Tuition and Aid Day student tuition: $32,106. Tuition installment plan (monthly payment plans, quarterly payment plan). Need-based scholarship grants available. In 2016–17, 14% of upper-school students received aid. Total amount of financial aid awarded in 2016–17: $1,365,483.

Admissions Traditional secondary-level entrance grade is 9. ISEE required. Deadline for receipt of application materials: November 13. Application fee required: $80. On-campus interview required.

Athletics Interscholastic: baseball (boys), basketball (b,g), cross-country running (b,g), dance squad (g), fencing (b,g), golf (b,g), indoor track & field (b,g), sailing (b,g), soccer (b,g), squash (b,g), swimming and diving (b,g), tennis (b,g), track and field (b,g), volleyball (g), winter (indoor) track (b,g); intramural: dance squad (g), indoor soccer (g); coed interscholastic: cross-country running, sailing; coed intramural: badminton, life saving, table tennis. 15 PE instructors, 41 coaches, 1 athletic trainer.

University of Chicago Laboratory Schools

Computers Computers are regularly used in business applications, mathematics, music, newspaper, science, writing, yearbook classes. Computer network features include on-campus library services, Internet access, wireless campus network. Student e-mail accounts and computer access in designated common areas are available to students. Students grades are available online. The school has a published electronic and media policy.

Contact Irene Reed, Executive Director of Admissions and Financial Aid. 773-702-9451. Fax: 773-702-7455. E-mail: ireed@ucls.uchicago.edu. Website: www.ucls.uchicago.edu/

UNIVERSITY PREP

8000 25th Avenue NE
Seattle, Washington 98115

Head of School: Matt Levinson

General Information Coeducational day college-preparatory and global education school. Grades 6–12. Founded: 1976. Setting: urban. 6-acre campus. 5 buildings on campus. Approved or accredited by Northwest Association of Independent Schools and Washington Department of Education. Member of National Association of Independent Schools and Secondary School Admission Test Board. Endowment: $9.7 million. Total enrollment: 545. Upper school average class size: 17. Upper school faculty-student ratio: 1:9. There are 169 required school days per year for Upper School students. Upper School students typically attend 5 days per week. The average school day consists of 6 hours and 50 minutes.

Upper School Student Profile Grade 6: 77 students (35 boys, 42 girls); Grade 7: 82 students (40 boys, 42 girls); Grade 8: 84 students (47 boys, 37 girls); Grade 9: 82 students (39 boys, 43 girls); Grade 10: 78 students (33 boys, 45 girls); Grade 11: 74 students (30 boys, 44 girls); Grade 12: 74 students (36 boys, 38 girls).

Faculty School total: 69. In upper school: 33 men, 35 women; 45 have advanced degrees.

Subjects Offered Civics, comparative politics, Pacific Northwest seminar, yoga.

Graduation Requirements Biology, health, Pacific Northwest seminar, physics.

Special Academic Programs Independent study; term-away projects; study abroad; programs in English, mathematics, general development for dyslexic students; special instructional classes for college-bound students with high intellectual potential who have diagnosed specific learning disability.

College Admission Counseling 77 students graduated in 2016; all went to college, including Occidental College; Santa Clara University; Syracuse University; University of Southern California; University of Washington; Wellesley College. Other: 3 had other specific plans. Median SAT critical reading: 620, median SAT math: 610, median SAT writing: 600, median combined SAT: 1865, median composite ACT: 28. 67% scored over 600 on SAT critical reading, 59% scored over 600 on SAT math, 67% scored over 600 on SAT writing, 57% scored over 1800 on combined SAT, 64% scored over 26 on composite ACT.

Student Life Upper grades have student council, honor system. Discipline rests equally with students and faculty.

Summer Programs Enrichment programs offered; held on campus; accepts boys and girls; not open to students from other schools. 40 students usually enrolled.

Tuition and Aid Day student tuition: $32,750. Tuition installment plan (monthly payment plans, individually arranged payment plans, Dewar Tuition Refund Plan). Need-based scholarship grants available. In 2016–17, 10% of upper-school students received aid. Total amount of financial aid awarded in 2016–17: $1,591,910.

Admissions Traditional secondary-level entrance grade is 9. For fall 2016, 206 students applied for upper-level admission, 85 were accepted, 32 enrolled. SSAT or SSAT, ERB, PSAT, SAT, PLAN or ACT required. Application fee required: $85. On-campus interview recommended.

Athletics Interscholastic: baseball (boys), basketball (b,g), cross-country running (b,g), flag football (b), Frisbee (b,g), soccer (b,g), softball (g), tennis (b,g), track and field (b,g), volleyball (g); intramural: golf (b,g), ultimate Frisbee (b,g); coed interscholastic: ultimate Frisbee; coed intramural: aerobics, aerobics/dance, backpacking, climbing, dance, fitness, hiking/backpacking, modern dance, outdoor activities, outdoor adventure, outdoor education, outdoor skills, outdoors, rock climbing, skiing (downhill), snowboarding, strength & conditioning, ultimate Frisbee, wall climbing, weight training, wilderness, yoga. 4 PE instructors, 35 coaches, 1 athletic trainer.

Computers Computers are regularly used in all academic, art, creative writing, English, foreign language, geography, history, information technology, journalism, library, mathematics, media, music, photography, publications, publishing, research skills, science, technology, writing, writing, yearbook classes. Computer network features include on-campus library services, online commercial services, Internet access, wireless campus network, Internet filtering or blocking technology, RYOD—Required Your On Device. Campus intranet, student e-mail accounts, and computer access in designated common areas are available to students. Students grades are available online. The school has a published electronic and media policy.

Contact Melaine Taylor, Associate Director of Admission. 206-832-1116. Fax: 206-525-5320. E-mail: admissionoffice@universityprep.org. Website: www.universityprep.org

UNIVERSITY SCHOOL OF JACKSON

232/240 McClellan Road
Jackson, Tennessee 38305

Head of School: Stuart Hirstein

General Information Coeducational day college-preparatory school. Grades PK–12. Founded: 1970. Setting: suburban. 130-acre campus. 4 buildings on campus. Approved or accredited by Southern Association of Colleges and Schools and Tennessee Department of Education. Member of National Association of Independent Schools. Endowment: $85,000. Total enrollment: 1,124. Upper school average class size: 18. Upper school faculty-student ratio: 1:13. There are 180 required school days per year for Upper School students. Upper School students typically attend 5 days per week. The average school day consists of 7 hours and 10 minutes.

Upper School Student Profile Grade 9: 69 students (34 boys, 35 girls); Grade 10: 63 students (37 boys, 26 girls); Grade 11: 94 students (57 boys, 37 girls); Grade 12: 86 students (42 boys, 44 girls).

Faculty School total: 100. In upper school: 15 men, 20 women; 26 have advanced degrees.

Subjects Offered 3-dimensional art, 3-dimensional design, accounting, acting, advanced biology, advanced chemistry, advanced math, Advanced Placement courses, advanced studio art-AP, algebra, American history, American literature, anatomy, anatomy and physiology, art, band, biology, biology-AP, broadcast journalism, calculus, calculus-AP, character education, chemistry, chemistry-AP, chorus, computer applications, computer programming, computer science, creative writing, current events, dramatic arts, ecology, economics, economics and history, English, English language-AP, English literature and composition-AP, English literature-AP, environmental science, environmental science-AP, European history, fine arts, French, geography, geology, geometry, government, government/civics, honors algebra, honors English, honors geometry, humanities, keyboarding, macroeconomics-AP, mathematics, music theory, music theory-AP, music-AP, performing arts, photography, physical education, physical science, physics, pre-calculus, psychology, science, social studies, Spanish, Spanish language-AP, studio art-AP, trigonometry, U.S. history, U.S. history-AP, vocal ensemble, world history, world religions, yearbook.

Graduation Requirements Arts and fine arts (art, music, dance, drama), computer science, English, foreign language, mathematics, science, social studies (includes history), 50 hours of community service.

Special Academic Programs 11 Advanced Placement exams for which test preparation is offered; honors section; academic accommodation for the gifted, the musically talented, and the artistically talented; ESL (6 students enrolled).

College Admission Counseling 82 students graduated in 2016; all went to college, including Mississippi State University; Rhodes College; Tennessee Technological University; The University of Tennessee; Union University; University of Arkansas. Median SAT critical reading: 550, median SAT math: 588, median SAT writing: 536, median combined SAT: 1674, median composite ACT: 26. 20% scored over 600 on SAT critical reading, 20% scored over 600 on SAT math, 20% scored over 600 on SAT writing, 20% scored over 1800 on combined SAT, 57% scored over 26 on composite ACT.

Student Life Upper grades have uniform requirement, student council, honor system. Discipline rests equally with students and faculty.

Summer Programs Remediation, enrichment, sports, art/fine arts, computer instruction programs offered; session focuses on enrichment and remediation; held on campus; accepts boys and girls; open to students from other schools. 700 students usually enrolled. 2017 schedule: June 1 to July 31. Application deadline: none.

Tuition and Aid Day student tuition: $7559–$10,373. Tuition installment plan (FACTS Tuition Payment Plan, monthly payment plans, quarterly payment plan). Tuition reduction for siblings, need-based scholarship grants, need-based financial aid available. In 2016–17, 3% of upper-school students received aid. Total amount of financial aid awarded in 2016–17: $180,000.

Admissions Traditional secondary-level entrance grade is 9. For fall 2016, 14 students applied for upper-level admission, 13 were accepted, 10 enrolled. Math Placement Exam, Otis-Lennon School Ability Test and writing sample required. Deadline for receipt of application materials: none. Application fee required: $50. On-campus interview required.

Athletics Interscholastic: baseball (boys), basketball (b,g), cheering (g), cross-country running (b,g), fitness (b,g), football (b), golf (b,g), physical fitness (b,g), soccer (b,g), softball (g), tennis (b,g), track and field (b,g), volleyball (g), weight lifting (b,g), weight training (b,g); intramural: bowling (b,g), in-line hockey (b); coed intramural: bowling. 2 coaches, 1 athletic trainer.

Computers Computers are regularly used in art, English, foreign language, history, journalism, keyboarding, music, science, technology, theater arts, word processing, writing, yearbook classes. Computer network features include on-campus library services, online commercial services, Internet access, wireless campus network, Internet filtering or blocking technology. Campus intranet and computer access in designated common areas are available to students. Students grades are available online. The school has a published electronic and media policy.

Contact Kay Shearin, Director of Admissions. 731-660-1692. Fax: 731-668-6910. E-mail: kshearin@usjbruins.org. Website: www.usjbruins.org

UPPER CANADA COLLEGE

200 Lonsdale Road
Toronto, Ontario M4V 1W6, Canada
Head of School: Mr. Sam McKinney
General Information Boys' boarding and day college-preparatory, arts, bilingual studies, technology, and International Baccalaureate school. Boarding grades 8–12, day grades K–12. Founded: 1829. Setting: urban. Students are housed in single-sex dormitories. 16-hectare campus. 4 buildings on campus. Approved or accredited by Canadian Association of Independent Schools, Conference of Independent Schools of Ontario, International Baccalaureate Organization, Ontario Ministry of Education, The Association of Boarding Schools, and Ontario Department of Education. Affiliate member of National Association of Independent Schools; member of Secondary School Admission Test Board. Language of instruction: English. Endowment: CAN$40 million. Total enrollment: 1,166. Upper school average class size: 20. Upper school faculty-student ratio: 1:8. There are 210 required school days per year for Upper School students. Upper School students typically attend 5 days per week. The average school day consists of 6 hours and 30 minutes.
Upper School Student Profile Grade 6: 80 students (80 boys); Grade 7: 120 students (120 boys); Grade 8: 125 students (125 boys); Grade 9: 145 students (145 boys); Grade 10: 159 students (159 boys); Grade 11: 165 students (165 boys); Grade 12: 165 students (165 boys). 15% of students are boarding students. 90% are province residents. 4 provinces are represented in upper school student body. 10% are international students. International students from China, Mexico, Russian Federation, Saudi Arabia, and United States; 17 other countries represented in student body.
Faculty School total: 138. In upper school: 57 men, 28 women; 35 have advanced degrees; 17 reside on campus.
Subjects Offered 3-dimensional design, advanced biology, advanced chemistry, advanced math, algebra, all academic, American history, art, athletics, biology, calculus, career and personal planning, chemistry, Chinese, civics, community service, computer multimedia, computer programming, computer science, creative arts, creative writing, digital art, drama, economics, English, English literature, environmental science, equality and freedom, European history, expository writing, film, film studies, fine arts, French, functions, geography, geometry, German, health, history, instrumental music, International Baccalaureate courses, Latin, mathematics, music, physical education, physics, science, social sciences, social studies, Spanish, theater, theater arts, theory of knowledge, trigonometry, visual arts, world history, writing.
Graduation Requirements English, foreign language, mathematics, science, social sciences, IB diploma requirements. Community service is required.
Special Academic Programs International Baccalaureate program; honors section; term-away projects; study abroad.
College Admission Counseling 165 students graduated in 2016; 157 went to college, including Dalhousie University; McGill University; Queen's University at Kingston; The University of Western Ontario; University of Toronto; University of Waterloo. Other: 3 had other specific plans.
Student Life Upper grades have uniform requirement, student council. Discipline rests equally with students and faculty.
Summer Programs Enrichment, advancement, art/fine arts, computer instruction programs offered; session focuses on enrichment and credit courses; held on campus; accepts boys and girls; open to students from other schools. 300 students usually enrolled. 2017 schedule: June 15 to August 30. Application deadline: none.
Tuition and Aid Day student tuition: CAN$33,550; 7-day tuition and room/board: CAN$54,510–CAN$61,010. Tuition installment plan (twice annual payment plan or full-payment discount plan). Merit scholarship grants, need-based scholarship grants, need-based financial assistance available. In 2016–17, 18% of upper-school students received aid, total upper-school merit-scholarship money awarded: CAN$50,000. Total amount of financial aid awarded in 2016–17: CAN$4,500,000.
Admissions Traditional secondary-level entrance grade is 9. SSAT or SSAT, ERB, PSAT, SAT, PLAN or ACT required. Deadline for receipt of application materials: none. Application fee required: CAN$200. Interview required.
Athletics Interscholastic: aquatics, badminton, baseball, basketball, crew, cricket, cross-country running, dance, football, golf, hockey, ice hockey, lacrosse, rowing, rugby, running, soccer, softball, squash, swimming and diving, tennis, track and field, volleyball; intramural: alpine skiing, backpacking, ball hockey, basketball, bicycling, canoeing/kayaking, climbing, combined training, cooperative games, fencing, field hockey, floor hockey, hiking/backpacking, hockey, ice hockey, in-line hockey, indoor hockey, indoor soccer, kayaking, martial arts, mountain biking, outdoor activities, outdoor adventure, outdoor education, outdoor recreation, outdoor skills, physical training, power lifting, rock climbing, ropes courses, self defense, skiing (downhill), snowboarding, soccer, softball, street hockey, strength & conditioning, volleyball, weight training, wilderness, winter soccer. 4 coaches, 1 athletic trainer.
Computers Computers are regularly used in business education, computer applications, digital applications, graphic arts, graphic design, graphics, media arts, technology classes. Computer network features include on-campus library services, online commercial services, Internet access, wireless campus network, Internet filtering or blocking technology, laptop school; laptop used across all subjects. Campus intranet, student e-mail accounts, and computer access in designated common areas are available to students. The school has a published electronic and media policy.
Contact Tricia Rankin, Associate Director of Admission. 416-488-1125 Ext. 2221. Fax: 416-484-8618. E-mail: trankin@ucc.on.ca. Website: www.ucc.on.ca

URSULINE ACADEMY

85 Lowder Street
Dedham, Massachusetts 02026-4299
Head of School: Ms. Rosann Whiting
General Information Girls' day college-preparatory and college preparatory school, affiliated with Roman Catholic Church. Grades 7–12. Founded: 1946. Setting: suburban. Nearest major city is Boston. 28-acre campus. 3 buildings on campus. Approved or accredited by Association of Independent Schools in New England, National Catholic Education Association, New England Association of Schools and Colleges, The College Board, and Massachusetts Department of Education. Member of National Association of Independent Schools. Total enrollment: 397. Upper school average class size: 18. Upper school faculty-student ratio: 1:9. Upper School students typically attend 5 days per week. The average school day consists of 5 hours and 45 minutes.
Upper School Student Profile Grade 7: 58 students (58 girls); Grade 8: 66 students (66 girls); Grade 9: 92 students (92 girls); Grade 10: 80 students (80 girls); Grade 11: 77 students (77 girls); Grade 12: 63 students (63 girls). 88% of students are Roman Catholic.
Faculty School total: 38. In upper school: 5 men, 31 women; 34 have advanced degrees.
Subjects Offered Advanced Placement courses, algebra, American history, American literature, anatomy and physiology, art, art history, arts, biology, biology-AP, calculus, calculus-AP, campus ministry, chemistry, chemistry-AP, church history, civics, communication arts, computer studies, English, English literature, English-AP, French, geography, geometry, government/civics, grammar, history, Latin, life science, mathematics, modern European history-AP, music, physical education, physical science, physics, pre-algebra, pre-calculus, psychology, public speaking, social studies, Spanish, Spanish language-AP, studio art, study skills, theology, trigonometry, U.S. history, U.S. history-AP, world history, world literature.
Graduation Requirements Arts and fine arts (art, music, dance, drama), computer science, English, foreign language, mathematics, physical education (includes health), religion (includes Bible studies and theology), science, social studies (includes history), study skills, senior year community service field project.
Special Academic Programs 7 Advanced Placement exams for which test preparation is offered; honors section.
College Admission Counseling 82 students graduated in 2016; all went to college, including Boston College; Boston University; College of the Holy Cross; Providence College; Stonehill College; University of Notre Dame. Mean SAT critical reading: 612, mean SAT math: 587, mean SAT writing: 619, mean combined SAT: 1818.
Student Life Upper grades have uniform requirement, student council, honor system. Discipline rests primarily with faculty. Attendance at religious services is required.
Tuition and Aid Day student tuition: $18,900. Tuition installment plan (Insured Tuition Payment Plan, FACTS Tuition Payment Plan, monthly payment plans, individually arranged payment plans, semester, quarterly, and monthly payment plans). Need-based scholarship grants available. In 2016–17, 15% of upper-school students received aid.
Admissions Traditional secondary-level entrance grade is 9. High School Placement Test or ISEE required. Deadline for receipt of application materials: December 16. Application fee required: $40. Interview recommended.
Athletics Interscholastic: alpine skiing, basketball, cross-country running, diving, field hockey, golf, hockey, ice hockey, indoor track, lacrosse, running, soccer, softball, swimming and diving, tennis, track and field, volleyball, winter (indoor) track; intramural: ballet, dance, golf, sailing, skiing (downhill), tennis, yoga. 2 PE instructors, 26 coaches, 1 athletic trainer.
Computers Computers are regularly used in all classes. Computer network features include on-campus library services, Internet access, wireless campus network, Internet filtering or blocking technology. Campus intranet, student e-mail accounts, and computer access in designated common areas are available to students. Students grades are available online. The school has a published electronic and media policy.
Contact Mrs. Maura Polles, Director of Admissions. 781-493 7727. Fax: 781-329-3926. E-mail: admissions@ursulineacademy.net. Website: www.ursulineacademy.net

THE URSULINE ACADEMY OF DALLAS

4900 Walnut Hill Lane
Dallas, Texas 75229
Head of School: Mrs. Andrea Shurley
General Information Girls' day college-preparatory school, affiliated with Roman Catholic Church. Grades 9–12. Founded: 1874. Setting: urban. 26-acre campus. 5 buildings on campus. Approved or accredited by Independent Schools Association of the Southwest and Texas Department of Education. Member of National Association of Independent Schools. Total enrollment: 843. Upper school average class size: 18. Upper school faculty-student ratio: 1:10. There are 180 required school days per year for Upper School students. Upper School students typically attend 5 days per week. The average school day consists of 7 hours.
Upper School Student Profile Grade 9: 214 students (214 girls); Grade 10: 222 students (222 girls); Grade 11: 216 students (216 girls); Grade 12: 192 students (192 girls). 78% of students are Roman Catholic.

Faculty School total: 103. In upper school: 20 men, 83 women; 73 have advanced degrees.

Subjects Offered 20th century history, 20th century world history, 3-dimensional design, acting, advanced biology, advanced chemistry, advanced computer applications, advanced math, Advanced Placement courses, advanced studio art-AP, algebra, American government, American history, American history-AP, anatomy, anatomy and physiology, Arabic, Arabic studies, art history, art history-AP, art-AP, athletics, band, Basic programming, biology, biology-AP, bookbinding, calculus, calculus-AP, campus ministry, ceramics, chemistry, chemistry-AP, Chinese, choir, Christian and Hebrew scripture, Christian scripture, clayworking, community service, comparative government and politics, comparative government and politics-AP, comparative religion, computer graphics, computer programming, computer science, computer science-AP, concert band, concert choir, costumes and make-up, creative dance, creative writing, current events, dance, digital imaging, digital photography, discrete mathematics, drama, drawing, economics, engineering, English language and composition-AP, English literature, English literature and composition-AP, environmental science, environmental science-AP, European history, European history-AP, filmmaking, fitness, forensics, French, French language-AP, geography, geology, geometry, government, government and politics-AP, government-AP, government/civics, health and wellness, honors algebra, honors English, honors geometry, human geography - AP, internship, intro to computers, introduction to theater, journalism, Latin, macroeconomics-AP, Mandarin, microeconomics-AP, music theory-AP, neuroscience, newspaper, oceanography, orchestra, painting, peer ministry, photography, physical education, physics, physics-AP, pre-calculus, printmaking, psychology, psychology-AP, set design, social justice, Spanish, Spanish language-AP, Spanish literature-AP, speech, speech communications, stage design, statistics, statistics-AP, student publications, studio art, studio art-AP, theater, theology, trigonometry, U.S. government, U.S. government and politics-AP, U.S. history, U.S. history-AP, U.S. literature, Web authoring, Web site design, wellness, Western civilization, world history, world literature, yearbook.

Graduation Requirements Arts and fine arts (art, music, dance, drama), computer science, English, foreign language, mathematics, physical education (includes health), religion (includes Bible studies and theology), science, social studies (includes history), speech. Community service is required.

Special Academic Programs Advanced Placement exam preparation; honors section; independent study.

College Admission Counseling 204 students graduated in 2016; 201 went to college. Other: 1 entered military service, 3 had other specific plans. Mean SAT critical reading: 614, mean SAT math: 603, mean SAT writing: 629, mean combined SAT: 1846, mean composite ACT: 28.

Student Life Upper grades have uniform requirement, student council, honor system. Discipline rests primarily with faculty. Attendance at religious services is required.

Summer Programs Remediation, advancement, art/fine arts, computer instruction programs offered; session focuses on remediation and advancement; held on campus; accepts girls; not open to students from other schools. 200 students usually enrolled. 2017 schedule: June 7 to June 28. Application deadline: February 14.

Tuition and Aid Day student tuition: $20,050. Guaranteed tuition plan. Tuition installment plan (FACTS Tuition Payment Plan, monthly payment plans, individually arranged payment plans, annual, semi-annual, and monthly (by bank draft) payment plans). Merit scholarship grants, need-based scholarship grants available. In 2016–17, 26% of upper-school students received aid; total upper-school merit-scholarship money awarded: $89,000. Total amount of financial aid awarded in 2016–17: $1,154,600.

Admissions Traditional secondary-level entrance grade is 9. For fall 2016, 400 students applied for upper-level admission, 220 enrolled. ISEE required. Deadline for receipt of application materials: January 6. Application fee required: $100. On-campus interview recommended.

Athletics Interscholastic: basketball, cheering, crew, cross-country running, drill team, golf, lacrosse, soccer, softball, swimming and diving, tennis, track and field, volleyball. 3 PE instructors, 15 coaches, 1 athletic trainer.

Computers Computers are regularly used in all classes. Computer network features include on-campus library services, online commercial services, Internet access, wireless campus network, 4-year technology support. Campus intranet and student e-mail accounts are available to students. Students grades are available online. The school has a published electronic and media policy.

Contact Mrs. Jill Tilden, Admissions Assistant. 469-232-1804. Fax: 469-232-1836. E-mail: jtilden@ursulinedallas.org. Website: www.ursulinedallas.org

VALLEY CHRISTIAN HIGH SCHOOL

100 Skyway Drive
San Jose, California 95111

Head of School: Dr. Clifford Daugherty

General Information Coeducational day college-preparatory, arts, religious studies, Conservatory of the Arts, and Applied Math, Science and Engineering Institute school, affiliated with Christian faith. Grades K–12. Founded: 1960. Setting: suburban. 53-acre campus. 6 buildings on campus. Approved or accredited by Association of Christian Schools International, Western Association of Schools and Colleges, and California Department of Education. Total enrollment: 2,668. Upper school average class size: 27. Upper school faculty-student ratio: 1:15. There are 175 required school days per year

for Upper School students. Upper School students typically attend 5 days per week. The average school day consists of 6 hours and 45 minutes.

Upper School Student Profile Grade 9: 422 students (217 boys, 205 girls); Grade 10: 413 students (224 boys, 189 girls); Grade 11: 402 students (199 boys, 203 girls); Grade 12: 362 students (192 boys, 170 girls). 80% of students are Christian.

Faculty School total: 110. In upper school: 55 men, 55 women; 74 have advanced degrees.

Subjects Offered Baseball, Bible as literature, business studies, choir, Christianity, community service, computer graphics, computer programming-AP, cultural geography, drama, English literature, English literature and composition-AP, entrepreneurship, environmental science, health and wellness, history-AP, integrated arts, jazz, lab/keyboard, language-AP, literature-AP, media production, music-AP, physical education, playwriting and directing, speech, telecommunications, theater production, U.S. literature, United States government-AP, video, world history-AP.

Graduation Requirements American history, American literature, art appreciation, Bible studies, biology, Christian and Hebrew scripture, Christian doctrine, Christian studies, computers, economics and history, English composition, English literature, global studies, physical science, religion (includes Bible studies and theology), science, U.S. government, U.S. history, world literature.

Special Academic Programs 23 Advanced Placement exams for which test preparation is offered; honors section; study at local college for college credit; academic accommodation for the musically talented and the artistically talented; remedial math; programs in English, mathematics, general development for dyslexic students.

College Admission Counseling 323 students graduated in 2016; all went to college, including California Polytechnic State University, San Luis Obispo; California State University, Chico; Pepperdine University; San Jose State University; University of California, Berkeley; University of California, Davis. Mean SAT critical reading: 570, mean SAT math: 580, mean SAT writing: 570, mean combined SAT: 1720, mean composite ACT: 26.

Student Life Upper grades have specified standards of dress, student council. Discipline rests primarily with faculty. Attendance at religious services is required.

Summer Programs Remediation, enrichment, advancement, sports, art/fine arts, computer instruction programs offered; session focuses on advancement, remediation, and enrichment; held on campus; accepts boys and girls; open to students from other schools. 500 students usually enrolled. 2017 schedule: June 12 to July 28. Application deadline: June 1.

Tuition and Aid Day student tuition: $19,955. Tuition installment plan (FACTS Tuition Payment Plan). Need-based scholarship grants available. In 2016–17, 15% of upper-school students received aid. Total amount of financial aid awarded in 2016–17: $2,500,000.

Admissions Traditional secondary-level entrance grade is 9. For fall 2016, 676 students applied for upper-level admission, 392 were accepted, 228 enrolled. Deadline for receipt of application materials: January 30. Application fee required: $70. Interview recommended.

Athletics Interscholastic: aquatics (boys, girls), badminton (b,g), baseball (b), basketball (b,g), cheering (b), cross-country running (b,g), dance squad (b,g), dance team (b), diving (b,g), football (b), golf (b,g), ice hockey (b,g), physical training (b,g), soccer (b,g), softball (g), swimming and diving (b,g), tennis (b,g), track and field (b,g), volleyball (b,g), water polo (b,g), weight training (b,g), wrestling (b); intramural: weight training (b,g); coed intramural: drill team. 7 PE instructors, 46 coaches, 2 athletic trainers.

Computers Computers are regularly used in business education, programming classes. Computer network features include on-campus library services, Internet access, wireless campus network, Internet filtering or blocking technology. Campus intranet, student e-mail accounts, and computer access in designated common areas are available to students. Students grades are available online. The school has a published electronic and media policy.

Contact Alana James, High School Admissions Coordinator. 408-513-2512. Fax: 408-513-2527. E-mail: ajames@vcs.net. Website: www.vcs.net

VALLEY CHRISTIAN SCHOOL

2526 Sunset Lane
Missoula, Montana 59804

Head of School: Mrs. Beth Howard

General Information Coeducational day and distance learning college-preparatory and general academic school, affiliated with Christian faith. Grades K–12. Distance learning grades 7–12. Founded: 1978. Setting: small town. Nearest major city is Spokane, WA. 5-acre campus. 2 buildings on campus. Approved or accredited by Montana Department of Education. Total enrollment: 211. Upper school average class size: 18. Upper school faculty-student ratio: 1:8. Upper School students typically attend 5 days per week.

Upper School Student Profile Grade 7: 26 students (10 boys, 16 girls); Grade 8: 17 students (7 boys, 10 girls); Grade 9: 25 students (13 boys, 12 girls); Grade 10: 15 students (5 boys, 10 girls); Grade 11: 9 students (1 boy, 8 girls); Grade 12: 12 students (5 boys, 7 girls). 98% of students are Christian.

Faculty School total: 30. In upper school: 6 men, 8 women; 5 have advanced degrees.

Subjects Offered Accounting, algebra, American history, American literature, art, arts, band, Bible studies, biology, biology-AP, business, business skills, chemistry, chorus, computer science, economics, English, English literature, environmental science, fine arts, geometry, German, government/civics, health, keyboarding, literature, mathematics, physical education, physics, science, social studies, Spanish, world history.

Special Academic Programs Advanced Placement exam preparation; honors section.

College Admission Counseling 13 students graduated in 2016; 6 went to college, including Montana State University; Montana State University Billings; The University of Montana Western; University of Richmond. Other: 2 went to work.

Student Life Upper grades have specified standards of dress, student council, honor system. Discipline rests primarily with faculty. Attendance at religious services is required.

Tuition and Aid Day student tuition: $4975. Tuition installment plan (FACTS Tuition Payment Plan, monthly payment plans, individually arranged payment plans). Tuition reduction for siblings, need-based scholarship grants, paying campus jobs available.

Admissions Traditional secondary-level entrance grade is 12. For fall 2016, 25 students applied for upper-level admission, 25 were accepted, 25 enrolled. Deadline for receipt of application materials: none. Application fee required: $100. Interview recommended.

Athletics Interscholastic: basketball (boys, girls), football (b,g), independent competitive sports (b,g), soccer (b), tennis (b,g), track and field (b,g), volleyball (b,g). 1 PE instructor, 10 coaches.

Computers Computers are regularly used in accounting, foreign language, information technology, journalism, library skills, multimedia classes. Computer network features include Internet access, Internet filtering or blocking technology. Campus intranet and computer access in designated common areas are available to students. Students grades are available online. The school has a published electronic and media policy.

Contact Sherry Cabrera, Office Manager. 406-549-0482 Ext. 230. Fax: 406-549-5047. E-mail: sherry.cabrera@valleychristian.org. Website: www.valleychristian.org

THE VALLEY SCHOOL

5255 S. Linden Rd.
Swartz Creek, Michigan 48473

Head of School: Kaye C. Panchula

General Information Coeducational day college-preparatory school. Grades PK–12. Founded: 1970. Setting: urban. Nearest major city is Flint. 5 acre campus. 1 building on campus. Approved or accredited by Independent Schools Association of the Central States. Total enrollment: 64. Upper school average class size: 18. Upper school faculty-student ratio: 1:8. There are 170 required school days per year for Upper School students. Upper School students typically attend 5 days per week. The average school day consists of 6 hours and 30 minutes.

Upper School Student Profile Grade 9: 3 students (2 boys, 1 girl); Grade 10: 5 students (2 boys, 3 girls); Grade 11: 4 students (2 boys, 2 girls); Grade 12: 4 students (2 boys, 2 girls).

Faculty School total: 15. In upper school: 4 men, 3 women; 4 have advanced degrees.

Subjects Offered Algebra, American history, American literature, anatomy, art, art history, biology, chemistry, current events, earth science, English, English literature, European history, expository writing, fine arts, geometry, government/civics, grammar, history, mathematics, music, physical education, physics, probability and statistics, SAT/ACT preparation, science, social sciences, Spanish, trigonometry, world cultures, world history, world literature, world religions, writing.

Graduation Requirements Arts and fine arts (art, music, dance, drama), biology, college counseling, English, foreign language, mathematics, science, social sciences, social studies (includes history), senior project off campus.

Special Academic Programs Honors section; study at local college for college credit; academic accommodation for the gifted and the artistically talented.

College Admission Counseling 6 students graduated in 2016; all went to college, including University of Michigan.

Student Life Upper grades have student council, honor system. Discipline rests equally with students and faculty.

Tuition and Aid Day student tuition: $9899. Tuition installment plan (FACTS Tuition Payment Plan). Tuition reduction for siblings, merit scholarship grants, need-based scholarship grants available. In 2016–17, 75% of upper-school students received aid; total upper-school merit-scholarship money awarded: $31,500. Total amount of financial aid awarded in 2016–17: $200,000.

Admissions Traditional secondary-level entrance grade is 9. For fall 2016, 5 students applied for upper-level admission, 3 were accepted, 2 enrolled. Brigance Test of Basic Skills, PSAT or school's own exam required. Deadline for receipt of application materials: none. No application fee required. On-campus interview required.

Athletics Interscholastic: basketball (boys, girls), golf (b), outdoor skills (b,g), outdoors (b,g), physical fitness (b,g), soccer (b,g), tennis (g), volleyball (g). 2 PE instructors, 3 coaches.

Computers Computers are regularly used in art, English, mathematics, science, social sciences, stock market, study skills, writing classes. Computer resources include

Internet access, wireless campus network. Computer access in designated common areas is available to students.

Contact Ms. Minka Owens, Director of Admissions. 810-767-4004. Fax: 810-655-0853. E-mail: email@valleyschool.org. Website: www.valleyschool.org

VALLEY VIEW SCHOOL

North Brookfield, Massachusetts
See Special Needs Schools section.

VALWOOD SCHOOL

4380 US Highway 41 North
Hahira, Georgia 31632

Head of School: Dr. Darren Pascavage

General Information Coeducational day college-preparatory school. Grades PK–12. Founded: 1969. Setting: rural. Nearest major city is Valdosta. 45-acre campus. 7 buildings on campus. Approved or accredited by Georgia Accrediting Commission, Georgia Independent School Association, Southern Association of Colleges and Schools, and Southern Association of Independent Schools. Member of National Association of Independent Schools and Secondary School Admission Test Board. Total enrollment: 509. Upper school average class size: 20. Upper school faculty-student ratio: 1:12. There are 180 required school days per year for Upper School students. Upper School students typically attend 5 days per week. The average school day consists of 7 hours and 30 minutes.

Upper School Student Profile Grade 6: 32 students (15 boys, 17 girls); Grade 7: 40 students (16 boys, 24 girls); Grade 8: 38 students (25 boys, 13 girls); Grade 9: 43 students (22 boys, 21 girls); Grade 10: 44 students (25 boys, 19 girls); Grade 11: 43 students (23 boys, 20 girls); Grade 12: 44 students (26 boys, 18 girls).

Faculty School total: 45. In upper school: 7 men, 8 women; 6 have advanced degrees.

Subjects Offered Algebra, American history, anatomy and physiology, art, biology, business skills, calculus, calculus-AP, chemistry, chemistry-AP, composition, drama, economics, English, English language-AP, English literature-AP, fitness, French, French-AP, geography, geometry, global issues, government/civics, health, honors algebra, honors English, honors geometry, instruments, Latin, literature, mathematics, model United Nations, music, music appreciation, physical education, physical science, physics, physics-AP, pre-calculus, psychology, science, senior project, Spanish, speech, strings, technology, trigonometry, U.S. history, U.S. history-AP, world history, world history-AP, yearbook.

Graduation Requirements Arts and fine arts (art, music, dance, drama), composition, computer science, English, foreign language, mathematics, physical education (includes health), science, social sciences, social studies (includes history), speech, technology, 20 hours of community service annually.

Special Academic Programs 15 Advanced Placement exams for which test preparation is offered; honors section; independent study; academic accommodation for the gifted and the musically talented.

College Admission Counseling 45 students graduated in 2016; all went to college, including Georgia Southern University; University of Georgia; Valdosta State University. Mean SAT critical reading: 554, mean SAT math: 528, mean SAT writing: 559, mean combined SAT: 1641, mean composite ACT: 24.

Student Life Upper grades have specified standards of dress, student council, honor system. Discipline rests primarily with faculty.

Tuition and Aid Day student tuition: $12,703. Tuition installment plan (monthly payment plans). Tuition reduction for siblings, merit scholarship grants, need-based scholarship grants available.

Admissions Traditional secondary-level entrance grade is 9. For fall 2016, 32 students applied for upper-level admission, 24 were accepted, 20 enrolled. ACT, Explore, latest standardized score from previous school, PSAT or SAT or Stanford Achievement Test required. Deadline for receipt of application materials: none. Application fee required: $50. Interview recommended.

Athletics Interscholastic: baseball (boys), basketball (b,g), cheering (g), cross-country running (b,g), football (b), golf (b,g), soccer (b,g), softball (g), tennis (b,g), track and field (b,g), volleyball (g), wrestling (b). 3 coaches, 1 athletic trainer.

Computers Computers are regularly used in creative writing, mathematics, science, technology, writing classes. Computer network features include on-campus library services, Internet access, wireless campus network, Internet filtering or blocking technology. Student e-mail accounts are available to students. Students grades are available online.

Contact Mrs. Val Gallahan, Director of Admissions. 229-242-8491. Fax: 229-245-7894. E-mail: admissions@valwood.org. Website: www.valwood.org

THE VANGUARD SCHOOL

Lake Wales, Florida
See Special Needs Schools section.

VENTA PREPARATORY SCHOOL

2013 Old Carp Road
Ottawa, Ontario K0A 1L0, Canada

Head of School: Ms. Marilyn Mansfield

General Information Coeducational boarding and day college-preparatory and music school. Boarding grades 1–10, day grades JK–10. Founded: 1981. Setting: small town. Students are housed in single-sex by floor dormitories and single-sex dormitories. 50-acre campus. 8 buildings on campus. Approved or accredited by Ontario Ministry of Education and Ontario Department of Education. Member of Secondary School Admission Test Board. Language of instruction: English. Total enrollment: 66. Upper school average class size: 12. Upper school faculty-student ratio: 1:6. There are 167 required school days per year for Upper School students. Upper School students typically attend 5 days per week. The average school day consists of 8 hours and 30 minutes.

Upper School Student Profile Grade 8: 11 students (7 boys, 4 girls). 5% of students are boarding students. 90% are province residents. 2 provinces are represented in upper school student body. 10% are international students. International students from China, Hungary, India, Nigeria, and Sweden.

Faculty School total: 29. In upper school: 4 men, 4 women; 7 have advanced degrees; 6 reside on campus.

Subjects Offered 3-dimensional art, 3-dimensional design, advanced biology, advanced chemistry, algebra, all academic, alternative physical education, applied arts, athletics, basketball.

Special Academic Programs Independent study; academic accommodation for the gifted; remedial reading and/or remedial writing; remedial math; programs in English, mathematics, general development for dyslexic students; ESL (2 students enrolled).

College Admission Counseling 20 students graduated in 2016.

Student Life Upper grades have uniform requirement, honor system. Discipline rests primarily with faculty.

Tuition and Aid Day student tuition: CAN$17,070–CAN$18,585; 5-day tuition and room/board: CAN$30,965–CAN$33,895; 7-day tuition and room/board: CAN$34,465–CAN$37,395. Tuition installment plan (monthly payment plans, individually arranged payment plans). Tuition reduction for siblings, merit scholarship grants available. Total upper-school merit-scholarship money awarded for 2016–17: CAN$6000.

Admissions Traditional secondary-level entrance grade is 8. For fall 2016, 1 student applied for upper-level admission, 1 was accepted, 1 enrolled. Psychoeducational evaluation, Wechsler Individual Achievement Test or Wechsler Intelligence Scale for Children III required. Deadline for receipt of application materials: none. Application fee required: CAN$150. On-campus interview required.

Athletics Coed Interscholastic: basketball, rugby, soccer; coed intramural: ball hockey, baseball, basketball, broomball, canoeing/kayaking, cross-country running, fitness, football, golf, handball, ice hockey, jogging, outdoor recreation, physical fitness, physical training, running, soccer, track and field, ultimate Frisbee, yoga. 1 PE instructor.

Computers Computers are regularly used in current events, geography, keyboarding, mathematics, research skills, science classes. Computer network features include Internet access, wireless campus network, Internet filtering or blocking technology. Student e-mail accounts and computer access in designated common areas are available to students. The school has a published electronic and media policy.

Contact Ms. Elizabeth Barnes, Manager of Admissions. 613-839-2175 Ext. 240. Fax: 613-839-1956. E-mail: ebarnes@ventaprep.com. Website: www.ventapreparatoryschool.com

VERDALA INTERNATIONAL SCHOOL

Fort Pembroke
Pembroke PBK1641, Malta

Head of School: Mr. Totty Aris

General Information Coeducational boarding and day college-preparatory and general academic school. Boarding grades 9–12, day grades PK–12. Founded: 1977. Setting: suburban. Nearest major city is Valletta, Malta. Students are housed in host family homes. 6-acre campus. 6 buildings on campus. Approved or accredited by International Baccalaureate Organization and Middle States Association of Colleges and Schools. Member of European Council of International Schools. Language of instruction: English. Endowment: €91,000. Total enrollment: 310. Upper school average class size: 17. Upper school faculty-student ratio: 1:7. There are 176 required school days per year for Upper School students. Upper School students typically attend 5 days per week. The average school day consists of 5 hours and 30 minutes.

Upper School Student Profile Grade 9: 28 students (15 boys, 13 girls); Grade 10: 31 students (14 boys, 17 girls); Grade 11: 33 students (16 boys, 17 girls); Grade 12: 27 students (11 boys, 16 girls).

Faculty School total: 48. In upper school: 5 men, 18 women; 7 have advanced degrees.

Subjects Offered Algebra, art, art history, biology, calculus, chemistry, computer science, drama, English, English literature, fine arts, French, geography, geometry, grammar, health, history, Italian, mathematics, music, physical education, physics, psychology, science, social studies, Spanish, theory of knowledge, trigonometry, world history, world literature, writing.

Graduation Requirements Arts and fine arts (art, music, dance, drama), computer science, English, foreign language, mathematics, physical education (includes health), science, social studies (includes history).

Special Academic Programs International Baccalaureate program; ESL (52 students enrolled).

College Admission Counseling 34 students graduated in 2016; all went to college. Median SAT critical reading: 500, median SAT math: 640, median SAT writing: 520.

Student Life Upper grades have specified standards of dress, student council, honor system. Discipline rests primarily with faculty.

Tuition and Aid Day student tuition: €6780; 7-day tuition and room/board: €7260. Tuition installment plan (monthly payment plans, individually arranged payment plans). Tuition reduction for siblings, need-based scholarship grants available. In 2016–17, 64% of upper-school students received aid. Total amount of financial aid awarded in 2016–17: $18,750.

Admissions Traditional secondary-level entrance grade is 9. Academic Profile Tests required. Deadline for receipt of application materials: none. No application fee required. On-campus interview required.

Athletics Interscholastic: basketball (boys), volleyball (b,g); intramural: physical fitness (b,g), soccer (b,g), swimming and diving (b,g), track and field (b,g); coed intramural: physical fitness, swimming and diving. 2 coaches, 1 athletic trainer.

Computers Computer resources include on-campus library services, online commercial services, Internet access. Computer access in designated common areas is available to students.

Contact Mrs. Daphne Baldacchino, Admissions Executive. 356-21375133. Fax: 356-21372387. E-mail: admissions@verdala.org. Website: www.verdala.org

VICKSBURG CATHOLIC SCHOOL

1900 Grove Street
Vicksburg, Mississippi 39183

Head of School: Dr. Virgil "Buddy" Strickland

General Information Coeducational day college-preparatory school, affiliated with Roman Catholic Church. Grades PK–12. Founded: 1860. Setting: urban. Nearest major city is Jackson. 8-acre campus. 2 buildings on campus. Approved or accredited by National Catholic Education Association, Southern Association of Colleges and Schools, and Mississippi Department of Education. Endowment: $350,000. Total enrollment: 536. Upper school average class size: 15. Upper school faculty-student ratio: 1:10. There are 180 required school days per year for Upper School students. Upper School students typically attend 5 days per week. The average school day consists of 5 hours and 50 minutes.

Upper School Student Profile Grade 7: 38 students (17 boys, 21 girls); Grade 8: 38 students (11 boys, 27 girls); Grade 9: 44 students (24 boys, 20 girls); Grade 10: 49 students (24 boys, 25 girls); Grade 11: 41 students (21 boys, 20 girls); Grade 12: 46 students (24 boys, 22 girls). 40% of students are Roman Catholic.

Faculty School total: 28. In upper school: 9 men, 19 women; 9 have advanced degrees.

Subjects Offered ACT preparation, algebra, anatomy and physiology, art, band, biology, biology-AP, calculus-AP, chemistry, chemistry-AP, choir, computer applications, desktop publishing, drama, earth science, economics, English, English language and composition-AP, environmental science, geography, geology, geometry, health, honors algebra, honors English, honors geometry, honors U.S. history, keyboarding, law, learning lab, literature, music, personal finance, physical education, physical science, physics-AP, pre-algebra, pre-calculus, psychology, sociology, Spanish, speech, state history, statistics, theology, trigonometry, U.S. government, U.S. history, world history, yearbook.

Graduation Requirements ACT preparation, algebra, American government, American history, art, biology, computer skills, economics, English, foreign language, geography, geometry, health, history, lab science, personal finance, physical education (includes health), state history, theology, U.S. government, U.S. history, world history, Mississippi state requirements, MAIS graduation requirements.

Special Academic Programs 5 Advanced Placement exams for which test preparation is offered; honors section; study at local college for college credit.

College Admission Counseling 41 students graduated in 2016; all went to college, including Hinds Community College; Louisiana State University and Agricultural & Mechanical College; Louisiana Tech University; Mississippi State University; University of Mississippi; University of Southern Mississippi. Median composite ACT: 23. 30% scored over 26 on composite ACT.

Student Life Upper grades have uniform requirement, student council, honor system. Discipline rests primarily with faculty. Attendance at religious services is required.

Tuition and Aid Day student tuition: $6900. Tuition installment plan (FACTS Tuition Payment Plan). Tuition reduction for siblings, need-based scholarship grants available. In 2016–17, 18% of upper-school students received aid. Total amount of financial aid awarded in 2016–17: $75,000.

Admissions Traditional secondary-level entrance grade is 7. For fall 2016, 24 students applied for upper-level admission, 22 were accepted, 22 enrolled. Admissions testing required. Deadline for receipt of application materials: none. Application fee required: $75. On-campus interview recommended.

Athletics Interscholastic: baseball (boys), basketball (b,g), cheering (g), cross-country running (b,g), dance squad (g), football (b), golf (b,g), power lifting (b), soccer (b,g), softball (g), swimming and diving (b,g), tennis (b,g), track and field (b,g); coed interscholastic: swimming and diving, tennis. 1 PE instructor, 1 coach.

Computers Computers are regularly used in technology, Web site design, yearbook classes. Computer network features include on-campus library services, online commercial services, Internet access, wireless campus network, Internet filtering or blocking technology. Student e-mail accounts are available to students. Students grades are available online. The school has a published electronic and media policy.

Contact Mrs. Patricia Rabalais, Registrar. 601-636-2256 Ext. 16. Fax: 601-631-0430. E-mail: patricia.rabalais@vicksburgcatholic.org. Website: www.vicksburgcatholic.org

VICTOR VALLEY CHRISTIAN SCHOOL

15260 Nisqualli Road
Victorville, California 92395

Head of School: Mrs. Deb Clarkson

General Information Coeducational day college-preparatory and community outreach and cultural sensitivity school, affiliated with Assemblies of God. Grades K–12. Founded: 1972. Setting: suburban. Nearest major city is Ontario. 10-acre campus. 5 buildings on campus. Approved or accredited by Association of Christian Schools International and Western Association of Schools and Colleges. Languages of instruction: English and Spanish. Total enrollment: 275. Upper school average class size: 22. Upper school faculty-student ratio: 1:16. There are 176 required school days per year for Upper School students. Upper School students typically attend 5 days per week. The average school day consists of 7 hours and 15 minutes.

Upper School Student Profile Grade 6: 20 students (11 boys, 9 girls); Grade 7: 17 students (8 boys, 9 girls); Grade 8: 22 students (11 boys, 11 girls); Grade 9: 18 students (8 boys, 10 girls); Grade 10: 26 students (12 boys, 14 girls); Grade 11: 17 students (13 boys, 4 girls); Grade 12: 15 students (10 boys, 5 girls). 30% of students are Assemblies of God.

Faculty School total: 18. In upper school: 5 men, 12 women; 5 have advanced degrees.

Subjects Offered Algebra, American government, American history, American literature, art, arts, ASB Leadership, Bible studies, biology, body human, calculus-AP, career/college preparation, chemistry, chorus, Christian education, computer literacy, computer science, drama, English, English as a foreign language, English language and composition-AP, English literature-AP, fine arts, geometry, government, health, mathematics, physical education, physics, pre-calculus, psychology-AP, religion, science, social sciences, social studies, Spanish, U.S. history, U.S. history-AP, word processing, world history, world history-AP, yearbook.

Graduation Requirements American history, arts and fine arts (art, music, dance, drama), career/college preparation, economics, English, foreign language, government, health, mathematics, physical education (includes health), religion (includes Bible studies and theology), science, social sciences, world history, community service.

Special Academic Programs 5 Advanced Placement exams for which test preparation is offered; honors section; accelerated programs; independent study; study at local college for college credit; domestic exchange program; academic accommodation for the gifted; remedial reading and/or remedial writing; remedial math; special instructional classes for students with learning disabilities (504 Plans); ESL (11 students enrolled).

College Admission Counseling 16 students graduated in 2016; 15 went to college, including California State University, San Bernardino; Grand Canyon University; University of California, Riverside; Vanguard University of Southern California. Other: 1 entered military service. Mean SAT critical reading: 395, mean SAT math: 497, mean SAT writing: 386, mean composite ACT: 21. 25% scored over 600 on SAT math, 15% scored over 1800 on combined SAT.

Student Life Upper grades have uniform requirement, student council. Discipline rests primarily with faculty.

Summer Programs Remediation, enrichment programs offered; session focuses on Remediation and Credit Recovery; held off campus; held at Options for Youth and Twinn Palms; accepts boys and girls; not open to students from other schools. 8 students usually enrolled. 2017 schedule: June 12 to August. Application deadline: June 1.

Tuition and Aid Tuition installment plan (FACTS Tuition Payment Plan, monthly payment plans, individually arranged payment plans). Tuition reduction for siblings, need-based scholarship grants available. In 2016–17, 51% of upper-school students received aid.

Admissions Traditional secondary-level entrance grade is 9. For fall 2016, 170 students applied for upper-level admission, 170 were accepted, 165 enrolled. Admissions testing required. Deadline for receipt of application materials: none. No application fee required. Interview recommended.

Athletics Interscholastic: baseball (boys), basketball (b,g), cheering (g), cross-country running (b,g), football (b), softball (g), track and field (b,g), volleyball (g), weight lifting (b); coed interscholastic: golf, self defense, soccer. 1 PE instructor, 10 coaches, 1 athletic trainer.

Computers Computers are regularly used in desktop publishing, graphic arts, journalism, yearbook classes. Computer network features include on-campus library services, Internet access, wireless campus network, Internet filtering or blocking technology, Google School. Campus intranet is available to students. Students grades are available online. The school has a published electronic and media policy.

Contact Mrs. Page Porter, Secretary. 760-241-8827. Fax: 760-243-0654. E-mail: pporter@vfassembly.org. Website: www.vvcs.org

VIEWPOINT SCHOOL

23620 Mulholland Highway
Calabasas, California 91302

Head of School: Mr. Mark McKee

General Information Coeducational day college-preparatory, arts, and technology school. Grades K–12. Founded: 1961. Setting: suburban. Nearest major city is Los Angeles. 40-acre campus. 5 buildings on campus. Approved or accredited by California Association of Independent Schools, Western Association of Schools and Colleges, and California Department of Education. Member of National Association of Independent Schools and Secondary School Admission Test Board. Endowment: $12 million. Total enrollment: 1,215. Upper school average class size: 18. Upper school faculty-student ratio: 1:10. There are 180 required school days per year for Upper School students. Upper School students typically attend 5 days per week. The average school day consists of 7 hours.

Upper School Student Profile Grade 9: 149 students (79 boys, 70 girls); Grade 10: 127 students (68 boys, 59 girls); Grade 11: 145 students (70 boys, 75 girls); Grade 12: 124 students (63 boys, 61 girls).

Faculty School total: 213. In upper school: 23 men, 37 women; 39 have advanced degrees.

Subjects Offered Adolescent issues, advanced chemistry, advanced computer applications, advanced studio art-AP, African literature, algebra, American history, American history-AP, American literature, American literature-AP, ancient history, ancient world history, animation, art, art appreciation, art history, art history-AP, art-AP, Asian history, Asian studies, ballet, Basic programming, basic skills, Bible as literature, biology, biology-AP, British literature, business skills, calculus, calculus-AP, California writers, ceramics, character education, chemistry, chemistry-AP, Chinese, Chinese studies, choir, choreography, chorus, college admission preparation, community service, comparative government and politics, comparative government and politics-AP, comparative political systems-AP, comparative politics, computer animation, computer programming, computer science, computer science-AP, concert band, contemporary women writers, CPR, creative writing, critical studies in film, dance, debate, decision making skills, diversity studies, drama, drama performance, dramatic arts, drawing and design, earth science, economics, English, English language-AP, English literature, English literature-AP, ensembles, environmental education, environmental science, environmental science-AP, European history, European history-AP, film, film appreciation, filmmaking, fine arts, French, French language-AP, French literature-AP, geometry, global science, government/civics, history, history-AP, Holocaust and other genocides, honors algebra, honors English, honors geometry, human development, humanities, instrumental music, international relations, jazz, jazz band, jazz dance, jazz ensemble, journalism, keyboarding, Latin, Latin American history, Latin History, Latin-AP, library skills, literary magazine, literature by women, mathematics, medieval history, multicultural literature, music, music composition, music history, music theory-AP, newspaper, oceanography, outdoor education, painting, performing arts, photography, physical education, physics, physics-AP, physiology, poetry, probability and statistics, psychology, psychology-AP, public speaking, robotics, science, sculpture, senior project, Shakespeare, short story, social studics, sociology, Spanish, Spanish language-AP, Spanish literature-AP, Spanish-AP, speech and debate, student publications, studio art, studio art-AP, study skills, swimming, theater, trigonometry, U.S. government and politics-AP, U.S. history-AP, video, vocal jazz, women's literature, word processing, world history, yearbook.

Graduation Requirements Arts and fine arts (art, music, dance, drama), computer science, English, foreign language, global studies, mathematics, physical education (includes health), science, social studies (includes history). Community service is required.

Special Academic Programs 28 Advanced Placement exams for which test preparation is offered; honors section; independent study; study abroad.

College Admission Counseling 111 students graduated in 2015; all went to college, including New York University; Stanford University; University of California, Berkeley; University of California, Los Angeles; University of Southern California; Washington University in St. Louis. Mean SAT critical reading: 653, mean SAT math: 651, mean SAT writing: 671, mean combined SAT: 1975, mean composite ACT: 30.

Student Life Upper grades have specified standards of dress, student council, honor system. Discipline rests primarily with faculty.

Tuition and Aid Day student tuition: $35,325. Tuition installment plan (Insured Tuition Payment Plan, monthly payment plans). Need-based scholarship grants available. In 2015–16, 20% of upper-school students received aid. Total amount of financial aid awarded in 2015–16: $2,801,010.

Admissions Traditional secondary-level entrance grade is 9. For fall 2015, 159 students applied for upper-level admission, 75 were accepted, 43 enrolled. ISEE or SSAT required. Deadline for receipt of application materials: December 15. Application fee required: $125. Interview required.

Athletics Interscholastic: baseball (boys), basketball (b,g), flag football (b), football (b), lacrosse (b), soccer (b,g), softball (g), volleyball (b,g); intramural: aerobics/dance (g), backpacking (b,g), ball hockey (b,g), ballet (b,g), baseball (b), basketball (b,g), soccer (b,g), volleyball (b,g); coed interscholastic: cross-country running, dance, dance squad, dressage, drill team, equestrian sports, golf, horseback riding, swimming and diving, tennis, track and field; coed intramural: cheering, cooperative games, cross-country running, dance, dance squad, dance team, football, hiking/backpacking, modern dance, outdoor activities, outdoor adventure, outdoor education, outdoor recreation, outdoor skills, outdoors, physical fitness, physical training, power lifting, strength & conditioning, table tennis, weight training, yoga. 14 PE instructors, 51 coaches, 2 athletic trainers.

Computers Computers are regularly used in animation, basic skills, college planning, English, foreign language, history, keyboarding, library skills, mathematics, multimedia, music, newspaper, publications, science, video film production, Web site design, word processing, yearbook classes. Computer network features include on-campus library services, online commercial services, Internet access, wireless campus network, Internet filtering or blocking technology, virtual desktop. Campus intranet, student e-mail accounts, and computer access in designated common areas are available to students. Students grades are available online. The school has a published electronic and media policy.

Contact Mr. Patrick LaBo, Admission and Financial Aid Coordinator. 818-591-6560. Fax: 818-591-0834. E-mail: admission@viewpoint.org. Website: www.viewpoint.org

VILLA DUCHESNE AND OAK HILL SCHOOL

801 S. Spoede Road
St. Louis, Missouri 63131
Head of School: Mr. Michael F. Baber

General Information Coeducational day college-preparatory school, affiliated with Roman Catholic Church. Boys grades JK–6, girls grades JK–12. Founded: 1929. Setting: suburban. 60-acre campus. 2 buildings on campus. Approved or accredited by Independent Schools Association of the Central States, Network of Sacred Heart Schools, and Missouri Department of Education. Member of National Association of Independent Schools. Total enrollment: 585. Upper school average class size: 15. Upper school faculty-student ratio: 1:8. There are 180 required school days per year for Upper School students. Upper School students typically attend 5 days per week. The average school day consists of 7 hours.

Upper School Student Profile 88% of students are Roman Catholic.

Faculty School total: 89. In upper school: 13 men, 44 women; 40 have advanced degrees.

Subjects Offered American government, American literature, American literature-AP, anatomy and physiology, art, biology, biology-AP, British literature, calculus, calculus-AP, campus ministry, ceramics, chemistry, chorus, civics, computers, creative writing, discrete mathematics, drawing, economics, English, European history, European history-AP, Far Eastern history, French, geography, geometry, health, integrated physics, math analysis, Middle East, music, newspaper, painting, personal development, physical education, physics, pre-algebra, pre-calculus, printmaking, psychology, public speaking, religion, scripture, sculpture, social justice, Spanish, studio art, studio art-AP, theater arts, U.S. history, U.S. history-AP, Western civilization, women's studies, world literature, yearbook.

Graduation Requirements All academic, career/college preparation, character education, college admission preparation, college counseling, electives, junior and senior seminars, mathematics, moral and social development, personal growth, religion (includes Bible studies and theology), science, senior thesis, social studies (includes history), technology, students must perform community service to graduate.

Special Academic Programs International Baccalaureate program; 13 Advanced Placement exams for which test preparation is offered; honors section; independent study; term-away projects; study at local college for college credit; domestic exchange program (with Network of Sacred Heart Schools); study abroad; academic accommodation for the gifted; remedial reading and/or remedial writing; remedial math.

College Admission Counseling 68 students graduated in 2016; all went to college, including Saint Louis University; Southern Methodist University; Texas Christian University; Tulane University; University of Mississippi; University of Missouri. Mean SAT critical reading: 568, mean SAT math: 549, mean SAT writing: 580, mean combined SAT: 1697, mean composite ACT: 27.

Student Life Upper grades have uniform requirement, student council, honor system. Discipline rests primarily with faculty. Attendance at religious services is required.

Summer Programs Enrichment, advancement, sports, art/fine arts, computer instruction programs offered; session focuses on enrichment and college preparation; held on campus; accepts boys and girls; open to students from other schools. 200 students usually enrolled. 2017 schedule: June 1 to August 14. Application deadline: May 1.

Tuition and Aid Day student tuition: $6258–$20,655. Tuition installment plan (SMART Tuition Payment Plan). Tuition reduction for siblings, merit scholarship grants, need-based scholarship grants available. In 2016–17, 20% of upper-school students received aid.

Admissions Traditional secondary-level entrance grade is 9. Standardized test scores required. Deadline for receipt of application materials: none. Application fee required: $50. On-campus interview required.

Athletics Interscholastic: basketball (girls), cross-country running (g), diving (g), field hockey (g), golf (g), lacrosse (g), racquetball (g), soccer (g), swimming and diving (g), tennis (g), track and field (g), volleyball (g). 5 PE instructors, 34 coaches, 1 athletic trainer.

Computers Computers are regularly used in all academic classes. Computer network features include on-campus library services, online commercial services, Internet access, wireless campus network, Internet filtering or blocking technology, students in grades 7 to 12 have personal tablet PCs. Campus intranet, student e-mail accounts, and computer access in designated common areas are available to students. Students grades are available online. The school has a published electronic and media policy.

Contact Mrs. Elaine Brooks, Admissions Assistant. 314-810-3566. Fax: 314-432-0199. E-mail: ebrooks@vdoh.org. Website: www.vdoh.org

VILLA JOSEPH MARIE HIGH SCHOOL

1180 Holland Road
Holland, Pennsylvania 18966
Head of School: Mr. Thomas Kardish

General Information Girls' day college-preparatory, arts, religious studies, technology, and drama school, affiliated with Roman Catholic Church. Grades 9–12. Founded: 1932. Setting: suburban. Nearest major city is Philadelphia. 55-acre campus. 3 buildings on campus. Approved or accredited by Middle States Association of Colleges and Schools and Pennsylvania Department of Education. Member of National Association of Independent Schools. Total enrollment: 363. Upper school average class size: 15. Upper school faculty-student ratio: 1:9. There are 170 required school days per year for Upper School students. Upper School students typically attend 5 days per week. The average school day consists of 6 hours and 45 minutes.

Upper School Student Profile Grade 9: 99 students (99 girls); Grade 10: 93 students (93 girls); Grade 11: 117 students (117 girls); Grade 12: 83 students (83 girls). 95% of students are Roman Catholic.

Faculty School total: 44. In upper school: 10 men, 34 women; 30 have advanced degrees.

Subjects Offered 3-dimensional art, acting, advanced biology, advanced chemistry, advanced math, Advanced Placement courses, American democracy, American literature, American literature-AP, anatomy, art-AP, band, bell choir, British literature, business, business studies, calculus, campus ministry, choral music, Christian and Hebrew scripture, church history, classical language, college counseling, community service, composition-AP, computer literacy, concert band, constitutional history of U.S., critical studies in film, current events, desktop publishing, digital art, DNA science lab, English language-AP, English literature and composition-AP, European history, film studies, fine arts, freshman seminar, government-AP, health education, history of the Catholic Church, honors algebra, honors English, honors geometry, human anatomy, human geography - AP, jazz band, literature by women, moral and social development, music theory, painting, portfolio art, social justice, Spanish-AP, U.S. government and politics-AP, U.S. history-AP.

Graduation Requirements Arts and fine arts (art, music, dance, drama), English, foreign language, mathematics, physical education (includes health), religion (includes Bible studies and theology), science, social sciences, social studies (includes history), service hours requirement.

Special Academic Programs 10 Advanced Placement exams for which test preparation is offered; honors section; independent study; study at local college for college credit; programs in general development for dyslexic students.

College Admission Counseling 97 students graduated in 2016; all went to college, including Penn State University Park; Saint Joseph's University; The University of Scranton; University of Pittsburgh; Villanova University; West Chester University of Pennsylvania. Mean SAT critical reading: 588, mean SAT math: 584, mean SAT writing: 610. 35% scored over 600 on SAT critical reading, 30% scored over 600 on SAT math, 38% scored over 600 on SAT writing, 30% scored over 1800 on combined SAT, 40% scored over 26 on composite ACT.

Student Life Upper grades have uniform requirement, student council, honor system. Discipline rests primarily with faculty. Attendance at religious services is required.

Summer Programs Enrichment, advancement, sports, art/fine arts programs offered; session focuses on enrichment; held on campus; accepts girls; open to students from other schools. 150 students usually enrolled. 2017 schedule: June 21 to August 14. Application deadline: June 1.

Tuition and Aid Day student tuition: $14,850. Guaranteed tuition plan. Tuition installment plan (monthly payment plans, individually arranged payment plans). Tuition reduction for siblings, merit scholarship grants, need-based scholarship grants available. In 2016–17, 25% of upper-school students received aid; total upper-school merit-scholarship money awarded: $300,000. Total amount of financial aid awarded in 2016–17: $180,000.

Admissions Traditional secondary-level entrance grade is 9. For fall 2016, 200 students applied for upper-level admission, 145 were accepted, 100 enrolled. High School Placement Test required. Deadline for receipt of application materials: November 15. Application fee required: $65. On-campus interview recommended.

Athletics Interscholastic: basketball, cheering, crew, cross-country running, field hockey, golf, indoor track, lacrosse, soccer, softball, swimming and diving, tennis, track and field, volleyball, winter (indoor) track; intramural: bowling, floor hockey. 1 PE instructor, 17 coaches, 1 athletic trainer.

Computers Computers are regularly used in all classes. Computer network features include on-campus library services, online commercial services, Internet access, wireless campus network, Internet filtering or blocking technology, Naviance - Guidance and college placement software. Computer access in designated common areas is available to students. Students grades are available online. The school has a published electronic and media policy.

Contact Mrs. Laura Lasky, Director of Admissions. 215-357-8810 Ext. 193. Fax: 215-357-2477. E-mail: llasky@vjmhs.org. Website: www.vjmhs.org

VILLA MADONNA ACADEMY

2500 Amsterdam Road
Covington, Kentucky 41017

Head of School: Mrs. Pamela McQueen

General Information Coeducational day college-preparatory, arts, business, technology, and STEM school, affiliated with Roman Catholic Church. Grades 7–12. Founded: 1904. Setting: suburban. Nearest major city is Cincinnati, OH. 234-acre campus. 3 buildings on campus. Approved or accredited by Commission on Secondary and Middle Schools, Southern Association of Colleges and Schools, and Kentucky Department of Education. Total enrollment: 421. Upper school average class size: 11. Upper school faculty-student ratio: 1:8. There are 177 required school days per year for Upper School students. Upper School students typically attend 5 days per week. The average school day consists of 6 hours and 30 minutes.

Upper School Student Profile Grade 7: 25 students (10 boys, 15 girls); Grade 8: 39 students (22 boys, 17 girls); Grade 9: 37 students (17 boys, 20 girls); Grade 10: 28 students (10 boys, 18 girls); Grade 11: 38 students (19 boys, 19 girls); Grade 12: 28 students (16 boys, 12 girls). 65% of students are Roman Catholic.

Faculty School total: 26. In upper school: 13 men, 13 women, 18 have advanced degrees.

Subjects Offered Advanced biology, advanced chemistry, Advanced Placement courses, advanced studio art-AP, algebra, American history, American history-AP, art, art history, biology, calculus, calculus-AP, chemistry, chorus, computer programming-AP, computer science, contemporary studies, digital photography, drama, economics and history, English, English language and composition-AP, English literature and composition-AP, English-AP, European history, French, French-AP, geometry, government/civics, graphic arts, health, honors English, human geography - AP, Latin, Latin-AP, macro/microeconomics-AP, media production, music, music theory-AP, photography, physical education, physics, physics-AP, pre-calculus, psychology-AP, religion, Spanish, Spanish-AP, speech communications, stagecraft, theater, U.S. history-AP.

Graduation Requirements Arts and fine arts (art, music, dance, drama), chemistry, electives, foreign language, health, mathematics, physical education (includes health), religion (includes Bible studies and theology), science, social studies (includes history). Community service is required.

Special Academic Programs Advanced Placement exam preparation; honors section; independent study; study at local college for college credit.

College Admission Counseling 42 students graduated in 2016; all went to college, including Miami University; University of Cincinnati; University of Kentucky; University of Louisville. Mean composite ACT: 28.

Student Life Upper grades have uniform requirement, student council, honor system. Discipline rests primarily with faculty. Attendance at religious services is required.

Tuition and Aid Tuition installment plan (FACTS Tuition Payment Plan). Tuition reduction for siblings, merit scholarship grants, need-based scholarship grants available. In 2016–17, 30% of upper-school students received aid.

Admissions Traditional secondary-level entrance grade is 9. Diocesan Entrance Exam and High School Placement Test required. Deadline for receipt of application materials: none. No application fee required. On-campus interview required.

Athletics Interscholastic: baseball (boys), basketball (b,g), bowling (b,g), cross-country running (b,g), golf (b,g), running (b,g), soccer (b,g), softball (g), swimming and diving (b,g), tennis (b,g), track and field (b,g), volleyball (g).

Computers Computers are regularly used in all academic classes. Computer network features include on-campus library services, Internet access, wireless campus network, Internet filtering or blocking technology. Campus intranet, student e-mail accounts, and computer access in designated common areas are available to students. Students grades are available online. The school has a published electronic and media policy.

Contact Mrs. Janet Baugh, Director of Admissions. 859-331-6333 Ext. 139. Fax: 859-331-8615. E-mail: admissions@villamadonna.net. Website: www.villamadonna.org/

VILLA VICTORIA ACADEMY

376 West Upper Ferry Road
Ewing, New Jersey 08628

Head of School: Sr. Lillian Harrington, MPF

General Information Girls' day college-preparatory school, affiliated with Roman Catholic Church. Grades K–12. Founded: 1933. Setting: suburban. Nearest major city is Trenton. 44-acre campus. 7 buildings on campus. Approved or accredited by Middle States Association of Colleges and Schools, National Catholic Education Association, New Jersey Association of Independent Schools, and New Jersey Department of Education. Member of National Association of Independent Schools. Total enrollment: 162. Upper school average class size: 12. Upper school faculty-student ratio: 1:8. There are 180 required school days per year for Upper School students. Upper School students typically attend 5 days per week. The average school day consists of 6 hours and 20 minutes.

Upper School Student Profile Grade 9: 19 students (19 girls); Grade 10: 14 students (14 girls); Grade 11: 16 students (16 girls); Grade 12: 16 students (16 girls). 65% of students are Roman Catholic.

Faculty School total: 20. In upper school: 3 men, 16 women; 12 have advanced degrees.

Subjects Offered Algebra, American literature, art, art history, art-AP, arts appreciation, athletics, Bible studies, biology, calculus, calculus-AP, campus ministry, career and personal planning, career exploration, career planning, career/college preparation, Catholic belief and practice, ceramics, character education, chemistry, chemistry-AP, Chinese studies, choir, choral music, chorus, Christian education, Christian ethics, Christianity, church history, clayworking, college admission preparation, college awareness, college counseling, college placement, college planning, college writing, communication skills, community service, computer science, concert band, concert choir, creative thinking, creative writing, critical thinking, critical writing, cultural arts, current events, drama, drawing, drawing and design, earth science, English, English composition, English language and composition-AP, English literature, English literature-AP, English-AP, ethics and responsibility, European history, fiction, fine arts, French, French language-AP, French studies, French-AP, gender and religion, general business, general math, general science, geography, geometry, global issues, government, government and politics-AP, government-AP, government/civics, government/civics-AP, grammar, health, health and safety, health and wellness, health education, history, history of music, history of religion, history of the Americas, history of the Catholic Church, history-AP, honors algebra, honors English, honors geometry, honors U.S. history, honors world history, humanities, independent study, interdisciplinary studies, Internet, Internet research, interpersonal skills, language and composition, Latin, leadership, leadership and service, library research, library skills, life management skills, Life of Christ, linguistics, literary magazine, literature, literature-AP, math analysis, math applications, math methods, math review, mathematics, mathematics-AP, mechanics of writing, modern history, modern languages, modern world history, money management, moral and social development, moral reasoning, moral theology, multimedia, music, music appreciation, music history, music performance, music theater, music theory, musical productions, musical theater, musical theater dance, oil painting, painting, participation in sports, peer ministry, performing arts, personal development, personal finance, personal fitness, personal money management, photography, physical education, physics, physics-AP, play production, poetry, portfolio art, pottery, prayer/spirituality, pre-algebra, pre-calculus, public service, public speaking, qualitative analysis, reading/study skills, religion, religion and culture, religious education, research, research skills, rhetoric, SAT preparation, SAT/ACT preparation, science, science and technology, sculpture, senior humanities, senior project, senior seminar, set design, Shakespeare, skills for success, social skills, social studies, society and culture, Spanish, Spanish language-AP, Spanish-AP, sports, sports conditioning, stage design, stagecraft, strategies for success, student government, student publications, theater, theater design and production, trigonometry, U.S. history, United States government-AP, values and decisions, visual and performing arts, visual arts, vocal ensemble, world civilizations, world cultures, world history, world issues, world literature, world religions, writing.

Graduation Requirements American literature, art history, arts and fine arts (art, music, dance, drama), biology, British literature, chemistry, computer science, English, foreign language, mathematics, physical education (includes health), physics, religion (includes Bible studies and theology), SAT/ACT preparation, science, social studies (includes history), world cultures, world literature, interdisciplinary humanities. Community service is required.

Special Academic Programs Advanced Placement exam preparation; honors section; independent study; academic accommodation for the gifted, the musically talented, and the artistically talented.

College Admission Counseling 13 students graduated in 2016; all went to college, including Boston University; Cornell University; Fordham University; The George Washington University; University of Virginia; Villanova University. Median combined SAT: 1767.

Student Life Upper grades have uniform requirement, student council, honor system. Discipline rests primarily with faculty. Attendance at religious services is required.

Tuition and Aid Day student tuition: $13,400. Tuition installment plan (FACTS Tuition Payment Plan, individually arranged payment plans, 2-payment plan). Tuition reduction for siblings, merit scholarship grants, need-based scholarship grants available. In 2016–17, 30% of upper-school students received aid; total upper-school merit-scholarship money awarded: $50,000.

Admissions Traditional secondary-level entrance grade is 9. High School Placement Test (closed version) from Scholastic Testing Service or school placement exam required. Deadline for receipt of application materials: none. Application fee required: $50. On-campus interview recommended.

Athletics Interscholastic: basketball, cross-country running, soccer, softball, tennis, track and field; intramural: dance, outdoor activities, outdoor education, walking. 1 PE instructor, 4 coaches.

Computers Computers are regularly used in art, English, foreign language, history, mathematics, music, SAT preparation, science, theater classes. Computer network features include on-campus library services, Internet access, wireless campus network, Internet filtering or blocking technology. Computer access in designated common areas is available to students. Students grades are available online. The school has a published electronic and media policy.

Contact Mrs. Colleen White, Director of Admissions. 609-882-1700 Ext. 19. Fax: 609-882-8421. E-mail: cwhite.villavictoria@gmail.com. Website: www.villavictoria.org

VILLA WALSH ACADEMY

455 Western Avenue

Morristown, New Jersey 07960

Head of School: Sr. Patricia Pompa

General Information Girls' day college-preparatory school, affiliated with Roman Catholic Church. Grades 7–12. Founded: 1967. Setting: suburban. Nearest major city is New York, NY. 130-acre campus. 4 buildings on campus. Approved or accredited by Middle States Association of Colleges and Schools, National Catholic Education Association, New Jersey Department of Education, and New Jersey Department of Education. Endowment: $6 million. Total enrollment: 238. Upper school average class size: 12. Upper school faculty-student ratio: 1:8. There are 176 required school days per year for Upper School students. Upper School students typically attend 5 days per week. The average school day consists of 6 hours and 30 minutes.

Upper School Student Profile Grade 9: 51 students (51 girls); Grade 10: 49 students (49 girls); Grade 11: 55 students (55 girls); Grade 12: 53 students (53 girls). 90% of students are Roman Catholic.

Faculty School total: 36. In upper school: 4 men, 32 women; 21 have advanced degrees.

Subjects Offered Advanced Placement courses, algebra, American history, American literature, anatomy and physiology, art, Bible as literature, biology, biology-AP, British literature, British literature (honors), calculus, calculus-AP, career/college preparation, chemistry, chemistry-AP, choral music, chorus, church history, college admission preparation, computer applications, computer graphics, computer literacy, computer processing, computer programming, computer science, computer skills, CPR, creative writing, desktop publishing, driver education, economics, English, English language and composition-AP, English literature, English literature-AP, ethics, European civilization, European history-AP, family living, first aid, French, French language-AP, French-AP, geometry, health education, honors English, honors geometry, honors U.S. history, Italian, mathematics, modern European history, moral theology, philosophy, physical education, physics, physics-AP, pre-calculus, psychology, psychology-AP, Spanish, Spanish-AP, statistics-AP, studio art, theology, U.S. government and politics, U.S. history, U.S. history-AP, voice ensemble, Web site design, world history, world literature.

Graduation Requirements Arts and fine arts (art, music, dance, drama), English, foreign language, mathematics, physical education (includes health), science, social studies (includes history), theology.

Special Academic Programs 14 Advanced Placement exams for which test preparation is offered; honors section; independent study; academic accommodation for the gifted, the musically talented, and the artistically talented.

College Admission Counseling 55 students graduated in 2016; all went to college, including Brown University; Bucknell University; Penn State University Park; University of Michigan; University of Notre Dame; University of Richmond. Mean SAT critical reading: 650, mean SAT math: 650, mean SAT writing: 660, mean combined SAT: 1960.

Student Life Upper grades have uniform requirement, student council, honor system. Discipline rests primarily with faculty. Attendance at religious services is required.

Tuition and Aid Day student tuition: $19,000. Tuition installment plan (Insured Tuition Payment Plan, individually arranged payment plans). Merit scholarship grants, need-based scholarship grants available. In 2016–17, 14% of upper-school students received aid; total upper-school merit-scholarship money awarded: $10,000. Total amount of financial aid awarded in 2016–17: $120,000.

Admissions Traditional secondary-level entrance grade is 9. For fall 2016, 140 students applied for upper-level admission, 60 were accepted, 51 enrolled. Math, reading, and mental ability tests and writing sample required. Deadline for receipt of application materials: none. Application fee required: $30. On-campus interview recommended.

Athletics Interscholastic: basketball, cross-country running, indoor track, lacrosse, soccer, softball, swimming and diving, tennis, track and field, volleyball, winter (indoor) track. 1 PE instructor, 32 coaches, 1 athletic trainer.

Computers Computers are regularly used in college planning, desktop publishing, independent study, keyboarding, library science, mathematics, newspaper, programming, SAT preparation, science, technology, Web site design, word processing, yearbook classes. Computer network features include on-campus library services, Internet access, wireless campus network, Internet filtering or blocking technology. Campus intranet is available to students. The school has a published electronic and media policy.

Contact Sr. Doris Lavinthal, Director. 973-538-3680 Ext. 175. Fax: 973-538-6733. E-mail: lavinthald@aol.com. Website: www.villawalsh.org

VIRGINIA EPISCOPAL SCHOOL

400 VES Road

Lynchburg, Virginia 24503

Head of School: Mr. Tommy Battle Jr.

General Information Coeducational boarding and day college-preparatory school, affiliated with Episcopal Church. Grades 9–12. Founded: 1916. Setting: small town. Nearest major city is Richmond. Students are housed in single-sex dormitories. 160-acre campus. 15 buildings on campus. Approved or accredited by The Association of Boarding Schools, Virginia Association of Independent Schools, and Virginia Department of Education. Member of National Association of Independent Schools and Secondary School Admission Test Board. Endowment: $18 million. Total enrollment: 262. Upper school average class size: 11. Upper school faculty-student ratio: 1:6. The average school day consists of 5 hours.

Upper School Student Profile Grade 9: 48 students (24 boys, 24 girls); Grade 10: 68 students (32 boys, 36 girls); Grade 11: 69 students (30 boys, 39 girls); Grade 12: 63 students (28 boys, 35 girls). 67% of students are boarding students. 49% are state residents. 10 states are represented in upper school student body. 22% are international students. International students from Bosnia and Herzegovina, China, Mexico, Republic of Korea, Turkey, and United States; 6 other countries represented in student body. 60% of students are members of Episcopal Church.

Faculty School total: 38. In upper school: 21 men, 17 women; 62 have advanced degrees; 42 reside on campus.

Subjects Offered 3-dimensional art, ACT preparation, acting, advanced biology, advanced chemistry, advanced math, algebra, American history, American history-AP, American literature, analysis, analysis and differential calculus, anatomy and physiology, ancient history, art, art history, art-AP, baseball, biology, biology-AP, calculus, calculus-AP, chemistry, choir, computer graphics, computer math, computer programming, computer programming-AP, computer science, computer science-AP, creative writing, drama, economics, English, English literature, English-AP, environmental science, ethics, European history, European history-AP, fine arts, French, French language-AP, geometry, grammar, graphic design, health education, history, honors algebra, honors English, honors geometry, honors U.S. history, honors world history, instrumental music, life issues, mathematics, medieval history, modern European history-AP, music, music history, music theory-AP, musical theater, physical education, physics, pre-calculus, religion, SAT preparation, science, Spanish, Spanish language-AP, sports medicine, theater, trigonometry, Web site design, world history, world literature, writing.

Graduation Requirements American government, American history, arts and fine arts (art, music, dance, drama), chemistry, computer science, English, foreign language, life issues, mathematics, physical education (includes health), religion (includes Bible studies and theology), science, social studies (includes history), world history.

Special Academic Programs Advanced Placement exam preparation; honors section; independent study; study abroad.

College Admission Counseling 61 students graduated in 2016; all went to college, including James Madison University; Penn State University Park; The College of William and Mary; The University of North Carolina at Chapel Hill; University of Virginia; Virginia Polytechnic Institute and State University.

Student Life Upper grades have specified standards of dress, student council, honor system. Discipline rests equally with students and faculty. Attendance at religious services is required.

Tuition and Aid Day student tuition: $21,450; 5-day tuition and room/board: $34,550; 7-day tuition and room/board: $46,400. Tuition installment plan (FACTS Tuition Payment Plan). Merit scholarship grants, need-based scholarship grants available. In 2016–17, 20% of upper-school students received aid; total upper-school merit-scholarship money awarded: $26,000. Total amount of financial aid awarded in 2016–17: $2,000,000.

Admissions Traditional secondary-level entrance grade is 9. For fall 2016, 230 students applied for upper-level admission, 130 were accepted, 79 enrolled. SSAT required. Deadline for receipt of application materials: none. Application fee required: $50. On-campus interview recommended.

Athletics Interscholastic: baseball (boys), basketball (b,g), field hockey (g), football (b), lacrosse (b,g), mountain biking (b), soccer (b,g), tennis (b,g), volleyball (g), wrestling (b); intramural: yoga (g); coed interscholastic: cross-country running, golf, swimming and diving, table tennis, track and field; coed intramural: bicycling, equestrian sports, horseback riding, strength & conditioning. 1 PE instructor, 31 coaches, 1 athletic trainer.

Computers Computers are regularly used in all academic classes. Computer network features include on-campus library services, online commercial services, Internet access, wireless campus network, Internet filtering or blocking technology. Campus intranet and student e-mail accounts are available to students. Students grades are available online. The school has a published electronic and media policy.

Contact Mrs. Justine Button, Director of Admissions and Financial Aid. 434-385-3622. Fax: 434-385-3603. E-mail: jbutton@ves.org. Website: www.ves.org

VISITATION ACADEMY

3020 North Ballas Road
St. Louis, Missouri 63131
Head of School: Mrs. Rosalie Henry

General Information Coeducational day (boys' only in lower grades) college-preparatory, arts, business, and technology school, affiliated with Roman Catholic Church. Boys grades PK–K, girls grades PK–12. Founded: 1833. Setting: suburban. 30-acre campus. 1 building on campus. Approved or accredited by Independent Schools Association of the Central States and Missouri Department of Education. Member of National Association of Independent Schools. Total enrollment: 553. Upper school average class size: 16. Upper school faculty-student ratio: 1:6. There are 176 required school days per year for Upper School students. Upper School students typically attend 5 days per week. The average school day consists of 7 hours.

Upper School Student Profile Grade 9: 53 students (53 girls); Grade 10: 87 students (87 girls); Grade 11: 82 students (82 girls); Grade 12: 84 students (84 girls). 81% of students are Roman Catholic.

Faculty School total: 80. In upper school: 8 men, 40 women.

Subjects Offered Adolescent issues, advanced biology, advanced chemistry, advanced math, Advanced Placement courses, algebra, American history, American history-AP, American literature, American literature-AP, anatomy, anatomy and physiology, art, art appreciation, art history, bell choir, biology, biology-AP, calculus, calculus-AP, character education, chemistry, chemistry-AP, choral music, chorus, church history, civics, classical language, computer math, computer programming, computer science, computer science-AP, concert choir, creative writing, digital applications, digital photography, drama, drawing and design, earth science, economics, engineering, English, English literature, English literature-AP, environmental science, European history, European history-AP, expository writing, fine arts, French, French-AP, genetics, geography, geometry, government/civics, grammar, graphic arts, graphic design, health, history, independent study, keyboarding, Latin, mathematics, music, music theory-AP, New Testament, photo shop, photography, physical education, physical science, physics, pre-calculus, psychology, robotics, science, social studies, Spanish, speech, statistics-AP, theater, theology, trigonometry, U.S. history-AP, Web site design, world geography, world literature.

Graduation Requirements Arts and fine arts (art, music, dance, drama), computers, electives, English, foreign language, mathematics, physical education (includes health), science, service learning/internship, social studies (includes history), theology, 120 hours of community service.

Special Academic Programs 13 Advanced Placement exams for which test preparation is offered; honors section; independent study; study at local college for college credit; special instructional classes for students with mild learning differences.

College Admission Counseling 99 students graduated in 2015; all went to college, including Emory University; Miami University; Saint Louis University; Texas Christian University; University of Arkansas; University of Missouri. Median SAT critical reading: 603, median SAT math: 593, median SAT writing: 591, median combined SAT: 1815, median composite ACT: 29.

Student Life Upper grades have uniform requirement, student council. Discipline rests primarily with faculty. Attendance at religious services is required.

Tuition and Aid Day student tuition: $18,860. Tuition installment plan (FACTS Tuition Payment Plan). Merit scholarship grants, need-based scholarship grants available. In 2015–16, 18% of upper-school students received aid. Total amount of financial aid awarded in 2015–16: $660,000.

Admissions Traditional secondary-level entrance grade is 9. For fall 2015, 37 students applied for upper-level admission, 33 were accepted, 23 enrolled. SSAT required. Deadline for receipt of application materials: January 15. Application fee required: $75. On-campus interview required.

Athletics Interscholastic: basketball, cheering, cross-country running, dance, diving, field hockey, golf, lacrosse, racquetball, soccer, swimming and diving, tennis, track and field, volleyball; intramural: cheering, dance. 4 PE instructors, 17 coaches, 1 athletic trainer.

Computers Computers are regularly used in all academic, art, English, foreign language, history, mathematics, science, theology classes. Computer network features include on-campus library services, online commercial services, Internet access, wireless campus network, Internet filtering or blocking technology. Campus intranet, student e-mail accounts, and computer access in designated common areas are available to students. Students grades are available online. The school has a published electronic and media policy.

Contact Mrs. Ashley Giljum, Director of Admission. 314-625-9102. Fax: 314-432-7210. E-mail: agiljum@visitationacademy.org. Website: www.visitationacademy.org

THE WALDORF SCHOOL OF SARATOGA SPRINGS

122 Regent Street
Saratoga Springs, New York 12866
Head of School: Mrs. Anne Maguire

General Information Coeducational day college-preparatory and general academic school. Grades PK–12. Founded: 1981. Setting: suburban. 5-acre campus. 1 building on campus. Approved or accredited by Association of Waldorf Schools of North America, New York State Association of Independent Schools, and New York Department of Education. Languages of instruction: English, French, and German. Total enrollment: 248. Upper school average class size: 13. Upper school faculty-student ratio: 1:13. There are 170 required school days per year for Upper School students. Upper School students typically attend 5 days per week. The average school day consists of 7 hours and 20 minutes.

Upper School Student Profile Grade 9: 13 students (8 boys, 5 girls); Grade 10: 14 students (5 boys, 9 girls); Grade 11: 8 students (2 boys, 6 girls); Grade 12: 14 students (8 boys, 6 girls). 8% of students are boarding students. 1% are state residents. 1 state is represented in upper school student body. 10% are international students. International students from Canada, Germany, and Republic of Korea.

Faculty School total: 40. In upper school: 8 men, 15 women; 5 have advanced degrees.

Subjects Offered 3-dimensional art, ACT preparation, acting, algebra, American government, American studies, analysis and differential calculus, analytic geometry, anatomy and physiology, ancient world history, applied arts, architecture, art, art history, astronomy, athletics, Bible as literature, biology, bookbinding, botany, ceramics, choir, drama, drawing, electives, English, eurythmy, fencing, fine arts, foreign language, French, geometry, medieval/Renaissance history, metalworking, North American literature, organic chemistry, painting, physics, practical arts, public speaking, SAT preparation, sculpture, senior career experience, senior thesis, service learning/internship, Shakespeare, stained glass, strings, track and field, woodworking, yearbook.

Graduation Requirements American history, American literature, analytic geometry, anatomy and physiology, Ancient Greek, ancient history, art, art history, astronomy, Bible as literature, biology, botany, calculus, calligraphy, career education internship, chemistry, choir, chorus, creative writing, critical writing, drama performance, drawing, earth science, English, English literature, eurythmy, foreign language, French, geology, geometry, German, history, history of architecture, human anatomy, human biology, human development, hydrology, life science, mathematics, medieval/Renaissance history, meteorology, modern world history, music, orchestra, organic chemistry, physical education (includes health), physics, printmaking, psychology, senior internship, Shakespeare, trigonometry, U.S. history, world cultures, zoology, juniors must complete an internship program, seniors must complete a senior project. Community service is required.

Special Academic Programs Independent study; study abroad; remedial reading and/or remedial writing; remedial math.

College Admission Counseling 8 students graduated in 2016; 14 went to college, including Bennington College; Binghamton University, State University of New York; Fashion Institute of Technology; Manhattanville College; Skidmore College.

Student Life Upper grades have specified standards of dress, honor system. Discipline rests primarily with faculty.

Tuition and Aid Day student tuition: $16,630. Tuition installment plan (monthly payment plans). Tuition reduction for siblings, need-based scholarship grants, tuition assistance program available. In 2016–17, 30% of upper-school students received aid.

Admissions Traditional secondary-level entrance grade is 9. For fall 2016, 1 student applied for upper-level admission, 1 was accepted, 1 enrolled. Non-standardized placement tests required. Deadline for receipt of application materials: none. No application fee required. Interview recommended.

Athletics Interscholastic: cross-country running (boys, girls), rowing (b,g), track and field (b,g); coed intramural: archery, ball hockey, basketball, climbing, crew, fencing, Frisbee, golf, hiking/backpacking, mountain biking, outdoor activities, outdoor adventure, outdoor education, outdoor recreation, outdoor skills, rock climbing, skiing (downhill), tennis, ultimate Frisbee, yoga. 1 PE instructor.

Computers Computers are regularly used in computer applications, graphic design, yearbook classes. Students grades are available online. The school has a published electronic and media policy.

Contact Mr. Richard Youmans, Enrollment Director. 518-587-2224. Fax: 518-581-1466. E-mail: admissions@waldorfsaratoga.org. Website: www.waldorfsaratoga.org/

WALLA WALLA VALLEY ACADEMY

300 South West Academy Way
College, Washington 99324-1283
Head of School: Brian Harris

General Information Coeducational day college-preparatory, arts, religious studies, and technology school, affiliated with Seventh-day Adventists. Grades 9–12. Founded: 1886. Setting: small town. Nearest major city is Tri Cities. 15-acre campus. 2 buildings on campus. Approved or accredited by National Council for Private School Accreditation and Washington Department of Education. Total enrollment: 178. Upper school average class size: 25. Upper school faculty-student ratio: 1:9. There are 180 required school days per year for Upper School students. Upper School students typically attend 5 days per week. The average school day consists of 7 hours and 30 minutes.

Upper School Student Profile 90% of students are Seventh-day Adventists.

Faculty School total: 16. In upper school: 10 men, 6 women; 7 have advanced degrees.

Subjects Offered Accounting.

Special Academic Programs Advanced Placement exam preparation; study at local college for college credit; remedial reading and/or remedial writing; remedial math; ESL (9 students enrolled).

Student Life Upper grades have uniform requirement, student council, honor system. Discipline rests primarily with faculty. Attendance at religious services is required.

Tuition and Aid Day student tuition: $9500. Tuition installment plan (monthly payment plans, individually arranged payment plans). Tuition reduction for siblings, merit scholarship grants, need-based scholarship grants, paying campus jobs available.

Admissions Traditional secondary-level entrance grade is 9. For fall 2015, 195 students applied for upper-level admission, 185 were accepted, 178 enrolled. High School Placement Test required. Deadline for receipt of application materials: June 1. Application fee required: $2000. Interview required.

Athletics Interscholastic: baseball (boys), basketball (b,g), cross-country running (b,g), golf (b,g), soccer (b,g), softball (g), track and field (b,g), volleyball (g); coed interscholastic: gymnastics, soccer; coed intramural: backpacking, basketball, flag football, ultimate Frisbee. 1 PE instructor, 12 coaches.

Computers Computer network features include on-campus library services, Internet access, wireless campus network, Internet filtering or blocking technology. Student e-mail accounts and computer access in designated common areas are available to students. Students grades are available online. The school has a published electronic and media policy.

Contact Elaine Hinshaw, Director of Recruitment & Marketing. 509-525-1050 Ext. 234. Fax: 509-525-1056. E-mail: hinsel@wwva.org. Website: www.wwva.org

WALNUT HILL SCHOOL FOR THE ARTS

12 Highland Street
Natick, Massachusetts 01760-2199

Head of School: Mr. Antonio Viva

General Information Coeducational boarding and day college-preparatory and arts school. Grades 9–PG. Founded: 1893. Setting: suburban. Nearest major city is Boston. Students are housed in single-sex dormitories and Gender Neutral Dormitory. 45-acre campus. 19 buildings on campus. Approved or accredited by Association of Independent Schools in New England, New England Association of Schools and Colleges, The Association of Boarding Schools, and Massachusetts Department of Education. Member of National Association of Independent Schools and Secondary School Admission Test Board. Endowment: $16 million. Total enrollment: 285. Upper school average class size: 16. Upper school faculty-student ratio: 1:6. Upper School students typically attend 5 days per week. The average school day consists of 8 hours.

Upper School Student Profile 73% of students are boarding students. 33% are state residents. 23 states are represented in upper school student body. 35% are international students. International students from China, Japan, Mexico, Republic of Korea, Russian Federation, and Taiwan; 10 other countries represented in student body.

Faculty School total: 51. In upper school: 24 men, 27 women; 47 have advanced degrees; 30 reside on campus.

Subjects Offered 20th century world history, 3-dimensional art, acting, advanced chemistry, advanced math, algebra, American history, American literature, art history, arts, ballet, ballet technique, biology, calculus, ceramics, chemistry, choral music, choreography, chorus, classical music, college counseling, community service, creative writing, dance, directing, drama, drawing, English, English literature, ESL, fine arts, French, geometry, health, history, history of dance, jazz dance, mathematics, modern dance, music history, music theory, musical theater, musical theater dance, opera, orchestra, painting, photography, physics, piano, poetry, pre-calculus, research seminar, science, sculpture, set design, Shakespeare, social studies, Spanish, stage design, technical theater, theater, theater design and production, theater production, U.S. history, visual and performing arts, visual arts, vocal music, voice, voice ensemble, world history, writing.

Graduation Requirements Arts, English, foreign language, mathematics, science, social studies (includes history), U.S. history, completion of arts portfolio, body of writing, or participation in performing arts ensembles and/or solo recital.

Special Academic Programs Independent study; study at local college for college credit; academic accommodation for the musically talented and the artistically talented; ESL (30 students enrolled).

College Admission Counseling 85 students graduated in 2016; 83 went to college, including Berklee College of Music; McGill University; New England Conservatory of Music; School of the Art Institute of Chicago; The Juilliard School; University of Cincinnati. Other: 2 had other specific plans.

Student Life Upper grades have student council. Discipline rests equally with students and faculty.

Summer Programs Art/fine arts programs offered; session focuses on theater, ballet, visual art,; held on campus; accepts boys and girls; open to students from other schools. 300 students usually enrolled. 2017 schedule: June 19 to August 16. Application deadline: none.

Tuition and Aid Day student tuition: $43,680; 7-day tuition and room/board: $57,880. Tuition installment plan (Tuition Refund Plan). Need-based scholarship grants available. In 2016–17, 39% of upper-school students received aid. Total amount of financial aid awarded in 2016–17: $3,500,000.

Admissions Traditional secondary-level entrance grade is 9. For fall 2016, 291 students applied for upper-level admission, 172 were accepted, 92 enrolled. Any standardized test, audition, TOEFL or SLEP or writing sample required. Deadline for receipt of application materials: January 15. Application fee required: $65. Interview recommended.

Athletics Coed Intramural: aerobics, aerobics/dance, ballet, basketball, boxing, combined training, dance, fitness, fitness walking, Frisbee, modern dance, outdoor activities, paddle tennis, physical training, strength & conditioning, yoga.

Computers Computers are regularly used in all classes. Computer network features include on-campus library services, Internet access, wireless campus network, Internet filtering or blocking technology. Student e-mail accounts and computer access in designated common areas are available to students. Students grades are available online. The school has a published electronic and media policy.

Contact Jason Hersom, Director of Admission and Financial Aid. 508-650-5020. Fax: 508-655-3726. E-mail: admissions@walnuthillarts.org.
Website: www.walnuthillarts.org/

WASATCH ACADEMY

120 South 100 West
Mt. Pleasant, Utah 84647

Head of School: Mr. Joseph Loftin

General Information Coeducational boarding and day college-preparatory and debate school. Grades 7–PG. Founded: 1875. Setting: small town. Nearest major city is Provo. Students are housed in coed dormitories. 40-acre campus. 31 buildings on campus. Approved or accredited by Northwest Association of Independent Schools, The Association of Boarding Schools, and Utah Department of Education. Member of National Association of Independent Schools. Endowment: $2 million. Total enrollment: 319. Upper school average class size: 12. Upper school faculty-student ratio: 1:10. There are 165 required school days per year for Upper School students. Upper School students typically attend 5 days per week. The average school day consists of 7 hours.

Upper School Student Profile Grade 9: 40 students (30 boys, 10 girls); Grade 10: 61 students (39 boys, 22 girls); Grade 11: 93 students (52 boys, 41 girls); Grade 12: 101 students (64 boys, 37 girls).

Faculty School total: 53. In upper school: 25 men, 26 women; 19 have advanced degrees; 48 reside on campus.

Subjects Offered 3-dimensional art, 3-dimensional design, acting, advanced computer applications, Advanced Placement courses, advanced studio art-AP, advanced TOEFL/grammar, algebra, American Civil War, American history, American history-AP, American literature-AP, anatomy, animation, art, athletic training, audio visual/media, ballet, biology, biology-AP, broadcast journalism, business mathematics, calculus-AP, ceramics, chemistry, chemistry-AP, Chinese, choir, cinematography, Civil War, college counseling, college placement, comedy, community garden, community service, dance, design, drama, drawing, drawing and design, driver education, earth science, electronic music, emerging technology, English, English language and composition-AP, English literature and composition-AP, English-AP, ensembles, environmental science-AP, equestrian sports, equine science, ESL, European history, European history-AP, film, filmmaking, fine arts, forensics, French, geography, geology, global issues, golf, guitar, honors algebra, honors English, honors U.S. history, jazz ensemble, jewelry making, Latin, learning strategies, martial arts, math applications, music, music theory, outdoor education, painting, performing arts, philosophy, photography, physical education, physical science, physics, physics-AP, piano, play production, pottery, pre-calculus, reading, SAT/ACT preparation, Spanish, Spanish-AP, speech and debate, stained glass, statistics-AP, student government, studio art-AP, study skills, theater, theater arts, theater design and production, TOEFL preparation, U.S. government, U.S. history, U.S. history-AP, United Nations and international issues, Vietnam War, weightlifting, Western civilization, woodworking, world religions, yearbook, yoga.

Graduation Requirements Arts and fine arts (art, music, dance, drama), computer literacy, English, foreign language, mathematics, physical education (includes health), science, social sciences, social studies (includes history), U.S. history, outdoor, cultural, community service, and recreational requirements.

Special Academic Programs 16 Advanced Placement exams for which test preparation is offered; honors section; accelerated programs; independent study; study at local college for college credit; programs in English, mathematics, general development for dyslexic students; ESL (29 students enrolled).

College Admission Counseling 105 students graduated in 2016; 100 went to college, including Boston University; Michigan State University; Parsons School of Design; Penn State University Park; Smith College; University of Utah. Median SAT critical reading: 500, median SAT math: 480, median composite ACT: 22. Mean SAT writing: 564, mean combined SAT: 1892. 13% scored over 600 on SAT critical reading, 9% scored over 600 on SAT math, 27% scored over 26 on composite ACT.

Student Life Upper grades have specified standards of dress, student council, honor system. Discipline rests primarily with faculty.

Summer Programs Remediation, enrichment, advancement, ESL programs offered; session focuses on academics and recreation; held on campus; accepts boys and girls; open to students from other schools. 50 students usually enrolled. 2017 schedule: June 26 to August 6. Application deadline: none.

Tuition and Aid Day student tuition: $30,000; 5-day tuition and room/board: $50,000; 7-day tuition and room/board: $54,900. Tuition installment plan (The Tuition

Plan, monthly payment plans, individually arranged payment plans). Merit scholarship grants, need-based scholarship grants, need-based loans available. In 2016–17, 44% of upper-school students received aid; total upper-school merit-scholarship money awarded: $3,857,580. Total amount of financial aid awarded in 2016–17: $3,857,580.

Admissions Traditional secondary-level entrance grade is 11. For fall 2016, 212 students applied for upper-level admission, 178 were accepted, 120 enrolled. Deadline for receipt of application materials: none. Application fee required: $100. On-campus interview required.

Athletics Interscholastic: alpine skiing (boys, girls), baseball (b), basketball (b,g), climbing (b,g), cross-country running (b,g), dance (b,g), dressage (b,g), equestrian sports (b,g), golf (b,g), horseback riding (b,g), outdoor activities (b,g), outdoor education (b,g), paint ball (b,g), physical training (b,g), rodeo (b,g), running (b,g), skiing (cross-country) (b,g), skiing (downhill) (b,g), snowboarding (b,g), snowshoeing (b,g), soccer (b,g), tennis (b,g), track and field (b,g), volleyball (g), weight training (b,g); intramural: alpine skiing (b,g), dance (b,g), skiing (downhill) (b,g), soccer (b,g), table tennis (b,g); coed interscholastic: aerobics/dance, backpacking, ballet, bicycling, canoeing/kayaking, cheering, climbing, combined training, cross-country running, dance, dressage, equestrian sports, fishing, golf, hiking/backpacking, horseback riding, kayaking, martial arts, modern dance, mountain biking, nordic skiing, outdoor activities, paint ball, physical training, rock climbing, rodeo, running, skiing (cross-country), skiing (downhill), snowboarding, snowshoeing, swimming and diving, table tennis, telemark skiing, tennis, track and field, weight training, yoga; coed intramural: aerobics/dance, aquatics, backpacking, badminton, ballet, bicycling, billiards, blading, bowling, canoeing/kayaking, climbing, combined training, cooperative games, dance team, equestrian sports, fishing, fitness, flag football, freestyle skiing, Frisbee, golf, hiking/backpacking, horseback riding, horseshoes, jogging, lacrosse, modern dance, mountain biking, nordic skiing, outdoor activities, paint ball, physical training, power lifting, rafting, rappelling, rock climbing, running, skateboarding, skiing (downhill), snowshoeing, swimming and diving, table tennis, telemark skiing, ultimate Frisbee, volleyball, weight lifting, weight training, yoga. 2 coaches, 1 athletic trainer.

Computers Computers are regularly used in all academic classes. Computer network features include on-campus library services, online commercial services, Internet access, wireless campus network, Internet filtering or blocking technology. Campus intranet and student e-mail accounts are available to students. Students grades are available online. The school has a published electronic and media policy.

Contact Dr. Brian McCauley, Assistant Head of School for Admissions and Marketing. 435-462-1400. Fax: 435-462-1450. E-mail: brian.mccauley@wasatchacademy.org. Website: www.wasatchacademy.org

WASHINGTON INTERNATIONAL SCHOOL

3100 Macomb Street NW
Washington, District of Columbia 20008

Head of School: Clayton W. Lewis

General Information Coeducational day college-preparatory and International Baccalaureate school. Grades PS–12. Founded: 1966. Setting: urban. 6-acre campus. 8 buildings on campus. Approved or accredited by Council of International Schools, International Baccalaureate Organization, Middle States Association of Colleges and Schools, and District of Columbia Department of Education. Member of National Association of Independent Schools, Secondary School Admission Test Board, and European Council of International Schools. Languages of instruction: English, French, and Spanish. Endowment: $5.5 million. Total enrollment: 920. Upper school average class size: 10. Upper school faculty-student ratio: 1:7. There are 176 required school days per year for Upper School students. Upper School students typically attend 5 days per week. The average school day consists of 5 hours and 25 minutes.

Faculty School total: 105. In upper school: 22 men, 22 women; 26 have advanced degrees.

Subjects Offered Advanced chemistry, advanced math, art, arts, biology, calculus, chemistry, chorus, community service, comparative government and politics, computer multimedia, computer science, contemporary history, drama, Dutch, economics, English, English literature, environmental science, fine arts, French, geography, history, information technology, integrated mathematics, International Baccalaureate courses, literature seminar, music, musical productions, physical education, physics, psychology, robotics, science, social sciences, Spanish, theater, theory of knowledge, world history.

Graduation Requirements Algebra, arts, arts and fine arts (art, music, dance, drama), biology, calculus, chemistry, economics, English, environmental science, foreign language, geography, geometry, physical education (includes health), physics, trigonometry, world history, world literature, International Baccalaureate program. Community service is required.

Special Academic Programs International Baccalaureate program.

College Admission Counseling 66 students graduated in 2016; all went to college, including New York University; Swarthmore College; University of California, Berkeley; University of California, Los Angeles; University of Chicago; University of Pennsylvania. Mean SAT critical reading: 655, mean SAT math: 656, mean SAT writing: 660, mean combined SAT: 1971, mean composite ACT: 31.

Student Life Upper grades have student council, honor system. Discipline rests primarily with faculty.

Tuition and Aid Day student tuition: $38,330. Tuition installment plan (monthly payment plans, 2-payment plan). Need-based scholarship grants available.

Admissions Traditional secondary-level entrance grade is 9. School's own exam required. Deadline for receipt of application materials: January 5. Application fee required: $75. Interview required.

Athletics Interscholastic: basketball (boys, girls), soccer (b,g), softball (g), tennis (b,g), track and field (b,g), volleyball (b,g); coed interscholastic: cross-country running, golf; coed intramural: swimming and diving. 3 PE instructors, 1 athletic trainer.

Computers Computers are regularly used in all classes. Computer network features include on-campus library services, online commercial services, Internet access, wireless campus network, Internet filtering or blocking technology. Campus intranet and student e-mail accounts are available to students. The school has a published electronic and media policy.

Contact Ms. Mary Hastings Moore, Director of Admissions and Financial Aid. 202-243-1831. Fax: 202-243-1807. E-mail: moore@wis.edu. Website: www.wis.edu

WASHINGTON WALDORF SCHOOL

4800 Sangamore Road
Bethesda, Maryland 20816

Head of School: Ms. Jennifer Page

General Information Coeducational day college-preparatory school. Grades PS–12. Founded: 1969. Setting: suburban. Nearest major city is Washington, DC. 6-acre campus. 1 building on campus. Approved or accredited by Association of Independent Maryland Schools and Maryland Department of Education. Member of National Association of Independent Schools. Total enrollment: 242. Upper school average class size: 18. Upper school faculty-student ratio: 1:7. There are 175 required school days per year for Upper School students. Upper School students typically attend 5 days per week. The average school day consists of 7 hours.

Upper School Student Profile Grade 9: 16 students (8 boys, 8 girls); Grade 10: 19 students (7 boys, 12 girls); Grade 11: 17 students (6 boys, 11 girls); Grade 12: 18 students (8 boys, 10 girls).

Faculty School total: 38. In upper school: 8 men, 8 women; 9 have advanced degrees.

Subjects Offered 3-dimensional art, African-American history, algebra, American Civil War, American literature, anatomy and physiology, ancient world history, art, art and culture, art history, biochemistry, biology, bookbinding, botany, British literature, calculus, calculus-AP, chamber groups, chemistry, choir, chorus, civil rights, classical civilization, crafts, critical thinking, critical writing, drama performance, ecology, epic literature, eurythmy, fine arts, general math, general science, geology, geometry, German, grammar, history of architecture, history of music, human anatomy, human development, lab science, medieval literature, metalworking, modern history, modern world history, mythology, oil painting, optics, physical education, pre-calculus, printmaking, research skills, sculpture, Shakespeare, Spanish, stone carving, trigonometry, U.S. constitutional history, weaving, Western literature, writing, zoology.

Graduation Requirements Arts and fine arts (art, music, dance, drama), comparative religion, constitutional history of U.S., crafts, English, eurythmy, foreign language, history of drama, history of music, mathematics, physical education (includes health), science, social studies (includes history).

Special Academic Programs 1 Advanced Placement exam for which test preparation is offered; study abroad; academic accommodation for the musically talented and the artistically talented.

College Admission Counseling 9 students graduated in 2016; 7 went to college, including Bennington College; Franklin & Marshall College; Hobart and William Smith Colleges; Oberlin College; Principia College; University of Maryland, College Park. Other 2 had other specific plans. Median SAT critical reading: 648, median SAT math: 578, median SAT writing: 652.

Student Life Upper grades have specified standards of dress, student council. Discipline rests primarily with faculty.

Summer Programs Sports programs offered; session focuses on basketball camps; held on campus; accepts boys and girls; open to students from other schools. 18 students usually enrolled.

Tuition and Aid Day student tuition: $27,900. Tuition installment plan (FACTS Tuition Payment Plan, monthly payment plans, individually arranged payment plans, self-insured tuition insurance). Tuition reduction for siblings, need-based scholarship grants, need-based assistance grants, tuition remission for children of faculty, one full scholarship for an inner-city student available. In 2016–17, 25% of upper-school students received aid. Total amount of financial aid awarded in 2016–17: $38,000.

Admissions Traditional secondary-level entrance grade is 9. Math and English placement tests required. Deadline for receipt of application materials: none. Application fee required: $60. On-campus interview required.

Athletics Interscholastic: baseball (boys), basketball (b,g), cross-country running (b,g), soccer (b,g), softball (g); coed intramural: golf, outdoor education, table tennis, volleyball, yoga. 1 PE instructor, 3 coaches.

Computers Computers are regularly used in architecture, art, classics, current events, drawing and design, English, foreign language, historical foundations for arts, humanities, mathematics, music, newspaper, philosophy, research skills, science, senior seminar, social studies, theater arts, woodworking, writing, yearbook classes. Computer resources include Internet access.

Contact Ms. Lezlie Lawson, Admissions/Enrollment Director. 301-229-6107 Ext. 154. Fax: 301-229-9379. E-mail: llawson@washingtonwaldorf.org. Website: www.washingtonwaldorf.org

THE WATERFORD SCHOOL

1480 East 9400 South
Sandy, Utah 84093

Head of School: Andrew Menke

General Information Coeducational day college-preparatory and visual arts, music, photography, dance, and theater school. Grades PK–12. Founded: 1981. Setting: suburban. Nearest major city is Salt Lake City. 42-acre campus. 10 buildings on campus. Approved or accredited by Northwest Association of Independent Schools, Northwest Association of Schools and Colleges, and Utah Department of Education. Member of National Association of Independent Schools. Endowment: $3.5 million. Total enrollment: 880. Upper school average class size: 16. Upper school faculty-student ratio: 1:4. There are 169 required school days per year for Upper School students. Upper School students typically attend 5 days per week. The average school day consists of 6 hours.

Upper School Student Profile Grade 9: 78 students (40 boys, 38 girls); Grade 10: 67 students (30 boys, 37 girls); Grade 11: 75 students (33 boys, 42 girls); Grade 12: 70 students (40 boys, 30 girls).

Faculty School total: 122. In upper school: 41 men, 37 women; 59 have advanced degrees.

Subjects Offered 20th century history, 3-dimensional design, acting, advanced math, Advanced Placement courses, aerobics, algebra, American history, American history-AP, American literature, art, Asian history, basketball, biology, biology-AP, British literature, calculus, calculus-AP, ceramics, chemistry, chemistry-AP, chorus, computer applications, computer art, computer graphics, computer programming, computer science, computer science-AP, creative writing, debate, drama, drama performance, drama workshop, drawing, ecology, economics, English-AP, European history, European history-AP, French, French-AP, genetics, geology, geometry, German, German-AP, Japanese, jazz ensemble, Latin, Latin American literature, music history, music performance, music theater, outdoor education, painting, philosophy, photography, physical education, physics, physics-AP, pre-calculus, probability and statistics, psychology, robotics, sculpture, Spanish, Spanish-AP, statistics-AP, strings, studio art-AP, trigonometry, voice ensemble, volleyball, weight training, wind ensemble, world literature, writing workshop, yearbook, zoology.

Graduation Requirements 20th century world history, algebra, American history, American literature, art, biology, British literature, calculus, chemistry, computer science, English, European history, foreign language, geometry, music performance, physics, pre-calculus, trigonometry, visual arts, world history, writing workshop, six terms of physical education or participation on athletic teams.

Special Academic Programs 15 Advanced Placement exams for which test preparation is offered; honors section; independent study; term-away projects; academic accommodation for the gifted, the musically talented, and the artistically talented.

College Admission Counseling 71 students graduated in 2016; all went to college. Mean SAT critical reading: 650, mean SAT math: 669, mean SAT writing: 629, mean combined SAT: 1949, mean composite ACT: 28.

Student Life Upper grades have uniform requirement, student council, honor system. Discipline rests equally with students and faculty.

Summer Programs Enrichment, advancement, sports, art/fine arts, rigorous outdoor training, computer instruction programs offered; session focuses on enrichment and advancement; held both on and off campus; accepts boys and girls; not open to students from other schools. 100 students usually enrolled. 2017 schedule: June 10 to August 15. Application deadline: March 15.

Tuition and Aid Day student tuition: $21,825. Tuition installment plan (Insured Tuition Payment Plan, monthly payment plans). Tuition reduction for siblings, need-based scholarship grants available. In 2016–17, 18% of upper-school students received aid. Total amount of financial aid awarded in 2016–17: $350,000.

Admissions Traditional secondary-level entrance grade is 9. For fall 2016, 42 students applied for upper-level admission, 32 were accepted, 25 enrolled. Admissions testing, school's own test and TOEFL required. Deadline for receipt of application materials: none. Application fee required: $35. On-campus interview recommended.

Athletics Interscholastic: basketball (boys, girls), crew (b,g), cross-country running (b,g), golf (b,g), lacrosse (b,g), soccer (b,g), tennis (b,g), volleyball (g); coed interscholastic: alpine skiing, ballet, dance, Frisbee, racquetball, ultimate Frisbee; coed intramural: aerobics, backpacking, climbing, crew, hiking/backpacking, outdoor activities, outdoor adventure, outdoor education, outdoor recreation, outdoor skills, outdoors, rock climbing, snowshoeing, strength & conditioning, weight training, yoga. 6 PE instructors, 15 coaches.

Computers Computers are regularly used in all academic, animation, college planning, graphic design, library, literary magazine, newspaper, photography, programming, publications, writing, yearbook classes. Computer network features include on-campus library services, online commercial services, Internet access, wireless campus network, Internet filtering or blocking technology. Campus intranet, student e-mail accounts, and computer access in designated common areas are available to students. Students grades are available online. The school has a published electronic and media policy.

Contact Mr. Todd Winters, Director of Admissions. 801-816-2213. Fax: 801-572-1787. E-mail: toddwinters@waterfordschool.org. Website: www.waterfordschool.org

WATKINSON SCHOOL

180 Bloomfield Avenue
Hartford, Connecticut 06105

Head of School: Mrs. Teriann Schrader

General Information Coeducational day college-preparatory, arts, and athletics, global studies school. Grades 6–PG. Founded: 1881. Setting: suburban. 40-acre campus. 5 buildings on campus. Approved or accredited by Association of Independent Schools in New England, New England Association of Schools and Colleges, and Connecticut Department of Education. Member of National Association of Independent Schools and Secondary School Admission Test Board. Endowment: $4.4 million. Total enrollment: 240. Upper school average class size: 12. Upper school faculty-student ratio: 1:6. There are 165 required school days per year for Upper School students. Upper School students typically attend 5 days per week. The average school day consists of 7 hours and 30 minutes.

Upper School Student Profile Grade 9: 38 students (24 boys, 14 girls); Grade 10: 40 students (18 boys, 22 girls); Grade 11: 46 students (25 boys, 21 girls); Grade 12: 44 students (19 boys, 25 girls); Postgraduate: 12 students (7 boys, 5 girls).

Faculty School total: 56. In upper school: 13 men, 30 women; 21 have advanced degrees.

Subjects Offered African history, algebra, American history, American literature, American sign language, anatomy, ancient world history, art, Asian history, biology, calculus, ceramics, chemistry, creative writing, dance, drama, drawing, earth science, English, English literature, environmental science, European history, expository writing, fine arts, forensics, French, geography, geometry, health, history, internship, mathematics, modern European history, painting, photography, physics, pottery, science, social studies, Spanish, theater, U.S. history, world history, world literature, writing.

Graduation Requirements Arts and fine arts (art, music, dance, drama), English, foreign language, health and wellness, mathematics, science, social studies (includes history), technology.

Special Academic Programs Independent study; study at local college for college credit; academic accommodation for the gifted, the musically talented, and the artistically talented; programs in English, mathematics, general development for dyslexic students; special instructional classes for deaf students.

College Admission Counseling 53 students graduated in 2016; 51 went to college, including Emerson College; Hampshire College; McGill University; Quinnipiac University; Salve Regina University; University of Connecticut. Other: 2 entered a postgraduate year. Median SAT critical reading: 530, median SAT math: 520, median SAT writing: 540, median combined SAT: 1615, median composite ACT: 25. 32% scored over 600 on SAT critical reading, 25% scored over 600 on SAT math, 32% scored over 600 on SAT writing, 20% scored over 1800 on combined SAT, 47% scored over 26 on composite ACT.

Student Life Upper grades have specified standards of dress, student council. Discipline rests equally with students and faculty.

Tuition and Aid Day student tuition: $37,925. Tuition installment plan (Insured Tuition Payment Plan, SMART Tuition Payment Plan). Need-based scholarship grants available. In 2016–17, 41% of upper-school students received aid. Total amount of financial aid awarded in 2016–17: $1,650,522.

Admissions Traditional secondary-level entrance grade is 9. For fall 2016, 172 students applied for upper-level admission, 49 were accepted, 31 enrolled. ISEE, SSAT, TOEFL or TOEFL Junior required. Deadline for receipt of application materials: February 1. Application fee required: $50. On-campus interview recommended.

Athletics Interscholastic: basketball (boys, girls), crew (b,g), cross-country running (b,g), ice hockey (b), lacrosse (b,g), rowing (b,g), soccer (b,g), tennis (b,g), track and field (b,g), volleyball (g); coed interscholastic: crew, cross-country running, tennis, ultimate Frisbee; coed intramural: aerobics, alpine skiing, ballet, Circus, combined training, dance, fencing, fitness, Frisbee, golf, horseback riding, outdoor activities, outdoor adventure, physical fitness, physical training, strength & conditioning, tennis, ultimate Frisbee, volleyball, weight lifting, yoga. 4 coaches.

Computers Computers are regularly used in creative writing classes. Computer network features include on-campus library services, online commercial services, Internet access, wireless campus network, Internet filtering or blocking technology. Campus intranet, student e-mail accounts, and computer access in designated common areas are available to students. Students grades are available online. The school has a published electronic and media policy.

Contact Mrs. Maryann Dupuis, Admissions Office Assistant. 860-236-5618 Ext. 136. Fax: 860-986-6146. E-mail: Maryann_Dupuis@watkinson.org. Website: www.watkinson.org

WAYNFLETE SCHOOL

360 Spring Street
Portland, Maine 04102

Head of School: Geoffrey Wagg

General Information Coeducational day college-preparatory school. Grades PK–12. Founded: 1898. Setting: urban. Nearest major city is Boston, MA. 37-acre campus. 10 buildings on campus. Approved or accredited by Association of Independent Schools in New England, Independent Schools of Northern New England, New England

Association of Schools and Colleges, The College Board, and Maine Department of Education. Member of National Association of Independent Schools. Endowment: $22.4 million. Total enrollment: 583. Upper school average class size: 11. Upper school faculty-student ratio: 1:11. There are 172 required school days per year for Upper School students. Upper School students typically attend 5 days per week. The average school day consists of 7 hours and 15 minutes.

Upper School Student Profile Grade 9: 58 students (25 boys, 33 girls); Grade 10: 75 students (38 boys, 37 girls); Grade 11: 57 students (27 boys, 30 girls); Grade 12: 69 students (26 boys, 43 girls).

Faculty School total: 85. In upper school: 24 men, 32 women; 35 have advanced degrees.

Subjects Offered 20th century American writers, 20th century history, 3-dimensional art, 3-dimensional design, acting, advanced biology, advanced math, African literature, algebra, American history, American literature, ancient/medieval philosophy, art history, astrophysics, bioethics, biology, British literature (honors), calculus, ceramics, chemistry, computer studies, constitutional history of U.S., creative writing, drama, drama workshop, English, English composition, English literature, environmental science, environmental studies, equality and freedom, European history, expository writing, French, geometry, government/civics, health, Islamic studies, Latin, Mandarin, marine biology, Middle Eastern history, modern European history, music, physical education, physics, pre-calculus, printmaking, psychology, Russian history, Spanish, statistics, studio art, trigonometry, U.S. constitutional history, Vietnam, world history, world literature.

Graduation Requirements American history, art, arts, biology, English, foreign language, historical research, history, mathematics, performing arts, physical education (includes health), science, U.S. history, writing, Seniors may design a month-long Senior Project, which allows them to pursue academic interests, potential careers, fine arts, or community service. Community service is required.

Special Academic Programs Independent study; term-away projects; study abroad.

College Admission Counseling 62 students graduated in 2016; 60 went to college, including Bard College; Bowdoin College; Oberlin College; Smith College; Tufts University; Wheaton College. Other: 1 went to work, 1 had other specific plans. Median SAT critical reading: 600, median SAT math: 580, median SAT writing: 580, median combined SAT: 1780, median composite ACT: 27. 49% scored over 600 on SAT critical reading, 40% scored over 600 on SAT math, 39% scored over 600 on SAT writing, 46% scored over 1800 on combined SAT, 59% scored over 26 on composite ACT.

Student Life Upper grades have student council. Discipline rests primarily with faculty.

Summer Programs Enrichment, sports, art/fine arts programs offered; session focuses on sports, gymnastics, martial arts, robotics, fine/performing arts, technology, sustainable ocean studies; held both on and off campus; accepts boys and girls; open to students from other schools. 2017 schedule: June 12 to July 28. Application deadline: none.

Tuition and Aid Day student tuition: $29,340. Tuition installment plan (Insured Tuition Payment Plan, FACTS Tuition Payment Plan). Need-based scholarship grants available. In 2016–17, 42% of upper-school students received aid. Total amount of financial aid awarded in 2016–17: $2,313,466.

Admissions Traditional secondary-level entrance grade is 9. For fall 2016, 61 students applied for upper-level admission, 35 were accepted, 24 enrolled. Deadline for receipt of application materials: February 10. Application fee required: $40. Interview recommended.

Athletics Interscholastic: baseball (boys), basketball (b,g), cross-country running (b,g), field hockey (g), golf (b), ice hockey (b,g), lacrosse (b,g), nordic skiing (b,g), skiing (cross-country) (b,g), soccer (b,g), tennis (b,g); good interscholastic: crew, rowing, sailing, swimming and diving, track and field; coed intramural: dance, fitness walking, golf, modern dance, physical fitness, sailing, swimming and diving, tennis, weight lifting, weight training, yoga. 3 PE instructors, 20 coaches, 1 athletic trainer.

Computers Computers are regularly used in all academic, computer applications, information technology, introduction to technology, programming classes. Computer network features include on-campus library services, online commercial services, Internet access, wireless campus network, Internet filtering or blocking technology, Google doc accounts; academic databases, including JSTOR and Schoology; Quizlet; and Noodle Tools. Student e-mail accounts and computer access in designated common areas are available to students. The school has a published electronic and media policy.

Contact Melissa Fox, Admission Office. 207-774-5721 Ext. 1224. Fax: 207-772-4782. E-mail: admissionoffice@waynflete.org. Website: www.waynflete.org

WEBB SCHOOL OF KNOXVILLE

9800 Webb School Drive
Knoxville, Tennessee 37923-3399

Head of School: Mr. Michael V. McBrien

General Information Coeducational day college-preparatory, arts, and religious studies school. Grades PK–12. Founded: 1955. Setting: urban. Nearest major city is Chattanooga. 114-acre campus. 8 buildings on campus. Approved or accredited by Southern Association of Colleges and Schools, Southern Association of Independent Schools, and Tennessee Department of Education. Member of National Association of Independent Schools and Secondary School Admission Test Board. Endowment: $40.3 million. Total enrollment: 989. Upper school average class size: 16. Upper school

faculty-student ratio: 1:11. There are 173 required school days per year for Upper School students. Upper School students typically attend 5 days per week. The average school day consists of 7 hours and 50 minutes.

Upper School Student Profile Grade 9: 101 students (50 boys, 51 girls); Grade 10: 109 students (56 boys, 53 girls); Grade 11: 126 students (68 boys, 58 girls); Grade 12: 113 students (50 boys, 63 girls).

Faculty School total: 96. In upper school: 14 men, 28 women; 34 have advanced degrees.

Subjects Offered 3-dimensional design, advanced math, algebra, anatomy and physiology, art history-AP, biology, biology-AP, calculus, calculus-AP, ceramics, chamber groups, chemistry, chemistry-AP, cinematography, civics, computer science-AP, concert choir, digital imaging, drama, drawing, economics, English, English language and composition-AP, English literature and composition-AP, English-AP, environmental science, forensics, French, French-AP, geometry, government and politics-AP, history of rock and roll, honors algebra, honors English, honors geometry, honors world history, journalism, Latin, Latin-AP, macroeconomics-AP, Mandarin, microeconomics-AP, modern European history-AP, modern world history, music theory-AP, painting, philosophy, photo shop, photography, physics, physics-AP, play/screen writing, pre-calculus, printmaking, probability and statistics, psychology-AP, robotics, sculpture, Spanish, Spanish-AP, speech, stage design, statistics-AP, strings, studio art-AP, theater arts, theater design and production, trigonometry, U.S. history, U.S. history-AP, video communication, wind ensemble, women in world history, world history, world history-AP, world issues, world religions, yearbook.

Graduation Requirements Algebra, American history, arts and fine arts (art, music, dance, drama), biology, chemistry, English, foreign language, geometry, history, mathematics, physical education (includes health), public service, science, world history, world religions, public speaking (two chapel talks), 15 hours of community service per year.

Special Academic Programs 25 Advanced Placement exams for which test preparation is offered; honors section; independent study; study abroad; remedial reading and/or remedial writing; remedial math.

College Admission Counseling 98 students graduated in 2016; all went to college, including Auburn University; Case Western Reserve University; The University of Alabama; The University of Tennessee; University of Colorado Boulder; University of Georgia. Mean SAT critical reading: 642, mean SAT math: 630, mean SAT writing: 623, mean combined SAT: 1896, mean composite ACT: 29. 77% scored over 600 on SAT critical reading, 72% scored over 600 on SAT math, 71% scored over 600 on SAT writing, 71% scored over 1800 on combined SAT, 70% scored over 26 on composite ACT.

Student Life Upper grades have uniform requirement, student council, honor system. Discipline rests equally with students and faculty.

Summer Programs Remediation, enrichment, advancement, art/fine arts programs offered; session focuses on academic; held on campus; accepts boys and girls; not open to students from other schools. 86 students usually enrolled. 2017 schedule: June 1 to July 31. Application deadline: June 1.

Tuition and Aid Day student tuition: $18,600. Tuition installment plan (monthly payment plans, individually arranged payment plans, tuition payments can also be paid in two installments-last calendar day in July and November). Need-based scholarship grants available. In 2016–17, 19% of upper-school students received aid. Total amount of financial aid awarded in 2016–17: $860,000.

Admissions Traditional secondary level entrance grade is 9. For fall 2016, 40 students applied for upper-level admission, 34 were accepted, 27 enrolled. ISEE required. Deadline for receipt of application materials: January 31. Application fee required: $75. On-campus interview required.

Athletics Interscholastic: baseball (boys), basketball (b,g), bowling (b,g), cheering (g), cross-country running (b,g), dance team (g), diving (b,g), field hockey (g), football (b), golf (b,g), lacrosse (b), soccer (b,g), softball (g), swimming and diving (b,g), tennis (b,g), track and field (b,g), volleyball (g), wrestling (b); intramural: archery (b,g), climbing (b,g), dance (b,g), Frisbee (b,g), hiking/backpacking (b,g); coed interscholastic: sailing. 45 coaches, 1 athletic trainer.

Computers Computers are regularly used in all academic classes. Computer network features include on-campus library services, Internet access, wireless campus network, Internet filtering or blocking technology, all students in grades 4-8 lease iPads through the school, all students in grades 9-12 lease laptops through the school. Student e-mail accounts are available to students. Students grades are available online. The school has a published electronic and media policy.

Contact Mrs. Christy Widener, Assistant Director of Admissions. 865-291-3830. Fax: 865-291-1532. E-mail: christy_widener@webbschool.org. Website: www.webbschool.org

THE WEBB SCHOOLS

1175 West Baseline Road
Claremont, California 91711

Head of School: Mr. Taylor Stockdale

General Information Coeducational boarding and day college-preparatory school. Grades 9–12. Founded: 1922. Setting: suburban. Nearest major city is Los Angeles. Students are housed in single-sex dormitories. 70-acre campus. Approved or accredited by The Association of Boarding Schools, Western Association of Schools and Colleges,

Western Catholic Education Association, and California Department of Education. Member of National Association of Independent Schools and Secondary School Admission Test Board. Endowment: $32 million. Upper school average class size: 16. Upper school faculty-student ratio: 1:8.

Upper School Student Profile Grade 9: 88 students (43 boys, 45 girls); Grade 10: 108 students (55 boys, 53 girls); Grade 11: 114 students (61 boys, 53 girls); Grade 12: 98 students (51 boys, 47 girls). 65% of students are boarding students. 70% are state residents. 13 states are represented in upper school student body. 20% are international students. International students from China, Hong Kong, Indonesia, Republic of Korea, Russian Federation, and Saudi Arabia; 18 other countries represented in student body.

Faculty School total: 58. In upper school: 47 have advanced degrees; 47 reside on campus.

Subjects Offered Algebra, American literature, art, astronomy, biology, biology-AP, calculus, calculus-AP, chamber groups, chemistry, chemistry-AP, Chinese, chorus, composition, computer programming, drawing, economics, English, English language and composition-AP, English literature and composition-AP, environmental science, environmental science-AP, foundations of civilization, French, French language-AP, health and wellness, history, humanities, integrated mathematics, introduction to literature, journalism, linear algebra, media arts, modern world history, oceanography, orchestra, painting, paleontology, physics, physics-AP, pre-calculus, psychology, sculpture, Spanish, Spanish language-AP, Spanish literature-AP, statistics, statistics-AP, theater, U.S. history, U.S. history-AP, world history-AP.

Graduation Requirements Arts and fine arts (art, music, dance, drama), English, foreign language, health, history, mathematics, physical education (includes health), science.

Special Academic Programs 15 Advanced Placement exams for which test preparation is offered; honors section; academic accommodation for the gifted.

College Admission Counseling 100 students graduated in 2015; 99 went to college, including Cornell University; Loyola Marymount University; New York University; Scripps College; University of California, San Diego; University of Southern California. Other: 1 had other specific plans. Median combined SAT: 2015.

Student Life Upper grades have specified standards of dress, student council, honor system. Discipline rests equally with students and faculty.

Tuition and Aid Day student tuition: $39,815; 7-day tuition and room/board: $55,985. Tuition installment plan (Insured Tuition Payment Plan, monthly payment plans). Need-based scholarship grants available. In 2015–16, 34% of upper-school students received aid. Total amount of financial aid awarded in 2015–16: $4,100,000.

Admissions Traditional secondary-level entrance grade is 9. ISEE, SSAT or TOEFL required. Deadline for receipt of application materials: January 15. Application fee required: $75. Interview required.

Athletics Interscholastic: baseball (boys), basketball (b,g), cross-country running (b,g), diving (b,g), football (b), golf (b,g), soccer (b,g), softball (g), swimming and diving (b,g), tennis (b,g), track and field (b,g), volleyball (b,g), water polo (b,g), wrestling (b); coed interscholastic: badminton; coed intramural: dance, fitness, outdoor activities, triathlon, yoga.

Computers Computers are regularly used in all academic classes. Computer network features include on-campus library services, online commercial services, Internet access, wireless campus network, Internet filtering or blocking technology. Campus intranet and student e-mail accounts are available to students. Students grades are available online. The school has a published electronic and media policy.

Contact Mr. Heidi Marti, Assistant Director of Admission. 909-482-5214. Fax: 909-445-8269. E-mail: hmarti@webb.org. Website: www.webb.org/admission

THE WEBER SCHOOL

6751 Roswell Road
Sandy Springs, Georgia 30328

Head of School: Rabbi Edward Harwitz

General Information Coeducational day college-preparatory school, affiliated with Jewish faith. Grades 9–12. Founded: 1997. Setting: suburban. Nearest major city is Atlanta. 20-acre campus. 2 buildings on campus. Approved or accredited by Georgia Independent School Association, Southern Association of Colleges and Schools, Southern Association of Independent Schools, The College Board, and Georgia Department of Education. Member of National Association of Independent Schools and Secondary School Admission Test Board. Languages of instruction: English, Hebrew, and Spanish. Total enrollment: 226. Upper school average class size: 15. Upper school faculty-student ratio: 1:6. There are 180 required school days per year for Upper School students. Upper School students typically attend 5 days per week. The average school day consists of 8 hours.

Upper School Student Profile Grade 9: 54 students (27 boys, 27 girls); Grade 10: 60 students (31 boys, 29 girls); Grade 11: 56 students (23 boys, 33 girls); Grade 12: 56 students (28 boys, 28 girls). 100% of students are Jewish.

Faculty School total: 38. In upper school: 17 men, 24 women; 35 have advanced degrees.

Subjects Offered 3-dimensional art, acting, anatomy and physiology, ancient world history, astronomy, ceramics, chorus, comparative religion, computer science-AP, creative dance, creative writing, dance, drama performance, drama workshop, economics-AP, English literature-AP, English/composition-AP, environmental science-

AP, finite math, forensics, government and politics-AP, history of rock and roll, Holocaust studies, jazz band, literary magazine, macro/microeconomics-AP, marketing, model United Nations, modern world history, personal fitness, probability and statistics, psychology-AP, robotics, senior seminar, softball, Spanish language-AP, studio art-AP, swimming, United States government-AP, video film production, volleyball, weight training, world history-AP, wrestling, yearbook, yoga.

Graduation Requirements Jewish Studies requirements, Hebrew language, Capstone Honors thesis.

Special Academic Programs 17 Advanced Placement exams for which test preparation is offered; honors section; independent study; study at local college for college credit; study abroad.

College Admission Counseling 55 students graduated in 2016; 50 went to college, including Indiana University Bloomington; Northwestern University; Tulane University; University of Georgia; University of Michigan; Washington University in St. Louis. Other: 1 entered military service, 4 had other specific plans. Mean SAT critical reading: 599, mean SAT math: 589, mean SAT writing: 617, mean combined SAT: 1805, mean composite ACT: 26.

Student Life Upper grades have specified standards of dress, student council. Discipline rests primarily with faculty.

Summer Programs Enrichment, advancement programs offered; session focuses on Academic subjects; held on campus; accepts boys and girls; open to students from other schools. 20 students usually enrolled. 2017 schedule: June 10 to July 20. Application deadline: June 1.

Tuition and Aid Day student tuition: $27,000. Tuition installment plan (FACTS Tuition Payment Plan, monthly payment plans, individually arranged payment plans, supplemental tuition assistance). Tuition reduction for siblings, need-based scholarship grants available. In 2016–17, 40% of upper-school students received aid.

Admissions Traditional secondary-level entrance grade is 9. For fall 2016, 123 students applied for upper-level admission, 104 were accepted, 70 enrolled. PSAT and SAT for applicants to grade 11 and 12 or SSAT required. Deadline for receipt of application materials: February 1. Application fee required: $125. On-campus interview recommended.

Athletics Interscholastic: baseball (boys), basketball (b,g), dance (g), dance team (g), modern dance (g), soccer (b,g), softball (g), tennis (b,g), volleyball (g), wrestling (b); coed interscholastic: cross-country running, fitness, golf, swimming and diving, track and field, weight training, yoga; coed intramural: aerobics/Nautilus, ultimate Frisbee. 14 coaches, 3 athletic trainers.

Computers Computers are regularly used in all academic classes. Computer network features include on-campus library services, online commercial services, Internet access, wireless campus network, Internet filtering or blocking technology, wireless lab, learning center. Campus intranet, student e-mail accounts, and computer access in designated common areas are available to students. Students grades are available online. The school has a published electronic and media policy.

Contact Ms. Rise Arkin, Director of Admissions. 404-917-2500 Ext. 117. Fax: 404-917-2501. E-mail: risearkin@weberschool.org. Website: www.weberschool.org

THE WELLINGTON SCHOOL

3650 Reed Road
Columbus, Ohio 43220

Head of School: Mr. Robert D. Brisk

General Information Coeducational day college-preparatory school. Grades PK–12. Founded: 1982. Setting: suburban. 21-acre campus. 1 building on campus. Approved or accredited by Independent Schools Association of the Central States, Ohio Association of Independent Schools, and Ohio Department of Education. Member of National Association of Independent Schools. Total enrollment: 668. Upper school average class size: 15. Upper school faculty-student ratio: 1:8. Upper School students typically attend 5 days per week. The average school day consists of 7 hours.

Faculty School total: 81. In upper school: 24 have advanced degrees.

Subjects Offered Advanced biology, advanced chemistry, advanced math, algebra, art and culture, band, biology, business skills, calculus, ceramics, chemistry, choir, chorus, computer graphics, creative arts, drama, drawing, earth and space science, economics, English, film, French, geometry, government, journalism, Latin, mathematics, modern history, music appreciation, painting, photography, physical education, physics, printmaking, Spanish, speech, strings, studio art-AP, U.S. history, visual arts, voice, Western civilization, word processing, writing, yearbook.

Graduation Requirements 3-dimensional art, arts and fine arts (art, music, dance, drama), English, foreign language, government, lab science, mathematics, physical education (includes health), science, social sciences, social studies (includes history), speech, senior independent project. Community service is required.

Special Academic Programs Advanced Placement exam preparation; honors section; accelerated programs; independent study; study at local college for college credit; study abroad; academic accommodation for the gifted, the musically talented, and the artistically talented; ESL.

College Admission Counseling 47 students graduated in 2016; they went to Emory University.

Student Life Upper grades have uniform requirement, student council, honor system. Discipline rests equally with students and faculty.

Summer Programs Enrichment, advancement, sports, art/fine arts programs offered; session focuses on enrichment/active learning; held both on and off campus; accepts boys and girls; open to students from other schools. Application deadline: none.

Tuition and Aid Day student tuition: $11,650–$22,750. Tuition installment plan (monthly payment plans, individually arranged payment plans, 2-, 6-, and 10-month payment plans). Merit scholarship grants, need-based scholarship grants available.

Admissions Traditional secondary-level entrance grade is 9. Admissions testing or ERB required. Deadline for receipt of application materials: none. Application fee required. On-campus interview required.

Athletics Interscholastic: baseball (boys), basketball (b,g), diving (b,g), fencing (b,g), golf (b,g), lacrosse (b,g), soccer (b,g), softball (g), tennis (b,g); intramural: basketball (b,g), independent competitive sports (g), lacrosse (g); coed interscholastic: fencing, swimming and diving; coed intramural: canoeing/kayaking, climbing, flag football, martial arts. 2 PE instructors, 15 coaches, 1 athletic trainer.

Computers Computer network features include on-campus library services, online commercial services, Internet access, wireless campus network, Internet filtering or blocking technology. Campus intranet, student e-mail accounts, and computer access in designated common areas are available to students. Students grades are available online. The school has a published electronic and media policy.

Contact Ms. Lynne Steger, Assistant Director of Admissions. 614-324-1647. Fax: 614-442-3286. E-mail: steger@wellington.org. Website: www.wellington.org

WELLSPRING FOUNDATION

Bethlehem, Connecticut
See Special Needs Schools section.

WESLEYAN ACADEMY

PO Box 1489
Guaynabo, Puerto Rico 00970-1489

Head of School: Rev. Fernando Vazquez

General Information Coeducational day college-preparatory school, affiliated with Wesleyan Church. Grades PK–12. Founded: 1955. Setting: urban. Nearest major city is San Juan. 6-acre campus. 1 building on campus. Approved or accredited by Association of Christian Schools International, Middle States Association of Colleges and Schools, and Puerto Rico Department of Education. Total enrollment: 903. Upper school average class size: 25. Upper school faculty-student ratio: 1:25. There are 180 required school days per year for Upper School students. Upper School students typically attend 6 days per week. The average school day consists of 7 hours.

Upper School Student Profile Grade 9: 58 students (27 boys, 31 girls); Grade 10: 71 students (32 boys, 39 girls); Grade 11: 62 students (28 boys, 34 girls); Grade 12: 54 students (28 boys, 26 girls). 30% of students are members of Wesleyan Church.

Faculty School total: 30. In upper school: 11 men, 17 women; 5 have advanced degrees.

Subjects Offered Accounting, advanced math, algebra, American history, anatomy and physiology, art, athletics, Bible, biology, calculus, career and personal planning, career planning, chemistry, choir, Christian education, college planning, computer skills, critical writing, dance, drama, earth science, English, English literature, French, general math, general science, geography, geometry, global studies, golf, guidance, guitar, handbells, health, history, Internet, intro to computers, jazz, jazz dance, keyboarding, lab science, library, mathematics, music, music appreciation, personal development, personal growth, physical science, piano, poetry, pre-algebra, pre-calculus, pre-college orientation, Puerto Rican history, science, self-defense, sewing, social sciences, Spanish, Spanish language-AP, swimming, trigonometry, U.S. government, volleyball, world affairs, world history, yearbook.

Graduation Requirements American government, American history, Bible, computer science, electives, English, foreign language, geometry, health, history, lab science, mathematics, physical education (includes health), science, service learning/internship, social sciences, social studies (includes history), Spanish, 84 accumulative hours of community service during high school years.

Special Academic Programs 3 Advanced Placement exams for which test preparation is offered; honors section; independent study; academic accommodation for the gifted.

College Admission Counseling 57 students graduated in 2016; all went to college, including Georgetown University; University of Puerto Rico, Mayagüez Campus; University of Puerto Rico, Río Piedras Campus; University of Puerto Rico in Cayey; University of Puerto Rico in Humacao. Median SAT critical reading: 540, median SAT math: 500, median SAT writing: 490, median combined SAT: 1560. 21% scored over 600 on SAT critical reading, 16% scored over 600 on SAT math, 11% scored over 600 on SAT writing, 16% scored over 1800 on combined SAT.

Student Life Upper grades have uniform requirement, student council, honor system. Discipline rests primarily with faculty.

Summer Programs Remediation, enrichment programs offered; session focuses on remediation and enrichment classes; held on campus; accepts boys and girls; open to students from other schools. 60 students usually enrolled. 2017 schedule: June 5 to June 30. Application deadline: May 30.

Tuition and Aid Day student tuition: $6700. Guaranteed tuition plan. Tuition installment plan (monthly payment plans, full payment discount plan, semester payment plan). Need-based scholarship grants available. In 2016–17, 2% of upper-school students received aid. Total amount of financial aid awarded in 2016–17: $1000.

Admissions Traditional secondary-level entrance grade is 9. For fall 2016, 152 students applied for upper-level admission, 128 were accepted, 111 enrolled. Academic Profile Tests, admissions testing, essay, mathematics proficiency exam and Metropolitan Achievement Short Form required. Deadline for receipt of application materials: none. Application fee required: $100. On-campus interview recommended.

Athletics Interscholastic: basketball (boys, girls), cheering (b,g), cross-country running (b,g), golf (b,g), indoor soccer (b,g), soccer (b,g), swimming and diving (b,g), tennis (b,g), track and field (b,g), volleyball (b,g); intramural: basketball (b,g), cheering (b,g), indoor soccer (b,g), soccer (b,g), track and field (b,g), volleyball (b,g); coed interscholastic: tennis. 2 PE instructors, 6 coaches.

Computers Computers are regularly used in all academic classes. Computer network features include on-campus library services, Internet access, wireless campus network, Internet filtering or blocking technology. Student e-mail accounts and computer access in designated common areas are available to students. Students grades are available online. The school has a published electronic and media policy.

Contact Mrs. Maeling Cardona, Admissions Clerk. 787-720-8959 Ext. 1235. Fax: 787-790-0730. E-mail: maeling.cardona@wesleyanacademy.org. Website: www.wesleyanacademy.org

WESLEYAN SCHOOL

5405 Spalding Drive
Peachtree Corners, Georgia 30092

Head of School: Mr. Chris Cleveland

General Information Coeducational day college-preparatory, arts, religious studies, and technology school, affiliated with Christian faith. Grades K–12. Founded: 1963. Setting: suburban. Nearest major city is Atlanta. 85-acre campus, 9 buildings on campus. Approved or accredited by Association of Christian Schools International, Georgia Independent School Association, Southern Association of Colleges and Schools, Southern Association of Independent Schools, and Georgia Department of Education. Member of National Association of Independent Schools and Secondary School Admission Test Board. Endowment: $16.5 million. Total enrollment: 1,132. Upper school average class size: 16. Upper school faculty-student ratio: 1:14. There are 180 required school days per year for Upper School students. Upper School students typically attend 5 days per week. The average school day consists of 6 hours and 55 minutes.

Upper School Student Profile Grade 6: 100 students (49 boys, 51 girls); Grade 7: 111 students (50 boys, 61 girls); Grade 8: 101 students (51 boys, 50 girls); Grade 9: 114 students (61 boys, 53 girls); Grade 10: 128 students (61 boys, 67 girls); Grade 11: 129 students (54 boys, 75 girls); Grade 12: 112 students (63 boys, 49 girls).

Faculty School total: 167. In upper school: 38 men, 37 women; 55 have advanced degrees.

Subjects Offered 20th century history, 20th century world history, 3-dimensional art, acting, advanced chemistry, advanced computer applications, advanced math, algebra, American government, American literature, art, art history-AP, band, Basic programming, Bible, biology, biology-AP, British literature, British literature (honors), calculus, calculus-AP, chemistry, chemistry-AP, choral music, chorus, Christian doctrine, Christian education, Christian ethics, Christian studies, computer science AP, economics, English literature and composition-AP, English literature-AP, environmental science, European history-AP, French, geometry, government, health and wellness, Latin, literary genres, modern world history, New Testament, photography, physical education, physics, pre-calculus, public speaking, Spanish, Spanish language-AP, studio art-AP, theater, U.S. history, U.S. history-AP, vocal ensemble, weight training, word processing, world literature.

Graduation Requirements Algebra, American history, American literature, analysis, arts and fine arts (art, music, dance, drama), Bible, biology, British literature, chemistry, economics, environmental science, foreign language, geometry, government, modern world history, physical education (includes health), physics, pre-calculus, statistics, world literature, writing.

Special Academic Programs Advanced Placement exam preparation; honors section.

College Admission Counseling 105 students graduated in 2015; all went to college, including Auburn University; Clemson University; Georgia College & State University; Samford University; University of Georgia; University of Mississippi. Median SAT critical reading: 580, median SAT math: 580, median SAT writing: 580, median composite ACT: 27. Mean combined SAT: 1791. 42% scored over 600 on SAT critical reading, 44% scored over 600 on SAT math, 47% scored over 600 on SAT writing, 63% scored over 26 on composite ACT.

Student Life Upper grades have uniform requirement, student council, honor system. Discipline rests equally with students and faculty. Attendance at religious services is required.

Tuition and Aid Day student tuition: $21,700. Tuition installment plan (Insured Tuition Payment Plan). Need-based scholarship grants available. In 2015–16, 22% of upper-school students received aid. Total amount of financial aid awarded in 2015–16: $1,551,511.

Admissions Traditional secondary-level entrance grade is 9. For fall 2015, 102 students applied for upper-level admission, 67 were accepted, 41 enrolled. PSAT, SSAT and writing sample required. Deadline for receipt of application materials: February 17. Application fee required: $85. Interview required.

Athletics Interscholastic: baseball (boys), basketball (b,g), cross-country running (b,g), diving (b,g), football (b), golf (b,g), lacrosse (b,g), soccer (b,g), softball (g), swimming and diving (b,g), tennis (b,g), track and field (b,g), volleyball (g), wrestling (b); intramural: cheering (g); coed intramural: strength & conditioning, water polo. 2 PE instructors, 2 athletic trainers.

Computers Computers are regularly used in all classes. Computer network features include on-campus library services, Internet access, wireless campus network, Internet filtering or blocking technology. Student e-mail accounts are available to students. Students grades are available online. The school has a published electronic and media policy.

Contact Mrs. Sylvia Pryor, Admissions Coordinator. 770-448-7640 Ext. 2267. Fax: 770-448-3699. E-mail: spryor@wesleyanschool.org.
Website: www.wesleyanschool.org

WESTBURY CHRISTIAN SCHOOL

10420 Hillcroft
Houston, Texas 77096

Head of School: Mr. Michael D. White

General Information Coeducational day college-preparatory school, affiliated with Church of Christ. Grades PK–12. Founded: 1975. Setting: urban. 13-acre campus. 1 building on campus. Approved or accredited by National Christian School Association, Southern Association of Colleges and Schools, Texas Private School Accreditation Commission, The College Board, and Texas Department of Education. Endowment: $300,000. Total enrollment: 464. Upper school average class size: 22. Upper school faculty-student ratio: 1:10. There are 180 required school days per year for Upper School students. Upper School students typically attend 5 days per week. The average school day consists of 7 hours and 45 minutes.

Upper School Student Profile Grade 9: 48 students (30 boys, 18 girls); Grade 10: 55 students (33 boys, 22 girls); Grade 11: 56 students (38 boys, 18 girls); Grade 12: 43 students (16 boys, 27 girls). 18% of students are members of Church of Christ.

Faculty School total: 59. In upper school: 18 men, 16 women; 10 have advanced degrees.

Subjects Offered Accounting, algebra, anatomy and physiology, art, athletics, band, basketball, Bible, biology, biology-AP, business, calculus-AP, cheerleading, chemistry, chemistry-AP, community service, computer applications, drama, economics, English, English language and composition-AP, English literature and composition-AP, geography, geometry, government, government-AP, health, human geography - AP, macro/microeconomics-AP, photography, physical education, physical science, physics, pre-calculus, psychology-AP, robotics, Spanish, speech, statistics-AP, studio art-AP, U.S. history, U.S. history-AP, vocal music, weight training, world history, world history-AP.

Graduation Requirements Arts and fine arts (art, music, dance, drama), Bible, electives, English, foreign language, geometry, mathematics, physical education (includes health), science, social studies (includes history), speech, continuous participation in student activities programs, community service each semester.

Special Academic Programs 15 Advanced Placement exams for which test preparation is offered; independent study; ESL (10 students enrolled).

College Admission Counseling 58 students graduated in 2016; 56 went to college, including Harding University; Houston Baptist University; Texas A&M University; Texas Tech University; The University of Texas at Austin; University of Houston. Other: 1 entered military service, 1 entered a postgraduate year. Mean SAT critical reading: 496, mean SAT math: 545, mean SAT writing: 495, mean combined SAT: 1536, mean composite ACT: 21. 9% scored over 600 on SAT critical reading, 25% scored over 600 on SAT math, 17% scored over 600 on SAT writing, 48% scored over 1800 on combined SAT, 36% scored over 26 on composite ACT.

Student Life Upper grades have uniform requirement, student council, honor system. Discipline rests primarily with faculty.

Summer Programs Enrichment, sports, art/fine arts programs offered; session focuses on week-long basketball, football, and volleyball instruction camps; held both on and off campus; accepts boys and girls; open to students from other schools. 200 students usually enrolled. 2017 schedule: June 3 to July 26. Application deadline: none.

Tuition and Aid Day student tuition: $14,360. Tuition installment plan (FACTS Tuition Payment Plan). Merit scholarship grants, need-based scholarship grants available. In 2016–17, 15% of upper-school students received aid; total upper-school merit-scholarship money awarded: $43,500. Total amount of financial aid awarded in 2016–17: $558,892.

Admissions Traditional secondary-level entrance grade is 9. For fall 2016, 65 students applied for upper-level admission, 51 were accepted, 41 enrolled. ISEE, Otis-Lennon School Ability Test and SLEP for foreign students required. Deadline for receipt of application materials: none. Application fee required: $75. Interview recommended.

Athletics Interscholastic: ballet (girls), baseball (b), basketball (b,g), cheering (g), cross-country running (b,g), football (b), golf (b,g), soccer (b,g), softball (g), strength &

conditioning (b,g), swimming and diving (b,g), tennis (b,g), track and field (b,g), volleyball (g). 1 PE instructor, 4 coaches, 1 athletic trainer.

Computers Computers are regularly used in all academic classes. Computer network features include on-campus library services, online commercial services, Internet access, wireless campus network, Internet filtering or blocking technology. Campus intranet and student e-mail accounts are available to students. Students grades are available online. The school has a published electronic and media policy.

Contact Mrs. Phylis Frye, Director of Admissions. 713-551-8100 Ext. 1018. Fax: 713-551-8117. E-mail: admissions@westburychristian.org.
Website: www.westburychristian.org

WEST ISLAND COLLEGE

7410 Blackfoot Trail SE
Calgary, Alberta T2H IM5, Canada

Head of School: Ms. Carol Grant-Watt

General Information Coeducational day college-preparatory, arts, business, bilingual studies, technology, and Advanced Placement school. Grades 7–12. Founded: 1982. Setting: urban. 18-acre campus. 2 buildings on campus. Approved or accredited by Canadian Association of Independent Schools and Alberta Department of Education. Languages of instruction: English and French. Total enrollment: 533. Upper school average class size: 21. Upper school faculty-student ratio: 1:17. There are 182 required school days per year for Upper School students. Upper School students typically attend 5 days per week. The average school day consists of 6 hours and 13 minutes.

Upper School Student Profile Grade 10: 81 students (40 boys, 41 girls); Grade 11: 65 students (33 boys, 32 girls); Grade 12: 83 students (41 boys, 42 girls).

Faculty School total: 45. In upper school: 20 men, 21 women; 15 have advanced degrees.

Subjects Offered Advanced Placement courses, anthropology, art, arts, biology, business, chemistry, choral music, communications, debate, drama, English, European history, experiential education, French, French studies, health, information processing, information technology, leadership, literature, mathematics, modern languages, music, outdoor education, philosophy, physical education, physics, political thought, politics, psychology, public speaking, science, social sciences, social studies, sociology, Spanish, standard curriculum, study skills, world geography, world history, world religions.

Graduation Requirements Alberta education requirements.

Special Academic Programs 10 Advanced Placement exams for which test preparation is offered; honors section; independent study; study abroad; academic accommodation for the gifted.

College Admission Counseling 67 students graduated in 2015; 66 went to college, including McGill University; Queen's University at Kingston; The University of British Columbia; University of Alberta; University of Calgary; University of Victoria. Other: 1 had other specific plans.

Student Life Upper grades have uniform requirement, student council, honor system. Discipline rests equally with students and faculty.

Tuition and Aid Day student tuition: CAN$12,800. Tuition installment plan (monthly payment plans).

Admissions Traditional secondary-level entrance grade is 10. For fall 2015, 24 students applied for upper-level admission, 23 were accepted, 19 enrolled. 3-R Achievement Test, CCAT, CTBS, OLSAT, Gates MacGinite Reading Tests or Otis-Lennon IQ Test required. Deadline for receipt of application materials: none. Application fee required: CAN$100. Interview required.

Athletics Interscholastic: basketball (boys, girls), field hockey (g), rugby (b), track and field (b,g), volleyball (b,g); intramural: aquatics (b,g), basketball (b,g), floor hockey (b,g), track and field (b,g), volleyball (b,g); coed interscholastic: badminton, climbing, cross-country running, soccer; coed intramural: alpine skiing, backpacking, badminton, bicycling, bowling, canoeing/kayaking, climbing, cross-country running, curling, dance, fitness, golf, hiking/backpacking, kayaking, mountaineering, nordic skiing, outdoor activities, outdoor education, physical fitness, physical training, rock climbing, sailing, skiing (cross-country), skiing (downhill), snowboarding, soccer, wilderness survival, wildernessways. 4 PE instructors, 10 coaches, 2 athletic trainers.

Computers Computers are regularly used in business, career education, career exploration, career technology, economics, English, French, independent study, mathematics, media arts, media production, multimedia, science, social studies, technology, word processing classes. Computer network features include on-campus library services, online commercial services, Internet access, wireless campus network, Internet filtering or blocking technology. Campus intranet, student e-mail accounts, and computer access in designated common areas are available to students. Students grades are available online. The school has a published electronic and media policy.

Contact Ms. Nicole Bernard, Director of Admissions. 403-444-0023. Fax: 403-444-2820. E-mail: admissions@westislandcollege.ab.ca. Website: www.westislandcollege.ab.ca

WESTMARK SCHOOL

Encino, California
See Special Needs Schools section.

WEST MEMPHIS CHRISTIAN HIGH SCHOOL

1101 North Missouri
West Memphis, Arkansas 72301

Head of School: Mrs. Mary Anne Pike

General Information Coeducational day college-preparatory school, affiliated with Christian faith. Grades K–12. Founded: 1970. Setting: small town. Nearest major city is Memphis, TN. 16-acre campus. 1 building on campus. Approved or accredited by Mississippi Private School Association and Arkansas Department of Education. Total enrollment: 208. Upper school average class size: 20. Upper school faculty-student ratio: 1:12. There are 178 required school days per year for Upper School students. Upper School students typically attend 5 days per week. The average school day consists of 6 hours.

Upper School Student Profile Grade 7: 19 students (7 boys, 12 girls); Grade 8: 26 students (12 boys, 14 girls); Grade 9: 15 students (7 boys, 8 girls); Grade 10: 13 students (10 boys, 3 girls); Grade 11: 21 students (14 boys, 7 girls); Grade 12: 14 students (9 boys, 5 girls). 80% of students are Christian.

Faculty School total: 20. In upper school: 6 men, 8 women; 6 have advanced degrees.

College Admission Counseling 18 students graduated in 2016; all went to college, including Arkansas State University; Harding University; University of Arkansas; University of Memphis. Mean composite ACT: 23. 33% scored over 26 on composite ACT.

Student Life Upper grades have uniform requirement, student council, honor system. Discipline rests primarily with faculty. Attendance at religious services is required.

Admissions Traditional secondary-level entrance grade is 7. Application fee required. On-campus interview recommended.

Athletics Interscholastic: baseball (boys), basketball (b,g), cheering (g), cross-country running (b,g), flag football (b), football (b), golf (b,g), physical fitness (b,g), running (b,g), softball (g), strength & conditioning (b,g), tennis (b,g), track and field (b,g), volleyball (g). 3 coaches.

Computers Computer resources include Internet access, wireless campus network, Internet filtering or blocking technology. Campus intranet, student e-mail accounts, and computer access in designated common areas are available to students. The school has a published electronic and media policy.

Contact Mrs. April Taylor, Principal. 870-400-4000. Fax: 870-735-0570. E-mail: amtaylor@wmcs.com. Website: www.wmcs.com

WESTMINSTER ACADEMY

5601 North Federal Highway
Fort Lauderdale, Florida 33308

Head of School: Dr. Leo Orsino

General Information Coeducational day college-preparatory, arts, religious studies, and technology school, affiliated with Presbyterian Church in America. Founded: 1971. 3 buildings on campus. Approved or accredited by Christian Schools of Florida, Middle States Association of Colleges and Schools, National Independent Private Schools Association, Southern Association of Colleges and Schools, and Florida Department of Education. Total enrollment: 966. Upper school average class size: 18. Upper school faculty-student ratio: 1:11.

Upper School Student Profile 30% of students are Presbyterian Church in America.

Student Life Upper grades have uniform requirement, student council. Attendance at religious services is required.

Admissions Application fee required: $100. Interview required.

Athletics Interscholastic: baseball (boys), basketball (b,g), cheering (g), cross-country running (b,g), diving (b,g), football (b), golf (b,g), soccer (b,g), softball (g), swimming and diving (b,g), tennis (b,g), track and field (b,g), volleyball (g), water polo (b,g).

Contact Mr. Jeffrey Jacques, Director of Admissions. 954-771-4615 Ext. 2529. E-mail: jacquesj@wa.edu. Website: www.wa.edu

WESTMINSTER CHRISTIAN ACADEMY

186 Westminster Drive
Opelousas, Louisiana 70570

Head of School: Mr. Scott Davis

General Information Coeducational day college-preparatory school, affiliated with Christian faith. Grades PK–12. Founded: 1978. Setting: rural. Nearest major city is Lafayette. 30-acre campus. 6 buildings on campus. Approved or accredited by Association of Christian Schools International and Louisiana Department of Education. Candidate for accreditation by Southern Association of Colleges and Schools. Member of National Association of Independent Schools. Endowment: $1.2 million. Total enrollment: 1,059. Upper school average class size: 23. Upper school faculty-student ratio: 1:13. There are 175 required school days per year for Upper School students. Upper School students typically attend 5 days per week. The average school day consists of 7 hours.

Upper School Student Profile Grade 9: 68 students (42 boys, 26 girls); Grade 10: 50 students (26 boys, 24 girls); Grade 11: 54 students (25 boys, 29 girls); Grade 12: 59 students (30 boys, 29 girls). 90% of students are Christian faith.

Faculty School total: 66. In upper school: 15 men, 15 women; 5 have advanced degrees.

Subjects Offered ACT preparation, advanced math, Advanced Placement courses, algebra, American history, art, athletics, Bible, biology, calculus, calculus-AP, ceramics, chemistry, chemistry-AP, civics, computer education, computer literacy, computer multimedia, concert choir, creative writing, desktop publishing, drama, drama workshop, economics, English, English-AP, fine arts, French, geometry, guitar, history, history-AP, honors English, Latin, music, physics, religion, Spanish, world history, yearbook.

Graduation Requirements Arts and fine arts (art, music, dance, drama), Bible, computer literacy, English, foreign language, mathematics, physical education (includes health), religion (includes Bible studies and theology), science, social studies (includes history).

Special Academic Programs 6 Advanced Placement exams for which test preparation is offered; honors section; accelerated programs; study at local college for college credit; special instructional classes for students with mild learning disabilities and Attention Deficit Disorder.

College Admission Counseling 58 students graduated in 2016; 55 went to college, including Louisiana State University and Agricultural & Mechanical College; Louisiana State University at Eunice; Louisiana Tech University; Southern University and Agricultural and Mechanical College; Tulane University; University of Louisiana at Lafayette. Other: 1 went to work, 2 had other specific plans. Mean composite ACT: 27. 32% scored over 26 on composite ACT.

Student Life Upper grades have uniform requirement, student council. Discipline rests primarily with faculty. Attendance at religious services is required.

Tuition and Aid Day student tuition: $6480. Tuition installment plan (Insured Tuition Payment Plan, monthly payment plans, individually arranged payment plans, annual, biannual, quarterly payment plans). Need-based scholarship grants, pastor discounts available. In 2016–17, 10% of upper-school students received aid. Total amount of financial aid awarded in 2016–17: $50,000.

Admissions Traditional secondary-level entrance grade is 9. For fall 2016, 19 students applied for upper-level admission, 13 were accepted, 12 enrolled. School's own exam and Terra Nova-CTB required. Deadline for receipt of application materials: none. Application fee required: $150. On-campus interview recommended.

Athletics Interscholastic: baseball (boys), basketball (b,g), cheering (g), cross-country running (b,g), football (b), soccer (b,g), softball (g), swimming and diving (b,g), tennis (b,g), track and field (b,g), volleyball (g); coed interscholastic: golf, hiking/backpacking, indoor track, outdoor adventure; coed intramural: archery, outdoor adventure, wilderness survival. 3 PE instructors, 2 coaches, 1 athletic trainer.

Computers Computers are regularly used in computer applications classes. Computer network features include on-campus library services, Internet access, wireless campus network, Internet filtering or blocking technology, one-to-one iPad program for grades 9-12. Student e-mail accounts and computer access in designated common areas are available to students. Students grades are available online. The school has a published electronic and media policy.

Contact Mrs. Michelle Nezat, Director of Institutional Advancement. 337-948-4623 Ext. 123. Fax: 337-948-4090. E-mail: mnezat@wcala.org. Website: www.wcala.org

WESTMINSTER CHRISTIAN SCHOOL

6855 Southwest 152nd Street
Palmetto Bay, Florida 33157

Head of School: Mr. Peter Cabrera

General Information Coeducational day college-preparatory school, affiliated with Reformed Presbyterian Church of North America. Grades PK–12. Founded: 1961. Setting: small town. Nearest major city is Miami. 31-acre campus. 9 buildings on campus. Approved or accredited by Christian Schools of Florida, Florida Council of Independent Schools, Southern Association of Colleges and Schools, and Florida Department of Education. Member of National Association of Independent Schools. Endowment: $2.2 million. Total enrollment: 1,244. Upper school average class size: 20. Upper school faculty-student ratio: 1:15. There are 175 required school days per year for Upper School students. Upper School students typically attend 5 days per week. The average school day consists of 7 hours.

Upper School Student Profile Grade 9: 107 students (55 boys, 52 girls); Grade 10: 128 students (58 boys, 70 girls); Grade 11: 132 students (62 boys, 70 girls); Grade 12: 134 students (71 boys, 63 girls). 15% of students are Reformed Presbyterian Church of North America.

Faculty School total: 120. In upper school: 27 men, 30 women; 40 have advanced degrees.

Subjects Offered Advanced Placement courses, algebra, American history, American literature, anatomy, art, Bible studies, biology, biology-AP, business law, business skills, calculus, ceramics, chemistry, chemistry-AP, community service, computer programming, computer science, creative writing, drama, economics, English, English literature, fine arts, French, French-AP, geometry, government-AP, government/civics, health, macroeconomics-AP, marine biology, mathematics, musical theater, organic chemistry, photography, physical education, physics, physiology, psychology, religion, SAT preparation, sculpture, sociology, softball, Spanish, Spanish-AP, speech, sports, statistics-AP, strings, study skills, swimming, theater, track and field, trigonometry, U.S. government, U.S. government and politics-AP, U.S. history, U.S. history-AP, vocal ensemble, volleyball, weightlifting, world history, world history-AP, world literature, wrestling, yearbook.

Graduation Requirements Arts and fine arts (art, music, dance, drama), Bible, electives, English, foreign language, health science, lab science, mathematics, physical education (includes health), science, social studies (includes history). Community service is required.

Special Academic Programs 21 Advanced Placement exams for which test preparation is offered; honors section; independent study; academic accommodation for the gifted, the musically talented, and the artistically talented; programs in English, mathematics for dyslexic students.

College Admission Counseling 134 students graduated in 2016; all went to college, including Florida International University; Florida State University; University of Central Florida; University of Florida; University of Miami. Mean SAT critical reading: 549, mean SAT math: 549, mean SAT writing: 536, mean combined SAT: 1634, mean composite ACT: 23. 50% scored over 600 on SAT critical reading, 50% scored over 600 on SAT math, 50% scored over 600 on SAT writing, 50% scored over 1800 on combined SAT, 50% scored over 26 on composite ACT.

Student Life Upper grades have uniform requirement, student council, honor system. Discipline rests primarily with faculty. Attendance at religious services is required.

Summer Programs Remediation, advancement, sports programs offered; session focuses on academics and athletics; held on campus; accepts boys and girls; not open to students from other schools. 50 students usually enrolled. 2017 schedule: June 7 to July 30.

Tuition and Aid Day student tuition: $20,000. Tuition installment plan (monthly payment plans, semiannual and annual payment plans). Need-based scholarship grants available. In 2016–17, 20% of upper-school students received aid. Total amount of financial aid awarded in 2016–17: $750,000.

Admissions Traditional secondary-level entrance grade is 9. For fall 2016, 150 students applied for upper-level admission, 81 were accepted, 61 enrolled. ISEE required. Deadline for receipt of application materials: none. Application fee required: $125. On-campus interview recommended.

Athletics Interscholastic: baseball (boys), basketball (b,g), cheering (g), cross-country running (b,g), football (b), golf (b,g), lacrosse (b), physical fitness (b,g), physical training (b,g), sailing (b,g), soccer (b,g), softball (b,g), swimming and diving (b,g), tennis (b,g), track and field (b,g), volleyball (b,g), weight lifting (b,g), weight training (b,g), wrestling (b). 5 PE instructors, 50 coaches, 2 athletic trainers.

Computers Computers are regularly used in all academic classes. Computer network features include on-campus library services, online commercial services, Internet access, wireless campus network, Internet filtering or blocking technology. Campus intranet, student e-mail accounts, and computer access in designated common areas are available to students. Students grades are available online. The school has a published electronic and media policy.

Contact Mrs. Lisa North, Director of Admission. 305-233-2030 Ext. 1246. Fax: 305-253-9623. E-mail: lnorth@wcsmiami.org. Website: www.wcsmiami.org

WESTMINSTER SCHOOL

995 Hopmeadow Street
Simsbury, Connecticut 06070

Head of School: Mr. William V.N. Philip

General Information Coeducational boarding and day college-preparatory school. Grades 9–PG. Founded: 1888. Setting: suburban. Nearest major city is Hartford. Students are housed in single-sex dormitories. 230-acre campus. 41 buildings on campus. Approved or accredited by Connecticut Association of Independent Schools, New England Association of Schools and Colleges, The Association of Boarding Schools, Virginia Association of Independent Specialized Education Facilities, and Connecticut Department of Education. Member of National Association of Independent Schools and Secondary School Admission Test Board. Endowment: $95 million. Total enrollment: 394. Upper school average class size: 12. Upper school faculty-student ratio: 1:5. There are 183 required school days per year for Upper School students. Upper School students typically attend 6 days per week. The average school day consists of 6 hours and 30 minutes.

Upper School Student Profile Grade 9: 75 students (37 boys, 38 girls); Grade 10: 109 students (55 boys, 54 girls); Grade 11: 106 students (58 boys, 48 girls); Grade 12: 92 students (53 boys, 39 girls); Postgraduate: 13 students (10 boys, 3 girls). 71% of students are boarding students. 47% are state residents. 31 states are represented in upper school student body. 16% are international students. International students from Canada, China, Hong Kong, Republic of Korea, Russian Federation, and Serbia and Montenegro; 23 other countries represented in student body.

Faculty School total: 60. In upper school: 29 men, 31 women; 45 have advanced degrees; 50 reside on campus.

Subjects Offered Acting, advanced chemistry, advanced computer applications, advanced math, Advanced Placement courses, advanced studio art-AP, African American history, algebra, American history, American history-AP, American literature, American literature-AP, anatomy and physiology, architecture, art, art history, art history-AP, art-AP, Asian history, astronomy, athletics, band, biology, biology-AP, calculus, calculus-AP, character education, chemistry, chemistry-AP, Chinese, choir, choral music, comparative government and politics-AP, computer programming, computer science-AP, creative writing, dance, discrete mathematics, drama, drama

workshop, drawing, drawing and design, driver education, ecology, economics, economics-AP, English, English literature, English-AP, English/composition-AP, environmental science-AP, ethics, ethics and responsibility, European history, European history-AP, female experience in America, fine arts, French, French language-AP, French literature-AP, geometry, graphic design, history, honors algebra, honors English, honors geometry, illustration, Latin, Latin-AP, literature and composition-AP, macro/microeconomics-AP, mathematics, mathematics-AP, mechanical drawing, modern European history-AP, music, music appreciation, music composition, music theory-AP, musical theater, painting, philosophy, photography, physics, physics-AP, pre-calculus, probability and statistics, psychology-AP, SAT preparation, SAT/ACT preparation, science, set design, social studies, Spanish, Spanish language-AP, Spanish literature, Spanish literature-AP, stagecraft, statistics, statistics-AP, student government, studio art-AP, theater, trigonometry, U.S. history-AP, world history, writing.

Graduation Requirements Art, arts, English, foreign language, historical research, history, mathematics, science.

Special Academic Programs 23 Advanced Placement exams for which test preparation is offered; honors section; independent study; term-away projects; study abroad.

College Admission Counseling 105 students graduated in 2016; all went to college, including Amherst College; Trinity College; Tufts University; University of Richmond; Wake Forest University. Median SAT critical reading: 608, median SAT math: 620, median SAT writing: 653, median combined SAT: 1881, median composite ACT: 27.

Student Life Upper grades have specified standards of dress, student council. Discipline rests primarily with faculty.

Tuition and Aid Day student tuition: $43,750; 7-day tuition and room/board: $58,300. Tuition installment plan (SMART Tuition Payment Plan). Need-based scholarship grants available. In 2016–17, 31% of upper-school students received aid. Total amount of financial aid awarded in 2016–17: $4,910,370.

Admissions Traditional secondary-level entrance grade is 9. For fall 2016, 1,134 students applied for upper-level admission, 298 were accepted, 130 enrolled. PSAT and SAT for applicants to grade 11 and 12, SSAT or TOEFL required. Deadline for receipt of application materials: January 15. Application fee required: $75. On-campus interview recommended.

Athletics Interscholastic: baseball (boys), basketball (b,g), cross-country running (b,g), diving (b,g), field hockey (g), football (b), golf (b,g), hockey (b,g), ice hockey (b,g), indoor hockey (b,g), lacrosse (b,g), soccer (b,g), softball (g), squash (b,g), swimming and diving (b,g), tennis (b,g), track and field (b,g); intramural: strength & conditioning (b,g); coed interscholastic: dance, martial arts, modern dance; coed intramural: aerobics/dance, ballet, canoeing/kayaking, dance, fitness, freestyle skiing, hiking/backpacking, kayaking, modern dance, mountain biking, outdoor activities, outdoor recreation, rugby, skiing (cross-country), skiing (downhill), snowboarding, table tennis, unicycling, weight lifting, weight training. 2 athletic trainers.

Computers Computers are regularly used in English, foreign language, history, mathematics, science classes. Computer network features include on-campus library services, online commercial services, Internet access, wireless campus network, Internet filtering or blocking technology. Campus intranet, student e-mail accounts, and computer access in designated common areas are available to students. Students grades are available online. The school has a published electronic and media policy.

Contact Mrs. Rhonda Smith, Admissions Assistant. 860-408-3060. Fax: 860-408-3042. E-mail: admit@westminster-school.org. Website: www.westminster-school.org

THE WESTMINSTER SCHOOL AT OAK MOUNTAIN

5080 Cahaba Valley Trace
Birmingham, Alabama 35252

Head of School: Rev. Robbie Hinton

General Information Coeducational day college-preparatory and general academic school, affiliated with Presbyterian Church; primarily serves individuals with Attention Deficit Disorder. Grades K–12. Setting: suburban. Students are housed in N/A. 17-acre campus. 1 building on campus. Approved or accredited by Southern Association of Colleges and Schools and Alabama Department of Education. Total enrollment: 508. Upper school average class size: 17. Upper school faculty-student ratio: 1:16. There are 175 required school days per year for Upper School students. Upper School students typically attend 5 days per week. The average school day consists of 6 hours and 40 minutes.

Upper School Student Profile 60% of students are Presbyterian.

Faculty School total: 25. In upper school: 17 men, 9 women; 13 have advanced degrees.

Graduation Requirements Senior thesis.

College Admission Counseling 28 students graduated in 2016; all went to college, including Auburn University; Mississippi College; Mississippi State University; Samford University; The University of Alabama; University of South Alabama. Other: 2 entered a postgraduate year. Median composite ACT: 29. 82% scored over 26 on composite ACT.

Student Life Upper grades have uniform requirement. Discipline rests primarily with faculty. Attendance at religious services is required.

Tuition and Aid Tuition reduction for siblings, need-based scholarship grants, OMPC church discount available.

Admissions Traditional secondary-level entrance grade is 7. Application fee required: $360. Interview recommended.

Athletics Interscholastic: basketball (boys, girls), cross-country running (b,g), fishing (b,g), golf (b,g), indoor track & field (b,g), soccer (b,g), swimming and diving (b,g), tennis (b,g), track and field (b,g), volleyball (b,g).

Computers Computer network features include wireless campus network. Students grades are available online. The school has a published electronic and media policy.

Contact Mrs. Kristen Williams, Director of Admissions. 205-995-9694. Fax: 205-980-9095. E-mail: kwilliams@westminsterknights.org. Website: www.westminsterknights.org/

THE WESTMINSTER SCHOOLS
1424 West Paces Ferry Road NW
Atlanta, Georgia 30327

Head of School: Mr. Keith Evans

General Information Coeducational day college-preparatory, arts, business, religious studies, bilingual studies, and technology school, affiliated with Christian faith. Grades K–12. Founded: 1951. Setting: suburban. 180-acre campus. 7 buildings on campus. Approved or accredited by Georgia Independent School Association, Southern Association of Colleges and Schools, and Southern Association of Independent Schools. Member of National Association of Independent Schools and Secondary School Admission Test Board. Endowment: $260.8 million. Total enrollment: 1,858. Upper school average class size: 16. Upper school faculty-student ratio: 1:8. There are 175 required school days per year for Upper School students. Upper School students typically attend 5 days per week. The average school day consists of 6 hours.

Upper School Student Profile Grade 9: 211 students (108 boys, 103 girls); Grade 10: 203 students (95 boys, 108 girls); Grade 11: 189 students (98 boys, 91 girls); Grade 12: 209 students (99 boys, 110 girls). 80% of students are Christian.

Faculty School total: 277. In upper school: 58 men, 57 women; 91 have advanced degrees.

Subjects Offered 3-dimensional art, 3-dimensional design, acting, advanced chemistry, advanced math, Advanced Placement courses, advanced studio art-AP, African American history, algebra, American history, American history-AP, American literature-AP, architecture, art, art history, Basic programming, Bible studies, biology, biology-AP, British literature-AP, calculus, calculus-AP, ceramics, chemistry, chemistry-AP, Chinese, choral music, Christian education, civil rights, computer math, computer programming, computer science, drama, driver education, earth science, economics, English, English language and composition-AP, English literature, English literature and composition-AP, entrepreneurship, environmental science-AP, ethics, European history, European history-AP, fine arts, French, French language-AP, French literature-AP, geometry, grammar, graphic design, health, history, Holocaust seminar, internship, Latin, Latin-AP, leadership education training, Mandarin, marine biology, mathematics, mathematics-AP, music, natural history, outdoor education, philosophy, photography, physical education, physics, physics-AP, political systems, psychology, religion, robotics, science, social studies, sociology, Spanish, Spanish language-AP, Spanish literature-AP, speech, speech and debate, statistics, statistics-AP, studio art-AP, theater, theater arts, trigonometry, U.S. history-AP, video film production, visual and performing arts, world history, writing.

Graduation Requirements Arts and fine arts (art, music, dance, drama), English, experiential education, foreign language, history, mathematics, physical education (includes health), religion (includes Bible studies and theology), science.

Special Academic Programs Advanced Placement exam preparation; honors section, independent study, term-away projects, study abroad, academic accommodation for the gifted, the musically talented, and the artistically talented.

College Admission Counseling 200 students graduated in 2015; all went to college, including Auburn University; Georgia Institute of Technology; University of Georgia; University of Virginia; Wake Forest University; Washington University in St. Louis.

Student Life Upper grades have specified standards of dress, student council, honor system. Discipline rests equally with students and faculty.

Tuition and Aid Day student tuition: $25,660. Tuition installment plan (Key Tuition Payment Plan, monthly payment plans). Need-based scholarship grants available. In 2015–16, 14% of upper-school students received aid. Total amount of financial aid awarded in 2015–16: $4,000,000.

Admissions Traditional secondary-level entrance grade is 9. For fall 2015, 181 students applied for upper-level admission, 36 were accepted, 23 enrolled. Admissions testing, Individual IQ, PSAT or SAT for applicants to grade 11 and 12 or SSAT required. Deadline for receipt of application materials: January 29. Application fee required: $75. On-campus interview required.

Athletics Interscholastic: baseball (boys), basketball (b,g), cheering (g), crew (g), cross-country running (b,g), diving (b,g), football (b), golf (b,g), gymnastics (g), lacrosse (b,g), soccer (b,g), softball (g), swimming and diving (b,g), tennis (b,g), track and field (b,g), volleyball (g), wrestling (b); intramural: crew (g), dance (g), equestrian sports (g), physical fitness (b,g), strength & conditioning (b,g); coed intramural: backpacking, climbing, dance squad, dance team, hiking/backpacking, paddle tennis, rappelling, rock climbing, ropes courses, squash, table tennis, tennis, ultimate Frisbee, water polo. 2 PE instructors, 4 coaches, 4 athletic trainers.

Computers Computers are regularly used in art, Bible studies, desktop publishing, economics, English, foreign language, history, mathematics, multimedia, music, religion, science, technology, video film production, writing classes. Computer network features include on-campus library services, online commercial services, Internet access, wireless campus network, Internet filtering or blocking technology, Math Lab staffed with faculty, Writing Lab staffed with students and faculty. Campus intranet, student e-mail accounts, and computer access in designated common areas are available to students. The school has a published electronic and media policy.

Contact Mrs. Julie Williams, Assistant Director of Admissions. 404-609-6202. Fax: 404-367-7894. E-mail: admissions@westminster.net. Website: www.westminster.net

WESTMINSTER SCHOOLS OF AUGUSTA
3067 Wheeler Road
Augusta, Georgia 30909

Head of School: Mr. Stephen D. O'Neil

General Information Coeducational day college-preparatory, arts, religious studies, bilingual studies, technology, and music, debate and drama school, affiliated with Presbyterian Church in America. Grades PK–12. Founded: 1972. Setting: suburban. 34-acre campus. 6 buildings on campus. Approved or accredited by Georgia Independent School Association, Southern Association of Colleges and Schools, and Southern Association of Independent Schools. Member of National Association of Independent Schools. Endowment: $290,000. Total enrollment: 605. Upper school average class size: 14. Upper school faculty-student ratio: 1:7. There are 180 required school days per year for Upper School students. Upper School students typically attend 5 days per week. The average school day consists of 7 hours and 30 minutes.

Upper School Student Profile Grade 9: 59 students (32 boys, 27 girls); Grade 10: 52 students (17 boys, 35 girls); Grade 11: 47 students (25 boys, 22 girls); Grade 12: 59 students (32 boys, 27 girls). 40% of students are Presbyterian Church in America.

Faculty School total: 63. In upper school: 20 men, 10 women; 16 have advanced degrees.

Subjects Offered 3-dimensional art, ACT preparation, advanced biology, advanced chemistry, Advanced Placement courses, advanced studio art-AP, algebra, analysis and differential calculus, analytic geometry, Ancient Greek, art, arts, band, Bible studies, biology, biology-AP, British literature (honors), calculus, calculus-AP, chemistry, chemistry-AP, choir, chorus, Christian scripture, classical Greek literature, computer programming, computer skills, computers, concert choir, drama, drama performance, dramatic arts, earth science, English, English language and composition-AP, English language-AP, English literature, English literature and composition-AP, English literature-AP, environmental science, family living, French, French language-AP, French-AP, geography, geometry, government/civics, Greek, guidance, health, health education, history, history-AP, honors algebra, honors English, honors geometry, honors U.S. history, keyboarding, lab science, Latin, Latin-AP, mathematics, modern European history-AP, modern history, modern world history, music, physical education, physical science, physics, physics-AP, pre-algebra, pre-calculus, religion, SAT preparation, science, social studies, Spanish, Spanish language-AP, Spanish-AP, speech, statistics-AP, studio art, study skills, swimming, trigonometry, U.S. government and politics-AP, U.S. history, U.S. history-AP, U.S. literature, United States government-AP, weight training, word processing, world history, world literature, writing, yearbook.

Graduation Requirements Arts and fine arts (art, music, dance, drama), electives, English, foreign language, mathematics, physical education (includes health), religion (includes Bible studies and theology), science, social studies (includes history).

Special Academic Programs 19 Advanced Placement exams for which test preparation is offered; honors section; study abroad; academic accommodation for the gifted; programs in general development for dyslexic students.

College Admission Counseling 42 students graduated in 2015; all went to college, including Augusta State University; Georgia Southern University; Kennesaw State University; Presbyterian College; University of Georgia; University of South Carolina. Median SAT critical reading: 580, median SAT math: 620, median SAT writing: 600, median combined SAT: 1800, median composite ACT: 25. 37% scored over 600 on SAT critical reading, 56% scored over 600 on SAT math, 37% scored over 600 on SAT writing, 49% scored over 1800 on combined SAT, 38% scored over 26 on composite ACT.

Student Life Upper grades have specified standards of dress, honor system. Discipline rests primarily with faculty.

Tuition and Aid Day student tuition: $13,900. Tuition installment plan (monthly payment plans). Tuition reduction for siblings, merit scholarship grants, need-based scholarship grants available. In 2015–16, 27% of upper-school students received aid. Total amount of financial aid awarded in 2015–16: $250,000.

Admissions Traditional secondary-level entrance grade is 9. For fall 2015, 36 students applied for upper-level admission, 27 were accepted, 22 enrolled. ERB - verbal abilities, reading comprehension, quantitative abilities (level F, form 1), mathematics proficiency exam and writing sample required. Deadline for receipt of application materials: none. Application fee required: $75. On-campus interview required.

Athletics Interscholastic: baseball (boys), basketball (b,g), cheering (g), cross-country running (b,g), football (b), golf (b,g), soccer (b,g), swimming and diving (b,g), tennis (b,g), track and field (b,g). 3 PE instructors, 4 coaches, 1 athletic trainer.

Computers Computers are regularly used in college planning, keyboarding, programming, SAT preparation, technology, yearbook classes. Computer network features include Internet access, wireless campus network, Internet filtering or blocking technology. Campus intranet, student e-mail accounts, and computer access in designated common areas are available to students. Students grades are available online. The school has a published electronic and media policy.

Contact Mrs. Aimee C. Lynch, Director of Admissions. 706-731-5260 Ext. 2220. Fax: 706-261-7786. E-mail: alynch@wsa.net. Website: www.wsa.net

WEST NOTTINGHAM ACADEMY

1079 Firetower Road
Colora, Maryland 21917-1599

Head of School: Dr. Thomas Banks

General Information Coeducational boarding and day college-preparatory and ESL school. Grades 9–PG. Founded: 1744. Setting: rural. Nearest major city is Baltimore. Students are housed in single-sex dormitories. 120-acre campus. 12 buildings on campus. Approved or accredited by Association of Independent Maryland Schools, Middle States Association of Colleges and Schools, National Commission of Accreditation of Special Education Services, The Association of Boarding Schools, and Maryland Department of Education. Member of National Association of Independent Schools and Secondary School Admission Test Board. Total enrollment: 117. Upper school average class size: 10. Upper school faculty-student ratio: 1:7. There are 170 required school days per year for Upper School students. Upper School students typically attend 5 days per week. The average school day consists of 7 hours.

Upper School Student Profile 80% of students are boarding students. 12 states are represented in upper school student body. International students from China, Indonesia, Nigeria, Rwanda, Saudi Arabia, and Viet Nam; 14 other countries represented in student body.

Faculty School total: 18. In upper school: 9 men, 9 women; 14 have advanced degrees; 12 reside on campus.

Subjects Offered Advanced chemistry, advanced math, advanced TOEFL/grammar, African-American history, algebra, American literature, anatomy, ancient world history, applied arts, art, art history, Asian history, astronomy, basic language skills, biology, biology-AP, body human, British literature, British literature (honors), calculus, calculus-AP, ceramics, chemistry, chemistry-AP, clayworking, college counseling, comparative religion, computer education, drama, drama performance, drawing, earth science, English, English literature, English literature-AP, English-AP, environmental science, equestrian sports, ESL, ethics, ethics and responsibility, European history, European history-AP, fine arts, French, French-AP, geography, geometry, government/civics, guitar, health, history, history-AP, honors algebra, honors English, honors geometry, honors U.S. history, human anatomy, human biology, humanities, independent study, instrumental music, journalism, Latin, marketing, mathematics, modern European history, modern European history-AP, multicultural studies, music, music appreciation, photography, physical education, physics, physics-AP, physiology, piano, play production, pottery, pre-calculus, psychology, religion, SAT preparation, science, senior humanities, senior project, senior thesis, social studies, Spanish, Spanish-AP, sports, stage design, student government, student publications, studio art, studio art-AP, U.S. history, U.S. history-AP, visual and performing arts, voice, voice ensemble, weight training, wellness, world history, world literature, world religions, wrestling, writing, yearbook.

Graduation Requirements Senior Research Project.

Special Academic Programs Advanced Placement exam preparation; honors section; independent study; study at local college for college credit; academic accommodation for the gifted, the musically talented, and the artistically talented; remedial reading and/or remedial writing; remedial math; programs in English, mathematics, general development for dyslexic students; ESL (15 students enrolled).

College Admission Counseling 37 students graduated in 2016; all went to college.

Student Life Upper grades have specified standards of dress, student council. Discipline rests primarily with faculty.

Summer Programs ESL programs offered; held on campus; accepts boys and girls; open to students from other schools. 2017 schedule: July 31 to August 13. Application deadline: June 1.

Tuition and Aid Day student tuition: $18,200; 5-day tuition and room/board: $48,500–$56,700; 7-day tuition and room/board: $48,500. Tuition installment plan (monthly payment plans, individually arranged payment plans). Need-based scholarship grants available. In 2016–17, 53% of upper-school students received aid. Total amount of financial aid awarded in 2016–17: $1,000,000.

Admissions Traditional secondary-level entrance grade is 9. ISEE, SSAT, TOEFL or TOEFL or SLEP required. Deadline for receipt of application materials: none. Application fee required: $50. On-campus interview required.

Athletics Interscholastic: baseball (boys), basketball (b,g), cheering (g), cross-country running (b,g), lacrosse (b,g), soccer (b,g), tennis (b,g), volleyball (g); intramural: badminton (b,g), bicycling (b), fitness (b,g), fitness walking (b,g), jogging (b,g), outdoor activities (b,g), physical training (b,g), running (b,g), yoga (b,g); coed interscholastic: cross-country running, tennis; coed intramural: badminton, baseball, fitness, fitness walking, horseback riding, jogging, outdoor activities, physical training, running, strength & conditioning, weight training, yoga. 6 coaches, 1 athletic trainer.

Computers Computers are regularly used in computer applications, introduction to technology, mathematics, SAT preparation, science classes. Computer network features include on-campus library services, online commercial services, Internet access,

wireless campus network, Internet filtering or blocking technology. Campus intranet, student e-mail accounts, and computer access in designated common areas are available to students. Students grades are available online. The school has a published electronic and media policy.

Contact Nancy Nolan, Director of Enrollment Management. 410-658-5556 Ext. 9224. Fax: 410-658-9264. E-mail: admissions@wna.org. Website: www.wna.org

WESTOVER SCHOOL

1237 Whittemore Road
Middlebury, Connecticut 06762

Head of School: Ms. Julie Faulstich

General Information Girls' boarding and day college-preparatory, science and rngineering, and art history school. Grades 9–12. Distance learning grades 11–12. Founded: 1909. Setting: small town. Nearest major city is New York, NY. Students are housed in single-sex dormitories. 145-acre campus. 11 buildings on campus. Approved or accredited by Association of Independent Schools in New England, Connecticut Association of Independent Schools, New England Association of Schools and Colleges, The Association of Boarding Schools, and Connecticut Department of Education. Member of National Association of Independent Schools and Secondary School Admission Test Board. Endowment: $61 million. Total enrollment: 210. Upper school average class size: 11. Upper school faculty-student ratio: 1:8. There are 183 required school days per year for Upper School students. Upper School students typically attend 6 days per week. The average school day consists of 6 hours.

Upper School Student Profile Grade 9: 41 students (41 girls); Grade 10: 63 students (63 girls); Grade 11: 47 students (47 girls); Grade 12: 51 students (51 girls). 60% of students are boarding students. 52% are state residents. 17 states are represented in upper school student body. 24% are international students. International students from China, Ecuador, Japan, Republic of Korea, Russian Federation, and Rwanda; 12 other countries represented in student body.

Faculty School total: 46. In upper school: 13 men, 31 women; 31 have advanced degrees; 33 reside on campus.

Subjects Offered Advanced chemistry, Advanced Placement courses, African-American studies, algebra, American history, American history-AP, American literature, art, art history, art-AP, astronomy, ballet technique, bell choir, biology, biology-AP, calculus, calculus-AP, ceramics, chemistry, clayworking, community service, computer literacy, computer science, computer science-AP, creative writing, dance, drama, drawing, English, English language and composition-AP, English literature, environmental science, ESL, etymology, European history, European history-AP, filmmaking, fine arts, French, French-AP, geography, geometry, grammar, health and wellness, journalism, Latin, mathematics, music, music theory-AP, musical productions, painting, performing arts, photo shop, photography, physics, physics-AP, poetry, politics, portfolio art, pre-calculus, religion, robotics, science, sculpture, Shakespeare, short story, social studies, Spanish, Spanish-AP, speech, studio art-AP, theater, trigonometry, wilderness education, women's studies, world history, writing.

Graduation Requirements American history, art, athletics, English, foreign language, lab science, mathematics, science, world history. Community service is required.

Special Academic Programs 25 Advanced Placement exams for which test preparation is offered; honors section; independent study; term-away projects; study abroad; academic accommodation for the gifted, the musically talented, and the artistically talented; special instructional classes for deaf students; ESL (13 students enrolled).

College Admission Counseling 52 students graduated in 2016; all went to college, including Brandeis University; Fordham University; The George Washington University; University of Connecticut; University of Vermont; Washington University in St. Louis. Median SAT critical reading: 625, median SAT math: 675, median SAT writing: 710, median combined SAT: 2205, median composite ACT: 27. 68% scored over 600 on SAT critical reading, 81% scored over 600 on SAT math, 81% scored over 600 on SAT writing, 82% scored over 1800 on combined SAT, 90% scored over 26 on composite ACT.

Student Life Upper grades have specified standards of dress, student council, honor system. Discipline rests equally with students and faculty.

Tuition and Aid Day student tuition: $39,100; 7-day tuition and room/board: $54,400. Tuition installment plan (SMART Tuition Payment Plan). Need-based scholarship grants available. In 2016–17, 50% of upper-school students received aid. Total amount of financial aid awarded in 2016–17: $3,600,000.

Admissions Traditional secondary-level entrance grade is 9. For fall 2016, 235 students applied for upper-level admission, 140 were accepted, 62 enrolled. ISEE, SSAT or TOEFL required. Deadline for receipt of application materials: January 15. Application fee required: $50. On-campus interview recommended.

Athletics Interscholastic: basketball, crew, cross-country running, field hockey, golf, independent competitive sports, lacrosse, rowing, soccer, softball, squash, swimming and diving, tennis, volleyball; intramural: aerobics, aerobics/dance, backpacking, ballet, canoeing/kayaking, climbing, dance, dance team, fitness, hiking/backpacking, jogging, kayaking, modern dance, outdoor activities, outdoor adventure, outdoor education, outdoor recreation, outdoor skills, outdoors, paddle tennis, physical fitness, physical training, rappelling, rock climbing, running, self defense, skiing (downhill), snowboarding, strength & conditioning, tennis, ultimate Frisbee, walking, wall climbing, weight lifting, weight training, wilderness, yoga. 2 PE instructors, 10 coaches, 1 athletic trainer.

Computers Computers are regularly used in all academic classes. Computer network features include on-campus library services, online commercial services, Internet access, wireless campus network, Internet filtering or blocking technology. Campus intranet, student e-mail accounts, and computer access in designated common areas are available to students. Students grades are available online. The school has a published electronic and media policy.

Contact Ms. Dawn Curtis, Associate Director of Admission. 203-577-4521. Fax: 203-758-1581. E-mail: admission@westoverschool.org. Website: www.westoverschool.org

WESTRIDGE SCHOOL

324 Madeline Drive
Pasadena, California 91105-3399

Head of School: Ms. Elizabeth J. McGregor

General Information Girls' day college-preparatory, arts, and technology school. Grades 4–12. Founded: 1913. Setting: suburban. Nearest major city is Los Angeles. 9-acre campus. 11 buildings on campus. Approved or accredited by California Association of Independent Schools, Western Association of Schools and Colleges, and California Department of Education. Member of National Association of Independent Schools. Endowment: $22 million. Total enrollment: 482. Upper school average class size: 11. Upper school faculty-student ratio: 1:7. There are 163 required school days per year for Upper School students. Upper School students typically attend 5 days per week. The average school day consists of 7 hours and 15 minutes.

Upper School Student Profile Grade 9: 74 students (74 girls); Grade 10: 74 students (74 girls); Grade 11: 74 students (74 girls); Grade 12: 74 students (74 girls).

Faculty School total: 62. In upper school: 15 men, 25 women; 30 have advanced degrees.

Subjects Offered Acting, Advanced Placement courses, algebra, American history, American literature, art, art history, biology, calculus, cell biology, ceramics, chemistry, Chinese, chorus, classical language, college counseling, computer applications, computer graphics, computer science, creative writing, dance, directing, drama, earth science, English, English literature, environmental science, European history, fine arts, French, geometry, government/civics, history, Latin, life science, Mandarin, mathematics, modern languages, music, orchestra, photography, physical education, physical science, physics, physiology, pre-calculus, science, Spanish, Spanish literature, statistics, studio art, theater, trigonometry, video, visual and performing arts, visual arts, world history, world literature.

Graduation Requirements Art, college counseling, cultural arts, English, foreign language, history, mathematics, music, physical education (includes health), science, senior project, statistics, Human Development & The College Process, Interim Program, culminating and comprehensive service project (CAP). Community service is required.

Special Academic Programs Advanced Placement exam preparation; honors section; independent study.

College Admission Counseling 47 students graduated in 2016; 46 went to college, including Boston University; Harvard University; New York University; University of Chicago; University of Southern California; Washington University in St. Louis. Other: 1 had other specific plans. Median SAT critical reading: 680, median SAT math: 640, median SAT writing: 690, median combined SAT: 2010, median composite ACT: 32. 82% scored over 600 on SAT critical reading, 71% scored over 600 on SAT math, 79% scored over 600 on SAT writing, 82% scored over 1800 on combined SAT, 96% scored over 26 on composite ACT.

Student Life Upper grades have uniform requirement, student council. Discipline rests primarily with faculty.

Tuition and Aid Day student tuition: $33,550. Tuition installment plan (monthly payment plans, full payment, two payment plan, 10-month tuition payment). Need-based scholarship grants available.

Admissions Traditional secondary-level entrance grade is 9. For fall 2016, 120 students applied for upper-level admission, 49 were accepted, 19 enrolled. ISEE or writing sample required. Deadline for receipt of application materials: January 13. Application fee required: $100. On-campus interview recommended.

Athletics Interscholastic: aerobics/dance, basketball, cross-country running, dance, diving, fencing, golf, lacrosse, martial arts, modern dance, physical fitness, soccer, softball, swimming and diving, tennis, track and field, volleyball, water polo, yoga. 4 PE instructors, 19 coaches, 1 athletic trainer.

Computers Computers are regularly used in art, English, foreign language, history, library skills, mathematics, newspaper, photography, science, yearbook classes. Computer network features include on-campus library services, online commercial services, Internet access, wireless campus network, Internet filtering or blocking technology, course Web sites, remote access to email and files, school Internet portal/Web site. Student e-mail accounts are available to students. The school has a published electronic and media policy.

Contact Ms. Sarah Jallo, Director of Admissions. 626-799-1153 Ext. 213. Fax: 626-799-9236. E-mail: sjallo@westridge.org. Website: www.westridge.org

WESTSIDE CHRISTIAN HIGH SCHOOL

8200 SW Pfaffle St
Tigard, Oregon 97223

Head of School: Dr. Debi Miller

General Information Coeducational day college-preparatory school, affiliated with Protestant-Evangelical faith. Grades 9–12. Founded: 1981. Setting: suburban. Nearest major city is Portland. 1 building on campus. Approved or accredited by Association of Christian Schools International and Oregon Department of Education. Total enrollment: 300. Upper school average class size: 20. Upper school faculty-student ratio: 1:12. There are 165 required school days per year for Upper School students. Upper School students typically attend 5 days per week. The average school day consists of 7 hours.

Upper School Student Profile 100% of students are Protestant-Evangelical faith.

Faculty School total: 211. In upper school: 11 men, 10 women.

Subjects Offered All academic.

Special Academic Programs Honors section.

College Admission Counseling 52 students graduated in 2016; they went to George Fox University.

Student Life Upper grades have specified standards of dress, honor system. Discipline rests primarily with faculty. Attendance at religious services is required.

Tuition and Aid Day student tuition: $11,800. Tuition installment plan (SMART Tuition Payment Plan). Tuition reduction for siblings, need-based scholarship grants available. In 2016–17, 25% of upper-school students received aid.

Admissions Deadline for receipt of application materials: January 31. Application fee required: $100. Interview recommended.

Athletics 2 PE instructors, 15 coaches.

Computers Computers are regularly used in all classes. Computer network features include on-campus library services, Internet access, wireless campus network, Internet filtering or blocking technology. Campus intranet, student e-mail accounts, and computer access in designated common areas are available to students. Students grades are available online. The school has a published electronic and media policy.

Contact Mr. Brett Meyers, Director of Admissions. 503-697-4711 Ext. 1249. Fax: 503-697-4605. E-mail: meyers@wchsonline.org. Website: www.wchsonline.org

WEST SOUND ACADEMY

16571 Creative Drive NE
Poulsbo, Washington 98370

Head of School: Ms. Barrie Hillman

General Information Coeducational boarding and day college-preparatory and International Baccalaureate school. Boarding grades 8–12, day grades 6–12. Founded: 1998. Setting: rural. Nearest major city is Seattle. Students are housed in single-sex by floor dormitories. 20-acre campus. 4 buildings on campus. Approved or accredited by International Baccalaureate Organization and Washington Department of Education. Total enrollment: 113. Upper school average class size: 13. Upper school faculty-student ratio: 1:6. There are 177 required school days per year for Upper School students. Upper School students typically attend 5 days per week. The average school day consists of 6 hours and 5 minutes.

Upper School Student Profile Grade 9: 23 students (14 boys, 9 girls); Grade 10: 20 students (8 boys, 12 girls); Grade 11: 15 students (5 boys, 10 girls); Grade 12: 15 students (6 boys, 9 girls). 21% of students are boarding students. 74% are state residents. 1 state is represented in upper school student body. 26% are international students. International students from China, France, Republic of Korea, and Viet Nam.

Faculty School total: 17. In upper school: 4 men, 10 women; 8 have advanced degrees.

Subjects Offered Advanced biology, algebra, art history, biology, calculus, chemistry, college counseling, community service, computer programming, drama performance, electives, English, English literature, experiential education, foreign language, French, geometry, history, International Baccalaureate courses, journalism, literary magazine, mathematics, music performance, oil painting, physical education, physics, pre-calculus, robotics, senior project, senior thesis, Spanish, theory of knowledge, TOEFL preparation, visual arts, yearbook.

Graduation Requirements Art, biology, chemistry, electives, English, experiential education, foreign language, history, mathematics, physics, senior project, theory of knowledge, visual arts, West Sound Academy has a 4-1-4 academic calendar; students complete a June-Term course each year, June Term has 3-week-long short courses of intense study in a variety of subjects outside the usual curriculum. Fall retreats, along with June Term trips to varied locations, teach leadership, environmental ethics, and technical skills.

Special Academic Programs International Baccalaureate program; independent study; term-away projects; academic accommodation for the gifted, the musically talented, and the artistically talented.

College Admission Counseling 18 students graduated in 2016; 17 went to college, including Oregon State University; Pomona College; Savannah College of Art and Design; University of Washington; Western Washington University; Whitman College. Other: 1 had other specific plans. Median SAT critical reading: 543, median SAT math: 617, median SAT writing: 531, median combined SAT: 1690, median composite ACT: 27. 53% scored over 600 on SAT critical reading, 60% scored over 600 on SAT math, 47% scored over 600 on SAT writing, 53% scored over 1800 on combined SAT, 50% scored over 26 on composite ACT.

Student Life Upper grades have specified standards of dress, student council, honor system. Discipline rests primarily with faculty.

Tuition and Aid Day student tuition: $17,356; 7-day tuition and room/board: $41,575–$44,875. Tuition installment plan (Insured Tuition Payment Plan, monthly payment plans). Merit scholarship grants, need-based scholarship grants available. In 2016–17, 37% of upper-school students received aid; total upper-school merit-scholarship money awarded: $149,550. Total amount of financial aid awarded in 2016–17: $242,891.

Admissions Traditional secondary-level entrance grade is 9. For fall 2016, 38 students applied for upper-level admission, 26 were accepted, 19 enrolled. International English Language Test or TOEFL required. Deadline for receipt of application materials: none. Application fee required: $175. Interview recommended.

Athletics Interscholastic: cross-country running (boys, girls), football (b), soccer (b,g), track and field (b), volleyball (g); intramural: ballet (b,g), dance team (g), equestrian sports (g), horseback riding (g), lacrosse (b,g); coed intramural: canoeing/kayaking, hiking/backpacking, outdoor activities, outdoor education, outdoor recreation, rafting, rappelling, rock climbing.

Computers Computers are regularly used in all classes. Computer network features include on-campus library services, Internet access, wireless campus network, Internet filtering or blocking technology, databases available through our library website: Gale, EBSCO, ProQuest, World Book, and others. Student e-mail accounts are available to students. Students grades are available online. The school has a published electronic and media policy.

Contact Ms. Lisa Gsellman, Director of Admissions. 360-598-5954. Fax: 360-598-5494. E-mail: lgsellman@westsoundacademy.org. Website: www.westsoundacademy.org/

WESTTOWN SCHOOL

975 Westtown Road

West Chester, Pennsylvania 19382-5700

Head of School: John W. Baird

General Information Coeducational boarding and day college-preparatory school, affiliated with Society of Friends. Boarding grades 9–12, day grades PK–12. Founded: 1799. Setting: suburban. Nearest major city is Philadelphia. Students are housed in single-sex dormitories. 600-acre campus. 38 buildings on campus. Approved or accredited by Friends Council on Education, Middle States Association of Colleges and Schools, Pennsylvania Association of Independent Schools, and Pennsylvania Department of Education. Member of National Association of Independent Schools and Secondary School Admission Test Board. Endowment: $86 million. Total enrollment: 636. Upper school average class size: 15. Upper school faculty-student ratio: 1:8. There are 168 required school days per year for Upper School students. Upper School students typically attend 5 days per week. The average school day consists of 9 hours and 20 minutes.

Upper School Student Profile Grade 9: 80 students (36 boys, 44 girls); Grade 10: 93 students (42 boys, 51 girls); Grade 11: 90 students (39 boys, 51 girls); Grade 12: 99 students (39 boys, 60 girls). 73% of students are boarding students. 58% are state residents. 17 states are represented in upper school student body. 17% are international students. International students from Canada, China, Germany, Republic of Korea, Spain, and Thailand; 13 other countries represented in student body. 15% of students are members of Society of Friends.

Faculty School total: 112. In upper school: 32 men, 34 women; 52 have advanced degrees; 62 reside on campus.

Subjects Offered 3-dimensional art, ACT preparation, advanced biology, advanced chemistry, advanced math, algebra, American culture, American foreign policy, American history, American literature, ancient history, art, Asian history, band, baseball, basketball, Bible, Bible studies, biology, botany, British literature, calculus, choir, choral music, Christian and Hebrew scripture, classical language, classical studies, comparative religion, computer applications, concert band, concert choir, crafts, creative dance, creative writing, dance, dance performance, digital art, drama, drama performance, drama workshop, drawing, drawing and design, earth science, Eastern religion and philosophy, ecology, ecology, environmental systems, electives, engineering, English, English as a foreign language, English composition, English literature, environmental science, environmental studies, environmental systems, ESL, European history, film and literature, folk art, foreign language, foreign policy, fractal geometry, French, functions, geometry, graphic design, Holocaust and other genocides, honors algebra, honors geometry, honors U.S. history, honors world history, jazz, jazz dance, jazz ensemble, lab science, language, Latin, Latin American history, leadership, library research, linear algebra, literature, literature seminar, Mandarin, mathematics, model United Nations, modern dance, music, music composition, music performance, music theater, musical theater, mythology, nature writers, non-Western literature, peace and justice, physics, piano, play production, playwriting and directing, pre-algebra, pre-calculus, Quakerism and ethics, religion, robotics, SAT preparation, science, senior project, senior seminar, set design, Shakespeare, Spanish, Spanish literature, stage design, statistics, student government, student publications, studio art, swimming, tennis, theater, theater design and production, theater history, theater production, trigonometry, U.S. history, U.S. literature, visual and performing arts, visual arts, vocal ensemble, vocal music, water color painting, weight fitness, Western civilization,

Western literature, Western religions, woodworking, world history, world literature, world religions, wrestling, writing, writing workshop, yearbook.

Graduation Requirements Arts and fine arts (art, music, dance, drama), English, foreign language, health education, history, mathematics, physical education (includes health), religion (includes Bible studies and theology), religious studies, science, senior project, service learning/internship, social sciences.

Special Academic Programs Advanced Placement exam preparation; honors section; independent study; study abroad; academic accommodation for the gifted, the musically talented, and the artistically talented; remedial math; ESL (18 students enrolled).

College Admission Counseling 98 students graduated in 2016; 97 went to college, including Guilford College; Hamilton College; Haverford College; University of Pennsylvania; University of Pittsburgh; Wesleyan University. Other: 1 had other specific plans. Median SAT critical reading: 620, median SAT math: 630, median SAT writing: 610, median combined SAT: 1865, median composite ACT: 28.

Student Life Upper grades have specified standards of dress, student council, honor system. Discipline rests equally with students and faculty. Attendance at religious services is required.

Tuition and Aid Day student tuition: $34,470; 7-day tuition and room/board: $55,240. Tuition installment plan (monthly payment plans). Merit scholarship grants, need-based scholarship grants available. In 2016–17, 45% of upper-school students received aid; total upper-school merit-scholarship money awarded: $126,500. Total amount of financial aid awarded in 2016–17: $5,511,681.

Admissions Traditional secondary-level entrance grade is 9. For fall 2016, 383 students applied for upper-level admission, 162 were accepted, 75 enrolled. SSAT or TOEFL required. Deadline for receipt of application materials: none. Application fee required: $50. Interview recommended.

Athletics Interscholastic: baseball (boys), basketball (b,g), cross-country running (b,g), field hockey (g), independent competitive sports (b,g), lacrosse (b,g), soccer (b,g), softball (g), swimming and diving (b,g), tennis (b,g), track and field (b,g); coed interscholastic: dance, dance team, golf, independent competitive sports, indoor track, indoor track & field; coed intramural: aquatics, ballet, basketball, canoeing/kayaking, combined training, dance, fitness, hiking/backpacking, indoor soccer, life saving, modern dance, outdoor activities, outdoor education, outdoor recreation, physical fitness, physical training, ropes courses, running, strength & conditioning, weight training, yoga. 18 coaches, 2 athletic trainers.

Computers Computers are regularly used in all academic classes. Computer network features include on-campus library services, online commercial services, Internet access, wireless campus network, Internet filtering or blocking technology. Campus intranet, student e-mail accounts, and computer access in designated common areas are available to students. Students grades are available online. The school has a published electronic and media policy.

Contact Nathan Bohn, Director of Admission. 610-399-7900. Fax: 610-399-7909. E-mail: admissions@westtown.edu. Website: www.westtown.edu

WHEATON ACADEMY

900 Prince Crossing Road

West Chicago, Illinois 60185

Head of School: Dr. Gene Frost

General Information Coeducational day college-preparatory and religious studies school, affiliated with Christian faith. Grades 9–12. Founded: 1853. Setting: suburban. Nearest major city is Chicago. 43-acre campus. 8 buildings on campus. Approved or accredited by Association of Christian Schools International, North Central Association of Colleges and Schools, and Illinois Department of Education. Total enrollment: 640. Upper school average class size: 21. Upper school faculty-student ratio: 1:15. There are 175 required school days per year for Upper School students. Upper School students typically attend 5 days per week. The average school day consists of 6 hours and 30 minutes.

Upper School Student Profile Grade 9: 167 students (81 boys, 86 girls); Grade 10: 164 students (77 boys, 87 girls); Grade 11: 160 students (78 boys, 82 girls); Grade 12: 165 students (81 boys, 84 girls). 96% of students are Christian faith.

Faculty School total: 55. In upper school: 29 men, 26 women; 33 have advanced degrees.

Subjects Offered ACT preparation, algebra, art, arts and crafts, band, Bible, Bible studies, biology, biology-AP, British literature, business, business applications, calculus, calculus-AP, ceramics, chemistry, chemistry-AP, child development, choir, Christian doctrine, Christian education, classics, comparative government and politics-AP, computer art, computer education, computer graphics, computer multimedia, computer processing, computer programming-AP, computer science, concert choir, consumer economics, creative writing, debate, desktop publishing, drama, drama workshop, drawing, driver education, earth science, economics, engineering, English, English language and composition-AP, English literature, English literature and composition-AP, environmental science, environmental science-AP, European history, European history-AP, family living, fiber arts, fine arts, foods, French, French language-AP, freshman seminar, geology, geometry, government/civics, graphic design, Greek, health, health and wellness, history, honors English, honors geometry, honors U.S. history, industrial arts, internship, journalism, keyboarding, leadership, literature, mathematics, multimedia design, music, music theory-AP, novels, orchestra, personal growth, physical education, physics, physics-AP, portfolio art, pre-algebra, psychology, publications, science, social sciences, social studies, sociology, Spanish, Spanish language-AP, speech, statistics, statistics-AP, student publications, theater, theology, trigonometry, U.S. government, U.S. government and politics-AP, U.S. history, U.S. history-AP, U.S. literature, world history, world history-AP, world literature, writing.

Graduation Requirements Arts and fine arts (art, music, dance, drama), English, mathematics, physical education (includes health), religion (includes Bible studies and theology), science, social sciences, social studies (includes history), Winterim (2-week period during January allowing students to take two classes beyond the typical curriculum).

Special Academic Programs 17 Advanced Placement exams for which test preparation is offered; honors section; independent study; term-away projects; study at local college for college credit; academic accommodation for the gifted, the musically talented, and the artistically talented; remedial reading and/or remedial writing; remedial math; special instructional classes for students with learning disabilities; ESL (50 students enrolled).

College Admission Counseling 164 students graduated in 2015; 160 went to college, including Biola University; Calvin College; Hope College; Taylor University; University of Illinois at Urbana–Champaign; Wheaton College. Other: 1 went to work, 3 had other specific plans. Median composite ACT: 25. 45% scored over 26 on composite ACT.

Student Life Upper grades have specified standards of dress, student council, honor system. Discipline rests primarily with faculty. Attendance at religious services is required.

Tuition and Aid Day student tuition: $15,000. Tuition installment plan (monthly payment plans, semester payment plan). Tuition reduction for siblings, merit scholarship grants, need-based scholarship grants, paying campus jobs available. In 2015–16, 35% of upper-school students received aid; total upper-school merit-scholarship money awarded: $15,000. Total amount of financial aid awarded in 2015–16: $700,000.

Admissions Traditional secondary-level entrance grade is 9. ACT-Explore and placement test required. Deadline for receipt of application materials: January 31. Application fee required: $50. On-campus interview required.

Athletics Interscholastic: baseball (boys), basketball (b,g), cheering (g), cross-country running (b,g), dance team (g), football (b), golf (b,g), ice hockey (b), lacrosse (b), pom squad (g), soccer (b,g), softball (g), tennis (b,g), track and field (b,g), volleyball (b,g); intramural: aerobics (g), flagball (g), ice hockey (b), wilderness survival (b); coed interscholastic: modern dance, physical training, running; coed intramural: climbing, floor hockey, hiking/backpacking, outdoor education, outdoor skills, power lifting, project adventure, riflery, rock climbing, skiing (cross-country), strength & conditioning, wall climbing, weight lifting, weight training. 2 PE instructors, 6 coaches, 1 athletic trainer.

Computers Computers are regularly used in Bible studies, graphic design, independent study, mathematics, multimedia, writing, yearbook classes. Computer network features include on-campus library services, online commercial services, Internet access, wireless campus network, Internet filtering or blocking technology. Student e-mail accounts are available to students. Students grades are available online. The school has a published electronic and media policy.

Contact Mr. Ryan Hall, Admissions Director. 630-562-7500 Ext. 7501. Fax: 630-231-1469. E-mail: rhall@wheatonacademy.org. Website: www.wheatonacademy.org

THE WHEELER SCHOOL

216 Hope Street
Providence, Rhode Island 02906

Head of School: Mr. Dan Miller, PhD

General Information Coeducational day college-preparatory, Community Action Program (service-based learning), and AERIE Program (individual academic enrichment grades 9-12) school. Grades N–12. Founded: 1889. Setting: urban. 5-acre campus. 8 buildings on campus. Approved or accredited by Association of Independent Schools in New England, New England Association of Schools and Colleges, and Rhode Island Department of Education. Member of National Association of Independent Schools. Endowment: $21.3 million. Total enrollment: 819. Upper school average class size: 15. Upper school faculty-student ratio: 1:7. There are 165 required school days per year for Upper School students. Upper School students typically attend 5 days per week. The average school day consists of 6 hours and 25 minutes.

Upper School Student Profile Grade 9: 95 students (44 boys, 51 girls); Grade 10: 96 students (46 boys, 50 girls); Grade 11: 90 students (46 boys, 44 girls); Grade 12: 93 students (55 boys, 38 girls).

Faculty School total: 124. In upper school: 29 men, 46 women; 36 have advanced degrees.

Subjects Offered 20th century American writers, 20th century world history, acting, Advanced Placement courses, advanced studio art-AP, algebra, American history, anatomy, art, art history, biology, biology-AP, biotechnology, Black history, broadcasting, business skills, calculus, calculus-AP, ceramics, chemistry, Chinese, Chinese studies, choral music, civil rights, computer programming, computer science, contemporary issues, dance, drama, drawing, economics, engineering, English, English literature, English-AP, environmental science, environmental science-AP, European

history, film studies, fine arts, forensics, French, geometry, guitar, Japanese, jazz ensemble, kinesiology, Latin, Latin American history, Latin American studies, mathematics, Middle Eastern history, music, nutrition, photography, physical education, physics, physiology, pre-calculus, printmaking, psychology, research, science, sculpture, social studies, Spanish, statistics, theater, trigonometry, Web site design, Western civilization.

Graduation Requirements Arts and fine arts (art, music, dance, drama), English, foreign language, history, mathematics, performing arts, physical education (includes health), science, community service, Unity and Diversity Curriculum.

Special Academic Programs 20 Advanced Placement exams for which test preparation is offered; honors section; independent study; term-away projects; study at local college for college credit; study abroad; academic accommodation for the gifted; programs in general development for dyslexic students.

College Admission Counseling 93 students graduated in 2016; all went to college, including Boston University; Brown University; Harvard University; The George Washington University; University of Rhode Island. Mean SAT critical reading: 640, mean SAT math: 650, mean SAT writing: 640, mean combined SAT: 1863, mean composite ACT: 27.

Student Life Upper grades have specified standards of dress, student council. Discipline rests equally with students and faculty.

Summer Programs Enrichment, sports, art/fine arts programs offered; session focuses on jazz camp, basketball camp, kayaking/voyager camps, sports academy; held on campus; accepts boys and girls; open to students from other schools. 175 students usually enrolled. 2017 schedule: June 19 to August 11. Application deadline: none.

Tuition and Aid Day student tuition: $33,865. Tuition installment plan (Key Tuition Payment Plan, monthly payment plans). Need-based scholarship grants available. In 2016–17, 24% of upper-school students received aid. Total amount of financial aid awarded in 2016–17: $2,093,652.

Admissions Traditional secondary-level entrance grade is 9. For fall 2016, 173 students applied for upper-level admission, 72 were accepted, 32 enrolled. ISEE or SSAT required. Deadline for receipt of application materials: January 13. Application fee required: $60. On-campus interview recommended.

Athletics Interscholastic: baseball (boys), basketball (b,g), cross-country running (b,g), field hockey (g), football (b), ice hockey (b,g), lacrosse (b,g), soccer (b,g), softball (g), swimming and diving (b,g), tennis (b,g), track and field (b,g), winter (indoor) track (b,g); coed interscholastic: golf, squash. 6 PE instructors, 48 coaches, 1 athletic trainer.

Computers Computers are regularly used in all classes. Computer network features include on-campus library services, online commercial services, Internet access, wireless campus network. Campus intranet, student e-mail accounts, and computer access in designated common areas are available to students. Students grades are available online. The school has a published electronic and media policy.

Contact Mrs. Jeanette Epstein, Director of Admission. 401-421-8100 Ext. 119. Fax: 401-751-7674. E-mail: jeanettepstein@wheelerschool.org.
Website: www.wheelerschool.org

WHITEFIELD ACADEMY

7711 Fegenbush Lane
Louisville, Kentucky 40228

Head of School: Mr. Gary W. Mounce

General Information Coeducational day college-preparatory, arts, religious studies, and technology school, affiliated with Southern Baptist Convention. Grades PS-12. Founded: 1976. Setting: suburban. 30-acre campus. 2 buildings on campus. Approved or accredited by Association of Christian Schools International, CITA (Commission on International and Trans-Regional Accreditation), Christian Schools International, Council of Accreditation and School Improvement, Southern Association of Colleges and Schools, and Kentucky Department of Education. Total enrollment: 711. Upper school average class size: 20. Upper school faculty-student ratio: 1:11. There are 179 required school days per year for Upper School students. Upper School students typically attend 5 days per week. The average school day consists of 6 hours and 25 minutes.

Upper School Student Profile Grade 9: 55 students (35 boys, 20 girls); Grade 10: 39 students (18 boys, 21 girls); Grade 11: 47 students (25 boys, 22 girls); Grade 12: 51 students (29 boys, 22 girls). 45% of students are Southern Baptist Convention.

Faculty School total: 47. In upper school: 9 men, 9 women; 12 have advanced degrees.

Subjects Offered Adolescent issues, advanced math, algebra, anatomy, art, arts, band, Bible studies, biology, calculus-AP, chemistry, choir, Christian education, Christian studies, college placement, college planning, college writing, composition, computer education, computers, drama, drama performance, economics, English, English composition, English literature, English literature-AP, foreign language, geometry, history, honors English, library, mathematics, music, political science, pre-calculus, reading, SAT/ACT preparation, science, science project, sex education, social sciences, Spanish, speech and debate, student government, student publications, U.S. history, U.S. history-AP.

Graduation Requirements Arts and fine arts (art, music, dance, drama), Bible, electives, English, foreign language, health, mathematics, physical education (includes health), science, social studies (includes history), religious studies.

Special Academic Programs 7 Advanced Placement exams for which test preparation is offered; honors section; independent study; study at local college for college credit; academic accommodation for the gifted.

College Admission Counseling 51 students graduated in 2015; 48 went to college, including Bellarmine University; Eastern Kentucky University; Jefferson Community and Technical College; University of Kentucky; University of Louisville; Western Kentucky University. Other: 1 went to work, 2 entered military service. Median composite ACT: 24. 20% scored over 26 on composite ACT.

Student Life Upper grades have uniform requirement, student council, honor system. Discipline rests primarily with faculty. Attendance at religious services is required.

Summer Programs Enrichment, sports, art/fine arts programs offered; session focuses on academic enrichment; held on campus; accepts boys and girls; open to students from other schools. 60 students usually enrolled.

Tuition and Aid Day student tuition: $6900. Tuition installment plan (FACTS Tuition Payment Plan, annual payment in full plan). Tuition reduction for siblings, need-based scholarship grants available. In 2015–16, 8% of upper-school students received aid. Total amount of financial aid awarded in 2015–16: $42,175.

Admissions Traditional secondary-level entrance grade is 9. For fall 2016, 17 students applied for upper-level admission, 13 were accepted, 13 enrolled. TerraNova required. Deadline for receipt of application materials: none. Application fee required: $100. On-campus interview required.

Athletics Interscholastic: aquatics (boys, girls), baseball (b), basketball (b,g), cheering (b,g), cross-country running (b,g), golf (b,g), soccer (b,g), softball (g), swimming and diving (b,g), tennis (b,g), track and field (b,g), volleyball (g); intramural: aerobics (g), fitness (b,g), outdoor activities (b,g), physical fitness (b,g), volleyball (g), weight lifting (b,g). 2 PE instructors.

Computers Computers are regularly used in all academic, college planning, library, newspaper, SAT preparation, theater arts, yearbook classes. Computer network features include on-campus library services, Internet access, wireless campus network, Internet filtering or blocking technology. Computer access in designated common areas is available to students. Students grades are available online. The school has a published electronic and media policy.

Contact Mrs. Lisa Sexton, Admissions Coordinator. 502-231-6261. Fax: 502-239-3144. E-mail: lisa.sexton@whitefield.org. Website: www.whitefield.org/

WHITFIELD SCHOOL

175 South Mason Road
St. Louis, Missouri 63141

Head of School: Mr. John Delautre

General Information Coeducational day college-preparatory, liberal arts, and STEM school. Grades 6–12. Founded: 1952. Setting: suburban. 26-acre campus. 4 buildings on campus. Approved or accredited by Independent Schools Association of the Central States. Member of National Association of Independent Schools. Endowment: $8 million. Total enrollment: 409. Upper school average class size: 14. Upper school faculty-student ratio: 1:7. There are 170 required school days per year for Upper School students. Upper School students typically attend 5 days per week. The average school day consists of 7 hours.

Upper School Student Profile Grade 6: 23 students (8 boys, 15 girls); Grade 7: 47 students (26 boys, 21 girls); Grade 8: 58 students (28 boys, 30 girls); Grade 9: 69 students (36 boys, 33 girls); Grade 10: 75 students (39 boys, 36 girls); Grade 11: 76 students (42 boys, 34 girls); Grade 12: 65 students (33 boys, 32 girls).

Faculty School total: 59. In upper school: 28 men, 38 women; 34 have advanced degrees.

Subjects Offered Advanced chemistry, algebra, American history, American literature, art, biology, calculus, calculus-AP, ceramics, chemistry, chemistry-AP, choir, college counseling, college placement, college planning, community service, computer science, concert band, earth science, English, European history, fine arts, French, French-AP, geometry, health, history, junior and senior seminars, Latin, Mandarin, mathematics, modern world history, music, painting, photography, physical education, physics, pre-algebra, pre-calculus, science, senior internship, social studies, sophomore skills, Spanish, Spanish-AP, symphonic band, theater, trigonometry, visual and performing arts, Western civilization, world cultures, world history, world literature.

Graduation Requirements Arts and fine arts (art, music, dance, drama), English, foreign language, mathematics, physical education (includes health), science, social studies (includes history), sophomore, junior, senior seminars.

Special Academic Programs Advanced Placement exam preparation; honors section; independent study; academic accommodation for the gifted; ESL (13 students enrolled).

College Admission Counseling 71 students graduated in 2016; all went to college, including Boston College; Kenyon College; Saint Louis University; University of Denver; Vanderbilt University; Washington University in St. Louis.

Student Life Upper grades have specified standards of dress, student council, honor system. Discipline rests primarily with faculty.

Tuition and Aid Day student tuition: $25,250. Tuition installment plan (Insured Tuition Payment Plan, monthly payment plans, 1-, 2-, and 10-payment plans). Merit scholarship grants, need-based scholarship grants available. In 2016–17, 26% of upper-school students received aid.

Admissions Traditional secondary-level entrance grade is 9. SSAT required. Deadline for receipt of application materials: January 17. Application fee required: $75. On-campus interview recommended.

Athletics Interscholastic: baseball (boys), basketball (b,g), cheering (g), cross-country running (b,g), dance team (g), field hockey (g), golf (b), ice hockey (b), lacrosse (b,g), soccer (b,g), squash (b,g), tennis (b), track and field (b,g), volleyball (g), wrestling (b); intramural: baseball (b), basketball (b,g), cheering (g), cross-country running (b,g), dance team (g), field hockey (g), soccer (b,g), volleyball (g), wrestling (b); coed interscholastic: dance team, golf, ice hockey, tennis; coed intramural: climbing, ice hockey, independent competitive sports, outdoor education, outdoor skills, wall climbing, yoga. 3 PE instructors, 2 coaches, 1 athletic trainer.

Computers Computers are regularly used in all classes. Computer network features include on-campus library services, online commercial services, Internet access, wireless campus network, Internet filtering or blocking technology, off-campus library and database searches, tablet PC program running Microsoft Windows. Campus intranet and student e-mail accounts are available to students. Students grades are available online. The school has a published electronic and media policy.

Contact Emily Chrysler, Director of Admission. 314-415-1270. Fax: 314-434-6193. E-mail: emily.chrysler@whitfieldschool.org. Website: www.whitfieldschool.org

WHITINSVILLE CHRISTIAN SCHOOL

279 Linwood Avenue
Whitinsville, Massachusetts 01588

Head of School: Lance B. Engbers

General Information Coeducational day college-preparatory school, affiliated with Christian Reformed Church. Grades PK–12. Founded: 1928. Setting: small town. Nearest major city is Worcester. 40-acre campus. 1 building on campus. Approved or accredited by Christian Schools International, New England Association of Schools and Colleges, and Massachusetts Department of Education. Endowment: $1.4 million. Total enrollment: 474. Upper school average class size: 13. Upper school faculty-student ratio: 1:8. There are 180 required school days per year for Upper School students. The average school day consists of 6 hours and 15 minutes.

Upper School Student Profile Grade 9: 44 students (21 boys, 23 girls); Grade 10: 48 students (18 boys, 30 girls); Grade 11: 51 students (19 boys, 32 girls); Grade 12: 33 students (16 boys, 17 girls). 35% of students are members of Christian Reformed Church.

Faculty School total: 60. In upper school: 14 have advanced degrees.

Special Academic Programs 5 Advanced Placement exams for which test preparation is offered; honors section; ESL (18 students enrolled).

College Admission Counseling 35 students graduated in 2015; 33 went to college, including Calvin College; Cedarville University; Gordon College; Messiah College; Palm Beach Atlantic University; University of Massachusetts Amherst. Other: 2 entered military service.

Student Life Upper grades have specified standards of dress, student council. Discipline rests primarily with faculty. Attendance at religious services is required.

Tuition and Aid Tuition installment plan (monthly payment plans). Tuition reduction for siblings available.

Admissions Deadline for receipt of application materials: none. Application fee required: $75. Interview required.

Athletics Interscholastic: baseball (boys), basketball (b,g), cross-country running (b,g), golf (b), indoor track & field (b,g), soccer (b,g), softball (g), tennis (b,g), track and field (b,g), volleyball (g). 2 PE instructors.

Computers Computer resources include Internet access, wireless campus network, Internet filtering or blocking technology. Student e-mail accounts are available to students. Students grades are available online. The school has a published electronic and media policy.

Contact 508-234-8211. Fax: 508-234-0624. Website: www.whitinsvillechristian.org

WICHITA COLLEGIATE SCHOOL

9115 East 13th Street
Wichita, Kansas 67206

Head of School: Mr. Tom Davis

General Information Coeducational day college-preparatory, arts, and technology school. Grades PS–12. Founded: 1963. Setting: urban. 42-acre campus. 1 building on campus. Approved or accredited by Independent Schools Association of the Southwest. Member of National Association of Independent Schools. Endowment: $7.8 million. Total enrollment: 935. Upper school average class size: 14. Upper school faculty-student ratio: 1:8. There are 174 required school days per year for Upper School students. Upper School students typically attend 5 days per week. The average school day consists of 7 hours.

Upper School Student Profile Grade 6: 65 students (37 boys, 28 girls); Grade 7: 69 students (31 boys, 38 girls); Grade 8: 50 students (25 boys, 25 girls); Grade 9: 70 students (33 boys, 37 girls); Grade 10: 68 students (40 boys, 28 girls); Grade 11: 73 students (42 boys, 31 girls); Grade 12: 78 students (36 boys, 42 girls).

Faculty School total: 108. In upper school: 16 men, 15 women; 17 have advanced degrees.

Subjects Offered Advanced Placement courses, algebra, American history, American history-AP, American literature, art, biology, biology-AP, calculus, calculus-AP, chemistry, chemistry-AP, computer programming, computer science-AP, drama, economics, economics-AP, English, English literature, English-AP, environmental science, European history, fine arts, French, French-AP, geometry, global studies, government-AP, government/civics, history, humanities, journalism, Latin, Latin-AP, macroeconomics-AP, mathematics, medieval/Renaissance history, music, photography, physical education, physics, physics-AP, science, social studies, Spanish, Spanish-AP, statistics, statistics-AP, theater, U.S. history-AP, United States government-AP, video, video film production, world history, writing, yearbook.

Graduation Requirements Arts and fine arts (art, music, dance, drama), computer science, economics, English, foreign language, humanities, mathematics, science, social studies (includes history).

Special Academic Programs 18 Advanced Placement exams for which test preparation is offered; study at local college for college credit; academic accommodation for the gifted.

College Admission Counseling 51 students graduated in 2015; all went to college, including Baylor University; Boston University; Kansas State University; The University of Kansas. Median SAT critical reading: 640, median SAT math: 660, median SAT writing: 640, median combined SAT: 1865, median composite ACT: 28. 62% scored over 600 on SAT critical reading, 76% scored over 600 on SAT math, 59% scored over 600 on SAT writing, 68% scored over 1800 on combined SAT, 81% scored over 26 on composite ACT.

Student Life Upper grades have specified standards of dress, student council, honor system. Discipline rests primarily with faculty.

Tuition and Aid Day student tuition: $16,840. Tuition installment plan (monthly payment plans, individually arranged payment plans, 3-payment plan). Need-based scholarship grants available. In 2015–16, 20% of upper-school students received aid. Total amount of financial aid awarded in 2015–16: $670,000.

Admissions Traditional secondary-level entrance grade is 9. Iowa Tests of Basic Skills, Otis-Lennon School Ability Test and writing sample required. Deadline for receipt of application materials: none. Application fee required: $35. Interview recommended.

Athletics Interscholastic: baseball (boys), basketball (b,g), cross-country running (b,g), dance squad (g), dance team (g), football (b), golf (b,g), soccer (g), strength & conditioning (b,g), swimming and diving (b,g), tennis (b,g), track and field (b,g), volleyball (g); coed interscholastic: bowling, cheering. 2 PE instructors, 16 coaches, 1 athletic trainer.

Computers Computers are regularly used in video film production, yearbook classes. Computer network features include on-campus library services, Internet access, wireless campus network. Student e-mail accounts and computer access in designated common areas are available to students. Students grades are available online. The school has a published electronic and media policy.

Contact Ms. Susie Steed, Director of Admission. 316-771-2203. Fax: 316-634-0598. E-mail: ssteed@wcsks.com. Website: www.wcsks.com

THE WILLISTON NORTHAMPTON SCHOOL

19 Payson Avenue
Easthampton, Massachusetts 01027

Head of School: Mr. Robert W. Hill III

General Information Coeducational boarding and day college-preparatory school. Boarding grades 9–PG, day grades 7–12. Founded: 1841. Setting: small town. Nearest major city is Northampton. Students are housed in single-sex dormitories. 125-acre campus. 57 buildings on campus. Approved or accredited by Association of Independent Schools in New England, New England Association of Schools and Colleges, and The Association of Boarding Schools. Member of National Association of Independent Schools and Secondary School Admission Test Board. Endowment: $44 million. Total enrollment: 528. Upper school average class size: 13. Upper school faculty-student ratio: 1:6. There are 160 required school days per year for Upper School students. Upper School students typically attend 5 days per week. The average school day consists of 8 hours and 30 minutes.

Upper School Student Profile Grade 9: 66 students (29 boys, 37 girls); Grade 10: 98 students (58 boys, 40 girls); Grade 11: 125 students (62 boys, 63 girls); Grade 12: 130 students (69 boys, 61 girls); Postgraduate: 12 students (11 boys, 1 girl). 67% of students are boarding students. 51% are state residents. 27 states are represented in upper school student body. 19% are international students. International students from Canada, China, Japan, Nigeria, Republic of Korea, and Taiwan; 26 other countries represented in student body.

Faculty School total: 73. In upper school: 35 men, 38 women; 48 have advanced degrees; 57 reside on campus.

Subjects Offered African-American history, algebra, American history, American literature, anatomy and physiology, animal behavior, art, art history, astronomy, biology, biology-AP, calculus, calculus-AP, chemistry, chemistry-AP, China/Japan history, Chinese, choral music, choreography, Christian and Hebrew scripture, comparative government and politics-AP, comparative politics, computer math, computer programming, computer science, computer science-AP, constitutional law, creative writing, dance, discrete mathematics, drama, economics, economics and history, economics-AP, English, English language-AP, English literature, English literature-AP, environmental science, ESL, ethics, European history, expository writing, fine arts, French, French language-AP, French literature-AP, French-AP, genetics, geometry, global studies, government/civics, health, history, history of jazz, honors algebra, honors English, honors geometry, Islamic studies, Latin, Latin American history, Latin-AP, mathematics, music, music theory, organic biochemistry, organic chemistry, philosophy, photography, photojournalism, physics, physics-AP, play production, playwriting, poetry, psychology, psychology-AP, religion, religion and culture, Russian history, science, sculpture, social studies, Spanish, Spanish language-AP, Spanish literature-AP, statistics-AP, theater, theology, trigonometry, U.S. history-AP, world history, world literature, writing workshop.

Graduation Requirements Arts and fine arts (art, music, dance, drama), English, foreign language, history, mathematics, science, participation in afternoon program.

Special Academic Programs 19 Advanced Placement exams for which test preparation is offered; honors section; independent study; term-away projects; study abroad; academic accommodation for the gifted, the musically talented, and the artistically talented; special instructional classes for deaf students; ESL (12 students enrolled).

College Admission Counseling 139 students graduated in 2015; 135 went to college, including Connecticut College; Cornell University; Hobart and William Smith Colleges; Syracuse University; The George Washington University; Trinity College. Other: 1 entered a postgraduate year, 3 had other specific plans. Median SAT critical reading: 580, median SAT math: 600, median SAT writing: 580, median combined SAT: 1770, median composite ACT: 25. 43% scored over 600 on SAT critical reading, 57% scored over 600 on SAT math, 45% scored over 600 on SAT writing, 47% scored over 1800 on combined SAT, 48% scored over 26 on composite ACT.

Student Life Upper grades have specified standards of dress, student council, honor system. Discipline rests equally with students and faculty.

Tuition and Aid Day student tuition: $37,500; 7-day tuition and room/board: $55,300. Tuition installment plan (Insured Tuition Payment Plan, monthly payment plans, individually arranged payment plans, Tuition Management Systems). Merit scholarship grants, need-based scholarship grants available. In 2015–16, 48% of upper-school students received aid; total upper-school merit-scholarship money awarded: $213,000. Total amount of financial aid awarded in 2015–16: $6,458,850.

Admissions Traditional secondary-level entrance grade is 9. For fall 2015, 873 students applied for upper-level admission, 313 were accepted, 113 enrolled. ACT, ISEE, PSAT or SAT for applicants to grade 11 and 12, SSAT or TOEFL required. Deadline for receipt of application materials: January 15. Application fee required: $50. Interview required.

Athletics Interscholastic: alpine skiing (boys, girls), baseball (b), basketball (b,g), crew (b,g), cross-country running (b,g), field hockey (g), football (b), golf (b,g), ice hockey (b,g), lacrosse (b,g), soccer (b,g), softball (g), squash (b,g), strength & conditioning (b,g), swimming and diving (b,g), tennis (b,g), track and field (b,g), volleyball (g), water polo (b,g), wrestling (b); intramural: self defense (g); coed interscholastic: dance, diving, physical training, ultimate Frisbee; coed intramural: aerobics, aerobics/dance, dance, dance team, equestrian sports, fitness, horseback riding, judo, martial arts, modern dance, mountain biking, snowboarding, weight lifting, weight training, yoga. 1 PE instructor, 5 coaches, 2 athletic trainers.

Computers Computers are regularly used in college planning, geography, graphic design, history, library, mathematics, newspaper, photography, photojournalism, programming, science, yearbook classes. Computer network features include on-campus library services, online commercial services, Internet access, wireless campus network, Internet filtering or blocking technology. Campus intranet, student e-mail accounts, and computer access in designated common areas are available to students. Students grades are available online. The school has a published electronic and media policy.

Contact Mr. Derek Cunha, Associate Director of Admission. 413-529-3241. Fax: 413-527-9494. E-mail: dcunha@williston.com. Website: www.williston.com

WILLOW HILL SCHOOL

Sudbury, Massachusetts
See Special Needs Schools section.

THE WILLOWS ACADEMY

1015 Rose Avenue
Des Plaines, Illinois 60016

Head of School: Mrs. Jeanne Petros

General Information Girls' day college-preparatory, arts, religious studies, and college preparatory school, affiliated with Roman Catholic Church. Grades 6–12. Founded: 1974. Setting: suburban. Nearest major city is Chicago. 4-acre campus. 1 building on campus. Approved or accredited by Illinois Department of Education. Total enrollment: 230. Upper school average class size: 18. Upper school faculty-student ratio: 1:10. Upper School students typically attend 5 days per week. The average school day consists of 6 hours and 30 minutes.

Upper School Student Profile Grade 6: 17 students (17 girls); Grade 7: 24 students (24 girls); Grade 8: 32 students (32 girls); Grade 9: 30 students (30 girls); Grade 10: 30

students (30 girls); Grade 11: 30 students (30 girls); Grade 12: 31 students (31 girls). 85% of students are Roman Catholic.

Faculty School total: 35. In upper school: 27 women; 17 have advanced degrees.

Subjects Offered Algebra, American history, American literature, art, biology, calculus, chemistry, choir, choral music, computer graphics, computer programming, computer science, economics, English, English literature, ethics, European history, fine arts, four units of summer reading, French, geography, geometry, government/civics, grammar, health, history, instrumental music, Latin, mathematics, music, music history, music theory, musical productions, philosophy, physical education, physics, precalculus, science, social studies, Spanish, statistics, theology, visual arts, vocal music, world history, world literature, writing.

Graduation Requirements Arts and fine arts (art, music, dance, drama), English, foreign language, four units of summer reading, mathematics, physical education (includes health), religion (includes Bible studies and theology), science, social studies (includes history), 40 hours of service work per year.

Special Academic Programs Advanced Placement exam preparation; honors section.

College Admission Counseling 43 students graduated in 2016; all went to college, including Marquette University; Northwestern University; University of Chicago; University of Dallas; University of Illinois at Urbana–Champaign; University of Notre Dame. Mean SAT critical reading: 690, mean SAT math: 670, mean SAT writing: 717, mean composite ACT: 28.

Student Life Upper grades have uniform requirement, student council, honor system. Discipline rests primarily with faculty.

Summer Programs Enrichment, sports programs offered; session focuses on athletic camps and enrichment; held on campus; accepts girls; open to students from other schools. 30 students usually enrolled. 2017 schedule: June 1 to July 31. Application deadline: none.

Tuition and Aid Day student tuition: $14,000. Tuition installment plan (Insured Tuition Payment Plan, monthly payment plans, quarterly, semiannual, and annual payment plans). Tuition reduction for siblings, need-based scholarship grants available. In 2016–17, 30% of upper-school students received aid.

Admissions Traditional secondary-level entrance grade is 9. Any standardized test, ISEE or school's own exam required. Deadline for receipt of application materials: none. Application fee required: $50. On-campus interview required.

Athletics Interscholastic: basketball, cross-country running, dance team, soccer, softball, swimming and diving, volleyball; intramural: strength & conditioning. 1 PE instructor, 8 coaches.

Computers Computers are regularly used in art, graphic design, history, mathematics, music, music technology, science classes. Computer network features include Internet access, Internet filtering or blocking technology. Computer access in designated common areas is available to students. Students grades are available online.

Contact Mrs. Kathryn Ferry, Director of Admissions. 847-824-6900 Ext. 208. Fax: 847-824-7089. E-mail: ferry@willowsacademy.org.

Website: www.willowsacademy.org

WILMINGTON CHRISTIAN SCHOOL

825 Loveville Road
Hockessin, Delaware 19707

General Information Coeducational day college-preparatory school, affiliated with Protestant faith. Grades PK–12. Founded: 1946. Setting: suburban. Nearest major city is Wilmington. 15-acre campus. 1 building on campus. Approved or accredited by Association of Christian Schools International, Middle States Association of Colleges and Schools, and Delaware Department of Education. Endowment: $400,000. Total enrollment: 500. Upper school average class size: 19. Upper school faculty-student ratio: 1:15. There are 177 required school days per year for Upper School students. Upper School students typically attend 5 days per week. The average school day consists of 6 hours and 40 minutes.

Upper School Student Profile Grade 9: 41 students (20 boys, 21 girls); Grade 10: 55 students (25 boys, 30 girls); Grade 11: 50 students (24 boys, 26 girls); Grade 12: 64 students (30 boys, 34 girls). 99% of students are Protestant.

Faculty School total: 57. In upper school: 13 men, 22 women; 16 have advanced degrees.

Subjects Offered Accounting, advanced math, algebra, American history, American history-AP, American minority experience, anatomy and physiology, art, band, biology, calculus, calculus-AP, chemistry, chorus, Christian doctrine, Christian ethics, church history, civics, computer applications, consumer mathematics, creative writing, democracy in America, driver education, ecology, economics, English, geometry, German, health, honors algebra, honors English, honors geometry, information processing, journalism, lab science, library assistant, marine biology, modern history, music theory, novels, physical education, physical science, physics, pre-calculus, Spanish, speech, study skills, trigonometry, world civilizations, world religions, yearbook.

Graduation Requirements Bible studies, English, foreign language, health education, mathematics, physical education (includes health), science, social studies (includes history), 40 hours of community service.

Special Academic Programs Advanced Placement exam preparation; honors section; study at local college for college credit; remedial reading and/or remedial writing; remedial math; programs in English, mathematics, general development for dyslexic students; special instructional classes for Learning Support Program; ESL (24 students enrolled).

College Admission Counseling 67 students graduated in 2016; 65 went to college, including Drexel University; Eastern University; Gordon College; Liberty University; Messiah College; University of Delaware. Other: 20 went to work.

Student Life Upper grades have uniform requirement, student council, honor system. Discipline rests primarily with faculty. Attendance at religious services is required.

Summer Programs Remediation, advancement programs offered; session focuses on to attract more students to the school; held on campus; accepts boys and girls; open to students from other schools. 12 students usually enrolled. 2017 schedule: June 15 to August 5.

Tuition and Aid Day student tuition: $14,630. Tuition installment plan (SMART Tuition Payment Plan). Tuition reduction for siblings, need-based scholarship grants available. In 2016–17, 47% of upper-school students received aid. Total amount of financial aid awarded in 2016–17: $325,000.

Admissions Traditional secondary-level entrance grade is 9. For fall 2016, 68 students applied for upper-level admission, 35 were accepted, 32 enrolled. Stanford Achievement Test required. Deadline for receipt of application materials: August 1. Application fee required: $125. On-campus interview required.

Athletics Interscholastic: baseball (boys), basketball (b,g), cross-country running (b,g), field hockey (g), golf (b,g), lacrosse (b), physical fitness (b,g), soccer (b,g), softball (g), track and field (b,g), volleyball (g), wrestling (b); coed interscholastic: running. 2 PE instructors, 16 coaches, 1 athletic trainer.

Computers Computers are regularly used in all academic, art, Bible studies, Christian doctrine, college planning, commercial art, computer applications, creative writing, design, English, ESL, foreign language, history, journalism, keyboarding, library, mathematics, media production, religion, remedial study skills, research skills, SAT preparation, science, senior seminar, social sciences, social studies, Spanish, theater, Web site design, writing, writing classes. Computer network features include on-campus library services, Internet access, wireless campus network, Internet filtering or blocking technology. Student e-mail accounts and computer access in designated common areas are available to students. Students grades are available online. The school has a published electronic and media policy.

Contact Mrs. Carol Allston-Stiles, Director of Enrollment. 302-239-2121 Ext. 3205. Fax: 302-239-2778. E-mail: admissions@WilmingtonChristian.org.

Website: www.wilmingtonchristian.org

WILMINGTON FRIENDS SCHOOL

101 School Road
Wilmington, Delaware 19803

Head of School: Kenneth E. Aldridge

General Information Coeducational day college-preparatory, peace and justice, theory of knowledge, web site design, and 3 dimensional art, environmental science, Quakerism & ethics school, affiliated with Society of Friends. Grades PS–12. Founded: 1748. Setting: suburban. Nearest major city is Philadelphia, PA. 57-acre campus. 4 buildings on campus. Approved or accredited by Friends Council on Education, International Baccalaureate Organization, Middle States Association of Colleges and Schools, Pennsylvania Association of Independent Schools, and Delaware Department of Education. Member of National Association of Independent Schools. Endowment: $28 million. Total enrollment: 736. Upper school average class size: 15. Upper school faculty-student ratio: 1:14. There are 169 required school days per year for Upper School students. Upper School students typically attend 5 days per week. The average school day consists of 7 hours.

Upper School Student Profile Grade 9: 74 students (39 boys, 35 girls); Grade 10: 57 students (34 boys, 23 girls); Grade 11: 78 students (40 boys, 38 girls); Grade 12: 71 students (33 boys, 38 girls). 3.8% of students are members of Society of Friends.

Faculty School total: 85. In upper school: 10 men, 18 women; 25 have advanced degrees.

Subjects Offered 3-dimensional art, advanced chemistry, art, biology, calculus, chemistry, community service, computer art, driver education, English, environmental science, European history, French, history, human development, improvisation, independent study, integrated mathematics, jazz ensemble, journalism, Mandarin, mathematics, music, music theory, peace and justice, physical education, physics, pre-calculus, programming, Quakerism and ethics, religion, science, social sciences, Spanish, studio art, theater, theater arts, theory of knowledge, U.S. history, Web site design, wellness, wind ensemble, world history.

Graduation Requirements Computer literacy, English, foreign language, history, mathematics, performing arts, Quakerism and ethics, science, social sciences, sports, 50 hours of community service (single organization) before senior year, Global Peace and Justice course, Visual and Performing Arts courses, Human Dynamics and Development course.

Special Academic Programs International Baccalaureate program; 2 Advanced Placement exams for which test preparation is offered; honors section; independent study; term-away projects; study abroad; academic accommodation for the gifted, the musically talented, and the artistically talented.

College Admission Counseling 69 students graduated in 2016; all went to college, including Boston University; Franklin & Marshall College; New York University; Penn State University Park; University of Delaware; University of Richmond. Median SAT critical reading: 600, median SAT math: 590, median SAT writing: 570, median combined SAT: 1795, median composite ACT: 26. 44% scored over 600 on SAT critical reading, 44% scored over 600 on SAT math, 36% scored over 600 on SAT writing, 49% scored over 1800 on combined SAT, 45% scored over 26 on composite ACT.

Student Life Upper grades have specified standards of dress, student council. Discipline rests primarily with faculty. Attendance at religious services is required.

Tuition and Aid Day student tuition: $27,000. Tuition installment plan (Tuition Management Systems (purchased Key Tuition Plan)). Need-based scholarship grants available. In 2016–17, 45% of upper-school students received aid. Total amount of financial aid awarded in 2016–17: $1,870,885.

Admissions Traditional secondary-level entrance grade is 9. For fall 2016, 74 students applied for upper-level admission, 32 were accepted, 20 enrolled. CTP, ERB or ISEE required. Deadline for receipt of application materials: none. Application fee required: $50. Interview required.

Athletics Interscholastic: baseball (boys), basketball (b,g), cross-country running (b,g), field hockey (g), football (b), lacrosse (b,g), soccer (b,g), swimming and diving (b,g), tennis (b,g), track and field (b,g), volleyball (g), wrestling (b); intramural: strength & conditioning (b,g); coed interscholastic: winter (indoor) track; coed intramural: aerobics. 3 PE instructors, 43 coaches, 1 athletic trainer.

Computers Computers are regularly used in art, English, French, library skills, literary magazine, mathematics, music, newspaper, science, social studies, Spanish, yearbook classes. Computer network features include on-campus library services, online commercial services, Internet access, wireless campus network, Internet filtering or blocking technology, 1:1 laptop program, Google Docs account, off-campus library services, online access to attendance, personalized Web site login for data driven Web site, open wireless network for personal devices, document storage, backup, and security. Campus intranet and computer access in designated common areas are available to students. Students grades are available online. The school has a published electronic and media policy.

Contact Ms. Melissa Brown, Director of Admissions and Financial Aid. 302-576-2932. Fax: 302-576-2939. E-mail: mbrown@wilmingtonfriends.org. Website: www.wilmingtonfriends.org/

WILSON HALL

520 Wilson Hall Road
Sumter, South Carolina 29150

Head of School: Mr. Frederick B. Moulton Sr.

General Information Coeducational day college-preparatory and arts school. Grades PS–12. Founded: 1966. Setting: small town. Nearest major city is Columbia. 17-acre campus. 6 buildings on campus. Approved or accredited by Southern Association of Colleges and Schools, Southern Association of Independent Schools, and South Carolina Department of Education. Endowment: $2 million. Total enrollment: 781. Upper school average class size: 18. Upper school faculty-student ratio: 1:13. There are 177 required school days per year for Upper School students. Upper School students typically attend 5 days per week. The average school day consists of 6 hours and 20 minutes.

Upper School Student Profile Grade 9: 50 students (30 boys, 20 girls); Grade 10: 66 students (26 boys, 40 girls); Grade 11: 65 students (32 boys, 33 girls); Grade 12: 64 students (32 boys, 32 girls).

Faculty School total: 83. In upper school: 15 men, 28 women; 23 have advanced degrees.

Subjects Offered 3-dimensional design, algebra, anatomy, biology-AP, calculus-AP, chemistry-AP, computer applications, computer programming, computer programming-AP, drawing, economics, English, English language-AP, English literature-AP, environmental science, European history-AP, French, French language-AP, government, government-AP, journalism, Latin, Latin-AP, Middle Eastern history, multimedia, music theory-AP, philosophy, physical education, physical science, physics-AP, pottery, sculpture, Spanish, Spanish language-AP, studio art-AP, trigonometry, U.S. history-AP, world history.

Graduation Requirements Arts and fine arts (art, music, dance, drama), computer science, English, foreign language, mathematics, physical education (includes health), science, social studies (includes history), acceptance into four-year college or university, 40 hours community service.

Special Academic Programs 17 Advanced Placement exams for which test preparation is offered; honors section.

College Admission Counseling 60 students graduated in 2016; all went to college, including Clemson University; College of Charleston; Furman University; The University of North Carolina at Chapel Hill; University of South Carolina; Wofford College. Mean SAT critical reading: 597, mean SAT math: 600, mean SAT writing: 605, mean combined SAT: 1802, mean composite ACT: 25.

Student Life Upper grades have specified standards of dress, honor system. Discipline rests primarily with faculty.

Summer Programs Remediation, enrichment, sports, art/fine arts, computer instruction programs offered; session focuses on enrichment; held on campus; accepts boys and girls; open to students from other schools. 250 students usually enrolled. 2017 schedule: June 1 to July 31. Application deadline: May 20.

Tuition and Aid Day student tuition: $4650–$6760. Tuition installment plan (monthly payment plans). Need-based scholarship grants available. In 2016–17, 4% of upper-school students received aid. Total amount of financial aid awarded in 2016–17: $150,000.

Admissions Traditional secondary-level entrance grade is 9. For fall 2016, 121 students applied for upper-level admission, 113 were accepted, 113 enrolled. ACT, CTBS, OLSAT, Iowa Tests of Basic Skills, PSAT and SAT for applicants to grade 11 and 12, school's own test or Stanford Achievement Test, Otis-Lennon School Ability Test required. Deadline for receipt of application materials: none. Application fee required: $150. Interview required.

Athletics Interscholastic: baseball (boys), basketball (b,g), bowling (b,g), cheering (g), cross-country running (b,g), fishing (b), football (b), golf (b,g), marksmanship (b), Nautilus (b,g), riflery (b), running (b,g), skeet shooting (b), softball (g), strength & conditioning (b,g), swimming and diving (b,g), tennis (b,g), track and field (b,g), trap and skeet (b), volleyball (g), wrestling (b); intramural: table tennis (b), weight lifting (b,g), weight training (b,g); coed interscholastic: climbing, equestrian sports, outdoor adventure, outdoor education, paint ball, riflery, skeet shooting, soccer; coed intramural: archery, outdoor adventure, rafting, rock climbing, ropes courses, table tennis. 4 PE instructors, 13 coaches.

Computers Computers are regularly used in computer applications, English, journalism, literary magazine, technology, yearbook classes. Computer network features include on-campus library services, online commercial services, Internet access, wireless campus network, Internet filtering or blocking technology. Students grades are available online. The school has a published electronic and media policy.

Contact Mr. Sean Hoskins, Director of Admissions and Public Relations. 803-469-3475 Ext. 107. Fax: 803-469-3477. E-mail: sean_hoskins@hotmail.com. Website: www.wilsonhall.org

THE WINCHENDON SCHOOL

172 Ash Street
Winchendon, Massachusetts 01475

Head of School: John Kerney

General Information Coeducational boarding and day college-preparatory school; primarily serves students with learning disabilities, individuals with Attention Deficit Disorder, and dyslexic students. Grades 9–PG. Founded: 1926. Setting: small town. Nearest major city is Boston. Students are housed in single-sex dormitories. 375-acre campus. 28 buildings on campus. Approved or accredited by Association of Independent Schools in New England, New England Association of Schools and Colleges, and The Association of Boarding Schools. Member of National Association of Independent Schools and Secondary School Admission Test Board. Languages of instruction: English, French, and Spanish. Endowment: $25 million. Total enrollment: 255. Upper school average class size: 8. Upper school faculty-student ratio: 1:8. The average school day consists of 7 hours.

Upper School Student Profile Grade 9: 26 students (11 boys, 15 girls); Grade 10: 59 students (36 boys, 23 girls); Grade 11: 71 students (51 boys, 20 girls); Grade 12: 70 students (48 boys, 22 girls); Postgraduate: 5 students (5 boys). 78% of students are boarding students. 30% are state residents. 21 states are represented in upper school student body. 50% are international students.

Faculty School total: 42. In upper school: 20 men, 22 women; 12 have advanced degrees; 34 reside on campus.

Subjects Offered Algebra, American history, American literature, anatomy, art, biology, calculus, ceramics, chemistry, computer programming, computer science, creative writing, drama, driver education, earth science, ecology, English, English literature, environmental science, ESL, European history, expository writing, French, geography, geometry, government/civics, grammar, health, history, mathematics, physical education, physics, physiology, psychology, science, social sciences, social studies, Spanish, speech, trigonometry, typing, world history, writing.

Graduation Requirements College admission preparation, computer science, English, experiential education, humanities, interdisciplinary studies, leadership and service, mathematics, physical education (includes health), science, social sciences, social studies (includes history).

Special Academic Programs Advanced Placement exam preparation; academic accommodation for the gifted; remedial reading and/or remedial writing; remedial math; programs in English, mathematics for dyslexic students; special instructional classes for students with learning disabilities and Attention Deficit Disorder; ESL (100 students enrolled).

College Admission Counseling 67 students graduated in 2016; 61 went to college, including Bentley University; Boston University; Curry College; Northeastern University; Penn State University Park; University of Massachusetts Amherst. Other: 1 entered military service, 5 entered a postgraduate year, 1 had other specific plans. Median SAT critical reading: 510, median SAT math: 550. 3% scored over 600 on SAT critical reading, 5% scored over 600 on SAT math.

Student Life Upper grades have specified standards of dress, student council. Discipline rests primarily with faculty.

Summer Programs Remediation, enrichment, advancement, ESL, sports, art/fine arts, rigorous outdoor training, computer instruction programs offered; session focuses on structured learning experience; held on campus; accepts boys and girls; open to students from other schools. 35 students usually enrolled. 2017 schedule: July 3 to August 11.

Tuition and Aid Day student tuition: $33,200; 7-day tuition and room/board: $58,500. Tuition installment plan (SMART Tuition Payment Plan). Need-based scholarship grants available. In 2016–17, 37% of upper-school students received aid. Total amount of financial aid awarded in 2016–17: $2,000,000.

Admissions Traditional secondary-level entrance grade is 9. For fall 2016, 615 students applied for upper-level admission, 250 were accepted, 72 enrolled. Deadline for receipt of application materials: none. Application fee required: $50. On-campus interview recommended.

Athletics Interscholastic: baseball (boys), basketball (b,g), ice hockey (b), lacrosse (b), soccer (b), tennis (b,g), volleyball (b,g); intramural: aerobics/dance (g), basketball (b,g), dance (g), ice skating (b,g), winter soccer (b); coed interscholastic: alpine skiing, bicycling, cross-country running, golf, running; coed intramural: aerobics, aerobics/Nautilus, alpine skiing, bicycling, cross-country running, equestrian sports, fitness, fitness walking, floor hockey, freestyle skiing, golf, horseback riding, in-line skating, indoor soccer, jogging, mountain biking, Nautilus, nordic skiing, outdoor activities, outdoor adventure, outdoor recreation, physical fitness, power lifting, running, skiing (cross-country), skiing (downhill), snowboarding, snowshoeing, strength & conditioning, swimming and diving, tennis, ultimate Frisbee, volleyball, walking, weight lifting, weight training, winter walking.

Computers Computer network features include on-campus library services, Internet access, wireless campus network, Internet filtering or blocking technology. Campus intranet and student e-mail accounts are available to students.

Contact Lesley Nesbitt, Director of Admissions & Financial Aid. 978-297-4476. Fax: 978-297-0352. E-mail: admissions@winchendon.org. Website: www.winchendon.org

WINCHESTER THURSTON SCHOOL

555 Morewood Avenue
Pittsburgh, Pennsylvania 15213-2899

Head of School: Mr. Gary J. Niels

General Information Coeducational day college-preparatory school. Grades PK–12. Founded: 1887. Setting: urban. 5-acre campus. 2 buildings on campus. Approved or accredited by Pennsylvania Association of Independent Schools, The College Board, and Pennsylvania Department of Education. Member of National Association of Independent Schools and Secondary School Admission Test Board. Endowment: $17 million. Total enrollment: 670. Upper school average class size: 15. Upper school faculty-student ratio: 1:8. There are 175 required school days per year for Upper School students. Upper School students typically attend 5 days per week. The average school day consists of 6 hours and 55 minutes.

Upper School Student Profile Grade 9: 59 students (33 boys, 26 girls); Grade 10: 62 students (34 boys, 28 girls); Grade 11: 65 students (29 boys, 36 girls); Grade 12: 56 students (29 boys, 27 girls).

Faculty School total: 91. In upper school: 16 men, 16 women; 20 have advanced degrees.

Subjects Offered Acting, advanced computer applications, Advanced Placement courses, algebra, American history, American history-AP, American literature, animal behavior, art, art history, art history-AP, biology, biology-AP, calculus, calculus-AP, ceramics, chemistry, Chinese, choir, chorus, classics, composition-AP, computer programming, computer science, computer science-AP, creative writing, dance, drama, drawing, economics, economics-AP, English, English literature, English literature-AP, English-AP, European history, European history-AP, expository writing, filmmaking, French, French-AP, geometry, government/civics, health, history, journalism, Latin, Latin-AP, linear algebra, mathematics, music, music theory, philosophy, photography, physical education, physics, physics-AP, pre-calculus, psychology, psychology-AP, SAT preparation, science, social studies, Spanish, Spanish-AP, speech, statistics-AP, visual arts, world history, world literature, writing, yearbook.

Graduation Requirements Arts and fine arts (art, music, dance, drama), computer science, computer skills, English, foreign language, mathematics, physical education (includes health), science, social studies (includes history), speech, City As Our Campus coursework, a unique program which connects our students with various educational opportunities within the city of Pittsburgh, (examples of these opportunities include courses taught collaboratively with over 100 area organizations).

Special Academic Programs Advanced Placement exam preparation; independent study; term-away projects; study at local college for college credit; study abroad; academic accommodation for the gifted, the musically talented, and the artistically talented; ESL (5 students enrolled).

College Admission Counseling 55 students graduated in 2016; all went to college, including New York University; Rochester Institute of Technology; Swarthmore College; Tulane University; University of Pennsylvania; University of Pittsburgh. Mean SAT critical reading: 627, mean SAT math: 620, mean SAT writing: 613, mean combined SAT: 1860, mean composite ACT: 26. 76% scored over 600 on SAT critical reading, 73% scored over 600 on SAT math, 67% scored over 600 on SAT writing.

Student Life Upper grades have specified standards of dress, student council. Discipline rests primarily with faculty.

Summer Programs Enrichment, sports, art/fine arts programs offered; session focuses on adventure and play, sports and physical fitness, creative arts, and academics; held on campus; accepts boys and girls; open to students from other schools. 500 students usually enrolled. 2017 schedule: June 19 to August 4. Application deadline: May 20.

Tuition and Aid Day student tuition: $26,500–$28,500. Tuition installment plan (monthly payment plans). Need-based scholarship grants available. In 2016–17, 33% of upper-school students received aid. Total amount of financial aid awarded in 2016–17: $1,750,000.

Admissions Traditional secondary-level entrance grade is 9. For fall 2016, 87 students applied for upper-level admission, 57 were accepted, 36 enrolled. ISEE, SSAT, TOEFL or TOEFL Junior required. Deadline for receipt of application materials: December 15. Application fee required: $50. Interview recommended.

Athletics Interscholastic: basketball (boys, girls), cross-country running (b,g), drill team (g), field hockey (g), lacrosse (b,g), rowing (b,g), running (b,g), soccer (b,g), tennis (b,g); intramural: squash (b); coed interscholastic: crew, fencing, golf, squash, track and field; coed intramural: basketball, dance, Frisbee, independent competitive sports, outdoor activities, physical fitness, physical training, strength & conditioning, ultimate Frisbee, weight training, winter soccer, yoga. 4 PE instructors, 24 coaches, 1 athletic trainer.

Computers Computers are regularly used in all academic, animation, art, college planning, computer applications, creative writing, English, foreign language, history, library, mathematics, music, photography, science, senior seminar, social studies, writing, writing, yearbook classes. Computer network features include on-campus library services, online commercial services, Internet access, wireless campus network, Internet filtering or blocking technology. Campus intranet, student e-mail accounts, and computer access in designated common areas are available to students. Students grades are available online. The school has a published electronic and media policy.

Contact Mr. Scot Lorenzi, Director of Upper School Admission. 412-578-3738. Fax: 412-578-7504. E-mail: lorenzis@winchesterthurston.org.
Website: www.winchesterthurston.org

WINDERMERE PREPARATORY SCHOOL

6189 Winter Garden-Vineland Road
Windermere, Florida 34786

Head of School: Thomas L. Marcy, EdD

General Information Boys' boarding and coeducational day college-preparatory and arts school. Boarding boys grades 9–12, day boys grades PK–12, day girls grades PK–12. Founded: 2000. Setting: suburban. Nearest major city is Orlando. Students are housed in single-sex dormitories. 48-acre campus. 3 buildings on campus. Approved or accredited by International Baccalaureate Organization, Southern Association of Colleges and Schools, Southern Association of Independent Schools, and Florida Department of Education. Upper school average class size: 18. Upper school faculty-student ratio: 1:14. There are 180 required school days per year for Upper School students. Upper School students typically attend 5 days per week. The average school day consists of 7 hours and 45 minutes.

Upper School Student Profile Grade 6: 88 students (43 boys, 45 girls); Grade 7: 87 students (42 boys, 45 girls); Grade 8: 78 students (44 boys, 34 girls); Grade 9: 118 students (66 boys, 52 girls); Grade 10: 116 students (57 boys, 59 girls); Grade 11: 105 students (66 boys, 39 girls); Grade 12: 123 students (68 boys, 55 girls). 19% of students are boarding students. 80% are state residents. 20% are international students. International students from Brazil, China, India, United Kingdom, Venezuela, and Viet Nam; 57 other countries represented in student body.

Faculty School total: 200. In upper school: 16 men, 23 women; 22 have advanced degrees; 1 resides on campus.

Subjects Offered 20th century history, 3-dimensional art, 3-dimensional design, acting, advanced biology, advanced chemistry, advanced math, Advanced Placement courses, advanced TOEFL/grammar, algebra, American government, American history, American literature, anatomy and physiology, art, band, biology, business, calculus, ceramics, chemistry, Chinese, choir, chorus, creative writing, dance, dance performance, digital art, digital imaging, drama, drama performance, economics, electives, English, English composition, English literature, entrepreneurship, environmental science, ESL, film, French, French as a second language, geometry, graphic design, honors algebra, honors English, honors U.S. history, honors world history, International Baccalaureate courses, jazz ensemble, Latin, life skills, marine science, music, music theory, personal fitness, physical education, physical fitness, physics, piano, pre-calculus, psychology, public speaking, social sciences, Spanish, speech and debate, sports medicine, theory of knowledge, U.S. history, weight training, wind ensemble, world history, world literature, writing, yearbook.

Graduation Requirements Arts and fine arts (art, music, dance, drama), biology, chemistry, electives, English, foreign language, mathematics, performing arts, physical fitness, science, social sciences, U.S. history, 26 credits are required for graduation. This is 2 credits higher than, the State of Florida graduation requirement. Community service is required.

Special Academic Programs International Baccalaureate program; 2 Advanced Placement exams for which test preparation is offered; honors section; independent study; study abroad; academic accommodation for the musically talented and the artistically talented; ESL (22 students enrolled).

College Admission Counseling 132 students graduated in 2015; all went to college, including Florida State University; Penn State University Park; Rollins College; University of Central Florida; University of Florida. Mean SAT critical reading: 536, mean SAT math: 573, mean SAT writing: 536, mean combined SAT: 1645, mean composite ACT: 24.

Student Life Upper grades have uniform requirement, student council, honor system. Discipline rests primarily with faculty.

Tuition and Aid Day student tuition: $18,950; 7-day tuition and room/board: $54,500. Tuition installment plan (monthly payment plans). Merit scholarship grants, need-based scholarship grants available. In 2015–16, 8% of upper-school students received aid; total upper-school merit-scholarship money awarded: $175,000. Total amount of financial aid awarded in 2015–16: $425,000.

Admissions Traditional secondary-level entrance grade is 9. For fall 2015, 153 students applied for upper-level admission, 110 were accepted, 76 enrolled. ERB (grade level), ISEE, school placement exam or TOEFL required. Deadline for receipt of application materials: none. Application fee required: $85. Interview recommended.

Athletics Interscholastic: baseball (boys), basketball (b,g), cheering (g), dance (g), football (b), golf (b,g), lacrosse (b,g), physical training (b,g), soccer (b,g), softball (g), strength & conditioning (b,g), swimming and diving (b,g), tennis (b,g), track and field (b,g), volleyball (g), weight lifting (b,g), weight training (b,g); coed interscholastic: aerobics/dance, aquatics, archery, crew, cross-country running, dance, dance team, track and field; coed intramural: flag football, golf. 9 PE instructors, 48 coaches, 1 athletic trainer.

Computers Computers are regularly used in all academic classes. Computer network features include on-campus library services, online commercial services, Internet access, wireless campus network, Internet filtering or blocking technology. Campus intranet and student e-mail accounts are available to students. Students grades are available online. The school has a published electronic and media policy.

Contact Mrs. Laura Lykins, Director of Admissions. 407-905-7737 Ext. 3228. Fax: 407-905-7710. E-mail: laura.lykins@windermereprep.com. Website: www.windermereprep.com

WINDERMERE SCHOOL

Browhead
Windermere LA23 1NW, United Kingdom

Head of School: Mr. Ian Lavender

General Information Coeducational boarding and day college-preparatory and water sports, outdoor education school. Grades 7–13. Founded: 1863. Setting: rural. Nearest major city is Manchester, United Kingdom. Students are housed in student apartments. 80 acre campus. 20 buildings on campus. Approved or accredited by Boarding Schools Association (UK), Department for Education and Skills (UK), Department of Education and Employment, United Kingdom, Headmasters' Conference, and Independent Schools Council (UK). Affiliate member of National Association of Independent Schools; member of European Council of International Schools. Language of instruction: English. Endowment: £4 million. Total enrollment: 375. Upper school average class size: 14. Upper school faculty-student ratio: 1:8. The average school day consists of 6 hours and 30 minutes.

Upper School Student Profile Grade 7: 36 students (15 boys, 21 girls); Grade 8: 34 students (15 boys, 19 girls); Grade 9: 37 students (10 boys, 27 girls); Grade 10: 37 students (19 boys, 18 girls); Grade 11: 35 students (7 boys, 28 girls); Grade 12: 25 students (6 boys, 19 girls); Grade 13: 28 students (8 boys, 20 girls). 50% of students are boarding students. 50% are state residents. 50% are international students. International students from Germany, Spain, and United Kingdom; 70 other countries represented in student body.

Faculty School total: 66. In upper school: 10 men, 31 women; 5 have advanced degrees; 12 reside on campus.

Subjects Offered Art, biology, ceramics, chemistry, computer programming, dance, drama, English, English literature, fabric arts, French, geography, German, government/civics, history, home economics, information technology, Latin, mathematics, music, physical education, physics, psychology, religion, science, Spanish, speech, theater.

Special Academic Programs Term-away projects; domestic exchange program (with The Athenian School, Bishop's College School, Sedbergh School); study abroad; academic accommodation for the gifted, the musically talented, and the artistically talented; remedial reading and/or remedial writing; remedial math; programs in English for dyslexic students; special instructional classes for deaf students; ESL (10 students enrolled).

College Admission Counseling 29 students graduated in 2016; all went to college. Other: 26 entered a postgraduate year.

Student Life Upper grades have uniform requirement, student council. Discipline rests equally with students and faculty.

Summer Programs Enrichment, sports, art/fine arts, rigorous outdoor training programs offered; session focuses on English and Outdoor education; held both on and off campus; accepts boys and girls; open to students from other schools. 140 students usually enrolled. 2017 schedule: July 1 to August 30. Application deadline: April 1.

Tuition and Aid Day student tuition: £6648–£7347; 5-day tuition and room/board: £11,898–£12,597; 7-day tuition and room/board: £12,597–£13,296. Tuition installment plan (monthly payment plans, individually arranged payment plans). Tuition reduction for siblings, bursaries, merit scholarship grants available.

Admissions Traditional secondary-level entrance grade is 7. Admissions testing and school's own exam required. Deadline for receipt of application materials: none. Application fee required: £50. Interview required.

Athletics Interscholastic: ballet (girls), football (b,g), netball (g), sailing (g), soccer (b,g); intramural: ballet (g), basketball (g), martial arts (g), netball (g), riflery (g), sailing (g), skiing (downhill) (g), soccer (g), softball (g), squash (g); coed interscholastic: aerobics, aerobics/dance, aquatics, artistic gym, backpacking, ball hockey, basketball, canoeing/kayaking, climbing, cricket, cross-country running, dance, equestrian sports, field hockey, fitness, football, golf, gymnastics, hiking/backpacking, hockey, horseback riding, kayaking, martial arts, modern dance, mountaineering, outdoor adventure, outdoor education, outdoor recreation, physical training, rafting, rock climbing, roller blading, rounders, sailboarding, skiing (downhill), soccer, speleology, squash, swimming and diving, table tennis, tennis, track and field, walking, wall climbing, windsurfing, winter soccer, winter walking. 5 PE instructors, 3 coaches.

Computers Computers are regularly used in all classes. Computer network features include Internet access, wireless campus network, Internet filtering or blocking technology. Student e-mail accounts are available to students. The school has a published electronic and media policy.

Contact Mrs. Rachel Akister, Registrar. 44-153-944-6164. Fax: 44-153-948-8414. E-mail: admissions@windermerschool.co.uk. Website: www.windermereschool.co.uk/

THE WINDSOR SCHOOL

37-02 Main St. / 3rd Floor
Flushing, New York 11354

Head of School: Mr. James Seery

General Information Coeducational day college-preparatory and ESL school. Grades 6–PG. Founded: 1969. Setting: urban. Nearest major city is New York. Students are housed in Homestay. 1 building on campus. Approved or accredited by Middle States Association of Colleges and Schools, New York Department of Education, New York State Board of Regents, The College Board, and New York Department of Education. Total enrollment: 110. Upper school average class size: 14. Upper school faculty-student ratio: 1:14. There are 185 required school days per year for Upper School students. Upper School students typically attend 5 days per week. The average school day consists of 6 hours and 5 minutes.

Upper School Student Profile Grade 8: 10 students (4 boys, 6 girls); Grade 9: 12 students (7 boys, 5 girls); Grade 10: 23 students (10 boys, 13 girls); Grade 11: 32 students (18 boys, 14 girls); Grade 12: 33 students (16 boys, 17 girls).

Faculty School total: 12. In upper school: 6 men, 6 women; 10 have advanced degrees.

Subjects Offered Advanced Placement courses, algebra, American history, American literature, art, basic skills, biology, business, calculus, chemistry, computer skills, creative writing, economics, English, English literature, environmental science, ESL, European history, fine arts, geometry, government/civics, grammar, health, marketing, mathematics, music, physical education, physics, pre-calculus, psychology, science, social sciences, social studies, Spanish, trigonometry, world affairs, world history.

Graduation Requirements Arts and fine arts (art, music, dance, drama), English, foreign language, health education, mathematics, physical education (includes health), science, social studies (includes history).

Special Academic Programs Advanced Placement exam preparation; honors section; accelerated programs; independent study; academic accommodation for the gifted, the musically talented, and the artistically talented; remedial reading and/or remedial writing; remedial math; ESL (27 students enrolled).

College Admission Counseling 34 students graduated in 2016; all went to college, including City College of the City University of New York; Michigan State University; Pace University; St. John's University; Stony Brook University, State University of New York. Median SAT critical reading: 440, median SAT math: 550, median SAT writing: 460. 10% scored over 600 on SAT critical reading, 35% scored over 600 on SAT math, 10% scored over 600 on SAT writing.

Student Life Upper grades have specified standards of dress, student council. Discipline rests primarily with faculty.

Summer Programs Remediation, enrichment, advancement, ESL programs offered; session focuses on advancement, enrichment, remediation; held on campus; accepts boys and girls; open to students from other schools. 450 students usually enrolled. 2017 schedule: July 1 to August 18. Application deadline: June 30.

Tuition and Aid Day student tuition: $26,000. Tuition installment plan (individually arranged payment plans). Tuition reduction for siblings available. In 2016–17, 5% of upper-school students received aid. Total amount of financial aid awarded in 2016–17: $20,000.

Admissions Traditional secondary-level entrance grade is 10. Traditional secondary-level entrance age is 14. For fall 2016, 80 students applied for upper-level admission, 76 were accepted, 73 enrolled. Achievement tests and school's own exam required. Deadline for receipt of application materials: none. No application fee required. On-campus interview recommended.

Athletics Interscholastic: basketball (boys, girls), soccer (b,g), table tennis (b,g), track and field (b,g); intramural: basketball (b,g), cooperative games (b,g), fitness (b,g), jump rope (g), physical fitness (b,g), soccer (b,g), strength & conditioning (b,g), table tennis (b,g), tennis (b,g), volleyball (b,g), yoga (b,g); coed interscholastic: basketball, soccer, table tennis, track and field; coed intramural: basketball, fitness, jump rope, physical fitness, soccer, strength & conditioning, table tennis, tennis, volleyball, yoga. 2 PE instructors, 2 coaches.

Computers Computers are regularly used in art, mathematics, research skills, yearbook classes. Computer network features include Internet access, Internet filtering or blocking technology. Campus intranet and computer access in designated common areas are available to students. The school has a published electronic and media policy.

Contact Ms. Emily Yu, Director of Admissions. 718-359-8300. Fax: 718-359-1876. E-mail: admin@thewindsorschool.com. Website: www.windsorschool.com

WINDWARD SCHOOL

11350 Palms Boulevard
Los Angeles, California 90066

Head of School: Tom Gilder

General Information Coeducational day college-preparatory school. Grades 7–12. Founded: 1971. Setting: urban. 9-acre campus. 11 buildings on campus. Approved or accredited by California Association of Independent Schools and Western Association of Schools and Colleges. Member of National Association of Independent Schools. Total enrollment: 541. Upper school average class size: 16. Upper school faculty-student ratio: 1:7. There are 165 required school days per year for Upper School students. Upper School students typically attend 5 days per week. The average school day consists of 7 hours.

Upper School Student Profile Grade 9: 94 students (47 boys, 47 girls); Grade 10: 93 students (46 boys, 47 girls); Grade 11: 93 students (46 boys, 47 girls); Grade 12: 93 students (46 boys, 47 girls).

Faculty School total: 65. In upper school: 32 men, 27 women; 37 have advanced degrees.

Subjects Offered 3-dimensional art, acting, advanced biology, advanced chemistry, Advanced Placement courses, algebra, American history, American literature, art, art history, ballet, biology, calculus, ceramics, chemistry, Chinese, chorus, computer science, creative writing, dance, drama, English, English literature, environmental science, European history, fine arts, French, geometry, government/civics, health, history, journalism, Latin, marine biology, mathematics, music, performing arts, photography, photojournalism, physical education, physiology, robotics, science, senior internship, social studies, Spanish, theater, trigonometry, world history.

Graduation Requirements Arts and fine arts (art, music, dance, drama), English, foreign language, mathematics, physical education (includes health), science, social studies (includes history).

Special Academic Programs 16 Advanced Placement exams for which test preparation is offered; honors section; independent study; study at local college for college credit.

College Admission Counseling 93 students graduated in 2016; all went to college, including New York University; Tufts University; University of California, Los Angeles; University of Southern California; Wesleyan University; Williams College. 98% scored over 26 on composite ACT.

Student Life Upper grades have specified standards of dress, student council, honor system. Discipline rests primarily with faculty.

Summer Programs Sports, art/fine arts, computer instruction programs offered; session focuses on skill development and team play; held on campus; accepts boys and girls; open to students from other schools. 550 students usually enrolled. 2017 schedule: June 18 to August 19. Application deadline: August 2.

Tuition and Aid Day student tuition: $34,215. Tuition installment plan (Key Tuition Payment Plan, monthly payment plans). Need-based scholarship grants, need-based loans available. In 2016–17, 17% of upper-school students received aid. Total amount of financial aid awarded in 2016–17: $1,980,066.

Admissions Traditional secondary-level entrance grade is 9. For fall 2016, 177 students applied for upper-level admission, 30 were accepted, 23 enrolled. ISEE required. Deadline for receipt of application materials: December 8. Application fee required: $150. On-campus interview required.

Athletics Interscholastic: baseball (boys), basketball (b,g), football (b); coed interscholastic: cross-country running, flag football. 5 PE instructors, 15 coaches, 2 athletic trainers.

Computers Computers are regularly used in art, English, history, mathematics, science classes. Computer network features include on-campus library services, online commercial services, Internet access, wireless campus network, Internet filtering or blocking technology. Student e-mail accounts and computer access in designated common areas are available to students. Students grades are available online. The school has a published electronic and media policy.

Contact Sharon Pearline, Director of Admissions. 424-2891010. Fax: 310-397-5655. Website: www.windwardschool.org

WINSTON PREPARATORY SCHOOL

New York, New York
See Special Needs Schools section.

THE WINSTON SCHOOL

Dallas, Texas
See Special Needs Schools section.

THE WINSTON SCHOOL SAN ANTONIO

San Antonio, Texas
See Special Needs Schools section.

WOODBERRY FOREST SCHOOL

10 Woodberry Station
Woodberry Forest, Virginia 22989

Head of School: Dr. Byron C. Hulsey

General Information Boys' boarding college-preparatory and liberal arts school. Grades 9–12. Founded: 1889. Setting: rural. Nearest major city is Charlottesville. Students are housed in single-sex dormitories. 1,200-acre campus. 38 buildings on campus. Approved or accredited by Southern Association of Colleges and Schools, Southern Association of Independent Schools, The Association of Boarding Schools, Virginia Association of Independent Schools, and Virginia Department of Education. Member of National Association of Independent Schools and Secondary School Admission Test Board. Endowment: $31.5 million. Total enrollment: 393. Upper school average class size: 10. Upper school faculty-student ratio: 1:6. There are 180 required school days per year for Upper School students. Upper School students typically attend 6 days per week. The average school day consists of 7 hours.

Upper School Student Profile Grade 9: 84 students (84 boys); Grade 10: 109 students (109 boys); Grade 11: 102 students (102 boys); Grade 12: 104 students (104 boys). 100% of students are boarding students. 30% are state residents. 27 states are represented in upper school student body. 10% are international students. International students from Canada, China, Germany, Republic of Korea, South Africa, and Viet Nam; 13 other countries represented in student body.

Faculty School total: 69. In upper school: 63 men, 8 women; 40 have advanced degrees; 62 reside on campus.

Subjects Offered Algebra, American history, American literature, art, art history, biology, calculus, chemistry, Chinese, community service, computer math, computer science, creative writing, drama, economics, English, English literature, environmental science, European history, expository writing, fine arts, French, geology, geometry, German, government/civics, health, Latin, mathematics, music, photography, physics, psychology, religion, science, social studies, Spanish, speech, theater, trigonometry, world history, world literature.

Graduation Requirements Arts and fine arts (art, music, dance, drama), English, foreign language, mathematics, physical education (includes health), religion (includes Bible studies and theology), science, social studies (includes history). Community service is required.

Special Academic Programs Advanced Placement exam preparation; honors section; independent study; study abroad; academic accommodation for the gifted, the musically talented, and the artistically talented.

College Admission Counseling 94 students graduated in 2016; all went to college, including The University of Alabama; The University of North Carolina at Chapel Hill; University of Mississippi; University of South Carolina; University of Virginia; Washington and Lee University. Mean SAT critical reading: 602, mean SAT math: 620, mean SAT writing: 597, mean combined SAT: 1819, mean composite ACT: 27.

Student Life Upper grades have specified standards of dress, student council, honor system. Discipline rests equally with students and faculty.

Tuition and Aid 7-day tuition and room/board: $53,500. Tuition installment plan (monthly payment plans). Need-based scholarship grants, need-based loans available. In 2016–17, 41% of upper-school students received aid. Total amount of financial aid awarded in 2016–17: $5,688,400.

Admissions Traditional secondary-level entrance grade is 9. For fall 2016, 432 students applied for upper-level admission, 182 were accepted, 122 enrolled. SSAT required. Deadline for receipt of application materials: January 15. Application fee required: $50. Interview recommended.

Athletics Interscholastic: baseball, basketball, cross-country running, diving, football, golf, indoor track, indoor track & field, lacrosse, running, skeet shooting, soccer, squash, swimming and diving, tennis, track and field, winter (indoor) track, wrestling; intramural: archery, backpacking, basketball, bicycling, billiards, boxing, canoeing/kayaking, climbing, combined training, cross-country running, fencing, fishing, fitness, fitness walking, flag football, golf, hiking/backpacking, jump rope, kayaking, lacrosse, mountaineering, outdoor activities, outdoor adventure, outdoor education, outdoor recreation, outdoor skills, outdoors, paint ball, physical fitness, physical training, power lifting, riflery, ropes courses, running, skeet shooting, skiing (cross-country), skiing (downhill), softball, squash, strength & conditioning, swimming and diving, tennis, track and field, trap and skeet, walking, wall climbing, weight lifting, weight training, wilderness, wilderness survival, winter walking. 1 athletic trainer.

Computers Computers are regularly used in art, English, foreign language, history, mathematics, science classes. Computer network features include on-campus library services, online commercial services, Internet access, Internet filtering or blocking technology. Student e-mail accounts and computer access are available to students. Students grades are available online. The school has a published electronic and media policy.

Contact Mr. Scott Schamberger, Assistant Headmaster for Admissions and College Counseling. 540-672-6023. Fax: 540-672-6471. E-mail: scott_schamberger@woodberry.org. Website: www.woodberry.org

THE WOODHALL SCHOOL

PO Box 550
58 Harrison Lane
Bethlehem, Connecticut 06751

Head of School: Matthew C. Woodhall

General Information Boys' boarding and day college-preparatory school. Grades 9–12. Founded: 1983. Setting: rural. Nearest major city is Waterbury. Students are housed in single-sex dormitories. 38-acre campus. 5 buildings on campus. Approved or accredited by Association of Independent Schools in New England, Connecticut Association of Independent Schools, New England Association of Schools and Colleges, and Connecticut Department of Education. Member of National Association of Independent Schools. Endowment: $450,000. Total enrollment: 42. Upper school average class size: 4. Upper school faculty-student ratio: 1:3. There are 184 required school days per year for Upper School students. Upper School students typically attend 6 days per week. The average school day consists of 6 hours.

Upper School Student Profile Grade 9: 8 students (8 boys); Grade 10: 6 students (6 boys); Grade 11: 11 students (11 boys); Grade 12: 12 students (12 boys). 100% of students are boarding students. 7% are state residents. 18 states are represented in upper school student body. 4% are international students. International students from Brazil, Canada, China, and United Kingdom.

Faculty School total: 15. In upper school: 14 men, 2 women; all have advanced degrees; 13 reside on campus.

Subjects Offered Algebra, American history, anatomy, art, biology, calculus, chemistry, comparative government and politics, creative writing, drama, English, environmental science, geometry, Greek, language and composition, Latin, physics, pre-calculus, Spanish, world civilizations.

Graduation Requirements Arts and fine arts (art, music, dance, drama), communication skills, English, foreign language, mathematics, physical education (includes health), science, social studies (includes history).

Special Academic Programs 6 Advanced Placement exams for which test preparation is offered; independent study; special instructional classes for We suport students with attention deficit disorder and non-verbal learning disabilities.

College Admission Counseling 9 students graduated in 2016; 7 went to college, including Champlain College; Curry College; Embry-Riddle Aeronautical University–Daytona; Goucher College; Manhattanville College; Rensselaer Polytechnic Institute. Other: 2 entered a postgraduate year. Median SAT critical reading: 560, median SAT math: 615, median SAT writing: 565, median combined SAT: 1695, median composite ACT: 26. 50% scored over 600 on SAT critical reading, 60% scored over 600 on SAT math, 30% scored over 600 on SAT writing, 40% scored over 1800 on combined SAT, 60% scored over 26 on composite ACT.

Student Life Upper grades have specified standards of dress, student council, honor system. Discipline rests primarily with faculty.

Tuition and Aid Day student tuition: $48,750; 7-day tuition and room/board: $65,000. Tuition installment plan (individually arranged payment plans).

Admissions Traditional secondary-level entrance grade is 10. For fall 2016, 51 students applied for upper-level admission, 14 were accepted, 14 enrolled. Deadline for receipt of application materials: none. Application fee required: $100. On-campus interview recommended.

Athletics Interscholastic: basketball, cross-country running, lacrosse, soccer, wrestling; intramural: basketball, canoeing/kayaking, cross-country running, fishing, fitness, fitness walking, hiking/backpacking, ice hockey, jogging, kayaking, lacrosse, outdoor activities, outdoor education, outdoor recreation, physical fitness, physical training, rafting, running, skiing (cross-country), soccer, strength & conditioning, ultimate Frisbee, volleyball, walking, wall climbing, weight lifting, winter walking, wrestling, yoga. 10 coaches, 2 athletic trainers.

Computers Computers are regularly used in art, English, foreign language, history, mathematics, science, social sciences classes. Computer network features include Internet access, wireless campus network, Internet filtering or blocking technology. Computer access in designated common areas is available to students. The school has a published electronic and media policy.

Contact Matthew C. Woodhall, Head of School. 203-266-7788. Fax: 203-266-5896. E-mail: mwoodhall@woodhallschool.org. Website: www.woodhallschool.org

THE WOODLANDS CHRISTIAN ACADEMY

5800 Academy Way
The Woodlands, Texas 77384

Head of School: Mrs. Julie H. Ambler

General Information Coeducational day college-preparatory, arts, religious studies, and technology school, affiliated with Christian faith. Grades PK–12. Founded: 1993. Setting: suburban. Nearest major city is Houston. 40-acre campus. 6 buildings on campus. Approved or accredited by Association of Christian Schools International, Southern Association of Colleges and Schools, and Texas Department of Education. Member of Secondary School Admission Test Board. Endowment: $100,000. Total enrollment: 579. Upper school average class size: 17. There are 177 required school days per year for Upper School students. Upper School students typically attend 5 days per week. The average school day consists of 7 hours and 30 minutes.

Upper School Student Profile Grade 6: 51 students (25 boys, 26 girls); Grade 7: 45 students (23 boys, 22 girls); Grade 8: 35 students (19 boys, 16 girls); Grade 9: 49 students (25 boys, 24 girls); Grade 10: 46 students (29 boys, 17 girls); Grade 11: 49 students (28 boys, 21 girls); Grade 12: 43 students (23 boys, 20 girls). 100% of students are Christian faith.

Faculty In upper school: 8 men, 16 women; 11 have advanced degrees.

Subjects Offered ACT preparation, Advanced Placement courses, art education, athletics, band, Bible, choir, computer applications, foreign language, theater arts.

Special Academic Programs Advanced Placement exam preparation; honors section; study at local college for college credit.

College Admission Counseling 36 students graduated in 2016; all went to college, including Baylor University; Oklahoma State University; Texas A&M University; Texas Christian University; Texas Tech University; Wheaton College. 50% scored over 26 on composite ACT.

Student Life Upper grades have uniform requirement, student council, honor system. Discipline rests primarily with faculty. Attendance at religious services is required.

Tuition and Aid Day student tuition: $16,995–$20,945. Tuition installment plan (Insured Tuition Payment Plan, FACTS Tuition Payment Plan, monthly payment plans, biannual payment plan). Need-based scholarship grants available. In 2016–17, 10% of upper-school students received aid.

Admissions Traditional secondary-level entrance grade is 9. For fall 2016, 76 students applied for upper-level admission, 37 were accepted, 31 enrolled. ISEE or SSAT, ERB, PSAT, SAT, PLAN or ACT required. Deadline for receipt of application materials: January 26. Application fee required: $275. Interview recommended.

Athletics Interscholastic: baseball (boys), basketball (b,g), cheering (g), cross-country running (b,g), football (b,g), golf (b,g), physical training (b,g), softball (g), swimming and diving (b,g), tennis (b,g), track and field (b,g), volleyball (g), weight training (b,g). 4 PE instructors, 17 coaches, 1 athletic trainer.

Computers Computers are regularly used in all academic classes. Computer network features include on-campus library services, Internet access, wireless campus network, Internet filtering or blocking technology. Student e-mail accounts are available to students. Students grades are available online. The school has a published electronic and media policy.

Contact Mrs. D'Anne P. Surber, Director of Enrollment. 936-273-2555. Fax: 936-271-3115. E-mail: dsurber@twca.net. Website: www.twca.net

WOODLYNDE SCHOOL

445 Upper Gulph Road
Strafford, Pennsylvania 19087

Head of School: Dr. Christopher M. Fulco, EdD

General Information Coeducational day college-preparatory and learning support and strategics for students with LD school. Grades K–12. Founded: 1976. Setting: suburban. Nearest major city is Philadelphia. 8-acre campus. 2 buildings on campus. Approved or accredited by Pennsylvania Association of Independent Schools and Pennsylvania Department of Education. Member of National Association of Independent Schools. Endowment: $559,699. Total enrollment: 270. Upper school average class size: 10. Upper school faculty-student ratio: 1:5. There are 168 required school days per year for Upper School students. Upper School students typically attend 5 days per week. The average school day consists of 6 hours and 55 minutes.

Upper School Student Profile Grade 9: 19 students (11 boys, 8 girls); Grade 10: 43 students (27 boys, 16 girls); Grade 11: 38 students (24 boys, 14 girls); Grade 12: 32 students (21 boys, 11 girls)

Faculty School total: 63. In upper school: 17 men, 20 women; 18 have advanced degrees.

Subjects Offered Advanced Placement courses, algebra, American history, American literature, architecture, art, art-AP, arts, biology, chemistry, creative writing, earth science, English, English literature, English-AP, European history, fine arts, French, geometry, government/civics, health, history, journalism, mathematics, music, photography, physical education, physics, political science, psychology, science, sign language, social studies, Spanish, studio art, world history, world literature, writing.

Graduation Requirements Arts and fine arts (art, music, dance, drama), English, foreign language, internship, mathematics, physical education (includes health), science, social studies (includes history), community service, senior project, senior speech.

Special Academic Programs Advanced Placement exam preparation; honors section; study at local college for college credit; remedial reading and/or remedial writing; remedial math; programs in English, mathematics, general development for dyslexic students.

College Admission Counseling 42 students graduated in 2016; 41 went to college, including American University; Cabrini University; Curry College; Landmark College; Montgomery County Community College; Towson University. Other: 1 had other specific plans.

Student Life Upper grades have uniform requirement, student council. Discipline rests primarily with faculty.

Summer Programs Remediation, enrichment, advancement, sports, art/fine arts, computer instruction programs offered; session focuses on mathematics and reading enrichment, college preparation; held on campus; accepts boys and girls; open to students from other schools. 75 students usually enrolled. 2017 schedule: June 19 to July 21. Application deadline: May 30.

Tuition and Aid Day student tuition: $35,625. Tuition installment plan (FACTS Tuition Payment Plan, monthly payment plans). Need-based scholarship grants available. In 2016–17, 40% of upper-school students received aid. Total amount of financial aid awarded in 2016–17: $1,000,000.

Admissions Traditional secondary-level entrance grade is 9. Individual IQ required. Deadline for receipt of application materials: none. Application fee required: $100. On-campus interview recommended.

Athletics Interscholastic: basketball (boys, girls), lacrosse (b), softball (g), tennis (b,g), volleyball (g); coed interscholastic: cross-country running, golf, indoor track, soccer; coed intramural: fitness, horseback riding, outdoor adventure, outdoors, physical fitness, strength & conditioning, ultimate Frisbee. 3 PE instructors, 12 coaches, 1 athletic trainer.

Computers Computers are regularly used in all academic, art, college planning, creative writing, drawing and design, English, foreign language, French, graphic arts, graphic design, health, history, journalism, Latin, learning cognition, mathematics, music, newspaper, photography, psychology, publications, science, social studies, Spanish, study skills, technology, word processing, writing, writing, yearbook classes. Computer network features include on-campus library services, online commercial services, Internet access, wireless campus network, Internet filtering or blocking technology. Campus intranet and student e-mail accounts are available to students. Students grades are available online. The school has a published electronic and media policy.

Contact Ms. Kristen Tabun, Director of Enrollment Management. 610-687-9660 Ext. 624. Fax: 610-687-4752. E-mail: tabun@woodlynde.org. Website: www.woodlynde.org

WOODSIDE PRIORY SCHOOL

302 Portola Road
Founders Hall
Portola Valley, California 94028-7897

Head of School: Mr. Tim J. Molak

General Information Coeducational boarding and day college-preparatory, arts, religious studies, and technology school, affiliated with Roman Catholic Church, Jewish faith. Boarding grades 9–12, day grades 6–12. Founded: 1957. Setting: suburban. Nearest major city is San Francisco/San Jose. Students are housed in single-sex dormitories. 50-acre campus. 25 buildings on campus. Approved or accredited by California Association of Independent Schools, National Catholic Education Association, The Association of Boarding Schools, The College Board, Western Association of Schools and Colleges, Western Catholic Education Association, and California Department of Education. Member of National Association of Independent Schools and Secondary School Admission Test Board. Endowment: $1.3 million. Total enrollment: 386. Upper school average class size: 18. Upper school faculty-student ratio: 1:9. There are 175 required school days per year for Upper School students. Upper School students typically attend 5 days per week. The average school day consists of 6 hours and 30 minutes.

Upper School Student Profile Grade 9: 79 students (41 boys, 38 girls); Grade 10: 70 students (37 boys, 33 girls); Grade 11: 61 students (34 boys, 27 girls); Grade 12: 68 students (29 boys, 39 girls). 18% of students are boarding students. 88% are state residents. 2 states are represented in upper school student body. 12% are international students. International students from China, Hungary, Nigeria, Republic of Korea, Taiwan, and Thailand; 6 other countries represented in student body. 40% of students are Roman Catholic, Jewish.

Faculty School total: 70. In upper school: 28 men, 27 women; 48 have advanced degrees; 16 reside on campus.

Subjects Offered 20th century physics, 3-dimensional art, 3-dimensional design, acting, advanced chemistry, advanced computer applications, advanced math, Advanced Placement courses, advanced studio art-AP, algebra, American democracy, American government, American history, American literature, analysis and differential calculus, animation, architecture, art, art history, art-AP, ASB Leadership, astronomy, Basic programming, biology, biology-AP, British literature, calculus, calculus-AP, ceramics, chemistry, chemistry-AP, choir, choral music, Christian and Hebrew scripture, church history, classics, college admission preparation, college counseling, community garden, community service, comparative cultures, computer applications, computer art, computer graphics, computer math, computer programming, computer science, computer science-AP, computer technologies, computers, constitutional history of U.S., contemporary issues, creative arts, creative writing, desktop publishing, drama, drama performance, earth and space science, earth science, ecology, economics, economics-AP, English, English composition, English literature, English literature-AP, English-AP, environmental science-AP, ethics, European history, European history-AP, expository writing, fine arts, French, French-AP, geography, geometry, government/civics, grammar, health and wellness, history of ideas, honors English, humanities, journalism, keyboarding, life science, mathematics, music, music appreciation, music performance, peer counseling, personal fitness, philosophy, photography, physical education, physics, physics-AP, play production, portfolio art, pre-algebra, pre-calculus, probability and statistics, psychology, religion, science, social sciences, social studies, sociology, Spanish, Spanish language-AP, Spanish literature-

AP, speech, studio art-AP, theater, theology, trigonometry, typing, U.S. history-AP, world history, world literature, world religions, writing.

Graduation Requirements 3-dimensional art, algebra, arts and fine arts (art, music, dance, drama), biology, British literature, calculus, chemistry, Christian and Hebrew scripture, comparative religion, computer science, earth science, English, environmental science, expository writing, foreign language, geometry, mathematics, physical education (includes health), physics, science, social sciences, social studies (includes history), theology. Community service is required.

Special Academic Programs 20 Advanced Placement exams for which test preparation is offered; honors section; independent study; academic accommodation for the gifted, the musically talented, and the artistically talented.

College Admission Counseling 65 students graduated in 2015; all went to college, including Massachusetts Institute of Technology; Santa Clara University; Stanford University; University of California, Berkeley; University of California, Los Angeles. Median SAT critical reading: 633, median SAT math: 641, median SAT writing: 653, median combined SAT: 1927. 31% scored over 600 on SAT critical reading, 31% scored over 600 on SAT math, 34% scored over 600 on SAT writing, 32% scored over 1800 on combined SAT.

Student Life Upper grades have specified standards of dress, student council, honor system. Discipline rests primarily with faculty.

Tuition and Aid Day student tuition: $39,900; 7-day tuition and room/board: $59,890. Tuition installment plan (monthly payment plans, individually arranged payment plans). Need-based scholarship grants available. In 2015–16, 21% of upper-school students received aid. Total amount of financial aid awarded in 2015–16: $2,170,538.

Admissions Traditional secondary-level entrance grade is 9. For fall 2015, 369 students applied for upper-level admission, 104 were accepted, 55 enrolled. High School Placement Test (closed version) from Scholastic Testing Service, ISEE, PSAT or SAT for applicants to grade 11 and 12, SSAT, TOEFL or writing sample required. Deadline for receipt of application materials: January 14. Application fee required: $95. On-campus interview required.

Athletics Interscholastic: baseball (boys), basketball (b,g), cross-country running (b,g), flag football (b), football (b), golf (b,g), soccer (b,g), softball (g), swimming and diving (g), track and field (b,g), volleyball (g), water polo (b); intramural: alpine skiing (b,g); coed interscholastic: cross-country running, dance, golf, outdoor education, tennis; coed intramural: alpine skiing, bowling, canoeing/kayaking, cross-country running, fitness, ropes courses. 4 PE instructors, 10 coaches, 1 athletic trainer.

Computers Computers are regularly used in all academic, animation, art, college planning, drafting, library, literary magazine, media arts, research skills, senior seminar, study skills, technology, yearbook classes. Computer network features include on-campus library services, online commercial services, Internet access, wireless campus network, Internet filtering or blocking technology. Campus intranet and student e-mail accounts are available to students. Students grades are available online. The school has a published electronic and media policy.

Contact Mr. Al Zappelli, Dean of Admissions and Financial Aid. 650-851-6101. Fax: 650-851-2839. E-mail: azappelli@prioryca.org. Website: www.PrioryCA.org

WOODSTOCK ACADEMY

57 Academy Rd
Woodstock, Connecticut 06281

Head of School: Mr. Christopher Sandford

General Information Coeducational boarding and day college-preparatory, arts, and STEM school; primarily serves students with learning disabilities and individuals with Attention Deficit Disorder. Grades 9–12. Distance learning grades 11–12. Founded: 1801. Setting: rural. Nearest major city is Hartford. Students are housed in single-sex dormitories. 190-acre campus. 12 buildings on campus. Approved or accredited by Association of Independent Schools in New England, New England Association of Schools and Colleges, and Connecticut Department of Education. Member of National Association of Independent Schools and Secondary School Admission Test Board. Endowment: $3 million. Total enrollment: 1,025. Upper school average class size: 20. Upper school faculty-student ratio: 1:14. There are 182 required school days per year for Upper School students. Upper School students typically attend 5 days per week. The average school day consists of 6 hours and 45 minutes.

Upper School Student Profile Grade 9: 250 students (125 boys, 125 girls); Grade 10: 250 students (125 boys, 125 girls); Grade 11: 250 students (125 boys, 125 girls); Grade 12: 250 students (125 boys, 125 girls). 10% of students are boarding students. 90% are state residents. 4 states are represented in upper school student body. 10% are international students. International students from China, Germany, Iraq, and Rwanda; 5 other countries represented in student body.

Faculty School total: 93. In upper school: 45 men, 48 women; 80 have advanced degrees; 20 reside on campus.

Subjects Offered 20th century history, 20th century world history, 3-dimensional design, accounting, acting, advanced biology, advanced chemistry, Advanced Placement courses, all academic.

Graduation Requirements American government, American history, arts and fine arts (art, music, dance, drama), English, foreign language, health education, mathematics, science, social studies (includes history).

Special Academic Programs Advanced Placement exam preparation; honors section; independent study; study at local college for college credit; study abroad; academic accommodation for the musically talented and the artistically talented; remedial reading and/or remedial writing; remedial math; programs in English, mathematics, general development for dyslexic students; special instructional classes for deaf students, full special education program; ESL (33 students enrolled).

College Admission Counseling 287 students graduated in 2016; 250 went to college, including American University; Arizona State University at the Tempe campus; Boston University; Northeastern University; University of California, Los Angeles; University of Connecticut. Other: 10 went to work, 7 entered military service, 2 entered a postgraduate year, 10 had other specific plans. Mean SAT critical reading: 511, mean SAT math: 511, mean SAT writing: 521. 62% scored over 600 on SAT critical reading, 60% scored over 600 on SAT math, 61% scored over 600 on SAT writing, 47% scored over 1800 on combined SAT.

Student Life Upper grades have specified standards of dress, student council. Discipline rests primarily with faculty.

Tuition and Aid Day student tuition: $14,500; 7-day tuition and room/board: $46,722. Tuition reduction for siblings, merit scholarship grants, need-based scholarship grants available. In 2016–17, 3% of upper-school students received aid. Total amount of financial aid awarded in 2016–17: $25,000.

Admissions Traditional secondary-level entrance grade is 10. For fall 2016, 230 students applied for upper-level admission, 180 were accepted, 90 enrolled. TOEFL or TOEFL Junior required. Deadline for receipt of application materials: none. Application fee required: $100. Interview recommended.

Athletics Interscholastic: baseball (boys), basketball (b,g), cross-country running (b,g), field hockey (g), football (b), golf (b,g), ice hockey (b), indoor track & field (b,g), lacrosse (b,g), soccer (b,g), softball (g), tennis (b,g), volleyball (b,g), winter (indoor) track (b,g); coed interscholastic: cheering, gymnastics, wrestling; coed intramural: badminton, bicycling, climbing, dance squad, fishing, hockey, project adventure, swimming and diving, table tennis, ultimate Frisbee, weight lifting. 4 PE instructors, 75 coaches, 1 athletic trainer.

Computers Computers are regularly used in all classes. Computer network features include on-campus library services, online commercial services, Internet access, wireless campus network, Internet filtering or blocking technology, all students have an iPad. Campus intranet and student e-mail accounts are available to students. Students grades are available online. The school has a published electronic and media policy.

Contact Mrs. Annaleise W. Radchenko, Admissions Assistant. 860-928-6575 Ext. 1168. Fax: 860-963-7222. E-mail: aradchenko@woodstockacademy.org.
Website: www.woodstockacademy.org

WOODSTOCK SCHOOL

Landour
Mussoorie
Uttarakhand 248 179, India

Head of School: Dr. Jonathan Long

General Information Coeducational boarding and day college-preparatory, arts, music, and science school, affiliated with Christian faith. Boarding grades 6–12, day grades 6–12. Founded: 1854. Setting: rural. Nearest major city is New Delhi, India. Students are housed in single-sex dormitories. 400-acre campus. 7 buildings on campus. Approved or accredited by Council of International Schools and Middle States Association of Colleges and Schools. Member of European Council of International Schools. Language of instruction: English. Total enrollment: 522. Upper school average class size: 18. Upper school faculty-student ratio: 1:15. There are 180 required school days per year for Upper School students. Upper School students typically attend 5 days per week. The average school day consists of 6 hours and 30 minutes.

Upper School Student Profile Grade 6: 40 students (20 boys, 20 girls); Grade 7: 50 students (25 boys, 25 girls); Grade 8: 60 students (30 boys, 30 girls); Grade 9: 80 students (40 boys, 40 girls); Grade 10: 80 students (40 boys, 40 girls); Grade 11: 90 students (45 boys, 45 girls); Grade 12: 80 students (40 boys, 40 girls). 93% of students are boarding students. 10 states are represented in upper school student body. 63% are international students. International students from Australia, Bhutan, Canada, India, Republic of Korea, and United States; 30 other countries represented in student body. 28% of students are Christian faith.

Faculty School total: 70. In upper school: 30 men, 30 women; 45 have advanced degrees; all reside on campus.

Subjects Offered Algebra, American history, American history-AP, American literature, American studies, art, art history, Asian studies, Bible, Bible studies, biology, biology-AP, calculus, calculus-AP, ceramics, chemistry, chemistry-AP, choir, choral music, Christianity, community service, comparative religion, computer science, concert band, drama, economics, English, English language-AP, English literature, English-AP, environmental science, environmental science-AP, ethics, European history, fine arts, French, French-AP, geometry, government, government and politics-AP, health education, Hindi, Indian studies, jazz band, journalism, macro/microeconomics-AP, macroeconomics-AP, mathematics, mathematics-AP, microeconomics-AP, music, philosophy, physical education, physics, physics-AP, religion, science, social studies, theater, trigonometry, U.S. government and politics-AP,

vocal music, world history, world history-AP, world literature, world religions, writing, yearbook.

Graduation Requirements Arts and fine arts (art, music, dance, drama), Christian studies, computer literacy, English, foreign language, mathematics, physical education (includes health), science, social studies (includes history). Community service is required.

Special Academic Programs 17 Advanced Placement exams for which test preparation is offered; independent study; domestic exchange program; study abroad; academic accommodation for the gifted, the musically talented, and the artistically talented; programs in English for dyslexic students; ESL (23 students enrolled).

College Admission Counseling 85 students graduated in 2016; 82 went to college, including Bard College; Columbia University; Mercyhurst University; Middlebury College; Northeastern University; Stanford University. Other: 3 had other specific plans. Median SAT critical reading: 566, median SAT math: 630, median SAT writing: 590, median combined SAT: 1810, median composite ACT: 27. 37% scored over 600 on SAT critical reading, 60% scored over 600 on SAT math, 48% scored over 600 on SAT writing, 56% scored over 1800 on combined SAT, 33% scored over 26 on composite ACT.

Student Life Upper grades have specified standards of dress, student council, honor system. Discipline rests equally with students and faculty. Attendance at religious services is required.

Summer Programs ESL programs offered; session focuses on ESL; held both on and off campus; accepts boys and girls, open to students from other schools, 10 students usually enrolled. 2017 schedule: July 7 to July 21. Application deadline: June 15.

Tuition and Aid 7-day tuition and room/board: $23,000. Tuition installment plan (individually arranged payment plans). Need-based scholarship grants available. In 2016–17, 25% of upper-school students received aid; total upper-school merit-scholarship money awarded: $1,000,000. Total amount of financial aid awarded in 2016–17: $1,000,000.

Admissions Traditional secondary-level entrance grade is 11. For fall 2016, 329 students applied for upper-level admission, 100 were accepted, 90 enrolled. Cognitive Abilities Test or school's own exam required. Deadline for receipt of application materials: none. Application fee required: $150. On-campus interview recommended.

Athletics Interscholastic: basketball (boys, girls), cricket (b), cross-country running (b,g), field hockey (b,g), soccer (b,g), strength & conditioning (b,g), swimming and diving (b,g), track and field (b,g); intramural: aerobics/dance (g), backpacking (b,g), badminton (b,g), basketball (b,g), climbing (b,g), cricket (b), cross-country running (b,g), field hockey (b,g), gymnastics (b,g), hiking/backpacking (b,g), hockey (b,g), outdoor activities (b,g), outdoor education (b,g), physical fitness (b,g), physical training (b,g), rock climbing (b,g), running (b,g), soccer (b,g), squash (b,g), strength & conditioning (b,g), swimming and diving (b,g), table tennis (b,g), tennis (b,g), track and field (b,g), volleyball (b,g), walking (b,g), wall climbing (b,g), weight training (b,g), wilderness survival (b,g); coed intramural: backpacking, hiking/backpacking, outdoor education, physical fitness, physical training, rock climbing. 4 PE instructors.

Computers Computers are regularly used in all academic classes. Computer network features include on-campus library services, Internet access, wireless campus network, Internet filtering or blocking technology. Campus intranet, student e-mail accounts, and computer access in designated common areas are available to students. Students grades are available online. The school has a published electronic and media policy.

Contact Mr. Marcus Shaw, Director of Admissions. 91-135-263-9105. Fax: 91-135-263-0897. E-mail: admissions@woodstock.ac.in. Website: www.woodstock.ac.in

WOODWARD ACADEMY

1662 Rugby Avenue
College Park, Georgia 30337

Head of School: Mr. Stuart Gulley, PhD

General Information Coeducational day college-preparatory school. Grades PK–12. Founded: 1900. Setting: suburban. Nearest major city is Atlanta. 112-acre campus. 50 buildings on campus. Approved or accredited by Georgia Independent School Association, Southern Association of Colleges and Schools, and Georgia Department of Education. Member of National Association of Independent Schools and Secondary School Admission Test Board. Endowment: $122 million. Total enrollment: 2,738. Upper school average class size: 16. Upper School students typically attend 5 days per week.

Faculty School total: 363. In upper school: 56 men, 81 women.

Subjects Offered 20th century world history, 3-dimensional art, 3-dimensional design, acting, Advanced Placement courses, algebra, American government, American history, American history-AP, anatomy and physiology, art, astronomy, audio visual/media, band, biology, biology-AP, calculus, calculus-AP, ceramics, chemistry, chemistry-AP, choir, choral music, chorus, comparative religion, computer education, computer programming, computer programming-AP, computer science, computer science-AP, concert band, contemporary history, contemporary issues, creative writing, dance, debate, digital music, drama, drama performance, drawing, drawing and design, earth science, ecology, economics, economics and history, economics-AP, English, English language and composition-AP, English literature, English literature and composition-AP, English-AP, environmental science, environmental science-AP, European history, European history-AP, fine arts, French, French language-AP, French-AP, geography, geometry, government and politics-AP, government/civics, grammar, health, history, history-AP, honors English, honors geometry, honors U.S. history, honors world history, independent study, Japanese, jewelry making, journalism, Latin, literature and composition-AP, marching band, marine ecology, mathematics, meteorology, microeconomics-AP, Middle East, modern European history-AP, multicultural literature, music, oceanography, performing arts, personal fitness, photography, physical education, physics, physics-AP, pre-calculus, probability and statistics, science, social studies, Spanish, Spanish language-AP, Spanish-AP, speech communications, statistics, statistics-AP, television, the Sixties, theater, trigonometry, U.S. government and politics, U.S. government and politics-AP, U.S. history, U.S. history-AP, video, voice ensemble, world history, world literature, world religions, yearbook.

Graduation Requirements Arts and fine arts (art, music, dance, drama), computer science, English, foreign language, mathematics, physical education (includes health), religion (includes Bible studies and theology), science, social studies (includes history).

Special Academic Programs 20 Advanced Placement exams for which test preparation is offered; honors section; independent study.

College Admission Counseling 245 students graduated in 2016; all went to college.

Student Life Upper grades have uniform requirement, student council, honor system. Discipline rests primarily with faculty.

Summer Programs Enrichment, advancement, sports, art/fine arts, computer instruction programs offered; held on campus; accepts boys and girls; open to students from other schools. 2,300 students usually enrolled.

Tuition and Aid Day student tuition: $25,800. Tuition installment plan (monthly payment plans, Your Tuition Solution—Springstone Financial, Sallie Mae). Need-based scholarship grants available.

Admissions Traditional secondary-level entrance grade is 9. SSAT required. Deadline for receipt of application materials: February 28. Application fee required: $75. On-campus interview recommended.

Athletics Interscholastic: baseball (boys), basketball (b,g), cheering (g), cross-country running (b,g), diving (b,g), football (b), golf (b,g), lacrosse (b,g), soccer (b,g), softball (g), swimming and diving (b,g), tennis (b,g), track and field (b,g), volleyball (g); intramural: basketball (b,g), cheering (g), football (b), soccer (b,g), softball (g), swimming and diving (b,g), tennis (b,g), track and field (b,g), volleyball (g); coed interscholastic: Frisbee, power lifting, riflery, skeet shooting, ultimate Frisbee, weight lifting; coed intramural: fencing, horseback riding, lacrosse. 4 PE instructors, 34 coaches, 2 athletic trainers.

Computers Computers are regularly used in creative writing, English, foreign language, graphic design, journalism, literary magazine, mathematics, media production, newspaper, science, yearbook classes. Computer network features include on-campus library services, online commercial services, Internet access, wireless campus network. Campus intranet and student e-mail accounts are available to students. Students grades are available online. The school has a published electronic and media policy.

Contact Rebecca Eckstein, Vice President for Admissions and Enrollment Management. 404-765-4001. Fax: 404-765-4009.
E-mail: rebecca.eckstein@woodward.edu. Website: www.woodward.edu

THE WOODWARD SCHOOL

1102 Hancock Street
Quincy, Massachusetts 02169

Head of School: Walter Hubley

General Information Girls' day college-preparatory school. Grades 6–12. Founded: 1869. Setting: urban. Nearest major city is Boston. 2-acre campus. 2 buildings on campus. Approved or accredited by Association of Independent Schools in New England, New England Association of Schools and Colleges, and Massachusetts Department of Education. Member of Secondary School Admission Test Board. Total enrollment: 120. Upper school average class size: 10. Upper school faculty-student ratio: 1:8. There are 165 required school days per year for Upper School students. Upper School students typically attend 5 days per week. The average school day consists of 6 hours and 50 minutes.

Upper School Student Profile Grade 6: 8 students (8 girls); Grade 7: 17 students (17 girls); Grade 8: 21 students (21 girls); Grade 9: 18 students (18 girls); Grade 10: 22 students (22 girls); Grade 11: 18 students (18 girls); Grade 12: 19 students (19 girls).

Faculty School total: 21. In upper school: 3 men, 9 women; 12 have advanced degrees.

Subjects Offered Advanced computer applications, algebra, American history, American literature, anatomy, art, arts, biology, calculus, calculus-AP, chemistry, chorus, classical studies, classics, community service, computer graphics, computer math, computer science, computer skills, constitutional law, drama, ecology, English, English language and composition-AP, environmental science, filmmaking, fine arts, French, health and wellness, health science, language arts, Latin, Latin-AP, law and the legal system, literature, literature and composition-AP, mathematics, media studies, music, music appreciation, physics, physics-AP, physiology, political science, portfolio art, pre-algebra, psychology, rhetoric, SAT preparation, science, senior project, social sciences, social studies, sociology, Spanish, study skills, theater arts, U.S. government, U.S. history, Web authoring, Web site design, world history, world literature, World War II, writing.

Graduation Requirements Arts and fine arts (art, music, dance, drama), computer science, English, foreign language, mathematics, science, senior project, social studies (includes history), Senior Project. Community service is required.

Special Academic Programs 5 Advanced Placement exams for which test preparation is offered; honors section; independent study; ESL (10 students enrolled).

College Admission Counseling 18 students graduated in 2016; all went to college, including Brown University; Emmanuel College; Pratt Institute; Suffolk University; The University of North Carolina Wilmington; Tufts University.

Student Life Upper grades have specified standards of dress, student council, honor system. Discipline rests primarily with faculty.

Tuition and Aid Day student tuition: $14,200. Tuition installment plan (SMART Tuition Payment Plan, monthly payment plans, individually arranged payment plans). Tuition reduction for siblings, merit scholarship grants, need-based scholarship grants available. In 2016–17, 39% of upper-school students received aid; total upper-school merit-scholarship money awarded: $4000. Total amount of financial aid awarded in 2016–17: $295,127.

Admissions Traditional secondary-level entrance grade is 9. Deadline for receipt of application materials: none. Application fee required: $50. Interview required.

Athletics Interscholastic: basketball, soccer, softball. 1 PE instructor, 1 coach, 1 athletic trainer.

Computers Computers are regularly used in all classes. Computer network features include on-campus library services, Internet access, wireless campus network, Internet filtering or blocking technology. Computer access in designated common areas is available to students. The school has a published electronic and media policy.

Contact Katie Carroll, Director of Admissions. 617-773-5610. Fax: 617-770-1551.
E-mail: kcarroll@thewoodwardschool.org. Website: www.thewoodwardschool.org

WOOSTER SCHOOL

91 Miry Brook Road
Danbury, Connecticut 06810

Head of School: Mr. Matthew J Byrnes

General Information Coeducational day college-preparatory, arts, and technology school, affiliated with Episcopal Church. Grades PK–12. Founded: 1926. Setting: suburban. 100-acre campus. 15 buildings on campus. Approved or accredited by Connecticut Association of Independent Schools, National Association of Episcopal Schools, New England Association of Schools and Colleges, and Connecticut Department of Education. Member of National Association of Independent Schools. Endowment: $8 million. Total enrollment: 383. Upper school average class size: 12. Upper school faculty-student ratio: 1:10. There are 173 required school days per year for Upper School students. Upper School students typically attend 5 days per week.

Upper School Student Profile Grade 9: 35 students (20 boys, 15 girls); Grade 10: 48 students (29 boys, 19 girls); Grade 11: 32 students (13 boys, 19 girls); Grade 12: 32 students (16 boys, 16 girls).

Faculty School total: 97. In upper school: 13 men, 11 women; 14 have advanced degrees.

Subjects Offered Accounting, algebra, American government, American history, American history-AP, ancient history, Arabic, art, art history-AP, art-AP, biology, biology-AP, calculus, calculus-AP, chemistry, community service, computer animation, computer science, computer science-AP, earth science, economics, English, English literature-AP, English/composition-AP, ESL, ethics, European history-AP, fine arts, French, French-AP, general science, geography, geometry, mathematics, music, music-AP, Pacific art, photography, physical education, physics, political science, pottery, religion, science, social studies, Spanish, Spanish-AP, statistics, statistics-AP, U.S. history-AP.

Graduation Requirements 20th century history, arts and fine arts (art, music, dance, drama), computer science, English, foreign language, mathematics, physical education (includes health), religion (includes Bible studies and theology), science, social studies (includes history), 100 hours of community service, senior independent study and Senior Seminar, Leadership in Self-help (jobs) program.

Special Academic Programs Advanced Placement exam preparation; honors section; accelerated programs; independent study; programs in English, mathematics, general development for dyslexic students.

College Admission Counseling 39 students graduated in 2015; all went to college, including Carnegie Mellon University; Sarah Lawrence College; Skidmore College; Tufts University; Vassar College. Mean SAT critical reading: 626, mean SAT math: 616, mean SAT writing: 638, mean combined SAT: 1881.

Student Life Upper grades have specified standards of dress, student council, honor system. Discipline rests equally with students and faculty. Attendance at religious services is required.

Tuition and Aid Day student tuition: $20,100–$34,350. Tuition installment plan (The Tuition Plan, Insured Tuition Payment Plan, monthly payment plans, individually arranged payment plans, school's own payment plan). Need-based scholarship grants available. In 2015–16, 28% of upper-school students received aid.

Admissions Traditional secondary-level entrance grade is 9. For fall 2015, 66 students applied for upper-level admission, 47 were accepted, 19 enrolled. ISEE or SSAT required. Deadline for receipt of application materials: February 1. Application fee required: $65. On-campus interview required.

Athletics Interscholastic: baseball (boys), basketball (b,g), cross-country running (b,g), football (b), ice hockey (b), lacrosse (b,g), soccer (b,g), tennis (b,g), volleyball (g); intramural: dance (g), weight training (g); coed interscholastic: alpine skiing, Frisbee, golf, outdoor education, skiing (downhill), strength & conditioning, yoga; coed intramural: outdoor education, ropes courses, weight lifting, weight training. 3 PE instructors, 15 coaches, 1 athletic trainer.

Computers Computers are regularly used in all classes. Computer network features include on-campus library services, Internet access, wireless campus network, Internet filtering or blocking technology. Campus intranet, student e-mail accounts, and computer access in designated common areas are available to students. The school has a published electronic and media policy.

Contact Ms. Melissa Haas, Database Manager and Admission Assistant. 203-830-3916. Fax: 203-790-7147. E-mail: melissa.haas@woosterschool.org. Website: www.woosterschool.org.

WORCESTER PREPARATORY SCHOOL

508 South Main Street
PO Box 1006
Berlin, Maryland 21811

Head of School: Dr. Barry W. Tull

General Information Coeducational day college-preparatory, arts, and technology school. Grades PK–12. Founded: 1970. Setting: small town. Nearest major city is Ocean City. 45-acre campus. 7 buildings on campus. Approved or accredited by Association of Independent Maryland Schools, Middle States Association of Colleges and Schools, and Maryland Department of Education. Member of National Association of Independent Schools. Total enrollment: 542. Upper school average class size: 15. Upper school faculty-student ratio: 1:9. There are 173 required school days per year for Upper School students. Upper School students typically attend 5 days per week. The average school day consists of 6 hours and 30 minutes.

Upper School Student Profile Grade 9: 56 students (26 boys, 30 girls), Grade 10: 51 students (33 boys, 18 girls); Grade 11: 50 students (16 boys, 34 girls); Grade 12: 56 students (29 boys, 27 girls).

Faculty School total: 62. In upper school: 12 men, 22 women; 29 have advanced degrees.

Subjects Offered Advanced Placement courses, algebra, American history, American literature, art, art appreciation, art history, athletics, band, biology, biology-AP, British literature, calculus, calculus-AP, chemistry, chemistry-AP, choir, choral music, computer programming, computer programming-AP, computer science, creative writing, dance, dance performance, digital applications, digital photography, drama, earth science, economics, English, English language and composition-AP, English language-AP, English literature, English literature and composition-AP, English literature-AP, English-AP, European history, fine arts, French, geography, geometry, government/civics, keyboarding, Latin, literature and composition-AP, literature-AP, mathematics, music, music theory, photography, physical education, physics, physics-AP, programming, psychology, robotics, SAT preparation, science, social sciences, social studies, Spanish, speech, statistics, technological applications, technology/design, theater, U.S. government, U.S. history, U.S. history-AP, vocal music, world history, world history-AP, world literature, writing, yearbook.

Graduation Requirements American government, American history, art appreciation, arts and fine arts (art, music, dance, drama), computer science, English, foreign language, mathematics, music appreciation, physical education (includes health), SAT preparation, science, social sciences, speech, technology, world history.

Special Academic Programs 9 Advanced Placement exams for which test preparation is offered; honors section; independent study; academic accommodation for the gifted, the musically talented, and the artistically talented.

College Admission Counseling 47 students graduated in 2016; all went to college, including Barnard College; Northwestern University; Savannah College of Art and Design; University of Delaware; University of Maryland, College Park; University of Richmond.

Student Life Upper grades have uniform requirement, student council, honor system. Discipline rests primarily with faculty.

Tuition and Aid Day student tuition: $14,075. Tuition installment plan (The Tuition Plan, Insured Tuition Payment Plan, monthly payment plans, individually arranged payment plans). Need-based scholarship grants available. In 2016–17, 1% of upper-school students received aid.

Admissions Traditional secondary-level entrance grade is 9. For fall 2016, 22 students applied for upper-level admission, 17 were accepted, 13 enrolled. Achievement/Aptitude/Writing and writing sample required. Deadline for receipt of application materials: none. Application fee required: $50. On-campus interview required.

Athletics Interscholastic: basketball (boys, girls), cross-country running (b,g), field hockey (g), lacrosse (b,g), soccer (b,g), tennis (b,g), volleyball (g), winter soccer (b,g); intramural: basketball (b,g), dance (b,g), dance squad (b,g), flag football (b,g), physical fitness (b,g), soccer (b,g), weight training (b,g); coed interscholastic: cheering, golf, tennis; coed intramural: dance, dance squad, physical fitness, weight training. 3 PE instructors, 21 coaches, 1 athletic trainer.

Computers Computers are regularly used in all academic classes. Computer network features include on-campus library services, online commercial services, Internet access, wireless campus network, Internet filtering or blocking technology. Campus intranet, student e-mail accounts, and computer access in designated common areas are available to students. Students grades are available online. The school has a published electronic and media policy.

Contact Tara F. Becker, Director of Admissions. 410-641-3575 Ext. 107. Fax: 410-641-3586. E-mail: tbecker@worcesterprep.org. Website: www.worcesterprep.org

WYOMING SEMINARY

201 North Sprague Avenue
Kingston, Pennsylvania 18704-3593

Head of School: Mr. Kevin P. Rea

General Information Coeducational boarding and day college-preparatory school, affiliated with United Methodist Church. Grades 9–PG. Founded: 1844. Setting: suburban. Nearest major city is Wilkes-Barre. Students are housed in single-sex dormitories. 22-acre campus. 13 buildings on campus. Approved or accredited by Middle States Association of Colleges and Schools, Pennsylvania Association of Independent Schools, The Association of Boarding Schools, The College Board, University Senate of United Methodist Church, and Pennsylvania Department of Education. Member of National Association of Independent Schools and Secondary School Admission Test Board. Endowment: $56.5 million. Total enrollment: 790. Upper school average class size: 14. Upper school faculty-student ratio: 1:8. There are 170 required school days per year for Upper School students. Upper School students typically attend 5 days per week. The average school day consists of 7 hours.

Upper School Student Profile Grade 6: 37 students (16 boys, 21 girls); Grade 7: 49 students (19 boys, 30 girls); Grade 8: 51 students (31 boys, 20 girls); Grade 9: 94 students (43 boys, 51 girls); Grade 10: 118 students (68 boys, 50 girls); Grade 11: 113 students (62 boys, 51 girls); Grade 12: 117 students (71 boys, 46 girls); Postgraduate: 13 students (12 boys, 1 girl). 35% of students are boarding students. 35% are state residents. 14 states are represented in upper school student body. 24% are international students. International students from Canada, China, Germany, Japan, Republic of Korea, and Viet Nam; 14 other countries represented in student body. 10% of students are United Methodist Church.

Faculty School total: 55. In upper school: 27 men, 28 women; 44 have advanced degrees; 34 reside on campus.

Subjects Offered 20th century world history, 3-dimensional design, algebra, alternative physical education, American Civil War, American history, American literature, analysis and differential calculus, analytic geometry, anatomy and physiology, ancient world history, art, art appreciation, art history, art history-AP, Bible studies, biology, biology-AP, botany, British literature, calculus, calculus-AP, ceramics, chemistry, chemistry-AP, choral music, college admission preparation, college counseling, computer programming, computer science, conceptual physics, creative writing, critical writing, discrete mathematics, drama, drawing and design, ecology, English, English literature, environmental science, environmental science-AP, ESL, European history, European history-AP, expository writing, fine arts, forensics, French, French-AP, geometry, health education, history, history of music, independent study, Judaic studies, Latin, Latin-AP, mathematics, music, music theory, music theory-AP, philosophy, photography, physics, poetry, pre-calculus, printmaking, psychology, psychology-AP, public speaking, religion, Russian, science, science research, Shakespeare, social studies, sociology, Spanish, Spanish-AP, statistics, statistics-AP, studio art-AP, theater, trigonometry, U.S. government and politics-AP, U.S. history-AP, women in literature, world civilizations, world cultures, world history, world literature, world religions, World War II, zoology.

Graduation Requirements Bible as literature, biology, music, music history, religion and culture, speech, U.S. history, world civilizations, 40 hours of community service, extracurricular participation.

Special Academic Programs 21 Advanced Placement exams for which test preparation is offered; honors section; independent study; term-away projects; study at local college for college credit; study abroad; ESL (35 students enrolled).

College Admission Counseling 126 students graduated in 2016; 123 went to college, including Fordham University; Lehigh University; Penn State University Park; Temple University; The University of Scranton; University of Pittsburgh. Other: 1 entered military service, 3 had other specific plans. Mean SAT critical reading: 559, mean SAT math: 605, mean SAT writing: 571, mean combined SAT: 1735, mean composite ACT: 24. 37% scored over 600 on SAT critical reading, 55% scored over 600 on SAT math, 45% scored over 600 on SAT writing, 40% scored over 1800 on combined SAT, 56% scored over 26 on composite ACT.

Student Life Upper grades have specified standards of dress, student council, honor system. Discipline rests equally with students and faculty.

Summer Programs Enrichment, advancement, ESL, sports, art/fine arts programs offered; session focuses on academics, performing arts and ESL; held on campus; accepts boys and girls; open to students from other schools. 385 students usually enrolled. 2017 schedule: June 25 to August 22. Application deadline: June 1.

Tuition and Aid Day student tuition: $24,300; 7-day tuition and room/board: $51,400. Tuition installment plan (FACTS Tuition Payment Plan, monthly payment plans). Merit scholarship grants, need-based scholarship grants available. In 2016–17,

50% of upper-school students received aid; total upper-school merit-scholarship money awarded: $878,025. Total amount of financial aid awarded in 2016–17: $8,500,000.

Admissions Traditional secondary-level entrance grade is 9. For fall 2016, 553 students applied for upper-level admission, 272 were accepted, 120 enrolled. TOEFL required. Deadline for receipt of application materials: none. Application fee required: $75. Interview recommended.

Athletics Interscholastic: baseball (boys), basketball (b,g), cross-country running (b,g), field hockey (g), football (b), ice hockey (b,g), lacrosse (b,g), soccer (b,g), softball (g), swimming and diving (b,g), tennis (b,g), wrestling (b); coed interscholastic: golf, strength & conditioning; coed intramural: ballet, combined training, dance, fitness, martial arts, modern dance, outdoor activities, outdoor recreation, physical training, rowing, wall climbing, yoga. 26 coaches, 2 athletic trainers.

Computers Computers are regularly used in art, English, foreign language, history, mathematics, music, science classes. Computer network features include on-campus library services, online commercial services, Internet access, wireless campus network, Internet filtering or blocking technology. Campus intranet, student e-mail accounts, and computer access in designated common areas are available to students. Students grades are available online. The school has a published electronic and media policy.

Contact Ms. Julie Bean, Dean of Admissions and Financial Aid. 570-270-2160. Fax: 570-270-2191. E-mail: admission@wyomingseminary.org. Website: www.wyomingseminary.org

XAVIER COLLEGE PREPARATORY

4710 North Fifth Street
Phoenix, Arizona 85012

Head of School: Sr. Joan Fitzgerald, BVM

General Information Girls' day college-preparatory, arts, religious studies, technology, Great Books, Advanced Placement, Dual College Enrollment, and STEM education school, affiliated with Roman Catholic Church. Grades 9–12. Founded: 1943. Setting: urban. 20-acre campus. 10 buildings on campus. Approved or accredited by National Catholic Education Association, North Central Association of Colleges and Schools, Western Catholic Education Association, and Arizona Department of Education. Endowment: $2.5 million. Total enrollment: 1,196. Upper school average class size: 24. Upper school faculty-student ratio: 1:22. There are 181 required school days per year for Upper School students. Upper School students typically attend 5 days per week. The average school day consists of 5 hours.

Upper School Student Profile Grade 9: 308 students (308 girls); Grade 10: 315 students (315 girls); Grade 11: 287 students (287 girls); Grade 12: 286 students (286 girls). 75% of students are Roman Catholic.

Faculty School total: 95. In upper school: 20 men, 75 women; 70 have advanced degrees.

Subjects Offered Accounting, advanced biology, advanced chemistry, advanced computer applications, advanced math, Advanced Placement courses, advanced studio art-AP, algebra, American government, American history, American history-AP, American literature, analysis and differential calculus, anatomy, anatomy and physiology, architecture, art, art history, art history-AP, astronomy, athletic training, audition methods, band, Basic programming, biology, biology-AP, calculus, calculus-AP, ceramics, cheerleading, chemistry, chemistry-AP, child development, Chinese, choir, church history, community service, computer programming-AP, computer science, computer studies, concert choir, contemporary issues, dance, dance performance, digital photography, drama, economics, English, English language and composition-AP, English literature-AP, environmental science-AP, ethics, European history-AP, family and consumer science, film studies, fine arts, French, French language-AP, geography, geometry, graphic design, great books, jazz band, Latin, Latin-AP, music, music theory-AP, musical theater, New Testament, newspaper, philosophy, physical education, physics, physics-AP, pre-calculus, psychology, sociology, Spanish, Spanish language-AP, Spanish literature-AP, sports medicine, stagecraft, statistics-AP, student government, theology, trigonometry, U.S. government and politics-AP, video and animation, visual arts, weight training, world history-AP, world literature.

Graduation Requirements American literature, arts and fine arts (art, music, dance, drama), computer programming, English, English literature-AP, foreign language, mathematics, physical education (includes health), religion (includes Bible studies and theology), science, social studies (includes history), Arizona History and Free Enterprise independent study, summer reading program, 50 hours of community service.

Special Academic Programs 24 Advanced Placement exams for which test preparation is offered; honors section; independent study; study at local college for college credit; study abroad; academic accommodation for the gifted and the artistically talented.

College Admission Counseling 286 students graduated in 2015; all went to college, including Arizona State University at the Tempe campus; Creighton University; Northern Arizona University; Santa Clara University; The University of Arizona; University of Southern California. Median composite ACT: 26. Mean SAT critical reading: 572, mean SAT math: 550, mean SAT writing: 567.

Student Life Upper grades have uniform requirement, student council, honor system. Discipline rests primarily with faculty. Attendance at religious services is required.

Tuition and Aid Day student tuition: $14,316–$18,312. Tuition installment plan (monthly payment plans, semester payment plan). Need-based scholarship grants, reduced tuition rate for Catholic families registered in Catholic parishes of the Diocese of Phoenix available. In 2015–16, 40% of upper-school students received aid. Total amount of financial aid awarded in 2015–16: $2,000,000.

Admissions Traditional secondary-level entrance grade is 9. For fall 2015, 500 students applied for upper-level admission, 360 were accepted, 325 enrolled. High School Placement Test required. Deadline for receipt of application materials: January 28. Application fee required: $50.

Athletics Interscholastic: aerobics/dance, badminton, basketball, cheering, crew, cross-country running, dance squad, dance team, danceline, diving, golf, lacrosse, pom squad, rowing, sand volleyball, soccer, softball, swimming and diving, tennis, track and field, volleyball, winter soccer; intramural: archery, crew, dance, fitness, floor hockey, modern dance, skeet shooting, strength & conditioning, tennis, weight training, yoga; coed interscholastic: ice hockey; coed intramural: flag football, mountain biking, tennis, volleyball. 4 PE instructors, 30 coaches, 2 athletic trainers.

Computers Computers are regularly used in all classes. Computer network features include on-campus library services, online commercial services, Internet access, wireless campus network, Internet filtering or blocking technology, Canvas, Naviance, Google Apps for Education. Student e-mail accounts and computer access in designated common areas are available to students. Students grades are available online. The school has a published electronic and media policy.

Contact Mrs. Paula Petrowski, Director of Admissions. 602-277-3772 Ext. 3104. Fax: 602-240-3175. E-mail: ppetrowski@xcp.org. Website: www.xcp.org

XAVIER HIGH SCHOOL

30 West 16th Street
New York, New York 10011

Head of School: Rev. John R. Raslowsky II

General Information Boys' day college-preparatory and Junior ROTC school, affiliated with Roman Catholic Church. Grades 9–12. Founded: 1847. Setting: urban. 2-acre campus. 5 buildings on campus. Approved or accredited by Jesuit Secondary Education Association, Middle States Association of Colleges and Schools, National Catholic Education Association, and New York State Association of Independent Schools. Endowment: $39 million. Upper school average class size: 23. Upper school faculty-student ratio: 1:14. There are 160 required school days per year for Upper School students. Upper School students typically attend 5 days per week. The average school day consists of 6 hours and 30 minutes.

Upper School Student Profile Grade 9: 258 students (258 boys); Grade 10: 266 students (266 boys); Grade 11: 274 students (274 boys); Grade 12: 278 students (278 boys). 85% of students are Roman Catholic.

Faculty School total: 67. In upper school: 51 men, 34 women; 71 have advanced degrees.

Subjects Offered 20th century history, acting, Advanced Placement courses, algebra, American government, American history, American history-AP, American literature, ancient/medieval philosophy, Arabic, art, art history, art-AP, arts, Bible, Bible studies, biology, British literature, British literature (honors), British literature-AP, business skills, calculus, Catholic belief and practice, chemistry, Christian and Hebrew scripture, Christian ethics, Christian scripture, community service, comparative government and politics-AP, computer art, computer graphics, computer math, computer programming, computer science, creative writing, drama, driver education, earth science, ecology, economics, English, English literature, English literature-AP, environmental science, ethics, European history, film appreciation, fine arts, French, geography, geology, geometry, German, global studies, government/civics, graphic design, Greek, health, history, history of the Catholic Church, human anatomy, Italian, jazz, jazz ensemble, JROTC, JROTC or LEAD (Leadership Education and Development), Latin, marine biology, mathematics, military science, music, New Testament, oceanography, peace and justice, philosophy, physical education, physics, physics-AP, prayer/spirituality, religion, robotics, science, set design, Shakespeare, social studies, software design, Spanish, Spanish-AP, stagecraft, theater, theology, trigonometry, U.S. government and politics-AP, U.S. history, U.S. history-AP, U.S. literature, vocal music, world history, world history-AP, world literature.

Graduation Requirements Arts and fine arts (art, music, dance, drama), business skills (includes word processing), computer science, economics, English, foreign language, mathematics, physical education (includes health), religion (includes Bible studies and theology), science, social studies (includes history), participation in Christian service program in sophomore, junior, and senior years. Community service is required.

Special Academic Programs Advanced Placement exam preparation; honors section.

College Admission Counseling 255 students graduated in 2016; 254 went to college, including Binghamton University, State University of New York; Fordham University; Loyola University Maryland; New York University; St. John's University; The University of Scranton. Other: 1 entered military service. Median SAT critical reading: 580, median SAT math: 600, median SAT writing: 580, median combined SAT: 1760, median composite ACT: 24. 44% scored over 600 on SAT critical reading, 52% scored over 600 on SAT math, 44% scored over 600 on SAT writing, 46% scored over 1800 on combined SAT, 42% scored over 26 on composite ACT.

Student Life Upper grades have specified standards of dress, student council. Discipline rests primarily with faculty. Attendance at religious services is required.

Tuition and Aid Day student tuition: $17,750. Tuition installment plan (FACTS Tuition Payment Plan, monthly payment plans, annual or semester payment plan). Merit scholarship grants, need-based scholarship grants available. In 2016–17, 42% of upper-school students received aid; total upper-school merit-scholarship money awarded: $673,650. Total amount of financial aid awarded in 2016–17: $3,400,000.

Admissions Traditional secondary-level entrance grade is 9. For fall 2016, 957 students applied for upper-level admission, 780 were accepted, 264 enrolled. Catholic High School Entrance Examination, Cooperative Entrance Exam (McGraw-Hill), High School Placement Test (closed version) from Scholastic Testing Service, ISEE, New York Archdiocesan Cooperative Entrance Examination, Newark or Paterson Diocesan Test or SSAT required. Deadline for receipt of application materials: none. No application fee required.

Athletics Interscholastic: baseball, basketball, bowling, cross-country running, diving, football, golf, ice hockey, JROTC drill, lacrosse, marksmanship, physical fitness, riflery, rugby, soccer, swimming and diving, tennis, track and field, volleyball, wrestling; intramural: bowling, football. 4 PE instructors, 20 coaches.

Computers Computers are regularly used in art, English, foreign language, history, JROTC, mathematics, music, science, theology classes. Computer network features include on-campus library services, online commercial services, Internet access, wireless campus network, Internet filtering or blocking technology. Student e-mail accounts and computer access in designated common areas are available to students. Students grades are available online. The school has a published electronic and media policy.

Contact Mr. Stephen Sanchez, Admissions Counselor. 212-924-7900 Ext. 1442. Fax: 212-924-0303. E-mail: admissions@xavierhs.org. Website: www.xavierhs.org

YOKOHAMA INTERNATIONAL SCHOOL

258 Yamate-cho, Naka-ku
Yokohama 231-0862, Japan

Head of School: Mr. Craig Coutts

General Information Coeducational day college-preparatory and IB PYP, MYP, DP school. Grades N–12. Founded: 1924. Setting: urban. 3-acre campus. 8 buildings on campus. Approved or accredited by Council of International Schools, East Asia Regional Council of Schools, International Baccalaureate Organization, and New England Association of Schools and Colleges. Language of instruction: English. Total enrollment: 644. Upper school average class size: 18. Upper school faculty-student ratio: 1:8. There are 179 required school days per year for Upper School students. Upper School students typically attend 5 days per week. The average school day consists of 7 hours.

Upper School Student Profile Grade 6: 50 students (34 boys, 16 girls); Grade 7: 47 students (29 boys, 18 girls); Grade 8: 63 students (30 boys, 33 girls); Grade 9: 68 students (29 boys, 39 girls); Grade 10: 68 students (33 boys, 35 girls); Grade 11: 65 students (31 boys, 34 girls); Grade 12: 57 students (30 boys, 27 girls).

Faculty School total: 78. In upper school: 25 men, 23 women; 27 have advanced degrees.

Subjects Offered Advanced biology, college counseling, design, dramatic arts, French as a second language, general science, global issues, health education, history, instrumental music, Japanese as Second Language, model United Nations, modern world history, music, outdoor education.

Graduation Requirements Arts, English, foreign language, information technology, mathematics, physical education (includes health), science, senior thesis, social studies (includes history), theory of knowledge.

Special Academic Programs International Baccalaureate program; ESL (80 students enrolled).

College Admission Counseling 56 students graduated in 2016; 50 went to college, including Berklee College of Music; Johns Hopkins University; New York University; Princeton University; University of Southern California. Other: 6 had other specific plans. Mean SAT critical reading: 496, mean SAT math: 576, mean SAT writing: 514, mean composite ACT: 24.

Student Life Upper grades have specified standards of dress, student council. Discipline rests primarily with faculty.

Summer Programs Remediation, enrichment, sports programs offered; session focuses on English, mathematics; held on campus; accepts boys and girls; open to students from other schools. 80 students usually enrolled. 2017 schedule: June 19 to June 30. Application deadline: May 1.

Tuition and Aid Day student tuition: ¥2,610,000.

Admissions Traditional secondary-level entrance grade is 9. For fall 2016, 310 students applied for upper-level admission, 204 were accepted, 167 enrolled. School's own test required. Deadline for receipt of application materials: none. Application fee required: ¥25,000. Interview required.

Athletics Interscholastic: badminton (boys, girls), baseball (b), basketball (b,g), cross-country running (b,g), field hockey (g), soccer (b,g), track and field (b,g), volleyball (b,g); coed interscholastic: dance team, tennis; coed intramural: skateboarding, yoga. 4 PE instructors.

Computers Computers are regularly used in all academic classes. Computer network features include on-campus library services, online commercial services, Internet access, wireless campus network, Internet filtering or blocking technology, 1:1 laptops from grades 3 - 12. Campus intranet and student e-mail accounts are available to students. Students grades are available online. The school has a published electronic and media policy.

Contact Ms. Susan Chen, Administrative Officer. 81-45-622-0084. Fax: 81-45-621-0379. E-mail: admissions@yis.ac.jp. Website: www.yis.ac.jp

YORK COUNTRY DAY SCHOOL

1071 Regents Glen Boulevard
York, Pennsylvania 17403

Head of School: Dr. Christine Heine

General Information Coeducational day college-preparatory school. Grades PS–12. Founded: 1953. Setting: suburban. Nearest major city is Baltimore, MD. 15-acre campus. 1 building on campus. Approved or accredited by Middle States Association of Colleges and Schools, Pennsylvania Association of Independent Schools, and Pennsylvania Department of Education. Member of National Association of Independent Schools. Endowment: $1.3 million. Total enrollment: 246. Upper school average class size: 12. Upper school faculty-student ratio: 1:6. There are 170 required school days per year for Upper School students. Upper School students typically attend 5 days per week. The average school day consists of 7 hours and 30 minutes.

Upper School Student Profile Grade 9: 25 students (13 boys, 12 girls); Grade 10: 25 students (13 boys, 12 girls); Grade 11: 19 students (10 boys, 9 girls); Grade 12: 12 students (6 boys, 6 girls).

Faculty School total: 42. In upper school: 10 men, 9 women; 17 have advanced degrees.

Subjects Offered Advanced biology, advanced chemistry, advanced studio art-AP, algebra, American history, American literature, art, art history, biochemistry, biology, calculus, chemistry, choral music, community service, creative writing, drama, English, English literature, European history, fine arts, French, geography, geometry, government/civics, health, history, Latin, literature, mathematics, music, physical education, physics, psychology, public speaking, robotics, SAT preparation, science, social studies, Spanish, studio art-AP, theater, world history, yearbook.

Graduation Requirements Arts and fine arts (art, music, dance, drama), English, foreign language, history, independent study, mathematics, physical education (includes health), public speaking, science, visual arts, 4 college classes. Community service is required.

Special Academic Programs Advanced Placement exam preparation; honors section; study at local college for college credit; academic accommodation for the gifted, the musically talented, and the artistically talented; ESL (6 students enrolled).

College Admission Counseling 15 students graduated in 2016; all went to college, including American University; Carnegie Mellon University; Rhode Island School of Design; University of Pennsylvania; University of Pittsburgh; Ursinus College. Mean SAT critical reading: 537, mean SAT math: 552, mean SAT writing: 533, mean combined SAT: 1638.

Student Life Upper grades have specified standards of dress, student council, honor system. Discipline rests equally with students and faculty.

Summer Programs Enrichment, sports, art/fine arts programs offered; session focuses on providing sports, arts, crafts, and swimming, robotics,; held both on and off campus; accepts boys and girls; open to students from other schools. 100 students usually enrolled. 2017 schedule: June 20 to August 15. Application deadline: June 15.

Tuition and Aid Day student tuition: $19,530. Tuition installment plan (Insured Tuition Payment Plan, monthly payment plans, semester payment plan). Need-based scholarship grants available. In 2016–17, 41% of upper-school students received aid. Total amount of financial aid awarded in 2016–17: $339,000.

Admissions Traditional secondary-level entrance grade is 9. Academic Profile Tests, ISEE or PSAT and SAT for applicants to grade 11 and 12 required. Deadline for receipt of application materials: none. Application fee required: $35. On-campus interview recommended.

Athletics Interscholastic: baseball (boys), basketball (b,g), cross-country running (b,g), field hockey (g), football (b), golf (b,g), soccer (b,g), softball (g), swimming and diving (b,g), tennis (b,g), volleyball (g), wrestling (b); intramural: basketball (b,g), soccer (b,g); coed intramural: soccer. 2 PE instructors, 6 coaches, 1 athletic trainer.

Computers Computers are regularly used in all academic classes. Computer network features include on-campus library services, online commercial services, Internet access, wireless campus network, Internet filtering or blocking technology. Student e-mail accounts are available to students. Students grades are available online.

Contact Mrs. Hannah Holliway, Director of Admission and Financial Aid. 717-815-6700. Fax: 717-815-6769. E-mail: hholliway@ycds.org. Website: www.ycds.org

YORK PREPARATORY SCHOOL

40 West 68th Street
New York, New York 10023-6092

General Information Coeducational day college-preparatory, arts, technology, music (practical and theory), and drama school. Grades 6–12. Founded: 1969. Setting: urban. 1 building on campus. Approved or accredited by Middle States Association of Colleges and Schools, National Independent Private Schools Association, and New

York Department of Education. Member of National Association of Independent Schools. Total enrollment: 358. Upper school average class size: 15. Upper school faculty-student ratio: 1:6. There are 158 required school days per year for Upper School students. Upper School students typically attend 5 days per week. The average school day consists of 6 hours and 30 minutes.

See Display on this page and Close-Up on page 610.

YORK SCHOOL

9501 York Road
Monterey, California 93940

Head of School: Chuck Harmon

General Information Coeducational day college-preparatory, arts, bilingual studies, and technology school. Grades 8–12. Founded: 1959. Setting: suburban. Nearest major city is San Jose. 126-acre campus. 6 buildings on campus. Approved or accredited by California Association of Independent Schools, National Association of Episcopal Schools, Western Association of Schools and Colleges, and California Department of Education. Member of National Association of Independent Schools. Endowment: $8 million. Total enrollment: 228. Upper school average class size: 13. Upper school faculty-student ratio: 1:7. Upper School students typically attend 5 days per week. The average school day consists of 7 hours.

Upper School Student Profile Grade 8: 22 students (9 boys, 13 girls); Grade 9: 55 students (25 boys, 30 girls); Grade 10: 56 students (20 boys, 36 girls); Grade 11: 55 students (22 boys, 33 girls); Grade 12: 50 students (24 boys, 26 girls).

Faculty School total: 33. In upper school: 18 men, 15 women; 26 have advanced degrees.

Subjects Offered Advanced studio art-AP, algebra, American history-AP, anatomy, ancient history, art, art history, Asian history, band, biology, biology-AP, calculus, calculus-AP, chemistry, chemistry-AP, choir, community service, computer science, creative writing, digital art, drama, English, English-AP, environmental science, film, fine arts, French, French language-AP, geometry, Greek, jazz, Latin, Latin-AP, marine biology, mathematics, music, music theory-AP, orchestra, painting, philosophy, photography, physical education, physical science, physics, physics-AP, physiology, pre-calculus, psychology-AP, science, social studies, Spanish, Spanish language-AP, statistics, studio art, U.S. history, U.S. history-AP, world history, yearbook.

Graduation Requirements Arts and fine arts (art, music, dance, drama), computer science, English, foreign language, mathematics, physical education (includes health), science, social studies (includes history), ensemble participation. Community service is required.

Special Academic Programs Advanced Placement exam preparation; honors section; independent study.

College Admission Counseling 47 students graduated in 2015; all went to college, including California Polytechnic State University, San Luis Obispo; University of California, Santa Barbara. Mean SAT critical reading: 649, mean SAT math: 635, mean SAT writing: 616, mean combined SAT: 1900.

Student Life Upper grades have specified standards of dress, student council, honor system. Discipline rests primarily with faculty.

Tuition and Aid Day student tuition: $31,150. Tuition installment plan (individually arranged payment plans, 2 payments, 10 payments). Need-based scholarship grants available. In 2015–16, 42% of upper-school students received aid. Total amount of financial aid awarded in 2015–16: $1,436,650.

Admissions Traditional secondary-level entrance grade is 9. For fall 2015, 115 students applied for upper-level admission, 92 were accepted, 61 enrolled. Admissions testing required. Deadline for receipt of application materials: February 1. Application fee required: $80. Interview required.

Athletics Interscholastic: basketball (boys, girls), cross-country running (b,g), diving (b,g), field hockey (g), golf (b,g), soccer (b,g), softball (g), swimming and diving (b,g), tennis (b,g), volleyball (g); coed interscholastic: dance, lacrosse; coed intramural: badminton, basketball, fitness walking, independent competitive sports, jogging, soccer, ultimate Frisbee, volleyball, walking, weight training, yoga. 18 coaches.

Computers Computers are regularly used in art, computer applications, technology, yearbook classes. Computer network features include on-campus library services, Internet access, wireless campus network. The school has a published electronic and media policy.

Contact Rebecca Geldmacher, Admission Associate and Registrar. 831-372-7338 Ext. 116. Fax: 831-372-8055. E-mail: becca@york.org. Website: www.york.org

THE YORK SCHOOL

1320 Yonge Street
Toronto, Ontario M4T 1X2, Canada

Head of School: Mr. Conor Jones

General Information Coeducational day college-preparatory and International Baccalaureate school. Grades JK–12. Founded: 1965. Setting: urban. 1-acre campus. 1 building on campus. Approved or accredited by Canadian Association of Independent Schools, Canadian Educational Standards Institute, Conference of Independent Schools of Ontario, International Baccalaureate Organization, and Ontario Department of Education. Member of Secondary School Admission Test Board. Language of

instruction: English. Total enrollment: 600. Upper school average class size: 18. Upper school faculty-student ratio: 1:16. Upper School students typically attend 5 days per week. The average school day consists of 7 hours.

Faculty School total: 80. In upper school: 12 men, 20 women.

Subjects Offered 20th century history, American history, biology, calculus, Canadian geography, Canadian history, Canadian law, careers, chemistry, civics, discrete mathematics, dramatic arts, economics, English, environmental systems, French, functions, geography, geometry, global issues, healthful living, instrumental music, Mandarin, physical education, physics, social sciences, society challenge and change, Spanish, theater arts, theory of knowledge, visual arts, vocal music, world history, world religions.

Graduation Requirements International Baccalaureate diploma exams.

Special Academic Programs International Baccalaureate program; honors section; independent study; study abroad; academic accommodation for the gifted, the musically talented, and the artistically talented.

College Admission Counseling 66 students graduated in 2015; all went to college, including Dalhousie University; McGill University; Queen's University at Kingston; The University of British Columbia; The University of Western Ontario; University of Toronto.

Student Life Upper grades have uniform requirement, student council, honor system. Discipline rests primarily with faculty.

Tuition and Aid Day student tuition: CAN$27,000. Tuition installment plan (monthly payment plans, individually arranged payment plans). Merit scholarship grants, need-based scholarship grants available. In 2015–16, 5% of upper school students received aid.

Admissions Traditional secondary-level entrance grade is 9. For fall 2015, 100 students applied for upper-level admission, 81 were accepted, 34 enrolled. School's own exam required. Deadline for receipt of application materials: December 4. Application fee required: CAN$200. Interview recommended.

Athletics Interscholastic: aerobics/dance (boys, girls), aerobics/Nautilus (b,g), alpine skiing (b,g), badminton (b,g), baseball (b,g), basketball (b,g), cooperative games (b,g), cross-country running (b,g), fitness (b,g), floor hockey (b,g), outdoor activities (b,g), outdoor education (b,g), running (b,g), soccer (b,g), softball (b,g), strength & conditioning (b,g), track and field (b,g); intramural: aerobics/Nautilus (b,g), badminton (b,g), baseball (b,g), basketball (b,g), outdoor education (b,g), volleyball (b,g); coed interscholastic: badminton, cooperative games, cross-country running, floor hockey, ice skating, outdoor activities, outdoor education, running, strength & conditioning, track and field, ultimate Frisbee; coed intramural: backpacking, badminton, curling, Frisbee, hiking/backpacking, outdoor adventure, outdoor education, outdoor skills, track and field, ultimate Frisbee. 4 PE instructors.

Computers Computers are regularly used in all academic classes. Computer network features include on-campus library services, Internet access, wireless campus network, Internet filtering or blocking technology. Campus intranet, student e-mail accounts, and computer access in designated common areas are available to students. Students grades are available online. The school has a published electronic and media policy.

Contact Ms. Julia Gordon, Admission Assistant. 416-646-5275. Fax: 416-926-9592. E-mail: admission@yorkschool.com. Website: www.yorkschool.com

ZURICH INTERNATIONAL SCHOOL

Steinacherstrasse 140
Wädenswil 8820, Switzerland

Head of School: Jeff Paulson

General Information Coeducational day college-preparatory and International Baccalaureate Diploma and Advanced Placement school. Grades PS–12. Distance learning grades 7–12. Founded: 1963. Setting: suburban. Nearest major city is Zurich, Switzerland. 6-acre campus. 1 building on campus. Approved or accredited by Council of International Schools, European Council of International Schools, and New England Association of Schools and Colleges. Member of European Council of International Schools. Language of instruction: English. Total enrollment: 1,422. Upper school average class size: 16. Upper school faculty-student ratio: 1:7. There are 175 required school days per year for Upper School students. Upper School students typically attend 5 days per week. The average school day consists of 7 hours.

Upper School Student Profile Grade 9: 116 students (64 boys, 52 girls); Grade 10: 132 students (61 boys, 71 girls); Grade 11: 130 students (65 boys, 65 girls); Grade 12: 135 students (64 boys, 71 girls).

Faculty School total: 224. In upper school: 33 men, 37 women; 40 have advanced degrees.

Subjects Offered Acting, Advanced Placement courses, art history, art history-AP, art-AP, biology, biology-AP, calculus, calculus-AP, chemistry-AP, concert band, concert choir, digital photography, drama, drama performance, economics, economics-AP, English, English language and composition-AP, English literature, English literature and composition-AP, ESL, European history-AP, fine arts, French, French language-AP, German, German-AP, health, history, history-AP, International Baccalaureate courses, journalism, macro/microeconomics-AP, macroeconomics-AP, mathematics, microeconomics-AP, music, philosophy, photography, physical education, physics-AP, pre-calculus, psychology-AP, public speaking, robotics, science, social studies, Spanish language-AP, statistics-AP, studio art, studio art-AP, theater, U.S. history-AP, visual arts, world history, world history-AP, writing.

Graduation Requirements Arts and fine arts (art, music, dance, drama), English, foreign language, mathematics, physical education (includes health), science, social studies (includes history), completion of a yearly service project. Community service is required.

Special Academic Programs International Baccalaureate program; 22 Advanced Placement exams for which test preparation is offered; honors section; independent study; remedial reading and/or remedial writing; remedial math; ESL (12 students enrolled).

College Admission Counseling 111 students graduated in 2016; 100 went to college, including Bard College; Cornell University; Florida Institute of Technology; Syracuse University; The University of Arizona; University of Southern California. Other: 2 went to work, 4 entered military service, 5 had other specific plans. Mean SAT critical reading: 579, mean SAT math: 595, mean SAT writing: 577, mean combined SAT: 1751. 36% scored over 600 on SAT critical reading, 46% scored over 600 on SAT math, 36% scored over 600 on SAT writing.

Student Life Upper grades have specified standards of dress, student council. Discipline rests primarily with faculty.

Tuition and Aid Day student tuition: 36,000 Swiss francs. Tuition installment plan (individually arranged payment plans, two installments (60% & 40%) of the annual tuition fee for the, 1st and 2nd semester of the school year). Need-based scholarship grants available.

Admissions Traditional secondary-level entrance grade is 9. For fall 2016, 107 students applied for upper-level admission, 81 were accepted, 63 enrolled. English for Non-native Speakers or math and English placement tests required. Deadline for receipt of application materials: none. Application fee required: 500 Swiss francs.

Athletics Interscholastic: basketball (boys, girls), rugby (b), soccer (b,g), softball (g), tennis (b,g), volleyball (g); coed interscholastic: alpine skiing, cross-country running, Frisbee, golf, nordic skiing, skiing (cross-country), skiing (downhill), swimming and diving, track and field, ultimate Frisbee; coed intramural: basketball, canoeing/kayaking, climbing, fitness, Frisbee, hiking/backpacking, indoor soccer, indoor track & field, juggling, kayaking, outdoor activities, physical fitness, physical training, rock climbing, running, snowboarding, strength & conditioning, wall climbing, yoga. 5 PE instructors, 8 coaches.

Computers Computers are regularly used in all classes. Computer network features include on-campus library services, online commercial services, Internet access, wireless campus network, one to one tablet program, Moodle, VHS, MAC lab, iPad pilot in upper school. Campus intranet, student e-mail accounts, and computer access in designated common areas are available to students. Students grades are available online. The school has a published electronic and media policy. **Contact** James Cooper, Head Admissions. 41-58 750 2531. Fax: 41-58 750 2501. E-mail: jcooper@zis.ch. Website: www.zis.ch

Traditional Day and Boarding School Close-Ups

BERKELEY PREPARATORY SCHOOL

Tampa, Florida

Type: Coeducational, independent, Episcopal-affiliated, college-preparatory day school
Grades: PK–12: Lower Division, Pre-Kindergarten–5; Middle Division, 6–8; Upper Division, 9–12
Enrollment: School total: 1,300; Lower Division: 400; Middle Division: 325; Upper Division: 575
Head of School: Joseph W. Seivold, Headmaster

THE SCHOOL

The Latin words *Disciplina, Diligentia,* and *Integritas* in Berkeley's motto describe the school's mission to nurture students' intellectual, emotional, spiritual and physical development so they can achieve their highest potential. Episcopal in heritage, Berkeley was founded in 1960, and opened for grades 7–12 the following year. Kindergarten through grade 6 was added in 1967, and Pre-Kindergarten began in 1988. Berkeley's purpose is to enable its students to achieve academic excellence in preparation for higher education and to instill in students a strong sense of morality, ethics, and social responsibility.

Berkeley is located on an 86-acre campus in Tampa, Florida, a location that attracts students from Hillsborough, Pinellas, Pasco, and Polk Counties and throughout the greater Tampa Bay area. Private bus transportation is available.

Berkeley is incorporated as a nonprofit institution and is governed by a 27-member Board of Trustees that includes alumni, parents of current students, and parents of alumni. The presidents of the Alumni Association and Parents' Club are also members of the Board.

ACADEMIC PROGRAM

The school year runs from the end of August to the first week of June and includes Thanksgiving, Christmas, and spring vacations. The curriculum naturally varies within each division.

In the Lower Division, the program seeks to provide appropriate, challenging learning experiences in a safe environment that reflects the academic, social, moral, and ethical values the school espouses in its philosophy. Curricular emphasis is on core subjects of reading and mathematics. An interdisciplinary approach is used in world language and social studies, and manipulatives are used extensively in the science and mathematics programs. Each student also receives instruction in library skills and integration of technology and learning.

Academic requirements in the Middle Division, where classes average 16 to 20 students, are English, English expression, mathematics, global studies, world language, science, technology, physical education, art, drama, and music. Classes meet five days a week on a rotating schedule. Extra help is available from teachers, and grades are sent to parents four times a year.

The Upper Division program, with an average class size of 15 to 20 students, requires students to take four or five credit courses a year, in addition to fine

arts and physical education requirements. To graduate, a student must complete 23 credits, including 4 in English, 4 in mathematics, and 3 in history, science, and foreign language. Students must also complete one year of personal fitness/health and an additional year of physical education, two years of fine arts, and two electives. In addition, Berkeley students are required to take a semester of religious studies each year and complete 76 hours of community service. More than 40 Advanced Placement, Honors, and Advanced Topics courses are offered. The Upper Division program is designed to provide students with the atmosphere and advantages of a small liberal arts college. Students are offered a choice of 100 student activities and clubs, and they may be selected to join several nationally recognized academic honor groups, including the Cum Laude Society and National Honor Society.

FACULTY AND ADVISERS

There are 300 full-time faculty and staff members. They hold baccalaureate, more than 150 graduate, and several doctoral degrees. Headmaster Joseph Seivold graduated Phi Beta Kappa from the University of North Carolina at Chapel Hill with a degree in history. He holds a master's degree in education administration from St. Mary's University of Minnesota. He came to Berkeley from The Blake School in Minnesota.

In addition to teaching responsibilities, faculty members are involved in Berkeley's co-curricular programs as coaches and student activity advisers. Berkeley faculty members receive support for professional development opportunities and several faculty members have been recognized as some of the top teachers among their peers nationally.

COLLEGE ADMISSION COUNSELING

Traditionally, 100 percent of Berkeley's graduating class goes on to attend college. Although Berkeley does not rank its students, more than 130 colleges visit the school each year to recruit its graduates. Berkeley's college counseling department works to assist students and their families in selecting colleges that best suit their academic, financial, and social needs.

Recent graduates are attending Boston College, Brown, Cornell, Dartmouth, Duke, Emory, Georgetown, Harvard, Northwestern, Notre Dame, NYU, Princeton, Stanford, Vanderbilt, Villanova, Yale, and the Universities of Florida, Miami, Michigan, North Carolina, Pennsylvania, and Virginia. Scholarship offers totaling more than $9 million were made to the Class of 2016.

STUDENT BODY AND CONDUCT

In all divisions, Berkeley students are expected to maintain high standards. Mature conduct and use of manners are expected, and an honor code outlines students' responsibilities. In exchange, students are entrusted with certain privileges, such as direct access to the administration and the opportunity to initiate school-sponsored clubs. Students wear uniforms to class.

CAMPUS FACILITIES

Berkeley is located on a beautiful 86-acre campus in Tampa, consisting of 29 buildings totaling 329,732 square feet that feature the following: three divisions housing modern classrooms and learning spaces; two libraries; the Technology Commons; a 425-seat dining café; the Early Childhood Center and playground; the Lower Division Makerspace; an outdoor environmental classroom; and a 75,000-square-foot center for the arts and sciences that includes a multimedia room with a green screen, sound booth, and multiple Mac stations using the latest digital editing software; a technology center featuring 3D printers, laser cutters, 3D imaging, and Mac stations; a design arts studio; a robotics lab; a 235-seat recital hall, a black box theatre; sound enhancing music performance spaces and classrooms; and state-of-the-art biology labs and project spaces.

The fine arts program is enhanced by the Lykes Center for the Arts, a 634-seat performing arts center, which also includes a gallery for visual arts displays, a flex studio for dance and small drama productions, dressing rooms, and an orchestra pit.

ATHLETICS

Varsity sports for boys include baseball, basketball, crew, cross-country, diving, football, golf, hockey, lacrosse, soccer, hockey, swimming, tennis, track, and wrestling. Girls compete in basketball, crew, cross-country, diving, golf, lacrosse, soccer, softball, swimming, tennis, track, and volleyball. Berkeley has been recognized as the Florida High School Athletic Association's overall 4A state academic champion for five consecutive years and has several individual and team champions.

Berkeley's athletic facilities include the 53,000 square-foot Straz Family Field House, two gymnasiums, a junior Olympic swimming pool, a wrestling/gymnastics room, a weight room, a rock-climbing wall, a varsity level soccer field, a tennis complex, a high- and low-ropes course, a baseball and softball complex, a state-of-the-art track, and practice fields for football, soccer, and lacrosse. Seasonal sports award banquets and a homecoming football game are scheduled annually.

EXTRACURRICULAR OPPORTUNITIES

In addition to its broad-based commitment to student organizations and clubs and its community service requirements, Berkeley offers its students a vast array of possibilities beyond the classrooms. Student artwork is accepted each year into national art shows and exhibits, and several students receive Gold Key Awards each year from the Alliance for Young Artists and Writers. An after-school Lower Division chess club attracts close to 100 students from Kindergarten through grade 5. Middle and Upper Division students, as well as many faculty members, participate in several international experiences, visiting countries such as England, New Zealand, the Dominican Republic, Ghana, Australia, China, France, Italy, Switzerland, and Spain.

DAILY LIFE

Students in Pre-Kindergarten through grade 5 attend classes from 8:00 a.m. to 3:05 p.m. Middle and Upper Division students also begin at 8:00 a.m. and end at 3:20 p.m. Teachers are available to assist students and offer extra help during activity periods, which are scheduled into each class day. Supervised study halls are also scheduled for some students.

SUMMER PROGRAMS

Berkeley hosts more than 100 sports, academic, and professional development camps and sessions during a six-week summer program for Bay-area students, prekindergarten through grade 12. More information is available online at www.berkeleyprep.org/summer.

COSTS AND FINANCIAL AID

The tuition schedule for 2016–17 is as follows: $17,560 for Pre-Kindergarten and Kindergarten, $19,720 for grades 1–5, $21,790 for grades 6–8, and $23,660 for grades 9–12. Tuition is payable in eight installments and must be paid in full by January 1. Tuition payments do not cover costs of uniforms, laptops, supplies, transportation, special event admission fees, or other expenses incurred in the ordinary course of student activities at Berkeley.

Berkeley makes all admission decisions without regard to financial status. Families who have reviewed their financial situation and feel that help may be needed in paying tuition should apply for aid. Financial aid awards are available at any grade level to students who demonstrate need. In determining need, the guidelines of the School and Student Service for Financial Aid (SSS) are used. Each award is individualized based upon the financial assessment of each applicant. It is important to note that Berkeley may not be able to accommodate all financial aid applications in a given year.

Berkeley is also fortunate to have a number of scholarships available to students. In addition to demonstrated financial need, specific criteria such as academic achievement and leadership potential are also components of a separate scholarship application process. Receiving a scholarship is a great honor; therefore, the process is both competitive and selective. A selection committee will review the completed applications and announce the scholarship recipients in early March.

ADMISSIONS INFORMATION

In considering applicants, Berkeley evaluates a student's talent, academic skills, personal interests, motivation to learn, and desire to attend.

Lower Division candidates visit age-appropriate classrooms and are evaluated through grade level assessments. Middle and Upper Division candidates are required to take the Secondary School Admissions Test (SSAT) and generally register for a November, December, or January test date. In addition to the SSAT, all applicants schedule an appointment with the Admissions Office for Otis-Lennon testing and a writing sample. Entering juniors and seniors may submit PSAT, SAT, PLAN, or ACT scores in place of sitting for the SSAT.

The admission process is selective and is based on information gathered from the application form, interviews, the candidate's record, admission tests, and teacher recommendations.

Berkeley admits students of any race, color, sex, religion, and national or ethnic origin and does not discriminate on the basis of any category protected by law in the administration of its educational policies, admission policies, and scholarship, financial aid, athletic, and other school-administered programs.

APPLICATION TIMETABLE

Applications should be submitted by the fall one year prior to the student's entrance into Berkeley. The Lower and Upper Division Admissions Committees begin evaluation of applicants in mid-February and decisions are made in March. The Middle Division Admissions Committee begins evaluation of completed files in mid-January with notification on a rolling basis from the end of January until vacancies are filled. All applications after the initial selection process are considered on a space-available basis.

Berkeley welcomes inquiries from families throughout the year. However, because of the competitive nature of the admission process, families are encouraged to visit the campus as early as possible to become familiar with the school, its programs, and its admission procedure.

ADMISSIONS CORRESPONDENCE

Janie McIlvaine
Director of Admissions
Berkeley Preparatory School
4811 Kelly Road
Tampa, Florida 33615
United States
Phone: 813-885-1673
Fax: 813-886-6933
E-mail: mcilvjan@berkeleyprep.org
Website: www.berkeleyprep.org/admissions

BERKSHIRE SCHOOL
Sheffield, Massachusetts

Type: Coeducational boarding and day college-preparatory school
Grades: 9–12 (Forms III–VI), postgraduate year
Enrollment: 399
Head of School: Pieter M. Mulder

THE SCHOOL

Berkshire School is a coed, college preparatory boarding and day school that prepares 399 ninth through twelfth graders and postgraduates for a global future. Signature programs—such as Advanced Math/Science Research, Advanced Humanities Research, and Sustainability—coexist with advanced sections and AP offerings in all disciplines. With a range of artistic and athletic offerings, a new Fine Arts Center, a state-of-the-art math and science center, a 117,000-square-foot athletic facility, and national recognition for its efforts in environmental conservation, Berkshire School is an extraordinary setting in which students are encouraged to embrace the school motto: *Pro Vita Non Pro Schola Discimus,* "Learning—not just for school but for life."

In 1907, Mr. and Mrs. Seaver B. Buck, graduates of Harvard and Smith respectively, rented the building of Glenny Farm at the foot of Mt. Everett and founded Berkshire School. The Bucks devoted themselves to educating young men with the values of academic excellence, physical vigor, and high personal standards. In 1969, this commitment to excellence was extended to include girls.

Situated at the base of Mt. Everett, Berkshire's campus spans 400 acres. It is a 75-minute drive to both Albany International Airport and Hartford's Bradley International Airport and just over two hours from Boston and New York City.

Berkshire School is incorporated as a not-for-profit institution, governed by a 27-member self-perpetuating Board of Trustees. The School has a $118-million endowment. Annual operating expenses exceed $26 million. The Annual Giving in 2015–16 surpassed $3 million. The Berkshire Chapter of the Cum Laude Society was established in 1942.

Berkshire School is accredited by the New England Association of Schools and Colleges and holds memberships in the Independent School Association of Massachusetts, the National Association of Independent Schools, the College Entrance Examination Board, the National Association for College Admission Counseling, the Secondary School Admission Test Board, and the Association of Boarding Schools.

ACADEMIC PROGRAM

Berkshire's academic program is firmly rooted in a college-preparatory curriculum that features advanced and AP courses across all disciplines. In addition, unique opportunities in humanities and math/science research, student-directed independent study, and electives in science, humanities, and fine arts allow students to pursue advanced study. As creative and agile problem solvers, strong critical thinkers, persuasive communicators, and active global citizens, Berkshire students are equipped with the skills required for the twenty-first century.

Berkshire requires the following credits: 4 years of English; 3 years each of mathematics, a foreign language, and history; 2 years of science; and 1 year of the visual or performing arts. All students are placed at a level commensurate with their skills and talent. Many take one or more of the seventeen Advanced Placement courses offered.

Students carry a minimum of five courses. The average number of students in a class is 12, and the student-teacher ratio is 4:1. The academic year is divided into two semesters, each culminating with an assessment period. Students receive grades and teacher comments twice a semester, and advisor letters twice a year. Berkshire uses a traditional letter-grading system of A–F (D is passing).

Berkshire has ten signature programs, which offer students the unique and wide-ranging opportunity to explore an intellectual passion or nurture a new interest. The School's signature programs are: Advanced Humanities Research, Advanced Math/Science Research, Aviation Science, Black Rock Scholars, Independent Study, Ritt Kellogg Mountain Program, Pro Vita Winter Session, Sabin Entrepreneurial Prize, STEAM, and Sustainability.

FACULTY AND ADVISORS

Berkshire has 63 teaching faculty, 91 including nonteaching faculty. Fifty-three teachers hold a master's degree and seven hold doctorates. Faculty members contribute to both the academic and personal development of each student. Each student is paired with a faculty advisor who provides guidance, monitors academic progress, and serves as a liaison to the student's family. Berkshire also retains the services of four pediatricians, five full-time registered nurses, and two certified athletic trainers.

In November 2013, Pieter M. Mulder was named Berkshire's sixteenth head of school. He holds a bachelor's degree in American studies from Williams College with minors in architecture and environmental science, and a master's degree in mathematics with a concentration in creative writing from Wesleyan University. Mr. Mulder came to Berkshire in 2005 and lives on campus with his wife, Lucia, and their two children.

COLLEGE ADMISSION COUNSELING

Berkshire School's six college counselors work closely with students and their parents in the search for an appropriate college or university. The formal process begins in junior year, with individual conferences with counselors, and the opportunity to meet with selected members of the approximately 100 college admissions representatives who visit the campus. Parents of sophomores are welcomed into the process with an overview from the College Counseling Office during Fall Parents' Weekend. In February, juniors and their parents attend a two-day seminar on the college admission process, in which admission strategies are discussed and specific institutions are identified for each student's consideration. During the summer, students are encouraged to visit colleges and draft their college application essays, while completing the Common Application. The application process is generally completed by winter vacation in the senior year.

Members of the classes of 2012–2016 enrolled at a variety of four-year colleges or universities, including: Amherst, Bates, Berkeley, Boston College, Boston University, Bowdoin, Brown, Bucknell, Colby, Colgate, College of Charleston, Colorado College, Columbia, Cornell, Dartmouth, Davidson, Denison, Dickinson, Duke, Elon, Emory, Franklin & Marshall, George Washington, Georgetown, Hamilton, Harvard, Johns Hopkins, Kenyon, Lafayette, Lehigh, Middlebury, NYU, Northeastern, Northwestern, Norte Dame, Occidental, Pitzer, Princeton, Providence College, RIT, Savannah College of Art and Design, Skidmore, Smith, SMU, St. Lawrence, Stanford, Syracuse, Trinity, Tufts, Union, United States Military Academy, United States Naval Academy, Vassar, Wake Forest, Wesleyan, Wheaton, Whitman, William and Mary, Williams, Yale, and the Universities of Connecticut, Colorado, Illinois, Miami, Michigan, New Hampshire, Pennsylvania, Richmond, Vermont, Virginia, and Wisconsin.

STUDENT BODY AND CONDUCT

In the 2016–17 academic year, there were 364 boarders and 35 day students. The student body is drawn from 31 states and 33 countries.

Students contribute directly to the life of the school community through involvement in Student Government, the Prefect Program, dormitory life, and various clubs and activities. Participation gives students a positive growth experience in keeping with the School's motto. The rules at Berkshire are simple and straightforward and are consistent with the values and ideals of the School. They are designed to help students live orderly lives within an environment of mutual trust and respect.

ACADEMIC FACILITIES

Berkshire Hall, the School's primary academic facility, built in 1930 and the centerpiece of the campus, reopened in the fall of 2008 after a full renovation. It houses larger classrooms with state-of-the-art technology, new administrative offices, a two-story atrium, and a Great Room for student study and special functions. A new music center and dance center opened in the fall of 2010, while in the fall of 2011, Allen Theater reopened after a complete renovation. This included new academic spaces for the Kenefick Center for Learning, classrooms for the theater and film department and the SAT tutoring program, as well as a studio for WBSL, the School's own radio station.

In October 2012, Berkshire inaugurated the state-of-the-art Bellas/Dixon Math and Science Center. This 48,000-square-foot LEED-Certified Gold building provides facilities that allow students to pursue academic excellence and innovation at the highest level while adhering to the School's commitment to sustainability. The 2013 school year saw the opening of the School's new Fine Arts Center, which includes a gallery, department offices, and classrooms for studio and digital art and ceramics.

In the fall of 2015, Berkshire completed a full renovation of its Geier Library, creating a comfortable, quiet study space of about 17,000 square feet, featuring ten Mac computers, half of which contain the Adobe Creative Cloud for design work and WiFi. Research is facilitated by access to JSTOR, an online database of more than 1,000 academic journals, containing literally millions of peer-reviewed articles, images, reviews, and primary sources. The library also holds a wide-ranging print collection. At the Dixon Observatory, computer synchronized telescopes make it possible to view and photograph objects in the solar system and beyond.

BOARDING AND GENERAL FACILITIES

Berkshire has ten residential houses, including two girls' dormitories completed in the fall of 2002. Three faculty families typically reside in each house, along with two prefects—seniors, whose primary responsibility is to assist dorm parents with daily routines, including study hall and room inspection. Dorm rooms all have Internet access and private phone lines. There is a common room in each house, where students may relax or study. Benson Commons features a dining hall, a post office, the School bookstore, the Music Center, the Student Life Office, and recreational spaces. In 2011 an 8-acre solar field was built on campus; it now provides approximately 40 percent of the School's energy needs. In the summer of 2015, Berkshire completed a project begun by students in the Sustainability class, installing an electric car charger on campus and making it available to the community.

ATHLETICS

Berkshire enjoys a proud tradition of athletic excellence. The School competes in the highly competitive New England Preparatory School Athletic Council (NEPSAC) offering 17 sports and 50 athletic team options. Students may also choose to participate in noncompetitive alternatives each afternoon, such as STEAM, the Ritt Kellogg Mountain Program, strength and conditioning, art, music, theater, or dance.

In January 2009, the 117,000-square-foot Jackman L. Stewart Athletic Center opened. The facility offers two ice rinks (one Olympic-size), 14 locker rooms, seating for 800 spectators, a 34 machine fitness center and athletic training rooms. It can also be used for indoor tennis and can accommodate all-school functions. A second athletic center features full-size courts for basketball and volleyball, four international squash courts, a climbing wall, and a dance studio. Other athletic facilities include the Thomas H. Young Field for baseball, softball fields, an all-weather track, a lighted football field, and two synthetic-turf fields. A twelve-court tennis facility was completed in the fall of 2010.

In September 2016, Berkshire opened a new squash center and renovated gymnasium. The 50,000-square-foot facility features new courts for basketball and volleyball, a newly renovated dance studio, new locker rooms, and 10 bright and airy, state-of-the-art squash courts.

EXTRACURRICULAR OPPORTUNITIES

Berkshire offers students a variety of opportunities to express their talents and passions. Students publish a newspaper, a yearbook, and both literary and scholarly journals featuring student writing, art, and photography. The Ritt Kellogg Mountain Program offers backcountry skills, boatbuilding, fly fishing, kayaking, rock climbing, and winter mountaineering.

There are a number of active clubs, including Afro-Latino Society, Bear-B-Q Club, Entrepreneurs Club, Gender and Sexuality Alliance, Berkshire Maple Syrup Corporation, Meditation Club, Philanthropy Club, and WBSL (radio station).

Berkshire students pursue the arts in the classroom and through extracurricular activities. The theater program offers a play in the fall and another in the spring, as well as a winter musical. There are four choral groups: Bear Tones, a coed *acapella* group; Ursa Major, an all-school chorus; Ursa Minor, a girls' *acappella* group; and Greensleeves, an all-male chorus. There are two music groups: jazz band and the chamber music ensemble. Students can also take private voice and instrument lessons. Each season, the Berkshire community looks forward to various performances, such as dance and music recitals, a jazz café, improv performances, and open mic nights. Visual arts include painting, drawing, sculpture, digital art, photography, and ceramics. Student artwork is displayed in the Student Center, Berkshire Hall Atrium, and The Warren Family Gallery.

DAILY LIFE

Berkshire follows a rotating schedule in which classes meet at different times each day. Within that rotation, there is a total of eight periods (including lunch). The school day begins at 8:15 a.m. and ends at 2:55 p.m., except on Wednesday and Saturday, when the school day ends at 11:40 a.m.

Athletics, outdoor experiences, and art activities occupy the afternoon. Clubs have a dedicated meeting time during the class day, once a week.

WEEKEND LIFE

Weekend activities are planned by a Director of Student Activities and include first-run movies, dances with live bands, and DJs. There are trips to local amusement parks and theaters, as well as shopping trips to Hartford and Albany. In addition, students and faculty members journey to New York and Boston to visit museums, attend theater and music productions, and take in professional sports events.

COSTS AND FINANCIAL AID

For the 2016–17 academic year, tuition was $58,500 for boarding students and $46,500 for day students. For most students, $100 a month is sufficient personal spending money. Ten percent of the tuition is paid upon enrollment, 50 percent is payable on June 30, and 40 percent is payable by October 31. Two tuition payment plans are available.

Financial aid is awarded on the basis of need to about 30 percent of the student body. The total financial aid spent in 2015–16 was $5.1 million. The School and Student Service (SSS) Parents Financial Statement and a 1040 form are required.

ADMISSIONS INFORMATION

Berkshire adheres to the principle that in diversity there is strength and therefore, actively seeks students from a broad range of geographic, ethnic, religious, and socioeconomic backgrounds. Admission is most common in the freshman and sophomore years, and the School enrolls a small number of juniors and postgraduates each year.

In order to assess a student's academic record, potential, character, and contributions to his or her school, Berkshire requires a personal interview, a transcript, test scores, and recommendations from English and mathematics teachers, along with the actual application. Candidates should have their Secondary School Admission Test (SSAT) scores forwarded to Berkshire School (school code 1612). International students are required to have their Test of English as a Foreign Language (TOEFL) scores forwarded in addition to their SSAT (school code 3252).

APPLICATION TIMETABLE

Interested families are encouraged to visit the campus in the fall or winter preceding the September in which admission is desired. Visits are arranged according to the academic schedule, Monday, Tuesday, Wednesday, Thursday, Friday, and Saturday. January 15 is the deadline for submitting applications. Berkshire adheres to the standard notification date of March 10 and the families' reply date of April 10. Applications to Berkshire School can be submitted using Gateway to Prep Schools and SSAT Standard Application Online.

ADMISSIONS CORRESPONDENCE

Andrew Bogardus, Director of Admission
Berkshire School
245 North Undermountain Road
Sheffield, Massachusetts 01257
United States
Phone: 413-229-1003
Fax: 413-229-1016
E-mail: admission@berkshireschool.org
Website: http://www.berkshireschool.org

DELBARTON SCHOOL

Morristown, New Jersey

Type: Boys' day college-preparatory school
Grades: 7–12: Middle School, 7–8; Upper School, 9–12
Enrollment: School total: 590; Upper School: 523
Head of School: Br. Paul Diveny, O.S.B., Headmaster

THE SCHOOL

Delbarton School was established in 1939 by the Benedictine monks of Saint Mary's Abbey as an independent boarding and day school. Now a day school, Delbarton is located on a 200-acre woodland campus 3 miles west of historic Morristown and 30 miles west of New York City. Adjacent to the campus is Jockey Hollow, a national historic park.

Delbarton School seeks to enroll boys of good character who have demonstrated scholastic achievement and the capacity for further growth. The faculty strives to support each boy's efforts toward intellectual development and to reinforce his commitment to help build a community of responsible individuals. The faculty encourages each boy to become an independent seeker of information, not a passive recipient, and to assume responsibility for gaining both knowledge and judgment that will strengthen his contribution to the life of the School and his later contribution to society. While the School offers much, it also seeks boys who are willing to give much and who are eager to understand as well as to be understood.

The School is governed by the 9-member Board of Trustees of the Order of Saint Benedict of New Jersey, located at Saint Mary's Abbey in Morristown. Delbarton's 2016–17 annual operating expenses totaled $23.2 million. It has an endowment of $37 million. This includes annual fund-raising support from 45 percent of the alumni.

Delbarton School is accredited by the Middle States Association of Colleges and Schools and approved by the Department of Education of the State of New Jersey. It is a member of the National Association of Independent Schools, the New Jersey Association of Independent Schools, the Council for Advancement and Support of Education, the National Catholic Educational Association, and the New Jersey State Interscholastic Athletic Association.

ACADEMIC PROGRAM

The academic program in the Upper School is college preparatory. The course of study offers preparation in all major academic subjects and a number of electives. The studies are intended to help a boy shape a thought and a sentence, speak clearly about ideas and effectively about feelings, and suspend judgment until all the facts are known. Course work, on the whole, is intensive and involves about 20 hours of outside preparation each week. The curriculum contains both a core of required subjects that are fundamental to a liberal education and various elective courses that are designed to meet the individual interests of the boys. Instruction is given in all areas that are necessary for gaining admission to liberal arts or technical institutions of higher learning.

The school year is divided into three academic terms. In each term, every boy must take five major courses, physical education, and religious studies. The specific departmental requirements in grades 9 through 12 are English (4 years), mathematics (4 years), foreign language (3 years), science (3 years), history (3 years), religious studies (2 terms in each of 4 years), physical education and health (4 years), fine arts (1 major course, 1 term of art, and 1 term of music), and computer technology (2 terms). For qualified boys in the junior and senior years, all departments offer Advanced Placement courses, and it is also possible in certain instances to pursue work through independent study or to study at neighboring colleges.

The grading system uses A to F (failing) designations with pluses and minuses. Advisory reports are sent to parents in the middle of each term as well as at the end of the three terms. Parents are also contacted when a student has received an academic warning or is placed on probation. The average class size is 15, and the student-teacher ratio is about 7:1, which fosters close student-faculty relations.

FACULTY AND ADVISERS

In 2016–17 the faculty consisted of 4 Benedictine monks and 75 lay teachers. Sixty-three are full-time members, with 59 holding advanced degrees.

Br. Paul Diveny, O.S.B., became Headmaster in July 2007. Br. Paul received his B.A. from the Catholic University of America in 1975; his diploma in Monastic Studies from the Pontificio Ateneo Sant'Anselmo in Rome, Italy in 1982; and his M.A. in German from Middlebury College in 1987. He has served the School previously as a teacher of Latin, German, ancient history, and religious studies, and as Assistant Headmaster.

The teaching tradition of the School has called upon faculty members to serve as coaches, counselors, or administrators. A genuine interest in the development of people leads the faculty to be involved in many student activities. Every boy is assigned to a guidance counselor, who advises in the selection of courses that meet School and college requirements as well as personal interests. Individual conferences are regularly arranged to discuss academic and personal development. The counselor also contacts the boy's parents when it seems advisable.

COLLEGE ADMISSION COUNSELING

Preparation for college begins when a boy enters Delbarton. The PSAT is given to everyone in the tenth and eleventh grades. Guidance for admission to college is directed by the senior class counselor. This process generally begins in the fall of the junior year, when the junior class counselor meets

with each boy to help clarify his goals and interests. Many college admissions officers visit the School annually for conferences. Every effort is made to direct each boy toward an institution that will challenge his abilities and satisfy his interests.

The mean SAT critical reading and math score for the class of 2016 was 1340. More than 25 percent of the young men in the classes of 2013, 2014, 2015, and 2016 have been named National Merit Scholars, Semifinalists, or Commended Students. In addition, 96 percent of the members of the class of 2016 were enrolled in at least one AP course.

All of the graduates of the classes of 2013, 2014, 2015, and 2016 went on to college, with 3 or more attending such schools as Boston College, Bucknell, Columbia, Georgetown, Hobart and William Smith, Middlebury, Notre Dame, Princeton, Tufts, Villanova, Vanderbilt, Williams, Yale, and the Universities of Pennsylvania and Virginia.

STUDENT BODY AND CONDUCT

The 2016–17 Upper School student body consisted of 132 ninth graders, 134 tenth graders, 131 eleventh graders, and 126 twelfth graders. The Middle School had 32 seventh and 35 eighth graders. All of the students are from New Jersey, particularly the counties of Morris, Essex, Somerset, Union, Bergen, Hunterdon, Passaic, and Sussex.

Regulations, academic and social, are relatively few. The School eschews the manipulative, the coercive, the negative, or the merely punitive approach to discipline. The basic understanding underlying the School's regulations is that each boy, entering with others in a common educational enterprise, shares responsibility with his fellow students and with faculty members for developing and maintaining standards that contribute to the welfare of the entire School community. Moreover, shared responsibility is essential to the growth of the community; at the same time, much of an individual boy's growth, the increase in his capacity for self-renewal, his sense of belonging, and his sense of identity spring from his eagerness and willingness to contribute to the life of the School. Each class has a moderator, who is available for advice and assistance. The moderator works closely with the boys, assisting them in their progress.

ACADEMIC FACILITIES

The physical facilities include two classroom buildings, a fine arts center, a science pavilion, a greenhouse, the church, and the dining hall. Academic facilities include thirty-seven classrooms, six science laboratories, art and music studios, and a library of more than 20,000 volumes. The five computer laboratories consist of 250 workstations in a networked system. The school recently adopted a one-to-one laptop program for the students and provides several charging stations throughout the campus. Three computer laboratories and dedicated classroom computers also provide over 100 workstations in a networked system. Some individual academic departments offer personal computers for advanced study in their discipline as well.

ATHLETICS

Sports at the School are an integral part of student life. The School holds the traditional belief that much can be learned about cooperation, competition, and character through participating in sports. Almost 85 percent of the boys participate on one or more interscholastic athletics teams. Varsity sports offered in the fall term are football, soccer, and cross-country; in the winter term, basketball, wrestling, track, hockey, squash, bowling, and swimming (in an off-campus pool); and in the spring, baseball, track, lacrosse, tennis, and golf. In most of these sports, there are junior varsity, freshman, and Middle School teams. Some intramural sports are available, depending upon interest, every year.

The facilities consist of two gymnasiums, eight athletics fields, six tennis courts, and an outdoor pool for swimming during warm weather. Students who join the golf team are able to play at nearby golf clubs.

EXTRACURRICULAR OPPORTUNITIES

The School provides opportunities for individual development outside the classroom as well as within. The faculty encourages the boys to express their intellectual, cultural, social, and recreational interests through a variety of activities and events. For example, fine arts at Delbarton are available both within and outside the curriculum. Studio hours accommodate boys after school, and students visit galleries and museums. In the music department, vocal and instrumental instruction is available. Performing ensembles include an orchestra, band, and chorus and smaller vocal and instrumental ensembles. Under the aegis of the Abbey Players, drama productions are staged three times a year, involving boys in a wide variety of experiences.

Other activities include Deaneries (student support groups promoting School unity and spirit), the *Courier* (the School newspaper), the *Archway* (the yearbook), *Schola Cantorum* (a vocal ensemble), the Abbey Orchestra, and the Model UN, Mock Trial, Speech and Debate, Junior Statesmen, Art, History, Chess, Cycling, Stock Exchange, and Future Business Leaders clubs. In addition, faculty moderators of the Ski Club

regularly organize and chaperone trips during School vacations.

To expose students to other cultures and to enhance their understanding of the world, faculty members have organized trips to Europe, Africa, and Latin America. The Campus Ministry office is active in sponsoring several outreach programs that lead boys to an awareness of the needs of others and the means to answer calls for help. The outreach programs include community soup kitchens, Big Brothers of America, Adopt-a-Grandparent, and Basketball Clinic for exceptional children.

Students' imagination and initiative are also given opportunities for expression through Student Council committees and assemblies. The students are also offered School-sponsored trips to cultural and recreational events at area colleges and in nearby cities.

DAILY LIFE

Classes begin at 8:10 a.m. and end at 2:41 p.m. The average number of classes per day for each student is six. Two classes are an hour long, while the remainder are 40 minutes each. The School operates on a seven-day cycle, and each class meets six days per cycle. Physical education classes are held during the school day. After classes, students are involved in athletics and the arts. Clubs and organizations also meet after school, while many meet at night.

COSTS AND FINANCIAL AID

Charges at Delbarton for the 2016–17 academic year were $36,900. These are comprehensive fees that include a daily hot lunch as well as library and athletics fees. The only other major expenses are the bookstore bill and transportation, the cost of which varies. Optional expenses may arise for such items as the yearbook, music lessons, or trips.

Because of the School's endowment and generous alumni and parent support, a financial aid program enables many boys to attend the School. All awards are based on financial need, as determined by the criteria set by the School and Student Service for Financial Aid. No academic or athletics scholarships are awarded. Financial aid is granted to boys in grades 7 through 12. In 2016, the School was able to grant $2.5 million to students.

ADMISSIONS INFORMATION

Delbarton School selects students whose academic achievement and personal promise indicate that they are likely to become positive members of the community. The object of the admissions procedure is for the School and prospective student to learn as much

as possible about each other. Admission is based on the candidate's overall qualifications, without regard to race, color, religion, or national or ethnic origin.

The typical applicant takes one of the three entrance tests administered by the School in October, November, and December. Candidates are considered on the basis of their transcript, recommendations, test results, and personal interview in addition to the formal application. In 2016–17, 385 students were tested for entrance in grades 7 and 9; of these, 161 were accepted. Ninety-one percent of the students who were accepted for the seventh grade were enrolled; 76 percent of those accepted for the ninth grade were enrolled. Delbarton does not admit postgraduate students or students who are entering the twelfth grade.

APPLICATION TIMETABLE

The School welcomes inquiries at any time during the year. Students who apply are invited to spend a day at Delbarton attending classes with a School host. Interested applicants should arrange this day visit through the Admissions Office. Tours of the campus are generally given in conjunction with interviews, from 9 a.m. to noon on Saturdays in the fall, or by special arrangement. The formal application for admission must be accompanied by a nonrefundable fee of $65. Application fee waivers are available upon request.

It is advisable to initiate the admissions process in the early fall. Acceptance notifications for applicants to grades 7 and 9 are made by the end of January. Applicants to all remaining grades, as well as students placed in a wait pool, are given acceptance notification as late as June. Parents are expected to reply to acceptances two to three weeks after notification. A refundable deposit is also required. Application for financial aid should be made as early as possible; the committee hopes to notify financial aid applicants by the middle of March.

ADMISSIONS CORRESPONDENCE

Dr. David Donovan
Dean of Admissions
Delbarton School
Morristown, New Jersey 07960
United States
Phone: 973-538-3231 Ext. 3019
Fax: 973-538-8836
E-mail: admissions@delbarton.org
Website: http://www.delbarton.org
 admissions

THE DERRYFIELD SCHOOL

Manchester, New Hampshire

Type: Coeducational, college-preparatory day school
Grades: Grades 6–12
Enrollment: Total: 397; Middle School: 127; Upper School: 270
Head of School: Mary Halpin Carter, Ph.D.

THE SCHOOL

The Derryfield School is an independent, coeducational, college-preparatory day school. It was founded by a group of Manchester families in 1964 to provide an outstanding secondary education, on par with the best boarding schools, where students could still be home for dinner each night.

Derryfield is a school built around its students—a school that cares about their points of view, their interests, how they learn, and their passions. Small enough and smart enough to truly personalize each learning experience, Derryfield invites students to come together to grow as individuals; to gain the skills and experience to be valued, dynamic, confident and purposeful members of any community.

Derryfield is accredited by the New England Association of Schools and Colleges and is a member of the National Association of Independent Schools (NAIS), the Association of Independent Schools of New England (AISNE), and the Independent Schools Association of Northern New England (ISANNE).

ACADEMIC PROGRAM

The promise of Derryfield's academic program is realized every day through small, engaged classes, taught by dynamic, dedicated teachers. In Derryfield classrooms, students feel safe to take intellectual risks. And what happens in the classroom is only the beginning. Derryfield's active style of learning brings Middle School science students into the woods, looking for animal tracks in the snow. It sends Upper School students to Manchester's immigrant communities for service learning. It encourages seniors to complete Independent Senior Projects that take them, in some cases, all over the world.

Derryfield's Middle School curriculum combines a seriousness of purpose with a sense of fun and love of learning, providing a firm background in skills and basic discipline areas in preparation for Upper School courses. All students in grades 6, 7, and 8 take English, mathematics, science, history, and a foreign language. In addition, all Middle School students participate in drama, music, wellness, physical education, and art.

Upper School students (grades 9–12) plan their course of study in the context of graduation requirements, college plans, and interests. A total of 18 academic credits is required with the following departmental distribution: 4 credits in English, 2 credits in history, 3 credits in mathematics, 3 credits in a world language, 2-1/3 credits in science, 1 credit in fine arts, and participation in either the alternative sports program or a team sport two seasons per year. Each student carries a minimum of five courses each term. The academic year consists of three terms.

The Independent Senior Project is an option for seniors during the final six weeks of the spring term. The project allows students to explore their interests and to gain practical experience outside of the classroom.

FACULTY AND ADVISERS

The Derryfield faculty consists of 49 members (24 men and 25 women). Master's degrees are held by 25 members and Ph.D.'s are held by 5 members. Twenty-five faculty members have taught at Derryfield for ten or more years, and annual faculty turnover is low. The student-faculty ratio is 8:1.

Faculty members are hired on the basis of a high level of expertise in their academic areas as well as enthusiasm to contribute to the overall success of their students and the School. In addition to their classroom obligations, faculty members advise approximately 8 students, coach Derryfield's athletic and academic teams, advise student activities, and make themselves available to counsel students in other areas of student life.

COLLEGE ADMISSION COUNSELING

The unique educational experience of Derryfield is evident in its graduates. Academically excellent, they are also energetic, empowered individuals. They've learned how to learn and how to make more of their college experiences and their lives.

A dedicated college counselor begins working with students in the fall of their junior year. College counseling is an active process that includes group seminars and individual meetings with students and their families. More than 100 college representatives visit Derryfield each year.

The average SAT scores for the class of 2016 were 605 in critical reading, 615 in math, and 610 in the writing section. Fifty-seven students graduated in 2016, with 100 percent of the class going to college. A sampling of the colleges and universities currently attended by 2 or more Derryfield graduates includes American, Bates, Boston College, Brown, Colby, Dartmouth, Elon, Emory, Georgetown, Goucher, Ithaca, Johns Hopkins, Macalester, Northeastern, NYU, Oberlin, Pace, Providence, Quinnipiac, RIT, St. Lawrence, Syracuse, Trinity, Tufts, William and Mary, and the Universities of Colorado–Boulder, Michigan, Southern California, and Vermont.

STUDENT BODY AND CONDUCT

Of the 397 students enrolled at The Derryfield School, 127 students attend the Middle School and 270 students attend the Upper School. Students come from fifty communities in New Hampshire and northern Massachusetts, as well as several foreign countries. To make the commute easier, bus transportation is available to five different regions of the state, including a route to the Seacoast.

Students are guided by five Fundamental Standards, and five Daily Guidelines for success at Derryfield. The Standards are:

1. Be honest.
2. Treat people and property with care and respect.
3. Take care of yourself in body, mind, and spirit.
4. Obey federal, state, and local laws.
5. Maintain the reputation and good nature of the school.

The Guidelines are:

1. Be present and engaged.
2. Be timely.
3. Be responsible, both on and off campus.
4. Dress appropriately.
5. Put forth your best effort.

While there is a dress code, it is not formal, and there is no uniform. Certain days during the year are dress-up days (Grandparents' Day in the fall, and sports teams' away games, for example), and there are also Spirit Days, on which students are invited to be creative in their dress.

ACADEMIC FACILITIES

Derryfield's academic facilities include classroom buildings with five fully equipped science laboratories, a STEM classroom, a technology center with workstations and laptops, a 95-seat multimedia lyceum, a 20,000-volume library with a large subscription database, two art studios, an art gallery, and a 400-seat performing arts center. Outdoor classroom facilities include several miles of cross-country trails, high and low ropes courses, and many acres of woods. A turf field, a full-sized gymnasium, weight-training area, and trainer's room are also valuable learning sites for courses in physical education and health and wellness. In addition, the School opened the 8,000-square-foot Gateway Building in 2011, which houses administrative offices, the Breakthrough Manchester Program, and additional teaching spaces.

ATHLETICS

"A sound mind in a healthy body" defined the Greek ideal and is the concept at the core of Derryfield's physical education, health and wellness, and athletics philosophy.

All Middle Schoolers (grades 6–8) take physical education and health and wellness. Seventh and eighth graders also have competitive athletic requirements. Offerings include alpine skiing, baseball, basketball, cross-country running, field hockey, lacrosse, Nordic skiing, soccer, softball, and tennis.

In the Upper School (grades 9–12), two levels of competitive sports teams (junior varsity and varsity), as well as some alternative physical activities (e.g., yoga, dance, weight training) are offered. Upper School athletics include alpine skiing, baseball, basketball, crew, cross-country running, equestrian, field hockey, golf, hockey, lacrosse, Nordic skiing, soccer, softball, swimming, bass fishing, and tennis. The School also honors areas of physical interest that it does not offer on site; students may request that an independent physical activity be a replacement for one of the two required seasons.

Derryfield is a member of the New Hampshire Interscholastic Athletic Association, participating in Divisions I, II, III, and IV, according to sport. Derryfield currently has the most athletic offerings of any Division IV school in New Hampshire and has garnered more than fifty-five state championships since 2000.

ARTS

Derryfield believes that an education designed to bring out the best in every student would not be complete without the arts, so the School's commitment to the arts is strong. Upper School students perform two large-scale theater productions each year, one musical and one play, while seventh and eighth graders stage their own musical. Each sixth grade drama class produces a junior musical. Instrumental ensembles that include classical, jazz, and orchestral instruments are active in both the Middle and Upper School. There are vocal groups in both schools, and Upper School students may audition for a select chorus or a cappella groups for men and women. All musicians participate in two concerts per year and frequently in talent shows and assemblies. Students are encouraged to audition for the New Hampshire All-State Chorus and Band. Visual art students regularly submit materials to the New Hampshire Student Artist Awards and the Boston Globe Scholastic Art Awards, and help organize displays of their own work in Derryfield's art gallery openings. Derryfield's campus also includes a sculpture garden, where student work is displayed each year.

EXTRACURRICULAR AND GLOBAL OPPORTUNITIES

In each of the two schools, Middle and Upper, students participate in more than a dozen student-organized clubs. Choices include School Council, Conservation Club, Art Club, Gay/Straight Alliance, Empower Women Club, Robotics Club, Social Media Ambassadors, and Chinese Culture Club, among others. Derryfield also offers competitive clubs, including Math Team, Mock Trial, Granite State Challenge, and Model United Nations. Student publications include newspapers, literary magazines, academic journals, and a yearbook.

Field trips, organized through classes or clubs, include regular visits to New York City, Boston, and Manchester museums, theaters, courtrooms, and outdoor areas of interest. Each year, different faculty members lead groups of students on cultural or service-learning outings. Upper School trips for the 2016–17 school year include two weeks exploring the culture of China, a Habitat for Humanity work project in North Carolina, and a service and trekking trip to Nepal. Middle School opportunities include an arts and culture trip to New York City and a service-oriented trip to a Native American reservation. Derryfield has also established an exchange program for ninth and tenth grade students with two South African high schools, the Durban Girls' College in Durban and the Wynberg Boys' School in Cape Town.

In its dedication to local and global communities, Derryfield's Key Club actively partners with more than a dozen organizations, including the New Hampshire Food Bank, the American Cancer Society, New Horizons Soup Kitchen, Boys and Girls Club, Special Olympics, and local immigrant/refugee programs.

Breakthrough Manchester, a year-round, tuition-free academic program, is also an important part of The Derryfield School. Breakthrough offers motivated students from Manchester's public middle schools the opportunity to learn from outstanding high school and college students. Several Derryfield faculty members work as mentor teachers, while a large number of Derryfield students teach for Breakthrough.

Traditional Derryfield events and celebrations include Founders' Day, Winter Carnival, Grandparents' Day, Head's Holiday, Country Fair, Moose Revue talent show, and the Prom.

DAILY LIFE

Because Derryfield students come from approximately fifty different surrounding towns, the School itself becomes a hub for learning, playing, serving, and socializing.

The school day begins at 7:55 a.m. and ends between 2:45 and 3:20 p.m. Departure times vary, depending on grade, level of involvement in extracurricular activities, or desire to obtain extra help from a teacher, use the library, or attend study hall.

The class schedule is a seven-period, seven-"day," rotating schedule, with blocks set aside each day for extracurricular meetings. Homeroom gatherings occur three mornings per week, and advisory groups meet three times per week. Monday's extracurricular block is an all-school assembly; the Tuesday and Friday blocks allow time for an activities period, during which clubs meet; and Thursday's is an academic block, when students may study independently, or seek extra help from their teachers. Athletic practices and games are held after the academic day ends.

SUMMER PROGRAMS

The Derryfield campus continues to be busy over the summer, when summer programs take over, including lacrosse, soccer, and a very popular theater camp. There are also a number of academic options, featuring robotics, academic skills, SAT preparation, creative writing, and writing for the college process.

COSTS AND FINANCIAL AID

Tuition and fees for 2016–17 were $30,950. In addition to the need-based Financial Aid Program and the Merit and Malone Scholarship Programs, which offer direct grants, the School offers installment payment options.

The Financial Aid Program is designed to make a Derryfield education accessible to qualified students who could not otherwise afford the cost of attending. On average, Derryfield provides financial assistance to 23 percent of the student body, with awards that vary from 5 to 95 percent of tuition. Derryfield awards nearly $2 million in financial aid grants annually.

The Merit Scholarship Program is designed to recognize students who demonstrate qualities that will add meaning and vitality to Derryfield's core values or are distinguished by a commitment to purposeful involvement in both the local and global community. Awards of up to $15,000 are made annually.

The Malone Scholars Program was established in 2012 with a $2 million award from the Malone Foundation in recognition of the School's academic program. The Foundation's goal is to improve access to quality education for gifted students who lack the financial resources to develop their talents. Currently, the school has five Malone Scholars.

ADMISSIONS INFORMATION

The Admission Committee considers applications from students entering grades 6 through 12. Although the largest number of students enters in grades 6, 7, and 9, spaces are often available in other grades as well.

Applicants are required to complete an on-campus interview and an online written application. The SSAT is required for all applications to grades 6 through 9. Applicants to grade 10, 11, and 12 have the option to submit their PSAT or SAT scores.

APPLICATION TIMETABLE

The priority deadline for applications is February 1. Tours and interviews are offered through the Admission Office. There is a $50 preliminary application fee for applicants.

Notification of acceptance is mailed on March 10, and families are expected to reply by April 10.

ADMISSION CORRESPONDENCE

Admission Office
The Derryfield School
2108 River Road
Manchester, New Hampshire 03104-1396
United States
Phone: 603-669-4524
Fax: 603-641-9521
E-mail: admission@derryfield.org
Website: http://www.derryfield.org

GRIER SCHOOL

Tyrone, Pennsylvania

Type: Girls' boarding and day college-preparatory school
Grades: 7–PG: Middle School, 7–8; Upper School: 9–12, postgraduate year
Enrollment: School total: 315
Heads of School: Douglas A. Grier, Director; Gina Borst, Head of School

THE SCHOOL

Grier School was founded in 1853 as the Mountain Female Seminary and was reincorporated in 1857 under the direction of Dr. Lemuel Grier. The School has been successfully operated under the management of four generations of the Grier family. In 1957, the School was reincorporated as a nonprofit foundation administered by an alumnae Board of Trustees. Grier is located on a 300-acre campus in the country, 3 miles from Tyrone, Pennsylvania, and halfway between State College (where Penn State University is located) and Altoona.

The School is committed to a highly supportive philosophy aimed at developing each girl's full potential as an individual. Competitive sports are offered but do not overshadow the many intramural, life-sports, and creative arts opportunities available to each girl. Grier does not seek an elitist or high-pressure label and is proud of its family-like environment. "Friendliness" is the word most often used by visitors to describe the atmosphere.

The current endowment stands at approximately $23 million, supplemented by $800,000 raised through the most recent Annual and Capital Giving program.

Grier School is accredited by the Middle States Association of Colleges and Schools. It has memberships in the National Association of Independent Schools, the Pennsylvania Association of Independent Schools, and the Secondary School Admission Test Board.

ACADEMIC PROGRAM

Grier offers a multi-track academic program. The Elite Scholars Program is well suited for high-achieving students interested in honors and AP courses. AP courses are offered in all subject areas as twenty class offerings. While all classes are college preparatory in nature, the Learning Skills and Student Support programs ensure that all students receive the support they need to empower themselves as learners. Every attempt is made to pace the curriculum to the needs of individual students, and crossover is encouraged between the academic tracks according to the abilities of the students.

Learning Skills, a course taught by 3 specialists, is available for students who require additional academic structure and provides opportunities for tutoring and the development of strong study habits. This program serves the needs of approximately 50 students at Grier. A comprehensive English as a second language program is offered to international students. Girls who test below 100 on the TOEFL Internet-based test are required to attend an international student orientation.

Students are encouraged to take at least one elective in the arts each year. The variety of course offerings is designed to provide students with the opportunity to pursue areas of interest and to develop and enhance their individual talents. Strong programs are offered in studio art, ceramics, jewelry making, photography, weaving, costume design, dance, music, and drama. Art faculty members help students assemble portfolios in preparation for higher education.

FACULTY AND ADVISERS

The full-time faculty consists of 48 women and 19 men, more than half of whom have received advanced degrees.

Douglas A. Grier, Director of the School for the past forty-eight years, is a graduate of Princeton and has an M.A. and a Ph.D. from the University of Michigan. Gina Borst is the Head of School. She has a B.S. and an M.Ed. from Penn State University. She has worked at Grier for twenty-four years.

Many faculty members live on campus, and 22 housemothers supervise the dormitories. Faculty members are available for extra academic help on a daily basis. Faculty members also serve as advisers to students and participate in various clubs and sports activities.

COLLEGE ADMISSION COUNSELING

The School has two full-time college counselors who work with students in their junior and senior years. College counseling begins in the winter term of the junior year with class discussions about colleges, admissions requirements, and application procedures. The college counselors then discuss specific colleges with each student individually and help the student develop a preliminary list of colleges to investigate and visit over the summer, thus refining the list. In the fall of the senior year, the counselors review each student's list again and encourage the student to apply to at least six colleges. Applications are usually sent by Thanksgiving (or before Christmas break at the latest).

Graduates of the class of 2016 were accepted at various colleges and universities, including University of California Berkeley, Boston College, Bryn Mawr, Carnegie Mellon, Cornell, Embry-Riddle Aeronautical University, Georgetown University, New York University, Rice University, Smith, and the University of Virginia.

STUDENT BODY AND CONDUCT

Students come from twenty-two states and fifteen other countries.

Students are expected to follow the rules as defined in the student handbook. A Discipline Committee composed of students, faculty members, and administrators handles all infractions. Grier believes that good citizenship should be encouraged through incentive, and girls earn merits for good conduct, honors grades, and academic effort.

The student government consists of a Student Council with representatives from each class. The council serves as a forum for student concerns and helps plan the weekend programs.

ACADEMIC FACILITIES

Trustees Building is a modern classroom facility that was completely remodeled in summer 2002. It houses academic classrooms and art studios for ceramics, batik, and photo printmaking. Adjoining buildings house computer studios, language classrooms, and the Landon Library, which houses 16,000 volumes. The Fine Arts Center, housing extensive facilities for music and art classes, opened in January 2002. The Science Center opened in August 2003. Grier's Performing Arts Center, containing practice and performance space for dance and drama, opened in June 2006. Four new classrooms were added to the academic facilities when a new dormitory was completed in September 2012. The Music Building opened in September 2015 and features classrooms for instrumental music, two grand piano studios, an orchestra rehearsal room, and a computer lab for video and music production.

BOARDING AND GENERAL FACILITIES

The living quarters consist of four dormitory areas and seven cottages. The dorms and cottages provide a modern private bath for every two rooms. Two girls share a room, and each combination of two rooms and bath is called a suite. All students must leave the campus for Thanksgiving, Christmas, and spring break, though the School does sponsor trips during Thanksgiving and spring break.

Multiple student lounges with TVs and games are available, and a School-operated snack bar is located in a remodeled eighteenth-century log cabin.

The Health Center is located on the campus and is staffed with registered nurses at all times for emergencies or any medical concern that may arise.

ATHLETICS

Students of all ability levels are encouraged to participate in either the interscholastic sports program, which includes riding, dance, basketball, soccer, volleyball, and tennis, or the life-sports program of riding, dance, swimming, tennis, fencing, archery, badminton, yoga, body sculpting, scuba diving, and skiing/snowboarding. Grier has an excellent horseback riding program with 3 full-time instructors and 2 part-time instructors. Four stables accommodate 33 School horses and up to 15 privately owned horses. Two indoor and two outdoor rings are located on the campus within an easy walking distance of the dorm. Grier's Western indoor ring was completed in September of 2012.

The School's gymnasium is well suited for basketball and volleyball. Grier's state-of-the-art fitness center opened in September 2006. Five tennis courts and ample playing fields round out the School's physical education facilities.

EXTRACURRICULAR OPPORTUNITIES

Student groups active on campus include Grier Dance; Grier Equestrians; the Athletic Association; drama, cooking, baking, outing, ecology, modern languages, and community service clubs; and the yearbook and School newspaper. In addition, students participate in "Green and Gold" intramural sports, which often include soccer, volleyball, basketball, softball, and horseback riding.

Creative arts play an important part in school life, and girls can participate in several activities for enjoyment and credit, including drama, photography, art, instrumental music, voice, and dance.

DAILY LIFE

Classes begin at 8 and run until 2:37, Monday through Friday; sports activities are scheduled during the next 3 hours. A 40-minute period is set aside daily for student-teacher conferences, and an all-school meeting is held monthly. Students have a 105-minute supervised study period in the dormitories Sunday through Thursday nights.

WEEKEND LIFE

Because most of Grier's students are boarders, a comprehensive program of weekend activities is planned. Approximately eight dances are planned annually, usually for Saturday evenings. The Outing Club uses the nearby facilities of Raystown Lake for camping and hiking, and canoeing and white-water rafting on the Youghiogheny River are also popular. Tussey Mountain Ski Resort is 40 minutes away.

Nearby Penn State University provides many cultural, social, and educational opportunities. A wide variety of field trips are offered each year, ranging from rock concerts to ski weekends to trips to Washington, D.C., Pittsburgh, and New York City. A regular schedule of visiting artists and a movie series complete the social activities.

COSTS AND FINANCIAL AID

Tuition, room, and board for the 2016–17 school year was $51,700. Books cost approximately $500 per year. Off-campus entertainment is optional, with additional costs charged based on individual participation. A deposit of $5,000 is due with the Enrollment Contract. Parents may elect to pay the entire tuition by July 1 or pay 75 percent in July and the balance in December.

Financial aid is based primarily on need. To apply, parents must submit the Parents' Financial Statement to the School and Student Service for Financial Aid in Princeton, New Jersey. In 2016–17, 55 percent of the student body received a total of $3.8 million in financial aid.

ADMISSIONS INFORMATION

Grier seeks college-bound students of average to above-average ability who possess interest in sports and the arts as well as a desire to work in a challenging yet supportive academic atmosphere. Applicants are accepted in grades 7 through 12 (and occasionally for a postgraduate year) on the basis of previous record, recommendations, and an interview. Grier School admits students of any race, nationality, religion, or ethnic background.

Approximately 50 percent of all applicants are accepted for admission.

APPLICATION TIMETABLE

Grier has rolling admissions, and the Selection Committee meets on a regular basis to consider students whose files are complete. Candidates are asked to file an application and transcript release form with a $50 application fee, submit two teacher's recommendations, and have a personal interview on campus. The Admissions Office is open for interviews and tours during both the academic year and the summer.

ADMISSIONS CORRESPONDENCE

Jennifer Nooly, Director of Admissions
Grier School
Tyrone, Pennsylvania 16686
United States
Phone: 814-684-3000
Fax: 814-684-2177
E-mail: admissions@grier.org
Website: http://www.grier.org

THE LAWRENCEVILLE SCHOOL

Lawrenceville, New Jersey

Type: Coeducational boarding and day college-preparatory school
Grades: 9–PG (Second–Fifth Forms): Lower School, Second Form; Circle/Crescent Level, Third–Fourth Forms; Fifth Form
Enrollment: 822
Head of School: Stephen S. Murray, Head Master

THE SCHOOL

The Lawrenceville School was founded in 1810 by Isaac Van Arsdale Brown as the Maidenhead Academy. Throughout the 1900s, Lawrenceville continued to develop as a leader in academic innovation, including early adoption of Advanced Placement (AP) courses and the introduction of nationally and internationally known guest speakers designed to broaden the intellectual horizons of young Lawrentians. Among the most-lasting changes was the introduction in 1936 of the Harkness method of education, which sought to bring the benefits of the House system to the classroom by providing an intimate environment for intellectual discourse.

Discussion of coeducation began in earnest in the 1970s, and after a lengthy, but thoughtful analysis of what it would mean both pedagogically and practically to the School, the Board elected to accept female students in 1985. The first girls arrived on campus in 1987 and brought a new vitality to the campus community. As the twentieth century drew to a close, the School embraced the ever-increasing diversity of its students in gender, geography, faith, race, and socioeconomic status, focusing on the need for a Lawrentian education to include broad exposure to all facets of the global community and an appreciation for and understanding of multiculturalism.

For more than 200 years, Lawrenceville graduates have gone on to success in their chosen fields, prepared by their education for the changing world around them. As the School enters its third century of educating students, it welcomes new students to join the legacy of Lawrenceville and discover what it means to be a Lawrentian in the 21st century.

The Lawrenceville School is located on 700 acres in the historic village of Lawrenceville, New Jersey.

Founded in 1810, through House and Harkness, Lawrenceville challenges a diverse community of promising young people to lead lives of learning, integrity, and high purpose. The School's mission is to inspire the best in each to seek the best for all.

Lawrenceville is accredited by the Middle States Association of Colleges and Schools and is a member of the Secondary School Admission Test Board, the National Association of Independent Schools, the New Jersey Association of Independent Schools, and the Council for Religion in Independent Schools.

ACADEMIC PROGRAM

The School's graduation requirements are designed to ensure students receive a strong foundation in all disciplines during their first two years that can be built upon in the upper forms. The requirements meet NCAA standards and are aligned with standard requirements for college admissions.

The requirements for entering Second Formers are: Arts 3 terms, English 9 terms, Humanities-English 3 terms, History 6 terms, Humanities-Cultural Studies 3 terms, Interdisciplinary 2 terms, Language through Level 3, Mathematics through Math 4 or precalculus, Religion & Philosophy 2 terms, Science 9 terms. If students have a compelling academic reason, they may opt to finish their coursework in one of three disciplines—Math, Science, and Language—after the foundational with approval of department chairs and the Dean of Academics. Students are also required to give at least 40 hours of community service before they graduate. Individual participation is encouraged in small classroom sections that average 12 students. Classes are grouped randomly and are taught around a large oval table called the Harkness table. Evening study periods, held in the Houses, are supervised by the Housemaster, the Assistant Housemaster, or an Associate Housemaster.

Individual participation is encouraged in small classroom sections that average 12 students. Classes are grouped randomly and are taught around a large oval table called the Harkness table. Evening study periods, held in the Houses, are supervised by the Housemaster, the Assistant Housemaster, or an Associate Housemaster.

Students may also apply for independent study, off-campus projects, or the Lawrenceville international programs. Recent destinations include China, the Dominican Republic, Mexico, Japan, France, Peru, Nicaragua, Ghana, the Galapagos, Great Britain, South Africa, and Tanzania. Other opportunities include language immersion trips, where students reside with host families. Driver's education is also available.

Lawrenceville uses a letter grading system (A–F) in which D– is passing and B+ qualifies for honors.

The school year is divided into three 10-week terms. Full reports are sent home at the end of each term, with interim reports at midterm. The full reports include comments and grades from each of a student's teachers indicating his or her accomplishments, efforts, and attitudes. Less formal progress reports are also written by teachers throughout the term as needed. Students in academic difficulty are placed on academic review, which entails close supervision and additional communication with parents.

FACULTY AND ADVISERS

There are 108 full-time and 4 part-time faculty members, and 4 teaching fellows, all of whom hold numerous degrees: 17 doctorates (15 Ph.D.'s, 2 J.D.'s); 70 master's; and 25 bachelor's. Most faculty members reside on the campus, and many serve as residential Housemasters, coaches, and club advisers. All are active in advising and counseling students.

Stephen S. Murray H'55 '65 P'16 became the Lawrenceville School's 13th Head Master on July 1, 2015. Murray came to the Lawrenceville School with deep independent school leadership experience. In his most recent role as Headmaster of University School in Shaker Heights and Hunting Valley, Ohio (a position he held for a decade), Murray was responsible for the overall management of the two-campus K–12 boys' school of 875 students and 235 faculty and staff. From 1990–2005, Murray led a distinguished career at Deerfield Academy including serving as Assistant Headmaster, Academic Dean, Dean of Students, and as teacher, coach, and faculty resident.

Murray received a B.A. in French and Political Science with honors in 1985 from Williams College, an Ed.M. from the Harvard Graduate School of Education in 1987, an M.A. in French Literature from the Harvard Graduate School of Arts and Sciences in 1990, and is a 1981 graduate of Phillips Exeter Academy.

Murray currently serves or has served on the boards of numerous nonprofit and civic institutions, including chairing the Board of the Center for the Study of Boys' and Girls' Lives (in collaboration with the University of Pennsylvania), chairing the Board of Citizens' Academy Charter School in Cleveland, and chairing and/or serving on the boards of the Cleveland Council of Independent Schools, the International Boys' School Coalition, and Camp Agawam, and was invited to participate in the civic engagement program Leadership Cleveland.

STUDENT BODY AND CONDUCT

For 2016–17, there are 822 students: boarding 568, day 254, male 429, and female 393. Students are from 31 states and 39 countries.

Lawrenceville expects its students to achieve good records and develop self-control, systematic study habits, and a clear sense of responsibility. The School has a high regard for energy, initiative, a positive attitude, and active cooperation. Students accepting this premise have no trouble following the basic regulations.

The student body elects five governing officers from among students in the Fifth Form, and each House elects its own Student Council.

COLLEGE ADMISSION COUNSELING

The College Counseling Office supports, informs, and encourages students and their families as they navigate the exciting, complex, and ever-changing process of college admissions. The counselors educate students and families about the nuances of admissions, advise students about college options that best suit their individual needs, and support and encourage students as they complete the application process.

Lawrenceville's college counselors offer students decades of professional experience as college counselors and college admissions officers. The counseling staff provides valuable and timely advice to families as the process unfolds and helps students present their abilities, talents, and experiences to colleges in the most appropriate manner. The six counselors carry a small average case load of 38 students, which allows for personal attention and sustained involvement in all aspects of the residential school community. Over the course of their Lawrenceville careers, families and students receive information through form-specific newsletters, class-wide meetings, and Parents' Weekend programming. They also have access to Naviance, an online college admission management tool. All of these resources help ensure that students and their families are well prepared to embrace the college counseling process when students are officially assigned to individual counselors in the middle of their Fourth Form year.

Median SAT scores are: 683 critical reading, 692 math, and 680 writing. Between 2014 and 2016, the twenty colleges most attended by Lawrenceville students were the following: Princeton, Georgetown, NYU, Columbia, University of Pennsylvania, Brown, Yale, Duke, University of Virginia, Cornell, Stanford, Harvard, Davidson, Dartmouth, Trinity, Williams, University of Chicago, Johns Hopkins, Boston College, and Colgate.

ACADEMIC FACILITIES

Lawrenceville's first rate, state-of-the art academic facilities, which include Fathers' Building, the Kirby Arts Center, Gruss Center of Visual Arts, the F. M. Kirby Math and Science Center, the Juliet Lyell Staunton Clark Music Center, Bunn Library, and the Noyes History Center, offer a unique opportunity for all students. Each building houses an entire academic discipline, so students are immersed within a particular subject from the minute they enter the building until the minute they leave.

Lawrenceville supports excellent teaching with outstanding educational and campus resources. The Bicentennial Campaign, completed in 2010 in honor of the School's 200th anniversary, demonstrated the intense willingness of alumni, parents, and friends to provide the absolute best facilities and support for students and faculty. This most ambitious campaign raised $218.5 million, exceeding the $200 million goal, for student financial aid, faculty support, academic programs, and student life. Among the campaign's successes were the new Al Rashid Health and Wellness Center, a state-of-the-art facility for both treatment and prevention; Carter House, a Crescent girls' residential house; and lighted turf fields of the Getz Sports Complex.

BOARDING AND GENERAL FACILITIES

Lawrenceville's most distinguishing feature is its House system. In each of the twenty Houses, the Housemaster maintains close contact with the residents. House athletics teams compete on an intramural level, and House identity is maintained through separate dining rooms in the Irwin Dining Center for the underformers. This distinctive system provides a small social environment in which each student's contribution is important and measurable.

Services in the Edith Memorial Chapel are nondenominational. The Al Rashid Health and Wellness Center offers inpatient and outpatient medical care, including psychological counseling services, and a consulting staff who offer gynecological care, orthopedic/sports medicine, and nutrition. Certified athletic trainers provide rehabilitation services for injuries. The Center's health professionals seek to educate and encourage students to develop the knowledge and skills needed to sustain a lifetime of healthy function.

ATHLETICS

Lawrenceville regards athletics as yet another educational opportunity for students and a valuable complement to the School's rigorous academic expectations. The importance of commitment; satisfaction of teamwork; hard lessons of failure; courage to surmount pain, fatigue, and frustration for a common goal; the virtue of physical conditioning; imperatives of sportsmanship; and the sheer joy of healthy competition are values Lawrenceville's athletic program is uniquely suited to teach. In addition, the School's proud interscholastic tradition and comprehensive intramural program, along with instruction in lifetime sports, ensure that each student experiences the challenge and reward of athletic competition.

The School takes pride in its first-class outdoor sports facilities: two FieldTurf artificial playing surfaces with lights for field hockey, lacrosse, and soccer; and eighteen other multipurpose natural grass athletic fields, including five intramural fields and two softball and two baseball diamonds. There are also twelve tennis courts, a nine-hole golf course, and a quarter-mile all-weather track. The crew program enjoys the use of a bay and other facilities at the Mercer Lake Rowing Association boathouse.

The Edward J. Lavino Field House is one of the finest athletic facilities at any independent school. The main arena has a Mondo surface with three combination basketball-volleyball-tennis courts; a four-lane 200-meter banked indoor track, with an eight-lane straightaway; and long jump, shot put, pole vault, and high jump areas. Along each side of the arena are two gymnasiums, a six-lane competition swimming pool, a wrestling room, a performance center, and an athletic training wellness room. A modern, enclosed ice hockey rink is attached to the Lavino Field House, and there are ten Anderson international squash courts. Nearby, a separate building houses the state-of-the-art, 4,500-square-foot Al Rashid Strength and Conditioning Center that is supervised by two certified coaches.

Students must participate in an approved form of athletic activity each term. Rehabilitation of athletic injuries and fitness testing are an important part of the athletic program and are available to students by Lawrenceville's two certified athletic trainers.

The School's outdoor, experientially based programs and initiatives educate students in responsible leadership, community membership, and character development and provide interactions in the outdoor environment, enhancing both academic and nonacademic skills development. Lawrentians have traveled the globe through outdoor program courses, scaling glaciers in Patagonia, trekking through the desert in South Africa, and sea kayaking among icebergs in Newfoundland. Athletic credit is given to participants.

Lawrenceville's ropes course offers students the opportunity to accept a challenge and work toward conquering it as a group. The course, created and built by an outdoor experiential education expert, is designed to help students listen to each other, trust each other, and work toward a common goal.

EXTRACURRICULAR OPPORTUNITIES

Lawrenceville provides a numerous opportunities for students to explore outside the classroom. There are more than 155 clubs and organizations specializing in interests such as writing, acting, debate, music, art, history, religion, science, photography, woodworking, and scuba diving.

Through the required Community Service Program, students serve as tutors, elementary school study center supervisors, and group activity counselors. The School sponsors organized educational and cultural trips to New York City and Washington, D.C.

Exhibits occur throughout the year. Several lecture programs bring speakers and artists to the campus. Annual events include Parents' Weekend in the fall, Parents' Winter Gathering, and Alumni Weekend in the spring.

DAILY LIFE

Lawrenceville students have their schedules packed full of classes, study hours, athletic practice, rehearsals, and time for friends, special events, eating, and sleeping. Students learn to manage their time, meet their commitments, and enjoy their friendships.

Classes begin at 8 a.m. on most days, and the dining center opens at 7 a.m. for breakfast. Each class meets four times a week for 55-minute sessions. Science and advanced classes have an additional 55-minute period each week for labs, extended discussions, test practice, writing workshops, etc. There are also three 40-minute periods each week for student-teacher consultations. Students are highly encouraged to take advantage of consultation periods.

The entire School eats lunch at the same time, and each House dines together. This tradition is yet another example of how the House system defines the Lawrenceville experience. On Mondays, students take lunch with their academic advisers. Each advisee group shares a table, and time is spent discussing both individual and group concerns; if needed, students can schedule a private meeting with their adviser.

The entire School assembles once a week for an all-School community meeting. These gatherings feature readings, reflections, and announcements. School meeting agendas include outside speakers, special guests, musical presentations, and opportunities to examine student issues.

Classes end at 3:05 p.m., but then there is more to do—sports or community service. On Wednesdays, classes end at 12:35 p.m., and students have the option of studying, rehearsing, practicing sports, working on publications, or fulfilling their community service requirement. Saturday classes end at 11:35 a.m.

Dinner is served from 5:30 to 7 p.m. All Forms eat in the Irwin Dining Center, except for the Fifth Form, which takes meals in the Abbott Dining Room. After dinner, there is time for clubs, activities, homework, and socializing. Check-in is at 8 p.m. for Lower School, 8:30 p.m. for Crescent and Circle Houses, and 9 p.m. for the Fifth Form, Sunday–Friday. Permission to leave the House after check-in to go to the library, rehearsals, club meetings, or to meet a teacher for consultation is granted after check-in time, but students must check back in with the Housemaster on duty by 10 p.m. (11 p.m. on Saturday).

WEEKEND LIFE

On weekends, at least one House sponsors an all-School social event, which may include carnivals, concerts, formal dinners, and dances. Faculty members are on hand to take trips to local shopping areas and movie theaters. Reach Out to the Arts is a faculty-led club that takes weekly trips to cultural events in New York. Day students are encouraged to attend all-campus activities.

COSTS AND FINANCIAL AID

The annual charges for 2017–18 are $59,860 for boarding students and $49,510 for day students.

Through the generosity of alumni, friends, and foundations, approximately $11.7 million in funds are available to provide financial assistance to qualified students. Currently, 29 percent of the student body receives assistance. Awards are made on the basis of character, ability, past performance, and future promise.

ADMISSIONS INFORMATION

All students who enter must be able to meet the academic standards. Lawrenceville also looks for students who possess the potential to become vitally interested members of the student body—students who make individual contributions.

Selection is based on all-around qualifications without regard to race, creed, or national origin. Character, seriousness of purpose, and future promise as well as past performance, the recommendation of a headmaster or principal, and SSAT results are all taken into consideration by the Admission Committee.

For fall 2016, 2,083 applications were submitted for grades 9–12, of which 249 enrolled. Required for admission is the formal application, which includes a written essay, a transcript of the applicant's school record, a letter of recommendation from the head of the current school, three reference letters, SSAT or ISEE and/or TOEFL scores, and an on-campus interview.

APPLICATION TIMETABLE

Campus tours and interviews are conducted during the week from 9 a.m. to 3 p.m. Monday, Tuesday, Thursday, and Friday. Applicants can also visit on Wednesdays from 9 a.m. to 11:30 a.m. and on Saturdays from 8:30 a.m. to 11:30 a.m. Interviews are not conducted on Saturdays during the summer months.

The application deadline is January 15 for boarding and day students, at which time all application materials must be submitted and interviews completed. The notification date is March 10, and parents reply by April 10.

ADMISSIONS CORRESPONDENCE

Dean of Admission
The Lawrenceville School
2500 Main Street
P.O. Box 6008
Lawrenceville, New Jersey 08648
United States
Phone: 609-896-2030
800-735-2030 (toll-free outside New Jersey)
Fax: 609-895-2917
E-mail: admission@lawrenceville.org
Website: http://www.lawrenceville.org

MAINE CENTRAL INSTITUTE
Pittsfield, Maine

Type: Coeducational traditional boarding and day college-preparatory and comprehensive curriculum
Grades: 9–12, postgraduate year
Enrollment: 500
Head of School: Christopher Hopkins

THE SCHOOL

Maine Central Institute is an independent college preparatory day and boarding school founded in 1866 by Free Will Baptists. Maine Central Institute (MCI) retains the inventive spirit and philosophy of its founders but no longer has a formal affiliation with the church. During the school's pioneer years, MCI served as a feeder school to Bates College in nearby Lewiston, Maine. Although adhering to upstanding and traditional educational values, MCI is progressive and broadminded, pledging to provide a comprehensive college-preparatory education to a multicultural student body diverse in talents, abilities, and interests.

MCI regards each student as an individual with individual needs and aspirations. In keeping with its belief in individuality, MCI strives to foster an overall environment of mutual respect, cooperation, and tolerance among all of its members and with the surrounding community. In a safe and caring atmosphere, students are encouraged to develop a moral and social consciousness, self-esteem, and social responsibility and to become globally aware, lifelong learners.

Maine Central Institute is located in a safe and scenic New England town approximately 40 minutes from Augusta (Capital City) and 3 hours from Boston, Massachusetts and Logan International Airport.

Pittsfield is a friendly, close-knit community which is nestled in between the Atlantic Ocean and the mountains of western Maine. It provides prime opportunities for hiking, skiing, biking, fishing, swimming, skating, and snowmobiling. The campus is within walking distance of local eateries, library, regional airport, recreational parks, shopping, hiking trails, and a movie theater. Students are involved with many community and volunteer causes throughout the year.

Maine Central Institute is accredited by the New England Association of Schools and Colleges and approved by the State of Maine Department of Education. MCI is also a member of the College Board and the National Association of Independent Schools.

ACADEMIC PROGRAM

MCI offers a rigorous comprehensive curriculum to accommodate various learning styles and academic abilities. MCI fosters the intellectual curiosities of its student body by offering accelerated and advanced placement courses in all core subject areas.

For grades 9–12, 20 credits are required for graduation. Students must successfully complete units in English (4), mathematics (4), social studies (3, including U.S. history), science (4), physical education (1), fine arts (1), computer science (½), and health (½). Students are required to take the equivalent of at least 6 units each semester. MCI also offers a postgraduate academic year with college prep and advanced placement courses.

MCI's math and science programs exceed national standards and utilize state-of-the-art technology and academic facilities. Students in MCI's well-known humanities program understand the culture of an era through a study of its history, literature, and art. The school has an award-winning music program.

The world language program includes four levels of French and Spanish. In 2009, MCI added a Chinese Mandarin program to the world languages, which is taught by a teacher from China. In addition to the traditional offerings, students may take courses in psychology, guitar, business, sociology, public speaking, computer-assisted drawing, vocational subjects, and piano.

MCI offers a structured ESL program for the international student who is planning for a university education. Students receive individual testing before placement at one of four levels of ESL. The extensive ESL program includes American history for international students and carefully structured math classes that focus on the development of math language skills. MCI also offers a two-week summer program for ESL which is required for all new international students.

SPECIAL ACADEMIC OFFERINGS

Students at MCI have access to several unique academic programs.

The **Manson Essay Program and Presentation** is a pre–college level project. Originating in the late 1800s, the Manson is a distinguished junior essay requirement. Juniors spend months researching and writing on a topic of their choice and end the assignment with an oral presentation of their essay in front of their peers. Following these presentations, 5 to 10 finalists are chosen to compete for the title of Manson Essay Winner.

The **Senior Project** is a capstone assessment, integrating students' mastery of communication skills, research techniques, public speaking conventions, and organization for independent, self-directed learning. Students devote five weeks to their chosen learning objectives, and then present their knowledge and product to peers, family, and community members.

Bossov Ballet Theatre offers MCI students a unique opportunity to study classical ballet as part of the academic curriculum. Ballet classes are taught by Natalya Nikolaevna Getman, a former dancer with the Moscow Ballet. The program allows students to earn full academic credit for ballet training. Students who complete the program are uniquely positioned either to matriculate to an outstanding college or join a professional ballet company.

MCI's **Academic Support Program** includes peer tutors, a writing center, and ESL. Faculty and students volunteer to assist international and domestic students, coach students on how to use all the resources available to them, and help them understand how to prepare for college applications and for testing.

MCI is excited to offer a **Flight School (aviation program)** in partnership with Central Maine Aviation and Curtis Air at the Pittsfield Municipal Airport to help students access the exciting world of aviation. Beginning in the spring of 2017 with a course surveying careers in aviation and the underlying math and science knowledge required for success in these fields, MCI will build credit-bearing courses that allow students to engage in formal ground school as part of their academic study. A new year-long course starting in 2017–18 during the regular school day will prepare students to pass the Federal Aviation Association (FAA) written knowledge tests for private pilot and commercial drone operator licenses. Students will have the opportunity to extend their study to private flight training based out of the Pittsfield Municipal Airport, within walking distance of the MCI campus.

FACULTY AND ADVISERS

The 2016–17 faculty consists of 60 full-time members. More than a quarter of the faculty and staff members reside on campus, while the rest live in nearby towns such as Newport, Waterville, and Bangor.

Faculty members are selected on the basis of three main criteria. They must possess a strong subject-matter background, the ability to relate to students, and an educational philosophy consistent with that of the institution and its mission. Faculty members are also expected to become actively involved in coaching, supervising dormitories, advising, counseling, and student affairs.

COLLEGE ADMISSION COUNSELING

A guidance team of 5 professional and experienced college counselors is available for students. Counselors are primarily responsible for helping students with postsecondary placement and academic program planning. Students receive one-on-one guidance from their counselors over the course of their four years. Counselors help students find colleges or universities that best meet students' interests, while guiding them through all steps of the application process. College Counselors also organize college fairs each year on campus. Approximately 90 college and university admission representatives visit Maine Central Institute's campus annually. Counselors also organize college tours for current students in all grades, allowing students to visit colleges and learn more about the programs offered. In addition, counselors also organize workshops for seniors, postgraduates, and parents regarding financial aid and scholarships.

Maine Central Institute also has an international college counselor who specifically helps global students find schools and guides them through the college application process.

Preparation for the SAT and ACT is offered within the math and English curricula. Supplemental SAT preparation is offered outside of the school day. Maine Central Institute is a registered SAT test center; students are able to register and take the SAT multiple times on MCI's campus throughout a year. Maine Central Institute Campus is also a TOEFL test center.

MCI has a strong history of placing students in post-secondary schools. Schools attended by recent graduates include Bates, Boston College, Boston University, Brown, Colby, Columbia, Cornell, Emerson, Emory, George Mason, George Washington, Hofstra, Maine Maritime Academy, Michigan State, Muhlenberg, Northeastern, NYU, Pace, Penn State, Princeton, Simmons, Syracuse, Tufts, UCLA, and the Universities of Connecticut, California, Maine, New England, New Hampshire, North Carolina–Chapel Hill, Rhode Island, Virginia, and Washington.

STUDENT BODY AND CONDUCT

The 2016–17 enrollment of 500 includes day and boarding students. Students come to MCI from six states and eighteen countries.

Students at MCI are expected to be good citizens and are held responsible for their behavior. The rules that provide the structure for the school community are written in the student handbook. Disciplinary issues are the responsibility of the administration, the faculty, and the residence hall staff.

ACADEMIC FACILITIES

There are eighteen buildings housed on the 23-acre campus. Visitors are greeted upon entrance with the stoic simplicity of the campus with its brick-front buildings and the historic bell tower of Founder's Hall.

The Math and Science Center is a recent addition to MCI. The 23,000-square-foot building includes fifteen instructional spaces and two computer classrooms which students utilize for AP computer science courses and on-campus SAT/TOEFL exams. A new media room includes a green screen and other equipment for students in film courses. Maine Central Institute also has an art studio, dark room, ballet studios, and a nearby greenhouse.

MCI adopted a one-to-one computer program in 2013, providing every student with an iPad for use at school and at home. Students can access Wi-Fi throughout campus and the dormitories. The school also has 100 additional computers available for student use. Students have access to the Powell Memorial Library on campus.

BOARDING AND GENERAL FACILITIES

Boarding students reside in three single-sex residence halls on campus, supervised by resident faculty and staff members. The school's highest-achieving residential students have the option of living in the Honors Dormitory. Each dormitory is outfitted with Wi-Fi, kitchenettes, washing machines, dryers, modern bathrooms, and a lounge area with a big-screen TV. Rooms include a bed, desk, wardrobe, dresser, bookshelf, and chair for each student. Students may have small refrigerators, TVs, stereos, irons, and personal computers in their rooms. The residential hall lounges are common areas for all boarding students and their guests to enjoy. Weymouth Hall houses the ESL Center, the Wellness Center, the school bookstore, and an additional student lounge.

MCI offers a unique Host Family Program. Participating students are paired with a family from the community that makes the student a part of its family for the school year. Students may spend time with their host family on weekends, after school, and during vacations.

ATHLETICS

MCI believes that athletics are an important part of the education process, a dynamic lesson in teamwork, and a hallmark of personal dedication. The school offers a comprehensive athletic program for student-athletes of varying levels of ability by offering JV, varsity, and club-level sports.

There are eighteen sports teams for boys and girls, including baseball, basketball, cheering, field hockey, football, golf, lacrosse, rifle, soccer, softball, tennis, track, and wrestling.

Wright Gymnasium and Parks Gymnasium are multiple-use athletic facilities, and each contains a weight room and locker facilities. Located on the main campus are a football field, a practice field, a ¼-mile track, and a rifle range. Manson Park has fields for soccer, lacrosse, field hockey, baseball, and softball as well as three tennis courts. The school has the use of a local golf course and ski areas for competitive teams and recreation.

EXTRACURRICULAR OPPORTUNITIES

MCI students may choose from forty-two campus organizations, which represent some of the following interests: drama production; world languages and travel to places such as Costa Rica, Spain, France, Italy, and Russia; chess; robotics; Kindness Krew; Outdoor adventure team, which includes hiking, biking, canoeing, and other activities; weight lifting; Key Club, which is the school's community service organization; computer science; and public speaking. Students may participate in Student Council; MCI's strong, award-winning music program includes concert band, concert choir, chamber choir, vocal jazz ensemble, instrumental jazz ensemble, jazz combo, percussion ensemble, and pep band; and the Math Team which competes locally and statewide.

DAILY LIFE

The school day begins at 7:45 a.m. and ends at 2:45 p.m., with a 40-minute lunch break. Classes run from Monday through Friday, with dinner served from 5 to 6:30 p.m. Sunday through Thursday, there is a mandatory supervised study hall from 7 to 8:30 p.m. for all boarding students. Honor Study is available to high-achieving students.

WEEKEND LIFE

Supervised weekend activities include trips to Canada, Boston, the nearby capital of Augusta, the city of Portland, historic ports, lighthouses and coastal towns along the Atlantic shoreline, and cultural and athletic events both on and off campus. Activities such as movies, whale watching, white-water rafting, and skiing at Sugarloaf Resort are also offered. With parental permission, students are allowed to go home on weekends or visit the home of their host family.

COSTS AND FINANCIAL AID

The 2016–17 tuition, room, and board are $42,750 for boarding students, and tuition is $11,000 for private day students. The cost for ESL support is $3,000 for the first class and $2,000 for each additional class. The nonrefundable deposit of $5,000 is due within two weeks of an offer of admission. A variety of payment plans are available.

Financial aid is awarded on a need basis, determined by information shown on the Parents' Confidential Statement and any additional financial information that is requested.

ADMISSIONS INFORMATION

MCI's Admissions Committee screens all applicants to determine their compatibility with MCI's philosophy that students should assume a mature responsibility for their own education. No entrance tests are required, but an on-campus or online video conference interview with each student and his or her parents is strongly recommended. School transcripts and results of standardized tests are used to determine academic ability and appropriate academic placement in classes in accordance with the student's individual needs, abilities, and interests.

Maine Central Institute does not discriminate on the basis of race, sex, age, religion, sexual preference, disability, or national or ethnic origin in the administration of its educational and admission policies, financial aid programs, and athletic or other school administered programs and activities.

APPLICATION TIMETABLE

Inquiries and applications are welcome at any time; however, applying by June 1 is recommended. Visits may be scheduled at any time during the year but are most effective when school is in session. Tours and interviews can be arranged by calling the Admissions Office, which is open Monday through Friday from 8 a.m. to 4:30 p.m. A nonrefundable application fee of $75 is required.

ADMISSIONS CORRESPONDENCE

Clint M. Williams, Dean of Admission
Maine Central Institute
295 Main Street
Pittsfield, Maine 04967
United States
Phone: 207-487-2282
Fax: 207-487-3512
E-mail: cwilliams@mci-school.org
Website: http://www.mci-school.org
Twitter: mciadmissions
Facebook: https://www.facebook.com/pages/
    MCI-Admissions/732239663517712
Skype: mciadmissions

MARYMOUNT SCHOOL OF NEW YORK

New York, New York

Type: Girls' independent college-preparatory Catholic day school
Grades: N–XII: Lower School, Nursery–II; Lower Middle School, III–V; Upper Middle School, VI–VIII, Upper School, IX–XII
Enrollment: School total: 758; Upper School: 247
Head of School: Concepcion R. Alvar

THE SCHOOL

Marymount School of New York is an independent Catholic day school that educates girls in a tradition of academic excellence and moral values. The School promotes in each student a respect for her own unique abilities and provides a foundation for exploring and acting on questions of integrity and ethical decision-making. Founded by Mother Marie Joseph Butler in 1926 as part of a worldwide network of schools directed by the Religious of the Sacred Heart of Mary, Marymount remains faithful to its mission "to educate young women who question, risk, and grow; young women who care, serve, and lead; young women prepared to challenge, shape, and change the world." Committed to its Catholic heritage, the School welcomes and values the religious diversity of its student body and seeks to give all students a deeper understanding of the role of the spiritual in life. The School also has an active social service program and integrates social justice and human rights into the curriculum.

Marymount occupies three adjoining landmark *Beaux Arts* mansions, located on Fifth Avenue's historic Museum Mile, a fourth mansion on East 82nd Street, and a recently renovated 42,000-square-foot facility on East 97th Street. The Metropolitan Museum of Art and Central Park, both located directly across the street from the Fifth Avenue Campus, provide resources that are integral to the School's academic and extracurricular programs. Several studio art classes meet in the Museum's Carroll Classroom. As part of the Class IX humanities curriculum and in advanced art history courses, Upper School students have classes in the Museum weekly. Central Park is used for science and fitness classes as well as extracurricular activities. Other city sites, such as the United Nations, Carnegie Hall, the American Museum of Natural History, MoMA, and the Guggenheim, are also frequent extensions of the classroom for Marymount students.

Since 1969, the School has been independently incorporated under the direction of a 30-member Board of Trustees made up of parents, alumnae, educators, and members of the founding order. The School benefits from a strong Parents' Association; an active Alumnae Association; the involvement of parents, alumnae, and student volunteers; and a successful Annual Giving Program.

Marymount is accredited by the New York State Association of Independent Schools (NYSAIS). The School holds membership in the National Association of Independent Schools (NAIS), NYSAIS, the Independent Schools Admissions Association of Greater New York (ISAAGNY), the National Catholic Education Association, the National Coalition of Girls' Schools (NCGS), and the Educational Records Bureau (ERB).

ACADEMIC PROGRAM

The study of classic disciplines at Marymount is dynamic and innovative. The rigorous college-preparatory curriculum emphasizes critical thinking, collaboration, communication, and creativity. Students are encouraged to question and explore topics in depth, to take intellectual risks, and to work independently and collaboratively to find alternative approaches to problems. With its focus on the education of young women, Marymount allows each student to find her own voice. Students develop the skills necessary to succeed in competitive colleges and in life beyond the classroom: self-confidence, leadership ability, a risk-taking spirit, and joy in learning.

A commitment to the study of science, technology, engineering, art, and mathematics (STEAM) is reflected in Marymount's curriculum, which fully integrates information and communication technologies into all subject areas. Students have access to desktop and laptop computers, iPads, and other mobile computing devices throughout the School. Students in Classes K through V use iPads for individual and collaborative exploration, creation, and communication. Students in Classes VI through XII and staff members each have a school-supplied MacBook, school email, and Google account and use digital media to carry out research, create presentations, publish work, communicate, and demonstrate ideas and concepts. Students learn a wide variety of authoring tools as well as programming languages to create and publish digital media. Using an array of interactive media, students extend discussions and collaborations beyond the classroom. Using online tools and video-conferencing, students collaborate on projects with other Marymount Schools and with students and researchers around the globe.

Marymount's position at the forefront of educational technology relies on more than the investment in laptops, iPads, interactive displays, software, and networks. To maintain its cutting-edge program—which has been recognized for excellence by NAIS, NCGS, littleBits, and Apple Inc.—the School offers technology workshops throughout the school year for the faculty and other NAIS-school faculty members. Sponsored in part by a generous grant from the E. E. Ford Foundation, Marymount established the Making and Learning Institute in 2014 to offer professional development to teachers in New York City interested in hands-on learning and innovative teaching.

The School offers honors and Advanced Placement courses as well as electives and studio courses, including art history, economics, classical Greek, introduction to acting, advanced drawing portfolio, 2-D design, critical thinking in the arts, Middle Eastern studies, physical computing, and entrepreneurship. In senior English, students choose from seminars that cover topics from slave narratives to contemporary American drama to women's literature. Most students elect to take a fourth year of math; advanced offerings include AP calculus AB, AP calculus BC, AP statistics, and calculus. Fourth-year science courses include advanced or AP courses in biology, chemistry, and physics, as well as molecular biology, atmospheric science, and engineering. The science program connects with and utilizes the research of numerous institutions, including Cold Spring Harbor Laboratory's DNA Learning Center in Manhattan, the New York Academy of Sciences, and Princeton University. The School also participates in the STEM Internship Program and the STEM Research Program. Class XII students may elect to take AP psychology or other advanced courses through Marymount's affiliate membership in Online School for Girls.

While a leader in science and technological education, Marymount is also committed to the study of humanities. All Class IX students take part in the Integrated Humanities program, an interdisciplinary curriculum that focuses on history, literature, and art history in the study of ancient civilizations. Classes are held at The Metropolitan Museum of Art at least once a week. The program includes a performance-based World Civilizations Festival and collaborative research projects in history and art history. As a culminating project, seniors submit an interdisciplinary writing portfolio of selected work from their last three years of high school.

The visual and performing arts offerings include studio art, media arts, AP 2-D design, AP drawing, ensemble music, choral music, chamber choir, and introduction to acting. The after-school chorus, Marymount Singers, performs regularly at masses and concerts, and the Marymount Players stage two productions annually.

The religious studies program includes comparative religions, Hebrew scriptures, the New Testament, social justice, and ethics. With a focus on moral and ethical decision-making, students analyze systemic social issues and immerse themselves in the community through numerous service projects, as well as the Marymount Philanthropy and Community Transformation (M-PACT) program. The Catholic-Jewish Initiative provides students with a deeper understanding of the Judeo-Christian tradition and includes Holocaust studies and a trip to the National Holocaust Museum in Washington, D.C.

High school graduation requirements include satisfactory completion of 4 years of English, 3 years of history, 3 years of math, 3 years of laboratory science, a 3-year sequence of a world language, 4 years of religious studies, 4 years of physical education, 3 semesters of visual/performing arts, and 2 semesters of health education. These requirements provide a broad, solid base of knowledge while sharpening problem-solving and research skills and promoting critical and creative thinking. Upper School students are formally evaluated four times a year, using an A–F grading scale. The evaluation process includes written reports and biannual parent/student/teacher conferences.

During the summer after junior year, each student participates in an off-campus internship to gain exposure to a career of interest. Students have interned at hospitals, research laboratories, law firms, financial organizations, theaters, schools, nonprofit organizations, and corporations. They also attend a career day, with visiting alumnae as guest speakers. A financial literacy program prepares graduates for the financial challenges of college and life.

As members of a worldwide network of schools, students may opt to spend the second semester of their sophomore year at a Marymount International School in London or Rome. There are also opportunities for shorter cultural or language exchanges at schools in Brazil, Colombia, Spain, and France. Annual concert and study tours and service trips extend the curriculum. Recent study tours have included researching sea turtles with Earthwatch in the Bahamas and exploring art and history in Italy. Recent service trips have brought students to advocate for Typhoon Haiyan victims on Capitol Hill and to build affordable housing in Florida. The Marymount Singers enjoy an annual concert tour and have performed domestically and abroad.

Housed in a newly renovated facility on East 97th Street, the Upper Middle School encourages, supports, and challenges early adolescent students as they continue to develop independence, leadership, and achievement. Experiential, inquiry-based learning offers students opportunities to question their thinking, shape their understanding, and explore varied points of view as they become critical thinkers and innovative problem-solvers. Studio courses allow students to tinker, explore, and practice creative expression. Students in the Upper Mid are expected to be both independent and collaborative, curious and compassionate, bold and reflective.

The Lower Middle School curriculum welcomes the diverse interests of young adolescents and is structured to channel their energy and natural love of learning. The integrated core curriculum gradually increases in the degree of departmentalization at each grade level, and challenging learning activities and flexible groupings in main subject areas ensure that the students achieve their full potential. Speech classes prepare the girls for dramatic presentations reflective of their social studies and literature curriculum, and Class V students visit The Metropolitan Museum of Art for studio art and social studies classes. Uptown Broadway, an extracurricular option, allows the students to participate in a full-scale musical production.

The Lower School provides child-centered, creative learning within a challenging, structured environment. The curriculum focuses on the acquisition of foundational skills, often through an interdisciplinary approach. Programs engage students in the exciting process of learning about themselves, their surroundings, and the larger world. Introductory lessons in Spanish complement the social studies curriculum. A hands-on science program; an emphasis on technology integration, including a study of robotics and coding; a popular School chorus; and an extensive after-school program are some highlights of the Lower School.

FACULTY AND ADVISORS

There are 126 full-time and 8 part-time faculty members, allowing for a 6:1 student-teacher ratio. Eighty-four percent of the faculty members hold master's degrees, and 9 percent hold doctoral degrees. In Nursery through Class II, each class has a head teacher and at least one assistant teacher. In Classes III through V, each class has three homeroom teachers. In Classes VI–XII, each student has a homeroom teacher and an advisor, usually one of her teachers, who follows her academic progress and provides guidance and support. Learning resource specialists, school nurses, an athletic trainer, artists-in-residence, and school psychologists work with students throughout the School.

Concepcion R. Alvar was appointed Headmistress in 2004 after serving thirteen years as the Director of Admissions and three years as a head teacher. She also served as the Director and Supervisor of Marymount Summer for sixteen years. Mrs. Alvar holds a B.S. from Maryknoll College (Philippines) and an M.A. from Columbia University, Teachers College.

COLLEGE ADMISSION COUNSELING

Under the guidance of the Director of College Counseling, Marymount's formal college counseling program begins during the junior year. Two College Nights are held for Class XI students and parents. Individual counseling throughout the semester directs each student to those colleges that best match her achievements and interests. Students participate in weekly guidance classes to learn about general requirements for college admission, the application process, and standardized tests. During the fall of their senior year, students continue the weekly sessions, focusing on essay writing, admissions interviews, and financial aid applications.

Graduates from recent classes are attending the following colleges and universities: Amherst, Barnard, Boston College, Boston University, Bowdoin, Brown, Columbia, Connecticut College, Cornell, Dartmouth, Davidson, Duke, Fairfield, Fordham, George Washington, Georgetown, Harvard, Holy Cross, Kenyon, Middlebury, NYU, Oberlin, Oxford University, Princeton, Sewanee, Skidmore, Smith, Stanford, Trinity, Tufts, Vanderbilt, Villanova, Wake Forest, Washington (St. Louis), Wellesley, Wesleyan, Wheaton, Williams, Yale, and the Universities of Notre Dame, Pennsylvania, St. Andrew's (Scotland), and Virginia.

STUDENT BODY AND CONDUCT

Marymount's enrollment is 758 students in Nursery through Class XII, with 347 girls in the Upper School. Most students reside in the five boroughs of New York City; however, Upper School students also commute from Long Island, New Jersey, and Westchester County. Students wear uniforms, except on special days; participate in athletic and extracurricular activities; and attend weekly chapel services, all-school masses, and annual class retreats.

Marymount encourages students to be active participants in their education and in the life of the School community. Students seek out leadership and volunteer opportunities, serving as advocates for one another through peer mentoring, retreat teams, and the Big Sister/Little Sister program. Student government and campus ministry provide social and service opportunities that enable students to broaden their perspectives, develop as leaders, sharpen public-speaking skills, and form lasting friendships. Teachers and administrators encourage each student to respect herself and others and to be responsible members of the community.

ACADEMIC FACILITIES

The *Beaux Arts* mansions on Fifth Avenue provide rooms for Lower and Upper School classes, and include four science laboratories, two art studios, a math center, an idea lab and tinker space, a gymnasium, an auditorium, a courtyard play area, a chapel, and a library complex. The East 82nd Street facility is the home of the Lower Middle School. Students in the Lower Mid, Upper Mid, and Upper Schools also attend classes at the East 97th Street campus. This renovated facility is the home of the Upper Middle School and includes a gymnasium, cafeteria, and three floors of classrooms. The fourth floor of the 97th Street Campus features several science classrooms and laboratories as well as a media-production lab and a fab lab where students can design, engineer, and fabricate an array of objects and solutions using 3-D printers, laser cutters, and other fabrication tools. The additional campus also offers space for visual and performing arts, dance, and fitness. All classrooms feature interactive boards and multimedia displays.

ATHLETICS

The athletics program promotes good health, physical fitness, coordination, skill development, confidence, and a spirit of competition and collaboration through its physical education classes, the electives program for Classes X–XII, and individual and team sports.

Marymount provides a full schedule for varsity and junior varsity sports, as well as competitive teams at the V/VI and VII/VIII class levels. Participants in Classes V/VI stay two days per week for an after-school sports program; students in Classes VII/VIII commit to three afternoons per week. The junior varsity and varsity teams compete within the Athletic Association of Independent Schools League (AAIS) in badminton, basketball, cross country, fencing, lacrosse, soccer, softball, swimming, tennis, track and field, and volleyball.

In addition to its gymnasia, Marymount has an athletics field and tennis court on East 97th Street for PE classes and sports practices, and the School uses facilities and field throughout New York City for some practices and competitions in field sports, track and field, tennis, and swimming.

EXTRACURRICULAR OPPORTUNITIES

A wide range of clubs and activities complement the academic program, promote student initiative, and provide opportunities to contribute to the school community and develop communication, cooperation, and leadership skills. Student-led clubs include affinity groups, book club, Global Awareness, Met club, Science Olympiad, forensics club, Mathletes, politics and philosophy club, set design/tech crew, student government, and Women in our World. Campus Ministry, CAMBIAS (Cultural Awareness Club), Marymount Singers, Marymount Players, Mock Trial, Model UN,

and National Honor Society offer additional opportunities for student service, leadership, and performance. Student publications include a yearbook (*Marifia*), a newspaper (*Joritan*), and an award-winning literary/arts journal (*Muse*).

Each year, the Upper School presents two dramatic productions, including a musical; organizes either a Harambee Celebration or a Bias Awareness Day; sponsors an Art Festival; and participates in numerous community service projects, local and national competitions, and conferences with other schools, including Model UN, Mock Trial, and the International Student Technology Conference. Students have the opportunity to interact with boys from neighboring schools through most of these activities, as well as at dances and other student-run social activities.

DAILY LIFE

Upper School classes are held from 8:00 a.m. to 2:50 p.m. Class periods are 45, 60, or 75 minutes in length and typically meet four days in an eight-day cycle. After classes have ended, most students remain for sports, extracurricular activities, and/ or independent study.

COSTS AND FINANCIAL AID

The tuition for the 2016–17 academic year ranges from $26,800 for Nursery to $47,085 for Class XII. In February, parents are required to make a deposit of $6,500, which is credited toward the November tuition. The Tuition Management System payment plan is available.

Roughly $4 million in financial aid was awarded in 2016–17 to students after establishing need through TADS. Twenty-one percent of Marymount students receive need-based financial aid.

ADMISSIONS INFORMATION

As a college-preparatory school, Marymount aims to enroll young women of academic promise and sound character who seek a challenging educational environment and opportunities for learning outside the classroom. Educational Records Bureau tests, School Readiness Task assessments, and interviews are used in selecting students.

The School admits students of any race, color, and national or ethnic origin to all the rights, privileges, programs, and activities generally accorded or made available to students at the School and does not discriminate on these bases in the administration of its educational policies, admissions policies, scholarship or loan programs, athletic programs, or other School programs.

APPLICATION TIMETABLE

Interested students are encouraged to contact the Admissions Office early in the fall for admission the following year. The application deadline is November 30, but may be changed at the discretion of the Director of Admissions. Notification of admissions decisions is sent in February, according to the dates established by the Independent School Admissions Association of Greater New York.

ADMISSIONS CORRESPONDENCE

Carolyn Booth
Director of Admissions
Marymount School of New York
1026 Fifth Avenue
New York, New York 10028
United States
Phone: 212-744-4486
Fax: 212-744-0716 (admissions)
E-mail: admissions@marymountnyc.org
Website: http://marymountnyc.org

MILTON HERSHEY SCHOOL

Hershey, Pennsylvania

Type: Coeducational, residential, college-preparatory, career and technical education school
Grades: PK–12: (Elementary School, PK–4; Middle School, 5–8; High School, 9–12)
Enrollment: School total: 2,016; High School: 923
Head of School: Peter Gurt, President

THE SCHOOL

Milton Hershey School (MHS), a cost-free educational boarding school, was founded in 1909 by Milton S. Hershey and his wife, Catherine. Milton and Catherine were unable to have children of their own and wanted to provide a home and school for children in need. In 1918, three years after Mrs. Hershey's death, Milton Hershey pledged his entire fortune derived from his chocolate business toward the support of the School. His generosity continues to provide a cost-free education and home for children from families of limited income. The School offers a secure, nurturing environment in which students of character and ability can learn and develop the skills necessary to prepare them for meaningful, productive, and successful lives. The comprehensive program supports each child's educational and growth needs to allow the student to reach his or her fullest potential.

The School's 4,200-acre campus is located in Derry Township in Dauphin County, Pennsylvania. The School is 12 miles east of the state capital of Harrisburg, 90 miles west of Philadelphia, 130 miles northwest of Washington, D.C., and 185 miles southwest of New York City. There are many cultural, amusement, and sports attractions in the Hershey/Harrisburg area. These include a nationally recognized theme park, HERSHEYPARK; a professional American League hockey team, the Hershey Bears; orchestral concerts and Broadway shows in the Hershey Theatre; a Museum of American History; and, of course, the largest chocolate manufacturing facility in the world. All of these attractions are located within a 3-mile radius of the Milton Hershey School campus. The community of Hershey is home to the Milton S. Hershey Medical Center and Medical School of The Pennsylvania State University. These excellent facilities are available to the students of Milton Hershey School should medical care be necessary.

Milton Hershey School is governed by a Board of Managers, with representation from the alumni and the Hershey enterprises. The School is totally funded by income generated by the trust established by the founders in 1909. The trust is administered by the Hershey Trust Company, established by Mr. Hershey in 1905.

Milton Hershey School is accredited by the Middle States Association of Colleges and Schools and the Pennsylvania Association of Private Academic Schools. The School is affiliated with the major associations of private schools in the United States, including the National Association of Independent Schools, the Pennsylvania Association of Independent Schools, the Pennsylvania Association of Private Academic Schools, the Association of Boarding Schools, and the National Middle School Association.

ACADEMIC PROGRAM

The strength of the Milton Hershey School experience is a strong, comprehensive, standards-based educational program with an emphasis on applied and experiential learning within a caring, family-like residential community.

Elementary students benefit from cooperative learning, individualized assistance, technology applications, field trips, and extracurricular activities. They attend classes in an elementary school equipped with the latest technology, two science labs, an outdoor atrium classroom, a library, a swimming pool, and age-appropriate play areas. Hands-on, activity-based experiential learning is the basis of the curriculum. The average class size is 15–17 students.

In the Middle School, students enhance their educational development through team-learning experiences from teachers of various disciplines. In addition, students learn the importance of goal setting, organizational skills, and time management. Students have the opportunity to explore career fields of their choice from a number of categories that represent diverse occupational clusters such as manufacturing, air and land transportation, industrial arts, communications, and consumer science, among others.

High school students engage in comprehensive, in-depth studies through the enhanced learning opportunities. The High School program provides all students with basic and advanced academic and career-technical courses (eleven career pathways) and offers applied learning, including internships, to prepare each student for entry-level work and further study. Temple University provides college classes on campus for high-achieving students.

From prekindergarten to grade 12, all students are involved in experiences to prepare them for the world of work. Practical and age-appropriate career technical exploratory experiences and hands-on curriculum activities broaden each student's understanding of the world of work and his or her own aptitudes and interests. Eleven career technical programs are offered to high school students, who gain entry-level job skills. Career and postsecondary counseling begins in the Middle School and continues into the High School.

Students also participate in the Agricultural and Environmental Education program, through which they learn about land use, animals, plants, and related resources. As an example, at the School's Environmental Center, students learn how to care for, conserve, and appreciate nature. As part of the career technical program, high school students can begin to focus their career paths in horticultural science occupations.

Because Milton Hershey School believes that all students can achieve at high levels, every student participates in a standards-based environment, where teaching and learning are tied to specific outcomes. Each program has an age-appropriate curriculum that is linked to national standards, which are designed to help children become productive, purposeful adults.

FACULTY AND ADVISERS

All of the 190 teachers hold baccalaureate degrees, and many have earned advanced degrees. Married houseparent couples staff 163 student homes, and guide and nurture an average of 8–12 students of similar ages. They are employed full-time and serve as the primary advocates and caregivers for the children in their care.

The School provides on-campus professional services for medical, dental, and counseling care for all students. The School also employs a staff for orientation of new students and for enrollment and family relations.

COLLEGE PLACEMENT

Once a student reaches high school, a counselor keeps him or her thinking about life after graduation. The counselor helps the student decide whether it would be best to attend college or a trade, technical, or business school; join the armed services; or enter the job market directly.

In 2016, 87 percent of the graduating seniors continued their education at postsecondary schools.

STUDENT BODY AND CONDUCT

Milton Hershey School seeks to maintain a diverse population among the School's students. The student body comes predominantly from Pennsylvania and the mid-Atlantic region and represents more than thirty states.

From the day they arrive at MHS, students are getting themselves ready for the day they graduate. Classroom learning builds knowledge. A solid home life and leadership experiences build character and confidence. Activities and other experiences build teamwork and time-management skills. Guided and nurtured at every step, MHS students are provided everything they need to succeed.

ACADEMIC FACILITIES

Milton Hershey School's campus includes five major classroom buildings, one each for elementary and middle, and three for high school; a Learning Resource Center; a student services center; a visual arts building; a performance gym; and agricultural and environmental education learning centers located near fields, streams, and woodland.

From high-tech smart classrooms to laptops and tablets for students, MHS is committed to providing the tools and the technological education each student needs to learn and prepare for the future.

BOARDING AND GENERAL FACILITIES

In each of approximately 163 student homes, an average of 10 students live with houseparents who have received specialized training in child care and child development. These adults play an important role in each student's development. In the student homes, students are responsible for doing household chores, participating in family activities, and completing homework. They also learn to respect the values and traditions of other cultures and gain life experiences through a wide range of opportunities and activities.

Students participate in planned activities and enjoy free and quiet times during the day for study and relaxation.

ATHLETICS

MHS fields varsity and junior varsity teams in baseball, basketball, cross-country (boys and girls), field hockey, volleyball, football, soccer, ice hockey, softball, swimming (boys and girls), track (boys and girls), and wrestling. Milton Hershey School teams compete locally with both public and private schools. Intramural and recreational athletics are offered as well.

In addition to a football stadium seating 7,000; the School has eight tennis courts, three indoor swimming pools, an ice skating rink, an all-weather track, field hockey and soccer fields, baseball and softball diamonds, and three gymnasiums. The Spartan Center is a state-of-the-art sports complex with tennis courts, strength-training and aerobics rooms, and an indoor jogging track. The center, with a seating capacity of 1,800, is also the venue for basketball games and wrestling matches and hosts competitive athletic events for both middle and high school teams.

EXTRACURRICULAR OPPORTUNITIES

The School offers a wide variety of activities, including a student yearbook; computer, environmental, animal, photography, science, and math clubs; Boy Scouts and Girl Scouts; and a number of music groups, ranging from a jazz ensemble and band to a varsity choir.

Community service programs, off-campus study, internships, and work programs are offered through several businesses and community organizations.

The Copenhaver Center includes a natatorium, providing swimming facilities for both middle and high school students; an ice skating rink; a social room; student government and club rooms; a student store; a snack area; student television production and radio studios; dance, drama, and music studios and theater, medical, dental, and psychological services; and the Religious Programs Office. Outdoor tennis courts and bicycle pathways are nearby. At no cost, students may enjoy the Hershey Museum, Hershey Gardens, and HERSHEYPARK in season, which is from May through September.

DAILY LIFE

The typical day for high school students begins at 6 a.m. Students eat morning and evening meals as a family group in the student residence. Classes begin at 7:30 and end between 2:30 and 2:45 p.m. A healthy lunch is provided for all students. The afternoon includes academic classes, a tutoring period, time for sports and activities, and afternoon chores. Following dinner and study hour, students may have free time if all homework is completed.

WEEKEND LIFE

Many students enjoy visiting hours with their parents and other approved visitors over the weekend. Students may participate in a wide variety of organized activities as their schedules permit. Students are encouraged to participate in as many activities as their schedules permit. Attendance at a nondenominational Sunday morning chapel service is required of all students.

SUMMER PROGRAMS

Because MHS provides a year-round experience, students have the option of remaining on campus during six weeks of the summer and attending a variety of educational programs and enjoyable activities, such as sports camps, field trips and camping, community service activities, part-time work, and internship and career exploration. Students who need extra help with classroom studies can take advantage of the program's tutoring and study skills offerings.

COSTS AND FINANCIAL AID

Milton Hershey School provides, at no cost, an education, housing in a student home, clothing, meals, medical and dental care, and recreational activities.

The Continuing Education Scholarship program provides graduates the opportunity to earn scholarship money, approximately $85,000, by solid academic achievement and good citizenship. This scholarship award may be applied to all kinds of accredited postsecondary education, including colleges, universities, trade and technical institutes, and business and computer schools.

ADMISSIONS INFORMATION

To be considered for enrollment, children must come from a family with limited income. (For example, the current income guideline for a family of three is $40,320.) Applicants must also be between the ages of 4 and 15 at the time of enrollment, have the potential for scholastic achievement, and be free of serious behavioral problems that disrupt life in the classroom or the home. Students must also be able to participate fully in the program offered.

Enrollment preference is given first to children born in the Pennsylvania counties of Dauphin, Lebanon, and Lancaster; followed by those from within the state of Pennsylvania; and then those from outside of Pennsylvania. Milton Hershey School does not discriminate in admissions or other programs on the basis of race, color, national or ethnic origin, ancestry, sex, religious creed, or disability.

APPLICATION TIMETABLE

Enrollment takes place primarily in August, September, and January. If space is available, students may enroll in October, November, February or March. Students accepted for August enrollment are notified between May and July.

ADMISSIONS CORRESPONDENCE

Admissions Office
Milton Hershey School
P.O. Box 830
Hershey, Pennsylvania 17033-0830
United States
Phone: 717-520-3600
800-322-3248 (toll-free)
Fax: 717-520-2117
E-mail: mhs-admissions@mhs-pa.org
Website: mhskids.org

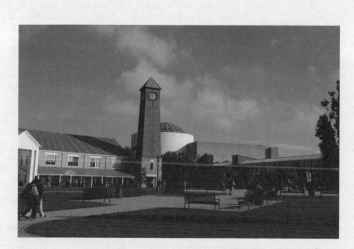

SOUTHWESTERN ACADEMY

Beaver Creek, Arizona and San Marino, California

Type: Coeducational boarding and day college-preparatory and general academic school
Grades: 6–12, postgraduate year
Enrollment: 144
Head of School: Kenneth R. Veronda, Headmaster

THE SCHOOL

Southwestern Academy offers achievement-based, departmentalized, and supportively structured classes limited to 9 to 12 students. Small classes allow for individualized attention in a noncompetitive environment. Southwestern was founded by Maurice Veronda in 1924 as a college-preparatory program "for capable students who could do better" in small, supportive classes. While maintaining that commitment, Southwestern Academy includes U.S. and international students with strong academic abilities who are eager to learn and strengthen English-language skills as well as pursue a general scholastic program in a small, supportive school structure. Southwestern Academy is accredited by the Western Association of Schools and Colleges (WASC).

Southwestern Academy offers students the opportunity to study at either of two distinctly different and beautiful campuses. The San Marino, California, campus is situated in a historic orange grove area near Pasadena. The Arizona campus, which is known as Beaver Creek Ranch, is located deep in a red-rock canyon in northern Arizona. Students may attend either campus and, if space permits, may divide the academic year between the two.

The San Marino campus occupies 8 acres in a residential suburb 10 miles from downtown Los Angeles and immediately south of Pasadena, home to the renowned Tournament of Roses Parade. The Beaver Creek campus is a 185-acre ranch located 100 miles north of Phoenix, 12 miles from the resort community of Sedona, and 45 miles south of Flagstaff. Although the program and philosophies are the same at both campuses, each offers a very different learning environment. Students at the California campus draw on the offerings of the urban setting. Students studying at the Beaver Creek Ranch campus enjoy a living and learning environment that takes full advantage of the rich cultural, scenic, and environmentally significant region.

A mix of U.S. and international students from several countries offers a unique blend of cultural, social, and educational opportunities for all. Every effort is made to enroll a well-balanced student body that represents the rich ethnic diversity of U.S. citizens and students from around the world. The student body consists of college-bound students who prefer a small, personalized education; above-average students who have the potential to become excellent academic achievers in the right learning environment; and average students who, with a supportive structure, can achieve academic success.

Southwestern Academy is incorporated as a not-for-profit organization. Operating expenses are approximately $5 million per annum and are met by tuition (93 percent) and grants and annual giving (7 percent). The Academy has no indebtedness.

ACADEMIC PROGRAM

Middle school students are placed in classes based on individual achievement levels. High school classes are divided by grade level, and students are assigned based on ability and achievement.

High school graduation requirements are based on University of California requirements and include completion of a minimum of 200 academic credits plus 40 credit hours of physical education. The academic term is mid-September through mid-June, with a summer quarter offered at both campuses. Requirements include 4 years of English, 3 years of mathematics, 2 years of a foreign language, 2 years of laboratory sciences, and 1 year each of U.S. history and world cultures, plus one semester of U.S. government and economics and 2 years of visual/performing arts. Proficiency exams in English, mathematics, and computer literacy, as well as community service hours, are also required for graduation.

A typical semester of course work includes six classes plus physical education. Advanced Placement classes are available in English, history, language, math, and science. Review and remedial classes are made available to students who need additional instruction. International students are offered three levels of classes in English as a second language (ESL), including an introductory class, to prepare them to enter and succeed in other academic areas.

Teachers are available daily during a midafternoon study period to work individually with students and meet with parents. There is no extra charge for this tutoring. Boarding students are required to attend a monitored evening study hall, where additional teacher assistance is available.

Student achievement is recognized with a grading system that ranges from A to F. Progress letters are sent monthly to parents and report cards are sent quarterly. The minimum college-recommending grade upon completion of academic requirements is a "C."

While studying at the Beaver Creek Ranch campus, students attend classes on a block schedule, Monday through Thursday. Each Friday, students participate in educational, project-oriented, and assignment-based field trips. Experiential learning allows students to apply knowledge from the classroom. It also supports an integrated academic element that links core subject areas in a practical, applied manner, promoting understanding and retention of key concepts.

FACULTY AND ADVISERS

Headmaster Kenneth Veronda was born at the San Marino campus that his father founded. Mr. Veronda attended classes at Southwestern, graduated, and completed undergraduate and graduate work in American history and foreign relations at Stanford University. The majority of 31 faculty members, 22 in California and 9 in Arizona, hold advanced degrees in their subject areas. Each teacher serves as a faculty adviser to a few students and meets with them individually throughout the school year. On-campus college and career counselors are also available to meet with and assist students in making post–high school graduation plans.

COLLEGE ADMISSION COUNSELING

The college counselors closely monitor the advisement and placement needs of each student. Beginning in the ninth grade, every effort is made to assist students in researching a variety of colleges and universities that match their interests and academic achievement levels. Students are provided a college planning handbook that offers helpful hints and suggestions regarding college application processes. A variety of college representatives are invited annually to visit each campus and meet with students.

Approximately 35 students graduate each year from Southwestern Academy. All enter a U.S. college or university. Some choose to attend a local two-year community college before transferring to a four-year college or university. In recent years, Southwestern Academy graduates have been accepted to the following schools: American University; Arizona State; Art Center College of Design; Azusa Pacific; Boston College; Boston University; Brown; Butler; California State, Fullerton, Monterey Bay, and Northridge; California State Polytechnic, Pomona; Columbia; Hampton; Howard; Loyola; Marymount; Menlo College; Mills; Occidental; Oregon State; Parsons; Penn State; Pepperdine; Pitzer; Temple; USC, Whittier; Woodbury; Wooster; Xavier; the Universities of California Berkeley, Davis, Irvine, Los Angeles, Riverside, Santa Barbara, San Diego, and Santa Cruz; and the Universities of Nevada, New Orleans, the Pacific, San Diego, San Francisco, St. Louis, Virginia, and Washington (Seattle).

ACADEMIC FACILITIES

The San Marino campus includes seven buildings encircling a large multisport athletic field. Lincoln Hall, the main academic building, houses morning assembly and study hall, ten classrooms, science and computer labs, and the library. Pioneer Hall includes several classrooms, a kitchen, dining rooms, and business offices. A separate building is home to large music and art studios and an additional science classroom and lab.

Newly renovated classrooms, a learning resource center, and the dormitories blend into the picturesque setting along Beaver Creek.

BOARDING AND GENERAL FACILITIES

Four dormitory halls are located on the San Marino campus. Each is designed to accommodate up to 20 boys in double and single rooms. Two off-campus dormitories (located within a mile) house a total of 34 girls. Dorm parents live in apartments adjoining each hall.

At Beaver Creek, seven stone cottages encircle the main campus area and provide faculty/staff housing. Four recently renovated residence halls accommodate up to 32 students. The Beaver Creek Ranch campus includes recreation rooms, a gymnasium, several large activity fields, and an indoor, solar-heated swimming pool.

ATHLETICS

Gyms and playing fields are available to all students at both campuses, where sports opportunities exist for physical education requirements and recreation. As a member of federated leagues in California and Arizona, Southwestern Academy fields teams at both campuses in all major sports except tackle football. Athletic events are held in late afternoon, following the regular school day.

EXTRACURRICULAR OPPORTUNITIES

Southwestern offers a wide range of co-curricular and extracurricular activities and opportunities, including art, drama, music, journalism, student government, and student clubs. Current clubs include chess, Interact, International, the Southwestern Arts Society, Southwestern Environmental Associates, and tennis. Frequent class trips to southern California and northern Arizona places of interest, such as tide pools, museums, archaeological sites, art galleries, and live theater, are great learning experiences for students at both campuses.

DAILY LIFE

Boarding students begin each school day with a breakfast buffet at 7:30 a.m. Following breakfast, day and boarding students meet for a required assembly at 8:10 a.m., with classes following from 8:30 a.m. to 2:45 p.m. Required study halls and optional clubs and athletic events are held between 2:50 and 4:30 p.m. Dinner is served at 6 p.m. and is followed by a monitored study hall lasting until 8 p.m. Lights out is at 10:30 p.m. for middle school students and 11 p.m. for high school students.

WEEKEND LIFE

Students in good standing may leave the campus, with permission, during any weekend. Many students take advantage of the planned activities that are arranged for them, including theater performances, shopping at the malls and Old Town Pasadena, barbecues, beach parties, and movies. Visits are planned to Disneyland, Magic Mountain, and Big Surf, and the other attractions of the two-state areas are a part of the social program at Southwestern Academy. Day students are welcome to attend all weekend activities if space permits.

SUMMER PROGRAMS

Summer school sessions are offered at both campuses. Both offer intensive yet enjoyable individualized classes in English and other subjects, plus educational and recreational trips to interesting places in southern California and northern Arizona.

The summer program in San Marino is an excellent opportunity for domestic students to catch up, if needed, or to move ahead academically in order to take more advanced courses before graduation. For non-English-speaking international students, the summer session can provide an entire semester of the appropriate ESL level necessary to successfully complete a college-preparatory curriculum.

Summer sessions at Beaver Creek Ranch combine review and enrichment courses with experiential learning and high-adventure activities in classwork, camp-type activities, and travel in northern Arizona. ESL is offered at the Beaver Creek campus during the summer.

COSTS AND FINANCIAL AID

Tuition for the 2016–17 school year for U.S. boarding students is $39,900. International student tuition is $47,850. The cost for a day student (U.S. citizens) is $19,750. An incidental account containing $2,000 for boarding students or $1,000 for day students is required of all students to cover expenses such as books, school supplies, physical education uniforms, and discretionary spending money. Payment is due in advance unless other arrangements are made with the business office.

Financial aid is awarded based on financial need. More than $440,000 was awarded in the 2016–17 school year.

ADMISSIONS INFORMATION

Southwestern Academy admits students of any race, color, national and ethnic origin, creed, or sex. A completed application packet is required, followed by a personal on-campus interview with students and parents. A daylong visit to classes (and an overnight for prospective boarding students) is strongly encouraged for prospective students already living in the United States. Interviews with prospective international students and parents are scheduled by the international admissions director and do not require a campus visit, although a visit, tour, and interview are encouraged.

Each campus offers exceptional learning opportunities. Prospective students are encouraged to seriously consider both campuses and apply to the one that seems better suited to them.

Admission materials and other information may be downloaded from the Southwestern Academy website. It can also be obtained by contacting the Office of Admissions.

APPLICATION TIMETABLE

Admission offers are made throughout the year, as space permits. Appointments are required for interviews and campus tours at both locations and/or via Skype. The admissions office for both campus locations is located in San Marino. Students should write or call the San Marino office for information on either campus.

ADMISSIONS CORRESPONDENCE

Office of Admissions
Southwestern Academy
2800 Monterey Road
San Marino, California 91108
United States
Phone: 626-799-5010 Ext. 5
Fax: 626-799-0407
E-mail: admissions@southwesternacademy.edu
Website:
    http://www.southwesternacademy.edu

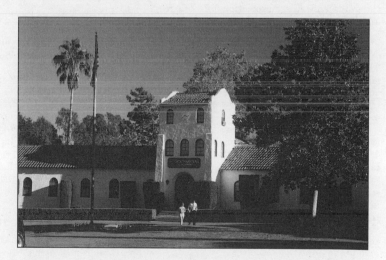

YORK PREPARATORY SCHOOL

New York, New York

Type: Coeducational day college preparatory school
Grades: 6–12: Middle School, 6–8; Upper School, 9–12
Enrollment: 340
Head of School: Ronald P. Stewart, Headmaster

THE SCHOOL

York Prep is a college preparatory school with a strong, academically challenging, traditional curriculum. In a city known for its diversity of private schools, York Prep has developed a unique program that leads students to their highest potential. The School's responsive approach emphasizes independent thought, builds confidence, and sends graduates on to the finest colleges and universities. At York, every student finds opportunities to flourish. York Prep believes that success breeds success, and excellence in academics, arts, or sports creates self-confidence that enhances all aspects of life, both in and out of the classroom.

York Prep was established in 1969 by its current Headmaster, Ronald P. Stewart, and his wife, Jayme Stewart, Director of College Guidance. Situated on West 68th Street between Columbus Avenue and Central Park West, the School is well served by public transportation. Therefore, it attracts students from all over the metropolitan area, creating a diverse community. York Prep takes full advantage of the prime location, with regular visits to museums, parks, and theaters, all of which are easily accessible.

York Prep is approved by the New York State Board of Regents and accredited by the Middle States Association of Colleges and Schools.

ACADEMIC PROGRAM

The curriculum is designed to develop the superior academic skills necessary for future success. Close attention to each student's needs ensures that progress toward personal excellence is carefully guided.

Students must complete 20 credits for graduation: 4 in English, 4 in math, 4 in science, 4 in history, and 4 in foreign language.

Eleventh and twelfth graders choose from a number of course offerings in every subject area. In addition to selecting one course from each required category, a student must choose an elective from a variety of options that range from the creative and performing arts to the analytical sciences.

York Prep is proud of its commitment to community service. Student volunteer work benefits others, helps students realize their full potential, builds a well-rounded individual, and establishes a closer relationship between the School and community. Colleges expect students to have volunteer experience and York Prep College Guidance strongly urges students to perform 25 hours of community service per year during high school as a mark of integrity, responsibility, and citizenship.

Classes at York are small—the average class has 15 students. There are close student-teacher relations and all students begin their day with a morning "house" period. Each student's academic and social progress is carefully monitored by the teachers, advisers, and deans of the Upper and Middle Schools. The deans, in turn, keep the Headmaster and Associate Head informed at weekly meetings. In addition, the Administration maintains close relationships with the students. All of York's administrators teach courses and are readily available to students and parents alike. At the close of each day, there is a period when students may go to faculty members or advisers for help.

Parents are kept informed of a student's progress through individual reports posted every Friday on "Edline," a component of the York Prep website. Each family signs in with a unique password to see their child's progress in all academic subjects. The annual Curriculum Night, during which parents become students for an evening by attending their child's abbreviated classes, provides a good overview of the course work and the faculty members. Parent involvement is encouraged, and there is an active Parents' Association.

FACULTY AND ADVISERS

York Prep is proud of having maintained a stable faculty of outstanding and dedicated individuals. New teachers join the staff periodically, creating a nice balance between youth and experience.

There are 70 full-time faculty members, including 2 college guidance counselors, an IT specialist, and reading and learning specialists.

Mr. Ronald P. Stewart, the founding Headmaster, is a graduate of Oxford University (B.A., 1965; M.A., 1966; B.C.L., 1968), where he also taught.

COLLEGE ADMISSION COUNSELING

York Prep has a notable college guidance program. Mrs. Jayme Stewart and Janet Rooney, Co-Directors of College Guidance, are well known for their expertise and experience. Jayme Stewart is the author of *How to Get into the College of Your Choice.* They meet with all ninth- and tenth-graders to outline the program and then meet individually with eleventh graders. Extensive meetings continue through the twelfth grade on an individual basis. In addition, the eleventh and twelfth graders take college guidance as a course where they write their essays, research colleges, and

complete their applications during school hours.

One hundred percent of York Prep's graduating students are accepted to college. The ultimate aim of the college guidance program is the placement of each student in the college best suited to him or her. More than 85 percent of York Prep graduates are accepted to, attend, and finish at their first- or second-choice college. Graduates are currently attending schools that include Babson, Brandeis, Brown, Carnegie Mellon, Colgate, Cornell, Dickinson, Franklin and Marshall, Georgetown, Hamilton, Harvard, Johns Hopkins, MIT, NYU (Tisch and Stern), Oberlin, Rhode Island School of Design, Skidmore, Swarthmore, UPENN Wharton, Vassar, Villanova, UCLA, and the University of Michigan. Numerous college representatives visit the School regularly to meet with interested students.

YORK PREP SCHOLARS AND JUMP START

York Prep Scholars is an enrichment program designed to address the needs of students who are already excelling in their standard honors curriculum. The York Scholars program provides a rich variety of opportunities to broaden and deepen students' academic perspectives. Courses include Contemporary Poetry, Geometric Sequences and Series, Modern Political Philosophy, Lincoln at Cooper Union, Euclid in the New World, and Microbiology.

York Prep's Jump Start Program enables students with different learning styles or specific learning differences to function successfully in an academically challenging mainstream setting. Students in the program work with a specialist in one or more of the following areas: language processing, reading, writing, math, and organizational skills.

STUDENT BODY AND CONDUCT

There are 340 students enrolled at York Prep. York students reside in all five boroughs of New York City as well as Long Island, northern New Jersey, and Westchester County. The School has a student code of conduct and a dress code. The elected student council is also an integral part of life at York Prep.

ACADEMIC FACILITIES

York is located near Lincoln Center on a safe and lovely tree-lined street, just steps from Central Park at 40 West 68th Street, in a seven-story granite building housing science laboratories, performance and art studios, and a sprung hardwood gymnasium with weight and locker room facilities. All classrooms have computers, audiovisual (AV) projectors, and interactive white boards. Wireless Internet access is available throughout the School and enables students to e-mail their teachers, review homework assignments, and extend learning to all areas of the School. Dance classes are held at a professional dance studio next to the School. The building is wheelchair accessible and meets ADA requirements.

ATHLETICS

All students are required to take courses in physical education and health each year. A varied and extensive athletic program offers students the opportunity to participate in competitive, noncompetitive, team, and individual sports. Sports include soccer, volleyball, basketball, golf, swimming, baseball, softball, track and field, and cross-country. York Prep participates in the ISAL, which it founded.

EXTRACURRICULAR OPPORTUNITIES

The School provides over fifty extracurricular clubs and activities, including Math Competition Club, Model UN, Broadway Club, chess and backgammon, Young Doctors Club, vocal and instrumental groups (including ukelele), beekeeping, hiking, pottery, sports broadcasting, a literary magazine, and a drama club. Upper School

students also have the opportunity to travel internationally to countries in Asia, Europe, and South America.

DAILY LIFE

The school day begins at 8:40 with a 10-minute house period. Academic classes of 42-minute duration begin at 8:54. There is a midmorning break at 10:22. Lunch period is from 12:06 to 12:58, Mondays through Thursdays, and classes end at 3:12. Following dismissal, teachers are available for extra help. During this time, clubs and sports teams also meet. The library is open until 7:30 p.m. Monday through Thursday as a study center for students. On Fridays the school day ends at 1:38.

SUMMER PROGRAMS

The School provides workshops during the summer, both in study skills and in academic courses, most of which are set up on an individual tutorial basis. In addition, the athletic department provides summer sports camps.

COSTS AND FINANCIAL AID

Tuition for the 2017–18 academic year ranges from $48,500 to $48,800. More than 12 percent of the student body receives some financial assistance. During the previous year, $1 million was offered in scholarship assistance.

ADMISSIONS INFORMATION

York Prep seeks to enroll students of above-average intelligence with the will and ability to complete college preparatory work. Students are accepted on the basis of their applications, teacher recommendations, ISEE or SSAT test scores, writing samples, and interviews.

APPLICATION TIMETABLE

York conforms to the notification guidelines established by the Independent Schools Admissions Association of Greater New York. Subsequent applications are processed on a rolling admissions basis. Requests for financial aid should be made at the time of application for entrance.

ADMISSIONS CORRESPONDENCE

Elizabeth Norton, Director of Enrollment
Tracy Warner, Director of Admissions
York Preparatory School
40 West 68th Street
New York, New York 10023
United States
Phone: 212-362-0400
Fax: 212-362-7424
E-mail: enorton@yorkprep.org
Website: http://www.yorkprep.org

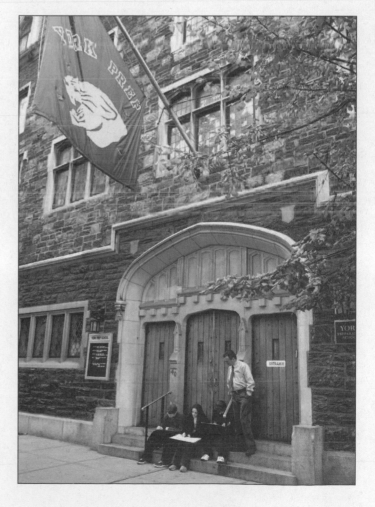

Special Needs Schools

ALPINE ACADEMY

1280 Whispering Horse Drive
Erda, Utah 84074

Head of School: Michele Boguslofski

General Information Girls' boarding college-preparatory, general academic, and equestrian, consumer sciences school; primarily serves underachievers, students with learning disabilities, individuals with Attention Deficit Disorder, individuals with emotional and behavioral problems, and dyslexic students. Grades 7–12. Founded: 2001. Setting: rural. Nearest major city is Salt Lake City. Students are housed in all girls school. Students live in houses on campus. 35-acre campus. 10 buildings on campus. Approved or accredited by National Association of Private Schools for Exceptional Children and Utah Department of Education. Total enrollment: 61. Upper school average class size: 8. Upper school faculty-student ratio: 1:4. There are 210 required school days per year for Upper School students. Upper School students typically attend 5 days per week. The average school day consists of 5 hours and 50 minutes.

Upper School Student Profile Grade 8: 3 students (3 girls); Grade 9: 9 students (9 girls); Grade 10: 11 students (11 girls); Grade 11: 15 students (15 girls); Grade 12: 19 students (19 girls). 100% of students are boarding students. 1% are state residents. 16 states are represented in upper school student body. 1% are international students. International students from Bermuda, Mexico, Thailand, and United States; 3 other countries represented in student body.

Faculty School total: 10. In upper school: 1 man, 9 women; 1 has an advanced degree; 14 reside on campus.

Subjects Offered ACT preparation, algebra, American government, American history, American sign language, art, arts, basic skills, biology, botany, chemistry, college admission preparation, costumes and make-up, CPR, dance, debate, drama, earth science, electives, English, equine science, geography, geometry, government, health, health education, history, honors English, journalism, life skills, mathematics, personal money management, physical education, pre-algebra, pre-calculus, psychology, SAT preparation, science, Spanish, weight training, women in world history.

Graduation Requirements Graduation is therapeutically, rather than academically, indicated.

Special Academic Programs Honors section; accelerated programs; independent study; study at local college for college credit; academic accommodation for the gifted; remedial reading and/or remedial writing; remedial math; special instructional classes for blind students, students with severe emotional disturbances.

College Admission Counseling 15 students graduated in 2016; 5 went to college. Other: 3 went to work.

Student Life Upper grades have specified standards of dress. Discipline rests primarily with faculty.

Summer Programs Remediation, enrichment, advancement, sports, art/fine arts programs offered; session focuses on making up or getting ahead on credits toward graduation (Year Round School); held on campus; accepts girls; not open to students from other schools. 65 students usually enrolled. 2017 schedule: May 2 to July 15. Application deadline: none.

Tuition and Aid Guaranteed tuition plan. Tuition installment plan (monthly payment plans, individually arranged payment plans). Need-based scholarship grants available. In 2016–17, 2% of upper-school students received aid.

Admissions Traditional secondary-level entrance grade is 10. Achievement tests or psychoeducational evaluation required. Deadline for receipt of application materials: none. No application fee required.

Athletics Interscholastic: aerobics, aerobics/dance, basketball, bicycling, climbing, cooperative games, dance, equestrian sports, fitness, fitness walking, Frisbee, golf, hiking/backpacking, horseback riding, outdoor activities, outdoor adventure, outdoor recreation, physical fitness, physical training, racquetball, rafting, rock climbing, running, snowshoeing, soccer, softball, strength & conditioning, swimming and diving, tennis, ultimate Frisbee, volleyball, walking, wall climbing, weight lifting, weight training, yoga. 1 PE instructor.

Computers Computers are regularly used in art, career education, career exploration, college planning, creative writing, dance, English, foreign language, geography, history, library, mathematics, psychology, science, study skills, theater arts, writing classes. Computer network features include on-campus library services, Internet access, Internet filtering or blocking technology. Campus intranet and computer access in designated common areas are available to students. Students grades are available online.

Contact Christian Egan, Admissions Director. 800-244-1113. Fax: 435-843-5416. E-mail: cegan@alpineacademy.org. Website: www.alpineacademy.org

ASSETS SCHOOL

One Ohana Nui Way
Honolulu, Hawaii 96818

Head of School: Mr. Paul Singer

General Information Coeducational day college-preparatory, arts, and technology school; primarily serves students with learning disabilities, individuals with Attention Deficit Disorder, dyslexic students, and gifted/talented students. Grades K–12. Founded: 1955. Setting: urban. 3-acre campus. 12 buildings on campus. Approved or accredited by The Hawaii Council of Private Schools, Western Association of Schools and Colleges, and Hawaii Department of Education. Member of National Association of Independent Schools. Endowment: $3.1 million. Total enrollment: 323. Upper school average class size: 8. Upper school faculty-student ratio: 1:8. There are 168 required school days per year for Upper School students. Upper School students typically attend 5 days per week. The average school day consists of 5 hours and 58 minutes.

Upper School Student Profile Grade 9: 40 students (32 boys, 8 girls); Grade 10: 40 students (25 boys, 15 girls); Grade 11: 23 students (13 boys, 10 girls); Grade 12: 19 students (14 boys, 5 girls).

Faculty School total: 68. In upper school: 7 men, 17 women; 18 have advanced degrees.

Subjects Offered 1 1/2 elective credits, algebra, American history, art, biology, business skills, calculus, chemistry, computer science, consumer education, creative writing, current events, earth science, economics, English, fine arts, fitness, general science, geometry, government/civics, health, humanities, independent study, integrated science, keyboarding, literature, marine biology, marine science, mathematics, music, music appreciation, philosophy, physical education, physics, pre-calculus, psychology, sign language, social studies, Spanish, statistics, theater, trigonometry, women's health, woodworking, word processing, world history, world literature.

Graduation Requirements Arts and fine arts (art, music, dance, drama), biology, business skills (includes word processing), computer science, English, foreign language, mathematics, physical education (includes health), science, social studies (includes history), study skills, participation in mentorship program in 9th–12th grades.

Special Academic Programs Academic accommodation for the gifted; remedial reading and/or remedial writing; remedial math; programs in English, mathematics, general development for dyslexic students.

College Admission Counseling 30 students graduated in 2015; 27 went to college, including Chaminade University of Honolulu; Hawai`i Pacific University; Oregon State University; University of Hawaii at Manoa; Washington State University. Other: 3 had other specific plans.

Student Life Upper grades have specified standards of dress, student council, honor system. Discipline rests primarily with faculty.

Tuition and Aid Day student tuition: $23,180. Tuition installment plan (FACTS Tuition Payment Plan, monthly payment plans, individually arranged payment plans, semester payment plan). Need-based scholarship grants, partial tuition remission for children of staff available. In 2015–16, 37% of upper-school students received aid. Total amount of financial aid awarded in 2015–16: $170,000.

Admissions Traditional secondary-level entrance grade is 9. WISC III or other aptitude measures; standardized achievement test required. Deadline for receipt of application materials: none. Application fee required: $75. On-campus interview required.

Athletics Interscholastic: baseball (boys), basketball (b,g), bowling (b,g), canoeing/kayaking (b,g), cheering (g), cross-country running (b,g), diving (b,g), football (b), golf (b,g), gymnastics (g), judo (b,g), kayaking (b,g), sailing (b,g), soccer (b,g), softball (g), swimming and diving (b,g), tennis (b,g), track and field (b,g), volleyball (b,g), water polo (b,g), wrestling (b,g); intramural: basketball (b,g), volleyball (b,g); coed intramural: basketball, dance, flag football, kickball, Newcombe ball, soccer, softball, tai chi, touch football, ultimate Frisbee, volleyball, whiffle ball, yoga. 2 PE instructors, 4 coaches.

Computers Computers are regularly used in English, mathematics, photography, science classes. Computer network features include on-campus library services, Internet access, wireless campus network, Internet filtering or blocking technology, assistive technology for learning differences. Student e-mail accounts and computer access in designated common areas are available to students. The school has a published electronic and media policy.

Contact Ms. Sandi Tadaki, Director of Admissions. 808-423-1356. Fax: 808-422-1920. E-mail: stadaki@assets-school.net. Website: www.assets-school.net

ATLANTIS ACADEMY

9600 Southwest 107th Avenue
Miami, Florida 33176

Head of School: Mr. Carlos Aballi

General Information Coeducational day general academic school; primarily serves underachievers, students with learning disabilities, individuals with Attention Deficit Disorder, individuals with emotional and behavioral problems, dyslexic students, and Autism Spectrum Disorder. Ungraded, ages 5–18. Founded: 1976. Setting: suburban. 3-acre campus. 1 building on campus. Approved or accredited by Florida Council of Independent Schools, Southern Association of Colleges and Schools, and Florida Department of Education. Total enrollment: 156. Upper school average class size: 9. Upper school faculty-student ratio: 1:8. The average school day consists of 6 hours and 15 minutes.

Faculty School total: 26. In upper school: 5 men, 9 women; 3 have advanced degrees.

Subjects Offered Art, computer skills, language arts, mathematics, physical education, reading, science, social studies, Spanish.

Special Academic Programs Remedial reading and/or remedial writing; remedial math; programs in English, mathematics, general development for dyslexic students; ESL (3 students enrolled).

College Admission Counseling 12 students graduated in 2015; 8 went to college, including Florida International University; Lynn University; Miami Dade College; New York Institute of Technology. Other: 4 went to work.

Student Life Upper grades have uniform requirement. Discipline rests primarily with faculty.

Tuition and Aid Day student tuition: $16,700–$18,100. Tuition installment plan (FACTS Tuition Payment Plan, monthly payment plans, semi-annual and annual payment plans). Need-based scholarship grants available. In 2015–16, 90% of upper-school students received aid. Total amount of financial aid awarded in 2015–16: $12,000.

Admissions Traditional secondary-level entrance age is 14. For fall 2015, 15 students applied for upper-level admission, 15 were accepted, 15 enrolled. Psychoeducational evaluation or school's own exam required. Deadline for receipt of application materials: none. No application fee required. On-campus interview required.

Athletics Interscholastic: basketball (boys, girls), flag football (b), tennis (b,g), volleyball (b,g); intramural: flag football (b); coed interscholastic: soccer, softball; coed intramural: basketball, golf, soccer, tennis, volleyball. 1 PE instructor, 2 coaches.

Computers Computers are regularly used in art, English, foreign language, history, mathematics, science, social sciences classes. Computer network features include Internet access.

Contact Mr. Eric Smith, Assistant Director/Director of Admissions. 305-271-9771. Fax: 305-271-7078. E-mail: esmith@esa-education.com. Website: www.atlantisacademy.com/

BALBOA CITY SCHOOL

525 Hawthorn Street
San Diego, California 92101

Head of School: Mr. Zachary C. Jones

General Information Coeducational day college-preparatory and general academic school; primarily serves underachievers. Grades 1–12. Founded: 1993. Setting: small town. 2-acre campus. 1 building on campus. Approved or accredited by California Association of Independent Schools and Western Association of Schools and Colleges. Member of Secondary School Admission Test Board. Total enrollment: 75. Upper school average class size: 12. Upper school faculty-student ratio: 1:10. There are 183 required school days per year for Upper School students. Upper School students typically attend 5 days per week. The average school day consists of 6 hours and 30 minutes.

Upper School Student Profile Grade 6: 9 students (4 boys, 5 girls); Grade 7: 30 students (20 boys, 10 girls); Grade 8: 36 students (15 boys, 21 girls); Grade 9: 25 students (10 boys, 15 girls); Grade 10: 15 students (9 boys, 6 girls); Grade 11: 7 students (5 boys, 2 girls); Grade 12: 8 students (3 boys, 5 girls).

Faculty School total: 26. In upper school: 11 men, 15 women; 10 have advanced degrees.

Subjects Offered Algebra, American literature, American sign language, art, arts, astronomy, biology, British literature, calculus, chemistry, computer graphics, computer literacy, construction, crafts, creative writing, drama, economics, English, foreign language, geometry, government, guitar, health, history, history of rock and roll, journalism, language, life science, life skills, literature, marine biology, mathematics, multicultural studies, music, outdoor education, painting, physical education, physical science, physics, piano, pre-calculus, psychology, reading, science, social sciences, social studies, sociology, Spanish, speech therapy, study skills, U.S. history, video film production, visual arts, vocational arts, world history, world literature, yearbook.

Graduation Requirements Arts and fine arts (art, music, dance, drama), computer science, English, foreign language, mathematics, physical education (includes health), science, social sciences, social studies (includes history). Community service is required.

Special Academic Programs ESL (44 students enrolled).

College Admission Counseling 17 students graduated in 2016; all went to college.

Student Life Upper grades have specified standards of dress, student council, honor system. Discipline rests primarily with faculty.

Summer Programs Remediation, enrichment, advancement, ESL, computer instruction programs offered; session focuses on academic training; held on campus; accepts boys and girls; open to students from other schools. 55 students usually enrolled. 2017 schedule: June 17 to July 30. Application deadline: May 1.

Tuition and Aid Day student tuition: $11,500. Guaranteed tuition plan. Tuition installment plan (monthly payment plans, individually arranged payment plans). Tuition reduction for siblings, merit scholarship grants, need-based scholarship grants available. In 2016–17, 5% of upper-school students received aid.

Admissions Traditional secondary-level entrance grade is 9. For fall 2016, 12 students applied for upper-level admission, 9 were accepted, 9 enrolled. Deadline for receipt of application materials: none. No application fee required. On-campus interview required.

Athletics Interscholastic: basketball (boys), soccer (b), volleyball (b). 1 PE instructor, 6 coaches.

Computers Computer network features include Internet access, wireless campus network, Internet filtering or blocking technology. Computer access in designated common areas is available to students. Students grades are available online. The school has a published electronic and media policy.

Contact Ms. Monica Castro, Registrar. 760-2944161. Fax: 760-2944209. E-mail: mcastro@balboaschool.com. Website: www.balboaschool.com

BRANDON HALL SCHOOL

1701 Brandon Hall Drive
Atlanta, Georgia 30350-3706

Head of School: Mr. Dean Fusto

General Information Coeducational boarding and day college-preparatory and ESL school. Boarding grades 7–12, day grades 6–12. Founded: 1959. Setting: suburban. Students are housed in single-sex by floor dormitories. 27-acre campus. 5 buildings on campus. Approved or accredited by Georgia Independent School Association, Southern Association of Colleges and Schools, Southern Association of Independent Schools, and Georgia Department of Education. Member of National Association of Independent Schools. Endowment: $100,000. Total enrollment: 155. Upper school average class size: 8. Upper school faculty-student ratio: 1:8. There are 180 required school days per year for Upper School students. Upper School students typically attend 5 days per week. The average school day consists of 7 hours and 15 minutes.

Upper School Student Profile Grade 9: 20 students (8 boys, 12 girls); Grade 10: 28 students (17 boys, 11 girls); Grade 11: 28 students (21 boys, 7 girls); Grade 12: 35 students (17 boys, 18 girls). 21% of students are boarding students. 73% are state residents. 10 states are represented in upper school student body. 11% are international students. International students from China, Georgia, Nigeria, Rwanda, Singapore, and Viet Nam.

Faculty School total: 40. In upper school: 21 men, 11 women; 16 have advanced degrees; 17 reside on campus.

Subjects Offered 20th century history, 3-dimensional art, acting, advanced biology, advanced chemistry, advanced math, Advanced Placement courses, advanced studio art-AP, advanced TOEFL/grammar, African American history, algebra, American government, American history-AP, American literature, American literature-AP, American sign language, analysis and differential calculus, anatomy and physiology, art, Asian history, astronomy, athletic training, audio visual/media, ballet, band, biology, British literature, British literature (honors), British literature-AP, calculus, calculus-AP, career/college preparation, chemistry, chemistry-AP, choir, choral music, choreography, chorus, cinematography, college admission preparation, college awareness, college counseling, college placement, college planning, college writing, computer science, computer science-AP, computer-aided design, contemporary issues, dance, desktop publishing, digital photography, drama, drama performance, driver education, earth science, economics, English, English as a foreign language, English composition, English literature and composition-AP, environmental science, environmental studies, ESL, ESL, fine arts, French, French as a second language, French-AP, geometry, government/civics, grammar, health education, history, honors English, honors geometry, honors U.S. history, honors world history, human anatomy, information technology, intro to computers, introduction to technology, introduction to theater, keyboarding, Latin, linear algebra, mathematics, microeconomics-AP, music, music history, music performance, musical theater, organic chemistry, painting, performing arts, philosophy, photography, physical education, physical fitness, physical science, physics, physics-AP, play production, play/screen writing, playwriting, playwriting and directing, poetry, politics, pre-algebra, pre-calculus, printmaking, probability and statistics, psychology, public speaking, reading/study skills, research skills, SAT/ACT preparation, science, sculpture, senior project, senior seminar, set design, sign language, social studies, Spanish, Spanish-AP, statistics-AP, student government, student publications, student teaching, technical theater, theater, TOEFL preparation, trigonometry, U.S government, U.S. history, U.S. literature, video film production, word processing, world history, world literature, writing, yearbook.

Graduation Requirements American government, arts and fine arts (art, music, dance, drama), computer applications, economics, English, foreign language, mathematics, physical education (includes health), science, social studies (includes history), community service hours.

Special Academic Programs 12 Advanced Placement exams for which test preparation is offered; honors section; accelerated programs; study at local college for college credit; study abroad; ESL (10 students enrolled).

College Admission Counseling 45 students graduated in 2016; they went to Appalachian State University; Georgia State University; Louisiana State University in Shreveport; Mercer University; Syracuse University; University of Georgia.

Student Life Upper grades have uniform requirement, student council, honor system. Discipline rests primarily with faculty.

Summer Programs Remediation, enrichment, advancement, ESL, sports, art/fine arts, computer instruction programs offered; session focuses on general academics; held on campus; accepts boys and girls; open to students from other schools. 150 students usually enrolled. 2017 schedule: May 30 to June 30.

Tuition and Aid Day student tuition: $29,750; 7-day tuition and room/board: $57,500. Tuition installment plan (Insured Tuition Payment Plan, monthly payment plans, individually arranged payment plans). Need-based scholarship grants available. In 2016–17, 10% of upper-school students received aid. Total amount of financial aid awarded in 2016–17: $250,000.

Admissions Traditional secondary-level entrance grade is 9. SSAT and TOEFL required. Deadline for receipt of application materials: none. Application fee required: $100. Interview required.

Athletics Interscholastic: baseball (boys), basketball (b,g), tennis (b,g), touch football (b), volleyball (g), wrestling (b); coed interscholastic: cheering, cross-country running, dance, equestrian sports, golf, soccer, swimming and diving, track and field; coed intramural: physical training.

Computers Computers are regularly used in all classes. Computer network features include on-campus library services, Internet access, wireless campus network, Internet filtering or blocking technology. Campus intranet, student e-mail accounts, and computer access in designated common areas are available to students. Students grades are available online. The school has a published electronic and media policy.

Contact Mrs. Kirsten Knowles Perdue, Director of Admissions. 770-394-8177 Ext. 201. Fax: 678-848-1444. E-mail: admissions@brandonhall.org. Website: www.brandonhall.org

BREHM PREPARATORY SCHOOL

950 S. Brehm Lane
Carbondale, Illinois 62901

Head of School: Mr. Brian P. Brown, PhD

General Information Coeducational boarding and day college-preparatory and general academic school; primarily serves students with learning disabilities, individuals with Attention Deficit Disorder, dyslexic students, and language-based learning differences. Grades 6–PG. Founded: 1982. Setting: small town. Nearest major city is St. Louis, MO. Students are housed in coed dormitories. 100-acre campus. 13 buildings on campus. Approved or accredited by Independent Schools Association of the Central States, North Central Association of Colleges and Schools, and Illinois Department of Education. Member of National Association of Independent Schools. Endowment: $900,000. Total enrollment: 85. Upper school average class size: 8. Upper school faculty-student ratio: 1:4. There are 185 required school days per year for Upper School students. Upper School students typically attend 5 days per week. The average school day consists of 7 hours and 30 minutes.

Upper School Student Profile Grade 9: 13 students (12 boys, 1 girl); Grade 10: 15 students (12 boys, 3 girls); Grade 11: 19 students (14 boys, 5 girls); Grade 12: 20 students (15 boys, 5 girls); Postgraduate: 8 students (8 boys).

Faculty School total: 24. In upper school: 8 men, 16 women; 15 have advanced degrees.

Subjects Offered 20th century American writers, 20th century history, ACT preparation, algebra, American history, American literature, anatomy and physiology, art, biology, British literature, calculus, career exploration, chemistry, communication skills, composition, computer graphics, computer programming, computer science, computer skills, consumer education, creative writing, current events, current history, desktop publishing, digital imaging, digital photography, earth science, economics, English, English literature, environmental science, geometry, government/civics, health, keyboarding, language, learning cognition, mathematics, photography, physical education, pragmatics, pre-algebra, pre-calculus, psychology, reading/study skills, science, Shakespeare, social studies, sociology, Spanish, speech, trigonometry, video and animation, weight training, world history, writing.

Graduation Requirements ACT preparation, computer science, consumer education, English, government, learning cognition, mathematics, physical education (includes health), science, social studies (includes history).

Special Academic Programs Study at local college for college credit; academic accommodation for the gifted; remedial reading and/or remedial writing; remedial math; programs in English, mathematics, general development for dyslexic students.

College Admission Counseling 24 students graduated in 2016; 10 went to college, including John A. Logan College; Lynn University; Marshall University; Southern Illinois University Edwardsville. Other: 10 entered a postgraduate year, 4 had other specific plans. Median composite ACT: 17. 7% scored over 26 on composite ACT.

Student Life Upper grades have specified standards of dress, student council, honor system. Discipline rests equally with students and faculty.

Summer Programs Remediation, enrichment, art/fine arts programs offered; session focuses on experiential learning/PBL; held on campus; accepts boys and girls; open to students from other schools. 32 students usually enrolled. 2017 schedule: June 25 to July 22. Application deadline: May 1.

Tuition and Aid Day student tuition: $45,300; 7-day tuition and room/board: $75,300. Tuition installment plan (individually arranged payment plans, Tuition Solution). Need-based scholarship grants available. In 2016–17, 8% of upper-school students received aid. Total amount of financial aid awarded in 2016–17: $99,300.

Admissions Traditional secondary-level entrance grade is 9. For fall 2016, 33 students applied for upper-level admission, 30 were accepted, 24 enrolled. Wechsler Individual Achievement Test, WISC or WAIS and Woodcock-Johnson required. Deadline for receipt of application materials: none. Application fee required: $75. On-campus interview required.

Athletics Interscholastic: basketball (boys, girls); coed interscholastic: soccer; coed intramural: aerobics, aerobics/dance, archery, basketball, billiards, bowling, dance, fishing, flag football, Frisbee, golf, hiking/backpacking, horseback riding, outdoor skills, paint ball, physical fitness, soccer, softball, strength & conditioning. 1 PE instructor, 1 coach.

Computers Computers are regularly used in all academic, career exploration, college planning, creative writing, design, desktop publishing, graphic arts, graphic design, keyboarding, learning cognition, photography, reading, remedial study skills, research

skills, study skills, typing, word processing, writing, writing, yearbook classes. Computer network features include Internet access, wireless campus network, Internet filtering or blocking technology. Student e-mail accounts are available to students. Students grades are available online. The school has a published electronic and media policy.

Contact Mr. Brian Taylor, Director of Admissions. 618-457-0371 Ext. 1303. Fax: 618-529-1248. E-mail: brian.taylor@brehm.org. Website: www.brehm.org

BRIDGES ACADEMY

3921 Laurel Canyon Boulevard
Studio City, California 91604

Head of School: Carl Sabatino

General Information Coeducational day college-preparatory, arts, technology, and music, drama, talent development, badges program school. Grades 4–12. Founded: 1994. Setting: suburban. Nearest major city is Los Angeles. 3.5-acre campus. 3 buildings on campus. Approved or accredited by California Association of Independent Schools, Western Association of Schools and Colleges, and California Department of Education. Member of National Association of Independent Schools. Total enrollment: 170. Upper school average class size: 8. Upper school faculty-student ratio: 1:8. There are 174 required school days per year for Upper School students. Upper School students typically attend 5 days per week. The average school day consists of 5 hours and 15 minutes.

Upper School Student Profile Grade 9: 26 students (24 boys, 2 girls); Grade 10: 23 students (21 boys, 2 girls); Grade 11: 19 students (18 boys, 1 girl); Grade 12: 19 students (16 boys, 3 girls).

Faculty School total: 28. In upper school: 19 men, 9 women; 10 have advanced degrees.

Subjects Offered 20th century history, algebra, American government, American literature, anatomy and physiology, art, biology, calculus, chemistry, drama, economics, European history, European literature, film, genetics, geometry, Japanese, modern European history, music, non-Western literature, photography, physics, pre-calculus, robotics, senior project, Spanish, statistics, study skills, technology, U.S. history, world history.

Graduation Requirements Economics, English, foreign language, government, history, mathematics, performing arts, science, senior seminar, visual arts.

Special Academic Programs Honors section; academic accommodation for the gifted.

College Admission Counseling 23 students graduated in 2016; 19 went to college, including California State University, Northridge; Chapman University; Indiana University Bloomington; The University of Arizona; University of California, Los Angeles; University of California, San Diego. Other: 4 had other specific plans. 57% scored over 600 on SAT critical reading, 23% scored over 600 on SAT math.

Student Life Discipline rests primarily with faculty.

Summer Programs Enrichment, sports, art/fine arts, computer instruction programs offered; session focuses on enrichment; held both on and off campus; accepts boys and girls; open to students from other schools. 2017 schedule: June 1 to June 30. Application deadline: none.

Tuition and Aid Day student tuition: $38,940. Tuition installment plan (Insured Tuition Payment Plan, monthly payment plans). Need-based scholarship grants available. In 2016–17, 18% of upper-school students received aid.

Admissions Traditional secondary-level entrance grade is 9. For fall 2016, 14 students applied for upper-level admission, 11 were accepted, 7 enrolled. Deadline for receipt of application materials: March 1. Application fee required: $150. On-campus interview recommended.

Athletics Coed Interscholastic: basketball, cross-country running, track and field. 3 PE instructors, 2 coaches.

Computers Computers are regularly used in all classes. Computer network features include Internet access, wireless campus network, Internet filtering or blocking technology. Campus intranet and student e-mail accounts are available to students. Students grades are available online. The school has a published electronic and media policy.

Contact Doug Lenzini, Director of Admissions. 818-506-1091. Fax: 818-506-8094. E-mail: doug@bridges.edu. Website: www.bridges.edu

CAMPHILL SPECIAL SCHOOL

1784 Fairview Road
Glenmoore, Pennsylvania 19343

Head of School: Mr. Bernard Wolf

General Information Coeducational boarding and day general academic, arts, and vocational school; primarily serves underachievers, intellectual and developmental disabilities, and mental retardation. Grades K–13. Founded: 1963. Setting: rural. Nearest major city is Philadelphia. Students are housed in on-campus single family homes. 88-acre campus. 1 building on campus. Approved or accredited by Association of Waldorf Schools of North America, Middle States Association of Colleges and Schools, National Council for Private School Accreditation, and Pennsylvania Department of Education. Total enrollment: 120. Upper school average class size: 11.

Upper school faculty-student ratio: 1:7. There are 180 required school days per year for Upper School students. Upper School students typically attend 5 days per week. The average school day consists of 8 hours.

Upper School Student Profile Grade 9: 9 students (6 boys, 3 girls); Grade 10: 13 students (9 boys, 4 girls); Grade 11: 10 students (6 boys, 4 girls); Grade 12: 11 students (7 boys, 4 girls); Grade 13: 24 students (15 boys, 9 girls). 76% of students are boarding students. 72% are state residents. 8 states are represented in upper school student body. 7% are international students. International students from Jamaica, Oman, Saudi Arabia, and United Arab Emirates.

Faculty In upper school: 2 men, 2 women; 2 have advanced degrees; 70 reside on campus.

Subjects Offered 20th century American writers, 20th century history, 20th century physics, 20th century world history, acting, agriculture, alternative physical education, American Civil War, American culture, American democracy, American government, American history, anatomy, Ancient Greek, ancient history, ancient world history, ancient/medieval philosophy, animal husbandry, animal science, art, art and culture, art appreciation, art history, astronomy, bell choir, biology, body human, bookbinding, botany, chemistry, choir, civil rights, Civil War, drama, drama performance, ecology, environmental education, eurythmy, gardening, geography, geometry, government, handbells, health and wellness, history, instruments, life skills, mathematics, medieval history, medieval literature, medieval/Renaissance history, meteorology, music, mythology, natural history, painting, physics, poetry, pottery, reading, science, Shakespeare, woodworking, zoology.

Special Academic Programs Remedial reading and/or remedial writing; remedial math.

Student Life Upper grades have student council. Discipline rests primarily with faculty.

Summer Programs Enrichment programs offered; session focuses on Extended School Year (ESY); held both on and off campus; accepts boys and girls; not open to students from other schools. 45 students usually enrolled. 2017 schedule: July 1 to July 29.

Tuition and Aid Need-based scholarship grants available.

Admissions Traditional secondary-level entrance grade is 9. Deadline for receipt of application materials: none. No application fee required. On-campus interview required.

Computers Computer resources include wireless campus network, Internet filtering or blocking technology. The school has a published electronic and media policy.

Contact Mr. Bernard Wolf, Director of Admissions. 610-469-9236. Fax: 610-469-9758. Website: www.camphillspecialschool.org

CHATHAM ACADEMY

4 Oglethorpe Professional Boulevard
Savannah, Georgia 31406

Head of School: Mrs. Carolyn M. Hannaford

General Information Coeducational day college-preparatory, general academic, and technology school; primarily serves underachievers, students with learning disabilities, individuals with Attention Deficit Disorder, dyslexic students, and different learning styles. Grades 1–12. Founded: 1978. Setting: suburban. 5-acre campus. 2 buildings on campus. Approved or accredited by Southern Association of Colleges and Schools, Southern Association of Independent Schools, and Georgia Department of Education. Endowment: $100,000. Upper school average class size: 10. Upper school faculty-student ratio: 1:10. There are 180 required school days per year for Upper School students. Upper School students typically attend 5 days per week. The average school day consists of 6 hours.

Upper School Student Profile Grade 9: 11 students (9 boys, 2 girls); Grade 10: 10 students (9 boys, 1 girl); Grade 11: 5 students (5 boys); Grade 12: 12 students (9 boys, 3 girls).

Faculty School total: 15. In upper school: 2 men, 6 women; 6 have advanced degrees.

Subjects Offered Algebra, American history, American literature, analytic geometry, ancient world history, art, basic skills, biology, body human, British literature, business communications, business mathematics, business studies, career exploration, career/college preparation, chemistry, college awareness, computer literacy, consumer economics, consumer mathematics, creative writing, earth science, ecology, ecology, environmental systems, economics, English, English literature, environmental science, expository writing, general math, geography, geology, geometry, government/civics, grammar, health and wellness, health education, health science, history, human biology, keyboarding, kinesiology, life science, life skills, literacy, literature, math applications, mathematics, organic chemistry, personal finance, personal fitness, personal money management, physical education, physical fitness, physical science, physics, pre-algebra, reading, reading/study skills, remedial study skills, remedial/makeup course work, SAT/ACT preparation, science, social sciences, social skills, social studies, Spanish, speech and debate, sports, U.S. history, weightlifting, work-study, world history, world literature, writing.

Graduation Requirements Algebra, American government, American history, biology, British literature, chemistry, civics, composition, consumer economics, earth science, economics, electives, English, English composition, English literature, foreign language, French, grammar, marine biology, mathematics, physical education (includes health), physical science, reading/study skills, science, social studies (includes history), U.S. history.

Special Academic Programs Independent study; study at local college for college credit; remedial reading and/or remedial writing; remedial math; programs in English, mathematics, general development for dyslexic students.

College Admission Counseling 9 students graduated in 2015; 3 went to college, including Armstrong State University; College of Charleston; Savannah College of Art and Design. Other: 4 went to work, 2 had other specific plans.

Student Life Upper grades have uniform requirement, student council, honor system. Discipline rests primarily with faculty.

Tuition and Aid Day student tuition: $16,274. Tuition installment plan (monthly payment plans, individually arranged payment plans). Tuition reduction for siblings, need-based scholarship grants, Georgia Special Needs Scholarship available. In 2015–16, 33% of upper-school students received aid. Total amount of financial aid awarded in 2015–16: $90,200.

Admissions Traditional secondary-level entrance grade is 10. For fall 2015, 10 students applied for upper-level admission, 7 were accepted, 5 enrolled. Achievement tests, Individual IQ, Achievement and behavior rating scale, school's own test, Stanford Binet, Wechsler Individual Achievement Test, Wechsler Intelligence Scale for Children III, WISC or WAIS, WISC-R, Woodcock-Johnson, Woodcock-Johnson Revised Achievement Test or writing sample required. Deadline for receipt of application materials: none. Application fee required: $50. Interview required.

Athletics Interscholastic: basketball (boys), flag football (b,g), yoga (g); intramural: soccer (b,g); coed interscholastic: basketball, cheering, fitness, fitness walking, flag football; coed intramural: canoeing/kayaking, cheering, cooperative games, fitness, fitness walking, flag football, jump rope, kickball, Newcombe ball, outdoor activities, outdoor recreation, paddle tennis, physical fitness, physical training, soccer, whiffle ball. 1 PE instructor, 2 coaches.

Computers Computers are regularly used in all academic classes. Computer network features include Internet access, Internet filtering or blocking technology. The school has a published electronic and media policy.

Contact Mrs. Carolyn M. Hannaford, Principal. 912-354-4047. Fax: 912-354-4633. E-mail: channaford@chathamacademy.com. Website: www.chathamacademy.com

CHELSEA SCHOOL

2970 Belcrest Center Drive, Suite 300
Hyattsville, Maryland 20782

Head of School: Frank Mills and Kristal Weems-Bradner

General Information Coeducational day college-preparatory and general academic school; primarily serves students with learning disabilities, individuals with Attention Deficit Disorder, and dyslexic students. Grades 5–12. Founded: 1976. Setting: suburban. 1 building on campus. Approved or accredited by Maryland Department of Education. Total enrollment: 65. Upper school average class size: 8. Upper school faculty-student ratio: 1:8. There are 185 required school days per year for Upper School students. Upper School students typically attend 5 days per week. The average school day consists of 6 hours and 30 minutes.

Upper School Student Profile Grade 6: 7 students (3 boys, 4 girls); Grade 7: 8 students (7 boys, 1 girl); Grade 8: 5 students (4 boys, 1 girl); Grade 9: 10 students (5 boys, 5 girls); Grade 10: 13 students (9 boys, 4 girls); Grade 11: 11 students (9 boys, 2 girls); Grade 12: 4 students (3 boys, 1 girl).

Faculty School total: 19. In upper school: 7 men, 12 women; 7 have advanced degrees.

Subjects Offered Algebra, American history, American literature, art, biology, calculus, career/college preparation, chemistry, community service, composition, computer graphics, computer technologies, computers, earth and space science, earth science, English, English literature, environmental science, foreign language, geometry, health, health and wellness, information technology, math review, music, personal fitness, physical education, pre-algebra, pre-calculus, reading, reading/study skills, remedial study skills, science, social skills, Spanish, state government, U.S. government, U.S. history, U.S. literature.

Graduation Requirements 20th century world history, algebra, American government, American history, art, biology, career/college preparation, chemistry, earth science, electives, English, English composition, English literature, general math, geometry, health and wellness, physical education (includes health), pre-algebra, Spanish, U.S. history.

Special Academic Programs Remedial reading and/or remedial writing; remedial math; programs in English, mathematics, general development for dyslexic students.

College Admission Counseling 14 students graduated in 2016; 12 went to college, including Eastern Connecticut State University. Other: 2 entered a postgraduate year.

Student Life Discipline rests primarily with faculty.

Summer Programs Remediation, enrichment, computer instruction programs offered; session focuses on remediation; held on campus; accepts boys and girls; open to students from other schools. 30 students usually enrolled. 2017 schedule: July to August. Application deadline: none.

Tuition and Aid Day student tuition: $37,572. Tuition installment plan (individually arranged payment plans). Need-based scholarship grants available.

Admissions Academic Profile Tests, Wechsler Individual Achievement Test, Wide Range Achievement Test, WISC III or other aptitude measures; standardized achievement test, WISC or WAIS, WISC-R or Woodcock-Johnson required. Deadline for receipt of application materials: none. Application fee required: $50. On-campus interview required.

Athletics Interscholastic: basketball (boys, girls); coed interscholastic: flag football, soccer, softball, track and field. 1 PE instructor.

Computers Computer network features include on-campus library services, Internet access, wireless campus network, Internet filtering or blocking technology. Campus intranet, student e-mail accounts, and computer access in designated common areas are available to students. The school has a published electronic and media policy.

Contact Debbie Lourie, Director of Admissions. 240-467-2100 Ext. 303. Fax: 240-467-2120. E-mail: dlourie@chelseaschool.edu. Website: www.chelseaschool.edu

COMMUNITY HIGH SCHOOL

1135 Teaneck Road
Teaneck, New Jersey 07666

Head of School: Scott Parisi

General Information Coeducational day college-preparatory school. Founded: 1968. Setting: suburban. Nearest major city is Hackensack. 1 building on campus. Approved or accredited by New Jersey Association of Independent Schools, New York Department of Education, and New Jersey Department of Education. Total enrollment: 181. Upper school faculty-student ratio: 1:5. There are 180 required school days per year for Upper School students. Upper School students typically attend 5 days per week. The average school day consists of 6 hours and 30 minutes.

Upper School Student Profile Grade 9: 37 students (24 boys, 13 girls); Grade 10: 52 students (34 boys, 18 girls); Grade 11: 43 students (31 boys, 12 girls); Grade 12: 43 students (30 boys, 13 girls).

Faculty School total: 44. In upper school: 10 men, 34 women.

Subjects Offered Algebra, American history, American literature, art, biology, business, calculus, chemistry, computer science, creative writing, drama, driver education, English, English literature, European history, expository writing, fine arts, forensics, geography, geometry, government/civics, grammar, history, journalism, mathematics, music, photography, physical education, physics, psychology, science, social sciences, social studies, sociology, Spanish, speech, study skills, theater, trigonometry, writing.

Graduation Requirements Arts and fine arts (art, music, dance, drama), English, mathematics, physical education (includes health), science, social sciences, social studies (includes history).

Special Academic Programs Remedial reading and/or remedial writing; remedial math; programs in English, mathematics, general development for dyslexic students.

College Admission Counseling 42 students graduated in 2016.

Student Life Upper grades have specified standards of dress, student council, honor system. Discipline rests primarily with faculty.

Tuition and Aid Day student tuition: $47,941.

Admissions Traditional secondary-level entrance grade is 9. For fall 2016, 200 students applied for upper-level admission, 60 were accepted, 41 enrolled. Deadline for receipt of application materials: none. Application fee required: $65. On-campus interview required.

Athletics Interscholastic: baseball (boys), basketball (b), soccer (b), softball (g); intramural: baseball (b), basketball (b,g), softball (g), table tennis (b,g), track and field (b,g), volleyball (b,g). 5 PE instructors, 8 coaches.

Computers Computers are regularly used in all academic classes. Computer network features include online commercial services, voice recognition systems. The school has a published electronic and media policy.

Contact Toby Braunstein, Director of Education. 201-862-1796 Ext. 18. Fax: 201-862-1791. E-mail: tbraunstein@communityhighschool.org. Website: www.communityschool.k12.nj.us

CROTCHED MOUNTAIN SCHOOL

1 Verney Drive
Greenfield, New Hampshire 03047

Head of School: Andra Hall

General Information Coeducational boarding and day arts, vocational, technology, and music school; primarily serves underachievers, students with learning disabilities, individuals with Attention Deficit Disorder, individuals with emotional and behavioral problems, dyslexic students, and students with multiple disabilities. Ungraded, ages 6–22. Founded: 1936. Setting: rural. Nearest major city is Manchester. Students are housed in group home, apartments. Approved or accredited by New Hampshire Department of Education. Endowment: $32 million. Upper school average class size: 8.

Faculty School total: 25. In upper school: 8 men, 13 women.

Subjects Offered Art, computers, desktop publishing, English, health, history, home economics, horticulture, mathematics, music, physical education, science, technology, vocational arts.

Graduation Requirements Arts and fine arts (art, music, dance, drama), business skills (includes word processing), computer science, English, mathematics, physical education (includes health), science, social sciences, social studies (includes history).

Special Academic Programs Remedial reading and/or remedial writing; remedial math; special instructional classes for deaf students, blind students.

Student Life Discipline rests primarily with faculty.

Summer Programs Session focuses on preventing regression in students' performance; held on campus; accepts boys and girls. 97 students usually enrolled. 2017 schedule: July 5 to August 29. Application deadline: none.

Tuition and Aid Funding from local districts and other agencies available.

Admissions Deadline for receipt of application materials: none. No application fee required. Interview recommended.

Athletics Coed Intramural: Special Olympics, swimming and diving. 1 PE instructor.

Computers Computers are regularly used in art, English, history, mathematics, music, science classes. Computer resources include Internet access. Student e-mail accounts are available to students. The school has a published electronic and media policy.

Contact David Etlinger, Director of Admissions. 603-547-3311 Ext. 1894. Fax: 603-547-2169. E-mail: david.etlinger@crotchedmountain.org.

DALLAS ACADEMY

950 Tiffany Way
Dallas, Texas 75218

Head of School: Mr. Jim Richardson

General Information Coeducational day college-preparatory and general academic school; primarily serves students with learning disabilities, individuals with Attention Deficit Disorder, and dyslexic students. Grades 1–12. Founded: 1965. Setting: suburban. 2-acre campus. 2 buildings on campus. Approved or accredited by Southern Association of Colleges and Schools and Texas Education Agency. Endowment: $250,000. Total enrollment: 165. Upper school average class size: 10. Upper school faculty-student ratio: 1:6. Upper School students typically attend 5 days per week. The average school day consists of 6 hours and 30 minutes.

Upper School Student Profile Grade 9: 23 students (14 boys, 9 girls); Grade 10: 14 students (10 boys, 4 girls); Grade 11: 22 students (15 boys, 7 girls); Grade 12: 22 students (14 boys, 8 girls).

Faculty School total: 34. In upper school: 3 men, 16 women; 5 have advanced degrees.

Subjects Offered Algebra, American history, art, computer science, computers, drawing, economics, English, fine arts, geography, government/civics, health, history, literature, mathematics, music, photography, physical education, physical science, pottery, science, social sciences, social studies, Spanish, speech, woodworking, world history, writing, yearbook.

Graduation Requirements Arts and fine arts (art, music, dance, drama), computer science, English, foreign language, mathematics, physical education (includes health), science, social sciences, social studies (includes history), 4 hours of community service per semester.

Special Academic Programs Study at local college for college credit; remedial reading and/or remedial writing; remedial math; programs in English, mathematics, general development for dyslexic students.

College Admission Counseling 21 students graduated in 2016; 20 went to college, including Richland College; Texas Tech University; The University of Texas at Arlington; University of Arkansas; University of North Texas; University of the Ozarks. Other: 1 went to work.

Student Life Upper grades have uniform requirement, student council. Discipline rests primarily with faculty.

Summer Programs Remediation, enrichment programs offered; held on campus; accepts boys and girls; open to students from other schools.

Tuition and Aid Day student tuition: $20,000. Tuition installment plan (semester payment plan). Need-based scholarship grants available. In 2016–17, 25% of upper-school students received aid.

Admissions Traditional secondary-level entrance grade is 9. Admissions testing and WRAT required. Deadline for receipt of application materials: none. No application fee required. On-campus interview recommended.

Athletics Interscholastic: baseball (boys), basketball (b,g), cheering (g), cross-country running (b,g), football (b), golf (b,g), physical fitness (b,g), soccer (b,g), track and field (b,g), volleyball (g), yoga (b,g); intramural: tennis (g); coed interscholastic: soccer. 3 PE instructors, 5 coaches, 1 athletic trainer.

Computers Computers are regularly used in English, geography, history, library, SAT preparation, science, typing, writing, yearbook classes. Computer network features include on-campus library services, online commercial services, Internet access, wireless campus network, Internet filtering or blocking technology. Students grades are available online. The school has a published electronic and media policy.

Contact Mr. Jim Richardson, Headmaster. 214-324-1481. Fax: 214-327-8537. E-mail: jrichardson@dallas-academy.com. Website: www.dallas-academy.com

DELAWARE VALLEY FRIENDS SCHOOL

19 East Central Avenue
Paoli, Pennsylvania 19301-1345

Head of School: Mr. Kirk Smothers

General Information Coeducational day college-preparatory and Orton-Gillingham based reading instruction school, affiliated with Society of Friends. Grades 5–12. Founded: 1986. Setting: suburban. Nearest major city is Philadelphia. 8-acre campus. 1 building on campus. Approved or accredited by Pennsylvania Association of Independent Schools and Pennsylvania Department of Education. Member of National

Association of Independent Schools. Endowment: $7 million. Total enrollment: 149. Upper school average class size: 12. Upper school faculty-student ratio: 1:5. There are 170 required school days per year for Upper School students. Upper School students typically attend 5 days per week. The average school day consists of 6 hours and 17 minutes.

Upper School Student Profile Grade 9: 26 students (18 boys, 8 girls); Grade 10: 31 students (25 boys, 6 girls); Grade 11: 31 students (21 boys, 10 girls); Grade 12: 33 students (20 boys, 13 girls). 6% of students are members of Society of Friends.

Faculty School total: 39. In upper school: 10 men, 19 women; 16 have advanced degrees.

Subjects Offered 20th century world history, advanced biology, algebra, American history, astronomy, biology, calculus, ceramics, chemistry, college counseling, college placement, computer-aided design, culinary arts, electives, engineering, English, geometry, health and wellness, human development, internship, language arts, language development, language structure, learning strategies, music, photography, physical education, physics, pre-calculus, printmaking, psychology, robotics, SAT/ACT preparation, science, sign language, social studies, sociology, Spanish, studio art, study skills, trigonometry, world history, writing.

Graduation Requirements Arts and fine arts (art, music, dance, drama), English, lab science, language arts, mathematics, physical education (includes health), science, senior internship, social studies (includes history), at least one Adventure Based Learning (A.B.L.E.) course. Community service is required.

Special Academic Programs Independent study; study at local college for college credit; academic accommodation for the artistically talented; remedial reading and/or remedial writing; remedial math; programs in English, mathematics, general development for dyslexic students.

College Admission Counseling 27 students graduated in 2016; 24 went to college, including Cabrini University; Franklin & Marshall College; Johnson & Wales University; McDaniel College; Penn State University Park; Temple University. Other: 3 went to work.

Student Life Upper grades have specified standards of dress, student council. Discipline rests primarily with faculty. Attendance at religious services is required.

Summer Programs Remediation, enrichment, art/fine arts, computer instruction programs offered; session focuses on individualized reading skills/writing tutoring using Orton-Gillingham methods; held on campus; accepts boys and girls; open to students from other schools. 50 students usually enrolled. 2017 schedule: June 26 to July 28. Application deadline: May 1.

Tuition and Aid Day student tuition: $38,500. Tuition installment plan (Insured Tuition Payment Plan, FACTS Tuition Payment Plan, monthly payment plans, individually arranged payment plans, 2-payment plan (66% due May 1, 34% due January 1)). Tuition reduction for siblings, need-based scholarship grants, need-based loans, middle-income loans available. In 2016–17, 36% of upper-school students received aid. Total amount of financial aid awarded in 2016–17: $892,650.

Admissions Traditional secondary-level entrance grade is 9. For fall 2016, 60 students applied for upper-level admission, 25 were accepted, 19 enrolled. Psychoeducational evaluation and WISC or WAIS required. Deadline for receipt of application materials: none. Application fee required: $100. On-campus interview recommended.

Athletics Interscholastic: basketball (boys, girls), cross-country running (b,g), lacrosse (b,g), soccer (b,g), tennis (b,g); coed interscholastic: golf, ultimate Frisbee; coed intramural: backpacking, bicycling, canoeing/kayaking, climbing, hiking/backpacking, rock climbing, ropes courses, sailing, skiing (cross-country), volleyball, yoga. 2 PE instructors, 5 coaches.

Computers Computers are regularly used in all classes. Computer network features include online commercial services, Internet access, wireless campus network, Internet filtering or blocking technology, adaptive technologies such as Kurzweil, Dragon/Mac Speech Dictate, etc., homework site, all students have school-supplied laptops (no additional cost). Student e-mail accounts and computer access in designated common areas are available to students. Students grades are available online. The school has a published electronic and media policy.

Contact Mary Ellen Trent, Director of Admissions. 610-640-4150 Ext. 2100. Fax: 610-560-4336. E-mail: maryellen.trent@dvfs.org. Website: www.dvfs.org

DENVER ACADEMY

4400 East Iliff Avenue
Denver, Colorado 80222

Head of School: Mr. Mark Twarogowski

General Information Coeducational day college-preparatory, general academic, and arts school; primarily serves underachievers, students with learning disabilities, individuals with Attention Deficit Disorder, dyslexic students, and unique learning styles. Grades 1–12. Founded: 1972. Setting: urban. 22-acre campus. 19 buildings on campus. Approved or accredited by Association of Colorado Independent Schools and Colorado Department of Education. Member of National Association of Independent Schools. Endowment: $3 million. Total enrollment: 378. Upper school average class size: 14. Upper school faculty-student ratio: 1:8. There are 169 required school days per year for Upper School students. Upper School students typically attend 5 days per week. The average school day consists of 6 hours and 15 minutes.

Upper School Student Profile Grade 9: 52 students (38 boys, 14 girls); Grade 10: 55 students (35 boys, 20 girls); Grade 11: 56 students (43 boys, 13 girls); Grade 12: 48 students (29 boys, 19 girls).

Faculty School total: 70. In upper school: 20 men, 23 women; 18 have advanced degrees.

Subjects Offered 3-dimensional art, ACT preparation, acting, adolescent issues, algebra, American history, American literature, anatomy, art, art history, arts, baseball, basic skills, basketball, biology, botany, business, calculus, ceramics, chemistry, comparative cultures, computer applications, computer graphics, computer math, computer processing, computer programming, computer science, computer skills, creative writing, drama, dramatic arts, earth science, English, English literature, environmental science, ethics, European history, film, filmmaking, fine arts, geography, geometry, government/civics, grammar, health, history, life skills, mathematics, music, philosophy, photography, physical education, physics, physiology, psychology, science, social sciences, social studies, Spanish, speech, theater, trigonometry, values and decisions, world history, world literature, writing, yearbook.

Graduation Requirements Arts and fine arts (art, music, dance, drama), English, mathematics, physical education (includes health), science, social sciences, social studies (includes history), community service hours.

Special Academic Programs Independent study; academic accommodation for the gifted; remedial reading and/or remedial writing; remedial math; programs in English, mathematics, general development for dyslexic students.

College Admission Counseling 44 students graduated in 2016; 33 went to college, including Fort Lewis College; Metropolitan State University of Denver; University of Colorado Boulder; University of Colorado Denver; University of Denver. Other: 4 went to work, 3 entered a postgraduate year, 4 had other specific plans. Median SAT critical reading: 700, median SAT math: 625, median SAT writing: 660, median combined SAT: 1985, median composite ACT: 21. 100% scored over 600 on SAT critical reading, 50% scored over 600 on SAT math, 100% scored over 600 on SAT writing, 100% scored over 1800 on combined SAT, 14% scored over 26 on composite ACT.

Student Life Upper grades have specified standards of dress, student council, honor system. Discipline rests primarily with faculty.

Summer Programs Remediation, enrichment, advancement, art/fine arts, rigorous outdoor training, computer instruction programs offered; session focuses on academics, remediation, and summer fun camp; held both on and off campus; accepts boys and girls; open to students from other schools. 130 students usually enrolled. 2017 schedule: June to August. Application deadline: June 1.

Tuition and Aid Day student tuition: $27,750. Tuition installment plan (monthly payment plans). Tuition reduction for siblings, need-based scholarship grants available. In 2016–17, 30% of upper-school students received aid. Total amount of financial aid awarded in 2016–17: $766,188.

Admissions For fall 2016, 45 students applied for upper-level admission, 40 were accepted, 31 enrolled. WISC or WAIS, Woodcock-Johnson and Woodcock-Johnson Revised Achievement Test required. Deadline for receipt of application materials: none. Application fee required: $75. On-campus interview required.

Athletics Interscholastic: baseball (boys), basketball (b,g), cross-country running (b,g), golf (b), soccer (b,g), track and field (b), volleyball (g); intramural: volleyball (g); coed interscholastic: physical fitness, physical training; coed intramural: backpacking, basketball, boxing, canoeing/kayaking, climbing, cooperative games, fishing, flag football, golf, indoor hockey, indoor soccer, indoor track, jump rope, mountaineering, outdoor activities, rafting, rock climbing, skiing (downhill), soccer, swimming and diving, track and field, wall climbing. 4 PE instructors, 4 coaches.

Computers Computers are regularly used in basic skills, career exploration, career technology, college planning, drawing and design, English, foreign language, independent study, introduction to technology, mathematics, media arts, media production, media services, multimedia, music, occupational education, SAT preparation, science, writing, yearbook classes. Computer network features include on-campus library services, online commercial services, Internet access, wireless campus network, Internet filtering or blocking technology. Student e-mail accounts and computer access in designated common areas are available to students. Students grades are available online. The school has a published electronic and media policy.

Contact Ms. Janet Woolley, Director of Admissions. 303-777-5161. Fax: 303-777-5893. E-mail: jwoolley@denveracademy.org. Website: www.denveracademy.org

EAGLE HILL SCHOOL

45 Glenville Road
Greenwich, Connecticut 06831

Head of School: Dr. Marjorie E. Castro

General Information Coeducational boarding and day college-preparatory and general academic school; primarily serves students with learning disabilities, dyslexic students, and language-based learning disabilities. Boarding grades 5–9, day grades 1–9. Founded: 1975. Setting: suburban. Nearest major city is New York, NY. Students are housed in single-sex dormitories. 16-acre campus. 4 buildings on campus. Approved or accredited by Connecticut Association of Independent Schools and Connecticut Department of Education. Member of National Association of Independent Schools and Secondary School Admission Test Board. Total enrollment: 250. Upper school average class size: 6. Upper school faculty-student ratio: 1:4. There are 180 required school days per year for Upper School students. Upper School students typically attend 5 days per week. The average school day consists of 7 hours and 40 minutes.

Upper School Student Profile 30% of students are boarding students. 50% are state residents. 4 states are represented in upper school student body.

Faculty School total: 65. In upper school: 15 men, 20 women; 33 have advanced degrees; 28 reside on campus.

Subjects Offered Art, English, health, history, mathematics, music, physical education, science, technology.

Graduation Requirements Arts and fine arts (art, music, dance, drama), computer science, English, mathematics, physical education (includes health), science, social sciences, social studies (includes history), study skills.

Special Academic Programs Remedial reading and/or remedial writing; remedial math; programs in English, mathematics, general development for dyslexic students.

College Admission Counseling 60 students graduated in 2016.

Student Life Upper grades have specified standards of dress, student council, honor system. Discipline rests primarily with faculty.

Tuition and Aid Day student tuition: $64,450; 5-day tuition and room/board: $85,365. Tuition installment plan (monthly payment plans). Need-based scholarship grants available.

Admissions For fall 2016, 179 students applied for upper-level admission, 90 were accepted, 70 enrolled. Psychoeducational evaluation and Wechsler Intelligence Scale for Children III required. Deadline for receipt of application materials: none. Application fee required: $100. On-campus interview required.

Athletics Interscholastic: baseball (boys), basketball (b,g), cheering (g), field hockey (g), lacrosse (b,g); intramural: aerobics (g), aerobics/dance (g), aerobics/Nautilus (b), flag football (b), football (b), lacrosse (g); coed interscholastic: basketball, cross-country running, ice hockey; coed intramural: basketball, bicycling, billiards, canoeing/kayaking, dance, fitness, fitness walking, floor hockey, Frisbee, golf, gymnastics, ice skating, jogging, judo, lacrosse, martial arts, outdoor activities, outdoor education, outdoor recreation, physical fitness, physical training, volleyball, yoga. 1 PE instructor, 1 athletic trainer.

Computers Computers are regularly used in English, history, mathematics, science classes. Computer network features include on-campus library services, online commercial services, Internet access, wireless campus network, Internet filtering or blocking technology, digital lab, iMovie, Active Boards. Campus intranet is available to students. The school has a published electronic and media policy.

Contact Mr. Thomas Cone, Director of Admissions and Placement. 203-622-9240 Ext. 648. Fax: 203-622-0914. E-mail: t.cone@eaglehill.org.

Website: www.eaglehillschool.org

EAGLE ROCK SCHOOL

2750 Notaiah Road
Estes Park, Colorado 80517

Head of School: Jeff Liddle

General Information Coeducational boarding and day college-preparatory and general academic school; primarily serves underachievers, students with learning disabilities, individuals with Attention Deficit Disorder, individuals with emotional and behavioral problems, dyslexic students, and students who are unsuccessful in a traditional high school. Founded: 1991. Setting: rural. Nearest major city is Boulder. Students are housed in single-sex by floor dormitories. 640-acre campus. 28 buildings on campus. Approved or accredited by Association for Experiential Education, Association of Colorado Independent Schools, North Central Association of Colleges and Schools, and Colorado Department of Education. Upper school average class size: 8. Upper school faculty-student ratio: 1:4. There are 273 required school days per year for Upper School students. Upper School students typically attend 6 days per week. The average school day consists of 7 hours.

Upper School Student Profile 100% of students are boarding students. 15% are state residents. 17 states are represented in upper school student body.

Faculty School total: 21. In upper school: 11 men, 10 women; 5 have advanced degrees; 26 reside on campus.

Subjects Offered Algebra, American history, art, arts, biology, business skills, computer science, English, environmental science, fine arts, geography, geometry, government/civics, history, literature, mathematics, music, personal development, physical education, physical science, science, social sciences, social studies, speech, technology.

Graduation Requirements Arts and fine arts (art, music, dance, drama), business skills (includes word processing), computer science, English, foreign language, health, health and wellness, mathematics, personal development, physical education (includes health), science, social sciences, social studies (includes history), personal growth.

Special Academic Programs Independent study; term-away projects; study abroad; academic accommodation for the gifted, the musically talented, and the artistically talented; remedial reading and/or remedial writing; remedial math; programs in English, mathematics, general development for dyslexic students.

College Admission Counseling 16 students graduated in 2016; 4 went to college. Other: 12 went to work.

Student Life Upper grades have student council, honor system. Discipline rests equally with students and faculty.

Tuition and Aid Tuition installment plan (full scholarship). Entire tuition paid by American Honda Education Corporation available. In 2016–17, 100% of upper-school students received aid.

Admissions Traditional secondary-level entrance age is 16. Deadline for receipt of application materials: none. No application fee required. Interview recommended.

Athletics Coed Intramural: aquatics, backpacking, ball hockey, basketball, bicycling, climbing, combined training, cross-country running, field hockey, fitness, floor hockey, Frisbee, hiking/backpacking, jogging, juggling, life saving, martial arts, mountain biking, outdoor activities, outdoor adventure, outdoor education, outdoor recreation, outdoor skills, physical fitness, physical training, rock climbing, running, self defense, skiing (cross-country), snowshoeing, soccer, softball, swimming and diving, ultimate Frisbee, volleyball, wall climbing, water polo, water volleyball, weight lifting, wilderness. 3 PE instructors.

Computers Computers are regularly used in art, business, college planning, creative writing, current events, data processing, digital applications, English, foreign language, geography, history, humanities, independent study, library, life skills, literacy, mathematics, music, photography, reading, research skills, SAT preparation, science, social sciences, social studies, Spanish, speech, study skills, typing, video film production, writing classes. Computer network features include on-campus library services, online commercial services, Internet access, wireless campus network. Campus intranet, student e-mail accounts, and computer access in designated common areas are available to students. The school has a published electronic and media policy.

Contact Megan Rebeiro, Director of Students. 970-586-0600. Fax: 970-586-4805. E-mail: mrebeiro@eaglerockschool.org. Website: www.eaglerockschool.org

EDMONTON ACADEMY

Unit 2, 810 Saddleback Road
Edmonton, Alberta T6J 4W4, Canada

Head of School: Laurie Oakes

General Information Coeducational day college-preparatory and arts school. Grades 3–12. Founded: 1983. Setting: urban. 2 buildings on campus. Approved or accredited by Association of Independent Schools and Colleges of Alberta and Alberta Department of Education. Language of instruction: English. Total enrollment: 69. Upper school average class size: 12. Upper school faculty-student ratio: 1:6. There are 175 required school days per year for Upper School students. Upper School students typically attend 5 days per week. The average school day consists of 7 hours and 10 minutes.

Upper School Student Profile Grade 10: 11 students (9 boys, 2 girls); Grade 11: 4 students (2 boys, 2 girls); Grade 12: 8 students (6 boys, 2 girls).

Faculty School total: 13. In upper school: 3 men, 5 women; 2 have advanced degrees.

Subjects Offered All academic.

Graduation Requirements All academic.

Special Academic Programs Academic accommodation for the gifted; remedial reading and/or remedial writing; remedial math; programs in English, mathematics for dyslexic students.

Student Life Upper grades have honor system. Discipline rests primarily with faculty.

Tuition and Aid Day student tuition: CAN$9600. Tuition installment plan (The Tuition Plan, individually arranged payment plans). Tuition reduction for siblings, bursaries available. In 2016–17, 3% of upper-school students received aid. Total amount of financial aid awarded in 2016–17: CAN$27,000.

Admissions Traditional secondary-level entrance grade is 10. For fall 2016, 6 students applied for upper-level admission, 6 were accepted, 6 enrolled. Battery of testing done through outside agency, Individual IQ, Achievement and behavior rating scale and WISC-R required. Deadline for receipt of application materials: August 31. Application fee required: CAN$50. On-campus interview recommended.

Athletics Coed Intramural: aerobics, badminton, ball hockey, basketball, cooperative games, fitness, flag football, golf, life saving, outdoor education, physical fitness, volleyball. 3 PE instructors.

Computers Computers are regularly used in all academic classes. Computer network features include Internet access, wireless campus network, Internet filtering or blocking technology. Campus intranet, student e-mail accounts, and computer access in designated common areas are available to students. The school has a published electronic and media policy.

Contact Elizabeth Richards, Executive Director. 780-482-5449. Fax: 780-482-0902. E-mail: e.richards@edmontonacademy.com. Website: www.edmontonacademy.com

FRANKLIN ACADEMY

140 River Road
East Haddam, Connecticut 06423

Head of School: A. Frederick Weissbach

General Information Coeducational boarding and day college-preparatory, college prep curriculum with emphasis on project and skills, and based learning. school. Grades 8–PG. Founded: 2001. Setting: rural. Nearest major city is Hartford. Students are housed in single-sex by floor dormitories and single-sex dormitories. 75-acre campus. 18 buildings on campus. Approved or accredited by Connecticut Association of Independent Schools, New England Association of Schools and Colleges, and

Connecticut Department of Education. Member of National Association of Independent Schools. Total enrollment: 85. Upper school average class size: 6. Upper school faculty-student ratio: 1:2. There are 180 required school days per year for Upper School students. Upper School students typically attend 6 days per week. The average school day consists of 6 hours and 30 minutes.

Upper School Student Profile Grade 8: 3 students (2 boys, 1 girl); Grade 9: 6 students (5 boys, 1 girl); Grade 10: 8 students (7 boys, 1 girl); Grade 11: 18 students (13 boys, 5 girls); Grade 12: 31 students (22 boys, 9 girls); Postgraduate: 7 students (5 boys, 2 girls). 95% of students are boarding students. 20% are state residents. 19 states are represented in upper school student body. 10% are international students. International students from Australia, China, Hong Kong, Mexico, Singapore, and United Arab Emirates; 2 other countries represented in student body.

Faculty School total: 44. In upper school: 18 men, 26 women; 32 have advanced degrees; 15 reside on campus.

Subjects Offered All academic.

Graduation Requirements Must take the "Individual and Community" or "Franklin Learning Institute 'Seminar Series'".

Special Academic Programs Honors section; independent study; term-away projects; study at local college for college credit; academic accommodation for the gifted; remedial reading and/or remedial writing; remedial math.

College Admission Counseling 24 students graduated in 2016; all went to college, including Fairleigh Dickinson University, College at Florham; Hampshire College; High Point University; Landmark College; Rochester Institute of Technology; University of Connecticut. Other: 2 entered a postgraduate year.

Student Life Upper grades have student council, honor system. Discipline rests equally with students and faculty.

Summer Programs Remediation, enrichment, art/fine arts, computer instruction programs offered; session focuses on social skills, special interest areas, summer camp; held both on and off campus; accepts boys and girls; open to students from other schools. 60 students usually enrolled. 2017 schedule: June 25 to July 22. Application deadline: June 1.

Tuition and Aid Day student tuition: $69,800; 7-day tuition and room/board: $79,800. Tuition installment plan (monthly payment plans, individually arranged payment plans, quarterly payment plans, pay in full discount). Merit scholarship grants available. In 2016–17, 10% of upper-school students received aid.

Admissions English for Non-native Speakers and psychoeducational evaluation required. Deadline for receipt of application materials: none. Application fee required: $75. On-campus interview recommended.

Athletics Coed Interscholastic: aerobics/dance, archery, basketball, bicycling, billiards, canoeing/kayaking, cooperative games, cross-country running, dance, fishing, fitness, fitness walking, flag football, Frisbee, golf, horseback riding, jogging, kayaking, kickball, outdoor recreation, outdoors, paddling, paint ball, physical fitness, running, sailing, soccer, softball, table tennis, ultimate Frisbee, walking, yoga.

Computers Computers are regularly used in all academic classes. Computer network features include on-campus library services, Internet access, wireless campus network, Internet filtering or blocking technology, Dragon Speak and other speech-to-text programs. Campus intranet, student e-mail accounts, and computer access in designated common areas are available to students. The school has a published electronic and media policy.

Contact Vincent Schmidt, Assistant Director of Admissions. 860-873-2700 Ext. 1154. Fax: 860-873-9345. E-mail: Vince@fa-ct.org. Website: www.fa-ct.org

FRASER ACADEMY

2294 West 10th Avenue
Vancouver, British Columbia V6K 2H8, Canada

Head of School: Mrs. Maureen Steltman

General Information Coeducational day college-preparatory, general academic, and BC Ministry of Education curriculum school; primarily serves students with learning disabilities and dyslexic students. Grades 1–12. Founded: 1982. Setting: urban. 1 building on campus. Approved or accredited by Canadian Association of Independent Schools and British Columbia Department of Education. Language of instruction: English. Total enrollment: 229. Upper school average class size: 10. Upper school faculty-student ratio: 1:3. There are 218 required school days per year for Upper School students. Upper School students typically attend 5 days per week. The average school day consists of 7 hours and 30 minutes.

Faculty School total: 90. In upper school: 10 have advanced degrees.

Graduation Requirements British Columbia Ministry of Education requirements.

Special Academic Programs Academic accommodation for the gifted; programs in English, mathematics, general development for dyslexic students; special instructional classes for Orton-Gillingham tutoring program.

College Admission Counseling 17 students graduated in 2016.

Student Life Upper grades have uniform requirement, student council, honor system. Discipline rests primarily with faculty.

Tuition and Aid Tuition installment plan (quarterly payment plan). Tuition reduction for siblings, bursaries available.

Admissions Traditional secondary-level entrance grade is 8. Academic Profile Tests, admissions testing and writing sample required. Deadline for receipt of application materials: none. Application fee required: CAN$500. On-campus interview recommended.

Athletics Interscholastic: volleyball (girls); intramural: volleyball (g); coed interscholastic: alpine skiing, basketball, canoeing/kayaking, cross-country running, field hockey, fitness, flag football, floor hockey, kickball, modern dance, outdoor activities, outdoor adventure, outdoor education, outdoor skills, physical fitness, running, skiing (downhill), snowboarding, soccer, softball, swimming and diving, track and field, wrestling; coed intramural: alpine skiing, ball hockey, basketball, bicycling, climbing, cross-country running, mountain biking, rock climbing, running, scuba diving, skiing (downhill), snowboarding, soccer, softball, track and field, wall climbing. 5 PE instructors, 10 coaches.

Computers Computers are regularly used in all academic classes. Computer network features include on-campus library services, Internet access, wireless campus network, Internet filtering or blocking technology, various learning disabilities/dyslexic-specific software. Student e-mail accounts and computer access in designated common areas are available to students. Students grades are available online.

Contact Ms. Brooke Ellison, Admissions Coordinator and Office Manager. 604-736-5575 Ext. 222. Fax: 604-736-5578. E-mail: bellison@fraseracademy.ca. Website: www.fraseracademy.ca

THE GLENHOLME SCHOOL, DEVEREUX CONNECTICUT

81 Sabbaday Lane
Washington, Connecticut 06793

Head of School: Maryann Campbell

General Information Coeducational boarding and day college-preparatory, arts, vocational, technology, social coaching and motivational management, and self-discipline strategies and character development school; primarily serves underachievers, students with learning disabilities, individuals with Attention Deficit Disorder, individuals with emotional and behavioral problems, High functioning ASD including Asperger's Syndrome; ADHD, PDD, and anxiet, depression and compulsive disorders. Founded: 1968. Setting: small town. Nearest major city is Hartford. Students are housed in single-sex dormitories. 105-acre campus. 30 buildings on campus. Approved or accredited by Association of Independent Schools in New England, Connecticut Department of Children and Families, Council of Accreditation and School Improvement, National Association of Private Schools for Exceptional Children, New England Association of Schools and Colleges, and Connecticut Department of Education. Member of National Association of Independent Schools. Total enrollment: 95. Upper school average class size: 10. Upper school faculty-student ratio: 1:10. There are 215 required school days per year for Upper School students. Upper School students typically attend 5 days per week. The average school day consists of 5 hours and 45 minutes.

Upper School Student Profile Grade 6: 6 students (6 boys); Grade 7: 3 students (3 boys); Grade 8: 10 students (7 boys, 3 girls); Grade 9: 7 students (3 boys, 4 girls); Grade 10: 15 students (10 boys, 5 girls); Grade 11: 17 students (11 boys, 6 girls); Grade 12: 25 students (16 boys, 9 girls); Grade 13: 6 students (2 boys, 4 girls); Postgraduate: 6 students (4 boys, 2 girls). 95% of students are boarding students. 28% are state residents. 15 states are represented in upper school student body. 5% are international students. International students from China, Costa Rica, Hong Kong, Mexico, and Panama; 4 other countries represented in student body.

Faculty School total: 22. In upper school: 4 men, 16 women; 12 have advanced degrees; 3 reside on campus.

Subjects Offered ADL skills, adolescent issues, aerobics, algebra, art, basketball, biology, career and personal planning, career education, career exploration, career/college preparation, character education, chemistry, choral music, chorus, college admission preparation, college planning, communication skills, community service, computer animation, computer applications, computer art, computer education, computer graphics, computer literacy, computer skills, creative arts, creative dance, creative drama, creative thinking, creative writing, culinary arts, dance, decision making skills, digital photography, drama, drama performance, earth science, English, equine management, fine arts, geometry, graphic arts, guidance, health, health and wellness, health education, Internet research, interpersonal skills, keyboarding, library, life skills, mathematics, media arts, moral and social development, music, participation in sports, performing arts, personal fitness, photography, physical education, piano, play production, radio broadcasting, SAT preparation, science, social sciences, Spanish, theater, U.S. history, video and animation, world history, writing, yearbook.

Graduation Requirements Art, electives, English, language, mathematics, physical education (includes health), science, social studies (includes history), students must meet either Glenholme graduation requirements or the requirements of their home state, depending on the funding source.

Special Academic Programs Academic accommodation for the gifted; remedial reading and/or remedial writing; remedial math; programs in English, mathematics, general development for dyslexic students; ESL (3 students enrolled).

College Admission Counseling 17 students graduated in 2015; 13 went to college. Other: 2 went to work, 2 entered a postgraduate year.

Student Life Upper grades have uniform requirement, student council, honor system. Discipline rests primarily with faculty.

Admissions Individual IQ, Achievement and behavior rating scale or psychoeducational evaluation required. Deadline for receipt of application materials: none. Application fee required: $150. On-campus interview required.

Athletics Intramural: aerobics (boys, girls), aerobics/dance (b,g), aquatics (b,g), archery (b,g), artistic gym (b,g), basketball (b,g), cheering (b,g), combined training (b,g), cooperative games (b,g), cross-country running (b,g), dance (b,g), dance team (b,g), equestrian sports (b,g), figure skating (b,g), fishing (b,g), fitness (b,g), fitness walking (b,g), flag football (b,g), Frisbee (b,g), golf (b,g), hiking/backpacking (b,g), horseback riding (b,g), ice skating (b,g), jogging (b,g), jump rope (b,g), kickball (b,g), modern dance (b,g), outdoor activities (b,g), outdoor recreation (b,g), paddle tennis (b,g), physical fitness (b,g), physical training (b,g), roller blading (b,g), ropes courses (b,g), soccer (b,g), softball (b,g), strength & conditioning (b,g), tennis (b,g), ultimate Frisbee (b,g), volleyball (b,g), walking (b,g), weight training (b,g), yoga (b,g); coed interscholastic: basketball, cross-country running, soccer, softball, tennis; coed intramural: aerobics, aerobics/dance, aquatics, archery, artistic gym, basketball, cheering, combined training, cooperative games, cross-country running, dance, dance team, equestrian sports, figure skating, fishing, fitness, fitness walking, flag football, Frisbee, golf, hiking/backpacking, horseback riding, ice skating, jogging, jump rope, kickball, modern dance, outdoor activities, outdoor recreation, paddle tennis, physical fitness, physical training, roller blading, ropes courses, soccer, softball, strength & conditioning, tennis, ultimate Frisbee, volleyball, walking, weight training, yoga. 1 PE instructor, 2 coaches, 1 athletic trainer.

Computers Computers are regularly used in all academic, technology classes. Computer network features include on-campus library services, Internet access, wireless campus network, Internet filtering or blocking technology, online learning, Web cam parent communications. Campus intranet, student e-mail accounts, and computer access in designated common areas are available to students. Students grades are available online. The school has a published electronic and media policy.

Contact Lauren Chilson, Admissions. 860-868-7377. Fax: 860-868-7413. E-mail: lchilson@devereux.org. Website: www.theglenholmeschool.org

THE GOW SCHOOL

2491 Emery Rd
South Wales, New York 14139-9778

Head of School: Mr. M. Bradley Rogers Jr.

General Information Coeducational boarding and day college-preparatory and reconstructive language school. Grades 6–12. Founded: 1926. Setting: rural. Nearest major city is Buffalo. Students are housed in single-sex dormitories. 120-acre campus. 22 buildings on campus. Approved or accredited by New York State Association of Independent Schools, New York State Board of Regents, The Association of Boarding Schools, and New York Department of Education. Member of National Association of Independent Schools. Endowment: $22 million. Total enrollment: 145. Upper school average class size: 5. Upper school faculty-student ratio: 1:4. There are 175 required school days per year for Upper School students. Upper School students typically attend 6 days per week. The average school day consists of 13 hours.

Upper School Student Profile Grade 6: 2 students (2 boys); Grade 7: 10 students (9 boys, 1 girl); Grade 8: 12 students (12 boys); Grade 9: 15 students (14 boys, 1 girl); Grade 10: 38 students (34 boys, 4 girls); Grade 11: 40 students (38 boys, 2 girls); Grade 12: 37 students (34 boys, 3 girls); Postgraduate: 1 student (1 boy). 91% of students are boarding students. 28% are state residents. 19 states are represented in upper school student body. 30% are international students. International students from Bermuda, Canada, Ecuador, Hong Kong, Saudi Arabia, and United Kingdom; 8 other countries represented in student body.

Faculty School total: 35. In upper school: 27 men, 7 women; 27 have advanced degrees; 29 reside on campus.

Subjects Offered Algebra, American history, American literature, art, biology, broadcast journalism, business, business applications, business skills, calculus, ceramics, chemistry, computer applications, computer literacy, computer programming, computer science, drama, earth science, economics, engineering, English, English literature, European history, expository writing, fine arts, geology, geometry, grammar, health, journalism, keyboarding, mathematics, metalworking, music, physics, reading, reconstructive language, robotics, science, social studies, theater, trigonometry, typing, video, world history, yearbook.

Graduation Requirements Arts and fine arts (art, music, dance, drama), English, mathematics, reconstructive language, research seminar, science, senior humanities, senior seminar, social studies (includes history). Community service is required.

Special Academic Programs Independent study; study at local college for college credit; academic accommodation for the musically talented; remedial reading and/or remedial writing; remedial math; programs in English, mathematics, general development for dyslexic students; ESL (5 students enrolled).

College Admission Counseling 34 students graduated in 2016; all went to college, including High Point University; Lynn University; Marshall University; Rochester Institute of Technology; The University of Arizona. Median composite ACT: 21. 2% scored over 26 on composite ACT.

Student Life Upper grades have specified standards of dress, student council. Discipline rests primarily with faculty.

Summer Programs Remediation, enrichment, advancement, ESL, sports, art/fine arts, computer instruction programs offered; session focuses on remediation and course

work; held both on and off campus; accepts boys and girls; open to students from other schools. 125 students usually enrolled. 2017 schedule: June 25 to July 29. Application deadline: none.

Tuition and Aid Day student tuition: $45,000; 7-day tuition and room/board: $64,000. Tuition installment plan (monthly payment plans, individually arranged payment plans). Need-based scholarship grants available. In 2016–17, 30% of upper-school students received aid. Total amount of financial aid awarded in 2016–17: $1,100,000.

Admissions Traditional secondary-level entrance grade is 10. For fall 2016, 39 students applied for upper-level admission, 38 were accepted, 34 enrolled. Wechsler Intelligence Scale for Children, WISC or WAIS, WISC/Woodcock-Johnson or Woodcock-Johnson Revised Achievement Test required. Deadline for receipt of application materials: none. Application fee required: $100. On-campus interview recommended.

Athletics Interscholastic: basketball (boys), wrestling (b); intramural: backpacking (b), basketball (b), bowling (b), climbing (b), cross-country running (b), Frisbee (b), handball (b), hiking/backpacking (b), ice hockey (b), jump rope (b), outdoor education (b), power lifting (b), rappelling (b), rock climbing (b), soccer (b), touch football (b); coed interscholastic: alpine skiing, crew, cross-country running, lacrosse, running, skiing (downhill), soccer, squash, tennis, volleyball; coed intramural: alpine skiing, fitness, flag football, floor hockey, freestyle skiing, golf, jogging, lacrosse, mountain biking, Nautilus, nordic skiing, paint ball, physical fitness, physical training, ropes courses, running, skiing (cross-country), skiing (downhill), snowboarding, snowshoeing, squash, strength & conditioning, tennis, ultimate Frisbee, weight lifting, weight training, whiffle ball. 25 coaches.

Computers Computers are regularly used in all academic, art classes. Computer network features include on-campus library services, online commercial services, Internet access, wireless campus network, Internet filtering or blocking technology, scanners, digital photography, voice recognition. Student e-mail accounts are available to students. The school has a published electronic and media policy.

Contact Mr. Douglas B. Cotter, Director of Admissions. 716-687-2001. Fax: 716-687-2003. E-mail: admissions@gow.org. Website: www.gow.org

THE HILL CENTER, DURHAM ACADEMY

3200 Pickett Road
Durham, North Carolina 27705

Head of School: Dr. Bryan Brander

General Information Coeducational day college-preparatory school; primarily serves underachievers, students with learning disabilities, individuals with Attention Deficit Disorder, and dyslexic students. Grades K–12. Founded: 1977. Setting: small town. 5-acre campus. 1 building on campus. Approved or accredited by National Association of Private Schools for Exceptional Children, North Carolina Association of Independent Schools, Southern Association of Colleges and Schools, Southern Association of Independent Schools, and North Carolina Department of Education. Member of National Association of Independent Schools. Endowment: $3.5 million. Total enrollment: 175. Upper school average class size: 4. Upper school faculty-student ratio: 1:4. There are 176 required school days per year for Upper School students. Upper School students typically attend 5 days per week. The average school day consists of 3 hours.

Upper School Student Profile Grade 9: 5 students (3 boys, 2 girls); Grade 10: 23 students (14 boys, 9 girls); Grade 11: 15 students (9 boys, 6 girls); Grade 12: 13 students (9 boys, 4 girls).

Faculty School total: 27. In upper school: 10 women; 9 have advanced degrees.

Subjects Offered Algebra, American literature, calculus, English, English literature, expository writing, geometry, grammar, mathematics, mechanics of writing, pre-algebra, pre-calculus, Spanish, writing.

Graduation Requirements Graduation requirements are determined by the student's home-based school.

Special Academic Programs Remedial reading and/or remedial writing; remedial math; programs in English, mathematics, general development for dyslexic students.

College Admission Counseling 14 students graduated in 2016; 12 went to college, including Appalachian State University; Colorado State University; Elon University; Guilford College; The University of North Carolina Wilmington; University of Mississippi. Other: 2 went to work.

Student Life Upper grades have student council. Discipline rests primarily with faculty.

Tuition and Aid Day student tuition: $18,200. Guaranteed tuition plan. Tuition installment plan (The Tuition Plan, Key Tuition Payment Plan, monthly payment plans, The Tuition Refund Plan). Need-based scholarship grants available. In 2016–17, 18% of upper-school students received aid. Total amount of financial aid awarded in 2016–17: $56,000.

Admissions Traditional secondary-level entrance grade is 9. For fall 2016, 27 students applied for upper-level admission, 22 were accepted, 18 enrolled. WISC or WAIS and WISC/Woodcock-Johnson required. Deadline for receipt of application materials: March 15. Application fee required: $50. On-campus interview required.

Computers Computers are regularly used in English, foreign language, mathematics, writing classes. Computer network features include Internet access, wireless campus network. Campus intranet and student e-mail accounts are available to students.

Contact Ms. Wendy Speir, Director of Admissions. 919-489-7464 Ext. 7545. Fax: 919-489-7466. E-mail: wspeir@hillcenter.org. Website: www.hillcenter.org

THE HOWARD SCHOOL

1192 Foster Street
Atlanta, Georgia 30318

Head of School: Ms. Marifred Cilella

General Information Coeducational day college-preparatory and general academic school; primarily serves students with learning disabilities, individuals with Attention Deficit Disorder, dyslexic students, and students with language learning disabilities and differences. Grades K–12. Founded: 1950. Setting: urban. 15-acre campus. 2 buildings on campus. Approved or accredited by Georgia Association of Private Schools for Exceptional Children, Georgia Independent School Association, Southern Association of Colleges and Schools, Southern Association of Independent Schools, and Georgia Department of Education. Member of National Association of Independent Schools. Total enrollment: 264. Upper school average class size: 9. Upper school faculty-student ratio: 1:8. There are 173 required school days per year for Upper School students. Upper School students typically attend 5 days per week. The average school day consists of 6 hours and 30 minutes.

Upper School Student Profile Grade 9: 16 students (12 boys, 4 girls); Grade 10: 19 students (12 boys, 7 girls); Grade 11: 27 students (20 boys, 7 girls); Grade 12: 24 students (17 boys, 7 girls).

Faculty School total: 72. In upper school: 11 men, 11 women; 11 have advanced degrees.

Subjects Offered Algebra, American history, American literature, American sign language, art, biology, communications, computer science, creative writing, ecology, economics, English, English literature, European history, film studies, geography, geometry, government/civics, grammar, history, journalism, mathematics, music, physical education, physical science, psychology, reading, science, service learning/internship, social studies, Spanish, study skills, trigonometry, world history, world literature, writing.

Graduation Requirements English, foreign language, health, mathematics, physical education (includes health), science, social studies (includes history).

Special Academic Programs Academic accommodation for the artistically talented; remedial reading and/or remedial writing; remedial math; programs in English, mathematics, general development for dyslexic students.

College Admission Counseling 20 students graduated in 2016; 15 went to college, including Georgia Southern University; Kennesaw State University; Lynn University; Reinhardt University; Savannah College of Art and Design; Young Harris College. Other: 3 went to work, 2 entered a postgraduate year.

Student Life Upper grades have specified standards of dress, student council, honor system. Discipline rests equally with students and faculty.

Summer Programs Remediation, advancement programs offered; session focuses on Make-up and advancement of academic courses for incoming and current students only; held on campus; accepts boys and girls; not open to students from other schools. 3 students usually enrolled. 2017 schedule: June 5 to June 30. Application deadline: April 1.

Tuition and Aid Day student tuition: $31,460. Tuition installment plan (FACTS Tuition Payment Plan, 1-, 2-, 3- and 8-payment plans). Need-based scholarship grants available. In 2016–17, 16% of upper-school students received aid.

Admissions Psychoeducational evaluation required. Deadline for receipt of application materials: none. Application fee required: $150. On-campus interview required.

Athletics Interscholastic: baseball (boys), basketball (b,g), soccer (b), track and field (b,g), volleyball (g); coed interscholastic: baseball, golf, soccer, track and field; coed intramural: flag football, Frisbee, weight training, yoga. 3 PE instructors.

Computers Computers are regularly used in all academic classes. Computer network features include online commercial services, Internet access, wireless campus network. Student e-mail accounts are available to students. Students grades are available online. The school has a published electronic and media policy.

Contact Ms. Dawn Splinter, Admissions Associate. 404-377-7436 Ext. 259. Fax: 404-377-0884. E-mail: dsplinter@howardschool.org. Website: www.howardschool.org

THE JOHN DEWEY ACADEMY

389 Main Street
Great Barrington, Massachusetts 01230

Head of School: Dr. Andrea E. Lein

General Information Coeducational boarding college-preparatory school; primarily serves underachievers, students with learning disabilities, individuals with Attention Deficit Disorder, individuals with emotional and behavioral problems, and gifted, underachieving, self-destructive adolescents. Grades 10–PG. Founded: 1985. Setting: small town. Nearest major city is Hartford, CT. Students are housed in single-sex dormitories. 90-acre campus. 3 buildings on campus. Approved or accredited by New England Association of Schools and Colleges and Massachusetts Department of Education. Total enrollment: 20. Upper school average class size: 6. Upper school

faculty-student ratio: 1:3. There are 330 required school days per year for Upper School students. Upper School students typically attend 7 days per week. The average school day consists of 6 hours.

Upper School Student Profile Grade 10: 2 students (2 boys); Grade 11: 11 students (10 boys, 1 girl); Grade 12: 5 students (3 boys, 2 girls); Postgraduate: 2 students (1 boy, 1 girl). 100% of students are boarding students. 10% are state residents. 11 states are represented in upper school student body. 10% are international students. International students from Canada.

Faculty School total: 8. In upper school: 3 men, 5 women; all have advanced degrees; 2 reside on campus.

Subjects Offered 20th century American writers, acting, adolescent issues, advanced chemistry, advanced math, algebra, American literature, analysis and differential calculus, art, art history, arts appreciation, athletic training, biology, calculus, character education, chemistry, cinematography, college admission preparation, college planning, computer programming, CPR, creative dance, creative writing, democracy in America, drama, English, English literature, environmental science, equality and freedom, ethics, European history, fine arts, foreign language, French, geometry, government/civics, grammar, health, health and wellness, history, independent study, Italian, leadership and service, life management skills, literary magazine, meditation, moral reasoning, organic chemistry, peer counseling, philosophy, physical education, physics, portfolio art, pre-algebra, psychology, remedial study skills, research skills, self-defense, senior internship, senior seminar, sexuality, social issues, sociology, Spanish, statistics, theater, trigonometry, world history, world literature, writing.

Graduation Requirements American history, arts and fine arts (art, music, dance, drama), biology, English, English literature, European history, foreign language, leadership, literature, mathematics, moral reasoning, physical education (includes health), science, social studies (includes history), moral leadership qualities, minimum 18 months residency, college acceptance.

Special Academic Programs Honors section; accelerated programs; independent study; study at local college for college credit; academic accommodation for the gifted and the artistically talented; remedial reading and/or remedial writing; remedial math; programs in general development for dyslexic students.

College Admission Counseling 7 students graduated in 2016; all went to college, including American University; Fordham University; Rose-Hulman Institute of Technology; Vassar College; Virginia Polytechnic Institute and State University. 95% scored over 600 on SAT critical reading, 95% scored over 600 on SAT math, 95% scored over 600 on SAT writing, 95% scored over 1800 on combined SAT.

Student Life Upper grades have specified standards of dress, student council, honor system. Discipline rests equally with students and faculty.

Summer Programs Remediation, enrichment, advancement programs offered; session focuses on continuing college preparatory program; held on campus; accepts boys and girls; not open to students from other schools. 25 students usually enrolled.

Tuition and Aid 7-day tuition and room/board: $92,000. Tuition installment plan (monthly payment plans, individually arranged payment plans). Need-based scholarship grants available. In 2016–17, 25% of upper-school students received aid.

Admissions Traditional secondary-level entrance grade is 11. Deadline for receipt of application materials: none. No application fee required. On-campus interview recommended.

Computers Computer resources include Internet access, Internet filtering or blocking technology. Campus intranet, student e-mail accounts, and computer access in designated common areas are available to students.

Contact Dr. Andrea Nathans, Executive Director/Admissions. 860-337-1104. E-mail: anathans@jda.org. Website: www.jda.org

THE JUDGE ROTENBERG EDUCATIONAL CENTER

250 Turnpike Street
Canton, Massachusetts 02021-2341

Head of School: Glenda Crookes

General Information Coeducational boarding general academic school; primarily serves underachievers, students with learning disabilities, individuals with Attention Deficit Disorder, individuals with emotional and behavioral problems, dyslexic students, and autism and developmental disabilities. Founded: 1971. Setting: suburban. Nearest major city is Boston. Students are housed in group homes. 2 buildings on campus. Approved or accredited by Massachusetts Department of Education and Massachusetts Department of Education. Upper school average class size: 10. Upper School students typically attend 5 days per week. The average school day consists of 6 hours.

Special Academic Programs Remedial reading and/or remedial writing; remedial math; special instructional classes for deaf students, blind students; ESL.

Student Life Upper grades have specified standards of dress, honor system. Discipline rests primarily with faculty.

Admissions Deadline for receipt of application materials: none. No application fee required. Interview recommended.

Athletics Intramural: basketball (boys, girls); coed intramural: aerobics/dance, physical fitness. 2 PE instructors.

Computers Computers are regularly used in all academic classes. Computer network features include Internet access, Internet filtering or blocking technology. Student e-mail accounts are available to students.

Contact Julie Gomes, Director of Admissions. 781-828-2202 Ext. 4275. Fax: 781-821-6020. E-mail: j.gomes@judgerc.org. Website: www.judgerc.org

KILDONAN SCHOOL

425 Morse Hill Road
Amenia, New York 12501

Head of School: Kevin Pendergast

General Information Coeducational boarding and day college-preparatory, general academic, arts, music, and design school; primarily serves students with learning disabilities, dyslexic students, and language-based learning differences. Boarding grades 6–PG, day grades 2–PG. Founded: 1969. Setting: rural. Nearest major city is New York. Students are housed in single-sex dormitories. 150-acre campus. 19 buildings on campus. Approved or accredited by New York State Association of Independent Schools. Member of National Association of Independent Schools. Endowment: $579,300. Total enrollment: 91. Upper school average class size: 8. Upper school faculty-student ratio: 1:2. There are 175 required school days per year for Upper School students. Upper School students typically attend 5 days per week. The average school day consists of 7 hours.

Upper School Student Profile Grade 6: 4 students (2 boys, 2 girls); Grade 7: 4 students (3 boys, 1 girl); Grade 8: 10 students (5 boys, 5 girls); Grade 9: 14 students (12 boys, 2 girls); Grade 10: 6 students (3 boys, 3 girls); Grade 11: 16 students (5 boys, 11 girls); Grade 12: 11 students (9 boys, 2 girls). 68% of students are boarding students. 44% are state residents. 15 states are represented in upper school student body. 9% are international students. International students from Bhutan, British Indian Ocean Territory, French Guiana, Micronesia, Qatar, and United Kingdom; 1 other country represented in student body.

Faculty School total: 56. In upper school: 26 men, 28 women; 15 have advanced degrees; 25 reside on campus.

Subjects Offered 3-dimensional art, 3-dimensional design, ACT preparation, acting, algebra, American history, American literature, anthropology, art, art history, biology, botany, business skills, calculus, ceramics, chemistry, computer programming, computer science, creative writing, earth science, ecology, economics, English, English literature, environmental science, European history, expository writing, fine arts, geography, geology, geometry, government/civics, grammar, health, history, mathematics, photography, physical education, physics, science, social studies, trigonometry, typing, world history, world literature, zoology.

Graduation Requirements Arts and fine arts (art, music, dance, drama), English, mathematics, physical education (includes health), science, social studies (includes history).

Special Academic Programs Independent study; remedial reading and/or remedial writing; programs in English, mathematics, general development for dyslexic students.

College Admission Counseling 11 students graduated in 2016; 13 went to college, including Curry College; Goucher College; Landmark College; Rhode Island School of Design; University of California, Davis.

Student Life Upper grades have uniform requirement, student council, honor system. Discipline rests primarily with faculty.

Summer Programs Remediation, enrichment, art/fine arts programs offered; session focuses on intensive academic tutoring for students with dyslexia; exciting, fun summer camp activities; held on campus; accepts boys and girls; open to students from other schools. 85 students usually enrolled. 2017 schedule: June 24 to August 5. Application deadline: none.

Tuition and Aid Day student tuition: $39,900–$51,000; 5-day tuition and room/board: $66,200; 7-day tuition and room/board: $68,900. Tuition installment plan (Tuition Management Systems). Need-based scholarship grants available. In 2016–17, 46% of upper-school students received aid. Total amount of financial aid awarded in 2016–17: $600,000.

Admissions Traditional secondary-level entrance grade is 9. For fall 2016, 60 students applied for upper-level admission, 43 were accepted, 23 enrolled. Wechsler Individual Achievement Test, WISC or WAIS, WISC/Woodcock-Johnson or Woodcock-Johnson Revised Achievement Test required. Deadline for receipt of application materials: none. Application fee required: $50. On-campus interview recommended.

Athletics Interscholastic: basketball (boys, girls); intramural: aerobics (g), basketball (b,g), dance (g); coed interscholastic: alpine skiing, lacrosse, skiing (downhill), snowboarding, soccer, softball, tennis, yoga; coed intramural: archery, basketball, bicycling, canoeing/kayaking, cross-country running, dressage, equestrian sports, fitness, fitness walking, flag football, freestyle skiing, golf, hiking/backpacking, horseback riding, lacrosse, martial arts, mountain biking, outdoor activities, physical fitness, rock climbing, running, skiing (cross-country), skiing (downhill), snowboarding, soccer, strength & conditioning, table tennis, touch football, walking, water skiing, weight lifting, weight training. 9 coaches.

Computers Computers are regularly used in design, drawing and design, English, humanities, mathematics, multimedia, music, writing classes. Computer network features include on-campus library services, Internet access, wireless campus network. Student e-mail accounts and computer access in designated common areas are available

to students. Students grades are available online. The school has a published electronic and media policy.

Contact Ms. Candie L. Fredritz, Admissions Assistant. 845-373-2012. Fax: 845-373-2004. E-mail: admissions@kildonan.org. Website: www.kildonan.org/

THE LAB SCHOOL OF WASHINGTON

4759 Reservoir Road NW
Washington, District of Columbia 20007

Head of School: Katherine Schantz

General Information Coeducational day college-preparatory, arts, and Students with learning differences and ADHD school. Grades 1–12. Founded: 1967. Setting: urban. 4-acre campus. 5 buildings on campus. Approved or accredited by Middle States Association of Colleges and Schools and District of Columbia Department of Education. Member of National Association of Independent Schools. Endowment: $3.5 million. Total enrollment: 375. Upper school average class size: 8. Upper school faculty-student ratio: 1:8. There are 180 required school days per year for Upper School students. Upper School students typically attend 5 days per week. The average school day consists of 6 hours and 30 minutes.

Upper School Student Profile Grade 9: 37 students (25 boys, 12 girls); Grade 10: 33 students (23 boys, 10 girls); Grade 11: 31 students (19 boys, 12 girls); Grade 12: 34 students (20 boys, 14 girls).

Faculty School total: 82. In upper school: 12 men, 15 women; 24 have advanced degrees.

Subjects Offered American democracy, ancient world history, environmental studies, personal money management, photography, physical fitness.

Graduation Requirements Arts and fine arts (art, music, dance, drama), career education internship, computer science, English, foreign language, mathematics, physical education (includes health), science, social sciences, social studies (includes history), senior thesis. Community service is required.

Special Academic Programs Study abroad; academic accommodation for the gifted, the musically talented, and the artistically talented; remedial reading and/or remedial writing; remedial math; programs in English, mathematics, general development for dyslexic students.

College Admission Counseling 30 students graduated in 2016; 22 went to college, including Columbia College Chicago; Guilford College; High Point University; Savannah College of Art and Design; St. Mary's College of Maryland; The University of Arizona. Other: 2 went to work, 1 entered a postgraduate year, 5 had other specific plans.

Student Life Upper grades have specified standards of dress, student council. Discipline rests primarily with faculty.

Summer Programs Advancement programs offered; session focuses on environmental studies; held both on and off campus; accepts boys and girls; not open to students from other schools. 15 students usually enrolled. 2017 schedule: June 12 to June 30.

Tuition and Aid Day student tuition: $41,995. Tuition installment plan (FACTS Tuition Payment Plan). Need-based scholarship grants, some students are funded by local public school systems available. In 2016–17, 9% of upper-school students received aid. Total amount of financial aid awarded in 2016–17: $164,700.

Admissions Traditional secondary-level entrance grade is 9. For fall 2016, 38 students applied for upper-level admission, 17 were accepted, 11 enrolled. Psychoeducational evaluation, WISC or WAIS or WISC-III and Woodcock-Johnson required. Deadline for receipt of application materials: January 15. Application fee required: $100. On-campus interview required.

Athletics Interscholastic: basketball (boys, girls), cross-country running (b,g), lacrosse (b,g), soccer (b,g), swimming and diving (b,g), track and field (b,g), volleyball (g); coed interscholastic: tennis. 2 PE instructors, 11 coaches.

Computers Computers are regularly used in all classes. Computer network features include on-campus library services, online commercial services, Internet access, wireless campus network, Internet filtering or blocking technology, iPads provided to all high school and eighth-grade students, access to tech support. Student e-mail accounts and computer access in designated common areas are available to students. Students grades are available online. The school has a published electronic and media policy.

Contact Dr. Robert Lane, Director of Admissions. 202-944-2214. Fax: 202-454-2338. E-mail: robert.lane@labschool.org. Website: www.labschool.org

LA CHEIM SCHOOL

55 East 18th Street
Antioch, California 94509

Head of School: Ms. Sue Herrera

General Information Coeducational day general academic and vocational school; primarily serves underachievers, students with learning disabilities, individuals with Attention Deficit Disorder, individuals with emotional and behavioral problems, and Bipolar. Boys grades 6–12, girls grades 2–12. Founded: 1974. Setting: suburban. 1 building on campus. Approved or accredited by California Department of Education. Total enrollment: 8. Upper school average class size: 10. There are 180 required school days per year for Upper School students. Upper School students typically attend 5 days per week. The average school day consists of 6 hours.

Faculty School total: 1. In upper school: 1 woman.

Subjects Offered Adolescent issues, American government, American history, art, basic skills, biology, economics, grammar, health, language arts, life science, life skills, mathematics, physical education, physical science, science, social studies, vocational skills, world history, writing.

Special Academic Programs Remedial reading and/or remedial writing; remedial math.

College Admission Counseling 1 student graduated in 2015 and went to Baldwin Wallace University. Other: 1 had other specific plans.

Student Life Upper grades have specified standards of dress. Discipline rests primarily with faculty.

Tuition and Aid Tuition installment plan (expenses covered by referring district and county agencies with no cost to parents).

Admissions Traditional secondary-level entrance grade is 9. Deadline for receipt of application materials: none. No application fee required. On-campus interview required.

Athletics Intramural: basketball (boys, girls), flag football (b,g).

Computers Computers are regularly used in all academic classes. Computer resources include Internet access.

Contact Ms. Sue Herrera, Director. 925-777-1133. Fax: 925-777-9933. E-mail: sue@lacheim.org. Website: www.lacheim.org/

LANDMARK EAST SCHOOL

708 Main Street
Wolfville, Nova Scotia B4P 1G4, Canada

Head of School: Peter Coll

General Information Coeducational boarding and day college-preparatory, arts, and technology school; primarily serves students with learning disabilities, individuals with Attention Deficit Disorder, and dyslexic students. Boarding grades 6–12, day grades 3–12. Founded: 1979. Setting: small town. Nearest major city is Halifax, Canada. Students are housed in single-sex dormitories. 5-acre campus. 4 buildings on campus. Approved or accredited by Nova Scotia Department of Education. Language of instruction: English. Endowment: CAN$1.3 million. Total enrollment: 71. Upper school average class size: 8. Upper school faculty-student ratio: 1:2. There are 180 required school days per year for Upper School students. Upper School students typically attend 5 days per week. The average school day consists of 6 hours and 45 minutes.

Upper School Student Profile Grade 6: 5 students (2 boys, 3 girls); Grade 7: 6 students (6 boys); Grade 8: 4 students (4 boys); Grade 9: 8 students (5 boys, 3 girls); Grade 10: 18 students (9 boys, 9 girls); Grade 11: 17 students (9 boys, 8 girls); Grade 12: 11 students (9 boys, 2 girls); Postgraduate: 1 student (1 girl). 40% of students are boarding students. 40% are province residents. 7 provinces are represented in upper school student body. 20% are international students. International students from Hong Kong, Japan, Nigeria, South Africa, Trinidad and Tobago, and United States.

Faculty School total: 35. In upper school: 10 men, 14 women; 2 have advanced degrees; 2 reside on campus.

Subjects Offered Accounting, art, biology, career and personal planning, chemistry, computer science, drama, economics, English, entrepreneurship, geography, geology, history, integrated science, law, mathematics, physics, strategies for success.

Graduation Requirements Canadian history.

Special Academic Programs Remedial reading and/or remedial writing; remedial math; programs in English, mathematics, general development for dyslexic students.

College Admission Counseling 17 students graduated in 2015; 14 went to college, including Saint Mary's University. Other: 2 went to work, 1 entered a postgraduate year.

Student Life Upper grades have uniform requirement, honor system. Discipline rests primarily with faculty.

Tuition and Aid Day student tuition: CAN$26,000–CAN$43,000; 7-day tuition and room/board: CAN$41,000–CAN$58,000. Tuition installment plan (monthly payment plans). Tuition reduction for siblings, bursaries, need-based scholarship grants available. In 2015–16, 50% of upper-school students received aid. Total amount of financial aid awarded in 2015–16: CAN$300,000.

Admissions Traditional secondary-level entrance grade is 10. Achievement tests, Cognitive Abilities Test and psychoeducational evaluation required. Deadline for receipt of application materials: none. Application fee required: CAN$100. Interview required.

Athletics Coed Interscholastic: cross-country running, running, track and field, volleyball, wrestling; coed intramural: aerobics, aerobics/dance, alpine skiing, aquatics, archery, badminton, ball hockey, basketball, bicycling, bowling, combined training, cooperative games, curling, dance, equestrian sports, fitness, fitness walking, flag football, floor hockey, Frisbee, handball, hiking/backpacking, horseback riding, ice skating, indoor soccer, jump rope, life saving, mountain biking, outdoor activities, outdoor education, outdoor recreation, rock climbing, running, skiing (cross-country), skiing (downhill), snowboarding, snowshoeing, soccer, softball, street hockey, strength & conditioning, table tennis, tennis, touch football, ultimate Frisbee, walking, weight lifting, weight training. 1 PE instructor.

Computers Computers are regularly used in art, English, mathematics, science classes. Computer network features include on-campus library services, online commercial services, Internet access, wireless campus network, Internet filtering or blocking technology. Student e-mail accounts and computer access in designated common areas are available to students. The school has a published electronic and media policy.

Contact Janet Cooper, Administrative Assistant. 902-542-2237 Ext. 227. Fax: 902-542-4147. E-mail: jcooper@landmarkeast.org. Website: www.landmarkeast.org

LANDMARK SCHOOL

PO Box 227
429 Hale Street
Prides Crossing, Massachusetts 01965-0227

Head of School: Robert J. Broudo

General Information Coeducational boarding and day college-preparatory, general academic, and language arts tutorial, skill-based curriculum school; primarily serves students with learning disabilities, dyslexic students, and language-based learning disabilities. Boarding grades 9–12, day grades 2–12. Founded: 1971. Setting: suburban. Nearest major city is Boston. Students are housed in coed dormitories. 50-acre campus. 24 buildings on campus. Approved or accredited by Association of Independent Schools in New England, Massachusetts Department of Education, Massachusetts Office of Child Care Services, National Association of Private Schools for Exceptional Children, New England Association of Schools and Colleges, and Massachusetts Department of Education. Member of National Association of Independent Schools. Endowment: $10 million. Total enrollment: 471. Upper school average class size: 8. Upper school faculty-student ratio: 1:3. There are 180 required school days per year for Upper School students. Upper School students typically attend 5 days per week. The average school day consists of 7 hours.

Upper School Student Profile Grade 9: 82 students (51 boys, 31 girls); Grade 10: 76 students (50 boys, 26 girls); Grade 11: 69 students (45 boys, 24 girls); Grade 12: 71 students (59 boys, 12 girls). 51% of students are boarding students. 78% are state residents. 22 states are represented in upper school student body. 3% are international students. International students from Australia, Christmas Island, Indonesia, Micronesia, Pakistan, and Senegal; 2 other countries represented in student body.

Faculty School total: 126. In upper school: 40 men, 56 women; 50 have advanced degrees; 24 reside on campus.

Subjects Offered Advanced math, algebra, American government, American history, American literature, anatomy and physiology, art, auto mechanics, biology, boat building, calculus, calculus-AP, chemistry, chorus, communications, composition, computer science, consumer mathematics, creative writing, cultural geography, dance, drama, early childhood, environmental science, expressive arts, filmmaking, geometry, grammar, health education, integrated mathematics, language and composition, language arts, literature, marine science, modern world history, multimedia design, oral communications, oral expression, photography, physical education, physical science, portfolio art, pragmatics, pre-algebra, pre-calculus, reading, reading/study skills, senior thesis, sociology, study skills, technical theater, technology, U.S. history, woodworking, world history, yearbook.

Graduation Requirements English, mathematics, physical education (includes health), science, social studies (includes history), Landmark School competency tests, minimum grade equivalents on standardized tests in reading and reading comprehension.

Special Academic Programs Study at local college for college credit; remedial reading and/or remedial writing; remedial math; programs in English, mathematics, general development for dyslexic students; special instructional classes for deaf students.

College Admission Counseling 89 students graduated in 2016; 85 went to college, including Bryant University; Champlain College; Suffolk University; University of Denver; University of Massachusetts Lowell; Westfield State University. Other: 1 entered military service, 3 had other specific plans. Mean SAT critical reading: 448, mean SAT math: 430, mean SAT writing: 441.

Student Life Upper grades have specified standards of dress, student council. Discipline rests primarily with faculty.

Summer Programs Remediation programs offered; session focuses on academic remediation and study skills; held on campus; accepts boys and girls; open to students from other schools. 160 students usually enrolled. 2017 schedule: June 30 to August 4. Application deadline: May 31.

Tuition and Aid Day student tuition: $55,900; 7-day tuition and room/board: $73,400. Tuition installment plan (Key Tuition Payment Plan). Need-based scholarship grants, community and staff grants available. In 2016–17, 5% of upper-school students received aid.

Admissions Traditional secondary-level entrance grade is 9. For fall 2016, 365 students applied for upper-level admission, 156 were accepted, 151 enrolled. Achievement tests, psychoeducational evaluation and WISC or WAIS required. Deadline for receipt of application materials: none. Application fee required: $150. On-campus interview recommended.

Athletics Interscholastic: baseball (boys), basketball (b,g), lacrosse (b,g), soccer (b,g), tennis (b,g), volleyball (g), wrestling (b); intramural: basketball (b,g), dance (g), floor hockey (b), weight lifting (b), weight training (b); coed interscholastic: cross-country running, golf, swimming and diving, track and field; coed intramural: ropes courses, sailing, skateboarding, skiing (downhill), yoga. 4 PE instructors, 1 athletic trainer.

Computers Computers are regularly used in graphic design, video film production, word processing classes. Computer network features include on-campus library services, Internet access, wireless campus network, Internet filtering or blocking technology. Student e-mail accounts are available to students. The school has a published electronic and media policy.

Contact Carol Bedrosian, Admission Liaison. 978-236-3420. Fax: 978-927-7268. E-mail: cbedrosian@landmarkschool.org. Website: www.landmarkschool.org

THE LAUREATE ACADEMY

100 Villa Maria Place
Winnipeg, Manitoba R3V 1A9, Canada

Head of School: Mr. Stino Siragusa

General Information Coeducational day college-preparatory and programs for students with learning disabilities school. Grades 1–12. Founded: 1987. Setting: suburban. 10-acre campus. 1 building on campus. Approved or accredited by Manitoba Department of Education. Language of instruction: English. Total enrollment: 80. Upper school average class size: 10. Upper school faculty-student ratio: 1:5. There are 183 required school days per year for Upper School students. Upper School students typically attend 5 days per week. The average school day consists of 6 hours and 15 minutes.

Upper School Student Profile Grade 9: 10 students (8 boys, 2 girls); Grade 10: 7 students (5 boys, 2 girls); Grade 11: 5 students (3 boys, 2 girls); Grade 12: 5 students (4 boys, 1 girl).

Faculty School total: 18. In upper school: 4 men, 4 women; 3 have advanced degrees.

Subjects Offered All academic.

Graduation Requirements Algebra, biology, Canadian geography, Canadian history, chemistry, communication skills, composition, computer skills, English, English literature, geometry, life issues, mathematics, physical education (includes health), physics, public speaking, science, social studies (includes history), writing, Department of Manitoba Education requirements, community service. Community service is required.

Special Academic Programs Academic accommodation for the gifted; remedial reading and/or remedial writing; remedial math; programs in English, mathematics for dyslexic students.

College Admission Counseling 5 students graduated in 2016; 3 went to college, including The University of Winnipeg; University of Manitoba. Other: 1 went to work, 1 entered a postgraduate year.

Student Life Upper grades have specified standards of dress, student council, honor system. Discipline rests primarily with faculty.

Tuition and Aid Day student tuition: CAN$19,200. Tuition installment plan (monthly payment plans, quarterly payment plan). Tuition reduction for siblings, bursaries available. In 2016–17, 15% of upper-school students received aid. Total amount of financial aid awarded in 2016–17: CAN$30,000.

Admissions Traditional secondary-level entrance grade is 9. For fall 2016, 9 students applied for upper-level admission, 4 were accepted, 3 enrolled. WISC or WAIS, WISC-III and Woodcock-Johnson and writing sample required. Deadline for receipt of application materials: none. Application fee required: CAN$75. On-campus interview recommended.

Athletics Interscholastic: basketball (boys), volleyball (b); intramural: badminton (b), ball hockey (b), basketball (b); coed interscholastic: badminton, cross-country running, soccer, track and field, volleyball; coed intramural: aerobics, alpine skiing, badminton, ball hockey, basketball, broomball, combined training, cooperative games, fitness, flag football, floor hockey, Frisbee, jogging, martial arts, outdoor activities, outdoor adventure, outdoor education, outdoor recreation, paddle tennis, physical fitness, physical training, running, self defense, skiing (downhill), snowboarding, soccer, softball, strength & conditioning, table tennis, touch football, track and field, ultimate Frisbee, volleyball, weight lifting, weight training. 2 PE instructors, 4 coaches.

Computers Computers are regularly used in career education, career exploration, computer applications, creative writing, English, mathematics, research skills, science, social studies, writing, yearbook classes. Computer network features include Internet access, wireless campus network, Internet filtering or blocking technology, Google Classroom, submitting assignments digitally. Campus intranet, student e-mail accounts, and computer access in designated common areas are available to students. The school has a published electronic and media policy.

Contact Mrs. Dora Lawrie, Admissions Coordinator. 204-831-7107. Fax: 204-885-3217. E-mail: dlawrie@laureateacademy.com. Website: www.laureateacademy.com

LAWRENCE SCHOOL

Upper School
10036 Olde Eight Road
Sagamore Hills, Ohio 44067

Head of School: Mr. Lou Salza

General Information Coeducational day college-preparatory school; primarily serves students with learning disabilities, individuals with Attention Deficit Disorder, and dyslexic students. Grades K–12. Founded: 1969. Setting: suburban. Nearest major city is Cleveland. 47-acre campus. 1 building on campus. Approved or accredited by Independent Schools Association of the Central States and Ohio Department of Education. Member of National Association of Independent Schools. Endowment: $2 million. Total enrollment: 344. Upper school average class size: 11. Upper school faculty-student ratio: 1:11. There are 185 required school days per year for Upper School students. Upper School students typically attend 5 days per week. The average school day consists of 6 hours.

Faculty School total: 32. In upper school: 12 men, 20 women; 4 have advanced degrees.

Subjects Offered 20th century history, accounting, Advanced Placement courses, algebra, American history, American sign language, anatomy, art, astronomy, biology, calculus, choir, chorus, college counseling, computer applications, consumer economics, creative writing, debate, drama, earth science, economics, English, English composition, forensics, geography, geometry, global studies, government, graphic arts, graphic design, health, integrated mathematics, journalism, keyboarding, language arts, Latin, law, life science, life skills, mathematics, meteorology, military history, music, mythology, painting, physical education, physical science, physics, physics-AP, poetry, pre-algebra, psychology, research skills, sign language, society, politics and law, sociology, Spanish, speech, speech communications, The 20th Century, U.S. history, U.S. history-AP, video, video communication, Web site design, weight training, world geography, world history, yearbook.

Graduation Requirements Arts and fine arts (art, music, dance, drama), business, English, foreign language, health, mathematics, physical education (includes health), science, social studies (includes history), technology, Independent Study Project for Seniors, service learning project.

Special Academic Programs Honors section; independent study; remedial reading and/or remedial writing; remedial math; programs in English, mathematics, general development for dyslexic students; special instructional classes for Lawrence is a certified provider of UCLA PEERS (Program for the Education and Enrichment of Relational Skills).

College Admission Counseling 40 students graduated in 2016; 31 went to college, including Baldwin Wallace University; Cleveland State University; John Carroll University; Michigan State University; Ohio University; University of Mount Union. Other: 4 went to work, 3 entered a postgraduate year, 2 had other specific plans.

Student Life Upper grades have specified standards of dress, student council, honor system. Discipline rests equally with students and faculty.

Summer Programs Enrichment, sports, art/fine arts, computer instruction programs offered; session focuses on Day Camp; held on campus; accepts boys and girls; open to students from other schools. 40 students usually enrolled. 2017 schedule: June 12 to August 11. Application deadline: May 31.

Tuition and Aid Day student tuition: $26,970–$29,192. Tuition installment plan (FACTS Tuition Payment Plan, monthly payment plans, individually arranged payment plans). Need-based scholarship grants available. In 2016–17, 30% of upper-school students received aid. Total amount of financial aid awarded in 2016–17: $1,214,000.

Admissions Traditional secondary-level entrance grade is 9. Admissions testing required. Deadline for receipt of application materials: none. Application fee required: $100. On-campus interview recommended.

Athletics Interscholastic: baseball (boys), basketball (b,g), cross-country running (b,g), softball (g), volleyball (g); coed interscholastic: golf, soccer, swimming and diving; coed intramural: badminton, bowling, cheering, cooperative games, fishing, fitness, flag football, floor hockey, outdoor activities, running, skiing (downhill), snowboarding, wall climbing. 1 PE instructor.

Computers Computers are regularly used in all academic classes. Computer network features include on-campus library services, Internet access, wireless campus network, Internet filtering or blocking technology, one-to-one notebook laptop program for grades 9 to 12, laptop program for grades 7-8, school-wide social networking through Saywire. Student e-mail accounts are available to students. Students grades are available online. The school has a published electronic and media policy.

Contact Mrs. Mary Beth Petzke, Admissions Assistant. 440-526-0717. Fax: 440-526-0595. E-mail: mpetzke@lawrenceschool.org. Website: www.lawrenceschool.org

THE LEELANAU SCHOOL

One Old Homestead Road
Glen Arbor, Michigan 49636

Head of School: Mr. Matthew B. Ralston

General Information Coeducational boarding and day college-preparatory, arts, and experiential program school; primarily serves students with learning disabilities, individuals with Attention Deficit Disorder, dyslexic students, Attention Deficit Hyperactivity Disorder, language-based learning differences, and non-verbal learning disabilities. Grades 9–12. Founded: 1929. Setting: rural. Nearest major city is Traverse City. Students are housed in single-sex dormitories. 50-acre campus. 12 buildings on campus. Approved or accredited by Independent Schools Association of the Central States, Midwest Association of Boarding Schools, National Independent Private Schools Association, The Association of Boarding Schools, The College Board, and Michigan Department of Education. Member of National Association of Independent Schools and Secondary School Admission Test Board. Endowment: $435,200. Total enrollment: 50. Upper school average class size: 6. Upper school faculty-student ratio: 1:5. There are 165 required school days per year for Upper School students. Upper

School students typically attend 5 days per week. The average school day consists of 5 hours and 50 minutes.

Upper School Student Profile Grade 9: 5 students (4 boys, 1 girl); Grade 10: 6 students (5 boys, 1 girl); Grade 11: 18 students (13 boys, 5 girls); Grade 12: 21 students (18 boys, 3 girls). 93% of students are boarding students. 25% are state residents. 9 states are represented in upper school student body. 18% are international students. International students from Angola, China, Puerto Rico, Turkey, and United Kingdom; 3 other countries represented in student body.

Faculty School total: 18. In upper school: 10 men, 5 women; 9 have advanced degrees; 11 reside on campus.

Subjects Offered 20th century history, acting, Advanced Placement courses, advanced TOEFL/grammar, algebra, American Civil War, American government, American history, American literature, anatomy and physiology, ancient history, ancient world history, animation, applied arts, applied music, art, art appreciation, arts, arts and crafts, arts appreciation, astronomy, athletics, audio visual/media, backpacking, basic language skills, biology, biotechnology, boat building, botany, British literature, business studies, calculus, calculus-AP, calligraphy, career and personal planning, career exploration, career/college preparation, cartooning/animation, ceramics, character education, chemistry, civil war history, classical civilization, clayworking, college admission preparation, college awareness, college counseling, college placement, college planning, college writing, comedy, computer animation, computer science, conflict resolution, conservation, constitutional history of U.S., CPR, critical thinking, critical writing, decision making skills, developmental language skills, digital art, digital imaging, digital music, digital photography, drama, drama performance, dramatic arts, drawing, drawing and design, earth science, ecology, electives, English, English as a foreign language, English composition, English literature, entrepreneurship, environmental education, environmental science, environmental studies, environmental systems, epic literature, equestrian sports, equine management, ESL, European history, experiential education, experimental science, expository writing, family living, fiction, field ecology, film and new technologies, filmmaking, fine arts, foreign language, general science, geography, geology, geometry, golf, government/civics, grammar, great books, guitar, history, honors English, human anatomy, human biology, human relations, illustration, improvisation, independent living, independent study, instruments, integrated arts, integrated science, interpersonal skills, jazz band, jazz ensemble, jewelry making, journalism, Korean culture, language, language and composition, language arts, languages, leadership, leadership education training, learning cognition, learning lab, learning strategies, life issues, life management skills, life science, life skills, literacy, literature, literature by women, marine biology, marine ecology, marine science, marine studies, mathematics, mentorship program, modern European history, modern history, modern world history, moral and social development, moral reasoning, multicultural literature, music, music appreciation, Native American history, Native American studies, nature study, nature writers, oil painting, organizational studies, outdoor education, painting, participation in sports, photography, physics, poetry, pottery, pre-calculus, printmaking, psychology, reading/study skills, relationships, religious studies, remedial study skills, remedial/makeup course work, SAT preparation, SAT/ACT preparation, science, science and technology, science project, science research, senior thesis, Shakespeare, silk screening, social studies, Spanish, speech, sports, statistics-AP, student government, studio art, study skills, theater, TOEFL preparation, travel, trigonometry, U.S. government, U.S. government and politics, visual arts, weight training, weightlifting, wellness, wilderness education, wilderness experience, world history, writing, yearbook.

Graduation Requirements Arts and fine arts (art, music, dance, drama), CPR, English, foreign language, mathematics, science, senior thesis, social studies (includes history), senior leadership orientation.

Special Academic Programs 3 Advanced Placement exams for which test preparation is offered; honors section; independent study; term-away projects; remedial reading and/or remedial writing; remedial math; ESL (5 students enrolled).

College Admission Counseling 28 students graduated in 2015; 27 went to college, including Curry College; Michigan Technological University; The College of Wooster; The Evergreen State College. Other: 1 had other specific plans.

Student Life Upper grades have specified standards of dress, student council. Discipline rests primarily with faculty.

Tuition and Aid Day student tuition: $30,625; 5-day tuition and room/board: $52,675; 7-day tuition and room/board: $61,350. Tuition installment plan (individually arranged payment plans). Tuition reduction for siblings, need-based scholarship grants, Beals Scholarship for legacy families available. In 2015–16, 25% of upper-school students received aid. Total amount of financial aid awarded in 2015–16: $200,000.

Admissions Traditional secondary-level entrance grade is 10. For fall 2015, 25 students applied for upper-level admission, 25 were accepted, 15 enrolled. Individual IQ, Achievement and behavior rating scale, psychoeducational evaluation, Stanford Test of Academic Skills, TOEFL or SLEP, Wechsler Intelligence Scale for Children, Wechsler Intelligence Scale for Children III, Woodcock-Johnson or writing sample required. Deadline for receipt of application materials: none. Application fee required: $50. On-campus interview required.

Athletics Interscholastic: basketball (boys), volleyball (g); coed interscholastic: dressage, equestrian sports, golf, soccer, tennis; coed intramural: alpine skiing, backpacking, bicycling, broomball, canoeing/kayaking, climbing, combined training, cross-country running, dance team, fishing, fitness, flag football, fly fishing, freestyle skiing, Frisbee, hiking/backpacking, horseback riding, independent competitive sports, jogging, kayaking, mountain biking, outdoor activities, outdoor adventure, outdoor education, outdoor recreation, outdoor skills, outdoors, paddling, paint ball, physical fitness, physical training, rock climbing, ropes courses, running, skiing (cross-country), skiing (downhill), snowboarding, snowshoeing, table tennis, triathlon, wall climbing, yoga. 1 PE instructor, 6 coaches, 1 athletic trainer.

Computers Computers are regularly used in all academic, animation, creative writing classes. Computer resources include on-campus library services, Internet access, wireless campus network, Internet filtering or blocking technology. Students grades are available online.

Contact Ms. Maleah R. Gluck, Director of Admission. 231-334-5824. Fax: 231-334-5898. E-mail: admissions@leelanau.org. Website: www.leelanau.org

LITTLE KESWICK SCHOOL

PO Box 24
Keswick, Virginia 22947

Head of School: Marc J. Columbus

General Information Boys' boarding arts school; primarily serves underachievers, students with learning disabilities, individuals with Attention Deficit Disorder, individuals with emotional and behavioral problems, and dyslexic students. Founded: 1963. Setting: small town. Nearest major city is Washington, DC. Students are housed in single-sex dormitories. 25-acre campus. 10 buildings on campus. Approved or accredited by Virginia Association of Independent Specialized Education Facilities and Virginia Department of Education. Total enrollment: 34. Upper school average class size: 7. Upper school faculty-student ratio: 1:3. There are 205 required school days per year for Upper School students. The average school day consists of 5 hours and 30 minutes.

Upper School Student Profile 100% of students are boarding students. 16 states are represented in upper school student body. 10% are international students. International students from Australia and Sweden.

Faculty School total: 6. In upper school: 3 men, 3 women; 5 have advanced degrees.

Subjects Offered Algebra, American history, biology, computer applications, earth science, English, geography, government/civics, health, industrial arts, mathematics, physical education, practical arts, social studies, world history.

Special Academic Programs Academic accommodation for the gifted; remedial reading and/or remedial writing; remedial math; programs in English, mathematics, general development for dyslexic students.

Student Life Upper grades have specified standards of dress. Discipline rests primarily with faculty.

Tuition and Aid 7-day tuition and room/board: $111,028. Tuition installment plan (monthly payment plans). Need-based scholarship grants available. In 2015–16, 2% of upper-school students received aid. Total amount of financial aid awarded in 2015–16: $20,000.

Admissions Psychoeducational evaluation, Rorschach or Thematic Apperception Test and WISC/Woodcock-Johnson required. Deadline for receipt of application materials: none. Application fee required: $350. On-campus interview required.

Athletics Interscholastic: basketball (boys), combined training (b), soccer (b); intramural: aquatics (b), backpacking (b), basketball (b), bicycling (b), canoeing/kayaking (b), climbing (b), cross-country running (b), equestrian sports (b), fishing (b), fitness (b), hiking/backpacking (b), horseback riding (b), lacrosse (b), outdoor activities (b), outdoor adventure (b), outdoor education (b), outdoor recreation (b), outdoor skills (b), outdoors (b), physical fitness (b), rock climbing (b), running (b), soccer (b). 1 PE instructor, 2 coaches.

Computers Computer network features include Internet access. Computer access in designated common areas is available to students. The school has a published electronic and media policy.

Contact Ms. Terry Columbus, Director. 434-295-0457 Ext. 14. Fax: 434-977-1892. E-mail: tcolumbus@littlekeswickschool.net. Website: www.littlekeswickschool.net

MAPLEBROOK SCHOOL

5142 Route 22
Amenia, New York 12501

Head of School: Miss Donna M. Konkolics

General Information Coeducational boarding and day college-preparatory, general academic, iPad program, and Executive Functioning school; primarily serves underachievers, students with learning disabilities, individuals with Attention Deficit Disorder, dyslexic students, and low average cognitive ability (minimum I.Q. of 70). Ungraded, ages 11–18. Founded: 1945. Setting: small town. Nearest major city is Poughkeepsie. Students are housed in single-sex dormitories. 100-acre campus. 25 buildings on campus. Approved or accredited by Independent Schools Association of the Central States, Middle States Association of Colleges and Schools, National Association of Private Schools for Exceptional Children, New York Department of Education, New York State Association of Independent Schools, New York State Board of Regents, The Association of Boarding Schools, and New York Department of Education. Member of National Association of Independent Schools. Endowment: $500,000. Total enrollment: 75. Upper school average class size: 6. Upper school faculty-student ratio: 1:8. There are 180 required school days per year for Upper School students. Upper School students typically attend 7 days per week. The average school day consists of 6 hours and 5 minutes.

Faculty School total: 55. In upper school: 12 men, 14 women; 26 have advanced degrees; 50 reside on campus.

Subjects Offered Career/college preparation, computer skills, environmental science, reading, relationships, remedial study skills.

Graduation Requirements Career and personal planning, computer science, English, mathematics, physical education (includes health), science, social sciences, social skills, social studies (includes history), attendance at Maplebrook School for a minimum of 2 years.

Special Academic Programs Study at local college for college credit; remedial reading and/or remedial writing; remedial math; programs in English, mathematics, general development for dyslexic students; ESL (3 students enrolled).

College Admission Counseling 15 students graduated in 2016; 4 went to college, including Curry College; Dutchess Community College; Mitchell College. Other: 3 went to work, 8 entered a postgraduate year.

Student Life Upper grades have specified standards of dress, student council, honor system. Discipline rests primarily with faculty.

Summer Programs Remediation, enrichment, sports, art/fine arts, computer instruction programs offered; session focuses on preventing regression of skills; held both on and off campus; held at various locations for New York City day and overnight trips; accepts boys and girls; open to students from other schools. 70 students usually enrolled. 2017 schedule: July 3 to August 13. Application deadline: none.

Tuition and Aid Day student tuition: $35,000; 5-day tuition and room/board: $58,000; 7-day tuition and room/board: $63,000. Tuition installment plan (Key Tuition Payment Plan, individually arranged payment plans, Tuition Management Systems Plan, Sallie Mae loans). Merit scholarship grants, need-based scholarship grants, need-based loans, middle-income loans, paying campus jobs, minority and cultural diversity scholarships, day student scholarships, merit scholarships available. In 2016–17, 20% of upper-school students received aid; total upper-school merit-scholarship money awarded: $10,000. Total amount of financial aid awarded in 2016–17: $100,000.

Admissions Traditional secondary-level entrance age is 15. For fall 2016, 179 students applied for upper-level admission, 68 were accepted, 31 enrolled. Achievement tests, Bender Gestalt, TerraNova, Test of Achievement and Proficiency or WISC or WAIS required. Deadline for receipt of application materials: none. No application fee required. Interview required.

Athletics Interscholastic: basketball (boys, girls), cheering (g), field hockey (g); coed interscholastic: cooperative games, cross-country running, equestrian sports, fitness, freestyle skiing, horseback riding, running, skiing (cross-country), skiing (downhill), soccer, softball, swimming and diving, tennis, track and field, weight lifting, weight training; coed intramural: aerobics/dance, alpine skiing, basketball, bicycling, bowling, cooperative games, cricket, dance, figure skating, fitness, fitness walking, flag football, floor hockey, freestyle skiing, gatorball, golf, hiking/backpacking, horseback riding, indoor hockey, martial arts, outdoor education, outdoor recreation, roller blading, skiing (cross-country), skiing (downhill), soccer, softball, Special Olympics, swimming and diving, table tennis, tennis, volleyball, weight lifting, weight training, wrestling. 1 PE instructor, 12 coaches.

Computers Computers are regularly used in all academic classes. Computer network features include on-campus library services, Internet access, wireless campus network, Internet filtering or blocking technology. Campus intranet, student e-mail accounts, and computer access in designated common areas are available to students. Students grades are available online. The school has a published electronic and media policy.

Contact Bekah Puddington, Admissions Associate. 845-373-8191. Fax: 845-373-7029. E-mail: admissions@maplebrookschool.org.
Website: www.maplebrookschool.org

MILL SPRINGS ACADEMY
13660 New Providence Road
Alpharetta, Georgia 30004

Head of School: Mr. Robert W. Moore

General Information Coeducational day college-preparatory school. Grades 1–12. Founded: 1981. Setting: suburban. Nearest major city is Atlanta. 85-acre campus. 5 buildings on campus. Approved or accredited by Georgia Association of Private Schools for Exceptional Children, Georgia Independent School Association, Southern Association of Colleges and Schools, and Southern Association of Independent Schools. Member of National Association of Independent Schools. Endowment: $140,000. Total enrollment: 355. Upper school average class size: 12. Upper school faculty-student ratio: 1:6. There are 180 required school days per year for Upper School students. Upper School students typically attend 5 days per week. The average school day consists of 7 hours.

Upper School Student Profile Grade 9: 55 students (39 boys, 16 girls); Grade 10: 42 students (29 boys, 13 girls); Grade 11: 38 students (29 boys, 9 girls); Grade 12: 38 students (25 boys, 13 girls).

Faculty School total: 56. In upper school: 11 men, 17 women; 20 have advanced degrees.

Subjects Offered Algebra, American history, American literature, anatomy and physiology, art, band, biology, British literature, British literature (honors), calculus,

career/college preparation, chemistry, Chinese, chorus, composition, creative writing, diversity studies, drama, ecology, economics, film, geometry, government, health, history, honors algebra, honors English, honors geometry, honors U.S. history, honors world history, journalism, literature, media, music theater, performing arts, physical education, physics, play production, play/screen writing, playwriting and directing, political science, pre-algebra, pre-calculus, psychology, sculpture, senior project, set design, Spanish, state government, studio art, symphonic band, technology, theater, theater design and production, trigonometry, U.S. history, values and decisions, visual and performing arts, voice, world literature, yearbook.

Graduation Requirements Algebra, American history, American literature, anatomy and physiology, biology, British literature, British literature (honors), calculus, chemistry, civics, composition, ecology, economics, foreign language, geometry, mathematics, physical education (includes health), physics, senior seminar, trigonometry, world history, world literature, senior English, 6 units of electives.

Special Academic Programs Honors section; study at local college for college credit; academic accommodation for the gifted, the musically talented, and the artistically talented; programs in English, mathematics, general development for dyslexic students.

College Admission Counseling 48 students graduated in 2016; 31 went to college, including Georgia College & State University; Georgia Perimeter College; Kennesaw State University; Reinhardt University; Savannah College of Art and Design; Young Harris College. Mean SAT critical reading: 504, mean SAT math: 477, mean SAT writing: 491, mean combined SAT: 1472, mean composite ACT: 19. 21% scored over 600 on SAT critical reading, 29% scored over 600 on SAT math, 14% scored over 600 on SAT writing, 29% scored over 1800 on combined SAT, 29% scored over 26 on composite ACT.

Student Life Upper grades have uniform requirement, student council, honor system. Discipline rests equally with students and faculty.

Summer Programs Enrichment, sports programs offered; session focuses on skills development or course credit; held on campus; accepts boys and girls; open to students from other schools. 160 students usually enrolled. 2017 schedule: May 30 to August 14. Application deadline: May 30.

Tuition and Aid Day student tuition: $22,926. Tuition installment plan (FACTS Tuition Payment Plan). Tuition reduction for siblings, need-based scholarship grants, Georgia Special Needs Scholarship, GA DoE available. In 2016–17, 14% of upper-school students received aid. Total amount of financial aid awarded in 2016–17: $110,000.

Admissions Traditional secondary-level entrance grade is 9. For fall 2016, 35 students applied for upper-level admission, 27 were accepted, 24 enrolled. Psychoeducational evaluation required. Deadline for receipt of application materials: none. No application fee required. On-campus interview recommended.

Athletics Interscholastic: baseball (boys), basketball (b,g), golf (b), lacrosse (b), tennis (b,g), volleyball (g), wrestling (b); intramural: cheering (g), strength & conditioning (b), weight training (b); coed interscholastic: cross-country running, soccer, swimming and diving, track and field; coed intramural: archery, dance, fencing, fishing, golf, mountain biking, outdoor activities, physical fitness, scuba diving, yoga. 1 PE instructor, 2 coaches.

Computers Computers are regularly used in all academic classes. Computer network features include on-campus library services, online commercial services, Internet access, wireless campus network, Internet filtering or blocking technology, all students 4-12th grades have laptops, electronic textbooks/literature books, assignments online. Student e-mail accounts are available to students. Students grades are available online. The school has a published electronic and media policy.

Contact Mrs. Sheila FitzGerald, Admissions Director. 770-360-1336 Ext. 1707. Fax: 770-360-1341. E-mail: sfitzgerald@millsprings.org. Website: www.millsprings.org

THE MONARCH SCHOOL
2815 Rosefield Drive
Houston, Texas 77080

Head of School: Patti Pace

General Information Boys' day and distance learning college-preparatory, general academic, arts, vocational, and technology school; primarily serves underachievers, students with learning disabilities, individuals with Attention Deficit Disorder, individuals with emotional and behavioral problems, dyslexic students, students with PDD spectrum disorders, mood disorders, Executive Functioning Disorder, other neurological-based disorders, and social coordination, and emotional regulation issues. Grades K–12. Distance learning grades 9–12. Founded: 1997. Setting: suburban. 11-acre campus. 5 buildings on campus. Approved or accredited by National Association of Private Schools for Exceptional Children and Southern Association of Colleges and Schools. Total enrollment: 135. Upper school average class size: 8. Upper school faculty-student ratio: 1:2. Upper School students typically attend 5 days per week. The average school day consists of 8 hours.

Faculty School total: 85. In upper school: 6 men, 12 women; 6 have advanced degrees.

Subjects Offered 20th century history, 20th century physics, 20th century world history, 3-dimensional art, 3-dimensional design, accounting, ADL skills, adolescent issues, advanced computer applications, advanced math, algebra, American Civil War, American culture, American government, American history, American legal systems, American literature, ancient history, ancient world history, animal behavior, applied music, art, art and culture, arts and crafts, athletics, automated accounting, banking, basic language skills, biology, boat building, body human, botany, business, business applications, business communications, business education, business mathematics, business skills, business studies, business technology, calculus, career and personal planning, career education, career education internship, career experience, career exploration, career planning, career/college preparation, carpentry, cell biology, chemistry, child development, civics, civics/free enterprise, civil rights, Civil War, civil war history, college admission preparation, college placement, comparative government and politics, competitive science projects, composition, computer animation, computer applications, computer education, computer graphics, computer literacy, computer skills, conflict resolution, conservation, construction, consumer economics, consumer education, consumer mathematics, contemporary history, crafts, creative arts, creative drama, culinary arts, current history, dance, decision making skills, democracy in America, developmental math, drawing, drawing and design, earth science, ecology, ecology, environmental systems, economics, English, English composition, entrepreneurship, environmental education, environmental geography, environmental science, environmental studies, epic literature, ethics, ethics and responsibility, European history, field ecology, fine arts, food and nutrition, food science, foods, foreign language, gardening, general science, geography, geology, geometry, government, government/civics, health, health and safety, health and wellness, health education, high adventure outdoor program, history, horticulture, independent living, inquiry into relationship, instrumental music, instruments, integrated physics, Internet, internship, interpersonal skills, Japanese, jewelry making, journalism, keyboarding, language arts, language development, language enhancement and development, leadership, leadership and service, leadership education training, learning lab, learning strategies, life skills, literacy, literature, logic, mathematics, mentorship program, moral and social development, moral reasoning, music appreciation, music performance, music theory, natural history, nature study, newspaper, North American literature, novels, nutrition, occupational education, outdoor education, peace and justice, peace education, personal and social education, personal development, personal finance, personal fitness, personal money management, physical education, physical fitness, physics, play production, play/screen writing, poetry, practical living, pre-algebra, pre-calculus, pre-vocational education, public speaking, publications, reading, reading/study skills, relationships, remedial study skills, SAT preparation, SAT/ACT preparation, science, senior project, service learning/internship, sexuality, skills for success, social issues, social skills, social studies, Spanish, speech communications, sports, standard curriculum, state government, strategies for success, student government, student publications, student teaching, techniques of living and coping, Texas history, the Presidency, the Sixties, transition mathematics, trigonometry, U.S. government, U.S. government and politics, U.S. history, values and decisions, video communication, vocational arts, vocational skills, vocational-technical courses, voice, wellness, Western civilization, wilderness education, wilderness experience, women's literature, wood lab, woodworking, work experience, work-study, world civilizations, world cultures, world geography, world history, writing, writing, yearbook.

Special Academic Programs International Baccalaureate program; Advanced Placement exam preparation; accelerated programs; independent study; study at local college for college credit; academic accommodation for the gifted and the artistically talented; remedial reading and/or remedial writing; remedial math; programs in English, mathematics, general development for dyslexic students; special instructional classes for student with autism.

College Admission Counseling 15 students graduated in 2016; 5 went to college, including Houston Baptist University; Houston Community College; St. Edward's University. Other: 10 went to work. Mean SAT critical reading: 690, mean SAT math: 605. 67% scored over 600 on SAT critical reading, 33% scored over 600 on SAT math.

Student Life Upper grades have uniform requirement, student council, honor system. Discipline rests equally with students and faculty.

Summer Programs Remediation, enrichment, art/fine arts, computer instruction programs offered; session focuses on relationship development, self-esteem, and executive functioning; held both on and off campus; accepts boys and girls; open to students from other schools. 100 students usually enrolled. 2017 schedule: June 14 to July 15. Application deadline: March 15.

Tuition and Aid Day student tuition: $26,000–$38,000. Tuition installment plan (monthly payment plans, individually arranged payment plans, quarterly, yearly payment plans). Need-based scholarship grants, need-based loans available. In 2016–17, 40% of upper-school students received aid. Total amount of financial aid awarded in 2016–17: $105,350.

Admissions Achievement tests and Individual IQ required. Deadline for receipt of application materials: none. Application fee required: $550. On-campus interview required.

Computers Computers are regularly used in business skills classes. Computer network features include Internet access, Internet filtering or blocking technology. Student e-mail accounts are available to students. The school has a published electronic and media policy.

Contact Ms. Jacquice Jones, Director of Admissions. 713-479-0800. Fax: 713-464-7499. E-mail: jjones@monarchschool.org. Website: www.monarchschool.org

NOBLE ACADEMY

3310 Horse Pen Creek Road
Greensboro, North Carolina 27410

Head of School: Linda Hale

General Information Coeducational day college-preparatory school. Grades K–12. Founded: 1987. Setting: suburban. Nearest major city is Greensboro/Winston-Salem. 40-acre campus. 3 buildings on campus. Approved or accredited by North Carolina Department of Exceptional Children, Southern Association of Colleges and Schools, and North Carolina Department of Education. Member of National Association of Independent Schools. Endowment: $2.5 million. Total enrollment: 160. Upper school average class size: 9. Upper school faculty-student ratio: 1:9. There are 180 required school days per year for Upper School students. Upper School students typically attend 5 days per week. The average school day consists of 6 hours and 45 minutes.

Upper School Student Profile Grade 10: 15 students (10 boys, 5 girls); Grade 11: 24 students (20 boys, 4 girls); Grade 12: 22 students (12 boys, 10 girls).

Faculty School total: 37. In upper school: 3 men, 14 women; 9 have advanced degrees.

Subjects Offered Algebra, American history, art, basic skills, biology, career and personal planning, career exploration, chemistry, civics, college counseling, drama, earth science, economics, English, environmental science, geometry, health, journalism, life management skills, political systems, pre-algebra, pre-calculus, reading, reading/study skills, Spanish, world history, world history-AP, yearbook.

Graduation Requirements Algebra, American history, biology, earth science, economics, English, environmental science, geometry, physical education (includes health), Spanish, world history, 8th grade end-of-grade test, 20th percentile score on standardized reading test, North Carolina Computer Competency Test.

Special Academic Programs Study at local college for college credit; remedial reading and/or remedial writing; remedial math; programs in English, mathematics, general development for dyslexic students.

College Admission Counseling 15 students graduated in 2016; 14 went to college, including Brevard College; Elon University; Guilford College; St. Andrews University; The University of North Carolina at Greensboro; William Peace University. Other: 1 went to work. Median SAT critical reading: 548, median SAT math: 454, median SAT writing: 496. Mean combined SAT: 1510. 22% scored over 600 on SAT critical reading, 11% scored over 600 on SAT writing.

Student Life Upper grades have student council, honor system. Discipline rests primarily with faculty.

Tuition and Aid Day student tuition: $19,960. Tuition installment plan (monthly payment plans, individually arranged payment plans). Need-based scholarship grants available. In 2016–17, 14% of upper-school students received aid. Total amount of financial aid awarded in 2016–17: $81,000.

Admissions Traditional secondary-level entrance grade is 10. For fall 2016, 9 students applied for upper-level admission, 5 were accepted, 3 enrolled. WISC/Woodcock-Johnson required. Deadline for receipt of application materials: none. Application fee required: $75. On-campus interview recommended.

Athletics Coed Interscholastic: basketball, cheering, cross-country running, flag football, Frisbee, golf, soccer, tennis, touch football, volleyball, weight lifting, weight training. 1 PE instructor, 7 coaches.

Computers Computers are regularly used in art, career education, career exploration, career technology, college planning, computer applications, current events, graphic arts, graphic design, history, information technology, introduction to technology, journalism, keyboarding, lab/keyboard, photography, social studies, Spanish, study skills, word processing, writing, writing, yearbook classes. Computer network features include on-campus library services, Internet access, wireless campus network, Internet filtering or blocking technology. Campus intranet and student e-mail accounts are available to students. Students grades are available online. The school has a published electronic and media policy.

Contact Christy Avent, Director of Advancement and Admissions. 336-282-7044. Fax: 336-282-2048. E-mail: cavent@nobleknights.org. Website: www.nobleknights.org

NORMAN HOWARD SCHOOL

275 Pinnacle Road
Rochester, New York 14623

Head of School: Paul Keller

General Information Coeducational day college-preparatory, general academic, arts, and outdoor education school; primarily serves underachievers, students with learning disabilities, individuals with Attention Deficit Disorder, dyslexic students, and autism (high functioning), anxiety. Grades 5–12. Founded: 1980. Setting: suburban. 2-acre campus. 1 building on campus. Approved or accredited by New York State Board of Regents and New York Department of Education. Total enrollment: 121. Upper school average class size: 10. Upper school faculty-student ratio: 1:3. There are 180 required school days per year for Upper School students. Upper School students typically attend 5 days per week. The average school day consists of 6 hours and 30 minutes.

Upper School Student Profile Grade 9: 19 students (12 boys, 7 girls); Grade 10: 26 students (20 boys, 6 girls); Grade 11: 17 students (10 boys, 7 girls); Grade 12: 20 students (15 boys, 5 girls).

Faculty School total: 42. In upper school: 13 men, 12 women; 17 have advanced degrees.

Subjects Offered 3-dimensional art.

Graduation Requirements Art.

Special Academic Programs Independent study; study at local college for college credit; remedial reading and/or remedial writing; remedial math; programs in English, mathematics, general development for dyslexic students; special instructional classes for deaf students.

College Admission Counseling 20 students graduated in 2016; 12 went to college, including Monroe Community College. Other: 5 went to work, 3 had other specific plans.

Student Life Upper grades have uniform requirement, student council, honor system. Discipline rests primarily with faculty.

Tuition and Aid Day student tuition: $28,600. Tuition installment plan (monthly payment plans, 60/40 payment option plan). Need-based scholarship grants, substantial financial aid to families who qualify available.

Admissions Traditional secondary-level entrance grade is 9. Deadline for receipt of application materials: none. Application fee required: $50. On-campus interview recommended.

Athletics Coed Intramural: outdoor adventure, outdoor education, physical fitness, skiing (downhill), swimming and diving. 2 PE instructors.

Computers Computers are regularly used in art classes. Computer network features include on-campus library services, Internet access, wireless campus network, Internet filtering or blocking technology, assistive technology. Campus intranet, student e-mail accounts, and computer access in designated common areas are available to students. The school has a published electronic and media policy.

Contact Julie Murray, Associate Director of Admissions and Special Events. 585-334-8010 Ext. 302. Fax: 585-334-8073. E-mail: jmurray@normanhoward.org. Website: www.normanhoward.org

OAKLAND SCHOOL

128 Oakland Farm Way
Troy, Virginia 22974

Head of School: Ms. Carol Williams

General Information Coeducational boarding and day general academic school; primarily serves underachievers, students with learning disabilities, individuals with Attention Deficit Disorder, dyslexic students, processing difficulties, and organizationa/executive functioningl challenges. Boarding grades 4–8, day grades 1–8. Founded: 1950. Setting: rural. Nearest major city is Richmond. Students are housed in single-sex dormitories. 450-acre campus. 25 buildings on campus. Approved or accredited by Virginia Association of Independent Specialized Education Facilities. Upper school average class size: 5. Upper school faculty-student ratio: 1:5. There are 180 required school days per year for Upper School students. Upper School students typically attend 5 days per week. The average school day consists of 6 hours and 45 minutes.

Upper School Student Profile 33% of students are boarding students. 76% are state residents. 21 states are represented in upper school student body. 1% are international students. International students from Indonesia; 1 other country represented in student body.

Faculty School total: 8. In upper school: 2 men, 6 women; 6 have advanced degrees.

Subjects Offered Algebra, American history, art, art and culture, art appreciation, art history, computer literacy, computer skills, consumer mathematics, drama, drama performance, earth science, English, English composition, expository writing, geometry, grammar, health, health and wellness, health education, history of the Americas, keyboarding, life science, mathematics, physical education, physical science, remedial study skills, study skills, U.S. and Virginia history, world history.

Graduation Requirements Skills must be at or above grade/ability level.

Special Academic Programs Remedial reading and/or remedial writing; remedial math; programs in English, mathematics, general development for dyslexic students.

College Admission Counseling 20 students graduated in 2016.

Student Life Upper grades have specified standards of dress, honor system. Discipline rests primarily with faculty.

Summer Programs Remediation, sports, art/fine arts, computer instruction programs offered; session focuses on academics; held on campus; accepts boys and girls; open to students from other schools. 110 students usually enrolled. 2017 schedule: June 26 to July 26.

Tuition and Aid Day student tuition: $29,175; 7-day tuition and room/board: $50,950. Tuition installment plan (SMART Tuition Payment Plan, individually arranged payment plans). Need-based scholarship grants available.

Admissions Wechsler Intelligence Scale for Children III required. Deadline for receipt of application materials: none. No application fee required. On-campus interview recommended.

Athletics Interscholastic: basketball (boys, girls), cross-country running (b,g), fitness (g), handball (b,g), horseback riding (b,g), running (b,g), soccer (b,g), wilderness (g); intramural: cheering (g), soccer (b,g); coed interscholastic: basketball, cross-country running, handball, horseback riding, running, soccer; coed intramural: aerobics/dance, archery, basketball, bicycling, billiards, cooperative games, cross-country running, dance, drill team, equestrian sports, fishing, fitness, Frisbee, hiking/backpacking, horseback riding, in-line skating, indoor soccer, jogging, kickball, lacrosse, mountain biking, outdoor activities, outdoor adventure, outdoor education, outdoor recreation, outdoor skills, outdoors, paddle tennis, physical fitness, physical training, roller blading, roller skating, running, skateboarding, soccer, softball, swimming and diving, table tennis, tennis, volleyball, walking, wilderness, yoga. 1 PE instructor, 4 coaches.

Computers Computers are regularly used in English, literacy, reading, remedial study skills, research skills, social studies, study skills, word processing, writing classes. Computer network features include Internet access. The school has a published electronic and media policy.

Contact Miss Abigail Sprague, Admissions Director. 434-293-9059. Fax: 434-296-8930. E-mail: admissions@oaklandschool.net. Website: www.oaklandschool.net

PACE/BRANTLEY HALL HIGH SCHOOL

3221 Sand Lake Road
Longwood, Florida 32779

Head of School: Ms. Pamela Tapley

General Information Coeducational day college-preparatory and general academic school; primarily serves underachievers and students with learning disabilities. Grades 2–12. Founded: 1972. Setting: suburban. Nearest major city is Orlando. 9-acre campus. 2 buildings on campus. Approved or accredited by Florida Council of Independent Schools. Total enrollment: 171. Upper school average class size: 12. Upper school faculty-student ratio: 1:12. There are 180 required school days per year for Upper School students. Upper School students typically attend 5 days per week. The average school day consists of 7 hours.

Faculty School total: 28. In upper school: 5 men, 8 women; 5 have advanced degrees.

Subjects Offered 1 1/2 elective credits, ACT preparation, algebra, American history, American literature, anatomy and physiology, anthropology, archaeology, art, basketball, biology, business skills, career and personal planning, career/college preparation, character education, chemistry, civics, college admission preparation, college awareness, college planning, communication skills, creative writing, criminology, critical thinking, critical writing, debate, drama, drama performance, drama workshop, economics, English, English literature, fine arts, fitness, forensics, gardening, geography, geometry, government, government/civics, grammar, health and wellness, health education, history of rock and roll, lab science, language arts, language of the theater, leadership, marine science, mathematics, physical education, physical science, psychology, public speaking, reading, science, social sciences, social studies, speech, theater, world geography, world history, writing, yoga.

Graduation Requirements Arts and fine arts (art, music, dance, drama), English, foreign language, mathematics, physical education (includes health), reading, science, social studies (includes history), high school competency test.

Special Academic Programs 1 Advanced Placement exam for which test preparation is offered; honors section; study at local college for college credit; academic accommodation for the gifted; remedial reading and/or remedial writing; remedial math; programs in English, mathematics, general development for dyslexic students.

College Admission Counseling 15 students graduated in 2016; 10 went to college, including Florida Atlantic University; Seminole State College of Florida; Stetson University; University of North Florida; Valencia College. Other: 1 went to work, 2 entered a postgraduate year, 2 had other specific plans.

Student Life Upper grades have uniform requirement, student council, honor system. Discipline rests primarily with faculty.

Summer Programs Remediation, enrichment, advancement, computer instruction programs offered; session focuses on course work and orientation for incoming students; held on campus; accepts boys and girls; not open to students from other schools. 25 students usually enrolled. 2017 schedule: June 12 to June 29. Application deadline: May 1.

Tuition and Aid Day student tuition: $15,685–$15,885. Tuition installment plan (monthly payment plans, individually arranged payment plans, semiannual payment plan). Tuition reduction for siblings, need-based scholarship grants, McKay Scholarship, PLSA, Step Up For Students available. In 2016–17, 90% of upper-school students received aid. Total amount of financial aid awarded in 2016–17: $28,000.

Admissions Traditional secondary-level entrance grade is 9. Traditional secondary-level entrance age is 14. For fall 2016, 55 students applied for upper-level admission, 42 were accepted, 178 enrolled. Academic Profile Tests, ACT, Cognitive Abilities Test, PSAT and SAT for applicants to grade 11 and 12, PSAT or SAT for applicants to grade 11 and 12, SAT and WRAT required. Deadline for receipt of application materials: none. Application fee required: $550. On-campus interview recommended.

Athletics Interscholastic: basketball (boys); coed interscholastic: physical fitness; coed intramural: fishing, flag football, jogging, kickball, outdoor activities, running, soccer, Special Olympics, tennis, track and field, volleyball, yoga. 1 PE instructor, 2 coaches.

Computers Computers are regularly used in business education, career exploration, college planning, desktop publishing, graphic arts, keyboarding, life skills, mathematics, science, social sciences, social studies, word processing, writing classes. Computer network features include on-campus library services, Internet access, wireless campus network, Internet filtering or blocking technology. Campus intranet, student e-mail accounts, and computer access in designated common areas are available to students. Students grades are available online. The school has a published electronic and media policy.

Contact Mrs. Pamela Bellet, Director of Admission. 407-869-8882. Fax: 407-869-8717. E-mail: pbellet@pacebrantley.org. Website: www.pacebrantley.org

THE PATHWAY SCHOOL

162 Egypt Road
Jeffersonville, Pennsylvania 19403

Head of School: Mr. David Schultheis

General Information Coeducational day general academic, technology, life skills/functional academics, and pre-vocational/career education school; primarily serves underachievers, students with learning disabilities, individuals with Attention Deficit Disorder, individuals with emotional and behavioral problems, students w/ Autism, students w/ neuropsychiatric disorders, Asperger's Syndrome, emotional disturbance, and students needing speech/language therapy and occupational therapy. Ungraded, ages 5–21. Founded: 1961. Setting: suburban. Nearest major city is Philadelphia. 12-acre campus. 12 buildings on campus. Approved or accredited by Pennsylvania Department of Education. Endowment: $1 million. Total enrollment: 135. Upper school average class size: 8. Upper school faculty-student ratio: 1:4. There are 182 required school days per year for Upper School students. Upper School students typically attend 5 days per week. The average school day consists of 5 hours and 30 minutes.

Faculty School total: 23. In upper school: 2 men, 8 women; 4 have advanced degrees.

Subjects Offered Algebra, art, biology, career education, career experience, career/college preparation, computer skills, consumer mathematics, creative arts, drama, earth science, electives, English, environmental science, general math, geometry, health education, history, horticulture, interpersonal skills, language arts, mathematics, money management, physical education, pre-vocational education, senior seminar, social skills, social studies, work experience, world history.

Graduation Requirements Graduation requirements are as specified by the sending school district.

Special Academic Programs Study at local college for college credit; remedial reading and/or remedial writing; remedial math; programs in general development for dyslexic students; special instructional classes for deaf students, blind students, emotional support program.

College Admission Counseling 6 students graduated in 2016; 1 went to college. Other: 5 went to work.

Student Life Upper grades have student council, honor system. Discipline rests equally with students and faculty.

Summer Programs Remediation, enrichment, sports, art/fine arts, computer instruction programs offered; session focuses on providing consistency for the entire calendar year; expanding on learning opportunities through experiences; held on campus; accepts boys and girls; open to students from other schools. 110 students usually enrolled. 2017 schedule: July 5 to August 15.

Tuition and Aid Day student tuition: $49,500–$51,000. Tuition installment plan (individually arranged payment plans).

Admissions Traditional secondary-level entrance age is 15. For fall 2016, 29 students applied for upper-level admission, 14 were accepted, 14 enrolled. Deadline for receipt of application materials: none. No application fee required. On-campus interview recommended.

Athletics Interscholastic: basketball (boys, girls), softball (b,g), Special Olympics (b,g); coed interscholastic: soccer, Special Olympics; coed intramural: basketball, flag football, soccer. 2 PE instructors, 2 coaches.

Computers Computers are regularly used in basic skills, business education, business skills, career education, college planning, data processing, English, history, life skills, mathematics, newspaper, research skills, senior seminar, typing, writing classes. Computer network features include Internet access, wireless campus network, Internet filtering or blocking technology, computer access in classroom, tablet technology provided to all students. Student e-mail accounts and computer access in designated common areas are available to students. Students grades are available online. The school has a published electronic and media policy.

Contact Mrs. Diana Phifer, Director of Admissions. 610-277-0660 Ext. 289. Fax: 610-539-1493. E-mail: dphifer@pathwayschool.org. Website: www.pathwayschool.org

PERKINS SCHOOL FOR THE BLIND

175 North Beacon Street
Watertown, Massachusetts 02172

Head of School: Dave Power

General Information Coeducational boarding and day college-preparatory and general academic school; primarily serves underachievers, students with learning disabilities, and blindness, vision impairment, and deafblindness. Grades K–12. Setting: suburban. Nearest major city is Boston. Students are housed in coed dormitories. 38-acre campus. 9 buildings on campus. Approved or accredited by Massachusetts Department of Education, New England Association of Schools and Colleges, and Massachusetts Department of Education. Member of National Association of Independent Schools. Upper school average class size: 5. There are 205 required school days per year for Upper School students. Upper School students typically attend 5 days per week. The average school day consists of 7 hours and 30 minutes.

Upper School Student Profile Grade 6: 14 students (10 boys, 4 girls); Grade 7: 7 students (5 boys, 2 girls); Grade 8: 8 students (5 boys, 3 girls); Grade 9: 8 students (3 boys, 5 girls); Grade 10: 9 students (5 boys, 4 girls); Grade 11: 27 students (19 boys, 8 girls); Grade 12: 43 students (27 boys, 16 girls). 55% of students are boarding students. 78% are state residents. 12 states are represented in upper school student body.

Faculty In upper school: 20 reside on campus.

Special Academic Programs Special instructional classes for blind students.

College Admission Counseling 12 students graduated in 2016; 2 went to college, including Lesley University; Northpoint Bible College. Other: 5 went to work, 1 entered a postgraduate year, 5 had other specific plans.

Student Life Upper grades have student council. Discipline rests primarily with faculty.

Summer Programs Held on campus; accepts boys and girls; open to students from other schools. 2017 schedule: June 26 to July 28.

Tuition and Aid Tuition installment plan (monthly payment plans).

Admissions Traditional secondary-level entrance grade is 9. No application fee required. On-campus interview recommended.

Contact Carol Kinlan, Director of Admissions and Enrollment. 617-972-7862. Fax: 617-972-7715. E-mail: admissions@perkins.org. Website: www.perkins.org

SEDONA SKY ACADEMY

PO Box 230
Rimrock, Arizona 86335

Head of School: Tammy Dehrmann

General Information Girls' boarding college-preparatory and general academic school; primarily serves students with learning disabilities, individuals with Attention Deficit Disorder, and individuals with emotional and behavioral problems. Grades 9–12. Founded: 1998. Setting: rural. Nearest major city is Sedona. Students are housed in single-sex dormitories. 30-acre campus. 8 buildings on campus. Approved or accredited by CITA (Commission on International and Trans-Regional Accreditation) and Arizona Department of Education. Total enrollment: 90. Upper school average class size: 8. Upper school faculty-student ratio: 1:7. Upper School students typically attend 5 days per week. The average school day consists of 6 hours.

Upper School Student Profile Grade 9: 6 students (6 girls); Grade 10: 6 students (6 girls); Grade 11: 6 students (6 girls); Grade 12: 6 students (6 girls). 100% of students are boarding students. 20% are state residents. 22 states are represented in upper school student body. 10% are international students. International students from Canada, Singapore, United Arab Emirates, and United States.

Faculty School total: 5. In upper school: 2 men, 3 women; 3 have advanced degrees; 1 resides on campus.

Subjects Offered ACT preparation, acting, adolescent issues, advanced math, algebra, American Civil War, American government, American history, American literature, ancient history, ancient world history, applied arts, applied music, art, art and culture, art appreciation, art education, art history, arts, athletic training, athletics, ballet, ballet technique, basketball, biology, botany, British literature, business, business communications, business mathematics, calculus, career planning, character education, chemistry, child development, choir, chorus, civics, Civil War, civil war history, college admission preparation, college awareness, college counseling, college placement, college planning, college writing, communication skills, communications, community garden, community service, comparative civilizations, composition, computer applications, computer education, computer graphics, computer literacy, computer math, computer science, computer skills, computers, consumer mathematics, contemporary art, contemporary history, contemporary issues, creative arts, creative dance, creative writing, current events, dance, dance performance, decision making skills, drama, drama performance, drama workshop, dramatic arts, drawing, drawing and design, earth science, economics, economics and history, electives, English, English composition, English literature, equality and freedom, equestrian sports, equine management, equine science, ethical decision making, European history, European literature, experiential education, female experience in America, film appreciation, fine arts, fitness, food and nutrition, foreign language, foreign policy, French, gender issues, general science, geography, geology, geometry, global studies, government, government/civics, grammar, graphic arts, health, health and safety, health and wellness, health education, health science, heritage of American Women, history, history of dance, history of drama, home economics, human biology, human development, human sexuality, independent living, international studies, intro to computers, jazz dance, journalism, lab/keyboard, language, language and composition, language arts, leadership, leadership education training, learning strategies, library, life issues, life management skills, life skills, linear algebra, literature, literature by women, math applications, mathematics, modern dance, modern languages, moral and social development, music, music appreciation, music composition, music history, music performance, musical productions, musical theater, nature study, news writing, newspaper, non-Western literature, nutrition, oil painting, parenting, participation in sports, peer counseling, performing arts, personal development, personal growth, physical education, physics, play production, poetry, political science, political systems, portfolio art, pre-calculus, psychology, SAT preparation, SAT/ACT preparation, science, sex education, sexuality, Shakespeare, Shakespearean histories, social issues, sociology, softball, Spanish, Spanish literature, speech, speech and debate, sports, sports conditioning, stage and body movement, state history, statistics, student government, student publications, studio art, study skills, tap dance, theater, theater arts, theater history, theater production, trigonometry, U.S. government, U.S. government and politics, U.S. history, U.S. literature, visual and performing arts, visual arts, vocal music, volleyball, water color painting, weight fitness, weightlifting, wellness, Western literature, women in literature, women's health, women's literature, world civilizations, world cultures, world geography, world history, world studies, writing, writing, yoga.

Graduation Requirements Option of traditional academic graduation as well as graduation from the therapeutic side of school.

Special Academic Programs Accelerated programs; independent study; study at local college for college credit; academic accommodation for the gifted, the musically talented, and the artistically talented; programs in English, mathematics for dyslexic students; special instructional classes for honor all IEP accomodations.

College Admission Counseling 15 students graduated in 2016; all went to college, including California State University, East Bay; California State University Channel Islands; Central Michigan University; College of Charleston; San Diego State University; University of Michigan.

Student Life Upper grades have student council, honor system. Discipline rests primarily with faculty.

Tuition and Aid Middle-income loans available. In 2016–17, 30% of upper-school students received aid. Total amount of financial aid awarded in 2016–17: $81,600.

Admissions Traditional secondary-level entrance grade is 10. For fall 2016, 250 students applied for upper-level admission, 150 were accepted, 60 enrolled. ACT or SAT required. Deadline for receipt of application materials: none. No application fee required.

Athletics Interscholastic: basketball, soccer, softball, volleyball; intramural: aerobics, aerobics/dance, badminton, ballet, basketball, cross-country running, dance, fitness, fitness walking, horseback riding, jogging, modern dance, physical fitness, physical training, soccer, softball, track and field, walking, yoga. 2 PE instructors, 1 coach, 1 athletic trainer.

Computers Computers are regularly used in all academic, career exploration, college planning, creative writing, current events, dance, drawing and design, foreign language, graphic arts, independent study, life skills, music, psychology, remedial study skills, research skills, SAT preparation, Spanish, study skills, writing classes. Computer network features include Internet access, Internet filtering or blocking technology. Student e-mail accounts are available to students. Students grades are available online. The school has a published electronic and media policy.

Contact Stephanie Coleman, Admissions Counselor. 877-617-1222 Ext. 116. Fax: 928-567-1323. E-mail: stephaniecoleman@sedonasky.org. Website: www.coppercanyonacademy.com

SHELTON SCHOOL AND EVALUATION CENTER

15720 Hillcrest Road
Dallas, Texas 75248

Head of School: Linda Kneese

General Information Coeducational day college-preparatory and general academic school; primarily serves students with learning disabilities, individuals with Attention Deficit Disorder, and dyslexic students. Grades PS–12. Founded: 1976. Setting: suburban. 1-acre campus. 1 building on campus. Approved or accredited by Independent Schools Association of the Southwest. Endowment: $6.7 million. Total enrollment: 895. Upper school average class size: 8. Upper school faculty-student ratio: 1:10. There are 166 required school days per year for Upper School students. Upper School students typically attend 5 days per week. The average school day consists of 6 hours.

Upper School Student Profile Grade 9: 86 students (50 boys, 36 girls); Grade 10: 70 students (43 boys, 27 girls); Grade 11: 75 students (44 boys, 31 girls); Grade 12: 69 students (43 boys, 26 girls).

Faculty School total: 138. In upper school: 14 men, 25 women; 16 have advanced degrees.

Subjects Offered All academic, American sign language, ethics, Spanish, theater arts.

Graduation Requirements Arts and fine arts (art, music, dance, drama), computers, English, ethics, foreign language, mathematics, physical education (includes health), reading, science, social studies (includes history), speech.

Special Academic Programs Programs in English, mathematics, general development for dyslexic students.

College Admission Counseling 51 students graduated in 2016; 49 went to college, including Albright College; Arkansas State University; Baylor University; Collin County Community College District; Savannah College of Art and Design; Texas Christian University. Other: 2 had other specific plans.

Student Life Upper grades have uniform requirement, student council, honor system. Discipline rests primarily with faculty.

Summer Programs Enrichment programs offered; session focuses on enrichment; held on campus; accepts boys and girls; open to students from other schools. 39 students usually enrolled. 2017 schedule: June 26 to July 20. Application deadline: May 5.

Tuition and Aid Day student tuition: $26,000. Tuition installment plan (SMART Tuition Payment Plan, FACTS Tuition Payment Plan, Sallie Mae). Need-based scholarship grants available. In 2016–17, 17% of upper-school students received aid. Total amount of financial aid awarded in 2016–17: $516,800.

Admissions Traditional secondary-level entrance grade is 9. For fall 2016, 61 students applied for upper-level admission, 26 were accepted, 22 enrolled. WISC/Woodcock-Johnson required. Deadline for receipt of application materials: none. No application fee required. On-campus interview required.

Athletics Interscholastic: baseball (boys), basketball (b,g), cheering (g), cross-country running (b,g), dance squad (g), drill team (g), football (b), tennis (b,g), track and field (b,g), volleyball (g); coed interscholastic: golf, physical training, soccer, strength & conditioning, swimming and diving. 4 PE instructors, 2 coaches, 1 athletic trainer.

Computers Computers are regularly used in all academic, English, foreign language, information technology, lab/keyboard, library, research skills, SAT preparation, video film production classes. Computer network features include on-campus library services, Internet access, wireless campus network, Internet filtering or blocking technology. Campus intranet, student e-mail accounts, and computer access in designated common areas are available to students. Students grades are available online. The school has a published electronic and media policy.

Contact Diann Slaton, Director of Admission. 972-774-1772. Fax: 972-991-3977. E-mail: dslaton@shelton.org. Website: www.shelton.org

THE SIENA SCHOOL

9727 Georgia Avenue
Silver Spring, Maryland 20910

Head of School: Ms. Jillian Darefsky

General Information Coeducational day college-preparatory, general academic, technology, and Experiential Education school; primarily serves students with learning disabilities, individuals with Attention Deficit Disorder, and dyslexic students. Grades 4–12. Setting: suburban. 3-acre campus. 1 building on campus. Approved or accredited by Middle States Association of Colleges and Schools and Maryland Department of Education. Member of National Association of Independent Schools. Upper school average class size: 10. Upper school faculty-student ratio: 1:10. There are 174 required school days per year for Upper School students. Upper School students typically attend 5 days per week. The average school day consists of 7 hours.

Upper School Student Profile Grade 6: 13 students (6 boys, 7 girls); Grade 7: 20 students (9 boys, 11 girls); Grade 8: 20 students (13 boys, 7 girls); Grade 9: 12 students (7 boys, 5 girls); Grade 10: 10 students (5 boys, 5 girls); Grade 11: 10 students (4 boys, 6 girls); Grade 12: 10 students (6 boys, 4 girls).

Faculty School total: 33. In upper school: 8 men, 7 women; 12 have advanced degrees.

Subjects Offered 20th century history, 20th century world history, 3-dimensional art, ACT preparation, acting, algebra, American government, American history, art, art history, audio visual/media, biology, calculus, carpentry, chemistry, college counseling, computer literacy, creative writing, digital photography, drama, earth science, ecology, environmental systems, English, experimental science, geometry, global studies, language arts, multimedia design, music composition, physical education, pre-algebra, pre-calculus, reading, senior internship, Spanish, trigonometry, U.S. history, world history.

Special Academic Programs Independent study; term-away projects; academic accommodation for the gifted; remedial reading and/or remedial writing; remedial math; programs in English, mathematics, general development for dyslexic students.

College Admission Counseling 10 students graduated in 2016; 8 went to college, including American University; Champlain College; Johnson & Wales University; McDaniel College; Towson University; University of Vermont. Other: 1 went to work, 1 had other specific plans. Median composite ACT: 21. 22% scored over 26 on composite ACT.

Student Life Upper grades have specified standards of dress. Discipline rests primarily with faculty.

Summer Programs Remediation, enrichment, art/fine arts programs offered; session focuses on review, reinforcement, and enhancement of academic skills; held on campus; accepts boys and girls; open to students from other schools. 50 students usually enrolled. 2017 schedule: June 29 to July 31. Application deadline: May 31.

Tuition and Aid Day student tuition: $38,281. Tuition installment plan (FACTS Tuition Payment Plan). Need-based scholarship grants available. In 2016–17, 33% of upper-school students received aid. Total amount of financial aid awarded in 2016–17: $270,000.

Admissions Traditional secondary-level entrance grade is 9. For fall 2016, 31 students applied for upper-level admission, 6 were accepted, 4 enrolled. WISC/Woodcock-Johnson required. Deadline for receipt of application materials: none. Application fee required: $110. On-campus interview required.

Athletics Interscholastic: basketball (boys, girls), cross-country running (b,g), flag football (b), judo (b,g), soccer (b,g), tennis (b,g), volleyball (g); coed interscholastic: horseback riding, softball, yoga. 1 PE instructor, 12 coaches.

Computers Computers are regularly used in all classes. Computer network features include Internet access, wireless campus network, Internet filtering or blocking technology. Student e-mail accounts and computer access in designated common areas are available to students. Students grades are available online. The school has a published electronic and media policy.

Contact Ms. Bekah Atkinson, Director of Admissions. 301-244-3600. Fax: 301-244-3601. E-mail: info@thesienaschool.org. Website: www.thesienaschool.org/

SMITH SCHOOL

131 West 86 Street

New York, New York 10024

Head of School: Mrs. Karen Smith

General Information Coeducational day college-preparatory, arts, and art, music, drama and technology programs school. Grades 7–12. Founded: 1990. Setting: urban. 1 building on campus. Approved or accredited by Middle States Association of Colleges and Schools, New York State Association of Independent Schools, New York State Board of Regents, and New York Department of Education. Total enrollment: 57. Upper school average class size: 4. Upper school faculty-student ratio: 1:4. There are 160 required school days per year for Upper School students. Upper School students typically attend 5 days per week. The average school day consists of 6 hours and 30 minutes.

Upper School Student Profile Grade 9: 10 students (4 boys, 6 girls); Grade 10: 11 students (4 boys, 7 girls); Grade 11: 9 students (4 boys, 5 girls); Grade 12: 12 students (5 boys, 7 girls).

Faculty School total: 14. In upper school: 6 men, 8 women; all have advanced degrees.

Subjects Offered Algebra, American history, anatomy and physiology, animation, applied music, art, arts and crafts, biology, calculus, career/college preparation, cartooning/animation, character education, chemistry, college admission preparation, college counseling, college placement, college writing, computer animation, computer programming, computer skills, drama, earth science, English, English literature, environmental science, environmental studies, European history, film, French, French as a second language, general science, geometry, health and wellness, interpersonal skills, lab science, life science, life skills, oceanography, peer counseling, physical education, physical science, physics, pre-calculus, service learning/internship, Spanish, speech therapy, student government, trigonometry, U.S. government, U.S. government and politics, U.S. history, Web site design, world history, world studies, yearbook, yoga.

Graduation Requirements Algebra, biology, conceptual physics, earth science, environmental science, European history, geometry, languages, physical science, pre-algebra, pre-calculus, trigonometry, mandatory extracurricular activity involvement, 100 hours of community service completed.

Special Academic Programs Honors section; accelerated programs; independent study; study at local college for college credit; academic accommodation for the musically talented and the artistically talented; remedial reading and/or remedial writing; remedial math; programs in English, mathematics, general development for dyslexic students; special instructional classes for peer mediation, socialization, and motivational issues.

College Admission Counseling 9 students graduated in 2016; all went to college, including American University; Binghamton University, State University of New York; City College of the City University of New York; Emerson College; Fordham University; Pratt Institute. Median SAT critical reading: 600, median SAT math: 620, median SAT writing: 620, median combined SAT: 600. 50% scored over 600 on SAT critical reading, 40% scored over 600 on SAT math, 50% scored over 600 on SAT writing, 45% scored over 1800 on combined SAT, 60% scored over 26 on composite ACT.

Student Life Upper grades have student council, honor system. Discipline rests primarily with faculty.

Summer Programs Remediation, enrichment, advancement, art/fine arts, computer instruction programs offered; session focuses on academic courses for enrichment, remediation, or credit; held both on and off campus; accepts boys and girls; open to students from other schools. 25 students usually enrolled. 2017 schedule: June 19 to August 2. Application deadline: June 1.

Tuition and Aid Day student tuition: $43,500–$45,500. Tuition installment plan (monthly payment plans, individually arranged payment plans, quarterly payment plan). Tuition reduction for siblings available. In 2016–17, 10% of upper-school students received aid.

Admissions Traditional secondary-level entrance grade is 9. Comprehensive educational evaluation, psychoeducational evaluation, school placement exam, Wide Range Achievement Test or writing sample required. Deadline for receipt of application materials: none. Application fee required: $50. On-campus interview recommended.

Athletics Coed Interscholastic: aerobics, basketball, cooperative games, dance, fitness, fitness walking, outdoor activities, physical fitness, physical training, running, ultimate Frisbee, volleyball, walking, yoga; coed intramural: basketball, cooperative games. 3 PE instructors, 3 coaches.

Computers Computers are regularly used in research skills, writing classes. Computer network features include Internet access, wireless campus network, Internet filtering or blocking technology, yearbook and monthly newsletter. Campus intranet, student e-mail accounts, and computer access in designated common areas are available to students. Students grades are available online. The school has a published electronic and media policy.

Contact Ms. Gladys Lopez, Executive Assistant. 212-879-6317. Fax: 212-879-0962. E-mail: glopez@smithschool.org. Website: www.smithschool.org

SUMMIT PREPARATORY SCHOOL

1605 Danielson Road

Kalispell, Montana 59901

Head of School: Todd Fiske, M.Ed

General Information Coeducational boarding college-preparatory and arts school; primarily serves students with learning disabilities, individuals with Attention Deficit Disorder, individuals with emotional and behavioral problems, dyslexic students, college-bound students with depression, anxiety, family conflict, and substance abuse, adoption issues, trauma, ADHD, mild learning disabilities. Grades 9–12. Founded: 2003. Setting: rural. Students are housed in single-sex dormitories. 540-acre campus. 1 building on campus. Approved or accredited by Association for Experiential Education, Northwest Association of Independent Schools, and Montana Department of Education. Total enrollment: 62. Upper school average class size: 10. Upper school faculty-student ratio: 1:8. Upper School students typically attend 5 days per week. The average school day consists of 5 hours.

Upper School Student Profile 100% of students are boarding students. 1% are state residents. 25 states are represented in upper school student body. 2% are international students. International students from Belgium, Honduras, and Mexico.

Faculty School total: 9. In upper school: 4 men, 5 women; 6 have advanced degrees.

Subjects Offered Algebra, American history, American literature, anatomy and physiology, art, astronomy, basketball, biology, British literature, calculus, ceramics, chemistry, choral music, composition, computer applications, drama, drawing, earth science, fitness, geometry, global studies, government, guitar, healthful living, interpersonal skills, journalism, painting, physical education, physics, poetry, portfolio art, pre-algebra, pre-calculus, SAT/ACT preparation, science fiction, sculpture, Shakespeare, Spanish, speech and debate, studio art, substance abuse, swimming, trigonometry, U.S. government, weight training, wilderness experience, world history.

Graduation Requirements Electives, English, government, history, mathematics, physical fitness, science, completion of therapeutic program, which includes individual, group, and family therapy, and follows the student through a series of four therapeutic stages.

Special Academic Programs Accelerated programs; independent study; study at local college for college credit; academic accommodation for the gifted; remedial reading and/or remedial writing; remedial math; programs in general development for dyslexic students.

College Admission Counseling 20 students graduated in 2015; 19 went to college, including Mississippi State University; Montana State University; New York University; Savannah College of Art and Design; The Ohio State University; University of Montana.

Student Life Upper grades have specified standards of dress, student council. Discipline rests primarily with faculty.

Tuition and Aid 7-day tuition and room/board: $99,600. Tuition installment plan (monthly payment plans, individually arranged payment plans). Need-based scholarship grants available. In 2015–16, 30% of upper-school students received aid. Total amount of financial aid awarded in 2015–16: $100,000.

Admissions Individual IQ, Achievement and behavior rating scale, psychoeducational evaluation, Rorschach or Thematic Apperception Test or WISC or WAIS required. Deadline for receipt of application materials: none. No application fee required. Interview recommended.

Athletics Interscholastic: basketball (boys, girls), indoor soccer (b,g), martial arts (b,g), soccer (b,g), tennis (b,g), volleyball (g), winter soccer (b,g); intramural: aerobics (b,g), alpine skiing (b,g), aquatics (b,g), backpacking (b,g), basketball (b,g), billiards (b,g), blading (b,g), bowling (b,g), broomball (b,g), canoeing/kayaking (b,g), climbing (b,g), cooperative games (b,g), cross-country running (b,g), fishing (b,g), fitness (b,g), floor hockey (b,g), fly fishing (b,g), Frisbee (b,g), golf (b,g), hiking/backpacking (b,g), horseback riding (b,g), ice skating (b,g), indoor soccer (b,g), indoor track (b,g), jogging (b,g), kayaking (b,g), lacrosse (b,g), martial arts (b,g), mountaineering (b,g), nordic skiing (b,g), outdoor activities (b,g), outdoor skills (b,g), physical fitness (b,g), physical training (b,g), rafting (b,g), rock climbing (b,g), roller blading (b,g), ropes courses (b,g), running (b,g), skateboarding (b,g), skiing (cross-country) (b,g), skiing (downhill) (b,g), snowboarding (b,g), snowshoeing (b,g), soccer (b,g), softball (b,g), strength & conditioning (b,g), swimming and diving (b,g), tennis (b,g), ultimate Frisbee (b,g), volleyball (b,g), walking (b,g), wall climbing (b,g), water polo (b,g), weight lifting (b,g), weight training (b,g), winter walking (b,g), wrestling (b), yoga (b,g); coed interscholastic: indoor soccer, mountain biking, tennis, winter soccer; coed intramural: bicycling, bowling, cooperative games, cross-country running, indoor soccer, mountain biking, outdoor activities, outdoor skills, rock climbing, tennis. 1 PE instructor, 3 coaches.

Computers Computers are regularly used in all academic, business, creative writing, writing classes. Computer network features include on-campus library services, Internet filtering or blocking technology, supervised access only to Internet. Students grades are available online.

Contact Judy Heleva, M.A., Director of Admissions. 406-758-8113. Fax: 406-758-8150. E-mail: jheleva@summitprepschool.org. Website: www.summitprepschool.org

SUNRISE ACADEMY

65 North 1150 West
Hurricane, Utah 84737

Head of School: Ms. Janette Thompson

General Information Girls' boarding college-preparatory and general academic school; primarily serves underachievers, students with learning disabilities, individuals with Attention Deficit Disorder, individuals with emotional and behavioral problems, and dyslexic students. Grades 7–12. Distance learning grades 7–12. Founded: 2000. Setting: small town. Nearest major city is St. George. Students are housed in single-sex dormitories. 6-acre campus. 1 building on campus. Approved or accredited by Utah Department of Education. Total enrollment: 32. Upper school average class size: 10. Upper school faculty-student ratio: 1:4. There are 199 required school days per year for Upper School students. Upper School students typically attend 5 days per week. The average school day consists of 7 hours.

Upper School Student Profile Grade 8: 6 students (6 girls); Grade 9: 10 students (10 girls); Grade 10: 21 students (21 girls); Grade 11: 13 students (13 girls); Grade 12: 10 students (10 girls). 100% of students are boarding students. 1% are state residents. 41 states are represented in upper school student body. 13% are international students. International students from Bermuda, Canada, Cayman Islands, Hong Kong, United Kingdom, and United States; 8 other countries represented in student body.

Faculty School total: 6. In upper school: 4 men, 2 women; 3 have advanced degrees.

Subjects Offered 20th century physics, 20th century world history, ACT preparation, addiction, adolescent issues, advanced biology, advanced chemistry, advanced math, aerobics, algebra, alternative physical education, American government, American history, American legal systems, American literature, American studies, anatomy, anatomy and physiology, ancient history, ancient world history, applied arts, art, arts, arts and crafts, athletic training, athletics, backpacking, basic skills, biology, body human, botany, calculus, career and personal planning, career and technology systems, career education, career experience, career exploration, career planning, career technology, career/college preparation, careers, chemistry, cinematography, civil rights, college awareness, college counseling, college planning, college writing, communication skills, community service, computer skills, computers, conflict resolution, consumer economics, consumer mathematics, crafts, creative arts, creative dance, creative drama, creative thinking, creative writing, critical studies in film, critical thinking, critical writing, culinary arts, current events, current history, dance, dance performance, decision making skills, digital photography, drama, drama performance, drawing, driver education, earth and space science, earth science, economics, electives, English, English composition, English literature, environmental science, equine management, equine science, ethical decision making, ethics, ethics and responsibility, European civilization, exercise science, experiential education, experimental science, family and consumer science, family living, family studies, film and literature, finance, first aid, fitness, food and nutrition, foods, foreign language, foundations of civilization, French, general science, geography, geology, geometry, government, government/civics, grammar, guidance, health, health and wellness, health education, health enhancement, health science, healthful living, high adventure outdoor program, history, history of the Americas, honors algebra, honors English, honors geometry, honors U.S. history, honors world history, human anatomy, human biology, human relations, human sexuality, independent living, independent study, integrated science, Internet research, internship, interpersonal skills, introduction to literature, introduction to theater, jewelry making, journalism, keyboarding, kinesiology, lab science, language and composition, language arts, Latin, leadership, learning cognition, learning lab, learning strategies, life issues, life management skills, life science, life skills, math applications, math methods, math review, mathematics, meditation, mentorship program, modern dance, modern history, modern politics, modern problems, modern Western civilization, modern world history, money management, moral and social development, moral reasoning, Native American history, Native American studies, nature study, nutrition, oral communications, outdoor education, parent/child development, participation in sports, peer counseling, performing arts, personal and social education, personal development, personal finance, personal fitness, personal growth, personal money management, photography, physical education, physical fitness, physical science, physics, physics-AP, political science, practical living, pre-algebra, pre-calculus, pre-college orientation, pre-vocational education, psychology, public service, reading, reading/study skills, relationships, remedial study skills, research, research and reference, research skills, SAT/ACT preparation, science, science research, senior career experience, service learning/internship, sex education, sexuality, Shakespeare, short story, skills for success, social education, social sciences, social skills, social studies, society and culture, sociology, softball, space and physical sciences, Spanish, sports medicine, strategies for success, student government, student publications, study skills, substance abuse, swimming, trigonometry, typing, U.S. constitutional history, U.S. government, U.S. government and politics, U.S. history, values and decisions, visual and performing arts, visual arts, vocational skills, vocational-technical courses, volleyball, weight fitness, weight training, weightlifting, wellness, Western civilization, women in literature, women in world history, women's health, women's studies, word processing, work-study, world civilizations, world geography, world history, writing, writing, writing workshop, yoga.

Graduation Requirements Therapeutic advancement and personal accountability.

Special Academic Programs Honors section; accelerated programs; independent study; study at local college for college credit; academic accommodation for the gifted;

remedial reading and/or remedial writing; remedial math; programs in English, mathematics, general development for dyslexic students.

College Admission Counseling 14 students graduated in 2016; all went to college, including Cornell University; Southern Utah University; The University of Arizona; University of California, Santa Barbara; University of Connecticut; Westminster College. Other: 6 went to work.

Student Life Upper grades have specified standards of dress, honor system. Discipline rests equally with students and faculty.

Summer Programs Remediation, enrichment, advancement, sports, art/fine arts, computer instruction programs offered; held both on and off campus; accepts girls; not open to students from other schools. 60 students usually enrolled. 2017 schedule: June 19 to July 28.

Tuition and Aid Guaranteed tuition plan. Tuition installment plan (The Tuition Plan, individually arranged payment plans).

Admissions Academic Profile Tests, ACT, admissions testing, battery of testing done through outside agency, Canadian Standardized Test, Cognitive Abilities Test, comprehensive educational evaluation, Diagnostic Achievement Battery-2 (for applicants from non-U.S. curriculum), Differential Aptitude Test, High School Placement Test, Individual IQ, Individual IQ, Achievement and behavior rating scale, math and English placement tests, Math Placement Exam, mathematics proficiency exam, non-standardized placement tests, Oral and Written Language Scales, placement test, PSAT, PSAT and SAT for applicants to grade 11 and 12, PSAT or SAT, PSAT or SAT for applicants to grade 11 and 12, PSAT, SAT, or ACT for applicants to grade 11 and 12 or psychoeducational evaluation required. Deadline for receipt of application materials: none. No application fee required. Interview required.

Athletics Interscholastic: aerobics, aerobics/dance, alpine skiing, aquatics, backpacking, ballet, basketball, bicycling, bowling, canoeing/kayaking, cheering, climbing, combined training, cooperative games, cross-country running, dance, equestrian sports, fishing, fitness, fitness walking, hiking/backpacking, horseback riding, independent competitive sports, jogging, modern dance, mountaineering, outdoor activities, outdoor adventure, outdoor education, outdoor recreation, outdoors, physical fitness, physical training, project adventure, rafting, rappelling, rock climbing, ropes courses, running, sand volleyball, skateboarding, skiing (downhill), snowboarding, soccer, softball, strength & conditioning, swimming and diving, volleyball, walking, weight lifting, weight training, yoga. 1 PE instructor, 1 coach, 1 athletic trainer.

Computers Computers are regularly used in all classes. Computer network features include on-campus library services, Internet access, wireless campus network, Internet filtering or blocking technology. Student e-mail accounts and computer access in designated common areas are available to students. Students grades are available online.

Contact Nicole Andra, Admissions Director. 435-635-1185. Fax: 435-635-1187. E-mail: nicolea@sunrisertc.com. Website: www.sunrisertc.com/

VALLEY VIEW SCHOOL

91 Oakham Road
PO Box 338
North Brookfield, Massachusetts 01535

Head of School: Dr. Philip G. Spiva

General Information Boys' boarding college-preparatory, general academic, arts, and vocational school; primarily serves underachievers, students with learning disabilities, individuals with Attention Deficit Disorder, individuals with emotional and behavioral problems, and difficulty socially adjusting to family and surroundings. Grades 6–12. Founded: 1970. Setting: small town. Nearest major city is Worcester. Students are housed in single-sex dormitories. 215-acre campus. 9 buildings on campus. Approved or accredited by Massachusetts Office of Child Care Services. Endowment: $675,000. Total enrollment: 33. Upper school average class size: 5. Upper school faculty-student ratio: 1:4. There are 191 required school days per year for Upper School students. Upper School students typically attend 5 days per week.

Upper School Student Profile 100% of students are boarding students. 10% are state residents. 25 states are represented in upper school student body. 15% are international students. International students from Canada, France, Kenya, Mexico, and United Arab Emirates; 3 other countries represented in student body.

Faculty School total: 11. In upper school: 6 men, 4 women; 4 have advanced degrees; 2 reside on campus.

Subjects Offered Algebra, American literature, anatomy, art, biology, chemistry, civics, composition, computer math, computer science, creative writing, drama, drama performance, drama workshop, dramatic arts, drawing, drawing and design, driver education, earth and space science, earth science, Eastern world civilizations, ecology, environmental systems, economics, economics and history, economics-AP, electronics, English, English composition, English language and composition-AP, English language-AP, English literature, English literature and composition-AP, English literature-AP, English-AP, English/composition-AP, environmental education, environmental geography, environmental science, environmental science-AP, epic literature, ethics and responsibility, ethnic studies, European history, European history-AP, general science, geography, geometry, government, grammar, health, history, life science, literature, mathematics, music, physical education, physical science, science,

social studies, Spanish, study skills, theater, U.S. history, Western civilization, world history, world literature, writing, zoology.
Graduation Requirements English, mathematics, physical education (includes health), science, social studies (includes history).
Special Academic Programs Remedial reading and/or remedial writing; remedial math.
College Admission Counseling 1 student graduated in 2015 and went to college.
Student Life Upper grades have specified standards of dress, student council, honor system. Discipline rests primarily with faculty.
Tuition and Aid 7-day tuition and room/board: $73,645. Tuition installment plan (quarterly payment plan).
Admissions Academic Profile Tests required. Deadline for receipt of application materials: none. No application fee required. On-campus interview required.
Athletics Interscholastic: basketball, cross-country running, golf, lacrosse, running, soccer, softball, tennis, ultimate Frisbee; intramural: alpine skiing, archery, backpacking, baseball, basketball, bicycling, billiards, blading, bocce, bowling, canoeing/kayaking, climbing, cross-country running, fishing, fitness, flag football, floor hockey, Frisbee, golf, hiking/backpacking, ice hockey, ice skating, in-line skating, indoor hockey, martial arts, mountain biking, outdoor recreation, outdoors, physical fitness, riflery, rock climbing, roller blading, running, skateboarding, skiing (cross-country), skiing (downhill), snowboarding, softball, street hockey, swimming and diving, table tennis, touch football, ultimate Frisbee, volleyball, wall climbing, weight lifting, whiffle ball. 2 PE instructors.
Computers Computers are regularly used in art, English, mathematics, science classes. Computer network features include Internet access, wireless campus network. Student e-mail accounts are available to students.
Contact Mr. Rick Bulger, Associate Director. 508-867-6505 Ext. 213. Fax: 508-867-3300. E-mail: r.bulger@valleyviewschool.org. Website: www.valleyviewschool.org

THE VANGUARD SCHOOL

22000 Highway 27
Lake Wales, Florida 33859-6858
Head of School: Mr. Harold Maready

General Information Coeducational boarding and day and distance learning college-preparatory, general academic, arts, and web design and digital design school; primarily serves underachievers, students with learning disabilities, individuals with Attention Deficit Disorder, dyslexic students, and non-verbal learning disabilities. Grades 6–12. Distance learning grades 9–12. Founded: 1966. Setting: small town. Nearest major city is Orlando. Students are housed in single-sex dormitories. 77-acre campus. 15 buildings on campus. Approved or accredited by Florida Council of Independent Schools, Southern Association of Colleges and Schools, The Association of Boarding Schools, and Florida Department of Education. Member of National Association of Independent Schools and Secondary School Admission Test Board. Endowment: $3.8 million. Total enrollment: 95. Upper school average class size: 7. Upper school faculty-student ratio: 1:6. There are 180 required school days per year for Upper School students. Upper School students typically attend 5 days per week. The average school day consists of 8 hours.
Upper School Student Profile Grade 6: 4 students (4 boys); Grade 7: 4 students (3 boys, 1 girl); Grade 8: 9 students (8 boys, 1 girl); Grade 9: 16 students (14 boys, 2 girls); Grade 10: 16 students (13 boys, 3 girls); Grade 11: 17 students (14 boys, 3 girls); Grade 12: 20 students (14 boys, 6 girls). 88% of students are boarding students. 50% are state residents. 11 states are represented in upper school student body. 33% are international students. International students from Bahamas, Barbados, Bermuda, British Virgin Islands, Cayman Islands, and Jamaica; 6 other countries represented in student body.
Faculty School total: 17. In upper school: 4 men, 13 women; 6 have advanced degrees.
Subjects Offered College admission preparation, college counseling, personal money management, remedial/makeup course work, social skills, visual and performing arts, volleyball, Web site design, weightlifting, world wide web design.
Graduation Requirements Arts and fine arts (art, music, dance, drama), biology, economics, English, government, life management skills, literature, mathematics, physical education (includes health), reading, science, social studies (includes history).
Special Academic Programs Independent study; study at local college for college credit; academic accommodation for the gifted; remedial reading and/or remedial writing; remedial math; programs in English, mathematics, general development for dyslexic students; special instructional classes for deaf students, blind students.
College Admission Counseling 24 students graduated in 2016; 22 went to college, including Florida Gulf Coast University; Johnson & Wales University; Lynn University; Nova Southeastern University; Santa Fe College; Savannah College of Art and Design. Other: 2 went to work.
Student Life Upper grades have uniform requirement, student council, honor system. Discipline rests primarily with faculty.
Summer Programs Remediation, enrichment programs offered; session focuses on academic enhancement and remediation; held on campus; accepts boys and girls; open to students from other schools. 30 students usually enrolled. 2017 schedule: July 9 to August 6. Application deadline: July 1.
Tuition and Aid Day student tuition: $24,500; 5-day tuition and room/board: $40,000; 7-day tuition and room/board: $46,000. Tuition installment plan (individually arranged payment plans, Your Tuition Solution). Tuition reduction for siblings, need-

based scholarship grants available. In 2016–17, 42% of upper-school students received aid. Total amount of financial aid awarded in 2016–17: $500,000.
Admissions Traditional secondary-level entrance grade is 9. For fall 2016, 50 students applied for upper-level admission, 35 were accepted, 22 enrolled. WISC/Woodcock-Johnson required. Deadline for receipt of application materials: none. Application fee required: $125. Interview recommended.
Athletics Interscholastic: basketball (boys, girls), golf (b), running (b,g), soccer (b), tennis (b), track and field (b,g), volleyball (g), weight lifting (b); intramural: basketball (b,g); coed interscholastic: cross-country running, golf, soccer, tennis; coed intramural: basketball, billiards, canoeing/kayaking, fishing, fitness, fitness walking, Frisbee, golf, kickball, paddle tennis, paint ball, physical fitness, sand volleyball, skateboarding, soccer, volleyball, walking, weight lifting. 1 PE instructor, 2 coaches, 1 athletic trainer.
Computers Computers are regularly used in all classes. Computer network features include on-campus library services, online commercial services, Internet access, wireless campus network, Internet filtering or blocking technology. Computer access in designated common areas is available to students. Students grades are available online. The school has a published electronic and media policy.
Contact Ms. Candi Medeiros, Director of Admissions. 863-676-6091 Ext. 1025. Fax: 863-676-8297. E-mail: candi.medeiros@vanguardschool.org. Website: www.vanguardschool.org

WELLSPRING FOUNDATION

21 Arch Bridge Road
PO Box 370
Bethlehem, Connecticut 06751
Head of School: Dan Murray

General Information Coeducational boarding and day college-preparatory, general academic, and arts school; primarily serves students with learning disabilities, individuals with Attention Deficit Disorder, individuals with emotional and behavioral problems, and depression, mood disorders, eating disorders, and Bipolar Disorder. Boarding boys grades 1–6, boarding girls grades 1–12, day boys grades 1–12, day girls grades 1–12. Founded: 1977. Setting: rural. Nearest major city is Hartford. Students are housed in single-sex dormitories. 13-acre campus. 7 buildings on campus. Approved or accredited by Connecticut Association of Independent Schools, Connecticut Department of Children and Families, New England Association of Schools and Colleges, and Connecticut Department of Education. Total enrollment: 51. Upper school average class size: 6. There are 189 required school days per year for Upper School students. Upper School students typically attend 5 days per week.
Faculty School total: 20.
Special Academic Programs Independent study; academic accommodation for the gifted; remedial reading and/or remedial writing; remedial math.
Student Life Upper grades have specified standards of dress. Discipline rests primarily with faculty.
Admissions Deadline for receipt of application materials: none. No application fee required. On-campus interview required.
Computers Computer network features include Internet access, Internet filtering or blocking technology. Campus intranet is available to students. The school has a published electronic and media policy.
Contact Nancy Thurston. 203-266-8002. Fax: 203-266-8030. E-mail: nancy.thurston@wellspring.org. Website: www.wellspring.org

WESTMARK SCHOOL

5461 Louise Avenue
Encino, California 91316
Head of School: Claudia Koochek

General Information Coeducational day college-preparatory, general academic, arts, and technology school; primarily serves students with learning disabilities, individuals with Attention Deficit Disorder, dyslexic students, and students with language-based learning disabilities. Grades 2–12. Founded: 1983. Setting: suburban. Nearest major city is Los Angeles. 5-acre campus. 6 buildings on campus. Approved or accredited by California Association of Independent Schools, Western Association of Schools and Colleges, and California Department of Education. Member of National Association of Independent Schools. Upper school average class size: 12. Upper school faculty-student ratio: 1:12. Upper School students typically attend 5 days per week. The average school day consists of 6 hours.
Faculty School total: 59. In upper school: 8 men, 20 women.
Subjects Offered Algebra, American history, American literature, anatomy, art, biology, career exploration, chemistry, community service, computer science, creative writing, drama, earth science, economics, English, environmental science, European history, fine arts, general science, geography, geometry, health, history, literature, mathematics, music, physical education, physical science, physics, physiology, science, sign language, social sciences, social studies, Spanish, theater, trigonometry, video, world history, writing.
Graduation Requirements Arts and fine arts (art, music, dance, drama), English, foreign language, mathematics, physical education (includes health), science, social

sciences, social studies (includes history), educational career plan. Community service is required.

Special Academic Programs Independent study; study at local college for college credit; remedial reading and/or remedial writing; remedial math; programs in English, mathematics, general development for dyslexic students.

College Admission Counseling 21 students graduated in 2016; 20 went to college. Other: 1 went to work.

Student Life Upper grades have uniform requirement, student council, honor system. Discipline rests primarily with faculty.

Summer Programs Remediation, enrichment, advancement, art/fine arts, computer instruction programs offered; session focuses on academic and social development; held on campus; accepts boys and girls; open to students from other schools. 50 students usually enrolled. 2017 schedule: July 7 to August 7. Application deadline: May 30.

Tuition and Aid Day student tuition: $42,100. Tuition installment plan (The Tuition Plan, Insured Tuition Payment Plan, monthly payment plans, individually arranged payment plans, Tuition Management Systems Plan). Need-based scholarship grants available.

Admissions Traditional secondary-level entrance grade is 9. Deadline for receipt of application materials: none. Application fee required: $125. On-campus interview recommended.

Athletics Interscholastic: baseball (boys), basketball (b,g), cheering (b,g), cross-country running (b,g), dance squad (g), equestrian sports (g), flag football (b), football (b,g), softball (g), volleyball (b,g); intramural: outdoor education (g); coed interscholastic: basketball, cross-country running, equestrian sports, flag football, golf, soccer, volleyball; coed intramural: fencing, outdoor education. 4 PE instructors, 7 coaches.

Computers Computers are regularly used in English, history, science, social studies classes. Computer network features include on-campus library services, Internet access, wireless campus network, Internet filtering or blocking technology, assistive and educational technology. Campus intranet, student e-mail accounts, and computer access in designated common areas are available to students. Students grades are available online. The school has a published electronic and media policy.

Contact Cindy Goodman, Director of Admissions. 818-986-5045 Ext. 303. Fax: 818-986-2605 Ext. 303. E-mail: cgoodman@westmarkschool.org. Website: www.westmarkschool.org

WILLOW HILL SCHOOL

98 Haynes Road
Sudbury, Massachusetts 01776

Head of School: Marilyn G. Reid

General Information Coeducational day college-preparatory, general academic, and visual and performing arts school; primarily serves underachievers, students with learning disabilities, individuals with Attention Deficit Disorder, dyslexic students, non-verbal learning disabilities, and Asperger's Syndrome. Grades 6–12. Founded: 1970. Setting: suburban. Nearest major city is Boston. 26-acre campus. 4 buildings on campus. Approved or accredited by Massachusetts Department of Education, New England Association of Schools and Colleges, and Massachusetts Department of Education. Member of National Association of Independent Schools. Total enrollment: 61. Upper school average class size: 8. Upper school faculty-student ratio: 1:3. There are 180 required school days per year for Upper School students. Upper School students typically attend 5 days per week. The average school day consists of 6 hours and 45 minutes.

Upper School Student Profile Grade 9: 12 students (9 boys, 3 girls); Grade 10: 10 students (5 boys, 5 girls); Grade 11: 14 students (11 boys, 3 girls); Grade 12: 12 students (9 boys, 3 girls).

Faculty School total: 22. In upper school: 10 men, 12 women; 21 have advanced degrees.

Subjects Offered 20th century world history, algebra, American government, American history, American literature, art, biology, career/college preparation, chemistry, computer science, computer technologies, conceptual physics, consumer mathematics, creative writing, decision making skills, drama, dramatic arts, earth science, English composition, English literature, geography, geometry, grammar, integrated science, keyboarding, library studies, life science, mathematics, outdoor education, physical education, physical science, pragmatics, pre-algebra, pre-calculus, science, senior composition, social studies, study skills, technology, U.S. history, U.S. literature, world history, World War II.

Graduation Requirements Art, drama, English composition, keyboarding, literature, mathematics, physical education (includes health), science, social studies (includes history), wilderness education, students must pass the Massachusetts Comprehensive Assessment System (MCAS), a state-mandated competency requirement, for public funded students.

Special Academic Programs 1 Advanced Placement exam for which test preparation is offered; independent study; study at local college for college credit; academic accommodation for the artistically talented; remedial reading and/or remedial writing; remedial math; programs in English, mathematics, general development for dyslexic students; special instructional classes for blind students.

College Admission Counseling 7 students graduated in 2016; 6 went to college, including Curry College; Dean College; Landmark College; University of Massachusetts Boston. Other: 1 entered a postgraduate year.

Student Life Upper grades have student council. Discipline rests primarily with faculty.

Tuition and Aid Day student tuition: $51,855.

Admissions Traditional secondary-level entrance grade is 9. Comprehensive educational evaluation and WISC or WAIS required. Deadline for receipt of application materials: none. No application fee required. On-campus interview recommended.

Athletics Coed Interscholastic: basketball, soccer, track and field, ultimate Frisbee; coed intramural: backpacking, basketball, bicycling, broomball, canoeing/kayaking, climbing, cooperative games, cricket, croquet, cross-country running, curling, fitness, flag football, floor hockey, Frisbee, hiking/backpacking, horseshoes, ice skating, kayaking, lacrosse, martial arts, mountain biking, outdoor activities, outdoor adventure, outdoor education, outdoor recreation, outdoor skills, outdoors, paddling, physical fitness, rappelling, rock climbing, ropes courses, rugby, running, snowshoeing, soccer, strength & conditioning, track and field, ultimate Frisbee, volleyball, wall climbing, weight lifting, wilderness, wilderness survival, yoga. 1 PE instructor.

Computers Computers are regularly used in all academic, animation, art, drafting, English, graphic design, keyboarding, library science, literary magazine, newspaper, photography, social studies, technology, writing, yearbook classes. Computer network features include on-campus library services, Internet access, wireless campus network, Internet filtering or blocking technology. Student e-mail accounts and computer access in designated common areas are available to students. The school has a published electronic and media policy.

Contact Tom Rimer, Director of Admissions. 978-443-2581. Fax: 978-443-7560. E-mail: trimer@willowhillschool.org. Website: www.willowhillschool.org

WINSTON PREPARATORY SCHOOL

126 West 17th Street
New York, New York 10011

Head of School: Mr. William DeHaven

General Information Coeducational day college-preparatory, general academic, arts, music, drama, sports, and skill-based instruction school; primarily serves underachievers, students with learning disabilities, individuals with Attention Deficit Disorder, dyslexic students, and non-verbal learning difficulties. Grades 4–12. Founded: 1981. Setting: urban. 1 building on campus. Approved or accredited by New England Association of Schools and Colleges and New York State Association of Independent Schools. Member of National Association of Independent Schools. Total enrollment: 227. Upper school average class size: 10. Upper school faculty-student ratio: 1:3. There are 166 required school days per year for Upper School students. Upper School students typically attend 5 days per week. The average school day consists of 6 hours and 45 minutes.

Upper School Student Profile Grade 6: 19 students (14 boys, 5 girls); Grade 7: 25 students (15 boys, 10 girls); Grade 8: 30 students (22 boys, 8 girls); Grade 9: 40 students (30 boys, 10 girls); Grade 10: 49 students (33 boys, 16 girls); Grade 11: 30 students (22 boys, 8 girls); Grade 12: 30 students (21 boys, 9 girls).

Faculty School total: 75. In upper school: 18 men, 57 women; 65 have advanced degrees.

Subjects Offered 3-dimensional art, acting, algebra, American Civil War, American history, American literature, art, athletic training, athletics, biology, community service, creative writing, drama, English, English literature, expository writing, geography, geometry, grammar, health, history, mathematics, music, physical education, science, social skills, speech, theater, trigonometry, U.S. history, writing.

Graduation Requirements Art, English, history, mathematics, physical education (includes health), science.

Special Academic Programs Study at local college for college credit; academic accommodation for the musically talented and the artistically talented; remedial reading and/or remedial writing; remedial math; programs in English, mathematics, general development for dyslexic students.

College Admission Counseling 26 students graduated in 2016; 23 went to college, including Adelphi University; Curry College; Landmark College; Lynn University; Manhattanville College; Pace University. Other: 3 had other specific plans.

Student Life Upper grades have specified standards of dress, student council, honor system. Discipline rests primarily with faculty.

Summer Programs Remediation, enrichment, sports, art/fine arts programs offered; session focuses on reading, writing, and math skill development as well as study skills; held on campus; accepts girls; open to students from other schools. 55 students usually enrolled. 2017 schedule: June 30 to August 20. Application deadline: June 1.

Tuition and Aid Day student tuition: $60,900. Tuition installment plan (SMART Tuition Payment Plan, individually arranged payment plans). Case-by-case financial aid available. In 2016–17, 20% of upper-school students received aid. Total amount of financial aid awarded in 2016–17: $500,000.

Admissions Traditional secondary-level entrance grade is 9. For fall 2016, 222 students applied for upper-level admission, 90 were accepted, 55 enrolled. Achievement tests, admissions testing, battery of testing done through outside agency, Wechsler Individual Achievement Test, Wechsler Intelligence Scale for Children, Wechsler Intelligence Scale for Children III and writing sample required. Deadline for receipt of application materials: none. Application fee required: $100. On-campus interview recommended.

Athletics Interscholastic: basketball (boys, girls); coed interscholastic: cross-country running, running, soccer, softball, track and field, wrestling; coed intramural: fencing, flag football, golf, outdoor education, physical fitness, physical training, running, sailing, skiing (cross-country), skiing (downhill), strength & conditioning, weight training, wrestling, yoga. 2 PE instructors, 6 coaches.

Computers Computers are regularly used in art, English, history, mathematics, music, science, writing classes. Computer network features include Internet access, wireless campus network, Internet filtering or blocking technology, online discussion group and course information, integrated technology—iPads, SmartBoards, Apple TVs, etc. Computer access in designated common areas is available to students. The school has a published electronic and media policy.

Contact Ms. Medry Rodriguez, Assistant to Director of Admissions. 646-638-2705 Ext. 619. Fax: 646-839-5457. E-mail: mrodriguez@winstonprep.edu. Website: www.winstonprep.edu

THE WINSTON SCHOOL

5707 Royal Lane
Dallas, Texas 75229

Head of School: Ms. Rebbie Evans

General Information Coeducational day college-preparatory, arts, and science, solar car program school; primarily serves students with learning disabilities, individuals with Attention Deficit Disorder, and dyslexic students. Grades K–12. Founded: 1975. Setting: suburban. 4-acre campus. 3 buildings on campus. Approved or accredited by Independent Schools Association of the Southwest and Texas Department of Education. Member of National Association of Independent Schools. Endowment: $6 million. Upper school average class size: 9. Upper school faculty-student ratio: 1:5. There are 169 required school days per year for Upper School students. Upper School students typically attend 5 days per week. The average school day consists of 6 hours and 10 minutes.

Upper School Student Profile Grade 9: 12 students (9 boys, 3 girls); Grade 10: 12 students (9 boys, 3 girls); Grade 11: 14 students (12 boys, 2 girls); Grade 12: 13 students (11 boys, 2 girls).

Faculty School total. 36. In upper school: 8 men, 9 women; 9 have advanced degrees.

Subjects Offered 3-dimensional art, algebra, American history, American literature, astronomy, athletics, biology, ceramics, chemistry, computer science, drama, economics, English, English literature, film, fine arts, foreign language, geometry, government/civics, grammar, health, keyboarding, photography, physical education, physics, Spanish, speech, student government, technical theater, theater, trigonometry, world history, world literature, writing.

Graduation Requirements Computer science, English, foreign language, mathematics, physical education (includes health), science, social sciences, social studies (includes history), 30 service hours per year (120 total).

Special Academic Programs Accelerated programs; independent study; study at local college for college credit; academic accommodation for the gifted and the artistically talented; remedial reading and/or remedial writing; remedial math; programs in English, mathematics, general development for dyslexic students.

College Admission Counseling 16 students graduated in 2016; 15 went to college, including Austin College; Fordham University; Pace University; Southern Methodist University; University of Arkansas; Westminster College. Other: 1 had other specific plans. Mean SAT critical reading: 547, mean SAT math: 510, mean SAT writing: 530, mean combined SAT: 1587, mean composite ACT: 22.

Student Life Upper grades have uniform requirement, student council, honor system. Discipline rests equally with students and faculty.

Summer Programs Remediation, enrichment, advancement, art/fine arts, computer instruction programs offered; session focuses on earning academic credit; held on campus; accepts boys and girls; open to students from other schools. 80 students usually enrolled. 2017 schedule: June 5 to July 23. Application deadline: June 1.

Tuition and Aid Day student tuition: $21,500–$28,000. Tuition installment plan (Insured Tuition Payment Plan, FACTS Tuition Payment Plan, monthly payment plans). Need-based scholarship grants available. In 2016–17, 24% of upper-school students received aid. Total amount of financial aid awarded in 2016–17: $229,000.

Admissions Traditional secondary-level entrance grade is 9. Traditional secondary-level entrance age is 14. For fall 2016, 14 students applied for upper-level admission, 9 were accepted, 8 enrolled. Psychoeducational evaluation required. Deadline for receipt of application materials: none. Application fee required: $195. On-campus interview required.

Athletics Interscholastic: baseball (boys), basketball (b,g), fitness (b,g), flag football (b), football (b), indoor soccer (g), softball (g), volleyball (g), winter soccer (b,g); coed interscholastic: bowling, cross-country running, dance team, fitness, golf, independent competitive sports, physical fitness, running, soccer, strength & conditioning, tennis, weight training, yoga. 2 PE instructors, 2 coaches.

Computers Computers are regularly used in all academic classes. Computer resources include on-campus library services, online commercial services, Internet access, wireless campus network, Internet filtering or blocking technology. Students grades are available online. The school has a published electronic and media policy.

Contact Rebbie Evans, Director of Admission and Financial Aid. 214-691-6950. Fax: 214-691-1509. E-mail: admissions@winston-school.org. Website: www.winston-school.org

THE WINSTON SCHOOL SAN ANTONIO

8565 Ewing Halsell Drive
San Antonio, Texas 78229

Head of School: Dr. Charles J. Karulak

General Information Coeducational day college-preparatory and general academic school; primarily serves underachievers, students with learning disabilities, individuals with Attention Deficit Disorder, and dyslexic students. Grades K–12. Founded: 1985. Setting: urban. 15-acre campus. 2 buildings on campus. Approved or accredited by Texas Department of Education. Member of National Association of Independent Schools. Total enrollment: 201. Upper school average class size: 9. Upper school faculty-student ratio: 1:8. There are 175 required school days per year for Upper School students. Upper School students typically attend 5 days per week. The average school day consists of 7 hours and 5 minutes.

Upper School Student Profile Grade 9: 23 students (17 boys, 6 girls); Grade 10: 22 students (14 boys, 8 girls); Grade 11: 17 students (11 boys, 6 girls); Grade 12: 28 students (20 boys, 8 girls).

Faculty School total: 31. In upper school: 8 men, 9 women; 11 have advanced degrees.

Subjects Offered Advanced math, algebra, American history, American literature, anatomy and physiology, art, athletics, basketball, biology, calculus, career experience, career/college preparation, cheerleading, chemistry, college admission preparation, college counseling, college planning, community service, computer applications, computer graphics, computer literacy, computer multimedia, computer skills, computer-aided design, conceptual physics, consumer mathematics, drama, economics, economics and history, English, English composition, English literature, environmental science, environmental studies, geography, geometry, government, government/civics, graphic arts, graphic design, health, health and wellness, health education, human anatomy, journalism, learning strategies, math methods, mathematical modeling, multimedia, music, photo shop, photography, physical education, physical fitness, physics, pre-calculus, reading, SAT/ACT preparation, Spanish, speech, speech communications, student publications, study skills, U.S. government, world geography, world history, yearbook.

Graduation Requirements Arts and fine arts (art, music, dance, drama), computer science, English, foreign language, history, mathematics, physical education (includes health), science, social sciences, 20 hours of community service per year, transition course, job shadowing program.

Special Academic Programs Independent study; study at local college for college credit; remedial reading and/or remedial writing; programs in English, mathematics, general development for dyslexic students.

College Admission Counseling 19 students graduated in 2016; 18 went to college, including Austin College; Boise State University; San Antonio College; Schreiner University; Texas A&M University; The University of Texas at San Antonio. Other: 1 went to work.

Student Life Upper grades have uniform requirement, student council, honor system. Discipline rests primarily with faculty.

Summer Programs Remediation, enrichment, advancement, sports, art/fine arts, computer instruction programs offered; session focuses on high school classes for credit; held on campus; accepts boys and girls; open to students from other schools. 110 students usually enrolled. 2017 schedule: June 19 to July 14. Application deadline: June 2.

Tuition and Aid Day student tuition: $17,795. Tuition installment plan (monthly payment plans, individually arranged payment plans, semester payment plan). Need-based scholarship grants available. In 2016–17, 25% of upper-school students received aid.

Admissions Traditional secondary-level entrance grade is 9. For fall 2016, 15 students applied for upper-level admission, 13 were accepted, 9 enrolled. Achievement tests, battery of testing done through outside agency, comprehensive educational evaluation, Individual IQ, Individual IQ, Achievement and behavior rating scale, psychoeducational evaluation, Wechsler Individual Achievement Test, Wechsler Intelligence Scale for Children, Wide Range Achievement Test or WISC or WAIS required. Deadline for receipt of application materials: none. Application fee required: $150. On-campus interview recommended.

Athletics Interscholastic: baseball (boys), basketball (b,g), football (b), volleyball (g); coed interscholastic: cheering, cross-country running, golf, outdoor education, physical fitness, physical training, soccer, strength & conditioning, track and field; coed intramural: golf, martial arts, outdoor education, physical fitness, physical training, soccer, strength & conditioning, tennis, track and field. 2 PE instructors.

Computers Computers are regularly used in all academic classes. Computer network features include on-campus library services, online commercial services, Internet access, wireless campus network, Internet filtering or blocking technology. Campus intranet and student e-mail accounts are available to students. Students grades are available online. The school has a published electronic and media policy.

Contact Mrs. Julie A. Saboe, Director of Admissions. 210-615-6544. Fax: 210-615-6627. E-mail: jsaboe@winston-sa.org. Website: www.winston-sa.org

Junior Boarding Schools

THE AMERICAN BOYCHOIR SCHOOL

75 Mapleton Road
Unit 4
Princeton, New Jersey 08540

Head of School: Dr. Kerry B. Heimann

General Information Boys' boarding and day general academic, choral music, and music theory and literacy school. Grades 4–8. Founded: 1937. Setting: rural. Students are housed in Homestay, with 2-4 students living at the homes of our local parents. 220-acre campus. 1 building on campus. Approved or accredited by Middle States Association of Colleges and Schools. Member of National Association of Independent Schools and Secondary School Admission Test Board. Endowment: $50,000. Total enrollment: 51. Upper school average class size: 8. Upper school faculty-student ratio: 1:3. There are 205 required school days per year for Upper School students. Upper School students typically attend 5 days per week. The average school day consists of 9 hours and 30 minutes.

Student Profile Grade 6: 6 students (6 boys); Grade 7: 7 students (7 boys); Grade 8: 10 students (10 boys). 50% of students are boarding students. 53% are state residents. 11 states are represented in upper school student body. 13% are international students. International students from Canada, China, and United States; 1 other country represented in student body.

Faculty School total: 10. In upper school: 4 men, 6 women; 9 have advanced degrees.

Subjects Offered Adolescent issues, Latin.

Graduation Requirements Algebra, applied music, character education, choir, choral music, concert choir, English, eurythmics (guard), eurythmy, general science, geography, mathematics, music, music appreciation, music composition, music performance, music technology, music theory, musicianship, physical education (includes health), piano, pre-algebra, social studies (includes history), Spanish, values and decisions, vocal music, voice, participation in the professional American Boychoir, extensive national and international touring with Boychoir.

Special Academic Programs Academic accommodation for the musically talented; remedial reading and/or remedial writing; remedial math.

Secondary School Placement 8 students graduated in 2016; they went to Avon Old Farms School; Peddie School; Phillips Exeter Academy; St. Andrew's School; The Pennington School.

Student Life Uniform requirement, honor system. Discipline rests equally with students and faculty.

Tuition and Aid Day student tuition: $29,500; 5-day tuition and room/board: $37,500; 7-day tuition and room/board: $37,500. Tuition installment plan (individually arranged payment plans). Tuition reduction for siblings, need-based scholarship grants available. In 2016–17, 80% of students received aid. Total amount of financial aid awarded in 2016–17: $37,500.

Admissions Audition and standardized test scores required. Deadline for receipt of application materials: none. No application fee required. On-campus interview recommended.

Athletics Intramural: ball hockey (boys), baseball (b), basketball (b), deck hockey (b), flag football (b), football (b), kickball (b), outdoor recreation (b), physical fitness (b), softball (b), tennis (b), touch football (b), volleyball (b), yoga (b). 1 PE instructor.

Computers Computers are regularly used in all academic classes. Computer network features include on-campus library services, Internet access, wireless campus network, Internet filtering or blocking technology, 1:1 iPad program. Campus intranet, student e-mail accounts, and computer access in designated common areas are available to students. The school has a published electronic and media policy.

Contact Ms. Melissa Keylock, Director of Admissions. 609-924-5858. Fax: 609-924-5812. E-mail: mkeylock@americanboychoir.org. Website: www.americanboychoir.org

ARTHUR MORGAN SCHOOL

60 AMS Circle
Burnsville, North Carolina 28714

Head of School: Jason Sterling

General Information Coeducational boarding and day college-preparatory, general academic, arts, service learning, and outdoor experiential learning school, affiliated with Society of Friends. Grades 7–9. Founded: 1962. Setting: rural. Nearest major city is Asheville. Students are housed in coed boarding homes. 100-acre campus. 7 buildings on campus. Approved or accredited by Friends Council on Education, North Carolina Department of Non-Public Schools, and North Carolina Department of Education. Member of Small Boarding School Association. Endowment: $1 million. Total enrollment: 27. Upper school average class size: 9. Upper school faculty-student ratio: 1:2. There are 180 required school days per year for Upper School students. Upper School students typically attend 5 days per week. The average school day consists of 8 hours.

Student Profile Grade 7: 8 students (4 boys, 4 girls); Grade 8: 11 students (5 boys, 6 girls); Grade 9: 3 students (3 boys). 100% of students are boarding students. 30% are state residents. 3 states are represented in upper school student body.

Faculty School total: 12. In upper school: 7 men, 5 women; 1 has an advanced degree; all reside on campus.

Subjects Offered 3-dimensional art, 3-dimensional design, acting, ADL skills, adolescent issues, African American history, African American studies, African history, agriculture, agroecology, algebra, alternative physical education, American culture, American government, American history, American literature, American minority experience, American studies, anatomy, ancient/medieval philosophy, animal behavior, animal husbandry, anthropology, applied skills, art, arts and crafts, astronomy, athletics, audio visual/media, audition methods, auto mechanics, backpacking, baseball, biology, bookbinding, botany, career education, career education internship, carpentry, ceramics, character education, chemistry, civics, civil rights, clayworking, communication skills, community garden, community service, comparative cultures, comparative politics, composition, computer skills, computers, conflict resolution, conservation, constitutional history of U.S., consumer education, crafts, creative arts, creative dance, creative drama, creative thinking, creative writing, critical thinking, culinary arts, current events, dance, debate, decision making skills, democracy in America, design, drama, drama performance, dramatic arts, drawing, earth science, ecology, English, English composition, English literature, entrepreneurship, ethical decision making, ethics, ethics and responsibility, evolution, experiential education, expressive arts, fabric arts, family and consumer science, family living, family studies, fiber arts, first aid, fitness, food and nutrition, foreign language, forestry, gardening, gender issues, general science, geography, geology, geometry, global issues, global studies, grammar, guitar, health and wellness, health education, high adventure outdoor program, history, horticulture, human rights, human sexuality, humanities, independent living, integrated mathematics, interpersonal skills, jewelry making, journalism, language arts, leadership, leadership and service, life issues, mathematics, media studies, medieval/Renaissance history, meditation, mentorship program, metalworking, music, mythology, Native American studies, natural history, natural resources management, nature study, North Carolina history, oil painting, organic gardening, outdoor education, painting, peace and justice, peace education, peace studies, peer counseling, permaculture, personal growth, photo shop, photography, physical education, physics, piano, playwriting, poetry, politics, pottery, practical living, printmaking, probability and statistics, reading/study skills, relationships, sex education, shop, social justice, social sciences, social skills, social studies, socioeconomic problems, Spanish, sports, stained glass, study skills, swimming, travel, values and decisions, Vietnam War, visual and performing arts, visual arts, weaving, wilderness education, woodworking, work experience, writing, yearbook, yoga.

Graduation Requirements Annual 18-day field service learning trip, annual 3-, 6- and 8-day outdoor education trips.

Special Academic Programs Independent study; programs in English, mathematics, general development for dyslexic students.

Secondary School Placement 9 students graduated in 2015; they went to Carolina Friends School; George School; The Meeting School; Westtown School.

Student Life Honor system. Discipline rests primarily with faculty.

Tuition and Aid Day student tuition: $13,517; 7-day tuition and room/board: $27,996. Tuition installment plan (40% by 8/15, 60% by Dec. 15; monthly payment 10% interest; full payment by 8/15- 2% discount). Need-based scholarship grants, individually negotiated barter arrangements may be made available. In 2015–16, 90% of students received aid. Total amount of financial aid awarded in 2015–16: $100,000.

Admissions Traditional entrance grade is 7. For fall 2015, 3 students applied for admission, 3 were accepted, 3 enrolled. Deadline for receipt of application materials: none. Application fee required: $35. On-campus interview required.

Athletics Coed Interscholastic: soccer; coed intramural: aquatics, backpacking, bicycling, billiards, blading, canoeing/kayaking, climbing, cooperative games, cross-country running, dance, fishing, Frisbee, hiking/backpacking, jogging, mountain biking, outdoor activities, rafting, rock climbing, running, skateboarding, soccer, swimming and diving, tai chi, ultimate Frisbee, wilderness, winter walking, wrestling, yoga.

Computers Computers are regularly used in current events, Spanish, writing, yearbook classes. Computer resources include supervised student access to computers for Web research, word processing, spreadsheet. Computer access in designated common areas is available to students.

Contact Bryan Freeborn, Admissions Coordinator. 828-675-4262. Fax: 828-675-0003. E-mail: admissions@arthurmorganschool.org. Website: www.arthurmorganschool.org

THE BEMENT SCHOOL

94 Old Main Street
PO Box 8
Deerfield, Massachusetts 01342

Head of School: Mr. Christopher H. Wilson

General Information Coeducational boarding and day college-preparatory school. Boarding grades 3–9, day grades K–9. Founded: 1925. Setting: small town. Nearest major city is Springfield. Students are housed in single-sex dormitories. 18-acre campus. 12 buildings on campus. Approved or accredited by Association of Independent Schools in New England. Member of National Association of Independent Schools and Secondary School Admission Test Board. Endowment: $7 million. Upper school average class size: 12. Upper school faculty-student ratio: 1:6. There are 163 required school days per year for Upper School students. Upper School students typically attend 5 days per week. The average school day consists of 8 hours and 30 minutes.

Student Profile Grade 6: 21 students (9 boys, 12 girls); Grade 7: 36 students (17 boys, 19 girls); Grade 8: 33 students (16 boys, 17 girls); Grade 9: 23 students (15 boys, 8

girls). 35% of students are boarding students. 6 states are represented in upper school student body. 30% are international students. International students from Brazil, China, Japan, Mexico, Republic of Korea, and Zimbabwe; 1 other country represented in student body.

Faculty School total: 41. In upper school: 10 men, 16 women; 18 have advanced degrees; 14 reside on campus.

Subjects Offered Algebra, American history, art, art history, biology, chemistry, Chinese, creative writing, drama, earth science, English, English literature, fine arts, French, geography, geometry, grammar, health, history, Latin, literature, mathematics, music, music history, physical education, physical science, physics, science, social studies, Spanish, theater, theater history, world history, world literature, writing.

Graduation Requirements Algebra, American history, art history, arts and fine arts (art, music, dance, drama), athletics, drama, English, foreign language, health, mathematics, music history, physics, science, social studies (includes history). Community service is required.

Special Academic Programs Study abroad; special instructional classes for deaf students; ESL (17 students enrolled).

Secondary School Placement 26 students graduated in 2016; they went to Deerfield Academy; Middlesex School; Northfield Mount Hermon School; Suffield Academy; The Williston Northampton School.

Student Life Specified standards of dress. Discipline rests primarily with faculty.

Tuition and Aid Day student tuition: $23,700; 5-day tuition and room/board: $45,975; 7-day tuition and room/board: $55,400. Tuition installment plan (monthly payment plans, individually arranged payment plans, 60%/40% payment plan). Need-based scholarship grants available. In 2016–17, 36% of students received aid. Total amount of financial aid awarded in 2016–17: $852,000.

Admissions Traditional entrance grade is 7. For fall 2016, 122 students applied for admission, 46 were accepted, 24 enrolled. SSAT or WISC III or Wechsler Intelligence Scale for Children required. Deadline for receipt of application materials: none. Application fee required: $50. On-campus interview recommended.

Athletics Interscholastic: alpine skiing (boys, girls); basketball (b,g), field hockey (g), lacrosse (b,g), soccer (b,g); coed interscholastic: cross-country running, diving, golf, squash, swimming and diving, tennis, track and field, ultimate Frisbee; coed intramural: ballet, dance, modern dance, nordic skiing, outdoor activities, skiing (cross-country), skiing (downhill), snowboarding, strength & conditioning, swimming and diving, tennis.

Computers Computers are regularly used in art, English, foreign language, history, mathematics, science classes. Computer network features include on-campus library services, Internet access, wireless campus network. Student e-mail accounts and computer access in designated common areas are available to students. Students grades are available online. The school has a published electronic and media policy.

Contact Ms. Kimberly Caldwell Loughlin, Director of Admission. 413-774-4209. Fax: 413-774-7863. E-mail: admit@bement.org. Website: www.bement.org/

CARDIGAN MOUNTAIN SCHOOL

62 Alumni Drive
Canaan, New Hampshire 03741-9307

Head of School: Mr. David J. McCusker Jr.

General Information Boys' boarding and day college-preparatory, arts, and technology school. Grades 6–9. Founded: 1945. Setting: rural. Nearest major city is Manchester. Students are housed in single-sex dormitories. 400-acre campus. 27 buildings on campus. Approved or accredited by Association of Independent Schools in New England, Independent Schools of Northern New England, Junior Boarding Schools Association, New England Association of Schools and Colleges, The Association of Boarding Schools, and New Hampshire Department of Education. Member of National Association of Independent Schools and Secondary School Admission Test Board. Endowment: $29.5 million. Total enrollment: 215. Upper school average class size: 12. Upper school faculty-student ratio: 1:4. There are 165 required school days per year for Upper School students. Upper School students typically attend 6 days per week. The average school day consists of 5 hours and 15 minutes.

Student Profile Grade 6: 11 students (11 boys); Grade 7: 38 students (38 boys); Grade 8: 71 students (71 boys); Grade 9: 95 students (95 boys). 89% of students are boarding students. 16% are state residents. 20 states are represented in upper school student body. 40% are international students. International students from Canada, China, Hong Kong, Japan, Mexico, and Republic of Korea; 14 other countries represented in student body.

Faculty School total: 59. In upper school: 38 men, 21 women; 28 have advanced degrees; 43 reside on campus.

Subjects Offered Algebra, American history, American literature, art, biology, ceramics, computer math, computer science, creative writing, drama, earth science, ecology, English, English literature, environmental science, ethics, European history, expository writing, fine arts, French, geography, geology, geometry, grammar, health, history, industrial arts, Latin, life skills, mathematics, music, physical science, reading, science, social studies, Spanish, speech, study skills, theater, trigonometry, typing, world history, world literature, writing.

Graduation Requirements Arts and fine arts (art, music, dance, drama), computer science, English, foreign language, mathematics, reading, science, social studies (includes history), study skills.

Special Academic Programs Honors section; independent study; academic accommodation for the gifted; remedial reading and/or remedial writing; remedial math; ESL (12 students enrolled).

Secondary School Placement 63 students graduated in 2015; they went to Avon Old Farms School; Berkshire School; Kent School; Salisbury School; St. Paul's School; Tabor Academy.

Student Life Specified standards of dress, student council, honor system. Discipline rests primarily with faculty.

Tuition and Aid Day student tuition: $31,220; 7-day tuition and room/board: $53,785. Tuition installment plan (The Tuition Plan, Insured Tuition Payment Plan, Academic Management Services Plan, Key Tuition Payment Plan, monthly payment plans). Need-based scholarship grants, need-based loans, prepGATE loans available. In 2015–16, 27% of students received aid. Total amount of financial aid awarded in 2015–16: $1,000,000.

Admissions For fall 2015, 220 students applied for admission, 155 were accepted, 80 enrolled. ISEE, SSAT, TOEFL or Wechsler Intelligence Scale for Children III required. Deadline for receipt of application materials: none. Application fee required: $50. Interview required.

Athletics Interscholastic: alpine skiing, baseball, basketball, climbing, cross-country running, football, freestyle skiing, ice hockey, independent competitive sports, lacrosse, mountain biking, nordic skiing, outdoor adventure, physical training, rock climbing, running, sailing, skiing (cross-country), skiing (downhill), snowboarding, soccer, strength & conditioning, tennis, track and field, wall climbing, weight training, wrestling; intramural: archery, bicycling, bowling, boxing, climbing, equestrian sports, fitness, golf, ice hockey, martial arts, mountain biking, outdoor activities, physical training, riflery, rock climbing, ropes courses, sailing, skiing (downhill), snowboarding, swimming and diving, tennis, trap and skeet, weight lifting, whiffle ball. 3 coaches, 2 athletic trainers.

Computers Computers are regularly used in English, history, mathematics, science, writing classes. Computer network features include on-campus library services, online commercial services, Internet access, wireless campus network, Internet filtering or blocking technology. Campus intranet, student e-mail accounts, and computer access in designated common areas are available to students. Students grades are available online. The school has a published electronic and media policy.

Contact Mrs. Sarah Sinclair, Admissions Coordinator. 603-523-3548. Fax: 603-523-3565. E-mail: ssinclair@cardigan.org. Website: www.cardigan.org

EAGLEBROOK SCHOOL

271 Pine Nook Road
P.O. Box #7
Deerfield, Massachusetts 01342

Head of School: Mr. Andrew C. Chase

General Information Boys' boarding and day college-preparatory, arts, and technology school. Grades 6–9. Founded: 1922. Setting: rural. Nearest major city is Springfield. Students are housed in single-sex dormitories. 775-acre campus. 26 buildings on campus. Approved or accredited by Association of Independent Schools in New England, Junior Boarding Schools Association, and The Association of Boarding Schools. Member of National Association of Independent Schools and Secondary School Admission Test Board. Endowment: $75 million. Total enrollment: 250. Upper school average class size: 10. Upper school faculty-student ratio: 1:4.

Student Profile Grade 6: 20 students (20 boys); Grade 7: 51 students (51 boys); Grade 8: 87 students (87 boys); Grade 9: 92 students (92 boys). 80% of students are boarding students. 35% are state residents. 22 states are represented in upper school student body. 36% are international students. International students from Bahamas, China, Hong Kong, Mexico, Republic of Korea, and Taiwan; 18 other countries represented in student body.

Faculty School total: 84. In upper school: 48 men, 36 women; 39 have advanced degrees; 55 reside on campus.

Subjects Offered Acting, African-American history, algebra, American studies, anthropology, architectural drawing, architecture, art, astronomy, band, batik, biology, ceramics, Chinese, Chinese history, chorus, Civil War, civil war history, community service, computer art, computer science, computer-aided design, concert band, CPR, creative writing, current events, desktop publishing, digital music, digital photography, drafting, drama, drawing, drawing and design, earth science, ecology, English, English literature, environmental science, ESL, European history, expository writing, fine arts, first aid, French, general science, geography, geometry, grammar, health, history, industrial arts, instrumental music, journalism, keyboarding, Latin, mathematics, medieval history, music, newspaper, photography, physical education, pottery, pre-algebra, public speaking, publications, Russian history, science, sex education, social sciences, social studies, Spanish, study skills, swimming, theater, typing, U.S. history, Web site design, woodworking, world history, writing.

Graduation Requirements Arts and fine arts (art, music, dance, drama), English, foreign language, mathematics, physical education (includes health), science, social sciences, social studies (includes history). Community service is required.

Special Academic Programs Honors section; academic accommodation for the gifted, the musically talented, and the artistically talented; ESL (15 students enrolled).

Secondary School Placement 81 students graduated in 2015; they went to Choate Rosemary Hall; Deerfield Academy; Northfield Mount Hermon School; Phillips Exeter Academy; The Hotchkiss School; The Taft School.

Student Life Specified standards of dress, student council. Discipline rests primarily with faculty.

Tuition and Aid Day student tuition: $36,100; 7-day tuition and room/board: $59,400. Tuition installment plan (individually arranged payment plans). Need-based scholarship grants available. In 2015–16, 30% of students received aid. Total amount of financial aid awarded in 2015–16: $1,650,000.

Admissions SSAT and Wechsler Intelligence Scale for Children required. Deadline for receipt of application materials: none. Application fee required: $50. On-campus interview required.

Athletics Interscholastic: alpine skiing, aquatics, baseball, basketball, cross-country running, diving, football, Frisbee, golf, hiking/backpacking, hockey, ice hockey, ice skating, in-line hockey, indoor hockey, indoor soccer, lacrosse, mountain biking, outdoor activities, outdoor recreation, ski jumping, skiing (downhill), snowboarding, soccer, squash, strength & conditioning, swimming and diving, tennis, track and field, triathlon, ultimate Frisbee, water polo, wrestling; intramural: backpacking, bicycling, broomball, canoeing/kayaking, climbing, deck hockey, fishing, fitness, floor hockey, fly fishing, hiking/backpacking, hockey, ice hockey, ice skating, in-line hockey, in-line skating, indoor hockey, indoor soccer, juggling, kayaking, life saving, mountain biking, nordic skiing, outdoor activities, physical training, rafting, riflery, rock climbing, roller blading, roller hockey, roller skating, ropes courses, scuba diving, ski jumping, skiing (cross-country), street hockey, surfing, table tennis, volleyball, wallyball, weight lifting, weight training, wilderness survival. 2 athletic trainers.

Computers Computer network features include on-campus library services, Internet access, wireless campus network, Internet filtering or blocking technology. Campus intranet, student e-mail accounts, and computer access in designated common areas are available to students. The school has a published electronic and media policy.

Contact Mr. Theodore J. Low, Director of Admission. 413-774-9111. Fax: 413-774-9119. E-mail: tlow@eaglebrook.org. Website: www.eaglebrook.org

See Display on this page and Close-Up on page 648.

FAY SCHOOL

48 Main Street
Southborough, Massachusetts 01772-9106

Head of School: Robert J. Gustavson

General Information Coeducational boarding and day general academic school. Boarding grades 7–9, day grades PK–9. Founded: 1866. Setting: small town. Nearest major city is Boston. Students are housed in coed dormitories. 66-acre campus. Approved or accredited by Association of Independent Schools in New England, Junior Boarding Schools Association, The Association of Boarding Schools, and Massachusetts Department of Education. Member of National Association of Independent Schools and Secondary School Admission Test Board. Endowment: $44 million. Total enrollment: 475. Upper school average class size: 14. Upper school faculty-student ratio: 1:6. There are 162 required school days per year for Upper School students. Upper School students typically attend 5 days per week. The average school day consists of 8 hours and 30 minutes.

Student Profile 50% of students are boarding students. 52% are state residents. 28% are international students. International students from Christmas Island, Hungary, Micronesia, Republic of Moldova, Rwanda, and Togo; 20 other countries represented in student body.

Faculty School total: 80. In upper school: 18 men, 22 women; 35 have advanced degrees; 40 reside on campus.

Subjects Offered 3-dimensional art, algebra, American history, ancient history, art, band, biology, ceramics, choir, creative thinking, English, French, geometry, Latin, life science, Mandarin, modern history, music, musicianship, painting, physical science, pre-algebra, pre-calculus, printmaking, Spanish, strings, technology, technology/design, wellness, world history.

Special Academic Programs ESL (36 students enrolled).

Student Life Specified standards of dress, student council, honor system. Discipline rests primarily with faculty.

Summer Programs Enrichment, ESL, sports, art/fine arts, computer instruction programs offered; held on campus; accepts boys and girls; open to students from other schools. 2017 schedule: June to August.

Tuition and Aid Day student tuition: $37,650–$39,440; 5-day tuition and room/board: $57,110–$58,900; 7-day tuition and room/board: $63,510–$65,300. Tuition installment plan (monthly payment plans). Need-based scholarship grants available. In 2016–17, 21% of students received aid. Total amount of financial aid awarded in 2016–17: $2,201,551.

Admissions Traditional entrance grade is 7. ISEE, SSAT, TOEFL or TOEFL Junior required. Deadline for receipt of application materials: none. Application fee required: $50. Interview required.

Athletics Interscholastic: baseball (boys), basketball (b,g), cross-country running (b,g), field hockey (g), football (b), ice hockey (b,g), independent competitive sports (b,g), lacrosse (b,g), soccer (b,g), softball (g), squash (b,g), tennis (b,g), track and field (b,g), volleyball (g), wrestling (b); coed intramural: dance, fitness, golf, outdoor adventure, skiing (downhill), snowboarding, tennis. 2 athletic trainers.

Computers Computers are regularly used in all classes. Computer network features include on-campus library services, online commercial services, Internet access, wireless campus network, Internet filtering or blocking technology. Campus intranet, student e-mail accounts, and computer access in designated common areas are available to students. Students grades are available online. The school has a published electronic and media policy.

Contact 508-485-0100. Fax: 508-481-7872. Website: www.fayschool.org

THE FESSENDEN SCHOOL

250 Waltham Street

West Newton, Massachusetts 02465-1750

Head of School: Mr. David Stettler

General Information Boys' boarding and day college-preparatory and general academic school. Boarding grades 5–9, day grades K–9. Founded: 1903. Setting: suburban. Nearest major city is Boston. Students are housed in single-sex dormitories. 41-acre campus. 25 buildings on campus. Approved or accredited by Association of Independent Schools in New England, National Independent Private Schools Association, The Association of Boarding Schools, and Massachusetts Department of Education. Member of National Association of Independent Schools and Secondary School Admission Test Board. Endowment: $33 million. Total enrollment: 475. Upper school average class size: 12. Upper school faculty-student ratio: 1:7. There are 162 required school days per year for Upper School students. Upper School students typically attend 5 days per week. The average school day consists of 8 hours.

Student Profile Grade 6: 72 students (72 boys); Grade 7: 71 students (71 boys); Grade 8: 88 students (88 boys); Grade 9: 44 students (44 boys). 50% of students are boarding students. 70% are state residents. 17 states are represented in upper school student body. 19% are international students. International students from Bermuda, China, Japan, Mexico, Republic of Korea, and United States; 7 other countries represented in student body.

Faculty School total: 91. In upper school: 40 men, 51 women; 54 have advanced degrees; 43 reside on campus.

Subjects Offered Advanced biology, algebra, American history, American literature, anatomy, art, astronomy, biology, ceramics, chemistry, computer math, computer programming, computer science, creative writing, drama, earth science, English, English literature, European history, expository writing, fine arts, French, geography, geometry, government/civics, grammar, health, history, human sexuality, Latin, library studies, mathematics, music, photography, physical education, physics, science, social sciences, social studies, Spanish, theater, typing, world history, writing.

Graduation Requirements Arts and fine arts (art, music, dance, drama), computer science, English, foreign language, mathematics, science, social sciences, social studies (includes history).

Special Academic Programs Honors section; academic accommodation for the gifted, the musically talented, and the artistically talented; remedial reading and/or remedial writing; remedial math; ESL (14 students enrolled).

Secondary School Placement 44 students graduated in 2016; they went to Middlesex School; Milton Academy; Noble and Greenough School; Phillips Exeter Academy; Tabor Academy.

Student Life Specified standards of dress, student council, honor system. Discipline rests primarily with faculty.

Summer Programs ESL programs offered; held on campus; accepts boys and girls; open to students from other schools. 40 students usually enrolled. 2017 schedule: June 27 to July 31. Application deadline: none.

Tuition and Aid Day student tuition: $26,100–$42,000; 5-day tuition and room/board: $53,400–$54,600; 7-day tuition and room/board: $61,200–$62,300. Tuition installment plan (FACTS Tuition Payment Plan, monthly payment plans). Need-based scholarship grants available. In 2016–17, 74% of students received aid. Total amount of financial aid awarded in 2016–17: $1,043,947.

Admissions Traditional entrance grade is 7. For fall 2016, 104 students applied for admission, 66 were accepted, 53 enrolled. ISEE, SSAT, TOEFL Junior, Wechsler Intelligence Scale for Children or writing sample required. Deadline for receipt of application materials: February 1. Application fee required: $50. On-campus interview recommended.

Athletics Interscholastic: baseball, basketball, cross-country running, football, ice hockey, lacrosse, soccer, squash, tennis, track and field, wrestling; intramural: alpine skiing, baseball, basketball, canoeing/kayaking, fencing, football, golf, ice hockey, mountain biking, racquetball, sailing, skiing (cross-country), skiing (downhill), snowboarding, soccer, strength & conditioning, swimming and diving, tennis, weight training. 3 PE instructors, 50 coaches, 1 athletic trainer.

Computers Computers are regularly used in all classes. Computer network features include on-campus library services, Internet access, Internet filtering or blocking technology. Campus intranet and student e-mail accounts are available to students. The school has a published electronic and media policy.

Contact Mr. Caleb Thomson, Director of Admissions. 617-630-2300. Fax: 617-630-2303. E-mail: admissions@fessenden.org. Website: www.fessenden.org

THE GREENWOOD SCHOOL

14 Greenwood Lane

Putney, Vermont 05346

Head of School: Ms. Caryl Frankenberger

General Information Boys' boarding and day general academic, arts, business, vocational, technology, woodshop, digital arts, and music school; primarily serves underachievers, students with learning disabilities, individuals with Attention Deficit Disorder, dyslexic students, and Executive Functioning Difficulties, Social Pragmatics. Grades 6–12. Founded: 1978. Setting: rural. Nearest major city is Hartford, CT. Students are housed in single-sex dormitories and Our middle school students are housed in a separate wing from the high school students. 100-acre campus. 13 buildings on campus. Approved or accredited by Association of Independent Schools in New England, Independent Schools of Northern New England, National Association of Private Schools for Exceptional Children, New England Association of Schools and Colleges, The Association of Boarding Schools, and Vermont Department of Education. Member of National Association of Independent Schools. Endowment: $840,000. Total enrollment: 50. Upper school average class size: 5. Upper school faculty-student ratio: 1:2. There are 208 required school days per year for Upper School students. Upper School students typically attend 7 days per week. The average school day consists of 7 hours and 30 minutes.

Student Profile Grade 6: 3 students (3 boys); Grade 7: 9 students (9 boys); Grade 8: 8 students (8 boys); Grade 9: 8 students (8 boys); Grade 10: 13 students (13 boys); Grade 11: 8 students (8 boys); Grade 12: 9 students (9 boys). 60% of students are boarding students. 7% are state residents. 13 states are represented in upper school student body. 6% are international students. International students from Bermuda, Dominican Republic, Malaysia, and Spain; 2 other countries represented in student body.

Faculty School total: 33. In upper school: 15 men, 14 women; 20 have advanced degrees; 15 reside on campus.

Graduation Requirements Community service is required.

Special Academic Programs Honors section; independent study; study at local college for college credit; academic accommodation for the gifted, the musically talented, and the artistically talented; remedial reading and/or remedial writing; remedial math; programs in English, mathematics, general development for dyslexic students.

Secondary School Placement 6 students graduated in 2016; 5 went to college. Other: 1 had other specific plans.

Student Life Specified standards of dress, student council, honor system. Discipline rests primarily with faculty.

Summer Programs Session focuses on community service travel; held both on and off campus; held at Maine, Washington, D.C., and Southwest and Alaska; accepts boys; not open to students from other schools. 6 students usually enrolled. 2017 schedule: June 29 to July 18.

Tuition and Aid Day student tuition: $53,475; 7-day tuition and room/board: $69,890. Tuition installment plan (individually arranged payment plans). Need-based scholarship grants available. In 2016–17, 12% of students received aid. Total amount of financial aid awarded in 2016–17: $249,290.

Admissions Traditional entrance grade is 9. For fall 2016, 60 students applied for admission, 27 were accepted, 25 enrolled. Wechsler Intelligence Scale for Children III or Woodcock-Johnson Revised Achievement Test required. Deadline for receipt of application materials: none. Application fee required: $75. On-campus interview required.

Athletics Interscholastic: baseball, basketball, climbing, cross-country running, rock climbing, soccer; intramural: alpine skiing, archery, backpacking, badminton, ball hockey, baseball, basketball, bicycling, billiards, blading, bowling, canoeing/kayaking, climbing, combined training, cooperative games, cricket, equestrian sports, fencing, fishing, fitness, fitness walking, flag football, floor hockey, fly fishing, football, freestyle skiing, Frisbee, golf, hiking/backpacking, hockey, horseback riding, horseshoes, ice hockey, ice skating, in-line skating, indoor hockey, indoor soccer, jogging, jump rope, kayaking, kickball, lacrosse, mountain biking, mountaineering, netball, nordic skiing, outdoor activities, outdoor adventure, outdoor education, outdoor recreation, outdoor skills, outdoors, physical fitness, physical training, rock climbing, roller blading, ropes courses, running, skateboarding, skiing (cross-country), skiing (downhill), snowboarding, snowshoeing, soccer, strength & conditioning, telemark skiing, ultimate Frisbee, volleyball, walking, weight lifting, weight training, wilderness, wilderness survival, winter soccer, yoga. 6 coaches.

Computers Computers are regularly used in all academic, animation, design classes. Computer network features include Internet access, wireless campus network, Internet filtering or blocking technology, individual laptop for each student, Assistive technologies in the classroom. Campus intranet and student e-mail accounts are available to students. Students grades are available online. The school has a published electronic and media policy.

Contact Ms. Tracy Wheeler, Admissions Assistant. 802-387-4545. Fax: 802-387-5396. E-mail: admissions@greenwood.org. Website: www.greenwood.org

HAMPSHIRE COUNTRY SCHOOL

28 Patey Circle
Rindge, New Hampshire 03461

Head of School: Bernd Foecking

General Information Boys' boarding college-preparatory and general academic school; primarily serves underachievers, individuals with Attention Deficit Disorder, unusually high intellectual ability, and non-verbal learning disabilities and Asperger's Syndrome. Grades 3–12. Founded: 1948. Setting: rural. Nearest major city is Boston, MA. Students are housed in single-sex dormitories. 1,700-acre campus. 8 buildings on campus. Approved or accredited by New England Association of Schools and Colleges and New Hampshire Department of Education. Member of National Association of Independent Schools. Endowment: $1 million. Total enrollment: 20. Upper school average class size: 4. Upper school faculty-student ratio: 1:2. There are 180 required school days per year for Upper School students. Upper School students typically attend 5 days per week. The average school day consists of 6 hours.

Student Profile Grade 6: 4 students (4 boys); Grade 7: 6 students (6 boys); Grade 8: 2 students (2 boys); Grade 9: 2 students (2 boys). 100% of students are boarding students. 7% are state residents. 9 states are represented in upper school student body. 20% are international students. International students from Bermuda, Hong Kong, and Mexico.

Faculty School total: 7. In upper school: 5 men, 2 women; all reside on campus.

Subjects Offered Algebra, civics, English, environmental science, geometry, German, history, life science, mathematics, pre-algebra, science, U.S. history, world history.

Graduation Requirements English, foreign language, mathematics, science, social studies (includes history).

Special Academic Programs Academic accommodation for the gifted; remedial reading and/or remedial writing; remedial math.

Student Life Specified standards of dress. Discipline rests primarily with faculty.

Tuition and Aid 7-day tuition and room/board: $57,500. Tuition installment plan (If a student does not complete a school year, the tuition is prorated for the time in attendance, and any overpayment is refunded).

Admissions Traditional entrance grade is 7. Academic Profile Tests, any standardized test or Individual IQ required. Deadline for receipt of application materials: none. No application fee required. On-campus interview recommended.

Athletics Intramural: alpine skiing, archery, basketball, bicycling, canoeing/kayaking, fishing, flag football, floor hockey, Frisbee, hiking/backpacking, kickball, outdoor activities, outdoor recreation, skiing (downhill), snowshoeing, soccer, table tennis, tennis, touch football, walking, winter walking.

Computers Computers are regularly used in writing classes.

Contact William Dickerman, Admissions Director. 603-899-3325. Fax: 603-899-6521. E-mail: admissions@hampshirecountryschool.net.
Website: www.hampshirecountryschool.org

HILLSIDE SCHOOL

404 Robin Hill Street
Marlborough, Massachusetts 01752

Head of School: Ed Chase

General Information Boys' boarding and day college-preparatory, technology, and leadership school; primarily serves students with learning disabilities, individuals with Attention Deficit Disorder, and dyslexic students. Grades 5–9. Founded: 1901. Setting: small town. Nearest major city is Boston. Students are housed in single-sex dormitories. 150-acre campus. 15 buildings on campus. Approved or accredited by Association of Independent Schools in New England, Junior Boarding Schools Association, The Association of Boarding Schools, and Massachusetts Department of Education. Candidate for accreditation by New England Association of Schools and Colleges. Member of National Association of Independent Schools and Secondary School Admission Test Board. Endowment: $4 million. Total enrollment: 150. Upper school average class size: 10. Upper school faculty-student ratio: 1:7. There are 160 required school days per year for Upper School students. Upper School students typically attend 5 days per week. The average school day consists of 9 hours.

Student Profile Grade 6: 19 students (19 boys); Grade 7: 32 students (32 boys); Grade 8: 57 students (57 boys); Grade 9: 39 students (39 boys).

Faculty School total: 32. In upper school: 19 men, 13 women; 14 have advanced degrees; 25 reside on campus.

Subjects Offered Algebra, American government, American history, ancient history, art, earth science, economics, English, English literature, environmental science, ESL, French, geography, geometry, international relations, leadership, life science, mathematics, music, physical education, science, social skills, social studies, Spanish, woodworking, writing.

Graduation Requirements Art, English, foreign language, leadership, mathematics, music, science, social studies (includes history).

Special Academic Programs Honors section; academic accommodation for the gifted; remedial reading and/or remedial writing; remedial math; programs in general development for dyslexic students; ESL (30 students enrolled).

Secondary School Placement 23 students graduated in 2016; they went to Avon Old Farms School; Dublin School; New Hampton School; Phillips Exeter Academy; St. Paul's School; The Williston Northampton School.

Student Life Specified standards of dress, student council, honor system. Discipline rests primarily with faculty.

Summer Programs ESL programs offered; session focuses on ESL; held on campus; accepts boys and girls; open to students from other schools. 75 students usually enrolled. 2017 schedule: July to August. Application deadline: none.

Tuition and Aid Day student tuition: $31,900; 5-day tuition and room/board: $48,200; 7-day tuition and room/board: $54,400. Tuition installment plan (SMART Tuition Payment Plan, monthly payment plans). Need-based scholarship grants available. In 2016–17, 30% of students received aid. Total amount of financial aid awarded in 2016–17: $1,500,000.

Admissions For fall 2016, 200 students applied for admission, 120 were accepted, 59 enrolled. Any standardized test, ISEE, SSAT, SSAT or WISC III, WISC III or other aptitude measures; standardized achievement test or WISC-III and Woodcock-Johnson required. Deadline for receipt of application materials: none. Application fee required: $50. Interview recommended.

Athletics Interscholastic: baseball, basketball, cross-country running, hockey, ice hockey, lacrosse, running, soccer, track and field, wrestling; intramural: alpine skiing, bicycling, canoeing/kayaking, climbing, crew, fishing, fitness, flag football, floor hockey, football, Frisbee, golf, hiking/backpacking, ice skating, indoor hockey, indoor soccer, mountain biking, outdoor activities, outdoor adventure, outdoor education, outdoor recreation, outdoor skills, physical training, rock climbing, ropes courses, rowing, running, sailing, skiing (downhill), snowboarding, soccer, swimming and diving, table tennis, tennis, touch football, ultimate Frisbee, volleyball, walking, weight lifting, weight training, whiffle ball, yoga. 1 athletic trainer.

Computers Computers are regularly used in all academic, art, music classes. Computer network features include on-campus library services, Internet access, Internet filtering or blocking technology. Student e-mail accounts and computer access in designated common areas are available to students.

Contact William J. Newman, Assistant Headmaster for Enrollment. 508-303-5731. Fax: 508-485-4420. E-mail: admissions@hillsideschool.net.
Website: www.hillsideschool.net

NORTH COUNTRY SCHOOL

4382 Cascade Road
Lake Placid, New York 12946

Head of School: David Hochschartner

General Information Coeducational boarding and day general academic, arts, outdoor education, and Experiential Learning school. Grades 4–9. Founded: 1938. Setting: rural. Nearest major city is Albany. Students are housed in coed dormitories and single-sex dormitories. 220-acre campus. 11 buildings on campus. Approved or accredited by New York State Association of Independent Schools, The Association of Boarding Schools, and New York Department of Education. Member of National Association of Independent Schools and Secondary School Admission Test Board. Endowment: $11 million. Total enrollment: 80. Upper school average class size: 10. Upper school faculty-student ratio: 1:3. There are 146 required school days per year for Upper School students. Upper School students typically attend 5 days per week. The average school day consists of 6 hours.

Student Profile Grade 9: 20 students (14 boys, 6 girls). 95% of students are boarding students. 30% are state residents. 6 states are represented in upper school student body. 45% are international students. International students from China, Guatemala, Sweden, and Togo.

Faculty School total: 25. In upper school: 13 men, 7 women; 6 have advanced degrees; 20 reside on campus.

Subjects Offered 3-dimensional art, acting, advanced math, African drumming, algebra, American history, art, audio visual/media, band, batik, biology, ceramics, clayworking, collage and assemblage, computer music, computer science, creative writing, culinary arts, dance, digital photography, directing, drama, drama performance, drama workshop, dramatic arts, drawing, drawing and design, earth and space science, earth science, electives, English, English as a foreign language, equestrian sports, ESL, fabric arts, fiber arts, film studies, fine arts, general science, geometry, guitar, history, instrumental music, jazz, jewelry making, justice seminar, language arts, life science, mathematics, metalworking, modern dance, music, music composition, music performance, musical theater, painting, performing arts, photo shop, photography, physical education, physical science, piano, play production, portfolio art, pottery, pre-algebra, pre-calculus, printmaking, public speaking, reading, robotics, set design, shop, social studies, Spanish, stage design, stagecraft, studio art, theater, theater arts, theater design and production, typing, video, visual and performing arts, water color painting, weaving, welding, wind instruments, woodworking, world cultures, world history, writing.

Special Academic Programs Remedial reading and/or remedial writing; remedial math; programs in English, mathematics, general development for dyslexic students; ESL (6 students enrolled).

Secondary School Placement 26 students graduated in 2016; they went to Dublin School; Kent School; Northwood School; Pomfret School; The Cambridge School of Weston; The Ethel Walker School.

Student Life Specified standards of dress, student council. Discipline rests primarily with faculty.

Tuition and Aid Day student tuition: $26,100; 5-day tuition and room/board: $47,600; 7-day tuition and room/board: $61,700. Tuition installment plan (monthly payment plans, individually arranged payment plans, 2-payment plan, Your Tuition Solutions). Need-based scholarship grants available. In 2016–17, 30% of students received aid. Total amount of financial aid awarded in 2016–17: $185,910.

Admissions Traditional entrance grade is 9. For fall 2016, 12 students applied for admission, 5 were accepted, 2 enrolled. Deadline for receipt of application materials: none. No application fee required. Interview recommended.

Athletics Coed Interscholastic: alpine skiing, basketball, biathlon, climbing, cross-country running, freestyle skiing, Frisbee, independent competitive sports, nordic skiing, rock climbing, running, skiing (cross-country), skiing (downhill), snowboarding, soccer, track and field, ultimate Frisbee; coed intramural: aerobics/dance, alpine skiing, backpacking, basketball, biathlon, bicycling, canoeing/kayaking, climbing, cross-country running, dance, drill team, equestrian sports, fishing, fitness walking, flag football, freestyle skiing, Frisbee, hiking/backpacking, hockey, horseback riding, indoor soccer, jogging, modern dance, mountain biking, mountaineering, nordic skiing, outdoor activities, outdoor adventure, outdoor education, outdoor recreation, outdoor skills, outdoors, paddle tennis, physical fitness, rock climbing, running, skateboarding, skiing (cross-country), skiing (downhill), snowboarding, snowshoeing, soccer, table tennis, telemark skiing, track and field, ultimate Frisbee, walking, winter walking.

Computers Computers are regularly used in all academic classes. Computer network features include on-campus library services, Internet access, wireless campus network, Internet filtering or blocking technology, Google Classroom. Student e-mail accounts and computer access in designated common areas are available to students. The school has a published electronic and media policy.

Contact David Damico, Director of Admissions. 518-523-9329 Ext. 6000. Fax: 518-523-4858. E-mail: admissions@northcountryschool.org. Website: www.northcountryschool.org

THE RECTORY SCHOOL

528 Pomfret Street
P. O. Box 68
Pomfret, Connecticut 06258

Head of School: Fred Williams

General Information Coeducational boarding and day and distance learning college-preparatory, general academic, arts, bilingual studies, technology, and music school; primarily serves underachievers, individuals with Attention Deficit Disorder, dyslexic students, OCD, and Executive Functioning. Boarding grades 5–9, day grades K–9. Distance learning grade 9. Founded: 1920. Setting: rural. Nearest major city is Hartford. Students are housed in coed dormitories. 138-acre campus. 25 buildings on campus. Approved or accredited by Junior Boarding Schools Association, National Independent Private Schools Association, The Association of Boarding Schools, and Connecticut Department of Education. Member of National Association of Independent Schools and Secondary School Admission Test Board. Endowment: $11 million. Total enrollment: 243. Upper school average class size: 12. Upper school faculty-student ratio: 1:4. There are 175 required school days per year for Upper School students. Upper School students typically attend 5 days per week. The average school day consists of 7 hours.

Student Profile Grade 6: 19 students (13 boys, 6 girls); Grade 7: 34 students (24 boys, 10 girls); Grade 8: 82 students (54 boys, 28 girls); Grade 9: 57 students (40 boys, 17 girls). 68% of students are boarding students. 30% are state residents. 13 states are represented in upper school student body. 40% are international students. International students from China, Japan, Mexico, Nigeria, Republic of Korea, and Thailand; 4 other countries represented in student body.

Faculty School total: 57. In upper school: 23 men, 34 women; 25 have advanced degrees; 27 reside on campus.

Subjects Offered Algebra, American Civil War, American history, American literature, ancient world history, art, biology, chorus, creative arts, creative writing, drama, earth science, ecology, English, English literature, environmental science, expository writing, fine arts, foreign language, French, general science, geography, geometry, grammar, history, journalism, Latin, life science, Mandarin, mathematics, music, photography, physical education, physical science, reading, science, social studies, Spanish, study skills, theater, vocal music, world history, world literature, writing.

Graduation Requirements Arts and fine arts (art, music, dance, drama), literature, mathematics, physical education (includes health), science, social studies (includes history).

Special Academic Programs Honors section; academic accommodation for the gifted, the musically talented, and the artistically talented; remedial reading and/or remedial writing; remedial math; programs in English, mathematics, general development for dyslexic students; special instructional classes for students with learning disabilities, Attention Deficit Disorder, dyslexia, and Executive Functioning; ESL (25 students enrolled).

Secondary School Placement 56 students graduated in 2016; they went to Kent School; Millbrook School; Northfield Mount Hermon School; Pomfret School; Tabor Academy; The Hotchkiss School.

Student Life Specified standards of dress, student council, honor system. Discipline rests primarily with faculty.

Tuition and Aid Day student tuition: $25,400; 5-day tuition and room/board: $45,600; 7-day tuition and room/board: $52,700. Tuition installment plan (monthly payment plans). Need-based scholarship grants available. In 2016–17, 38% of students received aid. Total amount of financial aid awarded in 2016–17: $1,600,000.

Admissions Traditional entrance grade is 8. For fall 2016, 225 students applied for admission, 148 were accepted, 82 enrolled. SSAT, TOEFL Junior or TOEFL or SLEP required. Deadline for receipt of application materials: none. Application fee required: $50. Interview required.

Athletics Interscholastic: baseball (boys), basketball (b,g), cross-country running (b,g), flag football (b), football (b), golf (b,g), lacrosse (b,g), soccer (b,g), softball (g), volleyball (g), wrestling (b); intramural: basketball (b,g), soccer (b); coed interscholastic: backpacking, cross-country running, dance, equestrian sports, fencing, golf, hockey, horseback riding, ice hockey, lacrosse, running, soccer, squash, strength & conditioning, tennis, track and field, yoga; coed intramural: basketball, bowling, climbing, cooperative games, cross-country running, dance, equestrian sports, fencing, fitness, flag football, golf, ice hockey, jogging, lacrosse, life saving, outdoor adventure, ropes courses, running, skiing (downhill), snowboarding, snowshoeing, soccer, softball, squash, street hockey, strength & conditioning, table tennis, tennis, touch football, ultimate Frisbee, volleyball, weight training, whiffle ball, yoga. 35 coaches, 1 athletic trainer.

Computers Computers are regularly used in English, French, history, mathematics, multimedia, music, science, Spanish, writing, yearbook classes. Computer network features include on-campus library services, online commercial services, Internet access, wireless campus network, Internet filtering or blocking technology. Campus intranet and student e-mail accounts are available to students. Students grades are available online. The school has a published electronic and media policy.

Contact John Seaward, Director of Enrollment. 860-928-1328. Fax: 860-928-4961. E-mail: admissions@rectoryschool.org. Website: www.rectoryschool.org

RUMSEY HALL SCHOOL

201 Romford Road
Washington Depot, Connecticut 06794

Head of School: Thomas W. Farmen

General Information Coeducational boarding and day college-preparatory and general academic school. Boarding grades 5–9, day grades K–9. Founded: 1900. Setting: rural. Nearest major city is Hartford. Students are housed in coed dormitories. 147-acre campus. 32 buildings on campus. Approved or accredited by Connecticut Association of Independent Schools, National Independent Private Schools Association, The Association of Boarding Schools, and Connecticut Department of Education. Member of National Association of Independent Schools and Secondary School Admission Test Board. Endowment: $14 million. Total enrollment: 420. Upper school average class size: 12. Upper school faculty-student ratio: 1:5. There are 180 required school days per year for Upper School students. Upper School students typically attend 6 days per week. The average school day consists of 6 hours and 40 minutes.

Student Profile 54% of students are boarding students. 21% are state residents. 15 states are represented in upper school student body. 20% are international students. International students from Bermuda, China, Mexico, and Republic of Korea; 11 other countries represented in student body.

Faculty School total: 58. In upper school: 28 men, 30 women; 25 have advanced degrees; 40 reside on campus.

Subjects Offered Algebra, American history, American literature, art, art history, biology, computer science, creative writing, drama, earth science, English, English literature, environmental science, European history, fine arts, French, geography, geometry, government/civics, grammar, health, history, Japanese history, Latin, mathematics, music, physical education, science, social studies, Spanish, theater, world history, writing.

Graduation Requirements Arts and fine arts (art, music, dance, drama), computer science, English, foreign language, mathematics, physical education (includes health), science, social studies (includes history).

Special Academic Programs Academic accommodation for the gifted; remedial reading and/or remedial writing; programs in English for dyslexic students; special instructional classes for students with learning disabilities and Attention Deficit Disorder; ESL (21 students enrolled).

Secondary School Placement 82 students graduated in 2016; they went to Avon Old Farms School; Berkshire School; Peddie School; St. George's School; The Lawrenceville School; The Taft School.

Student Life Specified standards of dress, student council, honor system. Discipline rests primarily with faculty.

Summer Programs Enrichment, ESL programs offered; session focuses on academic enrichment; held on campus; accepts boys and girls; open to students from other schools. 60 students usually enrolled. 2017 schedule: June 25 to July 30. Application deadline: May 1.

Tuition and Aid Day student tuition: $26,040; 7-day tuition and room/board: $55,665. Tuition installment plan (monthly payment plans, individually arranged payment plans). Need-based scholarship grants available. In 2016–17, 24% of students received aid. Total amount of financial aid awarded in 2016–17: $1,150,000.

Admissions Traditional entrance grade is 8. For fall 2016, 152 students applied for admission, 85 were accepted, 60 enrolled. Psychoeducational evaluation, SLEP, SSAT, Wechsler Intelligence Scale for Children III or writing sample required. Deadline for receipt of application materials: none. Application fee required: $100. Interview required.

Athletics Interscholastic: baseball (boys), basketball (b,g), crew (b,g), field hockey (g), football (b), ice hockey (b,g), lacrosse (b,g), soccer (b), softball (g), volleyball (g), wrestling (b); coed interscholastic: alpine skiing, cross-country running, horseback riding, skiing (downhill), soccer, tennis; coed intramural: alpine skiing, archery, backpacking, bicycling, broomball, canoeing/kayaking, climbing, cooperative games, equestrian sports, fishing, fly fishing, Frisbee, hiking/backpacking, ice skating, mountain biking, outdoor activities, outdoor recreation, outdoor skills, outdoors, physical fitness, physical training, project adventure, rock climbing, roller blading, ropes courses, running, skateboarding, skiing (downhill), snowboarding, street hockey, strength & conditioning, table tennis, tennis, track and field, triathlon, ultimate Frisbee, wall climbing, weight lifting, weight training, whiffle ball, winter soccer. 1 PE instructor, 28 coaches, 1 athletic trainer.

Computers Computers are regularly used in all academic, English, history, mathematics, science classes. Computer network features include on-campus library services, Internet access, wireless campus network, Internet filtering or blocking technology. Campus intranet, student e-mail accounts, and computer access in designated common areas are available to students. The school has a published electronic and media policy.

Contact Matthew S. Hoeniger, Assistant Headmaster. 860-868-0535. Fax: 860-868-7907. E-mail: admiss@rumseyhall.org. Website: www.rumseyhall.org

ST. CATHERINE'S ACADEMY

215 North Harbor Boulevard

Anaheim, California 92805

Head of School: Sr. Johnellen Turner, OP

General Information Boys' boarding and day college-preparatory, general academic, religious studies, leadership/military tradition, ESL, and military school, affiliated with Roman Catholic Church. Boarding grades 4–8, day grades K–8. Founded: 1889. Setting: suburban. Nearest major city is Los Angeles. Students are housed in single-sex dormitories and boys only. 8-acre campus. 8 buildings on campus. Approved or accredited by Military High School and College Association, National Catholic Education Association, The Association of Boarding Schools, Western Association of Schools and Colleges, Western Catholic Education Association, and California Department of Education. Total enrollment: 145. Upper school average class size: 16. Upper school faculty-student ratio: 1:14. There are 180 required school days per year for Upper School students. Upper School students typically attend 5 days per week. The average school day consists of 7 hours and 45 minutes.

Student Profile 74% of students are boarding students. 48% are state residents. 4 states are represented in upper school student body. 46% are international students. International students from China, Mexico, and Nigeria. 58% of students are Roman Catholic.

Faculty School total: 21. In upper school: 2 men, 13 women; 10 have advanced degrees; 7 reside on campus.

Subjects Offered Art, band, Catholic belief and practice, character education, choir, Civil War, computer applications, computer literacy, computer skills, conflict resolution, decision making skills, English, environmental systems, ESL, ethical decision making, ethics and responsibility, fine arts, fitness, grammar, guidance, guitar, health and wellness, health education, healthful living, history, instrumental music, instruments, interpersonal skills, keyboarding, lab/keyboard, leadership, leadership education training, life skills, marching band, mathematics, military history, military science, moral and social development, music, music appreciation, music history, music performance, participation in sports, personal development, personal fitness, personal growth, physical education, physical fitness, piano, pre-algebra, reading/study skills, religion, religious education, science, service learning/internship, single survival, social studies, Spanish, sports, survival training, swimming, volleyball, wind instruments, word processing, yearbook.

Special Academic Programs Special instructional classes for students with Attention Deficit Disorder and learning disabilities; ESL (20 students enrolled).

Secondary School Placement 48 students graduated in 2016; they went to Army and Navy Academy; Mater Dei High School; New Mexico Military Institute; Servite High School.

Student Life Uniform requirement, honor system. Discipline rests equally with students and faculty. Attendance at religious services is required.

Summer Programs Remediation, enrichment, ESL, sports, art/fine arts programs offered; session focuses on academics and outdoor activities; held both on and off campus; accepts boys; open to students from other schools. 100 students usually enrolled. 2017 schedule: July 1 to July 31. Application deadline: none.

Tuition and Aid Day student tuition: $12,100; 5-day tuition and room/board: $32,150; 7-day tuition and room/board: $42,835. Tuition installment plan (FACTS Tuition Payment Plan, monthly payment plans, individually arranged payment plans, 4 payments). Tuition reduction for siblings, need-based scholarship grants available. In 2016–17, 48% of students received aid. Total amount of financial aid awarded in 2016–17: $400,000.

Admissions Any standardized test required. Deadline for receipt of application materials: none. Application fee required: $100. Interview required.

Athletics Interscholastic: basketball, flag football, volleyball; intramural: ball hockey, baseball, basketball, bowling, cooperative games, cross-country running, drill team, equestrian sports, field hockey, fitness, flag football, golf, handball, life saving, physical fitness, physical training, soccer, softball, swimming and diving, touch football, track and field, volleyball, water volleyball, weight lifting. 1 PE instructor, 7 coaches.

Computers Computers are regularly used in English, history, science, social studies classes. Computer network features include Internet access, Internet filtering or blocking technology. Students grades are available online.

Contact Deisy Escobedo, Director of Admissions. 714-772-1363 Ext. 154. Fax: 714-772-3004. E-mail: admissions@stcatherinesacademy.org. Website: http://www.StCatherinesAcademy.org

ST. THOMAS CHOIR SCHOOL

202 West 58th Street

New York, New York 10019-1406

Head of School: Rev. Charles F. Wallace

General Information Boys' boarding college-preparatory, general academic, arts, religious studies, technology, music, and pre-preparatory school, affiliated with Episcopal Church. Grades 3–8. Founded: 1919. Setting: urban. Students are housed in single-sex dormitories. 1 building on campus. Approved or accredited by National Association of Episcopal Schools, The Association of Boarding Schools, and New York Department of Education. Member of National Association of Independent Schools and Secondary School Admission Test Board. Endowment: $18 million. Total enrollment: 29. Upper school average class size: 5. Upper school faculty-student ratio: 1:5. Upper School students typically attend 7 days per week. The average school day consists of 6 hours.

Student Profile Grade 6: 3 students (3 boys); Grade 7: 8 students (8 boys); Grade 8: 3 students (3 boys). 100% of students are boarding students. 40% are state residents. 11 states are represented in upper school student body. 85% of students are members of Episcopal Church.

Faculty School total: 8. In upper school: 6 men, 2 women; 6 have advanced degrees; 7 reside on campus.

Subjects Offered Algebra, applied music, art, choir, computers, English, French, Greek, history, Latin, mathematics, music theory, physical education, science, study skills, theology, visual arts.

Graduation Requirements Arts and fine arts (art, music, dance, drama), English, foreign language, mathematics, physical education (includes health), religion (includes Bible studies and theology), science, social studies (includes history).

Special Academic Programs Academic accommodation for the gifted and the musically talented; remedial reading and/or remedial writing; remedial math; programs in general development for dyslexic students.

Secondary School Placement 7 students graduated in 2015.

Student Life Uniform requirement. Discipline rests primarily with faculty. Attendance at religious services is required.

Tuition and Aid 7-day tuition and room/board: $14,875. Tuition installment plan (monthly payment plans, individually arranged payment plans). Need-based scholarship grants available. In 2015–16, 80% of students received aid. Total amount of financial aid awarded in 2015–16: $190,000.

Admissions Admissions testing and audition required. Deadline for receipt of application materials: none. No application fee required. On-campus interview required.

Athletics Interscholastic: basketball, soccer, track and field; intramural: baseball, basketball, fitness, flag football, floor hockey, independent competitive sports, indoor hockey, indoor soccer, kickball, lacrosse, Newcombe ball, outdoor recreation, physical fitness, running, soccer, softball, strength & conditioning, table tennis, track and field, ultimate Frisbee, volleyball. 1 PE instructor.

Computers Computers are regularly used in art, English, foreign language, history, library, mathematics, music, science classes.

Contact Mrs. Lily I. Scott, Director of Admissions. 212-247-3311 Ext. 504. Fax: 212-247-3393. E-mail: lscott@choirschool.org. Website: www.choirschool.org

Junior Boarding Schools
Close-Ups

EAGLEBROOK SCHOOL
Deerfield, Massachusetts

Type: Boys' day and boarding school
Grades: 6–9
Enrollment: 218
Head of School: Andrew C. Chase, Headmaster

THE SCHOOL

Eaglebrook School was opened in 1922 by its Headmaster and founder, Howard B. Gibbs, a former faculty member of Deerfield Academy. One of the earliest members of his faculty was C. Thurston Chase. When Mr. Gibbs died in 1928, Mr. Chase became Headmaster, a position he held for thirty-eight years. From 1966 to 2002, Stuart and Monie Chase assumed leadership of the School. While continuing to foster the School's traditional commitment to excellence, the Chases have encouraged and developed many components of a vital school: expansion of both academic and recreational facilities, emphasis on the arts, increased endowment and financial aid, student and faculty diversity, and a balanced, healthful diet. Stuart and Monie's son, Andrew C. Chase, now assumes leadership duties as Headmaster. Eaglebrook's goals are simple—to help each boy come into full and confident possession of his innate talents, to improve the skills needed for the challenges of secondary school, and to establish values that will allow him to be a person who acts with thoughtfulness and humanity.

The School owns more than 750 acres on Mt. Pocumtuck, overlooking the Deerfield Valley and the historic town of Deerfield. It is located 100 miles west of Boston and 175 miles north of New York City.

The Allen-Chase Foundation was chartered in 1937 as a charitable, educational trust. It is directed by a 40-member self-perpetuating Board of Trustees, representing alumni, parents, and outside professionals in many fields.

Eaglebrook is a member of the National Association of Independent Schools, the Association of Independent Schools of New England, the Valley Independent School Association, the Junior Boarding School Association, and the Secondary School Admissions Test Board.

ACADEMIC PROGRAM

Sixth graders are taught primarily in a self-contained setting. Subjects include English, mathematics, reading, Latin, history, science, and trimester-length courses in studio art, computers, music, and woodworking. Required classes for grades 7 through 9 each year include foreign language study in Latin, French, Mandarin Chinese, or Spanish; a full year of mathematics; a full year of Colonial history in seventh grade, followed by a self-selected history the next two years; a full year of English; two trimesters of geography; two trimesters of science in seventh grade, followed by a full-year laboratory course; one trimester of human sexuality in eighth grade; and one trimester of ethics in the ninth grade. The School offers extensive trimester electives, including band and instrumental instruction, computer skills, word processing, current events, conditioning, chess, film classics, drama, public speaking, industrial field trips, music appreciation, first aid, publications, and an extensive variety of studio arts. Drug and alcohol education is required of all students in every grade.

Class enrollment averages 8 to 12 students. Teachers report directly to a student's adviser any time the student's work is noteworthy, either for excellence or deficiency. This allows the adviser to communicate praise or concern effectively and initiate appropriate follow-up. Midway through each trimester, teachers submit brief written evaluations to the advisers of each of their students. Advisers stay in close touch with the parents of their advisees. Grades, along with full academic reports from each of the student's teachers, are given to advisers each trimester and then sent home. The reports are accompanied by a letter from the adviser discussing the student's social adjustment progress, athletic and activity accomplishments, and academic progress and study habits.

FACULTY AND ADVISERS

Andrew C. Chase, the current Headmaster, is a graduate of Deerfield Academy and Williams College. Along with his wife, Rachel Blain, a graduate of Phillips Andover Academy and Amherst College, Andrew succeeded his father as Headmaster in 2002.

Eaglebrook's full- and part-time faculty consists of 72 men and women, 46 of whom live on campus, many with families of their own. Seventy hold undergraduate degrees, and 30 also hold graduate degrees. Leaves of absence, sabbaticals, and financial assistance for graduate study are available. The ratio of students to faculty members is 4.9:1.

Teachers endeavor to make learning an adventure and watch over each boy's personal growth. They set the academic tone, coach the teams, serve as dorm parents, and are available for a boy when he needs a friend. They help each individual establish lifelong study habits and set standards for quality. Eaglebrook's teachers have the skill not only to challenge the very able but also to make learning happen for those who need close supervision. Faculty members are chosen primarily for their appreciation of boys this age, their character and integrity as role models, and competence in their subject areas. The fact that many are married and have children of their own helps to create a warm, experienced family atmosphere.

SECONDARY SCHOOL PLACEMENT

The Director of Placement assists families in selecting, visiting, and applying to secondary schools. He meets with parents and students in the spring of a boy's eighth-grade year to discuss which schools might be appropriate based on each boy's aptitude, interests, achievements, and talent. He arranges visits from secondary schools and helps with applications. Parents and the Director of Placement work together until the boy has decided upon his secondary school in April of his ninth-grade year.

Schools frequently attended by Eaglebrook School graduates include Deerfield Academy, Choate Rosemary Hall, the Hotchkiss School, Loomis Chaffee, Northfield Mount Hermon School, Phillips Andover Academy, Phillips Exeter Academy, Pomfret School, St. George's School, St. Paul's School, Taft School, and Westminster School.

STUDENT BODY AND CONDUCT

In the 2016–17 school year, of the 197 boarding students and 21 day students, 20 are in grade 6, 47 in grade 7, 94 in grade 8, and 87 in grade 9. Twenty-five states and twenty countries are represented.

There are specified standards of dress, which are neat and informal most of the time. Discipline is handled on an individual basis by those faculty members who are closely involved with the student.

ACADEMIC FACILITIES

The newly renovated C. Thurston Chase Learning Center contains classrooms, an audiovisual center, and an assembly area. It also houses the Copley Library, which contains 18,000 volumes and subscriptions to eighty-five publications, books on CDs, newspapers, and Internet access. The computer room is equipped with state-of-the-art computers, color printers, scanners, digital cameras, and a projection board. The Bartlett Assembly Room is an all-purpose area with seats for the entire School. The campus has a high-speed fiber-optic network with e-mail and access to the Internet for research.

Construction is underway on the new Science, Art, and Music building of the Edward P. Evans Academic Center, which opened in early 2017. This new facility houses the School's science laboratories; classrooms; studios for drawing, painting, stained glass, architectural design, computer-aided design, stone carving, ceramics, silk-screening, printmaking, and computer art; a darkroom for photography; a woodworking shop; a band rehearsal room; piano studios; piano practice rooms; musical instrument practice rooms; and a drama rehearsal room.

BOARDING AND GENERAL FACILITIES

Dormitories are relatively small; the five dormitories house between 40 students each, with at least one faculty family to every 8 to 10 boys.

Most students live in double rooms. A limited number of single rooms are available. After the first year, a boy may request a certain dormitory and adviser.

ATHLETICS

The athletics program is suitable for boys of all sizes and abilities. Teams are small enough to allow each boy a chance to play in the games, master skills, and develop a good sense of sportsmanship. The School's Athletic Director arranges a competitive schedule to ensure games with teams of equal ability. Fall sports include cross-country, tennis, mountain biking, football, water polo, and soccer. Winter sports include ice hockey, basketball, recreational and competitive skiing, ski patrol, swimming and diving, recreational and competitive snowboarding, squash, and wrestling. The School maintains the Easton Ski Area, consisting of several ski trails, the Macomber Chair Lift, and snowmaking equipment. Spring sports are baseball, track and field, golf, Ultimate Disc, lacrosse, Wilderness Rangers, and tennis. The School plays host to numerous students throughout the year in seasonal tournaments in ice hockey, soccer, skiing, basketball, Ultimate Disc, swimming, and wrestling. The Schwab Family Pool is a six-lane facility for both competitive and recreational swimming. The McFadden Rink at Alfond Arena features a state-of-the-art NHL-dimensioned 200-foot by 85-foot indoor ice surface. A multisport indoor surface is installed in the arena in the off-season to enable use of the facility for in-line skating, in-line hockey, soccer, lacrosse, and tennis. The Lewis Track and Field was dedicated in 2002.

EXTRACURRICULAR OPPORTUNITIES

Service and leadership opportunities build a sense of pride in the School and camaraderie in the student body. Elected Student Council representatives meet with the Headmaster as an advisory group and discuss School issues. Boys act as admissions guides, help with recycling, organize dances, serve as proctors in the dormitories and the dining room, act as headwaiters, and give the morning assemblies. Boys also assume responsibility, with faculty guidance, for the School newspaper, yearbook, and literary magazine.

Many of the students participate in numerous outdoor activities that are sponsored by the Eaglebrook Outdoor Program. They maintain an active weekend schedule that includes camping, hiking, backpacking, canoeing, kayaking, white-water rafting, fishing, rock climbing, and snowshoeing.

DAILY LIFE

On weekdays, students rise at 7:20 a.m.; breakfast is at 8. Academic class periods, including assembly, begin at 8:30. Lunch is at noon, and classes resume at 12:33. Study hall and special appointments begin at 2:15, athletics begin at 3:15, and tutorial periods and other activities begin at 5. Dinner is at 6, and evening activities are scheduled between 6:45 and 7:30; study hall is then held until 9:15 p.m. or later, according to the grade.

WEEKEND LIFE

A wide variety of weekend activities are available at Eaglebrook, both on campus and off, including community service, riflery, museum visits, dances, field trips, tournaments, movies, plays, concerts, town trips, Deerfield Academy games, bicycle trips, ski trips, hiking, camping, and mountain climbing. On Sunday, the Coordinator of Religion supervises a nondenominational and nonsectarian meeting for the student body. Attendance is required for boarding students. The aim is to share different beliefs and ways of worship. Transportation is provided for boys who wish to maintain their own religious commitment by attending local places of worship. Students with permission may leave the School for the weekend; 5–10 percent of the student body normally do so on a given weekend.

COSTS AND FINANCIAL AID

Eaglebrook School's tuition for the 2015–16 school year was $59,400 for boarding students and $36,100 for day students. Eaglebrook seeks to enroll boys from different backgrounds from this country and abroad, regardless of their ability to pay. Approximately 30 percent of the students receive financial aid. To apply for tuition assistance, a candidate must complete the School Scholarship Service's Parents' Financial Statement, which is obtainable from the Financial Aid Office.

ADMISSIONS INFORMATION

Most students enter in either the seventh or eighth grade, although students can be admitted to any grade. Information regarding required testing and transcripts can be obtained from the Admissions Office. A School visit and interview are required.

Eaglebrook welcomes boys of any race, color, religion, nation, or creed, and all share the same privileges and duties.

APPLICATION TIMETABLE

The School accepts applications throughout the year, but it is to the candidate's advantage to make application as early as possible. Decisions and notifications are made whenever a boy's file is complete. There is a $50 application fee ($100 for international students).

ADMISSIONS CORRESPONDENCE

Theodore J. Low
Director of Admissions
Eaglebrook School
271 Pine Nook Road, P.O. Box #7
Deerfield, Massachusetts 01342
United States
Phone: 413-774-9111 (admissions)
413-774-7411 (main)
Fax: 413-774-9119 (admissions)
413-772-2394 (main)
E-mail: admissions@eaglebrook.org
Website: http://www.eaglebrook.org

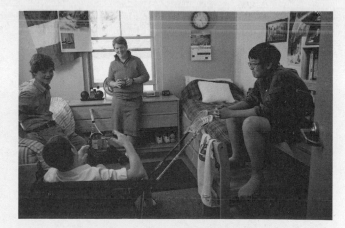

Specialized Directories

COEDUCATIONAL DAY SCHOOLS

Academy at the Lakes, FL
The Academy for Gifted Children (PACE), ON, Canada
Academy of Holy Angels, MN
Academy of Notre Dame, MA
Academy of the Sacred Heart, MI
Académie Ste Cécile International School, ON, Canada
Adelphi Academy, NY
Alabama Christian Academy, AL
Albuquerque Academy, NM
Alice Smith School, Malaysia
Allen Academy, TX
Allentown Central Catholic High School, PA
Allison Academy, FL
Alma Heights Christian High School, CA
Alpha Omega Academy, IA
American Christian Academy, AL
American Community School at Beirut, Lebanon
American Cooperative School of Tunis, Tunisia
The American Embassy School, India
The American International School, Austria
American International School Rotterdam, Netherlands
The American School Foundation, Mexico
The American School in Japan, Japan
The American School of Madrid, Spain
The American School of Puerto Vallarta, Mexico
American School of The Hague, Netherlands
Andrews Osborne Academy, OH
Archbishop Alter High School, OH
Archbishop Hoban High School, OH
Archbishop McNicholas High School, OH
Archbishop Mitty High School, CA
Arete Preparatory Academy, CA
Arizona Lutheran Academy, AZ
Arroyo Pacific Academy, CA
Asheville School, NC
Athens Academy, GA
Atlanta International School, GA
Augusta Christian School, GA
Aurora Central Catholic High School, IL
Austin Preparatory School, MA
Austin Waldorf School, TX
Bakersfield Christian High School, CA
Balboa City School, CA
Banbury Crossroads School, AB, Canada
Bangor Christian School, ME
Barnstable Academy, NJ
Battle Ground Academy, TN
Bavarian International School, Germany
Baylor School, TN
Bay Ridge Preparatory School, NY
The Bay School of San Francisco, CA
Bayview Glen School, ON, Canada
Bearspaw Christian School, AB, Canada
Beaufort Academy, SC
The Beekman School, NY
Bellevue Christian School, WA
The Bement School, MA
Ben Lippen Schools, SC
Bentley School, CA
Berean Christian High School, CA
Berkeley Carroll School, NY
Berkeley Preparatory School, FL
Berkshire School, MA
Beth Haven Christian School, KY
The Birch Wathen Lenox School, NY
Bishop Brossart High School, KY
Bishop Connolly High School, MA

Bishop Denis J. O'Connell High School, VA
Bishop Fenwick High School, OH
Bishop Foley Catholic High School, MI
Bishop Ireton High School, VA
Bishop John J. Snyder High School, FL
Bishop Kelly High School, ID
Bishop Kenny High School, FL
Bishop Machebeuf High School, CO
Bishop McGuinness Catholic High School, OK
Bishop O'Dowd High School, CA
Bishop's College School, QC, Canada
The Bishop's School, CA
Bishop Stang High School, MA
Bishop Verot High School, FL
Black Forest Academy, Germany
The Blake School, MN
Blanchet School, OR
Blessed Sacrament Huguenot Catholic School, VA
Blessed Trinity High School, GA
The Bolles School, FL
Boston Trinity Academy, MA
Boston University Academy, MA
Bradenton Christian School, FL
Brandon Hall School, GA
Brehm Preparatory School, IL
Brentwood College School, BC, Canada
Brethren Christian Junior and Senior High Schools, CA
Briarcrest Christian High School, TN
Briarwood Christian High School, AL
Bridges Academy, CA
Brimmer and May School, MA
British International School of Boston, MA
Brooks School, MA
Buckingham Browne & Nichols School, MA
The Buckley School, CA
Burr and Burton Academy, VT
Buxton School, MA
Cairo American College, Egypt
The Calhoun School, NY
California Crosspoint High School, CA
Calvin Christian High School, CA
Campbell Hall (Episcopal), CA
Camphill Special School, PA
Campion School, Athens, Greece
Canadian Academy, Japan
The Canterbury Episcopal School, TX
Canterbury School, CT
Canterbury School, FL
Canterbury School, IN
The Canterbury School of Florida, FL
Cape Cod Academy, MA
Cape Henry Collegiate School, VA
Capistrano Valley Christian Schools, CA
Cardinal Gibbons High School, NC
Cardinal Newman High School, FL
Cardinal Ritter High School, IN
Carnegie Schools Riverside, CA
Casady School, OK
Cascades Academy of Central Oregon, OR
Cascia Hall Preparatory School, OK
Cate School, CA
Catholic Central High School, NY
Catholic Central High School, WI
CCI The Renaissance School, Italy
Central Alberta Christian High School, AB, Canada
Central Catholic High School, LA
Central Catholic High School, MA
Chadwick School, CA

Chaminade College Preparatory, CA
Chaminade-Madonna College Preparatory, FL
Charles E. Smith Jewish Day School, MD
Charlotte Country Day School, NC
Charlotte Latin School, NC
Chase Collegiate School, CT
Chelsea School, MD
Cheverus High School, ME
Children's Creative and Performing Arts
    Academy of San Diego, CA
Choate Rosemary Hall, CT
Christa McAuliffe Academy School of Arts and Sciences, OR
Christ Church Episcopal School, SC
Christchurch School, VA
Christian Brothers Academy, NY
Christian Central Academy, NY
Chrysalis School, WA
City Christian Schools, OR
Clarksville Academy, TN
Colegio Bolivar, Colombia
Colegio Franklin D. Roosevelt, Peru
Collegedale Academy, TN
The Collegiate School, VA
Columbia Academy, TN
The Columbus Academy, OH
Commonwealth School, MA
Community High School, NJ
The Community School of Naples, FL
The Concept School, PA
Concord Academy, MA
Concordia Academy, MN
Concordia Lutheran High School, IN
Contra Costa Christian High School, CA
The Country Day School, ON, Canada
Covenant Canadian Reformed School, AB, Canada
Crawford Adventist Academy, ON, Canada
Crestwood Preparatory College, ON, Canada
Crotched Mountain School, NH
C.S. Lewis Academy, OR
The Culver Academies, IN
Currey Ingram Academy, TN
Cushing Academy, MA
Dalat School, Malaysia
Dallas Academy, TX
Darlington School, GA
Darrow School, NY
Davidson Academy, TN
Deerfield Academy, MA
De La Salle College, ON, Canada
DeLaSalle High School, MN
De La Salle North Catholic High School, OR
Delaware County Christian School, PA
Delaware Valley Friends School, PA
The Delphian School, OR
Denver Academy, CO
Denver Christian High School, CO
Desert Academy, NM
Detroit Country Day School, MI
Doane Academy, NJ
Dock Mennonite Academy, PA
The Dr. Miriam and Sheldon G. Adelson Educational Campus,
    The Adelson Upper School, NV
Donelson Christian Academy, TN
Donovan Catholic, NJ
Dowling Catholic High School, IA
Dublin Christian Academy, NH
Dublin School, NH

Duchesne High School, MO
Durham Academy, NC
The Dwight School, NY
Eagle Hill School, CT
Eagle Rock School, CO
Eastern Mennonite High School, VA
Eaton Academy, GA
Edgewood Academy, AL
Edgewood High School of the Sacred Heart, WI
Edison School, AB, Canada
Edmonton Academy, AB, Canada
Edmund Burke School, DC
Eldorado Emerson Private School, CA
Elgin Academy, IL
The English College in Prague, Czech Republic
The English School, Kuwait, Kuwait
The Episcopal Academy, PA
Episcopal Collegiate School, AR
Episcopal High School, TX
Episcopal High School of Jacksonville, FL
Erskine Academy, ME
Escola Americana de Campinas, Brazil
Escondido Adventist Academy, CA
Escuela Campo Alegre, Venezuela
Excel Christian Academy, GA
Ezell-Harding Christian School, TN
Faith Christian High School, CA
Faith Christian School, AZ
Faith Lutheran High School, NV
Falmouth Academy, MA
Father Lopez High School, FL
Father Yermo High School, TX
Fayetteville Academy, NC
Fay School, MA
The First Academy, FL
First Presbyterian Day School, GA
Flintridge Preparatory School, CA
Forsyth Country Day School, NC
Fort Worth Christian School, TX
Fort Worth Country Day School, TX
Foundation Academy, FL
Fountain Valley School of Colorado, CO
Fowlers Academy, PR
Franklin Academy, CT
Fraser Academy, BC, Canada
French-American School of New York, NY
Fresno Christian Schools, CA
Friends Academy, NY
Friends Select School, PA
The Frisch School, NJ
Front Range Christian High School, CO
Fuqua School, VA
Gabriel Richard Catholic High School, MI
The Galloway School, GA
Gann Academy (The New Jewish High School of
    Greater Boston), MA
Gaston Day School, NC
George Stevens Academy, ME
Glades Day School, FL
Glenelg Country School, MD
Good Hope Country Day School, VI
The Governor French Academy, IL
The Governor's Academy, MA
The Gow School, NY
Grace Baptist Academy, TN
Grace Christian School, AK
Grace Christian School, PE, Canada

The Grauer School, CA
Greater Atlanta Christian Schools, GA
Great Lakes Christian High School, ON, Canada
Greenfield School, NC
Green Fields Country Day School, AZ
Greenhill School, TX
Greenhills School, MI
Green Meadow Waldorf School, NY
Greenwood Laboratory School, MO
Griggs International Academy, MD
Guamani Private School, PR
Gulliver Preparatory School, FL
The Gunnery, CT
The Gunston School, MD
Halstrom Academy, Beverly Hills, CA
Halstrom Academy, Calsbad, CA
Halstrom Academy, Cupertino, CA
Halstrom Academy, Huntington Beach, CA
Halstrom Academy, Irvine, CA
Halstrom Academy, Los Angeles, CA
Halstrom Academy, Manhattan Beach, CA
Halstrom Academy, Mission Viejo, CA
Halstrom Academy, Orange, CA
Halstrom Academy, Pasadena, CA
Halstrom Academy, San Diego, CA
Halstrom Academy, San Mateo, CA
Halstrom Academy, Walnut Creek, CA
Halstrom Academy, Westlake Village, CA
Halstrom Academy, Woodland Hills, CA
Hammond School, SC
Hampton Roads Academy, VA
Harding Academy, AR
The Harker School, CA
The Harley School, NY
Harrells Christian Academy, NC
Harvard-Westlake School, CA
Hawaii Baptist Academy, HI
Hawai`i Preparatory Academy, HI
Hawken School, OH
Hawthorne Christian Academy, NJ
Hebrew Academy, CA
Hebron Academy, ME
Heritage Hall, OK
Highroad Academy, BC, Canada
The Hill Center, Durham Academy, NC
Hillcrest Christian School, CA
Ho'Ala School, HI
Holland Hall, OK
Holy Cross High School, CT
Holy Innocents' Episcopal School, GA
Holy Savior Menard Catholic High School, LA
Holy Trinity Diocesan High School, NY
Holy Trinity High School, IL
Holy Trinity School, ON, Canada
Hoosac School, NY
Hope Christian School, AB, Canada
Horizon Christian School, OR
The Hotchkiss School, CT
Houghton Academy, NY
The Howard School, GA
The Hun School of Princeton, NJ
Huntington-Surrey School, TX
Hyde Park Baptist School, TX
Hyde School, CT
Hyde School, ME
Hyman Brand Hebrew Academy of Greater Kansas City, KS
Illiana Christian High School, IL

Immaculata High School, KS
Immaculata High School, NJ
Immaculata-La Salle High School, FL
Independent School, KS
Indian Springs School, AL
Institut Monte Rosa, Switzerland
International College Spain, Spain
International High School, CA
International School Hamburg, Germany
International School Manila, Philippines
The International School of Aberdeen, United Kingdom
International School of Amsterdam, Netherlands
International School of Brussels, Belgium
International School of Kenya, Ltd., Kenya
The International School of London, United Kingdom
International School of Port-of-Spain, Trinidad and Tobago
Istanbul International Community School, Turkey
Jack M. Barrack Hebrew Academy, PA
Jackson Preparatory School, MS
Jean and Samuel Frankel Jewish Academy of Metropolitan
    Detroit, MI
Jewish Community High School of the Bay, CA
John Burroughs School, MO
The Journeys School of Teton Science School, WY
Kalamazoo Christian High School, MI
Kaohsiung American School, Taiwan
Kauai Christian Academy, HI
Keio Academy of New York, NY
Kent Denver School, CO
Kent School, CT
The Key School, MD
Kildonan School, NY
Kimball Union Academy, NH
Kimberton Waldorf School, PA
King School, CT
The King's Christian High School, NJ
King's-Edgehill School, NS, Canada
Kingswood-Oxford School, CT
Kolbe-Cathedral High School, CT
The Lab School of Washington, DC
La Grange Academy, GA
Lake Forest Academy, IL
Lakehill Preparatory School, TX
Lakeland Christian Academy, IN
Lake Ridge Academy, OH
Lakeview Academy, GA
La Lumiere School, IN
Lancaster Catholic High School, PA
Lancaster Mennonite High School, PA
Landmark Christian School, GA
Landmark School, MA
Lansdale Catholic High School, PA
La Salle Academy, RI
La Salle High School, CA
The Laureate Academy, MB, Canada
Laurinburg Institute, NC
Lawrence School, OH
The Lawrenceville School, NJ
Lawrence Woodmere Academy, NY
Lehigh Valley Christian High School, PA
Le Lycee Francais de Los Angeles, CA
Lexington Christian Academy, KY
Lexington Christian Academy, MA
Liberty Christian High School, CA
Liberty Christian School, CA
Lincoln Academy, ME
Linfield Christian School, CA

Livingstone Adventist Academy, OR
Long Island Lutheran Middle and High School, NY
Long Trail School, VT
Loudoun School for the Gifted, VA
Louisville Collegiate School, KY
The Lovett School, GA
Lower Canada College, QC, Canada
Loyola College Prep, LA
Lustre Christian High School, MT
Lutheran High North, TX
Lutheran High School, CO
Lutheran High School, MO
Lutheran High School Northwest, MI
Lutheran High School of Indianapolis, IN
Lutheran High School of San Diego, CA
Lutheran High School West, OH
Luther College High School, SK, Canada
Lycee Français La Perouse, CA
The Lycee International, American Section, France
Lycee Internationale de Boston/International School
   of Boston, MA
Lydia Patterson Institute, TX
Lyndon Institute, VT
Madison Academy, AL
Magnolia Heights School, MS
Manhattan Christian High School, MT
Maplebrook School, NY
Maranatha High School, CA
Marian Central Catholic High School, IL
Marian High School, MA
Marin Academy, CA
Marion Academy, AL
Marist High School, IL
Marist School, GA
Marshall School, MN
Martin Luther High School, NY
The Marvelwood School, CT
Mary Institute and St. Louis Country Day School (MICDS), MO
Massanutten Military Academy, VA
Mater Dei High School, IL
Mater Dei Prep, NJ
Matignon High School, MA
Maumee Valley Country Day School, OH
Maur Hill-Mount Academy, KS
Mayer Lutheran High School, MN
McDonogh School, MD
The McLean School of Maryland, Inc., MD
The Meadows School, NV
Memphis Catholic High School and Middle School, TN
Menlo School, CA
Mercersburg Academy, PA
Mercyhurst Preparatory School, PA
Mesa Grande Seventh-Day Academy, CA
The Miami Valley School, OH
Middlesex School, MA
Mid-Pacific Institute, HI
Millbrook School, NY
Mill Springs Academy, GA
Milton Academy, MA
MMI Preparatory School, PA
Moncton Wesleyan Academy, NB, Canada
Montclair Kimberley Academy, NJ
Monterey Bay Academy, CA
Moorestown Friends School, NJ
Mooseheart High School, IL
Moravian Academy, PA
Moreau Catholic High School, CA

Morris Catholic High School, NJ
Mountain View Academy, CA
Mountain View Christian High School, NV
Mount Dora Christian Academy, FL
Mount St. Agnes Academy, Bermuda
Mount Saint Charles Academy, RI
Mount Vernon Presbyterian School, GA
Nampa Christian Schools, ID
Nazareth Academy, IL
Nebraska Christian Schools, NE
New Covenant Academy, MO
New International School of Thailand, Thailand
New Roads School, CA
Newton's Grove School, ON, Canada
New York Military Academy, NY
Niagara Catholic Jr. /Sr. High School, NY
Niagara Christian Community of Schools, ON, Canada
Noble Academy, NC
Noble and Greenough School, MA
The Nora School, MD
Norman Howard School, NY
The North Broward Preparatory Upper School, FL
North Country School, NY
Northfield Mount Hermon School, MA
Northpoint Christian School, MS
North Shore Country Day School, IL
Northside Christian School, FL
North Toronto Christian School, ON, Canada
Northwest Academy, OR
Northwest Catholic High School, CT
The Northwest School, WA
North Yarmouth Academy, ME
The Norwich Free Academy, CT
Notre Dame-Cathedral Latin School, OH
Notre Dame High School, CA
Notre Dame High School, NJ
Notre Dame High School, NY
Notre Dame High School, TN
Notre Dame Junior/Senior High School, PA
Oak Grove Lutheran School, ND
Oak Grove School, CA
Oakland School, VA
Oak Ridge Military Academy, NC
The Oakridge School, TX
Ojai Valley School, CA
Oldenburg Academy, IN
The O'Neal School, NC
Oneida Baptist Institute, KY
Orangewood Adventist Academy, CA
Oregon Episcopal School, OR
Orinda Academy, CA
The Orme School, AZ
Pace Academy, GA
PACE/Brantley Hall High School, FL
Pacific Lutheran High School, CA
The Packer Collegiate Institute, NY
Padua Franciscan High School, OH
The Paideia School, GA
Paradise Adventist Academy, CA
The Park School of Baltimore, MD
The Park School of Buffalo, NY
The Pathway School, PA
Peddie School, NJ
The Pembroke Hill School, MO
Peninsula Catholic High School, VA
The Pennington School, NJ
Pensacola Catholic High School, FL

Peoples Christian Academy, ON, Canada
Perkins School for the Blind, MA
Perkiomen School, PA
Philadelphia-Montgomery Christian Academy, PA
Phoenix Christian Preparatory School, AZ
Phoenix Country Day School, AZ
Pickering College, ON, Canada
Pinecrest Academy, GA
Pine Tree Academy, ME
Pinewood Preparatory School, SC
The Pingree School, MA
The Pingry School, NJ
Pioneer Valley Christian Academy, MA
Plumstead Christian School, PA
Polytechnic School, CA
Pope Francis High School, MA
Pope John XXIII Regional High School, NJ
Portledge School, NY
Portsmouth Christian Academy, NH
The Potomac School, VA
Poughkeepsie Day School, NY
Powers Catholic High School, MI
Prestonwood Christian Academy, TX
Proctor Academy, NH
Professional Children's School, NY
Providence Country Day School, RI
Providence Day School, NC
Providence High School, CA
Providence School, FL
Punahou School, HI
Queen Margaret's School, BC, Canada
Quigley Catholic High School, PA
Quinte Christian High School, ON, Canada
Randolph-Macon Academy, VA
Ransom Everglades School, FL
Ravenscroft School, NC
Realms of Inquiry, UT
Redeemer Christian High School, ON, Canada
Redemption Christian Academy, MA
Redwood Christian Schools, CA
Regina Junior-Senior High School, IA
Regis High School, OR
Rejoice Christian Schools, OK
Rice Memorial High School, VT
Ridley College, ON, Canada
Riverdale Country School, NY
Rivermont Collegiate, IA
River Oaks Baptist School, TX
The Rivers School, MA
Rockland Country Day School, NY
Rock Point School, VT
Rockway Mennonite Collegiate, ON, Canada
Rocky Mount Academy, NC
The Roeper School, MI
Rolling Hills Preparatory School, CA
Ron Pettigrew Christian School, BC, Canada
Rosseau Lake College, ON, Canada
Rothesay Netherwood School, NB, Canada
Rotterdam International Secondary School, Wolfert
    van Borselen, Netherlands
Routt Catholic High School, IL
Rowland Hall, UT
Royal Canadian College, BC, Canada
Rudolf Steiner School of Ann Arbor, MI
Rumsey Hall School, CT
Rundle College, AB, Canada
Sacramento Country Day School, CA

Sacramento Waldorf School, CA
Sacred Heart/Griffin High School, IL
Sacred Heart High School, NY
Saddlebrook Preparatory School, FL
Sage Hill School, CA
Saint Agnes Academy–St. Dominic School, TN
Saint Albert Junior-Senior High School, IA
St. Andrew's Episcopal School, MD
Saint Andrew's Episcopal School, TX
Saint Andrew's School, FL
St. Andrew's School, GA
St. Andrew's–Sewanee School, TN
Saint Anthony High School, IL
St. Benedict at Auburndale, TN
St. Bernard's Catholic School, CA
St. Croix Schools, MN
St. Francis High School, KY
St. Francis School, GA
St. George's Independent School, TN
St. George's School, RI
Saint Ignatius College Prep, IL
St. John Neumann High School, FL
St. John's Catholic Prep, MD
St. John's International, BC, Canada
St. John's-Ravenscourt School, MB, Canada
Saint John's School, GU
Saint Joseph Academy, CA
St. Joseph Academy, FL
St. Joseph High School, CA
St. Joseph High School, CT
St. Joseph High School, TX
St. Joseph's Catholic School, SC
St. Luke's School, CT
Saint Mary of the Assumption High School, NJ
Saint Mary's Hall, TX
Saint Mary's High School, AZ
St. Mary's High School, CO
Saint Maur International School, Japan
St. Patrick's Regional Secondary, BC, Canada
Saint Paul Lutheran High School, MO
St. Pius X Catholic High School, GA
St. Pius X High School, TX
Saint Stephen's Episcopal School, FL
St. Stephen's Episcopal School, TX
St. Stephen's International School, Thailand
St. Stephen's School, Rome, Italy
St. Thomas Aquinas High School, FL
Saint Thomas Aquinas High School, KS
St. Thomas Aquinas High School, NH
Saint Thomas More Catholic High School, LA
Saint Vincent-Saint Mary High School, OH
Salem Academy, OR
Salpointe Catholic High School, AZ
San Francisco University High School, CA
Santa Fe Preparatory School, NM
Santa Margarita Catholic High School, CA
Sayre School, KY
Scattergood Friends School, IA
Scholar's Hall Preparatory School, ON, Canada
Schule Schloss Salem, Germany
SciCore Academy, NJ
Scotus Central Catholic High School, NE
Seabury Hall, HI
Seacrest Country Day School, FL
Seattle Academy of Arts and Sciences, WA
Second Baptist School, TX
Seton Catholic Central High School, NY

Seton Catholic High School, AZ
The Seven Hills School, OH
Shady Side Academy, PA
Shanley High School, ND
Shattuck-St. Mary's School, MN
Shawe Memorial Junior/Senior High School, IN
Shawnigan Lake School, BC, Canada
Shelton School and Evaluation Center, TX
Shorecrest Preparatory School, FL
Shoreline Christian, WA
The Siena School, MD
Sierra Canyon School, CA
Signet Christian School, ON, Canada
Smith School, NY
Sonoma Academy, CA
Southern Ontario Collegiate, ON, Canada
Southfield Christian High School, MI
Southwestern Academy, AZ
Springside Chestnut Hill Academy, PA
Springwood School, AL
Squaw Valley Academy, CA
The Stanwich School, CT
STAR Prep Academy, CA
Steamboat Mountain School, CO
Stevenson School, CA
The Stony Brook School, NY
The Storm King School, NY
Stratford Academy, GA
Stratton Mountain School, VT
Stuart Hall, VA
The Sudbury Valley School, MA
The Taft School, CT
Taipei American School, Taiwan
Takoma Academy, MD
Tandem Friends School, VA
TASIS The American School in England, United Kingdom
TASIS, The American School in Switzerland, Switzerland
The Tenney School, TX
Teurlings Catholic High School, LA
The Thacher School, CA
Thomas Jefferson School, MO
Thornton Academy, ME
Tilton School, NH
Timothy Christian High School, IL
TMI - The Episcopal School of Texas, TX
Tower Hill School, DE
Trevor Day School, NY
Tri-City Christian Academy, AZ
Trinity Academy, KS
Trinity Catholic High School, CT
Trinity College School, ON, Canada
Trinity Episcopal School, VA
Trinity High School, OH
Trinity Preparatory School, FL
United Mennonite Educational Institute, ON, Canada
United Nations International School, NY
University Lake School, WI
University of Chicago Laboratory Schools, IL
University Prep, WA
University School of Jackson, TN
Valley Christian High School, CA
Valley Christian School, MT
The Valley School, MI
Valwood School, GA
Venta Preparatory School, ON, Canada
Verdala International School, Malta
Vicksburg Catholic School, MS

Victor Valley Christian School, CA
Villa Duchesne and Oak Hill School, MO
Villa Madonna Academy, KY
Virginia Episcopal School, VA
The Waldorf School of Saratoga Springs, NY
Walnut Hill School for the Arts, MA
Wasatch Academy, UT
Washington International School, DC
Washington Waldorf School, MD
The Waterford School, UT
Watkinson School, CT
Waynflete School, ME
Webb School of Knoxville, TN
The Weber School, GA
The Wellington School, OH
Wesleyan Academy, PR
Westbury Christian School, TX
Westmark School, CA
West Memphis Christian High School, AR
Westminster Christian Academy, LA
Westminster Christian School, FL
Westminster School, CT
The Westminster School at Oak Mountain, AL
West Nottingham Academy, MD
Westside Christian High School, OR
West Sound Academy, WA
Westtown School, PA
The Wheeler School, RI
Whitefield Academy, KY
Whitfield School, MO
Willow Hill School, MA
Wilmington Christian School, DE
Wilmington Friends School, DE
Wilson Hall, SC
The Winchendon School, MA
Winchester Thurston School, PA
Windermere School, United Kingdom
The Windsor School, NY
Windward School, CA
Winston Preparatory School, NY
The Winston School, TX
The Winston School San Antonio, TX
The Woodlands Christian Academy, TX
Woodlynde School, PA
Woodstock Academy, CT
Woodstock School, India
Woodward Academy, GA
Worcester Preparatory School, MD
Wyoming Seminary, PA
Yokohama International School, Japan
York Country Day School, PA
Zurich International School, Switzerland

BOYS' DAY SCHOOLS

Academy of the New Church Boys' School, PA
The American Boychoir School, NJ
Archbishop Curley High School, MD
Archbishop Moeller High School, OH
Archbishop Shaw High School, LA
Army and Navy Academy, CA
Belen Jesuit Preparatory School, FL
Benedictine High School, OH
Brophy College Preparatory, AZ
Brother Martin High School, LA
The Browning School, NY

Coeducational in lower grades

Calvert Hall College High School, MD
Catholic Central High School, MI
Central Catholic High School, PA
Chaminade College Preparatory School, MO
Christian Brothers Academy, NJ
Christopher Columbus High School, FL
The Church Farm School, PA
Colegio San Jose, PR
Covington Catholic High School, KY
Crescent School, ON, Canada
Damien High School, CA
De La Salle High School, CA
Delbarton School, NJ
DeMatha Catholic High School, MD
Devon Preparatory School, PA
Eaglebrook School, MA
Father Duenas Memorial School, GU
The Fessenden School, MA
Fordham Preparatory School, NY
Gilman School, MD
Gonzaga College High School, DC
The Greenwood School, VT
The Haverford School, PA
Hillside School, MA
Holy Cross School, LA
Holy Ghost Preparatory School, PA
Jesuit College Preparatory School, TX
Jesuit High School of Tampa, FL
Junipero Serra High School, CA
Landon School, MD
La Salle Institute, NY
Loyola-Blakefield, MD
Malden Catholic High School, MA
Malvern Preparatory School, PA
The McCallie School, TN
Memphis University School, TN
Merchiston Castle School, United Kingdom
Monsignor Bonner and Archbishop Prendergast Catholic High
   School, PA
Montgomery Bell Academy, TN
Palma School, CA
The Phelps School, PA
Regis Jesuit High School, Boys Division, CO
Rockhurst High School, MO
The Roxbury Latin School, MA
St. Albans School, DC
Saint Augustine Preparatory School, NJ
St. Catherine's Academy, CA
St. Christopher's School, VA
Saint Francis High School, CA
St. George's School, BC, Canada
Saint John Bosco High School, CA
St. John's Jesuit High School, OH
St. John's Preparatory School, MA
Saint Joseph High School, NJ
Saint Joseph Regional High School, NJ
St. Joseph's Preparatory School, PA
St. Mary's Preparatory School, MI
Saint Patrick High School, IL
St. Paul's High School, MB, Canada
St. Stanislaus College, MS
Saint Thomas Academy, MN
Saint Xavier High School, KY
Subiaco Academy, AR
Trinity High School, KY
Trinity-Pawling School, NY
Upper Canada College, ON, Canada

The Woodhall School, CT
Xavier High School, NY

GIRLS' DAY SCHOOLS
Academy of Notre Dame de Namur, PA
Academy of Our Lady of Peace, CA
Academy of Saint Elizabeth, NJ
Academy of the Holy Cross, MD
Academy of the Holy Family, CT
Academy of the New Church Girls' School, PA
Academy of the Sacred Heart, LA
The Agnes Irwin School, PA
Alverno Heights Academy, CA
Atlanta Girls' School, GA
Balmoral Hall School, MB, Canada
The Bermuda High School for Girls, Bermuda
Bishop Kearney High School, NY
Branksome Hall, ON, Canada
Buffalo Seminary, NY
Carondelet High School, CA
Castilleja School, CA
Cathedral High School, NY
Chatham Hall, VA
Columbus School for Girls, OH
Dana Hall School, MA
Dominican Academy, NY
The Ellis School, PA
Elmwood School, ON, Canada
Flintridge Sacred Heart Academy, CA
Fontbonne Academy, MA
Fontbonne Hall Academy, NY
Foxcroft School, VA
Grier School, PA
The Harpeth Hall School, TN
The Hewitt School, NY
Immaculate Conception High School, NJ
Immaculate Heart Academy, NJ
Incarnate Word Academy, TX
Josephinum Academy, IL
La Pietra–Hawaii School for Girls, HI
Lauralton Hall, CT
The Linden School, ON, Canada
Louisville High School, CA
Ma'ayanot Yeshiva High School for Girls of Bergen County, NJ
Marlborough School, CA
Mary Help of Christians Academy, NJ
The Mary Louis Academy, NY
Marymount High School, CA
Maryvale Preparatory School, MD
Mercy High School, CT
Mercy High School, MI
Merion Mercy Academy, PA
Miss Edgar's and Miss Cramp's School, QC, Canada
Miss Porter's School, CT
Montrose School, MA
Mother McAuley High School, IL
Mount Carmel Academy, LA
Mount Mercy Academy, NY
Mount Notre Dame High School, OH
Nerinx Hall, MO
Newton Country Day School of the Sacred Heart, MA
Notre Dame High School, CA
Preston High School, NY
Queen of Peace High School, IL
Ramona Convent Secondary School, CA

Coeducational in lower grades

Regis Jesuit High School, Girls Division, CO
Sacred Heart Academy, NY
Sacred Heart High School, CA
St. Agnes Academy, TX
Saint Basil Academy, PA
Saint Dominic Academy, NJ
Saint Gertrude High School, VA
Saint Lucy's Priory High School, CA
St. Mary's Episcopal School, TN
Saint Teresa's Academy, MO
Saint Ursula Academy, OH
Saint Ursula Academy, OH
Salem Academy, NC
Santa Catalina School, CA
The Spence School, NY
Trafalgar Castle School, ON, Canada
Ursuline Academy, MA
The Ursuline Academy of Dallas, TX
Villa Joseph Marie High School, PA
Villa Victoria Academy, NJ
Villa Walsh Academy, NJ
Westover School, CT
Westridge School, CA
The Willows Academy, IL
The Woodward School, MA

SCHOOLS ACCEPTING BOARDING BOYS AND GIRLS

Académie Ste Cécile International School, ON, Canada†
Advanced Academy of Georgia, GA
Allen Academy, TX†
Alliance Academy, Ecuador
Andrews Osborne Academy, OH†
Asheville School, NC†
Baylor School, TN†
The Bement School, MA†
Ben Lippen Schools, SC†
Berkshire School, MA†
Bishop's College School, QC, Canada†
Black Forest Academy, Germany†
The Bolles School, FL†
Brandon Hall School, GA†
Brehm Preparatory School, IL†
Brentwood College School, BC, Canada†
Brockwood Park School, United Kingdom
Brooks School, MA†
Burr and Burton Academy, VT†
Buxton School, MA†
California Crosspoint High School, CA†
California Lutheran High School, CA
Camphill Special School, PA†
Canadian Academy, Japan†
Canterbury School, CT†
Cate School, CA†
CCI The Renaissance School, Italy†
Charles E. Smith Jewish Day School, MD
Children's Creative and Performing Arts Academy of San Diego, CA†
Choate Rosemary Hall, CT†
Christchurch School, VA†
Columbia International School, Japan
Concord Academy, MA†
Crotched Mountain School, NH
The Culver Academies, IN†
Cushing Academy, MA†

Dalat School, Malaysia†
Darlington School, GA†
Darrow School, NY†
Deerfield Academy, MA†
The Delphian School, OR†
Dock Mennonite Academy, PA†
Dublin Christian Academy, NH†
Dublin School, NH†
Eagle Hill School, CT†
Eagle Rock School, CO
Episcopal High School, VA
Fay School, MA†
First Presbyterian Day School, GA†
Forest Lake Academy, FL
Fountain Valley School of Colorado, CO†
Franklin Academy, CT†
Gem State Academy, ID
George Stevens Academy, ME†
Gilmour Academy, OH
Girard College, PA
The Governor French Academy, IL†
The Governor's Academy, MA†
The Gow School, NY†
Great Lakes Christian High School, ON, Canada†
The Gunnery, CT†
Harding Academy, AR†
The Harvey School, NY
Hawai`i Preparatory Academy, HI†
Hebron Academy, ME†
Hoosac School, NY†
The Hotchkiss School, CT†
Houghton Academy, NY†
The Hun School of Princeton, NJ†
Hyde School, CT†
Hyde School, ME†
Indian Springs School, AL†
Institut Monte Rosa, Switzerland†
The John Dewey Academy, MA
The Judge Rotenberg Educational Center, MA
Keio Academy of New York, NY†
Kent School, CT†
Kildonan School, NY†
Kimball Union Academy, NH†
King's-Edgehill School, NS, Canada†
Lake Forest Academy, IL†
Lake Mary Preparatory School, FL
La Lumiere School, IN†
Lancaster Mennonite High School, PA†
Landmark School, MA†
Laurinburg Institute, NC†
The Lawrenceville School, NJ†
Lexington Christian Academy, MA†
Leysin American School in Switzerland, Switzerland
Lincoln Academy, ME†
Lustre Christian High School, MT†
Luther College High School, SK, Canada†
Lyndon Institute, VT†
Maplebrook School, NY
Marianapolis Preparatory School, CT
The Marvelwood School, CT†
Massanutten Military Academy, VA†
Maumee Valley Country Day School, OH†
Maur Hill-Mount Academy, KS†
McDonogh School, MD†
Mercersburg Academy, PA†
Middlesex School, MA†
Midland School, CA

† Accepts day students

Millbrook School, NY†
Milton Academy, MA†
Milton Hershey School, PA
Monterey Bay Academy, CA†
Mooseheart High School, IL†
Nebraska Christian Schools, NE†
Neuchatel Junior College, Switzerland
New York Military Academy, NY†
Niagara Christian Community of Schools, ON, Canada†
Noble and Greenough School, MA†
The North Broward Preparatory Upper School, FL†
North Central Texas Academy, TX
North Country School, NY†
Northfield Mount Hermon School, MA†
The Northwest School, WA†
Oak Grove School, CA†
Oakland School, VA†
Oak Ridge Military Academy, NC†
Ojai Valley School, CA†
Oneida Baptist Institute, KY†
Oregon Episcopal School, OR†
The Orme School, AZ†
The Park School of Buffalo, NY†
Peddie School, NJ†
The Pennington School, NJ†
Perkins School for the Blind, MA†
Perkiomen School, PA†
Pickering College, ON, Canada†
Pine Tree Academy, ME†
Presbyterian Pan American School, TX
Proctor Academy, NH†
Randolph-Macon Academy, VA†
The Rectory School, CT
Redemption Christian Academy, MA†
Ridley College, ON, Canada†
Rockland Country Day School, NY†
Rock Point School, VT†
Rockway Mennonite Collegiate, ON, Canada†
Rosseau Lake College, ON, Canada†
Rothesay Netherwood School, NB, Canada†
Rumsey Hall School, CT†
Saddlebrook Preparatory School, FL†
Saint Andrew's School, FL†
St. Andrew's–Sewanee School, TN†
St. Bernard's Catholic School, CA†
St. Croix Schools, MN†
St. George's School, RI†
St. John's-Ravenscourt School, MB, Canada†
Saint John's School, GU†
Saint Paul Lutheran High School, MO†
St. Paul's School, NH
St. Stephen's Episcopal School, TX†
St. Stephen's School, Rome, Italy†
San Marcos Baptist Academy, TX
Scattergood Friends School, IA†
Schule Schloss Salem, Germany†
Shady Side Academy, PA†
Shattuck-St. Mary's School, MN†
Shawnigan Lake School, BC, Canada†
Southwestern Academy, AZ†
Squaw Valley Academy, CA†
Steamboat Mountain School, CO†
Stevenson School, CA†
The Stony Brook School, NY†
The Storm King School, NY†
Stratton Mountain School, VT†
Stuart Hall, VA†

The Taft School, CT†
TASIS The American School in England, United Kingdom†
TASIS, The American School in Switzerland, Switzerland†
The Thacher School, CA†
Thomas Jefferson School, MO†
Thornton Academy, ME†
Tilton School, NH†
TMI - The Episcopal School of Texas, TX†
Trinity College School, ON, Canada†
The Vanguard School, FL
Venta Preparatory School, ON, Canada†
Verdala International School, Malta†
Virginia Episcopal School, VA†
Walnut Hill School for the Arts, MA†
Wasatch Academy, UT†
Westminster School, CT†
West Nottingham Academy, MD†
West Sound Academy, WA†
Westtown School, PA†
The Winchendon School, MA†
Windermere School, United Kingdom†
Woodstock Academy, CT†
Woodstock School, India†
Wyoming Seminary, PA†

SCHOOLS ACCEPTING BOARDING BOYS

Academy of the New Church Boys' School, PA†
The American Boychoir School, NJ†
Army and Navy Academy, CA†
The Blue Ridge School, VA
Chaminade College Preparatory School, MO†
The Church Farm School, PA†
Eaglebrook School, MA†
The Fessenden School, MA†
The Greenwood School, VT†
Hampshire Country School, NH
Hillside School, MA†
Marine Military Academy, TX
The McCallie School, TN†
Merchiston Castle School, United Kingdom
The Phelps School, PA†
St. Albans School, DC†
St. Catherine's Academy, CA†
St. George's School, BC, Canada†
St. Lawrence Seminary High School, WI
St. Mary's Preparatory School, MI†
St. Michael's Preparatory School of the Norbertine Fathers, CA
St. Stanislaus College, MS†
Subiaco Academy, AR†
Trinity-Pawling School, NY†
Upper Canada College, ON, Canada†
Woodberry Forest School, VA
The Woodhall School, CT†

SCHOOLS ACCEPTING BOARDING GIRLS

Academy of the Holy Family, CT†
Academy of the New Church Girls' School, PA†
Alpine Academy, UT
Balmoral Hall School, MB, Canada†
Branksome Hall, ON, Canada†
Buffalo Seminary, NY†
Chatham Hall, VA†
Dana Hall School, MA†

† Accepts day students

Flintridge Sacred Heart Academy, CA†
Foxcroft School, VA†
Grier School, PA†
Hebrew Academy, CA†
The Hockaday School, TX
Miss Porter's School, CT†
Queen Margaret's School, BC, Canada†
Salem Academy, NC†
Santa Catalina School, CA†
Sedona Sky Academy, AZ
Sunrise Academy, UT
Trafalgar Castle School, ON, Canada†
Westover School, CT†

MILITARY SCHOOLS

Army and Navy Academy, CA
La Salle Institute, NY
Marine Military Academy, TX
Massanutten Military Academy, VA
New York Military Academy, NY
Oak Ridge Military Academy, NC
Randolph-Macon Academy, VA
St. Catherine's Academy, CA
Saint Thomas Academy, MN
TMI - The Episcopal School of Texas, TX

SCHOOLS WITH A RELIGIOUS AFFILIATION

Advent Christian Church
Schule Schloss Salem, Germany

American Baptist Churches in the U.S.A.
Liberty Christian High School, CA

Anglican Church of Canada
Holy Trinity School, ON, Canada
New York Military Academy, NY
Queen Margaret's School, BC, Canada
Ridley College, ON, Canada
Trinity College School, ON, Canada

Assemblies of God
Lustre Christian High School, MT
Mountain View Christian High School, NV
Victor Valley Christian School, CA

Association of Seventh-day Adventist Schools and Colleges
Griggs International Academy, MD

Baptist Church
American Christian Academy, AL
Bangor Christian School, ME
Ben Lippen Schools, SC
Berean Christian High School, CA
Beth Haven Christian School, KY
The First Academy, FL
Grace Baptist Academy, TN
Grace Christian School, PE, Canada
Hyde Park Baptist School, TX
Liberty Christian School, CA
Northside Christian School, FL
River Oaks Baptist School, TX
San Marcos Baptist Academy, TX

Second Baptist School, TX
Southfield Christian High School, MI
Tri-City Christian Academy, AZ
Whitefield Academy, KY

Bible Fellowship Church
California Crosspoint High School, CA

Brethren in Christ Church
Niagara Christian Community of Schools, ON, Canada

Calvinist
Manhattan Christian High School, MT

Christian
Alliance Academy, Ecuador
Alpha Omega Academy, IA
American Christian Academy, AL
Black Forest Academy, Germany
Bradenton Christian School, FL
Faith Christian High School, CA
Faith Christian School, AZ
Foundation Academy, FL
Front Range Christian High School, CO
Greater Atlanta Christian Schools, GA
Harrells Christian Academy, NC
Houghton Academy, NY
Lakeland Christian Academy, IN
Magnolia Heights School, MS
Marion Academy, AL
Nampa Christian Schools, ID
New Covenant Academy, MO
Niagara Catholic Jr. /Sr. High School, NY
Northpoint Christian School, MS
Peoples Christian Academy, ON, Canada
St. Croix Schools, MN
Valley Christian High School, CA
Valley Christian School, MT
West Memphis Christian High School, AR

Christian Churches and Churches of Christ
La Salle Academy, RI
Madison Academy, AL

Christian Nondenominational
Asheville School, NC
Augusta Christian School, GA
Bakersfield Christian High School, CA
Bearspaw Christian School, AB, Canada
Bellevue Christian School, WA
Boston Trinity Academy, MA
Briarcrest Christian High School, TN
City Christian Schools, OR
C.S. Lewis Academy, OR
Dalat School, Malaysia
Donelson Christian Academy, TN
Faith Christian High School, CA
Grace Christian School, AK
Hawthorne Christian Academy, NJ
Hillcrest Christian School, CA
Kauai Christian Academy, HI
The King's Christian High School, NJ
Landmark Christian School, GA
Linfield Christian School, CA
The Lovett School, GA
Maranatha High School, CA
Mount Vernon Presbyterian School, GA

Phoenix Christian Preparatory School, AZ
Portsmouth Christian Academy, NH
The Stony Brook School, NY
Trinity Academy, KS
Westminster Christian Academy, LA
The Woodlands Christian Academy, TX
Woodstock School, India

Christian Reformed Church
Central Alberta Christian High School, AB, Canada
Denver Christian High School, CO
Illiana Christian High School, IL
Kalamazoo Christian High School, MI
Shoreline Christian, WA
Timothy Christian High School, IL

Church of Christ
Alabama Christian Academy, AL
Columbia Academy, TN
Ezell-Harding Christian School, TN
Great Lakes Christian High School, ON, Canada
Harding Academy, AR
Mount Dora Christian Academy, FL
Westbury Christian School, TX

Church of the New Jerusalem
Academy of the New Church Boys' School, PA
Academy of the New Church Girls' School, PA

Episcopal Church
Berkeley Preparatory School, FL
The Bishop's School, CA
The Blue Ridge School, VA
Brooks School, MA
Campbell Hall (Episcopal), CA
The Canterbury Episcopal School, TX
Casady School, OK
Chatham Hall, VA
Christ Church Episcopal School, SC
Christchurch School, VA
The Church Farm School, PA
Doane Academy, NJ
The Episcopal Academy, PA
Episcopal Collegiate School, AR
Episcopal High School, TX
Episcopal High School of Jacksonville, FL
Holland Hall, OK
Holy Innocents' Episcopal School, GA
Hoosac School, NY
Kent School, CT
Oregon Episcopal School, OR
Rock Point School, VT
St. Albans School, DC
St. Andrew's Episcopal School, MD
Saint Andrew's Episcopal School, TX
Saint Andrew's School, FL
St. Andrew's–Sewanee School, TN
St. Christopher's School, VA
St. George's Independent School, TN
St. George's School, RI
Saint John's School, GU
St. Mary's Episcopal School, TN
St. Paul's School, NH
Saint Stephen's Episcopal School, FL
St. Stephen's Episcopal School, TX
Seabury Hall, HI
Shattuck-St. Mary's School, MN

Stuart Hall, VA
TMI - The Episcopal School of Texas, TX
Trinity Episcopal School, VA
Trinity-Pawling School, NY
Trinity Preparatory School, FL
Virginia Episcopal School, VA

Evangelical Christian Church
Capistrano Valley Christian Schools, CA

Evangelical
Peoples Christian Academy, ON, Canada

Evangelical Free Church of America
Hope Christian School, AB, Canada

Evangelical/Fundamental
Brethren Christian Junior and Senior High Schools, CA
California Crosspoint High School, CA
Christian Central Academy, NY

Evangelical Lutheran Church in America
Oak Grove Lutheran School, ND

Fellowship of Grace Brethren Churches
Brethren Christian Junior and Senior High Schools, CA

Free Will Baptist Church
Rejoice Christian Schools, OK

International Church of the Foursquare Gospel
Jean and Samuel Frankel Jewish Academy of Metropolitan Detroit, MI

Jewish
Charles E. Smith Jewish Day School, MD
The Dr. Miriam and Sheldon G. Adelson Educational Campus, The Adelson Upper School, NV
The Frisch School, NJ
Gann Academy (The New Jewish High School of Greater Boston), MA
Hebrew Academy, CA
Hyman Brand Hebrew Academy of Greater Kansas City, KS
Jack M. Barrack Hebrew Academy, PA
Jean and Samuel Frankel Jewish Academy of Metropolitan Detroit, MI
Jewish Community High School of the Day, CA
Ma'ayanot Yeshiva High School for Girls of Bergen County, NJ
The Weber School, GA

Lutheran Church
Long Island Lutheran Middle and High School, NY
Lutheran High School West, OH
Luther College High School, SK, Canada
Martin Luther High School, NY

Lutheran Church&-Missouri Synod
Concordia Academy, MN
Concordia Lutheran High School, IN
Faith Lutheran High School, NV
Lutheran High North, TX
Lutheran High School, CO
Lutheran High School, MO
Lutheran High School Northwest, MI
Lutheran High School of Indianapolis, IN
Lutheran High School of San Diego, CA
Mayer Lutheran High School, MN

Pacific Lutheran High School, CA
Saint Paul Lutheran High School, MO

Mennonite Church

Dock Mennonite Academy, PA
Eastern Mennonite High School, VA
Lancaster Mennonite High School, PA
Rockway Mennonite Collegiate, ON, Canada
United Mennonite Educational Institute, ON, Canada

Methodist Church

The Pennington School, NJ
Randolph-Macon Academy, VA

Moravian Church

Moravian Academy, PA
Salem Academy, NC

Pentecostal Church

Redemption Christian Academy, MA

Presbyterian Church

Ben Lippen Schools, SC
Presbyterian Pan American School, TX
The Westminster School at Oak Mountain, AL

Presbyterian Church in America

Briarwood Christian High School, AL
First Presbyterian Day School, GA
Shoreline Christian, WA

Protestant

Milton Hershey School, PA
Monsignor Bonner and Archbishop Prendergast Catholic High
    School, PA
Mooseheart High School, IL
Quinte Christian High School, ON, Canada
Redeemer Christian High School, ON, Canada
Wilmington Christian School, DE

Protestant-Evangelical

Delaware County Christian School, PA
Fresno Christian Schools, CA
Kauai Christian Academy, HI
Lehigh Valley Christian High School, PA
Nebraska Christian Schools, NE
North Toronto Christian School, ON, Canada
Salem Academy, OR
Westside Christian High School, OR

Reformed Church

Calvin Christian High School, CA
Covenant Canadian Reformed School, AB, Canada

Reformed Church in America

Academy of Notre Dame, MA
Illiana Christian High School, IL
Kalamazoo Christian High School, MI

Reformed Presbyterian Church of North America

Westminster Christian School, FL

Roman Catholic Church

Academy of Holy Angels, MN
Academy of Notre Dame de Namur, PA
Academy of Our Lady of Peace, CA
Academy of Saint Elizabeth, NJ

Academy of the Holy Cross, MD
Academy of the Holy Family, CT
Academy of the Sacred Heart, LA
Academy of the Sacred Heart, MI
Académie Ste Cécile International School, ON, Canada
Allentown Central Catholic High School, PA
Alverno Heights Academy, CA
Archbishop Alter High School, OH
Archbishop Curley High School, MD
Archbishop Hoban High School, OH
Archbishop McNicholas High School, OH
Archbishop Mitty High School, CA
Archbishop Moeller High School, OH
Archbishop Shaw High School, LA
Aurora Central Catholic High School, IL
Austin Preparatory School, MA
Belen Jesuit Preparatory School, FL
Benedictine High School, OH
Bishop Brossart High School, KY
Bishop Connolly High School, MA
Bishop Denis J. O'Connell High School, VA
Bishop Fenwick High School, OH
Bishop Foley Catholic High School, MI
Bishop Ireton High School, VA
Bishop John J. Snyder High School, FL
Bishop Kearney High School, NY
Bishop Kelly High School, ID
Bishop Kenny High School, FL
Bishop Machebeuf High School, CO
Bishop McGuinness Catholic High School, OK
Bishop O'Dowd High School, CA
Bishop Stang High School, MA
Bishop Verot High School, FL
Blanchet School, OR
Blessed Sacrament Huguenot Catholic School, VA
Blessed Trinity High School, GA
Brother Martin High School, LA
Calvert Hall College High School, MD
Cardinal Gibbons High School, NC
Cardinal Newman High School, FL
Cardinal Ritter High School, IN
Carondelet High School, CA
Cascia Hall Preparatory School, OK
Cathedral High School, NY
Catholic Central High School, MI
Catholic Central High School, NY
Catholic Central High School, WI
Central Catholic High School, MA
Central Catholic High School, PA
Chaminade College Preparatory, CA
Chaminade College Preparatory School, MO
Chaminade-Madonna College Preparatory, FL
Christian Brothers Academy, NJ
Christian Brothers Academy, NY
Christopher Columbus High School, FL
Colegio San Jose, PR
Convent of the Sacred Heart, CT
Covington Catholic High School, KY
Damien High School, CA
De La Salle College, ON, Canada
De La Salle High School, CA
DeLaSalle High School, MN
De La Salle North Catholic High School, OR
Delbarton School, NJ
DeMatha Catholic High School, MD
Devon Preparatory School, PA
Dominican Academy, NY

Donovan Catholic, NJ
Dowling Catholic High School, IA
Duchesne High School, MO
Edgewood High School of the Sacred Heart, WI
Father Duenas Memorial School, GU
Father Lopez High School, FL
Father Yermo High School, TX
Flintridge Sacred Heart Academy, CA
Fontbonne Academy, MA
Fontbonne Hall Academy, NY
Fordham Preparatory School, NY
Gabriel Richard Catholic High School, MI
Gilmour Academy, OH
Gonzaga College High School, DC
Holy Cross High School, CT
Holy Cross School, LA
Holy Ghost Preparatory School, PA
Holy Savior Menard Catholic High School, LA
Holy Trinity Diocesan High School, NY
Holy Trinity High School, IL
Holy Trinity School, ON, Canada
Immaculata High School, KS
Immaculata High School, NJ
Immaculata-La Salle High School, FL
Immaculate Conception High School, NJ
Immaculate Heart Academy, NJ
Incarnate Word Academy, TX
Jesuit High School of Tampa, FL
Josephinum Academy, IL
Junipero Serra High School, CA
Kolbe-Cathedral High School, CT
La Lumiere School, IN
Lancaster Catholic High School, PA
Lansdale Catholic High School, PA
La Salle Academy, RI
La Salle High School, CA
La Salle Institute, NY
Lauralton Hall, CT
Louisville High School, CA
Loyola-Blakefield, MD
Loyola College Prep, LA
Malden Catholic High School, MA
Malvern Preparatory School, PA
Marianapolis Preparatory School, CT
Marian Central Catholic High School, IL
Marian High School, MA
Marist High School, IL
Marist School, GA
Mary Help of Christians Academy, NJ
The Mary Louis Academy, NY
Marymount High School, CA
Marymount School of New York, NY
Maryvale Preparatory School, MD
Mater Dei High School, IL
Mater Dei Prep, NJ
Matignon High School, MA
Maur Hill-Mount Academy, KS
Memphis Catholic High School and Middle School, TN
Mercy High School, CT
Mercy High School, MI
Mercyhurst Preparatory School, PA
Merion Mercy Academy, PA
Monsignor Bonner and Archbishop Prendergast Catholic High
    School, PA
Monsignor Edward Pace High School, FL
Montrose School, MA
Mooseheart High School, IL

Moreau Catholic High School, CA
Morris Catholic High School, NJ
Mother McAuley High School, IL
Mount Carmel Academy, LA
Mount Mercy Academy, NY
Mount Notre Dame High School, OH
Mount St. Agnes Academy, Bermuda
Mount Saint Charles Academy, RI
Nazareth Academy, IL
Nerinx Hall, MO
Newton Country Day School of the Sacred Heart, MA
Northwest Catholic High School, CT
Notre Dame-Cathedral Latin School, OH
Notre Dame High School, CA
Notre Dame High School, CA
Notre Dame High School, NJ
Notre Dame High School, NY
Notre Dame High School, TN
Notre Dame Junior/Senior High School, PA
Oldenburg Academy, IN
Padua Franciscan High School, OH
Palma School, CA
Peninsula Catholic High School, VA
Pensacola Catholic High School, FL
Pinecrest Academy, GA
Pope Francis High School, MA
Pope John XXIII Regional High School, NJ
Powers Catholic High School, MI
Preston High School, NY
Providence High School, CA
Queen of Peace High School, IL
Quigley Catholic High School, PA
Ramona Convent Secondary School, CA
Regina Junior-Senior High School, IA
Regis High School, OR
Rice Memorial High School, VT
Routt Catholic High School, IL
Sacred Heart Academy, NY
Sacred Heart/Griffin High School, IL
Sacred Heart High School, CA
Sacred Heart High School, NY
St. Agnes Academy, TX
Saint Agnes Academy St. Dominic School, TN
Saint Albert Junior-Senior High School, IA
Saint Anthony High School, IL
Saint Augustine Preparatory School, NJ
Saint Basil Academy, PA
St. Benedict at Auburndale, TN
St. Bernard's Catholic School, CA
St. Catherine's Academy, CA
Saint Dominic Academy, NJ
Saint Francis High School, CA
Saint Gertrude High School, VA
Saint John Bosco High School, CA
St. John Neumann High School, FL
St. John's Catholic Prep, MD
St. John's Preparatory School, MA
Saint Joseph Academy, CA
St. Joseph Academy, FL
St. Joseph High School, CA
St. Joseph High School, CT
Saint Joseph High School, NJ
St. Joseph High School, TX
Saint Joseph Regional High School, NJ
St. Joseph's Catholic School, SC
St. Joseph's Preparatory School, PA
St. Lawrence Seminary High School, WI

Saint Lucy's Priory High School, CA
Saint Mary of the Assumption High School, NJ
Saint Mary's High School, AZ
St. Mary's High School, CO
St. Mary's Preparatory School, MI
Saint Maur International School, Japan
St. Michael's Preparatory School of the Norbertine Fathers, CA
Saint Patrick High School, IL
St. Patrick's Regional Secondary, BC, Canada
St. Paul's High School, MB, Canada
St. Pius X Catholic High School, GA
St. Pius X High School, TX
St. Stanislaus College, MS
Saint Teresa's Academy, MO
Saint Thomas Academy, MN
St. Thomas Aquinas High School, FL
Saint Thomas Aquinas High School, KS
St. Thomas Aquinas High School, NH
Saint Thomas More Catholic High School, LA
Saint Ursula Academy, OH
Saint Ursula Academy, OH
Saint Vincent-Saint Mary High School, OH
Saint Xavier High School, KY
Salpointe Catholic High School, AZ
Santa Catalina School, CA
Santa Margarita Catholic High School, CA
Scotus Central Catholic High School, NE
Seisen International School, Japan
Seton Catholic Central High School, NY
Seton Catholic High School, AZ
Shanley High School, ND
Shawe Memorial Junior/Senior High School, IN
Subiaco Academy, AR
Teurlings Catholic High School, LA
Trinity Catholic High School, CT
Trinity High School, KY
Trinity High School, OH
Ursuline Academy, MA
The Ursuline Academy of Dallas, TX
Vicksburg Catholic School, MS
Villa Duchesne and Oak Hill School, MO
Villa Joseph Marie High School, PA
Villa Madonna Academy, KY
Villa Victoria Academy, NJ
Villa Walsh Academy, NJ
The Willows Academy, IL
Xavier High School, NY

Roman Catholic Church (Jesuit Order)
Belen Jesuit Preparatory School, FL
Brophy College Preparatory, AZ
Cheverus High School, ME
Jesuit College Preparatory School, TX
Regis Jesuit High School, Boys Division, CO
Regis Jesuit High School, Girls Division, CO
Rockhurst High School, MO
Saint Ignatius College Prep, IL
St. John's Jesuit High School, OH

Schwenkfelder Church
Kolbe-Cathedral High School, CT

Seventh-day Adventist Church
Crawford Adventist Academy, ON, Canada
Escondido Adventist Academy, CA
Forest Lake Academy, FL
Gem State Academy, ID

La Sierra Academy, CA
Livingstone Adventist Academy, OR
Mesa Grande Seventh-Day Academy, CA
Monterey Bay Academy, CA
Mountain View Academy, CA
Orangewood Adventist Academy, CA
Pine Tree Academy, ME
Takoma Academy, MD

Seventh-day Adventists
Central Catholic High School, LA
Collegedale Academy, TN
Forest Lake Academy, FL
Paradise Adventist Academy, CA

Society of Friends
Delaware Valley Friends School, PA
Friends Academy, NY
Friends Select School, PA
Moorestown Friends School, NJ
Scattergood Friends School, IA
Westtown School, PA
Wilmington Friends School, DE

Southern Baptist Convention
Hawaii Baptist Academy, HI
Oneida Baptist Institute, KY
Prestonwood Christian Academy, TX

United Church of Christ
Massanutten Military Academy, VA

United Methodist Church
Lydia Patterson Institute, TX
Wyoming Seminary, PA

Wesleyan Church
Arizona Lutheran Academy, AZ
Moncton Wesleyan Academy, NB, Canada
Wesleyan Academy, PR

Wisconsin Evangelical Lutheran Synod
California Lutheran High School, CA
St. Croix Schools, MN

SCHOOLS WITH ELEMENTARY DIVISIONS
Academy at the Lakes, FL
Academy of Notre Dame de Namur, PA
Academy of the Sacred Heart, LA
Adelphi Academy, NY
The Agnes Irwin School, PA
Albuquerque Academy, NM
Allen Academy, TX
The American Boychoir School, NJ
The American International School, Austria
The American School Foundation, Mexico
The American School in Japan, Japan
The American School of Madrid, Spain
The American School of Puerto Vallarta, Mexico
Andrews Osborne Academy, OH
Army and Navy Academy, CA
Ashley Hall, SC
Athens Academy, GA
Atlanta Girls' School, GA
Atlanta International School, GA

Austin Preparatory School, MA
Balmoral Hall School, MB, Canada
Battle Ground Academy, TN
Baylor School, TN
Bay Ridge Preparatory School, NY
Bayview Glen School, ON, Canada
Beaufort Academy, SC
The Bement School, MA
Bentley School, CA
Berkeley Carroll School, NY
Berkeley Preparatory School, FL
The Birch Wathen Lenox School, NY
Bishop's College School, QC, Canada
The Bishop's School, CA
The Blake School, MN
The Bolles School, FL
Boston Trinity Academy, MA
Bradenton Christian School, FL
Brandon Hall School, GA
Branksome Hall, ON, Canada
Brehm Preparatory School, IL
Briarwood Christian High School, AL
Bridges Academy, CA
Brimmer and May School, MA
British International School of Boston, MA
The Browning School, NY
The Bryn Mawr School for Girls, MD
Buckingham Browne & Nichols School, MA
The Buckley School, CA
Cairo American College, Egypt
The Calhoun School, NY
Campbell Hall (Episcopal), CA
The Canterbury Episcopal School, TX
Canterbury School, FL
Canterbury School, IN
The Canterbury School of Florida, FL
Cape Cod Academy, MA
Cape Henry Collegiate School, VA
Casady School, OK
Cascades Academy of Central Oregon, OR
Castilleja School, CA
Chadwick School, CA
Chaminade College Preparatory School, MO
Charlotte Country Day School, NC
Charlotte Latin School, NC
Chase Collegiate School, CT
Christ Church Episcopal School, SC
Clarksville Academy, TN
Colegio Franklin D. Roosevelt, Peru
The Collegiate School, VA
The Columbus Academy, OH
Columbus School for Girls, OH
The Community School of Naples, FL
Convent of the Sacred Heart, CT
The Country Day School, ON, Canada
Crescent School, ON, Canada
Currey Ingram Academy, TN
Dana Hall School, MA
Darlington School, GA
Delaware County Christian School, PA
Delaware Valley Friends School, PA
Delbarton School, NJ
The Delphian School, OR
Denver Academy, CO
Desert Academy, NM
Detroit Country Day School, MI
Devon Preparatory School, PA

Doane Academy, NJ
The Dr. Miriam and Sheldon G. Adelson Educational Campus,
    The Adelson Upper School, NV
Donelson Christian Academy, TN
Durham Academy, NC
The Dwight School, NY
Eaglebrook School, MA
Eagle Hill School, CT
Eastern Mennonite High School, VA
Edmund Burke School, DC
Elgin Academy, IL
The Ellis School, PA
The Episcopal Academy, PA
Episcopal Collegiate School, AR
Episcopal High School of Jacksonville, FL
Escola Americana de Campinas, Brazil
Falmouth Academy, MA
Fayetteville Academy, NC
Fay School, MA
The Fessenden School, MA
The First Academy, FL
Flintridge Preparatory School, CA
Forsyth Country Day School, NC
Fort Worth Country Day School, TX
Franklin Academy, CT
French-American School of New York, NY
Friends Academy, NY
Friends Select School, PA
Fuqua School, VA
The Galloway School, GA
Gaston Day School, NC
Gilman School, MD
Gilmour Academy, OH
Girard College, PA
Glenelg Country School, MD
Good Hope Country Day School, VI
The Gow School, NY
The Grauer School, CA
Greater Atlanta Christian Schools, GA
Greenfield School, NC
Green Fields Country Day School, AZ
Greenhill School, TX
Greenhills School, MI
The Greenwood School, VT
Grier School, PA
Gulliver Preparatory School, FL
Hammond School, SC
Hampshire Country School, NH
Hampton Roads Academy, VA
The Harker School, CA
The Harley School, NY
The Harpeth Hall School, TN
Harvard-Westlake School, CA
The Harvey School, NY
The Haverford School, PA
Hawaii Baptist Academy, HI
Hawai`i Preparatory Academy, HI
Hawken School, OH
Hebron Academy, ME
Heritage Hall, OK
The Hewitt School, NY
The Hill Center, Durham Academy, NC
Hillside School, MA
The Hockaday School, TX
Holland Hall, OK
Holy Innocents' Episcopal School, GA
Holy Trinity School, ON, Canada

Hoosac School, NY
Houghton Academy, NY
The Howard School, GA
The Hun School of Princeton, NJ
Indian Springs School, AL
International High School, CA
International School Manila, Philippines
International School of Brussels, Belgium
Istanbul International Community School, Turkey
Jack M. Barrack Hebrew Academy, PA
Jackson Preparatory School, MS
John Burroughs School, MO
The Journeys School of Teton Science School, WY
Kent Denver School, CO
The Key School, MD
Kildonan School, NY
Kimberton Waldorf School, PA
King School, CT
Kingswood-Oxford School, CT
The Lab School of Washington, DC
La Grange Academy, GA
Lakehill Preparatory School, TX
Lake Mary Preparatory School, FL
Lake Ridge Academy, OH
Lakeview Academy, GA
Landmark School, MA
Landon School, MD
La Pietra–Hawaii School for Girls, HI
La Salle Academy, RI
Lawrence School, OH
Lawrence Woodmere Academy, NY
Le Lycee Francais de Los Angeles, CA
Lexington Christian Academy, MA
Lincoln School, RI
Long Island Lutheran Middle and High School, NY
Long Trail School, VT
Loudoun School for the Gifted, VA
Louisville Collegiate School, KY
The Lovett School, GA
Lower Canada College, QC, Canada
Lycee Français La Perouse, CA
Lycee Internationale de Boston/International
    School of Boston, MA
Malvern Preparatory School, PA
Marine Military Academy, TX
Marist School, GA
Marlborough School, CA
Marshall School, MN
Mary Institute and St. Louis Country Day School (MICDS), MO
Marymount School of New York, NY
Maryvale Preparatory School, MD
Massanutten Military Academy, VA
Maumee Valley Country Day School, OH
The McCallie School, TN
McDonogh School, MD
The McLean School of Maryland, Inc., MD
The Meadows School, NV
Memphis University School, TN
Menlo School, CA
The Miami Valley School, OH
Mid-Pacific Institute, HI
Mill Springs Academy, GA
Milton Academy, MA
Milton Hershey School, PA
Miss Edgar's and Miss Cramp's School, QC, Canada
MMI Preparatory School, PA
Montclair Kimberley Academy, NJ

Montgomery Bell Academy, TN
Montrose School, MA
Moorestown Friends School, NJ
Moravian Academy, PA
Mount Vernon Presbyterian School, GA
New Roads School, CA
Newton Country Day School of the Sacred Heart, MA
New York Military Academy, NY
Noble Academy, NC
Noble and Greenough School, MA
The North Broward Preparatory Upper School, FL
North Central Texas Academy, TX
North Country School, NY
Northpoint Christian School, MS
North Shore Country Day School, IL
Northwest Academy, OR
The Northwest School, WA
North Yarmouth Academy, ME
Oak Grove School, CA
Oak Ridge Military Academy, NC
The Oakridge School, TX
Ojai Valley School, CA
The O'Neal School, NC
Oregon Episcopal School, OR
The Orme School, AZ
Pace Academy, GA
The Packer Collegiate Institute, NY
The Paideia School, GA
The Park School of Baltimore, MD
The Park School of Buffalo, NY
The Pembroke Hill School, MO
The Pennington School, NJ
Perkins School for the Blind, MA
Perkiomen School, PA
The Phelps School, PA
Phoenix Country Day School, AZ
Pickering College, ON, Canada
Pinewood Preparatory School, SC
The Pingry School, NJ
Polytechnic School, CA
Portledge School, NY
The Potomac School, VA
Poughkeepsie Day School, NY
Professional Children's School, NY
Providence Country Day School, RI
Providence Day School, NC
Punahou School, HI
Queen Margaret's School, BC, Canada
Randolph-Macon Academy, VA
Ransom Everglades School, FL
Ravenscroft School, NC
The Rectory School, CT
Ridley College, ON, Canada
Riverdale Country School, NY
Rivermont Collegiate, IA
River Oaks Baptist School, TX
The Rivers School, MA
Rockland Country Day School, NY
Rocky Mount Academy, NC
The Roeper School, MI
Roland Park Country School, MD
Rolling Hills Preparatory School, CA
Rothesay Netherwood School, NB, Canada
Rowland Hall, UT
The Roxbury Latin School, MA
Rumsey Hall School, CT
Sacramento Country Day School, CA

Sacramento Waldorf School, CA
Saint Agnes Academy–St. Dominic School, TN
St. Albans School, DC
St. Andrew's Episcopal School, MD
Saint Andrew's Episcopal School, TX
Saint Andrew's School, FL
St. Andrew's School, GA
St. Andrew's–Sewanee School, TN
St. Christopher's School, VA
Saint Dominic Academy, NJ
St. George's Independent School, TN
St. George's School, BC, Canada
St. John's Preparatory School, MA
St. John's-Ravenscourt School, MB, Canada
Saint John's School, GU
St. Luke's School, CT
St. Mary's Episcopal School, TN
Saint Mary's Hall, TX
St. Stanislaus College, MS
Saint Stephen's Episcopal School, FL
St. Stephen's Episcopal School, TX
Saint Thomas Academy, MN
San Marcos Baptist Academy, TX
Santa Fe Preparatory School, NM
Sayre School, KY
Seabury Hall, HI
Seattle Academy of Arts and Sciences, WA
The Seven Hills School, OH
Shady Side Academy, PA
Shattuck-St. Mary's School, MN
Shawnigan Lake School, BC, Canada
Shorecrest Preparatory School, FL
The Siena School, MD
The Spence School, NY
Springside Chestnut Hill Academy, PA
The Stanwich School, CT
Stevenson School, CA
The Stony Brook School, NY
The Storm King School, NY
Stratford Academy, GA
Stratton Mountain School, VT
Stuart Hall, VA
Subiaco Academy, AR
Taipei American School, Taiwan
Tandem Friends School, VA
Thomas Jefferson School, MO
Thornton Academy, ME
TMI - The Episcopal School of Texas, TX
Tower Hill School, DE
Trafalgar Castle School, ON, Canada
Trevor Day School, NY
Trinity College School, ON, Canada
Trinity Episcopal School, VA
Trinity-Pawling School, NY
Trinity Preparatory School, FL
United Nations International School, NY
University Lake School, WI
University of Chicago Laboratory Schools, IL
University Prep, WA
University School of Jackson, TN
Upper Canada College, ON, Canada
Ursuline Academy, MA
Valwood School, GA
The Vanguard School, FL
Villa Duchesne and Oak Hill School, MO
Villa Victoria Academy, NJ
Wasatch Academy, UT

Washington International School, DC
Washington Waldorf School, MD
The Waterford School, UT
Watkinson School, CT
Waynflete School, ME
Webb School of Knoxville, TN
The Wellington School, OH
Westmark School, CA
Westminster Christian Academy, LA
Westminster Christian School, FL
Westridge School, CA
Westtown School, PA
The Wheeler School, RI
Whitfield School, MO
Willow Hill School, MA
Wilmington Friends School, DE
Winchester Thurston School, PA
Windermere School, United Kingdom
Windward School, CA
Winston Preparatory School, NY
The Winston School, TX
The Winston School San Antonio, TX
Woodlynde School, PA
Woodward Academy, GA
Worcester Preparatory School, MD
York Country Day School, PA

SCHOOLS REPORTING ACADEMIC ACCOMMODATIONS FOR THE GIFTED AND TALENTED

The Academy for Gifted Children (PACE), ON, Canada	G
Academy of Holy Angels, MN	G,M,A
Academy of Notre Dame, MA	G
Academy of Notre Dame de Namur, PA	G,M,A
Academy of the Holy Cross, MD	G,A
Academy of the Holy Family, CT	G,M
Academy of the New Church Boys' School, PA	G,M,A
Academy of the New Church Girls' School, PA	G,M,A
Academy of the Sacred Heart, MI	G,M,A
Académie Ste Cécile International School, ON, Canada	G,M,A
Adelphi Academy, NY	G,M,A
Advanced Academy of Georgia, GA	G,M,A
The Agnes Irwin School, PA	G
Allentown Central Catholic High School, PA	G
Alliance Academy, Ecuador	G
Allison Academy, FL	G,M,A
Alpine Academy, UT	G
Alverno Heights Academy, CA	G
The American Boychoir School, NJ	M
American School of The Hague, Netherlands	G,M,A
Andrews Osborne Academy, OH	G,M,A
Archbishop Hoban High School, OH	G,A
Archbishop Mitty High School, CA	G,M,A
Arete Preparatory Academy, CA	G
Arizona Lutheran Academy, AZ	G,M
Arroyo Pacific Academy, CA	G,M,A
Asheville School, NC	G
Ashley Hall, SC	G,M,A
Aurora Central Catholic High School, IL	G
Balmoral Hall School, MB, Canada	G
Banbury Crossroads School, AB, Canada	G
Barnstable Academy, NJ	G,M,A
Baylor School, TN	G
Bay Ridge Preparatory School, NY	G,M,A
Beaufort Academy, SC	G

G — gifted; M — musically talented; A — artistically talented

The Beekman School, NY	G,M,A	Cushing Academy, MA	G,M,A
Bellevue Christian School, WA	G,M,A	Darlington School, GA	M
The Birch Wathen Lenox School, NY	G	Darrow School, NY	G,M,A
Bishop Denis J. O'Connell High School, VA	G	Deerfield Academy, MA	G,M,A
Bishop Fenwick High School, OH	G	Delaware County Christian School, PA	G,M,A
Bishop Kearney High School, NY	G,M,A	Delaware Valley Friends School, PA	A
Bishop McGuinness Catholic High School, OK	G,A	The Delphian School, OR	G,M,A
Bishop O'Dowd High School, CA	G,M,A	DeMatha Catholic High School, MD	G,M,A
Bishop's College School, QC, Canada	G	Denver Academy, CO	G
Bishop Stang High School, MA	G	Detroit Country Day School, MI	G,M,A
Blueprint Education, AZ	M,A	Doane Academy, NJ	G,M,A
Boston University Academy, MA	G	The Dr. Miriam and Sheldon G. Adelson Educational	
Branksome Hall, ON, Canada	G,M,A	Campus, The Adelson Upper School, NV	G
Brehm Preparatory School, IL	G	Donovan Catholic, NJ	G,M,A
Brethren Christian Junior and Senior High Schools, CA	G	Dowling Catholic High School, IA	G,M,A
Briarcrest Christian High School, TN	G,M,A	Dublin Christian Academy, NH	M,A
Briarwood Christian High School, AL	G	Dublin School, NH	G
Bridges Academy, CA	G	Duchesne High School, MO	G
British International School of Boston, MA	G	The Dwight School, NY	G,M,A
Brockwood Park School, United Kingdom	G,M,A	Eaglebrook School, MA	G,M,A
Brother Martin High School, LA	G,M,A	Eagle Rock School, CO	G,M,A
The Browning School, NY	G,M	Eastern Mennonite High School, VA	G
The Bryn Mawr School for Girls, MD	G,M,A	Eaton Academy, GA	G,M,A
Buffalo Seminary, NY	G	Edison School, AB, Canada	G
Buxton School, MA	G,M,A	Edmonton Academy, AB, Canada	G
The Calhoun School, NY	G,M,A	Eldorado Emerson Private School, CA	G,M,A
California Crosspoint High School, CA	G	The Ellis School, PA	G,M,A
Calvert Hall College High School, MD	G,M,A	Elmwood School, ON, Canada	G
Campion School, Athens, Greece	M,A	The English College in Prague, Czech Republic	G,M,A
Cape Henry Collegiate School, VA	G,M,A	Episcopal High School of Jacksonville, FL	G
Cardinal Newman High School, FL	G	Excel Christian Academy, GA	G
Cardinal Ritter High School, IN	G,M,A	Explorations Academy, WA	G
Carondelet High School, CA	G	The Fessenden School, MA	G,M,A
Casady School, OK	G,M,A	Fontbonne Hall Academy, NY	G,M,A
Cascia Hall Preparatory School, OK	G	Forsyth Country Day School, NC	G
Castilleja School, CA	G	Fort Worth Country Day School, TX	G,M,A
Cate School, CA	G,M,A	Foxcroft School, VA	G,M,A
Catholic Central High School, WI	G,A	Franklin Academy, CT	G
Central Catholic High School, PA	G	Fraser Academy, BC, Canada	G
Chadwick School, CA	G,M,A	Friends Select School, PA	M,A
Chaminade College Preparatory School, MO	G	Front Range Christian High School, CO	G
Chaminade-Madonna College Preparatory, FL	G,M,A	Fuqua School, VA	G
Charles E. Smith Jewish Day School, MD	G	The Galloway School, GA	G,M,A
Charlotte Country Day School, NC	G	Gaston Day School, NC	G
Charlotte Latin School, NC	G	George Stevens Academy, ME	G,M,A
Chase Collegiate School, CT	G	Gilman School, MD	G,M,A
Chatham Hall, VA	G,M,A	Gilmour Academy, OH	G,M,A
Children's Creative and Performing Arts		Glenelg Country School, MD	G
Academy of San Diego, CA	G,M,A	The Governor French Academy, IL	G
Choate Rosemary Hall, CT	G,M,A	The Gow School, NY	M
Christa McAuliffe Academy School of Arts		The Grauer School, CA	G,M,A
and Sciences, OR	G,M,A	Greater Atlanta Christian Schools, GA	G,M,A
Christ Church Episcopal School, SC	G	Greenfield School, NC	G
Christchurch School, VA	G	The Greenwood School, VT	G,M,A
Christopher Columbus High School, FL	G	Grier School, PA	G,M,A
Chrysalis School, WA	G	Gulliver Preparatory School, FL	G,M,A
The Church Farm School, PA	G,M,A	The Gunnery, CT	G,M,A
City Christian Schools, OR	G,A	The Gunston School, MD	G,M,A
The Columbus Academy, OH	G	Halstrom Academy, Beverly Hills, CA	G,M,A
Commonwealth School, MA	G,M,A	Halstrom Academy, Calsbad, CA	G,M,A
The Community School of Naples, FL	G	Halstrom Academy, Cupertino, CA	G,M,A
The Concept School, PA	G	Halstrom Academy, Huntington Beach, CA	G,M,A
Concord Academy, MA	G,M,A	Halstrom Academy, Irvine, CA	G,M,A
Convent of the Sacred Heart, CT	G,A	Halstrom Academy, Los Angeles, CA	G,M,A
Crestwood Preparatory College, ON, Canada	G	Halstrom Academy, Manhattan Beach, CA	G,M,A
The Culver Academies, IN	G,M,A	Halstrom Academy, Mission Viejo, CA	G,M,A
Currey Ingram Academy, TN	G,M,A	Halstrom Academy, Orange, CA	G,M,A

G — gifted; M — musically talented; A — artistically talented

Halstrom Academy, Pasadena, CA	G,M,A	The Linden School, ON, Canada	G
Halstrom Academy, San Diego, CA	G,M,A	Linfield Christian School, CA	G
Halstrom Academy, San Mateo, CA	G,M,A	Loudoun School for the Gifted, VA	G
Halstrom Academy, Walnut Creek, CA	G,M,A	Loyola-Blakefield, MD	G,M,A
Halstrom Academy, Westlake Village, CA	G,M,A	Lutheran High School, CO	G,A
Halstrom Academy, Woodland Hills, CA	G,M,A	Lutheran High School, MO	A
Hammond School, SC	G,M,A	Lutheran High School West, OH	M
Hampshire Country School, NH	G	Luther College High School, SK, Canada	G
The Harker School, CA	G	Maranatha High School, CA	A
The Harpeth Hall School, TN	G,M,A	Marian Central Catholic High School, IL	G
Harvard-Westlake School, CA	G,M,A	Marin Academy, CA	G,M,A
The Haverford School, PA	G	Marine Military Academy, TX	G
Hebrew Academy, CA	G	Marist High School, IL	G,M,A
Hebron Academy, ME	G,M,A	Marshall School, MN	G
Heritage Hall, OK	G,M,A	Mary Institute and St. Louis Country Day	
Hillside School, MA	G	School (MICDS), MO	G
Ho'Ala School, HI	G,A	The Mary Louis Academy, NY	G,M,A
Holland Hall, OK	G,M,A	Marymount School of New York, NY	G
Holy Cross School, LA	G,M,A	Mater Dei High School, IL	G
Holy Innocents' Episcopal School, GA	G,M,A	Mater Dei Prep, NJ	G
Hoosac School, NY	M,A	Maumee Valley Country Day School, OH	G,M,A
The Hotchkiss School, CT	G,M,A	Maur Hill-Mount Academy, KS	G
The Howard School, GA	A	Mayer Lutheran High School, MN	G,M
The Hun School of Princeton, NJ	G	The McCallie School, TN	G
Huntington-Surrey School, TX	G	The McLean School of Maryland, Inc., MD	G
Hyde School, ME	G,M,A	The Meadows School, NV	G,M,A
Hyman Brand Hebrew Academy of Greater Kansas City, KS	G	Memphis University School, TN	G,M,A
Immaculata High School, NJ	M	Mercersburg Academy, PA	G,M,A
Independent School, KS	G,M,A	Merchiston Castle School, United Kingdom	G,M,A
Indian Springs School, AL	G,M	Mercyhurst Preparatory School, PA	G,M,A
International High School, CA	G,M,A	Merion Mercy Academy, PA	G,M,A
International School Manila, Philippines	G,M,A	The Miami Valley School, OH	G,M,A
International School of Amsterdam, Netherlands	G,A	Middlesex School, MA	G
International School of Brussels, Belgium	G,M,A	Mid-Pacific Institute, HI	G,M,A
International School of Port-of-Spain, Trinidad and Tobago	G	Mill Springs Academy, GA	G,M,A
Istanbul International Community School, Turkey	G	Milton Academy, MA	G,M,A
Jack M. Barrack Hebrew Academy, PA	G	Milton Hershey School, PA	M,A
Jackson Preparatory School, MS	G,M,A	Miss Porter's School, CT	G,M,A
Jean and Samuel Frankel Jewish Academy of Metropolitan		The Monarch School, TX	G,A
Detroit, MI	G	Montclair Kimberley Academy, NJ	G
The John Dewey Academy, MA	G,A	Mountain View Christian High School, NV	G,M,A
The Journeys School of Teton Science School, WY	G	Mount Carmel Academy, LA	A
Kalamazoo Christian High School, MI	G	Mount St. Agnes Academy, Bermuda	G
Kent School, CT	G,M,A	Neuchatel Junior College, Switzerland	G,M,A
The Key School, MD	G	Niagara Christian Community of Schools, ON, Canada	G
King School, CT	G,M,A	Noble and Greenough School, MA	G,M,A
The King's Christian High School, NJ	G,M,A	The Nora School, MD	G,A
King's-Edgehill School, NS, Canada	G	The North Broward Preparatory Upper School, FL	G,M,A
The Kiski School, PA	G	North Central Texas Academy, TX	G,M,A
The Lab School of Washington, DC	G,M,A	Northfield Mount Hermon School, MA	G,M,A
La Grange Academy, GA	G,M,A	Northpoint Christian School, MS	G
Lake Forest Academy, IL	G,M,A	Northside Christian School, FL	G
Lakeland Christian Academy, IN	G	Notre Dame-Cathedral Latin School, OH	G
Lake Mary Preparatory School, FL	G,M,A	Notre Dame High School, NY	G,A
Lake Ridge Academy, OH	G,M,A	Oak Grove Lutheran School, ND	G,M
Lakeview Academy, GA	G,M,A	Oak Ridge Military Academy, NC	G
La Lumiere School, IN	G,A	The Oakridge School, TX	G,M,A
Lancaster Catholic High School, PA	G,M,A	Ojai Valley School, CA	G,A
Lancaster Mennonite High School, PA	M	Oregon Episcopal School, OR	G
La Salle Academy, RI	G,M,A	Orinda Academy, CA	G
La Salle Institute, NY	M	Pace Academy, GA	G,M,A
La Sierra Academy, CA	G,M,A	PACE/Brantley Hall High School, FL	G
The Laureate Academy, MB, Canada	G	Pacific Lutheran High School, CA	G
Laurel Springs School, CA	G,M,A	Palma School, CA	G
Leysin American School in Switzerland, Switzerland	G,M,A	The Park School of Baltimore, MD	G,M,A
Liberty Christian School, CA	G	The Park School of Buffalo, NY	G
Lincoln Academy, ME	G,M,A	The Pembroke Hill School, MO	G,M,A

G — gifted; M — musically talented; A — artistically talented

Peninsula Catholic High School, VA	G	Saint Thomas More Catholic High School, LA	G
The Pennington School, NJ	G	Saint Vincent-Saint Mary High School, OH	G
The Phelps School, PA	G	Saint Xavier High School, KY	G,M,A
Philadelphia-Montgomery Christian Academy, PA	G,M,A	San Francisco University High School, CA	G,M,A
Phoenix Christian Preparatory School, AZ	G	San Marcos Baptist Academy, TX	G,M,A
Pinewood Preparatory School, SC	G	Santa Catalina School, CA	G,M,A
The Pingry School, NJ	G	Santa Fe Preparatory School, NM	G
Plumstead Christian School, PA	G	Santa Margarita Catholic High School, CA	G,M,A
Portledge School, NY	G,M,A	Sayre School, KY	G,A
Portsmouth Christian Academy, NH	G,M	Scattergood Friends School, IA	G
Poughkeepsie Day School, NY	G,M,A	Scholar's Hall Preparatory School, ON, Canada	G,M,A
Prestonwood Christian Academy, TX	G	Schule Schloss Salem, Germany	G,M,A
Proctor Academy, NH	G	SciCore Academy, NJ	G,A
Providence Country Day School, RI	G,M,A	Seabury Hall, HI	G
Providence Day School, NC	G,M,A	Seacrest Country Day School, FL	G,M,A
Providence High School, CA	M,A	Seattle Academy of Arts and Sciences, WA	G,M,A
Queen Margaret's School, BC, Canada	G,M,A	Sedona Sky Academy, AZ	G,M,A
Ramona Convent Secondary School, CA	G,M,A	Seton Catholic Central High School, NY	G,A
Randolph-Macon Academy, VA	G	The Seven Hills School, OH	G
Ravenscroft School, NC	G,M,A	Shady Side Academy, PA	G,M,A
Realms of Inquiry, UT	G,M,A	Shattuck-St. Mary's School, MN	G,M,A
The Rectory School, CT	G,M,A	Shawe Memorial Junior/Senior High School, IN	G
Redemption Christian Academy, MA	G	Shawnigan Lake School, BC, Canada	G
Rice Memorial High School, VT	G	Shorecrest Preparatory School, FL	G
Ridley College, ON, Canada	G,M,A	The Siena School, MD	G
Riverdale Country School, NY	G,M,A	Sierra Canyon School, CA	G,M,A
Rivermont Collegiate, IA	G,M,A	Smith School, NY	M,A
Rockland Country Day School, NY	G,M,A	Southwestern Academy, AZ	M,A
Rock Point School, VT	G,A	Springside Chestnut Hill Academy, PA	G,M,A
Rocky Mount Academy, NC	G	Squaw Valley Academy, CA	G,M,A
The Roeper School, MI	G,M,A	The Stanwich School, CT	G,M,A
Rolling Hills Preparatory School, CA	G	STAR Prep Academy, CA	G,M
Rothesay Netherwood School, NB, Canada	G,M,A	Steamboat Mountain School, CO	G
Rotterdam International Secondary School, Wolfert van Borselen, Netherlands	G	The Storm King School, NY	G,M,A
		Stuart Hall, VA	G,M,A
The Roxbury Latin School, MA	G,M,A	Subiaco Academy, AR	G,M,A
Rudolf Steiner School of Ann Arbor, MI	G	Sunrise Academy, UT	G
Rumsey Hall School, CT	G	The Taft School, CT	G,M,A
Sacred Heart/Griffin High School, IL	G,M,A	Tandem Friends School, VA	G
Sage Hill School, CA	G,M,A	TASIS The American School in England, United Kingdom	G
Saint Agnes Academy–St. Dominic School, TN	G,A	TASIS, The American School in Switzerland, Switzerland	G,M,A
Saint Albert Junior-Senior High School, IA	G		
St. Andrew's Episcopal School, MD	G	The Tenney School, TX	G,M,A
Saint Andrew's School, FL	G	The Thacher School, CA	G,M,A
St. Andrew's School, GA	G,M,A	Thomas Jefferson School, MO	G
St. Andrew's–Sewanee School, TN	G,M,A	Thornton Academy, ME	G,M,A
Saint Augustine Preparatory School, NJ	G,M,A	Tower Hill School, DE	G,M,A
St. Benedict at Auburndale, TN	G,M,A	Trafalgar Castle School, ON, Canada	G,M,A
St. Christopher's School, VA	G,M,A	Trevor Day School, NY	G,M,A
St. Croix Schools, MN	G,M,A	Trinity Academy, KS	G
St. Francis High School, KY	G,A	Trinity Episcopal School, VA	G,M,A
St. George's School, RI	G,M,A	Trinity High School, KY	G,M,A
St. George's School, BC, Canada	G	Trinity High School, OH	G,A
Saint John Bosco High School, CA	G,M,A	Trinity Preparatory School, FL	G,M,A
St. John Neumann High School, FL	G	United Nations International School, NY	G,M,A
St. Joseph Academy, FL	G,A	University Lake School, WI	G,M,A
St. Joseph High School, CT	G	University School of Jackson, TN	G,M,A
Saint Joseph High School, NJ	G	Valley Christian High School, CA	M,A
St. Joseph's Preparatory School, PA	G,M,A	The Valley School, MI	G,A
St. Luke's School, CT	G	Valwood School, GA	G,M
St. Mary's Episcopal School, TN	G,M,A	The Vanguard School, FL	G
St. Mary's Preparatory School, MI	M,A	Venta Preparatory School, ON, Canada	G
Saint Maur International School, Japan	G	Victor Valley Christian School, CA	G
St. Michael's Preparatory School of the Norbertine Fathers, CA	G	Villa Duchesne and Oak Hill School, MO	G
St. Paul's School, NH	G,M,A	Villa Victoria Academy, NJ	G,M,A
St. Pius X High School, TX	G	Villa Walsh Academy, NJ	G,M,A
Saint Thomas Aquinas High School, KS	G	Walnut Hill School for the Arts, MA	M,A

G — gifted; M — musically talented; A — artistically talented

Washington Waldorf School, MD	M,A
The Waterford School, UT	G,M,A
Watkinson School, CT	G,M,A
The Wellington School, OH	G,M,A
Wesleyan Academy, PR	G
Westminster Christian School, FL	G,M,A
West Nottingham Academy, MD	G,M,A
Westover School, CT	G,M,A
West Sound Academy, WA	G,M,A
Westtown School, PA	G,M,A
The Wheeler School, RI	G
Whitefield Academy, KY	G
Whitfield School, MO	G
Willow Hill School, MA	A
Wilmington Friends School, DE	G,M,A
The Winchendon School, MA	G
Winchester Thurston School, PA	G,M,A
Windermere School, United Kingdom	G,M,A
The Windsor School, NY	G,M,A
Winston Preparatory School, NY	M,A
The Winston School, TX	G,A
Woodberry Forest School, VA	G,M,A
Woodstock Academy, CT	M,A
Woodstock School, India	G,M,A
Worcester Preparatory School, MD	G,M,A
York Country Day School, PA	G,M,A

SCHOOLS WITH ADVANCED PLACEMENT PREPARATION

Academy at the Lakes, FL
The Academy for Gifted Children (PACE), ON, Canada
Academy of Holy Angels, MN
Academy of Notre Dame, MA
Academy of Our Lady of Peace, CA
Academy of Saint Elizabeth, NJ
Academy of the Holy Cross, MD
Academy of the New Church Boys' School, PA
Academy of the New Church Girls' School, PA
Academy of the Sacred Heart, LA
Academy of the Sacred Heart, MI
Académie Ste Cécile International School, ON, Canada
The Agnes Irwin School, PA
Alabama Christian Academy, AL
Albuquerque Academy, NM
Allen Academy, TX
Allentown Central Catholic High School, PA
Alliance Academy, Ecuador
Allison Academy, FL
Alma Heights Christian High School, CA
Alverno Heights Academy, CA
American Christian Academy, AL
The American Embassy School, India
The American School Foundation, Mexico
The American School in Japan, Japan
The American School of Puerto Vallarta, Mexico
American School of The Hague, Netherlands
Andrews Osborne Academy, OH
Archbishop Alter High School, OH
Archbishop Curley High School, MD
Archbishop Hoban High School, OH
Archbishop McNicholas High School, OH
Archbishop Mitty High School, CA
Archbishop Shaw High School, LA
Army and Navy Academy, CA
Arroyo Pacific Academy, CA

Asheville School, NC
Ashley Hall, SC
Athens Academy, GA
Augusta Christian School, GA
Aurora Central Catholic High School, IL
Austin Preparatory School, MA
Bakersfield Christian High School, CA
Balmoral Hall School, MB, Canada
Barnstable Academy, NJ
Battle Ground Academy, TN
Baylor School, TN
Bay Ridge Preparatory School, NY
Bayview Glen School, ON, Canada
Beaufort Academy, SC
The Beekman School, NY
Belen Jesuit Preparatory School, FL
Bellevue Christian School, WA
Benedictine High School, OH
Ben Lippen Schools, SC
Bentley School, CA
Berean Christian High School, CA
Berkeley Preparatory School, FL
Berkshire School, MA
The Birch Wathen Lenox School, NY
Bishop Connolly High School, MA
Bishop Denis J. O'Connell High School, VA
Bishop Fenwick High School, OH
Bishop Ireton High School, VA
Bishop John J. Snyder High School, FL
Bishop Kelly High School, ID
Bishop Kenny High School, FL
Bishop McGuinness Catholic High School, OK
Bishop O'Dowd High School, CA
Bishop's College School, QC, Canada
The Bishop's School, CA
Bishop Stang High School, MA
Bishop Verot High School, FL
Black Forest Academy, Germany
The Blake School, MN
Blanchet School, OR
Blessed Sacrament Huguenot Catholic School, VA
Blessed Trinity High School, GA
The Bolles School, FL
Boston Trinity Academy, MA
Bradenton Christian School, FL
Brandon Hall School, GA
Brentwood College School, BC, Canada
Brethren Christian Junior and Senior High Schools, CA
Briarcrest Christian High School, TN
Briarwood Christian High School, AL
Brimmer and May School, MA
Brooks School, MA
Brophy College Preparatory, AZ
Brother Martin High School, LA
The Browning School, NY
The Bryn Mawr School for Girls, MD
Buckingham Browne & Nichols School, MA
The Buckley School, CA
Buffalo Seminary, NY
Burr and Burton Academy, VT
Cairo American College, Egypt
California Crosspoint High School, CA
California Lutheran High School, CA
Calvert Hall College High School, MD
Calvin Christian High School, CA
Campbell Hall (Episcopal), CA
Canadian Academy, Japan

The Canterbury Episcopal School, TX
Canterbury School, CT
Canterbury School, FL
Canterbury School, IN
The Canterbury School of Florida, FL
Cape Cod Academy, MA
Cape Henry Collegiate School, VA
Capistrano Valley Christian Schools, CA
Cardinal Gibbons High School, NC
Cardinal Newman High School, FL
Carnegie Schools Riverside, CA
Carondelet High School, CA
Casady School, OK
Cascia Hall Preparatory School, OK
Castilleja School, CA
Cate School, CA
Cathedral High School, NY
Catholic Central High School, MI
Catholic Central High School, NY
Catholic Central High School, WI
Central Catholic High School, MA
Central Catholic High School, PA
Chadwick School, CA
Chaminade College Preparatory, CA
Chaminade College Preparatory School, MO
Chaminade-Madonna College Preparatory, FL
Charles E. Smith Jewish Day School, MD
Charlotte Latin School, NC
Chase Collegiate School, CT
Chatham Hall, VA
Cheverus High School, ME
Children's Creative and Performing Arts Academy
     of San Diego, CA
Choate Rosemary Hall, CT
Christa McAuliffe Academy School of Arts and Sciences, OR
Christchurch School, VA
Christian Brothers Academy, NJ
Christian Brothers Academy, NY
Christian Central Academy, NY
Christopher Columbus High School, FL
The Church Farm School, PA
Clarksville Academy, TN
Colegio Bolivar, Colombia
Colegio San Jose, PR
Collegedale Academy, TN
The Collegiate School, VA
Columbia Academy, TN
Columbia International School, Japan
The Columbus Academy, OH
Columbus School for Girls, OH
Commonwealth School, MA
The Community School of Naples, FL
Concordia Lutheran High School, IN
Contra Costa Christian High School, CA
Convent of the Sacred Heart, CT
The Country Day School, ON, Canada
Covington Catholic High School, KY
Crawford Adventist Academy, ON, Canada
Crescent School, ON, Canada
Crestwood Preparatory College, ON, Canada
The Culver Academies, IN
Cushing Academy, MA
Damien High School, CA
Dana Hall School, MA
Darlington School, GA
Darrow School, NY
Davidson Academy, TN

Deerfield Academy, MA
De La Salle College, ON, Canada
De La Salle High School, CA
DeLaSalle High School, MN
De La Salle North Catholic High School, OR
Delaware County Christian School, PA
Delbarton School, NJ
The Delphian School, OR
DeMatha Catholic High School, MD
Detroit Country Day School, MI
Devon Preparatory School, PA
Doane Academy, NJ
Dock Mennonite Academy, PA
The Dr. Miriam and Sheldon G. Adelson Educational Campus,
     The Adelson Upper School, NV
Dominican Academy, NY
Donelson Christian Academy, TN
Donovan Catholic, NJ
Dowling Catholic High School, IA
Dublin Christian Academy, NH
Dublin School, NH
Durham Academy, NC
The Dwight School, NY
Eastern Mennonite High School, VA
Edgewood Academy, AL
Edgewood High School of the Sacred Heart, WI
Edison School, AB, Canada
Edmund Burke School, DC
Eldorado Emerson Private School, CA
Elgin Academy, IL
The Ellis School, PA
The Episcopal Academy, PA
Episcopal Collegiate School, AR
Episcopal High School, TX
Episcopal High School, VA
Episcopal High School of Jacksonville, FL
Erskine Academy, ME
Escola Americana de Campinas, Brazil
Escondido Adventist Academy, CA
Excel Christian Academy, GA
Explorations Academy, WA
Ezell-Harding Christian School, TN
Faith Christian High School, CA
Faith Lutheran High School, NV
Falmouth Academy, MA
Father Duenas Memorial School, GU
Father Lopez High School, FL
Fayetteville Academy, NC
The First Academy, FL
First Presbyterian Day School, GA
Flintridge Preparatory School, CA
Flintridge Sacred Heart Academy, CA
Fontbonne Academy, MA
Fontbonne Hall Academy, NY
Fordham Preparatory School, NY
Forsyth Country Day School, NC
Fort Worth Christian School, TX
Fort Worth Country Day School, TX
Foundation Academy, FL
Fountain Valley School of Colorado, CO
Foxcroft School, VA
French-American School of New York, NY
Fresno Christian Schools, CA
Friends Academy, NY
Friends Select School, PA
The Frisch School, NJ
Front Range Christian High School, CO

Fuqua School, VA
Gabriel Richard Catholic High School, MI
The Galloway School, GA
Gann Academy (The New Jewish High School of
    Greater Boston), MA
Gaston Day School, NC
Gem State Academy, ID
George Stevens Academy, ME
Gilman School, MD
Gilmour Academy, OH
Girard College, PA
Glades Day School, FL
Glenelg Country School, MD
Gonzaga College High School, DC
Good Hope Country Day School, VI
The Governor French Academy, IL
The Governor's Academy, MA
Grace Baptist Academy, TN
Grace Christian School, AK
Grace Christian School, PE, Canada
Greater Atlanta Christian Schools, GA
Greenfield School, NC
Green Fields Country Day School, AZ
Greenhill School, TX
Greenhills School, MI
Grier School, PA
Guamani Private School, PR
Gulliver Preparatory School, FL
The Gunnery, CT
The Gunston School, MD
Halstrom Academy, Beverly Hills, CA
Halstrom Academy, Calsbad, CA
Halstrom Academy, Cupertino, CA
Halstrom Academy, Huntington Beach, CA
Halstrom Academy, Irvine, CA
Halstrom Academy, Los Angeles, CA
Halstrom Academy, Manhattan Beach, CA
Halstrom Academy, Mission Viejo, CA
Halstrom Academy, Orange, CA
Halstrom Academy, Pasadena, CA
Halstrom Academy, San Diego, CA
Halstrom Academy, San Matco, CA
Halstrom Academy, Walnut Creek, CA
Halstrom Academy, Westlake Village, CA
Halstrom Academy, Woodland Hills, CA
Hammond School, SC
Hampton Roads Academy, VA
Harding Academy, AR
The Harker School, CA
The Harley School, NY
The Harpeth Hall School, TN
Harrells Christian Academy, NC
Harvard-Westlake School, CA
The Harvey School, NY
Hawaii Baptist Academy, HI
Hawai`i Preparatory Academy, HI
Hawken School, OH
Hawthorne Christian Academy, NJ
Hebrew Academy, CA
Hebron Academy, ME
Heritage Hall, OK
The Hewitt School, NY
Hillcrest Christian School, CA
Ho'Ala School, HI
The Hockaday School, TX
Holland Hall, OK
Holy Cross High School, CT

Holy Cross School, LA
Holy Ghost Preparatory School, PA
Holy Innocents' Episcopal School, GA
Holy Savior Menard Catholic High School, LA
Holy Trinity Diocesan High School, NY
Holy Trinity High School, IL
Holy Trinity School, ON, Canada
Hoosac School, NY
The Hotchkiss School, CT
Houghton Academy, NY
The Hun School of Princeton, NJ
Hyde Park Baptist School, TX
Hyde School, CT
Hyde School, ME
Hyman Brand Hebrew Academy of Greater Kansas City, KS
Illiana Christian High School, IL
Immaculata High School, NJ
Immaculata-La Salle High School, FL
Incarnate Word Academy, TX
Independent School, KS
Indian Springs School, AL
Institut Monte Rosa, Switzerland
International School Manila, Philippines
International School of Brussels, Belgium
International School of Kenya, Ltd., Kenya
International School of Port-of-Spain, Trinidad and Tobago
Jack M. Barrack Hebrew Academy, PA
Jackson Preparatory School, MS
Jean and Samuel Frankel Jewish Academy of
    Metropolitan Detroit, MI
Jesuit College Preparatory School, TX
Jesuit High School of Tampa, FL
Jewish Community High School of the Bay, CA
John Burroughs School, MO
Josephinum Academy, IL
Junipero Serra High School, CA
Kalamazoo Christian High School, MI
Kaohsiung American School, Taiwan
Keio Academy of New York, NY
Kent Denver School, CO
Kent School, CT
The Key School, MD
Kimball Union Academy, NH
King School, CT
The King's Christian High School, NJ
Kingswood-Oxford School, CT
The Kiski School, PA
La Grange Academy, GA
Lake Forest Academy, IL
Lakehill Preparatory School, TX
Lake Mary Preparatory School, FL
Lake Ridge Academy, OH
Lakeview Academy, GA
La Lumiere School, IN
Lancaster Catholic High School, PA
Lancaster Mennonite High School, PA
Landmark Christian School, GA
Landon School, MD
Lansdale Catholic High School, PA
La Pietra–Hawaii School for Girls, HI
La Salle Academy, RI
La Salle High School, CA
La Salle Institute, NY
Laurel Springs School, CA
Lawrence Woodmere Academy, NY
Lehigh Valley Christian High School, PA
Le Lycee Francais de Los Angeles, CA

Lexington Christian Academy, KY
Lexington Christian Academy, MA
Lincoln Academy, ME
Lincoln School, RI
The Linden School, ON, Canada
Linfield Christian School, CA
Long Island Lutheran Middle and High School, NY
Loudoun School for the Gifted, VA
Louisville Collegiate School, KY
Louisville High School, CA
The Lovett School, GA
Lower Canada College, QC, Canada
Loyola-Blakefield, MD
Loyola College Prep, LA
Lutheran High North, TX
Lutheran High School, CO
Lutheran High School Northwest, MI
Lutheran High School of Indianapolis, IN
Lutheran High School of San Diego, CA
Lutheran High School West, OH
The Lycee International, American Section, France
Lydia Patterson Institute, TX
Lyndon Institute, VT
Ma'ayanot Yeshiva High School for Girls of Bergen County, NJ
Malden Catholic High School, MA
Malvern Preparatory School, PA
Manhattan Christian High School, MT
Maranatha High School, CA
Marianapolis Preparatory School, CT
Marian Central Catholic High School, IL
Marian High School, MA
Marin Academy, CA
Marine Military Academy, TX
Marist High School, IL
Marist School, GA
Marlborough School, CA
Marshall School, MN
Martin Luther High School, NY
The Marvelwood School, CT
Mary Help of Christians Academy, NJ
Mary Institute and St. Louis Country Day School (MICDS), MO
The Mary Louis Academy, NY
Marymount High School, CA
Marymount School of New York, NY
Maryvale Preparatory School, MD
Massanutten Military Academy, VA
Mater Dei High School, IL
Matignon High School, MA
Maumee Valley Country Day School, OH
Maur Hill-Mount Academy, KS
Mayer Lutheran High School, MN
The McCallie School, TN
McDonogh School, MD
The McLean School of Maryland, Inc., MD
The Meadows School, NV
Memphis University School, TN
Menlo School, CA
Mercersburg Academy, PA
Mercy High School, CT
Mercy High School, MI
Merion Mercy Academy, PA
The Miami Valley School, OH
Middlesex School, MA
Midland School, CA
Mid-Pacific Institute, HI
Millbrook School, NY
Milton Academy, MA

Milton Hershey School, PA
Miss Edgar's and Miss Cramp's School, QC, Canada
Miss Porter's School, CT
MMI Preparatory School, PA
The Monarch School, TX
Monsignor Bonner and Archbishop Prendergast Catholic High School, PA
Monsignor Edward Pace High School, FL
Montclair Kimberley Academy, NJ
Monterey Bay Academy, CA
Montgomery Bell Academy, TN
Montrose School, MA
Moorestown Friends School, NJ
Mooseheart High School, IL
Moravian Academy, PA
Moreau Catholic High School, CA
Mother McAuley High School, IL
Mountain View Academy, CA
Mount Carmel Academy, LA
Mount Dora Christian Academy, FL
Mount Mercy Academy, NY
Mount Notre Dame High School, OH
Mount St. Agnes Academy, Bermuda
Mount Saint Charles Academy, RI
Mount Vernon Presbyterian School, GA
Nazareth Academy, IL
Nerinx Hall, MO
Neuchatel Junior College, Switzerland
Newton Country Day School of the Sacred Heart, MA
Newton's Grove School, ON, Canada
New York Military Academy, NY
Noble and Greenough School, MA
The North Broward Preparatory Upper School, FL
Northfield Mount Hermon School, MA
Northpoint Christian School, MS
North Shore Country Day School, IL
Northside Christian School, FL
Northwest Catholic High School, CT
North Yarmouth Academy, ME
The Norwich Free Academy, CT
Notre Dame-Cathedral Latin School, OH
Notre Dame High School, CA
Notre Dame High School, CA
Notre Dame High School, NJ
Notre Dame High School, NY
Notre Dame High School, TN
Notre Dame Junior/Senior High School, PA
Oak Grove Lutheran School, ND
Oak Grove School, CA
The Oakridge School, TX
Ojai Valley School, CA
Oldenburg Academy, IN
The O'Neal School, NC
Oneida Baptist Institute, KY
Orangewood Adventist Academy, CA
Oregon Episcopal School, OR
Orinda Academy, CA
The Orme School, AZ
Pace Academy, GA
PACE/Brantley Hall High School, FL
Pacific Lutheran High School, CA
Padua Franciscan High School, OH
The Paideia School, GA
Palma School, CA
The Park School of Baltimore, MD
The Park School of Buffalo, NY
Peddie School, NJ

The Pembroke Hill School, MO
Peninsula Catholic High School, VA
The Pennington School, NJ
Pensacola Catholic High School, FL
Peoples Christian Academy, ON, Canada
Perkiomen School, PA
The Phelps School, PA
Philadelphia-Montgomery Christian Academy, PA
Phoenix Christian Preparatory School, AZ
Phoenix Country Day School, AZ
Pickering College, ON, Canada
Pinecrest Academy, GA
Pinewood Preparatory School, SC
The Pingree School, MA
The Pingry School, NJ
Pioneer Valley Christian Academy, MA
Polytechnic School, CA
Pope Francis High School, MA
Pope John XXIII Regional High School, NJ
Portsmouth Christian Academy, NH
The Potomac School, VA
Poughkeepsie Day School, NY
Powers Catholic High School, MI
Presbyterian Pan American School, TX
Preston High School, NY
Prestonwood Christian Academy, TX
Proctor Academy, NH
Providence Country Day School, RI
Providence Day School, NC
Providence High School, CA
Providence School, FL
Punahou School, HI
Queen Margaret's School, BC, Canada
Quigley Catholic High School, PA
Ramona Convent Secondary School, CA
Randolph-Macon Academy, VA
Ransom Everglades School, FL
Ravenscroft School, NC
Redemption Christian Academy, MA
Redwood Christian Schools, CA
Regina Junior-Senior High School, IA
Regis High School, OR
Regis Jesuit High School, Boys Division, CO
Regis Jesuit High School, Girls Division, CO
Rice Memorial High School, VT
Rivermont Collegiate, IA
The Rivers School, MA
Rockhurst High School, MO
Rockland Country Day School, NY
Rocky Mount Academy, NC
The Roeper School, MI
Roland Park Country School, MD
Rolling Hills Preparatory School, CA
Routt Catholic High School, IL
Rowland Hall, UT
The Roxbury Latin School, MA
Sacramento Country Day School, CA
Sacred Heart/Griffin High School, IL
Sacred Heart High School, CA
Sacred Heart High School, NY
Sage Hill School, CA
St. Agnes Academy, TX
Saint Agnes Academy–St. Dominic School, TN
St. Albans School, DC
Saint Albert Junior-Senior High School, IA
St. Andrew's Episcopal School, MD
Saint Andrew's School, FL

St. Andrew's–Sewanee School, TN
Saint Anthony High School, IL
Saint Augustine Preparatory School, NJ
Saint Basil Academy, PA
St. Benedict at Auburndale, TN
St. Bernard's Catholic School, CA
St. Christopher's School, VA
St. Croix Schools, MN
Saint Dominic Academy, NJ
Saint Francis High School, CA
St. Francis High School, KY
St. Francis School, GA
St. George's Independent School, TN
St. George's School, RI
St. George's School, BC, Canada
Saint Gertrude High School, VA
Saint John Bosco High School, CA
St. John Neumann High School, FL
St. John's Catholic Prep, MD
St. John's Jesuit High School, OH
St. John's Preparatory School, MA
St. John's-Ravenscourt School, MB, Canada
Saint John's School, GU
Saint Joseph Academy, CA
St. Joseph Academy, FL
St. Joseph High School, CT
Saint Joseph High School, NJ
St. Joseph High School, TX
Saint Joseph Regional High School, NJ
St. Joseph's Catholic School, SC
St. Joseph's Preparatory School, PA
Saint Lucy's Priory High School, CA
St. Luke's School, CT
St. Mary's Episcopal School, TN
Saint Mary's Hall, TX
Saint Mary's High School, AZ
St. Mary's High School, CO
St. Mary's Preparatory School, MI
Saint Maur International School, Japan
St. Michael's Preparatory School of the Norbertine Fathers, CA
Saint Patrick High School, IL
St. Patrick's Regional Secondary, BC, Canada
St. Paul's High School, MB, Canada
St. Paul's School, NH
St. Pius X Catholic High School, GA
St. Pius X High School, TX
St. Stanislaus College, MS
Saint Stephen's Episcopal School, FL
St. Stephen's Episcopal School, TX
St. Stephen's School, Rome, Italy
Saint Teresa's Academy, MO
Saint Thomas Academy, MN
St. Thomas Aquinas High School, FL
Saint Thomas Aquinas High School, KS
St. Thomas Aquinas High School, NH
Saint Thomas More Catholic High School, LA
Saint Ursula Academy, OH
Saint Vincent-Saint Mary High School, OH
Saint Xavier High School, KY
Salem Academy, NC
Salem Academy, OR
Salpointe Catholic High School, AZ
San Francisco University High School, CA
San Marcos Baptist Academy, TX
Santa Catalina School, CA
Santa Fe Preparatory School, NM
Santa Margarita Catholic High School, CA

Sayre School, KY
SciCore Academy, NJ
Seabury Hall, HI
Second Baptist School, TX
Seton Catholic Central High School, NY
Seton Catholic High School, AZ
The Seven Hills School, OH
Shady Side Academy, PA
Shanley High School, ND
Shattuck-St. Mary's School, MN
Shawe Memorial Junior/Senior High School, IN
Shawnigan Lake School, BC, Canada
Shorecrest Preparatory School, FL
Sierra Canyon School, CA
Sonoma Academy, CA
Southfield Christian High School, MI
Southwestern Academy, AZ
The Spence School, NY
Springside Chestnut Hill Academy, PA
Squaw Valley Academy, CA
The Stanwich School, CT
Steamboat Mountain School, CO
Stevenson School, CA
The Stony Brook School, NY
The Storm King School, NY
Stratford Academy, GA
Stuart Hall, VA
Subiaco Academy, AR
The Taft School, CT
Taipei American School, Taiwan
Takoma Academy, MD
Tandem Friends School, VA
TASIS The American School in England, United Kingdom
TASIS, The American School in Switzerland, Switzerland
The Tenney School, TX
The Thacher School, CA
Thomas Jefferson School, MO
Thornton Academy, ME
Tilton School, NH
Timothy Christian High School, IL
TMI - The Episcopal School of Texas, TX
Tower Hill School, DE
Trafalgar Castle School, ON, Canada
Trevor Day School, NY
Trinity Catholic High School, CT
Trinity College School, ON, Canada
Trinity Episcopal School, VA
Trinity High School, KY
Trinity High School, OH
Trinity-Pawling School, NY
Trinity Preparatory School, FL
University Lake School, WI
University of Chicago Laboratory Schools, IL
University School of Jackson, TN
Ursuline Academy, MA
The Ursuline Academy of Dallas, TX
Valley Christian High School, CA
Valley Christian School, MT
Valwood School, GA
Vicksburg Catholic School, MS
Victor Valley Christian School, CA
Villa Duchesne and Oak Hill School, MO
Villa Joseph Marie High School, PA
Villa Madonna Academy, KY
Villa Victoria Academy, NJ
Villa Walsh Academy, NJ
Virginia Episcopal School, VA

Wasatch Academy, UT
Washington Waldorf School, MD
The Waterford School, UT
Webb School of Knoxville, TN
The Weber School, GA
The Wellington School, OH
Wesleyan Academy, PR
Westbury Christian School, TX
Westminster Christian Academy, LA
Westminster Christian School, FL
Westminster School, CT
West Nottingham Academy, MD
Westover School, CT
Westridge School, CA
Westtown School, PA
The Wheeler School, RI
Whitefield Academy, KY
Whitfield School, MO
Willow Hill School, MA
The Willows Academy, IL
Wilmington Christian School, DE
Wilmington Friends School, DE
Wilson Hall, SC
The Winchendon School, MA
Winchester Thurston School, PA
The Windsor School, NY
Windward School, CA
Woodberry Forest School, VA
The Woodhall School, CT
The Woodlands Christian Academy, TX
Woodlynde School, PA
Woodstock Academy, CT
Woodstock School, India
Woodward Academy, GA
The Woodward School, MA
Worcester Preparatory School, MD
Wyoming Seminary, PA
Xavier High School, NY
York Country Day School, PA
Zurich International School, Switzerland

SCHOOLS REPORTING A POSTGRADUATE YEAR

The American Embassy School, India
Berkshire School, MA
The Bolles School, FL
Brehm Preparatory School, IL
Canterbury School, CT
Choate Rosemary Hall, CT
The Culver Academies, IN
Cushing Academy, MA
Darlington School, GA
Deerfield Academy, MA
Foxcroft School, VA
Franklin Academy, CT
Grier School, PA
The Gunnery, CT
Hawai`i Preparatory Academy, HI
Hebron Academy, ME
Hoosac School, NY
The Hotchkiss School, CT
The Hun School of Princeton, NJ
International School of Kenya, Ltd., Kenya
The John Dewey Academy, MA
Kent School, CT
Kildonan School, NY

Kimball Union Academy, NH
The Kiski School, PA
La Lumiere School, IN
Laurinburg Institute, NC
The Lawrenceville School, NJ
Leysin American School in Switzerland, Switzerland
Marianapolis Preparatory School, CT
Marine Military Academy, TX
Massanutten Military Academy, VA
Mercersburg Academy, PA
Northfield Mount Hermon School, MA
The Orme School, AZ
Peddie School, NJ
Perkiomen School, PA
The Phelps School, PA
Randolph-Macon Academy, VA
Redemption Christian Academy, MA
Ridley College, ON, Canada
St. Stephen's School, Rome, Italy
Shattuck-St. Mary's School, MN
Southwestern Academy, AZ
The Storm King School, NY
Stratton Mountain School, VT
The Taft School, CT
TASIS, The American School in Switzerland, Switzerland
Thomas Jefferson School, MO
Tilton School, NII
Trinity-Pawling School, NY
Walnut Hill School for the Arts, MA
Wasatch Academy, UT
Watkinson School, CT
Westminster School, CT
West Nottingham Academy, MD
The Winchendon School, MA
The Windsor School, NY
Wyoming Seminary, PA

SCHOOLS OFFERING THE INTERNATIONAL BACCALAUREATE PROGRAM

Academy of the Holy Cross, MD
Académie Ste Cécile International School, ON, Canada
Alma Heights Christian High School, CA
The American Embassy School, India
The American International School, Austria
American International School Rotterdam, Netherlands
The American School Foundation, Mexico
The American School of Madrid, Spain
American School of The Hague, Netherlands
Atlanta International School, GA
Bavarian International School, Germany
The Bermuda High School for Girls, Bermuda
The Bolles School, FL
Branksome Hall, ON, Canada
British International School of Boston, MA
Cairo American College, Egypt
California Lutheran High School, CA
Campion School, Athens, Greece
Canadian Academy, Japan
Cardinal Newman High School, FL
Central Catholic High School, MA
Charlotte Country Day School, NC
Christ Church Episcopal School, SC
Colegio Franklin D. Roosevelt, Peru
Colegio San Jose, PR
Desert Academy, NM

Detroit Country Day School, MI
Dublin Christian Academy, NH
The Dwight School, NY
Elmwood School, ON, Canada
The English College in Prague, Czech Republic
Escola Americana de Campinas, Brazil
Escuela Campo Alegre, Venezuela
Gulliver Preparatory School, FL
Hebrew Academy, CA
International College Spain, Spain
International High School, CA
International School Hamburg, Germany
International School Manila, Philippines
The International School of Aberdeen, United Kingdom
International School of Amsterdam, Netherlands
International School of Brussels, Belgium
International School of Kenya, Ltd., Kenya
The International School of London, United Kingdom
Istanbul International Community School, Turkey
The Journeys School of Teton Science School, WY
King's-Edgehill School, NS, Canada
Le Lycee Francais de Los Angeles, CA
Leysin American School in Switzerland, Switzerland
Long Trail School, VT
Luther College High School, SK, Canada
Lycee Internationale de Boston/International School of Boston, MA
Lydia Patterson Institute, TX
Mercyhurst Preparatory School, PA
Mid-Pacific Institute, HI
The Monarch School, TX
Mount Notre Dame High School, OH
New International School of Thailand, Thailand
New York Military Academy, NY
The North Broward Preparatory Upper School, FL
Pacific Lutheran High School, CA
Ridley College, ON, Canada
Rothesay Netherwood School, NB, Canada
Rotterdam International Secondary School, Wolfert van Borselen, Netherlands
St. Andrew's School, GA
Saint Anthony High School, IL
Saint Dominic Academy, NJ
Saint John's School, GU
St. Joseph's Preparatory School, PA
Saint Maur International School, Japan
Saint Paul Lutheran High School, MO
St. Stephen's School, Rome, Italy
Santa Margarita Catholic High School, CA
Schule Schloss Salem, Germany
Seisen International School, Japan
Shanley High School, ND
Shawe Memorial Junior/Senior High School, IN
Taipei American School, Taiwan
TASIS The American School in England, United Kingdom
TASIS, The American School in Switzerland, Switzerland
Trinity Episcopal School, VA
United Nations International School, NY
Upper Canada College, ON, Canada
Verdala International School, Malta
Villa Duchesne and Oak Hill School, MO
Washington International School, DC
West Sound Academy, WA
Wilmington Friends School, DE
Yokohama International School, Japan
Zurich International School, Switzerland

SCHOOLS REPORTING THAT THEY AWARD MERIT SCHOLARSHIPS

Academy of Notre Dame, MA
Academy of Notre Dame de Namur, PA
Academy of Our Lady of Peace, CA
Academy of Saint Elizabeth, NJ
Academy of the Holy Cross, MD
Academy of the Sacred Heart, LA
Academy of the Sacred Heart, MI
Académie Ste Cécile International School, ON, Canada
Adelphi Academy, NY
Advanced Academy of Georgia, GA
Allison Academy, FL
Alverno Heights Academy, CA
Andrews Osborne Academy, OH
Archbishop Alter High School, OH
Archbishop Curley High School, MD
Archbishop Hoban High School, OH
Archbishop McNicholas High School, OH
Archbishop Moeller High School, OH
Archbishop Shaw High School, LA
Aurora Central Catholic High School, IL
Austin Preparatory School, MA
Balboa City School, CA
Balmoral Hall School, MB, Canada
Barnstable Academy, NJ
Battle Ground Academy, TN
Baylor School, TN
Bay Ridge Preparatory School, NY
The Beekman School, NY
Benedictine High School, OH
Ben Lippen Schools, SC
Berean Christian High School, CA
Berkeley Preparatory School, FL
The Bermuda High School for Girls, Bermuda
The Birch Wathen Lenox School, NY
Bishop Brossart High School, KY
Bishop Connolly High School, MA
Bishop Denis J. O'Connell High School, VA
Bishop Fenwick High School, OH
Bishop Foley Catholic High School, MI
Bishop Ireton High School, VA
Bishop Kearney High School, NY
Bishop Machebeuf High School, CO
Bishop O'Dowd High School, CA
Bishop's College School, QC, Canada
Bishop Stang High School, MA
Bishop Verot High School, FL
The Blue Ridge School, VA
Branksome Hall, ON, Canada
Brethren Christian Junior and Senior High Schools, CA
British International School of Boston, MA
Brother Martin High School, LA
The Bryn Mawr School for Girls, MD
Buffalo Seminary, NY
California Crosspoint High School, CA
Calvert Hall College High School, MD
Campion School, Athens, Greece
Canterbury School, IN
Cape Cod Academy, MA
Cape Henry Collegiate School, VA
Capistrano Valley Christian Schools, CA
Cardinal Ritter High School, IN
Casady School, OK
Cascades Academy of Central Oregon, OR
Cathedral High School, NY
Catholic Central High School, MI

Catholic Central High School, WI
Central Catholic High School, MA
Central Catholic High School, PA
Chaminade College Preparatory, CA
Chaminade College Preparatory School, MO
Chaminade-Madonna College Preparatory, FL
Charlotte Latin School, NC
Chase Collegiate School, CT
Chatham Hall, VA
Cheverus High School, ME
Children's Creative and Performing Arts Academy of San Diego, CA
Christ Church Episcopal School, SC
Christian Brothers Academy, NJ
Christian Brothers Academy, NY
Christian Central Academy, NY
Columbia International School, Japan
The Columbus Academy, OH
Columbus School for Girls, OH
Concordia Academy, MN
Concordia Lutheran High School, IN
Convent of the Sacred Heart, CT
Covington Catholic High School, KY
Crescent School, ON, Canada
The Culver Academies, IN
Cushing Academy, MA
Damien High School, CA
Dana Hall School, MA
Darlington School, GA
DeLaSalle High School, MN
Delaware County Christian School, PA
The Delphian School, OR
DeMatha Catholic High School, MD
Denver Christian High School, CO
Devon Preparatory School, PA
Doane Academy, NJ
Dominican Academy, NY
Donovan Catholic, NJ
Duchesne High School, MO
Edgewood High School of the Sacred Heart, WI
Elgin Academy, IL
The Ellis School, PA
Elmwood School, ON, Canada
The English College in Prague, Czech Republic
Episcopal High School, TX
Episcopal High School, VA
Explorations Academy, WA
Falmouth Academy, MA
Father Duenas Memorial School, GU
Father Lopez High School, FL
First Presbyterian Day School, GA
Flintridge Sacred Heart Academy, CA
Fontbonne Academy, MA
Fontbonne Hall Academy, NY
Fordham Preparatory School, NY
Forest Lake Academy, FL
Forsyth Country Day School, NC
Fort Worth Country Day School, TX
Fountain Valley School of Colorado, CO
Foxcroft School, VA
Franklin Academy, CT
Fresno Christian Schools, CA
Front Range Christian High School, CO
Fuqua School, VA
Gabriel Richard Catholic High School, MI
Gaston Day School, NC
Gem State Academy, ID

Gilmour Academy, OH
Glenelg Country School, MD
Gonzaga College High School, DC
Good Hope Country Day School, VI
Great Lakes Christian High School, ON, Canada
Greenfield School, NC
Green Fields Country Day School, AZ
Green Meadow Waldorf School, NY
Grier School, PA
Gulliver Preparatory School, FL
The Gunnery, CT
The Gunston School, MD
Hammond School, SC
Hawai`i Preparatory Academy, HI
Hawken School, OH
Hawthorne Christian Academy, NJ
Hebron Academy, ME
Heritage Hall, OK
Ho'Ala School, HI
Holland Hall, OK
Holy Cross High School, CT
Holy Cross School, LA
Holy Ghost Preparatory School, PA
Holy Savior Menard Catholic High School, LA
Holy Trinity Diocesan High School, NY
Holy Trinity High School, IL
Hoosac School, NY
Hyde Park Baptist School, TX
Hyde School, ME
Immaculata-La Salle High School, FL
Immaculate Conception High School, NJ
Immaculate Heart Academy, NJ
Incarnate Word Academy, TX
International College Spain, Spain
The International School of Aberdeen, United Kingdom
International School of Kenya, Ltd., Kenya
International School of Port-of-Spain, Trinidad and Tobago
Jack M. Barrack Hebrew Academy, PA
Jesuit College Preparatory School, TX
Jesuit High School of Tampa, FL
Josephinum Academy, IL
Junipero Serra High School, CA
Kent School, CT
Kimball Union Academy, NH
The King's Christian High School, NJ
King's-Edgehill School, NS, Canada
Kingswood-Oxford School, CT
The Kiski School, PA
Kolbe-Cathedral High School, CT
La Grange Academy, GA
Lake Forest Academy, IL
Lake Mary Preparatory School, FL
Lake Ridge Academy, OH
Lakeview Academy, GA
La Lumiere School, IN
Lancaster Mennonite High School, PA
Lansdale Catholic High School, PA
La Salle Academy, RI
La Salle High School, CA
La Salle Institute, NY
La Sierra Academy, CA
Lauralton Hall, CT
The Lawrenceville School, NJ
Lawrence Woodmere Academy, NY
Le Lycee Francais de Los Angeles, CA
Lexington Christian Academy, MA
Leysin American School in Switzerland, Switzerland

Lincoln School, RI
The Linden School, ON, Canada
Linfield Christian School, CA
Long Island Lutheran Middle and High School, NY
Long Trail School, VT
Louisville Collegiate School, KY
Louisville High School, CA
Lower Canada College, QC, Canada
Loyola-Blakefield, MD
Loyola College Prep, LA
Lutheran High North, TX
Lutheran High School, MO
Lutheran High School Northwest, MI
Lutheran High School of San Diego, CA
Lutheran High School West, OH
Luther College High School, SK, Canada
Malden Catholic High School, MA
Malvern Preparatory School, PA
Maplebrook School, NY
Maranatha High School, CA
Marianapolis Preparatory School, CT
Marian High School, MA
Marine Military Academy, TX
Marist High School, IL
Martin Luther High School, NY
Mary Help of Christians Academy, NJ
Mary Institute and St. Louis Country Day School (MICDS), MO
The Mary Louis Academy, NY
Marymount High School, CA
Maryvale Preparatory School, MD
Massanutten Military Academy, VA
Mater Dei Prep, NJ
Matignon High School, MA
Maumee Valley Country Day School, OH
Maur Hill-Mount Academy, KS
The McCallie School, TN
Memphis Catholic High School and Middle School, TN
Mercersburg Academy, PA
Mercy High School, CT
Mercyhurst Preparatory School, PA
Merion Mercy Academy, PA
The Miami Valley School, OH
Mid-Pacific Institute, HI
Miss Edgar's and Miss Cramp's School, QC, Canada
Miss Porter's School, CT
MMI Preparatory School, PA
Monsignor Bonner and Archbishop Prendergast Catholic
    High School, PA
Montrose School, MA
Moorestown Friends School, NJ
Moreau Catholic High School, CA
Mountain View Academy, CA
Mount Carmel Academy, LA
Mount Mercy Academy, NY
Mount Notre Dame High School, OH
Nazareth Academy, IL
Nebraska Christian Schools, NE
Nerinx Hall, MO
Neuchatel Junior College, Switzerland
New York Military Academy, NY
Niagara Catholic Jr./Sr. High School, NY
Niagara Christian Community of Schools, ON, Canada
The North Broward Preparatory Upper School, FL
North Shore Country Day School, IL
Northwest Catholic High School, CT
Notre Dame-Cathedral Latin School, OH
Notre Dame High School, CA

Notre Dame High School, NY
Oak Grove Lutheran School, ND
Oak Ridge Military Academy, NC
Oldenburg Academy, IN
The O'Neal School, NC
Orangewood Adventist Academy, CA
Pacific Lutheran High School, CA
Padua Franciscan High School, OH
Palma School, CA
Paradise Adventist Academy, CA
The Park School of Buffalo, NY
Peddie School, NJ
The Pembroke Hill School, MO
The Pennington School, NJ
Perkiomen School, PA
The Phelps School, PA
Pickering College, ON, Canada
The Pingree School, MA
Presbyterian Pan American School, TX
Preston High School, NY
Providence Country Day School, RI
Providence High School, CA
Punahou School, HI
Queen Margaret's School, BC, Canada
Quigley Catholic High School, PA
Ramona Convent Secondary School, CA
Randolph-Macon Academy, VA
Ravenscroft School, NC
Realms of Inquiry, UT
Redemption Christian Academy, MA
Regis High School, OR
Regis Jesuit High School, Boys Division, CO
Regis Jesuit High School, Girls Division, CO
Ridley College, ON, Canada
Rockhurst High School, MO
Rocky Mount Academy, NC
Rolling Hills Preparatory School, CA
Rosseau Lake College, ON, Canada
Rothesay Netherwood School, NB, Canada
Routt Catholic High School, IL
Rowland Hall, UT
Royal Canadian College, BC, Canada
Rundle College, AB, Canada
Sacred Heart/Griffin High School, IL
Sacred Heart High School, CA
Sacred Heart High School, NY
St. Agnes Academy, TX
Saint Agnes Academy–St. Dominic School, TN
Saint Albert Junior-Senior High School, IA
Saint Andrew's School, FL
St. Andrew's–Sewanee School, TN
Saint Augustine Preparatory School, NJ
Saint Basil Academy, PA
St. Benedict at Auburndale, TN
St. Bernard's Catholic School, CA
St. Croix Schools, MN
Saint Dominic Academy, NJ
Saint Francis High School, CA
St. Francis High School, KY
St. George's School, BC, Canada
Saint Gertrude High School, VA
Saint John Bosco High School, CA
St. John Neumann High School, FL
St. John's Catholic Prep, MD
St. John's Jesuit High School, OH
St. John's Preparatory School, MA
St. John's-Ravenscourt School, MB, Canada

Saint John's School, GU
St. Joseph High School, CA
St. Joseph High School, CT
Saint Joseph High School, NJ
Saint Joseph Regional High School, NJ
St. Joseph's Catholic School, SC
St. Joseph's Preparatory School, PA
Saint Lucy's Priory High School, CA
Saint Mary of the Assumption High School, NJ
Saint Mary's Hall, TX
St. Mary's High School, CO
St. Mary's Preparatory School, MI
Saint Patrick High School, IL
St. Pius X High School, TX
Saint Teresa's Academy, MO
Saint Thomas Academy, MN
Saint Thomas Aquinas High School, KS
Saint Thomas More Catholic High School, LA
Saint Ursula Academy, OH
Saint Ursula Academy, OH
Saint Vincent-Saint Mary High School, OH
Saint Xavier High School, KY
Salem Academy, NC
Salpointe Catholic High School, AZ
Schule Schloss Salem, Germany
Second Baptist School, TX
Seton Catholic Central High School, NY
Seton Catholic High School, AZ
The Seven Hills School, OH
Shady Side Academy, PA
Shanley High School, ND
Shawnigan Lake School, BC, Canada
Squaw Valley Academy, CA
STAR Prep Academy, CA
Steamboat Mountain School, CO
Stratford Academy, GA
Stuart Hall, VA
Takoma Academy, MD
Thomas Jefferson School, MO
Thornton Academy, ME
Tilton School, NH
TMI - The Episcopal School of Texas, TX
Tower Hill School, DE
Trafalgar Castle School, ON, Canada
Trinity Catholic High School, CT
Trinity College School, ON, Canada
Trinity Episcopal School, VA
Trinity High School, KY
University Lake School, WI
Upper Canada College, ON, Canada
The Ursuline Academy of Dallas, TX
The Valley School, MI
Valwood School, GA
Venta Preparatory School, ON, Canada
Villa Duchesne and Oak Hill School, MO
Villa Joseph Marie High School, PA
Villa Madonna Academy, KY
Villa Victoria Academy, NJ
Villa Walsh Academy, NJ
Virginia Episcopal School, VA
Wasatch Academy, UT
The Wellington School, OH
Westbury Christian School, TX
West Sound Academy, WA
Westtown School, PA
Whitfield School, MO
Windermere School, United Kingdom

Woodstock Academy, CT
The Woodward School, MA
Wyoming Seminary, PA
Xavier High School, NY

SCHOOLS REPORTING A GUARANTEED TUITION PLAN

Academy of the Holy Family, CT
Alabama Christian Academy, AL
Alpine Academy, UT
Balboa City School, CA
Bangor Christian School, ME
Christa McAuliffe Academy School of Arts and Sciences, OR
City Christian Schools, OR
Erskine Academy, ME
Flintridge Sacred Heart Academy, CA
Gann Academy (The New Jewish High School of
    Greater Boston), MA
Girard College, PA
Green Meadow Waldorf School, NY
Hawaii Baptist Academy, HI
Hebrew Academy, CA
The Hill Center, Durham Academy, NC
Laurinburg Institute, NC
Loyola College Prep, LA
Marion Academy, AL
Middlesex School, MA
Mount Vernon Presbyterian School, GA
Nebraska Christian Schools, NE
Neuchatel Junior College, Switzerland
Pensacola Catholic High School, FL
Pope John XXIII Regional High School, NJ
Presbyterian Pan American School, TX
Saint Patrick High School, IL
St. Patrick's Regional Secondary, BC, Canada
Saint Paul Lutheran High School, MO
St. Thomas Aquinas High School, FL
San Marcos Baptist Academy, TX
Scholar's Hall Preparatory School, ON, Canada
Schule Schloss Salem, Germany
Southern Ontario Collegiate, ON, Canada
STAR Prep Academy, CA
Sunrise Academy, UT
Trinity High School, KY
Trinity High School, OH
The Ursuline Academy of Dallas, TX
Villa Joseph Marie High School, PA
Wesleyan Academy, PR

SCHOOLS REPORTING A TUITION INSTALLMENT PLAN

Academy at the Lakes, FL
The Academy for Gifted Children (PACE), ON, Canada
Academy of Holy Angels, MN
Academy of Notre Dame, MA
Academy of Notre Dame de Namur, PA
Academy of Our Lady of Peace, CA
Academy of Saint Elizabeth, NJ
Academy of the Holy Cross, MD
Academy of the Holy Family, CT
Academy of the New Church Boys' School, PA
Academy of the New Church Girls' School, PA
Academy of the Sacred Heart, LA

Academy of the Sacred Heart, MI
Académie Ste Cécile International School, ON, Canada
Adelphi Academy, NY
The Agnes Irwin School, PA
Alabama Christian Academy, AL
Albuquerque Academy, NM
Allen Academy, TX
Allentown Central Catholic High School, PA
Alliance Academy, Ecuador
Allison Academy, FL
Alma Heights Christian High School, CA
Alpha Omega Academy, IA
Alpine Academy, UT
Alverno Heights Academy, CA
The American Boychoir School, NJ
American Christian Academy, AL
American Community School at Beirut, Lebanon
American Cooperative School of Tunis, Tunisia
The American International School, Austria
American International School Rotterdam, Netherlands
The American School Foundation, Mexico
The American School in Japan, Japan
The American School of Madrid, Spain
The American School of Puerto Vallarta, Mexico
American School of The Hague, Netherlands
Andrews Osborne Academy, OH
Archbishop Alter High School, OH
Archbishop Curley High School, MD
Archbishop Hoban High School, OH
Archbishop McNicholas High School, OH
Archbishop Mitty High School, CA
Archbishop Moeller High School, OH
Archbishop Shaw High School, LA
Arizona Lutheran Academy, AZ
Arroyo Pacific Academy, CA
Asheville School, NC
Ashley Hall, SC
Athens Academy, GA
Atlanta Girls' School, GA
Atlanta International School, GA
Augusta Christian School, GA
Aurora Central Catholic High School, IL
Austin Preparatory School, MA
Austin Waldorf School, TX
Bakersfield Christian High School, CA
Balboa City School, CA
Dalmoral Hall School, MB, Canada
Banbury Crossroads School, AB, Canada
Bangor Christian School, ME
Barnstable Academy, NJ
Battle Ground Academy, TN
Bavarian International School, Germany
Baylor School, TN
Bay Ridge Preparatory School, NY
The Bay School of San Francisco, CA
Bayview Glen School, ON, Canada
Bearspaw Christian School, AB, Canada
Beaufort Academy, SC
The Beekman School, NY
Belen Jesuit Preparatory School, FL
Bellevue Christian School, WA
The Bement School, MA
Benedictine High School, OH
Ben Lippen Schools, SC
Bentley School, CA
Berean Christian High School, CA
Berkeley Carroll School, NY

Berkeley Preparatory School, FL
Berkshire School, MA
The Bermuda High School for Girls, Bermuda
Beth Haven Christian School, KY
The Birch Wathen Lenox School, NY
Bishop Brossart High School, KY
Bishop Connolly High School, MA
Bishop Denis J. O'Connell High School, VA
Bishop Fenwick High School, OH
Bishop Foley Catholic High School, MI
Bishop Ireton High School, VA
Bishop John J. Snyder High School, FL
Bishop Kearney High School, NY
Bishop Kelly High School, ID
Bishop Kenny High School, FL
Bishop Machebeuf High School, CO
Bishop McGuinness Catholic High School, OK
Bishop O'Dowd High School, CA
Bishop's College School, QC, Canada
The Bishop's School, CA
Bishop Stang High School, MA
Bishop Verot High School, FL
Black Forest Academy, Germany
The Blake School, MN
Blanchet School, OR
Blessed Sacrament Huguenot Catholic School, VA
Blessed Trinity High School, GA
The Blue Ridge School, VA
The Bolles School, FL
Boston Trinity Academy, MA
Boston University Academy, MA
Bradenton Christian School, FL
Brandon Hall School, GA
Branksome Hall, ON, Canada
Brehm Preparatory School, IL
Brentwood College School, BC, Canada
Brethren Christian Junior and Senior High Schools, CA
Briarcrest Christian High School, TN
Briarwood Christian High School, AL
Bridges Academy, CA
Brimmer and May School, MA
British International School of Boston, MA
Brockwood Park School, United Kingdom
Brooks School, MA
Brophy College Preparatory, AZ
Brother Martin High School, LA
The Bryn Mawr School for Girls, MD
Buckingham Browne & Nichols School, MA
The Buckley School, CA
Buffalo Seminary, NY
Burr and Burton Academy, VT
Buxton School, MA
The Calhoun School, NY
California Crosspoint High School, CA
California Lutheran High School, CA
Calvert Hall College High School, MD
Calvin Christian High School, CA
Campbell Hall (Episcopal), CA
Campion School, Athens, Greece
Canadian Academy, Japan
The Canterbury Episcopal School, TX
Canterbury School, CT
Canterbury School, FL
Canterbury School, IN
The Canterbury School of Florida, FL
Cape Cod Academy, MA
Cape Henry Collegiate School, VA

Capistrano Valley Christian Schools, CA
Cardinal Gibbons High School, NC
Cardinal Newman High School, FL
Cardinal Ritter High School, IN
Carnegie Schools Riverside, CA
Carondelet High School, CA
Casady School, OK
Cascades Academy of Central Oregon, OR
Cascia Hall Preparatory School, OK
Castilleja School, CA
Cate School, CA
Cathedral High School, NY
Catholic Central High School, MI
Catholic Central High School, NY
Catholic Central High School, WI
CCI The Renaissance School, Italy
Central Alberta Christian High School, AB, Canada
Central Catholic High School, LA
Central Catholic High School, MA
Central Catholic High School, PA
Chadwick School, CA
Chaminade College Preparatory, CA
Chaminade College Preparatory School, MO
Chaminade-Madonna College Preparatory, FL
Charles E. Smith Jewish Day School, MD
Charlotte Country Day School, NC
Charlotte Latin School, NC
Chase Collegiate School, CT
Chatham Hall, VA
Chelsea School, MD
Cheverus High School, ME
Children's Creative and Performing Arts Academy of San Diego, CA
Choate Rosemary Hall, CT
Christa McAuliffe Academy School of Arts and Sciences, OR
Christ Church Episcopal School, SC
Christchurch School, VA
Christian Brothers Academy, NJ
Christian Brothers Academy, NY
Christian Central Academy, NY
Christopher Columbus High School, FL
Chrysalis School, WA
The Church Farm School, PA
City Christian Schools, OR
Clarksville Academy, TN
Colegio Bolivar, Colombia
Colegio Franklin D. Roosevelt, Peru
Colegio San Jose, PR
Collegedale Academy, TN
The Collegiate School, VA
Columbia Academy, TN
Columbia International School, Japan
The Columbus Academy, OH
Commonwealth School, MA
The Community School of Naples, FL
The Concept School, PA
Concord Academy, MA
Concordia Academy, MN
Concordia Lutheran High School, IN
Contra Costa Christian High School, CA
Convent of the Sacred Heart, CT
Covenant Canadian Reformed School, AB, Canada
Covington Catholic High School, KY
Crawford Adventist Academy, ON, Canada
Crescent School, ON, Canada
Crestwood Preparatory College, ON, Canada
C.S. Lewis Academy, OR

The Culver Academies, IN
Currey Ingram Academy, TN
Cushing Academy, MA
Dallas Academy, TX
Damien High School, CA
Dana Hall School, MA
Darlington School, GA
Darrow School, NY
Davidson Academy, TN
Deerfield Academy, MA
De La Salle College, ON, Canada
De La Salle High School, CA
DeLaSalle High School, MN
De La Salle North Catholic High School, OR
Delaware County Christian School, PA
Delaware Valley Friends School, PA
Delbarton School, NJ
The Delphian School, OR
DeMatha Catholic High School, MD
Denver Academy, CO
Denver Christian High School, CO
Desert Academy, NM
Detroit Country Day School, MI
Devon Preparatory School, PA
Doane Academy, NJ
Dock Mennonite Academy, PA
The Dr. Miriam and Sheldon G. Adelson Educational Campus,
    The Adelson Upper School, NV
Dominican Academy, NY
Donelson Christian Academy, TN
Donovan Catholic, NJ
Dowling Catholic High School, IA
Dublin Christian Academy, NH
Dublin School, NH
Duchesne High School, MO
Durham Academy, NC
The Dwight School, NY
Eaglebrook School, MA
Eagle Hill School, CT
Eagle Rock School, CO
Eastern Mennonite High School, VA
Eaton Academy, GA
Edgewood Academy, AL
Edgewood High School of the Sacred Heart, WI
Edison School, AB, Canada
Edmonton Academy, AB, Canada
Edmund Burke School, DC
Eldorado Emerson Private School, CA
Elgin Academy, IL
The Ellis School, PA
Elmwood School, ON, Canada
The English School, Kuwait, Kuwait
The Episcopal Academy, PA
Episcopal Collegiate School, AR
Episcopal High School, TX
Episcopal High School, VA
Episcopal High School of Jacksonville, FL
Erskine Academy, ME
Escola Americana de Campinas, Brazil
Escondido Adventist Academy, CA
Escuela Campo Alegre, Venezuela
Excel Christian Academy, GA
Explorations Academy, WA
Ezell-Harding Christian School, TN
Faith Christian High School, CA
Faith Christian School, AZ
Faith Lutheran High School, NV

Falmouth Academy, MA
Father Lopez High School, FL
Father Yermo High School, TX
Fayetteville Academy, NC
Fay School, MA
The Fessenden School, MA
The First Academy, FL
First Presbyterian Day School, GA
Flintridge Preparatory School, CA
Flintridge Sacred Heart Academy, CA
Fontbonne Academy, MA
Fontbonne Hall Academy, NY
Fordham Preparatory School, NY
Forest Lake Academy, FL
Forsyth Country Day School, NC
Fort Worth Christian School, TX
Fort Worth Country Day School, TX
Foundation Academy, FL
Fountain Valley School of Colorado, CO
Fowlers Academy, PR
Foxcroft School, VA
Franklin Academy, CT
Fraser Academy, BC, Canada
French-American School of New York, NY
Fresno Christian Schools, CA
Friends Academy, NY
Friends Select School, PA
The Frisch School, NJ
Front Range Christian High School, CO
Fuqua School, VA
Gabriel Richard Catholic High School, MI
The Galloway School, GA
Gann Academy (The New Jewish High School of
    Greater Boston), MA
Gaston Day School, NC
Gem State Academy, ID
George Stevens Academy, ME
Gilman School, MD
Gilmour Academy, OH
Girard College, PA
Glades Day School, FL
Glenelg Country School, MD
Gonzaga College High School, DC
Good Hope Country Day School, VI
The Governor French Academy, IL
The Governor's Academy, MA
The Gow School, NY
Grace Baptist Academy, TN
Grace Christian School, AK
Grace Christian School, PE, Canada
The Grauer School, CA
Greater Atlanta Christian Schools, GA
Great Lakes Christian High School, ON, Canada
Greenfield School, NC
Green Fields Country Day School, AZ
Greenhills School, MI
Green Meadow Waldorf School, NY
Greenwood Laboratory School, MO
The Greenwood School, VT
Grier School, PA
Griggs International Academy, MD
Gulliver Preparatory School, FL
The Gunnery, CT
The Gunston School, MD
Halstrom Academy, Beverly Hills, CA
Halstrom Academy, Calsbad, CA
Halstrom Academy, Cupertino, CA

Halstrom Academy, Huntington Beach, CA
Halstrom Academy, Irvine, CA
Halstrom Academy, Los Angeles, CA
Halstrom Academy, Manhattan Beach, CA
Halstrom Academy, Mission Viejo, CA
Halstrom Academy, Orange, CA
Halstrom Academy, Pasadena, CA
Halstrom Academy, San Diego, CA
Halstrom Academy, San Mateo, CA
Halstrom Academy, Walnut Creek, CA
Halstrom Academy, Westlake Village, CA
Halstrom Academy, Woodland Hills, CA
Hammond School, SC
Hampshire Country School, NH
Hampton Roads Academy, VA
Harding Academy, AR
The Harley School, NY
The Harpeth Hall School, TN
Harrells Christian Academy, NC
Harvard-Westlake School, CA
The Harvey School, NY
The Haverford School, PA
Hawaii Baptist Academy, HI
Hawai`i Preparatory Academy, HI
Hawken School, OH
Hawthorne Christian Academy, NJ
Hebrew Academy, CA
Hebron Academy, ME
Heritage Hall, OK
The Hewitt School, NY
Highroad Academy, BC, Canada
The Hill Center, Durham Academy, NC
Hillcrest Christian School, CA
Hillside School, MA
Ho'Ala School, HI
Holland Hall, OK
Holy Cross High School, CT
Holy Cross School, LA
Holy Ghost Preparatory School, PA
Holy Innocents' Episcopal School, GA
Holy Savior Menard Catholic High School, LA
Holy Trinity Diocesan High School, NY
Holy Trinity High School, IL
Hoosac School, NY
Horizon Christian School, OR
The Hotchkiss School, CT
Houghton Academy, NY
The Howard School, GA
The Hun School of Princeton, NJ
Huntington-Surrey School, TX
Hyde Park Baptist School, TX
Hyde School, CT
Hyde School, ME
Hyman Brand Hebrew Academy of Greater Kansas City, KS
Illiana Christian High School, IL
Immaculata High School, NJ
Immaculata-La Salle High School, FL
Immaculate Conception High School, NJ
Immaculate Heart Academy, NJ
Incarnate Word Academy, TX
Independent School, KS
Indian Springs School, AL
International High School, CA
International School Hamburg, Germany
International School Manila, Philippines
The International School of Aberdeen, United Kingdom
International School of Amsterdam, Netherlands

International School of Brussels, Belgium
International School of Kenya, Ltd., Kenya
Istanbul International Community School, Turkey
Jack M. Barrack Hebrew Academy, PA
Jackson Preparatory School, MS
Jesuit College Preparatory School, TX
Jesuit High School of Tampa, FL
John Burroughs School, MO
The John Dewey Academy, MA
Josephinum Academy, IL
The Journeys School of Teton Science School, WY
Junipero Serra High School, CA
Kalamazoo Christian High School, MI
Kauai Christian Academy, HI
Keio Academy of New York, NY
Kent Denver School, CO
Kent School, CT
The Key School, MD
Kildonan School, NY
Kimball Union Academy, NH
Kimberton Waldorf School, PA
King School, CT
The King's Christian High School, NJ
King's-Edgehill School, NS, Canada
Kingswood-Oxford School, CT
The Kiski School, PA
Kolbe-Cathedral High School, CT
The Lab School of Washington, DC
La Grange Academy, GA
Lake Forest Academy, IL
Lakehill Preparatory School, TX
Lakeland Christian Academy, IN
Lake Mary Preparatory School, FL
Lake Ridge Academy, OH
Lakeview Academy, GA
La Lumiere School, IN
Lancaster Mennonite High School, PA
Landmark Christian School, GA
Landmark School, MA
Landon School, MD
Lansdale Catholic High School, PA
La Pietra–Hawaii School for Girls, HI
La Salle Academy, RI
La Salle High School, CA
La Salle Institute, NY
La Sierra Academy, CA
Lauralton Hall, CT
The Laureate Academy, MB, Canada
Laurel Springs School, CA
Laurinburg Institute, NC
Lawrence School, OH
The Lawrenceville School, NJ
Lawrence Woodmere Academy, NY
Lehigh Valley Christian High School, PA
Le Lycee Francais de Los Angeles, CA
Lexington Christian Academy, KY
Lexington Christian Academy, MA
Leysin American School in Switzerland, Switzerland
Liberty Christian High School, CA
Liberty Christian School, CA
Lincoln School, RI
The Linden School, ON, Canada
Linfield Christian School, CA
Livingstone Adventist Academy, OR
Long Island Lutheran Middle and High School, NY
Long Trail School, VT
Loudoun School for the Gifted, VA

Louisville Collegiate School, KY
Louisville High School, CA
The Lovett School, GA
Lower Canada College, QC, Canada
Loyola-Blakefield, MD
Loyola College Prep, LA
Lustre Christian High School, MT
Lutheran High North, TX
Lutheran High School, CO
Lutheran High School, MO
Lutheran High School Northwest, MI
Lutheran High School of Indianapolis, IN
Lutheran High School of San Diego, CA
Lutheran High School West, OH
Luther College High School, SK, Canada
Lycee Français La Perouse, CA
The Lycee International, American Section, France
Lycee Internationale de Boston/International
    School of Boston, MA
Lydia Patterson Institute, TX
Lyndon Institute, VT
Ma'ayanot Yeshiva High School for Girls of Bergen County, NJ
Madison Academy, AL
Magnolia Heights School, MS
Malden Catholic High School, MA
Malvern Preparatory School, PA
Manhattan Christian High School, MT
Maplebrook School, NY
Maranatha High School, CA
Marianapolis Preparatory School, CT
Marian Central Catholic High School, IL
Marian High School, MA
Marin Academy, CA
Marine Military Academy, TX
Marist High School, IL
Marist School, GA
Marlborough School, CA
Marshall School, MN
Martin Luther High School, NY
The Marvelwood School, CT
Mary Help of Christians Academy, NJ
Mary Institute and St. Louis Country Day School (MICDS), MO
The Mary Louis Academy, NY
Marymount High School, CA
Marymount School of New York, NY
Maryvale Preparatory School, MD
Massanutten Military Academy, VA
Mater Dei High School, IL
Mater Dei Prep, NJ
Matignon High School, MA
Maumee Valley Country Day School, OH
Maur Hill-Mount Academy, KS
Mayer Lutheran High School, MN
The McCallie School, TN
McDonogh School, MD
The McLean School of Maryland, Inc., MD
The Meadows School, NV
Memphis Catholic High School and Middle School, TN
Memphis University School, TN
Menlo School, CA
Mercersburg Academy, PA
Mercy High School, CT
Mercy High School, MI
Mercyhurst Preparatory School, PA
Merion Mercy Academy, PA
Mesa Grande Seventh-Day Academy, CA
The Miami Valley School, OH

Middlesex School, MA
Midland School, CA
Mid-Pacific Institute, HI
Millbrook School, NY
Mill Springs Academy, GA
Milton Academy, MA
Miss Edgar's and Miss Cramp's School, QC, Canada
Miss Porter's School, CT
MMI Preparatory School, PA
The Monarch School, TX
Moncton Wesleyan Academy, NB, Canada
Monsignor Bonner and Archbishop Prendergast Catholic High
    School, PA
Monsignor Edward Pace High School, FL
Montclair Kimberley Academy, NJ
Monterey Bay Academy, CA
Montgomery Bell Academy, TN
Montrose School, MA
Moorestown Friends School, NJ
Mooseheart High School, IL
Moravian Academy, PA
Moreau Catholic High School, CA
Mother McAuley High School, IL
Mountain View Academy, CA
Mountain View Christian High School, NV
Mount Carmel Academy, LA
Mount Dora Christian Academy, FL
Mount Mercy Academy, NY
Mount Notre Dame High School, OH
Mount St. Agnes Academy, Bermuda
Mount Saint Charles Academy, RI
Mount Vernon Presbyterian School, GA
Nampa Christian Schools, ID
Nazareth Academy, IL
Nebraska Christian Schools, NE
Nerinx Hall, MO
Neuchatel Junior College, Switzerland
New Covenant Academy, MO
New International School of Thailand, Thailand
New Roads School, CA
Newton Country Day School of the Sacred Heart, MA
Newton's Grove School, ON, Canada
New York Military Academy, NY
Niagara Catholic Jr./Sr. High School, NY
Niagara Christian Community of Schools, ON, Canada
Noble Academy, NC
Noble and Greenough School, MA
The Nora School, MD
Norman Howard School, NY
The North Broward Preparatory Upper School, FL
North Central Texas Academy, TX
North Country School, NY
Northfield Mount Hermon School, MA
Northpoint Christian School, MS
North Shore Country Day School, IL
Northside Christian School, FL
North Toronto Christian School, ON, Canada
Northwest Academy, OR
Northwest Catholic High School, CT
The Northwest School, WA
North Yarmouth Academy, ME
Notre Dame-Cathedral Latin School, OH
Notre Dame High School, CA
Notre Dame High School, CA
Notre Dame High School, NJ
Notre Dame High School, NY
Notre Dame High School, TN

Notre Dame Junior/Senior High School, PA
Oak Grove Lutheran School, ND
Oak Grove School, CA
Oakland School, VA
Oak Ridge Military Academy, NC
The Oakridge School, TX
Ojai Valley School, CA
Oldenburg Academy, IN
The O'Neal School, NC
Oneida Baptist Institute, KY
Orangewood Adventist Academy, CA
Oregon Episcopal School, OR
Orinda Academy, CA
The Orme School, AZ
Pace Academy, GA
PACE/Brantley Hall High School, FL
Pacific Lutheran High School, CA
The Packer Collegiate Institute, NY
Padua Franciscan High School, OH
The Paideia School, GA
Palma School, CA
Paradise Adventist Academy, CA
The Park School of Baltimore, MD
The Park School of Buffalo, NY
The Pathway School, PA
Peddie School, NJ
The Pembroke Hill School, MO
Peninsula Catholic High School, VA
The Pennington School, NJ
Pensacola Catholic High School, FL
Peoples Christian Academy, ON, Canada
Perkins School for the Blind, MA
Perkiomen School, PA
The Phelps School, PA
Philadelphia-Montgomery Christian Academy, PA
Phoenix Christian Preparatory School, AZ
Phoenix Country Day School, AZ
Pickering College, ON, Canada
Pinecrest Academy, GA
Pine Tree Academy, ME
Pinewood Preparatory School, SC
The Pingree School, MA
The Pingry School, NJ
Pioneer Valley Christian Academy, MA
Polytechnic School, CA
Pope Francis High School, MA
Pope John XXIII Regional High School, NJ
Portledge School, NY
Portsmouth Christian Academy, NH
The Potomac School, VA
Poughkeepsie Day School, NY
Powers Catholic High School, MI
Presbyterian Pan American School, TX
Preston High School, NY
Prestonwood Christian Academy, TX
Proctor Academy, NH
Professional Children's School, NY
Providence Country Day School, RI
Providence Day School, NC
Providence High School, CA
Providence School, FL
Punahou School, HI
Queen Margaret's School, BC, Canada
Quigley Catholic High School, PA
Quinte Christian High School, ON, Canada
Ramona Convent Secondary School, CA
Randolph-Macon Academy, VA

Ransom Everglades School, FL
Ravenscroft School, NC
Realms of Inquiry, UT
The Rectory School, CT
Redeemer Christian High School, ON, Canada
Redemption Christian Academy, MA
Redwood Christian Schools, CA
Regina Junior-Senior High School, IA
Regis High School, OR
Regis Jesuit High School, Boys Division, CO
Regis Jesuit High School, Girls Division, CO
Rejoice Christian Schools, OK
Rice Memorial High School, VT
Ridley College, ON, Canada
Riverdale Country School, NY
Rivermont Collegiate, IA
River Oaks Baptist School, TX
Rockhurst High School, MO
Rockland Country Day School, NY
Rock Point School, VT
Rockway Mennonite Collegiate, ON, Canada
Rocky Mount Academy, NC
The Roeper School, MI
Roland Park Country School, MD
Rolling Hills Preparatory School, CA
Rosseau Lake College, ON, Canada
Rothesay Netherwood School, NB, Canada
Rotterdam International Secondary School, Wolfert van Borselen,
    Netherlands
Routt Catholic High School, IL
Rowland Hall, UT
The Roxbury Latin School, MA
Rudolf Steiner School of Ann Arbor, MI
Rumsey Hall School, CT
Rundle College, AB, Canada
Sacramento Country Day School, CA
Sacramento Waldorf School, CA
Sacred Heart/Griffin High School, IL
Sacred Heart High School, CA
Sacred Heart High School, NY
Saddlebrook Preparatory School, FL
Sage Hill School, CA
St. Agnes Academy, TX
Saint Agnes Academy–St. Dominic School, TN
St. Albans School, DC
Saint Albert Junior-Senior High School, IA
St. Andrew's Episcopal School, MD
Saint Andrew's School, FL
St. Andrew's School, GA
St. Andrew's–Sewanee School, TN
Saint Anthony High School, IL
Saint Augustine Preparatory School, NJ
Saint Basil Academy, PA
St. Benedict at Auburndale, TN
St. Bernard's Catholic School, CA
St. Catherine's Academy, CA
St. Christopher's School, VA
Saint Dominic Academy, NJ
Saint Francis High School, CA
St. Francis High School, KY
St. Francis School, GA
St. George's Independent School, TN
St. George's School, RI
St. George's School, BC, Canada
Saint Gertrude High School, VA
Saint Ignatius College Prep, IL
Saint John Bosco High School, CA

St. John Neumann High School, FL
St. John's Catholic Prep, MD
St. John's Jesuit High School, OH
St. John's Preparatory School, MA
St. John's-Ravenscourt School, MB, Canada
Saint John's School, GU
Saint Joseph Academy, CA
St. Joseph Academy, FL
St. Joseph High School, CA
St. Joseph High School, CT
Saint Joseph High School, NJ
St. Joseph High School, TX
Saint Joseph Regional High School, NJ
St. Joseph's Catholic School, SC
St. Joseph's Preparatory School, PA
St. Lawrence Seminary High School, WI
Saint Lucy's Priory High School, CA
St. Luke's School, CT
Saint Mary of the Assumption High School, NJ
St. Mary's Episcopal School, TN
Saint Mary's Hall, TX
Saint Mary's High School, AZ
St. Mary's High School, CO
St. Mary's Preparatory School, MI
Saint Maur International School, Japan
St. Michael's Preparatory School of the Norbertine Fathers, CA
Saint Patrick High School, IL
St. Patrick's Regional Secondary, BC, Canada
Saint Paul Lutheran High School, MO
St. Paul's High School, MB, Canada
St. Paul's School, NH
St. Pius X Catholic High School, GA
St. Pius X High School, TX
St. Stanislaus College, MS
Saint Stephen's Episcopal School, FL
St. Stephen's Episcopal School, TX
St. Stephen's School, Rome, Italy
Saint Teresa's Academy, MO
Saint Thomas Academy, MN
St. Thomas Aquinas High School, FL
Saint Thomas Aquinas High School, KS
St. Thomas Aquinas High School, NH
Saint Thomas More Catholic High School, LA
Saint Ursula Academy, OH
Saint Ursula Academy, OH
Saint Vincent-Saint Mary High School, OH
Saint Xavier High School, KY
Salem Academy, NC
Salem Academy, OR
Salpointe Catholic High School, AZ
San Francisco University High School, CA
San Marcos Baptist Academy, TX
Santa Fe Preparatory School, NM
Santa Margarita Catholic High School, CA
Sayre School, KY
Scattergood Friends School, IA
Scholar's Hall Preparatory School, ON, Canada
Schule Schloss Salem, Germany
SciCore Academy, NJ
Scotus Central Catholic High School, NE
Seabury Hall, HI
Seacrest Country Day School, FL
Seattle Academy of Arts and Sciences, WA
Second Baptist School, TX
Seisen International School, Japan
Seton Catholic Central High School, NY
Seton Catholic High School, AZ

The Seven Hills School, OH
Shady Side Academy, PA
Shanley High School, ND
Shattuck-St. Mary's School, MN
Shawe Memorial Junior/Senior High School, IN
Shawnigan Lake School, BC, Canada
Shelton School and Evaluation Center, TX
Shorecrest Preparatory School, FL
Shoreline Christian, WA
The Siena School, MD
Sierra Canyon School, CA
Signet Christian School, ON, Canada
Smith School, NY
Sonoma Academy, CA
Southfield Christian High School, MI
Southwestern Academy, AZ
Springside Chestnut Hill Academy, PA
Squaw Valley Academy, CA
The Stanwich School, CT
STAR Prep Academy, CA
Steamboat Mountain School, CO
Stevenson School, CA
The Stony Brook School, NY
The Storm King School, NY
Stratford Academy, GA
Stratton Mountain School, VT
Stuart Hall, VA
Subiaco Academy, AR
Sunrise Academy, UT
The Taft School, CT
Taipei American School, Taiwan
Takoma Academy, MD
Tandem Friends School, VA
TASIS The American School in England, United Kingdom
TASIS, The American School in Switzerland, Switzerland
Teurlings Catholic High School, LA
The Thacher School, CA
Thomas Jefferson School, MO
Thornton Academy, ME
Tilton School, NH
Timothy Christian High School, IL
TMI - The Episcopal School of Texas, TX
Tower Hill School, DE
Trafalgar Castle School, ON, Canada
Trevor Day School, NY
Tri-City Christian Academy, AZ
Trinity Academy, KS
Trinity Catholic High School, CT
Trinity College School, ON, Canada
Trinity Episcopal School, VA
Trinity High School, KY
Trinity High School, OH
Trinity-Pawling School, NY
Trinity Preparatory School, FL
United Mennonite Educational Institute, ON, Canada
United Nations International School, NY
University Lake School, WI
University of Chicago Laboratory Schools, IL
University Prep, WA
University School of Jackson, TN
Upper Canada College, ON, Canada
Ursuline Academy, MA
The Ursuline Academy of Dallas, TX
Valley Christian High School, CA
Valley Christian School, MT
The Valley School, MI
Valwood School, GA

The Vanguard School, FL
Venta Preparatory School, ON, Canada
Verdala International School, Malta
Vicksburg Catholic School, MS
Victor Valley Christian School, CA
Villa Duchesne and Oak Hill School, MO
Villa Joseph Marie High School, PA
Villa Madonna Academy, KY
Villa Victoria Academy, NJ
Villa Walsh Academy, NJ
Virginia Episcopal School, VA
The Waldorf School of Saratoga Springs, NY
Walnut Hill School for the Arts, MA
Wasatch Academy, UT
Washington International School, DC
Washington Waldorf School, MD
The Waterford School, UT
Watkinson School, CT
Waynflete School, ME
Webb School of Knoxville, TN
The Weber School, GA
The Wellington School, OH
Wesleyan Academy, PR
Westbury Christian School, TX
Westmark School, CA
Westminster Christian Academy, LA
Westminster Christian School, FL
Westminster School, CT
West Nottingham Academy, MD
Westover School, CT
Westridge School, CA
Westside Christian High School, OR
West Sound Academy, WA
Westtown School, PA
The Wheeler School, RI
Whitefield Academy, KY
Whitfield School, MO
The Willows Academy, IL
Wilmington Christian School, DE
Wilmington Friends School, DE
Wilson Hall, SC
The Winchendon School, MA
Winchester Thurston School, PA
Windermere School, United Kingdom
The Windsor School, NY
Windward School, CA
Winston Preparatory School, NY
The Winston School, TX
The Winston School San Antonio, TX
Woodberry Forest School, VA
The Woodhall School, CT
The Woodlands Christian Academy, TX
Woodlynde School, PA
Woodstock School, India
Woodward Academy, GA
The Woodward School, MA
Worcester Preparatory School, MD
Wyoming Seminary, PA
Xavier High School, NY
York Country Day School, PA
Zurich International School, Switzerland

SCHOOLS REPORTING THAT THEY OFFER LOANS

Aurora Central Catholic High School, IL	N
Bishop's College School, QC, Canada	N
The Blake School, MN	N
Calvin Christian High School, CA	N
Canterbury School, CT	M,N
Chaminade-Madonna College Preparatory, FL	N
Commonwealth School, MA	N
Concord Academy, MA	N
Delaware Valley Friends School, PA	M,N
The Delphian School, OR	N
Explorations Academy, WA	N
Falmouth Academy, MA	N
Friends Select School, PA	N
Gilman School, MD	N
Gilmour Academy, OH	N
Great Lakes Christian High School, ON, Canada	M,N
Grier School, PA	N
The Gunnery, CT	N
Hawken School, OH	N
Heritage Hall, OK	N
The Hotchkiss School, CT	N
John Burroughs School, MO	N
Kent School, CT	N
Lawrence Woodmere Academy, NY	N
Lexington Christian Academy, KY	N
Lower Canada College, QC, Canada	N
Maplebrook School, NY	M,N
Massanutten Military Academy, VA	M,N
Maur Hill-Mount Academy, KS	N
The McCallie School, TN	N
Mercersburg Academy, PA	N
Mesa Grande Seventh-Day Academy, CA	M,N
Millbrook School, NY	N
The Monarch School, TX	N
Moorestown Friends School, NJ	N
Northfield Mount Hermon School, MA	N
North Shore Country Day School, IL	M,N
Ojai Valley School, CA	N
Pacific Lutheran High School, CA	M
Peddie School, NJ	N
The Pembroke Hill School, MO	N
The Pingree School, MA	N
Ravenscroft School, NC	N
Redemption Christian Academy, MA	M
Ridley College, ON, Canada	N
St. Albans School, DC	N
St. George's School, RI	M,N
Saint Ignatius College Prep, IL	N
Saint Joseph Regional High School, NJ	N
St. Joseph's Preparatory School, PA	M,N
St. Paul's High School, MB, Canada	N
Schule Schloss Salem, Germany	N
Sedona Sky Academy, AZ	M
Stratton Mountain School, VT	N
The Taft School, CT	N
Tilton School, NH	N
Trinity High School, OH	M
Trinity-Pawling School, NY	M,N
United Mennonite Educational Institute, ON, Canada	N
Wasatch Academy, UT	N
Windward School, CA	N
Woodberry Forest School, VA	N

M — middle-income loans; N — need-based loans

TOTAL AMOUNT OF UPPER SCHOOL FINANCIAL AID AWARDED FOR 2016–17

Academy of Holy Angels, MN	$1,300,000
Academy of Notre Dame, MA	$11,300
Academy of Notre Dame de Namur, PA	$1,078,519
Academy of Our Lady of Peace, CA	$2,600,000
Academy of the Holy Family, CT	$86,600
Academy of the New Church Boys' School, PA	$750,000
Academy of the New Church Girls' School, PA	$1,200,000
Academy of the Sacred Heart, LA	$342,850
Academy of the Sacred Heart, MI	$626,915
Adelphi Academy, NY	$125,000
Advanced Academy of Georgia, GA	$109,000
The Agnes Irwin School, PA	$1,771,400
Albuquerque Academy, NM	$2,385,154
Allen Academy, TX	$230,000
Allentown Central Catholic High School, PA	$923,830
Allison Academy, FL	$215,000
Alverno Heights Academy, CA	$63,920
The American Boychoir School, NJ	$37,500
American Christian Academy, AL	$95,000
The American School Foundation, Mexico	14,667,170 Mexican pesos
Andrews Osborne Academy, OH	$401,000
Archbishop Alter High School, OH	$200,000
Archbishop Hoban High School, OH	$1,550,000
Archbishop Mitty High School, CA	$3,800,000
Archbishop Moeller High School, OH	$1,400,000
Archbishop Shaw High School, LA	$100,000
Army and Navy Academy, CA	$382,500
Asheville School, NC	$1,803,000
Ashley Hall, SC	$1,215,000
Athens Academy, GA	$12,000,000
Bakersfield Christian High School, CA	$160,000
Balmoral Hall School, MB, Canada	CAN$291,000
Banbury Crossroads School, AB, Canada	CAN$10,500
Barnstable Academy, NJ	$200,000
Battle Ground Academy, TN	$963,689
Baylor School, TN	$5,900,000
Bearspaw Christian School, AB, Canada	CAN$111,354
Beaufort Academy, SC	$72,600
Belen Jesuit Preparatory School, FL	$514,810
Bellevue Christian School, WA	$900,000
The Bement School, MA	$852,000
Ben Lippen Schools, SC	$570,000
Berean Christian High School, CA	$286,000
Berkeley Carroll School, NY	$3,300,000
Berkshire School, MA	$5,100,000
The Bermuda High School for Girls, Bermuda	332,100 Bermuda dollars
Beth Haven Christian School, KY	$10,650
The Birch Wathen Lenox School, NY	$1,500,000
Bishop Denis J. O'Connell High School, VA	$2,100,000
Bishop Ireton High School, VA	$772,000
Bishop John J. Snyder High School, FL	$325,000
Bishop Kelly High School, ID	$1,398,238
Bishop McGuinness Catholic High School, OK	$237,350
Bishop O'Dowd High School, CA	$2,300,000
Bishop's College School, QC, Canada	CAN$900,000
Bishop Stang High School, MA	$600,000
The Blake School, MN	$2,321,797
Blanchet School, OR	$360,000
Blessed Sacrament Huguenot Catholic School, VA	$150,000
The Blue Ridge School, VA	$200,000
The Bolles School, FL	$3,878,650
Boston University Academy, MA	$1,514,582
Brandon Hall School, GA	$250,000
Branksome Hall, ON, Canada	CAN$600,000
Brehm Preparatory School, IL	$99,300
Brethren Christian Junior and Senior High Schools, CA	$7500
Briarwood Christian High School, AL	$30,000
Brimmer and May School, MA	$1,606,150
Brooks School, MA	$4,000,000
Brophy College Preparatory, AZ	$4,316,250
The Browning School, NY	$953,900
The Bryn Mawr School for Girls, MD	$1,664,085
Buckingham Browne & Nichols School, MA	$5,370,000
The Buckley School, CA	$530,000
Buffalo Seminary, NY	$1,074,305
Buxton School, MA	$1,600,000
The Calhoun School, NY	$2,000,000
California Crosspoint High School, CA	$520,000
California Lutheran High School, CA	$250,000
Calvert Hall College High School, MD	$2,668,735
Calvin Christian High School, CA	$275,000
Campbell Hall (Episcopal), CA	$5,400,000
Canadian Academy, Japan	¥3,350,000
Canterbury School, CT	$3,500,000
Canterbury School, FL	$1,747,197
The Canterbury School of Florida, FL	$1,014,852
Cape Cod Academy, MA	$1,600,000
Capistrano Valley Christian Schools, CA	$200,000
Cardinal Gibbons High School, NC	$1,400,000
Carondelet High School, CA	$1,100,000
Casady School, OK	$2,050,129
Cascades Academy of Central Oregon, OR	$152,000
Cascia Hall Preparatory School, OK	$75,000
Castilleja School, CA	$2,600,000
Cate School, CA	$3,200,000
Catholic Central High School, MI	$1,100,000
Catholic Central High School, NY	$240,000
Catholic Central High School, WI	$140,000
CCI The Renaissance School, Italy	€30,000
Central Catholic High School, LA	$167,512
Central Catholic High School, MA	$1,051,402
Central Catholic High School, PA	$1,600,000
Chadwick School, CA	$2,000,000
Chaminade College Preparatory, CA	$2,529,026
Chaminade College Preparatory School, MO	$1,600,000
Charles E. Smith Jewish Day School, MD	$5,000,000
Charlotte Country Day School, NC	$1,470,003
Charlotte Latin School, NC	$1,185,535
Chase Collegiate School, CT	$1,619,717
Cheverus High School, ME	$2,172,770
Children's Creative and Performing Arts Academy of San Diego, CA	$25,000
Choate Rosemary Hall, CT	$11,700,000
Christ Church Episcopal School, SC	$626,210
Christchurch School, VA	$2,578,000
Christian Brothers Academy, NJ	$700,000
Christian Central Academy, NY	$177,758
The Church Farm School, PA	$3,881,717
Colegio Franklin D. Roosevelt, Peru	$6200
Collegedale Academy, TN	$210,000
Columbia Academy, TN	$36,100
Columbia International School, Japan	¥3,360,000
The Columbus Academy, OH	$1,230,000
Columbus School for Girls, OH	$697,799
Commonwealth School, MA	$1,015,000
The Community School of Naples, FL	$1,212,598
Concord Academy, MA	$4,200,000
Concordia Academy, MN	$334,804
Concordia Lutheran High School, IN	$3,928,184
Covington Catholic High School, KY	$400,000

Crawford Adventist Academy, ON, Canada	CAN$40,000
Crescent School, ON, Canada	CAN$680,000
C.S. Lewis Academy, OR	$22,113
The Culver Academies, IN	$8,900,000
Currey Ingram Academy, TN	$1,750,000
Cushing Academy, MA	$3,500,000
Damien High School, CA	$495,000
Dana Hall School, MA	$4,090,422
Darlington School, GA	$2,566,200
Darrow School, NY	$1,400,000
Deerfield Academy, MA	$8,985,000
De La Salle High School, CA	$2,330,000
DeLaSalle High School, MN	$26,070,000
De La Salle North Catholic High School, OR	$294,820
Delaware County Christian School, PA	$800,000
Delaware Valley Friends School, PA	$892,650
Delbarton School, NJ	$2,605,000
The Delphian School, OR	$315,000
DeMatha Catholic High School, MD	$1,632,348
Denver Academy, CO	$766,188
Denver Christian High School, CO	$30,000
Desert Academy, NM	$180,000
Devon Preparatory School, PA	$1,030,000
Doane Academy, NJ	$8000
Dock Mennonite Academy, PA	$655,758
Donelson Christian Academy, TN	$217,000
Donovan Catholic, NJ	$400,000
Dowling Catholic High School, IA	$1,000,000
Dublin Christian Academy, NH	$125,000
Dublin School, NH	$1,490,000
Durham Academy, NC	$2,000,000
Eastern Mennonite High School, VA	$200,000
Edgewood High School of the Sacred Heart, WI	$641,388
Edmonton Academy, AB, Canada	CAN$27,000
Edmund Burke School, DC	$978,185
Eldorado Emerson Private School, CA	$50,000
Elgin Academy, IL	$1,590,000
Elmwood School, ON, Canada	CAN$250,000
Episcopal Collegiate School, AR	$482,000
Episcopal High School, TX	$2,229,200
Episcopal High School, VA	$6,600,000
Episcopal High School of Jacksonville, FL	$2,000,000
Escola Americana de Campinas, Brazil	$51,000
Escondido Adventist Academy, CA	$50,000
Explorations Academy, WA	$200,000
Ezell-Harding Christian School, TN	$136,000
Faith Christian High School, CA	$50,000
Faith Lutheran High School, NV	$635,000
Falmouth Academy, MA	$1,300,000
Father Lopez High School, FL	$1,230,000
Fayetteville Academy, NC	$562,297
Fay School, MA	$2,201,551
The Fessenden School, MA	$1,043,947
First Presbyterian Day School, GA	$874,000
Flintridge Preparatory School, CA	$2,286,100
Flintridge Sacred Heart Academy, CA	$558,450
Fontbonne Hall Academy, NY	$121,500
Fordham Preparatory School, NY	$3,600,000
Forest Lake Academy, FL	$347,000
Forsyth Country Day School, NC	$890,296
Fort Worth Christian School, TX	$111,000
Fort Worth Country Day School, TX	$1,087,387
Foundation Academy, FL	$200,000
Fountain Valley School of Colorado, CO	$2,354,978
Fowlers Academy, PR	$32,000
Foxcroft School, VA	$1,589,890
French-American School of New York, NY	$259,955
Fresno Christian Schools, CA	$262,944
Friends Select School, PA	$888,000
Front Range Christian High School, CO	$181,000
Fuqua School, VA	$67,636
The Galloway School, GA	$820,778
Gann Academy (The New Jewish High School of Greater Boston), MA	$2,300,000
Gaston Day School, NC	$203,858
George Stevens Academy, ME	$100,000
Gilman School, MD	$1,839,100
Gilmour Academy, OH	$4,539,858
Glenelg Country School, MD	$2,500,000
Gonzaga College High School, DC	$2,900,000
Good Hope Country Day School, VI	$311,550
The Governor's Academy, MA	$4,400,000
The Gow School, NY	$1,100,000
Grace Christian School, AK	$200,000
Grace Christian School, PE, Canada	CAN$20,000
The Grauer School, CA	$160,877
Great Lakes Christian High School, ON, Canada	CAN$225,000
Greenfield School, NC	$28,500
Greenhill School, TX	$1,812,250
Greenhills School, MI	$10,011,500
Greenwood Laboratory School, MO	$75,000
The Greenwood School, VT	$249,290
Grier School, PA	$2,000,000
The Gunnery, CT	$3,500,000
The Gunston School, MD	$1,400,000
Hammond School, SC	$1,400,000
Hampton Roads Academy, VA	$600,000
Harvard-Westlake School, CA	$6,859,500
The Harvey School, NY	$2,080,000
The Haverford School, PA	$3,438,700
Hawaii Baptist Academy, HI	$476,525
Hawai`i Preparatory Academy, HI	$3,651,310
Hawken School, OH	$5,102,962
Hawthorne Christian Academy, NJ	$175,000
Hebrew Academy, CA	$30,000
Hebron Academy, ME	$2,000,000
Heritage Hall, OK	$600,000
The Hewitt School, NY	$3,241,816
The Hill Center, Durham Academy, NC	$56,000
Hillcrest Christian School, CA	$12,700
Hillside School, MA	$1,500,000
Ho'Ala School, HI	$21,600
The Hockaday School, TX	$3,400,000
Holland Hall, OK	$928,525
Holy Cross High School, CT	$650,000
Holy Ghost Preparatory School, PA	$750,000
Holy Innocents' Episcopal School, GA	$1,465,280
Holy Savior Menard Catholic High School, LA	$150,000
Holy Trinity High School, IL	$600,000
Holy Trinity School, ON, Canada	CAN$50,000
Hoosac School, NY	$625,000
The Hotchkiss School, CT	$9,412,766
Houghton Academy, NY	$95,000
The Hun School of Princeton, NJ	$4,600,000
Hyde Park Baptist School, TX	$145,250
Hyde School, CT	$258,000
Hyde School, ME	$1,300,000
Hyman Brand Hebrew Academy of Greater Kansas City, KS	$97,107
Immaculata-La Salle High School, FL	$455,000
Immaculate Conception High School, NJ	$165,000
Indian Springs School, AL	$1,615,000
International College Spain, Spain	€17,600
International High School, CA	$748,000

International School of Brussels, Belgium	€395,232
International School of Kenya, Ltd., Kenya	$179,342
International School of Port-of-Spain, Trinidad and Tobago	$42,000
Jackson Preparatory School, MS	$210,000
Jesuit College Preparatory School, TX	$1,233,850
Jesuit High School of Tampa, FL	$1,655,648
John Burroughs School, MO	$2,527,400
The Journeys School of Teton Science School, WY	$240,150
Junipero Serra High School, CA	$2,400,000
Kauai Christian Academy, HI	$40,000
Kent Denver School, CO	$2,400,000
Kent School, CT	$8,400,000
The Key School, MD	$667,300
Kildonan School, NY	$600,000
Kimball Union Academy, NH	$3,201,052
Kimberton Waldorf School, PA	$164,250
King School, CT	$1,465,073
King's-Edgehill School, NS, Canada	CAN$900,000
Kingswood-Oxford School, CT	$2,300,000
The Kiski School, PA	$4,085,095
The Lab School of Washington, DC	$164,700
La Grange Academy, GA	$159,411
Lake Forest Academy, IL	$3,100,000
Lakeland Christian Academy, IN	$60,000
La Lumiere School, IN	$988,830
Lancaster Mennonite High School, PA	$3,000,000
Landon School, MD	$3,723,217
Lansdale Catholic High School, PA	$125,000
La Pietra–Hawaii School for Girls, HI	$406,000
La Salle Academy, RI	$2,200,000
La Salle High School, CA	$2,100,250
Lauralton Hall, CT	$534,630
The Laureate Academy, MB, Canada	CAN$30,000
Lawrence School, OH	$1,214,000
The Lawrenceville School, NJ	$11,533,470
Lehigh Valley Christian High School, PA	$17,387
Le Lycee Francais de Los Angeles, CA	$225,080
Lexington Christian Academy, MA	$739,135
Leysin American School in Switzerland, Switzerland Swiss francs	600,000
Liberty Christian School, CA	$20,000
Lincoln Academy, ME	$600,000
Lincoln School, RI	$2,000,000
The Linden School, ON, Canada	CAN$150,000
Long Island Lutheran Middle and High School, NY	$420,000
Long Trail School, VT	$99,599
Louisville High School, CA	$690,000
The Lovett School, GA	$1,760,366
Lower Canada College, QC, Canada	CAN$327,845
Loyola-Blakefield, MD	$2,510,301
Loyola College Prep, LA	$133,300
Lutheran High North, TX	$175,000
Lutheran High School, CO	$1,000,000
Lutheran High School, MO	$153,000
Lutheran High School Northwest, MI	$20,000
Lutheran High School of Indianapolis, IN	$207,000
Lutheran High School of San Diego, CA	$121,935
Lutheran High School West, OH	$1,100,000
Luther College High School, SK, Canada	CAN$165,000
The Lycee International, American Section, France	€30,000
Lydia Patterson Institute, TX	$15,795
Ma'ayanot Yeshiva High School for Girls of Bergen County, NJ	$1,446,363
Madison Academy, AL	$84,000
Malden Catholic High School, MA	$1,105,973
Manhattan Christian High School, MT	$50,000
Maplebrook School, NY	$100,000
Marian Central Catholic High School, IL	$288,816
Marian High School, MA	$600,000
Marin Academy, CA	$2,900,000
Marine Military Academy, TX	$1,000,000
Marist School, GA	$2,000,000
Marshall School, MN	$1,800,000
Martin Luther High School, NY	$1,955,670
The Marvelwood School, CT	$1,250,000
Mary Help of Christians Academy, NJ	$311,100
Mary Institute and St. Louis Country Day School (MICDS), MO	$2,587,645
The Mary Louis Academy, NY	$615,000
Marymount High School, CA	$1,320,000
Marymount School of New York, NY	$3,000,000
Mater Dei High School, IL	$120,000
Matignon High School, MA	$600,000
Maumee Valley Country Day School, OH	$454,900
Mayer Lutheran High School, MN	$280,000
The McCallie School, TN	$3,500,000
McDonogh School, MD	$3,340,390
The Meadows School, NV	$486,845
Memphis University School, TN	$2,500,000
Menlo School, CA	$5,600,000
Mercersburg Academy, PA	$6,178,725
Mercy High School, MI	$60,000
Mercyhurst Preparatory School, PA	$578,050
Mesa Grande Seventh-Day Academy, CA	$35,000
The Miami Valley School, OH	$1,070,670
Middlesex School, MA	$5,800,000
Midland School, CA	$1,500,000
Millbrook School, NY	$3,496,436
Mill Springs Academy, GA	$110,000
Milton Academy, MA	$9,900,000
Miss Edgar's and Miss Cramp's School, QC, Canada	CAN$135,000
Miss Porter's School, CT	$3,900,000
MMI Preparatory School, PA	$666,170
The Monarch School, TX	$105,350
Moncton Wesleyan Academy, NB, Canada	CAN$84,200
Montclair Kimberley Academy, NJ	$1,222,000
Monterey Bay Academy, CA	$240,000
Montgomery Bell Academy, TN	$2,150,000
Montrose School, MA	$500,000
Moorestown Friends School, NJ	$1,784,855
Moravian Academy, PA	$1,400,000
Moreau Catholic High School, CA	$2,100,000
Mother McAuley High School, IL	$1,000,000
Mountain View Academy, CA	$65,000
Mount St. Agnes Academy, Bermuda	$20,000
Mount Saint Charles Academy, RI	$750,000
Nampa Christian Schools, ID	$37,786
Nazareth Academy, IL	$300,000
Nebraska Christian Schools, NE	$140,000
Nerinx Hall, MO	$987,386
Neuchatel Junior College, Switzerland	CAN$393,000
New Roads School, CA	$4,800,000
Newton Country Day School of the Sacred Heart, MA	$1,080,000
New York Military Academy, NY	$355,000
Niagara Christian Community of Schools, ON, Canada	CAN$400,000
Noble Academy, NC	$81,000
Noble and Greenough School, MA	$3,985,500
The Nora School, MD	$177,000
North Country School, NY	$185,910
Northfield Mount Hermon School, MA	$9,400,000

Northpoint Christian School, MS	$70,000	Rice Memorial High School, VT	$650,000
North Shore Country Day School, IL	$1,750,000	Ridley College, ON, Canada	CAN$1,800,000
Northwest Academy, OR	$500,000	The Rivers School, MA	$3,727,504
Northwest Catholic High School, CT	$2,034,000	Rockhurst High School, MO	$2,200,000
The Northwest School, WA	$1,380,220	Rockland Country Day School, NY	$371,140
North Yarmouth Academy, ME	$900,000	Rock Point School, VT	$150,000
Notre Dame High School, CA	$120,000	Rockway Mennonite Collegiate, ON, Canada	CAN$191,200
Notre Dame High School, CA	$1,200,000	Rocky Mount Academy, NC	$186,005
Notre Dame High School, NJ	$720,000	The Roeper School, MI	$60,000
Notre Dame High School, NY	$600,000	Roland Park Country School, MD	$1,645,815
Notre Dame High School, TN	$1,600,000	Rolling Hills Preparatory School, CA	$1,200,000
Oak Grove Lutheran School, ND	$241,144	Rosseau Lake College, ON, Canada	CAN$160,000
Oak Grove School, CA	$80,000	Rothesay Netherwood School, NB, Canada	CAN$1,029,195
The Oakridge School, TX	$523,375	Rowland Hall, UT	$867,697
Ojai Valley School, CA	$347,360	The Roxbury Latin School, MA	$2,429,625
Oldenburg Academy, IN	$65,000	Royal Canadian College, BC, Canada	CAN$18,000
The O'Neal School, NC	$423,937	Rumsey Hall School, CT	$1,150,000
Orangewood Adventist Academy, CA	$200,000	Rundle College, AB, Canada	CAN$90,000
Oregon Episcopal School, OR	$1,051,590	Sacramento Country Day School, CA	$468,000
Orinda Academy, CA	$400,000	Sacramento Waldorf School, CA	$398,000
The Orme School, AZ	$1,200,000	Sacred Heart/Griffin High School, IL	$556,298
PACE/Brantley Hall High School, FL	$28,000	Sacred Heart High School, CA	$1,000,000
Pacific Lutheran High School, CA	$20,000	Sacred Heart High School, NY	$25,000
The Packer Collegiate Institute, NY	$7,400,000	Sage Hill School, CA	$2,093,974
Padua Franciscan High School, OH	$540,000	St. Agnes Academy, TX	$1,400,000
The Paideia School, GA	$1,481,011	St. Albans School, DC	$4,034,535
Palma School, CA	$700,000	Saint Albert Junior-Senior High School, IA	$390,000
Paradise Adventist Academy, CA	$30,000	St. Andrew's Episcopal School, MD	$2,708,400
The Park School of Baltimore, MD	$2,084,995	Saint Andrew's School, FL	$3,000,000
The Park School of Buffalo, NY	$533,061	St. Andrew's School, GA	$150,000
Peddie School, NJ	$7,000,000	St. Andrew's–Sewanee School, TN	$2,010,689
The Pembroke Hill School, MO	$466,410	Saint Augustine Preparatory School, NJ	$1,600,000
Peninsula Catholic High School, VA	$378,000	Saint Basil Academy, PA	$268,175
The Pennington School, NJ	$4,000,000	St. Benedict at Auburndale, TN	$35,000
Peoples Christian Academy, ON, Canada	CAN$30,000	St. Bernard's Catholic School, CA	$55,000
The Phelps School, PA	$1,100,000	St. Catherine's Academy, CA	$400,000
Philadelphia-Montgomery Christian Academy, PA	$650,000	St. Christopher's School, VA	$783,200
Phoenix Country Day School, AZ	$1,016,600	St. Croix Schools, MN	$850,000
Pickering College, ON, Canada	CAN$125,000	Saint Francis High School, CA	$1,000,000
The Pingree School, MA	$3,200,000	St. George's Independent School, TN	$975,000
The Pingry School, NJ	$2,711,787	St. George's School, RI	$42,000,000
Pioneer Valley Christian Academy, MA	$217,115	St. George's School, BC, Canada	CAN$1,000,000
Polytechnic School, CA	$2,219,233	Saint Ignatius College Prep, IL	$3,000,000
Pope Francis High School, MA	$150,000	Saint John Bosco High School, CA	$1,368,000
Portsmouth Christian Academy, NH	$225,000	St. John Neumann High School, FL	$300,000
Poughkeepsie Day School, NY	$550,000	St. John's Catholic Prep, MD	$800,000
Powers Catholic High School, MI	$400,000	St. John's Preparatory School, MA	$4,000,000
Presbyterian Pan American School, TX	$1,342,850	St. John's-Ravenscourt School, MB, Canada	CAN$262,250
Preston High School, NY	$510,000	Saint John's School, GU	$500,000
Prestonwood Christian Academy, TX	$734,381	Saint Joseph Academy, CA	$95,848
Proctor Academy, NH	$3,200,000	St. Joseph Academy, FL	$120,000
Professional Children's School, NY	$795,802	St. Joseph High School, CA	$525,000
Providence Country Day School, RI	$2,294,300	St. Joseph High School, CT	$1,400,000
Providence Day School, NC	$1,106,585	Saint Joseph High School, NJ	$750,000
Providence High School, CA	$942,250	St. Joseph High School, TX	$320,000
Punahou School, HI	$3,644,200	St. Joseph's Catholic School, SC	$805,000
Queen Margaret's School, BC, Canada	CAN$150,000	St. Joseph's Preparatory School, PA	$3,900,000
Quigley Catholic High School, PA	$299,953	St. Lawrence Seminary High School, WI	$778,110
Ramona Convent Secondary School, CA	$350,000	Saint Lucy's Priory High School, CA	$90,000
Randolph-Macon Academy, VA	$940,455	St. Luke's School, CT	$1,911,149
Ransom Everglades School, FL	$4,123,309	Saint Mary of the Assumption High School, NJ	$360,000
Realms of Inquiry, UT	$10,000	St. Mary's Episcopal School, TN	$674,412
The Rectory School, CT	$1,600,000	Saint Mary's Hall, TX	$621,990
Redwood Christian Schools, CA	$420,000	Saint Mary's High School, AZ	$3,800,000
Regina Junior-Senior High School, IA	$325,000	St. Mary's High School, CO	$750,000
Regis Jesuit High School, Boys Division, CO	$1,900,000	St. Michael's Preparatory School of the Norbertine Fathers, CA	$500,000
Regis Jesuit High School, Girls Division, CO	$1,900,000		

Saint Patrick High School, IL	$1,600,000
St. Patrick's Regional Secondary, BC, Canada	CAN$4000
Saint Paul Lutheran High School, MO	$273,555
St. Paul's High School, MB, Canada	CAN$355,200
St. Paul's School, NH	$11,200,000
St. Pius X Catholic High School, GA	$400,000
St. Stephen's Episcopal School, TX	$2,460,000
St. Stephen's School, Rome, Italy	€530,000
Saint Teresa's Academy, MO	$200,000
Saint Thomas Academy, MN	$2,800,000
Saint Thomas Aquinas High School, KS	$1,100,000
Saint Thomas More Catholic High School, LA	$100,000
Saint Ursula Academy, OH	$1,420,000
Saint Vincent-Saint Mary High School, OH	$809,720
Saint Xavier High School, KY	$2,100,000
Salem Academy, NC	$1,033,794
Salpointe Catholic High School, AZ	$1,848,925
San Francisco University High School, CA	$2,600,000
San Marcos Baptist Academy, TX	$50,000
Santa Catalina School, CA	$1,964,000
Santa Margarita Catholic High School, CA	$1,500,000
Sayre School, KY	$624,000
Scattergood Friends School, IA	$469,965
Scholar's Hall Preparatory School, ON, Canada	CAN$20,000
Scotus Central Catholic High School, NE	$176,709
Seabury Hall, HI	$935,850
Seacrest Country Day School, FL	$880,234
Sedona Sky Academy, AZ	$81,600
Seisen International School, Japan	¥4,500,000
Seton Catholic Central High School, NY	$200,000
Seton Catholic High School, AZ	$705,000
The Seven Hills School, OH	$1,357,434
Shady Side Academy, PA	$2,951,630
Shattuck-St. Mary's School, MN	$5,200,000
Shawe Memorial Junior/Senior High School, IN	$80,000
Shawnigan Lake School, BC, Canada	CAN$1,500,000
Shelton School and Evaluation Center, TX	$516,800
Shorecrest Preparatory School, FL	$739,305
Shoreline Christian, WA	$170,000
The Siena School, MD	$270,000
Sonoma Academy, CA	$3,000,000
Southwestern Academy, AZ	$240,000
The Spence School, NY	$2,260,164
Springside Chestnut Hill Academy, PA	$4,500,000
Squaw Valley Academy, CA	$175,000
STAR Prep Academy, CA	$500,000
Steamboat Mountain School, CO	$220,000
Stevenson School, CA	$3,475,000
The Storm King School, NY	$1,742,313
Stratton Mountain School, VT	$760,000
Stuart Hall, VA	$1,400,000
Subiaco Academy, AR	$475,550
The Taft School, CT	$8,000,000
TASIS The American School in England, United Kingdom	£223,600
Teurlings Catholic High School, LA	$84,000
The Thacher School, CA	$2,818,894
Thomas Jefferson School, MO	$700,000
Tilton School, NH	$4,100,000
Tower Hill School, DE	$1,300,000
Trafalgar Castle School, ON, Canada	CAN$43,000
Trevor Day School, NY	$5,884,000
Tri-City Christian Academy, AZ	$25,000
Trinity Academy, KS	$500,000
Trinity Catholic High School, CT	$477,260
Trinity College School, ON, Canada	CAN$2,407,200
Trinity High School, KY	$2,800,000
Trinity High School, OH	$150,000
Trinity-Pawling School, NY	$3,500,000
Trinity Preparatory School, FL	$1,800,000
United Mennonite Educational Institute, ON, Canada	CAN$46,000
University Lake School, WI	$272,000
University of Chicago Laboratory Schools, IL	$1,365,483
University Prep, WA	$1,591,910
University School of Jackson, TN	$180,000
Upper Canada College, ON, Canada	CAN$4,500,000
The Ursuline Academy of Dallas, TX	$1,154,600
Valley Christian High School, CA	$2,500,000
The Valley School, MI	$200,000
The Vanguard School, FL	$500,000
Verdala International School, Malta	$18,750
Vicksburg Catholic School, MS	$75,000
Villa Joseph Marie High School, PA	$180,000
Villa Walsh Academy, NJ	$120,000
Virginia Episcopal School, VA	$2,000,000
Walnut Hill School for the Arts, MA	$3,500,000
Wasatch Academy, UT	$3,857,580
Washington Waldorf School, MD	$38,000
The Waterford School, UT	$350,000
Watkinson School, CT	$1,650,522
Waynflete School, ME	$2,313,466
Webb School of Knoxville, TN	$860,000
Wesleyan Academy, PR	$1000
Westbury Christian School, TX	$558,892
Westminster Christian Academy, LA	$50,000
Westminster Christian School, FL	$750,000
Westminster School, CT	$4,910,370
West Nottingham Academy, MD	$1,000,000
Westover School, CT	$3,600,000
West Sound Academy, WA	$242,891
Westtown School, PA	$5,511,681
The Wheeler School, RI	$2,093,652
Whitefield Academy, KY	$42,175
Wilmington Christian School, DE	$325,000
Wilmington Friends School, DE	$1,870,885
Wilson Hall, SC	$150,000
The Winchendon School, MA	$2,000,000
Winchester Thurston School, PA	$1,750,000
The Windsor School, NY	$20,000
Windward School, CA	$1,980,066
Winston Preparatory School, NY	$500,000
The Winston School, TX	$229,000
Woodberry Forest School, VA	$5,688,400
Woodlynde School, PA	$1,000,000
Woodstock Academy, CT	$25,000
Woodstock School, India	$1,000,000
The Woodward School, MA	$295,127
Wyoming Seminary, PA	$8,500,000
Xavier High School, NY	$3,400,000
York Country Day School, PA	$339,000

SCHOOLS REPORTING THAT THEY OFFER ENGLISH AS A SECOND LANGUAGE

Academy at the Lakes, FL
Academy of Holy Angels, MN
Academy of the Holy Family, CT
Academy of the New Church Boys' School, PA
Academy of the New Church Girls' School, PA
Académie Ste Cécile International School, ON, Canada
Allen Academy, TX
Alliance Academy, Ecuador

Allison Academy, FL
Alma Heights Christian High School, CA
Alverno Heights Academy, CA
American Cooperative School of Tunis, Tunisia
The American Embassy School, India
The American International School, Austria
American International School Rotterdam, Netherlands
The American School of Madrid, Spain
American School of The Hague, Netherlands
Andrews Osborne Academy, OH
Arizona Lutheran Academy, AZ
Army and Navy Academy, CA
Ashley Hall, SC
Atlanta International School, GA
Augusta Christian School, GA
Balboa City School, CA
Balmoral Hall School, MB, Canada
Banbury Crossroads School, AB, Canada
Bangor Christian School, ME
Barnstable Academy, NJ
Bavarian International School, Germany
Bay Ridge Preparatory School, NY
The Beekman School, NY
Bellevue Christian School, WA
The Bement School, MA
Ben Lippen Schools, SC
Berkshire School, MA
Bishop Denis J. O'Connell High School, VA
Bishop Kearney High School, NY
Bishop's College School, QC, Canada
Black Forest Academy, Germany
Blanchet School, OR
The Blue Ridge School, VA
The Bolles School, FL
Boston Trinity Academy, MA
Brandon Hall School, GA
Branksome Hall, ON, Canada
British International School of Boston, MA
Brockwood Park School, United Kingdom
Burr and Burton Academy, VT
Buxton School, MA
Cairo American College, Egypt
California Crosspoint High School, CA
California Lutheran High School, CA
Campion School, Athens, Greece
Canadian Academy, Japan
Canterbury School, CT
Canterbury School, FL
The Canterbury School of Florida, FL
Cape Cod Academy, MA
Cape Henry Collegiate School, VA
Capistrano Valley Christian Schools, CA
Cardinal Ritter High School, IN
Carnegie Schools Riverside, CA
Catholic Central High School, NY
Chaminade College Preparatory School, MO
Charles E. Smith Jewish Day School, MD
Charlotte Country Day School, NC
Chase Collegiate School, CT
Chatham Hall, VA
Children's Creative and Performing Arts Academy of
    San Diego, CA
Christ Church Episcopal School, SC
Christchurch School, VA
Christian Central Academy, NY
City Christian Schools, OR
Colegio Bolivar, Colombia

Colegio Franklin D. Roosevelt, Peru
Columbia International School, Japan
Contra Costa Christian High School, CA
Crawford Adventist Academy, ON, Canada
Crestwood Preparatory College, ON, Canada
The Culver Academies, IN
Cushing Academy, MA
Damien High School, CA
Darlington School, GA
Darrow School, NY
Davidson Academy, TN
Delaware County Christian School, PA
The Delphian School, OR
Desert Academy, NM
The Dr. Miriam and Sheldon G. Adelson Educational Campus, The
    Adelson Upper School, NV
Dominican Academy, NY
Donelson Christian Academy, TN
Dublin School, NH
The Dwight School, NY
Eaglebrook School, MA
Eastern Mennonite High School, VA
Eaton Academy, GA
Eldorado Emerson Private School, CA
Elgin Academy, IL
Elmwood School, ON, Canada
The English College in Prague, Czech Republic
Erskine Academy, ME
Escola Americana de Campinas, Brazil
Escondido Adventist Academy, CA
Escuela Campo Alegre, Venezuela
Father Lopez High School, FL
Father Yermo High School, TX
Fay School, MA
The Fessenden School, MA
First Presbyterian Day School, GA
Forest Lake Academy, FL
Forsyth Country Day School, NC
Fountain Valley School of Colorado, CO
Fowlers Academy, PR
Foxcroft School, VA
French-American School of New York, NY
Friends Select School, PA
Fuqua School, VA
Gaston Day School, NC
George Stevens Academy, ME
The Governor French Academy, IL
The Gow School, NY
Grace Christian School, PE, Canada
The Grauer School, CA
Great Lakes Christian High School, ON, Canada
Green Fields Country Day School, AZ
Green Meadow Waldorf School, NY
Grier School, PA
The Gunnery, CT
The Gunston School, MD
Hammond School, SC
Hampton Roads Academy, VA
Hawai`i Preparatory Academy, HI
Hebron Academy, ME
Highroad Academy, BC, Canada
Hillcrest Christian School, CA
Hillside School, MA
The Hockaday School, TX
Holy Trinity High School, IL
Hoosac School, NY
Houghton Academy, NY

The Hun School of Princeton, NJ
Hyde School, CT
Hyde School, ME
Immaculate Conception High School, NJ
Institut Monte Rosa, Switzerland
International College Spain, Spain
International High School, CA
International School Hamburg, Germany
International School Manila, Philippines
The International School of Aberdeen, United Kingdom
International School of Amsterdam, Netherlands
International School of Brussels, Belgium
International School of Kenya, Ltd., Kenya
The International School of London, United Kingdom
International School of Port-of-Spain, Trinidad and Tobago
Istanbul International Community School, Turkey
The Judge Rotenberg Educational Center, MA
Kaohsiung American School, Taiwan
Keio Academy of New York, NY
Kent School, CT
The King's Christian High School, NJ
King's-Edgehill School, NS, Canada
The Kiski School, PA
Lake Forest Academy, IL
Lake Mary Preparatory School, FL
Lake Ridge Academy, OH
La Lumiere School, IN
Lancaster Mennonite High School, PA
La Salle Institute, NY
La Sierra Academy, CA
Lawrence Woodmere Academy, NY
Le Lycee Francais de Los Angeles, CA
Lexington Christian Academy, MA
Leysin American School in Switzerland, Switzerland
Lincoln Academy, ME
Long Trail School, VT
Lutheran High School, CO
Lutheran High School of San Diego, CA
Luther College High School, SK, Canada
Lycee Français La Perouse, CA
Lycee Internationale de Boston/International School of
    Boston, MA
Lyndon Institute, VT
Malden Catholic High School, MA
Maplebrook School, NY
Marianapolis Preparatory School, CT
Marian High School, MA
Marine Military Academy, TX
Martin Luther High School, NY
The Marvelwood School, CT
Massanutten Military Academy, VA
Mater Dei Prep, NJ
Matignon High School, MA
Maumee Valley Country Day School, OH
Maur Hill-Mount Academy, KS
Merchiston Castle School, United Kingdom
Mercyhurst Preparatory School, PA
Mesa Grande Seventh-Day Academy, CA
The Miami Valley School, OH
Mid-Pacific Institute, HI
Moncton Wesleyan Academy, NB, Canada
Monterey Bay Academy, CA
Mooseheart High School, IL
Moreau Catholic High School, CA
Mount Vernon Presbyterian School, GA
Nebraska Christian Schools, NE
New International School of Thailand, Thailand

Newton's Grove School, ON, Canada
New York Military Academy, NY
Niagara Christian Community of Schools, ON, Canada
The North Broward Preparatory Upper School, FL
North Central Texas Academy, TX
North Country School, NY
Northfield Mount Hermon School, MA
North Toronto Christian School, ON, Canada
The Northwest School, WA
The Norwich Free Academy, CT
Notre Dame-Cathedral Latin School, OH
Notre Dame High School, CA
Notre Dame High School, NJ
Oak Grove Lutheran School, ND
Oak Grove School, CA
Oak Ridge Military Academy, NC
Ojai Valley School, CA
Oldenburg Academy, IN
Oneida Baptist Institute, KY
Oregon Episcopal School, OR
Orinda Academy, CA
The Orme School, AZ
Pacific Lutheran High School, CA
The Park School of Buffalo, NY
Peninsula Catholic High School, VA
The Pennington School, NJ
Perkiomen School, PA
The Phelps School, PA
Philadelphia-Montgomery Christian Academy, PA
Phoenix Christian Preparatory School, AZ
Pickering College, ON, Canada
Pinewood Preparatory School, SC
Pope Francis High School, MA
Portledge School, NY
Portsmouth Christian Academy, NH
Poughkeepsie Day School, NY
Presbyterian Pan American School, TX
Proctor Academy, NH
Professional Children's School, NY
Queen Margaret's School, BC, Canada
Quinte Christian High School, ON, Canada
Randolph-Macon Academy, VA
The Rectory School, CT
Redemption Christian Academy, MA
Regina Junior-Senior High School, IA
Ridley College, ON, Canada
Rockway Mennonite Collegiate, ON, Canada
Roland Park Country School, MD
Rolling Hills Preparatory School, CA
Rosseau Lake College, ON, Canada
Rothesay Netherwood School, NB, Canada
Rotterdam International Secondary School, Wolfert
    van Borselen, Netherlands
Royal Canadian College, BC, Canada
Rudolf Steiner School of Ann Arbor, MI
Rumsey Hall School, CT
Saddlebrook Preparatory School, FL
Saint Albert Junior-Senior High School, IA
Saint Andrew's School, FL
St. Andrew's School, GA
St. Andrew's-Sewanee School, TN
St. Catherine's Academy, CA
St. Croix Schools, MN
Saint John Bosco High School, CA
St. John's International, BC, Canada
St. John's Jesuit High School, OH
St. John's-Ravenscourt School, MB, Canada

Saint John's School, GU
St. Joseph High School, CT
St. Mary's Preparatory School, MI
Saint Maur International School, Japan
St. Michael's Preparatory School of the Norbertine Fathers, CA
St. Patrick's Regional Secondary, BC, Canada
St. Stanislaus College, MS
St. Stephen's International School, Thailand
St. Thomas Aquinas High School, NH
Salem Academy, NC
Salem Academy, OR
San Marcos Baptist Academy, TX
Scattergood Friends School, IA
Scholar's Hall Preparatory School, ON, Canada
Schule Schloss Salem, Germany
SciCore Academy, NJ
Seisen International School, Japan
Shattuck-St. Mary's School, MN
Shawe Memorial Junior/Senior High School, IN
Shawnigan Lake School, BC, Canada
Signet Christian School, ON, Canada
Southern Ontario Collegiate, ON, Canada
Southwestern Academy, AZ
Squaw Valley Academy, CA
The Stony Brook School, NY
The Storm King School, NY
Stuart Hall, VA
Subiaco Academy, AR
Taipei American School, Taiwan
Tandem Friends School, VA
TASIS The American School in England, United Kingdom
TASIS, The American School in Switzerland, Switzerland
The Tenney School, TX
Thomas Jefferson School, MO
Thornton Academy, ME
Tilton School, NH
TMI - The Episcopal School of Texas, TX
Trafalgar Castle School, ON, Canada
Tri-City Christian Academy, AZ
Trinity Catholic High School, CT
Trinity College School, ON, Canada
Trinity-Pawling School, NY
United Nations International School, NY
University School of Jackson, TN
Venta Preparatory School, ON, Canada
Verdala International School, Malta
Victor Valley Christian School, CA
Walnut Hill School for the Arts, MA
Wasatch Academy, UT
The Wellington School, OH
Westbury Christian School, TX
West Nottingham Academy, MD
Westover School, CT
Westtown School, PA
Whitfield School, MO
Wilmington Christian School, DE
The Winchendon School, MA
Winchester Thurston School, PA
Windermere School, United Kingdom
The Windsor School, NY
Woodstock Academy, CT
Woodstock School, India
The Woodward School, MA
Wyoming Seminary, PA
Yokohama International School, Japan
York Country Day School, PA
Zurich International School, Switzerland

SCHOOLS REPORTING A COMMUNITY SERVICE REQUIREMENT

The Academy for Gifted Children (PACE), ON, Canada
Academy of Our Lady of Peace, CA
Academy of the Holy Family, CT
Academy of the Sacred Heart, LA
Academy of the Sacred Heart, MI
The Agnes Irwin School, PA
Allen Academy, TX
Allentown Central Catholic High School, PA
Allison Academy, FL
American Christian Academy, AL
American Community School at Beirut, Lebanon
Andrews Osborne Academy, OH
Archbishop Curley High School, MD
Archbishop McNicholas High School, OH
Archbishop Moeller High School, OH
Arizona Lutheran Academy, AZ
Aurora Central Catholic High School, IL
Austin Preparatory School, MA
Bakersfield Christian High School, CA
Balboa City School, CA
Battle Ground Academy, TN
Belen Jesuit Preparatory School, FL
Bellevue Christian School, WA
The Bement School, MA
Benedictine High School, OH
Ben Lippen Schools, SC
Bentley School, CA
Berkeley Carroll School, NY
Berkeley Preparatory School, FL
Berkshire School, MA
The Birch Wathen Lenox School, NY
Bishop Connolly High School, MA
Bishop Denis J. O'Connell High School, VA
Bishop Fenwick High School, OH
Bishop Ireton High School, VA
Bishop Kelly High School, ID
The Bishop's School, CA
Bishop Stang High School, MA
Black Forest Academy, Germany
Blanchet School, OR
Blessed Sacrament Huguenot Catholic School, VA
Boston University Academy, MA
Brandon Hall School, GA
Briarwood Christian High School, AL
Brimmer and May School, MA
Brophy College Preparatory, AZ
Brother Martin High School, LA
The Browning School, NY
The Bryn Mawr School for Girls, MD
Buckingham Browne & Nichols School, MA
The Buckley School, CA
Buffalo Seminary, NY
Burr and Burton Academy, VT
The Calhoun School, NY
Campbell Hall (Episcopal), CA
Canterbury School, FL
The Canterbury School of Florida, FL
Cape Cod Academy, MA
Cape Henry Collegiate School, VA
Cardinal Newman High School, FL
Cardinal Ritter High School, IN
Carnegie Schools Riverside, CA
Cascia Hall Preparatory School, OK
Catholic Central High School, WI
CCI The Renaissance School, Italy

Chaminade College Preparatory, CA
Chaminade College Preparatory School, MO
Chaminade-Madonna College Preparatory, FL
Charlotte Country Day School, NC
Cheverus High School, ME
Children's Creative and Performing Arts Academy of
    San Diego, CA
Choate Rosemary Hall, CT
Christian Brothers Academy, NJ
Christian Brothers Academy, NY
Christian Central Academy, NY
Christopher Columbus High School, FL
The Church Farm School, PA
City Christian Schools, OR
Colegio San Josc, PR
Collegedale Academy, TN
The Collegiate School, VA
The Columbus Academy, OH
Commonwealth School, MA
The Community School of Naples, FL
Concordia Lutheran High School, IN
Convent of the Sacred Heart, CT
Covington Catholic High School, KY
Crawford Adventist Academy, ON, Canada
The Culver Academies, IN
Currey Ingram Academy, TN
Dalat School, Malaysia
Dallas Academy, TX
Damien High School, CA
Dana Hall School, MA
Darlington School, GA
Delaware Valley Friends School, PA
The Delphian School, OR
Denver Academy, CO
Desert Academy, NM
Devon Preparatory School, PA
Donelson Christian Academy, TN
Dowling Catholic High School, IA
Duchesne High School, MO
Durham Academy, NC
The Dwight School, NY
Eaglebrook School, MA
Eastern Mennonite High School, VA
Edgewood Academy, AL
Edmund Burke School, DC
Eldorado Emerson Private School, CA
Episcopal High School of Jacksonville, FL
Escola Americana de Campinas, Brazil
Excel Christian Academy, GA
Explorations Academy, WA
Ezell-Harding Christian School, TN
Faith Lutheran High School, NV
Father Lopez High School, FL
Flintridge Sacred Heart Academy, CA
Fontbonne Academy, MA
Forest Lake Academy, FL
Forsyth Country Day School, NC
Fort Worth Christian School, TX
Fort Worth Country Day School, TX
Fountain Valley School of Colorado, CO
French-American School of New York, NY
Friends Academy, NY
Fuqua School, VA
Gaston Day School, NC
Gilmour Academy, OH
Glenelg Country School, MD
Gonzaga College High School, DC

Good Hope Country Day School, VI
The Governor's Academy, MA
The Gow School, NY
The Grauer School, CA
Greenfield School, NC
Greenhill School, TX
Greenhills School, MI
The Greenwood School, VT
Griggs International Academy, MD
Guamani Private School, PR
Gulliver Preparatory School, FL
The Gunston School, MD
Halstrom Academy, Beverly Hills, CA
Halstrom Academy, Calsbad, CA
Halstrom Academy, Cupertino, CA
Halstrom Academy, Huntington Beach, CA
Halstrom Academy, Irvine, CA
Halstrom Academy, Manhattan Beach, CA
Halstrom Academy, Mission Viejo, CA
Halstrom Academy, Orange, CA
Halstrom Academy, Pasadena, CA
Halstrom Academy, San Diego, CA
Halstrom Academy, Walnut Creek, CA
Halstrom Academy, Westlake Village, CA
Halstrom Academy, Woodland Hills, CA
Hampton Roads Academy, VA
The Harker School, CA
The Harley School, NY
Harvard-Westlake School, CA
Hawken School, OH
Heritage Hall, OK
Hillcrest Christian School, CA
The Hockaday School, TX
Holy Cross School, LA
Holy Ghost Preparatory School, PA
Holy Innocents' Episcopal School, GA
The Hun School of Princeton, NJ
Hyde Park Baptist School, TX
Hyman Brand Hebrew Academy of Greater Kansas City, KS
Immaculata-La Salle High School, FL
Incarnate Word Academy, TX
Independent School, KS
International College Spain, Spain
International School of Amsterdam, Netherlands
The International School of London, United Kingdom
Jack M. Barrack Hebrew Academy, PA
Jesuit College Preparatory School, TX
Jesuit High School of Tampa, FL
Josephinum Academy, IL
Junipero Serra High School, CA
Kalamazoo Christian High School, MI
Kent Denver School, CO
Kimberton Waldorf School, PA
Kingswood-Oxford School, CT
The Lab School of Washington, DC
Lake Forest Academy, IL
Lakeview Academy, GA
La Salle Academy, RI
La Sierra Academy, CA
Lauralton Hall, CT
The Laureate Academy, MB, Canada
The Lawrenceville School, NJ
Lawrence Woodmere Academy, NY
Lincoln Academy, ME
Linfield Christian School, CA
Long Trail School, VT
Louisville High School, CA

Lower Canada College, QC, Canada
Loyola College Prep, LA
Lutheran High School Northwest, MI
Malvern Preparatory School, PA
Manhattan Christian High School, MT
Maranatha High School, CA
Marin Academy, CA
Marist School, GA
Marshall School, MN
The Marvelwood School, CT
Mary Institute and St. Louis Country Day School (MICDS), MO
The Mary Louis Academy, NY
Marymount School of New York, NY
Maryvale Preparatory School, MD
Mater Dei Prep, NJ
Matignon High School, MA
Maumee Valley Country Day School, OH
McDonogh School, MD
The McLean School of Maryland, Inc., MD
The Meadows School, NV
Menlo School, CA
Mercy High School, CT
Mercy High School, MI
Mesa Grande Seventh-Day Academy, CA
The Miami Valley School, OH
Miss Porter's School, CT
Montclair Kimberley Academy, NJ
Moorestown Friends School, NJ
Moreau Catholic High School, CA
Mountain View Academy, CA
Mount Dora Christian Academy, FL
Mount St. Agnes Academy, Bermuda
Nerinx Hall, MO
New International School of Thailand, Thailand
Newton Country Day School of the Sacred Heart, MA
New York Military Academy, NY
Noble and Greenough School, MA
The Nora School, MD
The North Broward Preparatory Upper School, FL
North Shore Country Day School, IL
Northside Christian School, FL
North Toronto Christian School, ON, Canada
Northwest Academy, OR
Northwest Catholic High School, CT
Notre Dame High School, CA
Notre Dame High School, CA
Notre Dame High School, NJ
Oak Grove School, CA
Oak Ridge Military Academy, NC
The Oakridge School, TX
Oldenburg Academy, IN
The O'Neal School, NC
Orangewood Adventist Academy, CA
The Orme School, AZ
Pace Academy, GA
The Packer Collegiate Institute, NY
The Paideia School, GA
Palma School, CA
Paradise Adventist Academy, CA
The Park School of Buffalo, NY
Peddie School, NJ
The Pembroke Hill School, MO
Pensacola Catholic High School, FL
Perkiomen School, PA
The Phelps School, PA
Phoenix Country Day School, AZ
Pickering College, ON, Canada

Pinewood Preparatory School, SC
The Pingry School, NJ
Pioneer Valley Christian Academy, MA
Pope Francis High School, MA
Pope John XXIII Regional High School, NJ
Portledge School, NY
Poughkeepsie Day School, NY
Powers Catholic High School, MI
Providence Country Day School, RI
Punahou School, HI
Queen Margaret's School, BC, Canada
Ravenscroft School, NC
Regis Jesuit High School, Boys Division, CO
Regis Jesuit High School, Girls Division, CO
Riverdale Country School, NY
Rockhurst High School, MO
Rockland Country Day School, NY
Rock Point School, VT
Rocky Mount Academy, NC
Roland Park Country School, MD
Routt Catholic High School, IL
Sacramento Country Day School, CA
Sacramento Waldorf School, CA
Sacred Heart High School, CA
Sacred Heart High School, NY
St. Agnes Academy, TX
St. Albans School, DC
Saint Albert Junior-Senior High School, IA
St. Andrew's Episcopal School, MD
Saint Andrew's School, FL
St. Andrew's School, GA
St. Andrew's–Sewanee School, TN
Saint Basil Academy, PA
St. Bernard's Catholic School, CA
Saint Dominic Academy, NJ
Saint Francis High School, CA
St. Francis High School, KY
St. Francis School, GA
Saint Gertrude High School, VA
Saint Ignatius College Prep, IL
Saint John Bosco High School, CA
St. John Neumann High School, FL
Saint Joseph High School, NJ
St. Joseph's Catholic School, SC
St. Luke's School, CT
Saint Mary's Hall, TX
St. Mary's High School, CO
Saint Patrick High School, IL
Saint Paul Lutheran High School, MO
St. Paul's School, NH
St. Pius X High School, TX
Saint Stephen's Episcopal School, FL
St. Stephen's Episcopal School, TX
Saint Teresa's Academy, MO
Saint Thomas Academy, MN
St. Thomas Aquinas High School, NH
Saint Ursula Academy, OH
Salem Academy, OR
San Francisco University High School, CA
Santa Fe Preparatory School, NM
Sayre School, KY
Scattergood Friends School, IA
Schule Schloss Salem, Germany
Seabury Hall, HI
Seattle Academy of Arts and Sciences, WA
The Seven Hills School, OH
Shattuck-St. Mary's School, MN

Smith School, NY
Southwestern Academy, AZ
The Stony Brook School, NY
The Storm King School, NY
Stratford Academy, GA
Stratton Mountain School, VT
Subiaco Academy, AR
Tandem Friends School, VA
TASIS, The American School in Switzerland, Switzerland
Thomas Jefferson School, MO
Tilton School, NH
Timothy Christian High School, IL
TMI - The Episcopal School of Texas, TX
Tower Hill School, DE
Trevor Day School, NY
Trinity Catholic High School, CT
Trinity College School, ON, Canada
Trinity Episcopal School, VA
Trinity High School, KY
United Nations International School, NY
University of Chicago Laboratory Schools, IL
University School of Jackson, TN
Upper Canada College, ON, Canada
Ursuline Academy, MA
The Ursuline Academy of Dallas, TX
Valwood School, GA
Victor Valley Christian School, CA
Villa Duchesne and Oak Hill School, MO
Villa Madonna Academy, KY
Villa Victoria Academy, NJ
The Waldorf School of Saratoga Springs, NY
Wasatch Academy, UT
Washington International School, DC
Wayneflete School, ME
Webb School of Knoxville, TN
The Wellington School, OH
Wesleyan Academy, PR
Westbury Christian School, TX
Westmark School, CA
Westminster Christian School, FL
Westover School, CT
Westridge School, CA
The Wheeler School, RI
Wilmington Christian School, DE
Wilmington Friends School, DE
Wilson Hall, SC
The Winston School San Antonio, TX
Woodberry Forest School, VA
Woodlynde School, PA
Woodstock School, India
The Woodward School, MA
Wyoming Seminary, PA
Xavier High School, NY
York Country Day School, PA
Zurich International School, Switzerland

SCHOOLS REPORTING EXCHANGE PROGRAMS WITH OTHER U.S. SCHOOLS

Academy of the Sacred Heart, LA
Academy of the Sacred Heart, MI
Albuquerque Academy, NM
Andrews Osborne Academy, OH
Berkeley Preparatory School, FL
The Calhoun School, NY
The Canterbury Episcopal School, TX

Chadwick School, CA
Charlotte Country Day School, NC
Colegio San Jose, PR
Convent of the Sacred Heart, CT
Dalat School, Malaysia
Dominican Academy, NY
The Hockaday School, TX
Holy Savior Menard Catholic High School, LA
Josephinum Academy, IL
Keio Academy of New York, NY
Kimberton Waldorf School, PA
Liberty Christian High School, CA
Lower Canada College, QC, Canada
Maumee Valley Country Day School, OH
The McLean School of Maryland, Inc., MD
Miss Porter's School, CT
Montgomery Bell Academy, TN
Mount Vernon Presbyterian School, GA
Newton Country Day School of the Sacred Heart, MA
Niagara Catholic Jr./Sr. High School, NY
Pinewood Preparatory School, SC
St. Andrew's School, GA
St. Stephen's School, Rome, Italy
San Francisco University High School, CA
Schule Schloss Salem, Germany
The Spence School, NY
Victor Valley Christian School, CA
Villa Duchesne and Oak Hill School, MO
Windermere School, United Kingdom
Woodstock School, India

SCHOOLS REPORTING PROGRAMS FOR STUDY ABROAD

Academy of Notre Dame de Namur, PA
Advanced Academy of Georgia, GA
The Agnes Irwin School, PA
Albuquerque Academy, NM
American Christian Academy, AL
The American School Foundation, Mexico
Ashley Hall, SC
Atlanta Girls' School, GA
Atlanta International School, GA
Austin Waldorf School, TX
Baylor School, TN
Beaufort Academy, SC
The Bement School, MA
Benedictine High School, OH
Berkeley Carroll School, NY
Berkeley Preparatory School, FL
Berkshire School, MA
The Birch Wathen Lenox School, NY
Bishop's College School, QC, Canada
The Bishop's School, CA
The Blake School, MN
Brandon Hall School, GA
Brockwood Park School, United Kingdom
Brooks School, MA
Brophy College Preparatory, AZ
The Bryn Mawr School for Girls, MD
Buckingham Browne & Nichols School, MA
The Buckley School, CA
Burr and Burton Academy, VT
California Crosspoint High School, CA
Canterbury School, IN
Cape Cod Academy, MA

Casady School, OK
Cascia Hall Preparatory School, OK
Cate School, CA
CCI The Renaissance School, Italy
Chadwick School, CA
Charlotte Country Day School, NC
Charlotte Latin School, NC
Chase Collegiate School, CT
Chatham Hall, VA
Choate Rosemary Hall, CT
The Church Farm School, PA
City Christian Schools, OR
Columbia International School, Japan
Commonwealth School, MA
The Community School of Naples, FL
Concord Academy, MA
Convent of the Sacred Heart, CT
The Country Day School, ON, Canada
The Culver Academies, IN
Dana Hall School, MA
Darrow School, NY
Deerfield Academy, MA
DeLaSalle High School, MN
Delaware County Christian School, PA
The Dr. Miriam and Sheldon G. Adelson Educational Campus,
  The Adelson Upper School, NV
The Dwight School, NY
Eagle Rock School, CO
Eastern Mennonite High School, VA
The Ellis School, PA
The Episcopal Academy, PA
Episcopal High School, VA
Episcopal High School of Jacksonville, FL
Escola Americana de Campinas, Brazil
Falmouth Academy, MA
First Presbyterian Day School, GA
Fordham Preparatory School, NY
Fountain Valley School of Colorado, CO
Foxcroft School, VA
Gann Academy (The New Jewish High School of Greater Boston),
  MA
George Stevens Academy, ME
The Governor's Academy, MA
The Grauer School, CA
Greater Atlanta Christian Schools, GA
Green Fields Country Day School, AZ
Greenhill School, TX
Green Meadow Waldorf School, NY
Greenwood Laboratory School, MO
The Gunnery, CT
The Gunston School, MD
Hammond School, SC
The Harpeth Hall School, TN
Harvard-Westlake School, CA
The Haverford School, PA
Hawken School, OH
The Hewitt School, NY
The Hockaday School, TX
Holland Hall, OK
Holy Ghost Preparatory School, PA
Holy Innocents' Episcopal School, GA
The Hotchkiss School, CT
International High School, CA
Jack M. Barrack Hebrew Academy, PA
Jean and Samuel Frankel Jewish Academy of Metropolitan
  Detroit, MI
Josephinum Academy, IL

Kimball Union Academy, NH
Kimberton Waldorf School, PA
King's-Edgehill School, NS, Canada
The Lab School of Washington, DC
Lake Forest Academy, IL
Lakehill Preparatory School, TX
Lake Mary Preparatory School, FL
Landon School, MD
The Lawrenceville School, NJ
Leysin American School in Switzerland, Switzerland
Lincoln Academy, ME
Lincoln School, RI
Louisville Collegiate School, KY
The Lovett School, GA
Luther College High School, SK, Canada
Malvern Preparatory School, PA
Marin Academy, CA
Marist High School, IL
Marshall School, MN
Mary Institute and St. Louis Country Day School (MICDS), MO
The Mary Louis Academy, NY
Marymount School of New York, NY
Matignon High School, MA
Maumee Valley Country Day School, OH
The McCallie School, TN
Memphis University School, TN
Mercersburg Academy, PA
Merchiston Castle School, United Kingdom
The Miami Valley School, OH
Millbrook School, NY
Milton Academy, MA
Milton Hershey School, PA
Miss Porter's School, CT
Monsignor Edward Pace High School, FL
Montclair Kimberley Academy, NJ
Montgomery Bell Academy, TN
Montrose School, MA
Moorestown Friends School, NJ
Mount Notre Dame High School, OH
Mount Vernon Presbyterian School, GA
Neuchatel Junior College, Switzerland
Newton Country Day School of the Sacred Heart, MA
Noble and Greenough School, MA
Northfield Mount Hermon School, MA
North Shore Country Day School, IL
North Yarmouth Academy, ME
Oak Grove Lutheran School, ND
The Oakridge School, TX
Ojai Valley School, CA
Oldenburg Academy, IN
Oregon Episcopal School, OR
Pace Academy, GA
The Packer Collegiate Institute, NY
The Park School of Baltimore, MD
The Park School of Buffalo, NY
Peddie School, NJ
The Pembroke Hill School, MO
The Pennington School, NJ
Phoenix Country Day School, AZ
The Pingry School, NJ
Polytechnic School, CA
Portledge School, NY
Proctor Academy, NH
Providence Country Day School, RI
Providence Day School, NC
Punahou School, HI
Ramona Convent Secondary School, CA

Ravenscroft School, NC
Realms of Inquiry, UT
Rice Memorial High School, VT
Ridley College, ON, Canada
Riverdale Country School, NY
Rocky Mount Academy, NC
Roland Park Country School, MD
Rosseau Lake College, ON, Canada
The Roxbury Latin School, MA
Rudolf Steiner School of Ann Arbor, MI
Rundle College, AB, Canada
Sacramento Waldorf School, CA
St. Albans School, DC
Saint Andrew's School, FL
St. Andrew's School, GA
St. Andrew's–Sewanee School, TN
Saint Augustine Preparatory School, NJ
St. Francis High School, KY
St. George's School, RI
St. Joseph's Preparatory School, PA
St. Luke's School, CT
Saint Mary's Hall, TX
St. Paul's School, NH
St. Stephen's Episcopal School, TX
Saint Vincent-Saint Mary High School, OH
Salem Academy, NC
San Francisco University High School, CA
Santa Fe Preparatory School, NM
Schule Schloss Salem, Germany
Seattle Academy of Arts and Sciences, WA
Second Baptist School, TX
The Seven Hills School, OH
Shady Side Academy, PA
Sonoma Academy, CA
The Spence School, NY
Steamboat Mountain School, CO
Stevenson School, CA
The Taft School, CT
TASIS The American School in England, United Kingdom
TASIS, The American School in Switzerland, Switzerland
The Thacher School, CA
Trinity College School, ON, Canada
Trinity High School, KY
Trinity Preparatory School, FL
University Prep, WA
Upper Canada College, ON, Canada
Villa Duchesne and Oak Hill School, MO
Virginia Episcopal School, VA
The Waldorf School of Saratoga Springs, NY
Washington Waldorf School, MD
Waynflete School, ME
Webb School of Knoxville, TN
The Weber School, GA
The Wellington School, OH
Westminster School, CT
Westover School, CT
Westtown School, PA
The Wheeler School, RI
Wilmington Friends School, DE
Winchester Thurston School, PA
Windermere School, United Kingdom
Woodberry Forest School, VA
Woodstock Academy, CT
Woodstock School, India
Wyoming Seminary, PA

SCHOOLS REPORTING SUMMER SESSIONS OPEN TO STUDENTS FROM OTHER SCHOOLS

Academy at the Lakes, FL	A,C,S
Academy of Holy Angels, MN	S,O
Academy of Our Lady of Peace, CA	A,S,O
Academy of Saint Elizabeth, NJ	A,S
Academy of the Holy Cross, MD	A,C,S,O
Academy of the Holy Family, CT	A,O
Academy of the New Church Girls' School, PA	S
Académie Ste Cécile International School, ON, Canada	A,O
Adelphi Academy, NY	A,C,F,R,S,O
Advanced Academy of Georgia, GA	A,O
The Agnes Irwin School, PA	A,C,S,O
Albuquerque Academy, NM	A,C,S,O
Allen Academy, TX	S
Alliance Academy, Ecuador	A,S,O
Allison Academy, FL	A,O
Alpha Omega Academy, IA	A,C
Alverno Heights Academy, CA	A,C,F,R,S,O
The American School in Japan, Japan	A,C,O
The American School of Madrid, Spain	A,C,F,S,O
The American School of Puerto Vallarta, Mexico	A,O
Andrews Osborne Academy, OH	A,S,O
Archbishop Curley High School, MD	A,C,S
Archbishop Mitty High School, CA	A,C,S,O
Archbishop Moeller High School, OH	A,F,S,O
Arete Preparatory Academy, CA	A
Army and Navy Academy, CA	A,C,S,O
Arroyo Pacific Academy, CA	A,F
Ashley Hall, SC	A,C,F,S,O
Athens Academy, GA	A,C,S,O
Atlanta Girls' School, GA	A,C,F,O
Atlanta International School, GA	A,C,S,O
Austin Preparatory School, MA	A,F,S
Bakersfield Christian High School, CA	A,S
Balboa City School, CA	A,C,O
Barnstable Academy, NJ	A
Battle Ground Academy, TN	A,C,S,O
Bavarian International School, Germany	A,C,F,S,O
Baylor School, TN	A,C,R,S,O
Bearspaw Christian School, AB, Canada	S,O
Beaufort Academy, SC	A,S,O
The Beekman School, NY	A,O
Benedictine High School, OH	A,C,S,O
Berkeley Carroll School, NY	A,C,S,O
Berkeley Preparatory School, FL	A,C,F,S,O
Bishop Denis J. O'Connell High School, VA	A,C,S
Bishop Kearney High School, NY	A
Bishop O'Dowd High School, CA	A,C,S
Bishop's College School, QC, Canada	A,O
The Bishop's School, CA	A,C,S
Bishop Stang High School, MA	A,C,F,S,O
The Blake School, MN	A,S,O
Blanchet School, OR	A,S,O
Blessed Sacrament Huguenot Catholic School, VA	A,C,F,S,O
Blueprint Education, AZ	A,O
The Bolles School, FL	A,C,O
Boston Trinity Academy, MA	A
Brandon Hall School, GA	A,C,S,O
Brehm Preparatory School, IL	A,O
Brentwood College School, BC, Canada	S,O
Bridges Academy, CA	A,C,F,S,O
Brimmer and May School, MA	A,S,O
Brooks School, MA	A,C,O
Brophy College Preparatory, AZ	A,C,S,O
The Bryn Mawr School for Girls, MD	A,F,S,O
The Buckley School, CA	A,C,O

A — academic; C — computer instruction; F — art/fine arts; R — rigorous outdoor training; S — sports; O — other

Buffalo Seminary, NY	F,S,O	Durham Academy, NC	A,C,S,O
The Calhoun School, NY	F,O	Eaton Academy, GA	A,C,S,O
California Crosspoint High School, CA	A,S,O	Edgewood Academy, AL	O
Calvert Hall College High School, MD	A,C,S,O	Edmund Burke School, DC	A,C,O
Campbell Hall (Episcopal), CA	A,C,S,O	Eldorado Emerson Private School, CA	A,S
Canadian Academy, Japan	A,C,S,O	Elgin Academy, IL	A,F,S,O
Canterbury School, CT	S,O	Elmwood School, ON, Canada	A,S
Canterbury School, FL	A,S,O	The Episcopal Academy, PA	A,C,F,S,O
The Canterbury School of Florida, FL	A,C,S,O	Episcopal Collegiate School, AR	A,C,S,O
Cape Henry Collegiate School, VA	A,C,S,O	Episcopal High School, TX	A,F,S,O
Capistrano Valley Christian Schools, CA	A,F,S,O	Episcopal High School of Jacksonville, FL	A,C,R,S,O
Cardinal Gibbons High School, NC	A,F,S,O	Explorations Academy, WA	A,C,R,O
Cardinal Ritter High School, IN	A,O	Father Duenas Memorial School, GU	A
Carnegie Schools Riverside, CA	A	Fay School, MA	A,C,S
Carondelet High School, CA	A,S,O	The Fessenden School, MA	A
Casady School, OK	A,C,S	The First Academy, FL	A,F,S,O
Cascia Hall Preparatory School, OK	A,S,O	First Presbyterian Day School, GA	A,C,F,S,O
Cathedral High School, NY	A,S	Flintridge Preparatory School, CA	A,C,S,O
Catholic Central High School, WI	S,O	Fontbonne Academy, MA	A,C,S
Central Catholic High School, MA	A,C,F,O	Fontbonne Hall Academy, NY	S,O
Chadwick School, CA	C,S,O	Forest Lake Academy, FL	A
Chaminade College Preparatory, CA	A,C,S,O	Fort Worth Country Day School, TX	A,C,F,S,O
Chaminade College Preparatory School, MO	A,F,S	Foundation Academy, FL	A,F,S,O
Charlotte Country Day School, NC	A,C,S,O	Fowlers Academy, PR	A,O
Charlotte Latin School, NC	A,C,S,O	Franklin Academy, CT	A,C,O
Chase Collegiate School, CT	A,C,F,S,O	Friends Academy, NY	O
Chatham Hall, VA	S,O	Friends Select School, PA	A,C,O
Chelsea School, MD	A,C,O	Front Range Christian High School, CO	A,S,O
Cheverus High School, ME	A,S,O	Fuqua School, VA	A,F,S,O
Children's Creative and Performing Arts Academy of San Diego, CA	A,C,F,O	The Galloway School, GA	A,C,S,O
		Gaston Day School, NC	A,C,F,S,O
Choate Rosemary Hall, CT	A,S,O	Gilman School, MD	A,C,R,S,O
Christa McAuliffe Academy School of Arts and Sciences, OR	A,C,O	Gilmour Academy, OH	A,S,O
		Girard College, PA	A,C,S
Christ Church Episcopal School, SC	A,S,O	Glenelg Country School, MD	S,O
Christchurch School, VA	A,S,O	Gonzaga College High School, DC	A,O
Chrysalis School, WA	A,C,O	The Governor French Academy, IL	A,O
Clarksville Academy, TN	A,C,S,O	The Gow School, NY	A,C,S,O
Colegio San Jose, PR	A,O	The Grauer School, CA	A,C,R,S,O
Collegedale Academy, TN	A,O	Greater Atlanta Christian Schools, GA	A,F,S,O
The Collegiate School, VA	A,C,S,O	Greenhill School, TX	A,C,S,O
Columbia International School, Japan	A,C,S,O	Greenhills School, MI	A,F,S,O
The Columbus Academy, OH	A,C,O	Grier School, PA	A,F,S,O
Columbus School for Girls, OH	A,C,R,S,O	Griggs International Academy, MD	A
The Community School of Naples, FL	A,S,O	Guamani Private School, PR	A
Concordia Academy, MN	C,F,S	Gulliver Preparatory School, FL	A,C,F,R,S,O
Concordia Lutheran High School, IN	A,C,F,S,O	The Gunnery, CT	S,O
The Country Day School, ON, Canada	A,F,S,O	The Gunston School, MD	A,C,S,O
Crescent School, ON, Canada	A,O	Halstrom Academy, Beverly Hills, CA	A,O
The Culver Academies, IN	A,C,F,R,S,O	Halstrom Academy, Calsbad, CA	A,O
Cushing Academy, MA	A,C,F,S,O	Halstrom Academy, Cupertino, CA	A,O
Dallas Academy, TX	A	Halstrom Academy, Huntington Beach, CA	A
Damien High School, CA	A,C,S,O	Halstrom Academy, Irvine, CA	A
Dana Hall School, MA	A,O	Halstrom Academy, Los Angeles, CA	A,O
Darlington School, GA	A,C,F,S,O	Halstrom Academy, Manhattan Beach, CA	A,O
Davidson Academy, TN	A,S,O	Halstrom Academy, Mission Viejo, CA	A,O
Deerfield Academy, MA	A,O	Halstrom Academy, Orange, CA	A,O
De La Salle College, ON, Canada	A,O	Halstrom Academy, Pasadena, CA	A,O
DeLaSalle High School, MN	A	Halstrom Academy, San Diego, CA	A,C,O
Delaware County Christian School, PA	C,S	Halstrom Academy, San Mateo, CA	A,O
Delaware Valley Friends School, PA	A,C,O	Halstrom Academy, Walnut Creek, CA	A,O
Delbarton School, NJ	A,C,S,O	Halstrom Academy, Westlake Village, CA	A
The Delphian School, OR	A,C,F,S,O	Halstrom Academy, Woodland Hills, CA	A,O
DeMatha Catholic High School, MD	A,C,F,S,O	Hammond School, SC	A,C,F,S,O
Denver Academy, CO	A,C,F,R,O	The Harker School, CA	A,S,O
Detroit Country Day School, MI	A,C,F,S,O	The Harley School, NY	A,C,S,O
Dominican Academy, NY	A,O	The Harpeth Hall School, TN	A,C,S,O

A — academic; C — computer instruction; F — art/fine arts; R — rigorous outdoor training; S — sports; O — other

Harvard-Westlake School, CA	A,C,R,S,O	Lutheran High North, TX	A,C,S,O
The Harvey School, NY	A,O	Lydia Patterson Institute, TX	A,O
Hawaii Baptist Academy, HI	A,C,S,O	Malvern Preparatory School, PA	A,C,S,O
Hawai`i Preparatory Academy, HI	A,C,S,O	Maplebrook School, NY	A,C,S,O
Hawken School, OH	A,C,F,O	Maranatha High School, CA	A,F,S,O
Hebron Academy, ME	A,O	Marianapolis Preparatory School, CT	A
Heritage Hall, OK	A,C,F,S,O	Marian Central Catholic High School, IL	A,C,F,S,O
Hillside School, MA	A,O	Marine Military Academy, TX	A,R,S,O
The Hockaday School, TX	A,C,F,S,O	Marist High School, IL	A
Holland Hall, OK	A,C,F,S,O	Marist School, GA	A,S
Holy Cross High School, CT	S,O	Marshall School, MN	A,C,S,O
Holy Ghost Preparatory School, PA	A,C,S,O	Martin Luther High School, NY	A,C
Holy Innocents' Episcopal School, GA	A,C,S,O	The Marvelwood School, CT	A,F,O
Holy Trinity School, ON, Canada	A,C,S	Mary Institute and St. Louis Country Day School	
Hoosac School, NY	A,O	(MICDS), MO	A,C,R,S,O
The Hotchkiss School, CT	A,C,O	The Mary Louis Academy, NY	A,C,S,O
The Hun School of Princeton, NJ	A,C,S,O	Marymount High School, CA	A,C,F,S,O
Huntington-Surrey School, TX	A,O	Maryvale Preparatory School, MD	A,C,S
Hyde School, CT	A,R,S,O	Massanutten Military Academy, VA	A,C,S,O
Hyde School, ME	A,C,R,S,O	Matignon High School, MA	A,O
Illiana Christian High School, IL	F,S,O	Maumee Valley Country Day School, OH	A,C,S,O
Immaculata-La Salle High School, FL	A,O	Maur Hill-Mount Academy, KS	A,O
Incarnate Word Academy, TX	A,S,O	Mayer Lutheran High School, MN	A,C
Independent School, KS	A,C,S	The McCallie School, TN	A,R,S,O
Indian Springs School, AL	A,S,O	McDonogh School, MD	A,C,S,O
Institut Monte Rosa, Switzerland	A,S,O	The McLean School of Maryland, Inc., MD	A,O
International School Manila, Philippines	A,S,O	The Meadows School, NV	A,S,O
The International School of Aberdeen, United Kingdom	C,S	Memphis University School, TN	A,C,F,S,O
International School of Brussels, Belgium	A,C,S,O	Menlo School, CA	A,O
Jackson Preparatory School, MS	A,C,O	Mercersburg Academy, PA	A,R,S,O
Jesuit College Preparatory School, TX	A,C,S,O	Mercy High School, MI	A,O
Junipero Serra High School, CA	A,C,S,O	Mercyhurst Preparatory School, PA	A,C,F,O
Keio Academy of New York, NY	O	Merion Mercy Academy, PA	A,F,S,O
Kent Denver School, CO	A,C,S,O	Mesa Grande Seventh Day Academy, CA	S,O
Kent School, CT	A,C,O	The Miami Valley School, OH	A,R,S,O
The Key School, MD	A,C,R,S	Mid-Pacific Institute, HI	A,C,F,O
Kildonan School, NY	A,F,O	Mill Springs Academy, GA	A,S,O
Kimball Union Academy, NH	A,F,S,O	Miss Porter's School, CT	A,O
King School, CT	A,C,S,O	The Monarch School, TX	A,C,F,O
The King's Christian High School, NJ	A,S,O	Monsignor Edward Pace High School, FL	A,C,S,O
Kingswood-Oxford School, CT	A,S,O	Montclair Kimberley Academy, NJ	A,C,S
The Kiski School, PA	S,O	Montgomery Bell Academy, TN	A,C,R,S,O
Lake Forest Academy, IL	A,O	Montrose School, MA	A,S
Lakehill Preparatory School, TX	A,C,S,O	Moorestown Friends School, NJ	A,O
Lake Mary Preparatory School, FL	A,C,F,R,O	Moravian Academy, PA	A,S,O
Lake Ridge Academy, OH	A,C,F,S,O	Moreau Catholic High School, CA	A,S,O
Lakeview Academy, GA	A,C,F,S,O	Mother McAuley High School, IL	A,C,S,O
La Lumiere School, IN	A,S,O	Mount Carmel Academy, LA	A,C,S
Lancaster Mennonite High School, PA	A,F,S	Mount Mercy Academy, NY	A,O
Landmark School, MA	A,O	Mount Saint Charles Academy, RI	S,O
Landon School, MD	A,C,F,S,O	Nazareth Academy, IL	A,S,O
Lansdale Catholic High School, PA	A,S	New International School of Thailand, Thailand	A,C,S,O
La Salle Academy, RI	A,C,S	New Roads School, CA	A,S
La Salle High School, CA	A,C,F,S,O	Newton Country Day School of the Sacred Heart, MA	S,O
La Sierra Academy, CA	A,O	Newton's Grove School, ON, Canada	A,C,S,O
Laurel Springs School, CA	A,C,O	Niagara Christian Community of Schools, ON, Canada	A,O
Laurinburg Institute, NC	A,O	The North Broward Preparatory Upper School, FL	A,C,S,O
Lawrence School, OH	A,C,S,O	Northfield Mount Hermon School, MA	A,S,O
Le Lycee Francais de Los Angeles, CA	A,C,S,O	North Toronto Christian School, ON, Canada	A
Lexington Christian Academy, MA	A,S,O	The Northwest School, WA	A,C,S,O
Leysin American School in Switzerland, Switzerland	A,C,R,S,O	Notre Dame-Cathedral Latin School, OH	A,S
Lincoln Academy, ME	A,F,O	Notre Dame High School, CA	A,F,S,O
Long Island Lutheran Middle and High School, NY	C,S,O	Notre Dame High School, CA	A,O
Louisville Collegiate School, KY	A,C,F,S,O	Notre Dame High School, NJ	A,C,F,S,O
Louisville High School, CA	S,O	Oak Grove Lutheran School, ND	A,F,S
The Lovett School, GA	A,C,O	Oak Grove School, CA	A
Loyola-Blakefield, MD	A,C,F,S	Oakland School, VA	A,C,S,O

A — academic; C — computer instruction; F — art/fine arts; R — rigorous outdoor training; S — sports; O — other

Oak Ridge Military Academy, NC	A,R,O	Saint Francis High School, CA	A,C,S,O
The Oakridge School, TX	A,C,F,R,S,O	St. George's Independent School, TN	A,C,S,O
Ojai Valley School, CA	A,C,O	St. George's School, BC, Canada	A,C,S,O
Oneida Baptist Institute, KY	A,O	Saint Gertrude High School, VA	S
Orangewood Adventist Academy, CA	S,O	Saint Ignatius College Prep, IL	A,C,S
Oregon Episcopal School, OR	A,C,S,O	Saint John Bosco High School, CA	A,C,S,O
Orinda Academy, CA	A,O	St. John's International, BC, Canada	A,O
The Orme School, AZ	A,R,S,O	St. John's Preparatory School, MA	A,C,S,O
Pace Academy, GA	A,C,S,O	Saint John's School, GU	A,C,F,S,O
Pacific Lutheran High School, CA	A,S,O	St. Joseph High School, CT	A,C,F,S,O
Padua Franciscan High School, OH	A,C,F,S,O	Saint Joseph High School, NJ	A,C,S,O
Palma School, CA	A,C,R,S,O	St. Joseph High School, TX	S,O
The Park School of Baltimore, MD	C,S	St. Joseph's Catholic School, SC	A,S
The Park School of Buffalo, NY	A,F,S,O	St. Joseph's Preparatory School, PA	A,C,S,O
The Pathway School, PA	A,C,S,O	St. Luke's School, CT	A,C,S,O
Peddie School, NJ	A,C,S,O	Saint Mary of the Assumption High School, NJ	A,O
The Pembroke Hill School, MO	A,C,F,S,O	St. Mary's Episcopal School, TN	A,S,O
The Pennington School, NJ	A,S,O	Saint Mary's Hall, TX	A,C,S
Perkiomen School, PA	A,C,S	St. Mary's Preparatory School, MI	S,O
Phoenix Christian Preparatory School, AZ	A,S,O	Saint Maur International School, Japan	A,C,F,S,O
Phoenix Country Day School, AZ	A,C,S,O	Saint Patrick High School, IL	A,C,F,S,O
Pickering College, ON, Canada	A,O	St. Paul's High School, MB, Canada	S,O
The Pingry School, NJ	A,S,O	St. Paul's School, NH	A,O
Polytechnic School, CA	A,C,O	St. Pius X Catholic High School, GA	A,S
Portledge School, NY	A,C,S,O	St. Pius X High School, TX	A,C,S,O
Portsmouth Christian Academy, NH	A,S,O	St. Stanislaus College, MS	A,O
Poughkeepsie Day School, NY	A,F,O	Saint Stephen's Episcopal School, FL	A,C,S,O
Prestonwood Christian Academy, TX	A,C,R,S	St. Stephen's Episcopal School, TX	S,O
Providence Day School, NC	A,C,S,O	St. Stephen's School, Rome, Italy	A,F,O
Providence High School, CA	A,C,S,O	Saint Teresa's Academy, MO	A,C,S,O
Queen Margaret's School, BC, Canada	A,S,O	Saint Thomas Academy, MN	A,S,O
Ramona Convent Secondary School, CA	A,C,S,O	St. Thomas Aquinas High School, FL	A,C,O
Randolph-Macon Academy, VA	A,C,F,O	Saint Thomas Aquinas High School, KS	A,C,S,O
Ransom Everglades School, FL	A,C,O	Saint Ursula Academy, OH	A,C,F,S,O
Ravenscroft School, NC	A,C,S,O	Salpointe Catholic High School, AZ	A,C,S,O
The Rectory School, CT	A,C,F,S,O	Santa Catalina School, CA	A,S,O
Redemption Christian Academy, MA	A,R,S,O	Santa Margarita Catholic High School, CA	A,C,S,O
Regis Jesuit High School, Boys Division, CO	A,C,S	Scattergood Friends School, IA	O
Regis Jesuit High School, Girls Division, CO	A,C,S	Scholar's Hall Preparatory School, ON, Canada	A,C,F,O
Ridley College, ON, Canada	A,O	Schule Schloss Salem, Germany	A,S,O
Riverdale Country School, NY	A,O	SciCore Academy, NJ	A,C,O
Rivermont Collegiate, IA	A,C,F,S,O	Seabury Hall, HI	A,F,S,O
Rockhurst High School, MO	A,C,F,S,O	Seattle Academy of Arts and Sciences, WA	A,S
Rock Point School, VT	A,F,O	Seisen International School, Japan	A,C,S,O
Rocky Mount Academy, NC	A,C,F,S,O	Seton Catholic Central High School, NY	S,O
The Roeper School, MI	O	Seton Catholic High School, AZ	A,S,O
Rolling Hills Preparatory School, CA	A,O	The Seven Hills School, OH	A,O
Rosseau Lake College, ON, Canada	A,O	Shady Side Academy, PA	A,C,S,O
Rothesay Netherwood School, NB, Canada	A,S,O	Shattuck-St. Mary's School, MN	A,S,O
Rowland Hall, UT	A,C,S,O	Shawnigan Lake School, BC, Canada	S,O
The Roxbury Latin School, MA	A,C,S	Shelton School and Evaluation Center, TX	A,O
Rumsey Hall School, CT	A,O	Shorecrest Preparatory School, FL	A,F,S,O
Sacramento Country Day School, CA	A,C,S,O	The Siena School, MD	A,F,O
Sacred Heart/Griffin High School, IL	A,S,O	Smith School, NY	A,C,F,O
Saddlebrook Preparatory School, FL	A,S,O	Southwestern Academy, AZ	A,R,O
Sage Hill School, CA	A,S,O	Springside Chestnut Hill Academy, PA	A,C,S,O
Saint Agnes Academy–St. Dominic School, TN	A,C	Squaw Valley Academy, CA	A,S,O
St. Albans School, DC	A,C,R,S,O	Stevenson School, CA	A,S
St. Andrew's Episcopal School, MD	A,C,S,O	The Stony Brook School, NY	A,C,R,S,O
Saint Andrew's School, FL	A,C,S,O	The Storm King School, NY	A,O
St. Andrew's School, GA	A,S,O	Stratford Academy, GA	A,S
St. Andrew's–Sewanee School, TN	A,F,R,S,O	The Taft School, CT	A,S,O
Saint Augustine Preparatory School, NJ	A,F,R,S,O	Taipei American School, Taiwan	A,C,O
Saint Basil Academy, PA	A,S,O	Takoma Academy, MD	A,O
St. Catherine's Academy, CA	A,S,O	Tandem Friends School, VA	O
St. Christopher's School, VA	A,S,O	TASIS The American School in England, United Kingdom	
St. Croix Schools, MN	A,S,O	A,C,F,S,O	

A — academic; C — computer instruction; F — art/fine arts; R — rigorous outdoor training; S — sports; O — other

TASIS, The American School in Switzerland, Switzerland	
A,F,R,S,O	
The Tenney School, TX	A,O
Thornton Academy, ME	A,C,F,S
Tilton School, NH	A,C,S
Timothy Christian High School, IL	A,S,O
TMI - The Episcopal School of Texas, TX	A,R,S,O
Tower Hill School, DE	A,S,O
Trinity Academy, KS	A,F,S
Trinity Catholic High School, CT	A,O
Trinity College School, ON, Canada	A,O
Trinity Episcopal School, VA	A,C,R,S
Trinity High School, OH	A,S,O
Trinity Preparatory School, FL	A,C,F,S,O
United Nations International School, NY	A,C,S,O
University Lake School, WI	A,S,O
University of Chicago Laboratory Schools, IL	A,C,S,O
University School of Jackson, TN	A,C,S,O
Upper Canada College, ON, Canada	A,C,F,O
Valley Christian High School, CA	A,C,F,S,O
The Vanguard School, FL	A,O
Villa Duchesne and Oak Hill School, MO	A,C,S,O
Villa Joseph Marie High School, PA	A,F,S,O
Walnut Hill School for the Arts, MA	F,O
Wasatch Academy, UT	A,O
Washington Waldorf School, MD	S,O
Waynflete School, ME	A,S,O
The Weber School, GA	A,O
The Wellington School, OH	A,S,O
Wesleyan Academy, PR	A,O
Westbury Christian School, TX	A,S,O
Westmark School, CA	A,C,F,O
West Nottingham Academy, MD	A
The Wheeler School, RI	A,S,O
Whitefield Academy, KY	A,F,S,O
The Willows Academy, IL	A,S,O
Wilmington Christian School, DE	A,O
Wilson Hall, SC	A,C,F,S,O
The Winchendon School, MA	A,C,R,S,O
Winchester Thurston School, PA	A,S,O
Windermere School, United Kingdom	A,R,S,O
The Windsor School, NY	A,O
Windward School, CA	C,S,O
Winston Preparatory School, NY	A,F,S,O
The Winston School, TX	A,C,F,O
The Winston School San Antonio, TX	A,C,S,O
Woodlynde School, PA	A,C,S,O
Woodstock School, India	A,O
Woodward Academy, GA	A,C,S
Wyoming Seminary, PA	A,S,O
Yokohama International School, Japan	A,S,O
York Country Day School, PA	A,S,O

SCHOOLS REPORTING THAT THEY ACCOMMODATE UNDERACHIEVERS

Alpine Academy, UT
Balboa City School, CA
The Blue Ridge School, VA
Camphill Special School, PA
Crotched Mountain School, NH
Denver Academy, CO
Eagle Rock School, CO
Fowlers Academy, PR
The Greenwood School, VT
Halstrom Academy, Beverly Hills, CA

Halstrom Academy, Cupertino, CA
Halstrom Academy, Huntington Beach, CA
Halstrom Academy, Irvine, CA
Halstrom Academy, Los Angeles, CA
Halstrom Academy, Manhattan Beach, CA
Halstrom Academy, Orange, CA
Halstrom Academy, Pasadena, CA
Halstrom Academy, San Diego, CA
Halstrom Academy, San Mateo, CA
Halstrom Academy, Walnut Creek, CA
Halstrom Academy, Westlake Village, CA
Halstrom Academy, Woodland Hills, CA
Hampshire Country School, NH
The Hill Center, Durham Academy, NC
The John Dewey Academy, MA
The Judge Rotenberg Educational Center, MA
Maplebrook School, NY
Marine Military Academy, TX
The Monarch School, TX
Mooseheart High School, IL
Norman Howard School, NY
Oakland School, VA
PACE/Brantley Hall High School, FL
Pacific Lutheran High School, CA
The Pathway School, PA
Perkins School for the Blind, MA
The Rectory School, CT
Sunrise Academy, UT
The Vanguard School, FL
Willow Hill School, MA
Winston Preparatory School, NY
The Winston School San Antonio, TX

SCHOOLS REPORTING PROGRAMS FOR STUDENTS WITH SPECIAL NEEDS

Remedial Reading and/or Writing

Academy of the Holy Family, CT
Academy of the New Church Boys' School, PA
Academy of the New Church Girls' School, PA
Académie Ste Cécile International School, ON, Canada
Adelphi Academy, NY
Alliance Academy, Ecuador
Allison Academy, FL
Alpine Academy, UT
Alverno Heights Academy, CA
The American Boychoir School, NJ
The American Embassy School, India
The American International School, Austria
American International School Rotterdam, Netherlands
The American School Foundation, Mexico
The American School of Madrid, Spain
The American School of Puerto Vallarta, Mexico
American School of The Hague, Netherlands
Archbishop Curley High School, MD
Archbishop Hoban High School, OH
Archbishop McNicholas High School, OH
Archbishop Moeller High School, OH
Arete Preparatory Academy, CA
Arizona Lutheran Academy, AZ
Arroyo Pacific Academy, CA
Aurora Central Catholic High School, IL
Austin Waldorf School, TX
Barnstable Academy, NJ
Bavarian International School, Germany

Baylor School, TN
Bay Ridge Preparatory School, NY
The Beekman School, NY
The Bermuda High School for Girls, Bermuda
Bishop Ireton High School, VA
Bishop Kearney High School, NY
Bishop McGuinness Catholic High School, OK
Bishop O'Dowd High School, CA
Bishop's College School, QC, Canada
Bishop Stang High School, MA
Blueprint Education, AZ
The Blue Ridge School, VA
Brehm Preparatory School, IL
Brethren Christian Junior and Senior High Schools, CA
Briarcrest Christian High School, TN
Brockwood Park School, United Kingdom
Burr and Burton Academy, VT
Cairo American College, Egypt
California Crosspoint High School, CA
Calvin Christian High School, CA
Camphill Special School, PA
Capistrano Valley Christian Schools, CA
Cardinal Newman High School, FL
Cardinal Ritter High School, IN
Carnegie Schools Riverside, CA
Catholic Central High School, NY
Central Catholic High School, LA
Chaminade-Madonna College Preparatory, FL
Charles E. Smith Jewish Day School, MD
Chelsea School, MD
Children's Creative and Performing Arts Academy of
   San Diego, CA
Christa McAuliffe Academy School of Arts and Sciences, OR
Christ Church Episcopal School, SC
Christopher Columbus High School, FL
City Christian Schools, OR
Colegio Bolivar, Colombia
Columbia International School, Japan
Community High School, NJ
The Concept School, PA
Concordia Academy, MN
Concordia Lutheran High School, IN
Covenant Canadian Reformed School, AB, Canada
Crawford Adventist Academy, ON, Canada
Crestwood Preparatory College, ON, Canada
Crotched Mountain School, NH
Currey Ingram Academy, TN
Cushing Academy, MA
Dallas Academy, TX
De La Salle North Catholic High School, OR
Delaware Valley Friends School, PA
The Delphian School, OR
DeMatha Catholic High School, MD
Denver Academy, CO
Desert Academy, NM
Detroit Country Day School, MI
Doane Academy, NJ
Dock Mennonite Academy, PA
Donovan Catholic, NJ
Dowling Catholic High School, IA
Dublin Christian Academy, NH
The Dwight School, NY
Eagle Hill School, CT
Eagle Rock School, CO
Eastern Mennonite High School, VA
Eaton Academy, GA
Edmonton Academy, AB, Canada

The Ellis School, PA
Father Lopez High School, FL
The Fessenden School, MA
Franklin Academy, CT
Fresno Christian Schools, CA
Friends Academy, NY
The Frisch School, NJ
Front Range Christian High School, CO
George Stevens Academy, ME
The Gow School, NY
Greenfield School, NC
Green Meadow Waldorf School, NY
The Greenwood School, VT
Grier School, PA
The Gunnery, CT
Halstrom Academy, Beverly Hills, CA
Halstrom Academy, Calsbad, CA
Halstrom Academy, Cupertino, CA
Halstrom Academy, Huntington Beach, CA
Halstrom Academy, Irvine, CA
Halstrom Academy, Los Angeles, CA
Halstrom Academy, Manhattan Beach, CA
Halstrom Academy, Mission Viejo, CA
Halstrom Academy, Orange, CA
Halstrom Academy, Pasadena, CA
Halstrom Academy, San Diego, CA
Halstrom Academy, San Mateo, CA
Halstrom Academy, Walnut Creek, CA
Halstrom Academy, Westlake Village, CA
Halstrom Academy, Woodland Hills, CA
Hammond School, SC
Hampshire Country School, NH
The Haverford School, PA
Hebrew Academy, CA
The Hill Center, Durham Academy, NC
Hillside School, MA
Ho'Ala School, HI
Holy Trinity High School, IL
Hoosac School, NY
The Howard School, GA
Hyde School, CT
Hyde School, ME
Illiana Christian High School, IL
International School Manila, Philippines
International School of Amsterdam, Netherlands
International School of Brussels, Belgium
International School of Kenya, Ltd., Kenya
International School of Port-of-Spain, Trinidad and Tobago
Istanbul International Community School, Turkey
Jack M. Barrack Hebrew Academy, PA
Jean and Samuel Frankel Jewish Academy of Metropolitan
   Detroit, MI
The John Dewey Academy, MA
The Judge Rotenberg Educational Center, MA
Kauai Christian Academy, HI
Kildonan School, NY
The Lab School of Washington, DC
Lakeland Christian Academy, IN
Lakeview Academy, GA
Lancaster Catholic High School, PA
Lancaster Mennonite High School, PA
Landmark School, MA
Lansdale Catholic High School, PA
La Pietra–Hawaii School for Girls, HI
La Salle Institute, NY
The Laureate Academy, MB, Canada
Laurel Springs School, CA

Laurinburg Institute, NC
Lawrence School, OH
Le Lycee Francais de Los Angeles, CA
Liberty Christian School, CA
Lincoln Academy, ME
Lower Canada College, QC, Canada
Lutheran High School, CO
Lutheran High School of Indianapolis, IN
Lutheran High School West, OH
Lydia Patterson Institute, TX
Lyndon Institute, VT
Manhattan Christian High School, MT
Maplebrook School, NY
Maranatha High School, CA
Marian Central Catholic High School, IL
Marine Military Academy, TX
Marist High School, IL
Marshall School, MN
The Marvelwood School, CT
Mary Help of Christians Academy, NJ
Massanutten Military Academy, VA
Mater Dei High School, IL
Mater Dei Prep, NJ
Mayer Lutheran High School, MN
The McLean School of Maryland, Inc., MD
Memphis University School, TN
Merchiston Castle School, United Kingdom
Mercyhurst Preparatory School, PA
Merion Mercy Academy, PA
Milton Hershey School, PA
The Monarch School, TX
Monsignor Bonner and Archbishop Prendergast Catholic
    High School, PA
Mooseheart High School, IL
Mountain View Academy, CA
Mountain View Christian High School, NV
Mount St. Agnes Academy, Bermuda
New International School of Thailand, Thailand
Noble Academy, NC
The Nora School, MD
Norman Howard School, NY
The North Broward Preparatory Upper School, FL
North Country School, NY
Northpoint Christian School, MS
The Norwich Free Academy, CT
Notre Dame High School, NJ
Notre Dame High School, NY
Oak Grove Lutheran School, ND
Oakland School, VA
Ojai Valley School, CA
Oneida Baptist Institute, KY
PACE/Brantley Hall High School, FL
Pacific Lutheran High School, CA
Padua Franciscan High School, OH
Palma School, CA
The Pathway School, PA
The Phelps School, PA
Phoenix Christian Preparatory School, AZ
Pioneer Valley Christian Academy, MA
Plumstead Christian School, PA
Powers Catholic High School, MI
The Rectory School, CT
Redemption Christian Academy, MA
Redwood Christian Schools, CA
Regis High School, OR
Regis Jesuit High School, Boys Division, CO
Regis Jesuit High School, Girls Division, CO

Rice Memorial High School, VT
Rocky Mount Academy, NC
Routt Catholic High School, IL
Rudolf Steiner School of Ann Arbor, MI
Rumsey Hall School, CT
Sacred Heart High School, CA
Saint Albert Junior-Senior High School, IA
St. Andrew's School, GA
St. Andrew's–Sewanee School, TN
St. Benedict at Auburndale, TN
St. Bernard's Catholic School, CA
St. Croix Schools, MN
Saint Dominic Academy, NJ
St. Francis School, GA
St. George's School, BC, Canada
Saint John Bosco High School, CA
St. Joseph High School, CA
Saint Mary's High School, AZ
Saint Maur International School, Japan
Saint Patrick High School, IL
St. Pius X High School, TX
St. Stanislaus College, MS
St. Thomas Aquinas High School, FL
Saint Thomas Aquinas High School, KS
Saint Thomas More Catholic High School, LA
Saint Vincent-Saint Mary High School, OH
Saint Xavier High School, KY
Salpointe Catholic High School, AZ
Santa Margarita Catholic High School, CA
Sayre School, KY
Scholar's Hall Preparatory School, ON, Canada
Seattle Academy of Arts and Sciences, WA
Seisen International School, Japan
Seton Catholic Central High School, NY
Shattuck-St. Mary's School, MN
Shawe Memorial Junior/Senior High School, IN
Shawnigan Lake School, BC, Canada
Shoreline Christian, WA
The Siena School, MD
Smith School, NY
The Stanwich School, CT
The Storm King School, NY
Sunrise Academy, UT
Takoma Academy, MD
Tandem Friends School, VA
TASIS The American School in England, United Kingdom
The Tenney School, TX
Thornton Academy, ME
Tilton School, NH
Timothy Christian High School, IL
Trinity High School, KY
Trinity-Pawling School, NY
University Lake School, WI
The Vanguard School, FL
Venta Preparatory School, ON, Canada
Victor Valley Christian School, CA
Villa Duchesne and Oak Hill School, MO
The Waldorf School of Saratoga Springs, NY
Webb School of Knoxville, TN
Westmark School, CA
West Nottingham Academy, MD
Willow Hill School, MA
Wilmington Christian School, DE
The Winchendon School, MA
Windermere School, United Kingdom
The Windsor School, NY
Winston Preparatory School, NY

The Winston School, TX
The Winston School San Antonio, TX
Woodlynde School, PA
Woodstock Academy, CT
Zurich International School, Switzerland

Remedial Math

Academy of the Holy Cross, MD
Academy of the Holy Family, CT
Academy of the New Church Boys' School, PA
Academy of the New Church Girls' School, PA
Académie Ste Cécile International School, ON, Canada
Adelphi Academy, NY
Alliance Academy, Ecuador
Allison Academy, FL
Alpha Omega Academy, IA
Alpine Academy, UT
Alverno Heights Academy, CA
The American Boychoir School, NJ
American Cooperative School of Tunis, Tunisia
The American Embassy School, India
The American International School, Austria
American International School Rotterdam, Netherlands
The American School of Madrid, Spain
The American School of Puerto Vallarta, Mexico
American School of The Hague, Netherlands
Archbishop Curley High School, MD
Archbishop Hoban High School, OH
Archbishop McNicholas High School, OH
Archbishop Moeller High School, OH
Arete Preparatory Academy, CA
Arizona Lutheran Academy, AZ
Arroyo Pacific Academy, CA
Aurora Central Catholic High School, IL
Austin Waldorf School, TX
Barnstable Academy, NJ
Bavarian International School, Germany
Bay Ridge Preparatory School, NY
Bearspaw Christian School, AB, Canada
The Beekman School, NY
Bellevue Christian School, WA
Bishop Denis J. O'Connell High School, VA
Bishop Ireton High School, VA
Bishop Kearney High School, NY
Bishop McGuinness Catholic High School, OK
Bishop O'Dowd High School, CA
Bishop's College School, QC, Canada
Bishop Stang High School, MA
Black Forest Academy, Germany
Blueprint Education, AZ
The Blue Ridge School, VA
Brehm Preparatory School, IL
Brethren Christian Junior and Senior High Schools, CA
Briarcrest Christian High School, TN
Brockwood Park School, United Kingdom
Burr and Burton Academy, VT
Cairo American College, Egypt
Calvin Christian High School, CA
Camphill Special School, PA
Capistrano Valley Christian Schools, CA
Cardinal Newman High School, FL
Cardinal Ritter High School, IN
Carnegie Schools Riverside, CA
Catholic Central High School, NY
Central Catholic High School, LA
Chaminade-Madonna College Preparatory, FL
Charles E. Smith Jewish Day School, MD

Chelsea School, MD
Children's Creative and Performing Arts Academy
  of San Diego, CA
Christa McAuliffe Academy School of Arts and Sciences, OR
Christ Church Episcopal School, SC
City Christian Schools, OR
Colegio Bolivar, Colombia
Columbia International School, Japan
Community High School, NJ
The Concept School, PA
Concordia Academy, MN
Concordia Lutheran High School, IN
Covenant Canadian Reformed School, AB, Canada
Crotched Mountain School, NH
Currey Ingram Academy, TN
Cushing Academy, MA
Dallas Academy, TX
De La Salle High School, CA
De La Salle North Catholic High School, OR
Delaware Valley Friends School, PA
Denver Academy, CO
Desert Academy, NM
Doane Academy, NJ
Dock Mennonite Academy, PA
Donovan Catholic, NJ
Dowling Catholic High School, IA
Dublin Christian Academy, NH
The Dwight School, NY
Eagle Hill School, CT
Eagle Rock School, CO
Eastern Mennonite High School, VA
Eaton Academy, GA
Edmonton Academy, AB, Canada
Father Lopez High School, FL
The Fessenden School, MA
Franklin Academy, CT
Fresno Christian Schools, CA
Friends Academy, NY
The Frisch School, NJ
Front Range Christian High School, CO
George Stevens Academy, ME
The Gow School, NY
Grace Baptist Academy, TN
Greenfield School, NC
Green Meadow Waldorf School, NY
The Greenwood School, VT
Grier School, PA
The Gunnery, CT
Halstrom Academy, Beverly Hills, CA
Halstrom Academy, Calsbad, CA
Halstrom Academy, Cupertino, CA
Halstrom Academy, Huntington Beach, CA
Halstrom Academy, Irvine, CA
Halstrom Academy, Los Angeles, CA
Halstrom Academy, Manhattan Beach, CA
Halstrom Academy, Mission Viejo, CA
Halstrom Academy, Orange, CA
Halstrom Academy, Pasadena, CA
Halstrom Academy, San Diego, CA
Halstrom Academy, San Mateo, CA
Halstrom Academy, Walnut Creek, CA
Halstrom Academy, Woodland Hills, CA
Hampshire Country School, NH
The Haverford School, PA
Hebrew Academy, CA
The Hill Center, Durham Academy, NC
Hillside School, MA

Ho'Ala School, HI
Hoosac School, NY
The Howard School, GA
Hyde School, CT
Hyde School, ME
Illiana Christian High School, IL
International School Manila, Philippines
International School of Amsterdam, Netherlands
International School of Brussels, Belgium
International School of Kenya, Ltd., Kenya
International School of Port-of-Spain, Trinidad and Tobago
Istanbul International Community School, Turkey
Jack M. Barrack Hebrew Academy, PA
Jean and Samuel Frankel Jewish Academy of Metropolitan
    Detroit, MI
The John Dewey Academy, MA
The Judge Rotenberg Educational Center, MA
Kauai Christian Academy, HI
Kolbe-Cathedral High School, CT
The Lab School of Washington, DC
Lakeland Christian Academy, IN
Lakeview Academy, GA
Lancaster Mennonite High School, PA
Landmark School, MA
Lansdale Catholic High School, PA
La Pietra–Hawaii School for Girls, HI
La Salle Institute, NY
La Sierra Academy, CA
The Laureate Academy, MB, Canada
Laurel Springs School, CA
Laurinburg Institute, NC
Lawrence School, OH
Le Lycee Francais de Los Angeles, CA
Liberty Christian School, CA
Lincoln Academy, ME
Lower Canada College, QC, Canada
Lutheran High School, MO
Lutheran High School of Indianapolis, IN
Lutheran High School West, OH
Lyndon Institute, VT
Manhattan Christian High School, MT
Maplebrook School, NY
Maranatha High School, CA
Marian Central Catholic High School, IL
Marine Military Academy, TX
Marist High School, IL
Marshall School, MN
The Marvelwood School, CT
Mary Help of Christians Academy, NJ
Massanutten Military Academy, VA
Mater Dei High School, IL
Mater Dei Prep, NJ
Mayer Lutheran High School, MN
The McLean School of Maryland, Inc., MD
Memphis University School, TN
Merchiston Castle School, United Kingdom
Mercyhurst Preparatory School, PA
Merion Mercy Academy, PA
Mesa Grande Seventh-Day Academy, CA
Milton Hershey School, PA
The Monarch School, TX
Monsignor Bonner and Archbishop Prendergast
    Catholic High School, PA
Mooseheart High School, IL
Mountain View Academy, CA
Mount Mercy Academy, NY
Mount St. Agnes Academy, Bermuda

New International School of Thailand, Thailand
Noble Academy, NC
The Nora School, MD
Norman Howard School, NY
The North Broward Preparatory Upper School, FL
North Country School, NY
Northpoint Christian School, MS
The Norwich Free Academy, CT
Notre Dame High School, NJ
Notre Dame High School, NY
Oak Grove Lutheran School, ND
Oakland School, VA
Ojai Valley School, CA
Oneida Baptist Institute, KY
PACE/Brantley Hall High School, FL
Padua Franciscan High School, OH
Palma School, CA
The Pathway School, PA
The Phelps School, PA
Phoenix Christian Preparatory School, AZ
Pioneer Valley Christian Academy, MA
Plumstead Christian School, PA
Powers Catholic High School, MI
The Rectory School, CT
Redemption Christian Academy, MA
Redwood Christian Schools, CA
Regis High School, OR
Regis Jesuit High School, Boys Division, CO
Regis Jesuit High School, Girls Division, CO
Rice Memorial High School, VT
Rock Point School, VT
Rocky Mount Academy, NC
Routt Catholic High School, IL
Sacred Heart High School, CA
Saint Albert Junior-Senior High School, IA
St. Andrew's School, GA
St. Andrew's–Sewanee School, TN
Saint Anthony High School, IL
St. Benedict at Auburndale, TN
St. Bernard's Catholic School, CA
St. Croix Schools, MN
Saint Dominic Academy, NJ
St. Francis School, GA
Saint John Bosco High School, CA
St. Joseph High School, CA
Saint Mary's High School, AZ
St. Mary's High School, CO
Saint Patrick High School, IL
St. Paul's High School, MB, Canada
St. Pius X High School, TX
St. Stanislaus College, MS
St. Thomas Aquinas High School, FL
Saint Thomas Aquinas High School, KS
Saint Thomas More Catholic High School, LA
Saint Vincent-Saint Mary High School, OH
Saint Xavier High School, KY
Salpointe Catholic High School, AZ
Santa Margarita Catholic High School, CA
Sayre School, KY
Scholar's Hall Preparatory School, ON, Canada
Seattle Academy of Arts and Sciences, WA
Seisen International School, Japan
Seton Catholic Central High School, NY
Shattuck-St. Mary's School, MN
Shawnigan Lake School, BC, Canada
The Siena School, MD
Smith School, NY

The Stanwich School, CT
Sunrise Academy, UT
Takoma Academy, MD
Tandem Friends School, VA
The Tenney School, TX
Thornton Academy, ME
Tilton School, NH
Trinity High School, KY
Trinity High School, OH
University Lake School, WI
Valley Christian High School, CA
The Vanguard School, FL
Venta Preparatory School, ON, Canada
Victor Valley Christian School, CA
Villa Duchesne and Oak Hill School, MO
The Waldorf School of Saratoga Springs, NY
Webb School of Knoxville, TN
Westmark School, CA
West Nottingham Academy, MD
Westtown School, PA
Willow Hill School, MA
Wilmington Christian School, DE
The Winchendon School, MA
Windermere School, United Kingdom
The Windsor School, NY
Winston Preparatory School, NY
The Winston School, TX
Woodlynde School, PA
Woodstock Academy, CT
Zurich International School, Switzerland

Deaf Students

Allentown Central Catholic High School, PA
American Christian Academy, AL
The American School Foundation, Mexico
Archbishop Moeller High School, OH
The Bement School, MA
Bishop Kearney High School, NY
Blanchet School, OR
Brethren Christian Junior and Senior High Schools, CA
Brockwood Park School, United Kingdom
Burr and Burton Academy, VT
Cate School, CA
Concordia Academy, MN
Concordia Lutheran High School, IN
Crotched Mountain School, NH
Denver Christian High School, CO
The Dr. Miriam and Sheldon G. Adelson Educational Campus, The Adelson Upper School, NV
Eaton Academy, GA
Edgewood High School of the Sacred Heart, WI
The Frisch School, NJ
George Stevens Academy, ME
International School Manila, Philippines
Jack M. Barrack Hebrew Academy, PA
Jean and Samuel Frankel Jewish Academy of Metropolitan Detroit, MI
The Judge Rotenberg Educational Center, MA
Lake Ridge Academy, OH
Lancaster Mennonite High School, PA
Landmark School, MA
La Salle Institute, NY
Marian Central Catholic High School, IL
Marshall School, MN

Merchiston Castle School, United Kingdom
Monsignor Bonner and Archbishop Prendergast Catholic High School, PA
Norman Howard School, NY
The Pathway School, PA
Pensacola Catholic High School, FL
Portsmouth Christian Academy, NH
Saint Albert Junior-Senior High School, IA
St. Andrew's Episcopal School, MD
Saint Anthony High School, IL
Saint Augustine Preparatory School, NJ
St. Stanislaus College, MS
Saint Vincent-Saint Mary High School, OH
Santa Margarita Catholic High School, CA
Shawe Memorial Junior/Senior High School, IN
The Tenney School, TX
Tower Hill School, DE
Trinity High School, KY
The Vanguard School, FL
Watkinson School, CT
Westover School, CT
Windermere School, United Kingdom
Woodstock Academy, CT

Blind Students

Allentown Central Catholic High School, PA
Alpine Academy, UT
Alverno Heights Academy, CA
The American School Foundation, Mexico
Archbishop Moeller High School, OH
Bishop Kearney High School, NY
Brethren Christian Junior and Senior High Schools, CA
Brockwood Park School, United Kingdom
Burr and Burton Academy, VT
Concordia Lutheran High School, IN
Crotched Mountain School, NH
Dowling Catholic High School, IA
Edgewood High School of the Sacred Heart, WI
The Frisch School, NJ
George Stevens Academy, ME
Grace Baptist Academy, TN
Greenhills School, MI
Grier School, PA
Jean and Samuel Frankel Jewish Academy of Metropolitan Detroit, MI
The Judge Rotenberg Educational Center, MA
Lancaster Mennonite High School, PA
La Salle Institute, NY
Merchiston Castle School, United Kingdom
Monsignor Bonner and Archbishop Prendergast Catholic High School, PA
The Pathway School, PA
Pensacola Catholic High School, FL
Perkins School for the Blind, MA
Portsmouth Christian Academy, NH
Saint Augustine Preparatory School, NJ
St. Stanislaus College, MS
Saint Vincent-Saint Mary High School, OH
Santa Margarita Catholic High School, CA
Trinity High School, KY
University Lake School, WI
The Vanguard School, FL
Willow Hill School, MA

Index

Alphabetical Listing of Schools

In the index that follows, page numbers for school profiles are shown in regular type, page numbers for Close-Ups are shown in **boldface** type, and page numbers for Displays are shown in *italics*.

NOTES